GN00982736

reference
section
WEST
SUSSEX
COUNTY
COUNCIL
LIBRARY SERVICE
CWR

West Sussex Library Service
WITHDRAWN
For Sale

CONTEMPORARY DRAMATISTS

Contemporary Writers Series

Contemporary Dramatists
Contemporary Literary Critics
Contemporary Novelists
(including short story writers)
Contemporary Poets
Contemporary Popular Writers
Contemporary Southern Writers
Contemporary Women Poets
Contemporary World Writers

CONTEMPORARY DRAMATISTS

SIXTH EDITION

PREFACE TO THE THIRD EDITION

RUBY COHN

PREFACE TO THE FIFTH EDITION

MICHAEL BILLINGTON

PREFACE TO THE SIXTH EDITION

COLIN CHAMBERS

EDITOR

THOMAS RIGGS

ST. JAMES PRESS

AN IMPRINT OF GALE

DETROIT • NEW YORK

Thomas Riggs, *Editor*

Michael J. Tyrkus, *Project Coordinator*

Laura Standley Berger, Joann Cerrito, Dave Collins, Nicolet V. Elert,
Miranda Ferrara, Kristin Hart, Margaret Mazurkiewicz
St. James Press Staff

Peter M. Gareffa, *Managing Editor, St. James Press*

Mary Beth Trimper, *Production Director*
Deborah Milliken, *Production Assistant*

Cynthia Baldwin, *Product Design Manager*
Pamela A. E. Galbreath, *Senior Art Director*
Pamela A. Reed, *Photography Coordinator*
Randy Bassett, *Image Database Supervisor*
Robert Duncan, Mike Logusz, *Imaging Specialists*

ISBN 1-55862-371-X
ISSN 1050-3919

Printed in the United States of America
Published simultaneously in the United Kingdom

St. James Press is an imprint of Gale

10 9 8 7 6 5 4 3 2 1

CONTENTS

Preface to the third edition, 1982

This volume contains well over 300 entries for contemporary dramatists writing in English thousands of miles apart. It might seem then that English drama is alive and well, but for that to be true audiences should embrace drama. Do they? I have seen estimates ranging from 1 percent of the population (of America) to 5 percent (of England) who ever attend the theater, but regular attendance thins down to decimals of decimals. Will these dramatists continue to write for a diminishing audience?

How different from the burgeoning drama of the Elizabethans. And yet Burbage and Henslowe may also have worried about theater attendance. No language seems to sport more than one great age of drama, and other periods of English-language drama have looked pale by contrast with the Elizabethan. In later times English theater came to be a fabulous invalid, enjoying its several prognoses, diagnoses, and forecasts of doom. Such a forecast is again appropriate today, not because our contemporary drama is less skillful than that of any age since the Elizabethan or less plentiful. But because our drama, like that of no other period, has to survive in the noxious atmosphere of the mass media. Playwrights can defy the media, sidestep them, try to ignore them, or, as more often happens, use dramatic form as an entrée into the media, notably films and television.

In English-speaking countries, with their meager theater subsidies and their major technical resources, drama abounds on film and television. (Dublin's Abbey Theatre in 1922 became the first nationally subsidized theater in the English language, whereas the subsidized Comédie-Française dates from 1680.) If today's writer is inadequately nurtured by theater or publisher, he can turn to the media. But few media graduates have contributed significant dramas to live theater. Mass-media drama tends to appeal to the most facile reactions of an audience, and yet the techniques of the media can broaden the palette of the stage playwright. Since writing the preface to the first edition of *Contemporary Dramatists,* I have become aware of media writers who return sporadically but significantly to the stage and of Heathcote Williams's *AC/DC,* which grounds a frenzied strength in the weaknesses of a media civilization. The theater has always drawn upon other arts, crafts, and technologies, and it may arrive at a modes vivendi with the media.

Perhaps drama is dying in the form we have known for some 400 years—a fairly inflexible prompt copy that is eventually printed. However, the theater today—with or without promptbook—must recognize its uniqueness in that live actors play before live audiences. Each actor has a single instrument, the body that includes the voice. And for all the experimentation with nonverbal sounds, the voice has recourse to words, which are the province of the dramatist.

English drama is coeval with the printing press, and response to drama has for centuries been cumulative as a reader-spectator travels from stage to page and, all the more receptive, to stage again. This itinerary may be less frequent for today's spectators. Contemporary stage dialogue may include primitive nonverbal sounds and electronic post-verbal devices, but new dramas of verbal distinction are nevertheless being written and played. As long as that continues, in the full awareness of live theater as a minority art, drama will endure.

Prognosis pronounced, whom do we actually have in a volume on contemporary dramatists writing in English? Since "contemporary" has been defined for this volume as biologically alive, we find curious neighbors. Some dramatists have spent successful years appealing to middle-class entertainment seekers; others have tried to entertain while supporting worthy causes or baring social problems. As has been true for 400 years, certain plays were written to provide scope for the special talents of a particular actor. None of this sounds contemporary in an age when we take it for granted that we will fly faster than sound.

I have seen many, many plays and many kinds of plays in nearly 40 years of theater going. It seems only yesterday that I saw *The Iceman Cometh* in a production advised by Eugene O'Neill. (It was actually 1946.) Or *The Apple Cart,* crackling wittily, only shortly after Bernard Shaw's witticisms had ceased to crackle. (It was actually 1953.) But yesterday is far away in contemporary theater, so that Shaw and O'Neill belong to another age and another theater language. And since this is true of master playwrights, it is all the truer for their lesser colleagues. Even living playwrights are dead in today's theater: a windy would-be Elizabethan, a once angry young man turned surly, a once fragile young lyricist turned coy, a reacher for tragedy resigned to routine comedy, or various squatters in the Abbey Theatre, which nearly exploded under the impact of three different meteors. Such dramatists are less contemporary than Euripides or Shakespeare, not to mention John Whiting and Joe Orton, who died in midcareer. For there is no necessary convergence between biological and artistic life. I hope all playwrights live to be a hundred, but I cannot help exclaiming at some of the entries in this volume: "Is he still alive!"

Since midcentury we have seen specimens of English language theater labeled epic, angry, kitchen sink, absurd, ridiculous, radical, Third World, puppet, guerrilla, fact, nude, improvisational, perspectivist, alternative—all soon exploited by the mass media. It is small wonder that many of the contemporary dramatists in this volume seem either uncontemporary or undramatic, regardless of chronology or biology.

To shift abruptly to a positive note, we have among contemporary dramatists one giant, Samuel Beckett, who writes sometimes in English, sometimes in French, always in his own distinctive dramatic idiom. Beckett's plays are enduring masterpieces. They are also a terminus to the Western dramatic tradition, dissecting the parts of a play so that they can never again articulate innocently. Through the tension of play, Beckett probes the bases of Western culture—faith, reason, friendship, family. Through the skills of play, Beckett summarizes human action—word and pause, gesture and stillness, motion rising from emotion. Beckett's most celebrated play, *Waiting for Godot,* is striking in its stage presence. As Brecht called attention to the theater, Beckett calls attention to the play as play. Often pitched as polar opposites, Brecht and Beckett both reacted against the dominant illusionist drama of their time and ours, so that it is no longer so dominant. In spite of their differences, Beckett resembles Brecht in precision of language at the textural level and in integration of verbal rhythms into an original scenic whole.

Relentlessly digging his own way, Beckett has inspired two English-language playwrights, one on each side of the Atlantic: Harold Pinter and Edward Albee. From Beckett both younger dramatists have learned to convey the presence of stage action without before or after, exposition or resolution. Pinter capitalizes on the unverifiability of a past, and Albee fits the past obliquely into the stage present. Both playwrights create the stage present through carefully crafted dialogue. Their characters speak in stylized patterns that draw upon colloquial phrases of contemporary speech. Unlike the realists with whom they are sometimes confused, they use repetition and cross talk to probe beneath or beyond surface reality.

In their rejection of realism, other contemporary dramatists resemble Pinter and Albee. Since no stage designer can compete with the camera in photographic fidelity to surface appearance, many contemporary dramatists do not ask them to try. Departures from realism can be as diversified as John Arden's Brechtian songs in *The Ballygombeen Bequest,* Edward Bond's ghost in *Lear,* the penitential geometry of Kenneth H. Brown's *The Brig,* the seasonal symbolism of Ed Bullins's *In the Wine Time,* the eternal sparring in Maria Irene Fornés's *Tango Palace,* the opportunity for improvisation in Paul Foster's *Tom Paine,* the drug metaphor in Jack Gelber's *The Connection,* the mythic dimension in Amiri Baraka's *Dutchman,* the documentary absurdism of James Saunders's *Next Time I'll Sing to You,* the stretch toward Artaud in Peter Shaffer's *The Royal Hunt of the Sun,* the manic rock monologues of Sam Shepard's *The Tooth of Crime,* the tribal magic of Derek Walcott's *Dream on Monkey Mountain,* or the play organically within the play in Patrick White's *The Ham Funeral.* I am not saying that these plays are of equal quality, but I am saying that forays into nonrealistic modes provide richer possibilities of theatricalizing the profundities of contemporary experience.

Provided that audiences come to see the plays.

—Ruby Cohn

Preface to the fifth edition, 1993

Drama is an obstinate, if beleaguered, survivor. By all the laws of logic it should be tottering into its grave, killed off by mounting production costs, the media explosion, and massive competition for public attention. Yet, as the nearly 100 new entrants to the fifth edition of this volume testify, the urge to create plays remains irrepressible. There seems to be a fundamental need to tell stories, explore moral dilemmas, bear witness to great events, or simply make sense of an increasingly chaotic world. Even perhaps to make money. One of the entrants to this volume told me that, by her reckoning, there are half a dozen millionaire playwrights in Britain alone.

For all that, playwriting has, over the last decade, become an increasingly hazardous occupation. The first threat comes from the sanctification of the musical as the holy altar of theater. Travel to any major theatrical city in the world and you will find that a floating combination of hit musicals by Andrew Lloyd-Webber or the Boublil-Schönberg team is sure to be playing. They are as inescapable as fast-food joints or American hotel chains. But instead of sneering at *Cats* or moaning about *Les Misérables,* one should perhaps ask why it is that musicals are gradually supplanting drama, for many people, as the central theatrical experience. My own answer is that they offer, apart from the obvious attractions of melody, color, and spectacle, some kind of transcendent experience. We go to the theater seeking entertainment, enlightenment, and ecstasy, but the last of these is a quality that drama—with a few notable exceptions, such as Brian Friel's *Dancing at Lughnasa* or Tony Kushner's *Angels in America*—has lately forgotten how to supply.

Playwriting is under threat from other factors. An obvious one is the insatiate appetite of the cormorant media. In the English-speaking world theater is increasingly used as a nursery of talent by the film and television industries, which often devour writers before they have had a chance to develop. Obviously, film and television are valuable in that they help to keep writers off the breadline, and shrewd, mature talents like Harold Pinter and David Mamet bring the same verbal precision and technical craft to the screen as to the stage. The real problem is that television especially picks up young dramatists promiscuously and reduces them to the status of dialogue writers, leaving them ill equipped to handle the structural complexities of drama.

Another threat to playwrights is the perceptible cultural shift away from the present toward the past. It may be less true in America, Australia, New Zealand, or Africa. But certainly in Britain there is a feeling that new writing is no longer as sexy as it once was, that the smart, chic thing to do is to discover a neglected foreign classic from another century. It is partly a result of a gradual shift from a writer's to a director's theater and a realization by young directors that they can make their mark by offering a conceptual vision of a dead author rather than by serving a living writer. It is also tied up with a postmodernist belief that old texts exist to be reinvented, reinterpreted, even restructured. This has a gamy whiff of excitement very different from that of teasing out the meaning of a new play with the writer sitting next to you in the rehearsal room.

And yet, particularly when I survey the list of new entrants to this volume, it strikes me that drama is anything but dead. For a start it is good to see that the old Anglo-American hegemony is being increasingly challenged. Obviously those two countries, because of history and tradition, dominate the scene, and they have lately produced some exciting new dramatists, such as the morally exploratory Jon Robin Baitz or the alertly self-referential Martin Crimp. But a lot of the energy in recent years has been coming from other quarters. Ireland leaps to mind, with writers like Frank McGuinness and Billy Roche adding to the existing achievements of dramatists such as Brian Friel and Tom Murphy. But what exactly is it about Irish writers that gives them such global popularity? My own thesis is that, whether they are Protestant or Catholic, hail from north or south, they still deal with themes that have a universal, mythic resonance: the power of motherhood, the tenacity of land, the pathos of exile, the inescapable imprint of religion. Intriguingly, the things that unite Ireland seem even greater than those that divide it.

But other countries are also using drama as a means of self-definition. Australian colleagues tell me that their late 1960s theatrical renaissance—triggered partly by increased funding and partly by a need, in the light of the Vietnam experience, to discover a national identity—is tapering off. Yet frequent visits have convinced me that Australia still has an exploratory new drama, exemplified by works like Michael Gow's *Away,* which uses the structure of *A Midsummer Night's Dream* to describe the country's entry into global maturity, and Hannie Rayson's *Hotel Sorrento,* which argues that writers flourish best in their native soul. And in South Africa writers like Percy Mtwa, Mbongeni Ngema, and Barney Simon, linked by their association with Johannesburg's Market Theatre, have all deployed drama as a means not just of raising consciousness but of exploring national identity.

Drama is not just being enriched geographically. It is also heading in new directions formally. This is almost inevitable in the age of television, mass advertising, and pop videos. Given that we are used to receiving and absorbing information so much more quickly, the traditional theatrical structure of exposition, crisis, and denouement is bound to come in for a shake-up. To put it crudely, plays are becoming much shorter or much longer, and this in itself is a reflection of theater's increasing division into the powerfully intimate or the expansively epic. On the one hand, dramatists are discovering, not least in America, that they can pack into a single 90-minute act a particularly violent, intense, emotional experience. On the other hand, they are realizing that there is a renewed interest in narrative and that audiences today have a craving for inordinate, complex stories that take a long time to unravel. In classic theater we have seen it time and again with the popularity of productions like the Royal Shakespeare Company's *Nicholas Nickleby,* Mnouchkine's *Les Atrides,* and Brook's *The Mahabharata*. Now living writers, such as David Hare with his epic trilogy on the state of Britain or Tony Kushner with *Angels in America,* are realizing that long plays give you a chance to handle a multiplicity of themes and to depict the gradations of time. I suspect this is the way all theater is heading, either toward brief, powerful experiences in small spaces or toward daylong rituals in big public places.

The key question is whether drama is also heading in new directions thematically. One school of thought argues, quite ferociously, that it has to, that the drama of political and social commentary is dead, partly because audiences are bored with it and partly because, in this day and age, there are no visible utopias to hand. We need, runs the cry, a drama that reflects the fragmented, discontinuous, essentially private nature of modern experience. Well, maybe. But my antennae tell me that the opposite is true, that, if drama is to retain any hold on the attention of the public, it has to deal with the momentous issues that confront us at the end of the 20th century.

That is not simply a rhetorical phrase. Already it is possible to identify some of the issues that are bound to dominate drama in the 1990s. One obviously is AIDS, which, especially in the United States, has already yielded a substantial body of dramatic literature. What is heartening is that we have now moved from the slightly sentimental, consciousness-raising plays to works that relate this epidemic to prevailing moral attitudes and even treat it from a blackly comic standpoint.

A second key issue, particularly relevant to post-totalitarian societies, is our attitude to the past: whether it is right to seek revenge for criminal wrongs or to erase the memory of suffering. It is a subject that comes up time and time again in relation to the Nazi concentration camps (Peter Flannery's *Singer*), South American dictatorships (Ariel Dorfman's *Death and the Maiden*), South African apartheid (Athol Fugard's *Playland*), and European communism (Howard Brenton's *Berlin Bertie*). It is also a theme that throws up endless moral dilemmas. Should revenge be a legal or an individual act? By exercising forgiveness, do we cancel out the past? And how do we draw the line between punishment and vindictiveness? As more and more evidence of past iniquities comes to light, I suspect this will emerge as the major issue of our time.

But is it the business of drama to engage with public events? All one can say is that, historically, it has always done so. The *Lysistrata* of Aristophanes was both about the madness engulfing Greece because of the drawn-out war with Sparta and about the exclusively male domination of public life. Shakespeare's history plays are about the continuing tension between order and chaos. And there is a whole stream of plays, from Shaw's *Saint Joan* to Brecht's *Galileo,* about the conflict between the conscience of the individual and the authority of the state. If art is a response to life, then that response inevitably includes events in the public arena.

All of this, of course, begs the question raised by Ruby Cohn in an earlier preface to this volume: Is there still an audience that embraces drama? I suspect there is, even though that audience is clearly changing. Arthur Miller told me recently that when he started writing plays in the 1940s he assumed, idealistically, that he was addressing the whole nation. Now he knows that he is speaking to a select handful. My own hunch is that, in the commercial theater in all countries, there are a limited number of people prepared to pay high prices to see straight plays. But I still believe there is an audience in the subsidized venues, the studio spaces, and the regional theaters everywhere that has a hunger for drama. Everything is related to ability to pay. In Hungary a theater ticket costs no more than a bowl of soup. In Peter Brook's Paris theater, the Bouffes du Nord, a ticket costs the same as a decent bottle of wine. Result: never an empty seat. It is only when ticket prices reach unrealistic proportions that people start to question the value of a night at the theater. In my experience the appetite for drama still exists if only because people need some affirmation of their existence. The challenge for the future lies not just in keeping the plays coming—450 dramatists listed in this volume will see to that—but finally in ensuring that drama is affordable, available, and accessible to all.

—Michael Billington

Preface to the sixth edition, 1999

The recurring itch to order and catalog the chaos of human activity becomes overwhelming at landmark chronological times like this, when not only a century comes to an end but a millennium, too. Fortunately theater—itself a venerable form of ordering our chaos—always surprises, slips our grasp, and refuses to be measurable. Nevertheless, observation and critique of theater persists undaunted, moved by a similar impulse that impels the theater practitioner: the desire to make sense of the world. Even if theater can apparently be tamed by the wide-angled hindsight that is the common currency of the commentators—and also proves amenable to informed analysis and the tracing of patterns of its existence—theater robustly remains idiosyncratic and forever breaks the ties of those of us who stubbornly persevere in our attempts to package it in tidy parcels.

Theater refuses to lie down and die, however many times it is pronounced dead; it might be a little lumbering or dazed for a while, or it might be written off into the margins of history as irrelevant, overvalued, or simply past its sell-by date, but theater retains a vitality and awkwardness that continually brings it to astonishing life. Yet, the amazing capacity of this most human of art forms to be an obstinate, if beleaguered survivor—as Michael Billington put it in the preface to the fifth edition of *Contemporary Dramatists*—does not mean, and never has meant, that theater and its heartbeat, the playwrights, have ever had an easy time of it.

The world at the end of this millennium is a confused and confusing place. The collapse of the harsh variants of state socialism in central and eastern Europe has revealed a different brutality inherent in so-called free market capitalism and exposed the inadequacies of liberal politics to cope with the crushing eruption of petty dictators, civil wars, and ethnic cleansing that currently besmirches the international landscape. Globalization and local chauvinism race on, hand in hand, alongside poverty and disease. Polarization rooted in religion has accompanied the convergence and dissolution of ideologies at the end of a hundred years of extremes—unbridled subjectivity on the one hand and collectivist totalitarianism on the other. This anxious state of affairs may once again have brought into sharper relief the role and purpose of theater while robbing it of the certainties of the socially and politically conscious drama of recent times, but it has not quelled the rambunctious, nagging spirit of the dogged playwright.

Set against the horrors of this most traumatic of centuries, the theater of the 20th century represents a splendid and historic achievement. Even in the lean times, the diversity and extent of its playwriting are staggering, a constant reminder of the enduring power of that distinguishing human resource called imagination. Testimony to this can be found in the number and range of playwrights represented both in the forerunners to this volume and in the continual need to top up that list engendered by the feats of the dramatists themselves; hence this latest edition, the sixth. But, notwithstanding such a positive overall report, the environment in which playwrights in the English-speaking world survive and create is rarely as supportive as their societies' self-declared level of civilization would suggest, and, though not often openly hostile, it can certainly be sapping and unfriendly.

While mostly not having to face the legal restraint of pre-production censorship—though some theaters have continued to face enormous pressure over the content of plays, particularly from conservative and religious zealots—playwrights daily grapple with the debilitating trial of self-censorship in the face of the greater challenge posed by the unforgiving and, in today's climate, increasingly the ultimate judgment of the box office. Commercial values have become pervasive, in the public sector as well as in the private, exacerbating the habitual sense of isolation and dread already felt by playwrights. As Ruby Cohn says in the preface to the third edition of *Contemporary Dramatists,* the financing of theater in the English-speaking world does not nurture and protect the playwright, a situation that has not improved with the end of the cold war.

It is impossible to legislate for talent, but it should be possible to give it space to breathe and to look after it, yet few theaters are able to establish long-term relationships with writers, even if they manage to present new plays in their main programs in the first place. Where is the room for experiment and risk beyond the studio ghetto and away from the proliferation of workshops that audition writers in place of offering them production? This is not to attack either studio theaters or workshops, which do sustain and help many playwrights, but to question the responsibility of our societies toward the protection and promotion of the art form itself.

For the moment theater has lost its place as the conscience of a nation. It has been pushed into the sidelines by obsession with cartoons, films, fashion, sport, pop music, and home computer games. In this fast-changing world of ever more sophisticated electronic media, which are underpinning the ever extending global reach of both economics and culture, it is a difficult struggle for the playwrights of today to express their vision and passion and to make theater matter. Yet, while it is true that these new technological advances represent a major test for theater, looked at another way they present a tremendous opportunity for playwrights to show precisely why theater is special and why we need it. Not only can technology itself be harnessed to aid theatrical presentation but, more importantly, in the simplest or in the most complex of theatrical productions, the live use of language and silence, of movement and stillness, of sound, space, and light to tell a human story can demonstrate and emphasize the vital contrast between the mechanical fixities of the new media and the human fluidity of drama.

One response at the entertainment end of the profession has been the mass marketing and cloning of popular shows that allow productions of musicals such as *Cats* to be reproduced around the world, bringing in their train all the paraphernalia associated with them—the CDs, videos, T-shirts, and so forth. This international propagation is a paradoxical tendency given that theater is distinguished by the uniqueness of the un-reproducible moment and the live, ephemeral interaction between actor and audience. In similar vein, many theaters are being urged, and funded, to follow suit, often in the name of access, by making and distributing video versions of their performances. But no matter how many cameras are used or in what advantageous positions, such a process can result only in a degeneration of the original; the subsequent video will likely as not convince its viewers that they did not miss anything by missing the live performance, and just as likely it will put them off ever again thinking that it might be a good idea to go to a theater to see a live show. The video would probably be unexciting in video terms as well and may have value only as a documentary record for future researchers or as a nostalgic memento for those who did enjoy themselves at the live event. But, if this push for electronic exploitation undermines future audiences, can it avoid being a memento mori?

The popularity of the exportable, leviathan musical can be seen, however, as an understandable and even positive response to the atomization of our societies and the accompanying reduction in, and external control over, public space. (Witness, for example, the burgeoning of impersonal shopping malls patrolled by private uniformed guards under the blank stare of security cameras). Such shows do provide live, collective, and often socially aware experiences of celebration and enjoyment, but their rise has coincided with a serious consequence for playwrights—the decline of the large public play. Playwrights have had to make an accommodation with this insecure situation. Although generalizing, it can be said that thematically they have responded vigorously. They have redefined the political, which was seen as unfashionable, making it less direct and explicit; they have explored the urban as well as the rural nightmare, not always with optimism but usually with hard-won humor; and they have placed gender and individual identity center stage. They have found a new intensity in the drama of the small, tight focus and a new appreciation of the intimacy of the small space—a double-edged blessing, as the obvious and easy advantages of proximity can also lead to lack of concern for form. On the marketing front they have been further squeezed by the search for new audiences, which has necessarily been placed at the top of the agenda for many theaters without the most obvious means of achieving it being made available, namely the lowering of ticket prices. But at their sharpest the playwrights have fought their corner proudly. They have managed to find those elusive new audiences and have matched for them the intensity they have more usually been seeking and finding in popular music.

In different ways such reexaminations have happened throughout the century. Within dramaturgy playwrights (and others) have often engaged in this pursuit in order to discover an antidote and an alternative to the dominant strain of naturalism. In the late 20th century this line of inquiry has sometimes resulted in self-conscious displays of "theaterness" by writers and their collaborators—that is, overeager "look at me, this is theater, you can't find this anywhere else" types of gestures. When effective, however, this search has revealed a new awareness of the pleasure, of the eroticism even, that is fundamental to the communal act of performance and its reception. Furthermore, rediscovering the "play" element in playwriting has led some writers to exploit with intelligence and wit the popularity of other cultural forms, both from inside the theater, like revue or vaudeville, and from without, like fashion or film. Although occasionally allowing the archness of pastiche to stifle the energy of the original inspiration, dramatists have responded brightly to the challenges and have gloried in theater's eclecticism and particularity.

Playwriting has also had to face a challenge from the demotion and demolition of the word and from the concurrent rise of other primary sources and arbiters of artistic authority. Coeval with the explosion of interest in sexuality and the body that partnered the recent strong emergence of devised work (work devised in and through rehearsal without following a prewritten, singly authored text) and the accompanying faster dissolution of compartmentalized theatrical categories, there has been a significant crossover between forms that has seen new dramatic energies flow into music theater, dance theater, and the expanding world of site-specific installations and performance art. As a result, what was once a distinct branch of the fine arts is now subsumed under the voluminous umbrella of experimental theater.

In this situation, when classic texts are seen as merely a notation for performance, it is not surprising that new texts are viewed as dispensable or as molten artefacts to be molded not by the playwright but by the new auteurs—the director or the performer. Throughout the 20th century there has been a growing interest in the multiplicity of meanings that are made in the theater. Increasingly they have ceased to be identified as being made through conventional forms of representation fashioned by the unequivocal viewpoint of the writer and centered on directed, intended communication with the audience; the performance movement has denied the centrality of a single, guiding role in the creation of meaning and has, thereby, disrupted the dialogue from the stage with the audience in order to allow for a myriad of subjective interpretations made by the audience to be equally valid and significant. This has led to the progress and promotion of the abstract, a trend that has sometimes embraced and sometimes explicitly excluded the playwright, just as the assault on the traditional notion of the text and authorial intention has put further pressure on the playwright while, at the same time, offering new avenues for collaboration and expression, too.

Playwrights keep emerging regardless of the problems and the obstacles thrown up. This is general cause for optimism; especially gladdening is the fact that many writers in the last quarter century have not followed the traditional trajectory of success and decline but have gone on and on writing, becoming prolific and protean creators that have defied the usual pessimistic assumptions concerning the longevity of a modern playwright's career. Such a career is now also much more varied than was once the norm. Some writers, for example, decide to work in the under- or un-reported alternative drama of social engagement—community theater, youth theater, educational theater, theater for development, theater for the homeless, theater in prisons. Or, in order to survive, they might try to balance writing for the different media—and while theater loses some, many keep the faith. But whatever forum writers choose, and whether they are experienced or novices, they always face the same haunting challenge every time they sit down in front of a clear screen or blank sheet of paper: how to write the best play they can. And while this volume cannot provide the answer—for there is no answer, only continual striving—it can and does bear bold witness to the richness of the many temporary solutions that have thankfully been found by our unbowed band of contemporary dramatists.

—Colin Chambers

EDITOR'S NOTE

Contemporary Dramatists, now in its sixth edition, has been in print since 1973. Each edition has had the same goal: to provide biographical and bibliographic information, as well as brief critical essays, on some of the world's most important English-language dramatists.

The sixth edition has entries on 433 dramatists, all of whom, to the best of our knowledge, were alive at the beginning of our revision process (although two entrants who died late in the aforementioned process—John Hopkins and Johnny Speight—were included so that their entries could be brought up to date). Some of the entrants, such as Mark Ravenhill and Phyllis Nagy, were born in the 1960s and did not become prominent for their plays until the 1990s; others, such as Arthur Miller and Doris Lessing, have been listed in *Contemporary Dramatists* since its first edition.

Most of the sixth-edition entrants are from North America and the British Isles: 162 are classified as American; 24 as Canadian; 5 as Jamaican, Montserratian, or Trinidadian; 15 as Irish; and 158 as British, English, Scottish, or Northern Irish. The remaining entrants include 24 Australians, 13 New Zealanders, 2 Indians, 2 Singaporeans, and 2 Malaysians, as well as 27 dramatists from various countries in Africa.

All the entries have the same organization:

- *Biographical data,* listing, if known, the entrant's nationality, date and place of birth, education, military service, spouse and number of children, career, awards, significant memberships, agent, and address.

- *Bibliography,* listing all the dramatist's plays and other separately published work, including short-story and poetry collections, novels, books of nonfiction, and edited and translated books. Also listed are media adaptations, theatrical activities, and manuscript collections. The bibliography ends with a selected list of critical studies about the author's work.

- *Personal statement by the entrant (when available),* discussing the dramatist's work, approach to writing, early influences, or other topics related to his or her plays.

- *Critical essay on the entrant's plays,* written by a scholar or critic. Each essay ends with the contributor's byline.

St. James would like to thank the many people, including the advisers, who worked on this revision. The suggestions of the advisers were used to select the entrants and to help with other matters concerning the content and organization of the book. We would also like to thank the contributors, many of whom agreed to write for the book despite a heavy workload or prior publication commitments. Finally, we would like to express our appreciation to the dramatists who provided biographical and bibliographic information for their entries.

I would personally like to thank the people who worked with me in organizing the project and editing the book: Sally Cobau, who oversaw the compilation of the biographical and bibliographic sections and helped with many day-to-day tasks; Terry Bain, who helped with commissioning writers and handled much of the correspondence with them; Robert Rauch, who was the line editor for the majority of the essays and was essential in establishing many of the editing guidelines; Elizabeth Laskey and Susan Brown, who also edited essays; Elizabeth Oakes, who handled various tasks throughout the project; Janice Jorgensen, who edited essays and reviewed entries for last-minute problems; and Mike Tyrkus, who coordinated various in-house responsibilities, including the proofreading, and helped resolve problems with the project and with individual entries.

—Thomas Riggs
Editor

ADVISERS

Arthur H. Ballet
Martin Banham
Michael Benedikt
Eric Bentley
C.W.E. Bigsby
Michael Billington
Herbert Blau
John Bowen
Katharine Brisbane
Constance Brissenden
Alasdair Cameron
Richard Christiansen
Harold Clurman
Ruby Cohn
John Robert Colombo
Albert Cooke
Patricia Cooke
Robert W. Corrigan
Tish Dace
W.A. Darlington
John Elsom
Richard Gilman
Anthony Graham-White
Otis L. Guernsey, Jr.
Carole Hayman
Ronald Hayman
Nick Hern
John Istel
Stanley Kauffmann
Veronica Kelly
Naseem Khan
Bruce King
Laurence Kitchin
Richard Kostelanetz
Maurice Lindsay
Frank Marcus
E.A. Markham
Bonnie Marranca
Howard McNaughton
Walter J. Meserve
Benedict Nightingale
Richard Schechner
Joel Schechter
Alan Schneider
Michael T. Smith
John Spurling
Alan Strachan
J.L. Styan
Howard Taubman
John Russell Taylor
J.C. Trewin
Darwin T. Turner
Irving Wardie
Gerald Weales
Ross Wetzsteon
B.A. Young

CONTRIBUTORS

Elizabeth Adams
Addell Austin Anderson
Frances Rademacher Anderson
Gary Anderson
Thomas Apple
Arthur H. Ballet
Carol Banks
Clive Barker
Judith E. Barlow
Gene A. Barnett
Linda Ben-Zvi
Joss Bennathan
Eugene Benson
Gerald M. Berkowitz
Michael Bertin
C. W. E. Bigsby
Michael Billington
Walter Bode
John Bowen
Gaynor F. Bradish
Katharine Brisbane
Constance Brissenden
John Russell Brown
Joseph Bruchac
John Bull
Jarka M. Burian
Alasdair Cameron
Susan Carlson
Bernard Carragher
Ned Chaillet
D. D. C. Chambers
Bill Coco
Ruby Cohn
Clare Colvin
Judy Cooke
Patricia Cooke
Richard Corballis
Tish Dace

W. A. Darlington
Terence Dawson
Elin Diamond
Tony Dunn
Arnold Edinborough
Jane Edwardes
John Elsom
Mark W. Estrin
John V. Falconieri
Michael Feingold
Peter Fitzpatrick
Richard Fotheringham
Leah D. Frank
Melvin J. Friedman
Helen Gilbert
Reid Gilbert
Lizbeth Goodman
Lois Gordon
Martin Gottfried
Anthony Graham-White
Steve Grant
Frances Gray
Prabhu S. Guptara
Paul Hadfield
Jonathan Hammond
James Hansford
Ronald Hayman
Dick Higgins
Errol Hill
Harold Hobson
William M. Hoffman
Arthur Horowitz
Jorge Huerta
Christopher Innes
Esiaba Irobi
John Istel
C. Lee Jenner
Veronica Kelly
David E. Kemp
Burton S. Kendle
Helene Keyssar
Bruce King
H. Gustav Klaus
Richard Kostelanetz
John G. Kuhn
Bernd-Peter Lange
Paul Lawley
Michael T. Leech
Maurice Lindsay
Felicia Hardison Londré
Glenn Loney
James MacDonald
James Magruder
Paul Makeham
Frank Marcus
E. A. Markham
Thomas B. Markus
John Martin
John McCallum
Paul McGillick
Howard McNaughton
Walter J. Meserve
Geoffrey Milne
Louis D. Mitchell
Tony Mitchell
Christian H. Moe
Christopher Murray
Benedict Nightingale
Olu Obafemi
Garry O'Connor
Marion O'Connor
Osita Okagbue
John O'Leary
Judy Lee Oliva
M. Elizabeth Osborn
Eric Overmyer
Malcolm Page
Richard H. Palmer
Dorothy Parker
Don Perkins
William Peterson
Roxana Petzold
Rosemary Pountney
Henry Raynor
Leslie du S. Read
John M. Reilly
Sandra L. Richards
James Roose-Evans
Geoff Sadler
Arthur Sainer
Ellen Schiff
Adrienne Scullion
Elizabeth Shostak
Elaine Shragge
Michael Sidnell
Kirpal Singh
Christopher Smith
Michael T. Smith
A. Richard Sogliuzzo
John Spurling
Carol Simpson Stern
Alan Strachan
J. L. Styan
John Thomson
Peter Thomson
Joanne Tompkins
Darwin T. Turner
Elaine Turner
Victor I. Ukaegbu
Michelene Wandor
Erika J. Waters
Gerald Weales

LIST OF ENTRANTS

Michael Abbensetts
Ama Ata Aidoo
JoAnne Akalaitis
Edward Albee
Ted Allan
Robert Anderson
John Antrobus
John Arden
George Axelrod
Alan Ayckbourn

Thomas Babe
Jon Robin Baitz
Janis Balodis
Biyi Bandele-Thomas
Amiri Baraka
Howard Barker
Peter Barnes
Sebastian Barry
Neil Bartlett
J. P. Clark Bekederemo
Hilary Bell
Alan Bennett
Eric Bentley
Steven Berkoff
Barry Bermange
Kenneth Bernard
Stephen Bill
George Birimisa
Alan Bleasdale
Lee Blessing
Eric Bogosian
Carol Bolt
Chris Bond
Edward Bond
Andrew John Bovell
John Bowen
Howard Brenton
Lee Breuer
John Broughton
Kenneth H. Brown
Ed Bullins
John Burrows and John Harding
Charles Busch
Jez Butterworth
Alexander Buzo
John Byrne

David Campton
Lewis John Carlino
Lonnie Carter
Jim Cartwright
David Caute
Frank Chin
Caryl Churchill
Brian Clark
Sally Clark
Darrah Cloud
Barry Collins
Constance S. Congdon
Stewart Conn
Ray Cooney
Ron Cowen
Richard Crane
David Cregan
Martin Crimp
Michael Cristofer
Beverley Cross

Sarah Daniels
Nick Darke
Jack Davis
Ossie Davis
Alma De Groen
Phillip Hayes Dean
Nick Dear
Shelagh Delaney
Keith Dewhurst
Barry Dickins
Steven Dietz
Charles Dizenzo
J. P. Donleavy
Rosalyn Drexler
Martin Duberman
Nell Dunn
Christopher Durang
Charles Dyer

R. Sarif Easmon
David Edgar
David Edgecombe
Obi B. Egbuna
Ron Elisha
Kevin Elyot
Nick Enright
Marcella Evaristi
Stanley Eveling

Jules Feiffer
David Fennario
Harvey Fierstein
Peter Flannery
Horton Foote
Richard Foreman
María Irene Fornés
Michaelanne Forster
James Forsyth
Paul Foster
Brad Fraser
Mario Fratti

Michael Frayn
David Freeman
David French
Bruce Jay Friedman
Brian Friel
Terence Frisby
Christopher Fry
Athol Fugard
Charles Fuller
George Furth

Tsegaye Gabre-Medhin
Frank Gagliano
Tom Gallacher
Herb Gardner
David Geary
Larry Gelbart
Jonathan Gems
Pam Gems
William Gibson
Peter Gill
Frank D. Gilroy
John Godber
James Goldman
Steve Gooch
Clem Gorman
Philip Kan Gotanda
Michael Gow
Jack Gray
John Gray
Simon Gray
Spalding Gray
Richard Greenberg
David Greenspan
Trevor Griffiths
John Guare
A. R. Gurney
Michael Gurr

Wilson John Haire
John Hale
Roger Hall
Willis Hall and Keith Waterhouse
David Halliwell
Christopher Hampton
William Hanley
Chris Hannan
David Hare
Richard Harris
Tony Harrison
Ronald Harwood
Michael Hastings
William Hauptman
Allan Havis
Ronald Hayman
Iain Heggie
Tom Hendry
Beth Henley
James Ene Henshaw
John Herbert
Dorothy Hewett
Jack Hibberd
Dick Higgins

Tomson Highway
Errol Hill
Robert Hivnor
Stuart Hoar
William M. Hoffman
Joan Holden
Margaret Hollingsworth
Robert Holman
John Hopkins
Israel Horovitz
Debbie Horsfield
Donald Howarth
Tina Howe
Dusty Hughes
Ron Hutchinson
David Henry Hwang

Albert Innaurato
Debbie Isitt

Stephen Jeffreys
Ann Jellicoe
Len Jenkin
Terry Johnson
Keith Johnstone

Lee Kalcheim
Sarah Kane
Girish Karnad
John B. Keane
Charlotte Keatley
Kee Thuan Chye
Barrie Keeffe
Daniel Keene
Tom Kempinski
A. L. Kennedy
Adrienne Kennedy
Gibson Kente
Wendy Kesselman
Thomas Kilroy
Kenneth Koch
Arthur Kopit
Hone Kouka
H. M. Koutoukas
Kuo Pao Kun
Hanif Kureishi
Tony Kushner

Kevin Laffan
David Lan
Arthur Laurents
Bryony Lavery
Ray Lawler
Jerome Lawrence
Mike Leigh
Hugh Leonard
Doris Lessing
Deborah Levy
Wendy Lill
Romulus Linney
Liz Lochhead
Quincy Long
Earl Lovelace

Stephen Lowe
Craig Lucas
Doug Lucie
Ken Ludwig
Peter Luke
Tes Lyssiotis

Jackson Mac Low
Sharman Macdonald
Eduardo Machado
Yulisa Amadu Maddy
Karen Malpede
David Mamet
Matsemela Manaka
K. S. Maniam
Wolf Mankowitz
Emily Mann
Maishe Maponya
Patrick Marber
Tony Marchant
Donald Margulies
Jane Martin
William Mastrosimone
Mustapha Matura
Eugene McCabe
Anthony McCarten
Michael McClure
Martin McDonagh
Greg McGee
John McGrath
Tom McGrath
Frank McGuinness
Clare McIntyre
James McLure
Terrence McNally
Conor McPherson
Zakes Mda
Murray Mednick
Mark Medoff
Charles L. Mee, Jr.
Ronald Millar
Arthur Miller
Susan Miller
Ron Milner
Anthony Minghella
Adrian Mitchell
Julian Mitchell
Ken Mitchell
Loften Mitchell
Mavor Moore
Daniel Mornin
Bill Morrison
John Mortimer
Tad Mosel
Gregory Motton
David Mowat
Percy Mtwa
Rona Munro
Tom Murphy
Joanna Murray-Smith
John Murrell
Joseph Musaphia

Phyllis Nagy
N. Richard Nash
Richard Nelson
G. F. Newman
Mbongeni Ngema
Ngugi wa Thiong'o
Peter Nichols
Lewis Nkosi
John Ford Noonan
Marsha Norman
Louis Nowra

Meredith Oakes
Olu Obafemi
Wale Ogunyemi
Mary O'Malley
Michael O'Neill and Jeremy Seabrook
Femi Osofisan
Vincent O'Sullivan
Eric Overmyer
Rochelle Owens
Martin Owusu
OyamO

Louise Page
Suzan-Lori Parks
Gieve Patel
Robert Patrick
Caryl Phillips
John Pielmeier
David Pinner
Winsome Pinnock
Harold Pinter
Alan Plater
Stephen Poliakoff
Sharon Pollock
Bernard Pomerance
David Pownall

David Rabe
Mark Ravenhill
Hannie Rayson
James Reaney
Dennis J. Reardon
Barry Reckord
Keith Reddin
Christina Reid
Renée
Hanon Reznikov
Trevor D. Rhone
Ronald Ribman
Anne Ridler
Erika Ritter
Billy Roche
John Romeril
Ola Rotimi
David Rudkin
John Ruganda
Willy Russell

Arthur Sainer
Milcha Sánchez-Scott
James A. Saunders

Joan M. Schenkar
James Schevill
Murray Schisgal
David Selbourne
Stephen Sewell
Anthony Shaffer
Peter Shaffer
Ntozake Shange
John Patrick Shanley
Wallace Shawn
Jill Shearer
Sam Shepard
Martin Sherman
Stuart Sherman
Barney Simon
Neil Simon
Beverley Simons
Stephen Sinclair
Bernard Slade
Anna Deavere Smith
Michael T. Smith
Zulu Sofola
Octavio Solis
Bode Sowande
Wole Soyinka
Johnny Speight
John Spurling
David Starkweather
Barrie Stavis
John Steppling
Peter Stone
Tom Stoppard
David Storey
Mike Stott
Karen Sunde

George Tabori
Ted Tally
Ronald Tavel
Megan Terry
Peter Terson
Judith Thompson
Katherine Thomson
Sue Townsend
William Trevor

Alfred Uhry
Peter Ustinov

Luis Valdez
Jean-Claude van Itallie
Gore Vidal
Paula Vogel

Derek Walcott
George F. Walker
Joseph A. Walker
Naomi Wallace
Michelene Wandor
Douglas Turner Ward
Wendy Wasserstein
Arnold Weinstein
Michael Weller
Mac Wellman
Timberlake Wertenbaker
Arnold Wesker
Richard Wesley
Peter Whelan
Edgar Nkosi White
John White
Ted Whitehead
Hugh Whitemore
Christopher Wilkinson
Heathcote Williams
Nigel Williams
David Williamson
August Wilson
Doric Wilson
Lanford Wilson
Robert M Wilson
Snoo Wilson
George C Wolfe
Eleanor Wong
Charles Wood
Nicholas Wright
Olwen Wymark

Susan Yankowitz

Suzan L. Zeder
Paul Zindel

ABBENSETTS, Michael

Nationality: British. **Born:** British Guiana (now Guyana), 8 June 1938; became British citizen, 1974. **Education:** Queen's College, Guyana, 1952-56; Stanstead College, Quebec; Sir George Williams University, Montreal, 1960-61. **Career:** Security attendant, Tower of London, 1963-67; staff member, Sir John Soane Museum, London, 1968-71. Resident playwright, Royal Court Theatre, London, 1974; visiting professor of drama, Carnegie Mellon University, Pittsburgh, 1981. **Awards:** George Devine award, 1973; Arts Council bursary, 1977; Afro-Caribbean award, 1979. **Address:** c/o Heinemann Educational Books Ltd., Halley Court, Jordan Hill, Oxford OX2 8EJ, England.

PUBLICATIONS

Plays

Sweet Talk (produced London, 1973; New York, 1974). London, Eyre Methuen, 1976.
Alterations (produced London and New York, 1978; revised version produced London, 1985).
Samba (produced London, 1980). London, Eyre Methuen, 1980.
In the Mood (produced London, 1981).
Outlaw (produced Leicester and London, 1983).
El Dorado (produced London, 1984).
Living Together (includes *Roystony's Day, The Street Party*). Oxford, Heinemann, 1988.
The Lion (produced 1993).

Radio Plays: *Home Again*, 1975; *The Sunny Side of the Street*, 1977; *Brothers of the Sword*, 1978; *The Fast Lane*, 1980; *The Dark Horse*, 1981; *Summer Passions*, 1985.

Television Plays: *The Museum Attendant*, 1973; *Inner City Blues*, 1975; *Crime and Passion*, 1976; *Black Christmas*, 1977; *Roadrunner*, 1977; *Empire Road* series, 1977, 1979; *Easy Money*, 1982; *Big George Is Dead*, 1987.

Novel

Empire Road (novelization of television series). London, Panther, 1979.

*

Critical Study: "Taking Race for Granted" by Margaret Walters, in *New Society* (London), 16 November 1978.

Michael Abbensetts comments:

(1982) I once read something a black American playwright had written: he said his plays could not be understood by a white person. That is not the way I feel about my plays. It seems to me that if a play is good enough it should have something to say to everybody, once they are prepared to look for that something. However, having said that, I would like to add that I would never want to write a play that a black audience did not like, no matter how popular it was with a white audience. When my stage play *Alterations* was praised by critics of the *Sunday Times* and the *Financial Times*, it made me feel very pleased, but I was equally pleased that the reviewer in the *Jamaica Gleaner* liked the play as well.

Which brings me to the question I am sometimes asked. Why do I write so much for television? First, BBC-TV pays me well—okay, *reasonably* well—and second, my TV plays are bound to reach a larger black audience than my stage plays ever do.

Yet originally I had never even thought of writing for the theatre. Originally I wanted to be a novelist. Then while I was at university in Canada I saw a version of Osborne's *Look Back in Anger*, and suddenly I knew what I wanted to be—a playwright. So then I came to England. Other West Indians were coming to the UK to find jobs, I came here to find theatre. I'd read of a place called the Royal Court Theatre, and I vowed to myself to get one of my plays on there, even though, at that time, I hadn't even written a single play. Yet in time I did get a play on at the Royal Court, and I was made resident dramatist at the Court. A lot has happened to me since those first, heady days at the Royal Court Theatre.

* * *

Of the black British playwrights who emerged in the 1970s, Michael Abbensetts is quite simply the best. His first work to be widely noticed, the 1973 television play *The Museum Attendant,* struck the two notes that characterize all of his output. First, it worked out a tragic situation within a broad tradition of comedy; the humor arises primarily from incongruity, though there are fine instances of verbal felicity and wit. In the juxtaposition of tragedy and comedy Abbensetts goes back to English Renaissance drama, though the more immediate mentor is probably Edward Albee. Second, his work stood out because it was practically the first time that television drama had shown an accurate slice of immigrant life. A whole generation of television sitcoms (*Love Thy Neighbour* and *Mixed Blessings* were then the latest) had taken race as their main, if not sole, theme. With their appalling racial jokes, shown on the dubious grounds of "therapeutic value," these plays were deeply upsetting to many people. *The Fosters*, the only previous all-black comedy series, was welcomed by blacks but showed its American origins too clearly to be more than an aperitif. *Gangsters*, another television series, also with racial jokes and in an American blood-and-thunder movie tradition, was more controversial. Condemned as "vicious and vacuous," it was also praised for "somehow managing to suggest more of the corruption and reasons for racial tension than a score of more balanced and realistic programmes." It did not, however, affect the convention of cardboard blacks, who were a "problem" or who were pawns in arguments about British politics—e.g., in the automatic coupling of racism and fascism. Generally, blacks in plays were just plain stupid, as in *Curry and Chips* or *Till Death Us Do Part.* At best the presence of blacks on television consoled a liberal conscience.

Abbensetts's achievement in presenting a black viewpoint on black life in Britain allowed his characters to emerge as fully human beings for the very first time in the history of British performing media. He provides an honest picture of the diversity of black people, with individuals as sincere, muddled, feckless, wicked, or wonderful as might come from any other group. In contrast to the work of otherwise fine black playwrights such as Mustapha Matura, Abbensetts's work is free of defensive clowning.

Abbensetts has said that *Black Christmas* constitutes his claim to be taken seriously as a writer. In it a West Indian family under the peculiar strains of life in Britain holds together only by sheer will. Abbensetts can be seen, then, as working also in a tradition of domestic drama, though "domestic" needs to be understood in its extended Third World rather than nuclear Western sense. The concentrated impact of the concerns of *Black Christmas* was spun out into two series called *Empire Road.* Slicker if slighter than the single play, this established Abbensetts with the public. Especially in the second series he was able to match his writing to the personality and strength of the actors. "D.I.V.O.R.C.E.," the seventh episode of the second series, is generally considered the best; and in its most praised section two of the characters, who are drunk, reminisce about their life in Britain and especially those experiences that are traumatic or hideous. Abbensetts often presents middle-aged characters haunted by memory, a device that enables him to add irony and bite to his plays. In "D.I.V.O.R.C.E." this haunted hinterland of memory has a rich dramatic impact that itself comes to haunt viewers.

It is, however, the stage play *Alterations* that is Abbensetts's best complete work. Walker, a West Indian tailor, is desperately racing against the clock, trying to alter an immense number of trousers to sizes suitable for export to Japan If he can finish the work, he will earn enough money in time to pay the deposit and begin to realize a lifelong ambition of having his own shop. The pressures created by the situation impose a series of alterations in the lives, attitudes, and expectations of all the characters in the play: Walker himself; Horace and Buster, who intermittently help and hinder Walker; and Walker's discarded wife Darlene, to whom he is still attached in a strange West Indian way. All of Abbensetts's plays are, to a certain extent, parables. Though he tends to pack too much into his stage plays, they seem generally to be better constructed than his television plays.

His best television play is *Big George Is Dead.* At Big George's funeral Tony appears, having returned prosperous from Tobago to repay the money he owes his former friend Boogie. For old times' sake Tony and Boogie decide to relive their glorious past. Back in the swinging 1960s Boogie, Tony, and Big George had been three black desperadoes calling themselves "the wild bunch." Identities forged on the front line of Soho nightlife are tested in a London that now has punks, muggers, and drug dealers. As the night wears on, the two become more and more immersed in the tragic sense of loss in their lives—particularly Tony, whose girlfriend married Boogie when Tony was forced to disappear to Tobago. Tony's son has been adopted by Boogie, and no one wants the boy to realize the truth. It is an understated, atmospheric play, finely testifying to Abbensetts's reluctant cleavage from his earlier comic mode that made it possible for him richly to explore the muted tragedies of everyday people and everyday lives.

Abbensetts has been criticized by both black and white activists for his lack of political commitment. Over the years it has become clear that he does have a political vision, though it is not, of course, rendered in terms of British political allegiances. He has a larger vision of immigrant groups as incipiently one community, an all-embracing refuge that strengthens black people to tackle the problems presented by the alien white man's world in which they live. But Abbensetts also portrays the actualities of the relations between the different immigrant groups as well as between generations, and he raises the question of where this community is headed.

—Prabhu S. Guptara

AIDOO, (Christina) Ama Ata

Nationality: Ghanaian. **Born:** Abeadzi Kyiakor in 1942. **Education:** University of Ghana, Legon (Institute of African Studies fellowship), B.A. (honours) 1964; Stanford University, California. **Career:** Lecturer in English, University of Cape Coast, Ghana, 1970-82; PNDC Secretary (Minister) for Education, 1982-83; writer-in-residence, University of Richmond, Virginia, 1989. **Awards:** Fulbright scholarship, 1988.

Publications

Plays

The Dilemma of a Ghost (produced Legon, 1964; Pittsburgh, 1988). Accra, Longman, 1965; New York, Macmillan, 1971.
Anowa (produced London, 1991). London, Longman, and New York, Humanities Press, 1970.

Novels

Our Sister Killjoy; or, Reflections from a Black-eyed Squint. London, Longman, 1977; New York, NOK, 1979.
Changes—A Love Story. London, Women's Press, 1991.

Short Stories

No Sweetness Here. London, Longman, 1970; New York, Doubleday, 1971.
The Eagle and the Chickens and Other Stories. Enugu, Nigeria, Tana Press, 1986.
The Girl Who Can and Other Stories. Legon, Ghana, Sub-Saharan Publishers, 1996.

Poetry

Someone Talking to Sometime. Harare, College Press, 1985.
Birds and Other Poems. Harare, College Press, 1987.
An Angry Letter in January and Other Poems. Coventry, Dangaroo Press, 1992.

Other

Dancing Out Doubts. Enugu, Nigeria, NOK, 1982.

*

Critical Studies: *Ama Ata Aidoo: The Dilemma of a Ghost* (study guide) by Jane W. Grant, London, Longman, 1980; *Women Writers in Black Africa* by Lloyd Brown, Westport, Connecticut, Greenwood, 1981; *Ngambika: Studies of Women in African Lit-*

erature edited by Carole Boyce Davies and Anne Adams Greaves, Trenton, New Jersey, Africa World Press, 1986; *Diverse Voices: Essays on Twentieth-Century Women Writers in English* edited by Harriet Devine Jump, London, Harvester Wheatsheaf, 1991; *The Art of Ama Ata Aidoo: Polylectics and Reading Against Neocolonialsim* by Vincent O. Odamtten, Gainseville, University Press of Florida, 1994; "Clothing as Iconography: Examples of Ba, Aidoo, and Emecheta" by Chioma Opara, in *Feminism and Black Women's Creative Writing: Theory, Practice, and Criticism* edited by Aduke Adebayo, Ibadan, Nigeria, AMD, 1996; "National Identities, Tradition, and Feminism: The Novels of Ama Ata Aidoo Read in the Context of the Works of Kwame Nkrumah" by Elizabeth Willey, in *Interventions: Feminist Dialogues on Third World Women's Literature and Film,* New York, Garland, 1997.

* * *

Ama Ata Aidoo's two plays focus upon women's relationship to traditional values. In both the husband, the central male character, is ineffectual and unwilling to comprehend the effect of his actions or inaction on his wife.

A stock situation in African drama is the conflict between the modern ideas of the "been-to"—the man who has been to Europe for his education—and the traditions of his community. The title of Aidoo's first play, *The Dilemma of a Ghost*, comes from a song that children sing, that the university graduate Ato (the play's main character) loved as a child, and that he now sees as symbolizing his position:

> One early morning,
> When the moon was up
> Shining as the sun,
> I went to Elmina Junction
> And there and there,
> I saw a wretched ghost
> Going up and down
> Singing to himself
> "Shall I go
> To Cape Coast,
> Or to Elmina
> I don't know,
> I can't tell.
> I don't know,
> I can't tell."

The title character of Aidoo's other play, *Anowa*, has followed her own will in defiance of her community's expectations, and she also refers to herself as a ghost. The metaphor points to the isolation and strain felt by someone who has set himself or herself apart from the life and values of the community.

African playwrights have tended to identify with the been-to, but in *The Dilemma of a Ghost* Ato is almost unbelievably callow. He has not told his family that he married while in America. When the family becomes concerned about his wife's infertility—even when they subject her to curative herbal massage—he does not explain that he has insisted upon using contraception. Nor, it seems, has he prepared his wife, Eulalie, in any way for the attitudes she will encounter in his home village.

The other twist on the dramatic norm is that he has married not a white but a black woman—someone who is, to his family's horror, the descendant of slaves. She, too, is a rather unsympathetic figure, filled with false suppositions about "native" life and increasingly given to drinking too much.

Given such a central couple and the not altogether believable Americanisms that Eulalie is given, the vitality of the play lies in the women of Ato's village, in his mother and sister and in the two neighboring women who act as a chorus. It is from their perspective that the marriage and its conflicts are seen:

> My people have a lusty desire
> To see the tender skin
> On top of a child's scalp
> Rise and fall with human life.
> Your machines, my stranger-girl,
> Cannot go on an errand.
> They have no hands to dress you
> when you are dead. . . .

It is the compassion of Ato's mother that in the end leads her to rebuke her son and draw his wife into the family.

In Aidoo's second play Anowa is a beautiful but willful girl whose mother resists the vocation of priestess that others foresee for her daughter. For her part Anowa refuses the suitors of her parents' choice, marries a man the community considers a good-for-nothing, and leaves the village forever. With her aid her husband, Kofi, prospers in trade with the British, but Anowa, driven by an inner vision, refuses the perquisites and leisure that her husband and, as in the earlier play, a choral pair take for granted. Finally, after a quarrel in which Anowa guesses that the priest told Kofi she has destroyed his manhood and that he half believes her to be a witch, he shoots himself and she drowns herself.

It is remarkable that, in contrast to many other African plays, in Aidoo's works the historical events of the late nineteenth century are relegated to the background. The British, for example, are represented only by a picture of Queen Victoria hanging in Kofi's house. There is some suggestion that in her sensitivity to "the common pain and the general wrong," and especially in her acute discomfort with the institution of slavery, Anowa represents Africa. But more intensely felt and conveyed is the misery of her personal situation: self-exile from her community, childlessness, and profound alienation from her husband's way of life. Aidoo uses the historical setting to present freshly the call for a more liberated role for women. Anowa says, "I hear in other lands a woman is nothing. And they let her know this from the day of her birth. But here, O my spirit mother, they let a girl grow up as she pleases until she is married. And then she is like any woman anywhere: in order for her man to be a man, she must not think, she must not talk." But Aidoo avoids the overt didacticism of some other African plays on women's roles by placing her central character in another century, where her attitudes appear eccentric.

Aidoo's plays are individual, wry, sometimes poetic, and—in the case of *The Dilemma of a Ghost*—humorous. They deal with important themes, but these are secondary to the particular characters who are comfortable in or alienated from the community at the heart of the plays.

—Anthony Graham-White

AKALAITIS, JoAnne

Nationality: American. **Born:** Chicago, Illinois, 29 June 1937. **Education:** University of Chicago, B.A. in philosophy 1960; attended Stanford University. **Family:** Married Philip Glass in 1965 (divorced 1974); one daughter and one son. **Career:** Presented work and taught playwriting throughout North America, Europe, Australia, Nicaragua, Israel, and Japan. Co-founder of Mabou Mines, New York, 1970, and performer, designer, and director, 1970-90; playwright-in-residence, Mark Taper Forum, Los Angeles, 1984-85; artistic associate, Joseph Papp Public Theater, New York, 1990-91; artistic director, New York Shakespeare Festival, 1991-93. Co-founder and chef, Food restaurant. **Awards:** Obie award, 1976, 1977, 1979, 1984; Guggenheim fellowship, 1981; Rosemund Gilder award, 1981; Drama Desk award, 1983; Rockefeller grant, 1984. **Agent:** Flora Roberts, 157 West 57th Street, New York, New York 10019. **Address:** c/o New York Shakespeare Festival, 425 Lafayette Street, New York, New York 10003, U.S.A.

Publications

Plays

Southern Exposure (produced New York, 1979).

Dead End Kids: A History of Nuclear Power, music by David Byrne (produced New York, 1980).

Green Card (produced Los Angeles, 1986; New York, 1988). New York, Broadway Play Publishing, 1991.

The Voyage of the Beagle, (opera), music by Jon Gibson (produced New London, Connecticut, 1986).

Screenplay: *Dead End Kids: A History of Nuclear Power*, 1986.

*

Theatrical Activities:
Director: **Plays**—All her own plays; *Cascando* by Samuel Beckett, New York, 1976; *Dressed Like an Egg*, based on the writings of Colette, New York, 1977; *Request Concert* by Franz Xaver Kroetz, New York, 1981; *Red and Blue* by Michael Hurson, New York, 1982; *Through the Leaves* by Franz Xaver Kroetz, New York, 1984; *The Photographer* by Philip Glass, New York, 1984; *Endgame* by Samuel Beckett, Cambridge, Massachussetts, 1985; *Help Wanted* by Franz Xaver Kroetz, New York, 1986; *The Balcony* by Jean Genet, Cambridge, Massachusetts; *American Notes* by Len Jenkin, New York, 1988; *Leon & Lena (and Lenz)* by George Büchner, Minneapolis, 1989; *The Screens* by Jean Genet, Minneapolis, 1989; *Cymbeline* by Shakespeare, New York, 1989; *'Tis Pity She's a Whore* by John Ford, Chicago, 1990, and New York, 1992; *Henry IV, Parts One and Two* by Shakespeare, New York, 1991; *Prisoner of Love* by Jean Genet, New York, 1992; *Woyzeck* by Georg Büchner, New York, 1992. **Film**—*Dead End Kids*, 1986.

Actor: **Plays**—Role in *Dressed Like an Egg*, New York, 1977; *The Shaggy Dog Animation* by Lee Breuer, New York, 1977; *Dark Ride* by Len Jenkin, New York, 1981.

* * *

The title "avant-gardist" has stuck with JoAnne Akalaitis since she co-founded Mabou Mines. More anathema than blessing, it has prompted prejudice and a fundamental misunderstanding of her work. But Akalaitis is interested in the vicissitudes of human nature, a complex pursuit that requires her to delve deeply. Consequently, the theater of JoAnne Akalaitis has frequently been called "impenetrable" or "intimidating." Less interested in effect, she probes for cause. How does a noble quest become corrupt (*Dead End Kids*; *The Voyage of the Beagle*)? Wherefore man's inhumanity to man (*Green Card*)? To do this, Akalaitis writes and directs with the focus on key links within a chain of events. Once identified, the links are then viewed through a microscope. In much the same way that her physicists in *Dead End Kids* probe for the quintessence of an inanimate element, Akalaitis contemplates the cognizant animal.

One could take such a comparison further and say that, in a sense, to experience Akalaitis's theater is to sit in at the atomic level. At first sight it appears chaotic; it is consuming, frenetic, kinetic, volatile, and often unforgiving. She eschews plot and narrative, alternately flashing and contrasting theory and practice. Dubious of rhetoric, she renders dialogue almost secondary in the process. The preservation of temporal and spatial continuity does not always accurately reflect cause and effect, and when it does not, Akalaitis arranges her own chronology. Not satisfied with actors simply reading dialogue and making the occasional gesture, she synthesizes a variety of media. Thus choreographer, composer, and photographer are as integral to the play as the text. Her atomic stage is rich in both image and language and explicitly reflects the intensity of everyday life. The result is an almost successful transmogrification of theater, forming what critics have referred to as a "gestalt"—the creation of an environment in which it is impossible to distill any element from the play without radically altering the work.

Akalaitis's concern with the shortcomings of language is perhaps best reflected in *Green Card*, a rapid-fire montage of music, slides, songs, dance, words, and film. It is a caustic satire concerning superficial values, bringing face-to-face the Haves (citizens of the United States) and Have Nots (refugees seeking asylum in the States). The play demonstrates how language is a trap and how its subscribers are too easily held captive. Immigrants struggle to understand the subtleties of the English language. "Learn English! Learn English!" native speakers of Vietnamese, Yiddish, Spanish, Russian, and Chinese are warned, or be faced with ignorance and confusion—even death. Yet when they resolve to do so, what they learn is that they have not been adequately prepared to comprehend it. For example, when a student asks for an explanation of the "REAL difference between 'I was writing' and 'I have written,'" the response is an impatient "'I was writing' is the imperfect tense while 'I have written' is the present perfect tense." Not quite sure what to make of this answer, the student denigrates herself, acknowledging the inferiority of her race, until the evening school teacher responds grandly, "The imperfect tense refers to what WAS, while the present perfect tense refers to what HAS BEEN."

To obtain a green card, that precious document promising a life with dignity and reward to thousands of refugees, characters must compete on *The Green Card Show*, the "game you have to play if you want to stay." Mocking the consumer culture, Akalaitis transforms Ellis Island into a TV game show set complete with canned applause and neon lights. If they win, the prize, of course, is permission to stay in the country; to lose, however, is to "get sent back to where they belong." Akalaitis pummels characters and audience with idioms, building to a frenzy: what is the difference between "burn up," "burn down," and "burnt out"; how does one get "carried away" without movement; how do Zan and Rich "pull off" a joke—what is being removed and from where? Her questions are ambiguous and mischievous enough to confuse a native speaker of American English:

Q: What is the most contemporary use of the expression to TURN ONE ON or to TURN ONE OFF?

a: Pretty women certainly TURN Charlie ON?
b: Some of the Great Renaissance painters TURN me ON but some of the modern ones TURN me OFF.
c. Minimalist post-modern performance art of the 1980s is a real TURN OFF for me.

Finally, language becomes more than just a trap—a prison and a kind of torture—as an immigrant is grilled by officials to reveal his history and recent whereabouts. With search lights flashing across her stage and whistles singing at ear-piercing decibels, Akalaitis's immigration officials weed out the sick and undesirable and begin the examinations at breakneck speed. Struggling to keep up and misunderstanding the occasional trick question, the applicant begins blurting out responses half in English, half in Spanish.

This adroit manipulation of the traditional dramatic form is perhaps best experienced in *Dead End Kids*. Akalaitis has referred to the play as an "impassioned repudiation of nuclear ineptitude." In context it is a history of science, specifically physics, beginning with fifteenth-century alchemists and ending in the present with the careless and devastating misuse of nuclear power. *Dead End Kids* is concerned with how, in spite of the best intentions, the human journey for knowledge is doomed. Released from its narrative, the play shifts into a whirling multimedia extravaganza. It then switches to a variety show format circa 1962, and the host and hostess primp and pose and gloss over any potentially distressing news items. Scenes change, and time shifts. The hostess daydreams, and the magic potions of an alchemist bubble forth. There is another shift, and suddenly we are at a science fair where a young pupil and his perky teacher announce, "This is the H bomb." Producing ingredients and parts from a bag, they inform us, "It's a question of design, not ingredients." "Be careful," the older guide counsels, "it would be such a pity to have even the tiniest explosion." Slides of Hiroshima and Nagasaki remind us just what sort of pity. "Splllaaaaat! Nagasaki" reiterates Akalaitis. We witness explosion after explosion. In a flash a scene has changed, and fragments fall and form new vignettes. Akalaitis is as much an alchemist as the mysterious cloaked characters who mix potions and recite spells. The alchemist strives in vain to turn base metals into gold, while Akalaitis separates the elements of drama and recombines them to produce a strikingly original theater.

—Roxana Petzold

ALBEE, Edward (Franklin, III)

Nationality: American. **Born:** Virginia, 12 March 1928; adopted as an infant. **Education:** Rye County Day School, Lawrenceville, New Jersey, 1940-43; Valley Forge Military Academy, Pennsylvania, 1943-44; Choate School, Connecticut, 1944-46; Trinity College, Hartford, Connecticut, 1946-47; Columbia University, New York, 1949. **Military Service:** Served in the United States Army. **Career:** Radio writer, WNYC, office boy, Warwick and Legler, record salesman, Bloomingdale's, book salesman, G. Schirmer, counterman, Manhattan Towers Hotel, messenger, Western Union, 1955-58, all in New York; producer, with Richard Barr and Clinton Wilder, Barr/Wilder/Albee Playwrights Unit, later Albarwild Theatre Arts, and Albar Productions, New York. Founder, William Flanagan Centre for Creative Persons, Montauk, Long Island, New York, 1971, and Edward Albee Foundation, 1978. U.S. cultural exchange visitor to the U.S.S.R., 1963. Codirector, Vivian Beaumont Theater, New York, 1981; resident playwright, Atlantic Center for the Arts, New Smyrna Beach, Florida, 1982; Regents' professor of drama, University of California at Irvine, 1983-85. **Awards:** Berlin Festival award, 1959, 1961; Vernon Rice award, 1960; Obie award, 1960; Argentine Critics award, 1961; Lola D'Annunzio award, 1961; New York Drama Critics Circle award, 1964; Outer Circle award, 1964; London *Evening Standard* award, 1964; Tony award, 1964; Margo Jones award, 1965; Pulitzer prize, 1967, 1975; American Academy gold medal, 1980; Brandeis University Creative Arts award, 1983, 1984; inducted into Theater Hall of Fame, 1985; Pulitzer prize and New York Drama Critics Circle award, for *Three Tall Woman,* both 1994. D. Litt.: Emerson College, Boston, 1967; Litt.D.: Trinity College, 1974. **Member:** American Academy, 1966; Theater Hall of Fame, 1985. **Agent:** William Morris Agency, 1350 Avenue of the Americas, New York, New York 10019. **Address:** 14 Harrison Street, New York, New York 10013, U.S.A.

Publications

Plays

The Zoo Story (produced Berlin, 1959; New York and London, 1960). Included in *The Zoo Story, The Death of Bessie Smith, The Sandbox*, 1960.

The Death of Bessie Smith (produced Berlin, 1960; New York and London, 1961). Included in *The Zoo Story, The Death of Bessie Smith, The Sandbox*, 1960.

The Sandbox (produced New York, 1960). Included in *The Zoo Story, The Death of Bessie Smith, The Sandbox*, 1960.

The Zoo Story, The Death of Bessie Smith, The Sandbox: Three Plays. New York, Coward McCann, 1960; as *The Zoo Story and Other Plays* (includes *The American Dream*), London, Cape, 1962.

Fam and Yam (produced Westport, Connecticut, and New York, 1960). New York, Dramatists Play Service, 1961.

The American Dream (produced New York and London, 1961). New York, Coward McCann, 1961; London, French, 1962.

Bartleby, with James Hinton, Jr., music by William Flanagan, adaptation of the story by Melville (produced New York, 1961).

Who's Afraid of Virginia Woolf? (produced New York, 1962; London, 1964). New York, Atheneum, 1962; London, Cape, 1964.

The Ballad of the Sad Café, adaptation of the story by Carson McCullers (produced New York, 1963; Worcester, 1969). New York and Boston, Atheneum-Houghton Mifflin, 1963; London, Cape, 1965.

Tiny Alice (produced New York, 1964; London, 1970). New York, Atheneum, 1965; London, Cape, 1966.

Malcolm, adaptation of the novel by James Purdy (produced New York, 1966). New York, Atheneum, 1966; London, Cape-Secker and Warburg, 1967.

A Delicate Balance (produced New York, 1966; London, 1969). New York, Atheneum, 1966; London, Cape, 1968.
Breakfast at Tiffany's, music by Bob Merrill, adaptation of the story by Truman Capote (produced Philadelphia, 1966).
Everything in the Garden, adaptation of the play by Giles Cooper (produced New York, 1967). New York, Atheneum, 1968.
Box and Quotations from Chairman Mao Tse-tung (as *Box-Mao-Box*, produced Buffalo, 1968; as *Box and Quotations from Chairman Mao Tse-tung*, produced New York, 1968). New York, Atheneum, 1969; London, Cape, 1970.
All Over (produced New York, 1971; London, 1972). New York, Atheneum, 1971; London, Cape, 1972.
Seascape (also director: produced New York, 1975; Kingston on Thames, Surrey, 1980). New York, Atheneum, 1975; London, Cape, 1976.
Counting the Ways (produced London, 1976; also director: produced Hartford, Connecticut, 1977). Included in *Two Plays*, 1977.
Listening (broadcast 1976; also director: produced Hartford, Connecticut, 1977; Coventry, 1977; New York, 1979). Included in *Two Plays*, 1977.
Two Plays. New York, Atheneum, 1977.
The Lady from Dubuque (produced New York, 1980). New York, Atheneum, 1980.
Lolita, adaptation of the novel by Vladimir Nabokov (produced Boston and New York, 1981). New York, Dramatists Play Service, 1984.
Plays:
The Zoo Story, The Death of Bessie Smith, The Sandbox, The American Dream. New York, Coward McCann, 1981.
Alice, A Delicate Balance, Box and Quotations from Chairman Mao Tse-tung. New York, Atheneum, 1982.
Counting the Ways, Listening, All Over. New York, Atheneum, 1982.
Everything the Garden, Malcolm, The Ballad of the Sad Café. New York, Atheneum, 1982.
The Man Who Had Three Arms (also director: produced Miami, 1982; New York, 1983; Edinburgh, 1989).
Finding the Sun (produced 1983; New York, 1994). New York, Dramatists Play Service, 1994.
Envy, in *Faustus in Hell* (produced Princeton, New Jersey, 1985).
Marriage Play (produced Vienna, 1987; Princeton, New Jersey, 1992).
Three Tall Women (produced Vienna, 1991; New York, 1994). New York, Dutton, 1995.
Fragments: A Sit Around (produced Cincinnati, Ohio, 1993; New York, 1994). Published as *Edward Albee's Fragments: A Sit-Around,* New York, Dramatists Play Service, 1995.
A Delicate Balance: A Play. New York, Plume, 1997.

Screenplay: *A Delicate Balance*, 1976.

Radio Play: *Listening*, 1976 (UK).

Novel

Straight Through the Night. New York, Soho, 1989.

Other

Conversations with Edward Albee, edited by Philip C. Kolin. Jackson, University Press of Mississippi, 1988.

*

Bibliography: *Edward Albee at Home and Abroad: A Bibliography 1958-June 1968* by Richard E. Amacher and Margaret Rule, New York, AMS Press, 1970; *Edward Albee: An Annotated Bibliography 1968-1977* by Charles Lee Green, New York, AMS Press, 1980; *Edward Albee: A Bibliography* by Richard Tyce, Metuchen, New Jersey, Scarecrow, 1986.

Critical Studies: *Tradition and Renewal* by Gilbert Debusscher, translated by Anne D. Williams, Brussels, American Studies Center, 1967; *Edward Albee* by Richard E. Amacher, New York, Twayne, 1969, revised edition, 1982; *Edward Albee* by Ruby Cohn, Minneapolis, University of Minesota Press, 1969; *Edward Albee: Playwright in Protest* by Michael E. Rutenberg, New York, Drama Book Specialists, 1969; *Albee* by C.W.E Bigsby, Edinburgh, Oliver and Boyd, 1969, New York, Chip's Bookshop, 1978, and *Edward Albee: A Collection of Critical Essays* edited by Bigsby, Englewood Cliffs, New Jersey, Prentice Hall, 1975; *Edward Albee* by Ronald Hayman, London, Heinemann, 1971, New York, Ungar, 1973; *From Tension to Tonic: The Plays of Edward Albee* by Anne Paolucci, Carbondale, Southern Illinois University Press, 1972; *Edward Albee: The Poet of Loss* by Anita M. Stenz, The Hague, Mouton, 1978; *Who's Afraid of Edward Albee?* by Foster Hirsch, Berkeley, California, Creative Arts, 1978; *Edward Albee: An Interview and Essays* edited by Julian N. Wasserman, Houston, University of St. Thomas, 1983; *Edward Albee* by Gerald McCarthy, London, Macmillan, 1987; *Edward Albee: The Playwright of Quest* by C. P. Singh, Delhi, Mittal Publications, 1987; "Pure and Simple: The Recent Plays of Edward Albee" by Liliane Kerjan, in *New Essays on American Drama* edited by G. Debusscher, Amsterdam, Rodopi, 1989; in *Modern American Drama, 1945-1990* by C. W. E. Bigsby, Cambridge and New York, Cambridge University Press, 1992; "What's It All About Albee?" by David Blum, in *New York Magazine* (New York), November 1993, pp. 70-78; "Salvation or Damnation? Death in the Plays of Edward Albee" by Robert M. Post, in *American Drama* (Cincinnati, Ohio), Spring 1993, pp. 32-49; "American Variations on a British Theme: Giles Cooper and Edward Albee" by Peter Egri, in *Forked Tongues? Comparing Twentieth-Century British and American Literature,* edited by Ann Massa and Alistair Stead, London, Longman, 1994; in *The Playwright's Art: Conversations with Contemporary American Dramatists,* edited by Jackson R. Bryer, New Brunswick, New Jersey, Rutgers University Press, 1995; "Albee's Martha: Someone's Daughter, Someone's Wife, No One's Mother" by Bonnie Blumenthal Finkelstein, in *American Drama* (Cincinnati, Ohio), Fall 1995, pp. 51-70; "Albee and Me" by Marian Seldes, in *American Theatre,* September 1996, pp. 24-26.

Theatrical Activities:
Director: Several of his own plays.

Actor: Radio Play—Voice in *Listening*, 1988.

* * *

The signal success of Edward Albee as one of America's leading contemporary dramatists can be attributed to the thoroughly professional command of theatrical skills that he regularly employs for the expression of a personal vision of the human condition in which all thinking people will, at least to some degree, be able to recognize their own personal plight as individuals in the modern world. The basis of his art is an impressive command of the particular craft of writing dialogue. Readers need only leaf through his texts to recognize that his plays are for the most part made up of an interchange of short speeches, frequently between no more than two characters and rarely more than four. Generally they pronounce no more than one short sentence at a time, and a single word, even grunts and other noises (represented, e.g. as "Mmmmmmm") can often suffice to show a response or to provoke one. The style is too compressed and too articulate for it to be possible to characterize it as realistic, and Albee does not resist the temptation of inserting occasional general remarks on the human condition that have a portentous ring to them and interrupt the flow of conversation. Yet generally the syntax, vocabulary and idiom, even the pauses, echo the speech habits of intelligent educated middle-class people who can express themselves and who are also capable when necessary, of manipulating language so that they do not reveal more then they would wish at any particular juncture. As well as serving as a bridge between playwright and audience, Albee's language can serve powerful dramatic purposes. *Zoo Story* uses speech as a laconic, fragmented idiom precisely to lead up to the long speech that provides the climax of the play. In *Seascape* there is powerful symbolism in the fact that, after Nancy and Charlie have conversed in what we are easily persuaded is normal language, Sarah and Leslie continued in the same way, belying the very clear differences in their appearances to point to deeper similarities in thought as well as expression.

The simple staging of *Seascape*–a sand dune where a casually dragged couple settle down in sunshine to enjoy a seaside picnic undisturbed by anything other than the din of a passing jet aircraft until they are disturbed by two creatures emerging from the sea to talk with them–points to another aspect of Albee's stagecraft; its economy, aesthetically was well as in cash terms, which modern theatre manages to ignore. Sometimes two characters are enough, and, in *Who's Afraid of Virginia Woolf* and *Three Tall Women* as in *Seascape,* four are plenty, and they meet and interact on a single set that places few demands on the designer's skills. Leaving spectacle to the cinema, TV, and other sorts of drama, Albee embraces classical concepts of the theatre, relaying on the speech and body language of the actors as the expression of thought and emotion in conflicts that embody intellectual issues. The result is theatre not ashamed to appeal as much to the ear as to the eye and requiring attentive listening from an intelligent audience that responds knowledgeably to dramatic surprises but has no more need for traditional well-made plot than for elaborate scenery.

For many theatre-goers, *Who's Afraid of Virginia Woolf?* is the essence of Albee. There is nothing very extraordinary about the starting point. In an unremarkable home on a New England campus a late-middle-aged couple–she is a few crucial years older than her husband, whose career as a historian has not taken off although his wife is the daughter of the college president of a minor college–invite in for a last drink, after an official welcoming party, a biologist who has just joined the staff and his younger wife. It takes only moments for the sparks to start to fly. The relationship between the older couple seems to have crumbled, but they interrupt their squabbles as they set out to undermine the confidence of their guests. Conversation is cuttingly brilliant, embarrassment mounts as an apparent passion for self-revelation is linked with the desire to inflict psychological wounds, and the tension grows steadily throughout a long play whose very length and lack of external event are themselves expressions of these characters' dilemma until all our assumptions and interpretations are thrown into question by the suggestion that what we are witnessing is not a genuine response to events but rather a well-rehearsed game that is played out to wrong-foot newcomers. As if that were not enough, quotations from the *Dies Irae* hymn sung at Catholic requiem masses add an apocalyptic touch. Taken literally, *Who's Afraid of Virginia Woolf?* is a devastating portrayal of the disarray of American intellectuals in the modern age. Perhaps wider interpretations are called for, but what is certain is that the play provides a compelling account of the mechanisms of personal domination that serve inadequate people as a substitute for real achievement.

Inadequacies are also highlighted in *Tiny Alice,* another play that develops from uneasy subversive realism to something more symbolic. *Three Tall Women,* also neatly handled and with a title that gives away very little, seizes the attention of the audience by putting on stage the final hours in the life of an old lady who lied in bed watched over by a middle-aged woman and a younger one whose dialogue is crisp and assertive. It is only in the second half of the play that we appreciate that time has been turned topsy-turvy, for the three female characters are in fact simultaneous embodiments of successive phases int eh life of the old lady.

Albee's tendency to move on from the everyday to something less realistic and more imaginative in order to raise questions is exemplified in *Seascape.* Here a trip to the beach, a commonplace way of 'getting away from it all,' is given new dimensions as the picnickers, after a few moments of what we are given to understand is quite needless alarm, settle down to discuss the nature of life with two rather sensible creatures that emerge from the sea. Once again, the comment on contemporary attitudes is sharp, and the presentation is beguiling, inviting, if not requiring, imaginative interpretations. Development towards Absurdist tendencies traditions is even more pronounced in *Box* and *Quotations from Chairman Mao.* In a somewhat defensive prefatory note on these plays Albee proclaims his dual mission of commenting on the human condition in theatre and also of extending the bounds of drama before remarking that the audience must rid itself of preconceptions if it is to appreciate these starkly non-realistic works that focus on the unconscious.

Audiences that warmed to *Whose Afraid of Virginia Woolf?* have responded less enthusiastically to Albee's excursions into dramatic styles even further from the beaten track. Greatly to his credit, the dramatist has, however, declined the easy option of repeating the highly successful formula that he discovered early on. His career so far has been one more expression of the malaise that inspires his drama, and the hope that he will go on in the future delighting and puzzling audiences by expressing unsettling insights with outstanding theatrical artistry.

—Christopher Smith

ALLAN, Ted

Nationality: Canadian. **Born:** Alan Herman in Montreal, Quebec, 25 January 1916. **Education:** Baron Byng High School, Montreal. **Military Service:** Served in the International Brigade during the Spanish Civil War: colonel. **Family:** Married Kate Schwartz in 1939 (divorced 1966); one daughter and one son. **Career:** Store clerk, 1933-34; Montreal correspondent, Toronto *Daily Worker*, 1935; radio, television, and film actor; lived in London for nearly 30 years, now lives in Toronto and Los Angeles. **Awards:** Canada Council grant, 1956, 1970, Senior Arts grant, 1974, and travel grant, 1974; Berlin Film Festival Golden Bear, 1985; Stephen Leacock award, for fiction, 1985. **Agent:** Linda Butler, 31-501 Yonge Street, Toronto M4Y 1Y4, Canada.

Publications

Plays

The Money Makers (produced Toronto, 1954; as *The Ghost Writers*, produced London, 1955).
Legend of Pepito, adaptation of a story by B. Traven (produced London, 1955).
Double Image, with Roger MacDougall, based on a story by Roy Vickers (produced London, 1956). London, French, 1957.
The Secret of the World (produced London, 1962).
Oh What a Lovely War, with the Theatre Workshop (produced London and New York, 1964). London, Methuen, 1965.
Chu Chem: A Zen Buddhist-Hebrew Musical, music and lyrics by Mitch Leigh, Jack Haines, and Jack Wohl (produced Philadelphia, 1966; New York, 1988).
My Sister's Keeper (as *I've Seen You Cut Lemons*, produced London, 1969; revised version, as *My Sister's Keeper*, produced Lennoxville, Quebec, 1974; New York, 1979). Toronto, University of Toronto Press, 1976.
Love Streams, and The Third Day Comes (produced Los Angeles, 1984).
Lies My Father Told Me (produced New York, 1986). Toronto, Playwrights, 1984.

Screenplays: *1001 Arabian Nights*, with others, 1959; *The Webster Boy*, with Leo Marks, 1962; *Fuse*, 1970; *Them Damned Canadians*, 1973; *Lies My Father Told Me*, 1975; *Love Streams*, with John Cassavetes, 1984; *Bethune: The Making of a Hero*, 1990.

Radio Plays: *Canadian Mental Health* series, 1953; *Coloured Buttons*, 1958; *The Good Son*, 1969.

Television Plays: *Willie the Squowse*, 1954; *Go Fall in Love*, 1955; *Early to Braden* series, 1957-58; *Legend of Paradiso*, 1960; *Flowers at My Feet*, 1968.

Novels

This Time a Better Earth. London, Heinemann, and New York, Morrow, 1939.
Quest for Pajaro (as Edward Maxwell). London, Heinemann, 1957.
Chu Chem: A Zen Buddhist-Hebrew Novel. Montreal, Editions Quebec, 1973.
Lies My Father Told Me (novelization of screenplay; as Norman Allan). New York, New American Library, 1975.
Love Is a Long Shot. Toronto, McClelland and Stewart, 1984; London, Hale, 1986.

Short Stories

Don't You Know Anybody Else? Family Stories. Toronto, McClelland and Stewart, 1985.

Other

The Scalpel, The Sword: The Story of Dr. Norman Bethune, with Sydney Gordon. Boston, Little Brown, 1952; London, Hale, 1954; revised edition, New York, Monthly Review Press, 1973.
Willie the Squowse (for children). Toronto, McClelland and Stewart, and London, Cape, 1977; New York, Hastings House, 1978.
Dr. Ah Chu and Jonah's Egg. Montreal, R. Davies, 1996.

*

Critical Study: "*Oh What a Lovely War*: The Texts and Their Context" by Derek Paget, in *Critical Survey* (Oxford, England), 1990, pp. 117-27.

Ted Allan comments:

(1977) I find it difficult to appraise my work. At some moments I think they are the most underestimated plays of the 20th century. At other moments I think they all need to be rewritten.

They have been praised and damned but have not attained the fame I sought for them, with the exception of *Oh What a Lovely War*. But here my pleasure is mixed, for the director-producer threw out my main plot, kept my peripheral scenes, rewriting most of them, took my name off the play in England, and gave writing credits to a few hundred people, to indicate that nobody *wrote* it. I consider my original version a theatrical tour de force and hope to get it produced one day under a new title: *Smith and Schmidt*, directed by someone who will do it as I wrote it.

Outside of *Gog and Magog*, which began life as *Double Image*, and which ran for a year in London and almost five years in Paris, none of my plays ever achieved commercial success.

The Secret of the World (my major opus), which told the story of three generations of a Montreal family (the head of which goes mad), did get wild critical hosannas from most of London's critics, but was panned by Canadian critics when it was performed at Lennoxville in 1976.

I've Seen You Cut Lemons probed the problem of alleged insanity in those we, the so-called normal, like to call abnormal. It was cruelly savaged by most of London's critics. That sent me brooding for a few years and to writing screenplays. I will return to playwriting next year, after I finish a new screenplay, which will provide me with the wherewithal to write for the theatre.

I consider *Chu Chem* the happiest of my plays although it died an untimely death after six performances in Philadelphia. I keep hoping it will one day get the kind of imaginative production it needs. (We had an elderly and beloved lead who couldn't remember his lines. The poor man died soon after the play did.)

My wildest fantasy is called *Willie the Squowse*, which nobody wants to produce, although it's been done on both radio and television. I have a horrible feeling that my plays will start getting produced all over the world to be acclaimed with noisy popularity after I am dead. If that is the price I must pay to get my plays produced, I agree. I have decided to die before I am ninety. This is a concession, for I had planned to live to a hundred. When I finally go, I will let you know.

(1988) I'm finding it easier to appraise my work now that I have rewritten *The Secret of the World* for the thousandth time. With the off-Broadway production of *Lies My Father Told Me* and a scheduled production of *Willie the Squowse* I feel less neglected.

* * *

With his high octane-forcefulness and his formidable technical expertise, Ted Allan is a playwright who has been undeservedly neglected in the London theater since *The Secret of the World* was produced at Stratford East in 1962. His *I've Seen You Cut Lemons* is a far more interesting piece of theatrical writing than William Gibson's *Two for the Seesaw*, for instance, another two-character play that enjoyed considerable success.

The Secret of the World is rather like a Canadian *Death of a Salesman*, with the life of the central family set in a context of direct involvement in union politics during and after the upheaval caused by Khrushchev's revelations about Stalin. Chris Alexander (or Sam Alexander as he became at Stratford East) is an idealistic union leader who fails to get reelected when he breaks with the Communist party and who, from being successful, busy, and well-liked, declines further into loneliness, ineffectuality, and near madness. He is too honest to take advantage of an opportunity to get big money from a bus company in a settlement of an accident claim and hopes instead to make a fortune out of a crackpot invention—cuff links joined by elastic so that shirts can be put on without unfastening them.

The play's emotional brew is a rich one. The interlocking emotional problems of Chris's father, wife, son, daughter, and brother-in-law are all boiled up together, and the resulting soup would possibly be more digestible with a little more comedy and a little less meat. But there is an admirable sureness of touch in creating theatrical effects, even if this is done without letting the characters be conscious enough of their own theatricality. The old father is rather like a Montreal version of Ibsen's Old Ekdal. But the decline of Chris is powerfully plotted, and even when it is too obvious that Allan is trying to tug at the audience's heartstrings, the tugs are not usually fumbled.

In family plays especially an overly rich emotional mixture is often due to the presence of too much autobiographical material and too much residue of the guilt that family pressures create. The suspicion one has that Allan is drawing directly on his own experience is strengthened when we see how much Sarah in *I've Seen You Cut Lemons* resembles Susan in *The Secret of the World* and when we hear Sarah recalling incidents we actually saw in the earlier play—the mother, for instance, shouting "I believe in God, I believe in God! Atheists. Communists" outside the door of a room in her house where the Young Communist League was holding a meeting.

I've Seen You Cut Lemons is a more controlled, more economical play, and it succeeds in sustaining tension throughout the action by focusing on different aspects and different phases of a semi-incestuous brother-sister relationship. The action is set in the London bachelor flat of a Canadian university lecturer. His sister is a few years younger than he is. Like Susan, Sarah is a painter, but she blames the relationship with her brother for her partially deliberate failure to make more use of her talent, which they both regard as a very considerable one.

Both have children from broken marriages. As the action starts, the brother is on the point of taking his son to Corsica for a vacation when Sarah arrives unexpectedly, discharged early from the hospital. He lets her stay in the apartment, judging her mental health to be sufficiently restored to stand up to a period of being alone. Later, of course, he will regret this decision. When he returns, she tries harder and harder to monopolize his life, untruthfully informing his girlfriend (who is also called Susan) that they are having an incestuous relationship, and she goes all out to convince her brother that this is what he really wants as much as she does. Allan's dialogue measures up well to the difficult task of registering her oscillations between lucidity and hallucination. It even convinces the audience that she could play on her brother's guilt feelings cleverly enough to make him believe that her sanity could be fully and permanently restored if only he would devote a month of his life to looking after her. The play ends touchingly as she voluntarily goes back to the hospital and he emerges from the purgatory of their time together a wiser man than he was before.

Allan has also written prolifically for the screen and television, and he collaborated with Roger MacDougall on the stage play *Double Image*. He has also written *Chu Chem*, which he describes as a Zen Buddhist-Hebrew musical comedy. It owes as much to Brecht as to Zen Buddhism, and although the ingredients do not quite jell, there are some very amusing moments. The most inspired theatrical image is a seesaw with buckets attached to either end. A rock is put into one, and the villagers have to "balance the budget" by putting jewels and gold into the other.

—Ronald Hayman

ALLEN, Roland. *See* **AYCKBOURN, Alan.**

ANDERSON, Robert (Woodruff)

Nationality: American. **Born:** New York City, 28 April 1917. **Education:** Phillips Exeter Academy, Exeter, New Hampshire, 1931-35; Harvard University, Cambridge, Massachusetts, 1935-42, A.B. (magna cum laude) 1939, M.A. 1940. **Military Service:** Served in the United States Naval Reserve, 1942-46: lieutenant; Bronze Star. **Family:** Married 1) Phyllis Stohl in 1940 (died 1956); 2) the actress Teresa Wright in 1959 (divorced 1978). **Career:** Apprentice, South Shore Players, Cohasset, Massachusetts, summers 1937 and 1938. Assistant in English, Harvard University, 1939-42; teacher, Erskine School, Boston, 1941; teacher of playwriting, American Theatre Wing, New York, 1946-51, and Actors Studio, New York, 1955-56; member of the faculty, Salzburg Seminar in American Studies, 1968; writer-in-residence, University of North Carolina, Chapel Hill, 1969, and University of Iowa Writers Workshop, Iowa City, 1976. Member of the Playwrights Producing Company, 1953-60; president, New Dramatists Committee, 1955-56, and Dramatists Guild, 1971-73; member of the Board of Governors, American Playwrights Theatre, 1963-79. Member of the Council, 1965—; and vice-president, Authors League of America, 1980—. **Awards:** National Theatre Conference prize, 1945; Rockefeller fellowship, 1946; Writers Guild of America award, for screenplay, 1970; ACE award, for television, 1991; Last Frontier award, Valdez, Alaska, 1997. **Member:** Theater Hall of Fame, 1980. **Agent:** Jason Foggelson, William Morris, 1325 Avenue of the Americas, New York, New York 10018, U.S.A. **Address:** Roxbury, Connecticut 06783, U.S.A.

PUBLICATIONS

Plays

Hour Town, book, music and lyrics by Anderson (produced Cambridge, Massachusetts, 1938).
Come Marching Home (produced Iowa City, 1945; New York, 1946).
The Eden Rose (produced Ridgefield, Connecticut, 1949).
Sketches in *Dance Me a Song* (produced New York, 1950).
Love Revisited (produced Westport, Connecticut, 1951).
All Summer Long, adaptation of the novel *A Wreath and a Curse* by Donald Wetzel (produced Washington, D.C., 1952; New York, 1954). New York, French, 1955.
Tea and Sympathy (produced New Haven, Connecticut, and New York, 1953; London, 1957). New York, Random House, 1953; London, Heinemann, 1957.
Silent Night, Lonely Night (produced New Haven, Connecticut, and New York, 1959). New York, Random House, 1960.
The Days Between (produced Dallas, 1965; New York, 1979). New York, Random House, 1965.
You Know I Can't Hear You When the Water's Running (produced New York, 1967; London, 1968). New York, Random House, 1967.
I Never Sang for My Father (produced Philadelphia, 1967; New York, 1968; London, 1970). New York, Random House, 1968; screenplay published, New York, New American Library, 1970.
Solitaire/Double Solitaire (produced New Haven, Connecticut, Edinburgh, and New York, 1971). New York, Random House, 1972.
Free and Clear (produced New Haven, Connecticut, 1983).
The Last Act Is a Solo (televised 1991). New York, French, 1991.

Screenplays: *Tea and Sympathy*, 1956; *Until They Sail*, 1957; *The Nun's Story*, 1959; *The Sand Pebbles*, 1966; *I Never Sang for My Father*, 1970.

Radio Plays: *David Copperfield, Oliver Twist, Vanity Fair, The Glass Menagerie, Trilby, The Old Lady Shows Her Medals, The Petrified Forest, The Scarlet Pimpernel, A Farewell to Arms, Summer and Smoke, Arrowsmith*, and other adaptations, 1946-52.

Television Plays: *The Patricia Neal Story*, 1980; *The Last Act Is a Solo*, 1991; *Absolute Strangers*, 1991.

Novels

After. New York, Random House, and London, Barrie and Jenkins, 1973.
Getting Up and Going Home. New York, Simon and Schuster, 1978.

Other

Elements of Literature (textbook anthology). New York, Holt Rinehart, 6 vols., 1988.

*

Bibliography: *The Apprenticeship of Robert Anderson* by David Ayers, unpublished dissertation, Columbus, Ohio State University, 1969.

Manuscript Collection: Harvard University Theatre Collection, Cambridge, Massachusetts.

Critical Studies: *Life among the Playwrights* by John F. Wharton, New York, Quadrangle, 1974; *Playwrights Talk about Playwriting* edited by Lewis Funke, Chicago, Dramatic Publishing Company, 1975; *Robert Anderson* by Thomas Adler, Boston, Twayne, 1978; "A Dramatist's Inner Space," in *Dramatists Guild Quarterly* (New York), Spring 1979; *The Strands Entwined* by Samuel Bernstein, Boston, Northeastern University Press, 1980; *Represented by Audrey Wood* by Audrey Wood and Max Wilk, New York, Doubleday, 1981; *The Playwright's Art* edited by Jackson Bryer, New Brunswick, New Jersey, Rutgers University Press, 1995.

Robert Anderson comments:

(1973) It is difficult and dangerous for a writer to talk about his own work. He should move on to whatever he is impelled to write about next without looking back and trying to analyze his work. Recently I read a doctoral thesis written about me and my plays. In many ways I wish I hadn't read it. I don't think it is wise for a writer to think about his "continuing themes" and recurring attitudes.

When I was near the end of writing *Tea and Sympathy*, my first wife begged me to tell her something of the subject of my new play. (I never discuss my work with anyone while I am writing.) I gave in and simply told her it took place in a boys' school. She said, "Oh, my God, not another play about a boys' school!" This almost stopped me. At that moment I hadn't been consciously aware that I had written other (unproduced) work with a boys' school background. I simply knew that I wanted to write that play. My wife's making me aware that I had worked that vein before almost stopped me from finishing the play.

People sometimes say, "Why don't you write about something besides marriage?" Strangely, it is only after I have finished a play that I am aware that I have written again about marriage. Each time I start a play, I certainly don't have the feeling that I am going over old ground. I feel I have something new and different nagging at me to be written. I do not consciously say, "This is my theme. I have done it reasonably well before. Let's try it again."

And these "plays about marriage" are seldom just that. *Solitaire/Double Solitaire* was not about marriage in the present and in the future, as some critics described it. It was about the loneliness of being alone and the loneliness of marriage. *The Days Between* was not about an academic marriage on the rocks but about a man who was ruining his life and his marriage by being unable to live the ordinary, unexciting days of life, "the days between." Marriage is often the arena of the plays, but not always the real subject matter.

As a matter of fact, the plays are rarely "about" what critics say they are about. *Tea and Sympathy* has always been described as "a play about homosexuality." In effect, it has nothing to do with homosexuality. It has to do with an unjust charge of homosexuality and what follows such a charge. It has to do with responsibility, which must extend beyond giving tea and sympathy; it has to do again with loneliness; it has to do with questioning some popular definitions of manliness; and, most important, it has to do with judgment by prejudice . . . and a great deal more, I hope.

You Know I Can't Hear You When the Water's Running was said to be "about" sex. The plays were told in terms of sex, but they were not about sex. As Elia Kazan said when he first read the manuscript, "They're about the same things as your other plays except this time it came out funny" They are also very sad plays. As Walter Kerr said of them, "Laugh only when it hurts."

I seem to have written largely about the family, or rather to have used the family as the arena. By and large English critics feel that American playwrights rather overwork this area of concern. Still, our three finest plays are, probably, *The Glass Menagerie*, *Death of a Salesman*, and *Long Day's Journey into Night*. I am glad that Williams, Miller, and O'Neill didn't scare when and if someone said to them, "not another play about the family!"

I have been amused that I have sometimes been considered a "commercial" playwright. I am amused because each of my plays has had an enormous struggle to get on. Nobody has thought of them as "commercial" till after they were successful. *Tea and Sympathy* was turned down by almost every producer and was on its way back into my files when the Playwrights Company optioned it and started me on my career. *You Know I Can't Hear You When the Water's Running* was turned down by everyone until two new producers "who didn't know any better" took a chance on it. I waited something like seven years before someone "took a chance" on *I Never Sang for My Father*. I think I can't be blamed for being amused when I hear myself described as "commercial," especially inasmuch as three of my plays have premiered in very non-commercial regional theatres, one opened Off-Broadway, and one launched The American Playwrights Theatre, a project which seeks to get the plays of "established" playwrights into the regional and college theatres rather than into Broadway theatres.

At various times in my youth I wanted to be an actor and a poet. I acted in college and summer theatres, and I was elected Harvard Class Poet on graduation. I think it is only natural that with these two "bents" I should end up a playwright, because in playwriting one finds the same kind of compression and essentialization one finds in poetry. Poems and plays are both the tips of icebergs.

Finally, I admire form. I took a course at Harvard with Robert Frost. One evening he was asked why he didn't write free verse. He replied, "I don't like playing tennis with the net down." I think that a great deal of the excitement in the theatre comes from using the limitations of the theatre creatively. Most plays, when they are adapted as movies, "opened up," lose their effectiveness, because part of their attraction was the way the playwright had found intensity and a creative impulse in dealing with the limitations of the theatre. Compare the play and the film of *Our Town*. I believe that form can be challenged, changed, stretched. But some kind of form seems to me of the essence of theatre.

I would wish that a person coming on my plays for the first time would not have any preconceived idea as to what they are "about." Each reader or spectator is a new collaborator, and he will, in a sense, write his own play and arrive at his own meanings, based on his own experience of life.

(1988) It has never been easier to get a play done some- place. It has never been more difficult to get a play done where a playwright can earn enough money to write the next play. Many years ago I wrote something which has been endlessly quoted and is still true: "You can make a killing in the theatre but not a living." If I had not been able to write movies and television from time to time, I could not have continued as a playwright. Most playwrights I know are moonlighters. When *Tea and Sympathy* was done in 1953, it cost forty thousand dollars to produce, with Elia Kazan, Jo Mielziner, and Deborah Kerr, all superb and expensive talents. I am told that my six-character new play, *The Kissing Was Always the Best*, will probably cost close to a million dollars to produce on Broadway. I try not to think about this.

* * *

Robert Anderson first received limited recognition as a playwright in 1945 when his play *Come Marching Home* was awarded first prize in a National Theatre Conference contest. This was followed five years later by *Love Revisited*, which was performed at the Westport County Playhouse. But it was Alan Schneider's Washington Arena production of *All Summer Long* that marked his emergence as a writer of genuine power and considerable subtlety. Though it was not particularly well received when it eventually reached Broadway two years later, the success of *Tea and Sympathy* had by then established Anderson's reputation as a skillful and impressive playwright.

All Summer Long is a sensitive if somewhat portentously symbolic play about the loss of illusions and the inevitable dissolution of beauty, love, and innocence. The family, which is the focus for this elegy on human weakness, lives beside a river that is slowly eroding the bank under its home, a not very subtle image of the collapse of genuine feeling within the family itself. Willie, the youngest boy, is on the verge of adolescence, and his brother Don, a former college sports star who has been crippled in an automobile accident, tries to protect him from his emerging sexuality and from the cynicism and bitterness of the rest of the family. Ironically, however, Don is unable to come to terms with the change in his own life. Anderson piles on the agony, with parents who no longer care for each other or their children and with a girl who tries to produce an abortion by throwing herself on an electrified fence. Though Willie and Don spend the summer trying to build a wall to hold out the threatening floodwaters, the forces of nature can no more be controlled on this level than they can in the lives of individuals growing more self-centered and lonely as they grow older. The play ends as the house collapses, an obvious image of the family itself, which has long since disintegrated in human terms.

Though he has never since relied on such a melodramatic climax, Anderson's work is never entirely free of a certain dramatic overstatement. In *All Summer Long* Don is not only a crippled sports star, itself something of a cliché, but the accident that caused his injury had been a result of his father's inadequacy. Similarly, in a later play, *Silent Night, Lonely Night*, a child dies because her mother is at that very moment preoccupied with reading a letter that reveals her husband's adultery. Her subsequent plunge into insanity is perhaps understandable, but it serves to create a melodramatic setting for what is otherwise a subtle examination of human need. Nowhere, however, does Anderson control this tendency better than in what remains his best play, *Tea and Sympathy*, though even here there is a certain lack of subtlety in his portrait of a callous father and of a weak and therefore vindictive schoolmaster who may well share the very sexual deviancy he denounces in others.

Tea and Sympathy was Anderson's Broadway debut and earned him a deserved reputation for confronting delicate and even contentious issues with courage and effect, a reputation he was to parody in his later *You Know I Can't Hear You When the Water's Running*. The play is concerned with the plight of a 17-year-old boy in a New England boarding school who is accused of being homosexual. Unsure of himself and tormented by his fellow pupils, he turns to his housemaster's wife, whom he loves with adolescent passion and anguish. Horrified by her husband's inhumanity and genuinely concerned for the fate of the young boy, she finally allows him to make love to her, the only way she can see him regaining his sexual self-confidence and his faith in other people. The boy's father, long since divorced, has never offered his son the slightest affection, while the housemaster punishes the boy for his own suppressed fears. As a perceptive indictment of the witch-hunt, the play was produced at a particularly appropriate moment, the height of the McCarthy era. But it was a great deal more than this, and, despite the rather casual psychological assumptions underlying the portraits of both the father and housemaster, the play was a perceptive comment on the failure of compassion in a society that demanded conformity as the price of acceptance.

Anderson's next play, *Silent Night, Lonely Night,* again dealt with the anguish of those who are deprived of the affection and understanding of the people who should be closest to them. Katherine, temporarily separated from a husband whom she has just discovered to be unfaithful, finds herself alone in a New England inn on Christmas Eve. Upset and lonely, she dines with another guest whose wife is in a nearby mental hospital, driven there by his own infidelity. For this one night they manage to overcome their sense of guilt and self-concern in order to offer each other the momentary consolation of true compassion. The simple symmetry of the structure underlines the justice of those who see Anderson primarily as a constructor of well-made plays, but despite this and despite the melodramatic nature of the man's personal history the play remains a delicate study that compares well with Anderson's earlier work.

His next production, four one-act comedies presented under the title *You Know I Can't Hear You When the Water's Running,* was not staged until eight years later. Lightweight sketches that partly depend on and partly satirize the new vogue for sexual explicitness, they show little of his earlier sensitivity or skill. The same nostalgic regret for the decay of love and the passing of youth is manifested in two of the works, "The Footsteps of Doves" and "I'll Be Home for Christmas," but it now becomes the subject of rather tasteless jokes. The spectacle of Anderson mocking his earlier convictions is not an altogether attractive one, for the humor of the plays derives from precisely that cynical worldly wise detachment that he had previously seen as the enemy of the human spirit. When he briefly comes close to a moment of true pathos, as in "I'll Be Home for Christmas," the integrity of the scene is lost in the sophisticated banter of the rest of the play.

I Never Sang for My Father does little to redeem the weakness of his composite play. Centering on the almost neurotic need of a son to win the love of a bitter and virtually senile father, it reveals not only the terrifying gaps that can open up between those who should be drawn to one another by all the ties of natural affection and concern but also the desperate absence of love in a world full of people who choose to shelter and exile themselves in the fragile shell of their own personalities. Yet, despite the emotive nature of his subject, in the last resort Anderson fails to establish the tension he creates as anything more than a pathological study. The play is a compassionate and detailed examination of individuals who, despite the familiarity of their situations, remain case studies rather than evocative projections of a universal state.

In some respects Anderson suggests comparison with dramatists like William Inge, Carson McCullers, and Tennessee Williams. Like them he has chosen to describe the plight of those whose romantic dreams founder on the harsh realities of modern life. Emotionally scarred and sexually vulnerable, his protagonists try to find their way in a world that frightens and dismays them. In *All Summer Long* and *Tea and Sympathy* the central figure is, appropriately enough, an adolescent, for the boy confronting sexuality and cruelty for the first time serves to emphasize simultaneously the ideals of youth and the cynicism and disillusionment of middle age. For Anderson this contrast constitutes the key to individual anguish and the mainspring of a pathos that he seems to regard as the truest expression of human experience. This clearly is the stuff of which nostalgia and sentimentality are made, and his work is open to both charges. Whereas Williams balances his regret for the destruction of the innocent and the romantic with a grudging regard for the Prometheans who dominate their surroundings, Anderson offers only a romantic regret that things cannot be other than they are. Whereas Inge and McCullers see the growth away from innocence into experience as a painful but necessary human process, Anderson tends to see it as the first stage in the extinction of genuine feeling and human compassion. If some people can sustain their innocence into maturity, it seems that they do so in his world only at the cost of their ability to act. It is a paradox that Anderson is content to identify rather than examine with the kind of subtlety Williams brought to *The Glass Menagerie* and *Orpheus Descending.*

—C. W. E. Bigsby

ANTROBUS, John

Nationality: British. **Born:** Woolwich, London, 2 July 1933. **Education:** Bishop Wordsworth Grammar School, Salisbury, Wiltshire; Selhurst Grammar School, Croydon, Surrey; King Edward VII Nautical College; Royal Military Academy, Sandhurst, Camberley, Surrey. **Military Service:** Served in the British Army, East Surrey Regiment, 1952-55. **Family:** Married Margaret McCormick in 1958 (divorced 1980); two sons and one daughter. **Career:** Apprentice deck officer, Merchant Navy, 1950-52; supply teacher and waiter, 1953-54. Freelance writer, 1955—. Lives in London. **Awards:** George Devine award, 1970; Writers Guild award, 1971; Arts Council bursary, 1973, 1976, 1980, 1982; Banff Television Festival award, 1987. **Agent:** Pat White, Rogers, Coleridge, and White, 20 Powis Mews, London W11 1JN, England. **Address:** 13 Allfarthing Lane, London S.W. 18, England.

Publications

Plays

The Bed-Sitting Room, with Spike Milligan (also co-director: produced London, 1963). Walton on Thames, Surrey, Hobbs, 1970; revised version, as *The Bed-Sitting Room 2* (also director: produced London, 1983).

Royal Commission Review (produced London, 1964).

You'll Come to Love Your Sperm Test (also director: produced Edinburgh and London, 1965). Published in *New Writers 4,* London, Calder and Boyars, 1965.

Cane of Honour (produced London, 1965).

The Missing Links (televised 1965; produced London, 1977). Included in *Why Bournemouth? and Other Plays,* 1970.

Trixie and Baba (produced London, 1968). London, Calder and Boyars, 1969.
Why Bournemouth? (produced London, 1968). Included in *Why Bournemouth? and Other Plays*, 1970.
Captain Oates' Left Sock (produced London, 1969). London, French, 1974.
An Evening with John Antrobus (produced London, 1969).
Why Bournemouth? and Other Plays. London, Calder and Boyars, 1970.
An Apple a Day (televised 1971; produced London, 1974). Included in *Why Bournemouth? and Other Plays*, 1970.
Stranger in a Cafeteria, in *Christmas Present* (produced Edinburgh, 1971).
The Looneys (produced Edinburgh, 1971; London, 1974).
Crete and Sergeant Pepper (produced London, 1972).
The Dinosaurs, and Certain Humiliations (produced Edinburgh, 1973; London, 1974).
The Illegal Immigrant (produced London, 1974).
Mrs. Grabowski's Academy (produced London, 1975).
They Sleep Together (produced Leicester, 1976).
Sketches in *City Delights* (revue; produced Oxford, 1978; London, 1980).
Jonah (also director: produced Cambridge, 1979).
Hitler in Liverpool, One Orange for the Baby, Up in the Hide (produced London, 1980). London, Calder, and New York, Riverrun Press, 1983.
When Did You Last See Your Trousers?, with Ray Galton, adaptation of a story by Galton and Alan Simpson (produced Mold, Clwyd, 1986; London, 1987). London, French, 1988.

Screenplays: *Carry on Sergeant*, with Norman Hudis, 1958; *Idol on Parade*, 1959; *Jazzboat*, with Ken Hughes, 1960; *The Wrong Arm of the Law*, with others, 1962; *The Big Job*, with Talbot Rothwell, 1965; *The Bed-Sitting Room*, with Charles Wood, 1969.

Radio Writing: *Idiot Weekly* and *The Goon Show* series; *Brandy, Brandy*, 1972; *LMF (Lack of Moral Fibre)*, 1976; *Haute Cuisine*, 1977; *The Lie*, 1978; *In a Dry Place*, 1986; *Looneys*, 1987; *The Milligan Papers* series, 1987.

Television Writing: *Idiot Weekly* series; *A Show Called Fred* series; *The Army Game* series; *Bootsie and Snudge* series; for Eric Sykes, Arthur Haynes, Frankie Howerd, Jimmy Wheeler shows; *Lenny the Lion Show*, 1957; *Variety Inc. Show*, 1957; *For the Children Show*, 1957; *Early to Braden* series, 1957; *The April 8th Show (Seven Days Early)*, 1958; *The Deadly Game of Chess*, 1958; *The Missing Links*, 1965; *An Apple a Day*, 1971; *Don't Feed the Fish*, 1971; *Marty Feldman Show*, 1972; *A Milligan for All Seasons*, with Spike Milligan, 1974; episode in *Too Close for Comfort*, 1984 (USA); *The Last Laugh Before T.V. AM*, with Spike Milligan, 1985; *Room at the Bottom* series, with Ray Galton, 1986 and 1987; *Alfred Hitchcock Presents*, 1987 (USA).

Other (for children)

The Boy with Illuminated Measles. London, Robson, 1978.
Help! I Am a Prisoner in a Toothpaste Factory. London, Robson, 1978.
Ronnie and the Haunted Rolls Royce. London, Robson, 1982.
Ronnie and the Great Knitted Robbery. London, Robson, 1982.
Pirates, with Mike Wallis. London, Carnival, 1990.
Polo Time, with Mike Wallis. London, Carnival, 1990.
Spooky Time, with Mike Wallis. London, Carnival, 1990.
Picnic, with Mike Wallis. London, Carnival, 1990.
Ronnie and the High Rise. London, Robson, 1992.
Ronnie and the Flying Fitted Carpet. London, Robson, 1992.

*

Manuscript Collection: Mugar Memorial Library, Boston University.

Theatrical Activities:
Director: **Plays**—*The Bed-Sitting Room* (co-director, with Spike Milligan), London, 1963; *You'll Come to Love Your Sperm Test*, Edinburgh and London, 1965; *Savages* by Christopher Hampton, Aalsburg, Denmark, 1973; *Jonah*, Oxford, 1979; *One Orange for the Baby*, London, 1980; *The Bed-Sitting Room 2*, London, 1983.

Actor: **Plays**—*You'll Come to Love Your Sperm Test*, Edinburgh and London, 1965; *An Evening with John Antrobus*, London, 1969; Glendenning in *The Contractor* by David Storey, London, 1970; *Hitler in Liverpool*, London, 1980. **Film**—*Raising the Wind (Roommates)*, 1961; *Carry on Columbus*, 1992. **Radio**—*The Missing Links*, 1986. **Television**—*A Milligan for All Seasons*, 1974; *Squaring the Circle* by Tom Stoppard, 1986.

* * *

John Antrobus wrote his first play, *The Bed-Sitting Room*, with Spike Milligan, and though Antrobus's range has broadened, all of his work has retained characteristics that are as well examined through this first play as through any other.

World War III, apparently caused by a "Nuclear Misunderstanding," mutates Lord Fortnum of Alamein into the bed-sitting room of the title. His doctor moves into the premises instead of curing his patient, a trendy vicar in a Victorian bathing costume performs a marriage service by reading from *Lady Chatterley's Lover*, and Harold Wilson becomes a parrot. It is a surrealist mock-heroic fable, a shell-distorted mirror held up to an absurd society. The Milligan element is clearly crucial; as with *The Goon Show* the humor may or may not be tasteful, and the vaudeville cross talk moves from brilliant lunacy to dead trivialities. The work remains hilarious—indeed, it must be one of the funniest plays to come out of modern England—and it mixes gentleness with blasphemy, pathos, beauty, desperation, and innocent reverence. The exuberance of the play gives way to tenderness in the scene at the end, in which a mother cries, "Give me back my baby." But goonishness is a fraught context for simple or naive sincerity, especially when it leads to immediate wish fulfillment. Muddling through the ineptitude of the protagonists and the play is a strong moral concern addressed to the perennially urgent question of human survival. The play's satire, directed against politicians, vicars, advertising men, and all other regulators of modern life, is clearly rooted in Britain, as is its refusal to take itself seriously.

Ambivalence and tensions are rife in all of Antrobus's plays, and it is unclear whether these result from mere self-indulgence or from a lack of critical sense. At its worst Antrobus's lack of discipline leads to monotony, flabbiness, and garrulity. At his best Antrobus bids fair to rival Pinter, and usually, in spite of his lack of clarity and the faults of his dramatic structure, he manages to be profoundly disturbing and stimulating. From a formal or technical point of view his best work has been for radio. He is among the half dozen radio dramatists who manage to produce work that both understands and exploits the distinctive nature of the medium. Antrobus is best known, however, for his work on television, where both *The Army Game* and *Bootsie and Snudge* have acquired immortality.

Antrobus's Christian conversion, though a conversion to Jesus rather than to dogma or denomination, seemed out of character to observers who could only see in his work brilliant if anarchic satire of the establishment. Lying just under that hard and polished surface, however, has been a concern, usually expressed through irony, with the deepest issues of our time: the problems posed by the "advances" of science, the nature of militarism, the possibility of differentiating normalcy from madness, pretense and honesty in human relationships, and the wolfish and sheepish character of such religion as is tolerated (or connived at) by those in cultural and political power. His conversion seems to have had no discernible effect on his work, unless the relatively conservative form of *Crete and Sergeant Pepper* is part of a search for a new synthesis. If Antrobus can find a structure for his pyrotechnic fluidity and grow the body of his work from that inner womb or heart that is clearly sensitive to moral and even spiritual issues, his genius may be properly revealed. Overall, however, his work has shown him to be an individual, energetic, and zany playwright.

—Prabhu S. Guptara

ARDEN, John

Nationality: British. **Born:** Barnsley, Yorkshire, 26 October 1930. **Education:** Schools in Barnsley; Sedbergh School, Yorkshire, 1944-48; King's College, Cambridge, 1950-53, B.A. in architecture 1953; Edinburgh College of Art, 1953-55, diploma in architecture 1955. **Military Service:** Served in the British Army Intelligence Corps, 1949-50: lance-corporal. **Family:** Married the actress Margaretta Ruth D'Arcy in 1957; five sons (one deceased). **Career:** Architectural assistant, London, 1955-57; full-time writer, 1958—. Fellow in playwriting, Bristol University, 1959-60; visiting lecturer in politics and drama, New York University, 1967; Regents' lecturer, University of California, Davis, 1973; writer-in-residence, University of New England, Armidale, New South Wales, 1975. Cofounder, Committee of 100 anti-nuclear group, 1961; honorary chair *Peace News* pacifist weekly, London, 1966-70; cofounder, Corrandulla Arts and Entertainment, County Galway, Ireland, 1973; founding member, Theatre Writers' Group (now Theatre Writers' Union), 1975. Lives in Galway. **Awards:** BBC Northern Region prize, 1957; Encyclopaedia Britannica prize, 1959; *Evening Standard* award, 1960; Trieste Festival award, 1961; John Whiting award, 1973; PEN Macmillan Silver Pen award, 1992. **Agent:** Casarotto Ramsay Ltd., National House, 60-66 Wardour Street, London W1V 3HP, England.

Publications

Plays

All Fall Down (produced Edinburgh, 1955).

The Waters of Babylon (produced London, 1957; New York, 1965). Included in *Three Plays*, 1964.

When Is a Door Not a Door? (produced London, 1958). Included in *Soldier, Soldier and Other Plays*, 1967.

Live Like Pigs (produced London, 1958; New York, 1965). Published in *New English Dramatists 3*, London, Penguin, 1961; in *Three Plays*, 1964.

Serjeant Musgrave's Dance: An Unhistorical Parable (produced London, 1959; San Francisco, 1961; New York, 1966). London, Methuen, 1960; New York, Grove Press, 1962; revised version (produced London, 1972).

The Happy Haven, with Margaretta D'Arcy (produced Bristol and London, 1960; Kingston, Rhode Island, 1963; New York, 1967). Published in *New English Dramatists 4*, London, Penguin, 1962; in *Three Plays*, 1964.

Soldier, Soldier (televised 1960). Included in *Soldier, Soldier and Other Plays*, 1967.

The Business of Good Government: A Christmas Play, with Margaretta D'Arcy (also co-director: as *A Christmas Play*, produced Brent Knoll, Somerset, 1960; New York, 1970; as *The Business of Good Government*, produced London, 1978). London, Methuen, 1963; New York, Grove Press, 1967.

Wet Fish (televised 1961). Included in *Soldier, Soldier and Other Plays*, 1967.

The Workhouse Donkey: A Vulgar Melodrama (produced Chichester, 1963). London, Methuen, 1964; New York, Grove Press, 1967.

Ironhand, adaptation of a play by Goethe (produced Bristol, 1963). London, Methuen, 1965.

Armstrong's Last Goodnight: An Exercise in Diplomacy (produced Glasgow, 1964; London, 1965; Boston, 1966). London, Methuen, 1965; New York, Grove Press, 1966.

Ars Longa, Vita Brevis (for children), with Margaretta D'Arcy (produced Kirkbymoorside and London, 1964). In *Eight Plays 1*, edited by Malcolm Stuart Fellows, London, Cassell, 1965.

Three Plays. London, Penguin, 1964; New York, Grove Press, 1966.

Fidelio, adaptation of a libretto by Joseph Sonnleithner and Friedrich Treitschke, music by Beethoven (produced London, 1965).

Left-Handed Liberty: A Play about Magna Carta (produced London, 1965; Boston, 1968). London, Methuen, 1965; New York, Grove Press, 1966.

Friday's Hiding, with Margaretta D'Arcy (produced Edinburgh, 1966). Included in *Soldier, Soldier and Other Plays*, 1967.

The Royal Pardon; or, The Soldier Who Became an Actor (for children), with Margaretta D'Arcy (also co-director: produced Beaford, Devon, 1966; London, 1967). London, Methuen, 1967.

Soldier, Soldier and Other Plays. London, Methuen, 1967.

The True History of Squire Jonathan and His Unfortunate Treasure (produced London, 1968; New York, 1974). Included in *Two Autobiographical Plays*, 1971.

The Hero Rises Up: A Romantic Melodrama, with Margaretta D'Arcy (also co-director: produced London, 1968). London, Methuen, 1969.

The Soldier's Tale, adaptation of a libretto by Ramuz, music by Stravinsky (produced Bath, 1968).

Harold Muggins Is a Martyr, with Margaretta D'Arcy and the Cartoon Archetypical Slogan Theatre (produced London, 1968).

The Bagman; or, The Impromptu of Muswell Hill (broadcast 1970). Included in *Two Autobiographical Plays*, 1971.

Two Autobiographical Plays. London, Methuen, 1971.

Two Hundred Years of Labour History, with Margaretta D'Arcy and others (produced London, 1971).
Granny Welfare and the Wolf, with Margaretta D'Arcy (produced London, 1971).
My Old Man's a Tory, with Margaretta D'Arcy (produced London, 1971).
Rudi Dutschke Must Stay, with Margaretta D'Arcy (produced London, 1971).
The Ballygombeen Bequest, with Margaretta D'Arcy (produced Belfast and London, 1972; New York, 1976). Published in *Scripts 9* (New York), September 1972; revised version, as *The Little Gray Home in the West: An Anglo-Irish Melodrama* (produced Birmingham, 1982), London, Pluto Press, 1982.
The Island of the Mighty: A Play on a Traditional British Theme, with Margaretta D'Arcy (produced London, 1972; section produced, as *Handful of Watercress*, New York, 1976). London, Eyre Methuen, 1974; in *Performance* (New York), 1974.
The Devil and the Parish Pump, with Margaretta D'Arcy (produced Galway, 1974).
The Crown Strike Play, with Margaretta D'Arcy (produced Galway, 1974).
The Non-Stop Connolly Show: A Dramatic Cycle of Continuous Struggle in Six Parts, with Margaretta D'Arcy (also co-director: produced Dublin, 1975; London, 1976). London, Pluto Press, 5 vols., 1977-78; 1 vol. edition, London, Methuen, 1986.
Sean O'Scrudu, with Margaretta D'Arcy (produced Galway, 1976).
The Mongrel Fox, with Margaretta D'Arcy (produced Galway, 1976).
No Room at the Inn, with Margaretta D'Arcy (produced Galway, 1976).
Silence, with Margaretta D'Arcy (produced Galway, 1977).
Mary's Name, with Margaretta D'Arcy (produced Galway, 1977).
Blow-in Chorus for Liam Cosgrave, with Margaretta D'Arcy (produced Galway, 1977).
Plays 1 (includes *Serjeant Musgrave's Dance*, *The Workhouse Donkey*, *Armstrong's Last Goodnight*). London, Eyre Methuen, 1977; New York, Grove Press, 1978.
Vandaleur's Folly: An Anglo-Irish Melodrama, with Margaretta D'Arcy (also co-director: produced Lancaster, 1978). London, Eyre Methuen, 1981.
The Mother, with Margaretta D'Arcy, adaptation of a play by Brecht (produced London, 1984).
The Making of Muswell Hill, with Margaretta D'Arcy (produced London, 1984).
Whose Is the Kingdom?, with Margaretta D'Arcy (broadcast 1988). London, Methuen, 1988.

Radio Plays: *The Life of Man*, 1956; *The Bagman*, 1970; *Keep These People Moving!* (for children), with Margaretta D'Arcy, 1972; *Pearl*, 1978; *To Put It Frankly*, 1979; *Don Quixote*, from the novel by Cervantes, 1980; *The Winking Goose* (documentary), 1982; *Garland for a Hoar Head*, 1982; *The Old Man Sleeps Alone*, 1982; *The Manchester Enthusiasts*, with Margaretta D'Arcy, 1984; *Whose Is the Kingdom?*, with Margaretta D'Arcy, 1988; *A Suburban Suicide*, with Margaretta D'Arcy, 1994; *Little Novels of Wilkie Collins*, 1998.

Television Plays: *Soldier, Soldier*, 1960; *Wet Fish*, 1961; *Sean O'Casey: Portrait of a Rebel* (documentary), with Margaretta D'Arcy, 1973 (Ireland).

Novels

Silence among the Weapons: Some Events at the Time of the Failure of a Republic. London, Methuen, 1982; as *Vox Pop: Last Days of the Roman Republic*, New York, Harcourt Brace, 1983.
Books of Bale: A Fiction of History. London, Methuen, 1988.
Jack Juggler and the Emperor's Whore. London, Methuen, 1995.

Short Stories

Cogs Tyrannic. London, Methuen, 1991.

Other

To Present the Pretence: Essays on the Theatre and Its Public. London, Eyre Methuen, 1977; New York, Holmes and Meier, 1979.
Awkward Corners: Essays, Papers, Fragments, with Margaretta D'Arcy. London, Methuen, 1988.

*

Critical Studies: *John Arden* by Ronald Hayman, London, Heinemann, 1968, New York, Ungar, 1972; *Theatre Language: A Study of Arden, Osborne, Pinter, and Wesker* by John Russell Brown, London, Allen Lane, and New York, Taplinger, 1972; *John Arden* by Simon Trussler, New York, Columbia University Press, 1973; *John Arden* by Glenda Leeming, London, Longman, 1974; *Arden: A Study of His Plays* by Albert Hunt, London, Eyre Methuen, 1974; *Anger and Detachment: A Study of Arden, Osborne, and Pinter* by Michael Anderson, London, Pitman, 1976; *John Arden* by Frances Gray, London, Macmillan, and New York, Grove Press, 1982; *John Arden* by Malcolm Page, Boston, Twayne, 1984, and *Arden on File* edited by Page, London, Methuen, 1985; *John Arden and Margaretta D'Arcy: A Casebook* edited by Jonathan Wike, New York, Garland, 1995; "John Arden" by Michael L.Counts, in *British Playwrights, 1956-1995: A Research and Production Sourcebook*, Westport, Connecticut, Greenwood, 1996.

Theatrical Activities:
Director, with Margaretta D'Arcy: several of his own plays.

Actor: **Plays**—Wise Man in *A Christmas Play*, Brent Knoll, Somerset, 1960; Constable in *The Royal Pardon*, Beaford, Devon, 1966; Mr. Muggins in *Harold Muggins Is a Martyr*, London, 1968.

John Arden comments:

(1977) At the present time the gap between the playwright and the active life of the theatre seems as wide as it has ever been: and it shows no sign of closing. Figures such as the director and the scenic designer, whose relevance to good dramatic writing is at best marginal, have increased their power and influence in no small measure during the past few years: and they stand ominously between playwright and actors, inhibiting proper communication. The *content* of new plays is obscured and neutralized by overemphasis on aesthetic theatrical *form*. The dependence of the dramatic art upon subsidies from public funds has given rise to a bureaucratic intransigence on the part of directors, who are too often administrators as well, and are becoming less and less inclined to take the necessary risks demanded by adventurous and expanding experiment. The problem is similar to that faced by Ben Jonson in the 1620s, when he struck out against the dominance of Inigo Jones as designer-director of court entertainment, and lost his battle. The result of Jones's victory was the securing by the monarchy of the complete allegiance of the theatrical profession, followed by the closure of the theatres during the Cromwellian revolution. The playwrights, as a trade-grouping, never again recaptured the position of artistic strength and poetic potency which they had attained at the beginning of the 17th century. To forestall an equivalent disaster today, the modern dramatists must attempt two apparently contradictory tasks. 1) They must abandon their solitary status and learn to combine together to secure conditions-of-work and artistic control over the products of their imagination. 2) They must be prepared to combine not only with their fellows, but also with *actors*. It is not enough for the occasional author to *direct*; playwrights should be members of theatrical troupes, and take part in all aspects of production. In order to achieve goal 2, goal 1 must first be arrived at. The authors together must establish the importance of their written work as an essential *internal* element of the theatre, and then, individually, they must become absorbed into the theatre themselves as co-workers.

I am aware that these requirements go against all current trends. But the current trends are running towards the complete death of the modern drama. Remember, Shakespeare and Molière regarded themselves as men of the theatre rather than *literary* figures: and I believe it to be no accident that their works remain unequalled in the Western tradition.

* * *

A glance at John Arden's bibliography suggests that the entire opus of his work rests in his collaboration with his wife, Margaretta D'Arcy, for they have together produced a wealth of plays for both stage and radio. Arden himself has not written for the stage for some two decades. His handful of plays are generally acknowledged by both critics and contemporaries, however, to be seminal to the modern British theater and are arguably classics within the lifetime of their author.

Arden's plays break through the confinements of realism by using open staging, broad and poetic language, characters bordering on caricature, complex visual imagery, active social settings, and an appropriation of traditional popular forms like the music hall and medieval theater. They dramatize the interactive effects of concepts, ideas, and social organization on social, personal, and political life.

The scope and complexity of the plays, however, have often given rise to critical confusion. This is arguably owing to the very elements that have led to their acclaim, for a change in form necessarily signals changes in perspective and concern. Thus, realist readings of a nonrealist play invariably cause confusion and misunderstanding. Bemusement over Arden's plays seems to stem from the assumption that, whatever the form of the work, a play inevitably boils down to an elaboration of human emotion, eliciting sympathy for the individual and taking a clear, simple, literal moral stance. This is thought to be especially the case if the play deals with social and moral issues.

For example, critics became focused on deciding whether *Serjeant Musgrave's Dance* was propacifism. A more inclusive view of the play, however, renders the question irrelevant. The play patently is not promoting war. No argument is proposed to polarize pacifism against warmongering; rather, pacifism serves as the context, not the content of the play. That is, the play assumes that its audience finds war per se undesirable, and this premise establishes the terms by which the relationship between means and ends may be dramatized.

Since on the whole we agree that war is generally undesirable, we also agree that Musgrave's aim to put an end to all war is commendable. Assuming that the audience is in accordance with Musgrave's purpose, the play turns our attention from his intentions to his actions, from his desired goal, which we share, to the means by which he pursues it. His means, however, produce their own ends that are contradictory to his original goal. Hence, through Musgrave we experience the process by which even the finest of intentions become corrupted by the means employed for their accomplishment, and we are called on to assess the terms of their validity.

Our introduction to Musgrave through the effect he has on others prepares us to look toward action and consequence rather than explanation, to judge by effect rather than rationale. His soldiers prepare us for a man to admire, one who is organized, commanding, and demanding of respect. His uniform and his confident manner suggest qualities our society admires: order, organization, fear of God, and, above all, logic and reason. Alas, these are the very qualities that drive him to his horrifying conclusion. When Musgrave—steeped in simple, fundamental religious beliefs, a soldier's training and discipline, a life of careful order and authority, and, especially, a total faith in logical thought—is confronted with the horrible chaos of war, to which he has devoted his life, he inevitably uses the only means he has to create a plan to annihilate war. His solution is neat, ordered, and completely logical, and in his eyes it has the blessing of God. His intentions are good, but the result is destructive and insane. Musgrave's insight that the source of war lies with ordinary people who let their husbands and sons become cannon fodder has a certain validity, but his plan for eliminating war is both unacceptable and futile.

The opposition set up in *Serjeant Musgrave's Dance* is not between war and peace but between social ideals of order, organization, and logic in contrast to the "messy scribbling" of day-to-day existence, the erratic demands of emotion and need. The extreme opposite to Musgrave is the Bargee, an unattractive picture of daily survival unhampered by principle or design. Near Musgrave the Mayor and Parson organize fumblingly for their own ends. In the middle are the women and the miners with their needs, passions, and inconsistencies, their morals based more on experience than ideals. The play provides an analysis of the social precepts of order and reason as they are superimposed on the chaos of ordinary life.

Serjeant Musgrave's Dance also challenges the realist premises that good intentions mitigate behavior, and it calls into question the idea that reason can solve all human problems. Annie's importance, for example, is not that she will sleep with any man but that her act of lovemaking is an act of revivification. Arden neither promotes nor condemns promiscuity but contrasts the effect of Annie's actions with the imposed purity of Musgrave's orderliness.

Arden's vision is essentially anarchic. Ideals of organization and reason distort human life. War itself is the result of order imposed on human existence. The entrance of the Dragoons to restore order and to save us from Musgrave may bring some relief, but it also brings an inescapable sense of failure.

The playwright's organization subverts the audience's preconception of order. Arden's use of the open stage, his ballads and heightened language, and his frequent placing of more than one character at the center of the action are devices to turn attention away from personalization and simple moralizing toward an examination of the practical functioning of these moral precepts in the social context. In *The Workhouse Donkey,* for example, it is fruitless to complain that none of the politicians is blameless. "Misgoverned," says Sweetman; "Oh, it's not exactly misgoverned. It's just the wrong lot are the governers, that's all." The play assumes that power corrupts. The difference between Labour and Tory is not corruptibility but the form their corruption takes and to what end. The involvement of Feng, the incorruptible policeman, in this cozily untidy world takes us into an examination of the consequences of obsessive morality imposed on an imperfect world. As Arden says, Feng's absolute integrity causes infinitely more damage than Butterthwaite's bumbling dishonesty could ever manage to. Feng lacks warmth and compassion for the catch-as-catch-can bustle of ordinary life. Butterthwaite's warmth and human failings endear us to him despite his imperfections. Assuming a world of general imperfection, Arden attempts to turn attention away from abstract ideals of simplistic morality and toward the effect of these ideals when they are put into practice without regard for the fundamental anarchy of daily living.

Arden's theatrical devices distance the audience from the characters so they can be seen as active members of working societies. No better or worse than others, these societies run, as by implication all do, on moral precepts that have both weaknesses and strengths. When one of these little worlds is confronted by another that does not share its assumptions, the characters find themselves in extreme situations that threaten the social preconceptions. The consequences and effects of these actions dramatize the complex relationships between the individual and society, between social ideals and their practical application, between means and end.

Live Like Pigs can be read as a confrontation between two ways of living that are acceptable enough in themselves but mutually destructive in confrontation. This pattern is most richly and tragically elaborated in *Armstrong's Last Goodnight.* Through Lindsay and Armstrong the weaknesses and inner workings of their societies are set in relief. Neither Armstrong nor Lindsay is a villain. Each is the perfect representative of his society, but their worlds are different, with different ways of ordering and interpreting life, different moral concepts, and different ideals. Both can enlist our sympathy, Armstrong as a leader in an individualist world of action and Lindsay as a spokesman for the King in an integrated world of reason. On its own terms each society is perfectly viable, but they are entirely incompatible.

Though both live in Scotland, Lindsay and Armstrong inhabit realities so different that they can hardly speak to each other. The way each sees and evaluates the world excludes the world of the other. For example, when Lindsay tells Armstrong's wife that he has come from the King, she answers, "What King would that be?" Even a simple concept such as King is not shared. The play's scenes are juxtaposed to emphasize the misinterpretations and incompatibilities. The use of the stage itself—with James's court on one side and Armstrong's castle on the other—presents a visual image of the distance between the two worlds. Clothing imagery elaborates the social symbols of value and role and marks the opposing experiences of the characters. It is not that one is right and one wrong but rather that each, though wholly consistent within itself, is incompatible with the other. Yet Lindsay's quest is to integrate the two.

As they are forced to the surface in the confrontation, the moral precepts that have been the strengths of each society are shown also to be their weaknesses. Armstrong's dashing individualism leads him to his death. Lindsay's belief in reason is destroyed as his reasonable, organized society destroys Armstrong and the world he represents. We are not asked to judge the moral precepts informing these worlds so much as to wonder at the fact that, despite their opposing orders and moralities, they resort to exactly the same manner of dealing with threats. Wamphrey and Armstrong are executed on the same tree, victims of the same kind of treachery. Attention is turned from the superficialities of abstract moral judgment to the exacting examination of the execution of moral ideals in an imperfect world.

Arden's formal changes in his plays demand a shift from simplistic moralizing to dramatic investigation. It is a transfer from idealized expectations and easy judgments to responsible application and political analysis that transcends the simple taking of sides.

Since his disengagement with the conventional theater, Arden has collaborated with D'Arcy on a host of works for both the theater and radio. They are hard-hitting, energetic pieces that overtly draw on forms such as the music hall, melodrama, and living theater. They directly confront sociopolitical issues, their most salient quality being their expression of community. The plays not only confront community issues but also are often the product of community cooperation. Thus, both form and content reflect the sociopolitical commitments of their collaborators.

Arden has also written radio plays that make full use of the vast canvas offered by the medium and that continue his unblinkered investigation of sociopolitical dynamics, including, not surprisingly, the question of the artist's function in his society.

—Elaine Turner

ASKEW, Jack. *See* **HIVNOR, Robert (Hanks).**

AXELROD, George

Nationality: American. **Born:** New York City, 9 June 1922. **Military Service:** Served in the United States Army Signal Corps during World War II. **Family:** Married 1) Gloria Washburn in 1942 (divorced 1954), two sons; 2) Joan Stanton in 1954, one daughter. **Career:** Film director and producer. **Awards:** Writers Guild of America West award, for screenplay, 1962. **Agent:** Irving Paul Lazar Agency, 211 South Beverly Drive, Beverly Hills, California 90212, U.S.A.

Publications

Plays

Small Wonder (produced New York, 1948).

The Seven Year Itch: A Romantic Comedy (produced New York, 1952; London, 1953). New York, Random House, 1953; London, Heinemann, 1954.

Will Success Spoil Rock Hunter? (also director: produced New York, 1955). New York, Random House, 1956.
Goodbye Charlie (also director: produced New York, 1959). New York, French, 1959.
Breakfast at Tiffany's (screenplay). Hollywood, California, Paramount, 1960.
Souvenir, with Peter Viertel (produced Los Angeles, 1975).

Screenplays: *Phffft!*, 1954; *The Seven Year Itch*, with Billy Wilder, 1955; *Bus Stop*, 1956; *Rally 'round the Flag, Boys* (uncredited), 1958; *Breakfast at Tiffany's*, 1961; *The Manchurian Candidate*, 1962; *Paris When It Sizzles*, 1963; *How to Murder Your Wife*, 1964; *Lord Love a Duck*, with Larry H. Johnson, 1966; *The Secret Life of an American Wife*, 1968; *The Lady Vanishes*, 1979; *The Holcroft Covenant*, with Edward Anhalt and John Hopkins, 1982.

Radio Writer: *Midnight in Manhattan* program, 1940; material for *Grand Old Opry*, 1950-52.

Television Writer: *Celebrity Time*, 1950.

Night Club Writer: *All about Love*, New York, 1951.

Novels

Beggar's Choice. New York, Howell Soskin, 1947; as *Hobson's Choice*, London, Elek, 1951.
Blackmailer. New York, Fawcett, 1952; London, Fawcett, 1959.
Where Am I Now—When I Need Me? New York, Viking Press, and London, Deutsch, 1971.

*

Critical Study: "Bus Stop as Self-Reflexive Parody: George Axelrod on Its Adaptation" by Joanna E. Rapf, in *Film and Literature: A Comparative Approach to Adaptation,* edited by Wendell Aycock and Michael Schoenecke, Lubbock, Texas Tech University Press, 1988.

Theatrical Activities:
Director: **Plays**—*Will Success Spoil Rock Hunter?*, New York, 1955; *Once More, With Feeling* by Harry Kurnitz, New York, 1958; *Goodbye Charlie*, New York, 1959; *The Star-Spangled Girl* by Neil Simon, New York, 1966. **Films**—*Lord Love a Duck*, 1966; *The Secret Life of an American Wife*, 1968.

* * *

The playwriting career of George Axelrod well illustrates that dramatist of particular wit and imagination who manages to create marketable products for Broadway tastes and who for a brief period enjoys the fame and fortune that successful commercial comedy brings. His brief period was the decade of the 1950s. *The Seven Year Itch* ran nearly three years in New York with 1,141 performances, and *Will Success Spoil Rock Hunter?* lasted a year and had 444 performances. Prior to his first success he had learned his trade writing for radio and television. Since this decade of playwriting he has had some success as a director, effectively supervising such plays as Neil Simon's *The Star-Spangled Girl* for an audience acceptance that he was no longer able to reach as a dramatist.

In the history of American comic drama Axelrod might be mentioned as the author of two plays that say something about the country's tastes and attitudes during that post-World War II decade when audiences enjoyed a semi-sophisticated joke along with a semi-realistic view of themselves. Although the period for this enjoyment continued under the aegis of Simon, Axelrod's imagination for such playwriting dried up. A later novel, *Where Am I Now—When I Need Me?,* is an artless attempt to capitalize on free expression in writing as well as a pathetic admission. In the span of theater history in America the decade of the 1950s will be considered undistinguished, and Axelrod's contribution will be measured, if at all, as an instance of conscious yet effective technique on the Broadway scale of carefully analyzed entertainment.

Axelrod's success as a dramatist came with his ability to write clever, simply structured comedy that seemed a bit outrageous or naughty at first but was generally acceptable and comforting. Liberal circles have labeled him a writer of right-wing plays, in which conservative morality always triumphs, and have considered his success a disturbing feature of American comedy. Although such observations have their place in history, it is nonetheless true that such American comedy has a rich reputation, and for a decade Axelrod's polished and carefully tailored plays were the most imaginative of these slim pieces of professionally manufactured theater. His plays satisfied an audience's needs. *The Seven Year Itch* tells of a New York businessman, Richard Shermans, who combines a humorous reluctance and eagerness as he spends a night with a girl after his wife has left the hot city for the summer months. *Will Success Spoil Rock Hunter?* toys with the Faust theme as George MacCawley sells his soul 10 percent at a time for fame, fortune, and certain pleasures. But Axelrod always emphasized a definite, if sometimes late, morality. Richard is funny because his reluctance, his ineptness, and his remorse contrast hilariously with his view of himself as a seducer. At the final curtain a likable hero emerges from an educational experience; even the girl, who slept with him because he could not be serious with her, begins to think that marriage might be worth a try. George both has his cake and eats it too. His fantasies are dramatically fulfilled, but he does not lose his soul. In this manner Axelrod presented safe, conservative entertainment that would run for at least a year. A few years later it was out of date, and with another generation it has lost most of its appeal.

Technically, Axelrod used the accepted devices of unpretentious comic entertainment. Verbal and visual jokes were a major part of a play's success with an audience. Perhaps that is why Axelrod later substituted directing for playwriting. Topicality in the jokes was as much a part of a play's success as it was an appeal to snobbishness in the audiences. There are numerous local references to New York, and names were dropped in almost every scene. Axelrod obviously studied his audiences, considering them knowledgeable but not overly bright. Certain gags in *Will Success Spoil Rock Hunter?*—the positioning of the "Scarlet Letter" on a scantily clad model and the impossibility of making love in the sand—are repeated, and the staircase in *The Seven Year Itch*, described as giving "the joint a kind of Jean-Paul Sartre quality," is further explained as having "no exit." In *The Seven Year Itch* Axelrod enlivened his presentation with dramatic devices such as fantasy sequences, flashbacks, and soliloquies. Throughout all of his plays ridiculing, making witty comments, and satirizing man and his society are standard ploys for humor. But Axelrod was neither innovator nor reformer, merely a professional entertainer. He satirized the usual things—the movies, psychiatrists, sex, certain kinds of decadence, and so on. He had nothing to say to any thoughtful person, and he scarcely took himself seriously, suggesting as he did a thorough and comfortable acceptance of all that he ridiculed in his plays. John Gassner referred to his work as "imaginative fluff," and as such it has appeal for certain theater audiences at certain times.

—Walter J. Meserve

AYCKBOURN, Alan

Also writes as Roland Allen. **Nationality:** British. **Born:** London, 12 April 1939. **Education:** Haileybury, Hertford, 1952-56. **Family:** Married 1) Christine Roland in 1959 (divorced 1997), two sons; 2) Heather Stoney in 1997. **Career:** Stage manager and actor, Donald Wolfit's company, in Edinburgh, Worthing, Leatherhead, Scarborough, and Oxford, 1956-57; actor and stage manager, Stephen Joseph Theatre-in-the-Round, Scarborough, Yorkshire, 1957-62; associate director, Victoria Theatre, Stoke-on-Trent, Staffordshire, 1962-64; drama producer, BBC Radio, Leeds, 1964-70. Artistic director, Stephen Joseph Theatre, 1970—; associate director, National Theatre, London, 1986-88; professor of contemporary theatre, Oxford University, 1991-92. **Awards:** *Evening Standard* award, 1973, 1974, 1977, 1985, 1987, 1989, 1990; Olivier award, 1985; *Plays and Players* award, 1987; Evening Standard Best Play award, for *A Small Family Business,* 1987; Plays and Plays Best Director award, for *A View from the Bridge,* 1988; Evening Standard Best Comedy award, 1989, 1990; Drama-Logue Critics award, for *Henceforward,* 1991; TMA/MArtinin Regional Theatre award Best Show for children and Young People, for *Mr. A's Amazing Maze Plays,* 1993; Writer's Guild of Great Britain Lifetime Achievement award, 1993; John Ederyn Hughes Rural Wales Award for Literature, 1993; Birmingham Press Club Personality of the Year award, 1993; Yorkshire Man of the Year, 1994; Mont Blanc de la Culture Award for Europe, 1994; TMA Regional Theatre Awards Best Musical, 1996; Writers' Guild of Great Britain Best West End Play, 1996; Lloyds Private Banking Playwright of the Year, for *Things We Do For Love,* 1997. Honorary D.Litt.: University of Hull, Yorkshire, 1981; University of Keele, Staffordshire, 1987; University of Leeds, 1987; University of York, 1992; University of Bradford, 1994; Open University, 1998. C.B.E. (Commander, Order of the British Empire), 1987; Knighted for Services to the Theatre, 1997. **Agent:** Casarotto Ramsay Ltd., National House, 60-66 Wardour Street, London WIV 4ND, England.

PUBLICATIONS

Plays

The Square Cat (as Roland Allen) (produced Scarborough, 1959).
Love after All (as Roland Allen) (produced Scarborough, 1959).
Dad's Tale (for children; as Roland Allen) (produced Scarborough, 1960).
Standing Room Only (as Roland Allen) (also director: produced Scarborough, 1961).
Xmas v. Mastermind (produced Stoke-on-Trent, 1962).
Mr. Whatnot (also director: produced Stoke-on-Trent, 1963; revised version produced London, 1964).
Relatively Speaking (as *Meet My Father*, produced Scarborough, 1965; as *Relatively Speaking*, produced London, 1967; New York, 1984). London, Evans, and New York, French, 1968.
The Sparrow (also director: produced Scarborough, 1967).
How the Other Half Loves (also director: produced Scarborough, 1969; London, 1970; New York, 1971). London, Evans, and New York, French, 1972.
Countdown, in *We Who Are about to . . .*, later called *Mixed Doubles* (produced London, 1969). London, Methuen, 1970.
Ernie's Incredible Illucinations (for children; produced London, 1971). London, French, 1969; in *The Best Short Plays 1979*, edited by Stanley Richards, Radnor, Pennsylvania, Chilton, 1979.
The Story So Far (also director: produced Scarborough, 1970; revised version, as *Me Times Me Times Me*, produced Leicester, 1971; revised version, as *Family Circles*, produced Richmond, Surrey, 1978).
Time and Time Again (also director: produced Scarborough, 1971; London, 1972). London, French, 1973.
Absurd Person Singular (also director: produced Scarborough, 1972; London, 1973; New York, 1974). Included in *Three Plays*, 1977.
Mother Figure, in *Mixed Blessings* (produced Horsham, Sussex, 1973).
The Norman Conquests: Table Manners, Living Together, Round and Round the Garden (also director: produced Scarborough, 1973; London, 1974; Los Angeles and New York, 1975). London, Chatto and Windus, 1975; New York, Grove Press, 1979.
Absent Friends (also director: produced Scarborough, 1974; London, 1975; New Haven, Connecticut, 1977; New York, 1991). Included in *Three Plays*, 1977.
Confusions: Mother Figure, Drinking Companion, Between Mouthfuls, Gosforth's Fête, A Talk in the Park (also director: produced Scarborough, 1974; London, 1976). London, French, 1977.
Jeeves, music by Andrew Lloyd Webber, adaptation of works by P.G. Wodehouse (produced London, 1975).
Bedroom Farce (also director: produced Scarborough, 1975; London, 1977; New York, 1979). Included in *Three Plays*, 1977.
Just Between Ourselves (also director: produced Scarborough, 1976; London, 1977; Princeton, New Jersey, 1981). Included in *Joking Apart, Ten Times Table, Just Between Ourselves*, 1979.
Three Plays. London, Chatto and Windus, 1977; New York, Grove Press, 1979.
Ten Times Table (also director: produced Scarborough, 1977; London, 1978; Cleveland, 1983). Included in *Joking Apart, Ten Times Table, Just Between Ourselves*, 1979.
Joking Apart (also director: produced Scarborough, 1978; London, 1979). Included in *Joking Apart, Ten Times Table, Just Between Ourselves*, 1979.
Men on Women on Men, music by Paul Todd (produced Scarborough, 1978).
Joking Apart, Ten Times Table, Just Between Ourselves. London, Chatto and Windus, 1979; augmented edition, as *Joking Apart and Other Plays* (includes *Sisterly Feelings*), London, Penguin, 1982.
Sisterly Feelings (also director: produced Scarborough, 1979; London, 1980). With *Taking Steps*, London, Chatto and Windus, 1981.
Taking Steps (also director: produced Scarborough, 1979; London, 1980; Houston, 1983; New York, 1986). With *Sisterly Feelings*, London, Chatto and Windus, 1981.

Suburban Strains, music by Paul Todd (also director: produced Scarborough, 1980; London, 1981). London, French, 1982.
First Course, music by Paul Todd (also director: produced Scarborough, 1980).
Second Helping, music by Paul Todd (also director: produced Scarborough, 1980).
Season's Greetings (also director: produced Scarborough and London, 1980; revised version, also director: produced London, 1982; Berkeley, California, 1983; New York, 1985). London, French, 1982.
Way Upstream (also director: produced Scarborough, 1981; London, 1982). London, French, 1983.
Making Tracks, music by Paul Todd (also director: produced Scarborough, 1981; London, 1983).
Me, Myself, and I, music by Paul Todd (also director: produced Scarborough, 1981). London, French, 1989.
Intimate Exchanges (also director: produced Scarborough, 1982; London, 1984). London, French, 2 vols., 1985.
A Trip to Scarborough, adaptation of the play by Sheridan (also director: produced Scarborough, 1982).
Incidental Music (produced Scarborough, 1983).
It Could Be Any One of Us (also director: produced Scarborough, 1983).
The Seven Deadly Virtues, music by Paul Todd (also director: produced Scarborough, 1984).
A Cut in the Rates (televised 1984). London, French, 1991.
The Westwoods (also director: produced Scarborough, 1984; London, 1987).
A Game of Golf (produced London, 1984).
A Chorus of Disapproval (also director: produced Scarborough, 1984; London, 1985; New York, 1988). London, Faber, 1986.
Woman in Mind (also director: produced Scarborough, 1985; London, 1986; New York, 1988). London, Faber, 1986.
Boy Meets Girl, music by Paul Todd (also director: produced Scarborough, 1985).
Girl Meets Boy, music by Paul Todd (also director: produced Scarborough, 1985).
Mere Soup Songs, music by Paul Todd (also director: produced Scarborough and London, 1986).
Tons of Money, adaptation of the farce by Will Evans and Valentine (also director: produced London, 1986). London, French, 1986.
A Small Family Business (also director: produced London, 1987; New York, 1992). London, French, 1988.
Henceforward (also director: produced Scarborough, 1987; London, 1988; Los Angeles, 1991). London, Faber, 1988.
Vaudeville (produced Scarborough, 1988).
Mr. A's Amazing Maze Plays (for children) (also director: produced Scarborough, 1988). London, Faber, 1989.
Man of the Moment (also director: produced Scarborough, 1988, London 1990). London, Faber, 1990.
The Revengers' Comedies (also director: produced Scarborough, 1989; London 1991). London, Faber, 1991.
Invisible Friends (for children) (also director: produced Scarborough, 1989; London 1991). London, Faber, 1991.
Body Language (also director: produced Scarborough, 1990).
This Is Where We Came In (for children) (also director: produced Scarborough, 1990).
Callis to 5 (for children) (also director: produced Scarborough, 1990).
My Very Own Story (for children) (also director: produced Scarborough, 1991).
Wildest Dreams (also director: produced Scarborough, 1991).
Time of My Life (also director: produced Scarborough, 1992; London, 1993).
Dreams from a Summer House, music by John Pattison (produced Scarborough, 1992).
Communicating Doors (also director: produced Scarborô, 1994; London, 1995).
Haunting Julie (also director: produced Scarborô, 1994).
The Musical Jigsaw Play (for children; also director: produced Scarborô, 1994).
A Word from Our Sponsor, music by John Paltison (also director: produced Scarborô, 1995).
By Jeeves, music by Andrew Lloyd Webber (also director: produced Scarborô and London, 1996).
The Champion of Paribanou (for children; also director: produced Scarborô, 1996).
Things We Do for Love (also director: produced Scarborô, 1997; London, 1998).
Comic Potential (also director: produced Scarborô, 1998).
Gizmo (produced 1998).

Television Plays: *Service Not Included* (*Masquerade* series), 1974; *A Cut in the Rates*, 1984.

Other

Conversations with Ayckbourn, with Ian Watson. London, Macdonald, 1981.

*

Critical Studies: *Theatre in the Round* by Stephen Joseph, London, Barrie and Rockliff, 1967; *The Second Wave* by John Russell Taylor, London, Methuen, and New York, Hill and Wang, 1971; *Post-War British Theatre* by John Elsom, London, Routledge, 1976, revised edition, 1979; *The New British Drama* by Oleg Kerensky, London, Hamish Hamilton, 1977, New York, Taplinger, 1979; *Alan Ayckbourn* by Michael Billington, London, Macmillan, 1983, New York, Grove Press, 1984, revised edition, London, Macmillan, 1990; *File on Ayckbourn*, edited by Malcolm Page, London, Methuen, 1989; *Alan Ayckbourn: A Casebook* by Bernard F. Dukore, New York, Garland, 1991.

Theatrical Activities:
Director: **Plays**—Numerous productions at Victoria Theatre, Stoke-on-Trent, and Stephen Joseph Theatre, Scarborough, including *Miss Julie* by Strindberg, *Pygmalion* by Shaw, *A Man for All Seasons* by Robert Bolt, *Patriotic Bunting* and *Tishoo* by Brian Thompson, *Time and the Conways* by J. B. Priestley, *The Crucible* by Arthur Miller, *The Seagull* by Chekhov, *Thark* and *Rookery Nook* by Ben Travers, and many of his own plays; National Theatre, London: *Way Upstream*, 1982, *A Chorus of Disapproval*, 1985, *Tons of Money* by Will Evans and Valentine, 1986, *A View from the Bridge* by Arthur Miller, 1987, *A Small Family Business*, 1987, *'Tis Pity She's a Whore* by John Ford, 1988, and *The Haunt of Mr. Fossett* by Stephen Mallatratt, 1988. **Radio**—More than 100 productions, Leeds, 1964-70, and subsequently.

Actor: **Plays**—Roles with Stephen Joseph's touring company: The Cook in *Little Brother, Little Sister* by David Campton, Newcastle-under-Lyme, 1961; Victoria Theatre, Stoke-on-Trent: Fred in *The Birds and the Wellwishers* and Robert in *An Awkward Number* by William Norfolk, Aston in *The Caretaker*, James in *The Collection*, and Ben in *The Dumb Waiter*, by Harold Pinter, title role in

O'Flaherty, V.C. by G. B. Shaw, Roderick Usher in *Usher* by David Campton, Bill Starbuck in *The Rainmaker* by N. Richard Nash, The Crimson Gollywog in *Xmas v. Mastermind*, The Count in *The Rehearsal* by Anouilh, Vladimir in *Waiting for Godot* by Beckett, Thomas More in *A Man for All Seasons* by Robert Bolt, Jordan in *The Rainbow Machine* and Anderson in *Ted's Cathedral* by Alan Plater, Jerry Ryan in *Two for the Seesaw* by William Gibson, Mr. Manningham in *Gaslight* by Patrick Hamilton, The Interrogator in *The Prisoner* by Bridget Boland, and A Jew and Martin del Bosco in *The Jew of Malta* by Marlowe, 1962-64.

* * *

In the early part of Alan Ayckbourn's career, discussion often turned on his method of playwriting: announcing a title then, three or four days before rehearsals were due to start, shutting himself away to write. Ayckbourn responded by stressing that he was only a dramatist once a year, occasionally twice, and was primarily a director of the Stephen Joseph Theatre-in-the-Round in Scarborough. (He cleverly, and uniquely, appeared in print presenting his view of his writings in *Conversations with Ayckbourn* ahead of any books of criticism.)

Ayckbourn's early plays, such as *Relatively Speaking* and *Time and Time Again*, are polished and amusing. (Because Ayckbourn's titles rarely point unmistakably to the content, distinguishing between the plays is initially difficult.) His distinctive ingenuity was first shown in *How the Other Half Loves*, in which a couple attend two different dinner parties, on different days, at the same time. *Absurd Person Singular* has its three scenes on three consecutive Christmas Eves in three different kitchens and features the same three married couples, a fastidious tidiness. *The Norman Conquests* is a trilogy about the events of one weekend; it shows what is happening in a dining room, living room, and garden. The plays are designed to make sense in any order, or indeed by themselves. *Bedroom Farce* somehow steers eight people into three onstage bedrooms. *Sisterly Feelings* has alternative second and third acts, the choice of which is to be determined by tossing a coin at the end of the first and second acts, that lead to a fourth act. *Taking Steps* is set on different floors of a three-story house, but actually there is only one floor. In *It Could Be Any One of Us* Ayckbourn essays the comedy thriller, with five different endings that convict each of the suspects. *Intimate Exchanges* has two first acts, four second acts, eight third acts, and sixteen fourth acts. Each episode concludes with a choice, and Ayckbourn has written the scenes for both choices. Further, the time between acts is five days, then five weeks, and finally five years, and the fourth acts are all in a churchyard, variously following weddings, christenings, funerals, and harvest festivals. He makes his task even harder by writing the whole for one actor and one actress, each of whom plays two or three parts in every version.

Ayckbourn's first attempt to write, in his phrase, "a truly hilarious dark play" was *Absurd Person Singular*. In the middle act a woman attempts suicide by several methods while a stream of kind visitors fail to see her misery and instead clean her oven and mend her light. The comic-sinister ending has an obnoxious man dictatorially imposing party games on a group that wants nothing to do with him. In *Absent Friends*, Ayckbourn's most restrained and somber work, five people gather for a Saturday afternoon tea party to cheer Colin, whom they have not seen for some years and whose fiancée had drowned two months before. Colin proves to be cheerful, which exposes the unhappiness of the rest.

Just Between Ourselves was Ayckbourn's first so-called winter play, written for a January production when "the pressure that had always been on me to produce a play suited primarily to a holiday audience was no longer there." In this work he shows how a well-meaning husband drives his wife to insanity through relentless cheerfulness and optimism. The second scene ends with a disastrous tea party at which everyone tries not to focus on a forgotten birthday cake and the likelihood of accidents by the tense wife. In the extraordinary climax of the third scene, which is wildly funny and deeply tragic, the wife goes insane. While her husband has become entangled inside the car with the steering wheel, seat belts, and a neighboring woman, to whom he is demonstrating the vehicle, his wife quarrels with her mother-in-law and pursues her with a roaring electric drill. The car horn "blasts loudly and continuously" and then a birthday cake is carried in and lights switched on, "bathing the scene in a glorious technicolour." Four months later the wife is seen again, sitting silent in the garden in January. Throughout this chilling scene she stares out blankly, speechless, and motionless, as grim an image as any in Beckett.

Joking Apart sets its four scenes on special occasions: Guy Fawkes Night, Boxing Day, and an eighteenth birthday party. The scenes are four years apart, so that the seven characters are seen over twelve years, from their 20s to their 30s. *Joking Apart* studies winners and losers—a likable, generous, hospitable couple (who, significantly, have never bothered to get married) and their circle. Ayckbourn illuminates the sadness intrinsic to the fact that the world has born winners and the less obvious fact that other people shrink by contrasting themselves with the winners. Similar emotional bleakness and the same misgivings about the married state are found in *The Story So Far* and *Season's Greetings*.

Two plays represent changes of direction. *Way Upstream* is about three couples struggling with a cabin cruiser on a week's river trip. As their journey is to Armageddon Bridge, allegory is intended: the decent, unassertive moderates (perhaps Social Democrats) eventually realize that they must fight authoritarianism, capitalism, and the idle rich. *Woman in Mind* extends what has been called the comedy of pain. Hit on the head by a garden rake, a stunned wife copes with her unsympathetic family and fantasizes an ideal family as well, which may not be as delightful as it seems. Her husband is a vicar, and Ayckbourn is alluding to the failings of religion, with central themes of dislocation and unfulfilled existence.

A darker vision of society and of individuals has dominated in the plays from 1986 on. Ayckbourn's plays for children (or for families) have been described as "Stoppard for tots," playful approaches to reality and the illusion of theater. In 1974 Michael Billington tried to characterize Ayckbourn as "a left-wing writer using a right-wing form; even if there is nothing strident, obvious or noisy about his socialism, it is none the less apparent that he has a real detestation for the money-grubber, the status-seeker and the get-rich-quicker." Martin Bronstein emphasizes the feminism: "He's the only contemporary playwright who shows the real plight of the average woman in today's world." Ayckbourn himself has never admitted to such intentions; instead, he speaks of examining "the Chekhovian field, exploring attitudes to death, loneliness, etc.—themes not generally dealt with in comedy." All of Ayckbourn's work is amusing and ingenious, and his greatest moments are those that combine laughs and true seriousness about the human condition—or at least the contemporary condition of the English middle classes.

—Malcolm Page

B

BABE, Thomas

Nationality: American. **Born:** Buffalo, New York, 13 March 1941. **Education:** High school in Rochester, New York; Harvard University, Cambridge, Massachusetts, B.A. 1963 (Phi Beta Kappa), graduate work, 1965-68; St. Catharine's College, Cambridge (Marshall scholar, 1963-65), B.A. 1965; Yale University School of Law, New Haven, Connecticut, J.D. 1972. **Family:** Married Susan Bramhall in 1967 (divorced 1976), one daughter. **Career:** Operated the Summer Players, Agassiz Theatre, Cambridge, Massachusetts, with Timothy S. Mayer, 1966-68; speechwriter for John Lindsay, Mayor of New York City, 1968-69. **Awards:** CBS-Yale fellowship; Guggenheim fellowship, 1977; Rockefeller grant, 1978; National Endowment for the Arts fellowship, 1983. **Agent:** Agency for the Performing Arts, 888 Seventh Avenue, New York, New York 10016, U.S.A. **Address:** 103 Hoyt Street, Darien, Connecticut 06820, U.S.A.

Publications

Plays

Kid Champion, music by Jim Steinman (produced New York, 1974). New York, Dramatists Play Service, 1980.
Mojo Candy (produced New Haven, Connecticut, 1975).
Rebel Women (produced New York, 1976). New York, Dramatists Play Service, 1977.
Billy Irish (produced New York, 1977). New York, Dramatists Play Service, 1982.
Great Solo Town (produced New Haven, Connecticut, 1977). New York, Dramatists Play Service, 1981.
A Prayer for My Daughter (produced New York, 1977; London, 1978). New York, French, 1977.
Fathers and Sons (produced New York, 1978). New York, Dramatists Play Service, 1980.
Taken in Marriage (produced New York, 1979). New York, Dramatists Play Service, 1979.
Daniel Boone (for children; produced on tour, 1979).
Salt Lake City Skyline (produced New York, 1980). New York, Dramatists Play Service, 1980.
Kathleen (produced New York, 1980; revised version, as *Home Again, Kathleen*, produced Baltimore, 1981; New York, 1983).
The Wild Duck, adaption of a play by Ibsen, translated by Erik J. Friis (produced New York, 1981).
Buried Inside Extra (produced New York and London, 1983). New York, Dramatists Play Service, and London, Methuen, 1983.
Planet Fires (produced Rochester, New York, 1985). New York, Dramatists Play Service, 1987.
Carrying School Children (produced New York, 1987).
A Hero of Our Time (produced New York, 1988).
Demon Wine (produced Los Angeles, 1989). New York, Dramatists Play Service, 1989.
Down in the Dumps (produced Costa Mesa, California, 1989).
Casino Paradise, with Arnold Weinstein, music by William Bolcom (produced Philadelphia, 1990).
Junk Bonds (produced Denver, 1991). Los Angeles, Prima Facie, 1991.
Great Day in the Morning (produced Costa Mesa, California, 1992). New York, Broadway Play Publishing, 1998.
Born Every Minute (produced New York, 1997).
Singleton, the Medal Winner (produced Louisville, Kentucky, 1997).
Fever (musical), with Mildred Kayden and William Squier (produced New York, 1997).

Screenplays: *The Sun Gods*, with Mike Wadleigh, 1978; *The Vacancy*, 1979; *Kid Champion*, 1979; *Lincoln and the War Within*, 1991; *Junk Bonds*, 1991.

Radio Plays: *Hot Dogs and Soda Pop*, 1980; *The Volunteer Fireman*, 1981; *One for the Record*, 1986.

Ballet Scenarios: *When We Were Very Young*, music by John Simon, New York, 1980; *Twyla Tharp and Dancers*, 1980.

*

Manuscript Collection: Harvard University Theatre Collection, Cambridge, Massachusetts.

Theatrical Activities:
Director: **Plays**—*Two Small Bodies* by Neal Bell, New York, 1977; *Justice* by Terry Curtis Fox, New York, 1979; *Marmalade Skies* by M. Z. Ribalow, New York, 1983; *The Pornographer's Daughter* by Terry Curtis Fox, Chicago, 1984; *Life and Limb* by Keith Reddin, New York, 1985; *Voices in the Head* by Neal Bell, New York, 1986; *Finnegan's Funeral Parlor and Ice Cream Shoppe* by Robert Kerr, New York, 1989; *A Night with Doris* by Stephanie Brown, 1989; *Sleeping Dogs* by Neal Bell, New York, 1989; *Limbo Tales* by Len Jenkin, New York, 1990.

Thomas Babe comments:

(1982) My position as an American playwright has been realized in the tension between a longing for eternal verities and my perverse desire, like any writer who thinks he's worth his salt, to complicate things. I've gotten in a lot of critical trouble on my native turf, most of which I've tried to weather, because when you push at the edges of things that people really care about, you find the breaking point. This is not to say what I've written is best; only to mention that the theater, in bad money times, has become more conservative in its choices as the funding has dried up while ticket prices go on rising. I've never gotten a prize, and I don't expect one, but I would love to continue to work. And that is all the impetus behind what I've done—that, and a few bucks for the bills. There is a myth that has been promulgated about the suffering of American playwrights; it is neither true nor fair to their ability to survive. I most suspect that the ability to survive is what's behind the best work done by my contemporaries in the last decade, and nearly every one of them has upped the ante every time out.

* * *

A Prayer for My Daughter insists that social and political corruption depends upon coexisting individual corruption and that personal corruption depends upon preexisting social and political corruption. With this play Thomas Babe presents a pervasive, depressing, and compelling drama of post-Watergate, post-fall-of-Saigon America. We witness a complex crime committed by the four principals, hear of a murder, and finally hear of a suicide. We cannot imagine an end to the extreme behavior of Kelly and Jack (the cops) and Sean and Jimmy (the crooks), for the law keepers and the lawbreakers seem to have exchanged equally meaningless roles and to have annihilated the rule of law and morality and the law of nature. Such men exist in symbiosis; the terrors of blind selfishness permeate their common membrane and generate a composite cop-crook that becomes the dominant creature in the environment. When the play closes, the sentiment of the old standby "You Are My Sunshine"—sung intermittently by Jack throughout—becomes the lyric voice-over for Kelly's silent prayer "for [his] daughter," and it carries a terrible weight of meaning. Kelly and Jack function as the legal equivalent of Sean and Jimmy, whose end product is two deaths, four killers, six victims.

The condition "daughter" renders all male-male and male-female relations radically and dangerously ill-defined, especially to the daughters themselves. Babe introduces the notion that man is partly composed of woman and that the struggle between men and women cannot, therefore, be separated from the struggle within men. So long as human nature is misunderstood by the powerful, power will be destructive. Kelly's daughter kills herself with considerably less effect on Kelly than the elderly woman's murder that Sean and Jimmy are arrested for. And, although Sean and Jimmy seem at first to care for each other and to be more capable of caring than Kelly and Jack, neither has any loyalty, being perfectly ready to sell each other out when the moment comes. The love for his own daughter that Jimmy expresses in act 2 makes his being Sean's "daughter" strangely plausible, a plausibility reinforced when he becomes briefly Kelly's "daughter," whose vulnerability to Jimmy's "daughterliness" seems equally homosexual and paternal. The tenderness each realizes in the other, however, does nothing to mitigate the nasty course of their encounters, just as Kelly's initial "fatherly" concern for Margie does nothing to mitigate her despair—or ours. Law and love seem less compatible than love and crime, but love seems overwhelmed by both partners. Love is negated by partnerships of lawful and unlawful crime and by a partnership ordinarily thought to be above the law, the "natural" partnership of father and daughter. All power in this play, from the enforcement of the statutes to the beginnings of self-discovery, acts to make things worse.

Buried Inside Extra is a comic reverie on faith and duty with the absurd threat, taken seriously, of an A-bomb blast from within the *Times-Record* building on the morning of the paper's last edition; the sketchy love of the editor for the hard-nosed women's page editor; the "pill and placebo" love Jake gives his wife over the telephone; and the epidemic of compromising, lying, and unfaithfulness in the name of "twenty-five cents of the best writing that can be written in the full knowledge that the writing will be thrown out the next day." These reporters are driven to provide the public with a substitute for experience; those who "have weak hearts . . . and don't drink . . . [and] only fuck about twice a year" are promised "everything," which is defined as "true facts, clear impressions, informed guesses. . . . We will make our readers wear *our* shoes during the long night." Babe's newspeople possess little wisdom, little sympathy, little contentment, and little self-esteem. Their already moribund paper will be defunct after this extra edition to cover the atom bomb scare. The newsroom can only generate stories from within itself. Liz's hiding (and hidden) father, Culhane (himself a reporter), manufactures the bomb and phones the threat in because he knows that such news will cause Jake to print an extra edition. It is a way of prolonging life that Babe would have us consider to be the modus operandi of the press. Their own lives confused and conflicted, media people seek to clarify the lives of others by purveying the news, even if the clarity is fleeting and untrustworthy, even if the news moves society into yet more obscurity tomorrow, even if the headline proclaims and the columns elaborate a nonevent. When all stories are taken at face value and textualized as news, the distinction between true and false knowledge cannot function.

The edge to *Buried Inside Extra* lies along the blade joining realism to parody. The real atom bombs exploded decades ago over Nagasaki and Hiroshima, and reporters like these covered the story and made us a story, but not necessarily the true story. Babe uses Culhane's bomb as a device to explode any remaining fragments of trust in newspapers as truth-bearing instruments. Indeed, any trust in communication or in truth per se does not carry as far as Jake and Liz's choral, terminal "Write, you bastards." They know that everything beyond the headline article will not be read and will not be considered significant, that news will be "buried inside extra." This last edition will reconstruct events that might have led to they themselves being "buried inside extra." Their willingness to make news out of themselves, to make reality conform to autobiography, at once represents the news business and business as usual in the 1970s.

With *Junk Bonds* Babe offers a comparatively unfocused and largely unaccountable play, especially since the stronger *Demon Wine* was produced not long before. Pressing questions of personal morality are paramount in each, but substantial characters and a dynamic plot work only in *Demon Wine,* in which the parallel but opposing *éducation sentimentale* of an auto parts salesman and of a mobster's son are experienced. It turns out that the child of organized crime embodies honor, and the child of the people dishonor; power breeds authenticity, and powerlessness a dangerous inauthenticity. The laying out of full dilemmas seems to elicit Babe's strongest writing.

—Thomas Apple

BAITZ, Jon Robin

Nationality: American. **Born:** California, 1961. **Career:** Lived in Brazil, South Africa, and the United States. Playwright-in-residence, New York Stage and Film Company, 1986-89; formerly co-artistic director, Naked Angels, New York. **Awards:** Playwrights Horizons Revson fellowship, 1987; Rockefeller fellowship; New York *Newsday* Oppenheimer award, 1987; Playwrights U.S.A. award, 1988; Humanitas award, 1990; American Academy of Arts and Letters award, 1992; National Endowment for the Arts fellow, 1992. **Agent:** George Lane, William Morris Agency, 1325 Avenue of the Americas, New York, New York 10019, U.S.A.

Publications

Plays

The Film Society (produced Los Angeles, 1987; New York and London, 1988). New York, Theatre Communications Group, 1987.
Dutch Landscape (produced Los Angeles, 1989).
The End of the Day (produced Seattle, 1990; New York and London, 1992).
The Substance of Fire (produced New York, 1992). In *The Substance of Fire and Other Plays,* 1992.
The Substance of Fire and Other Plays. New York, Theatre Communications Group, 1992.
Three Hotels (produced New York, 1993; London, 1994). New York, Theatre Communications Group, 1993.
A Fair Country (produced New York, 1995). New York, Theatre Communications Group, 1994.
Mizlansky/Zilinsky: (Or 'Schmucks') (produced New York, 1997).

Television Play: *Three Hotels*, 1990.

* * *

Before his writing career was 10 years old, Jon Robin Baitz was already perceived as many things. First, he was that rarity, a Hollywood playwright concentrating on the stage when every waiter in town had pretensions to being a screenwriter. When his second play appeared, a sophisticated and knowledgeable piece about apartheid, he was seen as South African. At the time he was still well under 25. When that was followed by a disastrous new play at Los Angeles's Mark Taper Forum, he abandoned California for New York, where his reputation became a cosmopolitan one.

Not all of his audience was aware of it, but he was cosmopolitan from the first. From his birth in Beverly Hills to studies at Beverly Hills High School, his California credentials seemed impeccable. It was the time in between that gave him an international perspective.

As the son of an executive for Carnation Milk, Baitz spent most of his boyhood traveling, from Brazil to South Africa with spells in Israel, Holland, and England before returning to California. His earliest plays were reports from the vastly different front lines of Hollywood and South Africa.

His first substantial play, *Mizlansky/Zilinsky,* was propelled by dialogue that possessed the same earthy vigor as David Mamet's *Glengarry Glen Ross,* a point noted by several critics. There are similarities, most surprisingly in the authorial distance from characters who are allowed to present themselves sympathetically despite a catalog of obvious flaws. Then, too, like the real estate salesmen in Mamet's play, Baitz's characters Mizlansky and Zilinsky are deal makers. They are cynical, independent producers in the backwaters of Hollywood who have moved on from financing movies to creating tax shelters. If they make a record of children's Bible stories, they can guarantee that it will fail.

But Baitz's individuality is also apparent, and the play, produced when he was just 21, revealed his gifts of observation and empathy. In sharp, disjointed scenes that were described by the *Los Angeles Times* as a "little like listening to the Nixon tapes," he allowed his people to reveal their character as they themselves judged it. Mizlansky in particular, signing checks while facing bankruptcy and prison, must be taken on his own terms, while his morally quibbling partner Zilinsky finds that confession to the Internal Revenue Service does not cleanse his soul. For a dramatist beginning his career in Hollywood, such a clear-sighted view of the movie business could only be an advantage.

Baitz's second play, *The Film Society,* appeared to secure his reputation. He used his experience as a pupil in South Africa to create an all-white prep school like his own that served as an apparently benign model of the country's white society sealed off from the black majority culture. Through the character of a teacher, Jonathan Balton, who founds a film society in the school, Baitz dynamically illustrates the feebleness of neutrality. The effort to ignore the explosive realities of apartheid by projecting flickering images of Western civilization on the wall is doomed by the actuality of South Africa's real society, where the pent-up force of the subjugated black majority constantly threatens to explode.

The play was seen in New York and at London's Hampstead Theatre, and it attracted the interest of Hollywood filmmakers. For a time Baitz was the hottest dramatic talent produced by Los Angeles. With unusual and commendable loyalty, Baitz continued to write for the stage, but his next play, *Dutch Landscape,* was a famously unhappy experience for the playwright and his distinguished director, Gordon Davidson.

Perhaps prematurely, it attempted to confront his family life by compacting three continents' worth of experience into a muddled portrait of his relationship with his parents. Autobiographical conflict was partly buried by an uncomfortable return to the theme of apartheid, and the undigested nature of the piece drew vitriolic reviews.

His subsequent departure for New York proved a canny move. The confidence in his work that had been damaged by *Dutch Landscape* was restored, and the strength that all of his plays showed in portraying older men was reaffirmed when he created the character of a New York publisher resisting pressures to sell out.

The Substance of Fire was the play that finally gave Baitz his all-important New York credibility, earning him comparisons with Shakespeare, Chekhov, and Edward Albee. In the way of New York theatrical success nowadays, even off-Broadway success, it also brought him Hollywood deals ranging from commissions for adaptations to original screenplays that he would also direct. By the age of 29, Baitz was ready to put into practice the lessons of *Mizlansky/Zilinsky.*

—Ned Chaillet

BALODIS, Janis (Maris)

Nationality: Australian. **Born:** Tully, Queensland, 21 September 1950. **Education:** Townsville College of Advanced Education, Queensland, teaching diploma 1970; James Cook University, Townsville, 1973; East 15 Acting School, Loughton, Essex, 1976-77. **Family:** Married Pauline Walsh in 1982; one son and one daughter. **Career:** Primary school teacher, Tully, 1971, and Bambaroo, 1972, Queensland; assistant stage manager, Queensland Theatre Company, Brisbane, 1974; civil servant, Brisbane, 1975; teacher and director, East 15 Acting School, 1977-79. Freelance writer, Sydney, 1979—. Associate director, Melbourne Theatre Company, 1988—; chair, Australian National Playwrights' Centre, 1990-92. **Awards:** Australia Literature Board grant, 1981, 1983, and fellowship, 1985, 1987; Victorian Premier's award, 1986. **Agent:** Hilary Linstead and Associates, Suite 302, Easts Tower, 9-13 Bronte Road, Bondi Junction, New South Wales 2022. **Address:** 2/30 Barr Scott Drive, Lismore Heights, New South Wales 2480, Australia.

Publications

Plays

Backyard (produced Sydney, 1980).
Happily Never After (produced Brisbane, 1982).
Beginning of the End (produced Darwin, 1982).
Summerland (produced Brisbane, 1984).
Too Young for Ghosts (produced Melbourne, 1985). Sydney, Currency Press, 1985.
Wet and Dry (produced Darwin, 1986). Sydney, Currency Press, 1991.
Heart for the Future (produced Melbourne, 1989).
No Going Back (produced Melbourne, 1992).
My Father's Father (produced Melbourne, 1996).
The Ghosts Trilogy (includes *Too Young for Ghosts*; *No Going Back*; *My Father's Father*). Sydney, Currency Press, 1997.

Television Play: *A Step in the Right Direction*, 1981.

*

Critical Studies: Interview with Rudi Krausman, in *Aspect: Art and Literature*, 1985; "Projecting the Inner World onto an Existing Landscape" (interview with Veronica Kelly), in *Australasian Drama Studies* (St. Lucia), no.17, October 1990; "Falling between Stools: The Theatre of Janis Balodis" by Veronica Kelly, in *A Review of International English Literature* (Calgary, Canada), January 1992, pp. 115-32; "Ghosts in a Landscape: Louis Nowra's *Inside the Island* and Janis Balodis' *Too Young for Ghosts*" by Helen Gilbert, in *Southern Review: Literary and Interdisciplinary Essays* (Victoria, Australia), December 1994, pp. 432-47.

* * *

Janis Balodis was brought up in rural northern Queensland, the Australian son of Latvian parents, and he is distinguished from his fellow Australian playwrights on both counts. He is the first child of the generation of European displaced persons who went to Australia under the postwar immigration scheme to reach the front rank of the country's writers for the theater, and he is the first Queenslander of his generation to do so. His background is that of a frontier society, and his plays, not surprisingly, are inhabited by men and women cut off from their origins who cling together for self-preservation and who irrationally engage with a mutual destiny that they variously attempt to oppose or assimilate.

This theme is present in two minor allegorical works with local political overtones, *Happily Never After* and *Summerland,* both written for the TN Company in Brisbane. In the first a group of characters from the tales of the Brothers Grimm gather to rewrite their stories more favorably but are murdered severally in plots of self-interest. In the second Sinbad the Sailor is the narrator of a tale of a beggar transformed into a millionaire by learning to love himself. First he cheats and defrauds his way to power, and then by experience he comes to terms with the good and the bad within himself. But the sense of deracination, of malevolent intervention in the laws of man and nature, is more significantly present in the three plays upon which Balodis's reputation rests—*Backyard, Too Young for Ghosts,* and *Wet and Dry.*

The setting of *Backyard* is a shabby house in a small Queensland country town. The inhabitants are Pencil, a worker in a sugar mill, his wife Merlene, and her sister Dorothy. Their relationship is based largely on long familiarity and fear of change. Merlene regularly leaves home but never the town, and when she goes, Pencil takes Dorothy to bed. The betrayal comes to light when Dorothy becomes pregnant, and the play ends in a distorted, half-comic violence. Central to the theme is Sandshoeboots, an elderly backyard abortionist who sees herself as the instrument of a vengeful female God. On her first entrance she presents Pencil with the corpse of a pigeon she claims he shot, and the body follows the action like a talisman, at one point becoming an image of the aborted fetus. Written in a dense regional vernacular, the play shares with the early plays of Sam Shepard its portrayal of an inbred community.

Backyard is a chamber work, but Balodis's next play, *Too Young for Ghosts,* advances the dual theme of destiny and survival onto an epic scale. A group of refugees gather in a Stuttgart camp in 1947 to decide their future. One man has become a black marketer, one has returned from the front, grossly deformed by injuries, and the third is his wife's lover. The women have been surviving as best they can, mainly on the spoils from American GIs. We later find the group in a tin shed in northern Queensland, working out their two-year government bond as cane cutters. Their struggles with labor, loneliness, and the intractable language, climate, and culture are counterpointed with the colonial explorations of the German Ludwig Leichhardt, who died in 1848 while attempting to cross northern Australia. The setting is an open stage and the structure complex and inventive, with the action moving backward and forward in time on an emotional pendulum while the actors perform in rotation the roles of the immigrants and the explorers. *Too Young for Ghosts* is a dense, demanding play with the inevitable thrust of tragedy.

In 1992 and again in 1996 Balodis completed two further plays, collectively called *The Ghosts Trilogy,* that follow the Latvian exiles lives over 40 years. These plays are more domestic in scale and are darker, full of regret and unfulfilled dreams, and they are equally haunted by the ghost of Leichhardt. In *No Going Back* the characters come to the realization that they will never return "home," and in *My Father's Father* the next generation journeys in search of its family origins. The trilogy is the most significant exploration of Australia's postwar immigrant experience.

In what is probably Balodis's finest stage play, he makes an unexpected leap into comedy of manners. *Wet and Dry,* as the name implies, is a play of contrasts, using the language of comedy to hold emotion at bay while it examines the plight of urban men and women at war with nature, of displaced persons in the urban middle class. Pam and George are in their 30s; he is an estate agent, and she is a nurse. They have been unable to conceive a child. George is cynical and alienated, and he buries himself in his work. When his young brother Alex, an honest, uncomplicated country worker, comes to stay, Pam decides that he will father her baby. Alex flees to Darwin, sets up with a pragmatic older woman, and funds her hysterectomy. But finally Pam and Alex get together in a tropical storm, and the result is a son with which both men find they must—painfully—come to terms. Bisecting the play is a cyclone fence, another intervention in nature, which from scene to scene keeps at bay rabbits, neighbors, and the would-be suicides at Sydney's famous landmark, the Gap. The title refers in the first instance to the two seasons of tropical Australia and the opposing poles of north and south, bush and city, but more significantly it refers to the parallel struggle between nature and civilization in which the characters are engaged. *Wet and Dry* is one of the finest examples of a particularly indigenous form of urban comedy in which the characters batten down with tight, elegant, ironic dialogue the turbulent emotions and natural disasters of an ungovernable country to which white Australians are only now becoming reconciled.

Heart for the Future, Balodis's most complex work, combines live performance and video to examine again the shifting boundaries of reality and consciousness, the pressures of the past upon the present, and the postmodern preoccupation with image and visual fictions masquerading as fact. Helen is a marathon runner attempting to cross the Nullarbor Plain when her reflections upon the death of her mother and other pressures lead to a breakdown and she disappears. She joins a couple living in a bunker at Maralinga, the desert site of British nuclear bomb testing in the 1950s, which rendered the land uninhabitable. Meanwhile, the television producer broadcasting her run has replaced her on-screen by a double, an actress who in due course becomes Helen in a soap opera. The process of revising her life as fiction in this way leads Helen back to sanity.

—Katharine Brisbane

BANDELE-THOMAS, Biyi

Nationality: Nigerian. **Born:** Kafanchan, 1967. **Education:** University of Ife, Ile-Ife. **Career:** Writer and playwright. Lives in London. **Awards:** Best new play, London New Play Festival, 1994, for *Two Horsemen.*

Publications

Plays

Marching for Fausa. Oxford, Amber Lane Press, 1993.
Resurrections in the Season of the Longest Drought (produced 1994). London, Amber Lane Press, 1994.
Two Horsemen (produced Notting Hill, 1994). Charlbury, Amber Lane Press, 1994.
Way Past Cool (produced 1995).
Death Catches the Hunter (produced 1995).
Death Catches the Hunter and Me and the Boys. Charlbury, Amber Lane Press, 1995.
Things Fall Apart, adaptation of Chinua Achebe (produced London, 1997).
Rasselas, adaptation of Samuel Johnson (produced London, 1997).

Screenplay: *Not Even God Is Wise Enough, 1993*; *Bad Boys,* 1995; *Jam,* 1995.

Radio Play: *Thieves Like Us,* 1995; *Things Fall Apart,* adaptation of Chinua Achebe, 1998; *Ways of Dying,* adaptation of Zakes Mda, 1998.

Novels

The Man Who Came in From the Back of Beyond. London, Bellew Publishing, 1991.
The Sympathetic Undertaker and Other Dreams. London, Bellew Publishing, 1991.

*

Critical Study: "Biyi Bandele-Thomas: An Undertaker or a Dreamer?" by Dapo Adeniyi, in *Glendora Review,* June-August 1995, pp. 69-71.

* * *

'Biyi Bandele-Thomas, with Tess Onwueme, Gabriel Gbadamosi, and others, provides what Martin Banham calls "a significant extension to Nigerian theatre." A major quality of this group is that despite living and writing abroad, the inspiration for and concerns of these diasporic dramatists are essentially Nigerian; they write about the problems and state of the Nigerian nation. Bandele-Thomas is best known for his two very successful plays, the award-winning *Two Horsemen* (1994) and *Resurrections in the Season of the Longest Drought* (1994). His other notable plays are *Marching for Fausa* (1993), *Way Past Cool,* and *Death Catches the Hunter* (1995). Bandele-Thomas is a remarkably talented playwright and poet with a facility for easy and often witty dialogue (as in *Two Horsemen*), whose background is as multilayered as the texture of his dramatic works. His drama is informed and sustained by a humanist ideology and conviction that theater should be in the forefront in the fight for a more humane society. Little wonder that satire is his chosen mode of confronting and interrogating society.

Marching for Fausa, his first play, is about an investigative journalist, Telani Balarabe, who is in jail because she was about to expose the fact that Fausa, on whose behalf her schoolmates marched and were imprisoned, is, at 15 years old, to be the 11th wife of the very corrupt minister for culture. The play is a satiric indictment of Shonghai, where coups, counter-coups, and corruption follow on the heels of each other. For a first play Bandele-Thomas shows a competence and mastery of the dramatic form (he uses the flashback technique to reveal why Balarabe is in jail). His control of language and ability to create good dialogue and character are evident in this play.

His next play, *Resurrections,* is also set in a fictitious modern African state, but one in which ancient beliefs and myths are still active and very much part of the people's imagination. It is a society in which drug dealers, ghosts, lawyers, and vultures mix in a peculiarly African theatrical matrix in which different realms of existence and different beings are made to coexist comfortably with one another. In this play, which one of the resurrected characters describes as "Kafka on speed," Bandele-Thomas once again turns his attention to Nigeria, casting a sharp, satiric look at public morality; his unequivocal verdict is that corruption permeates every level of the society—a society where businessmen become rich by dealing in drugs, where the counsel for the defense bribes the presiding judge, and where all in positions of authority collude to pervert justice and undermine the ethics of public conduct.

The central character, BB, is a charismatic and kind criminal and master drug dealer out on probation, but, finding it difficult to resist returning to his drug trafficking ways, he attempts a major drug shipment and is caught. Against all expectation—there is an offer and acceptance of a hefty bribe to the judge who happens to be BB's girlfriend's father—he is condemned to death and executed. Even though *Resurrections* has three acts, it is structurally in two parts: the first deals with BB's fall, and the second is a fantasy epilogue of his resurrection and his "God"-given license to clean up society's mess. The play's final message seems to be that sometimes it is only the criminal hero, such as BB or Sanda (in Soyinka's *The Beatification of Area Boy*), who provides a means of escape or survival for the poor, and this is not a charming commentary on the state of the Nigerian nation.

The very Beckettian play *Two Horsemen* won Bandele-Thomas the award for the best new play at the London New Play Festival in 1994. It is a dialogue, in the manner of *Waiting for Godot*, between two street sweepers, Banza and Lagbaja, in which they cover subjects such as death, life, identity, resurrection, God, and sex. What characterizes this play is the essential limbo-like setting and an indeterminacy in the personalities of the two characters, firmly situating the play in the absurd tradition; so much is given, but the audience or reader is still left frustratingly wondering at the uncertainties, half-truths, unfinished ideas, and deep philosophical yet mundane utterances, such as Lagbaja's comment: "The more my life falls apart, the more my vocabulary seems to improve." The action of the play goes everywhere and yet nowhere as the two return to the same points and the same phrases. John Peter's comments in the *Sunday Times* (11 June 1994) aptly summarize the playwright's dramatic technique in the play: "Bandele-Thomas has an athletic, impudent imagination, freewheeling and ribald, full of eerie humour that pushes all the frontiers of the surreal. The writing bristles with jokes, both black and blue, and with flashes of poetry that reminds you of Beckett."

Death Catches the Hunter (first performed in 1995) is a three-character series of monologues spoken for the most part directly to the audience. It is about Prophet Emefa, who 15 years back had set up his Transcendental Church of God in Kafanchan and whose miracles cured Peteru's father of his blindness and Saratu (Peteru's wife) of her epilepsy. In spite and because of the church's success, there are tensions and suspicions that eventually lead to tragedy. Although simple on the surface, this is a thematically and structurally complex play, written in a language and tone that achieves sometimes an uncluttered poetic beauty and sometimes a racy colloquialism. It starts in the middle of the story and then skirts back to the beginning before skipping forward to the end. And it does this in a funny and rib-cracking sort of way. It is a measure of Bandele-Thomas's mastery of dramatic technique that a lot of the uncertainties and tensions are never fully resolved, leaving the audience to fill in the details for itself. He thus demands of his audience a creative investment in its encounter with his plays.

—Osita Okagbue

BARAKA, Amiri

Nationality: American. **Born:** Everett LeRoi Jones in Newark, New Jersey, 7 October 1934; took name Amiri Baraka in 1968. **Education:** Central Avenue School, and Barringer High School, Newark; Rutgers University, Newark, New Jersey, 1951-52; Howard University, Washington, D.C., 1953-54, B.A. in English 1954. **Military Service:** Served in the United States Air Force, 1954-57. **Family:** Married 1) Hettie Roberta Cohen in 1958 (divorced 1965), two daughters; 2) Sylvia Robinson (now Amina Baraka) in 1967, five children; also two stepdaughters and two other daughters. **Career:** Teacher, New School for Social Research, New York, 1961-64, and summers, 1977-79, State University of New York, Buffalo, Summer 1964, and Columbia University, New York, 1964 and Spring 1980; visiting professor, San Francisco State College, 1966-67, Yale University, New Haven, Connecticut, 1977-78, and George Washington University, Washington, D.C., 1978-79. Assistant professor, 1980-82, associate professor, 1983-84, professor of Africana studies, 1985—, State University of New York, Stony Brook. Founder, *Yugen* magazine and Totem Press, New York, 1958-62; editor, with Diane di Prima, *Floating Bear* magazine, New York, 1961-63; founding director, Black Arts Repertory Theatre, Harlem, New York, 1964-66. Founding director, Spirit House, Newark, 1966—; involved in Newark politics: member of the United Brothers, 1967, and Committee for Unified Newark, 1969-75; chair, Congress of Afrikan People, 1972-75. **Awards:** Whitney fellowship, 1961; Obie award, 1964; Guggenheim fellowship, 1965; Yoruba Academy fellowship, 1965; National Endowment for the Arts grant, 1966, award, 1981; Dakar Festival prize, 1966; Rockefeller grant, 1981; Before Columbus Foundation award, 1984; American Book award, 1984; PEN-Faulkner award, 1989; Langston Hughes medal, for outstanding contribution to literature, 1989; Ferroni award, Italy, and Foreign Poet award, 1993; Playwright's award, Black Drama Festival, Winston-Salem North Carolina, 1997. D.H.L.: Malcolm X College, Chicago, 1972. **Member:** Black Academy of Arts and Letters. **Address:** Department of Africana studies, State University of New York, Stony Brook, New York 11794-4340, U.S.A.

Publications (earlier works as LeRoi Jones)

Plays

A Good Girl Is Hard to Find (produced Montclair, New Jersey, 1958; New York, 1965).

Dante (produced New York, 1961; as *The 8th Ditch*, produced New York, 1964). Included in *The System of Dante's Hell*, 1965.

The Baptism (produced New York, 1964; London, 1971). With *The Toilet*, New York, Grove Press, 1967.

Dutchman (produced New York, 1964; London, 1967). With *The Slave*, New York, Morrow, 1964; London, Faber, 1965; in *Black Theatre USA*, New York, Free Press, 1996.

The Slave (produced New York, 1964; London, 1972). With *Dutchman*, New York, Morrow, 1964; London, Faber, 1965.

The Toilet (produced New York, 1964). With *The Baptism*, New York, Grove Press, 1967.

Experimental Death Unit #1 (also director: produced New York, 1965). Included in *Four Black Revolutionary Plays*, 1969.

Jello (produced New York, 1965). Chicago, Third World Press, 1970.

A Black Mass (also director: produced Newark, 1966). Included in *Four Black Revolutionary Plays*, 1969.

Arm Yrself or Harm Yrself (produced Newark, 1967). Newark, Jihad, 1967.

Slave Ship: A Historical Pageant (produced Newark, 1967; New York, 1969). Newark, Jihad, 1967.
Madheart (also director: produced San Francisco, 1967). Included in *Four Black Revolutionary Plays*, 1969.
Great Goodness of Life (A Coon Show) (also director: produced Newark, 1967; New York, 1969). Included in *Four Black Revolutionary Plays*, 1969.
Home on the Range (produced Newark and New York, 1968). Published in *Drama Review* (New York), Summer 1968.
Police, published in *Drama Review* (New York), Summer 1968.
The Death of Malcolm X, in *New Plays from the Black Theatre*, edited by Ed Bullins. New York, Bantam, 1969.
Rockgroup, published in *Cricket*, December 1969.
Four Black Revolutionary Plays. Indianapolis, Bobbs Merrill, 1969; London, Calder and Boyars, 1971.
Insurrection (produced New York, 1969).
Junkies Are Full of (SHHH . . .), and *Bloodrites* (produced Newark, 1970). Published in *Black Drama Anthology*, edited by Woodie King and Ron Milner, New York, New American Library, 1971.
BA-RA-KA, in *Spontaneous Combustion: Eight New American Plays*, edited by Rochelle Owens. New York, Winter House, 1972.
Black Power Chant, published in *Drama Review* (New York), December 1972.
Columbia the Gem of the Ocean (produced Washington, D.C., 1973).
A Recent Killing (produced New York, 1973).
The New Ark's a Moverin (produced Newark, 1974).
The Sidnee Poet Heroical (also director: produced New York, 1975). New York, Reed, 1979.
S-1 (also director: produced New York, 1976). Included in *The Motion of History and Other Plays*, 1978.
America More or Less, with Frank Chin and Leslie Marmon Silko, music by Tony Greco, lyrics by Arnold Weinstein (produced San Francisco, 1976).
The Motion of History (also director: produced New York, 1977). Included in *The Motion of History and Other Plays*, 1978.
The Motion of History and Other Plays (includes *S-1* and *Slave Ship*). New York, Morrow, 1978.
What was the Relationship of the Lone Ranger to the Means of Production? (produced New York, 1979).
At the Dim'crackr Convention (produced New York, 1980).
Boy and Tarzan Appear in a Clearing (produced New York, 1981).
Weimar 2 (produced New York, 1981).
Money: A Jazz Opera, with George Gruntz, music by Gruntz (produced New York, 1982).
Primitive World, music by David Murray (produced New York, 1984).
General Hag's Skeezag: A Play. In *Black Thunder New York*, New York, Mentor, 1992.
The Election Machine Warehouse. New York, Simon & Schuster, 1997.

Screenplays: *Dutchman*, 1967; *Black Spring*, 1967; *A Fable*, 1971; *Supercoon*, 1971.

Videos: *Dutchman*, 1967; *W. E. B Du Bois, a Biography in Four Voices*, with others, California Newsreel, 1995.

Novel

The System of Dante's Hell. New York, Grove Press, 1965; London, MacGibbon and Kee, 1966.

Short Stories

Tales. New York, Grove Press, 1967; London, MacGibbon and Kee, 1969.

Poetry

April 13. New Haven, Connecticut, Penny Poems, 1959.
Spring and Soforth. New Haven, Connecticut, Penny Poems, 1960.
Preface to a Twenty Volume Suicide Note. New York, Totem-Corinth, 1961.
The Disguise. Privately printed, 1961.
The Dead Lecturer. New York, Grove Press, 1964.
Black Art. Newark, Jihad, 1966.
A Poem for Black Hearts. Detroit, Broadside Press, 1967.
Black Magic: Collected Poetry 1961-1967. Indianapolis, Bobbs Merrill, 1969.
It's Nation Time. Chicago, Third World Press, 1970.
In Our Terribleness: Some Elements and Meaning in Black Style, with Fundi (Billy Abernathy). Indianapolis, Bobbs Merrill, 1970.
Spirit Reach. Newark, Jihad, 1972.
Afrikan Revolution. Newark, Jihad, 1973.
Hard Facts. Newark, Peoples War, 1976.
Selected Poetry. New York, Morrow, 1979.
AM/TRAK. New York, Phoenix Book Shop, 1979.
Spring Song. Privately printed, 1979.
Reggae or Not! Bowling Green, New York, Contact Two, 1981.
Thoughts for You! Nashville, Winston Derek, 1984.
LeRoi Jones–Amiri. New York, Thunder's Mouth Press, 1991.
An Amiri Baraka/LeRoi Jones Poetry Sampler. Satori Press, 1991.
Transbluency: The Selected Poems of Amiri Baraka/LeRoi Jones (1961-1995). New York, Marsilio, 1995.
Wise, Why's, Y's. Chicago, Illinois, Third World Press, 1995.
Funk Lore: New Poems, 1984-1995. Los Angeles, Sun & Moon Press, 1996.

Other

Cuba Libre. New York, Fair Play for Cuba Committee, 1961.
Blues People: Negro Music in White America. New York, Morrow, 1963; London, MacGibbon and Kee, 1965; Edinburgh, Payback Press, 1995.
Home: Social Essays. New York, Morrow, 1966; London, MacGibbon and Kee, 1968.
Black Music. New York, Morrow, 1968; London, MacGibbon and Kee, 1969.
Trippin': A Need for Change, with Larry Neal and A.B. Spellman. Newark, Cricket, 1969(?).
A Black Value System. Newark, Jihad, 1970.
Gary and Miami: Before and After. Newark, Jihad, n.d.
Raise Race Rays Raze: Essays since 1965. New York, Random House, 1971.
Strategy and Tactics of a Pan African Nationalist Party. Newark, National Involvement, 1971.
Beginning of National Movement. Newark, Jihad, 1972.
Kawaida Studies: The New Nationalism. Chicago, Third World Press, 1972.
National Liberation and Politics. Newark, Congress of Afrikan People, 1974.

Crisis in Boston!!!! Newark, Vita Wa Watu-People's War Publishing, 1974.
Afrikan Free School. Newark, Jihad, 1974.
Toward Ideological Clarity. Newark, Congress of Afrikan People, 1974.
The Creation of the New Ark. Washington, D.C., Howard University Press, 1975.
Selected Plays and Prose. New York, Morrow, 1979.
The Autobiography of LeRoi Jones/Amiri Baraka. New York, Freundlich, 1983.
Daggers and Javelins: Essays 1974-1979. New York, Morrow, 1984.
The Artist and Social Responsibility. N.p., Unity, 1986.
The Music: Reflections on Jazz and Blues, with Amina Baraka. New York, Morrow, 1987.
The LeRoi Jones/Amiri Baraka Reader, edited by William J. Harris, New York, Thunder's Mouth Press, 1991.
A Race Divided. New York, Emerge Communications, 1991.
The Afro American National Question. Newark, New Jersey, Unity & Struggle, 1992.
Heathens and Revolutionary Art: Poems and Lecture. Louisville, Kentucky, White Fields Press, 1994.
Conversations with Amiri Baraka, edited by Charlie Reilly. Jackson, University of Mississippi, 1994.
Eulogies. New York, Marsilio Publishers, 1996.
Home: Social Essays. Hopewell, New Jersey, Ecco Press, 1998.

Editor, *Four Young Lady Poets*. New York, Totem-Corinth, 1962.
Editor, *The Moderns: New Fiction in America*. New York, Corinth, 1963; London, MacGibbon and Kee, 1965.
Editor, with Larry Neal, *Black Fire: An Anthology of Afro-American Writing*. New York, Morrow, 1968.
Editor, *African Congress: A Documentary of the First Modern Pan-African Congress*. New York, Morrow, 1972.
Editor, with Diane di Prima, *The Floating Bear: A Newsletter, Numbers 1-37*. La Jolla, California, Laurence McGilvery, 1974.
Editor, with Amina Baraka, *Confirmation: An Anthology of African American Women*. New York, Morrow, 1983.

Recordings: *Amiri Baraka, Diane diPrima*, Naropa Institute, 1992; *Offbeat a Red Hot Sound Trip*, with others, Wax Trax!/TVT Records, 1996.

*

Bibliographies: *LeRoi Jones (Imamu Amiri Baraka): A Checklist of Works by and about Him* by Letitia Dace, London, Nether Press, 1971; *Ten Modern American Playwrights* by Kimball King, New York, Garland, 1982.

Manuscript Collections: Howard University, Washington, D.C.; Beinecke Library, Yale University, New Haven, Connecticut; Lilly Library, Indiana University, Bloomington; University of Connecticut, Storrs; George Arents Research Library, Syracuse University, New York.

Critical Studies: *From LeRoi Jones to Amiri Baraka: The Literary Works* by Theodore Hudson, Durham, North Carolina, Duke University Press, 1973; *Baraka: The Renegade and the Mask* by Kimberly W. Benston, New Haven, Connecticut, Yale University Press, 1976, and *Imamu Amiri Baraka (LeRoi Jones): A Collection of Critical Essays* edited by Benston, Englewood Cliffs, New Jersey, Prentice Hall, 1978; *Amiri Baraka/LeRoi Jones: The Quest for a Populist Modernism* by Werner Sollors, New York, Columbia University Press, 1978; *Amiri Baraka* by Lloyd W. Brown, Boston, Twayne, 1980; *To Raise, Destroy, and Create: The Poetry, Drama, and Fiction of Imamu Amiri Baraka (LeRoi Jones)* by Henry C. Lacey, Troy, New York, Whitston, 1981; *Theatre and Nationalism: Wole Soyinka and LeRoi Jones* by Alain Ricard, Ife-Ife, Nigeria, University of Ife Press, 1983; *Amiri Baraka: The Kaleidoscopic Torch* edited by James B. Gwynne, New York, Steppingstones Press, 1985; *The Poetry and Poetics of Amiri Baraka: The Jazz Aesthetic* by William J. Harris, Columbia, University of Missouri Press, 1985; "Some Thoughts on the Challenges Facing Black Gay Intellectuals" by Ron Simmons, in *Brother to Brother: New Writings by Black Gay Men* edited by Essex Hemphill, Boston, Alyson, 1991; "Discipline and Punish: The Case of Baraka's *Dutchman*" by Savas Patsalidis, in *North Dakota Quarterly* (Grand Forks, North Dakota), Summer 1992, pp. 101-13; "Jazz in the Poetry of Amiri Baraka and Roy Fisher" by Mary Ellison, in *Yearbook of English Studies* (London), 1994, pp. 117-45; "August Wilson and the Four B's: Influences" by Mark William Rocha in *August Wilson: A Casebook* edited by Marilyn Elkins, New York, Garland, 1994; "The Limits of African-American Political Realism: Baraka's *Dutchman* and Wilson's *Ma Rainey's Black Bottom*" by Eric Bergesen and William W. Demastes, in *Realism and the American Dramatic Tradition* edited by William W. Demastes, Tuscaloosa, University of Alabama Press, 1996; "Looking into Black Skulls: Amiri Baraka's *Dutchman* and the Psychology of Race" by George Piggford, in *Modern Drama* (Downsview, Ontario), Spring 1997, pp. 74-85.

Theatrical Activities:
Director: Several of his own plays.

Actor: Narrator in *W. E. B. DuBois, a Biography in Four Voices*, 1995.

Amiri Baraka comments:

My work changes as I change in a changing world.

* * *

In March 1964, when three one-act plays at different off-Broadway locales introduced Amiri Baraka (LeRoi Jones) to city audiences, black theater in America knew that it had found a compelling voice summoning black playwrights to a new and urgent mission.

The first of these plays, *The 8th Ditch*, was closed by action of civic authorities after a few days. Its fate foretold the playwright's continuing quarrel with officialdom. His second play, *The Baptism*, with its deliberate satire of subjects held sacred and taboo, served notice of Baraka's determination ruthlessly to strip the hypocritical masks that society wears to protect its vested interests. But it was in his third play and first professional production, *Dutchman*, that Baraka found his authentic voice to delineate a clearly perceived mission. The mission was nothing less than the cultural liberation of the black man in white America.

Dutchman, hailed by critic Clayton Riley as "the finest short play ever written in this country," spoke lucidly to black Americans of the savage destruction of their cultural identity should they continue to imitate or to flirt with an alien, though dominant, white lifestyle. White establishment critics praised Baraka's "fierce and blazing talent," the *Village Voice* awarded *Dutchman* an Obie as the best American play of the season.

Baraka's next professional production consisted of two plays. *The Slave,* a two-act drama, and *The Toilet,* another one-acter, were staged at Saint Mark's Playhouse in December 1964. *The Slave,* although it purports to speak of a coming race war between black and white and is called by Baraka "a fable," is frankly autobiographical in intent. Walker Vessels, a tall, thin Negro leader of a black army, enters the home where his former white wife, their two children, and her second husband are living together, apparently quite happily. The husband is a white liberal-minded professor who had taught Vessels in college. After a long, excoriating harangue in which he renounces his former life, Vessels shoots the white man, watches with indifference as his ex-wife is hit by a falling beam, and departs as shells from his black revolutionary forces demolish the house while the cries of children in an upstairs room mingle with the boom of guns and the shriek of falling debris. *The Toilet,* a curious work of teenage brutality and homosexual love set in a school lavatory, hints at the possibility of black and white coming together at some future time after the black man has earned his manhood and self-respect by defeating the white.

These two revolutionary plays were followed by an even more lurid and propagandistic work when *Experimental Death Unit #1* was staged at Saint Mark's Playhouse in New York in March 1965. In this short play Baraka concentrates on a nighttime encounter between two white homosexuals and a black whore in a seamy section of the city. The climax occurs when a death unit of marching black militants enters and executes the three degenerates. The men are beheaded and their heads stuck on pikes at the head of the procession. The black liberation army, Baraka seems to say, has a duty to rid society not only of the oppressor but also of the collaborator. Black skin does not save one from the due penalty for betraying the revolution.

Writing of this second group of plays, white critics who a few months earlier had hailed the rising star of playwright Baraka were now confounded. He had rejected the blandishments of popular white success held out to him and to them had become a bitter dramatist and violent propagandist preaching race hatred in virulent terms. In the main their attitude confirmed Baraka's suspicions that the white culture would allow nothing to have credence and value but what it approved of.

A month after the production of *Experimental Death Unit #1,* Baraka imitated the actions of his fictitious character, Walker Vessels, by breaking with his past life. He left his white wife and two children, moved to Harlem, and founded the Black Arts Repertory Theatre School. The aim of the school was to train and showcase black theatrical talent as well as to teach classes in remedial reading and mathematics. It lasted for only a short time.

In a forum on black theater held at the Gate Theatre in New York in 1969, Baraka articulated the philosophic premise of the black arts movement, giving credit to Ron Karenga of San Francisco for having helped in its formulation. Black art, he affirmed, is collective, functional, and committed, for it derives from the collective experience of black people, serves a necessary function in their lives, as opposed to the useless artifacts of most white art that adorn museums, and is committed to revolutionary change.

The short-lived Harlem-based theater produced only one new play by Baraka, *Jello,* a hard-hitting satire on the once popular Jack Benny radio program that advertised the product. The play, rejected by at least one established publisher because of its attack on a well-known stage personality, was performed on the streets of Harlem by the Black Arts Group. The straightforward plot casts Rochester, Benny's chauffeur and stereotyped black handyman, as a militant who demands and gets full redress for years of subservience and oppression. In the play Baraka is less interested in attacking the white man than in erasing the myth of black inferiority that decades of white-controlled entertainment have helped to perpetuate. From this point on Baraka became more conscious of addressing a black audience in his plays. His main characters were black, and whites were either pictured as the symbolic beast whose ritualistic death was necessary for the emergence of black consciousness and nationhood or were pilloried mercilessly as completely irrelevant to the black struggle. Baraka declared,

> The artist must represent the will, the soul of the black community. [His art] must represent the national spirit and the national will. . . . We don't talk about theatre down here, or theatre up there as an idle jest but because it is necessary to pump live blood back into our community.

When the Black Arts Repertory Theatre closed in 1966, Baraka returned to his native Newark, New Jersey, and formed the Spirit House Movers, a group of nonprofessional actors who performed his plays as well as the plays of other black writers.

In January 1969 Baraka formed the Committee for Unified Newark, which was dedicated to the creation of a new value system for the African American community. Aspects of this new system of values were evident in the wearing of traditional African dress, the speaking of the Swahili language in addition to English, the rejection of Christianity as a Western religion that has helped to enslave the minds of black people and the adoption of the Kawaida faith in its stead, and the assumption of Arabic names in place of existing Christian names. Jones became a minister of the Kawaida faith and adopted his new name of Amiri Baraka prefixed by the Swahili title Imamu (Spiritual Leader).

Baraka's work has continued to dwell on the themes of black liberation and the need to create a new sensibility by alerting audiences to the reality of their lives in a country dominated by a culture that Baraka passionately believes to be alien and hostile to blacks. The urgent need to root out white ways from the hearts and minds of black people is constantly reiterated. White error is seen in *A Black Mass* as the substitution of thought for feeling, as a curiosity for antilife. In *Home on the Range* the white family speaks a gibberish of unintelligible sounds and gazes glass-eyed at the television box like robots of the computer society they have created. In a glaring indictment of the hypocrisy of Christianity, the devils in *Bloodrites* eat of the host and chant a litany of love immediately after attempting to shoot blacks.

Baraka graphically dramatizes the problem by personifying the evil white lifestyle in the form of a devil or beast that must be slain if blacks are to gain their freedom. In *A Black Mass,* a play based on an Islamic fable, one of a trio of magicians persists in creating a wild white beast that he believes he can tame through love. The beast goes on a rampage and destroys everything in sight, including the magicians. *Madheart* has a Devil Lady who keeps a mother and sister of the Black Man in thrall, worshiping whiteness. In *Bloodrites* whites are gun-toting devils who masquerade as artists, musicians, and hipsters to seduce blacks struggling towards spiritual reconstruction.

Baraka has been accused of preaching race hatred and violence as a way of life. In 1967 he was given the maximum sentence of three years in prison by a county judge for possession of revolvers during the Newark riots, a conviction that was condemned as victimization by the American Council of Civil Liberties and was later overturned by a higher court. It is true that violence permeates his plays, that Baraka seems to revel in bloodletting, but the intensity of his feeling and the power of his language have the effect of lifting violence to the level of a holy war against evil forces of supernatural potency. When the Devil Lady in *Madheart* boasts that she can never die, the Black Man responds, "You will die only when I kill you," whereupon he stabs her several times, impales her with a stake and arrows, abuses her, stomps on her dead face, and finally drops her body into a deep pit from which smoke and light shoot up. Such needless overkill can only be understood in terms of magic and ritual.

Ritual, in fact, is the crucible that helps to transform the melodramatic incident in Baraka's plays into significant drama. Clay, the young black hounded by the vampire Lula in a subway train in *Dutchman,* realizes that the murder of a white is the only cure for the black man's neuroses, but he is too ingrained in white middle-class values to perform the rite that will liberate him. He dies as a result. Not so Walker Vessels in *The Slave*. When he shoots Easley, the white liberal professor, the latter's last words are "ritual drama, like I said, ritual drama." Similarly, when Court Royal, the weak-kneed assimilationist in *Great Goodness of Life* is forced to shoot his militant son, this, too, is a rite that must be performed, "a rite to show that you would be guilty, but for the cleansing rite." In keeping with his philosophy that black theater must be functional, Baraka has sought to make his plays identify with his audiences in form as well as content. Thus, *Bloodrites* calls for the sacrifice of a chicken whose blood is sprinkled into the audience. In *Police* the white cops are required to eat chunks of flesh from the body of the black policeman who has killed a member of his race and is forced by the black community to commit suicide. Such ritualistic acts reinforce the magical dimension of the struggle in which black people are engaged.

A second medium of identification is language. Baraka, the poet and litterateur, deliberately reaches for the vernacular and idiom of the urban black to pound home his message. *The Slave* is a fine example of the way in which college-educated Walker Vessels rejects the elegant but alienating discourse of which he is capable for the unifying language of the ghetto. The language in *Police* is pruned and compressed to a single drumbeat, with the syncopation and lyricism associated with that pervasive black musical instrument. The process of creating a new and appropriate language for black drama is pushed further in *Slave Ship,* where the narrative element relies heavily on action and music rather than language and where Yoruba instead of English is used in the first part of the production.

Finally, in his capacity as Spiritual Leader, Baraka uses the stage as a pulpit from which he exhorts his audiences to carry his message for revolutionary thinking and action into their daily lives. The Black Man in *Madheart* urges the audience to "think about themselves and about their lives when they leave this happening." A concluding narration in *A Black Mass* reminds the audience that the beasts are still loose in the world and must be found and slain. *Junkies Are Full of (SHHH ...)* begins with an address by an Italian dope dealer who informs the audience that he succeeds by getting "niggers to peddle dope." The audience at *Police* is expected to leap on stage at one point in the play and join the characters in demanding vengeance on the black cop who shot and killed a black brother.

Baraka's theater is blatantly agitprop drama on an elemental plane. Apart from *Slave Ship* the structure of his plays remains conventional, but the dynamic of message, the boldness of conception, and the lyricism of language give his dramas a fierceness on the stage that defies complacency. Critics may praise or damn him, but Baraka is no longer writing for critical acclaim.

—Errol Hill

BARKER, Howard

Nationality: British. **Born:** London, 28 June 1946. **Education:** Battersea Grammar School, London, 1958-64; Sussex University, Brighton, 1964-68, M.A. in history 1968. **Family:** Married Sandra Law in 1972; one son. **Career:** Resident dramatist, Open Space Theatre, London, 1974-75, and the Wrestling School, London, 1988—. **Awards:** Arts Council bursary, 1971; Sony award, Society of Authors award, and Italia prize, all for radio play, 1985. **Agent:** Judy Daish Associates, 83 Eastbourne Mews, London W2 6LQ, England.

Publications

Plays

Cheek (produced London, 1970). Published in *New Short Plays 3*, London, Eyre Methuen, 1972.
No One Was Saved (produced London, 1971).
Edward: The Final Days (produced London, 1971).
Faceache (produced London, 1971).
Alpha Alpha (produced London, 1972).
Private Parts (produced Edinburgh, 1972).
Skipper, and My Sister and I (produced London, 1973).
Rule Britannia (produced London, 1973).
Bang (produced London, 1973).
Claw (produced London, 1975; New York, 1976). With *Stripwell*, London, Calder, 1977.
Stripwell (produced London, 1975). With *Claw*, London, Calder, 1977.
Wax (produced Edinburgh and London, 1976).
Aces High (screenplay). London, Futura, 1976.
Fair Slaughter (produced London, 1977). London, Calder, 1978; with *Crimes in Hot Countries*, New York, Riverrun Press, 1985.
That Good Between Us (produced London, 1977). With *Credentials of a Sympathizer*, London, Calder, 1980; New York, Riverrun Press, 1981.
The Love of a Good Man (produced Sheffield, 1978; revised version produced Oxford and London, 1980). With *All Bleeding*, London, Calder, 1980; New York, Riverrun Press, 1981.
The Hang of the Gaol (produced London, 1978). With *Heaven*, London, Calder, 1982.
The Loud Boy's Life (produced London, 1980). Included in *Two Plays for the Right*, 1982.
Birth on a Hard Shoulder (produced Stockholm, 1980). Included in *Two Plays for the Right*, 1982.

No End of Blame: Scenes of Overcoming (produced Oxford, London, and New York, 1981). London, Calder, 1981; New York, Riverrun Press, 1982.
The Poor Man's Friend (produced Bridport, Dorset, 1981).
Two Plays for the Right. London, Calder, and New York, Riverrun Press, 1982.
Victory: Choices in Reaction (produced London, 1983). London, Calder, and New York, Riverrun Press, 1983.
A Passion in Six Days (produced Sheffield, 1983). With *Downchild*, London, Calder, and New York, Riverrun Press, 1985.
The Power of the Dog (produced Brentford, Middlesex, 1984; London, 1985). London, Calder, and New York, Riverrun Press, 1985.
Don't Exaggerate (produced London, 1984). London, Calder, 1985; New York, Riverrun Press, 1986.
Scenes from an Execution (broadcast 1984; produced London, 1990). With *The Castle*, London, Calder, 1985; New York, Riverrun Press, 1986.
Crimes in Hot Countries (produced London, 1985). With *Fair Slaughter*, London, Calder, 1984; New York, Riverrun Press, 1985.
Downchild (produced London, 1985). With *A Passion in Six Days*, London, Calder, and New York, Riverrun Press, 1985.
The Castle (produced London, 1985). With *Scenes from an Execution*, London, Calder, 1985; New York, Riverrun Press, 1986.
Pity in History (televised 1985; produced Edinburgh, 1986). With *Women Beware Women*, New York, Riverrun Press, 1987.
Women Beware Women, adaptation of the play by Thomas Middleton (produced London, 1986; New York, 1987). London, Calder, 1986; with *Pity in History*, New York, Riverrun Press, 1988; London, Calder, 1988.
The Last Supper (produced London, 1988). London, Calder, and New York, Riverrun Press, 1988.
The Bite of the Night (produced London, 1988). London, Calder, and New York, Riverrun Press, 1988.
The Possibilities (10 plays) (produced London, 1988). London, Calder, and New York, Riverrun Press, 1988.
Golgo (produced Leicester, 1989; London 1990). With *Seven Lears*, London, Calder, and New York, Riverrun Press, 1990.
Seven Lears (produced Sheffield, 1989; London, 1990). With *Golgo*, London, Calder, and New York, Riverrun Press, 1990.
The Europeans. With *Judith*, London, Calder, and New York, Riverrun Press, 1990.
Judith. With *The Europeans*, London, Calder, and New York, Riverrun Press, 1990.
Collected Plays 1 (includes *Claw, No End of Blame, Scenes from an Execution, The Castle, Victory*). London, Calder, 1990; New York, Riverrun Press, 1990.

Screenplays: *Made*, 1972; *Rape of Tamar*, 1973; *Aces High*, 1976.

Radio Plays: *One Afternoon on the North Face of the 63rd Level of the Pyramid of Cheops the Great*, 1970; *Henry V in Two Parts*, 1971; *Herman, with Millie and Mick*, 1972; *Scenes from an Execution*, 1984; *The Early Hours of a Reviled Man*, 1990; *A Hard Heart*, 1992.

Television Plays: *Cows*, 1972; *The Chauffeur and the Lady*, 1972; *Mutinies*, 1974; *Pity in History*, 1985.

Poetry

The Breath of the Crowd. London, Calder, 1986; New York, Riverrun Press, 1987.
Gary the Thief/Gary Upright. London, Calder, 1987; New York, Riverrun Press, 1988.
Lullabies for the Impatient. London, Calder, 1989.
The Ascent of Monte Grappa. London, Calder, and New York, Riverrun Press, 1991.
The Tortmann Diaries. London, Calder, 1996.

Other

Arguments for a Theatre (essays). London, Calder, 1989; third edition, Manchester, 1997.

*

Critical Studies: *The New British Drama* by Oleg Kerensky, London, Hamish Hamilton, 1977, New York, Taplinger, 1979; *Stages in the Revolution* by Catherine Itzin, London, Eyre Methuen, 1980; *Dreams and Deconstructions* edited by Sandy Craig, Ambergate, Derbyshire, Amber Lane Press, 1980; "Howard Barker Issue" of *Gambit* (London), vol. 11, no. 41, 1984; *Howard Barker: An Expository Study of His Poetry and Drama, 1969-1987* by David Ian Rabey, London, Macmillan, 1989; *Howard Barker's Theatre of Seduction* by Charles Lamb, London, Harwood Academic, 1998.

Theatrical Activities:
Director: **Play**—*Hated Nightfall*, 1996; *Judith*, 1997; *Uncle Vanya*, 1997; *Ursula–Fear of the Estuary*, 1998.

* * *

Having provided the high point of contemporary radical theater in the mid-1980s with a trilogy of plays (*Scenes from an Execution, Downchild, The Castle*) for the Royal Shakespeare Company at the small Pit theater in London, Howard Barker has continued to excoriate the pieties of art, sex, and politics in a series of dramatic works whose intransigence and theatrical inventiveness still appall the managements of the main subsidized theaters. No Barker play has been produced on the main stage at either the National Theatre or the Royal Shakespeare Company. Actors, however, recognize his talent, and an actors' company, The Wrestling School, was founded in 1988 exclusively to perform Barker. Other theaters, such as Almeida and Greenwich in London, Sheffield, and Leicester, have hosted Barker's extensive output. BBC Radio 3 has broadcast *The Early Hours of a Reviled Man*, his characterization of Céline as a splenetic doctor wandering the wastelands of Paris by night, and his libretto for Nigel Osborne's music to an opera on Goya.

In Barker's plays there is always a war on, and it is perhaps his emphasis on struggle, pain, and treachery that affronts and affrights the rational humanism of theater directors. *The Possibilities*, an evening of 10 short pieces, delights in cruel and abrupt reversals of lives and ideologies and proposes that all history is contemporary. In the eighth piece Judith, after beheading Holofernes, is lauded as the heroine of Israel. A patriot comes to persuade her to leave her retreat and return in triumph to Jerusalem, but Judith grows hot as she recalls sex with Holofernes. When the patriot is caustic about deriving private pleasure from state business, Judith's knife comes out again and slashes off the patriot's hand. Desire, as in so many Barker plays, tramples across politics. In the seventh piece a typist refuses to submit her body and her clothes to the dowdy dictates of puritanical feminism. In the third piece a young whore, while constructing herself through underwear, shoes, and a red dress, argues with an old, despairing female Stalinist that the zigzags of history show as well in the seams of falling stockings as in the sagas of liquidations, show trials, and barricades. In servicing the party's *nomenklatura,* she, too, is a revolutionary. In another piece a torturer turns on a young admirer and kills him because the young man lacked the courage to move from flattering his elder to usurping his position. In Barker the old maintain their position through cunning, not traditional respect. *Only Some Can Take the Strain* satirizes the position of the specialist bookseller in an era of populism. He remains so loyal to his stock that he refuses to sell any of his books, arguing that their knowledge will be misused in a time of censorship. The piece contains the most bitterly accurate exchange of the collection. "I'm from the Ministry of Education," says the censor. "There's no such thing," replies the bookseller.

The education of a king is the theme of *Seven Lears,* Barker's imaginative version of Shakespeare's original. Barker's Lear, trying desperately to be a good king in the midst of war and intrigue, shuttles between his lover Prudentia and his wife Clarissa, Prudentia's daughter. Prudentia bolsters Lear with her endless desire for him, while Clarissa reassures him with her clarity of motive and her leadership in war. Lear veers wildly between conscience and cruelty. The jail, a collective of the unjustly imprisoned, is always at hand to remind him of the poor, but he orders merciless slaughter after a battle. He confers the dukedom of Gloucester on a beggar but orders his most able minister to become his fool and sanctions the execution of Prudentia at the prompting of Clarissa. Building on an old legend, Barker has Lear attempt to fly, but he only causes the death of a boy he was very fond of. He tries to drown Cordelia in a vat of gin and finishes by playing chess with Kent, whom he hates. His desire for truth and honesty have caused mayhem and unhappiness.

The war continues in *A Hard Heart,* in which a Greek city is under siege and its queen, Praxis, appeals to the architect Riddler to save them. Like Clarissa in *Seven Lears,* Riddler is arrogant, imperious, and a rationalist. By the end of the play she will in some measure have been humbled by Seemore, a man of the streets who challenges her self-sufficient coldness and who, in a parody of the Pluto and Persephone myth, tries to drag her into the sewers to escape and be reborn. But Riddler's descent does not signal a subtle misogyny by Barker. Throughout the play Riddler has been stage center with a series of daring schemes to fool the enemy. The schemes fail not through her stupidity but through the treachery of her son, Attila, the only person she loves and whom, through special pleading, she has preserved from military service and starvation. No Barker characters are immune from the upheaval of passion into their ordered lives. Their hubris is that they imagine they are.

In *The Europeans* male and female are equally matched. The Viennese siege of 1684 has been lifted, and the Turks have been repulsed from Europe. The emperor and his court have returned to hail Vienna's military commander, Starhemberg, but Starhemberg refuses honors. He is searching for another self, one that can love, and he finds it with Katrin. She has undergone the extreme suffering that, in Barker's typology, alone can create a character of knowledge and equality. She has been raped by the Turks and her breasts cut off, but she is in the line of Barker's clear-eyed, crisp-talking women. She insists on a public examination of her body by the city's leading doctors and wants a mass distribution around the city of prints of her disfigurement. The birth of the product of the rape, a girl named Concilia by the mocking emperor, takes place in full public view. Katrin is in love with language and holds onto it even at moments of extreme stress: "Sometimes I find a flow and then the words go—torrent—cascade—cascade again. I used that word just now! I like that word now I have discovered it. I shall use it, probably ad nauseam, cascading!" But in the climatic third scene of act 2 she and Starhemberg are largely silent. Naked, they sit at a distance in a shuttered room and gaze at one another. Their bodies are imperfect, but their endurance has been equal, as are their minds. This is a brief equilibrium between lust and intelligence that could only be envisaged after extensive experience of thwarted passion and defeated reason. The shutters are opened by Katrin's sister Susannah, whose exasperated desire for the corrupt priest Orphuls has been blocked by his willful celibacy. In the final scene Concilia is given to the Turks so that there will be no false harmony between East and West. Katrin and Starhemberg, without children to distract them, finally kiss. The new Europe will be produced by war-weary adults.

Barker has continued to rewrite myths of the European past in a series of large-scale works that deconstruct received ideas. *Brutopia* envisages Thomas More's daughter constructing a countertext of pain and ecstasy to the idyllic humanism of her father's *Utopia,* while *Rome* excavates, through a number of antiphonal narratives, the noble and ignoble impulses toward divinity in the Hebraic, Greco-Roman, and Christian traditions. Barker renegotiates European cultural myths powerfully in his version of Chekhov's *Uncle Vanya.* He suspects that Chekhov's melancholy fits too well the current mood of fin de siècle indifference. So Barker's Vanya drops the cuddly title of uncle, actually kills Serebryakov, accuses Chekhov of cowardice in not fully using the gun he introduces into his play, and whirls around the stage in open pursuit of Helena. She begins with the stupefied eroticism of Chekhov's heroine but finishes with an extraordinary passage of Barkerian self-appraisal. At the beginning of act 3 she speaks into a giant mirror, where she sees her body as the perfect image of terminal longing: "My body is the end of thought. . . . I am the point and purpose of the world." She warns Vanya against touching her: "I am *a lethal object* careful you might cut your fingers and bleed from the caress." Helena is beautiful, but she is neither a neurotic aesthete nor a femme fatale. She is in full possession of what men see her as, and she then dares to anatomize their vision into skin and bone so as to reassemble her geometry of shoulder, neck, and thigh into a beauty that is even more dangerous. Vanya has to kill her as well. Her and her husband's egotism are an affront to this Vanya's struggles toward freedom and self-discovery. They are finally only a stage on Vanya's journey out of inertia and the play. He exits into a world without the miraculous life-creating sea conjured up earlier by Barker. Sonya and Marys rattle their dice, provincial torpor descends, and they murmur comfortably, "He'll be back."

—Tony Dunn

BARNES, Peter

Nationality: British. **Born:** London, 10 January 1931. **Education:** Stroud Grammar School, Gloucestershire. **Military Service:** Served in the Royal Air Force, 1949-50. **Family:** Married 1) Charlotte Beck in 1958 (died 1994); 2) C. Horn in 1995. **Career:** Worked for the London County Council, 1948 and 1950-53; critic, *Films and Filming*, London, 1954; story editor, Warwick Films, 1956. **Awards:** John Whiting award, 1969; *Evening Standard* award, 1969; Olivier award, 1985; Royal Television Society award, 1989, for *Nobody Here but Us Chickens*; Academy award nomination, 1992, for *Enchanted April*. **Agent:** Casarotto Ramsay Ltd., National House, 60-66 Wardour Street, London W1V 3HP. **Address:** 7 Archery Close, Connaught Street, London W2 2BE, England.

Publications

Plays

The Time of the Barracudas (produced San Francisco, 1963).

Sclerosis (produced Edinburgh and London, 1965).

The Ruling Class: A Baroque Comedy (produced Nottingham, 1968; London, 1969; Washington, D.C., 1971). London, Heinemann, and New York, Grove Press, 1969.

Leonardo's Last Supper, and Noonday Demons (produced London, 1969; *Noonday Demons* produced Los Angeles, 1977). London, Heinemann, 1970.

Lulu, adaptation of plays by Frank Wedekind, translated by Charlotte Beck (also co-director: produced Nottingham and London, 1970). London, Heinemann, 1971.

The Alchemist, with Trevor Nunn, adaptation of the play by Jonson (produced Nottingham and London, 1970; revised version produced Stratford-on-Avon and London, 1977).

The Devil Is an Ass, adaptation of the play by Jonson (also co-director: produced Nottingham, 1973; revised version produced Edinburgh, 1976).

The Bewitched (produced London, 1974). London, Heinemann, 1974.

The Frontiers of Farce, adaptation of the plays *The Purging* by Feydeau and *The Singer* by Wedekind (also director: produced London, 1976; *The Purging* produced New York, 1980). London, Heinemann, 1977.

For All Those Who Get Despondent (cabaret), adaptation of works by Brecht and Wedekind (also director: produced London, 1976; revised version, as *The Two Hangmen: Brecht and Wedekind*, broadcast 1978).

Antonio, adaptation of the plays *Antonio and Mellida* and *Antonio's Revenge* by Marston (broadcast 1977; also co-director: produced Nottingham, 1979).

Laughter! (produced London, 1978). London, Heinemann, 1978.

The Devil Himself (revue), adaptation of a play by Wedekind, music by Carl Davis and Stephen Deutsch (also director: produced London, 1980).

Barnes' People: Seven Monologues (broadcast 1981). Included in *Collected Plays*, 1981.

Collected Plays (includes *The Ruling Class*, *Leonardo's Last Supper*, *Noonday Demons*, *The Bewitched*, *Laughter!*, *Barnes' People*). London, Heinemann, 1981; as *Plays: One*, London, Methuen, 1989.

Somersaults (revue; also director: produced Leicester, 1981).

Barnes' People II: Seven Duologues (broadcast 1984). London, Heinemann, 1984.

Red Noses (produced London, 1985; Chicago, 1987). London, Faber, 1985.

Scenes from a Marriage, adaptation of a play by Feydeau (produced London, 1986).

The Real Long John Silver and Other Plays: Barnes' People III (as *Barnes' People III*, broadcast 1986). London, Faber, 1986.

The Real Long John Silver (produced London, 1989). Included in *The Real Long John Silver and Other Plays*, 1986.

Nobody Here But Us Chickens (televised 1989). With *Revolutionary Witness*, London, Methuen, 1989.

Revolutionary Witness (televised 1989). With *Nobody Here But Us Chickens*, London, Methuen, 1989.

The Spirit of Man (includes *A Hand Witch of the Second Stage*, *From Sleep and Shadow*, *The Night of the Simhat Torah*) (televised 1989; produced London, 1991). With *More Barnes' People*, London, Methuen, 1990.

More Barnes' People (broadcast 1989-90). With *The Spirit of Man*, London, Methuen, 1990.

Sunsets and Glories (produced Leeds, 1990). London, Methuen, 1990.

Tango at the End of Winter, adaptation of the play by Kunio Shimizu (produced London, 1991). Charlbury, Amber Lane, 1991.

Corpsing: Four One-Act Plays (includes *Humour Helps*; *Waiting for a Bus*; *Acting Exercize*; *Last Things*). N.p., n.d.

Plays (includes *Clap Hands, Here Comes Charlie*; *Heaven's Blessings*; *Revolutionary Witness*; *The Patriot, the Butcher, the Preacher, the Amazon*). London, Methuen, 1996.

Screenplays: *Violent Moment*, 1959; *The White Trap*, 1959; *Breakout*, 1959; *The Professionals*, 1960; *Off-Beat*, 1961; *Ring of Spies* (*Ring of Treason*), with Frank Launder, 1963; *Not with My Wife You Don't*, with others, 1966; *The Ruling Class*, 1972; *Enchanted April*, 1991.

Radio Plays: *My Ben Jonson*, 1973; *Eastward Ho!*, from the play by Jonson, Chapman, and Marston, 1973; *Antonio*, 1977; *The Two Hangmen: Brecht and Wedekind*, 1978; *A Chaste Maid in Cheapside*, from the play by Middleton, 1979; *Eulogy on Baldness*, from a work by Synesius of Cyrene, 1980; *For the Conveyance of Oysters*, from a work by Gorky, 1981; *The Soldier's Fortune*, from the play by Thomas Otway, 1981; *The Atheist*, from the play by Thomas Otway, 1981; *Barnes' People*, 1981; *The Singer*, from a work by Wedekind, 1981; *The Magician*, from a work by Gorky, 1982; *The Dutch Courtesan*, from the play by Marston, 1982; *A Mad World, My Masters*, from the play by Middleton, 1983; *Barnes' People II*, 1984; *The Primrose Path*, from a play by Feydeau, 1984; *A Trick to Catch the Old One*, from the play by Middleton, 1985; *The Old Law*, from the play by Middleton and Rowley, 1986; *Woman of Paris*, from a work by Henri Becque, 1986; *Barnes' People III*, 1986; *No End to Dreaming*, 1987; *The Magnetic Lady*, from the play by Jonson, 1987; *More Barnes' People* (series of monologues), 1989-90; *Billy and Me*, 1990; *Madame Zenobia*, 1990; *Slaughterman*, 1990; *The Road to Strome*, 1990; *Losing Myself*, 1990; *A True Born Englishman*, 1990; *Houdini's Heir*, 1991.

Television Plays: *The Man with a Feather in His Hat*, 1960; *Revolutionary Witness*, 1989; *Nobody Here But Us Chickens*, 1989; *More Than a Touch of Zen*, 1989; *Not as Bad as They Seem*, 1989; *The Spirit of Man*, 1990; *Bye Bye Columbus*, 1992.

*

Critical Studies: *The Theatre of Peter Barnes* by Bernard F. Dukore, London, Heinemann, 1981; *Landmarks of Modern British Drama: The Plays of the Sixties* edited by Roger Cornish and Violet Ketels, London, Methuen, 1986; *New Theatre Quarterly* (Cambridge), no. 21, 1990; *The Gothic Impulse* by Marybeth Inveso, Ann Arbor, University of Michigan Research Press, 1991; *Barnestorm: The Plays of Peter Barnes* by Bernard Frank Dukore, New York, Garland, 1995; "Peter Barnes" in *British Playwrights, 1956-1995: A Research and Production Sourcebook,* edited by William W. Demastes, Westport, Connecticut, Greenwood, 1996.

Theatrical Activities:
Director: **Plays**—Several of his own plays; *Bartholomew Fair* by Jonson, London, 1978 and 1987. **Film**—*Leonardo's Last Supper*, 1977. **Television**—*Nobody Here But Us Chickens*, 1989; *The Spirit of Man*, 1990; *Bye Bye Columbus*, 1992; *Hard Times*, 1994.

Peter Barnes comments:
Peter Barnes quotes from his programme note for *The Ruling Class*, 1968:

> The aim is to create, by means of soliloquy, rhetoric, formalized ritual, slapstick, songs, and dances, a comic theatre of contrasting moods and opposites, where everything is simultaneously tragic and ridiculous. And we hope never to consent to the deadly servitude of naturalism or lose our hunger for true size, weight, and texture.

* * *

Peter Barnes is one of the most consistently exciting and inventive of contemporary playwrights. He is a savage satirist and a glorious freebooter of past theatrical styles. Some of the more obvious influences are discernible in the adaptations of work by Marston, Jonson, and Wedekind, in particular in a magnificent version of Wedekind's *Lulu* plays. He is as implacably opposed to the dominant theatrical mode of naturalism as he is to the perpetuation of the status quo in the world in which he writes. His chief weapon is comedy, but a comedy always on the verge of nightmare. He first came to prominence with *The Ruling Class* in 1968, a play in which the delusion of the latest in a long line of insane Earls of Gurney that he is Christ serves as a perfectly reasonable representation of the continued appropriation of power by a self-perpetuating ruling class.

The play, the plot of which concerns the efforts of the earl's relations to get a male heir from him before having him certified, is a freewheeling farcical broadside on ruling-class excesses. A pervading sense of disgust at the way things are, however, is never balanced by any suggestion of a way out of the impasse. The only character who might seriously threaten the perpetuation of the old order is the butler, an ill-defined revolutionary completely unable to leave the world of privilege he would destroy despite the acquisition of a substantial inheritance from the previous earl. And this fascination with the ostensible object of attack is something that he shares with the play itself. For all its venom Barnes seemed at this juncture unable to do more than pick away at the scab.

The humor would subsequently be increasingly less cozy and the visions of society far bleaker if Barnes's plays were to offer an excess of blood, vomit, and excrement, guaranteed to offend the conventional West End audience, as was clearly intended, without ever offering the kind of positive analysis that might appeal to a more politically engaged audience. His work thus falls between the two extremes of contemporary theater, and as a result he has quite unfairly continued to struggle for productions. Indeed, it took him seven years to realize the 1985 production of *Red Noses*.

After *The Ruling Class* Barnes moved away from a fantasy version of the contemporary world, and his later plays offer a series of nightmare visions of climactic moments of an earlier civilization. The plays are inhabited by characters who speak a variety of inventive and historically unlocatable languages in ways that make the link between present crises and past roots never less than urgent and disturbing. In *Leonardo's Last Supper,* the great artist regains consciousness in a filthy charnel house, where he has been carried having been prematurely declared dead. His joy at his resurrection and at the further works of genius he will now be able to leave the world is not shared by the wretched family. They had seen their contract for the burial of the famous man as a way to worldly fame and success, and they simply carry on with the arrangements, having first ensured a real corpse by plunging Leonardo head first into a bucket of excrement, urine, and vomit. The wonders of the Renaissance mean nothing to this self-dependent family unit. The working model of the basic precepts of capitalist enterprise provided by the family acts also as a demonstration of the way in which everything represented by the aspirations of a man such as Leonardo is built on the usually mute sufferings of socially insignificant people.

In *The Bewitched* Barnes turned to a key moment in modern European history, the problem over the succession to the grotesquely inbred Philip IV of Spain. The effect of the transference of power on the lives of the powerless throughout Europe is heightened dramatically by the court's own total lack of concern for them. All interest in the court is centered on explanations of, and attempts to rectify, the ruler's impotence. It is a world in which spiritual salvation is sought for in the torture chamber and in the auto-da-fé as the political fate of Europe is decided by the crazy attempts of the institutions of church and state to create a rightful heir from the seed of an impotent and degenerate imbecile. The central metaphor that links a mad incapacity with political power is here used to far more telling effect, and the result is one of the most thrillingly disturbing plays of the modern period.

In *Laughter!* Barnes was to push the process a stage further with a series of carefully prepared theatrical shocks. The first part takes us back to another account of the insanity of rule, this time in the court of Ivan the Terrible. Terrifyingly comic though the opening is, it leaves the audience quite unready for what is to follow. The second part opens in an office that is dominated by an eight-foot-high stretch of filing cabinets and in which a poster of Hitler is prominent on the wall. As the dialogue develops, the audience is invited to laugh at the bureaucrats fighting for power and status among themselves, even as it becomes increasingly apparent that the office is responsible for organizing the finer details of the extermination program at the concentration camp at Auschwitz.

The wall of filing cabinets then opens to reveal an interior of gassed corpses being violently stripped of valuables by a sanitation squad in gas masks, and the dry statistics of the files are suddenly metamorphosed in a grotesque masque of death. The audience is forced to confront the reality behind the language of a petty officialdom that carries out the insane demands of its rulers without questioning or ever properly looking at what it is that is being administered. That Barnes should then finish his play with an epilogue in which two Jewish stand-up comedians go through their paces at the concentration camp Christmas concert is evidence of a writer who is prepared to tread a more dangerous tightrope than any of his contemporaries.

With *Red Noses* Barnes moved back into more distant history, continuing his exploration of the potential of laughter as a weapon against oppression. In the midst of a plague-torn Europe a group of self-appointed and papally sanctioned Red Noses take on the role of theatrical clowns and act out their parts on a politically repressive stage. They form an alliance with other more politically active groups in response to Barnes's own question: "Can we ever get laughter from comedy which doesn't accept the miseries of life but actually helps to change them? . . . Laughter linked with revolution might be the best of both worlds." But by the end of this remarkable play the passing of the plague is accompanied by the inevitable restoration of the old order of church and state.

The question that Barnes raises ever more urgently about the ability of the writer to affect change remains an open one, which makes his continuing problems in finding theaters to take his work the more depressing and in itself provides a reason for his continued use of past history as a source for his plots. He has a desire to write about the problems of the individual at odds with a corrupt society, but he is confronted with the worry that by the time his plays are produced any obviously contemporary references will have become dated. It was thus both peculiarly appropriate and very much to be welcomed that one of Britain's newest theaters, the West Yorkshire Playhouse in Leeds, should have opened in June 1990 with Barnes's *Sunsets and Glories.* For the first time the playwright presented the figure and struggles of a truly good man, the thirteenth-century Pope Celestine IV. The play is "about a man who was a saint, became pope, and because he was good, was bad for the job . . . the only pope ever voted out of office." The humor is as black as ever.

Barnes has continued to write as he wants rather than to bow to the economically diminishing demands of the theater of the new monetarist age for small-cast, small-scale domestic drama. As it is, however, the lack of regular productions of his work is nothing short of a national disgrace.

—John Bull

BARRY, Sebastian

Nationality: Irish. **Born:** Dublin, Ireland, 5 July 1955. **Education:** Trinity College, B.A. in 1977. **Award:** Honorary fellow in writing, University of Iowa, 1984. **Agent:** Anne McDermid, Curtis Brown, Ltd., 162-168 Regent Street, London W1R 5TB, England.

Publications

Plays

Boss Grady's Boys. Dublin, Raven Arts Press, 1989.
Prayers of Sherkin and Boss Grady's Boys. London, Methuen, 1991.
The Steward of Christendom. London, Methuen, 1995.
Plays (includes *Boss Grady's Boys*; *Prayers of Sherkin*; *White Woman Street*; *The Only True History of Lizzie Finn*; *The Steward of Christendom*). London, Methuen, 1997.

Novel

Macker's Garden. Irish Writer's Cooperative, 1982.

Short Stories

Time Out of Mind. Wolfhound Press, 1983.
Time Out of Mind and Strappado Square. Dublin, Wolfhound, 1985.

Poetry

The Water-Colourist. Dolmen Press, 1983.
The Rhetorical Town. Dolmen Press, 1985.
Fanny Hawke Goes to the Mainland Forever. Dublin, Raven Arts Press, 1989.
The Grammatical History of Everiu. Dolmen Press.

Other

Elsewhere: The Adventures of Belemus. (for children). Brogeen Books, 1985.
The Engine of Owl-Light. Paladin, 1987.
The Whereabouts of Eneas McNully. London, Picador, 1998.

*

Critical Study: "Such a Sense of Home: The Poetic Drama of Sebastian Barry" by Christopher Murray, in *Colby Quarterly* (Waterville, Maine), December 1991, pp. 242-48.

* * *

Sebastian Barry's writing is deeply elegiac without being baldly nostalgic, blackly absurd without being anything but wholly compassionate. He writes plays about Ireland and about history, and about emigration and the Irish diaspora, but mostly he writes about people and about their lives. His characters are the little people of history, simultaneously extraordinary and mundane, as Fintan O'Toole has observed, "the footnotes, the oddities, the quirks of history."

The people described in Barry's plays are a richly diverse band of loners, misfits, and eccentrics: aging farmers in rural Ireland; bold travelers struggling to remember a lost continent; devout members of a strange utopian sect; wild cowboys and aging desperadoes; dispossessed colonial warriors; daring music-hall dancers; fading gentry; rogues; vagabonds; and madmen and lunatics. They are also wholly human creations, flawed and damaged, certainly, but capable of great dignity, unquestioning love, physical tenderness, emotional truthfulness, and supreme linguistic elegance.

Barry's first great success as a dramatist was *Boss Grady's Boys* (1988), a bold and innovative variation on the theme of rural Ireland. The play tells of the lives of two brothers, Mick and Josey. They have grown old together and are struggling to keep their farm, located in the hills of the Cork-Kerry border, working. The play has a strange, dreamlike structure—scenes are not in chronological or narrative order and contain half-remembered flashbacks and fantastical imaginings based on memory and influenced by popular culture. The play cuts between the present setting of the brothers' lives to their childhood and adolescence, investigating, in particular, the flawed legacy of their domineering father, Boss Grady. The final image of the play is drawn from Barry's favorite metaphor of the mythic Wild West. It describes the brothers holed up in their last hideout watching the Indians circling for the kill: "We're surrounded. The Indians. You never see them, they shoot from behind boulders. It is very much as they say. I think I'm done for. I don't think I can wait for those cavalry horses. You hold out without me. You take my bullets. Don't waste your water on me. Don't let the Indians creep up on you. Keep your eyes peeled, Josey. Take my bullets. Is there no sign of them bloody horses?"

The Wild West is a motif of huge significance for Barry, repeated and replayed throughout his work: in *Prayers of Sherkin* (1990) the story of the James boys echoes throughout; in *The Only True History of Lizzie Finn* (1995) Buffalo Bill appears as a character; in *White Woman Street* (1992) the Englishman Blakely imagines buffalo grazing on the Sligo hills; and in *The Steward of Christendom* (1995) Mr. Smith, an asylum orderly, at one point dons the guise of Gary Cooper. Barry uses the metaphor to see the colonization of Ireland by England repeated in the genocide of westward expansion in the United States. As *White Woman Street*'s Trooper O'Hara—an immigrant from Sligo who earned his living as a cavalryman in the Indian wars—says, "The English had done it for us, I was thinking, and now we're doing it for the Indians." Barry has the Irish caught in a double bind of being both cowboys and Indians: on the one hand exploited by an expansive imperial power, on the other, complicit in the colonial exploitation of North America. It is an evocative resetting of the Irish dream of the United States as a nightmare of aggressive capitalism.

Barry is fundamentally concerned with ideas of nation, of community, of belonging, and of not belonging. His plays are full of ambiguous communities and idiosyncratic groupings—the end-of-Empire Anglo-Irish aristocracy, cowboys, Indians, Kitchener's army, Boers, music-hall performers, cultists, divided families, and obsessive lovers. Barry sets the debate around national identity and nationalism, colonialism and marginalization, Irishness, the English, and the promise of the United States in unique terms. He re-creates the metaphor of colonizer and colonized as duplicitous, quixotic, and more complex than Irish theater culture has, perhaps, traditionally allowed.

In contrast to *Boss Grady's Boys,* and again signaling something distinctive in contemporary Irish drama, both *Prayers of Sherkin* and *Lizzie Finn* have strong and lusty women at the center of the drama. Although the former is set in the 1890s and the latter in the early 1900s, Fanny Hawke and Lizzie Finn are truly modern women: independent of spirit and ready to love and to follow their passions. They are true partners for their equally independent lovers; they are "new Irish women." They are vital figures on stage, honest in their desires and hugely attractive because of it. Both characters are noble re-creations of Barry's own ancestors.

Barry's most assured and powerful play, *The Steward of Christendom,* also draws on the playwright's family history but transcends mere biography to produce a poetic and poignant paean for a closed chapter of Irish history. Thomas Dunne is a fallen, modern tragic hero, a broken man, a latter-day King Lear, and an inmate of a bare asylum. His faculties have failed and he is living in a mean room, paid for by "shillings" from his daughters. There he is visited by shades of his past life and relives the fall of a forgotten Ireland. Dunne is a quisling of Irish history: an Irish Catholic Loyalist whose son died in World War I and the last superintendent of the Dublin Metropolitan Police—a servant of English Ireland.

In Dunne, Barry has created one of the great acting roles of contemporary drama. The play offers more, however, than a bravura role for an actor. In a deep way the play is about the nation, about land, and about family. It contrasts ideas of a public and a private history, an authorized and a remembered history. The major public act of *The Steward of Christendom* is the surrender of Dublin Castle to Michael Collins in 1922. It is significant in the play because this official beginning of a modern Ireland marks also the end of Dunne's role on the public stage.

This pregnant tension between the great public acts of history and their private meanings and ramifications lies at the core of Barry's dramaturgy. In *White Woman Street* Clarke, the native American bartender, describes the Easter Rising to Trooper O'Hara:

"Place burning like Richmond, I hear. Some big mail depot or someplace. Fire and ruin in Dublin. Fellas put in jail and likely killed. Fighting the English." If Barry finds the United States re-created and mythologized in the Anglo-Irish imagination, the same historiographical distortions of Ireland itself must be exposed and deconstructed.

Barry's writing is, according to O'Toole, "evocative rather than explicit, poetic rather than realistic, intent, not on making the familiar conflicts of everyday life strange, but on making the strange familiar." In so doing, Barry fundamentally re-creates what contemporary Irish drama can achieve.

—Adrienne Scullion

BARTLETT, Neil

Nationality: British. **Born:** Hitchin, Hertfordshire, in 1958. **Education:** Magdalen College, Oxford, 1979-81, B.A. in English literature 1981. **Career:** Founder member, 1982 Theatre Company, London, 1982-84; staff member, Consenting Adults in Public, London, 1983, September in the Pink (London Lesbian and Gay Arts Festival), London, 1983, and International Aids Day, London, 1986; director, Théâtre de Complicité, London, 1985; M.C. for National Review of Live Art, London, Nottingham, and Glasgow, 1985-90; founder member, 1988, and director, writer and performer, 1988—, Gloria, London. **Awards:** Perrier award, 1985; *Time Out*/Dance Umbrella award, 1989; Writers Guild of Great Britain award, 1991; *Time Out* award, 1992. **Agent:** Gloria, 16 Chenies Street, London WC1E 7EX, England.

PUBLICATIONS

Plays

Dressing Up (produced London, 1983).
Pornography (produced London, 1984).
The Magic Flute, adaptation of the opera by Mozart (produced London, 1985).
A Vision of Love Revealed in Sleep, 1 (produced London, 1986).
Lady Audley's Secret, adaptation of the novel by Mary E. Braddon (produced London, 1988).
Le Misanthrope, adaptation of the play by Molière (produced Edinburgh, 1988; London, 1989; Chicago, 1989). Bath, Absolute Classics, 1990.
A Vision of Love Revealed in Sleep, 2 (produced London, 1989).
A Vision of Love Revealed in Sleep, 3 (produced London, 1990). Published in *Gay Plays 3*, edited by Michael Wilcox, London, Methuen, 1990.
The School for Wives, adaptation of the play by Molière (produced Derby, 1990; Washington, D.C., 1992). Bath, Absolute Classics, 1990.
Bérénice, adaptation of the play by Jean Racine (produced London, 1990). Bath, Absolute Classics, 1990.
Sarrasine, adaptation of the story by Honoré de Balzac (produced Edinburgh, 1990; London, 1990; New York, 1991).
Let Them Call It Jazz, adaptation of the story by Jean Rhys (produced London, 1991).
A Judgement in Stone, adaptation of the novel by Ruth Rendell, music by Nicolas Bloomfield (produced London, 1992).

Screenplay: *Now That It's Morning*, 1992.

Television Plays: *That's What Friends Are For*, 1988; *That's How Strong My Love Is*, 1989.

Video: *Where Is Love*, 1988; *Pedagogue* with Stuart Marshall, 1988.

Novels

Ready to Catch Him Should He Fall. London, Serpent's Tail, 1990; New York, Dutton, 1991.
Mr. Clive and Mr. Page. London, Serpent's Tail, 1996.

Short Stories

The Ten Commandments. London, Serpent's Tail, 1992.

Other

Who Was That Man? A Present for Mr. Oscar Wilde. London, Serpent's Tail, 1988.

*

Critical Studies: "Poaching and Pastiche: Reproducing the Gay Subculture" by Ross Chambers, in *Canadian Review of Comparative Literature,* March-June, 1994; "Who's Transgressing Now? Some Comments on Gay and Lesbian Literature" by Catherine R. Simpson, in *Authority and Transgression in Literature,* edited by Bonnie Braendlin and Hans Braendlin, Gainseville, Florida, University of Florida Press, 1996; "The Moment of Submission: Neil Bartlett in Conversation" by Alan Sinfield, in *Modern Drama* (Downsview, Ontario), Spring 1996, pp. 211-21.

Theatrical Activities:
Director: **Plays**—All his own plays; *More Bigger Snacks Now* by Théâtre de Complicité, London, 1985; *The Avenging Woman*, Riga, Australia, 1991; *Twelfth Night*, Chicago, 1992; *The Game of Love and Chance*, Poole, 1992.

Actor: **Plays**—Role in *Pornography*, London, 1984; Robert Audley in *Lady Audley's Secret*, London, 1988. **Television**—Roles in all his own television plays. **Video**—Roles in all his videos.

Neil Bartlett comments:

I do not consider my work "playwriting" because my performance work has its professional roots in collectively devised small-scale work, physical theatre, and performance art. I regard script as the documentation rather than origin of performance. I regard all my work as gay theatre whether it is solo performance, music theatre, or the re-invention of classic texts. I characteristically write, direct, light, and design all my pieces. I have been particularly influenced by my collaborations with: Banuta Rubess in Toronto and Riga; painter Robin Whitmore; vaudevillian Bette Bourne; and my colleagues in Gloria, producer, Simon Mellor, choreographer, Leah Hausman, and composer, Nicolas Bloomfield. I am particularly influenced by the unique traditions of British gay theatre in musicals, pub drag, pantomime, and contemporary activism. My favourite performer is Ethyl Eichelberger, my favourite play Racine's *Athalie*. My ambition is to produce a commercial pantomime, a classical tragedy, and a spectacular revue in the same season, in the same building, and with the same company.

* * *

Although he has completed only a few original dramatic texts, with them Neil Bartlett established himself as one of the most interesting drama writers working in Great Britain. He earned such a reputation precisely because he recognizes the limitations of the dramatist within the theater. It is his involvement with all aspects of a production that marks him as unique. He acts, directs, designs, and stage manages shows with equal aplomb—in the service of the performance as a complete work of art.

Bartlett draws his inspiration from many different forms of theater, from opera to performance art. Fortunately though, he does not make the mistake of so many performance artists of reacting against the dominance of text-based theater by devaluing the text. Bartlett loves the sound and the sensuality of words but seeks to present them with as much help as he can, enveloping them in beautiful music and illuminating them with startling visual images. His is also a theater of immediate and erotic impact and he revels in ornate Victorian theaters, lavish costumes, and shock. Much of this shock comes from the foregrounding of his gay sexuality. "I'm queer, I'm here, get used to it," is the message audiences have to accept before they can begin to appreciate Bartlett's work.

Bartlett is, above all, however, the most fastidious of theater artists. He constantly reworks a play until he is satisfied with it, accepting the challenge of re-creating a work for different venues and reshaping it until it seems to have been created as a site-specific piece of theater. His plays are feasts for the eyes, the ears, and the mind, but they are also accessible, controlled, and immaculate works of art with a backbone of political steel. It is this mixture of politics and aesthetics that won him his reputation in fringe theater and allowed him to tackle mainstream theater.

After completing his university studies and becoming involved as an actor and director with the 1982 Theatre Company (where he made a memorable Cleopatra in a little black frock), Bartlett presented his first piece, *Dressing Up* (1983), in London as part of a lesbian and gay festival called September in the Pink. It was on the same bill as Louise Kelly's *Antibody*, the first play about AIDS to be presented in Britain. *Dressing Up* was a piece of postmodern theater created before the term became fashionable. Weaving together fragments from the lives of gay men in London from the seventeenth to the nineteenth centuries, the piece was played out before a rack of costumes that mingled leather and lace, crinolines and codpieces. Bartlett declared the piece to be "a polemic guide to the splendours of the male body." Underlying the whole piece, however, was a serious political purpose that might best, but rather drearily, be described as reclaiming history and that revealed Bartlett as the marble fist in the gold lamé glove. The second part of *Dressing Up* was a series of reflections on the work and the words of the novelist Edmund White—an act of homage from disciple to master and one in which AIDS was touched upon at a time when it was hardly known in Britain.

Bartlett's next original piece was *Pornography*, created for the Institute of Contemporary Arts (ICA). It was, in part, a collective creation that used monologues woven around the personal memories of the actors in the piece, a device Bartlett was later to use to devastating effect in a reworked version for drag queens, *A Vision of Love Revealed in Sleep . . . Pornography* played with ideas of narrative, with memory, and with theater. It introduced a touch of red plush theatricality into the rather grim confines of the ICA, but at the heart of the piece were human stories of love and betrayal, raw and shocking, but delivered with such total honesty as to render them utterly compelling. *Pornography* began an association between Bartlett and the ICA that led to his producing a version of *The Magic Flute* for them. His gloss on Mozart's opera was his first step toward creating the all-embracing work of theater that exploits all that the stage has to offer to create that one ultimate performance.

Bartlett's interest in the hidden history of gay men (also evident in his much-praised book of meditations on Oscar Wilde *Who Was that Man?*) was used to overwhelming theatrical effect in his first one-man show, *A Vision of Love Revealed in Sleep*. Commissioned first by Nikki Milican for the Midland Group in Nottingham, it was later staged on the ornate Edwardian staircase of the old Battersea Town Hall, in a Docklands warehouse, in studio theaters, and in the incarnation mentioned above, as a large-scale theater piece expanded to include a chorus of lavishly costumed drag queens.

A Vision of Love Revealed in Sleep. is based upon the life of the Victorian painter and poet Simeon Solomon whose blossoming career was destroyed when he was prosecuted for gross indecency. Bartlett draws parallels between his own life and Solomon's and takes the audience through a series of variations on this theme. The play demonstrated Bartlett's combined virtuosity in writing and performing. He also gained some notoriety for performing in the nude, in order, he claimed, to prevent audiences from wasting time wondering whether he would take his clothes off. While audiences cannot fail to appreciate the skill with which Bartlett performs in his chosen environment, his paralleling of the nineteenth century and the present prevents the work from ever becoming a cozy biographical piece. His chilling evocation of what it meant to be a gay man in a 1980s London threatened by AIDS and by queer bashing made *A Vision of Love* as thought provoking as it was entertaining.

This skillful mixture of history, commentary, and unnerving immediacy—for example, the endless repetition of "young man, if you want to be happy, be careful,"—was also a feature of *Sarrasine*, Bartlett's reworking of Balzac, which introduced the audience to a world of baroque intrigue among cardinals and castrati. The play featured four actors and singers and evoked the murky interface between the glittering aristocracy and the infinitely more exciting underworld of eighteenth-century Rome. The piece is dominated by the figure of La Zambinella who is more than 200 years old when the play begins. La Zambinella is kept alive, like a vampire, by the devotion of continuing generations to the perfection of his voice. Through this unlikely figure, a tale of love and murder unfolds that fuses music hall and musical theater and explores obsession, the human need for art and admiration, and the similarity in response of the connoisseur to seventeenth-century opera and the man in the pub to a raunchy drag number. Bartlett also gives the play a political subtext that examines the erotic attraction of art and the sinister undercurrents of our worship of the artists who fulfill our sexual fantasies.

Bartlett is a prolific writer, but much of his stage work has been translations from Molière and Racine and adaptations of novels as diverse as *Lady Audley's Secret* and Ruth Rendell's *A Judgement in Stone*, as well as a story by Jean Rhys. Few other theater practitioners combine so successfully pleasure and politics, intellectual excitement and eroticism. Yet, as Bartlett would be the first to admit, although he may explore the heavens, he is always rooted on the stage—preferably in one of Frank Matcham's elaborate Edwardian theaters.

—Alasdair Cameron

BASS, Kingsley B., Jr. *See* **BULLINS, Ed.**

BASS, Rochelle. *See* **OWENS, Rochelle.**

BEKEDEREMO, J. P. Clark

Also wrote as John Pepper Clark. **Nationality:** Nigerian. **Born:** Kiagbodo, 6 April 1935. **Education:** Warri Government College, Ughelli, 1948-54; University of Ibadan, 1955-60, B.A. (honours) in English 1960, and graduate study (Institute of African Studies fellowship), 1963-64; Princeton University, New Jersey (Parvin fellowship). **Family:** Married to Ebun Odutola Clark; three daughters and one son. **Career:** Information officer, Government of Nigeria, 1960-61; head of features and editorial writer, Lagos *Daily Express*, 1961-62; research fellow, 1964-66, and professor of African literature, 1966-85, University of Lagos. Founding editor, *Horn* magazine, Ibadan; co-editor, *Black Orpheus*, Lagos, from 1968. Founding member, Society of Nigerian Authors.

Publications

Plays

Song of a Goat (produced Ibadan, 1961; London, 1965). Ibadan, Mbari, 1961; in *Three Plays*, 1964; in *Plays from Black Africa*, edited by Fredric M. Litto, New York, Hill and Wang, 1968.
Three Plays. London, Oxford University Press, 1964.
The Masquerade (produced London, 1965). Included in *Three Plays*, 1964; in *Collected Plays, 1964-1988*, 1991.
The Raft (broadcast 1966; produced New York, 1978). Included in *Three Plays*, 1964; in *Collected Plays, 1964-1988*, 1991.
Ozidi. Ibadan, London, and New York, Oxford University Press, 1966.
The Bikoroa Plays (includes *The Boat*, *The Return Home*, *Full Circle*) (produced Lagos, 1981). Oxford, Oxford University Press, 1985; in *Collected Plays, 1964-1988*, 1991.
Collected Plays, 1964-1988 (includes *Song of a Goat*, *The Masquerade*, *The Raft*, *Ozidi*, *The Boat*, *The Return Home*, *Full Circle*). Washington, D.C., Howard University Press, 1991.
The Wives' Revolt. Ibadan, University Press, 1991.

Screenplay: *The Ozidi of Atazi*.

Radio Play: *The Raft*, 1966.

Poetry

Poems. Ibadan, Mbari, 1962.
A Reed in the Tide: A Selection of Poems. London, Longman, 1965; New York, Humanities Press, 1970.
Casualties: Poems 1966-68. London, Longman, and New York, Africana, 1970.
Urhobo Poetry. Ibadan, Ibadan University Press, 1980.
A Decade of Tongues: Selected Poems 1958-1968. London, Longman, 1981.
State of the Union. London, Longman, 1985.
Mandela and Other Poems. Ikeja, Longman, 1988.
Collected Poems, 1958-1988. Washington, D.C., Howard University Press, 1991.

Other

America, Their America. London, Deutsch-Heinemann, 1964; New York, Africana, 1969.
The Example of Shakespeare: Critical Essays on African Literature. London, Longman, and Evanston, Illinois, North-western University Press, 1970.
The Hero as a Villain. Lagos, University of Lagos Press, 1978.

Editor and Translator, *The Ozidi Saga*, by Okabou Ojobolo. Ibadan, University of Ibadan Press, 1977.

*

Critical Studies: *John Pepper Clark* by Robert M. Wren, Lagos, Lagos University Press, 1984; *A Critical View of John Pepper Clark's "Three Plays"* by Martin Banham, London, Collins, 1985; *The Poetry of J.P. Bekederemo* by Isaac Irabor Elimimian, Ikeja, Longman, Nigeria, 1989; "J.P. Clark-Bekederemo and the Ijo Literary Tradition" by Dan S. Izevbaye, in *Research in African Literatures* (Bloomington, Indiana), Spring 1994, pp. 1-27.

* * *

J. P. Clark Bekederemo—or John Pepper Clark, as he once called himself—was awarded his B.A. by the University of Ibadan in 1960, the year of Nigerian independence, and his first play was produced and published two years later. His *Three Plays* was followed closely by *Ozidi,* but almost 20 years passed before *The Bikoroa Plays* appeared in 1985.

Bekederemo's first play, *Song of a Goat,* has been produced widely and is probably his most artistically successful. Its first lines state the theme:

> Masseur: Your womb
> Is open and warm as a room:
> It ought to accommodate many.
>
> Ebiere: Well, it seems like staying empty.
>
> Masseur: An empty house, my daughter, is a thing
> Of danger.

Ebiere's husband, Zifa, refuses to think of his sterility as permanent or of following the masseur's suggestion that the claims of fertility be honored by his brother Tonye. When, in her frustration, Ebiere seduces Tonye, Zifa perverts the ritual that would legitimize the surreptitious union; he makes Tonye force the head of the sacrificed goat into a pot, which shatters. By analogy this is, as they all realize, an assault upon Ebiere's womb. Tonye hangs himself, Zifa drowns himself, and Ebiere is left pregnant. The intensity of the conflict, in which each member of the trio is both victim and aggressor, sustains the short play and sweeps us through the trappings of Greek tragedy—a chorus of neighbors, a Cassandra-like aunt, a messenger speech telling of the final disaster—in which the playwright dresses the story. Despite some self-conscious writing, which is evident also in the etymological reference of the title, there is an extraordinary assurance in the play.

The playwright seems to have designed *The Masquerade* to offer relief from the intensity of *Song of a Goat.* He offers us "a real dance of the dragon-flies," the high-spirited wooing of Titi by a stranger who is Ebiere's son Tufa. Since he makes Tufa innocent of any knowledge of the tragedy surrounding his conception, the wooing can be lyrically joyful, a little in the spirit of Romeo and Juliet. Only as Titi's father investigates rumor and reveals the past does tragedy return. Unfortunately, one senses that the play's style and its denouement were willed into being. The language is full of Shakespearean echoes and conceits in the manner of Christopher Fry. Tufa has done nothing culpable, and, even with the intransigent hostility of Titi's father to the marriage, it takes a combination of misprision and accident to bring about the lovers' deaths.

The Raft, the third of *Three Plays,* presents four men drifting down a river on a raft of logs. Differences between the characters are subordinated to atmosphere as they drift through the fog, for the intent is, in the author's phrase, to convey the "human condition." Civil war overtook Nigeria and its constituent states not long after the play appeared, and some have read *The Raft* as a prescient allegorical vision. It is true that the raft splits and carries off one of the four men, but if the work suggests such a meaning, it is only as one metaphor among others. The play does not have the precision of an allegory.

The trilogy *The Bikoroa Plays* again traces the fate of a family through successive generations. This time Bekederemo focuses not on sexual relationships but, in the first play, on the differing ambitions of two brothers of contrasting character. They alternate in the use of the family boat, and irritations mount until there is a fatal quarrel. One is shot and the other condemned to death, and, ironically, the boat is split to carry each to his grave. The other two plays present the fatal quarrels of their two sons and two grandsons with such precise repetition that the action becomes predictable. Yet there is less sense of the author's self-conscious control of the action and of the language than in his earlier verse plays. The treatment is more relaxed, perhaps in part because the plays are in prose. More important, the brothers' behavior is seen, as the action in the earlier plays is not, from the viewpoint of the community within whose life they see their fulfillment. Metaphors are vivid but homely, using phrases that one can assume to be in everyday use. For example, the departure of an angry man evokes the comment "There goes a whirlwind with a lot of dust in its eye." Climactic scenes are trials and ceremonies. Beyond the community are the pressures of a changing colonial society that offers new opportunities but that has destroyed the traditional ideal of "the man, the fish, the vessel, all brought together in the one act of quest by man for fish over waters spilling into the sun."

Ozidi is based on an epic of Bekederemo's Ijaw people that, among them, is narrated and performed over seven days. In length, scope, and staging demands, it is unlike his other plays. It, too, deals with blood honor and the curse on a family, here worked out by a son avenging his father through his own strength abetted by his grandmother's magic. But the traditional story is refracted through the playwright's ironic consciousness. Ozidi is presented as a figure trapped in his destined role of warrior-avenger but at a loss to find himself. He is, like Goethe's Götz von Berlichingen, increasingly an outsider exemplifying anachronistic values. It has been suggested that the playwright created a "parable of the talented individual in Africa today," and, indeed, the modern storyteller Bekederemo changes Ijaw tradition in the play by having the storyteller take on the role of Ozidi.

Bekederemo's *The Wives' Revolt* is a comedy in which women walk out on their big-talking, overbearing husbands to protest the splitting of money from an oil company three ways—between the all-male elders, the men, and the women. Consensus is finally reached when it is agreed that the money will be used to build a school. The husbands are willing to compromise because they have proved inept at household duties and child rearing, the women because they have all returned with a venereal disease picked up in the unclean latrines of a nearby community. The disease is Bekederemo's original twist on an old theme: sexual reunion, such as is celebrated at the end of Aristophanes' *Lysistrata,* must be postponed. Because everything else is predictable, the comedy is only mildly amusing.

—Anthony Graham-White

BELL, Hilary

Nationality: Australian. **Born:** Stratford-Upon-Avon, England, 19 July 1966. **Education:** Australian Film, Television-Radio School, Sydney, Australia, 1990-92; Julliard School, New York, 1996-98. **Career:** Professional writer; playwright-in-residence, Shopfront Theatre for Young People, 1986-87; board member of World Interplay; tutor, African Regional Playwrights' Conference, Nairobi, 1996. **Awards:** Philip Parsons Memorial Young Playwrights' Award, 1994; Harold Park Short Play Competition, for *Wreckage,* 1996; Aurealis Award for Young Adult Fiction, for *Mirror, Mirror,* 1997; LeCompte du Nouy award, 1997, 1998; Greenroom award nominations, 1997, for *Wolf Lullaby*; Julliard Playwright fellow, 1997, 1998; Eric Kocher award, for *Eye of the Storm,* 1998; Jill Blewett Playwrights' Award, for *Wolf Lullaby,* 1998. **Member:** Dramatists Guild; Australian National Playwrights' Centre; Australian Writers' Guild. **Agent:** Jane Leigh, ICM, 40 West 57th Street, New York, New York 10019, U.S.A.; Robyn Gardiner Management, P.O. Box 128, Surry Hills NSW 2010, Australia.

Publications

Plays

Conversations with Jesus (produced Sydney, 1988).
Fortune (produced Honolulu, 1992). Currency Press, 1995.
Cockroach Opera, (libretti) music by Douglas Stephen Rae (produced Sydney, 1994).
The Wedding Song, (libretti) music by Douglas Stephen Rae (produced Sydney, 1994).
Eye of the Storm: A Shipwreck Tetralogy: Wreckage, The Bog Queen, Orilla Del Mundo, Tom and Eva (produced Melbourne, 1994).
The Frog Prince (produced 1996).
Wolf Lullaby (produced Sydney, 1996). Currency Press, 1997.
The Stronger, adaptation of August Strindberg (produced Adelaide, 1996).
Diviners (produced 1996).
Cheering Up Mother (produced Queensland, 1997).
Shot While Dancing (staged reading 1997, 1998).
Highway (cyberplay) (posted on web 1998).
Talk Show, (libretti) music by Elena Kats-Chermin (produced Sydney, 1998).

Radio Plays: *Cruisin',* 1988; *Wreckage,* 1996; *Wolf Lullaby,* 1997; *The Anatomy Lesson of Doctor Ruysch,* 1998.

Television Plays: *E Street,* 1992; *Mirror, Mirror,* 1993; *Reg Grundy Productions,* 1995; *Echo Point,* 1995.

Novel

Mirror, Mirror (for young adults). Hodder Headline, 1996.

Other

Translator, *Fortune,* by Isabelle Famchon, Belgium, Editions Lansman, 1995.

* * *

Hilary Bell, one of Australia's most accomplished young dramatists, studied playwriting at the National Institute of Dramatic Art, Sydney, and screenwriting at the Australian Film and Television School and has involved herself energetically in script development and workshops in Australia and abroad. She comes from a distinguished theatrical family; her father is the Shakespearean actor and director John Bell, and her mother Anna Volska and her sister Lucy Bell are actors. Her first short play, *Conversations with Jesus,* was commissioned by NIDA in 1987 and formed part of a program that toured to the 1988 Brisbane Expo. Written in a poetic and allusive style, it deals with the group of Theosophists who in 1923 built the amphitheater at Balmoral Beach, Sydney, in preparation for the second coming of Christ.

Bell writes libretti and lyrics for music theater, collaborating with dancers and composers. *A Pocketful of Hula Dreams,* which premiered in 1986 and was revived in 1992, is a cabaret-scaled musical pastiche of 1950s teen-romance surf movies that introduces her interest in the social patterns of modern multicultural Australia. With composer Graeme Dudley she created a children's opera, *The Young King* (1988), and in 1993 provided the lyrics for Belvoir Street's production of *The Cockroach Opera.* In 1994 her full-length musical *The Wedding Song* was performed by the NIDA Company and the Australian Musical Foundation, with a score by Douglas Stephen Rae and choreography by Stephen Page. It pits flesh against spirit in an allegory of colonialism with magical elements. A 1930s Australian couple voyage to the exotic Island of Drums, where their darker selves emerge in erotic interactions that bring about the destruction of the indigenous culture.

Bell's involvement with the experimental Kickhouse Theatre in Melbourne produced the dance piece *Wreckage,* which was given a promenade reading in 1994. In 1996 it received full production by the University of Melbourne Theatre Guild with music by Julian Ferretto and choreography by Glenn Rankin. *Wreckage* alludes to the wreck of the *Dunbar* off Sydney Heads in 1857; a tempest casts varied survivors onto the shores of their new country. Its complexities of class, displacement, and migration foreshadow the development of these ideas in *Fortune*. This play forms the first in the sequence *The Eye of the Storm : A Shipwreck Trilogy* (the following two being *The Bog Queen* and *Tom and Eva*), which received a staged reading at the National Playwrghts' Conference in Connecticut in 1997.

Bell came to national prominence in 1990 with her play *Fortune,* which was commissioned by NIDA, workshopped at the Royal Court Theatre, London, premiered at the Griffin Theatre, Sydney, and was subsequently widely produced in Australia. Its origin is the historical Chang the "Chinese Giant," who was exhibited in America and Australia in the nineteenth century. In *Fortune*, Chang is the Australian-born eleven-year-old freak, symbol of the young colony, who is exploited in bustling goldfields Australia by a German photographer and taken over by the tough but sometimes motherly Irish Kathleen and her dissolute Cockney lover, who all expect that Chang will make their fortune. Characters display various tensions arising from cultural displacement and hybridity. The play combines Bell's delineation of the ongoing Australian negotiation of identities in a migrant society and also her concern with the cycle of abuse, especially of the young: as Chang grows stronger than his exploiters, he chooses not to oppress them in turn. *Fortune*'s productions employ physicality and circus idioms, with the central child character played by an adult stiltwalker.

LullabyWolf was workshopped at the 1994 Australian National Playwrights' Conference, read at Adelaide during Red Shed's "Unplugged 1995" season, and premiered under the title *Wolf Lullaby* the next year at Griffin Theatre. Its inspiration came in 1993 from newspaper reports of a thirteen-year-old who had killed a four-year-old child and explores the fears and guilts that surround the issue of child murder. An intense play for four actors using both naturalistic and poetic devices, its central character is the eleven-year-old Lizzie, played by an adult actor, who fears possession by the dangerous "wolf," whose presence is heard rather than seen. Bell questions the sensationalism and moral panic surrounding such cases, exploring the thin psychological line separating violent impulses from normal behavior and truth from fantasy. Its disturbing subject matter and nonjudgmental treatment of evil, responsibility for violence, and questions of social and parental guilt, earned *Wolf Lullaby* several national awards.

Bell has written numerous scripts and storylines for commercial radio and television, including the popular children's program *The Ferals* and the long-running soap operas *GP* and *E Street.* Her children's television series *Mirror, Mirror* was novelized in 1996. Although a comparatively young writer, Bell has produced an impressive body of work in varied media, maintaining her commitment to exploring moral questions of contemporary society through a wide range of theatrical genres.

—Veronica Kelly

BENNETT, Alan

Nationality: British. **Born:** Leeds, Yorkshire, 9 May 1934. **Education:** Leeds Modern School, 1946-52; Exeter College, Oxford, 1954-57 (Open Scholar in History), B.A. (honors) 1957. National Service: Joint Services School for Linguists, Cambridge and Bodmin. **Career:** Temporary junior lecturer in history, Magdalen College, Oxford, 1960-62. **Awards:** *Evening Standard* award, 1961, 1968, 1971, 1985 (for screenplay); Tony award, 1963; Guild of Television Producers award, 1967; Broadcasting Press Guild award, for television play 1984, 1991; Royal Television Society award, 1984, 1986; Olivier award, 1990. D. Litt.: University of Leeds, 1990. Honorary Fellow, Exeter College, Oxford, 1987. **Agent:** Peters, Fraser, and Dunlop Group, 503/4 The Chambers, Chelsea Harbour, Lots Road, London SW10 0XF, England.

Publications

Plays

Beyond the Fringe, with others (produced Edinburgh, 1960; London, 1961; New York, 1962). London, Souvenir Press, and New York, Random House, 1963.

Forty Years On (produced Manchester and London, 1968). London, Faber, 1969.

Sing a Rude Song (additional material), book by Caryl Brahms and Ned Sherrin, music by Ron Grainer (produced London, 1969).

Getting On (produced Brighton and London, 1971). London, Faber, 1972.

Habeas Corpus (produced Oxford and London, 1973; New York, 1975). London, Faber, 1973.
The Old Country (produced Oxford and London, 1977). London, Faber, 1978.
Office Suite (includes *Green Forms*, televised as *Doris and Doreen*, 1978, and *A Visit from Miss Prothero*, televised 1978; produced London, 1987). London, Faber, 1981.
Enjoy (produced London, 1980). London, Faber, 1980.
Objects of Affection and Other Plays for Television (includes *Objects of Affection*: *Our Winnie, A Woman of No Importance, Rolling Home, Marks*, and *Say Something Happened*; and *A Day Out, Intensive Care, An Englishman Abroad)*. London, BBC Publications, 1982.
An Englishman Abroad (televised 1983; also director: produced London, 1988).
A Private Function (screenplay). London, Faber, 1984.
Forty Years On, Getting On, Habeas Corpus. London, Faber, 1985.
The Writer in Disguise (television plays; includes *Me, I'm Afraid of Virginia Woolf; Afternoon Off; One Fine Day; All Day on the Sands; The Old Crowd*; and an essay). London, Faber, 1985.
Kafka's Dick (produced London, 1986). Included in *Two Kafka Plays*, London, Faber, 1987.
The Insurance Man (televised 1986). Included in *Two Kafka Plays*, London, Faber, 1987.
Prick Up Your Ears (screenplay). London, Faber, 1987.
Talking Heads (includes *A Chip in the Sugar, Bed Among the Lentils, A Lady of Letters, Her Big Chance, Soldiering On, A Cream Cracker Under the Settee*) (televised 1987; produced London, 1992). London, BBC Publications, 1988; with *Single Spies*, New York, Summit, 1990.
A Question of Attribution (produced London, 1988).
Single Spies London, Faber, 1989; with *Talking Heads*, New York, Summit, 1990.
Single Spies and Talking Heads: Two Plays and Six Monologues. New York, Summit, 1990.
The Wind in the Willows (produced London, 1990). London, Faber, 1991.
Forty Years On and Other Plays (includes *Getting On, Habeas Corpus, Enjoy)*. London, Faber, 1991.
The Madness of George III (produced London, 1991). London, Faber, 1992.
The Clothes They Stood Up In. London, Faber, 1998.
Talking Heads 2. London, Faber, 1998.

Screenplays: *A Private Function*, 1984; *Prick Up Your Ears*, 1987.

Radio Plays: *Uncle Clarence* (a talk), 1986; *The Lady in the Van*, 1990; *The Clothes They Stood Up In,* 1997.

Television Plays: *On the Margin* series, 1966; *A Day Out*, 1972; *Sunset Across the Bay*, 1975; *A Little Outing*, 1977; *A Visit from Miss Prothero*, 1978; *Me, I'm Afraid of Virginia Woolf*, 1978; *Doris and Doreen*, 1978; *The Old Crowd*, 1979; *Afternoon Off*, 1979; *One Fine Day*, 1979; *All Day on the Sands*, 1979; *Intensive Care*, 1982; *Objects of Affection* (5 plays), 1982; *An Englishman Abroad*, 1983; *The Insurance Man*, 1986; *Talking Heads* (6 monologues), 1987; *102 Boulevard Haussmann*, 1990; *A Question of Attribution*, 1991; *Talking Heads 2,* 1998.

*

Critical Studies: *Beyond the Fringe . . . and Beyond: A Critical Biography of Alan Bennett, Peter Cook, Jonathan Miller, and Dudley Moore* by Roland Bergan, London, Virgin, 1990; "Talking Heads: 'Bed Among the Lentils' (Alan Bennett)" by Albert Hunt, in *British Television Drama in the 1980s,* Cambridge, Cambridge University Press, 1993; "North and South: Two Landscapes of Alan Bennett" by Daphne Turner, in *Modern Drama* (Downsview, Ontario), Winter 1994, pp. 551-67; "Fetishism and Fantasy in Bennett's *The Old Country* and *Single Spirits*" by Larry Langford, in *University of Mississippi Studies in English,* 1993-1995, pp. 361-75.

Theatrical Activities:
Director: **Plays**—*An Englishman Abroad*, London, 1988.

Actor: **Plays**—In *Better Late* (revue), Edinburgh, 1959; in *Beyond the Fringe*, Edinburgh, 1960, London, 1961, and New York, 1962; Archbishop of Canterbury in *The Blood of the Bambergs* by John Osborne, London, 1962; Reverend Sloley-Jones in *A Cuckoo in the Nest* by Ben Travers, London, 1964; Tempest in *Forty Years On*, London, 1968; Mrs. Swabb in *Habeas Corpus*, London, 1974; role in *Down Cemetery Road: The Landscape of Philip Larkin*, London, 1987; Tailor in *An Englishman Abroad*, London, 1988; Anthony Blunt in *A Question of Attribution*, London, 1988. **Films**—*Long Shot*, 1980; *The Secret Policeman's Ball*, 1986. **Radio**—In *The Great Jowett* by Graham Greene, 1980; *Dragon* by Don Haworth, 1982; Machiavelli in *Better Halves* by Christopher Hope, 1988. **Television**—Augustus Hare in *Famous Gossips*, 1965; *The Drinking Party*, 1965; *Alice in Wonderland*, 1966; *On the Margin*, 1966; Denis Midgley in *Intensive Care*, 1982; Shallow in *The Merry Wives of Windsor*, 1982; Housemaster in *Breaking Up*, 1986; narrator of *Man and Music*, 1986; *Fortunes of War*, 1987; narrator of *Dinner at Noon* (*By-Line* series), 1988; *A Chip in the Sugar*, 1988; narrator of *Portrait or Bust,* 1992; narrator of *The Abbey,* 1994.

* * *

> When we play language games, we do so rather in order to find out what game it is we are playing.
>
> —*Beyond the Fringe*

Whatever their ostensible themes, Alan Bennett's plays ultimately dramatize man's desire to define himself and his world through teasingly inadequate language, whether folk adages, government jargon, pronouncements from TV experts, or misapplied quotations from the greats. The resulting parodies simultaneously mock and honor the impulse to erect linguistic defenses in a frightening world. Bennett's comedy generally respects his characters, from aspiring intellectuals to northern ladies for whom "conversation is a conspiracy." But some works, like the TV plays collected as *The Writer in Disguise*, do not always resist the temptation to condescend: "Still our eldest girl's a manicurist and we've got a son in West Germany, so we haven't done too badly." Bennett's reliance on scatological humor, which reduces some characters to animals with pretensions to dignity, creates easy laughs. When focusing on professional writers like Kafka in later plays or Joe Orton in the film *Prick Up Your Ears*, Bennett sometimes overworks the audience's smug recognition of verbal and thematic allusions to these authors. Such distractions threaten to overwhelm his serious aims.

In *Beyond the Fringe* both Bennett's monologues and the sketches with Peter Cook, Jonathan Miller, and Dudley Moore focus on the game cliché, which trivializes the supposedly serious yet suggests that even inane values are better than none. A supposed lecture by the Duke of Edinburgh illustrates the precariousness of metaphorical language as well as an underlying desire for decency: "This business of international politics is a game . . . . It's a hard game, it's a rough game . . . sometimes, alas, it's a dirty game, but the point about a game, surely, is that there's no need to take it seriously . . . ." Other *Fringe* sketches brilliantly question the limits of discourse: a prison governor rebukes a condemned man who rejects an analogy between capital punishment and public school caning with "Come along, now, you're playing with words." Just as this semantic comedy foreshadows later plays like Hampton's *The Philanthropist* and Stoppard's *Jumpers*, "Aftermyth," a *Fringe* sketch on Britain during the Blitz, seems the spiritual parent of the many parodies of wartime England during the early 1970s. Bennett illuminates both the hilarious perversion of political rhetoric and the profound need to find attractive equivalents for painful reality.

The headmaster in *Forty Years On*, an ingenious play within a play that focuses on the annual performance by the boys and faculty of Albion School, indulges in similar rhetoric: "The more observant among you will have noticed that one of Bombardier Tiffin's legs was not his own. The other one, God bless him, was lost in the Great War. Some people lost other things, less tangible perhaps than legs, but no less worthwhile—they lost illusions, they lost hope, they lost faith . . . ." *Forty Years On* organizes a series of skits, similar in tone to "Aftermyth," on the cultural and political life of twentieth-century England. Wicked portraits of cultural heroes like Virginia Woolf and T. E. Lawrence are both outrageously unfair and deadly accurate. The best sketch is a Wilde pastiche in which Lady Dundowne, played by one of the masters in drag, advises her nephew to marry his spinster mother: "The arrangement seems so tidy that I am surprised it does not happen more often in society"—a perfect spoof of the archetypal Wilde plot and wit. "But then all women dress like their mothers, that is their tragedy. No man ever does. That is his," a parody of Wildean paradox, resonates with additional meaning from the elaborate pattern of homosexual allusion in the play; in this representative public school world, witty hyperbole equals literal statement. Bennett exposes the simultaneous idiocy and seductiveness of language on all levels, from the folk wisdom of a nanny to the devious rhetoric of Chamberlain, while the rude singing of the rugby team both undercuts and elevates the idealized game metaphor of the school anthem. Though only the headmaster emerges as a character, the cast of stereotypes is suitable for what is essentially a comic allegory of English life.

Getting On, an ambitious Chekhovian comedy, involves a fortyish Labour M.P., George Oliver, whose nostalgia for stability ("What we crave in life is order") and linguistic skill links him with the headmaster. His precarious illusion of order depends on an innocence of the sexual and political realities of his world: his son by a first marriage, his young second wife, and a Conservative homosexual M.P. form a strange triangle; his West Indian constituent who claimed that neighbors were poisoning her dog is not mad, as he had believed. Reality seems too complex for his categorizing, analytical mind, and, despite his belief in logic and language, he concludes, after a hilariously unsuccessful attempt to order a taxi, "Words fail me." Though continually confronted with proof of the pointlessness of work, George persists with established values. (His only radical action, from an English viewpoint, is throwing a bucket of water at a dog that perpetually fouls his doorstep.) Yet, as the punning title suggests, the ultimate reward for hard work is aging and death.

Habeas Corpus, which focuses on a sadly lecherous, aging general practitioner in Hove, somewhat uneasily balances a well-made farce plot with Bennett's verbal comedy, more elegiac than ever amid a frenzy of trouserless men, missed assignations, and a spinster with an artificial bust. The wit, frequently obsessed with the decline of England or of individual Englishmen, often slows down the crucial pacing of the farce, which, in turn, sometimes undercuts the impact of Bennett's parodies. The wistful tone of the comedy is apparent in the doctor's lament for his lacerated sensibility: "They parade before me bodies the color of tripe and the texture of junket. Is this the image of God, this sagging parcel of vanilla blancmange hoisted day after day on to the consulting table? Is this the precious envelope of the soul?" Though such disillusionment does not stop his pursuit of a nubile young patient, his later reference to "the long littleness of life" as he prepares to examine her attests to the general elegiac note of the play. This mood derives partly from the songs and verses, like those in Auden's verse plays, that allow characters to comment directly to the audience as the action stops: "So if you get your heart's desire,/our longings come to pass,/Remember in each other's beds,/ It isn't going to last." The resulting vaudeville atmosphere, however effective, softens the hard lines of the farce, a form that Bennett wisely abandoned in the plays that followed.

The Old Country, another comic elegy on the continuing decline of England, initially puzzles the viewer with its tricky setting, a country house outside Moscow in which a British defector, Hilary, and his wife, Bron, have tried to re-create the England he betrayed. A visit from Hilary's sister and her husband, Duff, ostensibly in Russia to lecture on Forster, brings the offer of a return to an England Hilary will no longer recognize. Hilary and Duff, like Bennett former Oxbridge men, conduct a typically loving yet satirical analysis of Forster *dicta* like "Only connect."

In the debate over the desirability of return Bron asks where in England they could leave their doors unlocked for long periods; her sister-in-law replies, "Wiltshire once. Not any more. There are muggers in Malmesbury." Hilary attempts a more balanced assessment of the overall situation: "No Gamages. No Pontins. No more trains from Kemble to Cirencester. No Lyons. On the other hand I read of the Renaissance of the small bakery; country breweries revive. Better bread, better beer. They come from Florence to shop in Marks and Spencer. It is not an easy decision." But Bron angrily rejects this supposed objectivity as another instance of his ability to argue both sides simultaneously. Certainly Hilary does seem the archetypal Bennett verbal juggler as he tries to define the English response to experience with a complex litany of familiar allusions: "Irony is inescapable. We're conceived in irony. We float in it from the womb. It's the amniotic fluid. It's the silver sea. It's the waters at their priestlike task washing away guilt and purpose and responsibility. Joking but not joking. Caring but not caring. Serious but not serious." *The Old Country*, Bennett's most successful play after *Forty Years On*, dramatizes the dangerous moral and political consequences of this semantic playfulness.

Green Forms, one of two television plays collected as *Office Suite*, satirizes the attempts of government workers to define the unknown with comforting jargon. Perplexed by the computerization of the system and the expendability of employees and whole offices, the workers display typical linguistic resourcefulness: "Southport is being wound down . . . . Wound down. Wound up. Phased out anyway. I hope she hasn't been made . . . you know . . . . Well . . . redundant. I wouldn't like to think she's been made redundant; she was very nicely spoken." *A Visit from Miss Prothero*, a one-acter, abounds in cozy malice as a retired bureaucrat gradually realizes the worthlessness of his life's work. In his world gossip masquerades as folk wisdom: Miss Prothero comments on an associate's eczema, "The doctor thinks it's nerves. I think it's those tights. Man-made fibers don't do for everybody. I pay if I wear crimplene."

Enjoy depicts a typical northern family, the son a transsexual social worker, the daughter a prostitute ("She's exceptional. You won't find girls like Linda stood on every street corner"), while the parents await the demolition of their home and speculate on their future residence: "It's a maisonette. They're built more on the human scale. That's the latest thing now, the human scale." Unfortunately, no authentic unifying tone emerges from the play's blend of folk comedy, parody, and satire on deranged social planners. That the old life with its family betrayals and vulgarities does not merit preservation, except as a historical curiosity, weakens concern for the fates of the couple, even though there are affecting moments.

The Writer in Disguise, a collection of plays Bennett wrote for television, is uneven in quality and sometimes relies on a familiar mixture of nostalgia for and broad satire of British seaside life (*All Day on the Sand* and *Afternoon Off*), but it does reveal his ability to write for film and videotape as well as for the stage. The best of the collection, *Me, I'm Afraid of Virginia Woolf*, develops Bennett's ambiguous views of Woolf and of high culture in general and through the career of a literature teacher mocks the futility of "further education." As is frequent with Bennett, the best lines are not necessarily those that reinforce the key themes but those that primarily display his impressive wit, as when the protagonist attempts to explain unorthodox sex to his mother: "Having tea in Marshall and Snelgrove's isn't lesbianism."

A series of monologues, *Talking Heads*, further displays Bennett's skill at conveying character through speech. Aside from the strained and clichéd *Her Big Chance*, these monologues magically fuse pathos with their comedy and generate sympathy even for upper-class ladies in decline (*Soldiering On*). The strongest is *Bed Among the Lentils*, a showcase for Maggie Smith as the alcoholic wife of a vicar saved by an affair with a Pakistani shopkeeper. Though it never quite transcends the stereotypes of warring female parishioners ("If you think squash is a competitive activity, try flower arrangement") and sexually adroit Third Worlders, the monologue brilliantly balances its compassion for the trapped wife with a satire of Christian values.

Single Spies, a program of one-acters, raises disturbing questions about patriotism and personal integrity in terms reminiscent of E. M. Forster, whose life seems of obsessive interest in a number of Bennett works. *An Englishman Abroad* derives from actress Coral Browne's encounter with Guy Burgess in Moscow, and *A Question of Attribution* wittily analyzes ethics and loyalties through conversations between Anthony Blunt, the "fourth man," and Elizabeth II: "I was talking about art. I'm not sure that she was." The play more than satisfies the uneasy anticipation created by the promise of a royal portrait: "If I am doing nothing, I like to be doing nothing to some purpose. That is what leisure means." With its Wildean echoes, the dialogue balances mockery of narrowness with insight into an impossible role. These two plays, while clearly sympathetic to their protagonists, differentiate between the physically and emotionally unkempt Burgess and the colder, more controlled, and provocatively ambiguous Blunt, for whom espionage may have been merely an elaborate game enabling him to savor his intellectual superiority to his compatriots. *Single Spies* reveals Bennett's increasing interest in biographical drama, a tendency evident in early works with references to the private lives of T. E. Lawrence or Forster and culminating in the plays on Kafka and George III.

The Insurance Man, written for television, wittily attempts to reconcile Kafka's career as both an insurance executive and partner in an asbestos factory with the view of the universe conveyed by his fiction. Kafka's concern for a laborer, Franz, suffering from a work-related malady, leads him to offer Franz a job in the factory. The bitter comedy of Bennett's version of Kafka's world ("Just because you're the injured party, it doesn't mean you are not the guilty party") ingeniously reveals a system in which even well-meaning officials like Kafka are doomed to intensify human suffering.

Less successful is *Kafka's Dick*, which traces Kafka's antiauthoritarian themes to his relationship with his father. The play is long for what it accomplishes and brilliant in some set pieces, but it is more a series of vaudeville skits than a coherent work. The Kafka who returns to life to learn that his writings have not been destroyed as he wished tries futilely to balance posthumous fame with the attendant loss of privacy (the title allusion especially disturbs him) and the rivalry with writers like Proust: "My room was noisy. It was next door to my parents. When I was trying to write I had to listen to them having sexual intercourse. I'm the one who needed the cork-lined room. And he's the greatest writer of the twentieth century. O God."

Even more ambitious is *The Madness of George III*. Bennett's earlier portrait of Elizabeth II demonstrated an ability to get inside the skin of unexpected characters, though George III's bad press makes him a special challenge. Bennett skillfully weaves in necessary exposition: "Pitt was on our side then. Now he has stitched himself into the flag and passed himself off as the spirit of the nation and the Tories as the collective virtue of England . . . ." But such speeches lack the force of parallel passages in Shakespeare's histories. Bennett's emphasis on scatological humor seems appropriate in an analysis of George's unfortunate physical symptoms, some of which result from the uninformed arrogance of his physicians and all of which reinforce his humanity, a humanity that seems especially vulnerable since his most private functions become matters of public interest and debate. Inviting comparison with such examples of royal madness as Lear and Caligula, George never approaches their tragic dimensions despite Bennett's reference to "tragic hero" in the preface. Bennett's king is too limited intellectually and spiritually for tragic stature, and the audience's continual awareness of his unpleasant symptoms establishes him primarily as a physical man, a Job without the spiritual capacity. Bennett also errs in introducing long passages from Shakespeare's play that, though touching in their picture of Lear's regeneration, underscore the limitations of his own psychology and language. The curtailing of George's mad speeches, which Bennett justifies in the preface, tends to minimize any sense of the king's mental and emotional complexity; it is thus difficult to know whether Bennett might have transcended his talent for making jokes about doctors and politicians to present a figure of real stature. Just as the copious prefaces and production notes for this play and others suggest another Shaw, so does Bennett's gift for debunking history; the portrait of a loquacious Burke who bored his auditors is especially amusing. Despite some problems this play represents real development for Bennett in its attempt to define a character in the context of a complex society, with the character a ruler and the society that of eighteenth-century English politics.

Bennett's ability to subordinate his verbal flourishes to some larger purpose is evident in his film scripts *Prick Up Your Ears* and *A Private Function*. In fact, the former unnecessarily downplays Joe Orton's genius with language in order to highlight more cinematic material about his sexual antics, and thus Orton's core, the rich talent that justified the biography, seems missing, though the film has some brilliant episodes. Less ambitious, *A Private Function* succeeds in its treatment of the social hierarchy in a postwar northern town as a chiropodist and his wife try to overcome class barriers and an unfair system of rationing with the help of an illegal pig for a dinner honoring the newly wed Princess Elizabeth. The polished dialogue and comic atmosphere suggest Chaucer's fabliaux, and Bennett's signature scatological humor seems exactly right in a work involving a pig, a chiropodist, a butcher, and a bizarre farm family. Like Bennett's best comedy the film creates a believable social world, and the dialogue reaffirms his status as England's preeminent comic dramatist. Impressively prolific and apparently eager to expand his thematic range, Bennett has, through a long career, continued to fulfill the dazzling promise of his early work.

—Burton S. Kendle

BENTLEY, Eric (Russell)

Nationality: American. **Born:** Bolton, Lancashire, England, 14 September 1916; moved to the United States, 1939; became citizen, 1948. **Education:** Bolton School; Oxford University, B.A. 1938, B.Lit. 1939; Yale University, New Haven, Connecticut, Ph.D. 1941. **Family:** Married 1) Maja Tschernjakow (marriage dissolved); 2) Joanne Davis in 1953; twin sons. **Career:** Teacher, Black Mountain College, North Carolina, 1942-44, and University of Minnesota, Minneapolis, 1944-48; Brander Matthews professor of dramatic literature, Columbia University, New York, 1952-69; freelance writer, 1970-73; Katharine Cornell professor of theatre, State University of New York, Buffalo, 1974-82. Professor of comparative literature, University of Maryland, College Park, 1982-89. Charles Eliot Norton professor of poetry, Harvard University, Cambridge, Massachusetts, 1960-61; Fulbright professor, Belgrade, 1980. Drama critic, *New Republic*, New York, 1952-56. **Awards:** Guggenheim fellowship, 1948; Rockefeller grant, 1949; American Academy grant, 1953; Longview award, for criticism, 1961; Ford grant, 1964; George Jean Nathan award, for criticism, 1967; CBS fellowship, 1976; Obie award, 1978; Theater Festival gold medal, 1985. D.F.A.: University of Wisconsin, Madison, 1975; Litt.D.: University of East Anglia, Norwich, 1979. **Member:** American Academy of Arts and Sciences, 1969. **Agent:** Jack Tantleff, 375 Greenwich Street, Suite 700, New York, New York 10013; or, Joy Westendarp, International Copyright Bureau, 22A Aubrey House, Maida Avenue, London W2 1TQ, England. **Address:** 194 Riverside Drive, Apartment 4-E, New York, New York 10025, U.S.A.

Publications

Plays

A Time to Die, and A Time to Live: Two Short Plays, adaptations of plays by Euripides and Sophocles (as *Commitments*, produced New York, 1967). New York, Grove Press, 1967.

Sketches in *DMZ Revue* (produced New York, 1968).

The Red White and Black, music by Brad Burg (produced New York, 1970). Published in *Liberation* (New York), May 1971.

Are You Now or Have You Ever Been: The Investigation of Show-Business by the Un-American Activities Committee 1947-1958 (produced New Haven, Connecticut, 1972; New York, 1973; Birmingham, 1976; London, 1977). New York, Harper, 1972.

The Recantation of Galileo Galilei: Scenes from History Perhaps (produced Detroit, 1973). New York, Harper, 1972.

Expletive Deleted (produced New York, 1974). Published in *Win* (New York), 6 June 1974.

From the Memoirs of Pontius Pilate (produced Buffalo and New York, 1976). Included in *Rallying Cries*, 1977.

Rallying Cries: Three Plays (includes *Are You Now or Have You Ever Been, The Recantation of Galileo Galilei, From the Memoirs of Pontius Pilate*). Washington, D.C., New Republic Books, 1977; as *Are You Now or Have You Ever Been and Other Plays*, New York, Grove Press, 1981.

The Kleist Variations: Three Plays. Baton Rouge, Louisiana, Oracle Press, 1982.

1. *Wannsee* (produced Buffalo, 1978).
2. *The Fall of the Amazons* (produced Buffalo, 1979).
3. *Concord* (produced Buffalo, 1982).

Larry Parks' Day in Court (produced New York, 1979).

Lord Alfred's Lover (produced Gainesville, Florida, 1979). Toronto, Personal Library, 1981; in *Monstrous Martyrdoms*, 1985.

Monstrous Martyrdoms: Three Plays (includes *Lord Alfred's Lover, H for Hamlet, German Requiem*). Buffalo, Prometheus, 1985.

Round Two. Published in *Gay Plays: Four*, edited by Michael Wilcox, London, Methuen, 1990.

Other

A Century of Hero-Worship: A Study of the Idea of Heroism in Carlyle and Nietzsche, with Notes on Other Hero-Worshipers of Modern Times. Philadelphia, Lippincott, 1944; as *The Cult of the Superman*, London, Hale, 1947.

The Playwright as Thinker: A Study of Drama in Modern Times. New York, Reynal, 1946; as *The Modern Theatre: A Study of Dramatists and the Drama*, London, Hale, 1948.

Bernard Shaw: A Reconsideration. New York, New Directions, 1947; London, Hale, 1950; revised edition as *Bernard Shaw 1856-1950*, New Directions, 1957; as *Bernard Shaw*, London, Methuen, 1967.

In Search of Theater. New York, Knopf, 1953; London, Dobson, 1954; New York, Applause Books, 1992.

The Dramatic Event: An American Chronicle. New York, Horizon Press, and London, Dobson, 1954.

What Is Theatre? A Query in Chronicle Form. New York, Horizon Press, 1956; London, Dobson, 1957.

The Life of the Drama. New York, Atheneum, 1964; London, Methuen, 1965; New York, Applause Theatre Books, 1991.

The Theatre of Commitment and Other Essays on Drama in Our Society. New York, Atheneum, 1967; London, Methuen, 1968.

What Is Theatre? Incorporating "The Dramatic Event" and Other Reviews 1944-1967. New York, Atheneum, 1968; London, Methuen, 1969.
Theatre of War: Comments on 32 Occasions. New York, Viking Press, and London, Eyre Methuen, 1972.
The Brecht Commentaries 1943-1980. New York, Grove Press, and London, Eyre Methuen, 1981.
The Pirandello Commentaries. Lincoln, University of Nebraska Department of Modern Languages and Literatures, 1985.
The Brecht Memoir. New York, Performing Arts Journal Publications, 1986; Northwestern University Press, 1991.
Thinking about the Playwright: Comments from Four Decades. Evanston, Illinois, Northwestern University Press, 1987.
Bertolt Brecht: A Study Guide. New York, Grove Press, 1995.

Editor, *The Importance of "Scrutiny": Selections from "Scrutiny," A Quarterly Review, 1932-1948*. New York, G.W. Stewart, 1948.
Editor and Part Translator, *From the Modern Repertory*. Denver, University of Denver Press, series 1 and 2, 1949-52; Bloomington, Indiana University Press, series 3, 1956.
Editor, *The Play: A Critical Anthology*. New York, Prentice Hall, 1951.
Editor, *Shaw on Music*. New York, Doubleday, 1955.
Editor and Part Translator, *The Modern Theatre*. New York, Doubleday, 6 vols., 1955-60.
Editor and Part Translator, *The Classic Theatre*. New York, Doubleday, 4 vols., 1958-61.
Editor and Translator, *Let's Get a Divorce! and Other Plays*. New York, Hill and Wang, 1958.
Editor and Part Translator, *Works of Bertolt Brecht*. New York, Grove Press, 1961.
Editor and Part Translator, *The Genius of the Italian Theatre*. New York, New American Library, 1964.
Editor, *The Storm over "The Deputy."* New York, Grove Press, 1964.
Editor, *Songs of Bertolt Brecht and Hanns Eisler*. . . . New York, Oak, 1966.
Editor, *The Theory of the Modern Stage: An Introduction to Modern Theatre and Drama*. London, Penguin, 1968; New York, Applause Books, 1997.
Editor and Part Translator, *The Great Playwrights: Twenty-Five Plays with Comments by Critics and Scholars*. New York, Doubleday, 2 vols., 1970.
Editor, *Thirty Years of Treason: Excerpts from Hearings before the House Committee on Un-American Activities 1938-1968*. New York, Viking Press, 1971.
Editor and Translator, *Dramatic Repertoire*. New York, Applause, 1985.

Translator, *The Private Life of the Master Race*, by Brecht. New York, James Laughlin, 1944.
Translator, *Parables for the Theatre: The Good Woman of Setzuan, and The Caucasian Chalk Circle*, by Brecht. Minneapolis, University of Minnesota Press, 1948; revised edition, University of Minnesota Press, and London, Oxford University Press, 1965.
Translator, with others, *Naked Masks: Five Plays*, by Pirandello. New York, Dutton, 1952.
Translator, *Orpheus in the Underworld* (libretto), by Hector Crémieux and Ludovic Halévy. New York, Program Publishing Company, 1956.
Translator, *The Wire Harp*, by Wolf Biermann. New York, Harcourt Brace, 1968.
Translator, *Two Plays*, by Brecht. New York, New American Library, 1983.
Translator, *Inspector and 3 Plays*, by Nikolai Gogol. New York, Applause Books, 1987.
Translator, *Woyzeck*, by Georg Buchner. New York, Samuel French, 1991.
Translator, *Pirandello's Major Plays*, by Luigi Pirandello. Evanston, Illinois, Northwestern University Press, 1991.
Translator, *The First Lulu*. New York, Applause Books, 1993.
Translator, *Spring's Awakening: Tragedy of Childhood*, by Frank Wedekind. New York, Applause Books, 1995.
Translator, *Pirandello: Plays*. Evanston, Illinois, Northwestern University Press, 1998.

Recordings (Folkways): *Bentley on Brecht*, Riverside, 1963; *Brecht Before the Un-American Activities Committee*, 1963; *A Man's a Man*, Spoken Arts, 1963; *Songs of Hanns Eisler*, 1965; *The Elephant Calf/Dear Old Democracy*, 1967; *Bentley on Biermann*, 1968; *Eric Bentley Sings The Queen of 42nd Street*, 1974.

*

Manuscript Collection: Boston University Library.

Critical Studies: *The Play and Its Critic: Essays for Eric Bentley* edited by Michael Bertin, Lanham, University Press of America, 1986; "In Praise of Eric Bentley" by Gordon Rogoff, in *Theater* (New Haven, Connecticut), Spring 1987, pp. 73-74; "Shaw 40 Years Later–Eric Bentley Speaks His Mind on Eleven Neglected Plays: Getting Married, Overruled, On the Rocks, and Others" by Alfred Turco, Jr., in *Shaw: The Annual of Bernard Shaw Studies* (University Park, Pennsylvania), 1987, pp. 7-29; "The Voice of America and the Voice of Eric Bentley," in *American Writing Today*, edited by Richard Kostelanetz, Troy, New York, Whitston, 1991.

Theatrical Activities:
Director: **Plays**—*Sweeney Agonistes* by T.S. Eliot, Salzburg, 1949; *Him* by e.e. cummings, Salzburg, 1950; *The House of Bernarda Alba* by García Lorca, Dublin, 1950; *The Iceman Cometh* (co-director) by Eugene O'Neill, Zurich, 1950; *Purgatory* by W.B. Yeats, and *Riders to the Sea* and *The Shadow of the Glen* by J.M. Synge, U.S. tour, 1951; *The Good Woman of Setzuan* by Brecht, New York, 1956.

Eric Bentley comments:

(1988) Eric Bentley quotes from an interview with Jerome Clegg:

> Clegg: Why on earth did you have to write a play? For you are nothing if not critical.
> Bentley: Maybe the impulse was to write a counter-play.
> Clegg: Counter to what?
> Bentley: A (good) performance of the Anouilh Antigone—in its integrity, not in the Galantiere adaptation-distortion—had riled me. So I had to write a "correct" Antigone; set Anouilh straight. The same with Brecht.
> Clegg: Meaning?

Bentley: He made such absurd demands upon his people. What else could Mother Courage have done?

Clegg: Galileo?

Bentley: Brecht wilfully chose to misunderstand him. The recantation could not possibly be taken as a betrayal of Marxism.

Clegg: So it was historical correctness you were after? Oh, you and your scholarly background!

Bentley: Rubbish. There would be no possible "historical correctness" for Antigone. It is a human correctness that interests me. Telling a story more honestly—truer to *our* time, if you will, not necessarily truer to some other time.

Clegg: Someone had called your dramatic works "no nonsense plays."

Bentley: Can one tell the Jesus story without nonsense? There would be no precedents.

Clegg: The New Testament nonsense?

Bentley: A very over-rated book.

Clegg: "Better than the New Testament"—is that a good description of your Jesus-Pilate play?

Bentley: I hope so. Shaw spoke of himself as "better than Shakespeare" with something like that in mind.

Clegg: He also put a question mark after the phrase.

Bentley: As I do.

Clegg: What was your first play? I want to know how all this got started.

Bentley: Which is the wickedest of all your wicked questions.

Clegg: Answer it.

Bentley: My first play wasn't a play of mine at all, it was other people's plays.

Clegg: Especially Bertolt Brecht's.

Bentley: Actually, my first-play-that-was-really-someone-else's-play was not a Brecht, it was a Meilhac and Halévy.

Clegg: Who dey?

Bentley: Jacques Offenbach. The first time I launched out on my own was when I re-did the libretto to Offenbach's *Orpheus* for the New York City Opera Company.

Clegg: Everyone loved it.

Bentley: The press hated it. Except the communist paper.

Clegg: So you took up the Commie cause in *Are You Now or Have You Ever Been*?

Bentley: Well, that was some centuries later, and it wasn't the commie cause.

Clegg: But you do champion causes. What came next?

Bentley: *Lord Alfred's Lover*?

Clegg: Exactly. Your gay liberation play.

Bentley: Touché.

Clegg: After which I lose you. No causes but lots of Heinrich von Kleist.

Bentley: My three Kleist Variations. In which lots of Kleist got thrown overboard—and not all causes were forgotten . . .

Clegg: No?

Bentley: No! Didn't you interview me on this point, and isn't your interview the preface to *The Kleist Variations*, published sometime, somewhere?

Clegg: Is it? Oh, yes. What's your latest?

Bentley: Another gay item.

Clegg: But prompted by a non-gay item, Schnitzler's *Reigen*? *La Ronde*?

Bentley: Transposed to the 1970s and New York. *Round Two*.

*   *   *

The majority of Eric Bentley's plays are history plays that deal with figures who have either attained the status of myth or who are on the verge of entering the popular imagination. He is consequently free to work on our assumptions about his characters, and he usually works toward a radical point—the shoring up of individual identity against the inroads of institutional power, be it of the church or the state.

Bentley is a Shavian dramatist in that not only does language matter but his talent makes it central to his plays. He may rely on a stage grouping, and he may use every available stage nuance, but in the end it is the pure dialectic of impassioned speech that gives his plays their force.

Bentley is Shavian as well in the less obvious sense of writing plays against the stage, the stage being but the reflection of our melodramatic lives. Against the commonly held belief that our enemies are evil personified and that ours is a kill-or-be-killed world, he grants the antagonist an argument and creates a scene in which both sides are right from their own perspective. His plays are thus historical tragedies, not mere spectacles of put-upon humanity.

We can see all of these ingredients at work in his early play *The Recantation of Galileo Galilei,* his response to the *Galileo* of Bertolt Brecht. A close comparison of the two makes for fascinating reading. If Brecht writes inspired science fiction, with a cast of inquisitors who are mostly clowns, Bentley carries the conviction of political reality, his play building to the climax of the trial that Brecht necessarily avoids. Brecht's *Galileo* may be the greater play, its epic scope, easy manner, and fine touch of folk wisdom bearing the marks of genius. Nevertheless, Bentley's mastery of the issues, his sense of the argument, and his scene of contention create a trial that is the best set piece since Shaw's *Saint Joan*.

As for the protagonists, if Brecht's appetitive man ends in cynicism and despair, his false confession before the threat of torture becoming his true confession of self-hatred for having caved in, Bentley reverses the human dilemma by making his Galileo lie for the greater good. His refined man is a naive intellectual headed for a rude awakening, but an awakening nevertheless. The cynicism of Brecht's protagonist is shifted in Bentley's play to the shoulders of a real antagonist, the Jesuit scientist and priest Scheiner.

If Bentley's Galileo is an ideological man who fights for the ideal, his Oscar Wilde, by contrast, fights for the right to be himself. The description nicely fits the title of the play, *Lord Alfred's Lover,* which implies, of course, that Wilde is not yet established as himself. The playwright's masterstroke is to "tell" the story of the trials through the expedient of the aging Bosie's confession to a priest. He thereby not only wins sympathy for Bosie but also subverts the intentions of those who would praise Wilde at Bosie's expense. (The adulation of Wilde when carried to an extreme sounds suspiciously like gay bashing, the Bosies of the world be damned!) By joining the two fates Bentley encompasses the scope of the homosexual journey that begins with Bosie, the man who never made peace with himself, and ends with Wilde, the man who did but at a cost.

Since the conventional audience reads the title for their definition of Wilde, Bentley establishes Wilde against their reading. The notorious homosexual is their creation, his notoriety being their contribution to the case. They would prefer the portrait of a self-destructive man, which absolves them of guilt. Instead, they get the portrait of their victim, which does not.

Of course, it is rash of Bentley to suggest that the gay Prime Minister Rosebery actively conspired against Wilde, but this is a mere quibble given the fine scene he creates for them at Reading Gaol. Threatened by association with Wilde, influential homosexuals may have helped bring him down. In any case, while we can argue that their "imaginary conversation" never took place, we can also imagine it as taking place every day in the minds of people who are forced into acting against themselves.

In a totally different key is a series of plays collectively known as *The Kleist Variations*. Contemporary readings of the plays of Heinrich von Kleist, they reveal the earlier playwright in a more metaphysical vein. To Kleist's astounding vision Bentley offers the challenge of a whole new world of sexual politics, political hatreds, and apocalyptic fears. *Concord,* the variation of Kleist's *Broken Jug,* is typical of the three plays. Set in Puritan New England, it turns the tables on a sexual bounder and instead makes him the victim of Puritan hatred (for which can be read "family values"). A "monstrous martyrdom" comically turned, it exposes the same hypocrisy that hit Wilde and Galileo, while it inspires the same hope.

—Michael Bertin

BERKOFF, Steven

Nationality: British. **Born:** Stepney, London, 3 August 1937. **Education:** Schools in Stepney; Hackney Downs Grammar School, London; Webber-Douglas Academy of Dramatic Art, London, 1958-59; École Jacques Lecoq, Paris, 1965. **Family:** Married Shelley Lee in 1976. **Career:** Actor in repertory in Nottingham, Liverpool, Coventry, and at Citizens' Theatre Glasgow, for six years. Founding director, London Theatre Group, 1973—. **Awards:** Los Angeles Drama Critics Circle award, for directing, 1983. **Agent:** Joanna Marston, Rosica Colin Ltd., 1 Clareville Grove Mews, London SW7 5AH, England.

Publications

Plays

In the Penal Colony, adaptation of a story by Kafka (produced London, 1968). Included in *The Trial, Metamorphosis, In the Penal Colony: Three Theatre Adaptations from Franz Kafka*, 1988.

Metamorphosis, adaptation of a story by Kafka (produced London, 1968; Los Angeles, 1982; New York, 1989). With *The Trial*, Ambergate, Derbyshire, Amber Lane Press, 1981.

The Trial, adaptation of a novel by Kafka (produced in the Netherlands, 1971; London, 1973). With *Metamorphosis*, Ambergate, Derbyshire, Amber Lane Press, 1981.

Agamemnon, adaptation of a play by Aeschylus (produced London, 1971; revised version produced London, 1976). Included in *East, Agamemnon, The Fall of the House of Usher*, 1977.

Knock at the Manor Gate, adaptation of a story by Kafka (produced Falmer, Sussex, and London, 1972).

Miss Julie Versus Expressionism, adaptation of a play by Strindberg (produced London, 1973).

Lunch (as *Mr. Prufrock's Songs*, produced London, 1974; revised version, as *Lunch*, produced London, 1981). Included in *West, Lunch, Harry's Christmas*, 1985.

The Fall of the House of Usher, adaptation of the story by Poe (produced Edinburgh, 1974; London, 1975). Included in *East, Agamemnon, The Fall of the House of Usher*, 1977.

East (produced Edinburgh and London, 1975). Included in *East, Agamemnon, The Fall of the House of Usher*, 1977.

East, Agamemnon, The Fall of the House of Usher. London, Calder, 1977; New York, Riverrun Press, 1982.

Greek (produced London, 1980; Los Angeles, 1982; New York, 1983). With *Decadence*, London, Calder, 1982; New York, Riverrun Press, 1983.

West (produced London, 1980). Included in *West, Lunch, Harry's Christmas*, 1985.

Decadence (produced London, 1981). With *Greek*, London, Calder, 1982; New York, Riverrun Press, 1983.

Harry's Christmas (produced London, 1985). Included in *West, Lunch, Harry's Christmas*, 1985.

The Tell-Tale Heart, adaptation of the story by Poe (produced London, 1985).

West, Lunch, Harry's Christmas. London, Faber, and New York, Grove Press, 1985.

Kvetch (produced Los Angeles, 1986; New York, 1987; Edinburgh and London, 1991). With *Acapulco*, London, Faber, 1986; New York, Grove Press, 1987.

Sink the Belgrano! (produced London, 1986). With *Massage*, London, Faber, 1987.

Acapulco (produced Los Angeles, 1986; London, 1992). With *Kvetch*, London, Faber, 1986; New York, Grove Press, 1987.

The Trial, Metamorphosis, In the Penal Colony: Three Theatre Adaptations from Franz Kafka. Oxford, Amber Lane, 1988.

Decadence and Other Plays (includes *East, West, Greek)*. London, Faber, 1989.

Short Stories

Gross Intrusion and Other Stories. London, Calder, and Dallas, Riverrun Press, 1979.

Other

Steven Berkoff's America. London, Hutchinson, 1988.

A Prisoner in Rio. London, Hutchinson, 1989.

I Am Hamlet. London, Faber, 1989; New York, Grove Press, 1990.

Theatre of Steven Berkoff. London, Methuen, 1992.

Wriolanus in Deutschland. Oxford, Amber Lane, 1992.

Meditations on Metamorphosis. London, Faber, 1995.

Free Associations—An Autobiography. London, 1996.

Graft: Tales of an Actor. London, Oberon Books, 1998.

*

Theatrical Activities:
Director: **Plays**—All his own plays; *Macbeth*, London, 1970; *The Zoo Story* by Edward Albee, Newcastle upon Tyne, 1973; *Coriolanus*, New York, 1988; *Salome* by Oscar Wilde, Dublin, 1988, Edinburgh, 1989, London 1989, Australia and Japan, 1992.

Actor: **Plays**—Most of his own plays; Gentleman Caller in *The Glass Menagerie* by Tennessee Williams, London, 1971; title role in *Hamlet*, London, 1980; Herod in *Salome* by Oscar Wilde, Dublin, 1988, Edinburgh and London, 1989, Australia and Japan, 1992. **Films**—*A Clockwork Orange*, 1971; *Barry Lyndon*, 1975; *The Passenger*, 1975; *Joseph Andrews*, 1977; *McVicar*, 1980; *Outland*, 1981; *Octopussy*, 1983; *Beverly Hills Cop*, 1984; *Rambo: First Blood, Part II*, 1985; *Revolution*, 1985; *Absolute Beginners*, 1986; *Under the Cherry Moon*, 1986; *The Krays*, 1990; *Decadence*, 1993; *Fair Game*, 1995; *Another 9 1/2 Weeks*, 1996. **Television**—*Charlie Was a Rich Man*, 1981; *Sins*, 1986; *War and Remembrance*, 1989; *Tell-Tale Heart*, 1991; *Silent Night*, adaptation of *Harry's Christmas*, 1991.

* * *

Through his appearances in three of Hollywood's most successful motion pictures—*Octopussy, Beverly Hills Cop,* and *Rambo*—Steven Berkoff became one of the cinema's favorite villains. For those who knew Berkoff through his stage work in Britain and in Los Angeles it was an unexpected transformation, as unlikely for a theatrical outsider as his subsequent embrace by Britain's National Theatre.

Long before he appeared in films, Berkoff had established his own dedicated following, an audience primed to admire the violent flow of his language as a dramatist and the physicality of his theatrical style. Where realism struggled to represent the inarticulacy of ordinary life, Berkoff gave his characters pages of poetic diatribe driven by profane imagery and obscene rhyme. He combined the street language of London's East End with Shakespearean grandiloquence. Through the threatening presence of motorcycles and muscular actors in leather and denim, his visual images shared the urgent violence of his language.

Berkoff's debt to classical theater in his original plays was made clear by his productions of classics, ranging from Aeschylus to Shakespeare, and his adaptations of Kafka and Edgar Allan Poe. But his originality was also poured in great measure into those plays. In Berkoff's *Agamemnon,* for instance, the arrival of the watchman at the beginning of the play required an actor to exhaust himself on a quarter-mile run before the play began and then collapse onto the stage with his message. When a chorus is required, in his original work or in his production of a classic, it is as organic as any of the leading characters.

Reassuringly for those who cherished his iconoclasm, Berkoff reinvested much of his Hollywood earnings in stage projects that remained faithful to his chosen theatrical prophets. Very early in his career he chose difficult masters, admiring, for instance, the discipline and formal skills of Bertolt Brecht as both playwright and director and noting with particular interest the way in which Brecht was able to develop his technique and beliefs through his own company, the Berliner Ensemble. It was a lesson he applied when he formed his own company, the London Theatre Group, where a Berkoff school of acting and presentation was carefully developed.

His next master was Antonin Artaud. All of Berkoff's theatrical work demonstrates Artaud's dedication to using the theater as a visceral art, drawing its energy from "the lower echelons of the body," from sexual and primal urges that can unleash profound feelings in actor and spectator. He once described his relationship with Artaud in clearly sexual terms when he said, "Since I started with Artaud I've never flirted with anyone else."

Like the Living Theatre of Julian Beck and Judith Malina, however, and rather unlike Artaud, Berkoff has found in the primal physicality of his theater a means of expressing political ideas. His disgust at Britain's conduct during the Falkland Islands War in 1982 was dramatized in his play *Sink the Belgrano!,* a diatribe in punk-Shakespearean verse. The play made no concessions to the sensibilities of his admirers, who knew him only for his film work. He scourged the audience with typically violent language, and as in his earliest work, he demanded of his actors extreme physical acts, portraying the dying sailors of the Argentine battleship *Belgrano* in screams and formalized agony. His indictment of the British government was expressed through coarse poetry and comedy that burlesqued the conventions of polite society.

Having demonstrated with *Sink the Belgrano!* that success would not soften his theater, Berkoff consolidated the achievements of his earlier plays. His adaptation of Kafka's *Metamorphosis,* originally tailored to his own athletic performance as the man who is transformed into a giant insect, has proved exceptionally durable. It has been staged by Berkoff in several languages, including a notable French production starring Roman Polanski. The adaptation has paved the way for his particular use of the human body and voice as the prime elements in his productions, powerfully demonstrating his concern for the expression of text through physical images that imprint themselves on the audience's memory. Visionary as his adaptations may be, however—with his use of Poe nightmarish in the extreme—it is the original writing that has proved most influential.

East, the play in which Berkoff first gave a violent representation to his vision of London life, has become a model for younger playwrights seeking to escape the limits of conversational drama. In the play he first mingled a Cockney corruption of Elizabethan-styled verse with sexual and aggressive prose speeches. Structured as a story of growing up in London's East End and with fights and fornication as major themes, the extreme imagery frequently grew into lyrical fantasias: "If I write a bit rationally, I know I fail. For instance, when I talk about a motorbike in *East,* it has to be the best, the shiniest. When I talk about a phallus, it is the largest. . . . Everything has to be extreme." The extreme view of London working-class life continued with the sequel *West* a few years later.

Berkoff's whole vision of drama is one of extremes, as was demonstrated again in his North London reworking of the *Oedipus Tyrannus* of Sophocles, which he called *Greek:* "In *Greek* every speech is an extreme feeling; of tenderness, of passion, of hate." It is typical that, despite the extremity of feeling when the hero Eddie discovers that he has married his mother, Berkoff dispenses with the tragic ending and lets Eddie continue as her husband. Wherever you find it, love is something worth keeping. It is by borrowing such themes as the Oedipus story and submitting them to his own vision that Berkoff achieves much of his intensity.

Decadence was Berkoff's first full-scale assault on the ruling classes, although his distaste for middle-class values was earlier evident in his comically vulgar portrayal of the insect's family in *Metamorphosis.* Gluttony and the buggery of public schools were indulgences ideally suited to gross physical imagery, and the coarse poetry he provided for the couple in evening dress was potently expressed by the man as if the words were vomit. The theatricality of the play was enhanced by his demand that the same actors portray a complementary working-class couple hopelessly in awe of decadence.

In Berkoff's one-man play *Harry's Christmas* he supplied a bitter corrective to the holiday spirit by showing a man whose loneliness leads him each year to recycle the few Christmas cards he has ever collected. Like his other work, the play was designed for sharp physical interpretations of the world rather than representations, and despite his work in Hollywood his plays have continued to be intended to tap the full potentiality of actors and to clear away the trivial routines and reenactments of ordinary activity. With the use of dialogue and monologues, "acting becomes a compulsive medium because I can touch primeval forces and release them—madness and maybe enlightenment." He occasionally finds an inspiration for such expression in existing sources, as in his internationally successful version of Oscar Wilde's *Salome,* first produced for Dublin's Gate Theatre.

Berkoff's Hollywood and other American experiences have been absorbed into his writing, both dramatically and in prose. This is notably so in his published imaginative "screenplay" *A Prisoner in Rio* and in the plays *Kvetch* and *Acapulco.* The latter in particular demonstrate Hollywood's vulnerability to individuals such as Berkoff. In the process of turning him into a star, it allowed him to bear close-range witness to the moviemaking megalomania of actors such as Sylvester Stallone in *Rambo.* Those experiences have been digested with customary bile to become the harsher entertainment of a Berkoff play.

—Ned Chaillet

BERMANGE, Barry

Nationality: British. **Born:** London, 7 November 1933. **Education:** An art school in Essex, 1947-52. **Military Service:** National service, 1952-54. **Family:** Married Maurine Jewel Bright in 1961. **Career:** Assistant designer, Perth Repertory Company, Scotland, 1955; actor and assistant stage manager, Swansea Repertory Company, 1956. **Awards:** Arts Council bursary, 1964; Ohio State University award, 1967; German Critics award, 1968; Karl Sczuka prize (Germany), 1981, 1987. **Address:** 35 Alexandra Park Road, London N10 2DD, England.

Publications

Plays

No Quarter (broadcast 1962; produced London, 1964). Included in *No Quarter and The Interview*, 1969.

Nathan and Tabileth (broadcast 1962; produced Edinburgh and London, 1967). With *Oldenberg*, London, Methuen, 1967.

The Cloud (produced London, 1964).

Four Inventions (includes *The Dreams, Amor Dei, The After-Life, The Evenings of Certain Lives*) (broadcast 1964-65; produced London, 1969).

Oldenberg (televised 1967; produced Edinburgh and London, 1967). With *Nathan and Tabileth*, London, Methuen, 1967.

The Interview (televised 1968; produced London, 1969). Included in *No Quarter and The Interview*, 1969.

Invasion (televised 1969). Included in *No Quarter and The Interview*, 1969.

No Quarter and The Interview (includes *Invasion*). London, Methuen, 1969.

Scenes from Family Life (televised 1969; produced Leatherhead, Surrey, 1974). Published in *Collection: Literature for the Seventies*, edited by Gerald and Nancy S. Messner, Boston, Heath, 1972.

Warcries (broadcast 1981; produced Donaueschingen, 1981).

The Soldiers (broadcast 1985; produced Frankfurt-am-Main, 1985).

The Dreams, Warcries, Kla[um]nge am Mikrophon (produced Kassel, 1987).

Radio Plays: *The Voice of the Peanut*, 1960; *Never Forget a Face*, 1961; *No Quarter*, 1962; *A Glass of Lemonade*, 1962; *Nathan and Tabileth*, 1962; *The Imposters* series, 1962; *Four Inventions*, 1964-65; *The Mortification*, 1964; *The Detour*, 1964; *Paths of Glory*, from the novel by Humphrey Cobb, 1965; *Letters of a Portuguese Nun*, 1966; *As a Man Grows Older*, 1967; *Neues vom Krieg*, 1969 (Germany); *S.O.S.*, 1977 (Netherlands), 1978 (UK); *Social Welfare*, 1979; *Warcries*, 1981 (Germany); *English Speaking People*, 1981 (Germany); *Scenario*, 1981 (Netherlands); *Four Inventions (Reconstruction 1)*, 1983 (Netherlands); *Kla[um]nge am Mikrophon*, 1985 (Germany); *The Soldiers*, 1985 (Germany); *Testament*, 1985 (Germany); *Le Désir*, 1986 (Germany); *Radioville*, 1987 (Germany); *Der gelbe Klang*, 1987 (Germany); *Annulamento*, 1987 (Germany); *4-Channels*, 1989 (Germany); *Big City Nightwork*, 1990 (Germany); *Cielo y Tierra*, 1991 (Germany).

Television Plays: *Oldenberg*, 1967; *The Interview*, 1968; *Tramp*, 1968 (Germany); *Invasion*, 1969; *Scenes from Family Life*, 1969; *International*, 1976; *Stars*, 1976.

*

Critical Studies: "Amor Dei" by Peter Faecke, in *Neues Hörspiel: Essays, Analysen, Gespräche* edited by Klaus Schöning, Frankfurt-am-Main, Suhrkamp, 1970; *Das englische "Radioplay" seit 1945: Typen, Themen, und Formen*, Berlin, Schmidt, 1978, *Barry Bermange: Eine Beschreibung seines Buhnen-, Funk-, und Fernsehdramatischen Werken*, Tubingen, Narr, 1986, and *Ut Pictura/Musica Poesis: Radiokom-position von Barry Bermange*, Giessen, Hoffman, 1986, all by Horst Priessnitz; "Warcries" in *Kirche und Rundfunk 82*, 24 October 1981.

Theatrical Activities:
Director: Most of his own plays.

* * *

The most remarkable characteristic of Barry Bermange's style as a dramatist is his ability to convey a powerful, universal theme with the utmost economy of means. His early plays, which were originally written for the stage, were first produced on radio, a medium ideally suited to capture the full evocativeness of the language, the symbolic power of the stories, and the graceful accuracy of each carefully calculated effect. Indeed, a live audience sometimes seems to disturb the precise timing on which his plays depend, for there is too little room for laughter or any other spontaneous reaction. Bermange has sometimes been compared to Beckett and Ionesco, and his plots are occasionally reminiscent of the theater of the absurd. In *No Quarter,* for example, a fat man and a quiet man seek lodging in a mysterious collapsing hotel. They eventually huddle together in a dark upper-story room, hoping that nothing will happen to them if they stay quite still. But, unlike Ionesco, Bermange rarely exploits dialogue for its own sake. His images do not carry the logic-shattering irrelevance of dadaism, and the plain meaning of *No Quarter* is too apparent for a dadaist work. The fat man and the quiet man represent two recognizable human reactions to the fear that their world is disintegrating. Nor is Bermange an iconoclastic writer. The collapsing hotel is not symbolic, say, of religion falling apart. Unlike the writers of the absurd, Bermange does not delight in pointing out the nonsense of cherished institutions, nor are his stories tantalizingly ridiculous. He does not attempt to give a pleasing frisson to the rational mind by rubbing it the wrong way. The themes of his plays are usually coherent and indeed logical, although they may contain many ambiguities. Bermange is a writer who defies easy categorizing simply because he chooses each technique carefully so as to express most directly his underlying themes. His plays can be absurdist, they can be naturalistic, and they can even include carefully maneuvered happenings. But the styles have always been selected for their appropriateness and not from any a priori assumptions about theater or dramatic art.

In the same way that he chooses his different styles with care, so Bermange distills each effect to its essential elements. Like Marguerite Duras, he sometimes presents an apparently small incident observed in precise detail and separates it from the surrounding life until it exists in significant isolation. In *The Interview* eight men wait in an outer office before being interviewed for a job. The audience never learns what the job is or who is finally selected. The play is solely concerned with the applicants' reactions to one another, and the small details—one man reading a newspaper, another looking at a picture—manage to convey an almost intolerable atmosphere of suspicion and rivalry. In *Nathan and Tabileth* an elderly couple feed the pigeons in the park, return home, and spend the evening by the fire. They are visited by a young man, Bernie, who says that he is their grandson, although they do not recognize him, and who talks of relatives they have forgotten. When Bernie leaves, the couple go to bed, and "darkness comes." Bermange manages to capture in the rambling, repetitive dialogue and in the intense, short soliloquies the shifting concentration of the old. Certain details—the hired boats on the lake, the pigeons, and the glowing fire—emerge in sharp focus, while others slide into a gray and closing background. The timing of the play is calculated to break up the normal pace of events, for the old people do not think consecutively, and the audience is not allowed to do so. Sometimes the characters ramble on about the past, and sometimes they try to cope with the present, with the breaking of a plate or with a scratched hand. With the possible exception of Beckett's *Happy Days,* no other contemporary play conveys with such agonizing plausibility the experience of old age.

The Interview and *Nathan and Tabileth* are both basically naturalistic plays. The observable details have been carefully selected and arranged to provide a particular impact, but the details are convincing on the level of external reality. In *Oldenberg,* however, Bermange caricatures the main characters. A man and a woman decide to let a room in their house. The tenant is a stranger, Oldenberg, whom they have never even met. At first they make considerable efforts to furnish the room comfortably, but then the possibility occurs to them that their tenant may not be English. In a fit of xenophobia, they destroy and desecrate the room they have so carefully prepared. But when he arrives, the stranger is English, and he is blind. *Oldenberg* is an allegory about the way in which people long for change but are afraid of the unfamiliar, of invasion. By using some of the techniques of absurdist writers, Bermange heightens the contradictory emotions caused by the intrusions of visitors.

But perhaps Bermange's most extraordinary achievement has been to compile four "sound inventions," originally for radio but afterward presented through loudspeakers in a darkened auditorium at the Institute of Contemporary Arts in London. The inventions were recorded extracts of interviews with ordinary men and women about their dreams, their reflections on old age, and their beliefs or skepticism about God and an afterlife. The speeches were carefully edited into short, revealing phrases, "orchestrated" with electronic music, and finally presented as totally original works of music drama. In these inventions Bermange's remarkable gift for effectively ordering sound—both ordinary speech patterns and electronic effects—was allied to themes that could scarcely have been expressed effectively any other way. He invented a new form of radio and theatrical experience, the only possible contemporary parallel being Berio's music drama for Italian radio. With equal ingenuity Bermange also wrote an improvisatory work for television, *Invasion,* in which a dinner party is gradually submerged by images of Vietnam flickering across a television screen. Bermange's inventiveness, his assurance in handling different styles and media, and the powerful intensity of his chosen themes have won him a unique position among British dramatists. No other writer can rival him for controlled daring and insight into the potentialities of experimental drama.

—John Elsom

BERNARD, Kenneth

Nationality: American. **Born:** Brooklyn, New York, 7 May 1930. **Education:** City College of New York, B.A. 1953; Columbia University, New York, M.A. 1956, Ph.D. 1962. **Military Service:** Served in the United States Army, 1953-55: private. **Family:** Married Elaine Reiss in 1952; two sons and one daughter. **Career:** Instructor, 1959-62, assistant professor, 1962-66, associate professor, 1967-70, and professor of English, 1971—, Long Island University, Brooklyn. Advisory editor, 1973-75, assistant editor, 1976-78, and fiction editor, 1979—, *Confrontation,* Brooklyn. Vice-president, New York Theatre Strategy, 1972-79. **Awards:** Rockefeller grant, 1971, 1975; Guggenheim fellowship, 1972; Creative Artists Public Service grant, 1973, 1976; National Endowment for the Arts grant, for fiction, 1977; Arvon poetry prize, 1980; Long Island University Trustees awards, for literary achievement, 1982, 1992; New York Foundation for the Arts award, for fiction, 1988. **Address:** 800 Riverside Drive, New York, New York 10032, U.S.A.

Publications

Plays

The Moke-Eater (produced New York, 1968). Included in *Night Club and Other Plays*, 1971.
The Lovers, published in *Trace* (London), May 1969; in *Night Club and Other Plays*, 1971.
Marko's: A Vegetarian Fantasy, published in *Massachusetts Review* (Amherst), Summer 1969.
Night Club (produced New York, 1970). Included in *Night Club and Other Plays*, 1971.
The Monkeys of the Organ Grinder (produced New Brunswick, New Jersey, and New York, 1970). Included in *Night Club and Other Plays*, 1971.
The Unknown Chinaman (produced Omaha, 1971). Published in *Playwrights for Tomorrow 10*, edited by Arthur H. Ballet, Minneapolis, University of Minnesota Press, 1973.
Night Club and Other Plays (includes *The Moke-Eater*, *The Lovers*, *Mary Jane*, *The Monkeys of the Organ Grinder*, *The Giants in the Earth*). New York, Winter House, 1971.
Mary Jane (also director: produced New York, 1973). Included in *Night Club and Other Plays*, 1971.
Goodbye, Dan Bailey, published in *Drama and Theatre* (Fredonia, New York), Spring 1971.
The Magic Show of Dr. Ma-Gico (produced New York, 1973). Published in *Theatre of the Ridiculous*, edited by Bonnie Marranca and Gautam Dasgupta, New York, Performing Arts Journal Publications, 1979; new expanded edition, 1998.
How We Danced While We Burned (produced Yellow Springs, Ohio, 1974). With *La Justice; or, The Cock That Crew*, Santa Maria, California, Asylum Arts, 1990.
King Humpy (produced New York, 1975). Published in *2Plus2* (Lausanne, Switzerland), 1985.
The Sensuous Ape, published in *Penthouse* (New York), September 1975.
The Sixty Minute Queer Show, music by John Braden (produced New York, 1977).
La Justice; or, The Cock That Crew, music by John Braden (produced New York, 1979). With *How We Danced While We Burned*, Santa Maria, California, Asylum Arts, 1990.
La Fin du Cirque (produced New York, 1984). Published in *Grand Street* (New York), 1982; *Clown at Wall* by Kenneth Bernard, New York, Confrontation Press, 1996.
The Panel (produced New York, 1984).
Play with an Ending; or, Columbus Discovers the World (produced New York, 1984).
We Should . . . (A Lie) (produced New York, 1992).

Short Stories

Two Stories. Mount Horeb, Wisconsin, Perishable Press, 1973.
The Maldive Chronicles. New York, Performing Arts Journal Publications, 1987.
From the District File. Boulder, Colorado, Fiction Collective 2, 1992.

Poetry

The Baboon in the Night Club. Santa Maria, California, Asylum Arts Press, 1994.

Other

Clown at Wall (an anthology of drama, poetry, and fiction). New York, Confrontation Press, 1996.

*

Manuscript Collections: Lincoln Center Library of the Performing Arts, New York; University of Minnesota, Minneapolis; Special Collections, Columbia University.

Critical Studies: Introduction by Michael Feingold to *Night Club and Other Plays*, 1971; "A Collaboration: Kenneth Bernard and John Vaccaro" by Gerald Rabkin, in *Performing Arts Journal* (New York), Spring-Summer 1978; *The Original Theatre of New York* by Stefan Brecht, Frankfurt am Main, Suhrkamp, 1978; *Contemporary American Dramatists 1960-1980* by Ruby Cohn, London, Macmillan, and New York, Grove Press, 1982; *The Darkness We Carry: The Drama of the Holocaust* by Robert Skloot, Madison, University of Wisconsin Press, 1988; article by Rosette LaMont in *Stages* (Norwood, New Jersey), 1992; "Cries and Whispers: An Introduction to the Art of Kenneth Bernard" by Gerald Rabkin, in *Clown at Wall* by Kenneth Bernard, New York, Confrontation Press, 1996; in *Theatre of the Ridiculous* by Gerald Rabkin, edited by B. Marranca, New York, 1998.

Theatrical Activities:
Director: **Play**—*Mary Jane*, New York, 1973.

Kenneth Bernard comments:

I like to think of my plays as metaphors, closer to poetic technique (the coherence of dream) than to rational discourse. I am not interested in traditional plot or character development. My plays build a metaphor; when the metaphor is complete, the play is complete. Within that context things and people do happen. I would hope the appeal of my plays is initially to the emotions only, not the head, and that they are received as spectacle and a kind of gorgeous (albeit frightening) entertainment. The characters in my plays can often be played by either men or women (e.g., *The Moke-Eater*, *Night Club*): only a living presence is necessary, one who reflects the character component in the play rather than any aspect of non-stage individuality: they are instruments to be played upon, not ego-minded careerists: they must "disappear" on stage. More important than technique, etc., are passion and flexibility. The defects of this preference are offset by strong directorial control: each play in effect becomes a training program. My plays use music, dance, poetry, rhetoric, film, sounds and voices of all kinds, costume, color, make-up, noise, irrationality, and existing rituals to give shape (e.g., the auction, the magic show). The audience must be authentically pulled into the play in spite of itself. It must not *care* what it all means because it is enjoying itself and feels itself involved in a dramatic flow. What remains with the audience is a totality, the metaphor, from which ideas may spring—not ideas from which it has (with difficulty) to recreate the dramatic experience.

* * *

Kenneth Bernard's major plays have been produced mainly by the Play-House of the Ridiculous and under John Vaccaro's direction. This collaboration provides the best avenue of approach to an understanding of Bernard's plays. The so-called Ridiculous style—with its shrilly pitched, frenzied extravagance, its compulsively and explicitly sexual interpretation of every action, its elaborate makeup and costumes that lend confusion to the antics of transvestites of both sexes, and its general aura of bleakness and violence that adds despair to even the company's most optimistic productions—is a reasonable physicalization of the world Bernard evokes.

The two interlocking themes of Bernard's drama are cruelty and entertainment. His characters are perpetually threatening one another with torture, mutilation, and particularly painful modes of execution. The vicissitudes are constantly placed in a theatrical frame of some sort, as intended for the amusement of a group, of the torture master, or of the audience itself, which is implicated by its silent consent to the proceedings. In Bernard's first full-length work, *The Moke-Eater,* the setting is a prototypical American small town and the hero the stock figure of a traveling salesman. Desperately ingenuous and jaunty, he suddenly finds himself, when his car breaks down, confronting the sinister, inarticulate townspeople and their malevolent boss, Alec. Alec alternately cajoles and bullies the salesman into submitting to a humiliating series of charades that are nightmarish parodies of small-town hospitality. The play reaches its climax as the salesman realizes that he is trapped, for when he drives off in the repaired auto, it breaks down outside the next town, which turns out to be exactly the same town he has just left. In the Ridiculous production an additional frisson was added at the point of the salesman's reentrance by having the townspeople attack and eviscerate him, a fate that Alec describes earlier in the play as having been inflicted on a previous visitor.

Later plays by Bernard present the spectacle of cruelty with the torturer, rather than the victim, as the protagonist. *Night Club* displays Western civilization as a hideous, inept cabaret show that is controlled by an androgynous master of ceremonies named Bubi. Like Alec in *The Moke-Eater,* Bubi cajoles and bullies both the audience and the performers into humiliating themselves. In fact, the theater audience first sees the company performing the show as a parody of itself. The grotesque nightclub acts all emerge out of the "audience," which meanwhile cheers, screams catcalls, attacks the club's one waitress, and generally behaves boorishly. The acts themselves include a male ventriloquist trapped in a virulent love-hate relationship with a female dummy who spouts obscenities; a juggler—recalling Destructive Desmond of Auden and Isherwood's *The Dog beneath the Skin*—who throws valuable antiques into the air and declines to catch them; an impersonator obsessed with his own virility and whose imitations veer from a sex-starved southern belle to a sadistic Nazi; and the Grand Kabuki Theatre of America, which lends the patina of Japanese ceremoniousness to a vulgar soap-opera-like story about a pregnant college girl. At Bubi's behest the nightclub show eventually culminates in mass copulation by the so-called audience, all accompanied by the *William Tell Overture.* The one member of the audience who declines to perform is summarily dragged onstage and decapitated while he repeatedly screams, "The menu says there's no cover charge!" In a similar vein Bernard's *The Magic Show of Dr. Ma-Gico* is a series of violent encounters. Based on fairy-tale and romance themes, it is more courtly in tone but just as unpleasant. For example, to test her lover's fidelity, a maiden transforms herself into a diseased old crone and forces him to make love to her, and a king is challenged to pick up a book without dropping his robe, orb, and scepter. In both cases the man fails. The unproduced play *Auction* is a surreal, aleatory version of a rural livestock auction whose items include a pig-woman and an invalid who sells off his vital organs one by one.

The world picture contained in these plays is essentially that of a continuous nightmare, and while the surface action and language change—with Bernard's language being exceptionally varied in texture, ranging from the loftiest politeness to the most degraded abuse—the emotional thrust of the material remains the same as it reveals the sheer ludicrous horror of existence. In his collaboration with the Play-House of the Ridiculous, Bernard has carried the Artaudian project of raising and exorcizing the audience's demons about as far as it is likely to get through the theatrical metaphor.

—Michael Feingold

BILL, Stephen

Nationality: British. **Born:** Birmingham, 16 January 1948. **Education:** Handsworth and Hales Owen grammar schools, 1952-67; Royal Academy of Dramatic Art, London, 1968-70. **Family:** Married Sheila Kelley in 1971; one son and one daughter. **Career:** Commis chef, Norfolk Hotel, Birmingham, 1966; ward orderly, Romsley Sanatorium, Romsley, Worcestershire, 1967-68; grave digger, Hales Owen Council, 1967; civil servant in tax office, Birmingham, 1968; writer-in-residence, Crucible Theatre, Sheffield, 1977-78. **Awards:** Thames Television award, 1977; John Whiting award, 1979; London *Evening Standard* award, 1987; *Plays and Players* award, 1987; *Drama* award, 1987; Writers Guild of Great Britain award, 1991. **Agent:** Judy Daish Associates, 83 Eastbourne Mews, London W2 6LQ, England.

Publications

Plays

Girl Talk (produced Sheffield, 1978; London, 1982).
Squeakers and Strags (produced Sheffield, 1978).
Final Wave (produced Sheffield, 1979).
The Old Order (produced Birmingham, 1979).
Piggy-Back Rider (produced Birmingham, 1981).
The Bottom Drawer (produced Oxford, 1982).
Naked in the Bull Ring (produced Birmingham, 1985).
Over the Bar (produced Derby, 1985).
Crossing the Line (produced Darlaston, West Midlands, 1987).
Curtains (produced London, 1987). London, Faber, 1988.
Heartlanders, with David Edgar and Anne Devlin (produced Birmingham, 1989). London, Hern, 1989.
Over a Barrel (produced Watford, 1990).
Stitched Up (produced Bolton, 1990).
The Antigone Project (produced Solihull, 1992).

Radio Play: *Worshipping the Ground*, 1988.

Television Plays: *Lyndsey*, 1980; *House Warming*, 1983; *Eh Brian, It's a Whopper* series, 1984; *Marjorie and the Preacher Man*, with Jim Broadbent, 1987; *Broke*, 1991.

*

Theatrical activities:
Actor: **Plays**—In repertory theatres and in London including: *The Silent Majority* by Mike Leigh, London, 1974; *Blood Sports* by David Edgar, London, 1975; *Blisters* by Sheila Kelley and Sarah Pia Anderson, London, 1976. **Film**—*Prick Up Your Ears*, 1987. **Television**—*Nuts in May* by Mike Leigh, 1976; *Spend, Spend, Spend* by Jack Rosenthal, 1977; *Stepping Out* by Sheila Kelley and Sarah Pia Anderson, 1977; *Days at the Beach* by Malcolm Mowbray, 1978.

Stephen Bill comments:

I feel like I am just a storyteller giving voice to the characters and situations that I have come across in everyday life. A voice to "ordinary" people whose stories I don't feel are normally told. I grew up in Handsworth, Birmingham. My father went from school into his father's small badge enamelling business in the jewellery quarter. They only employed women enamellers because they "couldn't pay enough to employ men." My mother died when I was about four and we never argued at home. I only mention these odd facts because everything I write relates back to upbringing. To pitting one set of values against another. To having the arguments in public that we didn't know how to have in private.

My theatre work falls into two categories: 1) intimate, character-based dramas; 2) broader, community based theatre. The character-based work often explores the values we hold in common—or don't. It looks at how "ordinary" people cope when placed in extraordinary situations. It tries to make sense of, or celebrate, the contradictions. My experience in community-based theatre stems from my time as resident writer at the Crucible Theatre, Sheffield. I worked with their Theatre Vanguard Company which toured the whole of South Yorkshire. The plays I wrote for them were specific to the area and were for specific audiences—children, teenagers, handicapped groups, etc. This strand of my work continued with: 2nd City Theatre Company, Theatre Foundry—the touring company for the Black Country; the *Heartlanders* project—a community play for Birmingham's centenary, co-written with Anne Devlin and David Edgar, with a cast of over a hundred local people; and in 1992 with *The Antigone Project* for the Royal Shakespeare Company. This is a retelling of the Sophocles play, *Antigone*, by 26 young people in the Chelmsley Wood area of Solihull. The story we tell will be out of their experience and will be in a language that is real to them.

* * *

Stephen Bill was an actor before he was a dramatist, and his first plays were written as a member of a company. As the resident writer at the Sheffield Crucible Theatre, he applied himself diligently to his job as a community playwright, researching issues and turning them into drama. His early plays, mainly based in South Yorkshire, are above average but conventional theater-in-education pieces about pigeons, delinquent teenagers, and the generation gap. One, *Final Wave*, is atypical of Bill's other works. It uses folk songs and folk rituals and is set on the remote island of Saint Kilda, with most of the action taking place in the eighteenth century and the characters frequently speaking Gaelic. No other Bill characters speak any foreign language. Though they are rooted in the past, it is a past that goes no further back than World War II. They are geographically located no farther south than Birmingham and no farther north than Doncaster, and they speak in the authentic voices of the British working class and petite bourgeoisie.

During the time at Sheffield, Bill's own voice was confident but not noticeably individual. The real Bill began with his three plays for the Birmingham Repertory Company—*The Old Order*, *Piggy-Back Rider*, and *Naked in the Bull Ring*. All are set in the Birmingham area, and all are based on his own family's experiences. The characters of *The Old Order* are the workers and management of a small factory like one once run by Bill's father. In *Piggy-Back Rider* a young accountant has taken over just such a factory from his own father, George, and is destroying the work of two generations by selling off the land in parcels and getting rid of the workforce. George and his wife Connie appear in *Naked in the Bull Ring* as the son and daughter-in-law of a woman of 90 who is strong willed but no longer confident in her mind or of her ability to control the conditions of her life. She is able to control the lives of her own family only by making those lives a nightmare.

The old woman, based on Bill's grandmother, appeared again five years later in what may be his finest play, *Curtains*. She has repeatedly asked to be helped to die and is killed at the beginning of the second act by one of her daughters, who is no longer able to cope with her. The rest of the family then attempts to behave as if the murder had not happened. The play was commissioned by the Hampstead Theatre Club and had considerable critical success, but it was transferred rather inappropriately to the Whitehall Theatre, home of the Whitehall farces. It may have bemused the regular Whitehall audiences and did not run for long although it has been performed by amateurs all over the world.

Bill's interest in communities persists throughout his work. In collaboration with David Edgar and Anne Devlin he wrote the community play *Heartlanders* for a cast of over 100, which was again performed in Birmingham. But his community usually is a family reacting to a family disaster—euthanasia in *Curtains* or the sudden announcement by a daughter in *The Bottom Drawer* that she intends to marry, the assumption being that she must be pregnant. Or it may be the community of the workplace. Besides the use of his father's factory in the Birmingham trilogy, Bill used a factory making ornamental barrels in *Over a Barrel* and the management of a football club in *Over the Bar*. His characters are invariably much concerned with possessions, either the accumulation of them or the encumbrance they represent.

Bill has a poet's concern with imagery. In *Stitched Up*, for example, a householder who is overwhelmed with debt simply goes into the kitchen cupboard and refuses to come out. He sees plays as conversations with an audience, which is why he enjoys working in regional theaters: "I know who I'm talking to." He is more interested in character than in narrative and likes to bring a group of people up against an idea or an event, or both, to see what comes of it. As a consequence the plays are more conversation than action. Though the subject may be of everyday concern, the locale an ordinary house or factory, and the language, the costumes, and the whole approach naturalistic, a Bill play has none of the self-indulgence of a semi-improvised piece by someone like Mike Leigh. Bill is naturalistic only in the sense that Pinter is naturalistic; he has a very sharp ear and a delight in the extraordinariness of demotic speech. Of all the present crop of British dramatists, he is the playwright of the inarticulate and confused. The characters of his later plays rarely finish a sentence.

—John Bowen

BIRIMISA, George

Nationality: American. **Born:** Santa Cruz, California, 21 February 1924. **Education:** Attended school to the ninth grade; studied with Uta Hagen at the Herbert Berghof Studios, New York. **Military Service:** Served in the United States Naval Reserve during World War II. **Family:** Married Nancy Linden in 1952 (divorced 1961). **Career:** Worked in a factory, as a disc jockey, health studio manager, clerk, salesman, bartender, page for National Broadcasting Company, bellhop; counterman, Howard Johnson's, New York, 1952-56; typist, Laurie Girls, New York, 1969-70. Artistic director, Theatre of All Nations, New York, 1974-76. **Awards:** Rockefeller grant, 1969. **Address:** 627 Page Street, Apartment 6, San Francisco, California 94117, U.S.A.

Publications

Plays

Degrees (produced New York, 1966).
17 Loves and 17 Kisses (produced New York, 1966).
Daddy Violet (produced Ann Arbor, Michigan, and New York, 1967). Published in *Prism International* (Vancouver), 1968.
How Come You Don't Dig Chicks? (produced New York, 1967). Published in *The Alternate* (San Francisco), January 1981.
Mister Jello (produced New York, 1968; London, 1969; revised version produced New York, 1974).
Georgie Porgie (produced New York, 1968). Published in *More Plays from Off-Off-Broadway*, edited by Michael T. Smith, Indianapolis, Bobbs Merrill, 1972.
Adrian (produced New York, 1974).
Will the Real Yogonanda Please Stand Up? (produced New York, 1974).
A Dress Made of Diamonds (produced Los Angeles, 1976).
Pogey Bait! (produced Los Angeles, 1976; New York, 1977). Published in *Drummer*, 1977.
A Rainbow in the Night (produced Los Angeles, 1978).
A Rose and a Baby Ruth (produced San Francisco, 1981).
The Man with Straight Hair (produced San Francisco, 1994). Dallas, Texas, Dialogus Play Service, 1994.
Looking for Mr. America (produced San Francisco, 1994; New York, 1995.) Dallas, Texas, Dialogus Play Service, 1994.

Screenplays: *Looking for Mr. America: A Portrait of George Birimisa,* produced by Jeffrey Winter and Jose Guevera, 1998.

*

Manuscript Collection: Joe Cino Memorial Library, Lincoln Center Library of the Performing Arts, New York.

Theatrical Activities:
Director: **Plays**—*The Bed* by Robert Heide, New York, 1966; *The Painter* by Burt Snider, New York, 1967; *Georgie Porgie*, New York, 1971; *A Buffalo for Brooklyn* by Anne Grant, Corning, New York, 1975.

George Birimisa comments:
(1973) I write about the people I know. At this point in my life many of my friends are homosexual. I try to write honestly about them. In writing honestly about them I believe that my plays (in particular *Georgie Porgie*) mirror the terror of a schizophrenic society that is lost in a world of fantasy. In *Daddy Violet* I believe I showed how the individual's fantasy can lead to the burning of women and children in Vietnam. The problem with my plays is that many critics label them as homosexual plays. In the United States we live at the edge of a civilization that is near the end of the line. I feel that it is important for me to throw away every fantasy and get down into the total terror of this insane society. Only then can I truly write a play that is God-affirming, that is full of light. In my new play, tentatively titled *It's Your Movie*, I'm trying to write about the only alternative left in a demonic society—the nitty-gritty love of brother for brother and sister for sister. I know I must go through the passions of the flesh before I can break through to love my brother and sister. Anything else is an illusion. I also believe that the American male is terrified of his homosexuality and this is one of the chief reasons why he is unable to love his brother. His repression creates fires of the soul and this is translated into wars and violence. If all the "closet queens" would step out into the sunshine it would be a different country. I believe the above is what I write about in my plays.

(1977) At last I have discovered that four letter word LOVE. My early plays were screams of anger and rage. I was really screaming at myself because I was a microcosm of the good and evil of the western world, and I finally realize that it is possible to walk through death and destruction, and care . . . really care.

(1992) I just re-read my comments of 1973 and 1977. *Pompous*. I gave up the theatre for the last 10 years but I'm back in it. This time it's for my personal enjoyment. Period.

(1998) My *Georgie Porgie* was a very homophobic play. It was also a scream for help out of unbearable pain. At 74 years of age I've finally been able to work through my own homophobia and let love into my life. I believe the greatest discovery of the 20th Century has been the 12 step program. It is not about getting over an addiction but is about becoming a responsible member of society. It is the only truly democratic organization that I know of.

* * *

George Birimisa's early play *Daddy Violet* is built on a series of cathartic acting exercises that, through a process of association and hallucinatory transformation, evoke a battle in the Vietnam War. The cruelty and destruction of the war are linked, using a technique based on improvisation, with the actor's self-loathing and sexual immaturity.

Birimisa is a fiercely moral writer; his plays are filled with compassionate rage against needless suffering, furious impatience with the human condition, and desperately frustrated idealism. He links the pain of human isolation to economic and social roots.

Mister Jello starts out with a mixed bag of characters: a waspish aging transvestite, a bitchy social worker, a dreamy boy flower child, a businesslike prostitute, and the fat, foolish Mister Jello, who pretends to be a little boy while the prostitute—his "mommy"—disciplines him. Birimisa sets their antagonisms in perspective by reference to the social philosopher Henry George.

Georgie Porgie is a series of vignettes about homosexual relationships. Almost all are bitter and ugly in tone, interspersed with choral episodes quoted from Friedrich Engels. The contrast between Engels's idealistic vision of human liberty and Birimisa's variously stupid, contemptible, pitiable, self-despising characters, all imprisoned in their own compulsions, is powerful and painful.

Birimisa's writing is often crude, the language vulgar, the humor cruel, the events shocking; the author has been preoccupied with psychic pain and the consequences of neurotic patterns, and his work makes up in self-examining integrity and emotional intensity what it eschews in seductiveness and beauty. In 1976 Birimisa moved from New York City to Los Angeles and then to San Francisco. In the more affirmative pre-AIDS climate of gay liberation there, he attempted to go beyond the rage and desperation of the earlier plays to a more positive view: *Pogey Bait!* was well received in Los Angeles and ran for several months.

—Michael T. Smith

BLEASDALE, Alan

Nationality: British. **Born:** Liverpool, Lancashire, 23 March 1946. **Education:** St. Aloysius Infant and Junior schools, Huyton, Lancashire, 1951-57; Wade Deacon Grammar School, Widnes, Lancashire, 1957-64; Padgate Teachers Training College, teachers certificate 1967. **Family:** Married Julia Moses in 1970; two sons and one daughter. **Career:** Teacher, St. Columbus Secondary Modern School, Huyton, 1967-71, King George V School, Gilbert and Ellice Islands, 1971-74, and Halewood Grange Comprehensive School, Lancashire, 1974-75; resident playwright, Liverpool Playhouse, 1975-76, and Contact Theatre, Manchester, 1976-78; joint artistic director, 1981-84, and associate director, 1984-86, Liverpool Playhouse. **Awards:** Broadcasting Press Guild award, 1982; Royal Television Society award, 1982; BAFTA award, 1982; *Evening Standard* award, for musical, 1985; ITV Achievement of the Decade award, 1989; Broadcasting Press Guild Television and Radio award, 1991. Lives in Liverpool. **Agent:** Lemon, Unna, and Durbridge, 24 Pottery Lane, Holland Park, London W11 4LZ, England.

Publications

Plays

Fat Harold and the Last 26 (produced Liverpool and London, 1975).
The Party's Over (produced Liverpool, 1975).
Scully, with others, adaptation of the novel by Bleasdale (produced Liverpool, 1975). London, Hutchinson, 1984.
Franny Scully's Christmas Stories, with Kenneth Alan Taylor (produced Liverpool, 1976).
Down the Dock Road (produced Liverpool, 1976).
It's a Madhouse (produced Manchester, 1976). With *Having a Ball*, London, Faber, 1986.
Should Auld Acquaintance (produced Manchester, 1976).
No More Sitting on the Old School Bench (produced Manchester, 1977). Todmorden, Yorkshire, Woodhouse, 1979.
Crackers (produced Leeds, 1978).
Pimples (produced Manchester, 1978).
Love Is a Many Splendoured Thing (for children; produced Redditch, Worcestershire, 1986). Published in *Act I*, edited by David Self and Ray Speakman, London, Hutchinson, 1979.
Having a Ball (produced Oldham, Lancashire, and London, 1981; revised version produced London, 1990). With *It's a Madhouse*, London, Faber, 1986.
Boys from the Blackstuff (televised 1982). London, Hutchinson, 1985.
Young People Today (sketch), in *The Big One* (produced London, 1983).
Are You Lonesome Tonight? (produced Liverpool and London, 1985; San Diego, 1989). London, Faber, 1985.
The Monocled Mutineer, adaptation of the book by William Allison and John Fairley (televised 1986). London, Hutchinson, 1986.
No Surrender: A Deadpan Farce (screenplay). London, Faber, 1986.
On the Ledge. London and Boston, Faber, 1993.

Screenplay: *No Surrender*, 1987.

Television Plays: *Early to Bed*, 1975; *Dangerous Ambition*, 1976; *Scully's New Year's Eve*, 1978; *The Black Stuff*, 1980; *The Muscle Market*, 1981; *Boys from the Blackstuff* series, 1982; *Scully* series, 1984; *The Monocled Mutineer*, 1986; *G.B.H.* series, 1991.

Novels

Scully. London, Hutchinson, 1975.
Who's Been Sleeping in My Bed? London, Hutchinson, 1977; revised edition, as *Scully and Mooey*, London, Corgi, 1984.

*

Critical Studies: *Dossier 20*, London, British Film Institute, 1984; *Boys from the Blackstuff: The Making of Television Drama* by Bob Millington and Robin Nelson, London, Comedia, 1986; "Boys from the Blackstuff (Alan Bleasdale)" by Bob Millington, in *British Television in the 1980s*, edited by George W. Brandt and David Rose, Cambridge, Cambridge University Press, 1993.

Alan Bleasdale comments:

I try *never* to look back and examine my work. I don't re-read the script or watch the video once the piece is finished. For what it's worth, I don't think a writer should know what he or she is doing! That's for the audience or critic to judge. I do know, however, that since I was a child all I have ever wanted was to be good and to do good. I should have been a social worker.

Notes such as these can sometimes become a playwright's first and last line of defence or explanation: "This is what my plays really mean!" My only explanation and defence lie between the first and last curtain.

Finally, the only three quotations I have ever managed to learn off by heart: "Any victim demands allegiance" (Graham Greene, *The Heart of the Matter*). "All my humor is based on destruction and despair. If the whole world was tranquil, without disease and violence, I'd be standing on the breadline, right behind J. Edgar Hoover" (Lenny Bruce). "Too much talking stinks up the room" (Duke Ellington).

* * *

Although he had been writing for the theater since the mid-1970s, it was his television series *Boys from the Blackstuff* that brought Alan Bleasdale wide recognition. In five successive episodes he traced, with mordant irony, the despair and madness of a group of unemployed Liverpool men and their families. The central battle is between the individual and the state. The unemployed struggle to supplement their dole money with casual earnings on building sites and in dockyards, while the Department of Employment, the social services, and the police combine to corral their clients within the government's regulations. Farce turns into tragedy that reverts to farce. While cars skid, crash, and overturn on Malloy's illegal building site at the end of the first episode, Snowy Malone, the plasterer who takes pride in his skills, falls to his death trying to escape the dole officials. Elsewhere, Chrissie Todd shoots his rabbits for food, Yosser Hughes is rescued from drowning by the police he has assaulted, and the sanctimonious priest at George Malone's funeral finishes up vomiting his whiskey down a grate after the reception. Bleasdale has no more sentimental regard for his characters than they have for one another. The children are as uncompromising as the parents. The scene in which Yosser's daughter Ann Marie butts the social worker Veronica is as comic as it is shocking.

Snowy's death is echoed by that of his father in the last episode. George Malone is respected throughout the community as a socialist and a battler for citizens' rights, but the structure of Bleasdale's series questions radically whether the Malones' ideology of class solidarity is still relevant to Britain. The Malones have an analysis of why mass unemployment has returned. Chrissie, Yosser, Dixie, and the rest have only their native wits, which, unsupported by any community or educational training, can flip over into hallucination. Yosser Hughes is a monomaniac, and his white face, staring red-rimmed eyes, and monotonous cry of "Gizza job" and "I can do that" immediately became the nation's most dramatic vision of unemployed misery. Chrissie's wife Angie sees clearly that jokes are not enough: "If you don't laugh, you'll cry—I've heard it for years—this stupid soddin' city's full of it." But when she screams at her husband to fight back, she has no more idea than he about how it can be done.

Bleasdale's view of the professional classes is equally acerbic. *Having a Ball*, a stage play of 1981, counterpoints the reactions of three men, Lenny, Ritchie, and Malcolm, waiting in a hospital for vasectomies. They are all middle class, and they are all terrified. With a woman surgeon and Malcolm's wife Doreen contemptuous of his army "bravery," the play exposes not woman, but man, as victim. And with three simultaneous areas for stage action—the waiting room, the preparation room, and the operating theater—Bleasdale exploits all of the possibilities for farcical encounters and concealments. But there is no harmonious resolution. The play ends with Lenny, like Yosser, screaming in despair. Through wit, mockery, and a kind of trickster role playing, he has exposed his own and everyone else's pretensions to control and confidence. "Most of us are cowards most of the time," he remarks. "Until we have no choice. And all the choices seem to be going." This is Bleasdale's savage double bind that Chrissie expresses in *Boys from the Blackstuff* as "It's a way of life. The only trouble is, it's no way to live."

With *Are You Lonesome Tonight?* Bleasdale moves away, to his cost, from the familiar territory of the northwest of England. Elvis Presley, in his last hours at Graceland, has the successes and betrayals of life portrayed to him upstage. He drools over his mother, curses Colonel Parker, and comes over as a good old southern boy of musical genius who was led astray by unscrupulous agents. Other accounts of Elvis's last years depict a drug-ridden, gun-obsessed monster, but Bleasdale was determined that this should be a tribute to what he called the "working class hero" of his youth. It was a West End hit, but it remains unique among Bleasdale's plays for its sentimentality and uncritical adulation. The London production was memorable not for the writing but for the electrifyingly accurate rendition of Elvis's great early hits by Simon Bowman.

In 1986 Bleasdale returned to his strengths, antiheroism and farce, with the four-part television series *The Monocled Mutineer* and the film *No Surrender*. The tricky career of Percy Toplis, a World War I conscript, is the subject of the television series. He leads an uprising of conscripted men against their atrocious conditions in the Etaples training camp in 1917. But he also impersonates officers and thoroughly enjoys their life of gambling, drinking, and whoring. Toplis is neither demogogue nor ideologue, and on several occasions he refuses to be called either a hero or a socialist. He is a working-class rebel who refuses all the clichés of such a figure. And he does not lead the Etaples uprising in any conventional way. Rather, he finds himself in a situation where he can inflict the maximum of mayhem on a class he both hates and simulates. "Don't get angry," he advises; "get even." Toplis is no Scarlet Pimpernel of the workers. After the war he is a poor man still hunted for his role at Etaples. He thinks he can live off a rich widow but finds that she is as big a poser as he is. Naturally he falls in love with her. When he rejoins the army, it is not just to get rich by black-marketing army supplies. He admits that he does not seem able to function outside the army's structure of command; its rigidity creates his flexibility. He is not therefore the roving outsider of the romantic tradition. To be that one has to have the money and class Toplis does not and never will have. The agents of the state finally eliminate this cultural hybrid on a deserted Cumbrian road, but his girlfriend's pregnancy indicates that he may be reborn. What Bleasdale has intuited is that Toplis's combination of cynicism, courage, and style is the true basis for oppositional politics in modern Britain. The man who invents himself from the debris all around him is the man who anticipates the new patterns of life.

No Surrender begins, continues, and ends in debris. A new manager comes to take over a decrepit nightclub in Liverpool and finds that it has been double booked by two parties of old age pensioners, one Catholic and the other Protestant. Infiltrated into this gathering is a Loyalist gunman on the run. Insults escalate from the verbal to the physical, the geriatrics take strength from the fires of religious fanaticism, and the film finishes in a mayhem of fists, bottles, the police, and a fancy dress competition.

G.B.H. is not only about physical violence, although throughout this 10-hour, seven-episode series for Channel 4 Bleasdale certainly features backstreet beatings and picket line intimidation. The last episode culminates in the firing of the town hall of a northern city by a mob of angry black citizens incited to revolt by a group of MI-5 agents posing as Trotskyite provocateurs. The central incident in the life of Michael Murray, Bleasdale's rabid Labour council leader, is an unwarranted beating he received from his primary school headmaster. The narrative proposes that this has bred in him a detestation of authority that has been the driving force behind his own authoritarian assumption of power in local politics. He is unable to cope with a humane, liberal headmaster like Jim Nelson, who keeps his school open during a strike maneuvered by Murray and who plays the good angel to Murray's devil throughout this political morality play. *G.B.H.*'s real interest, however, occurs when the personal and political collide without resolution. At these murky crossroads all is deceit and doubling.

Murray's real nemesis is one Eileen Critchley, rich when he was poor, at the same school as Murray, and a sadomasochist even as a child. She wants him to strangle her, her refrain being "You want to please me, don't you Michael?" But he cannot do her the violence she desires. Eileen, it emerges late in the series, committed suicide at Oxford in her 20s. But in a scene with her younger sister Barbara that repeats many times, she hisses, "Get Michael, he's easy," and Barbara, an upper-class blond of cool sexuality and a member of MI-5, pursues, seduces, and confuses Murray at the height of his power. The theme of our age, the absent father, is dramatized several times over in the crisscrossing stories of sex and politics that make up the series.

Jim Nelson also has a pathology. He is a hypochondriac with an irrational fear of bridges and a tendency to sleepwalk naked. He and his family represent the compassionate, middle-class socialism that Bleasdale clearly prefers to the conspiratorial fanaticism of Murray and his heavies. But Nelson's delusions remain farcical rather than psychological. His family is supportive, his sex life pure, and his morality impeccable. He is therefore dull (and woodenly acted by Michael Palin) and interesting only when he is the occasion for such scenes of hilariously black comedy as his nth interview with his doctor or his conversation in the storm with Grosvenor, a country gentleman with a bilious contempt for the guests at his holiday retreat, particularly if they are from the North.

G.B.H. is a many-layered narrative, full of the most abrupt cutting between farce and tragedy, childhood and adulthood, the personal and the political. It does not always succeed, but its ambition far outruns any contemporary television scripts, and its reading of the nature of obsession among public figures is sophisticated.

The father is only too present in Bleasdale's *Jake's Progress,* a four-part television drama of 1995. Jamie Diadoni is every liberal's dream of a househusband. He cooks, cleans, and obsessively cares for his six-year-old son Jake. His wife, Julie, is a nurse. The setting is a semirural area of North Yorkshire. Jamie appears content but can never forget his brief moment of bohemian freedom in the 1960s as the lead singer of a mediocre rock band called The Wanderers. And it is at a dreadful 1960s theme party that Jamie has his palm read by Monica, cool blond schoolteacher and amateur theater producer. She forecasts that he will have an affair just before he dies. Jamie becomes obsessed with this destiny and so adds superstition to the other typical female traits he displays, such as his smothering father's love for his son and his extreme emotional dependence on his wife. Jake develops into a highly disturbed child. He sets his grandmother's chair on fire, tries to hang himself, and does his best to injure his baby brother. Julie opens an old people's home to pay off their debts but finds herself saddled with her mother, who loads onto her all the resentments of an unfulfilled marriage.

Jamie is gradually attracted to Kate, a bold young woman who has returned to the village and who has her own history of sexual abuse and murder. The two climactic scenes are the suicide of Kate's father on the stairs outside her bedroom just before Jamie, full of trepidation, is about to make love to her, and the deaths of Jamie and Kate in a fall from a cliff. The two have finally made love and are standing by a flimsy fence on the cliff when Jake spots his father from a playground above, runs towards him, accelerates and jumps into his arms, and sends them all crashing through the fence and onto the rocks below. The last scene is of Julie prizing Jake out of his father's arms, the child slowly coming to life and for the first time in the saga saying, not "Play with me Daddy," but "Play with me Mummy."

The moral seems to be that illicit sex outside the family ends in disaster and that unconditional love for a child within the family can produce the Oedipal deformations that Jake obviously undergoes at his father's hands. As Julie puts it in the third episode, "You brought him up and you fucked him up." Mother and father are both in a kind of no-parents'-land in which role reversals breed pathology and traditional roles breed cruelty and unhappiness. This is a brave attempt by Bleasdale at an impossible issue, but Jamie is too wimpish for any admiration. Perhaps the playwright needs the public and the private to cross- fertilize his best imaginative work.

—Tony Dunn

BLESSING, Lee (Knowlton)

Nationality: American. **Born:** Minneapolis, Minnesota, 4 October 1949. **Education:** Schools in Minnetonka, Minnesota; University of Minnesota, Minneapolis, 1967-69; Reed College, Portland, Oregon, 1969-71, B.A. in English 1971; University of Iowa, Iowa City, 1974-79, M.F.A. in English 1976, M.F.A. in speech/theater 1979. **Family:** Married Jeanne Blake in 1986; two stepchildren. **Career:** Teacher of playwriting, University of Iowa, 1977-79, and Playwrights' Center, Minneapolis, 1986-88. **Awards:** American College Theater Festival award, 1979; Jerome Foundation grant, 1981, 1982; McKnight Foundation grant, 1983, 1989; Great American Play award, 1984; National Endowment for the Arts grant, 1985, 1988; Bush Foundation fellowship, 1987; American Theater Critics Association award, 1987; Marton award, 1988; Dramalogue award, 1988; Guggenheim fellowship, 1989. **Agent:** Lois Berman, Little Theatre Building, 240 West 44th Street, New York, New York 10036; or, Jeffrey Melnick, Harry Gold Agency, 3500 West Olive, Suite 1400, Burbank, California 91505. **Address:** 2817 West 40th Street, Minneapolis, Minnesota 55410, U.S.A.

Publications

Plays

The Authentic Life of Billy the Kid (produced Washington, D.C., 1979). New York, French, 1980.

Oldtimers Game (produced Louisville, Kentucky, 1982). New York, Dramatists Play Service, 1988.

Nice People Dancing to Good Country Music (produced Louisville, Kentucky, 1982; revised version produced St. Paul, Minnesota, 1984). New York, Dramatists Play Service, 1983; revised version included in *Four Plays*, 1990.

Independence (produced Louisville, Kentucky, 1984). New York, Dramatists Play Service, 1985; included in *Four Plays*, 1990; in *Plays for Actresses,* New York, Vintage Books, 1997.

Riches (as *War of the Roses*, produced Louisville, Kentucky, 1985). New York, Dramatists Play Service, 1986; included in *Four Plays*, 1990.

Eleemosynary (produced St. Paul, Minnesota, 1985; New York, 1989). New York, Dramatists Play Service, 1987; included in *Four Plays*, 1990.

A Walk in the Woods (produced La Jolla, California, 1987; New York and London, 1988). New York, New American Library, 1988.
Two Rooms (produced La Jolla, California, 1988). New York, Dramatists Play Service, 1990.
Cobb (produced New Haven, Connecticut, 1989). New York, Dramatists Play Service, 1991.
Down the Road (produced La Jolla, California, 1989). New York, Dramatists Play Service, 1991.
Four Plays (includes *Eleemosynary*, *Riches*, *Independence*, *Nice People Dancing to Good Country Music*). Oxford, Heinemann Educational Books, 1990; Portsmouth, New Hampshire, Heinemann, 1991.
Fortinbrass, adaptation of William Shakespeare. New York, Dramatists Play Service, 1992.
Lake Street Extension (produced New York, 1992). New York, Dramatists Play Service, 1993.
Patient A. New York, Dramatists Play Service, 1993.
Patient A, and Other Plays: Five Plays. Portsmouth, New Hampshire, Heinemann, 1995.

Television Play: *Cooperstown,* 1993.

* * *

A cast of characters that includes a foulmouthed nun who recites the back of cereal boxes instead of prayers, an eccentric grandmother who believes that she can fly using homemade wings, an American photographer who is taken hostage in Beirut, and a Russian diplomat who prefers talking about Willie Nelson instead of nuclear arms control reflects Lee Blessing's penchant for writing about the illogical state of the human condition. Themes embrace both public and private politics and center around the battle to establish, nurture, and maintain human relationships. The style and subject matter are eclectic, although Blessing's plays have certain features in common. His plays are usually short with small casts and sketchy plots.

The most interesting of Blessing's early works is *Nice People Dancing to Good Country Music.* A comedy set on a deck above a Houston bar, it pairs two unlikely women in order to explore the notions of discovery and acceptance. A would-be nun, Catherine, is asked to leave the convent because of inappropriate behavior and comes to stay with the raucous aunt who manages the bar. Catherine gets a secular education from her aunt and from a customer of the bar who advises her not "to remarry the world, just to date it a little." Understatement and double entendre help establish the environment necessary for the odd but realistic characters. There are a few instances in which the language is too clever and not in line with the character's personal voice. It is Blessing's creative use of language, however, that distinguishes much of his work.

Eleemosynary is also a one-act play with eccentric female characters, but here Blessing uses language both as a dramatic device and as an ongoing theme. Three generations of the Westbrook women tell their stories through recollections of their shared histories, each trying to find independence but each also wanting the security that dependence provides. The grandmother warns her daughter about having a child—"You'll just be something a child needs"—while the daughter reveals her thoughts about her mother—"I spent my free time being delighted not to be around my mother, and wondering how she was." The granddaughter, who uses a spelling bee to bring them all together, wins the contest with the word "eleemosynary" only to realize that words neither guarantee communication nor establish relationships. In fact, the characters use words to avoid communication. Most effective is Blessing's ability to use words both to engage and to disengage the characters' emotions and their relationships with one another.

Plot is subordinate to theme in *Eleemosynary*, but the structure is less traditional than in Blessing's other works. The exception is *Two Rooms,* a poignant dramatization of the imprisonment of an American hostage in Beirut and the effect it has on his wife. In this play Blessing uses symbolism to advantage, with light and darkness representing various issues and maintaining a comparison of the wife's situation with that of an African hornbill bird. Hers is a desperate attempt to maintain hope, while her husband's situation is exploited by the media and ignored by the government: "After they mate, the male walls the female up, in the hollow of a tree. He literally imprisons her. . . . After the eggs are hatched, he breaks down the wall again, and the whole family is united. . . . It hasn't been a prison at all. It's been . . . a fortress."

Blessing's concern about relationships is played out differently in *Independence* and in *Riches*. Like *Eleemosynary, Independence* explores female relationships in a family void of men. The burden of maintaining familial relationships is borne by three daughters and their mentally unstable mother. The mother, however, even though she is blatantly sardonic, is often remarkably lucid: "That's what family means—each generation destroying itself willingly, for what comes after." The linguistic rhythm is not as strong as it is in *Eleemosynary* and in *Two Rooms,* but the plot is more cohesive. Blessing often writes about the rituals that define and reflect individuality, and in *Independence* the oldest daughter forces the family to partake in a "tea time" ritual in the hope that the experience will change their behavior. It is a funny scene, but the exercise fails to effect change.

In *Riches* the husband's ritual of blowing his nose, "a big blow, then three little ones," prompts the wife's realization that she no longer wishes to be married. The play attempts to explore the notion that love is not enough to sustain a relationship. Unfortunately, the first act moves slowly, in contrast with a physically violent second act. There are interesting observations regarding human behavior, how people come to logical conclusions in rather illogical ways, for example, and creative contrasting images. Nonetheless, the play lacks substantive dramatic action. *Riches* is similar in treatment to *Down the Road,* a play about a husband and wife writing team who conduct a series of interviews with a serial killer. Like the husband and wife of *Riches,* in the end they suffer a failed marriage, in this case because of the unsuccessful results of their dealings with the murderer. The play seems truncated, but the issue of journalistic ethics serves as a unifying factor and makes the play dramatically more viable than *Riches*.

A Walk in the Woods is Blessing's most commercially successful play and has appeared on Broadway. It is based on an actual walk in the woods by the Russian and American diplomats Yuli A. Kvitsinsky and Paul H. Nitze. The play, however, is about personal politics and deals more with the process of how two superpowers negotiate rather than with the outcome. The plot is negligible and is subordinate to the theme of American idealism versus Russian pragmatism, a contrast underlying conversations on mundane topics that range from Italian shoes to the lyrics of country music. The play's structure is cyclical, which is problematic and which results in an unsatisfying ending since, in the end, nothing has changed. No agreement has been reached, and no revelations are made. It is similar in style to the earlier and lesser play *Oldtimers Game.* Both are vehicles for social and political issues, but neither explores these issues in any depth.

Blessing's work reflects an interest in characters whose past interferes with their future. Cyclical structures coupled with nontraditional plots create a unique style in which character and language are pivotal dramatic elements and in which unique observations about relationships create impassioned moments on the stage.

—Judy Lee Oliva

BOGOSIAN, Eric

Nationality: American. **Born:** Boston, Massachusetts, 24 April 1953. **Education:** Woburn High School and Woburn Drama Guild, Massachusetts, 1971-73; University of Chicago, 1973-74; Oberlin College, Ohio, 1975-76, B.A. in theater 1976. **Career:** Director of the dance program, The Kitchen, New York, 1977-81. **Awards:** National Endowment for the Arts and New York State Arts Council grants; Drama Desk award, 1986; Obie award, 1986, 1990, 1994; Berlin Film Festival Silver Bear, for *Talk Radio,* 1988. **Agent:** George Lane, William Morris Agency, 1325 Avenue of the Americas, New York, New York 10019, U.S.A.

Publications

Plays

Men Inside (produced New York, 1981; revised version produced New York, 1982).
Voices of America (produced Groningen, The Netherlands, and New York, 1982).
Funhouse (produced New York, 1983).
Talk Radio (produced Portland, 1985; revised version produced New York, 1987). New York, Vintage, 1988; London, Faber, 1989.
Blood on Canvas, recorded with Frank Zappa. 1986.
Drinking in America (produced Boston, New York, and London, 1986). New York, Vintage, 1987; London, Faber, 1988.
Sex, Drugs, Rock & Roll (produced New York, 1988). New York, Harper, 1990; New York, Theater Communications Group, n.d.
Pounding Nails in the Floor with My Forehead (produced New York, 1992). New York, Theater Communications Group, n.d.
Notes from Underground (produced New York, 1992).
Essential Bogosian. New York, Theater Communications Group, 1994.
SubUrbia (produced New York, 1994). New York, Theater Communications Group, 1994.
Wake Up and Smell the Coffee (solo tour, 1995).
31 Ejaculations (produced at St. Mark's Poetry Project, 1996).
Griller (produced Chicago, 1998).

Screenplay: *Talk Radio,* 1988; *Confessions of a Porn Star,* 1995; *High Incident,* 1995; *Substance of Fire,* 1995; *SubUrbia,* 1997.

*

Critical Study: "An Interview with Eric Bogosian" by Kay Bonetti, in *The Missouri Review* (Columbus, Missouri), 1996, pp. 95-116.

Theatrical Activities:
Actor: **Plays**—All his own plays. **Film**–Role in *Dolores Claiborne,* 1994; role in *Dark Territory,* 1994; role in *Deconstructing Harry,* 1997; role in *Office Killer,* directed by Cindy Sherman, 1996; voiceover for *The Beavis and Butthead Movie,* directed by Mike Judge, 1996. **Television**–Role in *Miami Vice,* 1984; role in *Twilight Zone,* 1985; role in *The Healer,* 1985; *Eric Bogosian Takes a Look at Drinking in America,* 1986; role in *Caine Mutiny Court Martial,* 1987; role in *Last Flight Out,* 1989; role in *Law and Order,* 1992; role in *Witchhunt,* 1994.

* * *

Eric Bogosian's theatrical work exemplifies a postmodern culture of simulation. Borrowing from the traditions of rock music, performance art, talk radio, and film noir, he performs numerous self-transformations to construct a brilliant array of monologues and plays that capture the darker side of life in contemporary America. His signature piece is the monologue, but he also excels as a playwright and storyteller. His work offers a study of representational tropes, many drawn from the media, film, rock culture, or the world of visual and performance artists. His in-your-face style of monologue, combined with dialogue peppered with obscenities in the manner of Lenny Bruce, is designed to affront and disgust the audience. His solo pieces—*Sex, Drugs, Rock & Roll,* and *Pounding Nails in the Floor with My Forehead*—offer his reflections on a culture in crisis. It is the frenetic energy of so many of his characters, his iconoclasm, and his outrageous wit that fuel his work and that account for much of his popularity. His bardic ambitions and his love/hate affair with America place him in the literary tradition of Walt Whitman, Jack Kerouac, and Allen Ginsberg. The American dream has failed him, but it has failed him grandly. For all the corrosiveness of his vision in the play *Griller,* its subject is still July 4, the promise of Independence Day and the hope of America's indigenous people. He writes of a badly damaged world and of deeply flawed and occasionally evil people, but he writes of them with deep feeling and humanity.

Bogosian's use of the monologue is quite similar to Cindy Sherman's treatment of photographs in her series *Untitled Film Stills.* Both artists, albeit in different media, experiment with self-portraiture with a twist. Sherman produces small black-and-white photographs in which she impersonates various female character types drawn from old B movies and film noir. She uses the image to explore the stereotype in unsettling ways. Bogosian draws on autobiography and his talents as an actor to construct solo pieces that allow him or other actors to inhabit the world of contemporary America's down-and-outers—drifters, punks, and prostitutes—as well as the world of the suburban backyard picnic.

Bogosian frequently mentions the strong influence of rock concerts, pop art, video art, happenings, and mixed media in his work. He is influenced by performance artists such as Cindy Sherman, Spalding Gray, Laurie Anderson, and Robert Longo. Working with alternative, experimental forms of theater, in the 1970s he developed his one-man show, dazzling and offending his audiences with his rogues' gallery of American males. The black stud, the spaced-out hippie, the virulently anti-Semitic caller on a radio talk show, the rock star, the gang bangers, the punks, and the homeless—all were played by this gifted theater artist in his black trousers, white oxford button-down shirt or T-shirt, and black referee shoes. At first his act was built around his imaginary entertainer-comedian

Ricky Paul, who ranted about the deplorable condition of the modern world. The set was generally sparse—a chair, table, microphone, and stand. Later, he eliminated Ricky Paul and simply played his medley of unlikely, zany, often nasty, but unforgettable characters. Like other monologists, he usually offered a warped, often angry quasi-autobiographical account of his dispossessed self.

Bogosian creates characters who challenge his vocal range, permitting him to play with the different accents and idioms of urban black English, a Texas drawl, burly ethnic American, or Hispanic speech. At its best the dialogue reflects the finely observed language of the hustler, druggie weirdo, Archie Bunker racist, or rock groupie. He laced together a stream of monologues and appropriated media images to create his satiric and parodic assemblages *Funhouse; Men Inside; Drinking in America; Talk Radio; Sex, Drugs, Rock & Roll;* and *An American Chorus.* A successful stand-up comic in Lower Manhattan's late-night clubs and also trained in dance, Bogosian energizes his monologues, propelling them with the power of a rock star and feeding off his audience's desire to be offended while being entertained.

Bogosian began offering his monologues in New York performance art spaces such as Performance Space 122, The Kitchen, Snafu Club, and Franklin Furnace. RoseLee Goldberg has described him as one of the founders of "artists' cabaret," a new genre spawned in New York discos. Beginning as a solo performer, Bogosian drew on Lenny Bruce, the New York deejay Alan Freed, the underground performer Brother Theodore, Bob Dylan, Jimi Hendrix, and Laurie Anderson for his inspiration. By 1982 his work had crossed over from the vanguard into the status of mass culture, twice winning best-play awards, becoming the subject of films and cable specials, and appearing in book form. Since the success of his first play, *Talk Radio,* Bogosian has written three additional plays—*Scenes from the New World,* published in *Notes from Underground, SubUrbia,* and *Griller.* His last two plays have been mounted on main stages across the United States as well as on numerous college campuses.

Influenced by the media age and what is known as the hyperreal, Bogosian's works are illuminated by reference to the writings of Roland Barthes and Jean Baudrillard. Barthes's dissection of mass culture and its mythologies has influenced Bogosian's exploration of a cross section of American cultural stereotypes. Baudrillard's analysis of the codes, structures, and practices of our consumer society are also helpful in situating Bogosian's themes.

Bogosian's works are full of advertising slogans—for Kronenbrau beer, Nyquil, and Remington cigarettes—and numerous references to McDonald's, BMWs, Volvos, a $3,000 griller, sportswear by Versace, Microsoft, Peruvian cocaine, Quaaludes, Jimi Hendrix, Janis Joplin, Cassius Clay, and other idols of American pop culture. His preoccupation with the media's ability to level all images and numb the mind informs his choice of the clichés and banalities uttered by his monologists.

Baudrillard defined the hyperreal as a condition in which simulations come to constitute reality itself. Drawing upon Marshall McLuhan's concept of implosion and his famous slogan "the medium is the message," Baudrillard argued that the boundary between image or simulation and reality implodes in the postmodern world; people cannot differentiate between the real and its simulations. He found ammunition to support this contention—one he has since modified—by citing the simulations of politics created by Ronald Reagan in which the public elected the image not the man, the simulations of religion foisted on people by television evangelists, and the simulations of rape, homelessness, or trials produced by television shows.

Bogosian's monologues can be read as simulations. Some of his callers on his talk show sentimentally echo the banal lyrics of Diana Ross to "reach out and touch" or Bruce Springsteen's "Arms across America" AIDS concerts as though these formed the basis of their moral beliefs. In *Sex, Drugs, Rock & Roll,* he ridicules the rock lyrics that revolutionized an era: "Freedom's just another word for nothing left to lose" or "Wanna die before I get old." Bogosian finds America's love affair with the confessional mode deeply disturbing, particularly as it is served by television, radio, and rock. With a humor that is often corrosive and with caustic wit, he offers his critique of American postmodern culture.

Barry Champlain, the radio host in *Talk Radio,* exploits the simulation. When a drugged caller pleads for help, saying that he cannot get his strung-out girlfriend to wake up, Champlain knows that the call is a hoax. He invites the caller onto the talk show, willing to take the risk that perhaps the caller might just really do what the killer of real-life Alan Berg did, namely, kill him. Berg was an ex-Chicago talk show host famous for his insulting and abusive manner. In 1984 he was machine-gunned to death in the driveway of his home in Denver by members of a neo-Nazi hate group angered by his radio persona. Bogosian intensifies the play's taut atmosphere by staging a moment when the caller in the studio reaches into his pocket and draws out a flash camera, not a gun, which he shoots. The moment is exactly of the kind that disturbs. Its hyperreality almost washes out the ground of reality. At one level it is possible that the crazy caller will kill the talk show host. Such events happen in life, but it is not clear that they are merely imitations of what has been staged on television or marketed on talk shows. Bogosian's play raises this troubling thought at the same time as it saturates the audience in the hyperreal. The portrait of the hyperactive, egocentric, abusive talk show host, mercurial in his mood and full of self-loathing, shows us a man just at the edge of a breakdown and as every bit as disturbing as some of the pathetic or chilling life stories confessed to him by his callers. Still more frightening is the way the play mirrors its audience, making it question its own insatiable appetite for sex, violence, trouble, and confession.

In the film version of *Talk Radio,* Oliver Stone changed the ending of Bogosian's stage version. The film's penultimate scene involves the shooting and death of Barry Champlain, while the final images show a postmodern mediascape in which the boundaries between information and entertainment, politics and image, implode. Callers are talking about Barry's death, which is incorporated into media patter. It has the same unreal feel about it that surrounded the television coverage of the Persian Gulf War, when images that played nightly on CNN threatened to replace the reality. Bogosian's stage play is even more effective. There is no dead talk show host; rather, there is a world of sound, of talk, and of narratives, most contrived and seemingly filled with beliefs for which there is no real referent. In this respect his stage play achieves some of the more nihilistic effects of Baudrillard's deeply pessimistic thinking of the 1970s.

In *Drinking in America* and *Sex, Drugs, Rock & Roll,* Bogosian refines his skill at portraiture, largely using the same male types and media clichés but focusing the image more sharply. Describing a schizoid America that wants to "live in piggish splendor and be ecologically responsible . . . wants to have the highest principles but win the popularity contest," Bogosian confesses to wanting both to be a big baby and a responsible citizen. In *Sex,*

Drugs, Rock & Roll he says that he has created 12 monologues that "take the nasty side of myself and put them out there for everyone to see." The play opens with a there-but-for-the-grace-of-God-go-I beggar panhandling the audience. The down-and-out ex-convict shamelessly pleads with the audience to do something, to give their money to him, not to the blacks in South Africa 10,000 miles away. His repeated "thank you" and "bless you" segue into the next piece, a hypocritical promotional spiel of a British rock and roll star and ex-druggie telling his imaginary talk show host how the youth of the day should avoid his mistakes and "just say no." The other monologues include a grubby derelict cursing at the gutter; a stud bragging about the size of his penis; the host of a stag party reveling in an evening of women, porn, and drugs; Candy, talking dirty to her phone sex caller; a wheeler-dealer; a paranoiac, a self-hating misogynist; and other equally obnoxious yet wholly believable types.

In both of Bogosian's later plays, *SubUrbia* and *Griller,* the line between simulation and reality continues to be blurred. In *SubUrbia* Bogosian writes about a group of suburban kids gathered by the corner store, awaiting the arrival of one of their pals who has made good as a national rock star and who is returning to his haunts to perform a concert. The waiting is followed by a night of drinking, bragging, and violence, both simulated and real. By morning one of the characters has overdosed on the roof, and the others have had to confront their own dreams and fears. Again and again throughout the play, a character threatens another with a gun; deaths are alluded to and then found out not to be true; hopes are dashed. The characters cannot find themselves, and they appear to have thrown away their chances. All are marked by the encounter with the ultimate simulation—the national rock star—and the reality behind the illusion.

Griller presents another variation on the theme of the American dream gone awry. It is also a play that treats the way in which the media and television have hopelessly corrupted American life. The play celebrates the 50th birthday of its self-made protagonist, Gussie, at the same time as it marks the country's anniversary on Independence Day. Four generations of Gussie's family are gathered at a picnic. Gussie and his family are trying to enact the American immigrant's dream of success. They have all the accoutrements of success, and yet failures of different kinds are all about. One of Gussie's sons is a heroin addict; the other is a driven, egotistical, impotent stockbroker, too enamored of himself to recognize why his marriage is failing and why his wife will have a fling with his druggie brother before the picnic is over. Gussie's mother is dying of cancer, and his sister wants to flee to warmer climes, leaving the caretaking to her brother. Worse yet, the play ends with Gussie killing Uncle Tony, his father's alcoholic friend, and pretending that it was an accident. The ending is not credible, with the audience asked to believe that the drowning in the pool can appear to be an accident. Since Gussie has clobbered Uncle Tony repeatedly with the huge novelty pepper mill that Grandma brought Gussie for his birthday, it is hard to believe that the police will accept the story that the family returned from the fireworks to find their friend drowned. The play exposes the toxicity of the media and of simulations, with its world a weird blend of simulated reality and life. Although the play is seriously flawed in its construction and met with quite critical reviews when it played in Chicago at the Goodman Theatre under the direction of Robert Falls, it has an uncanny way of claiming attention. Gussie, Tony, and Grandma are believable characters, and they are not easily forgotten.

Bogosian's solo pieces are raucous, often abrasive, rich in their specificity of character, and often capable of making their audience thoroughly uncomfortable. His plays treat many of the same themes he explores in his monologues. *SubUrbia* and *Griller* demonstrate that Bogosian can command the form of drama and that he can use it to depict the hyperreal and the culture of commodification. They also remind us why Bogosian is such a successful theater artist. He has a feel for our times, a zest for life, and a gift for language. All attest to man's humanity, albeit in a thoroughly damaged world.

—Carol Simpson Stern

BOLT, Carol

Nationality: Canadian. **Born:** Carol Johnson, Winnipeg, Manitoba, 25 August 1941. **Education:** University of British Columbia, Vancouver, 1957-61, B.A. 1961. **Family:** Married David Bolt in 1969; one son. **Career:** Researcher, Dominion Board of Statistics, London School of Economics, Market Facts of Canada, and Seccombe House, 1961-72; dramaturge, 1972-73, and chair of the Management Committee, 1973-74, Playwrights Co-op, Toronto; dramaturge, Toronto Free Theatre, 1973; writer-in-residence, University of Toronto, 1977-78. **Awards:** Canada Council grant, 1967, 1972; Ontario Arts Council grant, 1972, 1973, 1974, 1975. **Agent:** Great North Artists, 345 Adelaide Street West, Toronto, Ontario M5V 1R5. **Address:** 76 Herbert Avenue, Toronto, Ontario, Canada.

Publications

Plays

I Wish (as Carol Johnson; produced Toronto, 1966). Published in *Upstage and Down*, edited by D.P. McGarity, Toronto, Macmillan, 1968.

Daganawida (produced Toronto, 1970).

Buffalo Jump (as *Next Year Country*, produced Regina, Saskatchewan, 1971; as *Buffalo Jump*, produced Toronto, 1972). Toronto, Playwrights, 1972.

My Best Friend Is Twelve Feet High (for children), music by Jane Vasey (produced Toronto, 1972). With *Tangleflags*, Toronto, Playwrights, 1972.

Cyclone Jack (for children; produced Toronto, 1972). Toronto, Playwrights, 1972.

Gabe (produced Alcoma, Ontario, 1972). Toronto, Playwrights, 1973.

Tangleflags (for children; produced Toronto, 1973; St. Louis, 1977). With *My Best Friend Is Twelve Feet High*, Toronto, Playwrights, 1972; published separately, 1974.

The Bluebird, adaptation of a story by Marie d'Aulnoy (produced Toronto, 1973).

Pauline (produced Toronto, 1973).

Maurice (for children; produced Toronto, 1973). Toronto, Playwrights, 1975.

Red Emma, Queen of the Anarchists (produced Toronto, 1974). Toronto, Playwrights, 1974.

Shelter (produced Toronto, 1974). Toronto, Playwrights, 1975.

Finding Bumble (for children; produced Toronto, 1975).

Norman Bethune: On Board the S.S. Empress of Asia (produced Gravenhurst, Ontario, 1976).
Okey Doke (produced Kingston, Ontario, 1976).
Buffalo Jump, Gabe, Red Emma. Toronto, Playwrights, 1976.
One Night Stand (produced Toronto, 1977). Toronto, Playwrights, 1977.
Desperadoes (produced Toronto, 1977).
TV Lounge (produced Toronto, 1977).
Star Quality (produced Louisville, 1980). Excerpt published in *Acta Victoriana* (Toronto), vol. 102, no. 2, 1978.
Deadline (produced Toronto, 1979).
Escape Entertainment (produced Toronto, 1981). Toronto, Playwrights, 1982.
Love or Money (produced Blyth, Ontario, 1981).
Icetime. Markham, Ontario, Houghton Mifflin, 1994.
Famous. Toronto, PUC Play Service, 1997.

Screenplay: *Fidelity,* 1975.

Radio Play: *Fast Forward,* 1976.

Television Plays: *A Nice Girl Like You* (*Collaborators* series), 1974; *Distance,* 1974; *Talk Him Down,* 1975; *Red Emma,* 1976; *Cyclone Jack,* 1977; *One Night Stand,* 1978; *The Move,* 1978; *In a Far Country,* 1981; *Mayor Charlotte,* 1982; *I Don't Care,* 1983; *The Delinquent,* 1983; *Dungeons and Raccoons,* 1984.

Other

Drama in the Classroom. Toronto, Playwrights Canada, 1986.

*

Carol Bolt comments:

(1977) I've had a lot of opportunity to work in the theatre in the last four years, with twelve new plays commissioned. Much of this work has been inspired by the theatrical community, particularly work being done at the Toronto Free Theatre and the Théâtre Passe Muraille.

The plays often deal with "political" subjects, the characters often want to change the world, but I think my preoccupation is with the adventure, rather than the polemic, of politics. I think a play like *Red Emma* is about as political as *The Prisoner of Zenda.*

I'm interested in working in new forms of musical comedy and epic romance and in creating (or recreating) characters who are larger than life or mythic.

I'm also interested in exploring, recording, recreating, and defining Canadian concerns, characters, histories, cultures, identities. I want to create plays for this country, whether the plays are about the lost moments in Canada's past (like *Buffalo Jump*), whether they offer another view of an American mythic figure (like *Red Emma*), or whether they play at creating Canadian archetypes (*Shelter*).

I don't think this kind of cultural nationalism is parochial. I think our differences are our strengths, not our weaknesses, nationally and internationally, so I think the argument that if a Canadian play is any good the Americans or British will be happy to tell us via Broadway or the West End is specious and muddle-headed. I don't think Canadians will say anything of interest to the world until we know who Canadians are.

* * *

Through her prolific contribution to the theater Carol Bolt has shaped a unique form of social documentary that uses factual material to gain access to an imaginative Canadian mythology. Her best early plays are cohesive, rich in entertainment and dramatic values, politically inspired but romantically motivated, and imbued with a keen, sometimes riotous sense of social injustice.

Central to *Buffalo Jump, Gabe,* and *Red Emma* is an interest in combining theatrical styles and methods: a fluid interchange of locations loosely defined by props and emotional intensities, quick episodic scene changes, direct address to the audience, and the use of song to develop action or as a divertissement.

Both her adults' and children's plays have a free-form fluctuation of time, place, and space, enhanced by a strong entertainment factor that smooths abrupt or unlikely transitions with song, special lighting changes, or the emphasis of a significant prop—the train in *Buffalo Jump,* for example, or the banner of anarchy in *Red Emma.*

Bolt's ongoing transformations of original material also sift fiction, or rather an imaginative interpretation, into factual details that aim at a conscious redefinition of the time-blurred outlines of historical figures. Bolt has stated that she would rather be interesting than accurate and rather be one-sided than give a well-rounded viewpoint honed to dullness.

For example, the central character in *Buffalo Jump,* a play about the disastrous trek to Ottawa of unemployed Vancouver men during the Great Depression, combines two Canadian heroes, "Red" Walsh and "Slim" Evans, united for dramatic purposes into the single character Red Evans. A character develops not necessarily from what is true but from what might be true as the playwright understands it. The creation of myth and the reshaping of myth are more important to Bolt than the documentation of history. As she has said, "Myth is more appealing than fact. It postulates that heroism is possible, that people can be noble and effective and change things. . . . what we were doing in *Buffalo Jump* was making those characters tragic heroes. It was the same with the great Native Indian runner Tom Longboat, the central character of *Cyclone Jack* and others."

Gabe, based on the story of Louis Riel, the doomed Métis Indian leader of the Riel Rebellion, and his comrade in arms, Gabriel Dumont, is a constant interplay between memory images and the reality of the lives of the two modern namesakes who are the main characters of the play. The original Riel and Dumont have been refined by time into spiritual heroes who provide a constant source of romantic inspiration. The modern-day Louis says of his historic counterpart, "Louis Riel! Was the maddest, smartest, bravest Métis bastard ever wrote his own treaty. Ever fought for the rights of his people. For their land. Fought for representation. For his people and their children." In spite of courageous poses, the figures from the past did not achieve their political ideals or their romantic fantasies. The modern-day Louis must function within the context of a failed mythology. Where there was once a battle at Batoche, there is now a sports day and a camp meeting. And Louis has just finished a jail sentence.

Red Emma is more focused, dealing with one aspect of the life of the revolutionary Emma Goldman. Although the play is the least concerned with Canadian content, its style and sensibility link it *Buffalo Jump* and *Gabe.* Structurally, the play draws upon a fluid intermingling of scenes and juxtaposes caricature with real people. Set in New York in 1890, *Red Emma* glorifies the myth of freedom fighters, "the people and the things they can wish for, the beautiful radiant things." The clue to an interpretation of *Red*

Emma lies in the subtitle, *Queen of the Anarchists.* The Emma of the story is a young, idealistic woman given to histrionic poses and flamboyant gestures. But she is also a staunch supporter of women's emancipation, declaring, "Woman's development . . . must come from and through herself. . . . freeing herself from the fear of public opinion and public condemnation will set a woman free, will make her a force hitherto unknown in the world."

Bolt's first attempt to come to terms with such assumptions began tentatively with *Shelter,* the adult play following *Red Emma.* Dealing with five women, the social rituals of a funeral, a wedding, and an election campaign, and one woman's decision to run for office, *Shelter* shields its concerns with comedy. Painful decisions and reactions are given an almost surrealistic stylization, absurdity tops reality, and the women tend to be representative types instead of fully developed, deeply felt human beings. *Shelter* was followed by *One Night Stand,* Bolt's most aggressively modern play. In this award-winning work, Daisy, a young, lonely woman, celebrates her birthday with Rafe, a charming stranger who punctuates his lies with country-and-western songs. The consequences of their brief encounter—murder—are chillingly realistic.

Bolt's willingness to exhibit the theatrical process can also be found in her approach to children's plays. Two of her earliest, *Cyclone Jack* and *My Best Friend Is Twelve Feet High,* were formed completely in rehearsal. One of her most popular children's plays, *Ice Time,* is a depiction of a young girl who wants to play in a boy's hockey league. "Justine is a real person," Bolt has said, "a friend of my son, Alex. She successfully took her case to the Supreme Court of Canada. She was interesting, and the play grew out of that."

Bolt's later works for adults include *Famous,* the story of Kit, white, female, and the best friend of a multiple murderess. The two-hander includes Sheila, a black television researcher from San Francisco. Bolt has said, "The play is like *One Night Stand* in that it's about dark things, although it's meant to be funny." In the late 1990s her play *Mean to Me,* an original musical about a would-be torch singer, was in progress. The main character loves the old songs but wants to make them less negative toward women. "It will be amusing too, I hope," Bolt says.

—Constance Brissenden

BOND, Chris(topher Godfrey)

Nationality: British. **Born:** Sussex in 1945. **Education:** Child actor; educated at the Central School of Speech and Drama and the Drama Centre, both London. **Family:** Married to the writer Claire Luckham. **Career:** Actor, 1968-70, and resident dramatist, 1970-71, Victoria Theatre, Stoke-on-Trent, Staffordshire; artistic director, Everyman Theatre, Liverpool, 1976-78; director, Liverpool Playhouse, 1981-83; director, Half Moon Theatre, London, 1984-89. **Awards:** Arts Council grant, 1970. **Agent:** Blanche Marvin, 21-A St. John's Wood High Street, London NW8 7NG, England.

PUBLICATIONS

Plays

Sweeney Todd, The Demon Barber of Fleet Street (produced Stoke-on-Trent, 1970; London, 1973; New York, 1989). London, French, 1974.

Mutiny (produced Stoke-on-Trent, 1970).

Shem's Boat (for children; produced Stoke-on-Trent, 1971).

Downright Hooligan (produced Stoke-on-Trent, 1972; London, 1978).

Tarzan's Last Stand (produced Liverpool, 1973).

Judge Jeffreys (produced Exeter, 1973; London, 1976).

The Country Wife, adaptation of the play by William Wycherley (produced Liverpool, 1974).

Under New Management (produced Liverpool, 1975).

The Cantril Tales, with others (produced Liverpool, 1975).

George, in *Prompt One,* edited by Alan Durband. London, Hutchinson, 1976.

Scum: Death, Destruction, and Dirty Washing, with Claire Luckham (produced London, 1976).

Good Soldier Scouse (produced Liverpool, 1976).

The Beggar's Opera, based on the play by John Gay (also director: produced Liverpool, 1977).

A Tale of Two Cities, adaptation of the novel by Dickens (produced Liverpool, 1981).

Dracula (also director: produced London, 1984). Thomas Press.

Spend, Spend, Spend, with Claire Luckham, adaptation of the televison play by Jack Rosenthal (also director: produced London, 1985).

All the Fun of the Fair, with John McGrath and others (also director: produced London, 1986).

El Sid, music by Dave Watts, lyrics by Andrew Birtles, from an idea by Dave Barry (also director: produced London 1988).

The Mysterie of Maria Marten (produced London, 1991).

Novel

You Want Drink Something Cold. London, Joseph, 1969.

*

Theatrical Activities:
Director: **Plays**—*Flying Blind* by Bill Morrison, Liverpool, 1977, New York, 1979; *The Beggar's Opera,* Liverpool, 1977; *Stags and Hens* by Willy Russell, Liverpool, 1978; *Trafford Tanzi* by Claire Luckham, London, 1981 (and U.S. version, *Teaneck Tanzi,* New York, 1983); *Blood Brothers* by Willy Russell, Liverpool and London, 1983; *Dracula,* London, 1984; *Sweeney Todd* by Hugh Wheeler and Stephen Sondheim (musical adaptation of Bond's play), London, 1985; *Scrap!* by Bill Morrison, London, 1985; *Spend, Spend, Spend,* London, 1985; *Destiny* by David Edgar, London, 1985; *All the Fun of the Fair,* London, 1986; *Moll Flanders* by Claire Luckham, London, 1986; *Love on the Plastic* by Julia Schofield, London, 1987; *As Is* by William M. Hoffman, London, 1987; *Macbeth,* London, 1987; *El Sid,* London, 1988; *Poppy* by Peter Nichols, London, 1988; *Nativity* by Nigel Williams, London, 1989; musicals and revues, Tricycle Theatre, Sweden and Norway, 1990-97.

* * *

Chris Bond is one of several British dramatists who grew up under the spell of Joan Littlewood's Theatre Workshop in Stratford in East London. In his case, however, a primary attraction to the theater began almost from his cradle. His parents had run a touring company after World War II, and Bond himself was a child actor, playing at the Shakespeare Memorial Theatre in

Stratford-upon-Avon from the age of 11. He grew to love the rough-and-tumble of acting life, the performing skills, and the ability to contact audiences at all levels of appreciation. In his plays he loves to throw in effects that grab the attention—songs, dances, pieces of mime, and simple stage tricks such as the enlarged washing machine that the character Harold MacMillan in *Under New Management* mistakes for a minicar and thus gets spun around in with the rest of the laundry.

But the direction of Bond's work, its more serious side, derives from Littlewood. He has written social and historical documentaries such as *Under New Management* and *Judge Jeffreys,* and he seeks his audiences primarily from the young, working-class, left-wing public. Although not an overtly political writer, there is a strong vein of socialist thought within his work. It sometimes emerges into didactic messages but more usually is reflected in the handling of his themes—caricatures of establishment authority and sympathy with the underprivileged and the downtrodden.

The clearest and most striking example of this tendency is found in *Downright Hooligan,* first produced at the Victoria Theatre in Stoke-on-Trent, where Bond was the resident dramatist. The central character, Ian Rigby, is a sort of contemporary Wozzeck whose eyes, deep-set beneath a granite forehead, suggest a Neanderthal mentality. Permanently out of work and a fixture in the betting shop, Ian is surrounded by a society whose logical illogicalities he cannot comprehend. His mother bawls at him for masturbating in his bedroom, while her lover winks at him and tells him dirty jokes. He accidentally kills the school hamster and sticks drawing pins in its eyes for decoration. His headmaster is appalled by the atrocity, but he does not know that Ian has just paid his last respects to his grandmother, whose dead drawn face has been padded out with clutches of her own hair. One form of decorating the dead is socially acceptable, but Ian's treatment of the hamster is not. Confronted by the unpredictability of society, Ian asserts himself by hitting out savagely at an elderly man, and he is brought before the courts as a downright hooligan.

Thus Bond, without glamorizing his hero-victim, places the blame for his behavior on society at large. Some critics have claimed that his impression of repressive social forces is simplistic, belonging too much to a mentality of us and them. While his portrait of Ian Rigby's background is telling and convincing and was presented with marvelous detail by the Stoke company, *Under New Management* is almost a cartoon, agitprop documentary. It shows 12 cretinous general managers, one dressed as a schoolboy clutching a teddy bear, who mess up the Fisher-Bendix factory on the outskirts of Liverpool until the heroic workers, faced by mass lay-offs, take over. It was a thoroughly lively, enjoyable production, but it was inevitably one-sided, partly because Bond had deliberately not interviewed anyone from the management while conducting his research.

By trying to make his plays immediately entertaining, Bond also falls into the trap that snared some of Littlewood's productions. There is too much outer fun and too little inner content. The scenes are short and sketchlike, sometimes extended by horseplay and separated by songs and little dances, and the connecting themes are either lost or so heavily stressed that they seem merely repetitive. In the hands of a highly disciplined company, such as that of Stoke or of the old Liverpool Everyman, where Bond became artistic director, this music hall mixture could be pulled into a tight shape. His plays usually require the concentration supplied by a firm director and an experienced team.

While striving for a casual, easygoing, and lighthearted approach to the theater, Bond, in fact, usually demands great restraint and professionalism from his performers, an apparent contradiction that not all directors have realized. There was a luckless production of *Judge Jeffreys* at Stratford East in which the script seemed as banal as the performances, and *Tarzan's Last Stand,* about Enoch Powell the "ape man," seemed to miss its very broad, satirical target by not taking Powell's arguments sufficiently seriously. Like Alan Plater, a somewhat similar writer of social documentaries, Bond has perhaps not found that dramatic structure within which his talents and social insights can be best expressed.

—John Elsom

BOND, Edward

Nationality: British. **Born:** London, 18 July 1934. **Education:** Crouch End Secondary Modern School, 1944-49. **Military Service:** Served in the British Army, 1953-55. **Family:** Married Elisabeth Pablé in 1971. **Career:** Member of the English Stage Company Writers Group, Royal Court Theatre, London, from 1958. Founding member, Theatre Writers' Group (now Theatre Writers' Union), 1975; Northern Arts literary fellow, University of Newcastle-upon-Tyne and University of Durham, 1977-79; resident writer, University of Essex, Colchester, 1982; visiting professor, University of Palermo, Italy, 1983. **Awards:** George Devine award, 1968; John Whiting award, 1968; Obie award, 1976. D. Litt.: Yale University, New Haven, Connecticut, 1977. **Agent:** Casarotto Ramsay Ltd., National House, 60-66 Wardour Street, London W1V 4ND, England.

Publications

Plays

The Pope's Wedding (produced London, 1962). Included in *The Pope's Wedding* (collection), 1971.

Saved (produced London, 1965; New Haven, Connecticut, 1968; New York, 1970). London, Methuen, and New York, Hill and Wang, 1966.

A Chaste Maid in Cheapside, adaptation of the play by Middleton (produced London, 1966).

Three Sisters, adaptation of a play by Chekhov (produced London, 1967).

Narrow Road to the Deep North (produced Coventry, 1968; London and Boston, 1969; New York, 1972). London, Methuen, and New York, Hill and Wang, 1968.

Early Morning (produced London, 1968; New York, 1970). London, Calder and Boyars, 1968; New York, Hill and Wang, 1969; revised version in *Plays 1*, 1977.

Sketch in *The Enoch Show* (produced London, 1969).

Black Mass, part of *Sharpeville Sequence: A Scene, A Story, and Three Poems* (produced London, 1970). Included in *The Pope's Wedding* (collection), 1971; in *The Best Short Plays 1972*, edited by Stanley Richards, Philadelphia, Chilton, 1972.

Passion (produced London, 1971; New Haven, Connecticut, 1972). Published in *New York Times*, 15 August 1971; with *Bingo*, London, Eyre Methuen, 1974.

Lear (produced London, 1971; New Haven, Connecticut, 1973). London, Methuen, and New York, Hill and Wang, 1972.

The Pope's Wedding (collection; includes *Sharpeville Sequence* and the stories "Mr. Dog" and "The King with Golden Eyes"). London, Methuen, 1971.

The Sea (produced London, 1973; Chicago, 1974; New York, 1975). London, Eyre Methuen, 1973; with *Bingo*, New York, Hill and Wang, 1975.

Bingo: Scenes of Money and Death (and Passion) (produced Exeter, Devon, 1973; London, 1974; Cleveland, 1975; New York, 1976). London, Eyre Methuen, 1974; with *The Sea*, New York, Hill and Wang, 1975.

Spring Awakening, adaptation of a play by Wedekind (produced London, 1974; New York, 1978; Britain, 1992). Chicago, Dramatic Publishing Company, 1979; London, Eyre Methuen, 1980.

The Fool: Scenes of Bread and Love (produced London, 1975; Washington, D.C., 1976). With *We Come to the River*, London, Eyre Methuen, 1976; published separately, Chicago, Dramatic Publishing Company, 1978.

We Come to the River: Actions for Music, music by Hans Werner Henze (produced London, 1976). With *The Fool*, London, Eyre Methuen, 1976.

The White Devil, adaptation of the play by Webster (produced London, 1976).

A-A-America: Grandma Faust, and The Swing (produced London, 1976). Included in *A-A-America, and Stone*, 1976.

Stone (produced London, 1976; New York, 1981). Included in *A-A-America, and Stone*, 1976; in *Performing Arts Journal* (New York), Fall 1977.

A-A-America, and Stone. London, Eyre Methuen, 1976; revised edition, 1981.

Saved Early Morning, The Pope's Wedding. London, Eyre Methuen, 1977.

Lear, The Sea, Narrow Road to the Deep North, Black Mass, Passion. London, Eyre Methuen, 1978.

The Woman: Scenes of War and Freedom (also co-director: produced London, 1978; Baltimore, 1983). London, Eyre Methuen, 1979 (includes stories); New York, Hill and Wang, 1979.

The Bundle: Scenes of Right and Evil; or, New Narrow Road to the Deep North (produced London, 1978; New Haven, Connecticut, 1979). London, Eyre Methuen, 1978; Chicago, Dramatic Publishing Company, 1981.

The Worlds (also director: produced Newcastle upon Tyne and London, 1979). With *The Activists Papers*, London, Eyre Methuen, 1980.

Restoration: A Pastoral, music by Nick Bicât (also director: produced London, 1981). London, Eyre Methuen, 1981; Woodstock, Illinois, Dramatic Publishing Company, 1982; revised version, with *The Cat*, London, Methuen, 1982; revised version, published separately, 1988.

Summer: A European Play (also director: produced London, 1982; New York, 1983). London, Methuen, and Chicago, Dramatic Publishing Company, 1982.

Summer, with Fables, and Service: A Story. London, Methuen, 1982.

Derek (produced Stratford-on-Avon, 1982; London, 1984). With *Choruses from After the Assassinations*, London, Methuen, 1983.

The Cat (opera libretto), music by Hans Werner Henze (as *Die englische Katze*, produced Schwetzingen, West Germany, 1983; as *The English Cat*, produced Santa Fe, 1985; New York, 1986; Edinburgh, 1987). With *Restoration*, London, Methuen, 1982; as *The English Cat: A Story for Singers and Instrumentalists*, Mainz and London, Schott, 1983.

Choruses from after the Assassinations (produced Colchester, Essex, 1983). With *Derek*, London, Methuen, 1983.

The War Plays: A Trilogy (includes *Red Black and Ignorant* [produced London, 1984]; *The Tin Can People* [produced Birmingham, 1984]; and *Great Peace*; trilogy produced [also director] London, 1985). London, Methuen, 2 vols., 1985; revised edition (includes commentary on *The War Plays*), 1991.

Human Cannon (produced Edinburgh, 1986), London, Methuen, 1985.

Burns (dance theater for children; produced Birmingham, 1986).

Bingo, The Fool, The Woman. London, Methuen, 1987.

September (produced Canterbury, Kent, 1989). Included in *Two Post-Modern Plays*, 1989.

Jackets II (produced Leicester, 1989; London 1990). Included in *Two Post-Modern Plays*, 1989.

In the Company of Men (produced Avignon, 1992; Paris, 1997). Included in *Two Post-Modern Plays*, 1989.

Two Post-Modern Plays (includes Jackets *I* and *II*, *In the Company of Men*, *September*, "Notes on Post Modernism"). London, Methuen, 1989.

The Worlds, The Activists Papers, Restoration, Summer. London, Methuen, 1992.

Spring Awakening: A Children's Tragedy; Lulu: A Monster Tragedy, adaptations (with Elisabeth Bond-Pablé) of plays by Frank Wedekind (produced Britain, 1992). London, Methuen, 1993.

Olly's Prison. London, Methuen, 1993.

Tuesday. London, Methuen, 1993.

Coffee: A Tragedy (produced Paris, 1998). London, Methuen, 1995.

At the Inland Sea: A Play for Young People (produced Birmingham, prior to a tour of the Midlands, 1995). London, Methuen, 1997.

Human Cannon, The Bundle, Jackets, In the Company of Men. London, Methuen, 1996.

Eleven Vests (produced Birmingham, prior to a tour of the Midlands). London, Methuen, 1997.

The Crime of the Twenty-First Century. London, Methuen, 1998.

The War Plays, Choruses from After the Assassinations. London, Methuen, 1998.

Screenplays: *Blow-up*, with Michelangelo Antonioni and Tonino Guerra, 1967; *Laughter in the Dark*, directed by Tony Richardson, 1969; *Michael Kohlhaas*, 1969; *The Nun of Monza* (English dialogue), 1970; *Walkabout*, directed by Nicolas Roeg, 1971; *Nicholas and Alexandra*, with James Goldman, 1971; *Fury*, with Antonio Calenda and Ugo Pirro, 1973.

Televison Plays: *Olly's Prison*, 1993; *Tuesday*, 1993.

Ballet Scenario: *Orpheus*, music by Hans Werner Henze, Stuttgart and New York, 1979.

Poetry

The Swing Poems. London, Inter-Action, 1976.

Theatre Poems and Songs, edited by Malcolm Hay and Philip Roberts. London, Eyre Methuen, 1978.

Poems 1978-1985. London, Methuen, 1987.

Other

Edward Bond Letters, selected and edited by Ian Stuart (4 vols.). London, Harwood Academic Publishers, 1994.

*

Critical Studies: *Edward Bond* by Simon Trussler, London, Longman, 1976; *The Plays of Edward Bond* by Richard Scharine, Lewisburg, Pennsylvania, Bucknell University Press, 1976; *The Plays of Edward Bond: A Study* by Tony Coult, London, Eyre Methuen, 1977, revised edition, 1979; *Edward Bond: A Companion to the Plays*, London, TQ Publications, 1978, and *Bond: A Study of His Plays*, London, Eyre Methuen, 1980, both by Malcolm Hay and Philip Roberts, and *Bond on File* edited by Roberts, London, Methuen, 1985; *Edward Bond: A Study of His Plays* by Delia Donahue, Rome, Bulzoni, 1979; *Edward Bond* by David L. Hirst, London, Macmillan, 1985, New York, Grove Press, 1986; *The Art and Politics of Edward Bond* by Lou Lappin, New York, Peter Lang, 1987; *Dramatic Strategies in the Plays of Edward Bond* by Jenny S. Spencer, Cambridge, Cambridge University Press, 1992; *Politics in Performance: The Production Work of Edward Bond, 1978-1990* by Ian Stuart, New York, Peter Lang, 1996; *Edward Bond* by Michael Mangan, London, British Council, 1998.

Theatrical Activities:
Director: **Plays**—*Lear*, Vienna, 1973; *The Woman*, London, 1978; *The Worlds*, Newcastle upon Tyne and London, 1979; *Restoration*, London, 1981; *Summer*, London, 1982; *The War Plays*, London, 1985; *Tuesday*, London, 1993; *In the Company of Men*, London, 1996.

Actor: **Plays**—Aighard in *One Leg over the Wrong Wall* by Albert Bernel, London, 1960; Christ in *Black Mass*, London, 1970.

* * *

Edward Bond writes the most lapidary language in contemporary English theater, absorbing dialects, pastiches, metaphors, and questions into a rich mineral vein. Pithy phrases, swift scenes, and vivid characters are the building blocks for what he calls rational theater, theater dedicated to the creation of a rational society. Far from agitprop, however, his plays range through history and legend as well as the contemporary scene.

The early plays of surface realism shock by their pointless murders: young Scopey throttles an old hermit at the end of *The Pope's Wedding*; a group of youths stone a baby to death in the middle of *Saved*; at the beginning of *The Sea* Colin drowns while Hatch watches idly from the shore. Confrontation with these deaths, however, involves radical action on the part of Bond's protagonists. Behind its provocative title *The Pope's Wedding* dramatizes a young man's vain effort to understand fully another human being. Step by step, Scopey abandons companions, wife, and job in order to spend his time with the old hermit to learn "what yoo 'ere for?" Even in the old man's coat, communing with his corpse, he never learns.

As the title *Saved* suggests, Len is more successful. A loner, Len does not share in the bored activities of London youths who gamble, steal, and fornicate. They rub a baby's face in its diaper and then pitch stones into its carriage while Len, perhaps the baby's father, watches. The baby dies, and only later does Len admit, "Well, I should a stopped yer." Rejected by the baby's mother and flirting briefly with the grandmother, Len the loner is finally "saved" by the grandfather's barely articulate plea for him to remain in their household.

The Sea opens with Colin's drowning while his friend Willie pleads vainly for help from Evens, a drunken recluse, and Hatch, a paranoid coast guard watchman. Later Willie barely escapes a murderous attack by Hatch, who believes him to be an enemy from outer space. Despite his grief at Colin's death, in contrast with the satirized indifference of the townspeople, Willie comes to see that "the dead don't matter." Cumulatively, through these apparently realistic plays, "Life laughs at death."

For the most part Bond resembles Brecht in analyzing contemporary social injustice through parables based on legend or history. Both playwrights see war as the cruelest social injustice, and Bond explores that violence in violent plays. *Narrow Road to the Deep North* takes place in nineteenth-century Japan. Basho, the protagonist, follows the narrow road to the deep north in order to study, but he learns that "enlightenment is where you are." And where he is necessitates a choice between two evils, an English invader or a homegrown warlord. As the play ends, Basho is prime minister, his disciple falls disemboweled, and a stranger emerges from the river. Each man must make his own decisions in a time of war, and life goes on.

Of all Bond's protagonists his Lear experiences the most difficult enlightenment. From Shakespeare, Bond borrows the tragic conception intensified by grotesque humor. By way of Shakespeare, Bond reenforces his own dramatic concern with moral responsibility. As in Shakespeare, Lear is an absolute autocrat. Instead of dividing his kingdom, Bond's Lear encloses it within a wall built by forced labor. Lear's two daughters foment war, and both meet violent deaths. A composite of Kent and the Fool, Bond's Gravedigger's Boy has a wife named Cordelia. After he is shot and his wife raped by the daughter's soldiers, his ghost accompanies Lear on an infernal descent through madness and blindness. The ghost of the Gravedigger's Boy is slain, Lear attains wisdom, and Cordelia attains power as head of a new autocracy. In spite of Lear's age, he tries physically to dismantle Cordelia's wall, but he is shot. Like Shakespeare's Lear he has learned compassion, but he has also learned the necessity for socially responsible action.

In a later war parable Bond looks back to the cultural roots of the Western tradition, the Trojan War. *The Woman* (or "Scenes of War and Freedom") is a panoramic drama with the Trojan Hecuba as its protagonist. Part 1, set at the walls of Troy, condenses and revises Homer's *Iliad* to show a capitalist Greece attacking a feudal Troy ruled by Hecuba. Ismene, wife of the Greek commander Hero, speaks out so passionately for peace and mercy that she is buried alive in the Trojan wall. Part 2, set on an unnamed island 12 years later, finds blind Hecuba caring for her adopted daughter, the mentally crippled Ismene. War encroaches upon freedom when the Greeks invade the island. After wise old Hecuba perpetrates a ruse for freedom, she is killed in a storm. Ismene, crippled in mind, and a miner, crippled in body, face the new day together, strangers on an island.

Bond's nonwar plays derived from history and legend zigzag sharply from comic to tragic tones. *Early Morning* puns on mourning, but the play is grotesquely hilarious in its exposé of Victorian social injustice. Proper Queen Victoria has Siamese twin sons, Crown Prince George and the protagonist Arthur. The queen matches the former to Florence Nightingale, whom she then rapes.

Prince Albert, Disraeli, and Gladstone all plot against the queen. By midplay the whole cast is dead in heaven, where the main activity is cannibalism but where all flesh regenerates. Arthur alone refuses to accept the heavenly habit, starving himself to a second death.

Suicide also closes the grimmer *Bingo*, whose protagonist is William Shakespeare in retirement at Stratford. Aware that land enclosure means starvation for its victims, Shakespeare nevertheless fails to oppose enclosure so long as his own investments are guaranteed. After a visit from drunken Ben Jonson, Shakespeare's disgust at the cruelties of his fellow men shifts to self-disgust at his own failure to act: "How long have I been dead?" He answers the question by taking poison.

Like *Bingo*, *The Fool* indicts the cruelties of an acquisitive society. But unlike *Bingo*'s Shakespeare, the fool, poet John Clare, is exploited by his social "betters." Not only does he lose his money, his poems, and his evanescent mistress, but he also loses his sanity. Though Bond only sketches his two protagonist poets, Shakespeare and Clare, he dramatizes their society with deft economy.

Restoration dramatizes the life and death of another kind of fool, the honest servant Bob in the world of Restoration fops. Elegant, witty Lord Are deigns to marry a businessman's daughter for her dowry. She in turn has married him for entrance into the social whirl, an entrance he refuses her. In a preposterous scene she haunts him as a sourly unblithe spirit, and he stabs her dead and persuades faithful Bob to take the blame. In spite of the courage and protests of Bob's black wife, he is hanged for the crime he did not commit. *Summer* stages a private story, and the trilogy *The War Plays* is a postatomic epic with impassioned pleas for social responsibility.

Bond's violent scenes and cruel humor at first attracted attention rather than appreciation, but he gradually gathered admirers of his moral commitment theatricalized with verve and economy. He has spoken out against the theater of the absurd—"Life becomes meaningless when you stop *acting* on the things that concern you most." His rational theater does not preach a rational gospel, however, for he fills an almost bare stage with whole societies from which and against which heroes arise who learn through their suffering to act responsibly. This resembles the *pathos-mathos* of classical tragedy, but it is translated into a modern godless world.

—Ruby Cohn

BOVELL, Andrew John

Nationality: Australian. **Born:** Kalgoorlie, Western Australian, 23 November 1962. **Education:** University of Western Australian, Perth, 1980-83, B.A. 1983; Victorian College of the Arts, Melbourne, Victoria, 1984-86, B.A. in dramatic arts 1986. **Family:** Married Eugenia Fragos in 1988; 2 sons, 1 daughter. **Career:** Professional writer. Writer-in-residence Ensemble Theatre Project, 1986, Jigsaw Theatre Company, 1987, Melbourne Workers Theatre, 1987-88, and Melbourne Theatre Company, 1989-90. **Awards:** AFI nomination, for best television drama, for *Fisherman's Wake,* 1996; Premiers Literary Awards nomination and Awgie nomination, for *Scenes from a Separation,* 1996; Gold Medal for Drama at New York television and radio festival, for *Distant Lights from Dark Places,* 1997; Awgie award for best stage play, for *Speaking in Tongues,* 1997. **Agent:** Kate Richter, c/o Hilary Linstead and Associates, Level 18/ Plaza II, 500 Oxford Street, Bondi Junction NSW 2022, Australia.

Publications

Plays

An Ocean out My Window (produced Canberra, 1986).
State of Defence (produced Melbourne, 1987).
Ship of Fools (produced Adelaide and Melbourne, 1987).
After Dinner (produced 1988; New Zealand, England, and Ireland, 1997). Currency Press, 1997.
The Ballad of Lois Ryan (produced Melbourne, 1988).
Gulliver's Travels, adaptation of Jonathan Swift novel (produced Melbourne, 1992).
Like Whiskey on the Breath of a Drunk You Love (produced Melbourne, 1992).
Distant Lights from Dark Places (produced La Mama, 1994).
Scenes from a Separation, co-written with Hannie Rayson (produced Melbourne, 1995). Currency Press, 1997.
Shades of Blue (produced La Mama, 1996).
Speaking in Tongues (produced Sydney, 1996). Currency Press, 1998.
Confidentially Yours-Jane and Paula (produced 1998). Currency Press, 1998.
Who's Afraid of the Working Class-Trash (produced Melbourne, 1998).

Screenplays: *Piccolo Mondo,* 1992; *Strictly Ballroom,* co-written with Baz Lurhmann and Craig Pearce, 1992; *Lust,* 1993; *The Fisherman's Wake,* 1995; *The Riders,* adaptation of Tim Winton novel, 1997; *Head On,* adaptation of Christos Tsiolkas novel *Loaded,* 1997.

Radio Plays: *The Ballad of Lois Ryan,* 1989; *After Dinner,* 1993; *Distant Lights from Dark Places,* 1996.

* * *

Andrew Bovell emerged from what is sometimes called the second wave of Australian drama, a period beginning in the early 1980s and characterized by a more cosmopolitan worldview than that associated with the insular parochialism of the preceding new wave. While contemporaries such as David Williamson and Louis Nowra are better known, Bovell is nonetheless among the front rank of Australian playwrights. An acute observer and recorder of "ordinary people," he is one of Australia's most technically skilled dramatists, his plays consistently lauded for their precision of structure and their tightly woven, sharply naturalistic dialogue. Frequently his characters speak across one another, intercutting, overlaying, and repeating—weaving intricate patterns in dialogue. Common, too, in Bovell's work are sudden shifts in time, flashbacks, and other narrative manipulations; in particular, his reliance on coincidence and chance meetings is a trademark. Rather than straining credibility, this technique points up how accidental events can often precipitate crises. Bovell's dramas have strongly musical qualities. Structurally complex and emotionally rich, they are embellished with codas and harmonies, echoes and dissonances.

Dissenting views about Bovell's writing are rare; they center on perceptions of the plays as being rather too clinical, their structures too obviously neat and overly schematic. Moreover, the representational mode preferred by Bovell occasionally leaves observers wanting more theatrically adventurous work. This latter concern reflects in part a more generalized distaste for naturalistic drama common in some Australian critical circles.

Although best known for his "middle-class" plays, especially *After Dinner* (1988), Bovell's oeuvre charts remarkably diverse social territory. His collaborative work with the Melbourne Workers' Theatre (including *State of Defence*, 1987; *The Ballad of Lois Ryan*, 1988; and *Trash*, 1998) is grounded firmly in the worlds of the underprivileged and the marginalized: blue-collar laborers, homeless youth, street workers, and nightlifers. That said, the plays favored by main stage companies characteristically dissect the lives of middle-class characters in ways somewhat evocative of Pinter and Williams, writers to whom Bovell acknowledges a debt. Certainly classifiable as comedies and notable for their often brilliantly incisive humor, works such as *After Dinner, Shades of Blue* (1992), *Scenes from a Separation* (cowritten with Hannie Rayson, 1995), and *Speaking in Tongues* (1996) are also shot through with an ironic, sometimes despondent bleakness, their themes encompassing the stresses of modern life; the fragility of social masks; social and sexual inadequacies; and ultimately, the spiritual vacuity of contemporary culture. Such concerns, explored at the psychological level of the private and personal, are normally also contextualized within broader social complexities. Lois and Mick (*State of Defence*) carry their marital conflicts on into their shared workplace, while Mathew and Nina's alienation (*Scenes from a Separation*) is born of a deeper disease, one that is symptomatic of late twentieth-century materialism.

After Dinner, a black satire set in the twilight zone of Friday night singles' bars, became something of a standby for theater companies in the 1990s and was produced in New Zealand, England, and Ireland, as well as in Australia. Inspired by the pathos Bovell sensed as three women argued over splitting the bill in a Melbourne pub, the play centers on five office workers who come together at the end of the week ostensibly to let their hair down. Through their elaborately patterned dialogue, however, we sense their vulnerability, isolation, and pain. In *Scenes from a Separation*, Bovell and Rayson engage similar emotional themes, analyzing the breakdown of a middle-class marriage from two perspectives: the male and female. Bovell's one-act play *Like Whisky on the Breath of a Drunk You Love* (1992), a bitter portrayal of lust and disappointment, comments darkly on love in the 1990s.

Bovell is an experienced dramaturge, and, while his writing is always distinctive, he is also one of the best collaborators working in Australian theater. Much of his work involves close consultation with researchers, dramaturges (notably John Romeril at Melbourne Workers' Theatre), advisory groups, and students. He is much in demand as a scriptwriter for film and television, his biggest success coming with the hit film *Strictly Ballroom*, cowritten with Baz Luhrmann in 1992. His plays have also proved unusually well suited to radio. This is not surprising given that they are predominantly conversation driven, their key strengths residing at the level of dialogue, where, through language, people act upon—and against—one another.

—Paul Makeham

BOWEN, John (Griffith)

Nationality: British. **Born:** Calcutta, India, 5 November 1924. **Education:** Queen Elizabeth's Grammar School, Crediton, Devon; Pembroke College, Oxford (editor, *Isis*), 1948-51; St. Antony's College, Oxford (Frere Exhibitioner in Indian Studies), 1951-53, M.A. 1953; Ohio State University, Columbus, 1952-53. **Military Service:** Served in the Mahratha Light Infantry, 1943-47: captain. **Career:** Assistant editor, *Sketch* magazine, London, 1953-56; copywriter, J. Walter Thompson Company, London, 1956-58; head of the copy department, S.T. Garland Advertising, London, 1958-60; script consultant, Associated Television, London, 1960-67; drama producer, Thames Television, London, 1978-79, London Weekend Television, 1981-83, and BBC, 1984. **Awards:** Society of Authors traveling scholarship, 1986. **Agent:** (fiction) Christopher Sinclair-Stevenson, 3 South Terrace, London SW7 2TB, England; (theatre) Casarotto Ramsay Ltd., National House, 60-66 Wardour Street, London W1V 3HP, England. **Address:** Old Lodge Farm, Sugarswell Lane, Edgehill, Banbury, Oxfordshire OX15 6HP, England.

Publications

Plays

The Essay Prize, with A Holiday Abroad and The Candidate: Plays for Television. London, Faber, 1962.

I Love You, Mrs. Patterson (produced Cambridge and London, 1964). London, Evans, 1964.

The Corsican Brothers, based on the play by Dion Boucicault (televised 1965; revised version produced London, 1970). London, Methuen, 1970.

After the Rain, adaptation of his own novel (produced London, 1966; New York, 1967). London, Faber, 1967; New York, Random House, 1968; revised version, Faber, 1972.

The Fall and Redemption of Man (as *Fall and Redemption*, produced London, 1967; as *The Fall and Redemption of Man*, produced New York, 1974). London, Faber, 1968.

Silver Wedding (televised 1967; revised version, produced in *We Who Are about to . . .*, later called *Mixed Doubles*, London, 1969). London, Methuen, 1970.

Little Boxes (includes *The Coffee Lace* and *Trevor*) (produced London, 1968; New York, 1969). London, Methuen, 1968; New York, French, 1970.

The Disorderly Women, adaptation of a play by Euripides (produced Manchester, 1969; London, 1970). London, Methuen, 1969.

The Waiting Room (produced London, 1970). London, French, 1970; New York, French, 1971.

Robin Redbreast (televised 1970; produced Guildford, Surrey, 1974). Published in *The Television Dramatist*, edited by Robert Muller, London, Elek, 1973.

Diversions (produced London, 1973). Excerpts published in *Play Nine*, edited by Robin Rook, London, Arnold, 1981.

Young Guy Seeks Part-Time Work (televised 1973; produced London, 1978).

Roger, in *Mixed Blessings* (produced Horsham, Sussex, 1973). Published in *London Magazine*, October-November 1976.

Florence Nightingale (as *Miss Nightingale*, televised 1974; revised version, as *Florence Nightingale*, produced Canterbury, 1975). London, French, 1976.
Heil Caesar!, adaptation of *Julius Caesar* by Shakespeare (televised 1974). London, BBC Publications, 1974; revised version (produced Birmingham, 1974), London, French, 1975.
Which Way Are You Facing? (produced Bristol, 1976). Excerpts published in *Play Nine*, edited by Robin Rook, London, Arnold, 1981.
Singles (produced London, 1977).
Bondage (produced London, 1978).
The Inconstant Couple, adaptation of a play by Marivaux (produced Chichester, 1978). Published as *The Feigned Inconstancy* in *Marivaux Plays*, London, Methuen, 1988.
Spot the Lady (produced Newcastle upon Tyne, 1981).
The Geordie Gentleman, adaptation of a play by Molière (produced Newcastle upon Tyne, 1987).
The Oak Tree Tea Room Siege (produced Leicester, 1990).
Cold Salmon. French, 1998.

Radio Plays: *Digby* (as Justin Blake, with Jeremy Bullmore), 1959; *Varieties of Love* (revised version of television play *The First Thing You Think Of*), 1968; *The False Diaghilev*, 1988.

Television Plays: created the *Garry Halliday* series; episodes in *Front Page Story, The Power Game, Wylde Alliance*, and *The Villains* series; *A Holiday Abroad*, 1960; *The Essay Prize*, 1960; *The Jackpot Question*, 1961; *The Candidate*, 1961; *Nuncle*, from the story by John Wain, 1962; *The Truth about Alan*, 1963; *A Case of Character*, 1964; *Mr. Fowlds*, 1965; *The Corsican Brothers*, 1965; *Finders Keepers*, 1967; *The Whole Truth*, 1967; *Silver Wedding*, 1967; *A Most Unfortunate Accident*, 1968; *Flotsam and Jetsam*, 1970; *Robin Redbreast*, 1970; *The Guardians* series (7 episodes), 1971; *A Woman Sobbing*, 1972; *The Emergency Channel*, 1973; *Young Guy Seeks Part-Time Work*, 1973; *Miss Nightingale*, 1974; *Heil Caesar!*, 1974; *The Treasure of Abbott Thomas*, 1974; *The Snow Queen*, 1974; *A Juicy Case*, 1975; *Brief Encounter*, from the film by Noël Coward, 1976; *A Photograph*, 1977; *Rachel in Danger*, 1978; *A Dog's Ransom*, from the novel by Patricia Highsmith, 1978; *Games*, 1978; *The Ice House*, 1978; *The Letter of the Law*, 1979; *Dying Day*, 1980; *The Specialist*, 1980; *A Game for Two Players*, 1980; *Dark Secret*, 1981; *Honeymoon*, 1985; *Hetty Wainthrop Investigates*, with David Cook, 1996.

Novels

The Truth Will Not Help Us: Embroidery on an Historical Theme. London, Chatto and Windus, 1956.
After the Rain. London, Faber, 1958; New York, Ballantine, 1959.
The Centre of the Green. London, Faber, 1959; New York, McDowell Obolensky, 1960.
Storyboard. London, Faber, 1960.
The Birdcage. London, Faber, and New York, Harper, 1962.
A World Elsewhere. London, Faber, 1965; New York, Coward McCann, 1967.
Squeak: A Biography of NPA 1978A 203. London, Faber, 1983; New York, Viking, 1984.
The McGuffin. London, Hamish, Hamilton, 1984; Boston, Atlantic Monthly Press, 1985.
The Girls: A Story of Village Life. London, Hamish Hamilton, 1986; New York, Atlantic Monthly Press, 1987.
Fighting Back. London, Hamish Hamilton, 1989.
The Precious Gift. London, Sinclair-Stevenson, 1992.
No Retreat. London, Sinclair-Stevenson, 1994.

Other (for children)

Pegasus. London, Faber, 1957; New York, A. S. Barnes, 1960.
The Mermaid and the Boy. London, Faber, 1958; New York, A. S. Barnes, 1960.
Garry Halliday and the Disappearing Diamonds [*Ray of Death; Kidnapped Five; Sands of Time; Flying Foxes*] (as Justin Blake, with Jeremy Bullmore). London, Faber, 5 vols., 1960-64.

*

Manuscript Collections: Mugar Memorial Library, Boston University; (television works) Temple University Library, Philadelphia.

Critical Studies: *Writers on Themselves*, London, BBC Publications, 1964; "The Man Behind *The Disorderly Women*" by Robin Thornber, in *Guardian* (London), 19 February 1969; "Like a Woman They Keep Coming Back To" by Ronald Hayman, in *Drama* (London), Autumn 1970; "Bowen on the Little Box" by Hugh Hebert, in *Guardian* (London), 6 August 1971; "Author/Director," in *London Magazine*, December 1971, and "*The Guardians*: A Post Mortem," in *Plays and Players* (London), January 1972, both by Bowen.

Theatrical Activities:
Director: **Plays**—At the London Academy of Music and Dramatic Art since 1967; *The Disorderly Women*, Manchester, 1969, London, 1970; *Fall and Redemption*, Pitlochry, Scotland, 1969; *The Waiting Room*, London, 1970.

Actor: **Plays**—In repertory in North Wales, summers 1950-51; Palace Theatre, Watford, Hertfordshire, 1965.

John Bowen comments:

My plays, like my novels, are distinguished by a general preoccupation with myth (*The Truth Will Not Help Us, After the Rain, A World Elsewhere, Fall and Redemption, The Disorderly Women, Robin Redbreast*), and mainly with one particular myth, that of the Bacchae, which in my reading represents the conflict between Apollonian and Dionysiac ways of living more than the mere tearing to pieces of a Sacred King. This theme, the fight in every human being and between beings themselves, rationality against instinct, is to be found somewhere in almost everything I have written.

Another common theme is of manipulation, one person using another or others, not always consciously, and sometimes "for their good." This theme has been most clearly expressed politically in the episodes I wrote for the television series *The Guardians*, and in my novel *A World Elsewhere*. A third common theme, allied to the other two, is that of self-deceit.

I think of plays as constructions (as all literary forms are, but plays and poems perhaps most), and I enjoy theatricality. I like movement; plays are not talk, but action, though the talk may *be* action. I think that the cinema and television have helped the theatre in the twentieth century to rediscover some of the mobility it had in the sixteenth. Though I like above all naturalistic acting, I hate naturalistic settings, and try to avoid waits for scene changes: in most of my plays, the scenes flow into each other by a shift of light.

I have been influenced by Ibsen and Chekhov, probably by Coward, Anouilh, Pirandello, and Shaw. Of twentieth-century directors, I have most admired Sir Tyrone Guthrie.

* * *

Before his first major stage success with *After the Rain,* in 1966, John Bowen was already well known as a novelist and theater critic for the then prestigious *London Magazine*. His theater columns of that period reveal a sympathetic understanding of a large variety of dramatic modes, and so it is not surprising that his own plays have been criticized for stylistic eclecticism. Though *After the Rain* was based on one of Bowen's novels, its theatricality was immediately seen to reflect Weiss's *Marat/Sade*, particularly in the way each member of the cast is presented as being a criminal deviant hypnotized into the therapeutic reenactment of events related to the great deluge of the late twentieth century. The metatheatrical dimension is not developed at all, however, and Bowen's deeper interest emerges as lying in the use of archetype, particularly through sometimes startling diachronic collations.

After the Rain displays the emblems of epic theater from the start: a bare stage with a lectern, minimal props, placards identifying locations, and the first character (a lecturer) delivering his opening lines to the lighting technician. All of the barriers of the conventional theater seem to have dissolved. But within a few seconds the lecturer is referring to "life in 1968" as something prehistoric; elastic time has suddenly soared beyond the audience's experience. Early in the second act there appears a character whom audience members (but not the characters) recognize as Noah, and time bounces back violently in the other direction. The nine prisoners-characters, ostensibly drifting on a raft in the 1970s, find themselves in an arena in which the mythological merges with the futuristic and a primitive theocracy is generated by necessity, although the lecturer's skepticism is continually apparent. Satire of varying strength has been directed at the figures on the raft, stock types from the 1960s, and on his first appearance Noah also seems to be a target for iconoclastic ridicule. It quickly becomes apparent, however, that the Noah myth is not one of regeneration but of fossilization; the ark is full of rotting animals, and Noah survives alone as a demented Ancient Mariner, persecuted by the anonymous gods and crazed by drinking the blood of the Shetland pony. For the protection of humanity, the ark is incinerated with Noah aboard. A new totalitarian myth is, of course, emerging, but for the audience there remains the question of whether Arthur, the autocrat of the raft society, has annihilated the Noah myth or assimilated it. The ending differs in the 1972 revised version, but in both versions Arthur's divinity essentially is challenged when he demands the sacrifice of the first baby born; the result is a duel, with the death of the god and the birth of the new society that presents the play. At the same time, however, roles are also broken, and the play ends with the insistence that the theater has been invaded by reality.

Bowen's fascination with what he calls "myth" seems to derive from its defiance of chronology and conventional concepts of causation. His adaptation of Boucicault's *The Corsican Brothers* for television and then for the stage seems to have been stimulated by the telepathic link between the twins—and thus between Corsican and Parisian society. But the play also drops the morality of melodrama into a Brechtian limbo, heralded by the hobbyhorses of the first episode, developed by numerous flippantly sardonic songs, and culminating in a "moral finale." *Fall and Redemption* seems to consist of an iconoclastic pilfering of quaint details from the mystery cycles to create an acting exercise for LAMDA students, and its termination with the Crucifixion rather than doomsday, with which all the English cycles end, was interpreted as insensitivity to form. Yet its Brechtian rationale is evident at least when Cain and Abel are joined by a talking horse and is inescapable in the ending when the actors help Jesus off the cross and then come forward for applause. In another myth play for LAMDA, *The Disorderly Women*, Bowen knew that he was joining numerous playwrights of the 1960s in attempting a contemporary adaptation of *Bacchae.* Yet he was also trying to give a relatively sympathetic portrayal of Pentheus as a ruler committed to moderation, a principle neither understood by his father nor respected by Dionysus, whose cynicism, Bowen's introduction suggests, is substantiated by Auschwitz, Hiroshima, and Vietnam.

In the 1970s Bowen's interests and techniques developed variously, with *Singles*, a comedy about sexual mercenaries, achieving a modest critical success in London. The dilemma of Pentheus was expanded and domesticated in a play that did not reach London, *Which Way Are You Facing?*, a cerebral but aggressively theatrical contribution to the history of the problem play from the sympathetic perspective of the control room of the Samaritans, who monitor the unloveliest of humanity in every corner of the auditorium. By contrast, in the much praised *Robin Redbreast* Bowen exploits the savagery of the myth that leaps from prehistory into the life of a television script editor; the dialogue of the final scene even includes a reference to *The Golden Bough*, but the structure of the play depends on psychological realism, with its main impact being that of a thriller. In fact, although Bowen is best known for plays based on myth and using techniques of epic theater, he learned his dramatic craft writing for television, and his early plays, notably *A Holiday Abroad,* show a mastery of the subtleties of realism. One of his mature plays, *The Coffee Lace*, has even been interpreted as naturalistic in its portrayal of six veteran actors who have hermetically sealed themselves off from the world after a major theatrical failure 10 years previously; they are also fossilized grotesques, however, very similar in their situation to the figures of *After the Rain.* Ambivalent it may be, but the play and its companion piece *Trevor* must dispel the common complaint that Bowen is a humorless writer, for the gentle comedy in the portrayal of the social cripples in *The Coffee Lace* is rich but compassionate.

In the 1980s Bowen increasingly returned to his preferred early genre, fiction.

—Howard McNaughton

BOX, Edgar. *See* **VIDAL, Gore.**

BRENTON, Howard

Nationality: British. **Born:** Portsmouth, Hampshire, 13 December 1942. **Education:** Chichester High School; St. Catharine's College, Cambridge, B.A. (honours) in English 1965. **Family:** Married Jane Fry in 1970; two sons. **Career:** Stage manager in several repertory companies; resident dramatist, Royal Court Theatre, London, 1972-73. **Awards:** Arts Council bursary, 1969, 1970; John Whiting award, 1970; *Evening Standard* award, 1977, 1985. **Agent:** Casarotto Ramsay Ltd., National House, 60-66 Wardour Street, London W1V 3HP, England.

PUBLICATIONS

Plays

Ladder of Fools (produced Cambridge, 1965).
Winter, Daddykins (produced Dublin, 1965).
It's My Criminal (produced London, 1966).
A Sky-Blue Life, adaptation of stories by Gorky (produced London, 1967; revised version produced London, 1971). Included in *Three Plays*, 1989.
Gargantua, adaptation of the novel by Rabelais (produced Brighton, 1969).
Gum and Goo (produced Brighton, 1969; London, 1971). Included in *Plays for Public Places*, 1972.
Revenge (produced London, 1969). London, Methuen, 1970.
Heads, and The Education of Skinny Spew (produced Bradford, 1969; London, 1970). Included in *Christie in Love and Other Plays*, 1970.
Christie in Love (produced Brighton and London, 1969; Chicago, 1981). Included in *Christie in Love and Other Plays*, 1970.
Christie in Love and Other Plays. London, Methuen, 1970.
Fruit (produced London, 1970).
Wesley (produced Bradford, 1970). Included in *Plays for Public Places*, 1972.
Scott of the Antarctic; or, What God Didn't See (produced Bradford, 1971). Included in *Plays for Public Places*, 1972.
Lay By, with others (produced Edinburgh and London, 1971). London, Calder and Boyars, 1972.
Hitler Dances (produced Edinburgh and London, 1972). London, Methuen, 1982.
Plays for Public Places. London, Eyre Methuen, 1972.
How Beautiful with Badges (produced London, 1972). Included in *Three Plays*, 1989.
England's Ireland, with others (produced Amsterdam and London, 1972).
Measure for Measure, adaptation of the play by Shakespeare (produced Exeter, Devon, 1972). Included in *Three Plays*, 1989.
A Fart for Europe, with David Edgar (produced London, 1973).
The Screens, adaptation of a play by Jean Genet (produced Bristol, 1973).
Brassneck, with David Hare (produced Nottingham, 1973). London, Eyre Methuen, 1974.
Magnificence (produced London, 1973). London, Eyre Methuen, 1973.
Mug (produced Manchester, 1973).
Jedefrau, adaptation of a play by Hugo von Hofmannsthal (produced Salzburg, 1974).
The Churchill Play: As It Will be Performed in the Winter of 1984 by the Internees of Churchill Camp Somewhere in England (produced Nottingham, 1974; London, 1978; revised version, produced London, 1988). Included in *Plays 1*, 1986.
The Saliva Milkshake, adaptation of the novel *Under Western Eyes* by Conrad (televised 1975; produced London, 1975; New York, 1978). London, TQ Publications, 1977.
Government Property (produced Aarhus, Denmark, 1975).
Weapons of Happiness (produced London, 1976; Buffalo, 1983). London, Eyre Methuen, 1977.
Epsom Downs (produced London, 1977). London, Eyre Methuen, 1977.
Deeds, with others (produced Nottingham, 1978). Published in *Plays and Players* (London), May and June 1978.
Sore Throats (produced London, 1979; St. Louis, 1983; New York, 1985). With *Sonnets of Love and Opposition*, London, Eyre Methuen, 1979.
Warwickgate, with others (produced Warwick, 1979).
The Life of Galileo, adaptation of a play by Brecht (produced London, 1980). London, Eyre Methuen, 1980.
The Romans in Britain (produced London, 1980). London, Eyre Methuen, 1980; revised version, Methuen, 1982.
Plays for the Poor Theatre (includes *The Saliva Milkshake, Christie in Love, Heads, The Education of Skinny Spew, Gum and Goo*). London, Eyre, Methuen, 1980.
A Short Sharp Shock!, with Tony Howard (produced London, 1980). With *Thirteenth Night*, London, Eyre Methuen, 1981.
Thirteenth Night (produced London, 1981). With *A Short Sharp Shock!*, London, Eyre Methuen, 1981.
Nail Poems: 32 Haiku (produced London, 1981).
Danton's Death, adaptation of a play by Georg Büchner (produced London, 1982). London, Methuen, 1982.
The Thing (for children; produced Brackley, Northamptonshire, 1982).
Conversations in Exile, adaptation of a work by Brecht (produced London, 1982; New York, 1987).
The Genius (produced London, 1983; Los Angeles, 1984). London, Methuen, 1983.
Sleeping Policemen, with Tunde Ikoli (produced London, 1983). London, Methuen, 1984.
Bloody Poetry (produced Leicester and London, 1984; New York, 1987). London, Methuen, 1985.
Pravda: A Fleet Street Comedy, with David Hare (produced London, 1985; Minneapolis, 1989). London, Methuen, 1985.
Plays 1 (includes *Christie in Love, Magnificence, The Churchill Play, Weapons of Happiness, Epsom Downs, Sore Throats*). London, Methuen, 1986.
Dead Head (televised 1986). London, Methuen, 1987.
Plays 2 (includes *The Romans in Britain, Thirteenth Night, The Genius, Bloody Poetry, Greenland*). London, Methuen, 1988.
Greenland (produced London, 1988). London, Methuen, 1988.
Iranian Nights, with Tariq Ali (produced London, 1989). London, Hern, 1989.
Three Plays (includes *A Sky-Blue Life, How Beautiful with Badges, Measure for Measure*). Sheffield, Academic, 1989.
H.I.D. (Hess Is Dead) (produced London, 1989). London, Hern, 1989.
Moscow Gold, with Tariq Ali (produced London, 1990). London, Hern, 1990.
The Wall Dog, with Jane Brenton, adaptation of the play by Manfred Karge (produced London, 1990).

Berlin Bertie (produced London, 1992). London, Hern, 1992.
Faust Parts I & II: A New Version by Howard Brenton. London, Nick Hern, 1995.

Screenplay: *Skin Flicker*, 1973.

Television Plays: *Lushly*, 1972; *The Saliva Milkshake*, 1975; *The Paradise Run*, 1976; *A Desert of Lies*, 1984; *Dead Head* serial, 1986; *Faust, Part I & 11,* adaptation from Christa Weisman, 1995.

Novel

Diving for Pearls. London, Hern, 1989.

Poetry

Notes from a Psychotic Journal and Other Poems. Privately printed, 1969.

Other

Hot Irons: Diaries, Essays, Journalism. London, Nick Hern, 1995.

*

Critical Studies: Interview with Peter Ansorge, in *Plays and Players* (London), February 1972; *New British Political Dramatists* by John Bull, London, Macmillan, and New York, Grove Press, 1984; *File on Brenton* edited by Tony Mitchell, London, Methuen, 1988; *Brenton the Playwright* by Richard Boon, London, Methuen, 1991; *Howard Brenton: A Casebook,* edited by Ann Wilson, New York, Garland, 1992; "Making History: The Plays of Howard Brenton" by Hersh Zeifman, in *British and Irish Drama Since 1960,* edited by James Acheson, Houndmills, England, Macmillan, 1993; "Howard Brenton" by John E. O'Connor, in *British Playwrights, 1956-1995: A Research and Production Sourcebook,* edited by William W. Demastes, Westport, Connecticut, Greenwood, 1996.

Theatrical Activities:
Actor: **Plays**—With the Brighton Combination, 1969.

* * *

"It took me a long time," said Howard Brenton, after reading English at Cambridge University, "to get over being taught literature in that way." While at Cambridge, Brenton wrote a long, unworkable play called *Ladder of Fools,* but it was not until joining Brighton Combination as an actor and writer in 1968 that he began to find his feet in the theater. Adapting Rabelais's *Gargantua* for a group show led Brenton to experiment with style, and a shoestring budget while writing *Gum and Goo* in 1969 taught him to write with concentration. His first full-length play, *Revenge,* was produced by the Royal Court Theatre Upstairs in 1969, and he subsequently worked with Portable Theatre, writing *Lay By* and *Brassneck* in collaboration with David Hare and others.

In 1970 Brenton won the John Whiting Award for *Christie in Love.* The Rillington Place murderer is treated naturalistically, as a lover in search of a love object, while the police are essentially nonnaturalistic, giving the audience "a sense of moral vertigo." *Magnificence* turns on the impossibility of taking effective action against the establishment. In the final scene a would-be revolutionary, newly released from prison, fails to assassinate a cabinet minister because his gelignite mask has fused. When he tosses the mask away, it explodes, killing both himself and his victim, a final ineffectual act.

Brenton's early settings range from the South Pole (*Scott of the Antarctic*), to Epsom racecourse on Derby day (*Epsom Downs*), an internment camp (*The Churchill Play*), and a crisp factory (*Weapons of Happiness*). The plays are anarchic. *The Churchill Play,* for example, shows an army-operated internment camp for recalcitrant trade union members in the Britain of 1984. Warning against the possibility of a totalitarian Britain, *Weapons of Happiness* presents a black-and-white world of bosses and workers in which the workers, in a highly symbolic act, literally flee down the drain. Brenton's characters become signposts for good and evil. He describes the costumes for *Scott of the Antarctic* as "huge, gangling, gaudy apparitions—like adverts stepped down from the billboards of some rubbish world." It is a cartoon strip technique that is Brechtian in style.

During the 1970s Brenton emerged as a major political dramatist, his work increasingly in demand by establishment theaters. The National Theatre's 1980 production of *The Romans in Britain* caused a furor because of its prosecution by Mary Whitehouse on the grounds of indecency. The play is not a celebration of violence and degradation, however, but a serious exploration of the dubious nature of empire building. Brenton uses the homosexual rape of a Druid priest by a Roman soldier to demonstrate this theme and goes on to show the results of British incursions into Ireland.

Brenton's work includes the translation and adaptation of Brecht's *Galileo* and of Büchner's *Danton's Death,* both for the National Theatre. For the same theater he also wrote with David Hare the enormously successful Fleet Street satire *Pravda* (truth in Russian). Other plays have experimented with technique. In *Thirteenth Night* Brenton tried to "bury" the plot of *Macbeth,* while *The Genius* is a modern version of *Galileo* in which a twentieth-century mathematician who has discovered a formula that would destroy the universe if it were used to make a bomb attempts to hide his knowledge. Brenton's most innovative experiment is his collaboration with Tunde Ikoli for Foco Novo. Each wrote an entirely separate play, but both were set in Peckham and were about the same six characters. Working with director Roland Rees, the two plays were intercut to form the curiously dreamlike work *Sleeping Policemen.*

Iranian Nights was written with Tariq Ali early in 1989 in passionate support of free expression during the crisis over Salman Rushdie's *Satanic Verses.* It was followed by *H.I.D.,* which was commissioned by the Mickery Theatre in Amsterdam and which debated whether it was Hess or another who finally died in Spandau jail. The play explored the question "What is History? . . . that we bend, that we distort? From which we want . . . the truth?"

Brenton's first attempt at a play about utopia was *Sore Throats,* "the most violent writing I have ever done." He subsequently made an unsuccessful attempt to adapt William Morris's *News from Nowhere* and then shelved ideas for other utopias until Roland Rees requested a play about Shelley. Brenton realized that Shelley and his circle were "would-be Utopians" in both their work and lives, and he wrote *Bloody Poetry* "to salute them." In 1988 there followed *Greenland,* a play Brenton had been meditating on for a decade: "I have tried to dramatize how I hope my children or my children's children will live and think." Brenton realized that it was "a reckless undertaking" to try to describe a new world culture 700 years hence as free of conflict and oppression, but he finally found a model in Shakespearean romantic comedy, in which characters get lost and find themselves in an "alternative reality." Act 2 of *Greenland* catapults Brenton's characters from 1987 into a utopia in 2687:

> Joan: How is it organised? . . . There are no policies! No-one decides anything! . . . I just die for some authority!

In the final scene Joan returns to 1987 with a jewel from 2687, from which "light splinters across the stage and out over the auditorium." It is a surprisingly hopeful portent from Brenton for the future.

—Rosemary Pountney

BREUER, Lee

Nationality: American. **Born:** Philadelphia, Pennsylvania, 6 February 1937. **Education:** University of California, Los Angeles, B.A. 1958; San Francisco State University. **Family:** Married Ruth Maleczech in 1978; two children. **Career:** Director, San Francisco Actors' Workshop, 1963-65; free-lance director in Europe, 1965-70. Co-artistic director, Mabou Mines, New York, 1970—; staff director, New York Shakespeare Festival, 1982—; co-artistic director, Re Cher Chez studio. Teacher, Yale University School of Drama, New Haven, Connecticut, 1978-80, Harvard University Extension, Cambridge, Massachusetts, 1981-82, and New York University, 1981-82. Board member, Theatre Communications Group, New York. Lives in New York City. **Awards:** Obie award, 1978, 1980, 1984; Creative Artists Public Service grant, 1980; National Endowment for the Arts fellowship, 1980, 1982; Rockefeller grant, 1981; Los Angeles Drama Critics Circle award, 1986; Tony award, 1988. **Member:** Dramatists Guild. **Agent:** Lynn Davis, Davis-Cohen Associates, 513-A Avenue of the Americas, New York, New York 10011. **Address:** Mabou Mines, c/o Performing Arts Journal, 150 First Avenue, New York, New York 10009, U.S.A; 92 St. Marks Place, #3, New York, New York 10009, U.S.A.

Publications

Plays

The Red Horse Animation, music by Philip Glass (produced New York, 1970; revised version, produced New York, 1972). Published in *The Theatre of Images*, edited by Bonnie Marranca, New York, Drama Book Specialists, 1977.

The B-Beaver Animation, music by Philip Glass, adaptation of a work by Samuel Beckett (produced Waterford, Connecticut, and New York, 1974).

The Saint and the Football Players (produced New York, 1976).

The Lost Ones, adaptation of the fiction by Samuel Beckett (produced New York, 1977).

The Shaggy Dog Animation (produced New York, 1977).

Animations: A Trilogy for Mabou Mines. New York, Performing Arts Journal Publications, 1979.

A Prelude to Death in Venice (produced New York, 1980; Edinburgh and London, 1982). Published in *New Plays USA 1*, edited by James Leverett, New York, Theatre Communications Group, 1982.

Sister Suzie Cinema, music by Bob Telson (produced New York, 1980; Edinburgh and London, 1982). New York, Theatre Communications Group, 1987.

The Gospel at Colonus, music by Bob Telson, adaptation of *Oedipus at Colonus* by Sophocles (produced Edinburgh and London, 1982; New York, 1983). New York, Theatre Communications Group, 1989.

Hajj (produced New York, 1983). Published in *Wordplays 3*, New York, Performing Arts Journal Publications, 1984.

The Warrior Ant, music by Bob Telson (produced New Haven, Connecticut and New York, 1988).

Lear, adaptation of *King Lear* by Shakespeare (produced New York, 1990).

Other

The Warrior Ant: Poems. New York, Vincent Fitz Gerald & Company, 1992.

Recording: *An Ant Alone Songs from the Warrior Ant*, Gramavision, 1993.

*

Critical Studies: "Lee Breuer on Interculturalism" by Gabrielle Cody, in *Performing Arts Journal* (Baltimore, Maryland), 1989, pp. 59-66; "Lee Breuer" by Michael Goldbert, in *Bomb*, Summer 1996, pp. 24-29.

Theatrical Activities:
Director: **Plays**—All his own plays; *The House of Bernarda Alba* by García Lorca, San Francisco, 1963; *Mother Courage* by Brecht, Paris, 1967; *The Messingkauf Dialogues* by Brecht, Edinburgh, 1968; *Play* by Samuel Beckett, Paris, 1969, New York, 1970; *Come and Go* by Samuel Beckett, New York, 1975; *Mr. Frivolous* by Wallace Shawn, New York, 1976; *Earth Spirit* by Wedekind, New Haven, Connecticut, 1976(?); *Sunday Childhood Journeys to Nobody at Home* by Arthur Sainer, New York, 1980; *Lulu* by Wedekind, Cambridge, Massachusetts, 1980; *The Tempest*, New York, 1981; *From the Point of View of the Salt* by Liza Lorwin, New York, 1986.

Actor: **Play**—In *Wrong Guys* by Ruth Maleczech, New York, 1981.

Choreographer: **Play**—*Measure for Measure*, New York, 1976.

* * *

Lee Breuer is a dramatist as well as an auteur director. He was a founding member of the Mabou Mines experimental theater collective in New York, a company in which he has remained vitally active. His "performance poems," as he calls his play texts, merge the American tradition of the self-conscious, extended lyric poem of Whitman and Ginsberg with the main tendencies of modern European drama. After beginning his directorial work with the San Francisco Actors' Workshop, Breuer studied with the Berliner Ensemble and with actors who worked with Grotowski. Thus, he knows both "presence" and the complexities of self-conscious presentational form.

The greater part of Breuer's dramatic writing is structured in the form of a labyrinthine monologue that he then "animates" in a richly physicalized stage setting and performance. The monologues telescope many identities into a single voice that, in turn, splices together fragments of a number of linguistic worlds: street language, colloquialisms, phrases from sports, science, Latin, spiritualism, and, above all, pop imagery from the movies and the media. Through juxtaposition he develops a complex mode of irony that is dominated by a sophisticated use of punning. This artistic strategy allows the poem and its speakers to subvert the efficacy of the expressive language of emotion without denying the reality of the emotion itself. Breuer's approach to dramatic language plays with the illusions of performance, which is emphasized by the Bunraku puppets he admires and often uses in his stagings of the poems.

Breuer's early poems are brief modernist beast fables in which the animal figure tells a human story. A single voice is taken up by several performers to project a fragmented self. *The Red Horse Animation* is an interior monologue about a lone voice seeking a shape for its life, as performers gyrate in evocation of a message-carrying horse. In its struggle the horse's life is stifled by the father's ethos of drudge work and money. Just as the voice starts to feel mind and imagination coming together, the image of the horse—and potential poet—tears itself apart and dissolves into silence. *The B-Beaver Animation* tells of a stutterer, the artist who cannot get his words out. He seeks to build a dam to protect his Missus and The Brood, who function as a chorus for his thoughts, which are dammed up with the detritus of his everyday experience, his learning, and his fantasies.

While working on these animations, Breuer experimented with performance art, and both lines of work converged during the late 1970s to culminate in the hours-long *The Shaggy Dog Animation.* Here two distinct voices speak for a pair of Bunraku-style puppets in American contemporary dress that are supported by live performers who animate the puppets' bodies and their words. The story is that of the exploitative John Greed who falls in love with a faithful dog-woman who calls herself Your Dog Rose. She submits to him as one of the "bitches of the city" who are "prisoners of love." Her shaggy-dog life includes a trip to Venice, California, for moviemaking and a return to New York, where she enters the art world. At her opening she shows a painted fireplug, and the art establishment comes down on her for seeing only the surface of things. She goes on to have puppies, and after a last bitter street fight with John, she ends her relationship with him. Still, their voices merge to become one voice, as powerful in memory as they were in life.

With *A Prelude to Death in Venice* Breuer's stagings shifted to solo performance, here with a triple persona: the puppeteer Bill, the puppet John Greed, and the movie agent Bill Morris. Expanded from a brief section of *Shaggy Dog,* the play presents life as a succession of late-night calls into a pair of city street pay phones that frame the figure like the two thieves who framed Christ on Golgotha. He suffers the indignities of family and the movie world, with tirades against his mother, his agent—who is "into producing reality" and is, in fact, himself—and finally his father. Throughout, Thomas Mann's *Death in Venice* provides an overlay of imagery and ironic contrast. Exasperated by his failed plan to shoot a movie in Venice, California, Bill the puppeteer kills John his puppet self and thus is able to call down his father and deliver himself to momentary freedom.

A monologue of even greater complexity emerges with *Haji,* in which an American actress seated at her makeup table summons the memory of her eastern European father who committed suicide. They sleep together and suffer together, and he shoots himself before she can repay the money she had borrowed from him, which also stands for an emotional debt. In this fateful recollection that is her version of the Muslim's trip to Mecca, her father's image is superimposed upon her own and even upon that of her son. The effects are accomplished through a sophisticated interaction of live performer, mask, film, and video imagery. No unmasking will separate their identities, however, for they vibrate within one another.

Beginning in 1980, Breuer initiated a series of experiments in music theater with the composer Bob Telson that aimed for a synthesis of popular and high art on the order of the Brecht-Weill collaborations. Their first piece was *Sister Suzie Cinema,* a brief "Doo-Wop Opera" in which young black singers dream of a union with images on a movie house screen. Imagination becomes reality as the ground gives way and they ride to their paradise on a huge airplane wing.

In a major experiment with Telson, *The Gospel at Colonus,* Breuer ripped the Oedipus story from its Greek context and thrust it into the world of exultation that is American black gospel singing. While this radical adaptation maintains the central events and figures of Sophocles' final masterpiece, it augments the Greek conventions with the black preacher's dramaturgy of chanting and shouting together with an onstage congregation. By the end the audience too joins this great chorus, standing, clapping, and joyously singing along.

The transposition of the Sophoclean drama spin forward yet another strand of Breuer's auteur director's vision, which is, in his words, "to recreate [classic] texts through American lenses." In his *Lear,* as a company statement said, "Shakespeare's *King Lear* takes on a whole new aspect in a radical, matriarchal version transported to America's Deep South, circa 1957, updating with its interracial casting and gender-switching, to question the family unit, old age, and the traditional structure of power."

Breuer's most ambitious effort has been another collaboration with Telson, *The Warrior Ant.* A work in progress, it is projected as a 12-part mock epic poem to be played in four evening-long performances. Some parts have been performed. In this mythological biography, modeled upon Japanese samurai, the hero Ant is misconceived in rape and chooses the path of individuality over that of the society of the Hill. There is a Virgilian dream journey to hell in which he discovers that his true father is a termite and not an ant. Renouncing the world in order to transcend this essential war within himself produced by parental rape and his newly discovered identity, he moves toward the sky by climbing a redwood tree. Years later, after reaching the top, he copulates with the Death Moth and discovers that he loves death best. Drawing upon multiple and seemingly contradictory theatrical resources and cultures—including Japanese, Latino, and African—Breuer orchestrates a polyphonic cultural symphony in dramatic form with fabulous abandonment.

Most jubilantly in his collaborations with Telson, music and song have led Breuer into worlds of dramatic reconciliation. But even here, as in all his work, Breuer's poetry of the theater is predicated upon a radical synthesis of performance genres—illusory play that also is a feat of illumination.

—Bill Coco

BROUGHTON, John

Nationality: New Zealander. **Born:** Hastings, 19 March 1947. **Education:** Hastings Boys' High School; Massey University, Palmerston North, B.Sc. 1971; University of Otago, Dunedin, B.D.S. 1977. **Military Service:** Served in the New Zealand Territorial Army, 1971-92: captain. **Career:** Dental house surgeon, University of Otago Dental School, 1978; chair, Araiteuru Marae Council, Dunedin, 1984-90; dentist in general practice, Dunedin, 1979-89; Maori health lecturer, Department of Preventive and Social Medicine, University of Otago Medical School, Dunedin, 1989—. **Awards:** *Dominion Sunday Times* Bruce Mason award, 1990. **Agent:** Playmarket, P.O. Box 9767, Wellington, New Zealand. **Address:** Te Maraenui, 176 Queen Street, Dunedin, New Zealand.

Publications

Plays

Te Hokinga Mai (*The Return Home*) (also director: produced Dunedin, 1988). Dunedin, Aoraki Productions, 1990.
Te Hara (*The Sin*) (also director: produced Dunedin, 1988). Published in *He Reo Hou: 5 plays by Maori Playwrights*, edited by Simon Garrett. Wellington, Playmarket, 1991.
Peter's Pantomime (sketch; produced Dunedin, 1989).
Nga Puke (*The Hills*) (produced Wellington, 1990). Wellington, Aoraki Press, 1992.
Hokonui Jones and the Sword of Destiny (sketch; produced Dunedin, 1990).
The Private War of Corporal Cooper (produced Dunedin, 1991).
Michael James Manaia (produced Wellington and Edinburgh, 1991). Wellington, Aoraki Press, 1991.
Marae (produced Wellington, 1992).
Anzac (produced Dunedin, 1992).

Screenplay: *Tears of Stone*, 1992.

Video: *Nga Mahi Ora* (Careers in the Health Workforce), 1990.

Other

A Time Journal for Halley's Comet (for children), with G.T. Brown. Dunedin, Double B Productions, 1985.

*

Manuscript Collection: University of Otago, Dunedin.

Critical Study: "Einblicke in die Maori-Kultur" by A. R. Glaap, in *Der Fremdsprachliche Unterricht* (Seelze-Velber, Germany), July 1991.

John Broughton comments:

Theatre Marae has been part of Te Ao Maori (the Maori World) ever since the Maori has been in Aotearoa (New Zealand). The marae has always been an arena where real life drama is played out. However, by fusing the customs and practices of the marae with Western/European theatre a truly bicultural art form, unique to New Zealand, has evolved. This has been particularly active over the last 20 years and is still evolving and developing.

I have found that drama/theatre is a very powerful medium for the sharing of two cultures: Maori and Pakeha. It can embrace both without feeling threatening to one half. I like to think that the plays I have written, and their productions, cross both cultures in a way that is meaningful and relevant to both, resulting in enlightenment and hope for us all.

* * *

Since 1989 there has been an explosion of Maori theater in New Zealand. Building on Western traditions and writings in English, playwrights use the Maori language mainly for traditional forms of songs, greetings, and chants. Together with the universal themes of family life and love, Maori concerns are always tied to searching for and reclaiming the past and include the feeling of a special relationship with the land.

In a group of about a dozen Maori playwrights newcomer John Broughton (Kahungunu on his father's side, Kai Tahu on his mother's) holds a respected position for his treatment of sensitive issues as well as the widespread acceptance of his major work, *Michael James Manaia.*

Te Hara (*The Sin*), a short play for three women, tells how the building of a chicken house on sacred burial ground has terrible consequences. While a slight piece, it proved very moving in performance, and the theme of death is handled with great sensitivity. Broughton does not try to explain the beliefs held by his characters. He merely displays the beliefs in dramatic context, showing ordinary lives taking place in what remains of a holistic cultural tradition overlaid with so-called European belief systems.

Te Hokinga Mai (*The Return Home*) explores Maori and European differences by using Vietnam as a backdrop, a theater of war Broughton was to return to later on. Two soldiers, one Maori, the other European, become friends during the war. Afterward the European visits the tribal home (*marae*) of the Maori to present the family with a greenstone pendant, all that remains of their son. In flashbacks their friendship is shown to have had a rocky start but to have strengthened and become a bridge between their cultures. Broughton uses the situation to explore differences in values and, unashamedly didactic, to teach the European about Maori ways.

In *Nga Puke* (*The Hills*) two lonely people, a man and a woman, find love and friendship during World War II. Old-fashioned and attractively sentimental, the play reflects Broughton's continuing interest in war and its effects on people.

Broughton's first full-length play, *Michael James Manaia*, appeared in 1991. In this play for one actor he returns to Vietnam, which looms large in Broughton's mind because of his firsthand experience of the New Zealand army during the years following the conflict. The hero is a returned veteran who is suffering unexplained distress since his repatriation. He remembers and reenacts his experiences from childhood to the dreadful present during the course of the powerful and at times terrifying play, which shows how Broughton's command of the medium advanced in the four years after he began to write seriously.

The first half takes us through a youth spent in the country, where often harsh, often hilarious events are related. Broughton excels in giving a voice to the inarticulate, and a picture emerges of a brutal, even deprived life whose high points are lit by booze and brawling. A picture slowly emerges of the harsh father who fought at Monte Cassino in World War II but who never speaks of it. This looming presence is felt throughout, until the horrifying climax. The second half leads us through the hell of close combat in Vietnam and the ultimate fight with death in the form of Hine-Nui-te-Po (the goddess of death). The shattering climax, which combines the influences of clinging Maori myth and of creeping modern chemical warfare, shocks the audience.

The performance traveled well, to the Edinburgh Festival of 1991 in fact, where it was nominated for the *Independent* Fringe Award. Demanding and receiving an outstanding performance from the actor in the solo role (Jim Moriarty), *Michael James Manaia* is a gripping play about the brutalizing effects of war in a society in which brutality in men was once considered normal and manly. Although there are many moments of humor, the play is horrifying rather than moving, and, as with his other plays, Broughton still tends to overwrite. Cut by 15 minutes it would be greatly improved, as several critics remarked.

To continue his engagement with the wars of this century, Broughton has written a companion piece to *Nga Puke* entitled *The Private War of Corporal Cooper*, set during World War I. While on the surface it is a naive affirmation of the spiritual union between a nun knitting socks at home and a soldier who wears them in the trenches, the script has an unsophisticated but evocative power. In the television script *Tears of Stone* the breaking of a *tapu* again leads to disasters for a family.

Marae, a play written for the 1992 International Festival of the Arts in Wellington, was good on the page but failed to live up to its promise in performance. Dealing with the everyday life in a *marae*, the meetinghouse that forms the traditional center of the village in a Maori community, *Marae* tries to be too many things. Part myth, part love story, and part ecological treatise, the plot concerns the local council's plan to drive a new road through tribal land and the *marae* committee's efforts to stop it. Fund-raising is an issue, and a concert that is planned and performed seems to take over from the play. The audience was left with no sense of dramatic construction or focus, although the concert itself was enjoyable.

Broughton has been the quiet leader of one line of Maori playwriting in New Zealand.

—Patricia Cooke

BROWN, Kenneth H.

Nationality: American. **Born:** Brooklyn, New York, 9 March 1936. **Education:** A preparatory school in Brooklyn. **Military Service:** Served in the United States Marine Corps, 1954-57. **Career:** Mail clerk, 1951-54; bartender and waiter, New York and Miami, 1958-63; bank clerk, New York, 1960; cigarette sales-man, New York, 1961; resident playwright, Living Theatre, New York, 1963-67; private tutor, 1966-69, and resident playwright, 1968-69, Yale University School of Drama, New Haven, Connecticut; visiting lecturer (improvisational acting), Hollins College, Virginia, 1969; visiting lecturer (history of theatre), Hunter College, New York, 1969-70; associate professor in performance (theatrical production), University of Iowa, Iowa City, 1971. **Awards:** Venice Film Festival gold medal, 1964; Rockefeller fellowship, 1965, and grant, 1967; ABC-Yale University fellowship, 1966, 1967; Guggenheim fellowship, 1966; Creative Artists Public Service grant, 1974. **Agent:** Mary Yost, 59 East 54th Street, New York, New York 10022. **Address:** 150 74th Street, Brooklyn, New York 11209, U.S.A.

Publications

Plays

The Brig (produced New York, 1963; London, 1964). New York, Hill and Wang, and London, Methuen, 1965.
Devices (produced New York, 1965).
The Happy Bar (produced New York, 1967).
Blake's Design (produced New Haven, Connecticut, 1968; New York, 1974). Published in *The Best Short Plays 1969*, edited by Stanley Richards, Philadelphia, Chilton, 1969.
The Green Room (produced Iowa City, 1971).
The Cretan Bull (produced Waterford, Connecticut, 1972; New York, 1974).
Nightlight (produced Hartford, Connecticut, 1973; London, 1974). New York, French, 1973.

Screenplays: *The Brig*, 1965; *Devices*, 1967.

Novel

The Narrows. New York, Dial Press, 1970.

Other

You'd Never Know It from the Way I Talk (lectures and readings). Ashland, Ohio, Ashland Poetry Press, 1990.

Editor, *Masterpieces of the English Short Novel*. New York, Carroll and Graf, 1992.

*

Manuscript Collection: New York Public Library.

Critical Study: "Absurdity, Democracy and Love in Kenneth Brown's *The Big*" by Adam Janiszewski, in *Polish-American Literary Confrontations*, edited by Joanna Durczak and Jerzy Durczak, Lublin, Maria Curie-Sklodowska University Press, 1995.

Kenneth H. Brown comments:

I began as a playwright quite by accident. It was the best means to convey my experiences as a confined prisoner in a Marine Brig. All my plays since have been either direct or symbolic representations of my life experiences. As such, I have been classified by one theatre historian as an accidental playwright, a title I gladly accept since I adhere to the belief that all things of personal import in my life have come about as a result of pure chance. I do not take to writing as a daily chore that must be done. It is, for me, a labor of love and, as such, I engage in it only when moved to do so. As I get older, I am constantly amazed by the body of works accumulated through this philosophy.

* * *

Although Kenneth H. Brown has published poetry, the novel *The Narrows*, and the collection of lectures and readings titled *You'd Never Know It from the Way I Talk*, his most significant achievements have been in drama. *The Brig*, a stark and appalling indictment of militarism, stamped Brown as one of the more gifted and experimental of American dramatists of the 1960s. It placed him in a tradition with Artaud and proved him able to create what neither Artaud nor Ionesco accomplished, a "theater of cruelty" complete with a metaphysics of language. His next published play, *Blake's Design*, gave further support to the belief that Brown was a dramatist who defied labels. Moving away from the stark, purposefully flat prose of *The Brig*, Brown played with the catchy rhythms of vaudeville, embellished his prose to give it a lyrical quality, and turned away from naturalism to expressionism. Of *The Cretan Bull* Brown says that he produced a "very funny play about complete strangers who meet in Central Park at dawn and confront a very odd set of circumstances." Again Brown went in new directions, experimenting with another style and exploring different themes. In *Nightlight*, a play produced at the Hartford Stage Company to strong critical acclaim, Brown says that he wrote about "the elements of violence that are now threatening the safety of decent citizens in our big cities."

Though *The Brig* and *Blake's Design* are very different, they share many common elements. In both an egalitarianism makes Brown select characters for his drama who reflect the ethnic and racial mix that makes up American society. In both Brown draws on music and popular songs. In *Blake's Design* the songs and dances are handled in a manner reminiscent of a vaudeville skit. In *The Brig* music is subverted and becomes an instrument of torture. The sarcastic, strident, sneering tone of a guard's voice is played contrapuntally against a clear, impersonal, unaffected voice. The breaking of a command is answered by its own often inaudible flat echo. The hideous dissonant martial music that is the tool of the fascist or authoritarian state, the kind of music that breaks a man's mind and makes him crawl like a maggot at any command, is produced by clashing garbage can lids together as if they were cymbals. Yet more hellish music derives from the sound of a voice resonating against a toilet bowl as one of the prisoners, using the cubicle as his confessional, cries out his litany of wrongs in obedience to the guard's orders. Dance, too, figures in the plays. In *Blake's Design* Muvva and Zack sing of Zack's necrophilia with his dead black wife while they do a soft-shoe dance. In *The Brig* dance is a ritual in which the prisoners suffer repeatedly at the hands of the guards. The dance is one in which men shrink, recoil, and double over in response to the quick, sharp blows delivered by the truncheons of the warden or the guards. This violent dance is varied with a pattern of running across the stage and halting at every white line in conformity with the procedure outlined in the manual of the Marine Corps. Finally, both plays employ a point of view that is reminiscent of naturalism. A dispassionate, exact observer records precisely the world in all its minutiae, as if the reality being depicted were a hard surface that can only be penetrated once it has been fully sounded. But for all these seeming similarities the plays are, in fact, very different, both in style and in theme.

The Brig is a blatantly political play, or rather a "concept of theater" as Brown would call it. A penal institute in Camp Fuji, the brig is the place where marines are sent to be punished for any infraction of military orders. The set of the play duplicates as nearly as possible the specifications of the brig, and its actions reenact the rules that govern its workings as set down in the manual. The play opens with the waking of the prisoners at dawn, and it closes with the putting out of the lights at night. Between dawn and night the prisoners repeat again and again the same gestures and motions as they are forced to dress and undress, eat and march, and clean and stand at attention for no other reason than to fulfill an order and submit to power. Nameless (they are called by number—only the guards have names), the prisoners grovel, crawl, abuse themselves, whimper silently, and try desperately to carry out any order to the letter while the military guards sadistically delight in finding new indignities for them to suffer and new punishments for their supposed failures. The discipline is without restraint or reason. The prisoners are senselessly humiliated, beaten, and abused. The only logic that governs events is the relentless logic of power and physical force. In the course of the day one prisoner is released, a new one enters, and a third is released to an even worse form of institutional imprisonment, the asylum. After two weeks in the brig, which followed 16 years of honorable military service, number 26 finds himself, against all orders and common sense, crying out his name, James Turner, and in so doing demonstrating that in the brig seemingly sane behavior is in fact insane. For two hours the senses of the audience are assaulted as the prisoners are hollered at and harassed by the guards. Plot and character development in the ordinary sense are absent from the play. Language, stripped of all warmth, finally negates itself. The members of the audience are left responding to sounds, intonations, and incantations, not denotative meanings. The audience experiences an agony of feeling that derives from the immediacy of the violence unleashed both on the stage and in themselves and that has little reference to the world of reason that has systematically been destroyed by the extremes to which it has been pushed on the stage.

Blake's Design depicts Zack's struggle to free himself from both his past—the black woman whose dead body he has slept with for 10 years—and his illusions—Blake, or call him God, is one of them—in order to tell his son the truth, to live in the present, and to move upstairs from his dark basement apartment and into the light. Zack's mulatto son, Sweek, and his two women, Muvva, with whom he has shared his bed, his dead wife, and his son for 10 years, and Modrigal, his half-Oriental mistress, all talk rather self-consciously throughout the play about man's weakness, his lies, and that part of himself he does not know or understand and so calls God, or Blake. The play ends when Zack unburdens himself, tells the truth, closes the door on his past, and mounts the stairs. The symbolism is rather obvious, and the long talks about Blake tend to be tiresome. But the characters themselves are well imagined, and the quick staccato exchanges between Sweek and Zack and the shuffling dances and songs save the play.

Brown's talents are considerable, and he was one of the few genuinely original American dramatists to emerge in the early 1960s. It is the public's loss that Brown now finds the social and political environment in the United States inhospitable to writers of genuine creative talent. In his collection of lectures he laments the breakdown in the relationship between theater and community in the United States and starkly outlines the difficulties of trying to pursue the vocation of a writer in the modern era. He no longer finds his own art relevant to this crass, materialistic society. He finds this admission deeply sobering, not only because it speaks of his own failure but also because it speaks of a larger social loss. A society that does not nurture its own art also fails itself.

—Carol Simpson Stern

BRUNDAGE, John Herbert. *See* **HERBERT, John.**

BULLINS, Ed

Pseudonym: Kingsley B. Bass, Jr. **Nationality:** American. **Born:** Philadelphia, Pennsylvania, 2 July 1935. **Education:** Educated in Philadelphia public schools; at William Penn Business Institute, Philadelphia; Los Angeles City College, 1958-61; San Francisco State College, 1964-65, and M.F.A. candidate since 1990; Antioch University, San Francisco, B.A. 1989. **Military Service:** Served in the United States Navy, 1952-55. **Family:** Married Trixie Warner (marriage ended). **Career:** Playwright-in-residence and associate director, New Lafayette Theatre, New York, 1967-73; editor, *Black Theatre* magazine, New York, 1969-74; producing director, Surviving Theatre, New York, 1974—; writers unit coordinator, New York Shakespeare Festival, 1975-82; Mellon lecturer, Amherst College, Massachusetts, 1977—; public relations director, Berkeley Black Repertory, Berkeley, 1982; promotions director, Magic Theater, 1982-83; group sales coordinator, Julian Theater, 1983; playwriting teacher, Bay Area Playwrights Festival, and People's School of Dramatic Arts, 1983; instructor, City College of San Francisco, 1984-88; lecturer, Sonoma State University, California, 1987-89, and University of California, Berkeley, 1989. **Awards:** Rockefeller grant, 1968, 1970, 1973; Vernon Rice award, 1968; American Place grant, 1968; Obie award, 1971, 1975; Guggenheim grant, 1971, and fellowship, 1976; Creative Artists Public Service grant, 1973; National Endowment for the Arts grant, 1974, 1989; New York Drama Critics Circle award, 1975, 1977. D.L.: Columbia College, Chicago, 1976. **Address:** 3617 San Pablo Avenue, #118, Emeryville, California 94608, U.S.A.

PUBLICATIONS

Plays

Clara's Ole Man (produced San Francisco, 1965; New York, 1968; London, 1971). Included in *Five Plays*, 1969.

How Do You Do? (produced San Francisco, 1965; London, 1969; New York, 1980). Mill Valley, California, Illuminations Press, 1965.

Dialect Determinism, or, The Rally (produced San Francisco, 1965). Included in *The Theme Is Blackness*, 1973.

The Theme Is Blackness (produced San Francisco, 1966). Included in *The Theme Is Blackness*, 1973.

It Has No Choice (produced San Francisco, 1966; London, 1968). Included in *The Theme Is Blackness*, 1973.

A Minor Scene (produced San Francisco, 1966; London, 1968). Included in *The Theme Is Blackness*, 1973.

The Game of Adam and Eve, with Shirley Tarbell (produced Los Angeles, 1966).

In New England Winter (produced New York, 1967). Published in *New Plays from the Black Theatre*, edited by Bullins, New York, Bantam, 1969.

In the Wine Time (produced New York, 1968). Included in *Five Plays*, 1969.

A Son, Come Home (produced New York, 1968). Included in *Five Plays*, 1969.

The Electronic Nigger (produced New York and London, 1968). Included in *Five Plays*, 1969.

Goin' a Buffalo: A Tragifantasy (produced New York, 1968). Included in *Five Plays*, 1969; in *Black Theater USA*, New York, Free Press, 1996.

The Corner (produced Boston, 1968; New York, 1972). Included in *The Theme Is Blackness*, 1973.

The Gentleman Caller (produced New York and London, 1969). Published in *A Black Quartet*, edited by Clayton Riley, New York, New American Library, 1970.

Five Plays. Indianapolis, Bobbs Merrill, 1969; as *The Electronic Nigger and Other Plays*, London, Faber, 1970.

We Righteous Bombers (as Kingsley B. Bass, Jr.), adaptation of a work by Camus (produced New York, 1969).

The Man Who Dug Fish (produced Boston, 1969; New York, 1970). Included in *The Theme Is Blackness*, 1973.

Street Sounds (produced New York, 1970). Included in *The Theme Is Blackness*, 1973.

The Helper (produced New York, 1970). Included in *The Theme Is Blackness*, 1973.

A Ritual to Raise the Dead and Foretell the Future (produced New York, 1970). Included in *The Theme Is Blackness*, 1973.

The Fabulous Miss Marie (produced New York, 1970). Published in *The New Lafayette Theatre Presents*, edited by Bullins, New York, Doubleday, 1974.

Four Dynamite Plays: It Bees Dat Way, Death List, The Pig Pen, Night of the Beast (produced New York, 1970; *It Bees Dat Way* produced London, 1970). New York, Morrow, 1971.

The Duplex: A Black Love Fable in Four Movements (produced New York, 1970). New York, Morrow, 1971.

The Devil Catchers (produced New York, 1970).

The Psychic Pretenders (produced New York, 1972).

You Gonna Let Me Take You Out Tonight, Baby (produced New York, 1972).

Next Time, in *City Stops* (produced New York, 1972).

House Party, music by Pat Patrick, lyrics by Bullins (produced New York, 1973).

The Theme Is Blackness: The Corner and Other Plays (includes *Dialect Determinism, or, The Rally*; *It Has No Choice*; *The Helper*; *A Minor Scene*; *The Theme Is Blackness*; *The Man Who Dug Fish*; *Street Sounds*; and the scenarios and short plays *Black Commercial No. 2*, *The American Flag Ritual*, *State Office Bldg. Curse*, *One-Minute Commercial*, *A Street Play*, *A Short Play for a Small Theatre*, and *The Play of the Play*). New York, Morrow, 1973.

The Taking of Miss Janie (produced New York, 1975). Published in *Famous Plays of the '70s*, New York, Dell, 1980; In *Black Thunder New York*, New York, Mentor, 1992.

The Mystery of Phyllis Wheatley (produced New York, 1976).
I Am Lucy Terry (for children; produced New York, 1976).
Jo Anne!!! (produced New York, 1976).
Home Boy, music by Aaron Bell, lyrics by Bullins (produced New York, 1976).
Daddy (produced New York, 1977).
Sepia Star, or Chocolate Comes to the Cotton Club, music and lyrics by Mildred Kayden (produced New York, 1977).
Storyville, music and lyrics by Mildred Kayden (produced La Jolla, California, 1977; revised version produced Washington, D.C., 1979).
Michael (also director: produced New York, 1978).
C'mon Back to Heavenly House (produced Amherst, Massachusetts, 1978).
Leavings (produced New York, 1980).
Steve and Velma (produced Boston, 1980).
Bullins Does Bullins (also director: produced Oakland, California, 1988).
I Think It's Gonna Work Out Fine, with Idris Ackamoor and Rhodessa Jones (produced New York, 1990).
American Griot (produced New York, 1990).
Salaam, Huey Newton, Salaam (produced New York, 1991).Published in *Best Short Plays of 1990*, edited by Howard Stein and Glenn Young, New York, Applause, 1991.
Raining Down Stars: Sepia Stories of the Dark Diaspora, with Idris Ackamoor and Rhodessa Jones (produced San Francisco, 1992).
New/Lost Plays by Ed Bullins: An Anthology. Aiea, Hawaii, That New Publishing Company, 1993.

Screenplays: *Night of the Beast*, 1971; *The Ritual Masters*, 1972.

Novel

The Reluctant Rapist. New York, Harper, 1973.

Short Stories

The Hungered One: Early Writings. New York, Morrow, 1971.

Poetry

To Raise the Dead and Foretell the Future. New York, New Lafayette Publications, 1971.

Other

New Plays from the Black Theatre. New York, Bantam, 1969.

Editor, *The New Lafayette Theatre Presents: Plays with Aesthetic Comments by 6 Black Playwrights*. New York, Doubleday, 1974.

*

Bibliography: *Ten Modern American Playwrights* by Kimball King, New York, Garland, 1982.

Critical Studies: "Ed Bullins Was Steve Benson (But Who Is He Now?)" by Richard G. Scharine, in *Black American Literature Forum*, Fall 1979, pp. 103-9; "The (In) Humanity of Assassination: Plays by Albert Camus and Kingsley B. Bass, Jr." by Jack B. Moore, in *MELUS* (Amherst, Massachusetts), Fall 1981, pp. 45-56; *Drumbeats, Masks, and Metaphor: Contemporary Afro-American Theatre* by Geneviève Fabre, translated by Melvin Dixon, Cambridge, Massachusetts, Harvard University Press, 1983; *Toward Creation of a Collective Form: The Plays of Ed Bullins* by Nicholas Canaday, in *Studies in American Drama* (Erie, Pennsylvania), 1986; "Ed Bullins" by John L. DiGaetani, in *A Search for a Postmodern Theater: Interviews with Contemporary Playwrights*, edited by John L. DiGaetani, New York, Greenwood, 1991.

Theatrical Activities:
Director: **Play**—*Michael*, New York, 1978; *Bullins Does Bullins*, Oakland, California, 1988; *Savage Wilds*, Berkeley, California, 1988; *Tripnology* by J. Woodward, San Francisco, 1992.

Actor: **Play**—Role in *The Hotel Play* by Wallace Shawn, New York, 1981; role in *The Real Deal* by J. Woodward, San Francisco, 1988; role in *The Burial of Prejudice* by J. Woodward, San Francisco, 1991.

Ed Bullins comments:
I write plays for a number of reasons but the most simple and direct truth of the matter is that it is my work.

* * *

Although he is the most prolific figure, and one of the most active, in black American theater, Ed Bullins resists close identification with the prominent contemporary styles. With Black House and Black Arts/West in San Francisco he participated in projects to create a revolutionary theater, yet at the same time he was capable of satirizing revolutionary ideologues in *Dialect Determinism*. He can adapt the mode of realism for his Twentieth-Century Cycle but deflect a critic's attempt to discern its autobiographical theme with the remark that specific reference is not apt for symbolic writing like his own. Bullins's statements are often, in fact, less a commentary than an enactment of the theatrical devices of black language. There is the pretended innocence of "shuckin" that allows him to deny association with militants, the inflated language of the put-on self-description ("Ed Bullins, at this moment in time, is almost without peer in America—black, white or imported"), and the ironic humor that produces elaborate games about racial stereotypes in and around his plays. Like the originators of those linguistic techniques, Bullins stays loose so that he can survive the pressures of the moment and continue to evolve through performance after performance.

The best known of Bullins's works are set in the 1950s, a period that matches historically the personal deracination of the characters. They are urban people completely divorced from the southern past, the soil, and the traditional culture. Shown without the coloration of myth in either their own or their creator's consciousness, they are neither the idealized folk primitives so dearly beloved in the past to friendly white writers on the Negro nor the agents of imminent revolution ardently desired by some black spokespersons. Their ghetto is both physical and moral. Excluded from accomplishments beyond those of subsisting, they cannot transcend private passion or see any possibility of redemption in community. In *Clara's Ole Man*, for instance, a young student hoping to make out with a woman stumbles into a cast of grotesques who fulfill a projected sense of menace by calling in a street gang to beat him senseless.

Of the Twentieth-Century Cycle, Bullins has said, in his put-on voice, "There is already talk of this collective project surpassing greatness in its scope, though the work is not that astonishing, relative to Bullins' abilities." It develops its first installment, *In the Wine Time*, from a prologue in which a male narrator lyrically describes the beautiful woman who represents the goals he innocently hopes to achieve. As counterpoint the body of the play reveals through its slowly moving dialogue of a summer evening the disappointments of the youth's exhausted aunt, the frustrated hopes of her husband, and the diversion of their ambitions into a contest over the boy. Structured as an initiation play, *In the Wine Time* carries the protagonist to a point at which he destroys his own future with an act of casual violence. *In New England Winter* picks up the leading character, now free from the prison sentence he received for the pointless assault in the previous play, and juxtaposes him with yet another young man and a group of small-time hustlers. Scenes of a planned robbery are intermixed with memories of a love idyll that is at first attractive, like the prologue of *In the Wine Time,* but is then revealed to have been a period of desperate escape. The human needs that people have for one another issue in sadomasochistic relationships, gratuitous brutality, and a deadly lack of sustained feeling.

With *The Duplex,* subtitled *A Black Love Fable in Four Movements,* the theme of the cycle is fully established: the impossibility of love and, by implication, broader community and the reflexive self-destruction of character. Again the movement is of a young man gaining experience in the social world. Steve Benson hesitates between submission to the anodynes of alcohol and sex and the resolution to direct his own life. The forces for submission are so powerful that hesitation seems the only plausible action for him in the brief time of the play. Self-sufficiency would be too unlikely. Application of the playwright's naturalism is so overwhelming that race hardly seems the point of the plays in the cycle, though it certainly provides the circumstances that prod characters along their desperate ways. Cast out and angry, they invert their creativity. Social insignificance releases energy in violence and sexual dominance, and the contempt of an external society is mirrored in a lumpen style and contempt for life itself.

Still, Bullins stops short of dehumanizing his characters. In *The Fabulous Miss Marie* the vital and vulgar heroine demonstrates the vigor that sustains humanity, and in the other plays of the cycle Bullins rejects both a portrayal of characters as victims and the easy sentiment of pity that is equally dehumanizing. His identification with the plight of his people in the industrial slums of northeastern cities and the sunshine ghettoes of southern California instead advances the idea that the public world we know in terms of social and economic problems is lived in the experience of personal troubles and private feelings. If the inhabitants of the 1950s ghetto appear to be trapped, it is because Bullins sees in politics and the philosophy of art no release for their humanity. We have to see the problem, he says, in the depths of personality before we can honestly propose any solution.

The dramaturgy of Bullins's cycle, as well such a precycle play as *Goin' a Buffalo,* exploits the entire theatrical ambience for effect. The decor of *Goin' a Buffalo* consists of all-white walls and a crimson carpet. The set of *The Duplex* is a nonrealistic gradation of planes that contest with the realism of the dramatic action and dialogue to give credence to the view that the plays are, indeed, intended to be seen symbolically. Nearly all of the plays call for musical accompaniment attuned to situation and for shifting lighting effects to spot significant relationships, while the directions for movements on the stage suggest choreography.

In the late 1970s Bullins carried his interest in the associated stage arts into collaboration on the musicals *Storyville* and *Sepia Star.* At other times in his career he wrote sketches, one-act plays, children's dramas, scenarios, and even radio commercials. In this variety of production one sees the historical problem of the black playwright searching for a sympathetic audience. The expectations of white playgoers subtly educe, even against a writer's will, some accommodation, or else they create a strong need for defiance. Meanwhile, blacks who share the writer's cultural experience and language find their theater in the events of the church and in other institutions rather than on Broadway, which for more reasons than one has been called the "great white way." In an approach to the latter part of the problem Bullins became involved in the Black Arts Alliance on the West Coast, and he then invested 10 years of his time in New York attempting to establish in the contemporary city the New Lafayette Theatre as a successor to the original Lafayette Stock Company, which had laid the foundations of black legitimate theater from 1917 to 1932.

The creation of such political plays as those collected in *Four Dynamite Plays* can also be understood as part of Bullins's effort to engender in audiences the conviction that drama can be the arena for serious examination of black values. *Death List* from this collection portrays a rifleman intoning indictments of popular leaders while the play's other character, Blackwoman, explains the extenuating circumstances of each alleged betrayal of black interests. Getting no response to her pleas for mercy, Blackwoman asks if the potential assassin himself is not the actual enemy of the people. There is no resolution of the opposition, and the action simply ends with the offstage sound of shots. It is presumably time for the audience to debate the issue.

Bullins's confrontation of the white members of his dual audience generally takes the form of instructive, but not necessarily didactic, writing. The cycle plays are works meant to inform whites as much as to produce recognition for blacks. Then, too, a play such as *Daddy* can be taken, as it was by New York reviewers, to be an exploration of the feelings animating the man who abandons his family to better himself and the substitute father who replaces him. The abstracts of social science quantify the behavior that produces broken homes, something that Bullins tries to humanize.

The theater has taken a breather from militancy, and Bullins has assumed a retrospective attitude toward the revolutionary period. *House Party* satirizes political figures, and *The Taking of Miss Janie* converts the politics of the 1960s into a drama of interracial rape. All-black theater, too, seems to be a thing of the past for Bullins. Although there are several active companies in the United States and New York's Negro Ensemble Company looks to be the genuine successor to the famous American Negro Theater of the 1940s as well as the old Lafayette Players, Bullins sees community theater as being in a drift. For the present at least the outlet for his remarkable productivity remains the mainstream American theater. He has supervised the playwriting workshop of the New York Shakespeare Festival, recovered the roots of black show business for musical theater, and tried to shape his instructional plays into the style of domestic drama. Bullins has stayed loose, avoided getting backed into a corner, and survived to give the American stage in one or another of its forms his intensely dramatic vision.

—John M. Reilly

BURROWS, John and John Harding

BURROWS, John. Nationality: British. **Born:** London, 19 November 1945. **Education:** Manchester University, B.A. in drama. **Agent:** Alan Brodie, Alan Brodie Representation, 91 Regent Street, London W1R 7TB, England.

HARDING, John. Nationality: British. **Born:** Ruislip, Middlesex, 20 June 1948. **Education:** Pinner Grammar School; Manchester University, 1966-69, B.A. (honours) in drama 1969. **Family:** Married Gillian Heaps in 1968; one son. **Agent:** Michael Imison Playwrights, 28 Almeida Street, London N1 1TD, England.

Publications

Plays

For Sylvia (produced London, 1972). Published in *The Best Short Plays 1978*, edited by Stanley Richards, Radnor, Pennsylvania, Chilton, 1978.
The Golden Pathway Annual (produced Sheffield, 1973; London, 1974). London, Heinemann, 1975.
Loud Reports, with Peter Skellern (produced London, 1975).
Dirty Giant, music by Peter Skellern (produced Coventry, 1975).
The Manly Bit (produced London, 1976).

Television Play: *Do You Dig It?*, 1976.

Plays by John Burrows

Son of a Gun, with Sidewalk Theatre Company (produced London, 1976).
Cash Street, with Sidewalk Theatre Company (produced London, 1977).
Sketches in *Some Animals Are More Equal* (produced London, 1977).
Restless Natives, music by Rick Lloyd (produced London, 1978).
Dole Queue Fever, music by Rick Lloyd (produced London, 1978).
Sketches in *City Delights* (produced Oxford, 1978; London, 1980).
Freedom Point, music by Rick Lloyd (produced London, 1979).
The Last Benefit (produced London, 1980).
One Big Blow, music by Rick Lloyd (produced Bradford, 1981).
The Checkpoint, with the People Show (produced London, 1983).
Wartime Stories, music by Andrew Dickson, lyrics by Burrows (produced London, 1984).
It's a Girl!, music by Andy Whitefield (produced Lancaster and London, 1987). London, Methuen, 1988.
Viva España (produced Edinburgh, 1988).
Sweet Broken Heart, music by Andy Whitfield (produced London, 1991).

Radio Writings: *The Heath and Me*, 1985.

Television Plays: *Not the Nine O'Clock News* series, 1980.

Plays by John Harding

Radio Play: *Listen to My Voice*, 1987.

*

Theatrical Activities:
Director (BURROWS): **Plays**—All of his own plays, and *Big Square Fields* by John McGrath, London, 1979; *The Garden of England* by Peter Cox, Sheffield and London, 1985.

Actor (BURROWS): Several of his own plays, and television plays, including *Talkin' Blues* by Nigel Williams, 1977. (HARDING): **Plays**—All his own plays, and *Jack and Beanstalk*, Bromley, Kent, 1969; Whitaker in *The Long and the Short and the Tall* by Willis Hall, London, 1970; Pantalone in *Pinocchio* by Brian Way, London, 1971; James in *My Fat Friend* by Charles Laurence, London, 1972; Antipholus in *The Comedy of Errors*, Hornchurch, Essex, 1973; Sir Andrew Aguecheek in *Twelfth Night*, Sheffield, 1974; *Donkeys' Years* by Michael Frayn, London, 1976; Actors Company, London: *The Importance of Being Earnest* by Wilde and *Do You Love Me*? by R.D. Laing, 1977-78; *The Circle* by W. Somerset Maugham, Chichester and tour, 1978; National Theatre, London: *The Double Dealer* by Congreve, *Strife* by Galsworthy, *The Fruits of Enlightenment* by Tolstoy, *Undiscovered Country* by Tom Stoppard, *Richard III*, and *Amadeus* by Peter Shaffer, 1978-81; *Miranda* by Beverley Cross, Chichester, 1987. **Film**—*Little Dorrit*, 1987. **Television**—*Man of Mode* by Etherege, 1980; *Baby Talk* by Nigel Williams, 1981.

* * *

John Burrows and John Harding are two actors who evolved a distinctive revue style to look at British class society and at the effect its various myths have had on some of the inhabitants of the society. *For Sylvia* satirizes gently and almost nostalgically the postwar myth making of such 1950s epics as *The Dam Busters* and *Reach for the Sky*. In the original production Burrows played the central part of the pilot hero while Harding played everybody else. It was an accurate re-creation and parody of that genre of film and was performed with sensitivity and affection.

The Golden Pathway Annual is a more considerable work. It revolves around Michael Peters, a member of the postwar grammar school generation and the son of the working-class George and Enid, and traces him from his childhood through primary school, the 11-plus examination, grammar school, university, and the prospect of graduate unemployment. Burrows again played the central role in the first production, while Mark Wing-Davey and Maggie McCarthy played his parents and Harding everybody else. It is written in a series of short scenes—"Dad comes home from the war," "Michael at school," "The Coronation," "The Famous Five." *The Golden Pathway Annual* is a motif for the whole play. The annual is sold by a slick salesman to Michael's gullible parents for the boy's "education," and it becomes the trigger of Michael's fantasies both in boyhood and early adolescence. We see him imagining himself as one of Enid Blyton's middle-class "Famous Five" and then, a few years later, ironically realizing the fantasy's bourgeois content. The play is a gently ironic satire on the rise of the postwar meritocracy and is beautifully evocative for anyone of that generation.

Their third play, *Loud Reports*, done with the pop singer Peter Skellern, is about a blimpish brigadier, CorfePrater, and his resolute refusal to come to terms with modern-day social realities, whether it be the Great Depression of the 1930s, the advent of the welfare state in the 1940s, or affluence in the 1950s. Suez is a brief reminder of former glories, while he staggers on into the 1960s.

It is less original than *The Golden Pathway Annual,* though scarcely less entertaining.

—Jonathan Hammond

BUSCH, Charles (Louis)

Nationality: American. **Born:** New York City, 23 August 1954. **Education:** High School of Music and Art, New York, 1968-72; Northwestern University, Evanston, Illinois, 1972-76, B.S. **Career:** Worked as office temporary receptionist, quick sketch pastel portrait artist, ice-cream scooper, encyclopedia salesman, sports handicapper, 1976-84, New York and Chicago, Illinois. Co-founder, 1984, and playwright-in-residence, 1984—, Theatre-in-Limbo, New York. **Agent:** Jeffrey Melnick, Eight Square Entertainment, 606 North Larchmont #307, Los Angeles, California 90004, U.S.A.; or, Marc Glick, Glick and Weintraub, 1501 Broadway, Suite 2401, New York, New York 10036-5503, U.S.A.

Publications

Plays

Charles Busch, Alone with a Cast of Thousands (includes *Hollywood Confidential*, 1978, *A Theatrical Party*, 1980, *After You've Gone*, 1982, *Phantom Lovers*, 1983, produced on U.S. tours).
Before Our Mother's Eyes (produced New York, 1981).
Vampire Lesbians of Sodom (produced New York, 1984). Included in *Four Plays*, 1990.
Sleeping Beauty or Coma (produced New York, 1984). Included in *Four Plays*, 1990.
Theodora, She-Bitch of Byzantium (produced New York, 1984). Included in *Three Plays*, 1992.
Times Square Angel: A Hard-Boiled Christmas Fantasy (produced New York, 1984; revised version produced New York, 1985). Included in *Three Plays*, 1992.
Gidget Goes Psychotic (produced New York, 1986). New York, French, 1986.
Pardon My Inquisition; or, Kiss The Blood Off My Castanets (produced New York, 1986). Included in *Three Plays*, 1992.
Psycho Beach Party (produced New York, 1987). Included in *Four Plays*, 1990.
Ankles Aweigh, music and lyrics by Sammy Fain and Dan Shapiro (also co-director: produced East Haddam, Connecticut, 1987). New York, French, 1987.
The Lady in Question (produced New York, 1989). Included in *Four Plays*, 1990.
Four Plays. Garden City, New York, Fireside Theatre, 1990.
House of Flowers, adaptation of the libretto by Truman Capote (produced New York, 1991). New York, French, 1991.
Red Scare on Sunset (produced New York, 1991). Garden City, New York, Fireside Theatre, 1991.
Three Plays. Garden City, New York, Fireside Theatre, 1992.
You Should Be So Lucky (produced New York, 1994). New York, Samuel French, 1994; Garden City, New York, Fireside Theatre, 1994).
Swingtime Canteen (musical with book by Linda Thorson Bond, William Repicci and Charles Busch; produced New York, 1995). New York, French, 1997.
Flipping My Wig (one man show; produced New York, 1997).
The Green Heart (musical), music and lyrics by Rusty Magee (produced New York, 1997). New York, French, 1998.
Queen Amarantha (produced New York, 1997). New York, French, 1998.

Novel

Whores of Lost Atlantis. Hyperion Press, 1993; Penguin, 1995.

*

Manuscript Collection: Lincoln Center Library of Performing Arts, New York.

Critical Studies: *Downtown* by Michael Musto, New York, Vintage, 1986; "Naked in Pants: Drag Artist Charles Busch Writes Himself a Male Role" by Richard Niles, in *TheatreForum,* Summer-Fall 1995, pp. 66-73.

Theatrical Activities:
Director (with Dan Siretta): **Plays**—*Ankles Aweigh*, East Haddam, Connecticut, 1987.

Actor: **Plays**—All his own plays including: Virgin Sacrifice and Madeleine Astarte in *Vampire Lesbians of Sodom*; Irish O'Flanagan in *Times Square Angel*; Chicklet in *Psycho Beach Party*; title role in *Theodora, She-Bitch of Byzantium*; Maria Garbonza and the Marquesa Del Drago in *Pardon My Inquisition*; Gertrude Garnet in *The Lady in Question*; Fauna Alexander in *Sleeping Beauty*; Mary Dale in *Red Scare on Sunset*.

Charles Busch comments:

I identify strongly with the actor-managers of the nineteenth century. All of my plays have been written to give my company, Theatre-in-Limbo, and myself opportunities to act. Like the theatrical monsters I emulate, I believe passionately in the eternal power of melodrama, old-fashioned comedy rhythms, and the glamorous star vehicle. I've tried to celebrate these forms and conventions as well as parody them. An audience can be thrilled by the chase but also laugh at their own easy manipulation. However, I've also tried to employ old movie and theatrical genres as starting-off points to then reflect issues of importance to me, both personal and political. Ultimately, I remain hopelessly stagestruck and I write in order to act. It's not enough for an audience to read my stories, I am compelled to get up there and tell it to them myself.

* * *

Actor-playwright Charles Busch and his cohorts at Theatre-in-Limbo have proved themselves worthy successors to Charles Ludlam, whose death in 1987 was an irretrievable loss to the comic vein of American theater. In eight years Busch's work moved from burlesque sketch comedies performed for late-night coterie audiences to two-act off-Broadway productions with open runs. Less aesthetically dangerous and more intellectually accessible than Ludlam's sublime scavenging of Western art, Busch's deft fruit salads of B movie conventions, femme attitudes, and subversive politics are enormously popular with audiences and critics of all persuasions.

Although Busch insists in preface after preface that his heroines need not be performed by men in drag, much of the power in his work is derived from a cross-dressing, decidedly gay perspective. Without Busch himself expertly glossing—indeed, outdoing—Norma Shearer or Betty Hutton or Greer Garson on the stage, making us question the construction of gender and genre, his plays might seem of little more consequence than television spoofs of best-forgotten moments in American cinema. Yet no matter how outsized the role in Busch's menagerie, from a silent screen vamp to a 12-year-old Nazi, they are meant to be performed with a sincerity and a realism that forestalls any unwelcome complicity from the audience.

The double bill of *Sleeping Beauty or Coma* and *Vampire Lesbians of Sodom* started as a weekend party for friends and became one of the longest running plays in off-Broadway history. In *Sleeping Beauty*, a send-up of Carnaby Street in the swinging 1960s, a fashion designer, a supermodel, and a photographer hit the heights of mod London and crash semipermanently on shoddy tabs of acid. *Vampire Lesbians* travels through time from ancient Sodom to Hollywood in the 1920s to contemporary Las Vegas to tell the tale of rival succubi who wind up as competing entertainment divas. At the conclusion each discovers that she needs the other, if only to revile her. The rewards of feminine friendship, treated embryonically in this fairy tale, is a theme that runs through all of Busch's work.

Times Square Angel was Busch's first attempt at a cinematic saga, and he has continued to tailor roles for his troupe of regulars, much as Molière or Preston Sturges did. In this play Irish O'Flanagan goes from the slums of Hell's Kitchen to the top of the postwar entertainment industry, trading in her heart along the way. One Christmas Eve, with the help of a wayward angel, Irish learns the true meaning of life. Although this fantasia on *It's a Wonderful Life* overreaches itself narratively, *Times Square Angel* is full of Busch's deliriously hard-boiled dialogue.

Funnier still is *Psycho Beach Party*, an amalgam of 1960s beach movies, *Sybil*, and *Mommie Dearest*. In addition to all the surfboards, dance numbers, and petting sessions compulsory to the sand flick genre, Busch's characters are unconscious heralds of nonconformism. Chicklet must free herself by integrating her multiple personalities, and, rather than suppress their attraction for each other, beach rats Yo Yo and Provoloney openly declare their forbidden homosexual love. Liberation is again the theme when Busch returned to the 1940s with *The Lady in Question*, an anti-Nazi war melodrama. Like Irish O'Flanagan, the internationally acclaimed concert pianist Gertrude Garnet is an impossibly selfish woman who discovers her humanity only through sacrifice. After her sidekick Kitty is strangled by the evil Lotte Von Elsner, Gertrude rescues a political prisoner and escapes into Switzerland on skis with the man she loves. Busch's growth as a writer is impressive in the play. Familiarity with the intertexts, among them in this case Hitchcock's *Notorious* and the dreadful 1950s *Bad Seed*, enhances one's appreciation of *The Lady in Question*, but this knowledge is not necessary for one to laugh at its comedy or to be held in real suspense by its plot.

No less artful than Busch's other screen adaptations, *Red Scare on Sunset* was greeted with less enthusiasm. When Mary Dale, played by Busch, names names on the air in order to free Hollywood of the communist menace, audiences were confused by the author's intentions. In a culture that in a very short while has become increasingly hostile to homosexuals and to art, one can no longer afford to satirize the left with impunity. Busch is not a political writer per se, but his choice of material and his production style are an inherent critique of the American myths of family, assimilation, career, love, showbiz, power, and luxury. He celebrates personal freedom against the forces of evil implicitly gathering just beyond the footlights. In addition to his gay audience Busch is popular with aging baby boomers given over to refabricating the hoary artifacts and attitudes of their past. Yet, beneath the cartoon contours of his Hollywood tropes, Busch challenges an easy, ravenous predilection for camp by creating moments of genuine feeling. His insistence that his work be performed "straight" lends to his best plays an undeniable charm and a salutary tension.

—James Magruder

BUTTERWORTH, Jez

Nationality: British. **Born:** 1970. **Career:** Playwright. **Awards:** George Devine award, Writer's Guild award for best new comer, Evening Standard award for most promising playwright, The Critics' Circle award for best new writer, and Olivier award for best comedy, all 1995, all for *Mojo.* **Agent:** Nick Marston, Curtis Brown Group, Haymarket House, 28/29 Haymarket London SW1Y 4SP, England.

PUBLICATIONS

Plays

Huge (produced Edinburgh, 1994).
Mojo (produced London, 1995). London, Nick Hern, 1995.

Screenplays: *Christmas,* 1995; *Mojo,* 1997; *Birthday Girl,* with Tom Butterworth, 1997.

Television Plays: *The Night of the Golden Brain,* with Tom Butterworth, 1994.

Other

Mojo and a Film-maker's Diary. London, Faber, 1998.

*

Theatrical Activities:
Director: **Film**–*Mojo,* 1996.

* * *

Jez Butterworth established his credentials as an important contemporary dramatist with his play, *Mojo*, originally produced at London's Royal Court Theatre in 1995 when Butterworth was 25 years old. This staging marked the first time that the Royal Court produced a playwright's first effort since 1956, when John Osborne's *Look Back in Anger* ushered in the world of such angry young British playwrights as Joe Orton and Harold Pinter. Butterworth's play *Mojo* is heavily influenced by the work of these playwrights. Indeed, *Mojo* is even set in a seedy 1958 London nightclub, in a stark, male-dominated world of rock 'n roll, alcohol, amphetamines, and hazy dreams of making the big financial score. The playwright has said that the Cold War period of the late 1950s gave him the license he needed to create "characters that were very English and very postwar, suddenly experiencing these released desires that they didn't quite understand."

Along with Orton and Pinter, Butterworth's most obvious playwriting influence is David Mamet, particularly Mamet's 1975 play *American Buffalo*. Like Mamet, Butterworth confines his characters within a claustrophobic space as they try to act upon their plans for wealth and power. Like Mamet, Butterworth's comic impulses provide the energy that drives his characters. Butterworth's characters in *Mojo* speak in an obscene, pill-infused marriage of hipster and Cockney rhyming slang. Sweets and Potts are the luckless minions whose aimless and occasionally baffling commentary upon the play's off-stage action provides the framework for the play's developments. Early on they envision their future success hinging upon the nightclub's fledgling English Pop phenomenon, Silver Johnny:

> POTTS: Go down take a look at any picture Napoleon. Go take a butcher's at the Emperor Half the World. And you'll see it. You'll see. They got a lot of blokes *standing around*. Doers. Finders. Advisors. Acquaintances. Watchers. An *entourage*.
>
> SWEETS: Big fuckers in fur boots. On the payroll.
>
> POTTS: Napoleon's chums. And they're all there. Sticking around. Having a natter. Cleaning rifles. Chatting to cherubs. Waiting. Waiting for the deal to come off.
>
> SWEETS: They weren't there they wouldn't have fuckin' painted them.

The obscenity-laced comic naivete of Sweets and Potts, their inflated dreams of their own importance, and their deadpan, near stand-up comic repartee, juxtaposed against the play's brutality, provide the play with its irony, energy, and edge:

> SWEETS: Then they've had breakfast, gone round the bass player's and they've cut his thumb off. . . . Round his mum's. In front of his mum. Him in his Jimmy jams.
>
> POTTS: Thereby depriving him of his livelihood.
>
> SWEETS: Thereby depriving him of his *thumb*. The livelihood speaks for itself.

Mojo was awarded the 1995 Olivier award for best comedy, and Butterworth was given the George Devine and Evening Standard awards for most promising newcomer and the London Critics' award for best writer. Yet, while labeled a comedy, *Mojo* is vicious, brutal, and sadistic. Again, as in Mamet's work, the play's darkly comic core is located within a seamy, self-absorbed world of perverse acquisitiveness and decay. The play includes not only the appearance of a severed body distributed between a pair of garbage cans but a bet on which of the two cans contains the victim's head. Throughout the play characters are both physically and psychologically tortured, and the comedy concludes with a bullet to the head.

At this very early stage in his playwriting career, Butterworth's reputation rests solely on this explosive exercise in macabre humor, sadistic baiting and maiming, and precisely timed dialog. In *Mojo* Butterworth uses these devices in a provocative assault upon the senses and the values of his audience and his society.

—Arthur Horowitz

BUZO, Alexander (John)

Nationality: Australian. **Born:** Sydney, New South Wales, 23 July 1944. **Education:** Armidale School, New South Wales, 1956-60; International School of Geneva, 1962; University of New South Wales, Sydney, 1963-65, B.A. 1965. **Family:** Married Merelyn Johnson in 1968; three daughters. **Career:** Salesman, David Jones Ltd., Sydney, 1960; messenger, E.L. Davis and Company, Sydney, 1961; storeman-packer, McGraw-Hill Book Company, Sydney, 1967; clerk, New South Wales Public Service, Sydney, 1967-68; resident playwright, Melbourne Theatre Company, 1972-73; writer-in-residence, Sydney Teachers College, 1978, James Cook University, Townsville, 1985, University of Wollongong, 1989, and University of Central Queensland, 1991. **Awards:** Australian Literature Society gold medal, 1972; Commonwealth Literary Fund fellowship, 1973; Australia Council Literature Board grant, 1974, 1978; inaugural literary fellowship, University of South Wales, 1988. **Agent:** Margaret Connolly & Associates Pty Ltd, P.O. bpx 48 Paddington, New South Wales 2021, Australia.

Publications

Plays

The Revolt (produced Sydney, 1967).

Norm and Ahmed (produced Sydney, 1968; London, 1974).Included in *Norm and Ahmed, Rooted, and The Roy Murphy Show*, 1973.

Rooted (produced Canberra, 1969; Hartford, Connecticut, 1972; London, 1973). Included in *Norm and Ahmed, Rooted, and The Roy Murphy Show*, 1973.

The Front Room Boys (produced Perth, 1970; London, 1971). Published in *Plays*, Melbourne, Penguin, 1970.

The Roy Murphy Show (produced Sydney, 1971; London, 1983). Included in *Norm and Ahmed, Rooted, and The Roy Murphy Show*, 1973.

Macquarie (produced Melbourne, 1972). Sydney, Currency Press, 1971.

Tom (produced Melbourne, 1972; Washington, D.C., 1973).Sydney and London, Angus and Robertson, 1975.

Batman's Beach-head, adaption of a play by Ibsen (produced Melbourne, 1973).

Norm and Ahmed, Rooted, and The Roy Murphy Show: Three Plays. Sydney, Currency Press, and London, Eyre Methuen, 1973.

Coralie Lansdowne Says No (produced Adelaide, 1974). Sydney, Currency Press, and London, Eyre Methuen, 1974.

Martello Towers (produced Sydney, 1976). Sydney, Currency Press, and London, Eyre Methuen, 1976.

Vicki Madison Clocks Out (produced Adelaide, 1976; Louisville, 1980).

Makassar Reef (produced Melbourne and Seattle, 1978). Sydney, Currency Press, 1978.

Big River (produced Adelaide, 1980). With *The Marginal Farm*, Sydney, Currency Press, 1985.
The Marginal Farm (produced Melbourne, 1983). With *Big River*, Sydney, Currency Press, 1985.
Stingray (produced Sydney, 1987).
Shellcove Road (produced Sydney, 1989).
Pacific Union (produced Melbourne, 1995). Sydney, Currency Press, 1995.

Screenplays: *Rod*, 1972; *Norm and Ahmed*, 1988.

Radio Plays: *File on Rod*, 1972; *Duff*, 1980; *In Search of the New Class*, 1982; *East of Singapore*, 1986.

Television Writing (animated films): *A Christmas Carol*, 1982, *Great Expectations*, 1983, *David Copperfield*, 1984, and *The Old Curiosity Shop*, 1985, all from works by Dickens.

Novels

The Search for Harry Allway. Sydney, Angus and Robertson, 1985.
Prue Flies North. Melbourne, Mandarin, 1991.

Other

Tautology: I Don't Want to Sound Incredulous But I Can't Believe It. Melbourne, Penguin, 1981; revised edition, as *Tautology Too*, 1982.
Meet the New Class. Sydney, Angus and Robertson, 1981.
Glancing Blows. Melbourne, Penguin, 1987.
The Young Person's Guide to the Theatre and Almost Everything Else. Melbourne, Penguin, 1988.
Kiwese: A Guide, a Ductionary, a Shearing of Unsights. Port Melbourne, Mandarin, 1994.

Editor (Australian edition), *Real Men Don't Eat Quiche*, by Bruce Feirstein. Sydney, Angus and Robertson, 1982.
Editor with Jamie Grant, *The Longest Game*. Melbourne, Heinemann, 1990.

*

Manuscript Collections: Mitchell Library, Sydney; National Library, Canberra; University of New South Wales Library.

Critical Studies: Introduction by Katharine Brisbane to *Norm and Ahmed, Rooted, and The Roy Murphy Show*, 1973; *After "The Doll": Australian Drama since 1955* by Peter Fitzpatrick, Melbourne, Arnold, 1979; *Alexander Buzo's Rooted and Norm and Ahmed: A Critical Introduction* by T.L. Sturm, Sydney, Currency Press, 1980, and "Alexander Buzo: An Imagist with a Personal Style of Surrealism" by Sturm and "Aggressive Vernacular" by Roslyn Arnold, both in *Contemporary Australian Drama* edited by Peter Holloway, Currency Press, 1981, revised edition, 1987; interview in *Southerly* (Sydney), March 1986; *Buzo* by John McCallum, Sydney, Methuen, 1987; "Middle Class Dissenter: An Interview with Alexander Buzo" by Ron Verburgt, in *Australasian Drama Studies* (Queensland, Australia), April 1993, pp. 33-52; "Re-Orienting Australian Drama: Staging Theatrical Irony" by Joanne Tompkins, in *ARIEL: A Review of International English Literature* (Calgary, AB), October 1994, pp. 117-33.

Theatrical Activities:
Director: **Play**—*Care* by Daniel Hughes, Sydney, 1969.

Actor: **Plays**—*The Alchemist* by Jonson, Sydney, 1966; *Macbird* by Barbara Garson, Sydney, 1967.

Alexander Buzo comments:

My plays are, I hope, realistic poetic comedies set in contemporary times. They are not naturalistic. The mentality behind them could be described as humanist. Magritte is my favourite painter. When I started writing, the Theatre of the Absurd was a big influence. I place emphasis on verbal precision and visual clarity, and am not terribly interested in group anarchy. I believe in literacy, professionalism, and niceness. Nearly all my plays concentrate on one central character having problems with what's around and about.

* * *

Alexander Buzo's first short work, *Norm and Ahmed*, was something of a landmark on the route to the contemporary Australian play. It was only a decade from Ray Lawler's *Summer of the Seventeenth Doll* and seven years from Alan Seymour's *The One Day of the Year*, each of them regarded as quintessential Australian plays. But *Norm and Ahmed*, though not apparently revolutionary in form, gathered up a number of popular influences that began to take new writers in a different direction.

Norm, a middle-aged, lonely, and unimaginative storeman, stops Ahmed, a Pakistani student, on a street corner one night and engages him in reluctant conversation. Norm's character draws on caricatures of the conservative returned serviceman and portraits like Barry Humphries's Sandy Stone and Seymour's Alf Cook from *The One Day of the Year*. Buzo gives their xenophobia and their rigid daily rituals a new aspect by placing them in confrontation with an Asian hinterland. Norm's strikingly aggressive/defensive attitude, quite unprovoked by Ahmed, is crystallized in the final moment. Norm proffers his hand in farewell, and when Ahmed takes it, Norm smashes his head.

This is the only real moment of violence in all of Buzo's writing. After that he moved into the middle class for his context, and the violence turned inward into verbal persecution.

In common with other playwrights, in the late 1960s Buzo was attracted by the varieties of vernacular language and the loose rhythms of Australian life. Play by play he developed toward a comedy of manners that makes one listen afresh to familiar phrases and to his satirical embroidery of the colorful cliché. It has been said with justice that if his characters stopped talking they would scream. Buzo uses language both as a weapon against and as a shield between his people and an unpleasant or mundane reality.

For Buzo is more than a satirist. Behind the writing there are loneliness and a belief that in an older society with a stronger base of religious or social dogma things might be different. The absence of religious influence in Buzo's work is virtually unique among contemporary Australian playwrights. In its place is a strong poetic response to nature that the characters express in unguarded moments. Without exception Buzo's figures are alienated. Both Norm and Ahmed are aliens in the same land, trying fruitlessly to understand it. Bentley, the timid but ambitious public servant in *Rooted*, is singled out for persecution in the schoolboy gang games of the young executives for no better reason than that he is a bore. Beneath the parody of adolescent manners, the comic strip structure of the scenes, and the jargon of the beach, the art gallery, and the public service, *Rooted* is an allegory of every young man's sense of inadequacy in a society that has no roots but other people's acceptance. In *The Front Room Boys,* which satirically records in 12 scenes the tribal rituals of a city office, all of the front-room boys are hunted by the unexplained power of the backroom boys and in turn hunt one another. In *Tom,* Buzo presents a manufactured hero, an oil exploration troubleshooter who speaks in monosyllables and is surrounded by the camp followers of big business while his wife suffers suburban neurosis and toothache.

In *Macquarie* Buzo abandoned satire to deal with an early governor of New South Wales whose idealistic liberalism led to his downfall at the hands of the conservative power group. And in *Coralie Lansdowne Says No,* his most serious comedy of manners, a high-flying young rebel facing a bleak future on the other side of 30 settles for a tiresome public servant who offers durability. All of these characters are misfits, aliens like Norm in their own world, and they are swallowed up by the unquestioning values of their too modern society.

Buzo continued to pursue the problem of rootlessness in *Martello Towers* and *Makassar Reef,* the first about the immigrant consciousness in urban Australia and the second about the migrant habits of those who touch down in the resorts of Indonesia. The setting of *Martello Towers* is an island holiday house on the Hawkesbury River, near Sydney, where Edward Martello and his estranged wife and their parents gather by accident. The family is aristocratic, two generations Australian, but still with roots in Trieste, and old Martello has come to beg for a grandchild who will continue the family name. Edward says no, that there are plenty of Martellos in the phone book. None of the family is happy, though they have their comforts and their brief contact with the earth and the water. They are as alienated as Norm.

This is the last of the fierce, bitter Buzo wit in the theater and the last of the rebelliousness. With later works such as *Big River* and *The Marginal Farm,* Buzo entered a new phase, abandoning the brittleness for an overt romanticism in his examination of his characters' allegiance to their environment. He emerged with the realization that, when men and women put down their roots in the land, they find themselves not owners but servants of it.

Big River is a portrait of Australia at the time of federation, moving imperceptibly from the dramatic action of a frontier community to the gentler preoccupations of suburbia. The central image is the River Murray, which divides Victoria from New South Wales, with the protagonist a young widow returning to her father's vineyard for his funeral. As members of the family go their separate ways, we see Adele remain, her high-flying life force captured and domesticated into a quiet contentment. A similar prey of circumstances is Toby, the heroine of *The Marginal Farm,* who takes a job as governess in Fiji in a moment of romantic restlessness. Overwhelmed at first by the beauty of the sugarcane island, she soon finds her new community a band of itinerants who one by one fly away, leaving her stranded, clinging halfheartedly to the Indian lover she has taken on an impulse of defiant individualism.

Buzo's play *Shellcove Road* completes the cycle away from an assault on current manners into overt nostalgia. Set in the Sydney house in which he grew up, the play explores a family's decision to sell the long vacant family home. The father, a wealthy postwar immigrant, has learned how to live solely in the present, and for the mother the house is an inherited burden. But for the son, a financier, the house is haunted by the friendly ghosts of the past and gives a sudden reminder of different values from a more secure, less worldly way of life. The surface action revolves around the choice between development and conservation, and the elegiac tone is punctuated with a subdued but characteristic Buzo wit.

Although Buzo moved away from the theater to journalism and social satire, he returned in 1995 with *Pacific Union,* a drama about the founding in San Francisco of the United Nations and the political maneuverings of the brilliant, idealistic, and idiosyncratic Labor parliamentarian H. V. Evatt, who played a prominent role.

—Katharine Brisbane

BYRNE, John

Nationality: British. **Born:** Paisley, Renfrewshire, Scotland, 6 January 1940. **Education:** St. Mirin's Academy and Glasgow School of Art, 1958-63. **Family:** Married Alice Simpson in 1964; one son and one daughter. **Career:** Graphic designer, Scottish Television, Glasgow, 1964-66; designer, A.F. Stoddard, carpet manufacturers, Elderslie, 1966-68. Writer- in-residence, Borderline Theatre, Irvine, Ayrshire, 1978-79, and Duncan of Jordanstone College, Dundee, 1981; associate director, Haymarket Theatre, Leicester, 1984-85. Theatrical set and costume designer. **Awards:** *Evening Standard* award, 1978. **Agent:** Casarotto Ramsay Ltd., National House, 60-66 Wardour Street, London W1V 3HP, England. **Address:** 3 Castle Brae, Newport-on-Tay, Fife, Scotland.

PUBLICATIONS

Plays

Writer's Cramp (produced Edinburgh and London, 1977; revised version, produced London, 1980; New York, 1986). Published in *Plays and Players* (London), December 1977.

The Slab Boys Trilogy (originally called *Paisley Patterns*). London, Penguin, 1987.

1. *Slab Boys* (produced Edinburgh and London, 1978; Louisville, 1979; New York, 1980). Glasgow, Scottish Society of Playwrights, 1981; New York, French, 1982; revised version, Edinburgh, Salamander Press, 1982.
2. *Cuttin' a Rug* (as *The Loveliest Night of the Year*, produced Edinburgh, 1979; revised version, as *Threads*, produced London, 1980; as *Cuttin' a Rug*, produced London, 1982; Washington, D.C., 1986). *Threads* published in *A Decade's Drama: Six Scottish Plays*, edited by Richard and Susan Mellis, Todmorden, Lancashire, Woodhouse, 1981; *Cuttin' A Rug* published Edinburgh, Salamander Press, 1982.
3. *Still Life* (produced Edinburgh, 1982; Washington, D.C., 1986). Edinburgh, Salamander Press, 1982.

Normal Service (produced London, 1979). Published in *Plays and Players* (London), May-June 1979.

Hooray for Hollywood (produced Louisville, 1980).

Babes in the Wood, music by John Gould, lyrics by David Dearlove (produced Glasgow, 1980).

Cara Coco (produced Irvine, Ayrshire, 1981).

Candy Kisses (produced London, 1984).

The London Cuckolds, adaptation of the play by Edward Ravenscroft (produced Leicester and London, 1985). London, French, 1986.
Colquhoun and MacBryde. London, Faber and Faber, 1992.

Radio Plays: *The Staffie* (version of *Cuttin' a Rug*); *A Night at the Alex*, 1981; *The Nitshill Writing Circle*, 1984.

Television Plays: *The Butterfly's Hoof*, 1978; *Big Deal* (*Crown Court* series), 1984; *Tutti Frutti* series, 1987; *Your Cheatin' Heart* series, 1990.

Novels

Tutti Frutti (novelization of television series). London, BBC Publications, 1987.
Your Cheatin' Heart (novelization of television series). London, BBC Publications, 1990.

*

Critical Study: "Tutti Frutti (John Byrne)" by Hugh Herbert, in *British Television Drama in the 1980s*, edited by George W. Brandt, Cambridge, Cambridge University Press, 1993.

Theatrical Activities:
Designer (sets, costumes, and/or posters): **Plays**—*The Cheviot, The Stag, and the Black Black Oil* by John McGrath, Edinburgh and tour, 1973; *The Fantastical Feats of Finn MacCool* by Sean McCarthy, Edinburgh, 1974; *Writer's Cramp*, London, 1980; *Heaven and Hell* by Dusty Hughes, Edinburgh, 1981; *The Number of the Beast* by Snoo Wilson, London, 1982; *The Slab Boys Trilogy*, Edinburgh and London, 1982; *Other Worlds* by Robert Holman, 1982; *La Colombe* by Gounod, Buxton, Derbyshire, 1983; *McQuin's Metamorphosis* by Martyn Hobbs, Edinburgh, 1984; *The Cherry Orchard* by Chekhov, Leicester, 1984; *A Midsummer Night's Dream*, Leicester, 1984; *Candy Kisses*, London, 1984; *Dead Men* by Mike Stott, Edinburgh, 1985; *The London Cuckolds*, Leicester, 1985; *The Marriage of Figaro* by Mozart, Glasgow, 1986.

John Byrne comments:
(1982) I think I was 11 or 12 when I wrote my first piece . . . not for the theatre, although it was highly dramatic . . . about a cat that gets squashed under a bus. Accompanied by a linocut showing the young master in tears alongside the open coffin, it appeared in the pages of the school magazine. A slow fuse had been lit. 25 years later (in 1976) I wrote my first stage play, *Writer's Cramp*, a scherzo in J Minor for trio. This was followed by *The Slab Boys* (part 1 of a trilogy) based (but heavily embroidered) upon my own experience of working as a retarded teenager in the design studio of a carpet factory. Next came *Normal Service*, in the original draft densely packed with all sorts of motley stuffs like the haggis, but subsequently "opened up" for the stage, again based (however loosely) on a working experience, this time in television. I was trying in *Normal Service* to write a comedy without jokes, a comedy of manners, of character, the relationships within and without the office, the characters' attitudes towards one another, towards their own and each others' spouses, to their work. I can't be certain I've got the skill to cram all of that into two hours or so, which is part of the reason for my writing the aforementioned trilogy (in which the protagonists in Parts 1 and 2 are moved on 20-odd years in Part 3). In effect *The Slab Boys* trilogy will be one long play in three acts. In *Hooray for Hollywood* I transplanted the hero (F.S. McDade) of *Writer's Cramp* from Paisley to Los Angeles and looked on with mounting alarm as he proceeded to behave quite predictably. This was a ten-minute piece (part of an anthology) commissioned by the Actors' Theatre of Louisville. The distaff side of *Writer's Cramp*, *Cara Coco* (at present being rewritten), was presented by Borderline Theatre Co. in Scotland. Just now I am working on a play set in another country (other than Scotland, that is) and on one set in another time (not based on personal experience).

* * *

John Byrne, who was born in Paisley, a suburb of Glasgow, in 1940, draws heavily on his Scottish upbringing and adolescence for his stage writing. Unlike many of his contemporaries, Byrne did not have success as a writer until early middle age. Success came in 1977 with his first play, *Writer's Cramp,* which transferred to London from the Edinburgh Festival and was subsequently revived. Until then Byrne had earned his living as a designer and painter, having studied art before spells in carpet manufacturing and in television, periods on which he was to draw in subsequent plays. Byrne had dealings with the trendy world of art and pop music, particularly in the swinging 1960s, when he had an exhibition in London and was even accorded a profile in one of the Sunday supplements. Byrne also designed LP covers and dust jackets for contemporaries such as the comedian Billy Connolly and the singer Gerry Rafferty, and he worked as a scene painter with the celebrated Scottish touring group 7:84. His contempt for the art world has led him to quit it for good and to embrace the theatrical world not only as an alternative source of inspiration but, in his view, as a superior way of life. Nevertheless, his painter's preoccupation with detail and his gifts of observation are stamped boldly on his work for the stage.

Writer's Cramp is an often funny and accurate extended literary joke that parodies the styles and pretensions of arty Scotland through the life and times of one Francis Seneca McDade. A writer, painter, and belletrist possessing a lovable but irredeemable mediocrity, McDade is shown progressing from disaster to disaster—prep school, prison, literary Oxford, and swinging London—before his final demise clutching a hard-won but rather irrelevant wad of banknotes. Included among the send-ups and satires that are interspersed throughout the scenes in question are an article on work-shy pensioners and a disastrous musical on Dr. Spock, the latter, like much of McDade's canon, not advanced much further than the planning stage. As an artist McDade does acquire brief fame in the 1960s, however, after a typical review from the art critic of the *Scottish Field,* one Dermot Pantalone: "When I quizzed the artist as to why so many of his pictures were painted on Formica using household brushes, his answer was to pick up a pot of Banana Yellow Deep Gloss Enamel and proceed to draw the outline of a giraffe on my overcoat. . . ." McDade and his world of poseurs and eccentrics were a rather easy target for Byrne's obvious comic and linguistic gifts.

Byrne's second play, first seen at the Traverse Theatre in Edinburgh and later in London and on television, was a very different affair. *The Slab Boys,* a lively piece of social realism cum situation comedy set in the paint-mixing room of a Glasgow carpet factory in 1957, draws heavily on Byrne's own past as an apprentice. The play, which is fiercely idiomatic and full of pungent one-liners and shop floor banter, details a working day for three very different apprentices: Phil, the young, small rebel with a secret urge to be a painter; Spanky, the heavy and slow pal of Phil's; and Hector, the shy man who is domiciled with an overprotective mother. It is Hector's attempt to make himself ready and presentable for the forthcoming staff dance that provides the piece with most of its narrative drive. But it is Byrne's gift for recreating the trends and preoccupations of the period—from hit parade to comic book heroes and hairstyles—and his raucous sense of character and speech that made the play such a success.

Byrne's subsequent plays have also revealed an interest in character over narrative. *Threads,* originally *The Loveliest Night of the Year,* takes the action of *The Slab Boys* on to the evening of the "staffie," or firm dance. The dialogue is similarly colloquial, strident, and often witheringly amusing, but the action runs out of steam and relies on a series of farcical encounters in the dark that are poor compensation for the loss of the setting of the marvelously evocative slab room in the first play. Nevertheless, Byrne still manages to provide the occasional telling visual effect, such as the glaring imprint of a flatiron on the back of Phil's otherwise immaculate white tuxedo.

Normal Service, which equally obviously draws on Byrne's experiences, this time as a designer for Scottish Television in the early 1960s, is set in the design room of such an organization during a weekend in 1963 when the station's special 10th anniversary program is due to be recorded. It depicts the internecine strife of the assembled workers, who range from a cowardly, trendy media man with a kilt to a decrepit and hilariously unsuccessful repairman, a weedy expectant father, and a demonic trade union official of Italian descent who declares war every time he answers a ringing phone. Indeed, in the resulting chaos the characters and their interplay hold more sway over the audience than does any development of story line or message about technology and the chaotically minded people who service it daily.

Byrne's last substantial stage work, *Candy Kisses,* shows that his comic terrain can extend beyond Glasgow or London. It is set in 1963 in Italy, where the visit of Pope Paul VI to Perugia is greeted with murderous intent by a demented Fascist professor and two youthful locals with differing degrees of commitment to a Trotskyist terror group. There are varying supports: an East Coast American art student meets a draft-dodging West Coast twerp, and a German fräulein attempts restoration of a Perugino fresco. The local Italians speak with either Scots, Welsh, or Irish accents, a clever device that further isolates the cultural imperialists and foreigners. The plot unravels like a plate of spaghetti, although the play is hardly as substantial.

Byrne may not have kept up his steady output for the stage, but there is an amusing but insubstantial radio satire, *The Nitshill Writing Circle,* that takes us back to the territory of *Writer's Cramp.* He was acclaimed in 1987, however, for his television series *Tutti Frutti,* a wacky saga about the road tour of an aging Scottish rock-soul band that starred, among others, one of the original Slab Boys, Robbie Coltrane. Thus, Byrne has continued as one of Britain's more engaging and unpretentious comic talents.

—Steve Grant

BYRNE, John Keyes. *See* **LEONARD, Hugh.**

C

CAMPTON, David

Nationality: British. **Born:** Leicester, 5 June 1924. **Education:** Wyggeston Grammar School, 1935-41, matriculation 1940. **Military Service:** Served in the Royal Air Force, 1942-45; in the Fleet Air Arm, 1945-46. **Career:** Clerk, City of Leicester Education Department, 1941-49, and East Midlands Gas Board, Leicester, 1949-56. **Awards:** Arts Council bursary, 1958; British Theatre Association Whitworth prize, 1975, 1978, 1985; Japan prize, for radio play, 1977. **Agent:** ACTAC (Theatrical and Cinematic) Ltd., 15 High Street, Ramsbury, Wiltshire SN8 2PA, England. **Address:** 35 Liberty Road, Glenfield, Leicester LE3 8JF, England.

Publications

Plays

Going Home (produced Leicester, 1950). Manchester, Abel Heywood, 1951.

Honeymoon Express (produced Leicester, 1951). Manchester, Abel Heywood, 1951.

Change Partners (produced Leicester, 1952). Manchester, Abel Heywood, 1951.

Sunshine on the Righteous (produced Leicester, 1953). London, Rylee, 1952.

The Laboratory (produced Leicester and London, 1954). London, J. Garnet Miller, 1955.

Want a Bet? (produced Leicester, 1954).

Ripple in the Pool (produced Leicester, 1955).

The Cactus Garden (produced Reading, Berkshire, 1955). London, J. Garnet Miller, 1955.

Dragons Are Dangerous (produced Scarborough, 1955).

Idol in the Sky, with Stephen Joseph (produced Scarborough, 1956).

Doctor Alexander. Leicester, Campton, 1956.

Cuckoo Song. Leicester, Campton, 1956.

The Lunatic View: A Comedy of Menace (includes *A Smell of Burning, Then . . ., Memento Mori, Getting and Spending*) (produced Scarborough, *1957*; *New York, 1962*; *Then . . .* produced London, 1980). Scarborough, Studio Theatre, 1960; *A Smell of Burning*, and *Then . . .* published New York, Dramatists Play Service, 1971.

Roses round the Door (as *Ring of Roses*, produced Scarborough, 1958). London, J. Garnet Miller, 1967.

Frankenstein: The Gift of Fire, adaptation of the novel by Mary Shelley (produced Scarborough, 1959). London, J. Garnet Miller, 1973.

Little Brother, Little Sister (produced Newcastle-under-Lyme, Staffordshire, 1961; London, 1966). Leicester, Campton, 1960.

A View from the Brink (playlets: produced Scarborough, 1960). Section entitled *Out of the Flying Pan* included in *Little Brother, Little Sister; and Out of the Flying Pan*, 1970.

Four Minute Warning (includes *Little Brother, Little Sister*; *Mutatis Mutandis*; *Soldier from the Wars Returning*; *At Sea*) (produced Newcastle-under-Lyme, Staffordshire, 1960; *Soldier from the Wars Returning* produced London, 1961; *Mutatis Mutandis* produced London, 1967). Leicester, Campton, 4 vols., 1960.

Funeral Dance (produced Dovercourt, Essex, 1960). London, J. Garnet Miller, 1962.

Sketches in *You, Me and the Gatepost* (produced Nottingham, 1960).

Sketches in *Second Post* (produced Nottingham, 1961).

Passport to Florence (as *Stranger in the Family*, produced Scarborough, 1961). London, J. Garnet Miller, 1967.

The Girls and the Boys (revue; produced Scarborough, 1961).

Silence on the Battlefield (produced Dovercourt, Essex, 1961). London, J. Garnet Miller, 1967.

Sketches in *Yer What?* (produced Nottingham, 1962).

Usher, adaptation of the story "The Fall of the House of Usher" by Poe (also director: produced Scarborough, 1962; London, 1974). London, J. Garnet Miller, 1973.

Incident (produced 1962). London, J. Garnet Miller, 1967.

A Tinkle of Tiny Bells (broadcast 1963; produced Cumbernauld, Dumbartonshire, 1971).

Comeback (produced Scarborough, 1963; revised version, as *Honey, I'm Home*, produced Leatherhead, Surrey, 1964).

Don't Wait for Me (broadcast 1963; produced London, 1963). Published in *Worth a Hearing: A Collection of Radio Plays*, edited by Alfred Bradley, London, Blackie, 1967.

Dead and Alive (produced Scarborough, 1964). London, J. Garnet Miller, 1983.

On Stage: Containing Seventeen Sketches and One Monologue. London, J. Garnet Miller, 1964.

Resting Place (broadcast 1964; in *We Who Are about to . . .*, later called *Mixed Doubles*, produced London, 1969). London, Methuen, 1970.

The End of the Picnic (broadcast 1964; produced Vancouver, British Columbia, 1973). Included in *Laughter and Fear*, 1969.

The Manipulator (broadcast 1964; shortened version, as *A Point of View*, produced 1964; as *The Manipulator*, produced 1968). London, J. Garnet Miller, 1967.

Cock and Bull Story (produced Scarborough, 1965).

Where Have All the Ghosts Gone? (broadcast 1965). Included in *Laughter and Fear*, 1969.

Split Down the Middle (broadcast 1965; produced Scarborough, 1966). London, J. Garnet Miller, 1973.

Two Leaves and a Stalk (produced 1967). London, J. Garnet Miller, 1967.

Angel Unwilling (broadcast 1967; produced 1972). Leicester, Campton, 1972.

More Sketches. Leicester, Campton, 1967.

Ladies' Night: Four Plays for Women (includes *Two Leaves and a Stalk, Silence on the Battlefield, Incident, The Manipulator)*. London, J. Garnet Miller, 1967.

Parcel (broadcast 1968). London, French, 1979.

The Right Place (produced 1970). Leicester, Campton, 1969.

Laughter and Fear: *9 One-Act Plays* (includes *Incident, Then . . ., Memento Mori, The End of the Picnic, The Laboratory, A Point of View, Soldier from the Wars Returning, Mutatis Mutandis, Where Have All the Ghosts Gone?*). London, Blackie, 1969.

On Stage Again: *Containing Fourteen Sketches and Two Monologues*. London, J. Garnet Miller, 1969.

The Life and Death of Almost Everybody (produced London, 1970), Leicester, Campton, 1971; New York, Dramatists Play Service, 1972.

Now and Then (produced 1970). Leicester, Campton, 1973.
Little Brother, Little Sister; and Out of the Flying Pan. London, Methuen, and New York, Dramatists Play Service, 1970.
Timesneeze (produced London, 1970). London, Eyre Methuen, 1974.
Wonderchick (produced Bristol, 1970).
Jonah (produced Chelmsford, Essex, 1971). London, J. Garnet Miller, 1972.
The Cagebirds (produced Tunbridge Wells, Kent, 1971; London, 1977). Leicester, Campton, 1972.
Provisioning (produced London, 1971).
Us and Them (produced 1972). Leicester, Campton, 1972; Chicago, Dramatic Publishing Company, 1982.
Carmilla, adaptation of a story by Le Fanu (produced Sheffield, 1972). London, J. Garnet Miller, 1973.
Come Back Tomorrow. Leicester, Campton, 1972.
In Committee. Leicester, Campton, 1972.
Three Gothic Plays (includes *Frankenstein, Usher, Carmilla*). London, J. Garnet Miller, 1973.
Eskimos, in *Mixed Blessings* (produced Horsham, Sussex, 1973). Included in *Pieces of Campton*, 1979.
Relics (produced Leicester, 1973). London, Evans, 1974.
An Outline of History (produced Bishop Auckland, County Durham, 1974). Leicester, Campton, 1981.
Everybody's Friend (broadcast 1974; produced Edinburgh, 1975). London, French, 1979.
Ragerbo! (produced Peckleton, Leicestershire, 1975). Leicester, Campton, 1977.
The Do-It-Yourself Frankenstein Outfit (produced Birmingham, 1975). London, French, 1978.
George Davenport, The Wigston Highwayman (produced Countesthorpe, Leicestershire, 1975).
What Are You Doing Here? Leicester, Campton, 1976.
No Go Area. Leicester, Campton, 1976.
One Possessed (broadcast 1977). Leicester, Campton, 1977.
Oh, Yes It Is! (produced Braunston, Northamptonshire, 1977).
Zodiac, music by John Whitworth (produced Melton Mowbray, Leicestershire, 1977). London, French, 1978.
The Great Little Tilley (produced Nottingham, 1978).
After Midnight, Before Dawn (produced Leicester, 1978). London, French, 1978.
Dark Wings (produced Leicester, 1978). Leicester, Campton, 1980.
Pieces of Campton (dialogues; includes *According to the Book, At the Door, Drip, Eskimos, Expectation, Strong Man Act, Sunday Breakfast, Under the Bush, Where Were You Last Winter?*). Leicester, Campton, 1979.
Who Calls? (produced Dublin, 1979). London, French, and Chicago, Dramatic Publishing Company, 1980.
Under the Bush (produced London, 1980). Included in *Pieces of Campton*, 1979.
Attitudes (produced Stoke-on-Trent, 1981). Leicester, Campton, 1980.
Freedom Log. Leicester, Campton, 1980.
Star-station Freedom (produced Leicester, 1981).
Look—Sea, and Great Whales. Leicester, Campton, 1981.
Who's a Hero, Then? Leicester, Campton, 1981.
Apocalypse Now and Then (includes *Mutatis Mutandis* and *The View from Here*) (produced Leicester, 1982).
Olympus (produced Leicester, 1983).
But Not Here (produced Leicester, 1983). Leicester, Campton, 1984.
Two in the Corner (includes *Reserved, En attendant François, Overhearings*). Leicester, Campton, 1983.
En attendant François (produced Chelmsford, Essex, 1984). Included in *Two in the Corner*, 1983.
Who's Been Sitting in My Chair? (produced Chelmsford, Essex, 1984).
So Why? Leicester, Campton, 1984.
Mrs. Meadowsweet (as *Mrs. M.*, broadcast 1984; revised version, as *Mrs. Meadowsweet*, produced Ulverston, Lancashire, 1985). London, French, 1986.
Cards, Cups, and Crystal Ball (produced Broadway, Worcestershire, 1985). Leicester, Campton, and Chicago, Dramatic Publishing Company, 1986.
Singing in the Wilderness (produced Leicester, 1985). London, French, 1986.
Our Branch in Brussels. London, French, 1986.
The Spectre Bridegroom, adaptation of the play by W.T. Moncrieff (also director: produced Leicester, 1987). Leicester, Campton, 1987.
Can You Hear the Music? (produced Leicester, 1988). London, French, 1988.
The Winter of 1917 (produced Bognor Regis, West Sussex, 1989). London, French, and Chicago, Dramatic Publishing Company, 1989.
Smile (produced Colefore, 1990). London, French, and Chicago, Dramatic Publishing Company, 1990.
The Evergreens (produced Leicester, 1992). London, French, 1994.
Permission to Cry (produced Leicester, 1995). London, French, 1996.

Radio Plays: *A Tinkle of Tiny Bells*, 1963; *Don't Wait for Me*, 1963; *The Manipulator*, 1964; *Alison*, 1964; *Resting Place*, 1964; *The End of the Picnic*, 1964; *Split Down the Middle*, 1965; *Where Have All the Ghosts Gone?*, 1965; *Angel Unwilling*, 1967; *The Missing Jewel*, 1967; *Parcel*, 1968; *Boo!*, 1971; *Now You Know*, 1971 (Italy); *Ask Me No Questions* (Germany); *Holiday, As Others See Us, So You Think You're a Hero, We Did It for Laughs, Deep Blue Sea?, Isle of the Free, You Started It, Good Money, You're on Your Own, Mental Health, We Know What's Right, When the Wells Run Dry, Our Crowd, Nice Old Stick Really, On the Rampage, Victor, Little Boy Lost*, and *Tramps* (all in *Inquiry* series), from 1971; *Everybody's Friend*, 1974; *One Possessed*, 1977; *I'm Sorry, Mrs. Baxter*, 1977; *Our Friend Bimbo*, 1978, *Three Fairy Tales*, 1979, and *Bang! Wham!*, 1979 (all Denmark); *Community* series (5 episodes for schools), 1979; *Peacock Feathers*, 1982; *Kahani Apni Apni* series, 1983; *Mrs. M.*, 1984; *Cards, Cups, and Crystal Ball*, 1987.

Television Plays: *One Fight More*, with Stephen Joseph, 1956; *See What You Think* series, 1957; *Starr and Company* (serialization), 1958; *Tunnel under the World*, 1966; *Someone in the Lift*, 1967; *The Triumph of Death*, 1968; *A Private Place*, 1968; *Liar*, 1969; *Time for a Change*, 1969; *Slim John*, with others, 1971; *The Bellcrest Story*, 1972; *People You Meet*, 1972.

Other (for children)

Gulliver in Lilliput. London, University of London Press, 1970.
Gulliver in the Land of the Giants. London, University of London Press, 1970.

The Wooden Horse of Troy. London, University of London Press, 1970.
Modern Aesop Stories. Kuala Lumpur, Oxford University Press, 1976.
Vampyre, from a story by John Polidori. London, Hutchinson, 1986; New York, Barron's, 1988.
Frankenstein. London, Hutchinson, 1987.
Becoming a Playwright. London, Robert Hale, 1992.

*

Critical Studies: *Anger and After* by John Russell Taylor, London, Methuen, 1962, revised edition, 1969, as *The Angry Theatre*, New York, Hill and Wang, 1962, revised edition, 1969; *The Disarmers* by Christopher Driver, London, Hodder and Stoughton, 1964; "Comedy of Menace" by Irving Wardle, in *The Encore Reader*, London, Methuen, 1965; *Laughter and Fear* edited by Michael Marland, Glasgow, Blackie, 1969; *Investigating Drama* by Kenneth Pickering, Bill Horrocks, and David Male, London, Allen and Unwin, 1974.

Theatrical Activities:
Director: **Play**—*Usher*, Scarborough, 1962; *The Spectre Bridegroom*, 1987.

Actor: **Plays**—Roles with Stephen Joseph's Theatre in the Round, Scarborough and on tour, 1957-63, including Petey in *The Birthday Party* by Harold Pinter, Birmingham, 1959, Old Man in *Memento Mori*, London, 1960, Polonius in *Hamlet*, Newcastle-under-Lyme, Staffordshire, 1962, Noah in *The Ark* by James Saunders, Scarborough, 1962, and Harry Perkins in *Comeback*, Scarborough, 1963; Cinquemani in *The Shameless Professor* by Pirandello, London, 1959; Bread in *The Blue Bird* by Maeterlinck, London, 1963.

David Campton comments:

Realizing that a play in a drawer is of no use to anyone, and that, being an ephemeral thing, it will not wait for posterity to catch up with it, I have always written with production in mind.

The circumstances of production have varied from the village hall, through radio and television, to the West End stage. (Though representation on that last has been confined to one-act plays and sketches.) This has also meant that my plays have varied in kind from domestic comedy, through costume melodrama to—as Irving Wardle coined the phrase—"comedy of menace."

My profession is playwriting, and I hope I approach it with a professional mixture of art and business. The art of playwriting is of prime importance; I hope I have never relegated it to second place. I have never written a play "because it might sell." Everything I have written has been clamouring to be written and as long as I have been able to make marks on paper, there has always been a queue of a dozen or more ideas waiting their turn to achieve solid form. But an idea can always be developed towards a particular medium, be it experimental theatre in the round or an all-female group performing in a converted schoolroom.

I dislike pigeonholes and object to being popped into one. However, one label that might fit is the title of an anthology of my plays: *Laughter and Fear*. This is not quite the same as comedy of menace, which has acquired a connotation of theatre of the absurd. It is in fact present in my lightest domestic comedy. It seems to me that the chaos affecting everyone today—political, technical, sociological, religious, etc., etc.—is so all-pervading that it cannot be ignored, yet so shattering that it can only be approached through comedy. Tragedy demands firm foundations; today we are dancing among the ruins.

* * *

David Campton is a prolific writer of short plays. The nine plays in *Laughter and Fear* include some of his best. *On Stage* and *On Stage Again* are collections of revue-length sketches, and many of his short plays are slight, akin to traditional short stories that present two or three characters, reveal a significant event in the past to explain present eccentricities, and end with an unexpected twist. For example, in *Where Have All the Ghosts Gone?* a sensible young man intrudes on a drunken widow while looking for his girlfriend, who has been too ashamed of her mother to take him home. The mother does her best to break their attachment with a suicide attempt. She is dependent on her daughter, but she also blames her for the death of her husband in a car crash, though the daughter was only five years old at the time. The mother now plays upon her daughter's sense of guilt. The young man, however, proposes to the daughter, and in an epilogue the mother tells the audience that the house and garden are restored and that she is the grandmother of twins. But the twist is still to come: "Just one big happy family. In fact to see me now, you'd never imagine. . . . No, you'd never imagine that I was once a real person."

This is typical Campton territory: for the setting a crumbling house or dowdy flat, for a central character the middle-aged or elderly middle-class woman in reduced circumstances, and for a theme the fight to maintain independence and defend one's individuality. The combination is sometimes successful, as in *The Manipulator,* in which a Volpone-like bedridden woman uses gossip to blackmail, manipulate, and ensure that her daughters do not move her out of the flat. Since Campton's plays exploit the aching articulacies of the middle classes rather than the working-class inarticulacies explored by Harold Pinter, Edward Bond, and Stephen Lowe, they have lent themselves to radio productions.

Yet from his earliest work with Stephen Joseph's Theatre-in-the-Round in Scarborough, Campton has played with the inherent theatricality of the stage experience. This is particularly true of some of his later plays. In *The Life and Death of Almost Everybody* a stage sweeper conjures up characters from his imagination whom he then has trouble controlling. The committee of *In Committee,* meeting onstage, becomes aware but refuses to acknowledge that there is an audience present, even when "audience members" one by one replace committee members. And in *Who's a Hero, Then?* the stage is divided into an area representing a club and an "imagination area." At the club Norm is criticized for apparently letting his friend drown. Each of his critics enters the imagination area in turn, through which the drowning man's cries ring each time, and does no better. The artificiality of the theater experience is also implicit in *Timesneeze,* a play for youth performed by the National Theatre in 1970, in which a time machine moves the hero to different places and periods.

Another kind of theatricality that Campton exploits, and does so with more success, is linguistic. Like Pinter, he plays with proverbs, catchphrases, and clichés. *On Stage* includes four sketches about teenagers in which such phrases as "see you around" are by their repetition filled with all that is not being expressed. The committee members in *In Committee* are so tangled in procedural jargon that we never learn what the committee is considering. And in the high-level diplomatic encounter of *Out of the Flying Pan* the words themselves become garbled.

Campton acknowledges the influence of the theater of the absurd. Ionesco's Jack, who demands a bride who is well endowed, is first cousin to the new father who in *Mutatis Mutandis* has to break the news to his wife of their baby's precocious development of a full head of hair (green), teeth (pointed), and tail. The baby has inherited his eyes—fine brown eyes—all three of them. Similarly reminiscent of Ionesco is *Getting and Spending,* which follows a couple's progress from marriage to old age as they pursue mutual dreams that lead to the offstage proliferation of cots and prams in the nursery, while their dreams distract them from ever actually producing offspring.

It is when the absurd serves Campton's social conscience that he produces his best plays. *Incident* is a parable on racial prejudice in which an inn turns away a weary traveler because no one named Smith is to be admitted. The most interesting aspect of the play is the way in which Campton shows how Miss Smith's companion is drawn into negotiating a compromise, only to be (rightly) abandoned by Miss Smith. In *Soldier from the Wars Returning* a soldier boasts to a barmaid of his exploits, and she hands him an eye patch, a crutch, and so on until he leaves the bar a cripple. The play is a parable about war and perhaps an externalizing of the hidden psychological wounds that war inflicts on all participants. *Then . . .* is a play about nuclear holocaust. A physics teacher and the reigning Miss Europe are the sole survivors. Despite the social conventions they strive to follow, feelings that neither of them has ever had time for flow between them, but they dare not remove the brown paper bags they wear over their heads. These absurdly slight means of protection, like children's masquerades, along with their unperturbedly conventional responses to meeting, convey the frailty and limited vision of human beings, commenting more effectively in 10 minutes on the threat of nuclear war than any large-scale television dramatization of the future.

Of Campton's full-length plays the swift-moving *Jonah,* commissioned for performance at Chelmsford Cathedral in 1971, is the most interesting. Jonah is called on to warn everyone, from businessmen to the cathedral's cleaners, of the imminent destruction of their sinful city. He resists the call, knowing that he will be laughed at, and the destruction occurs, though—as he and the audience learn—only in a private vision for him. When he calls upon people to reform, they do. But they begin to demand to know when the destruction will occur, and they goad Jonah into declaring a date and time. When no destruction occurs, no one blames Jonah for false prophecy, but at the end of the play he feels humiliated. He has devoted his life to justice and punishment, not to the mercy God has shown.

Campton is a workmanlike—and sometimes workaday—playwright. *Jonah,* for example, could easily be performed with one professional as Jonah and amateurs in the numerous other roles. In his hands *Frankenstein* becomes an easily staged, almost domestic drama about Victor Frankenstein's complicated relationships with his fiancée and his best friend. Campton has also written a number of short plays for all-female casts, but they range, unfortunately, from the mechanical to the contrived. For example, in *Singing in the Wilderness* an ecologist and a folklorist come across Cobweb, Moth, Mustardseed, and their relatively new friend Tinkerbell, who are suffering from old age, the spraying of pesticides, and the destruction of hedgerows.

Campton is an unfashionable playwright. In an age that finds the tough-minded and difficult, the crabbed or elliptical, to be critically interesting, his inventions seem facile, especially in his full-length plays, and sometimes whimsical. His characters are usually articulate and understand one another fairly well, and his humane messages are clear. Some of his short plays deserve repeated production.

—Anthony Graham-White

CARLINO, Lewis John

Nationality: American. **Born:** New York City, 1 January 1932. **Education:** El Camino College, California; University of Southern California, Los Angeles, 1956-60, B.A. (magna cum laude) in film 1959 (Phi Beta Kappa), M.A. in drama 1960. **Military Service:** Served in the United States Air Force, 1951-55. **Family:** Married Denise Jill Chadwick; three children from previous marriage. **Career:** Playwright, screen and television writer. Lives in California. **Awards:** British Drama League prize, 1960; nominated for Academy award for best original screenplay, for *The Brotherhood,* 1968; Huntington Hartford fellowship; Yaddo fellowship; Rockefeller grant; Obie award. **Agent:** Gilbert Parker, William Morris Agency, 1350 Avenue of the Americas, New York, New York 10019, U.S.A.

Publications

Plays

The Brick and the Rose: A Collage for Voices (produced Los Angeles, 1957; New York, 1974; London, 1985). New York, Dramatists Play Service, 1959.

Junk Yard. New York, Dramatists Play Service, 1959.

Used Car for Sale. New York, Dramatists Play Service, 1959.

Objective Case (produced Westport, Connecticut, and New York, 1962). With *Mr. Flannery's Ocean*, New York, Dramatists Play Service, 1961.

Mr. Flannery's Ocean (includes *Piece and Precise*) (produced Westport, Connecticut, 1962). With *Objective Case*, New York, Dramatists Play Service, 1961.

Two Short Plays: Sarah and the Sax, and High Sign. New York, Dramatists Play Service, 1962.

The Beach People (produced Madison, Ohio, 1962).

Postlude, and Snowangel (produced New York, 1962).

Cages: Snowangel and Epiphany (produced New York, 1963; Leicester, 1964; *Epiphany* produced London, 1974). New York, Random House, 1963; New York, Dramatists Play Service, 1992.

Telemachus Clay: A Collage for Voices (produced New York, 1963). New York, Random House, 1964.

Doubletalk: Sarah and the Sax, and The Dirty Old Man (produced New York, 1964; *Sarah and the Sax* produced London, 1971). New York, Random House, 1964.

The Exercise (produced Stockbridge, Massachusetts, 1967; New York, 1968). New York, Dramatists Play Service, 1968.

Screenplays: *Seconds*, 1966; *The Fox*, with Howard Koch, 1967; *The Brotherhood*, 1968; *Reflection of Fear*, with Edward Hume, 1971; *The Mechanic*, 1972; *Crazy Joe*, 1973; *The Sailor Who Fell from Grace with the Sea*, 1976; *I Never Promised You a Rose Garden*, with Gavin Lambert, 1977; *The Great Santini*, 1980; *Resurrection*, 1981.

Television Plays: *And Make Thunder His Tribute* (*Route 66* series), 1963; *In Search of America*, 1971; *Doc Elliot* (pilot), 1972; *Honor Thy Father*, from the novel by Gay Talese, 1973; *Where Have All the People Gone?*, with Sandor Stern, 1974.

Video: *The Mechanic*, 1972; *The Sailor Who Fell from Grace with the Sea*, Anchor Bay Entertainment, 1976; *Honor Thy Father*, Front Row Entertainment, 1995; *Seconds*, Paramount, 1997.

Novels

The Brotherhood. New York, New American Library, 1968.
The Mechanic. New York, New American Library, 1972.

*

Theatrical Activities:
Director: **Films**—*The Sailor Who Fell from Grace with the Sea*, 1976; *The Great Santini*, 1980; *Class*, 1983.

* * *

Between June 1963 and May 1964—in a period of less than a year—four one-act plays and one full-length work by Lewis John Carlino were produced off-Broadway in New York. They ranged from the vast talent and imagination of *Telemachus Clay* to the burgeoning maturity of *Cages* to the unfulfilled *Doubletalk*. With these plays Carlino established himself as an American playwright of exceptional quality and promise. The theater did not hear from him again for four years as he turned to writing for the screen (*Seconds*, *The Brotherhood*). In 1968 he made his Broadway debut with the sloppy and self-indulgent *The Exercise*, and the catastrophe seems to have driven him permanently from the theater.

If critics, financial uncertainty, and the unpredictable duration of a play's run are the risk of the theater, film writing has its own dangers. Like too many artistic writers caught up in the American commercial maelstrom, Carlino was lost in the hurly-burly of a marketplace too busy to notice or care. Nevertheless, the originality and craftsmanship of his stage work endure. He is a playwright who should not forget or be forgotten.

Carlino's first notable New York production was *Cages*, a bill of one-act plays. The curtain-raiser, *Snowangel*, is a minor look at a constricted intellectual and an earthy prostitute that spells out the predictable point. The main work of the program, however, is devastating. Called *Epiphany*, it is about an ornithologist who is discovered by his wife in a homosexual act. In reaction he turns into a rooster. The Kafkaesque metaphor is theatrically powerful, visually striking, and provocative in context. But as he becomes a rooster, clucking and strutting, it turns out that he is laying eggs. Having really wanted to be a hen, he has suffered a breakdown only to find his wife all too willing to strip the coxcomb from the mask he has donned. He need no longer pretend to virility. She turns him into a female and intends to keep him that way. Although the play came at a time when every other drama seemed to condemn woman as man's archenemy, Carlino's imaginative story and powerful structure transcended the cliché. The dramatic scheme is faultless, and the writing is for actors, something too few playwrights seem capable of achieving.

As is often the case, a well-received play generates the production of a writer's earlier work, and within six months Carlino's *Telemachus Clay* was presented off-Broadway. One could only again ponder the judgment of producers, for here was a drama of tremendous poetry, artistry, and stage life. But it was a drama that would never have been presented had it not been for the notices *Cages* received.

Like so many first plays, *Telemachus Clay* is a story of the artist as a young man, in this case drawn parallel to Odysseus's son. It is subtitled *A Collage for Voices*, as indeed it is, with the actors perched on stools and facing the audience. The 11 actors play a host of characters, changing time and location with the magic of poetry that weaves the fabric of story, thought, event, and emotion in overlapping dialogue and sound. It is a device that risks pretension and artiness, but in *Telemachus Clay* it succeeds because of the sheer beauty of the language and the structural control. There are thoughts and dreams, flashbacks, memories, and overheard conversations—a score of effects beyond conventional structure and justifying the form. Like *Cages*, the play suffers from immature message making, but like it, too, there is a marvelous sense of theater, of dialogue, of fantasy, and of humor.

Doubletalk underlined the flaws rather than the strengths of these earlier plays. Instead of picking up on his technical finesse, strong dialogue, and sense of stage excitement, Carlino stumbled in his inclination toward point-making and his trouble with plots. These two one-act plays used coy notions instead of stories: an old Jewish woman who has a chance meeting with a black musician, and a virgin who has a chance meeting with an aged poet. This coyness came to a head with *The Exercise*, a play about actors, improvisations, reality, and theatricality. It threatened to bring Pirandello from his grave if only to blow up New York's Actors Studio, to which the play was virtually a bouquet.

Carlino's output has been slim and certainly inconsistent, and no peak of development has ever been achieved. Yet his playwriting is unmistakably artistic. Its uncertain flowering is tragically representative of too many American writers for the stage.

—Martin Gottfried

CARTER, Lonnie

Nationality: American. **Born:** Chicago, Illinois, 25 October 1942. **Education:** Loyola University, Chicago, 1960-61; Marquette University, Milwaukee, B.A. 1964, M.A. 1966; Yale University School of Drama, New Haven, Connecticut (Molly Kazan award, 1967; Shubert Fellow, 1968-69), M.F.A. 1969. **Family:** Married Marilyn Smutko in 1966 (divorced 1972). **Career:** Taught writing at Marquette University, 1964-65, Yale University School of Drama, 1974-75, Rockland Community College, Suffern, New York, University of Connecticut, Storrs, and New York University, 1979-86; Jenny McKean Moore Fellow, George Washington University, Washington, D.C., 1986-87. **Awards:** Peg Santvoord Foundation fellowship, 1969, 1970; Guggenheim fellowship, 1971; National Endowment for the Arts grant, 1974, 1983; CBS Foundation grant, 1974; Connecticut Commission on the Arts grant, 1976, 1988; Open Circle award, 1978; PEN grant, 1978. **Address:** Cream Hill Road, West Cornwall, Connecticut 06796, U.S.A.

PUBLICATIONS

Plays

Adam (produced Milwaukee, 1966).
Another Quiet Evening at Home (produced New Haven, Connecticut, 1967).
If Beauty's in the Eye of the Beholder, Truth Is in the Pupil Somewhere Too (produced New Haven, Connecticut, 1969).
Workday (produced New Haven, Connecticut, 1970).
Iz She Izzy or Iz He Ain'tzy or Iz They Both, music by Robert Montgomery (produced New Haven, Connecticut, 1970; New York, 1972). Included in *The Sovereign State of Boogedy Boogedy and Other Plays*, 1986.
More War in Store, and Time Space (produced New York, 1970).
Plumb Loco (produced Stockbridge, Massachusetts, 1970).
The Big House (produced New Haven, Connecticut, 1971).
Smoky Links (produced New York, 1972).
Watergate Classics, with others (produced New Haven, Connecticut, 1973). Published in *Yale/Theatre* (New Haven, Connecticut), 1974.
Cream Cheese (produced New York, 1974).
Trade-Offs (produced New Haven, Connecticut, 1976; New York, 1977).
Bleach (produced Chicago, 1977).
Bicicletta (produced New York, 1978). Included in *The Sovereign State of Boogedy Boogedy and Other Plays*, 1986.
Victoria Fellows (produced Baltimore, 1978).
Sirens (produced New York, 1979).
The Sovereign State of Boogedy Boogedy (produced Chicago, 1985; New York, 1986). Included in *The Sovereign State of Boogedy Boogedy and Other Plays*, 1986.
The Sovereign State of Boogedy Boogedy and Other Plays (includes *Iz She Izzy or Iz He Ain'tzy or Iz They Both, Waiting for G, Bicicletta, Necktie Party*). West Cornwall, Connecticut, Locust Press, 1986.
Mothers and Sons (produced Chicago, 1987).
Necktie Party (produced Chicago, 1987). Included in *The Sovereign State of Boogedy Boogedy and Other Plays*, 1986.
Gulliver (produced Pittsfield, Massachusetts, 1990).
Waiting for Lefty Rose (produced New York, 1991).
I.B. Randy Jr. (produced New York, 1992).
Plays by Lonnie Carter: The Gulliver Trilogy. New York, Broadway Play Publishing, 1997.

Radio Plays: *Certain Things about the Trombone*, 1982; *Lulu*, 1983.

Television Play: *From the Top*, 1976.

Video: *Visions of America*, with others, Film for the Humanities and Sciences, 1993.

* * *

While Lonnie Carter was studying playwriting at the Yale University School of Drama, he spent most of his time not writing plays but instead attending movie retrospectives of Buster Keaton, Charlie Chaplin, the Marx Brothers, and W. C. Fields. Spending hours watching these classic comedies, he saw something in the basic physiognomy of the characters that he was trying to do verbally in his own plays. He then decided to write his own slapstick farce, *The Big House,* using a Marx Brothers film as a springboard.

Employing the original plot of the film, in which three con men take over a prison and lock up the warden, Carter used the film's basic characters of Groucho, a Cockney Chico, Harpo, and a minister made up to look like Chaplin. Carter's only additions were a few songs and dances. What Carter basically ended up with was a hodgepodge of 1920s and 1930s movie comedies. The play is filled with low-comedy hijinks, pratfalls galore, and very broad burlesque humor. The action proceeds at such a furious pace that by the middle of the second act the audience is out of breath and the playwright out of plot. The main trouble with *The Big House* lies in the plot and structure. It would have been fine as a one-act play or as a minimusical, but it does not work as a full-length play.

Carter's most popular work is called *Iz She Izzy or Iz He Ain'tzy or Iz They Both.* It had its premiere at Yale in 1970 and has since been performed regularly by university and high school drama groups. *Izzy* is set in a chaotic contemporary courtroom where a schizoid judge—Justice "Choo-Choo" Justice, who is half male and half female—is on trial for having committed the premeditated murder of his female self. In *Izzy* Carter once again used many familiar movie gags, and the action is supplemented by songs with lovely lyrics that show off his audacious wit. A good example is the song sung by the frustrated justice near the end of the play: "I'd like to have a baby/A lass or little laddie/But when it saw its mommy/Would it say 'Daddy'?"

Smoky Links is about a revolution on a mythical Scottish golf course. The main revolutionary is a symbolic Oriental golf pro who threatens the whole club while turning the Scottish accent around with his pronunciation.

In *Smoky Links,* as in most of his plays, Carter wrestles with the subject of justice. All of his main characters—Wolfgang Amadeus Gutbucket in *The Big House,* Justice "Choo-Choo" Justice in *Izzy,* and the Oriental golf pro in *Smoky Links*—are in some way frustrated by the law. But the characters' attitude toward justice and the law remains mostly ambiguous, except in the case of the Marx Brothers in *The Big House*. The Marx Brothers are dyed-in-the-wool anarchists and never offer an alternative to total disruption.

Except for the highly derivative *The Big House,* Carter's sharp humor and verbal somersaults remind one more of Restoration comedy or the satires of Rabelais than of old-time Hollywood comedies. Although the influence of films is strong, Carter also has also a special, quite obvious talent.

—Bernard Carragher

CARTWRIGHT, Jim

Nationality: British. **Born:** Farnworth, near Manchester, Lancashire, 27 June 1958. **Family:** Married Angela Jones in 1984. **Awards:** George Devine award, 1986; Beckett award, 1987; *Drama* award, 1986; *Plays and Players* award, 1986; Monte Carlo Golden Nymph award for film, 1987; Golden Nymph award for Best Film, 1987; Manchester *Evening News* award for best new play, for *Two,* 1990; *Evening Standard* award for best comedy, for *The Rise and Fall of Little Voice,* 1992; Olivier award for best comedy, 1993; Samuel Beckett award, for *Road,* 1996; Drama magazine award, 1996; joint winner of George Devine award and Plays and Players award, 1996. **Agent:** Judy Daish Associates, 2 St. Charles Place, London W10 6EG, England.

Publications

Plays

Road (produced London, 1986; New York, 1988). London and New York, Methuen, 1986; revised version, 1990.
Bed (produced London, 1989). London, Methuen, 1991.
To (produced Bolton, Lancashire 1989; London, 1990). London. Methuen, 1991; as *Two*, Methuen, 1992.
The Rise and Fall of Little Voice (produced London, 1992). London, Methuen, 1992.
I Licked a Slag's Deodorant (produced London, 1996). New York, Methuen, 1996.

Radio Play: *Baths*, 1987.

Television Plays: *Vroom*, 1988; *June*, 1990; *Wedded*, 1990.

* * *

Jim Cartwright was the British theater's most exciting discovery of the 1980s, a genuinely original new voice. Comparisons have been made with Osborne, Bond, and, more fruitfully, Shelagh Delaney, but Cartwright is very much his own man. He is a shrewd observer of North Country working-class life, a poet of the underclasses, and a reactivator of demotic speech. In the course of four plays he moved geographically from the Royal Court's Theatre Upstairs to the West End and from a fragmented, episodic structure (*Road*) to something closely resembling a traditional well-made comedy (*The Rise and Fall of Little Voice*). Although the work has progressed, the voice has remained distinctive, that of a largely self-taught writer who loves the quirks and oddities of everyday speech and who has an enormous fund of sympathy for the discarded, the dispossessed, and the victims of an abrasive society.

Cartwright emerged virtually out of the blue in 1986 with *Road,* which was given a stunning promenade production, later televised, by the Royal Court. Under the guidance of a rum-soaked narrator, Scullery, it takes the audience on a kaleidoscopic tour of a grotty Lancastrian street, the last stop before the slag heap. One by one it introduces us to the characters in the road: an old woman locked into sexual reverie; a fanatical, keep-fit skinhead now converted to Buddhism; an unemployed ex-Royal Air Force conscript wondering, while doing the ironing, what happened to the days of jobs, courting, and the pictures three times a week; and, most tragically of all, a young boy and girl who get into bed and jointly commit anorexic suicide.

Road was variously compared to early Osborne, *Coronation Street*, *Under Milk Wood*, and *Our Town*. But what made the play unusual was partly Cartwright's ability to mix the realism of the streets with a heightened poetic language. An out-of-work office girl, for example, conveys her desperation by crying, "Every day's like swimming in ache." Even more remarkable was Cartwright's ability to cut through the spectator's intellectual defenses and flood the stage with feeling. In the remarkable final scene an unfulfilled double tryst, fueled by liquor and Otis Redding's recording of "Try a Little Tenderness," explodes into a song of desperate aspiration. Loose knit the play may have been. What finally bound the episodes together was Cartwright's compassion both for the confused, bewildered young and for the old, who nurse a collective memory of lost dignity and pleasure.

Cartwright's intuitive sympathy for the old is at the very heart of his next play, a slightly overwritten and whimsically surreal piece, *Bed.* This is a strange, dream-driven Dylanesque poem of a play that shows seven old people lying side by side in a vast bed, drifting through their memories. From a shelf above the bed a sleepless, red-eyed, disembodied head vituperatively abuses the snoozing elders in a Beckett-like manner. As in *Road*, there were elegiac memories of a lost and better England and signs of Cartwright's gift for language. But although the play is full of weird, wild images—including the sight of an old married couple descending through a hole in the bed to fetch a glass of water—it lacks any sense of imaginative rigor. As Paul Taylor wrote, "If *anything* can happen in the world of a play, then what actually does is robbed of dramatic necessity."

Cartwright was back on much surer ground in the cryptically entitled *To,* a sharp, salty, rapid-fire evocation of the surface gaiety and underlying melancholia of English pub life, with two actors playing both the publicans and their clientele. Once again, the structure is episodic. But Cartwright turned that to great advantage by catching, as in a series of lightning sketches, the oddity and pain behind the camaraderie of the saloon. He provided some wonderfully eccentric portraits, including that of a solitary widower summoning up his wife's departed spirit by touching a brown teapot and a vision of two Memphis-hooked fatties haunted by memories of the King ("Elvis died of a choked bum," one of them confidently asserts). But the Boltonian comic realism is counterpointed by a sense of the English pub as a place of gregarious solitude where, under the cheerful sluicing, one can hear the sound of breaking glass and relationships.

With *The Rise and Fall of Little Voice*, Cartwright finally harnessed all of his familiar characteristics—rich language, sympathy for the underdog, a streetwise wit—to a consecutive narrative. The Little Voice of the title is a painfully shy, waiflike agoraphobe with a hidden talent for doing impressions of Garland, Bassey, Fields, and Piaf in the privacy of her bedroom. Under pressure from her coarse, boozy, widowed mum and the mother's sleazy agent-boyfriend, the heroine is forced to expose her peculiar talent in a tatty Northern nightclub. But the irony is that by imitating others she finally finds her own voice.

There are obvious echoes here of other plays—*A Taste of Honey*, *Roots*, *Educating Rita*—in which a female protagonist discovers her true identity. But the particular appeal of the play lies in the contrast between the story's mythic, fairy-tale quality and the lewd, loud, lively language. Cartwright goes out of his way to emphasize the story's fablelike aspect, even showing Little Voice being rescued by a young engineer who rises outside her window on a British Telecom crane. The mother is a richly drawn vulgarian who curls her tongue around some choice Boltonian phrases. She remembers her late husband, for example, as "a length of dry stick that bored me bra-less." With *The Rise and Fall of Little Voice* Cartwright came up with an affirmative and wholly theatrical play, one that depends on the audience's spine-tingling realization that the actress playing Little Voice is really doing her own singing. It is easily the most optimistic play Cartwright has written, but it hinges, like its predecessors, on his rare ability to exploit the communal conspiracy of live theater.

—Michael Billington

CAUTE, (John) David

Nationality: British. **Born:** Alexandria, Egypt, 16 December 1936. **Education:** Edinburgh Academy; Wellington College, Crowthorne, Berkshire; Wadham College, Oxford, M.A. in modern history, D.Phil. 1962; Harvard University, Cambridge, Massachusetts (Henry Fellow), 1960-61. **Military Service:** Served in the British Army, in Africa, 1955-56. **Family:** Married 1) Catherine Shuckburgh in 1961 (divorced 1970), two sons; 2) Martha Bates in 1973, two daughters. **Career:** Fellow, All Souls College, Oxford, 1959-65; visiting professor, New York University and Columbia University, New York, 1966-67; reader in social and political theory, Brunel University, Uxbridge, Middlesex, 1967-70; Regents' lecturer, University of California, 1974; Benjamin Meaker visiting professor, University of Bristol, 1985. Literary and arts editor, *New Statesman*, London, 1979-80. Deputy chair, 1979-80, and co-chair, 1981-82, Writers Guild of Great Britain. **Awards:** London Authors' Club award, 1960; Rhys memorial prize, 1960. **Address:** 41 Westcroft Square, London W6 0TA, England.

PUBLICATIONS

Plays

Songs for an Autumn Rifle (produced Edinburgh, 1961).
The Demonstration (produced Nottingham, 1969; London, 1970). London, Deutsch, 1970.
The Fourth World (produced London, 1973).

Radio Plays: *Fallout*, 1972; *The Zimbabwe Tapes*, 1983; *Henry and the Dogs*, 1986; *Sanctions*, 1988; *Animal Fun Park*, 1995.

Television Documentary: *Brecht & Co.*, 1979.

Novels

At Fever Pitch. London, Deutsch, 1959; New York, Pantheon, 1961.
Comrade Jacob. London, Deutsch, 1961; New York, Pantheon, 1962.
The Decline of the West. London, Deutsch, and New York, Macmillan, 1966.
The Occupation. London, Deutsch, 1971; New York, McGraw Hill, 1972.
The Baby Sitters (as John Salisbury). London, Secker and Warburg, and New York, Atheneum, 1978.
Moscow Gold (as John Salisbury). London, Futura, 1980.
The K-Factor. London, Joseph, 1983.
News from Nowhere. London, Hamish Hamilton, 1986.
Veronica; or, The Two Nations. London, Hamish Hamilton, 1989; New York, Arcade, 1990.
The Women's Hour. London, Paladin, 1991.
Dr. Orwell and Mr. Blair. London, Weidenfeld, 1994.
Fatima's Scarf. London, Central Books, 1998.

Other

Communism and the French Intellectuals 1914-1960. London, Deutsch, and New York, Macmillan, 1964.
The Left in Europe since 1789. London, Weidenfeld and Nicolson, and New York, McGraw Hill, 1966.
Fanon. London, Fontana, and New York, Viking Press, 1970.
The Illusion. London, Deutsch, 1971; New York, Harper, 1972.
The Fellow-Travellers. London, Weidenfeld and Nicolson, and New York, Macmillan, 1973; revised edition, New Haven, Connecticut and London, Yale University Press, 1988.
Collisions: Essays and Reviews. London, Quartet, 1974.
Cuba, Yes? London, Secker and Warburg, and New York, McGraw Hill, 1974.
The Great Fear: The Anti-Communist Purge under Truman and Eisenhower. New York, Simon and Schuster, and London, Secker and Warburg, 1978.
Under the Skin: The Death of White Rhodesia. London, Allen Lane, and Evanston, Illinois, Northwestern University Press, 1983.
The Espionage of the Saints: Two Essays on Silence and the State. London, Hamish Hamilton, 1986.
Sixty-Eight: The Year of the Barricades. London, Hamish Hamilton, and New York, Harper, 1988.
Joseph Losey: A Revenge on Life. London, Faber, 1994; New York, Oxford UP, 1994.

Editor, *Essential Writings*, by Karl Marx. London, MacGibbon and Kee, 1967; New York, Macmillan, 1968.

*

Critical Studies: *Anger and After* by John Russell Taylor, London, Methuen, 1962, revised edition, 1969, as *The Angry Theatre*, New York, Hill and Wang, 1962, revised edition, 1969; "Rebels and Their Causes" by Harold Hobson, in *Sunday Times* (London), 23 November 1969; "Keeping Our Distance" by Benedict Nightingale, in *New Statesman* (London), 28 November 1969; in *Plays and Players* (London), February 1970; in *Times* (London), 22 July 1971.

David Caute comments:

With one exception, my plays have all been public plays. A "public" play, like a "private" play, is of course populated by individual characters with distinctive personalities, but the real subject lies elsewhere, in some wider social or political issue. Obviously the most elementary problem for the public playwright is to present characters who are not merely ciphers or puppets—words much cherished by critics hostile to didactic theatre.

Songs for an Autumn Rifle, written in 1960, is shaped in the spirit of banal realism. By the time I wrote my next play, *The Demonstration*, seven years later, my attitude towards both fiction and drama had changed. While the necessity of commitment still imposed itself, the old forms of naturalism, realism, and illusionist mimesis seemed incompatible with our present-day knowledge about language and communication. (These ideas are developed more fully in *The Illusion*, 1971.) One is therefore working to achieve a form of self-aware or dialectical theatre which is not only about a subject, but also about the play itself as a presentation—an inevitably distorting one—of that subject. The intention is to stimulate in the audience a greater critical awareness, rather than to seduce it into empathy and catharsis. In my view, for example, the lasting impact of Brecht's *Arturo Ui* consists less in what the play tells us about Hitler than what it tells us about *knowing about Hitler*.

The kind of writing I have in mind must pay far more attention to the physical possibilities of the theatre than did the old realism or well-made play. But whereas the author was once dictator, the modern playwright finds his supremacy challenged by directors or groups of actors. Up to a point this is healthy. But only up to a point! (See my "Author's Theatre," the *Listener*, 3 June 1971.)

One of my plays, *The Fourth World*, is different: a very private play, and, I hope a funny one. It was conceived and delivered all within a week.

* * *

While concern with social and political issues is no longer as rare among English dramatists as it was in the 1940s and early 1950s, there are still very few who are as deeply committed as David Caute or as deeply interested in European politics and in committed European playwrights like Sartre. Caute's first play, *Songs for an Autumn Rifle*, was a direct response to the dilemma that the Soviet treatment of the 1956 Hungarian uprising created for members of the Communist party. The central character is the editor of a British communist newspaper torn between his duty to the party and his duty to the truth as relayed to him by an honest correspondent. On a personal level he is being pressured by his wife, who is not a party member, by the doctrinaire daughter of a party leader who works on his paper and is in love with him, and, indirectly, by his son, a National Serviceman who brings the Cyprus question into the play, first going to military prison for refusing to serve there, then submitting to an intelligence officer's persuasions, and later being killed.

The play plunges right in to its subject matter. Several scenes are set in Hungary, showing the disillusioned correspondent of the English paper in argument not only with the Hungarian rebels but also with Russian soldiers, whose attitudes are not altogether at one with the orders they have to carry out.

The Demonstration is a much more sophisticated piece of playmaking that dramatizes the problems of student revolution among drama students at a university who rebel against the play their professor gives them to perform. They insist instead on substituting a play about their own experience of repressive authoritarianism at the university. Their play has the same title as the play the audience is watching, and we are often jerked from one level of theatrical reality to another. For instance, a scene between the women's dean and a student turns out to be a scene between two students, one of whom is playing the dean but who can come out of character to make comments about her.

There is a very funny scene about the rehearsal of a sequence of the professor's play, ironically representing a confrontation between a bearded guerrilla and a single peasant with interruptions from the students playing the parts who object that a bourgeois audience could take comfort from the satire. There is also an effective climax to the whole play when the police constables fail to respond to the professor's orders to remove the handcuffs from the students they have arrested and when the superintendent's mustache fails to come off when he pulls at it. Reality has taken over.

But there is more theatrical exploitation than dramatic exploration of the no-man's-land between reality and illusion, and the play is not fueled to fulfill the Pirandellian promise of its first few scenes. There are three main flaws. One is that the basic statement the play is making seems to have been too rigidly predetermined instead of being allowed to evolve during the course of the writing. The second is that, while there is an admirable sympathy in general for the victims of society—black women not admitted to hairdressing shops or students whose liberty is curtailed by rules that stem from pre-Victorian puritanism—there is not enough sympathy for the private predicaments of the characters, who remain too much like stereotypes. This applies even to the central character, Professor Bright. Caute, who himself resigned from All Souls College the year after he helped to organize an Oxford teach-in on Vietnam, has no difficulty in understanding the dilemma of a son who deplores the rule-worshiping bigotry of the university authorities, but he still cannot side with the rebellious students against them. It may then be a kind of personal modesty that makes Caute keep pulling Steven Bright away from the center of the action. It may be the technical failure to provide a character that Steven can confide in, or it may be a determination to focus on social and political rather than personal problems. But his failure to project Steven's ambivalence results in the third flaw—the lack of a firm moral and structural center. In act 2 Steven keeps disappearing to leave the stage free for the student actors. He makes two reappearances as an actor himself, but in disguise. In the first he is not recognized until after he has made a long speech—an effective coup de théâtre. But this does not reveal enough of what he is feeling. Instead he is crowded out by a host of peripheral characters. The stage direction at the beginning of the second scene of act 2 tells us that his "maliciously creative hand" can be detected in the presence on the stage of the hippies and dropouts who reject the political aims of the student revolutionaries and that he is seen prowling about while taking occasional notes and photographs. This is not enough. He should be holding the play together and carrying it forward, even when he is left by the students who take the initiative away from him.

—Ronald Hayman

CHIN, Frank (Chew, Jr.)

Nationality: American. **Born:** Berkeley, California, 25 February 1940. **Education:** University of California, Berkeley, 1958-61; University of Iowa, Iowa City, 1961-63; University of California, Santa Barbara, A.B. in English 1966. **Career:** Clerk, Western Pacific Railroad Company, Oakland, California, 1962-65; brakeman, Southern Pacific Railroad, Oakland, 1966; production writer and story editor, King-T.V. and King Screen Productions, Seattle, Washington, 1966-69; lecturer in Asian American Studies, University of California, Davis, San Francisco State College, 1969-70, and University of California, Santa Barbara, 1980; lecturer in creative writing, University of California, Berkeley, 1972, and lecturer in English, University of Oklahoma, Norman, 1988; film consultant, Western Washington State College, Bellingham, 1969-70; founder and artistic director, Asian American Theater Workshop, San Francisco, 1973-77. **Awards:** Joseph Henry Jackson award, 1965; James T. Phelan award, 1966; East-West Players award, 1971; Jack J. Flaks Memorial grant, 1972; San Francisco Foundation fellowship, 1974; Rockefeller grant, 1975; National Endowment for the Arts grant, 1975, 1980; Before-Columbus American Book award, 1981, 1989; Rockefeller American Generations grant, 1991. **Agent:** Dorothea Oppenheimer, 866 United Nations Plaza, New York, New York 10017, U.S.A. **Address:** 330 Union Street, San Francisco, California 94133, U.S.A.

Publications

Plays

The Chickencoop Chinaman (produced New York, 1972). With *The Year of the Dragon*, Seattle, University of Washington Press, 1981.
The Year of the Dragon (produced New York, 1974). With *The Chickencoop Chinaman*, Seattle, University of Washington Press, 1981.
Gee, Pop! (produced San Francisco, 1974).
America More or Less, with Amiri Baraka and Leslie Marmon Silko, music by Tony Greco, lyrics by Arnold Weinstein (produced San Francisco, 1976).
Lullaby, with Leslie Marmon Silko, from a story by Silko (produced San Francisco, 1976).
American Peek-a-Boo Kabuki, World War II and Me (produced Los Angeles, 1985).
Flood of Blood: A Fairy Tale (for children). Published in the *Seattle Review*, vol. 11 no. 1, 1988.

Television Plays: *Seattle Repertory Theatre: Act Two* (documentary), 1966; *The Bel Canto Carols* (documentary), 1966; *A Man and His Music* (documentary), 1967; *Ed Sierer's New Zealand* (documentary), 1967; *Seafair Preview* (documentary), 1967; *The Year of the Ram* (documentary), 1967; *And Still Champion . . .! The Story of Archie Moore* (documentary), 1967; *Mary*, 1969; *Rainlight Rainvision* (for *Sesame Street* series), 1969; *Chinaman's Chance* (documentary), 1971.

Novels

Donald Duk. Minneapolis, Coffee House Press, 1991.
Gunga Din Highway. St. Paul, Minnesota, Coffee House Press, 1994.

Short Stories

The Chinaman Pacific and Frisco R.R. Co. Minneapolis, Coffee House Press, 1988.

Other

Rescue at Wild Boar Forest (comic book). Calgary, Water Margin Press, 1988.
The Water Margin, or Shui Hu (comic book). Honolulu, Water Margin Press, 1989.
Lin Chong's Revenge (comic book). Vancouver, Water Margin Press, 1989.
Bulletproof Buddhists and Other Essays. Honolulu and Los Angeles, University of Hawaii Press, 1998.

Editor, with others, *Aiiieeeee! An Anthology of Asian American Writers*. Washington, D.C., Howard University Press, 1974.
Editor, with Shawn Wong, *Yardbird Reader, volume 3*. Berkeley, California, Yardbird Publishing Cooperative, 1974.
Editor, with others, *The Big Aiiieeeee!* Seattle, Washington University Press, 1991.

*

Critical Studies: "The Production of Chinese American Tradition: Displacing American Orientalist Discourse" by David Leiwei Li, in *Reading the Literatures of Asian America*, edited by Shirley Geok Lim and Amy Ling, Philadelphia, Temple University Press, 1992; "Dublin to Chinatown: James Joyce to Frank Chin" by Robert Murray Davis, in *Hungarian Journal of English and American Studies* (Debrecen, Hungary), 1996, pp. 117-22; "Tripmaster Monkey, Frank Chin, and the Chinese Heroic Tradition" by Patricia P. Chu, in *Arizona Quarterly: A Journal of American Literature, Culture, and Theory* (Tucson, Arizona), Autumn 1997, pp. 117-39.

Frank Chin comments:

Asian American theatre is dead without ever having been born, and American theatre, like American writing has found and nurtured willing Gunga Dins, happy white racist tokens, with which to pay their lip service to yellows and call it dues. No thanks.

My theatrical sense combined with my ruthless scholarly nature and need to make things right to produce ceremonial events that restored history and civility inside Japanese America, and between the Japanese Americans and Seattle and Portland. The events, called "Day of Remembrance," dramatically publicized the campaign to redress the constitutional grievances suffered by all persons of Japanese ancestry during World War II. I put together groups of Japanese-American leaders and activists to lead a return to the county fairgrounds outside of Seattle and Portland that had been converted into concentration camps for the Nikkei in 1942. The Day of Remembrance included participation by the National Guard, local politicians, a display of art and artifacts from the concentration camps, a huge pot luck dinner, and a couple thousand Japanese Americans in both cities.

Otherwise, I am out of theatre. I will not work with any theatre, producer, writer, director, or actor who has played and lives the stereotype. So, I write fiction, essays, and articles.

I have written extensively on Chinese- and Japanese-American history, culture, literature, and presence in popular local newsmagazines, television documentaries, and scholarly journals.

I have taught Asian-American history and ideas using storytelling, theatre, and writing games, in four- to five-week-long workshops for the Asian-American Studies Program at Washington State University, in Pullman, Washington; the American Thought and Literature Department at Michigan State University, in East Lansing, Michigan; in five Portland high schools for the Bilingual/ESL program of Portland Public Schools.

In response to American West Coast public schools teaching the white racist characterisation of Chinese fairytales and childhood literature as teaching misogynistic ethics and despicable morals as fact, I have, like the Cantonese and Chinese before me, wherever Chinese literature and language are banned, taken to the comic book as a tactic for making the real accessible in a hostile literary and learning atmosphere.

I am the principal editor and author of the introductory essays of *Aiiieeeee!: An Anthology of Asian American Writers*, the most influential critical work in Asian-American literature, and *The Big Aiiieeeee! The Big Aiiieeeee!* explores Chinese- and Japanese-American history and stereotyping through the history of western Christian thought and writing, Chinese- and Japanese-American writing, and the Asian fairytales and childhood literature that informed the immigrants and the structures of their political and artistic institutions from *tongs* and *tanemoshi* to railroad building and music.

* * *

Frank Chin's two full-length plays, *The Chickencoop Chinaman* and *The Year of the Dragon*, were presented at the American Place Theatre in New York in 1972 and 1974, and the latter was presented to a national television audience by the Public Broadcasting Service. The historical priority of his achievement might tempt one to call Chin the doyen of Asian-American playwrights, but that would be misleading, for he attacks his fellow writers—as he and his fellow editors put it in *The Big Aiiieeeee!*—for "ventriloquising the same old white Christian fantasy of little Chinese victims," victims of their own sadomasochistic culture and of their denial of their own identity in a quest for honorary whiteness. He also claims Maxine Hong Kingston, Amy Tan, and David Henry Hwang "fake all of Asian American history and literature." He attributes the success of Hwang's *M. Butterfly* to the portrayal of the central Chinese character as "the fulfillment of white male homosexual fantasy, literally kissing ass." He remains, then, something of the angry young man who is the central character in both his full-length plays.

Indeed, *The Chickencoop Chinaman* can be compared to *Look Back in Anger*. In both we are meant to recognize the truth of the central character's highly rhetorical attacks upon society, while in the course of the play the character himself is presented in such a way as to lose our sympathy. As Tam's friend Kenji says almost at the end of the play,

> I used to think it was funny, brave, man, the way you ripped everybody up with your tongue, showin' 'em up for clowns and bullshit. Your tongue was fast and flashy with the sounds, man, savin' your ass from this and that trouble, making people laugh, man, shooin' in the girls . . . . I used to know why you were mean and talkin' all the time. I don't anymore, and you're still talkin' the same crazy talk.

Tam acknowledges that he is a loner and a loser. Chin seems to try to save Tam from total alienation by having him end the play preparing Chinese food—perhaps because "food's our only common language" (*Year of the Dragon*)—while he reminisces about his grandparents. *Look Back in Anger* ends with a similarly sentimental turnaround.

The image of "the Chickencoop Chinaman making whooppee in a birdcage" recurs in both plays. The subject of Chin's plays is the difficulty Asian-American men have in establishing an independent and personal identity when doubly isolated, first, from a culture whose experiences the American-born Chinese has not directly known and of whose language he knows only a smattering and, second, from a dominant white society whose members see only stereotypes and seek to push one back—psychologically, if not physically—into the cage of Chinatown. Thus, Tam's speech "jumps between black and white rhythms and accents," for he has "no real language of [his] own to make sense with, so out comes everybody else's language that don't conceive." This metaphor links the sterility of the protagonist's language, however hyperactive, with a lack of manhood that all three Asian-American men in *The Chickencoop Chinaman* feel. Similarly, Fred, the corresponding slick-speaking central character in *Year of the Dragon*, swings between a phony Chinatown accent that he employs as a tourist guide and casual American English. Tam visits his friend Blackjap Kenji, who has adopted a black lifestyle and who is sheltering Lee, a woman who has had husbands of "all colors and decorator combinations." Although she passes for white, she is, in fact, part Chinese. Her Chinese ex-husband Tom turns up to claim her. Tam has told us that his own name has been miscorrected to Tom, and Tom is an obvious alter ego. (They are even given the same line about their visits—"I didn't mean to come/walk into no situation.") Tom represents the choice Tam has not made, to become a buttoned-down, assimilated, published writer. It is symbolic that Tam has married white, but both Tom and Tam are separated from their wives, as though neither staying in the culture nor leaving it is a satisfactory solution.

That dilemma is the subject of *The Year of the Dragon*. Again, there is a character—Fred's sister—who has "married out" and become a published author of a successful cookbook incorporating some of Fred's tourist patter. The ironic cultural contrasts pile up. Fred's "China-crazy" white brother-in-law speaks Mandarin and admires traditional Chinese culture, while Fred, who speaks a little Cantonese, is contemptuous of the Chinatown culture around him. Feeling the approach of death, Fred's father, to the dismay of his Chinese-American wife, has brought his first wife, Fred's mother, from China; since she speaks no English, however, she is a mostly silent reminder of the ties to the old country. In the younger generation Fred's brother is a juvenile delinquent, responsive to his peers rather than to the authority of the family.

Fred has always spoken of wanting to get out of Chinatown and to write. He helped his sister get out, and her success and his father's death at the end of the play give him that opportunity. But Chinatown is his subject, and he fears that, if he is away from it, his inspiration will dry up. Deeper than that, his decision is determined by his relationship to his father, the paterfamilias whom Chin names simply Pa. Pa disparages the one little magazine publication Fred has achieved and does not introduce Fred to his fellow seniors in Chinatown. (This is based on an incident in Chin's own life.) Pa is about to give a speech at the New Year's parade, in which he will acknowledge Fred's achievement in the community, but he collapses and dies in a confrontation with Fred:

> Fred: You gotta do somethin for me. Not for your son, but for me.
>
> Pa: Who you? You my son. Da's all. What else you ting you are.

The final irony is that he will continue as his father's son rather than pursue his individual dreams.

If *Chickencoop Chinaman* is akin to Osborne, *Year of the Dragon* is more like Odets in its tightly plotted family conflicts and in tone. The ideal seems to be, as Fred expresses it, that "[we] get together and we're talkin a universe, and sing." But in the hierarchical Chinese family that does not happen.

Flood of Blood: A Fairy Tale is a lively children's play performed by a traveling Chinese troupe in which Chin mixes the Flood story, the princess to be rescued from a dragon, and shades of Turandot.

—Anthony Graham-White

CHURCHILL, Caryl

Nationality: British. **Born:** London, 3 September 1938. **Education:** Trafalgar School, Montreal, 1948-55; Lady Margaret Hall, Oxford, 1957-60, B.A. in English 1960. **Family:** Married David

Harter in 1961; three sons. **Career:** Resident dramatist, Royal Court Theatre, London, 1974-75. **Awards:** Richard Hillary memorial prize, 1961; Obie award, 1982, 1983, 1988; Susan Smith Blackburn prize, 1983, 1988; *Time Out* award, 1987; Olivier award, 1987; *Plays and Players* award, 1987; *Evening Standard* award, 1987. **Agent:** Casarotto Ramsay Ltd., National House, 60-66 Wardour Street, London W1V 3HP. **Address:** 12 Thornhill Square, London N.1., England.

Publications

Plays

Downstairs (produced Oxford, 1958; London, 1959).
Having a Wonderful Time (produced Oxford and London, 1960).
Easy Death (produced Oxford, 1962).
The Ants (broadcast 1962). Published in *New English Dramatists 12*, London, Penguin, 1968.
Lovesick (broadcast 1967). Included in *Shorts*, 1990.
Abortive (broadcast 1971). Included in *Shorts*, 1990.
Not, Not, Not, Not, Not Enough Oxygen (broadcast 1971). Included in *Shorts*, 1990.
The Judge's Wife (televised 1972). Included in *Shorts*, 1990.
Schreber's Nervous Illness (broadcast 1972; produced London, 1972). Included in *Shorts*, 1990.
Owners (produced London, 1972; New York, 1973). London, Eyre Methuen, 1973.
Perfect Happiness (broadcast 1973; produced London, 1974).
Moving Clocks Go Slow (produced London, 1975).
Objections to Sex and Violence (produced London, 1975). Published in *Plays by Women 4*, edited by Michelene Wandor, London, Methuen, 1985.
Light Shining in Buckinghamshire (produced Edinburgh and London, 1976). London, Pluto Press, 1978.
Vinegar Tom (produced Hull and London, 1976). London, TQ Publications, 1978; New York, French, 1982.
Traps (produced London, 1977; Chicago, 1982; New York, 1988). London, Pluto Press, 1978.
The After Dinner Joke (televised 1978). Included in *Shorts*, 1990.
Floorshow, with others (produced London, 1978).
Cloud Nine (produced Cardiff and London, 1979; New York, 1981). London, Pluto Press, and New York, French, 1979.
Three More Sleepless Nights (produced London, 1980; San Francisco, 1984). Included in *Shorts*, 1990.
Top Girls (produced London and New York, 1982). London, Methuen, 1982; revised version, Methuen, and New York, French, 1984.
Fen (produced Wivenhoe, Essex, London, and New York, 1983). London, Methuen, 1983.
Softcops (produced London, 1984). London, Methuen, 1984.
Midday Sun, with Geraldine Pilgrim, Pete Brooks and John Ashford (produced London, 1984).
Plays 1 (includes *Owners*, *Vinegar Tom*, *Traps*, *Light Shining in Buckinghamshire*, *Cloud Nine*). London, Methuen, 1985.
A Mouthful of Birds, with David Lan (produced Birmingham and London, 1986). London, Methuen, 1987.
Softcops, and Fen. London, Methuen, 1986.
Serious Money (produced London and New York, 1987). London, Methuen, 1987; revised edition, 1990.
Icecream (produced London, 1989; New York, 1990). London, Hern, 1989.
Hot Fudge (produced London, 1989; New York, 1990). Included in *Shorts*, 1990.
Mad Forest (produced London, 1990). London, Hern, 1990.
Shorts (includes *Lovesick*; *Abortive*; *Not, Not, Not, Not, Not Enough Oxygen*; *Schreber's Nervous Illness*; *The Hospital at the Time of the Revolution*; *The Judge's Wife*; *The After Dinner Joke*, *Seagulls*; *Three More Sleepless Nights*; *Hot Fudge*). London, Hern, 1990.
Plays 2 (includes *Softcops*, *Top Girls*, *Fen*, *Serious Money*). London, Methuen, 1990.
Lives of the Great Poisoners (produced London, 1991).
Not Not Not Not Not Enough Oxygen and Other Plays. Harlow, Longman, 1993.
The Skriker. London, Nick Hern, 1994.
The After Dinner Joke and Three More Sleepless Nights. Cambridge, Cambridge University Press, 1995.
Blue Heart. New York, Theatre Communications Group, 1997.
Hotel: In a Room Anything Can Happen. London, Nick Hern, 1997.
Plays 3 (includes *Mouthful of Birds*; *Icecream*; *Mad Forest*; *Lives of the Great Poisoners*; *Skriker*; *Thyestes*). London, Nick Hern, 1998.

Radio Plays: *The Ants*, 1962; *Lovesick*, 1967; *Identical Twins*, 1968; *Abortive*, 1971; *Not, Not, Not, Not, Not Enough Oxygen*, 1971; *Schreber's Nervous Illness*, 1972; *Henry's Past*, 1972; *Perfect Happiness*, 1973.

Television Plays: *The Judge's Wife*, 1972; *Turkish Delight*, 1974; *The After Dinner Joke*, 1978; *The Legion Hall Bombing*, 1978; *Crimes*, 1982.

*

Critical Studies: *File on Churchill* edited by Linda Fitzsimmons, London, Methuen, 1989; *Caryl Churchill: A Casebook* edited by Phyllis R. Randall, New York, Garland, 1989; *Churchill the Playwright* by Geraldine Cousin, London, Methuen, 1989; *The Plays of Churchill* by Amelia Howe Kritzer, London, Macmillan, 1991; *The Plays of Caryl Churchill: Theatre of Empowerment* by Amelia Howe Kritzer, Houndmills, Macmillan, 1991; *Caryl Churchill, the Thatcher Years* (dissertation) by Janet E. Gardner, University of Massachusetts, 1995; *Caryl Churchill* by Elaine Aston, Plymouth, Northcote House, 1997.

* * *

London-born and Oxford-educated, Caryl Churchill is a highly successful playwright whose plays are designed to startle and instruct. In *The Plays of the Seventies* Roger Cornish and Violet Ketels note that she is in the unique and enviable position as a contemporary British playwright of having had three plays, *Fen, Cloud Nine,* and *Top Girls,* running simultaneously in New York in the same year, 1983. In the 1990s *Mad Forest* and *The Skriker* were highly acclaimed. Her plays are often gusty, outspoken, and sharp in their critique of social institutions. They are influenced by experimental movements in British theater growing up in the late 1960s. She writes an alternative theater, but one that is highly commercial while also controversial.

Recently Churchill has developed short, experimental one-act plays, pairing two plays in performance. In *Blue Heart* she presents *Heart's Desire* and *Blue Kettle.* Both explore familial relationships, in one case between a father and his daughter, in the other between a son and a number of putative mothers. The influence of Beckett and Ionesco on the plays is pronounced. *Hotel* is an experimental fragmented play/opera of everyday life. It consists of two plays, *Eight Rooms* and *Two Nights.* Music, words, and movement figure prominently, as they did in *The Striker* where Churchill wrote a little opera in one scene. In the first play eight hotel rooms are superimposed into one stage hotel bedroom, where the characters play the scene as if they were alone in just one bedroom. The play explores 16 hours in the life of occupants of the eight hotel bedrooms. In *Two Nights* there are two people who spend different nights in the same room; they are played by the silent characters of the first play. Throughout the piece the other speaking characters from the first play sing together from the text of a diary found in the hotel room. The theme of the play is disappearance. Churchill continues to have a highly productive collaboration with Orlando Gough, the composer, and Ian Spink, the choreographer. These experimental plays are far stronger in performance than when encountered as a written text.

Churchill has been writing plays for the radio, stage, and television for more than 30 years. *Shorts* offers a representative sample of ten of her short plays written between 1965 and 1989. Two of them have never been performed; several, such as *Lovesick* and *Abortive,* were written for radio; *The Judge's Wife* and *The After Dinner Joke* were written for television; and *Hot Fudge* was originally intended to be a companion to *Icecream.* One of her most successful early plays is *The Ants,* a profoundly disturbing work about identity and perspective broadcast on the BBC Third Program in 1962. Her early stage play *Owners,* produced by the Royal Court Theatre Upstairs in 1972, offered an indictment of the concept of property and ownership. In 1974 she became a writer-in-residence at the Royal Court, and in 1975 *Objections to Sex and Violence* was performed on their main stage. In 1976 she became the first woman dramatist invited to join the Joint Stock Theatre Group where she began working closely with two directors, Max Stafford-Clark and Les Waters, who have played an important part in her career ever since. Many of her subsequent plays have been produced either on the Royal Court's main stage or in the Theater Upstairs or in collaboration with Out of Joint. Originally Joseph Papp's matching grant to the Joint Stock made it possible for Churchill's plays to be brought to his Public Theater in New York. She also worked with the feminist theater group, Monstrous Regiment, where she produced *Vinegar Tom.* Some of her best and most commercially profitable plays, *Light Shining in Buckinghamshire, Cloud Nine,* and *Fen,* as well as some less successful albeit very interesting experiments such as *A Mouthful of Birds* and *Icecream,* have been developed for Joint Stock. *Fen,* a play about low-paid women potato pickers, won the distinguished Susan Smith Blackburn prize, which is awarded to outstanding women writers in the English language. Her plays have been performed at the National Theatre, the Barbican Pit, and the Royal Court Theatre as well as in repertory companies across England and Scotland and on stages across the United States.

Her plays usually take the British people, often working-class, for their subjects, but they travel well in part because of her feminist interests, topical themes, and socialist politics. In *Icecream* she charted the travels of an American couple to Britain in search of their ancestors, followed by the travels of the British distant cousins to America. The clash of the two cultures forms the backdrop to a chilling tale of murders and deaths that connects the families. The sociopolitical concerns expressed in her plays draw upon the thinking of such diverse minds as R. D. Laing, Frantz Fanon, and Michel Foucault. Her plays offer trenchant social commentaries upon the greedy decade of mergers and acquisitions, the appalling practices of colonialism and apartheid, and the theme of women's oppression, whether worked out in the seventeenth-century practice of witch-burning or the twentieth-century phenomenon of the battered wife or child. Others explore women's liberation showing both its gains and its losses. She often treats her themes with antic humor or ludicrous parody while making her audience consider how race, women-hating, and homophobia express themselves in our culture.

Churchill is well-schooled in the craft of theater, employing Brechtian devices, experimenting with the formal components of the play—the way it inhabits time and space—and most recently experimenting with dance and movement combined with music to enhance the theatricality of her stage images. Her experiences working in the medium of broadcast and with Joint Stock's method of writing have contributed importantly to the unusual texture, the overlapping of voices, and the often episodic structure of many of her plays. In *Traps* she keep rerunning the action while altering it, violating linear chronology, building a scene only to undercut its key elements, and leaving the audience perplexed about the exact relationships between characters and the nature of the action while absorbed by the psychological reality of the play. *Cloud Nine* takes similar liberties with time and the conventions of realistic theater.

Writing radio plays taught her much about narrative: discovering how characters can speak themselves, evoking the visual landscape while using words almost as musical notes, amplifying or diminishing the hearer's sense of space and time, and heightening the sense of anticipation. Her work in broadcast paved the way for her technique of overlapping characters' speeches on stage, a device she relies upon heavily since the writing of *Top Girls.* It also schooled her in the writing of dialogue. She often relies upon the exchange of short, staccato lines and a sparse, minimalist use of language in stage dialogue. Occasionally she uses language lavishly, giving characters long monologues. She opens *Serious Money* with a scene from Thomas Shadwell's *The Volunteers, or The Stockjobbers,* written in 1692. She then dazzles the audience with her own Shadwellian rhymed couplets throughout her play. She can also write tough, often sexually explicit dialogue. *Cloud Nine* shocked its audience with its talk of females masturbating and its use of cross-dressing and racial cross-casting to heighten the sense of the constructs of race and gender. One of its more outlandish stage pictures occurs when a young man crawls under the late-Victorian long gown of a woman in colonial Africa, grabbing at her parts while she tries to preserve genteel appearances; she is belied not only by the man under her dress but also by the whip she holds, a symbol of her none-too-latent desire to see men flogged.

Churchill's writing owes much to the protracted workshop experiences involving playwrights, actors, directors, and designers provided by the Royal Court Theatre Upstairs and Joint Stock. This format allows Churchill to work with the actors and directors in exploratory research to learn about the play's subject over a four-week period, followed by an interval of up to ten weeks in which she is left to script, and concluding with a six-week period of rehearsal prior to the play's opening. At other times she has scripted during the improvisational workshop stage, bringing in new text almost daily. In one instance she scripted collaboratively with David Lan, a playwright and anthropologist interested in rites of possession amongst Zimbabwe tribes. He scripted *A Mouthful of Birds* alongside her, both playwrights producing texts simultaneously. She seems to flourish in this setting. The workshop provides her rich thematic material and also immerses her in an environment, as it did in *Fen.* It gives her access to a wide range of characters and enables her to examine public and personal narratives, presenting private experiences set against a backdrop of historical time, institutional forces, and public events.

Churchill is a playwright of ideas. Although socialist in her political leanings, her stance is not predictable. Her work is lauded by feminists. She does not shy away from depicting powerful women corrupted by greed and ambition and deriving pleasure from the infliction of violence. She embarked on *A Mouthful of Birds* with David Lan, providing a modern-day Bacchae in order to show women in the thrall of violence. Responding to feminist environmentalists and women in the peace movement, Churchill explores images that show violence and pleasure as often integral to each other. Her play concludes with women who have known the power and pleasure of violence choosing not to use it. In *Owners* and *Serious Money* her protagonists, Marion, Scilla Todd, and Mary Lou Barnes are respectively property owners, London traders, and arbitrageurs. They thrill at the power of money, they like it to come fast, and their pursuit of it knows no limits.

Churchill's plays are often satiric. They explicitly condemn their characters and the capitalist social order, but they do it with gusto. Her women are brassy. While *Serious Money* questions traditional ideas about gender and mocks the crassly sexual way in which capitalists equate money with women, considering both something that ought to be exploited, the play also shows women who have been thoroughly appropriated. The fast money "Futures Song," bawdily shouting about cunts and money and concluding the first act of the play, caused a sensation when the play opened. Vulgar it is. And it is perhaps, in the end, not even necessary to Churchill's romp through the corrupt world of inside-trading, but its theatrical effect is visceral. The image conflates a chorus line with a drag ball played out in the traders' pits. Vamping in an orgy of excess, thrusting fists like pricks at the audience, and screaming out dirty words, the floor-traders, the insider dealers, the corporate raiders, and the arbitrageurs catch the audience up in a frenzy. *Softcops* is another play that revels in the nineteenth-century carnivalesque atmosphere where freakish side-shows are manipulated for their so-called instructional potential.

Often a topical matter of political importance is the impetus for Churchill's plays. *Serious Money* was her response to the financial scandals involving the takeover of Guinness and the arbitrageur Boesky, whose testimony finally led to the end of the era of insider-trading. Feminist concerns finding voice in the 1970s and 1980s inspired *Vinegar Tom* and *Light Shining in Buckinghamshire,* and they inform *The Skriker.* Cults of possession, demonic rites, the rise of alcoholism, particularly among women, and a growing concern with the abuse of the body—whether the result of eating disorders or violence—led to plays such as those cited above as well as *A Mouthful of Birds.* In the case of *Vinegar Tom,* Churchill was working with a feminist group, created in 1975, which was committed to exploring socialist themes. This play not only examines witchcraft and the scapegoating of women in the seventeenth century, with its obvious implications for the present day, but it examined the forces behind collectivities. In *Top Girls* Churchill looks at the liberated woman, the woman freed from housework, domesticity, and child-bearing. Marlene, the managing director of the Top Girls Employment Agency, celebrates her recent promotion by throwing a party to which she invites the most unlikely cast of guests—all women overachievers, some real, some invented. Pope Joan, Chaucer's Patient Griselda, Lady Nijo, a medieval courtesan-turned-nun, and Dull Gret, a figure from a Brueghel painting, all participate in Marlene's party. Their talk is trivial; they pay little attention to each other, speaking over each others' lines and all seemingly talking about their achievements. The play richly exploits all the trademarks of gender-bending for which Churchill is famous. She also plays fast and loose with time. In the second act, in ways reminiscent of *Cloud Nine,* the guests of the first act reappear, transformed into job applicants and interviewers in the personnel office. The play actually reveals the failure of the dream of liberation. These women are unhappy and miscast; their stories are ones of suffering, not success. The play is finally not as bleak as *Fen.* The women's suffering and sacrifices leave them incomplete and largely alone. The play's social context heightens the awareness of how gender constructs roles. Marlene is more than a victim of contemporary times—her victimhood is rooted in historical institutions.

Softcops was produced by the Royal Shakespeare Company at the Pit in 1984. As in many of her plays it probes the mainsprings of theater—spectacle, act, and audience—taking as its subject Foucault's examination of the spectacle of the scaffold and the modern institutions of discipline and punishments worked out so brilliantly in *Discipline and Punish: The Birth of the Prison.* The play contrasts different mechanisms of control: those brought about through the witnessing of terrible punishments inflicted upon the body of the transgressor and thereby teaching the public not to commit bad acts for fear that they will suffer the agonies of the body they have watched; and those produced by eliminating the audience of the spectacle and replacing it with a single central figure well positioned to conduct surveillance of guilty parties and exert control. This latter kind of control depends on men's terror of disobedience and a fear that they will be found out, which can be produced merely by curtaining off the surveillant so that he cannot be seen but can always see. Jeremy Bentham's architecture of the Panopticon, with its high, central watch tower, provided the ideal form of punishment, one in which very few in fact have to be imprisoned and the multitudes do not have to witness the spectacle of punishment. The consequence of the latter mechanism of control are demonstrated in the modern-day institutions of reformatories, prisons, hospitals, and school rooms. In a play that is often funny and sometimes rather preachy, Churchill explores the close interrelationship between criminals and law-enforcers, subverting the power of authority and finally posing the possibility that the entire institution of repressive authority might be toppled. This is a theme that she has advanced in a number of other plays from as early as *Objections to Sex and Violence.*

Mad Forest and *The Skriker* treat very different subjects: the Romanian Revolution and the overthrow of the Ceausescus in the first; the folk skriker and ancient, pagan lore in the other. *The Skriker* is a shape-shifter, ancient and wicked, taking on many identities and in the play preying on the two teenage girls, one of whom is pregnant. Both are extraordinarily strong and original works. *The Skriker* is wildly Joycean in its use of language. Its immersion in pagan lore provides marvelous spectacle. It revels in lore about witches and the underworld. The skriker was played by Katharyn Hunter, an actress famous for her depiction of monsters and hags. Churchill's imagination was fueled by writers such as Christina Rossetti in *Goblin Market,* Gertrude Stein, James Joyce in *Ulysses,* and Shakespeare in *Macbeth.* Both plays are full of the feminist sentiments and the critique of the environment and contemporary society that dominates most of Churchill's writings.

After more than 30 years of successful writing for the stage there are three book-length collections of Churchill's plays, and she is the subject of a spate of critical articles, several critical books, and some dissertations. Geraldine Cousin's book examines her use of the workshop format to develop her writing and offers an overview of her writing, considering in particular her handling of the theme of time and the possibility for revolutionary change in her plays. Chuchill continues to be a fine playwright not only because of the combination of daring and craft that is characteristic of her writing but also because of the keen intelligence behind her plays coupled with a high degree of wit.

—Carol Simpson Stern

CLARK, Brian (Robert)

Nationality: British. **Born:** Bournemouth, Hampshire, 3 June 1932. **Education:** Merrywood Grammar School, Bristol; Redland College of Education, Bristol, teaching certificate 1954; Central School of Speech and Drama, London, 1954-55; Nottingham University, B.A. (honours) in English 1964. **Military Service:** Served in the Royal Corps of Signals, 1950-52. **Family:** Married 1) Margaret Paling in 1961, two sons; 2) Anita Modak in 1983, one stepson and one stepdaughter; 3) Cherry Potter in 1990. **Career:** Schoolteacher, 1955-61 and 1964-66; staff tutor in drama, University of Hull, 1966-70. Founder, Amber Lane Press, Ashover, Derbyshire, 1978-79, Ambergate, Derbyshire, 1980-81, and Oxford, 1982—. **Awards:** Society of West End Theatres award, 1978; *Evening Standard* award, 1978; *Plays and Players* award, 1978; BAFTA Shell International Television award, 1979. Fellow, Royal Society of Literature, 1985. **Agent:** Judy Daish Associates, 83 Eastbourne Mews, London W2 6LQ, England.

Publications

Plays

Lay By, with others (produced Edinburgh and London, 1971). London, Calder and Boyars, 1972.

England's Ireland, with others (produced Amsterdam and London, 1972).

Truth or Dare? (produced Hull, 1972).

Whose Life Is It Anyway? (televised 1972; revised version produced London and Washington, D.C., 1978; New York, 1979). Ashover, Derbyshire, Amber Lane Press, 1978; New York, Dodd Mead, 1979.

Post Mortem (produced London, 1975). Published in *Three One-Act Plays,* Ashover, Derbyshire, Amber Lane Press, 1979.

Campion's Interview (produced London, 1976; New York, 1978-79).

Can You Hear Me at the Back? (produced London, 1979). Ashover, Derbyshire, Amber Lane Press, 1979.

Switching in the Afternoon or, As the Screw Turns (produced Louisville, 1980).

Kipling (produced London and New York, 1984).

All Change at the Wells, with Stephen Clark, music by Andrew Peggie (produced London, 1985).

The Petition (produced New York and London, 1986). Oxford, Amber Lane Press, 1986.

Hopping to Byzantium, with Kathy Levin (produced Osnabrück, Germany, 1990).

Screenplay: *Whose Life Is It Anyway?,* with Reginald Rose, 1981.

Television Plays: *Ten Torrey Canyons,* 1972; *Play in a Manger,* 1972; *Whose Life Is It Anyway?,* 1972; *Achilles Heel,* 1973; *Operation Magic Carpet,* 1973; *A Follower for Emily,* 1974; *Easy Go,* 1974; *An Evil Influence,* 1975; *The Saturday Party,* 1975; *The Eleventh Hour,* with Clive Exton and Hugh Whitemore, 1975; *Parole,* 1976; *A Working Girl,* 1976; *Or Was He Pushed,* 1976; *The Country Party,* 1977; *There's No Place . . . ,* 1977; *Happy Returns,* 1977; *Cat and Mouse,* 1977; *A Swinging Couple* (*Crown Court* series), 1977; *Out of Bounds* series, with Jim Hawkins, 1977; *Mirage,* with Jim Hawkins, 1978; *Houston, We Have a Problem,* with Jim Hawkins, 1978; *Telford's Change* series, 1979; *Horse Sense* (*All Creatures Great and Small* series), 1979; *Late Starter,* 1985; *Lord Elgin and Some Stones of No Value,* with others, 1985; *House Games,* with Cherry Potter.

Other

Group Theatre. London, Pitman, 1971; New York, Theatre Arts, 1972.

Out of Bounds (for children; novelization of television series), with Jim Hawkins. London, BBC Publications, 1979.

*

Critical Study: "Medical Technology on Stage" by Angela Belli, in *Ometeca,* 1996, pp. 291-303.

* * *

Having taught drama in a university and written on group theater, Brian Clark began his career as a playwright by collaborating with a number of younger radical dramatists on the antiestablishment political shockers *Lay By* and *England's Ireland* for Portable Theatre. There is no little irony in the fact that at about the same time he was writing the original television version of *Whose Life Is It Anyway?,* a play that six years later was to become the great "serious" West End hit of the late 1970s. Such was the critical and popular success of the play that it may be considered to have representative status. Here, it seemed, was a serious writer whose handling of an issue of contemporary relevance was, however entertaining, uncompromised by commercial success.

Whose Life Is It Anyway? concerns the claim by a man who lies in a hospital bed after a road accident, paralyzed from the neck down, to his right to die, that is, to commit suicide by choosing to be taken off the life-support machine. As its title suggests, the play's interest is in the moral argument, which culminates in the good-humored legal confrontation between the specialist, for whom life is an absolute, and the patient, who claims the right to choose suicide and who eventually wins his case. The personal relationships between the patient, Ken, and the hospital staff are economically handled and often touching, and the play provides the opportunity for a virtuoso performance of an unusual kind in the central role. (Tom Conti's performance was a major factor in its success in London.) The dialogue, which is alert, witty, and highly polished, is one of the play's most attractive features, yet its particular quality points to a major dramatic limitation. Clark is interested only in those elements of his chosen dramatic situation that can readily be verbalized. His dialectical resource is impressive, but the most interesting things about the paralyzed Ken's situation are those matters—most of them to do with psychological states—that are on the edges of the moral and legal dialectics. Ken has chosen to have his life ended and seeks to enforce his wishes with wit and pertinacity, but what of the frustration, anger, depression, and eventual self-resignation that he must be presumed to have experienced? The legal case turns on his mental state, yet psychology is unimportant to the play itself. The arguments are there, but what of the experience of being paralyzed?

The problem of verbalization is even more acute in Clark's second full-length stage play, *Can You Hear Me at the Back?*, though here, in a very different situation, the dramatist shows himself to be continually aware of the problem. The play deals with the attempts of the middle-aged chief architect of a new town to break out of a professional and personal, in this case marital, impasse. The professional planner feels that his life is "planned," devoid of spontaneity, his ideal being a "planned spontaneity." Although he finally leaves his wife, he had previously refused to take the easy way out by going away with his best friend's wife, who has confessed her love for him. The character himself is aware that he fits only too well the self-pitying cliché of the discontented middle-class, white-collar menopausal male, just as he acknowledges that the slickness and facility of his way of speaking is the verbal equivalent of what he abhors about his profession. In both cases a disorderly reality is made to submit to neat abstractions. Yet the necessary critique of the middle-class ethos represented—of which luxuriant self-scorn and guilt are an essential part—is entirely absent. Clark's own failure to reveal in the play a valid alternative way of speaking to that of his main character means that the only perspective on middle-class disillusionment offered by the work is that of the middle-class represented within it.

Implicit in Clark's attempts to combine moral argument with popular theatrical appeal is a keen awareness of an essentially middle-class liberal audience. This emerges explicitly in the quasi-biographical one-man show written for Alec McCowen, *Kipling*. Confronted by an audience composed largely of what he would term "wishy-washy liberals" and resisting crustily any demand for self-revelation, Kipling launches out on "a non-stop elegy of self-justification." The show invites the projected liberal audience to re-examine inherited assumptions about Kipling and to question its own beliefs and convictions, yet at least one reviewer saw it as an "accomplished exercise in audience ingratiation," carefully neutralizing a potentially disturbing subject.

Much the same could be said (and was) of Clark's two-hander *The Petition*. Here Clark returned to the issue play mode of *Whose Life Is It Anyway?*, except that in this instance the connection between the public issue ("in a way, the Bomb is the only thing worth writing about") and the private context is not ready-made. Clark's way of making the connection is thoroughly conventional. The discovery by a retired general that his wife has signed an antinuclear petition published in *The Times* prompts disclosure of her terminal illness and of an old sexual infidelity. Arguments about nuclear confrontation and the threat of universal annihilation are thus seen within the context of a purgative conflict within marriage. The characteristic facility of the dialogue tends only to confirm the cozy domestication of a disturbing issue, although the performances of Rosemary Harris and John Mills in London were remarkable. Reviewers mentioned William Douglas-Home and Terence Rattigan.

—Paul Lawley

CLARK, John Pepper. ***See* BEKEDEREMO, J. P. Clark**

CLARK, Sally

Nationality: Canadian. **Born:** Vancouver, British Columbia, 26 July 1953. **Education:** University of British Columbia, Vancouver, 1971-73; York University, Downsview, Ontario, 1973-75, B.A. in fine arts. **Career: Awards:** Canada Council, B Grant, 1985, 1991; Dora Mavor Moore Best play nomination, for *Moo,* 1989; Chalmers Best Play award, for *Moo,* 1990; Venture Fund, Ontario Arts Council, 1993; bronze award, Best Dramatic Short, 1994; N.A.F.T.A. grant, 1995; O.A.C. grant, 1995, 1997. **Agent:** Shain Jaffe c/o Great North Artists, 350 Dupont Street, Toronto, Ontario M5R 1V9, Canada.

Publications

Plays

Lost Souls and Missing Persons (produced Toronto, 1984). Vancouver, Talon Books, 1998.
Moo (produced Toronto, 1989). Playwrights Canada Press, 1989.
Trial of Judith K (produced Toronto, 1989). Playwrights Canada Press, 1991.
Jehanne of the Witches (produced Toronto, 1989). Playwrights Canada, 1993.
Life without Instruction (produced Toronto, 1989). Vancouver, Talon Books, 1994.
Saint Frances of Hollywood. N.p., n.d.
Wasps (produced Toronto, 1996). Vancouver, Talon Books, 1998.

Screenplays: *Lost Souls and Missing Persons,* 1990; *Ten Ways to Abuse an Old Woman,* 1992; *The Art of Conversation,* 1994; *Moo,* 1995.

Radio Plays: *McGowney's Miracle*; *Alligators in the Lake*; *The Shout*; *Moo.*

*

Theatrical Activities:
Director: **Play–***Wasps,* 1997.

Actor: **Plays**–*Trial of a Ladies Man,* 1986; *The Widow Judith,* 1998.

* * *

Sally Clark's plays stage women perceived to be weak but who are frequently invested with considerable strength. Clark often uses famous women, including the painter Artemisia Gentileschi, Joan of Arc (whom Clark accurately calls Jehanne), and Frances Farmer. The use of historical characters provides different ways of analyzing the positions of women: these women do not always change the world—or even their own situations—but they are provocative for contemporary women.

Clark's work generally attempts to provide several perspectives on recognized narratives. In *Moo* she offers various ways to see the relationship between a woman and her partner, the man her family deems to be a "rotter." Despite the separation of years and miles, Moo (short for Moragh) and Harry are inextricably bound together. Harry shoots Moo twice and commits her to a mental institution, but the complex nature of the relationship prevents the conclusion that Harry is simply bad and Moo is simply good. Yet it is also not possible to dismiss Moo as the "difficult woman" that her family labels her. Moo does as she pleases, caring little for the traditional family relationships that determine her sisters' lives. She is, however, prevented from maintaining this lifestyle by Harry's final bullet.

Jehanne of the Witches provides Clark with the opportunity to take the Joan of Arc story beyond the stereotyped figure. She tells the story through Jehanne's friend, Gilles de Rais, the historical figure also known as Bluebeard. Later burned at the stake himself, de Rais tries to recreate Jehanne's story in a play-within-a-play that raises questions of illusion versus reality and the ownership of the story, not to mention the role of women in the religion of the day. De Rais casts a young boy in the lead role of his "play," which underscores his own notorious sexual interest in boys and Jehanne's awkward position as a woman in an increasingly male-dominated world. Jehanne's voices are the women of the old religion, but she keeps their identity a secret because the growing power of the priests was relegating women to subservience. That de Rais continues to be haunted by Jehanne after her death suggests that her power (and the power of women) may not be limited after all.

Mental instability is a recurring feature of Clark's work, particularly in the contexts of misdiagnosis and wrongful incarceration. She returns to this trope in *Lost Souls and Missing Persons* and *Ten Ways to Abuse an Old Woman,* but it is most spectacular in *Saint Frances of Hollywood.* The play presents Frances Farmer's shifting relationship with her self-centered mother, her rise to stardom, her disastrous affair with the playwright Clifford Odets, and her increasing reliance on alcohol and Benzedrine. Rather than being treated for addiction, this very intelligent woman was committed to an asylum and peremptorily diagnosed as a paranoid schizophrenic. She spent years in and out of institutions, usually committed by her mother. Eventually put in a barbaric wing for "incurables" when she escaped her mother's care and refused to return to her movie career, she was forced to suffer nurses who delighted in tormenting their charges. The patient rebellion she organized resulted in her being given a lobotomy, which is staged very simply and effectively with an image of an ice pick. A victim of her family and social conventions, Frances tried to control her life in her way but was prevented from doing so. The play's conclusion presents the ultimate packaging of Hollywood conventionality, the *This Is Your Life* program, which produces real terror in Frances: having her life replayed according to her family's version is almost as traumatic as the life itself.

In later work Clark returns to trials as well as mental instability. She loosely adapted Franz Kafka's *The Trial* in *The Trial of Judith K.* Judith, an employee in a bank, finds herself accused of some sort of crime, the specifics of which keep eluding her. Ultimately her crime seems to be nothing more than wishing to live. The trial scene in Clark's *Life without Instruction* also bears little resemblance to democratic process: here the victim is tortured until she reveals the truth. The play is about Artemisia Gentileschi, who is raped by her father's friend. The trial, taken from historical accounts, provokes Artemisia to bend society's rules as much as possible to secure her independence. She achieves her autonomy by means of her paintings, which structure the play. Artemisia's two major paintings, the stories of Judith slaying Holofernes and Susannah and the Elders, come alive in a parallel of her own story. Artemisia's colorful, bloody portraits help her control men both on and off the canvas. *Life without Instruction,* like all Clark's plays about women challenging social conventions, relies on a strong, fluid structure and quick wit.

—Joanne Tompkins

CLOUD, Darrah

Nationality: American. **Born:** Illinois, 11 February 1955. **Education:** Goddard College, Plainfield, Vermont, B.A. 1978; University of Iowa, Iowa City, M.F.A. in creative writing 1980, M.F.A. in theater 1981. **Family:** Married David Emery Owens in 1992. **Career:** Writer. Lives in Catskill, New York. **Awards:** University of Iowa fellowship, 1978; National Endowment for the Arts grant, 1984; Drama League award, 1991. **Agent:** Peregrine Whittlesey Agency, 345 East 80th Street, New York, New York 10021, U.S.A.

Publications

Plays

The House across the Street (produced New York, 1982).
The Stick Wife (produced Los Angeles, 1987; New York and London, 1991). New York, Theatre Communications Group, 1987.
O, Pioneers! adaptation of the novel by Willa Cather, music by Kim D. Sherman (produced Seattle and New York, 1989). New York, Dramatic Publishing, 1996.
Obscene Bird of Night (produced Juneau, Alaska, 1989).
The Mud Angel (produced New York, 1990).
Genesis (produced Juneau, Alaska, 1992).

Screenplay: *The Haunted,* 1991.

*

Manuscript Collection: New Dramatists, New York.

Darrah Cloud comments:

I am haughty enough to think that I might be able to speak for people who can't speak for themselves, so I write plays. Since I began meeting tremendous and brilliant actresses with no good parts to play, I have been obsessed with writing parts for women. And as a woman, I have found a language within my gender that is secret and which I want to reveal, so that it becomes a part of the norm. For in language is perspective, and in perspective is a whole new way of looking at things. I want women's ways of looking at things to be more prevalent in the world.

I think that I always write for my mother. I imagine her in the audience and I know what makes her laugh, what affects her, what she'll believe and what she won't. In that sense, I am always writing my mother as well. I guess I am constantly showing my mother to my mother, in order to let her see herself as not alone, as understood and appreciated, if only by me. My male characters are my mother. And so, obviously, are my female characters. If there is a dog in the play, it's always the dog my mother picked out for us when we were little. I am currently writing a musical about the life of Crazy Horse. Crazy Horse, in his struggle against an encroaching white world, and toward his own fulfillment as a human being, Crazy Horse is my mother.

Sometimes I put my grandmother in because she's short and funny. I have yet to write my sister. This is a goal.

I grew up in the Midwest, and there too, is a unique language based not on what is said, but on what is not said. To be midwestern is to have to intuit the subtext of conversations. If one is talking about the weather, one might actually mean something quite different; something like, "I love you," or "my wife just died and I'm lost." The weather is a very important conversational tool in the Midwest. What is not said, but felt, implied in the moment, is what I love best to write. The congress of emotions that prevent the manifestation of explanations. That creates gestures that say more than words. Open mouths with nothing coming forth from them. This strikes me as always more honest than words. I am always trying to get at the truth of a moment. And so my characters rarely say what they feel, unless they're lying, which is more honest, to me.

I believe in ghosts. I believe that animals are so much more highly evolved than people that they have gotten over language and ambition and live to live. Sometimes I think they contain the spirits of dead people.

* * *

Darrah Cloud's best work focuses on everyday folks peripherally involved in notable historical events that give context to dark, satiric commentaries on American domestic bliss. Sometimes the result is an antic cartoonish realism that occasioned one critic to describe *The House across the Street,* an early "macabre comedy," as "'Father Knows Best' as written by Joe Orton." But Cloud's later plays, while sharing some of this loony-tune tone, tend more toward a surreal, Gothic tragicomedy than farce.

Fundamentally Cloud's plays explore the means by which the violence at the heart of American society reflects itself in the dysfunction of family life—and vice versa. Especially hard hit are the women characters, often portrayed as struggling valiantly but futilely amid a society that offers them little support or respect. Her plays, set in prototypical U.S. towns and cities—Birmingham, Alabama, rural Wisconsin, the suburbs of Chicago—invariably drop their sense of humor by the final fade-to-black, ending enigmatically but ultimately questioning the poverty of American lower- and middle-class life. These concerns are obviously evident in *The Sirens*, a documentary-style play focusing on five battered women, whose tragic stories are based on interviews Cloud conducted in women's shelters.

Cloud's dialogue often alternates passages of great lyrical beauty, reminiscent of the arias Sam Shepard often wrote for his characters, with scenes marked by the absurdity of a clipped, repetitious vernacular that, as David Mamet and Samuel Beckett before him discovered, creates its own powerful poeticism. All the plays contain central characters, most often female, whose struggle against their victimization tests their will, morality, and sanity. Cloud's focus on females caught in the grip of mid-American morality and restrictive social norms made her a natural choice to adapt Willa Cather's frontier fable *O Pioneers!* for the stage. Although filmed for television, the production had limited success. Perhaps Cloud felt her eccentric sense of humor was thwarted when harnessed to the slow-burn emotionalism of Cather's novel. Nevertheless, Cloud reteamed with Kim D. Sherman, whom she met while working on the Cather adaptation. They are responsible for two subsequent musical projects: *Honor Song for Crazy Horse*, a large-cast play with music that details the destruction of the West through the eyes of the eponymous Ogala Sioux warrior; and *Heart Land*, a musical about a terminally ill Iowa matriarch who summons her trio of daughters home to the farm after she has decided to commit suicide.

Mud Angel explores Cloud's feminist themes allegorically. In this surreal drama a rural Wisconsin farm family, symbolically named Malvetz, owns a horse named Shadow whose part is written as a speaking role to be portrayed by a female actor. The action centers around the tensions derived from the mother's threat to sell the valued yet victimized family pet. (A subsequent play, *The Braille Garden*, an unproduced Manhattan Theatre Club commission, seems a departure, focusing on a recently married couple and the consequences of the bridegroom's mysterious incapacitation that leaves him in bed, weak, and frightened.)

Cloud offers the most fully developed investigation of society's subjugation of women in *The Stick Wife*. The title refers to Jessie, a woman struggling against her domesticated, dominated (identity-less) status as spouse of the Ku Klux Klan member responsible for the bombing of a Birmingham church in 1963 that resulted in the murder of four young black girls. Cloud's parallel between sexism and racism is a conscious one; she once noted in an interview how women in a patriarchal society must deny their true feelings—a problem once shared by American slaves, who were forced to hide "their vibrant, inner life behind the 'Yes, Master' pose." The play begins with Ed leaving home to commit his despicable deed. Jessie prefers to ignore her husband's actions; when her neighbor tries to tell her that someone has bombed "a colored church," Jessie's responds by pulling her dress up over her head. Jessie pays a steep price for her willed ignorance: she has lost all contact with her two grown children; when alone she experiences delusions of self-importance, playing a movie star relating her life story to an imaginary Hollywood interviewer; and she hallucinates "white ghosts" (perhaps fleeting images of her husband's evil alternate identity). The action takes place exclusively in Jessie's backyard, dominated by the clothesline on which she hangs the white sheets that double as Ed's KKK costume and as symbols of her complicity in his crimes by virtue of their marriage bed. Based on a true incident, Jessie tries to free herself, not by divorcing her husband or running away but by secretly informing on him.

Cloud sets the action of the second act on the day of President Kennedy's assassination, two months after Ed has been indicted and imprisoned for murder. But the independence Jessie has gained from her surreptitious action dissipates—Ed is acquitted and returns home.

The ending mirrors the beginning: Ed says, "Here we go again," and although he senses something about Jessie has changed, he stalks out of the house as the lights fade on her repeatedly asking him, "Where are you going?" Jessie's helpless question mirrors the uncertainty felt by many Americans during a period marked by the violent murder of its moral and political leaders.

Cloud's earlier exploration of the violence of American life, *The House across the Street*, contains the seeds of many of these themes. The title refers to the home in which a mass-murderer, very loosely based on John Wayne Gacy, lived. The farcical black comedy focuses on the ironically named Fortune family, who never noticed anything amiss in their sedate suburban community even though their front window looked out on the murderer's house. Donald, a 13-year-old budding amateur scientist (he performs experiments on his comatose Grandma), and his kid sister, Donna, resemble characters from a Charles Addams cartoon. Impertinent, hip, and wizened choristers, they watch the police unearth more and more bodies across the street from their front window. For Donald this ghoulish activity is "like watchin' a movie." Donald's gleeful shouts accompanying each discovery of a body punctuate the play, much to his mother's frustration. Like Jessie in *The Stick Wife*, Lillian, the matriarch of the family, tries to shut out ugliness by insisting on shutting the front window's blinds, as if such willed ignorance offers protection from the terrors of contemporary reality.

Cloud humorously shows such efforts to be futile. The coroner Norman Bird (a nod here to Hitchcock's Norman Bates) enters late in the first act and to Lillian's horror tracks mud from the murder site all over the carpets. Unfortunately Cloud's antic dramatic energy soon spins out of control: as body bags sprout in the living room and the catatonic grandmother returns to consciousness, a heavy-handed Freudian family feud ensues that reads like a second-rate Albee one-act. Yet within this morass Cloud still manages to summon powerful imagery to state her themes—at one point Grandma crawls into a body bag, a succinct metaphor for America's willingness to view its elders as disposable. Although occurring in an early and uneven play, such hilarious and heartbreaking moments mark Cloud as a playwright of original and incisive vision.

—John Istel

COLLINS, Barry

Nationality: British. **Born:** Halifax, Yorkshire, 21 September 1941. **Education:** Heath School, Halifax, 1953-61; Queen's College, Oxford. **Family:** Married Anne Collins in 1963; two sons and one daughter. **Career:** Teacher, Halifax Education Committee, 1962-63; journalist, Halifax *Evening Courier*, 1963-71. **Awards:** Arts Council bursary, 1974; Edinburgh Festival award, 1980. **Agent:** Lemon, Unna, and Durbridge, 24 Pottery Lane, Holland Park, London W11 4LZ, England.

Publications

Plays

And Was Jerusalem Builded Here? (produced Leeds, 1972).

Beauty and the Beast (for children; produced Leeds, 1973).

Judgement (produced Bristol, 1974; London, 1975; Chicago and New York, 1980). London, Faber, 1974; revised version, Ambergate, Derbyshire, Amber Lane Press, 1980; New York, Urizen, 1981.

The Strongest Man in the World (produced Nottingham, 1978; London, 1980). London, Faber, 1980.

Toads (produced Nottingham, 1979).

The Ice Chimney (produced Edinburgh and London, 1980).

King Canute (broadcast 1985). Published in *Best Radio Plays of 1985*, London, Methuen, 1986.

Atonement (produced London, 1987).

Radio Play: *King Canute*, 1985.

Television Plays: *The Lonely Man's Lover*, 1974; *The Witches of Pendle*, 1975; *The Hills of Heaven* series, 1978; *Dirty Washing*, 1985; *Nada*, 1986; *Land*, 1987; *Lovebirds*, 1988.

*

Critical Study: "The Death of Nostalgia" by Craig Duffy, in *Canadian Theatre Review* (North York, Ontatio), Summer 1991, pp. 61-65.

* * *

Any script for solo theater makes extraordinary demands on the creative resources of the performer, especially when, as is common with the genre, there is a virtual absence of stage directions. Thus, Barry Collins's major work, *Judgement*, is deservedly also associated with the actors who have turned the 150-minute monologue into an engrossing theatrical debate: Peter O'Toole, Colin Blakely, and Richard Monette, to name the most successful of those who have done it in a dozen countries. Collins explains that the genesis of *Judgement* lay in an anecdote in George Steiner's epilogue to *The Death of Tragedy* concerning a war atrocity suggesting that God has grown weary of the savagery of man and, in withdrawing his presence, has precluded tragedy. In the anecdote a group of Russian officers imprisoned during World War II and abandoned by the Germans resort to cannibalism. Two survivors found by the advancing Russian forces are given a good ("decent") meal and then shot, which, with the incineration of their monastery prison, obliterates the evidence of man's potential for bestiality. Collins infers, although Steiner does not say so, that the survivors were insane, and he projects his play from the hypothesis that one of them preserved his sanity and was able, "dressed in white hospital tunic and regulation slippers," to deliver a Socratic apology to his judges, the theater audience. The man's implicit crime is not cannibalism (his fellow survivor would be equally culpable) but sanity: he will "defend obscenities that should strike reason dumb." At the end of the argument the speaker insists on his right to return to active service, and he speaks of himself as someone who has suffered greatly for his country.

That the play is polemical few would doubt; in fact, one way of responding to the speaker's sophistry is to interpret it as the manufacture of the warrior-hero. The play is also something of a milestone theatrically in that it may be seen as an extreme form of naturalism, in which the laboratory animal finds a voice and articulates its experiences before its extermination. This reading is supported by the context that Steiner gives the story: before the Germans left, they released some of their starving police dogs on the prisoners, so that the men's behavior is seen as conditioned on various animals. Read in this light, the play poses the question that obsessed writers from Cicero to Zola: what is there about man that places him above the brute beasts? That a taboo has been violated is taken for granted by the judges, whose tribal mentality insists that a scapegoat must be found so that the existence of the taboo may be reinforced and the dignity of man reasserted. Thus, in the theater there is the uncanny atmosphere of a voice coming from "the other side" and voicing extraterrestrial mysteries such as were presented in the medieval harrowing of hell or *danse macabre* dramas.

Collins's second attempt at a full-length monologue, *The Ice Chimney*, deals with an attempt by Maurice Wilson at a solo assault on Everest in 1936 and is thus another case of human fortitude braced against superhuman afflictions. Wilson's stature as a man of principle allows a sustained expositional analysis of the circumstances that led to his heroics, but the play never generates the urgency of *Judgement*, and its development seems an awkward amalgam of Milton, Auden, and Golding. In this play Collins's socialism is not organic to the action, and commitment appears to be to the self rather than to society.

Though best known for monologues, Collins has also written several large-cast works of epic theater that articulate dilemmas of socialism with a Brechtian flamboyance and a sometimes Hegelian complexity. His loose documentary about the Luddites, *And Was Jerusalem Builded Here?*, required two choruses, actors with circus skills and singing ability, projections, and costumes based on tarot cards. Nevertheless, the play does focus on one key character, a pamphleteer on whom there is centered a perplexing array of social and domestic responsibilities. Collins's most successful large-cast play has been *The Strongest Man in the World*, a parable for the theater about Ivan Shukhov, a Russian miner who wins an Olympic weight-lifting title as a consequence of being made to take steroids. The echoes of *Samson Agonistes* in *The Ice Chimney* become even more explicit here, as the dissident protagonist is initially discovered back in the mines considering the etiology of his condition of muscle-bound impotence, both physical and ideological. The argument of the play does have a close affinity with that of *Judgement*, for Shukhov is acutely conscious of his own state as a former Soviet hero descended from a line of such heroes. The retribution visited on him is once again extreme, and critics have predictably been divided in interpreting this as either a portrait of normal Soviet practice or as a black cartoon inflating a commonplace to an enormity. Collins's stagecraft would support the latter view.

—Howard McNaughton

CONGDON, Constance S.

Nationality: American. **Born:** Rock Rapids, Iowa, 26 November 1944. **Education:** Garden City High School, Kansas, 1963; University of Colorado, Colorado Springs, B.A. 1969; University of Massachusetts, Amherst, M.A., M.F.A. 1981. **Family:** Married Glenn H. Johnson, Jr. in 1971; one son. **Career:** Car hop, Bob's A & W Root Beer, 1960-63, columnist, Garden City *Telegram*, 1962-63, and grocery checker, Wall's IGA, 1963-65, all in Garden City; library clerk, Pikes Peak Regional District Library, 1965-66; library clerk, University of Colorado, 1966-69, and leather worker, What Rough Beast, 1969-70, all Colorado Springs; instructor in remedial writing, St. Mary's College of Maryland, St. Mary's City, 1974-76; instructor in rhetorical writing, University of Massachusetts, Amherst, 1977-81; instructor in English composition and theatre, Western New England College, Springfield, Massachusetts, 1981-83; literary manager, 1981-88, and playwright-in-residence, 1984-88, Hartford Stage Company, Connecticut, 1984-88. **Awards:** American College Theatre Festival National Playwriting award, 1981; Great American Play Contest prize, 1985; National Endowment for the Arts fellowship, 1986-87; Rockefeller award, 1988; Arnold Weissberger award, 1988; Dramalogue award, 1990; Oppenheimer award, 1990; Guggenheim fellowship, 1991. **Member:** New Dramatists Guild. **Agent:** Peter Franklin, William Morris Agency, 1325 Avenue of the Americas, New York, New York 10019, U.S.A. **Address:** 1423 Longmeadow Street, Longmeadow, Massachusetts 01106, U.S.A.

PUBLICATIONS

Plays

Gilgamesh (produced St. Mary's City, Maryland, 1977).

Fourteen Brilliant Colors (produced Amherst, Massachusetts, 1977).

The Bride (produced Amherst, Massachusetts, 1980).

Native American (produced Portland, Maine, 1984; London, 1988).

No Mercy (produced Louisville, Kentucky, 1986). New York, Theatre Communications Group, 1985; published in *Seven Different Plays*; edited by Mac Wellman, New York, Broadway Play Publishing, 1988.

The Gilded Age, adaptation of the novel by Mark Twain (produced Hartford, Connecticut, 1986).

Raggedy Ann and Andy (for children), adaptation of the books by Johnny Gruelle, music by Hiram Titus (produced Minneapolis, 1987).

A Conversation with Georgia O'Keeffe (produced Hartford, Connecticut, 1987).

Tales of the Lost Formicans (produced Woodstock, New York, 1988; New York City, 1990). New York, Broadway Play Publishing, 1990.

Rembrandt Takes a Walk (for children), adaptation of the book by Mark Strand and Red Grooms (produced Minneapolis, 1989). Published in *Plays in Process 4: Plays for Young Audiences* (New York), vol. 10, no. 12, 1989.

Casanova (produced New York, 1989). In *Tales of the Lost Formicans and Other Plays*, New York, Theatre Communications Group, 1994.

Time Out of Time (produced New York, 1990).

Mother Goose (for children), music by Hiram Titus (produced Minneapolis, 1990).

The Miser, adaptation of the play by Molière (produced Hartford, Connecticut, 1990).

Madeline's Rescue (for children), adaptation of the book by Ludwig Bemelmans, music by Mel Marvin (produced Minneapolis, 1990).

Beauty and the Beast (for children; produced Minneapolis, 1992).

Tales of Lost Formicans: And Other Plays (includes *Tales of the Lost Formicans*; *No Mercy*; *Casanova*; *Losing Father's Body*). New York, Theatre Communications Group, 1994.

*

Critical Studies: "An Interview with Constance Congdon" by Nancy Klementowski and Sonja Kuftinec, in *Studies in American Drama* (Columbus, Ohio), vol. 4, 1989; "Constance Congdon: A Playwright Whose Time Has Come" by Susan Hussey, in *Organica* (Tampa, Florida), Winter 1990; "Trying to Find a Culture: An Interview with Connie Congdon" by Lisa Wilde, in *Yale/Theatre* (New Haven, Connecticut), vol. 22, no. 1, Winter 1990; article by Craig Gholson, in *Bomb* (New York), Fall 1991; "Connie's *Casanova*" by M. Elizabeth Osborn, in *Theatre Week* (New York), June 3-9, 1991.

Constance Congdon comments:

I have an eclectic taste in theatre, although I usually hate everything I see on Broadway. My main influences are Thornton Wilder, The Wooster Group, Caryl Churchill, also rhythm and blues and country western music, Richard Wilbur, Joni Mitchell. The American critical scene is still culturally embarrassed and defensive and trying to be something it's not—cold, cynical, politically strident, trying to out-European the changing Europeans. The American art scene is still dominated by too many people from "good" schools who have intellectual agendas that have nothing to do with what I go to theatre for. I go to have an experience that taps the mystery of living, one that comes from great passion on the part of the artist, one that has something to do with awakening or calling up the spirit that is in every theatre.

I come from about as far away from the Ivy League as is possible and am proud of it. I see myself more as an "outside artist"—one of those people who makes sculpture out of car parts in their backyard. I don't live in New York although I enjoy going in to see the work of my friends which is very good and usually found in small theatres painted flat black with bad seats and great risk or big fun (or both) going on onstage.

When I start to write a play, I imagine an empty theatre space and see who or what turns up—this is my opening image and, if I mess with it, I always pay for it and lose my way in the play. I feel that the first things I create in a new play are like coded messages for the rest of the play, and I just return to them for clues about the rest of the play. The code is in metaphor, image, and given circumstances and I just need to see it. In *Native American*—the only naturalistic play I ever wrote—I saw, very clearly, the image of a cowboy lying face down on a couch with a sheet covering him. I also saw that the couch was outside on a porch. Then I saw an old Hudson automobile up on blocks. Some of these images were memories, I realize now, but at the time, they seemed all new and rich. Why the cowboy was on the couch, face down, gave me, bit by bit, the story and then the theme. I also knew that the play had to take place in consecutive real time. I trust these early strong impulses.

I need to entertain myself and surprise myself, so my plays are usually different from each other in style—I don't like to repeat myself. I make my living doing adaptations, and I don't recommend it to young playwrights, but it's better, for me, than teaching or trying to get media work.

* * *

Constance Congdon was a published poet before she was a playwright, and her plays have come to her as a series of images. They are made up of many small scenes, sometimes comic, often emotionally direct, with dialogue that goes straight to the heart of the matter. When these scenes are linked together, the result reflects the world's true complexity.

Though the lives of ordinary decent people, the pleasure and pain of sexuality, and the damaging effects of gender stereotypes are primary Congdon concerns, her central subject is loss. Her first play was a dramatization of the epic of Gilgamesh, at its heart the inconsolable grief of the hero at the death of his beloved friend Enkidu. The award-winning drama *No Mercy* deals with the testing of the first atomic bomb and its aftereffects, but the play is fundamentally about faith and the loss of faith in science, in religion, and in life itself. Watching the scientist J. Robert Oppenheimer cross and recross the stage—the play takes place in 1945 and 1985 simultaneously, and he is lost in time—we wonder if he is dreaming this world, whose other inhabitants are the kind of undistinguished Americans the writer lovingly brings to life. Our uncertainty about who rules the play's universe is part of the point: we are watching characters lose their certainty and then pick themselves up and go on.

By far the most successful of Congdon's plays is *Tales of the Lost Formicans*, which looks at the life of contemporary suburbia through the eyes of aliens, a perspective that shows this world, normally taken for granted, to be complicated, mysterious, and absurd. Behind this tragicomedy lies the death of Congdon's father many years ago from what we now call Alzheimer's disease, but the play is really about America's Alzheimer's. The father in *Formicans* is far from the only character who is confused, however. His recently divorced daughter has moved back home with her teenaged son, who expresses in pure form the anger and distress everyone in the play feels. By donning sunglasses the play's actors become aliens who are trying to make sense of a disoriented civilization; *Formicans* suggests that we ourselves are the aliens, attempting to distance ourselves from our own feeling. We are not finally sure whether or not real aliens are actually telling the story. As in *No Mercy*, not knowing reflects our actual position in the real world.

The opening words of Congdon's *Casanova* are the scream of a young woman in labor: "What—is—LOVE!" The playwright's answer to this most fundamental of questions is characteristically complex. An epic play not quite under control at its first showing, *Casanova* is Congdon's richest text, and it may one day be seen as a revelation of the way of our own world.

Casanova's focus on sexuality and gender was presaged by the early play *The Bride.* It brings to mind both *Our Town* and *Spring Awakening* in its depiction of the sexual awakening of four teenagers during the 1950s. In *Casanova* Congdon uses more than 60 years of her central character's life to present the full range of sexuality in men, women, and children. The famous lover is played by two actors: during the first act the old man who is writing his memoirs watches the irresistible boy he once was; after intermission the young Casanova is horrified to witness what he has become.

Congdon's *Casanova* is a feminist corrective to Casanova's one-sided memoirs. The author's deepest sympathy goes to the young girls the man loves and leaves. Yet the young Casanova is almost wholly appealing, for Congdon sees that his society gives him permission to behave as he does, that he is not so different from other men. She also shows us the complicity of women. Having no other power, mothers pimp their daughters, using their beauty and virginity for their own ends. The older Casanova commits monstrous acts, including rape and child seduction, but at the same time we see that he is aging and frightened, as trapped in his sexual role as any female.

In *Casanova* a bedrock biological difference inevitably makes women vulnerable. Yet there is hope in the play, and it lies in those characters who transcend the usual limits of gender. The two women who come through their encounters with Casanova unscathed are bisexual, and the play's exemplar of lasting devotion is Bobo, an aging transvestite. Once tutor to Casanova's daughter, Bobo is still taking care of her 30 years later. Bobo is Casanova's equal and opposite force and the most memorable incarnation of Congdon's special feeling for gay men.

Congdon's talent flows in many directions. Her poetic gift lends itself to opera librettos, and her comic sense has enlivened a series of delightful plays for the Children's Theatre of Minneapolis. Her one-woman piece about painter Georgia O'Keeffe lets her speak of her own love of the West and of her complicated feeling about the position of women artists. What knowledgeable theater people across the country said for years has become more widely known: Constance Congdon is one of the most original and revelatory writers in the contemporary American theater.

—M. Elizabeth Osborn

CONN, Stewart

Nationality: British. **Born:** Glasgow, Scotland, 5 November 1936. **Education:** Kilmarnock Academy and Glasgow University. **Military Service:** National Service: Royal Air Force. **Family:** Married Judith Clarke in 1963; two sons. **Career:** Appointed radio drama producer, 1962, became head of Drama (Radio), BBC Scotland, Edinburgh, resigned 1992. Literary adviser, Edinburgh Royal Lyceum Theatre, 1973-75. Lives in Edinburgh. **Awards:** Eric Gregory award, 1963; Scottish Arts Council poetry prize and publication award, 1968, award, 1978; Edinburgh Festival Fringe award, for drama, 1981, 1988; New York International Radio Festival drama award, 1991. **Agent:** Lemon, Unna, and Durbridge, 24 Pottery Lane, Holland Park, London W11 4LZ, England.

Publications

Plays

Break-Down (produced Glasgow, 1961).
Birds in a Wilderness (produced Edinburgh, 1964).
I Didn't Always Live Here (produced Glasgow, 1967). Included in *The Aquarium, The Man in the Green Muffler, I Didn't Always Live Here*, 1976.
The King (produced Edinburgh, 1967; London, 1972). Published in *New English Dramatists 14*, London, Penguin, 1970.
Broche (produced Exeter, 1968).
Fancy Seeing You, Then (produced London, 1974). Published in *Playbill Two*, edited by Alan Durband, London, Hutchinson, 1969.
Victims (includes *The Sword, In Transit*, and *The Man in the Green Muffler*) (produced Edinburgh, 1970). *In Transit*, published New York, Breakthrough Press, 1972; *The Man in the Green Muffler*, included in *The Aquarium, The Man in the Green Muffler, I Didn't Always Live Here*, 1976.
The Burning (produced Edinburgh, 1971). London, Calder and Boyars, 1973.
A Slight Touch of the Sun (produced Edinburgh, 1972).
The Aquarium (produced Edinburgh, 1973). Included in *The Aquarium, The Man in the Green Muffler, I Didn't Always Live Here*, 1976.
Thistlewood (produced Edinburgh, 1975). Todmorden, Lancashire, Woodhouse, 1979.
Count Your Blessings (produced Pitlochry, Perthshire, 1975).
The Aquarium, The Man in the Green Muffler, I Didn't Always Live Here. London, Calder, 1976.
Play Donkey (produced Edinburgh, 1977). Todmorden, Lancashire, Woodhouse, 1980.
Billy Budd, with Stephen Macdonald, adaptation of the novel by Melville (produced Edinburgh, 1978).
Hecuba (produced Edinburgh, 1979; revised version produced Glasgow, 1989).
Herman (produced Edinburgh, 1981; London, 1986).
Hugh Miller (produced Edinburgh, 1988).
By the Pool (produced Edinburgh, 1988; London 1989; Cleveland, Ohio, 1991).
The Dominion of Fancy (produced Pitlochry, Tayside, 1992).
Mission Boy (produced by Theatre for Africa and in Edinburgh, 1996).
Clay Bull (produced Edinburgh, 1998).

Radio Plays: *Any Following Spring*, 1962; *Cadenza for Real*, 1963; *Song of the Clyde*, 1964; *The Canary Cage*, 1967; *Too Late the Phalarope*, from the novel by Alan Paton, 1984; *Beside the Ocean of Time*, from the novel by George Mackay Brown, 1997.

Television Plays: *Wally Dugs Go in Pairs*, 1973; *The Kite*, 1979; *Blood Hunt*, 1986.

Poetry

Thunder in the Air. Preston, Lancashire, Akros, 1967.
The Chinese Tower. Edinburgh, M. Macdonald, 1967.
Stoats in the Sunlight. London, Hutchinson, 1968; as *Ambush and Other Poems*, New York, Macmillan, 1970.
Corgi Modern Poets in Focus 3, with others, edited by Dannie Abse. London, Corgi, 1971.
An Ear to the Ground. London, Hutchinson, 1972.
Under the Ice. London, Hutchinson, 1978.
In the Kibble Palace: New and Selected Poems. Newcastle upon Tyne, Bloodaxe, 1987.
The Luncheon of the Boating Party. Newcastle upon Tyne, Bloodaxe, 1992.
In the Blood. Newcastle upon Tyne, Bloodaxe, 1995.
At the Aviary. Cape Town, Snailpress, 1995.

Other

The Living Poet (radio broadcast). 1989.

Editor, *New Poems 1973-74*. London, Hutchinson, 1974.
Co-editor, *The Ice Horses*. Edinburgh, Scottish Cultural Press, 1996.

*

Manuscript Collection: Scottish National Library, Edinburgh.

Critical Studies: Interviews with James Aitchison in *Scottish Theatre* (Edinburgh), March 1969, Allen Wright in *The Scotsman*

(Edinburgh), 30 October 1971, and Joyce McMillan in *Scottish Theatre News* (Glasgow), August 1981; *Towards the Human* by Iain Crichton Smith, Edinburgh, M. Macdonald, 1987.

Theatrical Activities:
Director: **Radio**—Many plays, including *Armstrong's Last Goodnight* by John Arden, 1964; *The Anatomist* by James Bridie, 1965; *My Friend Mr. Leakey* by J.B.S. Haldane, 1967; *Mr. Gillie* by James Bridie, 1967; *Happy Days Are Here Again*, 1967, and *Good*, 1989, both by Cecil P. Taylor; *Wedderburn's Slave*, 1980, *The Telescope Garden*, 1986, and *Andromache*, 1989, all by Douglas Dunn; *Losing Venice* by John Clifford, 1987; *Dirt under the Carpet* by Rona Munro, 1987; *Not About Heroes*, and *In the Summer of 1918*, both by Stephen MacDonald; *Potestad* by Eduardo Pavlovsky; *Carver* by John Purser, 1991.

Stewart Conn comments:
(1973) My plays are about human beings, and about the dilemma of human choice. I interpret this dilemma in moral terms, and visualize the characters in the plays, and their relationships, as revolving around it. As Camus wrote (in *The Plague*), "On this earth there are pestilences and there are victims, and it's up to us, so far as possible, not to join forces with the pestilences." If there is a through line in what I have written so far, it might be a reminder that we do not live our lives in isolation—but that how we behave involves, and may cause hurt to, other people. At the same time the plays are explorations: they pose questions, rather than pretending to provide any easy answers. I do not wish to impose a set of values on an audience; but I like to think what I write might induce them to reassess their own. At the same time I am concerned with theatricality and with the use of words in the theatre, as also with the attempt to provide an instructive metaphor for the violence and betrayal, large and small, with which we must come to terms, within ourselves and in our society.

(1982) I find the above all rather pretentious—and rather than "comment" again I would prefer simply to get on with the plays: that is hard enough. "We must remember who we are . . ." (Lopakhin in *The Cherry Orchard*). Perhaps my main aim now is to send the audience out into the night, ideally both transformed and entertained, in time for the last bus!

* * *

Stewart Conn is a poet as well as a dramatist, and his best plays, like *The King, The Sword,* and *The Burning,* reveal this lyrical side. Of his full-length plays *Broche* and *I Didn't Always Live Here* are little more than solid, competent pieces of dramatic craftsmanship, but *The Aquarium* and *The Burning* are both of considerable merit.

The Aquarium is set in a lower-middle-class Scottish home and depicts a classical father-son confrontation. The father is imbued with the puritanical work ethic and has clearly defined attitudes and beliefs, based on an old-fashioned morality, that he attempts to impose on his teenage son. The son is restless, unsure of himself, and tentative in his approach to life, an attitude that is reflected in his flitting from job to job. Not unnaturally, he resists his father's attempts to make him conform, and they needle and taunt each other, with the mother ineffectually intervening, until matters come to a head when the father attempts to give his son a beating. This action triggers the son into a final breakaway from his family environment. The oppressive family atmosphere is particularly well and truthfully observed in the play, and the characters have a depth and power to them that belie their slightly clichéd conception. More than any other play of Conn's, *The Aquarium* reveals the influence of Arthur Miller, a playwright he greatly admires.

The Burning is perhaps Conn's most impressive work. It deals with the sixteenth-century power struggle between James VI of Scotland and his cousin, the Earl of Bothwell, and its theme can be deduced from Bothwell's line to James near the end of the play: "We are the upper and nether millstones, you and I. One way or another, it is those trappt in the middle must pay the price." The play is essentially about the brutality exercised toward those caught in the middle of any struggle for religious or political power, James standing for the divine right of kings and Bothwell for self-expression and individual freedom. But both treat the people under them as expendable and use them as pawns to advance their own positions. A subsidiary theme is that of witchcraft and superstition, but this is firmly placed within the context of the battle between authority and anarchy. The characters are vibrant with life, and in a powerful and an exact way they reflect the underlying moral and ethical problems posed by a commitment to one side or the other. Another remarkable feature of the play is the hard, sinewy Scottish language, which cleverly contrives to give an impression of late sixteenth-century speech.

Count Your Blessings revolves around Stanley, a man on the brink of death who is looking back over his life and regretting the lost opportunities for fulfilling his potentialities. A particularly powerful scene shows him as a boy berating his schoolmaster father for caving in to pressure from his headmaster employer and reneging on his commitment to address a Communist party rally in the 1930s on the effect of government cuts in education. *Thistlewood* is an impressionistic study of the 1820 Cato Street conspiracy of a group of radicals to assassinate the British cabinet. The play draws modern parallels in the continuing struggle between conservatism and radicalism in society.

Of Conn's short plays *The King* is a beautifully observed picture of two men fighting each other for the same girl, with a seduction scene between Attie and Lena that is replete with an unsentimental lyricism in the language. His trio of short plays, *Victims* (*The Man in the Green Muffler, In Transit,* and *The Sword*), are sharply and concisely drawn pictures of situations whose implications reverberate in the mind. The first play deals with an encounter between two pavement artists, one of whom has replaced someone who has died. The second is a macabre, Pinteresque exercise in violence between two men and an intruder whom they slowly dominate. *The Sword*, the best of the three, is a spooky psychological study of a man and a boy who are both obsessed, for different reasons, with the idea of military glory. The characterization in all of the plays is minutely and precisely accurate, qualities reflected in the taut dialogue, which has strong lyrical undertones, particularly in *The Sword,* and in the craftsmanlike attention to form.

The metaphorical connotations of Conn's best plays are strengthened by his feeling for dramatic construction, his understanding of individual psychology, and his basic interest in violence and its causes, both individual and in society at large. Allied with his quality of lyricism, they give his plays a peculiar power and depth.

—Jonathan Hammond

COONEY, Ray(mond George Alfred)

Nationality: British. **Born:** London, 30 May 1932. **Education:** Alleyn's School, Dulwich, London. **Military Service:** Served in the Royal Army Service Corps, 1950-52. **Family:** Married Linda Ann Dixon in 1962; two sons. **Career:** Actor, 1946—; theatrical director and producer, 1965—; director, Ray Cooney Presentations Ltd., London, 1966—; director and artistic director, Theatre of Comedy Company, London, 1983-91; owner, with George Borwick, The Playhouse Theatre, London, 1991—. **Address:** 1/3 Spring Gardens, London SW1A 2BD, England.

PUBLICATIONS

Plays

Dickory Dock, with Tony Hilton (produced Richmond, Surrey, 1959).
One for the Pot, with Tony Hilton (produced Wolverhampton, 1960; London, 1961). London, English Theatre Guild, 1963.
Who Were You with Last Night?, with Tony Hilton (produced Windsor, 1962).
How's Your Father? (produced Richmond, Surrey, 1963).
Chase Me, Comrade! (produced London, 1964). London, English Theatre Guild, and New York, Dramatists Play Service, 1966.
Charlie Girl, with Hugh and Margaret Williams, music and lyrics by David Heneker and John Taylor (produced London, 1965). London, Chappell, 1972.
Bang Bang Beirut; or, Stand by Your Bedouin, with Tony Hilton (produced Guildford, Surrey, 1966; as *Stand by Your Bedouin*, produced London, 1967). London, English Theatre Guild, 1971.
Not Now, Darling, with John Chapman (produced Richmond, Surrey, 1967; London, 1968; also director: produced New York, 1970). London, English Theatre Guild, 1970; New York, Dramatists Play Service, 1971.
My Giddy Aunt, with John Chapman (produced Wolverhampton, 1967; London, 1968). London, English Theatre Guild, 1970; revised edition, London, Chappell, 1987.
Move Over, Mrs. Markham, with John Chapman (produced Richmond, Surrey, 1969; also director: produced London, 1971). London, English Theatre Guild, and New York, French, 1972.
Why Not Stay for Breakfast?, with Gene Stone (produced Westcliff-on-Sea, Essex, 1970; also director: produced London, 1973). London, French, 1974.
Come Back to My Place, with John Chapman (produced Westcliff-on-Sea, Essex, 1973).
There Goes the Bride, with John Chapman (produced Birmingham and London, 1974). London, English Theatre Guild, 1975.
Her Royal Highness . . .?, with Royce Ryton (also director: produced London, 1981).
Two into One (produced Leicester, 1981; also director: produced London, 1984). London, French, 1985.
Run for Your Wife (also director: produced London, 1983; New York, 1989). London, French, 1984.
Wife Begins at Forty, with Arne Sultan and Earl Barret (also director: produced Guildford, Surrey, and London, 1985). London, French, 1986.
An Italian Straw Hat, adaptation of a play by Eugène Labiche (also director: produced London, 1986).
It Runs in the Family (also director: produced Guildford, Surrey, 1987; London, 1992). London, French, 1990.
Out of Order (also director: produced Leatherhead, Surrey, and London, 1990).
Funny Money: A Comedy. London, French, 1996.

Screenplays: *Not Now Comrade*, 1977; *There Goes the Bride*, with Terence Marcel, 1980; *Why Not Stay for Breakfast?*, with Terence Marcel, 1985.

Radio Plays: *Tale of the Repertory Actor*, 1971; *Mr. Willow's Wife*, with John Chapman, 1972; *Starring Leslie Willey*, 1987.

Television Plays (with Tony Hilton): *Boobs in the Wood*, 1960; *Round the Bend* (*Dial Rix* series), 1962.

*

Theatrical Activities:
Director: **Plays**—Many of his own plays, and *Thark* by Ben Travers, London, 1965; *In at the Death* by Duncan Greenwood and Robert King, London, 1967; *Press Cuttings* by Shaw, 1970; *The Mating Game* by Robin Hawdon, London, 1972; *Birds of Paradise* by Gaby Bruyère, London, 1974; *See How They Run* by Philip King, London, 1984; *Pygmalion* by Shaw, London, 1984; *Three Piece Suite* by Richard Harris, Hornchurch, Essex, 1986; *Holiday Snap* by Michael Pertwee, Guildford, Surrey, 1986. **Films**—*Not Now Darling*, with David Croft, 1973; *Not Now Comrade*, with Harold Snoad, 1977; *There Goes the Bride*, 1980.

Actor: **Plays**—Role in *Song of Norway* by Milton Lazarus, Robert Wright, and George Forrest, London, 1946; *Calcutta in the Morning* by Geoffrey Thomas, London, 1947; Larkin in *The Hidden Years* by Travers Otway, London, 1948; roles in repertory companies, 1952-56; *Dry Rot* by John Chapman, London, 1956; Corporal Flight in *Simple Spymen* by John Chapman, London, 1958; *One for the Pot*, London, 1961; Detective-Sergeant Trotter in *The Mousetrap* by Agatha Christie, London, 1964; Simon Sparrow in *Doctor at Sea* by Ted Willis, London, 1966; David Prosser in *Uproar in the House* by Anthony Marriott and Alistair Foot, London, 1967; Nicholas Wainwright in *Charlie Girl*, London, 1968; Timothy Westerby in *There Goes the Bride*, London, 1975; Willoughby Pink in *Banana Ridge* by Ben Travers, London, 1976; *Two into One*, Leicester, 1981, and Guildford, Surrey, 1985; *Run for Your Wife*, Guildford, Surrey, and London, both 1983, and New York, 1989; *Out of Order*, London, 1990; *It Runs in the Family*, London, 1992. **Films**—*Not Now Darling*, 1973; *Not Now Comrade*, 1977.

* * *

From the time of his first success with *One for the Pot* in 1960, Ray Cooney has sought to perfect his "talent to amuse." As one who has mastered the techniques of farce in the role of actor and producer as well as writer, he is perhaps more qualified than most. Certainly his varied abilities enable him to assess the likely response from the marketplace as well as the ivory tower, and over the years we have seen an increasingly imaginative use of his craft.

Farce is Cooney's chosen medium and one in which he excels. Its success has traditionally depended less on characterization or psychological insight than on swift and continuous action, and

Cooney's plays invariably fulfill these technical demands. Starting with a humdrum situation—a forthcoming society wedding, the collection of a mink coat, the decorating of an upmarket flat—the plays rapidly develop into a maze of misunderstandings, with the impending threat of potentially disastrous confrontations. Cooney shows great skill with his plots, neatly gauging the accelerating pace and eventual climax, and he matches the action with brittle, fragmented dialogue. He is also adept at exploiting such stock devices as the aside to the audience—Gilbert's comments on his partner Arnold in *Not Now, Darling* being a typical, and effective, example. A similar device is used in the same play when Arnold, confronted by a succession of irate spouses and girlfriends about to discover "proof" of infidelity, is repeatedly reduced to hurling the "evidence"—usually underwear—out the window. Read cold from a script, the effect appears tedious and mechanical, but onstage it works, lending added emphasis to the humor of the situation.

Repetition is a key element in Cooney's farces, the threat of discovery or catastrophic encounter continually recurring as the comic tension heightens and the possibilities grow more disastrous. *Run for Your Wife* has its bigamous taxi driver hero striving desperately to prevent the meeting of his two wives, his position rendered more comic by the use of a split stage that reveals both women and their thoughts at the same time. *Run for Your Wife* is one of Cooney's most striking works, the action ably measured, and the wit of the matching dialogue astute and keen. The same is true of *Not Now, Darling* and *Move Over, Mrs. Markham,* which show Cooney at his best. Like most of his plays, they are aimed at an upper-middle-class audience—"the tired businessman," as one reviewer puts it—and this is reflected in the locations, the former set in a high-class furrier's and the latter in "a very elegant top floor London flat." In *Not Now, Darling* Cooney contrasts the lecherous Gilbert and the prim Arnold in an escalating series of encounters as the former's amorous intrigues come home to roost. (Arnold's "I refuse to put all my bags in one exit!" must be one of Cooney's funniest lines.) *Move Over, Mrs. Markham* involves a publisher's family and friends and their liaisons, its climax a hilarious scene in which a prudish best-selling author is persuaded to sign for the firm by the publisher's wife while the publisher himself, as the butler, makes constant interruptions. All three plays are deftly executed, the interplay of character and situation sure and precise and the climaxes carefully weighted for maximum comic impact. *There Goes the Bride* is not quite equal to them. Polly Perkins, the 1920s flapper invisible to everyone but the dazed Timothy, is an overworked device, and the play lacks the "ordinariness" of Cooney's best settings. More effective is the Australian father-in-law, Babcock, in his role as that stock figure the "funny foreigner."

Farce, like the "tired businessman," is not noted for its taste, and Cooney's plays are no exception. On the face of it there would appear to be nothing very funny about Lebanon, but *Bang Bang Beirut,* which was produced in 1966, manages to wring comedy from the subject, much as Croft and Per'ry's *'Allo, 'Allo* has done with wartime France. Just as farce admits no unfunny locations, Cooney also regards minorities as fair game. The "funny foreigner" is repeatedly met with in his plays, either in person or by proxy, as with Linda's awful Austrian imitation in *Move Over, Mrs. Markham*. Cooney seems to find homosexuality unbelievably amusing, and he makes repeated use of its possibilities. The apparent "relationship" of Philip Markham and his partner is milked for laughs, the irony being their "discovery" by the effetely dressed Alistair, of whom Cooney seems unduly anxious to reassure us that "underneath his slightly arty exterior lurks a virile male." The bigamous husband of *Run for Your Wife* pretends to be gay himself at one point, and another camp character also makes an appearance. Many would contend that this kind of humor is on a par with racist jokes and that the author is playing for easy laughs. No doubt Cooney, as a performer, would contend that there is no such thing.

Later plays such as *It Runs in the Family, Wife Begins at Forty,* and *Out of Order* display all of Cooney's familiar skills and serve to confirm his reputation, *Out of Order* especially ranking with his finest work. A sequel to the earlier *Two into One*, it has a story that centers on the thwarted attempt by a junior government minister to secure a night of passion with an opposition secretary. The discovery in their hotel room of what appears to be the body of an intruder, trapped by a window with a faulty sash, is only the start of their troubles. Their unavailing efforts at hiding the "corpse" with the help of a bumbling PPS are further complicated by the unexpected arrival of both their spouses, the intrusive manager, a bribe-seeking waiter, and a private nurse. Cooney's script adroitly leads them—and us—through a frantic succession of hilarious scenes in which a cupboard and the faulty window figure prominently. The characters confront one another repeatedly in varying stages of undress and potentially outrageous situations, with the action matched throughout by the barbed wit of the author's dialogue. *Out of Order* provides an excellent example of Cooney's mastery of his chosen form.

Cooney's work has not been confined to the stage, and he has written for radio, television, and film. His radio play *Starring Leslie Willey,* which utilizes his flair for words effectively in the medium of sound, shows a rekindling of his interest in this form.

One feels that Cooney is not a particularly innovative writer. He is, rather, a master technician, a skilled manipulator of the conventions of his medium, where he operates to best effect. Attempts to move outside, as in *Why Not Stay for Breakfast?*, have been less satisfying. Within the limitations of his form, however, Cooney is altogether more impressive. Whether one laughs quite as loudly as the average businessman or winces on occasion, the fact remains that Cooney is one of the most capable and consistently successful writers in the medium of farce.

—Geoff Sadler

COWEN, Ron(ald)

Nationality: American. **Born:** Cincinnati, Ohio, 15 September 1944. **Education:** University of California, Los Angeles, B.A. in English 1966; Annenberg School of Communications, University of Pennsylvania, Philadelphia, 1967-68. **Career:** Taught classes in theatre at New York University, Fall 1969. Associate trustee, University of Pennsylvania. **Awards:** Wesleyan University fellowship, 1968; Vernon Rice award, 1968; Emmy award, 1986, and Peabody award, 1986, for television play. **Agent:** William Morris Agency, 151 El Camino, Beverly Hills, California 90212, U.S.A. **Address:** 147 West 79th Street, New York, New York 10024, U.S.A.

Publications

Plays

Summertree (produced Waterford, Connecticut, 1967; New York, 1968). New York, Random House, 1968.
Valentine's Day (produced Waterford, Connecticut, 1968; revised version, music by Saul Naishtat, produced New York, 1975).
Saturday Adoption (televised 1968; produced New York, 1978). New York, Dramatists Play Service, 1969.
Porcelain Time (produced Waterford, Connecticut, 1972).
The Book of Murder (televised 1974). New York, Dramatists Play Service, 1974.
Lulu, adaptation of plays by Wedekind (produced New York, 1974; as *Inside Lulu*, produced New York, 1975).
Unnatural Acts, with Daniel Lipman (produced Stockbridge, Massachusetts, 1975).

Television Plays: *Saturday Adoption*, 1968; *The Book of Murder*, 1974; *Paul's Case*, from the story by Willa Cather, 1977; *I'm a Fool*, from the story by Sherwood Anderson, 1979; *An Early Frost*, with Daniel Lipman, 1985; *The Love She Sought,* 1990; *Sisters* (series), 1991-96.

* * *

The ethical crisis arising from U.S. involvement in the Vietnam War was a major concern for American writers in the 1960s. *Summertree,* the most successful American play of the decade to deal with the subject, was written by Ron Cowen at the age of 20. (David Rabe's *The Basic Training of Pavlo Hummel* and *Sticks and Bones* may prove to be more significant works, but they appeared after the initial national tension over the war had peaked.) *Summertree,* which was widely produced and made into a Hollywood film, was perhaps successful more because of its timeliness than its intrinsic worth.

The play is an excessively sentimental telling of an inconsequential young man's death and life in Vietnam. As the protagonist (Young Man) lies fatally wounded under a jungle tree, he hallucinates flashback episodes from his civilian and military experience. Sometimes he is 20, and sometimes he is 10. The jungle tree becomes the backyard tree in which he once built a tree house. His recollections are of Mother and Father, Girl, and Buddy (Soldier). The characters are drawn by Cowen in broad strokes that critics of the production were prone to see as American archetypes, the essential constellation of personae. A critic of a less emotionally charged era is prone to see them as uninspired caricatures.

The play's most successful attribute is its three-act, cinematic structure, which provides a degree of dramatic irony and gives the work substance. Its least successful is its banal dialogue. When the Young Man says to his father late in the final act, "I want to tell the back yard goodbye," there is a cloying sentimentality that renders the moment bathetic. Yet for an audience tired of both the brutality of the war and the hysteria of the antiwar protests that shook the land in 1967, the play, and even its dialogue, struck sympathetic chords.

The play is a product of its cultural climate in yet another sense. It was written by Cowen while he was a student at the University of Pennsylvania. When the play was first presented, in the summer of 1967 at the Eugene O'Neill Memorial Theatre Foundation in Waterford, Connecticut, it underwent major rewriting at the request of the director. As it was prepared for production in New York by the Repertory Theater of Lincoln Center, additional changes were introduced. Thus, far more than the average commercial project, the play reflected the attitudes of many people who were concerned about the war. Small wonder that it found a receptive ear and was awarded the Vernon Rice Award for that turbulent year.

When the movie script was being prepared, the rewriting procedure got out of control, however. Cowen wrote a first screenplay, Rod McKuen was hired to do a second, and the shooting script was finally the work of Hollywood pros Edward Hume and Stephen Yafa. The final script owed shockingly little to Cowen's initial intentions, images, or characters.

Cowen's subsequent career has been somewhat erratic. In 1968 *Saturday Adoption* was telecast on CBS Playhouse, and in 1974 ABC aired *The Book of Murder*. Both were critical failures. The first deals with a socially-conscious young man's failure to change the world through his father's money or his pupil's achievements. The second is a coy murder mystery. Cowen's trademarks are easily seen in both: the cinematic structure, the sentimental and nostalgic tone, the domestic circumstance, and the conflict over money. His weaknesses are in evidence as well: the badly motivated actions, the clichéd characters, and the clumsy dialogue, which the critic for *Variety* called "goody two-shoes language." *I'm a Fool,* a television adaptation of the Sherwood Anderson story, was more successful, and *An Early Frost* won an Emmy.

Cowen has completed subsequent stage scripts, but none has been given major production. He assisted on the book for *Billy,* which flopped on Broadway in 1968. His musical *Valentine's Day* was showcased at the Manhattan Theatre Club in 1975 but reviewed as an "unsatisfying experience." It included the Cowensque line "I want to tell the apartment goodbye." *Inside Lulu* was a banal work, loosely based on the Wedekind plays and created by Section Ten, the off-off-Broadway improvisational group for which Cowen was the literary collaborator.

In retrospect *Summertree* appears very much to be in the tradition of television soap opera, and it is appropriate that Cowen should have continued to write for the television medium. His language, characters, and situations remain banal, autobiographical, and domestic, qualities that preclude a major work. *Summertree* appears to have been less the work of a wunderkind than a timely reflection of a culture's anxieties.

—Thomas B. Markus

COX, William Trevor. *See* **TREVOR, William.**

CRANE, Richard (Arthur)

Nationality: British. **Born:** York, 4 December 1944. **Education:** St. John's School, Leatherhead, Surrey, 1958-63; Jesus College, Cambridge, 1963-66, B.A. (honors) in classics and English 1966,

M.A. 1971. **Family:** Married Faynia Jeffery Williams in 1975; two sons and two stepdaughters. **Career:** Actor and director: founder member, Brighton Combination and Pool, Edinburgh. Fellow in theatre, University of Bradford, Yorkshire, 1972-74; resident dramatist, National Theatre, London, 1974-75; fellow in creative writing, University of Leicester, 1976, and University of East Anglia, Norwich, 1988; literary manager, Royal Court Theatre, London, 1978-79; dramaturg, Tron Theatre, Glasgow, 1983-84; associate director, Brighton Theatre, 1980-85; lecturer in English, University of Maryland, 1990; writer-in-residence, Birmingham Polytechnic, and tutor in playwriting, University of Birmingham, 1990-91. Member of the Board of Directors, Edinburgh Festival Fringe Society, 1973-89; writer-in-residence, H. M. Prison, Bedford, 1993. Lecturer in creative writing and literature development, University of Sussex, 1994—. **Awards:** Edinburgh Festival Fringe award, 1973, 1974, 1975, 1977, 1980, 1986, 1987, 1988, 1989; Thames Television bursary, 1974; Arts Council bursary, 1974. **Agent:** Tom Erhardt, Casarotto Ramsay Ltd, 60-66 Wardour Street, London W1V 3HP, London.

Publications

Plays

Footlights Revue, with others (produced Cambridge, 1966).
Three Ugly Women (produced Cork and London, 1967).
The Tenant (produced Edinburgh, 1971; London, 1972).
Crippen (produced Edinburgh, 1971). Colchester, School Play Ltd, 1990.
Tom Brown (produced Bradford, 1971).
Decent Things (produced Edinburgh, 1972; London, 1973).
The Blood Stream (produced Edinburgh, 1972).
Mutiny on the Bounty, music by Chris Mitchell (produced Bradford, 1972; revised version produced Brighton, 1980).
Bleak Midwinter (produced Edinburgh, 1972).
David, King of the Jews, music by Chris Mitchell (produced Bradford, 1973).
Thunder: A Play of the Brontës (produced Ilkley, Yorkshire, 1973; London, 1978). London, Heinemann, 1976.
Examination in Progress (produced Edinburgh, 1973).
Secrets (produced Belfast, 1973; London, 1974).
The Pied Piper, music by Chris Mitchell (produced Bradford, 1973).
The Quest, music by Chris Mitchell (produced Edinburgh, 1974).
The Route of All Evil (produced Edinburgh, 1974).
Humbug; or, Christmas Carol Backwards, music by Milton Reame-James (produced Bracknell, Berkshire, 1974).
Mystery Plays (produced Bracknell, Berkshire, 1974).
Mean Time (produced London, 1975).
Venus and Superkid (for children), music by Milton Reame-James (produced London, 1975).
Clownmaker (produced Edinburgh, 1975; London and Westport, Connecticut, 1976; New York, 1982).
Bloody Neighbours (produced London, 1975).
Manchester Tales (produced Manchester, 1975).
Gunslinger: A Wild West Show, music by Joss Buckley (produced Leicester, 1976; London, 1977). London, Heinemann, 1979.
Nero and the Golden House (produced Edinburgh, 1976).
The Perils of Bardfrod, with David Edgar (produced Bradford, 1976).
Satan's Ball, adaptation of a novel by Mikhail Bulgakov (produced Edinburgh, 1977; Davis, California, 1984).
Gogol (produced Brighton, 1978; London, 1979; New York, 1983).
Vanity, adaptation of *Eugene Onegin* by Pushkin (produced Edinburgh, 1980; London, 1983).
Sand (produced Brighton, 1981).
Brothers Karamazov, adaptation of a novel by Dostoevsky (produced Edinburgh and London, 1981).
Burke and Hare (produced Glasgow, 1983).
The Possessed, with Yuri Lyubimov, adaptation of a novel by Dostoevsky (produced Paris and London, 1985).
Mutiny!, with David Essex, music by Essex (produced London, 1985).
Envy, adaptation of a novel by Yuri Olesha, music by Donald Swann (produced Edinburgh, 1986).
Soldier Soldier, adaptation of a work by Tony Parker (produced Edinburgh, 1986).
Pushkin (produced Edinburgh and London, 1987).
Red Magic (produced Edinburgh and London, 1988).
Rolling the Stone (produced Edinburgh, 1989).
Phaedra, with Michael Glenny, adaptation of the play by Marina Tsvetayeva (produced London, 1990).
Baggage and Bombshells (produced Edinburgh 1991; London, 1992).
Under the Stars (produced London, 1993).

Screenplay: *Sebastian and the Seawitch* (for children), 1976.

Radio Plays: *Gogol*, 1979; *Decent Things*, 1984; *Optimistic Tragedy*, with Faynia Williams, adaptation of the play by Vsevolod Vishnevsky, 1986; *Anna and Marina*, 1991; *Plutopia*, music by Donald Swann, 1992; *Understudies*, 1992; *Vlad the Impaler*, adaptation of the play by Marin Sorescu, 1992; *The Sea, the Sea*, adaptation of the novel by Iris Murdoch, 1993.

Television Plays: *Nice Time* series, 1968-69; *The Billy West Show*, 1970; *Rottingdean*, 1980; *The Possessed*, with Yuri Lyubimov, 1986.

Recordings: *Mutiny!*, Phonogram, 1983, and Telstar, 1985 (and singles *Tahiti*, 1983, and *Welcome*, 1984, both Phonogram).

Other

The Sneak (novel).

Editor, *Poems from the Waiting Room*. N.p., n.d.
Editor, *The Last Minute Book*. University of Sussex, n.d.
Editor, *Pandora's Books*. University of Sussex, n.d.

*

Theatrical Activities:
Director of plays in Bradford, Edinburgh, and London, and actor from 1966 in London and in repertory, on television, and in films.

* * *

For three weeks each year Edinburgh is a world theatrical capital, with hundreds of performances taking place both in the International Festival and on the Fringe. Many a premiere sinks into instant obscurity, but the plays of Richard Crane have left an indelible mark, taking nine coveted Edinburgh Festival Fringe awards by 1992. Over 20 years of dedication to the Edinburgh Fringe is an unusual route to dramatic success, but there is a logic to it. By collaborating with his wife, the director Faynia Williams, and working with dedicated students from universities in Bradford, Essex, and East Anglia, Crane has been able to produce epic drama on a scale normally considered only by the National and Royal Shakespeare companies. Vast themes and a large theatrical canvas became economically feasible, and his work ranged from a retelling of the Arthurian legend to the full breadth of Mikhail Bulgakov's great novel *The Master and Margarita.*

It is interesting, then, that it was an intimate and intense play for four actors that finally elevated Crane's reputation nationally and internationally, and many of his later plays are highly refined miniatures for perhaps no more than a single actor. Although he had already had important posts as a playwright-in-residence at the National Theatre and with the Royal Court, it was his dramatization of *The Brothers Karamazov* in 1981 that consolidated Crane's reputation in London and in what was then the Soviet Union. It was no accident, however, that the play was quarried from Russian literature, for he and Williams had begun their exploration of the Russian greats well before it was fashionable.

Before turning to *The Brothers Karamazov* and Dostoevsky, Crane had presented a string of confrontations with Russian writers, including Bulgakov, Gogol, and Pushkin. This had followed investigations into British legends, English literature, and religion. At one point he had even written a children's play called *Venus and Superkid* that was described as a "trans-galactic rock supershow based on Greek legend."

Crane's dramatic interests have ranged from a music hall impression of the murderer Crippen to *Thunder,* a retelling of the Brontë family story, and *David, King of the Jews,* performed at Bradford Cathedral in 1973. His 1974 script for Bradford University, *The Quest,* offered the first serious rumblings of significant talent, in part because it was technically overambitious, and it was the Edinburgh Fringe success of that year. In the play he retold the legend of Arthurian England with opposing factions divided into prose and poetry speakers while the audience witnessed the rise and destruction of Camelot as if watching a jousting tournament.

The following year, which also saw the production of *Bloody Neighbours* in the National Theatre's studio season at the ICA Theatre, produced *Clownmaker*. Telling the story of the relationship between Diaghilev and Nijinsky, it was marked by shattering stage effects in Faynia Williams's production. The Ballets Russes forms the backdrop for the portrait of Diaghilev as puppet master, and the struggles of Nijinsky to establish a separate existence create the dramatic moments. Diaghilev produces Nijinsky's first sign of animation by providing the impetus to dance, and Nijinsky's rebellion against his homosexual relationship with Diaghilev provokes a virtual earthquake. Memorable scenes and moments of evocative dialogue did not quite jell into a total success, but the sheer theatricality was refreshing and unusual.

Crane's adaptation of Bulgakov's novel *The Master and Margarita* appeared two years later, after a series of somewhat less ambitious works. Called *Satan's Ball,* the play marked his first serious use of Russian material and formed a vast satirical and erotic canvas for Williams's staging, again on the Edinburgh Fringe. The next collaboration was on a markedly reduced scale—a monologue that was originally performed by Crane himself in a production by Williams for their own small company, the Brighton Actors' Workshop. Again, the subject was Russian, and the title, *Gogol,* was from the name of the author, with material taken from his writing, particularly "The Overcoat," and from his life. Crane's intention was to contrast the inner life with the outer appearance, to present the spiritual substance simultaneously with the surface indications and contradictions of the body, the clothes, and the published writing.

Before *The Brothers Karamazov* promoted him to the official Edinburgh Festival, Crane and Williams produced *Vanity* on the Fringe in 1980. It was a further investigation of Russian writing, described as a "response to *Eugene Onegin,*" and it cleared the way for the official invitation in 1981, which resulted in the London season and a tour of the Soviet Union.

The distinction of *The Brothers Karamazov* as an adaptation for the stage lies largely in the lucid retention of the moral and metaphysical ambiguities of Dostoevsky's novel. The originality of the work is largely in the ingenious structural emphases that significantly alter the tone of the original. Crane transforms introspective guilt into heady confessions, with each son eagerly displaying the reasons for which he might possibly have murdered his father. A familiarity with the novel helps clarify the multiple actions, but the multiple role playing of each character is theatrically engaging on its own. There is a playfulness in giving each of the four actors a principal characterization and then diverting them to play old Fyodor, always in a fur coat, or lounging women, which provides moment-to-moment entertainment. Crane thrives on challenges and more often than not meets them with original theatrical solutions.

The main developments of Crane's work have remained his collaborations with Faynia Williams, both with students and later in radio. His most visible production has been his collaboration with the pop star and actor David Essex on a West End musical based on *Mutiny on the Bounty. Mutiny!* had the merit of dispensing with the standard image of the leading mutineer, Fletcher Christian, as a recognizable hero. Instead, the character was approached as a confused romantic, longing for equality between officers and enlisted men. Unfortunately, the starry contributions by Essex were all too visible, keeping him moodily in view as sailors were flogged and involving him in erotic caresses with his island lover at every available chance.

Crane's most important collaboration has perhaps been his work with the exiled Soviet director Yuri Lyubimov on a European coproduction of a dramatization of Dostoevsky's *The Possessed* in 1985. The version reflected the director's highly personal vision of the book, but Crane's use of language was equally personal, and the heightened imagery was as evident in his concentrated English as in the director's vivid staging.

In other projects—from a lively dramatization of the Soviet classic *Envy* for the 1986 Edinburgh Festival to a radio version of the classic communist drama by Vsevolod Vishnevsky, *Optimistic Tragedy*—Crane has continued to explore the riches of Russian writing. He finally established a more personal tone with his impressionistic and intense study of the filmmaker Sergei Eisenstein, called *Red Magic* and written as the Soviet Union lumbered toward dissolution.

Many of Crane's plays have been designed for his own performances as an actor. They have ranged from his Gogol in an overcoat to a pun-rich retelling of the Sysyphus legend in *Rolling the Stone,* proving his value as an entertainer as well as a serious actor. The backstage knowledge he has accumulated as a theatrical all-rounder has been reflected in plays such as his script for radio, *Understudies,* a work about the jealousies and ambitions of actors waiting for terrible things to happen to the star. Naturally, the roles are tailor-made for those who are already stars.

Yet serious themes with political connotations have also made repeated appearances in his work, from his dramatization of Tony Parker's book about British soldiers and their wives, *Soldier Soldier,* to his 1991 play *Baggage and Bombshells,* a typically dense and imagistic shocker about women and war drawn from the rhetoric and propaganda of the Persian Gulf War. For all his vast and varied output over his writing career, Crane has showed little sign of flagging creativity, even if a single undisputed masterpiece has eluded him.

—Ned Chaillet

CREGAN, David (Appleton Quartus)

Nationality: British. **Born:** Buxton, Derbyshire, 30 September 1931. **Education:** Leys School, Cambridge, 1945-50; Clare College, Cambridge, 1952-55, B.A. in English 1955. **Military Service:** Served as an acting corporal in the Royal Air Force, 1950-52. **Family:** Married Ailsa Mary Wynne Willson in 1960; three sons and one adopted daughter. **Career:** Head of English, Palm Beach Private School, Florida, 1955-57; assistant English master, Burnage Boys' Grammar School, Manchester, 1957; assistant English master and head of drama, 1958-62, and part-time drama teacher, 1962-67, Hatfield School, Hertfordshire; salesman, and clerk at the Automobile Association, 1958. Worked with Royal Court Theatre Studio, London, 1964, 1968, and Midlands Arts Centre, Birmingham, 1971; conducted three-week studio at the Royal Shakespeare Company Memorial Theatre, Stratford-on-Avon, 1971. Member of the Drama Panel, West Midlands Arts Association, 1972, and Eastern Arts, 1980. **Awards:** Arts Council bursary, 1966, 1975, 1978, and grant, 1971; Foyle award, 1966; Sony award for radio, 1987. **Agent:** Casarotto Ramsay Ltd., National House, 60-66 Wardour Street, London W1V 3HP. **Address:** 76 Wood Close, Hatfield, Hertfordshire, England.

Publications

Plays

Miniatures (produced London, 1965). London, Methuen, 1970.
Transcending, and The Dancers (produced London, 1966). London, Methuen, 1967.
Three Men for Colverton (produced London, 1966). London, Methuen, 1967.
The Houses by the Green (produced London, 1968). London, Methuen, 1969.
A Comedy of the Changing Years (produced London, 1969).
Arthur, in *Playbill One*, edited by Alan Durband. London, Hutchinson, 1969.
Tipper (produced Oxford, 1969).
Liebestraum and Other Pieces (produced Birmingham, 1970). Included in *The Land of Palms and Other Plays*, 1973.
Jack in the Box; and If You Don't Laugh, You Cry (produced Birmingham, 1971). Included in *The Land of Palms and Other Plays*, 1973.
The Daffodil, and Sentimental Value (produced Birmingham, 1971).
How We Held the Square: A Play for Children (produced Birmingham, 1971; London, 1974). London, Eyre Methuen, 1973.
The Land of Palms (produced Dartington, Devon, 1972). Included in *The Land of Palms and Other Plays*, 1973.
George Reborn (televised 1973; produced Richmond, Surrey, 1973; London, 1977). Included in *The Land of Palms and Other Plays*, 1973.
Cast Off (produced Sheffield, 1973).
Pater Noster (in *Mixed Blessings*, produced Horsham, Sussex, 1973). Published in *Play Nine*, edited by Robin Rook, London, Arnold, 1981.
The Land of Palms and Other Plays (includes *Liebestraum*; *George Reborn*; *The Problem*; *Jack in the Box*; *If You Don't Laugh, You Cry*). London, Eyre Methuen, 1973.
The King (produced London, 1974).
Tina (produced Richmond, Surrey, 1975). With *Poor Tom*, London, Eyre Metheun, 1976.
Poor Tom (produced Manchester, 1976). With *Tina*, London, Eyre Methuen, 1976.
Tigers (produced Richmond, Surrey, 1978).
Young Sir (produced Richmond, Surrey, 1979).
Red Riding Hood (produced Stoke-on-Trent, 1979).
Getting It Right (produced Hatfield, Hertfordshire, 1980).
A Name Is More Than a Name, in *Play Nine*, edited by Robin Rook. London, Arnold, 1981.
Jack and the Beanstalk (pantomime), music by Brian Protheroe (produced London, 1982). London, French, 1987.
The Sleeping Beauty (pantomime), music by Brian Protheroe (produced London, 1983). London, French, 1984.
Red Ridinghood (pantomime), music by Brian Protheroe (produced London, 1984). London, French, 1986.
Crackling Angels (produced Beaminster, Dorset, 1987).
Beauty and the Beast (pantomime), music by Brian Protheroe (produced London, 1987).
Cinderella (pantomime), music by Brian Protheroe (produced London, 1989).
Aladdin (pantomime). London and New York, Samuel French, 1993.

Radio Plays: *The Latter Days of Lucy Trenchard*, 1974; *The Monument*, 1978; *Hope*, 1979; *Inventor's Corner*, 1979; *The Joking Habit*, 1980; *The True Story of the Public School Strike 1990*, 1981; *Diana's Uncle and Other Relatives*, 1982; *The Spectre*, 1983; *The Awful Insulation of Rage*, 1986; *A Butler Did It*, 1990; *From a Second Home in Picardy*, 1990; *What Happened with St. George*, 1991; *Eavesdropping*, 1992.

Television Plays: *That Time of Life*, 1972; *George Reborn*, 1973; *I Want to Marry Your Son*, 1973; *Pipkins*, with Susan Pleat, 1974; *Reluctant Chickens*, 1982; *Events in a Museum*, 1983; *Goodbye Days*, 1984; *A Still Small Shout*, 1985; *Goodbye, And I Hope We Meet Again*, 1989.

Novel

Ronald Rossiter. London, Hutchinson, 1959.

*

Critical Studies: *The Second Wave* by John Russell Taylor, London, Methuen, and New York, Hill and Wang, 1971; article by Timothy J. Kidd, in *British Dramatists since World War II* edited by Stanley Weintraub, Detroit, Gale, 1982.

David Cregan comments:

1. I am a socialist because there is no other reasonable thing to be. However, all problems, as well as all interesting thoughts, seem to stem from that one position. How much does the individual matter and how much the community? Can a contemporary community ever avoid becoming systematized, and anyway how much less traumatic is it living unsystematically than systematically? How simplistic can a government be before it must be opposed totally? If material poverty produces spiritual poverty, which, with special exceptions, it does, can material wealth produce spiritual wealth? How important *is* spiritual wealth, and on what does its value depend? Can the elevation of one working class be justified if it is achieved at the expense of another working class? If freedom is no longer a meaningful conception (and it only achieves any meaning by being opposed to some form of tyranny), which qualified freedom is the most important? Of thought or from hunger? If leaders are bad, are institutions worse? What is the basic nature of man as opposed to the animals, and can it be improved?

I doubt if any of this appears overtly in any of my writing, though the head of steam is always provided by acute anxieties felt on one score or another among these and similar peculiarly 20th-century questions.

2. Since for me the best plays seem to *be* rather than to be *about*, I personally prefer the episodic forms in which characters may be presented quickly and variously, so that the architecture provides the major insights.

3. Since I have this delight in form, I find no pleasure or virtue in personal rhetoric, self-indulgent self-revelation, or absolute naturalism.

4. Delight in construction also biases me against any form of expressionism or abstract symbolism, and increasingly I use songs, jazz, and a rough poetry spoken to music for various constructional purposes.

5. Since construction of the kind so far indicated is frequently a question of rhythm, there is a "playful" quality about my work. It has a musical quality, each scene sounding forward to another. This means the plays should be acted with a care for their surface, and anyone who acts them for any individual significance, the same shall surely lose it. There are frequently large alterations in emotional stance needed between the giving and receiving of the words, and there is much pleasure in watching this.

6. I have been much influenced by farce, Ibsen, Brecht, Beckett, and the directors I have been associated with at the Royal Court. Also by the intensely magical understanding of comedy shown by Keith Johnstone.

7. I am the fourth and youngest son of an Irish shirt manufacturer. My father fought and was gassed in World War I, and sought peace and prosperity in a small Derbyshire town, where he pursued a quiet Protestant way of life. My brothers fought, and one died, in World War II. I was largely brought up by a young working-class nursemaid.

8. Writer's notes about himself are alas more revealing when they fail to confirm the impression of his work than when they succeed. This happens to more of us than is generally supposed.

*   *   *

In David Cregan's earliest play, *Miniatures,* the deputy headmaster says, "If only one knew what every mind was thinking. If one had their habits of thought one could put in train the running of the school that way it ought to go. That's the way of achieving what is democratically best for everyone. One must have their minds, or else it is coercion." The common theme of Cregan's plays is the struggle for power and the manipulation of social conventions to achieve it. A more or less closed society that has developed its own conventions is often the setting: a school in *Miniatures* and again in *Tina,* a small town in *Three Men for Colverton,* an oasis in *The Land of Palms,* and a boardinghouse in *Poor Tom.* In other plays the characters act as if they are in a closed society. In *The Dancers* members of a middle-aged quintet dance and pair off in various combinations. In the "cozy circle" of *Liesbestraum* there are two mutually adulterous couples, but when Jane does not find herself attracted to the husband of her husband's lover, the others fear that she will seek a lover elsewhere, in which case "We'll find ourselves part of a larger community before we know where we are, with all the loss of sovereignty that will entail."

Often in Cregan's plays one set of conventions is brought into conflict with another. In his most complex play, *Three Men for Colverton,* the leader of a trio of evangelists seeks to take control of the town from the domineering Mrs. Carnock. She believes that Colverton "was meant to be a stagnant pool . . . and stagnant it will remain." The uncompromising vision of the evangelists, who "hate every lubricant of living" and decry "the stern virility of man [etiolated] in the black night of consumer goods," threatens the indulgence and manipulation of human relationships by which Mrs. Carnock maintains her dominance. Other power seekers are the liberal vicar and an Anglican monk who uses the confessional to his own advantage.

Where existing conventions are strained or broken, new conventions are invented. In *Liebestraum* the adulterous relationships are regularized. A strict alternation of days for sleeping with one's marriage partner and with one's lover is threatened by Jane's uncertain feelings. When she does fulfill expectations by completing the sexual cross-partnering, she does so on the wrong day, however, and is denounced for her carnality. In *The Land of Palms* several British have set up a community of peace and harmony at an oasis. Three former members of the foreign legion, all British, arrive with their military values. In *Transcending,* a short play of wonderful verve, a teenage girl escapes from the world of her parents and two of her neighbors, a young man and an older widower, all of whom have a role to offer her, by appearing at the end of the play dressed as a nun. She thus escapes by invoking a different set of conventions.

It would be interesting to produce *Transcending* alongside the very funny *Pater Noster,* in which a husband and wife are saying their bedtime prayers when the husband decides that he is God because he has created the child in her womb. He begins praying to himself despite his wife's arguments that there are other influences on conception, such as the availability of family allowances. The voice of the fetus is heard, apprehensive about the world it is to enter. We see the mother use the child to manipulate her husband and then, at the end of the play, threaten the fetus: "I'll tell him when he comes upstairs, and then you'll catch it." Even an infant is doomed in our world of manipulative conventions.

In Cregan's plays there are instinctive nonconformists. In *Miniatures,* for example, the climactic scene reveals the music teacher sitting in his store closet surrounded by the items that have been stolen from the school. He later tries to hang himself. In *The Land of Palms* the soldier who cannot adapt to the oasis community kills himself. In *Three Men for Colverton* one of the evangelists is homosexual. He declares, "One is one and all alone and ever more shall be so. Two bodies don't make one, two minds don't make one, and I'm one." In the last scene he throws himself from a clock tower and dies. Not borne up by angels, this individualist has unwittingly destroyed the leading evangelist's power. Meanwhile, Mrs. Carnock has died, and perhaps the play's other nonconformist, a teacher who fornicates with his pupils, will establish "that dreary venture, the Arts Centre," which Mrs. Carnock had opposed, as "an act of existential heroism." In much the same spirit he will marry his latest, pregnant teenage mistress.

In Cregan's later short plays the nonconformists are the central characters. Tina, a teacher, dresses in jeans and leather jacket to try to reach an abused 10-year-old whom Cregan has ironically named Dawn. In *Poor Tom,* Tom murders the owner of the boardinghouse to prevent him from selling it. In each play much of the interest is in how the other characters react to the tearing of the social fabric.

Cregan writes dry, wry comedies. Introducing *Three Men for Colverton,* he wrote, "The situations of most of the characters are too painful to make me laugh. However, most of the people are themselves aware of the silliness of their positions, and this frequently leads them to act in a sillier way than ever." So it is in all of his plays. The characters' self-consciousness effects a certain distancing from the audience. The characters often introduce themselves to the audience and sing choruses together. In *Three Men for Colverton* they move the revolving platforms Cregan envisions as the setting. In *The Dancers* different records are put on and taken off, accompanied by lighting changes, while in the brief comedy *George Reborn* the characters conduct an orchestra in snatches from well-known classical works.

The Houses by the Green is more farcical than Cregan's other full-length plays. It is a Plautine, or *commedia,* farce that involves the battle of two elderly men, the Commander and Mervyn Molyneux, who live in adjacent houses, for the hand of Molyneux's adopted daughter Susan. They are bested by her young lover, the serving man Oliver, whom they share. Molyneux woos Susan disguised as his own friend, and the Commander does likewise; neither is aware of the other's deception. Disguised as a land developer, Oliver threatens both men with their community's destruction. Susan disguises herself as the developer's trollop, and a puzzled Oliver tells the audience, "I must be impersonating a real person." Traditional forgiveness and marriage promises end the play when Susan, untraditionally pregnant, "is suddenly sick at the side of the stage."

—Anthony Graham-White

CRIMP, Martin (Andrew)

Nationality: British. **Born:** United Kingdom, in February 1956. **Education:** Cambridge University, graduated 1978. **Career:** Writer-in-residene, Royal Court Theatre, 1997-98. **Awards:** John Whiting award, 1993. **Agent:** Judy Daish Associates, 2 St. Charles Place, London W10 6E9, England.

Publications

Plays

Living Remains (produced London, 1982).

Four Attempted Acts (produced London, 1984).

A Variety of Death-Defying Acts (produced London, 1985).

Three Attempted Acts (broadcast 1985). Published in *Best Radio Plays of 1985,* edited by Richard Imison, London, Methuen, 1986.

Definitely the Bahamas (produced London, 1987).

A Kind of Arden (produced London, 1987).

Spanish Girls (produced London, 1987).

Dealing with Clair (produced London, 1988). London, Hern, 1988.

Play with Repeats (produced London, 1989). London, Hern, 1990.

No One Sees the Video (produced London, 1990). With *Getting Attention,* London, Hern, 1991.

Getting Attention (produced Leeds and London, 1991). With *No One Sees the Video,* London, Hern, 1991.

The Treatment (produced London and New York, 1993). London, Hern, 1993.

The Misanthrope, After Molière (produced London, 1996). London, Faber and Faber, 1996.

Attempts on Her Life (produced London 1997). London, Faber and Faber, 1997.

Roberto Zucco, adaptation of Kdtès (produced Stratford and London, 1997, 1998). London, Methuen, 1997.

The Chairs, adaptation of Ionesco (produced London and New York, 1997, 1998). London, Faber and Faber, 1997.

Radio Plays: *Three Attempted Acts,* 1985; *Six Figures at the Base of the Crucifixion,* 1986; *Definitely the Bahamas,* 1987; *The Country,* 1997.

* * *

In the short story "Stage Kiss," Martin Crimp's narrator, a well-known actor in middle age, visits the wife from whom he is "notoriously" divorced:

> The last thing my wife says to me is "Are you happy?" to which I reply "Are you?". In the theatre, these lines could prove unplayable, and I'd suggest a cut.

And yet it is in the discomforting area uncovered by this fundamental question and evasive answer that the action of Crimp's plays is developed. The appurtenances of comfort are all in place—television sets, cassette recorders, microwaves—but they are at best a distraction from, and at worst a substitute for, self-recognition. The emotional hollowness of the Thatcherite society of the 1980s is exposed catastrophically to the audience, while the characters in the play, those who survive the violation, struggle to keep their eyes closed to it.

Crimp characteristically sprinkles the closely observed dialogue of his plays with "faint laughs" and disconcerting pauses, enforcing a recognition of the unsaid beneath the generally civilized discourse of the brittle encounters of which the plays are composed. In *Dealing with Clair* the ostensible subject is usually the house that Mike and Liz, a monumentally unpleasant pair of libidinous yuppies, are trying to sell. Clair is their young estate agent, already inured to avarice and deception but not yet corrupted by it.

Patronized by both the vendors, she is an object of casual desire for Mike and of casual jealousy for Liz, but for the enigmatic cash buyer, James, desire is not enough. *Dealing with Clair* is unavoidably related to the disappearance in 1986 of a young estate agent, Suzy Lamplugh, who is presumed dead. More significant theatrically is the brilliantly sinister scene in which the solitary James conducts a soupy telephone conversation with Clair's mother while sitting on Clair's bed and emptying her handbag. With Clair and the cash buyer both gone, the vendors are pleased to learn from a colleague of Clair's that the house has been undervalued.

The craftsmanship of *Dealing with Clair,* its use of repetition and the aural leitmotiv of train sounds, is unobtrusive. In *Play with Repeats,* however, the playwright's craft is placed in the foreground. As he might have been in one of J. B. Priestley's time plays, Tony Steadman is given a chance to replay two crucial incidents in his unimpressive life. Not surprisingly, he makes a worse show of it the second time around. The play is more interesting for its creation and study of a casualty of competitive values than for its theatrical trickery. Tony pines for affection but earns none. He begins the play as a buttonholing pub bore, a role in which, on the reprise of his life, he is stabbed to death. His disappearance, like that of Clair in the earlier play, makes little difference to his workmates.

The self-conscious theatricality of *Play with Repeats* suggests a striving after effect. In *No One Sees the Video,* however, message and medium are finely synchronized. Crimp himself thinks of it as a "post-consumer play . . . it describes a world in which the equation of consumption with happiness is no longer debated, but is simply as axiomatic to everyday life as Newtonian mechanics." Intelligent and independent though she is, Liz is drawn into the confidence trickery of market research. The question of whether she can survive without self-hatred remains open at the end of the play. Crimp's ear for the quirks and blandness of contemporary speech is fully displayed. Under the barrage of consumerist interrogation and the intimidating technology of video recording, a sense of personal identity proves fragile. *No One Sees the Video* is a powerful documentary of our times.

Liz's troublesome teenage daughter Joanna is more resistant to the blandishments of consumerism than anyone else. A concern, tinged with anger, for the new generation is a feature of Crimp's work. The offstage crying of the daughter of Liz and Mike in *Dealing with Clair* signals the self-absorption of her repulsive parents. The future of even a daughter of privilege is bleak. For Sharon in *Getting Attention* the story is one of abuse that culminates, we have to assume, in death. This is a fine and deeply disturbing play. The setting is a block of South London flats, from any one of which the sounds that emanate eerily implicate the others. The configuration of the stage contributes crucially to the action. The main area is the interior of the flat in which Carol lives with her four-year-old daughter Sharon and her common-law husband Nick. They have a patch of garden in which Carol sunbathes and Nick does bodybuilding exercises. At the bottom of the garden, where it stretches out into the audience, the invisible Sharon is sometimes allowed to play. From the balcony running alongside the flats above, the lonely Bob looks at the scantily dressed Carol, and the lonely Milly tries to warn her that Sharon is eating mud. Most of the time, however, Sharon is locked in her room. The concrete evidence of her existence is the light that shows above her door when she is trying to attract her mother's attention. But the play is full of noises. Bob, drinking alone, falls over in his flat. (Or is it Nick dealing with Sharon?) Nick and Carol make love, and Bob listens to them and to the birds scratching in his chimney, although the scratching, we eventually learn, is Sharon's sad attempt to attract attention. Every Friday, Nick brings for Carol some new gadget for home comfort, and when the scratching stops, Sharon is probably dead.

—Peter Thomson

CRISTOFER, Michael

A pseudonym for Michael Procaccino. **Nationality:** American. **Born:** Trenton, New Jersey, 22 January 1945. **Education:** Catholic University, Washington, D.C., 1962-65; American University, Beirut, 1968-69. **Awards:** Los Angeles Drama Critics Circle award, for acting, 1973, for playwriting, 1975; Antoinette Perry award, 1977; Pulitzer prize, 1977; Tony award, 1977; Obie award, for acting, and American Theater Critics Award, both 1980. **Agent:** c/o Richard Lovett, 9830 Wilshire Boulevard, Beverly Hills, California 90212-1804.

Publications

Plays

The Mandala (produced Philadelphia, 1968).
Plot Counter Plot (produced New York, 1971).
Americomedia (produced New York, 1973).
The Shadow Box (produced Los Angeles, 1975; New York, 1977; London, 1979). New York, French, 1977.
Ice (produced Los Angeles, 1976; New York, 1979).
Black Angel (produced Los Angeles, 1978; New York, 1982; London, 1990). New York, Dramatists Play Service, 1984.
C.C. Pyle and the Bunyon Derby (produced Gambier, Ohio, 1978).
The Lady and the Clarinet (produced Los Angeles, 1980; New York, 1983; London, 1989). New York, Dramatists Play Service, 1985.
Love Me or Leave Me, adaptation of the screenplay by Isobel Lennart and Daniel Fuchs (produced Woodstock, New York, 1989).
Amazing Grace (produced Pittsburgh, 1995; New York, 1998).

Screenplays: *Falling in Love*, 1985; *The Witches of Eastwick*, 1987; *Bonfire of the Vanities,* 1990; *Mr. Jones,* 1991; *Breaking Up,* 1997; *GIA,* 1998.

*

Critical Studies: "Dying on Broadway: Contemporary Drama and Mortality" by Donald F. Duclow, in *Soundings, An Interdisciplinary Journal* (Knoxville, Tennessee), Summer 1981, pp. 197-216; "Images of the Gay Male in Contemporary Drama" by James W. Carleson, in *Gayspeak: Gay Male and Lesbian Communication,* edited by James W. Chesebro, New York, Pilgrim, 1981; "Medical Technology on Stage" by Angela Belli, in *Ometeca,* 1996, pp. 291-303.

Theatrical Activities:
Director: **Plays**—*Candida* by Shaw, New York, 1981; *Forty-Deuce* by Alan Bowne, New York, 1981.

Actor: **Plays**—Roles at the Arena Stage, Washington, D.C., 1967-68, Theatre of Living Arts, Philadelphia, 1968, and Beirut Repertory Company, Lebanon, 1968-69; in *Yegor Bulichov* by Gorky, New Haven, Connecticut, 1970-71; Jules in *The Justice Box* by Michael Robert Davis, New York, 1971; *The Tooth of Crime* by Sam Shepard, Los Angeles, 1973; *Ajax* by Sophocles, Los Angeles, 1974; Colin in *Ashes* by David Rudkin, Los Angeles, 1976; *The Three Sisters* by Chekhov, Los Angeles, 1976; *Savages* by Christopher Hampton, Los Angeles; Trofimov in *The Cherry Orchard* by Chekhov, New York, 1976; Charlie in *Conjuring an Event* by Richard Nelson, New York, 1978; title role in *Chinchilla* by Robert David MacDonald, New York, 1979; *Hamlet*, New York, 1993. **Films**—*An Enemy of the People*, 1976; *The Little Drummer Girl*, 1984; *Die Hard With a Vengeance*, 1994; *GIA*, 1998. **Television**—*Sandburg's Lincoln*, 1975; *Crime Club*, 1975; *The Last of Mrs. Lincoln*, 1975; *The Entertainer*, 1976; *Knuckle*, 1976.

* * *

Michael Cristofer's development as a playwright has included *Plot Counter Plot, The Mandala,* and *Americomedia.* It reached its climax, however, with *The Shadow Box,* which won the Pulitzer Prize and a Tony Award. His development is as instructive a lesson in how to become a playwright as *The Shadow Box* is an exciting addition to modern American drama. Like Harold Pinter and certain other contemporary dramatists, Cristofer also is a gifted actor and, with the Circle in the Square production of Shaw's *Candida,* a talented director, and his own practical experience in the theater is everywhere apparent in the skillful theatricality of *The Shadow Box*. In addition, his association with the Mark Taper Forum and its director Gordon Davidson has provided a unifying center. The coalescence of three one-act plays through a series of workshops into a single contrapuntal drama, *The Shadow Box* is a process seldom possible without a secure producing environment.

The play, apparently based on the terminal illness of two friends and on Elisabeth Kübler-Ross's research into the states of mind of dying patients, demonstrates how the shadow of death intensifies life, merges individuality into community, and reduces times and places into a single here and now. Perhaps reflecting its origin as three one-act draft plays, *The Shadow Box* is built on threes. Cristofer presents a trinity of characters, each surrounded by two other characters important in his personal life: Joe, a blue-collar worker, his wife, and his adolescent son; Brian, an extravagant writer and intellectual, his lover, and his former wife; and Felicity, a lady of uncertain age, and both her spinster daughter and her dead daughter, whose imaginary letters keep her alive. The play's set seems also to be in triplicate: three vacation cottages in the woods in a medically and psychologically controlled estate for the dying, each cottage with "a front porch, a living room area, and a large kitchen area." But it is through the set's omnipresent visual image, and the constant crosscutting this makes possible, that death's power to reduce diversity to communality and a common ground is constantly reiterated. The three cottages are, in effect, presented as one, and as the lights go down and come up, the trio of characters, who never actually meet, alternately inhabit the various playing areas. The pastoral setting and the domesticity made possible by the cottage also unobtrusively place death in the context of external nature and the echoes of everyday life.

If Cristofer has a sure theatrical sense and a feeling for essential dimensions of the human experience, he also has a sense for the other indispensable ingredient of drama—language. Like a number of contemporary playwrights, he has deliberately attempted to reverse the trend toward nonverbal theater—actually the concern of dance—that characterized so much drama in the 1960s and early 1970s. The movement made important contributions but forgot the necessity to be memorably articulate. Cristofer's concern for verbal complexity is apparent immediately in the title *The Shadow Box.* In modern drama especially, a title is an index to a play's concerns, and this one works on several complementary levels of reference. It refers to a late nineteenth-century device in which figures were superimposed against a chosen landscape or setting. The stationary quality of such scenes and their arbitrary arrangement express the predetermined situation of the terminally ill, who are placed in a deliberately arranged environment. The term, which refers as well to a method of covering a motion picture screen so that film can be shown in daylight, expresses the play's analysis of what is usually unseen, and the expression "to shadow box" suggests a fight, like the fight with death, that is ultimately an illusion. If the play begins with an emphasis on words, it ends with an extraordinary coda in which life is celebrated in the face of death. The characters speak in choral fashion, exchanging brief words and phrases and concluding with repetition of the affirmative yes, with the final comment being "This moment."

Ice is set in a cabin in Alaska and shows a trio of characters caught in a situation that symbolizes death in life. The subsequent *Black Angel* and *The Lady and the Clarinet* have been seen in New York, but these somewhat counterpart plays do not sustain the promise of *The Shadow Box*. The former studies a man, Martin Engel, an apparent Nazi war criminal, and analyzes hate, while the latter is a portrait of a woman, Luba, and her experiences with love. It is interesting that both plays suppress facts and narrative clarity and make use of simultaneous time, but in neither case are the central characters themselves created in enough depth or uniqueness to occasion or to support the playwright's relentless analyses of them. But the plays have continued Cristofer's important interest in the collaborative arts of theater.

—Gaynor F. Bradish

CROSS, (Alan) Beverley

Nationality: British. **Born:** London, 13 April 1931; son of the theatrical manager George Cross and the actor Eileen Williams. **Education:** Nautical College, Pangbourne, Berkshire, 1944-47; Balliol College, Oxford, 1952-53. **Military Service:** Served in the Royal Naval Reserve, 1944-48; British Army, 1948-50. **Family:** Married 1) Elizabeth Clunies-Ross in 1955 (marriage dissolved), two daughters; 2) Gayden Collins in 1965 (marriage dissolved), one son; 3) the actress Maggie Smith in 1975. **Career:** Seaman, Norwegian Merchant Service, 1950-52; actor, Shakespeare Memorial Theatre Company, 1954-56; production assistant for children's drama, BBC Television, 1956. Drama consultant, Stratford Festival Theatre, Ontario, 1975-80. **Awards:** Arts Council grant, 1957, and award, 1960. **Agent:** Curtis Brown Group, 162-168 Regent Street, London W1R 5TB, England.

PUBLICATIONS

Plays

One More River (produced Liverpool, 1958; London, 1959; New York, 1960). London, Hart Davis, 1959.
The Singing Dolphin (for children), based on an idea by Kitty Black (produced Oxford, 1959; London, 1963). With *The Three Cavaliers*, London, Hart Davis, 1960.
Strip the Willow (produced Nottingham and London, 1960). London, Evans, 1961.
The Three Cavaliers (for children; produced Birmingham, 1960). With *The Singing Dolphin*, London, Hart Davis, 1960.
Belle; or, The Ballad of Dr. Crippen, with Wolf Mankowitz, music by Monty Norman (produced London, 1961).
Boeing-Boeing, adaptation of a play by Marc Camoletti (produced Oxford, 1961; London, 1962; New York, 1965). London, Evans, and New York, French, 1967.
Wanted on Voyage, adaptation of a play by Jacques Deval (produced Canterbury, 1962).
Half a Sixpence, music by David Heneker, adaptation of the novel *Kipps* by H.G. Wells (produced London, 1963; New York, 1965). London, Chappell, 1967; Chicago, Dramatic Publishing Company, n.d.
The Mines of Sulphur, music by Richard Rodney Bennett (produced London, 1965; New York, 1968). Published in *Plays of the Year 30*, London, Elek, 1965.
The Pirates and the Inca Gold (produced Sydney, 1966).
Jorrocks, music by David Heneker, adaptation of novels by R.S. Surtees (produced London, 1966). London, Chappell, 1968.
All the King's Men (for children), music by Richard Rodney Bennett (produced Coventry and London, 1969). London, Universal Editions, 1969.
Phil the Fluter, with Donal Giltinan, music and lyrics by David Heneker and Percy French (produced London, 1969).
Victory, music by Richard Rodney Bennett, adaptation of the novel by Joseph Conrad (produced London, 1970). London, Universal Editions, 1970.
The Rising of the Moon, music by Nicholas Maw (produced Glyndebourne, Sussex, 1970). London, Boosey and Hawkes, 1971.
Catherine Howard (televised 1970). Published in *The Six Wives of Henry VIII*, edited by J.C. Trewin, London, Elek, 1972; revised version (produced York, 1972), London, French, 1973.
The Crickets Sing (produced Devizes, Wiltshire, 1971). London, Hutchinson, 1970.
The Owl on the Battlements (for children; produced Nottingham, 1971).
Where's Winkle? (for children; produced Liverpool, 1972).
The Great Society (produced London, 1974).
Hans Christian Andersen, with John Fearnley and Tommy Steele, music and lyrics by Frank Loesser (produced London, 1974; revised version produced London, 1976). New York, Music Theatre International, 1978.
The Mask of Orpheus, music by Nicholas Maw. London, Boosey and Hawkes, 1976.
Happy Birthday, adaptation of a play by Marc Camoletti (produced Brighton, 1978; London, 1979). London, French, 1980.
Haworth: A Portrait of the Brontës (produced Stratford, Ontario, 1978; Birmingham, 1981). Toronto, Theatre-books, 1978.
The Scarlet Pimpernel, adaptation of the novel by Baroness Orczy (produced Chichester, Sussex, and London, 1985). London, French, 1988.
Miranda, adaptation of a play by Goldoni (produced Chichester, 1987).

Screenplays: *Jason and the Argonauts*, with Jan Read, 1963; *The Long Ships*, with Berkely Mather, 1964; *Genghis Khan*, with Clarke Reynolds and Berkely Mather, 1965; *Half a Sixpence*, 1967; *The Donkey Rustlers*, 1969; *Mussolini: Ultimo Atto (Mussolini: The Last Act)*, with Carlo Lizzani, 1972; *Sinbad and the Eye of the Tiger*, 1977; *The Clash of the Titans*, 1981.

Television Plays: *The Nightwalkers*, from his own novel, 1960; *The Dark Pits of War*, 1960; *Catherine Howard*, 1970; *March On, Boys!*, 1975; *A Bill of Mortality*, 1975; *Miss Sugar Plum*, 1976 (Canada); *The World Turned Upside Down*, 1976 (USA).

Novels

Mars in Capricorn. London, Hart Davis, and Boston, Little Brown, 1955.
The Nightwalkers. London, Hart Davis, 1956; Boston, Little Brown, 1957.

*

Critical Studies: *Anger and After* by John Russell Taylor, London, Methuen, 1962, revised edition, 1969, as *The Angry Theatre*, New York, Hill and Wang, 1962, revised edition, 1969; introduction by J. C. Trewin to *The Mines of Sulphur*, in *Plays of the Year 30*, London, Elek, 1965.

Theatrical Activities:
Director: **Plays**—*Boeing-Boeing*, Sydney, 1964; *The Platinum Cat* by Roger Longrigg, London, 1965.

Actor: **Plays**—Agamemnon in *Troilus and Cressida*, Oxford, 1953; Soldier in *Othello*, Stratford-on-Avon, 1954; Mr. Fox in *Toad of Toad Hall* by A.A. Milne, London, 1954; Balthazar in *Much Ado about Nothing*, London, 1955; Herald in *King Lear*, London, 1955.

Beverley Cross comments:
Four main divisions of work: 1) for the commercial theatre, viz., books for musicals, boulevard comedies (i.e., *Boeing-Boeing*, *Half a Sixpence*); 2) librettos for modern opera (i.e., *The Mines of Sulphur*, *The Rising of the Moon*); 3) comedies and librettos for children (i.e., *The Three Cavaliers*, *All the King's Men*, *The Owl on the Battlements*); 4) fantasy movies (i.e., *Jason and the Argonauts*, *The Clash of the Titans*, etc).

* * *

Beverley Cross has become best known as a writer of books for popular musicals (*Half a Sixpence*, *Jorrocks*) and of librettos for operas (*Victory*, *The Rising of the Moon*). He has also translated a highly successful boulevard farce (*Boeing-Boeing*), contributed one of the better episodes to a highly successful television series, *The Six Wives of Henry VIII* (*Catherine Howard*), and written several lively, if less obviously successful, plays for children and a small number of commercially unsuccessful plays for adults. What generalizations can be made on the basis of such a spread of work?

First, at his best Cross is capable of writing a vigorous, muscular, masculine dialogue that many more pretentious writers might envy. Second, he is particularly interested in a spirit of adventure that, he feels, no longer exists in the contemporary world and, consequently, in the character of the adventurer himself. It is significant that many of his works are set in other periods. The light children's play *The Singing Dolphin,* for example, is set among pirates in the eighteenth century, and the serious opera *The Mines of Sulphur* takes place a remote country house at about the same time. This latter work, with its forceful language and vivid portrayal of a murderer who traps a troupe of wandering actors and is then trapped by them, shows Cross at his strongest. Another of his works is set in the future:

> No planes to spoil the view. No trippers to litter the grass. No stinking petrol fumes to poison the air. No silly women to bitch away your time with their gossip and intrigue. Nothing to read, nothing to see. Complete freedom for the first time in my life. It's wonderful!

These lines are spoken by a character in *Strip the Willow,* a rather inconclusive quasi-Shavian comedy of ideas that involves a tiny group of survivors of nuclear desolation who live deep in the English countryside and survive by their wits while the Russians and Americans divide the world between them. The sentiment, however, could be Cross's own.

Cross has written only one artistically successful play for adults, and that is his first, *One More River.* It is characteristic in that it occurs on a ship moored in a backwater on another continent and involves a mutiny. The seamen, among whom egalitarian notions have been circulating, turn on an unpopular officer and hang him on the false suspicion of having caused the death of one of their number. But they do not have the ability to exercise power and are ignominiously forced to get an apprentice officer to navigate them upriver. The story is excitingly told, and some of the characterization, notably that of a self-satisfied, popularity-seeking boatswain, is as good as some of it is melodramatic. But what makes the play interesting is its unfashionable viewpoint. Carefully and logically, it suggests that absolute democracy is mob rule, that some men are superior to others and that the others must submit to their authority. It is, of course, possible to pick holes in the argument as it emerges. For instance, Cross does not face the possibility that the seamen's apparent inferiority may be less innate than the result of an unjust environment. The achievement stands, however, for *One More River* is one of the very few intelligent right-wing plays that the modern theater has produced.

—Benedict Nightingale

D

DANIELS, Sarah

Nationality: British. **Born:** London in 1957. **Career:** Writer-in-residence, Royal Court Theatre, London, 1984. **Awards:** George Devine award, 1983. **Agent:** Alan Radcliff, ICM, Oxford House, 76 Oxford Street, London W1N OAX, England.

Publications

Plays

Penumbra (produced Sheffield, 1981).
Ripen Our Darkness (produced London, 1981). With *The Devil's Gateway*, London, Methuen, 1986.
Ma's Flesh Is Grass (produced Sheffield, 1981).
The Devil's Gateway (produced London, 1983). With *Ripen Our Darkness*, London, Methuen, 1986.
Masterpieces (produced Manchester and London, 1983). London, Methuen, 1984; revised version (produced London, 1984), 1984, revised version, 1986.
Neaptide (produced London, 1986). London, Methuen, 1986.
Byrthrite (produced London, 1986). London, Methuen, 1987.
The Gut Girls (produced London, 1988). London, Methuen, 1989.
Beside Herself (produced London, 1990). London, Methuen, 1990.
Plays One (includes *Ripen Our Darkness*; *The Devil's Gateway*; *Masterpieces*; *Neaptide*; *Byrthrite*). London, Methuen, 1991.
Head-Rot Holiday (produced London, 1992). London, Methuen, 1994.
Plays Two (includes *The Gut Girls*; *Beside Herself*; *Head-rot Holiday*; *The Madness of Esme and Shaz*). London, Methuen, 1994.
The Madness of Esme and Shaz (produced London, 1994).
Blow Your House Down (produced Newcastle-upon-Tyne, 1995).
Purple Side Coasters (radio play). Published in *Mythic Women, Real Woman,* edited by Lizbeth Goodman, London, Faber and Faber, 1998.

Radio Play: *Purple Side Coasters,* 1996.

*

Critical Studies: "Sarah Daniels: A Woman in the Moon" by Framji Minwalla, in *Theater* (New Haven, Connecticut), Summer-Fall 1990, pp. 26-29; "Doing the Dirty Work: Gendered Versions of Working Class Women in Sarah Daniels' *The Gut Girls* and Israel Horovitz's *North Shore Fish*" by Susan C. Haedicke, in *Journal of Dramatic Theory and Criticism* (Lawrence, Kansas), Spring 1994, pp. 77-88; "Extremities and Masterpieces: A Feminist Paradigm of Art and Politics" by Tracy C. Davis, in *Feminist Theatre and Theory,* edited by Helene Keyssar, New York, St. Martin's, 1996; "Return to the Mother: The Mother and Daughter Relationship in *Neaptide*" by Moonyoung Chung, in *Journal of English Language and Literature* (Korea), 1997, pp. 105-27.

* * *

When Sarah Daniels's work is mentioned in some critical and academic circles, discussion will often focus on politics rather than on form or style. But Daniels is, in fact, an innovative and gifted writer. Her work provides its own evidence of the stylistic force she brings to bear on her chosen subject. She also tends to choose controversial subjects.

There are those critics (mostly men) who find her work alarming in its representations of strong women, confused women, complicated women, and angry women. Daniels's plays rarely portray strong men, unless we count men who abuse their positions of power. In this she is accused of misconstruing the real, of allowing her feminist anger to stand in the way of writing "good theater." But Daniels's work is not purposefully angry or intentionally controversial in critical terms. She writes about issues of social importance. The urgency of her subject matter lends an urgency of tone to the work.

One suspects that a good deal of the critical alarm with which some of Daniels's work has been received is a reaction to the centrality of women in the plays and to Daniels's style, which tends to be informed by street smarts rather than by academic ideas about "aesthetic standards." Yet Daniels's plays need no apology, for her work is highly innovative in its self-consciously radical approach to the representation of social issues of relevance to her audiences. Daniels's work is powerful: sometimes raw, sometimes uncomfortably close to reality. Her writing is fueled by her awareness of the complexity of life in the modern world, of different forms of sexual and racial discrimination, and of class distinctions and divisions. Most importantly, however, Daniels's writing is invested with two qualities rare in contemporary play writing: a penchant for black humor and a strength and depth of vision—unacademic, straightforward, positioned, and determined—which allows Daniels to touch on subjects that others tend to gloss over or avoid altogether.

The best known and most controversial of her plays is *Masterpieces* (1984). The central character is Rowena, a woman who watches a snuff film and is so upset by it that she cannot separate the brutal sexual murder she witnessed on screen and the threat of real violence outside the cinema. When a stranger accosts her in the subway station, she reacts in automatic self-defense and pushes him away. He stumbles and falls to his death on the subway tracks. The play shifts back and forth between exchanges with Rowena, her partner, and friends. All have different experiences of pornography, and all have difficulty seeing the issue objectively. Finally, Rowena is tried for the murder of the stranger. She does not deny shoving him but cites legal precedents in which men found guilty of murder were let off due to "nagging wives." At the play's end, Rowena describes the snuff film in graphic detail to the policewoman who waits with her for the verdict. Her final words are chilling: "I don't want anything to do with men who have knives or whips or men who look at photos of women tied and bound, or men who say relax and enjoy it. Or men who tell misogynist jokes."

Masterpieces is unsettling, not only because it deals with the issue of pornography but because it challenges the distinction between "soft porn" and "hard porn." In Rowena's final words, the play suggests that the continuum from sexist jokes to real sexual violence against women is a dangerous and real one. In this way the play depicts and challenges aspects of contemporary controversy regarding pornography. Years after its first production *Masterpieces* continued to be frequently produced, particularly by student and community theater groups as an impetus to academic debate and social action.

Neaptide is, after *Masterpieces,* Daniels's best-known and most important play. In *Neaptide,* Daniels tells the story of Claire, a woman who hides her sexual identity in order to protect her job and thereby support her young daughter. Claire is a teacher in a small secondary school torn between defending the rights of a few lesbian pupils and remaining silent so as to keep her sexual preference secret from her peers. While she is involved in a potential child-custody case, the pressure to "appear normal" is great. Meanwhile, she reads the myth of Persephone. The ending of the play is optimistic but not overly so. Only individual women transcend such limitations: the lesbian pupils are saved when the principal of the school admits her own homosexuality and the mother comes out of the proverbial closet and decides to fight for her child. The myth functions as a convenient analogue to contemporary problems but not as an oversimplified model of a social corrective, nor as an all-encompassing statement about the function of roles.

In all her plays Sarah Daniels takes issues of real importance to women's lives and places them at center stage. Her plays are not easily pigeonholed. They cannot quite be called "great drama" and are sometimes difficult to justify for inclusion on university reading lists. Yet Daniels's plays teach more about the power of the theater, and of the written word, than do many of the texts studied in the average classroom. Her plays (*Esme and Shaz, Blow Your House Down,* and *Purple Side Coasters*) all have a great deal to say about the valuing of female experience in a society that claims to have addressed gender imbalances but still has a long way to go before that claim will be justified. Her work is difficult and controversial in the most positive, change-oriented sense.

—Lizbeth Goodman

DARKE, Nick

Nationality: British. **Born:** Wadebridge, Cornwall, 29 August 1948. **Education:** Newquay Grammar School, Cornwall; Rose Bruford College, Sidcup, Kent, 1967-70, diploma 1970. **Family:** Has two sons. **Career:** Actor in repertory, Belfast, 1970; actor and director, Victoria Theatre, Stoke-on-Trent, Staffordshire, 1971-79. **Awards:** George Devine award, 1979. **Agent:** Casarotto Ramsay Ltd., National House, 60-66 Wardour Street, London W1V 3HP. **Address:** St. Julians, Sevenoaks, Kent TN15 0RX, England.

Publications

Plays

Mother Goose (pantomime; also director: produced Stoke-on-Trent, 1977).
Never Say Rabbit in a Boat (produced Stoke-on-Trent, 1978).
Landmarks (produced Chester and London, 1979).
A Tickle on the River's Back (produced London, 1979).
Summer Trade (produced Ilfracombe, Devon, 1979).
High Water (produced Newcastle upon Tyne and London, 1980). Published in *Plays Introduction*, London, Faber, 1984.
Say Your Prayers, music by Andrew Dickson (produced Plymouth and London, 1981).
The Catch (produced London, 1981).
The Lowestoft Man (produced on tour, 1982).
The Body, music by Guy Woolfenden (produced London, 1983). London, Methuen, 1983.
Cider with Rosie, adaptation of the work by Laurie Lee (produced Manchester, 1983).
The Earth Turned Inside Out (produced St. Austell, Cornwall, 1984).
Bud (produced Newcastle upon Tyne and London, 1985). Included in *Ting Tang Mine and Other Plays*, 1987.
The Oven Glove Murders (produced London, 1986).
The Dead Monkey (produced London, 1986). Included in *Ting Tang Mine and Other Plays*, 1987.
Ting Tang Mine (produced St. Austell, Cornwall, 1987; revised version produced London, 1987). Included in *Ting Tang Mine and Other Plays*, 1987.
Ting Tang Mine and Other Plays (includes *The Dead Monkey, Bud*). London, Methuen, 1987.
Campesinos (produced Stratford-on-Avon, 1989).
Kissing the Pope (produced London, 1989). Included in *Kissing the Pope: A Play and a Diary for Nicaragua*, London, Hern, 1990.

Radio Plays: *Foggy Anniversary*, 1979; *Lifeboat*, 1981.

Television Play: *Farmers Arms*, 1983.

*

Theatrical Activities:
Director: **Plays**—Victoria Theatre, Stoke-on-Trent: *Mother Goose, Man Is Man* by Brecht, *The Miser* by Molière, *Absurd Person Singular* by Alan Ayckbourn, *The Scarlet Pimpernel,* and *A Cuckoo in the Nest* by Ben Travers, 1977-79.

Actor: Roles in more than 50 plays, Victoria Theatre, Stoke-on-Trent.

Nick Darke comments:

I consider my seven years as an actor to have been an apprenticeship for writing plays. By appearing in over 50 productions of new plays, classics, documentaries, children's plays, and community road-shows I learned firsthand the difference between good and bad dialogue, how to create characters and construct a world for the play to exist in. Most of my plays make people laugh, but I try to make an audience question its laughter. I have a low boredom threshold, and my interest in my plays lasts for exactly as long as it takes me to write them. I have strong ideas about how they should be cast and directed, and I watch them in performance to see how the audience reacts. After that my interest wanes and the next one has to be different in every respect to the last. I write quickly: the quicker it's written, the better the play. I think about a play for far longer than it takes me to write it. I type as fast as my brain works, so I dispense with the longhand stage and work straight onto the keyboard. I read my work out loud as I write it. For this reason I have to work entirely alone and out of earshot. I don't just mouth what I've written, if a scene demands decibels I supply them. If it's funny, I laugh. To see an audience laugh at something as much as I did when I first thought of it is a pleasure only another playwright could understand. I judge the success of my plays from the audience's response. My agent reads and sees my work, and I disregard her advice at my peril; she is my most valuable critic. I don't know what is a good play and what isn't. I don't know what makes some people like a play and others not. Some nights a whole audience will dislike a play, the next night they'll love it, with no perceptible change in the performance. My plays tend to be ambiguous, and because the style alters with each one, nobody knows what to expect. This makes for hair-raising volatility which I don't like, but can't help. My advice to a budding playwright: Cultivate your sense of rhythm, and never go into rehearsal without a good ending.

* * *

Nick Darke, who started his theatrical career as an actor at the Victoria Theatre in Stoke-on-Trent, seems to launch himself into writing plays rather as if he were working on new roles. Energetic, versatile, imaginative, inventive, eclectic, and insatiably hungry for identifications that let him disappear into a disguise, he slips unrecognizably from one style, one period, and one setting to another. *The Dead Monkey* is set in contemporary California, *Ting Tang Mine* goes back to an early nineteenth-century Cornish copper-mining community, and *A Tickle on the River's Back* takes place on a Thames barge, while the setting for *The Oven Glove Murders* is a Soho film production company. Darke lodges himself in contrasting idioms like an actor who is good at accents.

His plays, almost without exception, contain sequences that are extremely suspenseful and others that are extremely funny, but even in his best plays, such as *The Body* and *The Dead Monkey*, the writing sometimes sinks too far below the level he is capable of achieving. The funniest sequences in *The Body* occur in the first half, which climaxes in a hilarious scene involving a muddy, half-naked corpse, a farmer who is also muddy and half-naked because he is impersonating the corpse, a cat that has just been strangled, a rat trap, an old man wearing a gas mask, an old woman who believes that she may have been touched by divinity, three farmers who speak verse in unison, and a policeman who is trying to arrest all of the villagers simultaneously. Less amusing and more suspenseful, the second half of the play is set on a U.S. air base. It works toward a climax that centers on the probability of a nuclear explosion as a young Cornish farmer, brainwashed into believing that he is an American soldier, brandishes a loaded machine gun and hesitates whether to obey the orders of a sane sergeant or of a demented lieutenant who has been tied up and blindfolded but not—this was the sergeant's mistake—gagged.

The plot also introduces a rector who dresses as a mandarin, realizing that his parishioners pay no attention to him. They listen if he harangues them in Chinese, but all of this is not entirely irrelevant to the plot since it convinces the psychopathic lieutenant, who suspects Reds under the unlikeliest of beds, that Chinese infiltration is converting the villagers to Maoism. The solution is to ask them whether they are communist and to shoot them if they deny it.

Darke's hostility to nuclear weapons, Americans, policemen, soldiers, and capitalism is rather generalized, and his writing sags under its heavy burden of literary influences and bizarre jokes. The most obvious debt is to Brecht, who was himself indebted to Kipling for the three soldiers in *Mann ist Mann* who brainwash a civilian into taking on the identity of a missing comrade. The play also seems to have been influenced by the Auden and Isherwood of *The Dog beneath the Skin*, by the Stoppard of *After Magritte*, and by the T. S. Eliot of the verse plays.

The Dead Monkey is a funnier, more consistent play, more accomplished, less patchy, and less eclectic, though the rhythms of Tennessee Williams and Edward Albee are sometimes audible. We also feel that, as in some of the morbid coups de théâtre of *The Body*, Darke is trying to make us shudder. The play opens with the monkey dead on the table. Later on in the act we learn that Dolores, the wife of an unsuccessful commercial traveler, has been supplementing her income by performing sexual tricks with the monkey. Toward the end of the act the monkey, which may have died from the physical strain, is cooked and eaten by husband and wife.

It must be conceded, however, that, even if Darke is trying too hard to shock, he has succeeded better than any young playwright since Stephen Poliakoff and that the play is still richer in surprising dramatic twists than in shock effects. The plot pulls the couple through a taxing series of changing situations so that, as in a play by Strindberg, they become almost like new people as they react to changes in their partner. Lingering love gradually gives way to implacable hatred, but the savagery of Hank's physical attack on Dolores takes us by surprise. Eventually we see her lying dead on the table in the same position as the monkey, but the aggressive husband then starts talking to his dead wife, apologizing, pleading with her to come back, and reminding her of what she said after the animal's death. Perhaps it was looking down on them, and perhaps she is now too, while he pulls the dead body off the table and clings to it as if dancing.

Like the imaginary child in Albee's *Who's Afraid of Virginia Woolf?* the monkey and the Macedonian curly pig they adopt to replace it are emblems of what is missing from their relationship. The borrowing is unimportant, however, in comparison with the success achieved in the sharply written sequences of marital bickering and in the chemical changes that occur in Dolores's personality and in the relationship when a good-paying job lifts her into a position financially superior to Hank's. An acute observer of the effects that money and social prestige have on sexual relationships, Darke has taken his eclecticism into his stride.

—Ronald Hayman

DAVIS, Jack (Leonard)

Nationality: Australian; member of Bibbulmun tribe. **Born:** Perth, Western Australia, 11 March 1917. **Education:** Yarloop State School; Perth Technical College. **Career:** Worked as a stockman in North West Australia; director, Aboriginal Centre, Perth, 1967-71; managing editor, Aboriginal Publications Foundation, 1972-77; joint editor, *Identity* magazine, Perth, 1973-79; teacher of creative writing, Murdoch University, Western Australia. Director and president, Aboriginal Advancement Council, 1967 and 1972; first chair, Aboriginal Lands Trust, 1971; president, Aboriginal Writers and Dramatists Association, 1980-84; member, Australia Council Aboriginal Arts Board, 1983-1988. **Awards:** British Empire medal, 1977; Weickhardt award, 1980; Sidney Myer award, 1985; Australian Writers Guild award, 1986; BHP Bicentennial award, 1988; Federal creative fellowship, 1989; Ruth Adeney

Koori award, 1992. D. Litt.: Murdoch University, 1985. **Member:** A.M. (Order of Australia), 1985. **Address:** 22 Knutsford Avenue, Rivervale, Perth, Western Australia.

Publications

Plays

The Dreamers (produced 1973; revised version produced Perth, 1982; Portsmouth, Hampshire, 1987). With *Kullark (Home)*, Sydney, Currency Press, 1982.
Kullark (Home) (produced 1978). With *The Dreamers*, Sydney, Currency Press, 1982.
No Sugar (produced Perth, 1985). Sydney, Currency Press, 1986.
Honey Spot (for children; produced Adelaide, 1985).
Moorli and the Leprechaun (for children; produced 1986). Sydney, Currency Press, 1994.
Barungin (Smell the Wind) (produced Perth, 1988). Sydney, Currency Press, 1989.
In Our Town (produced Perth, 1990). Sydney, Currency Perth, 1992.

Poetry

The First-Born and Other Poems. Sydney and London, Angus and Robertson, 1970.
Jagardoo: Poems from Aboriginal Australia. Sydney, Methuen, 1977.
Black Life. St. Lucia, University of Queensland Press, 1992.

Other

Aboriginal Writing Today: Papers from the First National Conference of Aboriginal Writers. Canberra, Australian Institute of Aboriginal Studies, 1985.

Editor, with others, *Paperback: A Collection of Black Australian Writings*. St. Lucia, University of Queensland Press, 1990.

*

Critical Studies: "Black America and the Australian Aboriginal Literary Consciousness" by Emmanuel S. Nelson, in *Westerly: A Quarterly Review* (Nedlands, Australia), December 1985, pp. 43-54; "Aboriginal Australian Dramatists" by Cliff Watego, in *Community Theatre in Australia*, edited by Richard Fotheringham, Sydney, Methuen, 1987; *Jack Davis: A Life Story* by Keith Chesson, Melbourne, Dent, 1988; "Hybridity in Jack Davis's *No Sugar*" by Brian Dibble and Margaret MacIntyre, in *Westerly: A Quarterly Review* (Nedlands, Australia), Summer 1992, pp. 93-98; "Intercultural Exchange between Ethnic Minority and English Language Majority: The Writing of Jack Davis and Witi Ihimaera" by Dieter Riemenschneider, in *Imagination and the Creative Impulse in the New Literatures in English,* edited by M. T. Bindella and G. V. Davis, Amsterdam, Rodopi, 1993; "Jack Davis and the Emergence of Aboriginal Writing" by Bob Hodge, in *Critical Survey* (Oxford, England), 1994, pp. 98-104; *Brodie's Notes on Jack Davis's No Sugar* by Peter Carmody, South Melbourne, Victoria, Macmillan Education Australia, 1994; *Jack Davis: The Maker of History,* edited by Gerry Turcotte, Sydney, New South Wales, Angus & Robertson, 1994; "White Forms, Aboriginal Content" by Mudrooroo, in *The Post Colonial Studies Reader,* Routledge, 1995; *Australian Brodie's Notes on Jack Davis, Stephen Muecke, Mudrooroo Narogin, and Adam Shoemaker* by Phil Stabback, South Melbourne, Victoria, Macmillan, 1998.

* * *

Jack Davis was 56 years old before he tried his hand at playwriting and over 60 before he gained a professional production. He had published short stories and two books of poetry, but as a black activist in Australia he discovered late in life that the theater was the right forum for his work.

Davis's early childhood was spent in the forest country of southwestern Western Australia and his young adult life on sheep stations in the northern Gascoigne region. But part of his early life was also spent at the Moore River Native Settlement under the notorious Western Australian Aboriginal Protection Act, which once forced blacks onto government reserves, banned fraternization with whites, and separated families for the purpose of educating the children in the white way of life. These experiences are the material of his poetry and plays.

Since Davis first came to national attention with his play *Kullark* in 1978, his work has focused on bridging the gap of understanding between black and white values. For this he has received many awards from the white community, including an honorary doctorate in letters and the Order of Australia. He is not the first Aborigine to have worked in the theater, but he is the first to produce a body of work at the forefront of Australian drama. His plays have been the occasion for creating a training ground for black actors in Western Australia and a growing demand for their performances.

Davis's first play was *The Dreamers*, a short piece performed by an amateur group in 1973 and later revised into a full-length work. A meeting with the director Andrew Ross, then working in Perth, led to the production of *Kullark* in 1979 and to a long professional association that had an important influence upon Davis's new direction as a writer. *Kullark* is a polemical work that gathers together a variety of Aboriginal experiences at the hands of whites: fatal misunderstandings in the early settlement period; the evacuation of blacks from country towns during the Great Depression; life under the protection laws; the granting of citizenship rights to returned soldiers; and the round of grog, poverty, and prison that has customarily made up Aboriginal family life on the fringes of white society. What stands out from the basic narrative form of his early work are the revelations about the life he himself knew: the indigenous humor, the forbearance, and the brawling acts of frustration instinctively expressed in comic and dramatic dialogue.

These qualities show a marked advance in Davis's next play, *The Dreamers*, a domestic drama of the Wallitch family. It includes two school-age children coping with a white educational system, two layabouts on the dole and a young and ambitious public servant, and a dispirited father and a mother who, like all of the women in Davis's plays, bears the heat and burden of the day. Uncle Worru, patriarch and storyteller, is the family's link with their Aboriginal identity and heritage, and his death brings the play to a close. As he fades from his surroundings, his spirit retreats into the tribal past. This atavistic theme mingles with the modern in the form of a tribal dancer who haunts old Worru's thoughts and ritually signals his passing, demonstrating to the white audience that the familial and telepathic links of the old society are still an important element in black consciousness.

No Sugar returns to the theme of black oppression on the Moore River Native Settlement in a fuller and more refined form. The Millimurras are a happy-go-lucky family who live in a tent on the Northam reserve, about 60 miles east of Perth. Their peace is disrupted when they are ordered to Moore River, where they are subjected to many indignities in the name of hygiene and Christianity. Jimmy, the uncle, is a rebel and humorist who keeps the family's spirits up until he dies at an Australia Day ceremony; Gran is a reprobate who plays the system. In the center is the love story of Joe and Mary, who run away back to the old free life.

Concurrent with *No Sugar* came *Honey Spot*, a children's play about a white ranger's daughter and a black family who rendezvous in the bush to invent a dance for the girl's ballet examination. Each side is at sea with the other's form of dance, but together they learn a mutual accommodation.

Barungin deals with the death while in detention of a young man arrested on suspicion of receiving stolen goods. Along with *The Dreamers* and *No Sugar,* it completes a trilogy on the status of Aborigines called *The First-Born. Barungin* is the most directly political of Davis's plays. The theme is the high incidence of black deaths in police custody, the subject of a long-running judicial inquiry. It was first performed in the Australian bicentennial year of 1988, which Aborigines declared a year of mourning, and the play begins and ends with a funeral ritual. The name Wallitch means "nighthawk," the symbol of death, and the young man's life takes on the whole race memory of deaths at the hands of whites. The word *Barungin*, or "smell the wind," literally refers to Aboriginal sensibilities and survival skills and metaphorically to the stench of black corpses that have littered Australian history.

In Our Town again examines life in a country town and contrasts sterile white conformity with the humorous, generous, feckless nature of Aboriginal family life. The time is 1946. David Millimurra and his white mate Larry have just been discharged from the army. David is planning to start farm contract work and to buy a house for his extended family, which is still living on the Aboriginal reserve. Larry's sister Sue is attracted to David, but his status as a citizen and returned serviceman is soon undermined by the white community, which conspires against the friendships and David's plans. Sue takes up his cause, and together they resolve to face the town prejudice and work for better understanding.

—Katharine Brisbane

DAVIS, Ossie

Nationality: American. **Born:** Cogdell, Georgia, 18 December 1917. **Education:** Waycross High School, Georgia; Howard University, Washington, D.C., 1935-39; Columbia University, New York, 1948; studied acting with Paul Mann and Lloyd Richards. **Military Service:** Served in the United States Army, 1942-45: surgical technician. **Family:** Married Ruby Ann Wallace (i.e., the actress Ruby Dee) in 1948; two daughters and one son. **Career:** Janitor and clerk, New York, 1938-41; member of the Rose McClendon Players, Harlem, New York, 1940-42; then writer, actor, and director; off-Broadway stage manager, 1954-55; co-host, *Ossie Davis and Ruby Dee Story Hour* and *With Ossie and Ruby* television programs; founded Emmalyn Enterprises with his wife Ruby Dee. **Awards:** Frederick Douglass award, 1970; Emmy award, for acting, 1970; American Library Association Coretta Scott King award, for children's book, 1979; inducted into the NAACP Image Award Hall of Fame, 1989. **Agent:** The Artists Agency, 10000 Santa Monica Boulevard, Suite 305, Los Angeles, California 90067, U.S.A. **Address:** P.O. Box 1318, New Rochelle, New York 10802, U.S.A.

Publications

Plays

Goldbrickers of 1944 (produced in Liberia, 1944).
Alice in Wonder (produced New York, 1952; revised version, as *The Big Deal*, produced New York, 1953).
Purlie Victorious (produced New York, 1961). New York, French, 1961; revised version, with Philip Rose and Peter Udell, music by Gary Geld, as *Purlie* (produced New York, 1970), New York, French, 1970.
Curtain Call, Mr. Aldridge, Sir (produced New York, 1963). Published in *The Black Teacher and the Dramatic Arts*, edited by William R. Reardon and Thomas D. Pawley, Westport, Connecticut, Negro Universities Press, 1970.
Escape to Freedom: A Play about Young Frederick Douglass (for children; produced New York, 1976). New York, Viking Press, 1978.
Langston (for children). New York, Delacorte Press, 1982.
Bingo!, with Hy Gilbert, music by George Fischoff, lyrics by Gilbert, adaptation of a play by William Brashler (also director: produced New York, 1985).

Screenplays: *Gone Are the Days!*, 1963; *Cotton Comes to Harlem*, with others, 1970; *Black Girl*, with J. E. Franklin, 1973; *Countdown at Kusini*, with others, 1976.

Television Writing: *Schoolteacher*, 1963; *Just Say the Word*, 1969; *Today Is Ours*, 1974; *For Us the Living*, 1983; scripts for *Bonanza*; *NYPD*; *East Side, West Side*; and *The Eleventh Hour* series.

Other

Just Like Martin (novel). Simon and Schuster, n.d.

*

Critical Study: "An Interview with Ossie Davis" by Dwight E. Greer, in *High Plains Literary Review* (Denver, Colorado), Spring 1994, pp. 74-80.

Theatrical Activities:
Director: **Plays**—*Take It from the Top* by Ruby Dee, New York, 1979; *Bingo!*, New York, 1985. **Films**—*Cotton Comes to Harlem*, 1970; *Kongi's Harvest*, 1970; *Black Girl*, 1973; *Gordon's War*, 1973; *Countdown at Kusini*, 1976. **Television**—*The Perpetual People Puzzle* (co-director), 1972; *Today Is Ours*, 1974.

Actor: **Plays**—In *Joy Exceeding Glory*, New York, 1941; title role in *Jeb* by Robert Ardrey, New York, 1946; Rudolf in *Anna Lucasta* by Philip Yordan, toured, 1947; Trem in *The Leading Lady* by Ruth Gordon, New York, 1948; Lonnie Thompson in *Stevedore* by George Sklar and Paul Peters, New York, 1948; Stewart in *The Smile of the World* by Garson Kanin, New York, 1949; Jacques in *The Wisteria Trees* by Joshua Logan, New York, 1950, 1955; Jo in *The Royal Family* by George S. Kaufman and Edna Ferber, New York, 1951; Gabriel in *The Green Pastures* by Marc Connelly, New York, 1951; Al in *Remains to be Seen* by Howard Lindsay and Russel Crouse, New York, 1951; Dr. Joseph Clay in *Touchstone* by William Stucky, New York, 1953; The Lieutenant in *No Time for Sergeants* by Ira Levin, New York, 1955; Cicero in *Jamaica* by E. Y. Harburg and Fred Saidy, New York, 1957; Walter Lee Younger in *A Raisin in the Sun* by Lorraine Hansberry, New York, 1959; Purlie in *Purlie Victorious*, New York, 1961; Sir Radio in *Ballad for Bimshire* by Loften Mitchell, New York, 1963; in *A Treasury of Negro World Literature*, toured, 1964; Johannes in *The Zulu and the Zayda* by Howard DaSilva and Felix Leon, New York, 1965; *Take It from the Top* by Ruby Dee, New York, 1979; Midge in *I'm Not Rappaport* by Herb Gardner, New York, 1987. **Films**—*No Way Out*, 1950; *Fourteen Hours*, 1951; *The Joe Louis Story*, 1953; *The Cardinal*, 1963; *Gone Are the Days!*, 1963; *Shock Treatment*, 1964; *The Hill*, 1965; *A Man Called Adam*, 1966; *The Scalphunters*, 1968; *Slaves*, 1969; *Sam Whiskey*, 1969; *Let's Do It Again*, 1975; *Countdown at Kusini*, 1976; *Hot Stuff*, 1980; *Harry and Son*, 1984; *Avenging Angel*, 1985; *I'm Not Rappaport* by Herb Gardner, 1986; *School Daze*, 1988; *Do the Right Thing*, 1989; *Jungle Fever*, 1991; *Grumpy Old Men*; *The Client*; *Get On the Bus*. **Television**—*The Green Pastures* (*Showtime* series), 1951; *The Emperor Jones* (*Kraft Theater* series), 1955; *The Defenders* series, 1961-65; *Death Is the Door Price* (*The Fugitive* series), 1966; *The Outsider*, 1967; *The Third Choice* (*The Name of the Game* series), 1969; *Night Gallery* series, 1969; *Teacher, Teacher*, 1969; *The Sheriff*, 1971; *Billy: Portrait of a Street Kid*, 1980; *Roots: The Next Generation*, 1981; *King*, 1981; *The Tenth Level*, 1984; *Seven Times Monday*; *The Doctors*; *The Nurses*; *Twelve O'clock High*; *Bonanza*; *Hawaii Five-O*; *All God's Children* series; *Evening Shade*; *The Stand*; *Mrs. Evers Boys*.

* * *

Ossie Davis is extraordinary on two counts. Loften Mitchell says in *Black Drama*, "This tall, intelligent, graying, proud man came into the theater, interested in writing. Fortunately and unfortunately, it was learned that he is a good actor—a phenomenon rare for a writer, and detrimental as well. Mr. Davis went on to job after job working regularly as a Negro actor, never quite getting as much writing done as he wanted to do." Despite his greater acclaim as director and actor, however, two of his plays are lasting contributions to dramatic literature.

The early 1950s were difficult years for black playwrights to try to get their works produced. One of the plays that did happen to make the boards—directed and produced in September 1952 in Harlem by the playwright and his friends Maxwell Glanville, Julian Mayfield, and Mitchell, among others—was Davis's *Alice in Wonder*. The production, impoverished as it was, also included two of Mayfield's one-acters, *A World Full of Men* and *The Other Foot*. At the Elks Community Theater the talented group of spirited black artists "ushered in a hit show with few people in the audience," as Mitchell put it in *Crisis* in March 1972. Davis's charming play was eventually optioned off to Stanley Greene and produced successfully in downtown New York. Davis later expanded it into a full piece, *The Big Deal*.

Alice in Wonder, a reputable beginning for a gifted man, is a delightful piece. It is set in upper Harlem, "Cadillac country," as Davis calls it. Alice (Ruby Dee in the original production) sees her husband Jay (Glanville) given a sizable contract by one of the leading television networks. In the meantime Alice's brother (Ed Cambridge) has involved himself in a number of political affairs, one of which is an effort to restore the passport of a militant black singer. The network director asks Jay to go to Washington to testify before a government committee and to denounce the singer. Complications arise and Alice, who refuses to compromise her principles, sees that Jay is about to "sell out." She packs up and leaves. The ethos of this play is racial tension and all that it means, and it showed what Davis could do as a writer.

Purlie Victorious, which was warmly received by the alert New York critics at its opening at the Cort Theater on 29 September 1961, moved beyond an embryonic idea of laughter as a cure for racial bigotry to became a dramatic experiment and an artistic dream. The play is farcical, mocking, sparkling, resounding in ethnic wit, rapid, and unyielding as satire. Purlie Judson, a man of impatience with a flowery evangelical style and moved by a messianic mission for his race ("Who else is they got?") goes south determined to turn Big Bethel, an old barn, back into a church as an integrated symbol of freedom. Every racial cliché of southern and of northern life—the white pro-Confederate colonel, the Jim Crow system, the colored mammy and all the image brings to mind, the Uncle Tom figure, the plantation store, the parochial cop, the stalking country sheriff, the NAACP, the Supreme Court, the church—and all they symbolize in both the white man's and the black man's psychology—integration, constitutional rights—are given a Swiftian examination. *Purlie Victorious* is a series of irresistible mirrors in which men are forced to see the folly of hatred, the insanity of bigotry, and the fruitlessness of theories of racial supremacy. As Davis himself has said, "What else can I do but laugh? . . . The play is an attempt, a final attempt to hold that which is ridiculous up to ridicule—to round up all the indignities I have experienced in my own country and to laugh them out of existence."

The dialogue is scintillating, poetic, and realistic. There are many puns, ironic uses of idiomatic expressions, and an acute awareness of the black American's sense of melody and rhythm. The satire is sharply focused with the clever use of malapropisms and misnomers:

> This is outrageous—This is a catastrophe! You're a disgrace to the Negro profession! . . . That's just what she said all right—her exactly words. . . . When I think of his grandpaw, God rest his Confederate soul, hero of the Battle of Chickamauga. . . . My ol' Confederate father told me on his deathbed: Feed the Negroes first—after the horses and cattle—and I've done it evah time! . . . You know something, I've been after these Negroes down here for years: Go to school, I'd say, first chance you get—take a coupla courses in advanced cotton picking. But you'd think they'd listen to me: No sireebob. By swickety!

Like many other comic works *Purlie Victorious* is an angry play. Davis allows his anger to smolder through a gem-lit comedy, and he permits his work to romp and bound through southern settings and bromidic racial situations of the most impoverished and demeaning variety. But Davis is ever in control. Like Molière he knows that people laugh at beatings, mistaken identities, disguises, clever repartee, buffoonery, indecency, and themselves when taken off guard. Thus, the satire, which is ever corrective in the hands of an artist, is both crude and polished in aiming its fire at personal and general prejudices.

The struggle to keep the mask in place in comedy becomes a conflict between intelligence and character, craft and habit, art and nature. In Davis's principles of writing and performing there is a beautiful balance between poetry and realism.

—Louis D. Mitchell

De GROEN, Alma

Nationality: New Zealander. **Born:** Alma Mathers, Foxton, 5 September 1941. **Education:** Mangakino District High School, Waikato, 1954-57. **Family:** Married Geoffrey De Groen in 1965; one daughter. **Career:** Library assistant, New Zealand National Library Service, Wellington and Hamilton, 1958-64; library assistant, Sydney University library, Australia, 1964-65; librarian, New Zealand Trade Commission, Sydney, 1965; writer-in-residence, West Australian Institute of Technology, Perth, 1986; dramaturg, Griffin Theatre Company, Sydney, 1987; writer-in-residence, University of Queensland, St. Lucia, 1989, and Rollins College, Florida, 1989. **Awards:** Canada Council grant, 1970; Australian Writers Guild award, 1985; New South Wales Premier's award, 1988; Victorian Premier's award, 1988; Australian Writers' Guild award, 1993. **Agent:** Hilary Linstead & Associates, Suite 302, Easts Tower, 9-13 Bronte Road, Bondi Junction, New South Wales 2022, Australia.

PUBLICATIONS

Plays

The Joss Adams Show (produced Toronto, 1970; London, 1974; Brisbane, 1974; Nimrod, 1975). Included in *Going Home and Other Plays*, 1977.
The Sweatproof Boy (produced Sydney, 1972; Perth, 1973).
Perfectly All Right (produced Adelaide, 1973). Included in *Going Home and Other Plays*, 1977.
The After-Life of Arthur Cravan (produced Sydney, 1973; Perth, 1974).
Going Home (produced Melbourne, 1976). Included in *Going Home and Other Plays*, 1977.
Chidley (produced Melbourne, 1977). Published in *Theatre Australia* (Sydney), January/February, 1977; Montmorency, Victoria, Yackandandah Playscripts, 1993.
Going Home and Other Plays. Sydney, Currency Press, 1977.
Vocations (produced Melbourne, 1981). Sydney, Currency Press, 1983. In *Australian Women's Drama: Texts and Feminisms*, 1997.
The Rivers of China (produced Sydney, 1987). Sydney, Currency Press, 1988; in *Australian Plays*, 1989.
The Girl Who Saw Everything (produced Melbourne, 1991).
The Woman in the Window (produced Melbourne, 1998).

Radio Play: *Available Light* (two monologues for women), both 1991; *Stories in the Dark* (ABC radio), 1995.

Television Plays: *Man of Letters*, adaptation of the novel by Glen Tomasatti, 1985; *Chris* (episode) in *Singles* series, 1986; *After Marcuse*, 1986; *The Women* (episode) in *Rafferty's Rules* series, 1987.

*

Critical Studies: *The Plays of Alma De Groen* by Elizabeth Perkins, Amsterdam and Atlanta, Rodopi, 1994.

* * *

Swathed in bandages, the figure of a hospital patient is featured in Alma De Groen's most acclaimed play, *The Rivers of China,* and it provides an appropriate icon for much of her work, which focuses on the more painful moments of human existence while generally rejecting nihilism or despair. Always interested in relationships between the sexes, De Groen frequently foregrounds art as the contested ideological space on and through which male/female conflicts are enacted. She is deeply concerned with the role of the female artist in patriarchal society, exploring this issue not only through dialogue but also in structure that she aims to make exactly parallel to the audience's experience of a particular play. Although she has experimented with naturalism and episodic realism, De Groen's best works achieve a fluidity of form that characterizes the feminist aesthetic in its ability to break down boundaries and challenge conventional expectations.

The Joss Adams Show, an early but very accomplished one-act play, exhibits precisely this fluid movement between time and place, reality and the surreal, as it presents the biting story of a young woman who beats her baby to death while those around her fail to notice how unhappy, trapped, and desperate she feels. Framed by its introduction as a television show, Joss's story positions her husband and relatives, as well as the audience, as voyeuristic accomplices to the baby's beatings. Understated and at times even funny, the narrative clearly lays much of the blame for Joss's actions on the shoulders of an uncaring patriarchal society that provides women with few real economic and social options to cope with neglect and violence.

Going Home and *Vocations* also explore the contemporary woman's search for a meaningful "home," a position or reference point from which to act without being overwhelmed by the demands of a male-dominated society. *Going Home,* which focuses on the relationships among a group of Australians living in Canada, uses the physical exile of its antagonists to stress their alienation from one another and their lack of a sense of identity rooted in place. While the men are caught up in bombast and petty rivalries over their successes and failures as expatriate artists, the women show their dislocation more elliptically through compulsive spending and eating. These symptoms point not only to general unhappiness but also to deeply felt pain that can be linked to emotional trauma and, in Molly's case, even to rape. Although most of the characters idealize the environments they have left behind, the play suggests that "going home" is clearly a problematic process that involves not just physical relocation but also some kind of resolution to the enacted gender conflicts.

Vocations extends some of these themes in its representation of two couples struggling to maintain a meaningful relationship while developing their individual careers. Though the four find some kind of home in artistic expression, the struggle for recognition and independence is clearly much harder for the women. For them home remains an elusive place best posited as a feeling of connectedness with the universe and the self, a space fiercely defended but always vulnerable. In particular, Vicki's profession as an actor is not only compromised by her pregnancy but also by her partner Ross, who is bent on managing the pregnancy, the baby, and everything else. Her friend Joy, a writer, faces similar usurpation when her husband uses her as the subject of his feminist novel, "packag[ing] all her pain" without first feeling it. Much of the dramatic energy of the play results from the women's efforts to resist this appropriation of their space, their vocations, and indeed their bodies. Though richly comic in its depiction's of the battle of the sexes, *Vocations* nonetheless poses some complex questions about what men, as well as women, should be allowed to be.

The Rivers of China marks an important point in De Groen's development as a dramatist. It brings together many of her earlier themes, dealing even more incisively with contemporary sexual politics while merging content with form to create a visually exciting and intellectually provocative play. Indulging her interest in "walking around in other times," here De Groen follows two earlier pieces on historical figures, *Chidley* and *The After-Life of Arthur Cravan,* with an account of the last few months in the life of Katherine Mansfield. Although its major thrust is undoubtedly feminist, *The Rivers of China* also offers powerful moments for postcolonial readings through Mansfield's efforts to delineate a position for the nascent colonial woman artist immured in the territorialized spaces of the imperial patriarchal canon. To recover Mansfield as a historical figure is only one aim of the play. Her story is interwoven with, and indeed transformed by, a contemporary narrative set in a feminist dystopia in present-day Sydney. In this "brave new world" women have physical, economic, and cultural power, while the men continually struggle for recognition and freedom of expression. But the play never suggests that this dystopia is preferable to patriarchal society. Rather, it problematizes simple inversions of the current power structure by re-creating Mansfield's mind and spirit in the body of a young man who wakes up in a hospital after trying to commit suicide. Structurally, the narrative disrupts chronology, taking the audience on a difficult journey that emphasizes slippages between the past and present, masculine and feminine, and sickness and health. Above all the play is about ways of seeing.

De Groen's play *The Girl Who Saw Everything* similarly focuses on ways of interpreting the world, but its characters are more questioning of the aesthetic refractions of reality that art provides, especially when they are faced with marital breakdown and midlife crises. Witty as always but less complex and challenging than *The Rivers of China,* this critique of patriarchy also avoids polemic and demonstrates a great deal of sympathy for the position of men as well as women in our society.

—Helen Gilbert

DEAN, Phillip Hayes

Nationality: American. **Born:** Chicago, Illinois. **Education:** Schools in Pontiac, Michigan. **Career:** Taught acting at the University of Michigan, Ann Arbor. **Awards:** Dramatists Guild Hull-Warriner award, 1972; Drama Desk award, 1972. **Address:** c/o Dramatists Play Service, 440 Park Avenue South, New York, New York 10016, U.S.A.

Publications

Plays

This Bird of Dawning Singeth All Night Long (produced New York, 1968). New York, Dramatists Play Service, 1971.
The Sty of the Blind Pig (produced New York, 1971). New York Dramatists Play Service, 1972.
American Night Cry (includes *Thunder in the Index, This Bird of Dawning Singeth All Night Long, The Minstrel Boy*) (produced New York, 1974). *Thunder in the Index* and *The Minstrel Boy* published New York, Dramatists Play Service, 1972.
Freeman (produced New York, 1973). New York, Dramatists Play Service, 1973.
The Owl Killer. New York, Dramatists Play Service, 1973.
Every Night When the Sun Goes Down (produced Waterford, Connecticut, 1974; New York, 1976). New York, Dramatists Play Service, 1976.
If You Can't Sing, They'll Make You Dance (also director: produced New York, 1978).
Paul Robeson (produced New York and London, 1978). New York, Doubleday, 1978.
Moloch Blues. New York, Dramatists Play Service, 1996.

*

Theatrical Activities:
Director: **Play**—*If You Can't Sing, They'll Make You Dance*, New York, 1978.

* * *

Phillip Hayes Dean, who had been working intermittently as a playwright since the 1950s, emerged as a dramatist to watch when the Negro Ensemble Company produced *The Sty of the Blind Pig* late in 1971. The title is the name of the red-light house in which Blind Jordan, one of the last of the blind street singers, was born and that he describes in a graphic passage as a place of blood and violence and the "smell of butchered pig." (Pork would figure more directly as an image of black self-corruption in *Every Night When the Sun Goes Down.*) Blind Jordan's presence emphasizes the condition of the other three characters, whose worlds are collapsing: Weedy, the acid-tongued churchwoman, sure of her own righteousness despite a long affair with her minister and who goes on the annual convocation to Montgomery just in time for the 1955 bus boycott to find the new church unrecognizable; her brother Doc, who imagines that if he can get a little money together he can become Sportin' Jimmy Sweet again in a Memphis that has disappeared; and Alberta, Weedy's daughter. The last is the central figure in the play, a woman caught between a past she never really had and a future she cannot embrace; at the end she assumes the voice and manner of her mother. The offstage event, the burgeoning civil rights movement, is putting an end to whatever community Weedy and Doc know, although the characters never see anything other than a bunch of "young folks" with "nappy hair" heading south for some reason. In the most effective scene in *The Sty of the Blind Pig,* Alberta reenacts a funeral service in which her fervor is clearly sexual, a mark of the personal and social repression in which she lives. The strength of the piece, however, lies in the characters as a group, the querulous sense of family even in a state of disintegration, and in the mysterious and disquieting presence of Blind Jordan.

The three plays that make up *American Night Cry*, some of which predate *The Sty of the Blind Pig*, are fables of white fear and black oppression, images of mutuality that end in madness, murder, and suicide. *Thunder in the Index*, *This Bird of Dawning Singeth All Night Long*, and *The Minstrel Boy* are all long on accusation, but the confrontations, despite Dean's talent for grotesque game-playing, are too obviously in the service of the ideational thrust of the plays. The programmatic quality of the work and the assumption of inevitable violence prepare the way for the Moloch plays. Both *Freeman* and *Every Night When the Sun Goes Down* are set in Moloch, a small industrial city in Michigan obviously suggested by Pontiac, where Dean lived for a time, but appropriately named Moloch because that god was worshiped through the sacrificial burning of children; both plays end in fire. *Freeman* is a family play in which the titular protagonist is an ambitious and bright man constantly defeated by his inability to work in the practical world of compromise; he is thwarted by his working-class family, his frightened wife, and his foster brother, who has become a successful doctor. In the end he torches the community center that he sees as a symbol of accommodation to white power and is saved from arrest at the cost of incarceration in a mental hospital. A more fully developed version of the main character in *Thunder in the Index*, Freeman is interesting dramatically as a man whose best impulses are self-destructive and harmful to those around him. Such a description may be an act of white liberal co-option, softening Dean for the mainstream of American theater, for the play is more ambiguous about Freeman. It suggests, primarily through the belated understanding of his father, that Freeman is not an instance of black hubris but of a man driven mad by an uncongenial society whose final act of violence is the inevitable end of his frustrated quest. Such a reading is certainly suggested by *Every Night When the Sun Goes Down*. Set in a decrepit bar-hotel peopled by whores, pimps, drunks, and crazies, it brings Blood back from prison, inspirited by a new sense of self, as a prophet who enlists this motley crew in a firebomb attack on their own environment: "And God gave Noah the Rainbow sign. No more water, the fire next time."

Paul Robeson is an unusual play in the Dean canon unless one sees the destruction of the political activist in the second act as the inevitable end of the black hero who outwitted the forces of oppression in the first act to become a football star, a lawyer, a famous singer, and an actor. Yet the celebratory frame of the play belies so Dean-like a movement. Neither convincingly Paul Robeson nor effectively Phillip Hayes Dean, it remains an anomaly in the playwright's work, perhaps because Dean had his dramatic image forced on him by Robeson's biography. One of Dean's theatrical virtues is that he has a knack for nonrealistic fables in which his best characters have room to develop realistically. At his weakest the expected development never takes place; such is the case with *If You Can't Sing, They'll Make You Dance*, in which an unlikely triangle allows the protagonist's ineffectuality to expose his macho self-image. At the other extreme is *The Sty of the Blind Pig*, in which the fable, implicit in Alberta's wondering if Blind Jordan was "ever really here," gains power from those who act it out. It is not that "every character comes from some man or woman," as Dean has said, but that every character becomes a man or woman. The other plays lie between these two, at their strongest when invention and idea are less visible than the people who embody them.

—Gerald Weales

DEAR, Nick

Nationality: British. **Born:** Portsmouth, Hampshire, 11 June 1955. **Education:** Various schools in Southampton; University of Essex, Colchester, B.A. (honors) 1977. **Family:** Lives with Penny Downie; two children. **Career:** Has worked as messenger boy, laundry van driver, bakery worker, garage attendant, town sergeant at Southampton Guildhall, film company administrator, and tutor in film and photography; playwright-in-residence, University of Essex, 1985; Arts Council playwright-in-residence, Royal Exchange Theatre, Manchester, 1987-88. **Awards:** Pye Radio award, 1980; John Whiting award, 1987; BAFTA award for best single drama, for *Persuasion,* 1996; Broadcasting Press Guild award, 1996. **Agent:** Rosica Colin Ltd., 1 Clareville Grove Mews, London SW7 5AH, England.

PUBLICATIONS

Plays

The Perfect Alibi (produced Colchester, Essex, 1980).

Pure Science (broadcast 1983; revised version produced Stratford-on-Avon, 1986).

Temptation (produced London, 1984; New York, 1985).

In the Ruins (broadcast 1984; revised version produced Bristol, 1989; London, 1990). With *The Art of Success*, London, Methuen, 1989.

The Art of Success (produced Stratford-on-Avon, 1986; London, 1987; New York, 1989). With *In the Ruins*, London, Methuen, 1989.

Food of Love (produced London, 1988).

A Family Affair, adaptation of a play by Ostrovsky (produced London, 1988). Bath, Absolute Press, 1989.

The Last Days of Don Juan, adaptation of a play by Tirso de Molina (produced Stratford-on-Avon, 1990; London, 1991). Bath, Absolute Press, 1990.

Le Bourgeois Gentilhomme, adaptation of the play by Molière (produced London, 1992). Bath, Absolute Press, 1992.

A Family Affair (opera; with music by Julian Grant, produced London, 1993).

Siren Song (opera; with music by Jonathan Dove, produced London, 1994).

Zenobia (produced London, 1995). London, Faber, 1995.

Screenplays: *Memo*, with Ann Foreman, 1980; *The Monkey Parade*, with Ann Foreman, 1982; *The Ranter*, 1988; *Persuasion,* adaptation of the Jane Austin novel, 1995; *The Gambler,* adaptation of Dostoyevsky, 1997.

Radio Plays: *Matter Permitted*, 1980; *Pure Science*, 1983; *In the Ruins*, 1984; *Jonathan Wild*, adaptation of the novel by Fielding, 1985; *Free*, 1986; *Swansong*, with David Sawer, 1989.

*

Nick Dear comments:

I mistrust writers' statements about their own work. I think there are two types of plays and of playwriting. One is concerned with money, glory, and a lot of invitations to dinner. The other is concerned with finding out something about oneself and one's place in the world—that old story—and attempting to communicate it honestly. Success is easily measured on the first count; less so on the second.

* * *

Sex, greed, disgust, and greatly heightened language are four of the basic elements that Nick Dear regularly mixes in his theatrical alchemy. His voice is a powerfully original one and is at its most intense in his best-known play, *The Art of Success,* a savage portrait of the great painter, engraver, and caricaturist William Hogarth. But even in his minor plays, where he playfully borrows form and style from the likes of Steven Berkoff, Joe Orton, and Harold Pinter, as in *Pure Science,* there is no mistaking the fierceness of Dear's own vision.

Because it flirts with form, *Pure Science* is particularly revealing of Dear's influences. The elderly couple whose private life is invaded by a young Mr. Perkins could be the couple in Pinter's *A Slight Ache,* thrown off balance by the presence of the matchseller at their gate, or the flirtatious Mr. Perkins could be said to resemble Orton's Mr. Sloane, importing sexual and criminal danger into the house. When he speaks, Mr. Perkins uses the rough rhyme of a Berkoff East Ender, grandly elevating his larcenous inclinations through doggerel.

The moral arguments, however, are pure Dear. The chemical smells that have wafted up the stairs from the basement for the past 50 years are the evidence of unceasing experiments in alchemy, the time-honored art of transmuting base elements into higher elements, for example, lead into gold. It is this prospect that attracts the attention of Mr. Perkins, who fails to find interest in what has been achieved by his host—eternal life.

Although the latter was the grand aim of alchemy, Dear himself is clearly not convinced that scientific advancement will improve the lot of mankind. He calls on J. Robert Oppenheimer, the father of the atomic bomb, as a witness to the dangers of science and drives the Four Horsemen of the Apocalypse through the play. But it remains a comedy, with a workshop full of entrails for predicting the future, and it offers a cheerful reversal when the greedy, villainous, and seductive Mr. Perkins is drowned by the elderly wife—"There should be more comeuppance." The couple decide to take their secret knowledge into hiding, like many unknown others, rather than to share it with a wicked world.

In Dear's play *Temptation,* in which a schoolteacher hopelessly trots out examples of zoological variety to his pupils while reminding them that man destroys a species every month whereas evolution takes 1,000 years, the bitter view of humanity is even more specific. On his way toward suicide, the teacher blurs his unspoken thoughts with his lessons, telling the children that the headmistress "has little knowledge of the world, she's not even frightened of it." His own state of mind is best summed up with the thought that he is "aware that there are 3,000 million starving and he has not gone mad." But perhaps he has, for his own grip on life has slipped through the ordinary muddle of an unwise affair and a damaged marriage.

Perhaps as evidence for the prosecution of humanity, Dear has turned to history more than once, providing a harrowing portrait of the declining George III in *In the Ruins* but making his greatest impact with *The Art of Success.* Hogarth's chosen form of expression, the harsh morality pictures that make up such series as *The Rake's Progress, The Harlot's Progress,* and *Marriage à la Mode,* has obviously found a sympathizer in Dear, but Hogarth's own morality faces a rigorous test in the play.

Dear's great achievement in the play is to enter into Hogarth's world. By trawling with the artist through the whoring and hypocrisy of his era, he etches his own series of images: Hogarth debasing a condemned murderer by sketching her in her cell against her will; Hogarth seeking degradation with prostitutes; Hogarth's wife uncovering a sheaf of drawings depicting her in sexual acts with other men. The murky desires of Hogarth's deepest imaginings are shown dramatically as the force behind his own condemnations of corruption.

For all its power to shock, its darkness of tone, and its violent, vigorous language, *The Art of Success* is also comic and knowing. With its portrayal of the powers and movers of the time, of Hogarth's coup in achieving copyright for his work, it also comments on the 1980s and the commerce of art. For the duration of the play author and subject seem to share a common vision.

Adaptation has also provided Dear with rich modes of expression, unleashing the extravagant theatrical gestures of Russian and Spanish drama through his extremely vivid English versions of classic plays. Although skilled in writing miniatures such as *Temptation,* he seems most at home when given the scope of classical drama.

—Ned Chaillet

DELANEY, Shelagh

Nationality: British. **Born:** Salford, Lancashire, 25 November 1939. **Education:** Broughton Secondary School. **Family:** One daughter. **Career:** Worked as salesgirl, usherette, and photographer's laboratory assistant. **Awards:** Foyle New Play award, 1959; Arts Council bursary, 1959; New York Drama Critics Circle award, 1961; BAFTA award, 1962; Robert Flaherty award, for screenplay, 1962; Encyclopaedia Britannica award, 1963; Writers Guild award, for screenplay, 1969; Cannes Film Festival award, 1985. **Member:** Royal Society of Literature, 1985. **Agent:** Tessa Sayle, 11 Jubilee Place, London SW3 3TE, England.

Publications

Plays

A Taste of Honey (produced London, 1958; New York, 1960). London, Methuen, and New York, Grove Press, 1959.

The Lion in Love (produced Coventry and London, 1960; New York, 1963). London, Methuen, and New York, Grove Press, 1961.

The House That Jack Built (televised 1977; produced New York, 1979). London, Duckworth, 1977.
Don't Worry about Matilda (broadcast 1983; produced London, 1987).

Screenplays: *A Taste of Honey*, with Tony Richardson, 1961; *The White Bus*, 1966; *Charlie Bubbles*, 1968; *Dance with a Stranger*, 1985.

Radio Plays: *So Does the Nightingale*, 1981; *Don't Worry about Matilda*, 1983.

Television Plays: *Did Your Nanny Come from Bergen?*, 1970; *St. Martin's Summer*, 1974; *The House That Jack Built* series, 1977; *Find Me First*, 1981.

Other

Sweetly Sings the Donkey. New York, Putnam, 1963; London, Methuen, 1964.

*

Critical Studies: *Anger and After* by John Russell Taylor, London, Methuen, 1969; *Feminist Theatre* by Helene Keyssar, London, Macmillan, 1984; *Look Back in Gender* by Michelene Wandor, London, Methuen, 1987; *Shelagh Delaney: A Taste of Honey* by Loreto Todd, London, Longman, 1992; "Shelagh Delaney" by Colette Lindroth, in *British Playwrights, 1956-1995: A Research and Production Handbook,* edited by William W. Demastes, Westport, Connecticut, Greenwood, 1996.

* * *

Shelagh Delaney's *A Taste of Honey* is usually considered as part of the "angry" upsurge of the late 1950s that shook the British theater out of its complacency and boredom. But it equally belongs with a contemporaneous spate of novels and plays from the industrial north of England whose rootedness in raw working-class experience, faithfulness to actual speech, and concern for young people are not captured by the label "angry." Delaney's hometown of Salford had already produced Walter Greenwood, who wrote the celebrated unemployment novel *Love on the Dole* (1933), and it was in the Manchester-Salford region that Joan Littlewood was first active in the Workers' Theatre Movement before she moved her Theatre Workshop to London's East End (where Delaney's career was launched).

A Taste of Honey is set in a squalid single-room flat in a rundown area of Manchester, surrounded by "tenements, cemetery, slaughter-house," as one character caustically remarks. But the two new lodgers, a not exactly respectable or harmonious mother and daughter, are not warped by this environment. Their zest for life and plebeian *savoir vivre* never deserts them. Helen, the mother, has had many lovers in her time and soon darts off with her latest flame, a heavy-drinking car salesman with pockets full of money, to a more comfortable setup in suburbia. Jo, an astute and quick-witted teenager, also has an affair, partly to compensate for her loneliness, partly to enjoy, much like her mother, the here and now. But hers ends in pregnancy, with her black sailor boyfriend at large.

Despite these blows Jo manages to hold on. In act 2 we find her mothered by Geof, a homosexual art student, whose advances she refuses. Shortly before the confinement Helen returns and drives Geof out. The play succeeds in presenting the "immoral" behavior and unsentimental attitudes of the two struggling independent women as perfectly valid and with the same frankness introduces Jo's racially and sexually different friends. Present-day audiences, familiar with the claims of feminism, are perhaps better equipped to appreciate the domestic centering and implicit sexual politics of the play. There is no spectacular action, intensity of dramatic conflict, or discussion of ideas, only the absorbing interest and vitality of the two strong female characters.

Naturalist elements abound in the play, but it is a matter of choice for directors whether to bring the naturalism to the fore or balance it, as Littlewood did, with music hall elements and the addressing of the audience.

The Lion in Love continues the questioning of gender roles and conventional family structures as well as reiterating the point that "young people mature quicker these days." There is the same pervasive restlessness and disorder. Yet we get a much larger picture of the rough end of a northern working-class community: three generations instead of two, the public space of a street market instead of merely the interior of a house, a large cast with a constantly shifting focus of attention. Though the action is again slight—the younger people quit the milieu and seek their fortunes elsewhere, whereas those who have reached "the chaos of middle age" remain ineluctably stuck in it—it is difficult to say why this clearly more ambitious play is so rarely produced. It has a comparable zestful female protagonist in the figure of boozing and riotous Kit, the male characterization is undoubtedly an advance over the earlier play, it offers a larger vista of the pressures and frustrations to which the socially marginal are exposed, and it again has its dreamlike poetic moments that temper the general picture of social disorganization.

Given this history, Delaney's celebration of marriage in the television serial *The House That Jack Built*, written after a lapse of 15 years, came as a surprise. But it is easily overlooked that beneath the interminable rows between mother and daughter in *A Taste of Honey* or the ill-matched couple in *The Lion in Love* there remained a common wavelength, a possibility of understanding and a capacity for caring. This helps to explain why the break in neither case was final and why *The House That Jack Built* was not such a departure.

By contrast, a situation with a grim end is to be found in the script for the prizewinning film *Dance with a Stranger*, if only in its re-creation of the real-life tragedy of barmaid Ruth Ellis, who murdered her upper-class lover and who was the last woman to be hanged in Britain. Delaney wrote the scenario in close collaboration with director Mike Newell, who had chosen to dwell on the destructive internal dynamics of the relationship rather than the class issues involved. Ellis, the woman living the fast life, bears some resemblance to Delaney's earlier hedonistic protagonists. She is reluctantly drawn to the man who wants to possess her but who then rejects her for a fiancée more befitting his social station. The film does not evade the class attitudes that impregnate the relationship from the start, nor does it ignore the repressive social mores of Britain in the mid-1950s. But the film's thrust is not social or documentary. The unfolding horror story of lust and obsession, jealousy and despair, and ugly behavior and deadly revenge has a more timeless dimension.

—H. Gustav Klaus

DEWHURST, Keith

Nationality: British. **Born:** Oldham, Lancashire, 24 December 1931. **Education:** Rydal School, 1945-50; Peterhouse, Cambridge, 1950-53, B.A. (honours) in English 1953. **Family:** Married 1) Eve Pearce in 1958 (divorced 1980), one son and two daughters; 2) Alexandra Cann in 1980. **Career:** Yarn tester, Lancashire Cotton Corporation, Romiley, Cheshire, 1953-55; sports writer, Manchester *Evening Chronicle*, 1955-59; presenter, Granada Television, 1968-69, and *Review* arts programme, BBC, 1972; arts columnist, the *Guardian*, London, 1969-72. Writer-in-residence, West Australian Academy of Performing Arts, Perth, 1984. **Award:** Japan prize, for television play, 1968. **Agent:** Alexandra Cann Representation, 12 Abingdon Road, London W8 6AF.

Publications

Plays

Running Milligan (televised 1965). Published in *Z Cars: Four Scripts from the Television Series*, edited by Michael Marland, London, Longman, 1968.
Rafferty's Chant (produced London, 1967). Published in *Plays of the Year 33*, London, Elek, 1967.
The Last Bus (televised 1968). Published in *Scene Scripts*, edited by Michael Marland, London, Longman, 1972.
Pirates (produced London, 1970).
Brecht in '26 (produced London, 1971).
Corunna! (produced London, 1971). Published in *War Plays*, London, Oberon Books, 1996.
Kidnapped, adaptation of the novel by Robert Louis Stevenson (produced Edinburgh, 1972).
The Miser, adaptation of a play by Molière (produced Edinburgh, 1973).
The Magic Island (produced Birmingham, 1974).
The Bomb in Brewery Street (produced Sheffield, 1975). Published in *War Plays*, London, Oberon Books, 1996.
One Short (produced Sheffield, 1976).
Luggage (produced London, 1977).
Lark Rise, adaptation of works by Flora Thompson (produced London, 1978). Included in *Lark Rise to Candleford*, 1980.
The World Turned Upside Down, adaptation of the work by Christopher Hill (produced London, 1978). Published in *War Plays*, London, Oberon Books, 1996.
Candleford, adaptation of works by Flora Thompson (produced London, 1979). Included in *Lark Rise to Candleford*, 1980.
Lark Rise to Candleford (includes *Lark Rise* and *Candleford*). London, Hutchinson, 1980.
San Salvador (produced Louisville, 1980).
Don Quixote, adaptation of the novel by Cervantes (produced London, 1982). Oxford, Amber Lane Press, 1982.
Batavia (produced Perth, Western Australia, 1984).
Black Snow, adaptation of a novel by Mikhail Bulgakov (produced London, 1991). Bath, Absolute Press, 1991.

Screenplays: *The Empty Beach*, 1985; *The Land Girls*, with David Leland, 1998.

Radio Plays: *Drummer Delaney's Sixpence*, 1971; *That's Charlie George Over There*, 1972; *Dick Turpin*, 1976; *Mother's Hot Milk*, 1979.

Television Plays: *Think of the Day*, 1960; *A Local Incident*, 1961; scripts for *Z Cars* series, 1962-67; *Albert Hope*, 1962; *The Chimney Boy*, 1964; *The Life and Death of Lovely Karen Gilhooley*, 1964; *The Siege of Manchester*, 1965; *The Towers of Manhattan*, 1966; *Softly Softly* series, 1967, 1975-76; *The Last Bus*, 1968; *Men of Iron*, 1969; *Why Danny Misses School*, 1969; *It Calls for a Great Deal of Love*, 1969; *Helen*, from the play by Euripides, 1970; *The Sit-In*, 1972; *Lloyd-George*, 1973; *End Game*, 1974; *The Great Alfred* (*Churchill's People* series), 1975; *Our Terry*, 1975; *Just William* series, from books by Richmal Crompton, 1977; *Two Girls and a Millionaire*, 1978; *The Battle of Waterloo*, 1983; *What We Did in the Past*, 1986; *Joe Wilson* series, from short stories by Henry Lawson 1987 (Australia); and for *Knight Errant*, *Skyport*, *Love Story*, *Front Page Story*, *The Villains*, *The Emigrants*, *Boy Dominic*, *Juliet Bravo*, *Van der Valk*, *Casualty*, and *Making News* series.

Novels

Captain of the Sands. New York, Viking Press, 1981; London, Cape, 1982.
McSullivan's Beach. London, Angus and Robertson, 1985.

*

Keith Dewhurst comments:

One day in June 1986 I walked into a discount bookshop in Sydney and flicked through an encyclopaedic television guide compiled by Leslie Halliwell, whom I remember with gratitude from my Cambridge days (when he managed the Rex Cinema), and the critic Phillip Purser. Two of my own television plays were accorded entries: *Men of Iron* and *The Siege of Manchester*, which had an asterisk admitting it to "Halliwell's Hall of Fame." This stunned me, in an amiable sort of way, and seems to me to be a classic example of the random fates that await the plays people write.

The Siege of Manchester was a broken-backed epic, for which I have a very soft spot, as I suppose one does for anything half-regretted, and I am delighted that Phillip Purser remembers it, but it does not seem to me to be in the same class as some other television plays I have written, such as *Albert Hope*, *It Calls for a Great Deal of Love*, *Our Terry*, *Lloyd-George*, *Men of Iron* itself, and an episode of *Juliet Bravo* called *Oscar*.

Similarly, *Lark Rise*, which was performed at the National Theatre and subsequently in various countries around the world has, I hazard, been recognised as an interesting piece, and the one in which the director Bill Bryden and myself best expressed a modern genre—the promenade play with music, that tries to make the theatre an event again. Yet the plays by which one arrived at that destination, especially *Corunna!*, aren't even in a vestibule of fame. They're out in the car park, where it's pissing with rain.

This damp obscurity I attribute mainly to the plays in question never having been published. Nor was *The Bomb in Brewery Street*, which additionally suffered from radical chic reviewers who thought that, being set in the Belfast troubles, it should provide solutions that eluded Elizabeth I, Oliver Cromwell, Henry Grattan, Gladstone, Parnell, Lloyd-George, and de Valera. In fact it is a funny and carefully researched work whose sub-text clearly favours colonial disengagement, and I wish I could hustle it into *somebody's* "Hall of Fame," but I don't suppose I will.

I can, however, close with an appropriate "Hall of Fame" reminiscence. There was an extra in *The Siege of Manchester* who was supposed to be dead in a battle scene but kept getting up. Four years later, when the director Herbert Wise and I were working on *Men of Iron*, we met this same extra in the studio corridor, clearly wearing a costume for our new play.

Herbert gripped my wrist and said: "It's George!"

George said: "Hello, Mr. Wise. I never thought I'd work for you again!"

"You wouldn't have," said Herbert, "if I'd remembered your other name."

Maybe the car park does have consolations, after all.

(1998) Ten years on, or whatever it is, and the fates have been ever more random: episode after episode of one's past output floats by on cable television, plays have been published twenty years after they seemed to have sunk without a trace, and through the director of one of them, David Leland, I find myself writing in the cinema. And behind this soap opera there is a serious drama.

Many of the British-born writers in this book learned their trade and earned much of their livelihoods in public-service television. In my previous personal statement I made comic complaint about TV plays I had written–today there is no likelihood of such work ever being commissioned again for English television.

Assaults upon TV by politicians who hated its independent voice, and the compliance of the bureaucratic Lackeys who run it, have destroyed something unique in modern culture. How the careers of English writers will fare in a local arena that is but a glove with Hollywood's hand inside it, and in a theatre struggling to make ends meet, remains to be seen. But it is a struggle that is sure to be reflected in future pages of this book.—London, April, 1998.

* * *

Keith Dewhurst is a highly skilled and conscientious dramatic craftsman. He has been prepared to write in a number of different dramatic styles, readily accepting the challenges of working for the technically demanding medium of television and of preparing for the stage adaptations of works of fiction that a large proportion of his audience already know well and love in their original form. For television he has adopted the realistic manner that is the current norm for popular entertainment, and his *Van der Valk* detective series has been well received. For the stage, however, he has often preferred to experiment with ideas taken up from Bertolt Brecht's epic theater, with the illusion of reality broken in order to facilitate a more direct address to the audience and to accommodate subjects that might prove unduly resistant to conventional treatment.

As well as scaling down his work so that it fits comfortably onto the small screen, Dewhurst has used a number of different forms of staging, including arena style, the thrust stage with the audience seated on either side of a long ramp, and what he calls "promenade production." This last type of staging goes a long way toward abolishing the traditional—or to be more accurate, the 19th-century—distinction between the public and the actors in order to create a greater degree of intimacy and involvement. Dewhurst uses it even at the cost of some spoiling of the sight lines that used to be thought so important. Music is not treated as a mere incidental or just to emphasize atmosphere but in many instances serves as an essential part of the dramatic presentation.

Dewhurst never loses sight of the need for the theater to entertain, but when he comments on this, he is not just repeating a commonplace and far less is he making the facile distinction of some old-fashioned critics between a theater of entertainment and a theater of ideas. Instead, he insists that drama can and ought to be an artistic medium that appeals to a wide range of people in a number of different ways. In this, as in his choice of dramatic mentor, Dewhurst proclaims a wide sympathy with the great mass of humanity.

Dewhurst's talents and his sympathy are clearly revealed in *Running Milligan,* an outstanding contribution to the BBC's epoch-making series *Z Cars*. Milligan is shown leaving prison, let out on parole to attend his wife's funeral. The policemen on patrol see him, and their immediate suspicions set the perspectives of a tragedy that is inevitable. At home Milligan predictably finds no support and cannot resist the crazy temptation of trying to run away. It is to no avail, and Barlow, who has presided over the usual police station subplot, arrives to arrest him. To some extent this is conventional enough, but Dewhurst contrives to bring out all of the pathetic helplessness of Milligan, suggesting that the blame lies not with him but with his impossible situation and that society's response to his problems is no less bungling and ineffectual than his own efforts at escape. The dialogue is pared down to essentials, but in a scene near the end, when Milligan tries to comfort a drink-sodden tramp whose memory is fuddled by memories of fighting in the war by telling him a fairy story, there is a sudden and disturbingly apt touch of poetry.

Rafferty's Chant, which was produced at the Mermaid Theatre in London, has a great deal more humor in its portrayal of the life and downfall of a wonderfully plausible con man in the used car trade. The dialogue is crisp and laconic, but there is a wonderful touch of romance in Rafferty's patter as he sells old bangers as if they were dream machines. The skimpy plot of this play, which has more than a touch of farce to it, is no more than a thread to hold together closely observed characters in a number of sketches that explore their motivations as they try to cope with one of those vitally important little matters in present-day life, the buying of a car. As we laugh with Rafferty at mankind's foibles, there is no danger of our taking any more seriously than he does the stern words he imagines a judge speaking to him before pronouncing a stiff sentence for preying on gullibility.

Following a line of development that probably owes its origins to the experiments of the French director Jean-Louis Barrault and that was certainly influenced to some extent by the work of Ariane Mnouchkine, whose production of *1789* with the Théâtre du Soleil he witnessed at the Cartoucherie de Vincennes in Paris, Dewhurst has done some of his most original work in adaptations. For instance, *Corunna!* dramatized episodes from the Napoleonic Wars as a ballad opera with no more than five actors reinforced by a five-piece rock band. *Kidnapped,* after Robert Louis Stevenson, was also notable for its freedom of dramatic treatment. The same quality was in evidence when, in an impressive feat of compression, Dewhurst fashioned a satisfying drama out of Cervantes's *Don Quixote,* which was all the more remarkable since the dramatist insisted on the rather different tone of the second, more reflective part of the novel. The dialogue was based on the first English translation, produced by Thomas Shelton in 1612 and 1620. In a prefatory note Dewhurst scrupulously points out that the printed text of the play is not quite identical with the version that was performed at the National Theatre's Olivier Theatre.

If the problem with *Don Quixote* was an excess of text, that with *Lark Rise,* after Flora Thompson's celebrated portrait of village life in Victorian Oxfordshire, was a lack of narrative and a consequent lack of a clear central focus of attention. Dewhurst does not try to remedy this. His approach is rather to let the images of the village and its people develop before the eyes of the audience so that the succession of glimpses may add together almost as they do when we look in on real life. In this way *Lark Rise* serves as a prelude to the rather more obviously shaped *Candleford.* These texts do not read particularly well, but this criticism is no more just here than when it is leveled at television scripts. Flora Thompson's book, like the novels of Cervantes or Stevenson, remains intact for those who wish to read it.

Dewhurst's aim is to find a dramatic representation of these works that functions in performance with all of the different means of communication that are available in the theater. Without the trammels and clutter of old-fashioned realism, the imagination can be engaged and provoked into providing whatever may be sensed as needed to color the pictures that are sketched before our eyes. The success of the productions of *Lark Rise* and *Candleford* is ample justification for the enterprise that Dewhurst has embarked upon.

—Christopher Smith

DICKINS, Barry

Nationality: Australian. **Born:** Regent, Victoria, in 1949. **Education:** Preston Institute of Technology, diplomas in fine arts and education 1974. **Career:** Worked at various factory jobs and as a scenic artist for television; writer-in-residence, La Mama, 1980, Victoria College of the Arts, and Playbox Theatre, 1982, all Melbourne. **Awards:** Radio Broadcasting grant, 1976; APG Playwriting prize, 1978; Australia Council fellowship, 1984; Victorian Premier's Award for Drama, 1995. **Address:** 63 Illawara Road, Flemington, Victoria 3031, Australia.

Publications

Plays

Ghosts (produced Melbourne, 1975).
The Interview (produced Melbourne, 1976).
Only an Old Kitbag (produced Melbourne, 1977).
The Great Oscar Wilde Trial (produced Melbourne, 1977).
Mag and Bag (as *The Horror of Suburban Nature Strips*, produced Melbourne, 1978). With *The Bridal Suite*, Montmorency, Victoria, Yackandandah, 1985.
The Rotten Teeth Show (produced Melbourne, 1978).
The Fool's Shoe Hotel (produced Melbourne, 1978). Montmorency, Victoria, Yackandandah, 1985.
The Bridal Suite (produced Melbourne, 1979). With *Mag and Bag*, Montmorency, Victoria, Yackandandah, 1985.
Banana Bender (produced Melbourne, 1980). With *The Death of Minnie*, Sydney, Currency Press, 1981.
The Ken Wright Show (produced Melbourne, 1980).
The Death of Minnie (produced Melbourne, 1980). With *Banana Bender*, Sydney, Currency Press, 1981.
The Golden Goldenbergs (produced Melbourne, 1980). Montmorency, Victoria, Yackandandah, 1986.
Lennie Lower (produced Melbourne, 1981). Montmorency, Victoria, Yackandandah, 1982.
One Woman Shoe (produced Melbourne, 1981). Montmorency, Victoria, Yackandandah, 1984.
A Couple of Broken Hearts (produced Melbourne, 1982).
Graeme King Lear (produced Melbourne, 1983).
Greenroom (produced Melbourne, 1985).
Beautland (produced Adelaide, 1985). Sydney, Currency Press, 1985.
More Greenroom (produced Melbourne, 1986).
Reservoir by Night (produced Melbourne, 1986).
Royboys (produced Melbourne, 1987). Sydney, Currency Press, 1987.
Eat Your Greens (produced Melbourne, 1987).
Between Engagements (produced Melbourne, 1988).
Bedlam Autos (produced Melbourne, 1989).
Perfect English (produced Melbourne, 1990).
Hymie (produced Melbourne, 1991).
Dear Suburbia (produced Melbourne, 1992).
A Dickens Christmas (produced Melbourne, 1992). Sydney, currency Press, 1992.
The Foibles (produced Melbourne, 1992).
Remember Ronald Ryan (produced Melbourne, 1994). Sydney, Currency Press, 1994.
Dame Joan Green (produced Melbourne, 1995).

Novels

Crookes of Epping. Fairfield, Victoria, Pascoe, 1984.
Ron Truffle: His Life and Bump Out. Alphington, Pascoe, 1987.
My Grandmother: Years of Wit, Warmth and Laughter. Melbourne, Penguin, 1989.

Other

What the Dickins 1-2 (humour). Melbourne, Penguin, 2 vols., 1987-89.
Gift of the Gab (humour). Melbourne, McPhee Gribble, 1988.

Illustrator, *The Barracker's Bible: A Dictionary of Sporting Slang* by Jack Hibberd and Garrie Hutchinson. Melbourne, McPhee Gribble, 1983

* * *

While not all of his plays are specifically set in his hometown, Barry Dickins is very much a Melbourne writer, and much of his contribution to popular culture chronicles the passing parade of everyday life in that city, mostly in a warmly humorous vein if often tinged with bitter poignancy. Even in Melbourne, however, his plays have sometimes been criticized for their waywardness, lack of discipline, and unorthodox dramatic structure.

Most of Dickins's work is certainly antinaturalistic. Much of it resembles the so-called larrikin style of La Mama and the Pram Factory in the late 1960s and early 1970s, while some of it recalls the surrealism and absurdism of even earlier periods. The best of Dickins's work is in a broad cartoon style that is very much his own. In particular, he has developed the form of the dramatic monologue—and at times of true monodrama—to a high level of achievement.

The majority of Dickins's plays deal with down-and-outs, or "Aussie battlers," of one kind or another. In *Royboys* the fluctuating fortunes of the battling, working-class, and ambiguously named Noble family are chronicled in parallel with those of their beloved and equally battling Fitzroy Football Club. The team is of working-class origins but is now languishing at the bottom of a competition dominated by wealthy, sophisticated clubs that have changed the style of the game and the nature of the football league itself. Dickins uses the changing and, in his bitingly satirical view, deteriorating face of football as a metaphor for the gradual passing of a more leisurely and dignified lifestyle that is rapidly being supplanted by a fast-paced, impersonal world. In the end it is the Nobles' courage and determination rather than their poverty that we remember.

Similarly, the exploits of a pair of unashamedly shadowy but struggling used-car salesmen are celebrated, albeit with less satirical confidence, in *Bedlam Autos*, while *Mag and Bag* portrays a pair of elderly suburban sisters whose life together is reduced, like that of Beckett's tramps in *Waiting for Godot,* to insulting each other as a way of passing the time. Images of a birdcage and a trapeze serve to emphasize the two women's up-and-down relationship.

In *The Death of Minnie* and *The Bridal Suite* the sad and broken solo female characters, Minnie and Vera, rail with considerable vigor, and with alternating humor and bitterness, against the bad hand life has dealt them, but they still succumb to their unhappy fate. In a use of stage properties that is typical of Dickins, Minnie's failure in life is poignantly underlined by the failure of a pop-up toaster that finally functions (triumphantly!) only at the moment of her death. Indeed, in the later monodrama *Hymie,* partly based on the life of an actual left-wing Melbourne Jewish artist, Hymie Slade is already dead and regales us with anecdotes about his life and death from an elaborate and well-appointed coffin. It is significant that the eponymous Hymie was not a great artist, but what Dickins values is the indomitable spirit—"the bullshit artistry"—of the melancholy, solitary character.

Other plays portray theatrical artists. In *The Golden Goldenbergs* a family of down-on-their-luck Melbourne Jewish comedians gather for a grand night of mad reminiscences, theatrical feats, and feasting. In *Fool's Shoe Hotel* the hotel of the title is actually a sort of asylum for a troupe of battling actors and other show business has-beens who, in a bizarre and highly surrealist soiree, display skills and tricks that were better recognized and valued in days gone by.

More effective, however, in their exploration of comic performers are two further monodramas: the early *Lennie Lower* and the later *Between Engagements.* In Lennie Lower, the real-life eccentric journalist of 1930s Sydney, Dickins found a genuine soulmate for what is arguably one of his finest plays. In a strongly developed monodrama, the physically and emotionally crippled Lower spends what turns out to be the last night of his life in 1947 in a working-class pub putting together the next day's funnies column for his daily paper, reminiscing about his past—with the usual Dickins alternation of nostalgia, bitterness, and surreal, ribald humor—suffering from a terminal case of writer's block, and drinking himself to life and to death. Along the way, Lower portrays his longtime colleague, the cartoonist WEP, as well as his boss, Sir Frank Packer. Again, it is the vibrant if idiosyncratically perverse life of the character rather than his pitiful death that we remember. *Lennie Lower* has been often revived in Australian theaters.

Equally poignant is *Between Engagements,* which portrays a perennially unemployed actor who, apart from a telephone, is stuck in his flat alone. The telephone serves as his sole lifeline to a hostile outside world, and he hopes that it will bring him work. Needless to say, the telephone is reluctant to ring despite the encouragement, threats, and wonderful "audition pieces" (speeches from his possibly remembered, possibly imagined past career in Melbourne's most illustrious theaters) he lavishes upon the recalcitrant instrument. It is not unlike Minnie and her uncooperative toaster.

A huge number of other monologues—such as the various evenings at La Mama written for the actor Peter Green and bearing punning references to his name, for example, *Greenroom*—are examples of Dickins's contribution to Melbourne's burgeoning comedy and cabaret circuit. The interconnected series of monologues for a female performer, *One Woman Shoe,* and the rather bitter later monodrama, *Dear Suburbia,* reveal his frequently insightful and sympathetic writing for women actors.

But the play that has won Dickins his most acclaim, *Remember Ronald Ryan,* is vastly different in style, structure, and character from the majority of his works. Based on detailed research into the real life of the last man to be hanged in Australia—allegedly for fatally shooting a prison warder during a daring escape from the notorious Pentridge Prison in 1965—this is a tightly structured semidocumentary, semirealistic drama of highly ambitious proportions. It portrays more than 30 named characters, who are intentionally doubled by a cast of 9, over a period of 20 years in scenes spanning the days prior to Ryan's and his mate Walker's breakout to their recapture and trial and Ryan's subsequent execution. Interspersed are flashbacks to Ryan's days as a boy and as a largely amateur bungling criminal. Along the way, his marriage to the upper-class Dorothy George and his equally bungled attempts to forge a decent family life are sketched in fragmentary but confidently worked-up vignettes. While the play clearly speaks out against capital punishment and casts a generally sympathetic light on the despicable but lovable rogue Ryan, Dickins never sentimentalizes his subject, revealing him to be a victim of a benighted era in Victorian politics and of his own amateurish ambitions. The play won the Premier's Literary Award for Drama in 1995.

Dramaturgically unorthodox though some of them may be, Dickins's plays nevertheless teem with life as much as with death, and at their best they are vigorously entertaining portraits of Australian battlers.

—Geoffrey Milne

DIETZ, Steven

Nationality: American. **Born:** Denver, Colorado, 23 June 1958. **Education:** University of Northern Colorado, Greeley, 1976-80, B.A. 1980. **Career:** Member, Playwrights' Center, 1980-91, co-founder, Quicksilver Stage, 1983-86, and artistic director, Midwest PlayLabs, 1987-89, all Minneapolis; resident director, Sundance Institute, Utah, 1990; associate artist, A Contemporary Theatre, Seattle, 1990-91. **Awards:** Jerome Foundation fellowship, 1982, 1984; McKnight fellowship in directing, 1985, in playwriting

1989; Theatre Communications Group fellowship in directing, 1987; Society of Midland Authors award, 1988; National Endowment for the Arts fellowship, 1989. **Agent:** Wiley Hausam, International Creative Management, 40 West 57th Street, New York, New York 10019. **Address:** 4416 Thackeray North East, Seattle, Washington 98105, U.S.A.

Publications

Plays

Brothers and Sisters, music by Roberta Carlson (produced Minneapolis, 1982).
Railroad Tales (produced Minneapolis, 1983).
Random Acts (produced Minneapolis, 1983).
Carry On (produced Minneapolis, 1984).
Wanderlust (also director: produced Minneapolis, 1984).
Catch Me a Z, music by Greg Theisen (produced Minneapolis, 1985).
More Fun Than Bowling (produced St. Paul, Minnesota, 1986; New York, 1992). New York, French, 1990.
Painting It Red, music by Gary Rue, lyrics by Leslie Ball (produced St. Paul, Minnesota, 1986). New York, French, 1990.
Burning Desire (produced St. Paul, Minnesota, 1987).
Foolin' Around with Infinity (produced Los Angeles, 1987). New York, French, 1990.
Ten November, music and lyrics by Eric Bain Peltoniemi (produced Chicago, 1987). Published in *Plays in Process* (New York), vol. 9 no. 4, 1987; New York, French, 1990.
God's Country (produced Seattle, 1988; New York, 1992). New York, French, 1990.
Happenstance, music by Eric Bain Peltoniemi (produced Seattle, 1989).
After You (produced Louisville, 1990; New York, 1991). Published in *More Ten-Minute Plays from Actor's Theatre of Louisville*, edited by Michael Dixon, New York, French, 1992.
To the Nines (produced Seattle, 1991). Published in *The Twentieth Century*, edited by Dan Fields, Seattle, Rain City Press, 1991.
Halcyon Days (produced Seattle, 1991). Seattle, Rain City Press, 1991.
Trust (produced Seattle, 1992). Seattle, Rain City Press, 1992.
Lonely Planet (produced Seattle, 1992). New York, Dramatists Play Service, 1994; in *Actor's Book of Gay and Lesbian Plays*, New York, Penguin, 1995.
The Rememberer (produced Seattle, 1994). Seattle, Washington, Rain City Projects, 1993.
The Nina Variations: A Play. Seattle, Washington, Rain City Projects, 1996.
Dracula, adaptation of Bram Stoker. New York, Dramatists Play Service, 1996.
Still Life with Iris: A Play (produced Seattle). Seattle, Washington, Rain City Projects, 1997.

Screenplay: *The Blueprint*, 1992.

*

Critical Study: "Risking Sentiment" by John Istel, in *American Theatre*, December 1995, pp. 38.

Theatrical Activities:
Director: **Plays**—Many of his own plays; *Standing on My Knees* by John Olive, St. Paul, Minnesota, 1982; *21-A* by Kevin Kling, Minneapolis, 1984, New York, 1986; *The Voice of the Prairie* by John Olive, Minneapolis, 1985; *Harry and Claire* by Jaime Meyer, Minneapolis, 1985; *A Country Doctor* by Len Jenkin, Minneapolis, 1986; *Auguste Moderne* by Kevin Kling, Minneapolis, 1986; *T Bone N Weasel* by Jon Klein, Minneapolis, 1986, Louisville, Kentucky, 1987; *Lloyd's Prayer* by Kevin Kling, Minneapolis, 1987; *The Einstein Project* by Paul D'Andrea and Jon Klein, Minneapolis, 1987, Washington, D.C., 1992; *The Wild Goose Circus* by Russell Davis, Sundance, Utah, 1990; *Tears of Rage* by Doris Baizley, Seattle, 1991; *New Business* by Tom William, Denver, Colorado, 1991; *Home and Away* by Kevin Kling, Chicago and Minneapolis, 1992; and many readings and workshops at the Playwrights' Center, Minneapolis, 1980-91. **Opera**—*Saint Erik's Crown* by Eskil Hemberg, St. Peter, Minnesota, 1989.

Steven Dietz comments:

At the core of my interest in the theatre is a quote from Bertolt Brecht: "The modern theatre musn't be judged by whether it manages to interest the spectator in the theatre itself—but whether it manages to interest him in the world."

To that end, I have devoted many of my plays to investigations of factual events. I believe the theatre is a rehearsal of the concerns of the present moment. I believe that, as workers in this marvelous grand accident of an art form, we have a mandate to be the explorers, not the curators, of our society. Our daunting challenge, one we seldom rise to meet, is to run through the minefields before our culture does. To make the mistakes, confront the idiocy and revel in the excesses (social, sexual, religious, political) of our culture in the metaphorical safety of the theatre (where we can watch, learn, and judge)—before these same things hit us head-on in the bloody maelstrom of the world.

I believe that, at its best, the theatre can serve as a social forum, a place where members of a community can gather to confront those things which affect them. A place for reasoning and rage, laughter and loss, recognition and discussion.

I believe that, at its best, the theatre is a combustible mix of fun, fury, and eloquence.

* * *

Of the generation of young dramatists coming of age in the 1990s, Steven Dietz is unique in a number of ways. Although he works largely out of Seattle, his plays are frequently seen in theaters around the country, including those in New York City. He is prolific and diverse, and he has a voice that is always changing and yet recognizable as his own. Dietz pays careful attention to an issue that most playwrights of his generation and background tend to ignore or glide over—politics.

Dietz's dramaturgy came to public attention a few years ago in a theater in Saint Paul, Minnesota, with *More Fun Than Bowling*. The theater company is now defunct, but the voice of Dietz in the play is unmistakable: macabre, funny, lunatic, hard-hitting, and finally disturbing in a way that many other plays of his contemporaries fail to be. Dietz showed, almost proudly, that he cared, that he had compassion, that he was not just another cool observer. The promise of *More Fun Than Bowling* has been realized since then in even more compelling work.

God's Country captured a good deal of attention because it dared to take on the headlines. The murder of radio talk show host Alan Berg by neo-Nazis is the mainspring of the play, in which Dietz tackles thorny questions and comes up with lucid explanations. A fairly small cast is called on to play a wide range of characters in this courtroom docudrama. The play dramatizes Voltaire's statement that "anyone who has the power to make you believe absurdities has the power to make you commit injustices," which Dietz quotes in the published text. Berg, described as "a bleeding heart with an acid tongue," had outraged the far right with his Denver talk show and his challenges to make-believe "facts," and he was murdered for attempting to be reasonable and sane. As with much modern docudrama, Dietz unfortunately resorts too often to having his characters tell us the play rather than show it to us. There is a plethora of speeches directly to the audience, but montages of voices and images work well to create the atmosphere and the sense of irrationality that the madmen-murderers palm off as "salvation." The Jew-haters are themselves pathetic and dangerous, believing the "absurdities" their leaders manufacture out of whole cloth.

In later plays Dietz has resorted to direct addresses to the audience even more frequently. While the speeches themselves are interesting and even fascinating, they replace dramatic conflict between characters on the stage that might have been more effectively achieved through dialogue and action.

In *Halcyon Days* Dietz turns his attention to the American invasion of Grenada. Here he again relies on long speeches that are essentially narrative rather than theatrical. Too, there is a montage of short, snappy scenes and representative characters that range from senators to goofy, laid-back medical students, from gift shop clerks to presidential speechwriters. While the central issue of the invasion of the tiny island became moot almost instantly, what saves the play as theater and should guarantee it a future life is its wit. As Senator Eddie notes, "There are no comics in D.C. Comics would be redundant." Sadly, the senator's own life is engulfed by the tragedy, and comedy itself becomes redundant. Dietz proves over and over again that he can write very funny material, as when he has a character attack the murder of language, which he calls "linguicide." Euphemisms hide reality: "The old are chronologically gifted. The hungry are nourishment-free. And the homeless are architecturally-inconvenienced . . . . Murdered civilians become collateral damage, and the starving thousands . . . become disenfranchised indigenous people of color." Strong stuff emerges from hilarious spoofery, but Dietz, like many Americans, is outraged at the way his country's leaders behave and speak and lie. Such political stands are rare in American drama, but by and large Dietz makes them work.

Trust once again uses the open stage to represent a variety of essentially cinematic settings. When Dietz lets his dialogue rip along, he is absolutely first-rate, but he frequently slips back into monologue that relates the action to the audience. The fault, if it is a fault at all, is common enough in his generation of playwrights, but in *Trust* it seems intrusive. Yet Dietz has the jargon, attitude, value system, and casual but twitchy behavior of the 1990s generation down pat.

Dietz's later play *Lonely Planet* seems very different from the preceding works, but the language is absolutely on the mark and the point being made is sadly only too recognizable. Two men, Jody and Carl, play games of truth and lies with each other in a map store, with the world as seen by the astronauts hanging behind them. In the play Dietz pays direct homage to Ionesco's *The Chairs*, and in time his stage is filled with chairs, with memories that may or may not be true. Carl complains that he is bored, but we eventually learn that his boredom is with death, which the chairs symbolize. The two characters duel with maps and play with the world, but their inner struggle emerges as we see their fear and share their anxiety. AIDS is out there, waiting, and the chairs are the chairs of their dead friends. The play is heavy in symbolism, but despite its grim center there is wit and irony, which is "the penicillin of modern thought." Dietz is at his best when he has Jody ponder, "We remember the wrong things. We remember the combination to our high school gym locker, we forget the name of the woman who taught us to swim. We remember the capitals of states and forget our parents' birthdays." In the end on our lonely planet we have only memory, however faulty, and one another.

In *Lonely Planet* Dietz treats the audience as a character to be addressed, to have things directed at. But here the device is relevant and important since it integrates the audience as a part of the action. We should not remain passive.

—Arthur H. Ballet

DIZENZO, Charles (John)

Nationality: American. **Born:** Hackensack, New Jersey, 21 May 1938. **Education:** New York University, B.A. 1962. **Family:** Married Patricia Hines in 1964. **Career:** Instructor in playwriting, New York University 1970-71, and Yale University, New Haven, Connecticut, 1975-76. **Awards:** Yale University-ABC fellowship, 1966, and CBS fellowship, 1975; Guggenheim fellowship, 1967; National Endowment for the Arts grant, 1972. **Member:** Dramatists Guild; New Dramatists Committee. **Agent:** Helen Harvey Associates, 110 West 57th Street, New York, New York 10011, U.S.A. **Address:** 106 Perry Street, New York, New York 10014, U.S.A.

Publications

Plays

The Drapes Come (televised 1965; produced New York, 1965; Liverpool, 1973; London, 1982). New York, Dramatists Play Service, 1966; in *Off-Broadway Plays 1*, London, Penguin, 1970.

An Evening for Merlin Finch (produced New York, 1968; Coventry, 1969). New York, Dramatists Play Service, 1968; in *Off-Broadway Plays 1*, London, Penguin, 1970.

A Great Career (produced New York, 1968). New York, Dramatists Play Service, 1968.

Why I Went Crazy (produced Westport, Connecticut, 1969; New York, 1970; as *Disaster Strikes the Home*, produced Edinburgh, 1970; London, 1971).

The Last Straw, and Sociability (produced New York, 1970). New York, Dramatists Play Service, 1970.

Big Mother and Other Plays (includes *An Evening for Merlin Finch* and *The Last Straw*). New York, Grove Press, 1970.

Big Mother, music by John Braden (produced New York, 1974). Included in *Big Mother and Other Plays*, 1970.

Metamorphosis, adaptation of works by Kafka (produced New York, 1972). New York, Dramatists Play Service, 1977.
The Shaft of Love (produced New York, 1975).

Television Play: *The Drapes Come*, 1965.

Other

Phoebe (for children), with Patricia Dizenzo. New York, Bantam, 1970.

* * *

Charles Dizenzo's plays were first produced in the off-off-Broadway workshop movement of the 1960s. Since then they have been presented by the Repertory Company of Lincoln Center, the David Merrick Arts Foundation, and the American Place Theater in New York, as well as in theaters in Europe.

A good example of Dizenzo's work is a pair of one-act comedies first presented at Lincoln Center's experimental Forum Theater. The first play, *A Great Career,* is a work built on the assumption that office life is impossible but that, for all the meaningless work and the petty quarrels among employees, it is as much "womb as tomb" or, as the heroine snarlingly calls it as the play opens, "a home away from home." The play is about a harried clerical worker named Linda who has a report to prepare. During the course of the action she explodes, gets herself fired, and then, realizing that there is no place else to go that is not the same, literally begs to be taken back. This description makes the play sound more painful than funny, and Dizenzo obviously wants his audience to hang on to that side of the story, which the ending certainly encourages them to do. As a fellow employee tells her about the new bookkeeper who tried unsuccessfully to commit suicide in the men's room, we see Linda crawling around the stage and picking up the papers she scattered during her defiant scene. In *A Great Career* Dizenzo shows the emasculating nature of office life by having men play women and women turning out to be men.

In *An Evening for Merlin Finch* the sterility of the office gives way to the silent violence of the home. Darlene Finch, an insensitive middle-class, middle-American housewife, is plagued by a vengeful mother who materializes in the shape of her son Merlin. This becomes her vision of hatred and guilt. As he demonstrates in all of his plays, Dizenzo is fascinated with the normality within a sick society. His plays point up the compromises that sink the soul of modern man into a dismal acceptance of everyday predicaments. Merlin, the focus of concern, is forced to play his bassoon for company. Each observation his parents make is a body blow and each gesture of contact a refusal. Merlin's life turns out to be an eternal adolescence, and as he blows away on his bassoon, his slim identity evaporates before our eyes. His mother's ignorance and hostility continuously undercut the comic image of Merlin's silly instrument. Here Dizenzo's dry black humor, together with a carefully constructed situation, exposes and explodes the Finches' severely distorted family life.

Another Dizenzo play that in its own bizarre and comic way explodes the quiet violence of family life is *Disaster Strikes the Home,* which has also been presented under the title *Why I Went Crazy.* In this play Dizenzo submerges his audience in a complete and outrageous comic world. Once again the sexes are changed: wives are played by men, and husbands by women. The reversal is not a gimmick but rather a surrealistic view of the sexual strangulation that exists in the American household. Dizenzo counterpoints these outlandish images with careful, but empty, colloquial speech. The violent role reversals that take place in weak marriages epitomize Dizenzo's nightmare view of American family life.

Dizenzo's playwriting is always startlingly inventive and for the most part consistently amusing. By distorting the real world he illuminates the dark emotional silences between people, which is something many contemporary playwrights attempt but seldom achieve. Although his writing has none of the manicured edge of Albee's or Ionesco's, and in places is in serious need of tightening, Dizenzo has a keen ear for the truthful phrase and a fine farceur's instinct for pace. His theatrical vision is controlled and iconoclastic. He imitates no one, relying totally on his own creative talents and thereby fostering a theatrical voice that is both unique and thoroughly American.

—Bernard Carragher

DONLEAVY, J(ames) P(atrick)

Nationality: Irish. **Born:** Brooklyn, New York, United States, 23 April 1926; became Irish citizen, 1967. **Education:** A preparatory school, New York; Trinity College, Dublin. **Military Service:** Served in the United States Naval Reserve during World War II. **Family:** Married 1) Valerie Heron (divorced), one son and one daughter; 2) Mary Wilson Price in 1970 (divorced), one daughter and one son. **Awards:** London *Evening Standard* award, 1961; Brandeis University Creative Arts award, 1961; American Academy award, 1975; Woldfest Houston Gold award, 1992; Cine Golden Eagle award for writer and narrator, 1993. **Address:** Levington Park, Mullingar, County Westmeath, Ireland.

Publications

Plays

The Ginger Man, adaptation of his own novel (produced London and Dublin, 1959; New York, 1963). New York, Random House, 1961; as *What They Did in Dublin, with The Ginger Man: A Play*, London, MacGibbon and Kee, 1962.
Fairy Tales of New York (produced Croydon, Surrey, 1960; London, 1961; New York, 1980). London, Penguin, and New York, Random House, 1961.
A Singular Man, adaptation of his own novel (produced Cambridge and London, 1964; Westport, Connecticut, 1967). London, Bodley Head, 1965.
The Plays of J.P. Donleavy (includes *The Ginger Man*, *Fairy Tales of New York*, *A Singular Man*, *The Saddest Summer of Samuel S*). New York, Delacorte Press, 1972; London, Penguin, 1974.
The Beastly Beatitudes of Balthazar B, adaptation of his own novel (produced London, 1981; Norfolk, Virginia, 1985).

Radio Play: *Helen*, 1956.

Novels

The Ginger Man. Paris, Olympia Press, and London, Spearman, 1955; New York, McDowell Obolensky, 1958; complete edition, London, Corgi, 1963; New York, Delacorte Press, 1965.

A Singular Man. Boston, Little Brown, 1963; London, Bodley Head, 1964.

The Saddest Summer of Samuel S. New York, Delacorte Press, 1966; London, Eyre and Spottiswoode, 1967.

The Beastly Beatitudes of Balthazar B. New York, Delacorte Press, 1968; London, Eyre and Spottiswoode, 1969.

The Onion Eaters. New York, Delacorte Press, and London, Eyre and Spottiswoode, 1971.

A Fairy Tale of New York. New York, Delacorte Press, and London, Eyre Methuen, 1973.

The Destinies of Darcy Dancer, Gentleman. New York, Delacorte Press, 1977; London, Allen Lane, 1978.

Schultz. New York, Delacorte Press, 1979; London, Allen Lane, 1980.

Leila. New York, Delacorte Press, and London, Allen Lane, 1983.

DeAlfonce Tennis: The Superlative Game of Eccentric Champions: Its History, Accoutrements, Conduct, Rules and Regimen. London, Weidenfeld and Nicolson, 1984; New York, Dutton, 1985.

Are You Listening Rabbi Löw. London, Viking, 1987.

That Darcy, That Dancer, That Gentleman. London, Viking, 1990; New York, Atlantic Monthly Press, 1991.

Short Stories

Meet My Maker the Mad Molecule. Boston, Little Brown, 1964; London, Bodley Head, 1965.

The Lady Who Liked Clean Rest Rooms: The Chronicle of One of the Strangest Stories Ever to Be Rumoured Around New York. New York, Thornwillow Press, 1995.

An Author and His Image: The Collected Shorter Pieces. London and New York, Vintage, 1997.

Other

The Unexpurgated Code: A Complete Manual of Survival and Manners, drawings by the author. New York, Delacorte Press, and London, Wildwood House, 1975.

Ireland: In All Her Sins and in Some of Her Graces. London, Joseph, and New York, Viking, 1986.

A Singular Country, illustrated by Patrick Prendergast. Peterborough, Ryan, 1989; New York, Norton, 1990.

The History of the Ginger Man. London, Viking, 1994.

Wrong Information Is Being Given Out at Princeton. London, Little Brown, 1998.

*

Bibliography: By David W. Madden, in *Bulletin of Bibliography* (Westport, Connecticut), September 1982.

Critical Studies: *J. P. Donleavy: The Style of His Sadness and Humor* by Charles G. Masinton, Bowling Green, Ohio, Popular Press, 1975; *Isolation and Protest: A Case Study of J. P. Donleavy's Fiction* by R. K. Sharma, New Delhi, Ajanta, 1983; "American Readings of J. P. Donleavy's *The Ginger Man*" by Donald E. Morse, in *Eire Ireland: A Journal of Irish Studies* (St. Paul, Minnesota), Fall 1991, pp. 128-38.

* * *

Although J. P. Donleavy is better known as a novelist, he has adapted his novels *The Ginger Man* and *A Singular Man* into plays that have received fairly successful productions, and his original stage play, *Fairy Tales of New York,* won the *Evening Standard*'s Most Promising Playwright Award for 1961. In adjusting to the medium of the theater, Donleavy faced two particular problems. His prose style is rich and idiosyncratic, with a quality that encourages cult enthusiasms, but it was not clear to what extent this verbal power could be incorporated into stage dialogue without leaving the impression of overwriting. Too, his novels are usually written from the standpoint of one man, an antihero such as Sebastian Dangerfield or George Smith, but in a play the audience is necessarily aware of other characters simply because they are on the stage. If the central character talks too much, the audience's sympathy may be drawn toward the reactions of other people to him. A single angle of vision, easy to maintain in a novel, is often hard to achieve in the theater, which is a multidimensional medium.

Donleavy's first play, *The Ginger Man,* revealed an uncertain control of these difficulties. The story concerns Sebastian Dangerfield, an impoverished American living with his English wife, Marion, in Dublin. He is supposedly studying law at Trinity College, but his main efforts are directed toward staving off creditors, avoiding the responsibilities of fatherhood, and raking together enough money to get drunk. In the novel Sebastian's sheer wildness, his refusal to settle down, is exciting; it is an archetypal rebellion against dreary conformity. But in the play we are unavoidably aware of the pain Sebastian causes others, particularly Marion, who leaves him, and a genteel spinster, Miss Frost, whom he seduces. And the fine, uninhibited imagination of Sebastian, which provides so much fun in the book, is in the play relentlessly controlled by the physical surroundings of the set: the squalid flat at One Mohammed Road, and the prim suburban house at 11 Golden Vale Park. "*The Ginger Man*," concluded Richard Gilman, "desperately requires: song, dance, lyrical fragments, voices from nowhere, shapes, apparitions, unexplainable gestures." In the format of a naturalistic play it lost many of the qualities that made the book so remarkable. Even the theme seemed less original, and the relationship between O'Keefe and Sebastian recalled the boozing friendship between Joxer and Captain Boyle in O'Casey's *Juno and the Paycock.*

Fairy Tales of New York is much more successful. It is a sequence of four related anecdotes that almost seem to continue the ginger man's career. An American returns to his native city with his English wife, who dies on the voyage. Cornelius Christian is in the same state of desolation as was Sebastian at the close of the earlier play. He is harassed by poverty, and he is guilty and grief stricken. The four scenes illustrate Cornelius's gradual rehabilitation: the burial of his wife and his job at the funeral parlor, his entry into the American business world, his workouts at a gymnasium, and finally his successful, though imaginary, conquest of a snobbish head waiter and an embarrassed girlfriend. Unlike Sebastian, however, Cornelius is a reserved, quiet man who observes others and sometimes pokes gentle fun at them. This changed role for the central character, together with the much greater flexibility of form, allows Donleavy's great gifts for caricature, witty dialogue, and buoyant fun to be more evident. Nor are the episodes as unrelated and superficial as they may appear. Donleavy stresses the contrast between the democratic ideals of American society and rigidly class-structured and snobbish habits. Christian is employed because he has been to Europe and acquired "breeding." He dazzles the head waiter, who refused to serve him because he wore peach shoes, by dressing as a visiting Eastern potentate wearing no shoes at all. The spurious emotionalism of the funeral parlor is related to Christian's moving grief, and the sheer falseness of an overcommercialized society is exposed with a delicate skill that only Evelyn Waugh and Edward Albee have matched.

Although *A Singular Man* lacks some of the moral seriousness and the fun of *Fairy Tales of New York*, it, too, is a rewarding play. It is centered around the life of a fairly successful New York businessman, George Smith, and his friendships and affairs with three women—Ann Martin, Sally Tomson, and Shirl. Smith is a fall guy who always misses out on the opportunities he dreams about. "The only time the traffic will stop for me," he confesses to Shirl, "is when I'm dead." His sexual fantasies focus on Sally Tomson, a gorgeous secretary who is protected by her tough-guy brother and many other lovers. Her death at the end of the play, just before her marriage to a rich tycoon, crystallizes Smith's sense of cosmic defeat. But Smith never quite gives up hope, and his resilience through successive embarrassments and failures provides the mainspring for the play. *A Singular Man* is similar in construction to *Fairy Tales of New York*. It has a sequence of 12 anecdotal scenes that work both on the level of isolated and very amusing revue sketches and together as a group, with the insights of one episode being carried forward to the next until the full picture of the society and the central man emerges. In the first scene Smith opts out of a conversation with a boring friend just by answering, "Beep beep," but in the seventh he tries the same tactics with Shirl only to discover that his relationship with her is too charged and complex to admit such an evasion.

Donleavy's style of humor is reminiscent both of *New Yorker* cartoons and of the American dramatist Murray Schisgal, whose plays are also popular in Britain. But his jokes are never flippant, although they do sometimes seem whimsical. They succeed because they are based on detailed observation and a rich command of language. Although Donleavy may not have lived up to the promise of *Fairy Tales of New York*, he has been an exciting dramatist.

—John Elsom

DREXLER, Rosalyn

Pseudonym: Julia Sorel. **Nationality:** American. **Born:** New York City, 25 November 1926. **Education:** Self-educated. **Family:** Married Sherman Drexler in 1946; one daughter and one son. **Career:** Painter, sculptor, singer, and wrestler; taught at the University of Iowa, Iowa City, 1976-77. **Awards:** Obie award, 1965, 1979, 1985; Rockefeller grant, 1965 (2 grants), 1968, 1974; *Paris Review* fiction prize, 1966; Guggenheim fellowship, 1970; Emmy award, 1974. **Member:** New Dramatists; Dramatists Guild. **Agent:** Georges Borchardt Inc., 136 East 57th Street, New York, New York 10022, U.S.A.

Publications

Plays

Home Movies; and Softly, and Consider the Nearness, music by Al Carmines (produced New York, 1964). Included in *The Line of Least Existence and Other Plays*, 1967.

Hot Buttered Roll (produced New York, 1966; London, 1970). Included in *The Line of Least Existence and Other Plays*, 1967; with *The Investigation*, London, Methuen, 1969.

The Investigation (produced Boston and New York, 1966; London, 1970). Included in *The Line of Least Existence and Other Plays*, 1967; with *Hot Buttered Roll*, London, Methuen, 1969.

The Line of Least Existence (produced New York, 1967; Edinburgh, 1968). Included in *The Line of Least Existence and Other Plays*, 1967.

The Line of Least Existence and Other Plays. New York, Random House, 1967.

The Bed Was Full (produced New York, 1972). Included in *The Line of Least Existence and Other Plays*, 1967.

Skywriting, in *Collision Course* (produced New York, 1968). New York, Random House, 1968.

Was I Good? (produced New York, 1972).

She Who Was He (produced New York, 1973).

The Ice Queen (produced Boston, 1973).

Travesty Parade (produced Los Angeles, 1974).

Vulgar Lives (produced New York, 1979).

The Writers' Opera, music by John Braden (produced New York, 1979).

Graven Image (produced New York, 1980).

Starburn, music by Michael Meadows (produced New York, 1983).

Room 17-C (produced Omaha, 1983).

Delicate Feelings (produced New York, 1984).

Transients Welcome (includes *Room 17-C*, *Lobby*, *Utopia Parkway*) (produced New York, 1984). New York, Broadway Play Publishing, 1984.

A Matter of Life and Death (produced New York, 1986).

What Do You Call It? (produced New York, 1986).

The Heart That Eats Itself (produced New York, 1987).

Dear: A New Play. New York, Applause Books, 1997.

Video: *The Lily Tomlin Special*, with others, 1973.

Novels

I Am the Beautiful Stranger. New York, Grossman, 1965; London, Weidenfeld and Nicolson, 1967.

One or Another. New York, Dutton, 1970; London, Blond, 1971.

To Smithereens. New York, New American Library, 1972; London, Weidenfeld and Nicolson, 1973; as *Submissions of a Lady Wrestler*, London, Mayflower, 1976.

The Cosmopolitan Girl. New York, Evans, 1975.

Dawn: Portrait of a Teenage Runaway (as Julia Sorel). New York, Ballantine, 1976.

Alex: Portrait of a Teenage Prostitute (as Julia Sorel). New York, Ballantine, 1977.

Rocky (novelization of screenplay; as Julia Sorel). New York, Ballantine, 1977.

See How She Runs (novelization of screenplay; as Julia Sorel). New York, Ballantine, 1978.

Starburn: The Story of Jenni Love. New York, Simon and Schuster, 1979.

Forever Is Sometimes Temporary When Tomorrow Rolls Around. New York, Simon and Schuster, 1979.

Bad Guy. New York, Dutton, 1982.

Other

Rosalyn Drexler: Intimate Emotions. New York, Grey Art Gallery, 1986.
Art Does (Not!) Exist. Norman, Illinois, FC2, 1996.

*

Critical Study: "Rosalyn Drexler's Semiotics of Instability" by Rosette C. Lamont, in *Theater* (New Haven, Connecticut), Winter 1985, pp. 70-77.

Rosalyn Drexler comments:

I try to write with vitality, joy, and honesty. My plays may be called absurd. I write to amuse myself. I often amuse others.

Almost all my reviews have been excellent, but I am not produced much. It seems that every theatre wants to premiere a play. (That's how they get grants.) Therefore, if a play is done once, good or bad, that's it for the playwright—unless she is Ibsen, Shaw . . . etc.

Playwriting is my first love, I'm considered established, but I have just begun.

* * *

Rosalyn Drexler came to prominence as a novelist and playwright at a time when the absurdist symbolism of Albee was very much in vogue. Her own work of the 1960s has sometimes been called "pop art," and it has also been billed as "An Evening of Bad Taste." Whatever it is called, it seems very much a reaction against the intellectualism and pretentiousness that surrounded the theater of the absurd. By the 1980s, remaining true to her early style, she had found sympathetic and emphatically alternative production milieus with groups like the Omaha Magic Theater.

Bad taste is often both the subject and the style of Drexler's plays as she manipulates the audience into compromising corners. *The Investigation* presents itself as a simple if not naive parable about a police interrogation of an adolescent murder suspect, a timid, puritanical boy who is eventually bullied by the police into suicide. Some critics found it a fashionable tract against police brutality and hence a very slight work. The characters are, as is usual in Drexler, two-dimensional, but the boy is so colorless that he fails to be engaging as an object of sympathy. The detective, on the other hand, is so resourceful that his techniques of sadistic attrition become the main theatrical dynamic. Much of the detective's imaginative energy is invested in verbal reconstruction of the grotesque rape and murder, putting the boy in the central role. Because the audience receives no evidence from any external source, there remains the possibility that the facts the detective narrates may be correct and that what appears to be his sadism is, in fact, nausea at an outrageous crime. In the second scene there is a surprising technical twist when the murder victim's twin sister introduces herself to the audience and volunteers to reenact the crime, using a boyfriend of hers as the accused boy. That this is parodic is obvious—they congratulate each other on their performances and show no sadness that a girl has been killed—but the mechanics of the parody are obscure. Does the scene represent the detective's hypothesis? The boy's nightmare? Or public assumptions about what happens when repression meets precociousness? The only possibility to be eliminated is that the scene shows what really happened. When questions like these are left open at the end of a play, the author can hardly be accused of triteness.

If she generated questions prodigally, Drexler also seems to have many techniques for ensuring that her plays do not become too meaningful. The title piece of her collection *The Line of Least Existence*, for example, may consist of profundity or malapropism. Verbal vandalism certainly does exist in the play but so does an utterly unpretentious playfulness in which words are discovered and traded just for their phatic values. Because Drexler's dramatic world is never remotely naturalistic, the reference of words is often totally unclear. One wonders if "least existence" actually defines the dramatic cosmos as a kind of limbo, especially when at the end the central character, with a heroic irresponsibility, commits his wife and himself to a mental asylum. In *Hot Buttered Roll,* Mr. Corrupt Savage, a senile, bedridden billionaire, exercises his waning appetites with the assistance of a call girl and an Amazonian bodyguard who from time to time throws him back into bed. The cast also includes two pimps, a "purveyor of girly girls" and a "purveyor of burly girls," but the essential action seems to be in a bunker, where all connections and relationships have been severed and the use of appetite is tentative and vicarious. As with the detective in *The Investigation*, the more scabrous parts of the dialogue sometimes have a vatic quality, so that the impact is often in its vagueness or suggestiveness. Thus, the play's central image is never clearly stated, but it seems to be that of (gendered) man as a kind of transplant patient, his facilities being monitored externally, his needs being canvassed through a huge mail order system, and his responses being tested by the bizarre performances by the call girl at the foot of the bed. Very similar in rationale is *Softly, and Consider the Nearness*, in which a woman uses a television set as a surrogate world of experience.

In the later play *Skywriting* there are only two characters, and their referential functions are trimmed back even further. The unnamed man and woman seem to be archetypes, and as such they make this an important work, a transition from the pop plays of the 1960s toward the mythical work of the 1970s. Beyond the fact that the diction seems closer to Drexler's Bronx than to Eden, the play is not located in any time or place. The two characters, who are segregated on either side of the stage, argue about the possession of a huge (projected) picture postcard of clouds. As in Shepard, the sky is perceived as a fantasy arena, and the characters instinctively take a territorial attitude toward it, invading each other's minds as they defend their sexuality. This is a very clever and economical play, in which the primordial merges with the futuristic before dissolving in a throwaway ending. *She Who Was He* investigates the world of myth and ritual in an exotic, distant past; the style is lavish and operatic, but the attempt at transcendence has been problematic for audiences. In her Obie-winning *The Writers' Opera* Drexler returns to a more familiar mode, the perversely illogical associative collage of stereotypical items. The pretentiousness and fickleness of the art world is the satirical target in the play, and this world is reflected in the domestic behavior of the central characters, with a transsexual finding himself in an Oedipal relationship with his son. Such events differ only in degree, however, from the ingredients of her first stage success, *Home Movies*, in which outrageous farcical grotesquerie revolves round the prodigal and inventive sexuality of the characters. There, as throughout Drexler's large output of plays, novels, and novelizations, her most characteristic trait, the ridiculous pun, typifies an author who defies critical assessment while at the same time—in her own inimitable phrasing—she "shoots the vapids."

—Howard McNaughton

DUBERMAN, Martin (Bauml)

Nationality: American. **Born:** New York City, 6 August 1930. **Education:** Yale University, New Haven, Connecticut, 1948-52, B.A. 1952 (Phi Beta Kappa); Harvard University, Cambridge, Massachusetts, 1952-57, M.A. 1953, Ph.D. 1957. **Career:** Tutor, Harvard University, 1955-57; instructor and assistant professor (Morse Fellow, 1961-62), Yale University, 1957-62; assistant professor, 1962-65, associate professor, 1965-67, and professor of history, 1967-71, Princeton University, New Jersey. Distinguished professor, Lehman College Graduate Center, 1971—, and founder, 1986, Center for Lesbian and Gay Studies, City University of New York. **Awards:** Bancroft prize, for history, 1962; Vernon Rice award, 1964; American Academy award, 1971; Manhattan Borough Presidents gold medal, 1988; George Freedley prize, 1990; Lambda Book award, 1990 (twice); Myer award, 1990. **Address:** 475 West 22nd Street, New York, New York 10011, U.S.A.

Publications

Plays

In White America (produced New York, 1963; London, 1964). Boston, Houghton Mifflin, 1964; London, Faber, 1965.
Metaphors, in *Collision Course* (produced New York, 1968). New York, Random House, 1968.
Groups (produced New York, 1968).
The Colonial Dudes (produced New York, 1969). Included in *Male Armor*, 1975.
The Memory Bank: The Recorder, and The Electric Map (produced New York, 1970; *The Recorder* produced London, 1974). New York, Dial Press, 1970.
Payments (produced New York, 1971). Included in *Male Armor*, 1975.
Soon, music by Joseph Martinez Kookoolis and Scott Fagan, adaptation of a story by Kookoolis, Fagan, and Robert Greenwald (produced New York, 1971).
Dudes (produced New York, 1972).
Elagabalus (produced New York, 1973). Included in *Male Armor*, 1975.
Male Armor: Selected Plays 1968-1974 (includes *Metaphors*, *The Colonial Dudes*, *The Recorder*, *The Guttman Ordinary Scale*, *Payments*, *The Electric Map*, *Elagabalus*). New York, Dutton, 1975.
Visions of Kerouac (produced New York, 1976). Boston, Little Brown, 1977.
Mother Earth: An Epic Drama of Emma Goldman's Life. New York, St. Martin's Press, 1991.
Posing Naked (produced New York, 1997).

Screenplays: *The Deed*, 1969; *Mother Earth*, 1971.

Other

Charles Francis Adams 1807-1886. Boston, Houghton Mifflin, 1961.
James Russell Lowell. Boston, Houghton Mifflin, 1966.
The Uncompleted Past (essays). New York, Random House, 1969.
Black Mountain: An Exploration in Community. New York, Dutton, 1972; London, Wildwood House, 1974; revised edition, New York, Norton, 1992.
About Time: Exploring the Gay Past. New York, Seahorse, 1986; revised edition, New York, Dutton, 1992.
Paul Robeson. London, Bodley Head, and New York, Knopf, 1989.
Cures: A Gay Man's Odyssey. New York, Dutton, 1991.
Stonewall. New York, Dutton, 1993.
Midlife Queer. New York, Scribner's, 1996.

Editor, *The Antislavery Vanguard: New Essays on the Abolitionists*. Princeton, New Jersey, Princeton University Press, 1965.
Editor with Martha Vicinus and George Chauncey, Jr., *Hidden from History: Reclaiming the Gay and Lesbian Past*. New York, New American Library, 1989; London, Penguin, 1991.
Editor, *A Queer World*. New York, New York University Press, 1997.
Editor, *Queer Representations*. New York, New York University Press, 1997.

*

Critical Studies: "The Hairpin Drop Heard 'round the Academy: A Review of Teaching Texts in Lesbian and Gay Studies" by Kathleen Kennedy, in *GLQ: A Journal of Lesbian and Gay Studies* (Langhorne, Pennsylvania), 1994, pp. 349-58.

* * *

Martin Duberman's *In White America* was first produced in October 1963, the era of the New Frontier and a time of great optimism in American social consciousness. The play was an immediate, sustained, and internationally acclaimed success. Its author, however, was a playwright by avocation only, and in subject matter, theory of communication, and evolution his subsequent theatrical productivity has proved to reflect his true profession. Long a professor of history at Lehman College, Duberman is a professional historian of recognized accomplishment and the author of several works in that field: *James Russell Lowell, Charles Francis Adams, The Uncompleted Past, Black Mountain: An Exploration in Community,* and *About Time*.

In White America is less a play in a traditional literary sense than what might be called an evening of theater. It is an assemblage of documents from the history of the black American's experience of 200 years of suffering. As a historical event reflecting the social fabric of its time, the piece is significant, and at the time of its presentation it was a moving experience for all audiences. It weaves together dialogues, documents, songs, and narration with impressive sensitivity for theatrical construction, and it suggests a possible form for playwrights to explore. In the 1963 essay "Presenting the Past" Duberman argued that "the past has something to say to us . . . a knowledge of past experience can provide valuable guidelines, though not blueprints, for acting in the present." It is clear that his professional concern for history provided him with his subject matter. He did not create material but rather selected, edited, and shaped it. His teaching duties, moreover, led him to a belief in the theatrical and dramatic potential of oral communication, the belief that a lecturer can be more than informative. "The benefits of a union between history and drama," Duberman has written, "would not by any means be all on one side. If theater, with its ample skill in communication, could increase the immediacy of past experience, history, with its ample material on human behavior, could broaden the range of theatrical testimony." In his preface to the printed play he added, "I chose to tell this story on the stage, and through historical documents, because I wanted to combine the evocative power of the spoken word with the confirming power of historical fact." It was the assessment of critics of the time that Duberman had succeeded in all respects. The play stimulated an awakening social consciousness, was vital in its enactment, and communicated its thesis most effectively.

In the late 1960s Duberman's attitudes toward the uses of the past and the efficacy of wedding history to theater began to change. Perhaps the disenchantment of the New Left that followed the Kennedy and King assassinations influenced his thinking. His work for the theater abandoned the path suggested by *In White America*, and he began to write fictional, or invented, drama.

Male Armor collected seven plays written between 1968 and 1974. Two are full-length, and four of the one-acts had been published previously. None had received successful production in the commercial theater. In his introduction to the collection Duberman professed that the plays explore a common theme—"What does it mean to be a 'man'?" The collection's title, he explained, was meant to recall Wilhelm Reich's concept of "character armor"—the devices we employ to protect ourselves from our own energy, particularly our sexual energy. Each of the plays investigates the way in which we build protective roles that then dominate us. For Duberman the way to destroy these confining roles apparently is through androgyny, either practiced or metaphorical.

Metaphors, The Electric Map, and *The Recorder* are all highly literate sparrings between consenting adults that explore the themes of power struggle and homosexuality. In *Metaphors* a young applicant to Yale University nearly seduces his admissions interviewer. *The Electric Map* and *The Recorder,* which had an unsuccessful off-Broadway production under the title *The Memory Bank,* are also duologues. The former is set before an elaborate electrified map of the battle of Gettysburg, and it self-consciously uses the visual analogue to puff up a foolish domestic quarrel between two brothers into what the author hopes will be something akin to universality. There is a predictable undertone of latent homosexuality to the trite and poorly motivated action. *The Recorder* is an interview of the friend of a great man by an academic historian. In it Duberman is intrigued by the ineffectiveness and inaccuracy of historical inquiry, and the play unquestionably reflects his growing disenchantment with the study of history as well as his growing use of sexuality as a dramatic subject. By the time of these plays Duberman was referring to himself as "more a writer than a historian."

The latest play in *Male Armor* is *Elagabalus,* a six-scene realistic play about Adrian, a self-indulgent and affluent androgynist. Duberman writes, "Adrian is playful and daring. His gaiety may be contaminated by petulance and willfulness, but he *is* moving toward an *un*-armored territory, moving out so far that finally he's left with no protection against the traditional weaponry brought to bear against him . . . other than the ultimate defense of self-destruction." In his quest for self, Adrian stabs himself fatally in the groin, and the final image the writer offers is a gratuitous freeze-frame from the porno film *Big Stick,* in which a teenage girl sucks sensuously on a Popsicle. This reader was reminded of the adage that many people—perhaps Adrian or Duberman—who are looking for themselves may not like what they find. Adrian is a boring character whose self-destruction does not seem significant.

The Uncompleted Past is a collection of Duberman's critical and historical essays that concludes with an expression of his disenchantment with the study of history and reveals why his theatrical development moved toward fiction, in which area he appears undistinguished, and away from the documentary, in which his initial acclaim was achieved. He writes:

> For those among the young, historians and otherwise, who are chiefly interested in changing the present, I can only say . . . they doom themselves to bitter disappointment if they seek their guides to action in a study of the past. Though I have tried to make it otherwise, I have found that a "life in history" has given me very limited information or perspective with which to understand the central concerns of my own life and my own times.

It seems probable that *In White America* will stand as Duberman's major writing for the theater and that it will prove more significant as an event of cultural history than as either an innovation in theatrical form or the first work in the career of a significant playwright. It thus belies the very attitudes toward history and the theater that Duberman has come to hold.

—Thomas B. Markus

DUNN, Nell (Mary)

Nationality: British. **Born:** London in 1936. **Education:** A convent school. **Family:** Married the writer Jeremy Sandford in 1956 (marriage dissolved); three sons. **Awards:** Rhys Memorial prize, 1964; Susan Smith Blackburn prize, for play, 1981; *Evening Standard* award, for play, 1982; Society of West End Theatre award, 1982. **Agent:** Curtis Brown, 162-168 Regent Street, London W1R 5TB. **Address:** 10 Bell Lane, Twickenham, Middlesex, England.

PUBLICATIONS

Plays

Steaming (produced London, 1981; Stamford, Connecticut, and New York, 1982). Ambergate, Derbyshire, Amber Lane Press, 1981; New York, Limelight, 1984.

Sketches in *Variety Night* (produced London, 1982).

I Want, with Adrian Henri, adaptation of their own novel (produced Liverpool, 1983; London, 1986).

The Little Heroine (produced Southampton, 1988).

My Silver Shoes. London, Bloomsbury, 1996.

Screenplay: *Poor Cow,* with Ken Loach, 1967.

Television Plays: *Up the Junction*, from her own stories, 1965; *Every Breath You Take*, 1988.

Novels

Poor Cow. London, MacGibbon and Kee, and New York, Doubleday, 1967.
The Incurable. London, Cape, and New York, Doubleday, 1971.
I Want, with Adrian Henri. London, Cape, 1972.
Tear His Head Off His Shoulders. London, Cape, 1974; New York, Doubleday, 1975.
The Only Child: A Simple Story of Heaven and Hell. London, Cape, 1978.

Short Stories

Up the Junction. London, MacGibbon and Kee, 1963; Philadelphia, Lippincott, 1966.

Other

Talking to Women. London, MacGibbon and Kee, 1965.
Freddy Gets Married (for children). London, MacGibbon and Kee, 1969.
Grandmothers. London, Chatto and Windus, 1991.

Editor, *Living Like I Do*. London, Futura, 1977; as *Different Drummers*, New York, Harcourt Brace, 1977.

* * *

Nell Dunn was best known in the 1960s and 1970s as a chronicler of the lives of working-class women. The child of a securely middle-class background and with a convent school education, she became fascinated by the haphazard lives of women who existed without the safety net of money or education to sustain them. In 1963 she published a collection of short stories, *Up the Junction,* that consisted of vignettes of life as she had observed it among the young in Clapham. The book, which she later adapted for television, emphasized the vitality and sharpness of perception of the women together with their acceptance of the fate life had mapped out for them—a few short butterfly days followed by a hopeless and unrewarding existence.

In her first novel, *Poor Cow,* Dunn centered on one woman, Joy, whose life from early on is set on a downward spiral. At 22 she has gone through one broken marriage and has a young son, Jonny. As her own life deteriorates, she transfers her hopes onto her son, trusting that his life at least will be better. Her epitaph on her own is "To think when I was a kid I planned to conquer the world and if anyone saw me now they'd say, 'She's had a rough night, poor cow.'" A film was made of the book by director Ken Loach.

Dunn's stage play *Steaming* continues her fascination with working-class women and with the character on whom Joy was based in particular, the woman who lives for freedom and fun but in reality remains a prisoner of her lack of self-confidence and the hard brutalities of life. Josie, the Joy figure in the play, is lively and earthy, and she enjoys leading her men in dance, but she invariably ends up the worse for it. "How come I always get hit on the left side?" she asks after yet another beating up.

Steaming is set in a London Turkish bath, which provides Dunn with the background for what she is best at—women talking among themselves without the constraints of a male presence. The only male, the caretaker of the baths, is dimly glimpsed through a glass door, unable to enter the female domain. The six characters are a mixture of age and class. Apart from Josie, there is Mrs. Meadow, a repressive mother who will not let her retarded, overweight daughter take her "plastics" off, even in the shower. There are two middle-class women—Jane, a mature student with a bohemian past, and Nancy, who shops at Peter Jones and whose husband has just left her after 22 years of marriage. The baths are presided over by Violet, in her 40s, who has worked there as an attendant for 18 years and who is threatened with early retirement if the council goes ahead with its intention to close the building.

Not a great deal happens in the play, but the humor and conversation sustain the evening. Without their clothes and in the steamy companionship of the baths, the women develop a sisterhood that transcends class barriers. The new entrant, Nancy, who at first is nervous of the milieu, is drawn in and at one point breaks down and talks about her broken marriage and the pressures that have kept her dependent on a man. Josie reveals that her seeming sexual freedom is also tied to dependence on a man's finances. Their campaign against the closure of the baths gives them a new lease on life, and by the end Josie, after making a brilliant, if disregarded, speech at a public meeting, says that she is going to get an education. Nancy, the rejected wife, announces that she is "going to get fucked," and Dawn asserts herself against her overprotective mother.

Whether the ending is anything more than a way of giving an upbeat finale to the play is a matter for debate, and Dunn's characters probably find that they are not able to change their lives greatly after their temporary euphoria. The dialogue of the working-class women has far more of a ring of truth about it than the dialogue of the middle-class women, but the author has always found a richness and rhythm in working-class speech that she fails to find in the more educated voice. *Steaming* can be regarded as a gentle piece of female consciousness-raising. It must also be one of the few feminist plays to have brought large numbers of male chauvinists in, attracted by the fact that the cast members are nude for much of the time.

I Want, written in 1972 in collaboration with Adrian Henri, is about a love affair between a well-bred, convent-educated girl but "with the devil in her" and a scholarship boy from a Liverpool terrace home. They meet in the 1920s, and the play charts the course of their relationship over the next 60 years. It has moments of humor but lacks the strength of *Steaming.* Dunn also published a book of interviews, *Talking to Women,* in 1965. It is of interest for its recording of the stirrings of female consciousness among divergent women. In 1991 she published a sequel in *Grandmothers.* Dunn, herself a grandmother, drew on her own experiences as well as on those of her friends to investigate the pleasures and pains of being a grandmother. Based on conversations with 14 of her friends, the book is particularly interesting because of the variety of backgrounds from which her subjects come and because of the contrast between the traditional image of a grandmother and present-day reality.

Dunn's play *The Little Heroine,* which deals with a young woman's addiction to heroin, was produced during the same year as Granada Television produced her *Every Breath You Take.* The latter play deals with the effect on a newly divorced woman,

Imogen, of finding her 13-year-old son diagnosed as diabetic. Obsessed with Tom's diet and insulin injections, she is unable to concentrate on anything else. In the end it is Tom, mature and sensible for his age, who restores her sense of proportion and helps her rebuild the life and career she had seemed ready to abandon.

—Clare Colvin

DURANG, Christopher (Ferdinand)

Nationality: American. **Born:** Montclair, New Jersey, 2 January 1949. **Education:** Harvard University, Cambridge, Massachusetts, 1967-71, A.B. in English 1971; Yale University School of Drama, New Haven, Connecticut, 1971-74, M.F.A. in playwriting 1974. **Career:** Drama teacher, Southern Connecticut College, New Haven, 1975, and Yale University, 1975-76. **Awards:** CBS fellowship, 1975; Rockefeller grant, 1976; Guggenheim grant, 1979; Obie award, 1980, 1985; Lecomte de Nouy Foundation grant, 1981; Dramatists Guild Hull-Warriner award, 1985; Lila Wallace Readers Digest Writing award, 1994-96. **Agent:** Helen Merrill Ltd., 425 West 23rd Street #1F, New York, New York 10011, U.S.A.

PUBLICATIONS

Plays

The Nature and Purpose of the Universe (produced Northampton, Massachusetts, 1971; New York, 1975). Included in *The Nature and Purpose of the Universe; Death Comes to Us All, Mary Agnes; 'dentity Crisis*, 1979.

'dentity Crisis (as *Robert*, produced Cambridge, Massachusetts, 1971; as *'dentity Crisis*, also director: produced New Haven, Connecticut, 1975; London, 1986). Included in *The Nature and Purpose of the Universe; Death Comes to Us All, Mary Agnes; 'dentity Crisis*, 1979.

Better Dead Than Sorry, music by Jack Feldman, lyrics by Durang (produced New Haven, Connecticut, 1972; New York, 1973).

I Don't Generally Like Poetry But Have You Read "Trees"?, with Albert Innaurato (produced New Haven, Connecticut, 1972; New York, 1973).

The Life Story of Mitzi Gaynor; or, Gyp, with Albert Innaurato (produced New Haven, Connecticut, 1973).

The Marriage of Bette and Boo (produced New Haven, Connecticut, 1973; revised version produced New York, 1979). New Haven, Connecticut, *Yale/Theatre*, 1973; revised version (produced New York, 1985; London, 1987), New York, Dramatists Play Service, 1985.

The Idiots Karamazov, with Albert Innaurato, music by Jack Feldman, lyrics by Durang (produced New Haven, Connecticut, 1974). New Haven, Connecticut, *Yale/Theatre*, 1974; augmented edition, New York, Dramatists Play Service, 1981.

Titanic (produced New Haven, Connecticut, 1974; New York, 1976). New York, Dramatists Play Service, 1983.

Death Comes to Us All, Mary Agnes (produced New Haven, Connecticut, 1975). Included in *The Nature and Purpose of the Universe; Death Comes to Us All, Mary Agnes; 'dentity Crisis*, 1979.

When Dinah Shore Ruled the Earth, with Wendy Wasserstein (produced New Haven, Connecticut, 1975).

Das Lusitania Songspiel, with Sigourney Weaver, music by Mel Marvin and Jack Gaughan (produced New York, 1976; revised version produced New York, 1976; revised version produced New York, 1980).

A History of the American Film, music by Mel Marvin (produced Hartford, Connecticut, 1976; New York, 1978). New York, Avon, 1978.

The Vietnamization of New Jersey (produced New Haven, Connecticut, 1977). New York, Dramatists Play Service, 1978.

Sister Mary Ignatius Explains It All for You (produced New York, 1979; London, 1983). New York, Dramatists Play Service, 1980.

The Nature and Purpose of the Universe; Death Comes to Us All, Mary Agnes; 'dentity Crisis: Three Short Plays. New York, Dramatists Play Service, 1979.

Beyond Therapy (produced New York, 1981; revised version produced New York and London, 1982). New York, French, 1983.

The Actor's Nightmare (produced New York, 1981; London, 1983). With *Sister Mary Ignatius Explains It All for You*, New York, Dramatists Play Service, 1982.

Christopher Durang Explains It All for You (includes *The Nature and Purpose of the Universe, 'dentity Crisis, Titanic, The Actor's Nightmare, Sister Mary Ignatius Explains It All for You, Beyond Therapy*). New York, Avon, 1982; New York, Grove Press, 1990.

Baby with the Bathwater (produced Cambridge, Massachusetts, and New York, 1983; Colchester, Essex, 1984; London, 1991). New York, Dramatists Play Service, 1984; with *Laughing Wild*, New York, Grove, 1989.

Sloth, in *Faustus in Hell* (produced Princeton, New Jersey, 1985).

Laughing Wild (produced New York, 1987; London, 1988) With *Baby with the Bathwater*, New York, Grove, 1989.

Cardinal O'Connor and *Woman Stand-up*, in *Urban Blight* (musical revue), based on an idea by John Tillinger, music by David Shire, lyrics by Richard Maltby Jr. (produced New York, 1988).

Chris Durang and Dawne (cabaret; produced New York, 1989).

Naomi in the Living Room (produced New York, 1991).

Media Amok (produced Cambridge, Massachusetts, 1992).

For Whom the Southern Belle Tolls (produced New York, 1994).

Durang/Durang (6 one acts; produced New York, 1994).

Christopher Durang: 27 Short Plays. Lyme, New Hampshire, Smith and Kraus Book, 1995.

Sex and Longing (produced New York, 1996).

Christopher Durang: Complete Full-Length Plays, 1975-1995. Lyme, New Hampshire, Smith and Kraus Book, 1997.

Screenplay: *Beyond Therapy*, with Robert Altman, 1987.

Television Writing: *Comedy Zone* series; *Carol Burnett Special*; *Trying Times Series;* episode "The Visit," for PBS, 1988.

*

Critical Study: "Metatheatre as Antitheatre: Durang's Actor's Nightmare" by Suzanne Burgoyne Dieckman, in *American Drama* (Cincinnati, Ohio), Spring 1992, pp. 26-41.

Theatrical Activities:
Director: **Plays**—*'dentity Crisis*, New Haven, Connecticut, 1975; *And the Air Didn't Answer* by Robert Kerr, New York, 1989.

Actor: **Plays**—At Yale University School of Drama, New Haven, Connecticut: Gustaf in *Urlicht* by Albert Innaurato, 1971, Darryl in *Better Dead Than Sorry*, 1972, Performer in *The Life Story of Mitzi Gaynor; or, Gyp*, 1973, Bruce in *Happy Birthday, Montpelier Pizz-zazz* by Wendy Wasserstein, 1974, and Emcee in *When Dinah Shore Ruled the Earth*, 1975; at Yale Repertory Theatre: Chorus in *The Frogs* by Burt Shevelove and Stephen Sondheim, 1974, Student in *The Possessed* by Camus, 1974, and Alyosha in *The Idiots Karamazov*, 1974; Performer in *I Don't Generally Like Poetry But Have You Read "Trees"?*, New York, 1973; Performer in *Das Lusitania Songspiel*, New York, 1976, 1980; Young Cashier in *The Hotel Play* by Wallace Shawn, New York, 1981; Matt in *The Marriage of Bette and Boo*, New York, 1985; role in *Laughing Wild*, New York, 1987; Ubu's Conscience in *Ubu Roi*, adaptation of Alfred Jarry's play by Larry Sloan and Doug Wright, New York, 1989; *Chris Durang and Dawne*, 1990; *Putting it Together*, 1993; *Call Me Madman*. **Films**—*The Secret of My Success*, 1987; *Housesitter*, 1992; *Butcher's Wife*; *Mr. North*; *The Cowboy Way*; *Penn and Teller Get Killed.*

*   *   *

Handsomely surviving a Catholic boyhood in New Jersey and an Ivy League education at Harvard and Yale, where he received an M.F.A. in playwriting, Christopher Durang has been critically ranked in the top echelon of American playwrights. Most of his plays, which have been popular with regional groups and theaters outside the mainstream, reflect the author's penchant for parody, with favorite targets being drama and film, literature, American social history and popular culture, parochial religion, and the middle-class family. He achieved national recognition with the 1978 Broadway production of *A History of the American Film*. Most critics applauded Durang's satiric skills in this inventive, multilevel profile of the films and social history of the previous 50 years.

Using a revue-type format and song lyrics by the playwright, *American Film* trots out the clichés, stereotypes, and superficial attitudes toward events that bombarded American culture from *Orphans of the Storm* to *Earthquake*. The characters interchange as screen spectators and actors while the audience follows the thorny path of the naively innocent heroine from poverty with a callous Cagney-like lover through speakeasies, prison, high society, and wartime to heavenly ascension. The play spoofs specific films of the 1930s and 1940s, film genres, and screen stars personifying ideals of toughness or innocence. The audience watches itself identifying with the black-and-white morality of the Western, the jingoism of World War II, and the neurotic narcissism of the postwar period. More than a revue with skits that wear thin by the second act, this satiric farce is impudently effective.

Literature and drama, respectively, fall under attack in *The Idiots Karamazov,* written with Albert Innaurato, and *The Vietnamization of New Jersey*. The first is an irreverent send-up of Dostoevskii's novel, one of Western literature's great books. Its action combines chaotic slapstick with a profusion of literary allusions that are largely comprehensible only to the cognoscenti. Displaying sharper comedic ability, the second play is an absurdist parody of David Rabe's anti-Vietnam play *Sticks and Bones* and of American antiwar dramas generally that thrust collective guilt upon docile audiences. Comic recognition, however, rests too heavily on a knowledge of Rabe's drama.

The theater and drama as satirical subjects again surface in *The Actor's Nightmare,* a hilarious curtain-raiser in which a befuddled accountant clad as Hamlet, without benefit of lines or rehearsal, finds himself onstage in a phantasmagoric play whose actors veer from Noël Coward's *Private Lives* and Samuel Beckett to *Hamlet* and Robert Bolt's *A Man for All Seasons*. Ultimately thrust into a scene from the Bolt play, the baffled hero becomes Sir Thomas More facing a suddenly realistic execution, and, despite his last-minute, out-of-character recanting, he is not seen on stage for the curtain call. It is an end resembling that of Tom Stoppard's *Rosencrantz and Guildenstern Are Dead.*

Setting his sights on personal relationships and the deficiencies of psychiatrists, in *Beyond Therapy* Durang chronicles the tale of two Manhattan singles in their 30s, a bisexual male lawyer and a female journalist concerned about getting married, who meet through a personals ad. The curious couple are ineptly coached through a courtship of insults, rejections, and threats by their respective psychiatrists. The woman's doctor is a male chauvinist who seduces his female patients, and the man's is a daffy woman who carries a Snoopy doll and confuses words. In a more optimistic ending than Durang normally gives, the couple jointly reject their therapists and consider having a continuing relationship, which might even lead to marriage. The play has a dazzling display of funny lines and jokes on contemporary mores, gender identity, and psychiatry. Credibility is stretched, however, by having two such divergent lovers even consider a relationship, a problem not mitigated by the lack of a final resolution scene or a well-developed plot to connect the many short two-character scenes. Yet these shortcomings have not prevented the play from becoming a favorite with community and regional theaters.

Dogmatic parochial education receives barbs in Durang's Obie-winning *Sister Mary Ignatius Explains It All for You.* The title character is a sin-smelling nun who tyrannizes her students. During a lecture she is interrupted by the return of four former students who loathe her. The group ranges from a happy homosexual and an unwed mother to a rape victim and a suicidal alcoholic. Their recriminations rouse the nun to shoot them, and class servility is restored. The satire is sharp and wildly funny in this gem of black humor.

Absurdist portraits of the American family abound in five Durang plays. *The Nature and Purpose of the Universe; Death Comes to Us All, Mary Agnes;* and *'dentity Crisis* are three short black comedies that treat victimized females who lose their life, sanity, or identity at the hands of callous families and the traditional Catholic view of women. Although the plays lose their bite in farcical chaos, they project subjects more maturely developed in two later works. One of these, *Baby with the Bathwater,* is a satirical farce on parenting in which two self-absorbed parents idiotically raise a male child, confusing his true gender for 15 years. He survives to young adulthood desperate to avoid the mistakes of his own upbringing when he becomes a father himself. The play's string of cartoonlike scenes progressively palls, despite the satirical feast they offer, and the work would profit from sharper variety and a greater buttressing by reality. More effective is the revised (1985) Obie-winning *The Marriage of Bette and Boo,* a trenchantly amusing dissection of the contemporary Catholic family. In 33 inventive scenes related by the family's only son and treated with farcical brilliance, a marriage moves through three decades of alcoholism and divorce, with relatives who represent failures of the married and single state and a priest who dodges counseling session questions by imitating frying bacon. At the center stand the dipsomaniac Boo and the dimwit Bette, who, after a first child survives, persists against medical advice in producing babies, all of whom are stillborn. Admitting an autobiographical connection, the playwright gives an outrageously satiric view of society that characterizes his best work.

Durang's satiric concern with the perils of modern urban life continues in two later works. *Laughing Wild* consists of two monologues delivered by a man and a woman who expose the dreams and frustrations resulting from their daily lives in which they encounter rude taxi drivers, waiting in line, inane talk shows, attitudes of the Catholic Church toward sexual matters, and each other as they clash over a purchase of canned tuna fish in a supermarket aisle. In the play's final section the two strangers meet to reenact the supermarket incident with varying interpretations, and they reach a hesitant truce. It is an inventive comedy that has proved popular with regional theaters. The less successful *Naomi in the Living Room* is a dark absurdist comedy that treats a self-absorbed, psychotic middle-class mother who rejects her cross-dressing son and his wife after they visit.

Durang continued his satirical bent in the 1990s. *Media Amok* is a flippant send-up of television talk show characters whose favorite topics are abortion, gay rights, and racial tension. In the six playlets that make up *Durang Durang,* he takes swipes at fellow playwrights. *For Whom the Southern Belle Tolls* parodies Tennessee Williams's *The Glass Menagerie,* with Laura now a man, Lawrence, with a collection of glass cocktail stirrers and a mother who wants him to marry a "feminine caller" who turns out to be a lesbian. *A Stye in the Eye* lampoons Sam Shepard's existential cowboys and John Pielmeier's *Agnes of God.* Other pieces make targets of David Mamet, Peter Shaffer, and Chekhov. Critics have expressed reservations about the works but overall have found them amusing.

Critics were not as sanguine, however, about *Sex and Longing,* which in its 1996 production starred Sigourney Weaver as Lulu, a sexually compulsive woman attacked by a serial killer only to be saved and converted by a sex-obsessed minister of the religious right who then rapes her. Accompanied by his puritanical wife, a sleazy politician who was once rejected by Lulu becomes president and brings her to trial. Jesus comes to testify, but when he later is revealed to be the serial killer, he murders Lulu. The play succeeds neither as an absurdist cartoon nor as an effective satirical attack on the religious right and literary icons. (Characters and plot threads from Frank Wedekind's *Pandora's Box* and Somerset Maugham are apparent.)

Durang's work rises above collegiate-like preciosity to reveal a gifted satirist and farceur whose American absurdist view of the world is most delightfully successful when he furnishes a floor of reality under the dance of his characters. As a satirist writing for the stage, he is a member of an endangered species who deserves the theater's nurturing in order to flourish. His is a talent that is needed in the American theater.

—Christian H. Moe

DYER, Charles (Raymond)

Also writes as C. Raymond Dyer and R. Kraselchik. **Nationality:** British. **Born:** Shrewsbury, Shropshire, 7 July 1928. **Education:** Highlands Boys' School, Ilford, Essex; Queen Elizabeth's School, Barnet, Hertfordshire. **Military Service:** Served in the Royal Air Force, 1944-47: flying officer. **Family:** Married Fiona Thomson in 1959; three sons. **Career:** Actor and director; chair and artistic director, Stage Seventy Productions Ltd. **Address:** Old Wob, Gerrards Cross, Buckinghamshire, England.

Publications

Plays

Clubs Are Sometimes Trumps (as C. Raymond Dyer) (produced Wednesbury, Staffordshire, 1948).
Who on Earth! (as C. Raymond Dyer) (produced London, 1951).
Turtle in the Soup (as C. Raymond Dyer) (produced London, 1953).
The Jovial Parasite (as C. Raymond Dyer) (produced London, 1954).
Single Ticket Mars (as C. Raymond Dyer) (produced Bromley, Kent, 1955).
Time, Murderer, Please (as C. Raymond Dyer) (produced Portsmouth, Hampshire, and London, 1956). London, English Theatre Guild, 1962.
Wanted—One Body! (as C. Raymond Dyer) (produced on tour, 1956). London, English Theatre Guild, 1961.
Poison in Jest (as C. Raymond Dyer) (produced Oxford, 1957).
Prelude to Fury (as C. Raymond Dyer) (produced London, 1959).
Red Cabbage and Kings (as R. Kraselchik) (produced South-sea, Hampshire, 1960).
Rattle of a Simple Man (produced London, 1962; New York, 1963). London and New York, French, 1963.
Gorillas Drink Milk, adaptation of a play by John Murphy (produced Coventry, 1964).
Staircase (produced London, 1966; New York, 1968). London, Penguin, 1966; New York, French, 1967.
Mother Adam (produced York, 1971; also director: produced London, 1971). London, Davis Poynter, 1972.
A Hot Godly Wind (produced Manchester, 1975). Published in *Second Playbill 3*, edited by Alan Durband, London, Hutchinson, 1973.
Futility Rites (produced in Germany, 1980).
Lovers Dancing (produced London, 1983). Oxford, Amber Lane Press, and New York, French, 1984.

Screenplays: *Rattle of a Simple Man*, 1964; *Staircase*, 1969; *Brother Sun and Sister Moon*, 1970.

Novels

Rattle of a Simple Man. London, Elek, 1964.
Charlie Always Told Harry Almost Everything. London, W.H. Allen, 1969; as *Staircase; or, Charlie Always Told Harry Almost Everything*, New York, Doubleday, 1969.
Under the Stairs. Berlin, Langen Müller, 1991.

*

Manuscript Collection: Manchester Central Library.

Critical Studies: In *Sunday Times* (London), 14 April 1966, 5 December 1971, and 29 April 1973; *Drama* (London), Winter 1967;

L'Avant Scène (Paris), 15 January 1968; *New Yorker*, 20 January 1968; *Sipario* (Rome), August 1969; *Irish Tatler* (Dublin), December 1969; "Nobody Is Anything Without Someone: Charles Dyer's *Mother Adam* and *The Trilogy of Loneliness*" by Moylan C. Mills, in *Mid Hudson Language Studies* (Poughkeepsie, New York), 1983, pp. 81-91.

Theatrical Activities:
Director: **Plays**—In London, Amsterdam, Rotterdam, Paris, Berlin; recently, *Mother Adam*, London, 1972, Stratford-on-Avon and London, 1973, Paris, 1981 and 1986.

Actor: **Plays**—Roles in 250 plays; debut as Lord Harpenden in *While the Sun Shines* by Terence Rattigan, Crewe, Cheshire, 1947; Duke in *Worm's Eye View* by R.F. Delderfield, London and tour, 1948-50; Digger in *The Hasty Heart* by John Patrick, toured, 1950; Wilkie in *No Trees in the Street* by Ted Willis, toured, 1951; Turtle in *Turtle in the Soup*, London, 1953; Launcelot Gobbo in *The Merchant of Venice*, London, 1954; Freddie Windle in *The Jovial Parasite*, London, 1954; Maitre d'Hotel in *Room for Two* by Gilbert Wakefield, London, 1955; Keith Draycott in *Pitfall* by Falkland L. Cary, London, 1955; Dr. John Graham in *Suspended Sentence* by Sutherland Scott, London, 1955; Horace Grimshaw in *The Imperfect Gentleman* by Harry Jackson, London, 1956; Wishee Washee in *Aladdin*, London, 1956; Syd Fish in *Painted Sparrow* by Guy Paxton and E.V. Hoile, Cork, Ireland, 1956; Flash Harry in *Dry Rot* by John Chapman, London and tour, 1958; Shylock in *The Merchant of Venice*, Bromley, Kent, 1959; Viktor in *Red Cabbage and Kings*, Southsea, Hampshire, and tour, 1960; Percy in *Rattle of a Simple Man*, London, 1963; Mickleby in *Wanted—One Body!*, Guildford, Surrey, 1966. **Films**—Include *Cuptie Honeymoon*, 1947; *Naval Patrol*, 1959; *The Loneliness of the Long Distance Runner*, 1962; *Rattle of a Simple Man*, 1964; *The Knack*, 1965; *How I Won the War*, 1967. **Television**—*Hugh and I* series, 1964; Charlie in *Staircase*, 1986.

Charles Dyer comments:

Outside bedtime, no one truly exists until he is reflected through the mind of another. We exist only as we think others think of us. We are not real except in our own tiny minds according to our own insignificant measurement of thought.

Animals adapt to their inadequacies without shame or discernible consciousness. Eventually, they wither to nothing, wagging their minds behind them, and die unsurprised—like frogs. Man is different, and is measured according to breadth of chest, amount of hair, inside leg, bosom and backside. He is insulted by death. He cares. And he cares more about what is seen than is hidden; yet unseen differences have greatest emotional effect.

Such as loneliness.

And I write about loneliness.

Obviously, Man is progressing towards a life, a world of Mind. Soon. Soon, in terms of creation. But with physicalities dismissed, the mind is lonelier than ever. Mind was God's accident. An unfortunate bonus. We should be more content as sparrows, spring-fluttering by the clock; a sudden day, tail-up; then the cock-bird, and satisfaction matter-of-factually; a search for straw; eggs and tomorrow automatic as the swelling of string in water. It happens for sparrows, that is all! Anything deeper is Mind. And Mind is an excess over needs. Therefore Mind is loneliness.

Rattle of a Simple Man and *Staircase* and *Mother Adam* form a trilogy of loneliness, three plays enacted on Sundays, Bells are so damned lonely. Duologues, they are, because two seems the most sincere symbolic number, especially as man plus woman may be considered physically One. My plays have no plots, as such. Action cannot heal loneliness: it is cured only by *sharing* an action, and is emphasised by reduction of plot. And reduction of stage setting—which should, I feel, be expendable once the play is written. I detail a setting for the preparation of each duologue, that its dialogue may relate to a particular room; then, as a casting reflects its mould, the setting becomes irrevocably welded into and between the lines. The potency of these duologues is greater in drapes.

They reprimand me, occasionally, for handicapping my characters either physically or mentally: Cyrenne the prostitute and Percy, male virgin, in *Rattle of a Simple Man*; schizophrenic Adam and arthritical Mammles in *Mother Adam*; homosexual Charlie and nakedly-bald Harry in *Staircase*. And as the Trilogy grew, I locked them into barber shops and attics, depriving them even of a telephone to outside realities. This was a private challenge; yet what interest in an even face? what fault in a crooked smile? I love the courage of my imperfect characters, I despair with them—so small in a world of mindless faces, and faceless minds driving science to God's borders. In *Staircase*, man plus man situation, Charlie and Harry are lost without one another. But Charlie is too proud to admit such a fatal interdependence. He patronises Harry, taunts him, and drops "exciting" names which are anagrams of his own; he refuses to reflect anything of Harry; thus, Harry becomes an anagram, too; and even me, as their author. Charlie, Harry and me, become one; because there is no reality until we are reflected through someone else's eyes.

My characters have hope with their imperfections. They are dismayed by today's fading simplicity; today's lack of humility—no one ever wrong, always an excuse; kissing footballers without respect for the losers; and people who, from the safety of secret conscience, dismiss others as "them."

Man's disease is loneliness; God's is progress.

* * *

The opening performance of Charles Dyer's *Rattle of a Simple Man* was given at the Garrick Theatre on 19 September 1962. I had heard that it consisted of a dialogue between a mug and a tart and, knowing nothing of Dyer's delicacy and integrity, assumed that it would be full of equivocal situations. Before the end of the first act I realized that I was in the presence of a new and valid talent, possessed to an astonishing degree of the capacity to find pearls among swine. In drunken football fans, in middle-aged, failing homosexual hairdressers, and in the half-paralyzed relics of tambourine-banging religiosity, Dyer finds not the debris of humanity but unforgettable gleams of tenderness and self-sacrifice:

> Cyrenne: Been on holiday?
>
> Percy: I went to Morecambe. There were lots of married couples at the digs.
>
> They took a fancy to me. I was always making them laugh. It was marvellous. I think I'll go somewhere else next year, though.

Dyer shows his skill in using the simplest words to change the whole mood of a scene. One can tell the very moment the light went out for Percy.

For many years Dyer traveled the country as an actor in provincial productions of London successes, and in Percy's unhappy seaside memories there may well be recollections of drab theatrical lodgings. The two homosexual barbers in *Staircase* are exceptionally bitter on this subject:

> Charlie: Even me honeymoon was a—a—a holocaust: one night of passion and food-poisoning for thirteen. Maggots in the haddock, she claimed.
> (Harry giggles)
> Oh, I was laughing, dear. Yes. What! Lovely—your blushing bride all shivering and turgid in the promenade shelter; hurricanes whipping the shingle. Couldn't even paddle for a plague of jelly-fish.

Dyer considers and reconsiders very aspect of his work, and he does not let it go until he has got out of it everything that it contains. Unlike most other eminent contemporary dramatists, he is ready, even delighted, to discuss his work, its meaning, and its origin. It is clear that what he puts into his plays is but a small part of his knowledge of the people he writes about. He has written two novels, which have had considerable success, and both are treatments of themes dealt with in the plays *Rattle of a Simple Man* and *Staircase*. Most people suppose that the novels are rewritings of the plays, but this is not true. The novels were the original works, and the plays followed after.

Thus, though *Rattle of a Simple Man* has an effect similar to that of the *nouveau roman* in that it leaves the audience with a question unanswered, Dyer is really at the opposite pole from writers like Alain Robbe-Grillet and Marguerite Duras. They leave questions open because their philosophy tells them that human knowledge is limited, whereas Dyer ends with an uncertainty only because the wealth of information with which he could resolve the matter would blur the clear outline of what he wishes to say.

Long before the end of *Rattle* we understand and love Cyrenne and Percy. They are characters who are bruised, resilient, and in their ridiculous way curiously dignified, and they make for righteousness because they manifest sympathy and consideration for others. They are, in fact, people of honor.

That they are so is the basis of Dyer's outlook on the drama. He writes his plays, which are spare and austere in form, according to a classic formula of abiding power. The question with Dyer is not what his characters appear to be but what they will do in the circumstances in which he places them. It is in my opinion a mistake to consider *Staircase* as primarily a study of homosexuality. It is essentially a study of how under great stress a man's character may crumble and then rebound to a level it never attained before.

In fact, Dyer is the complement to Anouilh, whom in many ways he rivals in theatrical expertise. Whereas it is with bitter distress that Anouilh discovers the sordidness of purity, Dyer—in this resembling Maupassant—comes upon purity in sordidness. Against dispiriting odds people are capable of behaving unexpectedly well. This is one reason Dyer's work is so much more exhilarating than that of even his most distinguished contemporaries. He is a dramatist who indulges neither in self-pity nor in recrimination.

In *Staircase,* presented by the Royal Shakespeare Company in 1966-67, Dyer did a very curious thing. He gave his own name to the character played by Paul Scofield. This was the introduction of his theory that everybody is alone. He carried his theme into *Mother Adam,* but in *Staircase* all characters, on- and offstage, are woven into patterns of the name Charles Dyer. It is a dramatic device to pinpoint the lack of substance in a man-man relationship in which Charlie could not exist without Harry or Harry without Charlie. All is loneliness. And each without the other, says Dyer, would be like "a golfer holing-in-one by himself. Nobody to believe him. Nobody to prove his moment ever truly existed." Dyer is at his best when dealing with commonplace aspects of life and discerning in them the emotional depths of their apparent shallowness. There is something both ludicrous and touching in the way Harry broods over the distresses he suffered as a scoutmaster. Patrick Magee brought real humanity to his task of making tea for Scofield's Dyer—prissy, pampered, pomaded, a ruined god awaiting a summons for indecent behavior. To his lurking terror Scofield gave a fine touch of injured vanity.

The actor who plays this splendid part, which is one of the best in modern drama, can be riveting, revolting, and masterly all at the same time, for he has sudden bursts of panic, vain boastings of a largely imaginary past as a pantomime dame, irritability, and readiness in his own terror to wound his pitiably vulnerable companion.

Mother Adam is Dyer's most ambitious play. Adam's paralyzed mother is a tyrant of extreme power, and she brings it to bear on her son, who longs—he thinks—to escape and marry. Despite its consciousness that, in one of Dyer's shining phrases, "There aren't so many silk-loined years," the play is as full of laughter as it is of heartbreak. Its dialogue is rich in curious eloquence and stirring images.

Fine as these things are, it is not in them that Dyer's mastery is to be found but rather in his capacity to hold in his mind two conflicting rights and to see, with a true compassion, that their confrontation cannot be resolved. It is because of this capacity that he has written in *Mother Adam* one of the few tragedies of our time. Adam cannot be free unless his mother is deserted; his mother cannot be cared for unless her son's life is ruined. It is this situation that Charles Dyer observes with a dancing eye and a riven heart.

I say, with the same absolute confidence with which I wrote of Pinter's *The Birthday Party* in 1958, that in the history of the contemporary theater *Mother Adam* will rank as a masterpiece.

Dyer had previously written two fine and successful plays—*Rattle of a Simple Man* and *Staircase*. *Mother Adam* is better than either. It is more disturbing; it has deeper resonance; it is more beautifully written, with an imagination at once exotic and desperately familiar; and it has a profounder pity and a more exquisite falling close.

Loneliness haunts Dyer's imagination. Is there any solution to this terrible problem? Dyer says that there is. Loneliness is the product of selfishness, and where there is no selfishness, there is no loneliness. The condition of unselfishness is not easy to attain. It is within reach only of the saints. But sanctity is not an unattainable goal, and we should all aim for it.

In *Mother Adam* Dyer seeks the continuing theme of oneness in man and mother, almost to the edges of Oedipus. The moment at which Adam falls to his knees at her bedside, hugging his mother, dragging her crippled knuckles to his face, and begging "Hug me! hug me! I dream of love. I need love," should represent the climax not only of *Mother Adam* but of the whole Loneliness Trilogy.

In two of his plays Dyer dealt with subjects that, when the plays were first produced, were considered daring. The Lord Chamberlain made 26 cuts in *Staircase,* including the scene in which Harry explains his hatred of the physical side of life. The *Report on Censorship 1967* mentioned *Staircase* throughout 25 of its 200 pages. Dyer likes to feel that he is ahead of trends but not excessively so: "In terms of eternity, the interval between Adam and Eve's nakedness and the Moment when God cast them forth in animal skins is but a finger click. The serious, most important period is what happens *after* they put on clothes."

We clothe our inadequacies. This is what Dyer's plays are all about.

—Harold Hobson

E

EASMON, R(aymond) Sarif

Nationality: Sierra Leonean. **Born:** Freetown, Sierra Leone, 1913. **Education:** Newcastle University, England, received M.B. and B.S. degrees. **Career:** Practicing doctor.

PUBLICATIONS

Plays

Dear Parent and Ogre (produced Ibadan, Nigeria, 1961). London and New York, Oxford University Press, 1964.
The New Patriots. London, Longman, 1966.

Novel

The Burnt-Out Marriage. London, Nelson, and New York, Humanities Press, 1967.

Short Stories

The Feud and Other Stories. London, Longman, 1981.

* * *

With his unfailing sense of the comic potential in any situation, it seems likely that R. Sarif Easmon is, as Bernth Lindfors has put it, "the first African offspring of Oscar Wilde and Noël Coward." His witty, urbane plays deal with the romance of politics and the politics of romance—two areas dear to the heart of an African audience—and they move with the grace of a dancer from one finely choreographed scene to the next.

There has been criticism of the language used by Easmon's upper-class characters, a pure Oxford English of the type that has proven so satisfying to a generation of word-conscious and Western-educated Africans. Yet when a person sees one of Easmon's plays in production, there is no doubt that the language is perfectly suited to both the personalities and the social positions of the characters. After all, not all Africans speak continually in proverbs. Moreover, when Easmon introduces characters from different social backgrounds, he fits their speech to their class. One need only compare the words of Dauda Touray, the "parent and ogre" of Easmon's first play—"Our gratitude shall transcend champagne, Saidu!"—with those of the hired ruffian Charles Randall—"Lord 'ave mercy—Oh! For de name way me daddy and mammy gave me!"—to see the difference.

There is nothing stock about the characters in Easmon's delightful comedies. The two roguish politicians of his second play, *The New Patriots,* who are struggling for the hand of the same woman, are as alive as Dauda Touray, the main character of *Dear Parent and Ogre,* yet they are not in any way a copy of the earlier character. Easmon's figures have unorthodox turns to their nature. Sekou, the young hero of *Dear Parent and Ogre,* is a son of a Yalie, a class given over to singing, quite literally, the praises of the noble Touray family. Yet he has found success in Europe as a recording star and has returned, replete with impeccable French and a Rolls-Royce, to claim the hand of Dauda's daughter.

Because they deal with the themes of a new Africa, an Africa where the two suitors can be a descendant from former slaves on the one hand and from a lowly class of minstrels on the other, an Africa where champagne, moonlight, Joloff rice, and hired thugs can be blended into a scene of high comedy, Easmon's plays have attracted large audiences whenever they have been performed in West Africa. Because Easmon manages, while developing these themes, to present us with vital human characters and situations that have larger universal implications, it seems safe to say that his appeal need not be limited to African audiences.

—Joseph Bruchac

EDGAR, David

Nationality: British. **Born:** Birmingham, Warwickshire, 26 February 1948. **Education:** Oundle School, Northamptonshire, 1961-65; Manchester University, 1966-69, B.A. (honours) in drama 1969. **Career:** Reporter, Bradford *Telegraph and Argus*, Yorkshire, 1969-72; Yorkshire Arts Association fellow, Leeds Polytechnic, 1972-73; resident playwright, Birmingham Repertory Theatre, 1974-75; lecturer in playwriting, Birmingham University, 1974-78; literary adviser, Royal Shakespeare Company, 1984-88. Honorary senior research fellow, Birmingham University, 1988— . Lives in Birmingham. **Awards:** John Whiting award, 1976; Bicentennial Exchange fellowship, 1978; Society of West End Theatre award, 1980; New York Drama Critics Circle award, 1982; Tony award, 1982. **Agent:** Michael Imison Playwrights, 28 Almeida Street, London N1 1TD, England.

PUBLICATIONS

Plays

Two Kinds of Angel (produced Bradford, 1970; London, 1971). Published in *The London Fringe Theatre*, edited by V.E. Mitchell, London, Burnham House, 1975.
A Truer Shade of Blue (produced Bradford, 1970).
Still Life: Man in Bed (produced Edinburgh, 1971; London, 1972).
The National Interest (produced on tour, 1971).
Tedderella (produced Edinburgh, 1971; London, 1973).
Bloody Rosa (produced Edinburgh, 1971).
Acid (produced Bradford, 1971).
Conversation in Paradise (produced Edinburgh, 1971).
The Rupert Show (produced on tour, 1972).
The End (produced Bradford, 1972).
Excuses, Excuses (produced Coventry, 1972; London, 1973; as *Fired*, produced Birmingham, 1975).
Rent; or, Caught in the Act (produced on tour and London, 1972).
State of Emergency (also director: produced on tour and London, 1972).
Not with a Bang But a Whimper (produced Leeds, 1972).

Death Story (produced Birmingham, 1972; New York and London, 1975).
The Road to Hanoi, in *Point 101* (produced London, 1972).
England's Ireland, with others (produced Amsterdam and London, 1972).
A Fart for Europe, with Howard Brenton (produced London, 1973).
Gangsters (produced London, 1973).
Up Spaghetti Junction, with others (produced Birmingham, 1973).
Baby Love (produced Leeds and London, 1973). Included in *Shorts*, 1989.
The Case of the Workers' Plane (produced Bristol, 1973; shorter version, as *Concorde Cabaret*, produced on tour, 1975).
Operation Iskra (produced on tour and London, 1973).
Liberated Zone (produced Bingley, Yorkshire, 1973; London, 1974).
The Eagle Has Landed (televised 1973; produced Liverpool, 1973).
Man Only Dines (produced Leeds, 1974).
The Dunkirk Spirit (produced on tour, 1974).
Dick Deterred (produced London, 1974; New York, 1983). New York, Monthly Review Press, 1974.
The . . . Show (produced Bingley, Yorkshire, 1974).
The Midas Connection (televised 1975). Included in *Shorts*, 1989.
O Fair Jerusalem (produced Birmingham, 1975). Included in *Plays 1*, 1987.
The National Theatre (produced London, 1975). Included in *Shorts*, 1989.
Summer Sports: Beaters, Cricket, Shotputters, Cross Country, Ball Boys (produced Birmingham, 1975; as *Blood Sports*, produced London, 1976; New York, 1987; revised version of *Ball Boys* produced London, 1977). *Ball Boys* published London, Pluto Press, 1978; in *The Best Short Plays 1982*, edited by Ramon Delgado, Radnor, Pennsylvania, Chilton, 1982; as *Blood Sports with Ball Boys*, included in *Shorts*, 1989.
Events Following the Closure of a Motorcycle Factory (produced Birmingham, 1976).
Destiny (produced Stratford-on-Avon, 1976; London, 1977). London, Eyre Methuen, 1976; revised version (produced London, 1985), Methuen, 1986.
Welcome to Dallas, J.C., adaptation of a play by Alfred Jarry (produced London, 1976).
The Perils of Bardfrod, with Richard Crane (produced Bradford, 1976).
Saigon Rose (produced Edinburgh, 1976; New York, 1982). Included in *Plays 1*, 1987.
Wreckers (produced Exeter and London, 1977). London, Eyre Methuen, 1977.
Ecclesiastes (broadcast 1977). Included in *Plays 2*, 1990.
Our Own People (produced London, 1977). With *Teendreams*, London, Methuen, 1987.
Mary Barnes (produced Birmingham, 1978; London, 1979; New Haven, Connecticut, 1980). London, Eyre Methuen, 1979; revised version, Methuen, 1984.
The Jail Diary of Albie Sachs, adaptation of the work by Sachs (produced London, 1978; New York, 1979). London, Collings, 1978.
Teendreams, with Susan Todd (produced Bristol and London, 1979). London, Eyre Methuen, 1979; revised edition, with *Our Own People*, London, Methuen, 1987.
The Life and Adventures of Nicholas Nickleby, adaptation of the novel by Dickens (produced London, 1980; New York, 1981). New York, Dramatists Play Service, 2 vols., 1982; included in *Plays 2*, 1990.
Maydays (produced London, 1983). London, Methuen, 1983; revised version, 1984.
Entertaining Strangers: A Play for Dorchester (produced Dorchester, Dorset, 1985; revised version produced London, 1987). London, Methuen, 1986.
That Summer (produced London, 1987). London, Methuen, 1987.
Plays 1 (includes *The Jail Diary of Albie Sachs, Mary Barnes, Saigon Rose, O Fair Jerusalem, Destiny*). London, Methuen, 1987.
Vote for Them, with Neil Grant (televised 1989). London, BBC Publications, 1989.
Shorts: Short Plays (includes *Blood Sports with Ball Boys, Baby Love, The National Theatre, The Midas Connection*). London, Hern, 1989.
Heartlanders, with Stephen Bill and Anne Devlin (produced Birmingham, 1989). London, Hern, 1989.
The Shape of the Table (produced London, 1990). London, Hern, 1990.
Plays 2 (includes *Ecclesiastes, The Life and Adventures of Nicholas Nickleby, Entertaining Strangers: A Play for Dorchester*). London, Methuen, 1990.
Plays 3 (includes *Our Own People*; *Teendreams*; *Maydays*; *That Summer*). London, Methuen, 1991.
The Strange Case of Dr. Jekyll and Mr. Hyde, adaptation of the story by Robert Louis Stevenson. London, Hern, 1991.
Pentecost (produced Stratford-upon-Avon, 1994). London, Nick Hern Books, 1995.

Screenplay: *Lady Jane*, 1986.

Radio Plays: *Ecclesiastes*, 1977; *Saigon Rose*, 1979; *A Movie Starring Me*, 1991.

Television Plays: *The Eagle Has Landed*, 1973; *Sanctuary*, from his play *Gangsters*, 1973; *I Know What I Meant*, 1974; *The Midas Connection*, 1975; *Censors*, with Hugh Whitemore and Robert Muller, 1975; *Vote for Them*, with Neil Grant, 1989.

Other

The Second Time as Farce: Reflections on the Drama of Mean Times. London, Lawrence and Wishart, 1988.

*

Critical Studies: *David Edgar, Playwright and Politician* by Elizabeth Swain, New York, Peter Lang, 1986; *File on Edgar* edited by Simon Trussler, London, Methuen, 1991; "Adapting Dickens to the Modern Eye: *Nicholas Nickleby* and *Little Dorrit*" by Christopher Innes, in *Novel Images: Literature in Performance*, edited by Peter Reynolds, 1993; *Edgar: The Playwright* by Susan Painter, London, Methuen, 1996; "David Edgar" by Art Borrega, in *British Playwrights, 1956-1995: A Research and Production Sourcebook*, edited by William W. Demastes, Westport, Connecticut, Greenwood, 1996.

Theatrical Activities:
Director: **Plays**—*State of Emergency*, tour and London, 1972; *The Party* by Trevor Griffiths (co-director, with Howard Davies), London, 1985.

* * *

A glance at the titles of David Edgar's many plays of the early 1970s will suggest readily enough to anyone who was aware of the chief social and political issues of the time in Britain (and not only there) the nature of his early work. Edgar himself has described his work with General Will between 1971 and 1974 as "pure unadulterated agit-prop," designed to convey information in an entertaining way and from a socialist standpoint by using satirically the forms of popular culture—pantomime, comic strip, and the like. The aim was to elucidate political and economic conditions in general by reference to particular incidents. In 1973-1974 Edgar turned from agit-prop to "become a social realist," feeling the necessity to "inculcate consciousness" more forcefully and in so doing to create a truly radical "theatre of public life." Several documentary plays preceded *Destiny,* which, through television and radio adaptations, brought his work before the widest possible audience.

Edgar describes *Destiny* as having an "agit-prop structure"—the dramatic unit is, as in Brechtian epic theater, the presentational scene rather than the traditional long act. It is the creation of convincing characters, however, (without the "psychologism" that is anathema to the socialist playwright) rather than demonstration-room puppets that enables it to communicate so powerfully a sense of crisis. Though the play spans in epic fashion the period from 1947 (the year of Indian Independence and the consequent return home of the colonial army) to the mid-1970s, its main action takes place against the background of a West Midland by-election campaign and the concurrent unofficial strike of Asian workers at a local foundry. The growth of the fascist Nation Forward party, through the power of its racist rhetoric to manipulate widely differing groups and individuals into a shallow yet dangerous unity of purpose, is coolly examined, and its relation to Conservatism in its many varieties precisely analyzed. Nation Forward gains increasing popular support and the new, tough Toryism, bitter at the loss of empire, shakes off old-style sentimental-paternalist Conservatism, secretly joining forces with the fascists in order to break the Asian strike and to ensure a formidable economic basis for the hard right. The cruel irony of its final plot twist crystallizes the play's message in terms of the individual: the pathetic local antique dealer (and before that, soldier in India) whose misdirected bitterness had driven him to join Nation Forward and who—as their adopted candidate in the by-election—has been exploited by the party to such good effect, finds out by accident that his shop was taken away from him not by Jewish property speculators (as his mentors had insinuated) but by the same businessmen who are now concluding a secret agreement with his own party leaders.

Wreckers (written for and with 7:84) and *Teendreams* (written with Susan Todd for the feminist group Monstrous Regiment) confirm Edgar's continuing belief in the validity and usefulness of collectively devised agit-prop-type work in the late 1970s. His best work of this period, however, shows a growing interest in the relation between politics and psychology—especially the psychology of suffering. This interest emerges first in *The Jail Diary of Albie Sachs*, an adaptation that is still very much Edgar's own play. For the Jewish lawyer Albie, detained under the "90-day" law in his native South Africa, the suffering inflicted upon him by the state is merely destructive, depriving him of moral strength and crushing his will to political action. For the eponymous heroine of *Mary Barnes,* the suffering caused by mental illness is something to be gone *through* (in her case in a Christ-like way). Alternative therapy, unlike conventional psychiatry, helps her to "go through" her schizophrenia towards the attainment of a stable self. In this way she becomes capable, as many "normal" people are not, of real human relationships. The play avoids the simplistic rubric of the antipsychiatry fashion of the 1960s—that only the mad are truly sane—while allowing an implicit sociopolitical critique to emerge from Mary's schizophrenia and the treatment of it. Yet it is also honest about the dilemmas and conflicts within the alternative community and the causes of its eventual dissolution. *Mary Barnes* is technically an adaptation, but it is one that—like the immensely popular and widely seen version of *Nicholas Nickleby*, and the more recent post-Freudian *The Strange Case of Dr. Jekyll and Mr. Hyde*—brings into question the value of conventional distinctions between adaptation and original play.

After his adaptation of *Nicholas Nickleby* (for the Royal Shakespeare Company), Edgar continued to work on plays with and for particular groups, such as *Entertaining Strangers.* Written as a community play for Dorchester (by a "stranger" and on the subject of the rightness of "entertaining strangers" of different kinds), it is nonetheless a rich dramatic text in its own right, sharing significant formal characteristics with a slightly earlier play, Edgar's most important one of the 1980s, *Maydays.*

With an epic structure resembling that of *Destiny* (though without the feel of agit-prop), *Maydays* deals with the course of socialism since World War II. With special concentration on the impact of the crucial dates 1956 and 1968 and ending in the election year of 1979, the play attempts to articulate the shifting relations between history, ideology, and personal belief and commitment by charting the ironically interconnected progress of three men: the radical son of a vicar who becomes a Trotskyist but who, in the aftermath of 1968, grows disillusioned, is ejected from the party, and ends up in the 1980s Tory think-tank; a working-class communist who, feeling himself to have been born too late and into the wrong class, comes in the 1970s to embrace unquestioningly the authoritarian nationalism of the hard right; and a Russian army officer who, having been jolted by his experience in Hungary in 1956, is imprisoned as a dissident in the 1970s and then is exiled to the West—where he finds his views being coopted and himself used by the same right-wing authoritarian grouping. The play ends with two very different acts of protest: the subtle disruption by the Russian exile of a public function organized by the right to honor him and the stand of the women on Greenham Common. The many ironies built into the plot are characteristic of Edgar's drama as a whole. Their pointedness and inevitability are intensified by the rich pattern of echo and counterpoint—in both phrase and idea—that is created by the continual juxtaposition of the three narrative strands. The intensity is both dialectical and emotional: in a play that (among other things) examines the opposition in political discourse between thought and feeling, Edgar succeeds in provoking both.

Despite his advocacy of urban "festivals of the oppressed" as the necessary future for theater, Edgar's own creative practice seemed to become, in the late 1980s and early 1990s, ever more social-realist. His play about the 1984 miners' strike, *That Summer*, is not the wide-ranging public drama that might have been expected, but an intimate, even domestic, piece. Indeed, the miners' strike—although the desperate reality of it is registered forcefully in an indirect way—is less the subject of the play than the occasion for a witty and even poignant revaluation of late 1960s radicalism and its relevance in the Thatcher era. When a generation-of-'68 Oxford history don and his family play host in a North Wales holiday house to two teenage girls from the Welsh coalfields, the class- and culture-clashes that inevitably ensue resolve themselves, through a shift of emphasis away from class towards a shared culture of dissent, in a modest affirmation of the continuity of a tradition of radical noncompliance. ("That summer" is both 1984 and 1968.) Gay, feminist, and antinuclear protesters are not the closest political cousins of the striking miner.

Edgar's response to revolution in Eastern Europe was, dramatically speaking, a direct one. Although *The Shape of the Table* is "based on events in a number of countries, it draws most from Czechoslovakia, and is thus about a negotiated, essentially pacific and ultimately decisive overthrow of communist rule." The focus is on "high politics" rather than popular dissent or events on the street; the excitement of the play is in the maneuverings of the incumbent party leaders in their negotiations for survival with a radical "Public Platform" opposition led by a Havel-like dissident writer. It is a play of argument and debate, which clarifies the differing experiences of oppression on all sides and quietly qualifies the future delights of Western-style democracy. Yet it is also Edgar's most "playful" piece. The very inevitability of the outcome promotes in us the awareness of a pattern and irony that are even more pervasive than in *Destiny* or *Maydays*. The action is shadowed by the characteristic structures and motifs of fairy tales, which are consistently invoked by the opposition leader Prus, and the progress of negotiations is imaged wittily by the (literal) change of shape of the table that dominates the set. The ironic reversals of plot and situation are acknowledged by the characters themselves. In the final debate, between dissident-become-president Prus and hard-line ex-first secretary, the bluntly sarcastic ex-Titoite Lutz, Prus offers a deal for Lutz's pardon that echoes the one he himself was offered in the very first scene. (Lutz refuses, thereby accepting individual responsibility and imprisonment.) And when the discrediting of an ambitious younger minister of the old regime reveals a Soviet "master-script" for large-scale liberalization without loss of party domination, the wryly conciliatory former prime minister points out to the Dubcék figure—an elderly "ghost" at this table from the projected "New Morning" of 1968—that "this revolution was set in train by the very people who put paid to yours. As Marx perceptively reminds us, the events of history occurring twice. First time as tragedy, the second time as farce."

Pentecost is Edgar's response to the growth of nationalist sentiment that has ravaged postcommunist Eastern Europe. The play is heavily yet elegantly ironic, presenting a babel of languages among which the sole, often grotesque, lingua franca is American English. The setting is potently symbolic: "an abandoned church of the Romanesque period in an unnamed south-east European country," variously used for centuries by successive dominant cultures, Christian and Islamic. It is at once a "battlement" of Europe and a "frontier" between the medieval and modern worlds. The action concerns the authenticity of a recently discovered fresco of the Lamentation on the church-wall, potentially "the biggest art find since the unearthing of Pompeii." An English art-historian and a local art-curator argue that it predates and anticipates Giotto, and with the connivance of the state they plan its removal to a local museum; an American art-historian is skeptical, and with local priests (Orthodox and Catholic) argues for its maintenance *in situ*. After armed asylum-seekers of various Eastern nationalities burst in, take the Westerners hostage, and negotiate their demands, the church is stormed by commandos and the Englishman is killed—but not before realizing the true cultural significance of the fresco: it is not pre-Giottan but the work of an *Arab* artist engaging freshly and powerfully with a great Christian subject. Inevitably, during the storming of the church, this great symbol of intercultural "hospitality" is utterly destroyed.

—Paul Lawley

EDGECOMBE, David

Nationality: Montserratian. **Born:** Montserrat, 4 February 1952. **Education:** Niagara College, Welland, Ontario, diploma in radio and television arts, 1973; Concordia University, Montreal, Canada, B.A. in 1976, M.A. in 1983; Thomson Foundation, London, diploma in journalism, 1988. **Family:** Married Leonie Lee in 1991. **Career:** Radio announcer and journalist, Montserrat, 1970-71; radio announcer, Antilles radio corporation, 1971; administrator, Lagos Festival, 1976-77; director of education, Antilles radio corporation, 1977-80; manager, WE Garments, 1983-85; editor, *Montserrat Reporter*, 1985-90; instructor of speech and theater, University of the Virgin Islands, 1990-92. Director of the Reichhold Center for the Arts, University of the Virgin Islands, St. Thomas, 1992—. **Address:** P.O. Box 3328, Veteran's Drive Station, St Thomas, Virgin Islands 00803.

Publications

Plays

For Better, For Worse (produced Montserrat, 1973).
Sonuvabitch (produced St. Thomas, 1975; as *Making It* Montreal, 1993). Montserrat, Offset Commercial Printers, 1975; as *Making It* in *Heaven and Other Plays,* Frederikstes, Virgin Islands, Eastern Caribbean Institute, 1993.
Strong Currents, adaptation of Austin Clarke (produced Legos, Nigeria, 1977).
View from the Bridge, adaptation of Arthur Miller (produced Montserrat, 1979).
Coming Home to Roost: A Play in Two Acts (produced Montserrat, 1978). Plymouth, Summit Communications, 1988.
Kiernon's Kingdom (produced St. Thomas, 1981).
Heaven (produced St. Thomas, 1991).
Heaven and Other Plays (includes *Heaven*; *Making It*; *For Better, For Worse*). Frederiksted, Virgin Islands, Eastern Caribbean Institute, 1993.
Marilyn (produced St. Thomas, 1992).

Radio Plays: *Sonuvabitch*; *Coming Home to Roost*; *Tangled Web,* adaptation of Dorbrene O'Marde; *Nice Box,* adaptation of Alwin Bully; *Kirnon's Kingdom.*

*

Theatrical Activities:
Director: **Plays**—Many of his own plays. *Ceremonies in Dark Old Men* by Lonnie Elder III; *A Calabash of Blood* by Eric Roach; *Dance Bongo* by Errol Hill; *the Dover Road* by A.A. Milne; *Old Story Time* by Trevor Rhone; *Goose and Gander* by Wilfred Redhead.

Actor: **Plays**–Bono in *Fences* by August Wilson; the valet in *The Blacks* by Jean Genet; Macuri in *The Swamp Dwellers* by Wole

Soyinka; Polonius in *Hamlet* by William Shakespeare; the philosopher in *Forced Marriage* by Molière.

* * *

One of the foremost Caribbean playwrights of his generation, David Edgecombe examines contemporary Caribbean life, particularly the interchange between American and Caribbean peoples and the recent transformation of the islands. His themes, however, are decidedly universal and include the nexus of wealth, evil, and power and the corruptibility of man. Edgecombe often centers his plays around an evil man who uses his power to corrupt others.

Edgecombe's first play, *For Better for Worse,* exposes the hypocrisies of marriage in two families and features a prototype of his immoral, evil man in the character of a wealthy legislator. In his second play, *Sonuvabitch* (later renamed *Making It*), Edgecombe uses a variety of neurotic personalities to explore obsessive love and classism on a Caribbean island. The play, however, focuses on one man who is driven to achieve economic success at any cost.

Edgecombe's next two plays were adaptations. *Strong Currents,* based on two novels by Austin Clarke, was commissioned as the Canadian contribution to FESTAC 77, the Second World Black and African Festival, held in Nigeria in 1977. (At the time Edgecombe was at a university in Canada.) It is significant that the hero of the play, which garnered several awards at the festival, is a doomed poet. Back home in Montserrat, Edgecombe wrote and produced a *View from the Bridge,* a Caribbean adaptation of Arthur Miller's play. Edgecombe found the parallel between immigrant Italians and immigrant West Indians to be compelling.

In his next play, *Coming Home to Roost,* Edgecombe dealt with an archetypal Caribbean pattern—a man returns to his island home after 10 years in England. The play follows the man's efforts to reclaim his role in the family as he is thwarted by a jealous, manipulative older brother, the corrupt man of Edgecombe's earlier plays.

In *Kiernon's Kingdom,* as Edgecombe reacted to events occurring in the Caribbean, for the first time the clash between good and evil took on racial implications. The play, which was chosen in a competition among Caribbean playwrights for production at the University of the Virgin Islands, is set in the 1960s and tells of a prime minister who is influenced by a white investor to introduce real estate development to his island. He is ultimately defeated by his own son, a symbolic statement that the younger generation may well reject ill-considered economic success. The play was also a departure for Edgecombe in that it is told entirely in flashback, from the perspective of a journalist interviewing the defeated prime minister.

Edgecombe's next play, *Heaven,* has as its base a love triangle, but it is an allegory of good and evil with political reverberations. The play is set in a discotheque called Heaven, where a powerful, depraved businessman named Sam tries to seduce or destroy the other characters. While Sam is clearly a devil figure (he is repeatedly called a snake), through the use of the name Edgecombe appears to equate the United States with the devil in its attempts to exploit the Caribbean islands. As critic Patricia Harkins-Pierre has pointed out, Sam's rejection at the end of the play is seen as only temporary, for the tempter is always waiting.

Edgecombe became director of the Reichhold Theatre at the University of the Virgin Islands in 1992 and immediately formed the Reichhold Caribbean Repertory Company with the intention of producing Caribbean plays. Among the works he has produced is his *Marilyn,* named for the hurricane that devastated Saint Thomas in 1995. Five characters, one called Marilyn and another being the familiar immoral businessman, represent the diverse ethnic groups on the island. In *Marilyn* Edgecombe openly confronts racism, exposes the ascendancy of business on Saint Thomas, and comes to grips with the incipient paternalism extant in the relations between the races. In what is his most ambitious staging, Edgecombe juxtaposes past and present as the characters relive the night of the hurricane.

Marilyn is a controversial play, but Edgecombe, who writes firmly in the realistic tradition, has never refrained from straightforwardly expressing his observations of contemporary Caribbean life. He has remained a fervent advocate for Caribbean theater. He is outspokenly critical about the lack of support Caribbean theater generally receives and argues with conviction that a vibrant Caribbean theater is the best defense against cultural imperialism.

—Erika J. Waters

EGBUNA, Obi B(enedict)

Nationality: Nigerian. **Born:** 1938. **Education:** A university in England; University of Iowa, Iowa City, M.A. in English 1978; Howard University, Washington, D.C., Ph.D. in English 1986. **Career:** High school teacher, Bishop Shanahan College, Orlu, 1955-56, and Beaver College, Glenside, Pennsylvania, 1967; writer-in-residence and director, East Central State Writers Workshop and ECBS television, Enugu, 1973-76; honorary fellow, University of Iowa, 1976; teacher, department of African studies, 1979-81, department of German-Russian studies, 1981-86, and writer-in-residence, 1987, Howard University. **Address:** Apartment #B705, 3636 16th Street, NW, Washington, D.C. 20010, U.S.A.

Publications

Plays

Divinity (broadcast 1965). Published in *New Africa* (London), August and September 1965; Stuttgart, Ernst Klett, 1985.
The Anthill. London and New York, Oxford University Press, 1965.
Wind Versus Polygamy (televized 1966; produced Dakar, 1966).
Theatre of Power (produced Copenhagen, 1967).
The Agony (produced London, 1970).

Radio Plays: *Divinity*, 1965; *Daughters of the Sun*, 1970; *The Rape of Lysistrata,* 1980; *The Madness of Didi,* 1980; *Black Candle for Christmas,* 1980.

Television Play: *Wind Versus Polygamy*, 1966.

Novels

Wind Versus Polygamy: Where "Wind" Is the "Wind of Change" and "Polygamy" Is the "Change of Eves." London, Faber, 1964; as *Elina*, London, Fontana, 1978.

The Madness of Didi. London, Fontana, 1980.
The Rape of Lysistrata. Enugu, Fourth Dimension, 1980.

Short Stories

Daughters of the Sun and Other Stories. London, Oxford University Press, 1970.
Emperor of the Sea and Other Stories. London, Fontana, 1974.
The Minister's Daughter. London, Fontana, and New York, Watts, 1975.
Diary of a Homeless Prodigal. Enugu, Fourth Dimension, 1976.
Black Candle for Christmas. Enugu, Fourth Dimension, 1980.

Other

The Murder of Nigeria: An Indictment. London, Panaf, 1968.
Destroy This Temple: The Voice of Black Power in Britain. London, MacGibbon and Kee, and New York, Morrow, 1971.
The ABC of Black Power Thought. Apapa, Nigeria, di Nigro Press, 1973.

*

Theatrical Activities:
Actor: **Play**—Sizwe Bansi in *Sizwi Bansi Is Dead* by Athol Fugard, Iowa City, 1977.

* * *

Although Obi B. Egbuna's efforts as a dramatist include a number of radio dramas and a play entitled *Wind Versus Polygamy*, his light and frothy comedy *The Anthill* remains the only drama that he has published as such, his earlier works having been rewritten into short stories and a novel. It seems that Egbuna has chosen well, for of all his dramatic works *The Anthill* seems to be the most entertaining and the best constructed, displaying the sort of witty comedy that has made Wilde's *The Importance of Being Earnest* a perennial favorite.

The play is the tale of a young African painter, Bobo, who for some reason paints only anthills. Except for Bobo, all of the characters are British and white, and Egbuna draws them to be just substantial enough to interest us and just stock enough to be taken less than seriously, which is necessary in any comedy that centers around a series of deaths, two real and one pretended. Even the landlady and mother of the young British soldier, Tommy, who dies from a heart attack when confronted by Bobo, does not seem to be overly disturbed by her own son's death. She is more concerned that people admire her appendix, which she keeps in a jar on her mantel.

Egbuna presents us with a full house of coincidences—that the policeman who visits their room just happens to be the father of the girl who has matrimonial intentions on Bobo's friend Nigel, that Tommy dies because Bobo resembles a young African whose death Tommy caused while stationed in Tongo, which is Bobo's home country, that Bobo is the deceased African's twin brother, and so on. But such coincidences are in keeping with this kind of frolic, as are the puns, which flow fast and freely. The verdict of the judge that Tommy's death was his own fault—"All young British soldiers must behave like English gentlemen at home and abroad. Under no circumstances must you kill a man to whom you are not properly introduced"—is the perfect sort of climax to a story that another writer might have turned into a heavy-handed tragedy.

Underneath it all, of course, there is a deep undercurrent of seriousness. Comedy is the other side of the mask of tragedy. Egbuna himself is a serious writer, as *Destroy This Temple*, essays written while he was locked in an English prison, indicates. His other plays have dealt with the conflict between tribal ways and Christianity and the resultant agonies in the hearts of young men who are the sons of Christian Africans but advocates of black power. When Egbuna has Bobo describe himself as "a typical Tongolese gentleman . . . a dedicated vindicator of African personality and I've got my Anglo-Saxon political and academic titles to prove it," the laughter is as bitter as it is sweet.

—Joseph Bruchac

ELISHA, Ron

Nationality: Australian. **Born:** Jerusalem, Israel, 19 December 1951; brought to Australia, 1953. **Education:** Melbourne High School, 1966-69; Melbourne University, 1970-75, B.Med., B.Surgery 1975. **Family:** Married Bertha Rita Rubin in 1981; one son and one daughter. **Career:** General practitioner, Melbourne, 1977—. **Awards:** Australian Writers Guild award, for *Einstein*, 1982; Australian Writers Guild award, for *Two*, 1984; Australian Writers Guild Major award, 1982; Australian Writers Guild award for television, for *Death Duties*, 1992; Houston International Film Festival Gold award, for *By My Own Authority*, 1990. **Agent:** Barbara Gange Management, 128 Rupert Street, Collingwood, Victoria 3066, Australia. **Address:** 4 Bruce Court, Elsternwick, Victoria 3185, Australia.

Publications

Plays

In Duty Bound (produced Melbourne, 1979). Montmorency, Victoria, Yackandandah, 1983.
Einstein (produced Melbourne, 1981; New York, 1982; London, 1986). Melbourne, Penguin, 1986; Belgium, Lansman Publishers, 1995.
Two (produced Perth, 1983; London, 1987). Sydney, Currency Press, 1985; Chicago, Dramatic Publishing Company, 1990.
Pax Americana (produced Perth, 1984). Montmorency, Victoria, Yackandandah, 1990.
The Levine Comedy (produced Melbourne, 1986). Montmorency, Victoria, Yackandandah, 1987.
Safe House (produced Melbourne, 1989). Sydney, Currency Press, 1989.
Esterhaz (produced Melbourne, 1990). Sydney, Currency Press, 1990.
Impropiety. Sydney, Currency Press, 1993.
Choice. Sydney, Currency Press, 1994.
Unknown Soldier. Random House, 1997.

Screenplay: *By My Own Authority*, 1989.

Radio Play: *Einstein*, 1982.

Television Play: *Death Duties*, 1991.

Other

Pigtales (for children). Sydney, Random Century, 1992.
Too Big (for children). Sydney, Random House, 1997.

*

Manuscript Collections: University College, University of New South Wales; Australian Defence Forces Academy Library, Canberra.

Critical Study: Article by Helen Thompson, in *Australian Drama Studies* (St. Lucia), April 1987.

Ron Elisha comments:

Life is crammed with merciless irony. Generally speaking, we humans prefer to remain blind to this most glaring aspect of our existence choosing, instead, to imbue the workings of the universe with some profound and basic meaning. As a playwright, I'll take irony over meaning every time.

My writing is motivated by anger—anger at the poverty of human imagination that allows us to ascribe the random viciousness of existence to the perverse, backhanded machinations of some Grand Architect. We value human life far too little if we believe that it depends, for its meaning, upon the existence of a Divine Referee.

The purpose of all my writing is to restore the value of human life to its rightful place. This value is self-referential. Life is its own meaning. There is only one field of human endeavour which drives home this message with any real power: drama. And there is only one tool which is sharp enough to enable drama to rise to the occasion: irony. Taking as its foundation the twin pillars of the precepts "Live and let live" and "Do unto others . . . ," the foregoing underpins all that I have written.

* * *

As a Jewish intellectual in Melbourne, the most multicultural city in Australia, Ron Elisha has been able to write for an extensive university-educated audience in daily contact with the pressures and barriers of cross-cultural hybridization. Melbourne also presents itself as the "comedy capital of Australia," but because Elisha's work exploits comedy with unusual strategies, he has been called the victim of his own cleverness.

The problematic responses of a defensive migrant population were apparent even in *In Duty Bound*, which prompted some to call Elisha an anti-Semite essentially because he wrote about racism. It was felt that Australia's first major Jewish playwright should deal in terms of the "normal" and the "positive" and not expose the embittered reactionary attitudes of an older generation toward mixed marriages. Persisting with what he called "rational" drama, treating the serious in a fundamentally serious way, Elisha wrote *Two* and *Pax Americana*, works that left him bracketed with Louis Nowra as one of Australia's new "internationalists." The nature of *Pax* has been blurred by debate over production approaches, but the play may be seen as a satirical excursion into postmodernism, as a kaleidoscopic vision of postwar, media-constructed America. *Two* takes its title from its number of characters but also from the problems of the Manichaean worldview of recurrent Elisha characters. Set in Germany in 1948, the play centers on a woman who is learning Hebrew so that she can go to Israel but who turns out to be a former SS member, and the binaries of Jew and Arab, good and evil, self and other are exposed to erosion.

Elisha's refusal to deal in terms of trite polarization meant that audience prejudices were simply confirmed by his early plays. In *The Levine Comedy* he decided on a technique of audience "seduction" by packaging his serious thrust in "irrational" forms and styles. Most blatantly, the title character can acknowledge here his dialogic style by invoking the name of Woody Allen at the point of domestic tragedy, but the irrational also obtrudes in the form of abrupt changes of tone, the sudden death of story elements (a device from *In Duty Bound*), and a sequence of secondary but pivotal characters who are all called Hope. If this last is in part a device from the morality play tradition, it is also reflective of Elisha's interest in psychoanalytical dissection and in the representation of universal, macrocosmic elements through single characters on stage.

Central to both *Einstein* and *Safe House* is a displaced male character who is represented in a schizoid manner so that an older self can collide with a younger self within the character's mind and bring "recollections from the future." Three actors play Einstein: one in 1955 at the point of death, one from 1919 until Hiroshima, and one retrogressively from 1919 to the formulation of the theory of relativity in 1905. Throughout, Einstein speaks to another lawgiver, Moses (not represented by an actor), and the finale fuses the epiphanic motif of the burning bush with a projection of the Hiroshima explosion. Einstein's interrogation of Moses recalls that of the aging Freud, and here, too, is the ambivalence of the man who kills his brother while in search of revelation. Other less specific facets of Hebrew history permeate the play, which opens with women's lamentations echoing the exilic Rachel, the generic mother of Israel, "weeping for her children, refusing to be comforted, because they were not."

Safe House proceeds by a series of brilliant swivels, starting with Marx in dialogue with Tolstoy—who turns out to be one of the lesser-known Tolstoys thinking of defecting to Australia (as a "safe house") in 1956. The first act ends with Marx administering a game of 20 questions and concluding that Tolstoy is schizoid, something that is realized in the second act, where he is represented as both Tolstoy and as a professor. Now, 30 years later, he is institutionalized, apparently in Melbourne, and the rich texture of comedy offers a backhanded gloss on Australia from a migrant perspective. A final game of 20 questions reverses all of the answers given earlier and is preceded by a long vatic speech in which Tolstoy cries out to Australia in the manner of a Hebrew prophet, with the inference that Australia does not hear him.

Several of Elisha's plays use music as a structuring or symbolic device; three violins, for example, reflect the conflict of the Einsteins. Only in *Esterhaz*, however, does a whole play hinge on the semiotics of music in the way that *Two* does on the Hebrew language. Here Haydn, in the employment of Esterhazy in 1772, is surrounded by musical espionage that accentuates the political dimension to composition, authorship, and authority, rather as Stalin does in Pownall's *Master Class*. For Elisha, however, the parallel is not starkly allegorical but instead metonymic, so that the irrational absurdities of the antics around the palace seduce the audience from the larger applications of music, as happened, for example, in twentieth-century fascism. When the death of a starving peasant is choreographed to the second movement of the *Emperor* Quartet, gothic politics invade an art world that is trying to stay innocently rococo.

—Howard McNaughton

ELYOT, Kevin

Nationality: English. **Born:** Kevin Ronald Lee, Birmingham, England, 18 July 1951. **Education:** King Edward's School, Birmingham, England, 1962-96; University of Bristol, 1970-73, B.A. (special honours) 1973. **Career:** Actor, 1973—. **Awards:** Writer's Guild of Great Britain Best TV Play, for *Killing Time,* 1991; Samuel Beckett award, for *Coming Clean,* 1982; Writer's Guild Best Fringe Play, for *My Night with Reg,* 1995; Evening Standard Best Comedy, for *My Night with Reg,* 1995; Laurence Olivier Best Comedy, for *My Night with Reg,* 1995; London Critic's Circle Most Promising Newcomer, for *My Night with Reg,* 1995. **Address:** c/o Sebastian Born, The Agency, 24 Pottery Lane, London W11 4LZ, England.

Publications

Plays

Coming Clean (produced London, 1982). London, Faber and Faber, 1984.
Consent (produced Basingstoke, 1989).
The Moonstone, adaptation of Wilkie Collins (produced Worcester, 1990).
Artists and Admirers, new version of Ostrovskyes (produced London, 1992).
My Night with Reg (produced London, 1994). London, Nick Hern Books, 1994.
The Day I Stood Still (produced London, 1998). London, Nick Hern Books, 1998.

Radio Plays: *According to Plan,* 1987; *The Perfect Moment,* 1988; *The Double Dealer,* 1995.

Television Plays: *Killing Time,* 1990; *The Moonstone,* from the novel by Wilkie Coollins, 1996; *My Night with Reg,* 1997.

*

Theatrical Activities:
Actor: Twenty years experience as an actor in productions in the West End, The London Fringe, Manchester Royal Exchange, and other regional theatres as well as in film, television and radio.

* * *

Kevin Elyot achieved enormous popular success with his 1994 play *My Night with Reg*—it was the first Royal Court play to transfer directly from the Royal Court Upstairs to the West End since *The Rocky Horror Show* in 1972. Elyot's follow-up play, *The Day I Stood Still,* premiered at the National Theatre in 1998. Although he had a number of other significant successes—his first play *Coming Clean* (1982) and *Killing Time* (1991), his first television play—it is *My Night with Reg* and *The Day I Stood Still,* both comedies of modern gay manners that have secured Elyot's reputation.

My Night with Reg is a funny, closely observed and occasionally moving contemporary farce set in London in the post-AIDS era. Elyot describes six gay male characters—five friends approaching middle age and the young house painter who comes to decorate a conservatory and remains as a friend. Although the characters are in some measure underwritten and at times rather clichéd, they are also capable of wit, humor, and some emotional depth. They are at their most effective not when dealing with sex (although this is at the core of the play) but when they confront and discuss aging. The characters lament their fading status as a golden generation and express their fears about loss of looks and declining heath with a sentimental poignancy and linguistic authenticity that hints at (but somehow fails to deliver) a deep emotional truth.

The central figure of *My Night with Reg* is Guy, a warm and caring character and the reliable fixed point in a community of impermanent and casual relationships. He is much liked by everyone but desired by none: "I sometimes think I'd rather be fancied than liked," he reflects. Guy carries a torch for John, his friend from university who at the opening of the play is having a secret affair with Reg, the lover of their friend Daniel. John turns to Guy to confide his affair, but he does so without understanding or even allowing the possibility that Guy has his own complex emotions and desires. Guy is constrained from expressing his true feelings regarding John and, more generally, from confronting his own emotional and sexual life. His identity and, in particular, his sexuality is limited by a general lack of self-worth and confidence but above all—and rather like the central character in Paul Rudnick's *Jeffrey*—by a debilitating fear of the risks of sex.

The setting of the play is Guy's flat and the action takes place over an unspecified number of years. It begins with a flat-warming party, shifts to the wake for Reg, and ends the morning after Guy's own funeral. The play charts the shifting relationship between the characters—the central conceit being that all except Guy have had sex with Reg. This suggests that the play is quite open and honest about representing and discussing gay sex and to an extent this is the case: all the characters refer to and talk about their sexual histories naturally and without affectation; Daniel cruises Hampstead Heath for casual and anonymous sexual encounters, while Guy indulges in role-playing telephone sex. Nevertheless, in Guy's one physical sexual act—he is all but raped by his partner—he contracts HIV. By the beginning of act 3 he is dead. It is a very determinist representation of AIDS in Britain, and it has been used by critics to argue that the central figures of both Elyot's major plays—Guy in *My Night with Reg* and Horace in *The Day I Stood Still*—represent, and in narrative terms are locked into, a version of homosexuality that is in some measure self-loathing.

The Day I Stood Still, too, is concerned with aging and sexuality. Like *My Night with Reg,* it focuses on a character who is not really at ease with expressing his sexuality and who is cast by his straight friends into an asexual role of physical impotence. Like Guy, Horace has an undeclared but hugely obsessive love for another man, here his straight school friend Jerry. The play begins with a 30-something Horace in his flat. He is lonely and has no outside social life. He is waiting for the arrival of Terence, a young male prostitute. The unexpected entrance, however, of Jerry's widow, Judy, causes some degree of panic. The arrival of this old friend and her lover ensures that Horace's transaction with Terence fails and Horace again falls into a habitual pattern of asexuality and impotence.

The action then cuts forward some 13 years to find Horace again waiting in the same flat when another unexpected arrival appears—Jimi, Judy and Jerry's 17-year-old son (and Horace's godson). Jimi is the image of his father (in production Jimi and Jerry are played by the same actor), and Horace is immediately attracted to him.

Jimi is more or less unaware of this, as he is distraught at being left by his boyfriend. The scene ends rather uneasily with Horace perhaps set to have a chance with Jimi.

Finally, in the third scene, the play cuts back to the '60s and the day Horace attempted to declare his true sentiments to Jerry. Jerry fails to comprehend the magnitude of Horace's feelings, while Horace himself is disconcerted and embarrassed by the overtly sexual presence of Jerry new girlfriend, Judy. Certainly it is an act of some insensitivity that Jerry turns from Horace's small but significant declaration of love to a passionate coupling with Judy.

Elyot produces an almost seamless text in which there are no loose ends. The play sets up conventions and habits and "explains" their origins—a lost necklace, a broken chair, Horace's obsessive eating of Mars bars. Such adroit plotting can be seen as both the success and the failure of the piece: the neatness of the plotting verges on the mechanical. Nevertheless, the play survives and flourishes because the conversation along the way is very fluid and dynamic and is enormously witty and diverting.

The Day I Stood Still explores much the same territory as *My Night with Reg.* Both plays are chamber pieces about the evolution of long-standing relationships between a group of old friends. The plays focus on a desexualized central character, each with a mostly unrealized desire for another, while simultaneously exploring the appeal and sexual potential of youth. In parallel with those similarities, the plays comment on the effects of the untimely deaths of characters and the responsibilities and restrictions of maturity. Both plays ably demonstrate Elyot's expert ear for contemporary dialogue and, in particular, the emotional and linguistic shorthand used by friends. While he is perhaps less successful in the description of fully delineated characters and the creation of original and unexpected situations, Elyot's theater pieces are fun, witty and, at times, truthful and touching reflections on contemporary sexualities.

—Adrienne Scullion

ENRIGHT, Nick (Nicholas Paul)

Nationality: Australian. **Born:** Newcastle, New South Wales, 22 December 1950. **Education:** St. Ignatius College, Riverview, New South Wales, 1962-67; Sydney University, 1968-71, B.A. 1971; New York University School of the Arts, 1975-77, M.F.A. 1977. **Career:** Associate director, State Theatre Company of South Australia, Adelaide, 1978-81; teacher of acting, 1978, 1989-92, and head of acting, 1982-84, National Institute of Dramatic Art, Sydney; member, Australia Council literature board, Sydney, 1986-89; host, *Play into Opera* series, ABC-FM, 1987; cabaret performer, Tilbery Hotel, Sydney, 1989. Regular host/narrator for Sydney Symphony Orchestra, 1988-92; regular contributor of verse and features to the Sydney *Morning Herald*, the *Australian*, the *National Times*, *Theatre Australia*, and *Vogue Australia*; regular reviewer for ABC Radio, *Books and Writing* and *First Edition.* **Awards:** New South Wales Premier's award, 1983; Australia Council grant, 1975-76, 1984, 1991; Australia Writers' Guild award, for radio, for television, and for best script in any medium, 1990. **Agent:** Hilary Linstead & Associates, Suite 302, Easts Tower, 9-13 Bronte Road, Bondi Junction, New South Wales 2022, Australia; or Intertalent, Suite 300, 131 South Rodeo Drive, Beverly Hills, California 90212, U.S.A. **Address:** 20 Chalder Street, Newtown, New South Wales 2042, Australia.

Publications

Plays

Electra, with Frank Hauser, adaptation of the play by Sophocles (produced Melbourne, 1978).
The Servant of Two Masters, with Ron Blair, adaptation of the play by Carlo Goldoni (produced Adelaide, 1978).
Oh, What a Lovely War, Mate!, adaptation of Australian scenes in the play created by Joan Littlewood and her Theatre Workshop Company (produced Adelaide, 1979).
The Venetian Twins, adaptation of the play by Carlo Goldoni, music by Terence Clarke (produced Sydney, 1979; revised version, Brisbane, 1990).
King Stag, adaptation of the play by Carlo Gozzi (produced Adelaide, 1980).
On the Wallaby (produced Adelaide, 1980). Sydney, Currency Press, 1982.
Music Is (for children; produced Adelaide, 1981).
Fatal Johnny (for children; produced Adelaide, 1982).
First Class Women (produced Sydney, 1982).
Variations, music by Terence Clarke (produced Sydney, 1982).
The Marriage of Figaro, adaptation of the play by Beaumarchais (produced Adelaide, 1983).
Summer Rain, music by Terence Clarke (produced Sydney, 1983; revised version, Sydney, 1989).
Don Juan, adaptation of the play by Molière (produced Adelaide, 1984). Sydney, Currency Press, 1984.
The Snow Queen, adaptation of the story by H. C. Andersen, music by Graham Dudley (produced Adelaide, 1985).
Daylight Saving (produced Sydney, 1989). Sydney, Currency Press, 1990.
Carnival of the Animals, music by Saint-Saens (produced Sydney, 1989). Sydney, ABC Publications, 1991.
Mongrels (produced Sydney, 1991).
St. James Infirmary (produced Penrith, New South Wales, 1992). Sydney, Currency Press, 1992.
A Property of the Clan (produced Newcastle, New South Wales, 1992).
Good Works (produced Queensland and New Zealand, 1995; Bristol, United Kingdom, 1997).
The Quartet from Rigoletto (produced 1995).
Black Rock (produced Sydney, 1995).
The Way I Was (produced Sydney, 1995).
Miracle City, music by Max Lambert (produced Sydney, 1995).
The Voyage of Mary Bryant (produced Perth, 1996).
The Female Factory (produced Sydney, 1997).
Cloudstreet, adaptation of Tim Winton novel, with Justin Monjo (produced Sydney, 1998).
The Boy from Oz (produced 1998).
Chasing the Dragon (produced Sydney, 1998).

Screenplay: *Lorenzo's Oil*, with George Miller, 1992.

Television Plays: *Come In Spinner* series, with Lissa Benyon, adaptation of the novel by F. James and D. Cusack, 1989; *Breaking Through*, adaptation of *No Longer a Victim* by Cathy-Ann Matthews, 1990.

Radio Plays: *Ship Without a Sail* (documentary), 1985; *The Trojan Women*, adaptation of the play by Euripides, 1989; *Watching Over Israel*, 1990; *St. James Infirmary*, 1992; *Blackrock*, 1997.

Poetry

The Maitland and Morpeth String Quartet (for children). Sydney, David Ell Press, 1980.

Recordings: *The Venetian Twins*, Sydney, Larrikin Records, 1981; *Carnival of the Animals* with *Peter and the Wolf*, music by Saint-Saens, Polygram Records, 1989.

*

Manuscript Collection: Australian Defence Forces Academy Library, Canberra.

Critical Study: "'A Form of Music': An Interview with Nick Enright" by Veronica Kelly, in *Australasian Drama Studies* (Queensland, Australia), April 1994, pp. 58-76.

Theatrical Activities:
Director: **Plays**—*American Buffalo* by David Mamet, *Twelfth Night* by Shakespeare, *Arms and the Man* by Shaw, all Adelaide, 1979; *Traitors* by Stephen Sewell, *On the Wallaby*, *A Month in the Country* by Turgenev, all Adelaide, 1980; *A Hard God* by Peter Kenna, *As You Like It* by Shakespeare, both Adelaide, 1981; *The Real Thing* by Tom Stoppard, Sydney, 1985; *Measure for Measure* by Shakespeare, Sydney, 1986.

Actor: **Plays**—With State Theatre Company of South Australia, Adelaide, 1978-81; Elyot in *Private Lives* by Noël Coward, Newcastle, 1985; Tocky in *A Happy and Holy Occasion* by John O'Donoghue, Newcastle, 1986; Saul in *As Is* by William Hoffman, Sydney, 1987; Godfrey in *Vocations* by Alma De Groen, Sydney, 1987; Max de Winter in *Rebecca* by Daphne du Maurier, Sydney, 1991. **Radio**—Regular drama and feature performances since 1972; narrator, *Australia* series, 1988. **Television**—Roles in *Breaking Up*, 1985; *Princess Kate*, 1987; *Willessee's Australians*, 1988; *Brotherhood of the Rose*, 1988; *Come in Spinner*, 1989; *The Paper Man*, 1990.

Nick Enright comments:

I came to playwriting through my work as performer and director, devising, editing, adapting, or translating works for schools, community groups, and regional theatre companies. The strongest influence on the work was the circumstances of its performance. Music was usually part of the pieces which were often in a "popular theatre" vein. I was and am a pragmatist and a natural collaborator.

Recently I have moved towards more personal work, though I have never been much interested in autobiographical revelation. Much of my work has dealt with the Australian past; that concern now seems to be coalescing with some aspects of personal history.

I have no commitment to particular form or tone, preferring to allow the material to dictate both. My writing for stage and screen is always conceived rhythmically; and I like to think about form in musical terms.

* * *

Nick Enright understands the way theater works from experience in every facet of the medium, including that of performing and directing. Because his grounding is in theater rather than in literature, film, or television, Enright's plays have a technical craftsmanship and assuredness that are satisfying for both the audience and the players. Much of his generation's writing—in the United States, in Australia, and in Britain—reveals ignorance of the basic elements of a theatrical event: action, characters who show us that action, a setting in which the action takes place, and an audience that shares in the event. In short, Enright's plays may seem slightly old-fashioned inasmuch as they invariably have a strong story to show us, characters who are three-dimensional, and even a beginning, a middle, and an end, where the pieces are more or less tied together. There is about Enright's work, over and above almost everything else, an unmistakable theatricality.

In *On the Wallaby,* for example, Enright combines a poor Irish-Australian family struggling during the Great Depression, docudrama and Brechtian agitprop shenanigans, and traditional British and Australian music hall nonsense. The play reveals a masterly command of the theater as an instrument to entertain, inform, and move us. If the politics seem black-and-white today and if the promises of the labor movements and of communism itself have failed, never mind. The play as a play grips us with its action and its relevance. It holds the stage, which is true of almost all of Enright's work.

Much of the time Enright apparently writes for specific actors, and in *Daylight Saving* he has concocted a completely different series of theatrical conventions. Very modern, even trendy, and certainly very jokey, the play is a farce of manners, of characters, and of today. Enright has slyly slipped in hilarious comments on the United States in the 1970s, when he himself was studying there, and Australia in the 1990s. Aging yuppies and their parents, neighbors, clients, and schedules all collide in a swiftly paced, magnificently plotted series of events that boisterously amuse and reflect giddily a world far different from that of *On the Wallaby.* Enright is not Noël Coward, but he comes close.

With *Mongrels* the playwright enters quite different territory, yet he always keeps a tight hold on what the theater is and can do best. In fact, a play is being enacted within a play, and the characters are intertwined. The witty dialogue, which is largely centered in gay chatter and allusions, is overshadowed here by a kind of darkness. Theater is a business and a dirty business at that. Who is doing what to whom at any given moment is up for grabs, it would seem, as we watch an evolution of characters from prison cells to high-rise Sydney apartments. It rings true because it is rooted in actions and situations that we know to be true, whether we are of the theater or not. The mirror Enright holds up to the world in *Mongrels* reflects a less pleasant scene than the play pretends, for a shadow hangs over the gags and the jabs.

St. James Infirmary is in a way furthest from the jamboree of *On the Wallaby,* for in this play Enright attempts to show us both morality and art, which may be closer than we think but which are very hard to portray on stage. We are asked to believe that a snotty young man at a Catholic school for boys is "brilliant" as an artist but that the forces pulling at him—a priest, a nurse, some adoring adolescent boys—could destroy him. As in all melodrama, however, the hero is stronger than these forces and in time goes out on his own, gloriously and flamingly. The issues are less interesting than the characters or the mastery of technique that the playwright displays. It sometimes seems that the technique shows through, but it is always admirable craftsmanship.

Although he is called an Australian playwright, Enright's plays work on the stage anywhere. Some of the lingo may seem foreign, but the drift, the ideas, and the people come across without strain. His skill and devotion to the theater have launched him on a handsome career in the English-speaking world.

—Arthur H. Ballet

EVARISTI, Marcella

Nationality: British. **Born:** Glasgow, 19 July 1953. **Education:** Notre Dame High School for Girls, Glasgow, to 1970; University of Glasgow, 1970-74, B.A. (honours) in English and drama. **Family:** Married Michael Boyd in 1982; one son and one daughter. **Career:** Playwright-in-residence, University of St. Andrews, Fife, 1979-80; creative writing fellow, University of Sheffield, Yorkshire, 1979-80; writer-in-residence, universities of Glasgow and Strathclyde, 1984-85. **Awards:** BBC Student Verse Competition prize, 1971; Arts Council bursary, 1975-76; Pye award, 1982. **Agent:** Andrew Hewson, John Johnson Authors' Agent, 45/47 Clerkenwell House, Clerkenwell Green, London EC1R 0HT, England.

Publications

Plays

Dorothy and the Bitch (produced Edinburgh, 1976).
Scotia's Darlings (produced Edinburgh, 1978).
Sugar and Spite (revue), with Liz Lochhead (produced Edinburgh, 1978).
Mouthpieces (revue; produced St. Andrews, 1980).
Hard to Get (produced Edinburgh, 1980).
Commedia (produced Sheffield, 1982; London, 1983). Edinburgh, Salamander Press, 1983.
Thank You for Not in *Breach of the Peace* (revue; produced London, 1982).
Checking Out (produced London, 1984).
The Works (produced Edinburgh, 1984). Published in *Plays Without Wires*, Sheffield, Sheffield Academic Press, 1989.
Terrestrial Extras (produced Glasgow, 1985).
Trio for Strings in 3 (sketch; produced, Glasgow, 1987).
Visiting Company (produced Glasgow, 1988).
The Offski Variations (produced Glasgow, 1990).

Radio Plays: *Hard to Get*, 1981; *Wedding Belles and Green Grasses*, 1983; *The Hat*, 1988; *The Theory and Practice of Rings*, 1992; *Troilus and Cressida and La-di-da-di-da*, 1992.

Television Plays: *Eva Set the Balls of Corruption Rolling*, 1982; *Hard to Get*, 1983.

*

Theatrical Activities:
Actor: **Plays**—Roles in *Dorothy and the Bitch*, Edinburgh, 1976; *Twelfth Night*, Glasgow, 1979; *Sugar and Spite*, Edinburgh, 1981; *Mystery Bouffe*, Sheffield, 1982; *The Works*, Glasgow, 1985; *Terrestrial Extras*, Glasgow, 1985; Rhona Andrews in *Visiting Company*, Glasgow, 1988; *The Offski Variations*, Glasgow, 1990. **Radio**—Roles in *The Works*, 1985; *The Hat*, 1988.

* * *

A rare but consistently recognizable sensibility marks the work of Marcella Evaristi. To explain it, she has frequently remarked on her heritage—part Italian Catholic, part Jewish, altogether Glaswegian. It is a blend that has kept her a significant part of the Scottish theater scene since her first play, *Dorothy and the Bitch,* in 1976, although her most important plays have had life south of the border in England as well.

Her qualities are seen at their most harmonious in her emotionally powerful play *Commedia.* Set partly in Evaristi's native Glasgow and partly in Bologna, the drama marries the passionate domesticity of an Italian home in Scotland to the volatile politics of Italy in 1980. As in all of her work, she reveals the most intimate details of her characters' private lives with a coroner's attention to opening up wounds, but her concerns in *Commedia* are also the ways in which the broader world determines the fate of the individual.

The play begins with edgy comedy as the adult sons of the widowed Elena bring their wives to her house for their usual Chianti Hogmanay, a Scottish New Year's Eve full of "pasta, pollo alla cacciatore and wine" and seemingly lacking in the traditional whisky and tall, dark stranger "first-footing it" through the door at midnight. But there is a handsome stranger, Davide, a young teacher from Bologna working in the Glasgow schools and working on Elena's heart.

An affair between Davide and Elena, for all its uncertainties caused by a 20-year age gap, brings up less generational conflict than might be expected, for the lovers are prepared to work at their differences. Typically for Evaristi, conflict erupts from within the family, from the jealousy of one of Elena's sons. The men in Evaristi's plays regularly cling to boyhood, while the women accept whatever responsibility is required.

There are fairy-tale elements that promise a happy ending, and Elena is entertainingly eccentric from the first and engages the audience's sympathy. She receives the support of an "outsider"—Lucy, the American wife of the jealous son, Stefano. Davide's radical left politics provide a philosophy and a circle of friends that accommodate his relationship with Elena. But there is a bitterness in the writing. When Elena and Davide take a holiday in Bologna, for example, it provokes a family showdown that inadvertently leads to the death of the gentler son, Cesare, one of the innocent people killed in the Fascist bombing of Bologna's railway station.

The relationship subsequently fails, Lucy leaves Stefano, Elena's late-life freedom is curtailed when Cesare's widow and her daughter move in, and, in effect, all of the women return to a world without men. A happy ending will remain a fairy tale until male and female relationships can survive without illusion.

There is a poetic grace and imagination in the best of Evaristi's writing that elevates the most domestic of themes. In *Commedia* Elena's conflicts are encapsulated in a song, "Tin Mags the Kitchen Witch," that divides her character into disciplinarian mother and libertarian witch, making her a kind of lady of misrule. In a play such as *Wedding Belles and Green Grasses* Evaristi follows two sisters and their half sister through childhood to puberty and their first boyfriends and to jobs, marriage, and divorce, lyrically raising the familiar material into ironic understanding through the musical repetition of themes with subtle variations for each character.

Evaristi's poetic imagination makes even greater leaps in her major radio play *The Hat*. The world of the play is full of objects that are given voice. An elegant old-world mirror, for example, observes the troubled relationship of Marianne and her lover, the artist Crispin, and, to Marianne's dismay, comments on it. Other inanimate characters develop conversational relationships with her, including her compact mirror and, most importantly, her cloche hat. The hat, which is despised by Crispin, can be seen symbolically as Marianne's sexuality, but the imagery of the play transcends Freud. Crispin's great achievement as an artist is a collage that represents Marianne's free spirit. As Marianne establishes her own independence, the collage deteriorates in its gallery, and Crispin's only hope of retaining his artistic reputation is to sexually subjugate her once again.

Women remain at the mercy of men in another of Evaristi's radio plays, a potent reworking of the Troilus and Cressida story titled *Troilus and Cressida and La-di-da-di-da*. Fine, elevated sentiments from the two lovers begin the play, with a beautiful statement of bodily and spiritual commitment from each partner. When war intervenes, Troilus reluctantly becomes a soldier and continually restates his love, but Cressida is deprived of his words by other men who prostitute her. Corruption of ideals is again the natural product of male society.

Evaristi also writes well for herself as a performer, and she has appeared in one-woman shows such as *The Offski Variations*, in which she further investigates the seemingly endless separations of people, from abandoned child to divorcing parents and departing partners. Her best work, however, transcends the strong persona of her own character. She is a lyric dramatist of intense subjectivity, constantly observing the impact of society on the individual.

—Ned Chaillet

EVELING, (Harry) Stanley

Nationality: British. **Born:** Newcastle upon Tyne, Northumberland, 4 August 1925. **Education:** Rutherford College; Samuel King's School; King's College, Durham University (William Black Noble Student, 1950-51), B.A. (honors) in English 1950, B.A. (honors) in philosophy 1953; Lincoln College, Oxford, D. Phil. 1955. **Military Service:** Served in the Durham Light Infantry, 1944-47. **Family:** Married to Kate Eveling. **Career:** Assistant lecturer, Department of Logic and Metaphysics, King's College, University of Aberdeen, 1955-57; lecturer, Department of Philosophy, University College of Wales, Aberystwyth, 1957-60. Senior lecturer, 1960-83, and teaching fellow in philosophy, University of Edinburgh, 1984—. Television critic, the *Scotsman*, Edinburgh, 1970—. **Awards:** Earl Grey fellowship, 1955. **Agent:** Lemon, Unna and Stephen Durbridge, 24 Pottery Lane, Holland Park, London W11 4LZ, England. **Address:** 30 Comely Bank, Edinburgh EH4 LAJ, Scotland.

PUBLICATIONS

Plays

The Balachites (produced Edinburgh, 1963). With *The Strange Case of Martin Richter*, London, Calder and Boyars, 1970.

An Unspeakable Crime (produced London, 1963).

Come and Be Killed (produced Edinburgh, 1967; London, 1968). With *Dear Janet Rosenberg, Dear Mr. Kooning*, London, Calder and Boyars, 1971.

The Strange Case of Martin Richter (produced Glasgow, 1967; London, 1968). With *The Balachites*, London, Calder and Boyars, 1970.

The Lunatic, The Secret Sportsman, and the Woman Next Door (produced Edinburgh, 1968; London, 1969). With *Vibrations*, London, Calder and Boyars, 1970.

Dear Janet Rosenberg, Dear Mr. Kooning (produced Edinburgh and London, 1969; New York, 1970). With *Come and Be Killed*, London, Calder and Boyars, 1971.

Vibrations (produced Edinburgh, 1969; London, 1972). With *The Lunatic, The Secret Sportsman, and the Woman Next Door*, London, Calder and Boyars, 1970.

Dracula, with others (produced Edinburgh, 1969; London, 1973).

Mister (produced Edinburgh, 1970; London, 1971). Published in *A Decade's Drama*, Huddersfield, Woodhouse Books, 1980.

Sweet Alice (as *Jakey Fat Boy*, produced New York 1970; as *Sweet Alice*, produced Edinburgh and London, 1971). Published in *Plays and Players* (London), March 1971.

Better Days, Better Knights (produced Edinburgh, 1971; London, 1972).

Our Sunday Times (produced Edinburgh and London, 1971).

Oh Starlings (produced Edinburgh, 1971). Published in *Plays and Players* (London), March 1971.

The Laughing Cavalier (produced London, 1971).

He Used to Play for Hearts, in *Christmas Present* (produced Edinburgh, 1971).

Caravaggio, Buddy (produced Edinburgh, 1972; London, 1977).

Union Jack (and Bonzo) (produced Edinburgh and London, 1973).

Shivvers (produced London, 1974).

The Dead of Night (produced Edinburgh, 1975).

The Buglar (sic) *Boy and His Swish Friend* (produced Edinburgh, 1983). Edinburgh, Salamander Press, 1983.

The Albright Fellow (produced Edinburgh, 1995).

Radio Plays: *Dance ti Thy Daddy*, 1964; *The Timepiece*, 1965; *A Man Like That*, 1966; *The Devil in Summer*, with Kate Eveling, from a play by Michel Faure, 1971; *The Queen's Own*, 1976.

Television Plays: *A Man Like That*, 1970; *Ishmael*, 1973.

Poetry

Poems. Oxford, Fantasy Press, 1956.

Other

The Total Theatre. Edinburgh, Heriot Watt University, 1972.

*

Manuscript Collections: Mugar Library, Boston University; National Library of Scotland, Edinburgh.

Stanley Eveling comments:

My plays seem, very roughly speaking, to oscillate between reality and unreality, between moral dramas and plays in the absurdist, or, better, Dickensian, tradition. I hanker after the former and still think that *Mister*, a sort of dramatic interface between the fantastic and the real, is the play that says most, though it doesn't have the inventive duplicity and cunning of *Dear Janet* and some others.

If I had to say what theme hovers around in all, it would be that they all seem to have something to do with beleaguered human beings, most often male ones, in circumstances that precisely don't call for his (or her) particular virtues. In *Mister*'s case these are heroic virtues, Nelsonian virtues; in the case of the Oblomovian Jim in *Come and Be Killed*, it is as if he were called upon to exercise the "wrong" virtues, mundane virtues that go with domesticity and responsibility, like asking Shelley to wash the nappies or the Ford Cortina, or so Jim construes it. Alec, in *Dear Janet*, is asked to play a romantic role in a young girl's dream as she is required to fulfil a dreamed-up bit of him. In *The Buglar Boy and His Swish Friend* (the most complicated play, perhaps), the characters themselves, called down from the eternal library of the imagination, attempt and fail to fulfil the tragic requirements of the play's theme, attempt and fail to take on a tragic role at a time, in an age, and with qualities that belong to comedy. This is as close as I want to get. In the play *Impossible People* (revised as *The Albright Fellow*), I see that the theme is that of a man called upon to perform the last male role, that of being subservient to his wife's genius. Naturally he does not succeed.

What is "ridiculous" or "absurd" is that the wrong qualities are also the right qualities, that tragic predicaments happen in comic circumstances, that is, outside the environment which would give them tragic significance. As Janet says of her own work, at the end of the play, it is carried along on "the last ripple left by the receding impulse of tragedy."

* * *

Stanley Eveling is a prolific and at first sight a somewhat baffling playwright. He writes in a variety of styles and almost always adopts a veiled, even blurred approach to his subject matter. Although he is a professional moral philosopher as well as a playwright and although his characters often involve themselves in philosophical argument and speculation, his plays are by no means intellectual in the sense of being elaborately constructed to act as working models of some abstract thesis. Eveling's approach is veiled not because he is hiding the machinery but because, on the contrary, he himself seems to write in the act of watching the machinery at work. He sits almost painfully close to the characters, feels them rather than thinks them, and uses one style or another, as he might use one stage or another, as at most a temporary accommodation for his stubborn and chaotic material.

This material is presented in its simplest versions in the two plays *Come and Be Killed* and *Dear Janet Rosenberg, Dear Mr. Kooning*. The first concerns an abortion, the second an abortive relationship between an aging novelist and his female fan. The muddled, narrowly confined, squalid situations in which the characters find themselves in both plays are compounded by their own muddled, limited, and selfish reactions. "You're not wicked, you're just ignorant," says one character to another in *Come and Be Killed*, which might be a motto for all of Eveling's work. Creation in general is messy, cruel, and blind, and the lords of creation are no more and no less. In *The Balachites* Eveling shows a pair of innocents, a modern Adam and Eve, corrupted not by Satan but by the ghosts of dead men. In his nearest thing to an absurdist play, *The Lunatic, The Secret Sportsman, and the Woman Next Door*, he shows the pathetic innocence of mental and sexual aberration.

Naturally, the idea that there are such creatures as heroes in such a world is a fruitful source of still further pain and confusion. The story of Donald Crowhurst, who made it appear that he was winning the *Sunday Times* single-handed yacht race around the world but who turned out to have disappeared, almost certainly overboard, without ever having sailed beyond the Atlantic, forms the basis of Eveling's play *Our Sunday Times*. But he extends the story, as the title implies, to cover a much more widespread form of bogus heroism, of cheaply bought superiority over trivial circumstances, the vicarious act of reading newspapers or watching television. The play's effect is weakened by this attempt at generalization, for Eveling steps back too far from his characters. But *Mister,* in which he again treats a would-be sailor-hero, the owner of an antique shop who acts out his fantasy of being Lord Nelson but with the unfortunate complication of having a Lady Hamilton on the premises who is not content with a sexual relationship confined to fantasy, is perhaps Eveling's best play. It is certainly his saddest and funniest and his finest example of what Janet Rosenberg calls "the curious mixture of farce and misery which is the slight ripple left by the receding impulse of tragedy."

Nevertheless, although Eveling's dramatic outlook is on the whole more sad than angry, reminiscent of those world-weary but intermittently kindly doctors in Chekhov's plays, he has written at least one work in which the mixture of farce and misery is replaced by that of savage humor and despair. In *The Strange Case of Martin Richter* a German industrialist employs three ex-Nazis as household servants, not realizing or not caring what this means for his butler, who is of "Swebish" origin and whose father was murdered during the Third Reich for being Swebish. The butler's solution is to pretend that he himself was a prominent Nazi, claim acquaintance with Hitler, constitute himself the leader of a neo-Nazi party, and pretend to eliminate the industrialist for being Swebish. The play ends, after several twists of fortune and a marvelously composed drunken party, with everything as it was, the industrialist once more on top of the evil heap. *Martin Richter* is the nearest thing in Eveling's work to a straight political and moral fable. It is compact and clear, a powerful and bitterly comic outcry against the nastiness, brutishness, and shortness of human life.

Shivvers; *Caravaggio, Buddy*; and *The Dead of Night* all deal with suicide in one form or another. The central character of *Shivvers,* having for a time assuaged his own sense of guilt by imposing vicious behavior on a vicar and a whore, commits suicide when they shake off his domination. *Caravaggio, Buddy* is an ambitious comic fantasy, an episodic quest play somewhat reminiscent of *Peer Gynt* whose hero fails in many attempts to commit suicide and ends up reconciled with society. The play's complex and carefully controlled shifts of style establish in dramatic rather than intellectual terms the reality and humanity of the misfit as against the unreality and inhumanity of the "organized." It is full of delightful comic inventions, such as the colloquy between Buddy and a yeti on the slopes of Mount Everest, while just offstage innumerable international expeditions make more or less disastrous assaults on the summit. *The Dead of Night* is a somber piece, enlivened by a German general trying to disguise himself as a woman, that is set beside Hitler's bunker in Berlin and features the archsuicide himself.

All three plays show Eveling sharpening his lines and clarifying his construction without losing his closeness to the characters. His themes remain the same, but his methods of exploring them become more precise and versatile.

—John Spurling

F

FEIFFER, Jules (Ralph)

Nationality: American. **Born:** The Bronx, New York, 26 January 1929. **Education:** James Monroe High School, New York; Art Students' League, New York, 1946; Pratt Institute, Brooklyn, 1947-48, 1949-51. **Military Service:** Served as a cartoon animator and graphic artist in the United States Army Signal Corps, 1951-53: private. **Family:** Married 1) Judith Sheftel in 1961 (separated 1971, divorced 1983), one daughter; 2) Jennifer Allen in 1983, one daughter. **Career:** Assistant to the cartoonist Will Eisner, 1946-51 (ghostwriter, *The Spirit* comic, 1949-51); drew cartoon *Clifford*, 1949-51; freelance cartoonist and artist, 1951-56. Cartoonist (*Feiffer*), *Village Voice*, New York, 1956—, and syndicated in other newspapers and magazines, 1959—. Faculty member, Yale University School of Drama, New Haven, Connecticut, 1973-74; senior fellow, National Arts Journalism Program, Columbia University, 1997-98. President, Dramatists Guild Foundation, 1982-83. Director, Corporation of Yaddo, Saratoga Springs, New York, 1976—. **Awards:** Oscar, for cartoon, 1961; George Polk Memorial award, 1962; London Theatre Critics award, 1968; Obie award, 1968; Outer Circle award, 1968, 1969; Pulitzer prize, for cartoon, 1986; Los Angeles Critics Circle award, 1988; Venice Film Festival award, for screenplay, 1989. **Member:** American Academy of Arts and Letters. **Address:** 325 West End Avenue, New York, New York 10023, U.S.A.

PUBLICATIONS

Plays

The Explainers (produced Chicago, 1961; New York, 1964).

Crawling Arnold (produced Spoleto, London, and Cambridge, Massachusetts, 1961; New York, 1979). Published in *Best Short Plays of the World 1958-1967*, edited by Stanley Richards, New York, Crown, 1968.

The World of Jules Feiffer (produced Hunterdon Hills, New Jersey, 1962).

Interview, published in *Harper's* (New York), June 1962.

You Should Have Caught Me at the White House, published in *Holiday* (Indianapolis), June 1963.

Little Murders (produced New Haven, Connecticut, 1966; London and New York, 1967). New York, Random House, 1968; London, Cape, 1970.

The Unexpurgated Memoirs of Bernard Mergendeiler (produced Los Angeles, 1967; New York, 1968; Glasgow, 1969; London, 1972). Published in *Collision Course*, New York, Random House, 1968.

God Bless (produced New Haven, Connecticut, and London, 1968). Published in *Plays and Players* (London), January 1969.

Feiffer's People (produced Edinburgh and London, 1968; Los Angeles, 1971).

Dick and Jane, in *Oh! Calcutta!* (produced New York, 1969; London, 1970). New York, Grove Press, 1970.

The White House Murder Case (produced New York, 1970). New York, Grove Press, 1970.

Munro (produced New York, 1971).

Carnal Knowledge: A Screenplay (revised version produced, Houston, 1988). New York, Farrar Straus, and London, Cape, 1971.

Silverlips, in *VD Blues* (televised 1972). New York, Avon, 1973.

Watergate Classics, with others (produced New Haven, Connecticut, 1973).

Cohn of Arc, published in *Partisan Review* (New Brunswick, New Jersey), vol. 40, no. 2, 1973.

Knock, Knock (produced New York, 1976). New York, Hill and Wang, 1976.

Hold Me! (produced New York, 1977). New York, Dramatists Play Service, 1977.

Grown Ups (produced Cambridge, Massachusetts, and New York, 1981). New York, French, 1982.

A Think Piece (produced New York, 1982).

Rope-a-Dope, in *Urban Blight* (musical revue), based on an idea by John Tillinger, music by David Shire, lyrics by Richard Maltby, Jr. (produced New York, 1988).

Elliot Loves (produced New York, 1989). New York, Grove Press, 1989.

Bernard and Huey. New York, RC Publications, 1995.

Anthony Rose (produced Philadelphia, 1989). New York, Lantz Office, 1996.

Screenplays: *Munro* (animated cartoon), 1960; *Carnal Knowledge*, 1971; *Little Murders*, 1971; *Popeye*, 1980; *I Want to Go Home*, 1989.

Television Plays: *Silverlips* in *VD Blues*, with others, 1972; *Kidnapped* (*Happy Endings* series), 1975.

Novels

Harry, The Rat with Women. New York, McGraw Hill, and London, Collins, 1963.

Ackroyd. New York, Simon and Schuster, 1977; London, Hutchinson, 1978.

Tantrum: A Novel-in-Cartoons. New York, Knopf, 1979; London, Sidgwick and Jackson, 1980.

Other

Sick, Sick, Sick. New York, McGraw Hill, 1958; London, Collins, 1959.

Passionella and Other Stories. New York, McGraw Hill, 1959; London, Collins, 1960.

The Explainers. New York, McGraw Hill, 1960; London, Collins, 1961.

Boy, Girl. Boy, Girl. New York, Random House, 1961; London, Collins, 1962.

Hold Me! New York, Random House, 1963.

Feiffer's Album. New York, Random House, 1963.

The Unexpurgated Memoirs of Bernard Mergendeiler. New York, Random House, 1965; London, Collins, 1966.

The Penguin Feiffer. London, Penguin, 1966.

Feiffer on Civil Rights. New York, Anti-Defamation League of B'nai B'rith, 1966.

Feiffer's Marriage Manual. New York, Random House, 1967.
Pictures at a Prosecution: Drawings and Text from the Chicago Conspiracy Trial. New York, Grove Press, 1971.
Feiffer on Nixon: The Cartoon Presidency. New York, Random House, 1974.
Jules Feiffer's America from Eisenhower to Reagan, edited by Steven Heller. New York, Knopf, and London, Penguin, 1982.
Outer Space Spirit 1952, with Will Eisner and Wallace Wood, edited by Denis Kitchen. Princeton, Wisconsin, Kitchen Sink Press, 1983.
Marriage Is an Invasion of Privacy and Other Dangerous Views. Fairway, Kansas, Andrews McMeel and Parker, 1984.
Feiffer's Children. Fairway, Kansas, Andrews McMeel and Parker, 1986.
Ronald Reagan in Movie America: A Jules Feiffer Production. Fairway, Kansas, Andrews McMeel and Parker, 1988.
Feiffer: The Collected Works:
Clifford. Seattle, Fantagraphics, 1989.
Munro. Seattle, Fantagraphics, 1989.
Sick, Sick, Sick. Seattle, Fantagraphics, 1991.
Passionella. Seattle, Fantagraphics, 1993.
The Man in the Ceiling (for children). New York, HarperCollins, 1993.
A Barrel of Laughs, a Vale of Tears (for children). New York, HarperCollins, 1995.
Meanwhile (for children). New York, HarperCollins, 1997.
I Lost My Bear (for children). New York, Morrow Junior Books, 1998.

Editor, *The Great Comic Book Heroes*. New York, Dial Press, 1965; London, Allen Lane, 1967.

Illustrator, *Phantom of the Tollbooth*, by Norton Juster.

*

Critical Studies: "Jules Feiffer and the Comedy of Disenchantment" by Stephen J. Whitfield, in *From Hester Street to Hollywood: The Jewish American Stage and Screen*, edited by Sarah Blacher Cohen, Bloomington, Indiana, Indiana University Press, 1983; "Jules Feiffer" by John DiGaetani, in *A Search for a Postmodern Theater: Interviews with Contemporary Playwrights*, New York, Greenwood, 1991.

* * *

Jules Feiffer is, first of all, a cartoonist. Long before he began to write plays, he had made a reputation as a satirist with an uncanny knack for catching the psychological, social, and political clichés that are the refuge and the cross of the college-educated middle class, which provides him with an audience as well as a subject matter. His talent has always been as much verbal as visual, his ear as good as his hand. His cartoons ordinarily are strips in which two characters pursue a conversation, panel by panel, until the congenial platitudes dissolve into open aggression, naked greed, impotence, ineffectuality, and pain; a variation is the strip in which a single figure—I almost said performer—speaks directly to the reader. The line between this kind of cartoon and the revue sketch is a narrow one, and a great many of Feiffer's early cartoons have crossed that line. Most of the material in *Feiffer's People* and *Hold Me!* presumably began as cartoon dialogue. Even those short works written for the theater—*Dick and Jane*, the Feiffer sketch from *Oh! Calcutta!*, or the early one-acter *Crawling Arnold*—seem little more than extended cartoons, with the stage directions standing in for the drawing.

Inevitably, Feiffer's full-length plays have been viewed—and condemned in some cases—as the work of a cartoonist. There is justice in the viewing, if not in the condemnation, for—as so often with satirists—Feiffer works in terms of stereotypes, of those figures identified by a single idiosyncrasy or a pattern of related compulsions. Even the two young men in *Carnal Knowledge* are social types rather than psychological studies, although the labels by which we identify them may be written in the kind of psychological language that one expects to find in the balloons of Feiffer's cartoons. Feiffer tends to see his figures as more realistic than my description suggests. Just before the off-Broadway revival of *Little Murders*, Feiffer told an interviewer that his characters "are very, very real to me. I care about them as people." Yet, elsewhere in the same interview he identified the family in the play as "a nice, Andy Hardy type family," and the Hardy family films were straight stereotype. If we read "real" in the Feiffer quotation as "true"—that is, identifiable—the characters are real, as is Andy Hardy and as are the figures in his cartoons. We look at them and say, "Oh yes, I know him," meaning "Oh yes, I know the type."

The important thing about Feiffer as a playwright is that he produces unified dramatic structures—related in some of their elements to his cartoons and to revue sketches—in which apparently disparate material is held together by a controlling idea. In *Little Murders* the random violence that is the ostensible subject is simply the most obviously theatrical evidence of a general collapse reflected in technological malfunction (the failed electricity) and the impotence of traditional power and virtue figures (the comic turns of the judge, the detective, and the priest). When Feiffer's nice American family begins to shoot people on the street, the event is not so much a culmination of the action as an open statement of what has been implicit all through the play. The last scene of the play; the disintegration, both physical and political, in *The White House Murder Case*; and the sexual ignorance and failure that calls itself carnal knowledge—all these suggest that Feiffer has about as black a view of American society and of human possibility as one can find in the contemporary theater.

After *Knock, Knock*, an uncharacteristic fantasy of commitment, *Grown Ups* comes home to familiar Feiffer territory with a self-pitying protagonist who is faced with personal and professional collapse and a parental support system that is the presumed cause of his misery; on stage his daughter, used as a weapon by all of the adults, is something of a trial for the audience, but the television version of the play, ending with the camera on the little girl, successfully emphasizes the child as victim and the continuity of loving destructiveness within the family. *A Think Piece* concentrates on the trivia of daily existence to show, as the author says, "the nothingness that constitutes so much of our lives."

Elliot Loves and *Anthony Rose* explore familiar Feiffer themes, once again in darkly comic contexts. The titular hero of *Elliot Loves*, a nonrealistic gathering of four sketchlike scenes, is a man so unable to stop questioning, teasing, and testing his love that he ends with only a telephone cord holding him, tentatively, to his beloved. Anthony Rose is a successful playwright who turns up at a rehearsal of *The Parent Lesson*, a 25-year-old hit of his, and proceeds to rewrite it to conform to his new view of the world; the villainous father and the wronged sons exchange guilt and innocence. In the process the playwright takes over the production, undermining the company even as he calls them his family—a scary label since he has destroyed his own family and every theater group with which he has worked. *Elliot Loves* is the more polished script, but *Anthony Rose* is more interesting—particularly in its assumption that an author, at whatever age, uses his art to get back at the real world.

—Gerald Weales

FENNARIO, David

Nationality: Canadian. **Born:** David William Wiper in Montreal in 1947. **Education:** Dawson College, Montreal, 1969-71. **Family:** Married Elizabeth Fennario in 1976; one child. **Career:** Worked odd jobs including work as a packer and mail clerk; playwright-in-residence, Centaur Theatre, Montreal, 1973—. Cofounder, Cultural Workers Association. **Awards:** Canada Council grant, 1973; Chalmers award, 1979. **Address:** c/o Centaur Theatre Company, 453 St. François Xavier Street, Montreal, Quebec H2Y 2TI, Canada.

Publications

Plays

On the Job (produced Montreal, 1975). Vancouver, Talonbooks, 1976.
Nothing to Lose (produced Montreal, 1976). Vancouver, Talonbooks, 1977.
Toronto (produced Montreal, 1978).
Without a Parachute, adaptation of his own book (produced Toronto, 1978).
Balconville (produced Montreal, 1979; Bath and London, 1981). Vancouver, Talonbooks, 1980.
Changes, adaptation of his journal *Without a Parachute* (produced Ottawa, 1980).
Moving (produced Montreal, 1983).
Blue Mondays, poems by Daniel Adams. Verdun, Quebec, Black Rock Creations, 1984.
Joe Beef (produced Montreal, 1985). Vancouver, Talonbooks, 1991.
Doctor Neil Cream (produced Toronto, 1988). Vancouver, Talonbooks, 1993.
The Murder of Susan Parr (produced Montreal, 1989).
The Death of René Lévesque (produced Montreal, 1991).

Other

Without a Parachute (journal). Privately printed, 1972; Toronto, McClelland and Stewart, 1974.

*

Critical Study: "Fennario and Ryga: Canadian Political Playwrights" by Marvin Gilman, in *Australasian Drama Studies* (Queensland), October 1996, pp. 180-86.

* * *

It is difficult to consider David Fennario's work without reference to the man himself. The issues and attitudes of his plays arise from and consistently express his social background and his politics. This is as true of the later work as of the early autobiographical writing, and it explains his discomfort at working for established theaters such as Montreal's Centaur Theatre, where he was first staged and where his most successful plays have been mounted.

Fennario comes from a working-class immigrant area of Montreal. In this subculture he learned to be streetwise in a city divided between French and English factions and further stressed by an increasingly obvious and vocal ethnic mosaic. His personal story, which was dramatized in the one-man show *Changes,* has become a literary artifact itself, since it was the publication of his diary memoir, *Without a Parachute,* that led Fennario to an unprecedented residency with Centaur, the production of his first play, and an immediate popular success. Although his popularity has declined since then, he remains well known in Anglophone Quebec.

An extended sense of self has become characteristic of Fennario's plays. *On the Job* and *Balconville* move further from it than, say, *Nothing to Lose,* in which a protagonist exactly like the author returns to a slum exactly like his home and talks to friends exactly like his own about how it has been to become a famous playwright and media personality. But even the less autobiographical plays exhibit the familiar setting, figures, and tone of the author's background. In fact, his late work *Banana Boots* is again directly autobiographical, recounting his experiences in going to Ireland for a production of *Balconville,* and here Fennario also performed himself. When he distanced himself from his milieu in the play *Toronto,* where he set aside his own territory and moved across the border into English Canada, he wrote his least convincing play.

On the Job established the themes central to Fennario's writing. The play is set in the packing room of a clothing factory on Christmas Eve, with the action initiated by a special rush order from the Eaton department store, a megabusiness that is a symbol of the Canadian establishment in this work as in other Canadian writing. The order requires the shipping crew to remain through the usual half day holiday and brings to the surface the workers' feelings of exploitation and powerlessness. It also allows their representative personalities to emerge: the old worker aware of his political weakness; the foreman, a Quebecois who has risen to a position of impotent power in the English management; a young punk who wishes only to drink and avoid working; a young radical who tries to incite revolution by organizing an illegal strike, which ends in the firing of the employees.

The notion of revolution is pivotal, for it introduces Fennario's Marxist politics, a consistent ideology that continues in *Joe Beef* and explains his decision not to alter the text of *Balconville* for a 1992 remounting. As he said in an interview in the *Toronto Globe and Mail,* "Times haven't really changed."

In *On the Job* the political discussion among the men is reproduced in extremely effective dialogue. Fennario has an ear for the dialects of Montreal, and in large part the accurate, powerful vernacular accounts for his early local success. The play is full of vulgar songs and of fights, props, and business, which makes it lively and engaging in production. In print, however, it presents a situation that has been explored before, and it suffers from a political vision that seems shallow.

Balconville is Fennario's most successful play, and the first production broke attendance records and received ecstatic newspaper reviews. Although some critics have reconsidered this popularity, attributing it to the relation of the play to the social milieu of Montreal in 1979 and to its bold experiment in bilingualism, its appeal also lies in a strong dramatic structure and in Fennario's excellent ear for naturalistic dialogue.

The play is set in Pointe St. Charles, the working-class district so familiar in Fennario's work. In this setting, represented onstage by two double-storied apartment buildings with balconies that face each other, family groups of Quebecois and English workers display iconic traits, establishing the linguistic and social differences between the French and English within an otherwise similar society. These people cannot afford to travel south to the sun in the freezing winter or away from the inner-city heat in the humid summer, hence "vacation" in "Balconville," the crowded verandas of their tenements. Here each observes the other, and petty jealousies and language barriers explode under pressure into family and social hatreds. This allegorization of Canadian society is amplified by the use of untranslated passages in both languages. The theatrical effect of the bilingual dialogue is significant. Just as the characters cannot understand one another, neither can portions of the audience, and the viewer is trapped by the text into participating in a dramatic distillation of the frustrations of the nation. Since the work's first production, this device has been used in other Canadian plays.

Once again, characters fulfill political stereotypes of little depth. The slum landlord and politician are monsters; the unemployed are self-destructive victims of capitalist exploitation. The ending, in which the *quartier* burns down while the inhabitants struggle to find some common support, offers a facile solution to the dilemma but does offer dim hope for social cooperation. The figures are more rounded than those of *On the Job.* In Thibault, Fennario creates a true clown, and the rhythms of the dialogue, punctuated by lonely guitar music, are well crafted and disciplined. The play also presents female characters for the first time, figures much more deeply drawn than the male characters who are Fennario's normal subjects.

When he became disillusioned with mainstream theater, Fennario began to work with an amateur community group. *Joe Beef* and *Doctor Neil Cream,* both written for this group, have been poorly received. *The Murder of Susan Parr,* which concerns the splintering of the Pointe St. Charles community, returned Fennario to an established playhouse but did not alter his subject.

In *Joe Beef (A History of Pointe St. Charles),* a tavern keeper who fed a thousand workers and their families for six weeks during an organized strike in 1887, acts as the master of ceremonies for a revisionist history of Montreal. The revue is lively, sometimes funny, and often moving, but, once again, it is single-minded in its protest. Further, it presents no solutions to the history of the oppression it documents except for a vague call to "stand together" and the possibility of revolution: "Because. . . . Like this, we are nothing. But this . . . *(closes his hand into a fist)* we are Everything." The play may be successful in depicting the 19th-century history of the district, but it does not offer much to audiences in the late 20th century.

In *The Death of René Lévesque*, Fennario examines changes to the separatist movement in Quebec in an anniversary celebration of the death of its most charismatic leader. Using Francophone actors to speak English lines, Fennario again plays with the accented tensions of language in the society. Characters representing a union leader, a terrorist turned bourgeois, a folksinger, and a politician depict the slide to the right of the Parti Québécois and question the ideology that might form a new nation. The play received a mixed response, partly because it insulted some Francophone viewers and partly because it mixed analysis of the struggle for independence with the Marxist polemic that is Fennario's repetitive focus.

The monologue *Banana Boots* describes Fennario's trip to Ireland, mixing personal anecdote with political analysis. Fennario sees links between the Irish struggle and the larger struggle of the working class emblematized by his own neighbors in Verdun. The one-man show is often, in the words of Maurice Podbrey in the documentary *Fennario: His World on Stage,* genuinely "charming," and it revealed Fennario as an accomplished performer, but it also creates a fiction of Ireland even as it perpetuates the author's fiction of a working-class Montreal.

Fennario's interest in community theater evolved from his preoccupation with place and class. Fennario sees community theater as "being put together right there by [the citizens] themselves, for themselves . . . like a weapon." He hopes to find in such theater an honesty and immediacy that he believes cannot be achieved in commercial drama, "stuck up on a stage over and above whatever an audience might want to do about its own situation." Again, the vision is political—"to create theatre that can be used to fight back with."

A viewer is drawn to Fennario's desire to mold theater into an instrument of local proletarian action, but somehow the message seems stale. *Banana Boots* is, after all, a memory. Ironically, his call for community action falters because he draws not on materialist evidence but on his own fictionalized and static subjectivity.

—Reid Gilbert

FIERSTEIN, Harvey (Forbes)

Nationality: American. **Born:** Brooklyn, New York, 6 June 1954. **Education:** Pratt Institute, Brooklyn, B.F.A. 1973. **Career:** Founding actor in Gallery Players Community Theater, Brooklyn, 1965; drag performer and actor from 1970: professional debut at Club 82 and La Mama Experimental Theatre Club, New York, 1971; roles in more than 60 plays and in several films. **Awards:** Rockefeller grant; Ford grant; Creative Artists Public Services grant; Obie award, 1982; Tony award, 1983 (for writing and acting), 1984; Oppenheimer award, 1983; Drama Desk award, 1983 (for writing and acting); Dramatists Guild Hull-Warriner award, 1983; Los Angeles Drama Critics Circle award, 1984; Ace award, 1988. **Agent:** George Lane, William Morris Agency, 1325 Avenue of the Americas, New York, New York 10019, U.S.A.

Publications

Plays

In Search of the Cobra Jewels (produced New York, 1972). New York, Author, 1972.

Freaky Pussy (produced New York, 1973).

Flatbush Tosca (produced New York, 1975). New York, Author, 1975.

Torch Song Trilogy (produced New York, 1981; London, 1985). New York, Gay Presses of New York, 1981; London, Methuen, 1984.
1. *The International Stud* (produced New York, 1978).
2. *Fugue in a Nursery* (produced New York, 1979).
3. *Widows and Children First!* (produced New York, 1979).
Spookhouse (produced New York, 1982; London, 1987). Published in *Plays International* (London), July 1987.
La Cage aux Folles, music and lyrics by Jerry Herman, adaptation of the play by Jean Poiret (produced Boston and New York, 1983; London, 1986).
Manny and Jake (produced New York, 1987).
Safe Sex (includes *Manny and Jake*, *Safe Sex*, *On Tidy Endings*; produced New York, 1987; London, 1991). New York, Atheneum, 1987.
Forget Him (produced New York, 1988).
Legs Diamond, with Charles Suppon, music and lyrics by Peter Allen (produced New York, 1988).
Untold Decades: Seven Comedies of Gay Romance. New York, St. Martin's Press, 1988.

Screenplay: *Torch Song Trilogy*, 1989.

Television Play: *Tidy Endings*, 1988.

Video: *The International Stud*, 1988.

Recording: *This Is Not Going to Be Pretty*, with Lenny Babbish, Plump Records, 1995.

*

Critical Study: "Coming Up for Air: Three AIDS Plays" by Gregory D. Gross, in *Journal of American Culture* (Bowling Green, Ohio), Summer 1992, pp. 63-67.

Theatrical Activities:
Actor: **Plays**–*Pork*, by Andy Warhol, 1971; *Xircus: The Private Life of Jesus Christ*; *The Trojan Women*; *Vinyl Visits an FM Station*; *International Stud*; *Fugue in a Nursery*; *Widows and Children First*; *Torch Song Trilogy*; *Safe Sex Trilogy*; *The Haunted Host*. **Films**–*Garbo Talks*, 1984; *Torch Song Trilogy*, 1988; *The Harvest*, 1992; *Mrs. Doubtfire*, 1993; narrator for *The Times of Harvey Milk*. **Television**–*Tidy Endings*, 1988; *In the Shadow of Love*, 1991; appearances in *Cheers* and *The Simpsons*, 1992.

* * *

The actor and drag queen Harvey Fierstein began writing plays at age 20 so as to create roles for himself. His first attempt concerned his efforts to clean Harry Koutoukas's apartment, a horrifying task he undertook so that the playwright would write a script for him. Instead, Fierstein wrote about the housecleaning experience in the musical *In Search of the Cobra Jewels*, complete with a chorus of cockroaches, in which both writers appeared as themselves. Because Fierstein wanted to play a whore, he wrote *Freaky Pussy*, whose seven cross-dressing hookers live in a subway men's room. Then, longing to sing Tosca, he wrote *Flatbush Tosca*. His next play, *Cannibals*, anticipated a plot element in *La Cage aux Folles*, as two kids run off and bring shame on their tribe because they want to be straight.

Fierstein created his Tony award-winning role Arnold Beckoff (i.e., "beckon" versus "back off") in the first of the *Torch Song Trilogy* plays, *The International Stud.* With this work the plump pixie, wit, political activist, and outspoken critic of a heterosexist society finally began attracting the attention of audiences beyond the confines of the experimental off-off-Broadway La Mama. In dialogue at once droll, direct, and distressing ("A thing of beauty is a joy till sunrise"), Arnold compulsively carries the torch for bisexual Ed, but his winning the stud degrades him nearly as much as does the initial pursuit and the eventual loss. Yet he accompanies each act of dependence, each self-destructive kvetch with which he pushes Ed away from him, with a laconic quip that lets us know that Arnold understands what he is doing. Like the torch singer who capitalizes on her pain with "music to be miserable by," Arnold often allows his vulnerability to careen crazily into masochistic self-pity.

Fierstein suited his form to his content by employing presentational styles in the first two plays. Thus, Arnold's egocentricity finds expression when he gazes into a mirror during the opening of *The International Stud*, which also isolates Arnold and Ed in a series of self-absorbed monologues. Although this is a two-character play (plus torch singer), they appear together only in the last scene, after Fierstein has created the effect of a backroom orgy by employing Arnold alone. *Fugue in a Nursery* picks up Arnold and ex-lover Ed a year after the end of their affair as Arnold and his new flame, Alan, visit Ed and the "other woman" Laurel at Ed's summer home. Only slightly matured out of pure narcissism, the four, in contrapuntal scenes played upon a giant bed, engage in frequently rearranged pairings with occasionally intersecting dialogue. They are sophisticated enough to suit the fugal accompaniment (by string quartet) and plot construction but sufficiently infantile for Arnold's bedroom to be termed "the nursery."

If *Fugue*'s duologues seem to be an experimental version of Noël Coward or William Wycherley, the representational domestic drama *Widows and Children First!* begins with more conventional sitcom plotting and balances the deflation of sentiment with effective sentimentality. Five years after *Fugue*, we find Arnold, in a period of widowhood following Alan's death, bludgeoned with baseball bats by homophobes. Ed has left Laurel; and Arnold mothers his "hopelessly homo" foster son, 15-year-old David; while visiting Mrs. Beckoff who rebukes her own homosexual son, Arnold; giving us, therefore, two mothers, two widows, two sons, and two referees for fights—yet only four characters. Although Arnold and Ed have matured to some degree, Ed still does not know what he wants, and Arnold still displays a penchant for acting in ways not in his own best interest. In a moving microcosm of human paradox, Mrs. Beckoff disapproves of David when she, in a hilarious scene, mistakes him for Arnold's lover, but she grows still more shocked when she learns that the tie is filial. Arnold demands respect from his mother without necessarily giving it in return. David waxes wise about how to help Arnold, yet he does not apply much insight to himself. Arnold objects to his mother's distress at homosexuality, yet he loves an equally fearful man.

Fierstein's rich thematic panoply—including loneliness, loss, self-esteem, homophobia, and honesty ("What's the matter? Catch your tongue in the closet door?")—numbers among its concerns frequent allegiance to the sort of family values to which right-wing zealots love to claim sole proprietorship. Arnold cannot be impersonal about sex, longing instead for romance, commitment, monogamy, and children to mother. Such conventional values imbue most of Fierstein's work ever since his groundbreaking trilogy and contribute to his popularity among heterosexual as well as gay audiences.

Spookhouse embodies contradictory attitudes toward the possibility of raising decent kids. The conscientious but destructively naive gay social worker believes in the social system and the future. As in Tennessee Williams's *The Glass Menagerie*, the obnoxious mother's grit provides the only glue holding together her neurotic, and in this case lower-class, family, but she knows that the system has failed her kids and wants her sociopathic son imprisoned. Set in a disintegrating Coney Island amusement park ride and the home above it, *Spookhouse* serves as metaphor for the horrors in lives we cannot control. ("Life's scary enough without paying for added attractions.") These haunt us even in our safe places, as in our homes, and pop out at us when we are unable to cope with them. This black comic melodrama, replete with rape, incest, murder, and arson, taps into our anxieties, particularly our pessimism about parenting and urban bureaucracy, which victimizes both its clients and its employees.

The dysfunctional but straight Janiks in *Spookhouse* contrast with the stable gay family in *La Cage aux Folles*, a musical that provides a refreshing perspective refuting homophobic stereotypes. Married in all but law, Albin and Georges exceed their devotion to each other only in their love for son Jean-Michele, who poorly repays Albin's mothering by banishing him from the family flat when the boy's fiancée and her right-wing parents visit to inspect their future in-laws. Unlike Jean Poiret in the original French farce, Fierstein poignantly focuses on Jean-Michele's insensitivity and ingratitude and celebrates the commitment between the two middle-aged men, a nightclub owner and his androgynous drag queen star. In addition to dramatizing loving domestic relationships, Fierstein again stresses the importance of being oneself ("I Am What I Am") and respecting oneself and others, particularly parents.

Although this tender comedy ran on Broadway for four and a half years, Fierstein's second foray onto the musical stage proved less successful, probably because he merely attempted to salvage the work of an inexperienced librettist. When Fierstein inherited clothing designer Charles Suppon's book for the 1940s gangster musical *Legs Diamond*, scored by the Australian Peter Allen, he revised characters and dialogue but retained the structure. The less said about this disastrous vanity production for the composer-star the better. The one-act, pre-AIDS comedy *Forget Him*, on the other hand, deserves an audience. The Fierstein stand-in, Michael, has paid a finder's fee for the perfect lover—handsome, rich, smart, athletic, and attentive. Yet he demands his money back because Eugene's blindness and deafness—or Michael's own insecurities—leave him troubled that someone even better, the title's "him," will come along.

With the *Safe Sex* trilogy Fierstein turned to the effect of AIDS on gay men's lives, representing the impact in part by means of presentational set metaphors (like *Fugue*'s bed and the spooks in *Spookhouse*). In *Manny and Jake* he dramatizes disease-carrying Manny's ex-lovers—many now corpses—with dummies. In the title play he visualizes for us how the men's relationship has been thrown off-balance by placing them on a seesaw, although a later New York revival put them in bed, which made the seductiveness and terrors more real.

Indeed, fear informs all three plays. Manny, who used to live for sex, paralyzes himself with worry over infecting more men, even while praying for the renewal of the romantic possibilities he regards as now blighted by his HIV status. He implicitly rejects the option of safer sex and simply laments his loss. His parallel in the title play, Ghee (played by Fierstein), also permits fears to inhibit him. HIV-negative, the terrified Ghee avoids sex by means of verbal attacks, retreats, and reprises that actually mask a greater problem—fear of intimacy. The teeter-totter metaphor expresses a relationship out of balance from scares about AIDS, fears of letting a lover get close and of the potential loss of both lover and life. Despite the pain at their core, *Manny and Jake* offers a lyrical elegy to sexual joy, while *Safe Sex* satirically mocks both Ghee's anxieties and his macho lover's unwashed ardor.

In his final treatment of fear, loss, and—dare we?—trust, *On Tidy Endings*, Fierstein employs a fully representational style and setting, repeating in this trilogy the same progression from presentational to realistic he first used in *Torch Song*. The Fierstein character, Arthur, mourns his lover's death from AIDS while confronting Colin's ex-wife with legal papers for their shares of the inheritance. Part of the legacy turns out to be the disease, which ironically has spared Arthur but stricken the woman. She has worked hard to win Arthur's trust not only for her sake but also for that of her son, who needs to overcome his own grief, rage, and homophobia so as to continue to benefit from Arthur's maternal care. Like *Torch Song Trilogy*, *On Tidy Endings* prompts laughter and tears at a son and at alternately bickering and affectionate widows.

—Tish Dace

FLANNERY, Peter

Nationality: British. **Born:** Jarrow, Tyne and Wear, 12 October 1951. **Education:** University of Manchester, B.A. (honours) in drama 1973. **Career:** Director, actor, and stage manager, Manchester, 1974-76; playwright-in-residence, Royal Shakespeare Company, London, 1979-80. Member, North West Arts Association drama panel, 1980-85. **Awards:** London *Sunday Times* Student Play award, 1978; Thames Television award, 1979; Arts Council bursary, 1980, 1984; John Whiting award, 1982; Beckett award, 1989. **Agent:** Stephen Durbridge, Lemon, Unna and Durbridge, 24 Pottery Lane, Holland Park, London W11 4LZ, England.

Publications

Plays

Heartbreak Hotel (produced Manchester, 1975). Todmorden, Woodhouse, 1979.

Last Resort (produced London, 1976).

Are You with Me? (produced Nottingham, 1977).

Savage Amusement (produced London, 1978; New York, 1981). London, Rex Collings, 1978.

The Boy's Own Story (produced Manchester, 1978; London, 1980; New York, 1983).

The Adventures of Awful Knawful, with Mick Ford (for children; produced London, 1978). London, Eyre Methuen, 1979.

Jungle Music (produced Manchester, 1979).

Our Friends in the North (produced Stratford-on-Avon and London, 1982). London, Methuen, 1982.

Heavy Days (produced Stratford-on-Avon, 1982).
Silence on My Radio (produced Newcastle-upon-Tyne, 1983).
Blind Justice: Five Screenplays (includes *Crime and Punishment*; *White Man, Listen*; *The One About the Irishmen*; *A Death in the Family*; *Permanent Blue*) (televised, 1988). London, Hern, 1990.
Singer (produced Stratford-on-Avon, 1989; London, 1990). London, Hern, 1989.

Screenplay: *Funny Bones*, with Peter Chelsom, 1995.

Radio Plays: *Small Talk*, with Elizabeth Gamlin, 1986; *Singer*, 1992.

Television Plays: *Our Friends in the North: Seven Screenplays* (includes *One Man, One Vote*; *Public Relations*; *Honour*; *Conspiracies*; *Pictures*; *Power*; *Mysteries*), 1984; *Warhill*, 1985; *Blind Justice: Five Screenplays*, 1988; *Shoot the Revolution*, 1990.

* * *

Peter Flannery, son of two generations of Jarrow shipyard workers, studied drama at Manchester University, planning to be a director. He was soon writing, however: *Heartbreak Hotel*, a rock musical; the 75-minute *Last Resort*, in which a peculiar group of people meet beside a Punch-and-Judy show on Blackpool beach; the one-character *The Boy's Own Story*, in which a goalkeeper explains himself between saves; and *Jungle Music*, Brecht's *In the Jungle of the Cities* as a musical, updated and moved to Manchester.

Flannery first drew attention with *Savage Amusement*, staged by the Royal Shakespeare Company at the Warehouse in 1978. Set in 1982 after a Tory election victory (then in the future), four young dropouts squatting in Hulme in south Manchester realize their dependence on a strange, detached working-class youth and, more important, reveal a crumbling, frightening environment. Flannery explained his subject in *The Warehouse Papers*: "I was concerned about what young people in Hulme might grow up thinking and hoping. . . . Whose fault is Hulme? Can or should people from outside get involved with the place? What happens if Hulme continues to deteriorate? . . . If I am living in a society founded on civilised values, then what went wrong? . . . Though I am aware that poverty *is* a political issue, the play attempts no political solutions." Michael Billington noted that, though Flannery sympathized with his characters, he also showed "their powerlessness in the face of disintegration." More than this, Flannery created a unique and disturbing world of fear and threat, of wilderness and concentration camp, of a collapsing social fabric.

Small Talk, a sensitive 1986 study of childlessness for radio, was followed in 1988 by the five-part *Blind Justice*, among the very few television scripts to be published. Two "alternative" lawyers, a man and a woman, deal with various cases that raise awkward questions about the legal system. Flannery visited Romania in 1990 before writing, again for television, *Shoot the Revolution*, about the fall of Ceau escu in December 1989. Using news film and a narrator, he illustrates the situation in Romania through a secret policeman, his ineffectual liberal teacher brother, a peasant girl, and an actress representing intellectuals.

In his introduction to the text of *Blind Justice* Flannery says that he belongs "among that small band of writers which still wants to write about the big picture." This is what he has done in his two epic condition-of-England plays, *Our Friends in the North* and *Singer*.

Our Friends, episodic and ambitious, spans the period from 1964 to 1979 and has scenes in Newcastle, Soho, Scotland Yard, Parliament, and Rhodesia. Flannery expects his audience to know its British history for the period and to pick up on his allusions to the scandals surrounding Poulson and Dan Smith in the northeast in the 1960s. The three main plot threads are the ties between an unprincipled architect and the complacent local Labour Party, corrupt police failing to act against vice in London, and the pretense that genuine sanctions were imposed on Rhodesia after its unilateral declaration of independence in 1965. The threads are linked by the parallel biographies of two Newcastle boys, one disillusioned after experiences of Labour politics, the other somehow educated to understand power through crime and a spell as a mercenary in Rhodesia. The play ends with the latter and a prostitute apparently about to machine-gun a man as he leaves a restaurant and perhaps also to shoot an M.P., an oil executive, a civil servant, and three top policemen, all heard but not seen in the closing minutes. *Our Friends* is about the decline and disappearance of principles and how even innocents become involved in corruption. Parliamentary democracy appears ineffective. *Our Friends* was rewritten as an 11-part TV serial for the BBC, but it appears to have been blocked because of the possible legal implications of the fact that its characters were based on real people.

Flannery was prompted to write *Singer* by reading Shirley Green's biography of Peter Rachman, who became notorious nationally at the end of the 1950s as an unscrupulous and wealthy slum landlord. From the biography Flannery learned that Rachman was a survivor of concentration camps. This led him into a year's research, a strong response to the books of Primo Levi, and so to a play about "a man's rapaciousness and the reasons behind it." The scale was Jacobean, five acts with a prologue and epilogue, and *Singer* was well suited to be the first modern play staged in the Royal Shakespeare Company's Swan Theatre at Stratford-upon-Avon.

Chorus speeches briefly give us the dates, from wartime ("a time, and what a time, when war was not a crime but a crusade"), through Harold Wilson's 1960s ("Now the white heat of technological revolution dazzles the eyes and all the youth of England are on fire") to the Thatcherite 1980s, the years of "the Great Housekeeper, with fox-like cunning, lion's strength, and matching crocodile accessories."

Singer, a Polish Jew, is first seen as a prisoner in Auschwitz, already a wheeler-dealer with his nephew Stefan and the German communist Manik, both of whom accompany him to Britain after the war. Soon he is dealing in nylons and frying pans from a public telephone box in Bayswater, charming young women (he resembles Krank in John Arden's *Waters of Babylon*), then rising to riches in property deals, and finally evicting elderly sitting tenants. He obtains British citizenship, entertains the upper classes at a party, and at the end of act 3 drowns in a Hampstead pond. Reappearing, he woos a girl whose crippled father proves to have been a guard at Auschwitz. He delivers soup to the homeless on the South Bank but then is led into a scheme to provide "camps" for the homeless. Meanwhile, he has found Stefan, now a photographer who also paints scenes from the camps so that the Holocaust will be remembered and who finally kills himself.

The drama is memorable for the huge title role originally played by Antony Sher. *Singer* explores the immigrant experience, the legacy of Nazism, and the need to remember Auschwitz, the

Rachman era, and the failure of the 1980s to learn from Rachman's exploitation. For Neil Taylor *Singer* was "a parable to explain the nature of modern Britain and, at the same time, the moral significance of such universals as memory and guilt."

Flannery's major stage plays require enormous casts, while all of his work is controversial and antiestablishment. One hopes that both the Royal Shakespeare Company and television companies will continue to find a place for his necessary and challenging work.

—Malcolm Page

FOOTE, (Albert) Horton (Jr.)

Nationality: American. **Born:** Wharton, Texas, 14 March 1916. **Education:** Pasadena Playhouse Theatre, California, 1933-35; Tamara Daykarhanova Theatre School, New York, 1937-39. **Family:** Married Lillian Vallish in 1945; two daughters and two sons. **Career:** Actor with American Actors Theatre, New York, 1939-42; theater workshop director and producer, King-Smith School of Creative Arts, 1944-45, and manager, Productions Inc., 1945-48, both Washington, D.C. Lives in New York City and Wharton, Texas. **Awards:** Oscar, for screenplay, 1963, 1983; honored for contribution to American Theatre, Ensemble Studio Theatre Gala, 1985; Capostelo award, Brooklyn, New York, 1987; elected to the Fellowship of Southern Writers, 1988; Dickinson College Arts award, 1989; William Inge award, for lifetime achievement in theater, 1989; Evelyn Burkey award, Writers Guild East, 1989; Alley Theatre award, Houston, Texas, 1991; Headliners' Club award, Houston, 1991; Touch of Hope award, Barbara Barondess Theatre Lab Alliance, New York, 1992; Laurel award, The Writer's Guild West, Beverly Hills, 1993; Lontinkle Award from the Texas Institute of Letters, Dallas, 1994; Lucille Lortel Award, New York, 1995; Pulitzer prize for drama, 1995; Special Achievement award, Outer Critics Circle, New York, 1995; Lifetime Achievement award, Heartland Film Festival, Indianapolis, Indiana, 1995; induction to the Theater Hall of Fame, New York, 1996; Best Teleplay award, for *Lily Dale,* Lone Star Film and Television, Dallas, 1997; Humanitas Winner and Christopher award, both for *Old Man,* 1997. D.Litt.: Austin College, Sherman, Texas, 1987; Drew University, Madison, New Jersey, 1987; American Film Institute, Los Angeles, California; Spalding University. **Member:** American Academy of Arts and Letters, 1995. **Agent:** Lucy Kroll Agency, 390 West End Avenue, New York, New York 10024, U.S.A.

Publications

Plays

Wharton Dance (produced New York, 1940).
Texas Town (produced New York, 1941).
Out of My House (also co-director: produced New York, 1942).
Only the Heart (produced New York, 1942). New York, Dramatists Play Service, 1944.
Two Southern Idylls: Miss Lou, and The Girls (produced New York, 1943).
The Lonely (produced New York, 1943).
Goodbye to Richmond (produced New York, 1943).
Daisy Lee, music by Bernardo Segall (produced New York, 1944).
Homecoming, In My Beginning, People in the Show, The Return (produced Washington, D.C., 1944).
Themes and Variations (produced Washington, D.C., 1945?).
Celebration (produced New York, 1948).
The Chase (produced New York, 1952). New York, Dramatists Play Service, 1952.
The Trip to Bountiful (televised 1953; produced New York, 1953; London, 1956; Austin, Texas, 1990; Louisville, Kentucky, 1991; Perth, Australia, 1992; Upper Montclair, New Jersey, 1993; Purchase, New York, 1993). New York, Dramatists Play Service, 1954; in *Texas Plays,* edited by William B. Martin, Southern Methodist University, 1990.
The Oil Well (televised 1953; produced New York, 1991).
The Midnight Caller (televised 1953; produced New York, 1958). New York, Dramatists Play Service, 1959.
John Turner Davis (televised 1953; produced New York, 1958). Included in *A Young Lady of Property*, 1955.
The Dancers (televised 1954; produced Los Angeles, 1963). Included in *A Young Lady of Property*, 1955.
The Travelling Lady (produced New York, 1954). New York, Dramatists Play Service, 1955.
A Young Lady of Property: Six Short Plays (includes *A Young Lady of Property, The Dancers, The Old Beginning, John Turner Davis, The Death of the Old Man, The Oil Well*). New York, Dramatists Play Service, 1955.
Harrison, Texas: Eight Television Plays (includes *The Dancers, The Death of the Old Man, Expectant Relations, John Turner Davis, The Midnight Caller, The Tears of My Sister, The Trip to Bountiful, A Young Lady of Property*). New York, Harcourt Brace, 1956.
Flight (televised 1957). Published in *Television Plays for Writers*, edited by A. S. Burack. Boston, The Writer, 1957.
Old Man, adaptation of a story by Faulkner (televised 1958). Included in *Three Plays*, 1962.
Roots in a Parched Ground (as *The Night of the Storm*, televised 1960). Included in *Three Plays*, 1962.
Tomorrow, adaptation of the story by Faulkner (televised 1960). Included in *Three Plays*, 1962.
Three Plays. New York, Harcourt Brace, 1962.
The Screenplay of To Kill a Mockingbird. New York, Harcourt Brace, 1964.
Gone with the Wind, music and lyrics by Harold Rome, adaptation of the novel by Margaret Mitchell (produced London, 1972; Los Angeles, 1973).
The Roads to Home (includes *The Dearest of Friends, A Nightingale, Spring Dance*) (also director: produced New York, 1982 and 1992). New York, Dramatists Play Service, 1982.
Courtship (produced Louisville, 1984). Included in *Courtship, On Valentine's Day, 1918*, 1987.
1918 (televised 1984). Included in *Courtship, On Valentine's Day, 1918*, 1987.
On Valentine's Day (televised 1985). Included in *Courtship, On Valentine's Day, 1918*, 1987.
Tomorrow (television play) and *Tomorrow* (screenplay), in *Tomorrow and Tomorrow and Tomorrow* (also includes Faulkner's story "Tomorrow"), edited by David G. Yellin and Marie Conners. Jackson, University Press of Mississippi, 1985.
The Road to the Graveyard (produced New York, 1985). New York, Dramatists Play Service, 1988.

Blind Date (produced New York, 1986). New York, Dramatists Play Service, 1986; in *The Best Short Plays*, edited by Ramon Delgado, Applause Theatre Book Publishers, 1988.
Lily Dale (produced New York, 1986). Included in *Roots in a Parched Ground, Convicts, Lily Dale, The Widow Claire*, 1988.
The Widow Claire (produced New York, 1986). Included in *Roots in a Parched Ground, Convicts, Lily Dale, The Widow Claire*, 1988; in *The Best Plays of 1986-1987*, edited by Otis L. Guernsey, Jr., Dodd, Mead & Co., 1987.
Courtship, On Valentine's Day, 1918. New York, Grove Press, 1987.
Roots in a Parched Ground, Convicts, Lily Dale, The Widow Claire. New York, Grove Press, 1988.
The Man Who Climbed the Pecan Trees (produced New York, 1988). New York, Dramatists Play Service, 1989; in *The Best American Short Plays*, Applause Theatre, 1990.
Selected One-Act Plays, edited by Gerald C. Wood. Dallas, Texas, Southern Methodist University Press, 1988.
Habitation of Dragons (also director: produced Pittsburgh, 1988).
Cousins, and The Death of Papa. New York, Grove Press, 1989.
To Kill a Mockingbird, Tender Mercies, The Trip to Bountiful: Three Screenplays. New York, Grove Press, 1989.
Dividing the Estate (produced Princeton, New Jersey, 1989; Winston Salem, North Carolina, 1991).
Talking Pictures (produced Florida, 1990; Houston, Texas, 1991; New York, 1994).
Nineteen-Eighteen (produced San Francisco, 1992).
Night Seasons (produced Teaneck, New Jersey, 1993; New York, 1994).
Four New Plays (includes *Habitation of Dragons*; *Night Seasons*; *Dividing the Estate*; *Talking Pictures*). Lyme, New Hampshire, Smith and Kraus, 1993.
The Young Man from Atlanta (produced New York, 1995).
Laura Dennis (produced New York, 1995).
Collected Plays (includes *The Trip to Bountiful*; *The Chase*; *The Traveling Lady*; *The Roads to Home*). Lyme, New Hampshire, Smith and Kraus, 1996.
The Death of Papa (produced Chapel Hill, 1997).

Radio Play: *Vernon Early*, 1997.

Screenplays: *Storm Fear*, 1955; *To Kill a Mockingbird*, 1962; *Baby, The Rain Must Fall*, 1964; *Hurry Sundown*, with Thomas Ryan, 1966; *Tomorrow*, 1972; *Tender Mercies*, 1983; *1918*, 1984; *The Trip to Bountiful*, 1985; *On Valentine's Day*, 1985; *Courtship*, 1986; *Convicts*, 1989; *Of Mice and Men*, 1991.

Television Plays: *Ludie Brooks*, 1951; *The Travelers*, 1952; *The Old Beginning*, 1952; *The Trip to Bountiful*, 1953; *A Young Lady of Property*, 1953; *The Oil Well*, 1953; *Rocking Chair*, 1953; *Expectant Relations*, 1953; *The Death of the Old Man*, 1953; *The Tears of My Sister*, 1953; *John Turner Davis*, 1953; *The Midnight Caller*, 1953; *The Dancers*, 1954; *The Shadow of Willie Greer*, 1954; *The Roads to Home*, 1955; *Drugstore: Sunday Noon*, 1956; *Flight*, 1957 (UK title: *Summer's Pride*, 1961); *Member of the Family*, 1957; *Old Man*, 1958; *Tomorrow*, 1960; *The Shape of the River*, 1960; *The Night of the Storm*, 1960; *The Gambling Heart*, 1964; *The Displaced Person*, from a story by Flannery O'Connor, 1977; *Barn Burning*, from the story by Faulkner, 1980; scripts for *Gabby Hayes Show*, 1950-51; *Habitation of Dragons*, 1991; *Lily Dale*, 1996; *Old Man*, adaptation of William Faulkner, 1997; *Alone*.

Novel

The Chase. New York, Rinehart, 1956.

*

Critical Studies: "On Valentine's Day" by Samuel G. Freedman, in the New York *Times* Magazine, 9 February 1986; "Roots in a Parched Ground: An Interview with Horton Foote" by Ronald L. Davis, in *Southwest Review* (Dallas, Texas), Summer 1988; in *The Writer's Mind: Interviews with American Authors*, edited by Irv Broughton, Fayetteville, University of Arkansas Press, 1990; "Horton Foote's Southern Family in Roots in a Parched Ground" by Carter Martin, in *The Texas Review* (Huntsville, Texas), Spring-Summer 1991, pp. 76-90; "Beyond the Commercial Media: Horton Foote's Procession of Defeated Men" by Charles S. Watson, in *Studies in American Drama, 1945-Present* (Columbus, Ohio), 1993, pp. 175-87; "You Can Go Home Again: The Focus on Family in the Works of Horton Foote" by Rebecca Luttrell Briley, New York, Peter Lang, 1993.

Theatrical Activities:
Director: **Plays**—*Out of My House* (co-director, with Mary Hunter and Jane Rose), New York, 1942; *Goodbye to Richmond*, New York, 1946.

Actor: **Plays**—Role in *The Eternal Road* by Franz Werfel, New York, 1937; with One-Act Repertory Company: Robert Emmet in *The Coggerers*, Lorenzo in *The Red Velvet Goat*, and Chief Outourou's Brother in *Mr. Banks of Birmingham*, New York, 1939; *Railroads on Parade*, New York, 1939; *Yankee Doodle Comes to Town*, toured, 1940; *The Fifth Column* by Ernest Hemingway, New York, 1940; Pharmacist in *Texas Town*, New York, 1941.

* * *

In *1918* Horace Robedaux, the principal character of Horton Foote's Orphans' Home cycle, asks Foote's rich and perennial question: "How can human beings stand all that comes to them?" A little later his mother-in-law indirectly answers him: "You just stand it. You keep going." Between the question and the answer lies Foote's deeply realized Texan world, where the fundamentals and the universals of many kinds of relationships are played out. We see and hear in the accents of everyday talk how sons and daughters, mothers and fathers, lovers, drunks, and crazies "stand" it and "keep going." We are not preached at, nor are the scenes or characters calculated to point morals. Instead, the plays—each of which can stand on its own dramatically—present the stuff of life simply and inexorably. And since the cycle is set in the earlier parts of the twentieth century, our sense acts unconsciously to join that past to our own. Thus, the past becomes actual, both in its differences and in its similarities. There are few large-scale events. World War I, for instance, seems very far from, yet very much a part of, *1918*. The central characters engage in getting and losing jobs, missing trains, and flunking out of school, as well as fathering and losing children and marrying the ones they love. Although life can be very bleak, Foote somehow justifies the bleakness; despite ourselves, we do not feel desperate or depressed. Through the cycle Texas becomes our world, and Horton Foote's people become our people.

The rhetoric of Foote's work suggests that the language we regularly use be taken as fully adequate to our condition and that our condition consists precisely of the people we know, the work we do, and the era in which we live. Things like a new dress (*Roots in a Parched Ground*) are significantly related to flu epidemics (*1918*), and Foote's methodical vision delineates the relationship and discovers the particulars of its reality. Nothing and no one is unrelated, even by choice. The Texas of 1912 and the New York City of 1992 work in the same categories of truth and falsehood, love and death, happiness and unhappiness, and rejection and acceptance. The cycle lives through the coming-of-age of Horace Robedaux. In the days just before his father's early death we become part of his family, and we know him at the beginning of self-definition and experience with him the sorrows and the joys. He never assumes the role of representative, however, for Foote has made his character a living one that now and again makes surprising decisions. The familiarity we have established does not breed contempt but rather respect. Horace endures partly on our behalf, and our response to that endurance is to understand ourselves better, a classical purpose of theater.

Much of Foote's drama treats the common man and woman realistically in disturbing but strangely comforting stories. The pathos that ordinary people undergo, the nobility of the neglected and the forgotten, the profound humor in unsuspected houses and families, the suffering around every corner, the substantiality of what is taken for granted, the high stakes wagered in backstairs games—these constitute his subject. Foote's realism pertains to times and places he has both lived in and imagined, and his ear for speech is true and his characters recognizable and individualized. The Orphans' Home cycle offers us aspects of life itself, and it deserves to be staged as a cycle so that its full subtlety and strength can be realized.

Foote is a writer schooled in the television screenplay. He is a regional writer, a folk writer, and a miniaturist. But, thanks to all that, he is a writer of considerable power. His one-act *The Man Who Climbed the Pecan Trees* treats only part of the subject of the cycle, namely, the spiritual barrenness of an arid Texas landscape. Much like Horace, Stanley has grown up in a family devoid of judgment and passion. Stanley's family still functions, however, for his mother keeps it alive despite its breakup. (By contrast, Horace's mother moves to Houston and leaves him to fend for himself.) The husband and father is dead before the play begins, but the mother (Mrs. Campbell) keeps him alive too in a series of inane sentimentalities that function to deaden him further and to stultify memory itself. This is so much so in Stanley's case that he cannot finally say where in the world he is or where he has been, a fate that might well have been Horace's.

As it turns out, the same source of energy by which Mr. Campbell has gone on living since his death will now sustain his son, Mr. Stanley Campbell. Mrs. Campbell's platitudes deny even the truth of sentiment in Stanley's obsessive lyric "In the gloamin', Oh, my darlin'." The mother's manner of speaking will pen him (is penning him) in a dead end. At the play's end he sits beside his mother, firmly on the ground but no longer of this earth. Ironically, until he "falls" back into infantile dependency, Stanley, among the evaders and euphemists, has been the truth-teller, one who sees things for what they are even if the facts are partial. Foote's "facts" may be partial, too, but the impartiality of the theater allows him to give an almost complete version of American society.

—Thomas Apple

FOREMAN, Richard

Nationality: American. **Born:** New York City, 10 June 1937. **Education:** Scarsdale High School, Scarsdale, New York; Brown University, Providence, Rhode Island, 1955-59, B.A. 1959; Yale University School of Drama, New Haven, Connecticut, 1959-62, M.F.A. 1962. **Family:** Married 1) Amy Taubin in 1962 (divorced 1971); 2) Kate Manheim in 1992. **Career:** Writer with New Dramatists and Actors Studio, both New York, 1962-65; associate director, Film-Maker's Cinematheque, New York, 1967-68. Founding director, Ontological-Hysteric Theatre, New York, 1968—. **Awards:** Obie award, 1970, 1973, 1983, 1987, sustained achievement award for playwrighting, 1976, 1986, 1988; National Opera Institute grant, 1971; Guggenheim fellowship for playwrighting, 1972; National Endowment for the Arts grant, 1972, 1974, and distinguished artists fellowship, 1989; Creative Artists Public Service award, 1972, 1974; Rockefeller grant, 1974; Ford Foundation grant, 1980; American Academy and Institute of Arts and Letters award, 1992; MacArthur fellowship, 1995-2000; Edwin Booth award, 1996. **Agent:** Gregor F. Hall, Bookport International, 429 Third Street, Suite 2B, Brooklyn, New York 11215. **Address:** 152 Wooster Street, New York, New York 10012, U.S.A.

Publications

Plays

Angelface (also director: produced New York, 1968).
Elephant-Steps, music by Stanley Silverman (also director: produced Lenox, Massachusetts, 1968; New York, 1970).
Ida-Eyed (also director: produced New York, 1969).
Real Magic in New York, music by Stephen Dickman (produced New York, 1969).
Total Recall: Sophia [equals] (Wisdom) Part 2 (also director: produced New York, 1970).
Dream Tantras for Western Massachusetts, music by Stanley Silverman (also director: produced Lenox, Massachusetts, 1971).
HcOhTiEnLa; or, Hotel China (also director: produced New York, 1971). Excerpts published in *Performance 2* (New York), April 1972.
Evidence (also director: produced New York, 1972; selection, as *15 Minutes of Evidence*, produced New York, 1975).
Dr. Selavy's Magic Theatre, music by Stanley Silverman, lyrics by Tom Hendry (also director: produced Lenox, Massachusetts, and New York, 1972; Oxford, 1978).
Sophia [equals] (Wisdom) Part 3: The Cliffs (also director: produced New York, 1972). Published in *Performance 6* (New York), May-June 1973.
Particle Theory (also director: produced New York, 1973).
Honor (also director: produced New York, 1973).
Classical Therapy; or, A Week under the Influence . . . (also director: produced Paris, 1973).
Pain(t) (also director: produced New York, 1974).
Vertical Mobility: Sophia [equals] (Wisdom) Part 4 (also director: produced New York, 1974). Published in *Drama Review 63* (New York), June 1974.
RA-D-IO (Wisdom); or, Sophia [equals] (Wisdom) Part 1, music by David Tice (produced New York, 1974).

Pandering to the Masses: A Misrepresentation (also director: produced New York, 1975). Published in *The Theatre of Images*, edited by Bonnie Marranca, New York, Drama Book Specialists, 1977.
Hotel for Criminals, music by Stanley Silverman (also director: produced New York, 1975).
Rhoda in Potatoland (*Her Fall-starts*) (also director: produced New York, 1975).
Thinking (One Kind) (produced San Diego, 1975).
Le Théâtre de Richard Foreman, edited by Simone Benmussa and Erika Kralik. Paris, Gallimard, 1975.
Plays and Manifestos, edited by Kate Davy. New York, New York University Press, 1976.
Livre de Splendeurs (Part I) (produced Paris, 1976).
Lines of Vision, music by George Quincy, lyrics by María Irene Fornés (produced New York, 1976).
Slight (produced New York, 1977).
Book of Splendors (Part II): Book of Levers: Action at a Distance (also director: produced New York, 1977). Published in *Theater* (New Haven, Connecticut), Spring 1978.
Blvd. de Paris (I've Got the Shakes) (produced New York, 1978).
The American Imagination, music by Stanley Silverman (produced New York, 1978).
Luogo [plus] *Bersaglio* (Place [plus] Target) (produced Rome, 1979).
Madame Adare, music by Stanley Silverman (produced New York, 1980).
Penguin Touquet (also director: produced New York, 1981).
Café Amérique (produced Paris, 1982).
Egyptology: My Head Was a Sledgehammer (produced New York, 1983).
George Bataille's Bathrobe (produced Paris, 1984).
Miss Universal Happiness (also director: produced New York, 1985).
Reverberation Machines: The Later Plays and Essays. Barrytown, New York, Station Hill Press, 1985.
Africanis Instructus, music by Stanley Silverman (also director: produced New York, 1986).
The Cure, music by Foreman (produced New York, 1986). Included in *Unbalancing Acts*, 1992.
Film Is Evil, Radio Is Good (also director: produced New York, 1987). Included in *Unbalancing Acts*, 1992.
Love and Science (also director: produced Stockholm, 1987; Stockbridge, Massachusetts, 1990). New York, Theatre Communications Group, and London, Hern, 1991.
Symphony of Rats (also director: produced New York, 1988). Included in *Unbalancing Acts*, 1992.
What Did He See? (also director: produced New York, 1988). Included in *Unbalancing Acts*, 1992.
Lava (also director: produced New York, 1989). Included in *Unbalancing Acts*, 1992.
Eddie Goes to Poetry City: Part 1 (also director: produced Seattle, Washington, 1990).
Eddie Goes to Poetry City: Part 2 (also director: produced New York, 1991).
The Mind King (also director: produced New York, 1992).
Unbalancing Acts: Foundations for a Theater. New York, Pantheon, 1992.
Samuel's Major Problems (also director: produced New York, 1993).
My Head Was a Sledgehammer (also director: produced New York, 1994).
I've Got the Shakes (also director: produced New York, 1995).
My Head Was a Sledgehammer and Other Plays. New York, Overlook Press, 1995.
The Universe (also director: produced New York, 1996).
Permanent Brain Damage (also director: produced New York and London, 1996).
Pearls for Pigs (also director: produced Hartford, Connecticut, New York, Paris, and Rome, 1997).
Benita Canova (also director: produced New York, 1997).

Screenplays: *Out of the Body Travel*, 1975; *City Archives*, 1977; *Strong Medicine*, 1978.

Other

No-Body: A Novel in Parts. New York, Overlook Press, 1996.

*

Manuscript Collections: Lincoln Center Library of the Performing Arts, New York; Anthology Film Archives, New York.

Critical Studies: "Richard Foreman's Ontological-Hysteric Theatre" by Michael Kirby, in *Drama Review* (New York), June 1973; *Richard Foreman and the Ontological-Hysteric Theatre* by Kate Davy, Ann Arbor, Michigan, UMI Research Press, 1981; *The Director's Voice*, New York, Theater Communications Group, 1988; *In Their Own Words*, New York, Theater Communications Group, 1988; *Directions in Rehearsal* by Susan Cole, New York, Routledge, 1992; *Theater at the Margins* by Erik MacDonald, Ann Arbor, University of Michigan Press, 1993; *The Other American Drama* by Marc Robinson, Cambridge University Press, 1994; *Postmodernism and Performance* by Nick Kage, Macmillan, 1995.

Theatrical Activities:
Director: **Plays**—Most of his own plays (also designer); *The Threepenny Opera* by Brecht, New York, 1976; *Stages* by Stuart Ostrow, New York, 1978; *Don Juan* by Molière, Minneapolis, 1981; *Three Acts of Recognition* by Botho Strauss, New York, 1982; *Die Fledermaus* by Johann Strauss, Paris, 1984; *Dr. Faustus Lights the Lights* by Gertrude Stein, Paris, 1984; *Golem* by H. Levick, New York, 1984; *My Life My Death* by Kathy Acker, Paris, 1985; *The Birth of the Poet* by Kathy Acker, New York, 1985; *Largo Desolato* by Va lav Havel, New York, 1986; *End of the World* by Arthur Kopit, Cambridge, Massachusetts, 1987; *The Fall of the House of Usher* by Arthur Yorinks and Philip Glass, Louisville, Kentucky, 1988, New York, 1989, and revised version, Florence, 1992; *Where's Dick?* by Michael Korie and Stewart Wallace, Houston, Texas, 1989; *Woyzeck* by Georg Büchner, Hartford, Connecticut, 1990; *Don Giovanni* by Mozart, Lille, France, 1991; *Venus* by Suzan-Lori Parks, New York Shakespeare Festival, 1996.

Richard Foreman comments:

In 1968 I began to write for the theatre which I wanted to see, which was radically different from any style of theatre that I had seen. In brief, I imagined a theatre which broke down all elements into a kind of atomic structure—and showed those elements of story, action, sound, light, composition, gesture, in terms of the smallest building-block units, the basic cells of the perceived experience of both living and art-making.

The scripts themselves read like notations of my own process of imagining a theatre piece. They are the evidence of a kind of effort in which the mind's leaps and inventions may be rendered as part of a process not unique to the artist in question (myself) but typical of the building-up which goes on through all modes of coming-into-being (human and non-human). I want to refocus the attention of the spectator on the intervals, gaps, relations, and rhythms which saturate the objects (acts and physical props) which are the "givens" of any particular play. In doing this, I believe the spectator is made available (as I am, hopefully, when writing) to those most desirable energies which secretly connect him (through a kind of resonance) with the foundations of his being.

* * *

Richard Foreman has said, "I have developed a style that shows how it is with us, in consciousness. I don't speak in generalities. I show the mind at work, moment-by-moment." This is perhaps the best starting point from which to approach his theater. In the attempt to dramatize the process of thinking itself, his plays eschew plot, characters, development, and even emotions. Each moment in the theater corresponds to a moment in consciousness, and the relationships between them, or between the moments in the theater, may not be immediately obvious. In *Rhoda in Potatoland* actors discuss writing but digress to a dinner of potatoes. As in any train of thought—"Do you think using the associative method," says Foreman's Voice in *Pandering to the Masses*. "Everybody does you know."—potatoes become part of the freight, and the play begins to compare everything to a potato. After a digression for an all-girl band and a shoe store, a sign announces "THE RETURN OF THE POTATOES," and with the entrance of four human-sized potatoes, the Voice says,

> Now this is where the interesting part of the
> evening begins. Everything up to now was
> Recognizable.
>
> Now, however
> The real potatoes are amongst us
> And a different kind of understanding is possible
> for anybody who wants a different kind of
> understanding.

Thereafter "potato" becomes a kind of counter, a word that can replace another word or form comparisons and links with other objects. Even when the word is replaced by other words, Foreman follows the linguistic philosophy of Ludwig Wittgenstein as he interprets it: "Use anything, to mean anything, but the system must have a rigor."

To perform consciousness rigorously, Foreman has developed techniques that allow tight control over the presentation. He directs his plays using a core of performers who have little or no training in classical theater. Foreman's actors speak their lines flatly, without inflection. In some of the performances the actors murmur only key words of their prerecorded dialogue. Their words are frequently repeated, the sentences broken into fragments, and the phrases echoed by another actor. Foreman further ends the identity of actor and character through movement. The actors' gestures are repeated in a hieratic style until they lose their original significance and acquire a new one from the course of the play.

The visual side of Foreman's theater is crucial. Backdrops are used to present a fleeting image, to introduce a stray thought. Small stages reproduce the larger scene, and the actors themselves freeze into tableaux. Strings, ropes, and pieces of wood or paper stretch across the stage, link props or actors, or divide the stage into smaller frames. Buzzers, lights, and noises create other aural and visual frames to isolate words and actions.

No description of this odd theater can suggest the power that Foreman's slow, measured plays build. As the performances progress, the incomprehensible actions and incidents take their place in the overall design not with a logical inevitability but with a psychological appropriateness. As in Gertrude Stein's landscape plays, dialogue and incident are meant to be seen together and simultaneously, not as a sequential development. A part of the power of the plays arises from the effort of the spectator in deciphering each individual moment, like the facet in a cubist painting, and then assembling them into a whole. Foreman has described his plays as being what happens in his mind as he is writing.

Since Foreman has increasingly been directing other playwright's works, it is possible that this expansion of his artistic universe has infected his playwriting. *Egyptology* hints at a real setting and includes Louis XIV, who may have come from Foreman's having directed Molière's *Don Juan*. *Miss Universal Happiness* is topical in including Central American guerrillas even as it asserts that "the self you seek is inside you." *The Cure* not only provides a moment of emotional contact but also makes a hesitant attempt at synthesis and statement. "The pain is the cure," says one of the characters. All of this is undoubtedly happening in Foreman's mind, and while we may debate whether such a detailed presentation of one man's mind is appropriate to the theater, that is precisely the kind of debate Foreman would enjoy: "The play's over. You're left with your own thoughts. Can you really get interested in them or are they just occurring."

—Walter Bode

FORNÉS, María Irene

Nationality: American. **Born:** Havana, Cuba, 14 May 1930; immigrated to the United States, 1945; became citizen, 1951. **Education:** Educated in Havana public schools. **Career:** Lived in Europe, 1954-57; painter and textile designer; costume designer, Judson Poets Theatre and New Dramatists Committee productions, 1965-70; teacher at the Teachers and Writers Collaborative, New York, privately, and at numerous drama festivals and workshops, 1965—. President, New York Theatre Strategy, 1973-80. **Awards:** Whitney fellowship, 1961; Centro Mexicano de Escritores fellowship, 1962; Office for Advanced Drama Research grant, 1965; Obie award, 1965, 1977, 1979, 1982, 1984, 1985, 1988; Cintas Foundation fellowship, 1967; Yale University fellowship, 1967, 1968; Rockefeller fellowship, 1971, 1985; Guggenheim fellowship, 1972; Creative Artists Public Service grant, 1972, 1975; National Endowment for the Arts grant, 1974; American Academy award, 1985; Home Box Office award, 1986. **Agent:** Helen Merrill Ltd., 435 West 23rd Street, 1A, New York, New York 10011. **Address:** 1 Sheridan Square, New York, New York 10014, U.S.A.

Publications

Plays

The Widow (produced New York, 1961). Published, as *La Viuda*, in *Teatro Cubano*, Havana, Casa de las Américas, 1961.

Tango Palace (as *There! You Died*, produced San Francisco, 1963; as *Tango Palace*, produced New York, 1964; revised version produced Minneapolis, 1965). Included in *Promenade and Other Plays*, 1971.

The Successful Life of Three: A Skit for Vaudeville (produced Minneapolis and New York, 1965). Included in *Promenade and Other Plays*, 1971.

Promenade, music by Al Carmines (produced New York, 1965; revised version produced New York, 1969). Included in *Promenade and Other Plays*, 1971.

The Office (produced New York, 1966).

A Vietnamese Wedding (produced New York, 1967). Included in *Promenade and Other Plays*, 1971.

The Annunciation (also director: produced New York, 1967).

Dr. Kheal (produced New York, 1968; London, 1969). Included in *Promenade and Other Plays*, 1971.

The Red Burning Light; or, Mission XQ3 (produced Zurich, 1968; New York, 1969). Included in *Promenade and Other Plays*, 1971.

Molly's Dream, music by Cosmos Savage (produced Lenox, Massachusetts, 1968; also director: produced New York, 1968). Included in *Promenade and Other Plays*, 1971.

Promenade and Other Plays. New York, Winter House, 1971; revised edition, New York, Performing Arts Journal Publications, 1987.

The Curse of the Langston House, in *Baboon!!!* (produced Cincinnati, 1972).

Dance, with Remy Charlip (also co-director: produced London, 1972).

Aurora, music by John FitzGibbon (also director: produced New York, 1974).

Cap-a-Pie, music by José Raúl Bernardo (also director: produced New York, 1975).

Lines of Vision (lyrics only), book by Richard Foreman, music by George Quincy (produced New York, 1976).

Washing (produced New York, 1976).

Fefu and Her Friends (also director: produced New York, 1977). Published in *Wordplays 1*, New York, Performing Arts Journal Publications, 1980.

Lolita in the Garden, music by Richard Weinstock (also director: produced New York, 1977).

In Service (also director: produced Padua Hills, California, 1978).

Eyes on the Harem (also director: produced New York, 1979).

Blood Wedding, adaptation of a play by García Lorca (produced New York, 1980).

Evelyn Brown: A Diary (also director: produced New York, 1980).

Life Is Dream, adaptation of a play by Calderón, music by George Quincy (also director: produced New York, 1981).

A Visit, music by George Quincy (also director: produced Padua Hills, California, and New York, 1981).

The Danube (also director: produced Padua Hills, California, 1982; New York, 1983). Included in *Plays*, 1986.

Mud (also director: produced Padua Hills, California, and New York, 1983; revised version, also director: produced Omaha, 1985; London, 1988). Included in *Plays*, 1986.

Sarita, music by Leon Odenz (also director: produced New York, 1984; London, 1988). Included in *Plays*, 1986.

Abingdon Square (produced Seattle, 1984; New York, 1987; London, 1989).

The Conduct of Life (also director: produced New York, 1985; London, 1988). Included in *Plays*, 1986.

Cold Air, adaptation of a play by Virgilio Piñera (also director: produced New York, 1985). New York, Theater Communications Group, 1985.

Drowning, adaptation of a story by Chekhov, in *Orchards* (produced Urbana, Illinois, 1985; New York, 1986). New York, Knopf, 1986.

The Trial of Joan of Arc on a Matter of Faith (also director: produced New York, 1986).

Lovers and Keepers, music by Tito Puente and Ferrando Rivas, lyrics by Fornés (also director: produced New York, 1986). New York, Theatre Communications Group, 1987.

Art, in *Box Plays* (produced New York, 1986).

The Mothers (also director: produced Padua Hills, California, 1986).

Plays. New York, Performing Arts Journal Publications, 1986.

A Matter of Faith (produced New York, 1986).

Uncle Vanya, adaptation of the play by Anton Chekhov (also director: produced New York, 1987).

Hunger (also director: produced New York, 1988).

And What of the Night? (also director: produced Milwaukee, Wisconsin, 1989).

Oscar and Bertha (produced San Francisco, 1991).

*

Manuscript Collection: Lincoln Center Library of the Performing Arts, New York.

Critical Studies: Interviews with Rob Creese in *Drama Review* (New York), December 1977, with Gayle Austin in *Theatre Times* (New York), March 1984, with Allen Frame in *Bomb* (New York), Fall 1984, and with Scott Cummings in *Theater* (New Haven, Connecticut), Winter 1985; "The Real Life of María Irene Fornés," in *Theatre Writings* by Bonnie Marranca, New York, Performing Arts Journal Publications, 1984; "Creative Danger" by Fornés, in *American Theatre* (New York), September 1985; preface by Susan Sontag to *Plays*, 1986; "The Search for Identity in the Theater of Three Cuban American Female Dramatists" by Maida Watson, in *The Bilingual Review* (Tempe, Arizona), May-December 1991, pp. 188-96; "Fornés's Odd Couple: Oscar and Bertha at the Magic Theatre" by Scott T. Cummings, in *Journal of Dramatic Theory and Criticism* (Lawrence, Kansas), Spring 1994, pp. 147-56; *How Shall I Live?: Community and Moral Vision in Selected Plays by María Irene Fornés* (dissertation) by Diane Rao, Bowling Green, Ohio, Bowling Green State University, 1995; *María Irene Fornés and Her Critics* by Assunta Bartolomucci Kent, Westport, Connecticut, Greenwood Press, 1996; *Fornés: Theater in Present Tense* by Diane Lynn Moroff, Ann Arbor, University of Michigan Press, 1996: *Invasion of the Temple: Women Speaking on the Ground of the Abject in the Plays of María Irene Fornés* (dissertation) by Julia Jeanette Norstrand, Los Angeles, UCLA, 1996; "Wordscapes on the Body: Performative Language as Gestus in María Irene Fornés's Plays" by Deborah R. Geis and "Drama and the Dialogic Imagination: *The Heidi Chronicles* and *Fefu and Her Friends*" by Helene Keyssar, both in *Feminist Theatre and Theory*, edited by Helene Keyssar, New York, St. Martin's, 1996; "Feminism, Metatheatricality, and Mise-en-scene in María Irene Fornés's *Fefu and Her Friends*" by Penny Farfan, in *Modern Drama* (Canada), Winter 1997, pp. 442-53.

Theatrical Activities:
Director: **Plays**—Several of her own plays; *Exiles* by Ana Maria Simo, New York, 1982; *Uncle Vanya* by Anton Chekhov, New York, 1987; *Going to New England* by Ana Maria Simo, New York, 1990.

* * *

Eight Obie awards, including 1982's "sustained achievement" distinction, honor playwright-director Maria Irene Fornés, who has insisted on her own risky vision while walking the stylistic edges of Off-Broadway's experimentation since her earliest plays. Steadily current and cosmopolitan, enriched by Latin sensibilities and an exploratory feminism, her plays bypass psychological, sociological, and realistic expectations. Bright, intensely performed words and actions—serious and comic—fill her stages. Characters are characteristically, or become momentarily, "dangerous" or "safe," dominant or dominated. No one else onstage dares interrupt the frantic (or manic) line, monologue, or dance of someone afoot with a vision. Scripts often seem cryptic because they pivot on an objectifying abstraction of myth or metaphysics (like Burt's in *Terra Incognita)*, on a realistic detail exhaustively wrung dry, or on free-floating pronouns and unstated constructs in dialogue or movement. Among these discontinuous images lurk shadows, and in creeps Fornés's tragic sense of a threatening entropy or some critical missing pieces. From the first, Fornés's considered but playful attention to verbal and visual imagery poked audiences with freakish or theatrically exalted characters. In her morally passionate plays the comic provocations of a laugh or grimace reveal her fresh point of view. Even the fairly consistent, selective realism of many of her later, more substantial works moves with the odd undulations of an idiosyncratic heart and mind, which can give rise to magic startlings. Fornés is a sometimes poignant, often humorous, and always intense playwright. This Cuban-born master-teacher—by way of her own plays, projects, and workshops—has helped develop powerful, new Hispanic American playwrights and repertory.

An antic symbiosis of sadism and masochism, in life and art, locks the naive Leopold and the strenuous Isidore into *The Tango Palace*. The arrogant harangue of *Dr. Kheal*, the raucous road show of *The Red Burning Light*, and the Jarry-Beckett scatology of *Oscar and Bertha* now seem too familiar as comic-didactic theater. With songs and the Crosby-Hope *Road*-show format of *Promenade*, Prisoners 105 and 106 journey from cell back to cell constantly tricking or eluding the pursuant Jailer—a dumb, sexually overactive beast. They tunnel out of prison into a snooty Banquet, meet Miss Cake, ally themselves with the Servant (who seeks the meaning of life), and escape after robbing the rich Guests who nod off from stupid self-indulgence. Seeking her lost babes, mother, too, joins the lengthening line of the prisoners' pursuers. She and the fugitives play a tender double pietà with two soldiers on the battlefield, before the tyrannical mayor sends them back to jail—to escape again. The cruelty and criminality are casual. After mother's tucking-in and the servant's fond farewell, the prisoners remain alone, neither informed nor changed by their adventures.

Molly's Dream uses Dietrich poses and the bar-setting of Hollywood westerns to ridicule the machismo and romance of male myths found in *Bus Stop* and *The Misfits*. When a young couple and an older man act with movie timing and allusion through 10 semi-burlesque scenes of *The Successful Life of 3,* their looks at each other (He "disdainful"; She "stupid") become part of the dialogue. Later such "looks" become whole scenes in *Abingdon Square*. The patterns and figures—an older man, a casual stranger, a self-loathing woman, a mysteriously ill person—of these 1960s plays recur with permutations throughout her works.

The Hispanic family and religious heritage informs the musical chronicle *Sarita* (set in South Bronx, 1939-47) and the viciously spare *The Conduct of Life* (set in a Latin American country). Trapped in poverty between Cuban and Yankee values, and Catholic and pagan gods, the title character of *Sarita,* from age 13, tries to ignore her incinerating passion for Julio but cannot, despite his ruthless betrayals and the understanding of her "nice" new American husband, Mark. Momentary vignettes and songs lead her through deepening self-hatred, and she eventually stabs her lover-destroyer to death. Is Mark's holding her hand in the hospital any hope for healing? *The Conduct of Life* distributes the male-dominated woman's role among three in relation to the character Orlando. Rising on the mutilated minds and bodies of his victims to become state torturer for a fascist Latin American government, he ridicules the intellectual, spiritual aspirations of his wife, Leticia, who tolerates his humiliations and betrayals. He ignores the older servant, Olimpia (who seethes with anger but will survive); but he rapes, enslaves, and installs in his cellar (as servant) 12-year-old Nena, who "receives" those who hurt her "since maybe they are in worse pain than me." Adaptively resisting her knowledge of his evil, Leticia grovels toward her husband and remains petulantly childish with Olimpia—until she must finally accept her identity in relation to both Orlando and his victims. She shoots him and gives Nena the gun—so that the child will shoot her? or, as in a later version's stage direction, "hoping she will take the blame"? These are fascinating consequences of moral distancing from one's actions.

With a European perspective *The Danube* creates a bloated horror of America's naive international meddling. In Budapest—1938 to whenever—nice American Paul meets sweet Eve. Chronicled in units (scenes) of Hungarian-English lessons, the play shows them marrying, declining with a mysterious sickness, and blaming each other. Puppet shows and human scenes then repeat the last two, most difficult lessons—until, contorted and red-spotted, Paul and Eve exit in a white-flash explosion of either a pistol shot or a nuclear blast. That violence is much like Fefu's in *Fefu and Her Friends*; and the destructively contaminating and cautionary vision of evil in the play coincides with that of Rob and Steve (Fra Bartolome de las Casas) in *Terra Incognita* and that of the driven Ray in "Springtime," "Lust," and "Hunger" of *What of the Night?*

Seven accomplished women arrive to plan a panel on education in *Fefu and Her Friends*. Fefu, who considers herself alternately bright and "loathsome," proves herself always "outrageous" by fixing toilets and shooting (only blanks?) at her always-offstage husband through the window with a rifle. She reports that, after falling, he dusts himself off—men are lucky. Fefu's friend Julia, who observes that only ballerinas lack the heavy female insides, is crippled and dying of a "malady" and suffers from hallucinations. After the first living-room scene, Fornés quarters her audience, which is led backstage to stand by the kitchen, backyard, study, and Julia's bedroom, in intimate proximity to actors performing their brief scene four times intensely; then audience and actors return to auditorium and stage, respectively. Even the ferocious Fefu, who for her own self-respect and survival must save Julia, cannot do so. Fefu shoots her husband again outside, and Julia dies behind her with a Shepardian red-cross of blood on her forehead.

Introduced at age 10 in "Nadine," the character Rainbow returns, at age 29, in "Springtime," the second and most tender of the four acts in *What of the Night?*, Fornés's powerful epic drama of human hunger and aspirations, incest and degradations. Rainbow's domestic serving rituals and her narrated adventures can only sustain the deep love between her and the convalescent Gretchen a short while against their own fragilities and the world's antagonism, as personified in the brief appearance in their bedroom of Rainbow's lost brother, Ray, 27.

In print the 19-page "Springtime" of *What of the Night?* consists of 14 titled scenes, and the 16 pages of Act III, "Lust," is made up of 12 moments or beats. This type of short-scene construction tends to fragment the more linear *Abingdon Square* (two acts, 32 scenes), a frequently moving chronicle of the love and marriage between poor Marion, 15, and wealthy Juster, 50, from 1908 to 1917. Though "outrageousness" again leads to liberation, *Abingdon Square* ends with the angelically illuminated Michael (loving son, war-casualty) appearing behind the pietà of Marion cradling dead old Juster.

Unlike *Abington Square,* however, the short-scene construction of the opera *Terra Incognita* (24 labeled beats) or the similarly cut units of *Mud* accumulate considerable force in single settings. Three young American tourists pause at an outdoor Spanish café in *Terra Incognita.* Through meandering arias and recitative, each employs individual strategies—such as compulsive diary-keeping, looking at their guidebooks and maps, serving others drinks, or deconstructing Albee's *Zoo Story,* Sondheim's red "hat," or a postcard picture with Foucault-like calculus—to fathom betrayals, miscommunications, the historic virginity of Henry the Navigator, or the horrors of the Gulf War. Two fascinating "natives" who wander in complicate/implicate all: a crazy bum with inconsistent visions of discoveries by Columbus or Eratosthenes or of capitalism or Christian mystics; and a stolid, fixated monk who relentlessly recites the sixteenth-century atrocities in the Indies and gives a lesson in sailing in doing so. The play becomes a landslide of history, legend, and humanism. The young women and man are no rocks, only pebbles in a grand mosaic.

In *Mud,* too, Fornés compassionately represents the intricacies of relationships among three characters: Mae and Lloyd (both 25) and an older Henry. Behind their ignorant and repetitiously brutal language, both Mae and Lloyd yearn for nourishment and to nourish: through dinner, health, sex, or learning. By exiting one scene to pivot visibly in the doorway to re-enter for the next, the actors reflect their attempt to recreate themselves out of the red mud of situation and linguistics into a next phase. Mae brings semi-literate Henry in to read a pamphlet on Lloyd's sickness and to teach her to read. Not wanting to live like an animal, Mae mistakes the meaner-spirited Henry for "heaven." Lloyd weeps but learns to read, cure himself, and nurse Henry, who becomes more greedy, mocking, and crippled. "Lloyd is good, Henry. And this is his home," she says before fleeing it and the men's destructive combat. Lloyd chases her, shoots her, and brings her back—to die like a starfish.

The playwright's compassionate concern with another three characters cannot redeem *Enter the Night* from being an unpersuasive redaction of *No Exit* set during the epidemic of AIDS and homophobia. As Fornés's plays seem sometimes to imply—with *Enter the Night,* or that eternal game of euchre occupying the four characters at the end of the grotesque little *Oscar and Bertha,* or the bleak heap that may finally absorb all in *What of the Night?*—is depriving others the necessary conduct of life? Not in her later play, *Summer in Gossensass.* This work exuberantly celebrates American actress Elizabeth Robins's acquisition of an Ibsen script in 1891. The enthusiasm is infectious as Robins and Marion Lea explore *Hedda Gabler.* As performers starved for recognition as women and for challenge as artists, they secure and prepare the play's first London production with increasing insight and an exhilarating, growing feminism.

—John G. Kuhn

FORSTER, Michaelanne

Nationality: New Zealander (originally American; emmigrated to New Zealand, 1973, naturalized citizen, 1995). **Born:** Michelanne Forster, Santa Monica, California, 26 April 1953. **Education:** Aukland University, B.A. (with distinction) 1975; Aukland Secondary Teachers College, Diploma in Teaching, 1976. **Family:** Married Paul Corwin (separated 1996), two sons; partner with Nigel Dunlop. **Career:** Has worked as a script editor, writer, and studio/film director, Television New Zealand, 1980-89. Teacher at New Zealand School of Broadcasting at Christchurch Polytechnic, 1996—. **Awards:** QEII Playwrights Bursary, 1993; finalist, Adam Foundation Playwright award, 1994; Buckland award for Literature, for *Daughters of Heaven,* 1994; Winner, Takahe Short Story Competition, 1996; Best Dramatic Production, Radio New Zealand, 1996; Best Dramatic Production RNZ, 1997. **Address:** c/o Playmarket, P.O. Box 9767, Te Aro, Wellington, New Zealand.

Publications

Plays

A Dream Romance (produced Court Theatre, 1986).
Songs My Mother Taught Me (also director: produced Court Theatre, 1993).
Daughters of Heaven (produced Court Theatre, 1991). Victoria Press, 1992.
Larnach—Castle of Lies (produced Court Theatre, 1993).
The Other Eden (produced Court Theatre, 1996).

Radio Plays:*Daughters of Heaven,* 1993; *Larnach,* 1996; *The Rosenberg Sisters,* 1997.

Television Plays: *Play School, Spot On, Once Upon A Story, Sesame Street, After School, What Now, Sunday, The Third Wife of Larnach, The Posy Narkers, Bumble, The Big Chair, Bingo and Molly,* 1997; *Emerald and the Fairyfolk of Gemstone Valley,* 1998.

Plays for Children

The Bungling Burglars. N.p., n.d.
Mean Jean the Pirate Queen. N.p., n.d.

Arabella and the Amazing Wardrobe. N.p., n.d.
Musical Beasts. N.p., n.d.

Other

Rodney the Rat and the Sunken Treasure. Hodder and Stoughton, 1983.
The Four-Legged Prince. Hodder and Stoughton, 1985.
Rodney the Rat and the Sneaky Weasel Gang. Hodder and Stoughton, 1985.
Rodney Rat and the Space Creatures. Hodder and Stoughton, 1989.
A Passion for Travel. Tandem Press, 1998.
When It's Over. Penguin, 1998.

* * *

Michaelanne Forster is best known for three full-length plays—*Daughters of Heaven* (1991), *Larnach—Castle of Lies* (1993), and *This Other Eden* (1996)—and the one-act play *The Rosenberg Sisters* (1992); all have a unifying principle of historical revisionism, or "re-staging history," not as much by way of documentary representation but by exploring the undersides of official or popular accounts. Despite her subjects' basis in reality, she emphasizes the subjective nature of her work: "It is my imagination which is being revealed, my version of events."

The Rosenberg Sisters is a tightly constructed "memory play," which, while located in the present, moves between World War II Germany and postwar New Zealand through the reminiscences of sisters who formed an Andrews Sisters-style singing group. Musicality and counterpoint govern the dramatic structure, dialogue, and tone of this play, which, although fictional, holds a mirror up to a society whose complacency about its status as a refuge from the evils of war is questioned as insistently as the sisters' varying responses to their identification as Jews.

Forster's most successful work is *Daughters of Heaven,* whose action relates to the 1954 murder by teenagers Juliet Hulme and Pauline Parker of Parker's mother in Victoria Park, Christchurch (also the basis of Peter Jackson's film *Heavenly Creatures*). Unlike the film's preoccupation with fantasy, the play situates the girls and the murder itself within the dual frame of the imaginative-spiritual world in which they believed themselves most real and their incarceration in separate prisons. The play opens and closes in 1959 as, awaiting release, the girls are subject to the interfering machinations of a (fictional) Irish-Catholic housekeeper to the Hulmes, now a treacherous intermediary between the girls. Most of the play's action explores the girls' domestic backgrounds and their relationship and fantasies, leading to the murder at its center and interspersed with short scenes from the trial. The girls' story is enacted between two poles of commentary: the historic recorded legal discourse on their act; and social gossip, represented in condensation through the housekeeper, who is the constant mediator between stage and audience, the instrument of audience implication. The audience must accept or question her often intimate and conspiratorially delivered judgements. The play does not resolve into easy answers: the murder took place and is not excused, but its meaning remains suspended among questions of evil, insanity, and love beyond reason, and among the respective roles of the imaginary world and the unimaginative world of 1950s provincial Christchurch with its class and gender rigidities and its social and sexual hypocrisies.

Controversy has also surrounded the play's production decisions, such as representations of the physical relationship between the girls, and the mode of staging (or not) the murder. But there has also been debate about the ethics of Forster mixing historical/factual events with fictional material without clear indications of the boundaries. Nevertheless, the same approach characterizes *Larnach—Castle of Lies* about William Larnach, colonial banker, landowner, and politician who committed suicide in Parliament House in 1898. The play works imaginatively through the private regions beneath the public face of power and ambition to uncover a more complex and personal basis to Larnach's turmoil, finding family tragedies and rivalries that supplement the official explanation of his death as "business failure." While drawing on research and information from Larnach's descendants and extended family, Forster invents characters and condenses others; a household of 46 servants becomes the one fictional butler whose "loyal" connivances help precipitate the crisis. The domestic drama interweaves plots and subplots, melodramatic elements and dramatic irony, as well as the ball scene, alongside of which Forster develops intrigue, suspicions, and betrayals that suit the nineteenth-century setting in an isolated, eccentric, and extant Otago castle. The play treads a fine line between questions of accountability raised by the fictional representation of real events and real characters whose descendants are still living and questions of sustaining interest to a contemporary audience beyond the parochial.

Written with the cultural advice of Maori cast members and set just before British colonization, *This Other Eden* explores the complex relationship of the missionary Thomas Kendall and chief Hongi Hika. While "cultural difference" may define their encounter, Forster's play does not sustain a trite binary situation. Kendall is in conflict with the Church Missionary Society, while his marriage collapses under the pressure of his obsessions. Hongi's tribal authority is unstable, and his rivalries with other chiefs draw him to Kendall for muskets; their final mutual disillusionment is a sobering provocation to examine realities of contemporary New Zealand discourses of biculturalism. In production the play problematically tended to represent Maori, in terms of "culture," as a collectivity alongside European individual inwardness and alienation. The set, burdened with the dual representation of European romanticized nature and the more literal physical situation of the Maori, is not necessarily inherent in the script but nonetheless provokes useful questions about the possibilities of bicultural theater.

—Chris Prentice

FORSYTH, James (Law)

Nationality: British. **Born:** Glasgow, Lanark, 5 March 1913. **Education:** Glasgow High School, graduated 1930; Glasgow School of Art, diploma in drawing and painting 1934. **Military Service:** Served in WWII (1940-46); Scots Guard and 53rd Welsh Division, Normandy; Captain Signals Officer; Bronze Cross of the Netherlands. **Family:** Married 1) Helen Steward in 1938 (divorced 1953), two sons; 2) Louise Tibble in 1955. **Career:** Worked with the General Post Office Film Unit, 1937-40; dramatist-in-residence, Old Vic Company: worked with the Old Vic School and the Young Vic, 1946-48; dramatist-in-residence, Howard University, Washington, D.C., 1962; guest director and lecturer, Tufts University,

Medford, Massachusetts, 1963; distinguished professor-in-residence, Florida State University, Tallahassee, 1965; director, Tufts University Program in London, 1967-71. Artistic director, The Forsyths' Barn Theatre, Ansty, Sussex, 1972—. Member of the Executive Council, League of Dramatists and Radio Writers Association, 1954-64; founding member, Theatres Advisory Council, **Awards:** Arts Council bursary, 1980. **Agent:** Claire Evans Associates, 11 Gifford House, Eastney Street, Greenwich, London SE10 9NT, England. **Address:** Grainloft, Ansty, Haywards Heath, Sussex RH17 5AG, England.

PUBLICATIONS

Plays

Trog (broadcast 1949; produced Coventry, 1959; Tallahassee, Florida, 1964).
Brand, adaptation of the play by Ibsen (broadcast 1949; produced London, 1964). London, Heinemann, and New York, Theatre Arts, 1960.
The Medicine Man (produced London, 1950).
Emmanuel: A Nativity Play (broadcast 1950; produced London and New York, 1960). London, Heinemann, 1952; New York, Theatre Arts, 1963.
Héloïse (broadcast 1951; produced Southsea, Hampshire, and London, 1951; New York, 1958). Included in *Three Plays*, 1957; New York, Theatre Arts, 1958.
The Other Heart (broadcast 1951; produced London, 1952; also director: produced Medford, Massachusetts, 1963). Included in *Three Plays*, 1957; New York, Theatre Arts, 1964; revised version, as *Villon* (opera), music by Gardner Read (produced New Orleans, 1981).
Adelaise (broadcast 1951; produced Ashburton, Devon, 1953). Included in *Three Plays*, 1957.
Three Plays. London, Heinemann, 1957.
The Pier (televised 1957; produced Bristol Old Vic Theatre, 1958).
The Road to Emmaus: A Play for Eastertide. London, Heinemann, 1958; New York, Theatre Arts, 1972.
Joshua, music by Franz Waxman (produced Dallas, 1960). New York, Ricordi, 1959.
Dear Wormwood, adaptation of *The Screwtape Letters* by C.S. Lewis (produced Brighton, 1965). Chicago, Dramatic Publishing Company, 1961; as *Screwtape*, 1973.
Fifteen Strings of Money, adaptation of a play by Guenther Weisenhorn based on a story by Chu Su-chen (produced Pitlochry, Perthshire, 1961).
Everyman (produced Coventry, 1962).
Defiant Island (produced Washington, D.C., 1962). Chicago, Dramatic Publishing Company, 1975.
Seven Scenes for Yeni (produced Boston, 1963).
Cyrano de Bergerac, adaptation of the play by Edmond Rostand (produced Sarasota, Florida, 1963; London, 1967; New York, 1968). Chicago, Dramatic Publishing Company, 1968.
If My Wings Heal (produced Stroud, Gloucestershire, 1966).
Four Triumphant (televised 1966; as *Festival of Four*, produced Ansty, Sussex, 1976).
What the Dickens, adaptation of the novel *The Pickwick Papers* by Dickens (produced Ansty, Sussex, 1974).
Lobsterback (produced Boston and Ansty, Sussex, 1975).
No Crown for Herod (as *Christmas at Greccio*, produced Ansty, Sussex, 1976). Chicago, Dramatic Publishing Company, 1977.
The Play of Alban (produced St. Albans, 1977).
"N" for Napoleone (produced Ansty, Sussex, 1978).
When the Snow Lay Round About (broadcast 1978; as *Wenceslas*, produced Ansty, Sussex, 1980).
A Time of Harvest (produced Ansty, Sussex, 1981; as *The Threshing Floor*, broadcast 1982).
One Candle (unproduced, 1996).
The Bridge Between (unproduced, 1997).

Screenplays: *The End of the Road*, with Geoffrey Orme, 1954; *Francis of Assisi*, with Eugene Vale and Jack Thomas, 1961.

Radio Plays: *The Bronze Horse*, 1948; *Trog*, 1949; *Brand*, 1949; *Emmanuel*, 1950; *Seelkie*, music by Brian Easdale, 1950; *The Seal Woman* (radio opera); *The Other Heart*, 1951; *Adelaise*, 1951; *Héloïse*, 1951; *The Nameless One of Europe*, 1951; *For He's a Jolly Good Fellow*, 1952; *Pig*, 1953; *The Festive Spirit*, 1955; *Lisel*, 1955; *Christophe*, 1958; *Every Pebble on the Beach*, 1963; *When the Snow Lay Round About*, 1978; *The Threshing Floor*, 1982.

Television Plays: *Old Mickmack*, 1955; *The Pier*, 1957; *Underground*, from a novel by Harold Rein, 1958; *Four Triumphant*, 1966; *The English Boy*, 1969; *The Last Journey*, 1972; *The Old Man's Mountain*, 1972.

Other

Tyrone Guthrie: A Biography. London, Hamish Hamilton, 1976.
Back to the Barn. Ansty, Sussex, Grainloft, 1986.

*

Manuscript Collection: Lincoln Center Library of the Performing Arts, New York.

Theatrical Activities:
Director: **Plays**—*The Other Heart*, Medford, Massachusetts, 1963; *Trog*, Coventry, 1961.

James Forsyth comments:

(1982) The plays themselves being the playwright's *more than* personal statement to the public, I am reluctant to make other statements. I say "more than personal" and I say "play*wright*" (not playwrite) for these reasons: That Theatre, where it is more than a show for Entertainment or Propaganda purposes, is an Art—an all-arts Art—and in Art the thing wrought out of the raw material is a thing in itself and speaks for itself. I *wright* for the Theatre as a performing place for the Art of Theatre, a tough and practical and popular art. The *writing* of the playwright is only the recording art which ends up with a script. The script ends up with "the thing itself" which is the event, the production. And it is all *wrought* out of the many arts of the playwright in the fields of sight, sound, touch, etc., realized in any playhouse by all the contributory arts of those who were once, and accurately, referred to as "artistes."

I had started life as an artist painter and sculptor, and my apprenticeship to the art of the theatre, with the Old Vic Company of Guthrie and Olivier, gave me a taste for the all-arts theatre and also for epic theatre. I am a playwright because I have found that the live event of the play is the best occasion in the world for the communion with—the sharing of artistic experience with—an audience; and the art of Theatre is the best medium for creation of the concepts worth sharing.

But the all-arts theatre is a hard road in a world of theatre brutally constricted by cash considerations, a constriction relieved only a bit by subsidy of certain playhouses and the heroism of "fringe" and "off-off" companies. That is why I have directed, for the last ten years, my own plays in my own barn which is a natural playhouse with an enthusiastic audience and a company of so-called "amateurs" who have become professed to the Art of Theatre to a professional degree. But in turning away in some despair from the world of the professional theatre and showbiz in its present state to this limited but real local success in the art, I have not of course "made a living" from it, which begins to make this statement more "personal" than necessary. But by the subsidy of an Arts Council bursary I have been able to complete what could be my most important play, *The Spanish Captain*, 1981.

(1998) When my wife died in 1983, *The Spanish Captain* had not had a production. And crippled by the loss of my wife I retreated into poetry and painting and some sculpture, doing no work in or "wrighting" for theatre until 1996 *One Candle* and 1997 *The Bridge Between.* Both have been given rehearsed readings (Brighton, London, and York), but not yet committed to production.

* * *

Craft is fundamental to all art, even though not all craftsmen are artists any more than every artist is a craftsman. Indeed today, in a time when artists are promoted by public relations, craft has become somewhat unfashionable. Hence, the well-made play has come to be regarded as something slightly old-fashioned. Yet the virtue of a well-made play is that it knows how to tell a story and how to hold an audience, which is an essential part of the dramatist's craft.

James Forsyth is such an old-fashioned playwright, a term that is perhaps the most pat of all for an author who himself said in 1972: "I have yet to wright my best play. And 'wright' is right, I am not a 'dramatist,' I am a 'playwright.' Drama is the stuff, plays are the works, and I am professed to works." His works are prolific. There has been a steady output over the years, from the Old Vic production of *The Other Heart* to a television series on the patron saints of England, Scotland, Ireland, and Wales, to *The Last Journey,* a 90-minute television play on Tolstoi.

The Other Heart is one of Forsyth's strongest and most powerfully constructed plays. It is full of excellent character studies such as that of Marthe, the servant, who, when asked why she risks her life in coming to Paris during the plague, replies, "I need to help." In the character of the romantic poet, François Villon, Forsyth catches marvelously the impetuosity of young love and the radiant recklessness of the visionary and poet. They are qualities that seem to attract him again and again. While he is drawn to "wrighting" plays about historical characters, it is noticeable how many of them are variations on the theme of a pair of star-crossed lovers. In this play there are Villon and Catherine de Vausselles, and there are Francis and Clare in *If My Wings Heal* and Héloïse and Abelard in *Héloïse.* In *The Last Journey,* a study of the last days of Tolstoi, Forsyth has written brilliantly of the tragic gap between a husband and wife.

The clash of the idealist with reality, however, is perhaps the profoundest recurring theme in all Forsyth's work. It has attracted him to a powerful adaptation of Ibsen's *Brand,* and in *If My Wings Heal* he sets out to explore the conflict between Saint Francis of Assisi, the creative artist, poet, and visionary, and Brother Elias, the ambitious administrative genius of the Franciscan order. It was Brother Elias who wanted to turn the Friars Minor into the most powerful order within the church "for the sake of possession, for the possession of power." As one of the friars remarks, "It was never Brother Francis's idea that we should be other than small bands, always on the move. We were to be the salt which is scattered."

This is a tougher and less sentimental rendering of the story of Francis of Assisi than the *Little Plays of St. Francis* by Laurence Housman or the five-act devotional drama by Henri Ghéon, *The Marriage of St. Francis.* Only the scene of the stigmata fails, but it may be impossible to put a mystical experience on the stage. Perhaps only a major poet such as T. S. Eliot, whose insight into the transcendental was close to that of the great mystics themselves, could really tackle such a scene. If Forsyth is a proven playwright, he is, I think, a poet manqué. His weakest writing almost always stems from a tendency to poeticize, to lapse into obvious rhyming blank verse. Yet in terms of theater one can see what he is about, for the steady beat and rhythm of these passages serve to carry the story forward.

David, Andrew, Patrick, and *George* (*Four Triumphant*) are four full-length plays envisaged as a cycle to be performed over two days. They embody not merely the history of the four patron saints but also are a study of the pioneers of Christianity. Each play is self-sufficient, and yet each gains from its relation to the others.

Perhaps Forsyth's most memorable play is *Defiant Island,* the story of Henri Christophe, the self-proclaimed black king of northern Haiti. It is a deeply moving tragedy of an idealist who is led astray by his fanatical devotion to his own ideals, so that the man is destroyed at the expense of the image of himself as the first black monarch. Finally, when Napoleon insists on "nothing less than the total extinction of every adult black, male and female," Henri Christophe, who had naively believed that all men could meet in equal justice, has to admit to himself, "I asked too much. It is a fault in me."

Christophe, Brand, Abelard, Villon, Francis of Assisi—all are men of thought suffused with passion. They are the solitary visionaries, the reckless romantics, the uncomfortable reformers. They are heroes in the true sense of the word. Forsyth belongs to that great tradition of bardic poets who sang the exploits and epics of heroes. It is a tradition that is at present a little out of fashion, but fashions change, and the wheel comes full circle. When that happens, Forsyth will find that he has wrought his best play.

—James Roose-Evans

FOSTER, Paul

Nationality: American. **Born:** Penns Grove, New Jersey, 15 October 1931. **Education:** Schools in Salem, New Jersey; Rutgers University, New Brunswick, New Jersey, 1950-54, B.A. 1954; St. John's University Law School, New York, 1954, 1957, LL.B. 1958. **Military Service:** Served in the United States Naval Reserve, 1955-57. **Career:** Co-founder and president, La Mama Experimental Theater Club, New York, 1962—. U.S. Department of State lecturer, 1975, 1976, 1977; Fulbright lecturer, Brazil, 1980; taught at University of California, San Diego, 1981, and New York University, 1983. **Awards:** Rockefeller fellowship, 1967; Irish Universities award, 1967, 1971; New York Drama Critics Circle award, 1968; Creative Artists Public Service grant, 1972, 1974; National Endowment for the Arts grant, 1973; Arts Council of Great Britain award, 1973; Guggenheim fellowship, 1974; Theatre Heute award, 1977; Bulandra Foreign Play award, 1983. **Address:** 242 East 5th Street, New York, New York 10003, U.S.A.

PUBLICATIONS

Plays

Hurrah for the Bridge (produced New York, 1962; Edinburgh, 1967). Bogotá, Colombia, Canal Ramirez, 1965; in *Balls and Other Plays*, 1967.
The Recluse (produced New York, 1964; Edinburgh, 1967). Included in *Balls and Other Plays*, 1967.
Balls (produced New York, 1964; Edinburgh, 1967). Included in *Balls and Other Plays*, 1967.
The Madonna in the Orchard (produced New York, 1965). Published as *Die Madonna im Apfelhag*, Frankfurt, Fischer, 1968; as *The Madonna in the Orchard*, New York, Breakthrough Press, 1971; in *Elizabeth I and Other Plays*, 1973.
The Hessian Corporal (produced New York, 1966; Edinburgh, 1967). Included in *Balls and Other Plays*, 1967.
Balls and Other Plays. London, Calder and Boyars, 1967; New York, French, 1968.
Tom Paine (produced New York, 1967; expanded version produced Edinburgh and London, 1967; New York, 1968). London, Calder and Boyars, 1967; New York, Grove Press, 1968.
Heimskringla; or, The Stoned Angels (televised 1969; produced New York, 1970). London, Calder and Boyars, and New York, French, 1970.
Satyricon (produced New York, 1972). Published in *The Off-Off-Broadway Book*, edited by Bruce Mailman and Albert Poland, Indianapolis, Bobbs Merrill, 1972; in *Elizabeth I and Other Plays*, 1973.
Elizabeth I (produced New York, 1972; London, 1973). New York, French, 1972; in *Elizabeth I and Other Plays*, 1973.
Elizabeth I and Other Plays. London, Calder and Boyars, 1973.
Silver Queen Saloon (as *Silver Queen*, music by John Braden, lyrics by Foster and Braden, produced New York, 1973; revised version, as *Silver Queen Saloon*, produced New York, 1978; London, 1982). New York, French, 1976; with *Marcus Brutus*, London, Calder, 1977.
Rags to Riches to Rags (produced New York, 1974).
Marcus Brutus (produced Springfield, Massachusetts, 1975). New York, French, 1976; with *Silver Queen Saloon*, London, Calder, 1977.
A Kiss Is Just a Kiss (televised 1980; produced New York, 1983).
The Dark and Mr. Stone 1-3 (produced New York, 1985-86).

Screenplay: *Cinderella Story*, 1985.

Television Plays: *Heimskringla, or, The Stoned Angels*, 1969; *A Kiss Is Just a Kiss*, 1980 (Denmark); *Mellon*, 1980; *Smile*, 1981; *The Cop and the Anthem*, from the story by O. Henry, 1984.

Short Stories

Minnie the Whore, The Birthday Party, and Other Stories. Caracas, Venezuela, Zodiaco, 1962.

Other

The Buddhist Influence in T. S. Eliot's "Four Quartets." Frankfurt, Haag und Herchen, 1977.
Beckett and Zen: A Study of Dilemma in the Novels of Samuel Beckett. Boston, Wisdom Publications, 1989.

Translator, *Kasimir and Karoline*; *Faith, Hope, and Charity*; *Figaro Gets a Divorce*; *Judgement Day*, by Ödön Von Horváth. New York, PAJ Publications, 1986.

*

Manuscript Collection: Lincoln Center Library of the Performing Arts, New York.

Critical Studies: *The New Bohemia* by John Gruen, New York, Shorecrest, 1966; "The Theatre of Involvement" by Richard Atcheson, in *Holiday* (New York), October 1968; "The World's a Stage," in *MD Publications* (New York), October 1968; *Foster, Robbe-Grillet, Bergson: Teatro, Novela, Tiempo* by Gustavo Majia, unpublished doctoral dissertation, University of the Andes, Bogotá, 1969; *Up Against the Fourth Wall* by John Lahr, New York, Grove Press, 1970; *Le Nouveau Théâtre Américan* by Franck Jotterand, Paris, Seuil, 1970; *Selvsyn-Aktuel Litteratur og Kulturdebat* by Elsa Gress, Copenhagen, Gyldendal, 1970; *Now: Theater der Erfahrung* by Jens Heilmeyer and Pia Frolich, Cologne, Schauberg, 1971; *The Off-Off-Broadway Book* edited by Bruce Mailman and Albert Poland, Indianapolis, Bobbs Merrill, 1972.

* * *

The theatrical reputation of Paul Foster essentially belongs to the 1960s, when, as a highly innovative contributor to the off-off-Broadway movement, he showed greater audacity than Albee and at one point appeared to be the mentor to the emergent Sam Shepard. The diversity of Foster's early work is much greater than his often-argued debt to Beckett would suggest. As well as abstraction, symbolism, and existentialism—for which European models may be suggested—his plays up to *Tom Paine* all have a highly idiosyncratic lyrical vein that was peculiarly suited to the ensemble techniques of the La Mama Experimental Theater Club, where all of his best work was premiered. In *Hurrah for the Bridge* an old waif, who is pulling a cart piled high with junk, appears to be victimized by an expressionistic group of leather-jacketed urban predators, though their autonomy is demonstrated by his eventual death at their hands, at which point he is visited by the down-and-out angel he idolizes. *The Recluse* is more distinctively American in style in its presentation of an old basement grotesque accompanied by her semianimate mannequins and her pet cat, which is stuffed and which she hides in a drawer and keeps the best milk for. Foster's sympathies with the happening and with kinetic art, hinted at in these earliest plays, became rather more explicit in *Balls*, strictly a puppet play in which two pendant table tennis balls swing in and out of light. Human representation comes only through recorded voice-overs, a nostalgic dialogue between the two cadavers remaining in a coastal cemetery that is being eroded by the sea.

Foster's first approach to an ostensibly nonfictional subject was *The Hessian Corporal.* Although it is subtitled "a one-act documentary play," it is more like a parable for the theater on the theme of the immorality of war, historicized by the Hessian recruitment of 1776. Though this was an important new development for Foster, it differs from his later "historical" works in that its focus is not a famous individual. His concern in the play is with the exploited nonentity, and it has a social resonance that approaches the sentimental, although its relevance to Vietnam disguised this in the premiere. Even Foster's most famous play, *Tom Paine*, is only superficially a historical portrait, however. In the face of surging ensemble playing and an insistent line of lyrical narrative, individuality crystallizes only briefly before dissolving back into a faceless collective context. The play poses questions about individuality. It presents conflicting elements in the traditional portrait of Paine, the visionary and the alcoholic, but by theatricality (such as fragmenting Paine and sharing him among several actors) there arises the implicit question whether such elements can coexist in the world of history or whether such a Paine is just a monster from myth. Several prominent critics felt that the play was not about a person but about a way of looking at a society, about collective impulses toward revolution. Paine himself is, theatrically and metatheatrically, a trigger device for a commonsense reappraisal of the world that matters, a world that comes into focus haphazardly through the blurring devices of Paine's alcoholism and the ensemble performance.

Nor is *Elizabeth I* any more a history play or documentary. Again, two actors play the title role, but this time not to achieve schizoid characterization. One actress does Queen Elizabeth, while the other does Elizabeth the Player Queen, a member of an itinerant company presenting a fairy tale, a cartoon-style play about the queen in the late sixteenth century. A few episodes, such as those concerning the death of Mary of Scotland, have some urgency, but the sterner tone and historical momentum of *Tom Paine* are all but absent. This play is generally much more frolicsome, and there is no sense of continuity between the events depicted and the world of the modern audience. A similar tone of historical vandalism permeates the earlier television play *Heimskringla*, in which Leif Eriksson's discovery of Newfoundland is initially presented with the aura of a dramatized saga, with a massed choric incantation generating the action. An anachronistic flippancy soon permeates the action, however, with a diagram showing how to fill the stage with bubbles, and by the second-act "love-in" all intellectual pretensions have been abandoned. From this perspective *Satyricon* would seem an almost logical development for Foster: a stage embellishment of Petronius's work in which the decadence of the *Cena* is supplemented by appearances from various bacchants, Petronius himself, and Nero and Agrippina, who together enact the foundation of Rome, with the emperor playing Romulus while she plays the she-wolf. The comic grotesquerie of the play moves beyond cartoon caricature into theatrical pop art, an appropriate contribution to the theater of the ridiculous. A later play with a Roman setting, *Marcus Brutus*, attempts to return to an individual focus but again fails to target contemporary issues.

Foster's subsequent plays have been diverse and have included film scripts, but the stylistic assurance that marked his work up to *Tom Paine* has not been seen again. His sole work to attract substantial critical interest has been *A Kiss Is Just a Kiss,* in which Humphrey Bogart sits center stage and splices together personal memory and public film clips. Like Tom Paine, Bogey seems intended to offer a lens to our world, but in performance the play has lacked cohesion. Foster has never been a playwright in any conventional sense; he has been a literary collaborator in group-developed work, and his idiosyncratic habit of writing stage directions as imperatives defies any acceptance of his scripts as literature.

—Howard McNaughton

FRASER, Brad

Nationality: Canadian. **Awards:** Alberta Culture playwrighting competition, 1978, 1979, 1987, 1988, 1989; Laura May Kutney Stylings award, best new play, Calgary, 1989; Floyd S. Chalmers award, best Canadian play, 1991, for *Unidentified Human Remains and the True Nature of Love,* 1996, for *Poor Super Man*; London Evening Standard award, 1992; Time Out award, 1992; Genie award for best adapted screenplay, for *Love and Human Remains,* 1994; Dpra Mavor Moore award, Toronto, 1995; Los Angeles Critics award, 1995.

Publications

Plays

Wolf Boy (produced 1981).
Unidentified Human Remains and the True Nature of Love (produced 1989).
The Ugly Man (produced 1991).
Poor Super Man (produced 1994).
Martin Yesterday (produced Toronto, 1997).

Screenplays: *Beauty,* 1994; *Love and Human Remains,* 1994; *Parade,* 1995; *Our Man in Manila,* 1996; *Zircon Love,* 1997; *Poor Super Man,* 1998.

Radio Plays: *Hip Check Harry's,* 1989; *King of Another Place,* 1991; *The Ugly Man,* 1995; *The Killer Inside Me,* 1996; *Martin Yesterday,* 1996.

Television Plays: *Killing Time,* 1991; *Insomnia,* 1995.

* * *

Brad Fraser's plays are written for the television generation. Full of references to the popular culture of television, movies, music videos, and comic books, they weave a complex intertextual framework that sometimes heightens a particular mood and sometimes deliberately undercuts the tensions of the moment. *Poor Super Man* is subtitled *A Play with Captions,* with the captions (operating sometimes as scene location devices and sometimes as "thought bubbles" that have the capacity to supplement and contradict the characters' dialogue) projected onto various stage surfaces.

Sexuality is one of the most important topics to shape the plays because Fraser sees sexuality as a central aspect of life. Sex in

Fraser's plays can be very liberating, particularly for his male characters who are declaring their homosexuality for the first time. One of the results of this focus on male homosexuality is that some female characters are less well-developed. Balancing the celebration of homosexuality is, of course, AIDS, which occupies a role in several of his plays. His attempt to depict graphic sex—particularly homosexual sex—sometimes sits uncomfortably with theater administrations. Fraser has a reputation for being difficult to work with and for initiating strong public actions to counter cancellations of his shows on homophobic grounds.

If sex is one of the central realities of life for Fraser, another is violence. Most of the characters in his work are the victims of at least one form of abuse: sexual, emotional, or physical. Many are broken young people who live—barely—on the fringes of society. The brutality that is perpetrated on the characters is generally not the subject of the plays; rather it tends to be the backdrop for the action of the plays. The patterns of abuse frequently become cyclical, with victims of abuse continuing to be abused or becoming abusers themselves.

The play for which Fraser is probably best known is *Unidentified Human Remains and the True Nature of Love,* which was filmed by Denys Arcand under the title *Love and Human Remains* (for which Fraser wrote the screenplay). *Unidentified Human Remains* is about David, a one-time child-actor now waiting on tables who learns that his best friend, Bernie, is a serial killer of young women. The play also addresses the awkward and painful dilemma of determining one's sexual preference: the characters Candy and Kane both have homosexual and heterosexual encounters in their search for love. The unidentified remains of the title refer to Bernie's victims and to most of the characters who would barely be missed if they too were killed. Benita, a dominatrix, tells horror stories, but the lives of many of the play's characters rival her grisly tales.

The names of two characters from *Unidentified Human Remains* are recycled in *Wolfboy,* about two abused and neglected teenagers, David and Bernie, who are incarcerated in a psychiatric hospital. David purports to be a werewolf, an image that Fraser uses in several plays. While this "medical condition" is disproved, he kills Bernie in a form of werewolf communion that he believes will give him the strength to survive in the world.

The supernatural world is also central to *The Ugly Man,* which is based on Middleton and Rowley's *The Changeling* (including the bed trick) as well as the Archie comics, *Big Valley,* and *Star Wars.* It takes the already contorted view of humanity and evil from *The Changeling* and pushes it further to explore the limits to humans' capacity for greed. The skull of a murdered man rolls on stage to wreak revenge. The play unleashes an anger that is not dispelled by the very bloody resolution.

Poor Super Man is very fast paced—with even more of a staccato effect than usual for Fraser—and is about a famous painter, David, whose muse has temporarily deserted him; he takes a job in a restaurant to see if he can recover it. He shares a house with a would-be transsexual, Shannon, who is dying of AIDS. The death of Superman in the serial comic book structures the plot and offers the opportunity for the audience to speculate just how super-human the male characters are.

Fraser's plays are non-naturalistic, highly fractured and episodic, imagistic, and frequently very funny. The dialogue, often more like a short-hand that the audience must decipher, does not turn on artifice or metaphor. His plots are often convoluted, relying on many locations, simple staging, and few detailed characterizations: instead of adhering to theatrical rules (either traditional rules or rules of practicality), he creates what he considers to be contemporary theater.

—Joanne Tompkins

FRATTI, Mario

Nationality: American. **Born:** L'Aquila, Italy, 5 July 1927; immigrated to the United States, 1963; became citizen, 1974. **Education:** Ca'Foscari University, Venice, 1947-51, Ph.D. in language and literature 1951. **Military Service:** Served in the Italian Army, 1951-52: lieutenant. **Family:** Married 1) Lina Fedrigo in 1953 (marriage dissolved); 2) Laura Dubman in 1964; three children. **Career:** Translator, Rubelli Company, Venice, 1953-63; drama critic, *Sipario*, Milan, 1963-66, *Paese Sera*, Rome, 1963-73, *L'Ora*, Palermo, 1963-73, and *Ridotto*, Venice, 1963—, Rome. Taught at Adelphi University, Garden City, New York, and New School for Social Research, New York, 1964-65, Columbia University, New York, 1965-66, and Hofstra University, Hempstead, New York, 1973-74. Member of the Department of Romance Languages, Hunter College, New York, 1968—. **Awards:** RAI-Television prize, 1959; Ruggeri prize, 1960, 1967, 1969; Lentini prize, 1964; Vallecorsi prize, 1965; Unasp-Enars prize, 1968; Arta-Terme award, 1973; O'Neill Selection award, Richard Rodgers award, The Outer Critics Circle award, the Leone di San Marco Literary award, the Heritage and Culture award, eight Drama Desk awards, and five Tony awards, all for *Nine*; Carm-Cosenza Literary award, for *Sacrifici,* 1996. **Agent:** Samuel French Inc., 45 West 25th Street, New York, New York 10010, U.S.A. **Address:** 145 West 55th Street, Apartment 15-D, New York, New York 10019, U.S.A.

Publications

Plays

Il Campanello (produced Milan, 1958). Published in *Ridotto* (Venice), 1958; as *The Doorbell* (produced New York, 1970; London, 1972), in *Ohio University Review* (Athens), 1971.

La Menzogna (The Lie) (produced Milan, 1959). Published in *Cynthia* (Florence), 1963.

A (produced Rome, 1965). Published in *Ora Zero* (Rome), 1959; translation in *Fusta* (New Jersey), 1976.

La Partita (The Game) (produced Pesaro, 1960). Published in *Ridotto* (Venice), 1960.

Il Rifiuto (produced Mantua, 1960). Published in *Il Dramma* (Turin), October 1965; as *The Refusal* (produced New York, 1972; London, 1973), in *Races*, 1972.

In Attesa (produced La Spezia, 1960). Rome, EIST, 1964; as *Waiting* (produced New York, 1970), in *Poet Lore* (Boston), Autumn 1968.

Il Ritorno (produced Bologna, 1961). Published in *Ridotto* (Venice), 1961; as *The Return* (produced New York, 1963; London, 1972), New York, French, n.d.; in *Four by Fratti*, 1986.

La Domanda (The Questionnaire) (produced La Spezia, 1961). Published in *La Prora* (Rome), 1962.

Flowers from Lidice, published in *L'Impegno* (Bari), 1961; in *Dramatics* (Cincinnati), October 1972.

L'Assegno. Cosenza, Pellegrini, 1961; translated by Adrienne S. Mandel as *The Third Daughter* (produced New York, 1978), New York, French, n.d.

Confidenze (produced Rome, 1962). Rome, EIST, 1964; as *The Coffin* (produced New York, 1967). Published in *Four Plays*, 1972; in *Intermission* (Chicago) 1967.

Gatta Bianca al Greenwich (produced Rome, 1962). Published in *Il Dramma* (Turin), March 1962, as *White Cat*, in *Races*, 1972.

Il Suicidio (produced Spoleto, 1962). Published in *Cynthia* (Florence), 1962; as *The Suicide* (produced New York, 1965; London, 1973), in *Four by Fratti*, 1986.

La Gabbia (produced Milan, 1963). Published in *Cynthia* (Florence), 1962; as *The Cage* (produced New York, 1966). Published in *The New Theater of Europe* (New York), 1964; in *The Cage, The Academy, The Refrigerators*, 1977.

The Academy (produced New York, 1963). As *L'Accademia*, Rome, EIST, 1964; as *The Academy*, in *The Cage, The Academy, The Refrigerators*, 1977; as *Academy-Return*, in *Masterpieces of the Italian Theater* (New York) 1967.

La Vedova Bianca (produced Milan, 1963). Published in *Ridotto* (Rome), 1972; as *Mafia* (produced Tallahassee, Florida, 1966), Newark, Delaware, Proscenium Press, 1971.

La Telefonata (produced Rome, 1965). Rome, EIST, 1964; as *The Gift* (produced New York, 1966; London, 1972), in *Four Plays*, 1972.

I Seduttori (produced Venice, 1972). Published in *Il Dramma* (Turin), 1964; as *The Seducers*, music and lyrics by Ed Scott (produced New York, 1974), with *The Roman Guest*, Rome, Ora Zero, 1972.

I Frigoriferi (produced Pistoia, 1965). Published in *Ora Zero* (Udine), 1964; as *The Refrigerators* (produced New York, 1971), in *The Cage, The Academy, The Refrigerators*, 1977.

Le Spie (produced Pescara, 1967). Published as *The Spies*, in *Fusta* (New Jersey), 1978.

Eleonora Duse (produced Sarasota, Florida, 1967; New York, 1980). New York, Breakthrough Press, 1972.

Il Ponte (produced Pesaro, 1967). Published in *Ridotto* (Rome), 1967; as *The Bridge* (produced New York, 1972; London, 1980), New York, McGraw Hill, 1970.

The Victim (produced Sacramento, California, 1968; New York, 1973). As *La Vittima*, Rome, Lo Faro, 1972; as *The Victim*, in *Eleonora Duse, The Victim, Originality*, 1980.

Che Guevara (produced Toronto, 1968; New York, 1971). Published in *Enact* (New Delhi), April 1970; New York, French, 1980.

Unique (produced Baltimore, 1968). Published in *Ann Arbor Review* (Ann Arbor, Michigan), 1971.

L'Amico Cinese (produced Fano, 1969). Published in *Ridotto* (Rome), 1969; as *The Chinese Friend* (produced New York, 1972), in *Enact* (New Delhi), October 1972.

L'Ospite Romano (produced Pesaro, 1971). Rome, ENARS, 1969; as *The Roman Guest*, with *The Seducers*, Rome, Ora Zero, 1972.

La Panchina del Venerdi (produced Milan, 1970); as *The Friday Bench* (produced New York, 1971), in *Four Plays*, 1972.

Betrayals. Cosenza, Pellegrini, 1970; in *Drama and Theatre* (Fredonia, New York), 1970.

The Wish (produced Denton, Texas, 1971; London, 1972). Included in *Four Plays*, 1972.

The Other One (produced New York, 1971). Included in *Races*, 1972.

The Girl with a Ring on Her Nose (produced New York, 1971). Published in *Janus* (Seaside Park, New Jersey), 1972.

Too Much (produced New York, 1971). Published in *Janus* (Seaside Park, New Jersey), 1972.

Cybele (produced New York, 1971).

The Brothel (produced New York, 1972). Published in *Mediterranean Review* (Orient, New York), 1971.

Three Plays in Japanese (includes *Chile 1973, The Bridge, Che Guevara*) (produced in Japan). Tokyo, Mirai Sha, 1972.

The 75th (produced Florence, 1974; New York, 1980). Published in *Arcoscenico* (Rome), January 1972; in *Dramatika* (New York), 1976.

Notti d'amore, published in *Tempo Sensibile* (Novara), July 1972.

The Letter (produced New York, 1978). Published in *Tempo Sensibile* (Novara), September 1972; in *Wind* (Kentucky), 1974.

The Family (produced New York, 1972). Published in *Enact* (New Delhi), October 1972.

Four Plays. Houston, Edgemoor, 1972.

Three Minidramas, published in *Janus* (Seaside Park, New Jersey), 1972.

Rapes (produced New York, 1972). Included in *Races*, 1972.

Races: Six Short Plays (includes *Rapes, Fire, Dialogue with a Negro, White Cat, The Refusal, The Other One*). Newark, Delaware, Proscenium Press, 1972.

Dialogue with a Negro (produced New York, 1975). Included in *Races*, 1972.

Teatro Americano (includes *Fuoco, Sorelle, Violenze, Fami- glia*). Casale Monferrato, Tersite, 1972.

L'Ungherese (produced Florence, 1974). Published in *Tempo Sensibile* (Novara), 1972.

Dolls No More (produced London and Lafayette, Indiana, 1975). Published in *Drama and Theatre* (Fredonia, New York), Winter 1972-73.

Chile 1973 (produced Parma and New York, 1974). Published in *Enact* (New Delhi), October, November, and December 1973; in *Parola del Popolo* (Chicago), 1974.

New York: A Triptych (produced New York, 1974).

Patty Hearst, published in *Enact* (New Delhi), 1975; in *Parola del Popolo* (Chicago), 1975.

Madam Senator, music and lyrics by Ed Scott (produced New York, 1975).

Originality (produced New York, 1975). Included in *Eleonora Duse, The Victim, Originality*, 1980.

The Only Good Indian . . ., with Henry Salerno (produced New York, 1975). Published in *Drama and Theatre* (Fredonia, New York), 1975.

Tania, music by Paul Dick (produced New York, 1975).

Scene Americane (7 plays). Frascati-Roma, Tusculum, 1975.

Kissinger (produced California, 1976). Published in *Enact* (New Delhi), 1976.

Messages, published in *Dramatika* (New York), 1976.

The Cage, The Academy, The Refrigerators. New York, French, 1977.

Lunch with Fratti: The Letter, Her Voice, The Piggy Bank (produced New York, 1978). *The Piggy Bank* published in *Scholia Satyrica* (Tampa, Florida), 1977.

La Croce di Padre Marcello. Turin, Elle Di Ci, 1977.

The Biggest Thief in Town (produced New York, 1978).

Birthday. New York, French, n.d.

David, Son of Sam, published in *Ars-Uomo* (Rome), 1978.

Six Passionate Women, published in *Enact* (New Delhi), 1978.

Two Women (produced New York, 1981). Published in *Zone Press* (New York), 1978.
Sette Commedie. Frascati, Tusculum, 1979.
The Fourth One (produced New York, 1980). Published in *Il Ponte* (New York), May 1991.
Caccia al Morto, Mafia. Frascati, Tusculum, 1980.
The Pill (produced New York, 1980). Published in *Scholia Satyrica* (Tampa, Florida), 1980. Published in *Magazine* (Rome), 1981.
Eleonora Duse, The Victim, Originality. New York, French, 1980.
Nine, book by Arthur Kopit, music and lyrics by Maury Yeston, adaptation of the screenplay 81/2 by Federico Fellini (produced Waterford, Connecticut, 1981; New York, 1982). New York, French, 1983.
Half, published in *Other Stages* (New York), 1981.
Elbow to Elbow, adaptation of a play by Glauco Disalle (produced New York, 1982).
Il Pugnale Marocchino (produced L'Aquila, 1982). L'Aquila, Teatrama, 1982.
Viols, Feu (two plays) (produced Paris, 1983).
Four by Fratti (includes *The Suicide*, *The Return*, *The Victim*, *Eleonora Duse*). New York, French, 1986.
Our Family, Toys (two plays). New York, Griffin House Publications, 1986.
A.I.D.S. (produced London, 1987).
V.C.R. (produced Rome, 1988).
Thank you, Gorbachev!. New York, Wall to Wall Press, 1990.
Encounter (musical; produced Schenectady, New York, 1989). New York, French, 1992.
Two Centuries, with Penelope Bradford (produced New York, 1990). New York, French, 1992.
Lovers (produced New York, 1992). Published in *La Follia* (New York) 1991.
Six Plays by Fratti. Rome, E. R.G. Publishers, 1992.
2 Monologos, 2 Obras Cartas. Madrid, La Avispa Publishers, 1992.
Friends. Published in *The Bridge* (New York) Spring 1993.
Leningrado, L'Ungherese, Il Salvadanaio, Video (produced New York, Messina, L'Aquila, 1996). Published in *Ridotto* (Rome), 1996.
Beata, the Pope's Daughter (produced New York, 1996). New York, *Wall to Wall Press*, 1996.
Eight Plays in Russian. St. Petersburg, AC Publisher, 1996.
Sacrifici (five plays). Italy, Cosenza, 1996; as *Sacrifices*, in *Gradiva* (New York) 1997.
Sister (produced New York, 1997).
Le Promesse di San Michele. Published in *Drama Review–Wall to Wall* (New York) 1997.
Seven Minipiezes (*Alexia, Dina y Alba, Porno, Hermanas, Sinceridad, Fuego, Violencias)*. Valencia, Art Teatral, 1998.

Translations for Italian television: plays by David Shaw, Reginald Rose, Thomas W. Phipps, R. O. Hirson, J. P. Miller.

Poetry

Volti: Cento Poesie (Faces: 100 Poems). Bari, Mariano, 1960.

*

Bibliography: In *Ora Zero* (Udine), 1972; in *Four Plays*, 1972.

Manuscript Collection: Lincoln Center Library of the Performing Arts, New York.

Critical Studies: By Robert W. Corrigan, in *New Theatre of Europe II*, New York, Dell, 1964, and in *Masterpieces of the Modern Italian Theatre*, New York, Collier Macmillan, 1967; by Paul T. Nolan, in *Ora Zero* (Udine), 1972, and in *La Vittima*, 1972; *Mario Fratti* by Jane Bonin, Boston, Twayne, 1982; "Italian-American Playwrights on the Rise" by G. C. Di Scipio, in *Journal of Popular Culture* (Bowling Green, Ohio), Winter 1985; "The Way of the World According to Mario Fratti" by Nina Da Vinci Nichols, in *Modern Drama* (Downsview, Ontario), December 1993, pp. 519-28.

Mario Fratti comments:

I keep writing plays, at least one a year, because I have something to say. It is my way of being involved with the world that surrounds me. It is my way to comment on the jungle we are living in. Greed and hatred prevail today. I am trying to create characters who are the victims of greed and hatred. I indicate ways to unmask them.

* * *

Mario Fratti arrived in New York in 1963 as a foreign correspondent for the Italian press. He had already achieved some distinction in Italy as a playwright, and he made his American debut that same year with productions of *The Academy* and *The Return* at the Theatre De Lys. Although a critical success, the productions failed to establish Fratti as an important New York playwright. Undaunted, he continued writing. Translations of his plays appeared in prominent American literary journals and anthologies, and his works were produced throughout the United States and abroad and were evaluated in several academic studies. Fratti was an unusual phenomenon—a European playwright based in New York achieving national and international recognition without being produced in New York. While most playwrights struggled to crack the New York theatrical scene, Fratti imposed himself upon the city by the weight of his international success of more than 300 productions.

Fratti is fascinated with the idea of life as theater. Existing in an unknowable universe and caught in social systems beyond his control, man becomes an actor wearing an endless array of public and private masks as a means of survival. In such a world deceit, treachery, and violence are commonplace. While this theme has been explored by other modern writers, Fratti is unique for embracing clarity rather than obscurity in the theater. He is convinced that the playwright must be the "quintessence of clarity" both for the actor and the audience. Otherwise he is only "an hysterical poet talking to himself in front of a mirror." Fratti's rich theatrical imagination and impeccable craftsmanship assure clarity.

Comparable to the plots of the *commedia dell'arte,* many of Fratti's plays hinge on a deception, but the results are frequently pathetic or tragic rather than comic. While the characters are passionate and the situation tense, the structure is coldly logical and tight, progressing like a mystery thriller. The audience's sympathies shift from one character to another, for each seems to be on the side of right, and the truth is elusive. The conclusion, however, is not the revelation of a murderer but rather a provocative idea regarding the human condition. "I want to open a door in the minds of the audience," Fratti has said.

In *The Cage* Cristiano's pessimism is convincing, and his isolation seems justified. Ultimately, however, his moralizing proves destructive, and his murder of Pietro, the presumably cruel husband, is the megalomaniacal act of a man who would play God with other people's lives. Sanguemarcio, the invalid degenerate of *The Coffin,* pays to hear lurid tales of violence and perversion and is aided by his trusted friend Paoletto, who provides him with storytellers. But the tales are lies, and Paoletto is a thief and parasite using the old degenerate for profit. Sanguemarcio dies when he discovers that his one trusted friend was just another of life's frauds. Fratti, however, never moralizes. Deceived and deceiver are caught in a hopeless struggle for survival.

The dominant metaphor in Fratti's plays is the trap. Characters are trapped in situations they attempt to escape by violence or deception. Most of the plays are set indoors, in oppressive rooms or in a cage, which are concrete images of entrapment. Even the short, percussive titles of his plays suggest traps that have been sprung. But Fratti is not another modern pessimist. Although he dramatizes life's inferno, he believes in man's basic goodness: "I believe in man, man notwithstanding." In *The Bridge* a courageous policeman risks his life to save potential suicide victims, recalling a biblical parable that it is better to save one lost sheep than to keep a flock. The priest of *The Roman Guest* learns a new liberalism in America, confronts a prejudiced mob, and returns to Italy with a more profound sense of Christianity. *Che Guevara* is a heroic yet realistic depiction of the Argentine revolutionary, a man who views his actions as expedient rather than superhuman, which are necessary steps toward the positive evolution of society.

Fratti also has a subtle sense of comedy. Works such as *The Academy* and *Waiting* are humorous explorations of deceit and self-deception. In *The Academy,* which is set in postwar Italy, a Fascist attempts to revenge himself upon the United States by maintaining an academy for gigolos in pursuit of wealthy American women. The heroine of *Waiting* feigns docility in order to lure her seducer into marriage and then punish him by making his future life a hell. *The Refrigerators,* a dark comedy, is a bizarre parable of contemporary American life and technology, which is a unique departure from the essential realism of Fratti's drama. Transvestism and perversion are rampant, and the madcap events have a Marx Brothers quality.

The United States has had a significant influence on Fratti: "This society with all its problems and conflicts is fascinating. It's the ideal society for a modern dramatist." He now writes in English as well as Italian, and he evidences a remarkable ear for American speech, with a terseness and directness that suit the compactness of his dramatic structure. Living in the heart of Manhattan's theater district, Fratti has been continually stimulated by the city and inspired by the most seemingly insignificant event or occurrence around him: "I am a great observer. Faces are incredibly revealing. Just an expression can give me an idea for a play." He has described the scene that provided him with the idea for *The Chinese Friend,* a one-act masterpiece of racial prejudice that is filled with nuances regarding America's foreign policy in the Asia: "A very handsome, and elegantly attired American family passed me on the street. They seemed to be overly solicitous to a Chinese gentleman, who was, apparently, their guest."

The theme of cynicism has tended to come to override Fratti's humanism. The world is too much with him of late, embittered as he has become by the cruelty, violence, and obsessive war mentality of the post-Vietnam period. But he has remained deeply concerned about the poor, the underdog, and the perennially helpless victims of life's more skillful and deceptive players. A recurring metaphor is exposure—men and women enmeshed in a futile battle of the sexes and exposing their penchant for foolishness, deceit, and treachery. In his darker plays the exposure concerns buried guilts, jealousies, and hatreds that end in senseless tragedy.

In the comedy *Six Passionate Women* voyeurism and self-exposure dominate the lives of the film industry characters of the play. A man hater, appropriately named Mrs. Gunmore, sets out to avenge herself upon a film director, Nino, for what she regards as the male chauvinism and contempt for women evident in his work. *Nine* also centers on the travails of a film director, Guido Contini, but he is treated more sympathetically than is Nino. "Sometimes I neglect you," Guido tells his suffering wife, but he asks her to forgive him for his waywardness and exposure of their private life on film, which is his way of "creating and recreating." Adapted from Fellini's *8 1/2, Nine* dramatizes the central character's attempts toward self-understanding by exploring his guilts, desires, and fantasies through his characters. The work also satirizes the film industry's incongruous marriage of crass materialism and art through the character of the German financier Weissnicht, who backs Guido's latest film.

The Third Daughter and *Birthday* are two dark plays concerned with the theme of a father's incestuous desire for his daughter. In *The Third Daughter* Ilario decides to avenge himself on his adulterous wife by having the offspring of her infidelity, their third daughter, have an affair with a young man, thus destroying the girl's purity and tormenting his wife. The sordid tale is complex in its implications regarding family ties, hatreds, jealousies, and desires. Ilario's own daughters are acting out a love-hate relationship with their father, hating him for his cruel treatment of their mother and for his preferring their stepsister to them. He has not only denied them paternal love but also has aroused their jealousy, which is based on their own repressed incestuous desires. *Birthday* is a fascinating dramatization of incest that becomes madness. A father annually enacts the imagined return of his runaway daughter on her birthday. Women are brought in to assume the role coached by the servant, who encourages them to please the man and satisfy his incestuous desires.

In *The Piggy Bank* deception and exposure again prevail. A clever prostitute frightens off clients who have paid in advance by pretending to have venereal disease. She uses her victims and is in turn used by her husband in a vicious game of survival with no real winners. *The Letter* is one of Fratti's short chamber plays and is an excellent acting vehicle—brief, intense, and ambivalent.

Fratti is one of off-off-Broadway's most frequently performed playwrights, a tribute to his originality and willingness to explore uncomfortable truths about contemporary life. He finds fertile ground for his drama in the most apparently insignificant moments in the passing scene of everyday life, and he has a notebook filled with ideas for plays. "Look, I'll never be able to use them all in my lifetime." Let us hope that he is wrong.

—A. Richard Sogliuzzo

FRAYN, Michael

Nationality: British. **Born:** Mill Hill, London, 8 September 1933. **Education:** Sutton High School for Boys; Kingston Grammar

School, Surrey; Emmanuel College, Cambridge, B.A. 1957. **Military Service:** Served in the Royal Artillery and Intelligence Corps, 1952-54. **Family:** Married 1) Gillian Palmer in 1960 (marriage dissolved 1990), three daughters; 2) Claire Tomalin in 1993. **Career:** Reporter, 1957-59, and columnist, 1959-62, the *Guardian*, Manchester and London; columnist, the *Observer*, London, 1962-68. Lives in London. **Awards:** Maugham award, 1966; Hawthornden prize, 1967; National Press award, 1970; *Evening Standard* award, for play, 1976, 1981, 1983, 1985; Society of West End Theatre award, 1977, 1982; British Theatre Association award, 1981, 1983; Olivier award, 1985; New York Drama Critics Circle award, 1986; Emmy award, 1990; *Sunday Express* Book of the Year award, 1991. Honorary fellow, Emmanuel College, 1985. **Agent:** Elaine Greene Ltd., 37 Goldhawk Road, London W12 8QQ, England.

PUBLICATIONS

Plays

Zounds!, with John Edwards, music by Keith Statham (produced Cambridge, 1957).

Jamie, On A Flying Visit (televised 1968). With *Birthday*, London, Methuen, 1990.

Birthday (televised 1969). With *Jamie, On a Flying Visit*, London, Methuen, 1990.

The Two of Us (includes *Black and Silver, The New Quixote, Mr. Foot, Chinamen*) (produced London, 1970; Ogunquit, Maine, 1975; *Chinamen* produced New York, 1979). London, Fontana, 1970; *Chinamen* published in *The Best Short Plays 1973*, edited by Stanley Richards, Radnor, Pennsylvania, Chilton, 1973; revised version of *The New Quixote* (produced Chichester, Sussex, and London, 1980).

The Sandboy (produced London, 1971).

Alphabetical Order (produced London, 1975; New Haven, Connecticut, 1976). With *Donkeys' Years*, London, Eyre Methuen, 1977.

Donkeys' Years (produced London, 1976; New York, 1987). With *Alphabetical Order*, London, Eyre Methuen, 1977.

Clouds (produced London, 1976). London, Eyre Methuen, 1977.

The Cherry Orchard, adaptation of a play by Chekhov (produced London, 1978). London, Eyre Methuen, 1978.

Balmoral (produced Guildford, Surrey, 1978; revised version, as *Liberty Hall*, produced London, 1980; revised version, as *Balmoral*, produced Bristol, 1987). London, Methuen, 1987.

The Fruits of Enlightenment, adaptation of a play by Tolstoy (produced London, 1979). London, Eyre Methuen, 1979.

Make and Break (produced London, 1980; Washington, D.C., 1983). London, Eyre Methuen, 1980.

Noises Off (produced London, 1981; New York, 1983). London, Methuen, 1982; New York, French, 1985.

Three Sisters, adaptation of a play by Chekhov (produced Manchester and Los Angeles, 1985; London, 1987). London, Methuen, 1983.

Benefactors (produced London, 1984; New York, 1985). London, Methuen, 1984.

Wild Honey, adaptation of a play by Chekhov (produced London, 1984; New York, 1986). London, Methuen, 1984.

Number One, adaptation of a play by Jean Anouilh (produced London, 1984). London, French, 1985.

Plays I (includes *Alphabetical Order, Donkey's Years, Clouds, Make and Break, Noises Off*). London, Methuen, 1986.

The Seagull, adaptation of a play by Chekhov (produced Watford, Hertfordshire, 1986; London, 1990). London, Methuen, 1986.

Clockwise (screenplay). London, Methuen, 1986.

Exchange, adaptation of a play by Yuri Trifonov (broadcast 1986; produced Southampton, Hampshire, 1989; London, 1990). London, Methuen, 1990.

Uncle Vanya, adaptation of a play by Chekhov (produced London, 1988). London, Methuen, 1987.

Chekhov: Plays (includes *The Seagull, Uncle Vanya, Three Sisters, The Cherry Orchard*, four vaudevilles). London, Methuen, 1988.

The Sneeze, adaptation of works by Chekhov (produced Newcastle-upon-Tyne and London, 1988). London, Methuen, and New York, French, 1989.

First and Last (televised 1989). London, Methuen, 1989.

Look Look (as *Spettattori*, produced Rome, 1989; as *Look Look*, produced London, 1990). London, Methuen, 1990.

Listen to This: 21 Short Plays and Sketches. London, Methuen, 1991.

Plays: Two (includes *Benefactors*; *Balmoral*; *Wild Honey*). London, Methuen, 1992.

Audience. French, 1991.

Here (produced Donamr Warehouse, 1993). London, Methuen, 1993.

Now You Know (produced Hampstead Theatre, 1995). London, Methuen, 1995.

La Belle Vivette (opera libretto). ENO, 1995.

Screenplays: *Clockwise*, 1986; *Remember Me?*, 1997.

Radio Play: *Exchange*, adaptation of a play by Yuri Trifonov, 1986.

Television Plays and Documentaries: *Second City Reports*, with John Bird, 1964; *Jamie, on a Flying Visit*, 1968; *One Pair of Eyes*, 1968; *Birthday*, 1969; *Beyond a Joke* series, with John Bird and Eleanor Bron, 1972; *Laurence Sterne Lived Here* (*Writers' Houses* series), 1973; *Imagine a City Called Berlin*, 1975; *Making Faces*, 1975; *Vienna: The Mask of Gold*, 1977; *Three Streets in the Country*, 1979; *The Long Straight* (*Great Railway Journeys of the World* series), 1980; *Jerusalem*, 1984; *First and Last*, 1989; *Jamie on a Flying Visit & Birthday*, 1990; *Magic Lantern: Prague*, 1993; *Budapest: Written in Water*, 1996.

Novels

The Tin Men. London, Collins, 1965; Boston, Little Brown, 1966.

The Russian Interpreter. London, Collins, and New York, Viking Press, 1966.

Towards the End of the Morning. London, Collins, 1967; as *Against Entropy*, New York, Viking Press, 1967.

A Very Private Life. London, Collins, and New York, Viking Press, 1968.

Sweet Dreams. London, Collins, 1973; New York, Viking Press, 1974.

The Trick of It. London, Viking, 1989; New York, Viking, 1990.

A Landing on the Sun. London, Viking, 1991; London, Penguin, 1992; New York, Viking, 1992.

Now You Know. London, Viking, 1992; London, Penguin, 1993; New York, Viking, 1993; New York, Penguin, 1994.

Other

The Day of the Dog (*Guardian* columns). London, Collins, 1962; New York, Doubleday, 1963.
The Book of Fub (*Guardian* columns). London, Collins, 1963; as *Never Put Off to Gomorrah*, New York, Pantheon, 1964.
On the Outskirts (*Observer* columns). London, Fontana, 1967.
At Bay in Gear Street (*Observer* columns). New York, Fontana, 1967.
Constructions (philosophy). London, Wildwood House, 1974.
Great Railway Journeys of the World, with others. London, BBC Publications, 1981; New York, Dutton, 1982.
The Original Michael Frayn: Satirical Essays, edited by James Fenton. Edinburgh, Salamander Press, 1983.
Speak after the Beep (collection of columns). London, Methuen, 1995.

Editor, *The Best of Beachcomber*, by J. B. Morton. London, Heinemann, 1963.

*

Critical Studies: "Farce and Michael Frayn" by Katharine Worth, in *Modern Drama* (Downsview, Ontario), March 1983, pp. 47-53; introduction by Frayn to *Plays 1*, 1986; "Why This Farce?" by Vera Gottlieb, in *New Theatre Quarterly* (Cambridge, England), August 1991, pp. 217-28; "Michael Frayn and the World of Work" by Karen C. Blansfield, in *South Atlantic Review* (Atlanta, Georgia), November 1995, pp. 111-27; "Michael Frayn" by Karen C. Blansfield, in *British Playwrights, 1956-1995: A Research and Production Guide*, edited by William W. Demastes, Westport, Connecticut, Greenwood, 1996.

* * *

Michael Frayn deplored the so-called didactic drive of the 1970s because it replaced drama with ideology. Like his contemporary Alan Ayckbourn, Frayn consciously distinguished his work from the political drama that was sweeping the English stage at the beginning of the 1970s, asserting a return to traditional comic values. In contrast to Joe Orton, who treated tragic material as farce for shock effect, Frayn made farce a way of exposing the insensitivity of stock responses by showing potential tragedy beneath the comic surface. Laughter in Frayn is therefore frequently ambiguous, as in *Alphabetical Order:*

> Lucy: (*. . . starts to laugh again*) . . . I'm sorry. It's not funny!
> Nora: It's not at all funny.
> John: It's what one might call tragic irony. (*He starts to laugh*)

Frayn deals with society in terms of organizations—the news media, the manufacturing industry, the commercial theater—that intrinsically threaten the survival of humanity. Deadening order is always subverted, however unintentionally, and the life force triumphs, though at the expense of what the individuals concerned are striving for. Thus, the newspaper library of *Alphabetical Order* is overwhelmed by the accretion of trivia in the piles of yellowing newsprint. While the instant redundancy of the facts recorded in the clippings satirizes the illusory nature of what our news-fixated culture considers important, the confusion of the library files is presented as organic, a sign of individualism surviving even in what is, to take newspaper slang literally, a "morgue."

According to Frayn, what his plays "are all about . . . is the way in which we impose our ideas upon the world around us. In *Alphabetical Order* it is by classification, in *Make and Break* by consumption." This approach takes the form of challenging the way audiences perceive what they see on stage and is closely related to the subjects of his plays: the way news reportage categorizes events in *Alphabetical Order*, or the difference between socialist and capitalist views of the world, as in *Clouds,* which reflects Frayn's disorienting experiences as a journalist in Cuba.

His most successful play, *Noises Off,* applies this to the theater itself, taking as its title the technical term for behind-the-scenes activity that breaks the theatrical illusion. It juxtaposes backstage action with the rehearsal and performance of a mirror text, *Nothing On*, a highly artificial farce that echoes Ben Travers's *Rookery Nook.* The characters are stock figures on two overlapping levels. As actors they are the drunken old stager, the shortsighted sex symbol, and the fading television star investing in her own show to finance retirement. And they are cast as Shavian Burglar (à la *Heartbreak House*), dumb blond, and comic servant (duplicating the television soap role in which the aging actress made her name).

The catalyst on both back- and onstage levels is the director. His casual affairs with both the sex symbol and the assistant stage manager, hired because her father's firm is sponsoring the production, are a real-life version of the onstage characters' sexual activities. This behind-the-scenes promiscuity progressively disrupts the performance that he has so carefully organized in the rehearsal.

The act 1 dress rehearsal of *Nothing On* demonstrates the fragility of the ordered precision on which the performance of farce depends. Lines are forgotten, entries missed, doors jam at crucial moments or will not close, and the comedy misfires completely. It is the incompetence of the actors, not the antics of the characters, that is funny.

In the second act, when the perspective is reversed to show us the set from behind, the humor comes from mistaken motives and a series of emotional crises (typical of farce) that afflict the actors in the wings. The complete silence imposed on them by the ongoing performance on the other side of the thin scenery magnifies their misunderstandings and frustrations into hysterical comedy. In fact, *Noises Off* outdoes *Nothing On* in every way. The activity behind the scenes results in double the number of men with trousers round their ankles (including the director) and two seminude girls instead of the one in *Nothing On.* The chaos distorts the unseen performance, finally eclipsing it when the assistant stage manager's announcement of her pregnancy rings out through the theater just after the curtain lines, which are greeted with a deadly silence from the imaginary audience of *Nothing On.*

As Frayn has commented, "The fear that haunts [the cast] is that the unlearned and unrehearsed—the great dark chaos behind the set, inside the heart and brain—will seep back on to the stage. . . . Their performance will break down, and they will be left in front of us naked and ashamed." This fear is realized in the final act when, some months later in the tour, the mayhem behind the scenes has indeed spread onto the stage. As the performers hit each other over the head or are tripped and fall down the backstage stairs, the stage manager is forced to enter as a stand-in for one after another, only to have the injured actor stagger into view while he is still on the set. This culminates in no fewer than three comic burglars appearing when the old soak misses his entry. Believing him to be drunk, the stage manager dashes onstage to say his crucial lines, as does the director, believing that the stage manager is already on in another role, followed by the drunken actor himself. Under the pressure of such physical chaos the dialogue, uncertain at the best of times, disintegrates. In desperation the cast drags down the curtain between them and the audience.

This open theatrically—in which people are presented as performers and their social context as a stage set, so that everything is related to drama—is characteristic of the most inventive contemporary comedy. It is shared with Trevor Griffiths, Peter Barnes, and Tom Stoppard.

—Christopher Innes

FREEMAN, David

Nationality: Canadian. **Born:** Toronto, Ontario, 7 January 1945; palsied from birth. **Education:** Sunnyview School for the Handicapped, Toronto, 1951-61; McMaster University, Hamilton, Ontario (news features editor, university newspaper), 1966-71, B.A. in political science 1971. **Career:** Public relations officer, IBM, Don Mills, Ontario, 1970. **Awards:** Ontario Council for the Arts grant, 1971; Canada Council grant, 1972, 1974; Chalmers award, 1972; Drama Desk award, 1973; Edinburgh Fringe Festival first, 1979; Los Angeles Critics Circle award (three), 1983. **Agent:** Agence Goodwin, 839 Shrebrooke East, Suite 2, Montreal, Quebec H2L 1K6, Canada.

Publications

Plays

Creeps (produced Toronto, 1971; Washington, D.C., and New York, 1973; Edinburgh, 1979; London, 1981). Toronto, University of Toronto Press, 1972; New York and London, French, 1975.

Battering Ram (produced Toronto, 1973; New York, 1975; revised version as *Le Bélier*, produced Montreal, 1984). Toronto, Playwrights, 1972.

You're Gonna Be Alright, Jamie-Boy (produced Toronto, 1974; New York, 1977; London, 1990). Vancouver, Talonbooks, 1974.

Flytrap (produced Montreal, 1976). Toronto, Playwrights, 1980.

Radio Plays: *Year of the Soul*, in Quebec Heroes and Anti-Heroes series, 1982.

Other

A Hollywood Life. Joseph, 1991.

*

Critical Study: Article by G. Anthony, in *Stage Voices*, edited by Anthony, Toronto, Doubleday Canada, 1978.

David Freeman comments:

(1973) *Creeps* is an autobiographical play which takes place one afternoon in the men's washroom of a sheltered workshop for the cerebral palsied. It has four main characters: Tom, Jim, Pete, and Sam. The four congregate in the washroom in order to get away from such menial and boring tasks as sanding blocks, separating nuts and bolts, folding boxes, and weaving rugs. The main conflict is between Tom, who considers himself an abstract artist and wants to leave the workshop to devote more time to his painting, and Jim, who has recently been promoted to office work and would prefer that Tom stay in the workshop where life is less complicated. Pete is lazy and is content to let the world wait on him, while Sam is bitter, cruel, foul-mouthed, and lecherous. This afternoon they talk about sexual frustration, broken dreams, and rage at a society which has condemned them to the mercy of false charity and at themselves for accepting it. The play came out of my own experiences in such a place ten years ago, for I myself am afflicted with cerebral palsy.

(1993) *Battering Ram*, a play which explores emotional and sexual taboos, followed *Creeps*. My third work, *You're Gonna Be Alright, Jamie-Boy*, allowed me to look at the taboos and emotional trauma of the nuclear family. In *Flytrap*, I threw my audience a curve when I created a family where there should never have existed one; a middle-aged childless couple tries to play parent to a young man in his twenties.

Presently, I continue to work on a number of scripts and novels. The plays are periodically workshopped and receive readings. The novel which I am now revising tells the story of young people caught up in the changes of the late 1960s. The setting is a rural university campus. The action is a concoction of truth and the exaggerations of youth.

* * *

David Freeman's world is one of cripples, both physical and psychological, and one that mirrors the equally crippled morality, aspirations, and institutions of the real world that surrounds his fictional world and that causes or assists in the deforming of his various victims. It follows, therefore, that his characters and plots are naturalistic, although dramatic hyperbole often breaks into the otherwise naturalistic conception in the form of stereotype leading to caricature, as in *You're Gonna Be Alright, Jamie-Boy,* or of intensely theatrical and fantastic vignettes superimposed on the plot, as in the circus interludes of *Creeps*. The result in *Creeps* is the creation of a shockingly powerful dramatic vehicle for Freeman's bitter but balanced attack on his audience, its physical normality, its ignorance of the humiliation experienced by an adult trapped in the crippled body of a hideous child, and, finally and most unrelentingly, its pity. It is in the dramatic rather than the thematic elements that Freeman most devastatingly exposes the shallow and self-gratifying attempts of the charitable institutions to invade this "sheltered" world. In its virtually terroristic design, the play hurls its washroom set, sexual frustration, unremittingly obscene language, and grotesque mime at the audience in a coup de théâtre that the more controlled and mature later plays cannot approach. The design is so compelling and dramatically so powerful that in production the audience, stunned by Freeman's ferocity, accepts elements—the exaggeration of the foul language, for example—that it would not credit in print. In the later plays, where his personal anger becomes less acute, Freeman cannot assume the same overwhelmed acceptance by his audience, although, regrettably, he sometimes does so.

Battering Ram reworks the theme of sexual frustration, and in its removal of the physically repulsive loses much of the dramatic strength of *Creeps*. Still, the play makes an arresting statement and, more importantly, builds it around a full characterization of the protagonist. In this focus and in its largely successful execution, Freeman evidences his growth as a playwright, moving as he does into more literary and less personal devices. The play is also a movement into the more commercial theater, employing themes that become more popular as they become less personal.

In *You're Gonna Be Alright, Jamie-Boy,* Freeman created a play in the neonaturalistic school that became popular in Canadian drama in the 1970s. In moving completely from his physically crippled familiars, Freeman unfortunately created rather clichéd North American types working out a predictable pattern based on the emptiness of television-oriented lives. After the strength of the earlier plays, this reworking of a commonplace situation seems facile, and in many respects it seems more like a first play than the third in a series. In its investigation of the psychology of the characters, however, it holds together well given the shallow range of personality each exhibits. Freeman looks at stereotypical characters, but he looks at them reasonably well, especially through dialogue that often picks up the verve of *Creeps* and sometimes leaps into moments of real comedy and pathos.

Freeman's fourth play, *Flytrap,* moves further into the realm of the commercial, and it does so with considerable success. In its first production in Montreal in 1976, Myron Galloway of the *Montreal Star* called the play "straightforward, well crafted, entertaining and unpretentious," and it has been seen as a significant example of a movement in contemporary Canadian theater away from self-consciously social themes and into middle-class issues with a broad base of appeal. This is particularly interesting in the case of Freeman because of the very specialized concerns of *Creeps* that had previously obsessed him. The dramatic tone and staging of the play also differs. It moves at a leisurely pace through the struggle of a married but childless couple to come to terms with the new presence in their troubled marriage of a surrogate son of mature years. This strange triangle is explored without the bombast of the early work—until the end, at least, when the principals finally fight out their frustration—and the treatment is much lighter and more ironic than in the previous plays. The critical dilemma is to determine whether a more controlled discussion of average material is more or less laudable than an uncontrolled scream through the highly unusual and astonishing world of *Creeps*.

Freeman has proved himself a professional man of the theater. He has not, however, matched the brilliance of his first play by incorporating its energy in a fully mature framework.

—Reid Gilbert

FRENCH, David

Nationality: Canadian. **Born:** Coley's Point, Newfoundland, 18 January 1939. **Education:** Harbord Collegiate High School; Oakwood Collegiate High School, Toronto, graduated 1958; studied acting at Al Saxe Studio, Toronto, 1958, Pasadena Playhouse, California, 1959, and Lawlor School of Acting, Toronto, 1960. **Family:** Married Leslie Gray in 1979. **Career:** Actor in Toronto, 1960-65; post office worker, 1967-68. Lives in Toronto. **Awards:** Chalmers award, 1973; Lieutenant-Governor's award, 1974; Canada Council grant, 1974, 1975; Dora award, 1985; Hollywood Drama-Logue Critics award, 1985, and Hollywood Drama League award, 1985, both for *Salt-Water Moon*; Canadian Authors Association award, 1986. **Agent:** Shain Jaffe, Great North Artists, 350 DuPont Street, Toronto, Ontario M5R 1V9, Canada.

Publications

Plays

Leaving Home (produced Toronto, 1972; New York, 1974). Toronto, New Press, 1972; New York and London, French, 1976.

Of the Fields, Lately (produced Toronto, 1973; New York, 1980). Toronto, Playwrights, 1973; New York, French, 1975.

One Crack Out (produced Toronto, 1975; New York, 1978). Toronto, Playwrights, 1975; Toronto, New Press, 1976.

The Seagull, adaptation of a play by Chekhov (produced Toronto, 1977). Toronto, Playwrights, 1977; Vancouver, Talon Books, 1993.

Jitters (produced Toronto and New Haven, Connecticut, 1979). Toronto, Playwrights, 1980; Vancouver, Talon Books, 1980.

The Riddle of the World (produced Toronto, 1981).

Salt-Water Moon (produced Toronto, 1984; Costa Mesa, California, 1985; Edinburgh, 1986). Toronto, Playwrights, 1985; New York, Dramatists Play Service, 1988; Vancouver, Talon Books, 1988.

The Forest, adaptation (produced Toronto, 1987).

1949 (produced Toronto, 1989). Vancouver, Talon Books, 1989.

Silver Dagger (produced Toronto, 1992).Vancouver, Talon Books, 1993.

Radio Plays: *Angeline*, 1967; *Invitation to a Zoo*, 1967; *Winter of Timothy*, 1968.

Television Plays: *Beckons the Dark River*, 1963; *The Willow Harp*, 1964; *A Ring for Florrie*, 1964; *After Hours*, 1964; *Sparrow on a Monday Morning*, 1966 (USA); *A Token Gesture*, 1970; *The Tender Branch*, 1972; *The Happiest Man in the World*, from a short story by Hugh Garner, 1972; scripts for *Razzle Dazzle* children's series.

*

Critical Study: "David French" by Cynthia Zimmerman, in *Profiles in Canadian Literature* (Toronto), 1982.

* * *

The first of David French's stage plays, *Leaving Home,* concerns the sense of displacement and frustration of a family of Irish immigrants who have been torn from their roots, not once but twice, first from Ireland to Newfoundland and then from Newfoundland to Toronto. They carry with them the luggage of their past—Catholic-Protestant antagonisms, family loyalties and bitter dissension, a salty vituperation, and a habit of convivial overdrinking. Because of their double displacement the past has become meaningless, yet the older generation retains it and struggles to relate it to the future. The play's theme is the ancient one of a son's need to free himself from his father, which is paralleled and reinforced by the theme of the alienation of the immigrant from his children in the new land.

The Mercer family organization is not unlike that in Arthur Miller's *Death of a Salesman,* with Mary Mercer loving but ineffectual in her efforts to keep the family peace and to protect her husband, Jacob, and eldest son, Ben, from hurting each other. Jacob's life has been damaged by a brutal, uncaring father, the early death of his mother, and an interrupted education. In Ben, Jacob dreams of living again, successful in a socially esteemed profession and with a warm father-son relationship, yet he sneers at the university education that is his son's path to a better life.

The action of the play takes place in the Mercer kitchen and parlor, rendered with an effect of cramped and unlovely realism, on the wedding day of the younger son, Billy, who has gotten his high school girlfriend pregnant. She is Catholic and the daughter of Minnie Jackson, a sweetheart of Jacob's youth, a woman he did not marry because of her religion and because of her randy and slipshod behavior, which still both attracts and repels him. Instead he married Protestant Mary, who was pretty, austere, and middle-class. The wedding triggers a series of painful reminiscences and violent reactions in Jake, not against Billy, who is marrying a Catholic, abandoning school, and the traditional prejudices of the Irish in general, but against Ben, whose leaving home Jacob regards with anguish as the death of all his hopes.

The sequel to this play, *Of the Fields, Lately,* deals with Ben's return home after two futile years in the prairies, ostensibly summoned for the funeral of his aunt but actually because of the growing frailty of his father. The play is permeated with a sense of death, but the funeral device does not create as tight a dramatic unity as does the wedding in *Leaving Home*. The same temperamental antagonisms arise between Jacob and Ben and complete their alienation, which is shown by the use of soliloquies of reminiscence by both characters at the beginning of the play and by Ben alone after his father's death at the end. This single departure from realism frames the play, declaring symbolically at the opening and reaffirming at the closing the sense of isolation felt by each character.

Yet rejection and alienation are not the whole story. Jake has a vitality lacking in his sons, although it has been warped into boasting, empty heroics at his job and by heavy drinking. Ben instinctively recognizes his father's superiority and feels a dogged sense of duty and even respect, but he cannot bear to be enslaved by Jacob's disappointments and dead values.

The realism of the first two works is pushed to greater extremes in French's third play, *One Crack Out,* which deals with the tawdry life of petty criminals and pool hall gamblers. The set is divided between the squalid pool hall and adjoining lavatory and the equally squalid bed-sitting-room of Charlie, a pool shark, and his wife Helen, a stripper. These claustrophobic interiors, plus 11 short scenes tumbling upon one another, build up tension as the deadline approaches for Charlie to pay the collector the $3,000 he owes or get his hands broken.

As all of his efforts to raise the money by borrowing and hustling fail, Charlie emerges as not only devious and frantic but also as one who is capable of loyalty and unselfish feeling. With his losing streak ended through an act of pure devotion by Helen, he is able to resolve his problem on his own terms by a duel of skill. In creating Charlie's dilemma and preventing any avenue of escape, French has overplotted the play, and its emotional power is diffused by melodramatic effects such as the breathlessly approaching deadline, the complication of Charlie's sexual impotence with his wife, and the unprepared-for conversion of the collector to accepting Charlie's challenge debt. Despite the fact that the play is less strong than French's first two, it marks a forward step in his development by moving away from the autobiographical into an invented, objective world.

French's first comedy was *Jitters,* the title of which reflects the feelings of a group of Canadian actors as they rehearse a play they expect to be seen by an important New York director. He will, they hope, pave their way to Broadway, the necessary seal of success in Canada. During the action they reveal the uncertainty and inferiority felt by Canadian artists in the shadow of the United States.

The play begins with a trompe l'oeil effect of a play within a play that the audience thinks is the real thing until, after several minutes, the director leaps up from a theater seat with "cut, cut!" This sudden break from "theatrical" harmony to "real life" rivalry points up the personal antagonism between Jessica, who has star billing, and Patrick, the leading actor who is outraged that his long, successful career in Canada counts for less than Jessica's two flops on Broadway. It is her former director in New York who operates as a nemesis, increasing both the hopes and jitters of everyone, including the playwright. The director's failure to attend the performance is the final irony of Canadian-American relations, in theater as in everything, underscoring the Canadian sense of American imperviousness and indifference.

In *Salt-Water Moon* French returns to Newfoundland and autobiographical themes with a play that, in time, precedes *Leaving Home* by depicting the courtship of Jacob Mercer and Mary Snow. The play is set on the front porch and in the yard of the summer home of the local M.P., where Mary is in service, and is confined to the 90-minute running time of the action. (There is no intermission.) It focuses narrowly on Jacob and Mary, their frustrated love, their poverty, and their poignant struggle in different ways to help their families: Mary to save her sister from the brutality of an orphan asylum, and Jacob to spare his father the humiliation of being "in collar," a pernicious employment system devised by the local fishing bosses.

The play's tension arises not from suspense about whether the lovers will finally resolve their differences but about how they will do so. Their meeting after a year's absence begins in recrimination—hers for his sudden departure and his for her having become engaged to his archenemy's son. The evening proceeds with a series of explanations that reveal their experiences of suffering, death, and poverty along with their strength and tenacity. It ends with harmony being reestablished under the "salt-water moon." As always, French's dialogue is affecting and funny, nostalgic and poetic, with the resonance of Newfoundland Irish idiom.

—Dorothy Parker

FRIEDMAN, Bruce Jay

Nationality: American. **Born:** New York City, 26 April 1930. **Education:** De Witt Clinton High School, Bronx, New York; University of Missouri, Columbia, 1947-51, Bachelor of Journalism 1951. **Military Service:** Served in the United States Air Force, 1951-53: lieutenant. **Family:** Married 1) Ginger Howard in 1954 (divorced 1977), three children; 2) Patricia J. O'Donohue in 1983, one daughter. **Career:** Editorial director, Magazine Management Company, publishers, New York, 1953-56; visiting professor of literature, York College, City University, New York, 1974-76. **Address:** P.O. Box 746, Water Mill, New York 11976, U.S.A.

Publications

Plays

23 Pat O'Brien Movies, adaptation of his own short story (produced New York, 1966).
Scuba Duba: A Tense Comedy (produced New York, 1967). New York, Simon and Schuster, 1968.
A Mother's Kisses, music by Richard Adler, adaptation of the novel by Friedman (produced New Haven, Connecticut, 1968).
Steambath (produced New York, 1970). New York, Knopf, 1971.
First Offenders, with Jacques Levy (also co-director: produced New York, 1973).
A Foot in the Door (produced New York, 1979).
Have You Spoken to Any Jews Lately? (produced New York, 1995).

Screenplays: *The Owl and the Pussycat*, 1971; *Stir Crazy*, 1980; *Doctor Detroit*, with others, 1983; *Splash*, with others, 1984.

Novels

Stern. New York, Simon and Schuster, 1962; London, Deutsch, 1963.
A Mother's Kisses. New York, Simon and Schuster, 1964; London, Cape, 1965.
The Dick. New York, Knopf, 1970; London, Cape, 1971.
About Harry Towns. New York, Knopf, 1974; London, Cape, 1975.
Tokyo Woes. New York, Fine, 1985; London, Abacus, 1986.
The Current Climate. New York, Atlantic Monthly Press, 1989.
A Father's Kisses. New York, Fine, 1995.

Short Stories

Far from the City of Class and Other Stories. New York, Frommer-Pasmantier, 1963.
Black Angels. New York, Simon and Schuster, 1966; London, Cape, 1967.
Let's Hear It for a Beautiful Guy and Other Works of Short Fiction. New York, Fine, 1984.
The Collected Stories of Bruce Jay Friedman. New York, Fine, 1995.

Other

The Lonely Guy's Book of Life. New York, McGraw Hill, 1978.
The Slightly Older Guy. New York, Simon and Schuster, 1994.

Editor, *Black Humor*. New York, Bantam, and London, Corgi, 1965.

*

Critical Studies: *Bruce Jay Friedman* by Max F. Schulz, New York, Twayne, 1974; "Bruce Jay Friedman's Fiction: Black Humour and After" by David Seed, in *Thalia: Studies in Literary Humor* (Ottawa, Ontario), Spring-Summer 1988, pp. 14-22.

Theatrical Activities:
Director: **Play**—*First Offenders* (co-director, with Jacques Levy), New York, 1973.

* * *

It has always been the temptation of fiction writers to turn to the theater. From Balzac through Henry James nineteenth-century novelists tried their hand at playwriting, with quite mixed results. Most of us are now interested in only one of Balzac's plays, *Mercadet*, and that probably because of its influence on *Waiting for Godot*. James's plays are readily available in Leon Edel's fine edition, but only specialists seem to bother to read them. The same is true for most of the plays of the other nineteenth-century novelists-turned-dramatist. This rule of thumb applies also to certain of our contemporaries. Saul Bellow and John Hawkes, for example, have turned from first-rate fiction to the theater, with results that have been somewhat frustrating and disappointing.

The case of Hawkes is instructive, for his plays seem largely extensions of his novels and elaborate on certain of their themes. Hawkes had already published four superb novels by the time he brought out his collection of plays, *The Innocent Party*, in 1966. It would seem that he turned to the theater only after he felt that his position as a novelist was fairly assured. Bruce Jay Friedman appeared to follow the same pattern, although he turned to playwriting earlier in his career than did Hawkes. His change from fiction to drama was also managed, from all indications, with fewer problems. *Scuba Duba* and *Steambath* are clearly more stageable, if less literary, than Hawkes's plays.

But, like the plays in *The Innocent Party*, Friedman's work for the theater is thematically very much tied to his fiction. *Scuba Duba* and *Steambath* use the ambience, character types, and other literary props familiar to readers of Friedman's novels and collections of stories. Guilt, failure, and frustration are words that come to mind when we look at any part of his oeuvre.

Scuba Duba bears the subtitle "a tense comedy." This might be said of almost everything Friedman has written, for laughs come at the expense of overbearing psychic pain in all of his work. Harold Wonder, a 35-year-old worrier who uses a scythe as an aggressive kind of security blanket, has rented a chateau in the south of France. As the play opens, he laments the fact that his wife has just run off with a black man. Harold's urban Jewish intonation is evident even in his first speech: "I really needed this. This is exactly what I came here for." He feels the need to communicate his *tsuris* to anyone who will listen. An attractive young woman, Miss Janus, is all too willing to help out, but Harold, like most of Friedman's heroes, seems especially drawn to his psychiatrist and his mother. The former, aptly named Dr. Schoenfeld, who appears in the first act as a "cut-out" and returns in the flesh in act 2, warns him in accustomed psychiatric fashion, ". . . you've never once looked at life sideways. . . ." Harold's mother seems cut from the same cloth as the mothers in Friedman's novels *Stern*, *A Mother's Kisses*, and *The Dick*. Harold speaks to her long-distance, and the telephone conversation that takes place should be familiar to readers of the fiction of Philip Roth, Wallace Markfield, Herbert Gold, and other American Jewish writers. Harold's mother's voice is perfectly tuned: "That's all right, Harold. I'll just consider that my payment after thirty-six years of being your mother."

As the play, develops the stage becomes more and more crowded. A name-dropping French landlady, an American tourist who demands proximity to a Chinese restaurant, a thief with an aphoristic turn ("All men are thieves"), an anti-American gendarme, a "wild-looking blonde" named Cheyenne who prefers "Bernie" Malamud and "those urban Jews" to C. P. Snow—all appear at one time or another. The main confrontation occurs in the second act when Harold's wife appears, followed shortly by two black men, one of whom is her lover. Harold's reaction involves much of the ambivalence experienced by Friedman's Jews when in the company of blacks. The hero of Friedman's first novel, for example, went out of his way to express an affection he was never certain to be compelling enough: ". . . Stern, who had a special feeling for all Negroes, hugged him [Crib] in a show of brotherhood."

Harold, schlemiel that he is, ends up by losing his wife and vows to "get started in my new life." Stern and Kenneth LePeters, the hero of *The Dick,* make similar resolutions, and LePeters even goes to the point of leaving his wife and planning an extended trip with his daughter.

Friedman has been grouped with the so-called black humorists on several occasions. In a foreword he wrote for the collection of stories *Black Humor,* which included his own story "Blank Angels," he remarked, "There *is* a fading line between fantasy and reality. . . ." This is evident in *Scuba Duba* but perhaps even more so in *Steambath.* Almost half way through the first act, the protagonist Tandy makes the shocked discovery that ". . . We're dead? Is that what you were going to say? That's what I was going to say. That's what we are. The second I said it, I knew it. Bam! Dead! Just like that! Christ!" Until this point in the play all indications are that this is a real steam bath. Everything then suddenly dilates into symbol and fantasy, with no noticeable change in the dramatic movement. (John Hawkes used a steam bath in the fifth chapter of his novel *The Lime Twig* with somewhat the same symbolic intent.)

Tandy is clearly not quite ready for death and protests the attendant's (God's) decision through the remainder of the play. He seems very much like Kenneth LePeters at the end of *The Dick.* After having divorced his wife and given up his job "teaching art appreciation over at the Police Academy," he is on the verge of doing things he likes—writing a novel about Charlemagne, working for a charity to help brain-damaged welders, courting a Bryn Mawr girl who makes shish kebab. Tandy shares his frustration with a blond girl named Meredith in somewhat the way Harold Wonder shared his plight, conversationally, with Miss Janus in *Scuba Duba.*

Max Schulz, in a very good book on the American Jewish novel, *Radical Sophistication,* speaks of Friedman's manner as having something "of the stand-up comic." This is especially noticeable in *Steambath.* Its humor favors the incongruous and unlikely. One can almost hear Woody Allen pronouncing some of the lines with considerable relish, for example, Tandy's incredulous response when he realizes that God is a Puerto Rican steam bath attendant or when he discovers what he stands to lose by being dead: "No more airline stewardesses . . . *Newsweek* . . . Jesus, no more *Newsweek.*"

Much of the humor has to do with popular culture. Bieberman, who makes intermittent appearances, is very much taken with the actors and baseball players of the 1940s. Other characters refer to the impact made by such essentials of television as the *David Frost Show* and pro football (American style). Names of every variety, including those of defeated political candidates (Mario Procaccino) and editors of magazines (Norman Podhoretz), are introduced incongruously and irreverently in the conversations. Theodore Solotaroff believes that

> nostalgia has a particular attraction for many Jewish writers: some of them, like Gold or Bruce Jay Friedman or Wallace Markfield or Irwin Faust, seem to possess virtually total recall of their adolescent years, as though there were still some secret meaning that resides in the image of Buster Brown shoes, or Edward G. Robinson's snarl, or Ralston's checkerboard package.

How much to the point of this remark is *Steambath.*

There is a good deal of the spirit of the second-generation American Jew in Friedman's plays as well as in his novels. He has caught this verbal rhythm and pulse beat in much the way that Philip Roth and Woody Allen have.

—Melvin J. Friedman

FRIEL, Brian (Bernard Patrick Friel)

Nationality: Irish. **Born:** Killyclogher, County Tyrone, 9 January 1929. **Education:** St. Columb's College, Derry, 1941-46; St. Patrick's College, Maynooth, 1946-49, B.A. 1949; St. Mary's Training College (now St. Joseph's College of Education), Belfast, 1949-50. **Family:** Married Anne Morrison in 1954; four daughters and one son. **Career:** Schoolteacher in primary and intermediate schools in Derry, 1950-60. Full-time writer, 1960—. Founder, with Stephen Rea, Field Day Theatre Company, Northern Ireland, 1980. Observer, for five months in 1963, Tyrone Guthrie Theatre, Minneapolis. Member of Irish Senate, 1987. **Awards:** Irish Arts Council Macauley fellowship, 1963; Christopher Ewart-Biggs Memorial award, 1982; New York Drama Critics Circle award, 1989, 1991; Olivier award, 1991; *Evening Standard* award, 1991; *Plays and Players* award, 1991; Writers Guild of Great Britain award, 1991; Tony award, 1992. D.Litt.: Rosary College, Chicago, 1979; National University of Ireland, Dublin, 1983; University of Ulster, Coleraine, 1986; Queen's University, Belfast, 1992; Trinity College, Dublin, 1992. Honorary senior fellow, University College, Dublin, 1998. **Member:** Irish Academy of Letters, 1972; Aosdana, 1983; and American Academy of Arts and Letters, 1996. **Agent:** The Agency, 24 Pottery Lane, Holland Park, London W11 4LZ, England. **Address:** Drumaweir House, Greencastle, County Donegal, Ireland.

Publications

Plays

The Francophile (produced Belfast, 1960; as *The Doubtful Paradise*, produced Belfast, 1960).

The Enemy Within (produced Dublin, 1962). Dublin, Gallery Press, and Newark, Delaware, Proscenium Press, 1979.

The Blind Mice (produced Dublin, 1963; Belfast, 1964).

Philadelphia, Here I Come! (produced Dublin, 1964; New York, 1966; London, 1967). London, Faber, 1965; New York, Farrar Straus, 1966.

The Loves of Cass McGuire (broadcast 1966; produced New York, 1966; Belfast, 1968; London, 1970). London, Faber, and New York, Farrar Straus, 1967.
Lovers: Part One: Winners; Part Two: Losers (produced Dublin, 1967; New York, 1968; London, 1969). New York, Farrar Straus, 1968; London, Faber, 1969.
Crystal and Fox (produced Dublin, 1968; Los Angeles, 1970; New York, 1973). London, Faber, 1970; with *The Mundy Scheme*, New York, Farrar Straus, 1970.
The Mundy Scheme (produced Dublin and New York, 1969). With *Crystal and Fox*, New York, Farrar Straus, 1970.
The Gentle Island (produced Dublin, 1971). London, Davis Poynter, 1974.
The Freedom of the City (produced Dublin, London, and Chicago, 1973; New York, 1974). London, Faber, 1974; New York, French, 1979.
Volunteers (produced Dublin, 1975). London, Faber, 1979.
Living Quarters (produced Dublin, 1977; New York, 1983). London, Faber, 1978; in *Selected Plays*, 1984.
Faith Healer (produced New York, 1979; London, 1981). London, Faber, 1980; in *Selected Plays*, 1984.
Aristocrats (produced Dublin, 1979; London, 1988; New York 1989). Dublin, Gallery Press, 1980; in *Selected Plays*, 1984.
Translations (produced Derry, 1980; New York and London, 1981). London, Faber, 1981; in *Selected Plays*, 1984.
American Welcome (produced Louisville and New York, 1980). Published in *The Best Short Plays 1981*, edited by Stanley Richards, Radnor, Pennsylvania, Chilton, 1981.
Three Sisters, adaptation of a play by Chekhov (produced Derry, 1981). Dublin, Gallery Press, 1981.
The Communication Cord (produced Derry, 1982; London, 1983; Seattle, 1984). London, Faber, 1983.
Selected Plays (includes *Philadelphia, Here I Come!*; *The Freedom of the City*; *Living Quarters*; *Aristocrats*; *Faith Healer*; *Translations*). London, Faber, 1984; Washington, D.C., Catholic University of America Press, 1986.
Fathers and Sons, adaptation of a novel by Turgenev (produced London, 1987). London, Faber, 1987.
Making History (produced Derry and London, 1988; New York, 1991). London, Faber, 1989.
Dancing at Lughnasa (produced Dublin and London, 1990; New York, 1991). London, Faber, 1990.
The London Vertigo, adaptation of a play by Charles MacKlin (produced Dublin, 1992).
A Month in the Country, adaptation of the play by Turgenev (produced Dublin, 1992).
Wonderful Tennessee (produced Dublin, 1993; New York, 1994). Penguin, n.d.
Give Me Your Answer, Do! (produced Dublin, 1997). Oldcastle, Ireland, Gallery Books, 1997.

Screenplay: *Philadelphia, Here I Come!*, 1970.

Radio Plays: *A Sort of Freedom*, 1958; *To This Hard House*, 1958; *The Founder Members*, 1964; *The Loves of Cass McGuire*, 1966.

Short Stories

The Saucer of Larks. New York, Doubleday, 1962; London, Gollancz, 1963.
The Gold in the Sea. London, Gollancz, and New York, Doubleday, 1966.
A Saucer of Larks: Stories of Ireland (selection). London, Arrow, 1969.
Selected Stories. Dublin, Gallery Press, 1979.
The Diviner. Dublin, O'Brien Press, and London, Allison and Busby, 1983.

Other

The Last of the Name, by Charles McGlinchey. Belfast, Blackstaff Press, 1986.

*

Bibliography: *Ten Modern Irish Playwrights* by Kimball King, New York, Garland, 1979.

Critical Studies: *Brian Friel* by D. E. S. Maxwell, Lewisburg, Pennsylvania, Bucknell University Press, 1973; *Brian Friel: The Growth of an Irish Dramatist* by Ulf Dantanus, Gothenburg, Sweden, Gothenburg Studies in English, 1985, London, Faber, 1987; *The Achievement of Brian Friel*, edited by Alan Peacock, Colin Smythe, 1989; *Brian Friel* by Ulick O'Conner, Elo Publications, 1989; *Brian Friel* by George O'Brien, Dublin, Gill and Macmillan, and Boston, Twayne, 1990; *Brian Friel and Ireland's Drama* by Richard Pine, London, Routledge, 1990; *The Art of Brian Friel* by Elmer Andrews, MacMillan, 1995.

* * *

Brian Friel began as a writer of short stories, and the art of the short story permeates all of his dramatic work. His drama is lyrical, intimate, and understated in ways perhaps more common to the short story form than to the stage. Yet Friel has proved, during a career spanning 30 years, his theatrical skill in arousing and maintaining audience interest, and his narrative power, therefore, cannot be described satisfactorily in terms of the short story writer. One should recall that Chekhov, the writer with whom Friel is most often compared, also had two strings to his bow.

After a few radio plays written for BBC Northern Ireland, Friel's first significant stage play, *The Enemy Within*, was written for the Abbey Theatre. The significance lies less in the play itself, a history play set in the seventh century, than in its introduction of Friel as an Abbey playwright. This tradition, which was founded by Yeats and Synge and carried on by O'Casey, was by 1962 much attenuated, yet the role it provided for Irish playwrights was still nominally, if problematically, available to mediate between individual vision and social or sociopolitical reality. Friel's originality lay in his perception of the critical state of this relationship in modern Irish life. For Friel there was an unacknowledged gap between the individual mind and experience and a social reality that was crumbling at an alarming rate, so that old beliefs, old values, and settled lifestyles, heretofore rendered coherent by the patriarchal nature of Irish authority, no longer retained a satisfying viability. A major statement on this alienated condition appeared in *Philadelphia, Here I Come!*, one of Friel's best and most enduring plays. It is significant that the play was not staged at the Abbey Theatre, to which Friel did not return until 1973. In the meantime he worked out his experimental and revolutionary ideas in alternative theaters in Dublin and elsewhere and under directors such as Tyrone Guthrie who were not tied to conventional notions of production.

Philadelphia, Here I Come! might at first sight appear to be just one more Irish peasant play addressing topics familiar from the canon of Irish drama. But in effect Friel subverts the tradition. His play is not mainly concerned with a conventional theme such as emigration, the land, or a love match. Its primary concentration is on the alienated consciousness of a young man, Gareth O'Donnell, whose relationship with his widowed father is an image of a new, privatized awareness of human isolation. Friel divides the character in two, Private and Public, to be played by two actors, "two views of the one man." Private Gar, the "alter ego," is invisible to all onstage but serves to articulate for the audience the inner thoughts and feelings of the young hero. These thoughts and feelings give a Hamlet-like dimension to the characterization, and this is where the real power of the play lies, though it is also supremely well balanced in its use of comedy and pathos.

Friel himself has said that the two plays that followed, *The Loves of Cass McGuire* and *Lovers*, share with *Philadelphia* the common theme of love. It is perhaps truer to observe that they are about loneliness and the futility of communication. Each is also theatrically experimental. After 1972, however, a different emphasis made its appearance in Friel's work. In January 1972 the political situation in Northern Ireland took a turn for the worse as British paratroopers shot 13 civilians on a civil rights march in Derry. Like many another Irish writer, Friel was outraged, particularly as Derry was his adopted city. He wrote *The Freedom of the City* to express his anger at the whitewashing Widgery Report, which exonerated the British army. Its premiere at the new Abbey Theatre marked Friel's return to nationalist concerns. The play, while not among Friel's best, is remarkably skillful in its adaptation of Brechtian techniques of storytelling to a current political situation, even though critics in London and New York faulted it on political grounds. On these grounds it is a play to be linked with *Translations* and *Making History*, as Friel became increasingly preoccupied with the crisis in Northern Ireland. *Translations* was staged by the Field Day Theatre Company, established by Friel and actor Stephen Rea to intervene culturally in the crisis by touring with plays that addressed specific issues. To some degree Friel became a political dramatist.

Translations, a history play set in the year 1833, is one of Friel's best plays and one of his works most often performed internationally. The action takes place in a hedge school and uses two distinct but interrelated issues to explore a community in crisis and a native culture at the point of dissolution. The issues are education and cartography, which in a colonial situation are related specifically to language and identity. Though the implications of the play are far ranging, there is, as always in Friel, a simple human situation at its core: a love story between the English soldier Yolland and the Irish woman Máire, who is deemed to be speaking only Gaelic throughout. The tragic failure of the affair recounts a national disaster.

Dancing at Lughnasa, perhaps Friel's most successful play, shows how inadequate and even falsifying it is to categorize him as a political playwright. The fact that it was premiered by the Abbey Theatre rather than by Field Day suggests that Friel himself felt the need to escape the confines of the Field Day ideology. *Dancing at Lughnasa* is a reminder that Friel is first and foremost an artist, a storyteller, a playwright for whom nuances of emotional experience take priority over ideas. Even in the 1970s, when his work seemed to point inevitably to the writing of *Translations,* he could confound the critics with such essentially nonpolitical plays as *The Gentle Island, Living Quarters, Aristocrats,* and, above all, *Faith Healer*. The latter, occupied with the ambivalent powers of the eponymous artist figure, stands out as one of Friel's most original and poetic plays. If *Dancing at Lughnasa* filters the doomed perfection of the past through the imagination of a boy about to develop into a writer, *Faith Healer* goes to the root of the mature artist's guilt for his failure to intervene in that doom.

Faith Healer is comprised of four monologues, two from Frank and one each from his wife Grace and his impresario Teddy. In Pirandellian fashion the audience must sift the truth from the contradictions of the characters' narrations. The stories they tell not only reinforce Friel's skill, but the climax also returns us to Ballybeg, the village invented for *Philadelphia, Here I Come!* In a sense the exile of that play returns to his place of birth and is destroyed in *Faith Healer*. Thus, Friel's plays are interrelated in patterns that tell not only the story of Ireland and its wounds but also the timeless story of human longing for completion, forgiveness, and love.

—Christopher Murray

FRISBY, Terence

Nationality: British. **Born:** New Cross, London, 28 November 1932. **Education:** Dobwalls Village School; Dartford Grammar School; Central School of Speech Training and Dramatic Art, London, 1955-57. **Family:** Married Christine Vecchione in 1963 (divorced); one son. **Career:** Worked as a salesman, capstan lathe operator, factory hand, waiter, chauffeur, checker-out at the Hammersmith Palais, etc.; professional actor, 1957—; also a producer. Resident director, New Theatre, Bromley, Kent, 1963-64. **Awards:** Writers Guild of Great Britain award, for screenplay, 1970; BBC Giles Cooper award, best radio plays, 1988; Houston International Film Festival gold award, for comedy, 1991. **Agent:** The Agency, 24 Pottery Lane, Holland Park, London W11 4LZ, England. **Address:** 72 Bishops Mansions, Bishops Park Road, London SW6 6DZ, England.

PUBLICATIONS

Plays

The Subtopians (also director: produced London, 1964). London, French, 1964.

There's a Girl in My Soup (produced London, 1966; New York, 1967). London and New York, French, 1968.

The Bandwagon (produced London, 1969). London, French, 1973.

It's All Right If I Do It (produced Leicester and London, 1977). London, French, 1977.

Seaside Postcard (also director: produced London, 1977). London, French, 1978.

First Night (produced London, 1987).

Just Remember Two Things: It's Not Fair and Don't Be Late (broadcast 1988). Published in *Best Radio Plays of 1988*, London, Methuen, 1988.

Screenplay: *There's a Girl in My Soup*, 1970.

Radio Play: *Just Remember Two Things: It's Not Fair and Don't Be Late*, 1988.

Television Plays: *Guilty*, 1964; *Public Eye* series, 1964; *Take Care of Madam*, 1965; *Adam Adamant* series, 1966; *More Deadly Than the Sword*, 1966; *Don't Forget the Basics*, 1967; *Lucky Feller* series, 1976; *That's Love* series, 1988-92.

Other

Autobiographical Story: Outrageous Fortune. London, First Thing Publications, 1998.

*

Critical Studies: *Anger and After* by John Russell Taylor, London, Methuen, 1962, revised edition, 1969, as *The Angry Theatre*, New York, Hill and Wang, 1962, revised edition, 1969; *The Season* by William Goldman, New York, Harcourt Brace, 1969, revised edition, New York, Limelight, 1984.

Theatrical Activities:
Director: **Plays**—In various repertory companies, including plays at Bromley, Kent, 1963-64; *The Subtopians*, London, 1964; *Seaside Postcard*, London, 1977.

Actor (as Terence Holland, 1957-66): **Plays**—Over 200 roles in repertory theatres in Bromley, Guildford, Lincoln, Richmond, York; London debut as Charlie Pepper in *Gentleman's Pastime* by Marion Hunt, 1958; in *A Sense of Detachment* by John Osborne, London, 1973; *X* by Barry Reckord, London, 1974; Clive Popkiss in *Rookery Nook* by Ben Travers, London, 1979; Father Mullarkey in *Once a Catholic* by Mary O'Malley, toured, 1980-81 and 1986; Birdboot in *The Real Inspector Hound* by Tom Stoppard, and Leslie in *Seaside Postcard*, toured, 1983-84; Archie Rice in *The Entertainer* by John Osborne, Sonning, Berkshire, 1984; David Bliss in *Hay Fever* by Noel Coward, Manchester, 1985; other roles in London and on tour. **Radio**—Narrator in *Just Remember Two Things: It's Not Fair and Don't Be Late*, 1988. **Television**—*Play School*, 1964-66; *It Must Be Something in the Water* by Alan Plater, 1973; *Two Townsmen*, adaptation of Thomas Hardy's work by Douglas Livingstone, 1974; *Leeds—United!* by Colin Welland, 1974; *When the Boys Come out to Play* by Richard Harris, 1975; *The Brothers*, 1976; *The Madness Museum* by Ken Campbell, 1986; *Signals*, 1990; *A Strike Out of Time*, 1991; *That's Love*, 1992.

* * *

Terence Frisby's first play, *The Subtopians*, was greeted with eulogies when, in 1964, it was seen for the first time. It was, critics decided, funny but complex, accurately worked out, deeply felt in spite of its genuine comedy, and serious in intention but almost painfully hilarious, and it had an unbreakable grip on the realities of social life in the 1960s.

Frisby was 32 when *The Subtopians* arrived to signal a newcomer whose gifts were, to say the least, so interesting that his future activities were sure to demand close attention. At least part of the technical neatness of his first play was due to his work at the Central School of Speech Training and Dramatic Art and to his work as an actor in repertory, musicals, and films, as an entertainer in nightclubs and cabaret, and as a director. There is a solid foundation of technique beneath the sometimes unkind observation and harsh comedy.

In 1966 *There's a Girl in My Soup* brought Frisby one of the greatest commercial successes in the modern theater. It ran for six years in the West End and at the same time pleased most of the critics. Like *The Subtopians* it has beautifully efficient machinery and precision of observation. Its hero has the sort of position in life—he is an expert on food who writes for intellectual periodicals—that once would have pointed him out as a figure of fun. In 1966, however, this assured an audience that he was a leader of thought and fashion whose familiarity with the best restaurants is intrinsically romantic and enviable. He is thus in a position to follow an exhausting, eventful career as an amorist whose endless successes are with the young who find his expertise, and the attitude toward him of those whose efforts he criticizes, altogether glamorous. It is less the dialogue or anything explicit in the play than the form it takes and the succession of events which indicate that behind the parade of insatiable appetite for change and his pride in his sexual prowess he is at the same time both lonely and uncertain of his attractiveness to those whom he regards as victims. Frisby naturally chooses to study the girl whose victim he becomes, in whose life he is only a pleasant interlude. The trendiness and contemporaneity of *There's a Girl in My Soup* carried the play round a triumphal tour of the world's theaters, with productions not only throughout the English-speaking theater but in most European countries as well and also in Turkey, Israel, and Mexico.

The course of events that led to the production of Frisby's third play, *The Bandwagon*, rose out of his success as a scriptwriter. *Guilty*, a 1964 piece for the BBC, was followed by a comedy, *Don't Forget the Basics*, done for Independent Television, and contributions to various series, notably to *Public Eye*, which at its best gave an almost Continental seediness to the activities of a provincial private detective, and *Adam Adamant*, in which adventure stories that might almost have come to birth in a boys' comic were treated with unusual and preposterous elegance and elaboration. *The Bandwagon*, originally *Some Have Greatness Thrust upon Them*, was to be one of the BBC's socially conscious Wednesday plays. It chose to imagine the situation of a stupid, ugly, graceless teenage girl, a member of a family of almost appalling fecundity—her mother and her sister are both pregnant when the play begins—who discovers that, though unmarried, she is to become the mother of quintuplets. Her fecundity, before drugs inducing multiple births had won any special attention, reaches the ears of popular newspapers, who make her a heroine, and television, which interviews her. The interview comes to an end when Aurora (the most unfortunately named heroine) explains the physiological misinformation and ignorance that are responsible for her plight. Frisby's refusal to alter a line that the BBC believed would give unnecessary offense led to its refusal to produce the play.

The BBC was perhaps entirely wrong. The line—"My friend Syl told me it was safe standing up"—is all of a piece, with a matter-of-fact simplicity that makes Aurora almost unexploitable. Aurora is maneuvered into marriage and has to be hurried from the church into childbed, and so have her mother and sister. The play belongs to the tradition of broad farce, and its final scene, as the womenfolk depart from the altar in agonized haste, sacrifices the precarious dignity and simplicity that have won the sympathy of the audience. *The Bandwagon*, in the good old days of curtain-raisers, could have stopped at its natural end, the silent, almost unnerving confrontation of two essentially pathetic victims of exploitation—Aurora and her husband-to-be—and have retained its integrity.

Although when it was new *The Bandwagon* seemed likely to follow Frisby's earlier plays and become an outstanding success, it did not do so. Possibly its depressing social milieu and its unfriendly view of what we have been taught to call the "media," as well as its combination of farce with serious moral concern, simply bothered audiences who found Aurora to be no more than a heroine of farce. In the same way neither *It's All Right If I Do It* nor *Seaside Postcard* won any startling success. Frisby's gift for comic incident and comic dialogue, obviously rooted in a serious view of society, has not perhaps found its audience when he applies it to areas outside the provinces and the glossy West End world of *There's a Girl in My Soup*.

—Henry Raynor

FROY, Herald. *See* **WATERHOUSE, Keith (Spencer).**

FRY, Christopher

Nationality: British. **Born:** Christopher Fry Harris in Bristol, 18 December 1907. **Education:** Bedford Modern School, 1918-26. **Military Service:** Served in the Non-Combatant Corps, 1940-44. **Family:** Married Phyllis Marjorie Hart in 1936 (died 1987); one son. **Career:** Teacher, Bedford Froebel Kindergarten, 1926-27; actor and office worker, Citizen House, Bath, 1927; schoolmaster, Hazelwood School, Limpsfield, Surrey, 1928-31; secretary to H. Rodney Bennett, 1931-32; founding director, Tunbridge Wells Repertory Players, 1932-35; lecturer and editor of schools magazine, Dr. Barnardo's Homes, 1934-39; director, 1939-40, and visiting director, 1945-46, Oxford Playhouse; visiting director, 1946, and staff dramatist, 1947, Arts Theatre Club, London. Also composer. **Awards:** Shaw Prize Fund award, 1948; Foyle poetry prize, 1951; New York Drama Critics Circle award, 1951, 1952, 1956; Queen's Gold medal, 1962; Royal Society of Literature Heinemann award, 1962. D.A.: Manchester Polytechnic, 1966. D.Litt.: Oxford University, 1988. Honorary fellow, Manchester Polytechnic, 1988. Fellow, Royal Society of Literature. **Agent:** ACTAC Ltd, 15 High Street, Ramsbury, Wiltshire SN8 2PA. **Address:** The Toft, East Dean, near Chichester, West Sussex PO18 0JA, England.

Publications

Plays

Youth and the Peregrines (produced Tunbridge Wells, Kent, 1934).

She Shall Have Music (lyrics only, with Ronald Frankau), book by Frank Eyton, music by Fry and Monte Crick (produced London, 1934).

To Sea in a Sieve (as Christopher Harris) (revue; produced Reading, 1935).

Open Door (produced London, 1936). Goldings, Hertfordshire, Printed by the Boys at the Press of Dr. Barnardo's Homes, n.d.

The Boy with a Cart: Cuthman, Saint of Sussex (produced Coleman's Hatch, Sussex, 1938; London, 1950; New York, 1953). London, Oxford University Press, 1939; New York, Oxford University Press, 1951.

The Tower (produced Tewkesbury, Gloucestershire, 1939).

Thursday's Child: A Pageant, music by Martin Shaw (produced London, 1939). London, Girls' Friendly Society, 1939.

A Phoenix Too Frequent (produced London, 1946; Cambridge, Massachusetts, 1948; New York, 1950). London, Hollis and Carter, 1946; New York, Oxford University Press, 1949.

The Firstborn (broadcast 1947; produced Edinburgh, 1948). Cambridge, University Press, 1946; New York, Oxford University Press, 1950; revised version (produced London, 1952; New York, 1958), London and New York, Oxford University Press, 1952, 1958.

The Lady's Not for Burning (produced London, 1948; New York, 1950). London and New York, Oxford University Press, 1949; revised version, 1950, 1958.

Thor, With Angels (produced Canterbury, 1948; Washington, D.C., 1950; London, 1951). Canterbury, Goulden, 1948; New York, Oxford University Press, 1949.

Venus Observed (produced London, 1950; New York, 1952). London and New York, Oxford University Press, 1950.

Ring round the Moon: A Charade with Music, adaptation of a play by Jean Anouilh (produced London and New York, 1950). London and New York, Oxford University Press, 1950.

A Sleep of Prisoners (produced Oxford, London, and New York, 1951). London and New York, Oxford University Press, 1951.

The Dark Is Light Enough: A Winter Comedy (produced Edinburgh and London, 1954; New York, 1955). London and New York, Oxford University Press, 1954.

The Lark, adaptation of a play by Jean Anouilh (produced London, 1955). London, Methuen, 1955; New York, Oxford University Press, 1956.

Tiger at the Gates, adaptation of a play by Jean Giraudoux (produced London and New York, 1955). London, Methuen, 1955; New York, Oxford University Press, 1956; as *The Trojan War Will Not Take Place* (produced London, 1983), Methuen, 1983.

Duel of Angels, adaptation of a play by Jean Giraudoux (produced London, 1958; New York, 1960). London, Methuen, 1958; New York, Oxford University Press, 1959.

Curtmantle (produced in Dutch, Tilburg, Netherlands, 1961; Edinburgh and London, 1962). London and New York, Oxford University Press, 1961.

Judith, adaptation of a play by Jean Giraudoux (produced London, 1962). London, Methuen, 1962.

The Bible: Original Screenplay, assisted by Jonathan Griffin. New York, Pocket Books, 1966.

Peer Gynt, adaptation of the play by Ibsen (produced Chichester, 1970). London and New York, Oxford University Press, 1970.

A Yard of Sun: A Summer Comedy (produced Nottingham and London, 1970; Cleveland, 1972). London and New York, Oxford University Press, 1970.

The Brontës of Haworth (televised 1973). London, Davis Poynter, 2 vols., 1974.
Cyrano de Bergerac, adaptation of the play by Edmond Rostand (produced Chichester, 1975). London and New York, Oxford University Press, 1975.
Paradise Lost, music by Penderecki, adaptation of the poem by Milton (produced Chicago, 1978). London, Schott, 1978.
Selected Plays (includes *The Boy with a Cart, A Phoenix Too Frequent, The Lady's Not for Burning, A Sleep of Prisoners, Curtmantle*). Oxford and New York, Oxford University Press, 1985.
One Thing More; or, Caedmon Construed (produced Chelmsford, Essex, 1986; London, 1988). New York, London, King's College, and New York, Dramatists Play Service, 1987.
The Seasons, poems to accompany Julie Cooper's adaptation of Vivaldi's *The Four Seasons* (produced London, 1990).
A Journey into Light, music by Robert Walker (produced Chichester, 1992).

Screenplays: *The Beggar's Opera*, with Denis Cannan, 1953; *A Queen Is Crowned* (documentary), 1953; *Ben Hur*, 1959; *Barabbas*, 1962; *The Bible: In the Beginning*, 1966.

Radio Plays: for *Children's Hour* series, 1939-40; *The Firstborn*, 1947; *Rhineland Journey*, 1948.

Television Plays: *The Canary*, 1950; *The Tenant of Wildfell Hall*, 1968; *The Brontës of Haworth* (four plays), 1973; *The Best of Enemies*, 1976; *Sister Dora*, from the book by Jo Manton, 1977.

Poetry

Root and Sky: Poetry from the Plays of Christopher Fry, edited by Charles E. and Jean G. Wadsworth. Cambridge, Rampant Lions Press, and Boston, Godine, 1975.

Other

An Experience of Critics, with *The Approach to Dramatic Criticism* by W.A. Darlington and others, edited by Kaye Webb. London, Perpetua Press, 1952; New York, Oxford University Press, 1953.
The Boat That Mooed (for children). New York, Macmillan, 1966.
Can You Find Me: A Family History. London, Oxford University Press, 1978; New York, Oxford University Press, 1979.
Death Is a Kind of Love (lecture). Cranberry Isles, Maine, Tidal Press, 1979.
Genius, Talent and Failure: The Brontës (lecture). London, King's College, 1987.
Looking for a Language (lecture). London, King's College, 1992.

Editor, *Charlie Hammond's Sketchbook*. Oxford, Oxford University Press, 1980.

Translator, *The Boy and the Magic*, by Colette. London, Dobson, 1964.
Translator, with Timberlake Wertenbaker, *Jean Anouilh: Five Plays*. London, Heinemann, 1986.

Incidental Music: *A Winter's Tale*, London, 1951; recorded by Caedmon.

*

Bibliography: By B. L. Schear and E. G. Prater, in *Tulane Drama Review 4* (New Orleans), March 1960.

Manuscript Collection: Harvard University Theatre Collection, Cambridge, Massachusetts.

Critical Studies: *Christopher Fry: An Appreciation*, London, Nevill, 1950, and *Christopher Fry*, London, Longman, 1954, revised edition, 1962, both by Derek Stanford; *The Drama of Comedy: Victim and Victor* by Nelson Vos, Richmond, Virginia, John Knox Press, 1965; *Creed and Drama* by W. M. Merchant, London, SPCK, 1965; *The Christian Tradition in Modern British Verse Drama* by William V. Spanos, New Brunswick, New Jersey, Rutgers University Press, 1967; *Christopher Fry* by Emil Roy, Carbondale, Southern Illinois University Press, 1968; *Christopher Fry: A Critical Essay*, Grand Rapids, Michigan, Eerdmans, 1970, and *More Than the Ear Discovers: God in the Plays of Christopher Fry*, Chicago, Loyola University Press, 1983, both by Stanley M. Wiersma; *Poetic Drama* by Glenda Leeming, London, Macmillan, 1989; *Christopher Fry* by Glenda Leeming, Boston, Twayne Publishers, 1990.

Theatrical Activities:
Director: **Plays**—*How-Do, Princess?* by Ivor Novello, toured, 1936; *The Circle of Chalk* by James Laver, London, 1945; *The School for Scandal* by Sheridan, London, 1946; *A Phoenix Too Frequent*, Brighton, 1950; *The Lady's Not for Burning*, toured, 1971; and others.

Actor: **Plays**—In repertory, Bath, 1937.

Christopher Fry comments:

The way a man writes for the theatre depends on the way he looks at life. If, in his experience, direction and purpose seem to be all-pervading factors, pattern and shape are necessary to his writing. The verse form is an effort to be true to what Eleanor, in *Curtmantle*, calls "the silent order whose speech is all visible things." No event is understandable in a prose sense alone. Its ultimate meaning (that is to say, the complete life of the event, seen in its eternal context) is a poetic meaning. The comedies try to explore a reality behind appearances. "Something condones the world incorrigibly" says Thomas Mendip in *The Lady's Not for Burning*—in spite of the "tragic" nature of life. The problem, a long way from being solved, is how to contain the complexities and paradoxes within two hours of entertainment: how to define the creative pattern of life without the danger of dogmatic statement. Dogma is static; life is movement. "La vérité est dans une nuance."

* * *

Christopher Fry's work was doubtless overrated in the fruitful years of *The Lady's Not for Burning* and *A Sleep of Prisoners,* and it is most certainly underrated today. This is in part due to an integrity and consistency in the work of a playwright who has pursued his own style of the seriocomic and chosen to ignore fashion. It is as if Beckett and the theater of the absurd had not existed, nor Brecht and the practice of epic theater, with its oblique devices of structure and technique, nor the socially and politically committed drama following Osborne's *Look Back in Anger.* Fry's reputation has paid the price. It remains to be seen whether his neglect of contemporary trends matters in the final verdict.

In *A Yard of Sun* Fry is still writing in that highly idiosyncratic, all-but-verse idiom of loose pentameters that drew attention to his earliest plays. Characteristically mixing the colloquial and the allusive, a minor character can say, "I pick words gingerly like a rose out of thorns," and at a stroke he equalizes his role with that of a major, thus by prosaic kitchen-sink standards making all the parts equally literate and classless. Or Angelino Bruno, one of the two central characters whose families are unexpectedly united after World War II, can come out with a startling turn of expression that fixes and underscores the general statement of the stage:

> What a settling-up God's having this week!
> Both of us within two days. Well, once
> The bit's between His teeth things start to move.

Although it may not bear close analysis as poetry on the page, verbal panache of this kind keeps Fry's stage alive when a situation is static. It is often spendthrift with the necessary economy of the action, and the idiom that refreshed the grim postwar years and dazzled the critics can now seem irrelevant, even facile.

But Fry was seeking a spiritual idiom for a contemporary and unobtrusively Christian verse drama after T. S. Eliot had prepared the ground with *Murder in the Cathedral* (1935) and *The Family Reunion* (1939). Whereas Eliot was concerned to find a spare and unobtrusive verse form designed to control the speech and movement of modern martyrs on a stage, Fry, in a less certain style but with more sense of the stage, aimed with abandon at a general mood to match his themes. There are times in *A Sleep of Prisoners*, possibly the best antiwar play of its period, when the verse achieves the richness of both tonal and physical embodiment of the stage moment while exploring a verbal idea:

> How ceaseless the earth is. How it goes on.
> Nothing has happened except silence where sound was,
> Stillness where movement was . . .

These lines are spoken by the figure of Adam just after he has witnessed the murder of his son Abel, and they enact both the father's horror and the scene's meaning.

Whereas, however, Eliot's profundity of vision carried him through his own inadequacies as a dramatist—notably his inability to create character that did not suffer the atrophy of symbolism—Fry came to lean on an explosive central situation that was fruitful in itself. This situation might lack the qualities of conflict, tension, and development yet still be capable of holding attention. Thus *A Sleep of Prisoners* consists of a pattern of reenacted Old Testament stories chosen to illustrate facets of the idea of violence. Each story is not only informed by the audience's own memories of the Bible but also, because it is dreamed by a modern soldier held prisoner in a church, automatically granted a contemporary relevance. Within the structure of the play the spectator himself works to supply the missing factor in the dramatic equation, and the teaching element of a morality play is actively deduced by our application of the fiction to the fact. Nevertheless, the play suffers, as only morality plays can, from the static preconception by which morality characters tend to be fixed in their symbolic attitudes.

This play in its time startled and delighted audiences by the free use of its church setting, where at a glance the chancel could be Adam's jungle or the pulpit Abraham's mountain. As they were for *Murder in the Cathedral*, audiences were both theatergoers and congregation and were unusually exercised by the multiplicity of association felt within the performance. There are no such props for a dramatic experience in Fry's other plays, although *The Boy with a Cart* is a simple mystery play of spontaneous charm, *The Firstborn* explores the tragic dilemma of Moses and the plagues, and *Curtmantle* draws upon legend and history in parallel attempts to bring the remote closer to home. *Curtmantle*, too neglected a play, was his most sustained attempt at a serious character study. A chronicle play of Henry II in conflict with his archbishop, Becket, it is set out in a sequence of vivid episodes more in the simple manner of Bolt's episodic *A Man for All Seasons* than with the prismatic counterpoint of Brecht's epic theater. The scenes are designed to illustrate the wit, the wisdom, and the complex passions of the title part as Henry searches for a rational unity of divine and secular law.

Fry creates a drama of color and flair, choosing a situation for its imaginative potential, often one of implicit crisis involving a clash of strong, bright personalities. His situation enables him to demonstrate a compassionate affirmation of life, an optimism that inevitably seemed escapist beside the bleak absurdist landscape of the postwar years in spite of the tragic mode of *The Firstborn*, *Thor, With Angels* (the 1948 Canterbury Festival play), and *The Dark Is Light Enough*, plays that exemplify Fry's philosophy of maturing through crisis:

> We reach an obstacle, and learn to overcome it;
> our thoughts or emotions become knotted, and we
> increase ourselves in order to unknot them; a
> state of being becomes intolerable, and, drawing
> upon a hidden reserve of spirit, we transform it.

But he is nevertheless remembered for those early comedies of mood touched with the wit and fantasy by which he could express his most gentle and humane thinking. The prototype for this kind of comedy, and still the most regularly revived, was the one-act *A Phoenix Too Frequent*. This was taken from the ancient tale of the young Roman widow romantically committed to a fast to the death in her husband's tomb until she and an equally romantic young soldier agree to substitute the husband's body for the corpse the soldier was guarding with his life. With the lightest of touches the widow decides for life, and youth and love supplant social convention and death, a joyful illustration of the life force at work.

The springtime comedy that made Fry's name and competed for London's attention with Eliot's *The Cocktail Party* in 1949 was his best-known play, *The Lady's Not for Burning*, an extension of the style and spirit of *A Phoenix Too Frequent*. His verbal pyrotechnics were at their most assured, and the medieval color on his stage lifted the play into a rarefied atmosphere that forced comparison with Giraudoux and the lighter Anouilh of *L'Invitation au château*, which Fry was later to translate beautifully as *Ring round the Moon*. A simple crisis again sets the play in motion when one Thomas Mendip, desiring but denied death, is confronted with Jennet Jourdemayne, who wants to live but must die as a witch. She envies his death wish and he her "damnable mystery" until, to test his sincerity and her courage, Fry impudently arranges for them one last "joyous" evening together before Jennet's execution. The result is to dramatize with graceful irony Fry's sense of cosmic purpose.

His other plays designed to celebrate the seasons followed irregularly in an unpredictable range of moods, some unexpectedly somber—*Venus Observed* (autumn), *The Dark Is Light Enough* (winter), and *A Yard of Sun* (summer). *Venus Observed* is a comedy of middle-aged disillusionment, but it is pleasingly balanced and without fashionable cynicism. *The Dark Is Light Enough,* however, selects 1848, the year of revolutions, for its darker setting, and it secures its unity in the compassionate and gracious presence of an Austrian countess, a part created by Edith Evans. With the countess's "divine non-interference" it is demonstrated:

how apparently undemandingly
She moves among us; and yet
Lives make and unmake themselves in her
neighbourhood
As nowhere else.

The theme is thus one of providence, and, through the wisdom of the countess as she recognizes the imminence of death, it embodies the necessity of our respect for every human personality in its touch of grace.

To set side by side plays as contrasting as *The Lady's Not for Burning* and *The Dark Is Light Enough* is inescapably to be impressed by Fry's versatility and by the integrity of a writer who uses his chosen medium as a way of searching out his personal philosophy, whether in the vein of farce or tragedy, spring or winter. Eliot notwithstanding, Fry's is the most sustained attempt in English to write an undogmatic Christian drama in modern times.

—J. L. Styan

FUGARD, (Harold) Athol (Lannigan)

Nationality: South African. **Born:** Near Middleburg, Cape Province, 11 June 1932. **Education:** Marist Brothers College, Port Elizabeth, 1938-45; Port Elizabeth Technical College, 1946-50; University of Cape Town, 1950-53. **Family:** Married Sheila Meiring in 1956; one daughter. **Career:** Seaman, *S.S. Graigaur*, 1953-54; journalist, Port Elizabeth *Evening Post*, 1954; reporter, South African Broadcasting Corporation, Port Elizabeth and Cape Town, 1955-57; clerk, Fordsburg Native Commissioner's Court, Johannesburg, 1958; stage manager and publicity agent, National Theatre Organization, 1958; worked as cleaner in London, 1960. Co-founder, Circle Players theatre workshop, Cape Town, 1957, African Theatre Workshop, Sophiatown, 1958-59, New Africa Group, Brussels, 1960, Ijinle Company, London, 1966, and The Space experimental theatre, Cape Town, 1972; director, Serpent Players, Port Elizabeth, 1963—; director of and actor in many of his own plays. Lives in Port Elizabeth. **Awards:** *New York Times* award, 1965; Obie award, 1971; London Theatre Critics award, 1974; Locarno Film Festival Ernest Artaria award, 1977; Berlin Film Festival Golden Bear, 1980; Yale University fellowship, 1980; New York Drama Critics Circle award, 1981, 1988; London *Evening Standard* award, 1984; Common Wealth award, 1984; Drama League award, 1986; Helen Hayes award, for direction, 1990. D.Litt.: University of Natal, Durban, 1981; Rhodes University, Grahamstown, 1983; University of Cape Town, 1984. D.F.A.: Yale University, New Haven, Connecticut, 1983. D.H.L.: Georgetown University, Washington, D.C., 1984. **Agent:** Esther Sherman, William Morris Agency, 1325 Avenue of the Americas, New York, New York 10019, U.S.A.

Publications

Plays

No-Good Friday (also director: produced Johannesburg, 1958; Sheffield, 1974). Included in *Dimetos and Two Early Plays*, 1977.

Nongogo (also director: produced Cape Town, 1959; Sheffield, 1974; New York, 1978). Included in *Dimetos and Two Early Plays*, 1977.

The Blood Knot (also director: produced Johannesburg, 1961; London, 1963; New York, 1964). Cape Town, Simondium, 1963; New York, Odyssey Press, 1964; in *Three Port Elizabeth Plays*, 1974.

Hello and Goodbye (also director: produced Johannesburg, 1965; New York, 1968; Leicester, 1971; London, 1973). Cape Town, Balkema, 1966; in *Three Port Elizabeth Plays*, 1974.

The Coat (produced Port Elizabeth, 1966). With *The Third Degree*, by Don MacLennan, Cape Town, Balkema, 1971.

People Are Living There (produced Glasgow, 1968; also director: produced Cape Town, 1969; New York, 1971; London, 1972). Cape Town, Buren, 1969; London, Oxford University Press, 1970.

The Occupation: A Script for Camera, in *Ten One Act Plays* edited by Cosmos Pieterse. London, Heinemann, 1968.

Boesman and Lena (also director: produced Grahamstown, 1969; revised version produced New York, 1970; London, 1971). Cape Town, Buren, 1969; New York, French, 1972; London, Oxford University Press, 1973.

Orestes (produced Cape Town, 1971). Published in *Theatre One: New South African Drama*, edited by Stephen Gray, Johannesburg, Donker, 1978.

Statements after an Arrest under the Immorality Act (also director: produced Cape Town, 1972; London, 1974; New York, 1978). Included in *Statements*, 1974.

Sizwe Bansi Is Dead, with John Kani and Winston Ntshona (also director: as *Sizwe Banzi Is Dead*, produced Cape Town, 1972; as *Sizwe Bansi Is Dead*, produced London, 1973; New Haven, Connecticut, and New York, 1974). Included in *Statements*, 1974; in *Two Plays*, 1976.

The Island, with John Kani and Winston Ntshona (also director: as *Die Hodoshe Span* produced Cape Town, 1973; as *The Island* produced London, and New York, 1974). Included in *Statements*, 1974; in *Two Plays*, 1976.

Three Port Elizabeth Plays: The Blood Knot, Hello and Goodbye, Boesman and Lena. New York, Viking Press, and London, Oxford University Press, 1974.

Statements: Three Plays. London, Oxford University Press, 1974.

Dimetos (also director: produced Edinburgh, 1975; revised version produced Nottingham, London, and New York, 1976). Included in *Dimetos and Two Early Plays*, 1977.

Two Plays: Sizwe Bansi Is Dead, and The Island, with John Kani and Winston Ntshona. New York, Viking Press, 1976.

Dimetos and Two Early Plays. London, Oxford University Press, 1977.

The Guest: An Episode in the Life of Eugène Marais, with Ross Devenish (as *The Guest at Steenkampskraal*, televised 1977). Johannesburg, Donker, 1977.

A Lesson from Aloes (also director: produced Johannesburg, 1978; New Haven, Connecticut, New York, and London, 1980). New York, Random House, and Oxford, Oxford University Press, 1981.
Boesman and Lena, and Other Plays (includes *The Blood Knot, People Are Living There, Hello and Goodbye*). London, Oxford University Press, 1978.
The Drummer (produced Louisville, 1980).
"Master Harold" and the Boys (also director: produced New Haven, Connecticut, and New York, 1982; London, 1983). New York, Knopf, 1982; Oxford, Oxford University Press, 1983.
Marigolds in August (screenplay), with Ross Devenish. Johannesburg, Donker, 1982.
The Road to Mecca (produced New Haven, Connecticut, 1984; London, 1985; also director: produced New York, 1988). London, Faber, 1985.
A Place with the Pigs (also director: produced New Haven, Connecticut, 1987, London, 1988). London, Faber, 1988.
Selected Plays (includes *"Master Harold" and the Boys, The Blood Knot, Hello and Goodbye, Boesman and Lena*). Oxford, Oxford University Press, 1987.
My Children! My Africa! (also director: produced Johannesburg and New York, 1989; London, 1990). London, Faber, 1990.
Playland (produced Cape Town, 1992).
Marigolds in August and The Guest (screenplays). New York, Theatre Communications Group, 1992.
The Township Plays. Oxford, Oxford University Press, 1993.
Valley Song (produced Johannesburg and Princeton, New Jersey, 1995). New York, Samuel French, 1996.
Plays (includes *The Road to Mecca*; *A Place with the Pigs*; *My children! My Africa!*; *Playland*; *Valley Song*). London, Faber, 1998.

Screenplays: *Boesman and Lena*, 1973; *Marigolds in August*, with Ross Devenish, 1980; *The Road to Mecca,* 1991.

Television Plays: *Mille Miglia*, 1968 (UK); *The Guest at Steenkampskraal*, with Ross Devenish, 1977.

Novel

Tsotsi. Johannesburg, Donker, and London, Collings, 1980; New York, Random House, 1981.

Other

Notebooks 1960-1977, edited by Mary Benson. Johannesburg, Donker, and London, Faber, 1983; New York, Knopf, 1984.
Writer and Region: Athol Fugard (essay). New York, Anson Phelps Stokes Institute, 1987.
Cousins: A Memoir. New York, Theatre Communications Group, 1994.

*

Bibliography: *Athol Fugard: A Bibliography, Biography, Playography* by Russell Vandenbroucke, London, TQ Publications, 1977; *Athol Fugard: A Source Guide* by Temple Hauptfleisch, Johannesburg, Donker, 1982.

Manuscript Collection: National English Literary Museum, Rhodes University, Grahamstown.

Critical Studies: *Athol Fugard* by Stephen Gray, Johannesburg, McGraw Hill, 1982; *Athol Fugard* by Dennis Walder, London, Macmillan, 1984, New York, Grove Press, 1985; *Truths the Hand Can Touch: The Theatre of Athol Fugard* by Russell Vandenbroucke, New York, Theatre Communications Group, 1985; "Wilson and Fugard" by Joanne Gordon, in *August Wilson: A Casebook,* edited by Marilyn Elkins, New York, Garland, 1994; "Potatoes, Beets and Radishes?: A Divergence of Critical Opinion Concerning Imagery and the Character of Marius in Fugard's *Road to Mecca*" by James McCoy, in *Notes on Contemporary Literature* (Carrollton, Georgia), March 1994, pp. 2-3; "Challenge and Response: The Changing Face of Theatre in South Africa" by Andre Brink, in *Twentieth Century Literature* (Hempstead, New York), Summer 1997, pp. 162-76; *Athol Fugard and Barney Simon: Bare Stage, a Few Props, Great Theatre* by Mary Benson, Randburg, South Africa, Ravan Press, 1997.

Theatrical Activities:
Director: **Plays**—Many of his own plays; *The Cure*, adaptation of *Mandragola* by Machiavelli, Grahamstown, 1963; *Woyzeck* by Georg Büchner, South Africa, 1964; *Antigone* by Sophocles, Cape Town, 1965; *The Trials of Brother Jero* by Wole Soyinka, London, 1966; *Statements after an Arrest under the Immorality Act,* 1974; *Dimetos,* 1975; *A Lesson from Aloes,* 1978; *The Road to Mecca,* 1988; *My Children! My Africa!,* 1991. **Film**–*The Road to Mecca,* 1991.

Actor: **Plays**—Roles in most of his own plays in South Africa; Okkie the Greek in *A Kakamas Greek* by David Herbert, Brussels, 1960; Morrie in *The Blood Knot*, New York, 1962 and 1985, London, 1966; *A Place with the Pigs*, New Haven, Connecticut, 1987; role in *The Road to Mecca*, New York, 1988. **Films**—*Boesman and Lena*, 1973; *Meetings with Remarkable Men*, 1979; *Marigolds in August*, 1980; *Gandhi*, 1982; *The Killing Fields*, 1984. **Television**—*The Blood Knot*, 1967 (UK); *The Guest at Steenkampskraal*, 1977.

* * *

Athol Fugard is a playwright in the fullest sense of the word; he is a builder of plays in the way that a shipwright is a builder of ships. Although the solitude of writing has produced a number of his finest dramas, plays at once highly personal and particular about his native South Africa and internationally accessible and meaningful, he has also used his skills as an actor and a director to forge collaborations that have had a profound effect on the development of South African culture. By continuing to direct his plays himself—in South Africa, the United States, and Britain—he has also continued to control the shape and expression of his ideas far more than have most dramatists.

What has given particular force to Fugard's plays, individual or collaborative, is the consistent demonstration that private lives are political. His belief that this is so was formed under apartheid, an imposed division of people that made apolitical existence impossible, but dramatizing that belief means that his plays show the real dimensions of human society to a degree seldom achieved by his contemporaries in British and American theater.

Fugard's collaborative plays appeared in the early 1970s when the very act of collaborating with black African actors was political. Some of the plays during that period were written in much the same way as earlier successes like *The Blood Knot.* Thus,

Statements after an Arrest under the Immorality Act, a key drama examining the carnal relations between a man and a woman whose contact was forbidden under the racial laws of South Africa, was fully scripted by him. But, in terms of their impact on the development of black South African theater, his most significant plays at that time were the two he wrote in collaboration with Winston Ntshona and John Kani, *Sizwe Bansi Is Dead* and *The Island.*

These plays opened a dialogue with the world, presenting, as *The Blood Knot* had done earlier, such theatrically exact metaphors for South Africa's racial strife that the human situation transcended the politics while at the same time it illuminated the nature of the conflict. In addition, the final shape of the plays, with many roles performed by two actors, was to provide an economical model for further exploration of the South African situation by Barney Simon, Percy Mtwa, and others. *Sizwe Bansi* has remained a particularly powerful statement about the effect of repression on individuals subjected to South Africa's laws. Its examination of the problem of individual identity gives a haunting, nearly mythological power.

The South African division of humanity into three groups—whites, coloreds, and blacks—always had its absurdities as well as its tragedies. *Sizwe Bansi* seizes on both aspects, beginning with an actual death and ending with a symbolic transfer of identities with a dead man. In a society in which access was determined by bureaucratic interpretations of race and by the possession of the right identity card, a new card could mean a new life.

Fugard's expansion of the idea into a full-length play was given additional reality through the improvisational work of Kani and Ntshona under his direction. They contributed in a similar way to *The Island,* which is set in a prison, and they undoubtedly endowed both plays with elements of speech and observed details that deepened the impact. There is, nonetheless, a dominant sense of form that evokes the two brothers of *The Blood Knot,* one light skinned and the other black, who share an identity while appearing to the world to be different. It is Fugard's clear theatrical structuring, combined with an exceptional literacy, that gives each of his plays a recognizable voice.

While most of Fugard's plays operate within the context determined by the politics and racial situation of apartheid in South Africa and while most of his characters, regardless of race, are shown as victims of those policies, he has extended his work equally bravely into mythic dimensions. *Dimetos,* which was commissioned by the Edinburgh Festival and subsequently performed in London, followed some of his most political pieces and attempted to explore a mythic fragment that had lodged itself in his memory. Using contemporary dress along with lengthy literal discussions, the work explored the subject of a guilty love, but while the touch of a major playwright was always evident, it was a considerably more literary touch than that of his more specifically South African works.

Unlike any other playwright of comparable stature, Fugard has identified the work of the Polish director Jerzy Grotowski as a major influence on his work. Grotowski was notable for extending the physical and vocal range of actors and for productions that obscured the language and texts at their centers. In a similar manner one of the major experiments made by Fugard in Cape Town was almost completely physical. He described the experiment, *Orestes,* as "an experience which lasted about eighty minutes and which had a 'text' of about four hundred words. The rest was space, silence, and action."

Neither *Orestes* nor *Dimetos* could be described as typical. Rather, they are extremes of Fugard's approach to theater, which he might have explored further had he not obviously found the problems and contradictions of his country so pressing. The work beginning with *A Lesson from Aloes* is far more representative of his usual concerns and prepared the way for the differently autobiographical dramas *"Master Harold" and the Boys* and *The Road to Mecca,* which appeared in the 1980s, and for his later drama *Playland,* the first of his plays to be premiered in South Africa for some years.

Reflecting notes Fugard had made in 1961, *A Lesson from Aloes* was based on actual people caught in the closing trap of apartheid. It graphically and poignantly examines the decision of an Afrikaaner of conscience who decides to cling to South Africa, drawing what sustenance he can from his native earth while he bids farewell to a Cape coloured friend who has been forced out. The play clearly suggests Fugard's private debate on the importance and effectiveness of remaining bound to South Africa. *"Master Harold" and the Boys,* however, was to bring an even more personal expression of conflict, being the self-confessedly true story of Fugard's own temptation into the assertion of racial superiority when he was a boy. The irony in the title, with the "master" being a foolish youth and the "boys" being African men of wit, generosity, and sympathy, is a statement of Fugard's guilt, and the play painfully accepts responsibility for an unforgivable act of contempt to a black man who had been like a father to him.

The Road to Mecca, like *A Lesson from Aloes,* is more of a biographical portrait than autobiography, but the subtext is always the intolerant society of South Africa. The eccentric heroine is modeled on Fugard's mother, who had sacrificed to give him an education and who had reached her 70s while building her own extremely private version of Mecca. In the play she confronts the repressive community in her village of New Bethlehem in the Great Karoo, where Fugard maintains a home. When they wish to confine her to an old people's home, she turns for support to a young friend who is finding it hard to come to grips with a recent abortion and with her encounter with an African woman and child she met on the road to New Bethlehem.

In *A Place with the Pigs* Fugard finally seemed to be moving away from his South African setting and themes. Based on the true story of a Soviet deserter in World War II who lived in secret for 40 years among the pigs on his family farm, the play is about the man's struggle to preserve his humanity while denied all human contact except that of the wife who hid him. Considered by some to form a metaphor for political repression, Fugard himself said that it was an expression of his struggle with alcoholism.

Fugard's next play, *My Children! My Africa!,* was a powerful return to South Africa. A three-hander, it reflects the struggle between forces for knowledge and argument, on the one hand, and revolutionary violence, on the other. The central character is a black teacher who tries to persuade his brightest student that reason can win the struggle. He offers the student the choice of all the knowledge, all the words, in a dictionary, which he contrasts to the single word "stone," one of which he holds in his other hand. His reward for his position is death by "necklacing," that is, by having a burning tire placed around his neck.

Reconciliation makes a more hopeful appearance in Fugard's next work, *Playland.* It takes place at an amusement park on New Year's Eve in 1989, a month before President F. W. de Klerk announced the death of apartheid. The two characters are a black watchman, Martinus, and a white visitor to the park, Gideon. It is Gideon's alcohol-fueled rantings, including the boast of having killed dozens of blacks in a South African border war, that bring forth Martinus's story of having killed a white man who demanded sex from his servant, Martinus's fiancée. Their sharing of shadowy histories is finally positive, offering hope of future peaceful settlement, and as usual the story transcends its locality. Fugard has described the play as being about "the karma of violence."

Nothing Fugard has written declines to the didactic, and although he remains a political author of the first rank, he is even more consistently a humanist. The body of his work is a glowing testament to the human spirit.

—Ned Chaillet

FULLER, Charles (H., Jr.)

Nationality: American. **Born:** Philadelphia, Pennsylvania, 5 March 1939. **Education:** Villanova University, 1956-58, and La Salle College, 1965-67, both Philadelphia. **Military Service:** Served as a petroleum lab technician in the United States Army in Japan and Korea, 1959-62. **Family:** Married Miriam A. Nesbitt in 1962; two sons. **Career:** Bank loan collector, counselor at Temple University, and city housing inspector, all Philadelphia, 1960s; co-founder and co-director, Afro-American Arts Theatre, Philadelphia, 1967-71; writer and director, *The Black Experience* program, WIP Radio, Philadelphia, 1970-71; professor of African-American Studies, Temple University, until 1993. Lives in Philadelphia. **Awards:** Creative Artists Public Service grant, 1975; Rockefeller grant, 1976; National Endowment for the Arts grant, 1976; Guggenheim fellowship, 1977; Obie award, 1981; Audelco award, 1981, 1982; Pulitzer prize, 1982; New York Drama Critics Circle award, 1982; Outer Circle award, 1982; Hazelitt award, 1983; Mystery Writers of America Edgar Allan Poe award, for screenplay, 1985. D.F.A.: La Salle College, 1982; Villanova University, 1983. **Agent:** Esther Sherman, William Morris Agency, 1325 Avenue of the Americas, New York, New York 10019, U.S.A.

Publications

Plays

The Village: A Party (produced Princeton, New Jersey, 1968; as *The Perfect Party*, produced New York, 1969).
The Rise, in *New Plays from the Black Theatre*, edited by Ed Bullins. New York, Bantam, 1969.
In My Many Names and Days (produced New York, 1972).
Candidate (produced New York, 1974).
In the Deepest Part of Sleep (produced New York, 1974).
First Love (produced New York, 1974).
The Lay Out Letter (produced Philadelphia, 1975).
The Brownsville Raid (produced Waterford, Connecticut, 1975; New York, 1976).
Sparrow in Flight, music by Larry Garner, based on a concept by Rosetta LeNoire (produced New York, 1978).
Zooman and the Sign (produced New York, 1980). New York, French, 1982.
A Soldier's Play (produced New York, 1981; Edinburgh, 1984). New York, Hill and Wang, 1982.
We (includes *Sally*, *Prince*) (produced New York, 1988).
Eliot's Coming, in *Urban Blight* (musical revue), based on an idea by John Tillinger, music by David Shire, lyrics by Richard Maltby, Jr. (produced New York, 1988).
Jonquil (produced New York, 1990).

Screenplay: *A Soldier's Story*, 1984.

Television Plays: *Roots, Resistance, and Renaissance* series, 1967; *Mitchell*, 1968; *Black America* series, 1970-71; *The Sky Is Gray*, from the story by Ernest J. Gaines (*American Short Story* series), 1980; *A Gathering of Old Men*, 1987.

*

Critical Studies: "The Descent of Charlie Fuller into Pulitzerland and the Need for African-American Institutions" by Amiri Baraka, in *Black American Literature Forum* (Terre Haute, Indiana), Summer 1983, pp. 51-54; *Images of America: Four Contemporary Playwrights* (dissertation) by Esther Harriott, Ann Arbor, Michigan, 1984; "The Role of Detective in *A Soldier's Play*" by Linda K. Hughes and Howard Faulkner, in *Clues: A Journal of Detection* (Bowling Green, Ohio), Fall-Winter 1986, pp. 83-97; *Contemporary African American Theater: Afrocentricity in the Works of Larry Neal, Amiri Baraka and Charles Fuller* by Nilgun Anadolu-Okur, New York, Garland, 1997.

* * *

An angry, consuming energy that propels the protagonist toward violence and an irony that humanizes him while depriving the viewer of easy categorizations are elements characterizing Charles Fuller's style. Within the American theater tradition Fuller's work both acknowledges the seminal position of Amiri Baraka and extends the vision of the tumultuous 1960s beyond a rigid, racial schematization that, in conferring upon blacks the status of victims of oppression, seemingly robbed them of any responsibility for or power over the circumstances in which they find themselves.

A former bank loan collector, college counselor, and city housing inspector, Fuller initially gained national recognition in 1976 with *The Brownsville Raid*. Though it went out of circulation, the play is of interest because it prefigures the approach adopted in the later *A Soldier's Play*. *The Brownsville Raid* is a dramatization of the investigation into a 1906 shooting spree that culminated in President Theodore Roosevelt's unwarranted dishonorable discharge of an entire black infantry brigade. With historical accounts as his starting point, Fuller skillfully interweaves a whodunit plot with a compelling portrait of a black corporal who has his faith in the army shattered when he refuses to comply with his officers' demand for a scapegoat. Both the black and the white men are presented with strengths and faults, and what emerges is a composite picture of men and of a society whose vision is distorted by racism.

In both *Zooman and the Sign* and *A Soldier's Play* racism does not appear as a specific, external event to which the black protagonists must react. Rather, its negative values have been so internalized that, propelled by their own frantic despair, the characters move relentlessly toward self-destruction. In the first play, which is about a father's search for the person who killed his daughter, a knife-toting and drug-running 15-year-old, Zooman, casually admits to the audience at the outset that he is the killer. Although Zooman attempts to mask a mounting sense of entrapment with calculated bravado, his direct conversations with the audience about familial disintegration, unwanted homosexual encounters, and detention for uncommitted crimes characterize him as an alienated youth whose experiences have taught him that "niggahs can't be heroes," that blacks seemingly have no control over the atrophy engulfing their families and communities. The monologues, delivered in a frenetic streetwise style that is nonetheless reminiscent of black toasting traditions and of Muhammad Ali's alliterative poetry, have the effect of humanizing Zooman, of placing him in a context in which his asocial behavior becomes more understandable and his affinity to the larger society more apparent.

Just as Zooman believes that blacks are helpless, so too do the neighbors of the slain girl, for no one will come forth as witnesses to the crime. The father's act of erecting a sign accusing them of moral complicity only triggers hostile recriminations from the neighbors and arguments within the family itself. Symbolic of a community's failure to foster a more active, ennobling sense of its own possibilities, the sign occasions the final violence when Zooman is accidentally killed in his attempt to tear it down. Another black child lies dead in the street, another family grieves, and another sign goes up as a momentary monument to incredible waste.

An ultimately pervasive irony that empties the landscape of possible victors and reveals instead a society maimed by racism is equally evident in *A Soldier's Play*. Unlike Zooman, Sergeant Waters espouses the black middle-class values of hard work, education, and racial pride as the means of self-advancement. Like Zooman, Waters seeks a sphere in which to exercise a masculine sense of control and dignity, but he has had only limited success, for he operates within the segregated army of World War II. The search for his killer triggers a series of flashbacks that reveal him as a vicious, petty tyrant bent on literally ridding the race of those blues-singing, hoodoo-oriented men who, he says, prevent advancement. Yet the flashbacks also create a measure of sympathy for this ambitious man who is consumed by misplaced faith, self-hatred, and guilt.

The eventual identification of two black recruits as Waters's murderers defies the expectation, carefully nurtured by the playwright, that overt white hostility was the motivating factor. In addition, it raises questions concerning the definition of justice, for the infantrymen have just received their long-awaited orders to ship out, in effect being granted license to kill in Europe a tyranny similar to what Waters represented at home. Compounding the irony further, Fuller provides a postscript that subverts the dramatic experience. The investigating officer reveals that the entire incident is recorded in military documents as a meaningless black-on-black crime, Waters is inadvertently listed as a heroic war casualty, and the entire company is destroyed in combat. Thus, the army learns nothing from this sorry episode.

Fuller's dramatic world is dominated by driven, destructive men trying to carve out a viable place within a hostile environment. Though his characters inhabit a bleak landscape, his audiences need not, for through the dramatic experience they can appreciate how racism distorts a society and can choose to stop the human destruction.

—Sandra L. Richards

FURTH, George

Nationality: American. **Born:** George Schweinfurth in Chicago, Illinois, 14 December 1932. **Education:** Northwestern University, Evanston, Illinois, B.S. in speech 1954; Columbia University, New York, 1955-56, M.F.A. 1956. **Military Service:** Served in the United States Navy, 1958-62. **Career:** Stage, film, and television actor from 1956; member of the Drama Department, University of Southern California, Los Angeles, 1979. **Awards:** New York Drama Critics Circle award, 1970; Outer Circle award, 1970; Drama Desk award, 1970; Tony award, 1971. **Agent:** The Lantz Office, 888 Seventh Avenue, New York, New York 10106. **Address:** 3030 Durand Drive, Hollywood, California 90068, U.S.A.

Publications

Plays

Company, music and lyrics by Stephen Sondheim (produced New York, 1970; London, 1972). New York, Random House, 1970.

Twigs (includes *Emily, Celia, Dorothy, Ma*) (produced New York, 1971; Coventry, 1973). New York, French, 1972.

The Act, music by John Kander, lyrics by Fred Ebb (produced New York, 1977). New York, French, 1987.

Merrily We Roll Along, music and lyrics by Stephen Sondheim, adaptation of the play by George S. Kaufman and Moss Hart (produced New York, 1981; London, 1983).

The Supporting Cast (produced New York, 1981). New York, French, 1982.

Precious Sons (produced New York, 1986). New York, French, 1988.

Getting Away with Murder, with Stephen Sondheim. New York, Theatre Communications Group, 1997.

Recording: *Precious Sons,* Theatre Works, 1995.

*

Manuscript Collection: Northwestern University School of Speech, Evanston, Illinois.

Theatrical Activities:
Director: **Plays**—*The Supporting Cast*, Chicago, 1986; *Precious Sons*, Chicago, 1988.

Actor: **Plays**—Jordan in *A Cook for Mr. General* by Steve Gethers, New York, 1961; Junior Tubbs in *Hot Spot*, 1963; Skip in *Tadpole* by Jules Tasca, Los Angeles, 1973; Butler in *Tiny Alice* by Edward Albee; Arnold in *The Supporting Cast*, Los Angeles, 1982. **Films**—*The Best Man*, 1964; *The New Interns*, 1964; *A Rage to Live*, 1965; *A Very Special Favor*, 1965; *The Cool Ones*, 1967; *Games*, 1967; *Tammy and the Millionaire*, 1967; *The Boston Strangler*, 1968; *How to Save a Marriage—And Ruin Your Life*, 1968; *Nobody's Perfect*, 1968; *P.J.*, 1968; *What's So Bad about Feeling Good?*, 1968; *Butch Cassidy and the Sundance Kid*, 1969; *Myra Breckinridge*, 1970; *Blazing Saddles*, 1974; *Shampoo*, 1975; *Airport '77*, 1977; *Cannonball Run*, 1981; *MegaForce*, 1982; *The Man with Two Brains*, 1983; *Doctor Detroit*, 1983. **Television**—*Tammy*,

Broadside, *Mary Hartman, Mary Hartman* and *The Dumplings* series.

* * *

George Furth's career, his book for Stephen Sondheim's *Company* excepted, has been a tantalizing series of near misses. Adroit as his work is, especially when he has risked innovations with the actual form of mainstream playwriting, he has rarely strayed from the narrow range of concerns that can occupy the successful Broadway play.

Twigs is essentially four one-act plays with a linking thread that provide a versatile actress with the chance to play three different sisters and their mother in the course of the evening. Taking its title from Alexander Pope ("Just as the twig is bent, the tree's inclined"), the plays are set in four different kitchens all on the same day before Thanksgiving. All of the sisters have their problems, seen mainly through a comedic lens, although the slick lines and sight gags of the first playlet, in which the garrulous, recently widowed Emily finds a possible new romance, are in sharp contrast to the second, in which Celia, married to a crudely unfeeling slob whose ex-army buddy joins them for Thanksgiving, trembles on the verge of another nervous breakdown. This play begins in a vein of rambunctious comedy but gradually reveals an undertow of bleak pain. Furth does not always have time to paint in the subtlest of brush strokes, one of the hazards of the one-act format. Perhaps unsurprisingly, the most successful episode is the final one, in which the sisters' terminally ill mother, a formidable old lady, decides that before she dies the "Pa" with whom she has lived for so long will do right by her and marry her. The ensuing wedding scene with an understandably flustered priest may be fairly broad comedy, but it also has a gleeful relish, skirting the boundaries of taste, that fuels it with zest.

Furth, with an actor's background, gives all of his cast good opportunities, as well as providing a virtuoso showcase for the central performer. The play had a moderate Broadway success, which was more than he achieved with *The Supporting Cast.* Set in a luxurious Malibu beach house, with a brushfire and a minor earthquake among the traumas of the day, the play is happiest in the realms of a wisecracking or visual comedy; it milks a recurring sight gag of characters walking into glass patio doors, and the dialogue is crammed with sardonic one-liners, the most pungent coming from the sharp-tongued Mae. Like all of the characters, all friends of the first-time novelist Ellen, whose novel's publication requires waivers from the real-life prototypes of her characters, Mae represents East Coast unease with Californian living. (As Florrie from Brooklyn puts it, "Someone must have tipped this country on its end and everything that wasn't screwed down fell into California."). The play's slight plot rests on the mixed reactions to the book before outrage turns to ego preening. Aiming to be a high-octane zany comedy, the play becomes progressively more desperate in its contrivances simply to keep events moving.

All of which made Furth's later play perhaps somewhat surprising. *Precious Sons* managed only a short run, even in a Broadway season starved of good new plays. It has many of the hallmarks of an autobiographical play. Set in Furth's native Chicago in the summer of 1949, it is a solidly naturalistic play centered on the lower-middle-class household of Fred Small, a hardworking and tough father in poor health; Bea, his slapdash, indomitably optimistic wife; and their two very different sons, the younger with dreams of becoming an actor, the elder sneaking off to wed his prom sweetheart, for both of whom Fred is desperate for better lives. It is a long and sometimes flawed play, somewhat confused over Bea's motives at crucial points, especially her attitude toward a projected promotion of Fred's, but it offers magnificent acting opportunities, particularly in the loving, brawling volatile relationship between Fred and Bea. The play, set as it is in 1949, inevitably recalls the playwrights of that period—Inge, Miller, Williams (indeed, Williams figures strongly in the story, with Freddy, the younger son, auditioning for the touring company of *A Streetcar Named Desire*, producing a wonderful scene in which Bea has to read Blanche to Freddy's newspaper boy). The work deserved a more considered critical reaction than the faint praise it received on Broadway.

Furth has had considerable success with his streamlined books for various musicals, including *Company. The Act,* however, required little more than linking dialogue between Liza Minnelli's numbers. Sadly the failure of *Precious Sons* on Broadway, a bitter disappointment, seems to have atrophied Furth's talent. This was especially regrettable when revivals of *Company* in both London and New York reminded audiences of his tart, laconic dialogue and his gift for framing both comic and dramatic scenes.

—Alan Strachan

G

GABRE-MEDHIN, Tsegaye

Nationality: Ethiopian. **Born:** Ambo, Shewa, 17 August 1936. **Education:** Zema and Kine Ethiopian Orthodox Church Schools, 1945-48; Ambo Elementary School, 1948-52; General Wingate and Commercial Secondary schools, 1952-56; Blackstone School of Law, Chicago, LL.B. 1959. **Family:** Married Laketch Bitew in 1961; three daughters. **Career:** Studied British theatre at the Royal Court Theatre, London, and French theatre at the Comédie Française, Paris, 1959-60; director, 1961-71, and general manager, 1967-74, Haile Selassie I Theatre (now Ethiopian National Theatre), Addis Ababa; editor, Oxford University Press, Addis Ababa, 1971; research fellow, University of Dakar, Senegal, 1971—; permanent secretary, Ministry of Culture and Sports, Addis Ababa, 1975-76; assistant professor of theatre arts, Addis Ababa University, 1977; secretary general, Ethiopian Peace, Solidarity and Friendship House, 1979. Currently adviser, Ministry of Culture, Addis Ababa. **Awards:** Unesco fellowship, 1959; International Theatre Institute fellowship, 1965; Haile Selassie I prize, 1966; Fulbright fellowship, 1966, 1971, 1975, 1985; Gold Mercury award, 1982. Commander, Senegal National Order, 1971. **Address:** Ministry of Culture, P.O. Box 1907, Addis Ababa, Ethiopia.

Publications

Plays

Belg (Autumn) (produced Addis Ababa, 1957). Addis Ababa, Berhanena Selam, 1962.

Yeshoh Aklil (Crown of Thorns) (produced Addis Ababa, 1958). Addis Ababa, Berhanena Selam, 1959.

Askeyami Lijagered (The Ugly Girl) (produced Addis Ababa, 1959).

Jorodegif (Mumps) (produced Addis Ababa, 1959).

Listro (Shoe Shine Boy) (produced Addis Ababa, 1960).

Igni Biye Metahu (Back with a Grin) (produced Addis Ababa, 1960).

Chulo (Errand Boy) (produced Addis Ababa, 1961).

Kosho Cigara (Cheap Cigarettes) (produced Addis Ababa, 1961).

Yemama Zetegn Melk (Mother's Nine Faces) (produced Addis Ababa, 1961).

Tewodros (in English; produced Addis Ababa, 1962; revised version produced Addis Ababa, 1983; London, 1987). Published in *Ethiopian Observer* (Addis Ababa), vol. 10, no. 3, 1966.

Othello, adaptation of the play by Shakespeare. Addis Ababa, Oxford University Press, 1963.

Tartuffe, adaptation of the play by Molière (produced Addis Ababa, 1963).

The Doctor in Spite of Himself, adaptation of a play by Molière (produced Addis Ababa, 1963).

Oda Oak Oracle: A Legend of Black Peoples, Told of Gods and God, Of Hope and Love, Of Fears and Sacrifices (produced Addis Ababa, 1964). London and New York, Oxford University Press, 1965.

Azmari (in English; produced Addis Ababa, 1964). Published in *Ethiopian Observer* (Addis Ababa), vol. 10, no. 10, 1966.

Yekermo Sew (The Seasoned) (produced Addis Ababa, 1966). Addis Ababa, Berhanena Selam, 1967.

Petros (produced Addis Ababa, 1968).

King Lear, adaptation of the play by Shakespeare (produced in part, Addis Ababa, 1968).

Macbeth, adaptation of the play by Shakespeare (produced in part, Addis Ababa, 1968). Addis Ababa, Oxford University Press, 1972.

Hamlet, adaptation of the play by Shakespeare (produced in part, Addis Ababa, 1968). Addis Ababa, Oxford University Press, 1972.

Kirar Siker (Kirar Tight-Tuned) (produced Addis Ababa, 1969).

Ha Hu Besidist Wer (A-B-C in Six Months) (produced Addis Ababa, 1974). Addis Ababa, Berhanena Selam, 1975.

Enat Alem Tenu (Mother Courage), adaptation of the play by Brecht (produced Addis Ababa, 1975). Addis Ababa, Berhanena Selam, 1975.

Atsim Beyegetsu (Skeleton in Pages) (produced Addis Ababa, 1975).

Abugida Transform (produced Addis Ababa, 1976).

Collision of Altars. London, Collings, 1977.

Melikte Proletarian (produced Addis Ababa, 1979).

Mekdem (Preface) (produced Addis Ababa, 1980).

Gamo (produced Addis Ababa, 1981).

Zeray (produced Asmara, Eritrea, 1981).

Zikegna Abera (produced Addis Ababa, 1986).

Poetry

Issat Woy Ababa (Fire of Flower). Addis Ababa, Berhanena Selam, 1973.

Other

Ethiopia: Footprint of Time (travel), photographs by Alberto Tessore. Udine, Italy, Magnus, 1984.

*

Tsegaye Gabre-Medhin comments:

I do not think in English or French but in Ethiopian first. My cultural personality is formed out of a background that consciously resists being re-created in the image of any and all supremacist alien values. I write for a people who for many thousands of years have developed a conscious taste for their own poetic heritage, in one of their own scripts, and in one of their own indigenous languages. I write in the literature of one of the children of Kam: of Meroe, of Nubia, of Egypt, of Ethiopia—of the cradles of the world's earliest civilization. The people are still the judges of my plays that mirror them. They are still the critics of the poetry and culture that make them, and that in turn they themselves make.

If for instance a British poet *naturally* felt hard put to think or dream his verse in Chinese it is because a.) Chinese is not the natural expression of British culture; b.) Chinese literature forms the Chinese personality, makes and develops first a Chinese universal man and not first a Briton or a British personality; and c.) the said British poet is not yet re-created in the image of the Chinese. Can any African artist-poet or playwright (unless of course his culture is already killed in him and replaced by something else) afford to think or dream his verse in anything less than what is his indigenous African expression FIRST? Just like *no* Chinese literature can make a truly British culture, so there is *no* English, French, Dutch, or Portuguese, etc., literature that can make a truly African culture.

* * *

Tsegaye Gabre-Medhin has written and directed plays in Amharic, including versions of Shakespeare and Molière. In his English plays both the phrasing and the poetic conception suggest that he is experimenting with the transferal of devices alien to modern English. This can be seen in *Oda Oak Oracle*, for instance:

Loneliness is
When the ripe fruit fails,
To make the bird
Aware of its existence.
Loneliness is
When the avoided heart,
Growing stale every night,
Wears a mask of bitterness,
While the tense veins
Growing frantic and mad
Scratch at the mask
Of a stricken heart.
Loneliness is
When the aged mule
Rubs its flank
Against the deserted trunk
Of a dead bush.
Loneliness is
When the moon is left cold
Among a glowing
Jungle of stars.

The rich elaboration contributes to the florid, torrid melodrama.

In *Oda Oak Oracle* the oracle has decreed marriage between Shanka and Ukutee and the sacrifice of their firstborn to the ancestors. To avoid this, Shanka refuses to consummate the marriage. In humiliation and frustration Ukutee offers herself to Shanka's friend Goaa. He brings to the play the perspective of another society, for he had once been taken away by strangers and instructed by them in the Gospel. His criticism of the oracle and traditional beliefs feeds Shanka's doubts. By the last act Ukutee is in labor. Clouds darken the valley, and there is perturbation among the elders at the lack of sun. The oracle commands a combat between Goaa and Shanka, the victor to be flogged from the valley by Ukutee. Goaa is killed, and Ukutee consents to whip Shanka since the oracle has promised that she will then bear a fine son. In fact, she dies giving birth to a daughter, and the play ends with Shanka holding the child as a mob approaches to stone both of them to death.

In his *Four African Literatures* (1971) Albert Gerard finds this doom-laden play to be "one of the finest plays to have been written in Africa." I find the extremely short lines awkward, however, and their divisions of little help to the speaker. Moreover, the climax of the play seems to pile up punishments overingeniously.

The resignation of a sixth-century emperor after he has lost his army to disease, the political impotence of his sons, and the disintegration of the empire from religious sectarianism are the subjects of *Collision of Altars*. Gabre-Medhin's theatrical experience is evident in the ingeniously complex setting and epic scale, but character development seems precluded by the number of representatives of different religions and political interests and by the public nature of most of the scenes. In any case the author is interested in presenting the conflicts in a symbolic dimension. The ultimate effect is one of a vast threnody.

More interesting, I believe, are two short plays that appeared in the *Ethiopia Observer*. *Tewodros* is an account of a mid-nineteenth-century commoner who rose to be emperor. He had a vision of uniting Ethiopia, but his rule was troubled by various revolts and ended with a British invasion. Showing both concern for the welfare of the common people and bloody ruthlessness, Tewodros is an ambiguous figure, and the interest of Gabre-Medhin's play lies not in his Tamerlane-like career but in the doubts expressed by his first and second wives and by others around him:

> Washing my hands in other's blood and watching mine flow out has occupied the best years of my life. The one exciting activity I can remember of my only son is the lashing of his paper sword and his shouting of the war-cry "zeraf" . . . until finally I heard him repeat the same thing on the battlefield once and for all . . . then he bled to death in my arms. What has the poor peasant to live for, Princess, if he can't afford to question why his children should sing war songs and not read the Book of Life?

The same note is struck in *Collision of Altars*.

The most successful of Gabre-Medhin's plays is *Azmari*. *Azmaris* are professional singers, and female *azmaris* are considered little better than courtesans. The play portrays the tensions in a family, each generation of which has a member who is called to be "the expressive medium for Nature's passions." It is thus that Lulu considers herself. The center of the play is Lulu's clash with her mother, who resents her being "out with that moaning harp of hers day and night, and never lifting a finger to help the family" and who maintains that a minstrel's is "no decent folk's way of life." Who is betraying whom—the member of the family who rejects the call of music or the artist who does not help support it?

Unlike Gabre-Medhin's other plays *Azmari* has only one violent action, the smashing of Lulu's harp. As in Chekhov, the significant action takes place offstage—Lulu has played at the marriage of the man she loved, who has jilted her for a socially acceptable bride—and no resolution is offered. The use of music as an emotional punctuation of the scenes is dramatically relevant. Grandiloquence, too, is used dramatically, for it is set off against the everyday speech of those in the family who refuse music's call.

—Anthony Graham-White

GAGLIANO, Frank (Joseph)

Nationality: American. **Born:** Brooklyn, New York. **Education:** Queens College, New York, 1949-53; University of Iowa, Iowa

City, B.A. 1954; Columbia University, New York, M.F.A. 1957. **Military Service:** Served in the United States Army, 1954-56. **Family:** Married Sandra Gordon in 1958; one son. **Career:** Freelance copywriter, New York, 1958-61; promotion copywriter, McGraw-Hill Text-Film Division, New York, 1962-65. Associate professor of drama, Florida State University, Tallahassee, 1969-72; lecturer in playwriting and director of the E. P. Conkle Workshop, University of Texas, Austin, 1972-75. Benedum professor of playwriting, University of West Virginia, Morgantown, 1976—. Visiting professor, University of Rhode Island, Providence, 1975. Lives in Pittsburgh. **Awards:** Rockefeller grant, 1965, 1966; Wesleyan University-O'Neill Foundation fellowship, 1967; National Endowment for the Arts grant, 1973; Guggenheim fellowship, 1974; Pennsylvania Playwrighting fellowship, 1990; yearly $2,000 Benedum Grant (1986-97). **Agent:** Gilbert Parker, William Morris Agency, 1325 Avenue of the Americas, New York, New York 10019, U.S.A. **Address:** Theatre Arts Center, University of West Virginia, Morgantown, West Virginia 26506, U.S.A.

Publications

Plays

Night of the Dunce (as *The Library Raid*, produced Houston, 1961; revised version, as *Night of the Dunce*, produced New York, 1966). New York, Dramatists Play Service, 1967.
Conerico Was Here to Stay (produced New York, 1965). Included in *The City Scene*, 1966.
The City Scene (includes *Paradise Gardens East* and *Conerico Was Here to Stay*) (produced New York, 1969). New York, French, 1966.
Father Uxbridge Wants to Marry (produced Waterford, Connecticut, and New York, 1967). New York, Dramatists Play Service, 1968.
The Hide-and-Seek Odyssey of Madeleine Gimple (produced Waterford, Connecticut, 1967). New York, Dramatists Play Service, 1970.
The Prince of Peasantmania (Inny), music by James Reichert (produced Waterford, Connecticut, 1968; revised version produced Milwaukee, 1970). New York, Agency for the Performing Arts, 1968.
Big Sur (televised 1969; revised version produced Tallahassee, Florida, 1970). New York, Dramatists Play Service, 1971.
In the Voodoo Parlour of Marie Laveau: Gris-Gris, and The Comedia World of Byron B (produced Waterford, Connecticut, 1973; as *Gris-Gris, and The Comedia World of Lafcadio Beau*, produced New York, 1974; revised version, as *Voodoo Trilogy*, produced New York, 1977; revised version, as *In the Voodoo Parlour of Marie Laveau*, produced New York, 1983).
Congo Square, music by Claibe Richardson (produced Providence, Rhode Island, 1975).
The Resurrection of Jackie Cramer, music by Raymond Benson (produced Providence, Rhode Island, and New York, 1976).
The Private Eye of Hiram Bodoni (produced New York, 1978).
The Total Immersion of Madeleine Favorini (produced Las Vegas, Nevada, 1981).
San Ysidro (cantata), music by James Reichert (produced Milwaukee, 1985).
From the Bodoni County Songbook Anthology, Book 1 (produced Morgantown, West Virginia, 1986).
My Chekhov Light and *Hanna* (produced Pittsburgh, 1991; New York, 1992).
The Last Hurrah of Harold Hubris (produced New York, 1993).
Smells (produced Pittsburgh).
Eulogy (produced 1994).
The Farewell Concert of Irene and Vernon Pallazzo (produced 1994).
The Kafka Furies (produced 1996).

Television Play: *Big Sur*, 1969.

*

Manuscript Collections: Lincoln Center Library of the Performing Arts, New York; O'Neill Theatre Center Library, Waterford, Connecticut.

Critical Studies: *Stages: The Fifty-Year Childhood of the American Theatre* by Emory Lewis, Englewood Cliffs, New Jersey, Prentice Hall, 1969; *The Nature of Theatre* by Vera M. Roberts, New York, Harper, 1971.

* * *

Frank Gagliano is an experimental artist who is uncompromising in his quest for a dramatic form that synthesizes his passion for music, language, and metaphysical themes of Christian idealism in an age of terror, disorder, perversion, and violence. "Mindlessness scares me and I'm in a mindless age," cries the heroine of *The Total Immersion of Madeleine Favorini*. Her words express the playwright's own torment. But Gagliano resembles a medieval dramatist, theatricalizing the terrors of hell to effect salvation yet fascinated by the evils he deplores. In his plays images of decay, violence, and death prevail over those of transcendence and salvation.

Gagliano is at war with himself. His drama is often an unresolved battleground of contradictory themes, language, and structure; winged allegories soar toward some unperceived light, burdened by the very demons they hope to evade. It is a brilliant, painful quest for truth, a journey for playwright and spectator in which the ridiculous and sublime combine in uneasy balance. Gagliano never plays it safe, which is his great virtue as an artist.

Gagliano's two-act opera *Inny* exemplifies the allegories of his earlier work. The dominant metaphor is that of the odyssey toward some form of self-realization, although the play's structure is far more logical and compact than that of his later plays. Innocent Inny, the rightful heir to the throne of Peasantmania, is prevented from ruling by the forces of political, social, and religious corruption that dominate the country. In his struggle to obtain power Inny journeys from innocence to wisdom. Despite the evils endured, Inny remains spiritually pure, a Christ on the throne ready to suffer for man's transgressions and leading him to salvation: "I must stay . . . I'll never understand this—the ones who chased me, beat me, betrayed me . . . I love them all."

Inny is a grand operatic spectacle of pageants, processions, dances, choruses, and battles. There is an entourage of jaded and cruel aristocrats, hags, heroines, and fools, as well as a wise jester, a symbol of art, who ultimately dies a horrid death with Inny's beloved, Glorabella. The dominant image of the play is a huge, foreboding eye that hangs overhead. "God's surrealistic yo-yo?" cries the jester; "But where's the string?" Is the horror heaven sent, the cruel plaything of a less than benign God, or is it the devil's toy? The ultimate answers are beyond us. All we know for certain is that man pursues senseless evil and that the innocent and wicked suffer alike. All we can hope for is that wise, beneficent, and courageous leaders like Inny may ultimately triumph.

The Private Eye of Hiram Bodoni is a flawed, sprawling work intended for television that is part comedy, part surrealistic nightmare. Bodoni, a private eye, is hired to discover the cause of the unexplained death of the star of a television soap opera. The plot, however, is merely a device to explore the lives of the characters through their personal recollections, flashbacks, and fantasies. Although it offers some imaginative visual images and poetic dialogue, the play is confused and unresolved.

In the Voodoo Parlour of Marie Laveau, "an unsung chamber opera," is a three-character play in which a man and woman seek help and revenge from a voodoo sorceress. Under Marie Laveau's spell, the two characters give vent to nightmares and sexual fantasy:

> I wish that was me
> being humped by a donkey
> while the chic of New Orleans
> marveled at me.

The woman's gross allusion revolts the man, who dreams of pure, idealized love. Verbal images of lurid sexuality dominate the play's language, but they do so only as essential to theme and action and never gratuitously. Marie Laveau's parlor is a microcosm of New Orleans at the turn of the century, a city of Mardi Gras, witchcraft, perversion, racial hatred, and violence. The play gains its intensity by the very limitations of its theme. Rather than Gagliano's usual depiction of the characters' torments as symptomatic of a vaster social malaise, *Marie Laveau* concentrates on the characters as ends in themselves. The parallel to nineteenth-century melodramatic plots of love and revenge—a self-contained world of passion, violence, and death—is deliberate. The settings and costumes are simple yet theatrically effective: a bare space, masks, skulls, bizarre headgear, the horrid implements of the voodoo ritual. The hypnotic spell of the ritual is perfectly suited to Gagliano's odyssey metaphor, the evocation of nightmare and fantasy. Through an imaginative use of scenery, costumes, and operatic dialogue, Gagliano creates a Genet-like transcendence through evil. *Marie Laveau* is powerful drama that lends itself naturally to music.

In *The Total Immersion of Madeleine Favorini* Gagliano again uses the metaphor of the journey into the self through the protagonist's total immersion in fantasy, nightmares, and dreams. Madeleine, a timid librarian locked in a gynecologist's stirrups for two weeks, wanders back in fantasy to Sicily, the land of her ancestors. On her journey she encounters various forms and characters: a Stalactite, the Wax Prometheus, the Goddess Materna. The actress playing Madeleine transforms herself into each of them, with the other actor and actress also assuming a variety of identities. Madeleine becomes imbued with the Dionysian and Christian spirit of this ancient land, an earth mother absorbing all humanity into her giant womb. In a brilliant sequence of dialogues Madeleine and her deceased grandfather, Pazzotesto (Crazy Head), rhapsodize over the wonders of the basil that covers the landscape of Sicily, creeping "up from the bottom of the green Mediterranean . . . on the beach . . . the roads, rooftops. The toilets have basil seats. The bells of the great cathedrals are covered with basil and cushion their clang." At the conclusion of the play Madeleine is freed from the restrictions of the harsh, decadent society that nurtured her. She ascends to freedom on a crescendo of pure language: "Yes! Yes! I know what I want. I know what I mean! I want to become—language! Language!"

These final moments of the play seem to represent Gagliano's desire to free himself from the limits of drama. The work is a form of theatricalized literature or poetry rather than drama. Action becomes the exploration of character and theme instead of the resolution of some essential dramatic conflict. Gagliano's emphasis on language as the dominant structural element of his drama can become excessive and unfocused. He has a tendency to use dialogue for the sheer richness of sound and imagery. Yet his dialogue can also be stirring or even frightening, revealing a character's desperate need for freedom and salvation.

Gagliano's drama has been in transition. Nonetheless, he has remained one of the most daring, imaginative, and poetic playwrights of the American theater.

—A. Richard Sogliuzzo

GALLACHER, Tom

Nationality: British. **Born:** Alexandria, Dunbartonshire, Scotland, 16 February 1934. **Career:** Writer-in-residence, Pitlochry Festival Theatre, Perthshire, 1975-78, and Royal Lyceum Theatre, Edinburgh, 1978-80. **Awards:** Scottish Arts Council award, 1983, 1986. **Address:** 25 Linn Walk, Garelochhead, Dunbartonshire G84 ODS, Scotland.

Publications

Plays

Our Kindness to Five Persons (produced Glasgow, 1969). Glasgow, Scottish Society of Playwrights, 1980.

Mr. Joyce Is Leaving Paris (produced London, 1970; revised version produced Dublin, 1971; London, 1972; New York, 1978). London, Calder and Boyars, 1972.

Revival! (produced Dublin, 1972; London, 1973). With *Schellenbrack*, Glasgow, Molendinar Press, 1978.

Three to Play: Janus, Pastiche, Recital (produced Montrose, Angus, 1972; *Recital* produced London, 1973).

Schellenbrack (produced London, 1973). With *Revival!*, Glasgow, Molendinar Press, 1978.

Bright Scene Fading (produced London, 1973).

The Only Street (produced Dublin and London, 1973). Glasgow, Scottish Society of Playwrights, 1980.

Personal Effects (produced Pitlochry, 1974).

A Laughing Matter (produced St. Andrews, 1975).

Hallowe'en (produced Dundee, 1975). Glasgow, Scottish Society of Playwrights, 1980.

The Sea Change (produced Edinburgh, 1976). Glasgow, Scottish Society of Playwrights, 1980.

A Presbyterian Wooing, adaptation of the play *The Assembly* by Archibald Pitcairne (produced Pitlochry, 1976).

The Evidence of Tiny Tim, with Joan Knight (produced Perth, 1977).
Wha's Like Us—Fortunately (produced Dundee, 1978).
Stage Door Canteen, with John Scrimger (produced Perth, 1978).
Deacon Brodie, adaptation of the play by Robert Louis Stevenson and W.E. Henley (produced Edinburgh, 1978).
An Enemy of the People, adaptation of a play by Ibsen (produced Edinburgh, 1979).
Jenny (produced Pitlochry, 1979). London, French, 1980.
Natural Causes (produced Perth, 1980).
The Father, adaptation of a play by Strindberg (produced Dundee, 1980).
A Doll's House, adaptation of a play by Ibsen (produced Edinburgh, 1980).
The Parole of Don Juan (produced Perth, 1981).
The Treasure Ship, adaptation of the play by John Brandane (produced Pitlochry, 1981).
The Wild Duck, adaptation of a play by Ibsen (produced Perth, 1987).

Radio Plays: *Progress to an Exile*, 1970; *The Scar*, 1973; *Hunting Shadows*, 1975; *The Man with a Hatchet*, 1976; *Portrait of Isa Mulvenny*, 1978; *Perfect Pitch*, 1979; *Store Quarter*, 1983; *The Previous Tenant*, 1986.

Television Plays: *The Trial of Thomas Muir*, 1977; *If the Face Fits*, 1978.

Novels

Apprentice. London, Hamish Hamilton, 1983.
Journeyman. London, Hamish Hamilton, 1984.
Survivor. London, Hamish Hamilton, 1985.
The Wind on the Heath. London, Hamish Hamilton, 1987.

Short Stories

Hunting Shadows. Helensburgh, Jeffrey, 1981.
The Jewel Maker. London, Hamish Hamilton, 1986.

Uncollected Short Stories

"In Defiance of Miss Hetty" in *The Herald*, 1992.
"The Hermit" in *The Herald*, 1993.
"Lord Help the Sister" in *The Herald*, 1994.
"Our Missives Now Are Concluded" in *The Herald*, 1996.
"The Transformation of Walden Sunter" in *The Herald*, 1996.
"The Extravagances of Sir Robert Morton" in *The Herald*, 1996.
"Post Early for Crisis" in *The Herald*, 1996.
"Pride Accounts for Everything" in *The Herald*, 1997.
"The Ascent of Dumbarton Rock" in *The Herald*, 1997.

Other

To Succeed at Home. Edinburgh, Chapman, 1986.
The Way to Write for the Stage. London, Elm Tree, 1987.

*

Tom Gallacher comments:

(1977) Mainly, the plays deal with exceptions. Sometimes the exceptions are artists; sometimes it is another kind of outsider, a genius, a catalyst, or a singular man. All of them are in some way seeking to extend the meaning of their lives or the boundaries of reality.

An illustration of this can be gained from my book *The Jewel Maker*, which is a fictional account of a playwright at work. There it is made clear how the work is influenced by people and events, and how the conflict of illusion and reality extends the boundaries of the human spirit. That is the testing ground where human evolution continues to progress.

All the plays celebrate the individual. The protagonists are unmoved by Class, Party, or Movement, but they are acutely conscious of the interior actions of emotion, spirit, and reason. The crises—whether sad or funny—are person to person. The conflict in comedy and drama arises from an effort to make a workable connection—between the accepted and the potential, between what we are and what we may be, between what is degrading and what is exalting.

"Only connect" was the motto which E. M. Forster placed as guardian over his novel *Howards End*. I can't think of a better motto for a writer because the motto leads to a concept of great courage and enterprise. The characters in my plays do not always master the concept or gain its acceptance by others. But if they go down they go down knowing which way is forward.

(1998) After many years writing fiction, my return to drama with *Of Time and Loss* shows, for the first time, a political dimension. This coincides with the return of a Scottish parliament after 300 years of London domination. Yet, I would like to think the play's themes of atavism and repatriation will not obscure the more essential preoccupations of the characters.

Certainly, the play now in progress is all character, and the character is William Somerset Maugham. For in this dramatised biography, once more the conflict of reality and illusion is my main interest.

* * *

At the end of Tom Gallacher's first play, *Our Kindness to Five Persons*, an alcoholic Glaswegian author pours himself another drink and proposes a solitary toast: "Should auld acquaintance be forgot and *never* brought to mind? Yes. Please God. Yes." The play has just demonstrated a denial of the prayer, but the question and the artist's special rights of adjudication over it are constant threads through the plays Gallacher has written since.

Gallacher's preoccupation with art and artists is immediately obvious on the surfaces of his plays. Writers are the central characters of at least half of them, and Gallacher often points a passage of dialogue toward the epigrammatic use of a quotation or builds a scene around the recitation of poetry or the singing of ballads. Literary sources and models are of even greater substantive and structural importance for some of Gallacher's work. *The Sea Change* and the short radio play *The Scar* are both dream plays within plays in which the stuff of the central character's imagination comes from Shakespeare. *A Presbyterian Wooing* descends from literary obscurity, and *The Assembly* is a Jacobite's dramatic satire on the ecclesiastical politics and personal morals of the Edinburgh Kirk. Trimmed and embroidered into a neo-Restoration comedy of sexual hypocrisy, *A Presbyterian Wooing* demonstrates Gallacher's sensitivity to earlier dramatic modes and his ability to tune his invention and idiom to the same key. The same knack belabors

Ibsen's dramaturgy and Kierkegaard's ontology in *Revival!*, the aim of which seems to be to tease the audience into reading the complete works of both Scandinavians. In *Hallowe'en,* on the other hand, Fraser's account of that ritual in pagan times is compactly reincarnated in contemporary Glasgow, and the literary *drame à clé* is cleanly unlocked in the dialogue.

The thematic purposes to which Gallacher puts these and other of his "auld acquaintance" in literature are remarkably repetitive, although the dramatic techniques he uses vary considerably. He is occupied to the edge of obsession with the dual nature of the remembered past—omnipresent in influence and irretrievable in fact. Every one of his original plays is in large measure focused on the relationship between dramatic past and present. In some cases a radical time change is built into the play, its point of departure being the out-of-time introduction of the central character. *The Sea Change, Bright Scene Fading,* and the unproduced *A Lady Possessed* are all constructed as flashbacks in time and space through the consciousness of the central character, while *Mr. Joyce Is Leaving Paris* brings the personages of Joyce's past to the front of his present consciousness. The other plays, while preserving naturalistic time schemes and the convention of the fourth wall, investigate events and relationships anterior to the action of the play, reenact them, or exorcise them.

For Gallacher the memory that matters is the artistic statement of a perception about personal experience. Such a statement stands for him as evidence of the essentials of observed and observer and as an imposition of order and connection among these essentials. "Witness" and "pattern" are terms that often turn up in the dialogue, and another is "signpost," an indication of where someone has been and a directive to those who follow. When the plays incorporate such overt expositions of their author's understanding of art, it is not surprising that several draw attention to their own artificiality. Nor is it surprising that so many celebrate the triumph of artistic insight over technology, biographical data, time, and the perceptions of the pedestrian majority of mankind.

Though the penultimate victory supplies him with some fairly strong stuff, Gallacher finds his best dramatic material in the last. Only here does he create any real competition, and only here are his aesthetic concerns communicated by more than interpretative glosses and plot gimmickry. The axis along which Gallacher most characteristically depicts these conflicts is that of an intense relationship between a gifted figure and a sympathetic sibling or comrade left behind: James and Stanislaus Joyce in *Mr. Joyce Is Leaving Paris*, Martin and Richard in *The Only Street*, and Otto and Steve in *Bright Scene Fading*. The high price of giftedness also hovers over the presentation of parent-child, husband-wife, and mentor-pupil relationships in these and other plays, but Gallacher plays a better game for higher stakes when he is dealing with doubles and shadows.

Gallacher's own practice of art as witness and as pattern is apparent in his plays and illuminates some of their more idiosyncratic aspects. His writing of dialogue is distinguished on the one hand by an accurate reproduction of spoken rhythms, with particularly precise variations for local, professional, social, and even situational idiom, and on the other by a wit that specializes in paradoxes, perfect squelches, and the literalization of abstractions and figures of speech. Gallacher rarely loses this balance of an attentive ear and orderly invention.

Gallacher's patterning of his materials betrays a taste for symmetry, a mastery of plot mechanics, and an ability to exploit exposition, complication, reversal, and resolution in traditional well-made ways or to invert them for the sake of emphasis. (The exceptions to this rule of flexibility are found in his act endings, for he seems incapable of placing an interval anywhere but on the edge of a cliff in the plot.) His fascination with pattern is perhaps most easily perceived in miniature in the tidy and playful plots of his three one-acts for three players—*Janus, Recital,* and *Pastiche*. The patterning is, however, so apparent in the full-length plays as well that it is impressively ironic that Gallacher's best and best-known play, *Mr. Joyce Is Leaving Paris,* should be, superficially, his most untidy. The second half of the play saw production first, and its order is not dictated by traditional dramaturgy but, as is pointed out by one of the figures that haunt the aging Joyce, by the order of events at an Irish wake. That the "corpse" is the sole survivor of the wake is a good instance of how Gallacher can plot a joke to great thematic purpose. The order of the first half, set much earlier in Joyce's career but written slightly later in Gallacher's, is one of the playwright's confrontations of gifted and ungifted, moving from mutual challenge, though routines long familiar to both, toward acceptance. Although Stanislaus turns up, much muted, in the second half, the two patterns converge only through the consciousness of Joyce, formal confirmation of his and, behind him, of Gallacher's claim to sole mastery of the remembered situations.

In fact, *Mr. Joyce Is Leaving Paris* typifies Gallacher's dramatic writing as a whole as well as at its best. The qualitative difference between its parts is the difference between commendably accomplished craftsmanship and irresistibly imaginative insight. An analogous difference may be discerned in the use of theatrical resources. To these Gallacher is always attentive, using them to supplement the scripted action and dialogue in his fourth-wall dramas and pulling off some stunning isolated effects in the process. At best, however, Gallacher makes the technical parts of theatrical production indispensable to his dramatic statement. The lighting in the second half of *Mr. Joyce Is Leaving Paris,* for example, and the set for *The Sea Change* serve as visual indexes to the central character's control of his memories and thus as evidence of the truth of his vision. In *The Sea Change* that vision, despite its ingenious presentation, remains derivative and diffuse. But when, as in the second half of *Mr. Joyce Is Leaving Paris,* Gallacher aligns tradition and his individual talent in perfect focus, he creates a resonant work.

—Marion O'Connor

GARDNER, Herb(ert)

Nationality: American. **Born:** Brooklyn, New York, 28 December 1934. **Education:** High School of Performing Arts, New York, graduated 1952; Carnegie Institute of Technology, Pittsburgh; Antioch College, Yellow Springs, Ohio. **Career:** Cartoonist: created *The Nebbishes* syndicated cartoon strip. Lives in New York City. **Awards:** Oscar nomination for Best Picture, Best Screenplay, 1965; Screenwriters Guild award, 1966; Tony award, 1986; Outer Critics Circle award, 1986; John Gassner award, 1986. **Address:** c/o Samuel French Inc., 45 West 25th Street, New York, New York 10010, U.S.A.

Publications

Plays

The Elevator (produced New York, 1952). New York, French, 1952.

A Thousand Clowns (produced New York, 1962; London, 1964). New York, Random House, 1962.

The Goodbye People (produced New York, 1968). New York, Farrar Straus, 1974; revised version (produced Los Angeles and New York, 1979), included in *A Thousand Clowns, Thieves, The Goodbye People*, 1979.

Who Is Harry Kellerman and Why Is He Saying Those Terrible Things about Me? (screenplay). New York, New American Library, 1971.

Thieves (produced New York, 1974). Included in *A Thousand Clowns, Thieves, The Goodbye People*, 1979.

Three One Act Plays (includes *How I Crossed the Street for the First Time All By Myself*; *The Forever Game*; *I'm With Ya Duke*). *Duke* published in *Best American Short Plays*, New York, Applause Books, 1996.

Life and/or Death (produced New York, 1979).

A Thousand Clowns, Thieves, The Goodbye People. New York, Doubleday, 1979.

I'm Not Rappaport (produced Seattle and New York, 1985; Birmingham and London, 1986). New York, Doubleday, 1986.

Conversations with My Father (produced New York, 1992). New York, Pantheon Books, 1994.

Screenplays: *A Thousand Clowns*, 1965; *Who Is Harry Kellerman and Why Is He Saying Those Terrible Things about Me?*, 1971; *Thieves*, 1976; *The Goodbye People*, 1982; *I'm Not Rappaport*, 1995.

Television Play: *Happy Endings*, with others, 1975.

Novel

A Piece of the Action. New York, Simon and Schuster, 1958; London, W.H. Allen, 1959.

*

Critical Study: "The Struggle to Affirm: The Image of Jewish-Americans on Stage" by Glenda Frank, in *Staging Difference: Cultural Pluralism in American Theatre and Drama,* edited by Marc Maufort, New York, Peter Lang, 1995.

* * *

Critics keep trying to point out serious ideas in Herb Gardner's plays, but the playwright consistently wards off their attempts with a comic flourish. Clearly a thoughtful man, obviously stimulated by certain prevailing attitudes of mankind, he insists that he is a writer of comedy and that his objective is to entertain audiences. Surely this is a noble and inspiring trait in a modern dramatist, particularly during a period in history when social issues are forcibly intruded into theaters at every opportunity. Unlike Robert Sherwood, who, though concerned with the human condition, hid his serious thoughts behind a facade of light comedy, the like-minded Gardner looks carefully around. And, like Chekhov, he is genuinely amused by what he sees—the fancied and the futile attempts of man to escape the real world and the indefatigable quality of old age. Gardner, then, proceeds to use the comic techniques that bring his plays—*A Thousand Clowns, The Goodbye People, Thieves*, and *I'm Not Rappaport*—to Broadway.

The world that seems funny to Gardner, however, sometimes arrests the attention of others as extremely sad. There is Max Silverman in *The Goodbye People*. This exuberant but completely unrealistic old gentleman wants to erase 20 years from passing time, rebuild his hot dog stand on Coney Island, and bring his "Hawaiian Ecstasies" to an eager public. Moreover, he wants to do this in February, so convinced is he that his dreams can awaken ecstasy in a dull world. There is old Nat in *I'm Not Rappaport,* a defiant, irascible Jewish radical who refuses to be intimidated by either the establishment or the underworld and who rejects any movement that intrudes upon his independence. There are all the pathetic people around the apartment building in *Thieves,* each with a problem to which no one listens, each a thief, and each being robbed by passing time. And from *A Thousand Clowns* there are Murray, who is tortured by the world he sees, Leo, who wants to believe in himself but cannot, and Arthur, who purposefully surrenders to the establishment but survives by catching the wind and going with it. Gardner's characters mainly appear to catch the cold wind straight in their faces, defiantly, stubbornly, and disastrously, and they die, in one sense or another, romantically and in the glow of stage sentiment.

The comic appeal of Gardner's plays comes from his mastery of comic technique and his philosophy as a writer. Although not a storyteller and, as his plays show, somewhat contemptuous of traditional plotting, he likes to hear people talk. He is also a dreamer who, like Nat, can make up little scenes that may appear as a line, a speech, or an incident—a joke, a monologue, or an episode. Like Max Silverman, Gardner does not believe in standing around and watching. One must act, wage battle even while knowing that victory is impossible. Like Murray, he is afraid of "dying alive." Although called a "laureate of losers," Gardner has a sense of comic balance that contradicts this description. He sees humor, not sadness. Losers stand around, while fighters keep the soul alive, and Gardner's characters, synthetic and romanticized or caricatured as they may be, are ever hopeful, even in their fantastic, ridiculous, or childishly recalcitrant attempts to escape whatever worlds surround them. Gardner sees his people as survivors, and in juxtaposing their acts with those of others in the world he experiences he creates dramatic tension in silly-serious, comic-tragic, and pathetic-horrible situations while revealing a real comic irony.

Structurally, Gardner's plays include a lavishly encumbered stage and a love story. As visual metaphors there are the incredibly messy room in *A Thousand Clowns,* the beach that sprouts fireworks in *The Goodbye People,* the terrace in *Thieves,* and the bench in *I'm Not Rappaport*. Gardner truly loves the long monologue, the quick repartee of stand-up comedians, and the one-line gag. Jewish humor, local New York humor, visual jokes, absurd comparisons, and the unexpected retort vie for attention in a selected accumulation of odd people. In *Thieves* a character complains that "all I ever got from this neighborhood was four knife scars, two broken noses and a fruitcake wife! And they all hurt when it rains." Gardner's comedies are assuredly enhanced by good actors. His monologues are a comedian's food and wine, and his dialogue can be as sprightly and as touching as the actor can make it. Music also is significant in his plays, and it may please or assault the ear as the clutter onstage may accost the eye. Within this grand expression of comic theater, where dreams cannot be answered but believing in dreams is deemed necessary, Gardner presents his characters mainly in episodes involving the rituals of lovemaking in the modern world. Then he stops, for conclusions are not his métier.

The comic possibilities that brought Gardner success during most of his career are fleeting and mainly overshadowed by a dour bitterness in *Conversations with My Father*. Perhaps this was inevitable. During the 1960s audiences applauded the rebellious youth's single-minded escape into fantasy from a real world where they found people living as "fakes." Today's audiences are more interested in contending with this real world. Carlton, the young thief in *Thieves,* is not funny to them, nor is Sally, who contends seriously and unsuccessfully with a stubbornly inhuman father. It is scarcely funny to a generation concerned with people starving in the streets that a doorman is not sleeping but dead. When Gardner presents father-daughter relationships in *The Goodbye People, Thieves,* and *I'm Not Rappaport,* all funny to him, each one is geared to the comic sense of a different audience. Unfortunately, his success in catching the balance between pathos and comedy eluded him in *Conversations with My Father*.

Jewish humor may intrude effectively, but by and large the world portrayed in *Conversations with My Father* is not comic. Even the conversations are looked upon as "bouts," a prizefighter's term indicative of the atmosphere created. A frame play in which Charlie remembers his past with his father, an ex-boxer who owns a bar in Brooklyn, *Conversations* painfully yet vividly annotates the difficulties of being a Jew. Full of violence, anger, greed, jealousy, and aggressive defensiveness, Charlie's memories span the years from 1936 to 1976 as his father contends with his family and his Jewish God. Echoing Gardner's dramaturgy in earlier plays, *Conversations with My Father* includes Jewish jokes and monologues with great success, music is basic to its development, and spectacular scenes such as the Flamingo Lounge enhance its production. Gardner's people, too, are still survivors, still reluctant to accept blame. "Sure," says the father, "I screwed up, now it's your turn. . . . End of conversation." But the play creates a deep sense of loss. It is clearly a work of very personal reflection for the dramatist. Gardner sees the sadness, not the humor, and he still draws no conclusions.

—Walter J. Meserve

GEARY, David

Nationality: New Zealander. **Born:** Fielding, New Zealand, 19 September 1963. **Education:** Victoria University, Wellington, 1982-85, B.A. in 1986; New Zealand Drama School, Wellington, 1986-87, drama diploma, 1987. **Career:** Story executive, Melody Rules, Auckland, 1995-96. Freelance actor and writer for theatre, television, and film, 1988—. **Awards:** Bruce Mason Playwright award, 1992; Adam Foundation award, 1996. **Agent:** Playmarket, P.O. Box 9767, Te Aro, Te Wharganui-a-Tara, Wellington, New Zealand. **Address:** 20 Aitken Terrace, Kingsland, Auckland, New Zealand.

Publications

Plays

Gothic Butstauner (produced Wellington, 1988). Wellington, Playmarket, 1988.
Dry, White & Friendly (produced Wellington, 1988). Wellington, Playmarket, 1988.
Pack of Girls (produced Wellington, 1988). Wellington, Playmarket, 1990.
Lovelock's Dream Run (produced Auckland, 1993). Wellington, Victoria University Press, 1993.
Savage Hearts/Manawa Taua (produced Auckland, 1994). Wellington, Playmarket, 1994.
Learner's Stand (produced Wellington, 1994). Wellington, Playmarket, 1994.
Backstage with the Quigleys (produced Wellington, 1994). Wellington, Playmarket, 1994.
The Rabbitter's Daughter (produced Wellington, 1995). Wellington, Playmarket, 1995.
King of Stains (produced Wellington, 1996). Wellington, Playmarket, 1996.
Ruapehu (produced Wellington, 1996). Wellington, Playmarket, 1996.
The Farm (produced Palmerston North, 1997). Palmerston North, Playmarket, 1997.
Solid Gold Hits (produced Palmerston North, 1998). Palmerston North, Playmarket, 1997.

Television Plays: *The Smell of Money,* 1992; *Melody Rules,* 1994; *Shortland Street* (10 episodes), 1997-98; *Queerie and Pete,* 1998.

*

Manuscript Collection: Victoria University Drama Department.

Theatrical Activities:
Director: **Plays**–*Backstage with the Quigleys,* 1994; *The Rabbitter's Daughter,* 1994.

Actor: **Plays**–Larry in *Burn This* by Lanford Wilson, 1989; Barry in *Ladies Night* by Sinclair, 1989; Brent in *Sex Fiend* by Sinclair, 1990; in *Twelfth Night* by Shakespeare, 1991; in *Conquest of the South Pole,* 1992; Oliver in *Art of Success* by Nick Dear, 1993.

David Geary Comments:
The greatest influence on my work has been Samuel Beckett. His "Godot" I threw across the room as a student. Now I consider this play, and him, as the chief contributor to theatre this century. Pinter, Miller, Williams, Chekhov, Mamet, and Shepherd I would also name as strong influences. I consider playwrighting as the documenting of a tribe, its workings and rituals as revealed through plot. I lean towards comedy with black humour probably because this is how I perceive life in general.

* * *

Born in 1963 and growing up in a hill country village in the Manawatu district of New Zealand, David Geary was influenced early on by agriculture and male figures. His father, who ran a shearers' gang, introduced him to drama through storytelling; yarns told over a few beers after work were his bedtime stories. At Victoria University of Wellington he began by studying law but was lured into creative writing and drama and switched to an arts degree. He entered the New Zealand School of Drama in 1987 and upon graduating worked as an actor in Wellington and Palmerston North.

His writing started with late-night plays on topical issues, written in collaboration with other actors: *Gothic but Staunch* with Alan Brough, a skillful, comic, but anarchic look at teenage suicide, in 1988; and *Dry, White and Friendly* with John Leigh, another comic look at male bonding in the empty lives of two chartered accountants, in 1989. Both had something more than just youthful high spirits, which made critics sit up and watch. In 1991 Geary was awarded the Dominion *Sunday Times* Bruce Mason award for young playwrights.

Although his concerns are with tribal rituals observed by groups of men, his first full-length play, in 1991, was *Pack of Girls,* a domestic look at the Amazon girls who play "Rugby-without-balls" as a defense against their men's absence at own their "footy." In a society so obsessed with the game that an item about rugby frequently takes first place on the main television news, this was both daring and dangerous. That it did not completely come off was not surprising, but it was entertaining and ambitious, attempting to dissect almost dysfunctional male-female relationships and the bonding that the "girls" felt in getting together to play.

Geary was back to cooperative work in 1992, this time with Tim Spite and Mick Rose for the comedy *Backstage with the Quigleys,* about two brothers' deep-seated rivalry as they jockey for position in the backbiting world of little theaters. Another collaboration with Mick Rose brought *The Rabbiter's Daughter* in 1993, a more serious discussion of literary integrity and the place of life vis-à-vis art, woven around a thriller, all of which unfolds in a little over an hour.

Geary's most ambitious work is *Lovelock's Dream Run,* first produced in Auckland in 1993. Lovelock was an actual New Zealand hero who won a gold medal at the Berlin Olympics in 1936 and later died mysteriously on a railway line. Geary's play centers around a boy at boarding school who is obsessed with Lovelock and has finally come to the school his hero attended. There is an oak tree, given by Hitler to the runner, planted in the school's grounds. The boy, Howard, befriends Nick, a Maori. Their story, with its undeclared love of one boy for the other, is run in parallel with Lovelock's life, all against the background of the Berlin Olympics; the play examines Fascism, race, boys' school ethics, and the pursuit of heroes and demons. A demanding play to stage, it puzzled many in the audience who shied away from the implied homosexuality and had to face a few unwelcome demons of their own culture; but the play is well-structured and satisfying in the questions it raises and the theatricality of the treatment. It was published by Victoria University Press in 1993.

After writing *Savage Hearts/Manawa Taua* in 1994 with Wiremu Davis, the early influence of the shearer's shed re-asserted itself as a primal influence and resulted in *The Learner's Stand,* about the beauty and mateship of shearing sheep and the rituals of the shearing gang (including cross-dressing). As Geary said, "shearing 200 sheep in a day is one of the rites on the way to manhood that follows getting your driver's licence and losing your virginity." Hilariously funny, it was probably the play that led to his being awarded the Adam Foundation Playwriting award in 1994, his second major award. *The Learner's Stand* is Geary's most popular play and has been performed all around New Zealand.

Two less successful forays into different areas followed with *King of Stains* and *Ruapehu* (part of a double bill devised by the actors) in 1996, leading back to the area that he knows and depicts so well, backblocks New Zealand, with *The Farm* in 1997. Here a desperate young couple with a failing farm becomes involved with two Russian trampers and scheme for self-support.

Film and television scripts have engaged Geary's skills in situation and dialogue, and he has been involved with some documentary filmmaking. His screenplay *The Smell of Money,* a documentary about redundant freezing workers, won a New Zealand Film Accolade in 1993.

Geary's 1998 play, *Solid Gold Hits,* tells of an international rock star who has a breakdown and retreats from the world of sex, drugs, and rock 'n' roll to the obscurity of a late-shift DJ, yet another world Geary is exploring. Geary, though, is perhaps at his best observing the tribal initiation rites of the country male Kiwi. The main attraction of his plays is the humor and dexterity with which he displays these New Zealanders to us and the occasional subtlety that brings into sharp and very human focus characters who otherwise might be stereotypes. Unlike others writing in this field, he has stayed and continues to stay the course, finding new depths and fresh stories to dramatize.

—Patricia Cooke

GELBART, Larry

Nationality: American. **Born:** Chicago, Illinois, 25 February 1928. **Education:** John Marshall High School, Chicago; Fairfax High School, Los Angeles. **Military Service:** Served in the United States Army, 1945-46. **Family:** Married Pat Marshall in 1956; two daughters and three sons. **Career:** Radio and television writer from 1947; producer or co-producer of television series including *The Marty Feldman Comedy Machine*, 1971, *M*A*S*H*, 1972-76, *Karen*, 1975, *United States*, 1980, and the *Academy Awards Show*, 1985. Artist-in-residence, Northwestern University, Evanston, Illinois, 1984-85. **Awards:** Sylvania award, 1958; Emmy award, 1958, 1973; Tony award, 1963, 1990 (twice); Peabody award, 1964, 1975; Montreux Television Festival Golden Rose award, 1971; Humanitas award, 1976; Edgar Allan Poe award, 1977, 1990; Writers Guild of America award, 1977, 1978, 1982; Christopher award, 1978; Laurel award, 1981; Los Angeles Film Critics award, 1982; New York Film Critics award, 1982; National Society of Film Critics award, 1982; Pacific Broadcasting Pioneers award, 1987; Lee Strasberg award, 1990; Outer Critics Circle award, 1990 (twice); Drama Desk award, 1990; New York Drama Critics Circle award, 1990; Beverly Hills Theater Guild Spotlight award, 1991. D. Litt: Union College, Schenectady, New York, 1986. **Member:** Motion Picture Academy of Arts and Sciences. **Address:** 807 North Alpine Drive, Beverly Hills, California 90210, U.S.A.

Publications

Plays

My L.A. (revue; produced Los Angeles, 1948).

The Conquering Hero, with Burt Shevelove, adaptation of the work by Preston Sturges, music by Moose Charlap, lyrics by Norman Gimbel (produced New York, 1960).

A Funny Thing Happened on the Way to the Forum, with Burt Shevelove, music and lyrics by Stephen Sondheim, adaptation of plays by Plautus (produced New York, 1962; London, 1963; revised version produced Los Angeles, 1971, New York, 1972). New York, Dutton, 1963.
Jump (produced London, 1971).
Sly Fox, adaptation of *Volpone* by Ben Jonson (produced New York, 1976). New York, French, 1978.
Mastergate (produced Cambridge, Massachusetts, and New York, 1989). New York, French, 1990.
City of Angels, music by Cy Coleman, lyrics by David Zippel (produced New York, 1989; London, 1993). New York, Applause, 1990.
Power Failure (produced Cambridge, Massachusetts, 1991).
Peter and the Wolf (narration for ballet) (produced New York, 1991).

Screenplays: *The Notorious Landlady*, 1962; *The Thrill of It All*, with Carl Reiner, 1963; *The Wrong Box*, with Burt Shevelove, 1966; *Not with My Wife, You Don't*, with Norman Panama and Peter Barnes, 1966; *Oh, God*, 1977; *Movie Movie*, 1978; *Neighbors*, 1981; *Tootsie*, 1982; *Blame It on Rio*, 1984; *Barbarians at the Gate*, 1992.

Radio Writing: *Danny Thomas* ("Maxwell House Coffee Time"), 1945; *The Jack Paar Show*, 1945; *Duffy's Tavern*, 1945-47; *The Eddie Cantor Show*, 1947; *Command Performance* (Armed Forces Radio Service), 1947; *The Jack Carson Show*, 1948; *The Joan Davis Show*, 1948; *The Bob Hope Show*, 1948.

Television Writing: *The Bob Hope Show*, 1948-52; *The Red Buttons Show*, 1952; *"Honestly, Celeste!"* (*The Celeste Holm Show*), 1953; *The Patrice Munsel Show*, 1954-62; *The Pat Boone Show*, 1954; *Caesar's Hour*, 1955-57; *The Art Carney Specials*, 1958-59; *The Danny Kaye Show* (consultant), 1963; *The Marty Feldman Comedy Machine*, 1971; *M*A*S*H* series, 1972-76; *Karen*, 1975; *United States*, 1980; *Academy Award Show*, 1985, 1986; *Mastergate*, 1992.

Recordings: *Peter and the Wolf*, Philips Records, 1971; *Gulliver*, adaptation of the novel by Swift, Soundwings Records, 1989.

Other

Laughing Matters. New York, Random House, 1998.

*

Critical Study: "Larry Gelbart" by John L. DiGaetani, in *A Search for a Postmodern Theater: Interviews with Contemporary Playwrights*, edited by John L. DiGaetani, New York, Greenwood, 1991.

Theatrical Activities:
Director: **Play**—*A Funny Thing Happened on the Way to the Forum*, Chichester and London, 1986. **Television**—Several episodes of *M*A*S*H* series.

Larry Gelbart comments:

If anything I've ever written in any way reflects this dreamlike existence that passes for life, I can only hope that the mirror I've held up to it is sufficiently cracked.

* * *

In an age of often homogenized comedy Larry Gelbart has helped to keep the tradition of American satirical writing alive. He has more than a trace of George S. Kaufman's lean, sharp style, and like Kaufman he has also written for the musical theater, undoubtedly helping the economic style and satiric thrust of his plays.

He is, in fact, one of the few book writers of musicals whose scripts could survive without the music. *A Funny Thing Happened on the Way to the Forum*, coauthored with Burt Shevelove, was a glorious reminder in 1962, at a time when the musical tended toward refinement, that the American musical stage had one foot in its indigenous past of vaudeville and burlesque as well as one in European operetta. *Funny Thing* exploited with gleeful zest the happy marriage between the staples of Plautine farce and those of the Orpheum Circuit's world of top bananas and bump-and-grind. Its fusion of low comedy and high-precision plotting makes it one of the endearingly funny musical comedies.

Gelbart, working solo, also later restored faith in the comedy element of musical comedy in his book for *City of Angels*, which opened in 1989 at the close of a decade dominated by the sung-through spectacles of the Lloyd Webber-dominated British ascendancy. The show came out of Gelbart's collaboration on the flop revue *My L.A.*, which showed him "just how theatrically marvellous that marvellously theatrical city was." His wry evocation of the mean streets of Los Angeles contrasted with the poolsides of Bel Air, filtered through a pastiche of classic detective fiction and film noir, helped give his script its acrid wit. It is an extremely layered script, building up complex levels of irony but always moving the story forward, which is essential for a musical. It tells the story of a novelist (Stine) gradually selling out to Hollywood crassness, while simultaneously presenting scenes from his work that mirror those in his life. His work is an adaptation of one of his movies into a screenplay built around a fictional ex-cop turned private eye (Stone), the Stone scenes creating onstage a classic private eye movie. The Hollywood of the 1940s is created in Technicolor, while the movie is staged in monochrome, with the two worlds coalescing as the levels of reality and fantasy combine into a hall of mirrors. Again, Gelbart's script was genuinely funny—not least in its portrait of a wonderfully monstrous movie mogul, Buddy Fidler—as it joyfully skewered Tinseltown pretensions.

Gelbart's other big theatrical success was also a study of human duplicity, greed, and gullibility—his nimble 1976 reworking of *Volpone* set in the rambunctious Barbary Coast world of San Francisco at the turn of the century. *Sly Fox* has a satirical energy that gives Jonson's original some key twists. Purists might carp that he diminishes a masterpiece, but Gelbart actually uses Jonson's play as a trampoline for some fast and furious fun. His language—a sinewy, muscular prose—finds a bold American equivalent for Jonson's verse, not least in his reworking of Volpone's great speeches to his gold as Foxwell S. Sly hymns his treasure chest. And the trial scene, with a no-nonsense judge (played by the same actor who plays Sly) presiding over a courtroom filled with cheats and chiselers, is sidesplitting, especially in the evidence of the venal good-time girl Merrilee Fancy, who gives her occupation to the court as "a pleasure engineer."

Gelbart's other theatrical efforts have been less successful. *Jump*, a frenetic farce centered round a zany New York family, sank under a dismal London production, and *Mastergate* flopped on a Broadway no more hospitable than usual to political satire. Both were uneven pieces, but it is hoped that these failures will not keep Gelbart away from the theater.

—Alan Strachan

GEMS, Jonathan (Malcolm Frederick)

Nationality: British. **Born:** London, 7 January 1952; son of Pam Gems, *q.v.* **Education:** Stowe School, Buckinghamshire, 1965-67; Holland Park Comprehensive, London, 1967-68; Sandown Grammar, Isle of Wight, 1968-69; Royal Academy of Dramatic Art, London, 1970-71; Exeter College of Art, 1971-72. **Family:** Married Catherine Hall in 1981. **Career:** Founder, with Richard Branson, *Student* magazine, 1969-70; managing director, Capricorn Graphics, founder, Jonny and the Gemstones music group, and editor, *It's All Lies* (adult comic), 1970-73; deputy manager, Portobello Hotel, and managing director, Holland Mirrors, both London, 1973-75; stage manager, Open Space Theatre, London, and managing director, Jean Collette Seel fashion company, 1975-76; stage manager, Half Moon Theatre, London, 1976-77. Lives in Los Angeles. **Awards:** George Devine award, 1980; Critics Circle award, 1986; Aspen Film Festival award, 1992. **Agent:** Sebastian Born, Curtis Brown, 161-168 Regent Street, London W1R 5TB, England.

Publications

Plays

Jesus Rides Out (produced London, 1978).
The Shithouse of the August Moon (produced London, 1978).
Rinni Bootsie Tutti Frutti (produced London, 1978).
The Dentist (produced London, 1979).
The Tax Exile (produced London, 1979). London, Playwrights Press, 1986.
The Secret of the Universe (produced London, 1980).
Naked Robots (produced London, 1980). With *Susan's Breasts* and *The Paranormalist*, 1989.
The Paranormalist (produced London, 1982). With *Naked Robots* and *Susan's Breasts*, 1989.
Doom Doom Doom Doom (produced London, 1984).
Susan's Breasts (produced London, 1985). With *Naked Robots* and *The Paranormalist*, 1989.
Naked Robots, Susan's Breasts, The Paranormalist. Birmingham, Oberon, 1989.

Screenplays: *White Mischief*, with Michael Radford, 1985; *The Dress*, 1990; *Mars Attacks!*.

Novel

Mars Attacks!, based on his screenplay. New York, Signet, 1996.

*

Theatrical Activities:
Director: **Plays**—Some of his own plays; *The Treat* by Pam Gems, London, 1982 (co-director); *These Foolish Things* by Philip Davis, London, 1983. **Film**—*The Dress*, 1990.

Jonathan Gems comments:
I wanted to be a great playwright but instead I've ended up writing movie scripts in Los Angeles.

* * *

It would seem that Jonathan Gems has become one more in a line of younger British dramatists (Antony Minghella is another) wooed away from the theater by movies. However skilled Gems's writing for the screen may be, it would be sad to lose his special talent from the theater.

Perhaps he became disillusioned by the fact that none of his plays of the 1980s made the breakthrough into the mainstream. However successful he may have been in filling small theaters on the London fringe, he clearly wanted to reach a wider audience, not to mention make a decent living, which is hardly possible on fringe royalties even with packed houses. But the fact remains that few dramatists managed to pin down with such lethal accuracy and comedic flair the subcultures of the 1980s.

Gems made a big stir with *The Tax Exile*, a rarity of modern high comedy that traces the destruction of a decent middle-aged man by the venality of his family. High comic spirits and a strongly moral core made an unusual combination in a young writer in 1979, and all of his plays of the 1980s were fueled by this fusion. In *Naked Robots*, as he admitted, "I wrote about me and my friends." There was a subsequent lack of enthusiasm when he started showing the script around, everyone rejecting it on the grounds that the characters were disgusting and the situations unbelievable ("I was baffled. This was my life!"). The Royal Shakespeare Company rescued the play, and its 1980 production remains one of the company's key achievements in new writing. It is set in a warehouse dominated by a bed comprised of 10 stacked mattresses, and its characters are predominantly young, either drifting, like the middle-class punk Gemma, or trying to carve out careers in fashion or the music industry, like the central couple Desna and Nudy. The play, tracing the shifting relationships that develop, covers a world of squatters, casual sex, abortion, pop music, and drugs. (Gems's dealer, Ray, is often a hilariously inept figure.) He neither judges nor sentimentalizes his characters, and the play remains one of the most clear-eyed of its period.

The family seems less than a cozy unit in most of Gems's plays; characters like Desna and Gemma seem totally detached from their parents. In *The Paranormalist* we seem initially to be once again in the midst of the postnuclear family, with the paranormalist grandfather Sonny resented by his mixed-up psychiatrist daughter Barbara, at odds in turn with her dropout daughter Mopsa, who is recovering from an abortion as the play begins. *The Paranormalist* is hardly short on action, for it involves several paranormal experiments, Sonny's levitation, and an exorcism. Partly this was Gems's attempt to move beyond the technical restrictions of studio theaters, but it also reflected his sense of the inexplicable and the unknown that underlies most lives. Sonny's serenity casts an increasing spell over the action, which ends, after the violence of the exorcism that casts out Barbara's demons, with a beguiling scene of unity as the characters sing a harmonized version of "The Melody Lingers On" while the lights fade.

Gems's *Susan's Breasts* is a later play. He wanted to tackle the theme of love, but, except for the mysterious character of Lemon, a disturbed but passionate young man who gives the play its emotional resonance, it "became predominantly a play about people *not* falling in love." The play focuses on another group of young Londoners, some more affluent and distinctly less appealing than those in *Naked Robots*, with the men mostly a brutish, sexist lot interested solely in financial and social success. The women—the aspiring actress Susan, the American model Pookie, and the drug addict Carol—all seem to connive with the males' sexism in a mid-1980s world in which love is sex and relationships are business deals. Opening with a superbly written scene at a picnic in a London park, the play moves into a different gear as Lemon's love for and obsession with Susan increases. Susan has been diagnosed as sterile, but she casually sleeps once with Lemon and becomes pregnant. (The breasts of the title now increase in size.) Although Lemon escapes from the asylum in which he has been committed to plead with her, the closing implication is that Susan, faced with the loss of a movie role, will abort the child. The play's final image of Susan being comforted by the increasingly addicted Carol is another instance of Gems's ability to fuse strong theatrical images with the dialogue of his splendidly varied casts of characters. Gems in the 1990s has lived in the United States and has concentrated exclusively on movies, with some success–his script for *Mars Attacks!* had some of the wonderfully inventive comedy of his 1980s plays. His particularly satiric voice has been missed in the British theater of the 1990s.

—Alan Strachan

GEMS, (Iris) Pam(ela)

Nationality: British. **Born:** Pamela Price, Bransgore, Dorset, 1 August 1925. **Education:** Brockenhurst County High School, 1936-41; Manchester University, 1946-49, B.A. (honours) in psychology 1949. **Military Service:** Served in the Women's Royal Naval Service, 1944-46. **Family:** Married Keith Gems in 1949; two sons, including Jonathan Gems, *q.v.*, and two daughters. **Career:** Research assistant, BBC, London, 1950-53. **Address:** c/o Bloomsbury Publishing Ltd., 2 Soho Square, London W1V 5DE, England.

Publications

Plays

Betty's Wonderful Christmas (for children; produced London, 1972).
My Warren, and After Birthday (produced London, 1973).
The Amiable Courtship of Miz Venus and Wild Bill (produced London, 1973).
Sarah B. Divine! (additional material), by Tom Eyen, music by Jonathan Kramer (produced London, 1973).
Go West Young Woman (produced London, 1974).
Up in Sweden (produced Leicester, 1975; London, 1980).
Dusa, Fish, Stas, and Vi (as *Dead Fish*, produced Edinburgh, 1976; as *Dusa, Fish, Stas, and Vi*, produced London, 1976; Los Angeles, 1978; New York, 1980). London, French, and New York, Dramatists Play Service, 1977.
The Project (produced London, 1976).
Guinevere (produced Edinburgh and London, 1976).
The Rivers and Forests, adaptation of a play by Marguerite Duras (produced London, 1976).
My Name Is Rosa Luxemburg, adaptation of a play by Marianne Auricoste (produced London, 1976).
Franz into April (produced London, 1977).
Queen Christina (produced Stratford-on-Avon, 1977; London, 1979; revised version produced London, 1982). London, St. Luke's Press, 1982.
Piaf (produced Stratford-on-Avon and London, 1978; New York, 1981). Ashover, Derbyshire, Amber Lane Press, 1979; New York, French, 1983.
Ladybird, Ladybird (produced London, 1979).
Sandra (produced London, 1979).
Uncle Vanya, adaptation of a play by Chekhov (produced London, 1979; San Francisco, 1983). London, Eyre Methuen, 1979.
A Doll's House, adaptation of a play by Ibsen (produced Newcastle upon Tyne, 1980).
Sketches in *Variety Night* (produced London, 1982).
The Treat (produced London, 1982).
Aunt Mary (produced London, 1982). Published in *Plays by Women 3*, edited by Michelene Wandor, London, Methuen, 1984.
The Cherry Orchard, adaptation of a play by Chekhov (produced Leicester, 1984).
Loving Women (produced London, 1984). Included in *Three Plays*, 1985.
Camille, adaptation of a play by Dumas fils (produced Stratford-on-Avon, 1984; London, 1985; New Haven, Connecticut, 1986). Included in *Three Plays*, 1985.
Pasionaria, music by Paul Sand, lyrics by Gems and Sand (produced Newcastle upon Tyne, 1985).
Three Plays (includes *Piaf, Camille, Loving Women*). London, Penguin, 1985.
The Danton Affair, adaptation of a work by Stanislawa Przybyszewska (produced London, 1986).
The Blue Angel, adaptation of a novel by Heinrich Mann (produced Stratford-on-Avon, 1991; London, 1992).
Deborah's Daughter. London, Nick Hern, 1995.
Stanley. London, Nick Hern, 1996.
The Seagull, adaptation of Chekhov.

Television Plays: *A Builder by Trade*, 1961; *We Never Do What They Want*, 1979.

Novels

Mrs. Frampton. London, Bloomsbury, 1989.
Bon Voyage, Mrs. Frampton. London, Bloomsbury, 1990.

*

Critical Studies: "The Return of a Sacred Monster: Pam Gems' *Camille*" by Gabrielle H. Cody, in *Theater* (New Haven, Connecticut), Fall-Winter 1987, pp. 78-80; "The Plays of Pam Gems" by Katherine H. Burkman, in *British and Irish Drama Since 1960*, edited by James Acheson, Houndmills, Macmillan, 1993; "The Church of Me" by Simon Schama, in *New Yorker*, February 1997, pp. 50-61.

Theatrical Activities:
Actress: **Film**—*Nineteen Eighty-Four*, 1984.

* * *

Contemporary women playwrights explore areas of experience that the stage has traditionally ignored and have developed styles designed as a radical contrast to the standard dramatic forms. Indeed, from a feminist viewpoint the category of woman writer defines "a species of creativity that challenges the dominant image," since "the very concept of the 'writer' implies *maleness*." Like Caryl Churchill, however, Pam Gems has rejected this extreme position, declaring that "the phrase 'feminist writer' is absolutely meaningless because it implies polemic, and polemic is about changing things in a direct political way. Drama is subversive."

Also like Churchill, Gems developed her vision and theatrical techniques through dealing with historical subjects, and their example has been influential, making the history play characteristic of women's drama over the past several years. The tension between received ideas of the past—reinforcing the subservient status of women by relegating them to invisibility—and the very different feminist perspective contributes to the thematic complexity of such plays.

Like many women dramatists Gems came to the theater late, after 20 years of marriage and raising children. She started on the fringe, and her early work for feminist theater groups included an autobiographical piece together with two monologues about female isolation and abortion and a satiric pantomime. *Queen Christina*, her first major play, struck a new note and established her central themes.

As in this play, Gems's most characteristic work dramatizes the human reality of women who have been transformed into cultural symbols. These range from the seventeenth-century Swedish queen who renounced her crown, to a nineteenth-century courtesan, to a modern nightclub singer, to *The Blue Angel* image of Marlene Dietrich as vampire sexuality. In each case the character is set against a familiar and highly romanticized picture. The source for the earliest of Gems's historical dramas was the classic Garbo film of an ethereal and intellectual beauty who abdicates for love and then finds consolation in religion when the man for whom she has sacrificed everything is killed in a duel. *Piaf* turns from Hollywood myth to the sanitized commercial image of a vulnerable street sparrow, a purely emotional being whose songs are the direct expression "of unhappiness . . . of being made helpless by love . . . of being alone." *Camille* is a reversal of both Dumas's sentimentally tragic *La Dame aux camélias* and Verdi's operatic idealization in *La Traviata*.

The deforming pressures of society are most fully explored in *Queen Christina*, which provides a test case for issues of sexual definition, biological determinism, and social programming. As the sole heir to a kingdom at war, this historical figure has been "reared as a man . . . And then, on her accession, told to marry and breed, that is to be a woman. By which time, of course, like males of her era, she despised women as weak, hysterical, silly creatures." For Gems, "It is a confusion which seems as apposite as ever." Forced to abdicate, she searches Europe for a way of life in which she can be herself. She is hailed as an inspiration to man-hating feminists, in the shape of eighteenth-century French bluestockings, in their campaign for control over their bodies through abortion. She finds herself repulsed, however, by their life-denying warfare against the opposite sex, which she recognizes as the mirror image of male domination. She seeks spiritual emancipation in the Catholic Church, but, finding that the pope is interested only in exploiting her celibacy as religious propaganda, she asserts that "We won't deny the body." Offered the kingdom of Naples, she attempts to return to her masculine role. But when it forces her to kill her lover for betraying her invading armies, she rejects the whole male ethos, setting herself against domination in all its forms, master/servant as well as man/woman. Finally, when she is too old to bear children, she discovers the value of maternal instincts and affirms her biological nature.

For Gems, "Whichever way we look at it, the old norms won't do any more." The play asks what it means to be female, and Christina's example implies that a valid definition can be reached only through "the creation of a society more suited to both sexes," which Gems has described as her aim in writing. Her concept of drama as subversive rather than confrontational means working on public consciousness indirectly. In line with this her protagonist comes to realize that positive change can be achieved only through the specifically female, undervalued qualities of weakness, nonviolent resistance, and maternal nurture: "Half the world rapes and destroys—must women, the other half, join in?"

Gems typically creates an opposition between what is depicted on the stage and the audience's expectations. This is most obvious in *Piaf*, in which incidents from the Parisian singer's life are interpolated with renditions of her popular lyrics. The gutter milieu, prostitution and involvement in murder, drunkenness, and drugs contrast with the glittering public persona. Piaf disintegrates under the contradiction, and when the gap between idol and real woman can no longer be disguised, society preserves the false image by divorcing musical soul from female body.

At the same time the way the songs rise out of the scenes emphasizes that Piaf's unconventional art and her physical crudity are inseparable. Her rise to stardom is a process of continual exploitation by the men who manage or marry her and by the public—by extension the audience for Gems's play—that projects its desires onto her. Yet it is also her status as a star that enables her to assert a personal autonomy, however provisional. This is expressed through her sexual freedom, which overturns all the moral codes. And the same reversal of conventional values is reflected in the play itself, which shows Piaf not only copulating but also ostentatiously urinating onstage. Physicality at its most basic, a stock way of representing reality, demolishes the socially acceptable female stereotype promoted and imposed by men and thus provides an example of alternative values.

—Christopher Innes

GIBB, Lee. ***See*** **WATERHOUSE, Keith (Spencer).**

GIBSON, William

Nationality: American. **Born:** New York City, 13 November 1914. **Education:** City College of New York, 1930-32. **Family:** Married Margaret Brenman in 1940; two sons. **Career:** Co-founding president, Berkshire Theatre Festival, Stockbridge, Massachusetts, 1966—. **Awards:** Harriet Monroe Memorial prize (*Poetry*, Chicago), 1945; Sylvania award, for television play, 1957. **Agent:**

Flora Roberts Inc., 157 West 57th Street, New York, New York 10019. **Address:** Stockbridge, Massachusetts 01262, U.S.A.

PUBLICATIONS

Plays

I Lay in Zion (produced Topeka, Kansas, 1943). New York, French, 1947.

Dinny and the Witches: A Frolic on Grave Matters (produced Topeka, Kansas, 1945; revised version produced New York, 1959). With *The Miracle Worker*, New York, Atheneum, 1960.

A Cry of Players (produced Topeka, Kansas, 1948; New York, 1968). New York, Atheneum, 1969.

The Ruby (as William Mass), libretto based on the play *A Night at an Inn* by Lord Dunsany, music by Norman Dello Joio. New York, Ricordi, 1955.

The Miracle Worker: A Play for Television (televised 1957). New York, Knopf, 1957; stage version (produced New York, 1959; London, 1961). With *Dinny and the Witches*, New York, Atheneum, 1960; published separately London, French, 1960.

Two for the Seesaw (produced New York and London, 1958). Published in *The Seesaw Log: A Chronicle of the Stage Production*, New York, Knopf, 1959; London, Corgi, 1962.

Golden Boy, with Clifford Odets, adaptation of the play by Odets, music by Charles Strouse, lyrics by Lee Adams (produced New York, 1964). New York, Atheneum, 1965.

American Primitive (as *John and Abigail*, produced Stockbridge, Massachusetts, 1969; as *American Primitive*, produced Washington, D.C., 1971). New York, Atheneum, 1972.

The Body and the Wheel: A Play Made from the Gospels (produced Lenox, Massachusetts, 1974). New York, Atheneum, 1975.

The Butterfingers Angel, Mary and Joseph, Herod the Nut, and the Slaughter of 12 Hit Carols in a Pear Tree: A Christmas Entertainment (produced Lenox, Massachusetts, 1974; London, 1979; New York, 1980). New York, Dramatists Play Service, 1975.

Golda (produced New York, 1977). Published as *How to Turn a Phoenix into Ashes: The Story of the Stage Production, with the Text, of Golda*, New York, Atheneum, 1978; *Golda* published London, French, 1978.

Goodly Creatures (produced Washington, D.C., 1980). New York, Dramatists Play Service, 1986.

Monday after the Miracle (produced Pretoria, South Africa, Charleston, South Carolina, and New York, 1982; Northampton, 1986; London, 1990). New York, Atheneum, 1983.

Handy Dandy (produced New York, 1984). New York, Dramatists Play Service, 1986.

Raggedy Ann and Andy, music and lyrics by Joe Raposo (produced Albany, New York, 1984; as *Rag Dolly*, produced Albany, 1985; as *Raggedy Ann*, produced New York City, 1986).

Screenplays: *The Cobweb*, 1954; *The Miracle Worker*, 1962.

Television Play: *The Miracle Worker*, 1957.

Novel

The Cobweb. New York, Knopf, and London, Secker and Warburg, 1954.

Poetry

Winter Crook. New York, Oxford University Press, 1948.

Other

A Mass for the Dead. New York, Atheneum, 1968.

A Season in Heaven, Being a Log of an Expedition after that Legendary Beast, Cosmic Consciousness. New York, Atheneum, 1974.

Shakespeare's Game. New York, Atheneum, 1978.

* * *

William Gibson began as a novelist and poet, earning a reputation with the best-selling novel *The Cobweb* and the collection of verse *Winter Crook*. An early playwriting interest resulted in a short verse drama about the apostle Peter (*I Lay in Zion*), a work well tailored for church groups and one that predicted larger dramas to come.

Gibson's first success on the Broadway stage came in 1958 with *Two for the Seesaw*, a two-character drama about an embittered and lonely Nebraska lawyer in New York who is separated from his wife and who has an affair with a generous-hearted Bronx gamine down on her luck as a dancer. Although mutual love and dependency develop between these two disparate people, the lawyer's home ties are strong enough ultimately to draw him back to his wife. The drama's chief appeal lies in its engaging portrait of the dancer, whose colorful individuality and guileless love in the face of what she realizes is a doomed relationship grasps one's attention and sympathy. The role marked the author's uncommon ability to create strong parts for women and brought recognition to the actress Ann Bancroft, who continued to portray other Gibson heroines. The play won praise from the critics and a substantial Broadway run that resulted in a film contract for Gibson. It was later adapted by others as the basis of the successful musical *Seesaw*. In *The Seesaw Log* Gibson chronicles with liveliness the page-to-stage odyssey of *Two for the Seesaw* and reveals his disenchantment with the professional production process without minimizing the significant contribution of his collaborators.

In 1959 Gibson's short-lived off-Broadway production of *Dinny and the Witches*, a satirical fantasy with song whose good intentions exceeded its effectiveness, was followed by his greatest success, *The Miracle Worker*. Originally written as a teleplay, the biographical drama portrays the teacher Anne Sullivan's turbulent but triumphant struggle to free her savagely recalcitrant pupil, Helen Keller, from the prison of a sightless and soundless body. Encompassing the time it takes the young teacher to gain mastery over the seemingly ungovernable child in order to teach her language, the play is brought to a poignant resolution when Helen, having had her hand repeatedly doused under the water pump, excitedly discovers the connection between words and things as she writes the word "water" in her teacher's palm. A somewhat uneven and clumsy structure results from an insufficient transformation of the drama from its television form. Although critics faulted the play for its sentimentality and deficiencies in craft, they and the public agreed on its theatrical impact in presenting a compassionate portrait of the heroic teacher who made possible the greatness of Helen Keller. The play's success led to a 1962 film scripted by Gibson. Less critically successful was the 1982 sequel *Monday after the Miracle*, which focuses on the lively courtship and marriage of Anne Sullivan, still Helen Keller's companion and protector 17 years later, to the journalist John Macy, who comes to live in the Boston-area household of the two women and unavoidably disturbs their dependent relationship. Macy, unable to subordinate his private and professional needs to the now famous and articulate Helen, who is first in his wife's priorities and also sexually awakened by his presence, must leave. Critically indicted for being less emotionally powerful in material and effect than its predecessor, this thoughtful play about the difficult choices between duty and happiness offers compelling characterizations of its three leading figures and deserved better than its brief Broadway run.

Extending his experience in 1965 by collaborating on the book for a musical version of Clifford Odets's *Golden Boy*, Gibson transformed the white violinist-turned-boxer hero into a nonmusical black pugilist. Aided by Sammy Davis, Jr., in the title role and by a well-adapted book, the musical's New York production won moderate success.

A return to biography in the late 1960s was marked both by *American Primitive*, a lively documentary portraying John and Abigail Adams through their letters over three stormy years, and *A Cry of Players*, Gibson's dramatization of the young William Shakespeare's scantily recorded Stratford years and those of his wife Anne, who emerges as a full-bodied character enlisting our compassion. Shakespeare is characterized as a restless, free-living profligate, frustrated by the limitations of his village and the constricting ties of his family, who survives public punishment for poaching to join Will Kempe's troupe of players for the destiny that awaits him in London. Critics validly observed that the writer's penchant for poetic speech was marred by his lapses into either pretentious or prosaic dialogue, and they did not offer sufficient approval to let the play endure on Broadway. This did not diminish the drama's popularity with community and college theaters, however.

Less successful than his other ventures into biography, Gibson's *Golda* offers the decisive days of the so-called Yom Kippur war of 1973 as a dramatic frame to surround an episodic portrait of Israel's Golda Meir. As the prime minister deals with strategy crises and conflicting generals, she recalls in a series of flashbacks key public and private moments in her life stretching from her childhood to her ultimately troubled marriage and strong commitment to Zionism. Despite several strong scenes and a periodically enlivening profile of the protagonist's humor and humanity, the play fails to compress sufficiently the abundant scope of the material and to disclose the private person behind the public one. Yet Gibson merits credit for attempting to dramatize so worthy and so difficult a subject, who was then still living.

In the 1980s Gibson wrote two works considerably slighter than *Monday after the Miracle. Handy Dandy* is a thematically pointed comedy about a conservative judge and a radical antiarmaments nun who is constantly brought into his court. The book for the musical *Raggedy Ann* concerns a doll springing to life to solve a sick young girl's parental problems, but its 1986 New York production lasted only briefly.

Gibson's work in several media demonstrates both his literary and dramatic gifts, which have resulted in important plays of sensitivity and substance. Largely successful in dramatizing actual figures, Gibson has secured his place in American letters as an effective writer of biographical dramas.

—Christian H. Moe

GILL, Peter

Nationality: British. **Born:** Cardiff, Glamorgan, 7 September 1939. **Education:** St. Illtyd's College, Cardiff. **Career:** Actor, 1957-65; associate director, Royal Court Theatre, London, 1970-72; director, Riverside Studios, Hammersmith, London, 1976-80. Associate director, National Theatre, London, 1980—, and director, National Theatre Studio, 1984—. **Awards:** Belgrade International Theatre Festival prize, for directing, 1968; George Devine award, 1968; British Theatre Association award, for directing, 1985. O.B.E. (Officer, Order of the British Empire), 1980. **Agent:** Casarotto Ramsay Ltd., National House, 60-66 Wardour Street, London W1V 3HP, England.

Publications

Plays

The Sleepers Den (produced London, 1965; revised version produced London, 1969). With *Over Gardens Out*, London, Calder and Boyars, 1970.

A Provincial Life, adaptation of a story by Chekhov (produced London, 1966).

Over Gardens Out (produced London, 1969). With *The Sleepers Den*, London, Calder and Boyars, 1970.

The Merry-Go-Round, adaptation of the play by D.H. Lawrence (produced London, 1973). London, Theatreprint, 1973.

Small Change (produced London, 1976). With *Kick for Touch*, London, Boyars, 1985.

The Cherry Orchard, adaptation of a play by Chekhov (produced London, 1978).

Kick for Touch (produced London, 1983). With *Small Change*, London, Boyars, 1985.

In the Blue (produced London, 1985). With *Mean Tears*, Birmingham, Oberon, 1987.

As I Lay Dying, adaptation of the novel by Faulkner (produced London, 1985).

Mean Tears (produced London, 1987). Published in *Plays International* (London), August 1987; with *In the Blue*, Birmingham, Oberon, 1987.

The Look Across the Eyes. London, Oberon, 1997.

Cardiff East. London, Faber, 1997.

*

Critical Studies: "Eliot, Epipsychidion, and the Post-Modern Wasteland: Allusion in Simon Gray's *Butley* and Peter Gill's *Mean*" by John M. Clum, in *Text and Presentation,* Lanham, Maryland, UP of America, 1989.

Theatrical Activities:
Director: **Plays**—All his own plays, and *A Collier's Saturday Night* by D. H. Lawrence, London, 1965, 1968; *The Dwarfs* by Harold Pinter, Glasgow, 1966; *The Ruffian on the Stair* by Joe Orton, London, 1966; *O'Flaherty, V. C.* by Shaw, London, 1966; *The Local Stigmatic* by Heathcote Williams, London, 1966; *The Soldier's Fortune* by Thomas Otway, London, 1967; *The Daughter-in-Law* by D. H. Lawrence, London, 1967, 1968, and Bochum, 1972; *Crimes of Passion* by Joe Orton, London, 1967, 1972; *June*

Evening by Bill Naughton, toured, 1967; *The Widowing of Mrs. Holroyd* by D. H. Lawrence, London, 1968; *Life Price* by Michael O'Neill and Jeremy Seabrook, London, 1969; *Much Ado about Nothing*, Stratford, Ontario, 1969, London, 1981; *Hedda Gabler* by Ibsen, Stratford, Ontario, 1970; *Landscape and Silence* by Harold Pinter, New York, 1970; *The Duchess of Malfi* by Webster, London, 1971; *Macbeth*, Stratford, Ontario, 1971; *Cato Street* by Robert Shaw, London, 1971; *A Midsummer Night's Dream*, Zurich, 1972; *Crete and Sergeant Pepper* by John Antrobus, London, 1972; *Twelfth Night*, Stratford-on-Avon, 1974; *Fishing* by Michael Weller, New York, 1975; *The Fool* by Edward Bond, London, 1975; *As You Like It*, Nottingham and Edinburgh, 1975, London, 1976; *The Changeling* by Middleton and Rowley, London, 1978; *Measure for Measure*, London, 1979; *Julius Caesar*, London, 1980; *Scrape Off the Black* by Tunde Ikoli, London, 1980; *A Month in the Country* by Turgenev, London, 1981; *Don Juan* by Molière, London, 1981; *Major Barbara* by Shaw, London, 1982; *Danton's Death* by Georg Büchner, London, 1982; *Tales from Hollywood* by Christopher Hampton, 1983; *Venice Preserv'd* by Thomas Otway, London, 1984; *Antigone*, London, 1984; *Fool for Love* by Sam Shepard, London, 1984; *A Twist of Lemon* by Alex Renton, London, 1985; *The Garden of England* by Peter Cox, 1985; *Bouncing* by Rosemary Wilton, London, 1985; *Up for None* by Mick Mahoney, London, 1985; *Mrs. Klein* by Nicholas Wright, London, 1988; *Juno and the Paycock* by Sean O'Casey, London, 1989. **Opera**—*The Marriage of Figaro* by Mozart, Leeds, 1987. **Television**—*Girl* by James Robson, 1973; *Grace* by David Storey, 1974; *A Matter of Taste* by Alex La Guma, 1974; *Fugitive* by Sean Walsh, 1974; *Hitting Town* by Stephen Poliakoff, 1976.

Actor: **Plays**—Customer in *Last Day in Dreamland* by Willis Hall, London, 1959; Plato in *The Trial of Cob and Leach* by Christopher Logue, London, 1959; Mangolis in *The Kitchen* by Arnold Wesker, London, 1959; Marcus and A Postcard Seller in *This Way to the Tomb* by Ronald Duncan, London, 1960; Silvius in *As You Like It*, 1962; in *The Caucasian Chalk Circle* by Brecht, London, 1962. **Films**—*H.M.S. Defiant* (*Damn the Defiant!*), 1962; *Zulu*, 1964.

* * *

For Peter Gill playwriting has always been incidental to his profession as a director. Indeed, he is still better known as the director who first realized the theatrical potential of D. H. Lawrence's plays than as the author of any of his own works, all of which he has also directed. His special skill, both as a director and dramatist, derives from the naturalistic exploitation of subtext, usually in association with relatively inarticulate proletarian characters, so that the simplest domestic situations are weighted and economically developed for their dramatic potential.

The Sleepers Den illustrates this method well. The Shannon family, immured in an apparently condemned Cardiff slum flat, suffers variously from claustrophobia and agoraphobia. Cornered, defensive, and scared to come to grips with their real dangers, they gradually expose themselves to emotional decomposition until their whole pattern of life collapses. The subtext becomes of paramount importance because of the characters' severely limited capacity even to begin to understand their problems. The Shannons are a fragmented family that includes an adult brother and sister, their bedridden mother, and a daughter. There is no explanation as to how this situation evolved, and there is no evidence that anyone understands it. Across the three generations power and defense are manipulated by trivial, but effective, gestures of bribery, blackmail, and threats. Two outsiders—a debt collector and a Catholic social worker—function as catalysts to the situation, but the revelations that are offered seem ridiculous irrelevancies. The brother confesses to the social worker that he has been working overtime and not telling his sister, and no one seems to understand the seriousness of court action for debt. It is clear that the characters' mental states are a reflection of their environment, that their lethargy and low self-esteem have a century of conditioning behind them. The dramatic crisis comes at the end of the second act when the sister barricades herself inside the flat as a response to a situation that is too complicated for her to understand, let alone solve. The very short last act consists in her ignoring the pleadings of her brother and the daughter, who are now forced to sleep with friends. In Gill's 1969 production it was clear that old Mrs. Shannon is dead in the last act, so that the sister has shut herself in with the corpse. It is possible to interpret the play in such a way that, far from presenting a grotesque family incident, it suggests a recurrent pattern. The now insane sister usurps her dead mother's role at the end, with a family's inherited state of introverted lethargy on the verge of reenactment. The omission of an apostrophe from the play's ambiguous title, which has been observed in all editions, may be calculated to hint at this.

The single sealed-in set of *The Sleepers Den* is an ideal laboratory for naturalism, but in *Over Gardens Out* Gill developed similar assumptions about character evolution while setting the action in two domestic and several exterior locations. Again, several generations are represented, and surprise and vagueness about the processes of physical decay and growth are intermittently felt. But the structures of authority and rebellion between the generations are relatively unambiguous here, and mindless behavior, though plentiful, seems attributable to individual characters rather than to a collective force. This means that particular antisocial gestures can be isolated as particular problems, so that even through some of the severities of the action a rich vein of wry comedy persists. The central characters are two adolescent Cardiff boys of widely differing propensities, though both are intellectually limited, whose leisure hours are filled with acts of vandalism that range from the trivial to the alarming. The picaresque tone of the play is more typical of the 1960s than is *The Sleepers Den*, but the play does show an advance in terms of its warmly sympathetic characterization.

A similar technique is deployed more adventurously in *Small Change*, in which two Cardiff boys are again followed through boyhood and adolescence into manhood. For the premiere Gill even used one of the lead actors from *Over Gardens Out*, an actor he would use again in *Kick for Touch*. Such an expansive chronology means that the play's naturalistic cogency is not comparable with the earlier plays, and Gill allows himself rather more intelligent and perceptive characters who deliver nostalgic, poetical monologues, the quality of which has been questioned by critics. By 1976 Gill could include a climactic scene of adult anagnorisis and recrimination in which the boyhood relationship is explicitly perceived as homosexual.

Gill's later plays use very similar material that is dissected with increasingly audacious techniques. *Kick for Touch* has two Cardiff brothers who are war babies reminiscing haphazardly across a kitchen table. A woman who is married to one of them and has been the lover of both is the linking device for a series of interior monologues and duologues, with uninvolved characters simply moving a yard or two away and freezing. Again, there is a bond of something approaching love between the men, although the finale does not pivot on this but on the mystery of a domestic tragedy. *In the Blue* has only two male characters, both homosexual, one of whom is articulate and educated. The technical novelty of the play consists in the hypothetical reinterpretation of scenes, with alternative performances introduced just by the word "or" so that there is some uncertainty as to which version represents reality and which fantasy. Gill's naturalism has here been obscured completely, and the play is almost purely expressionistic. In *Mean Tears* chronological structuring is denied in a collation of short segments of time in which three men and two women intersect, collide, and form fragile relationships.

Gill has also successfully written and directed numerous adaptations, but mention should be made of one heroic failure whose technical effrontery resembles that of his original plays. *As I Lay Dying* theatricalizes the innovative narrative method of Faulkner's novel, resulting in a pattern of monologues with varying perspectives that are traded across the body of the characters' mother. Such a jigsaw of monologues epitomizes a tendency in Gill's plays, and the maternal catalyst is also recurrent, especially in *Small Change*.

—Howard McNaughton

GILROY, Frank D(aniel)

Nationality: American. **Born:** New York City, 13 October 1925. **Education:** De Witt Clinton High School, Bronx, New York; Dartmouth College, Hanover, New Hampshire, B.A. (magna cum laude) 1950; Yale University School of Drama, New Haven, Connecticut, 1950-51. **Military Service:** Served in the United States Army, 1943-46. **Family:** Married Ruth Dorothy Gaydos in 1954; three sons. **Career:** Member of the council, 1964—, (president) 1969-71, Dramatists Guild, New York. Lives in Monroe, New York. **Awards:** Obie award, 1962; Outer Circle award, 1964; Pulitzer prize, 1965; New York Drama Critics Circle award, 1965; Berlin Film Festival Silver Bear, 1971. D. Litt.: Dartmouth College, 1966. **Address:** c/o Dramatists Guild, 1501 Broadway, Suite 701, New York, New York 10036, U.S.A.

Publications

Plays

The Middle World (produced Hanover, New Hampshire, 1949).
A Matter of Pride, adaptation of the story "The Blue Serge Suit" by John Langdon (televised 1957). New York, French, 1970.
Who'll Save the Plowboy? (produced New York, 1962; London, 1963). New York, Random House, 1962.
The Subject Was Roses (produced New York, 1964). New York, French, 1962; included in *About Those Roses; or, How Not to Do a Play and Succeed, and the Text of "The Subject Was Roses,"* New York, Random House, 1965.
Far Rockaway (televised 1965). With *That Summer—That Fall*, New York, Random House, 1967.
That Summer—That Fall (produced New York, 1967). With *Far Rockaway*, New York, Random House, 1967.
The Only Game in Town (produced New York, 1968). New York, Random House, 1968.
Present Tense (includes *Come Next Tuesday, Twas Brillig, So Please Be Kind, Present Tense*) (produced New York, 1972). New York, French, 1973.
The Next Contestant (produced New York, 1978). New York, French, 1979.
Dreams of Glory (produced New York, 1979). New York, French, 1980.
Last Licks (produced New York, 1979; as *The Housekeeper*, produced Brighton and London, 1982).
Real to Reel (produced New York, 1987).
Match Point (produced New York, 1990).
A Way with Words (produced New York, 1991).

Screenplays: *The Fastest Gun Alive*, with Russel Rouse, 1956; *Texas John Slaughter*, 1958; *Gunfight at Sandoval*, 1959; *The Gallant Hours*, with Beirne Lay, Jr., 1960; *The Subject Was Roses*, 1968; *The Only Game in Town*, 1969; *Desperate Characters*, 1971; *From Noon till Three*, 1976; *Once in Paris*, 1978; *The Gig*, 1985.

Television Plays: *A Matter of Pride*, 1957; *Who Killed Julie Greer?* and *Up Jumped the Devil (Dick Powell Show)*, 1960-61; *Far Rockaway*, 1965; *The Turning Point of Jim Malloy*, 1975; *Gibbsville* series, from stories by John O'Hara, 1976; *Nero Wolfe*, from the novel *The Doorbell Rang* by Rex Stout, 1979; *Burke's Law* series; and since 1952 plays for *U.S. Steel Hour*, *Omnibus*, *Kraft Theater*, *Studio One*, *Lux Video Theatre*, and *Playhouse 90*.

Novels

Private. New York, Harcourt Brace, 1970.
From Noon till Three: The Possibly True and Certainly Tragic Story of an Outlaw and a Lady Whose Love Knew No Bounds. New York, Doubleday, 1973; as *For Want of a Horse*, London, Coronet, 1975.

Other

Little Ego (for children), with Ruth G. Gilroy. New York, Simon and Schuster, 1970.

*

Theatrical Activities:
Director: **Films**—*Desperate Characters*, 1971; *From Noon till Three*, 1976; *Once in Paris*, 1978; *The Gig*, 1985. **Television**—*The Turning Point of Jim Malloy* (pilot film), 1975; *Gibbsville* series, 1976; *Nero Wolfe*, 1979; *Money Plays*, 1997.

* * *

Frank D. Gilroy's bittersweet comedies consider men and male rituals: their alienation and loneliness, their difficulty communicating with and understanding women, and their insecurities in dealing with one another.

In Gilroy's first commercial success, *Who'll Save the Plowboy?*, the characters set the pattern of relationships found in his later work. Gilroy introduces us to three lives characterized by frustration, failure, and an inability to communicate honestly. Albert, the plowboy of the title, and Helen, his wife, confront Larry, the man who saved the plowboy's life during the war and who is now dying. Albert builds a castle of lies to impress his war buddy with nonexistent postwar success and accomplishment, with fantasies of a happy marriage, and with an imaginary strong and healthy son. Albert struts through the script like a rooster who does not notice that the henhouse is empty. In *Plowboy* Gilroy begins to delineate the little humiliations, the deceits, and the burdensome pretenses of being a man. He also introduces us to the sexually unresponsive, adulterous woman who talks incessantly about insignificant and inappropriate things. These are the characters who populate all of Gilroy's work. In spite of *Plowboy*'s exposition and plot development, the shorthand that later became a trademark of a Gilroy script is apparent: the short, snappy repartee; the one-liner insights; the quick expressions of anger and bitterness.

The Subject Was Roses, which won the Pulitzer Prize, is still the epitome of Gilroy's style and thematic concerns. Elegant in its spareness, the play all but eliminates plot and concentrates on a moment of precisely outlined dramatic time. The World War II experiences of Timmy, another veteran, are a backdrop for the parental battlefield in his home, where his warring parents alternately use him as the cannon with which to shoot one another down. Gilroy hones his ability to communicate a complex set of emotions by focusing in exquisite detail on ordinary objects. When Nettie's waffles stick in the waffle iron, spoiling the first breakfast she's made for her son in three years, her tears have less to do with a hungry son than they do with her fear of ruining an already tenuous mother-son relationship, her sense of inadequacy as a woman, and her inability to cope with losing her baby to an adult world.

Because of their terror of exposing their inner selves, Gilroy's characters are divided rather than united by emotions. They smash into one another and spin away without pausing to examine the damage. Toward the end of *The Subject Was Roses,* Timmy says, "I suspect that no one's to blame. . . . Not even me." This disavowal of any responsibility for the mess they have made of their lives is a common factor among all of Gilroy's characters.

Impressed with his Pulitzer Prize and subsequent personal publicity, Gilroy admits to having felt a pressure to write something worthy of his newfound fame. The result was the disastrous *That Summer—That Fall,* in which he tried to wed the Phaedra and Hippolytus legend to modern characters living in Manhattan's Little Italy. The play had 12 performances, and as Gilroy has said, "It proved that a boy from the Bronx shouldn't mess with the Greeks." The experience released him from what he perceived as the burden of being a Pulitzer Prize-winning playwright and enabled him to return to his own ideas and terse dramaturgy.

It is in his one-act plays that Gilroy is best able to concentrate the power of his simple, descriptive style. He takes an incident and rapidly sets time, mood, and place by zeroing in on the minutest detail. In *The Next Contestant,* for example, a man who is about to be married becomes a guest on a television game show and is challenged to call up an ex-girlfriend, who knows that he is engaged, and to get a date with her. If he achieves his goal, he will win a washer and dryer, a bedroom suite, a radio, a television, a stereo, wall-to-wall carpeting, luggage, an all-expenses-paid vacation in Miami Beach, and more. The heart of this very short play is the quick and emotionally painful telephone conversation between the contestant and the jilted ex-girlfriend. Gilroy shows the manipulation, the deceit, and the subsequent devastating disillusionment.

Gilroy is an idea man more than a plot man, and this can and does hinder him in his full-length work. *Last Licks* presents a variation on his stock characters, who are involved with a one-act's worth of idea. A father, a son, and in this case the father's mistress present a typical Gilroy triangular relationship filled with deception, emotional and physical sadism, drinking bouts, and tales of extramarital affairs.

Gilroy builds entire lives around rebuke and repentance. *Last Licks* is resplendent with repressed emotions and bitter speeches. Like so many of his plays, it is an often comic but more often quite painful skirmish between the sexes in which the primary sympathy is with the men's involvement with the world and with one another.

—Leah D. Frank

GODBER, John (Harry)

Nationality: British. **Born:** Upton, Yorkshire, 15 May 1956. **Education:** Minsthorpe High School, South Elmsall, Yorkshire; Bretton Hall College, West Bretton, Yorkshire, 1974-78, Cert. Ed. 1977, B. Ed. (honours) 1978; Leeds University, 1978-79, M.A. in theatre 1979, graduate study, 1979-83. **Career:** Teacher, Minsthorpe High School, 1981-83. Artistic director, Hull Truck theatre company, 1984—. **Awards:** Edinburgh Festival award, 1981, 1982, 1984; Olivier award, 1984; Los Angeles Drama Critics Circle award, 1986. **Address:** Hull Truck, Spring Street Theatre, Spring Street, Hull, Yorkshire HU2 8RW, England.

Publications

Plays

A Clockwork Orange, adaptation of the novel by Anthony Burgess (produced Edinburgh, 1980; London, 1984).

Cry Wolf (produced Rotherham, Yorkshire, 1981).

Cramp (produced Hull, 1981; revised version, music by Tom Robinson and Hereward K, produced Edinburgh and London, 1986).

E.P.A. (produced Hull, 1982).

Happy Jack (produced Hull, 1982; London, 1985). Included in *Five Plays*, 1989.

Young Hearts Run Free: Ideas Towards a Play (produced West Bretton, Yorkshire, 1983).

September in the Rain (produced Edinburgh, 1983; London, 1984; New York, 1985). Included in *Five Plays*, 1989.

Bouncers (produced Edinburgh and London, 1984; Los Angeles, 1986; New York, 1987). With *Shakers*, London, Chappell, 1987.

Up 'n' Under (produced Edinburgh and London, 1984; New York, 1989). Oxford, Amber Lane Press, 1985.

Shakers, with Jane Thornton (produced Hull and London, 1985). With *Bouncers*, London, Chappell, 1987; as *Shakers Re-stirred,* London, Warner Chappell Plays, 1993.

Up 'n' Under II (produced Edinburgh, 1985; New York, 1989). London and New York, Samuel French, 1994.

Blood, Sweat and Tears (produced Hull and London, 1986). London and New York, 1995.
The Ritz (televised 1987; as *Putting on the Ritz*, produced Leicester, 1987).
Teechers (produced Edinburgh and London, 1987). London, French, 1989.
Oliver Twist (for children), adaptation of the novel by Charles Dickens (produced Hull, 1987).
Salt of the Earth (produced Hull and London, 1988). London, French, 1989.
Five Plays (includes *Up 'n' Under, Bouncers, Teechers, September in the Rain, Happy Jack*). London, Penguin, 1989.
On the Piste (produced Leeds, 1990).
Happy Families (produced at 49 theatres around the United Kingdom, including London, 1991).
The Office Party (produced Hull and London, 1992). London, Warner Chappell Plays, 1995.
April in Paris (produced Hull, 1992). London, Samuel French, 1993.
Passion Killers. London and New York, Samuel French, 1995.
Lucky Sods. London, Samuel French, 1995.

Television Plays: series scripts for *Grange Hill*, 1981-83, *Brookside*, 1983-84, and *Crown Court*, 1983; *The Rainbow Coloured Disco Dancer*, from work by C.P. Taylor, 1984; *The Ritz* series, 1987; *The Continental*, 1987; *My Kingdom for a Horse*, 1991.

*

Theatrical Activities:
Director: **Plays**—All of his own plays; *Imagine* by Stephen Jeffreys, *Hedda Gabler* by Ibsen, and *The Dock* by Phil Woods, Hull, 1987; *Twelfth Night* by Shakespeare, London, 1989; *Sweet Sorrow* by Alan Plater, London, 1990.

* * *

John Godber is very clear about his particular theatrical style: "The dancer and not the poet is the father of the theatre." Reading his plays gives little sense of the energy and pace of the pieces in performance, which have an energy and a pace deriving from his resolute refusal to separate the role of writer from that of director. His involvement with the Hull Truck Company has been a happy one. Their commitment to a theater based on contemporary and community-related issues and a long pedigree of theater derived from improvisation and intense collaboration between writer and actors have allowed him the room to experiment with an exhilarating mixture of theatrical techniques. The result has been some very funny and enjoyable evenings spent in a theater.

Plot in Godber's work is kept to a minimum, and the plays frequently have a strong, if deliberately jokey, documentary feel to them. In *Bouncers* the action takes place in a provincial disco, where the events of a typical night are interspersed with flashback scenes of anxious preparation for the great night out by the lads and girls. Nothing particularly unusual occurs. The bouncers rehearse various degrees of aggression toward the punters; copious amounts of tears, beer, and vomit are spilt; and the characters are united in a macabre attempt to shut off the grim realities of their lives, an attempt that will, as always, be doomed. All of the many characters, both male and female, are played by the same four male bouncers, and the effect is to enlarge the comic potential of the events but also to stress their nonparticularity. Godber is not interested in creating unique, psychologically realized characters. They are representative, standing in for an audience who may very well proceed from the theater to such a disco, the more particularly since Godber is intent on attracting audiences that would not normally regard theater as a part of their cultural experience. The club, then, acts as a gently symbolic location of the contemporary world at play, looking for a dreamworld of alcoholic oblivion and easy sex but finding instead a continuation of the daytime regime that is ruled over by arbitrary bouncers free to admit or refuse entrance to a fun palace in which there are strict rules about dress, an expensive bar, and complete limitations on the celebration of any conceivable excess.

Shakers, written in collaboration with Jane Thornton, changes the sexual perspective. Set in a provincial wine bar run by four waitresses, who again play all of the other male and female characters, it offers an even bleaker account of the urge to escape. We see four young girls at work in a supermarket and fantasizing about a birthday party to come, agonizing over the choice of clothes, and seeing as the limit of their dreams the joy of actually working in a cocktail bar. But the life at Shakers as presented by the four waitresses is no different from any other work situation. The hours are long, the pay is bad, and sexual harassment is not only rife but is also effectively encouraged by the unseen management. That they are better able to analyze their situation than are their male counterparts in *Bouncers* is typical of Godber's work. His strong feminist line demands this distinction. His plays are all about politically marginalized people, those who are failures and victims of the system. For the women the victimization is made worse by their sense of being underdogs in a world of underdogs, and they are given a stronger oppositional voice.

The pace of the productions and the constant role switching does little to disguise, however, a certain literalness of political analysis. Everything fits too neatly into place. Godber's concentration on marginalized characters in an urban wasteland brings with it an inability to look beyond the boundaries of marginalization, although it must be admitted that in performance it is a weakness that is less apparent than on more sober reflection. For these reasons his most successful play is *Up 'n' Under,* for here Godber has been able to use the buildup to and the actual enactment onstage of a Rugby League Sevens match as a far less prosaic metaphor of a modern world of male competition and machismo. Down-at-the-heels Arthur is conned into a large bet with a businessman that he cannot train the worst amateur pub team in Yorkshire to beat the top dogs, the Cobblers Arms from Castleford. Arthur's team is dragged, understrength and unwillingly, into a training program supervised by, horror of horrors, a woman. The scene is set for a *Rocky*-style conclusion—Arthur's favorite movies being the *Rocky* films—in which the underdog gets up off his backside at the last possible moment and wins. The presentation of the game, with seven actors, including their female trainer, acting out the play, is the most exciting piece of total theater I have ever seen, and tension as to the outcome is kept up throughout. This is not Hollywood, however, and the heroes lose. But Godber's characters, although inveterate losers, always retain an optimistic strain, and the play ends with the team planning a double-or-nothing bet on the result of a further match, a match that duly takes place in *Up 'n' Under II.*

The sporting theme is reexplored in *On the Piste,* the very title proclaiming its seaside postcard antecedence, which played at the Leeds Grand in the summer of 1990. This was followed by one of the most unusual events in theatrical history. In 1991 the Little Theatre Guild of Great Britain commissioned a play for the first time. Suitably enough, they turned to Godber, and on October 12 his *Happy Families* received 49 simultaneous first performances by different U.K. companies. The story, which follows the rise of John Taylor, a bright small-town lad on the make, is a typical Godber mix of sex and class warfare, and it is hard to think of a writer, at the same time both populist and popular, more suited for the guild's ambitious commission.

—John Bull

GOLDMAN, James

Nationality: American. **Born:** Chicago, Illinois, 30 June 1927. **Education:** University of Chicago, Ph.B. 1947, M.A. 1950; Columbia University, New York, 1950-52. **Military Service:** Served in the United States Army, 1952-54. **Family:** Married 1) Marie McKeon in 1962 (divorced 1972), one daughter and one son; 2) Barbara Deren in 1975. **Career:** Member of the Council, Dramatists Guild, 1966—, and member of the Council, Authors League of America, 1967—. **Awards:** Oscar, 1969; Writers Guild of America West award, 1969; Writers Guild of Great Britain award, 1969; New York Film Critics award, 1969; New York Drama Critics Circle award, 1972; Olivier award, 1987; *Evening Standard* award, 1987; Society of West End Theatres award, 1987. **Agent:** Owen Laster, William Morris Agency, 1325 Agency of the Americas, New York, New York 10019, U.S.A.

Publications

Plays

They Might Be Giants (produced London, 1961). New York, Bantam, 1970.

Blood, Sweat and Stanley Poole, with William Goldman (produced New York, 1961). New York, Dramatists Play Service, 1962.

A Family Affair, with William Goldman, music by John Kander (produced New York, 1962).

The Lion in Winter (produced New York, 1966). New York, Random House, and London, French, 1966.

Follies, music and lyrics by Stephen Sondheim (produced New York, 1971; revised version produced London, 1987). New York, Random House, 1971.

Robin and Marian (screenplay). New York, Bantam, 1976.

Tolstoy (produced London, 1996).

Screenplays: *The Lion in Winter*, 1968; *They Might Be Giants*, 1970; *Nicholas and Alexandra*, 1971; *Robin and Marian*, 1976; *White Nights*, with Eric Hughes, 1985.

Television Plays: *Evening Primrose*, music and lyrics by Stephen Sondheim, 1966; *Oliver Twist*, 1983; *Anna Karenina*, from the novel by Tolstoy, 1985; *Anastasia: The Mystery of Anna Anderson* series, 1986.

Novels

Waldorf. New York, Random House, 1965; London, Joseph, 1966.

The Man from Greek and Roman. New York, Random House, 1974; London, Hutchinson, 1975.

Myself as Witness. New York, Random House, 1979; London, Hamish Hamilton, 1980.

Fulton County. New York, Morrow, and London, Bantam, 1989.

* * *

James Goldman at his best is a second-rate Neil Simon. Both are dramatists who entertain rather than engage their audiences. Whether he is writing situation comedies in collaboration with his brother (*A Family Affair* and *Blood, Sweat and Stanley Poole*), historical dramas (*The Lion in Winter* and *Nicholas and Alexandra*), or a musical (*Follies*), his work is always predictable, never ranging outside the already tested limits of the form. Only his skillful handling of dialogue occasionally redeems his plays, but even this cannot compensate for his deficiency in imagination. Nor can it conceal that his characters are stock, his plots mechanical, and his themes imperfectly realized.

A Family Affair and *Blood, Sweat and Stanley Poole* play like the pseudocomedies that could be seen between 6 and 10 P.M. any weeknight on American television throughout the late 1950s and early and middle 1960s. One concerns itself with the bustle and bickering that typically occur when two families attempt to plan a wedding and the guardian of the bride wants a simple, elegant family affair, while the mother of the groom longs for something a bit fancier. The other involves an army officer, Lieutenant Stanley Poole, who has been bribing the education officer, Malcolm, with goods from the supply room to pass him on the army proficiency tests. The hero of the day is Private Robert Oglethorpe, who runs a cram course for the army officers, making it possible for Poole to replace the pilfered supplies, free himself from his bondage to Malcolm, and retain his military rank by passing the proficiency exams. The plot is mechanical, the jokes are stale, the characters are too familiar, and the situation—Oglethorpe's classroom for the army's dunderheads—plays like a classroom scene from *Our Miss Brooks* or *Sergeant Bilko*, replete with all the cute gimmicks and mnemonics that teach the adult student to learn the names of the five Great Lakes or to recognize "the Symphony that Schubert wrote and never finished." Even the two Goldmans' sense of theatricality falters in this play. The slapstick accident, in which the good guys mangle and mutilate the villainous Captain Malcolm's coveted Jaguar, takes place offstage and can only be recounted, supposedly hilariously, by the conspirators on the stage. The climax of the play comes when the clumsy Private Oglethorpe, who previously got headaches whenever the word "bayonet" was even mentioned, catches the rifle Malcolm throws at him and brilliantly executes the manual of arms. The first action better fits a movie or television program than a play; the second simply lacks enough intrinsic importance to carry even the climax of a silly piece of canned comedy.

Goldman finds better success in another genre, the history or chronicle play, which had its revival in the 1960s with *Luther*, *Lawrence of Arabia*, and, most successfully, *A Man for All Seasons*. Well done, the chronicle play examines and revitalizes characters from the past whose significance is unchallenged. It brings the past to life, and, more importantly, it shows how the present has worked upon the past, making it relevant. Goldman, however, seems to have overlooked this most important aspect of historical drama. It is not surprising that the dramatist of *They Might Be Giants* left the contemporary world and looked to the past to supply him with the heroes he sought, but it is regrettable that he went to the past only to acquire material and not to relate it to modern concerns. In *The Lion in Winter* Henry II of England and Eleanor of Aquitaine engage in a battle of wits as each attempts to outdo the other and settle the questions of succession, which son will marry the king's mistress and which son will inherit the Vexin and Aquitaine. Henry, the aging monarch but still the roaring, regal lion, seeks to possess both his mistress and his wife, and he wants both of their lands in order to pass England and that portion of France which is England's to John, his youngest and weakest son. Eleanor fights fiercely to hold Henry and, failing that, to guarantee that England and her precious Aquitaine are willed to Richard Coeur de Lion. Geoffrey, the middle and cleverest son, plays brother against brother and son against father as he, too, struggles to protect what he believes should be his own. Alais, the lovely mistress, is pawn to Henry and his aged and imprisoned wife throughout the play. The dialogue is witty, intelligent, pithy, and often mercurial. Henry and Eleanor alternately rage at each other and ask for pity in a manner reminiscent of George and Martha's quarrels in *Who's Afraid of Virginia Woolf?* Finally, however, the play is too contrived, the games of one-upmanship grow stale, and the audience begins to doubt that anything so real as the fate of the kingdom is at stake. The play ends in a stalemate; the question of succession is postponed to another year, and Eleanor and Henry conclude by acknowledging to each other that their real enemy is time and that it will win. Goldman, meanwhile, seems to have forgotten that there was ever a real historical question raised in the play. History, and not the play, is left to tell us how the question of succession was resolved. The natures of the regal pair and not succession seem to have been the stuff of the play, but Goldman never demonstrates why these natures matter or who this king and queen are.

Goldman later tried his hand at musical comedy, but he seems no more likely to be successful with this form than with the others. The book for *Follies* suffers from the same flaws that plagued his earlier works. The occasion is a reunion called by an impresario of the Weismann Follies. Back to the crumbling music hall that had its heyday 30 years earlier come the showgirls who had danced in the era between the wars. Among the guests are two women, Sally and Phyllis, and their husbands, Buddy and Ben. As the evening progresses, we watch these pairs when they were young and in love and also see the women now that they are old and discontented and flirting with the possibility that they can undo time and return to the men who had jilted them before they married. The soap opera tale can be guessed. After an evening in which the couples dance and sing down memory lane and exorcise their regrets, the couples leave their fancied past and return to drab realities and each other. The lyrics and music do much to redeem the play, and the gauzy interplay of past and present, of shadows and substance, is well handled visually and extremely well suited to a musical that has taken sentimentality and nostalgia for its theme. A revised version of *Follies*, which Goldman and Stephen Sondheim worked on together, was a 1987 hit in London.

Goldman's difficulty in creating fully realized characters of his own fresh imagining and his lack of a significant theme have continued to plague his work.

—Carol Simpson Stern

GOOCH, Steve

Nationality: British. **Born:** Surrey, 22 July 1945. **Education:** Emanuel School, London, 1956-63; Trinity College, Cambridge, 1964-67, B.A. (honors) in modern languages 1967; St. John's College, Cambridge (Harper-Wood Scholar), 1967; Birmingham University, 1968-69. **Career:** Assistant editor, *Plays and Players* magazine, London, 1972-73; resident dramatist, Half Moon Theatre, London, 1973-74, Greenwich Theatre, London, 1974-75, Solent People's Theatre, Southampton, 1981-82, Theatre Venture, London, 1983-84, Croydon Warehouse Theatre, Surrey, 1986, and Gate Theatre, London, 1990-91. **Awards:** Arts Council bursary, 1973; Thames Television award, 1974. **Agent:** Micheline Steinberg Playwrights, 409 Triumph House, 187-191 Regent Street, London W1R 7WF, England.

Publications

Plays

The NAB Show (produced Brighton, 1970).
Great Expectations, adaptation of the novel by Dickens (produced Liverpool, 1970).
Man Is Man, adaptation of the play by Brecht (produced London, 1971; New Haven, Connecticut, 1978).
It's All for the Best, adaptation of the novel *Candide* by Voltaire (produced Stoke-on-Trent, 1972; London, 1979).
Big Wolf, adaptation of a play by Harald Mueller (produced London, 1972). London, Davis Poynter, 1972.
Will Wat; If Not, What Will? (produced London, 1972). London, Pluto Press, 1975.
Nicked (produced Exeter, 1972).
The Mother, adaptation of a play by Brecht (produced London, 1973). London, Eyre Methuen, 1978.
Female Transport (produced London, 1973; Louisville, 1975; New York, 1976). London, Pluto Press, 1974.
Dick (produced London, 1973).
The Motor Show, with Paul Thompson (produced Dagenham, Essex, and London, 1974). London, Pluto Press, 1975.
Cock-Artist, adaptation of a play by Rainer Werner Fassbinder (produced London, 1974). Published in *Gambit 39-40* (London), 1982.
Strike '26, with Frank McDermott (produced London, 1975).
Made in Britain, with Paul Thompson (produced Oxford, 1976).
Landmark (as *Our Land Our Lives*, produced London, 1976; revised version, as *Landmark*, produced Wivenhoe, Essex, 1980). Colchester, Theatre Action Press, 1982.
Back-Street Romeo (produced London, 1977).
Rosie, adaptation of a play by Harald Mueller (also director: produced London, 1977).
The Women Pirates: Ann Bonney and Mary Read (produced London, 1978). London, Pluto Press, 1978.
In the Club (produced London, 1979).
Future Perfect, with Michelene Wandor and Paul Thompson (produced on tour, 1980).
Fast One (produced Southampton, 1982). Southampton, Solent People's Theatre, 1982.
Fuente Ovejuna, adaptation of the play by Lope de Vega (produced London, 1982).

Flotsam, adaptation of a play by Harald Mueller (produced Croydon, Surrey, 1985). Published in *Gambit 39-40* (London), 1982.
Home Work, adaptation of a play by Franz Xaver Kroetz (produced London, 1990). Published in *Gambit 39-40* (London), 1982.
Taking Liberties (produced London, 1984).
Good for You (produced Leicester, 1985).
Mister Fun (produced Sheffield and London, 1986).
Star Turns (produced London, 1987).
Massa (produced London, 1989). London, New Cross, 1990.
Our Say (produced Wednesbury, West Midlands, 1989).
Lulu, adaptation of *Earth Spirit* and *Pandora's Box* by Frank Wedekind (produced Edinburgh and London, 1990).
The Marquis of Keith, adaptation of the play by Frank Wedekind (produced London, 1990).
Dark Glory (produced Southhampton, 1994).
Free Time (public readings in London and Krakow, 1994).

Radio Plays: *The Kiosk*, from a play by Ludvík Askenazy, 1970; *Delinquent*, from a play by Harald Mueller, 1978; *Santis*, from a play by Martin Walser, 1980; *What Brothers Are For*, 1983; *Bill of Health*, 1987.

Other

All Together Now: An Alternative View of Theatre and the Community. London, Methuen, 1984.
Writing a Play. London, A & C Black, 1988.

Translator, *Poems and Ballads*, by Wolf Biermann. London, Pluto Press, 1977.
Translator, with Paul Knight, *Wallraff, The Undesirable Journalist*, by Günter Wallraff. London, Pluto Press, 1978; New York, Overlook Press, 1979.

*

Critical Studies: Interviews in *Renaissance and Modern Studies* (Nottingham), 1977, and *Hard Times 12* (Berlin), 1980; *Alternativen im britischen Drama der Gegenwart* by Günther Klotz, Berlin, Akademie, 1978; *Stages in the Revolution* by Catherine Itzin, London, Eyre Methuen, 1980; "The Surveyor and the Construction Engineer" by Gooch, in *Theatre Quarterly 36* (London), 1980.

Theatrical Activities:
Director: **Plays**—*Work Kills!* by Bruce Birchall, London, 1975; *Consensus* by Michael Gill, London, 1976; *Rosie*, London, 1977; *Night Shift* by John Derbyshire, London, 1983.

Steve Gooch comments:

My work has developed over the years from an attempt to articulate the voice of working-class and other dispossessed sections of British society towards a general aesthetic in which the personal struggle to take control of one's life is given full emotional value within an open-eyed depiction of the social nexus surrounding it.

This has often been expressed through historical analogy and the portrayal of "hidden history," and frequently by means of multiple protagonists or groups engaged in a common, though variegated, purpose. In these plays I have attempted to reflect the increasingly collective nature of modern life, confronting the dilemma of pluralism within an ordered democratic progress.

Crucial to this "group" aesthetic is the gap between experience and thought, specifically in the way individual characters in groups "think" each other. This has also been important in my smaller-cast plays during the 1980s, where wider social conflict has tended to be treated through the microcosm of man-woman relationships. In each of these contexts language becomes the fine-tuning of communication between conflicting social aspirations and judgements. In exploring this, my translation and adaptation of European works has been invaluable in sensitising my understanding of language as the barometer of social will.

* * *

In contrast to other British playwrights of his generation, Steve Gooch has not, in spite of being a prolific and versatile writer, found a firm foothold in either the major subsidized theater companies or the mass media. This is not due to a lack of talent or a lack of successful productions of his plays, or even to a decline of the British alternative theater scene, but rather to Gooch's adherence to a theater for the community. From the beginning of Gooch's career as a writer for the stage, a great deal of artistic energy has gone into the mediation, by translations or adaptations, of plays and theatrical ideas from the Romance and German languages. Gooch shows particular skill in his translations of German dramatists of the classical modernist period like the early Brecht and, more recently, Frank Wedekind and of those contemporary playwrights (Kroetz, Harald Mueller, Martin Walser) whose preoccupation with political aspects of subjectivity mirrors his own, but he has also adapted classic authors like Dickens, Voltaire, Lope de Vega, and Terence.

In his original work for the stage Gooch early on found a congenial venue in the Half Moon Theatre in London's East End. One of the first results of workshop projects there was Gooch's dramatization, as *Will Wat; If Not, What Will?*, of Wat Tyler's 1381 peasant uprising, the first protosocialist movement in English history. In this attempt "to show what the history books usually leave out," Gooch draws on contemporary documents and alternative versions of medieval history to present the peasants' point of view in their opposition to royal militarism and their exploitation by old feudal and emerging merchant interests. The play acutely balances the eventual defeat of the peasants, led by John Ball and Tyler, against the positive growth of self-awareness of an oppressed class. History is brought onstage as a collective process whose dramaturgy has to preempt individual identification by anti-illusionist techniques such as double casting, songs, and quotes from historical documents. Similar Brechtian techniques are employed in Gooch's next historical play, also produced by the Half Moon Theatre, *Female Transport*. Again, it is history from below, this time in the more familiar scenery of early nineteenth-century Britain. The play gives a realistic account of the voyage to Australia of six female convicts who gradually gain insight into the necessity of resistance against a patriarchal class society. This socialist-feminist line in Gooch's work is elaborated in an early text that ended up as a Royal Shakespeare Company production of *The Women Pirates: Ann Bonney and Mary Read*. In this epic portrait of two women at the turn of the eighteenth century, Gooch charts, in a loose configuration of scenes interspersed with many songs, a successful if seemingly peripheral liberation from hegemonic law and morality.

While developing his Brechtian style of historical plays with a socialist, humanist, and feminist slant, Gooch collaborated on theatrical projects that concerned sections of the contemporary working class in a more direct way. It was here that Gooch came nearest to his declared aim of writing "about working-class experience and history, and for a working-class audience and readership." In *The Motor Show* (written with Paul Thompson) Gooch tried to create a working-class community theater from within. After local research at the Dagenham Ford plant by the group called Community Theatre, the play turned into a 24-scene documentation, done in a deft cartoonlike style mixing documentary, realistic, and music hall elements, of 60 years of struggle between the company and its workers. The Community Theatre failed to set itself up in Dagenham, but the unashamedly agitprop techniques—rescued from preachiness by witty dialogue—of *The Motor Show*, largely retained in *Strike '26* and in *Made in Britain*, a documentary about British Leyland (again written with Thompson), became a model for many similar attempts by other writers. In *Our Land, Our Lives* Gooch's concern with issues involving specifically contemporary communities was placed on a more general level by being given a fictional focus in a reunion of young married people in a village barn that had served them as a meeting place in their school days. The play shows the encroachment of agribusiness on traditional village life, but in its reworking at the Essex University Theatre (under the title *Landmark*) it came to include the theme of nuclear threat. In the revised version the fields against whose sale the young people have been rallying opposition are bought up by the Ministry of Defence to be converted into a site for nuclear missiles.

In the austerity of the 1980s Gooch apparently redefined the range of his dramatic themes, even though he remained faithful to the small companies and theater groups of the dwindling alternative circuit. The move away from agitprop didacticism is obvious even in his *Taking Liberties*, written in the genre of the historical play, which lends itself most readily to political discourse with clear-cut messages. In this play we get an unusually broad social panorama, from patricians to plebeians, bound up in the radical agitation of the late eighteenth century. The carnivalesque action focuses on the mock election of a mayor of Garratt and reflects John Wilkes's creation of a new type of populist politics involving the London masses. The play also indicates a change in the post-1979 political atmosphere in that it does not rescue the utopian perspectives from the historical setting but rather ends in the temporary defeat of plebeian aspirations for political participation. The widening of thematic range and intended appeal finds expression in a reappropriation of realist and even naturalist theatrical approaches. This development accompanies the synthesis in Gooch's conception of his own work between John McGrath's purist reliance on popular traditions and David Edgar's more eclectic attitude toward mainstream theatrical codes. The new approach characterizes even a play with a seemingly exotic setting like *Fast One*, in which a merchant seaman is caught up in an international intrigue about the sale of arms in an unspecified South American country.

Mister Fun, written for a Sheffield-based touring group, goes even further in the direction of a naturalist tradition that the author had never completely excluded from his theater language. The play concentrates on the lives of a young couple working at a traditional fairground. The action shows the inevitable takeover of the fair by the electronics branch of the leisure industry after a local council's abortive attempts to give it a permanent site. This process is traced in its divisive effects on the young couple's lives. In their drifting apart the girl achieves some degree of independence, whereas the eponymous hero becomes a kind of walking ad for what was once popular entertainment but now usurps people's work and minds.

—Bernd-Peter Lange

GORMAN, Clem (Brian Gorman)

Nationality: Australian. **Born:** Perth, Western Australia, 18 October 1942. **Education:** St. Louis School, 1955-56, and Aquinas College, 1957-60, both Perth; University of Sydney, 1963-67, B.A., Dip. Ed.; Polytechnic of Central London, diploma in arts administration 1975. **Family:** Married Sandra Dent in 1967 (divorced 1986). **Career:** Free-lance stage manager and theatre administrator, Sydney, 1967-68: founder, Australian Free Theatre Group; co-founder, *Masque* theatre magazine, 1968; lived in London, 1970-79; deputy administrator, Round House Trust, London, 1975-76; administrator, Moving Being dance company, Cardiff, 1976-77; administrator, Australian National Playwrights Conference, Sydney, 1982; lecturer in playwriting, Victorian College of the Arts, Melbourne, 1984, and Adelaide University, 1985; training officer, Australian Book Publishers Association, Sydney, 1986. Freelance journalist, 1966—. **Awards:** Australia Council Literature Board grant, 1980, and fellowship, 1981. **Agent:** Anthony Williams, 55 Victoria Street, Potts Point, New South Wales 2011, Australia.

Publications

Plays

I Love Your Sailor (produced London, 1976).

Let Me In, I'm a Friend of the Band (produced London, 1978).

A Manual of Trench Warfare (produced Adelaide, 1978). Sydney, Currency Press, 1979.

The Harding Women (produced Adelaide, 1980). With *A Night in the Arms of Raeleen*, Sydney, Currency Press, 1983.

The Motivators (produced Sydney, 1981). Montmorency, Victoria, Yackandandah, 1983.

A Night in the Arms of Raeleen (produced Melbourne, 1982). With *The Harding Women*, Sydney, Currency Press, 1983.

A Fortunate Life, adaptation of the autobiography by A.B. Facey (produced Melbourne, 1984). Sydney, Currency Press, 1987.

The Journey Home (for children; produced Adelaide, 1985).

A Face from the Street (produced Canberra, 1985).

The Last Night-Club. Montmorency, Victoria, Yackandandah, 1985.

Screenplay: *The Swans Away* (documentary), 1986.

Other

The Book of Ceremonies. Bottisham, Cambridgeshire, Whole Earth Tools, 1969; revised edition, as *Making Ceremonies*, 1972; revised edition, as *The Book of Ceremony*, 1972.

Making Communes: Survey/Manual. Bottisham, Cambridgeshire, Whole Earth Tools, 1971.

People Together. St. Albans, Hertfordshire, Paladin, 1975.
Backstage Rock: Behind the Scenes with the Bands. London, Pan, 1978.
National Report on Script Consultancy in the Theatre. Wollongong, New South Wales, Scarp Publications, 1992.

Editor, *The Larrikin Streak: Australian Writers Look at the Legend*. Sydney, Pan Macmillan, 1990.

*

Manuscript Collection: University of Queensland Press, St. Lucia.

Critical Study: "Gallipoli Revisited: Historicity in Plays by Alan Seymour and Clem Gorman" by Bill Dunstone, in *ACLALS,* 1986, pp. 11-18.

Clem Gorman comments:

It may be—and a writer is not necessarily the best person to know—that my work is about the struggle between the female and male sides of my own nature.

* * *

Though it was only in 1978 with *A Manual of Trench Warfare* that he achieved recognition as an Australian playwright, Clem Gorman had been working in the Australian and English theater since the mid-1960s and had written books on several aspects of the counterculture as well as organizing an experimental group in Sydney. In view of this background his original published plays are surprising in that they are stylistically muted, mostly using a naturalistic structure of human relationships broken only by intermittent songs and direct audience address. Moreover, in his plays with male subjects the ostensible central theme is the traditional Australian one of mateship, questioned, tested, and analyzed but not absolutely rejected. *A Manual of Trench Warfare* actually begins with a male chorus of Australian voices singing a hymn to mateship, an assertion of both working-class and nationalistic solidarity, and the first scene opens with a young soldier alone in a trench at Gallipoli writing a letter to his mother about how he killed the Turk who had killed his mate. A new mate, a more garrulous Irish larrikin soldier, brings a different bond in terms of whisky, antiauthoritarianism, and comradeship in battle, but gradually Gorman's focus shifts from this traditional model of mateship to an examination of the support system that evolves between the two men and that is ultimately expressed in physical love. In the poignant final scene the Australian's patriotism has been completely displaced by his loyalty to his dying Irish mate, to the extent that he offers to shoot the corporal who has interrupted their lovemaking.

In *A Night in the Arms of Raeleen* the solitary female character is a catalyst for the delusory concept of mateship that 20 years previously had bound together the four males who are now having a reunion and trying to regress to their Bodgie identities in talk and dress. Raeleen, however, has recently told herself that she has got to make her "own support system now," and she defiantly asserts the sober values of middle age, forcing the men away from mutual congratulation and myth mongering toward a rudimentary awareness of themselves and their needs. A series of monologues from various characters, done directly to the audience under a single spotlight, shows how with a brutal cauterizing of emotions Raeleen was used as the pivotal commodity in their adolescent camaraderie. But the naturalistic context of these addresses shows her emergent self-knowledge dissolving all relationships and the whole support structure, forcing them to find independence as a precondition for new, honest relationships.

In *The Harding Women* all three characters are female, held together by their various relationships to the dead paterfamilias, dramaturgically a male equivalent of Raeleen, whom they have known as wife, as housekeeper-mistress, and as daughter. Each character has at least three monologues and songs that deal with personal crises and explain how the present situation of distrust and exploitation evolved. For these the widow dresses in clothes of the early 1960s and speaks accusingly to her dead husband, while the other two women speak directly to the audience in a more reflective manner. A Strindbergian web of entrapment is sketched, with the acerbic, hypochondriac mother venting her histrionic bitterness on the housekeeper, who had been paradoxically snared by the dead man's intended generosity, and on the daughter, who feels an irrational piety toward her mother even though she can state, "I don't need a man to look after me. I don't need a support system except my friends and colleagues at work. I don't need a system of beliefs to buttress me." But both mother and daughter have a dependence on alcohol and drugs, and the ending is intensely pessimistic. Whereas the reunion at Raeleen's occurred once in 20 years, never to be repeated, for the Harding women it is an annual ritual with no prospect of relief or resolution, at least until another death occurs. The poignancy of dependence recurs in Gorman's less-known works, particularly *The Motivators*, which presents itself as two revue-style monologues that unexpectedly intersect at the end. The woman, a middle-aged "training officer," and the man, a drunken "motivator," both assert their independence but emerge as pathetically inadequate.

The playwright Jack Hibberd has astutely observed that the Harding mother "embodies the awful oppressiveness of the 1950s in Australia" and that she has a strong affinity to the recurrent type of "the great Australian emptiness" in the plays and novels of Patrick White of that period. Gorman's pessimism is reinforced because the oppressiveness has invaded and infected the 1970s, and this implication underlies the ironies of his other major work, a stage adaptation of A. B. Facey's autobiography, *A Fortunate Life*. In this play Old Bert narrates from the stage the story of his life, which is episodically acted out by a large cast. The narrator's persistence in refusing to see that the extraordinary saga of abandonment and deprivation is anything other than fortunate, coupled with a simplistic delivery style and a magnification of the most meager happiness, brings an extreme pathos. Even at Gallipoli, where Bert sees the deaths of not only his mate but also his brother, there is expression of neither anger nor grief, and when his son is killed in World War II, Bert's response does not go beyond losing faith in God. The terrible stoicism that accepts oppressiveness ironically belies Gorman's assertion that Australians "are a very direct and often publicly emotional people." The impregnable satisfaction of the old Facey, the obdurate larrikin, would have few answers to the emotional directness of the middle-aged Raeleen.

—Howard McNaughton

GOTANDA, Philip Kan

Nationality: American. **Born:** Stockton, California, 17 December 1949. **Education:** University of California, Santa Barbara, B.A. in Asian studies; Hastings College, Nebraska, J.D. **Career:** Co-founder, Asian American Musicians Organization; artist-in-residence, Okada House, Stanford University, California. **Awards:** Rockefeller grant, 1980-81.

Publications

Plays

Bullet Headed Birds (produced New York, 1981).
A Song for a Nisei Fisherman (produced Los Angeles, 1982; New York, 1983).
The Dream of Kitamura (produced New York, 1985). Published in *West Coast Plays* (San Francisco), 15/16, 1983.
The Wash (produced Los Angeles, 1985). Published in *West Coast Plays,* 1987; in *Between Worlds: Contemporary Asian-American Plays*, edited by Misha Berson, New York, Theatre Communications Group, 1990; Portsmouth, New Hampshire, Heinemann, 1992.
Yankee Dawg, You Die (produced San Francisco, 1987; New York, 1989). New York, Dramatists Play Service, 1989.
Fish Head Soup (produced San Francisco, 1987).
Fish Head Soup and Other Plays. Seattle, Washington, University of Washington Press, 1995.
Ballad of Yachiyo. New York, Theatre Communications Group, 1996.
Day Standing on Its Head. New York, Dramatists Play Service, 1994; in *But Still, Like Air, I'll Rise,* Philadelphia, Temple University Press, 1997.

Recordings: *Ballad of Yachiyo,* Los Angeles, Theatre Works, 1996.

*

Critical Study: "Choice and Chance" by Nina Siegal, in *American Theatre,* February 1996, p. 26.

* * *

Philip Kan Gotanda's earliest published play, *The Dream of Kitamura,* seems to borrow from the No theater the reenactment of a crucial act from the past that haunts the central character. At the beginning of the play, over the chanting of a Buddhist sutra, we hear a voice that tells us, "A crime has been committed. A robbery. A double murder. There was a witness." We find Rosanjin enthroned like Beckett's Hamm, so fearful of the vengeance of the demon mask Kitamura—though in the end we learn that Rosanjin was not the murderer—that he has hired guards to protect him. Gotanda's ritualized presentation suggests Rosanjin's state of mind even though the action does not take place within his consciousness. Gotanda's next two plays are realistic in their action, though *The Wash* has three locations simultaneously present throughout, and *Yankee Dawg, You Die,* like *The Dream of Kitamura,* uses an abstract set of shoji screens. But in his later plays he returns to the reenacting of the past and to the sense that one of the characters is the controlling intelligence of the play.

The Wash takes us deep into the psyches of a married but now separated couple, who are perceived with deep sympathy, and totally involves us in their parallel situations. After decades of marriage, in which she played a traditional supportive role, Masi has walked out on her husband, Nobu. Every week she comes by to collect his dirty washing and to return his clean clothes. He barely acknowledges her visits, but he expresses his hurt by focusing on building an elaborate kite such as he flew in his childhood. Masi seeks a new relationship with a widower, and Nobu is drawn into tentative communication with a widow who runs a neighborhood restaurant, where he now eats. When Masi announces her remarriage, however, Nobu isolates himself in his apartment, refusing to answer the door or the telephone. Yet Gotanda suggests hope for Nobu. One of his two daughters has married a black man, something Nobu has considered to be a disgrace, but when she visits with her young son, he slowly accepts the child and gives him the kite.

On the one hand, anyone can identify with Masi's struggles for self-fulfillment, even if dramatists only rarely present them among retired people in their 60s. On the other hand, *The Wash* has particular significance for Japanese-Americans. First, the central problem is Nobu's internalized prohibition against the expression of emotion, perhaps particularly strong among Nisei (second-generation Japanese-Americans) because of their difficult lives, notably the wartime internment to which Nobu's mind keeps returning. Even in the scene in which he asks Masi to stay the night, he is able to do so only indirectly by asking her to make him breakfast the next morning. This same inhibition makes him embarrassed by the restaurant owner's small advances. Second, because of a sense of obligation to the family, Masi has taken a long time to face up to the recognition of her own needs. Only now that her children are in their 30s does she feel free to consider herself. Third, as Michael Toshiyuki Uno, the director of the 1988 film of *The Wash,* has suggested, "[In] Asian-American images in the past, there is no sexuality," yet *The Wash* deals openly with sexual needs.

Yankee Dawg, You Die is a smaller play in cast and in subject. It is a series of encounters between two Japanese-American film actors, the elder of whom took a Chinese name in the 1940s to improve his acceptability. This is one of the professional compromises the play addresses. The young actor, who is about to move from an Asian-American theater company to "the industry," expresses a mixture of admiration for the older actor's success and contempt for the compromises he made to achieve it. At the play's end the two friends, as they have become, are offered roles in the same movie. The young actor takes the part of Yang, the evil one—the kind of stereotyped role he has attacked the older man for accepting—while the older actor chooses to appear instead in an independent, low-budget Asian-American film.

A Song for a Nisei Fisherman and *Fish Head Soup* center on basically the same couple as *The Wash,* an emotionally constricted Nisei and his anxious and protective wife. Introducing a collection of the three plays, Michael Omi spoke of an unconsciously wrought family trilogy. Rather, the same marital relationship is explored from the perspective of a different family member—the wife in *The Wash,* the husband in *A Song for a Nisei Fisherman,* and a son in *Fish Head Soup.* In *A Song* an old man, in a reverie while fishing, reviews the events of his life. Not only do the events closely parallel those of Gotanda's father, but the fisherman's two sons are a doctor and a law school dropout turned writer. Gotanda, who once intended to be a psychiatrist, earned a law degree.

The play written from the son's perspective, *Fish Head Soup,* is the most searing. It begins after the funeral of the younger son, Mat, and has a complex structure. To everyone's shock Mat walks in, but as the action proceeds, the audience realizes that it is watching a reenactment of his last visit home together with incidents from each family member's past life. A number of the incidents involve racism. Mat's brother was wounded in the Vietnam War and is mentally impaired. He is repairing, or dismantling, the house. The father is mentally and physically incapacitated. The mother is having an affair with a white man who pushes her into the role of an imagined Japanese woman. Mat himself has tried to make it in movies. His achievement has been to play a stud in a porn flick, which his mother sees in a hotel room with her lover. The family is falling apart, and at the end of the play the walls of the house collapse, "revealing the clean framework of the house—pipes, wiring—pristine and glowing" under a full moon. But one feels that the play cannot be resolved by a striking visual image.

Gotanda's *Ballad of Yochiyo* is explicitly about his own family—about his father's sister, Yochiyo, who had an affair, became pregnant, killed herself, and was never spoken of. (Gotanda seems to use the words "ballad" and "song" to indicate a nonrealistic style.) In the play the teenage Yochiyo goes from her Hawaiian village to work for a Japanese potter. Gotanda seems to want us to believe that in allowing the potter to have an affair with her she is sacrificing herself for his art. Inspired by her, as he never has been by his wife, he produces pottery of rare elegance. Yochiyo is like the bird that has nested in the chimney of the kiln and flies away in flames when the pots are fired. If, indeed, his plays are inspired by the relationships within his own family, the metaphor might be extended to Gotanda himself, who has flown from it with flames in his heart.

—Anthony Graham-White

GOW, Michael

Nationality: Australian. **Born:** Sydney in 1955. **Education:** Sydney University, B.A. 1980. **Career:** Founder-member, Thalia Theatre Company, Sydney; chair of the board, Griffin Theatre Company, Sydney, 1986—; board member, Australian Theatre for young people, 1989-95; currently associate director, Sydney Theatre Company. **Awards:** New Writers fellowship, 1986; New South Wales Premier's award, 1986, 1995; Sydney Theatre Critics Circle award, 1986, 1991; Green Room award for best play, 1986; Australian Writers Guild award, 1987; Australian film institute award for best mini-series, 1989. **Address:** c/o Robyn Gardiner Management, 2/397 Riley Street, Surry Hills, NSW 2010, Australia.

Publications

Plays

The Kid (produced Sydney, 1983). Sydney, Currency Press, 1983.
The Astronaut's Wife (produced Sydney, 1984).
Away (produced Sydney, 1986; Sacramento, California, 1989). Sydney, Currency Press, 1986.
On Top of the World (produced Sydney, 1986; London, 1992).
Europe (produced Sydney, 1987; Leatherhead, Surrey, 1989). Sydney, Currency Press, 1988.
1841 (produced Adelaide, 1988). Sydney, Currency Press, 1988.
Furious (produced Sydney, 1991). Sydney, Currency Press, 1994.
All Stops Out (for children) (produced Sydney, 1991).
Sweet Phoebe (produced Sydney, 1994; London, 1995; Portland, USA, 1997). Sydney, Currency Press, 1995.
Live Acts on Stage (produced Sydney, 1996).

Radio Plays: *The Astronaut's Wife,* 1986; *Europe,* 1987.

Television Plays: *Art 'n Life,* 1985; *Eden's Lost,* 1988; *The Ten Commandments,* 1997.

*

Critical Studies: "An Interview with Michael Gow" by John M. Pearson, in *Southerly: A Review of Australian Literature,* June 1992, pp. 116-31; *Michael Gow's Plays: A Thematic Approach* by Luke Simon, Sydney, Currency Press, 1991; "Monumental Moments: Michael Gow's *1841, Stephen Sewell's Hate, Louis Nowra's Capricornia and Australia's Bicentenary*" by Helen Gilbert, in *Australasian Drama Studies* (Queensland, Australia), April 1994; The *NEAP Guide to Away* by Jane Tibby, Carlton, Victoria, NEAP, 1997.

Theatrical Activities:
Director: **Plays**–*The Secret House,* 1987; *Live Acts on Stage* 1996; *1841,* 1988; *Fire on the Snow Day* by Douglas Stewart, 1996; *Away,* 1989, 1992; *Phadra* by Racine, 1991; *Furious,* 1991, 1994; *Women of Troy* by Euripides, 1992; *Angels in America Part 1 and 2* by Tony Kushner, 1992; *Titus Andronicus* by Shakespeare, 1993; *Oleanna* by David Mamet, 1993; *The Visit* by Durrenmatt, 1993; *Sweet Phoebe,* Sydney, 1994, 1995; *Broken Glass* by Arthur Miller, Sydney, 1996; *Iphigenie en Tauride* by Gluck, 1997; *The Birth Day Party* by Harold Pinter, Sydney, 1997; *Welcome to Broome,* Perth, 1998; *Xpo: The Human Factor* by John Romeril, 1998.

* * *

With the success of his play *Away* and its numerous productions in Australia and abroad, Michael Gow was considered the most exciting new writing talent in 1980s Australian theater. The clear, sparse dialogue and sure theatrical sense of his plays owe something to his experience as an actor and a director. His textual references to and citations of European models, particularly Greek and French classical tragedy and Shakespeare, led many critics to hail his plays as exemplars of a new internationalism in Australian theater. Yet behind the Greek allusions, Gow's main subject in *Away* and *The Kid* is the intergenerational and sexual tensions of the nuclear family, more specifically the lower-middle-class 1960s generation, alienated by international media culture and the very suburban affluence that their Depression-era parents worked so hard to bequeath to them.

Gow's first play, *The Kid,* is an extraordinarily assured debut, a kind of Wagnerian road movie initiating his themes of the precariousness of the family and the death of the young. The "kid" is Aspro, whose tough sister Snake and brother Dean take him to Sydney in search of compensation for a head injury. On the road to the big city, Dean picks up the gentle Donald but becomes fascinated by the abused waif Desiree's deluded allegiance to "Gard's word," apocalyptic nuclear visions from fundamentalist America. Atop a Sydney high rise with the city ringed by apocalyptic bushfires, the quest fails, and the precarious "family" of kids is shattered by the pressures of an uncomprehending official world. The tersely witty scenes are framed by operatic allusions to Valhalla and other grandiose European cultural expressions. These allusions lend context and comment to the kids' alienation and constricted lives amidst a plethora of postmodernist packaged "culture" offered by adults, whether religious paranoias, opera albums, or fatuous coffee-table Australiana books.

Although written before *Away*, *On Top of the World* was produced in the following year and shows a family's precarious reestablishment in the face of disease, emotional pain, and death. A daringly funny play, *On Top* deals with the tormented children of Clive, a widowed patriarch who is dying of cancer in his high-rise Gold Coast apartment building. His estranged and probably gay son Marcus brings to the family reunion the elderly Baby, a motherly working-class woman who eventually overcomes the hostility of his vehement sister Stephanie to find a home and function as Clive's wife. The play ends in hilarious savagery when Marcus phones to berate Baby's own ungrateful and selfish relatives, inducing the family to join in a ritual of cathartic abuse. Echoes of the Atreidae story combine with Gow's typical use of tirade and stichomythia to endow the play with classical structure and mythic resonance.

In *Away,* Gow's most renowned play, a school production of Shakespeare's *Midsummer Night's Dream* frames the story of the effect of the dying boy Tom's life on three 1960s families, each with some grief in need of healing. The suburban rituals of the Australian Christmas seaside family holiday are rudely shattered by storms (played by the Fairies), by various tensions caused by generational conflict, and, in the case of the fragile Coral, by the loss of her son in the Vietnam War. References to *The Tempest* and *Twelfth Night* lend a tone of comic regeneration, punctured by the final recitation of the first scene of *King Lear.* Gow altered the play's ending for his 1992 production to clarify that Tom has really died. His keen satire of the human and environmental costs of creeping postwar affluence and lower-middle-class gentrification is typified in the Greek chorus of campers demanding fatuous "improvements" to the natural beauty of the beach caravan site that would turn it into a replica of conformist suburbia.

In the Australian bicentennial year of 1988 Gow wrote for the Adelaide Festival the historical melodrama *1841.* A damning indictment of Australia's penal past and blinkered present, the play is a dystopian and quite uncelebratory version of the history play genre. This neorevolutionary pageant explores the penal state of early Australia through the character of Aurora, the spirit of European revolution who fails to inspire a society already infected with European violence, acquisitiveness, and public corruption. Deadening apathy and cynicism prevent most of its inhabitants from responding to Aurora's call to resistance, and the pious charade of "civilization" continues. This play was savagely condemned by the very critics who had earlier hailed the writer as an apostle of harmony and reconciliation; his subsequent silence was broken in 1991 by *Furious*, a fractured and powerful play in which a famous playwright must deal with the furies of both his lost family and his own creative vision.

Australia's ambivalent relationship to European high culture is cleverly dramatized in the romantic comedy *Europe*. Douglas has become infatuated with Barbara, a European actor with whom he had a fling while she was acting in an international festival in Sydney. To her horror Douglas follows her to Europe and demands the continuation of the relationship. Douglas and Barbara project on to each other their various culturally constructed longings and frustrations: his fascination with and resentment of European glamour and prestige and her irritation with and longing for Australian innocence and possibility. As these stereotypes are stripped away (Douglas proves both complicated and tenacious), the couple move toward a less illusioned and more hopeful phase of their relationship. *All Stops Out* (1989), written for the Australian Theatre for Young People, maintained Gow's interest in the problems of young people by examining the pressures caused to high school students and families by the HSC, the all-important matriculation examination upon whose syllabus *Away* so often depends.

In *Furious* (1991) Gow again used classic models, particularly allusions to the *Eumenides,* to create a play of concentrated power and confrontational force. As the successful playwright Roland inherits from a dying woman a quest for his lost sister and her family, he becomes possessed by them as his creative furies, beings who invade his consciousness demanding his energy and allegiance. Meanwhile, his love affair with the young Chris develops, only to be terminated by vengeful society. The overt gay theme of *Furious* has been implicit in his writing since *The Kid,* and here it suggests a fragile alternative to the endemic fracturing of the nuclear family. Gow has been at some pains to reject the mantle of family values and heterosexual niceness bestowed by the success of *Away*, which retains its popularity in the educational and theatrical repertory by being positioned as a play of healing and optimism. In 1997 he directed Gluck's *Iphigenie en Tauride* for the Australian Opera, a text that picks up his own themes of the lost sister and the central gay relationship.

In 1994 *Sweet Phoebe* showed anew Gow's control of his medium in a comic play for two actors about two self-obsessed young professionals who must find the strayed dog entrusted to their care. Their quest for the lost dog takes them all over Sydney, encountering people whose situation and attitudes change their own lives and relationships. His 1996 play *Live Acts on Stage* is a queer and darkly comic vaudeville romp through Greek legend. In revenge for Zeus' dalliance with Ganymede, a vengeful, power-suited Hera sets off the train of events that leads to the Trojan War, amidst scenes and reworked classical characters inspired by urban life in contemporary Sydney.

Gow's popularity and literary reputation remained high in the late 1990s, as he continued to be one of the most assured and adventurous writers working. His own theater writing established a uniquely theatricalized view of Australian life, wherein bold mise-en-scènes and thematic intertextuality transcend a merely naturalistic account of human interaction. Gow used these techniques to contextualize historical forces and interrogate postcolonial and postmodern suburban culture with its gender normativity and conformist pressures.

—Veronica Kelly

GRAY, Jack

Nationality: Canadian. **Born:** Detroit, Michigan, 7 December 1927. **Education:** Primary and secondary schools in Ontario; Queen's University, Kingston, Ontario; University of Toronto,

B.A., M.A. **Family:** Married Araby Lockhart in 1952; three sons and two daughters. **Career:** Assistant editor, *Maclean's Magazine*, Toronto, 1953-57; executive director and resident playwright, Neptune Theatre, Halifax, Nova Scotia, 1963; professor of integrated studies, University of Waterloo, Ontario, 1969-71; secretary general, Canadian Theatre Centre, Toronto, 1971-73; president, Association of Canadian Television and Radio Artists (ACTRA), 1978-82; special consultant on cultural policy, Department of Communications, Ottawa, 1982-83; president, League for Canadian Communications, 1984. President, International Writers Guild, and John Gray Productions Ltd.; editor, Canadian Play Series, University of Toronto Press. **Agent:** Elspeth Cochrane Agency, 11-13 Orlando Road, London SW4 0LE, England. **Address:** 65 Pine Street, Brockville, Ontario K6V 1G6, Canada.

Publications

Plays

Bright Sun at Midnight (produced Toronto, 1957).
Ride a Pink Horse, music by Louis Applebaum (produced Toronto, 1958).
The Teacher (produced Stratford, Ontario, 1960).
Chevalier Johnstone (as *Louisbourg*, produced Halifax, 1964; revised version, as *Chevalier Johnstone*, produced Halifax, 1966). Toronto, Playwrights, 1972.
Emmanuel Xoc (produced Toronto, 1965).
Godiva! (produced Coventry, 1967).
Susannah, Agnes, and Ruth (broadcast 1969). Toronto, Playwrights, 1972.
Striker Schneiderman (produced Toronto, 1970). Toronto, University of Toronto Press, 1973.

Radio Plays: *To Whom It May Concern*, 1958; *The Lost Boy*, 1959; *Susannah, Agnes, and Ruth*, 1969; *The Cracker Man*, 1970; *And I Mayakovsky*, 1976.

Television Plays: *The Ledge*, 1959 (UK); *The Glove*, 1961 (UK); *Man in Town*, 1962; *The Enemy*, 1962 (UK); *The Guard*, 1963; *Miss Hanago*, 1964 (UK).

Other

The Third Strategy: A Canadian Primer of Sensible Proposals for the Solution of Insoluble Problems, with André Fortier. Ottawa, Canadian Conference of the Arts, 1984.

*

Manuscript Collection: Metropolitan Toronto Library.

Theatrical Activities:
Director: **Play**—*Clap Hands* (revue), London, 1962.

* * *

Jack Gray is a Shavian with a taste for the baroque. Most of his plays inhabit the world of witty altercation, occasionally to the detriment of their dramatic form. But they are on the whole well made, and the aphoristic quality of many of the speeches indicates more than superficial wit. In *Susannah, Agnes, and Ruth* the repartee is brittle:

> Ian: He'll never get over it.
> Susannah: He never got over being born.

But it is more than brittle. Gray has listened to the ghastly maxims of middle-class Methodism with an attentive ear: "Don't be smart," or "A responsible parent can never be said to be interfering." Both speak for the world of O'Neill's *Ah, Wilderness!* with all the exuberance removed, a world in which we expect to hear that "the Attorney-General says that dancing on Sunday must stop in Ontario." This is only just the day before yesterday, and it does Gray credit not only that he can capture it so exactly without cause or rancor but also that he can give to Susannah, the grandmother figure who is its spokesperson, a toughness and a life that even the men in the play have missed. In a passage reminiscent of Strether's impassioned speech to Little Bilham in Henry James's *The Ambassadors*, Bob, one of the uncles, says to Ruth, "We've evaded life—sidestepped it—it's like a dance—one-two-side-step—one-two-step aside. . . . Don't be like we are, Ruth—take hold of life." But it is Susannah more than the rest who realizes the importance of seizing upon life and denying death. She rebukes the simpering vicar who speaks of her son and others as having died heroic deaths in France in World War I:

> They did not. They died dirty, lonely blasphemous deaths. Each year on that anniversary, Mr. Smith, I take off my mourning, I wear my gayest clothes. It's all I can do to protest the shallow sham you men make of life. It's how I would meet God—singing! We must never celebrate such deaths.

It is this festivity in the face of bleakness and heroism in spite of itself that characterizes the lead in Gray's later play *Striker Schneiderman*, probably his best-known work. But there is a set-piece quality about the play, a sense of its being written for an occasion or to a prescription that does not allow for much more than an entertaining piece of theater. Its elements are too predictable, even down to the tailor joke from *Endgame*.

This criticism is valid to some degree for *Chevalier Johnstone* as well, but although it too seems very much written for an occasion (not to say for television), it has a greater toughness about it, and the ending seems somehow less forced. Part of this is due to the hardheadedness of the dialogue—the absence of sentimentality and Jewish melodrama—and part to a sense that the world described, though it is two centuries away from our own, is closer to our preoccupations than are those of *Schneiderman*. The play has a curiously Brechtian quality, partly the result no doubt of the rapid shifting of scenes and the extravagant stage directions: "We lose the woods and stream and follow them as they walk back to, and then through, the fortress." But this Brechtian character is most obvious in the restraint of sentiment by a wit that keeps us at a distance. The wit is directed against our prejudices regarding, for instance, flabby democracy and literary superstition. "I'm an Indian, not a gentleman," says Samuel, the scout who attaches himself to Johnstone while repulsing any foolish notion of mere equality. And in response to Johnstone's explanation that for recreation he reads "Pascal . . . Molière. And, of course, Voltaire," his superior Drucour asks, "What do you do for healthy recreation?"

Emmanuel Xoc and *The Teacher* both suffer from flaws not so evident in the other plays. In fact, in spite of certain turns of phrase in *Emmanuel Xoc*—"fifty years' caution in a man is a kink"—the play is not a good omen. It is like a combination of Puccini's *Gianni Schicchi* and Tennessee Williams's *The Milk Train Doesn't Stop Here Anymore*. But its host of characters—Tweedie, Xoc, Baptist, Fink, Fingers, Arnold, and Morgan—is too much like something out of an old Bowery Boys film for us to take the play as more than a sort of baroque exercise.

There is a similar element of fantasy in *The Teacher* (like *Emmanuel Xoc*, it has a ghost), though the fantasy is not grotesque but lyrical in a way that easily becomes sentimental. Indeed, there is a studied quality about the play that, coupled with the absence of the sort of wit so evident in the later plays, gives it an unfortunate flatness. Its gestures are both toward Dylan Thomas's *Under Milk Wood* and Joyce's *The Dead*, but it fails to get beyond the sort of artificial melodrama, complete with folk songs, that used to be a favorite of the CBC.

Fortunately Gray has come a great way since then. His later plays show both an eye for detail and an ear for wit that are badly needed. None of his plays is great, but some of them are very good indeed.

—D. D. C. Chambers

GRAY, John (MacLachlan)

Nationality: Canadian. **Born:** Ottawa, Ontario, 26 September 1946. **Education:** Mount Allison University, Sackville, New Brunswick, B.A. 1968; University of British Columbia, Vancouver, M.A. in theatre 1972. **Family:** Married to Beverlee, two sons. **Career:** Founding director, Tamahnous Theatre, Vancouver, 1971-74; freelance director, 1972-76: directed 40 productions throughout Canada. Currently writer of weekly column, *The Vancouver Sun*. **Awards:** Los Angeles Drama Critics Circle award, 1981; Governor-General's award, 1983; Vancouver award, 1988; 2 Dora Mavor Moore awards, Toronto; Chalmers award, Toronto; Canadian Authors Association Medal; Golden Globe award; ACTRA award; Canadian Film and Television award; Gold Medal, New York Film and Television Festival; Silver Hugo, Chicago; National Magazine award; 6 Western Magazine awards. **Address:** 3392 West 37th Avenue, Vancouver, British Columbia V6N 2V6, Canada.

Publications

Plays

Salty Tears on a Hangnail Face (lyrics only, with Jeremy Long), book by Long, music by Gray (produced Vancouver, 1974).
18 Wheels, music and lyrics by Gray (also director: produced Toronto, 1977). Included in *Local Boy Makes Good*, 1987.
Billy Bishop Goes to War, music and lyrics by Gray (also director: as *Billy Bishop*, produced Vancouver, 1978; as *Billy Bishop Goes to War*, produced Washington, D.C., New York, and Edinburgh, 1980; London, 1981). Vancouver, Talonbooks, 1981.
Rock and Roll (also director: produced Ottawa, 1981). Published in *Canadian Theatre Review* (Downsview, Ontario), Summer 1982; included in *Local Boy Makes Good*, 1987.
Bongo from the Congo (for children; produced Vancouver, 1982).
Balthazaar and the Mojo Star (produced Vancouver, 1982).
Better Watch Out, You Better Not Die (produced Halifax, Nova Scotia, 1983).
Don Messer's Jubilee (produced Halifax, Nova Scotia, 1985). Included in *Local Boy Makes Good*, 1987.
The B.C. Review (produced Vancouver, 1986).
Local Boy Makes Good: Three Musicals (includes *18 Wheels, Rock and Roll, Don Messer's Jubilee*). Vancouver, Talonbooks, 1987.
Health, the Musical (produced Vancouver, 1989).
Amelia (produced Ottawa, 1995).
The Tree, the Tower, the Flood (produced Vancouver, 1997).

Screenplays: *Billy Bishop Goes to War*, 1982; *The King of Friday Night*, 1984.

Television Plays: *Eyes of a Cowboy*, 1998.

Novel

Dazzled. Toronto, Irwin, 1984.

Other

I Love Mom: An Irreverent History of the Tattoo. Key Porter, 1994.
Lost in North America: The Imaginary Canadian in the American Dream. Talonbooks, 1994.

Recording: *Billy Bishop Goes to War*, Tapestry, 1979.

*

Critical Studies: "John Gray's Progress" by Judy Steed, in *Toronto Life*, May 1981; *The Work: Interviews with English-Canadian Playwrights* by Robert Wallace and Cynthia Zimmerman, Toronto, Coach House Press, 1982; *Second Stage: The Alternative Theatre Movement in Canada* by Renate Usmiani, Vancouver, University of British Columbia Press, 1983; article by David Cruise, in *Atlantic Insight* (Halifax, Nova Scotia), August 1983; *"Billy Bishop Goes to War* and *Maggie and Pierre*: A Matched Set" by Mary Jane Miller, in *Theatre History in Canada du Theatre au Canada* (Toronto, Ontario), Fall 1989, pp. 188-98.

Theatrical Activities:
Director: **Plays** (selection)—Most of his own plays; *The Bacchae* by Euripides, Vancouver, 1972; *Dracula Two*, Vancouver, 1974; *The Tempest*, Vancouver, 1974; *Bull Durham* by Jeremy Newson, Toronto, 1974; *Canadian Heroes Series 1* (co-director with Paul Thompson), Toronto, 1975; *Preparing* by Beverley Simons (co-director with Buzz Bense), Vancouver, 1975; *The Imaginary Invalid* by Molière, Vancouver, 1975; *Herringbone* by Thomas Cone, Vancouver, 1975 and 1976, and Lennoxville, Quebec, 1978.

Composer: music for all his own plays, and: *Bull Durham* by Jeremy Newson, Toronto, 1974; *The Imaginary Invalid* by Molière, Vancouver, 1975; *The False Messiah* by Rick Salutin, Toronto, 1975; *The Horsburgh Scandal* by Betty Jane Wylie, Toronto, 1976; *1837: The Farmer's Revolt* by Rick Salutin, Toronto, 1976; *The Farm Show* by Theatre Passe Muraille (music with Jimmy Adams), Toronto, 1976; *The Olympics Show* by Theatre Passe

Muraille, Toronto, 1976; *The Great Wave of Civilization* by Herschel Hardin, Lennoxville, Quebec, 1976; *Money* by Rick Salutin, Toronto, 1976; *Le Temps d'une vie* by Roland Lepage, Toronto, 1978.

John Gray comments:

I write populist musicals in which regional and Canadian themes are placed in the broader context of the world and the human spirit. In *18 Wheels* the Canadian truck driver is the central focus for the Canadian preoccupation with physical distance and the enormous space between things and people. *Billy Bishop Goes to War* is about the World War I flying ace, and explores the various ironies that result from colonial success in an imperial war. *Rock and Roll* is about youth culture in a small Canadian town in the 1960s, from the point of view of the local rock and roll band. *Better Watch Out, You Better Not Die* is a satire on left-right attitudes in the face of old age and violent death. *Bongo from the Congo* is an afro-musical about a man's search for a mystical African animal and for the grace that that animal both embodies and bestows. *Balthazaar and the Mojo Star* is a nativity jazz musical about the odyssey of a Parthian magus. *Don Messer's Jubilee* is a musical about traditional rural culture: its purpose, how it develops, and how it is destroyed in favour of international stereotypes. *Dazzled*, the novel, is a comic Bildungsroman, a cultural satire in which a Vancouver ex-hippie makes the adjustment from the romanticism of the 1960s to the neoconservatism of the 1970s. As he makes the adjustment he attempts to see beyond the media hallucinations of both eras and to understand what is really going on around him.

* * *

Although he can be said to belong to the large school of playwrights who chronicle Canadian social and political history, John Gray strikingly differs from other such playwrights in style and often in subject matter. He searches for signifiers of the Canadian psyche and finds them not only in conventional heroes like the World War I aviator Billy Bishop but also in an array of small-town heroes—band leaders, high school rock stars—who speak directly to the audience's local identification with the social and musical rhythms of its country. The fact that Gray writes pop musical theater is not coincidental to the success his work has found with audiences. The national sense he presents is young, unsure, energetic, and discordant, and his theatrical design itself forms a major part of the social myths he creates. His is a satirical vision, but it is a satire full of affection. He presents documentary history, but as Jamie Portman has said, "This kind of history is part cartoon, part musical hall." While his early work in plays such as *18 Wheels,* a musical about truckers, presents issues and sounds to be heard throughout North America, there is a consistent Canadian texture to his images and attitudes. In *Don Messer's Jubilee*, which was generally well received, Gray attempts to make an icon of a homely CBC variety show that ran on radio and television for 40 years and that Gray suggests is part of the Canadian personality, even if viewers of Gray's own age deplored it in their teens as old-fashioned and corny. Yet Gray ignores the generation younger than himself for whom Don Messer holds no meaning. Gray's work, which to some extent mirrors his own maturation, tends to speak directly and powerfully to a predominantly middle-aged audience. But he has not explored issues unrelated to specific periods of time in Canadian social history, nor is his style in the avant-garde.

Gray first came to major international attention with his second musical, *Billy Bishop Goes to War*, a one-man show about the most celebrated Canadian wartime aviator. Accompanied by a pianist who doubles as occasional foil (Gray himself in the early productions), the narrator-actor impersonates 18 characters, including Bishop. The debt is obvious to the improvisational technique of Paul Thompson's Theatre Passe Muraille, in whose ensemble Gray worked as a young musician and from which influence *18 Wheels* first grew. In *Billy Bishop*, however, Gray finds his own voice both in the score and in his reading of history, an interpretation of Bishop that is endearing while iconoclastic. It is ironic that, while showing Bishop to be "a sort of small town juvenile delinquent who, though just scraping to survive and hang on, became the toast of London," Gray makes him a hero of tremendous power and appeal. In Gray's version Bishop becomes the peculiar hero most suited to the Canadian self-image, a hero who is swept into fame almost against his will but who is not, in the end, unaware of his new status nor above using it to his own advantage. Bishop realizes, "I really was Number One now," but his enjoyment of the adulation does not change him or endow him with any new sense of personal purpose. In this sense he is a hero without guile, perhaps even the "hero as anti-hero," as Allan Massie called him in the *Scotsman.* He is also still the small-town boy, able to call himself "a dignitary" but ever aware that he is "a colonial dignitary, Bishop. There is a difference." He remains, as his sophisticated London benefactress, Lady St. Helier, sings, "a typical Canadian/You're modesty itself." Indeed, as Bishop himself comments, "Nobody starts no wars on Canada/Where folks tend to wish each other well." It is only "once . . . in the air, [that Bishop feels] a lot better. In fact, [he feels] like a King." In this complex characterization Gray has captured a personality who seeks security in the knowledge that he is second-best and yet who alone in an environment he can control can scream "at the top of my lungs, I win, I WIN, I WIN!" As the astounding commercial success of the play attests, such a hero appeals to the Canadian sense of self. Its similar success in other Commonwealth countries and its commercial failure in New York, despite marked critical support, underlines the point: in his subtle portrait Gray has captured a hero for the colonial mind. And if that character is also likable and embodies fears and hopes with which the audience can empathize—and if he sings and makes airplane noises—the resulting relationship is certain to be intense and positive. As contemporary Canadian literature develops a postmodern and postcolonial discourse, however, Gray's hero begins to appear dated. His vision remains a popular one rather than one that challenges or initiates.

The play exploits its economical design. The sparse set and multiple characterizations force an audience to imagine most of the action and, in doing so, compel its involvement. The pace, the comic and often cruel caricatures, the sentiment and bravado and charm of the protagonist, the adventure of a World War I setting, and the acting tour de force required of the principal actor all work together to engage an audience.

In *Rock and Roll* Gray presents a personal memoir in a play about the members of a small-town rock and roll band meeting again in middle age to restage their youth while preparing for a reunion concert. The script exists largely to allow the music to tell the story, as it does in *18 Wheels*, but the songs are Gray's best work, and the predictable plot is happily lost in the highly theatrical staging and hard-driving rock music. The show is pure nostalgia for those who were teenagers in the 1950s. It displays a spectrum of easy emotion—love, jealousy, a manic sense of humor, the pathos of ruined dreams, and the triumph of maturity over adolescent insecurities. If the play can be criticized for its failure to develop any emotion or, in fact, any plot event past the surface, it survives in performance because the mood swings are naturalistic to the teenage characters and appropriate to the highly wrought emotions of those caught up in memory and because the design of the play is episodic, built around the musical numbers. The play is great fun to watch and, like *Billy Bishop,* presents involved patterns of music and action, establishing Gray as firmly in control of score and staging.

In *Don Messer's Jubilee* Gray is more self-conscious about memory, more intent upon exploring the reasons for the cancellation of the popular television show than in truly re-creating one of Messer's programs. But in his version of the old show he presents an entertainment that Martin Knelman in *Saturday Night* called "a lot livelier than an evening of true Messer music would be." Gray is guilty of polishing the hero to give him more big-time glitz, but in doing so he is clearly mythmaking; he seeks to secure the older folklore in a more contemporary aesthetic.

Gray also wrote and performed a series of parodic and satiric television vignettes for the CBC that capitalized on his own popularity and a 1980s cynicism about social and political issues. He explored the aging process in his musical *Health,* which, like the TV spots, recognizes that his audience has reached middle age. The play presents an urban everyman who is recently divorced, stressed at work, and suddenly ill. He is accompanied by a chorus of personified body parts—his brain, bowels, and phallus—that urge him in various directions, seeking mastery. Faced with the reality of his mortality, the man attempts to redefine himself and his sense of family and politics. The play is vaudevillian in design, and the chorus presents songs and dances against sketches of the man's life, all against a grotesque proscenium of mechanized human organs. It is a highly visual show and often amusing, but the discussion is trite and relies on the allegorical device more than on internal tension.

Gray is an important spokesman for Canadian culture, a role in which his widespread popularity has given him considerable influence. He also has continued to enjoy a major success with audiences, although his television spots have not received uniform praise. He has uniquely been able to capture the temperament of his nation.

—Reid Gilbert

GRAY, Simon (James Holliday)

Nationality: British. **Born:** Hayling Island, Hampshire, 21 October 1936. **Education:** A school in Montreal; Westminster School, London; Dalhousie University, Halifax, Nova Scotia, 1954-57, B.A. (honours) in English 1957; Trinity College, Cambridge, 1958-61, B.A. (honours) in English 1961, M.A. **Family:** Married Beryl Mary Kevern in 1965; one son and one daughter. **Career:** Harper-Wood student, 1961-62, and research student, 1962-63, Trinity College; lecturer in English, University of British Columbia, Vancouver, 1963-64; supervisor in English, Trinity College, 1964-66; lecturer in English, Queen Mary College, London, 1965-85. Since 1964 editor, *Delta* magazine, Cambridge. Lives in London. **Awards:** Recipient; *Evening Standard* award, 1972, 1976; New York Drama Critics Circle award, 1977; Cheltenham prize for literature, 1982. Honorary fellow, Queen Mary College, 1985. **Agent:** Judy Daish Associates, 2 St. Charles Place, London W10 6EG, England.

Publications

Plays

Wise Child (produced London, 1967; New York, 1972). London, Faber, 1972.

Molly (as *Death of a Teddy Bear*, televised 1967; revised version, as *Molly*, produced Watford, Hertfordshire, and London, 1977; New York, 1978). Included in *The Rear Column and Other Plays*, 1978; in *The Rear Column, Dog Days, and Other Plays*, 1979.

Sleeping Dog (televised 1967). London, Faber, 1968.

Spoiled (televised 1968; produced Glasgow, 1970; London, 1971; New York, 1972). London, Methuen, 1971.

Dutch Uncle (produced Brighton and London, 1969). London, Faber, 1969.

Pig in a Poke (televised 1969). With *Close of Play*, London, Eyre Methuen, 1980.

The Idiot, adaptation of a novel by Dostoevsky (produced London, 1970). London, Methuen, 1971.

Butley (produced Oxford and London, 1971; New York, 1972). London, Methuen, 1971; New York, Viking Press, 1972.

Man in a Side-Car (televised 1971). Included in *The Rear Column and Other Plays*, 1978; in *The Rear Column, Dog Days, and Other Plays*, 1979.

Otherwise Engaged (produced Oxford and London, 1975; New York, 1977). Included in *Otherwise Engaged and Other Plays*, 1975.

Plaintiffs and Defendants (televised 1975). Included in *Otherwise Engaged and Other Plays*, 1975.

Two Sundays (televised 1975). Included in *Otherwise Engaged and Other Plays*, 1975.

Otherwise Engaged and Other Plays. London, Eyre Metheun, 1975; New York, Viking Press, 1976.

Dog Days (produced Oxford, 1976). London, Eyre Metheun, 1976; in *The Rear Column, Dog Days, and Other Plays*, 1979.

The Rear Column (produced London and New York, 1978). Included in *The Rear Column and Other Plays*, 1978; in *The Rear Column, Dog Days, and Other Plays*, 1979.

The Rear Column and Other Plays. London, Eyre Methuen, 1978.

The Rear Column, Dog Days, and Other Plays. New York, Viking Press, 1979.

Close of Play (produced London, 1979; New York, 1981). With *Pig in a Poke*, London, Eyre Methuen, 1980; published separately, New York, Dramatists Play Service, 1982.

Stage Struck (produced London, 1979; Chicago, 1984). London, Eyre Methuen, 1979; New York, Seaver, 1981.

Quartermaine's Terms (produced London, 1981; New Haven, Connecticut, 1982; New York, 1983). London, Eyre Methuen, 1981; revised version, Methuen, and New York, French, 1983.

Chapter 17 (produced Guildford, Surrey, 1982).

Tartuffe, adaptation of the play by Molière (produced Washington, D.C., 1982). With *The Holy Terror*, London, Faber, 1990.

The Common Pursuit: Scenes from Literary Life (produced London, 1984; New Haven, Connecticut, 1985; also co-director: produced New York, 1986; revised version, produced New York, 1987; also director: produced London, 1988). London, Methuen, 1984; New York, Dramatists Play Service, 1987.
Play 1 (includes *Butley, Otherwise Engaged, The Rear Column, Quartermaine's Terms, The Common Pursuit*). London, Methuen, 1986.
Melon (produced London, 1987; revised version, as *The Holy Terror*, broadcast 1989; also director: produced New York, 1992). London, Methuen, 1987; as *The Holy Terror*, with *Tartuffe*, London, Faber, 1990.
After Pilkington (televised 1987). London, Methuen, 1987.
Hidden Laughter (also director: produced Brighton and London, 1990). London, Faber, 1990.
Old Flames and A Month in the Country. London, Faber, 1990.
Cell Mates (produced London, 1995).
Simply Disconnected (produced Chichester, 1996).
Life Support (produced London, 1997).
Just the Three of Us (produced Guildford, 1997).

Screenplays: *Butley*, 1976; *A Month in the Country*, 1987.

Radio Plays: *Up in Pigeon Lake*, from his novel *Colmain*, 1963 (Canada); *The Holy Terror* (revised version of *Melon*), 1989; *The Rector's Daughter*, 1992; *With a Nod and a Bow*, 1993; *Suffer the Little Children*, 1993.

Television Plays: *The Caramel Crisis*, 1966; *Death of a Teddy Bear*, 1967; *A Way with the Ladies*, 1967; *Sleeping Dog*, 1967; *Spoiled*, 1968; *Pig in a Poke*, 1969; *The Dirt on Lucy Lane*, 1969; *Style of the Countess*, 1970; *The Princess*, 1970; *Man in a Side-Car*, 1971; *Plaintiffs and Defendants*, 1975; *Two Sundays*, 1975; *After Pilkington*, 1987; *Old Flames*, 1990; *They Never Slept*, 1991; *Running Late*, 1992; *Femme Fatale*, 1993; *Unnatural Pursuits*, 1994.

Novels

Colmain. London, Faber, 1963.
Simple People. London, Faber, 1965.
Little Portia. London, Faber, 1967.
A Comeback for Stark (as Hamish Reade). London, Faber, 1968.
Breaking Hearts. London, Faber, 1997.

Other

An Unnatural Pursuit and Other Pieces: A Playwright's Journal. London, Faber, 1985; New York, St. Martin's Press, 1986.
How's That for Telling 'Em, Fat Lady? A Short Life in the American Theatre. London, Faber, 1988.
Fat Chance. London, Faber, 1995.

Editor, with Keith Walker, *Selected English Prose*. London, Faber, 1967.

*

Critical Studies: "The Fool as Hero: Simon Gray's *Butley* and *Otherwise Engaged*" by Katherine H. Burkman, in *Theatre Journal* (Baltimore, Maryland), May 1981, pp. 163-72; "Simon Gray's Comedy of Bad Manners" by Anne Nothof, in *Essays in Theatre* (Guelph, Ontario), May 1988, pp. 109-112; "Light Heavy-Weight? The Plays of Simon Gray" by Timothy Kidd, in *Encounter*, January/February 1990, pp. 42-46; "The Unhappy Mean in Simon Gray's *Otherwise Engaged*" by Byron Nelson, in *Contemporary British Drama, 1970-90*, edited by Hersh Zeifman and Cynthia Zimmerman, Toronto, University of Toronto Press, 1993; "Simon Gray" by Tony J. Stafford, in *British Playwrights, 1956-1995: A Research and Production Sourcebook*, edited by William W. Demastes, Westport, Connecticut, Greenwood, 1996.

Theatrical Activities:
Director: **Plays**—*Dog Days*, Vienna, 1980; *The Common Pursuit* (co-director, with Michael McGuire), New York, 1986; *Hidden Laughter*, Brighton and London, 1990; *Cell Mates*, London, 1995.

* * *

Simon Gray is a witty, intelligent, literary playwright who writes about marriage and infidelities and human friendship and betrayal with a flair for the topical and a gift for creating memorable characters. He writes comedies of manners, or rather bad manners. He frequently combines elements from the bedroom farce with features of the whodunit. In *The Rear Column* and *Cell Mates* he draws on historical figures for his subjects. The lives of Simon Hench and his friend Jeff Golding are treated in a number of different plays. Butley's savage wit, Hench's arch reserve, Quartermaine's kindly vacancy, Melon's mental suffering, Ronnie's words about the divine, the human spirit, and hidden laughter, and J. G.'s ruminations about love at the bedside of his wife on life support—all live in the landscape of the mind long after the details of the plays have been forgotten. Gray's dialogue—witty, derisive, colloquial, syntactically lively, often irreverent, and sometimes heartbreaking—rarely fails him.

Gray's portrait of Butley bears favorable comparison with Kingsley Amis's hero in *Lucky Jim*. One critic has faulted Gray for his lack of "magnanimity of spirit and largeness of vision." No doubt his often corrosive humor contributes to this judgment, but his poignant depiction of the protagonist of *Quartermaine's Terms* should silence those who argue that he lacks heart. If anything, Gray feels too keenly and requires humor and friendship to make life more tolerable. His two sequels to *Otherwise Engaged* give ample demonstration of his depth of feeling and seriousness of mind.

Gray's plays have appeared regularly in the West End since *Wise Child* opened in 1967, shocking its London audience. In 1972 *Butley* won the *Evening Standard* Award as the best play. Nonetheless, his detractors gave most of the credit to the superior actors and directors—including Alec Guinness, Simon Ward, Alan Bates, and Harold Pinter—who lent their talents to his plays. In 1979 James Fenton of the *Sunday Times* announced nastily that Gray had committed "public suicide" in his thriller *Stage Struck* and gloated that *Close of Play*, an "overblown domestic tragedy," had itself closed at the Lyttelton in less than 10 days. *Quartermaine's Terms*, an international success and the only play to win the Cheltenham Prize for literature, was similarly savaged by a San Francisco radio reviewer.

Not one quick to forget or forgive slights, Gray opened *An Unnatural Pursuit and Other Pieces* with a quote of Fenton's: "Ladies and Gentlemen, the play's the thing, as Shakespeare put it. But Ladies and Gentlemen, there isn't a play here! No play at all, ladies and gentlemen." Gray later defiantly boasted that his play *The Common Pursuit* "has no plot." Ambiguously named after F. R. Leavis's book, the play takes revenge upon Gray's unkindly reviewers and includes a rude joke at the expense of the *Sunday Times.* Gray feared that the joke would cost him dearly and, if his account of the play's reviews and fate is accurate, his fears were warranted. His producers ultimately backed out of plans to move the play from the Lyric in Hammersmith to the West End. The play later traveled to the United States, where it was performed in New Haven, with a revised version staged in Los Angeles.

Gray has had more than his share of flops and negative reviews. His adaptation of Dostoevsky's *The Idiot* entertained his audience, but the critics immodestly displayed their expertise on the Russian master and ignored Gray's talents. *Dutch Uncle* was depressing, and the critics deplored its lack of taste. *Spoiled,* with its touching exploration of a homosexual encounter between pupil and teacher—an encounter that is reworked in a number of Gray's plays and films for television—simply failed to stir any interest. *Close of Play* did not work.

Butley, however, was a stunning success, capturing the bitchiness, vanity, and all too fragile ego of a thoroughly jaundiced university lecturer. The protagonists of *Otherwise Engaged* and *Stage Struck,* also played by Alan Bates, possess many of the traits that made Ben Butley unforgettable. Both plays had long runs in the West End.

Gray's thrillers do not take advantage of a period setting. Instead they capitalize on kinky sexuality and psychologically perverse behavior. His BBC screenplay *After Pilkington* shows him at his best. He calls it a Jamesian ghost thriller and exploits games from childhood to chilling ends. But his stage plays in this genre lack the marvelous visual effects that made Paul Giovanni's Sherlock Holmes play *The Crucifer of Blood* such a favorite. Instead, they depend on the ingenuity of their plots and the psychological intricacies of their characters for their success.

Gray's early domestic comedies compare favorably with Alan Ayckbourn's, but, with the important exception of *Quartermaine's Terms,* they have the same limitations. They pander to popular taste, make too much of sexual peccadilloes, be they between members of the same or of the opposite sex, and often lack love. None equals Peter Shaffer's *Black Comedy.*

Otherwise Engaged is about a snobbish, cynical, Oxford-educated publisher, Simon Hench, who lives with his schoolteacher wife, Beth, and their upstairs tenant, Dave. On a day when he hopes to listen quietly to Wagner while Beth is away on an outing with her foreign students and a colleague, Ned, Simon is repeatedly interrupted by a string of visitors, most unexpected and all needy. His visitors include his tenant; his brother; his boisterous college friend Jeff Golding; Davina, Jeff's current mistress; and Wood, an old schoolmate, Strapley of Windale, previously known as "Wanker" Strapley. The old rivalries between the brothers are explored; Simon is propositioned by a bare-breasted Davina after she quarrels with Jeff; he admits to a fling with Joanna, a young girl in his office who happens to be living with Wood; and he learns that his wife is pregnant and has been having an affair with Ned, whom she says she wishes to marry. Wood wildly accuses Simon of heartlessly screwing his fiancée Joanna. When Simon unfeelingly confirms the accusation, Wood flees and later leaves a message on Simon's voice mail saying that he is killing himself. Simon shuts off the machine in midspeech and attempts to return to his quiet afternoon listening to music. At the play's close Jeff and Simon retreat from life and listen to *Parsifal.*

Dog Days treats the same situations and themes, but the characters have different names. Peter is a junior editor whose wife Hilary is having an affair that threatens to destroy their marriage. His brother Charles is married to a vegetarian earth mother, Alison, who has produced four children and is expecting more. After accusing Hilary of "replacing mechanical sex with spontaneous frigidity," Peter walks out to join Joanna, a young illustrator in his publishing house. When postcoital depression mars his affair, he returns contritely to Hilary, who says that she will no longer have him. Peter and Charles live a dog's life, both groveling to people they loathe, both dependent on others in ways they had not predicted. Hilary cannot contemplate spending any more years in a marriage with a man who likes neither himself nor her. In Gray's two television plays about Peter and Charles, the marriages withstand Peter's infidelities and Alison's endless cooing.

The Rear Column is a fascinating play based on Stanley's march to the relief of Emin Pasha in 1887. It deals with the fate of the rear column and of the 5 white men left behind in the encampment in the Congo, with 300 "niggers" inside and hoards of cannibals without. The play is about Major Barttelot who, left to guard the rear column, ends up flogging, shooting, and eating the natives, while Jameson, the British naturalist left behind with him, also loses all moral purpose. In his final decadence he watches a "nigger girl" killed, cooked, and eaten so that he can sketch the rite of cannibalism with the same scientific accuracy he devotes to sketching African bird life.

Gray's plays are peopled with men discontented with themselves and ill suited to their roles. Often these men are homosexuals. In their self-loathing they resort to transvestism (*Wise Child*), bondage (*Sleeping Dog*), and sadomasochistic games (*Sleeping Dog, Dutch Uncle,* and *Stage Struck*). Butley has married to escape his homosexuality, only to leave his wife six months later and return to his male student-lover turned colleague. Butley constantly belittles his wife, colleague, and lover. Ultimately, his corrosive humor drives them all away, leaving him too worn out and full of self-dislike to initiate yet another affair with one of his students. Butley uses words to kill. Although he cuts to the quick those who need or love him, ultimately it is he who is the victim. The nasty cut on his chin that he dabs throughout the play makes physical the depth of his self-dislike.

Mr. Godboy, the protagonist of *Dutch Uncle,* courts punishment at the hands of a police constable noted for his strict ways. Mr. Godboy is unsuccessful in his attempt to gas his wife and upstairs tenant, but he experiences vicariously the humiliations practiced by the constable. In *Molly,* Molly and her lover kill her rich old husband, a man whose habit of spanking his "naughty" wife finally infuriates the lover. In *Sleeping Dog* a retired colonial officer torments a West Indian for being too familiar with his wife. He chains the Jamaican in the cellar of his English house, makes him confess to crimes against his wife and to homosexuality, and finally forces the man to service his wife. *Stage Struck* develops the cat-and-mouse game of *Dutch Uncle* into an extravagant panoply of stage tricks masterminded by the stage director husband who uses suicide and murder to revenge himself upon his domineering actress wife.

Quartermaine's Terms, one of Gray's finest plays, and *The Common Pursuit* depart in significant ways from the mode of *Butley,* although both take teachers and literary types for their characters. Butley and Simon Hench use language and wit trenchantly—Butley to lash out to deflect his self-hatred against others, Hench more sparingly as an armor to prevent others from touching him.

In contrast, Sir John Quartermaine, a teacher in a Cambridge public school training foreign boys in English, is a man of halting phrases, few words, and nearly vacant silences. The play traces the fortunes of the school and its small staff. It is also about the death of an old tradition. Sir John retreats from his world into a drowsy sleep where he can no longer remember when or what he is teaching or even the swans on the pond near his aunt's home. He drifts in and out of reminiscences, weaving the words of Yeats's "The Wild Swans at Coole" with his own vague memories, reproducing in his own diminished way the sense of radical dislocation and displacement of Yeats's poem.

Gray's treatment of Quartermaine and the staff is richly comic in the manner of Chekhov. Mr. Meadle is the play's Two-and-Twenty-Misfortunes; Quartermaine's yearnings for another era echo Anya's and Gaef's nostalgia in *The Cherry Orchard;* Gray's characters cannot remember one another's names; they murmur reassuring pleasantries, while underneath they are confused and in emotional pain. Melanie is a frustrated spinster driven to kill her sickly, hate-ridden mother and do penance through her Christian conversion. Mr. Meadle, the accident-prone new instructor from the North Country, struggles desperately to secure both a permanent position in the school and a wife. There are the marital infidelities and complications and the suicide that often figure in Gray's plays, but this play's mood is different. When Quartermaine is finally dismissed by the new principal on the eve of the Christmas break, it is wrenching. All of Windscape's reasons for the firing are legitimate: Quartermaine has not been teaching for years, and the other staff simply carried him, not having the heart to do anything else. It is unconscionable to pretend that Quartermaine has a role to play in an instructional institution, yet the play asks, "Why not let him linger in the staff lounge, teaching almost not at all, rather than displace him utterly?" The play ends with a gentle good night exchanged between the two men, followed by Quartermaine's lapse into silence. Echoes of Yeats's poem hover in the air. It is Gray's best ending.

The Common Pursuit departs from *Butley* in its treatment of time and its reliance on cinematic techniques for its staging and its plot development. Gray calls it a play about friendship, "English, middle-class, Cambridge-educated friendship." Its control of time grew out of the television play *Two Sundays.* The play covers 20 years and closes with a scene set 15 minutes later than the opening scene, 20 years before. Gray's treatment of time in the play has been accused of being derivative of Pinter's in *Betrayal,* but in fact the debt goes the other way. *The Common Pursuit* is episodic, tracing the fortunes of the Cambridge friends and their literary enterprise. Many of its characters are Gray's typical academic misfits and literary opportunists. Stuart is what Gray calls "the spine of the play." The play's sweeping movement over the lives of the six Cambridge friends is akin in structure to Virginia Woolf's novel *The Waves.* Gray feared that the play might be too precious, too literary, and too elitist, but it has stood up well. Its control of time is superb, and its startling epilogue is a stunning piece of theater.

Melon is based on an actual psychiatric case history. It is a memory play presented from the perspective of its protagonist, a successful literary publisher who discovers one day that the ground has opened up under his feet. The entire routine of success around which his life has been fashioned collapses, and he finds himself in the midst of a mental breakdown, recounting to his psychiatrist how it all came to be. The themes of the play are familiar: marital infidelity and breakdown, thwarted ambition, and confused sexual identity. Melon's overbearing presence, his infidelities, and his contempt for others finally undo him, but his agony is intensified because we see the play through his perspective. He has the unbearable task of trying to rebuild himself and trying to speak the moment when his world came apart. Gray has a deep understanding of this state of mind and captures it brilliantly. He employs a musical metaphor, with its capacity to embrace both harmony and discord, to unite his protagonist's memories. The play is fluid, evocative, and disturbing. Alan Bates again played the lead. *The Holy Terror: Melon Revised* works well on the screen and in the theater.

Hidden Laughter is a very funny and yet at the same time a deeply sad play about redemption that teases out T. S. Eliot's treatment of childish laughter and the garden in *The Four Quartets.* The play's action covers 13 years, tracing the happenings in the life of a successful literary agent, his novelist wife, and two children as they seek a retreat in the life of the country. The years are full of strange happenings, near accidents, and near deaths. The garden that offers its owners the promise of a pastoral idyll becomes the site of a tentative, troubled present, full of strained relationships before it again provides the characters a possibility of transcendence. The most memorable character in the play is the tolerant and yet good vicar whose life touches and alters all the others.

In *Simply Disconnected* Gray explores the life of Simon Hench roughly 25 years after the Sunday afternoon depicted in *Otherwise Engaged.* Beth has died four years earlier, and Simon is trying to have sex with Mandy, a young woman who sang in the choir with Beth and who is cleaning house for Simon while living with a husband who jealously adores her. In the climax of act 1 Julian Wood points a pistol at Simon, demanding that he account for what happened 31 years ago with Joanna. Act 2 opens with Wood, pistol still in hand, having it out with Simon. Wood wants to believe that he is the fruit of Simon and Joanna's affair, which resulted in his putative father's suicide. Simon is still being tormented by his brother, the so-called public school pederast, who continues to squeak through his scrapes and remain with his nurturing wife and children. Simon's longtime friend Jeff is now a successful writer of travel books, living a turbulent life with his drunken wife, who resents the celibacy that accompanied his sobriety and subsequent success. Whereas *Otherwise Engaged* ended with Jeff and Simon turning to Wagner's *Parsifal,* this play closes with Jeff and Simon listening quietly to a CD of Beth and Mandy's choral singing. Simon's studied life of careless indifference to the world around him leaves him howling. Beth alive was a Beth he could not satisfy or properly love, and the dead wife's flat voice is now the music he seeks to comfort himself. Moral triumph in this play lies with the younger Wood and Mandy and with Stephen. They all experience love, something Simon has never allowed himself to express, and they resist Simon's attempt to use them.

Gray's experience with his play *Cell Mates* afforded him the natural subject for another frank journal about life in the theater. *Fat Chance: 'Stephen Fry quits' drama* chronicles the collapse of the play, occasioned by the selfish, rash departure of Fry during the first week of its London opening. Even though Simon Ward was brought in to take over Fry's part, the play did not recover from the bad press. Having opened with all of the promise of a true West End hit, it closed in less than six weeks.

Cell Mates explores the relationship between Sean Bourke, a renegade Irishman played by Rik Mayall, and George Blake, a

Russian spy. They meet each other in Wormwood Scrubs prison in the early 1960s when one has been jailed for 42 years as a spy and the other has been convicted for sending a letter bomb to an investigator who had "set him up." Blake befriends Bourke and draws him into his plot to make a successful prison break. Little does Bourke realize that Blake is simply using him to escape prison and luring him to the safety of Moscow so that Blake can return to the protection of the KGB.

Mayall's performance was brilliant. As Gray has stated, he was deeply and wholly present in the character he played. Fry, who was hired to bring star power to the production, had the difficult task of playing the duplicitous KGB spy gifted in counterespionage. He relied on his actor's tricks but, according to Gray, could never actually be present in the character. Fry's fears about his own talents as an actor caused him to leave the production within the first week of its London opening, proving himself a traitor, albeit on a lesser scale, of the same sort as Blake, the character he could not play. Gray had worked on the play for more than five years, had retitled it many times, and had mastered the form that could contain the story of the two men's friendship and the subsequent betrayal by Blake. It is a play that is inherently dramatic and that provides superb parts for gifted actors.

In *Life Support* Gray again demonstrates his ability to drill deeply into a character in moments of extremis. Set in an intensive care ward of a London hospital, the play shows how J. G. copes with the final weeks and months of his wife's dying, before he permits the plug of the life-support machine to be pulled. The play further fleshes out the life of Jeff Golding and Gwen, his wife, two characters that Gray has treated in his other plays about Simon Hench. Gray is at the top of his comic form, while treating one of the most difficult situations life poses. His treatment of J. G. and Gwen is full of compassion and pathos, as well as being exquisitely funny. It is a heartrending play, full of pathos and inventiveness and written with an emotional honesty that is truly rare.

Gray is among Britain's most talented and literarily sophisticated playwrights working in the traditional genre of the comedy of manners. He is well schooled in his craft, original, and able to create unforgettable characters. He has mellowed over the years, and he has come to make his plea for the irrational and his religious musings more explicit in his writing.

—Carol Simpson Stern

GRAY, Spalding

Nationality: American. **Born:** Providence, Rhode Island, 5 June 1941. **Education:** Fryeburg Academy, Maine; Emerson College, Boston, B.A. 1965. **Family:** Married Renee Shafransky in 1991 (divorced). **Career:** Actor in summer stock, Cape Cod, Massachusetts, and in Saratoga, New York, 1965-67; with Performance Group, New York, 1969-75; founder, with Elizabeth LeCompte, the Wooster Group, New York, 1975. Visiting instructor, University of California, Santa Cruz, Summer 1987, and Columbia University, New York, 1985; artist-in-residence, Mark Taper Forum, Los Angeles, 1986-87. **Awards:** National Endowment for the Arts fellowship, 1977; Rockefeller grant, 1980; Guggenheim fellowship, 1985; Edward Albee fellowship, 1985; Obie award, for *Swimming to Cambodia,* 1985. **Agent:** Suzanne Gluck, International Creative Management, 40 West 57th Street, New York, New York 10019. **Address:** c/o The Wooster Group, Box 654, Canal Street Station, New York, New York 10013, U.S.A.

Publications

Plays and Monologues

Scales (also director: produced Northampton, Massachusetts, 1966; New York, 1975).

Sakonnet Point, with Elizabeth LeCompte (produced New York, 1975).

Rumstick Road, with Elizabeth LeCompte (also co-director: produced New York, 1977).

Nayatt School, with Elizabeth LeCompte (produced New York, 1978).

Three Places in Rhode Island (includes *Sakonnet Point, Rumstick Road, Nayatt School*), with Elizabeth LeCompte (produced New York, 1978).

Point Judith: An Epilog, with Elizabeth LeCompte (produced New York, 1979).

Sex and Death to the Age 14 (produced New York, 1979). Included in *Sex and Death to the Age 14* (collection), 1986.

Booze, Cars, and College Girls (produced New York, 1979). Included in *Sex and Death to the Age 14*, 1986.

India and After (America) (produced New York, 1979).

Nobody Wanted to Sit Behind a Desk (produced New York, 1980). Included in *Sex and Death to the Age 14*, 1986.

A Personal History of the American Theater (produced New York, 1980).

Interviewing the Audience (produced New York, 1981).

47 Beds (produced New York, 1981). Included in *Sex and Death to the Age 14*, 1986.

In Search of the Monkey Girl, with Randal Levenson (produced New York, 1982). New York, Aperture, 1982.

8 x Gray (produced New York, 1982).

Swimming to Cambodia, parts 1 and 2 (produced New York, 1984; London, 1985). New York, Theatre Communications Group, 1985; in *Swimming to Cambodia: The Collected Works*, 1987.

Travels Through New England (produced Cambridge, Massachusetts, 1984).

Rivkala's Ring, adaptation of a story by Chekhov, in *Orchards* (produced Urbana, Illinois, 1985; New York, 1986). New York, Knopf, 1986.

Terrors of Pleasure: The House (produced Cambridge, Massachusetts, 1985; New York, 1986; London, 1987; as *Terrors of Pleasure: The Uncut Version*, produced New York, 1989). Included in *Sex and Death to the Age 14*, 1986.

Sex and Death to the Age 14. New York, Random House, 1986; augmented edition, including *Swimming to Cambodia*, parts 1 and 2, as *Swimming to Cambodia: The Collected Works*, London, Pan, 1987.

Monster in a Box (produced New York, 1990). New York, Vintage, 1992.

Gray's Anatomy (produced New York, 1993). New York, Vintage, 1994.

It's a Slippery Slope (produced New York, 1996). New York, Noonday Press, 1997.

Screenplay: *Swimming to Cambodia*, 1987.

Television Play: *Bedtime Story*, with Renée Shafransky, 1987.

Film Adaptations: *Monster in a Box*, 1992; *Gray's Anatomy*, 1997.

Short Stories

Seven Scenes from a Family Album. Benzene Press, 1981.

Novel

Impossible Vacation. London, Picador, 1992.

*

Critical Studies: "Spalding Gray's *Swimming to Cambodia*: A Performance Gesture" by Jessica Prinz, in *Staging the Impossible: The Fantastic Mode in Modern Drama*, edited by Patrick D. Murphy, Westport, Connecticut, Greenwood, 1992; "Sidebar Excursions to Nowhere: The Vernacular Storytelling of Errol Morris and Spalding Gray" by John D. Dorst, in *Folklore, Literature, and Cultural Theory: Collected Essays*, edited by Carol Lynn Preston, New York, Garland, 1995; *Mirrors of the Self: The Myth of Narcissus in the Monologues of Spalding Gray* (dissertation), by Diane Allene Merchant, Ann Arbor, 1996; "Talking His Way Back to Life: Spalding Gray and the Embodied Voice" by Gay Brewer, in *Contemporary Literature* (Madison, Wisconsin), Summer 1996.

Theatrical Activities:
Director: **Plays**—*Scales*, Northampton and Amherst, Massachusetts, 1966; *Rumstick Road* (co-director, with Elizabeth LeCompte), New York, 1977.

Actor: **Plays**—Roles in all of his own plays and in numerous other plays; Hoss in *The Tooth of Crime* by Sam Shepard, New York, 1973; role in *North Atlantic* by Jim Strahs, New York, 1984; Stage Manager in *Our Town* by Thornton Wilder, New York, 1988. **Films**—*The Killing Fields*, 1984; *True Stories*, 1986; *Swimming to Cambodia*, 1987; *Clara's Heart*, 1989; *Monster in a Box*, 1992; *Straight Talk*, 1992; *King of the Hill*, 1993; *The Pickle*, 1993; *The Paper*, 1994; *Bad Company*, 1995; *Beyond Rangoon*, 1995; *Bliss*, 1997. **Television**—*The American Dream*, 1986; *Bedtime Story*, 1987; *Spalding Gray: Terrors of Pleasure*, 1987; *Our Town*, 1989; *Caffe Lena*, 1990; *The Image*, 1990; *To Save a Child*, 1991; *Zelda*, 1993.

* * *

Like Eugene O'Neill—also a New England playwright—Spalding Gray creates histrionic exorcisms of private demons. An autobiographical dramatist who cheerfully admits to narcissism, Gray—again like O'Neill—is obsessed in his early work with family and doctors. Although Gray's subjects have evolved, his work always unabashedly concerns himself. An actor before he began writing roles, Gray appears in his pieces as well.

Gray initially created personal plays in collaboration with the director Elizabeth LeCompte, with whom he constructed four works named after places from his boyhood. *Sakonnet Point* recalls discontinuous images of his preschool summer beach vacations, and it is as nonverbal as the infant Gray. It is a quiet piece built around objects and simple activities, in contrast to the often frenetic and noisy *Rumstick Road*, which includes tape recordings of actual family members and of the psychiatrist who treated his mother before her suicide. So important are the recordings that the operator of the tape machine sits in full view above the set. Below is a doctor's examination table, on either side of which is a room. One room, containing a window through which we see a tent, is primarily associated with Gray's reenacted past, while the other, containing a screen and slide projector, is associated more often with Gray's probing of the past through the stimulation of his memories with mementos and tapes. The most interesting is a recording of the insensitive doctor who tells Gray that his mother's insanity is hereditary, "but don't be frightened."

Although still more fragmented and surreal, the third of Gray's *Three Places in Rhode Island* is called *Nayatt School*, after a childhood school. It begins with a seemingly straightforward lecture on T. S. Eliot's *The Cocktail Party*, from which Gray and LeCompte's script derives at least half its dialogue. While it deconstructs the Eliot play, *Nayatt School*'s imagery remains that of *Rumstick Road*: a red tent, insanity, death, Christian Science's suspicion of doctors, and the preservation of past experiences on tapes, film, and records—although the latter eventually are destroyed. Gray's earnest academician, a pedant intoning without emotion his passion for the Eliot play, sits at a long table midway between the audience above and the playing space below, where one of the rooms in *Rumstick Road* has been turned around so that we peer into it through the window. From quiet beginnings *Nayatt School* increases its speed, ferocity, iconoclasm, and discontinuity. Farcical chases punctuate scenes with a mad doctor and a parody of a horror film in which a scientist lets a giant blob of protoplasm run amok ("Get me a rewrite man quick—it's still growing"). The mindless antisocial amenities of alcohol, cigarettes, and disco music are partaken by children dressed as sophisticated adults until the characters strip and literally climb the walls.

Even more apocalyptic is the Gray and LeCompte part of the Rhode Island trilogy's epilogue, *Point Judith*, which also incorporates a send-up of machismo by Jim Strahs called *Rig*. Once more there recurs the red tent and the room frame, the preservation of the past on records and film, windows that invite us in yet cut us off, and madness. This time madness is conveyed in part by the deconstruction of O'Neill's *Long Day's Journey into Night*, which is drowned out by a buzzer, wind, and Berlioz and accompanied by frantic farce in which objects (particularly a reversed vacuum cleaner billowing exhaust), writhing ribbons of light, and whirling bodies create cataclysmic discord. As a quieter coda a film of men dressed as nuns and the trademark room frames conclude the piece.

After *Point Judith* Gray tired of fragmentation and deconstruction. In search of a controlled narrative form, he returned to the monologue format he had employed in the opening of *Nayatt School* and constructed three intensely personal solo pieces. In these and his subsequent experiments in unilateral repartee, Gray reflects upon such intimate, often embarrassing details of his private life as what sort of things he did with his penis at the age of 12. (A variation is *Interviewing the Audience*, in which, after speaking candidly of his own life, he grills spectators on their experiences.) Although he condenses time and occasionally embellishes details, Gray does not fabricate. "A poetic journalist," as he terms himself, may rearrange events to increase the humor or drama, but candor compels him to confess in *Swimming to Cambodia*, which is about both national and personal corruption, that he vomited on the beach, made half as much money as others in *The Killing Fields*, was obsessed about losing his money, and patronized prostitutes. *Terrors of Pleasure* examines memories of being outfoxed by a con artist and of humiliation in Hollywood.

Whereas in those monologues Gray is largely victimized, in others he reveals his ineptitude at getting laid. Among his Woody Allen-style tales of anxious bumbling toward the sack and fumbling in it is the account of his ineffectual attempt to escape his confirmed heterosexuality in sex with another man. "I figured no one will know about it," Gray muses—and 200 spectators laugh.

This self-deprecatory raconteur carries a dozen "public memories" around in his head, a nearly Homeric achievement, and writes of shame—"pretty hard to maintain in New York City"—and pain, of fear, freaks, and failure, of embarrassment, banality, discomfort, and death, of greed and exploitation. With minimalist means he confronts his paranoia, and, employing a Buddhist idea, he recycles negative energy, a healing process for us as well as for him.

—Tish Dace

GREENBERG, Richard

Nationality: American. **Born:** East Meadow, New York, 22 February 1958. **Education:** Local schools; Princeton University, Princeton, New Jersey, 1976-80, A.B. in English 1980; Harvard University, Cambridge, Massachusetts, 1980-81; Yale University School of Drama, New Haven, Connecticut, 1982-85, M.F.A. in drama 1985. **Career:** Member, Ensemble Studio Theater, New York. **Awards:** Oppenheimer award, 1985; Dramalogue award, 1991. **Agent:** George Lane, William Morris Agency, 1325 Avenue of the Americas, New York, New York 10019, U.S.A.

Publications

Plays

The Bloodletters (produced New York, 1984).

Life under Water (produced New York, 1985). New York, Dramatists Play Service, 1985.

Vanishing Act (produced New York, 1986). New York, Dramatists Play Service, 1987.

The Author's Voice (produced New York, 1987). New York, Dramatists Play Service, 1987.

The Maderati (produced New York, 1987). New York, Dramatists Play Service, 1987.

The Hunger Artist, with Martha Clarke and company, adaptation of a work by Franz Kafka (produced New York, 1987).

Eastern Standard (produced Seattle, 1988; New York, 1988). New York, Grove, 1989.

Neptune's Hips (produced New York, 1988).

The American Plan (produced New York, 1990). New York, Dramatists Play Service, 1990.

The Extra Man (produced Costa Mesa, California, 1991; New York, 1992).

Jenny Keeps Talking (produced New York, 1992). New York, Dramatists Play Service, 1995.

Pal Joey, adaptation of the musical by Rodgers and Hart (produced Boston, Massachusetts, 1992).

Night and Her Stars. New York, Dramatists Play Service, 1997.

Screenplays: *Ask Me Again*, 1989; *Life under Water*, 1989.

Television Play: *The Sad Professor*, in the *Trying Times* series, 1989.

*

Richard Greenberg comments:

Self-indulgently, I consider all my work to date to constitute a public apprenticeship. My last several plays have had quite classically constructed stories. This is a deliberate process of self-teaching, an effort to master the fundamentals of story-telling as a kind of jumping-off place for whatever the future brings. I'm non-ideological but I prefer plays that *become* ideas to those that provide forums for ideas.

* * *

Richard Greenberg's plays explore what it is to be young, semi-gifted, white, and wealthy in contemporary East Coast America, with all the attendant education, anxiety, and ennui that such status confers. Exclusively set in New York City or some fashionable nearby resort, Greenberg's exquisitely structured plays are populated by females with names better suited for pets—Minna, Rena, Dewy, Lina, and Jinx— and WASPy, dithering men saddled with names that are the inheritance of their "hegemony"—Keene, Kip, Pip, Spence, and Sky. (Who else would have a character name his son "Walker" because the father always fantasized about being a *flaneur*?) Greenberg treats his characters with a mixture of fascination, cynicism, and envy. Often an uneasy tension exists: are they adorable but misguided eccentrics or despicably vacuous victims of their wealth and breeding?

Greenberg's characters are articulate to a fault. Where exceptions occur, the inability to properly express oneself becomes a character flaw open to ridicule or running jokes—in *The Maderati* the "Method Actor" Danton mumbles inaudibly while mediocre poet Keene never finishes his similes. In *Three Days of Rain* Ned not only stutters but, he says, "I know all the great . . . stu-stutterers in hi-history, I have their calendar."

Greenberg's fixation with the power of language, syntax, and literacy is evident throughout his work. Responding to the formal elocution of Eva, a German emigre nicknamed "Czarina" in *The American Plan*, Gil exclaims: "What a sentence—wonderful!—Americans take grammar to that kind of extreme." In *Life under Water* Kip tries to seduce Amy-Beth by describing a fictitious green light at the end of her dock. She responds: "That's the goddamn 'Great Gatsby.' I can read! Oh, you sensitive boys with your quotations." This is an example not only of Greenberg's propensity for making literary references but for having other characters—and therefore the audience—recognize them. Given this obsession with wielding knowledge and wit as a way to power, it is little wonder that Greenberg would select the 1950s television quiz show scandals as a subject in *Night and Her Stars*. The three-hander focuses on a trio of historic characters: Charles Van Doren, the handsome son of a famous poet from Columbia University; Herbert Stempel, the nebbishy winner who must purposefully lose to the more glamorous Van Doren; and the master manipulator, producer Dan Enright. Their struggle to publicly strut their intelligence and the humiliation they suffer for their efforts encapsulate the arc of many characters in Greenberg's plays.

Greenberg's one-act comedies are original, intriguing works with an appealing fairy-tale tone and surreal quality. *Vanishing Act* is a Pirandellian experiment that unfolds in a dreamy landscape peopled by wealthy but largely useless characters searching for ways to prevent physical or emotional dissipation. In the play Minna brushes her younger sister Anya's hair while telling her a bedtime story about a woman named Carla whose husband is murdered and dismembered. The last scene jumps ahead several years to find Carla, the character in Minna's story, onstage telling her daughter a bedtime tale about Minna's family. As one narrative "vanishes" into another, Greenberg's structural sleight-of-hand jostles the audience's sense of reality, making manifest the infuriatingly ephemeral nature of life and art.

Life under Water uses 17 short scenes to evoke incisively the emotionally submerged existence of pampered young people at a fashionable Hamptons beach house. Kip, a hapless teenager, runs away from home and meets Amy-Joy and her friend Amy-Beth, recently released from a mental institution. Although a short romance flares up between Kip and Beth, Kip cannot sustain any sense of commitment—emblematic of so many Greenberg characters.

The Maderati is a broad farce satirizing a crowd of self-involved New York artists and pseudo-intellectuals. Greenberg fully embraces the traditional farce form, concluding with a *faux* murder and the couples neatly arrayed in a final tableaux. The genre and the subject allow Greenberg to give full rein to his verbal games. After the depressed poet Charlotte has been committed to an insane asylum, Dewy erroneously believes she has died, while Keene thinks she is hospitalized for an abortion. Both believe Danton should not be out of town:

> Keene: He should be by her bedside.
> Dewy: You mean by her *bier.*
> Keene: Buying her beer, buying her flowers, buying her anything she wants.

Both *The American Plan* and *The Extra Man* feature strong, slightly demonic figures—the Miss Haversham-like Eva and the blocked writer Keith, respectively—who destructively manipulate the love affairs of those they care for most, ostensibly out of some subliminal jealousy (although sheer boredom and lack of amusement is offered as a more frightening, though unconvincing, motivation). Both plays describe the difficulty of loving another person because of the accouterments necessary—honesty, strength, determination, commitment, and openness—qualities invariably lacking in cynical times. Often, however, the characters are so spineless and emotionally witless that they fail to generate much sympathy.

Eastern Standard most successfully details its characters struggles to commit. The first act's three scenes occur at the same lunch hour and at the same restaurant, but with three different couples center stage. In this way the action that was peripheral in one scene becomes central in another. The main character, Stephen, an architect specializing in monstrous postmodern office towers ("I am urban blight"), meets his gay friend, Drew, a painter of some renown, while the girl he has loved only from a distance, Phoebe, waits to meet her brother, Peter, a television writer recently diagnosed with AIDS. When May, a mentally unstable homeless woman hits Peter with her Perrier bottle, Stephen has his excuse to meet his love object as he and Drew come to Peter's rescue. Act Two takes place at Stephen's Hamptons beach house, to which he has invited everyone present at the restaurant that day—eventually including May, the bag lady, and Ellen, the waitress. Here all the characters struggle, not always convincingly, with commitment—Ellen to her acting career, May to sanity, Peter to the solitude imposed by the discovery he has AIDS, Drew to his artwork and his cynicism, and Stephen and Phoebe to their love for each other. Unusual for a Greenberg play, they also actively struggle with their liberal guilt, trying to gauge their personal responsibility for homelessness, an assessment occasioned by May's presence. But once it is clear that no one can prevent her return to the streets, May steals their valuables and disappears. The play ends a bit glibly, with Drew breaking through Peter's emotional defenses, and Stephen and Phoebe engaged to each other and a decision to design and finance buildings for the homeless.

While *Hurrah at Last* and *Safe as Houses* seem to be fairly standard Greenberg comedies in the mold of those already described, *Three Days of Rain* may turn out to be his most produced play. A completely revised version of one of his earliest drama school scripts, it resembles *Eastern Standard* in two ways: a central character is an architect, and it boldly plays with narrative structure. Act One begins in a present-day New York City apartment where Walker and his sister, as well as childhood friend Pip (the son of their deceased father's partner), meet before and after hearing their father's will read. Act Two takes place 30 years before when their parents (played by the same actors as Walker and his sister) meet. Constructed as suavely and solidly as one of the houses the father became famous for designing, the play concerns itself with the characters' internal architecture. The reverse chronological structure reinforces the sense that Walker, who had disappeared to Europe, is now on an archaeological dig into the family's emotional history, trying to find the source of his anguish. Of course the anguish is only intensified by the patriarch architect's true Greenbergian primordial sin: he never communicated well, verbally or in writing. The character is so taciturn that the words "Three Days of Rain" serve as the father's sole journal entry during the most momentous week in his life. As in most Greenberg's plays, any transgression can be forgiven but that one.

—John Istel

GREENSPAN, David

Nationality: American. **Born:** Los Angeles, California, 17 March 1956. **Education:** Beverly Hills High School, graduated 1974; University of California, Irvine, B.A. in drama 1978. **Family:** Lives with William Kennon. **Career:** Playwright-in-residence, HOME for Contemporary Theatre and Art, New York, 1987-90; director and playwright-in-residence, New York Shakespeare Festival, 1990-92. **Awards:** Brooklyn Arts and Cultural Association award, 1984; Art Matters grant, 1987, 1988, 1989, 1992; Revson fellowship, 1989; Rockefeller fellowship, 1989; Albee Foundation residency, 1989; Yaddo residency, 1991; Jerome Foundation, 1993; McKnight Fellowship, 1993; New York State Council on the Arts, 1993, 1994; New Jersey State Council on the Arts, 1998. **Agent:** Judy Boals Berman, Berman, Boals and Flynn, 208 West 30 Street #401, New York, New York 10001, U.S.A.

Publications

Plays

Vertices, Man in a/the Chair, Pieces in the Dark, Recent Hemispheres (monologues and short pieces; produced New York, 1981-86).
The Horizontal and the Vertical (produced New York, 1986).
Dig a Hole and Bury Your Father (produced New York, 1987).
Jack (produced New York, 1987). Published in *The Way We Live Now*, edited by M. Elizabeth Osborn, New York, Theatre Communications Group, 1990.
Principia (produced New York, 1987).
The Home Show Pieces (includes *Doing the Beast, Too Much in the Sun, Portrait of the Artist, The Big Tent*) (produced New York, 1988; Glasgow, 1992). Published in *Plays in Process* (New York), 1993.
The Closet Piece (produced New York, 1989).
2 Samuel 11, Etc. (also director: produced New York, 1989; London, 1991). Published in *Plays in Process* (New York), 1990.
Dead Mother, or Shirley Not All in Vain (produced New York, 1991). Published in *Grove New American Theatre Anthology*, New York, Grove Weidenfeld, 1992.
Dog in a Dancing School (produced New York, 1993).
Son of an Engineer (produced New York, 1994).

*

Critical Study: "Four Writers" by Marc Robinson, in *Theater* (New Haven, Connecticut), 1993, pp. 31-42.

Theatrical Activities:
Director: **Plays**—*Sexual Perversity in Chicago* by David Mamet, New York, 1984; *Danny and the Deep Blue Sea* by John Patrick Shanley, New York, 1986; *Kate's Diary* by Kathleen Tolan, 1989; *Wanking 'Tards* by Nicky Silver, New York, 1990; *Gonza the Lancer* by Chikamatsu Monzaemon, New York, 1990; *The Way of the World* by William Congreve, New York, 1991; *Subterraneans* by Carlos Murillo, 1995.

* * *

David Greenspan is the most nakedly personal of playwrights. He became a writer for the theater when he started performing excerpts from his journals, and he often takes the central role in his pieces, which he also invariably directs. Greenspan's mother died of lupus when he was a boy. Her specter shadows his entire body of work, and the tensions of a troubled family are dramatized again and again. Homoerotic fantasy is another key component of Greenspan's writing, but here, as elsewhere, his real focus is the mind and not the body. His true subject is not sex but obsession and longing. He seeks to capture the process of thinking, especially thinking about feeling.

Yet Greenspan's highly emotional art has always been formally experimental. Samuel Beckett, Gertrude Stein, and Robert Wilson are his acknowledged masters. Greenspan has described his early pieces as "very abstract—word-associated, fragmented, stream-of-consciousness, nonsensical in the strictest sense of the word." To include performers other than himself, he used numbers to indicate who was to speak which lines of the texts. There is little sense of character. What is dramatized is a single consciousness.

Greenspan's later texts resemble plays more closely, and they contain vivid characters who often have their own convincing voices. Yet the playwright still identifies them as Character 1 or Speaker 2, emphasizing the distance between actors and characters on the one hand and between characters and the actual people who inspired them on the other. Any sort of actor might play any sort of character. Various actors can play the same character at different points in the play. Actors can stop playing their characters and start discussing them. Identity is fluid. Transformation, role-playing, and pretending are paramount.

The one-act *Jack* is a good introduction to Greenspan's work. It is an AIDS play, a lovely and elegiac piece for three women speakers who stand upstage at music stands—"Ideally, the image is one of floating busts," writes Greenspan—and a male, Character 8, who sits surrounded by seven empty chairs. On the page the speakers' words are printed in three columns; in the theater they are overlapping waves of sound. In this verbal music repetition and variation gradually build a portrait of the dead Jack. At other moments one voice breaks clear to deliver a monologue, long or short, as often about Jack's difficult mother as about Jack himself. At the center of the piece is a depiction of a primal Greenspan location: a dark park where men come for sex. It is a locus of longing, a fallen Eden, a trap. Late in the play Character 8—Jack—finally speaks, telling about getting lost as a small boy on a crowded beach and about finally seeing his father and embracing him, crying.

The Home Show Pieces and *Dead Mother, or Shirley Not All in Vain* are much bigger works, uneven, ungainly, and fascinating. *Home* contains some of the writer's wittiest scenes. In its opening section Character 1 is in bed, first trying to read and then trying to hump the mattress between the interruptions of a series of phone calls that reveal his loneliness. Some years later Character 1 sits on the toilet, indulging in fantasies of fame, a playwright claiming not to read his reviews while revealing extensive knowledge of them.

The central character in *Dead Mother* is a young man, Harold, who impersonates his mother to help his brother win the woman he wants to marry. There is comedy in this *Charley's Aunt* situation, of course, but also intense drama. In one remarkable scene Harold looks into a mirror, at once accusing the mother whose identity he has taken on and, as the mother, striking back. The unexpected appearance of Harold's father, who thinks that he is seeing his dead wife's ghost, gives Harold the opportunity to attack his father, expressing his mother's grievances along with his own. The masquerade enables Harold not only to speak long hidden truths to his family but also to know himself. In the end he leaves his marriage and the family business to disappear into a homosexual life.

Greenspan's most impressive and successful piece is *2 Samuel 11, Etc.*, which retells the David and Bathsheba story from the woman's point of view. It is set against a complex contemporary narrative that works its way to the story of a young man's encounter with a sexually predatory old man. Both narratives are evolving in the mind of Character 1, a writer who spends the second half of the play standing in his shower recounting the second story and telling it through the dialogue of 11 characters.

Character 1 is also onstage during the first half, but all the speaking is done by Character 2, Bathsheba as she is reimagined by the writer. As the expression of the male writer's mind, the female character speaks not only Bathsheba's story—which is wonderfully told and filled with a complex mixture of revulsion and sympathy for the old king who seduces her, has her husband killed, and takes her into his harem—but also the homoerotic fantasies that overwhelm the writer and the telephone conversations that represent the intrusion of everyday realities.

It is all the audience can do to keep up with the complicated postintermission narrative, but the first half of *2 Samuel 11* is utterly clear, and there is space for rich comedy. "I've got to find a way to get this down on paper," says Character 2, speaking for her author, who is masturbating with one hand and writing with the other. Bathsheba's jaundiced view of Old Testament patriarchy also brings wicked laughter, and there is shocking power in the juxtaposition of the Bible and what Greenspan himself calls the "pornographic ruminations" coming out of her mouth. This time the author has embodied his ideas and obsessions in a context so potent that the result is unforgettable theater.

—M. Elizabeth Osborn

GRIFFITHS, Trevor

Nationality: British. **Born:** Manchester, Lancashire, 4 April 1935. **Education:** St. Bede's College, Manchester, 1945-52; Manchester University, 1952-55, B.A. in English 1955. **Family:** Married 1) Janice Elaine Stansfield in 1960 (died 1977), one son and two daughters; 2) Gillian Cliff in 1992. **Career:** Lecturer in liberal studies, Stockport Technical College, Cheshire, 1962-65; further education officer, BBC, Leeds, 1965-72. Co-editor, *Labour's Northern Voice*, 1962-65, and series editor for Workers Northern Publishing Society. Lives in Yorkshire. **Awards:** BAFTA Writer's award, 1982; Writers' Guild of America award for Best Screenplay, for *Reds*, 1982; Royal Television Society award for regional programme, for *Food for Ravens*, 1998. **Agent:** Peters, Fraser and Dunlop Group, 503/4 The Chambers, Chelsea Harbour, Lots Road, London SW10 0XF, England.

Publications

Plays

The Wages of Thin (produced Manchester, 1969; London, 1970).

The Big House (broadcast 1969; produced Newcastle upon Tyne, 1975). With *Occupations*, London, Calder and Boyars, 1972.

Occupations (produced Manchester, 1970; London, 1971; New York, 1982). With *The Big House*, London, Calder and Boyars, 1972; revised version, published separately, London, Faber, 1980.

Apricots (produced London, 1971). With *Thermidor*, London, Pluto Press, 1978.

Thermidor (produced Edinburgh, 1971). With *Apricots*, London, Pluto Press, 1978.

Lay By, with others (produced Edinburgh and London, 1971). London, Calder and Boyars, 1972.

Sam, Sam (produced London, 1972; revised version produced London, 1978). Published in *Plays and Players* (London), April 1972.

Gun (also director: produced Edinburgh, 1973).

The Party (produced London, 1973; revised version produced Coventry, 1974). London, Faber, 1974.

All Good Men (BBC 1974; produced London, 1975). Included in *All Good Men, and Absolute Beginners*, 1977.

Comedians (produced Nottingham and London, 1975; New York, 1976; BBC television, 1981). London, Faber, and New York, Grove Press, 1976; revised version, Faber, 1979.

The Cherry Orchard, adaptation of the play by Chekhov, translated by Helen Rappaport (produced Nottingham, 1977; BBC television, 1981). London, Pluto Press, 1978; revised edition, London, Faber, 1989.

All Good Men, and Absolute Beginners: Two Plays for Television. London, Faber, 1977.

Through the Night, and Such Impossibilities: Two Plays for Television. London, Faber, 1977.

Deeds, with others (produced Nottingham, 1978). Published in *Plays and Players* (London) May and June 1978.

Country: A Tory Story (televised 1981). London, Faber, 1981.

Sons and Lovers, adaptation of the novel by D. H. Lawrence (televised 1981). Nottingham, Spokesman, 1982.

Oi for England (televised 1982; produced London, 1982). London, Faber, 1982.

Real Dreams, adaptation of the story "Revolution in Cleveland" by Jeremy Pikser (also director: produced Williamstown, Massachusetts, 1984; London, 1986). London, Faber, 1987 (includes "Revolution in Cleveland" by Pikser).

Judgement over the Dead: The Screenplays of The Last Place on Earth, (televised 1985). London, Verso, 1986.

Fatherland (screenplay). London, Faber, 1987.

Collected Plays for Television (includes *All Good Men*; *Absolute Beginners*; *Through the Night*; *Such Impossibilities*; *Country*; *Oi for England*). London, Faber, 1988.

Piano (produced London, 1990). London, Faber, 1990.

The Gulf Between Us: The Truth and Other Fictions (also director: produced Leeds, 1992). London, Faber, 1992.

Thatcher's Children (produced Bristol, 1993). London, Farber, 1994.

Hope in the Year Two. London, Farber, 1994.

Who Shall Be Happy...? (produced Belfast, 1995).

Plays One: Collected Theatre Plays (includes *The Party*; *Comedians*; *Real Dreams*). London, Farber, 1996.

Food for Ravens. London, Oberon, 1998.

Screenplays: *Reds*, with Warren Beatty, 1981; *Fatherland*, 1987.

Radio Plays: *The Big House*, 1969; *Jake's Brigade*, 1971.

Television Plays: *Adam Smith* series (as Ben Rae), 1972; *The Silver Mask*, from a story by Horace Walpole (*Between the Wars* series), 1973; *All Good Men*, 1974; *Absolute Beginners* (*Fall of Eagles* series), 1974; *Don't Make Waves* (*Eleventh Hour* series), with Snoo Wilson, 1975; *Through the Night*, 1975; *Bill Brand* series, 1976; *Sons and Lovers*, 1981; *Country: A Tory Story*, 1981; *Oi for England*, 1982; *The Last Place on Earth*, 1985; *The Party*, 1988; *Hope in the Year Two*, 1994.

Other

Tip's Lot (for children). London, Macmillan, 1972.

*

Manuscript Collection: British Film Institute, London.

Critical Studies: *Stages in the Revolution: Political Theatre in Britain Since 1968* by Catherine Itzin, London, Eyre Methuen, 1980; *An Introduction to Fifty Modern British Plays* by Benedict Nightingale, London, Pan, 1982; *Powerplays: Trevor Griffiths in Television* by Mike Poole and John Wyver, London, British Film Institute, 1984; "The Caretaker and the Classroom Setting in Trevor Griffiths' Comedians" by Neal A. Lester, in *Notes on Contemporary Literature* (Carrollton, Georgia), May 1990, pp. 5-6; "The Cherry Orchard: A New Version by Trevor Griffiths" by David Allen, in *Chekhov on the British Stage,* edited by Patrick Miles, Cambridge, Cambridge University Press, 1993; "Trevor Griffiths" by Stanton B. Garner, Jr., in *British Playwrights, 1956-1995: A Research and Production Sourcebook,* edited by William W. Demastes, Westport, Connecticut, Greenwood, 1996; "Politics over the Gulf: Trevor Griffiths in the Nineties" by Stanton B. Garner, Jr., in *Modern Drama* (Downsview, Ontario), Fall 1996, pp. 381-91.

Theatrical Activities:
Director: **Plays**—*Gun,* Edinburgh, 1973; *Real Dreams,* Williamstown, Massachusetts, 1984; *Saint Oscar* by Terry Eagleton, Derry, 1989, London, 1990; *The Gulf Between Us,* Leeds, 1992; *Who Shall Be Happy...?,* 1995. **Television**—*Food for Ravens,* 1997.

* * *

Trevor Griffiths is unique for the remarkable consistency with which he has probed into critical phases and issues of the international labor movement. Earlier social and political dramatists portrayed individual labor struggles or dealt with the brutal consequences of fascism, but never before have the crucial questions of socialist strategy and morality been so forcefully examined on the stage. While assuming the desirability of socialism, Griffiths is anxious to distinguish and analyze the different positions hammered out by various brands of socialism and communism and the personal dilemmas arising out of absorbing engagement in one of these movements.

It is significant that Griffiths started with a number of plays about Continental rather than British crises. *Occupations* is set in Turin at the height of the revolutionary upsurge after World War I when factories were taken over and soviets formed in many Italian cities. The play shows the workers of Turin addressed in two moving speeches by Gramsci, but its focus is less on the confrontation between capital and labor than on the controversy between Gramsci and Kabak, a secret envoy of the Comintern, over the correct estimate and handling of the situation. Kabak, who has the experience and prestige of a successful revolution behind him, stands for a communist realpolitik; by contrast Gramsci embodies a hesitant, if fervent, revolutionary idealism that is always guided by a consideration, even love, for the people he leads.

The strategic differences between these two exponents of communism are also reflected in their personal outlooks. At the end Kabak leaves behind his mistress, who is dying of cancer, while Gramsci goes to Sardinia to attend to his sister on her deathbed. The political and the personal, it is suggested, should not be seen as separate concerns. This dual perspective is also expressed by the play's title (Griffiths has a predilection for succinct, ambiguous titles), which refers not only to the action taken by the Fiat workers but also to the private undertakings of the protagonists.

One of several future historical developments hinted at toward the end of *Occupations* is Stalinism. It can be seen germinating in Kabak's ruthless pragmatism and is summed up in Gramsci's ominous words "Treat masses as expendable, as fodder, during the revolution, you will always treat them thus." *Thermidor* gives us a glimpse of Soviet Russia in the throes of Stalinism during the purges of 1937. This one-act play is named after the summer month of the French revolutionary calendar, in which Robespierre himself fell victim to the terror he had unleashed in the defense of the Revolution. Here it is Anya, formerly a loyal member of the Communist party, who will disappear in the cellars of the NKVD. The play shows her at the mercy of her interrogator, Yukhov, who twists her sentences and fabricates absurd charges. Here there is even less doubt than in the altercations between Gramsci and Kabak as to where the author's sympathies lie. Yukhov's phrase "Enemies . . . are no longer people" disqualifies him and a whole system from speaking in the name of a humanist socialism. But when Anya finally pleads innocent and Yukhov asks the rhetorical question "Are you?" this is as much the voice of the author, who cannot absolve a once diligent and influential party member like Anya of historical guilt.

In contrast to these two analytical and descriptive plays, *The Party* introduces an ironical note. An assortment of noncommunist and almost exclusively non-working-class leftists meet at the instigation of a progressive television producer, Joe Shawcross, to discuss the possibilities of joint revolutionary action in Britain, all against the backdrop of Parisian students mounting the barricades in May 1968. The ironic nature of the whole radical chic congregation and the impotence of the British intellectual left are suggested from the beginning through the appearance in the prologue of Groucho Marx musing at a picture of his political namesake and by Joe's masturbation prior to the arrival of the leftist partygoers. Neither of the two conflicting analyses of the situation offered by a sociology lecturer and a veteran Trotskyist, respectively, the latter pointing to the necessity of building the party, is entirely wrong, but, equally, neither is free of empty revolutionary phrasemaking and worn-out slogans, as the debunking comments of a drunk writer, who is accidentally present, point out.

Occupations, *Thermidor*, and *The Party* were all conceived and written for the stage. So was *Comedians*, which is often regarded as Griffiths's best work. It is certainly his funniest, even though one finds oneself often painfully aware of the impropriety of one's laughs. For this is a comedy about the social uses of stand-up comedy and of working-class entertainment, a comedy about the proper function of the performer and, by implication, of the dramatist. Humor for Griffiths is too serious a business to be left in the hands of mindless word jugglers who insult people's intelligence or pander to ethnic and sexual stereotypes.

Since the mid-1970s Griffiths's career has, however, been primarily and deliberately that of a television playwright. Few critics and scholars have appreciated this decision, and some on the left have even accused him of opportunism. The author has sought this medium out of a deep conviction that a socialist dramatist today cannot afford to address only the theatergoer, whether in the West End or on the fringe. While the one kind of theater reaches only a middle-class audience, the other too often ends by preaching to the converted. As Raymond Williams has pointed out, for the vast majority of the population "drama in a dramatised society" like ours means television drama, and as one character in *Through the Night* puts it, "Whoever does not reach the capacity of the common people and fails to make them listen to him, misses his mark."

Yet what Griffiths has called the "strategic penetration" of the central channel of communication proved initially difficult. *Such Impossibilities*, commissioned by the BBC as part of a series entitled *The Edwardians*, was rejected, ostensibly on grounds of cost but more probably because its hero, the militant labor leader Tom Mann, and its theme, the 1911 transport strike in Liverpool, a social conflict of almost civil-war-like dimensions, fitted awkwardly into an ancestral gallery composed of such establishment figures as Baden-Powell, Horatio Bottomley, and Charles Stewart Rolls.

Not surprisingly, therefore, *All Good Men*, Griffiths's first major television play to be produced, shows the author fully alert to the power of the medium to forge consensus and to mystify. A television producer who wants to conduct an interview with the elderly Labour politician Edward Waite, a former cabinet minister now to be made a peer, is attacked by William, the politician's son, precisely for his seemingly disinterested, value-free pose. William, a left-wing research student, is equally critical of the historical record of the Labour Party, and the dispute between father and son over its successes, as the former sees it, or purely minor reforms ultimately solidifying capitalism, as the latter argues, forms the climax of the play. But true to his familiar oppositional setup, Griffiths, though sharing many of William's reservations about "Labourism," distributes the arguments fairly evenly. Moreover, Waite—like so many of Griffiths's totally committed figures—has paid a heavy price for his lifelong dedication to working-class politics. He has been deserted by his wife and is now betrayed by his son, who supplies the interviewer with compromising material about his father's past, not out of personal vindictiveness but in order to bring the internal political machinations of the Labour Party into the open.

All Good Men, like its 11-part successor, *Bill Brand*, questions the parliamentary road to socialism and scrutinizes the role of the Labour Party without writing off either completely. But as the revolutionary optimism of much of the British socialist drama of the 1970s subsided and experienced a definite check under the realities of Thatcher's Britain, Griffiths found other themes more pertinent, among them the situation of unemployed urban youths (*Oi for England*) and the construction of national myths (*The Last Place on Earth*).

Country, Griffiths's strongest play of the 1980s, is about a significant moment in the history of British socialism, namely, Labour's landslide victory in 1945. But the play looks at it from an unexpected angle, an upper-class estate in Kent, where the members of the Carlion dynasty have assembled for the annual family gathering, at which a successor to the aging Sir Frederic, baronet and chairman of the board of the Carlion brewery empire, will have to be found. As the devastating election results come in and the common people themselves symbolically lay claim to the property by trespassing and occupying a barn, incredulity and consternation alternate with wrath. But Philip, one Carlion not affected by the general stupefaction, an outsider among the pretenders for the succession not least because of his bohemian lifestyle, now energetically assumes responsibility. Philip's victory over the "old gang," his efficient and smooth dealing with the squatters, indicates the capacity of the ruling class to renew itself and adapt to unforeseen circumstances—a point already made in *Occupations*, where the Fiat manager envisages a whole paternalistic welfare program as a palliative against future social unrest.

Griffiths's work also includes screenplays. Chief among these are *Reds* (directed by Warren Beatty), about the American journalist John Reed's involvement in the October Revolution, and *Fatherland* (directed by Ken Loach), an intriguing story of German partition and a song maker's search for his father, who left East Germany for the West 30 years before his son.

With *Real Dreams* Griffiths returned to the stage and to an earlier preoccupation. Like *The Party* this play about the American student movement in the late 1960s highlights the feelings of isolation and frustration behind the leftward move of many intellectuals. The attempt of a commune of white middle-class students to move out of the protected world of the campus and form a fighting alliance with Puerto Rican working people fails dismally, hampered as it is by all kinds of ethnic, cultural, sexist, and psychic blocks. But the play ends on an optimistic note as the real historical contradictions are dissolved into an anticipatory dream of perfect unity, grace, and victory, all symbolized by a trancelike Tai Chi exercise. The limitations and self-indulgence as well as the potential power and promise of this phase of radicalism are thus brought alive. If the conclusion appears somewhat forced, the play demonstrates once again Griffiths's masterly building up of tension and testifies to his continuing concern for the global struggle for liberation.

Perhaps the most important single theatrical influence on the later Griffiths is Chekhov, whose *The Cherry Orchard* he adapted to shrill screams of protest from critics, who took issue with the downgrading of the central figure Ranevsky and the consequent shift of emphasis from plangent sorrow over the loss of property to the acute anticipation of a revolutionary situation. Chekhov also looms large in *Piano*, which is based on the Russian's early unfinished play *Platonov* and equally set in turn-of-the-century rural society. A kindred atmosphere of imminent historical change hangs over the characters, most of them finely graded members of the blasé upper class, who are enmeshed in a web of failure and frustration, confusion and apathy, stalemate and deadlock. It is a mental and psychological state not at a great remove from that of radical intellectuals of the present day after the collapse of socialist hopes.

—H. Gustav Klaus

GUARE, John (Edward)

Nationality: American. **Born:** New York City, 5 February 1938. **Education:** Joan of Arc Elementary School, and St. John's Preparatory School, New York; Georgetown University, Washington, D.C., 1956-60, A.B. 1960; Yale University School of Drama, 1960-63, M.F.A. 1963. **Military Service:** Served in the United States Air Force Reserve, 1963. **Family:** Married Adele Chatfield-Taylor in 1981. **Career:** Assistant to the manager, National Theatre, Washington, D.C., 1960; member, Barr/Wilder/Albee Playwrights Unit, New York, 1964; founding member, Eugene O'Neill Playwrights Conference, Waterford, Connecticut, 1965; playwright-in-residence, New York Shakespeare Festival, 1976-77; adjunct professor of playwriting, Yale University, 1978; visiting artist, Harvard University, 1990-91; fellow, Julliard School, 1993-94; lecturer, New York University and City College of New York. Council member, Dramatists Guild, 1971; vice-president, Theatre Communications Group, 1986. Lives in New York City. **Awards:** ABC-

Yale University fellowship, 1966; Obie award, 1968, 1971; *Variety* award, 1969; Cannes Film Festival award, for screenplay, 1971; New York Drama Critics Circle award, 1971, 1972; Tony award, 1972, 1986; Joseph Jefferson award, 1977; Venice Film Festival Golden Lion, National Society of Film Critics award, New York Film Critics Circle award, and Los Angeles Film Critics award, all for screenplay, 1980; American Academy Award of Merit Medal, 1981; named Literary Lion, New York Public Library, 1986; New York Institute for the Humanities fellowship, 1987. **Address:** c/o R. Andrew Boose, Collyer and Boose, 1 Dag Hammarskjold Plaza, New York, New York 10017-2299, U.S.A.

Publications

Plays

Theatre Girl (produced Washington, D.C., 1959).
The Toadstool Boy (produced Washington, D.C., 1960).
The Golden Cherub (produced New Haven, Connecticut, 1962?).
Did You Write My Name in the Snow? (produced New Haven, Connecticut, 1963).
To Wally Pantoni, We Leave a Credenza (produced New York, 1965).
The Loveliest Afternoon of the Year, and *Something I'll Tell You Tuesday* (produced New York, 1966; *The Loveliest Afternoon of the Year* produced London, 1972). New York, Dramatists Play Service, 1968.
Muzeeka (produced Waterford, Connecticut, 1967; New York and Edinburgh, 1968; London, 1969). Included in *Off-Broadway Plays*, London, Penguin, 1970; in *Cop-Out, Muzeeka, Home Fires*, 1971.
Cop-Out (produced Waterford, Connecticut, 1968; New York, 1969). Included in *Off-Broadway Plays*, London, Penguin, 1970; in *Cop-Out, Muzeeka, Home Fires*, 1971.
Home Fires (produced New York, 1969). Included in *Cop-Out, Muzeeka, Home Fires*, 1971.
Kissing Sweet (televised 1969). With *A Day for Surprises*, New York, Dramatists Play Service, 1971.
A Day for Surprises (produced New York, 1970; London, 1971). With *Kissing Sweet*, New York, Dramatists Play Service, 1971.
The House of Blue Leaves (produced New York, 1971; London, 1988). New York, Viking Press, 1972.
Two Gentlemen of Verona, with Mel Shapiro, music by Galt MacDermot, lyrics by Guare, adaptation of the play by Shakespeare (produced New York, 1971; London, 1973). New York, Holt Rinehart, 1973.
Cop-Out, Muzeeka, Home Fires. New York, Grove Press, 1971.
Taking Off (screenplay), with others. New York, New American Library, 1971.
Optimism; or, The Misadventures of Candide, with Harold Stone, based on a novel by Voltaire (produced Waterford, Connecticut, 1973).
Rich and Famous (produced Lake Forest, Illinois, 1974; New York, 1976). New York, Dramatists Play Service, 1977.
Marco Polo Sings a Solo (produced Nantucket, Massachusetts, 1976; revised version produced New York, 1977). New York, Dramatists Play Service, 1977.
Landscape of the Body (produced Lake Forest, Illinois, and New York, 1977). New York, Dramatists Play Service, 1978.
Take a Dream (produced New York, 1978).
Bosoms and Neglect (produced Chicago and New York, 1979). New York, Dramatists Play Service, 1980.
In Fireworks Lie Secret Codes (produced in *Holidays*, Louisville, 1979; also director: produced separately, New York, 1981). New York, Dramatists Play Service, 1981.
Nantucket series:
Lydie Breeze (produced New York, 1982). New York, Dramatists Play Service, 1982.
Gardenia (produced New York, 1982; London, 1983). New York, Dramatists Play Service, 1982.
Women and Water (produced Los Angeles, 1984; revised version produced Washington, D.C., 1985). New York, Dramatists Play Service, 1990.
Three Exposures (includes *The House of Blue Leaves*, *Landscape of the Body*, *Bosoms and Neglect*). New York, Harcourt Brace, 1982.
Hey, Stay a While, music by Galt MacDermot, lyrics by Guare (produced Chicago, 1984).
Gluttony, in *Faustus in Hell* (produced Princeton, New Jersey, 1985).
The Talking Dog, adaptation of a story by Chekhov, in *Orchards* (produced Urbana, Illinois, 1985; New York, 1986). New York, Knopf, 1986.
The House of Blue Leaves and Two Other Plays (includes *Landscape of the Body* and *Bosoms and Neglect*). New York, New American Library, 1987.
Moon over Miami (produced New Haven, Connecticut, 1989).
Six Degrees of Separation (produced New York, 1990; London, 1992). New York, Vintage, 1990; London, Methuen, 1992.
Four Baboons Adoring the Sun (produced New York, 1992). Published in *Antaeus* (New York), 1992.
The War Against the Kitchen Sink. Lyme, New Hampshire, Smith and Kraus, 1996.

Screenplays: *Taking Off*, with others, 1971; *Atlantic City*, 1980.

Television Play: *Kissing Sweet* (*Foul!* series), 1969.

Film Adaptation: *Six Degrees of Separation.*

*

Manuscript Collection: Beinecke Library, Yale University, New Haven, Connecticut.

Critical Studies: Article and checklist by John Harrop, in *New Theatre Quarterly 10* (Cambridge), May 1987; "John Guare" by John DiGaetani, in *A Search for a Postmodern Theater: Interviews with Contemporary Playwrights,* edited by John DiGaetani, New York, Greenwood, 1991; "Fierce Love and Fierce Response: Intervening in the Cultural Politics of Race, Sexuality, and AIDS" by David Roman, in *Critical Essays: Gay and Lesbian Writers of Color,* edited by Emmanuel S. Nelson, New York, Haworth, 1993; "Life Is a Silken Net: Mourning the Beloved Monstrous in Lydie Breeze" by Robert F. Gross, in *Journal of Dramatic Theory and Criticism* (Lawrence, Kansas), Fall 1994, pp. 21-43.

Theatrical Activities:
Director: **Play**—*In Fireworks Lie Secret Codes*, New York, 1981.

* * *

In dramatizing *philos/aphilos,* the love/hate relationships in the American family, John Guare locates sources of humor in suffering by penning stinging satires, corrosive black comedies, and screwball farces about such subjects as bereavement, humiliation, betrayal, and guilt. An ironist who frequently eschews pathos, the fantasist Guare speaks to our brutal realities, and his comedies can move us to tears. His freewheeling imagination is unfettered by the constraints of realism as he employs such presentational devices as narration, soliloquies and asides to the audience, and poetic speech. Nonetheless, Guare grounds his plays in contemporary American life, especially in the sudden end of a family unit.

This paradoxical playwright has described one of his plays as a union of Feydeau and Strindberg. Not surprisingly, since narcissism precludes nurturing, Guare depicts marriage as bondage between self-absorbed people who cannot care for others. When egocentric misfits nevertheless marry and breed, they create nightmares that frequently culminate in death. Women, who are often more sympathetic than this dramatist's men, suffer especially from romantic or domestic ties, but sons also are victimized by family life.

Guare's early one-acts provide the characters with bizarre backgrounds that distance them from us. The wayward husband in *The Loveliest Afternoon of the Year*, "a seeing eye person for blind dogs," recounts his sister's dismemberment by a polar bear and his father's death by scalding from a calliope's steam. "You're from Ohio," he explains to his mistress. "You come from a nice family. You don't understand the weirdness, the grief that people can spring from." Perhaps she gains that understanding when she dies, for the man's wife shoots and kills them both.

Guare's early neoabsurdist plays also include the dreadful marital squabbles of *Something I'll Tell You Tuesday,* characters so removed from humanity in *A Day for Surprises* that Pringle is pregnant not with a baby but with *The Complete Works of Dr. Spock,* and the eradication of reproductive capacity in the S&M *Cop-Out*. In *Home Fires* Guare mocks the lengths to which the Schmidts go to avoid acknowledging their family name and ties. *Muzeeka*'s short Brechtian episodes and scene titles indict marriage, which causes Argue (an anagram for Guare) to sell out his creativity, flee to kinky sex, and then ultimately escape via suicide. Marriage proves one of the rotten institutions comprising the American dream.

The House of Blue Leaves keeps the pain at a distance with increasingly antic farce as nuns in Artie Shaughnessy's Queens apartment pursue a soldier disguised as an altar boy, prompting him to toss a bomb into the arms of the deaf movie star. In order to dramatize familial resentments of the humiliations that relatives inflict on one another, Guare creates Artie, a zookeeper/composer whose singing voice is as cracked as his wife's mind. Artie's son Ronnie hates Uncle Billy for having made a fool of him, and he loathes his father for never ceasing to remind him of it. Instead of murdering his real father, Ronnie resorts to symbolic patricide by trying to kill the pope. Because Artie cannot stand having his wife Bananas witness his failures and having her know that he has plagiarized his songs, he kills her. Among a group of hopeless narcissists, only Bananas can love others, and she is therefore "mad." Guare dramatizes this family as unreal, phony, illusory, and impermanent, like the bare tree in which blue birds momentarily perch. The family home, not the mental institution, constitutes the real "house of blue leaves."

In the cartoon *Rich and Famous*, one of the plays replete with arctic imagery, Bing turns to his parents for comfort, but he encounters not warmth but ice. They shoot him—and he shoots back—because he has failed to fulfill their own dreams. They would prefer a mentally retarded son to one who wants his own life.

In the even more baroque *Marco Polo Sings a Solo*, set in the Arctic Circle, icy images dominate, although they are mixed with metaphors of fire. The characters, narcissists who live only for themselves, engage in solos or in quests alone. Stony McBride even owes his birth to a transsexual impregnated by her own sperm—the ultimate image of self-absorption. Guare describes the play as a "comedy coming out of each character's complete obsession with self." In a house carved out of ice, all three marriages disintegrate, but it is as though Ibsen's Nora (one wife has attended 41 productions of *A Doll's House*) has been walled in by a gigantic igloo without doors—or egress.

Landscape of the Body dramatizes relatives as helpless victims, or, as Guare puts it, "people drifting with their heads cut off." Here family members long for love, but their insecurities destroy them. After his father abandons them, Bert and his mother Betty try to begin a new life in New York, but he fears that his mother will not return from a search for a husband, grabs a friend in his terror, and dies because his pal, misinterpreting this as a homosexual pass, in his own turn panics and kills and decapitates Bert. Betty's own anxieties had sent her away on a trip with an unsuitable admirer, and her fears thus cost her the only person with whom she could share love, a parallel to Artie's murdering Bananas, his loving wife.

Bosoms and Neglect likewise concerns loss, anxiety, egomania, and aching loneliness. Despite the farce with which Guare maneuvers Scooper, his aging mother, and new girlfriend, *Bosoms* forces us to experience the excruciating pain of family life. Scooper worries more about neglected authors than about his neglect of his mother or her neglect of her breast and uterine cancer, the areas of her body where he was gestated and nurtured. After Scooper tries to murder his mother, she lays bare her own regrets, anguish, and humiliation in an effort to offer him salvation, but his selfishness already has prompted him to leave the room. It is horrifying that, as she provides him with the key to understanding his recurrent nightmare, his blind mother cannot know that he is not there to hear her.

Such images of loneliness, frequent throughout his career, achieve especial poignancy in *Landscape of the Body*, *Bosoms and Neglect*, and most of Guare's subsequent work. Even as he honed his ability to dramatize people cut off from other's affections, however, Guare shifted direction in another respect. While he tended to focus in the first couple of decades on families with sons, thereafter, with one exception, he has written also about daughters and sisters in his full-length plays.

The exception, *Moon over Miami,* resembles the playwright's work of 20 years earlier in its blistering, Ortonesque satire that targets corruption among FBI agents, politicians, and religious con artists (a salesman of Bibles that "leave out the sad parts," such as the fact that Jesus dies). The characters comprise such grotesques as the agent Otis Flimbsby, who is weird because he is honest, the con man Shelley Slutsky, his mother, who sings only lewd and scatological songs in her nightclub act, and a chorus of mermaids. Beginning in Alaska and then shifting to Miami, *Moon* features more images of ice and heat as well as extravagant efforts to connect with others. Agent Wilcox even recognizes that disillusioning people or leaving them can kill them. Suggested by the ABSCAM federal sting operation, *Moon* indicts fraud and deception. Flimsby encounters only unscrupulous charlatans except for his girlfriend, who hopes "to find a better world where Bambi runs free and Dumbo flies high and Pinocchio tells the truth and Sleeping Beauty is wide awake."

Guare originally undertook *Moon over Miami* as a film for John Belushi, who died inopportunely as though he were a character in one of the dramatist's black comedies. Guare encountered better luck with another violent but amusing film script, the award-winning *Atlantic City*. Initially it depicts a bleak view of families: Sally's husband has run away with and impregnated her sister Chrissy. Yet Lou becomes a surrogate father for Sally, and Chrissy finds a surrogate mother in Grace. Perhaps substitute or chosen families nurture more tenderly and effectively than biological relatives.

In two 1980s one-acts Guare examined alienation between lovers without offspring. *In Fireworks Lie Secret Codes* concerns belonging or not belonging on the part of a gay male couple and their friends. *The Talking Dog* dramatizes the unsuitable mating of a woman and her boyfriend; she agrees to both physical and emotional risk taking while he hang glides but hangs back from commitment.

Sabotaging or betraying relationships likewise figures prominently in Guare's full-length plays of the 1980s and early 1990s. The ambitious Nantucket trilogy evokes comparison to Eugene O'Neill's New England plays. Beginning during the Civil War and continuing through the subsequent three decades, these melodramas offer an American fable that illuminates the country's origins, nature, and future direction, just as Guare's William Dean Howells urges the aspiring writer Joshua to do. The presentational and episodic *Women and Water* moves fluidly back and forth across time and permits Lydie Breeze to confide her thoughts directly to the audience. Guare dramatizes murder, rape, arson, and suicide in a melodrama that veers off into both satire and Senecan tragedy of blood guilt and a ghost's vengeance. Moving between hope and disillusion, Guare touches upon betrayal, patricide, greed, lies, and the punishment of sins, as well as the healing of wounds and the ideals of a golden age. He balances water as a life-sustaining force against the image of the watery grave. Out of the Battle of Cold Harbor, in which 17,000 men died, and other misery grows Lydie's resolution to take three men—Joshua, Dan, and Amos—to found the commune of Aipotu (Utopia spelled backwards).

The more realistic and linear *Gardenia*, though it also features murder, takes as its central image blossoms: their birth and nurturance with water and their flowering, deflowering, and withering. Other emblematic details include Lydie's conviction that her patient's baby died in punishment of the parents (innocence and guilt and sin and redemption figure prominently) and Joshua's prison assurance to the Brighton Mauler that going home constitutes a happy ending, an ironic view considering what lies ahead of Joshua. As Guare further examines ideals and disillusionment, hope and its loss, the healing of old wounds and the inflicting of new ones, and the loneliness that engulfs Lydie, he maintains suspense by withholding from the audience the cause of the killing.

To learn the cause we need *Lydie Breeze*, replete with more murder, rape, and suicide as well as madness and syphilis. Yet this summer on Nantucket provides a sunny ending, permitting peace with the past and hope for Lydie's daughter, even while clearly suggesting a future fraught with further narcissism and corruption. This coming-of-age play of Lydie Hickman ends on the significant word "alone."

Six Degrees of Separation depicts a man singularly alone, an outsider in several senses. Black, gay, self-educated, poor, and homeless, Paul is totally separated from the pampered and privileged residents of condos bordering Central Park. Yet, in scenes both searing and amusing, he cons them into accepting him as one of them. In this touching and hilarious commentary on human interconnections—often the disconnections that separate us from ourselves as well as one other—society matron Ouisa Kittredge figures that "Everybody on this planet is separated by only six people." Ouisa fears the failure to forge links but also appears anxious about letting people get close, past those distancing devices at which the Kittredges and their friends excel.

As he did with *Landscape of the Body*, Guare lifted found materials from newspaper headlines. An African American, claiming that he is both Sidney Poitier's son and a friend of the Kittredges' college student offspring, arrives at their posh apartment saying that he has been mugged in the park. When the Kittredges and several friends learn that they all have, after hearing the same tale, given overnight lodging and small sums to the man, they figure that they have been victimized by a con artist. Yet he has spent their money on them, plus a male hustler, and he has stolen nothing. His goal was to become one of them, part of the family, and to receive parental love from Ouisa and her husband. With dramaturgy that sports monologues, dreams, jumps in time and place, and chats with the audience, Guare shows Paul's impressive bid for a foster family and the Kittredges' eventual failure to provide the affection and approval he craves.

As double-sided as the Kittredges' Kandinsky, *Six Degrees* has multiple ironies and a dual tone that have won it many admirers. Less popular but rich in its own right, *Four Baboons Adoring the Sun* flashes both forward (although Guare clarifies the chronology only on the page, not the stage) and backward to the courtship of Penny and Philip. The present portrays their married life in Sicily, where they dig up artifacts of the past, ostensibly archeological finds but actually the damage to their lives that may render their union too fragile to endure.

Within 24 hours, in a classical Italian setting, events evolve that we know will end tragically, for the god Eros predicts disaster in the first lines: "The start of another perfect day./Something will go wrong." The newlyweds are joined by their total of nine children from their former marriages. Eros targets their firstborn, Wayne and Halcy, at 13 craving the romantic and sexual bliss secured by their parents, who try to thwart their youngsters' wishes. The title, which refers to a statue in which the eyes have been burned out from worshiping the sun, suggests both the ecstatic joy of love and the danger of worshipping Eros. In each pair of lovers the men depart, and the women remain to survive tragedy and respond affirmatively to Eros's injunction "From out of the part of your soul that's not broken, adore the Sun." If Guare in this and other plays offers hope of battered spirits reviving and flourishing, clearly they will spring from among his resilient women.

—Tish Dace

GURNEY, A(lbert) R(amsdell)

Nationality: American. **Born:** Buffalo, New York, 1 November 1930. **Education:** St. Paul's School, Concord, New Hampshire, 1944-48; Williams College, Williamstown, Massachusetts, 1948-

52, B.A. 1952; Yale University School of Drama, New Haven, Connecticut, 1955-58, M.F.A. 1958. **Military Service:** Served in the United States Naval Reserve, 1952-55. **Family:** Married Mary Goodyear in 1957; two sons and two daughters. **Career:** Member of the faculty, Massachusetts Institute of Technology, Cambridge, 1960—; professor of literature, Massachusetts Institute of Technology, Cambridge, 1970-1996. **Awards:** Drama Desk award, 1971; Rockefeller grant, 1977; National Endowment for the Arts award, 1982; American Academy and Institute of Arts and Letters award of merit, 1987. D.D.L.: Williams College, 1984; Buffalo State University, 1992. **Agent:** Gilbert Parker, William Morris Agency, 1325 Avenue of the Americas, New York, New York 10019, U.S.A. **Address:** 40 Wellers Bridge Road, Roxbury, Connecticut 06783, U.S.A.

PUBLICATIONS

Plays

Three People, in *The Best Short Plays 1955-56*, edited by Margaret Mayorga. Boston, Beacon Press, 1956.

Turn of the Century, in *The Best Short Plays 1957-58*, edited by Margaret Mayorga. Boston, Beacon Press, 1958.

Love in Buffalo (produced New Haven, Connecticut, 1958).

The Bridal Dinner (produced Cambridge, Massachusetts, 1962).

The Comeback (produced Cambridge, Massachusetts, 1965). New York, Dramatists Play Service, 1967.

The Rape of Bunny Stuntz (produced Cambridge, Massachusetts, 1966; New York, 1967; Richmond, Surrey, 1976). London, French, 1976.

The David Show (produced Tanglewood, Massachusetts, 1966; New York, 1968). New York, French, 1968.

The Golden Fleece (produced New York, 1968; London, 1982). Published in *The Best Short Plays 1969*, edited by Stanley Richards, Philadelphia, Chilton, 1970.

The Problem (produced Boston, 1969; London, 1973; New York, 1978). New York, French, 1968; London, French, 1973.

The Open Meeting (produced Boston, 1969). New York, French, 1969.

The Love Course (produced Boston, 1970; New York, 1973; London, 1974). Published in *The Best Short Plays 1970*, edited by Stanley Richards, Philadelphia, Chilton, 1971; published separately, London, French, 1976.

Scenes from American Life (produced Tanglewood, Massachusetts, 1970; New York, 1971; revised version produced New Haven, Connecticut and Edinburgh, 1988). Included in *Four Plays*, 1985.

The Old One-Two (produced Waltham, Massachusetts, 1973; London, 1974). New York, French, 1971; London, French, 1976.

Children, suggested by the story "Goodbye, My Brother" by John Cheever (produced London, 1974; Richmond, Virginia, and New York, 1976). London, French, 1975; included in *Four Plays*, 1985.

Who Killed Richard Cory? (produced New York, 1976; Edinburgh, 1988). New York, Dramatists Play Service, 1976; revised version, as *Richard Cory* (produced Williamstown, Massachusetts, 1984), 1985.

The Middle Ages (produced Los Angeles, 1977; New York, 1982). Included in *Four Plays*, 1985.

The Wayside Motor Inn (produced New York, 1977). New York, Dramatists Play Service, 1978.

The Golden Age, suggested by the story "The Aspern Papers" by Henry James (produced London, 1981; New York, 1984). New York, Dramatists Play Service, 1985; included in *Love Letters and Two Other Plays*, 1990.

What I Did Last Summer (produced New York, 1981). New York, Dramatists Play Service, 1983; included in *Love Letters and Two Other Plays*, 1990.

The Dining Room (produced New York, 1982; London, 1983). London, French, 1982; included in *Four Plays*, 1985.

Four Plays. New York, Avon, 1985.

The Perfect Party (produced New York, 1986; London, 1987). New York, Dramatists Play Service, 1986; included in *The Cocktail Hour and Two Other Plays*, 1989.

Another Antigone (produced San Diego, 1986; New York, 1988). New York, Dramatists Play Service, 1988; included in *The Cocktail Hour and Two Other Plays*, 1989.

Sweet Sue (produced Williamstown, Massachusetts, 1986; New York, 1987). New York, Dramatists Play Service, 1987.

White Walls, in *Urban Blight* (musical revue), based on an idea by John Tillinger, music by David Shire, lyrics by Richard Maltby, Jr. (produced New York, 1988).

The Cocktail Hour (produced San Diego and New York, 1988; London, 1990). Included in *The Cocktail Hour and Two Other Plays*, 1989.

Love Letters (produced New Haven, Connecticut, 1988; New York, 1989; London, 1990). Included in *Love Letters and Two Other Plays*, 1990.

The Cocktail Hour and Two Other Plays (includes *The Perfect Party, Another Antigone*). New York, Plume, 1989.

Love Letters and Two Other Plays (includes *The Golden Age, What I Did Last Summer*). New York, Plume, 1990.

The Snow Ball, adaptation of his own novel (produced Hartford, 1991; Los Angeles, 1992; Boston, 1992).

The Old Boy (produced New York, 1991).

The Fourth Wall (produced Westport, 1992; Chicago, 1993).

Later Life (produced New York, 1993).

A Cheever Evening (produced New York, 1994).

Sylira (produced New York, 1995).

Overtime (produced San Diego, 1995; New York, 1996).

Let's Do It! (produced New Haven, 1996).

Labor Day (produced San Diego, 1998; New York, 1998).

Far East (produced Williamstown, 1998).

Nine Early Plays, 1961-1973. Lyme, New Hampshire, Smith and Kraus.

Collected Plays, 1974-1983. Lyme, New Hampshire, Smith and Kraus.

Screenplays: *The House of Mirth*, 1972; *The Hit List*, 1988; *Love Letters*, 1993; *Sylira*, 1996.

Television Play: *O Youth and Beauty*, from a story by John Cheever, 1979.

Novels

The Gospel According to Joe. New York, Harper, 1974.

Entertaining Strangers. New York, Doubleday, 1977; London, Allen Lane, 1979.

The Snow Ball. New York, Arbor House, 1985.

*

Manuscript Collection: Sterling Library, Yale University, New Haven, Connecticut.

A. R. Gurney, Jr., comments:

What attracts me about the theatre are its limitations as well as its possibilities. Indeed, its best possibilities may lie in its limitations. I am as much concerned about what to leave out as about what to put in. Offstage characters and events give a kind of pressure and resonance to what is shown onstage. In fact, offstage comprises the infinite possibilities and resources of film and television. Anyone who writes plays these days is forced to explore the very restrictions of this enduring old medium. I am particularly drawn to it because I like to write about people who themselves are beginning to stretch out and push against the walls.

(1998) Over the years I've tried to wear a tapestry of plays having to do with the world I grew up in and how it has attempted to respond to these rapidly changing times.

* * *

A. R. Gurney, Jr.'s reputation in his native United States has risen sharply, and his work also continues to be performed in Britain. This has been partly due to changes in the organization of the American theater. Gurney's first full-length play, *Scenes from American Life,* was produced at the Forum Theatre at Lincoln Center in 1971, but after the theater's regime changed, he had virtually nowhere else to go with his work, especially at a time when his main concern—WASP manners and mores—was out of fashion. But with a changing society that produced the yuppie generation, Gurney's plays, especially *The Dining Room,* which marked his breakthrough in the United States, finally found their audiences. He also formed a continuing and productive link with the Playwrights Horizons group in New York. His work continues to expand the technical skill and the fascination with theatrical flexibility that has marked it from the outset.

As the title implies, *Scenes from American Life* is a kind of montage of Americana. With a small cast that includes an onstage pianist who provides the links, it uses an almost cinematic technique of dissolving and overlapping scenes. The play builds a series on WASP life from the 1930s to the immediate future—a christening, a debutant dance, a modern encounter therapy session, and so on. Its ingenious structure at points recalls Thornton Wilder, but in its concern with archetypal American rituals and family ties, not to mention the device of an offstage character (the omnipresent Snoozer), the play indicated that Gurney had his own voice.

To a great extent offstage characters dominate Gurney's one-act plays. *The Golden Fleece* is about a suburban couple, friends of Jason and Medea, whom the audience never sees, and in the very funny *The Open Meeting* a discussion group discovers startling new relationships while awaiting the arrival of a vanished founding member. Much of the edge of the plays derives from characters who never appear. As in Greek drama, the gods remain offstage, although people are influenced by them—or, as Gurney has said, "people find their gods in other people"—and he often uses or adapts classical motifs. *The Love Course* and *The Old One-Two* are both sharp satires on liberal academic attitudes, but *The Old One-Two* develops a strain of Plautine farce as a hip young college dean discovers an unexpected relationship with his adversary, an old-fashioned professor.

Children, first produced in London during the fallow years at home for Gurney, was "suggested by" John Cheever's 1940s story "Goodbye, My Brother." Like the story, the play takes place in a New England summer home, and it has a violent confrontation between two brothers, a crucial offstage event. In structure the play is much tighter than *Scenes from American Life,* covering one Saturday on a July 4 weekend in the lives of a well-to-do WASP family on vacation. It is a deceptively simple study of the tensions caused by the eldest son, Pokey, who rules his family as an offstage presence. (He is only one of the offstage "gods" in the piece, with the dead father a kind of god to all of the characters.) In a long final speech the mother reverses her decision to remarry and talks to Pokey, finally visible as a shadow on the terrace on which the play takes place, casting him out to preserve the family. The scene is a fitting summation to the play, which subtly exposes, not least in its aptly sparse dialogue devoid of metaphor, a culture in erosion.

Who Killed Richard Cory? is an exploration revolving around a WASP lawyer who finds "liberation" in middle age. It is a more confident handling of the techniques of *Scenes from American Life,* confirming Gurney's special ability to suggest the unease under the surface of average America. *The Dining Room,* a long-running New York success later produced widely in regional theaters and abroad, is even more confident, a sign that Gurney's world is less recondite than it had seemed when he began his career. The dining room in which the play is set represents many such rooms in different places and times from the Depression to the present, and the play is both a dissection of and an elegy to a civilization in flux, a world centered around rituals and family occasions. It uses a small cast to represent a large canvas of characters—children, patriarchs, servants, and adulterous adults alike—and its stagecraft is breathtakingly assured. The play can move from sharply observed social comedy, as a Thanksgiving lunch collapses into disarray when the grandmother slides into happy senility, to a poignant late scene in which an upright dying father instructs his son in the arrangements for his funeral.

Gurney has continued to be encouragingly prolific. *What I Did Last Summer* is a touching and often very funny play centered around an adolescent boy who spends a wartime summer with his mother and family on the Canadian border and befriends a dynamic, eccentric woman while the family's father, another of Gurney's potent offstage presences, is away in the Pacific. *The Golden Age,* an updated version of Henry James's *The Aspern Papers,* faintly reminiscent of the kind of star vehicle of Gurney's childhood, was less successful. Despite an intriguing central situation—James's Juliana transformed into Isobel Hastings Hoyt, a fabled New York legend, possibly the original of Daisy in *The Great Gatsby* and the possessor of Fitzgerald manuscripts—the play never quite worked either in London or New York despite Constance Cummings and Irene Worth, respectively. This was mainly because of Gurney's inability to create a satisfactory character for his variation on James's investigative scholar.

But Gurney was quickly back to form with both *Another Antigone,* a full-length return to the cultural clash of the academic world of his one-act plays, and *The Perfect Party,* a successful example of that rarity, an American artificial comedy of manners. The latter is set in the house of a college professor hosting what he plans as the perfect party reflecting late 20th-century American life, the event to be reviewed by a critic from "a leading New York newspaper." The play spirals into Wildean comedy as the professor, trying to keep the beautiful critic's interest, finds himself embroiled in a plot with distinct echoes of *The Importance of Being Earnest.*

Gurney also adapted his novel *The Snow Ball* for the stage, an ambitious play with a large cast that is centered around the final revival of the tradition of the Snow Ball, a winter dance in Buffalo, and that incorporates several scenes involving ballroom dancing. The play traces various characters across several decades, with the central pair consisting of the socially different Jack and the rich girl Kitty, champion dancers whose lives go separate ways. Gurney again subtly conveys the changes in a city and a culture.

Gurney's autobiographical *The Cocktail Hour* is a social comedy in the Philip Barry tradition that tells of a playwright's return to his family in Buffalo to tell them about his new play. To some consternation, the play is based on the family, and the visit opens up old resentments and secrets. Gurney had an extraordinary runaway success with *Love Letters,* a simple two-handed piece in which actors seated at a desk read letters over a 40-year period between a WASP couple, a buttoned-up man with political leanings and a more bohemian, mixed-up woman. Once again, in this understated play Gurney manages to cover a lot of ground as he traces the pair's relationship, beginning with formal notes after childhood parties and following them through marriages, her divorce and love affairs, and their own brief affair to her death. The play was not successful in England, where misconceived casting made the piece seem sentimentally trite.

Gurney charted new ground in *The Old Boy,* an unsettling piece that handles its time shifts with considerable skill. In the play a WASP politician revisits his old private school and has to face the truth, which might compromise his career ambitions, that the man who was his roommate has died of AIDS. Gurney's handling of WASP traditions and mores is as subtle as ever, but there is a new astringency in the play. Gurney reworked it extensively following its first production in New York at Playwrights Horizons, which has continued to be a welcoming home for his work.

Playwrights Horizons and similar small but vibrant New York theaters, the Manhattan Theatre Club included, have continued to be hospitable to Gurney, although the 1990s have been an oddly checkered decade for him. Playwrights Horizons' production of his beautifully crafted and ingenious mosaic of episodes from Cheever's stories in *A Cheever Evening* was as devoted and technically superb as its treatment of *Later Life,* a touching, rueful piece set at a smart party in a Boston high-rise apartment, during which a mysterious woman emerges out of the past of Austin, one of Gurney's best quintessential WASP heroes. The play stretches Gurney's delight in playing with the resources of the theater, an aspect of his work that clearly strikes a chord with the similarly technically adventurous Alan Ayckbourn, who has directed both *The Dining Room* and *Later Life* at his Scarborough Theatre. All of the many other guests at the party are played by only two actors, providing virtuoso showcases without overly dominating the central couple's story.

Gurney's *The Fourth Wall,* in a more Pirandellian vein, was a less successful experiment. *Sylvia,* a buoyant jeu d'esprit that puts a smart spin on the eternal triangle (a man, his wife, and, in this instance, a stray Manhattan mutt—played by an actress—with which the husband becomes obsessed) was first produced at Manhattan Theatre Club. It made potent use of popular music—Cole Porter—also using one of the actors to play a variety of wildly contrasting roles, including one in drag, a familiar Gurney device here given new twists. Unfortunately, *Sylvia* continued Gurney's unhappy relationship with the London theater. In New York its particular tone—very wry, very *New Yorker*—was superbly handled, and the play breathed the right air. In London, given a slap-up West End production (London's lack of a real equivalent to off-Broadway has been tricky for writers such as Gurney, Tina Howe, and Terrence McNally), it feel foul of the London critics and closed remarkably quickly.

—Alan Strachan

GURR, Michael

Nationality: Australian. **Born:** Melbourne, 20 October 1961. **Education:** Melbourne high school; National Theatre Drama School. **Career:** Playwright-in-residence, Melbourne Theatre Company, 1982; Artistic Counsel, Playbox theatre, Melbourne, 1993-95. **Awards:** Victorian Premier's Literary award for drama, 1993, for *Sex Diary of an Infidel,* 1997, for *Jerusalem*; Green Room award for Best Play, 1992, for *Sex Diary of an Infidel*, 1996, for *Jerusalem*; NSW State Literary award for drama. **Agent:** Curtis Brown Pty. Ltd., P.O. Box 19, Paddington, 2021 NSW, Australia.

Publications

Plays

Magnetic North (produced Melbourne, 1982). Montmorency, Victoria, Yackandandah, 1982.
A Pair of Claws (produced Melbourne, 1982). Montmorency, Victoria, Yackandandah, 1983.
Dead to the World (produced Melbourne, 1986). Montmorency, Victoira, Yackandandah, 1986.
Worlds Apart (produced Melbourne, 1987).
These Days (produced Melbourne, 1988).
The Hundred Year Ambush (produced Melbourne, 1990).
Sex Diary of an Infidel (produced Melbourne, 1992). Sydney, Currency Press, 1992.
Desirelines (produced Melbourne, 1993).
Underwear, Perfume, and Crash Helmet (produced Melbourne, 1994). Sydney, Currency Press, 1994.
Jerusalem (produced Melbourne, 1996). Sydney, Currency Press, 1996.
Shark Fin Soup (produced Melbourne, 1998).

Screenplay: *Departure,* 1986.

Radio Play: *World's Apart,* 1986.

Television Play: *Emmett Stone,* 1984.

*

Critical Studies: "Occidental (Sex) Tourists: Michael Gurr's *Sex Diary of an Infidel*" by Helen Gilbert, in *Australasian Drama Studies,* October 1994, pp. 177-88; "Pulling the Rug out from Under Your Feet: An Interview with Michael Gurr" by Helen Gilbert and Melinda Mawson, in *Australasian Drama Studies*, April 1995, pp. 22-35.

* * *

The Melbourne playwright Michael Gurr is obsessed with actions and the consequences of those actions. Nina, the straight-talking, 30-something doctor in his 1996 play *Jerusalem* could be speaking for the playwright when she asserts, "I don't believe that justice is something you light a candle for. It's just the way you behave." Gurr's plays present the spectator with a broad tapestry of characters whose lives are inextricably linked through the moral choices made by each individual. As the playwright observed in a 1994 interview, "I think it's about 'how do you live' and 'what do you live by?'" Gurr's best-known plays of the 1990s—*Sex Diary of an Infidel; Underwear, Perfume and Crash Helmet;* and *Jerusalem*—show us a series of deeply flawed, sometimes well-meaning, but just as often malevolent or confused characters who collide with one another in a series of short, rigorously constructed scenes that reach a coda with the jury still out.

Sex Diary of an Infidel (1991) placed Gurr squarely on the map of Australian theater, in part owing to the play's topical concern with sexual imperialism in Asia. Australian sex tourism in the Philippines, however, is merely the structural mechanism for a far richer exploration into the psychosocial and sexual exchanges among an award-winning female journalist with a black heart, an Australian pimp trading in Filipino flesh, a male photographer with conflicted sexual feelings, and a young Filipino transsexual named Toni who serves as the play's moral center. Toni ultimately chooses to fight against economic, cultural, and sexual imperialism, while each of the Australians profit in various ways from their economic and sexual exchanges with the Filipino people.

Gurr's social conscience and his thematic concerns are fed by the need to expose the values that people choose to live by. Thus, his seeming preoccupation with Australian party politics in *Underwear, Perfume and Crash Helmet* and in *Jerusalem* serves as a backdrop for the larger issue of moral choice. Though clearly no fan of Australia's conservative Liberals, who took over from the Labor government in 1996, his characterization of Labor backbencher Cameron Rickman in *Jerusalem* suggests that, while the Liberals may have given over choice to the forces of the global marketplace, Labor long ago stopped communicating with a generation of young people, thus sealing their fate as a minority party. Similarly, in his 1990 play *The Hundred Year Ambush,* Japanese property developers and Australians worshiping at the altar of market forces collude when people stop taking responsibility for their actions. While politics and social justice are central concerns of the playwright, a play's outcome is always determined by what individuals do or do not believe in.

Stylistically, Gurr's best-known work is characterized by a striking and skillful use of polyphony in the construction of dialogue and action. Characters collide through their actions, and the connections between them are underscored in scenes in which multiple characters are simultaneously present in different areas of the stage. Conversations taking place in "real" stage time, tape-recorded conversations, and the greetings and messages left on answering machines overlap and intertwine, connecting characters both concretely and metaphorically as they implicate themselves, lie, confess, and insinuate themselves into one another's lives.

Gurr believes that "it's the mess of humanity that's attractive." Indeed, one of Gurr's greatest achievements is his uncanny ability to create despicable characters who are as utterly fascinating and irresistible to watch as a train wreck. The character of Patrick in his play *Underwear, Perfume and Crash Helmet* serves as the rudderless, amoral motivating force behind many of the key actions that drive the play forward. At one point the clever, glib, and uncontainable Patrick urges his malleable friend Nicholas to join him in raping a young homeless woman, posing the key question "What's stopping you?" As Gurr asserted in a 1994 interview, "If you don't find what you believe in, then you're vulnerable to any articulate thug who shows up on your doorstep, in his [Nicholas's] case in the form of Patrick. So they end up raping the homeless girl because 'why not?'" Gurr's contribution to Australian theater is his ability to make spectators interested in the "mess of humanity" and, in the process, to make them better able to question and evaluate their own moral choices.

—William Peterson

H

HAIRE, Wilson John

Nationality: British. **Born:** Belfast, Northern Ireland, 6 April 1932. **Education:** Clontonacally Elementary School, Carryduff, County Down, 1939-46. **Family:** Married 1) Rita Lenson in 1955 (marriage dissolved), five children; 2) Sheila Fitz-Jones in 1974 (marriage dissolved); 3) Karen Mendelsohn in 1979 (marriage dissolved). **Career:** Actor, Unity Theatre, London, 1962-67; co-director, Camden Group Theatre, London, 1967-71; resident dramatist, Royal Court Theatre, London, 1974; resident dramatist, Lyric Theatre, Belfast, 1976. **Awards:** George Devine award, 1972; *Evening Standard* award, 1973; Thames Television award, 1974; Leverhulme fellowship, 1976. **Address:** 61 Lulot Gardens, London N19 5TS, England.

PUBLICATIONS

Plays

The Clockin' Hen (produced London, 1968).
The Diamond, Bone and Hammer; and Along the Sloughs of Ulster (produced London, 1969).
Within Two Shadows (produced London, 1972; New York, 1974). Published in *Scripts 9* (New York), September 1972; published separately, London, Davis Poynter, 1973.
Bloom of the Diamond Stone (produced Dublin, 1973). London, Pluto Press, 1979.
Echoes from a Concrete Canyon (produced London, 1975).
Lost Worlds: Newsflash, Wedding Breakfast, Roost (produced London, 1978). London, Heinemann, 1978.
Worlds Apart, with J. P. Dylan (produced Glasgow, 1981).

Television Plays: *Letter from a Soldier*, 1975; *The Dandelion Clock*, 1975.

*

Wilson John Haire comments:

(1988) I first began writing about Northern Ireland back in 1960. I wrote three short stories for a monthly paper called the *Irish Democrat*. My first story was called "Refuge from the Tick-Man" and I went under the pen name of "Fenian." "Fenian" is a derogatory name for Catholic in Northern Ireland. When I began writing the story of how my family fled the city of Belfast for the countryside to escape the debt collectors I became proud of that name. To me it meant someone who resists corruption and sectarian bullying. The editor of the paper persuaded me to use my real name for my second story, "The Screening"—a teenage boy, pretending to be a Protestant, survives interrogation and taunts about Catholicism and gets the job for which he is applying. The third story was "The Beg." "Beg" is bag or sack in Ulster dialect. The local shipyard sheds a quarter of its workers, and the story is told through the eyes of an apprentice carpenter.

I took to writing drama in 1968 with a one-act play *The Clockin' Hen.* A broody hen hatches out her eggs under a darkening sky—in 1968 the Reverend Paisley attempts to lead a demonstration, with protection, through a Catholic ghetto and is resisted. A Catholic and Protestant are put on trial. The Catholic sees no hope of justice in a court that openly loathes him.

After that I wrote *The Diamond, Bone and Hammer; and Along the Sloughs of Ulster.* It is a sort of "Fear and Misery in the Third Reich." This play sequence was produced at the Hampstead Theatre, and later transfered to the Unity Theatre. This was not a professional production, and no reviewer appeared except for D.A.N. Jones of the *Listener*, who gave it an intelligent review. It was this one and only review that made me want to go on writing.

On opening night, Friday, 8 August 1969, the Bogside riots began, and Ulster became a topic of conversation in London. On 12 April 1972 *Within Two Shadows* opened at the Royal Court Theatre. The media said it was the first play on the Ulster crisis to open in London. I come from a parentage of both Catholic and Protestant. I saw this as the "two shadows" in my life, and I told the tale from within the family.

* * *

Wilson John Haire, born in the Shankill Road area of Belfast, the son of a Catholic mother and a Protestant father, has drawn much of the background material for his plays from that stark area of the tortured city. Even when the actual turmoil of Northern Ireland is not part of a play, as in *Echoes from a Concrete Canyon,* one can still feel the claustrophobic atmosphere of an unfriendly town beyond the walls of a lonely flat. Four of Haire's plays, however, are set against the background of sectarian violence, bigotry, and loneliness. He conveys the tragedy of Ulster more directly and vividly than any other contemporary playwright, drawing upon memories that reach far back into his childhood.

Haire is not a polemical writer. Political ideas interest him, particularly as part of the environments from which they come, but he is concerned more with the nature and extent of Ulster's suffering than with easy moralizing. His best-known play, *Within Two Shadows,* is also the most autobiographical. It deals with a working-class Belfast family, dog-eared with poverty and torn apart by prejudices that they try to exclude but that gradually eat into their lives. In the play the mother is a Protestant, the father a Catholic, and we feel that both at some time in their lives have made conscientious efforts to leap over the religious barriers dividing them. But the pressure of events, the opinions of their neighbors, and the growing violence are too much for them. They try to stay away from conflict, if only to protect their children, but the children, who are now teenagers, are growing up and are quick to enter into the rivalries as part of their puppy play, but with fangs bared.

In *Bloom of the Diamond Stone* Haire shows what could almost have been the beginnings of that marriage, a Romeo-and-Juliet love affair in which a young couple from opposite sides fall in love and then have to battle against their families, the restrictions set at work, and the rigid outlooks of their former friends. In both plays Haire conveys a sense of inner honesty and goodness corrupted by circumstance. In this way he can be an optimistic writer. His characters are not vicious in themselves but are only made so by a historical backlog of revenge, fear, and defensiveness. To that extent Ulster's torment seems to be the result of a curable mixture of follies rather than the dark nightmare of the soul as other dramatists, including David Rudkin, have sometimes presented it. The British soldier searching for a "terrorist" in *Bloom of the Diamond Stone* is shown to be a likable human being until his fears and his job prompt him to be otherwise.

But the follies extend in all directions. They are sometimes rooted in sheer lack of understanding of the awfulness of the situation. In his first television play, *Letter from a Soldier,* Haire merely describes a soldier's effort to make his family in England understand what a tour of duty in Ulster is like. His second, *The Dandelion Clock,* concerns the particular problems facing a young girl growing up in Belfast. What sort of future can she plan for herself? The problems, however, are not just ones of comprehension. They also stem from a social organization that is out of touch with the lives people lead.

The Clockin' Hen, Haire's first stage play, concerns a court case in which two shipyard workers of different religions are put on trial following a Paisleyite demonstration in 1966. How do they react to the presence of the law? Do they regard law in any meaningful sense? And if they do not, where does an Ulsterman go? "Emotionally," Haire has said, "I am a Catholic, but intellectually I am a Protestant." The conflict is reflected in his plays. Haire perceives the need for a formal social order, but he is sympathetic to the resentments caused by the existing order. To be out of touch with society, to defy, ignore, or simply have an ingrained distrust of the ordering forces that are there, is equivalent to dropping out. Haire's sympathy with Irish dropouts, tramps, and drunkards is shown in *The Latchicoes of Fort Camden*, an unperformed play set in a London doss-house.

Haire's skill as a dramatist reveals the strength and weaknesses of someone who chooses subjects so close to his personal experience. He can write vigorously and directly and usually naturalistically, but he does so without the detachment needed to ensure that his plays have a clear form and that each point is made dramatically and concisely. Although he has indicated an intention to break away from his concentration on Northern Ireland, in *Echoes from a Concrete Canyon,* which concerns the mental breakdown of a woman estranged from her husband and living with her daughter in a block of flats, the clotted verbosity that often accompanies autobiography is still present. Lightening touches of humor are rare, and the frequent poeticisms add heaviness rather than variety to the language.

Haire might gain maturity as a dramatist by becoming less dependent on his background, but at the same time he might also lose the force of reality that adds power to his Ulster plays. He speaks as a witness and a survivor of a continuing drama of stupidity, cruelty, and resentment. That has been his main role, and it is not an insignificant one in contemporary British theater.

—John Elsom

HALE, John

Nationality: British. **Born:** Woolwich, Kent, 5 February 1926. **Education:** Army schools in Egypt, Ceylon, and Malta; Borden Grammar School, Sittingbourne, Kent; Royal Naval College, Greenwich. **Military Service:** Served in the Fleet Air Army, 1941-51: boy apprentice to petty officer, later commissioned. **Family:** Married Valerie June Bryan in 1950; one son and one daughter. **Career:** Stage hand, stage manager, and electrician, in variety, touring, and repertory companies, 1952-55; founder, and artistic director, Lincoln Theatre, 1955-58; artistic director, Arts Theatre, Ipswich, 1958-59 and Bristol Old Vic, 1959-61; freelance director, 1961-64; member of the Board of Governors, 1963-71, associate artistic director, 1968-71, and resident playwright, 1975-76, Greenwich Theatre, London. Freelance writer and director, 1964—. **Awards:** Golden Globe award, 1970; Royal Television Society award, for *Children of the North,* 1992. **Agent:** (for plays and screenplays) The Agency, 24-32 Pottery Lane, Holland Park, London W11 4LZ, England; (for novels) Aitken and Stone Ltd., 29 Fernshaw Road, London SW10 0TG, England.

Publications

Plays

The Black Swan Winter (as *Smile Boys, That's the Style*, produced Glasgow, 1968; as *The Black Swan Winter*, also director: produced London, 1969). Published in *Plays of the Year 37*, London, Elek, 1970.
It's All in the Mind (also director: produced London, 1968).
Spithead (also director: produced London, 1969). Published in *Plays of the Year 38*, London, Elek, 1971.
Here Is the News (produced Beaford, Devon, 1970).
Lorna and Ted (also director: produced London, 1970).
Decibels (produced Liverpool, 1971). Published in *Prompt Three*, edited by Alan Durband, London, Hutchinson, 1976.
The Lion's Cub (televised 1971). Published in *Elizabeth R*, edited by J.C. Trewin, London, Elek, 1971.
In Memory of. . . Carmen Miranda (also director: produced London, 1975).
Love's Old Sweet Song (also director: produced London, 1976).
The Case of David Anderson, Q.C. (produced Manchester and Edinburgh, 1980; London, 1981).

Screenplays: *The Mind of Mr. Soames*, with Edward Simpson, 1969; *Anne of the Thousand Days*, with Bridget Boland, 1970; *Mary Queen of Scots*, 1972.

Radio Writing: *Micah Clarke* series, 1966.

Television Plays: *The Rules That Jack Made*, 1965; *The Noise Stopped*, 1966; *Light the Blue Touch Paper*, 1966; *Thirteen Against Fate* series, 1966; *Samson and Delilah, Strike Pay*, and *Her Turn*, all from short stories by D.H. Lawrence, 1966-67; *The Queen's Traitor* (5 parts), 1967; *Retreat*, 1968; *The Picnic*, 1969; *The Distracted Preacher*, 1969; *The Lion's Cub*, in *Elizabeth R* series, 1971; *The Bristol Entertainment*, 1971; *Anywhere But England*, 1972; *Ego Hugo: A Romantic Entertainment*, 1973; *Lorna and Ted*, 1973; *The Brotherhood*, 1975; *An Impeccable Elopement*, 1975; *Goodbye America*, 1976; *The Grudge Fight*, from his own novel, 1981; *The Whistle Blower,* 1986; *Children of the North*, 1991; *Nostromo,* adaptation of the Joseph Conrad novel (4 part, 6 hour film for television), 1997.

Novels

Kissed the Girls and Made Them Cry. London, Collins, 1963; Englewood Cliffs, New Jersey, Prentice Hall, 1966.

The Grudge Fight. London, Collins, 1964; Englewood Cliffs, New Jersey, Prentice Hall, 1967.
A Fool at the Feast. London, Collins, 1966.
The Paradise Man. London, Rapp and Whiting, and Indianapolis, Bobbs Merrill, 1969.
Mary, Queen of Scots (novelization of screenplay). London, Pan, 1972.
The Fort. London, Quartet, 1973.
The Love School. London, Pan, 1974; New York, St. Martin's Press, 1975.
Lovers and Heretics. London, Gollancz, 1976.
The Whistle Blower. London, Cape, 1984; New York, Atheneum, 1985.

*

Theatrical Activities:
Director: **Plays**—About 150 plays in Lincoln, Ipswich, Bristol and elsewhere, including several of his own plays, and *An Enemy of the People* by Arthur Miller, Lincoln, 1958; *Cyrano de Bergerac* by Edmond Rostand, Bristol, 1959; *The Merry Wives of Windsor*, London, 1959; *The Tinker* by Laurence Dobie and Robert Sloman, Bristol and London, 1960; *The Rehearsal* by Anouilh, Bristol and London, 1961; *The Killer* by Ionesco, Bristol, 1961; *Sappho* by Lawrence Durrell, Edinburgh, 1961; *Mother Courage* by Brecht, Hiram, Ohio, 1966. **Television**—About 16 plays, 1961-64, including *The Fruit at the Bottom of the Bowl* by Ray Bradbury, and *Drill Pig* by Charles Wood; *The Rules That Jack Made*, 1965. **Recordings**—13 Shakespeare plays, including *The Taming of the Shrew*, *Richard II*, and *Henry V*, FCM Productions.

John Hale comments:
I am both a playwright and a novelist. The plays and novels are written alternately; I buy the time with screenplays for television and films. If I have anything to say only part of it is in the plays: all of it, whatever it is, is in the plays and the novels taken together.

* * *

As a playwright John Hale seems to share what is a common quality of actors, the ability to take up a theme, immerse himself in it, work it out, and leave it. It can be recognized that the same actor is performing, if one's concern is to look for him, yet the characters are different creations. Whereas other writers may work through and within an obsession, in some cases (Strindberg and Tennessee Williams) becoming trapped by it so that their plays are like a series of studies of a vast central object too large to be contained in any one work, Hale seems to make a fresh start in each case. It is as if he were saying: "Here is my subject. I give myself to it. I use this particular piece of my own experience for it. I build it from inside, and shape it from the outside. I have made a play. I move on."

The Black Swan Winter, Hale's first stage play, was written after his own father's death and uses memories of his father and himself. In a later play, *Love's Old Sweet Song,* Hale and his father appear again along with his grandfather, but they appear as supporting characters in what seems to be primarily an examination of two appalling castrating women, a mother and daughter jointly devoted to the destruction of all of the men around them. His novel *The Grudge Fight* used his experiences in the navy, and when he wanted to return to the subject in *Spithead,* he used instead the secondary experience of history. *It's All in the Mind* is Hale's only excursion into politics, *Lorna and Ted* the only one into Suffolk, and his one-act monologue *In Memory of . . . Carmen Miranda* the only one into Samuel Beckett country, which is just as well since he seems not to be happy there.

Yet there is a moral being, Hale himself, who made all of this work, even though he is modest as well as moral and requires that one search for him. *Kissed the Girls and Made Them Cry, The Black Swan Winter,* and *Love's Old Sweet Song* all share a theme, the attempt to get back into one's past and to find out what went wrong. The shadow of his father, a warrant officer in the army, lies upon his work and is shown in Hale's concern for fairness and his admiration of discipline, most of all self-discipline. If Forster can be boiled down to "only connect," then Hale's two words are "soldier on." Fairness for him means most of all fairness to other people, a decent recognition of the right to difference, but it can also mean, as in *Lorna and Ted,* fairness to oneself, an assertion of one's own rights, and an acceptance of responsibility.

Hale's plays are well made in the manner of a play by Shakespeare or, nowadays common, a television play, with a number of scenes running into each other and a fragmented set. They are thoughtful, observed, humane, and only rarely self-indulgent. Their fault, which is commonly found in company with these virtues, is an occasional overexplicitness. Like Priestley's, Hale's characters too often say what they should only mean, though this is not a fault of the two-hander *Lorna and Ted,* which is his most interesting play. He seems always to have been happiest when writing duologues since too many characters at once appear to worry him. In this play, with only a nonspeaking voluptuous lady in support, his construction has been most at ease, most relaxed, least stiff.

—John Bowen

HALL, Roger (Leighton)

Nationality: New Zealander. **Born:** England, 17 January 1939. **Education:** University College School, London, 1952-55; Victoria University, Wellington, 1963-68, M.A. (honours). **Family:** Married Mavis Dianne Sturm in 1968; one daughter and one son. **Career:** Worked in insurance, as a wine waiter, in factories, and as a teacher before becoming a freelance writer and editor. Teaching fellow, University of Otago, Dunedin, 1979-91; guest artist, New Mexico State University, Las Cruces, 1983. **Awards:** Arts Council of New Zealand travel grant, 1975; Robert Burns fellowship, University of Otago, 1977, 1978; Turnovsky Arts award, 1987; Queen's Service Order (Q.S.O.), 1987; Commemoration medal, 1990. **Agent:** Casarotto Ramsay Ltd., National House, 60-66 Wardour Street, London W1V 3HP, England; or, Playmarket, P.O. Box 9767, Wellington, New Zealand.

Publications

Plays

Glide Time (produced Wellington, 1976; as *Roll On, Friday*, produced Southampton, 1985). Wellington, Victoria University Press, 1978.

Middle-Age Spread (produced Wellington, 1977; London, 1979). Wellington, Victoria University Press, 1978; London, French, 1980.
State of the Play (produced Wellington, 1978). Wellington, Victoria University Press, 1979.
Cinderella (produced Auckland, 1978).
Robin Hood (produced Auckland, 1979).
Prisoners of Mother England (produced Dunedin, 1979). Wellington, Playmarket, 1980.
Fifty-Fifty (produced Auckland, 1981). Wellington, Victoria University Press, 1982.
The Rose (produced Auckland, 1981).
The Quiz (broadcast 1982; produced Dunedin, 1983). Published in *On Stage 1*, edited by David Dowling, Auckland, Longman Paul, 1983.
Hot Water (produced Auckland, 1982). Wellington, Victoria University Press, 1983.
Footrot Flats, music by Philip Norman, lyrics by A.K. Grant, based on works by Murray Ball (produced Christchurch, 1983). Wellington, Playmarket, 1984.
Multiple Choice (produced Las Cruces, New Mexico, 1983; Guildford, Surrey, 1984).
Dream of Sussex Downs (produced Auckland, 1986).
Love Off the Shelf, music by Philip Norman, lyrics by Hall and A.K. Grant (produced Dunedin, 1986; Southampton, 1988).
The Hansard Show, songs by Nigel Eastgate and John Drummond (produced Wellington, 1986).
The Share Club (produced Dunedin, 1987).
After the Crash (produced Dunedin, 1988).
Mr. Punch (produced Dunedin, 1989).
You Must Be Crazy (produced Wellington, 1989).
Conjugal Rites (produced Palmerston North and Watford, Hertfordshire, 1990).
Making It Big, music by Philip Norman (produced Dunedin, 1991).
By Degrees (produced Dunedin, 1993).
Market Forces (produced Wellington, 1995).
Social Climbers (produced Dunedin, 1995).
C'mon Black (produced Dunedin, 1996).
Dirty Weekends, with music and lyrics by Philip Norman (produced Dunedin, 1998).

Radio Plays: *Gliding On* series, 1977-80; *Hark, Hark, The Harp!*, 1981; *Last Summer*, 1981; *The Quiz*, 1982; *Conjugal Rites* series, 1991; *The Dream Factory*, 1992; *By Degrees* series, 1992.

Television Plays: *Clean Up*, 1972; *The Bach*, 1974; *Some People Get All the Luck*, 1974; *The Reward*, 1974; *Gliding On* series, 1982-86; and series episodes for *In View of the Circumstances*, 1970-71, *Pukemanu*, 1972, *Buck House*, 1974, and *Neighbourhood Watch*, 1991; *Conjugal Rites*, 1993; *Market Forces* series, 1998.

Other

Captain Scrimshaw in Space (for children). Adelaide, Rigby, 1979; London, Arnold, 1981.
How the Crab Got a Hard Back, adaptation of a West Indian folktale (for children). Adelaide, Rigby, 1979; London, Arnold, 1981.
Sam, Max, and Harold Meet Dracula (for children). Wellington, Nelson, Price, 1990.
Penguin Trouble (for children). Wellington, Nelson Price, 1991.
My Aunt Mary Went Shopping (for children). Auckland, Ashton Scholastic, 1991.
The Theatre Writers' Guide–Hot Tips for Good Scripts. Wellington, Playmarket, 1998.

*

Manuscript Collections: Alexander Turnbull Library, Wellington; Hocken Library, University of Otago, Dunedin.

* * *

Within the network of community theaters, the intimate professional theaters situated near the center of each of New Zealand's major cities, the writing of Roger Hall has been of organic importance. His works reflect their growth, their economic constraints, and especially their audience composition. His earliest theater writing, which were satirical revues, dates back to the foundation period of the first of these groups, and his first major success, *Glide Time,* marked the point at which most of them had gathered sufficient momentum to regard locally written scripts as a possible commercial venture. *Glide Time's* extended seasons throughout the country had a major unifying effect on the community theaters, as well as creating a sense of a national drama audience. Hall's farces of the late 1980s—*The Share Club, After the Crash,* and the television spin-off *Neighbourhood* Watch—used the same cluster of characters from the world of spare-time stock market punters. This seemed precisely to correlate with the world of the audiences the theaters were then drawing, one that was substantially different from the students who queued up for the early satirical revues.

Hall's ability to read his dominant audience has always been astute, as has been his careful development of his craft without betraying that audience's expectations and tolerances. The satirical vein has never completely left his work, but neither has he ever overstepped his audience's inclination to laugh at itself. With *Glide Time,* the satirical target was easy. Setting the satire on the public service in the capital, and premiering it there, meant easy recognition of the absurdities of the daily battle against the institutional system. In *Middle-Age Spread* the institution is marriage, but the main character's gesture of anarchy, a solitary case of marital infidelity, foreshadowed elements of the domestic farce that would be the mode of works such as *Hot Water* and *Conjugal Rites.* Even in the wording of the titles—"glide" and "spread"—there was embedded the idea of escapism or beating the system and the audience's vicarious complicity.

An inclination to move toward the more serious dramatic statement has been apparent intermittently in Hall's work, from an attempt at psychoanalytical complexity in *State of the Play,* about a playwriting class, to *The Rose,* inspired by the 1981 Springbok rugby tour, and *Multiple Choice,* a play about education, Hall's own early career. But even in *Glide Time* there is a filament of seriousness and poignancy in the case of a migrant for whom the office is a partial refuge from a domestic world that is getting progressively bleaker in the face of cultural displacement. He developed this motif into a full-length work, *Prisoners of Mother England,* using mainly the revue techniques of his apprenticeship. The title characters are 8 of the 1,100 assisted migrants on the *Captain Cook,* sailing to New Zealand with visions of walking the Milford Track, big game fishing, and a land of opportunity and cheap living with people who are "more English than the English." The play shows the collapse of these delusions within the varyingly successful process of assimilation, but the scrapbook effect of the 59 short scenes and the blatantly stereotypical presentation of many New Zealand characters through only five actors emphasize that this is how the migrants saw, and were partially encouraged to see, them. The play, which is broadly autobiographical, frankly acknowledges the migrant perspective that informs much of Hall's best satire. One further treatment of the migration theme was a critical success but had a limited stage history. *Dream of Sussex Downs* returned to a more conventional form, fuller characterization, and a somber Chekhovian tone derived from *Three Sisters*.

Throughout this period radio and television series that had been developed from *Glide Time* continued, and with *Footrot Flats,* from a popular New Zealand cartoon strip, Hall emerged as a writer of musicals. He continued with *Love off the Shelf,* a musical parody of Mills and Boon, and *The Hansard Show,* ingeniously derived from New Zealand's parliamentary archives and ranging from the grotesque to the compassionate in its glimpses of the country's emergent national identity through the lenses of politics. Since he became commercially successful, Hall has continued to be actively supportive of innovative work by younger playwrights, especially through workshops and his playwriting course at the University of Otago.

Hall is best known internationally for the long London run of *Middle-Age Spread,* which encouraged him to script another play for the West End, *Fifty-Fifty.* Although there is relatively little satire in the latter play, its strength lies in two areas in which some critics have found Hall defective: female characterization and intergenerational dynamics. The central character is an unorganized, unassertive middle-aged failure who is dividing up matrimonial property in the face of divorce. He encounters his adult children, including a son whose Ph.D. stands as a barrier to employment, and an assertively independent woman who is moving into his flat. The play's engagingly equivocal mood derives from the fragmentation of precisely the values that were a source of complacency to the characters of *Middle-Age Spread.*

—Howard McNaughton

HALL, Willis and Keith (Spencer) Waterhouse

HALL, Willis. Nationality: British. **Born:** Leeds, Yorkshire, 6 April 1929. **Education:** Cockburn High School, Leeds. **Military Service:** National Service 1947-52: radio playwright for the Chinese Schools Department of Radio Malaya. **Family:** Married 1) the actress Jill Bennett in 1962 (marriage dissolved 1965); 2) Dorothy Kingsmill-Lunn (marriage dissolved); 3) Valerie Shute in 1973; four sons. **Career:** Writer of children's fiction, plays, and screenplays. Lives in Ilkley, West Yorkshire. **Awards:** *Evening Standard* award, 1959; BAFTA award, 1988. **Agent:** c/o Alexandra Cann Representation, 337 Fulham Road, London SW10 5TW, England.

WATERHOUSE, Keith (Spencer). Pseudonyms: Herald Froy and Lee Gibb. **Nationality:** British. **Born:** Leeds, Yorkshire, 6 February 1929. **Education:** Osmondthorpe Council Schools, Leeds. **Military Service:** Served in the Royal Air Force. **Family:** Married 1) Joan Foster in 1951 (divorced 1968), one son and two daughters; 2) Stella Bingham (divorced 1989). **Career:** Freelance journalist and writer in Leeds and London, 1950—; columnist, *Daily Mirror*, 1970-86, and *Daily Mail,* 1986—, both London. Member, Kingman Committee on Teaching of English Language, 1987-88. **Awards:** Recipient (for journalism): Granada award, 1970, and special award, 1982; IPC award, 1970, 1973; British Press award, 1978; *Evening Standard* award, for play, 1991. Honorary fellow, Leeds Polytechnic. **Member:** Fellow, Royal Society of Literature. **Agent:** London Management, 235 Regent Street, London W1A 2JT. **Address:** 29 Kenway Road, London, S.W.5, England.

Publications

Plays

Billy Liar, adaptation of the novel by Waterhouse (produced London, 1960; Los Angeles and New York, 1963). London, Joseph, 1960; New York, Norton, 1961.

Celebration: The Wedding and The Funeral (produced Nottingham and London, 1961). London, Joseph, 1961.

England, Our England, music by Dudley Moore (produced London, 1962). London, Evans, 1964.

Squat Betty (produced London, 1962; New York, 1964). With *The Sponge Room*, London, Evans, 1963.

The Sponge Room (produced Nottingham and London, 1962; New York, 1964). With *Squat Betty*, London, Evans, 1963; in *Modern Short Plays from Broadway and London*, edited by Stanley Richards, New York, Random House, 1969.

All Things Bright and Beautiful (produced Bristol and London, 1962). London, Joseph, 1963.

The Sponge Room, and Squat Betty. London, Evans, 1963.

Come Laughing Home (as *They Called the Bastard Stephen*, produced Bristol, 1964; as *Come Laughing Home*, produced Wimbledon, 1965). London, Evans, 1965.

Say Who You Are (produced Guildford, Surrey, and London, 1965). London, Evans, 1966; as *Help Stamp Out Marriage* (produced New York, 1966), New York, French, 1966.

Joey, Joey, music by Ron Moody (produced Manchester and London, 1966).

Whoops-a-Daisy (produced Nottingham, 1968). London, French, 1978.

Children's Day (produced Edinburgh and London, 1969). London, French, 1975.

Who's Who (produced Coventry, 1971; London, 1973). London, French, 1974.

Saturday, Sunday, Monday, adaptation of a play by Eduardo De Filippo (produced London, 1973; New York, 1974). London, Heinemann, 1974.

The Card, music and lyrics by Tony Hatch and Jackie Trent, adaptation of the novel by Arnold Bennett (produced Bristol and London, 1973).

Filumena, adaptation of a play by Eduardo De Filippo (produced London, 1977; New York, 1980). London, Heinemann, 1978.

Worzel Gummidge (for children), music by Denis King, adaptation of stories by Barbara Euphan Todd (produced Birmingham, 1980; London, 1981). London, French, 1984.

Lost Empires, music by Denis King, adaptation of the novel by J.B. Priestley (produced Darlington, County Durham, 1985).

Budgie, music by Mort Shuman, lyrics by Don Black (produced London, 1988).

Screenplays: *Whistle Down the Wind*, 1961; *The Valiant*, 1962; *A Kind of Loving*, 1963; *Billy Liar*, 1963; *West Eleven*, 1963; *Man in the Middle*, 1963; *Pretty Polly* (*A Matter of Innocence*), 1967; *Lock Up Your Daughters*, 1969.

Television Plays: *Happy Moorings*, 1963; *How Many Angels*, 1964; *Inside George Webley* series, 1968; *Queenie's Castle* series, 1970; *Budgie* series, 1971-72; *The Upper Crusts* series, 1973; *Three's Company* series, 1973; *By Endeavour Alone*, 1973; *Briefer Encounter*, 1977; *Public Lives*, 1977; *Worzel Gummidge* series, from stories by Barbara Euphan Todd, 1979; *The Reluctant Dragon* (animated), 1988.

Other

The Television Adventures [and *More Television Adventures*] *of Worzel Gummidge* (for children). London, Penguin, 2 vols., 1979; complete edition, as *Worzel Gummidge's Television Adventures*, London, Kestrel, 1981.
Worzel Gummidge at the Fair (for children). London, Penguin, 1980.
Worzel Gummidge Goes to the Seaside (for children). London, Penguin, 1980.
The Trials of Worzel Gummidge (for children). London, Penguin, 1980.
Worzel's Birthday (for children). London, Penguin, 1981.
New Television Adventures of Worzel Gummidge and Aunt Sally (for children). London, Sparrow, 1981.
The Irish Adventures of Worzel Gummidge (for children). London, Severn House, 1984.
Worzel Gummidge Down Under (for children). London, Collins, 1987.

Editor, *Writer's Theatre*. London, Heinemann, 1967.

Plays by Willis Hall

Final at Furnell (broadcast 1954). London, Evans, 1956.
Poet and Pheasant, with Lewis Jones (broadcast 1955; produced Watford, Hertfordshire, 1958). London, Deane, and Boston, Baker, 1959.
The Gentle Knight (broadcast 1957; produced London, 1964). London, Blackie, 1966.
The Play of the Royal Astrologers (produced Birmingham, 1958; London, 1968). London, Heinemann, 1960.
Air Mail from Cyprus (televised 1958). Published in *The Television Playwright: Ten Plays for BBC Television*, edited by Michael Barry, London, Joseph, and New York, Hill and Wang, 1960.
The Long and the Short and the Tall (produced Edinburgh, 1958; London, 1959; New York, 1962). London, Heinemann, 1959; New York, Theatre Arts, 1961.
A Glimpse of the Sea, and Last Day in Dreamland (produced London, 1959). Included in *A Glimpse of the Sea: Three Short Plays*, 1961.
Return to the Sea (televised 1960; produced London, 1980). Included in *A Glimpse of the Sea: Three Short Plays*, 1961.
Chin-Chin, adaptation of the play by François Billetdoux (produced London, 1960).
A Glimpse of the Sea: Three Short Plays. London, Evans, 1961.
Azouk, with Robin Maugham, adaptation of a play by Alexandre Rivemale (produced Newcastle upon Tyne, 1962).
Yer What? (revue), with others, music by Lance Mulcahy (produced Nottingham, 1962).
The Days Beginning: An Easter Play. London, Heinemann, 1964.
The Love Game, adaptation of a play by Marcel Achard, translated by Tamara Lo (produced London, 1964).
The Railwayman's New Clothes (televised 1971). London, French, 1974.
They Don't All Open Men's Boutiques (televised 1972). Published in *Prompt Three*, edited by Alan Durband, London, Hutchinson, 1976.
Walk On, Walk On (produced Liverpool, 1975). London, French, 1976.
Kidnapped at Christmas (for children; produced London, 1975). London, French-Heinemann, 1975.
Stag-Night (produced London, 1976).
Christmas Crackers (for children; produced London, 1976). London, French-Heinemann, 1976.
A Right Christmas Caper (for children; produced London, 1977). London, French-Heinemann, 1978.
The Wind in the Willows, music by Denis King, adaptation of the story by Kenneth Grahame (produced Plymouth, 1984; London, 1985).
Treasure Island, music by Denis King, adaptation of the novel by Robert Louis Stevenson (produced Birmingham, 1984).
The Water Babies, adaptation of the novel by Charles Kingsley (produced Oxford, 1987).
Jane Eyre, adaptation of the novel by Charlotte Bronte. Samuel French, 1994.
Mansfield Park, adaptation of the novel by Jane Austen. London, Samuel French, 1994.
The Three Muskateers, adaptation of the novel by Alexandre Dumas. London, Samuel French, 1995.

Screenplays: *The Long and the Short and the Tall* (*Jungle Fighters*), with Wolf Mankowitz, 1961.

Radio Plays: *Final at Furnell*, 1954; *The Nightingale*, 1954; *Furore at Furnell*, 1955; *Frenzy at Furnell*, 1955; *Friendly at Furnell*, 1955; *Fluster at Furnell*, 1955; *Poet and Pheasant*, with Lewis Jones, 1955; *One Man Absent*, 1955; *A Run for the Money*, 1956; *Afternoon for Antigone*, 1956; *The Long Years*, 1956; *Any Dark Morning*, 1956; *Feodor's Bride*, 1956; *One Man Returns*, 1956; *A Ride on the Donkeys*, 1957; *The Calverdon Road Job*, 1957; *The Gentle Knight*, 1957; *Harvest the Sea*, 1957; *Monday at Seven*, 1957; *Annual Outing*, 1958; *The Larford Lad*, 1958; *The Case of Walter Grimshaw*, with Leslie Halward, 1958.

Television Plays: *Air Mail from Cyprus*, 1958; *Return to the Sea*, 1960; *On the Night of the Murder*, 1962; *The Ticket*, 1969; *The Railwayman's New Clothes*, 1971; *The Villa Maroc*, 1972; *They Don't All Open Men's Boutiques*, 1972; *Song at Twilight*, 1973; *Friendly Encounter*, 1974; *The Piano-Smashers of the Golden Sun*, 1974; *Illegal Approach*, 1974; *Midgley*, 1975; *Match-Fit*, from a story by Brian Glanville, 1976; *A Flash of Inspiration*, 1976; *Secret Army* series, 1977; *The Fuzz* series, 1977; *Hazell Gets the Boot* (*Hazell* series), 1979; *Danedyke Mystery*, from a work by Stephen Chance, 1979; *National Pelmet*, 1980; *Minder* series, 1980-86; *Christmas Spirits*, 1981; *Stan's Last Game*,

1983; *The Road to 1984*, 1984; *The Bright Side* series, 1985; *The Return of the Antelope*, and *The Antelope Christmas Special*, from his own stories, 1986.

Plays by Keith Waterhouse

Steafel Variations (songs and sketches), with Peter Tinniswood and Dick Vosburgh (produced London, 1982).
Mr. and Mrs. Nobody, adaptation of *The Diary of a Nobody* by George and Weedon Grossmith (produced London, 1986).
Jeffrey Bernard Is Unwell (produced Brighton and London, 1989). London and New York, Samuel French, 1991.
Bookends, adaptation of *The Marsh Marlowe Letters* by Craig Brown (produced London, 1990).
Our Song, adaptation of his novel (produced London, 1992).

Radio Plays: *The Town That Wouldn't Vote*, 1951; *There Is a Happy Land*, 1962; *The Woolen Bank Forgeries*, 1964; *The Last Phone-In*, 1976; *The Big Broadcast of 1922*, 1979.

Television Plays: *The Warmonger*, 1970; *The Upchat Line* series, 1977; *The Upchat Connection* series, 1978; *Charlie Muffin*, from novels by Brian Freemantle, 1979; *West End Tales* series, 1981; *The Happy Apple* series, from a play by Jack Pulman, 1983; *This Office Life*, from his own novel, 1984; *Charters and Caldicott*, 1985; *The Great Paper Chase*, from the book *Slip Up* by Anthony Delano, 1988; *Andy Capp* series, 1988.

Novel by Willis Hall

The Fuzz (novelization of TV series). London, Coronet, 1977.

Novels by Keith Waterhouse

There Is a Happy Land. London, Joseph, 1957.
Billy Liar. London, Joseph, 1959; New York, Norton, 1960.
Jubb. London, Joseph, 1963; New York, Putnam, 1964.
The Bucket Shop. London, Joseph, 1968; as *Everything Must Go*, New York, Putnam, 1969.
Billy Liar on the Moon. London, Joseph, 1975; New York, Putnam, 1976.
Office Life. London, Joseph, 1978.
Maggie Muggins; or, Spring in Earl's Court. London, Joseph, 1981.
In the Mood. London, Joseph, 1983.
Thinks. London, Joseph, 1984.
Our Song. London, Hodder and Stoughton, 1988.
Bimbo. London, Hodder and Stoughton, 1990.

Other by Willis Hall

They Found the World (for children), with I.O. Evans. London and New York, Warne, 1960.
The Royal Astrologer: Adventures of Father Mole-Cricket or the Malayan Legends (for children). London, Heinemann, 1960; New York, Coward McCann, 1962.
The A to Z of Soccer, with Michael Parkinson. London, Pelham, 1970.
The A to Z of Television, with Bob Monkhouse. London, Pelham, 1971.
My Sporting Life. London, Luscombe, 1975.
The Incredible Kidnapping (for children). London, Heinemann, 1975.
The Summer of the Dinosaur (for children). London, Bodley Head, 1977.
The Last Vampire (for children). London, Bodley Head, 1982.
The Inflatable Shop (for children). London, Bodley Head, 1984.
Dragon Days (for children). London, Bodley Head, 1985.
The Return of the Antelope (for children). London, Bodley Head, 1985.
The Antelope Company Ashore [*At Large*] (for children). London, Bodley Head, 2 vols. 1986-87.
Spooky Rhymes (for children). London, Hamlyn, 1987.
Henry Hollins and the Dinosaur (for children). London, Bodley Head, 1988.
Doctor Jekyll and Mr. Hollins (for children). London, Bodley Head, 1988.
The Vampire's Holiday (for children). London, Bodley Head, 1992.
The Vampire's Revenge (for children). London, Bodley Head, 1993.
The Vampire's Christmas (for children). London, Bodley Head, 1994.

Editor, with Michael Parkinson, *Football Report: An Anthology of Soccer.* London, Pelham, 1973.
Editor, with Michael Parkinson, *Football Classified: An Anthology of Soccer.* London, Luscombe, 1975.
Editor, with Michael Parkinson, *Football Final.* London, Pelham, 1975.

Other by Keith Waterhouse

The Café Royal: Ninety Years of Bohemia, with Guy Deghy. London, Hutchinson, 1955.
How to Avoid Matrimony: The Layman's Guide to the Laywoman, with Guy Deghy (as Herald Froy). London, Muller, 1957.
Britain's Voice Abroad, with Paul Cave. London, Daily Mirror Newspapers, 1957.
The Future of Television. London, Daily Mirror Newspapers, 1958.
How to Survive Matrimony, with Guy Deghy (as Herald Froy). London, Muller, 1958.
The Joneses: How to Keep Up with Them, with Guy Deghy (as Lee Gibb). London, Muller, 1959.
Can This Be Love?, with Guy Deghy (as Herald Froy). London, Muller, 1960.
Maybe You're Just Inferior: Head-Shrinking for Fun and Profit, with Guy Deghy (as Herald Froy). London, Muller, 1961.
The Higher Jones, with Guy Deghy (as Lee Gibb). London, Muller, 1961.
O Mistress Mine: or, How to Go Roaming, with Guy Deghy (as Herald Froy). London, Barker, 1962.
The Passing of the Third-Floor Buck (Punch sketches). London, Joseph, 1974.
Mondays, Thursdays (Daily Mirror columns). London, Joseph, 1976.
Rhubarb, Rhubarb, and Other Noises (Daily Mirror columns). London, Joseph, 1979.
Daily Mirror Style. London, Mirror Books, 1981; revised, edition as *Waterhouse on Newspaper Style*, London, Viking, 1989.
Fanny Peculiar (Punch columns). London, Joseph, 1983.
Mrs. Pooter's Diary. London, Joseph, 1983.
Waterhouse at Large (journalism). London, Joseph, 1985.

The Collected Letters of a Nobody (Including Mr. Pooter's Advice to His Son). London, Joseph, 1986.
The Theory and Practice of Lunch. London, Joseph, 1986.
The Theory and Practice of Travel. London, Hodder and Stoughton, 1989.
English Our English (and How to Sing It). London, Viking, 1991.
Unsweet Charity. London, Hodder and Stoughton, 1992.
Sharon and Tracy and the Rest: The Best of Keith Waterhouse in the Daily Mail. London, Spectre, 1992.
City Lights: A Street Life. London, Hodder and Stoughton, 1994.
Streets Ahead: Life After City Lights. London, Hodder and Stoughton, 1995.

* * *

Willis Hall and Keith Waterhouse have written so many stage plays and television and film scripts that critics are wont to regard them as the standby professionals of British theater. Their technical skill has never been doubted, but their artistry and originality often have. They were both born in Leeds in 1929 and have therefore shared a similar Yorkshire background. Both were successful individually before their long-standing collaboration began. Hall's *The Long and the Short and the Tall,* which was premiered by the Oxford Theatre Group in 1958, was described by Kenneth Tynan as "the most moving production of the [Edinburgh] festival." Waterhouse's novel *Billy Liar* was well received in 1957. The stage version of *Billy Liar* was their first joint effort, and its success in London, where it helped to establish the names of the two actors who played the title role, Albert Finney and Tom Courtenay, encouraged them to continue in the vein of "purely naturalistic provincial working-class comedy," to quote T. C. Worsley's description. *Celebration, All Things Bright and Beautiful,* and *Come Laughing Home,* together with the one-act plays *The Sponge Room* and *Squat Betty,* allowed critics to regard them as the true successors of Stanley Houghton and Harold Brighouse. This convenient label stuck to their work until 1965, when their farce *Say Who You Are,* set in Kensington and concerning a middle-class *ménage à quatre,* proved an unexpected success of the season. This lively, and in some respects ambitious, sexual comedy demonstrated that their talents were not confined to one style of humor or their sense of place to the North of England. When this barrier of mild prejudice was broken, it was remembered that Hall was responsible for perhaps the best British adaptation of a contemporary French comedy, Billetdoux's *Chin-Chin* (1960), and that both had contributed widely to revues and satirical programs such as the BBC's *That Was the Week That Was* and had written modern versions of Greek tragedies, such as Hall's *Afternoon for Antigone*. Their range as writers and their sophistication obviously extended beyond the narrow limits that had brought them their reputations.

Nor is technical skill so common a quality among contemporary dramatists that it can be dismissed as unimportant. Hall and Waterhouse have the merits of good professionals. When they write satirically, their polemic is sharp, witty, and to the point. When they write naturalistically—whether about a provincial town in Yorkshire, a seaside amusement arcade, the war in Malaya, or Kensington—they take the trouble to know the surroundings in detail. Their groundwork enables them to discover possibilities that other writers overlook. For example, *Celebration,* set in a working-class suburb of a Yorkshire town, presents two contrasting family events—a marriage and a funeral. There is no main story to hold the episodes together, nor is there a theme or even a clearly identifiable climax. But the play triumphs because the distinctive flavor of each "celebration" is captured and because the 15 main characters are each so well drawn. The slender threads of continuity that bind the episodes together reveal a sensitive insight into the nature of the society. The first act is about the wedding preparations in the back room of a pub. Rhoda and Edgar Lucas are determined to do well by their daughter, Christine, who is marrying Bernard Fuller. But Rhoda has decided to economize by not employing Whittaker's, the firm in the town that specializes in weddings. Her efforts to ensure that the wedding breakfast does not let her daughter down are helped and hindered by the other members of the family. Despite the tattiness of the scene, the collapsible tables, the grease-proof paper, and the dirty cups, the audience eventually is drawn to see the glowing pride and family self-importance that surround the event. Christine and Bernard survey the transformed room at the end of the act, and their contented happiness justifies the efforts. The second act is about the funeral of Arthur Broadbent, Rhoda's great-uncle and the best known eccentric of the family, who has been living in sin for years with May Beckett. The funeral is over, and the pieties continue in the living room of the Lucas house. Although the family does not want to acknowledge May Beckett, she invades the house both physically, since they try to prevent her from coming, and emotionally, by expressing a grief that the conventional sentiments of the family cannot match. May's nostalgic tribute to her lost lover, so carefully prepared for in the script and emerging with an easy naturalness, is one of the truly outstanding moments of postwar British naturalistic drama and ranks with Beatie's speech at the end of Wesker's *Roots*.

This assured handling of naturalistic details is a feature of all of the best plays of Hall and Waterhouse. What other writers would have used the pub and the telephone box as so important a part of a sex comedy, replacing the more familiar stage props of a settee and a veranda? Or caught the significance of a backyard for a lonely introvert like Billy Liar? Or surrounded the pregnant unmarried girl, Vera Fawcett, in *Come Laughing Home* with a family whose stultifying complacency offer a convincing example of the wasteland from which she is trying unsuccessfully to escape? With this unusual skill in capturing an exact milieu, Hall and Waterhouse are also adept at writing those single outstanding roles that actors love to play. The part of Private Bamforth in *The Long and the Short and the Tall* gave Peter O'Toole his first opportunity, which he seized with relish. Hayley Mills was "discovered" in their film *Whistle Down the Wind*, with the then underrated actor Alan Bates. Hall and Waterhouse were once criticized for writing "angry young man" parts without providing the psychological insight or rhetoric of Osborne's Jimmy Porter. John Russell Taylor wrote that

> The central characters, Bamforth and Fentrill [in *Last Day in Dreamland*], are almost identical: the hectoring angry young man who knows it all and stands for most of the time in the centre of the stage, aquiver as a rule (whether the situation warrants it or not) with almost hysterical intensity, berating the other characters, who in each case, rather mysteriously, accept him as a natural leader and the life and soul of the party. The indebtedness to *Look Back in Anger* is unmistakable. . . .

This description may apply to Fentrill, whose anger at the rundown amusement arcade seems somewhat strained since he is not forced to stay there. But it applies less so to Bamforth, whose bitterness derives from claustrophobic jungle war, and scarcely at all to the other main characters of their plays. The distinctive strength of their protagonists lies not in volubility or complexity of character but in their reactions to unsympathetic surroundings. Vera Fawcett is not a stock rebel. Billy Liar does not rebel at all, for he is too satisfied with fantasies about escape. Unlike John Osborne, Hall and Waterhouse rarely offer "mouthpiece" characters, people whose insight and rhetoric about their own problems justify their presence on the stage. The central characters emerge from their surroundings, and the environment shapes the nature of their rebellion. Their dilemmas are a typical part of their societies and are not superimposed upon their families as a consequence of too much intelligence or education.

A fairer criticism of the work of Hall and Waterhouse might run along these lines: while their dialogue is always lively and accurate, it rarely contains flashes of intuition. Much of the humor of *Celebration, Billy Liar,* and *Say Who You Are* depends on carefully calculated repetition. The characters are sometimes given verbal catchphrases—Eric Fawcett teases his son Brian endlessly for ordering "whisky and Scotch" in a pub—but more frequently they are given habits that become irritating after a time. Fawcett's life in *Come Laughing Home* centers around making model boats. Edgar continually chides Rhoda for not arranging the wedding through Whittaker's, while his son Jack greets every newcomer with the same question, "Lend us a quid?" The reiteration often makes a valid dramatic point, if only to illustrate the poverty of the relationships, but it sometimes seems to be just an easy way of establishing a person by constantly reminding the audience of an obsession. Hall and Waterhouse often fail to reveal any deeper cause behind the nagging habit, and this lack of depth prevents the characters from seeming sympathetic. In *Say Who You Are* the two men, David and Stuart, are both self-opinionated male chauvinists, credible enough but rather uninteresting because they have so little self-knowledge. Valerie, who invents a marriage so that she can have an affair without getting too involved, is a more engaging creation, but she, too, seems superficial when we learn that her objections to marriage rest on a dislike of "togetherness"—"toothbrushes nestling side by side"—and on little else. Sometimes when Hall and Waterhouse try to give an added dimension to their characters, the effect seems strained. As Vera Fawcett resigns herself to an arid future with the family from whom she cannot escape, she says, "I wanted to reach out for something, but I couldn't reach far enough. It's something you need—for living—that I haven't got. I haven't really looked, but I wanted to, I was going to." This statement of her defeat does not dramatically match or rise to the opportunity the play provides for her.

This superficiality has often been explained as the reverse side of the authors' facility; writers who produce so many scripts cannot be expected to be profound as well. But there may be another reason. Hall and Waterhouse share a remarkable sense of form and timing, which partly accounts for the success of *Say Who You Are* and *Celebration.* Intending to ring each other up, David and Sarah go to two different telephones at the same time, with the result that the numbers are always engaged and they jump to the wrong conclusion. The scenes are based on a clever use of parallels and counterpoint, but this also depends on the characters behaving with a mechanical predictability. We know what they are really going to do, and the fun comes from seeing their stock reactions fail to achieve the expected results. The formalism of the scripts, in short, sometimes prevents the characters from having an independent life, and this is the result not so much of technical facility as of an overzealous care in the construction that shortsightedly ignores other possibilities. Despite these limitations, however, Hall and Waterhouse have an expertise that few other writers of the new wave of British drama can match and that accounts for the continuing popularity of their best plays.

—John Elsom

HALLIWELL, David (William)

Nationality: British. **Born:** Brighouse, Yorkshire, 31 July 1936. **Education:** Bailiff Bridge Elementary School; Victoria Central Secondary Modern School, Rastrick; Hipperholme Grammar School; Huddersfield College of Art, Yorkshire, 1953-59; Royal Academy of Dramatic Art, London, diploma 1961. **Career:** Founder, with Mike Leigh, Dramagraph production company, London, 1965; director and committee member, Quipu group, London, 1966-76; visiting fellow, Reading University, 1969-70; resident dramatist, Royal Court Theatre, London 1976-77, and Hampstead Theatre, London, 1978-79. Co-director, Vardo Productions Ltd. Director, playwriting workshops, The Actor's Centre, London, 1991—. Member Charlbury Town Council, 1991— (vice chairperson, 1996-97). **Awards:** *Evening Standard* award, 1967; John Whiting award, 1978; Hawthornden fellow, 1995. **Member:** Fellow, Royal Society of Literature. **Address:** 8 Crawborough Villas, Charlbury, Oxford OX7 3TS, England.

Publications

Plays

Little Malcolm and His Struggle Against the Eunuchs (produced London, 1965). London, French, 1966; as *Hail Scrawdyke!* (produced New York, 1966), New York, Grove Press, 1967.
A Who's Who of Flapland (broadcast 1967; produced London, 1969). Included in *A Who's Who of Flapland and Other Plays*, 1971.
The Experiment, with David Calderisi (also co-director: produced London and New York, 1967).
A Discussion (produced Falmouth, 1969). Included in *A Who's Who of Flapland and Other Plays*, 1971.
K. D. Dufford Hears K. D. Dufford Ask K. D. Dufford How K. D. Dufford'll Make K. D. Dufford (produced London, 1969). London, Faber, 1970.
Muck from Three Angles (produced Edinburgh and London, 1970). Included in *A Who's Who of Flapland and Other Plays*, 1971.
The Girl Who Didn't Like Answers (produced London, 1971).
A Last Belch for the Great Auk (produced London, 1971).
A Who's Who of Flapland and Other Plays. London, Faber, 1971.
An Amour, and A Feast (produced London, 1971).
Bleats from a Brighouse Pleasureground (broadcast 1972; produced London, 1972).
Janitress Thrilled by Prehensile Penis (also director: produced London, 1972).
An Altercation (also director: produced London, 1973).
The Freckled Bum (also director: produced London, 1974).
Minyip (also director: produced London, 1974).

Progs (also director: produced London, 1975).
A Process of Elimination (also director: produced London, 1975).
Meriel the Ghost Girl (televised 1976; also director: produced London, 1982). Published in *The Mind Beyond*, London, Penguin, 1976.
Prejudice (also director: produced Sheffield, 1978; as *Creatures of Another Kind*, produced London, 1981).
The House (produced London, 1979). London, Eyre Methuen, 1979.
A Rite Kwik Metal Tata (produced Sheffield and London, 1979).
Was It Her? (broadcast 1980; also director: produced London, 1982).
A Tomato Who Grew into a Mushroom (produced on Oxfordshire tour, 1987).
Bonds. In *Norwegian Journal of Group Analysis*, 1995.

Radio Plays: *A Who's Who of Flapland*, 1967; *Bleats from a Brighouse Pleasureground*, 1972; *Was It Her?*, 1980; *Spongehenge*, 1982; *Grandad's Place*, 1984; *Shares of the Pudding*, 1985; *Do It Yourself*, 1986; *Bedsprings*, 1989; *Parts*, 1989; *There's a Car Park in Witherton*, 1992; *Crossed Lines*, 1992.

Television Plays: *A Plastic Mac in Winter*, 1963; *Cock, Hen and Courting Pit*, 1966; *Triptych of Bathroom Users*, 1972; *Blur and Blank via Checkheaton*, 1972; *Steps Back*, 1973; *Daft Mam Blues*, 1975; *Pigmented Patter*, 1976, and *Tree Women of Jagden Crag*, 1978 (*Crown Court* series); *Meriel the Ghost Girl* (*The Mind Beyond* series), 1976; *There's a Car Park in Witherton*, 1982; *Speculating about Orwell*, 1983; *Arrangements*, 1985; *Doctor Who* series (2 episodes), 1985; *The Bill* (1 episode), 1989; *Bonds*, 1990.

*

Critical Study: Article in *The Gothic Impulse In Contemporary Drama* by Mary Beth Inverso, Ann Arbor, Michigan, UMI Research Press, 1990.

Theatrical Activities:
Director: **Plays**—Quipu group: many of his own plays, and *The Dumb Waiter* by Harold Pinter, *Keep Out, Love in Progress* by Walter Hall, *The Stronger* by Strindberg, and *A Village Wooing* by Shaw, 1966; *The Experiment* (co-director, with David Calderisi), London and New York, 1967; *A Day with My Sister* by Stephen Poliakoff, Edinburgh, 1971; *The Hundred Watt Bulb* by George Thatcher, *I Am Real and So Are You, A Visit from the Family*, and *Crewe Station at 2 A.M.* by Tony Connor, 1972; *The Only Way Out* by George Thatcher, 1973; *We Are What We Eat* by Frank Dux, *The Knowall* by Alan C. Taylor, and *The Quipu Anywhere Show* (co-director, with Gavin Eley), London, 1973; *The Last of the Feinsteins* by Tony Connor, London, 1975; *Paint* by Peter Godfrey, London, 1977; *Lovers* by Brian Friel, Kingston, Surrey, 1978; *Jelly Babies* by Glenn Young, London, 1978.

Actor: **Plays**—Vincentio in *The Taming of the Shrew* and Seyton in *Macbeth*, Nottingham, 1962; Hortensio in *The Taming of the Shrew*, Leicester, 1962; Sydney Spooner in *Worm's Eye View* by R.F. Delderfield, Colchester, 1962; General Madigan in *O'Flaherty, V.C.* by Shaw, and Jim Curry in *The Rainmaker* by N. Richard Nash, Stoke-on-Trent, 1962; Hero in *The Rehearsal* by Anouilh, Pozzo in *Waiting for Godot* by Beckett, and The Common Man in *A Man for All Seasons* by Robert Bolt, Stoke-on-Trent, 1963; Scrawdyke in *Little Malcolm and His Struggle Against the Eunuchs*, London, 1965; Jackson McIver in *The Experiment*, London, 1967; Policeman in *An Altercation*, London, 1973; Botard in *Rhinoceros* by Ionesco, London, 1974; Frankie in *Birdbath* by Leonard Melfi, Bristol, 1975. **Films**—*Defence of the Realm*, 1986; *Mona Lisa*, 1986. **Radio**—Landlord in *Spongehenge*, 1982; Interrogator in *Bedsprings*, 1989; Hitler in *The Eagle Has Landed*, 1989, and *The Eagle Has Flown*, 1992, by Jack Higgins; Prison Officer in *Crossed Lines*, 1992.

David Halliwell comments:

Since the last edition of this book I have arrived at the essence of what I want to do as a dramatist. I have developed the means of expressing the conflicts and harmonies between the inner and outer parts of characters that I have been selecting and moving towards from the beginning of my dramatic career. Means organically centred on actors and performances which, although they can be adapted to any medium, require, in essence, no mechanical or electronic equipment.

* * *

David Halliwell's dramatic territory is Flapland; his perennial subject, the Hitler syndrome; the motive force of his central characters, that childish outburst of King Lear's: "I will do such things,/ What they are, yet I know not, but they shall be/The terrors of the earth." Malcolm Scrawdyke, the hero of *Little Malcolm and His Struggle against the Eunuchs*, models himself explicitly on the early Hitler, except that he wears a Russian anarchist's greatcoat in place of Hitler's raincoat. Expelled from art school, Scrawdyke enlists three variously inadequate siblings into his Party of Dynamic Erection, plans a ludicrous revenge (which never gets beyond the fantasy stage) on the man who expelled him, and succeeds only in two petty, but nonetheless unpleasant, acts of terror—the "trial" of his most articulate and independent sibling and the beating up of a girl who has taunted him with sexual cowardice. Scrawdyke is only a phantom Hitler, his rabble-rousing speeches confined to the inside of his Huddersfield garret and his grasp of reality so tenuous as to constitute little danger even to his specific enemies, let alone the community at large. But the hero of Halliwell's other full-length play, *K. D. Dufford Hears K. D. Dufford Ask K. D. Dufford How K. D. Dufford'll Make K. D. Dufford,* who actually wears a raincoat, sets his sights lower than Scrawdyke. His recipe for instant notoriety is to murder a child, and he is entirely successful. Halliwell makes an ambitious attempt in this play not simply to suggest the interplay between fantasy and reality but actually to display it, chapter and verse, on the stage, with several different versions of each scene—the real event compared with the event as imagined to his own advantage by K. D. Dufford and by each of the other main characters.

Halliwell explores the possibilities and limitations of this device in a series of short plays—*Muck from Three Angles, A Last Belch for the Great Auk, Bleats from a Brighouse Pleasureground,* and *Janitress Thrilled by Prehensile Penis*. The effect is often clumsy and ultimately superfluous since the shades of fantasy and reality pursue one another with such unerring clarity through his virtuoso monologues that an audience must grow restive at being told by means of explicit technical devices what it has already grasped implicitly through intense dramatic sympathy.

For however faceless, talentless, witless, loveless, and lacking in courage and moral compunction these characters may be, Halliwell's comic view of them makes them irresistibly sympathetic. Something similar happens in the plays of Halliwell's contemporary Joe Orton, as well as in those of the master from whom they both learned, Samuel Beckett. The fact that these characters would be, if met in real life, virtually subhuman, certainly pitiable or despicable to an extreme degree, is beside the point. In Halliwell's, as in Orton's and Beckett's plays, they are exaggerated dramatic representations of universal human weaknesses, and Halliwell has found and shown that, in this age of overpopulation and social disorientation, we are peculiarly vulnerable to paranoia. In *The Experiment,* partly devised by himself, partly improvised by the actors, Halliwell acted an avant-garde theatrical director "of international repute" rehearsing his company in "a modern epic translated from the Icelandic entitled *The Assassination of President Garfield.*" The efforts of the director to drive his cast toward the nadir of art, to discover in the purposeless murder of a forgotten American politician deeper and deeper levels of insignificance, satirized the gullibility of audiences as much as the inflated self-admiration of certain members of the theatrical profession. But there was above all a direct demonstration of Halliwell's own special subject—the banal striving to be the unique, the insignificant the significant, the squalid reality the dream of power.

In his lightest and most charming play, *A Who's Who of Flapland,* originally written for radio but successfully translated to lunchtime theater, Halliwell closes the circle by confronting one paranoiac with another who is his equal if not his master at the gambits and routines of Flapland. Here, as in *Little Malcolm,* Halliwell relies entirely on his mastery of dramatic speech, using his native industrial Yorkshire idiom as a precision instrument to trace complex patterns of aggression, alarm, subterfuge, humiliation, triumph, and surrender. The later plays *A Rite Kwik Metal Tata, The House,* and *Prejudice* are all what one might call "polyphonic" developments of this technique, adding, for example, a Cockney girl and an upper-class M.P. to the Yorkshire characters in *Metal Tata* and a Bradford Pakistani and an exiled Zulu to those in *Prejudice. The House,* set in a country mansion requisitioned as a hospital during World War I, is the least successful, since Halliwell's command of regional idioms is not matched by any sense of period, and the action is too desultory. But in *Prejudice* and *Metal Tata* the plots are strong enough to allow him to turn his characters around and inside out in relation to one another without losing the momentum of the play. Of course, this is only what the best playwrights have always done, but good methods decay into tired conventions, and it is clear that Halliwell's struggle has been to remove the deadwood and to reconstitute traditional polyphonic drama in the fresh terms of his own ideas and idiosyncrasies.

—John Spurling

HAMPTON, Christopher (James)

Nationality: British. **Born:** Fayal, the Azores, 26 January 1946. **Education:** Schools in Aden and Alexandria, Egypt; Lancing College, Sussex, 1959-63; New College, Oxford, 1964-68, B.A. in modern languages (French and German) 1968, M.A., honorary fellowship, 1997. **Family:** Married Laura Margaret de Holesch in 1971; two daughters. **Career:** Resident dramatist, Royal Court Theatre, London, 1968-70. **Awards:** *Plays and Players* award, 1970, 1973, 1985; *Evening Standard* award, 1970, 1984, 1986; Los Angeles Drama Critics Circle award, 1974, 1989; Olivier award, 1986; New York Drama Critics Circle award, 1987; BAFTA award for television, 1987, for screenplay, 1990; Writers Guild of America award, 1989; Prix Italia, 1989; Academy award, 1989. Fellow, Royal Society of Literature, 1976; Tony awards (2), 1995; Special Jury Prize, Cannes Festival, 1995; Scott Moncrielt Translation prize, 1997. **Member:** Royal Society of Literature, 1984-90. **Agent:** Casarotto Ramsay Ltd., National House, 60-66 Wardour Street, London W1V 3HP. **Address:** 2 Kensington Park Gardens, London W.11, England.

Publications

Plays

When Did You Last See My Mother? (produced Oxford and London, 1966; New York, 1967). London, Faber, and New York, Grove Press, 1967.

Marya, adaptation of a play by Isaak Babel, translated by Michael Glenny and Harold Shukman (produced London, 1967). Published in *Plays of the Year 35,* London, Elek, 1969.

Total Eclipse (produced London, 1968; Washington, D.C., 1972; New York, 1974). London, Faber, 1969; New York, French, 1972; revised version (produced London, 1981), Faber, 1981.

Uncle Vanya, adaptation of a play by Chekhov, translated by Nina Froud (produced London, 1970). Published in *Plays of the Year 39,* London, Elek, 1971.

The Philanthropist: A Bourgeois Comedy (produced London, 1970; New York, 1971). London, Faber, 1970; New York, French, 1971; revised version, Faber, 1985.

Hedda Gabler, adaptation of a play by Ibsen (produced Stratford, Ontario, 1970; New York, 1971; London, 1984). New York, French, 1971; with *A Doll's House,* London, Faber, 1989.

A Doll's House, adaptation of a play by Ibsen (produced New York, 1971; London, 1973). New York, French, 1972; with *Hedda Gabler,* London, Faber, 1989.

Don Juan, adaptation of a play by Molière (broadcast 1972; produced Bristol, 1972; Chicago, 1977). London, Faber, 1974.

Savages (produced London, 1973; Los Angeles, 1974; New York, 1977). London, Faber, 1974; revised version, New York, French, 1976.

Treats (produced London, 1976; New York, 1977; revised version produced London, 1988). London, Faber, 1976.

Signed and Sealed, adaptation of a play by Georges Feydeau and Maurice Desvallières (produced London, 1976).

Able's Will (televised 1977). London, Faber, 1979.

Tales from the Vienna Woods, adaptation of a play by Ödön von Horváth (produced London, 1977; New Haven, Connecticut, 1978). London, Faber, 1977.

Ghosts, tranalation of a play by Ibsen (produced on tour, 1978). New York, French, 1983.

Don Juan Comes Back from the War, adaptation of a play by Ödön von Horváth (produced London, 1978; New York, 1979). London, Faber, 1978.

The Wild Duck, adaptation of a play by Ibsen (produced London, 1979). London, Faber, 1980; New York, French, 1981.

Geschichten aus dem Wiener Wald (screenplay), with Maximilian Schell. Frankfurt, Suhrkamp, 1979.

After Mercer, based on works by David Mercer (produced London, 1980).

The Prague Trial, adaptation of a work by Patrice Chéreau and Ariane Mnouchkine (broadcast London, 1980).

A Night of the Day of the Imprisoned Writer, with Ronald Harwood (produced London, 1981).

The Portage to San Cristobal of A.H., adaptation of the novel by George Steiner (produced London and Hartford, Connecticut, 1982). London, Faber, 1983.

Tales from Hollywood (produced Los Angeles, 1982; London, 1983). London, Faber, 1983.

Tartuffe; or, The Impostor, adaptation of the play by Molière (produced London, 1983). London, Faber, 1984.

Les Liaisons Dangereuses, adaptation of the novel by Choderlos de Laclos (produced Stratford-on-Avon, 1985; London, 1986; New York, 1987). London, Faber, 1985.

The Ginger Tree, adaptation of the novel by Oswald Wynd (televized 1989). London, Faber, 1989.

Faith, Hope, and Charity, adaptation of a play by Ödön von Horváth (produced London, 1989). London, Faber, 1989.

Dangerous Liaisons: The Film. London, Faber, 1989.

White Chameleon (produced London, 1991). London, Faber, 1991.

The Philanthropist and Other Plays (includes *Treats*, *Total Eclipse*). London, Faber, 1991.

Sunset Boulevard, with Don Black (produced London, 1993; Los Angeles, 1994; New York, 1995). London, Faber, 1993, revised version, 1996.

Alice's Adventures Under Ground, adapted from the writings of Lewis Carroll (produced London, 1994). London, Faber, 1995.

Art, adaptation of a play by Yasmina Reza (produced London, 1996; New York, 1998). London, Faber, 1996.

Christopher Hampton Plays 1. London, Faber, 1997.

An Enemy of the People, adaptation of a play by Isben (produced London, 1997; Los Angeles, 1998). London, Faber, 1997.

The Unexpected Man, adaptation of a play by Yasmina Reza (produced London, 1998). London, Faber, 1998.

Screenplays: *A Doll's House*, 1973; *Geschichten aus dem Wiener Wald* (*Tales from the Vienna Woods*), with Maximilian Schell, 1981; *Beyond the Limit* (*The Honorary Consul*), 1983; *The Good Father*, 1986; *Wolf at the Door*, 1986; *Dangerous Liaisons*, 1989; *Carrington*, 1995; *Total Eclipse*, 1995; *Mary Reilly*, 1996; *The Secret Agent* and *Nostromo* (adapted from the novel *Secret Agent* by Joseph Conrad), 1996.

Radio Plays: *2 Children Free to Wander* (documentary), 1969; *Don Juan*, 1972; *The Prague Trial 79*, from a work by Patrice Chéreau and Ariane Mnouchkine, 1980.

Television Plays: *Able's Will*, 1977; *The History Man*, from the novel by Malcolm Bradbury, 1981; *Hotel du Lac*, from the novel by Anita Brookner, 1986; *The Ginger Tree*, adaptation of the novel by Oswald Wynd, 1989.

*

Critical Studies: *Theatre Quarterly 12* (London), October-December 1973; *Christopher Hampton: A Casebook*, edited by Robert Gross, New York, Garland, 1990; "Christopher Hampton" by John L. DiGaetani, in *A Search for a Postmodern Theater: Interviews with Contemporary Playwrights*, edited by John L. DiGaetani, New York, Greenwood, 1991; "Makers of Real Shapes: Christopher Hampton and His Story-Tellers" by Sebastain Black, in *Contemporary British Drama, 1970-90*, edited by Hersh Zeifman and Cynthia Zimmerman, Toronto, University of Toronto Press, 1993; "The Narcissist and the Mirror in *Les Liaisons dangereuses:* Laclos, Hampton, Muller" by Christine Kiebuzinska, in *The Comparatist: Journal of the Southern Comparative Literature Association* (Knoxville, Tennessee), May 1993, pp. 81-100; "Christopher Hampton" by William J. Free, in *British Playwrights, 1956-1995: A Research and Production Sourcebook*, Westport, Connecticut, Greenwood, 1996.

Theatrical Activities:
Director: **Film**–*Carrington*, 1995; *The Secret Agent*, 1996.

Actor: **Play**—Role in *When Did You Last See My Mother?*, Oxford, 1966; role in *Total Eclipse*, 1995.

* * *

Dangerous Liaisons preserves the original title of a French epistolary novel as adroitly dramatized by Christopher Hampton to applause on Broadway, in the West End, and on the screen. The title aptly summarizes Hampton's own theatrical focus. Although he is not an overtly political playwright, he suggests that one of the dangers to the self-absorbed partners of the liaison is their very indifference to politics.

At age 18, while still an Oxford undergraduate reading French and German, Hampton wrote his first play, *When Did You Last See My Mother?* It received a bare-boards Sunday night production at the Royal Court Theatre and was immediately snapped up for the West End. Hampton's cruel and articulate protagonist adheres to the tradition of the angry young man established by John Osborne, but all three of the play's characters are involved in dangerous liaisons—a love/hate ménage between two teenage boys and a brief affair between one of the boys and the mother of the other. Unlike Broadway's *Tea and Sympathy*, however, the latter emotion is absent from Hampton's stage. In six swift, pitiless scenes the teenage lovers circle back to their ménage after an automobile accident in which the self-reproachful mother is killed.

In *Total Eclipse* the cruelly brilliant teenager is the French poet Arthur Rimbaud, who formed a dangerous liaison with Paul Verlaine, a married poet nearly twice his age. Hampton steeped himself in scholarly sources about their two-year relationship in order to be able to dramatize its tempestuous quality, which he does, again, in six scenes. This time it is Verlaine who pivots between wife and lover, again and again, until Mme. Verlaine divorces him. Lies, drink, and drugs exacerbate the homosexual liaison, which erupts twice into violence. Rimbaud coolly stabs Verlaine's hands, and on another occasion Verlaine accidentally shoots Rimbaud in the hand, for which he is imprisoned for two years. Hampton's final scene bears witness to his title, since both poetic talents suffer total eclipse. A derelict Verlaine is visited by the sister of the dead Rimbaud, and he fantasizes an idyllic liaison.

In spite of the fact that Hampton had had two productions by the age of 21, he toyed with the idea of graduate study after taking his degree in 1968. At that point, however, Bill Gaskill created for him the position of resident dramatist at the Royal Court, with only a slender income but with no duties. Hampton proceeded to work simultaneously on translations, adaptations, and his own *The Philanthropist*, conceived as a rebuttal to Molière's

Le Misanthrope. While the latter is an aristocratic comedy in rhyme, Hampton's play is a bourgeois comedy in prose. Since the protagonist Philip is a philologist as well as a philanthropist, Hampton has marked him thrice as a lover (the meaning of "philo"). True to Hampton's focus, Philip involves himself in dangerous liaisons with the woman he wants to marry and with a woman who does not attract him. Spurned by both, he starts a wooing letter to still a third woman. By the end of the play, when all have rejected his love, Philip reaches into a drawer for a gun, but when he pulls the trigger, a flame shoots out to light his cigarette. His will be a slower death, with sophisticated London as an analogue of the desert island to which Molière's misanthrope resolved to flee.

Incisive and obliquely moral about the worlds of his experience, Hampton reaches out globally in *Savages*. Triggered by the genocide of Brazilian Indians, the play indicts cultured Europeans and radical South Americans for their complicity in the systematic decimation of the natives in order to acquire their land. Painting on a large canvas, Hampton parallels the public tragedy with a private one. A British embassy official and minor poet, significantly named West, is taken hostage by Brazilian radicals who hope to trade him for their imprisoned colleagues. As the confinement of West stretches on, Hampton shows the past in flashbacks—embassy dinners, an anthropologist's distress, a pious and callous American mission, mercenaries who kill wholesale, preparations for the ceremonial gathering of Indian tribes, and West's poems based on Indian legends. Then, abruptly, the two plots coalesce in disaster. A bourgeois radical proves his revolutionary fervor by shooting West, a light plane bombs the Indians at their ceremony, and the pilot descends to shoot survivors. But the pilot burns all trace of the massacre, whereas West, dead, becomes a hero of the media.

Hampton retreated to another lover's triangle in *Treats*. A private term for sexual favors, the title points to the desires of two different men for Ann, who is married to the psychologically sadistic Dave and intermittently living with the flaccid Patrick. When the play ends, Ann has replaced Patrick with Dave, and the sadomasochistic merry-go-round will presumably continue.

While producing these plays, Hampton worked on an unusually wide range of translations of Ibsen, Chekhov, Molière, and the lesser-known Austrian playwright Ödön von Horváth, who fired his imagination. Fleeing to Paris after the Anschluss, Horváth was killed at the age of 37 when a freak storm felled a tree under which he had taken shelter. In *Tales from Hollywood* Hampton invents a life for Horváth among anti-Nazi central European refugees in Hollywood. Mixing both easily and uneasily with the Mann family and with Brecht and others, Horváth is unable to toe a party line, just as he is unable to fulfill a woman's needs. Unlike earlier Hampton heroes, Horváth is too humane and compassionate for dangerous liaisons. He withdraws from his putative afterlife and is killed instantly by the falling tree, as recorded in history.

Rooted in his own life, *White Chameleon* was a new departure for Hampton. Set in Alexandria from 1952 to 1956, the play traces the effects of Egyptian social conflicts on an English family. The protagonist, Christopher, is split in two—a boy of Hampton's own age at the time and an adult looking back in memory. In *White Chameleon* a liaison of sympathy between young Christopher and the family servant Ibrahim proves ultimately dangerous to the latter. Little people are devoured by cataclysmic events.

Hampton is a playwright in the old sense of the word "wright"—a craftsman who hones his tools even as he molds increasingly large structures. As witty as his contemporaries, Hampton is more serious than most of them in his incisive dramas of the cruelties of people's private and public lives.

—Ruby Cohn

HANLEY, William

Nationality: American. **Born:** Lorain, Ohio, 22 October 1931. **Education:** Cornell University, Ithaca, New York, 1950-51; American Academy of Dramatic Arts, New York, 1954-55. **Military Service:** Served in the United States Army, 1952-54. **Family:** Married 1) Shelley Post in 1956 (divorced 1961); 2) Patricia Stanley in 1962 (divorced 1978); two daughters. **Career:** Worked as bank clerk, mail clerk, factory worker, and book salesman; playwright and novelist. **Awards:** Vernon Rice award, 1963; Outer Circle award, 1964. **Agent:** Georges Borchardt Inc., 136 East 57th Street, New York, New York 10022.

Publications

Plays

Whisper into My Good Ear (produced New York, 1962; London, 1966). Included in *Mrs. Dally Has a Lover and Other Plays*, 1963.
Mrs. Dally Has a Lover (produced New York, 1962; revised version, produced New York, 1988). Included in *Mrs. Dally Has a Lover and Other Plays*, 1963.
Conversations in the Dark (produced Philadelphia, 1963).
Mrs. Dally Has a Lover and Other Plays. New York, Dial Press, 1963.
Today Is Independence Day (produced Berlin, 1963; New York, 1965). Included in *Mrs. Dally Has a Lover and Other Plays*, 1963.
Slow Dance on the Killing Ground (produced New York, 1964; London, 1991). New York, Random House, 1964.
Flesh and Blood (televised 1968). New York, Random House, 1968.
No Answer, in *Collision Course* (produced New York, 1968). New York, Random House, 1968.
Whisper Into My Good Ear, Mrs. Dally Has a Lover: Two Plays. New York, Dramatists Play Service, 1991.

Screenplay: *The Gypsy Moths*, 1969.

Radio Play: *A Country Without Rain*, 1970.

Television Plays: *Flesh and Blood*, 1968; *Testimony of Two Men*, with James and Jennifer Miller, from the novel by Taylor Caldwell, 1977; *Who'll Save Our Children*, from a book by Rachel Maddox, 1978; *The Family Man*, 1979; *Too Far to Go*, from stories by John Updike, 1979; *Father Figure*, 1980; *Moviola: The Scarlett O'Hara War* and *The Silent Lovers*, from the novel by Garson Kanin, 1980; *Little Gloria . . . Happy at Last*, from the book by Barbara Goldsmith, 1982; *Something about Amelia*, 1984; *Celebrity*, 1984.

Novels

Blue Dreams; or, The End of Romance and the Continued Pursuit of Happiness. New York, Delacorte Press, and London, W.H. Allen, 1971.
Mixed Feelings. New York, Doubleday, 1972.
Leaving Mt. Venus. New York, Ballantine, 1977.

* * *

With a trio of one-act plays and one full-length drama, William Hanley achieved a reputation in American drama that seems to have satisfied him. During a three-year period he made his appearance, created a play—*Slow Dance on the Killing Ground*—that not only reflected relevant contemporary issues but also provided three acting vehicles, and disappeared from the New York theater scene.

In spite of some serious dramaturgical weaknesses in his work, Hanley was one of the few American playwrights who infused a certain amount of vitality into American drama in the early 1960s. His one-act plays are somewhat unstructured, talky, two-character plays. They are essentially conversations, but they involve perceptive thought, poetic tenderness, and the problems and feelings of generally believable people. Hanley's major concern is communication, that sometimes impossible connection between two people. Language, therefore, is important to him, and his plays occasionally show a too luxuriant use of it, just as these same plays become overly concerned with discussion. Understandably, then, his sense of humanity, which is allied to his feelings for communication, frequently erupts in a distasteful sentimentality. He believes in the optimism that such sentiment suggests, however, and although his characters seem to stumble around in an unhappy world, they do see something better. It is this vague idea of something better that he once explained as the major thought he wished his audiences for *Slow Dance on the Killing Ground* would take with them. It was a shrewd comment, for throughout man's history such points of view have not only been acceptable but also ardently desired, especially in the theater.

Whisper into My Good Ear presented the conversation of two old men who are contemplating suicide but change their minds. One can find a good ear for ones problems; friends have value. Hanley's most popular one-act play, *Mrs. Dally Has a Lover*, is a conversation between a middle-aged Mrs. Dally and her 18-year-old lover. Before they part when the curtain falls and their affair ends, the difficulty of conversation is dramatized as they are drawn in and out of their respective psychological shells. The sympathy created in the play for Mrs. Dally is further explored in *Today Is Independence Day,* in which she talks with her husband, Sam, who almost leaves her but decides to stay. Mrs. Dally also makes decisions about her own attitudes, and although the ending of the play is sad and essentially unhappy, it is an affirmation of living.

The same comment can be made for *Slow Dance on the Killing Ground*, his only full-length Broadway success. (*Conversations in the Dark*, a discussion of the problems of husband-wife infidelity, closed in Philadelphia.) Act 1 of *Slow Dance* introduces us to three characters. None of the three—a young black genius, a middle-class white girl, a Jew who has denied his heritage and his family—can escape the violence of the world, the killing ground. In act 2 each is unmasked, and in act 3 a mock trial shows that each one guilty. Although the play suggests that nothing can be done, there is a cohesiveness among the characters, a joint decision toward commitment and responsibility on this killing ground, that tends to remove the play from sentimental and simply clever melodrama. Instead, Hanley's insight into his characters and his obvious theme of contemporary significance have challenged critics to see *Slow Dance* as a quite substantial theater piece.

—Walter J. Meserve

HANNAN, Chris(topher John)

Nationality: British. **Born:** Glasgow, 25 January 1958. **Education:** St. Aloysius' College, Glasgow, 1969-75; University College, Oxford, 1975-78. **Career:** Voluntary worker, Simon Community, Glasgow, 1978-80. Lives in Edinburgh. **Awards:** *Time Out* award, 1991; *Plays and Players* award, 1991; Charrington London Fringe award, 1991.

PUBLICATIONS

Plays

Purity (produced Edinburgh, 1984).
Klimkov: Life of a Tsarist Agent (produced Edinburgh, 1984).
Elizabeth Gordon Quinn (produced Edinburgh, 1985). London, Hern, 1990.
The Orphans' Comedy (produced Edinburgh, 1986).
Gamblers, with Christopher Rathbone, adaptation of a play by Nikolai Gogol (produced Glasgow, 1987; London, 1992).
The Baby (produced Glasgow, 1990). London, Hern, 1991.
The Evil Doers (produced London, 1990). London, Hern, 1991.
The Pretenders, adaptation of the play by Henrik Ibsen (produced London, 1991).
The Evil Doers and the Baby. London, Nick Hern, 1991.
Shining Souls. London, Nick Hern, 1996.

*

Chris Hannan comments:

I'm attracted to mess; chaos. I read a couple of books about chaos theory, which I enjoyed. I can get quite into the philosophy of science. I suppose it gives me a way to think about form, patterns, order and disorder.

I like characters who believe in things however ridiculous the belief. Elizabeth Gordon Quinn, for example, is a woman who refuses to believe she's poor. To prove to herself that she's someone grand—an individual—she has a piano. Unfortunately this means she can't eat or pay the rent. She's a ridiculous and destructive woman in conflict with her family and community but also sort of heroic.

Elizabeth Gordon Quinn is quite melodramatic. Whatever I write I like the thing to have a heightened quality, a language. I admire language which is mesmeric even when it's nonsense, like in Gogol or Ben Jonson where words dance in front of the characters' eyes like the fires of hell.

I suppose I write about people who are trying to save themselves, in deformed or exotic ways. Like Macu in *The Baby* who confronts Pompey and the entire Roman State singlehandedly in a misplaced attempt to exorcise her private hurts. Or like Sammy and Tracky in *The Evil Doers* who try to save themselves from the chaos in their lives by creating more chaos.

* * *

Chris Hannan writes complex narrative plays about people of strong principle and strong feeling that, nevertheless, sometimes exist on the verge of social chaos and emotional desperation. His great skill is in creating remarkably complex characters and then placing those characters in surroundings that test their mettle and morality. Hannan, however, never abandons his creations for the audience's voyeuristic indulgence. His plays are deeply and poetically moral and spiritually generous. They are precariously, but enticingly, balanced between what the actor and playwright Simon Donald identifies as the populist and the intellectual.

From *Elizabeth Gordon Quinn* (1985) to *The Evil Doers* (1990) and *Shining Souls* (1996), the conventions of the genre of working-class familial drama, character types, environment, and social agenda remain pervasive and ubiquitous. Within the conventions of Scottish writing, such images and ideas maintain their potency to the extent that writers can refer with confidence to a set of shorthand indicators and familiar images in order to reassess the mythology. The most sustained example of this tendency is his radical deconstruction in *Elizabeth Gordon Quinn* of a Scottish urban mythology. This play disects the seemingly impermeable stereotypes of Scottish popular culture: the strong and suffering working-class mother; the community spirit of the tenement; the tradition of the uniquely brave Scottish soldier; and the mythology of Red Clydeside. Hannan depicts a whirl of social activity and political organization bubbling around the aloof and solitary figure of Elizabeth. Denying sentimentalism and effacing heroicism, Hannan creates a character at odds with her environment and our perceived images of that environment. Although she lives in a tenement, Elizabeth rejects a legacy of representation that insists on the ethos of collectivism and togetherness. Hannan describes a flat, a room, and a character surrounded by life but determinedly separate from it: "Please come in, Mrs Shaw. This is a tenement after all. We have no alternative but to enter into the spirit of it."

But Hannan's heroine does disown the "spirit" associated with the tenement. Elizabeth's front door may be open, but the egalitarian ideology that this might suggest is rejected. She consistently denies the existence of community in two directions. Primarily she defies the community of the working-class environment around her (the close, the street), but she also repudiates the ideal of the nurturing, mutually supportive community of family. Around Elizabeth movements of collective activity (a rent strike organized by the women of the district and the national military mobilization) threaten the ideal of splendid isolation Elizabeth has constructed. These two points of shared responsibility are symbolized in her relations with her children. Aidan and Maura attempt to embrace community, mostly to spite and to escape their mother. Maura works with her neighbors in what develops as a highly politicized rent strike, while Aidan has first joined and then deserted an Irish regiment.

Analyzing the tradition of working-class drama as contributing to and supporting social protest, Hannan offers a character who transgresses not just gender roles but refuses the identity imposed by politics, economics, and convention: "I refuse to learn how to be poor," declares the defiant Elizabeth at the end of the play, countering a version of Scottish drama that sustains, if not celebrates, a dominant mythology of a staunch working-class identity united within an aggressive and ignoble capitalist hierarchy. Hannan's play is a complex psychological minefield in which his central character steadfastly refuses the myth of collective and socialist responsibility while paralleling the practical success of the recognition and politicization of community and shared responsibility.

Hannan's play, while concentrating on this individual at odds with her family and society, still offers the ideal of the group as a valid and effective force for social organization and political change. While Elizabeth denies her commonality with the striking women, their joint action is successful: rents do fall. *Elizabeth Gordon Quinn* is radical in the emotional and intellectual complexities it unearths within the myth of the family and the tenement community. It still acknowledges and allows, however, for characters finding strength and power in the celebration and mobilization of their commonalities.

The idea of the individual at odds with the community also appears in Hannan's revisionary city comedies, *The Evil Doers* and *Shining Souls,* each offering very bleak views of contemporary urban Glasgow. *The Evil Doers* is an idiosyncratic comedy about money and the pursuit of it. Its central characters, Tracky and Susan, are teenage girls, more or less abandoned by the adults in their lives and engaged in a strange, and even mythic, journey through inner-city Glasgow, reinvented in its guise as the 1990 "City of Culture." Tracky, a teenage heavy-metal music fan, pursues and is pursued by her alcoholic mother, while she tries to win some degree of attention and love by attempting to sabotage her father's taxi business. Meanwhile, Susan tracks a seductive loan shark who is, in his turn, chasing her father. It is a grim, disordered environment but one where friendship can survive and, indeed, must endure.

A similar world of loan sharks and addiction (this time a gambling addiction) is described in the black comedy *Shining Souls*. Again Hannan references the genre of the Jonsonian city comedy, and the core of the play is the pursuit of money. The vestiges of family are represented by the mother and daughter, Ann and Mandy; friends Max and Charlie; Charlie's estranged wife, Margaret Mary; and Mandy's two suitors, Billy I and Billy II. The play confronts the regrets and sorrows of family and of faith, with a central concern being the role of fate and self-determination within a chaotic, urban present and a central motif being Ann's question to Mandy, "Do you not believe in happy endings . . . ?"

—Adrienne Scullion

HARE, David

Nationality: British. **Born:** Bexhill, Sussex, 5 June 1947. **Education:** Lancing College, Sussex; Jesus College, Cambridge, M.A. 1968. **Family:** Married 1) Margaret Matheson in 1970 (divorced 1980); two sons and one daughter; 2) Nicole Farhi in 1992. **Career:** Founding director, Portable Theatre, 1968-71; literary manager, 1969-70, and resident dramatist, 1970-71, Royal Court Theatre, London; resident dramatist, Nottingham Playhouse, 1973; co-founder, 1973, and director, 1975-80, Joint Stock Theatre Company; founder, Greenpoint Films, 1982. Associate director, National Theatre, London, 1984—. Lives in London. **Awards:** Variety London Critics Poll, 1970; Evening Standard Drama award, 1970, 1985; John Llewellyn Rhys award, 1974; BAFTA Best Play of the Year, 1978; New York Critics Circle award, 1983, 1997; Berlin Golden Bear, for Best Film, 1985; Plays and Players Best Play, 1985, 1988, 1990; City Limits Theatre award, 1985; Fellow of the Royal Society of Literature, 1985; Drama Magazine award, 1988; London Critics Poll, for Best Play, 1990; Time Out Theatre award, 1990; Laurence Olivier award, for Best Play, 1990, 1995; Drama-Logue award, 1992; Officier de l'Ordre des Arts et Lettres, 1997. **Agent:** Casarotto Ramsay Ltd., National House, 60-66 Wardour Street, London W1V 3HP, England.

PUBLICATIONS

Plays

Inside Out, with Tony Bicât, adaptation of the diaries of Kafka (also director: produced London, 1968).
How Brophy Made Good (produced London, 1969). Published in *Gambit 17* (London), 1971.
What Happened to Blake? (produced London, 1970).
Slag (produced London, 1970; New York, 1971). London, Faber, 1971.
The Rules of the Game, adaptation of a play by Pirandello (produced London, 1971).
Deathsheads (sketch), in *Christmas Present* (produced Edinburgh, 1971).
Lay By, with others (produced Edinburgh and London, 1971). London, Calder and Boyars, 1972.
The Great Exhibition (produced Hampstead, 1972). London, Faber, 1972.
England's Ireland, with others (also director: produced Amsterdam and London, 1972).
Brassneck, with Howard Brenton (also director: produced Nottingham, 1973). London, Eyre Methuen, 1974.
Knuckle (produced Oxford and London, 1974; New York, 1975). London, Faber, 1974; revised version, 1978.
Fanshen, adaptation of the book by William Hinton (produced London, 1975; Milwaukee, 1976; New York, 1977). London, Faber, 1976.
Teeth 'n' Smiles, music by Nick Bicât, lyrics by Tony Bicât (also director: produced London, 1975; Washington, D.C., 1977). London, Faber, 1976.
Plenty (also director: produced London, 1978; Washington, D.C., 1980; New York, 1982). London, Faber, 1978; New York, New American Library, 1985.
Deeds, with others (produced Nottingham, 1978). Published in *Plays and Players* (London), May and June 1978.
Licking Hitler (televised 1978). London, Faber, 1978.
Dreams of Leaving (televised 1980). London, Faber, 1980.
A Map of the World (also director: produced Adelaide, Australia, 1982; London, 1983; New York, 1985). London, Faber, 1982; revised version, 1983.
Saigon: Year of the Cat (televised 1983). London, Faber, 1983.
The Madman Theory of Deterrence (sketch), in *The Big One* (produced London, 1983).
The History Plays (includes *Knuckle, Licking Hitler, Plenty*). London, Faber, 1984.
Pravda: A Fleet Street Comedy, with Howard Brenton (also director: produced London, 1985; Minneapolis, 1989). London, Methuen, 1985.
Wetherby (screenplay). London, Faber, 1985.
The Asian Plays (includes *Fanshen, Saigon: Year of the Cat, A Map of the World*). London, Faber, 1986.
The Bay at Nice, and Wrecked Eggs (also director: produced London, 1986; New York, 1987). London, Faber, 1986.
The Knife (opera), music by Nick Bicât, lyrics by Tim Rose Price (also director: produced New York, 1987).
Paris by Night (screenplay). London, Faber, 1988.
The Secret Rapture (produced London, 1988; New York, 1989). London, Faber, 1988; New York, Grove Weidenfeld, 1989.
Strapless (screenplay). London, Faber, 1990.
Racing Demon (produced London, 1990; New York, 1995). London, Faber, 1990.
Murmuring Judges (produced London, 1992). London, Faber, 1991.
Heading Home (televized 1991). With *Wetherby* and *Dreams of Leaving*, London, Faber, 1991.
Heading Home, Wetherby, Dreams of Leaving. London, Faber, 1991.
The Early Plays (includes *Slag, Teeth 'n' Smiles, Dreams of Leaving*). London, Faber, 1992.
The Absence of War (produced London, 1993).
The Life of Galileo, adaptation of Brecht (produced Almeida, 1994).
Mother Courage and Her Children, adaptation of Brecht (produced London, 1995).
Skylight (produced London, 1995; New York, 1996).
Ivanov, adaptation of Chekhov (produced Almeida and New York, 1995).
La Ronde, adaptation of Schnitzler (produced 1998).
Amy's View (London, 1997; Aldwych, 1998).
The Judas Kiss (Almeida and New York, 1998).
Via Dolorosa (produced 1998).

Screenplays: *Wetherby*, 1985; *Plenty*, 1985; *Paris by Night*, 1989; *Strapless*, 1990; *Damage*, adapted from the novel by Josephine Hart, 1992; *The Secret Rapture,* 1993; *Feasting with the Panthers,* 1996.

Television Plays: *Man above Men*, 1973; *Licking Hitler*, 1978; *Dreams of Leaving*, 1980; *Saigon: Year of the Cat*, 1983; *Heading Home*, 1991; *The Absence of War* (BBC), 1995.

Other

Writing Left-Handed. London, Faber, 1991.

*

Critical Studies: By John Simon, in *Hudson Review* (New York), 1971; *The New British Drama* by Oleg Kerensky, London, Hamish Hamilton, 1977, New York, Taplinger, 1979; *Dreams and Deconstructions* edited by Sandy Craig, Ambergate, Derbyshire, Amber Lane Press, 1980; *Stages in the Revolution* by Catherine Itzin, London, Eyre Methuen, 1980; "Breaking the Bond with Edward Bond" by Marc Robinson, in *Theater* (New Haven, Connecticut), Winter-Spring 1989-1990, pp. 23-28; "Saint Isobel: David Hare's *the Secret Rapture* as Christian Allegory" by Liorah Anne Golomb, in *Modern Drama* (Downsview, Ontario), December 1990, pp. 563-74; *File on Hare* edited by Malcolm Page, London, Methuen, 1990; "Freedom and Form in David Hare's Drama" by James Gindin, in *British and Irish Drama Since 1960,* edited by James Acheson, Houndmills, England, Macmillan, 1993; "Interview: David Hare" by Georg Gaston, in *Theatre Journal* (Baltimore, Maryland), May 1993, pp. 213-25; *The Plays of David Hare* by Carol Homden, Cambridge, Cambridge University Press, 1995; "David Hare" by Judy Lee Oliva, in *British Playwrights, 1956-1995: A Research and Production Sourcebook,* Westport, Connecticut, Greenwood, 1996; "Nostalgic Rapture: Interpreting Moral Commitments in David Hare's Drama" by John J. Su, in *Modern Drama* (Downsview, Ontario), Spring 1997, pp. 23-37.

Theatrical Activities:
Director: **Plays**—*Inside Out*, London, 1968; *Christie in Love* by Howard Brenton, Brighton and London, 1969; *Purity* by David Mowat, Canterbury, 1969; *Fruit* by Howard Brenton, London, 1970; *Blowjob* by Snoo Wilson, Edinburgh and London, 1971; *England's Ireland*, Amsterdam and London, 1972; *The Provoked Wife* by Vanbrugh, Watford, Hertfordshire, 1973; *Brassneck*, Nottingham, 1973; *The Pleasure Principle* by Snoo Wilson, London, 1973; *The Party* by Trevor Griffiths, tour, 1974; *Teeth 'n' Smiles*, London, 1975; *Weapons of Happiness* by Howard Brenton, London, 1976; *Devil's Island* by Tony Bicât, Cardiff and London, 1977; *Plenty*, London, 1978, New York, 1982; *Total Eclipse* by Christopher Hampton, London, 1981; *A Map of the World*, Adelaide, 1982, London, 1983, New York, 1985; *Pravda*, London, 1985; *The Bay at Nice, and Wrecked Eggs*, London, 1986; *King Lear*, London, 1986; *The Knife*, New York, 1987; *The Designated Mourner* by Wallace Shawn, London, 1996; *Heartbreak House* by Bernard Shaw, Almeida, 1997. **Film**—*Wetherby*, 1985; *Paris by Night*, 1989; *Strapless*, 1990; *The Designated Mourner* by Wallace Shawn, 1996. **Television**—*Licking Hitler*, 1978; *Dreams of Leaving*, 1980; *Saigon: Year of the Cat*, 1983; *Heading Home*, 1990.

* * *

David Hare's early plays show a bright young man drawing on his education, writing of Kafka and Blake, and on his experience. *Teeth 'n' Smiles* is about a Cambridge May ball, audaciously linking a rock band with a serious play while giving Helen Mirren a memorable part. *Slag,* which is superficially about women teachers, in fact reflects Hare's view of how institutions shape people. While in his 20s, Hare also gained practical theater experience with the Portable Theatre and accepted invitations to write, collaborating on *Lay By* and *England's Ireland.* His left-wing political convictions—always scrutinized, flexible, and rarely dogmatic—began to show in *The Great Exhibition,* the study of a burned-out Labour M.P. who sold out. Hare's political self-education continued in his adaptation of *Fanshen,* showing that the condition of Chinese peasants clearly improved after the revolution and implying a roughly comparable need for change in Britain. *Fanshen* was, however, as much a Joint Stock collective effort as a distinct Hare work.

From *Brassneck* on, nearly all of Hare's writing has been engaged with the condition of England, and his scripts for film and television are also usually a part of his unfolding, expanding, and increasingly complex views. With two pieces especially, *A Map of the World* and *Saigon,* Hare's subject broadens from Britain to the world. Cowritten with Howard Brenton, *Brassneck* is an epic about the rise of a new style of capitalism in the Midlands from 1945 on, including the operation of strip clubs and the importing of heroin, to a final toast to "the last days of capitalism."

Plenty, probably Hare's best play and one that survived reasonably faithfully in the film version, starts with World War II. Full of a sense of mission, young Susan operates in occupied France, and on a sunny hillside in August she optimistically looks ahead: "There will be days and days and days like this." Said in a flashback, this is the last line of the drama, but earlier we have seen Susan's disillusion as the play counterpoints her private life with such public events as the Festival of Britain in 1951, changed to the 1953 coronation in the film, and the British attack on Suez in 1956. Her friend Alice appears to be more successful at discovering a purpose in her life in peacetime.

Hare's preoccupation with how the war shaped postwar Britain is reflected also in his *Licking Hitler,* which was written for television. *Pravda,* also coauthored with Brenton, is polemical, a ferocious, energetic attack on sensational newspapers and their owners, who are motivated only by profit. Anthony Hopkins memorably played the unprincipled magnate.

Some of Hare's later writing highlights the personal, notably two domestic one-acters—*Wrecked Eggs* and *The Bay at* Nice—and three film scripts—*Wetherby,* reflecting Hare as a Londoner puzzled by middle-class life in the small Yorkshire market town, *Strapless,* and *Paris by Night.* In the introduction to the latter, Hare wrote, "Although there has been a considerable body of films and plays about the economic results of Thatcherism, there has been almost nothing of consequence about the characteristics and personalities of those who have ruled over us during these last eight years." He remedied this in *The Secret Rapture,* which contrasts a Conservative woman M.P., a kind of attempt to understand Margaret Thatcher, and her good sister, "a portrait of absolute goodness," wrote Michael Ratcliffe. In a rather similar way *Skylight* juxtaposes a wealthy Thatcherite, a restaurant owner, and an idealistic teacher who has been his mistress. Beyond the specifics of political attitudes, in these works Hare continues his exploration of love and goodness.

The link between such works and *The Judas Kiss* is Hare's preoccupation with betrayal and unrequited love. Oscar Wilde seems at first an unexpected subject for Hare. He focuses on two episodes—Wilde's failure to avoid arrest by fleeing the country and Wilde in Naples after his release from prison.

Hare's 1990-93 trilogy at the National Theatre examining the Church of England (*Racing Demon*), the legal system (*Murmuring Judges*) and politics (*The Absence of War*), with the last focusing on Labour's campaign in the 1992 election, is his most ambitious study of the condition of England. Most critics have found *Racing Demon* to be the best play. Hare emphasized the documentary element of the works by publishing an account of his research. Michael Billington summed up his achievement by saying that the trilogy "not only offers a vigorous, bracing, provocative portrait of modern Britain, but also a coherent vision: Hare pins down, with mordant wit, the institutional clubbiness, the increasing reliance on P.R., the sclerotic ancestor-worship, the decay of any core belief, that he sees as symptoms of our current malaise."

Each of Hare's mature works has greater resonance when placed in sequence and in context. More than any other British dramatist, he has scrutinized the state of the nation for the past quarter of a century.

—Malcolm Page

HARRIS, Richard

Nationality: British. **Born:** London, 26 March 1934. **Awards:** London *Evening Standard* award, 1979, for best comedy, 1984; Molière award, Paris, 1990; New York Film and Television Festival gold medal, 1990. **Agent:** Lemon, Unna, and Durbridge, 24 Pottery Lane, Holland Park, London W11 4LZ, England.

Publications

Plays

Partners: A Comedy (produced Edinburgh, 1969). London, Evans 1973.
Albert: A One-Act Comedy (produced London, 1971). London, Evans, 1972.
You Must Be Virginia (produced London, 1971).
No, No, Not Yet, with Leslie Darbon (produced Windsor, 1972).
Two and Two Make Sex, with Leslie Darbon (produced Windsor and London, 1973). London, French, 1973.
Who Goes Bare?, with Leslie Darbon (produced Windsor, 1974).
Conscience Be Damned (produced London, 1975).
Correspondents' Course, with Leslie Darbon (produced Westcliff, Essex, 1976). London, French, 1976.
The Pressures of Life: Four Television Plays. London, Longman, 1977.
Outside Edge (produced London, 1979). London, French, 1980.
The Dog It Was (produced Richmond, Surrey, 1980).
The Business of Murder (produced Windsor and London, 1981). Oxford, Amber Lane, 1985.
Is It Something I Said? (produced London, 1982). London, French, 1982.
Local Affairs (produced Leicester, 1982). London, French, 1982.
Stepping Out (produced Leatherhead, Surrey and London, 1984). Oxford, Amber Lane, 1985.
The Maintenance Man (produced Leatherhead, Surrey, 1986; London, 1986). London, French, 1987.
Three Piece Suite (produced Hornchurch, Essex, 1986).
Visiting Hour (includes *Plaster*, *Keeping Mum*, *Show Business*, *Going Home*, *Waiting*, *Magic*) (produced London, 1987; revised version produced Richmond, Surrey, 1990). London, French, 1991.
Party Piece (produced Basingstoke, 1990). London, French, 1990.
Keeping Mum. New York, Samuel French, 1991.
Mixed Blessing (musical), with Keith Strachan (produced Westcliff, Essex, 1991).
Dead Guilty. London, Samuel French, 1996.

Screenplays: *Strongroom*, with Max Marquis, 1965; *I Start Counting*, adaptation of the novel by Audrey Erskine Lindop, 1969; *The Lady in the Car with Glasses and a Gun*, adaptation of the novel by Sebastian Japrisot, 1970; *Orion's Belt*, adaptation of the novel by Jan Michelet, 1988; *Stepping Out*, 1991.

Radio Play: *Was It Something I Said?*, 1978.

Television Plays: *Who's a Good Boy Then? I Am*; *You Must Be Virginia*; *Saving It for Albie*; *When the Boys Come Out to Play*; *Sunday in Perspective*; *Occupier's Risk*; *Time and Mr. Madingley*; *I Can See Your Lips Move*; *A Slight Formality*; *Jack's Trade*; *Dog Ends*; *Searching for Senor Duende* and *This for the Half, Darling*, in *About Face* series, 1989; *Murder Most English*, adaptation of *The Flaxborough Chronicles* by Colin Watson; *The Prince and the Pauper*, adaptation of the novel by Mark Twain; *Plain Murder*, adaptation of the novel by C. S. Forester; *Sherlock Holmes*, adaptation of the novel by Arthur Conan Doyle; *The Darling Buds of May*, adaptation of the novel by H. E. Bates, 1991; *A Touch of Frost*, adaptation of the novels by R. D. Wingfield; *Shoestring* series; *Man in a Suitcase* series; *The Gamblers* series.

* * *

Few playwrights can boast one of the longest-running comedies in London as well as one of the longest-running thrillers. With *The Business of Murder* and *Stepping Out,* Richard Harris has had both. But then Harris has always been a skilled professional. His work delivers exactly what it promises for the most part, but with two plays—*Outside Edge* and *Stepping Out*—he staked a claim to be regarded as an original comic talent rather than the second-league Ayckbourn he has sometimes been dubbed.

Harris seems at home in most theatrical genres. In collaboration with Leslie Darbon, he has written a clever farce with the misleadingly sniggering title *Two and Two Make Sex.* A typical piece of British farcical comedy—menopausal man pursing younger girl, her boyfriend attracting the older man's wife, both pairs ignorant of the complications until a late scene of near confrontations—it naturally featured sex deferred rather than sex consummated, but, within the limitations of the genre, characteristic Harris insights into women's points of view could be glimpsed underneath the mechanics of telephone calls and close encounters on a split-level set. And *The Maintenance Man,* a fairly formula comedy centered around an eternal triangle, again provided two rounded roles for women.

Women dominated *Outside Edge* and *Stepping Out.* Set in a local cricket club, *Outside Edge* is a deceptively small-scale play. Underneath the cricket jokes and sight gags there gradually emerges a sense of real pain in the midst of this suburban haven, and cracks in supposedly happy marriages and relationships begin to appear like weeds on the club's lawn. Harris has again written especially good female roles, and he has created an original and endearing double act in the shape of a role-reversing couple. She, memorably played by Maureen Lipman in London, is tall and lusty and copes with all of the heavy building work at home, while he is tiny and domestic and takes over the cooking and the polishing. They are the happiest couple in the play.

Stepping Out has a single male role, the shy widower who is the only man in attendance at the weekly tap dance class in a North London church hall. Mavis, the ex-chorus girl instructor, the redoubtable and temperamental pianist, together with seven very contrasting pupils, make up the rest of the cast. In the course of the play, following the class through until their appearance at the finale in which they step out at a charity performance to Irving Berlin, Harris traces the patterns behind these separate lives. All is obliquely handled, with much being revealed in throwaway clues rather than in confessional speeches. This is especially so in the case of Vera, another Harris original, an apparently bright, confident wife of an older and much absent businessman husband given to cheery aphorisms ("It may be February outside but it's always August under the armpits"). Her marriage, we gradually sense, is driving her into increasing isolation. Harris does not have room to develop all of his characters to the same extent, but the play has an authenticity and sureness of rhythm that make it more than a formula hit. When the core to the play was readjusted, as for the glitzy Broadway version or for the movie, it was much less successful.

Later Harris work has included the revue-style book for *Mixed Blessings,* a musical on marriage involving several contrasting couples that was poorly staged in its regional premiere, and several reworkings, under various titles, of the comedy *Party Piece,* set in the adjoining back gardens of two socially different couples and with a memorable portrait of a possessive mother. All of this suggests that Harris's drive not to repeat himself is unimpaired.

Harris's prolific work for television, including a successful series based on the *Outside Edge* characters, seems to have stifled his theatrical drive, however. Another excursion into the theater, the book of the small-scale musical version of *Stepping Out,* was efficient enough but did nothing to his original play to suggest that it was worth musicalization in the first place.

—Alan Strachan

HARRISON, Tony

Nationality: British. **Born:** Leeds, Yorkshire, 30 April 1937. **Education:** Cross Flatts County Primary, Leeds, 1942-48; Leeds Grammar School, 1948-55; University of Leeds, 1955-60, B.A. in classics 1958, postgraduate diploma in linguistics. **Family:** Married 1) Rosemarie Crossfield in 1962, one daughter and one son; 2) Teresa Stratas in 1984. **Career:** Schoolmaster, Dewsbury, Yorkshire, 1960-62; lecturer in English, Ahmadu Bello University, Zaria, Northern Nigeria, 1962-66, and Charles University, Prague, 1966-67; editor, with Jon Silkin and Ken Smith, *Stand* magazine, Newcastle-upon-Tyne, 1968-69; resident dramatist, National Theatre, London, 1977-79. U.K.-U.S. Bicentennial fellow, New York, 1979-80. President, Classical Association of Great Britain, 1987-88. **Awards:** Northern Arts fellowship, 1967, 1976; Cholmondeley award, 1969; UNESCO fellowship, 1969; Faber memorial award, 1972; Gregynog fellowship, 1973; U.S. Bicentennial fellowship, 1979; European Poetry translation prize, 1983; Whitbread Poetry prize, 1992. Fellow, Royal Society of Literature, 1984. **Agent:** Gordon Dickerson, 2 Crescent Grove, London SW4, England.

PUBLICATIONS

Plays

Aikin Mata, with James Simmons, adaptation of *Lysistrata* by Aristophanes (produced Zaria, Nigeria, 1965). Ibadan, Oxford University Press, 1966.

The Misanthrope, adaptation of a play by Molière (produced London, 1973; Washington, D.C. and New York, 1975). London, Rex Collings, 1973; New York, Third Press, 1975.

Phaedra Britannica, adaptation of a play by Racine (produced London, 1975; New York, 1988). London, Rex Collings, 1975.

Bow Down, music by Harrison Birtwistle (produced London, 1977). London, Rex Collings, 1977.

The Passion, from the York Mystery Plays (produced London, 1977; with *The Nativity* and *Doomsday*, as *The Mysteries*, London, 1985). London, Rex Collings, 1977; in *The Mysteries*, 1985.

The Bartered Bride, adaptation of an opera by Sabina, music by Smetana (produced New York, 1978). New York, Schirmer, 1978; in *Dramatic Verse*, 1985.

The Nativity, from the York Mystery Plays (produced London, 1980; with *The Passion* and *Doomsday*, as *The Mysteries*, 1985). In *The Mysteries*, 1985.

The Oresteia, music by Harrison Birtwistle, adaptation of the plays by Aeschylus (includes *Agamemnon*; *Choephori*; *Eumenides*) (produced London, 1981). London, Rex Collings, 1981.

Yan Tan Tethera, music by Harrison Birtwistle (produced London, 1983). In *Dramatic Verse*, 1985.

The Big H, music by Dominic Muldowney (televised, 1984). Included in *Dramatic Verse*, 1985.

Dramatic Verse 1973-1985 (includes *The Misanthrope*; *Phaedra Britannica*; *Bow Down*; *The Bartered Bride*; *The Oresteia*; *Yan Tan Tethera*; *The Big H*; *Medea: Sex War*). Newcastle-upon-Tyne, Bloodaxe, 1985; as *Theatre Works 1973-1985*, London, Penguin, 1986.

Doomsday, from the York Mystery Plays (with *The Nativity* and *The Passion*, as *The Mysteries*, produced London, 1985). In *The Mysteries*, 1985.

The Mysteries, adaptation of the York Mystery Plays (includes *The Passion*, *The Nativity*, *Doomsday*) (produced London, 1985). London, Faber, 1985.

Medea: Sex War (produced London, 1991). Included in *Dramatic Verse*, 1985.

The Trackers of Oxyrhynchus (produced Delphi, 1988; London, 1990). London, Faber, 1990.

The Common Chorus. London, Faber, 1992.

Square Rounds (also director: produced London, 1992). London, Faber, 1992.

Poetry or Bust. Salts Mill, Saltaire, 1993.

The Kaisers of Carnuntum (produced Carnuntum, Austria, 1995).

The Labourers of Herakles (produced Delphi, Greece, 1995). Published in *Plays 3,* New York, Faber.

The Prince's Play (produced New York, 1996).

Prometheus. New York, Faber, 1998.

Television Pieces: *Arctic Paradise*, 1981; *The Big H*, music by Dominic Muldowney, 1984; *Loving Memory* series, 1987; *V.*, 1987; *The Blasphemers' Banquet*, 1989; *The Gaze of the Gorgon*, adaptation of *The Oresteia* and *The Mysteries*, 1992; *A Maybe Day in Kazakhstah, The Shadow of Hiroshima.*

Poetry

Earthworks. Leeds, Northern House, 1964.

Newcastle Is Peru. Newcastle-upon-Tyne, Eagle Press, 1969.

The Loiners. London, London Magazine Editions, 1970.

Corgi Modern Poets in Focus 4, with others, edited by Jeremy Robson. London, Corgi, 1971.

Ten Poems from the School of Eloquence. London, Rex Collings, 1976.

From the School of Eloquence and Other Poems. London, Rex Collings, 1978.

Looking Up, with Philip Sharpe. West Malvern, Worcestershire, Migrant Press, 1979.

Continuous: 50 Sonnets from the School of Eloquence. London, Rex Collings, 1981.
A Kumquat for John Keats. Newcastle-upon-Tyne, Bloodaxe, 1981.
U.S. Martial. Newcastle-upon-Tyne, Bloodaxe, 1981.
Selected Poems. London, Viking Press, 1984; revised edition, London, Penguin and New York, Random House, 1987.
The Fire-Gap: A Poem with Two Tails. Newcastle-upon-Tyne, Bloodaxe, 1985.
V. (single poem). Newcastle-upon-Tyne, Bloodaxe, 1985; with press articles, 1989.
Anno 42. N.p., Michael C. Caine, 1987.
Ten Sonnets from the School of Eloquence. London, Anvil Press Poetry, 1987.
V. and Other Poems. New York, Farrar Straus, 1989.
A Cold Coming: Gulf War Poems. Newcastle-upon-Tyne, Bloodaxe, 1991.
The Gaze of the Gorgon. Newcastle-upon-Tyne, Bloodaxe, 1992.
The Shadow of Hiroshima and Other Film/Poems. New York, Faber and Faber, 1995.
Permanently Bard. Newcastle, Bloodaxe, 1995.

Other

Poems, by Palladas. London, Anvil Press Poetry, 1975.

*

Bibliography: *Tony Harrison: A Bibliography 1957-1987* by John R. Kaiser, London, Mansell, 1989.

Manuscript Collections: University of Newcastle-upon-Tyne; Newcastle Literary and Philosophical Society.

Critical Studies: *Essays on Tony Harrison* edited by Neil Astley, Newcastle-upon-Tyne, Bloodaxe, 1990; *Ancient Sun, Modern Light* by Marianne McDonald, New York, Columbia University Press, 1992; "Postmodern Classics: The Verse Drama of Tony Harrison" by Romana Huk, in *British and Irish Drama Since 1960*, edited by James Acheson, London, Macmillan and New York, St. Martin's Press, 1993; *The Poetry of Tony Harrison* by Luke Spencer, Harvester, 1994; *Tony Harrison* by Joe Kelleher, 1996; *Tony Harrison: Loiner,* edited by Sandie Byrne, Oxford University Press, 1996.

Tony Harrison comments:

It seems to me no accident that some of the world's best poetry is to be found in some of the world's best drama, and comes from those periods when poets, and I emphasise poets, worked directly with actors and wrote their pieces for specific players and spaces. This is to be found in the ancient Greek drama, for which I have had a lifelong passion, when the poet was regarded as the "didaskalos" the "teacher" of his work, and the term would involve everything now taken over by the function of director. The relationship is to be found also in the theatre of Shakespeare, the Jacobeans, Molière, Racine, Goethe, Yeats, Brecht, or in the anonymous poets who worked and reworked their texts with their illiterate players in the medieval Mysteries. My at least 25-year quest for a space for myself as a poet in the theatre, involved me in seeking the help of some of these ancients and using their stylistic resources to discover new ones for myself. And I have always thought in terms of "theatre" rather than in the compartmentalised genres of drama, music theatre, opera, remembering that opera originated when artists thought they were rediscovering Greek drama. I have always found working with composers very congenial.

I have never for a moment been interested in antique reproduction only in finding styles and conventions to confront modern issues and conflicts that the predominantly naturalistic styles seemed unable to encompass. When I first started out on my quest I found only what has been called "poetry in the theatre rather than of it" that is in works like Eliot and Fry. And indeed even the great verse classics were often played in pedestrian prose translations so far had the theatre left behind that tradition. What kept verse alive for me as a theatrical medium was not only my immersion in great theatrical poets of the past, whose styles and language I studied and often translated, but also an early appetite and relish for the verse of the music-hall recitation and the pantomime which were still vigorous enough when I was a child for me to have been influenced by them. Indeed they were my earliest experiences of theatre. I have sometimes used the resources I found in these popular forms to "unlock" or "reoriginate" the classics of the past and bring the energy of the so-called "low" art forms into the so-called "high" art forms. Sometimes I believe that there is not that great a difference between the two, and that our culture has falsely made them seem too irreconcilably distinct.

My close work with actors from the beginning of my theatrical career has led me, project by project, deeper into the everyday practicalities of theatrical production until I have reached the position of preferring to direct my own theatre pieces and to collaborate with known actors in known spaces, whether conventional theatres or not. *The Trackers of Oxyrhynchus* was devised in the National Theatre Studio with actors I had worked with on other projects, and was premiered in the unique space of the ancient stadium of Delphi in Greece. When it played subsequently in the Olivier Theatre at the National, it was radically rewritten for the new space. When the production toured to Salts Mill, Saltaire, Art Carnuntum, Vienna, the Gasworks Theatre, Copenhagen, and the Brighton Festival I was with the company for every performance and went on making local variations in the text.

* * *

If his status as England's best-known contemporary theater poet will probably always be controversial, Tony Harrison's achievement as a brilliant and innovative translator can scarcely be contested. Audacity that sometimes hovers on the edge of verbal vandalism has characterized some of his verse, both in his collections of poetry and in his plays, but works like his *Misanthrope* and *Oresteia* have satisfied even those with a conservative concept of the translator's role. He is, however, also thoroughly conversant with current translation theory, and in other works he extends the logic of transposition and refraction to move far beyond any suggestion of the play as a statement of faith to an original.

From the first Harrison has been acutely aware of the need to read both the original and the target audience. He always regarded *Aikin Mata,* his Nigerian *Lysistrata,* as unplayable except in West Africa. Though it has been successfully staged even by the Sydney Theatre Company, *The Trackers of Oxyrhynchus* was written for a single performance at Delphi. And even the apparently conventional *The Misanthrope* was written to an audience for whom 1968 was a recent memory. It was *Phaedra Britannica,* however, that confronted London with the principle of cultural transposition as an integral function in contemporary translation.

The politicization of Racine by grounding the play in India just before the mutiny was a brilliant piece of audience manipulation. Denied the consolation of reading the play as an object "back there" in French literature or even as an archaeological exhibit from Greek prehistory, London theatergoers found it folded into their own imperial history, the more fragile because its cultural sequel had already been written. Reading Racine by taking a detour through India thus became an ingeniously contrived exercise in Orientalism in the theater, a point illustrated by the response of unwitting critics who complained of the absence of (consolingly meaningless) Greek gods. In their place Harrison offered some specifically Indian deities and also a collective they, a dark, menacing colonial sense of otherness. Thomas (Hippolytus), a half-caste, is rejected by his father as an "animal," his Indian blood a "lower self" that sooner or later will emerge from its "lair."

Harrison has always been conscious of himself as a Yorkshire poet, and his interest in regional material is combined with his training in comparative linguistics in *Bow Down,* a savage theatricalization of several treatments of the "Two Sisters" ballad. Here his technique may be compared with what Walter Benjamin, whom he admires, saw as an ideal in translation, the interlinear, for Harrison collates the versions, leaving the Danish, for example, in its original. This inclination to leave "ready-mades" embedded throughout a work is more pronounced in the "sex-war" opera *Medea* and would itself become the subject of a play in *Oxyrhynchus*.

Defiantly regionalist is *The Mysteries,* in which a darts mat represents the palm-strewn road into Jerusalem and Herod's son reads the York telephone directory before his father tears it to bits, a gesture of macho physicality that has no precedent in the Herod of the cycle plays. The initial entrance of God on a forklift seems appropriate in what Harrison sees as the "post-Christian" era, but the structural awkwardness of the play, an amalgam of all four cycles, reflects the fact that it was written first just as an Easter Passion and eight years later bulked out with a Nativity, which includes a lot of Wakefield material like Cain and Noah, and a Doomsday. Between the two versions Harrison wrote the television play *The Big H,* a highly stylized treatment of Herod in contemporary Leeds that incorporates some of the precise stylistic features of the "Slaughter of the Innocents" from the cycles. Formal boasting speeches from Herod and lamentation sequences from the mothers coexist with startling liberties such as the fact that all three Herods are local schoolteachers with secret selves (called Jekyll and Hyde) with a propensity for fascism and "kiddicide." Although clearly written as a Christmas play, it was premiered by BBC2 on Boxing Day.

The Trackers of Oxyrhynchus is a work of virtuosity that fittingly combines the proclivities of all of Harrison's best work. Grenfell and Hunt, the pioneer British papyrologists, are digging through Egyptian compost heaps and find the fragments of a satyr play, which is then realized with themselves in the central roles of Apollo and Silenus. Harrison's keen sense of prosody is wittily indulged here as his characteristic rhyming couplets are filled out with blanks around the papyrus word fragments and as a caryatid maiden, a powerlifter carrying a pediment, enters and launches into a pastiche of Victorian translationese. The performance is contextualized within the frame of the Pythian Games, which are then synchronized with the world of the audience with the intrusion of "new generation" satyrs as football hooligans. The play thus re-creates the coexistence of the high and the low, the sacred and the profane, which Harrison's brilliant introduction argues was integral to classical Greek drama. His detractors, who have called his work kitsch, are given some substance here insofar as compost is kitsch. But, as Silenus shrewdly observes, the full subtleties of that kitsch are accessible only to readers with a very good reading knowledge of Greek.

—Howard McNaughton

HARWOOD, Ronald

Nationality: British. **Born:** Ronald Horwitz in Cape Town, South Africa, 9 November 1934. **Education:** Sea Point Boys' High School, Cape Town; Royal Academy of Dramatic Art, London. **Family:** Married Natasha Riehle in 1959; one son and two daughters. **Career:** Joined Donald Wolfit's Shakespeare Company in London, 1953; actor, 1953-59; presenter, *Kaleidoscope* radio programme, 1973, and television series *Read All About It*, 1978-79, and *All the World's a Stage*, 1984; artistic director, Cheltenham Festival, 1975; visitor in theatre, Balliol College, Oxford, 1986. Chairman, Writers' Guild of Great Britain, 1969; member of the Literature Panel, Arts Council of Great Britain, 1973-78. President, English PEN, 1989-93; president, International PEN, 1993-97; governor, Central School of Speech and Drama. **Awards:** Royal Society of Literature Winifred Holtby prize, for fiction, 1974; *Evening Standard* award, 1980; Drama Critics Circle award, 1980. Fellow, Royal Society of Literature, 1974; Jewish Quarterly Prize for Fiction, 1994; Chevalier National Order of Arts and Letters, France, 1996. **Agent:** Judy Daish Associates, 83 Eastbourne Mews, London W2 6LQ, England.

Publications

Plays

Country Matters (produced Manchester, 1969).

One Day in the Life of Ivan Denisovich (screenplay). London, Sphere, 1970; New York, Ballantine, 1971.

The Good Companions, music by André Previn, lyrics by Johnny Mercer, adaptation of the novel by J. B. Priestley (produced Manchester and London, 1974). London, Chappell, 1974.

The Ordeal of Gilbert Pinfold, adaptation of the novel by Evelyn Waugh (produced Manchester, 1977; London, 1979). Oxford, Amber Lane Press, 1983.

A Family (produced Manchester and London, 1978). London, Heinemann, 1978.

The Dresser (produced Manchester and London, 1980; New York, 1981). Ambergate, Derbyshire, Amber Lane Press, 1980; New York, Grove Press, 1981.

A Night of the Day of the Imprisoned Writer, with Christopher Hampton (produced London, 1981).

After the Lions (produced Manchester, 1982). Oxford, Amber Lane Press, 1983).

Tramway Road (produced London, 1984). Oxford, Amber Lane Press, 1984.

The Deliberate Death of a Polish Priest (produced London 1985). Oxford, Amber Lane Press, and New York, Applause, 1985.

Interpreters: A Fantasia on English and Russian Themes (produced London, 1985). Oxford, Amber Lane Press, 1985.
J.J. Farr (produced Bath and London, 1987). Oxford, Amber Lane Press, 1988.
Another Time (produced Bath and London, 1989; also director: Chicago, 1991). Oxford, Amber Lane Press, 1989.
Reflected Glory (produced Darlington, Durham and London, 1992). London, Faber, 1991.
Poison Pen (produced 1993).
The Collected Plays of Ronald Harwood. London and Boston, Faber & Faber, 1993.
Taking Sides (produced 1995).
Ronald Harwood: Plays 2. London and Boston, Faber & Faber, 1995.
The Handyman (produced 1996).

Screenplays: *The Barber of Stamford Hill*, 1962; *Private Potter*, with Casper Wrede, 1962; *A High Wind in Jamaica*, with Denis Cannan and Stanley Mann, 1965; *Drop Dead Darling* (*Arriverderci, Baby!*), with Ken Hughes, 1966; *Diamonds for Breakfast*, with N.F. Simpson and Pierre Rouve, 1968; *Eyewitness*, 1970; *Cromwell*, with Ken Hughes, 1970; *One Day in the Life of Ivan Denisovich*, 1972; *Operation Daybreak*, 1975; *The Dresser*, 1984; *The Doctor and the Devils*, 1986; *The Browning Version,* 1994; *Cry, The Beloved,* 1995.

Radio Plays: *All the Same Shadows*, from his own novel, 1971; *Goodbye Kiss,* 1997.

Television Plays: *The Barber of Stamford Hill*, 1960; *Private Potter*, with Casper Wrede, 1961; *Take a Fellow Like Me*, 1961; *The Lads*, 1963; *Convalescence*, 1964; *Guests of Honour*, 1965; *The Paris Trip*, 1966; *The New Assistant*, 1967; *Long Lease of Summer*, 1972; *The Guests*, 1972; *A Sense of Loss* (documentary on Evelyn Waugh), with John Selwyn, 1978; *The Way Up to Heaven*, 1979, *Parson's Pleasure*, 1986, and *The Umbrella Man*, 1986 (all in *Tales of the Unexpected* series); *Evita Péron*, 1981; *Mandela*, 1987; *Breakthrough at Reykjavik*, 1987; *Countdown to War*, 1989.

Novels

All the Same Shadows. London, Cape, 1961; as *George Washington September, Sir!*, New York, Farrar Straus, 1961.
The Guilt Merchants. London, Cape, 1963; New York, Holt Rinehart, 1969.
The Girl in Melanie Klein. London, Secker and Warburg, 1969; New York, Holt Rinehart, 1973.
Articles of Faith. London, Secker and Warburg, 1973; New York, Holt Rinehart, 1974.
The Genoa Ferry. London, Secker and Warburg, 1976; New York, Mason Charter, 1977.
César and Augusta. London, Secker and Warburg, 1978; Boston, Little Brown, 1979.
Home. London, Secker and Warburg, 1993.

Short Stories

One. Interior. Day. Adventures in the Film Trade. London, Secker and Warburg, 1978.

Other

Sir Donald Wolfit, C.B.E.: His Life and Work in the Unfashionable Theatre. London, Secker and Warburg, and New York, St. Martin's Press, 1971.
All the World's a Stage. London, Secker and Warburg, 1984; Boston, Little Brown, 1985.
Mandela. London, Boxtree, and New York, New American Library, 1987.

Editor, with Francis King, *New Stories 3*. London, Hutchinson, 1978.
Editor, *A Night at the Theatre*. London, Methuen, 1982.
Editor, *The Ages of Gielgud: An Actor at Eighty*. London, Hodder and Stoughton, and New York, Limelight, 1984.
Editor, *Dear Alec: Guinness at Seventy-Five*. London, Hodder and Stoughton, and New York, Limelight, 1989.
Editor, *The Faber Book of the Theatre*. London, Faber & Faber, 1993.

*

Critical Study: "State Terror and Dramatic Countermeasures" by Mary Karen Dahl, in *Terrorism and Modern Drama,* edited by John Orr and Dragan Klaic, Edinburgh, Edinburgh University Press, 1990.

Theatrical Activities:
Director: **Plays**—*The Odd Couple*, Manchester, 1989; *Another Time*, Chicago, 1991.

Actor: **Plays**—With Donald Wolfit's Shakespeare Company in London: roles in *Macbeth*, *The Wandering Jew* by E. Temple Thurston, *The Taming of the Shrew*, *1 Henry IV*, *Hamlet*, *Volpone* by Jonson, *Twelfth Night*, *A New Way to Pay Old Debts* by Massinger, and *The Clandestine Marriage* by Garrick and Colman, 1953; Third Jew in *Salome* by Oscar Wilde, London, 1954; Captain Arago in *The Strong Are Lonely* by Fritz Hochwalder, London, 1955; repertory seasons in Salisbury and Chesterfield.

* * *

Ronald Harwood is both a popular and a populist writer with a diverse list of works—novels, television plays, screenplays, and stage plays. If there is any theme or common denominator in his work, it must focus on his own deep love of the theater (*The Dresser*, *After the Lions*, and *Reflected Glory* all have theatrical settings) and his concern to show how people feel rather than how they think. Most of the plays turn on a central anguished relationship based on conflict and have the acute sense of character to be expected only in a novelist and dramatist brought up as an actor.

Harwood went to Britain from South Africa in 1953 and joined Donald Wolfit's Shakespeare Company as an actor and as a dresser to the great man himself. His early work included theatrical adaptations of Alexander Solzhenitsyn (*One Day in the Life of Ivan Denisovich*) and Evelyn Waugh (*The Ordeal of Gilbert Pinfold*) as well as the book for an André Previn-Johnny Mercer musical adaptation of J. B. Priestley's *The Good Companions*. *The Ordeal of Gilbert Pinfold* is probably the best of his early works. It is an excellent adaptation of Waugh's late novel, based on the author's actual experiences, about an invalid on a cruise who is bedeviled by figments of his own imagination. *Gilbert Pinfold* was produced at the Royal Exchange Theatre in Manchester in 1977 and reached London in 1979. The Manchester-London progression was repeated in 1978 with *A Family*, which played at the Haymarket Theatre. This play is designed to show that a family, however possessive, has the inner resources to remain true to itself in spite of adversity. Good though the writing is, especially the delineation of character, there is an odd sense that this is another adaptation from a novel, a hangover perhaps from earlier work.

The play that established Harwood as an international success was *The Dresser*, which transferred from Manchester to the Queen's Theatre in London in 1980. The play re-creates with wonderful detail and fidelity the kind of classical touring theater that must have all but disappeared by the time Harwood first joined Donald Wolfit's company in 1953. It has a wonderful and poignant quality about it of the end of an era. An aging actor-manager, simply called Sir, struggles to play up to eight major Shakespearean roles a week as his company tours Britain in the middle of World War II. Emotionally and creatively spent, Sir performs each night only with the help of his dresser, Norman, who cajoles, bullies, protects, and cossets his highly strung employer. The central relationship between Sir and Norman is superbly realized and does much to make *The Dresser* one of the most significant and best-loved plays of the 1980s. This is despite the fact that the play has no overriding social message, an attribute considered essential at the time. It should be stressed that Sir is not a portrait of Sir Donald Wolfit, but rather an amalgam of several actor-managers known and read about by the author. The central role of Sir is a mosaic, a symbol of the age of actor-managers, who were often remarkable men dedicated not only to the classical repertoire but also to a surprisingly high degree of performance. As Sir acts King Lear on what proves to be the last night of his life, other stories of ambition, loyalty, loneliness, and betrayal are played out offstage, acting as a counterpoint and making this the most moving and empathetic of all Harwood's work.

The Dresser proved to be a hard act to follow, and, indeed, although *After the Lions* shares the same backstage setting, it did not transfer to London after its Manchester premiere. This latter play deals with a grim period in the life of the great Sarah Bernhardt, the point in her career at which her leg was amputated. The main focus of the play is the attempt of Pitou, Bernhardt's secretary, to get the great actress to retire and not face a humiliating American tour. Skillful though the writing is, the play does not have the atmospheric immediacy of *The Dresser*, although the major roles must be coveted by the acting establishment.

Tramway Road, seen briefly in London in 1984, is a fine play. Two of its major characters are a married expatriate English couple trapped in a bitter relationship. The man teaches elocution to a South African youth who dreams of the theater in London. But the boy is "reclassified" as a half-caste, and his future is destroyed. Faced with the boy's dilemma, the husband acts with a weakness it is difficult to forgive. The play is essentially a clash between the wistfulness of what might have been and the reality of the cruelty of bigotry. Written with deep conviction and truth, the play reminds one of the works of Athol Fugard, and it is interesting to note what Ronald Harwood himself had to say about the piece in a 1992 interview in *Plays and Players*: "My stand (the condemnation of South Africa) was honourable, and it was certainly fashionable at the time. But it is easy to pontificate when one is 6000 miles away. I think Athol Fugard is a wonderful writer and a proper witness to what happened there. I'm not a proper witness, I wasn't there." In spite of Harwood's protests, *Tramway Road* remains the most undervalued of all his plays.

The year 1985 was a prolific one. *The Deliberate Death of a Polish Priest* was presented at the Almeida Theatre in London. This documentary play was based on the transcripts of a trial and other material arising out of the murder of Father Jerzy Popieluszko in 1984. The priest was a political activist, and all of the words of Father Popieluszko and the witnesses are their own. Disarmingly simple, the tragic story and its attempted cover-up have a deep emotional impact. On a totally different emotional level, *Interpreters*, which enjoyed a long London run, also looks at the last days of the Cold War. The play's focus is the visit to England by the Soviet president. As the itinerary is carefully examined, the English translator Nadia, who is of Russian descent, and the Russian Victor face each other at the conference table. Nadia and Victor were embroiled in a passionate affair a decade earlier, and we eagerly watch the renewal of this romance even though we suspect the rejuvenated liaison cannot last.

In *Another Time*, presented in London in 1989, Harwood returned both to a South African setting and to a reexploration of the themes of the family. Initially set in Cape Town in the 1950s, the play examines the life of Leonard Lands, 17 years old, the only child of immigrant parents, and a gifted pianist. In order to achieve success commensurate with his talent, Leonard must study in Europe. Act 2 takes place in London 35 years later, when Leonard has reached another turning point in his life. Harwood skillfully examines the price Leonard has paid for his single-minded devotion to his music and the effect this has had on his relationship to his family.

Harwood's *Reflected Glory* opened in London in 1992. Like much of his work, the play turns on a central, troubled relationship. Here the struggle is between two brothers. Michael is a playwright whose latest script exposes the deepest personal secrets of his family. The other brother, restaurateur Alfred, has tried and failed to enjoin the play, causing a long and acrimonious rift with his sibling. *Reflected Glory* concerns the attempt by Michael to effect a reconciliation, although, in fact, he is trying to clear the ground for his latest play, which will examine his relationship with Alfred. Funny, heartfelt, and with autobiographical overtones, *Reflected Glory* is in many ways Harwood's best play since *The Dresser*.

—David E. Kemp

HASTINGS, Michael (Gerald)

Nationality: British. **Born:** Lambeth, London, 2 September 1938. **Education:** Alleyn's School, 1949-53; apprentice, Kilgour French and Stanbury, bespoke tailors, London, 1953-56. **Family:** Married Victoria Hardie in 1975; two sons and one daughter from previous marriage. **Awards:** Arts Council award, 1956; Encyclopaedia Britannica award, 1965; Maugham award, 1972; Writers Guild award, 1972; Emmy award, 1973; British Screenwriters Guild award, 1975; *Evening Standard* award, 1979. **Member:** Fellow, Royal Geographical Society. **Agent:** Andrew Hewson, John Johnson Ltd., Clerkenwell House, 45-47 Clerkenwell Green, London EC1R 0HT. **Address:** 2 Helix Gardens, London S.W.2, England.

Publications

Plays

Don't Destroy Me (produced London, 1956; New York, 1957). London, Nimbus, 1956.
Yes, and After (produced London and New York, 1957). Included in *Three Plays*, 1966.
The World's Baby (produced London, 1965). Included in *Three Plays*, 1966.
Lee Harvey Oswald: A Far Mean Streak of Indepence Brought on by Negleck (as *The Silence of Lee Harvey Oswald*, produced London, 1966). London, Penguin, 1966.
Three Plays (includes *Don't Destroy Me*; *Yes, and After*; *The World's Baby*). London, W.H. Allen, 1966.
The Silence of Saint-Just (produced Brighton, 1971). London, Weidenfeld and Nicolson, 1970.
The Cutting of the Cloth (produced London, 1973).
For the West (Uganda) (produced London, 1977). Included in *Three Plays*, 1980.
Gloo Joo (produced London, 1978). Included in *Three Plays*, 1980.
Full Frontal (produced London, 1979). Included in *Three Plays*, 1980.
Carnival War (as *Carnival War a Go Hot*, produced London, 1979). With *Midnite at the Starlite*, London, Penguin, 1981.
Midnite at the Starlite (as *Midnight at the Starlight*, televised 1980; as *Midnite at the Starlite*, produced Birmingham, 1981). With *Carnival War*, London, Penguin, 1981.
Three Plays. London, Penguin, 1980.
Two Fish in the Sky (produced New York, 1982).
The Miser, adaptation of a play by Molière (produced Cambridge, 1982).
Tom and Viv (produced London, 1984; New York, 1985). London, Penguin, 1985.
Going to a Party (for children; produced London, 1984).
The Emperor, with Jonathan Miller, adaptation of a novel by Ryszard Kapuscinski (also co-director: produced London, 1987). London, Penguin, 1988.
A Dream of People (produced London, 1990).
Three Political Plays (includes *The Emperor*, *For the West (Uganda)*, *Lee Harvey Oswald*). London, Penguin, 1990.
Death and the Maiden, adaptation of the play by Ariel Dorfman (produced London, 1991; New York, 1992). London, Hern, 1991.
Unfinished Business and Other Plays (includes *Unfinished Business*; *A Dream of People*; *Stars of the Roller State Disco*). London, Penguin, 1994.

Screenplays: *Bedtime*, 1968; *The Nightcomers*, 1972; *Tom and Viv*, 1991.

Television Plays: *The Game*, from his novel, 1961, revised version, 1973; *For the West* (*Congo*), 1965; *Blue as His Eyes the Tin Helmet He Wore*, 1967; *Camille '68*, 1968; *Ride, Ride*, 1970; *The Search for the Nile* (documentary), with Derek Marlowe, 1971; *Auntie Kathleen's Old Clothes*, 1977; *Murder Rap*, 1980; *Midnight at the Starlight*, 1980; *Michael Hastings in Brixton* (documentary), 1980; *Stars of the Roller State Disco*, 1984.

Novels

The Game. London, W.H. Allen, 1957; New York, McGraw Hill, 1958.
The Frauds. London, W.H. Allen, 1960; New York, Orion Press, 1961.
Tussy Is Me: A Romance. London, Weidenfeld and Nicolson, 1970; New York, Delacorte Press, 1971.
The Nightcomers. New York, Delacorte Press, 1972; London, Pan, 1973.
And in the Forest the Indians. London, Hodder and Stoughton, 1975.
The Brothers. Piatkus, 1992.

Short Stories

Bart's Mornings and Other Tales of Modern Brazil. London, Hodder and Stoughton, 1975.

Poetry

Love Me, Lambeth, and Other Poems. London, W.H. Allen, 1961.

Other

The Handsomest Young Man in England: Rupert Brooke: A Biographical Essay. London, Joseph, 1967.
Sir Richard Burton: A Biography. London, Hodder and Stoughton, 1978.

*

Manuscript Collections: Princeton University, New Jersey; University of Texas, Austin.

Critical Study: *The Author of the Boards: Intertextuality and Literary Biographical Drama* (dissertation) by Robert Joseph Hubbard, Bowling Green State University, 1996.

Theatrical Activities:
Director: **Play**—*The Emperor* (co-director, with Jonathan Miller), London, 1987.

* * *

Michael Hastings's first play was produced at the now defunct New Lindsey Theatre in Notting Hill when he was only 18, winning him instant fame as one of the youngest dramatists ever to have had his work performed. *Don't Destroy Me* showed an ear for the casual but revealing remark, though the dialogue was never fully controlled. Hastings's second play, *Yes, and After*, was three times as long (i.e., four and a half hours), indicating an increasing ease with the medium. It was also a mature work in many respects. He exploited his ability at dialogue, his minor characters were well observed, and, significantly, the female characters came at least as fully to life as the male ones, the daughter in the play being one of his finest creations. Both these plays were considered significant additions to the new drama of the angry young men.

Hastings returned to the stage only after nine years. For five years he had not written at all, having spent time educating himself while living frugally in France, Germany, and Spain. In dramatic terms the education was less digested than was desirable. *The World's Baby* is a skeptical chronicle of British life from the 1920s to the 1950s. The central character, Anna, begins as a

Dionysian dispenser of sex. While her Cambridge boyfriends change as a result of wartime experiences, Anna's antibourgeois convictions remain intact. Hastings's Jewish and working-class background might lead one to expect sympathy with Anna's views, but their effect is pitilessly to transform her from charming, if childish, impetuousness to menopausal crankiness. Is Anna to be seen as a victim of circumstances, as a symbol of her times, or simply as an individual? She is a little of each but not enough of any to be quite convincing. If Hastings's technique had not grown any more coherent, he certainly had come better to understand how people behave under emotional stress.

Hastings discovered the vein that he was to mine most successfully with his first popular success, *The Silence of Lee Harvey Oswald*. The playwright's background had given him an undeniable instinct for character, his self-education gave him a sense of what was topical, and he rightly focused on the person rather than on history. He had read through the 26-volume report of the Warren Commission, but the purpose of his play was to understand what was enigmatic in the alleged assassin. The play is structured around Oswald's declining marriage, and its emotional power is generated by the explosive brutality of Oswald's treatment of his wife. When she attempts to desert him, their sense of loneliness and exhaustion, which prompts Oswald to plead for her return, is equally tellingly handled. The play moves from verbatim transcripts of evidence by Oswald's wife and mother to dramatizations of episodes described by them. The two women hold different views of the man, his mother believing him to be a framed CIA agent, his wife thinking that he killed Kennedy to gain notoriety. (The work's popularity may also have come from the perpetually appealing techniques and suspense of cross-examination, which has a key place in the technique of the play.) The two views are, however, presented flatly. Oswald remains impenetrable, and Hastings's concern for truth is precisely what prevents the play from achieving the insight of art.

In his play on Saint Justin, Hastings violently couples the documentary material with invented dialogue about twisted revolutionary heroes. Saint Justin's powerful and mysterious silence for the 30 hours preceding his execution is made into the play's crucial anticlimax, showing Hastings at his technically adventurous best. *For the West*, on Idi Amin, is a better blend of documentary and imaginative material, and it is assisted by the fact that a large part of it takes place in Amin's dreams.

In the third stage of his playwriting career, Hastings was preoccupied with racial themes. *Gloo Joo* and *Carnival War* are perhaps the best known of the plays on these themes, but Hastings's undoubtedly serious concern is undercut by the farcical mode in which he chooses to treat strongly divisive issues. *Carnival War* combines mischief about the Notting Hill carnival with buffoonery aimed against the police. It is reminiscent of some of Hastings's earlier plays, especially the television play *Blue as His Eyes the Tin Helmet He Wore*. Notwithstanding this, Hastings's plays about blacks have enjoyed considerable success in Africa and the Caribbean.

Tom and Viv is based on the allegation that T. S. Eliot's first wife, Vivien Haigh-Wood, was committed to an asylum not because she was a lunatic but because, emotionally troubled as she was, she indulged in behavior that Eliot and his Bloomsbury friends found embarrassing. The controversial nature of the thesis was compounded by the uncertainty regarding its factual basis, and only history can reveal the truth of the matter. This satirical and sometimes sickening play succeeds as a startling re-creation of the period and of period characters, eloquently portraying the savagery of the two societies—the landed merchant class of her origin and her husband's glittering literary set who considered her a boor—that destroyed Vivien.

Hastings is a dramatist of ever widening range, extended even further in his later *The Emperor*, but he still seems in search of a completely congenial dramatic form. There remains a gulf between the inner and outer worlds of his plays.

—Prabhu S. Guptara

HAUPTMAN, William (Thornton)

Nationality: American. **Born:** Wichita Falls, Texas, 26 November 1942. **Education:** Wichita Falls Senior High School, graduated 1961; University of Texas, Austin, B.F.A. in drama 1966; Yale University School of Drama, New Haven, Connecticut, M.F.A. in playwriting 1973. **Family:** Married 1) Barbara Barbat in 1968 (divorced 1977), one daughter; 2) Marjorie Erdreich in 1985, one son. **Career:** Instructor in playwriting, Adelphi College, 1973-75 and Yale University School of Drama, 1976; associate professor, Texas Center for writers, 1996. **Awards:** CBS grant, 1976; National Endowment for the Arts grant, 1977; Obie award, 1977; Guggenheim grant, 1978; Boston Theatre Critics Circle award, 1984; Tony award, 1985; San Diego Drama Critics Circle award, 1985; Drama-Logue award, 1986; Jesse Jones award, for fiction, 1986. **Agent:** Gloria Loomis, Watkins-Loomis Agency, 133 East 35th Street, New York, New York 10016, U.S.A. **Address:** 240 Warren Street, Apartment E, Brooklyn, New York, New York 11201, U.S.A.

Publications

Plays

Heat (produced New Haven, Connecticut, 1972; revised version produced New York, 1974). New York, French, 1977.

Shearwater (produced New Haven, Connecticut, 1973; New York, 1974). Published in *Performance* (New York), vol. 1, no. 5, March-April 1973.

Domino Courts (produced New York, 1975). With *Comanche Cafe*, New York, French, 1977.

Comanche Cafe (produced New York, 1976). With *Domino Courts*, New York, French, 1977.

The Durango Flash (produced New Haven, Connecticut, 1977).

Big River, music and lyrics by Roger Miller, adaptation of the novel *Adventures of Huckleberry Finn* by Mark Twain (produced Cambridge, Massachusetts, 1984; New York, 1985). New York, Grove Press, 1986.

Gillette (produced Cambridge, Massachusetts, 1985; revised version produced La Jolla, California, 1986). New York, Theatre Communications Group, 1985.

Television Play: *A House Divided* series (3 episodes), 1981.

Novel

The Storm Season. New York, Bantam, 1992.

Short Stories

Good Rockin' Tonight. New York, Bantam, 1988.

*

William Hauptman comments:

I find as I get older I'm more interested in writing what I know about, and what I really know about is working class, because that's where I'm from. . . . When you get older you realize that there's a reason why the forms exist; they've been created by a process that's hundreds of years long. Story and character are still the most important things. The style comes and goes, but stories about people remain.

* * *

There is a remarkable wholeness about William Hauptman's dramatic writing that transcends the working-class milieu in which his plays are set. His characteristic preoccupations surface even in *Big River,* his Tony Award-winning book for the 1985 Broadway musical based on Mark Twain's *Adventures of Huckleberry Finn.* An awareness of the outdoors, the land, and the forces of nature permeates the writing and generates some striking scenic images. The visual sensibility is supplemented by his strongly imagistic use of sound: the distant dog bark that ends *Domino Courts,* the low rumble that seems to comment on Carroll's line "Now we can have some peace and quiet, right, honey?" in *Heat,* a passing train, the howl of a coyote, droning cicadas, and specific musical selections that often mock a character's pipe dreams.

All of Hauptman's plays are episodically constructed. Like the early Tennessee Williams, he might be better described as a "scenewright" than a playwright. The loose construction, however, is metaphorically appropriate for his studies of characters infected by wanderlust. The car on the road or the raft on the river offer them an aimless mobility that might bring "the answer" to drifters like Huck and Jim in *Big River,* Mickey and Bobby in *Gillette,* and Roy in *Domino Courts* or to those who merely dream of travel, like Ronnie in *Comanche Cafe* and Joe Billy in *Heat.* Above all, Hauptman's characters seem to be in search of their own identities. Huck Finn declares in song his determination "to be nobody but himself." "Hell—let's be ourselves," Floyd pleads with Roy, whom he accuses of flaunting a "phony personality." In *Heat* Carroll says, "I've got a club. When you belong you can be anyone you want." Mickey, the fortyish drifter in *Gillette,* says, "You look at that town and you see all the towns that ever were, and every person you've ever been. . . . There's somebody inside me who's bigger and better than I've ever been yet." But his young friend Bobby, a novice on the road, seeks to define himself in terms of an occupation.

Friendship between two men is the basis for all of Hauptman's full-length plays as well as for the one-act *Domino Courts.* Huck and Jim, Mickey and Bobby, Carroll and Harley, and Floyd and Roy all experience a pattern of alternating closeness and estrangement in their relationships. Each craves self-sufficiency but fears loneliness. The pattern is reiterated structurally by an alternation of scenes set in town with scenes set on the river or prairie or desert. When they are in town, the men feel trapped and have to get away from "civilization," but out in the country, with the town's lights twinkling in the distance, they feel as if they are missing out on some action. Similarly, they are often torn between their need for freedom and their desire for the comfort of a woman's love. Mickey sums up the conflict most of them have faced: "Long time ago, I decided not to go for the house and kids. I was going for the other dream—freedom and a big score at the end of the road."

Women cause the greatest stress on the men's friendships. *Gillette* deals most directly with this problem, for both Mickey and Bobby must choose between binding themselves to the women who seem to be so right for them or remaining buddies as before. In *Domino Courts* Floyd and Roy get at each other through their women. In both of these plays and in *Heat* the men often behave like little boys showing off for the women or for each other. They speak of "staying up all night" as if it were a special affirmation of manhood. This sort of bonding between women is rare in Hauptman's plays, for they are usually too afraid of losing their men. Their wariness occasionally is dissolved in a spontaneous appreciation of having something in common, as in *Heat* when Susan and Billie find that they have both shoplifted. As Ronnie says in *Domino Courts,* they devote much effort to learning "how to deal with men" even as they tell one another, "Don't cry, honey, no man's worth it." It is a major breakthrough when a woman like Jody in *Gillette* learns that she need not be dependent on a man.

Hauptman's best writing is probably *Gillette,* a play about a couple of oil rig roughnecks who dream of making "big coin" in a northeastern Wyoming boomtown. Originally published in Theatre Communications Group's Plays in Process series in 1985, it was extensively revised by Hauptman for its 1986 production at La Jolla Playhouse. *Variety*'s review sums up the appeal of this compelling portrait of blue-collar America: "It is earthy, rousing, contemporary and tough-minded—a very funny, well-written, well-staged, well-played serious comedy with a Saroyanesque strain in oddly touching moments. And like Saroyan, Hauptman's long suit is dialog and the creating of strong, highly individual, often eccentric characters."

—Felicia Hardison Londré

HAVIS, Allan

Nationality: American. **Born:** New York City, 26 September 1951. **Education:** City College, New York, B.A. 1973; Hunter College, New York, M.A. 1976; Yale University, New Haven, Connecticut, M.F.A. 1980. **Family:** Married Cheryl Riggins in 1982. **Career:** Film instructor in children's program, Guggenheim Museum, New York, 1974-76; writer-in-residence, Case Western Reserve University, Cleveland, Ohio, 1976; theatre critic, *Our Town*, New York, 1977; playwriting instructor, Foundation of the Dramatists Guild, New York, 1985-87, Ulster County Community College, Stone Ridge, New York, 1986-88, Old Dominion University, Norfolk, Virginia, 1987, Sullivan County Community College, Loch Sheldrake, New York, 1987, and University of California at San Diego, La Jolla, 1988—. **Awards:** John Golden award, 1974, 1975; Case Western Reserve University Klein award, 1976; Dramatists Guild/CBS award, 1985; Playwrights USA award, 1986; National Endowment for the Arts fellowship, 1986; Rockefeller fellowship, 1987; Guggenheim fellowship, 1987; New York State Foundation for the Arts fellowship, 1987; Albee Foundation for the Arts fellowship, 1987; Kennedy Center/American Express grant, 1987; MacDowell fellowship, 1988; McKnight fellowship, 1989;

Hawthornden fellowship, 1989; University of California Faculty Summer fellowship, 1989; California Arts Council fellowship, 1991; Rockefeller residency, Bellagio Centre, Italy, 1991. **Agent:** William Craver, Writers & Artists, 19 West 44th Street, Suite 1000, New York, New York 10036, U.S.A.; or Peters, Fraser, and Dunlop Group, 503/4 The Chambers, Chelsea Harbour, Lots Road, London SW10 0XF, England. **Address:** 531 Palomar Avenue, La Jolla, California 92037, U.S.A.

PUBLICATIONS

Plays

The Boarder and Mrs. Rifkin (produced New York, 1974).
Oedipus Again (produced Cleveland, 1976).
Watchmaker (produced New York, 1977).
Heinz (produced New Haven, Connecticut, 1978).
Interludes (produced New Haven, Connecticut, 1978).
Family Rites (produced New Haven, Connecticut, 1979).
The Road from Jerusalem (produced New York, 1984).
Holy Wars (produced Cambridge, Massachusetts, 1984).
Morocco (produced New York, 1984). Included in *Plays in Process* (New York), 1985; in *Morocco, Mink Sonata, Hospitality*, 1989.
Mink Sonata (also director: produced New York, 1986). In *Morocco, Mink Sonata, Hospitality*, 1989.
Duet for Three (produced New York, 1986).
Mother's Aria (also director: produced New York, 1986).
Einstein for Breakfast (produced New York, 1986).
Haut Goût (produced Norfolk, Virginia, 1987). Published in *Plays in Process* (New York), vol. 8, no. 5, 1987.
Hospitality (produced Philadelphia, 1988; London, 1989). In *Morocco, Mink Sonata, Hospitality*, 1989.
Morocco, Mink Sonata, Hospitality. New York, Broadway Play Publishing, 1989.
A Daring Bride (produced New Haven, Connecticut, 1990).
Lilith (produced New York, 1990). New York, Broadway Play Publishing, 1991.

Other

Albert the Astronomer (for children). New York, Harper, 1979.

*

Theatrical Activities:
Director: **Plays**—Some of his own plays.

* * *

"We had a passion for strange dark risks," says Claire, the modern-day demon lover in Allan Havis's *Lilith*, getting at the essence of the mysterious and disturbing work of this American playwright. Havis's plays tend toward the Kafkaesque. Their worlds are nightmares of unreason in which a well-off white American male, often Jewish, is lured by the siren song of the other, a woman or a man of dark skin such as an Arab or a Haitian. Whether or not a formal investigation is taking place, dialogue is filled with the threat of attack, the tension of defense. The white man is victimized, betrayed. He may be goaded to murder, but his antagonist always wins.

Havis is a cryptic storyteller. Critic James Leverett wrote of one of his plays that characters "encounter one another in circumstances that are fraught but far from clear." This is generally true, and the playwright's elegant and elliptical language resists reduction to straightforward meaning or moral. Still, the sexual and racial tensions at the heart of Havis's plays are uncomfortably familiar, and the dramatist's most important achievement may prove to be the revelation of what it feels like to be a white American male in an age in which he senses that his long ascendancy is coming to an end.

Morocco, Havis's best and most successful play, was described by Mel Gussow in the *New York Times* as "an absorbing cat-and-mouse game in which one cannot always distinguish the cat from the mouse." The first act consists of 10 brief scenes representing 10 days during which Kempler, a Jewish-American architect, attempts to secure his wife's release from a Moroccan jail. Kempler's antagonist, the nameless Arab colonel who runs the prison, is given to remarks like "Is this secrecy Jewish?" Havis knows that his audience will think the worst of the Moroccan and the best of the architect and his banker wife. They will therefore assume that the charge of prostitution and diagnosis of syphilis have been trumped up, at least until they witness the tension-filled second-act conversation between the husband and wife that takes place at an expensive restaurant in Spain "some days later." Increasingly, it seems possible that Mrs. Kempler, who is part Arab and part Spanish gypsy, is in fact promiscuous; it is also apparent that her husband is inclined to jealousy, paranoia, and masochism. The third act finds him back in the colonel's office confessing to the murder of his wife, who promptly appears to collect her husband. She takes him away only after her exchanges in Arabic with the colonel show that Kempler is the odd man out. The play takes place—the phrase is Gussow's—in "a Morocco of the mind."

Haut Goût mines similar terrain. Gold, a rich Jewish doctor insists on taking leave from his New York suburban life to spend several months in Haiti to test a milk formula he has developed to combat infant mortality. An innocent abroad, he promptly finds himself entangled with the ruler of the island, who incarnates Americans' most prejudicial notions about such figures. Le Croix is an army general, a communist, a torturer, a heroin addict, and a homosexual, and as Gold discovers, he has AIDS (though that term is not used). Gold resists Le Croix's persistent sexual advances but is nonetheless under his spell. The doctor is less successful in standing up to Latch, the U.S. State Department official who pressures him to murder the general. (Latch, we are given to understand, arranged for the deaths of seven babies in Gold's study, deaths the doctor naively blames himself for.) Gold gives Le Croix a lethal injection and returns home a broken man, but in the last scene the general turns up in Scarsdale with his perpetual attendant, a woman said to be able to raise the dead. They poison Gold, and Le Croix ends the play with talk of togetherness in death. Filled with the guilt of the privileged, the American has sought his own destruction.

A sinister view of the U.S. government is central to the ironically titled *Hospitality*, in which two immigration agents—one white, one black—work to break two detainees—one a female Colombian journalist, the other a right-wing Israeli politician. They induce diarrhea in the woman, she gives them names, and finally she is released, though it is now impossibly dangerous for her to return home. The Jew is beaten and his insulin withheld, and he dies of a stroke. Happy Logan, the agent who administered the beating, is in a neat reversal the designated victim of the subsequent investigation. His presumed buddy, the black agent Fuller, will not help him and may, in fact, have set him up. His personal as well as professional life a shambles, Logan kills himself. He is a particularly clear example of a white American destroyed through his dealings with the other.

Mink Sonata, at least initially, attempts a lighter tone. The most absurdist of these plays, it focuses on the relationship between an affluent father and his troubled daughter, Roberta. She has an alter ego, Blake, "stylish, self-confident and very attractive." Played by the same actress, Blake enables sexual fantasies to surface. Nearly every relationship in a Havis play is notable for talk about what would ordinarily be subliminal sexual tension.

There is considerable comedy, too, in the first act of *Lilith*, in which Adam and his pre-Eve wife wrangle before a voice, that of an archangel conducting the hearing that will result in the couple's separation and the creation of Adam's new mate. "Strindberg as directed by Mike Nichols" is Havis's description of his postintermission depiction of present-day Claire's power to disrupt family life by seducing Arnold (the act's Adam), sexually initiating his 10-year-old son, and, at moments, casting her spell over Eppy, the wife and mother who is the act's Eve. Throughout the play Adam is inept and helpless in the face of Lilith's determination to have children, and once again male power is shown to be illusory.

—M. Elizabeth Osborn

HAYMAN, Ronald

Nationality: English. **Born:** Bournemouth, 4 May 1932. **Education:** Cambridge University, 1951-54, B.A. in 1954, M.A. in 1962. **Military Service:** Royal Air Force, 1950-51; education branch sergeant. **Family:** Married 1) Monica Lorimer in 1969 (divorced 1985), one daughter. One daughter with Sue Trenchard. **Career:** Director and writer. Formerly director, Arts Theatre, Stratford East and Welwyn Garden City, and assistant producer, Northampton Repertory Company. Stage and television actor, 1957-61. **Agent:** Peters, Fraser & Dunlop, 503-4 The Chambers, Chelsea Harbour, London SW10 0XF, England.

Publications

Plays

The End of an Uncle (produced Wimbledon, 1959).
The Last Real Thing (also director: produced Hampstead, 1976).
Playing the Wife (produced Belfast, 1992). London, Samuel French, 1996.

Radio Plays: *The Last Tea Dance*, 1988; *Such Rotten Luck* (series), 1989-91.

Biography

Harold Pinter. London, Heinemann, 1968.
John Arden. London, Heinemann, 1968.
John Osborne. London, Heinemann, 1968.
Samuel Beckett. London, Heinemann, 1968.
John Whiting. London, Heinemann, 1969.
Robert Bolt. London, Heinemann, 1969.
Arnold Wesker. London, Heinemann, 1970.
Arthur Miller. London, Heinemann, 1970.
Tolstoy. London, Routledge & Kegan Paul, 1970.
Edward Albee. London, Heinemann, 1971.
John Gielgud: A Biography. London, Heinemann, 1971.
Eugene Ionesco. London, Heinemann, 1972.
Tom Stoppard. London, Heinemann, 1977.
De Sada: A Critical Biography. London, Constable, 1978.
Nietzche: A Critical Life. New York, Oxford University Press, 1980.
Kafka: A Biography. New York, Oxford University Press, 1982.
Brecht: A Biography. New York, Oxford University Press, 1983.
Fassbinder Film Maker. New York, Simon & Schuster, 1984.
Writing Against: A Biography of Sartre. London, Weidenfeld & Nicolson, 1986.
Proust: A Biography. New York, HarperCollins, 1990.
The Death and Life of Sylvia Plath. London, Heinemann, 1991.
Tennessee Williams: Everyone Else Is an Audience. New Haven, Connecticut, Yale University Press, 1993.
Thomas Mann: A Biography. New York, Scribners, 1995.
Hitler & Geli. London, Bloomsbury, 1997.

Other

Techniques of Acting. London, Methuen, 1969.
Arguing with Walt Whitman: An Essay on His Influence on Twentieth-Century American Verse. London, Covet Garden Press, 1971.
Playback. New York, Horizon Press, 1973.
The Set-Up: An Anatomy of the English Theatre Today. London, Methuen, 1973.
Playback II. New York, Horizon Press, 1974.
The First Thrust: The Chichester Festival Theatre. London, Davis-Poytner, 1975.
The Novel Today, 1967-1975. Harlow, Longman for the British Council, 1976.
Leavis. London, Heinemann, 1976.
How to Read a Play. London, Methuen, 1977.
Artaud and After. New York and Oxford, Oxford University Press, 1977.
British Theatre Since 1955: A Reassessment. New York and London, Oxford University Press, 1979.
Theatre and Anti-Theatre: New Movements Since Beckett. New York, Oxford University Press, 1979.
Bertolt and Brecht: The Plays. London, Heinemann, 1984.
Gunter Grass. London, Methuen, 1985.
Secrets: Boyhood in a Jewish Hotel, 1932-1954. London, Owen, 1985.
Nietzche's Voices. London, Weidenfeld, 1997.

Editor, *The Collected Plays of John Whiting.* London, Heinemann, 1969.
Editor, *The German Theatre: A Symposium.* London, Wolff, 1975.
Editor, with Ann Thwaite, *My Oxford, My Cambridge: Memories of University Life by Twenty-four Distinguished Graduates.* New York, Taplinger, 1977.

*

Manuscript Collection: Boston University, Mugar Memorial Library.

Theatrical Activities:
Director: **Plays**–*Deathwatch* by Jean Genet, 1961; *Jungle of the Cities* by Bertolt Brecht, 1962; *An Evening with G.B.S.*, Edinburgh, 1966; *My Foot My Tutor* by Peter Handke, 1971; *Home Front* by Martin Walser, 1971; *Bremen Coffee* by Rainer Werner Fassbinder, Edinburgh, 1974; *The Servant* by Robin Maugham, Guildford; *The Real Thing*, 1976.

* * *

Ronald Hayman is best known as the author of a remarkably long list of valuable critical biographies, studies, and editions that testify to his lifelong interest in English, American, and continental European literature, especially drama, in the 19th and 20th centuries. His writings also include works on practical aspects of theatrical production. In addition to undertaking the direction of a number of plays, some of which were at the time reckoned advanced and "difficult," Hayman has also shown his creative side by writing several plays of his own. Although the text of the first two—*The End of an Uncle*, produced in 1959, and *The Last Real Thing*, which received its premiere in 1976–is not available in print, the text of *Playing the Wife*, first performed at the Otranmillis Theatre in Belfast in 1992 and subsequently revived with Derek Jacobi in the lead at Chichester's Minerva Theatre in 1995, has been published.

The basis for *Playing the Wife* is an intriguing investigation of the psychology of the anguished Swedish playwright August Strindberg (1849-1912) through a study of his problematic relationships with two of his wives, the not particularly gifted actress Siri von Essen and Harriet Bosse, who was more accomplished and who scored successes in a number of roles, some of them in plays by her husband. There is rich material here, especially as Strindberg's reputed misogyny was linked with a profound desire for a rewarding and enduring marriage that would sustain him in his endless struggles with the literary establishment. It is, however, arguable that Hayman may be to some extent mistaken in assuming that, as a whole, his English-speaking public not only shares his interest in Strindberg but is also as thoroughly acquainted as he is with the Swedish dramatist's works and career. As a consequence, although the play develops speedily and explores issues with acumen and with techniques that have affinities with those of Luigi Pirandello, many in the audience are likely to feel, if not exactly puzzled about what is at issue, at least somewhat concerned that they are missing finer points. This feeling, like a certain uneasiness about the precise balance between documentary accuracy and dramatic license, can be disconcerting and even irritating.

Using admirable economy, *Playing the Wife* calls for only four characters: the 52-year-old Strindberg; the attractive young figure of the actress Harriet Bosse, with "dark soulful eyes" and "almost Oriental" features; the actor Bengt, described as being "in his middle or late twenties, fair, slim, tall, good-looking, working-class in origin but not in accent"; and the 40ish, bespectacled, good-natured Gertrud. The setting, on a wintry day when spring is still a distant hope, is a late 19th-century Stockholm playhouse that has been damaged by fire. The images of crumbling decay betoken a hostile environment that challenges the creativity of Strindberg. The action centers around the developing relationship between Strindberg and Harriet, with further dimensions added by the fact that Bengt, too, is in love with the actress, with whom he is rehearsing scenes under the direction of the dramatist who has written them.

Though by no means without precedent, the device of using a theater as the scene of the play serves particularly well for the portrayal of a man whose whole life was bound up with the stage. In much the same way, the equally familiar device of elaborating the plot out of what purports to be a rehearsal of a play, which in this instance is of a distinctly autobiographical nature, and from the breaks that inevitably occur during its course conveys well the sense of the gradual integration of fragments of the performers' actions and utterances into a coherent whole under the commanding presence of the director-playwright.

What adds tension and vitality to this situation is the constant overstepping of the borderline between theatricality and reality, in other words, between what has already been fictionalized and is now being prepared for vicarious expression in the theatrical mode and what is gradually and at first almost imperceptibly growing not into the perfected performance of a stage role but into the comprehending acquiescence to a genuine and actual personal experience of love. This blurring of firm borderlines is especially apt for the portrayal of a dramatist renowned for putting his psychological problems into his plays. As Hayman's Strindberg puts it, "The only stories a man can tell are stories he's lived."

As is suggested by the rich ambiguities latent in its title, *Playing the Wife* emerges as an intriguingly multitiered work played out in overlapping time sequences that suggest the way memories flood back into the present. Quite careful reading is often required to discriminate between the various layers of expression. In the theater, however, where Harriet, for instance, can chose one tone of voice when acting her stage role and, say, a rather less obviously projected one when speaking for herself, a distinction between different aspects can be initially established. The audience is all the more struck as it becomes clear that the worlds of theater and of emotional life cannot be kept apart.

Presented largely in a language of an everyday style, *Playing the Wife* is full of lines that have a rich resonance. Harriet's opening speech runs "Listen to yourself. Listen to your voice—what you do to it. You try to unbalance yourself. Listen to yourself." Not particularly remarkable in themselves, these few short sentences highlight major themes for future exploration. A little later, after Harriet has, not without justification, accused Strindberg of seeking revenge on Siri in his play and asserted that it is all "nothing to do with me," the rejoinder "I think you'll find it is" has a chilling prophetic ring. In an effort to persuade Bengt to interpret his role in a less conventional fashion, Strindberg bursts out,

> You're still trying to be a character. People aren't characters. We're inconsistent, out of joint. . . . You'll never be any good till you learn not to think [in terms of character]. Am I always consistent? Is there a clear-cut outline all around me? Or her? Or you? Nothing about us is static. We're improper fractions, top-heavy, ramshackle assemblages from scraps of feeling and thought. Sometimes we do things, and if there's a reason for them, we have no idea what it is.

From such disturbingly negative concepts Hayman's Strindberg goes on to try once more to find a meaning for life in the love of a woman. The result in *Playing the Wife* is an intellectually demanding play that has some grim humor to season its emotional power and that makes for fascinating theater.

—Christopher Smith

HEGGIE, Iain

Nationality: British and Scottish. **Born:** John Hamilton Heggie, Glasgow, 23 April 1953. **Education:** Wolverhampton Poly, Wolverhampton, England, 1974-77. Degrees in English and Geography, 1977. **Career:** Health club instructor, Olympic health, Glasgow; drama teacher, London, 1981-83. Acting teacher, Glasgow, 1990—. **Awards:** Mobil award, 1985, for *Wholly Healthy Glasgow*; John Whiting award and Manchester Evening news award for best new play, both 1987, both for *American Bagpipes*. **Address:** 158 Whitehill Street, Glasgow GBL 2LU.

Publications

Plays

Wholly Healthy Glasgow (produced Manchester, 1987). London, Methuen, 1987.
American Bagpipes (produced Manchester, 1988). London, Penguin, 1988.
Sex Comedies (produced Edinburgh, 1992).
American Bagpipes and Other Plays (includes *American Bagpipes*; *Waiting for Shuggie's Ma*; *Politics in the Park*). London, Penguin, 1989.
Lust (produced Edinburgh, 1993).
Tourist Variations (produced Edinburgh, 1994).
Experienced Woman Gives Advice (produced Manchester, 1995). London, Methuen, 1995.
Funf in der Luft (produced Glasgow, 1997).
Politics in the Park (produced Liverpool, 1996). London, Penguin, 1988.
Don Juan, adaptation (produced Glasgow, 1998).

Screenplay: *The Pen,* 1995.

*

Theatrical Activities:
Director: **Play**–*Sex Comedies,* 1993.

Iain Heggie comments:
My main influences have been David Mamet, Harold Pinter, Edward Albee, stand up comedy, my own teaching work, particularly improvisation.

* * *

Iain Heggie left school at age 16. He worked in a Glasgow health club as a part-time instructor and then moved to Birmingham, where he had a similar job. There he took a degree in humanistic studies at Wolverhampton Polytechnic, followed by teacher training. He held several teaching jobs in London and became a full-time playwright in 1984. In addition to writing, he teaches at the Royal Scottish Academy of Music and Drama.

Outside Scotland Heggie is regarded as a controversial playwright. His work falls into at least two strands, one dealing with class mores and another with comic views of sex. Although he lives in Glasgow, he takes a pessimistic view of the prospects for drama in Scotland. "Far too much is spent on theatre buildings in Scotland," he has commented, "and not enough on production. The first essential is a full time Repertory Company in Scotland, which does not at present exist."

Heggie has acknowledged that when he began writing he was more interested in dialogue than in story. Since then, however, he has become more concerned with the story of his plays. "It begins with a situation," he explains, "out of which the characters emerge." He views the purpose of drama as being "to produce order out of chaos," which is, of course, one of the purposes of all art. He also believes that drama has the function of widening people's understanding of the situations that others—indeed, sometimes they themselves—must face.

The first play to bring Heggie to wide public notice was *A Wholly Healthy Glasgow,* a comedy of life in a Scottish massage parlor. The play speaks the language of working-class Glasgow, and it was described as "raucous and rambly" when it was staged at the Royal Court Theatre in London in February 1988. *The London Theatre Record* found it "depressing, unambitious" but praised Heggie's ear for "the invective grammar and defiant vulgarity of the Glasgow streets." *The Independent* praised the play's "baroque festival of foul language that is, for once, soaringly eloquent." The critic Dominic Gray thought the "humour, language and the characters finely wrought," but the *Jewish Chronicle* attacked it as a largely unlikeable play. . . . Heggie makes some sharp and funny observations but he goes on making them again and again." Perhaps the critics' reservations were not altogether surprising, London being described in the play as "that shitbag, esoteric work hole down South." The play won the 1985 Mobil Award for comedy.

Scottish critics were much more favorable. *The Scotsman* called the play "a gamy slice of low life . . . a comic extravagance wildly funny at times, outwardly realistic, but in fact carefully stylised. So, indeed, is the obsessive verbal rudery."

Heggie's second major play was *American Bagpipes.* It was thought by the *Financial Times* to be a "powerful, questioning, funny and virtually Euripidean domestic comedy" that "surprises as much as it delights." Although in Scotland it did not receive quite the acclaim of Heggie's previous play, it has been translated into several European languages, including Finnish and German. The work has also been staged, less successfully, in the United States.

Heggie's full-length 1996 play *An Experienced Woman Gives Advice* has been performed in Manchester, where the playwright feels that he is most warmly received. "In Manchester," he says, "they are perhaps nearer to the working class and their ear is more attuned to the Glasgow speech than in the South." He has noted that in Manchester, too, the audience is to some extent stratified by days of the week, Saturday, for example, being the day for students and the young.

Heggie has done translations of several Russian plays, and he also has written several short plays, the most widely acclaimed being those that make up the so-called sex comedies. When the sex comedies were staged in 1997, a *Herald* critic wrote, ". . . what's surprising is that when finally the two characters reach their futile end, and the room is filled with indifferent neighbours, we do feel a sense of loss, a sense of real people ignored, neglected and misunderstood and a feeling there is a quality in both production and play that will return to haunt us." The works have elsewhere been described as a round of "destruction and self-destruction."

—Maurice Lindsay

HENDRY, Tom

Nationality: Canadian. **Born:** Winnipeg, Manitoba, 7 June 1929. **Education:** Bishop Taché School and Norwood Collegiate Institute, St. Boniface, Manitoba; Kelvin Technical High School, Winnipeg, graduated 1947; University of Manitoba, Winnipeg, 1947; Manitoba Institute of Chartered Accountants, admitted to membership 1955. **Family:** Married 1) Irene Chick in 1958 (divorced 1963); 2) Judith Carr in 1963; two sons and one daughter. **Career:** Owner, Thomas Hendry, C.A., 1956-58, and partner, Hendry and Evans, 1958-61, Winnipeg; founder and partner, Theatre 77, Winnipeg, 1957-58; manager and producer, Rainbow Stage, Winnipeg, 1958-60; founder and general manager, Manitoba Theatre Centre, Winnipeg, 1958-63; secretary-general, Canadian Theatre Centre, Toronto, 1964-69; editor, *Stage in Canada*, Toronto, 1965-69; literary manager, Stratford Festival, Ontario, 1969, 1970; founding director, Playwrights Co-op, 1971-79 and Playwrights Canada, 1979-82, Toronto; co-founder and producer, Toronto Free Theatre, 1971-82; co-founder, Banff Playwrights Colony, and head of the Playwriting Department, Banff Centre, Alberta, 1974-76; audit officer, Department of National Revenue, Toronto, 1982-84; chair, Task Force on National Arts Centre, Ottawa, 1986. Consultant, 1984-85, policy director, 1985—, Toronto Arts Council; Barker Fairley distinguished visitor in Canadian culture, University College, Toronto, 1986—. Lives in Toronto. **Awards:** Canada Council travel grant, 1963, Senior Arts grant, 1973, and grant, 1977; Centennial medal, 1967; Lieutenant-Governor's medal, 1970; Queen's Silver Jubilee medal, 1977; Toronto Drama Bench award, 1982. Fellow, Bethune College, York University, Downsview, Ontario, 1978. **Address:** 34 Elgin Avenue, Toronto, Ontario M5R 1G6, Canada

PUBLICATIONS

Plays

Do You Remember? (televised 1954; revised version, music by Neil Harris, produced Winnipeg, 1957).

Trapped! (for children; produced Winnipeg, 1961).

Do Not Pick the Flowers (mime play; produced Winnipeg, 1962).

All about Us (revue), with Len Peterson, music by Allan Laing (produced Winnipeg, 1964).

Fifteen Miles of Broken Glass (televised 1966). Published in *A Theatre Happening*, Toronto, Nelson, 1968; revised version (produced Toronto, 1970), Toronto, Playwrights, 1972; Vancouver, Talon Books, 1975.

Satyricon, music by Stanley Silverman, adaptation of the work by Petronius (produced Stratford, Ontario, 1969).

How Are Things with the Walking Wounded? (as *The Walking Wounded*, produced Lansing, Michigan, 1970; as *How Are Things with the Walking Wounded?*, produced Toronto, 1972). Toronto, Playwrights, 1972.

That Boy—Call Him Back (produced Lansing, Michigan, 1970; Toronto, 1971). Published in *Performing Arts in Canada* (Toronto), Winter 1972.

You Smell Good to Me, and Séance (produced Toronto, 1972). Toronto, Playwrights, 1972.

The Missionary Position (produced Vancouver, 1972). Toronto, Playwrights, 1972.

Dr. Selavy's Magic Theatre (lyrics only), with Richard Foreman, music by Stanley Silverman (produced Lenox, Massachusetts, and New York, 1972; Oxford, 1978).

Aces Wild, music by Hendry and Stephen Jack, lyrics by Hendry (also director: produced Hamilton, Ontario, 1972).

Friends and Lovers (includes *You Smell Good To Me* and *The Missionary Position*). Toronto, Playwrights, 1972.

Gravediggers of 1942, music by Stephen Jack, lyrics by Hendry (produced Toronto, 1973; London, 1984). Toronto, Playwrights, 1973.

The Dybbuk (lyrics only), book by John Hirsch, music by Allan Laing, adaptation of the play by S. Ansky (produced Winnipeg, 1974; Los Angeles, 1975). Winnipeg, Peguis, 1975.

Naked at the Opera (produced Banff, Alberta, 1975). Toronto, Co-opera, 1976.

A Memory of Eden (produced Banff, Alberta, 1975).

Apart from Everything, Is Anything the Matter? (produced Banff, Alberta, 1975).

Byron, music by Stephen Jack (produced Toronto, 1976).

Confidence (produced Banff, Alberta, 1976).

Séance II, published in *Quarry* (Kingston, Ontario), Winter 1978-79.

Hogtown: Toronto the Good, music by Paul Hoffert (produced Toronto, 1981).

East of the Sun, West of the Moon (produced Toronto, 1986).

Not in My Back Yard (produced Toronto, 1994).

Screenplays: *Box Car Ballet* (documentary), 1955; *A City in White* (documentary), 1956; *A House Divided* (documentary), 1957; *The Day the Freaks Took Over*, 1972; *Aces Wild*, 1974; *Private Places*, with Ron Kelly, 1976.

Radio Plays: *Wolf, Adolph, and Benito*; *The Steps Behind Her*; *Sea and Sky*, 1951-59.

Television Plays: *Do You Remember?*, 1954; *The Anniversary*, from a short story by Chekhov, 1965; *Fifteen Miles of Broken Glass*, 1966; *Last Man on Horseback*, 1969; *I Was Never in Kharkov*, 1972; *Pickles*, 1976; *Royal Suite* series (3 episodes), 1976; *Santa Claus from Florida*, 1976; *King of Kensington* series (6 episodes), 1977-78, 1981; *Welcome to Canada*, 1977; *The Central Tech Tiger*, 1977; *Volcano*, 1978; *Please Say You're Real*, 1978.

Other

The Canadians (on English-Canadian theatre). Toronto, Macmillan, 1967.

Theatre in Canada: A Reluctant Citizen. Toronto, Committee for an Independent Canada, 1972.

Cultural Capital: The Care and Feeding of Toronto's Artistic Assets. Toronto, Toronto Arts Council, 1985.
L'École/The School with Michel Garneau. Montréal, Stanke, 1985.
Task Force on the National Arts Centre: Accent on Access/Favoriser l'accessibilité (English and French texts). Ottawa, Government of Canada, 1986.

*

Manuscript Collections: Public Archives of Canada, Ottawa; Toronto Public Library.

Critical Study: *The Work: Conversations with English-Canadian Playwrights* by Robert Wallace and Cynthia Zimmerman, Toronto, Coach House Press, 1982.

Theatrical Activities:
Director: **Play**—*Aces Wild*, Hamilton, Ontario, 1972.

Actor: Roles in *The Jacksons and Their Neighbours* and other radio and television series, early 1950s.

Tom Hendry comments:

I cannot explain why I write plays, or why I choose the subjects that I do. The people in the plays reflect the people in my life—mostly they are outsiders. Paradoxically, I believe that if you examine anyone closely you will find that in some important area of his life he is an outsider, a non-participant. I believe that civilized society is a system of institutionalized violence directed at the individuals who make it up, and that to some extent each of us is aware of and opposes this violence. I believe that how people behave is as important as why they behave as they do. I believe that the damage we do to each other will only abate and finally cease when more perfect forms of communication—akin to ESP—are discovered and taught to everyone. Therefore I believe that dreams and nightmares and fairy tales are the only things worth writing or writing about. My plays say what I have to say.

* * *

Tom Hendry fills the plays from his most prolific period of writing for the stage with articulate and sophisticated characters—with artists, models, literati, and successful businessmen. His is a world of chic parties, brittle dialogue, liquor, drugs, and sexual freedom of a marked homosexual ambiance—a world of falsity. In expressing a set of attitudes typical of young urbanites of the 1970s, these plays also present central themes and figures that can be found in Hendry's earliest plays and that recur in later work. In this world of stereotypes the very shallowness of the fictional personalities is true to the real world they represent, and Hendry draws them accurately. His world is less erudite than Waugh's, but it is also less guilty and self-indulgent than Crowley's and, therefore, more credible. At times Hendry draws elements out of even these predictable characters that bring them to life, but the strains of the mannered drawing room comedy are more than reminiscent, and when Hendry is imitative, he is as shallow as his characters and as boring. In a play like *How Are Things with the Walking Wounded?* an unevenness arises between those sections that work out an original pattern and those that seem superimposed snatches of Noël Coward, a difficulty in integrating material, especially lyrics, that persists through the later musical collaborations. This is unfortunate, since a maturation of craft can be seen throughout this period, and, apart from the sense of déjà vu that besets it, *Walking Wounded* is a fine play. Unfortunately also, however, Simone is correct in remarking of herself and her fellow characters, "We do tend to talk a lot, darling."

The plays produced at the Toronto Free Theatre rework the related themes of the outsider, the "non-participant" as Hendry has called him, and the prostitute he becomes in a world based on selling out as a solution to loneliness or failure. The figure first appears in the television play *Fifteen Miles of Broken Glass* in the person of an underaged air force cadet who is left out when the war ends three years before he can join it. The bombing of Hiroshima ends the protagonist's heroic dreams, forcing him to connect with reality. The outsider becomes representative of Canada in this war play and, even more strongly, in the later *Gravediggers of 1942*, which overlays a campy musical comedy subplot on the shocking events of the Dieppe raid. Here the thesis is a more intellectual statement of the Hendry theme, with the prostitution symbolically extended to a cynical self-destruction of the Canadian psyche in the person of the ingenue Judy, who finally capitulates to Hitler's offers of wealth and power. Kept outside the principal action and sacrificed by stronger powers and made as ineffectual as the naive Canadian kids in the subplot trying to become part of the war effort by putting on a show to sell war bonds, "Our Lady of the Peace Tower" accepts one solution to being outside: she learns to prostitute herself. By doing so she completes the series of characters in *You Smell Good to Me*, *The Missionary Position*, and *Walking Wounded.* Seen from various vantages, Albert-Steven-Willy is the same character, and Regan-Rene-Barbara-Judy, although they display different external characteristics and even genders, are simply facets of the hustler figure.

Gravediggers suffers from often clumsy lyrics and an uneven relationship of song to plot, a problem that caused the later musical collaboration *Hogtown: Toronto the Good* to fail in production though its concept is sound and its scale ambitious. *Hogtown* presents a dialectic on the legislation of public morality, and once again it presents the struggle as a battle between the establishment and the outsider. Here, too, the outsider is a prostitute, a famous brothel keeper from Toronto's past. Like *Gravediggers* and a series of musical collaborations after *Satyricon*, this play attempts to join a debate on heroism through often hopeless action, a theme explored most completely in *Byron,* to the apparatus of the Broadway musical. Each of these entertainments is an exciting cooperative project, but each remains in need of further revision and completion. Hendry has not achieved the complex mix of cynicism and froth he seeks, and he has not brought his highly interrelated plays together to produce the one play to which all the others point.

Hendry's work as an arts administrator has included the preparation of a pivotal report on cultural funding. He has turned away from writing for the stage, but he did adapt *Fifteen Miles of Broken Glass* for film.

—Reid Gilbert

HENLEY, Beth

Nationality: American. **Born:** Jackson, Mississippi, 8 May 1952. **Education:** Southern Methodist University, Dallas, B.F.A. 1974; University of Illinois, Urbana, 1975-76. **Career:** Actress, Theatre Three, Dallas, 1972-73, with Southern Methodist University Directors Colloquium, 1973, and with the Great American People Show, New Salem, 1976; teacher, Dallas Minority Repertory Theatre, 1974-75, University of Illinois, Urbana, 1975-76. Lives in Los Angeles. **Awards:** Co-winner of Great American Playwriting contest, 1978; Pulitzer prize, for *Crimes of the Heart,* 1981; New York Drama Critics Circle award, 1981; Oppenheimer award, 1981. **Agent:** Gilbert Parker, William Morris Agency, 1325 Avenue of the Americas, New York, New York 10019, U.S.A

PUBLICATIONS

Plays

Am I Blue? (produced Dallas, 1973; revised version produced Hartford, Connecticut, 1981; New York, 1982). New York, Dramatists Play Service, 1982.
Crimes of the Heart (produced Louisville, 1979; New York, 1980; London, 1983). New York, Viking Press, 1982.
The Miss Firecracker Contest (produced Los Angeles, 1980; London, 1982; New York, 1984). New York, Dramatists Play Service, 1985.
The Wake of Jamey Foster (produced Hartford, Connecticut, and New York, 1982). New York, Dramatists Play Service, 1983.
The Debutante Ball (produced Costa Mesa, California, 1985; New York, 1988; London, 1989). Jackson, University of Mississippi Press, 1991.
The Lucky Spot (produced New York, 1987; London, 1991). New York, Dramatists Play Service, 1987.
Abundance (produced Costa Mesa, California, 1989; New York, 1990). In *Plays for the South Coast Repertory,* New York, Dramatists Play Service, 1993.
Control Freaks (also director: produced Chicago, 1992).
Monologues for Woman. Toluca Lake, California, Dramaline Publications, 1992.
Beth Henley: Four Plays (includes *The Wake of Jamey Foster*; *The Miss Firecracker Contest*; *The Lucky Spot*; *Abundance*). Portsmouth, New Hampshire, Heinemann, 1992.

Screenplays: *The Moon Watcher*, 1983; *True Stories*, with Stephen Tobolowsky, 1986; *Crimes of the Heart*, 1987; *Nobody's Fool*, 1987; *Miss Firecracker*, 1990.

Television Plays: *Morgan's Daughters,* 1979; *Survival Guides,* 1985; *How to Survive a Family Tree,* 1987.

*

Critical Studies: *Commercial Theatre and the Female Script: A Case Study of Beth Henley's Crimes of the Heart* (dissertation) by Cynthia L. Allan, University of Georgia, 1992; *Women's Identity and the Intersecting Concepts of Gender, Race, and Class in the Plays of Ntozake Shange, Beth Henley, and Cherrie Moraga* (dissertation) by Julia De Foor Jay, Houston, Texas, University of Houston, 1994.

* * *

Portraying women who seek to define themselves outside their relationships with men and beyond their family environment is a unifying factor in all of Beth Henley's plays.

Her first play to be produced in New York, *Crimes of the Heart,* won the Pulitzer Prize, and most of her work continues to be compared to it. There are strong similarities between her plays, not only in theme but also in plot, but it is Henley's characters that provide unique contributions to the dramaturgy. The McGrath sisters in *Crimes of the Heart* are probably the most traditionally well developed of her characters in that each has a strong connection to the plot, each grows from her experience, and each comes to understand others better. In *The Debutante Ball, The Wake of Jamey Foster,* and *Abundance,* however, Henley masterfully creates characters who explore their identities within a complex plot and who transcend their experience with uncertain and unexpected results.

The Debutante Ball is a quirky play filled with Henley's typical southern humor and Chekhovian characters. The play includes action that is not often dramatized, such as women cutting themselves shaving, and an unsympathetic treatment of a deaf girl. The ball serves as a structural device for all of the characters to come together in hopes of reestablishing their place in society. Teddy, the debutante, cannot go through with the facade, however, and in the end she is left bleeding all over her ball gown, having aborted a child. Pregnant by a one-armed man with a scarred face, whom Teddy had called ugly, she explains that, "I kinda just did it to be polite. I couldn't take on any more, ah, bad feelings, guilt."

In *The Wake of Jamey Foster* the occasion is the burial of Marshael's husband, Jamey. The unhappy and bitter widow eventually resolves her feelings and, like the debutante, is actually empowered by the difficulties and troubled feelings that the death has brought to light. In *Abundance* two pioneer women, Macon Hill and Bess Johnson, are also empowered by the unexpected twists of fate that in the end leave them both looking like freaks, a powerful physical representation of disfigured dreams.

Death, disaster, and freakish accidents play a major role in all of Henley's plays. Henley's treatment of this recurring motif is often humorous, however. Most of her southern characters accept such events matter-of-factly, so that when Babe shoots her husband in *Crimes of the Heart,* Bess is kidnapped by the Indians in *Abundance,* or orphan Carnelle in *The Miss Firecracker Contest* speaks nonchalantly about people dying—"It seems like people've been dying practically all my life, in one way or another"—it is never maudlin.

Structurally, Henley relies on storytelling, especially those stories in which female characters can turn to other females for help. She often employs one or two female characters as the center of her story, usually an occasion of some sort, and then adds dimension to the plot with minor characters who are bleakly comic or mildly eccentric. Leon, the slow-witted brother in *The Wake of Jamey Foster*; Cassidy, the pathetic tomboy teenager in Henley's least successful play, *The Lucky Spot*; or Delmount, the mentally unstable cousin in *The Miss Firecracker Contest,* are all good examples. These secondary characters reinforce a comic pathos established by the central characters. The cruelties of life befall all of Henley's characters, and the playwright is adept in dramatizing their sadness with a rare duality of expression that creates laughter and tears. One of the most memorable examples is that of Cassidy, who clings to a dream in which a "furry animal" pledged his love for her.

Male characters often serve as plot devices and are rarely fully developed. Especially problematic is the character of Elmore in *Abundance,* an opportunist who shows up late in the play to help Bess write about her ordeal of being kidnapped and living with the Indians for five years. Brighton in *The Debutante Ball* and Doc in *Crimes of the Heart* are necessary to advance the plot but remain one-dimensional. Male characters rarely take any definite positive action but serve as the impetus for action by the female characters. Will in *Abundance* and, to a lesser degree, Brocker in *The Wake of Jamey Foster* are exceptions.

Linguistically, Henley's style couples witty dialogue with poetic colloquial speech that at its best produces a powerful personal voice for her characters, especially when the playwright trusts the simplicity and honesty of her southern characters. Language becomes forced when Henley moves beyond descriptions of experience. When characters reveal how they feel, Henley makes good use of her own strong feelings and observations. She is less successful, however, in descriptive metaphors, which are especially clumsy in the opening scenes of *Abundance,* an epic play that spans 25 years beginning in the late 1860s. The dialogue creates a forced rhythm that is unnatural and uncharacteristic of Henley. For example, in the early moments of the play Bess says, "Thanks kindly. I'm near pined t'death with famine." Later in the play Henley overuses metaphor, as when Bess says, "I try not to show my hurt. I hide it in different parts of the house. I bury jars of it in the cellar; throw buckets of it down the well; iron streaks of it into the starched clothes and hang them in the closet."

In terms of dramatic elements, *Crimes of the Heart* is Henley's most fully integrated play, but *Abundance* is her most ambitious. The latter contains many elements of earlier plays, including freak accidents, female bonding, and the exploration of identity. It also shares one of the less successful dramaturgical strategies seen in other plays, in which too much happens between scenes. Character transformations happen in mental space so that it is difficult to believe the changes that occur, especially in the character of Bess. The problem is more pervasive in *Abundance* because of the epic nature of the play. Still, the play is Henley's most sober and explicit work, filled with a strong sense of irony and uncompromising in its depiction of the evils that befall women who sell out their identities to men.

—Judy Lee Oliva

HENSHAW, James Ene

Nationality: Nigerian. **Born:** Calabar, 29 August 1924. **Education:** Christ the King College, Onitsha; National University of Ireland, Dublin, M.B. 1949; University of Wales, T.D.D. 1954. **Family:** Married Caroline Nchelem Amadi in 1958; five sons and three daughters. **Career:** Physician: medical consultant to Government of Eastern Nigeria, 1955-78: controller of medical services in Southern Eastern State (now Cross River State), 1968-72, and senior consultant on tuberculosis control, Rivers State, 1973-78. Member, National Council on Health, 1968-72, and Nigerian Medical Council, 1970-72. **Awards:** Henry Carr Memorial Cup, 1953. Knight, Order of St. Gregory the Great, 1965; Officer, Order of the Niger, 1977. **Address:** Itiaba House, 4 Calabar Road, P.O. Box 1249, Calabar, Nigeria.

Publications

Plays

This Is Our Chance (produced Dublin, 1947). Published in *This Is Our Chance*, 1957.

This Is Our Chance: Plays from West Africa (includes *The Jewels of the Shrine*, *A Man of Character*, *This Is Our Chance*). London, University of London Press, 1957; *The Jewels of the Shrine* published in *Plays from Black Africa*, edited by Fredric M. Litto, New York, Hill and Wang, 1968.

A Man of Character (produced Ilorin, 1970). Published in *This Is Our Chance*, 1957.

Children of the Goddess and Other Plays (includes *Companion for a Chief* and *Magic in the Blood*). London, University of London Press, 1964.

Magic in the Blood (produced Newcastle-upon-Tyne, 1987). Published in *Children of the Goddess and Other Plays*, 1964.

Medicine for Love. London, University of London Press, 1964.

Dinner for Promotion. London, University of London Press, 1967.

Enough Is Enough: A Play of the Nigerian Civil War (produced Benin City, Nigeria, 1975). Benin City, Ethiope, 1976.

A Song to Mary Charles, Irish Sister of Charity (produced Owerri, 1981). Calabar, Etewa, 1984.

*

Critical Studies: "Modern Drama in West Africa" by O. Ogunba, in *Perspectives in African Literature*, edited by Christopher Haywood, London, Heinemann, 1971; "Drama and Theatre in Nigeria" by Y. Ogunbiyi, in *Nigeria Magazine* (Lagos), 1982; *The Resilience of Religious Tradition in the Dramas of Wole Soyinka and James Ene Henshaw* by Rosemary N. Edet, Rome, n.p., 1984; "The Politics of Literary Syllabus: The Marginalization of James Ene Henshaw's Plays" and "Ene Henshaw and the Beginnings of Popular Plays in Nigeria" by A. Bamikunie, in *Nigeria Magazine* (Lagos), vol. 53, no.1, 1985.

James Henshaw comments:

(1988) I usually try (as much as I can) to make sure that those people who watch my plays do not return to their homes sadder than they have been. That is why the plays are mostly described as "comedies," even though there are more tragic situations in some of them than in some "tragic" plays. The comedy medium has, however, worked well for the type of audiences I have always had in mind, namely the youths, especially Nigerian youths.

Through many of my plays and the introductory essays that accompany them I have tried to make it clear that I was writing about Africans and for Africans. To me the preoccupation of making the "white man" understand the "black man" through African writing has never been as important as the need to make one Nigerian understand the other, or one African understand the other better. The plays are therefore always relevant to the culture and environment of the play goers. In addition to introductory essays, I usually give simple instructions to help players who might not have someone to direct them. Occasionally I am invited to see the plays and I think I enjoy them like anyone else in the audience. I have been particularly impressed by the variety of productions.

* * *

James Ene Henshaw occupies a unique position in African/Nigerian literary drama, coming as he does between the "coarse plays" of the Onitsha Market literary tradition of the 1950s and early 1960s and the more sophisticated and better constructed plays of Wole Soyinka and the other university-trained dramatists. One thing for which Henshaw should be remembered is the fact that his was the first attempt to write what could be regarded as authentic African drama to be performed by African people. He set out, as he says in the preface to *This Is Our Chance*, to write plays "whose scenes take place in surroundings" not "far removed from the African's own" and in which things spoken about have a "relationship with the problems of the African audience."

As a playwright Henshaw captures the pulse and moments of his West African society. It is quite possible to see his plays as chronologically reflecting the moral concerns and social development of his region, for they usually deal with the prevailing political and ethical preoccupations of certain moments in West African history. In *This Is Our Chance* Henshaw looks at a West Africa before colonialism and before Christianity. Koloro is almost virgin Africa with all its traditions intact, even if there already are cracks and friction represented by the indomitable Bambulu, the rebellious Princess Kudaro, and the moderately radical Enusi. Here Henshaw begins his exploration of the theme of tradition in conflict with modernity, a theme that dominates his consciousness in later plays like *Children of the Goddess* and *Companion for a Chief*. One key statement that Henshaw seems to be making in these plays is that societies are capable of generating change from within and that, where there are external influences, compromise and accommodation should become the watchwords. This, coming as it did in the 1950s and 1960s when the norm was a wholesale sweeping away of traditional African value systems for foreign Euro-Christian ones, was a new kind of thinking. This may well explain Henshaw's popularity across a wide spectrum of West African society, for his audiences can relate to his concerns, which in a sense are their concerns.

Henshaw's plays can be divided into two broad categories, the traditional plays and the contemporary plays. In the first group Henshaw seems concerned with exploring the tensions that arise when African traditions are faced with new "modernizing" influences from outside, and to this extent these plays depict an Africa caught in the throes of transition. Henshaw's voice strikes a middle ground since for him, much as we do not have to remain static by clinging to outmoded traditional practices—the killing of twins in *Children of the Goddess*, the silly superstitions of *This Is Our Chance*, and the sacrificing of human beings to accompany great chiefs when they die, as in *Companion for a Chief*—neither should we abandon all traditional codes of behavior so as to make way for a strange and undigested modernity.

It is obvious that, while Henshaw accepts that the missionaries, the Mcphails and Wilberforce, are agents of good, he cautions that these "good Christians" can become destabilizing if they show no respect for the culture and opinions of the people they have come to Christianize. For Henshaw the traditional African culture and the Euro-Christian culture can learn from each other and thus avoid the unnecessary tensions that a stubborn rejection and a callous denigration can give rise to. Does this make Henshaw a traditionalist or a modernist? I think that he is neither, for he is both, and this, I believe, is why his plays escape the tag of being moral tracts or a preaching theater. While his ambivalence tends to deprive his plays of a deeper significance, it allows him a measure of distance from his subjects and characters, which in the end ensures the delightful comic spirit that is never absent from a Henshaw play. It is this and the fact of his being a pioneer of African literary drama that ensured his popularity in the 1950s, 1960s, and 1970s.

In the contemporary plays the themes range from Kobina's stubborn honesty and integrity in the face of domestic and social pressure in *A Man of Character*, the confrontation between the filial irresponsibility of youth and the crafty doggedness of the old in *The Jewels of the Shrine*, to the mild feminism, blind hero worship, and judicial corruption of *Magic in the Blood*. It also includes the corrupt politics and social excesses of *Medicine for Love*, the cool and devious manipulations in *Dinner for Promotion*, and the more serious and somber reflections of the post-civil war play *Enough Is Enough*. What one notices in the progress of Henshaw's drama is that, as he moved away from traditional concerns, his plays also began to lose the pervading sense of community that characterized *This Is Our Chance* and *Children of the Goddess*. The feeling of the possible communal catastrophe and chaos of these two is replaced by a detached vision of individuals struggling through personal dilemmas and mishaps, as do Ewia and Kobina in *Medicine for Love* and *A Man of Character*, respectively.

In both phases, however, Henshaw manages to show his highly developed sense for the comic through deft twists in situations, delightful turns of phrase, and character manipulations for effect. Some of his characters are so memorable that they become household names. Who can forget Bambulu, the artist and master of the big phrase and pose? His comic antics and exuberant pedantry provided ample elocutionary meat for many budding actors and actresses. His famous salvo to Princess Kudaro—"This is the child of my brain, the product of my endeavour, and the materialisation of my inventive genius"—is a popular speech that became synonymous with African drama and acting in the 1960s. Most of us growing up then knew Bambulu and his famous speech by heart before we chanced on *This Is Our Chance*.

Henshaw is thus important for giving us the first truly stageable African plays, and, simple as these plays were, they are filled with memorable African characters and situations.

—Osita Okagbue

HERBERT, John

A pseudonym for John Herbert Brundage. **Nationality:** Canadian. **Born:** Toronto, Ontario, 13 October 1926. **Education:** Educated in public schools, 1932-43; Art College of Ontario, Toronto, 1947-49; New Play Society School of Drama, Toronto, 1955-58; Volkoff Ballet School, Toronto, 1956; National Ballet School of Canada, 1957. **Career:** Commercial artist, Toronto, 1943-46; served 6-month sentence in reformatory, Guelph, Ontario, 1946; worked at various jobs in the U.S.A., 1947, 1950-54; artistic director, Adventure Theatre, 1960-62, and New Venture Players, 1962-65, both Toronto; artistic director and producer, Garret Theatre Company, Toronto, 1965-71; artistic director, Medusa Theatre, 1972-74; associate editor, Arteditorial Company, Toronto, 1975-82; resident dramatist and associate director, Smile Company, Toronto, 1984-85. Lecturer in drama, Ryerson Polytechnical School, Toronto, summers 1969-70, York University, Downsview, Ontario, Summer 1972, New College, University of Toronto, summers 1973-76, Three Schools of Art, Toronto, 1975-81, and Tappa School of Art, 1982-83. Dancer, Garbut Roberts's Dance Drama Company; actor, dancer, and set and costume designer with other companies. **Awards:** Dominion Drama Festival Massey award, 1968 (refused); Chalmers award, 1975. **Agent:** Ellen Neuwald Inc., 905 West End Avenue, New York, New York 10025, U.S.A. **Address:** Suite B-1, 1050 Yonge Street, Toronto, Ontario M4W 2L1, Canada.

Publications

Plays

They Died with Their Boots On: *A Marsh-Melodrama* (produced Canoe Lake, Ontario, 1942).
Private Club (also director: produced Toronto, 1962).
A Household God (also director: produced Toronto, 1962).
A Lady of Camellias, adaptation of a play by Dumas fils (also director: produced Toronto, 1964).
Closer to Cleveland (also director: produced Toronto, 1967).
Fortune and Men's Eyes (produced New York, 1967; London, 1968). New York, Grove Press, 1967; in *Open Space Plays*, edited by Charles Marowitz, London, Penguin, 1974.
World of Woyzeck, adaptation of a play by Georg Büchner (also director: produced Toronto, 1969).
Beer Room (produced Toronto, 1970). Included in *Some Angry Summer Songs*, 1976.
Close Friends (produced Toronto, 1970). Included in *Some Angry Summer Songs*, 1976.
Born of Medusa's Blood (also director: produced Toronto, 1972).
Omphale and the Hero (produced Toronto, 1974). Published in *Canadian Theatre Review 3*, (Toronto), Summer 1974.
Some Angry Summer Songs (includes *Pearl Divers*, *Beer Room*, *Close Friends*, *The Dinosaurs*) (also director: produced Toronto, 1974). Vancouver, Talonbooks, 1976.

Screenplay: *Fortune and Men's Eyes*, 1971.

Other

Belinda Wright and Jelko Yuresha (biography). London, Kaye Bellman, 1972.

*

Manuscript Collection: University of Waterloo, Ontario.

Critical Studies: By Nathan Cohen, in *Canadian Writing Today* edited by Mordecai Richler, London, Penguin, 1970; "Damnation at Christmas" by Ann P. Messenger, in *Dramatists in Canada* edited by W.H. New, Vancouver, University of British Columbia Press, 1972; "Sexuality and Identity in *Fortune and Men's Eyes*" by Neil Carson, in *Twentieth Century Literature* (Los Angeles), July 1972.

Theatrical Activities:
Director: **Plays**—*Mourning Becomes Electra* by O'Neill, Toronto, 1957; Adventure Theatre, Toronto: *The Chalk Garden* by Enid Bagnold, 1961, and *Dear Brutus* by J.M. Barrie, 1962; New Venture Players, Toronto: *Private Club* and *A Household God*, 1962, and *A Lady of Camellias*, 1964; Garret Theatre, Toronto: *The Maids* by Jean Genet and *Escurial* by Michel de Ghelderode, 1965, *The Sea Gull* by Chekhov, 1966, *Closer to Cleveland*, 1967, *Doberman* by David Windsor and *Gin Rummy* by S. Bordenvik, 1968, and *World of Woyzeck*, 1969; *Born of Medusa's Blood*, Toronto, 1972; *Some Angry Summer Songs*, Toronto, 1974; *The Gnädiges Fräulein* by Tennessee Williams, Toronto, 1976; *Close Friends*, Toronto, 1976.

Actor: **Plays**—Shylock in *The Merchant of Venice*, Toronto, 1939; Thisbe in *A Midsummer Night's Dream*, Toronto, 1939; Juliet in *Romeo and Juliet*, Toronto, 1949; Father in *The Monkey's Paw* by W.W. Jacobs and L.N. Parker, Toronto, 1941; Farmer in *The Arkansas Traveller*, Toronto, 1942; Singer in *The Rising of the Moon* by Lady Gregory, Canoe Lake, Ontario, 1942; Carmen in *They Died with Their Boots On*, Canoe Lake, Ontario, 1942; Dancer in *Paris after Midnight* by Betty Rohm, Canadian tour, 1953; Tom in *The Glass Menagerie* by Tennessee Williams, Toronto, 1956: Octavius and Doctor in *The Barretts of Wimpole Street* by Rudolf Besier, Toronto, 1957; Orin in *Mourning Becomes Electra* by O'Neill, Toronto, 1957; Trigorin in *The Sea Gull* by Chekhov, Toronto, 1958; Dr. Sloper in *The Heiress* by Ruth and Augustus Goetz, Toronto, 1958; Professor Tobin in *The Druid Circle* by John van Druten, Toronto, 1959; Mental Patient in *The Wall* by Vyvyan Frost, Toronto, 1960; Rhangda in *A Balinese Legend* by Garbut Roberts, Toronto, 1967; title role in *The Gnädiges Fräulein* by Tennessee Williams, Toronto, 1976.

John Herbert comments:
(1973) My life in theatre goes back as far as I can remember, for I fell in love with the art as a small child. I saw Leonide Massine dance the Cuban Sailor in a production of *Gaîté Parisienne* with a touring company. I saw and heard some of the greatest artists of the theatre at Toronto's Royal Alexandra, in the days when all artists of magnitude travelled the world for us, and I have never lost my passion as a member of the audience. I visit the theatre constantly to see and hear what others are thinking, feeling, and doing. Occasionally, the original thrilling convulsion of surprise returns, as when the Bolshoi Ballet dances, or when Laurence Olivier plays the father in O'Neill's *Long Day's Journey into Night*, or whenever I encounter a new young voice in the theatre, whether it belong to playwright, director, or player. I cannot say that I care more about writing a play than for directing, acting, designing, or dancing. I try to live in the theatre as one would revel as a swimmer in the ocean. The tides must always be felt, powerful, endless, timeless, and terrible as life itself.

* * *

John Herbert's reputation as the enfant terrible of Canadian drama arose almost entirely from the acclaim with which his *Fortune and Men's Eyes* was first greeted. That it was well written and without the worst aspects of nationalistic theater recommended it highly to audiences weary of the sentimental quest for the great Canadian play.

Having said that, however, it is necessary to say that *Fortune and Men's Eyes* is not a great play. Its attractions are that it can easily be performed by a small cast with a modest competence and few resources for sets. Its weakness is that, for all its Sartrean setting, it is sentimental in another way—in its depiction of good and evil in Western terms. Smitty, the first-time criminal who is at the center of the play, is essentially a Victorian character. He is corrupted not by defects present in his own character but by the circumstances of his confinement. In fact, we have very little sense of what sort of person he is, and in that sense his transformation from bewildered innocence to black awareness is artificial. His last speech—"I'll pay you all back"—reminds us of Malvolio's "I'll be revenged on the whole pack of you." But the comparison reveals the thinness of the conflict.

Something of this artifice is manifested in Smitty's diction. To Mona, the Blanche DuBois of this underworld whose brutalization is the moment of Smitty's awakening, he says, "You keep your secrets, like Greta Garbo—under a hat." And his revulsion from Mona is too articulate for the character that he is meant to be: "Let me out of here! I'll go to the bloody concert—anywhere—where there is life."

It is the tendency toward caricature that weakens the play and exposes it as trading both in a fashionable subject and on the need for social reform. Neither of these things would in itself have prevented the play from retaining some permanent stature—Ibsen's *Ghosts* is an example of similar defects—were it not for the fact that the characters seem manufactured. Mona is too weak, with a penchant for great books that is too exaggerated. (It is from Mona's attempt to make analogies between the banal life of Kingston Pen and Shakespeare's relation to Southampton that the somewhat precious title comes.) Queenie is credible enough as a caricature but not as a person. "Her" vocabulary is just not credible. "Does Macy's bother Gimbel's?" is not a phrase that we believe he, as a Canadian, in a Canadian prison, would use. The author is coming through. It is, in fact, in precisely this absence of particular places and definable voices that the play is weakest. To be everywhere is to be nowhere.

This is not to say that the play is without dramatic force. In its first production and again in its London premiere, it was shocking in the forthrightness of its language and action. But more than shock and a passable narrative are required in a play of stature. And not even these are present in *Omphale and the Hero*, in which an archetypal whore-meets-hustler situation is the venue for a great deal of bathetic language and a plot that creaks at every joint. It is sad to see Herbert's talent wasted on bad Tennessee Williams.

—D. D. C. Chambers

HEWETT, Dorothy (Coade)

Nationality: Australian. **Born:** Perth, Western Australia, 21 May 1923. **Education:** Perth College; University of Western Australia, Perth, 1941-42, 1959-63, B.A. 1961, M.A. 1963. **Family:** Married Lloyd Davies in 1944 (marriage dissolved 1949), one son (deceased); lived with Les Flood, 1950-59, three sons; married Merv Lilley in 1960, two daughters. **Career:** Millworker, 1950-52; advertising copywriter, Sydney, 1956-58; senior tutor in English, University of Western Australia, 1964-73. Writer-in-residence, Monash University, Melbourne, 1975, University of Newcastle, New South Wales, 1977, Griffith University, Nathan, Queensland, 1980, La Trobe University, Bundoora, Victoria, 1981, Magpie Theatre Company, Adelaide, 1982, Rollins College, Florida, 1988, and Edith Cowan University, Washington, 1990. Poetry editor, *Westerly* magazine, Nedlands, Western Australia, 1972-73. Member of the editorial board, *Overland* magazine, Melbourne, 1970—, and *Sisters* magazine, Melbourne, 1979—; editor and director, Big Smoke Books, and review editor, *New Poetry*, both Sydney, 1979—. **Awards:** Australian Broadcasting Corporation prize, for poetry, 1945, 1965; Australia Council grant, 1973, 1976, 1979, 1981, 1984, lifetime emeritus fellowship, 1988; Australian Writers Guild award, 1974, 1982, 1986; International Women's Year grant, 1976, Australian prize, for poetry, 1986; Grace Levin prize, for poetry, 1988; Mattara Butterfly Books prize, for poetry, 1991; Nettie Palmer prize, for non-fiction, 1991; Victorian Premier's award, 1991. **Member:** A.M (Order of Australia), 1986. **Agent:** Hilary Linstead and Associates, 302 Easts Towers, 9-13 Bronte Road, Bondi Junction, New South Wales 2022. **Address:** 496 Great Western Highway, Faulconbridge, New South Wales 2776, Australia.

Publications

Plays

Time Flits Away, Lady (produced 1941).

This Old Man Comes Rolling Home (produced Perth, 1966; revised version produced Perth, 1968). Sydney, Currency Press, 1976.

Mrs. Porter and the Angel (produced Sydney, 1969). Included in *Collected Plays 1*, 1992.

The Chapel Perilous; or, The Perilous Adventures of Sally Banner, music by Frank Arndt and Michael Leyden (produced Perth, 1971). Sydney, Currency Press, 1972; London, Eyre Methuen, 1974.

Bon-Bons and Roses for Dolly (produced Perth, 1972). ith *The Tatty Hollow Story*, Sydney, Currency Press, 1976.

Catspaw (produced Perth, 1974).

Miss Hewett's Shenanigans (produced Canberra, 1975).

Joan, music by Patrick Flynn (produced Canberra, 1975). Montmorency, Victoria, Yackandandah, 1984.

The Tatty Hollow Story (produced Sydney, 1976). With *Bon-Bons and Roses for Dolly*, Sydney, Currency Press, 1976; included in *Collected Plays 1*, 1992.

The Beautiful Miss Portland, published in *Theatre Australia* (Sydney). November-December and Christmas 1976.

The Golden Oldies (produced Melbourne, 1976; London, 1978). With *Susannah's Dreaming*, Sydney, Currency Press, 1981.

Pandora's Cross (produced Sydney, 1978). Published in *Theatre Australia* (Sydney), September-October 1978.

The Man from Mukinupin (produced Perth, 1979). Sydney, Currency Press, 1980.

Susannah's Dreaming (broadcast 1980). With *The Golden Oldies*, Sydney, Currency Press, 1981.

Golden Valley (for children; produced Adelaide, 1981). With *Song of the Seals*, Sydney, Currency Press, 1985.

The Fields of Heaven (produced Perth, 1982).

Song of the Seals (for children), music by Jim Cotter (produced Adelaide, 1983). With *Golden Valley*, Sydney, Currency Press, 1985.

Christina's World (opera libretto; produced Sydney, 1983).

The Rising of Peter Marsh (produced Perth, 1988).

Zoo with Robert Adamson (produced Wagga Wagga, New South Wales, 1991).

Collected Plays 1 (includes *This Old Man Comes Rolling Home, Mrs. Porter and the Angel, The Chapel Perilous, The Tatty Hollow Story*). Sydney, Currency Press, 1992.

Screenplays: *For the First Time*, with others, 1976; *Journey among Women*, with others, 1977; *The Planter of Malata*, with Cecil Holmes, 1983.

Radio Plays: *Frost at Midnight*, 1973; *He Used to Notice Such Things*, 1974; *Susannah's Dreaming*, 1980.

Novels

Bobbin Up. Sydney, Australasian Book Society, 1959; revised edition, London, Virago Press, 1985.
The Toucher. Ringwood, Victoria, McPhee Gribble, 1994.

Short Stories

The Australians Have a Word for It. Berlin, Seven Seas, 1964.

Poetry

What about the People, with Merv Lilley. Sydney, Realist Writers, 1962.
Windmill Country. Sydney, Edwards and Shaw, 1968.
The Hidden Journey. Newnham, Tasmania, Wattle Grove Press, 1969.
Late Night Bulletin. Newnham, Tasmania, Wattle Grove Press, 1970.
Rapunzel in Suburbia. Sydney, New Poetry, 1975.
Greenhouse. Sydney, Big Smoke, 1979.
Journeys, with others, edited by Fay Zwicky. Melbourne, Sisters, 1982.
Alice in Wormland. Newcastle-upon-Tyne, Bloodaxe, 1987.
A Tremendous World in Her Head. Sydney, Dangaroo Press, 1989.
The Upside Down Sonnets. Springwood, New South Wales, Butterfly Books, 1991.
Peninsula. South Fremantle, W.A., Fremantle Arts Centre Press, 1994.
Collected Poems, 1940-1995. South Fremantle, W.A., Fremantle Arts Centre Press, 1995.

Other

Wild Card (autobiography). Melbourne, McPhee Gribble, and London, Virago, 1990.

Editor, *Sandgropers: A Western Australian Anthology.* Nedlands, University of Western Australia Press, 1973.

*

Manuscript Collections: Australian National Library, Canberra; Fisher Library, University of Sydney; Flinders University, Adelaide, South Australia.

Critical Studies: "Quest or Question? Perilous Journey to the Chapel" by Reba Gostand, in *Bards, Bohemians, and Bookmen* edited by Leon Cantrell, St. Lucia, University of Queensland Press, 1976; "Confession and Beyond" by Bruce Williams, in *Overland* (Sydney), 1977; *After "The Doll"* by Peter Fitzpatrick, Melbourne, Arnold, 1979; *Contemporary Australian Playwrights* edited by Jennifer Palmer, Adelaide, University Union Press, 1979; interview with Jim Davidson, in *Meanjin* (Melbourne), 1979; articles by Brian Kiernan and Carole Ferrier, in *Contemporary Australian Drama* edited by Peter Holloway, Sydney, Currency Press, 1981, revised edition, 1986; *Dorothy Hewett: The Feminine as Subversion* by Margaret Williams, Sydney, Currency Press, 1992; *Setting the Stage, a Semiotic Re-reading of Selected Australian Plays by Dorothy Hewett, Jack Hibberd, Louis Nowra, and Stephen Sewell* (dissertation) by Joanne Tompkins, York University, 1992; "Golden Girls and Bad Girls: The Plays of Dorothy Hewett" by Elizabeth Schafer, in *Critical Survey* (Oxford, England), 1994, pp. 140-45; "Dealing It Out: Dorothy Hewett's *Wild* Card" by Joan Newman, in *Critical Survey* (Oxford), 1994, pp. 133-39; *Dorothy Hewett: Selected Critical Essays,* edited by Bruce Bennett, South Fremantle, W.A., Fremantle Arts Centre Press, 1995.

* * *

It is hard to be indifferent to the work of Dorothy Hewett. Everything she has goes into it, provoking in the observer anger, distaste, admiration, extravagant praise and partisanship, and, on two occasions, threat of court action. First a poet and the author of an important novel and much left-wing journalism, she turned to playwriting in 1965. Her materials are the female psyche and the burden that men and society lay on the romantic imagination and the artistic soul. She disclaims any autobiographical intention, bending her mind as she does to the universal experience of the woman as artist through her own painful experience of the role, but it is nevertheless true that most of her characters can be identified by a style of language and imagery that refers noticeably to her own life and literary experience.

The progress of Hewett's work shows a steady movement from dramatic narrative to ritual poetry, and much of the discomfort she causes stems from her defiant intrusion of the private nature of the poetic experience into the naked public arena of the theater.

Her first play, *This Old Man Comes Rolling Home,* remains her most immediately accessible and contains some of her best dramatic writing. It is the story of a household of communist activists in Redfern, an inner Sydney suburb, in the early 1950s, the fierce time of the unsuccessful attempt by Sir Robert Menzies to ban the Communist party. The play was a response to her own time in Redfern and is an acknowledgement of what she calls her "love affair with the working class."

Two early dramatic influences were Patrick White and Tennessee Williams, both of them moving out of realism toward a poetic interpretation of the ordinary man and woman. Like them but in her own way, she has since progressed into a landscape not real in the accepted sense but born of and reflecting the mind and sensibilities of Hewett and her characters. She made a leap into this landscape with *Mrs. Porter and the Angel,* a play in which a deranged woman teacher wanders through the gathering dark to the houses of her colleagues in search of an imaginary dog. The play is replete with black-dog images of impotence and closet sexuality, of men and women destroying one another out of their own fantasies. And yet the play adds up to a kind of celebration of the good and evil in all of them. It shares the optimism of *This Old Man,* a comedy of poverty that pays tribute to the forces of life and laughter.

Journeys are endemic to Hewett's writing. The major journey is that taken by Sally Banner in *The Chapel Perilous,* her most widely performed play. In it she audaciously compares to the questing of Malory's heroes a woman's search for spiritual truth through literary striving, sexual adventures, marriage, communism, and public recognition. In *Bon-Bons and Roses for Dolly* her heroine is a teenager of the 1940s, indulged by her emotionally starved parents and grandparents and fed on the fairy floss of the Hollywood movie. In the second act Dolly returns, middle-aged, to the now crumbling Crystal Palace, a meeting of two empty and neglected monuments to secondhand dreams.

In a different style Hewett's rock opera *Catspaw* offers a dropout guitar player in search of the real Australia. In a ribald grand parade of legendary characters the author postulates that most of these enlightened minds were stick-in-the-mud conservatives.

The Tatty Hollow Story and *Joan* return to the theme of the female predicament and demonstrate how women rise to the roles men create for them. The former ritually brings together the five lovers of the mysterious Tatty Hollow, whom each remembers in a different fantasy. At last, in retaliation for what she sums up as a wasted life, Tatty takes revenge on them and dissolves—and the play with her—into a poetic madness. *Joan* is the Joan of Arc story as a rock opera with four eponymous heroines—Joan the peasant, Joan the soldier, Joan the witch, and Joan the saint.

The Golden Oldies, a savage mood piece on the round of domestic duty and mutual exploitation that is the lot of many women, emerges in retrospect as a turning point for Hewett's imagination, an exorcism of the past. Leaving us with the image of an old woman's death and her daughter sifting through the flotsam of a lifetime, Hewett moves away from her exploration of isolation toward unifying the elements of life. In the work that follows she begins to live down the old defiance and absorb the destructive forces, which had hitherto preoccupied her, into a total creative vision.

Pandora's Cross is a nostalgic attempt to rally the old creative forces of the once bohemian Kings Cross, later a haunt of drug addicts and racketeers. The play contains some of Hewett's best poetry but suffers, like other work from this middle period, from unresolved dramatic action. In 1979, however, the challenge of writing a festive work for Western Australia's sequicentennial celebrations, drew from her a play that changed her fortunes and reconciled her with the state of her birth. *The Man from Mukinupin* mingles childhood memories of the wheat-farming district in which she grew up with a dense education in Shakespeare and the English and Australian romantics. Like many small communities Mukinupin hides a dark secret, and the mad water diviner Zeek Perkins is its guardian. In an allegory of good and evil, of women journeying from romance to reality, pretty Polly Perkins, the grocer's daughter, and her handsome sweetheart enter the dark world of their outcast siblings, the whore and the rebel.

This was the beginning of what has come to be known as Hewett's pastoral period. In close succession it produced *Susannah's Dreaming,* a radio play about the tragic intrusion of adult brutality into the magical sea world of a retarded innocent; *The Fields of Heaven,* about the takeover of a farming community by an ambitious escapee from Mussolini's Italy; and two children's plays, *Golden Valley,* set in the wheat fields, and *Song of the Seals,* set in a mystical sub-Antarctic bay, which use the forces of nature in the form of people transmuted into birds and fish to fight the intrusion of acquisitive outsiders into their rural harmony.

Hewett's work is informed by a strong literary background and an incorrigible romanticism that contrasts oddly with her critical armory. Part of the romanticism is an attention-getting daring and a determination to prove that life can be beautiful, a desire so strong in some plays that the energy consumes an often shaky structure. The source of her romanticism can be traced to the artistic isolation of her girlhood in Western Australia and her private schooling, which together encouraged poetry and idealism. Her long allegiance to the Communist party was an emotional, even a religious, commitment, and her expulsion in 1968 left her isolated, bereft of beliefs, and newly aware of her mortality, a sense confirmed by the senility and death of her mother. These factors are strongly represented in the work of her middle period and come to an end with the sudden force of *The Man from Mukinupin.* Hewett's subsequent works still take the same journey through idealism to understanding, but they carry a new optimism and a new acceptance of the follies of life, a new recognition of the splendor and the resilience of the human spirit.

—Katharine Brisbane

HIBBERD, Jack

Nationality: Australian. **Born:** Warracknabeal, Victoria, 12 April 1940. **Education:** Marist Brothers College, Bendigo, Victoria; University of Melbourne, M.D. 1964. **Family:** Married 1) Jocelyn Hibberd in 1969 (divorced 1977), one daughter and one son; 2) Evelyn Krape in 1978, one son. **Career:** Practicing physician, 1965-66, 1970-73, and 1986—. Member, Australia Council Theatre Board, 1977-79; first president, Melbourne Writers' Theatre; editor, "Performing Arts in Australia" issue of *Meanjin,* Melbourne, 1984. Currently wine columnist, Melbourne *Age.* **Awards:** Australia Council fellowship, 1973, 1977, 1981. **Address:** 125 Wooralla Drive, Mount Eliza, Victoria 3930, Australia.

PUBLICATIONS

Plays

Brain Rot (produced Carlton, Victoria, 1967; augmented version produced Melbourne, 1968). Section *Who?* published in *Plays,* Melbourne, Penguin, 1970; *Just Before the Honeymoon* in *Kosmos II* (Clayton, Victoria), 1972; *One of Nature's Gentlemen* in *Three Popular Plays,* 1976; selections in *Squibs,* 1984.

White with Wire Wheels (produced Melbourne, 1967). Published in *Plays,* Melbourne, Penguin, 1970.

Dimboola: A Wedding Reception Play (produced Carlton, Victoria, 1969). Melbourne and London, Penguin, 1974.

Marvellous Melbourne, with John Romeril (produced Melbourne, 1970). Published in *Theatre Australia* (Potts Point, New South Wales), July-September 1977.

Customs and Excise (also director: produced Carlton, Victoria, 1970; augmented version, as *Proud Flesh,* produced Carlton, Victoria, 1972).

Klag (produced Melbourne, 1970).

Aorta (produced Melbourne, 1971).

A Stretch of the Imagination (also director: produced Carlton, Victoria, 1972; London, 1982; Richmond, Virginia, 1983). Sydney, Currency Press, 1973; London, Eyre Methuen, 1974.

Women!, adaptation of a play by Aristophanes (produced Carlton, Victoria, 1972).

Captain Midnight V.C., music by Lorraine Milne (produced Carlton, Victoria, 1973). Montmorency, Victoria, Yackandandah, 1984.

The Architect and the Emperor of Assyria, adaptation of a play by Fernando Arrabal (produced Carlton, Victoria, 1974).

The Les Darcy Show (produced Adelaide, 1974). Included in *Three Popular Plays,* 1976.

Peggy Sue; or, The Power of Romance (produced Carlton, Victoria, 1974; revised version produced Melbourne, 1983). Montmorency, Victoria, Yackandandah, 1982.

Goodbye Ted, with John Timlin (produced 1975). Montmorency, Victoria, Yackandandah, 1983.

A Toast to Melba (also director: produced Adelaide, 1976). Included in *Three Popular Plays*, 1976.

The Overcoat, music by Martin Friedel, adaptation of a story by Gogol (produced Carlton, Victoria, 1976; London, 1978). With *Sin*, Sydney, Currency Press, 1981.

Three Popular Plays. Melbourne, Outback Press, 1976.

Memoirs of a Carlton Bohemian, published in *Meanjin* (Melbourne), no. 3, 1977.

Sin (opera libretto), music by Martin Friedel (produced Melbourne, 1978). With *The Overcoat*, Sydney, Currency Press, 1981.

A Man of Many Parts (produced Perth, 1980).

Mothballs (produced Melbourne, 1981). Published in *Meanjin* (Melbourne), no. 4, 1980.

Liquid Amber (produced Wodonga, Victoria, 1982). Included in *A Country Quinella*, 1984.

Lavender Bags, published in *Aspect*, no. 25, 1982.

Glycerine Tears (produced Melbourne, 1983; London, 1985). Published in *Meanjin* (Melbourne), no. 4, 1982; with *The Old School Tie*, as *Duets*, 1989.

Squibs: A Collection of Short Plays (includes selections from *Brain Rot* and *Asian Oranges*, *A League of Nations*, *The Three Sisters*, *Death of a Traveller*). Brisbane, Phoenix, 1984.

A Country Quinella: Two Celebration Plays (includes *Dimboola* and *Liquid Amber*). Melbourne, Penguin, 1984; as *Dimboola and Liquid Amber*, Melbourne, Penguin, 1994.

Death Warmed Up, published in *Scripsi* (Melbourne), vol. 2, no. 4, 1984.

Odyssey of a Prostitute, published in *Outrider* (Indooroopilly, Queensland), 1985.

Duets (includes *The Old School Tie*, *Glycerine Tears*) (produced Melbourne, 1989). Montmorency, Victoria, Yackandandah, 1989.

Slam Dunk. Sydney, Currency Press, 1996.

Novels

Memoirs of an Old Bastard. Melbourne, McPhee Gribble, 1989.

The Life of Riley. Melbourne, Mandarin, 1991.

Perdita. Ringwood, Victoria, McPhee Gribble, 1992.

Other

The Barracker's Bible: A Dictionary of Sporting Slang, with Garrie Hutchinson. Melbourne, McPhee Gribble, 1983.

Translator, *Le vin des amants: Poems from Baudelaire*. Toorak, Victoria, Gryphon, 1977.

*

Manuscript Collections: Australian National Library, Canberra; Melbourne University Archives; La Trobe University Library, Bundoora, Victoria; Eunice Hanger Collection, University of Queensland, St. Lucia.

Critical Studies: "Snakes and Ladders" by Margaret Williams, in *Meanjin* (Melbourne), no. 2, 1972; "Assaying the New Drama" by A. A. Phillips, in *Meanjin* (Melbourne), no. 2, 1973; *After "The Doll"* by Peter Fitzpatrick, Melbourne, Arnold, 1979; interviews in *Contemporary Australian Playwrights* edited by Jennifer Palmer, Adelaide, University Union Press, 1979, *Sideways from the Page* by Jim Davidson, Sydney, Fontana, 1983, and with Elizabeth Perkins in *Linq* (Townsville, Queensland), vol. 11, no. 1, 1983; articles by Peter Pierce, Charles Kemp, and Paul McGillick, in *Contemporary Australian Drama* edited by Peter Holloway, Sydney, Currency Press, 1981; *Hibberd* by John Hainsworth, Melbourne, Methuen Australia, 1987; *Jack Hibberd* by Paul McGillick, Amsterdam, Rodopi, 1988; "Jack Hibberd and Australian Popular Theatre" by John Tittensor, in *Commonwealth Essays and Studies* (Dijon, France), Autumn 1989, pp. 81-86; "The Ocker in Australian Drama" by Lisa Jacobson, in *Meanjin Parkville* (Victoria), Autumn 1990, pp. 137-47; "A Conversation with Jack Hibberd" by Julianne Lochner, in *Antipodes: A North American Journal of Australian Literature* (Brooklyn, New York), December 1995, pp. 131-34.

Theatrical Activities:
Director: **Plays**—Several of his own plays, and *Bedfellows* by Barry Oakley, Carlton, Victoria, 1975.

Jack Hibberd comments:

(1977) I have striven over the last ten years to write specifically of an Australian experience on matters of social aberration and folly, history, politics, popular myth, and individual torment. As a playwright, I believe implacably in the necessity for practical involvement in theatre. Though my plays do not evolve out of laboratory and workshop situations, I believe theatre is the best context in which to attempt dramaturgical diversity and innovation.

(1988) Over the last ten years I have been less concerned to write specifically of Australian experience but more sweepingly of human conduct in a context of comico-tragic formal experiment, especially in my monodramas and other theatrical sorties into the actor-audience farce.

* * *

Jack Hibberd's work consistently explores the formal possibilities of the theater. This alone would make him unique among Australian playwrights. But the fact that his formal explorations reflect a clearly articulated philosophy of the nature and function of the theater, together with his fascination with language, makes his position in the Australian theater all the more distinctive. Hibberd's plays successfully marry form and content within the context of two key ideas: the theater as a place for communal celebration and the theater as a metaphor for life. He aims to speak directly in a distinctively theatrical language that requires no translation. A Hibberd play is always primarily a theatrical experience, and the audience is never allowed to forget that it is in a theater and participating in a social event.

The other distinguishing feature of his work has been its recursive nature. The themes and formal concerns of his earliest plays weave their way through his whole output to re-emerge, with greater sophistication, in his later work.

Hibberd's first period (1967 to 1976) was where he quickly found his own voice and made preliminary experiments with the theatrical issues that have come to dominate his writing. Early short plays like *Who?* worked through the influences of Pinter and Beckett, applying their typical situations and linguistic conceits to an Australian setting, using Australian English. The menace of the early Pinter plays surfaced in Hibberd in the form of a simmering violence that he implies is endemic to mateship—violence towards anyone who opts out of the tribe, towards women, towards any of the refinements that contradict the exaltation of crudity characteristic of "ocker" mateship. These same themes inform Hibberd's first full-length play, *White with Wire Wheels*. It is also his first explicitly anti-naturalistic play, using nightmare sequences and one actress to play three female roles (later, in *Peggy Sue*, he has one man play all three male roles).

The most important play from this first period is *A Stretch of the Imagination*. It is a monodrama (where one character re-enacts his own life, unlike a monologue where the character merely relates his life to the audience)—a form Hibberd has repeatedly returned to and refined. In this play Monk O'Neill is an embittered recluse living in a hut in the Australian outback. With Monk Hibberd goes beyond merely satirizing the "ocker" to an exploration of the existential alienation that produces sociopaths like ockers, soccer hooligans, and Hitlers. Through the particularity of this very Australian character who relives, presumably often fictionalizing, the events that have led to his miserable condition (although Monk insists he is happy in his rejection of people), Hibberd achieves a universality that has resulted in the play being performed around the world in different languages despite its apparent cultural specificity.

Hibberd's other major success from this period is *Dimboola*, which has also been performed around the world and is the most-performed Australian play ever. Its origins were twofold—Hibberd's interest in exploring the viability of audience participation and his attempt to create a truly "popular" theater that would embody his notion of theater as social celebration. In *Dimboola* the audience members are guests at a country wedding reception, and the play is a comic exploration of the rituals of the wedding, such as the testing of strength of "the two recently conjugated tribes," as Hibberd describes it—in this case, one Catholic, the other Protestant. The play allows for improvisation and the active participation of the audience on the dance floor. *Dimboola* probably signals Hibberd's discovery of himself as a comic writer. Like Gogol (a writer he admires), Hibberd combines an existential vision with comic inspiration, his characters coping with an absurd and hostile world through laughter.

Hibberd produced two more "popular" plays, each of which used famous and archetypal Australians to explore the myths by which Australians tried to explain themselves. He then abandoned the genre, complaining that it had been hijacked by others.

With his free adaptation of Gogol's *The Overcoat* in 1976—described as "a theatrical double somersault and half-pike from the springboard of Gogol's insane prose"—Hibberd moved into a new phase. His formal explorations took on a musical quality. The formal properties of character and language became as important as their representational function. He now heightened the Australian-ness of his characters and their language as a kind of de-familiarizing device to draw attention to his vision of an absurd and contradictory world.

Music is always important in Hibberd's work, often acting as a Brechtian commentary on the action. It plays a more explicit role in *A Toast to Melba* (about the Australian opera singer Nellie Melba) and in *Sin*, his parodistic opera based on the seven deadly sins (inspired by Kurt Weil's oratorio) with music by Martin Friedl, a spoof that plays with ideas about the artist's role in society.

In his seven monodramas Hibberd develops the idea of the theater as a metaphor, although the finest expression of that idea, *Odyssey of a Prostitute*, is not a monodrama. Based on a Maupassant story about an abandoned country girl forced into prostitution, the play is essentially a farce with a dark underbelly, celebrating the theater as entertainment but using it also as a metaphor for a menacingly unpredictable universe. Set in a square in Paris, which the characters use as a performance area to act out their intertwined stories, the play simultaneously draws attention to its own theatricality and satirizes it, using a variety of Shakespearean conceits and songs to comment on the action.

Hibberd stopped writing plays in 1984, enraged that his plays had suddenly become unfashionable and with the fact that, when they were performed, they were performed badly. During the next ten years he returned to practicing medicine and produced a book on allergies, three novels, and a volume of poetry.

He returned to playwriting in 1994 and produced a series of plays that reexplored earlier themes, such as threats to individual and cultural identity and what he terms the psychopathology of everyday life. This work aspires quite explicitly to the condition of music, with formal elements like rhythms, tempi, phrasings, and counterpoint integral to the thematic concerns. He has also reconceived the monodramas and the two- and three-character plays into a grand musical scheme he calls *Musical Parts*. The plays are now termed male/female sonatinas and sonatas, duets, and trios. He plans to write five quartets, six quintets, a sextet, a septet, an octet, and a nonet, culminating in a symphony featuring all the characters and many lines from the previous plays and resulting in "an orchestrated performance of a very structured swansong play, dawn to dusk, birth to death." Hibberd sees this as an allegorical journey, moving from single voices to a cacophony, a Babel signifying an insane and overpopulated world.

—Paul McGillick

HIGGINS, Dick

Nationality: American. **Born:** Cambridge, England, 15 March 1938. **Education:** St. Paul's School, Concord, New Hampshire, 1950-55; Yale University, New Haven, Connecticut, 1955-57; Columbia University, 1958-60, B.S. 1960; New York University, 1975-79, M.A. 1977. **Family:** Married Alison Knowles in 1960, two daughters. **Career:** Camera man, Zaccar Offset, New York, 1963; customer service representative, Book Press, 1963-65; production director, Russell and Russell, New York, 1964-65; president, Something Else Press, New York, 1964-73; president, Unpublished Editions, Barton, Vermont, 1971-78; president, Printed Editions, Barrytown, New York, 1981-86. Free-lance designer and consultant, Barrytown, New York, 1971—. **Awards:** New York State Council on the Arts, 1968; Dwutcher Akademischer Austauschdienst–Künstlerprogramm Berlin: residency in Berlin, 1975, 1981-82; Purchase College Foundation: grants for pattern poetry projects, 1984-86, 1988; Collaborations Grant from the Visual Arts Program, New York State Council on the Arts, 1989; Banff Centre residency grant, 1990; Pollock-Krasner grant to paint, 1993. **Address:** P.O. Box 27, Barrytown, New York 12507, U.S.A.

Publications

Plays

27 Episodes for the Aquarian Theatre (also director: produced New York, 1959).

What Are Legends. New York, Bern Porter Books, 1960.
Stacked Deck, music by Richard Maxfield (produced New York, 1960; revised production with new score by Pauline Oliveros, Los Angeles, 1982).
Cabarets, Contributions, Einschluß (produced New York, 1960).
St. Joan at Beaurevoir (produced New York, 1961).
Graphis 82 (also director: produced New York, 1961).
The Peaceable Kingdom and *The Stacked Deck* (produced New York, 1961).
Inroads Rebuff'd or The Disdainful Evacuation (also director: produced New York, 1962).
Colloquial and Sentimental Edifices (produced Köln, 1962).
Jefferson's Birthday/Postface. New York, Something Else Press, 1964; /new York, Smith, 1984.
The Tart, Solo for Florence and *Celestials* (produced Queens, New York, 1965).
Vanity Fair (also director: produced South Hadley, Massachusetts, 1967).
foew&ombwhnw. New York, Something Else Press, 1969.
Incomprehensible Act (also director; produced Newhall, California, 1970).
Parade (also director: produced Claremont, California, 1971).
amigo. Barton, Vermont, Unpublished Editions, 1972.
The Ladder to the Moon. Barton, Vermont, Unpublished Editions, 1973.
Le petit Cirque au Fin du Monde, un Opera Arabasque. Liège, Belgium, Aarevue/Aafondation, 1973.
Spring Game (puppet opera) (produced Montreal, 1974). Barton, Vermont, Unpublished Editions, 1973.
City with All the Angles. Barton, Vermont, Unpublished Editions, 1974.
Act (produced New York, 1974, 1978; Iowa City, 1980; San Francisco, 1994).
Gilles (produced New York, 1976).
Classic Plays. West Glover, Vermont, Unpublished Editions, 1976.
Legends and Fishnets. West Glover, Vermont, Unpublished Editions, 1976.
Cat Alley. Willis, California, Tuumba Press, 1976.
The Epitaphs/Gli Epitath. Napoli, Studio Morra, 1977.
The Importance of Caravaggio, composed with Alison Knowles (produced Montreal, 1977; Pavia, Italy, 1978; Lexington, New York, 1989).
Clown's Way (produced Genève, 1977).
The Epickall Quest of the Brothers Dichtung and Other Outrages. West Glover, Vermont, Unpublished Editions, 1977.
Graphis 64 (produced New York, 1978; Taos, New Mexico and Los Angeles, 1981-82).
An Evening with Dick Higgins and Alison Knowles (also director with Alison Knowles and Michel Oren, Amherst, Massachusetts, 1979).
Some Recent Snowflakes (and Other Things). New York, Printed Editions, 1979.
Of Celebration of Morning. New York, Printed Editions, 1980.
Art Performances by Dick Higgins (also director, Hanover, New Hampshire, 1980).
26 Mountains for Viewing the Sunset From. Barrytown, New York, Printed Editions, 1981.
Selected Early Works. Berlin, Galerie Ars Viva, 1982.
Ten Ways of Looking at a Bird (produced Berlin, 1983). Barrytown, New York, Printed Editions, 1981.
1959/60 (produced New York, 1985). Verona, Edition Francesco Conz, 1982.
Metadramas (produced København, Denmark, 1986).
The Journey (produced Poughkeepsie, New York, 1988). Barrytown, New York, Left Hand Books, 1991.
Two Double Helixes that Aren't for Sale (produced New York, 1990).
Ebb Tide (produced Poughkeepsie, New York, 1991).
The Autobiography of the Moon, translated by George Brecht, Menotr, Ohio, Generator, 1992.
Octette. Providence, Rhode Island, Woodbine Press, 1994.
Buster Keaton Enters into Paradise. Barrytown, New York, Left Hand Books, 1994.
American Asbestos (produced Chicago, 1995).
Life Flowers, or Shadow of the Wind. Providence, Rhode Island, Woodbine Press, 1997.

Performance Scores: *Piano Album: Short Piece, 1962-1984,* 1980; *Sonata for Prepared Piano,* 1981; *Variations on a Natural Theme for Orchestra,* 1981; *Sonata No. 2 for Piano,* 1983; *Song for Any Voice(s) and Instrument(s),* 1983.

Screenplays: *A Tiny Movie,* 1959; *the Flight of the Florence Bird,* 1960; *The Flaming City,* 1961-62; *Invocation of Canyons and Boulders,* 1962; *Plunk,* 1964; *For the Dead,* 1965; *Scenario,* 1968; *Hank and Mary Without Apologies,* 1969; *Mysteries,* 1969; *Men & Women & Bells,* 1970.

Radio Plays: *Die Fabelhafte Geträume von Taifun-Willi,* 1970; *City With All Angles,* 1973; *Scenes Forgotten and Otherwise Remembered,* 1985; *Was er 1st: eine Girlande für John,* 1987; *Five Professional Whom You Can Trust,* 1989; *Three Double Helixes that Aren't for Sale,* 1990.

Television Plays: *Gentle Talk,* 1977; *The Something Else Press and Since,* 1981; *Fluxes at Williams,* 1987.

Poetry

Modular Poems. Barton, Vermont, Unpublished Editions, 1975.
George Herbert's Pattern Poems: in their Tradition. West Glover, Vermont, Unpublished Editions, 1977.
Poems, Plain & Fancy. Barrytown, New York, Station Hill Press, 1986.

Other

Die fabelhafte Geträume von Taifun-Willi. Stuttgart, Reflexion Press, 1969.
Computers for the Arts. Somerville, Massachusetts, Abyss Editions, 1970.
A Book About Love & War & Death. Barton, Vermont, Something Else Press, 1972.
For Eugene in Germany. Barton, Vermont, Something Else Press, 1973.
A Dialect of Centuries: Notes Towards a Theory of the New Arts. New York, Printed Editions, 1978.
Horizons: the Poetics and Theory of the Intermedia. Carbondale, Illinois, Southern Illinois University Press, 1983.
Intermedia. Warszawa, Poland, Akademia Ruchu, 1985.
Pattern Poetry: Guide to an Unknown Literature. Albany, New York, State University of New York Press, 1987.

Happytime the Medicine Man (for children). Genève, 1992.
Modernism Since Postmodernism. San Diego, San Diego State University Press, 1997.

Editor, *Pop Architektur.* Düsseldorf, Droste Verlag, 1969; US edition *Fantastic Architecture,* Millerton and New York, Something Else Press, 1971.
Editor, *On the Composition of Images, Signs and Ideas,* by Giordano Bruno, translated by Charles Doria. New York, Willis, Locker, and Owen, 1991.

*

Manuscript Collections: Sohm Archiv, Stuttgart (to 1970); Getty Art Institute (1970-1993).

Critical Study: "Dick Higgins on His Work" by Dick Higgins, in *American Writing Today,* edited by Richard Kostelanetz, Troy, New York, Whitston, 1991.

Theatrical Activities:
Director: **Plays**–Many of his own plays.

* * *

One of the founders of the 1960s-era fluxus movement, Dick Higgins used his varied talents in music and visual expression to challenge conventional theater during an era of intense experimentation. A musical composer, painter, translator, art theorist, and publisher, Higgins drew on his disparate interests in helping to create the fluxus movement's unstructured theater "happenings" in the early 1960s.

Fluxus began in 1962 as a way in which artists could take words, sounds, images, and so on out of their normal contexts and arrange them in startling new ways. The happenings of Higgins and other fluxus artists (among them Claes Oldenburg, John Cage, Yoko Ono, and Allen Kaprow, who coined the term *happenings* in 1959) deliberately challenged rationality and convention and blurred distinctions between genres and between actor and observer.

Happenings often used new technologies—slide projections or audio recordings—as integral parts of the performance and incorporated music, dance, and images into the work.

Happenings were not fully scripted plays; they were staged events with little formal structure.

They brought together in open areas (parking lots, street corners, galleries, studio lofts, or stages) groups of participants and spectators who reacted together to various stimuli organized by the happening creator. Though happenings, like improvisations, were meant to be one-time performances, they were more controlled than true improvisations.

Although most happenings were not meant to be repeated, Higgins's *Cowboy Plays* has been performed several times since it originated in 1967. It was updated in 1994 and staged by Joe De Marco's Fluxus Theater Group at the Marilyn Monroe Memorial Theater in San Francisco with Higgins himself in the audience. The revised piece incorporated music, narration, and slide projections in what Fluxus described as a "vaudeville style game of '52 Pick-Up.'" Nine performers move into and out of 52 different onstage mini-dramas in this piece, giving it a quality both slapstick and surreal.

In a more recent work, *Buster Keaton Enters Into Paradise,* Higgins played 11 scoreless games of Scrabble with Alison Knowles and Bryan McHugh to generate lists of words that became the play's 11 scenes. "Buster Keaton" was spelled out in the center of the board at the beginning of each game, becoming what one reviewer called a "free radical, to be portrayed on stage by a dancer." Clips from Buster Keaton films were projected during each scene, and Higgins also used a chorus to comment on the dancer's and the performer's actions.

Though happenings began as rather elitist events that attracted the artistic avant garde, they soon became associated in American popular culture with the 1960s-era mass gatherings known as be-ins or love-ins. Among artists, however, happenings and other fluxus events provided inspiration for a wide range of new work in performance art. Although few works after the mid-1960s involved the interaction of participants and spectators as true happenings did, theater through the next few decades showed the influence of happenings. In the 1970s, such artists as Carolee Schneeman, Joseph Beuys, and Chris Burden created performance pieces influenced by fluxus principles, and performance art has continued to be a cutting-edge expressive form.

In music and dance, artists such as Merce Cunninghan, John Cage, and Meredith Monk created new works that showed the fluxus influence in their use of new technologies and in their combining of music, images, and gesture. Although some critics considered happenings artificial or even banal, the movement was important in that it expanded and reshaped the boundaries between the visual arts and performance.

—Elizabeth Shostak

HIGHWAY, Tomson

Nationality: Canadian. **Born:** Northern Manitoba, 6 December 1951. **Education:** Boarding school, The Pas, Manitoba; University of Western Ontario, London, graduated 1975. **Career:** Concert pianist; worked with Native organizations and cultural programs around Canada; founder and artistic director, Native Earth Performing Arts, 1983-93. **Awards:** Dora Mavor Moore award, 1987; Floyd S. Chalmers Canadian Play award, for Outstanding New Play, 1989; Governor General's Literary award for Drama, 1989; Wang Festival award, 1989. **Agent:** Suzanne DePoe, Creative Technique Inc., P.O. Box 311, Station F, Toronto, Ontario M4Y 2L7, Canada.

Publications

Plays

A Ridiculous Spectacle in One Act (produced West Bay, Ontario, 1985).
The Rez Sisters (produced Toronto, 1986). Saskatoon, Fifth House Publishers, 1988.
Aria (produced Toronto, 1987).
New Song...New Dance (produced 1988).
The Sage, the Dancer, and the Fool (produced Toronto, 1989).
Annie and the Old One (produced Montreal, 1989).

Dry Lips Oughta Move to Kapuskasing (produced Toronto, 1989). Saskatoon, Fifth House Publishers, 1989.
Kiss of the Fur Queen. Toronto, Doubleday, 1998.

*

Critical Studies: "Native Playwright: Tomson Highway" by Gitta Honegger, in *Theater* (New Haven, Connecticut), Winter 1992, pp. 88-92; "Absortption, Elimination, and the Hybrid: Some Impure Questions of Gender and Culture in the Trickster Drama of Tomson Highway" by Sheila Rabillard, in *Essays in Theatre* (Guelph, Ontario), November 1993, pp. 3-27; "Twenty-One Native Women on Motorcycles: An Interview with Tomson Highway" by Joanne Tompkins and Lisa Male, in *Australasian Drama Studies* (Queensland), April 1994, pp. 13-28; "On the Road with Tomson Highway's Blues Harmonica in Dry Lips Oughta Move to Kapuskasing" by Roberta Imboden, in *Canadian Literature* (Vancouver), Spring 1995, pp. 113-24.

* * *

Tomson Highway's biography is extraordinary. He is a Cree-speaking native from remote northern Manitoba whose first career was as a concert pianist. He is the first major native playwright in Canada and is also important as the founder of the Native Earth Performing Arts company in 1983, where he served as artistic director for 10 years. This has directly and indirectly encouraged other First Nations dramatists, among them Daniel David Moses, Drew Hayden Taylor, Marie Clements, Margo Kane, and Monique Mojica.

In *The Rez Sisters,* an accomplished and successful first play, Highway shows seven women from the "rez" (reservation) on Manitoulin Island in Ontario. The women are, in fact, sisters, sisters-in-law, and a daughter by adoption. Their names are variously English, French, Indian, Indian in translation, and nonsense words. They include a bisexual biker; a would-be country-and-western singer; Marie-Adele, who is dying of cancer; and the retarded Zhaboonigan, who was once viciously raped. The women decide to make the long journey to the world's largest bingo game, in Toronto, and they succeed in raising money for the trip. Their night journey is mysterious, even magical, with an audacious scene of changing a tire in complete darkness. The game and the return are almost anticlimactic.

This is far from a documentary of reservation life, and Highway adds Nanabush, the trickster, who is without gender, often silently present, and so more conspicuous on the stage than in the text. Highway explains that "the trickster is the central figure in the dream world, the articulation of the dream life of a culture. In the same way that Christianity has Christ as the central figure, the mediator between man and God, we have the trickster—except that ours has a sense of humor." Nanabush's presence asserts that First Nations peoples have beliefs and traditions worth maintaining or reestablishing. Highway records, "I'm writing about a socio-economic condition we find ourselves in as Indian people. . . . Life on a reserve is mundane and boring." He chose to write of women because "women have such an ability to express themselves emotionally. Men are all clogged up. And as a writer, you want to express emotion." Further, "the very center of our belief is the earth as the ultimate source of creation and procreation. Earth is a very feminine energy." He claims also that the sonata form shapes his play: "Characters in their various keys, one staccato in rhythm, one lyrical in rhythm. Then you go on to development."

Dry Lips Oughta Move to Kapuskasing is even more ambitious and more problematic. Complementary to *The Rez Sisters,* there are seven men and a female Nanabush. The title refers to the women of the reserve who form an ice hockey team and to the males' reactions. Along the way Highway shows rival business schemes, sexual comedy, revelations about men, an account of a horrific birth of a baby with fetal alcohol syndrome, and an even more horrific rape with a crucifix. Because the script focuses on the rapist rather than the victim, Highway has been accused of misogyny. Stylistically, the play moves from sitcom to tragedy to comic resolution. Highway looks variously at alcoholism, religion, and parental responsibility. Indeed, as Jerry Wasserman has observed, Highway is "examining the possibility of spiritual renewal for contemporary Native culture."

Highway's *The Sage, the Dancer and the Fool* portrays a day in the life of a native in Toronto. The character is divided into three: the mind (the sage), the dream (the dancer), and the desires (the fool). The work uses English and Cree, with music composed and performed by Highway and with choreography by his brother, Rene.

—Malcolm Page

HILL, Errol (Gaston)

Nationality: American. **Born:** Trinidad, 5 August 1921; naturalized U.S. citizen. **Education:** Royal Academy of Dramatic Art (British Council scholar), London, diploma 1951; University of London, diploma in dramatic art 1951; Yale University, New Haven, Connecticut, B.A., M.F.A. 1962, D.F.A. 1966. **Family:** Married Grace L. E. Hope in 1956; four children. **Career:** Drama tutor, University of the West Indies, Kingston, Jamaica, 1952-58; creative arts tutor, University of the West Indies, Trinidad, 1958-65; teaching fellow in drama, University of Ibadan, Nigeria, 1965-67; associate professor of drama, Richmond College, City University, New York, 1967-68. Associate professor of drama, 1968-69, professor of drama, 1969-76, Willard professor of drama and oratory, 1976-89, and emeritus professor, 1989—, drama department, Dartmouth College, Hanover, New Hampshire. Chancellor's distinguished professor, University of California, Berkeley, 1983. Visiting Mellon professor, Tulane University, New Orleans, 1994. Founder, Whitehall Players, Trinidad; editor, Caribbean Plays series, University of the West Indies, 1954-65. Editor, *ATA Bulletin of Black Theatre*, Washington, D.C., 1971-76. **Awards:** Rockefeller fellowship, 1958, 1959, and teaching fellowship, 1965-67; Theatre Guild of America fellowship, 1961; Bertram Joseph award for Shakespeare Studies, 1985; Barnard Hewitt award, for theatre history, 1985; Guggenheim fellowship, 1985; Fulbright fellowship, 1988; Honoree, American Society for Theatre Research, 1989; Presidential Medal for Outstanding Leadership and Achievement, Dartmouth College, 1991; Robert Lewis Medal for lifetime achievement in Theatre Research, Kent State University Libraries, Ohio, 1996. **Address:** 3 Haskins Road, Hanover, New Hampshire 03755, U.S.A.

Publications

Plays

Oily Portraits (as *Brittle and the City Fathers*, produced Trinidad, 1948). Port-of-Spain, Trinidad, University of the West Indies, 1966.
Square Peg (produced Trinidad, 1949). Port-of-Spain, Trinidad, University of the West Indies, 1966.
The Ping Pong: A Backyard Comedy-Drama (broadcast 1950; produced Trinidad, 1953). Port-of-Spain, Trinidad, University of the West Indies, 1955.
Dilemma (produced Jamaica, 1953). Port-of-Spain, Trinidad, University of the West Indies, 1966.
Broken Melody (produced Jamaica, 1954). Port-of-Spain, Trinidad, University of the West Indies, 1966.
Wey-Wey (produced Trinidad, 1957). Port-of-Spain, Trinidad, University of the West Indies, 1958.
Strictly Matrimony (produced New Haven, Connecticut, 1959; London, 1977). Port-of-Spain, Trinidad, University of the West Indies, 1966; in *Black Drama Anthology*, edited by Woodie King and Ron Milner, New York, New American Library, 1971.
Man Better Man (produced New Haven, Connecticut, 1960; London, 1965; New York, 1969). Published in *The Yale School of Drama Presents*, edited by John Gassner, New York, Dutton, 1964; in *Plays for Today*, edited by Hill, London, Longman, 1986.
Dimanche Gras Carnival Show (produced Trinidad, 1963).
Whistling Charlie and the Monster (carnival show; produced Trinidad, 1964).
Dance Bongo (produced New York, 1965). Port-of-Spain, Trinidad, University of the West Indies, 1966; in *Caribbean Literature: An Anthology*, edited by G. R. Coulthard, London, University of London Press, 1966.

Radio Play: *The Ping Pong*, 1950.

Other

The Trinidad Carnival: Mandate for a National Theatre. Austin, University of Texas Press, 1972.
Why Pretend? A Conversation about the Performing Arts, with Peter Greer. San Francisco, Chandler and Sharp, 1973.
Shakespeare in Sable: A History of Black Shakespearean Actors. Amherst, University of Massachusetts Press, 1984.
The Jamaican Stage 1655-1900. Amherst, University of Massachusetts Press, 1992.
The Cambridge Guide to African and Caribbean Theatre, with Martin Banham and George Wordyard, Cambridge, Cambridge University Press, 1994.

Editor and Contributor, *The Artist in West Indian Society: A Symposium*. Port-of-Spain, Trinidad, University of the West Indies, 1964.
Editor, *A Time and a Season: 8 Caribbean Plays*. Port-of-Spain, Trinidad, University of the West Indies, 1976.
Editor, *Three Caribbean Plays for Secondary Schools*. Port-of-Spain, Trinidad, Longman, 1979.
Editor, *The Theater of Black Americans: A Collection of Critical Essays*. Englewood Cliffs, New Jersey, Prentice Hall, 2 vol., 1980.
Editor, *Plays for Today*. London, Longman, 1986.
Editor, *Black Heroes: Seven Plays*. New York, Applause, 1989.

*

Bibliography: *Black Theatre and Performances: A Pan-African Bibliography* by John Gray, New York, Greenwood Press, 1990.

Manuscript Collection: Baker Library, Dartmouth College, Hanover, New Hampshire.

Theatrical Activities:
Director: **Plays**—More than 120 plays and pageants in the West Indies, England, the United States, and Nigeria.

Actor: **Plays**—More than 40 roles in amateur and professional productions in the West Indies, England, the United States, and Nigeria.

Errol Hill comments:

I was trained first as an actor and play director. I began writing plays when it became clear to me, as founder of a Trinidad theatre company (the Whitehall Players, later merged with the New Company to become the Company of Players), that an indigenous West Indian theatre could not exist without a repertoire of West Indian plays. The thrust of my work as playwright has been to treat aspects of Caribbean folk life, drawing on speech idioms and rhythms, music and dance, and to evolve a form of drama and theatre most nearly representative of Caribbean life and art. As drama tutor for the University of the West Indies I carried this message to every part of the Caribbean and have written plays by way of demonstrating what could be done to provide a drama repertoire for Caribbean theatre companies.

* * *

Errol Hill demonstrates a remarkable talent in two separate but closely associated artistic fields, namely, playwriting and literary criticism. Long a member of the faculty of the department of drama at Dartmouth College, he is the author of one-act plays and full-length dramas, has edited the Caribbean Plays series, and is the author of many articles and reports. *The Trinidad Carnival: Mandate for a National Theatre* is a definitive contribution to the study of a rich folklore.

Man Better Man, Hill's most outstanding theatrical success, tells of a young suitor for the hand of Petite Belle Lily. The suitor's method is to challenge the village stick-fighting champion to a decisive duel. The young lover resorts to the supernatural means of his vibrant culture. He goes to the village obeahman, Diable Papa, and is subsequently cheated by the quack magician. He receives a herb, Man Better Man, known as a cure guaranteeing invincibility. With characteristic humility, Hill once wrote to me the following explanation:

> It [*Man Better Man*] was for me little more than an experiment in integrating music, song, and dance into dramatic action, and using the calypso form with its rhymed couplets to carry the rhythm and make the transitions occur more smoothly. . . . I never had an orchestral score of the music for the play. Since most of it is traditional-based, with a few numbers "composed by

me," . . . I simply provided a melodic line and left it to each production to create their own orchestration. Much of the music should appear to be improvised anyway with, ideally, the musicians carrying their instruments as part of the chorus on stage.

Hill's play celebrates, in a ritualized form, the triumphal pleasure of comedy. When the play received its New York production in 1969, Richard F. Shepard said in the *New York Times:* "Mr. Hill has encapsuled an authentic folk tale flavor, letting us know something about a people, his people, whose history antedates steel drum bands. It is quaint, yet not condescending; ingenuous, yet not silly." On the surface the musical play gleams with a tropical panache; beneath are the threatened subtleties and hidden meanings. Thus, that magic, that mystery the festive Greeks knew very well, is engaged—or released—by Hill on a richly set Caribbean stage. The connection between the author's skill in portraying effects obtained by the juxtaposition of the real with the assumed, which is one of the several functions of comedy, and his symbolic comic vision is the dynamic element of the work.

C. L. R. James was deeply moved when Hill produced and directed a lengthy skit in Trinidad of dramatic, musical, festive, and political impact. He observed that the audience enjoyed it while "the authorities" did not approve. Hill's venture to me is completely West Indian and completely Greek. Sir William Ridgeway, in *The Origin of Tragedy* (1910) and *The Dramas and Dramatic Dances of Non-European Races* (1915), could have been speaking of West Indian drama as well as Greek tragedy when he stated that the heavy emphasis on ghosts, burial rites, and ancestor worship could not be derived from such a deity as Dionysus alone. The art must be related to hero and ancestor worship and to the cult of the dead. In *Man Better Man,* for example, Hannibal is a calypsonian who enjoys a position roughly analogous to the Anglo-Saxon court scop. He immortalizes the island's heroes in song, and his repertoire constitutes a veritable oral chronicle. Pogo's Homeric cataloguing of famous stick fighters displays the continuity of the heroic tradition. Villagers manifest an awareness that they see tradition in the making, "Excitement for so/More trouble and woe/A day to recall/When you grow old."

Medieval courtly conventions are carried off to the Caribbean setting in the most graceful and lyrical moods. Courtly love comes forward, and all of the action stems from Tim Briscoe's desire to win a woman's affection through a demonstration of physical prowess. He expresses his longing for Petite Belle Lily in courtly love terms. Tim displays the familiar symptoms of heroes, the conventional lover's malady, when he says, "I cannot eat by day, come the night/Cannot sleep, what a plight." Petite Belle Lily shows her indifference—perhaps medieval, perhaps Petrarchan—to her lover's sorry state, which is fitting and proper to her courtly, heroine-like state. The stick fight itself—traditionally accompanied by a *calinda*—between Tim and Tiny Sata is reminiscent of a medieval tournament, whose proceedings were governed by ritualized and rigid customs. Aspects of trial by combat are ever present, along with a strong emphasis on personal honor and its defense. Indeed, stick fighting is envisioned among the island dwellers as a folk institution. The fighter is a true folk hero, like Beowulf or Achilles, who embodies not only the primitive drive of the islanders but also the qualities they esteem most highly—physical courage, prowess in battle, and personal honor. The reigning champion becomes a personification of the communal ideal.

The tension between Diable Papa—a fake and a counterfeit who, by means of voodoo, makes money from the primitive fears of the people—and Portagee Joe supplies the intellectual focus of the drama. The obeahman—the holder of all of the local rituals, spells, and incantations—represents the power of illusion and mass deception. Portagee Joe, who successfully challenges Diable Papa's authority, is the typical village atheist whose cynicism or rationalism keeps him outside the circle of communal belief. "The social significance of the play lies in the relationship between Portagee Joe and his customers: They were not 'niggers' to him and he is not 'white' to them," Mrs. Stanley Jackson wrote in a letter to the *New York Times*. "A man could be judged as a man seventy years ago in Trinidad. . . . The author of *Man Better Man* knew his material extremely well."

Lastly, Diable Papa, who is a fraud, nevertheless reflects picaresque influences. He is reminiscent of the medieval and Tudor horrific-comic depiction of stock diabolic figures. But the obeahman is balanced against the broader irony of the play's resolution. Tim Briscoe qua antihero, although defeated, emerges as a hero in spite of himself. Diable Papa, confounded by supposedly supernatural happenings and spectral visitations, is actually victimized by the very beliefs he has fostered in the villagers.

The drama is a picture of thoughtful delight. The audience, even the reader, becomes an extension of the stage. One cannot help recalling throughout the work Michael Rutenberg's advice to directors, "Break through the proscenium!" The ceremonial interaction of chorus, dancers, actors, and calypsonian sequences—responsive in nature, with countermelodies used by Diable Papa and Minee—and the lively verse—incantatory in quality and reflecting the natural rhythmic delivery of the West Indian speech pattern—all go to picture and reemphasize the profundity of life, dying, and existence when tragic and comic values meet in confrontation.

—Louis D. Mitchell

HIVNOR, Robert (Hanks)

Pseudonyms: Jack Askew; Osbert Pismire. **Nationality:** American. **Born:** Zanesville, Ohio, 19 May 1916. **Education:** University of Akron, Ohio, A.B. 1936; Yale University, New Haven, Connecticut, M.F.A. 1946; Columbia University, New York, 1952-54. **Military Service:** Served in the United States Army, 1942-45. **Family:** Married Mary Otis in 1947; two sons and one daughter. **Career:** Political cartoonist and commercial artist, 1934-38; instructor, University of Minnesota, Minneapolis, 1946-48, and Reed College, Portland, Oregon, 1954-55; assistant professor, Bard College, Annandale-on-Hudson, New York, 1956-59. **Awards:** University of Iowa fellowship, 1951; Rockefeller grant, 1968. **Address:** 420 East 84th Street, New York, New York 10028, U.S.A.

PUBLICATIONS

Plays

Martha Goodwin, adaptation of the story "A Goat for Azazel" by Katherine Anne Porter (produced New Haven, Connecticut, 1942; revised version broadcast, 1959).

Too Many Thumbs (produced Minneapolis, 1948; New York, 1949; London, 1951). Minneapolis, University of Minnesota Press, 1949.
The Ticklish Acrobat (produced New York, 1954). Published in *Playbook: Five Plays for a New Theatre*, New York, New Directions, 1956.
The Assault upon Charles Sumner (produced New York, 1964). Published in *Plays for a New Theatre: Playbook 2*, New York, New Directions, 1966.
Love Reconciled to War (produced Baltimore, 1968). Published in *Break Out! In Search of New Theatrical Environments*, edited by James Schevill, Chicago, Swallow Press, 1973.
"I" "Love" "You" (produced New York, 1968). Published in *Anon* (Austin, Texas), 1971.
DMZ (includes the sketches *Uptight Arms*, *How Much?*, *"I" "Love" "You"*) (as Osbert Pismire and Jack Askew; produced New York, 1969).
A Son Is Always Leaving Home. Published in *Anon* (Austin, Texas), 1971.
Apostle/Genius/God. Published in *Bostonia* (Boston), January/February, 1990.

*

Critical Studies: "The Pleasure and Pains of Playgoing" by Saul Bellow, in *Partisan Review* (New York), May 1954; *The Theatre of the Absurd* by Martin Esslin, New York, Doubleday, 1961, London, Eyre and Spottiswoode, 1962, revised edition, London, Penguin, 1968, Doubleday, 1969; *American Drama since World War II* by Gerald Weales, New York, Harcourt Brace, 1962; *The New American Arts* edited by Richard Kostelanetz, New York, Horizon Press, 1965; by Albert Bermel, in *New Leader* (New York), 1966; by A. W. Staub, in *Southern Review* (Baton Rouge, Louisiana), Summer 1970.

* * *

The economics of the theater are too cruel to art. Because a play costs so much more to produce than, say, a novel, many important texts are rarely if ever presented. Those particularly victimized by such economic discrimination include older playwrights who have neither the time nor the energy necessary to launch noncommercial productions on their own. There is no doubt in my judgment that Robert Hivnor has written two of the best and most original American postwar dramas, but it is lamentable that our knowledge of them as well as his reputation must be based more upon print than performance and that lack of incentive keeps yet other plays half finished. The first, called *Too Many Thumbs*, is more feasible, requiring only inventive costuming and masks to overcome certain difficulties in artifice. It tells of an exceptionally bright chimpanzee possessed of a large body and a small head who in the course of the play moves up the evolutionary ladder to become, first, an intermediate stage between man and beast and, then, a normal man and, ultimately, a godlike creature with an immense head and a shriveled body. The university professors who keep him also attempt to cast him as the avatar of a new religion, but unending evolution defeats their designs. Just as Hivnor's writing is often very funny, so is the play's ironically linear structure also extremely original. (It precedes Ionesco's use of it in *The New Tenant.*) By pursuing the bias implicit in evolutionary development to its inevitable reversal, the play coherently questions mankind's claim to a higher state of existence. Although *The Ticklish Acrobat* is a lesser work, it nonetheless exhibits some true originality and typically Hivnorian intellectual comedy. Here, however, the practical difficulty lies in constructing a set whose period recedes several hundred years in time with each act.

Hivnor is fundamentally a dark satirist who debunks myths and permits no heroes, but, unlike other playwrights without protagonists, he is less interested in absurdity than in comprehensive ridicule. *The Assault upon Charles Sumner* is an immensely sophisticated history play, regrettably requiring more actors and scenes than an unsubsidized theater can afford and an audience more literate than Broadway offers. Its subject is the supreme example of liberal intellectuality in American politics—the nineteenth-century senator from Massachusetts, Charles Sumner, who had been a distinguished proponent of abolition and of the Civil War. Like Sumner's biographer David Donald, Hivnor finds that Sumner, for all his saintliness, was politically ineffectual and personally insufferable. The opening prologue, which contains some of Hivnor's most savage writing, establishes the play's tone and thrust as it deals with the funeral and possible afterlife of the last living Negro slave. "Sir, no American has ever been let into heaven." "Not old Abe Lincoln?" the slave asks. "Mr. Lincoln," Sumner replies, "sits over there revising his speech at the Gettysburg. . . ."

Extending such negative satire, Hivnor feasts upon episodes and symbols of both personal and national failure in the attempt to define a large historical experience in a single evening. While much of the imagery is particularly theatrical, such as repeating the scene in which Preston Brooks assaults Sumner with a cane, perhaps the play's subject and scope are finally closer, both intrinsically and extrinsically, to extended prose fiction.

—Richard Kostelanetz

HOAR, Stuart (Murray)

Nationality: New Zealander. **Born:** New Plymouth, 17 June 1957. **Education:** James Cook High School, Auckland, 1970-74. **Career:** Clerk, Department of Education, Auckland, 1975; film sound recordist, Television New Zealand, Auckland, 1976-81; part-time cleaner, Auckland, 1982-87; literary fellow, Auckland University, 1990. **Awards:** Bruce Mason award, 1988. **Agent:** Playmarket, Box 9767, Wellington, New Zealand.

Publications

Plays

Squatter (produced Auckland, 1987). Wellington, Victoria University Press, 1988.
American Girl (broadcast 1988; produced Dunedin, 1992). Published in *Three Radio Plays*, edited by Michael Peck, Wellington, Victoria University Press, 1989.
Exile (produced Auckland, 1990).
Scott of the Antarctic (broadcast 1988; produced Wellington, 1990).
A Long Walk Off a Tall Rock (produced Wellington, 1991).
Cool Gangs (produced Auckland, 1992).
The Pulp Explosion (produced Christchurch, 1992).
The Boat (produced Auckland, 1992).

Screenplay: *Lovelock*, 1992.

Radio Plays: *The Birdwatchers*, 1983; *Sea Pictures*, 1984; *Emmet City*, 1984; *The Tigers, the Man on the Vine, and the Wild Strawberry*, 1985; *Crystal of Life*, 1985; *The Man Who Would Be Perfect*, 1986; *Contact*, 1986; *The Second Crusade*, 1986; *Horses*, 1986; *American Girl*, 1988; *Rios Negroes*, 1988; *Hank Williams Laid Down in the Back of My Car and Died*, 1988; *Scott of the Antarctic*, 1989; *Terror and Virtue*, 1989; *Past Lives, Present Mind*, 1990; *The Boat*, 1990; *The Chinese Figure*, 1990; *The Voyage*, 1991; *Ohura*, 1991; *Appointment with Samarra*, 1992; *Travels of the Ship's Surgeon Zuynprit in and about Neu Zeelandt*, 1992.

*

Stuart Hoar comments:

I believe in plays which contain outsights rather than insights, which are aligned outwards into society rather than inwards into the individual, which will make an attempt to apprehend the rational and irrational behaviour contained within any situational frame. Such analysis need not be mechanical, indeed its particular strength, in dramatic form, will be the way imagination, emotion, and thought are used to build each unique situation that a play is, or should be. I believe in plays which actually liberate the imagination from its fetters of an anticipated and expected response. Instead of a closed (and ultimately comfortable) system in which a play generates empathetic reaction to the sum of its representations, there are the potential and the precedent for an open theatre of poetry, paradox, and parable in which the sum of the play's disrepresentations add up to a whole greater than its parts.

* * *

After a short stay at a university Stuart Hoar worked as a film sound recordist, which may be where he developed his ear for the rhythms of dialogue. Apart from this there is little that is autobiographical in his work; his settings range all over the known world and across time. He began his playwriting with radio plays at the age of 24, and between 1983 and 1992 Radio New Zealand broadcast 26 of his plays.

His first full-length stage play, *Squatter*, was produced in Auckland in 1987 and the following year in Wellington. Apart from being set in recognizably historic times, Canterbury in the 1890s when the Liberal government was forcibly breaking up the bigger sheep stations, *Squatter* is deliberately nonnaturalistic. Hoar insists that complete identification with his characters is not required from his actors, and he seeks critical detachment rather than suspension of disbelief from his audience. His occasional didacticism almost demands an exchange of ideas.

Squatter investigates generational political struggles between greedy capitalists—the Bilstrode family, who are landowners, or squatters—and rather disorganized revolutionaries consisting of Elisabeth the cook, Tuckler the idealistic socialist, Wade the ineffectual manager, and Snape, a farcical grotesque of a butler. These four plan to oust Bilstrode, his wily son William, and his daughter Florence, but, as well as being unable to organize themselves, they are diverted by the activities of a couple of roving characters—Bracken, a photographer, and Olive, a murderer. Florence is also accompanied by Amy, who is looking for security of her own.

The plot is violent, and even the props include dead sheep and rabbits. There is an early murder of a roustabout by Olive, Elisabeth is bloodily killed offstage, a hasty hanging is rigged on stage for Tuckler (wrongly thought to have killed Elisabeth), and finally a fatal shooting and devastating fire bring all their plans to nothing more than "floating telegrams of ash."

Sons' memories of their fathers is a theme running through the soliloquies in which several characters address the audience. Bilstrode and his son demonstrate their own relationship, and the feeling between Olive and Bracken is very much like that between father and son. These generational exchanges underline the political theme of old systems having to give way to the new.

The final scene emphasizes Hoar's Brechtian allegiance, with the four dead characters carrying placards displaying slogans while the remaining actors scavenge in the ruins and find pieces of human bone. The last sound is of hunting dogs closing in on the murderer, as the placards give their message: This Space For Hire. The image that remains is of the eternal land, scraped and burned to the bone by exploiters of several kinds.

A fascinating play that was welcomed critically but was too demanding to become popular, *Squatter* contains elements of farce, parable, social satire, comedy of manners, and melodrama. Hoar uses modern colloquial language whose incongruity in the mouths of period figures is acceptable since he is more interested in exploring ideas—in this case "how people face moral ideas, whether to make a stand or just talk about it, whether to act on principle or look after oneself. Most do the latter."

Hoar is perhaps not a typical New Zealand playwright, for he does not write about local concerns in contemporary settings. His next work was a version of Alexander Dumas's *The Three Musketeers* that combined the high romance of the original with a fast-moving action-packed plot. Indeed, one critic described it as a seventeenth-century *Star Wars*.

Exile, originally called *Exile in Stonehurst*, emerged in 1990. Set in 1939, it is a satire on literary attitudes and their inability to bring about change in society. Three German exiles arrive in Auckland to escape Hitler and are at first welcomed enthusiastically by the tiny literary community. Consisting of recognizable caricatures, the play is dryly amusing as the local community dances from bed to bed with and around the newcomers. By contrasting the indigenous writers with the exotic arrivals and a staunch, local everyman who is cheerfully going off to war, Hoar shows New Zealand's isolation and narrow-mindedness and the futility of literary pretensions. Lines such as "Brush away the shallow fripperies of mateship and behold the ice-people of the South Pacific" mark *Exile* as a play that has moved on from celebrating the specialness of being a New Zealander to the critical assessment of just what that means.

Branching into opera librettos and turning one of them—*A Long Walk Off a Tall Rock*—into a full-length play have given Hoar experience in dealing with grand emotions. This play tells a story of the fate of pure and unrequited love in a society that is driven purely by profit. The idea came from an actual event in Auckland in 1984 in which a stripper, trapped in a violent marriage, had an affair with a dwarf. The lovers hired a member of the Mongrel Mob to kill the husband. It is on this story that Hoar based his play, written entirely in verse, which became both operatic and surreal in a dynamic student production.

Hoar deliberately prevents the audience from getting excited and involved with characters and therefore suffers the risk of audience indifference. Perhaps *American Girl*, first broadcast in 1988 and staged at Otago University, shows a change to a more sympathetic style, however.

—Patricia Cooke

HOFFMAN, William M.

Nationality: American. **Born:** New York City, 12 April 1939. **Education:** City University, New York, 1955-60, B.A. (cum laude) in Latin 1960 (Phi Beta Kappa). **Career:** Editorial assistant, Barnes and Noble, publishers, New York, 1960-61; assistant editor, 1961-67, and associate editor and drama editor, 1967-68, Hill and Wang, publishers, New York; literary adviser, *Scripts* magazine, New York, 1971-72; visiting lecturer, University of Massachusetts, Boston, Spring, 1973; playwright-in-residence, American Conservatory Theatre, San Francisco, 1978, and La Mama, New York, 1978-79. Star professor, Hofstra University, Hempstead, New York, 1980—. **Awards:** MacDowell Colony fellowship, 1971; Colorado Council on the Arts and Humanities grant, 1972; Carnegie Fund grant, 1972; PEN grant, 1972; Guggenheim fellowship, 1974; National Endowment for the Arts grant, 1975, 1976; Drama Desk award, 1985; Obie award, 1985; New York Foundation for the Arts grant, 1985. **Agent:** International Creative Management, 40 West 57th Street, New York, New York 10019, U.S.A. **Address:** 199 Prince Street, New York, New York 10012, U.S.A.

Publications

Plays

Thank You, Miss Victoria (produced New York, 1965; London, 1970). Published in *New American Plays 3*, edited by Hoffman, New York, Hill and Wang, 1970.
Saturday Night at the Movies (produced New York, 1966). Published in *The Off-Off-Broadway Book*, edited by Albert Poland and Bruce Mailman, Indianapolis, Bobbs Merrill, 1972.
Good Night, I Love You (produced New York, 1966).
Spring Play (produced New York, 1967).
Three Masked Dances (produced New York, 1967).
Incantation (produced New York, 1967).
Uptight! (produced New York, 1968).
XXX (produced New York, 1969; as *Nativity Play*, produced London, 1970). Published in *More Plays from Off-Off-Broadway*, edited by Michael T. Smith, Indianapolis, Bobbs Merrill, 1972.
Luna (also director: produced New York, 1970). As *An Excerpt from Buddha*, published in *Now: Theater der Erfahrung*, edited by Jens Heilmeyer and Pia Frolich, Cologne, Schauberg, 1971.
A Quick Nut Bread to Make Your Mouth Water (also director: produced New York, 1970). Published in *Spontaneous Combustion: Eight New American Plays*, edited by Rochelle Owens, New York, Winter House, 1972.
From Fool to Hanged Man (produced New York, 1972). Published in *Scenarios* (New York), 1982.
The Children's Crusade (produced New York, 1972).
Gilles de Rais (also director: produced New York, 1975).
Cornbury, with Anthony Holland (produced New Haven, Connecticut, 1977). Published in *Gay Plays*, edited by Hoffman, New York, Avon, 1979.
The Last Days of Stephen Foster (televised 1977). Published in *Dramatics* (Cincinnati), 1978.
A Book of Etiquette, music by John Braden (produced New York, 1978; as *Etiquette*, produced New York, 1983).
Gulliver's Travels, music by John Braden, adaptation of the novel by Swift (produced New York, 1978).
Shoe Palace Murray, with Anthony Holland (produced San Francisco, 1978). Published in *Gay Plays*, edited by Hoffman, New York, Avon, 1979.
The Cherry Orchard, Part II, with Anthony Holland (produced New York, 1983).
As Is (produced New York, 1985; London, 1987). New York, Random House, 1985; in *Best American Plays, 1983-1992,* New York, Crown, 1993.
Ghosts of Versailles, (opera libretto, music by John Corigliano; produced New York, 1991).

Television Writing: *Notes from the New World: Louis Moreau Gottschalk*, with Roger Englander, 1976; *The Last Days of Stephen Foster*, 1977; *Whistler: 5 Portraits*, 1978.

Poetry

The Cloisters: A Song Cycle, music by John Corigliano. New York, Schirmer, 1968.
Wedding Song. New York, Schirmer, 1984.

Other

New American Plays 2, 3 and 4. New York, Hill and Wang, 3 vols., 1968-71.

Editor, *Gay Plays: The First Collection*. New York, Avon, 1979.

*

Manuscript Collections: University of Wisconsin, Madison; Lincoln Center Library of the Performing Arts, New York.

Critical Studies: "AIDS Enters the American Theater: *As Is* and *The Normal* Heart" by Joel Shatzky, in *AIDS: The Literary Response,* edited by Ammanuel S. Nelson, New York, Twayne, 1992; The *Ghosts of Versailles: A Character Study of the Opera by John Corigliano and William M. Hoffman* (dissertation) by William Ladd Higgins, University of Oklahoma, 1995; "Toxic Bodies and the Performance of Mourning in American AIDS Drama" by Nancy Plooster, in *JAISA–The Journal of the Association for the Interdisciplinary Study of the Arts* (Carrollton, Georgia), 1996, pp. 103-10.

Theatrical Activities:
Director: **Plays**—*Thank You, Miss Victoria*, New Brunswick, New Jersey, 1970; *Luna*, New York, 1970; *A Quick Nut Bread to Make Your Mouth Water*, New York, 1970, Denver, 1972; *XXX*, New York, 1970; *First Death* by Walter Leyden Brown, New York, 1972; *Gilles de Rais*, New York, 1975.

Actor: **Plays**—Frank in *The Haunted Host* by Robert Patrick, New York, 1964; Cupid in *Joyce Dynel* by Robert Patrick, New

York, 1969; Twin in *Huckleberry Finn*, New York, 1969. **Film**—*Guru the Mad Monk*, 1970.

William M. Hoffman comments:

(1982) In 1980 the Metropolitan Opera commissioned me to write a libretto for their 1983-84 season. The composer chosen was John Corigliano. We decided to complete the trilogy of operas on Figaro, using Beaumarchais's last play, *La Mère coupable* (*The Guilty Mother*), as our port of embarkation.

This libretto capped a decade of work with historical materials. My subjects included Gilles de Rais, the actual Bluebeard of 15th-century France; *Gulliver's Travels* and Emily Post's *Book of Etiquette* (1934 edition), in musical adaptation; James McNeill Whistler, Stephen Foster, and Louis Moreau Gottschalk, in plays for television; and Jesus.

My three collaborations with Anthony Holland were also historically founded. *Cornbury* is based on the life of the transvestite English governor of New York in the early 18th century. *Shoe Palace Murray* is located in New York in the 1920s. And *The Cherry Orchard, Part II* is set in Russia of the 1905-17 era.

But now after finishing the libretto, I have returned to the more personal material of my earliest plays, which all took place in contemporary times. I am currently working on a semiautobiographical play and a novel set in my neighborhood, SoHo.

* * *

William M. Hoffman's early work *Spring Play* is about a young man leaving his home, girlfriend, and innocence and going to New York City, where he meets a variety of exciting, corrupting people and experiences and comes to some grief in growing up. The style of the play is romantic and poetic, a kind of hallucinatory naturalism. Since then Hoffman has edited several anthologies of new American plays, and his awareness of contemporary styles and modes of consciousness is reflected in his own work. *Thank You, Miss Victoria* is a brilliant monologue in which a mother-fixated young business executive gets into a bizarre sadomasochistic relationship on the telephone. *Saturday Night at the Movies* is a bright, brash comedy, and *Uptight!* a musical revue. The eccentrically titled play *XXX* has as characters Jesus, Mary, Joseph, the Holy Ghost, and God. It retells the story of Jesus's life in a personal, free-form, associative, hip, provocatively beautiful fashion. The play is conceived as an ensemble performance for five actors. *Luna* is a light show. *A Quick Nut Bread to Make Your Mouth Water* is an ostensibly improvisatory play for three actors constructed in the form of a recipe, and the nut bread is served to the audience at the finish of the performance. In one production the author himself directed, he incorporated a group of gospel singers into the play.

Hoffman has explored forms other than drama, seeking a renewal of dramatic energies and attempting to expand theatrical possibilities and the audience's awareness. *From Fool to Hanged Man* is a scenario for pantomime, based on imagery from the tarot. By contrast with much of Hoffman's earlier work, which makes a point of the possibility of enlightenment in which innocence is at least rewarded with edifying experience, here the innocent hero moves blindly, almost passively, through a bleak succession of destructive encounters and is finally hanged. The beauty of the work only emphasizes its despair. Characteristically, the forces at work are not worldly or political but seem to exist in the individual state of mind. *The Children's Crusade* is another dance pantomime of naive and sentimental innocence brought down by the mockery and hostility of the corrupt, historically worn-out world. The theme parallels a widespread shift of attitude in the United States, and to follow Hoffman's work is to observe a representative contemporary consciousness.

Gilles de Rais, which seems to embrace depravity, was followed by three collaborations with the late Anthony Holland, a veteran of the improvisational comedy troupe Second City. *The Cherry Orchard, Part II* satirically traces the evolution between 1903 and 1918 of a group of Moscow intellectuals from Tolstoian pacifism to Bolshevism. *Shoe Palace Murray* takes place in a New York footwear store in 1926, while *Cornbury* dramatizes the life of an early governor of New York, a transvestite who ruled in Queen Anne's leftover clothing. With the songwriter John Braden, Hoffman wrote two musicals, *Gulliver's Travels* and *A Book of Etiquette*.

As Is (1985) made a powerful impact as one of the first serious plays to deal with AIDS. Blending humor with rage and sorrow and playing freely with time and place, Hoffman's play created a much copied model by dramatizing illness and larger social issues in the context of a single love story. In 1991, when his opera *Ghosts of Versailles,* written in collaboration with composer John Corigliani, opened at the Metropolitan Opera, he succeeded in bringing a Caffe Cino sensibility into the highest hall of culture.

—Michael T. Smith and C. Lee Jenner

HOLDEN, Joan

Nationality: American. **Born:** Berkeley, California, 18 January 1939. **Education:** Reed College, Portland, Oregon, B.A. 1960; University of California, Berkeley, M.A. 1964. **Family:** Married 1) Arthur Holden in 1958 (divorced); 2) Daniel Chumley in 1968, three daughters. **Career:** Waitress, Claremont Hotel, Berkeley, 1960-62; copywriter, Librairie Larousse, Paris, 1964-66; research assistant, University of California, Berkeley, 1966-67. Playwright, 1967—, publicist, 1967-69, and business manager, 1978-79, San Francisco Mime Troupe. Editor, Pacific News Service, 1973-75; instructor in playwriting, University of California, Davis, 1975, 1977, 1979, 1983, 1985, 1987. **Awards:** Obie award, 1973; Rockefeller grant, 1985. **Address:** San Francisco Mime Troupe, 855 Treat Street, San Francisco, California 94110, U.S.A.

Publications

Plays

L'Amant Militaire, adaptation of a play by Carlo Goldoni, translated by Betty Schwimmer (produced San Francisco and New York, 1967). Published in *The San Francisco Mime Troupe: The First Ten Years*, by R. G. Davis, Palo Alto, California, Ramparts Press, 1975.

Ruzzante; or, The Veteran, adaptation of a play by Angelo Beolco, translated by Suzanne Pollard (produced Hayward, California, 1968).

The Independent Female; or, A Man Has His Pride (produced Los Angeles, 1970). Included in *By Popular Demand*, 1980.

Seize the Time, with Steve Friedman (produced San Francisco, 1970).

The Dragon Lady's Revenge, with others (produced San Francisco, 1971; New York, 1972). Included in *By Popular Demand*, 1980.

Frozen Wages, with Richard Benetar and Daniel Chumley (produced San Francisco, 1972). Included in *By Popular Demand*, 1980.

San Fran Scandals, with others (produced San Francisco, 1973). Included in *By Popular Demand*, 1980.

The Great Air Robbery (produced San Francisco, 1974).

Frijoles; or, Beans to You, with others (produced San Francisco, 1975). Included in *By Popular Demand*, 1980.

Power Play (produced San Francisco, 1975).

False Promises/Nos Engañaron (produced San Francisco, 1976; New York, 1978). Included in *By Popular Demand*, 1980.

The Loon's Rage, with Steve Most and Jael Weisman (produced on tour, 1977). Published in *West Coast Plays 10* (Berkeley, California), Fall 1981.

The Hotel Universe, music by Bruce Barthol (produced La Rochelle, France, 1977). Published in *West Coast Plays 10* (Berkeley, California), Fall 1981.

By Popular Demand: Plays and Other Works by The San Francisco Mime Troupe (includes *False Promises/Nos Engañaron*; *San Fran Scandals*; *The Dragon Lady's Revenge*; *The Independent Female*; *Frijoles*; *Frozen Wages* by Holden, and *Los Siete* and *Evo-Man*). San Francisco, San Francisco Mime Troupe, 1980.

Factperson, with others (produced San Francisco, 1980). Published in *West Coast Plays 15-16* (Berkeley, California), Spring 1983.

Americans; or, Last Tango in Huahuatenango, with Daniel Chumley (produced Dayton, Ohio, and London, 1981; New York, 1982).

Factwino Meets the Moral Majority, with others (produced San Francisco, 1981; New York, 1982). Published in *West Coast Plays 15-16* (Berkeley, California), Spring 1983.

Factwino vs. Armaggedonman (produced San Francisco, 1982). Published in *West Coast Plays 15-16* (Berkeley, California), Spring 1983.

Steeltown, music by Bruce Barthol (produced San Francisco, 1984; New York, 1985).

1985, with others (produced San Francisco, 1985).

Spain/36, music by Bruce Barthol (produced Los Angeles, 1986).

The Mozamgola Caper, with others (produced San Francisco, 1986). Published in *Theater* (New Haven, Connecticut), Winter 1986.

Ripped van Winkle, with Ellen Callas (produced San Francisco, 1988).

Seeing Double, with others (produced San Francisco and New York, 1989).

Back to Normal, with others (produced San Francisco, 1990).

The Marriage of Figaro, adaptation of a play by Beaumarchais (produced San Francisco, 1990).

*

Manuscript Collection: University of California, Davis.

Critical Studies: "*Hotel Universe*: Playwriting and the San Francisco Mime Troupe" by William Kleb, in *Theater* (New Haven, Connecticut), Spring 1978; "Joan Holden and the San Francisco Mime Troupe," in *Drama Review* (New York), Spring 1980, and *New American Dramatists 1960-1980*, London, Macmillan, and New York, Grove Press, 1982, both by Ruby Cohn; "Woman as Citizen in Satiric Melodrama: Joan Holden and the San Francisco Mime Troupe" by Donna Jean Zane, in *Gramma: Journal of Theory and Criticism*, 1994, pp. 213-26.

Joan Holden comments:

I write political cartoons. For years, I was ashamed of this. I agreed meekly with those critics who said, "*mere* political cartoons." To please them, and led astray by well-wishers who'd say, "You can do more—you could write *serious* plays," I've tried my hand, from time to time, at realism. Each time I've been extremely impressed, at first, with the solemnity of what I've written. Rereading those passages, I always find I've written melodrama. The fact is, I'm only inspired when I'm being funny. Writing comedy is not really a choice: it's a quirk. On a certain level, making things funny is a coward's way of keeping pain at arm's length. But that same distance allows you to show certain things clearly: notably, characters' social roles, their functions in history. These generalities, not the specifics which soften them, interest caricaturists—who have serious reasons for being funny, and in whose ranks I now aspire to be counted.

For 20 years, I've written for a permanent company, for particular actors, directors, and composers, and in collaboration with them. This has put conditions on my writing; it has also supplied a nearly constant source of ideas, and a wonderful opportunity to learn from mistakes.

* * *

Joan Holden has been the principal playwright of the San Francisco Mime Troupe, which has always performed with words as well as gestures. Although chance led to the association, a 30-year career developed.

The Holden/Goldoni *Military Lover/L'Amant Militaire* drew large audiences to nearly 50 park performances. Holden wrote, "Comedy, which in its basic action always measures an unsatisfactory reality against its corresponding ideal, may be the revolutionary art form *par excellence*." It became Holden's art form par excellence, pitting satirized establishment figures of unsatisfactory reality against the satisfactory dream of working-class harmony and celebration.

After the Mime Troupe became a collective in 1970, *The Independent Female* expressed the new spirit. *Commedia* characters gave way to those of soap opera with satiric telltale names—Pennybank for a business tycoon, Heartright for a junior executive, Bullitt for a militant feminist. As in soap opera, a pair of lovers is faced with an obstacle to their marriage. But subverting the genre, Holden identifies the obstacle as the young ingenue's growing independence. Instead of dissolving the obstacle for a happy curtain clincher, Holden sees a happy ending in sustained feminist revolt that the audience is asked to link to working-class revolt.

The Dragon Lady's Revenge is grounded in another popular form, the comic strip, with assists from B movies. Its intricate plot involves a corrupt American ambassador, his soldier son, the CIA agent Drooley, and the titular Dragon Lady, as well as the honest Blossom, a native revolutionary. Holden shifted from global to local politics with *San Fran Scandals*, depicting housing problems through vaudeville. She then exploited science fiction and the detective story for *The Great Air Robbery*.

In the mid-1970s the San Francisco Mime Troupe reached out beyond the white middle class, actively recruiting Third World members, and Holden's scripts reflected the new constituency. *Frijoles* (beans) zigzags between Latin American and North American couples, joining them at a food conference in Europe and through identical class interests. Just as *Frijoles* travels through space, *Power Play* travels through time in order to indict the antiecological monopoly of the Pacific Gas and Electric Company.

By the late 1970s Holden was in firm command of her style: a specific issue attacked through a popular art form; simple language and a clean story line; and short scenes that often culminated in a song. For 1976, the bicentennial year of the United States, the troupe wanted to present a work on the uncelebrated aspects of American history—the role of workers, minorities, and women. Using collective research, Holden scripted *False Promises,* which deviated from her usual satiric formula in presenting working-class characters with heightened realism. The characters continued to appear in such subsequent plays as *Steeltown* and the final play of the Factwino trilogy.

In *Factperson* the person of the title is an old black bag lady with the power to cite facts that contradict the lies of the media. In *Factwino vs. Armaggedonman* "the double-headed dealer of doom," the military-industrial complex, subjugates an old black wino with alcohol, but in a later Factwino play he emerges triumphant through his own research into lies: "Everybody has to find their own power." *Ripped van Winkle* is a hilarious reversion to satire, in which a 1960s hippie awakens from a 20-year acid trip to find himself adrift in Reaganomics. Whether dealing with local or global issues, probing character, or tickling caricatures, Holden theatricalizes current events with verve.

—Ruby Cohn

HOLLINGSWORTH, Margaret

Nationality: Canadian. **Born:** Sheffield, England, in 1940; immigrated to Canada, 1968; became citizen, 1974. **Education:** Hornsey High School, London; Loughborough School of Librarianship, Leicestershire, A.L.A.; Lakehead University, Thunder Bay, Ontario (gold medal), B.A. 1972; University of British Columbia, Vancouver, M.F.A. in theatre and creative writing 1974. **Career:** Journalist, editor, librarian, and teacher in England, 1960-68; chief librarian, Fort William Public Library, Ontario, 1968-72. Since 1972 freelance writer. Assistant professor, David Thompson Centre, University of Victoria, Nelson, British Columbia, 1981-83; writer-in-residence, Concordia University, Montreal, 1985-86, Stratford Festival Theatre, Ontario, 1987, and University of Western Ontario, London, Ontario, 1989-90; assistant professor of creative writing, University of Victoria, British Columbia, 1992—. Lives in Victoria. **Awards:** Association of Canadian Television and Radio Artists award, 1979; Chalmers award, 1985; Dora Mavor Moore award, 1986, 1987; Jessie Richardson award for Outstanding play produced in Vancouver, 1995. **Address:** c/o Playwrights Union of Canada, 54 Wolseley Street, Toronto, Ontario M5T 1A5, Canada.

Publications

Plays

Bushed (produced Vancouver, 1974). With *Operators*, Toronto, Playwrights, 1981.

Operators (produced Vancouver, 1975; revised version produced 1981). With *Bushed*, Toronto, Playwrights, 1981.

Dance for My Father. Vancouver, New Play Centre, 1976.

Alli Alli Oh (produced Vancouver, 1977). Toronto, Playwrights, 1979.

The Apple in the Eye (broadcast 1977; produced Vancouver, 1983). Included in *Willful Acts*, 1985.

The Writers Show (revue), with others (produced Vancouver, 1978).

Mother Country (produced Toronto, 1980). Toronto, Playwrights, 1980.

Ever Loving (produced Victoria, British Columbia, 1980). Toronto, Playwrights, 1981.

Islands (produced Vancouver, 1983). Toronto, Playwrights, 1983.

Diving (produced Vancouver, 1983). Included in *Willful Acts*, 1985.

War Babies (produced Victoria, British Columbia, 1984). Included in *Willful Acts*, 1985.

It's Only Hot for Two Months in Kapuskasing (produced Toronto, 1985). Included in *Endangered Species*, 1989.

Willful Acts (includes *The Apple in the Eye*, *Ever Loving*, *Diving*, *Islands*, *War Babies*). Toronto, Coach House Press, 1985.

The Green Line (produced Stratford, Ontario, 1986).

Poppycock (produced Toronto, 1987).

Endangered Species (includes *The House That Jack Built*, *It's Only Hot for Two Months in Kapuskasing*, *Prim and Duck, Mama and Frank*). Toronto, One Act Press, 1989.

Prim and Duck, Mama and Frank (produced Toronto, 1991). Included in *Endangered Species*, 1989.

Alma Victoria (produced Nanaimo, British Columbia, 1990).

There's a Few Things I Want to Tell You (produced Vancouver, 1992).

Making Greenpeace (produced Vancouver, 1992).

Numbrains (produced Vancouver, 1993). Victoria, Reference West, 1995.

In Confidence (produced Vancouver, 1993). Vancouver, Scirocco Drama, 1994.

Blowing Up Toads (produced Calgary, 1996).

Radio Plays: *Join Me in Mandalay*, *Prairie Drive*, *As I Was Saying to Mr. Dideron*, *Wayley's Children*, and *War Games*, from 1973; *The Apple in the Eye*, 1977; *Webster's Revenge*, 1977; *Operators*, 1986; *Alli Alli Oh*, 1986; *Responsible Party*, 1986; *Woman on the Wire*, 1986; *Surreal Landscape*, *The Cloud Sculptors of Coral D*, *Sailing Under Water*, *A Mother in India*, from 1986; *Mussomeli-Dusseldorf*, adaptation of the radio play by Dacia Maraini, 1991.

Television Plays: *Ole and All That*, 1968 (UK); *Sleepwalking* (*AirWaves* series), 1986; *Scene from a Balcony*, 1987; *The Last Demise of Julian Whittaker*, 1989.

Short Stories

Sailing Under Water. Vancouver, Lazara Press, 1989.

*

Critical Studies: "Margaret Hollingsworth," in *The Work: Conversations with English Canadian Playwrights*, edited by Cynthia Zimmerman, Toronto, Coach House Press, 1982; introduction by Ann Saddlemyer to *Willful Acts*, 1985; "Readings in Review: *Willful Acts*," by Rina Fraticelli, in *Canadian Theatre Review* (Downsview, Ontario), Summer 1986; "Alienation and Identity: The Plays of Margaret Hollingsworth," in *Canadian Literature* (Vancouver), no. 118, Autumn 1988; "Margaret Hollingsworth," in *Fair Play: 12 Women Speak/ Conversations with Canadian Playwrights*, edited by Judith Rudakoff and Rita Much, Toronto, Simon and Pierre, 1990.

Margaret Hollingsworth comments:

(1988) My work is very wide-ranging in style and subject. Constantly recurring themes are the search for a home, sex roles and sexual stereotypes, and war. My latest plays are *The Green Line* which is set on the green line in Beirut, and *Marked for Marriage*, a 3-act farce set against the background of the survival games which are an extremely popular pseudo-military outdoor activity among Canadian men.

Some of my more experimental work, such as *Prim and Duck, Mama and Frank*, has yet to get beyond the workshop production stage, since there are very few outlets for experimental work in Canada at this time.

* * *

Margaret Hollingsworth, born in England, immigrated to Canada at the age of 28. She has insisted that "Canada is what I write about. Canada is where I come from; it's what feeds me. My plays always, in some way, come out of Canada." She believes, as she said in a 1982 interview, that her distinctive style accounts for the infrequent staging of her work: "It tends to read flat but it isn't flat in production. Often directors are very tentative about how to handle it because it doesn't fall into any category. It isn't like what anyone else is doing. My work has got a surreal level to it. That's the way I see life. I see it in a very surreal way but rooted in practical realism." The broad trend of Hollingsworth's work ranges from relatively conventional drama, perhaps shaped by the assumptions of the New Play Centre in Vancouver, to more obscure styles and techniques linked to the gradual evolution of her own female aesthetic.

Bushed and *Operators*, early one-act plays, are set in northern Ontario. *Bushed* depicts tired immigrant men in a Laundromat, and *Operators* features two women night-shift workers whose long-term friendship is disrupted by a newcomer. These are pieces of mood, of place, and of displacement.

Ever Loving, which is an ironic title, is her most accessible drama. In 38 scenes, starting in 1970 and going back as far as 1938, we see three war marriages between near strangers: a Dundee fisherwoman with an Ontario millworker of Irish descent, a posh Englishwoman with a Ukrainian prairie farmer, and an Italian aristocrat with a would-be musician in Nova Scotia. Hollingsworth includes prewar life, first meetings, courtship, crossing the Atlantic, and the ups and downs of 25 years. "Canada's roots," wrote Helen Thomson, are shown as in "other and older cultures," while "Canadian nationalism excludes its women, and is only a spurious emotion in men." *Ever Loving* explores an important aspect of modern Canadian experience, and although it is about romance, it avoids all the clichés. It is unobtrusively adventurous structurally, showing two or three separate actions onstage at the same time, interweaving dates and comments with 29 popular songs, and juxtaposing different accents and speech rhythms.

The murder of Francis Rattenbury by his wife's toy boy, perhaps aided by the wife, was a sensation in England in 1935. Rattenbury, an architect, worked mostly in British Columbia. The story prompted two other plays, *Cause Célèbre* by Terence Rattigan and, distantly, *Molly* by Simon Gray. Hollingsworth's treatment, *Alma Victoria*, was commissioned for the 1990 Nanaimo Festival. It occurs largely before the murder, with the first half in the 1920s promisingly sketching the English-style middle-class way of life in Victoria, British Columbia. Rattenbury, at 58, abandons his wife for young Alma, a successful New York pianist who has already been twice married. The more routine conclusion in Bournemouth has Rattenbury drinking and in decline while his wife composes songs. The focus becomes a troubled woman circumscribed by her times.

Though Hollingsworth was active in the Campaign for Nuclear Disarmament in Britain, her political principles become overt only in *Woman on the Wire*. She explained her lack of confidence in writing explicitly on political subjects for a long time as "part of being a woman. You don't feel that your voice is important enough to matter. It takes a lot of writing to be able to get to the point where I feel confident enough to do that." In *Woman on the Wire* Kate, a Canadian wife and mother, is drawn to the peace camp at the missile base at Greenham Common. The tension of night beside the barbed wire is created with a lonely male sentry on one side and a female lookout on the other. Both are tired, jumpy, and afraid. We learn in snippets how Kate had to accompany her manager husband to London, how an English friend first took her to Greenham Common, and how the commitment becomes more vital than the marriage. Another camper is a teacher who found that she could teach war because it was history but not peace, because it was politics. Kate proclaims polemically, "Just being here can make a difference to life on this planet." *Woman on the Wire* shows the usual enterprise in structure, as when the husband's "I love you" and the trial judge's "How do you plead?" are intercut and overlapped.

Mother Country shows Hollingsworth attempting to create on both a literal and a superrealistic level. The characters are an English émigré family, three daughters returning to celebrate their dominating mother's 65th birthday, on an island off the British Columbia coast. The themes were stated succinctly by Cynthia Zimmerman: it is a play "about country and culture, about belonging and home."

Hollingsworth believes, as she told the *Vancouver Sun* in 1984, that women's drama is "unlinear, concerned with getting inside people's heads, into the thought process. There's an earthy rhythmic sense to a lot of female writing, an effort to be more universal, to find a wholeness, a diffusing quality." She later explained that she seeks "a poetic drama that isn't self-conscious." In a 1985 article she probed further into the problems of the woman dramatist: the domination of men as decision makers in the theater, and the tendency for women to write for ensembles, "always a stumbling block to smooth production" but also the way a woman defies the rules of playwriting ("The concept of a hero is perhaps a male invention, a male need"). Women prefer to write of "inner states and tensions," which often do not "fit neatly into an accepted dramatic form."

An early piece such as *The Apple in the Eye* shows concern with the differences between a woman's public and private voice together with puzzles about precisely what the apple represents.

The four self-published short scripts collected as *Endangered Species* reveal Hollingsworth clearly pushing in new directions, ignoring the expectations of mainstream theater. One of these, *Poppycock*, developed from work with masks and clowning. Here time is "scrambled," and three well-researched relationships are brought together—H. D. and Ezra Pound, Dora Maar and Picasso, and Winifred Wagner and Hitler—with the same actor playing the three men. The semiabsurdist *Prim and Duck, Mama and Frank* has four characters in four different rooms, with the movements of the play entitled "Feet," "Hands," "Body," and "Head."

While commentators have examined Hollingsworth's work in the light of her degree in psychology and through the influence of Pinter, neither provides the key, nor is she precisely absurdist or surrealistic. She uses short forms and evolves her own kind of nonrealism, and her work is increasingly individualistic, even idiosyncratic. Her writing is characterized by care for language, by focus on women in a man's world, and by a continuing restless search for something new, the perfect form of self-expression. But will these plays be produced—preferably without the restrictions of low budgets and short rehearsal periods—before she is discouraged?

—Malcolm Page

HOLMAN, Robert

Nationality: British. **Born:** Guisborough, Cleveland, 25 August 1952. **Education:** Lawrence Jackson School, Guisborough, 1963-69; Prior Pursglove Sixth Form College, Guisborough, 1969-71. **Career:** Bookstall assistant, Paddington Station, London, 1972-74; resident dramatist, National Theatre, London, 1978-80, and Royal Shakespeare Company, Stratford-on-Avon, 1984. **Awards:** Arts Council bursary, 1974; George Devine award, 1978; Fulbright fellowship, 1988. **Agent:** Casarotto Ramsay Ltd., National House, 60-66 Wardour Street, London W1V 3HP, England.

PUBLICATIONS

Plays

The Grave Lovers (produced Edinburgh, 1972).
Progress in Unity (produced Teesside, 1972).
Coal (produced London, 1973).
The Natural Cause (produced London, 1974).
Mud (produced London, 1974). With *German Skerries*, London, Heinemann, 1977.
Outside the Whale (produced Edinburgh, 1976; London, 1978). With *Rafts and Dreams*, London, Methuen, 1991.
German Skerries (produced London, 1977). With *Mud*, London, Heinemann, 1977.
Emigres, adaptation of the play by Slawomir Mrozek (produced London, 1978; New York, 1979). Published in *New Review* (London), 1979.
Rooting (produced Edinburgh, 1980).
Other Worlds (produced London, 1983). London, Methuen, 1983.
Today (produced Stratford-on-Avon, 1984; London, 1985). London, Methuen, 1985.
The Overgrown Path (produced London, 1985). London, Methuen, 1985.
Making Noise Quietly: A Trilogy (includes *Being Friends*, *Lost*, *Making Noise Quietly*) (produced London, 1986; Los Angeles, 1989). London, Methuen, 1987.
Across Oka (produced Stratford-on-Avon, 1988; London, 1989). London, Methuen, 1988.
Rafts and Dreams (produced London, 1990). With *Outside the Whale*, London, Methuen, 1991.
Bad Weather. London, Nick Hern, 1998.

Television Plays: *Chance of a Lifetime*, 1979; *This Is History, Gran*, 1984.

Novel

The Amish Landscape. London, Hern, 1992.

* * *

Allusive and carefully crafted, Robert Holman's plays explore the interpenetration of ordinary lives and large historical events. The Great Depression, the Spanish Civil War, World War II, the Holocaust, the destruction of Nagasaki, and the continuation of research on the hydrogen bomb—such realities darken the worlds shaping and shaped by his characters, worlds that in turn illuminate the contradictions and complexities of these realities. History is not a backdrop, nor even a stage, for these characters but rather a sense of pattern that reveals, and is revealed by, their action or inaction. Time and again his protagonists articulate this simple truth: "It's important. History. Our lives."

Perhaps his strongest and most ambitious play is *The Overgrown Path*. The work opens with a playlet performed by primary school children in modern-day Nagasaki. It recounts the experience of a girl called Etsuko on the day the atomic bomb was dropped. When the playlet ends, Etsuko is identified as the children's schoolteacher. The rest of the drama takes place on the Greek island of Tinos, where Daniel Howarth, a 73-year-old British academic, has retired from the world with Beth, his second wife. Four years his junior, she is American and a doctor. As a member of a medical relief team in Nagasaki in 1945, she had witnessed the effects of the bomb and during her time there had befriended a 10-year-old orphan of the blast called Etsuko. Daniel's career had been in atomic physics, and he had led the research program on the hydrogen bomb throughout the 1950s. They met and married in the 1960s. To their escape on Tinos come Daniel's daughter by his first marriage and a bright, questioning disciple in his late 30s who is hesitating before embarking on what clearly could be a brilliant academic career. From the lives of these four people come stories and processes of learning that reveal patterns of design and accident that help to bring both characters and historical "facts" into a felt relationship. As Daniel says to his inquisitive disciple, "I'm not a historian, but it seems to me we look at history in the wrong way. We have to look at ourselves first. At our own stories. When we stop repeating our own failings, and take responsibility for our actions, maybe we have a chance."

This need to "take responsibility" is a recurring motif. It is something Joe Waterman, in the earlier play *Other Worlds*, is running away from. It is something his betrothed, at their last tragic meeting, insists upon:

Joe: It's other people messed it up, not us.
Emma: It's us.

It is something that, by the end of the play, Joe learns to do. *Other Worlds* takes place during the final decades of the eighteenth century, when enclosure by private acts of Parliament was dividing communities and challenging custom. The barriers of enmity and suspicion raised by one such act, separating the world of the fishers and the world of the farmers on an isolated stretch of the north Yorkshire coast, are reinforced by the threat of an invasion from France. Fear of the unknown and of the reciprocal violence engendered by enclosure is portrayed through such vivid stage imagery as the unexpected irruption of a shipwrecked gorilla dressed in a blue woolen sailor's jumper, his capture in a fishing net, and his imprisonment and eventual execution as a Frenchman alongside a vagrant girl who, dressed in boy's clothes, is thought to be a French spy and whose protestations of gender are not believed. The absurdity of such images highlights how in a collision of closed worlds any sense of identity, shared humanity, or responsibility to otherness becomes constrained. Against these implosive forces are posited a belief in education and learning, hope—"When you've lost hope, you've lost everything"—and the need not to drift or run away but to take on the responsibility for one's actions.

In all of Holman's work a care for detail is balanced by an impressionistic style designed to engage an audience in a continual process of inference, surprise, reassessment, and understanding concerning both events and people. In many of his plays events move backward and forward in time, as, for example, in *Today*, where they move from 1936 to 1920 to 1922 to 1937 to 1946. In this drama we are drawn into the experiences of the relatives, friends, and casual acquaintances of Victor Ellison, a Yorkshire music teacher who, struggling to compose something out of his life, goes to fight in Spain. Their experiences articulate differences in opportunities, aspirations, economics, class, and region before and during the Great Depression. The shifts in time sharpen our sense of the choices and restrictions facing these figures as well as highlighting how chance and accident can affect the direction of events. The shifts in perspective involve the audience in seeing and revising why and how these things happened. Holman's approach to characterization deepens this involvement. New, often contradictory facets of character are continually juxtaposed, making us modify, even change outright, our sense of what motivates each person.

We get to know Holman's characters through partial and accidental revelations and encounters. This allusive approach is best exemplified in *Lost*, the shortest of the one-act plays comprising the trilogy *Making Noise Quietly*. A young naval lieutenant visits his sister's mother-in-law to commiserate on her son's death in the Falkland Islands. They have not met before, and she does not know who he is. The mother has not heard that her son is dead; she does not even know that he was married. These facts—along with details of family relationships, their social backgrounds, and respective pasts—are disclosed in a seemingly haphazard way that exposes an emotional muddle of "little lies" in the front room of a small terraced house in Redcar, a muddle that parallels and illuminates the moral murk of the Falklands War.

—Leslie du S. Read

HOPKINS, John (Richard)

Nationality: British. **Born:** London, 27 January 1931. **Education:** Raynes Park County Grammar School; St. Catharine's College, Cambridge, B.A. in English. **Military Service:** Served in the British Army (national service), 1950-51. **Family:** Married 1) Prudence Balchin in 1954; 2) the actress Shirley Knight in 1970; two daughters. **Career:** Worked as television studio manager; writer, BBC Television, 1962-64. Freelance writer, 1964—. **Awards:** Two Screenwriters Guild awards. **Agent:** William Morris Agency, 31-32 Soho Square, London W1V 6AP, England. **Died:** 23 July 1998.

Publications

Plays

A Place of Safety (televised 1963). Published in *Z Cars: Four Scripts From the Television Series*, edited by Michael Marland, London, Longman, 1968.

Talking to a Stranger: Four Television Plays (includes *Anytime You're Ready I'll Sparkle, No Skill or Special Knowledge Is Required, Gladly My Cross-Eyed Bear, The Innocent Must Suffer*) (televised 1966). London, Penguin, 1967.

A Game—Like—Only a Game (televised 1966). Published in *Conflicting Generations: Five Television Plays*, edited by Michael Marland, London, Longman, 1968.

This Story of Yours (produced London, 1968; New Haven, Connecticut, 1981). London, Penguin, 1969.

Find Your Way Home (produced London, 1970; New York, 1974). London, Penguin, 1971; New York, Doubleday, 1975.

Economic Necessity (produced Leicester, 1973; New York, 1976).

Next of Kin (produced London, 1974).

Losing Time (produced New York, 1979). New York, Broadway Play Publishing, 1983.

Absent Forever (produced Cleveland, Ohio, 1987).

Screenplays: *Two Left Feet*, with Roy Baker, 1963; *Thunderball*, with Richard Maibaum, 1965; *The Virgin Soldiers*, with John McGrath and Ian La Fresnais, 1969; *Divorce—His, Divorce—Hers*, 1972; *The Offence*, 1973; *Murder by Decree*, 1980; *The Holcroft Covenant*, with George Axelrod and Edward Anhalt, 1982; *The Power*, with John Carpenter and Gerald Brach, 1983.

Television Plays: *Break Up*, 1958; *After the Party*, 1958; *The Small Back Room*, 1959; *Dancers in Mourning*, 1959; *A Woman Comes Home*, 1961; *A Chance of Thunder* (6 parts), 1961; *By Invitation Only*, 1961; *The Second Curtain*, 1962; *Look Who's Talking*, 1962; *Z Cars* series (53 episodes), 1962-65; *The Pretty English Girls*, 1964; *I Took My Little World Away*, 1964; *Parade's End* (serialization), from the novel by Ford Madox Ford, 1964; *Time Out of Mind*, 1964; *Houseparty* (ballet scenario), 1964; *The Make Believe Man*, 1965; *Fable*, 1965; *Horror of Darkness*, 1965; *A Man Like Orpheus*, 1965; *Talking to a Stranger* (4 parts), 1966; *Some Place of Darkness*, music by Christopher Whelen, 1966; *A Game—Like—Only a Game*, 1966; *The Gambler* (serialization), from a novel by Dostoevsky, 1968; *Beyond the Sunrise*, 1969; *The Dolly Scene*, 1970; *Some Distant Shadow*, 1971; *That Quiet Earth*, 1972; *Walk into the Dark*, 1972; *The Greeks and Their Gifts*, 1972; *A Story to Frighten the Children*, 1976; *Double Dare*, 1976; *Fathers and Families* (6 plays), 1977; *Smiley's People*, with John le Carré, from the novel by le Carré, 1982.

* * *

With well over 50 scripts for the television series *Z Cars* and several short television plays behind him, John Hopkins is not primarily a writer for the stage. It was on the newer medium that his reputation was made and continues to stand at its highest. Indeed, one important critic called his tetralogy *Talking to a Stranger* "the first authentic masterpiece written directly for television," and there must be many others who, though perhaps charier of the word "masterpiece," would agree that no finer dramatic work has yet been seen on it. The work is undeniably impressive in itself, and it also makes a helpful introduction to the first plays Hopkins was subsequently to write for the theater, *This Story of Yours* and *Find Your Way Home*.

Each of the four plays of *Talking to a Stranger* involves approximately the same day, and each is written from the stance of a different member of the same family—the father, the mother, and their two grown-up children, Alan and Teresa. They are characterized in striking depth. With the possible exception of the son, all are thoroughly self-absorbed, more inclined to talk in monologues than dialogues, and, again except for the son, all stand in danger of being overwhelmed by their own self-destructive feelings. All, including the son, are lonely and dissatisfied. The tetralogy opens with Teresa, bustling with frantic neurosis, and ends with the mother, dead by her own hand, and between the two Hopkins avoids none of the emotional collisions and unpleasantness that his plot generates. Whereas most contemporary writers would hedge, tread warily, or retreat into irony, he strides in wholeheartedly and sometimes repetitively, using straightforward, unpretentious, naturalistic language. Not surprisingly, he has been accused of dramatic overstatement, even melodrama.

But melodrama occurs when a writer presents extremes of feeling that are neither justified by his material nor empathetically understood by himself. In *Talking to a Stranger* the emotions on display are no more than the objective correlative of the dramatic situation that is so painstakingly assembled, and it is equally the case that Hopkins has a thorough grasp of the people he has created. He gives the impression of knowing instinctively how they would react to any new event. The question is, Can we say as much for his stage plays? And the proper answer would seem to be not quite.

This Story of Yours seems almost to be accusing Hopkins's scripts for *Z Cars* of romanticizing their subject, the police, although in fact they were widely admired for their wry realism. It is a study of the mind of Detective Sergeant Johnson, trapped in an unfulfilling marriage and at once disgusted and fascinated by work that Hopkins characteristically describes in lurid detail. He breaks and, in a scene of considerable dramatic intensity, beats to death an alleged child rapist, an act that is doubly self-destructive since it wrecks his career and is clearly a way of sublimating his loathing for his own hideous thoughts and corrupt desires. *Find Your Way Home* mainly concerns two homosexuals—one young, unhappy, and apparently a part-time prostitute, the other a married man—and ends with their settling down seriously to live together after having confessed their mutual love. By bringing on a distraught wife and by accentuating the crudity and sadness of the homosexual subculture, Hopkins is at pains to make this decision as difficult as possible. But his view evidently is that it is the right one. The older man has "found his way home" to a more honest and fulfilling way of life.

From this it will be seen that Hopkins's view of the world is bleak, and what seems melodramatic in his work is often only his way of emphasizing his belief that people are lonely and perverse, full of black thoughts and longings. If a relationship is capable of any success at all, which is doubtful, it can be only after each partner has accepted his own and the other's emotional inadequacies, as the protagonists of *Find Your Way Home* are beginning to do. It is an outspoken, unfashionable moral stance that may need the more thorough characterization we find in *Talking to a Stranger* to be persuasive. There are psychological gaps left open in the stage plays and notably in *Find Your Way Home,* whose scheme forces Hopkins to the dubious assumption that a young man who has gone very far in self-destructive promiscuity may be capable of sustained affection in a mature relationship. Hopkins achieves his effects by accumulating the emotional evidence as thickly as he can, and he may, therefore, need more space and more time than other contemporary writers in order to do so.

—Benedict Nightingale

HOROVITZ, Israel (Arthur)

Nationality: American. **Born:** Wakefield, Massachusetts, 31 March 1939. **Education:** Royal Academy of Dramatic Art, London, 1961-63; City College, New York, M.A. in English 1972. **Family:** Married 1) Elaine Abber in 1959 (marriage annulled 1960); 2) Doris Keefe in 1961 (divorced 1972), one daughter and two sons; 3) Gillian Adams in 1981, twin daughter and son. **Career:** Stage manager, Boston and New York, 1961-65; playwright-in-residence, Royal Shakespeare Company, London, 1965; instructor in playwriting, New York University, 1967-69; professor of English, City College, 1968-73; Fanny Hurst professor of theatre, Brandeis University, Waltham, Massachusetts, 1973-75. Founder, New York Playwrights Lab, 1977; founder, 1980, and producer and artistic director, Gloucester Stage Company, Massachusetts. Columnist, *Magazine Littéraire*, Paris, 1971-77. **Awards:** Obie award, 1968, 1969; Rockefeller fellowship, 1969; Vernon Rice award, 1969; Drama Desk award, 1969; *Jersey Journal* award, 1969; Cannes Film Festival Jury prize, 1971; New York State Council of Arts fellowship, 1971, 1975; National Endowment for the Arts fellowship, 1974, 1977; American Academy award, 1975; Fulbright fellowship, 1975; Emmy award, 1975; Christopher award, 1976; Guggenheim fellowship, 1977; French Critics prize, 1977; Los Angeles Drama Critics Circle award, 1980; Goldie award, 1985; Eliot Norton Prize, 1986; Boston Best Play award, 1987; Literature Prize of Washington College, 1996. Honorary degree: Salem State College. **Agents:** Jason Fogelson, c/o William Morris Agency, 1325 Avenue of the Americas, New York, New York 10019, U.S.A.; and c/o Jane Annakin, London Management, 2-4 Noel Street, London W1V3RB, England.

Publications

Plays

The Comeback (produced Boston, 1958).
The Death of Bernard the Believer (produced South Orange, New Jersey, 1960).

This Play Is about Me (produced South Orange, New Jersey, 1961).
The Hanging of Emanuel (produced South Orange, New Jersey, 1962).
Hop, Skip, and Jump (produced South Orange, New Jersey, 1963).
The Killer Dove (produced West Orange, New Jersey, 1963).
The Simon Street Harvest (produced South Orange, New Jersey, 1964).
The Indian Wants the Bronx (produced Waterford, Connecticut, 1966; New York and Watford, Hertfordshire, 1968; London, 1969). Included in *First Season*, 1968; in *Off-Broadway Plays*, London, Penguin, 1970.
Line (produced New York, 1967; London, 1970; revised version produced New York, 1971). Included in *First Season*, 1968.
It's Called the Sugar Plum (produced Waterford, Connecticut, 1967; New York and Watford, Hertfordshire, 1968; London, 1971). Included in *First Season*, 1968; in *Off-Broadway Plays*, London, Penguin, 1970.
Acrobats (produced New York, 1968; London, 1980). New York, Dramatists Play Service, 1971.
Rats (produced New York, 1968; London, 1969). Included in *First Season*, 1968.
Morning (in *Chiaroscuro* produced Spoleto, Italy, 1968; in *Morning, Noon, and Night* produced New York, 1968). Published in *Morning, Noon, and Night*, New York, Random House, 1969.
First Season: Line, The Indian Wants the Bronx, It's Called the Sugar Plum, Rats. New York, Random House, 1968.
The Honest to God Schnozzola (produced Provincetown, Massachusetts, 1968; New York, 1969). New York, Breakthrough Press, 1971.
Leader (produced New York, 1969). With *Play for Trees*, New York, Dramatists Play Service, 1970.
Play for Trees (televised 1969). With *Leader*, New York, Dramatists Play Service, 1970.
Shooting Gallery (produced New York, 1971). With *Play for Germs*, New York, Dramatists Play Service, 1973.
Dr. Hero (as *Hero*, produced New York, 1971; revised version, as *Dr. Hero*, produced Great Neck, New York, 1972; New York City, 1973). New York, Dramatists Play Service, 1973.
The Wakefield Plays (produced New York, 1978). Included in *The Wakefield Plays* (collection), 1979.
Alfred the Great (also director: produced Paris and Great Neck, New York, 1972; New York City, 1973). New York, Harper, 1974.
Our Father's Failing (produced Waterford, Connecticut, 1973; New York, 1974).
Alfred Dies (produced New York, 1976).
Play for Germs (in *VD Blues*, televised 1972). With *Shooting Gallery*, New York, Dramatists Play Service, 1973.
The First, The Last, and The Middle: A Comedy Triptych (produced New York, 1974).
The Quannapowitt Quartet (produced New Haven, Connecticut, 1976). 3 plays in *The Wakefield Plays* (collection), 1979.
Hopscotch (also director: produced Paris and New York, 1974; London, 1980). With *The 75th*, New York, Dramatists Play Service, 1977.
The 75th (produced New York, 1977). With *Hopscotch*, New York, Dramatists Play Service, 1977.
Stage Directions (produced New York, 1976; Richmond, Surrey, 1978). With *Spared*, New York, Dramatists Play Service, 1977.
Spared (also director: produced Paris and New York, 1974). With *Stage Directions*, New York, Dramatists Play Service, 1977.
Turnstile (produced Hanover, New Hampshire, 1974).
The Primary English Class (produced Waterford, Connecticut, 1975; also director: produced New York, 1975; Richmond, Surrey, 1979; London, 1980). New York, Dramatists Play Service, 1976.
Uncle Snake: An Independence Day Pageant (produced New York, 1975). New York, Dramatists Play Service, 1976.
The Reason We Eat (produced Stamford, Connecticut, and New York, 1976).
The Lounge Player (produced New York, 1977).
Man with Bags, adaptation of a play by Eugène Ionesco, translated by Marie-France Ionesco (produced Baltimore, 1977). New York, Grove Press, 1977.
The Former One-on-One Basketball Champion (produced New York, 1977). With *The Great Labor Day Classic*, New York, Dramatists Play Service, 1982.
Cappella, with David Boorstin, adaptation of the novel by Horovitz (produced New York, 1978).
The Widow's Blind Date (produced New York, 1978). New York, Theatre Communications Group, 1981.
Mackerel (produced Hartford, Connecticut, 1978; revised version produced Washington, D.C., 1978). Vancouver, Talonbooks, 1979.
A Christmas Carol: Scrooge and Marley, adaptation of the story by Dickens (produced Baltimore, 1978). New York, Dramatists Play Service, 1979.
The Good Parts (produced New York, 1979). New York, Dramatists Play Service, 1983.
The Great Labor Day Classic (in *Holidays*, produced Louisville, 1979; produced separately New York, 1984). With *The Former One-on-One Basketball Champion*, New Dramatists Play Service, 1982.
The Wakefield Plays (collection; also includes *The Quannapowitt Quartet* except for *The 75th*). New York, Avon, 1979.
Sunday Runners in the Rain (produced New York, 1980).
Park Your Car in Harvard Yard (produced New York, 1980).
Henry Lumper (produced Gloucester, Massachusetts, 1985; New York, 1989). New York, Dramatists Play Service, 1990.
Today, I Am a Fountain Pen, adaptation of stories by Morley Torgov (produced New York, 1986). New York, Dramatists Play Service, 1987.
A Rosen by Any Other Name, adaptation of a novel by Morley Torgov (produced New York, 1986). New York, Dramatists Play Service, 1987.
The Chopin Playoffs, adaptation of stories by Morley Torgov (produced New York, 1986). Included in *An Israel Horovitz Trilogy*, 1987.
North Shore Fish (produced Gloucester, Massachusetts, and New York, 1986). New York, Dramatists Play Service, 1989.
Year of the Duck (produced Portland, Maine, 1986; New York, 1987). New York, Dramatists Play Service, 1988.
An Israel Horovitz Trilogy (includes *Today, I Am a Fountain Pen*; *A Rosen by Any Other Name*; *The Chopin Playoffs*). New York, Nelson Doubleday, 1987.
Faith, Hope, and Charity (three one-acts) with Terrence McNally and Leonard Melfi (produced New York, 1988). New York, Dramatists Play Service, 1989.
Strong-Man's Weak Child (also director: produced Los Angeles, 1990).

Fighting over Beverly (produced Gloucester, Massachusetts, 1993).
My Old Lady (produced Gloucester, Massachusetts, 1996; New York, 1997; London, 1998).
Lebensraum (produced Gloucester, Massachusetts, 1996; New York, 1997; London, 1998).
One Under (produced Gloucester, Massachusetts, 1997).

Screenplays: *Machine Gun McCain* (English adaptation), 1970; *The Strawberry Statement*, 1970; *Believe in Me* (*Speed Is of the Essence*), 1970; *Alfredo*, 1970; *The Sad-Eyed Girls in the Park*, 1971; *Camerian Climbing*, 1971; *Acrobats*, 1972; *Fast Eddie*, 1980; *Fell*, 1982; *Berta*, 1982; *Author! Author!*, 1982-83; *Light Years*, 1985; *A Man in Love*, with Diane Kurys, 1988; *James Dean*; *A Star Is Born*; *Captain Courageous*; *Strong-Man's Weak Child*; *North Shore Fish*; *The Widow's Blind Date*; *Fighting Over Beverly*; *The Taste of Sunshine*.

Radio Plays: *The Chips Are Down*; *Fighting Over Beverly*.

Television Plays: *Play for Trees*, 1969; *VD Blues*, with others, 1972; *Start to Finish*, 1975; *The Making and Breaking of Splinters Braun*, 1976; *Bartleby the Scrivener*, from the story by Melville, 1978; *A Day with Conrad Green*, from a story by Ring Lardner, 1978; *The Deer Park*, from the novel by Norman Mailer, 1979.

Novels

Cappella. New York, Harper, 1973.
Nobody Loves Me. Paris, Minuit, 1975; New York, Braziller, 1976.

*

Manuscript Collections: Lincoln Center Library of the Performing Arts, New York; Sawyer Free Library, Gloucester, Massachusetts.

Critical Studies: *Thirty Plays Hath November* by Walter Kerr, New York, Simon and Schuster, 1969; *Opening Nights* by Martin Gottfried, New York, Putnam, 1970; *The Playmakers* by Stuart W. Little and Arthur Cantor, New York, Dutton, 1970, London, Reinhardt, 1971; in *Études Anglaises* (Paris), Summer 1975; *Israel Horovitz: A Collection of Critical Essays*, edited by Leslie Kane, Westport, Connecticut, Greenwood, 1994.

Theatrical Activities:
Director: **Plays**—Several of his own plays in English and French, and *Chiaroscuro: Morning, Noon and Night*, by Horovitz, Leonard Melfi, and Terrence McNally, Spoleto, Italy, 1968; *Mighty Bad Day*, by Nicole Burdette. **Film**—*Acrobats*, 1972. **Television**—*VD Blues*, 1972.

Actor: **Film**—*The Strawberry Statement*, 1970; *Dead Letters Don't Die*, *Trifecta*; *Subway Stories*; *Corps Plongés*; *The First Seven Years*.

Israel Horovitz comments:

(1988) Much of life has changed for me.

I used to aspire to run 10 kilometers under 30 minutes. Breaking 40 minutes for the same distance is now quite satisfactory.

My family and my work remain as they were to me before: holy.

(1993) Not much has changed. Happy to break 45 minutes for 10 kilometers.

* * *

Since the 1970s Israel Horovitz has produced a large volume of work, leaving audiences with the impression of a writer with broad concerns, varying aesthetic impulses, and an impish overview of the human condition. The Horovitz work wants to reach out to the American community, and, using rudimentary terms, buoyant cadences, and colloquial jargon that changes with the times, it often addresses that community about the perverse innocence of the New World and the blatant, if also diluted, examples of good and evil within it. All of this is revealed in good-humored fashion by an older brother who can speak to that afternoon headache known to us as the "land of the free and the home of the brave." "Morning in America" is not to be recycled, but "afternoon in America" is having its extended, slightly sickening nap. Israel is somewhat inducing it to sleep on and somewhat inducing it to get on its feet, and Horovitz is positioned as a kind of Puckish moralist-voyeur over an uneasy, fitfully napping, sometimes racist Gulliver.

First performed in 1968 at the Astor Place Theatre in New York City, *The Indian Wants the Bronx* presents a luminous title, suggesting what in fact it is not. This Indian is not a Native American demanding the return of ancestral lands that have been renamed the Grand Concourse and Tremont Avenue. Instead, he is a Hindu momentarily trapped in Manhattan by two juvenile hoods while waiting for a bus to take him to his English-speaking son somewhere in the bombed-out vista still known as the Bronx. The Indian, named Gupta, has just landed in the United States and has a working knowledge neither of what passes for English nor of the habits of white slum kids idling between self-induced bouts of trouble. Unfortunately dependent on the kindness of strangers to help him locate the son he is visiting and from whom he has momentarily been separated, Gupta is caught in a luckless encounter. We gather from the moment Horovitz's two louts, Joey and Murph, come careening into view, disturbing the silence of a September night on upper Fifth Avenue with their aggressive rendition of a rock and roll number—the import of which is that "Baby, you don't care"—that Gupta is in for an ugly encounter or at least a touch of misery before he is ever reunited with his son. The louts, before they turn their attention to Gupta, have been trying to make the September night unbearable for a lady they call Pussyface, a social worker whose caseload has included Joey and Murph. Pussyface's apartment apparently faces the aforementioned bus stop, and the lady is being serenaded with snippets and variations from the "Baby, you don't care" cycle. We deduce that she is either out of town, fast asleep, or indifferent to or highly annoyed at the public attention being showered on her. The impromptu concert goes on intermittently as the boys curse, sulk, and play ugly physical games, but in due time they begin to terrorize the Indian. Why do they terrorize him? He is an innocent, an alien, and the play needs tension.

The work's major problem is that it is essentially an anecdote that Horovitz has to loosen into movement. An anecdote is a self-enclosed organism that is perfectly satisfied with itself. It moves nowhere on its own; one has to make something of it. The anecdote may have threads, but, having been unraveled, even threads need to be transformed. In *Indian* there is no plausible reason for the fact that the bus never arrives except that it is necessary for

Horovitz's story. It also is necessary that Gupta speak not a word of English and that he be on his own in a strange city, unable to make contact with his son except through a phone number that he cannot read. Horovitz sets up the conditions whereby Gupta has to be terrorized. But the terrorizing is an arbitrary development, and one has to ask what we learn from it other than the fact that human actions are sometimes arbitrary.

Albee's *Zoo Story* can be viewed as a similarly arbitrary work. That is, the writing of the narrative takes on an arbitrariness, and it pushes the story into another arbitrariness. In the Horovitz play there is even less necessity than in the Albee. People in the world do sometimes, but not always, terrorize one another. One would think that something in Joey and Murph, which might only be understood viscerally, has to give way and take over in order to manifest the terror. In André Gide's *Lafcadio's Adventures* there is an arbitrary murder, but it is a willed arbitrariness; Gide's hero wants not to resist the impulse to arbitrariness. Perhaps Horovitz needed to employ arbitrariness for the sake of theatricality.

Henry Lumper, written some two decades later, begins with necessity. Horovitz creates, sets, and produces the play in Gloucester. It deals with serious concerns of the Gloucester townspeople that are familiar to many: drugs, mass unemployment, deception, alcoholism, violence, community dislocation, and, as in *Indian,* our relationships to those we see as aliens. In the 1970s disciples of Sun Myung Moon, more popularly known as Moonies, moved into the fishing village of Gloucester, creating much tension and bitterness among townspeople who envisioned the cult movement destabilizing the village. As Horovitz tells it, the area was also invaded by condo developers buying up precious waterfront property and drug runners moving in on the fishing industry. Overlaid on this contemporary drama is Shakespeare's *Henry IV,* with the Bolingbrokes and the Percys as principal players and with Prince Hal—here the alcoholic loser Hal Boley—as the principal among principals. Boley cannot find himself. It is post-Vietnam, and he cannot make a commitment and is into drugs, booze, and erotic pleasures. He will, however, eventually redeem himself, tackle the issues, become a responsible Boley, put the town back on its feet, and provide moral clarification for a community under siege.

Horovitz has given us a contemporary morality play, a work that has to do both with economics and with saving the soul of a people. In its best moments, and there are many of them, *Henry Lumper* is a moving, heartfelt work with clarity and believable people. Horovitz uses an open stage and cinematic devices, with quick dissolves between characters, so that a whole layer of subjectivity is beautifully present. One might argue that Shakespeare simply gets in the way of the story, so that one wastes time hunting for parallels. But the work has fine strengths, and here Horovitz has moved far beyond the arbitrariness and unconvincing staginess of *Indian.* It is a play, perhaps too heavily coated with morality, that nevertheless moves as if under its own steam, and that is a significant movement.

—Arthur Sainer

HORSFIELD, Debbie

Nationality: British. **Born:** Manchester, 14 February 1955. **Education:** Eccles Grammar School, Manchester, 1966-73; Newcastle University, B.A. (honours) in English literature 1977. **Career:** Assistant administrator, Gulbenkian Studio Theatre, Newcastle-upon-Tyne, 1978-80; assistant to the artistic director, Royal Shakespeare Company, London, 1980-83; writer-in-residence, Liverpool Playhouse, Liverpool, 1983-84. **Awards:** Thames Television award, 1983. **Agent:** Julia Kreitman, The Agency Ltd, 24 Pottery Lane, Holland Park, London W11 4LZ, England.

PUBLICATIONS

Plays

Out on the Floor (produced London, 1981).
Away from It All (produced London, 1982).
The Next Four Years, Parts 1-2 (produced Liverpool, 1983).
All You Deserve (produced London, 1983).
Red Devils (produced Liverpool, 1983; London, 1984; New York, 1989). Included in *Red Devils Trilogy*, 1986.
True Dare Kiss (produced Liverpool, 1983; London, 1985). Included in *Red Devils Trilogy*, 1986.
Command or Promise (produced Liverpool, 1983; London, 1985). Included in *Red Devils Trilogy*, 1986.
Touch and Go (produced London, 1984).
Revelations (produced Chichester, Sussex, 1985).
Red Devils Trilogy. London, Methuen, 1986.
Royal Borough (produced London, 1987).
In Touch (produced Coventry, 1988).
Making Out (televised 1989). London, Transworld, 1989.

Radio Play: *Arrangements*, 1981.

Television Plays: *Face Value*, in *Crown Court* series, 1982; *Out on the Floor*, 1983; *Making Out* 3 series, 1989-91; *The Riff-Raff Element,* 2 series, 1993-94; *Born to Run* series, 1997; *Sex and Chips* series, 1998.

* * *

Since the 1980s Debbie Horsfield has led the way in creating strong female characters for the stage and for television. She is among the most successful of Britain's female playwrights, primarily because of the popularity of her television drama writing. Her original idea for the television program *Making Out* was to focus on working-class women's issues. Horsfield sets the series in a factory. Thus, rather than putting one woman at the center of a largely male world, she created a community of women who live and work with men yet who are not primarily identified through their relationships (social or sexual) with those men. *Making Out* reached a wide audience eager to see reflections of real women on television. Significantly, the series is not only written by a woman but has tended to be directed and produced by women as well.

The same focus on strong, realistic women is what fuels Horsfield's writing for the theater. Her best-known theater work is *The Red Devil's Trilogy* (published by Methuen in 1986). All three plays in the trilogy focus on the same four characters: Alice, Nita, Phil, and Beth. These four young women grow up together and develop their relationships, careers, hopes, and fears as they share their experiences and their love of football (Manchester United, to be precise). Of course, Manchester United is not only the name of a football team but is also an accurate phrase to describe the relationship between the four central female characters: all are from Manchester; their friendship, which stems from common roots and shared experiences, unites them.

In this trilogy of comic plays, the same idea that gives energy to *Making Out* likewise fuels the power of the theater performance: women working and playing together; women who share non-stereotypically "feminine" interests; women who like each other and enjoy each other's company; and women who know how to make each other laugh, just as Horsfield clearly knows how to make her audiences laugh. The working-class setting invites men as well as women into the worlds of the plays, as working-class situations are so rarely well portrayed in the theater.

In the first play, *Red Devils* (first published in 1984), the four central characters are school girls on their way to the 1979 Cup Final at Wembley Stadium. The action takes place in Manchester before the game, in London during the game, and at a motorway service station between the two locations after the game. The cast of characters is laid out on the page of the published version in the shape of a football formation, with Horsfield's name as author in the goal box. This playful presentation of the "facts" of the performance are in keeping with the mood of the play. *Red Devils,* like much of Horsfield's work (including several of her earlier plays), emphasizes female friendship and the enjoyment that women, like men, find in each other's company. Petty differences are presented in a humorous rather than a "catty" way.

The same positive spirit enlivens the second two plays in the trilogy: *True Dare Kiss* and *Command or Promise,* both staged in London's Cottesloe Theatre (The Royal National Theatre) in 1985. In both these plays the four characters are adults. They have remained friends, sharing different aspects of their adult lives and their continued love of football. The plays have been criticized for being "too much like soap opera": a criticism that says as much about our cultural expectations as it does about the plays. It is true that the depiction of the young women's lives in these later plays is channeled through multiple story lines that are familiar from televised soap operas and serials. Yet to identify the form of the plays as a fault is misleading—they are episodic because they deal with the conflicting and overlapping stories of four different women's lives. Relationships are represented between women and men, women and work, women and higher education, and women and cultural trends (punk culture and football). Yet the uniting thread of the four stories in the three plays of *The Red Devils Trilogy* is the relationship between the four women. That focus on women's friendship is still uncommon on the stage. Horsfield has begun to make it more acceptable and has thereby opened the way for other playwrights to experiment with a wide range of common but little-represented experiences in contemporary theater.

—Lizbeth Goodman

HOWARTH, Donald

Nationality: British. **Born:** London, 5 November 1931. **Education:** Grange High School for Boys, Bradford; Esme Church Northern Children's Theatre School, 1948-51. **Career:** Stage manager and actor in various repertory companies, 1951-56. Literary manager, Royal Court Theatre, London, 1975-76. **Awards:** Encyclopaedia Britannica award, 1961; George Devine award, 1971. **Agent:** Casarotto Ramsay Ltd., National House, 60-66 Wardour Street, London W1V 3HP, England.

Publications

Plays

Lady on the Barometer (also co-director: produced London, 1958; as *Sugar in the Morning*, produced London, 1959).
All Good Children (produced Bromley, Kent, 1960; also director: produced London, 1964). London, French, 1965.
Secret of Skiz, adaptation of a play by Zapolska (produced Bromley, Kent, 1962).
A Lily in Little India (televised 1962; also director: produced London, 1965). London, French, 1966.
Ogodiveleftthegason (also director: produced London, 1967).
School Play, in *Playbill One*, edited by Alan Durband. London, Hutchinson, 1969.
Three Months Gone (produced London, 1970). London, French, 1970.
Othello Sleges Blankes, adaptation of the play by Shakespeare (also director: produced Cape Town, 1972).
Scarborough (also director: produced Cape Town, 1972).
The Greatest Fairy Story Ever Told, adaptation of a play by Kathleen Housell-Roberts (also director: produced New York, 1973).
Meanwhile, Backstage in the Old Front Room (produced Leeds, 1975).
Ibchek (also director: produced Grahamstown, South Africa, 1979).
Adventures of a Black Girl, adaptation of the novel *Adventures of a Black Girl in Her Search for God* by Shaw (also director: produced Cape Town, 1980).

Screenplay: *Gates to Paradise*, 1968.

Television Plays: *A Lily in Little India*, 1962; *Stanley*, 1972; *A Taste of Tony*, 1992-93.

*

Critical Study: Introduction by Michael Billington to *New English Dramatists 9*, London, Penguin, 1966.

Theatrical Activities:
Director: **Plays**—Several of his own plays, and *This Property Is Condemned* by Tennessee Williams, London, 1960; *Miniatures* by David Cregan, London, 1965; *Play Mas* by Mustapha Matura, London, 1974; *Mama, Is Terry Home for Good?* by James Edward Shannon, Johannesburg, 1974; *Parcel Post* by Yemi Ajibade, London, 1976; *Rum an' Coca Cola* by Mustapha Matura, London, 1976, New York, 1977; *Waiting for Godot* by Beckett, London, Cape Town, and New York, 1981.

Actor: **Plays**—Roles in reportory, 1951-56; Salvation Army Captain in *Progress to the Park* by Alun Owen, London, 1959.

Donald Howarth comments:
Art is what you don't do. Less is more.

* * *

One of the pleasures of reading through Donald Howarth's earlier plays in sequence—*Sugar in the Morning*, *All Good Children*, *A Lily in Little India*, *Ogodiveleftthegason*, and *Three Months Gone*—is seeing a playwright finding his way to an individual and successful compromise between naturalism and freewheeling expressionism by dint of returning again and again to the same themes and the same characters but never to the same style. He has worked hard, and at its worst his writing is laborious, but he has been capable from the beginning of sustaining passages of comedy that deftly combine truthfulness with elegant and compelling theatrical rhetoric. Finally, in *Three Months Gone* he achieved a sureness of touch that enabled him to tie fantasy material down to solid surfaces and to draw dividends from his earlier stylistic experiments. *Ogodiveleftthegason* is the play in which he takes the most expressionistic shortcuts and that spans the greatest amount of human experience. It is his least successful play, however, not because it is the least comic or the least realistic but because it is the most shapeless and the least able to gain an audience's sympathy for the characters or to sustain its interest in them—partly because their identity keeps changing. *Three Months Gone*, while no less remote from the slow development of the conventional naturalistic three-act play, has a story line strong enough to keep the colorful balloons of fantasy that both main characters fly tethered securely to a solid matter-of-factness.

Mrs. Broadbent, the sexually frustrated landlady in *Sugar in the Morning*, and Grannie Silk, her obstinately vulgar, cheerful, warmhearted, interfering mother, are both rough prototypes of Mrs. Hanker in *A Lily in Little India* and *Three Months Gone*. Mrs. Hanker combines the main characteristics of both of them without having Mrs. Broadbent's pretensions to gentility or her ineptness at finding food for her sexual appetites. A clear picture of suburban life emerges in *Sugar in the Morning*, but much of the basic energy is spent on drawing it. Decisions about which lodgers to take, clipping the privet hedge, arguments about noisy radios and washing hung up outside windows, rent collecting, drinking cups of tea in the landlady's room, hurrying for the 7:40 bus, finding a shilling for the gas meter, discussing whether to have a baby—in using episodes like these as its currency, the play makes them all seem equally important. None of the characters in *Sugar in the Morning* reappears in *All Good Children*, but Rev. Jacob Bowers and his daughter and son, Anna and Maurice, are in both *All Good Children* and *A Lily in Little India*, which introduces Mrs. Hanker and her son Alvin, who are to reappear in *Three Months Gone* together with Anna and Maurice. The whole of the action of *All Good Children* is set in a converted farmhouse in South Yorkshire, but the 60-year-old minister is about to retire and to move his family to the suburb where we find them in the two subsequent plays. The new theme introduced in *All Good Children*, which will recur persistently in the later work, is the relationship between Protestant morality and sexual deprivation. Jacob Bowers, now a devout antisensualist, was very different when younger, and he became a minister only because of guilt feelings after his affair with a minister's daughter had caused the old man's death. Unlike his younger brother, Clifford, who has been more of a conformist, Maurice has reacted violently against his puritanical upbringing, and he becomes a sailor. His letters, with their juicy descriptions of local brothels, have been Anna's main lifeline, and the love she feels for Maurice verges on the incestuous. After her mother's death, caused by an onstage fall down a staircase, she rejects her chance of breaking out of the family cage, however, and condemns herself, after 20 years of imprisonment, to staying with her father.

The plot of *All Good Children* is developed mostly through speeches that rake over the past. *A Lily in Little India* is a less Ibsenesque play, and physical action bulks larger in it. The action, like the stage, is divided between the houses of the Bowerses and the Hankers. We see Anna waiting on the old father who has spoiled her life by his narrowness and writing letters to the brother through whom she is still vicariously living; in the other house a selfishly sensual landlady is trapping a reluctant postman into an affair regardless of the harm done to her sensitive son, who finds happiness only in growing a lily and in his encounters with Anna. When the mother, poised on a ladder outside his bedroom window, threatens to destroy his beloved lily, he throws water in her face, causing her to fall backward, and moves into Anna's house when his mother goes to the hospital. The characters win considerable sympathy and interest, and there are some very funny and touching moments, but the comedy and the seriousness do not quite balance or reinforce each other as one comes to feel they should. Although the dialogue has been praised by Michael Billington as "a just sufficiently heightened version of ordinary speech," it sinks sometimes into self-consciousness and just occasionally into sentimentality.

But the dialogue of *Three Months Gone* is virtually unflawed. The rapid shifts in and out of Anna's and, later, Alvin's fantasies give Howarth the opportunity to penetrate funnily but compassionately their private views of themselves, each other, and the two other main characters, Maurice and Mrs. Hanker, who are sexually so much more robust. There is a hilarious scene in which Mrs. Hanker, bullying Alvin to find the pluck to make Anna marry him, makes him propose to her while she pretends to be Anna, and this is followed by a sequence in which Maurice makes a pass at him under guise of teaching him how to make a woman submit. The audience's uncertainty about which sequence represents fantasy and which reality is often an advantage.

The later plays are different and less successful. *The Greatest Fairy Story Ever Told* is a skittish pantomime full of arch chinoiserie. There are characters called Much Too Yin and Too Much Yang and jokes about Pon-Ting's fabric hall and the Royal Courtyard. *Meanwhile, Backstage in the Old Front Room* is highly serious, ambitiously moving further away from naturalism than any of Howarth's earlier works. It leans on both Beckett and Genet, with *Endgame* being feminized in the relationship between the dominating old woman who never leaves her wheelchair and the blind younger women, possibly her daughter, who lives with her. The power games and the extremism in making the characters speak out their thoughts are reminiscent of Genet's *The Maids*. The influence is domesticated into a family setting but not altogether digested.

—Ronald Hayman

HOWE, Tina

Nationality: American. **Born:** New York City, 21 November 1937. **Education:** Sarah Lawrence College, Bronxville, New York, B.A. 1959; Chicago Teachers College, 1963-64; Columbia University. **Family:** Married Norman Levy in 1961; one son and one daughter. **Career:** Adjunct professor, New York University, 1983—;

visiting professor, Hunter College, City University of New York, 1990—. **Awards:** Rosamond Gilder award, 1983; Rockefeller grant, 1983; Obie award, 1983; Outer Critics Circle award, 1983, 1984; John Gassner award, 1984; National Endowment for the Arts grant, 1984; Guggenheim fellowship, 1990; American Academy of Arts and Letters award in literature, 1993. Honorary degree: Bowdoin College, Brunswick, Maine, 1988. **Agent:** Flora Roberts Inc., 157 West 57th Street, New York, New York 10019, U.S.A.

Publications

Plays

Closing Time (produced Bronxville, New York, 1959).
The Nest (produced Provincetown, Massachusetts, 1969; New York, 1970).
Museum (produced Los Angeles, 1976; New York, 1977). New York, French, 1979.
Birth and After Birth, in *The New Women's Theatre*, edited by Honor Moore. New York, Random House, 1977.
The Art of Dining (produced Washington, D.C., and New York, 1979). New York, French, 1980.
Appearances (produced New York, 1982).
Painting Churches (produced New York, 1983; Southampton, 1991; London, 1992). New York, French, 1984.
Three Plays (includes *Museum*, *The Art of Dining*, *Painting Churches*). New York, Avon, 1984.
Coastal Disturbances (produced New York, 1986). New York, French, 1987.
Approaching Zanzibar (produced New York, 1989). New York, Theatre Communications Group, and London, French, 1989.
Coastal Disturbances: Four Plays (includes *Painting Churches*, *The Art of Dining*, *Museum*). New York, Theatre Communications Group, 1989.
Teeth. Published in *Antaeus* (New York), no.66, Spring 1991.
Swimming (produced New York, 1991).
One Shoe Off. New York, Samuel French, 1993.
Approaching Zanzibar and Other Plays (includes *Approaching Zanzibar*; *Birth and After Birth*; *One Shoe Off*). New York, Theatre Communications Group, 1995.
Pride's Crossing. New York, Theatre Communications Group, 1998.

*

Critical Studies: *Creating Theater: The Professionals' Approach to New Plays* by Lee Alan Morrow and Frank Pike, New York, Vintage, 1986; *Interviews with Contemporary Women Playwrights* edited by Kathleen Betsko and Rachel Koenig, New York, Beech Tree Books, 1987; "The Art of Tina Howe" by Judith E. Barlow, in *Feminine Focus: The New Women Playwrights*, edited by Enoch Brater, Oxford, Oxford University Press, 1989; *A Search for Postmodern Theater: Interviews with Contemporary Playwrights* by John L. DiGaetani, New York, Greenwood Press, 1991; "Tina Howe and Feminine Discourse" by Kenneth E. Johnston, in *American Drama* (Cincinnati, Ohio), Spring 1992, pp. 15-25; "Tina Howe's Secret Surrealism: Walking a Tightrope" by Rosette C. Lamont, in *Modern Drama* (Downsview, Ontario), 1993, pp. 27-37; "Tina Howe" by Judith E. Barlow, in *Speaking on Stage: Interviews with Contemporary American Playwrights*, edited by Philip C. Kolin and Colby H. Kullman, Tuscaloosa, University of Alabama Press, 1996.

* * *

Tina Howe is a marvelously perceptive observer of contemporary mores, and much of the pleasure one receives from her plays comes from her comic skewering of pretentious art critics, couples moaning orgasmically over the yuppie menu of their dreams, costume designers with nothing to wear, and thoroughly enlightened parents wholly unable to cope with their monstrous four-year-old. Her best works, however, probe beneath the surface to reveal the inextricable mixture of the humorous and horrific that has always defined human existence. In Howe's theatrical world, parlor games raise metaphysical questions, and playfulness teeters on the edge of pathos.

Although it already hints of better things to come, *The Nest* is the least satisfying of Howe's full-length plays. The influence of Ionesco and Beckett, whose work she admires, is evident here in the use of repetition as well as in the heavy reliance on verbal and physical farce. Still, this comedy about a trio of female roommates lacks the satirical and emotional force of her next play, *Birth and After Birth*. "Family life has been over-romanticized; the savagery has not been seen enough in the theatre and in movies," Howe once complained. She attempts to fill this gap with *Birth and After Birth*, a sometimes hilarious, often frightening portrait of the Apples. As their name implies, the Apples, including a four-year-old son played by an adult actor, are a parody of the all-American television family, continually declaring how happy they are and continually belying this claim. What keeps *Birth* from being simply another burlesque of Ozzie and Harriet is not only Howe's accurate portrait of the physical and emotional brutality inherent in family life but also her disturbingly negative exploration of why women choose to have—or not to have—children. Despite the often broad slapstick, *Birth* is one of Howe's darkest comedies, which may explain why it had to wait more than two decades for its first professional productions.

Museum is less a plotted play than a wonderful series of comic turns as visitors—singly and in groups—wander through an exhibit entitled "The Broken Silence." As Howe has acknowledged in interviews, all of her plays are about art, and *Museum* examines the complex interrelationships among creator, creation, and viewers. On one level *Museum* reveals what fools art makes of us (witness the young woman painstakingly copying an all-white canvas). On another level, however, it shows that artworks cannot fully exist except in the presence of an audience, foolish or not. In one of the comically horrific monologues that seem to be an essential part of the Howe landscape, a museumgoer recounts a foraging expedition she took with the artist Agnes Vaag. Vaag may well be Howe's archetypal artist, at once a mysterious genius who makes "menacing constructions" out of animal carcasses and a ludicrous figure who lugs suitcases through state parks.

Another loosely knit comedy, *The Art of Dining* combines Howe's obsession with food, first manifest in *The Nest* and carried through *One Shoe Off*, and her concern with art and its consumption. Because the fragility of art is a repeated motif throughout Howe's canon, in a sense food is for her the ultimate artistic medium: it must be destroyed to be appreciated. Set in a restaurant, *Dining* contains one of Howe's most brilliant creations, Elizabeth Barrow Colt, a wonderfully comic and pathetic figure who embodies every cliché about writers. Comfortable only in the world of the imagination, she is a genius with a pen but a total failure with a soupspoon. In *Dining*'s spectacular conclusion, with all of the restaurant's guests gathered around a flaming platter of crepes tended by the female chef, Howe uses Elizabeth to point out the connection between art and ritual as well as the redemptive power of artistic creation, a recurrent theme in her work.

Howe's biggest critical success is *Painting Churches,* in some ways her most conventional play as well as one of her most lyrical. Returning to the favorite subject of the American playwright—the nuclear family—Howe gives us a comedy about the necessity of acceptance: a daughter accepting the inevitable decline of her aging parents, and parents accepting their daughter as a capable adult and artist. Howe's quirky sense of humor and her distinctive verbal and visual idiom mark the work as uniquely her own, however familiar her starting point. Although Howe denies that she is an autobiographical writer, there is obviously a kinship between the playwright and Mags Church, the young artist who learns that the picture she is painting of her parents is a self-portrait as well. In a moving final tour-de-force that erases the line between Mags's painting and Howe's play, the stripped-bare stage becomes the portrait, the aging characters rescued from decline for the space of a magical moment.

Howe favors unusual settings, and the beach locale of *Coastal Disturbances* is as much metaphor as place. Like human beings and their relationships, the sand and ocean remain essentially the same over millennia yet change from moment to moment. The main character is a young woman photographer; appropriately, the play is divided into numerous short scenes that rely heavily on visual effects, resembling, in other words, a sequence of snapshots. Although the central situation, a love triangle, is not Howe's most original, her verbal and especially her visual wit are amply in evidence.

In the late 1980s and the 1990s Howe continued to write a new work roughly every three years. *Approaching Zanzibar* is a "road play" that follows a family of four on a cross-country trip to visit a dying relative, an elderly artist reminiscent of Georgia O'Keeffe. The Blossoms' journey is both physical and metaphysical as they engage in hilarious—and often cruel—travel games while wrestling with anxieties about change, loss, and death. Not only is this the first of Howe's plays to exploit multiple settings, but its relatively large cast represents a deliberate attempt on the playwright's part to include a wider range of characters in terms of class and ethnicity as well as age. Much smaller in scale although not in scope is the poignant *One Shoe Off,* which returns to a domestic setting. But whereas the stately home in *Painting Churches* was being dismantled by its departing owners, Leonard and Dinah's Greek Revival farmhouse in *Shoe* is dismantling itself: full-size trees grow in the living room, mushrooms and broccoli sprout in the closets, while arugula unfurls on the stairs. In the midst of this threatening fecundity, five adults try to come to terms with career disappointments and personal betrayals. Literature and language are among the weapons the characters use in their attempts to bring order to the chaos, desperately reciting everything from nursery rhymes to excerpts from *Henry V*. Despite being among Howe's most complex and rich works, both *Approaching Zanzibar* and *One Shoe Off* received mixed reviews and had relatively short runs in New York.

Pride's Crossing, Howe's latest play, is a journey through time rather than space as 7 actors play 20 roles of varying ages, genders, and ethnicities. Actress Cherry Jones won critical raves as Mabel Tidings Bigelow, a 90-year-old former Channel swimmer who relives her attempts to escape the narrow boundaries set by her upper-class New England family. The Fourth of July croquet match that ends the play is an ironic tribute to Mabel's declaration of independence from gender and class rules in the "game" of her life, even if the declaration is inevitably limited.

Howe acknowledges her debt to absurdist writers, a debt more apparent in her earlier than in her later works, although her fondness for their techniques—particularly manic farce and extravagant wordplay—remains. Like many American playwrights, Howe does not entirely share the nihilistic vision of her European absurdist counterparts, and although salvation is transitory and more likely to be aesthetic than religious or social, there are moments of redemption in most of her plays. As the numerous references to Shakespeare and Chekhov in *One Shoe Off* suggest, her later works are also tempered by more traditional theatrical influences, leading to a greater emotional depth in her drama. At the same time her perspective has grown more clearly feminist as she has continued to weave her plays around women artists and other female iconoclasts. In a 1998 address entitled "Women's Work: White Gloves or Bare Hands," Howe said that she had come to realize that "my gender defines my work and its reception." Her work over the past three decades has also been defined by a splendidly anarchic sense of humor, the courage to take theatrical risks, a growing interest in the social construction of roles onstage and offstage, and a rare sensitivity to the terrifyingly comic dimensions of the human condition.

—Judith E. Barlow

HUGHES, Dusty

Nationality: British. **Born:** Boston, Lincolnshire, 16 September 1947. **Education:** Queen Elizabeth Grammar School, Wakefield, Yorkshire, 1957-65; Trinity Hall, Cambridge, 1965-68, M.A. (honours) in English. **Family:** Has one daughter. **Career:** Assistant director, Birmingham Repertory Theatre, 1970-72; theatre editor, *Time Out*, London, 1973-76; artistic director, Bush Theatre, London, 1976-79; script editor, *Play for Today* series, BBC Television, 1982-84. Member, Arts Council Drama panel, 1975-80. **Awards:** London Theatre Critics award, 1980; Edinburgh Festival award, 1981.

Publications

Plays

Grrr (produced Edinburgh, 1968).

Commitments (produced London, 1980). With *Futurists*, London, Faber, 1986.

Heaven and Hell (produced Edinburgh and London, 1981).

Molière; or, The Union of Hypocrites, adaptation of a play by Mikhail Bulgakov (produced Stratford-on-Avon, 1982; London, 1983). London, Methuen, 1983.

From Cobbett's Urban Rides, in *Breach of the Peace* (produced London, 1982).

Bad Language (produced London, 1983).

Philistines, adaptation of a play by Maxim Gorky (produced Stratford-on-Avon, 1985; London, 1986). Oxford, Amber Lane Press, 1985; New York, Applause, 1986.
Futurists (produced London, 1986). With *Commitments*, London, Faber, 1986.
Jenkin's Ear (produced London, 1987). London, Faber, 1987.
Metropolis, music by Joe Brooks, adaptation of the Fritz Lang film (produced London, 1989).
A Slip of the Tongue (produced Chicago and London, 1992).

Screenplays: *Cries from the South*, 1986; *In Hiding*, 1987; *Tom*, 1991; *Crimes of Passion*, 1992.

Television Play: *The Secret Agent*, adaptation of the novel by Joseph Conrad, 1992.

*

Theatrical Activities:
Director: **Plays**—Bush Theatre, London: *The Soul of the White Ant* by Snoo Wilson, 1976; *Blood Sports* by David Edgar, 1976; *Vampire* by Snoo Wilson, 1977; *Happy Birthday, Wanda June* by Kurt Vonnegut, Jr., 1977; *In at the Death* by Snoo Wilson and others, 1978; *A Greenish Man* by Snoo Wilson, 1978; *Wednesday* by Julia Kearsley, 1978.

* * *

Dusty Hughes emerged in the 1980s with several dramatic works to his credit. An early experience with the left wing did not transform him into a "good Bolshevik," and this has shaped the subject and concerns of his produced plays. The plays pursue the theme of disenchantment with Marxist and socialist ideals that have turned sour or repressive, as well as with middle-class aspirations that disclose emptiness and produce social and personal inertia.

Examples are Hughes's three best works: *Commitments*, *Futurists*, and the adaptation *Molière; or, The Union of Hypocrites*. *Commitments* introduces a small group of left-wing activists in 1973 who are using as their live-in headquarters the London flat of a tolerant bourgeois dilettant reluctant to join their cause. Forming a focal and substantially dimensionalized triumvirate are the charming but undirected benefactor, an actress strongly committed to the party, and her working-class actor-lover. Fellow workers drop in as the group discusses politics and strategies and performs menial party tasks, while outside the 1974 Labour government comes to power owing little to the party's efforts or workers. Malaise affects the group's relationships. The flat owner, now motivated to become politically active, ends up returning to his wastrel ways, persuaded that the party is "authoritarian and not a little unrealistic." The politically committed actress loses her lover, who returns to his wife. The drama offers a trenchant picture of disillusioned leftists whose cause and commitments have seemed wasted efforts.

In *Futurists* Hughes goes to 1921 postrevolutionary Petrograd, where great and mediocre artists, journalists, political hacks, striking sailors, and Bolshevik informers mingle in a sweaty nightclub. The drama centers on the futurist poets—the figures of Mandelstam, Mayakovsky, Anna Akhmatova, and others are vividly re-created—who are drawn together by a fervent revolutionary belief that they have something to say. They are initially unaware that their individualistic, unconventional thought and expression will eventually doom them. They proclaim their art and reveal their loss of equilibrium in the excitement of revolutionary confusion, while beyond the nightclub the revolution has gone wrong. The poets have relied for protection on their hero Gorky, friend of Lenin, who presides over them like a one-man arts council but finds that he cannot save them from the firing squads or from being otherwise silenced. In the new society the artist is an endangered species; the mediocre survive, and the talented grow silent or die. Central to the action, the tubercular Gorky becomes a tragic figure. As he becomes increasingly powerless to help his friends and is even warned by Lenin to leave the country, he loses his self-assured belief that "people don't kill poets." Hughes fills his characters and their world with vibrant life and a dire meaning, which was tellingly visualized in the 1986 London production as the colorfully grotesque futurist trappings of the artists' cabaret were progressively stripped away to reveal the ominous black and red banners of Stalin. Yet with Akhmatova's final recitation of a forbidden poem, Hughes reminds us that poetry outlasts revolutions.

That the playwright was drawn to adapt Mikhail Bulgakov's *Molière* is understandable. The play focuses on Molière's relationship to Louis XIV as a sardonic paradigm of the Russian Bulgakov's position as a writer under Stalin, who in 1936 banned the play after seven performances. In his portrayal of a freethinking Molière incurring the wrath of the church in mounting *Tartuffe* and suffering its banishment and his own fall from grace, Hughes demonstrates how the artist must demean himself before tyrannical and faction-influenced authority. Rejecting his long-time mistress Madeleine for a disastrous marriage with her supposed younger sister, Molière is informed upon by a dismissed actor in his company. This allows the religious cabal unscrupulously to engineer Molière's fall from favor by extracting Madeleine's confession that his wife is actually their mutual daughter, thus forcing the King's disapproval and his capitulation to their condemnation of the artist. The lively portrait of Molière, who switches from the impetuous actor-manager-writer backstage to a groveling sycophant when in the presence of his sovereign, is both thematically lucid and dramatically powerful, if perhaps historically exaggerated, as is the use of the unproved incest rumor. Molière underestimates the power of church and state, with its near omnipotent king and informer-ridden society resembling Stalinist Russia. The play is effective as theater and as political statement.

Several further works also are underscored by sociopolitical themes. Hughes's wrote an uninspired libretto for a musical adaptation of Fritz Lang's 1927 film *Metropolis* that presents a futuristic vision of a city where workers toil in subterranean factories under the dictatorship of an aboveground capitalist elite. A workers' revolt blows up the city, paving the path for a less harsh future in which the power structure may or may not be significantly changed for the better. Although the play was not a critical success, its 1989 London production was visually spectacular. In *A Slip of the Tongue* the question is whether freedom obligates a sense of responsibility to the political world or gives license to indulge hedonistic impulses. The theme is embodied in the actions of a noted dissident and womanizing writer who leaves the long harassment of a unspecified eastern European country after the Berlin Wall crumbles to become a globe-trotting lecturer rather than a needed helper in framing a new government. This imperfect play drew popular attention in a 1992 Chicago world premiere with John Malkovitch as the antihero protagonist. *Jenkin's Ear* focuses on a disillusioned ex-foreign correspondent who pursues a missing female friend in a Central American country like Honduras. It explores the moral issue of whether getting a story is worth people's lives. The inertness of middle-class values, which rapidly infect the generations, underlines *Bad Language*, a wryly comic survey of Cambridge undergraduates touched by the malady of sameness. *Philistines* is an adaptation of Gorky's flawed yet compelling first play, in which Hughes incisively presents a blackly comic portrait of a turn-of-the-century petit bourgeois provincial family in Russia unable to change their ineffectual lives, thus foreshadowing national upheaval.

Hughes has earned recognition as a playwright committed to creating dramas of substance that thoughtfully examine and offer parallels to the sociopolitical tapestry of his time.

—Christian H. Moe

HUTCHINSON, Ron

Nationality: British. **Born:** Near Lisburn, County Antrim, Northern Ireland; brought up in Coventry, Warwickshire. **Education:** Schools in Coventry. **Career:** Worked at various jobs, including fish gutter, carpet salesman, scene shifter, and bookseller, all Coventry; clerk, Ministry of Defence and Ministry of Labour, Coventry; social worker and claims investigator, Department of Health and Social Security, Coventry, 5 years. Resident writer, Royal Shakespeare Company, London, 1978-79. Moved to Los Angeles in 1988. **Awards:** George Devine award, 1978; John Whiting award, 1984; Emmy award, 1989; Ace award, 1989. **Agents:** Judy Daish Associates, 83 Eastbourne Mews, London W2 6LQ, England; and Merrily Kane, The Artists Agency, 10000 Santa Monica Boulevard, #305, Los Angeles, California 90067, U.S.A.

Publications

Plays

Says I, Says He (produced Sheffield, 1977; London, 1978; New York, 1979). Part 1 published in *Plays and Players* (London), March and April 1978; complete play published Newark, Delaware, Proscenium Press, 1980.
Eejits (produced London, 1978).
Jews/Arabs (produced London, 1978).
Anchorman (produced London, 1979).
Christmas of a Nobody (produced 1979).
The Irish Play (produced London, 1980).
Into Europe (produced London, 1981).
Risky City (broadcast 1981; produced Coventry, 1981).
The Dillen, adaptation of a work by Angela Hewins (produced Stratford-on-Avon, 1983).
Rat in the Skull (produced London, 1984; New York, 1985). London, Methuen, 1984.
Mary, After the Queen, with Angela Hewins (produced Stratford-on-Avon, 1985).
Curse of the Baskervilles, from a story by Arthur Conan Doyle (produced Plymouth, 1987).
Babbit: A Marriage, adaptation of a novel by Sinclair Lewis (produced Los Angeles, 1987).
Pygmies in the Ruins (produced Belfast, 1991; London, 1992).

Radio Plays: *Roaring Boys*, 1977; *Murphy Unchained*, 1978; *There Must Be a Door*, 1979; *Motorcade*, 1980; *Risky City*, 1981; *Troupers*, 1988; *Larkin*, 1988.

Television Plays: *Twelve Off the Belt*, 1977; *Deasy Desperate*, 1979; *The Last Window Cleaner*, 1979; *The Out of Town Boys*, 1979; *Deasy*, 1979; *The Winkler*, 1979; *Bull Week*, 1980; *Bird of Prey* series, 1982 and 1984; *Connie* series, 1985; *The Marksman*, from the novel by Hugh C. Rae (*Unnatural Causes* series), 1987; *The Murderers Among Us: The Simon Wiesenthal Story*, 1988; *Dead Man Walking*, 1988; *Red King, White Knight*, 1990; *The Josephine Baker Story*, 1990; *Prisoners of Honor*, 1991; *Blue Ice*, 1992.

Novel

Connie (novelization of television series). London, Severn House, 1985.

*

Critical Study: "The Bite of Exiled Love: Abjective Protagonists in Some Contemporary Anglo-Irish Dramas" by David Ian Rabey, in *Essays in Theatre* (Guelph, Ontario), November 1994, pp. 29-43.

* * *

The value of Ron Hutchinson's drama derives largely from its consistent concentration on the Irish experience outside Ireland, an experience that serves in his plays to crystallize native Irish problems. The focus is only incidentally social in character. *Risky City* offers a forceful account, in the form of deathbed flashbacks, of the wasting of a Coventry-Irish youth by his inner-city environment, but his experience is not presented as a specifically Irish one. More characteristic is Hutchinson's first stage play, *Says I, Says He,* in which the "Old Firm" of two picaresque Ulster navvies, the "roaring boy" Hannafin and the "clean-shave" Phelan, leave their terrorist siblings and the beautiful dancer for whose hand they are rivals to conquer London. Financial success for Phelan, which is gained, ironically, not without obscure threats of Ulster-style violence, attracts the attention of the terrorists but turns out to be illusory, a matter of the "gab." Reunited, the two plan to leave for England again but are gunned down.

With its musical numbers—some of them uproariously obscene, all of them broadly ironic—*Says I, Says He* resembles a navvies' version of Stewart Parker's *Catchpenny Twist,* another Irish play in which the aspiring heroes ultimately fail to escape political violence. Whereas Parker has musicians, Hutchinson, as his title suggests, has talkers, but they are no less performers. The play consists of a series of comic sketches-episodes in which the humor is not often a matter of inflection and that are crowned by Phelan's final fibbing performance—"You took *me* in. With *your* act." In the play Hutchinson is content, however, to revel in his characters' gift of the gab rather than to reflect upon it. The comedy is not of the serious kind.

Eejits also focuses on performers. But here the four violently argumentative members of a London-based *ceilidh* band are not under threat from terrorists; rather, they carry their nationalist factionalism around with them. The same predicament receives thorough and hilarious treatment, again in connection with a performance, in *The Irish Play*. In a broken-down Midlands Irish club, the embattled President O'Higgins, striving to retain his control and dignity in the face of the machinations of the opposing Roche faction, endorses the presentation of a nationalistic historical play (agitprop Ferguson) as part of his plan to endow the bibulous membership with a "historical perspective." As to history, he discovers that "it's all around us, that's the trouble," when, in debate, committee, and finally rehearsal, the ancient alignments of civil war emerge: "Constitutionals versus Hill-men"; Collins versus De Valera; Kerry versus Wexford. In a comic metaphor of internecine self-destruction, the building is jointly wrecked by the warring factions, leaving only the bewildered step dancer who "plays recorder and dances in the rubble."

The playwright Ruari in *The Irish Play* declares that he is "trying to understand my country . . . my countrymen . . . myself." Hutchinson himself has said of his most successful and best play, *Rat in the Skull,* "I wanted to write this play to sort out my personal reactions to what is going on in Ireland. . . . You find out who you are in the process." This certainly feels like a work energized by a personal imperative. For the first time Hutchinson's abrasively comic dialogue and his preoccupation with performance are concentrated into a sustained scrutiny of the self-awareness and self-understanding catalyzed within an Irishman by his presence in England.

Rather than a plot, *Rat in the Skull* presents a situation and poses a question. The framework is not naturalistic. Under a screen that shows clinical photographs of Michael Patrick De Valera Demon Bomber Roche after his clinical beating by Detective-Inspector Nelson of the Royal Ulster Constabulary in Paddington Green police station, there are played out the interrogation of Roche by Nelson, which led up to the beating, and the consequent interviews by the Irish "specialist," Superintendent Harris of Nelson, and of the young policeman detailed to be present at the interrogation. The case had been "stitched up," and Nelson had come to London only because of the possibility of the prisoner's turning informer. Why then the very deliberative act of violence? The weary Harris reaches for extenuating personal circumstances—an unfaithful wife and a recently dead father—persuading Nelson to accept an "unfit discharge," but neither he nor the baffled, indifferent Constable Naylor can conceive of the complex relation between history and personal identity that renders these Irishmen intimate in conflict—to the exclusion of the Englishman—and that alone points to the explanation. Nelson's fierce parodies of sectarian rhetoric and his sudden changes of tone and address turn the interrogation into a terrible comic performance, one calculated not only to "get inside" and break Roche but also to discomfit an English public that, he senses, stereotypes him in the role of "unclean" Paddy. As Naylor, the "audience" to the interrogation, says, "Roche hasn't said a word the sod, but he's straight man to Nelson . . . it's him and Roche on me." But Nelson is also inflicted with the performer's self-scrutinizing distance. The eponymous rat in the skull images the doubt and self-awareness that persuade him to "break step" for the first time with his Protestant forebears by acknowledging through this calculated gesture of violence that he is not a state-sanctioned fighter in a holy war but rather one of "two fellas in a ditch, clubbing each other, till the one dropped dead." *Rat in the Skull* capitalizes thematically on the talent for punchy, stylized dialogue that has always been apparent in Hutchinson's work for both stage and television (*Bird of Prey* and *Connie*), and in so doing it enriches that most vital tradition within Irish drama, its concern with the nature and power of rhetoric.

Since the late 1980s Hutchinson has lived and worked in the United States, writing scripts for film and television. His stage play, *Pygmies in the Ruins,* can be seen as an apologia, a treatment of the playwright's "quarrel with himself" over his having left Ireland. For D. I. Nelson there is no way out, and his decisive act of violent (self-) confrontation condemns him to an inevitably violent death. But for Harry Washburn in *Pygmies in the Ruins* an even more intricate acknowledgment of the guilty historical roots of his own personal identity sanctions self-justification and release, so that emigration—a "going *to*" America—can be distinguished from exile—a "running *from*" Ireland. Act 1 of *Pygmies* "takes place simultaneously in Belfast 1991 and Belfast 1871." Again, a mystery informs the action. When Washburn, a police photographer with artistic pretensions, cracks up after working on yet another apparently sectarian murder, he becomes obsessed with the unsolved murder in 1871 of a pathetic domestic servant girl. In 1871 we see Dr. Mulcahy's investigation of that earlier case; though thwarted, it nonetheless reveals the dark underside of that "progress" that has earned Belfast prosperity and civic pride. The police photographer and the physician from Dublin are both examples of the artist as witness, intimate with yet professionally detached from their surroundings. The double whodunit changes radically when, in act 2, the two "meet" in Washburn's hallucinatory consciousness to play out a nightmare trial scene. Mulcahy joins with the play's other characters to embody the sick man's feelings of guilt at not only his own life and calling, with its "aesthetic of extinction," but also at the "bloody knot of rope" that binds the identity of a whole culture—"the idea of the North," "the mystery of us." They are pygmies in the ruins of a city. Suicide is arrested and recovery begins only when Washburn comes to realize that the very strenuousness of his self-confrontation is a mark of the "voluntary man," the free individual. Reality returns, and Washburn, defying the charge of "quitting," prepares to leave for America with his lover and "a kind of peace."

—Paul Lawley

HWANG, David Henry

Nationality: American. **Born:** Los Angeles, California, 11 August 1957. **Education:** Stanford University, California, 1975-79, A.B. in English 1979; Yale University School of Drama, New Haven, Connecticut 1980-81. **Family:** Married Kathryn Layng in 1993; one son. **Awards:** Dramalogue award, 1980, 1986; Obie award, 1981; Golden Eagle award, for television writing, 1983; Rockefeller fellowship, 1983; Guggenheim fellowship, 1984; National Endowment for the Arts fellowship, 1985; Tony award, 1988; Outer Critics Circle award, 1988; Drama Desk award, 1988; Obie award, 1997. **Agent:** William Craver, Writers and Artists Agency, 19 West 44th Street #1000, New York, New York 10036, U.S.A.

Publications

Plays

FOB (produced Stanford, California, 1978; New York, 1980). Included in *Broken Promises: Four Plays*, 1983.

The Dance and the Railroad (produced New York, 1981; in *Broken Promises*, produced London, 1987). Included in *Broken Promises: Four Plays*, 1983.
Family Devotions (produced New York, 1981). Included in *Broken Promises: Four Plays*, 1983.
Sound and Beauty (includes *The House of Sleeping Beauties* and *The Sound of a Voice*) (produced New York, 1983; *The House of Sleeping Beauties* in *Broken Promises*, produced London, 1987). *The House of Sleeping Beauties* included in *Broken Promises: Four Plays*, 1983; *The Sound of a Voice* published New York, Dramatists Play Service, 1984.
Broken Promises: Four Plays. New York, Avon, 1983.
Rich Relations (produced New York, 1986).
As the Crow Flies (produced Los Angeles, 1986).
Broken Promises (includes *The Dance and the Railroad* and *The House of Sleeping Beauties*) (produced London, 1987).
1000 Airplanes on the Roof, music by Philip Glass (produced Vienna, Philadelphia, and New York, 1988; Glasgow, 1989). Layton, Utah, Gibbs Smith, 1989.
M. Butterfly (produced New York, 1988; Leicester and London, 1989). New York, New American Library, 1989; London, Penguin, 1989.
FOB and Other Plays (includes *The Dance and the Railroad, The House of Sleeping Beauties, 1000 Airplanes on the Roof, Family Devotions, The Sound of a Voice*). New York, New American Library, 1990.
The Voyage, music by Philip Glass (produced New York, 1992).
Face Value (produced Boston, 1993).
Peer Gynt (produced Providence, 1998),
Golden Child (produced New York, 1996 and 1998). New York, Theater Communications Group, 1998.

Screenplays: *M. Butterfly*, 1993; *Golden Gate*, 1994.

Television Play: *Blind Alleys*, 1985.

*

Critical Studies: "David Hwang's *M. Butterfly:* Perpetuating the Misogynist Myth" by Gabrielle Cody, in *Theater* (New Haven, Connecticut), Spring 1989, pp. 24-27; "*M. Butterfly:* An Interview with David Henry Hwang" by John Louis DiGaetani, in *the Drama Review: A Journal of Performance Studies* (Cambridge, Massachusetts), Fall 1989, pp. 141-53; "David Henry Hwang" by Devorah Frockt, in *The Playwright's Art: Conversations with Contemporary American Dramatists*, edited by Jackson R. Bryer, New Brunswick, New Jersey, Rutgers University Press, 1995; "New Theatrical Statements: Asian Western Mergers in the Plays of David Henry Hwang" by Robert Cooperman, in *Staging Difference: Cultural Pluralism in American Theatre and Drama,* edited by *Marc Maufort*, New York, Peter Lang, 1995; "In the Shadows of a Diva: Committing Homosexuality in David Henry Hwang's *M. Butterfly*" by David L. Eng, in *Amerasia Journal* (Los Angeles, California), 1994, pp. 93-116; "Ethnic Fiction and Survival Ethics: Toni Morrison, Louise Erdrich, David H. Hwang" by Alfred Hornung, in *Ethics and Aesthetics: The Moral Turn of Postmodernism,* edited by Gerhard Hoffman and Alfred Hornung, Heidelberg, 1996.

Theatrical Activities:
Director: **Plays**—*A Song for a Nisei Fisherman*, 1980, and *The Dream of Kitamura*, 1982, both by Philip Kan Gotanda, San Francisco; *FOB*, New York, 1990.

David Henry Hwang comments:

I'm interested in the dust that settles when worlds collide. Sometimes these worlds are cultural, as in my explorations of a Chinese past meeting an American present. Sometimes they are spiritual, as in *Rich Relations*, where the gung-ho materialism of a California family struggles with its Christian mysticism. Most of the time I also try to walk the fine line between tragedy and comedy. I'm fascinated by America as a land of dreams—people pursue them and hope some day to own one.

* * *

"The element it shares with my previous work has to do with a concern for identity," says David Henry Hwang in the introduction to *1000 Airplanes on the Roof.* "To me, all the really interesting human dilemmas are basically internal searches." His comment is as misleading as it is true, for the internal searches in his plays are hedged by external pressures and prejudices. This fact is obvious in the title (*Broken Promises*) Hwang gave to the collection of his first four plays. Historically, the promise that was broken for so many Chinese immigrants was the golden dream of an America where fortunes could be picked up off the street. Hwang, the son of immigrants and conventionally educated at choice American universities, is not only interested in the broken promises of the past but also is concerned about the loss implicit in an embracing of the emblems of American success and the confusions embodied in being a hyphenated person, a Chinese-American.

Essentially a nonrealistic dramatist, Hwang does not develop his characters in the conventional way by the accumulation of psychological details. They emerge through formal presentational modes as varied as Chinese opera (*The Dance and the Railroad*) and the television sitcom (*Family Devotions*). Neither the opera nor the sitcom is allowed to retain its classic form, however, for artistically as well as ideationally Hwang is preoccupied in the early plays with the ground on which the hyphenated American struggles to define himself. The tension of inclusion and exclusion that marks these plays operates in a less narrowly ethnic context in the later work, and the early use of nonrealistic techniques—the role playing in *FOB*, for instance—prepares the way for the extreme theatricality of *M. Butterfly* and *1000 Airplanes*, in which Jerome Sirlin's projections come close to upstaging both Philip Glass's music and Hwang's text.

FOB is a three-way struggle between Dale, who is (almost) accepted as something other than "a Chinese, a yellow, a slant, a gook"; Grace, his first-generation cousin who has been in the United States since she was a child; and Steve, the bumptious newcomer, the FOB (fresh off the boat). The final pairing of Steve and Grace, who sometimes become the hero Gwan Gung and the woman warrior Fa Mu Lan, suggests that the Chinese in America must hold onto some sense of being Chinese, but it is instructive that at the end they are heading for a fashionable disco in a rented limousine. There is a similar but more moving crossover in *The Dance and the Railroad*, in which Lone tries to separate himself from his fellow immigrant workers by going to the mountaintop to practice the movements of Chinese opera. With Lone's blessing Ma, who wants both to dance with Lone and to be one of the "guys" down below, improvises an opera, at once comic and touching, that uses the vocabulary of traditional art in a new American context and that frees Lone of his need to stand apart. In *Family Devotions* it is the visiting uncle from the mainland, more Chinese than communist, who teaches his great-nephew that before he can escape the twin traps of materialism and Christianity his family represents he must recognize his face, reflected in the back of the violin that will open his path to the future, and carry his Chinese self into his American world.

Between *Family Devotions* and *M. Butterfly*, which appeared seven years later, there were several plays, including the elegantly suggestive, Japanese-based *Sound and Beauty,* but it was with *M. Butterfly* that Hwang scored his greatest success. Much of the success came from the surface slickness of the work, in part the contributions of the director and the designer, and the somewhat lurid content of the story around which the play is built. Yet *M. Butterfly* is Hwang's most complex treatment of the crises of identity, one that allows for political, sexual, and social considerations more convoluted than those in the early work. The scandalous story, borrowed from a real event, is the account of a French diplomat and his mistress, a Chinese actress with whom he thought he had fathered a child and who is charged with spying. The trial reveals, to the apparent surprise of the diplomat, that the mistress is a man. In the end the diplomat dons the robes discarded by his lover and, like Madame Butterfly, kills himself to prove that there is a love deep enough to die for. The suicide is simply an audience-pleasing charade unless playgoers recognize the act as an illustration of the arbitrariness and elusiveness of sexual and ethnic stereotypes. The assumptions underlying the affair—Western male assumptions—are that both women and Asians are submissive, accepting the invasion of the male, the Westerner. It is an admonitory tale for a time in which such assumptions are under attack.

With *1000 Airplanes on the Roof* Hwang's protagonist is stripped of ethnic identification. He or she (the role was designed to be played by either a man or a woman) is ill at ease in the ordinary world in which he presumably lives, constantly on the run from both the here and now and from a half-remembered encounter with extraterrestrials, a painful but transcendent event. An interview with a doctor allows him to disown all extraordinary elements in his life, frees him from the threat implied in recurrent lines ("It is better to forget. It is pointless to remember. No one will believe you. You will have spoken heresy. You will be outcast"), and lets him see "only the glow of neon" in the sky but robs him of the sound like a thousand airplanes on the roof. Although the "science fiction music-drama" gives Hwang his most experimental vehicle, his text is largely a platitude about the contemporary sense of alienation. Neither his text nor Glass's music has the force or the imagination of Sirlin's design. Perhaps it is time for Hwang to jump (space)ship and get back to the land of broken promises and broken butterflies.

—Gerald Weales

I-J

INNAURATO, Albert

Nationality: American. **Born:** Philadelphia, Pennsylvania, 2 June 1947. **Education:** Temple University, Philadelphia, B.A.; California Institute of the Arts, Valencia, B.F.A. 1972; Yale University School of Drama, New Haven, Connecticut, M.F.A. 1975. **Career:** Playwright-in-residence, Playwrights Horizons, New York, 1983. Professor at Columbia University, New York, 1985—. **Awards:** Guggenheim grant, 1975; Rockefeller grant, 1977; Obie award, 1977; National Endowment for the Arts grant, 1986, 1989; Drama League award, 1987. **Agent:** Helen Merrill, 337 West 22nd Street, New York, New York 10011, U.S.A. **Address:** 325 West 22nd Street, New York, New York 10011, U.S.A.

PUBLICATIONS

Plays

Urlicht (produced New Haven, Connecticut, 1971; New York, 1974). Included in *Bizarre Behavior*, 1980.

I Don't Generally Like Poetry But Have You Read "Trees"?, with Christopher Durang (produced New Haven, Connecticut, 1972; New York, 1973).

The Life Story of Mitzi Gaynor; or, Gyp, with Christopher Durang (produced New Haven, Connecticut, 1973).

The Transfiguration of Benno Blimpie (produced New Haven, Connecticut, 1973; New York, 1975; London, 1978). New Haven, Connecticut, Yale/Theatre, 1976; London, TQ Publications, 1977.

The Idiots Karamazov, with Christopher Durang, music by Jack Feldman, lyrics by Durang (also director: produced New Haven, Connecticut, 1974). New Haven, Connecticut, Yale/Theatre, 1974; augmented edition, New York, Dramatists Play Service, 1981.

Earth Worms (produced Waterford, Connecticut, 1974; New York, 1977). Included in *Bizarre Behavior*, 1980.

Gemini (produced New York, 1976). New York, Dramatists Play Service, 1977.

Ulysses in Traction (produced New York, 1977). New York, Dramatists Play Service, 1978.

Passione (also director: produced New York, 1980). New York, Dramatists Play Service, 1981.

Bizarre Behavior: Six Plays (includes *Gemini*, *The Transfiguration of Benno Blimpie*, *Ulysses in Traction*, *Earth Worms*, *Urlicht*, *Wisdom Amok*). New York, Avon, 1980.

Coming of Age in SoHo (also director: produced Seattle and New York, 1984; revised version produced New York, 1985). New York, Dramatists Play Service, 1985.

Best Plays (includes *Coming of Age in SoHo*, *The Transfiguration of Benno Blimpie*, *Gemini*). New York, Gay Presses of New York, 1987.

Gus and Al (produced Denver, Colorado, 1987; New York, 1988). New York, Dramatists Play Service, 1989.

Magda and Callas (produced Philadelphia, 1988). New York, Theatre Communications Group, 1989.

Recordings: *Death in Venice*, 1993; *La forza del destino*, 1996.

*

Critical Studies: "An Interview with Albert Innaurato" by John Louis DiGaetani, in *Studies in American Drama* (Columbus, Ohio), 1987, pp. 87-95; "Innaurato and Pintauro: Two Italian-American Playwrights" by Carol Bonomo Ahearn, in *The Journal of the Society for the Study of Multi-Ethnic Literature of the United States* (Amherst, Massachusetts), Fall 1989-90, pp. 113-25; "Albert Innaurato" by John Louis DiGaetani, in *Speaking on Stage: Interviews with Contemporary American Playwrights*, edited by Philip C. Kolin, Tuscaloosa, University of Alabama Press, 1996.

Theatrical Activities:
Director: **Plays**—*The Idiots Karamazov*, New Haven, Connecticut, 1974; *Passione*, New York, 1980; *The Transfiguration of Benno Blimpie*, New York, 1983; *Herself as Lust*, New York, 1983; *Coming of Age in SoHo*, Seattle 1984, New York, 1984 and 1985.

Actor: **Play**—*I Don't Generally Like Poetry But Have You Read "Trees"?*, New York, 1973.

* * *

In the introduction to his collection of plays *Bizarre Behavior*, the extraordinarily talented Albert Innaurato expresses understandable annoyance at the frequency with which critics misunderstand his plays or insist upon discussing connections between them. But to misread is always the critic's risk and to search out the connections, when they do indeed exist, one of his obligations. When considered together, Innaurato's individual plays delineate, as the work of such an important and promising dramatist must, a unique, powerfully held vision of the human condition. The vision is characterized by the skillful manipulation of vividly contrasting dramatic elements that ignite the plays' tensions and yield to their reconciliations. Most prominent among these are satiric farce, comedy, and pathos; the beauty-and-the-beast combination of the grotesque and the beautiful; and the religious and the blasphemous. Among a rather extensive list of more specific dualities are his characters' outward appearances and contrasting inner realities, their often bizarre behavior and their rather different inner impulses, and a frequent doubling of times and places that parallel these dichotomies of character and action. Innaurato also explores the psychological terrain of sexual ambiguity, seems to exploit aspects of the disease of overeating known as bulimia, with the necessary purgation here Aristotelian rather than a Roman orgy in nature, and borrows from music the concepts of aria and counterpoint.

The multiple dualities of *Gemini*, his most commercially successful play, with a run of over four years at a small Broadway house, are indicated by the title from which the hero Francis Geminiani, "plump" and "a little clumsy," derives his name. At the time of his 21st birthday, his fellow Harvard students, the attractive and very WASPish Judith Hastings and her freshman younger brother, arrive for an unexpected visit to his Italian and Catholic South Philadelphia home. At his symbolic coming of age, climaxed by a disastrous birthday feast, Francis is forced to investigate openly his inner life and to admit that he is attracted emotionally not only to the sister but to her brother as well. But despite the potential pathos of the central situation, as Harvard and South Philadelphia, his college friends and his overfed, rough-talking, but good-hearted neighbors collide, the results are a raucous comic festival as lively as an Italian street *festa* and funnier than anything Neil Simon could devise. In *Passione* Innaurato returns to South Philadelphia to explore the emotional problems of a middle-aged couple and to contrast the parents with their happy son, a clown who is incongruously married to the fat lady of the circus.

Innaurato's later, more interesting, and less successful play *Coming of Age in SoHo* is a kind of counterpart or sequel to *Gemini* and brings to the foreground some of its preoccupations. The hero Bartholomew Dante has left his wife to write in a loft in SoHo and like his predecessor also comes of age, this time at age 36. There is again much wild humor, triggered here by his wife's South Philadelphia family that is headed by her father, the Mafia don Cumbar' Antonio, and the unexpected entrance of three boys: the brothers Odysseus ("WASP culture") and Trajan from Saint Paul's and Harvard, and his own forgotten son Puer, the result of a long-ago affair with a German terrorist. But the play's intent is serious. The brothers with classical names, poor Puer (boy), who seeks a brother and finds his father (*puer* complex), and the Dante-Beatrice allusions index the play's assemblage of elements of what might be called the Gemini concept: the linkage of narcissism, dual or ambivalent identity, and creativity. Aspects of this concept underlie Albee's much earlier *The American Dream* and are present in the plays of Peter Shaffer, particularly *Equus*.

But the brilliant, darkly beautiful *The Transfiguration of Benno Blimpie,* Innaurato's finest work, belongs to a differently imagined South Philadelphia than *Gemini* and is more characteristic of his other plays. The fat, unattractive Benno, with his delicate inner life, is eating himself to death. As he controls the play's dramatic time, he comments on and verbally participates in scenes of his past emotional yearnings and rejections. The play ends with a startling cannibalistic image as Benno, before the quick blackout, "*lowers the meat cleaver as though to cut off some part of himself.*"

The same dark intensity is present in *Earth Worms,* one of the most wildly imaginative plays by any contemporary dramatist. Arnold Longese, the sexually ambiguous hero, manages to beget a child with a country girl from the south. He brings her back to South Philadelphia, and there they are surrounded by his blind grandmother who lives on the floor, two transvestites, and a group of hustlers. At the end of the play the grandmother dies, the family home is becoming a whorehouse, and the hero is mutilated by three vindictive nuns. Perhaps these are ingredients for an unintended comedy, but here they combine into Magritte-like fragments of a vivid tragicomic nightmare. The short play *Urlicht,* belonging to a similar dramatic world, features outrageously comic religious situations, and is peopled in part by incongruous nuns.

Innaurato's plays clearly make allusions to his awareness of the grandeur and comedy of the classical past. *Gemini* and *Ulysses in Traction,* the latter with its implications of inhibited enterprise, make the suggestions in their titles. The mad nuns who become like giant cockroaches as they swarm over the hero of *Earth Worms* recall the Furies. But in their effects the plays bring to mind that modern gothic playwright Michel de Ghelderode, and they seem more properly gothic and medieval. Francis in *Gemini* and Arnold in *Earth Worms* wander like modern everymen through their distorted worlds, and Innaurato's most memorable characters resemble frightening or wildly comic gargoyles. But in the familiar phrases of Shakespeare and Yeats, most of his characters have "that within which passeth show"; they have Dionysus's "beating heart" rather than stone "in the midst of all."

—Gaynor F. Bradish

ISITT, Debbie

Nationality: British. **Born:** Birmingham, 7 February 1966. **Education:** Lordswood Girls' School, Birmingham, 1977-82; Coventry Centre for the Performing Arts, 1983-85. **Career:** Dancer, Unique, Birmingham, 1978-82; receptionist, Hendon Business Association, Birmingham, 1982-83; actor, Cambridge Experimental Theatre Company, European tour, 1985-86; co-founder and artistic director, 1986—, Snarling Beasties Theatre Company, Longford, Coventry; guest director, Coventry Centre for Performing Arts, 1991, Other Theatre of Comedy Trust, London, 1992, and Repertory Theatre, Heilbronn, Germany, 1992. **Awards:** *Scottish Daily Express* award, 1988; Independent Theatre award, 1989; Perrier Pick of the Fringe award, 1989, 1990; *Time Out* Theatre award, 1990-91; Edinburgh Fringe Festival first, 1992. **Agent:** Nick Marston, A. P. Watt Ltd., 20 John Street, London WC1N 2DR. **Address:** c/o Snarling Beasties Coventry Touring Theatre Co-op Ltd., 36 Sydnall Road, Longford, Coventry CV6 6BW, England.

PUBLICATIONS

Plays

Gangsters (produced Edinburgh, 1988).
Punch and Judy: The Real Story (also director: produced Edinburgh and London, 1989).
Valentino (also director: produced Birmingham and London, 1990).
Femme Fatale (also director: produced Edinburgh and London, 1990).
The Woman Who Cooked Her Husband (produced Warwick and London, 1991).
You Never Know Who's Out There (produced London, 1992).
Matilda Liar!. London, Warner Chappell Plays, 1994.
Nasty Neighbours. London, Warner Chappell Plays, 1995.

Television Play: *The Lodger*, 1992.

*

Theatrical Activities:
Director: **Plays**—All her own plays; *East* by Steven Berkoff, Edinburgh, 1986.

Actor: **Plays**—All her own plays; *A Midsummer Night's Dream*, European tour, 1985-86.

Debbie Isitt comments:

Writing for me has to have a purpose and that purpose is usually to reach people and hopefully make them feel something, see something, hear something, think something, and maybe even do something. In my experience writing for the theatre is vitally important; I am not reliant very often on producers, publicists, marketing machines, sponsors, donors, editors, censors, men in suits and women in shoulder pads to be able to create and get my work seen. Part of this freedom comes from directing and appearing in my own work; I only have to find a willing person to let me have a space, find others willing to push themselves and take a few risks and put it on. This is the most important bit—to put it on and say—this is what I wanted to say and it's how I wanted to say it—it is a truthful interpretation of what I intended and let people take from it what they wish. I could not stand to be part of a system that compromised my plays, that shaped them and bent them and formed them into someone else's. If a writer is not herself behind the words then she is not a writer. She should put herself on the line and create dramas that draw people into her world just for the duration of the play; even if the world is one from her imagination it is HER imagination and no one else's that we should be sharing. So much emphasis is put on criteria for funding, fitting in, opting out. I would like to think I can maintain control of my writing, although as I move some way into film I begin to see that things are very difficult, there seems to be little room for guts, imagination, and risk.

I tend to choose themes that are at once personal and close to home while smacking of larger social issues. Heterosexual relationships and the dark forces seething behind contemporary marriage is a theme that I am drawn to time and again. Social myths and secrets that we hide and disguise and twist to fit in and conform. Domestic violence, tranvestism, betrayal, phobias, lies are the stuff my plays are made of. They are real and surreal fusing together. Music is a massive influence, especially the great works of contemporary heros like Frank Sinatra, Ella Fitzgerald, Patsy Cline. The woman's psyche being put centre stage is another of my interests; I like to put women into certain situations to see how they react and then make them do things and think things and say things that we're not supposed to and see how the men react. It's really a very interesting process. I also like to leave room for movement and mime and visual techniques often influenced by films and incorporate it on the stage. Above all I think I like to be truthful to the characters, the situation, and myself. The plays are usually funny even though they are often dark. I cannot stand to get depressed—we need to recognize the funny side of pain and guilt and grief. We also need fight and spirit and punch and my plays must be performed with pace and vitality. I am not the sentimental type—just the mental type.

* * *

Debbie Isitt's plays are inextricably linked to her company's productions, in which she usually also acts. The company was formed in 1986 and called Snarling Beasties (Steven Berkoff's creative slang for testicles) because Isitt fancied the idea of strait-laced bureaucrats unwittingly referring to male genitalia in the course of deciding whether or not to give the company money. After their inaugural production of Berkoff's *East* at Edinburgh, it fell upon Isitt to come up with follow-up material. Not for her the luxury of dwelling on every syllable, and her best work has been produced under the pressure of the deadlines of the Edinburgh Festival. *Punch and Judy, Femme Fatale,* and *The Woman Who Cooked Her Husband* are a trio of plays exploring the underbelly of heterosexual relationships on the themes, respectively, of wife battering, transvestism, and adultery. In production her words are supported by an expressionistic, mimetic presentation of character, loud popular music, and a set that hits the audience between the eyes. The effect is intensely theatrical and reminiscent of Berkoff in the aggressive use of rhyming couplets. Such an up-front presentation is exhilarating to watch, although sometimes one wonders whether it is the raucous music that is providing the uplift rather than Isitt's words.

Judging from Isitt's work, she is not a woman in need of courses in assertiveness. Her approach is unashamedly partisan, and men appear as boorish, unimaginative wimps with little or nothing to recommend them. *The Woman Who Cooked Her Husband* was inspired by the real-life case of Nicholas Boyce, who in 1985 chopped his wife up and distributed the pieces because he could no longer stand her nagging. In summing up, the judge said that Boyce was sorely provoked, and he served only six years for manslaughter. In contrast, Sara Thornton received a life sentence for killing her husband after being abused for years. Such an imbalance of justice fuels Isitt's anger. *The Woman Who Cooked Her Husband* depicts a triangular relationship between Kenneth, his wife Hilary, and Laura, his mistress. Kenneth is torn between Laura's skills in bed and Hilary's in the kitchen. Hilary has devoted her life to serving up tempting delicacies in the belief that a well-fed man will never leave her. Through flashback we see Kenneth's first encounters with the sulky Laura, who can hardly summon up enough energy to open a packet of fish sticks. Cringing, shifty, and a poor liar, Kenneth continues to meander between the two until Laura takes matters into her own hands and spills the beans to Hilary, forcing Kenneth to leave her. At a strange reunion Kenneth salivates as he anticipates his first good meal for a long time, but Hilary, finally supported by Laura, has other ideas for the menu.

There is no doubt that Kenneth is the most unpleasant character onstage, and there can be few audiences who would not cheer Hilary on in her grisly deed. But Isitt also criticizes the wife's tendency to blame "the other woman" instead of her spouse. The woman, it seems, is seen as inadequate if she is left and criticized as a home wrecker if she does the leaving. Isitt does not see that marriage has much to offer a woman. So one-sided and dogmatic is her approach that it can inspire resistance in an audience, and it is the black humor that transforms the bile into something more memorable.

Femme Fatale, the second play in the trilogy, is more complex since for once Isitt does not have all of the answers. Georgia and Jimmy could be a model couple, with lots of disposable income and a good sex life, but Jimmy is drawn irresistibly toward a black cubicle at the back of the stage, where he is transformed into Jessica. Apart from the shock and distaste, what enrages Georgia is that Jessica should be such a paragon of femininity, lying on the sofa painting her nails and eager to do all she can to make their domestic life run smoothly. Her perfection challenges Georgia's refusal to be a slave to the sink or her husband. Jimmy likes to dress up because he says that it makes him feel "free from pressure." But being a woman is far from being free of pressure. Isitt tentatively explores why transvestites are drawn to such stereotypical images of femininity, tottering around on high heels and crowned with their beehive hairdos, everything that feminists are trying to escape. As Georgia gets more aggressive, so Jimmy becomes more passive. Beneath the feminist rhetoric there is sympathy for the man who feels that he has to adopt the clothes of a woman in order to explore the more feminine side of his nature.

But Isitt never loses sight of the fact that discovering one's husband dressed in a pair of one's knickers does have a funny side.

Since the trilogy the Other Theatre of Comedy Trust commissioned *You Never Know Who's Out There,* which explores the seedy, racist, and misogynist world of the Northern club and is reminiscent of Trevor Griffiths's *Comedians.* A power struggle among the performers results in much spilling of blood but little illumination. Snarling is Isitt's hallmark. Now that we know that she is not afraid to show her teeth, it would make a change if she occasionally concealed them.

—Jane Edwardes

JEFFREYS, Stephen

Nationality: British. **Born:** London, 22 April 1950. **Education:** Stationers' Company's School, London, 1961-68; Southampton University, B.A. (honours) in English language and literature 1972, and research student for M.Phil 1972-74. **Career:** Driver for Silexeine Paints, London, 1969, and Jeffreys Brothers (Billiards) Ltd., London, 1972-74; teacher, Upton House Comprehensive School, London, 1974-75; lecturer in drama and English, Cumbria College of Art and Design, 1975-78; writer-in-residence, Brewery Arts Centre, and founder, Pocket Theatre, Cumbria, 1978-80; writer-in-residence, Paines Plough, London, 1987-89. Part-time literary associate, Royal Court Theatre, London, 1991—. **Awards:** *Sunday Times* National Student Drama award, 1977; Edinburgh Fringe first, 1978, 1984; *Evening Standard* award, 1989; Critics Circle award, 1989; *Plays and Players* award, 1989. **Agent:** Tom Erhardt, Casarotto Ramsay Ltd., National House, 60-66 Wardour Street, London W1V 3HP, England.

PUBLICATIONS

Plays

Where the Tide Has Rolled You (produced Southampton, 1973).
Counterpoint (produced Southampton, 1975).
Like Dolls or Angels (produced Carlisle, Cumbria and London, 1977).
Mobile 4 (produced Carlisle, Cumbria and London, 1978). London, French, 1979.
Darling Buds of Kendal (produced Kendal, Cumbria, 1978).
Year of the Open Fist (for children; produced Kendal, Cumbria, 1978).
The Vigilante Trail (produced Kendal, Cumbria, 1979).
Jubilee Too (produced Warwick and London, 1980).
Watches of the Night (broadcast, 1981; produced Kendal, Cumbria, 1981).
Imagine (produced Edinburgh, 1981).
Peer Gynt with Gerry Mulgrew, adaptation of the play by Henrik Ibsen (produced Kendal, Cumbria, 1981).
Hard Times, adaptation of the novel by Dickens (produced Kendal, Cumbria, 1982; London and New York, 1987). London, French, 1987.
Futures (produced Kendal, Cumbria, 1984).
Carmen 1936, adaptation of the novel by Prosper Mérimée (produced Edinburgh, 1984; Baltimore and London, 1985).
Clearing House (produced Kendal, Cumbria, 1984).
Returning Fire (produced London, 1985).
Desire (produced Edinburgh, 1986).
The Garden of Eden (produced Carlisle, Cumbria, 1986).
Valued Friends (produced London, 1989; New Haven, Connecticut, 1990). Published in *First Run 2*, edited by Kate Harwood, London, Hern, 1990.
The Clink (produced Plymouth and London, 1990). London, Hern, 1990.
A Jovial Crew, adaptation of the play by Richard Brome (produced Stratford-on-Avon and London, 1992).
A Going Concern (produced London, 1993). London, Nick Hern, 1993.
The Libertine (produced London, 1994; Chicago, 1996). London, Nick Hern, 1994; The Dramatic Publishing Company, 1997.

Radio Plays: *Like Dolls or Angels*, 1979; *Watches of the Night*, 1981; *Absolute Decline*, 1984; *Carmen 1936*, 1992; *The Libertine,* 1996.

*

Theatrical Activities:
Director: **Plays**—For the Pocket Theatre, Cumbria, 1979: *Stone* by Edward Bond; *Games* by James Saunders; *The Vigilante Trail.*

Stephen Jeffreys comments:

I think of myself in the widest sense as an entertainer, and I write plays partly out of a desire to create exciting events. I like audiences to laugh, to be moved, and to be confronted—to have a big experience. I am interested in telling stories and use different techniques—naturalism, epic theatre—in the service of narrative. As a playwright working in live theatre I want to give audiences an evening they cannot have in front of the television or in the cinema, an experience which depends on their sharing a space with live actors.

* * *

The plays of Stephen Jeffreys invite comparison because his facility for capturing the sounds and techniques of others and the range of styles he uses obscure any distinct voice or dominant theme. Critics at various times have seen in Jeffreys similarities to David Edgar (*Hard Times*), to Doug Lucie and Alan Ayckbourn (*Valued Friends*), and to Peter Barnes, Trevor Griffiths, and Howard Barker (*The Clink*). Not surprisingly, given his keen ear for diverse styles and idioms, adaptations have been among his most popular work: a much-produced version of Dickens's *Hard Times*, mixing narrative and dramatization and designed to be played by four actors; and an adaptation for the Royal Shakespeare Company of Richard Brome's 1641 play *A Jovial Crew.* He also dramatized Prosper Mérimée's nineteenth-century novel *Carmen*, resetting it to the 1936 Spanish Civil War for a production by the Scottish Communicado Theatre Company.

As do so many other contemporary British playwrights, Jeffreys draws on historical material to comment on contemporary social issues but with a gentler voice than his predecessors. He also seems more interested in using period literary and dramatic forms than in writing historical drama per se. *The Clink* is set during the final days of the reign of Elizabeth I; but the characters are fictional, and the archaism comes principally from the successful mimicry of Jacobean drama complete with sections of polished blank verse, couplet tags, slang, virtuoso punning, multiple plot lines, and an abundance of violence and death. Forty-five percent of the text for the adaptation of *A Jovial Crew* was invented by Jeffreys, but his additions are so much in the idiom and spirit of the original that the dialogue swings seamlessly between Brome and Jeffreys.

His biographical drama about the Second Earl of Rochester, *The Libertine*, was performed at The Royal Court in repertory with another play based on the life of Rochester, George Etherege's Restoration comedy *The Man of Mode* (1676), which also figures into *The Libertine*. The Royal Court in 1988 had similarly staged Timberlake Wertenbaker's *Our Country's Good* in repertory with its play-within-a-play, George Farquhar's *The Recruiting Officer* (1706). *The Libertine* shares some of the belief in the redemptive power of theater developed in *Our Country's Good*.

A sense of period extends even to his more realistic plays in modern settings. *Valued Friends* depicts the dawn of entrepreneurship among four upwardly mobile roommates who capitalize on the mid-1980s property boom in London to the detriment of their communal relations. When the Hampstead Theatre revived the play a year after its 1989 premiere, a recession had caused a decline in London property values, and critics complained that the play already seemed dated. Jeffreys places *A Going Concern* in 1966, drawing on his own family background in billiard table manufacturing for the setting for a play about generational conflict in a family business. The personal and social issues seem less defined by the year than the style, which uses the straightforward realism of 1960s domestic drama.

Because of the adroit handling of plot and character and the droll comic dialogue, these realistic plays were popular, but some critics complained that Jeffreys lacked the radical voice expected in the fringe theater for which he principally wrote. Both *The Clink* and *The Libertine* are more experimental in form and more cynical in tone than the realistic plays, but Jeffreys's social criticism is still less strident than that of writers half a generation older. Critics saw in *The Clink* parallels between the entropy of Elizabeth's dying court and the fall of Margaret Thatcher, but if so, the satire is very generalized.

Jeffreys seems more concerned with humanistic value than social order. His major plays demonstrate how social pressures, often economic or political, destroy personal relationships. A quest for material success destroys the figurative family in *Valued Friends* and a literal family in *A Going Concern*. As Queen Elizabeth takes her own time to die in *The Clink*, the struggle for power and position of all the characters results in their virtual self-destruction. Rochester carries Restoration self-indulgence to its logical extreme and consequently destroys his ability to sustain any meaningful relations with other people and, more devastatingly, his own love for life. Even the adaptations develop this theme. In *Carmen 1936* Jeffreys transforms Carmen from a life-loving gypsy into a gun runner interested only in money who destroys José, a Basque trying to remain neutral in the midst of the ideologically driven Spanish Civil War. The adaptation of *Hard Times* emphasizes the conflict between materialism and the ways of the heart, showing the destructiveness of a doctrinaire society.

—Richard H. Palmer

JELLICOE, (Patricia) Ann

Nationality: British. **Born:** Middlesbrough, Yorkshire, 15 July 1927. **Education:** Polam Hall, Darlington, County Durham; Queen Margaret's, Castle Howard, Yorkshire; Central School of Speech and Drama, London (Elsie Fogarty prize, 1947), 1944-47. **Family:** Married 1) C. E. Knight-Clarke in 1950 (marriage dissolved 1961); 2) Roger Mayne in 1962, one son and one daughter. **Career:** Actress, stage manager, and director, in London and the provinces, 1947-51; founding director, Cockpit Theatre Club, London, 1952-54; lecturer and director, Central School of Speech and Drama, 1954-56; literary manager, Royal Court Theatre, London, 1973-75; founding director, 1979-85, and president, 1986, Colway Theatre Trust. **Award:** O.B.E. (Officer, Order of the British Empire), 1984. **Agent:** Casarotto Ramsay Ltd., National House, 60-66 Wardour Street, London W1V 3HP, England.

Publications

Plays

Rosmersholm, adaptation of the play by Ibsen (also director: produced London, 1952; revised version produced London, 1959). San Francisco, Chandler, 1960.

The Sport of My Mad Mother (also co-director: produced London, 1958). Published in *The Observer Plays*, London, Faber, 1958; revised version, London, Faber, 1964; with *The Knack*, New York, Dell, 1964.

The Lady from the Sea, adaptation of a play by Ibsen (produced London, 1961).

The Knack (produced Cambridge, 1961; also director: London, 1962; Boston, 1963; New York, 1964). London, Encore, and New York, French, 1962; Faber and Faber, 1964.

The Seagull, with Adriadne Nicolaeff, adaptation of a play by Chekhov (produced London, 1964).

Der Freischütz, translation of the libretto by Friedrich Kind, music by Weber (produced London, 1964).

Shelley; or, The Idealist (also director: produced London, 1965). London, Faber, and New York, Grove Press, 1966.

The Rising Generation (produced London, 1967). Published in *Playbill 2*, edited by Alan Durband, London, Hutchinson, 1969.

The Giveaway (produced Edinburgh, 1968; London, 1969). London, Faber, 1970.

You'll Never Guess (also director: produced London, 1973). Included in *3 Jelliplays*, 1975.

Two Jelliplays: Clever Elsie, Smiling John, Silent Peter, and A Good Thing or a Bad Thing (also director: produced London, 1974). Included in *3 Jelliplays*, 1975.

3 Jelliplays (for children; includes *You'll Never Guess*; *Clever Elsie, Smiling John, Silent Peter*; *A Good Thing or a Bad Thing*). London, Faber, 1975.

Flora and the Bandits (also director: produced Dartington, Devon, 1976).

The Reckoning (also director: produced Lyme Regis, Dorset, 1978).

The Bargain (also director: produced Exeter, 1979).

The Tide (also director: produced Axminster, Devon, 1980).

The Western Women, music by Nick Brace, (also director: produced Lyme Regis, Dorset, 1984).

Mark og Mont (Money & Land) (also director: produced Holbaek, Denmark, 1988).
Under the God, music by Andrew Dickson (also director: produced Dorchester, Dorset, 1989.).
Changing Places (also director: produced Woking, Surrey, 1992).

Other

Some Unconscious Influences in the Theatre. London and New York, Cambridge University Press, 1967.
Devon: A Shell Guide, with Roger Mayne. London, Faber, 1975.
Community Plays: How to Put Them On. London, Methuen, 1987.

*

Critical Studies: "Learn to Play the Game: Learning and Teaching Strategies in Ann Jellicoe's *The Knack*" by Laura Snyder, in *Modern Drama* (Downsview, Ontario), Fall 1994, pp. 451-60; "Ann Jellicoe" by Janice Oliver, in *British Playwrights, 1956-1995: A Research and Production Sourcebook,* edited by William W. Demastes, Westport, Connecticut, Greenwood, 1996.

Theatrical Activities:
Director: **Plays**—*The Confederacy* by Vanbrugh, London, 1952; *The Frogs* by Aristophanes, London, 1952; *Miss Julie* by Strindberg, London, 1952; *Rosmersholm* by Ibsen, London, 1952; *Saint's Day* by John Whiting, London, 1953; *The Comedy of Errors*, London, 1953; *Olympia* by Feren Molnár, London, 1953; *The Sport of My Mad Mother* (co-director, with George Devine), London, 1958; *For Children* by Keith Johnstone, London, 1958; *The Knack* (director, with co-director Keith Johnstone), London, 1962; *Skyvers* by Barry Reckord, London, 1963; *Shelley*, London, 1965; *You'll Never Guess*, London, 1973; *Two Jelliplays*, London, 1974; *A Worthy Guest* by Paul Bailey, London, 1974; *Six of the Best*, London, 1974; *Flora and the Bandits*, Dartington, Devon, 1976; *The Reckoning*, Lyme Regis, Dorset, 1978; *The Bargain*, Exeter, 1979; *The Tide*, Axminster, Devon, 1980; *The Poor Man's Friend* by Howard Barker, Bridport, Dorset, 1981; *The Garden* by Charles Wood, Sherborne, Dorset, 1982; *The Western Women* (director, with co-directors Chris Fog and Sally-Ann Lomax), Lyme Regis, Dorset, 1984; *Entertaining Strangers* by David Edgar, music by Andrew Dickson, Dorchester, Dorset, 1985.

* * *

The major plays by new young writers in London between 1956 and 1959 included *Look Back in Anger*, *The Birthday Party*, *Roots*, *Serjeant Musgrave's Dance*, *A Resounding Tinkle*, *The Long and the Short and the Tall*, *Flowering Cherry*, *Five Finger Exercise*, *The Hostage*, *A Taste of Honey*, and Ann Jellicoe's *The Sport of My Mad Mother* at the Royal Court, the heart of this activity.

After this impressive debut Jellicoe wrote only three other full-length stage plays, two of them slight. The 16 brief scenes of *Shelley* take the poet from his Oxford years through two marriages, to Harriet Westbrook and Mary Godwin, to his drowning in Italy. *Shelley*, subtitled "the Idealist," is written as though for a nineteenth-century touring company of 12: heavy, walking gentleman, juvenile, and so on. Jellicoe remarks that as a writer she is tackling a new set of problems, working "within a set narrative framework—partly for the sheer technical discipline involved." Shelley interests her because he is very young and trying to be good: "the problems of goodness which are so much more interesting than those of evil." He is tragic because of "his blindness to the frailty of human nature." *Shelley* is a flat work, with conspicuous explanatory sections in which the poet talks like a letter or tract.

The Giveaway turns on a suburban housewife who wins a competition prize of 10 years' supply of cornflakes (which are conspicuously on stage); she has had to pretend to be under 14. While the only production may not have done it justice, *The Giveaway* seems to be a clumsy attempt to write a farce, with a hint of satire on consumerism and a touch of the kind of nonverbal comedy Jellicoe had written earlier.

Jellicoe's best play, *The Knack*, is an exuberant, liberating, youthful comedy. Three young men share a flat: Tolen (he has only this one curious name), who has "the knack" of success with women; likable Colin, who lacks it and envies Tolen; and the garrulous Tom, half outside the sex war. Enter Nancy, a lost, gawky, 17-year-old northerner looking for the YWCA, who will give Tolen a chance to demonstrate his knack. The staccato, repetitive dialogue skims along like jazz and is sometimes hard to follow on the page. A bed provides comic business (they pretend that it is a piano), as do entries through the window. An undercurrent is Tolen's Nazi characteristics—and whether negotiation is possible with such people. (The film, scripted by Charles Wood and directed by Richard Lester, was substantially changed but also great fun.)

Jellicoe's succès d'estime, *The Sport of My Mad Mother*, is much more unusual and demanding. It is about four London teenagers and three people they come across: a liberal American, a retarded girl of 13, and Greta, an Australian who comes to represent also the Hindu goddess of destruction and creation, Kali. Yet character, plot, and dialogue hardly matter. This is a piece to be brought to life by a director, and, to make reading really difficult, stage directions are few. The form is nonlinear; Jellicoe writes in the preface to the revised text of 1964 that the play "was not written intellectually according to a prearranged plan. It was shaped bit by bit until the bits felt right in relation to each other and to the whole. It is an anti-intellect play not only because it is about irrational forces and urges but because one hopes it will reach the audience directly through rhythm, noise and music. . . . Very often the words counterpoint the action or intensify the action by conflicting with it." *The Sport of My Mad Mother* is highly original (especially for Britain and for the 1950s) in its Artaudian use of ritual, its stress on physical expressiveness, its use of speech and drums for rhythms, its audacious nonliterary form and apparent shapelessness, and its search for the roots of arbitrary violence. Proper recognition and appreciation would require a readily available film version.

In 1972 Jellicoe told Carol Dix in the *Guardian:* "Directing, as I see it, is an interpretative art, and writing is a creative art, and it's a bloody relief not to have to be creative any longer. The impulse to create is linked with the aggressive instinct."

A 10-year silence ended when in 1978 Jellicoe moved to Lyme Regis in Dorset; she has since staged numerous community plays in the southwest. These ambitious works involve many local people (up to 180 onstage), use the town as the setting, and have a promenade production. Jellicoe wrote the first, *The Reckoning*, about the Monmouth Rebellion of 1685. Allen Saddler described it in *Plays and Players* as follows: "It is all action. The mayor and his cronies scramble about in a frenzy, people rush by in terror, beg for mercy or confide strange secrets in your ear. A girl who is pregnant by a Catholic finds herself in a strange dilemma, proclamations are read from various parts of the hall. Soldiers burst in. Bands play. Prisoners are dragged off screaming. Brawls break out just where you are standing. Events proceed so quickly that there is no time to examine the Catholic or the Protestant case." *The Western Women*, about the part played by women in the siege of Lyme in the English Civil Wars, was rewritten by Jellicoe from a script by Fay Weldon. Another local history piece, *The Bargain*, concerned Judge Jeffreys and was commissioned by the Southwest Music Theatre. In her essay in *Women and Theatre* Jellico writes of the satisfaction of this community activity: "It was extraordinary, the people of Lyme, in rehearsal and in performance, watching a play about themselves. There is a unique atmosphere. It's partly the promenade style of performance, partly that the play is specially written for the town, but it has never failed, that excitement, they just go wild. . . . What I love about it is slowly building something in the community."

In May 1992 Jellicoe took up the challenge of devising a community play for Woking in Surrey, a place lacking much history or sense of identity. Her *Changing Places* focused on women, on Ethel Smythe, a composer and militant suffragette, contrasting her with a working-class woman—outside the middle-class movement for votes for women—who achieves self-realization as a nurse in World War I. Jellicoe appears unlikely to return to the Royal Court or to the West End, for her fulfillment now comes from her community work in the West Country.

—Malcolm Page

JENKIN, Len

Nationality: American. **Born:** New York City, 2 April 1941. **Education:** Columbia University, New York, 1958-63, 1969-71, B.A. in English 1962, M.A. 1963, Ph.D. in English 1972. **Family:** Has one daughter. **Career:** Lecturer in English, Brooklyn College, New York, 1965-66; associate professor of English, Manhattan Community College, 1967-79. Associate professor, Tisch School of the Arts, New York University, 1980—. Associate artistic director, River Arts Repertory Company, Woodstock, New York, 1983—. **Awards:** Yaddo fellowship, 1975; National Endowment for the Arts fellowship, 1979, 1982; Rockefeller fellowship, 1980; Christopher award, 1981; American Film Festival award, 1981; Creative Artists Public Service grant, 1981; Obie award, 1981 (for writing and directing), 1984; MacDowell fellowship, 1984; Guggenheim fellowship, 1987. **Agent:** Scott Hudson, Writers and Artists Agency, 19 West 44th Street, Suite 1000, New York, New York 10036, U.S.A.

Publications

Plays

Kitty Hawk (produced Stratford, Connecticut, 1972; New York, 1974; London, 1975).

Grand American Exhibition (produced New York, 1973).

The Death and Life of Jesse James (produced Los Angeles, 1974; New York, 1978).

Mission (produced New York, 1975).

Gogol: A Mystery Play (also director: produced New York, 1976). Published in *Theatre of Wonders: Six Contemporary American Plays*, edited by Mac Wellman, Los Angeles, Sun and Moon Press, 1986.

Kid Twist (produced San Francisco, 1977; New York, 1983). New York, Broadway Play Publishers, 1987.

New Jerusalem (produced New York, 1979).

Limbo Tales (includes *Highway*, *Hotel*, *Intermezzo*) (also director: produced New York, 1980; London, 1982). New York, Dramatists Play Service, 1982.

Five of Us (produced Seattle, 1981; New York, 1984). New York, Dramatists Play Service, 1986.

Dark Ride (also director: produced New York, 1981). New York, Dramatists Play Service, 1982.

Candide; or, Optimism, adaptation of the novel by Voltaire (produced Minneapolis, 1982). New York, Theatre Communications Group, 1983.

A Country Doctor, adaptation of a story by Kafka (also director: produced San Francisco, 1983; New York, 1986).

My Uncle Sam (also director: produced New York, 1984). New York, Dramatists Play Service, 1984.

Madrigal Opera, music by Philip Glass (produced Los Angeles, 1985).

American Notes (also director: produced Los Angeles, 1986; New York, 1988). New York, Dramatists Play Service, 1988.

A Soldier's Tale, adaptation of a libretto by Ramuz, music by Stravinsky (produced New York, 1986).

Poor Folks Pleasure (also director: produced Seattle, 1987).

Pilgrims of the Night (also director: produced Seattle, 1991). New York, Theatre Communications Group, 1991.

Careless Love. Los Angeles, Sun & Moon Press, 1993.

Dark Ride and Other Plays. Los Angeles, Sun & Moon Press, 1993.

Ramona Quimby, adaptation of the book by Beverly Cleary (for children). Woodstock, Illinois, Dramatic Publishing, 1994.

The Secret Life of Billie's Uncle Myron. New York, H. Holt, 1996.

Screenplays: *Merlin and Melinda*, 1977; *Blame It on the Night*, 1985; *Welcome to Oblivion*, 1989; *Nickel Dreams*, 1992.

Television Plays: *More Things in Heaven and Earth*, 1976, and *See-Saw*, 1977 (*Family* series); *Road Show* (*Visions* series), 1976; *Eye of the Needle* (*Quincy* series), 1977; *Games of Chance* (*Incredible Hulk* series), 1979; *Family of Strangers*, 1980; *Days and Nights of Molly Dodd*, 1989.

Novel

New Jerusalem. Los Angeles, Sun and Moon Press, 1986; London, Harper Collins, 1990.

Other

Survival Printout. New York, Random House, 1973.

*

Critical Study: "Desultory Structures: Language as Presence in the Works of Overmyer, Wellman, and Jenkin" by Paul C. Castagno, in *The Journal of the Comparative Drama Conference* (Gainseville, Florida), 1991, pp. 1-7.

Theatrical Activities:
Director: Some of his own plays.

Len Jenkin comments:

I always like the opening: the houselights fade, the room goes black, the voices around me quiet, the first lights come up in the toybox, and the figures start to move.

Once that's over, for something to hold me, as author or audience, there needs to be a continuing sense of *wonder*, as powerful as that in fairy tales, moonlight, or dreams. This can be present in any sort of work for the stage—realistic to sublimely outrageous—and it's a quality that can't be fused into or onto something with clever staging or sideways performances. It's gotta be there, in the text and through and through.

The other thing that needs to be there for what I'd consider to be "Theatre" to exist is what I call *heart*. This doesn't mean I want to look at people struggling bravely through their emotional problems. It means that the author is not primarily an entertainer; that he/she is instead a preacher, and a singer, and a human being. And that the deep twined nature of what binds us and what makes us free is going to be out there on the stage.

I want to see theatre energetically stomping around the U.S.A. and the rest of the world. Put on plays by the highway side. I want to see tractor-trailers full of men in hats and beautiful women, pulling into town and setting up on the high school football field. I'll be glad to be in the cab of the first truck in line—the one that says "ALIVE" in a bullet on its side.

* * *

In Len Jenkin's *American Notes* one character says, "You have fallen through an American crack, and them is deep." This might be said of most of his characters. Another says, "You know, there's a lot of people who think their life is what happens to them. Get a job, get married, eat an ice cream cone. It's a great life. There's another kind of people who don't connect what happens to them with their lives at all. Their life is something else . . . hopefully." It is about the latter that Jenkin writes.

Yearning for something outside their lives, Jenkin's characters are interested in the sleazy dreams offered by supermarket tabloids and carnival pitchmen. Isolated beings, they are as likely to address the audience in monologues as to engage with other characters. Jenkin's play *Careless Love* is a fantastic rhapsody about his usual drifters and loners: "Everything you always wanted to see, but were afraid to look. The back side of town, down by the railroad yards, near the Shawnee Tavern. Girl in blue jeans vomits into the sink. Next room, an old man watches *Ironside* on TV. . . ." The alternative, offered by a seedy singing duo, is to get on "the DREAM EXPRESS." But Jenkin is not really offering that to his audience, which is observing those who proffer and those who need the dream.

The central characters of *Gogol, Five of Us,* and *Dark Ride* are artists of a kind: a playwright, a writer more successful at writing pseudonymous pornographic romances than the artistic novel in his desk drawer, and a translator of a meaningless and perhaps fake Chinese mystical work. Journalists, would-be writers, lounge room singers, and an ex-director of slasher films haunt the margin of Jenkin's works. Other purveyors of dreams are salesmen of encyclopedias, love potions, or novelties that trick and surprise people.

This last salesman, the eponymous Uncle Sam, might speak for Jenkin: "These gags break the rule in people's heads. If there weren't any rules I'd be outta business." Jenkin plays with theatrical conventions and seems to disclaim any deeper intention. At the end of *Dark Ride,* 10 characters repeat, one after another, "I'm not interested in philosophy. Just tell me how it ends." But Jenkin's epigraph to *American Notes*—"Tho' obscur'd, this is the form/Of the angelic land," from Blake's "America: A Prophecy"—suggests otherwise. This is spelled out most clearly in *American Notes:*

> Last few weeks, I've seen a lot of dreams with my eyes open, just riding down the road. I drive through these towns, one after the other, and they all got a main street, and on it is a place to buy groceries, Food Town—a place to eat, Marv's Broiler—and a place to get fucked-up, Hi-Hat Tavern. And when you go through these places in America, the question is always "Anybody home?" The answer is obvious. No. Basically, there is nobody home in America, Pauline. Except you.

Whimsical but symbolically, in *Careless Love* Jenkin has human tumbleweeds suspended above the stage.

Jenkin's plays, which might be called *drames noirs,* commonly center upon quests that are presented wryly, even mockingly. *Gogol, Dark Ride,* and *My Uncle Sam* all portray absurd quests in which gangsters or policemen dog the central character as he stumbles toward an unclear goal. And in *Pilgrims of the Night* irreligious pilgrims wait through the night for a ferry to nowhere in the hope of contacting extraterrestrials who are reported to have crashed in the forest across the river. All of these plays have narrator figures and an episodic structure full of seedy eccentrics who typically offer the audience an introductory account of themselves. *My Uncle Sam,* one of Jenkin's most fascinating plays, has various levels of commentary on the action—from the author, from Uncle Sam in old age, from Sam when young and on his quest, from an audio cassette from the Universal Detective Agency that instructs him step by step, and from a series of narrators who are dressed appropriately for the successive settings. Jenkin's version of *Candide,* which might be described as a nonquest play, has an equally elaborate set of narrative devices and characters. Both *Candide* and *Gogol* include a play within a play, and in *Pilgrims of the Night* the characters while away the time by telling stories, which we see enacted.

This overt, sometimes flamboyant theatricality brings a joyous aesthetic pleasure that can give an audience something of the transfiguring experience whose want Jenkin's characters unconsciously or consciously feel. For example, in "Hotel," one of his *Limbo Tales,* a "starved, stalled, and stranded" salesman talks to the audience from his hotel room. On either side of him are two other rooms, with only a large audio speaker in each. From one we hear a writer painfully composing "Kubla Khan," interrupted not by a person from Porlock but by a lightning rod salesman, and from the other a teenage drug addict visited by acquaintances who leave with her last $20. The salesman gets a phone call from his dead father, and as he leaves, ahead of eviction, he quotes the Bible: "For ye shall go out with joy, and be led forth with peace: the mountains and the hills shall break forth before you into singing, and all the trees of the field shall clap their hands." Finally, with his room and the stage empty, we see the shadow of a dove briefly on the window shade and hear the writer begin to type again. Like *Waiting for Godot,* Jenkin's plays are about the inability of man not to hope.

—Anthony Graham-White

JOHNSON, Terry

Nationality: British. **Born:** 20 December 1955. **Education:** Queens School, Bushey, Hertfordshire; University of Birmingham, 1973-76, B.A. in drama 1976. **Career:** Actor in late 1970s, and director. Lives in London. **Awards:** *Plays and Players* award, 1982; *Evening Standard* award, 1983; John Whiting award, 1991. **Agent:** Phil Kelvin, Goodwin Associates, 12 Rabbit Row, London W8 4DX, England.

Publications

Plays

Amabel (produced London, 1979).
Days Here So Dark (produced Edinburgh and London, 1981).
Insignificance (produced London, 1982; New York, 1986). London, Methuen, 1982; New York, Methuen, 1986.
Bellevue (produced on tour, 1983).
Unsuitable for Adults (produced London, 1984; Costa Mesa, California, 1986). London, Faber, 1985.
Cries from the Mammal House (produced Leicester and London, 1984).
Tuesday's Child, with Kate Lock (televised 1985; produced London, 1986). With *Time Trouble*, London, Methuen, 1987.
Time Trouble (televised 1985). With *Tuesday's Child*, London, Methuen, 1987.
Imagine Drowning (produced London, 1991). London, Methuen, 1991.
Plays One (includes *Insignificance*; *Unsuitable for Adults*; *Cries from the Mammal House*). London, Methuen, 1993.
Hysteria: Or Fragments of an Analysis of an Obsessional Neurosis. London, Methuen, 1994.
Dead Funny. London, Methuen Drama, 1994.

Screenplays: *Insignificance*, 1985; *Killing Time*, 1985.

Television Plays: *Time Trouble*, 1985; *Tuesday's Child*, with Kate Lock, 1985; *Way Upstream*, adaptation of the play by Alan Ayckbourn, 1988.

*

Theatrical Activities:
Director: **Plays**—*The Woolgatherer* by William Mastrosimone, London, 1985; *I've Been Running* by Clare McIntyre, London, 1986; *Candy and Shelley Go to the Desert* by Paula Cizmar, London, 1986; *Bedroom Farce* by Alan Ayckbourn, Bolton, 1987; *Children of the Dust* by Anne Aylor, London, 1988; *Rag Doll* by Catherine Johnson, Bristol, 1988; *Sleeping Nightie* by Victoria Hardie, London, 1989; *Death of a Salesman* by Arthur Miller, York, 1989; *Just Between Ourselves* by Alan Ayckbourn, 1991. **Television**—*Time Trouble*, 1985; *Way Upstream* by Alan Ayckbourn, 1988; *Rag Doll* by Catherine Johnson, 1988; *The Lorelei* by Nick Dunning, 1989; *Man in Heaven* (episode 3: *Falling in Love*), 1990; *Ball on the Slates* by Bryan Elsley, 1990.

* * *

Boldness of conception and a subtle control in execution are richly combined in Terry Johnson's drama. *Insignificance*, despite all the potential for lurid sensation in a scenario that brings together an Einstein-figure, a Marilyn Monroe-figure, a Joe DiMaggio-figure, and a Senator McCarthy-figure in a New York hotel room in 1953, impresses as a sustained dramatic scrutiny, within a basically naturalistic framework, of the nature of celebrity and of the human need for celebrities. It is a play about wants. The far-from-dumb-blond Actress arrives at the Professor's hotel room wanting to talk to him, to prove her knowledge (of his theories especially), and finally to sleep with him. The Ballplayer wants the Actress to come home and *make* a home. The Senator, meanwhile, wants the Professor to cooperate with him and his committee and to back an anti-Soviet nuclear program. The Professor himself wants only to be left alone to retreat with his calculations about the shape of the universe. Johnson articulates a theory of existential relativity concerning the need of each individual to feel a center of identity. In modern Western culture this need results in the erection of "false gods" as guarantors and measures of personal wholeness: the neon-lit image of the Actress's famous skirt-blown-up pose; the Ballplayer immortalized on a million bubble-gum cards; the omniscient Professor dubbed "True Child of the Universe." Yet the Actress, whose desperate desire for a child is thwarted even within the play itself (she miscarries when the Senator strikes her), ultimately recognizes the despair implicit in the Professor's refusal to confront his own fear of an impending nuclear devastation for which he feels responsible. The repulsive Senator, self-proclaimed "gentleman and . . . solipsist," is the extreme embodiment of the "madman's scheme of things" that the Professor and the Actress, in their different ways, both diagnose as general: so convinced is he of a self-centered universe that he can claim to have invented them all to fulfill his purposes.

The ability of Johnson to dramatize fully and powerfully complex ideas and arguments is also evident in *Unsuitable for Adults*. The setting—an upstairs pub-theater in Soho—is very different from that of *Insignificance*, but the concentration is again upon a vital lack of personal identity in modern culture. The resolution is gender based. The feminist alternative comedian Kate attempts to convince the asthmatic lunchtime stripper Tish of her unthinking collusion with a culture that turns women into images and potential objects of violence; however, Kate's real experience of feminism and her extrication from her own hopeless involvement with Nick, a brilliant impressionist whose pretense and avoidance of moral responsibility in his private life are an extension of his act, can take place only with self-acknowledgment and self-understanding. Although the other acts—Tish's schoolgirl strip, Nick's impressions, the magician Keith's feeble escapism—provide images of fantasy or compensation for an audience that as a result remains "captive," Kate attempts aggressively to confront both them and herself with her scabrous Lenny Bruce-style act (a considerable opportunity for the performer). But her routine gradually falls apart, and verbal violence comes to a cathartic physical climax when she deliberately mutilates a finger: "the body turns against the mind and says, 'Enough. I want to stop this now.'" In the play's epilogue Kate withdraws to a Dartmoor cottage with Tish (who is recovering from a serious asthma attack). The performances are over, and the stripping is now a discovery of truth, both moral and physical: it reveals an essentially natural identity in which both women partake.

The very considerable philosophical ambition of *Insignificance* and *Unsuitable for Adults* is fully disclosed only as the carefully worked dramatic pattern of each play becomes apparent. Each is notable for a stylistic texture that is varied and flexible, natural and uninsistent; climaxes are violent, but there are no shocks of structure or style. In *Cries from the Mammal House*, however, there is a clear relation between philosophical ambition and theatrical experiment. Hitherto in Johnson's work, metaphor provided a crucial means of dialectical organization within a broadly naturalistic structure; but in this play a single, diagnostic dramatic metaphor is proposed at the outset and subsequently explored in a theatrical mode replete with bizarre detail, blackly comic juxtaposition, and stylistic variation. The point of reference is expressionism—in plot as in style. When a half-Celtic, bastard bird-conservationist arrives at the zoo kept by his brother for the funeral of their father, the zoo's founder, he finds it in a state of terminal decay. Despite the efforts of his wife, Anne (who falls in love with the visitor), the despairing brother Alan is impotent to reverse the trend of death and morbid preservation begun by the morally corrupt founding father himself, and the zoo is sold. Renewal comes only after the "Birdman" David has undertaken a "dreamlike" journey to Mauritius in search of the pink pigeon and returns to England, having experienced the company of strange colonial survivors and been kidnapped by a Creole tribe with a real live Dodo. The zoo animals have by now been killed, prior to his suicide, by Alan; however, as the play ends David and Anne, together with her daughter Sally (formerly traumatized but now released) and his three Mauritian companions, plan a "new lease of life" for the zoo—under the sign not of the decadent Western father but of an Eastern enlightenment (and with the "absurd cry" of the Dodo).

Imagine Drowning also has a richly symbolic setting with much characteristically grotesque detail: a chaotic guest-house on the Cumbrian coast in the shadow (or "glow") of Sellafield Nuclear Power station. Into this modern "haunted house," with its bizarre menagerie, comes a young woman called Jane, who is in search of her radical journalist husband David. An intricately worked double time scheme enables the intertwined presentation of the crises of self undergone by both David (a few weeks earlier) and Jane. David gives way to a reactionary individualist pessimism and confronts the "cold, black nugget" of the homicidal impulse within himself; Jane experiences the depressive "schism" of mind and body. The play's resolution, however, is unconvincing because the full dramatic realization of the "journey of the soul" is limited by the presence of two figures of ethical authority through whom the playwright offers explicit diagnosis and commentary. Both figures are, inevitably, marginal to society, if not actually outside it: The severely disabled Tom, whose political activism is presented with affectionate (self-) irony, attempts to stir the couple to political action and catalyses Jane's confrontation of her relation to David. Buddy, "grounded" American former astronaut and now mystical beach-bum, forces each to be "baptized into the new age" by immersion in the sea, thus effecting a death-and-rebirth consonant with his holistic philosophy. The dominance of these figures inhibits exploration of the play's most interesting character, the mysterious, eccentric survivor Brenda, "a very slow woman" who keeps the guest house. Buddy's philosophy recognizes "connection," but the causal link made by the playwright between the deathly effects, moral and physical, of Sellafield and the homicidal activities of Brenda's imprisoned mass-murderer husband seems rather a matter of ideological correctness than of the fresh perception of the relation between self and society of which we know Johnson to be capable. The large symbolic ambitions of this "dream play about the pain we're all immersed in" are frustrated by the very urgency of the need to deliver a message about the "moral, political and sexual confusion" of the 1980s and the possibility of renewal in the future.

Johnson's interest in the seriousness of comedy issued in the 1990s in two farces. "Farce," he has said, "is about that which is hidden having to come to light to resolve the lie" and "you don't have to push it far to get to the true horrors." The true horror in *Hysteria* is the dying Freud's continuing concealment, in bad faith, of actual child abuse, rather than infantile fantasy, as an endemic cause of mental illness. The importunate, naked young woman whom the psychoanalyst seeks to hide in the closet from both his doctor and none other than Salvador Dali is revealed, through a whirling *Rookery Nook*-style action, to be the daughter of a former patient who committed suicide after an apparently successful analysis. As Freud continues to resist the reality of child-abuse in his patients'—and ultimately his own—experience, the action enters into the repetitive loop of his final morphine-induced hallucination, with its surreal revelation of the cultural significance of his (self-)betrayal. The next play, *Dead Funny,* brings to light the lies lived by the members of a comedy appreciation society as they gather to commemorate Benny Hill on the night of Frankie Howerd's death. A gay member pluckily comes out, but the ritually reenacted sketches, the naughty undies, and the custard-pie mêlée at the climax do little to resolve the self-delusions and half-hearted betrayals that create a sexual stalemate in the lives of the major characters.

—Paul Lawley

JOHNSTONE, Keith

Nationality: British. **Born:** Brixham, Devon. **Family:** Married to Ingrid Johnston. **Career:** Director of the Theatre Studio, 1965-66, and associate director, 1966, Royal Court Theatre, London; director, Theatre Machine Improvisational Group; taught at Royal Academy of Dramatic Art, London, and Statens Teaterskole, Copenhagen. Currently associate professor of drama, University of Calgary. Codirector, Loose Moose Theatre Company, Calgary. **Address:** Department of Drama, University of Calgary, Calgary, Alberta T2N 1N4, Canada.

Publications

Plays

Brixham Regatta, and For Children (produced London, 1958).
The Nigger Hunt (produced London, 1959).
Gloomy Go Round (produced London, 1959).
Philoctetes, adaptation of the play by Sophocles (produced London, 1964).
Clowning (produced London, 1965).
The Performing Giant, music by Marc Wilkinson (also co-director: produced London, 1966).
The Defeat of Giant Big Nose (for children; also director: produced on Welsh tour, 1966).
Instant Theatre (produced London, 1966).
Caught in the Act (produced London, 1966).
The Time Machine (produced London, 1967).
The Martians (produced London, 1967).

Moby Dick: A Sir and Perkins Story (produced London, 1967).
Wakefield Mystery Cycle (also director: produced Victoria, British Columbia, 1968).
Der Fisch (also director: produced Tübingen, 1971).
The Last Bird (produced Aarhus, Denmark, 1973). Toronto, Playwrights, 1981.
Shot by an Elk (produced Kingston, Ontario, 1974).
Robinson Crusoe (produced Calgary, Alberta, 1976).

Other

Impro: Improvisation and the Theatre. London, Faber, and New York, Theatre Arts, 1979; revised edition, London, Eyre Methuen, 1981.
Don't Be Prepared: Theatresports for Teachers. Calgary, Loose Moose Theatre, 1994.

*

Theatrical Activities:
Director: **Plays**—*Eleven Plus* by Kon Fraser, London, 1960; *The Maimed* by Bartho Smit, London, 1960; *The Triple Alliance* by J.A. Cuddon, London, 1961; *Sacred Cow* by Kon Fraser, London, 1962; *Day of the Prince* by Frank Hilton, London, 1962, 1963; *The Pope's Wedding* by Edward Bond, London, 1962; *The Knack* by Ann Jellicoe (co-director, with Jellicoe), London, 1962; *Edgware Road Blues* by Leonard Kingston, London, 1963; *The Cresta Run* by N.F. Simpson, London, 1965; *The Performing Giant* (co-director, with William Gaskill), London, 1966; *The Defeat of Giant Big Nose*, Welsh tour, 1966; *Wakefield Mystery Cycle*, Victoria, British Columbia, 1968; *Der Fisch*, Tübingen, 1971; *Waiting for Godot* by Beckett, Alberta, 1972.

Keith Johnstone comments:

(1973) I began writing plays when the Royal Court commissioned me in 1957. They were about physical sensations, often sensations experienced in infancy, expressed in visual images.

When I began writing again in 1966 it was only to provide suitable scripts for improvisors and short "entertainment" pieces. Most of my work from 1965 to 1970 was with my group Theatre Machine. We toured in many parts of England, gave demonstrations to teachers and trainee teachers, and hammered out an effective formula. *Instant Theatre* was the Theatre Machine in an early show. We were the only British group to be invited to Expo 67 in Montreal, and toured in Denmark, Germany, Belgium, Yugoslavia, and Austria.

I am at present writing an account of my improvisational methods, and am returning to writing "real" plays. *Brixham Regatta* was given a Sunday night production at the Mermaid in about 1969 and it looked O.K. to me. This has made me feel that there might be some point in trying a serious work again.

I dislike "sets." I think theatre should be popular. I think theatre should "freak-out" the audience rather than offer conversation pieces. Favourite play—*Do It!* performed by the Pip Simmons Group.

* * *

Keith Johnstone's work has been relatively little exposed, and it can hardly be claimed that he has had much direct influence on the British theater. But in a more subtle and pervasive manner his work played an important role in the British theater of the 1960s. To a large extent this was initially confined to his work at the Royal Court for the English Stage Company during one of its most creative periods. Associated with the Royal Court from 1957, he was a codirector of the 1965-66 season and director of the Theatre Studio, from which emerged Johnstone's Theatre Machine Group, whose work, based on improvisations, has influenced a large number of younger English actors and writers.

The first efforts of the Theatre Studio to gain widespread attention consisted of a 1965 Christmas show, *Clowning*. Designed for both children and adults, each performance was unpredictable and different, basing itself on mime and improvisational exercises that originated in the Royal Court's acting classes. Broadly put, the show's theme was the making of clowns, examining whether and how they can be trained. Using a few basic situations from which the actors could take off into improvisation, the show intriguingly experimented with that sense of the unexpected and dangerous, which Johnstone evidently sees as a major clowning skill, in its concentration on the immediacy of the theatrical moment.

Some aspects of the work were elaborated in Johnstone's most interesting play, *The Performing Giant*, produced on a double bill with Cregan's *Transcending* at the Royal Court in 1966. The play received a poor reception at the time, for critics seemed to lack a critical vocabulary with which to cope with a kind of theater that many other experimental groups were later to make easier for them. The play is an allegory of the adolescent's attempt to understand the mysteries and puzzles of the outside world as well as the processes of the developing body. A group of adolescents encounters a giant and explores the terrain of his inside as a potential Disneyland only to have the giant rebel and defeat them with the aid of the girl he falls in love with. To most critics the play seemed merely strange and extravagant; charging it with whimsical obscurity in its initial premise, they missed the denseness of the developing fantasy and the way in which Johnstone's allegory worked. The play is not planned as a series of concepts but as an immediate theatrical experience that uses a loose basic structure as a starting point. It does so in a manner parallel to the work of another Royal Court dramatist, Ann Jellicoe, in *The Sport of My Mad Mother*. It would be interesting to see *The Performing Giant* revived, for it is a more important play than thought at the time.

Johnstone's other work in England has been mainly in the shape of further Theatre Machine Group shows, each one progressively more adventurous, or of adaptations, such as his excellent version of Sophocles' *Philoctetes*. His sense of the possibilities of theater, coupled with his ability to work within the terms of fantasy without sentimentality or whimsy, marks him as an original voice too rarely heard.

—Alan Strachan

K

KALCHEIM, Lee

Nationality: American. **Born:** Philadelphia, Pennsylvania, 27 June 1938. **Education:** Trinity College, Hartford, Connecticut, B.A.; Yale University School of Drama, New Haven, Connecticut, one year. **Awards:** Rockefeller grant, 1965; Emmy award, 1973. **Agent:** Susan Schulman, 454 West 44th Street, New York, New York 10036. **Address:** RD #2, West Center Road, West Stockbridge, Massachusetts 01266, U.S.A.

PUBLICATIONS

Plays

A Party for Divorce (produced New York, 1963).
Match Play (produced New York, 1964). Published in *New Theatre in America*, edited by Edward Parone, New York, Dell, 1965.
. . . And the Boy Who Came to Leave (produced Minneapolis, 1965; New York, 1973). Published in *Playwrights for Tomorrow 2*, edited by Arthur H. Ballet, Minneapolis, University of Minnesota Press, 1966.
An Audible Sigh (produced Waterford, Connecticut, 1968).
The Surprise Party (produced New York, 1970).
Who Wants to Be the Lone Ranger (produced Los Angeles, 1971).
Hurry, Harry, with Jeremiah Morris and Susan Perkis, music by Bill Weeden, lyrics by David Finkle (produced New York, 1972).
Prague Spring (produced Providence, Rhode Island, 1975; New York, 1976).
Win with Wheeler (produced Waterford, Connecticut, 1975). New York, French, 1984.
Winning Isn't Everything (produced New York, 1978).
Breakfast with Les and Bess (produced New York, 1983). New York, French, 1984.
Friends (produced New York, 1984; also director: revised version, produced New York, 1989).
Moving (produced Lenox, Massachusetts, 1991). New York, French, 1991.
The Tuesday Side of the Street (produced Lenox, Massachusetts, 1991).

Television Plays: *Reunion*, 1967; *Let's Get a Closeup of the Messiah*, 1969; *Trick or Treat*, 1970; *All in the Family* series, 1971-72; *Is (This) Marriage Really Necessary*, 1972; *The Class of '63*, 1973; *The Bridge of Adam Rush*, 1974; *The Comedy Company*, 1978; *Marriage Is Alive and Well*, 1980.

*

Lee Kalcheim comments:

I am a realist. So, my plays are realistic. Comic. Dramatic. Strongly based on characters. I grew up with the realistic writers of the 1950s. Found myself sitting in the middle of the avant garde movement with an inherited style. And then as the theatre began to be less faddish (in New York) it became apparent that I could indeed maintain my love of character—of reality—and survive as a playwright. My work in improvisational theatre and film began to broaden my work. My later work became more fragmented or film like. Less . . . livingroomish. But I realized that for all the excitement of theatrical effects (I have tried various experiments with mixed media), the thing that still moved me most, standing in rehearsal watching my plays, were those one to one scenes. Those scenes where two people faced each other, wanting something from each other. Those scenes where something happened between people. They washed out all the media effects, or unusual transitions, or whatever. They were theatre at its strongest. And I suppose I keep coming back to those in my plays. I do write film. But I keep coming back to the theatre for the excitement of those live, vibrant scenes—that put flesh and blood out there in front of you.

*   *   *

"It makes me very sad and very happy to be a playwright" was Lee Kalcheim's answer to a request for a statement that could introduce this piece about him. It serves well. Kalcheim is indeed a melancholy and a joyful chronicler. But what made him unusual among the American dramatists of his generation was his ability to bustle, hustle, and earn his own way as a writer. While most young playwrights were weaving their tortured ways through the mazes of foundations and endowments and theater boards seeking grants, honoraria, subsistences, and other encouraging handouts, Kalcheim energetically and quite successfully went into the business of writing.

He has a good mind and an intelligence that reflects both cool observations and warm insights into the characters he creates. More than storytelling, Kalcheim does "peopletelling." His plays, he says, are about "human ideas." As a playwright he is less concerned with the usual ideas per se than he is with the humanness of the ideas, with the humanity that generates the ideas.

Moreover, as even a quick reading or viewing of his work for the stage reveals, Kalcheim is fascinated by human loneliness. What for other, more abstract writers is a concern with the condition of loneliness for Kalcheim becomes both a compassionate and an uninvolved concern for the human being as an alone creature. Yes, he is both passionate and uninvolved, both sad and happy. People trying—desperately, lazily, sadly, hopefully, hilariously, pathetically, ridiculously—to make contact with other people is what his plays not only are but are about.

At the end of *An Audible Sigh* one of the characters, Gale, says, "You see . . . I want to be loved, but I don't want to have strings attached." And, indeed, there is the rub. Kalcheim's people are lonely, loving but afraid of being loved and even of not being lonely. They sometimes seem to enjoy their loneliness and find sanctuary in their state of not being loved. Driven in part by the fear of being possessed and by the desire to possess, the characters are intensely vulnerable. Their bulwarks all seem terribly sturdy and well planned but facing in the wrong direction.

Kalcheim examines these qualities in play after play. Even more personally, he exhibits a unique ability to watch and be part of the action and to double the effect, to watch the watchers, himself included, and the actors. Again and again Kalcheim seems to be writing much the same play, each time in a different guise but each time about the same qualities and sensibilities. If the feelings and events—love, divorce, joining, separation, regret, hope, need, fear, tenacity, escape—are indeed his own experiences, he is excellent at turning that experience into theatrical action, for Kalcheim the writer is a very astute observer of Kalcheim the man.

Moreover, his technique works unusually well. He juxtaposes comedy and drama with almost metronomic regularity. But at the critical heart of the matter is a much more important and profound juxtaposition—the fear of death poised against an immortality assured.

Kalcheim has been writing since he was 11 years old, and he has said that when his first playlet was produced he wept at the recognition of his own voice "up there." If he has turned more and more to film and television to earn a living, his first and enduring love is perhaps not, ironically, a person but the theater. As with many media writers, Kalcheim plays the game of running down his own television writing, but he nonetheless speaks with justified pride about the way his voice is heard on the stage.

—Arthur H. Ballet

KANE, Sarah

Nationality: British. **Born:** 1971. **Career:** Writer-in-residence, Paines Plough Theatre Company. **Agent:** Casarotto Company, National House, 60-66 Wardour Street, London W1V 4ND England.

Publications

Plays

Blasted (produced London, 1995).
Phaedra's Love (produced London, 1996).
Cleansed (produced London, 1998).
Blasted and Phaedra's Love. London, Methuen, 1996.
Crave (produced Edinburgh, 1998).

Television Play: *Skin.*

*

Critical Study: "Truth and Dare: Sarah Kane's *Blasted*" by Tom Sellar, in *Theater* (New Haven, Connecticut), 1996, pp. 29-34.

* * *

Following a trilogy of monologues titled *Sick,* Sarah Kane rose to notoriety with performances of her first full-length drama, *Blasted* (1995), a coruscating litany of tension, violence, and atrocity that attracted almost unanimous disapprobation from critics. Some were led to offer unfavorable comparisons with Edward Bond's *Saved,* which had also premiered at the Royal Court Theatre (1965), and the Royal National Theatre's staging of Howard Brenton's *The Romans in Britain* (1980). Kane's play is arguably less well focused than Bond's and less richly layered than Brenton's, although all three are engaged with problems of violence and gender politics, with power and depersonalization in a more or, in Kane's case, less well-defined social and political context.

This lack of specificity is signaled at the outset, the setting being a "very expensive hotel room in Leeds—the kind that is so expensive it could be anywhere in the world." Ian, a middle-aged, cancerous hack, racist, and misogynist, is reestablishing exploitative sexual relations with Cate, a young, infantile, epileptic woman who is as capable of sudden expressions of lust and affection as is Ian of embarrassed protestations of love and dependence. The abiding pressures, however, are competing ones and the prevailing circumstance—Ian, in fear of vengeful attack from secret service personnel with whom he once worked, is armed—one of siege. It is indicated that an unspecified civil conflict is taking place in the streets outside.

The outside irrupts midway through the drama as an unnamed soldier breaches the defenses, which room service has thus far done much to shore up, and a complementary world recontextualizes what has so far been affirmed and denied. Earlier scenes of graphic sexual violence and desperation give way to homosexual rape, cannibalism, and suicide prompted by the soldier's vengeful feelings in respect of Col, a woman brutalized abroad. Meanwhile, Cate, whose exit coincided with the soldier's incursion, returns from war-torn streets clutching a dying baby that, buried beneath the floorboards, is finally food for Ian, who, eyeless, ekes out an existence amid what has become at best merely a bombed-out shelter.

The play transposed Bosnia, the signal case in the 1990s, to middle England, with private griefs and desires counterpointing public and political atrocity and showing the banality of evil. "A gratuitous welter of carnage" was a representative critical comment. But there is an intensity, an integrity, and a discipline to the writing and to the play's form, its dramatic parameters, that ought to temper a response undeniably governed by visceral assault. Kane constructs dialogue with a perverse kind of tact that makes suppressed and inverted feelings of affection between her characters and yearnings for the ineffable within them subjects for serious attention.

The frustrations of feeling and desire thwarted by political and cultural anesthesia and isolation are given classical counterpoint in Kane's second play, *Phaedra's Love* (1996), a reworking of the story told by Euripides, Sophocles, and Racine. Hippolytus's chastity and allure in Kane's version, however, is the cauterized indifference of the overindulgent, and the play itself is a study, as is *Blasted,* of the relation between excess and impoverishment. Phaedra's suicide and Hippolytus's subsequent self-incrimination allow for mutual sacrifice and for the laconic, Nietzschean complaint that there should have been "more moments like this." Personal sacrifice—"She really did love me"—is set beside family and public scapegoating. The service of institutional credibility in a broadly satiric fashion is no more convincing a contextualization here than is war-torn Europe in *Blasted* but no less schematic than in Kane's more illustrious classical predecessors. Religion and royalty—the priest's hypocrisy, Theseus's rape of his daughter Strophe—are equally complicit in the inversions of desire and control the play dramatizes. One critic at the time called the dialogue "dismayingly flat and prone to bathos," while another observed it to be "full of reeking toughness . . . the right comic inflections and [a] dark comic edge."

Universality in *Cleansed* (1998) is predicated upon a university setting, a Foucaultian world of surveillance and punishment inhabited by the socially deviant and dysfunctional.

Incest, infantilism, homosexuality, and drug addiction are its conspicuous manifestations, and Tinker, the presiding dealer/doctor, is himself implicated in the savage loves and terrors he observes, orchestrates, and unleashes. In a series of color-coded institutional spaces, all within the fence of the perimeter, couples (Grace/Graham, Carl/Rod, Tinker/Woman) work out patterns of desire, possession, and commitment to flesh out the incompleteness of individual identity. Meanwhile, Tinker emasculates, mutilates, and transposes body parts as if to destroy or locate the perimeters of affective energy. Short tableau scenes make few inroads into the future when the excoriating pain or ecstasy of the here and now is to be celebrated in moments of purification to which the play's title alludes. Kane's *Cleansed,* unlike Bond's *Saved,* however, pares away the social, political, and even conventionally moral parameters to expose more or less attenuated states of being and becoming.

Artaud's theater of cruelty and Howard Barker's theater of catastrophe lie behind much of Kane's drama, and her directorial work on Büchner's *Woyzeck* registered a comparable affinity. But there is a declamatory economy and austerity to Kane's writing that is not found in these other theoreticians and practitioners. These qualities are precisely what have given Kane's work in the theater such chaste, visceral power.

—James Hansford

KARNAD, Girish (Raghunath)

Nationality: Indian. **Born:** Matheran, Maharashtra, 19 May 1938. **Education:** Karnataka University, Dharwad, 1954-58, B.A. in mathematics and statistics 1958; Bombay University (Dakshina fellow), 1958-59; Magdalen College, Oxford University (Rhodes scholar), 1960-63, M.A. in philosophy, politics, and economics 1963. **Family:** Married Saraswathy Ganapathy in 1980; one daughter and one son. **Career:** Assistant manager, 1963-69, and manager, 1969-70, Oxford University Press, Madras; director, Film and Television Institute of India, Pune, 1974-76; president, Karnataka State Nataka Academy, 1976-78; visiting professor and Fulbright scholar-in-residence, University of Chicago, 1987-88. Member, Ministry of Information and Broadcasting Special Commission on Film, 1976; Indian co-chair, Indo-U.S. Sub-Commission on Education and Culture, Joint Media Committee, 1984-93, and chair, Sangeet Natak Akademi (National Academy of the Performing Arts), 1988-93. **Awards:** Mysore Rajyotsava award, 1970; Homi Bhabha fellowship, for folk theatre, 1970-72; President's gold medal, for film *Samskara*, 1970; National award, for film direction, 1972, for screenplay, 1978; Sangeet Natak Akademi award, 1972; Kamaladevi award, 1972; President's silver medal, for feature film, 1974; Karnataka State award, for acting, 1991; Golden Lotus award, for documentary, 1989. Padma Shri, 1974; Padma Bhushan, 1992; National Award for the Best Film on Environment/Conservation, for *Cheluvi,* 1993; Gubbi Veeraune Award by the Government of Karnataka, 1996. Honorary degrees: Doctor of Letters, Karnatak University, Dharwad, 1994; fellow, Sangeet Natak Akademi, New Delhi, 1996. **Address:** 697 15th Cross Road, J.P. Nagar Phase II, Bangalore 560078, India.

Publications

Plays

Yayati (produced in Hindi, Bombay, 1967). Published in Kannada, Dharwad, Manohara Grantha Mala, 1961.
Ma Nishada (broadcast in Kannada, 1963). Published in Kannada, New Delhi, Sahitya Akademi, 1986.
Tughlaq (produced in Urdu, Delhi, 1966; in English, Bombay, 1970; in Kannada, Bangalore, 1971). Published in Kannada, Dharwad, Manohara Grantha Mala, 1964; in English, New Delhi, Oxford University Press, 1972.
Hayavadana (produced in Kannada, Bangalore, 1972; in Hindi, Bombay, 1972; in English, Madras, 1972; London, 1988). Published in Kannada, Dharwad, Manohara Grantha Mala, 1971; in English, Calcutta, Oxford University Press, 1975.
Evam Indrajit, translation of the play by Badal Sircar (produced Bombay, 1985). New Delhi, Oxford University Press, 1974.
Anjumallige (produced in Kannada, Bangalore, 1978). Published in Kannada, Dharwad, Manohara Grantha Mala, 1977.
Hittina Hunja (produced in Hindi as *Bali*, Bombay, 1987). Published in Kannada, Dharwad, Manohara Grantha Mala, 1980.
Nagamandala (produced in English by Guthrie Theatre, Minneapolis, 1993). Published in Kannada, Dharwad, Manohara Grantha Mala, 1989; in English, New Delhi, Oxford University Press, 1990.
Taledanda (produced in Kannada, Gadag, 1991). Published in Kannada, Dharwad, Manohara Grantha Mala, 1990; in English, New Delhi, Ravi Dayal Publishers, 1993.
Agni Mattu Malé (produced in Hindi as *Agni Aur Barkha,* Delhi, 1997). Published in Kannada, Dharwad, Manohara Grantha Mala, 1994; in English as *The Fire and the Rain,* New Delhi, Oxford University Press, 1998.

Screenplays: In Kannada—*Samskara*, 1969; *Vamsha Vriksha* with B.V. Karanth, 1971; *D.R. Bendre* (documentary), 1973; *Kaadu*, 1973; *Tabbaliyu Neenade Magane*, with B.V. Karanth, 1977; *Bhumika*, 1977; *Kondura*, 1977; *Ondanondu Kaladalli*, 1978; in Hindi: *Utsav*, 1984; in English: *Kanaka-Purandara* (documentary), 1973; *Kalyug*, 1980; *The Lamp in the Niche 1-2* (documentary), 1989.

Radio Play: *Ma Nishada* (in Kannada), 1963; *The Dreams of Tipu Sultan* (in English), broadcast from London, by B.B.C. Radio, 1997.

*

Critical Studies: "New Visions in Indian Cinema: Interviews with Mrinal Sen, Girish Karnad, and Ketan Mehta" by Udayan Gupta, in *Cineaste: America's Leading Magazine on the Art and Politics of the Cinema* (New York), 1982, pp. 18-24; "Once Upon a Time There Was an 'Emperor'": A Reading of *Tughlaq,* a Modern Indian Play by Girish Karnad" by R.P. Rama, in *Journal of the South Pacific Association from Commonwealth Literature and Language Studies* (Murdoch, Australia), 1993, pp. 330-35.

Theatrical Activities:
Director: **Plays**—With the Madras Players, 1964-69. **Films**—*Vamsha Vriksha*, 1971; *Kaadu*, 1973; *Tabbaliyu Neenade Magane*, with B.V. Karanth, 1977; *Ondanondu Kaladalli*, 1978; *Utsav*, 1984;

Cheluvi (in Hindi), 1992. **Television**—*Woh Ghar* (in Hindi) by Kirtinath Kurtkoti, 1984.

Actor: **Plays**—With the Madras Players, 1964-69; lead roles in *Oedipus Rex* and *Jokumaraswamy*, Bangalore, 1972. **Film**—*Samskara*, 1969; *Vamsha Vriksha*, 1971; *Manthan*, 1977; *Swami*, 1977; also several Hindi feature films. **Television**—Several Hindi television films and serials, including those by Satyajit Ray and Mrinal Sen.

Girish Karnad comments:

My generation was the first to come of age after India gained independence. It therefore had to face tensions that had been suppressed but now had come to the surface and demanded resolution: tensions between the country's cultural past and its colonial experience, between the attractions of the Western mode of thought and our own traditions.

In my first play I automatically turned to the *Mahabharata* for source material and have since then continued to borrow from mythology, history, legends, and oral tales. These narrative traditions are still alive in India and widely shared, even in the cities. The problem was to find a theatrical form which could do justice to this inheritance.

Such theatre as existed in our cities in the 1960s, derived from Victorian models and later from naturalistic drama, was clearly inadequate. I turned to the traditional theatre of my childhood, still surviving in small towns and villages, from which the urban playwright felt divorced. The aim was to identify the structure of expectations and conventions about entertainment underlying these forms on which one could base a fresh rapport with the audience.

To my delight, I have found that these various devices—half-curtains, masks, music, mime, the mixing of human and non-human elements—allow for greater technical complexity and hence a more sensitive exploration of contemporary issues. They permit a simultaneous viewing of alternative points of view without which one could not handle the immense contradictions of life in India today.

* * *

Girish Karnad is one of a handful of playwrights who have completely reshaped the form and content of theater in India since its independence. In doing this, they have rejected the British theatrical structures that existed until 1947 and the agitprop styles that developed with the struggle for independence. This group, writing in various Indian languages, have drawn from the epics, religious stories, and folktales of India for modern metaphors. Moreover, they have reinterpreted this material by using conventions and structures of Indian classical and folk drama to forge a dynamic new national style.

Of this group Karnad is the only one to translate his work into English, and the three plays that have been translated give a wonderful insight into his abilities and his vision. He writes in Kannada, the language of his culturally rich native state of Karnataka, and his plays have been translated into many other Indian languages. In all of his work he treats traditional material as a metaphor, but he teasingly avoids giving a moral message, preferring to open up a challenge for the audience to make its own decisions. The seriousness of his dilemmas is without doubt, for he is an intellectual observer of his society, but his ability as a man of the theater to draw from the clownlike and the traditional relationship of storyteller to audience that is found in Indian folk drama gives a wonderful lightness of touch to his subject matter. Masks, music, dance, and song enrich his verbal structures to create highly accessible theater.

Karnad's earliest play in English, *Tughlaq* (1970), was an immediate success. The play takes place in Delhi in 1327 and follows the reign of the Muslim ruler of northern India, Sultan Muhammad Tughlaq. It is not a historical chronicle, however, but rather an allegory of power and idealism. It charts the labyrinthine efforts of Tughlaq to achieve, and be seen to achieve, his ideal liberal society. The play follows the trickery, deceit, force, and violence in which he indulges to attain this. The contradiction between his methods and his ideal destroys him.

The opening scene shows a Muslim *dhobi* paid to pose as a Hindu Brahman to demonstrate that it is possible for a Hindu to bring a successful case against a Muslim ruler. This character, Aziz, and his friend, Aazam, are like the clowns of the traditional *nataka* drama. Aziz, using blatant deceit to achieve success, mirrors Tughlaq's less honest attempts. As similar events occur, we uncover the layers of the play from historical myth to modern allegory, which was conceived in the days after Nehru's era of idealism led to political disillusionment.

Hayavaduna, Karnad's next play to be translated into English, had a curious genesis. He took the theme from Thomas Mann's *The Transposed Heads*, but Mann had taken the story from the Sanskrit *Katha-saritsagara*. The central story is that of two close friends, Devadatta and Kapila, the former a refined philosopher and poet and the latter a "man of the body." When Devadatta falls in love with and marries Padmini, Kapila is also drawn to her. They try to solve these complications in a hilarious scene in which both men behead themselves and Padmini obtains a boon from the bored goddess Kali to restore their heads and their lives. In the dark she mistakes the heads and places them on the wrong bodies. The resulting confusion leads to essential questions as to who is her husband and the father of her expected child. Karnad explore the question of head versus body, but he also goes further to question the tangled identities within a relationship. Finally, the two composite men die again, this time in a duel. None of this is shown as tragic, and to underline this the play is set within the framework of a storyteller who at the beginning meets a sad creature, half man and half horse—Hayavadana of the title—who longs to be whole. The storyteller sends him off to a temple, and at the end of the play the creature returns and has been made whole, a whole horse.

In *Nagamandala*, which is subtitled *Play with a Cobra*, Karnad mixes two folktales and presents his material using all of the energy of Indian folk theater. The first story, which again provides the framework for the whole piece, concerns a man in a temple telling us that he will die if he cannot stay awake the whole night. A chorus of flames, from the lights that are put out at night, introduces a character called Story, who can exist only if someone will listen to her and pass on the story. The man agrees, and her story is the central portion of the play. The story concerns a young woman, Rani, who marries Apanna, who locks her in their new home and returns only at midday to eat. Unhappy, she resorts to a magic potion to make her husband love and stay with her. She cannot go through with it, however, and pours the mixture on an anthill. It is drunk by a king cobra, Naga, who falls in love with her and visits her each night in her husband's shape. She thus sees her husband as a cruel tyrant by day and a caring lover by night and cannot understand. When she becomes pregnant, her husband accuses her of infidelity before the village court, but she chooses trial by plunging her hand into the snake's lair while proclaiming that she has touched none of the male sex except her husband and the snake. It is the truth, and the cobra does not bite her but spreads his hood over her in view of everyone. It is proclaimed a miracle, and she is seen as a goddess incarnate. Her husband is obliged to spend the rest of his life in her service, and the cobra dies of sorrow. The story has been told, and the man has listened all night and has been saved by hearing the story. And, of course, it has been passed on to us.

Nagamandala is perhaps the least demanding of the three Karnad plays translated into English, but it celebrates the folk idiom and shows how it allows for many ways of seeing. It is this complex seeing that is the effective core of his work. And he clothes the core with the entertainment implicit in traditional Indian theater. In this way he challenges us with entertainment.

—John Martin

KEANE, John B(rendan)

Nationality: Irish. **Born:** Listowel, County Kerry, 21 July 1928. **Education:** Saint Michael's College, Listowel, graduated 1947. **Family:** Married Mary O'Connor in 1955; three sons and one daughter. **Career:** Chemist's assistant, 1946-51; street sweeper and furnace operator, Northampton, England, 1952-54. Pub owner-operator, Listowel, 1955—. Weekly columnist Limerick *Leader* and Dublin *Evening Herald*. President, Irish PEN, 1973—. **Awards:** D. Litt: Trinity College, Dublin, 1977; D.F.A.: Marymount Manhattan College, New York, 1984. **Address:** 37 William Street, Listowel, County Kerry, Ireland.

PUBLICATIONS

Plays

Sive (produced Listowel, County Kerry, 1959; London, 1960). Dublin, Progress House, 1959; Elgin, Illinois, Performance, n.d.

Sharon's Grave (produced Cork, 1960; New York, 1961; London, 1988). Dublin, Progress House, 1960; Elgin, Illinois, Performance, n.d.

The Highest House on the Mountain (produced Dublin, 1961). Dublin, Progress House, 1961.

Many Young Men of Twenty (produced Cork, 1961; London, 1987). Dublin, Progress House, 1961; in *Seven Irish Plays 1946-1964*, edited by Robert Hogan, Minneapolis, University of Minnesota Press, 1967.

No More in Dust (produced Dublin, 1962).

Hut 42 (produced Dublin, 1963). Dixon, California, Proscenium Press, 1963.

The Man from Clare (produced Cork, 1963). Cork, Mercier Press, 1963.

The Year of the Hiker (produced Cork and Chicago, 1964). Cork, Mercier Press, 1964.

The Field (produced Dublin, 1965; New York, 1976). Cork, Mercier Press, 1967.

The Roses of Tralee (produced Cork, 1966).

The Rain at the End of the Summer (produced Cork, 1967). Cork, Mercier Press, 1967.

Big Maggie (produced Cork, 1969; New York, 1973). Cork, Mercier Press, and New York and London, French, 1969.

Faoiseamh (produced Dublin, 1970). Dublin, Avel Linn, n.d.

The Change in Mame Fadden (produced Cork and Chicago, 1971). Cork, Mercier Press, 1973.

Moll (produced Killarney, County Kerry, 1971; New York, 1977). Cork, Mercier Press, 1971, revised edition, 1991.

The One-Way Ticket (produced Listowel, County Kerry, 1972). Elgin, Illinois, Performance, 1972.

Values: The Spraying of John O'Dovey, Backwater, and The Pure of Heart (produced Cork, 1973; *The Pure of Heart* produced London, 1985). Cork, Mercier Press, 1973.

The Crazy Wall (produced Waterford, 1973). Cork, Mercier Press, 1974.

Matchmaker (produced Dublin, 1975).

The Good Thing (produced Limerick, 1976). Cork, Mercier Press, 1976; Newark, Delaware, Proscenium Press, 1978.

The Buds of Ballybunion (produced Cork, 1979). Cork, Mercier Press, 1979.

The Chastitute (produced Dublin, 1980). Cork, Mercier Press, 1981.

Three Plays (includes *Sive, The Field, Big Maggie*). Cork, Mercier Press, 1990.

The Field and Other Irish Plays. Niwot, Colorado, Roberts Rinehart Publishers, 1994.

Sharon's Grave, The Crazy Wall, The Man from Clare. Cork, Mercier Press, 1995.

Radio Plays: *Barbara Shearing*, 1959; *A Clutch of Duckeggs*, 1970; *The War Crime*, 1976 (UK); *The Talk Specific*, 1979; *The Battle of Ballybooley*, 1980.

Novels

The Bodhrán Makers. Dingle, County Kerry, Brandon, 1986; New York, Vanguard Press, 1988.

The Ram of God. Boulder, Colorado, Roberts Rinehart Publishers, 1991.

Durango. Boulder, Colorado, Roberts Rinehart Publishers, 1992.

The Contractors. Dublin, Mercier Press, 1993.

A High Meadow. Cork, Mercier Press, 1994.

Short Stories

Death Be Not Proud and Other Stories. Cork, Mercier Press, 1976.

Stories from a Kerry Fireside. Cork, Mercier Press, 1980.

More Irish Short Stories. Cork, Mercier Press, 1981.

Love Bites and Other Stories. Cork, Mercier Press, 1991.

Innocent Bystanders and Other Stories. Cork, Mercier Press, 1994.

More Irish Stories for Christmas. Boulder, Colorado, Roberts Rinehart Publishers, 1995.

The Voice of an Angel and Other Christmas Stories. Cork, Mercier Press, 1995.

Inlaws and Outlaws and Other Stories. Cork, Mercier Press, 1995.

A Warm Bed on a Cold Night and Other Stories. Cork, Mercier Press, 1997.

Under the Sycamore Tree and Other Tales. Cork, Mercier Press, 1997.

Poetry

The Street and Other Poems. Dublin, Progress House, 1961.

Other

Strong Tea. Cork, Mercier Press, 1963.
Self-Portrait. Cork, Mercier Press, 1964.
Letters of a Successful T.D. [*an Irish Parish Priest, an Irish Publican, a Love-Hungry Farmer, a Matchmaker, an Irish Civic Guard, a Country Postman, an Irish Minister of State*]. Cork, Mercier Press, 8 vols., 1967-78.
The Gentle Art of Matchmaking. Cork, Mercier Press, 1973.
Is the Holy Ghost Really a Kerryman? Cork, Mercier Press, 1976.
Unlawful Sex and Other Testy Matters. Cork, Mercier Press, 1978.
Stories from a Kerry Fireside. Cork, Mercier Press, 1980.
Unusual Irish Careers. Cork, Mercier Press, 1982.
Man of the Triple Name. Dingle, County Kerry, Brandon, 1984.
Owl Sandwiches. Dingle, County Kerry, Brandon, 1985.
The Bodhrán Makers. Boulder, Colorado, Roberts Rinehart, 1986.
Letters to the Brain. Dingle, County Kerry, Brandon, 1993.

*

Bibliography: *Ten Modern Irish Playwrights* by Kimball King, New York, Garland, 1979.

Critical Studies: In *Seven Irish Plays 1946-1964* edited by Robert Hogan, Minneapolis, University of Minnesota Press, 1967, and *After the Irish Renaissance* by Hogan, University of Minnesota Press, 1967, London, Macmillan, 1968; *Fifty Years Young: A Tribute to John B. Keane* edited by John M. Feehan, Cork, Mercier Press, 1979; *Festival Glory in Athlone* by Gus Smith, Dublin, Aherloe, 1979; *The Irish Theatre* by Christopher Fitz-Simon, London, Thames and Hudson, 1983; *Modern Irish Drama 1891-1980* by D. E. S. Maxwell, Cambridge, Cambridge University Press, 1984; "The Wall and the Wanderer: Unresolved Domestic Conflict in the Plays of John B. Keane" by Marie Hubert Kealy, in *Notes on Modern Irish Literature* (Butler, Pennsylvania), 1990, pp. 74-78; *The Life and Work of John B. Keane: An Overview* (dissertation) by Lucia Capell, Drew University, 1991; "John B. Keane: The Writer as Irishman" by Paul Deane, in *Notes on Modern Irish Literature* (Butler, Pennsylvania), Spring 1995, pp. 24-33; "Traditional Satire in the Novels of John B. Keane" by Marguerite Quintelli Neary, in *Notes on Modern Irish Literature* (Butler, Pennsylvania), Fall 1995, pp. 29-35; "John B. Keane" by Sister Marie Hubert Kealy, in *Irish Playwrights, 1880-1995: A Research and Production Handbook*, edited by Bernice Schrank and William W. Demastes, Westport, Connecticut, Greenwood, 1997.

John B. Keane comments:

I regard the playwright of today as a man who must speak for his people, to speak up and to speak out, to say what vested interests, politicians, and big business are afraid to say. I believe that men should be tried for not speaking out when doing so would benefit their fellows and ultimately save lives. Those guilty of not doing so are criminals in every sense of the word. Most men have moral courage, but moral courage without skill to impose one's views is like a steed without a rider. I feel strongly about exploring the ills of modern Ireland and the world, for the anguish of our times is the Frankenstein monster that has been created by our convenient and long silences. We reap this anguish because we have encouraged its growth by pulling the bedclothes over our heads, hoping that the ogres might go away and that dawn might purify all. That is why we are fast approaching a post-Christian era. This is why speaking out early and often is so essential if there is to be a decent quality of life. I look to life as it is lived around me and listen to a language that is living. It would be against my nature to ignore a living speech and a living people. I sometimes feel I would die without these to sustain me. Playwriting is my life. Just as a tree spreads its roots into the earth, I spread my recording impulses around the breasts of my people and often into their very cores. People need to be recorded, to be witnessed; they expect and deserve it. I feel a responsibility to my people, a duty to portray them accurately and with dignity lest they are falsely delineated. There is a lot of love and humour in my plays, for without love and humour there is nothing. Where there is love there is every virtue you care to think of: love begets all that is great and constant. Think of that word "constant." That's what love is. That is the rock to which I have anchored myself, and I think my best is to come.

* * *

The distinction between "amateur" and "professional" has been a defining characteristic of the Irish stage from Yeats onward. It is this fact alone that has led to the failure to balance John B. Keane's immense and continuing success with audiences with the low level of critical interest in his achievements. In 1953, the year that the ageing professional Shakespearean actor Anew McMaster made his celebrated attack on the resurgent amateur stage, Keane had yet to write a drama. But in the years between 1959 and 1981 he wrote and published 24 plays, many of which have become *de riguer* in the Irish theater company repertoire.

The Abbey and RTE (the Irish Broadcasting Service) originally rejected the script of *Sive*, Keane's first play. But Keane followed the advice of Michael O'hAodha (at the time an executive with RTE and later with the Abbey), and *Sive* became a huge success on the amateur circuit. Although in the 1990s the context has much changed, it should be recognized that many rural communities in Ireland rarely experienced professional theater. In contrast, amateur dramatic productions were regularly performed in local venues for adjudication on a competitive circuit. When the performance was over, adjudication was given, usually by a "celebrity" from the professional stage. However ambivalent the "professionals" were, few were too proud to turn down the invitation, the fee, the fortnight's free board, and the local attention that went with the role.

Equivocation in Keane's achievements was evident from the outset. The premiere of *Sive* was described by O'hAodha as "a carbon copy of an Abbey production." Tomas McAnna, amateur thespian turned artistic director at the Abbey, was even less ambiguous. The obvious success of the play was due, he said, to the fact that it had been "rewritten in the way suggested by the Abbey Theater," a point that Keane himself has always rebutted.

Keane is self-effacing about his dramatic technique abilities: "There is no character that I haven't actually seen through my own eyes," he has said. Michael Billington, however, in his largely complimentary review of the November 1997 revival of *Sive* at Ben Barnes's Palace Theater in Watford, describes Keane's play in terms of its "characteristic Irish emotionalism . . . [and] unashamed theatricality." In focusing on "character," Keane diverts attention from his characters' successful interaction with their mainly west-of-Ireland settings. He has experimented with other locales, especially in *Hut 42*, Keane's Abbey premiere. The play is, however, one of his least successful, at best "a sentimental perspective of Ireland from a North of England building site." But he has also been criticized for the "prehistoric" quality of his pieces. D. E. S. Maxwell, in writing about *The Field*, observed that while the character Bull McCabe "emanates a brooding menace . . . , the play never brings him, its story, and the telling of it . . . into 'The Present.'"

James N. Healy, creator of many of Keane's major roles, offers a synthesis of the alternating views of the playwright's work by suggesting that the rural background of the plays is a part of the "living present." By way of illustration, the central theme in *The Field* dramatizes an immutable relationship between Man and the space he inhabits: "When you'll be gone Father, to be a Canon . . . Tadgh's children will be milking cows and keeping donkeys out of the ditches. . . . If there's no grass, there's the end of me and mine."

Keane generates with his Irish landscapes an extraordinary concatenation of domesticity and mythic power. In this setting his characters appear—like Hieronymus Bosch figures—distorted but definably real. But Keane's sophisticated and acute powers of observation are sublimated in his creations: his "character" plays (*The Field, Big Maggie, Sive, Sharon's Grave*) reveal the playwright at his most confident and expressive.

In *Sharon's Grave,* for instance, Keane creates a grotesque double-headed monster, which he dismembers as a coup-de-theater at the end of the play. At the point where Dinzie Conlee—the malignant cripple—and his hulking brother Jack—on whose back he is forcibly borne—are both about to mutilate the girl Trassie, Jack sets Dinzie down to settle a score with Trassie's fiancé. Set against this situation, the exposing of the cripple's impotence only serves to underline Keane's ability to exercise remarkable control over the tone of his plays.

Perhaps the most precise assessment of Keane is to describe him as a genuinely "popular" writer. He once declared that his "best is to come." If this is the case, then it will most likely emerge in the form of a more balanced and practical criticism on the revisiting of his plays. This is happening already, not least because Ben Barnes, the erstwhile Abbey director, has laid down some seminal and critically acclaimed professional productions of Keane's major plays. Of these, the British premiere of *Sive* at Watford and its production at the Tricycle Theater Kilburn are the most significant.

—Paul Hadfield

KEATLEY, Charlotte

Nationality: British. **Born:** London in 1960. **Education:** Manchester University, B.A. in drama 1982; University of Leeds, M.A. in theatre arts 1983. **Career:** Theatre critic for the Yorkshire *Post*, *Times Educational Supplement*, *Plays and Players*, Glasgow *Herald*, 1981-85, and for the *Financial Times*; writer, actor, and director in performance art and community theatre in Leeds and Manchester, 1982-84; teacher in drama in primary and secondary schools around Britain, 1985-86; Judith E. Wilson visiting fellow in English, Cambridge University, 1988-98; lecturer in playwriting and theatre skills, University of London, Royal Court Young People's Theatre and Women's National Touring Theatre, London, University of Birmingham, and Vassar College, Poughkeepsie, New York, 1988-92. **Awards:** *Sunday Times* award, for acting, 1980; Manchester *Evening News* award, 1987; George Devine award, 1987; *Plays and Players* award, 1989; Edinburgh Fringe first, for direction, 1991. **Agent:** Rod Hall Agency Ltd., 7 Goodge Place, London W1P 1FL, England.

Publications

Plays

Underneath the Arndale (produced Manchester, 1982).

Dressing for Dinner (produced Leeds, West Yorkshire, 1982).

An Armenian Childhood, with Pete Brooks and Steve Schill (produced Leeds, 1983).

The Legend of Padgate, music by Mark Vibrans (also director: produced Warrington, Cheshire, 1986). London, Methuen, 1994.

Waiting for Martin (produced Manchester and London, 1987).

My Mother Said I Never Should (produced Manchester, 1987; London, 1989; New York, 1990). London, Methuen, 1988; revised version, London, Methuen, 1989.

You're a Nuisance Aren't You, in *Fears and Miseries of the Third Term*, with others (produced Liverpool and London, 1989).

The Singing Ringing Tree (for children), music by Errollyn Wallen (produced Manchester, 1991).

Our Father (produced 1998).

Radio Plays: *My Mother Said I Never Should*, 1989; *Citizens* series, with others, 1989-90; *North and South,* 1997.

Television Play: *Badger* (for children), 1989.

*

Critical Studies: "Art Form or Platform? On Women and Playwrighting" by Lizbeth Goodman, in *New Theatre Quarterly* (Cambridge, England), May 1990, pp. 128-40; "Feminist Drama: The Politics of the Self: Churchill and Keatley" by Jasbir Jain, in *Women's Writing: Text and Context,* edited by Jasbir Jain, Jaipur, India, Rawat, 1996.

Theatrical Activities:
Director: **Plays**—*The Legend of Padgate*, Warrington, Cheshire, 1986; *Autogeddon* by Heathcote Williams, Edinburgh, 1991.

* * *

Charlotte Keatley's play *My Mother Said I Never Should* received widespread acclaim and many subsequent revivals (across the United Kingdom and abroad) after its premier run in London at the Royal Court. With its unique time structure, the play was described in *The Guardian* as "the equivalent to breaking the four minute mile in terms of playwriting for women." *My Mother Said I Never Should* is one of the most widely performed plays by a female playwright. It has been translated and produced in 17 languages and is a curriculum set text in schools and universities in Britain and India.

While the huge success of *My Mother Said I Never Should* is what most often comes to mind when Keatley's name is mentioned, she has had a prodigious and creative output throughout her career, both before the play became so successful and since. Keatley has also written *Underneath the Arndale* (1982) and *Dressing for Dinner* (1983–84). In addition, she was one of the writers for the television serial *Citizens* (1987–88). In an interview in 1989, Keatley compared her work to that of the early feminist and alternative theaters noting that "When you start making plays about your own experiences and in your own language, there is so much to say that the temptation is to say it all quickly and crudely, and so you throw up big signs. After that, you can become more sophisticated and more subtle in the way you say things, which I would say started happening in the late seventies."

Keatley's own work has developed in a similar way, from the dark humor of *Dressing for Dinner* to the more sophisticated balance of humor and drama found in *My Mother Said I Never Should.* Keatley performed in her play *Dressing for Dinner* in a production staged in 1983–84 by The Royal Balle, her own company. The highly visual play centers on the image of the feminine woman and that essential item of apparel—the "little black number." It experiments with images and ideas as well as movement and gesture in a form that reflected 1980s feminist thought and satirized the performance and visual theater styles of the period. Visual tricks such as comparing—through innuendo and layered symbolism—the dressing of a woman and a recipe for dressing chicken in aspic served as shock techniques to first made the audience laugh and then to make them question the source of their laughter. Keatley continued to experiment with shock techniques in her later work, most notably in *My Mother Said I Never Should.* In the later works, however, the "shock" is primarily directed at audience empathy and is not necessarily meant to provoke the audience into a radical questioning of their values and motives.

Both *Dressing for Dinner* and *My Mother Said I Never Should* explore the relationships between generations of women and their shared experiences and memories. Yet *My Mother Said I Never Should* is a much more sophisticated piece of writing and of theater. It can be studied as a script or literary text, chronicling the lives of four generations of British society during the twentieth century. It can be seen also as a political play in the way it pinpoints moments of change. In addition, it is radical in its structure and in its use of female characters.

It can also be studied in larger terms as a performance of self in society; that is, it can be analyzed as a play informed by feminist politics and theories, played out in the differences between generations of women. Keatley, of course, is part of one of those generations. Her skill as a playwright, however, has transcended the limitations of the author's own perspective, offering instead a play which can be—and often is—seen to be filtered through the perspective of different generations. In fact, as Keatley herself once observed after watching her own play, audience members tended to identify with a particular character and with that character's generation. The critical conception of "the gaze" is manipulated in terms of generational difference rather than gender difference. Gender is, however, also a crucial consideration in the play. No male characters appear on stage. Yet unlike many women's plays that are criticized for a lack of male characters, Keatley seems somehow to have sidestepped that kind of red-herring criticism: partly through her use of humor and partly through a skillful manipulation of audience expectations in regard to the invisible male characters. While no men appear on stage in *My Mother Said I Never Should,* Keatley incorporates references to men in the script: husbands and partners are mentioned and at times seem to be present in the wings as the women on stage shout questions and comments to them. This manipulation of audience expectations is used for comic effect but also has a more serious purpose. In Keatley's words: "I finally decided to do the play without men at all because I wanted to present whole ways of being for women which only happen when the men have gone out of the room." That introduction to female characters as they appear when no men are present is one of Keatley's greatest contributions. That men seem to enjoy the play is a tribute to the quality of Keatley's writing. With or without male characters, the creation of plays that deal intelligently with the performance of gender roles makes Keatley a playwright whose work should be read and seen.

—Lizbeth Goodman

KEE Thuan Chye

Nationality: Malaysian. **Born:** Penang, 25 May, 1954. **Education:** Francis Light Primary School; Peang Free School; Universiti Sains Malaysia. Penang; Essex University, M.A. in drama 1987. **Family:** Married, two children. **Career:** Playwright; literary editor, *The National Echo,* 1977-79. Literary editor, *New Straight Times,* 1979—. Contributor to *Asiaweek, Far Eastern Economic Review,* and *The Asia Magazine.*

PUBLICATIONS

Plays

Oh, But I Don't Want to Go; Oh, But I Have To (produced 1974).
Eyeballs, Leper and a Very Dead Spider (produced 1977).
1984 Here and Now (produced 1985). Petaling Jaya, Selangor, K. Das Ink, 1987.
The Big Purge (also director: produced 1988).
*We Could **** You Mr. Birch.* Kuala Lumpur, Academe Art and Print Services, 1995.

Other

Old Doctors Never Fade Away. Kuala Lumpar, Teks Publishing, 1988.
Just in So Many Words. Singapore, Heinemann, 1992.

Editor, *Haunting the Tiger and Other Stories.* Kuala Lumpar, 1991.

*

Critical Study: "Political Theatre in Maylasia: *1984 Here and Now*" by Jacqueline Lo, in *Australasian Drama Studies* (Queensland), April 1993, pp. 54-61.

Theatrical Activities:
Actor: **Plays**–Willy Loman in *Death of a Salesman*; Bill in *Gulls.* **Television**–Acted in 200 episodes of series City of the Rich.

* * *

Though basically known for two plays, Kee Thuan Chye is probably the most sought after dramatist in Malaysia today—writing in English, that is. In Malaysia the national language is Bahasa Malaysia, and it is very hard for those not writing in the national language to become known. But Kee has managed to challenge that by writing two of the most daring and powerful plays in recent Malaysian theater history. Having both directed and acted in plays, Kee has a very strong sense of what makes the piece work on stage, and he exploits this knowledge admirably in his own plays. His university studies in English as well as a master's degree in drama from Essex University in the United Kingdom have no doubt helped in the shaping of his dramatic technique.

Kee came into the limelight with the staging of *1984 Here and Now* (1984), a play he affectionately calls his "notorious agitprop play." This is a play about political oppression and racial discrimination. Kee does not pretend that he was unaware of the sensitivities surrounding the writing and the staging of a play of this nature in a country with declared national agendas. *1984 Here and Now* was a huge success (and continues to be) and made people aware of the more insidious dangers and evils of Big Brotherism and racism. Adapted from Orwell's celebrated novel, Kee's play demonstrated that political awareness is possible through clever inventiveness, witty dialogue, and elaborate stage configurations. The play stated publicly what many Malaysians felt privately; dangerous and sensitive issues were being thrown on stage, and the play's blunt political stand attracted the attention of everyone who was English-educated and in the contemporary political climate. The play marked a milestone in Malaysian theater: no play before this had tackled head-on the directions being set by the political establishment. Using as it did obvious examples of "bad management," the play proved how viable political theater was as a mode of expression in Malaysia. The play spoke directly to the people of their aspirations and frustrations, and there was a resonance that struck deep chords. It was an appropriate play for the times and showed Kee's astute grasp of the more subtle (and sometimes not-so-subtle) aspects of Malaysian political life.

*We Could **** You Mr Birch,* with its deliberate and tantalizing title into which, says Kee, one could insert any appropriate four-letter word, is ostensibly a play about Birch, the British Resident of Perak (one of the bigger states in Malaysia) in Colonial times who was assassinated by the natives (of course the natives had to pay dearly for this) in the nineteenth century. But history, according to Kee, is what we are made to know and made to believe and may not tell the truth, certainly never the whole truth. Thus this play, performed first in 1994, cut the great Birch down to size, destroying the myths of elevation on which thousands of Malaysians had been brought up by the British history textbooks. By using a familiar historical figure and a familiar historical event (which by some was always seen to have been a blot on Malaysia's otherwise peaceful past), Kee cleverly subverts received notions of traditional truths and obliquely, therefore, criticizes current parallel situations. The clash of cultures that led to trouble for Mr. Birch continues to haunt Kee, too, though for the playwright the "haunting" is easy to exorcize if we seek truth with all its discomforts. History is not always reliable, says Kee, and as his actors step aside from their character roles and critique the play on stage, the audiences begin to get a better idea of Kee's dramatic technique of alienating in order to reaffirm. The basic issue is, after all, universal: we are all creatures of history, subject to how others consider the same truths or history—but memories shape histories, which shape identities. Kee is deeply concerned about identity, more so as he continues to live and work in a country where the memory of the horrible events of 13 May 1969 (Malaysia's worst racial riots) is still alive.

There is no doubt whatsoever that Kee's professional career as a journalist (he is the literary editor of Malaysia's *New Straits Times*) has helped tremendously his intellectual fervor. Combining skillfully the theater conventions of both East and West, Kee has given the Malaysian theater in English two major plays (many others of his have been broadcast over the radio) that have so far not been challenged by any other playwright.

—Kirpal Singh

KEEFFE, Barrie (Colin)

Nationality: British. **Born:** London, 31 October 1945. **Education:** East Ham Grammar School, London. **Family:** Married 1) Dee Truman in 1969 (divorced 1979); 2) the writer Verity Bargate in 1981 (died 1981), two stepsons; 3) Julia Lindsay in 1983. **Career:** Actor, at Theatre Royal Stratford East, London, 1964, and National Youth Theatre, 3 years; reporter, *Stratford and Newham Express*, London, to 1969, and for news agency to 1975; dramatist-in-residence, Shaw Theatre, London (Thames TV Playwright scheme), 1977, and Royal Shakespeare Company, 1978; associate writer, Theatre Royal Stratford East, 1986-1991. Member of the Council, National Youth Theatre, 1977—; member of the Board of Directors, Soho Poly Theatre, London, 1978—. **Awards:** French Critics prize, 1978; Mystery Writers of America Edgar Allan Poe award, for screenplay, 1982. **Agent:** Lemon, Unna, and Durbridge, 24 Pottery Lane, Holland Park, London W11 4LZ; and, Gilbert Parker, William Morris Agency, 1325 Avenue of the Americans, New York, New York 10019, U.S.A. **Address:** 110 Annandale Road, London SE10 0JZ, England.

Publications

Plays

Only a Game (produced London, 1973).

A Sight of Glory (produced London, 1975).

Gimme Shelter: Gem, Gotcha, Getaway (*Gem* produced London, 1975; *Gotcha* produced London, 1976; trilogy produced London, 1977; New York, 1978). London, Eyre Methuen, 1977; New York, Grove Press, 1979.

My Girl (produced London, 1975; revised version produced London, 1989). With *Frozen Assets*, London, Methuen, 1989.

A Certain Vincent, with Jules Croiset, adaptation of letters of Vincent Van Gogh (also director: produced Amsterdam and London, 1975).

Scribes (produced Newcastle upon Tyne, 1975; London, 1976; New York, 1977).

Here Comes the Sun (produced London, 1976). Published in *Act 3*, edited by David Self and Ray Speakman, London, Hutchinson, 1979.

Barbarians: *A Trilogy: Killing Time, Abide with Me, In the City* (*Abide with Me* produced London, 1976; trilogy produced London, 1977). London, Eyre Methuen, 1978.

Up the Truncheon (produced London, 1977).
A Mad World, My Masters (produced London, 1977; San Francisco, 1978; revised version produced London, 1984). London, Eyre Methuen, 1977.
Frozen Assets (produced London and San Francisco, 1978; revised version produced London, 1987). London, Eyre Methuen, 1978.
Sus (produced London, 1979; New York, 1983). London, Eyre Methuen, 1979.
Heaven Scent (broadcast 1979). Published in *Best Radio Plays of 1979*, London, Eyre Methuen, 1980.
Bastard Angel (produced London, 1980). London, Eyre Methuen, 1980.
Black Lear (produced Sheffield, 1980).
She's So Modern (produced Hornchurch, Essex, 1980).
Chorus Girls, music by Ray Davies (produced London, 1981).
A Gentle Spirit, with Jules Croiset, adaptation of a story by Dostoevsky (also director: produced Amsterdam, 1981; London, 1982).
The Long Good Friday (screenplay). London, Methuen, 1984.
Better Times (produced London, 1985). London, Methuen, 1985.
King of England (produced London, 1988). With *Bastard Angel*, London, Methuen, 1989.
Not Fade Away (produced London, 1990). In *Wild Justice, Not Fade Away, Gimme Shelter*, 1990.
Wild Justice (produced London, 1990). In *Wild Justice, Not Fade Away, Gimme Shelter*, 1990.
Wild Justice, Not Fade Away, Gimme Shelter: Three Plays. London, Methuen, 1990.
The Long Good Friday (screenplay). London and New York, Methuen, 1998.

Screenplay: *The Long Good Friday*, 1981.

Radio Plays: *Good Old Uncle Jack*, 1975; *Pigeon Skyline*, 1975; *Self Portrait*, 1977; *Heaven Scent*, 1979; *Paradise*, 1989.

Television Plays: *The Substitute*, 1972; *Nipper*, 1977; *Not Quite Cricket*, 1977; *Champions*, 1978; *Hanging Around*, 1978; *Waterloo Sunset*, 1979; *No Excuses* series, 1983; *King*, 1984; *Betty*, 1990.

Recording: *A Certain Vincent*, RCA; *No Excuses*, CBS.

Novels

Gadabout. London, Longman, 1969.
No Excuses (novelization of his television series). London, Methuen, 1983.

Other

The 1984 Verity Bargate Award Short Plays. London, Methuen, 1985.

Editor, *The Verity Bargate Award New Plays 1986*. London, Methuen, 1987.
Editor, *The Verity Bargate Award New Plays 1988*. London, Methuen, 1987.

*

Critical Study: "Barrie Keefe" by John L. DiGaetani, in *A Search for a Postmodern Theater: Interviews with Contemporary Playwrights*, New York, Greenwood, 1991.

Theatrical Activities:
Director: **Plays**—*A Certain Vincent*, Amsterdam and London, 1975; *A Gentle Spirit*, Amsterdam, 1981, London, 1982.

* * *

In the days when Barrie Keeffe worked for a local newspaper in East London, one of his assignments was an astrology column that, even more than most astrology columns, was a piece of total imagination written under the byline of Kay Sera. The random assignment of different fates to his readers must have given his employers some indication of his developing dramatic gifts, but it was another assignment that profoundly colored his future work. At the end of an interview with the procensorship campaigner Mary Whitehouse, later to be the recognizable target of his satire *She's So Modern,* he asked her who the people were that she professed to speak for. With a metaphorical pat on the head, she replied, "Ordinary, decent people; like you and me." The plays that followed the interview, whether comedies or dramas, frequently troubled Whitehouse, particularly when broadcast on television, but Keeffe's explorations of British racism and alienated youth certainly followed his own concerns with decency. What is remarkable for a writer so very much of his time and place is how successful the plays have been in other countries and how they have endured.

Revivals began in the mid 1980s when Keeffe found that *Frozen Assets,* his play written for the Royal Shakespeare Company in 1978, was being performed and revalued. His radio version of the play, somewhat less profane but no less powerful than the stage version, was broadcast by the BBC in his own updated adaptation, and stage revivals were scheduled in acknowledgment that the basic story of a Borstal boy on the run in London had survived with its comical cynicism intact. Indeed, the picture the play paints of East London as a community destroyed by property speculation was provided with additional poignancy in the wake of the yuppie invasion of dockland.

Similarly, 1986 saw revivals of Keeffe's 1977 trilogy of one-act plays *Gimme Shelter,* which included the play *Gotcha,* about a schoolboy who took his teachers hostage with matches held over the open petrol tank of a motorcycle. The arguments in the play had not dated nor had the level of resentment he had first measured in schools that were dumping pupils, unprepared, into a society that could not provide them with jobs. Another apparently topical play was *Sus,* about a black man arrested under the so-called sus law, since abolished, by which people could be held by the police on grounds of suspicion alone. It has also survived the progress of time and continues to appear in various productions both in Britain and abroad, even though it was specifically set on the night of Margaret Thatcher's first electoral victory. At the heart of its survival is the recognizable human pain of the man falsely accused of his wife's death.

Despite the continued interest in Keeffe's early plays and the undoubted influence of his plays about disaffected British youth, the flood of his stage plays in the 1970s subsided to a trickle in the mid-1980s. The plays that appeared in the 1980s were notably different from the scripts of the 1970s, as with the short-lived musical he wrote with Ray Davies of The Kinks, *Chorus*

Girls, a political entertainment taken from an obscure comedy by Aristophanes, *Thesmophoriazusae*. Similar in some ways to the satirical comedy he wrote in 1977 for the Joint Stock Company, *A Mad World, My Masters*—with the title and the spirit of the free-flowing plot borrowed from the Jacobean writer Thomas Middleton—the play tapped a classical source for a current inspiration concerning the kidnapping of Prince Charles by dedicated feminists. The play was ill directed, and it had only a local success in London's Theatre Royal, Stratford East, the theater for which it was designed. It was, nonetheless, witty, often uproariously so, with several excellent songs from Davies, and its presentational format marked a breakthrough in Keeffe's technique.

The play that followed four years later, *Better Times,* was another departure, part documentary about a historic rent strike in East London and part East End comedy in the mood of *A Mad World.* The play was meticulous in its re-creation of the courtroom scenes and back room dramas surrounding an important moment in British socialist history, with the most telling demonstration of Keeffe's talent being the imaginary scenes with his patented version of an East End Keystone Kop. Though cheered by East London audiences, the play was received with bemusement by several critics. It has often been the wayward force of his comedy that has bewildered reviewers, but the touch of absurdism in his work remains another of the qualities that keeps the apparently topical subject matter of the plays alive.

Keeffe's work has long benefited from associations with specific companies, beginning with the National Youth Theatre and achieving a major impetus from Verity Bargate's support at London's Soho Poly Theatre. It was in this small venue that both of his youthful trilogies, *Gimme Shelter* and *Barbarians,* were developed, and something of the claustrophobic power of these pictures of aimless young Londoners can probably be ascribed to their original performance space, which he exploited to its full. The trilogies boldly gave his inarticulate and angry young men a rich imagistic language, both abusive and tender, that has been much imitated by younger writers. Keeffe, however, has varied his dramatic offerings much more than has his followers, and his own influences range visibly from Plautus—the twins in *She's So Modern*—to Chekhov.

Bastard Angel was written for the Royal Shakespeare Company. Belying its own gutsy story of a female rock singer rattling painfully through despair in the mansion she has bought in order to humiliate servants who humiliated her when she was a young singer, the play took its inspiration from Chekhov's *Platonov,* and key images from each of the four acts of the Russian play have been retained. More cataclysmic by far than the Chekhov original, with the rock star entering into a sexual relationship with her own son, the play manages to retain autumnal beauty in the midst of violent events and blasting music. The later television version, *No Excuses,* carried the story further but lacked the focus of the stage version, which is a major work.

Throughout the 1980s Keeffe developed a successful relationship with London's Theatre Royal, Stratford East, once the home of Joan Littlewood. A split with the theater came in 1991, but his work with Philip Hedley there produced two of his best plays, *My Girl* and *Wild Justice,* both written for the actor Karl Howman.

My Girl is a claustrophobic comedy, highly impassioned and often painful, about the relationship between a social worker and his wife. The constant caring for strangers that is his job seems to deprive him of the devotion appropriate to his heavily pregnant wife and their child, but a crisis is reached when his attraction to a client threatens their marriage. Never simply about the relationship, since the fundamental anxiety concerns Sam's inability to reconcile his own ideals with the stress of his underpaid job, it is a powerful love story nonetheless. *Wild Justice* is a modern revenge play, triggered by the death of a child and as blackly insistent as any Jacobean revenge tragedy. It contains some of the very best of Keeffe's writing.

With the success of his screenplay *The Long Good Friday,* a film that seized the initiative from American crime movies to mingle East End villainy, the IRA, international crime, and a unique political perspective, Keeffe moved into the rank of writers constantly courted by Hollywood, a not altogether happy arrangement given the tendency of moviemakers to demand a Hollywood version of his vision. Prior to that he had contributed notably to British television, particularly with his audacious comedy *Waterloo Sunset,* with its portrait of an elderly white woman who walks out of a home for old folks and moves in with a black family in South London. It later became the stage play *Not Fade Away.*

Keeffe's short prizewinning radio play *Heaven Scent,* about crime and perfume, is a model of radio technique and beautifully demonstrates his gift for characterization and storytelling. Radio also saw the premiere of his epic drama about Robespierre, *Paradise,* a play of great power and historical clarity that recognizes, as few other sources do, the extreme youth of the makers of the French Revolution. Vast in its intention and achievement, the play has yet to find a stage performance.

Adept in all areas of drama, Keeffe has also written the novel *No Excuses,* which provides interesting commentary on the intentions of the story. It loses the touch of Chekhov, however, that made the original play so effective. With his exuberant language and uninhibited vision of the potential of the stage, Keeffe's greatest gifts are theatrical, and few writers have his ability to create searing images through the speech of their characters.

—Ned Chaillet

KEENE, Daniel

Nationality: Australian. **Born:** 1955. **Career:** Teacher, Swinburne University, Melbourne, 1990-92. **Awards:** Best feature, Banff International Television Festival, 1986, for *The Hour Before My Brother Dies*; Louis Esson prize for drama, 1989, for *Silent Partner*; Green room award, best new Australian play, 1996, for *All Souls*; Wal Cherry play of the year award, 1996, for *Beneath Heaven*; Jill Blewitt playwright's award and Australian National Playwrights' Center award, 1996, for *Because You Are Mine.*

Publications

Plays

Skelta (produced Melbourne, 1981).
Horseplay (produced Melbourne, 1982).
Car Crash at the O.K. Corral (produced Melbourne, 1982).
Ruby Dark (produced Melbourne, 1983). In *Exiles in Paradise,* Fringe Network, 1983.
The Snake Pit (produced Melbourne, 1984).

Cho Cho San (produced Melbourne, 1984). Sydney, Currency Press, 1987.
Isle of Swans (produced Melbourne, 1985; New York, 1987).
The Hour Before My Brother Dies (produced New York, 1986).
The Fighter (produced Melbourne, 1986; New York, 1988).
Silent Partner (produced Melbourne, 1989).
Estrella! (produced Melbourne, 1990).
Low (produced Perth, 1991).
Adjacent Rooms, with score by Michale Smetanin (produced 1993).
All Souls (produced Adelaide, 1993). Sydney, Currency press, 1995.
Skinless Kiss of Angels, with score by Michale Smetanin (produced Melbourne, 1993).
Beneath Heaven (produced 1995).
Because You Are Mine (produced Adelaide, 1996).
Terminus (produced Adelaide, 1996).
The Prisoner and His Keeper (produced Adelaide, 1997).
Homeland & A Glass of Twilight (produced Melbourne, 1997).
Seeing in the Dark (produced Melbourne, 1998).
The Architect's Walk (produced Adelaide, 1998).
Untitled Monologue (produced Melbourne, 1998).
Night, A Wall, Two Men & Neither Lost Nor Found (produced Melbourne, 1998).
Custody, What Remains & To Whom It May Concern (produced Melbourne, 1998).

Screenplays: *Cold Love*, 1988; *Riding Down the Sky*, 1989; *Isle of Swans,* 1990; *Silent Partner,* 1992; *Low,* 1992; *Juke,* with Laurie McInnes, 1995; *Remembering Babylon,* adapted from the novel by David Malouf, 1995.

Television Plays: *The Hour Before My Brother Dies,* 1986.

Poetry

Nocturnes. North Fitzroy, Victoria, Black Pepper, 1997.

*

Critical Study: "*Cho Cho San:* A Triumph of Collaboration" by Geoffrey Milne, in *Australasian Drama Studies* (Queensland), 1988, pp. 85-101.

Theatrical Activities:
Director: Many of his own plays.

* * *

Since beginning his playwriting career in 1979, Melbourne-based Daniel Keene has had more than 20 plays professionally produced, some of them as many as five or six times, and these productions have appeared in every state of Australia. He has also written libretti for experimental music-theater pieces and contributed short dramatic pieces and lyrics to other larger works. In addition, 10 productions or public readings of Keene's plays have been seen in New York, Paris, and Edinburgh, as well as in Poland and China. By 1998 Keene was the ninth-most-produced playwright in Australia in the 1990s, tying Anton Chekhov.

Although Keene has written about a wide variety of topics in different forms, his plays can be loosely grouped into four categories: intense, small-cast examinations of contemporary Australian working-class "battlers" in mostly realistic form; larger-scale plays dealing with wider social issues in a more surreal, "fantastic" style; music-theater and mixed-form pieces; and plays dealing with international figures and events in a highly imaginative, fictionalized style. In most of his work, it is the underdog, the misunderstood, and the downtrodden who excite our sympathy, no matter how reprehensible their behavior may be. Likewise, in all of his work—including the most ostensibly realistic of the plays—the language of his characters is imbued with a heightened poeticism, while dreams, role-playing, and flashbacks to the past play an important role in revealing the truth about present realities.

His small-scale plays about the growing Australian underclass are arguably his most successful. In *The Hour Before My Brother Dies* (premiered in Melbourne in 1985), Sally and her brother Martin have just one hour together in which to settle scores and to reassess their lives before Martin is to be hanged for a murder to whose details we are not made privy. What emerges in the steamy and impassioned role-play of the dreamlike flashbacks is that both have been abused by other members of their dysfunctional family and that, in seeking refuge in each other, they have had an incestuous relationship. Despite the unpalatable and even sordid nature of its subject, the play evokes our sympathy for its inarticulate and brutalized characters through the unsentimentalized compassion of the author's treatment.

In *Low* (premiered in Sydney in 1991 but seen since in five separate productions in Australia), Emma and Jay are also desperately in search of meaning, love, and affection in their petty lives together but find little solace in their routine drinking sprees. But when they embark on a career of holding up corner stores (first at knifepoint, later with a gun, and still later wearing absurdly playful-looking pig masks), they suddenly feel, in their inarticulate way, as good as anyone with a proper career. Again, the characters' actions are indefensible, but the underlying reason for their behavior is clear: the dispossessed, uneducated pair turn to drink and crime because the inexorable march of economic rationalism has left them with nothing else to do. The theme of betrayal is also explored in two plays set in the shadowy world of fringe, working-class sport. In *Silent Partner* (which won the Victorian Premier's Literary Award for Drama in 1989 and later appeared in four other cities), a pair of gullible, small-time punters see their dream of owning a racing greyhound come true, but the dream turns sour along with their mateship (the only decent thing they have) when the crooked realities of the racing game take over. *The Fighter* (1986) is about a drink-soaked ex-boxer, Joey, who is haunted by dreams of his failed career and by the ghosts of his (possibly murdered) girlfriend and his brother, who was killed in the Vietnam war. Like Martin in *The Hour*, Joey tries uncomprehendingly to reconstruct the meaning of his life as it nears its end.

The blend of gritty realism, dreams, and fantasy does not work as successfully in the larger-scale plays about misfits and arbitrary violence, like *All Souls* and *Terminus*, both commissioned by the Red Shed Theatre Company in Adelaide in 1993 and 1996, respectively. These have been criticized as overwritten and risking self-parody in their overblown mysticism, but his music-theater works have won wide acclaim and high praise. *Cho Cho San* (which was premiered in Melbourne in 1984) is an imaginative reworking of the *Madame Butterfly* story in the form of an opera for actors, singers, and life-sized "Bunraku-style" puppets. In this play the yearning for love and the themes of oppression, betrayal, and dispossession reach their highest statement in this author's work. Some of Keene's plays about international issues also reveal great passion and forceful rage, especially *Because You Are Mine* (another Red Shed commission in 1994), which deals with the violence, deprivation, and dislocation that are the daily stuff of ordinary people's lives in a Bosnia wracked by civil war.

In writing with rage and compassion about the dispossessed underclass of society, Daniel Keene honors a class that is too often neglected or ridiculed on the Australian stage.

—Geoffrey Milne

KEMPINSKI, Tom

Nationality: British. **Born:** London, 24 March 1938. **Education:** Hall School; Abingdon Grammar School; Cambridge University (open scholar). **Family:** Married. **Career:** Actor, 1960-71. **Awards:** London Drama Critics award, 1980. **Agent:** Alan Brodie Representation, ICM, 8942 Wilshire Boulevard, Beverly Hills, California 90026, U.S.A.

Publications

Plays

The Peasants Revolt (produced Essex, 1971).
The English Civil War (produced London, 1972).
Moscow Trials (produced London, 1972).
Pageant of Labour History (4 plays; produced London, 1973).
The Ballad of Robin Hood, with Roger Smith (produced London, 1973).
October, with Roger Smith (produced 1973).
Sell-Out (1931), with Roger Smith, music by Kempinski and Smith (produced London, 1974).
Flashpoint (as Gerrard Thomas) (produced London, 1978).
What about Borneo? (produced London, 1978).
The Workshop, adaptation of a play by Jean-Claude Grumberg (produced London, 1979; as *The Workroom*, produced New Haven, Connecticut, 1982).
Japanese Noh Plays (for children; produced Leicester, 1979).
Mayakovsky, adaptation of a work by Stefan Schütz (produced London, 1979).
Duet for One (produced London, 1980; New York, 1981). London, French, 1981.
Dreyfus, adaptation of the play by Jean-Claude Grumberg (produced London, 1982).
The Beautiful Part of Myself (produced Watford, Hertfordshire, 1983).
Life of Karl Marx, with Roger Smith (produced London, 1984).
Self-Inflicted Wounds (produced Mold, Clwyd, 1985).
Separation (produced London, 1987). London, French, 1989.
Sex Please, We're Italian (produced London, 1991).
A Free Country, adaptation of a play by Jean-Claude Grumberg (produced London, 1991).
When the Past Is Still to Come (produced London, 1992).

Screenplay: *Duet for One*, with Jeremy Lipp and Andrei Konchalovsky, 1987.

*

Tom Kempinski comments:

There are two kinds of oppression in the world: the oppression of one group in society by another, and the oppression of one part of a person by another part of the same person. I write about both kinds, because I have experienced both—and also studied and struggled to change both.

My historical plays are influenced by English radio comedy of the 1950s, and include songs and music which I compose.

My "personal" plays are characterised by attempts to penetrate beneath the surface of people's deeds to their inner, and often concealed motives. These plays are written in a "naturalistic" "style," and—in a country that keeps a stiff upper lip (since 1800?) in order not to show weakness to wogs, niggers, wops, and other human beings which Britain has conquered—are found to be just a touch emotional.

Top people—whether parents or dictators—prefer lies of all kinds, because they invent these lies to maintain their superior status in the world.

* * *

Tom Kempinski writes about strong people under unbearable pressure, charting the process of their bravely resisted but inevitable collapse. Stephanie Abrahams in *Duet for One* is a classical musician struck down by multiple sclerosis and compelled to face a life without the music that has been the center of it; Isaac Cohen in *Self-Inflicted Wounds* is a dedicated Nazi hunter who finds his courage faltering when it comes time to publish his research; Carter in *Flashpoint* is a wisecracking soldier whose method of coping with army routine is tested in a crisis.

Given these outlines, it is not surprising that Kempinski's plays sometimes skirt the edge of soap opera and melodrama. *Duet for One*, which consists entirely of Stephanie's sessions with an overly wise psychologist, at least in part follows a predictable emotional outline. One knows from the minute she enters, bravely denying a psychological problem, that she will eventually break down and cry ("I-can-never-never-play-the-the-the-violin again" at the end of act 1), just as one can predict that the laconic psychologist will eventually make an eloquent pull-yourself-together speech (in act 2). *Self-Inflicted Wounds* is also a bit schematic in the way Cohen's affair with a young girl and his own family secrets are twisted back on the main plot to be used against him by his enemies. And the action of *Flashpoint*, which involves an armed soldier going berserk and taking his platoon hostage in an attempt to stop the execution of a deserter, threatens to lose sight of its ideas in the melodramatic action.

But while these dangers are not always avoided, they are almost inevitable given Kempinski's determination to find the sources and limits of his protagonists' strength. It is notable that the process is not simple or direct, and the discoveries made are complex and sometimes surprising. Stephanie Abrahams does not go from bold defiance to simple despair; the predictable breakdown is only the end of the first act. Kempinski sees that despair is a step, not a conclusion. It is followed by self-denial and self-abasement as Stephanie tries to convince herself that she does not care about her loss of dignity and self-control, by self-deceit as the fear of losing her husband is raised to deflect the psychologist from deeper probing, and only then by the loss of all defenses and the admission of the elementary fears that everything else was covering, an admission that Kempinski sees as the bravest step of all and the basis for hope.

Similarly, Cohen's perplexing hesitancy to publish the damning results of his research is not explained or exposed simply. Each revelation gives a little more true than the one before it, but not the entire truth. Even at the end, when Cohen admits that he might have deliberately sabotaged himself by giving his enemies the means to discredit him, his reasons are a subtle mixture of weakness and strength, betrayals of his own morality and higher affirmations of it. And Carter is also shown to be more complex than one might first expect; his wise guy attitude does not keep him from being the strongest participant in the hostage crisis or bar him from sympathy for his weaker comrades. It is only after the crisis is over and he learns how those outside had manipulated both gunman and hostages that Carter momentarily breaks, showing in his sense of betrayal a core of faith in the military that his sneers had hidden.

Kempinski's one attempt at comedy, *Sex Please, We're Italian*, merely proves that his talents do not lie in that area. This would-be romp about townsfolk trying to hide their many sexual peccadilloes from a visiting clergyman is leadenly unfunny, without the manic energy or insane internal logic that successful farce demands.

Duet for One remains the strongest of Kempinski's plays, largely because it is such a successful theatrical piece, and its effectiveness as a vehicle for a sensitive actress disguises or counterbalances its weaknesses. It is also the most tightly focused of his plays. Making the enemy a disease frees Kempinski from having to create melodramatic events and also eliminates any potentially distracting political overtones. Like many well-meaning political writers, Kempinski tends to become less controlled and more simplistic the closer he comes to his own passionate convictions. To the extent that *Self-Inflicted Wounds* is about Nazism, *Flashpoint* about the British military presence in Northern Ireland, or *Dreyfus* about anti-Semitism, they are at their weakest and most diffuse. Kempinski's strengths are always in the personal dramas.

—Gerald M. Berkowitz

KENNEDY, A(lison) L(ouise)

Nationality: Scottish. **Born:** Dundee, 1965. **Education:** Warwick University, degree in drama. **Career:** Administrative appointments in two creative writing programs. Full-time writer. **Awards:** Saltire Award for Best First Book, for *Night Geometry and the Garscadden Trains*; Mail on Sunday/John Llewellyn Rhys Prize; Somerset Maugham Award, for *Looking for the Possible Dance*; Encore Award and joint winner of Saltire Scottish Book of the Year award, for *So I Am Glad.*

Publications

Plays

Delicate. Leamington Spa, Motionhouse, 1996.
The Life and Death of Colonel Blimp (screenplay). London, British Film Institute, 1997.
The Audition (produced Edinburgh, 1997).

Screenplay: *Stella Does Tricks.*

Novels

Looking for the Possible Dance. London, Secker and Warburg, 1993.
So I Am Glad. London, J. Cape, 1995.

Short Stories

Night Geometry and the Garscadden Trains. London, Phoenix, 1990.
Now That You're Back. London, Vintage, 1994.
Original Bliss. London, Jonathan Cape, 1997.

Other

Editor, with James McGonigal. *A Sort of Hot Scotland.* Aberdeen, Association for Scottish Literary Studies, 1994.
Editor, with Hamish Whyte. *The Ghost of Liberace.* Aberdeen, Association for Scottish Literary Studies, 1993.

* * *

Alison Louise Kennedy was born in Dundee, Scotland, and educated at the high school there and at Warwick University, where she took a degree in drama. While she was still a student, she wrote "stage pieces whenever they were required" and also involved herself in acting and production. After leaving the university, she held two appointments in creative writing before settling enthusiastically in Glasgow as a full-time writer.

In a sense Kennedy's verbal preoccupation makes her a natural for writing for the screen, especially television, and it is in this sphere that most of her work has been concentrated. To an interviewer who once asked her if studying drama had influenced her writing, she replied, "Being the kind of writer I am, it was probably the best training I could have had, because I'm very ear-related. I hear the language. I'm not actually good with seeing things. I learn a lot with my ear and I understand writing by ear. Writing is very aural. If you think about all the language that describes literature, it's all about rhythm and music and pace and timing—things that don't actually exist on the page but that exist within the reader's mind." She herself trained to be an actor but eventually had to come to terms with failure in that sphere. "I went through the whole thing of being obsessed with the theatre, being in love with it, and it just didn't work. . . ."

Kennedy's only stage drama, *The Audition,* was written for Mike Haywood and was a spectacular success, although its humor is characteristically grim. The play, which aroused both admiration and expectations, deals with the idea that all the world is a stage, although "subverting it with characteristic unflinching starkness." It was staged by Borderline Theatre in 1997 at the Edinburgh International Festival Fringe, the seedbed of much fresh talent, and it was very well received, being voted a Fringe first. For television she wrote the feature film *Stella Does Tricks* and a number of plays for the BBC Education Department on historical topics, an experience that, she says, gave her "an ear for dialogue."

One English critic hailed *The Audition* as "a remarkable debut from a talented novelist who looks set to become a playwright of distinction." Writing in Glasgow's *Herald,* Gerard Seeman observed that "her films and her stage plays are far less serious than her prose, perhaps because there is a director to provide a second strand of creative input, or perhaps because her apparent preoccupation with stylistics cannot be transferred to this medium. She does, however, take her screen and stage writing very seriously."

Since that time Kennedy has become one of the most enthusiastically hailed younger novelists and story writers in Britain. The chorus of acclaim with which her fiction has been greeted seems, for the time being at least, to have diverted her from writing for the stage and television.

—Maurice Lindsay

KENNEDY, Adrienne (Lita)

Nationality: American. **Born:** Adrienne Hawkins, Pittsburgh, Pennsylvania, 13 September 1931; grew up in Cleveland, Ohio. **Education:** Educated in Cleveland public schools; Ohio State University, Columbus, B.A. in education 1953; Columbia University, New York, 1954-56. **Family:** Married Joseph C. Kennedy in 1953 (divorced 1966); two sons. **Career:** Joined Edward Albee's workshop in 1962. Lecturer in playwriting, Yale University, New Haven, Connecticut, 1972-74, Princeton University, New Jersey, 1977, and Brown University, Providence, Rhode Island, 1979-80; chancellor's distinguished lecturer, University of California, Berkeley, 1986; visiting professor, Harvard University, Cambridge, Massachusetts, fall 1997. Member of the Board of Directors, PEN, 1976-77. **Awards:** Obie award, 1965; Guggenheim fellowship, 1967; Rockefeller grant, 1967, 1969, 1973; New England Theatre Conference grant; National Endowment for the Arts grant, 1972; CBS-Yale University fellowship, 1973; Creative Artists Public Service grant, 1974; Academy award in Literature, American Academy of Arts and Letters, 1994; Lilla Wallace-Reader's Digest Fund Writers' award, 1994; Pierre LeComte duNouy Foundation award, for *The Ohio State Murders,* 1994. **Agent:** Bridget Aschenberg, 40 West 57th Street, New York, New York 10019, U.S.A. **Address:** 325 West 89th Street, New York, New York 10024, U.S.A.

PUBLICATIONS

Plays

Funnyhouse of a Negro (produced New York, 1964; London, 1968). New York, French, 1969.

The Owl Answers (produced Westport, Connecticut, and New York, 1965). Included in *Cities in Bezique*, 1969.

A Beast's Story (produced New York, 1965). Included in *Cities in Bezique*, 1969.

A Rat's Mass (produced Rome, 1966; New York and London, 1970). Published in *New Black Playwrights*, edited by William Couch, Jr., Baton Rouge, Louisiana State University Press, 1968.

The Lennon Play: In His Own Write, with John Lennon and Victor Spinetti, adaptation of works by Lennon (produced London, 1967; revised version produced London, 1968; Albany, New York, 1969). London, Cape, 1968; New York, Simon and Schuster, 1969.

A Lesson in Dead Language (produced New York and London, 1968). Published in *Collision Course*, New York, Random House, 1968.

Boats (produced Los Angeles, 1969).

Sun: A Poem for Malcolm X Inspired by His Murder (produced London, 1969). Published in *Scripts 1* (New York), November 1971.

Cities in Bezique: 2 One-Act Plays: The Owl Answers and A Beast's Story. New York, French, 1969.

An Evening with Dead Essex (produced New York, 1973).

A Movie Star Has to Star in Black and White (produced New York, 1976). Published in *Wordplays 3*, New York, Performing Arts Journal Publications, 1984.

Orestes and Electra (produced New York, 1980). Included in *In One Act*, 1988.

Black Children's Day (produced Providence, Rhode Island, 1980).

A Lancashire Lad (for children; produced Albany, New York, 1980).

In One Act (includes *Funnyhouse of a Negro, The Owl Answers, A Lesson in Dead Language, A Rat's Mass, Sun, A Movie Star Has to Star in Black and White, Electra, Orestes*). Minneapolis, University of Minnesota Press, 1988.

She Talks and Beethoven: 2 One-Act Plays. Published in *Antaeus* (New York), no.66, Spring 1991.

The Alexander Plays. Minneapolis, University of Minnesota Press, 1992.

In One Act (includes *Funnyhouse of a Negro*; *The Owl Answers*; *A Lesson in Dead Language*; *A Rat's Mass*; *Sun*; *A Movie Star Has To Star in Black and White* and adaptations of *Electra* and *Orestes*). Minneapolis, University of Minnesota Press.

Other

People Who Led to My Plays (memoirs). New York, Knopf, 1987.

Deadly Triplets: A Theatre Mystery and Journal. Minneapolis, University of Minnesota Press, 1990.

*

Critical Studies: *Intersecting Boundaries, The Theater of Adrienne Kennedy,* edited by Paul K. Bryant-Jackson and Lois More Overbeck, Minneapolis, University of Minnesota Press, 1992; in *The Subject's Tragedy: Political Poetics, Feminist Theory, and Drama* by Linda Kintz, Ann Arbor, University of Michigan Press, 1992; *Shackles on a Writer's Pen: Dialogism in Plays by Alice Childress, Lorraine Hansberry, Adrienne Kennedy, and Ntozake Shange* (dissertation) by Elizabeth Barnsley Brown, University of North Carolina at Chapel Hill, 1996; "Dividing Cultures: Racially Unresolved Identities in Adrienne Kennedy's Drama" by Avra Sidiropoulou, in *Nationalism and Sexuality: Crises of Identity,* edited by Yiorgos Kalogeras, Thessaloniki, Greece, Aristotle University, 1996; "Realism, Narrative, and the Feminist Playwright–A Problem of Reception" by Jeanie Forte, in *Feminist Theatre and Theory,* edited by Helene Keyssar, New York, St. Martin's, 1996; "Gods and Owls: The Sacred and the Profane in Adrienne Kennedy's *The Owl Answers*" by Carla J. McDonough and "A Prison of Object Relations: Adrienne Kennedy's *Funnyhouse of a Negro*" by Claudia Barnett, both in *Modern Drama* (Canada), Fall 1997; "Her Dissonant Selves: The Semiotics of Plurality and Bisexuality in Adrienne Kennedy's *Funnyhouse of a Negro*" by Obododimma Oha, in *American Drama* (Cincinnati, Ohio), Spring 1997, pp. 67-80.

Adrienne Kennedy comments:

My plays are meant to be states of mind.

* * *

As the black power movement gathered strength in the United States in the 1960s, the dramatist Adrienne Kennedy was discovering more uses for the word "Negro." She marked the beginnings of celebrating blackness with *Funnyhouse of a Negro* (1962), in which a character's history of miscegenation, rape, and madness records the larger history of black experience in white America, a history that Americans now sanitize and democratize under the rubric "race relations." Kennedy makes no claim to represent anyone, but the play's motifs resonate sharply with collective history.

In her New York apartment Kennedy's Negro-Sarah enshrines an enormous statue of Queen Victoria and, in the course of the play, splits into a hunchbacked Jesus, the duchess of Hapsburg, the African liberation leader Patrice Lumumba, and even Queen Victoria Regina, each denoted as "One of Herselves." This is history and identity in a fun house of distorted mirrors whose reflections are as unthinkable in a racist America emerging from the 1950s as Sarah herself, child of a light-skinned woman raped by her missionary husband in Africa. Inexorably Sarah's incarnations emerge from darkness to narrate bits of the original trauma: the missionary zeal of the father who "wanted the black man to rise from colonialism"; the mother who "didn't want him to save the black race and spent her days combing her hair . . . and would not let him touch her in their wedding bed and called him black"; the daughter conceived in violence who rejects the father but who resembles him and watches her mother lapse into madness and then death, the remembered sign for which is hair that falls out.

Throughout the play shining hairless skulls appear in dialogue and enacted fantasy until Sarah tries to stifle her father's, and her race's, claim on her by bludgeoning him with an ebony mask. Yet he returns: "He keeps returning forever, coming back ever and keeps coming back forever." Sarah's white friends, who "keep [her] from reflecting too much upon the fact that [she is] a Negro," cannot protect her from this recurring, repressed racial memory, signified by the repeated sound of knocking and the obsessively repeated images of fallen hair, both kinky and straight, on a white pillow; of yellowness, the mixed-race pallor of Sarah's skin; and of swarming ravens and of death heads. The surrealistic "funnyhouse" of Sarah's memory defies linear logic. Her father hangs himself or does not—in the two versions of the story—but the last image of the play shows Sarah herself hanged, reclaimed by the jungle that engulfs the stage.

Sarah's split subjectivity bears the scars of African American history. Her identification with her mother and murderous repression of her father's culture engage the discourses of feminism and psychoanalysis and reveal the desire and exclusion embodied in Kennedy's Negro. *Funnyhouse of a Negro* won an Obie in 1964, the year that *Dutchman* by LeRoi Jones (Amiri Baraka) won the same award.

The Owl Answers (1965) brilliantly extends these issues through the laminated identities of Kennedy's protagonist, SHE who is CLARA PASSMORE who is the VIRGIN MARY who is the BASTARD who is the OWL, whose history generates another violently skewed family romance, this time with a poor black mother and the RICHEST WHITE MAN IN THE TOWN. Gradually a story emerges of a bastard daughter of a mixed-race union who is adopted by the Reverend Passmore and renamed Clara. She carries her black mother's color and a passion for her white father's culture, "the England of dear Chaucer, Dickens and dearest Shakespeare," whose works she reads as a child in the Passmore library and later disseminates as a "plain, pallid" schoolteacher in Savannah. The glorious fathers of literary history merge with those of Christian myth as God's white dove, which is associated with Passmore's preaching, replaces the jungle father's black ravens in *Funnyhouse of a Negro*. The adopted Clara identifies her black mother, called a whore, with the Virgin Mary. But on a fantasy visit to England the white fathers who have colonized her desire refuse Clara access to St. Paul's, where she imagines burying her own white father, and lock her in the Tower of London. Rejected by her father but unable to bury or repress him, Clara is imprisoned in her own history. In the play's associative logic the tower is also a New York subway car in which the adult Clara, lost in guilt and rage, picks up a Negro man, introduces herself as Mary, addresses him as God, and tries to stab him.

The Tower of London (dominant white culture) and the high altar (sacrificial Christianity) are the phallic edifices against which Clara Passmore measures her being. She is ultimately transformed into a screeching owl, a symbol of her black mother and her criminal origins: "The Owl was [my] beginning." Although her adopted status allows her to "pass more," Clara belongs to the owls, for she cannot belong to the world of "Buckingham Palace, . . . the Thames at dusk, and Big Ben" or to the "Holy Baptist Church . . . on the top of the Holy Hill." Near the end of the play Clara kneels to pray: "I call God and the Owl answers."

This summary conveys nothing of Kennedy's surrealistic spectacle: "There is the noise of the train, the sound of moving steel on the track." "The WHITE BIRD's wings should flutter loudly"—a cacophony that should evoke, says Kennedy "a sense of exploding imprisonment."

Two shorter works, *Lesson in a Dead Language* (1968) and *A Rat's Mass* (1966), added new elements to Kennedy's bestiary. In the first, Western culture in the form of a Latin lesson and a schoolteacher, costumed from the waist up as a White Dog, and Christian doctrine in the form of enormous statues of Jesus, Joseph, Mary, the Wise Men, and a shepherd instruct and overwhelm seven little girls whose initiation into menstruation marks them and their white dresses as guilty. In *A Rat's Mass* redemptive authority resides in a schoolmate, Rosemary, who refuses to expiate the incestuous crime of Brother and Sister Rat. The sister goes mad. In this as in all of Kennedy's beautifully crafted plays, cultural exclusion translates into sexual terror and guilt, the signs of Negro womanhood.

In *A Movie Star Has to Star in Black and White* (1976) Kennedy explores the fantasy incursions of cinema stars and scenarios into the life of a young black woman named, as in *The Owl Answers,* Clara. Sharing with earlier American dramatists such as Elmer Rice, Sophie Treadwell, Clifford Odets, and Tennessee Williams a fascination with film technique, Kennedy goes beyond occasional references to important films. Her cast list calls for actors who resemble Bette Davis and Paul Henreid of *Now Voyager*; Marlon Brando and Jean Peters of *Viva Zapata!,* and Montgomery Clift and Shelley Winters of *A Place in the Sun,* as well as actors who evoke Clara's personal family photos. Real life and cinematic life are interwoven, with movie stars adopting the rhythms of their film roles but narrating key scenes of Clara's family history. Familiar Kennedy themes—family trauma, sexual guilt, isolation, racial terror—mingle with allusions to earlier Kennedy texts as, the playwright informs us, "[Clara] lets her movie stars speak for her."

The 1990s witnessed a second florescence of Kennedy's dramatic writing. In 1992 the University of Minnesota Press issued *The Alexander Plays,* bringing together four one-act works—*Ohio State Murders, She Talks to Beethoven, The Film Club (A Mono-*

logue by Suzanne Alexander), and *The Dramatic Circle*—in which the memories and fantasies of a mature woman writer, Suzanne Alexander, are represented by, among other works, Beethoven's *Fidelio,* Napoleon and Josephine's love letters, Eisenstein's *Potempkin,* Hardy's *Tess of the D'Urbervilles,* Bram Stoker's *Dracula,* and Frantz Fanon's *The Wretched of the Earth.* Except for the longest play, *The Ohio State Murders,* which is an allegory of racist university life in the 1950s, Kennedy's world-traveled Suzanne Alexander finds herself in London, Accra, and Washington, D.C., mourning the absence of her husband David whose work with Fanon takes him to dangerous places. If violent images of psychic and social horrors dominated Kennedy's early plays, the retrospective tone of *The Alexander Plays* produces effects no less shocking. Signs and symbols proliferate, disappear, transmogrify, and reappear with the cadence of certain dread and growing paranoia. Kennedy has written in "Theatre Journal," appended to her novel *Deadly Triplets,* "Despite the enchantment there was a subplot in England that I couldn't perceive."

The winner of numerous grants and awards, Kennedy was honored by the Signature Theatre Company of New York City when it produced a season of her plays in 1995-96. While all were enthusiastically received, *June and Jean in Concert* and *Sleep Deprivation Chamber,* the latter written in collaboration with her son Adam, won a second Obie for Kennedy.

In 1987 Kennedy produced one of that decade's most brilliant examples of postmodern writing, her autobiography *People Who Led to My Plays.* Designed to answer the frequently asked question "Who or what influenced you to write the way you do?" the text is an informative yet elusive self-portrait that intercalates family snapshots, movie studio glossies, and press photography with brief lines of text. Distinctions between subjectivity and social formation, foreground and background, history and fantasy, and word and image are slippery or continually displaced. Even as one learns of Kennedy's childhood fascination with Lon Chaney's Wolf Man and the terror of metamorphosis, clues to the transformations in *Funnyhouse of a Negro* and *The Owl Answers,* the text's gaps and silences are equally telling. No unified reading of Kennedy's life is possible or even desirable.

—Elin Diamond

KENTE, Gibson

Nationality: South African. **Born:** 1932. **Career:** Director and theater manager. Imprisoned for political reasons, 1976-77.

Publications

Plays

Manana, the Jazz Prophet (n.d.).
Sikalo (produced by Union Artists at The Great Hall of Witwatersrand University, December 1965 and July 1966).
Life (produced 1967-70).
Zwi (produced 1967-70).
How Long (produced in Soweto, December 1973).
I Believe (produced April 1974).
Too Late (produced in Soweto, February 1975).
Can You Take it? (produced 1977).
Hard Road (produced 1978).
Lobola (produced 1980).
Mama and the Load (produced 1981).

Other

South African People's Plays: Ons phola hi (plays by Kente and others). London, Heinemann, 1981.

* * *

Gibson Kente approaches drama and theater from a musical and business perspective. He is the one artist who popularized the genre of the township musical in South Africa. *King Kong* (1959), although written and directed by whites, was the first musical to have caught the attention of black audiences and performers alike, and Kente and others who followed him adopted its musical comedy style and melodramatic content. His foray into playwriting was not by choice, as he was trained neither in drama nor in literature. But after the success of *King Kong,* Kente was inspired to set up his own theater business, and he approached some African writer friends for suitable scripts. When these were not forthcoming, he proceeded to write his own—the first of which was the not-so-successful *Manana, the Jazz Prophet.* Not much is known of this first play because, unlike his other plays, it has never been revived.

By the time he wrote his second play, *Sikalo,* he had perfected what has become the township musical format: a simple township story, a *shebeen* (drinking house) and its queen, gangsters and *tsotsis,* dancing girls, the brutish but comic policeman, corrupt priests with nothing to preach, and the traditional comic Zulu boy with his broken English. These stock characters and their situations are then melodramatically sensationalized to much popular music and dancing. *Sikalo* is set within the culture and rhythm of township life. Sikalo, a "typical township youth," struggles to survive in a society being terrorized by gangs, but he ends up arrested and imprisoned. One cannot but agree with theater critic Robert Kavanagh (1985) that there is a certain superficiality in the analysis and social vision of this play, which makes no connection between apartheid and the deprivation and oppression that breeds the gangs or that makes life generally hard for blacks in the townships. It is thus the *tsotsis* (roughnecks) and not the agents of apartheid who terrorize the townships. In later plays however, Kente succeeds in making this connection and sets the terrorism of the gangs in the context of the apartheid that engenders it.

How Long is about Asinamali Thwala (We-Have-No-Money Carry-A-Burden), a poor municipal dustman struggling to put his son, Africa, through school. One can see the significance of Kente's allegory in this play, given that it was written and performed at a time in South Africa when the apartheid Bantu education policy was causing explosive situations in the townships, culminating in the Soweto uprising of 1976. Little wonder that it is regarded as Kente's most political play. Its title, as theater critic David Kerr suggests, is politically significant because it contains presentiments of the riots that broke out two years later. Kente next wrote *I Believe,* a plea for unity among the township dwellers whose interethnic divisions and rivalries—Zulu against Xhosa, for example—blinker their perceptions of who the real enemy is. The play advocates that blacks should reach out to one another in their daily encounters with the racist and oppressive laws of apartheid. The central character, Zwelithsa, has problems that are mainly created by tribal prejudice; for example, even his love for Kurula, a Shangana, is not approved by his Xhosa mother. It is also significant that in *I Believe* Kente attempts to change the musical formula of the township play by cutting out the melodrama and the burlesque elements while retaining the political overtone developed in *How Long*.

In 1975, Kente wrote *Too Late,* arguably his best play. It is about Saduwa, an orphan from Northern Transvaal who comes to the township to live with his aunt, Madinto (a *shebeen* queen) and her crippled daughter, Ntanana. He meets and falls in love with Totozi, Ntanana's friend. But Saduwa is having difficulty getting the appropriate permit to enable him to work in Johannesburg. In his effort to acquire this all-important pass, he is assisted by Mfundisi, a priest. Pelepele, the overzealous and vindictive local policeman, not only harasses him but also arrests Madinto for selling liquor illegally. She is eventually imprisoned, leading to Saduwa and Ntanana becoming destitute. If that were not bad enough, Saduwa himself is arrested, and, in trying to prevent the arrest, Ntanana is killed by Pelepele. Saduwa, on coming out of prison, nearly kills Pelepele and is only stopped by Offside, his good friend. The play ends with Saduwa, his aunt, and his girlfriend united. One theme that runs through Kente's plays is the idea of human interest and hope in times of trouble, with family and community always being there to support the individual.

Kente's theater of hope explores the idea of individual survival in spite of enormous obstacles. For this and for his shallow sociostructural analysis of South African society, he has been criticized—and rightly too. His other plays include *Mama and the Load*, *Can You Take It*, *Hard Road*, *Life*, *Zwi*, and *Lobola*. *Can You Take It* was written after his release from detention in 1977—he had been arrested while working on a film version of *How Long* in 1976. It is therefore hardly surprising that in the new play he completely steers clear of politics, and in subsequent plays, such as *Mama and the Load*, he returns to the earlier apolitical and ideologically bland dramaturgy of *Sikalo*. But whatever criticism is made of Kente's drama, one must bear in mind that his interest is in music, which was the dominant medium in the township musical, and that his literary merits come second to his musical talent and ambition. His plays can therefore be thin in literary merit, and Kavanagh has heavily criticized them for "their superficiality and lack of provocation, intellectual stimulation, deeper meaning and message." However, in performance they have been praised "for their ability to entertain" by presenting and engaging the audience in a moving experience.

—Osita Okagbue

KESSELMAN, Wendy (Ann)

Nationality: American. **Born:** 1940. **Career:** Teaching fellow, Bryn Mawr College, Pennsylvania, 1987. Also a composer and songwriter. **Awards:** Meet the Composer grant, 1978, 1982; National Endowment for the Arts fellowship, 1979; Sharfman award, 1980; Susan Smith Blackburn prize, 1980; Playbill award, 1980; Guggenheim fellowship, 1982; Ford Foundation grant, 1982; McKnight fellowship, 1985; ASCAP Popular award, for musical theatre, 1992. **Agent:** George Lane, William Morris Agency, 1325 Avenue of the Americas, New York, New York 10019; and, Jane Annakin, William Morris Agency Ltd., 31-32 Soho Square, London W1V 6AP, England. **Address:** P.O. Box 680, Wellfleet, Massachusetts 02667, U.S.A.

Publications

Plays

Becca (for children), music and lyrics by Kesselman (produced New York, 1977). New Orleans, Anchorage Press, 1988.
Maggie Magalita (produced Washington, D.C., 1980; New York, 1986). New York, French, 1987.
My Sister in This House, music by Kesselman (produced Louisville and New York, 1981; revised version produced Leicester and London, 1987). New York, French, 1982.
Merry-Go-Round (produced Louisville, 1981; New York, 1983).
I Love You, I Love You Not (one-act version produced Louisville, 1982; New York, 1983; full-length version produced St. Paul, 1986; New York, 1987). New York, French, 1988.
The Juniper Tree: A Tragic Household Tale, music and lyrics by Kesselman (produced Lenox, Massachusetts, 1982; New York, 1983). New York, French, 1985.
Cinderella in a Mirror (produced Lenox, Massachusetts, 1987).
The Griffin and the Minor Cannon, music by Mary Rodgers, lyrics by Ellen Fitzhugh (produced Lenox, Massachusetts, 1988).
A Tale of Two Cities, adaptation of the novel by Dickens (produced Louisville, 1992).
The Butcher's Daughter (produced Cleveland, Ohio, 1993).

Fiction (for children)

Franz Tovey and the Rare Animals. New York, Quist, 1968.
Angelita. New York, Hill and Wang, 1970.
Slash: An Alligator's Story. New York, Quist, 1971.
Joey. New York, Lawrence Hill, 1972.
Little Salt. New York, Scholastic Press, 1975.
Time for Jody. New York, Harper, 1975.
Maine Is a Million Miles Away. New York, Scholastic Press, 1976.
Emma. New York, Doubleday, 1980.
There's a Train Going by My Window. New York, Doubleday, 1982; London, Hodder and Stoughton, 1983.
Flick. New York, Harper, 1983.
Sand in My Shoes. Westport, Connecticut, Hyperion, 1993.

*

Critical Studies: "Wendy Kesselman: Transcendence and Transformation" by Jay Dickson, in *Harvard Advocate* (Cambridge, Massachusetts), 1986; "Disturbing Women: Wendy Kesselman's *My Sister in This House*" by Bette Mandl, in *Modern American Drama: The Female Canon,* edited by June Schlueter, Rutherford, Fairleigh Dickinson University Press, 1990; "Locked behind the Proscenium: Feminist Strategies in *Getting Out* and *My Sister in This House*" by Patricia Schroeder, in *Feminist Theatre and Theory,* edited by Helene Keyssar, New York, St. Martin's Press, 1996; "The Agoraphobic Imagination: The Protagonist Who Murders and the Critics Who Praise Her" by Nancy L. Nester, in *American Drama* (Cincinnati, Ohio), Spring 1997.

Theatrical Activities: Actor: **Play**—Role in *The Juniper Tree*, New York, 1983.

* * *

Already an author of children's books, Wendy Kesselman began her playwriting career with *Becca*, a play ostensibly for a young audience, though older spectators responded to the implicit subtext of parental neglect and a brother's abuse of his sister. Kesselman charms tiny tots with her book, lyrics, and music, particularly the songs for caged animals (parrot, salamander, grasshopper, and bullfrog) and the creatures (rats, Ida the Spider, escaped snake, and witches) who terrify Becca when her bullying brother Jonathan, as a means of controlling her, locks her in the closet. Yet Kesselman teaches as well as entertains. Relegated to his room by parents who never appear but by implication both ignore him and dictate his every move, Jonathan mirrors their behavior by neglecting to provide his pets with food and water and by tyrannizing his sister, treating her like a toy doll rather than a person. He eventually learns to respect others, relinquishes his pets (after Becca tells them that they can free themselves), and stops hitting and threatening his sister. Jonathan changes because Becca changes first by finding the courage to put a stop to his dehumanizing treatment, to take control of her own life, and to toss onto the closet floor the long white dress that reduced her to a mere object. The most amazing moment in this startling feminist parable occurs when Becca rebels against her tormentor and it finally dawns on us that she is not a doll.

Becca prefigures Kesselman's later dramas in its use of her own music, its parallels (Becca and the pets) and contrasts (the pets versus the creatures, Becca versus Jonathan), and its themes of loneliness, maturation, violence to soul and body, fear, family relations, control, and courage. Kesselman has continued to write about children and adolescents and about gender inequities, while expanding this exploration to include conflicts fueled by disparities of class, age, and culture. Further, she imbues her plays with a feminist sensibility to the ways patriarchal, social, and economic structures stunt women's minds and stifle their souls.

Kesselman's early masterpiece *My Sister in This House* exemplifies the way in which she keeps her viewpoint implicit, never preaching, always dramatizing. She constructs the play in a dazzling series of parallels and contrasts, satirizing life in the drawing room and dining room while portraying with compassion life in the kitchen and garret. Conversations between the maids and between the mother and daughter for whom they slave frequently intersect, the concerns of each economic class reflecting those of the other. But so great is the social stratification separating them that not until the play's bloody climax do the two sets of women converse across class lines. Instead, the Danzards beckon or point or nod or, when the white glove detects dust, scowl. Yet the sisters and the two women who employ them share a common obstacle to their humanity and self-actualization: female existence in a time and place—France in the early 1930s—that permit their sex only a domestic function. Conservative arbiters of conduct require women without men to repress their sexuality as well as their need for personal and professional fulfillment. While the women in both social strata lead empty lives, at least the sisters provide each other with the tender love and sex missing from their vacuous employers' existence. Yet the young women's inability to control their own economic destinies dooms both them and their bourgeois nemeses as the impulse toward aggression, though stifled, builds and builds on both sides.

When Jean Genet based *The Maids* on the same horrendous Le Mans double murder committed by incestuous sisters, he was not attempting to create sympathetic portraits of the killers, but Kesselman accepts that challenge. She succeeds by depicting impoverished innocents trapped in a claustrophobic world devoid of stimulation, affection, or purpose except for each other's solace. After the mutual enthusiasm of the Danzards and the sisters gives way to suspicion and fear, the mother explodes with a venomous denunciation that guarantees that the sisters will be thrown onto the street without references, food, or shelter. The tragedy can end only in the destruction of all four bleak lives.

A prizewinning composer as well as a dramatist, Kesselman has supplied music for most of her texts. By the end of *My Sister* we are already deeply affected by the play's action, but Kesselman enhances its impact by the recurrence of the musical refrain "Sleep my little sister, sleep." In *The Juniper Tree: A Tragic Household Tale,* Kesselman renders the drama's macabre murder, dismemberment, cannibalism, revenge, and resurrection both funnier and more horrifying by describing and enacting events with lovely solos and eerie duets. As usual, Kesselman takes a child's perspective in dramatizing this Grimms' fairy tale about parental abuse. Both narrating and acting out the plot in the style of story theater, *The Juniper Tree* portrays the irrational but compulsive murder of a child by, as in *Cinderella in a Mirror,* a wicked stepmother, who then compounds the crime by blaming her own daughter for the boy's death and cooking him and serving him as soup for supper. Among Kesselman's funny, folksy touches are the men's descriptions of their personal activities, the father's ravenous appetite—gruesomely comic—and the daughter's disgust at her father's gross table manners while he unknowingly devours his son.

Merry-Go-Round, which uses only the title song as music, considers childhood largely by depicting its outcome in young adults as we see a similar child within each quite different grown-up. The play's structure jumps from present to past, not with flashbacks but with the adults reenacting the earlier scenes. After they reconnect with their past selves, their roots, the powerful early bond broken by their parents, and their loneliness after Michael moved away, Daisy and Michael consummate sexually their earlier relationship, thus coming full circle as the title suggests. Kesselman keeps all of this understated, implicit, and subtle, but she authentically evokes the feelings engendered by a reunion of former soul mates.

In *Maggie Magalita* Kesselman depicts an adolescent immigrant struggling to win acceptance from her classmates in New York City while responding with embarrassment to her Spanish-speaking grandmother. Their cultural clash eventually educates them both, but only after screaming arguments, sullen rejection, and cruelties to the aging Abuela that correspond to what her tormentors inflicted upon little Magalita before she became Americanized into Maggie. In addition to her characteristic theme of loneliness—Magalita's as well as Abuela's—Kesselman dramatizes such values as respect for those who are different, self-acceptance, and courage when confronting pressures to conform. Although set largely in the family apartment, the episodes shift freely from present to past and among such other locales as the zoo, the seashore, and Maggie's high school. The playwright visually expresses her protagonist's transformation from Latin American to North American when the teenager dons flashy sunglasses and earrings and a baggy T-shirt bearing a photo of a rock group.

In *I Love You, I Love You Not* the dramatist narrows this confrontation of cultures and generations to its essentials: the willful adolescent Daisy (perhaps a favorite name), and Nana, her grandmother from the Old World. Jewish rather than Hispanic, Daisy (the name of the flower used in playing the game referred to by the play's title) actually wants to learn the language of her heritage, in this case German, so as to deprive her parents of their ability to speak privately in her presence. Nana, however, is a Holocaust survivor and hates the tongue of those who persecuted her and killed her sisters and parents. As in *Becca*, Kesselman keeps Daisy's parents offstage, but she employs them as a formidable hostile presence. Like the playwright's other domestic dramas, this work also compels our attention to the love/hate relationships within a family. While the high-strung teenager spends the weekend in her rites of passage to maturity by skirmishing with her grandmother, her parents intrude by telephone as they attempt to remove her from her grandmother's nurturing care. "Care" is the operative word. Never maudlin—indeed, Daisy proves spoiled, narcissistic, self-indulgent, childish—*I Love You, I Love You Not* dramatizes the volatile but nurturing relationship between an emotionally needy, insecure youngster and the woman who can develop this fragile flower into hardier stock with survival skills, capable of overcoming her intolerance, guilt, and especially fears.

In the late 1980s Kesselman began work on two more musical plays, each set in France during the Revolution. Both again in some part concern young people, contrast classes, and dramatize events in brief episodes, and each ends with execution by guillotine. In *A Tale of Two Cities* she adapts Dickens's novel, whereas *The Butcher's Daughter* breaks audacious new ground. *A Tale of Two Cities* employs the parallels of Charles and Sydney, young Thérèse and young Lucie, the burning of shoemaking tools and the burning of the Bastille, and Lucie's imprisoned father and then little Lucie's imprisoned father. Kesselman also uses flashbacks to build suspense about events we cannot fully comprehend when we first observe them, until we finally grasp how Thérèse Defarge's sister was raped on her wedding day by the Évremondes, who killed her husband, father, and brother. The latter's moving song, "Quieting the Frogs," proves one of the best among Kesselman's extraordinary compositions for musical theater.

The parallels of *The Butcher's Daughter* constitute the play's whole structure. We follow the destinies of two young women, one adopted by a butcher, the other the daughter of the executioner who decapitates the butcher's daughter at the end, when the executioner's daughter hangs herself. A grandmother lives in each household. Images of blood permeate the play, which indicts such male-driven acts as capital punishment and incest. Once more, the world proves pernicious to women of any talent or spirit, so utterly denying them autonomy and equity that they cannot survive. Kesselman selects as one of her central figures the pioneering playwright and feminist Olympe de Gouges, and both women's spirits soar. The women interact only twice for a few wordless but indelible moments. Linking the two protagonists, the street singer Pierrot knows, loves, and celebrates them both, just as Kesselman herself sings of women young and old, timid and bold. She has created some of the most memorable female characters in contemporary drama.

—Tish Dace

KILROY, Thomas

Nationality: Irish. **Born:** Callan, County Kilkenny, 23 September 1934. **Education:** Christian Brothers School, Callan; St. Kieran's College, Kilkenny; University College, Dublin, 1953-59, B.A. 1956, higher diploma in education 1957, M.A. in English 1959. **Family:** Married 1) Patricia Cobey in 1963 (divorced 1980), three sons; 2) Julia Lowell Carlson in 1981. **Career:** Headmaster, Stratford College, Dublin, 1959-64; visiting lecturer in English, University of Notre Dame, Indiana, 1962-63; visiting professor of English, Vanderbilt University, Nashville, 1964-65; assistant lecturer, Department of Modern English and American Literature, University College, Dublin, 1965-73; lecturer, School of Irish Studies, Dublin, 1972-73. Visiting professor, Sir George Williams University and McGill University, both Montreal, 1973, University College, Galway, 1975-76 and 1979, Dartmouth College, Hanover, New Hampshire, 1976, University College, Dublin, 1977-78; Professor of Modern English, University College Galway, 1979-89; visiting professor, Bamberg University, West Germany, 1984; Examiner in Modern English, Trinity College, Dublin, and Thomond College, Limerick, 1983. Lives in Kilmaine, Mayo, Ireland. **Awards:** *Guardian* prize, for fiction, 1971; Royal Society of Literature Heinemann award, for fiction, 1972; Irish Academy prize, 1972; American-Irish Foundation award, 1974; Arts Council of Ireland bursary, 1976; Bellagio Study Centre grant, 1986; Rockefeller grant, 1986. **Member:** Royal Society of Literature, (fellow 1972, member, 1973, and member of the council, 1979); Irish Academy of Letters; Aosdana, 1986. **Agent:** Casarotto Ramsay Ltd., National House, 60-66 Wardour Street, London W1V 3HP, England.

Publications

Plays

The Death and Resurrection of Mr. Roche (produced Dublin, 1968; London, 1969; New York, 1978). London, Faber, and New York, Grove Press, 1969.

The O'Neill (produced Dublin, 1969). Gallery Press, 1995.

Tea and Sex and Shakespeare (produced Dublin, 1976). Gallery press, 1998.

Talbot's Box (produced Dublin and London, 1977). Dublin, Gallery Press, and Newark, Delaware, Proscenium Press, 1979.

The Seagull, adaptation of a play by Chekhov (produced London, 1981). London, Eyre Methuen, 1981; Gallery Press, 1993.

Double Cross (produced Derry and London, 1986). London, Faber, 1986.

Ghosts, adaptation of the play by Henrik Ibsen (produced Dublin, 1988).

The Madame MacAdam Travelling Theatre (produced Derry, 1991; New York, 1992). London, Methuen, 1991.

Six Vharacters in Search of an Author, adaption of a play by Luigi Pirandello (produced Dublin, 1996).

The Secret Fall of Consvance Wilde (produced Dublin, 1997). Gallery Press, 1997.

Illusions Comiqués à l'lrlandaise. Septentrion Presse, 1998.

Radio Plays: *The Door*, 1967; *That Man, Bracken*, 1986.

Television Plays: *Farmers*, 1978; *The Black Joker*, 1981; *Gold in the Streets*, 1993.

Novel

The Big Chapel. London, Faber, 1971.

Other

Sean O'Casey: A Collection of Critical Essays. Englewood Cliffs, New Jersey, Prentice Hall, 1975.

*

Bibliography: *Ten Modern Irish Playwrights* by Kimball King, New York, Garland, 1979.

Critical Studies: Articles by Christopher Murray, in *Ireland Today* (Dublin), 1982, and by Gerald Dawe, in *Theatre Ireland 3* (Belfast), 1982; "The Fortunate Fall: Two Plays by Thomas Kilroy" by Anthony Roche, in *The Writer and the City* edited by Maurice Harmon, Gerrard's Cross, Buckinghamshire, Smythe, 1984; in *A Critical History of Modern Irish Drama* by D.E.S. Maxwell, Cambridge UP, 1984; "A Haunted House: The Theatre of Thomas Kilroy" by Frank McGuinness, in *Irish Theatre Today* edited by Barbara Hayley and Walter Rix, Würzburg, Königshausen & Neumann, 1985; "Thomas Kilroy" by Anthony Roche, in *Post-War Literatures in English: A Lexicon*, Groningen, Netherlands, Noordhoff, 1989; "A Voice from the Trees: Thomas Kilroy's Version of Chekhov's *The Seagull*" by Frank McGuinness, in *Irish University Review: A Journal of Irish Studies* (Dublin, Ireland), Spring-Summer 1991, pp. 3-14; in *Contemporary Irish Drama* by Anthony Roche, Dublin, Gill and MacMillan, 1994; "Worlds Elsewhere: The Plays of Thomas Kilroy" by Christopher Murray, in *Eire Ireland: A Journal of Irish Studies* (St. Paul, Minnesota), Summer 1994, pp. 123-38; in *Twentieth Century Irish Drama* by Christopher Murray, Manchester University Press, 1997.

* * *

Thomas Kilroy is probably best known on both sides of the Atlantic for *The Death and Resurrection of Mr. Roche,* a tragicomedy that demonstrates his flair for funny yet trenchant dialogue in a style reminiscent of O'Casey. In this play, as well as in his historical portraits of Matt Talbot in *Talbot's Box* and of William Joyce and Brendan Bracken in *Double Cross,* his characters are strongly defined, and his sense of dramatic structure is adroit. He is quite eclectic in his dramaturgy, and his plays have little in common except an apparent rejection of the strong naturalistic tradition of many Abbey playwrights. His first play, *Mr. Roche,* is basically realistic in style, while his second, *The O'Neill,* is a historical work about Owen Roe O'Neill, the Irish opponent of Queen Elizabeth I. *Talbot's Box* is a penetrating psychological study notable for its use of expressionistic devices. *Tea and Sex and Shakespeare* is a thin comedy that teeters on the edge of absurdist theater. *Double Cross* is a curious dramatic diptych, a study of two political opposites who figured prominently in the propaganda battles of England and Germany during World War II. A decade separated a fine adaptation of Chekhov's *The Seagull* from a brilliant updating of Ibsen's *Ghosts*. Kilroy's *The Madame MacAdam Travelling Theatre* is a meditation on acting and the theater that is imposed on a humorous account of a down-at-the-heels company of actors touring rural Eire in the early 1940s. Some of Kilroy's themes are traditionally Irish, while others like the aloneness of spiritual isolation and the theater as a doubling of reality are universal.

In *The Death and Resurrection of Mr. Roche* an all-male drinking party seemingly turns tragic when one of the group suddenly dies, or so it appears. Kelley, a mid-30s civil servant of peasant background, has extended a casual invitation to assorted patrons of Murray's Bar to return to his small, desolate Dublin flat for further drinking. Last to arrive is Mr. Roche, the oldest of the lot and a known homosexual, to whom Kelley is openly hostile. After they are even further into their cups, they begin to torment him, and he suddenly "dies" after they have forced him into a cubbyhole of a cellar. While two of the drinkers, Doc and Kevin, are out attempting to dispose of the body, Kelley and Seamus have what is thematically the most significant scene of the play. In an account of a sexual encounter with Roche, Kelley reveals his homosexual tendencies, and Seamus confesses that he is trapped in marriage to a girl whose "sameness is beginning to drive me mad." At a carefully chosen moment Doc and Kevin reappear with a very live Mr. Roche and an explanation that never quite includes how Doc could have pronounced him dead in the first place.

The central theme is the stultifying effect, the spiritual and cultural sterility, that contemporary urban life has had on young Irish men who were able to leave small family farms and villages and make careers in Dublin. They are descendants of the early "peasant play" characters who, unconsciously at least, longed to leave behind the hard life on the land, the narrow provinciality of the village, and the stifling influence of parents and clergy for the headier life of Dublin, England, or America. Kilroy's Irish are cousins to Brian Friel's Gar, who leaves the small family business for the United States in *Philadelphia, Here I Come!* Kilroy's characters have put the father-son conflict, the Irish generational gap, well behind them. They have made their escape and feel lucky. They have, however, as they sadly admit, lost contact with their families. Kelley thinks that he has a very good job, and Seamus, with whom he grew up, is proud of being a teacher and, until he thinks about it, is happily married. Their reunion over several pints becomes a melancholy baring of the soul in which Seamus admits that he is not just attempting to recapture the pleasure of their last reunion two years ago: "Twas more like I was trying to get back to ten years ago. What was healthy then is sick now. . . . Why haven't you changed even a little? . . . You're in the same situation as you were when you came to Dublin"—Kelley angrily insists that he is "the success of my family," while Seamus concludes sadly that he is "as happy as ever I'll be." Their conversation concludes with Kelley's unwelcome revelation that he had, in fact, invited Roche to the apartment before and that they once had sexual relations.

Homosexuality is Kilroy's second theme, along with Irish hypocrisy. Kelley's hostile attitude toward Roche is made clear quite early so as to underline his hypocrisy: "I won't let the likes of him over that step. . . ." After Roche's "death" Kelley is terrified that their acquaintance will come out: "Prison I can take. It's the bad name that leaves me wake at the knees." Roche is, however, in Kevin's words, "not a bad auld skin." In fact, Roche speaks for Kilroy in a plea for sympathy and understanding for all of his characters, for homosexuality is here the playwright's metaphor for aloneness. Through Roche, Kilroy strongly condemns their lifestyle, their drinking bouts to assuage loneliness and uncertainty, the waste of their lives. When Kelley condescendingly rejects Roche's sympathy, the homosexual makes a plea for all of them: "We all need sympathy now and again. . . . There's little comfort as it is, in this world. . . . Who am I or you to deny someone the single object which makes each day bearable?" Writing in 1968, Irving Wardle praised *Mr. Roche* as "the most important new work ever presented by the Dublin Theatre Festival."

Tea and Sex and Shakespeare was Kilroy's contribution to the 1976 Dublin Festival. It involves the fantasies of a blocked writer named Brien. In one fruitless day spent in his Dublin attic workroom, he plays out his dreams involving his wife Elmina, who is, in fact, at work; his neighbor Sylvester, who finds him a nuisance but fancies his wife; his comic landlady and her nubile daughter Deirdre, to whom he is tutor; and finally Mummy and Daddy, his in-laws, who might have escaped from a short play by Edward Albee. Brien's dreamworld centers around dramatic suicides and seductions, with dialogue quoted or paraphrased from Shakespeare, the subject of his tutorials with the buxom Deirdre. The plot and characters are exceedingly thin. The play ends on a poignantly serious note as the long-suffering wife remonstrates with Brien. "You build your absurd jokes around you like a high wall so that no one can reach you," she charges. Brien responds that he is only trying to say, "I'm alone." Her reply—"And who in this world isn't alone?"—reiterates the theme of spiritual isolation that Kilroy mined far more effectively and dramatically in *Talbot's Box*. This comedy of the frustrated, haunted creative person is only moderately successful.

Talbot's Box rarely matches the humor of *Mr. Roche,* but in its central character there is a highly effective study of religious zealotry, a subject the dramatist had dealt with in his novel *The Big Chapel* a few years earlier. Matt Talbot was a Dublin workman and mystic who died in 1925, and as early as 1931 a movement was under way for his canonization. On his death it was discovered that for many years he had been wearing heavy chains and cords around his body, arms, and legs and that some of the rusty chains had sunk into the flesh. The play is an inquiry into the psyche of Talbot. The action comes through four actors who portray a variety of different roles, with costume changes made onstage. The playwright touches a number of social bases. Talbot's role in the transport strike of 1913, for example, sets his unique vision against the background of labor troubles, just as his encounters with the church demonstrate that in his zealous humiliation of the flesh he is as unmanageable as Shaw's Saint Joan. In the key scene of the play Talbot tells the priest: "I knows the darkness! . . . 'Tis in every man, woman 'n child born inta the world." For him "the darkness is Gawd," and "there's no peace till ya walk through it inta some kinda light." The humiliation of the flesh is "only the way for me to know the darkness of me own body." In Kilroy's own words *Talbot's Box* is a play "about aloneness, its cost to the person and the kind of courage required to sustain it."

Kilroy's next work for the stage was a highly effective adaptation of Chekhov's *The Seagull.* Set on an estate in the west of Ireland, this transplanted Russian classic showed no signs of a sea change in its passage from one predominantly rural nineteenth-century culture to another.

Double Cross is concerned with the problem of "doubleness or doubling, . . . the way things repeat themselves in life or attract their opposites." This is the "basis of acting or role-playing," Kilroy wrote in the introduction, as well as the impetus behind "the universal desire . . . to make up and tell stories, thereby inventing a reality which may reflect everyday life but is still distinct from it." *Double Cross* attempts "to move along the lines from role-playing and fiction-making to the act of political treason." William Joyce, born in Brooklyn in 1906, arrived in England via Ireland and Northern Ireland in 1921. By 1933 he had become a member of Sir Oswald Mosley's British Union of Fascists. In 1939 he went to Germany, where he joined German Radio. Before the year was out, he had become the infamous Lord Haw-Haw, probably Goebbels's best-known radio commentator and apologist for the Nazi regime. Kilroy finds Joyce's opposite in Brendan Bracken, born in 1901 in Tipperary, who by dint of systematic cultivation of the rich, famous, aristocratic, and politically powerful rose, by 1939, to be Churchill's parliamentary private secretary at the Admiralty. By 1941 he was minister of information, whose responsibility it was to counteract the effect of Lord Haw-Haw's broadcasts.

Double Cross is divided into two halves: "The Bracken Play: London" and "The Joyce Play: Berlin." The first scene of the Bracken play introduces both Joyce and Bracken, played by the same actor, as well as an actor and actress who both narrate and play a variety of characters, most notably Churchill and Lord Beaverbrook and the two women in the lives of Joyce and Bracken. Structurally, each play is made up of a series of free-flowing scenes that chronicle, in the case of Bracken, his political maneuverings and his affair with a woman called Popsie, while still allowing him to look back at his modest beginnings in Ireland and ahead to his own death by cancer in 1958. Joyce's Berlin play focuses on his relations with his second wife, Margaret, and on an interview, after his capture by the Allies, with Lord Beaverbrook. He was hanged as a war criminal in 1946.

For Kilroy this is a play about "two men who invented themselves," Bracken as an actor on the English political scene in the late 1930s and the war years and Joyce as "a creator of fictions" driven to an invented self by a "deep, angry impatience" with life. Both came of unremarkable Irish backgrounds, both invented lives for themselves in English society, and both tried to imitate his oppressor, Joyce by his anti-British propaganda and Bracken by his very "English" attitude toward Ireland. Each of the plays is a tour de force for both the dramatist and the actor, although the first play is the better of the two. Yet, as Irving Wardle wrote in *The Times,* Kilroy's idea that "social play-acting in some way leads to fascism and treason" is not effectively projected. The play remains, however, a fascinating study of "doubles/opposites." Kilroy followed *Double Cross* with a radio play on the same subject—the Bracken half of it—called *That Man, Bracken,* which is an effective distillation of material used in the earlier work.

Kilroy's adaptation of Ibsen's *Ghosts* is a highly effective updating, justifiably received with enthusiasm in its first production at the 1988 Dublin Theatre Festival. The scene is a provincial Irish town, but more importantly the time has been moved up to the late 1980s. Certain changes, which are both natural and effective, make the play highly contemporary. First, Oliver Aylward, like Ibsen's Oswald Alving, has come home to die, for he is in the final stages of AIDS. Second, there is a hint that his father introduced him to drugs, probably marijuana, in his childhood. (This is Kilroy's variation on Oswald's story of how, when a small boy, he became ill by smoking his father's pipe.) Third, Oliver's rejection of the ghosts theme—that the sins of the fathers are visited on the children—is more forceful, coupled as it is with his assertion of personal responsibility. Fourth, the euthanasia theme is far more acceptable now than it would have been for much of the life of Ibsen's play, and since Helen Aylward (Ibsen's Helene Alving) seems a more "liberated" woman than her original, there is reason to suppose that Oliver will not be allowed to suffer long. All four characters, even Father Manning (Pastor Manders), are drawn with greater precision than in most translations of Ibsen. Further, Kilroy's excoriation of the social hypocrisies surrounding marriage and the family are more trenchant in the adaptation. "There is more evil propagated inside family life than in any other human organisation that I know of," says Oliver. Finally, even the image and symbol of the sun is employed with more resonance in the final moment of the play. This adaptation is so timely and effective that a modern classic becomes a brand-new play.

Kilroy's later work *The Madame MacAdam Travelling Theatre* is a highly original play that generated a negative critical response at the 1991 Dublin Theatre Festival. The play is not strong in either plot, which is quite complex, or characterization, although it certainly is adequate. Set in a small town in rural Ireland during the so-called emergency, the World War II years when the country was neutral, *Madame MacAdam* concerns a third-rate, traveling British theater company that, by the merest chance, winds up in the Free State. With only five members, they are depleted in number, and they have run out of petrol. Unable to move on, they become involved in a crooked greyhound race, through which they hope to obtain petrol, the search for a missing child, the seduction of a local teenager by a young actor in the company, and, somewhat incidentally, a performance of an Irish melodrama dealing with the eighteenth-century patriot Robert Emmet and his love, Sarah Curran.

Interweaving these various strands of plot, Kilroy sometimes satirizes and sometimes parodies as he employs the most hackneyed materials of melodrama in a setting that only occasionally hints at realism, for example, the drone overhead of warplanes that may be either German or English. As Madame MacAdam says in her first speech: "Tonight we offer the usual fare. A love story. A lost child. Villainy at large. While in the background the drums of war. And at the end, that frail salvation of the final curtain. What else is there?"

Kilroy employs projected scene headings of a melodramatic nature that evoke silent film subtitles but that also recall the scene captions employed to quite a different end in Brechtian theater. Their function is, of course, not only to acknowledge and so mitigate the episodic nature of the plot but also to gently tease the banal ingredients. Madame MacAdam's speech above finally seems directed more to the audience in the real theater than to the rural Irish who watch Robert Emmet court Sarah.

The various plot strands form a context for a running commentary by several characters on the acting profession and the nature and function of the theater. This is really what the play is about: the actor's artistic urge for expression; his triumph in making an audience believe; the ephemeral nature of his achievement; the healing and transforming power of theater; "the greatest mystery of all"—becoming another person; "human error and human frailty . . . and the second-rate" as the foundation for "the miracle of theatre." Madame MacAdam, thought to be based on the famous actor-manager of the period Anew McMaster, is comically pompous, but she can also be wisely succinct: "To keep at bay the principle of chaos. That is what is urgent." Although not necessarily his best, *Madame MacAdam* is Kilroy's most complex and demanding play.

—Gene A. Barnett

KOCH, Kenneth

Nationality: American. **Born:** Cincinnati, Ohio, 27 February 1925. **Education:** Harvard University, Cambridge, Massachusetts, A.B. 1948; Columbia University, New York, M.A. 1953, Ph.D. 1959. **Military Service:** Served in the United States Army, 1943-46. **Family:** Married 1) Mary Janice Elwood in 1955 (divorced 1981), one daughter; 2) Karen Steinbrink in 1994. **Career:** Lecturer in English, Rutgers University, New Brunswick, New Jersey, 1953-54, 1955-56, 1957-58, and Brooklyn College, 1957-59; director of the Poetry Workshop, New School for Social Research, New York, 1958-66. Lecturer, 1959-61, assistant professor, 1962-66, associate professor, 1966-71, and professor of English, 1971—, Columbia University. Associated with *Locus Solus* magazine, Lans-en-Vercors, France, 1960-62. **Awards:** Fulbright fellowship, 1950, 1978; Guggenheim fellowship, 1961; National Endowment for the Arts grant, 1966; Ingram Merrill Foundation fellowship, 1969; Harbison award, for teaching, 1970; Frank O'Hara prize (*Poetry*, Chicago), 1973; American Academy award, 1976; American Academy of Arts and Letters award of merit, 1987; Bollingen Prize for American Poetry, 1995; Bobbitt National Poetry award, Library of Congress, 1996. **Address:** Department of English, 602 Philosophy Hall, Columbia University, New York, New York 10027, U.S.A.

Publications

Plays

Bertha, (produced New York, 1959). Included in *Bertha and Other Plays*, 1966.

The Election (also director: produced New York, 1960). Included in *A Change of Hearts*, 1973.

Pericles (produced New York, 1960). Included in *Bertha and Other Plays*, 1966.

George Washington Crossing the Delaware (in *3 x 3*, produced New York, 1962; produced separately, London, 1983). Included in *Bertha and Other Plays*, 1966.

The Construction of Boston (produced New York, 1962). Included in *Bertha and Other Plays*, 1966.

Guinevere; or, The Death of the Kangaroo (produced New York, 1964). Included in *Bertha and Other Plays*, 1966.

The Tinguely Machine Mystery; or, The Love Suicides at Kaluka (also co-director: produced New York, 1965). Included in *A Change of Hearts*, 1973.

Bertha and Other Plays (includes *Pericles*, *George Washington Crossing the Delaware*, *The Construction of Boston*, *Guinevere; or, The Death of the Kangaroo*, *The Gold Standard*, *The Return of Yellowmay*, *The Revolt of the Giant Animals*, *The Building of Florence*, *Angelica*, *The Merry Stones*, *The Academic Murders*, *Easter*, *The Lost Feed*, *Mexico*, *Coil Supreme*). New York, Grove Press, 1966.

The Gold Standard (produced New York, 1969). Included in *Bertha and Other Plays*, 1966.

The Moon Balloon (produced New York, 1969). Included in *A Change of Hearts*, 1973.

The Artist, music by Paul Reif, adaptation of the poem "The Artist" by Koch (produced New York, 1972). Poem included in *Thank You and Other Poems*, 1962.

A Little Light (produced Amagansett, New York, 1972).
A Change of Hearts: Plays, Films, and Other Dramatic Works 1951-1971 (includes the contents of *Bertha and Other Plays*, and *A Change of Hearts*; *E. Kology*; *The Election*; *The Tinguely Machine Mystery*; *The Moon Balloon*; *Without Kinship*; *Ten Films*: *Because*, *The Color Game*, *Mountains and Electricity*, *Sheep Harbor*, *Oval Gold*, *Moby Dick*, *L'Ecole Normale*, *The Cemetery*, *The Scotty Dog*, and *The Apple*; *Youth*; and *The Enchantment*). New York, Random House, 1973.
A Change of Hearts, music by David Hollister (produced New York, 1985). Included in *A Change of Hearts* (collection), 1973.
Rooster Redivivus (produced Garnerville, New York, 1975).
The Art of Love, adaptation by Mike Nussbaum (produced Chicago, 1976).
The Red Robins, adaptation of his own novel (produced New York, 1978). New York, Performing Arts Journal Publications, 1979.
The New Diana (produced New York, 1984).
Popeye among the Polar Bears (produced New York, 1986).
One Thousand Avant-Garde Plays (produced New York, 1987). New York, Knopf, 1988.
The Construction of Boston, music by Scott Wheeler (produced Boston, 1989).
Some Avant Garde Plays (produced Portland, Maine, 1990).
The Gold Standard, A Book of Plays (includes *The Gold Standard*; *George Washington Crosses the Delaware*; *The Construction of Boston*; *The Red Robins and the Death of Sir Brian Caitskill*; *The Strangers from the Sea*; *The Banquet*; *A Heroine of the Greek Resistence*; *Edward and Christine*). New York, Knopf, 1996.
The Banquet, music by Marlello Panni (produced Bremen, 1998).

Screenplays: *The Scotty Dog*, 1967; *The Apple*, 1968.

Novel

The Red Robins. New York, Random House, 1975.

Short Stories

Interlocking Lives, with Alex Katz. New York, Kulchur Press, 1970.
Hotel Lambosa and Other Stories. Minneapolis, Coffee House Press, 1993.

Poetry

Poems. New York, Tibor de Nagy, 1953.
Ko; or, A Season on Earth. New York, Grove Press, 1960.
Permanently. New York, Tiber Press, 1960.
Thank You and Other Poems. New York, Grove Press, 1962.
Poems from 1952 and 1953. Los Angeles, Black Sparrow Press, 1968.
When the Sun Tries to Go On. Los Angeles, Black Sparrow Press, 1969.
Sleeping with Women. Los Angeles, Black Sparrow Press, 1969.
The Pleasures of Peace and Other Poems. New York, Grove Press, 1969.
Penguin Modern Poets 24, with Kenward Elmslie and James Schuyler. London, Penguin, 1973.
The Art of Love. New York, Random House, 1975.
The Duplications. New York, Random House, 1977.
The Burning Mystery of Anna in 1951. New York, Random House, 1979.
From the Air. London, Taranman, 1979.
Days and Nights. New York, Random House, 1982.
Selected Poems 1950-1982. New York, Random House, 1985.
On the Edge. New York, Viking, 1986.
Seasons on Earth. New York, Viking, 1987.
Selected Poems. Manchester, Carcanet, 1991.
One Train. New York, Knopf, 1994.
On the Great Atlantic Rainway. New York, Knopf, 1994.
Straits. New York, Knopf, 1998.

Other

John Ashbery and Kenneth Koch (A Conversation). Tucson, Interview Press, 1965(?).
Wishes, Lies, and Dreams: Teaching Children to Write Poetry. New York, Random House, 1970.
Rose, Where Did You Get That Red? Teaching Great Poetry to Children. New York, Random House, 1973.
I Never Told Anybody: Teaching Poetry Writing in a Nursing Home. New York, Random House, 1977.
Making It Up, with Allen Ginsburg. New York, Catchword Papers, 1994.
The Art of Poetry. Ann Arbor, University of Michigan Press, 1996.
Making Your Own Days, The Pleasure of Reading and Writing Poetry. New York, Scribner, 1998.

Editor, with Kate Farrell, *Sleeping on the Wing: An Anthology of Modern Poetry, with Essays on Reading and Writing*. New York, Random House, 1981.
Editor, with Kate Farrell, *Talking to the Sun: An Illustrated Anthology of Poems for Young People*. New York, Holt Rinehart, 1985; London, Viking Kestrel, 1986.

*

Critical Studies: "An Interview with Kenneth Koch" by John Tranter, in *Scripsi* (Parkville, Australia), November 1986, pp. 177-85; "Comic Fantasy in Two Postmodern Verse Novels: *Slinger* and *Ko*"by Nancy Lang, in *The Poetic Fantastic: Studies in an Evolving Genre*, Westport, Connecticut, Greenwood, 1989; "Frank O'Hara and His Poetry: An Interview with Kenneth Koch" in *American Writing Today*, edited by Richard Kostelanetz, Troy, New York, Whitston, 1991; "Dr. Fun" by David Lehman, in *The American Poetry Review* (Philadelphia, Pennsylvania), November/December 1995, pp. 53-59; "Kenneth Koch" by Jordan Davis, in *The American Poetry Review* (Philadelphia, Pennsylvania), November/December 1996, pp. 45-53.

Theatrical Activities:
Director: **Plays**—*The Election*, New York, 1960; *The Tinguely Machine Mystery* (co-director, with Remy Charlip), New York, 1965.

* * *

Kenneth Koch is a genuine man of letters, although that epithet seems inappropriate for a writer whose natural instincts are comic and parodic. In addition to writing much first-rate poetry and some striking fiction, he has been one of America's best teachers of writing, not only inspiring several promising younger poets but also popularizing the idea of poetry writing in elementary education. His book *Wishes, Lies, and Dreams,* which details his own experience in the New York City public schools, established a pedagogical example that has come to be imitated throughout the United States. Koch has also written short plays, most of which originated as responses to his personal experience as a graduate student of literature, college professor, serious poet, and participant in the New York art scene. Perhaps because of their occasional inspiration, many of these shorter works remained too attached to their original circumstances to be presented more than once. His second collection of plays, *A Change of Hearts,* included several new pieces, all of which are typically Kochian but none particularly better than his earlier work.

On the one hand Koch is a bemused absurdist and a giggler, incapable of taking anything too seriously, and his plays exploit situations and subjects for their available humor. On the other hand he is a poet of the New York school, capable of extraordinary acoherent, as distinct from incoherent, writing, such as the marvelous nonsense of these concluding lines from his early play *Pericles:*

> And we stood there with pure roots
> In silence in violence one two one two
> Will you please go through that again
> The organ's orgasm and the aspirin tablet's speechless spasm.

In terms of structure, his plays tend to be collections of related sketches strung together in sequences of varying duration, allowing imaginative leaps between the scenes. The best also reveal his debt, both as playwright and as poet, to the French surrealists and dadaists.

Bertha and Other Plays collects most of Koch's early works in chronological order. The very best, *George Washington Crossing the Delaware,* originated as a response to Larry Rivers's painting of the same title, and the play is dedicated to the artist. Koch's compressed historical play ridicules several kinds of clichés: the myths of American history, the language of politicians, war films, military strategies, patriotism, and much else. The theme of Koch's multiple burlesques, here and elsewhere, is that the accepted familiar versions are no more credible than his comic rewritings. By scrambling space and time, the play also reveals Koch's love of Apollinaire's great poem *Zone* (1918). The British general refers at one point to "the stately bison," which did not enter popular mythology until the 19th century and certainly could not be seen on the East Coast, and the play takes place in Alpine, New Jersey, which is not near the Delaware River.

In the 10 very short scenes of his earlier miniepic, *Bertha,* whose text runs less than 10 pages, Queen Bertha of Norway uses power to assuage her evident madness, attacks Scotland but halts at the frontier, and shoots lovers for their sins only to win the confidence of both her armies and their captives. The historical source of this burlesque is less obvious than for *George Washington,* although there are several possibilities. Koch's book also includes *Guinevere,* an early work with some marvelous nonsense writing, and "Six Improvisational Plays," four of which are prose texts that suggest a performance, much like a script for a happening. The book closes with scenes from *Angelica,* an opera about 19th-century French poetry that was written for the American composer Virgil Thomson but never performed.

Koch's later plays are likewise filled with marvelous moments. In *The New Diana,* essentially a satire of the myth of poets and their muses, he has live turkeys appear, speaking an apparently indigenous language:

> CAGED TURKEY: Mishiki wai nowuga gan! Ish tang.
> TURKEY ON TABLE: Nai shi mai ghee itan, korega.

Popeye among the Polar Bears, likewise a series of vignettes, has the wit and representational freedom that have come to be associated with Koch's verse plays. By contrast, *The Red Robins* is an adaptation of Koch's sole novel, published a few years before, and it differs from Koch's other theatrical works in having considerably longer speeches.

In the mid-1980s Koch developed a working relationship with Barbara Vann and her colleagues at the Medicine Show, a New York off-Broadway theater that produced an operatic version of *A Change of Hearts,* from his second collection. Perhaps because his writing is so strong sentence by sentence and thus need not depend upon linear continuity, Koch's texts have been used as librettos for contemporary operas. The composer Scott Wheeler adapted *The Construction of Boston* into an opera that was performed in Boston in 1989 and 1990, while Marcello Panni made another Koch text into *The Banquet,* an opera that premiered in Bremen, Germany, in June 1998. Perhaps the greatest tragedy of Koch's libretto career was that the collaboration with Thomson in the late 1950s did not bear fruit.

There is a case to be made for Koch as the master conceptual playwright of our time. He is the author of texts that are meant to be read as plays even if they are not actually performed, in a contemporary update of not just Goethe's *Faust* but also of certain of Gertrude Stein's dramatic texts. His book *One Thousand Avant-Garde Plays* (1988), whose title alone is classic, includes "Tadeusz Kantor and the Duck," which is in its entirety a prose description of the noted Polish director interacting with "a large DUCK dressed in black." To the duck's direction Kantor staggers around the stage and dies in its center. "Then, to loud, funereal music, KANTOR is reborn. He and the DUCK go to opposite ends of the stage, then run into each other with a crash. Both fall dead. Then each gets up and, with an ordinary walk, leaves the stage." After another round of music, "the play begins again," implying that it continues into infinity—or until the reader turns the page. Another text in the book, "The Return of Odysseus," has Penelope and Odysseus reciting only one word apiece in alternation. Perhaps it is needless to say that, in the great tradition of conceptual literature, the book contains, contrary to its title, only 112 discrete texts.

Whereas Koch is clearly a major American poet, the question remains whether he should be regarded as a comparably major playwright. His dramatic texts are unique in the ways that all major work is unique. They are radical enough for Ruby Cohn to have written in *New American Dramatists 1960-1980* (1982), "I find the plays of poet Kenneth Koch, which I have never seen performed, too childish to examine in a book intended for adults." Such dismissal would not occur unless Koch's texts took risks with theatrical language, and yet, to my senses, they do not take enough risks within their premises and do not sustain their innovations to sufficient length. There is nothing in Koch's theater equal to his two book-length poems, *When the Sun Tries to Go On* (written in 1953 but not published until 1969) and *Ko; or, A Season on Earth,* but symptoms of such ambition abound in his work. It should also be noted that Koch, like his poetic colleagues John Ashbery and Frank O'Hara, both of whom also wrote plays, belongs to the countertradition of American playwriting—a theater of poets and novelists that emphasizes not naturalism but fantasy, not character but circumstance, not events but essence.

—Richard Kostelanetz

KOPIT, Arthur (Lee)

Nationality: American. **Born:** New York City, 10 May 1937. **Education:** Lawrence High School, New York, graduated 1955; Harvard University, Cambridge, Massachusetts, A.B. (cum laude) 1959 (Phi Beta Kappa). **Family:** Married to Leslie Ann Garis; two sons and one daughter. **Career:** Playwright-in-residence, Wesleyan University, Middletown, Connecticut, 1975-76; CBS fellow, 1976-77, adjunct professor of playwriting, 1977-80, Yale University, New Haven, Connecticut. Adjunct professor of playwriting, City College, New York, 1981—. Council member, Dramatists Guild, 1982—. Lives in Connecticut. **Awards:** Shaw Travelling fellowship, 1959; Vernon Rice award, 1962; Outer Circle award, 1962; Guggenheim fellowship, 1967; Rockefeller grant, 1968, 1977; American Academy award, 1971; National Endowment for the Arts grant, 1974; Wesleyan University Center for the Humanities fellowship, 1974; Italia prize, for radio play, 1979; Tony award, 1982. **Agent:** Audrey Wood, International Creative Management, 40 West 57th Street, New York, New York 10019, U.S.A.

PUBLICATIONS

Plays

The Questioning of Nick (produced Cambridge, Massachusetts, 1957; New York, 1974; London, 1981). Included in *The Day the Whores Came Out to Play Tennis and Other Plays*, 1965.

Gemini (produced Cambridge, Massachusetts, 1957).

Don Juan in Texas, with Wally Lawrence (produced Cambridge, Massachusetts, 1957).

On the Runway of Life, You Never Know What's Coming Off Next (produced Cambridge, Massachusetts, 1957).

Across the River and into the Jungle (produced Cambridge, Massachusetts, 1958).

To Dwell in a Place of Strangers, Act 1 published in *Harvard Advocate* (Cambridge, Massachusetts), May 1958.

Aubade (produced Cambridge, Massachusetts, 1958).

Sing to Me Through Open Windows (produced Cambridge, Massachusetts, 1959; revised version produced New York, 1965; London, 1976). Included in *The Day the Whores Came Out to Play Tennis and Other Plays*, 1965.

Oh Dad, Poor Dad, Mamma's Hung You in the Closet and I'm Feelin' So Sad: A Pseudoclassical Tragifarce in a Bastard French Tradition (produced Cambridge, Massachusetts, 1960; London, 1961; New York, 1962). New York, Hill and Wang, 1960; London, Methuen, 1962.

Mhil'daim (produced New York, 1963).

Asylum; or, What the Gentlemen Are Up To, And As for the Ladies (produced New York, 1963; *And As for the Ladies* produced, as *Chamber Music*, London, 1971). *Chamber Music* published in *The Day the Whores Came Out to Play Tennis and Other Plays*, 1965.

The Conquest of Everest (produced New York, 1964; London, 1980). Included in *The Day the Whores Came Out to Play Tennis and Other Plays*, 1965.

The Hero (produced New York, 1964; London, 1972). Included in *The Day the Whores Came Out to Play Tennis and Other Plays*, 1965.

The Day the Whores Came Out to Play Tennis (produced Cambridge, Massachusetts, 1964; New York, 1965). Included in *The Day the Whores Came Out to Play Tennis and Other Plays*, 1965.

The Day the Whores Came Out to Play Tennis and Other Plays. New York, Hill and Wang, 1965; as *Chamber Music and Other Plays*, London, Methuen, 1969.

Indians (produced London, 1968; Washington, D.C., and New York, 1969). New York, Hill and Wang, 1969; London, Methuen, 1970.

An Incident in the Park, in *Pardon Me, Sir, But Is My Eye Hurting Your Elbow?*, edited by Bob Booker and George Foster. New York, Geis, 1968.

What's Happened to the Thorne's House (produced Peru, Vermont, 1972).

Louisiana Territory; or, Lewis and Clark—Lost and Found (also director: produced Middletown, Connecticut, 1975).

Secrets of the Rich (produced Waterford, Connecticut, 1976). New York, Hill and Wang, 1978.

Wings (broadcast 1977; produced New Haven, Connecticut, and New York, 1978; London, 1979). New York, Hill and Wang, 1978; London, Eyre Methuen, 1979.

Nine (book), music and lyrics by Maury Yeston, from an adaptation by Mario Fratti of the screenplay *8* by Federico Fellini (produced Waterford, Connecticut, 1981; New York, 1982). New York, French, 1983.

Good Help Is Hard to Find (produced New York, 1981). New York, French, 1982.

Ghosts, adaptation of a play by Ibsen (produced New York, 1982; Southampton, 1986). New York, French, 1984.

End of the World (produced New York, 1984; as *The Assignment*, produced Southampton, 1985). New York, Hill and Wang, and London, French, 1984; in *Best American New Plays, 1983-1992*, New York, Crown, 1993.

Bone-the-Fish (produced Louisville, Kentucky, 1989; revised version as *The Road to Nirvana*, produced New York, 1991). New York, Hill and Wang, 1991.

Phantom, music and lyrics by Maury Yeston (produced Houston, 1991).

The Day the Whores Came Out to Play Tennis, and Other Plays. New York, Samuel French, 1993.

Three Plays (includes *Oh Dad, Poor Dad, Mamma's Hung You in the Closet and I'm Feelin' So Sad*; *Indians*; *Wings*). New York, Hill and Wang, 1997.

Radio Play: *Wings*, 1977.

Television Plays: *The Conquest of Television*, 1966; *Promontory Point Revisited*, 1969; *Starstruck*, 1979; *Hands*, 1987; *Hands of a Stranger* series; *Phantom of the Opera* series; *In a Child's Name*.

*

Bibliography: *Ten Modern American Playwrights* by Kimball King, New York, Garland, 1982.

Critical Studies: *Sam Shepard, Arthur Kopit, and the Off Broadway Theater* by Doris Auerbach, Boston, Twayne, 1982; "Waging Nuclear War Rationally: Strategic Thought in Arthur Kopit's *End of the World*" by Daniel L. Zins, in *The Nightmare Considered: Critical Essays on Nuclear War Literature,* edited by Nancy Anisfeld, Bowling Green, Ohio, Popular, 1991; "Two Kinds of Alaska: Pinter and Kopit Journey through Another Realism" by Norman J. Myers, in *The Pinter Review* (Frankfurt, Kentucky), 1992-93, pp. 11-19; "A Gynocratic Feminist Perspective in the Case of Kopit's *Indians*" by Linda Walsh Jenkins, in *Theatre and Feminist Aesthetics,* Madison, New Jersey, Dickinson University Press, 1995; "The Puritan Ideology of Wilderness Projected on American Nature" by Hoon Sung Hwang, in *The Journal of English Literature and Language* (Seoul, Korea), 1996, pp. 179-96; "The Larger Perspective: Arthur Kopit's *Indians* and the Vietnam War" by Karl Gross, in *Modern War on Stage and Screen,* Lewiston, New York, Mellen, 1997.

Theatrical Activities:
Director: **Plays**—*Oh Dad, Poor Dad, Mamma's Hung You in the Closet and I'm Feelin' So Sad*, Paris, 1963; *Louisiana Territory*, Middletown, Connecticut, 1975. **Television**—*The Questioning of Nick*, 1959.

* * *

"Do I exaggerate?" asks Michael Trent in his first speech in *End of the World.* "Of course. That is my method. I am a playwright." The line is a comic one that becomes ironic in the face of a theme—the prospect of global annihilation—that turns even the grandest theatrical exaggeration into austere understatement. Out of context the words provide a suitable description of the way Arthur Kopit works.

At 23, fresh out of Harvard, Kopit escaped—or appeared to escape—the cocoon of university production when *Oh Dad, Poor Dad, Mamma's Hung You in the Closet and I'm Feelin' So Sad* was published by a house that specializes in serious drama and went on to productions in London and New York. A fashionable success, it established Kopit as a dramatist, but it also saddled him with the label "undergraduate playwright," which stayed with him long after the playfulness of *Oh Dad* had given way to the mixed-genre method that marks his best and most complex plays. One reason the epithet stuck is that the work that immediately followed *Oh Dad* lacked the flash of that play and offered little substance in consolation. *The Day the Whores Came Out to Play Tennis and Other Plays*, which contained some of his student work along with his post-*Oh Dad* efforts, seemed to confirm the critics who saw him simply as a clever young man noodling around.

Such a judgment is far too dismissive. Although some of *Oh Dad*'s games—the parody references to Tennessee Williams, for instance—seem too cute in retrospect, it is an early indication of the dramatic virtues that have become increasingly apparent in Kopit's work: a facility with language, an ear for the clichés of art and life, an eye for the effective stage image (the waltz scene in which Madame Rosepettle breaks Commodore Roseabove, for instance), a strategic use of caricature, and the talent for being funny about a subject that is not at all comic. All of these are in evidence in *Oh Dad,* and all of them are in the service of a serious theme (or one that seemed serious in 1960)—the emasculation of the American male by the too protective mother, the iron maiden temptress, and the little girl as seducer.

In a 1962 interview in *Mademoiselle,* Kopit said, "Comedy is a very powerful tool. . . . You take the most serious thing you can think of and treat it as comically as you can." Although he invoked Shaw, *Oh Dad* is the immediate reference. Since then he has thought of more serious things—war, death, nuclear destruction—and has treated them both seriously and comically, as *Indians* and *End of the World* indicate. The Bantam edition of *Indians* (1971) prints a long interview with John Lahr in which Kopit identifies his play as a response to "the madness of our involvement in Vietnam," but he chose to approach the subject obliquely by going back to the eviction of the American Indian from his land. The play shows the distance between official words and deeds, the power of platitude, and the way in which myths are made and used. The central figure is Buffalo Bill, who begins as a friend of the Indians and ends—a star of his own show—as an apologist for slaughter. The play moves back and forth between comic and serious scenes, from the broad farce of the play within the play and the cartoon Ol' Time President to the powerful accusatory ending in which the Wild West Show is invaded by the dead Indians. For some the funny scenes fit uncomfortably with the solemn subject matter, but they are not simply entertaining decoration. The comedy is thematic. The disastrous production of the Ned Buntline melodrama at the White House is both an instance of the creation of myth and a critique of it.

End of the World is a similar fusion of genres. It concerns a playwright who is commissioned to write a play about the dangers of nuclear proliferation—as Kopit was, in fact—and finds that he can only do so by writing a play about a playwright who . . . . The parody of the private eye frame of the play (the playwright as detective), the agents' lunch at the Russian Tea Room, and the three interviews in which the rationale of nuclear stockpiling and scenarios of destruction are presented as comic turns are all central to the play's assumption that there are personal, artistic, and official ways of not facing up to the impending horror. What Michael Trent learns in the play is that all the nuclear strategists know the situation to be hopeless but do not believe what they know, and he finds out that he was chosen to write the play because, like the men he interviews, he has an attraction to evil and destruction. A painful and funny play, it provides no solution, only an insistence on the probability of catastrophe, and, unlike the conventional postbomb melodrama, no promise of rebirth.

If *Indians* and *End of the World* share dramatic method, *Wings* is an indication of Kopit's unpredictability. There are funny lines in the play, but it is primarily a lyric exploration of death. It is about a woman who suffers a stroke, struggles to make her fragmented speech fit her still coherent thoughts, and after a second stroke becomes eloquent as she sees herself flying into the unknown. She was a wing walker in her youth, and her profession/art provides the main metaphor for her final sense of exhilarating discovery. The play evokes both the concerned narrowness of medicine's perception of the woman and the imagination that continues to carry her above her stammering exasperation with herself and those around her. It is an indication—along with *Indians* and *End of the World*—that Kopit is wing walking far above the bravura flight of *Oh Dad.*

—Gerald Weales

KOUKA, Hone

Nationality: New Zealander (Maori). Affiliated with Ngati Porou, Ngati Kahungungu, and Ngati Raukawa tribes. **Born:** Balcutha, 1968. **Education:** Otago University, Dunedin, graduated in 1988; Toi Whakaari o Aotearoa: The New Zealand Drama School, graduated in 1990. **Career:** Actor, director, journalist, and playwright. Writer-in-residence, Canterbury University, 1996; artistic director, Taki Rua Productions, Wellington. **Awards:** Most promising newcomer, Chapman Tripp Theatre awards, 1991; most original play, Chapman Tripp Theatre awards, 1992; Bruce Mason Playwrighting award, most original play, 1992; Te Ha Drama award, best New Zealand play, 1993; best new New Zealand play, Chapmann Tripp Theatre awards, 1994.

Publications

Plays

Mauri Tu (produced Dunedin, 1991). Christchurch, Aoraki Press, 1992.
He Waki, with Apirana Taylor and Erina Toi Paku (produced Australian University tour, 1992).
Remembrance of Things to Come, with sue Morrison (produced Taki Rua, 1992).
Hide 'n' Seek, with Hori Ahipene (produced Taki Rua, 1992).
Mokemoke (produced Dunedin, 1993).
Five Angels (produced Taki Rua, 1993).
Nga Tangata Toa (produced Taki Rua, 1994). Wellington, Victoria University Press, 1994.
Whakakotahi (produced Berlin, 1994).
Tuakana (produced Wellington, 1995).
King Hits (produced Taki Rua, 1995).
Waiora (produced Wellington, 1996). Huia Publishers, 1997.
Grey (produced Taki Rua, 1997).
Peach and Terry (produced Dunedin, 1997).
Taiki E, with John Vakidis (produced New Zealand tour, 1997).
Homefires (produced 1998).

*

Critical Study: "Ta Matou Mangai/Our Own Voices: A Discussion" by Howard McNaughton and Hone Kouka, in *Post-Colonial Stages: Critical and Creative Views on Drama, Theatre and Performance in Colonised Cultures,* Hebden Bridge, England, Dangaroo Press, 1998.

* * *

As the leading playwright to emerge within the context of Maori cultural self-determination, Hone Kouka has worked with specifically Maori philosophies of performance, identity, and personal interaction from the first: his *Mauri Tu* is a short autoperformance developed at drama school, but it premiered at Taki Rua, at the time the leading laboratory of Maori and bicultural theater in Aotearoa New Zealand. Important determinants in this theater practice have been the attendance of tribal elders throughout rehearsals to observe and authorize cultural practice, as well as "whanau" nights, on which special performances would be done for the extended family of the cast; these performances bring a deep cultural literacy and often a radically different response to the play, partly because Kouka does not build English translations of Maori speech into his dialogue as other Maori playwrights have done.

Although his earlier, short plays were contemporary in setting and youthful in their focus, Kouka first attracted international attention with an inter-generational drama with a historicized action. *Nga Tangata Toa* [The Warrior People] was "derived" from Ibsen's *Vikings at Helgeland,* but it emerged in the theater as a cross-cultural exploration, facilitated by a Norwegian dramaturge. The play's epic sweep and the urgency of its historical occasion have been central to its success, but so too has Kouka's concern to unsettle a tendency towards stereotype in the action and characterization of some Maori plays of the 1980s. In this play the action pivots on a strong Maori woman of low birth status whose destructive resentment undermines custom and audience expectation, especially as the play's supernatural texture is heightened by her curses and uncanny premonitions of death. Publicity aside, few theatergoers would associate this with one of Ibsen's less-known plays, but there is an important territorial similarity in that both plays have crucial scenes in communal meeting houses and on the shore or coast: the indoor scenes emphasize the importance of oral transmission of knowledge and oratory; and the seaside scenes present a terrain of economic and spiritual importance to both peoples, while serving as the primary contact zone with other cultures and other tribes. The historical setting of the play—in 1919, with a family group gathering to meet a returning war hero—accentuates this further, because Maori participation in the war had itself been contentious.

The most important stereotype that Kouka was contesting in *Nga Tangata Toa*, however, was that of the warrior, at the time a concept foregrounded by Alan Duff's novel *Once Were Warriors* (1990) and its subsequent screen version in which urban violence was related to a warrior tradition. Kouka went further in modifying this warrior figure in *Waiora*, where toughness and resilience are central male qualities but are not confused with brutality. Here the occasion seems quite innocent—a family birthday celebration on a beach in 1965—and the action is continuous and unified, a contrast with the fragmented, sometimes frenetic texture of *Nga Tangata Toa.* At its core is the patriarch, outwardly a grumpy middle-aged man, but more deeply a repository of tensions generated by a life of cultural denial and territorial displacement. His status in turn has a strong bearing on the play's historical situation, just before the Maori cultural revival of the 1970s, a time when the future of Maori seemed very fragile; this is contextualized by the prominence of the European mill manager, who has some control over the characters' dignity as well as their economic status. The sharpness of this historical grounding, however, is tempered by the presence of four ancestors—a vestigial presence through much of the play—who are seen and accepted as a continuous part of the present community by the Maori characters. They, voicing the claim of tradition, construct the agonistic finale over the body of a drowned girl. It is typical of Kouka's practice that by this stage in the play, management of the action is entirely in traditional Maori performance terms of haka, waiata tangi, karanga, and karakia, even when tradition itself is being contested.

—Howard McNaughton

KOUTOUKAS, H. M.

Nationality: American. **Born:** Endicott, New York, 4 June 1947. **Education:** Harpur College, Binghamton, New York; Maria Ley-Piscator Dramatic Work-shop, New School for Social Research, New York, 1962-65; Universalist Life Church, Modesto, California, Ph.D. **Career:** Associated with the Electric Circus and other theatre groups in New York; founder Chamber Theatre Group, New York; member, the Ridiculous Theatrical Company, New York. **Awards:** Obie award, 1966; National Arts Club award; Professional Theatre Wing award. **Agent:** Nino Karlweis, 250 East 65th Street, New York, New York 10021.

PUBLICATIONS

Plays

The Last Triangle (produced New York, 1965).
Tidy Passions; or, Kill, Kaleidoscope, Kill (produced New York, 1965). Published in *More Plays from Off-Off-Broadway*, edited by Michael T. Smith, Indianapolis, Bobbs Merrill, 1972.
All Day for a Dollar (produced New York, 1966).
Medea (produced New York, 1966).
Only a Countess (produced New York, 1966).
A Letter from Colette (also director: produced New York, 1966).
Pomegranada, music by Al Carmines (produced New York, 1966).
With Creatures Make My Way (produced New York, 1967).
When Clowns Play Hamlet (also director: produced New York, 1967).
View from Sorrento (produced New York, 1967).
Howard Kline Trilogy (produced New York, 1968).
Christopher at Sheridan Squared (produced New York, 1971).
French Dressing (revue), with others (produced New York, 1974).
Grandmother Is in the Strawberry Patch (produced New York, 1974).
The Pinotti Papers (produced New York, 1975).
One Man's Religion (produced New York, 1975).
Star Followers in an Ancient Land, music by Tom O'Horgan and Gale Garnett (also director: produced New York, 1975).
The Legend of Sheridan Square (produced New York, 1976).
Turtles Don't Dream (also director: produced New York, 1977).
Too Late for Yogurt (also director: produced New York, 1978).
The Butterfly Encounter, music by David Forman (produced New York, 1978).
A Hand Job for Apollo (produced New York, 1988).
When Lightning Strikes Twice (includes *Awful People Are Coming Over So We Must Be Pretending to Be Hard at Work and Hope They Will Go Away, Only a Countess May Dance When She's Crazy*) (produced New York, 1991).
Skin of the Night (produced New York, 1992).
Songs Lucifer Sang to Me as I Made Love to a Dutch Male (produced New York, 1995).
Prostitute (produced New York, 1995).
Enough's Enough (produced New York, 1995).
All for Art (produced New York, 1995).

*

Theatrical Activities:
Director: **Plays**—Several of his own plays.

* * *

H. M. Koutoukas's plays have a special tone and flavor that are all his own and are immediately recognizable. He often writes in verse, and the characters and situations are the product of a fancifully perverse imagination and an elaborately refined sensibility. Most of his plays are designated as "camps" rather than dramas or comedies. The style is flamboyantly romantic, innocently idiosyncratic, self-satirizing, full of private references and inside jokes, precious, boldly aphoristic, and disdainful of preconceptions of sense, taste, or fashion. Koutoukas is perhaps the last of the aesthetes. Underlying the decorative surface, however, there characteristically are portraits of people or creatures so strange—the deformed, the demented, the rejected, the defiant—that they have lost touch with ordinary life, yet their feelings are all the more tender and vulnerable.

Koutoukas's adaptation of *Medea* is set in a laundromat, and, in the author's production at the Caffe Cino, Medea was played by a man, Charles Stanley. Only ridiculous on the surface, the play depicts a woman from a more primitive, natural, expressive culture trapped among the overcivilized, calculating Greeks and makes her desperation sympathetic. *Tidy Passions; or, Kill, Kaleidoscope, Kill* is peopled by a high priestess and several witches of a broken-down cobra cult, a dying dove, Narcissus, and Jean Harlow, who proclaims, "Glamour is dead." *With Creatures Make My Way* is set in a sewer where the single character, neither man nor woman, consummates eternal love with a passing lobster. *A Letter from Colette,* written in a naturalistic mode, sweetly conjures romance between an aging woman and a handsome young delivery boy. *Pomegranada,* an opera with music by Al Carmines, opens in the Garden of Eden and is about tarnish. *Christopher at Sheridan Squared* is a hallucinatory documentary about the Greenwich Village street where Koutoukas has always lived.

In the mid-1980s Koutoukas reemerged as an actor and theatrical personality. He presented his students, the School for Gargoyles, in *A Hand Job for Apollo* and appeared at La Mama in *The Birds.* Joining the Ridiculous Theatrical Company, he won acclaim for his performances in revivals of several plays by the late Charles Ludlam, appearing in London as well as New York. Koutoukas's plays *Awful People Are Coming Over So We Must Be Pretending to Be Hard at Work and Hope They Will Go Away* and *Only a Countess May Dance When She's Crazy* were presented by the Ridiculous, starring Everett Quinton, in 1991. *Skin of the Night* followed, since which Koutoukas has done *Songs Lucifer Sang to Me as I Made Love to a Dutch Male Prostitute, Enough's Enough,* and *All for Art,* a monster trilogy done separately.

—Michael Smith

KRASELCHIK, R. *See* **DYER, Charles (Raymond).**

KUO Pao Kun

Nationality: Singaporean. **Born:** Hebei Province, China, 27 June 1939; brought to Singapore in 1949. **Education:** National Institute of Dramatic Art, Sydney, graduated 1964; advanced course in theatre, 1971. **Family:** Married Goh Lay Kuan. **Career:** Cofounder with his wife, Practice Performing Arts School, 1965; detained without trial by the Singapore Government under Internal Security Act, March 1976-October 1980; founding artistic director, The Theatre Practice, 1986; founding artistic director, The Substation (Singapore's first arts center), 1990-95. Adjunct associated professor of drama and performance, National Institute of Education, Nanyang Technological University, 1994—. Fulbright professional exchange fellowship, 1989. **Awards:** National Cultural Medallion, Singapore, 1990; Culture award for Japan Chamber of Commerce and Industry, Singapore, 1992; ASEAN Cultural award, 1993; Chevalier des Arts et des Letters by the French government, 1997; Asian leadership fellowship program, Japan, 1997.

Publications

Plays

Caucasian Chalk Circle, adaptation of Bertolt Brecht (produced 1967).
A Raisin in the Sun, adaptation of Lorraine Hansberry (produced 1968).
Hey, Wake Up! (produced 1968).
The Struggle (produced 1969).
The Spark of Youth (produced 1970).
Growth (produced 1974).
Atop Roof, Tile Roof, adaptation of Kala Dewata (produced 1981).
The Little White Sailing Boat (produced 1982).
The Coffin is Too Big For the Hole (produced Hong Kong,1984). Times Books International, 1990.
The Island, adaptation of Athol Fugard (produced 1985).
Kapai Kapai, adaptation of Arifin C. Noer (produced 1986).
No Parking on Odd Days (produced Hong Kong, 1986). Times Books International, 1990.
Kopitiam (produced 1986).
The Fire Teasers, adaptation of Max Frisch (produced 1987).
The Silly Little Girl and the Funny Old Tree (produced 1987). Times Books International, 1990.
Day I Met the Prince (produced 1988). Times Books International, 1990.
Mama Looking For Her Cat (produced 1988). Times Books International, 1990.
The Eagle & The Cat (produced 1990).
The Coffin Is Too Big for the Whole and Other Plays. Singapore, Times Books, International. 1990.
Lao Jiu (produced 1990).
OZero01 (produced 1991).
The Evening Climb (produced 1992).
Descendants of the Eunuch Admiral (produced 1995).
Geylang People in the Net (produced 1997).
The Spirits Play (produced 1998).

*

Critical Study: "Theater in Singapore: An Interview with Kuo Pao Kun" by Jacqueline Lo, in *Australasian Drama Studies* (Queensland), October 1993, pp. 135-46.

* * *

The form, content, and linguistic complexity of the work for the Singaporean theater of the Chinese-born playwright Kuo Pao Kun reflects the profound political, economic, and social shifts that have taken place in that country during the postindependence era. Fluent in both Mandarin and English, Kuo studied theater production at the National Institute of Dramatic Art in Sydney in the early 1960s and returned to Singapore in 1965, the year of its break from the Malaysian Federation. That same year, along with his wife, the choreographer Goh Lay Kuan, he formed the Practice Performing Arts School, the country's oldest theater company and training institution.

In the early 1970s Kuo's company embraced the "Go into Life" campaign, which involved sending young artists and intellectuals into the factories, rice fields, pineapple farms, and fishing villages of Singapore and peninsular Malaysia. Large working-class audiences witnessed the company's variety show-style productions, which featured songs, poetry, dance, and Chinese cross-talk routines. This radical theater movement came to an end in 1976 when thousands were arrested in a massive purge of the left. Kuo himself was detained under the provisions of Singapore's Internal Security Act from 1976 to 1980, a period he now regards as "a very, very deep education process."

When Kuo emerged in 1980, both the world and Singapore had changed enormously. The perceived communist threat to the rest of Southeast Asia had been eliminated, and Singapore had become the principal transshipment center for a part of the world that was experiencing rapid economic growth. English had emerged as the language that dominated in Singapore's educational, business, and financial spheres, while the country's ruling Political Action Party, under the firm hand of Lee Kuan Yew, had virtually eliminated all vestiges of domestic dissent. Thus, the political and social criticism imbedded in Kuo's work since the early 1980s has become metaphoric, indirect, and laced with humor and Singaporean colloquialisms. During the 1980s Kuo wrote and staged a series of one-act plays in both English and Mandarin that reflected the social pressures and cultural dislocation many were experiencing as the nation rapidly redefined its sense of self.

In Kuo's monologue *The Coffin Is Too Big for the Hole* (1985), a grandson finds himself having to take on a humorless and rigid bureaucracy on the day of his grandfather's funeral when the coffin is found to be too large for the regulation size hole. The uniform size of burial plots functions as an apt metaphor for stifling conformity and the many social controls that govern the lives of regulation-bound Singaporeans. Similarly, in Kuo's *No Parking on Odd Days* (1986) a father, goaded by his son's sense of justice, takes on the judiciary over a parking offense for which he feels the state shares responsibility. Unlike the dutiful grandson who successfully fulfills his filial obligation toward his grandfather in *Coffin,* the father in *No Parking* ultimately loses the battle and finds that his son "became more and more quiet and gradually the questions didn't come any more." What the father interprets as "a sign of him growing up" can also be read as a triumph of the state over the individual.

Although Kuo has written largely in English or Mandarin, the country's other cultural and linguistic streams (Chinese dialects, Malay, South Indian/Tamil) are also prominently featured in his plays. *Mama Looking for Her Cat*(1988), created in workshops with a group of 11 actors and performed in English, Mandarin, Tamil, and the Chinese dialects of Hokkien, Cantonese, and Teochew, is one of Singapore's most aggressively multilingual plays. The use of Malay words and Chinese and Malay sentence structure even when speaking English has resulted in a form known as Singlish, constituting yet another language that enters into both Kuo's and Singapore's linguistic mix.

Much of Kuo's work in the 1990s has directly or indirectly dealt with aspects of Singaporean identity that have been lost as the country joins the race to make it to the top of the economic heap in an age dominated by Western culture and mediated by the values of global capitalism. In *Lao Jiu* (Ninth Son) the first boy to be born after a long line of girls turns down a future in which prosperity and status are virtually guaranteed to pursue the dying art of Hokkien hand puppetry. It is Kuo's 1995 work *Descendants of the Eunuch Admiral,* however, that best exemplifies his ability to express social and political criticism so deftly and subtly that it not only falls within Singapore's established censorship guidelines but also speaks across cultural boundaries. The play uses the historical figure of the powerful 15th-century eunuch Admiral Zhenghe as a device for asserting an inverse relationship between sex and power. Integrated into the play are detailed and chilling descriptions of methods of castration that are just open enough textually to be read as metaphors for other kinds of power freely given over to one's masters in the pursuit of material pleasure. The play thus provides piquant social criticism, though in a manner that is artfully indirect.

Kuo's is one of the few voices in Singapore that have come forth to question publicly the wisdom behind the government's decision to place significant resources behind what he terms "the theatre that consumes." While the government is committed to building a home for Western-style musicals as it races to complete the Esplanade, one of the world's largest and most sophisticated performing arts centers, Kuo has used theater to develop and express a uniquely Singaporean vision. In a world in which cultural and linguistic differences are being rapidly assimilated and transformed into a kind of postmodern depthlessness or an empty nostalgia for a fictional past, Kuo's plays remind Singapore and the world that multiple identity and linguistic complexity are strengths that theater can explore and celebrate.

—William Peterson

KUREISHI, Hanif

Nationality: British. **Born:** London, 5 December 1954. **Education:** King's College, University of London, B.A. in philosophy. **Career:** Writer-in-residence, Royal Court Theatre, London, 1981 and 1985-86. **Awards:** George Devine award, 1981; *Evening Standard* award, for screenplay, 1985. **Agent:** Lemon, Unna, and Durbridge, 24 Pottery Lane, Holland Park, London W11 4LZ, England.

Publications

Plays

Soaking the Heat (produced London, 1976).
The Mother Country (produced London, 1980).
The King and Me (produced London, 1980). Included in *Outskirts, The King and Me, Tomorrow—Today!*, 1983.
Outskirts (produced London, 1981). Included in *Outskirts, The King and Me, Tomorrow—Today!*, 1983.
Tomorrow—Today! (produced London, 1981). Included in *Outskirts, The King and Me, Tomorrow—Today!*, 1983.
Cinders, from a play by Janusz Glowacki (produced London, 1981).
Borderline (produced London, 1981). London, Methuen, 1981.
Artists and Admirers, with David Leveaux, from a play by Alexander Ostrovsky (produced London, 1982).
Birds of Passage (produced London, 1983). Oxford, Amber Lane Press, 1983.
Outskirts, The King and Me, Tomorrow—Today! London, Calder, and New York, Riverrun Press, 1983.
Mother Courage, adaptation of a play by Brecht (produced London, 1984).
My Beautiful Laundrette (screenplay; includes essay "The Rainbow Sign"). London, Faber, 1986.
Sammy and Rosie Get Laid (screenplay). London, Faber, 1988.
London Kills Me (screenplay). London, Faber, 1991.
Sleep with Me. London, Faber.

Screenplays: *My Beautiful Laundrette*, 1985; *Sammy and Rosie Get Laid*, 1988; *London Kills Me*, 1991; *My Son The Fanatic,* n.d.

Radio Plays: *You Can't Go Home*, 1980; *The Trial*, from a novel by Kafka, 1982.

Novels

The Buddha of Suburbia. London, Faber, 1990; New York, Penguin, 1991.
The Black Album. London, Faber, 1995.
Intimacy. London, Faber.

Short Story Collection

Love in a Blue Time. London, Faber, 1997.

* * *

Hanif Kureishi is often assumed to be a purely Asian writer, but for the most part his earlier plays look at events through the eyes of characters who are white. Kureishi himself was born in London of mixed parentage, with an English mother and a Pakistani father. He grew up without feeling that he was different from his classmates and has always thought of himself as an Englishman. The need for an Asian voice in contemporary theater and the current concern with problems that affect Asians have caused him, however, to examine this other aspect of his heritage.

After two early plays produced in 1980, *The Mother Country* at Riverside Studios and *The King and Me*—about a couple's obsession with Elvis Presley—at the Soho Poly, Kureishi's more ambitious play *Outskirts* received a production at the Royal Shakespeare Company Warehouse in 1981. It centers on two men who grew up together in the straggling suburbs around Orpington and on the eventual divergence of their lives. Del, who has always tagged along with the more dominant Bob, makes the break from their dead-end working-class background and trains as a teacher. Bob, who leaves school early for a well-paid job, finds himself on the unemployment scrap heap. In his bitterness he turns to the

National Front, where, he says, "We're strong men, together. Men worn down by waiting. Abused men. Men with no work. Our parents made redundant. Now us. . . ." But the racism he expresses is a reminder of an evening 10 years before when he and Del had beaten up a Pakistani. On that occasion Del had taken the initiative in violence, and the shadow of the incident haunts him now that he is a respectable teacher.

Outskirts has an awkwardness of construction in the way it moves from past to present and back again, and the appearance at intervals of Bob's mother is not always successfully dealt with. Nonetheless, Kureishi gets inside the skin of young men who thought that with the end of school and a wage packet each week the world would be theirs. "I tell you," says Bob, "it's all waiting for a boy like me. Cars, clothes, crumpet." Kureishi also illuminates the lot of the women. When Bob's wife Maureen returns from having had an abortion rather than bring up a child in a home with no money, she is told by Bob's mother, who is prematurely old: "You did the right thing. Sometimes I wish I'd done the same. I know it's wicked to say that. But I think it. I do."

In *Borderline,* written after a workshop collaboration with Joint Stock and produced at the Royal Court in 1981, Kureishi turns to the problems of Asian immigrants. The idea of writing about Asians in Britain came from the theater's artistic director, Max Stafford-Clark, and Kureishi was at first nervous about writing from outside his own experience. His misgivings proved unnecessary, and, with the combination of several weeks of meeting and talking with Asians in Southall and the inspiration of his imagination and his own past, he was able to write a play about the Asian dilemma in England. For him writing about Pakistanis in England is also a way of writing about the English and the way England has changed.

Borderline is concerned with the lives of several Asians who are trying to survive in an indifferent or hostile community. An English observer, Susan, a journalist who is writing an article on Asians in England, at times takes the role of commentator on what Kureishi himself heard during his research: "All the people I've spoken to have been beaten or burnt or abused at some time. You speak to them, they say they like England, it is democratic, or just or good. And then say what's been done to them here. Such viciousness in England." The play also deals with conflict among the Asians, between those who try to maintain an Asian way of life and those who adopt English morals and attitudes. The parents of Amina decide to send her back to an arranged marriage in Pakistan, but she realizes that she has become English and that, whether she likes it or not, England is her home.

Birds of Passage deals with a lower-middle-class family in Sydenham that has fallen on hard times. There are resonances of Chekov's *The Cherry Orchard* as the family is forced to sell its house to an Asian former lodger. Until he loses his job, the father of the family, a self-educated Labour councillor, does not realize that times have changed. Despite her education his daughter has taken to prostitution on the side, and his wife's sister and her husband, at one time affluent from the proceeds of selling central heating, suddenly find that the bottom has dropped out of the market. Kureishi writes about his ineffectual characters with affection, and there is what amounts to a hymn of praise to suburbia from the father: "Out here we live in peace, indifferent to the rest of the world. We have no sense of communal existence but we are tolerant, not cruel." The least sympathetic character is Asif, the spoiled, indolent son of rich Asian parents. Asif despises poor Pakistani immigrants and is smugly upwardly mobile. The play is not primarily about racial attitudes but about the effect of the recession on people in Britain who believed in the optimism of the 1960s and then had to face unemployment in the early 1980s.

Kureishi's script for the film *My Beautiful Laundrette* brought him to the attention of a wider public. A small-budget movie directed by Stephen Frears, it caught the imagination of critics and audiences. Several of the characters and situations of his stage plays are enlarged on here. The outwardly modest but sexually experienced Amina of *Borderline* has her counterpart in the film as does the amoral young entrepreneur Asif of *Birds of Passage*, while the intense, and in the film's case homosexual, relationship of the two boys who grew up together echoes the relationship of Del and Bob in *Outskirts*.

Kureishi's second film, *Sammy and Rosie Get Laid,* was larger, more diffuse, and in the end less satisfactory. It featured polemical discussions on drugs, and the gay incidents seemed to be extraneous rather than a development of the story. Sammy, an Asian, and the English Rosie, living in Brixton, have an uneasy relationship. Sammy's Pakistani politician father arrives in London to find that the pleasant and gentlemanly England he remembers has vanished. He is haunted by the ghost of a man with a battered face, a reminder of his responsibility for torture in Pakistan. The film has strong, raw images, but it suffers from Kureishi's ambition to give a dissertation on everything that was wrong in Britain in the Thatcherite 1980s.

Kureishi directed his next film, *London Kills Me,* which narrows its theme to the London drug scene. Clint, a young member of a drug-dealing posse, is half in love with the heroin addict Sylvie, but she is stolen from him by the posse leader Muffdiver. The small-time posse tries to get in with the big-time dealers but ends only by alienating them. Clint, having been unlucky in love and crime, decides to go straight and takes a job as a waiter in a diner. His first ingratiating smile at a customer implies that he will be a success in his new occupation. Although the film is set against the drug scene, it concentrates on the triangular relationship and the symbolic search by Clint for the "true shoe" after his own have been stolen when he is beaten up by a couple of dealers to whom he owes money. The ending is ambiguous. The spontaneous street hustler has turned into a paid performer in waiter's costume, yet there is an air of futility about his friends, who decide to continue the life of flight and disguise.

Kureishi's novel *The Buddha of Suburbia* has an autobiographical element. It is the story of Karim Amir, "an Englishman born and bred—almost," who lives with his English mother and Indian father in a dull South London suburb. It is his dream to escape to London proper and to the world of sex and drugs. His father, "the Buddha of Suburbia," finally leads the way with his glamorous mistress, Eva, and introduces him to the exciting life of the city. Karim becomes an actor and falls under the influence of the charismatic theater director Matthew Pike, star of the flourishing alternative theater. The play that Karim is appearing in transfers to New York, where he encounters his old schoolfriend Charlie, now a rock star and into sadomasochism. The book is strong on dialogue and characters, some of which are clearly borrowed from real life. It is episodic in construction and reads at times like a source book for the recurring themes in Kureishi's plays.

—Clare Colvin

KUSHNER, Tony

Nationality: American. **Born:** New York City, 16 July 1956. Grew up in Lake Charles, Louisiana. **Education:** Columbia University, New York, B.A. 1978; New York University, M.F.A. in directing 1984. **Career:** Guest artist, New York University Graduate Theatre Program, Yale University, New Haven, Connecticut, and Princeton University, New Jersey, 1989—; director, Literary Services, Theatre Communications Group, New York, 1990-91; playwright-in-residence, Juilliard School of Drama, New York, 1990-92. Lives in Brooklyn. **Awards:** National Endowment for the Arts directing fellowship, 1985; Princess Grace award, 1986; New York State Council on the Arts playwriting fellowship, 1986; New York Foundation for the Arts playwriting fellowship, 1987; John Whiting award, 1990; Kennedy Center/American Express Fund for New American Plays award, 1990, 1992; National Arts Club Kesselring award, 1991; Will Glickman playwriting prize, 1992; *Evening Standard* award, 1992; Pulitzer prize for drama, Tony award for best play, and New York Drama Critics Circle award for best new play, all 1993, all for *Millennium Approaches,* part 1 of *Angles in America*; American Academy of Arts and Letters award, 1994; Tony award for *Perestroika,* part two of *Angles in America,* 1994; Lambda Literary award, Lesbian and Gay drama, 1996, for *Thinking About the Longstanding Problems of Virtue and Happiness.* **Agent:** Joyce Ketay, 1501 Broadway, Suite 1910, New York, New York 10024, U.S.A.

Publications

Plays

Yes, Yes, No, No (for children; produced St. Louis, Missouri, 1985). Published in *Plays in Process* (New York), vol. 7, no. 11, 1987.

Stella, adaptation of the play by Goethe (produced New York, 1987).

A Bright Room Called Day (produced San Francisco, 1987; London, 1988; New York, 1991). New York, Broadway Play Publishing, 1991.

Hydriotaphia (produced New York, 1987).

The Illusion, adaptation of a play by Pierre Corneille (produced New York, 1988; revised version produced Hartford, Connecticut, 1990). New York, Broadway Play Publishing, 1991.

Widows, with Ariel Dorfman, adaptation of the novel by Dorfman (produced Los Angeles, 1991).

Angels in America, Part One: Millennium Approaches (produced San Francisco, 1991; London, 1992; New York, 1993). London, Hern, 1992; with *Angels in America, Part Two: Perestroika*, New York, Theatre Communications Group, 1993.

Angels in America, Part Two: Perestroika (produced Los Angeles, 1992; London and New York, 1993). With *Angels in America, Part One: Millennium Approaches*, New York, Theatre Communications Group, 1993; revised version, New York, Theatre Communications Group, 1996.

Other

Thinking About the Longstanding Problems of Virtue and Happiness. London, Nick Hern Books, 1995.

A Prayer (excerpt from *Slavs!: Thinking About the Longstanding Problems of Virtue and Happiness*). New York, Theatre Communications Group, 1995.

Tony Kushner in Conversation, edited by Robert Vorlicky. Ann Arbor, University of Michigan Press, 1998.

Translator, *A Dybbuk.* New York, Theatre Communications Group, 1998.

*

Critical Studies: "Tony Kushner Considers the Longstanding Problems of Virtue and Happiness" by David Savran, in *American Theatre,* 1994, pp. 20-27, 100-04; *Essays on Kushner's Angels,* edited by Per K. Brask, Winnipeg, Blizzard Publishing, 1995; "The Angels of Fructification: Tennessee Williams, Tony Kushner, and Images of Homosexuality on the American Stage" by James Fisher, in *Mississippi Quarterly: The Journal of Southern Culture,* Winter 1995-96, pp. 13-32; "*Angels in America:* Tony Kushner's Theses on the Philosophy of History" by Charles McNully, in *Modern Drama* (Downsview, Ontario), Spring 1996; "Authors in America: Tony Kushner, Arthur Miller, and Anna Deveare Smith" by Iris Smith, in *The Centennial Review* (East Lansing, Michigan), Winter 1996, pp. 125-42; *Approaching the Millennium: Essays on Angels in America,* edited by Deborah R. Geis and Steven F. Kruger, Ann Arbor, University of Michigan Press, 1997.

Theatrical Activities:
Director: **Plays**–*Yes Yes Yes No No: The Solace-of-Solstice, Apogee/Perigee, Bestial/Celestial Holiday Show,* St. Louis, Missouri, 1985; *In Great Eliza's Golden Time,* St. Louis, Missouri, 1986; *Golden Boy,* St. Louis, Missouri, 1986.

Actor: **Play**–*Letter from New York to Sarajevo,* 1995. **Television**–*The 47th Annual Tony Awards,* 1993; *In Search of Angles,* 1994

* * *

Tony Kushner dreams on a grand scale. He creates manifestations of Satan, death, and the soul as readily as other dramatists invent ordinary humans. A gay activist and passionate political thinker and a devoted student of Bertolt Brecht, Kushner writes plays suffused with historical consciousness and often filled with political argument. Behind the torrents of his language lie models of extravagant prose—his play *Hydriotaphia* was inspired by the seventeenth-century essayist Sir Thomas Browne—and the poetry of centuries. Though Kushner has an acute ear for the ways in which all sorts of people speak, his dialogue frequently breaks into poetry, which can rhyme or be very free. He is a romantic whose work is haunted by death, yet full of hope.

Kushner has shot to prominence with his two-part, roughly seven-hour *Angels in America. Angels,* the first significant Kushner play to be rooted wholly in contemporary life, depicts the catastrophe of AIDS in New York City. This emotionally powerful subject works to bring the recondite material of Kushner's earlier plays to a much larger audience.

The Illusion, freely adapted from Corneille's *L'illusion comique*, shows Kushner reveling in romance. The play is full of poetic hyperbole at once indulged in and mocked but above all enjoyed. Kushner's braggart soldier Matamore is a Don Quixote, the embodiment of the play's absurd and melancholy beauty. The love of theater, of its magic and its transformations, at the play's heart is a key element in *Angels* as well.

Kushner wrote his first important play, *A Bright Room Called Day*, in "deepest-midnight Reagan America"; since then it has been extensively revised. In the Weimar Germany of 1932-33 a circle of friends disintegrates under the pressures of Hitler's rise to power, one after another forced into hiding or exile until just one woman, Agnes, is left cowering in her apartment. The story is periodically interrupted by Zillah Katz, a contemporary American "with Anarcho-Punk tendencies," who in the version staged at New York's Public Theater in 1991 comes to Berlin and lands in the same apartment; finally she and Agnes inhabit each other's dreams. Kushner keeps rewriting Zillah's lines because she is there to draw parallels with the contemporary political situation in the United States. "Overstatement is your friend: use it," advises Zillah, comparing Reagan and Bush to Hitler. For subsequent productions, Kushner has written, he "will cheerfully supply new material, drawing appropriate parallels between contemporary and historical monsters and their monstrous acts, regardless of how superficially outrageous such comparisons may seem. To refuse to compare is to rob history of its power to inform present action."

One of the bravest of *Bright Room*'s characters, a woman artist named Gotchling, says that "the dreams of the Left are always beautiful." Her words catch at the essence of Kushner's art: "As an artist I am struck to the heart by these dreams. These visions. We progress. But at great cost." Words very like these recur at the end of *Angels in America*.

Subtitled "A Gay Fantasia on National Themes," *Angels* is an epic play for eight actors, its theatricality heightened by casting them in a number of roles—often characters of the opposite sex—in addition to their primary parts. Twin plots center on two troubled couples. Prior has AIDS, and his lover Louis, unable to cope, leaves him. Joe and Harper are Mormons whose marriage is falling apart. Joe is losing his lifelong battle to repress his homosexuality, and Harper's way of dealing is to retreat into Valium-assisted visions. As in a nineteenth-century novel, the two stories interweave: Louis and Joe become lovers, and Harper and Prior meet in a mutual hallucination. Joe and Louis both work at a federal court building in Brooklyn, giving scope for plenty of political argument between the conservative Mormon and the liberal Jew.

Even more important to the play's political nexus is Roy M. Cohn, Joe's father figure and the embodiment of the naked desire for power that underlies politics and corrupts it. Kushner has made of this historical figure a monster—a profane, bigoted, brazen criminal. He is also the life force incarnate. Cohn fights the whole world and revels in the struggle. A gay man dying of AIDS—however closeted, however much he insists that he has liver cancer—he is furious and unafraid. He brings to *Angels in America* acid comedy and demonic energy, he summons complicated feelings, and after he dies, he comes back to dominate yet additional scenes.

Millennium Approaches is not only the first part's title, but it is also the feeling that underlies the entire work. Prior's illness seems to open him to a sense of apocalypse, and at the end of part 1 an angel crashes through his bedroom ceiling. In the second part, *Perestroika*, Prior journeys to heaven to reject the role of prophet, to reject the angel's message of stasis, and to ask for more life. By the January 1990 epilogue, set at the Bethesda angel's fountain in Central Park, where no water flows in winter, he has been living with AIDS for five years. Prior and his friends tell the story of the original fountain of Bethesda: when the Millennium comes—"not the year two thousand, but the capital M Millennium"—the waters that heal all pain will flow again.

Angels in America is a work of such size and scope and is so filled with poetry and felt thought that it brings to mind *Faust* and *Peer Gynt*. It is one of the most ambitious, exciting, and talented plays ever written in America. In it one encounters an enormously gifted writer coming into his full power.

—M. Elizabeth Osborn

L

LAFFAN, Kevin (Barry)

Nationality: British. **Born:** Reading, Berkshire, 24 May 1922. **Family:** Married Jeanne Lilian Thompson in 1952; three sons. **Career:** Repertory actor and director until 1950; director of productions, Pendragon Company, 1950-52, and Everyman Theatre Company, 1953-58, both Reading. **Awards:** ATV Television award, 1959; Irish Life award, 1969; National Union of Students award, 1969; *Sunday Times* award, 1970. **Agent:** ACTAC (Theatrical and Cinematic) Ltd., 16 Cadogan Lane, London S.W.1, England.

Publications

Plays

Ginger Bred (as Kevin Barry) (produced Reading, 1951).
The Strip-Tease Murder (as Kevin Barry), with Neville Brian (produced Reading, 1955).
Winner Takes All (as Kevin Barry) (produced Reading, 1956).
First Innocent (as Kevin Barry) (produced Reading, 1957).
Angie and Ernie, with Peter Jones (produced Guildford, Surrey, 1966).
Zoo Zoo Widdershins Zoo (produced Leicester, 1969). London, Faber, 1969.
It's a Two-Foot-Six-Inches-above-the-Ground World (produced Bristol, 1969; London, 1970). London, Faber, 1970.
The Superannuated Man (produced Watford, Hertfordshire, 1971).
There Are Humans at the Bottom of My Garden (produced London, 1972).
Adam and Eve and Pinch Me (produced London, 1974).
Never So Good (produced London, 1976).
The Wandering Jew (produced London, 1978).
The Dream of Trevor Staines (produced Chichester, 1983).
Adam Redundant (also director: produced London, 1989).

Screenplays: *It's a Two-Foot-Six-Inches-above-the-Ground World* (*The Love Ban*), 1973; *The Best Pair of Legs in the Business*, 1973.

Radio Play: *Portrait of an Old Man*, 1961.

Television Plays: *Lucky for Some*, 1969; *The Best Pair of Legs in the Business*, 1969; *You Can Only Buy Once*, 1969; *Castlehaven* series, 1970; *Kate* series, 1970; *A Little Learning*, 1970; *The Designer*, 1971; *Decision to Burn*, 1971; *Fly on the Wall* (trilogy), 1971; *The General*, 1971; *Emmerdale Farm*, 1972, 1977; *Justice* series, 1973; *The Reformer*, 1973; *Getting Up*, 1973; *Beryl's Lot* series, with Bill McIlwraith, 1973, 1977; *After the Wedding Was Over*, 1975; *It's a Wise Child*, 1975; for Bud Flanagan programme.

Novel

Amos Goes to War with M. Mitchell. Molesey, Surrey, Venus Publications, 1987.

* * *

Anybody leaving the theater after the first performance of Kevin Laffan's *Zoo Zoo Widdershins Zoo* would probably have been amazed to discover that the writer was a man in his 40s. Laffan's study of a group of young people—the eldest are in their early 20s—sharing a house and everything in it while refusing to work and turning to petty crime—shoplifting, robbing telephone booths, and cheating gas meters—when money is scarce seems to have come exactly out of the way of life it re-creates.

Laffan, however, was born in 1922, and *Zoo Zoo Widdershins Zoo* was his first real success. It won an award from the National Union of Students, which wanted a play for production in universities. If the occasion of the play suggested its theme, only Laffan's complete understanding of his characters, their idioms, and their attitudes and rejection of social responsibility can account for the play's authenticity and for its cool, morally neutral tone. It captures and makes comprehensible a gaiety that seems to grow out of the apparently depressing lifestyle these people have adopted. It is a clever play entirely about a minute community, and there is a feeling that the audience, as well as the squatters, is betrayed when the couple whose house has become a home for the group maneuver the others out and suddenly revert to conventional bourgeois habits.

Zoo Zoo Widdershins Zoo, which is almost plotless, is carefully designed to seem as aimless as the way of life it observes, and its alternations of intensity and relaxation are all conveyed in the limited, inexplicit dialogue that exploits its young people's idiom.

This was by no means Laffan's first play. He began his career in the theater as an actor. With others he helped to found the Everyman Theatre Company in Reading, and in 1959 he won an award from ATV for the television play *Cut in Ebony,* which was never produced because it deals with problems of race and color in terms of comedy. Abandoning acting and direction, Laffan earned the time to write plays by undertaking any other writing that would pay, including a not very successful series of television programs for the comedian Bud Flanagan. His television plays—*Lucky for Some*, *You Can Only Buy Once*, and *The Best Pair of Legs in the Business*—established him as a playwright in this medium, however, and *Castlehaven*, a television serial that did for a Yorkshire community what *Coronation Street* did for Lancashire, became a fixed part of commercial television schedules outside London.

Laffan's stage play *Angie and Ernie* was produced outside London. *The Superannuated Man* won an Irish Life award in 1969 but was produced only in 1971. But *Zoo Zoo Widdershins Zoo*, after its university production, was given a successful commercial production in London and impressed the critics. The result was that *It's a Two-Foot-Six-Inches-above-the-Ground World,* first seen at the Theatre Royal in Bristol, was able to travel to London and make a distinct impression there. Using a highly individual tone of tough, angry, affectionate hilarity, the play considers the effects on a young Catholic husband and wife of their church's refusal to permit any means of birth control. Catholics complained that Laffan's play misrepresents the church's attitude, but in its own terms, as a work for the theater, it is entirely successful.

The marriage of a young Liverpool Catholic is falling into ruins. His wife, a Protestant girl who was converted to Catholicism only in order to marry him, has provided him with three sons; another child would probably kill her, while sexual abstinence, which suits the wife even less than it suits the husband, is destroying the marriage. The voice of the church is transmitted by a young priest who expresses the Catholic prohibition at its most extreme and unyielding. A totally permissive view is offered by an outsider, a van driver making a delivery at the middle son's Catholic primary school. The father's prudery had prevented him from teaching his children anything about their physical functions, so that the van driver's use of the school lavatory, arousing the child's interest in an adult masculine body, costs the unfortunate driver—an energetic and undeviating lecher—his job.

These people argue their cases with great energy, and the play dresses the situation in continual high spirits. When all else fails, the wife's surreptitiously acquired and so far unused collection of contraceptive pills comes in useful; they can, for example, be mistaken for aspirins. It would not be fair to accuse Laffan of pulling his punches in the interests of good taste or of scrupulous intellectual fairness in his presentation of opposed points of view. He is, however, far more deeply involved through his emotions than through any desire to solve intellectual arguments, and under the hard-edged hilarity of its presentation there is a touching awareness of the painful situation of two simple, good, likable people trapped by the husband's earnest conviction.

Laffan's progress has been slow. *There Are Humans at the Bottom of My Garden* did not rival the success of its predecessor, and his later work for television, notably the skillfully written *Emmerdale Farm* and the more predictable *Justice* series, won a loyal television following without suggesting any of the tougher moral and social implications of his work for the theater. A handful of television plays and two unusual comedies, differing so widely in tone and aim as *Zoo Zoo Widdershins Zoo* and *It's a Two-Foot-Six-Inches-above-the-Ground World*, suggest that his other plays deserve careful study by some enterprising theater manager.

—Henry Raynor

LAN, David

Nationality: South African and British. **Born:** Cape Town, 1 June 1952. **Education:** University of Cape Town, 1970-72, B.A. in English 1972; London School of Economics, 1973-76, B.Sc. in social anthropology 1976, Ph.D. 1983; research associate, University of Zimbabwe, Harare, 1980-82. **Career:** Moved to England, 1972; lived in Zimbabwe, 1980-82. Writer-in-residence, Royal Court Theatre, 1996-97. **Awards:** John Whiting award, 1977; George Orwell Memorial award, 1983. **Agent:** Judy Daish Associates, 2 St. Charles Place, London W1O 6E9, England.

PUBLICATIONS

Plays

Painting a Wall (produced London, 1974; New York, 1980). London, Pluto Press, 1979.
Bird Child (produced London, 1974).
Homage to Been Soup (produced London, 1975).
Paradise (produced London, 1975).
The Winter Dancers (produced London, 1977; Los Angeles, 1978; New York, 1979). Included in *Desire and Other Plays*, 1990.
Not in Norwich (produced London, 1977).
Red Earth (produced London, 1978).
Sergeant Ola and His Followers (produced London, 1979; New York, 1986). London, Methuen, 1980; revised version in *Desire and Other Plays*, 1990.
Flight (produced Stratford-on-Avon, 1986; London, 1987; New York, 1992). London, Methuen, 1987.
A Mouthful of Birds, with Caryl Churchill (produced Birmingham and London, 1986). London, Methuen, 1986.
Ghetto, adaptation of the play by Joshua Sobol (produced London and New York, 1989). London, Hern, 1989.
Desire (produced London, 1990). Included in *Desire and Other Plays*, 1990.
Desire and Other Plays (includes *The Winter Dancers*, *Sergeant Ola and His Followers*). London, Faber, 1990.
Hippolytos, adaptation of the play by Euripides (produced London, 1991). London, Almeida Theatre Scripts, 1991.
Ion, adaptation of the play by Euripides (produced London, 1993). London, Methuen, 1994.
The She Wolf, adaptation of the play by Giovanni Verga (produced Glasgow, 1995).
The Ends of the Earth (produced London, 1996). London, Faber, 1996.
Uncle Vanya, adaptation of the play by Anton Chekov (produced London, 1998). London, Methuen, 1998.
Collected Plays, Volume 1 (includes *Painting a Wall*; *Red Earth*; *Flight, Desire*; *The Ends of the Earth*). London, Methuen, 1998.

Radio Play: *Charley Tango,* 1995.

Television Plays: *The Sunday Judge*, 1985; *The Crossing*, 1988; *Streets of Yesterday*, 1989; *Welcome Home Comrades*, 1989; *Dark City*, 1990.

Other

Guns and Rain: Guerrillas and Spirit Mediums in Zimbabwe. London, Currey, and Berkeley, University of California Press, 1985.

*

Theatrical Activities:
Director: **Plays—***A New Way to Pay Old Debts* by Massinger, Cape Town, 1971; *The Sport of My Mad Mother* by Ann Jellicoe, Cape Town, 1972; *Pericles to Shakespeare,* London, 1997. **Television–***Artist Unknown,* 1997; *Royal Court Diaries,* 1997.

* * *

David Lan is South African, and so he begins with a subject. His one-act *Painting a Wall* and his full-length play *Bird Child* both deal with aspects of apartheid. The first is, like a short story, slight and impressionistic. Two colored men and an Indian, helped by a colored boy, paint a wall. The Indian has lost his child and makes an unsuccessful attempt at suicide by drinking paint. The boy runs away. The men paint pictures on the wall but must paint over them. They talk and paint. The wall is finished. They leave.

In *Bird Child* the characters are white, mostly students in collision with the police. In protesting against the denial of freedom to her mother's maid, the heroine discovers the nature of freedom for herself. The other protagonists are locked by the system into predetermined attitudes. This is Lan's most immediately accessible play, owing particularly to his handling of Krou, the colonel of police, an intelligent, logical, and resourceful man and by no means a target for the scoring of liberal easy points.

Lan's next play, the one-act *Homage to Been Soup,* is only 12 pages long, no more than a technical exercise. *Paradise,* which followed, is more ambitious and interesting. Lan appears to have been inspired by Goya's *Horrors of War,* for he set the play in northern Spain in 1808, the year of Bonaparte's invasion. His characters—deserters from the French army and Spanish peasants and their landlord with his wife and schoolteacher daughter—have no particularity of time and place, and the play might more suitably have been set in a nonparticular Whiting-Land, into which his two most successful images, a simpleton who teaches the others his private, unintelligible nonlanguage and the birds that move their nests from trees about to be chopped down, might fit more successfully. Lan's concern with the nature of freedom is noble and his images striking, and his own search for a language and ideas more complex than those of his earlier plays is admirable.

A new direction came with *The Winter Dancers* and *Sergeant Ola and His Followers,* the first two of a trilogy of anthropological plays. (Lan had taken a doctorate in social anthropology at the London School of Economics.) In *The Winter Dancers* he used the work of Franz Boas on the Kwakiutl of Vancouver Island and for *Sergeant Ola* Peter Worsley's research into cargo cults in Papua New Guinea. Both plays use ritual and magic, and both are concerned with the statement, explicit in *The Winter Dancers,* "White men are eating up the world."

In *The Winter Dancers* the shaman, Carver, knows that he cures the sick by trickery and sleight of hand. Others believe in his power, but he knows that he has none. Yet the cures are genuine. When he finally comes to believe in his own power, he has already lost it, for the white men have destroyed the people's belief, and he is killed by the chief of the tribe in order to preserve the legend. In *Sergeant Ola* there is no longer any power in the people but only in the "wetmen" who have taken away the people's ancestors and offered them Adam and Eve instead. The wetmen have all the cargo (riches), the people are merely offered pay (which is not cargo) for doing the wetmen's work, and the wetmen manifestly do no work at all. The attempts of the people to make cargo come again by ignorant imitation, amounting to parody, of what they have observed of the wetmen's ways is both comic and piteous.

Lan's next play, *Flight,* is more complex. The narrative is neither strong nor straightforward, with the action moving between 1930, when a Jewish family flees from persecution in Lithuania, to 1980, when the next generation is leaving Zimbabwe. The title and a prologue to the play suggest that its theme is the perpetual uprooting, settlement elsewhere, and subsequent uprooting of Jews under persecution, but my own view is that the title may be ironic and that the real flight may be from political reality. In this view the centuries of persecution that have made the Jews politically aware and active have also contributed to the development of a family loyalty that occludes political vision and vitiates action. Because of its complexity the play demands to be seen more than once.

In 1980 Lan went to live in Zimbabwe and work with the Shona. From this time comes the third play, *Desire,* of the anthropological trilogy. The play is set in the Zambezi Valley. The war is over and freedom won. The spirit of a dead girl, a guerrilla shot during the war by soldiers, possesses her friend, Rosemary, who becomes ill every time she tries to live with her husband. The possession is ended—ritually, with ancestors participating, as one would expect from Lan—when it is discovered that the dead girl's own father, Rosemary's father, and Rosemary's husband were all involved in causing the girl's death. *Desire,* like the other two plays of the trilogy, is lively and energetic. Lan has a talent for expressing in language and action the behavior and beliefs of people whom the West would call primitive. He has said that he does not want his plays to be "lectures with feet," but to some extent they have become so. They are illustrative, and the illustrations of primitive behavior are formed into parables that are themselves illustrations.

About the time *Desire* was produced, Lan wrote two other works. The first, done with Jeremy Sams, is *Ghetto,* a play with dancing and music by the Israeli playwright Joshua Sobol about the last two years of the ghetto at Vilna before the last occupants were murdered by the Germans. The second is a version of the *Hippolytos* of Euripides. *Ghetto,* a play about a society in destruction, is full of passion and bitter laughter and uses ritual and music, as Lan's own work does. It is admirably suited to his methods. This cannot be said, however, of *Hippolytos.*

—John Bowen

LAUNKO, Okinba. ***See* OSOFISAN, Femi.**

LAURENTS, Arthur

Nationality: American. **Born:** Brooklyn, New York, 14 July 1917. **Education:** Cornell University, Ithaca, New York, B.A. 1937. **Military Service:** Served in the United States Army, 1940-45: sergeant; radio playwright, 1943-45 (Citation, Secretary of War, and *Variety* radio award, 1945). **Career:** Stage director. Director, Dramatists Play Service, New York, 1961-66. Council member, Dramatists Guild, 1955—. **Awards:** American Academy award, 1946; Sidney Howard Memorial award, 1946; Tony award, for play, 1967, for directing, 1984; Vernon Rice award, 1974; Golden Globe award, 1977; Screenwriters Guild award, 1978; elected to the Theatre Hall of Fame, 1983; Sydney Drama Critics award, for directing, 1985. **Agent:** Peter Franklin, c/o William Morris Agency, 1325 Avenue of the Americas, New York, New York 10019, U.S.A. **Address:** P.O. Box 582, Quogue, New York 11959, U.S.A.

PUBLICATIONS

Plays

Now Playing Tomorrow (broadcast 1939). Published in *Short Plays for Stage and Radio,* edited by Carless Jones, Albuquerque, University of New Mexico Press, 1939.

Western Electric Communicade (broadcast 1944). Published in *The Best One-Act Plays of 1944*, edited by Margaret Mayorga, New York, Dodd Mead, 1944.
The Last Day of the War (broadcast 1945). Published in *Radio Drama in Action*, edited by Erik Barnouw, New York, Farrar and Rinehart, 1945.
The Face (broadcast 1945). Published in *The Best One-Act Plays of 1945*, edited by Margaret Mayorga, New York, Dodd Mead, 1945.
Home of the Brave (produced New York, 1945; London, 1948; as *The Way Back*, produced London, 1949). New York, Random House, 1946.
Heartsong (produced New Haven, Connecticut, 1947).
The Bird Cage (produced New York, 1950). New York, Dramatists Play Service, 1950.
The Time of the Cuckoo (produced New York, 1952). New York, Random House, 1953.
A Clearing in the Woods (produced New York, 1957). New York, Random House, 1957; revised version, New York, Dramatists Play Service, 1960.
West Side Story, music by Leonard Bernstein, lyrics by Stephen Sondheim (produced New York, 1957; London, 1958). New York, Random House, 1958; London, Heinemann, 1959.
Gypsy, music by Jule Styne, lyrics by Stephen Sondheim, adaptation of a book by Gypsy Rose Lee (produced New York, 1959; also director: produced London, 1973). New York, Random House, 1960.
Invitation to a March (also director: produced New York, 1960; Hereford, 1965). New York, Random House, 1961.
Anyone Can Whistle, music by Stephen Sondheim (also director: produced New York, 1964; Cheltenham, Gloucestershire, 1986). New York, Random House, 1965.
Do I Hear a Waltz?, music by Richard Rodgers, lyrics by Stephen Sondheim (produced New York, 1965). New York, Random House, 1966.
Hallelujah, Baby!, music by Jule Styne, lyrics by Betty Comden and Adolph Green (produced New York, 1967). New York, Random House, 1967.
The Enclave (also director: produced Washington, D.C., and New York, 1973). New York, Dramatists Play Service, 1974.
Scream (also director: produced Houston, 1978).
The Madwoman of Central Park West, with Phyllis Newman, music by Peter Allen and others, adaptation of the play *My Mother Was a Fortune Teller* by Newman (also director: produced Buffalo and New York, 1979).
A Loss of Memory (produced Southampton, New York, 1981). Published in *The Best Short Plays* 1983, edited by Ramon Delgado, Radnor, Pennsylvania, Chilton, 1983.
Nick and Nora, music by Charles Strowse, lyrics by Richard Maltby, Jr. (also director: produced New York, 1991).
Jolson Sings Again (produced Seattle, Washington, 1993).
The Radical Mystique (produced New York, 1995). New York, Samuel French, 1996.
My Good Name (produced Sag Harbor, 1997).

Screenplays: *The Snake Pit*, with Frank Partos and Millen Brand, 1948; *Rope*, with Hume Cronyn, 1948; *Anna Lucasta*, with Philip Yordan, 1949; *Caught*, 1949; *Anastasia*, 1956; *Bonjour Tristesse*, 1958; *The Way We Were*, 1973; *The Turning Point*, 1977.

Radio Plays: *Now Playing Tomorrow*, 1939; *Hollywood Playhouse*, *Dr. Christian*, *The Thin Man*, *Manhattan at Midnight*, and other series, 1939-40; *The Last Day of the War*, *The Face*, *Western Electric Communicade*, and other plays for *The Man Behind the Gun*, *Army Service Force Presents* and *Assignment: Home* series, 1943-45; *This Is Your FBI* series, 1945.

Television: *The Light Fantastic*, 1967.

Novels

The Way We Were. New York, Harper, 1972; London, W.H. Allen, 1973.
The Turning Point. New York, New American Library, 1977; London, Corgi, 1978.

*

Manuscript Collection: Brandeis University, Waltham, Massachusetts.

Theatrical Activities:
Director: **Plays**—*Invitation to a March*, New York, 1960; *I Can Get It for You Wholesale* by Jerome Weidman, New York, 1962; *Anyone Can Whistle*, New York, 1964; *The Enclave*, Washington, D.C., and New York, 1973; *Gypsy*, London, 1973, New York, 1974 and 1989; *My Mother Was a Fortune Teller* by Phyllis Newman, New York, 1978; *Scream*, Houston, 1978; *The Madwoman of Central Park West*, Buffalo and New York, 1979; *So What Are We Gonna Do Now?* by Juliet Garson, New York, 1982; *La Cage aux Folles* by Jean Poiret, adapted by Harvey Fierstein, Boston and New York, 1983, Sydney, 1985, London, 1986; *Birds of Paradise* by Winnie Holtzman and David Evans, New York, 1987; *Nick and Nora*, New York, 1991; *Jolson Sings Again*, 1993; *The Radical Mystique*, 1995; *My Good Name*, 1997.

Arthur Laurents comments:

Too much of today's theatre brings "The Emperor's New Clothes" to my mind. Style is considered content; formlessness is considered new technique; character is reduced to symbol and/or type; and story has been banished—not necessarily a loss—in favor of incident which is usually too thin and too undramatic to fuse an entire play. Moreover, the dominant tone is modish pessimism or militancy, both of which can be as sentimentally romantic as effulgent optimism.

All a matter of taste, of course. My own is for a heightened theatricality and for new forms—but I still believe that form is determined by content and requires control. I want characters in a play, I want to be emotionally involved; I want social content; I want language and I want a *level* of accessibility. (I suspect obscurantism of being the refuge of the vague, the uncommitted, and the chic.) Although I do not demand it, I prefer optimism—even if only implied. For I think man, naturally evil or not, is optimistic. Even the bleakest has hope: why else does he bother to write?

For the United States, for New York, I want subsidized theatres with permanent companies playing repertory. I think that is the most important need of the American playwright and would be of the greatest aid in his development.

* * *

Arthur Laurents was one of the most promising dramatists appearing immediately after World War II. His first success in New

York, *Home of the Brave*, showed both his skill as a dramatist and his insight into human nature as he depicted the ethnic and individual problems of a Jewish soldier in a battle situation. During the following 15 years Laurents wrote four plays—*The Bird Cage*, *The Time of the Cuckoo*, *A Clearing in the Woods*, and *Invitation to a March*—that continued to demonstrate his theatrical powers and his inclination to write serious drama. Unfortunately, in neither area—theatricality or intellectual penetration—was he able to sustain or develop a first-rate drama for the American commercial theater. Perhaps he recognized either a personal or public impasse. At any rate, toward the end of this period Laurents had begun to devote more of his talents to musical comedy and with considerable success. His creation of the books for *West Side Story* and *Gypsy* gave these works the careful integration and character development that distinguish them among modern musicals. During the next decade he collaborated on musicals but without significant success and seemed to abandon his career in legitimate drama, a disappointment for critics who had felt his earlier promise.

Laurents's seriousness as a dramatist was most evident in the themes that he chose to develop. The fearful uncertainty of the lonely person trying to find a meaningful identity in a world full of frustrations and strangers is a dominant theme in his works. His major characters were generally trying to discover the essentials of love, which Laurents seemed to believe would lead to a revelation of self. Although the psychological penetration into his major characters suggests a generally acute perception of humanity, his dramatized solutions tend more consistently toward theatricality than a probing concern for mankind. In other words, the problems he considers—a person's fears, frustrations, and feelings of alienation—place Laurents among these seriously concerned with modernity, but his insistence that sex is fundamental to all such problems limits both his psychology and his insight.

In three of the four plays since his initial success his major characters have been women whose psychological problems have driven them toward disaster. (The other play, *The Bird Cage*, tells the story of Wally, a vicious egomaniac and owner of a nightclub whose abuse of everyone stems from his own sexual frustrations.) In *The Time of the Cuckoo* Leona Samish is a warm but lonely woman whose pathos rests in her inability to know and have faith in herself or to accept the love of others. Sorry for herself and bitter toward life and thus unable to get what she most desires, she is that dangerous person who destroys. Virginia, the heroine of *A Clearing in the Woods*, sees herself as a destroyer although she wants desperately to be loved. Discovering that someone does truly care, she can work toward a position in which she accepts both herself and the world around her. *Invitation to a March* tells of a girl who at first wants to "march" along with the ordinary world and its seemingly inherent problems of love, sex, and divorce. But she changes, rejects the march, and finds love with one who said, "Come dance with me." Uncharacteristically for a Laurents work, the climax of this play is a strongly made decision, and perhaps both the author and his characters abandon the ordinary world as idealism seems a possible alternative to drudgery. Unfortunately, no further step has been dramatized.

Although Laurents has not been an innovator in technical theater, he has courageously employed distinctive techniques in his plays. *The Bird Cage* employs a rather obvious use of theatrical symbols, but the "clearing in the woods" with its "magic circle" is well integrated into the structure of the play, in which three characters—Ginna, Nora, and Jigee—act out particular ages in the heroine's life and tease her for her inability to accept what they contribute to her present problems. The frequent front delivery to the audience in an attempt to indicate unspoken and personal feelings was unsuccessful even in a semifantasy such as *Invitation to a March*. Music becomes a dominant part of several of his plays, as might be expected of a dramatist interested in musical comedy. In all of Laurents's theater works his care in the creation of his characters is a major asset. Whether in musical comedy or straight drama, through an integration of theme and theatrical technique Laurents has tried to express his views on psychological and social life in the modern world.

—Walter J. Meserve

LAVERY, Bryony

Nationality: British. **Born:** Wakefield, Yorkshire, 21 December 1947. **Education:** University of London, 1966-69, B.A. (honours) in English 1969. **Career:** Artistic director, Les Oeufs Malades, 1976-78, Extraordinary Productions, 1979-80, and Female Trouble, 1981-83, all London. Resident dramatist, Unicorn Theatre for Young People, London, 1986-88; artistic director, Gay Sweatshop, London, 1989-91. **Agent:** St. John Dunlop, Peters, Fraser, and Dunlop, 503/4 Chelsea Harbour, London SW10 0XF, England. **Address:** 17 Maitland Road, London E15 4EL, England.

Publications

Plays

Of All Living (produced London, 1967).
Days at Court (produced London, 1968).
Warbeck (produced London, 1969).
I Was Too Young at the Time to Understand Why My Mother Was Crying (also director: produced London, 1976).
Sharing (also director: produced London, 1976).
Germany Calling, with Peter Leabourne (produced London, 1976).
Grandmother's Footsteps (also director: produced London, 1977).
Snakes (produced London, 1977).
The Catering Service (also director: produced London, 1977).
Floorshow, with others (produced London, 1978).
Helen and Her Friends (also director: produced London, 1978).
Bag (also director, produced London, 1979).
Time Gentlemen Please (cabaret; produced London, 1979).
The Wild Bunch (for children; produced London, 1979). Published in *Responses*, edited by Don Shiach, London, Thomas Nelson, 1990.
Sugar and Spice (for children; produced Ipswich, Suffolk, 1979).
Unemployment: An Occupational Hazard? (for children; also director: produced London, 1979).
Gentlemen Prefer Blondes, adaptation of the novel by Anita Loos (produced London, 1980).
The Joker (for children; also director: produced London, 1980).
The Family Album (also director: produced London, 1980).
Pamela Stephenson One Woman Show (cabaret; produced London, 1981).
Missing (also director: produced Colchester, Essex, and London, 1981).

Zulu, with Patrick Barlow (produced London, 1981).
Female Trouble (cabaret; produced London, 1981).
The Black Hole of Calcutta, with Patrick Barlow (produced London, 1982).
Götterdämmerung; or, Twilight of the Gods, with Patrick Barlow and Susan Todd (produced London, 1982).
For Maggie, Betty and Ida, music by Paul Sand (produced London, 1982).
More Female Trouble (cabaret), music by Caroline Noh (produced London, 1982).
Uniform and Uniformed, and Numerical Man (broadcast 1983). Published in *Masks and Faces*, edited by Dan Garrett, London, Macmillan, 1984.
Hot Time (produced London, 1984).
Calamity (produced London, 1984).
Origin of the Species (produced Birmingham, 1984; London, 1985). Published in *Plays by Women: Six*, edited by Mary Remnant, London, Methuen, 1987.
The Wandsworth Warmers (cabaret; also director: produced London, 1984).
The Zulu Hut Club (for children; produced London, 1984).
The Wandsworth Warmers Christmas Carol Concert (cabaret; also director: produced London, 1985).
Over and Out (also director: produced on tour, 1985).
Witchcraze (produced London, 1985). Published in *Herstory*, edited by Gabrial Griffin and Elaine Aston, Sheffield, Sheffield Academic Press, 1991.
Getting Through (additional lyrics only), by Nona Shepphard, music by Helen Glavin (produced on tour, 1985; London, 1987).
The Wandsworth Warmers in Unbridled Passions (cabaret; also director: produced London, 1986).
Sore Points (for children; produced London, 1986).
Mummy, with Sally Owen and L. Ortolja (produced London, 1987).
Madagascar (for children; also director: produced London, 1987).
The Headless Body, music by Stephanie Nunn (produced London, 1987).
The Dragon Wakes (for children; produced London, 1988).
Puppet States (produced London, 1988).
The Drury Lane Ghost, with Nona Shepphard (produced London, 1989).
Two Marias (produced London, 1989). Included in *Her Aching Heart, Two Marias, Wicked*, 1991.
Wicked (produced London, 1990). Included in *Her Aching Heart, Two Marias, Wicked*, 1991.
Her Aching Heart (produced London, 1990). Included in *Her Aching Heart, Two Marias, Wicked*, 1991.
Kitchen Matters (produced London, 1990).
Her Aching Heart, Two Marias, Wicked. London, Methuen, 1991.
Flight (produced London, 1991).
Peter Pan, with Nona Shepphard (produced London, 1991).
The Sleeping Beauty, with Nona Shepphard (produced London, 1992).
Ophelia (produced Milton Keynes, 1996). Selected scenes published in *Mythic Women/Real Woman*, edited by Lizbeth Goodman, London, Faber and Faber, 1998.
Goliath (produced 1997).
More Light. N.p., n.d.
Bryon Lavery: Plays One. London, Methuen, 1998.

Radio Plays: *Fire the Life-Giver*, 1979; *Changes at Work* series, 1980; *Let's Get Dressed*, 1982; *Uniform and Uniformed*, 1983; *Numerical Man*, 1983; *Magical Beasts*, 1987; *Cliffhanger* series, 1990; *Laying Ghosts*, 1992; *No Joan of Arc*, 1997.

Television Plays: *Revolting Women* series, with others, 1981; *Rita of the Rovers*, 1989; *The Cab Wars*, 1989.

Video: *The Lift*, 1988; *Twelve Dancing Princesses*, 1989.

*

Critical Study: "But Will Men Like It; or, Living as a Feminist Writer Without Committing Murder" by Lavery, in *Women and Theatre* edited by Susan Todd, London, Faber, 1984.

Theatrical Activities:
Director: **Plays**—Most of her own plays; *More Female Trouble* (revival), London, 1983; *Homelands: Under Exposure* by Lisa Evans, and *The Mrs. Docherties* by Nona Shepphard (co-director, with Shepphard), London, 1985; *Hotel Destiny* by Tasha Fairbanks, London, 1987.

* * *

Bryony Lavery's plays tend to be both comic and controversial: they are funny and engaging at a popular level, although her subject matter is not mainstream. Lavery has worked in British alternative theater for many years. She was one of the early contributors to the work of both Gay Sweatshop and Monstrous Regiment. In the 1970s Lavery collaborated with Caryl Churchill and Michelene Wandor on *Floorshow*, the Monstrous Regiment's cabaret. She also worked on the Regiment's cabaret *Gentlemen Prefer Blondes* and on comic shows such as *Female Trouble* and *More Female Trouble*. She worked with the Women's Theatre Group and in children's theater and the Theatre in Education program. In addition, she taught playwriting at Birmingham University.

By drawing on this wide range of experience, Lavery developed a voice quite unique in British theater and a style that reaches beyond the typical middle-class forms of farce and drawing-room humor. Her style is intelligent and comic without being too sarcastic or snide, and her writing reveals a certain jolly approach to important issues. Lavery achieves a balance between parody and celebration that is politically effective, because it makes her plays engaging and enjoyable to read and watch.

Origin of the Species is one of Lavery's best-known plays and illustrates her skill for combining humor with serious social commentary. *Origin of the Species* was first produced by Monstrous Regiment in 1984 with Gillian Hanna as Molly, an anthropologist who unearths a living creature-woman (played by Mary McCusker). Directed by Nona Shepphard, this play was ambitious in its scope (all of history) but remarkably unambitious in its use of resources: two actors, minimal sets and props, and a small performance space. The power of the play resides in its language and its use of humor.

Her Aching Heart is also a sophisticated piece of writing that combines wit and parodies of courtly and poetic language with the representation of social issues. *Her Aching Heart* was first produced in 1990 at the Oval House in London, directed by Claire Grove and performed by Nicola Kathrens and Sarah Kevney. The play is a "lesbian historical romance" that casts two modern-day women as the readers of bodice-ripping fiction and concurrently as the heroines and heroes of that fiction. Modern-day characters

Molly and Harriet enter into a budding romance in "real life" that parallels the stories in the novel of the servant girl Molly and the fiery aristocrat Lady Harriet of Helstone Hall. Molly and Harriet read the novel and engage in the fictional romance, while they begin to know each other through telephone conversations. The audience becomes acquainted with the story and the course of their romance through the narratives and songs of these two central characters. Their songs of love are enriched by references to stereotypical images of romance lifted from fiction and fairy tales. That the two lovers are both women is important, but it is not the key to the play's politics. Rather, the interweaving of the modern and the "historical," the real and the fictional, and the serious and the silly results in a delightful and complicated play.

Her Aching Heart toured twice with the Women's Theatre Group in 1990 and 1991, both times with great success. That the play is so accessible and so amusing—and so beautifully constructed—makes the choice of a lesbian story line all the more significant. Similarly, the play identifies gender, class, and power as issues intrinsic to an informed examination of the historical romance as a popular form and to the expectations involved in reading such fiction. Yet all these important considerations are represented as parts of the whole rather than as "politically correct" issues to be evaluated in and of themselves.

Some of Lavery's work is much larger in scale, and some is immediately linked to contemporary social issues. In 1991, for instance, Lavery wrote *Kitchen Matters,* a play for Gay Sweatshop (a feminist theater company that has promoted women's work since its founding in 1974). Sweatshop's economic struggle for survival became the subject of the play, which Lavery wrote as an "epic comedy." In a humorously self-referential scene, *Kitchen Matters* opens with a narrator (a woman at a typewriter) discussing her decision to write a (the) play:

> There were some kids in a touring theatre company.
> They were Gay they were Poor they were Minority
> but they wanted a show.
> I had to help them out.
> I'm a writer with a Large Soul and Big Bills.
> My brain met up with my heart and they took a walk
> down into my guts to see what was there.
> The place was full of undigested matter.
> I chewed it over.
> A heavenly light shone on my blank A4 paper.
> I lit my two hundred and thirty-fourth cigarette.
> I started to write.

Lavery's enjoyment of and facility with language is evident even in this short extract. So is her dedication to the theater. The narrator of this scene, like Lavery, wrote for the benefit of the theater company. The play was quite successful and attracted a diverse audience. Although it was a political play with a point to make, the comedy made the point and the self-conscious nature of the humor made it all the more powerful.

Lavery's 1996–97 play for the Sphinx Theatre, *Goliath,* was widely hailed as a tour de force of writing and performance. This one-woman show, performed by Nicola McAuliffe and directed by Annie Castledine, was based on the book by Bea Campbell and breathed life into the documentary story of class and race conflict in working-class England. The play makes serious political points, but it conveys its messages through emotion and through the vision (and the visionary quality of writing) of a set of characters trapped in time and place. Lavery allows the characters the freedom to strive for means of change, yet she does not offer any easy solutions.

—Lizbeth Goodman

LAWLER, Ray(mond Evenor)

Nationality: Australian. **Born:** Footscray, Melbourne, Victoria, in 1921. **Education:** Left school at age 13. **Family:** Married Jacklyn Kelleher; three children. **Career:** Worked in a foundry, 1934-45; actor, Sid Turnbull's Melbourne Repertory Company, 1946-49; actor and producer, National Theatre Company, Melbourne, 1950-54; director, Union Theatre Repertory Company, Melbourne University, 1954-55; lived in Denmark, England, and mainly in Ireland, early 1960s-75; director and literary adviser, Melbourne Theatre Company, 1976-86. **Awards:** Playwrights Advisory Board prize, 1955; London *Evening Standard* award, 1958. O.B.E. (Officer, Order of the British Empire), 1981. **Agent:** Curtis Brown, 27 Union Street, Paddington, New South Wales 2021, Australia.

Publications

Plays

Cradle of Thunder (produced Melbourne, 1949).

Summer of the Seventeenth Doll (produced Melbourne, 1955; London, 1957; New York, 1958). London, Angus and Robertson, and New York, Random House, 1957.

The Piccadilly Bushman (produced Melbourne, 1959; Liverpool, 1965). London, Angus and Robertson, 1961.

The Unshaven Cheek (produced Edinburgh, 1963).

A Breach in the Wall (televised 1967; produced Canterbury, Kent, 1970).

The Man Who Shot the Albatross (produced Melbourne, 1972).

Kid Stakes (produced Melbourne, 1975). Included in *The Doll Trilogy*, 1978.

Other Times (produced Melbourne, 1976). Included in *The Doll Trilogy*, 1978.

The Doll Trilogy (includes *Kid Stakes, Other Times, Summer of the Seventeenth Doll*). Sydney, Currency Press, 1978.

Godsend (produced Melbourne, 1982).

Television Plays: *A Breach in the Wall*, 1967; *Sinister Street* serial, from the novel by Compton Mackenzie, 1968; *Cousin Bette* serial, from the novel by Balzac, 1971; *The Visitors* serial, from the novel by Mary McMinnies, 1972; *Two Women* serial, from a novel by Alberto Moravia, 1972; *Mrs. Palfrey at the Claremont*, from the novel by Elizabeth Taylor, 1973; *After the Party*, from the story by W. Somerset Maugham, 1974; *Seeking the Bubbles* (*The Love School* series), 1975; *True Patriots All*, 1975; *Husband to Mrs. Fitzherbert*, 1975.

*

Critical Studies: *A Text Response to Ray Lawler's Summer of the Seventeenth Doll,* Ballart, Wizard Books, 1994; "Is It a Boy or a Girl? Gendering the *Seventeenth Doll*" by Kerryn Goldsworthy, in *Southerly: A Review of Australian Literature,* Autumn 1995, pp. 89-105.

Theatrical Activities:
Actor: **Play**—Barney Ibbot in *Summer of the Seventeenth Doll,* Melbourne, 1955, London, 1957.

* * *

Ray Lawler's reputation as one of Australia's most distinguished playwrights is still based largely on a single extremely successful play, *Summer of the Seventeenth Doll.* The play came at a crucial time not only for the narrow world of the Australian theater but also for Australian culture generally. The 1950s were a time of national self-consciousness when former ideas of "Australianness" were, to a certain extent, being reassessed. *Doll* took the traditional legend of the laconic, hard-bitten Australian bushman, which had been an important part of the national self-image since the 1890s, and almost literally dragged it kicking and screaming into the cities to face the realities of postwar urban Australia.

The play had a sudden popular impact when it first appeared. Its warm portrayal of distinctive bush and city character types was greeted with delighted recognition by middle-class audiences for whom the original legend had, in fact, been only an exotic dream. The two tough cane cutters, Roo and Barney, who come down from the Queensland cane fields each year to spend the "layoff" season whooping it up in Melbourne, represented a vanishing national type with whom the city audiences liked to identify.

Doll shows these two legendary characters failing to deal with the new urban Australia. The romantic dream of the layoffs—times of innocent, loving fun for the men and their barmaid girlfriends—is already beginning to fail as the play opens. Olive, Roo's woman, tries to sustain her vision of a nobler life than what the "soft city blokes" have to offer, and she clings to it even when it brings personal tragedy for her. But the world of the soft city blokes wins, practically if not emotionally. Perhaps for contemporary audiences the portrayal of Olive as a foolish woman who refuses to grow up, which is confirmed in the expanded *The Doll Trilogy,* has dated. There is some justice in her claim to have found a serious alternative to marriage, but after a series of reversals at the end we are left with a final ironic triumph of the legend as Roo and Barney stagger out to head back north, leaving Olive alone in her grief.

Doll's appeal, even for foreign audiences who know nothing of the bush legend, is based in the solid, old-fashioned virtues of well-made realism: detailed and consistent characterization, a wonderfully rich use of vernacular, and a complex and carefully plotted action. These were virtues that Lawler showed he was still a master of when he came, 20 years after the original appearance of *Doll*, to write the two additional plays making up the trilogy, *Kid Stakes* and *Other Times.*

The extraordinary success of *Doll* meant that Lawler's next plays, before the completion of the trilogy, were bound to be received with disappointment. *The Piccadilly Bushman* is a technically competent play that explores the self-image of an Australian expatriate who has achieved success as an actor in England and returns to confront what he now sees as his embarrassing "colonial" past. *The Man Who Shot the Albatross* is a historical play about a much treated subject in Australian drama: the colonial Governor Bligh, struggling to deal with mutinous local bigwigs, and haunted by the memory of the other more famous mutineers on the *Bounty.* The play presents its subject largely in terms of personal conflict between Bligh and the politically astute landowner, John Macarthur, and avoids any wider historical or political exploration. It is for this reason perhaps that it seemed rather old-fashioned in 1972. Neither of these two plays has had much impact in the Australian theater.

Lawler lived abroad during the great upsurge in Australian drama in the early 1970s, but he returned in the mid-1970s to produce two plays that revived his reputation—*Kid Stakes* and *Other Times.* These plays are set prior to *Doll.* They go back to the first and the ninth layoffs, introducing the appealing character of Nancy, whose memory so dominates *Doll,* and generally filling in the background to what had by the mid-1970s become a well-known and well-loved part of the national heritage. *Kid Stakes* is a play of great charm. Its delightful portrait of an innocent young Australian society before World War II showed Lawler at his full strength, lamenting the loss of a simpler world. *Other Times,* set in winter during the war, is written in a minor key, introducing a note of bitterness that anticipates the tragedy of *Doll.*

Ironically, the effect of the trilogy was to lessen the impact of the original play. The new plays take so much trouble to plant hints anticipating the action of *Doll* that the brilliant Ibsenesque exposition in the original becomes rather pointless and the story and characters move into a new world of sophisticated soap opera. Again, however, the warmth and richness with which these familiar characters are developed make this one of the most charming works in the new wave of Australian drama.

In 1982 Lawler produced his first major work since the trilogy, *Godsend.* The godsend is the discovery in a small rural church in Kent of the lost tomb of Saint Thomas à Becket. Each of the four central characters—a traditionalist Catholic bishop, the Anglican archbishop, an idealistic parson, and his agnostic wife—has a different interest in the holy remains, and through their conflict the play explores the nature of religious faith and the difficulties of sustaining it. The play is a stylistic departure from the well-made realism of *The Doll Trilogy,* especially in its complex use of direct audience address. It is the work of a mature dramatist with accomplished skills and has not yet had the impact it deserves.

Lawler's place in the development of Australian drama is still assured by *Doll.* If he has never repeated that success, it is perhaps partly because his dramatic interests have become less relevant to the issues that now involve Australian audiences, but he remains one of the most technically capable of all Australian dramatists and one who has contributed some of the best-loved characters in the culture.

—John McCallum

LAWRENCE, Jerome

Pseudonym: Jerome Schwartz. **Nationality:** American. **Born:** Cleveland, Ohio, 14 July 1915. **Education:** Ohio State University, Columbus, B.A. 1937; University of California, Los Angeles, 1939-40. **Career:** Director of summer stock, Connellsville, Pennsylvania, then Pittsfield, Massachusetts, summers 1934-37; reporter and telegraph editor, Wilmington *News-Journal,* Ohio, 1937; editor, New Lexington *Daily News,* Ohio, 1937-38; continuity editor, KMPC Radio, Beverly Hills, California, 1938, 1939;

senior staff writer, Columbia Broadcasting System, Hollywood and New York, 1939-41; scenario writer, Paramount Pictures, Hollywood, 1941. Expert consultant to the Secretary of War during World War II: co-founder of Armed Forces Radio Service, and radio correspondent in North Africa and Italy (wrote and directed the official Army-Navy programs for D-Day, VE Day and VJ Day). Partner, Lawrence and Lee, 1942—, and president, Lawrence and Lee Inc., New York and Los Angeles, 1955—. Founder and national president, Radio Writers Guild; co-founder and president, American Playwrights Theatre, 1970-85; co-founder and judge, Margo Jones award; founder and board member, Writers Guild of America; council member, Dramatists Guild and Authors League of America; member of the advisory board, Eugene O'Neill Foundation, American Conservatory Theatre, 1970-80, Board of Standards of the Living Theatre, Plumstead Playhouse, Stella Adler Theater, and Ohio State University School of Journalism. Professor, Banff School of Fine Arts, Alberta, Canada, 1950-53; member, U.S. State Department Cultural Exchange Panel, 1962-70. Master playwright, New York University, 1967, 1968; visiting professor of playwriting, Ohio State University, 1969; lecturer, Salzburg Seminar in American Studies, 1972; visiting professor, Baylor University, Waco, Texas, 1976; William Inge lecturer, Independence Community College, Kansas, 1983, 1986-91; professor of playwriting, University of Southern California, Los Angeles, 1984-92. Contributing editor, *Dramatics* magazine, Cincinnati. **Awards:** New York Press Club award, 1942; *Radio-TV Life* award, 1948, 1952; Peabody award, 1949, 1952; *Radio-TV Mirror* award, 1952, 1953; *Variety* award, 1954, 1955; Donaldson award, 1955; Outer Circle award, 1955; British Drama Critics award, 1960; Moss Hart Memorial award, 1967; Ohio State University Centennial award, 1970, and Alumni medal, 1985; American Theatre Association award, 1979; International Thespian Society Directors award, 1980; William Inge award, 1983; Valentine Davies award, 1984; Emmy award, 1988 (twice); Southeastern Theater Conference award, 1990; elected to Theater Hall of Fame and College of Fellows of the American Theatre, 1990; national theater conference honorary member, 1993. D.H.L.: Ohio State University, 1963. D.Litt.: Fairleigh Dickinson University, Rutherford, New Jersey, 1968; College of Wooster, Ohio, 1983. D.F.A.: Villanova University, Pennsylvania, 1969. **Agent:** Robert Freedman Dramatic Agency, 1501 Broadway, New York 10036; and, Mitch Douglas, International Creative Management, 40 West 57th Street, New York, New York 10019. **Address:** P.O. Box 2770, Malibu, California 90265, U.S.A.

PUBLICATIONS

Plays

Laugh, God!, in *Six Anti-Nazi One-Act Plays*. New York, Contemporary Play Publications, 1939.

Tomorrow, with Budd Schulberg, in *Free World Theatre*, edited by Arch Oboler and Stephen Longstreet. New York, Random House, 1944.

Inside a Kid's Head, with Robert E. Lee, in *Radio Drama in Action*, edited by Erik Barnouw. New York, Farrar and Rinehart, 1945.

Look, Ma, I'm Dancin', with Robert E. Lee, music by Hugh Martin, conceived by Jerome Robbins (produced New York, 1948).

The Crocodile Smile, with Robert E. Lee (as *The Laugh Maker*, produced Hollywood, 1952; revised version, as *Turn on the Night*, produced Philadelphia, 1961; revised version, as *The Crocodile Smile*, also director: produced Flatrock, North Carolina, 1970). New York, Dramatists Play Service, 1972.

Inherit the Wind, with Robert E. Lee (produced Dallas and New York, 1955; London, 1960). New York, Random House, 1955; London, Four Square, 1960.

Shangri-La, with Robert E. Lee and James Hilton, music by Harry Warren, adaptation of the novel *Lost Horizon* by Hilton (produced New York, 1956). New York, Morris Music, 1956.

Auntie Mame, with Robert E. Lee, adaptation of the work by Patrick Dennis (produced New York, 1956; London, 1958). New York, Vanguard Press, 1957; revised version, music by Jerry Herman, as *Mame* (produced New York, 1966; London, 1969), New York, Random House, 1967.

The Gang's All Here, with Robert E. Lee (produced New York, 1959). Cleveland, World, 1960.

Only in America, with Robert E. Lee, adaptation of the work by Harry Golden (produced New York, 1959). New York, French, 1960.

A Call on Kuprin, with Robert E. Lee, adaptation of the novel by Maurice Edelman (produced New York, 1961). New York, French, 1962.

Sparks Fly Upward, with Robert E. Lee (as *Diamond Orchid*, produced New York, 1965; revised version, as *Sparks Fly Upward*, produced Dallas, 1967). New York, Dramatists Play Service, 1969.

Live Spelled Backwards (produced Beverly Hills, California, 1966). New York, Dramatists Play Service, 1970.

Dear World, with Robert E. Lee, music by Jerry Herman, based on *The Madwoman of Chaillot* by Giraudoux (produced New York, 1969).

The Incomparable Max, with Robert E. Lee (also director: produced Abingdon, Virginia, 1969; New York, 1971). New York, Hill and Wang, 1972.

The Night Thoreau Spent in Jail, with Robert E. Lee (produced Columbus, Ohio, and 154 other theatres, 1970). New York, Hill and Wang, 1970.

Jabberwock: Improbabilities Lived and Imagined by James Thurber in the Fictional City of Columbus, Ohio, with Robert E. Lee (produced Columbus, Ohio, 1972). New York, French, 1974.

First Monday in October, with Robert E. Lee (also director: produced Cleveland, 1975; New York, 1978). New York, French, 1979.

Whisper in the Mind, with Norman Cousins and Robert E. Lee (produced Tempe, Arizona, 1990).

The Plays of Lawrence and Lee, edited by Alan Woods (includes: *Inherit the Wind, Auntie Mame, The Gang's All Here, Only in America, A Call on Kuprin, Diamond Orchid, The Night Thoreau Spent in Jail, First Monday in October*). Columbus, Ohio, Ohio State University Press, 1992.

The Angels Weep. Published in *Studies in American Drama: 1945 to the Present*. (Columbus, Ohio), 1992.

The Selected Plays of Jerome Lawrence and Robert E. Lee (includes *Inherit the Wind*; *Auntie Mame*; *The Gang's All Here*; *Only in America*; *A Call on Kuprin*; *Diamond Orchid*; *The Night Thoreau Spent in Jail*; *First Monday in October*). Columbus, Ohio State University Press, 1995.

Screenplays, with Robert E. Lee: *My Love Affair with the Human Race*, 1962; *The New Yorkers*, 1963; *Joyous Season*, 1964; The *Night Thoreau Spent in Jail*, 1972; *First Monday in October*, 1982.

Radio Plays: *Junior Theatre of the Air* series, 1938; *Under Western Skies* series, 1939; *Nightcap Yarns* series, 1939, 1940; *Stories from Life* series, 1939, 1940; *Man about Hollywood* series, 1940; *Hollywood Showcase* series, 1940, 1941; A *Date with Judy* series, 1941, 1942; *They Live Forever* series, 1942; *Everything for the Boys* series, 1944; *I Was There* series; with Robert E. Lee—*Columbia Workshop* series, 1941-42; *Armed Forces Radio Service Programs*, 1942-45; *The World We're Fighting For* series, 1943; *Request Performance* series, 1945-46; *Screen Guild Theatre* series, 1946; *Favorite Story* series, 1946-49; *Frank Sinatra Show*, 1947; *Dinah Shore Program*, 1948; *The Railroad Hour*, 1948-54; *Young Love* series, 1949-50; *United Nations Broadcasts*, 1949-50; *Halls of Ivy* series, 1950-51; *Hallmark Playhouse* series, 1950-51; *Charles Boyer Show*, 1951; other freelance and special programs, 1941-50.

Television Plays: *Lincoln, The Unwilling Warrior*, 1975; with Robert E. Lee—*The Unexpected* series, 1951; *Favorite Story* series, 1952-53; *Song of Norway*, 1957; *West Point*, 1958; *Actor*, music by Billy Goldenburg, 1978.

Other

Oscar the Ostrich (for children; as Jerome Schwartz). New York, Random House, 1940.
Actor: The Life and Times of Paul Muni. New York, Putnam, 1974; London, W.H. Allen, 1975.

Editor, *Off Mike: Radio Writing by the Nation's Top Radio Writers*. New York, Essential, 1944.

*

Bibliography: In *Studies in American Drama: 1945 to the Present* (Columbus, Ohio). 1992.

Manuscript Collections: Lawrence and Lee Theatre Research Institute, Ohio State University, Columbus; Lincoln Center Library of the Performing Arts, New York; Kent State University, Ohio; Widener Library, Harvard University, Cambridge, Massachusetts; Ziv-United Artists film and transcription library.

Critical Studies: "Literature, Medicine, and the Magic Lie" by Lawrence Schneiderman, in *Kaleidoscope: International Magazine of Literature, Fine Arts, and Disability*, Summer-Fall 1987, pp. 12-15; in *The Playwright's Art: Conversations with Contemporary American Dramatists*, edited by Jackson R. Bryer, New Brunswick, New Jersey, Rutgers University Press, 1995; "Jerome Lawrence and Robert E. Lee" by Nena Couch, in *Speaking on Stage: Interviews with Contemporary American Playwrights*, edited by Philip C. Kolin and Colby H. Kullman, Tuscaloosa, University of Alabama Press, 1996.

Theatrical Activities:
Director: **Plays**—*You Can't Take It with You* by George S. Kaufman and Moss Hart, *The Imaginary Invalid* by Molière, *Anything Goes* by Howard Lindsay and Russel Crouse, *The Green Pastures* by Marc Connelly, *Boy Meets Girl* by Bella and Sam Spewack, *H.M.S. Pinafore* and *The Pirates of Penzance* by Gilbert and Sullivan, and *Androcles and the Lion* by Shaw, in summer stock, 1934-37; *Mame*, Sacramento, California, 1969; *The Incomparable Max*, Abingdon, Virginia, 1969; *The Crocodile Smile*, Flatrock, North Carolina, 1970; *The Night Thoreau Spent in Jail*, Dublin, 1972; *Jabberwock*, Dallas, 1974; *Inherit the Wind*, Dallas, 1975; *First Monday in October*, Cleveland, 1975.

Jerome Lawrence comments:
Robert E. Lee and I have been called by various critics: "the thinking man's playwrights." In our plays and in our teaching we have attempted to be part of our times. We have done all we can to encourage truly national and international theatre, not confined to a few blocks of real estate in Manhattan or London's West End. Thus, we have sought to promote the growth of regional and university theatres through the formation of American Playwrights Theatre, to bring new and vital and pertinent works to all of America and all of the world.

It has been my privilege to travel to more than a hundred countries, often on cultural-exchange missions. At home, through the years, we have tried to encourage new and untried playwrights, stimulating their work through teaching and through the annual Margo Jones Award.

In our plays we have hoped to mirror and illuminate the problems of the moment—but we have attempted to grapple with universal themes, even in our comedies. We have tried for a blend between the dramatic and the entertaining: our most serious works are always leavened with laughter (*Inherit the Wind* is an example) and our seemingly frivolous comedies (*Auntie Mame*, *Mame*, *Jabberwock*) have sub-texts which we hope say something important for the contemporary world. We are pleased and gratified that our plays have been translated and produced in 34 languages.

We are lovers of the living theatre and intend to continue working and living in it.

* * *

"Eatable things to eat and drinkable things to drink," comments a shocked character in Dickens's short story "Mugby Junction" in describing a visit to France. The British railway station buffet is the object of Dickens's scorn, and the news that French railways provide edible and easily assimilated food causes the staff of Mugby Junction's restaurant to come close to catatonic fits.

Many a critic, professional or amateur, might, in snobbish chorus, make similar comments about the works of the collaborators Jerome Lawrence and Robert E. Lee. "Playable plays to play—or readable plays to read!" might be their disbelieving cry. The expressions of disapproval and disdain might be almost as extreme as those of the nineteenth-century railway grotesques, for both playability and readability are cardinal points of the works of Lawrence and Lee. Their plots are tight, their characters cleanly developed, and their dialogue smooth. Actors like them, for they present strong speeches and well-developed scenes, and although this might be considered old-fashioned playwriting, it is clear that audiences like it too.

Lawrence and Lee's most successful work, *Inherit the Wind*, was first presented at the National Theatre in New York on April 1955 after a run in Dallas under a great encourager of new talent, Margo Jones. It became the third-longest-running serious play in the history of Broadway. The play was based on the famous Scopes trial in Tennessee, sometimes referred to as the "monkey trial," in which Darwinism and traditional religion had a head-on crash in a rural American setting. The production featured Paul Muni and Ed Begley, who made the dialogue of this solid courtroom drama flow back and forth like a mounting tide. The script is very readable, and although not deep, it is most engaging in a theatrical, if not an intellectually involving, way. The effect of putting two great contemporary orators, pitted one against the other, at the core of the play makes for compelling speeches, and the device of the trial itself provides a rounded dramatic vehicle, still open-ended enough to allow one of the protagonists to stand at the end weighing copies of the Bible and Darwin while planning the appeal. Today's audiences, even though we would like to think of ourselves as beyond quaint beliefs, can still become emotionally involved over God versus monkey. Good and forceful fare, it has been produced around the world.

Many of the works of Lawrence and Lee are lighter, mirroring their ability to zero in on the essentially sentimental underbelly of the average Broadway audience. Their evident enjoyment of the sentimental is one of their secrets. By far the largest part of the Broadway audience is out for fun, a pleasurable look at a never-never land, which is why the musical, when successful, is always such a huge money spinner. Lawrence and Lee pull off a clever trick with *Inherit the Wind,* for it has many elements of the musical yet gives patrons the self-importance of feeling that they have seen something serious.

Lawrence and Lee are also at home in creating an impossible character like *Auntie Mame,* first produced in New York in 1956. This giddy American dame was adored onstage, although she probably would not have been tolerated for more than a moment beyond Manhattan or Wilshire Boulevard. Many of the members of the audience would have come from suburban patios like the satirized Upsons, whose house in Connecticut is called "Upson Downs"—Lawrence has a weakness for rather ponderous puns in conversation, with his own California house called "Writers to the Sea"—but the social comment is kept gentle and the medicine never too strong. An amusing evening and intended to be nothing more no doubt, yet for this writer the play only sparked into life when Beatrice Lillie played the part in the London production.

Auntie Mame became the very successful musical *Mame,* which Lawrence and Lee also wrote and which featured the then relatively unknown Angela Lansbury. Their collaboration on a monolithic musical called *Dear World,* based on the Giraudoux play *The Madwoman of Chaillot,* was less successful. It is hard, however, to find fault with writers when faced with the complexities of producing musicals in New York City, where music, lyrics, choreography, special songs, production numbers, direction, elaborate costumes, and staggering scenery—along with equally staggering costs—seem often to overwhelm the basic book.

Nevertheless, Lawrence and Lee seem happier when they are away from the big-time musical stage, as witnessed by their commitment to a play entitled *The Night Thoreau Spent in Jail.* This play, first presented at Ohio State University in 1970, was an interesting experiment. Some years ago, intent on trying to circumvent the sterile Broadway scene so far as serious plays were concerned, the partners set up American Playwrights Theatre in Columbus. It was a deliberate move away from New York in a laudable attempt to develop new audiences for serious drama, with the plays of dramatists, known and unknown, presented in a new "circuit"—a network of resident and university theaters across the United States. Each writer was guaranteed a number of different productions in various spots on the circuit, and many were produced before Lawrence and Lee launched one of their own—*Thoreau.* This was a subject of particular interest to young audiences, for it dealt with one of the first cases of civil disobedience in America. Later collaborations included *Jabberwock* and *First Monday in October.*

Their hand with humor can, unfortunately, be a little heavy, and when tackling such a delicate exponent of the art as Max Beerbohm in *The Incomparable Max,* they became caught in a morass that was anything but Maxian. There are times when the pair cleaves dangerously close to the jungle of clichés.

Lawrence and Lee collaborate easily. Each has a veto, "but it's a positive one," says Lawrence. They both feel that they can and do learn from criticism. Their contribution to American drama is perhaps most significant when one looks at the number of countries that know them from the many translations of their principle works. *Inherit the Wind* has been translated into well over two dozen languages, while the citizens of Ireland, Israel, Holland, Germany, Bangladesh, and Russia, among others, have been given an eye-opening view of a Yankee philosopher's protest in *Thoreau.*

—Michael T. Leech

LEIGH, Mike

Nationality: British. **Born:** Salford, Lancashire, 20 February 1943. **Education:** North Grecian Street County Primary School; Salford Grammar School; Royal Academy of Dramatic Art, London, 1960-62; Camberwell School of Arts and Crafts, London, 1963-64; Central School of Art and Design, London, 1964-65; London Film School, 1965. **Family:** Married the actress Alison Steadman in 1973; two sons. **Career:** Founder, with David Halliwell, Dramagraph production company, London, 1965; associate director, Midlands Arts Centre for Young People, Birmingham, 1965-66; actor, Victoria Theatre, Stoke-on-Trent, Staffordshire, 1966; assistant director, Royal Shakespeare Company, 1967-68; lecturer, Sedgley Park and De La Salle colleges, Manchester, 1968-69, and London Film School, 1970-73. Member of advisory council, Independent Broadcasting Authority, 1980-82. **Awards:** Chicago Film Festival and Locarno Film Festival awards, 1972; George Devine award, 1974; *Evening Standard* award, 1982, 1989; Venice Film Festival Critics award, 1988; Stars de Demain Coup de Coeur, 1989; Peter Sellers Comedy award, 1989; National Society of Film Critics Best Film award, 1991; Cannes Film Festival award, 1993, for *Naked.* Honorary degrees: M.A., University of Salford, 1991. Decorated Officer, Order of British Empire, 1993. **Agent:** Peters, Fraser, and Dunlop Group, 503/4 The Chambers, Chelsea Harbour, Lots Road, London SW10 0XF, England.

Publications

Plays

The Box Play (produced Birmingham, 1965).
My Parents Have Gone to Carlisle (produced Birmingham, 1966).
The Last Crusade of the Five Little Nuns (produced Birmingham, 1966).
Waste Paper Guards, (produced Birmingham, 1966).
NENAA (produced Stratford-on-Avon, 1967).
Individual Fruit Pies (produced Loughton, Essex, 1968).
Down Here and Up There (produced London, 1968).

Big Basil (produced Manchester, 1969).
Epilogue (produced Manchester, 1969).
Glum Victoria and the Lad with Specs (produced Manchester, 1969).
Bleak Moments (produced London, 1970).
A Rancid Pong (produced London, 1971).
Wholesome Glory (produced London, 1973).
The Jaws of Death (produced Edinburgh, 1973; London, 1978).
Dick Whittington and His Cat (produced London, 1973).
Babies Grow Old (produced Stratford-on-Avon, 1974; London, 1975).
The Silent Majority (produced London, 1974).
Abigail's Party (produced London, 1977). With *Goose-Pimples*, London, Penguin, 1983.
Ecstasy (produced London, 1979). With *Smelling a Rat*, London, Hern, 1989.
Goose-Pimples, (produced London, 1981). With *Abigail's Party*, London, Penguin, 1983.
Smelling a Rat (produced London, 1988). With *Ecstasy*, London, Hern, 1989.
Greek Tragedy (produced Sydney, 1989; Edinburgh and London, 1990).
Career Girls. London, Faber and faber, 1997.

Screenplays: *Bleak Moments*, 1972; *The Short and Curlies*, 1987; *High Hopes*, 1988; *Life Is Sweet*, 1991; *Naked*, 1993; *Career Girls*, 1997.

Radio Play: *Too Much of a Good Thing*, 1979 (banned).

Television Plays: *A Mug's Game*, 1973; *Hard Labour*, 1973; "Five Minute Films": *The Birth of the 2001 FA Cup Final Goalie*, *Old Chums*, *Probation*, *A Light Snack*, and *Afternoon*, all 1975; *The Permissive Society*, 1975; *Nuts in May*, 1976; *Knock for Knock*, 1976; *The Kiss of Death*, 1977; *Who's Who*, 1979; *Grown-Ups*, 1980; *Home Sweet Home*, 1982; *Meantime*, 1983; *Four Days in July*, 1985.

*

Critical Studies: *The Improvised Play: The Work of Mike Leigh* by Paul Clements, London, Methuen, 1983; "Four Days in July (Mike Leigh)" by Paul Clements, in *British Television in the 1980s*, edited by George W. Brandt, Cambridge, Cambridge University Press, 1993; "Mike Leigh: Beyond Embarrassment" by Andy Medhurst, in *Sight and Sound*, November 1993, pp. 6-10; "Mike Leigh" by Gordon Bette, in *BOMB*, Winter 1994, pp. 30-33.

Theatrical Activities:
Director of all his own plays and films.

* * *

"My work," Mike Leigh once said in an interview, "is always very strictly scripted with serious literary considerations." Such words should be taken into account when assessing his plays, for a misconception has grown up, caused perhaps by Leigh's well-known improvisational method, that his work is simply a slice of life. Nothing could be further from the truth, although, as anyone who has seen his plays can attest, this method does give his pieces a highly recognizable form and flavor.

Leigh produces his work through a process that is, broadly speaking, collaborational. A group of actors is selected, and each is presented with the germ of a character. They are then asked to go away and develop the characters by using their own experience and imagination. At the end of several weeks or even months, they are reassembled, and a play is put together under Leigh's direction. The emphasis here is under Leigh's direction, for although he welcomes, and indeed expects, creative input from his actors, Leigh remains very much in control. "I function as author and director," he has said. "There's no committee involved."

Such a process produces a particular kind of play. Plots are simple, almost nonexistent, and the language is idiomatic, even vulgar. There are no great dramatic moments, no soaring lyrical flights, indeed little that is theater in the usual sense. What there is is a close and exact study of suburban angst that uses the smallest words and actions to highlight undercurrents of malice and frustration. It is Artaud moved to Pinner, one might say, or Beckett in Brooklyn. What it is not is simply a slice of life.

Leigh's first major success, and still his most popular play, was *Abigail's Party*. The eponymous Abigail is having a thrash. Intimidated, her mother Sue retreats to the lurid drawing room of her neighbor Beverley, a former beautician, and of her estate agent husband Laurence. Two other guests arrive, and what should be a lovely evening degenerates into a hilariously grotesque nightmare of jealousy, cruelty, and indifference. We laugh at Leigh's characters, but we laugh uneasily, for in their material wealth and spiritual poverty they are perhaps a little too close for comfort.

Ecstasy, Leigh's next play, stands somewhat apart from his other pieces. Here the characters are working-class rather than lower-middle-class, and, though desperate, Jean and Dawn and Mike and Len manifest a clumsy warmth and sympathy quite absent from, say, *Abigail's Party*. Particularly moving are the songs that end the play, songs whose sweetness and occasional indecency accentuate the characters' human pathos to an almost unbearable degree.

Two years later came *Goose-Pimples*, a return, at least in tone, to the world of *Abigail's Party*. Jackie, a trainee croupier and lodger, brings home Muhammed, a small-time Arab businessman, for a drink. He thinks that she is a prostitute, and she thinks that he is an oil sheikh. Into this misunderstanding barges her landlord, a car dealer, a colleague of his from work, and the colleague's wife. What follows is a parody of West End farce, with exits and entrances and muddles galore. At the end of the piece the two Englishmen, in a fit of drunken and entirely spurious gallantry, assault and humiliate Muhammed, a graphic depiction of the violence and xenophobia undercutting British society. It is a brutal moment, with the shadow of Pinter, one feels, hovering nearby.

After several years of film and television work Leigh returned to the stage with *Smelling a Rat*. More a playlet than a play, it is perhaps the slightest of his pieces. Of greater substance is *Greek Tragedy*, which Leigh directed in Australia in 1989. This project was something of a risk, for by his own admission he knew nothing of Greek-Australian society. Using a cast drawn entirely from this ethnic group, however, he overcame the difficulty and produced by his collaborational method a play every bit as accurate and discomforting as his British pieces. A tragedy in more than one sense—it observes, for example, the classical unities—*Greek Tragedy* portrays the sterile, loveless marriage of Kalliope and Alex, two workers in the rag trade for whom the Australian dream has scarcely come true. Into their stifled lives burst Larry and Vicki, immigrant success stories and monsters par excellence. The stage is then set for another of Leigh's studies in suburban cruelty and frustration. If it all sounds a little familiar—*Goose-Pimples,* as it were, translated Down Under—it is still horribly unerring.

—John O'Leary

LEONARD, Hugh

A pseudonym for John Keyes Byrne. **Nationality:** Irish. **Born:** Dublin, 9 November 1926. **Education:** Presentation College, Dun Laoghaire, 1941-45. **Family:** Married Paule Jacquet in 1955; one daughter. **Career:** Civil servant, Dublin, 1945-59; script editor, Granada Television, Manchester, 1961-63; literary editor, Abbey Theatre, Dublin, 1976-77; programme director, Dublin Theatre Festival, 1978-80; weekly columnist, *Sunday Independent.* **Awards:** Italia prize, for television play, 1967; Writers Guild of Great Britain award, 1967; Tony award, 1978; New York Drama Critics Circle award, 1978; Outer Circle award, 1978; Vernon Rice award, 1978; Sagittarius prize. D.H.L.: Rhode Island College, Providence, 1980. D. Litt.: Trinity College, Dublin, 1989. **Agent:** Lemon, Unna, and Durbridge, 24 Pottery Lane, Holland Park, London W11 4LZ, England. **Address:** 6 Rossaun, Pilot View, Dalkey, County Dublin, Ireland; e-mail: panache@ iol.ie.

PUBLICATIONS

Plays

The Italian Road (produced Dublin, 1954).
The Big Birthday (produced Dublin, 1956).
A Leap in the Dark (produced Dublin, 1957).
Madigan's Lock (produced Dublin, 1958; London, 1963; Olney, Maryland, 1970). With *Pizzazz*, Dublin, Brophy, 1987.
A Walk on the Water (produced Dublin, 1960).
The Passion of Peter Ginty, adaptation of the play *Peer Gynt* by Ibsen (produced Dublin, 1961).
Stephen D, adaptation of the works *A Portrait of the Artist as a Young Man* and *Stephen Hero* by James Joyce (produced Dublin, 1962; London, 1963; New York, 1967). London, Evans, 1965.
Dublin One, adaptation of the stories *Dubliners* by James Joyce (produced Dublin, 1963).
The Poker Session (produced Dublin, 1963; London, 1964; New York, 1967). London, Evans, 1963.
The Family Way, adaptation of a play by Eugène Labiche (produced Dublin, 1964; London, 1966).
The Late Arrival of the Incoming Aircraft (televised 1964). London, Evans, 1968.
A View from the Obelisk (televised 1964; in *Scorpions*, produced Dublin, 1983).
The Saints Go Cycling In, adaptation of the novel *The Dalkey Archives* by Flann O'Brien (produced Dublin, 1965).
Mick and Mick (produced Dublin, 1966; as *All the Nice People*, produced Olney, Maryland, 1976; New York, 1984). London, French, 1966.
A Time of Wolves and Tigers (televised 1967; produced in *Irishmen*, Olney, Maryland, and Dublin, 1975). Included in *Suburb of Babylon*, 1983.
The Quick, and The Dead (produced Dublin, 1967).
The Au Pair Man (produced Dublin, 1968; London, 1969; New York, 1973). Published in *Plays and Players* (London), December 1968; New York, French, 1974.
The Barracks, adaptation of the novel by John McGahern (produced Dublin, 1969).
The Patrick Pearse Motel (produced Dublin and London, 1971; Olney, Maryland, 1972; New York, 1984). London, French, 1972.
Da (produced Olney, Maryland, and Dublin, 1973; London, 1977; New York, 1978). Newark, Delaware, Proscenium Press, 1976; revised version, London, French and New York, Atheneum, 1978.
Summer (produced Olney, Maryland, and Dublin, 1974; London, 1979; New York, 1980). London, French, 1979.
Suburb of Babylon (includes *A Time of Wolves and Tigers*, *Nothing Personal*, *The Last of the Last of the Mohicans*) (as *Irishmen*, produced Olney, Maryland, and Dublin, 1975). London, French, 1983.
Great Expectations (produced Dublin, 1975).
A Tale of Two Cities (produced Dublin, 1976).
Some of My Best Friends Are Husbands, adaptation of a play by Eugène Labiche (produced London, 1976).
Liam Liar, adaptation of the play *Billy Liar* by Keith Waterhouse and Willis Hall (produced Dublin, 1976).
Time Was (produced Dublin, 1976). Included in *Da, A Life, Time Was*, 1981.
A Life (produced Dublin, 1979; London and New York, 1980). London, French, 1980; New York, Atheneum, 1981.
Da, A Life, Time Was. London, Penguin, 1981.
Kill (produced Dublin, 1982; New York, 1986.)
Pizzazz (produced Dublin, 1983). London, French, 1986.
Scorpions (includes *A View from the Obelisk*, *Roman Fever*, *Pizzazz*) (produced Dublin, 1983).
The Mask of Moriarty, based on characters by Arthur Conan Doyle (produced Dublin, 1985; Leicester, 1987).
Moving (produced Dublin, 1992).
Magic (produced 1997).
Love in the Title (produced 1998).

Screenplays: *Great Catherine*, 1967; *Interlude*, with Lee Langley, 1967; *Whirligig*, 1970; *Percy*, with Terence Feely, 1970; *Our Miss Fred*, 1972; *Widows' Peak*, 1986; *Da*, 1989; *Mattie,* 1998.

Radio Plays: *The Kennedys of Castleross* series; *Ending It,* 1976.

Television Plays: *The Irish Boys* (trilogy), 1962; *Saki* series, 1962; *A Kind of Kingdom*, 1963; *Jezebel Ex-UK* series, 1963; *The Second Wall*, 1964; *A Triple Irish*, 1964; *Realm of Error*, 1964; *My One True Love*, 1964; *The Late Arrival of the Incoming Aircraft*, 1964; *Do You Play Requests?*, 1964; *A View from the Obelisk*, 1964; *The Hidden Truth* series, 1964; *Undermind* series, 1964; *I Loved You Last Summer*, 1965; *Great Big Blond*, 1965; *Blackmail* series, 1965; *Public Eye* series, 1965; *Simenon* series: *The Lodger* and *The Judge*, 1966; *Insurrection* (8 parts), 1966; *Second Childhood*, 1966; *The Retreat*, 1966; *Silent Song*, from a story by Frank O'Connor, 1966; *The Liars* series, 1966; *The Informer* series, 1966; *Out of the Unknown* series, 1966-67; *A Time of Wolves and Tigers*, 1967; *Love Life*, 1967; *Great Expectations* (serialization), from the novel by Dickens, 1967; *Wuthering Heights* (serialization), from the novel by Emily

Brontë, 1967; *No Such Things as a Vampire*, 1968; *The Corpse Can't Play*, 1968; *A Man and His Mother-in-Law*, 1968; *Assassin*, 1968; *Nicholas Nickleby* (serialization), from the novel by Dickens, 1968; *Conan Doyle* series: *A Study in Scarlet* and *The Hound of the Baskervilles*, 1968; *Hunt the Peacock*, from a novel by H.R.F. Keating, 1969; *Talk of Angels*, 1969; *The Possessed* (serialization), from a novel by Dostoevsky, 1969; *Dombey and Son* (serialization), from the novel by Dickens, 1969; *Somerset Maugham* series: *P & O*, 1969, and *Jane*, 1970; *A Sentimental Education* (serialization), from a novel by Flaubert, 1970; *The Sinners* series, 1970-71; *Me Mammy* series, 1970-71; *White Walls and Olive Green Carpets*, 1971; *The Removal Person*, 1971; *Pandora*, 1971; *The Virgins*, 1972; *The Ghost of Christmas Present*, 1972; *The Truth Game*, 1972; *Tales from the Lazy Acres* series, 1972; *The Moonstone* (serialization), from the novel by Wilkie Collins, 1972; *The Sullen Sisters*, 1972; *The Watercress Girl*, from the story by H.E. Bates, 1972; *The Higgler*, 1973; *High Kampf*, 1973; *Milo O'Shea*, 1973; *Stone Cold Sober*, 1973; *The Bitter Pill*, 1973; *Another Fine Mess*, 1973; *Judgement Day*, 1973; *The Travelling Woman*, 1973; *The Hammer of God*, *The Actor and the Alibi*, *The Eye of Apollo*, *The Forbidden Garden*, *The Three Tools of Death*, and *The Quick One* (*Father Brown* series), 1974; *London Belongs to Me*, from the novel by Norman Collins, 1977; *Bitter Suite*, 1977; *Teresa*, *The Fur Coat*, and *Two of a Kind*, from stories by Sean O'Faolain, 1977; *The Last Campaign*, from the novel *The Captains and the Kings* by Jennifer Johnston, 1978; *The Ring and the Rose*, 1978; *Strumpet City*, from the novel by James Plunkett, 1980; *The Little World of Don Camillo*, from a novel by Giovanni Guareschi, 1981; *Good Behaviour*, from a work by Molly Keane, 1983; *O'Neill* series, 1983; *The Irish R.M.* series, 1985; *Hunted Down*, from a story by Dickens, 1985; *Troubles*, 1987; *Parnell and the Englishwoman* (serialization), from his own novel, 1991.

Novel

Parnell and the Englishwoman. New York, Atheneum, 1990.

Other

Leonard's Last Book (essays). Enniskerry, County Wicklow, Egoist Press, 1978.
A Peculiar People and Other Foibles (essays). Enniskerry, County Wicklow, Tansy, 1979.
Home Before Night: Memoirs of an Irish Time and Place. London, Deutsch, 1979; New York, Atheneum, 1980.
Leonard's Year (journalism). Dublin, Canavaun, 1985.
Out After Dark (memoirs). London, Deutsch, 1989.
Rover and Other Cats (memoirs). London, Deutsch, 1992.

*

Bibliography: *Ten Modern Irish Playwrights* by Kimball King, New York, Garland, 1979.

Critical Studies: "Insubstantial Fathers and Consubstantial Sons: A Note on Patrimony and Patricide in Friel and Leonard" by Thomas B. O'Grady, in *Canadian Journal of Irish Studies* (Saskatoon, Saskatchewan), July 1989, pp. 71-79; "Q. And A. with Hugh Leonard" by S. F. Gallagher, in *Irish Literary Supplement: A Review of Irish Books*, Spring 1990, pp. 13-14.

Theatrical Activities:
Actor: **Play**—In *A Walk on the Water*, Dublin, 1960.

Hugh Leonard comments:

(1973) Being an Irish writer both hampers and helps me: hampers, because one is fighting the preconceptions of audiences who have been conditioned to expect feyness and parochial subject matter; helps, because the writer can utilise a vigorous and poetic idiom which enables him to combine subtlety with richness. Ireland is my subject matter, but only to the degree in which I can use it as a microcosm; this involves choosing themes which are free of Catholicism and politics, both of which I detest, and which deprive one's work of applicability outside Ireland.

For many years I was obsessed with the theme of betrayal (*A Walk on the Water* and *The Poker Session*)—its effects and its inevitability. My work then began to reflect a preoccupation with defining and isolating the essence of the new prosperity, which I used as the subject for satire (*The Patrick Pearse Motel* and *Thieves*, as yet unproduced). By and large—and after the event—my work reflects Ibsen's observation that to be a writer is to sit in judgment on oneself; and perhaps for this reason I now want to write a play which, like *A Walk on the Water* and *Pandora*, is autobiographical. Like most writers I am involved in seeking a form. A play takes me a long time to write, and my methods involve—partly deliberately, partly because of how I work—various subterranean levels. At times this leads to an excess of cleverness, stemming perhaps from a lack of faith in one's own powers. Now that I have learned both the requirements and the uses of the dramatic form I would like to use a simplicity of style combined with visual situations—the image in my mind is the scene in which Lavinia confronts her mother across her father's corpse in *Mourning Becomes Electra*.

Like all writers who achieve middle-age, I am conscious of having wasted time, and also of having at last arrived at a sense of identity. Ideally, I would now like to write my "failures"; i.e., plays written as pure acts of self-expression, without any hope of their being staged. I am conscious that my main faults are the cleverness (in the structural sense) which I have mentioned and at times an irresponsible sense of comedy, which is not so much out of place as inclined to give my work an unintended lightness. These faults at least I know and can guard against. I regard myself as an optimist, and the theme that emerges from my plays is that life is good if it is not misused. But this is only an impression which—again after the event—I have gleaned from revisiting my work. As Moss Hart has said, one begins with two people on a stage, and one of them had better say something pretty damn quick! One starts to write, and one's own character and beliefs—not consciously defined—shapes, limits, enriches, pauperises, and defines one's work. Choice of subject and form are the cartridge case which contains the bullet. A play is an accident: often one writes the right play at the wrong time in one's life, and vice-versa; often one begins to write it that vital fraction in time before it has ripened in one's skull—or a moment too late, when it has gone cold. One goes on trying.

* * *

In the masterful autobiography of his early years, *Home Before Night*, Hugh Leonard tells of his gradual progress into the stifling prize of a job in the Irish civil service. The book is an eloquent statement of reconciliation that explores his illegitimacy and family relationships, and it is a rich lode of characters and personalities that are developed further in his plays. There is a passage toward the end in which he records his first serious experience of theatergoing, when he visited the Abbey's production of Sean O'Casey's *The Plough and the Stars*. His prose crystallizes the experience and communicates the personal epiphany that made him a playwright. Rushing from the theater to a train, he found himself in a compartment with a courting couple who sulked at his presence: "The pair of them could strip to their skins for all he cared. He looked away from them through the window and saw his reflection in the dark glass. It was amazing how calm he looked. His breath in the unheated compartment threw a mist upon the glass, but even then he could see, as if it was out there by the tracks, the door he would escape through."

Since O'Casey Irish playwrights have made Ireland their major subject. Leonard has claimed his place in that tradition, but there are essential differences, and he has always looked for broader applicability. He works mainly through the emergent middle classes of Ireland, with conflicts more suburban than urban and politics and religion as mere ghosts in the background. They are, of course, inescapable ghosts.

Leonard's best plays explore the characters of his own life and stretch from *A Walk on the Water* to *A Life,* with 20 years of experience between the works and a rare, deepening texture that demonstrates his own increased understanding of the past. Memory is also the form of many of his adaptations, including his first international success, *Stephen D,* a dramatization of James Joyce's autobiographical books. Using both *A Portrait of the Artist as a Young Man* and Joyce's earlier, more straightforward version of the book, *Stephen Hero,* Leonard showed his sympathy for the metaphysical flight of Dedalus—Joyce's own exile from church, family, and Ireland—as directly as if telling his own story.

His earliest plays found him more within the Irish dramatic tradition, even showing a concern with politics, but the form of *A Leap in the Dark* suggested his alienation from the violent course Irish politics often took. On a New Year's Eve in Dublin a father and son fall out over the new troubles in Northern Ireland, with the son opposing the violence so completely that his best friend tries to show the reasoning behind the border raids by confessing his own part in them. The son, Charles, then discovers that another raid is in the making, and he sets out to inform the police. On his return to the house he is shot.

It is rare that such scenes are depicted in Leonard's work, but his private path has wandered in many directions. After his start in the theater writing plays for the Dublin Theatre Festival, he learned the discipline of prolificacy by writing a serial called *The Kennedys of Castlerosse* for commercial radio. He went from Irish radio to British television, editing scripts, writing dramas, and churning out numerous series. In the midst of this work, and while providing a steady stream of original plays for the stage, he continued adapting the work of other writers. Before *Stephen D* there was the Irish *Peer Gynt,* which he called *The Passion of Peter Ginty*. Flann O'Brien's surreal humor in *The Dalkey Archives* went to the stage as *The Saints Go Cycling In,* and *Billy Liar* was transformed into an Irish play for the Abbey as *Liam Liar*.

Leonard, who is known to most of Ireland as Jack Byrne or as plain Jack, since the Irish reject the pseudonym of Hugh Leonard, is quick to point out that an Irish literary movement occurs when two playwrights are on speaking terms. Nonetheless, he has found himself at the center of Irish letters on several occasions, including the stormy year he spent as literary manager of the Abbey and during his spell of literary management as one of the directors of the important Dublin Theatre Festival. These positions were dignified by his presence, for there is no doubt that he is a major playwright of international importance.

For a long time Leonard had a rewarding relationship with a theater in Olney, Maryland, just outside Washington, D.C. Plays such as *The Patrick Pearse Motel* and *Da* were mounted in Olney well before New York took notice. New York, however, finally did with *Da* what London regularly refused to do with Leonard's critically well-regarded work—give him a major popular success.

The play *Da* is a joyous one, undisguisedly about the death of Leonard's own stepfather, the Da of the title. At the father's death the son flies from London to Dublin for the funeral, only to find that the old man wanders in to discuss the funeral and to claim his place in his stepson's heart and mind. Leonard links past and present with the son's younger self, who is also on hand, reliving the traumas of adolescence, fighting it out with his mother, and getting furiously annoyed with Da. The memories of the past and the details of the present, which include putting the meager effects of the father into order, are so ingeniously layered that farce, understanding, and frustrated fury all manage to coexist. From Leonard's precise evocation of individuals at different points in time is conveyed the love that comes from understanding.

A minor figure from *Da* is the character of Drumm, a man figuring in the autobiography as the civil servant who brings Leonard into the civil service. In *Da* he complains of "tummy trouble," which is revealed as cancer in the next memory play, *A Life*. Again, past and present coexist, with Drumm irascibly trying to make his peace with the girl he failed to marry in his youth while witnessing his younger self making all of the original mistakes that foretold his old age as a bundle of attitudes and principles. The delicacy of Leonard's imagery and the richness of his comedy deflect the maudlin potential of the story, and the affirmation of life is reflected even in the final sentence as Drumm confronts the imminence of death and says to his wife, "Let's make a start." In these plays Leonard is a writer at the height of his powers, and he confirms his ability to extend the specific to a large audience. It is as if he were a master of the spectator's memories as well as his own.

A spectacular Dublin story about money siphoned out of his accounts saw to it that Leonard spent the greater part of his time for a few years after *A Life* concentrating on the more lucrative expression of films, but he never abandoned the theater. His most notable advance was *Kill*, a dinner party metaphor about Irish politics with some acidly presented characters all too recognizable to the Irish audience. His presentation of the Irish government as covert collaborators with terror alienated some of his audience, although not permanently. His Sherlock Holmes adventure, *The Mask of Moriarty,* was the hit of the 1985 Dublin Theatre Festival despite a notorious interview with the play's leading actor that gave away the twist in the play before it opened.

Although a number of friendly notices greeted an English production of *The Mask of Moriarty* at Leicester's Haymarket Theatre the following year, with the twist that it was widely publicized again that Holmes's enemy Moriarty had had surgery to become Holmes's double, the play failed to find a West End home. Leonard's subsequent successes included a movie version of *Da* and a major television series, *Parnell and the Englishwoman,* a story about the Irish leader Charles Stewart Parnell and an adulterous affair that destroyed his career. Perhaps the lurking point, that without the affair Parnell's leadership might have kept Ireland from later years of bloodshed, was not finely enough expressed, but Leonard's novel of the same story won him the Sagittarius Prize for a first novel by an author over 60.

Leonard's 1992 play *Moving* saw him in the familiar geographical territory of the Dublin seaside town of Dalkey, but his attempt to chart an ordinary suburban family's rise over the 30 years from 1957 to 1987 showed its scheme rather too clearly. From the childish skipping of mass to gay rights years later, from household pride to high pretension, the family called Noone represents an Ireland that cannot find its way. Overall, however, Leonard's art represents a potent expression of Ireland as he sees it and from where it molds the individual.

—Ned Chaillet

LESSING, Doris (May)

Nationality: British. **Born:** Doris Taylor, Kermansha, Persia, 22 October 1919; moved with her family to England, then to Banket, Southern Rhodesia, 1924. **Education:** Dominican Convent School, Salisbury, Southern Rhodesia, 1926-34. **Family:** Married 1) Frank Charles Wisdom in 1939 (divorced 1943), one son and one daughter; 2) Gottfried Lessing in 1945 (divorced 1949), one son. **Career:** Au pair, Salisbury, 1934-35; telephone operator and clerk, Salisbury, 1937-39; typist, 1946-48; clerk, Cape Town *Guardian*, 1949; moved to London, 1949; member of the editorial board, *New Reasoner*, 1956. **Awards:** Maugham award, for fiction, 1954; Médicis prize (France), 1976; Austrian State prize, 1981; Shakespeare prize (Hamburg), 1982; W.H. Smith Literary award, 1986; Palermo prize (Italy), 1987; Mondello prize (Italy), 1987; Cavour award (Italy), 1989. Honorary fellow, Modern Language Association (U.S.A.), 1974; distinguished fellow in literature, University of East Anglia, Norwich, 1991. Honorary degrees: Princeton University, New Jersey, 1989; University of Durham, 1990; Harvard University, Cambridge, Massachusetts, 1997; Oxford, Warwick, 1997. **Member:** American Academy, 1974. **Agent:** Jonathan Clowes Ltd., Iron Bridge House, Bridge Approach, London, NW1 8BD, England.

Publications

Plays

Each His Own Wilderness (produced London, 1958). Published in *New English Dramatists*, London, Penguin, 1959.
Play with a Tiger (produced Brighton and London, 1962; New York, 1964). London, Joseph, 1962; in *Plays by and about Women*, edited by Victoria Sullivan and James V. Hatch, New York, Random House, 1973.
The Storm, adaptation of a play by Alexander Ostrovsky (produced London, 1966).
The Singing Door (for children), in *Second Playbill 2*, edited by Alan Durband. London, Hutchinson, 1973.
The Making of the Representative for Planet 8 (opera libretto), music by Philip Glass, adaptation of the novel by Lessing (produced London, 1988).
The Marriages between Zones Three, Four, and Five (opera libretto).
Play with a Tiger, and Other Plays. London, Flamingo, 1996.

Television Plays: *The Grass Is Singing*, from her own novel, 1962; *Care and Protection* and *Do Not Disturb* (both in *Blackmail* series), 1966; *Between Men*, 1967; *In the Habit of Loving* (co-author on a Maupassant series).

Novels

The Grass Is Singing. London, Joseph, and New York, Crowell, 1950.
Children of Violence:
Martha Quest. London, Joseph, 1952; with *A Proper Marriage*, New York, Simon and Schuster, 1964.
A Proper Marriage. London, Joseph, 1954; with *Martha Quest*, New York, Simon and Schuster, 1964.
A Ripple from the Storm, London, Joseph, 1958; with *Landlocked*, New York, Simon and Schuster, 1966.
Landlocked. London, MacGibbon and Kee, 1965; with *A Ripple from the Storm.* New York, Simon and Schuster, 1966.
The Four-Gated City. London, MacGibbon and Kee, and New York, Knopf, 1969.
The Golden Notebook. London, Joseph, and New York, Simon and Schuster, 1962.
Briefing for a Descent into Hell. London, Cape, and New York, Knopf, 1971.
The Summer Before the Dark. London, Cape, and New York, Knopf, 1973.
The Memoirs of a Survivor. London, Octagon Press, 1974; New York, Knopf, 1975.
Canopus in Argos: Archives:
Shikasta. London, Cape, and New York, Knopf, 1979.
The Marriages Between Zones Three, Four, and Five. London, Cape, and New York, Knopf, 1980.
The Sirian Experiments. London, Cape, and New York, Knopf, 1981.
The Making of the Representative for Planet 8. London, Cape, and New York, Knopf, 1982.
The Sentimental Agents. London, Cape, and New York, Knopf, 1983.
The Diaries of Jane Somers. New York, Vintage, and London, Joseph, 1984.
The Diary of a Good Neighbour (as Jane Somers). London, Joseph, and New York, Knopf, 1983.
If the Old Could—(as Jane Somers). London, Joseph, and New York, Knopf, 1984.
The Good Terrorist. London, Cape, and New York, Knopf, 1985.
The Fifth Child. London, Cape, and New York, Knopf, 1988.

Short Stories

This Was the Old Chief's Country. London, Joseph, 1951; New York, Crowell, 1952.
Five: Short Novels. London, Joseph, 1953.
No Witchcraft for Sale: Stories and Short Novels. Moscow, Foreign Language Publishing House, 1956.
The Habit of Loving. London, MacGibbon and Kee, and New York, Crowell, 1957.
A Man and Two Women. London, MacGibbon and Kee, and New York, Simon and Schuster, 1963.
African Stories. London, Joseph, 1964; New York, Simon and Schuster, 1965.
Winter in July. London, Panther, 1966.

The Black Madonna. London, Panther, 1966.
Nine African Stories, edited by Michael Marland. London, Longman, 1968.
The Story of a Non-Marrying Man and Other Stories. London, Cape, 1972; as *The Temptation of Jack Orkney and Other Stories*, New York, Knopf, 1972.
Collected African Stories. New York, Simon and Schuster, 1981.
This Was the Old Chief's Country. London, Joseph, 1973.
The Sun Between Their Feet. London, Joseph, 1973.
(*Stories*), edited by Alan Cattell. London, Harrap, 1976.
Collected Stories: To Room Nineteen and *The Temptation of Jack Orkney.* London, Cape, 2 vols., 1978; as *Stories*, New York, Knopf, 1 vol., 1978.
London Observed. London, Cape, 1991.
The Real Thing. New York, HarperCollins, 1991.

Poetry

Fourteen Poems. Northwood, Middlesex, Scorpion Press, 1959.

Other

Going Home. London, Joseph, 1957; revised edition, London, Panther, and New York, Ballantine, 1968.
In Pursuit of the English: A Documentary. London, MacGibbon and Kee, 1960; New York, Simon and Schuster, 1961.
Particularly Cats. London, Joseph, and New York, Simon and Schuster, 1967.
A Small Personal Voice: Essays, Reviews, Interviews, edited by Paul Schlueter. New York, Knopf, 1974.
Prisons We Choose to Live Inside. Montreal, CBC, 1986; London, Cape, and New York, Harper, 1987.
The Wind Blows Away Our Words, and Other Documents Relating to Afghanistan. London, Pan, and New York, Vintage, 1987.
The Doris Lessing Reader. London, Cape, and New York, Knopf, 1989.
African Laughter: Four Visits to Zimbabwe (memoir). London and New York, HarperCollins, 1992.
Under My Skin (Volume 1 of autobiography). London and New York, HarperCollins, 1996.
Walking in the Shade (Volume 2 of autobiography). New York, HarperCollins, 1997.

*

Bibliographies: *Doris Lessing: A Bibliography* by Catharina Ipp, Johannesburg, University of the Witwatersrand Department of Bibliography, 1967; *Doris Lessing: A Checklist of Primary and Secondary Sources* by Selma R. Burkom and Margaret Williams, Troy, New York, Whitston, 1973; *Doris Lessing: An Annotated Bibliography of Criticism* by Dee Seligman, Westport, Connecticut, Greenwood Press, 1981; *Doris Lessing: A Descriptive Bibliography of Her First Editions* by Eric T. Brueck, London, Metropolis, 1984.

Critical Studies (selection): *Doris Lessing* by Dorothy Brewster, New York, Twayne, 1965; *Doris Lessing*, London, Longman, 1973, and *Doris Lessing's Africa*, London, Evans, 1978, New York, Holmes and Meier, 1979, both by Michael Thorpe; *Doris Lessing: Critical Studies* edited by Annis Pratt and L.S. Dembo, Madison, University of Wisconsin Press, 1974; *Notebooks/Memoirs/Archives: Reading and Re-reading Doris Lessing* edited by Jenny Taylor, London and Boston, Routledge, 1982; *Doris Lessing* by Lorna Sage, London, Methuen, 1983; *Doris Lessing* by Mona Knapp, New York, Ungar, 1984; *Doris Lessing* edited by Eve Bertelsen, Johannesburg, McGraw Hill, 1985; *Critical Essays on Doris Lessing* edited by Claire Sprague and Virginia Tiger, Boston, Hall, 1986; *Doris Lessing: The Alchemy of Survival* edited by Carey Kaplan and Ellen Cronan Rose, Athens, Ohio University Press, 1988; *Doris Lessing* by Ruth Whittaker, London, Macmillan, 1988; *Doris Lessing* by Jeannette King, London, Arnold, 1989; *Understanding Doris Lessing* by Jean Pickering, Columbia, University of South Carolina Press, 1990; *Wolf and Lessing: Breaking the Mold,* edited by Ruth Saxton and Jean Tobin, 1994; *Doris Lessing* by Margaret Moan Rowe, 1994; *Doris Lessing: The Poetics of Change* by Gayle Greene, 1994.

* * *

In any theater a deal of talent must go to waste, especially among playwrights, but it is a great pity that Doris Lessing's career as a playwright should have been abortive. One of the failures of George Devine's successful regime at the Royal Court was its not helping her to go on from *Each His Own Wilderness*, which was given a Sunday night production in 1958. Though it was dismissed by many of the critics as a novelist's play can so readily be dismissed, simply by describing it as "a novelist's play," in fact it was remarkably free from the flaws that might have been expected—flat characters, overly leisurely development, verbal analysis written out as dialogue, or lack of dramatic drive. On the contrary Lessing had a very keen instinct for how to ignite a situation theatrically.

By building the play around a mother-son conflict and empathizing successfully with the son, she steered clear of the pitfall of subordinating the other characters to the woman she could most easily identify with. Myra Bolton is an attractive middle-aged campaigner for left-wing causes, warm, well-meaning, but gauche in human relationships. She is liable to inflict unintended pain not only on her son but also on the three men in the play she has had relationships with—two of her own generation, one of her son's. The muddles and misunderstandings of these involvements are all developed in a way that contributes richly to the play's dramatic texture, and the untidiness we see on the set—the hall of her London house—contributes visually to the impression of an inability to keep things under control.

The men are all well characterized—the sad, aging, lonely politician, the architect trying to embark on a new marriage with a young girl, the opportunistic 22-year-old son of a woman friend, and above all the son Tony who returns from National Service to find that Myra did not know what day to expect him. His pained anger at his own inability to commit himself to any outside reality and at the lack of understanding between him and his mother mounts effectively throughout the play. It reaches a climax when he discovers that Myra has sold the house he loves more than anything, intending to help him by raising money to set him up on his own in a flat. It may be a well-made play, but it is made remarkably well, with an unusual talent for keeping a number of relationships simultaneously on the boil, and it catches the flavor of the life of left-wing intellectuals in the 1950s. Showing private people devoting their lives to protesting about public issues, Lessing successfully merges personal and political themes. Like the characters in John McGrath's play, these people are all "plugged-in to history."

Lessing had started writing for the theater five years earlier, in 1953, and of the three plays she turned out *Mr. Dollinger* was also produced in 1958, earlier in the year, at the Oxford Playhouse, and *The Truth about Billy Newton* was produced in 1960 at Salisbury. But the only play of hers to receive a full-scale London production was *Play with a Tiger,* which was written in 1958 and had a seven-and-a-half-week run at the Comedy in 1962.

Lessing was determined to turn her back on both naturalism and realism. "It is my intention," she wrote in a 1963 note on the play,

> that when the curtain comes down at the end, the audience will think: Of course! In this play no one lit cigarettes, drank tea or coffee, read newspapers, squirted soda into Scotch, or indulged in little bits of "business" which indicated "character." They will realize, I hope, that they have been seeing a play which relies upon its style and its language for its effect.

But it starts off naturalistically in an underfurnished room with a litter of books and cushions, paraffin heaters, a record player, and a telephone. There are also sound effects of traffic noises. Anna Freeman is a woman of "35 or so" who lives as a literary freelancer, has a son by a broken marriage, and has recently decided not to marry an Englishman who is about to settle for a safe job on a women's magazine. She is in love with an American Jew who would never settle down, and if she had been entertaining ideas of marrying him, these would be killed off in the first act by the visit of a nice young American girl who announces that she is going to have Dave's baby.

In other words the play's starting points are all naturalistic, and there is even a naturalistic cliché neighbor who fusses about an invisible cat. But toward the end of the first act the walls disappear, and though the neighbor is going to reappear and the play is still going to make gestures toward satisfying the audience's expectations that its first half hour has aroused, its center has shifted. With only a few interruptions from other characters, more than 60 pages of the 92-page script are taken up with a dialogue between Anna and Dave. But the language and the style cannot depart completely from those of the naturalistic beginning. Some of the writing in it is very good, and some of it is bad and embarrassing, especially when the characters play games reminiscent of the psychoanalytical situation.

Even the best sections of the dialogue, which make a defiant and articulate declaration of rights on behalf of the woman against the male predator, tend to generalize the play away from its roots in the specific predicament of a specific woman. In reacting against naturalism, Lessing is renouncing all of its disciplines, some of which were very useful to her in *Each His Own Wilderness*. *Play with a Tiger* may look more like a public statement, and it was seized on by feminist groups whose performances unbalanced the central relationship by failing to give Dave equal weight with Anna. Lessing complained about this in a 1972 postscript, but the fault is basically in the play. It actually is more private than *Each His Own Wilderness,* and because the dialogue is spun too directly out of personal preoccupations, it is more self-indulgent.

—Ronald Hayman

LEVY, Deborah

Nationality: British. **Born:** South Africa in 1959. **Education:** Dartington College of Arts, Devon, 1978-81, B.A. (honours) in theatre language 1981; fellow in creative arts, Trinity College, Cambridge, 1989-91. **Career:** Writer and director for MANACT Theatre Company, Cardiff and London, 1992—.

Publications

Plays

Pax (produced Edinburgh and London 1984: Baltimore, 1985). London, Methuen, 1985.
Clam (produced London, 1985). London, Methuen, 1985.
Our Lady (produced Edinburgh and London, 1986).
Heresies (produced London, 1987). With *Eva and Moses*, London, Methuen, 1987.
Eva and Moses. With *Heresies*, London, Methuen, 1987.
Blood Wedding, (libretto) adaptation of the play by Federico García Lorca (produced London, 1992). London, Novello, 1992.
The B File (also director: produced Cardiff, 1992). London, Methuen, 1992.
Call Blue Jane (produced London, 1992).
Swallowing Geography. London, Vintage, 1993.
The Unloved. London, J. Cape, 1994.
Billy and Girl. London, Bloomsbury, 1996.
Diary of a Steak. London, Books Works, 1997.

Television Plays: *Celebrating Quietly*, 1988; *Lickin' Bones*, 1990; *The Open Mouth*, 1991.

Novel

Beautiful Mutants. London, Cape, 1987; New York, Viking, 1989.

Short Stories

Ophelia and the Great Idea. London, Cape, and New York, Viking, 1986.

Poetry

An Amorous Discourse in the Suburbs of Hell. London, Cape, 1990.

Other

Walks on Water: Five Performance Texts. London, Methuen, 1992.

*

Critical Study: "Questions of Survival: Towards a Postmodern Feminist Theatre" by Irini Charitou, in *New Theatre Quarterly* (Cambridge, England), August 1993, pp. 225-32.

Deborah Levy comments:

I now mostly direct my own texts for the theatre, working with ensemble companies who come from diverse arts backgrounds and cultures. I hope to create with them as writer and director, work that is visual, visceral, kinetic, and physical.

* * *

A female world without patriarchy can be deduced from Deborah Levy's dramatic work. Its primary substances are bread, fruit, and eggs; its primary symbols are fish, the sea, and the moon; and its religion is a combination of goddess worship and the ritual aspects of Catholicism and Judaism. Female children are parented by the whole community, which is itself intergenerational and the collective guardian of a herstory of revolutionary élan as well as domestic drudgery. The wisest women are witches and eccentrics like the Keeper in *Pax* and Leah in *Heresies*. Moneymaking is the most abhorred activity; the making of art the best. Even the betrayers can be redeemed, as is Mayonnaise (*Heresies*), who is the beautiful wife and mistress, respectively, of a securities dealer (Edward) and a commercial architect (Pimm) and who forces her lover's ex-wife and child to return to Budapest. Her hair falls out, and, it is implied, she loses Pimm, but she is welcomed into the circle of women at the end who gather to hear Leah's final composition. The Domesticated Woman's presence in *Pax* is intensely resented by the fiercely independent and autocratic Keeper, but she is accepted by the other younger women—the Mourner, who is a geologist, and H. D., the hidden daughter of the Keeper but also presumably a reference to the American modernist writer Hilda Doolittle. When the Mourner leaves at the end, she gives an egg to the Domesticated Woman; it is a symbol not just of fertility but also of professional expertise, for the Mourner specializes in the egg fossils of dinosaurs. The two older women come to look on the younger generation with a wry affection. "We have," observes the Keeper, "two young women between us. Mad as nettles in a storm." In an endnote to the play Levy admits that she began by detesting what the Domesticated Woman represented and finished with respect and even liking for her. Perhaps Mary, the devout Catholic servant of Pimm, best sums up the ideal existence: "I'd like a house with a garden and a tree." Active, mobile women are respected in the plays, but the settings are all interiors, with rapid movements of flight or travel made either in retrospect or prospect.

Such matters, along with emotionally numb men and distracted hunts for fathers and mothers, are the commonplaces of second-wave feminist utopias. Indeed, there are distinct echoes of the first, Edwardian wave. The posed eccentricity of Leah playing the piano in a hat rimmed with lighted candles and of her companion Violet trampling a tub of grapes recalls the desperate bohemianism of Gudrun and Ursula in *Women in Love*. Mayonnaise's staccato statements of inconsequent desires ("I want to be a Catholic") echo the disjointed utterances of Evelyn Waugh's Agatha Runcible, and H. D., with her fishing rod and her cigars, can trace her ancestry back to Una Troubridge and Vita Sackville-West. But Levy defamiliarizes these themes by a persistent preoccupation with Eastern Europe as both the site of terrible history and of a more humane community. In *Clam* the domestic couple Alice and Harry, who double as Lenin and Krupskaya, another domestic couple, play out a history of the defeat of revolution. As in *Heresies*, a fish tank is a key prop, a cornucopia of objects to provoke fantasies. Alice imagines the sea bringing in Poland and Latvia and other Eastern-bloc countries like fish so that "a little boy kissed the Ukraine . . . a woman in a bikini put Poland on her belly." For Cholla, a domestic cleaner and the mother of Pimm's child, Hungary is her lost homeland of song and fecundity, a culture she rejected for that of the frozen English and to which she now wishes to return. Leah remembers the Russians as beautiful in their revolution, and the Keeper counterpoints a refrain of "I want to go back to Vienna/Prague etc." with horrific recollections of the Holocaust. Cholla fled from Hungary at the age of 17 because of the claustrophobia of family life, but now she dreams of her mother standing on Liberty Bridge "in her red shoes . . . calling me." Cholla sums up East/West relations in the prescient line "The West only likes Eastern Europe when she cries."

Levy is both of and not of the performance art movement of the 1980s. She has an interest in visual theater, and her symbol for the imagined funeral of H. D.'s father, one bright light on a polished marble column, effectively condenses a multiplicity of signs. Music strains to become a language in its own right under Leah's promptings, and the abrupt emotional shifts of Mayonnaise and Krupskaya are typical of the distrust of continuous narrative in much performance art. But Levy also has a traditional interest in plot and character conflict. The histories that are recounted indicate a concern for verbal language that many performance artists would consider quite outmoded. One suspects that Levy is struggling to reconcile her commitment to a distinctive female voice in theater with her determination to find her own voice. Too often her characters, particularly male, mouth attitudes rather than dramatize situations. With the decline of feminism and the collapse of communism she will be forced back onto her own linguistic resources, although, in true postmodernist fashion, she may find her way to them through the words of others. Her libretto version of Lorca's *Blood Wedding* for the Women's Theatre Trust would seem to indicate just this.

—Tony Dunn

LILL, Wendy

Nationality: Canadian. **Born:** Vancouver, 1950. **Family:** Married; two children. **Career:** Writer for magazines, radio, film, television, and stage. **Awards:** ACTRA award, for Radio Documentary, 1981; Floyd S. Chalmers Canadian Play award nomination, 1989; Governor General's Literary award for drama finalist, 1987, 1996.

Publications

Plays

The Fighting Days (produced 1982). Vancouver, Talon Books, 1985.

The Occupation of Heather Rose (produced 1985). In *NeWest Plays for Women,* Edmonton, NeWest Publishers, 1987.

Memories of You (produced Winnipeg, 1988). Blizzard Publishing, 1989.

Sisters (produced Parrsboro, Nova Scotia, 1989). Vancouver, Talon Books, 1991.

All Fall Down (produced Edmonton, 1993). Vancouver, Talon Books, 1994.

Glace Bay Miners Museum (produced 1995). Vancouver, Talon Books, 1996.

*

Critical Study: "The Glace Bay Miners' Museum by Wendy Lill" by Joanne Tompkins, in *Australasian Studies* (Queensland), October 1996, pp. 115-54.

* * *

Wendy Lill's plays typically present "a strong woman squaring off against an apparently immovable force over an issue with clear currency in the world beyond the theatre," writes Robert Everett-Green. Her recurring subject, in her own words, is "How did these women get the courage to do what they wanted to do?" Writing from a moderate feminist standpoint, she may be the leading Canadian dramatist with an overt social conscience.

After *On the Line,* based on a strike by immigrant women in Winnipeg, Lill wrote *The Fighting Days,* portraying women's struggle for the vote in Manitoba before and during World War I. Specifically, the subject is Francis Beynon, usually overshadowed by the more famous campaigner Nellie McClung. Beynon, a visionary, is shown relating to her sister, to the man she loves, and also to causes and to her career. Kim McCaw, who directed the first production, in Winnipeg, describes the drama as a "portrait of courage and integrity." The need for contemporary women to fight too is implicit.

In the powerful monologue *The Occupation of Heather Rose* a young nurse describes her experiences and disillusion in a northern native reserve, an environment of snow, alcohol, boredom, and loneliness. While the monologue is revealing about relations between whites, who are often well-meaning, and First Nations people, *Occupation* also presents Rose's self-discovery as she comes to terms with herself as an adult and discovers her attitudes toward poverty and indigenous people.

Memories of You, Lill's least political work, is linked with others by its focus on the dilemmas faced by women in the 20th century. The subject is Elizabeth Smart, known for her novel *By Grand Central Station I Sat Down and Wept* and for her lifelong passionate love for the English poet George Barker. Although she had four children by Barker, he moved erratically in and out of her life. Lill has explained, "Because the play is about memory, both the sets and the scenes have the unfinished floating qualities of memories." The merits of *Memories* have been disputed. Judith Fitzgerald, for example, found it "a rather passionless play with a handful of selfish and one-dimensional figures," while Reg Skene judged it to be "Lill's most mature and effectively written play."

Sisters is associated with the previous drama as, in Lill's words, "a reconstruction/memory play." The issue here is the widely publicized one of abuse in native residential schools. The form is intriguing. A nun, charged in 1969 with setting fire to the school where she had worked, is questioned by her lawyer. The nun discovers her true feelings as she recalls how nearly 20 years earlier she had entered the order and come to accept the school's tyrannical ways. Lill's particular spin is in showing the nuns to have been almost as victimized as the children they abused.

The issue in *All Fall Down* is again abuse of the young, this time at a day care center, with unanswered questions about what really happened. Lill is not simply looking at a much discussed current issue but rather is showing the development of a witch-hunt, similar to that in Arthur Miller's *The Crucible*. She remarks that the point is "protecting the search for truth in a society in great upheaval." The narrative unfolds ingeniously with only four characters. A neurotic single mother, uneasy about her child, goes to a social worker, who initiates an inquiry. A man is convinced of the innocence of the unseen day care worker, but his wife is undecided. Lill insists that the man is the key: "It is the story of a man struggling to hold his family together and understand the truth in the midst of the growing intolerance and hysteria which surrounds him."

The Glace Bay Miner's Museum, based on a short story of the same title by Sheldon Currie, tells of life in the coal mines of Cape Breton in Nova Scotia in the 1940s and of the surviving Scottish heritage. Two women, mother and daughter, are central, the girl finally defying the limited roles assigned to women in this society. The later drama *Corker* presents a woman deputy minister who is engaged in reducing government services and whose sister gives her responsibility for a mentally handicapped man.

Lill decided to act on her principles, and she ran successfully in the 1997 election to become the New Democrat M.P. for Dartmouth, Nova Scotia. She has stated that she will not write plays while she is an M.P., and so we will have to wait for further explorations of heroic women and of problems in society.

—Malcolm Page

LINNEY, Romulus

Nationality: American. **Born:** Philadelphia, Pennsylvania, in 1930. **Education:** Oberlin College, Ohio, A.B. 1953; Yale University School of Drama, New Haven, Connecticut, M.F.A. 1958. **Military Service:** Served in the United States Army, 1954-56. **Career:** Actor and director in stock for 6 years; stage manager, Actors Studio, New York, 1960; has taught at the Manhattan School of Music, University of North Carolina, Chapel Hill, University of Pennsylvania, Philadelphia, Brooklyn College, Princeton University, New Jersey, Columbia University, New York, Hunter College, New York, and Connecticut College, New London. Currently teaching at The New School University, New York. Lives in New York City. **Awards:** National Endowment for the Arts grant, 1974; Obie award, 1980, for sustained achievement, 1992; Guggenheim fellowship, 1980; Mishima prize, for fiction, 1981; American Academy award, 1984; Rockefeller fellowship, 1986; American Theater Critics Association award, 1988, 1990; Helen Hayes award, 1990. Honorary degrees: Oberlin College, Ohio, 1994; Appalachian State University, 1996; Wake Forest University, 1998. **Member:** Dramatists Guild; fellowship of Southern Writers; American Academy of Arts and Letters. **Agent:** Peter Hagen, The Gersh Agency, 130 West 42th Street #1000, New York, New York 10036, U.S.A.

Publications

Plays

The Sorrows of Frederick (produced Los Angeles, 1967; Birmingham, 1970; New York, 1976). New York, Harcourt Brace, 1966.

The Love Suicide at Schofield Barracks (produced New York, 1972). With *Democracy and Esther*, New York, Harcourt Brace, 1973; one-act version (produced Louisville, 1984), in *The Best Short Plays 1986*, edited by Ramon Delgado, New York, Applause, 1986.
Democracy and Esther, adaptation of the novels by Henry Adams (as *Democracy*, produced Richmond, Virginia, 1974; revised version produced Milwaukee, 1975). With *The Love Suicide at Schofield Barracks*, New York, Harcourt Brace, 1973; as *Democracy*, New York, Dramatists Play Service, 1976.
Holy Ghosts (produced New York, 1974). With *The Sorrows of Frederick*, New York, Harcourt Brace, 1977.
Appalachia Sounding (produced on tour, 1975).
Old Man Joseph and His Family (produced New York, 1977). New York, Dramatists Play Service, 1978.
Childe Byron (produced Richmond, Virginia, 1977; revised version produced Louisville, New York, and London, 1981). New York, Dramatists Play Service, 1981.
Just Folks (produced New York, 1978).
The Death of King Philip, music by Paul Earls (produced Boston, 1979). New York, Dramatists Play Service, 1984.
Tennessee (produced New York, 1979). New York, Dramatists Play Service, 1980.
El Hermano (produced New York, 1981). New York, Dramatists Play Service, 1981.
The Captivity of Pixie Shedman (produced New York, 1981). New York, Dramatists Play Service, 1981.
Goodbye, Howard (produced New York, 1982). Included in *Laughing Stock*, 1984.
F.M. (also director: produced Philadelphia, 1982; New York, 1984). Included in *Laughing Stock*, 1984.
April Snow (produced Costa Mesa, California, 1983; New York, 1987). Included in *Three Plays*, 1989.
Laughing Stock (includes *Goodbye, Howard*; *F.M.*; *Tennessee*) (produced New York, 1984). New York, Dramatists Play Service, 1984.
Wrath, in *Faustus in Hell* (produced Princeton, New Jersey, 1985).
Sand Mountain (includes *Sand Mountain Matchmaking* and *Why the Lord Come to Sand Mountain*) (produced New York, 1986). New York, Dramatists Play Service, 1985.
A Woman Without a Name (produced Denver, 1986). New York, Dramatists Play Service, 1986.
Pops (includes *Can Can, Claire de Lune, Ave Maria, Gold and Silver Waltz, Battle Hymn of the Republic, Songs of Love*) (produced New York, 1986). New York, Dramatists Play Service, 1987; *Ave Maria* produced as *Hrosvitha* in *Three Poets*, 1989.
Heathen Valley, adaptation of his own novel (produced Denver, 1986). New York, Dramatists Play Service, 1988.
Yancey (produced New York, 1988). Included in *Three Plays*, 1989.
Juliet (produced New York, 1988). Included in *Three Plays*, 1989.
Pageant, with others, music and lyrics by Michael Rice (produced Little Rock, Arkansas, 1988).
Precious Memories, adaptation of a story by Chekhov (also director: produced New York, 1988); as *Unchanging Love* (produced New York, 1991), New York, Dramatists Play Service, 1991.
Three Plays (includes *Juliet, Yancey, April Snow*). New York, Dramatists Play Service, 1989.
Three Poets (includes *Komachi, Hrosvitha, Akhmatova*; also director: produced New York, 1989). New York, Dramatists Play Service, 1990.
2 (produced Louisville, 1990). Included in *Six Plays*, 1993.
Ambrosio (produced New York, 1992). Included in *Seventeen Short Plays*, 1992.
Seventeen Short Plays (includes *Ambrosio*; *The Love Suicide at Schofield Barracks*; *Sand Mountain Matchmaking*; *Why the Lord Come to Sand Mountain*; *Komachi, Hrosvitha*; *Akhmatova*; *Can Can*; *Claire de Lune*; *Gold and Silver Waltz*; *Songs of Love*; *Juliet, Yancey*; *The Death of King Philip*; *El Hermano*; *The Captivity of Pixie Shedman*; *Goodbye; Howard*). Newbury, Vermont, Smith and Kraus, 1992.
Six Plays (includes *F.M.*; *Childe Byron*; *Tennessee*; *2*;*April Snow*; *Heathen Valley*). New York, Theatre Communications Group, 1993.
Spain (produced New York, 1993). New York, Dramatists Play Service, 1994.
Shotgun (produced Stamford, Connecticut, 1995).
Oscar over Here (produced New York, 1995).
True Crimes (produced New York, 1996). New York, Dramatists Play Service, 1996.

Television Plays: *The 34th Star*, 1976; episodes for *Feelin' Good* series, 1976-77.

Novels

Heathen Valley. New York, Atheneum, 1962; London, Cassell, 1963.
Slowly, By Thy Hand Unfurled. New York, Harcourt Brace, 1965; London, Cassell, 1966.
Jesus Tales. San Francisco, North Point Press, 1980.

Other

Ten Plays for Radio. Minneapolis, Burgess, 1954.

Editor, with Norman A. Bailey and Domenick Cascio, *Radio Classics*. Minneapolis, Burgess, 1956.

*

Manuscript Collection: Lincoln Center Library for the Performing Arts, New York.

Critical Studies: "An Interview with Romulus Linney" by Don B. Wilmeth, in *Studies in American Drama, 1945-Present* (Columbus, Ohio), 1987, pp. 71-84; "Romulus Linney" by John L. DiGaetani, in *A Search for a Postmodern Theatre: Interviews with Contemporary Playwrights*, edited by John L. DiGaetani, New York, Greenwood, 1991; "The Low-Down on a High Place: Family Matters in Heathen Valley" by D.F. Hurley, in *Appalachian Journal: A Regional Studies Review* (Boone, North Carolina), Winter 1993, pp. 176-81; "Storyteller in the Wilderness: The American Imagination of Romulus Linney" by James F. Schlatter, in *The Southern Quarterly: A Journal of the Arts in the South* (Hattiesburg, Missouri), Winter 1994, pp. 63-78; "Romulus Linney" by Don B. Wilmeth, in *Speaking on Stage: Interviews with Contemporary American Playwrights*, Tuscaloosa, University of Alabama Press, 1996.

Theatrical Activities:
Director: **Plays**— *F.M.*, Philadelphia, 1982; *Sand Mountain Matchmakers*, New York, 1989; *F.M.*, Philadelphia, 1982; *Sand Moun-*

tain, Montclair, New Jersey, 1985; *Love suicide at Schofield Barracks,* New York, 1991; *True Crimes,* New York, 1996.

Romulus Linney comments:

My plays and novels are drawn from either historical subjects or memories of my childhood in Tennessee and North Carolina, or direct personal experiences.

* * *

Romulus Linney has worked at the writer's trade as playwright, novelist, and television scriptwriter. His dramatic writing has garnered awards and resulted in more than 15 plays produced on and off Broadway, in American regional theaters, and in other countries. Ranging widely in subject and structure, Linney's plays show him to be a distinctive writer of uncommon literacy.

Linney often develops in his dramas a pattern of action in which his protagonists enter into or mature in environments where they confront values repressive of their own worth as individuals. Usually tempted or victimized by such values, the characters experience them while testing or evaluating them against their own needs and beliefs, ultimately reaching a decision to accept or reject them. This pattern is evident in at least six plays: *The Love Suicide at Schofield Barracks, Democracy, Holy Ghosts, A Woman without a Name, Tennessee,* and *The Sorrows of Frederick.*

Within the framework of a military inquiry, *The Love Suicide at Schofield Barracks* reveals the events behind the bizarre double suicide in 1970 of an army general and his wife in Hawaii. As witnesses testify, a compassionate portrait emerges of a patriotic professional soldier whose beliefs become so shattered by Vietnam that with his wife he perpetrates—in the guise of a classic Japanese drama—a ritualistic suicide expressing disapproval of the war and America's conduct. The play generates considerable tension as the event is finally pieced together, and it makes a strong statement about war and individual responsibility for national morality. The author also has written an equally powerful one-act version that preserves the original's skillfully orchestrated characters.

Democracy, a combined dramatization of two of Henry Adams's 19th-century novels, introduces a wealthy widow and an agnostic photographer, two attractive and intelligent women who enter Washington's 1875 presidential society during the corruption-ridden Grant administration. They are individually charmed, courted, and proposed to by two attractive men of high station whose beliefs they abhor, and they courageously reject the men and leave Washington. Major characters are richly drawn, and the values of 19th-century American democracy are examined in a manner both provocative and dramatic.

In *Holy Ghosts* a runaway wife flees a boorish husband to find sanctuary with a Pentecostal sect whose members seek redemption from self-loathing by surviving the handling of poisonous snakes. When the husband angrily comes to reclaim his newly converted wife and lets his low self-esteem turn him into a convert during the cult's ritual, the wife abandons the sect, resolving to achieve independence and self-realization. This theatrically intriguing drama of redemption colorfully re-creates its rural southern milieu and its dispossessed.

Also rising above domestic strife and despair by achieving self-recognition is the title character in *A Woman without a Name,* a drama adapted from Linney's novel *Slowly, by Thy Hand Unfurled.* The woman is an uneducated, small-town southern wife and mother tormented both by her turn-of-the-century family's afflictions and by its unfair calumny of her regarding its travails. With despairing self-doubt she records memories of family experiences in a journal as characters come forward to reenact events and interact with her as participant. She becomes progressively literate and liberated as she absolves herself of guilt and discovers her self-worth in a starkly yet imaginatively conceived portrait of feminine endurance and self-discovery.

Similarly effective is the Obie-winning *Tennessee,* which portrays an elderly 1870s Appalachian woman, her family's sole survivor, who recalls her youth and realizes that her late husband cheated her of independence by tricking her into the stern service of a frontier marriage. The richly rounded protagonist and vividly detailed exposition create a definitive world of the past with parallels to the present. Appearing in a short-play trilogy collectively entitled *Laughing Stock, Tennessee* accompanies two effective comedies—*Goodbye, Howard,* about three sisters' confused deathwatch over a brother, and *F.M.*, focusing on a talented rough-diamond student writer who shocks dilettante classmates in a creative writing course.

The Sorrows of Frederick offers a psychological portrait of Prussia's philosopher-king Frederick the Great. In a series of sharply etched scenes, Linney unravels the chronicle of a father-dominated prince who as a king forsakes great artistic and intellectual gifts to pursue power and finds himself a victim of his life at its end. Enriched by elevated dramatic language and fully rounded characterizations, the drama revivifies Frederick and, like the aforementioned dramas, exemplifies Linney's concern with characters who resolve their destinies by their choice of values. Treating a less regal tyrant, *2* thoughtfully examines the character of Hermann Göring during the 1945-46 Nuremberg trials as he reveals the self-deception and unrepentant Nazi prejudices existing within all nations and all would-be world conquerors.

Apparent in Linney's work is a penchant for comedy, romance, and the one-act form, which is demonstrated by two collective works of short plays, *Sand Mountain* and *Pops*. Strong in homespun humor, *Sand Mountain* encompasses two Appalachian folklore yarns about, respectively, a discriminating young widow who rejects a bragging band of eligible men for a truth-telling widower and the visit of Jesus and Saint Peter, in human disguise, to a mountaineer family. *Pops,* consisting of six comically rich one-acts, treats forms of love, young and old, from the romantic to the aesthetic. Among the collection's funniest works are those of a romance between oldsters that is opposed by their progeny (*Songs of Love*) and a 10th-century abbess's defense of Hrosvitha's and her own right to create art (*Ave Maria*). The latter, retitled *Hrosvitha,* accompanies *Komachi,* an adapted Japanese No drama, and *Akhmatova,* demonstrating the Russian poetess's calm ethical courage in confronting a Stalinist inquisition, in an admirable short-play collection entitled *Three Poets*.

Two later works in a darker mode trenchantly depict the tight rural world of Appalachia. *Unchanging Love,* based on a Chekhov story and formerly entitled *Precious Memories,* exposes the corruption and lack of social compassion within a merchant family. In Linney's adaptation of his novel *Heathen Valley,* the narrator-protagonist disavows and opposes church hierarchy and dogmatism to advocate his community's need for social goodness. Also set in Appalachia, *True Crimes* (1996), adapted from Tolstoi's *The Power of Darkness,* details the degradation of a young, shiftless backwoods stud motivated by greed and lust and by murderous maternal advice. He beds a married neighbor, poisons her husband, impregnates the dead man's daughter, and kills the offspring. When guilt strikes him, he rejects confession for fear of endangering a profitable marriage. Critics have been reservedly supportive of this play of amorality, with some praising Linney for never turning his Appalachian characters into caricatures or sentimentalized pastels.

Two further plays of the 1990s represent a departure in subject and setting. *Spain* encompasses three playlets (*Torquemada, Anna Rey, Escobedo de la Aixa)* that are linked by the 15th-century Abbot Escobedo, who humanely treats the insane and is persecuted by the Spanish Inquisition, which desecrates his memory after his death. His life provides an example that restores a depressed psychiatrist to normalcy. *Spain* compels a probative look at religiosity and crises of conscience. Also treating the Inquisition, *Ambrosio* centers on a 16th-century monk condemned to burning because his vows of celibacy did not withstand temptations. The drama, adapted from Matthew Lewis's *The Monk,* deftly touches contemporary concerns with sexuality and crises of faith.

A writer of substance and range, Linney creates plays that crackle with challenging issues and theatricality and that, by the spectrum of their structural variety, evince an imaginative craftsman. He is a major talent among contemporary dramatists.

—Christian H. Moe

LOCHHEAD, Liz

Nationality: Scottish. **Born:** Motherwell, Lanarkshire, 26 December 1947. **Education:** Dalziel High School, Motherwell, 1960-65; Glasgow School of Art, 1965-70, diploma in art. **Career:** Art teacher at Bishopbriggs High School, Glasgow, and other schools in Glasgow and Bristol. **Awards:** BBC Scotland prize, 1971; Scottish Arts Council award, 1973, and fellowship, 1978. **Address:** 11 Kersland Street, Glasgow G12 8BW, Scotland.

PUBLICATIONS

Plays

Blood and Ice (produced Edinburgh, 1982; revised version, produced London, 1984). Edinburgh, Salamander Press, 1982; New York, Methuen, 1983.
Tickly Mince (revue), with Tom Leonard and Alisdair Gray (produced Glasgow, 1982).
The Pie of Damocles (revue), with others (produced Glasgow, 1983).
A Bunch of Fives, with Tom Leonard and Sean Hardie (produced Glasgow, 1983).
Silver Service. Edinburgh, Salamander Press, 1984.
Dracula, adaptation of the novel by Bram Stoker (produced Edinburgh, 1985). With *Mary Queen of Scots Got Her Head Chopped Off*, London, Penguin, 1989.
Tartuffe, adaptation of the play by Molière (produced Edinburgh, 1985). Edinburgh, Polygon, 1985.
Mary Queen of Scots Got Her Head Chopped Off (produced Edinburgh and London, 1987). With *Dracula*, London, Penguin, 1989.
The Big Picture (produced Glasgow, 1988).
Patter Merchant (produced Edinburgh, 1989).
Jock Tamson's Bairns, with Gerry Mulgrew (produced Glasgow, 1990).
Quelques Fleurs (produced Edinburgh and London, 1991).

Screenplay: *Now and Then*, 1972.

Radio Play: *Blood and Ice*, 1990.

Television Play: *Sweet Nothings* in *End of the Line* series, 1984.

Poetry

Memo for Spring. Edinburgh, Reprographia, 1972.
The Grimm Sisters. London, Next Editions, 1981.
Dreaming Frankenstein, and Collected Poems. Edinburgh, Polygon, 1984.
True Confessions and New Clichés. Edinburgh, Polygon, 1985.
Bagpipe Muzak. London, Penguin, 1991.

*

Critical Studies: "Feminist Nationalism in Scotland: *Mary Queen of Scots Got Her Head Chopped Off*" by Ilona S. Koren-Deutsch, in *Modern Drama* (Toronto), September 1992; *Liz Lochhead's Voices,* edited by Robert Crawford, Edinburgh, Edinburgh University Press, 1993; "Desire and Difference in Liz Lochhead's *Dracula*" by Jennifer Harvie, in *Essays in Theatre Etudes* (Canada), May 1993, pp. 133-43; "The Devil Is Beautiful: *Dracula:* Freudian Novel and Feminist Drama" by Jan McDonald, in *Novel Images: Literature in Performance,* edited by Peter Reynolds, London, Routledge, 1993; "The Mirror and the Vamp: Liz Lochhead" by Anne Varty, in *A History of Scottish Women's Writing,* edited by Douglas Gifford and Dorothy McMillan, Edinburgh, Edinburgh University Press, 1997.

Theatrical Activities:
Actor: **Play**—*The Complete Alternative History of the World, Part 1*, Edinburgh, 1986.

* * *

> Once upon a time there were *twa queens* on the wan green island, and the wan green island was split inty two kingdoms. But no equal kingdoms, naebody in their richt mind would insist on that.
>
> —La Corbie, *Mary Queen of Scots Got Her Head Chopped Off*

Liz Lochhead is a teller of tales, the author of strongly narrative plays, dramatic monologues, and poetry. The stories she recounts are often drawn from popular memory and folk culture but are retold with a distinctively female voice. History, myth, and memory interconnect and are analyzed and deconstructed in a body of work that finds reference in both literary and popular culture. In common with other contemporary women writers Lochhead has been attracted to the images and the conventions of the gothic and has discovered in fairy tales and in childhood rhymes a new set of metaphors for the role of women in society. Like Angela Carter, Lochhead twists the familiar to find a dark and bloody unconscious with new perspectives on the assumed truths of our society.

Lochhead's plays retell the stories of Mary Shelley and Frankenstein, Mary Queen of Scots and Elizabeth I, Tartuffe, and Dracula with a compelling mix of traditional Scots, contemporary vernacular dialogue, and a subtle lyricism that contemporary theater writing often effaces in favor of bald realism. Lochhead is not afraid to mix the prosaic and the poetic in one play, one scene, one speech. This combination brings to her already credible and recognizable characters new heights of tragedy or pathos. In *Quelques Fleurs* the extended monologues of Verena and Derek, her husband who works on an oil rig—characters as recognizable in a Scottish context as Mike Leigh's characters are within English culture—are written in a mordantly idiomatic and scathingly witty prose to blackly comic effect.

Across a range of genres and subjects Lochhead writes about women and about monsters. Rarely, however, does she write about monstrous women. Focusing on the experiences of women in history, in literature, and in the contemporary world, Lochhead's writing uncovers society's fears of the *unheimlich* aspects of the feminine. Her plays foreground the social and domestic and the sexual and creative roles of women within societies that politically and culturally marginalize and devalue their work and their lives. Lochhead takes the common view of these women—Mary as femme fatale and Elizabeth as scheming politician in *Mary Queen of Scots Got Her Head Chopped Off* and Mary Shelley as daughter of Mary Wollstonecraft and William Godwin and lover and wife of Percy Bysshe Shelley, with Elise as mere downtrodden maid, in *Blood and Ice*—and peels back the mythology to draw out the essential humanity of the person. She strives to find in each of her creations a more empowering identity than has traditionally been projected.

Lochhead's plays reset the role of women within both historical and contemporary society with a ubiquity of language that draws on her skills as poet and performer. The subjects of her plays may be historically diverse, but they are united by an energetic, vibrant, and precise use of language.

Blood and Ice, her first full-length play, was achieved after several revisions. It is essentially a memory play with characters and spirits emerging from the life and imagination of Mary Shelley. Time, place, and degree of reality are all signaled in the prose and the verse of the text. In a play dealing with Mary Shelley's creativity and the writing process, with commentary on the lives of both Shelley and Byron, there is a deliberate overemphasis on the importance of words. Language is used to mark shifts in time and space and in memory and imagination. Variations in tone suggest in turn the lyricism of the idyll of Lake Geneva, the artificiality of the conversation and society of Mary's romantic companions, the prosaic language of domestic duties and responsibilities, and the obsessive and violent nature of her imagination and her creativity.

The nature and value of creativity is also examined by presenting alternative visions of Mary Shelley as mother and author. The process of writing the novel is mirrored in her role as mother to her children and in her increasingly maternal relationships with Shelley and her half sister Claire and as creator of the fiction of *Frankenstein*. This is further compared to the character of Frankenstein bringing life to his monster. Society's restricting expectations of roles of wife/lover and mother are described as problematic, particularly to the creative and powerful woman. *Blood and Ice* shows that society demands a heavy price from the woman who steps outside the framework of family and wants to be more than muse to another's imagination. At the end of the play Mary Shelley may be left isolated and alone, but Lochhead has recovered her and her life from a distraction of myths and received ideas to posit an impression of her heroine as a person, as a mother, and as a writer in her own right.

As with *Blood and Ice*, the demands of society upon woman to be wife and mother is a central theme of *Mary Queen of Scots Got Her Head Chopped Off*. In this play, however, the dramatic conflict is not played out in private places or in the psyche of one woman but in the public sphere and in the political conflicts of two nations. La Corbie, the play's narrator, chorus, and sometime conscience, poses the central riddle of the play: ". . . I ask you, when's a queen a queen/And when's a queen juist a wummin?"

Plays like *Blood and Ice*, *Mary Queen of Scots Got Her Head Chopped Off*, and *Dracula*, although written with a strongly narrative spine, are structurally dense, with complex layerings of temporal, geographic, and psychological spaces. Lochhead uses doubling with psychological intent, actors being required to play two, three, or even four different but fundamentally linked characters. Mary and Elizabeth are matched at each step by parallel and complementary characters, each time played by the same actors. The pairings of the maids Marian and Bessie, the beggars Mairn and Leezie, and the children Marie and Wee Betty reveal another facet of Lochhead's project to show the similarities in the problems faced by Mary and Elizabeth in particular but also by other women both in the time frame of the drama and in our own age.

Scottish theater writing is often criticized for its essential nostalgia and preoccupation with the nation's history, and certainly *Mary Queen of Scots Got Her Head Chopped Off* is a play about a privileged moment in Scotland's political development. Typical of Lochhead, however, the play energizes the discourse of nostalgia through the use of rhymes and games. It uses doppelgänger for all the main players in the drama and an omnipresent narrator who speaks in an eclectic version of sixteenth-century Scots and also introduces parallel scenes within contemporary culture. Her use of the past is very much more precise and focused, however, than is the case with plays that offer a more straightforward version of historical drama. Lochhead sets out to reinterpret the past and to draw out a new and political agenda for contemporary audiences. She mixes the introspection of much of Scottish culture with a desire to develop a new set of images and a new system of metaphors for the depiction of domestic and psychological drama. The activation of memory as well as history is again reflected in her use of language. The play ends with the characters of the drama transformed into children playing a demonic game in which Mary/Marie is again the victim of prejudice and group hysteria.

Just as the received images society holds of Mary Shelley are dissected in *Blood and Ice*, so in *Mary Queen of Scots Got Her Head Chopped Off* Lochhead reexamines the mythology associated with both Mary and Elizabeth. She again finds disturbing parallels between the demands made of the women in the play and the prejudices that still limit their expectations and ambitions. The play functions as an explicit metaphor for contemporary society.

Lochhead's plays reexamine the deeply rooted prejudices and assumptions held by our culture. Using the conventions of historical drama in *Mary Queen of Scots Got Her Head Chopped Off*, restoring the real horror and tragedy of *Dracula*, and revealing the isolation of women as different as Mary Shelley and Verena,

Lochhead rewrites the myths of our culture to reinstate the experiences and the voices of women.

—Adrienne Scullion

LONG, Quincy

Nationality: American. **Born:** Youngstown, Ohio, 26 October 1945. **Education:** Hiram College, Hiram, Ohio, 1967-70, B.A. in 1970; Yale Drama School, New Haven, Connecticut, 1983-86, M.F.A. in 1986. **Military Service:** USMCR, 1963-69. **Family:** Married 1986. **Career:** Reporter, *Painesville Telegraph*, Painesville, Ohio, 1971-73; tech director, School of Fine Arts, Willoughby, Ohio, 1973-76; actor, New York, 1976-83. Professional writer, 1983—, living in New York. Guest lecturer, University of California at San Diego, 1992. **Agent:** Scott Yoselow.

Publications

Plays

The Sex Organ (produced 1982).
Bascombe & Bascombe (produced 1983).
Korea (produced 1983).
The Johnstown Vindicator (produced New York, 1984). New York, Dramatists Play Service, 1989.
Yokohama Duty (produced New York, 1985).
Something About Baseball (produced New York,1985).
Instructions to the Phantom of the Opera (produced Brooklyn, New York, 1985).
The Virgin Molly (produced Berkeley, 1986).
Shaker Heights (produced Washington D.C., 1986; New York, 1994).
Dirty Work (produced 1987).
Whole Hearted (produced 1989).
The Year of the Baby (produced 1989).
The Adventures of Por Quinly, musical for children (produced 1991).
Gamboling on the Game, musical (produced San Francisco, 1994).
The Joy of Going Somewhere Definite (produced New York, 1996). New York, Dramatists Play Service, 1998.
The Song of the Carpet (produced 1996).
The Sixth Floor Museum (produced 1998).
The Lively Lad (produced 1998).

Screenplays: *Marlon Brando's Roommate,* 1986; *The Miami Messiah,* 1993.

Television Plays: *The Sportswriter,* adaptation of Richard Ford novel, 1988; *The Man Who Fell In Love with a Pigeon,* 1988.

* * *

Whether writing about subjects as varied as consumerism, gender identity, baseball, political corruption, or romance, Quincy Long zeroes in on the follies of contemporary men and women but understands their frailties and strengths as well. With a canny awareness of the absurdities of human behavior, he spoofs social mores in plays that flirt with the bizarre yet never entirely depart from traditional emotional values. His writing, too, is firmly traditional; he eschews abstraction and experimentation, and although his perspective is always slightly askew, his work is never truly threatening and is accessible to a wide audience.

Long's themes are as all-American as his treatment of them is irreverent. In his full-length comedy, *Yokohama Duty*, for example, the plot centers on the revelation of the identity of the unknown soldier—a subject Long handles without a trace of heaviness or cliché. His one-act piece, *Something About Baseball,* puts a fresh new twist on America's favorite pastime: a German intellectual baseball fan wants to break into the major leagues. Long tweaks convention but with cheekiness rather than contempt.

Several of Long's plays focus on romantic themes, and the playwright is adept at exposing both the exhilaration and the absurdity of mating rituals and human bonding. In *The Joy of Going Somewhere Definite,* which Long wrote originally as a radio play, characters go through several strange levels of emotional involvement. Three unemployed loggers in Minnesota encounter a drunken man who offends them. After they shoot the stranger, they discover a note from his wife who has abandoned him and run off to Canada with a new lover. This outrages the loggers even more, but when the trio sets out to reunite the victim with his wife, nothing goes quite as planned. Although the pace of the action sometimes lags, the play is always engaging. Both wildly absurd and quietly moving, it reflects what Peter Marks of the *New York Times* considered to be "a truly original sensibility."

Although he has written several domestic comedies, Long is no stranger to more controversial themes. *The Virgin Molly,* for example, which debuted at the Berkeley Repertory Theatre in 1990, explores the delicate issue of homosexuality in the Marine Corps. Quincy's *A Por Quinly Christmas* is nothing less than a full-scale attack on rampant commercialism, set during that most sacred shopping season, Christmas. In this scathingly funny one-hour musical, the play's hero, the young Por Quinly, is whisked off to his first shopping mall by a talking Christmas tree. At the mall the evil Doktor Shopperlifter imprisons the boy, while Quinly's father, a political radical, reluctantly plays Santa Claus as part of his community service sentence for prior civil disobedience. Although the play's anticommercial message is certainly blunt—perhaps to a fault—its humor reaches occasional heights of incisive satiric irreverence and absurdity.

—Elizabeth Shostak

LOVELACE, Earl

Nationality: Trinidadian. **Born:** Toco, Trinidad, 13 July 1935. **Education:** Scarborough Methodist primary school, Tobago; Nelson Street boys Roman Catholic school, Port of Spain; Ideal High School, 1948-53; Eastern Caribbean Institute of Agriculture and Forestry, Centeno, Trinidad, 1961-62; Johns Hopkins University, M.A. in English 1974. **Family:** Married; three children. **Career:** Proofreader, *Trinidad Guardian,* 1953-54; field assistant and agriculture assistant, Department of Agriculture, 1956-66; editorial writer, columnist and reviewer, *Trinidad and Tobago Express,* 1967-71; lecturer, University of the District of Columbia, Washington, D.C., and visiting novelist, Johns Hopkins University, 1971-73; teacher of creative writing and literature, University of the West Indies, St. Augustine, 1977. Writer-in-residence, Howard University, Washington, D.C., 1966-67; participant in the International Writing Program, University of Iowa, 1980; writer-in-residence, Hartwick College, Oneonta, New York, 1986. **Awards:** British Petroleum Independence Literary award, 1964, for *While Gods Are Falling*; Pegasus Literary award for outstanding contributions to the arts in Trinidad and Tobago, 1966; Guggenheim fellowship, 1980. **Agent:** c/o Andre Deutsch, 105 Great Russell Street, London WC1B 3LJ, England.

Publications

Plays

The New Boss (produced Trinidad, 1962).
My Name Is Village (produced Port of Spain, 1976).
Pierrot Ginnard (produced 1977).
Jestina's Calypso (produced Trinidad, 1978; revised production Northhampton, Massachusetts, 1988).
The New Hardware Store (produced London, 1985).
Jestina's Calypso and Other Plays (includes *The New Hardware Store*; *My Name Is Village*; *Jestina's Calypso*). Heinemann, 1984.
The Dragon Can't Dance, adapted from the novel (produced Port of Spain, 1986).
The Wine of Astonishment, adapted from the novel (Produced Port of Spain, 1987).

Novels

While Gods Are Falling. London, Collins, 1965.
The Schoolmaster. London, Collins, 1968.
The Dragon Can't Dance. London, Deutsch, 1979.
The Wine of Astonishment. London, Deutsch, 1982.
Salt. London and Boston, Faber, 1996.

Short Stories

Brief Conversion and Other Stories. Oxford, Heinemann, 1988.

*

Critical Studies: "Spirited Bodies in Earl Lovelace's *The Wine of Astonishment*" by Renu Juneja, in *Reading the Social Body,* edited by Catherine Burroughs and Jeffrey David Ehrenreich, Iowa City, University of Iowa Press, 1993; "Masculinity, National Identity, and the Feminine Voice in *The Wine of Astonishment"* by Sandhya Shetty, in *The Journal of Commonwealth Literature* (London), 1994, pp. 65-79; *Orality Versus Literacy: A Study of the Nature and Role of the African Oral Tradition in Selected Works of Earl Lovelace* (dissertation) by Elsa P. Rogers, University of Southwestern Louisiana, 1995; "Strategies for Survival: Anti-Imperialist Theatrical Forms in the Anglophone Caribbean" by Elaine Savory, in *Imperialism and Theatre: Essays on World Theatre, Drama and Performance,* edited by Ellen J. Gainor, London, Routledge, 1995.

* * *

Earl Lovelace emerged in the late 1960s as one of the most characteristic voices of Caribbean anticolonialism, expressing his views in novels and stories as well as in drama. Although drama cannot be said to be his favorite mode of literary expression, his theater has genuine quality and a distinct personal tone. Not all of his plays are available in print, but the three that are included in *"Jestina's Calypso" and Other Plays* (1984) are evidence of a considerable and unusual talent. Not content merely to profit from a remarkable ear for West Indian dialogue, Lovelace makes in his dramatic productions a significant place for song and dance. These elements lift the events from their everyday settings as they give a collective role to a community that, without dehumanizing the individuals who work out their lives and personal misfortunes within it, is nonetheless envisioned as the greater value in the final analysis.

Song and dance underpin the action in every one of the five short but vivid scenes of Caribbean rural life in the two-act play *My Name Is Village.* Roy embodies the discontent of a group of young people who find scant purpose in life. "What's my thing/ Who am I/Where am I going/What's my future," they chant, nostalgically envying guerrillas in the hills in the past not on account of the cause that inspired their military action but because fighting gave sense to existence. They are unwilling to accept the suggestion—expressed through the figures of the attractive Elena and her ambitious mother Angelina—that the best way out is the conventional one of studying for high school qualification exams. Town Test and his pair of Yes Men—figures combining caricature with allegory—pass through, peddling encyclopedias and crass urban culture but to no avail. Roy's frustrations burst out in the cry "Tell me how to be a winner. Tell me how to be a man. I don't want to play dolly house with my life. I don't want to go around being my head and saying 'Excuse me!' I want to be a man." His father, significantly called Cyril Village, is not a particularly prepossessing figure, but he points the way to contentment in the present and in fulfilling human relationships: "Living people are not machines." The theme is presented as the lights slowly brighten and everybody starts singing the village song.

The dramatic method employed in *Jestina's Calypso* adds dimensions to the intriguing realistic problem that it confronts. At 39 and living "in this narrow prison of an island," Jestina is growing old and knows that she is losing her looks. Realizing that her prospects of finding a husband are bleak, she has struck up and maintained by post a relationship with an expatriate Trinidadian. The long-distance relationship has developed so far that the couple plan to marry. Beginning on the day his plane is expected to arrive, the play cleverly builds up suspense in two ways. In the lively opening scene Lovelace presents Jestina's neighbors singing and dancing as they comment, in a fairly disabused fashion, on what is about to unfold. Matters become more tense when next, with a distinct slowing of tempo for more serious considerations, we see Jestina, alone at first, in her bedroom as she reflects on what she has done and her crippling doubts about her future. She is then joined by Laura, and the two women's conversation gives important further insights. The situation becomes all the more fraught when it is revealed that, though Jestina sent a phonograph to her fiancé, it was not one of herself but something she believed he would find more attractive. All the same, declaring that "I do not have to hide from them [the other members of the community]. I do not have to be ashamed of living," she sets off in some hope. It is in the interval between the two acts that the inevitable occurs, and after dashing our expectations in this way, Lovelace also deals with the aftermath in a strikingly original fashion. Our curiosity about what actually happened is very quickly satisfied, and then act 2 is largely devoted to the neighbors' comments that focus not so much on trying to apportion blame to individuals as to grasp the social, cultural, and political significance of this painful failure in human relations. Not appearing until far later than in act 1, Jestina at last comes onstage with "a kind of tall calm" and observes that the time has not yet come when changed attitudes would enable her to realize her potential. Appearances are as much a lie as the photograph had been, but there is a worth beneath the surface.

The New Hardware Store is also a play that begins with an ordinary, everyday situation and develops to have far wider implications. The first act portrays Mr. A. A. Ablack, the proprietor of a store he has acquired from an earlier white owner. It does not take long for it to become apparent that the store's change of ownership does not really betoken any great improvement for the people who are employed in it. Ablack is an unattractive and unintelligent figure with a tendency to bully his staff of three whenever occasion offers. As his bookkeeper Miss Calliste puts it, "I feel like I is only a piece of machine, like the work I doing ain't have nothing to do with me. Everything is a fuss, the littlest thing, you make them big rules, regulations, sign out for lunch. . . . Even when the books correct you have this smile like it ain't true, like you suspect something. I not comfortable." When the challenge to his authority comes from people and Rooso declares that he is battling for his life, Ablack's outburst speaks volumes: "Hear the word: Life! The new word in the lexicon of black dictionary." As playacting mingles confusingly with reality, Lovelace again confronts the alternative lifestyles available in a postcolonial situation in yet another play that has space for song to complement its realism.

Lovelace records that it was at the insistence of the celebrated Caribbean actor Errol Jones that he fashioned *The Dragon Can't Dance* out of his 1979 novel of the same name. Throughout it, too, is heard the music of carnival that is the expression of the temperament of the ordinary people of Trinidad.

—Christopher Smith

LOWE, Stephen

Nationality: British. **Born:** Nottingham, 1 December 1947. **Education:** University of Birmingham, 1966-70, B.A. (honours) in English 1969. **Career:** Actor and director, Stephen Joseph Theatre-in-the-Round, Scarborough, Yorkshire, 1975-78; senior lecturer, Dartington College of Arts, Devon, 1978-82; resident playwright, Riverside Studios, London, 1984. Artistic director, Meeting Ground Theatre Company, Nottingham, 1984—. **Awards:** George Devine award, 1977. **Agent:** Judy Daish Associates, 83 Eastbourne Mews, London W2 6LQ, England.

Publications

Plays

Comic Pictures (includes *Stars* and *Cards*) (produced London, 1972; revised version produced Scarborough, 1976; London, 1982). *Cards* published London, French, 1983; *Stars* included in *Moving Pictures: Four Plays*, 1985.

Touched (produced Nottingham, 1977). Todmorden, Yorkshire, Woodhouse, 1977; revised version (produced London, 1981; New York, 1982), London, Eyre Methuen, 1981.

Shooting, Fishing and Riding (produced Scarborough, 1977).

Sally Ann Hallelujah Band (produced Nottingham, 1977).

The Ragged Trousered Philanthropists, adaptation of the novel by Robert Tressell (produced Plymouth and London, 1978; New York, 1987). London, Joint Stock, 1978; revised version (produced London, 1983), London, Methuen, 1983.

Fred Karno's Bloody Circus (produced London, 1980).

Moving Pictures (as *Glasshouses*, produced London, 1981; as *Moving Pictures*, produced Leeds, 1985). Included in *Moving Pictures: Four Plays*, 1985.

Tibetan Inroads (produced London, 1981). London, Eyre Methuen, 1981.

Strive (produced Exeter, 1983; London, 1987). Included in *Moving Pictures: Four Plays*, 1985.

The Trial of Frankenstein (produced Plymouth, 1983).

Seachange (produced London, 1984). Included in *Moving Pictures: Four Plays*, 1985.

Keeping Body and Soul Together (produced London, 1984) Published in *Peace Plays 1*, edited by Lowe, London, Methuen, 1985.

Moving Pictures: Four Plays. London, Methuen, 1985.

Desire (produced Nottingham, 1986).

Demon Lovers (produced Loughborough, Leicestershire and London, 1987).

The Storm, adaptation of a play by Alexander Ostrovsky (produced London, 1987).

Divine Gossip (produced London, 1988). With *Tibetan Inroads*, London, Methuen, 1988.

William Tell, adaptation of the play by Schiller (produced Sheffield, 1989).

Paradise (musical; produced Nottingham, 1990).

The Alchemical Wedding (produced Salisbury, 1998).

Television Plays: *Cries from a Watchtower*, 1979; *Shades*, 1982; *Kisses on the Bottom*, 1985; *Albion Market* series, 1986; *Coronation Street* series, 1989; *Families* series, 1990; *Ice Dance*, 1990; *Flea Bites*, 1992; *In Suspicious Circumstances*, 1992; *Tell-Tale Hearts*, 1992.

Other

Peace Plays 1. London, Methuen, 1985.

Editor, *Peace Plays 2*. London, Methuen, 1989.

*

Critical Studies: "Letters from a Workshop: *The Ragged Trousered Philanthropists*," in *Dartington Papers 2* (Totnes, Devon), 1978, and "Peace Plays: Peace as a Theatrical Concern," in *Englische Amerikanische Studien* (Munich), nos. 3-4, 1986, both by Lowe.

Stephen Lowe comments:

The best introductions to my work are, of course, the plays. But some central concerns, or obsessions, are clear even to me and have taken me into plays set in the past and into plays set on the other side of the world—in Tibet. One concern is to explore moments of real change in society, to discover perhaps an optimistic vision that might inspire us through the present moment of change. A large number of them *I* would call political love stories; these have often led me into an exploration of "inner language" through dreams and fairy and folk tale elements.

As Joyce pointed out, there are probably only three subjects worth writing about—politics, religion, and sex. I have discovered in my work that the clear divisions between these create a false perspective, and the interrelation of all these elements is, to me, a crucial theatrical concern, in both form and content.

* * *

Stephen Lowe's career as a professional playwright started with the production of two short plays, *Cards* and *Stars,* at the Library Theatre in Scarborough while Lowe was employed there as an actor. Since then his plays have been regularly premiered and performed on all the major British stages, on radio, and on television. He has also completed filming for a major network production in New Zealand.

Lowe's work as a playwright is characterized by a sustained interest in exploration and experiment both in dramatic technique and in the processes of production. Largely because of this, his work is hard to classify. His career follows, nonetheless, a pattern familiar to most working playwrights: an early interest in acting; the application of his experience of stage technique to writing for the stage; and the subsequent engagement with film and television production. He has had singular successes in all the genres to which he has applied himself. A longer perspective, however, suggests that there is an underlying tension that informs most of his significant work. This can best be expressed as the need to divide his genius between, on the one hand, an "organic" creativity, and on the other, a creativity that derives from cerebral interchange between research and the imagination.

It is tempting to see this distinction as a division between traditional theater work—where rehearsal and production usually proceed in a linear, people-oriented, and compacted manner—and the film or television production—where the process is more three-dimensional, technical, and fragmented. This is a neat rather than exact distinction. During Lowe's contract with Granada for the record-breaking television "soap" *Coronation Street*, priority was placed on collective development of the story lines by the scriptwriting team. New writing for television, however, usually requires something of the order of a "complete" script before a production can begin, unlike new writing for the theater. Hence it is largely the case that Lowe's film and video commissions are sourced more frequently from a process of research and imagination rather than collaboration.

This distinction is further emphasized by other tensions implicit in Lowe's work. He clearly owes a debt to his Nottingham origins, even though his imagination and his traveling have taken him across the world. His early and substantial work therefore derives from being born in and spending most of his life around Nottingham. In this respect his plays not uncommonly deal with issues that broadly overlap with those of D. H. Lawrence before him: local dialect; intense interest in sexuality; and, above all, the preoccupations of working-class people. At the same time Lowe fundamentally subscribes to the view that only through the application of the imagination is the individual liberated from the constrictions of convention, parochialism, or the material strictures that hold one in thrall. In practice Lowe's disciplined and structured use of metaphor and allusion sustains dramas of resonance and wide applicability. Complementary to this, in his theatrical interests and activities Lowe's consciousness to confront a rooted predisposition for his own "place" enables him to maintain a balance between a sense of responsibility to his own community and the larger thematic awareness in his writing of "a world elsewhere."

Touched, his first major successful play, is a recognizable paradigm of Lowe's "organic" creativity. Described by *Times* critic Benedict Nightingale (27 January 1992) as (arguably) his "finest stage play," *Touched* was first directed at the Nottingham Playhouse by Richard Eyre, taken on tour, and then revived by Bill Gaskill for the Royal Court in 1981. The play is set in the 100-day period between May and August 1945—between the end of the war in Europe and the dropping of the atomic bomb on Hiroshima. Against a collage of extraneous sounds and images of a "world gone wrong" Lowe reveals the quiet, relentless tragedy of an extended family through a structured defoliation of the private hopes and fears of the women left at home to sustain the life of a community unmanned by the war.

The burden of *Touched* rests on Sandra, a married woman in her mid-30s who sees the chance to confront the old hierarchies with her decision to carry a child begotten out of an opportunistic relationship with an Italian prisoner of war. The plot is complicated by the presence of an 18-year-old epileptic boy. He makes an unsolicited declaration to Sandra's family that he is the father of her child. It transpires that his admission of paternity arises from a wish to offer Sandra a measure of protection from the stigma of straying outside the tribe. He also wishes to expiate his own sin of spying on Sandra's illicit lovemaking. In gratitude Sandra presents herself to Johnny: he is unable to "touch" her. Like all the men in the play, where the values of a homocentric world are inverted, he can no longer function as a "man." This theme permeates the play, with the increasingly desolate and unrelieved vision of the impending return of men at the end of the war. The ambiguous nature of the piece is reflected in the audience's final realizations that Sandra's pregnancy also is an illusion, ratified in the final ironies of General MacArthur's voice-over: "Men everywhere walk upright in the sun. . . . The entire world is at peace. . . . The Holy Mission is completed."

Touched is important in that it prefigures most of Lowe's thematic concerns. Not the least of these is the belief that in order to deal with the myths history embodies, it cannot be treated like a "theme park," detached from the present. The historic "moment" or "turning point" as Lowe now describes his creative springboard is the mainspring of dramatic action. The "moments" he employs to test his hypothesis are generally accessible ones, though in the earlier plays they inevitably carry a personal resonance. In the later plays there is a discernible shift towards a larger dialectical confrontation—to the point at which the surface of the play and the life of the imagination "turns." In *Touched*, however, his personal interest in the theme grew out of extended discussions with his aunt and his mother and of his father's trials in the 8th Army Corps. In *Moving Pictures*, perhaps the most autobiographical of his plays, the "moment" is relatively diffuse: 1963 to 1964, the age of mobility and the growth of the nuclear family, the shift from street community to high-rise flat.

Strive is a short play based on the "turning point" of the Falklands War. Lowe develops this with more complexity in *Seachange*, also based on the Falklands War and again linked to a personal odyssey—a trip across the Aegean Sea, which Lowe some years earlier had made. His grandfather was killed when his ship sank after aerial bombardment during the ill-fated Gallipoli Campaign during World War I. In the introduction to *Seachange* Lowe imagined that on his odyssey, "I might have passed over the clear waters of my grandfather's grave," thus re-enacting "the uncertain intimacy of those who love each other through blood but (who) are only too aware of the Seas of Time that divide them."

Although the link between history and the imagination is fully present in *Touched*, it is given more detailed examination in *Tibetan Inroads, Moving Pictures, Demon Lovers,* and *Divine Gossip. Demon Lovers* is in fact an imaginative construction of the relationship between the Moors murderers Ian Brady and Myra Hindley. He juxtaposes their love for each other with the Gothic horror of an art piece (in this case a video) worked out of the suffering they inflicted on their victims.

Lowe's recurring interest in the relationship between imagination, creativity, and art is present in most of his plays. In *Demon Lovers*, as earlier in *The Trial of Frankenstein*, he alludes to the negative power of an imagination denied expression. *Divine Gossip* reveals a more positive though no less potent manifestation of creativity in action. The play has an historical setting: 1929, the year in which three of Lowe's heroes (George Orwell, Harry Crosby, and D. H. Lawrence) were all in Paris. It overlays aspects of maleness—in art, sexuality, and the desire for death—upon Louise Brooks's story "Pandora's Box" and a French prostitute aspiring to be Louise Brooks.

Although through *Touched* Lowe earned an early reputation for being a writer of women's plays, many other pieces—*The Ragged Trousered Philanthropist* and *Divine Gossip* in particular—clearly contradict this view. Between these poles lies *Shooting, Fishing and Riding*, a play about rape that was inspired by the feminist writer Susan Brownmiller's book *Against Our Will.* While he considers this piece to have been unsuccessful, it is characteristic of Lowe's method that he obsessively reworks themes that interest him to the point where he is able, fully and effectively, to exploit them. Hence in *Tell-Tale Hearts*, a psychological thriller about a reformed child-murderer set in Edinburgh and Glasgow, he revisits the issue of sexual abuse within relationships—extrapolated from the themes of *Demon Lovers*—to create a stunningly successful, redemptive three-part work for television.

Lowe is at his most articulate and assured when writing about personal relationships. *Tibetan Inroads* is an exemplary work from a number of perspectives. The play is based around the vicissitudes of natural love and the penalties and consequences of disrupting social convention. If *Tibetan Inroads* makes any single statement about people it is that they are endlessly unknowable, possessing in equal measure the mystical, intangible capacities for compassion and abuse. But above all his characterization has revealed a care for and a love of the extraordinary richness, diversity, and complexity across the spectrum of human behavior. Characteristic of this is his uproariously comic, plangent scene from *Moving Pictures* in which adolescent brothers and sisters tried to construct a Lawrentian sex movie in a studio improvised in the parents' front parlor.

Although, earlier, a distinction is drawn between the organic and the imaginative processes that are distributed across the range of Lowe's writing, these qualities are also powerfully connected through his interest in the human psyche. Regardless of whether he is writing new material, as in *Flea Bites* or *Tell-Tale Hearts*; whether he is adapting other writers' work, as in his critically praised script of Stendhal's *Rouge et Noir* (*Scarlet and Black*); or whether he is working within the strictures of an existing television series (*Pascoe and Dalziel*), Lowe's work centers on the elucidation of "character" as infinitely and psychologically complex.

This interest is psychological complexity is the continuum over which Lowe's stage work and an ever-expanding media portfolio passes. Television drama seems, in particular, to suit his genius, as it also reveals the extent to which he is prepared to "take on" the genre. Lowe is especially interested in the portrayal of characters on boundaries of psychological probability. Benedict Nightingale describes *Flea Bites* as "a highly improbable idea . . . [that Lowe] somehow bounces us into believing." At the same time the critic commends the play's audacity "for the kind of contradiction that wins an author trust and respect." In the play Lowe develops themes of "perseverance and mutual dependency" around a story of an 80-year-old man who teaches a 12-year-old boy to catch, harness, and train fleas in the back streets of Nottingham. For *Tell-Tale Hearts,* in pursuit of acquiring an insight into the mentality of the child murderer, Lowe spent more than two years talking to the parents of children who had been murdered or gone missing. But his later work shows that he is equally happy in dealing with themes far removed from his origins. He has completed the epic series *Greenstone*—a co-production (involving Television New Zealand and Robin Scoles, producer of Alan Duff's *Once Were Warriors*)—for screening in the autumn of 1998. The "turning point" in *Greenstone*, Lowe notes, is "two world's meeting": the British colonization of New Zealand.

Much of Lowe's work is informed by the paradox that the more one seeks knowledge the less one truly knows. His thematic interest in psychology is always contrasted with the view that despite the reductive view of human degeneracy there is a corresponding capacity for transcendence. In other words the "magic," exhilaration, joy, and completeness that one person can discover in a relationship with another—and that must therefore lie at the heart of human interaction—is always inherently possible. In this Lowe shares interesting philosophical parallels with the Irish playwright Tom Murphy. Whereas in Murphy's *The Gigli Concert* transcendence loosens the character J. P. W. King from the strictures of a world of "too many facts," Lowe's stage play *The Alchemical Wedding,* in an imaginative fusion of theme and process, develops the metaphor of alchemy where the facts themselves are spellbinding.

Hence in *The Alchemical Wedding,* which premiered at the Salisbury Theatre in April 1998, Lowe characterizes his theme in the form of an historical figure, John Dee (1527-1608). Dee, the Elizabethan mystic, mathematician, and alchemist, has enjoyed considerable vogue at the hands of a number of innovative and creative artists who are fascinated as much by the chimerical aspects as in the substance of the man; these artists include Snoo Wilson, Alan Drury, and the late Derek Jarman. Lowe's interest, characteristically, is the exploration of a bizarre but nonetheless material confrontation between Dee and Edward Kelley (his erstwhile assistant at the Court of Rudolph II in Prague in the 1590s). Kelley's reputation rests in his claim to have discovered "the philosopher's stone" in the ruins of Glastonbury Abbey.

The play operates at an interface where fact and fancy are interchangeable, and again it was developed both out of a period of sustained research on Dee and through immersion in the city itself that, 400 years ago, had been the alchemical capital of Europe. By all accounts Kelley was a rogue. He arrived in Prague with ears cropped, after the fashion for forgery; and he lost his life in fleeing from the city. The "turning point" of *The Alchemi-*

cal Wedding is a fantastical and consummate conjunction: the secrets of alchemy are bestowed in exchange for Dee and Kelley's consent to the Magic Covenant—"the request from the angels to share wives in common."

In balancing out the requirement to be faithful to history and to his art, Lowe emphasizes the integrity of his own method while continuing to push his imaginative and creative capacities to the limit. Such strategies are not free from risk. It is worth remarking that while Lowe has over the years shown a high degree of consistency in the quality of his output, his best work has invariably happened at the hands of actors and directors of unquestioned talent. That his work should interest and attract actors and directors from the top drawer is a tribute to his professional skill. That he should need them is a measure of his artistic modesty.

—Paul Hadfield

LUCAS, Craig

Nationality: American. **Born:** Atlanta, Georgia, 29 April 1951. **Education:** Boston University, Massachusetts, B.F.A. (cum laude) 1973. **Career:** Associate artist, South Coast Repertory, Costa Mesa, California, 1987—. Lives in New York City. **Awards:** Drama-Logue award 1986; Los Angeles Drama Critics award, 1986; George and Elizabeth Marton award, 1986; Guggenheim fellowship, 1987; Rockefeller grant, 1989; Tony award, 1989; Outer Critics Circle award, 1989; Obie award, 1990; Sundance Film Festival Audience award, 1990. **Agent:** Peter Franklin, William Morris Agency, 1325 Avenue of the Americas, New York, New York 10019, U.S.A.

Publications

Plays

Marry Me a Little, with Norman Rene, music and lyrics by Stephen Sondheim (produced New York, 1980; London, 1982).

Blue Window, music by Craig Carnelia (produced New York, 1984; London, 1989). With *Reckless*, New York, Theatre Communications Group, 1989.

Three Complaints, music by Stewart Wallace (produced New York, 1985).

Missing Persons (produced New York, 1985; revised production New York, 1994).

Three Postcards, music and lyrics by Craig Carnelia (produced Costa Mesa, California and New York, 1987; Edinburgh, 1992).

Prelude to a Kiss (produced Costa Mesa, California, 1988; New York, 1990). New York, Dutton, 1990.

Reckless, music by Craig Carnelia (produced New York, 1988). With *Blue Window*, New York, Theatre Communications Group, 1989.

Orpheus in Love (libretto), music by Gerald Busby (produced New York, 1992).

Throwing Your Voice (produced New York, 1992).

God's Heart (produced New York, 1997). New York, Theater Communications Group, 1998.

The Dying Gaul (produced New York, 1998). New York, Theater Communications Group, 1998.

Screenplays: *Reckless*, directed by Norman René, 1987; *Longtime Companion*, with Norman René, 1990; *Prelude to a Kiss*, with Norman René, 1991.

Television Play: *Blue Window*, with Norman René, 1987.

*

Manuscript Collection: Boston University, Special Collections, Boston, Massachusetts.

Critical Studies: "Craig Lucas" by Billy Hopkins, in *BOMB*, Summer 1989, pp. 56-59; "Craig Lucas" by John L. DiGaetani, in *A Search for a Postmodern Theatre: Interviews with Contemporary Playwrights*, edited by John L. DiGaetani, New York, Greenwood, 1991.

Theatrical Activities:
Actor: **Plays**—Role as Confederate Sniper in *Shenandoah* by James Lee Barrett, New York, 1975, and Nathan, 1976-77; Gentleman of the Court in *Rex*, book by Sherman Yellen, music by Richard Rodgers, lyrics by Sheldon Harnick, New York, 1976; male singer and standby Max Jacobs in *On the Twentieth Century*, book and lyrics by Betty Comden and Adolph Green, music by Cy Coleman, New York, 1978; member of the company, *Sweeney Todd, the Demon Barber of Fleet Street*, book by Hugh Wheeler, music and lyrics by Stephen Sondheim, New York, 1979; *Marry Me A Little* by Lucas and Norman Rene, music and lyrics by Stephen Sondheim, New York, 1980.

* * *

Several of Craig Lucas's plays are prefaced by epigraphs from other authors that give pointers to the journeys taken in his work. W. H. Auden's aptly titled "Leap Before You Look" provides the motto for *Reckless*, at the startling opening of which the heroine Rachel, a happy suburban housewife anticipating a happy Christmas with her husband and kids, is suddenly told by her husband that he has taken out a contract on her life. As an intruder breaks in downstairs, Rachel climbs out of the bedroom window. Windows in Lucas's world have something of the mystery of the nursery window in *Peter Pan*, and in *Reckless* Rachel's defenestration begins one of the roller coaster journeys on which Lucas takes his audiences.

Reckless is an unusual Christmas fable. Fleeing into the snowy night, Rachel is given a lift by Lloyd, who takes her to the Springfield, Massachusetts, home he shares with the crippled Pooty, who is also deaf and dumb. But as Pooty reveals to Rachel later, she so adored Lloyd when she first saw him at the center for the physically handicapped where he works that she has only pretended to be deaf and dumb; she felt that only if she were somehow needier than others would she get special attention from him. This is only one of several revelations in the play; that Lloyd walked out on a wife with multiple sclerosis is another ("The past is the nightmare you wake up to every day," he says). It traces Rachel's journey through a wacky parody of television game shows ("Your Money or your Wife?") and her encounters with different doctors, all played by the same actor (Lucas has some sharp fun at psychiatry's expense in these sections), to eventual self-discovery and maturity. It ends with Rachel as a doctor herself interviewing her now adolescent son, who, of course, does not recognize her and who, troubled by his family's past, has had problems sleeping. The scene reaches a climax in a curiously affecting sense of reconciliation at another Christmastime.

The audience goes on another journey in *Blue Window*, a play of dazzling technical achievement that takes place in five separate New York apartments simultaneously. It is Sunday night, and Libby is preparing to give a party, relying on her friend Griever for telephonic advice; other guests include a lesbian couple and a composer and his girl. Before, during, and after the party, Lucas weaves their conversations into a complex mesh of overlapping dialogue, scoring verbal music against an abstract blue setting. Against this slightly sterile background he builds up the patterns of youngish professionals in mid-1980s Manhattan, anxious and self-defensively wry (especially in Griever's often outrageous cadenzas), with some splendid running sight gags (Libby's encounter with a caviar jar breaks off a cap on a tooth, forcing her to mask her mouth for much of the evening). On the page it might seem overwistful and fatally arch, but in performance *Blue Window* combines social comedy with a melancholy substrain to potent effect.

Lucas's association with the Circle Repertory Company in New York continued with the play *Prelude to a Kiss*, which then moved to Broadway for a long run. E. M. Forster's aperçu from *Howards End* that "Death destroys a man, but the idea of death is what saves him" suggests the dark urban fairy tale at the center of the play.

Prelude to a Kiss represents the boldest of Lucas's journeys. A young man (Peter) falls in love with a young girl (Rita) he meets at a party in Manhattan. There are just a few clues—Rita's insomnia, for example—that suggest perils lurking behind the idyll of their courtship. At their wedding at the home of Rita's parents in New Jersey, an unsettling incident occurs when an uninvited old man kisses Rita and then goes on his way. Rita seems oddly affected by the encounter, and her oddness increases on the couple's Jamaican honeymoon. By the disturbing close of act 1, we have begun to realize that a transmigration of souls has taken place, and act 2 traces Peter's dilemma; with Rita's soul residing in the body of an old man dying of cancer, can he still love her? Love makes Peter resourceful enough to engineer a way by which to regain Rita's soul, and the play ends with their reunion after a typical Lucas tragicomic journey. The play occasionally falls into the trap of becoming overslick, even fey, but obliquely, as he does in much of his work, Lucas reaffirms the power of love in an age of fears that compromise it. And the hairpin bends Lucas has to negotiate in the rides he creates give his best work a sense of exhilarating adventure.

—Alan Strachan

LUCIE, Doug

Nationality: British. **Born:** Chessington, Surrey, 15 December 1953. **Education:** Tiffin Boys' School, 1965-72: Worcester College, Oxford, 1973-76, B.A. (honours) in English 1976. **Career:** Resident playwright, Oxford Playhouse Company, 1979-80; visiting playwright, University of Iowa, Iowa City, 1980. **Awards:** *Time Out* award, 1988. **Agent:** Michael Imison Playwrights, 28 Almeida Street, London N1 1TD, England.

Publications

Plays

John Clare's Mad, Nuncle (produced Edinburgh, 1975).
Rough Trade (also director: produced Oxford, 1977).
The New Garbo (produced Hull and London, 1978).
We Love You (also director: produced London, 1978).
Oh Well (also director: produced Oxford, 1978).
Heroes (also director: produced Edinburgh and London, 1979).
Fear of the Dark (produced London, 1980).
Poison (also director: produced Edinburgh, 1980).
Strangers in the Night (produced London, 1981).
Hard Feelings (produced Oxford, 1982; London, 1983). With *Progress*, London, Methuen, 1985.
Progress (produced London, 1984; New Haven, Connecticut, 1986; New York, 1989). With *Hard Feelings*, London, Methuen, 1985.
The Key to the World (produced Leicester and London, 1984).
Force and Hypocrisy (produced London, 1986).
Fashion (produced Stratford-on-Avon, 1987; London, 1988; Chicago, 1992). London, Methuen, 1987.
Doing the Business (produced London, 1990).
Fashion; *Progress*; *Hard Feelings*; *Doing the Business*. London, Methuen, 1991.
Grace (produced London, 1993). London, Nick Hern, 1993.
The Shallow End. London, Methuen, 1997.
Plays (includes *Progress*; *Fashion*; *Grace*; *Gaucho*). London, Methuen, 1998.

Television Plays: A *Class of His Own*, 1984; *Funseekers*, with Nigel Planer, 1987.

*

Theatrical Activities:
Director: **Plays**—Some of his own plays; student productions of *The Duchess of Malfi* by Webster, *The Comedy of Errors*, and *Hitting Town* by Stephen Poliakoff.

Actor: **Plays**—*We Love You*, London, 1978; *Oh Well*, Oxford, 1978.

* * *

Wherever people congregate there are rich pickings for those with an ear for the nuances of speech and a nose for the ridiculous. Since comedy of manners was invented, the drawing room has provided the playwright with a suitable microcosm for bourgeois society. Where once there were drawing rooms, there are now communal living spaces. At some point in the 1970s Doug Lucie moved into yours or mine. He has captured the social mores and hypocrisies of a particular social strata, both in the university and beyond, and pilloried us on stage for our general amusement and embarrassed recognition.

Lucie has not dealt exclusively with the cynicism, power games, and capacity for self-delusion of his contemporaries. *The New Garbo* anticipated the interest in the actress Frances Farmer. *Strangers in the Night* flirted with a lurid expressionism redolent of midperiod Sam Shepard. But it is as the persistent chronicler of his peers that Lucie has gained his reputation. *We Love You* deals with adolescent rebel posturing. *Heroes* shows six undergraduates in a shared house in Oxford and contrasts them with a different group living there 10 years before. *Hard Feelings* is set in Brixton in 1981, where inside another shared house the characters bicker and pose, while outside they riot. *Progress* is about marriage and careers and sexual politics, with Will a Channel 4 researcher and Ronee a social worker. What with the lodger, the battered wife they adopt, the phone calls from Ronee's lesbian lover, and Will's men's group ("We're trying to change our attitudes by being open and supportive without resorting to traditional, hierarchical structures"), their living room achieves honorary communal status.

Lucie's plays unfold with an ease and grace that belie a precise construction and rigorous comic technique. He has an insidious way with exposition. Scenes end at precisely the right moment, with the structure never sagging, and the comic effect derives from incongruous juxtaposition and savage undercutting. With a good designer to capture the latest nuances of interior decor and personal accessories, an evening at a Lucie play can provide an irresistible but excruciating portrait of the way we carry on. Our foibles are exposed in a relentlessly funny and viciously acute way.

Is it replication or exaggeration? There are those who say that Lucie lacks subtlety. It is true that he assembles predictable characters in unsurprising combinations. *Progress* is a title with heavy-handed irony. In *Hard Feelings* the living room blinds are always down, which is perhaps an overemphatic metaphor. But unless Lucie aspires to subtlety, lack of it is neither here nor there. One cannot scourge discreetly. Yet who is being scourged and why? It may be that Lucie feels himself an interloper in the world he describes, but his sympathies are always with the outsiders regardless of their actions and attitudes. When Tone, the outsider in *Hard Feelings,* bellows, "People aren't kind of things, they're people," he articulates the author's, and the audience's, outrage. But in *Progress* the outsiders are Mark and Lenny. Mark is a gutter-press journalist with a spectacular line in sexist banter. Lenny uses his wife "as a sparring partner and she doesn't box." He also rapes her. Being bereft of privilege or pretense does not accord integrity by default, and it seems untypically naive of Lucie even to hint that this is the case.

I do not think, as some do, that Lucie is trivial, but he does often trivialize. Comedy of manners is, almost by definition, concerned with surfaces. Too often the dictates of this comic form constrain Lucie. When human beings are reduced to plot functionaries, however brilliantly, it is difficult to care much about what happens to them. Points are half raised and then, lest the pace slacken, abandoned. Despite his huge talent Lucie often seems willfully insubstantial.

Lucie is a dramatist of rare wit and exceptional powers of observation. It would be necessary, however, for him to transcend the civilizing parameters he has set himself in order to attain the coruscating heights of great satire. In this respect it is interesting to note that his 1984 play *The Key to the World* moved out of the drawing room and toward a more humane and less comic vision.

—Joss Bennathan

LUDWIG, Ken

Nationality: American. **Born:** York, Pennsylvania, 15 March 1950. **Education:** York Suburban High School, 1968; Haverford College, Pennsylvania, B.A. (magna cum laude) 1972; Trinity College, University of Cambridge, England, LL.M. 1975; Harvard Law School, Cambridge, Massachusetts, J.D. 1976. **Family:** Married Adrienne George in 1976; one daughter and one son. **Career:** Attorney (Of Counsel), Steptoe and Johnson, law firm, Washington, D.C., 1976-89. Lives in Washington, D.C. **Awards:** New Play Committee of the National Endowment for the Arts award, 1995; Pennsylvania's Governor's award for Excellence in the Arts, 1997; Edwin Forest award for Outstanding Achievement in Drama, Walnut Street Theatre, 1998. Honorary degree: York College of Pennsylvania, 1993. **Agent:** Gilbert Parker and Peter Franklin, William Morris Agency, 1325 Avenue of the Americas, New York, New York 10019, U.S.A.

Publications

Plays

Class Night (sketches) (produced Haverford and Bryn Mawr, Pennsylvania, 1970 and 1972).

Divine Fire (produced Washington D.C., 1979; New York, 1980).

Sullivan and Gilbert (produced Milford, New Hampshire, 1983; New York, 1984). New York, French, 1989.

Postmortem (produced Milford, New Hampshire, 1984). New York, French, 1989.

Dramatic License (produced Cleveland, Ohio, 1985).

Lend Me a Tenor (as *Opera Buffa*, produced Milford, New Hampshire, 1985; as *Lend Me a Tenor*, produced London, 1986; New York, 1989). London, French, 1986; New York, French, 1989.

Crazy for You, adaptation of *Girl Crazy* by George and Ira Gershwin (produced Washington, D.C., 1991; New York, 1992; London, 1993).

Moon over Buffalo (produced Boston, 1996; Hew York, 1996). New York, French, 1997.

*

Theatrical Activities:
Director: **Play—***Who's Afraid of Virginia Woolf* by Edward Albee, Haverford and Bryn Mawr, Pennsylvania, 1972.

Ken Ludwig comments:

The tradition of stage comedy that I admire most is what scholars call "high comedy" and what I like to call "muscular comedy." It's the kind of comedy that, while firmly rooted in reality and the emotions of the characters, bursts off the stage, has a story filled with unexpected twists and turns, contains a broad range of characters from different levels of society, and abounds in word play—all in all, a reflection of our real lives but somehow "bigger." The most distinguishing hallmark of this kind of comedy is some form of confusion, deception, or mistake, either in the workings of the plot or at the core of the structure.

The tradition began about 2,000 years ago with that irreverent Roman, Plautus. It re-emerged in the comedies of Shakespeare where mistaken identities and deception abound (*viz*., in my opinion, the greatest comedies ever written, *Twelfth Night, As You Like It, Much Ado About Nothing*, and *A Midsummer Night's Dream*). Then came Goldsmith and Sheridan (*She Stoops to Conquer* and *The Rivals*) in the eighteenth century. In the nineteenth century the tradition is best seen in the comic operas of Rossini and

Donizetti. And in our own century the tradition re-emerges in the stage comedies of Kaufman and Hart, Hecht and MacArthur, the screen comedies of Lubitsch and Sturges, and in the uniquely American musical comedies that were written in the 1920s and 1930s.

This is the form of drama that, when it has greatness about it, touches me most deeply. My goal as a writer is to reinvent this tradition for our own times.

* * *

It is hardly surprising that Ken Ludwig should have achieved his biggest success with *Crazy for You,* his 1990s reworking of the 1930s book to the old Gershwin musical *Girl Crazy*. Music runs like a seam through Ludwig's plays, and it was surely his musical sense and his sharp ear for the rhythm and shaping of a scene that made him the ideal choice to reconstruct the show's libretto affectionately.

Sullivan and Gilbert, Ludwig's play about the volatile relationship between Gilbert and Sullivan, may not tread any noticeably new ground. But it integrates the accompanying Savoy Opera songs with adroit smoothness, and the play has some astute scenes revealing the pitfalls of artistic collaboration.

Lend Me a Tenor is that rarity, a completely successful modern farce. Leading comedy writers have either failed signally in this tricky field (Neil Simon with *Rumors*) or skirted it with homage to the form (as with Alan Ayckbourn's tribute to Ben Travers in *Taking Steps*). In Britain at least only Ray Cooney is left to fly the flag for farce. So *Lend Me a Tenor* was doubly welcome—a farce that had all the classic Swiss watch precision of plotting as it handled the spiraling complexities of its initially simple central situation while retaining wit and heart.

In a hotel suite in 1930s Cleveland, an imperious opera house manager faces disaster when the Italian tenor (Il Stupendo) booked to sing Otello at an important charity gala falls into a drunken stupor and is presumed dead. (The scene of this assumption, involving the misunderstanding of a good-bye note from the tenor's jealous wife, may be a familiar staple of farce—Ayckbourn uses it, too, in *Taking Steps*—but here it is superbly funny because it is so credibly plotted and planted.) To save the day, the impresario's dogsbody, Max, besotted by his employer's daughter, gets the chance to realize his operatic ambitions when he puts on blackface to win acclaim as Otello. Of course, Il Stupendo awakens and dresses in costume, leading to a postperformance second act of hairbreadth near misses as the real and substitute Otellos enter and exit through the suite's multiple doors, while the aphrodisiacs of fame and seductive music figure more strongly as various swooning females crowd the suite.

The play works well (it achieved an especially buoyant success in Jerry Zaks's high-octane New York production) not just because of its meticulous timing and passages of climactic lunacy, which reach the heights of some vintage Marx Brothers sequences, but also because of the spine of the plot, the old standby of the understudy blossoming into star, which is given extra mileage here by a genuinely appealing central character. The audience moves progressively toward Max throughout the play as it looks as if he will win both his girl and musical fame.

Theatrical ambitions are also at the heart of Ludwig's expert book for *Crazy for You.* His hero, Bobby Childs, dreams of a dancing career in the Zangler Follies in 1930s New York but is forced to act for his affluent family law firm to repossess a bankrupt Western township. In Deadrock, Nevada, there just happens to be an unused theater, and Bobby falls for the owner's daughter. Ludwig then cheekily reworks his central *Tenor* device, with Bobby impersonating the flamboyant Zangler, only for the real Zangler to turn up. The script has a blithe, spring-heeled invention that no doubt had producers besieging Ludwig for more of the same, but his next venture brought back the kind of native farcical comedy so rare on Broadway these days.

Moon over Buffalo, a backstage comedy set in the 1950s and revolving around an affectionately portrayed theatrical couple fallen on lean touring times but with a movie comeback beckoning, is a rarity—a farce with a heart, like George S. Kaufman in an unlikely but intriguing alliance with Frank Capra. The play lays its groundwork very well and has some strong supporting roles, but what should be its high spot—a second-act mix-up when the hungover actor-manager confuses *Private Lives* and *Cyrano de Bergerac* at a vital matinee while his family and staff try to save the day—never quite delivers as it promises, while the plotting turns heavy and the jokes strain with increasing artifice. It also ends surprisingly tamely. With big box office insurance from Carol Burnett's star name, the play managed a decent Broadway run, but it did not deliver the delight of *Lend Me a Tenor*.

—Alan Strachan

LUKE, Peter (Ambrose Cyprian)

Nationality: British. **Born:** St. Albans, Hertfordshire, 12 August 1919. **Education:** Eton College; Byam Shaw School of Art, London; Atelier André Lhote, Paris. **Military Service:** Served in the Rifle Brigade, in the Western Desert, Italy, and Northwest Europe, 1940-46: Military Cross, 1944. **Family:** Married 1) Carola Peyton-Jones (died); 2) Lettice Crawshaw (marriage dissolved), one son (deceased) and one daughter; 3) the actress June Tobin in 1963, two sons and three daughters. **Career:** Sub-editor, Reuters, 1946-47; worked in the wine trade, 1947-57; book critic, *Queen* magazine, London, 1957-58; story editor, *Armchair Theatre* programme, 1958-60, and editor, *Bookman* programme, 1960-61, and *Tempo* arts programme, 1961-62, all for ABC Television, London; drama producer, BBC Television, London, 1963-67. Freelance writer, producer, and director, 1967—; director, Gate Theatre, Dublin, 1977-80. **Awards:** Italia prize, for television production, 1967; Tony award, 1969. **Agent:** Lemon, Unna, and Durbridge, 24 Pottery Lane, Holland Park, London W11 4LZ, England.

Publications

Plays

Hadrian VII, based on *Hadrian the Seventh* and other works by Frederick Rolfe, "Baron Corvo" (produced Birmingham, 1967; London, 1968; New York, 1969). Published as *The Play of Hadrian VII*, London, Deutsch, 1968; New York, Knopf, 1969.

Bloomsbury (produced London, 1974). New York and London, French, 1976.

Rings for a Spanish Lady, adaptation of a play by Antonio Gala (also director: produced Dublin, 1977).

Proxopera, adaptation of the novel by Benedict Kiely (produced Dublin, 1978).
Married Love: The Apotheosis of Marie Stopes (produced Leatherhead, Surrey, 1985; London, 1988).
Yerma, adaptation of the play by Federico García Lorca (produced London, 1987). Published in *Lorca, Plays: One*, edited by Gwynne Edwards, London, Methuen, 1987.

Radio Plays: *Nymphs and Satyrs Come Away*, 1985; *The Last of Baron Corvo*, 1989; *The Other Side of the Hill* (includes *The Road to Waterloo* and *It's a Long Way to Talavera*), 1991.

Television: *Small Fish Are Sweet*, 1959; *Pig's Ear with Flowers*, 1960; *Roll On, Bloomin' Death*, 1961; *A Man on Her Back*, from a story by William Sansom, 1966; *The Devil a Monk Wou'd Be*, from a story by Daudet, 1967; *Anach Cuan: The Music of Sean O Riada*, 1967; *Black Sound—Deep Song: The Andalusian Poetry of Federico García Lorca*, 1968; *Honour, Profit, and Pleasure*, with Anna Ambrose, 1985.

Novel

The Other Side of the Hill. London, Gollancz, 1984.

Short Stories

Telling Tales: The Short Stories of Peter Luke. The Curragh, County Kildare, Goldsmith Press, 1981.

Other

Sisyphus and Reilly: An Autobiography. London, Deutsch, 1972.
Paquito and the Wolf (for children). The Curragh, County Kildare, Goldsmith Press, 1981.
The Mad Pomegranate and the Praying Mantis: An Andalusian Adventure, London, Mantis Press, 1984.

Editor, *Enter Certain Players: Edwards-MacLiammóir and the Gate 1928-1978*. Dublin, Dolmen Press, 1978.

*

Critical Studies: By Ronald Bryden in *Observer* (London), 21 April 1968; by Harold Hobson in *Sunday Times* (London), 21 April 1968; "Peter Luke Used to Be a Television Producer. Then He Escaped" by Luke, in *Listener* (London), 12 September 1968; by Clive Barnes in *New York Times*, 9 January 1969; "*Hadrian VII* Is Alive and a Hit" by John Chapman, in *San Francisco Examiner*, 5 October 1969.

Theatrical Activities:
Director: **Plays**—*Hadrian VII*, Dublin, 1970; *Rings for a Spanish Lady*, Dublin, 1977. **Television**—*Hamlet at Elsinore*, 1963; *A Passage to India*, 1966; *Silent Song*, 1967; *Anach Cuan: The Music of Sean O Riada*, 1967; *Black Sound—Deep Song: The Andalusian Poetry of Federico García Lorca*, 1968.

Peter Luke comments:

(1977) To write an introduction to my work as a playwright is difficult because to date there is relatively little of it. I did not write my first play until I was nearly forty. The oeuvre, such as it is to date, consists of four original plays for television and one dramatization of a novel by William Sansom for the same medium. In addition there are two films d'auteur commissioned by the BBC. They are respectively, and perhaps significantly, about a musician and a poet. Then there is the stage play, *Hadrian VII*, which was first written in 1961 but was not produced until 1967. *Bloomsbury*, produced by Richard Cottrell in 1974, ran for only five weeks due to the American recession as it affected Throgmorton Street and the tourist trade and a petulant notice from Harold Hobson (anagram: Dora Snobhol). (1988: Since then *Married Love* has had an airing, but has not yet reached the West End.)

I would like to be able to give some indication of the direction in which I think I am going, but this is difficult. Certainly I am more than ever interested in poetry, which is not to say that I am immediately contemplating a play in verse. But if I can see a development in my work, it is towards the articulate. Language is my preoccupation and I feel that the theatre, now as in the past, and quite irrespective of present day vogues and trends, should be the place to use it in.

The choice of medium was made for me. My father, Harry Luke, was a writer but early on I decided that I wanted to paint and I had already spent two years studying when the war broke out in 1939. Nineteen—nearly twenty—years later, in 1959, my first television play, *Small Fish Are Sweet*, starring Donald Pleasence and Katherine Blake, was produced. Several others followed hard upon. What happened in between is told in an essay in autobiography, *Sisyphus and Reilly*.

I did not intend to become a playwright. It happened by accident. I do not even now consider myself to be solely a writer of plays, though I suppose few writers can have been so fortunate as to have had an international success on the scale of *Hadrian VII*. Indeed, how many playwrights have had a major success which began as a flop? Thanks to Hadrian, however, I am now free to write what I want to and my intention for the foreseeable future is to alternate plays with books. This I find very therapeutic and my one concern now is that the results will justify the therapy, and that the therapy will give me a long life in which to write a great deal more.

* * *

Peter Luke was almost 40 years old when, in 1958, he became a story editor for ABC Television and began writing television plays. In 1963 he joined the BBC, where he stayed until 1967. Since then he has worked as a freelance writer, producer, director, and translator and has also written a historical novel, short stories, and two autobiographical reminiscences.

In 1967 Luke adapted Frederick Rolfe's novel *Hadrian the Seventh* for the stage. In an otherwise faithful rendering, he made one major change. In the novel the protagonist is a young man called George Arthur Rose. Luke has described his play as "a biography of Rolfe himself in terms of his 'Hadrian' fantasy."

Hadrian VII begins with Rolfe being visited by two bailiffs. They present him with a writ resulting from a series of petty debts, but he refuses to sign. Left alone to his imagining, he fantasizes that the two bailiffs are a bishop and a cardinal come to persuade him to accept ordination. They invite him to Rome, where he learns that he has been elected pope. He calls himself Hadrian VII and immediately announces his intention of dissolving the temporal church and selling the Vatican's treasure and real estate. The cardinals are outraged. Meanwhile, Jeremiah Sant, who knew Rolfe before his election, tries to wheedle money out of him. Hadrian refuses to give him money but offers to help save his soul instead. Sant thereupon draws a revolver and shoots Hadrian, who dies requesting that Sant be forgiven his crime. The final scene shows the bailiffs confiscating Rolfe's belongings, among them the manuscript of his masterpiece. The play's enormous success in the late 1960s can be attributed to two factors. The contrast between the "real" Rolfe in his seedy garret and Rolfe as he imagines himself is dramatically very effective, and the theme of individuality versus authority is perennial.

Luke's next play, *Bloomsbury,* portrays the group of friends surrounding Lytton Strachey as seen through the eyes of Virginia Woolf. Toward the end of the play she says, "Yes, I have created an art form out of them all. . . . I have orchestrated their movements like the waves." Although the concept is clever, the various relationships and attitudes explored lack the dramatic interest of his previous work.

Proxopera (coined from "operation proxy") was adapted from a novel by Benedict Kiely, who described his story as "a condemnation of the interference by violent men in the lives of the innocent." A group of IRA men are holding a family at gunpoint. They threaten to kill the women and child if Binchey, a retired schoolmaster, does not drive a bomb into town for them. He agrees and sets off to do so, but when he sees his town in the early morning light, he cannot bring himself to aid in the murder of any of its citizens. He tells two soldiers what he is carrying. They rescue his family, but Binchey dies of a heart attack after safely exploding the bomb.

Married Love: The Apotheosis of Marie Stopes opens lightheartedly, contrasting Stopes's academic brilliance and her emotional immaturity. After chasing a Japanese professor to no avail, she marries a man who is impotent. As a result she comes to think that contraception could be used to produce a better species. George Bernard Shaw persuades her that contraception would be better employed to help women avoid unwanted pregnancies. Her subsequent achievement in promoting contraception is set against her sense of personal emptiness. Early in the play she tells Shaw, "I only know that I haven't got something that I feel I ought to have." She never acquires it. She is never settled and never satisfied. The play maintains a fine balance between comedy and domestic tragedy, and it is certainly Luke's best work since *Hadrian VII.*

Ez, commissioned by the Hampstead Theatre Company is about the nontrial for treason of Ezra Pound. The first act is set in a cage in a prison in Pisan, Italy, and the second in Saint Elizabeth's Hospital in Washington, D.C., where Pound spent more than a decade. Some of Pound's best work belongs to this period, but Luke is more concerned with the contradictions inherent in his character. He was an egotist, but he would share his scraps of food with a cat, and he was a racist who made friends easily with blacks. Pound emerges as a victim of a genius inseparable from irresponsibility. But when he is eventually released, he is no longer so sure that what he believed in was right, and his confession that he was at fault brings the play to a close. The work is a plea for tolerance.

Luke has also written many successful television plays and documentaries, from *Small Fish Are Sweet* in 1959 to *Honour, Profit, and Pleasure,* a 1985 work about Handel that was cowritten with Anna Ambrose. He has made two excellent translations from the Spanish. *Rings for a Spanish Lady,* from a prizewinning play by Antonio Gala, is the story of how El Cid's widow, who represents Spain, is compelled by the king to forego her love for Don Minaya and accept her widowhood. Luke has described his translation of Lorca's *Yerma* as "the first unbowdlerized version."

Although Luke's subjects vary widely, their themes are closely related. In all of his plays the main characters' dreams or plans are threatened by a society that has no place for their kind of individuality. His work is a call for greater understanding between individuals.

—Terence Dawson

LYSSIOTIS, Tes

Nationality: Australian. **Education:** Rusden State College, Melbourne, degree in teaching. **Family:** Married in 1974; two children. **Career:** Secondary school teacher, from 1975-81, and 1983; drama consultant for the Knox Region, 1980; playwright-in-residence, La Mama, 1984, and LaTrobe University, 1991, both Melbourne. **Address:** 33 Lorraine Drive, East Melbourne, Victoria 3151, Australia.

Publications

Plays

I'll Go to Australia and Wear a Hat (produced Melbourne, 1982).
Come to Australia They Said (produced Melbourne, 1982).
Hotel Bonegilla (produced Melbourne, 1983).
On the Line (produced Melbourne, 1984).
The Journey (produced Melbourne, 1985).
Café Misto (produced Melbourne, 1986).
A White Sports Coat (produced Melbourne, 1988).
The Forty Lounge Café (produced Melbourne, 1990). Sydney, Currency, 1990.
The Past Is Here (produced Melbourne, 1991).
Zac's Place (for children; produced Melbourne, 1991).
A White Sports Coat & Other Plays. Sydney, Currency Press, 1996.

Radio Play: *A Small Piece of Earth,* 1990.

*

Critical Studies: "Interview: Going to the Source: Tes Lyssiotis Talks to Tony Mitchell" by Tony Mitchell, in *Australasian Drama Studies* (Queensland, Australia), 1988, pp. 5-15; "The Past Is Here: An Interview with Tes Lyssiotis" by Carolyn Pickett, in *Australasian Drama Studies* (Queensland, Australia), April 1996, pp. 79-85.

* * *

Biculturalism is at the heart of the multilingual plays of the Greek-Australian writer-director Tes Lyssiotis: "I grew up aware that I wasn't just Greek and I wasn't just Australian—I'm both." The daughter of a proxy bride who went to Australia in 1949 from the island of Cythera, she draws on her own background in exploring the historical experiences of southern European migrant women. *I'll Go to Australia and Wear a Hat* contrasts the bleak and barren reality of low-paying menial work that awaited migrant women in the 1950s with their expectations of Australia as "a paradise, a place where men made money and women got to be ladies with fine jewellery and sophisticated hats." Presented in a workshop with an all-female cast, this semidocumentary play incorporated extracts from parliamentary debates, editorials, and letters from newspapers of the period expressing the prevalent, often openly racist, Anglo-Australian attitudes toward migrants of non-English-speaking backgrounds. It also showed the value of migrant oral history as dramatic material: "It dawned on me that my mother had so many stories to tell. I believe the most ordinary people have the most extraordinary stories to tell if you talk to them."

Come to Australia They Said examined the experiences of Italian migrants in Australia during World War II, including their internment as enemy aliens as well as the widening generation gap within Italo-Australian families. Lyssiotis drew on the experiences of the Italian actors in her cast, and although she does not speak Italian herself, she stressed the importance of developing the material in workshops with non-English-speaking actors in their native languages. *Hotel Bonegilla,* which was developed with actors of Greek, Italian, and German backgrounds, dealt with the infamous eponymous migrant camp formed from temporary army huts in 1947. As many as 10,000 migrants of 32 different nationalities lived at Bonegilla until more permanent housing and employment could be found for them. The play opens with a slow-motion imagistic sequence inspired by Theodoros Angelopoulos's film *The Travelling Players*—a strong influence on Lyssiotis's work—in which a group of migrants carrying suitcases enter through the audience to form a tableau. The alienation of the different language groups becomes a vehicle for comedy. Italian, Greek, and German families forced to share cramped adjacent cubicles attempt with disastrous results to discuss the misfortunes of communal living, and a Greek girl looking for the place where her brother sleeps is misunderstood as wanting to sleep with her brother, while a camp official asks if anyone can speak "European" to interpret for her. *Hotel Bonegilla* also reenacts the riots that occurred in the camp when poor food, lack of work and money, the remote and alienating environment, and racist attitudes became too much to bear and tanks were sent in to quell the violence.

In 1984 Lyssiotis formed the Filiki Players with the actors Nikos Zarkadas and Lu Beranek, and as the writer in residence at La Mama Theatre in Melbourne she was commissioned to write *On the Line* about migrant factory workers. She had spent a year working with a group of women suffering from repetitive strain injuries from jobs on production lines, and she built their experiences at home and at work into the play. The following year she devised *The Journey,* a "collage of events" selected from her four previous plays that then transferred to the larger Universal Theatre in Melbourne and later toured other states of Australia. This brought national attention to her work for the first time, although the critical response to the play's inevitable discontinuities was not always positive. It was not until the German periodical *Theater Heute* described the play as "a synthesis, by minimal means, of history and individual fates, of stage play and reality, as it is seldom seen in Germany" that the importance of her work began to be fully recognized.

Playbox Theatre in Melbourne commissioned her to write *The Forty Lounge Café.* Using songs and sections of dialogue in Greek, it draws on the sometimes comic experiences of Lyssiotis's mother in working in her brother-in-law's fish-and-chips shop in rural Australia as a basis for flashbacks to the protagonist Elefteria's childhood and adolescence in Greece. As she states to her sister when she returns to Greece for her mother's funeral in the play's final scene, Elefteria's whole life has been a sacrifice:

> I was working in the orphanage, so Irini could have some kind of dowry. I worked so my younger sister could marry. . . . She sent me away, I didn't ask to be married to a stranger. Did anyone ever ask me what I wanted? Why did she send me away? I curse the day I set foot on that plane. For years I was a servant to this family.

Because of Elefteria's forced subjugation to the welfare of others, she is determined to provide an upbringing for her daughter Toula that makes the most of her cultural heritage. She counters Toula's dismissal of Greece as "just a bunch of old rocks" and her adoption of Anglo-Australian attitudes by insisting on passing on to her Greek skills and traditions. In a play dominated by mourning, sadness, and deprivation, the briskness of the café scenes provide welcome moments of levity.

In the monologue *A White Sports Coat* a pregnant playwright reminisces about her mother, her Greek family home, and her Australian childhood while desperately trying to finish a play before she gives birth to her child. *Zac's Place* focuses on the dilemmas of a young Greek-Australian torn between the romanticized notions of Greece of his father, who wants to close the family milk bar and go back to their homeland, and the peer pressure of his Australian friends. Lyssiotis presents Greek-Australian migrant experience "from the inside out," but she avoids the ghetto of much non-Anglophonic Australian community theater and rejects the tokenism of multiculturalism: "I don't want to be labelled as 'multicultural.' I want to be regarded as an artist, and the fact that I am working on things to do with migrants is irrelevant. It could just as well be elephants or disabled people."

—Tony Mitchell

M

MAC LOW, Jackson

Nationality: American. **Born:** Chicago, Illinois, 12 September 1922. **Education:** University of Chicago, 1939-43, A.A. 1941; Brooklyn College, New York, 1955-58, A.B. (cum laude) in Greek 1958. **Family:** 1) Married the painter Iris Lezak (divorced), two children; 2) the painter, poet, and composer Anne Taxdos. **Career:** Freelance music teacher, English teacher, translator, and editor, 1950-66; reference book editor, Funk and Wagnalls, 1957-58, 1961-62; editor, Unicorn Books, 1958-59; copy editor, Alfred A. Knopf, 1965-66, all in New York. Member of the editorial staff, and poetry editor, 1950-54, *Now, Why?* (later *Resistance*), a pacifist-anarchist magazine; instructor, American Language Institute, New York University, 1966-73; instructor, Mannes College of Music, 1966; instructor, State University of New York, Albany, 1984; visiting professor of creative writing, State University of New York, Binghamton, 1989; visiting writer, Temple University, Philadelphia, 1989; Regents' Lecturer, University of California, San Diego, 1990; lecturer, seminar participant, and reader of his own poetry, State University of New York, Buffalo, 1990, 1997; writing teacher and lecturer, Schule für Dichtung in Wien, Vienna, 1992, 1993; teacher in M.F.A. program, Bard College, Annandale-on-Hudson, New York, 1994; teacher of creative writing, Naropa Institute, Boulder, Colorado, 1975, 1991, 1994; teacher of creative writing, Brown University, Providence, Rhode Island, 1994; participant in translation seminar, Foundation Royaumont Asnières, Oise, France, 1996; reader, seminar participant, University of Pennsylvania, Philadelphia, 1997. **Awards:** Grant from American Academy of Arts and Letters, 1971; grant from PEN, 1974, 1982; Madeline Sadin award for poetry, New York Quarterly, 1974; Creative Artists Public Service fellowship in Multimedia, 1973-74; CAPS fellowship in poetry, 1976-77; fellowship in creative writing, National Endowment for the Arts, 1979; Guggenheim fellowship for poetry, 1985; co-winner, award for book published, San Francisco State University Poetry Center, 1984, 1985; Fulbright grant, 1986; composer's grant from Queen Elizabeth II Arts Council, New Zealand, 1986; fellowship in poetry, New York Foundation for the Arts, 1988; unsolicited grant by the Fund for Poetry, 1988, 1998; co-awardee, the American Awards for Literature, 1994. **Address:** 42 North Moore Street, New York, New York 10013-2441, U.S.A.

Publications

Plays

The Marrying Maiden: A Play of Changes, music by John Cage (produced New York, 1960). Los Angeles, Sun and Moon, 1999.

Verdurous Sanguinaria (produced New York, 1961; Exeter, 1968). Baton Rouge, Louisiana, Southern University, 1967; Los Angeles, Sun and Moon, 1999.

Thanks: A Simultaneity for People (produced Wiesbaden, 1962).

Letters for Iris, Numbers for Silence (produced Wiesbaden, 1962; New York, 1962).

A Piece for Sari Dienes (produced Wiesbaden, 1962; New York, 1982).

Thanks II (produced Paris, 1962).

The Twin Plays: Port-au-Prince, and Adams County, Illinois (produced New York, 1963; Exeter, 1968). New York, Mac Low and Bloedow, 1963; New York, Something Else Press, 1966.

Questions and Answers. . . : A Topical Play (produced New York, 1963). New York, Mac Low and Bloedow, 1963.

Asymmetries No. 408, 410, 485 (produced New York, 1965). New York, Printed Editions, 1980.

Asymmetries, Gathas and Sounds from Everywhere (produced New York, 1966).

A Vocabulary for Carl Fernbach-Flarsheim (produced New York, 1977). New York, Mac Low, 1968.

Performance Scores and Broadsides (published New York, Mac Low): *A Vocabulary for Sharon Belle Mattlin* [*Vera Regina Lachman, Peter Innisfree Moore*], 1974-75; *Guru-Guru Gatha*, 1975; *1st Milarepa Gatha*, 1976; *1st Sharon Belle Mattlin Vocabulary Crossword Gatha*, 1976; *Homage to Leona Bleiweiss*, 1976; *The WBAI Vocabulary Gatha*, 1977, revised edition, 1979; *A Vocabulary Gatha for Pete Rose*, 1978; *A Notated Vocabulary for Eve Rosenthal*, 1978; *Musicwords (for Phill Niblock)*, 1978; *A Vocabulary Gatha for Anne Tardos*, 1980; *Dream Meditation*, 1980; *A Vocabulary Gatha for Malcolm Goldstein*, 1981; *1st* [*2nd*] Happy Birthday, Anne, Vocabulary Gatha, 1982; *Unstructured Meditative Improvisation for Vocalists and Instrumentalists on the Word "Nucleus,"* 1982; *Pauline Meditation*, 1982; *Milarepa Quartet for Four Like Instruments*, 1982; *The Summer Solstice Vocabulary Gatha*, 1983; *Two Heterophonics from Hereford Bosons 1 and 2*, 1984; *Phonemicon from Hereford Bosons 1*, 1984. Published in *Baker's Dictionary of Musicians.*

Words and Ends from Ez (derived by diastic text-selection, from Ezra Pound's *Cantos*). Bolinas, California, Avenue B, 1989.

Two Plays (includes *The Marrying Maiden* and *Verdurous Sanguinaria*). Sun and Moon Press, 1999.

Radio Writing: *Dialog unter Dichtern/Dialog among Poets*, 1982; *Thanks/Danke*, 1983; *Reisen/Traveling*, 1984 (all Germany); *Locks*, 1984.

Composer (selection): incidental music for *The Age of Anxiety* by W.H. Auden, produced New York, 1954; for *The Heroes* by John Ashbery, produced New York, 1955; *The Ten Bluebird Asymmetries*, 1967; *Tranverse Flute Mime Piece*, 1981; *A Bean Phenomenon for Alison Knowles*, 1984; *The Birds of New Zealand*, 1986; *Iran-Contra Hearings*, 1987; *Ezra Pound and 99 Anagrams*, 1989; *Fieldpiece*, 1996; *Dream Other People Different*, 1997.

Poetry

The Pronouns: A Collection of 40 Dances—for the Dancers—6 February-22 March 1964. New York, Mac Low, 1964; London, Tetrad Press, 1971; Barrytown, New York, Station Hill Press, 1979.

August Light Poems. New York, Caterpillar, 1967.

22 Light Poems. Los Angeles, Black Sparrow Press, 1968.
23rd Light Poem: For Larry Eigner. London, Tetrad Press, 1969.
Stanzas for Iris Lezak. Barton, Vermont, Something Else Press, 1972.
4 Trains, 4-5 December 1964. Providence, Rhode Island, Burning Deck, 1974.
36th Light Poem: In Memoriam Buster Keaton. London, Permanent Press, 1975.
21 Matched Asymmetries. London, Aloes, 1978.
54th Light Poem: For Ian Tyson. Milwaukee, Membrane Press, 1978.
A Dozen Douzains for Eve Rosenthal. Toronto, Gronk, 1978.
Phone. New York, Printed Editions, 1978; Amsterdam, Kontexts.
Asymmetries 1-260: The First Section of a Series of 501 Performance Poems. New York, Printed Editions, 1980.
Antic Quatrains. Minneapolis, Bookslinger, 1980.
From Pearl Harbor Day to FDR's Birthday. College Park, Maryland, Sun and Moon, 1982; second edition, Los Angeles, Sun and Moon Press, 1995.
"Is That Wool Hat My Hat?" (produced New York, 1980, 1986; Buffalo, 1997; Boston, 1998). Milwaukee, Membrane Press, 1983.
Bloomsday. Barrytown, New York, Station Hill Press, 1984.
French Sonnets, Composed Between January 1955 and April 1983. Tucson, Black Mesa Press, 1984; second edition, Milwaukee, Membrane Press, 1998.
The Virginia Woolf Poems. Providence, Rhode Island, Burning Deck, 1985.
Representative Works 1938-1985. New York, Roof, 1986.
Twenties: 100 Poems: 24 February 1989-3 June 1990, with computer-aided cover art by Anne Tardos. New York, Roof Books, 1991.
Pieces o' Six: Thirty-three Poems in Prose, with computer-aided cover art and videographics by Anne Tardos. Los Angeles, Sun and Moon Press, 1992.
in Memoriam, with computer-aided painting of Schwitters by Anne Tardos. Barrytown, Station Hill Press, 1994.
Barnesbook, from works by Djuna Barnes, cover art by Anne Tardos. Los Angeles, Sun and Moon Press, 1996.

Recordings: *Blackbox,* Düsseldorf/München, S Press Tonband Verlag, 1975; *Simultaneities,* New York, New Wilderness Foundation, 1977; *Breathing Space/77, Black Box 15,* Washington D.C., The Watershed Foundation, 1978; *Gatherings,* New York, New Wilderness Foundation, 1982; *A Reading of Primitive and Archaic Poems,* with others, Broadside; *From a Shaman's Notebook,* with others, Broadside; *The Museum inside the Telephone Network,* Tokyo, 1991; *Open Secrets,* New York, Experimental Intermedia, 1993; *A Chance Operation: The John Cage Tribute,* Westbury, New York, Koch International Classics, 1993; *The Little Magazine, Volume 21* (CD-ROM anthology), Albany, 1995.

*

Critical Studies: "Jackson Mac Low Issue" of *Vort 8* (Silver Spring, Maryland), 1975, and *Paper Air* (Blue Bell, Pennsylvania), vol. 2, no. 3, 1980; "Jackson Mac Low: Gristlier Translations, Arcane Pronouns" in *Compulsory Figures* by Henry Taylor, Baton Rouge, London, Louisiana State UP, 1992, pp. 245-66; "Zarthathustran Pataphysics" by Steve McCaffey, in *Open Letter: A Canadian Journal of Writing and Theory: Ninth Series, number 7, Winter 1997: Millennial Paraphysics,* edited by Christian Bök and Darren Wershler-Henry, London, Ontario, Open Letter, 1997; *Crayon Premier Issue: Festschrift for Jackson Mac Low's 75th Birthday,* edited by Andrew Levy and Bob Harrison, Brooklyn, New York, Crayon, 1997.

Theatrical Activities:
Director: **Plays**–*Faustina* by Paul Goodman, New York, 1949; *Jonah* by Paul Goodman, New York, 1950.

Actor: **Plays**—In *Tonight We Improvise* by Pirandello, New York, 1959, and other plays; *Verdurous Sauguinaria,* 1961. Later performed in all his radio works and performance works (New York, Cologne, Vienna, San Francisco, 1961-1998).

* * *

Jackson Mac Low is recognized as America's leading dramatist of the aleatoric school, which uses chance-structured materials and which is best known by its principal musical exponent, John Cage. Mac Low's works for the theater have been performed in the United States, Canada, Germany, Brazil, and England, although few have ever been commercially published in a complete form.

Mac Low's original interest was musical composition, but after 1939 he became increasingly involved in poetry. During the 1940s he contributed to such anarchist publications as *Now, Why?* (later called *Resistance*) and was poetry editor for *WIN* (a publication of the Workshop In Nonviolence). Most of his poems are, however, designed for live performance, and Mac Low once described himself as a "Writer and Composer of Poetry, Music, Simultaneities, and Plays."

The most active phase of Mac Low's theater activity began in 1949 with Prester John's Company in New York, one of the most interesting early off-off-Broadway groups. He was a codirector and actor in various Paul Goodman plays, and in 1952 he began a long association with the Living Theatre, originally as a composer for productions of John Ashbery's *The Heroes*, W. H. Auden's *The Age of Anxiety*, and other plays but also as an actor and eventually as dramatist.

The major phase of Mac Low's dramatic corpus also began with his association with the Living Theatre and, at about the same time, with John Cage. There are two sets of "Biblical Poems" and a *Biblical Play,* performed in 1955, and a major play called *Lawrence*, based on writings by D. H. Lawrence. These pieces are extremely static and resemble Gagaku oratorios of words. The climax of this group of works is *The Marrying Maiden,* performed in repertoire by the Living Theatre in 1960-61 with a sound score by John Cage. This play is totally lyrical and abstract, and it includes actions to be determined by the performers by using a randomizing process. The Living Theatre's production was extremely conventional and inappropriate. It failed to bring out the uniqueness of the piece, and as a result the play was unpublished except as an acting script and was not performed again. About the works of this time, Mac Low has written,

> All during the 1940s and 1950s, many poems of mine in all modes express a pacifistic and libertarian political viewpoint strongly related to religious attitudes derived from Taoism, Buddhism, and mystical Judaism (Chassidism and Cabala). . . . These religious and political

views, along with the more libertarian schools of psychotherapy [e.g. Paul Goodman], helped make me receptive to the use of chance operations and to the interpenetration of art works and the environment. . . .

Mac Low's performance works are structured as social models in which each participant is a coequal and in which direction is achieved by self-guidance and the working out of ideas rather than along doctrinaire, authoritarian, or imposed visionary lines. The sound of the lines is as important as the sense (the sound often is the sense), resulting in a uniquely musical theater experience.

After *The Marrying Maiden* the plays became more choric—there is action, usually repetitive and in unison—though the texts remain more musical than semantic. As with *Lawrence,* the pieces take their names from some aspect of their source material. For instance, one major work of this period is *Verdurous Sanguinaria,* which is derived from a botanical text on wildflowers. *The Twin Plays* consists of two plays with identical action in all respects, but one of them uses combinations of the letters in the name Port-au-Prince and the other proverbs collected from Adams County, Illinois, which become the names for their respective plays. Another of these works is *Questions and Answers Incredible Statements the Litany of Lies Action in Freedom Statements and Questions All Round Truth and Freedom in Action; or, Why Is an Atom Bomb Like a Toothbrush? A Topical Play* takes political texts reflecting Mac Low's views, treats them as a litany, and then randomizes the actions.

Simultaneous with his theater work, and not necessarily completely separate from it, are Mac Low's poems that developed in parallel blocks. There are early works such as *Peaks and Lamas* (1957), included in the magazine *Abyss* (spring 1971). There is *Stanzas for Iris Lezak,* a massive cycle of over 400 pages written more or less immediately after *The Marrying Maiden* and in some ways paralleling it. His work then developed into *Asymmetries,* another large cycle that, although unpublished in any complete form, is, like *Stanzas,* often performed. These poems are overwhelmingly oriented toward the ear. They include long silences that are difficult to approximate on a printed page apart from performance. They may be poetry, but they partake of theater, especially in their heard elements. Many are "simultaneities," to use Mac Low's term, but in fact they are theater.

Starting in the late 1950s the theater of happenings began to develop, with its emphasis on the simple image. The acme of happenings was the Fluxus group, which performed many works by George Brecht, Ben Vautier, Ay-o, Dick Higgins, Bob Watts, Wolf Vostell, Yoko Ono, Chieko Shiomi, and others in Europe, Japan, and the United States. In 1962 and the years immediately following, the Fluxus group published and performed a number of Mac Low pieces, and his third major body of performance works is related to the Fluxus kind of piece. As scripts many of these works, such as *Thanks* or *Questioning,* have sets of directions and intentions that are filled in improvisationally by the performer. Others such as *Gathas,* a series begun in 1961, are purely choric simultaneities in which the performers read the sounds in any direction. Still other performance pieces are buried in cycles, an example being *8th Light Poem,* a scenario written in a fairly typical happenings vein. There also exist film scenarios from this period and style. The best known is *Tree,* in which the cameraman is asked to photograph a tree, unmoving and static, throughout a day.

Mac Low's cycle of odes, highly personal poems in classical form, do not use chance in any direct way and suggest a more direct and semantic phase in his work.

—Dick Higgins

MacDONALD, Sharman

Nationality: British. **Born:** Glasgow, Scotland in 1951. **Education:** Edinburgh University. **Family:** Married to Will Knightley; two children. **Career:** Thames Television writer-in-residence, The Bush Theatre, London, 1984-85. **Awards:** *Evening Standard* award, 1984. **Agent:** Patricia MacNaughton, MacNaughton Lowe Representation, 200 Fulham Road, London SW10 9PN, England.

Publications

Plays

When I Was a Girl, I Used to Scream and Shout . . . (produced London, 1984; Costa Mesa, California, 1989). London, Faber, 1985.
The Brave (produced London, 1988). Included in *When I Was a Girl, I Used to Scream and Shout . . . , When We Were Women,* 1990.
When We Were Women (produced London, 1988). Included in *The Brave, When I Was a Girl, I Used to Scream and Shout . . . ,* 1990.
When I Was a Girl, I Used to Scream and Shout . . . , The Brave, When We Were Women: Three Plays. London, Faber, 1990.
All Things Nice (produced London, 1991). London, Faber, 1991.
Shades (produced London, 1992). London, Faber, 1992.
Winter Guest (produced London, 1993). London, Faber, 1993.
Sharman MacDonald: Plays (includes *When I Was a Girl, I Used to Scream and Shout...*; *When We Were Women*; *The Winter Guest*; *Borders of Paradise*). London, Faber, 1995.

Television Play: *Wild Flowers,* 1990.

Novels

The Beast. London, Collins, 1986.
Night, Night. London, Collins, 1988.

*

Critical Study: "Listening to Women Talk" by Carol Anderson, in *The Scottish Novel Since the Seventies,* edited by Gavin Wallace and Randall Stevenson, Edinburgh, Edinburgh University Press, 1993.

* * *

Sharman Macdonald is one of the most successful contemporary Scottish playwrights. In contrast, however, to the many contemporary writers working in Scottish theater—Sue Glover, Rona Munro, Liz Lochhead—Macdonald's career has been predominantly metropolitan. Although many of her plays are set in Scotland, she achieved a much more visible production profile in England, both in the West End and in Leeds: *When I Was a Girl, I Used to Scream and Shout* (1984) premiered at the Bush; *When we Were Woman* (1989) at the Cottesloe; *All Things Nice* (1991) at the Royal Court; *Shades* (1992) in the West End; *Borders of Paradise* (1995) at Watford Palace; and *The Winter Guest* (1995) at West Yorkshire Playhouse.

The lack of production success in Scotland was even more perplexing, as her characters speak a shockingly realistic, completely familiar Scots-English. The subtlety of the language marks it as both affectingly truthful and achingly poetic, rooting the characters to Scotland in terms of class and geography and language and imagery. Thematically, too, her plays touch on issues deeply resonant within Scottish culture——mothers entangled in puzzling and even destructive relationships with their children (particularly their daughters); absent or problematic fathers; confused adolescents; and an immediate and deeply affecting physical world. Exploration of the nature of memory, nostalgia, and regret are all common in Macdonald's work.

Macdonald's first play, *When I was a Girl I Used to Scream and Shout,* is set in a small seaside town on the Scottish east coast. It shifts easily and poignantly between contemporary action and memory, between 1983 (the present) and 1955, 1959, 1960, and 1966. It charts three sets of relationships: that between Fiona and her mother Morag; between Fiona and her friend Vari; and between Fiona and her boyfriend Ewan, who only appears in the earlier flashbacks. The play is something of a rites-of-passage narrative with Fiona's relationship with Ewan at the center of that. Despite the significance of that relationship, however, the play's focus is on the mother/daughter relationship, exploring the secrets they keep from each other and the compromises necessary within families.

The Winter Guest adopts a much more classical structure—one day in the lives of the characters—but is equally evocative. All but plotless, it is an assured study in mood and feeling. It is set one February day in a seaside town on the west coast of Scotland. The beach is covered with a chilly layer of frost—a forthright metaphor for the stalled relationships the play describes and the characters' preoccupations with death. At its core is the relationship between a mother, Elspeth, and her recently widowed adult daughter, Frances. Their conversation is locked in a cycle of adolescent petulance and nostalgic regret but tempered by feelings of love and responsibility. Their relationship is matched by three other pairings: that of Frances's son Alex and his girlfriend Nita; the truant schoolboys Tom and Sam; and the elderly women, Chloe and Lily. It is a wholly human play with a chilly denouement of innocence lost. Despite all its restrained emotion and its taut theatrical structure, *The Winter Guest* was made into a film. MacDonald and the film's director, Alan Rickman, wrote the screenplay, and the film won a significant degree of interest from the Scottish press.

In 1996, Perth Theatre produced *When We Were Women*, and in 1997 Brunton produced *When I was a Girl.* In 1998, the Tron Theatre, Glasgow, in association with Dundee Repertory, presented the stage premiere of Macdonald's *Sea Urchins. Sea Urchins* is again about a remembered childhood past. It is set in Wales in June 1966 on a pebbled beach below a precipitous cliff. The play reveals family secrets and passions through the eyes of 11-year-old Rena, the daughter of Ailsa (who is Scottish) and John (who is Welsh). Each year the family goes on holiday with John's brother David and his family. In the course of one hot day the façade of familiarity—the habits, rituals, and traditions that hold the family together—is tested to its breaking point. John's less-than-secret affair with his sister-in-law Dora is exposed, hastening the revelation that John is the father of two of Dora's children, Rhiannon and Noelle. We learn of the death at birth of Rena's twin brother, a tragedy that continues to affect Ailsa and John, and we see Rhiannon's departure to live with her married lover in London.

The play is, then, about the lies, the concessions, and the negotiations that keep all relationships going. This is beautifully evoked in one of the play's most powerful speeches. David and his son Gareth see John and Dora making love in the long grass by the beach. Gareth is appalled, but David reveals not only that he knows about John and Dora's affair but that he has come to accept it:

> I'd add this to the marriage vows. Keep your secrets. Never breathe. Never hint. Don't tell at the moment of parting or on the day of a death. Don't let a fight pull it out of you. If you sin. It's your sin. Never cast your sin on another for their forgiveness and your relief. Bear your guilt yourself forever. Confession only injures the hearer. Lock it up. Lock it all inside you. See that? That back there. Who's to say that's not my fault? If that's what your mother needs to give me fifty week of her year. So be it. I don't want her to tell me about it. Don't want that ever. The day she tells me's the day I lose her. The longer the time that passes and her silent the more sure I am that she'll never speak. That I'll keep her.

The speech is a remarkable acknowledgment of responsibility, of need, of love, and of the necessity of compromise and forgiveness. It is all the more powerful in the play because it is spoken by, to, and about adults.

The convention of the childish voyeur and narrator has been a significant and successful feature of Macdonald's work. Very frequently her plays are about children watching adults with much of the drama resting on the vision and the telling of children. Although this is certainly the key structuring theme of *Sea Urchins*—the figures of Rena and, to a lesser degree, Noelle, carry the full weight of the drama—one might also detect in the play a straining at this convention. The deeply felt crises in the play are not for the children, and they are not seen, overheard, or told to them. Instead there are private moments—like that between David and Gareth—where adults struggle to achieve communication with each other. This struggle is the stuff of real and demanding drama.

Macdonald's is a unique and oddly detached voice within Scottish theater. By conjuring and representing hugely personal memories, her plays achieve a distinctive emotional immediacy, geographical localism, and linguistic specificity. They are utterly assured in their narrativity, occasionally breathtaking in their emotional ruthlessness but always utterly honest in their representations of family.

—Adrienne Scullion

MACHADO, Eduardo

Nationality: American. **Born:** Havana, Cuba in 1953. Moved to the United States in 1956. **Career:** Writer; lives in New York.

Agent: William Craver, The Writers and Artists Agency, 19 West 44th Street, Suite 1000, New York, New York 10036, U.S.A.

Publications

Plays

Rosario and the Gypsies, music by Rick Vartorella (produced New York, 1982).
The Modern Ladies of Guanabacoa (produced New York, 1983). Included in *The Floating Island Plays*, 1991.
Broken Eggs (produced New York, 1984). Published in *On New Ground* (an anthology of Hispanic plays), edited by Betty Osborne, New York, Theatre Communications Group, 1986.
Fabiola (produced New York, 1985). Included in *The Floating Island Plays*, 1991.
When It's Over, with Geraldine Sher (produced New Haven, Connecticut, 1986).
Wishing You Well (produced New York, 1987).
Why to Refuse (produced New York, 1987).
A Burning Beach (produced New York, 1988).
Don Juan in New York City (produced New York, 1988).
Garded (opera libretto) (produced Philadelphia, 1988).
Once Removed (produced New Haven, Connecticut, 1992). Published in *Plays in Process* (New York) vol. 9, no. 3, 1988.
The Day You'll Love Me, adaptation of the play by José Ignacio Cabrujas (produced Los Angeles, 1989; London, 1990).
Cabaret Bambu (produced New York, 1989).
Related Retreats (also director: produced New York, 1990).
Pericones (produced New York, 1990).
Stevie Wants to Play the Blues, music by Fredric Myrow, lyrics by Machado and Myrow (produced Los Angeles, 1990).
In the Eye of the Hurricane (produced Louisville, 1991). Included in *The Floating Island Plays*, 1991.
The Floating Island Plays (includes *The Modern Ladies of Guanabacoa, Fabiola, Broken Eggs, In the Eye of the Hurricane*). New York, Theatre Communications Group, 1991.

Television Plays: *Death Squad*, 1989: *China Rios, HBO*, 1989; *In the Heat of Saturday Night*, 1990.

Recording: *Broken Eggs*, 1996.

*

Critical Studies: "Eduardo Machado" by Stuart Spencer, in *BOMB*, Winter 1990, pp. 26-28; "Of Small Conquests and Big Victories: Gender Constructs in *The Modern Ladies of Guanabacoa*" by Elias Miguel Munoz, in *The Americas Review: A Review of Hispanic Literature and Art of the USA* (Houston, Texas), Summer 1992, pp. 105-11.

Theatrical Activities:
Actor: **Play**—Role in *A Visit* by Maria Irene Fornés, New York, 1981.

* * *

With his teacher and mentor Irene Fornés, Eduardo Machado stands at the forefront of Hispanic-American drama, an increasingly important component of theater in the United States. His plays, unlike those of Fornés, are not innovative in form. Machado is prolific and his work uneven. The best of his plays bring Chekhov to mind, for in the tempestuous and yet ordinary life of a household may be seen the end of an era, the remaking of a society. The highly individual characters are viewed with a critical yet compassionate eye. The plays are tragicomic, filled with absurdity, pettiness, energy, and grief.

Sent from his homeland as a child, the Havana-born Machado knows firsthand the loss of privilege and the experience of exile. In all his major work he seeks the meaning of his people's history. *A Burning Beach* symbolically represents Cuban society in the late nineteenth century, at the time of the short-lived uprising led by the poet José Martí; this decadent world of Yankee imperialists, landowners of Spanish descent, and Afro-Cuban servants is clearly doomed. The Bay of Pigs debacle is the background event in *Once Removed*, which chronicles the misadventures of an emigrant family in Florida and then in Texas. Machado's most satiric play, it is also full of affectionate admiration for the bumbling perseverance of its displaced persons. But the richest of Machado's works is the quartet published as *The Floating Island Plays*. Based on autobiography, they make up an epic twentieth-century drama that encompasses the stories of several Cuban families linked by marriage and then by exile in the United States. This is poetic history, in which details of characters' lives shift to meet the needs of an individual play, and it is high comedy, laying bare personal and social shortcomings at every turn.

Each of the *Floating Island* plays shows an extended family struggling with fundamental change. Set in the Cuba of 1928-31, *The Modern Ladies of Guanabacoa* depicts the domestic rituals of a society that is conservative, Catholic, and patriarchal. As the title suggests, these values are under siege, and in the end the head of the household, a proud Basque who excels at womanizing rather than moneymaking, is shot dead—possibly by an enraged husband, possibly by a government displeased by the expansion of the family's bus routes, possibly at the instigation of his son-in-law, a taxi driver who is using the family money and his own ability to make their fortune. Remarkably fair to all of his characters, the playwright nonetheless exhibits throughout his work a special sympathy for those out of power: women, homosexual men, and all those from a lower class and with darker skin. Not that such Machado creations are weak people. Women, here and in other plays, are the survivors, and they frequently get what they want. In these home-centered plays they are often dominant figures.

Fabiola covers the period 1955-67 and introduces *Floating Island*'s central catalytic, though offstage, event—the rise of Fidel Castro. Portraying a wealthy family related by marriage to that of the previous play, this work is the quartet's least comic and most daring. Its terrain is gothic, at its heart the desperate love of one brother for another. The less committed partner in this incestuous relationship must flee the country; his needier brother finally slits his wrists as yet more family members leave for the United States. Years of luxury end in anguish and guilt.

In the Eye of the Hurricane dramatizes the nationalization of the bus company established in the first play. It is 1960, and the taxi driver, in his climb to wealth, has apparently forgotten where he came from. He and his wife, attempting to keep their buses through public protest, are shocked when their efforts are made ludicrous by a lack of support. The populace cheers the takeover. Family members who lent romantic support to Castro's revolution come to see what it really means.

The resolution, if that is the right word, of this epic story takes place in 1979 when three generations of displaced Cubans gather for a wedding at a country club in suburban Los Angeles. *Broken Eggs* is the blackest of comedies. Though these Cuban-Americans are once again reasonably well-off, their tight family structure has come apart. The bride's parents have divorced, and her father is remarried to an Argentinean. Nearly everyone is dependent on drugs; the older generation downs Valium and alcohol, and the younger snorts cocaine. Though family lives throughout *The Floating Island Plays* are filled with squabbles, tensions, and power struggles, nastiness has reached a new level. For all this, however, we see that both the family and Cuba are inescapable. More than one character in more than one play quotes Christopher Columbus: "This is the most beautiful land that human eyes have seen." The loss of Eden is the quintessential American theme. Machado knows that you cannot go home again.

—M. Elizabeth Osborn

MADDY, Pat Amadu. *See* **MADDY, Yulisa Amadu.**

MADDY, Yulisa Amadu

Also writes as Pat Amadu Maddy. **Nationality:** Sierra Leonean. **Born:** Freetown, 27 December 1936. **Education:** Schools in Sierra Leone; Rose Bruford College, Sidcup, Kent, diploma 1965; City of London University, postgraduate diploma in arts administration; research fellow, Leeds University, from 1986. **Family:** Married Abibatu Kamara in 1986; six children. **Career:** Worked for Sierra Leone Railways; radio producer, Denmark and Britain, early 1960s; director and dancer, Comedia Hus, Copenhagen, 1966; director and actor, British Council Theatre, Freetown, 1968-69; tutor in drama and African literature, Evelyn Hone College, University of Zambia, Lusaka, 1969-70; artistic director, Keskidee Arts Centre, London, 1971-73; acting director, Sierra Leone Ministry of Tourism and Culture, Freetown, 1974-77; instructor in dance and drama, Morley College, London, 1979-80; fellow in theatre arts, Ibadan University, Nigeria, 1980-81; senior lecturer in performing arts, Ilorin University, Nigeria, 1981-83; visiting professor of performing arts, Special Education Resource Center, Bridgeport, Connecticut, 1983-85; Fulbright senior scholar, University of Maryland, College Park, and Morgan State College, Baltimore, 1985-86. Artistic director, Gbakanda Afrikan Tiata, Leeds, 1986—. **Awards:** Sierra Leone National Arts Festival prize, for fiction, 1973; Gulbenkian grant, 1978; Edinburgh Festival award, 1979. **Address:** 19 Francis Street, Leeds, Yorkshire LS7 4BY, England.

PUBLICATIONS (EARLY WORKS AS PAT AMADU MADDY)

Plays

Alla Gbah (produced London, 1967). Included in *Obasai and Other Plays*, 1971.

Obasai and Other Plays. London, Heinemann, 1971.

Gbana-Bendu (produced London, 1973; Baltimore, 1986). Included in *Obasai and Other Plays*, 1971.

Yon-Kon (televised 1982; produced Bridgeport, Connecticut, 1984). Included in *Obasai and Other Plays*, 1971.

Life Everlasting (produced London, 1972). Published in *Short African Plays*, edited by Cosmo Pieterse, London, Heinemann, 1972.

Big Breeze Blow (produced Freetown, 1974). Privately printed, 1984.

Take Tem Draw di Rope (produced Freetown, 1975).

Put for Me (produced Freetown, 1975).

Nah We Yone Dehn See (produced Freetown, 1975).

Big Berrin (in Krio: Big Death) (produced Freetown, 1976; Washington, D.C., 1984). Privately printed, 1984.

A Journey into Christmas (produced Ibadan, 1980).

Drums, Voices and Words (produced London, 1985).

Radio Plays: *If Wishes Were Horses*, 1963 (UK); and plays for Cross River Broadcasting, Sierra Leone Broadcasting, and Zambia Broadcasting.

Television Writing: *Saturday Night Out* series, 1980 (Nigeria); *Yon-Kon*, 1982 (Nigeria); and plays for Sierra Leone Broadcasting.

Novel

No Past, No Present, No Future. London, Heinemann, 1973.

Short Stories

Ny Afrikansk Prose, edited by Ulla Ryum. Copenhagen, Vendelkaer, 1967.

Other

African Images in Juvenile Literature: Commentaries on Neocolonialist Fiction. Jefferson, North Carolina, McFarland, 1996.

*

Critical Studies: *The Development of African Drama* by Michael Etherton, London, Hutchinson, 1982; "Empathy with the Deprived" by Chris Dunton, in *West Africa* (London), May 1988, pp. 968-969.

Theatrical Activities:
Director: **Plays**—All of his own plays; *The Trials of Brother Jero* by Wole Soyinka, Copenhagen, 1966, Freetown, 1969; *Theatre of Power* by Obi B. Egbuna, Copenhagen, 1967; *The Road* by Wole Soyinka, Freetown, 1968, Lusaka, 1970; *Dalabani* by Mukhtarr Mustapha, London, 1972; *Anansi and Bra Englishman* by Manley Young, London, 1972; *Onitsha Market Play*, London, 1973; *Cherry and Wine* by Jimi Rand, London, 1973; *Sighs of a Slave's Dream* by Lindsey Barrett, London, 1973; *Alla Gbah*, Freetown, 1974; *Gbakfest* (National Theatre Festival), Freetown, 1976; *Pulse* by Alem Mezgebe, London, 1979, Ibadan, 1980; *The Refund*, Ilorin, Nigeria, 1982; *The Chattering and the Song* by Femi Osofisan, Ilorin, Nigeria, 1983; *Gbana-Bendu*, Ilorin, Nigeria, 1983; *12 Days at the Round House*, London, 1986. **Television**—*Saturday Night Out* series, 1980; *Yon-Kon*, 1982.

Actor: **Plays**—Chume in *The Trials of Brother Jero* by Wole Soyinka, Copenhagen, 1966; Student in *Theatre of Power* by Obi B. Egbuna, Copenhagen, 1967; Professor in *The Road* by Wole Soyinka, Freetown, 1968, Lusaka, 1970; Brother Jero in *The Trials of Brother Jero*, Freetown, 1969; *Dalabani* by Mukhtarr Mustapha, London, 1972; *Life Everlasting*, London, 1972; *Onitsha Market Play*, London, 1973; *Sighs of a Slave's Dream* by Lindsey Barrett, London, 1973; *Alla Gbah*, Freetown, 1974; *Big Breeze Blow*, Freetown, 1974; *Take Tem Draw di Rope*, Freetown, 1975; *Put for Me*, Freetown, 1975; *Nah We Yone Dehn See*, Freetown, 1975; Awoko in *Big Berrin*, Freetown, 1976, Washington, D.C., 1984; Dictator in *Pulse* by Alem Mezgebe, London, 1979, Ibadan, 1980; *A Journey into Christmas*, Ibadan, 1980; Bobby in *Big Breeze Blow*, Ibadan, 1981; Student in *The Refund*, Ilorin, Nigeria, 1982; *Drums, Voices and Words*, London, 1985; *12 Days at the Round House*, London, 1986; Shadow in *Gbana-Bendu*, Baltimore, 1986. **Television**—Pagu in *Yon-Kon*, 1982.

Yulisa Amadu Maddy comments:

To make a statement introducing my work as a playwright is not easy for I am still asking questions which have yet to be answered; questions which demand honest, direct, and altruistic answers from publishers, critics, distributors, and a great many institutions and individuals. These people have yet to come to terms with the history, traditions, social, political, and economic background of this playwright; who and what he is; what he represents—this African from the so-called Third World.

I have always held Dylan Thomas in great esteem, not only because he was a great poet but because without him, the world would never have known, experienced, and enjoyed the wealth of knowledge and greatness in Amos Tutuola's Yoruba folktale, *The Palm-Wine Drinkard.* Tutuola's work, written in his own cryptic pidgin English, was looked upon with disdain and rejected as non-literary by his own countrymen and other African men of letters ("Euro-Afros"). Things haven't changed much—or have they? I am very happy that I am recognised as an "Afrikan Writer"; but first as a Sierra Leonean. I do not strive to satisfy American or European academics, researchers or Africanists. My direction is Africa—the people; whatever I write identifies with the people I know, from whom I came.

It will never be easy for most critics to be enthusiastic about my plays because they cannot discuss my characters without destroying them. My critics expose their own limitations with regard to their ignorance of the grassroots, the vital human relationships that I share very closely with those characters in their own world.

I took to creative writing, especially playwriting, because it gives me the freedom to experiment with the senses and emotions, the foibles and frailties of people, but mostly because I enjoy probing the fears, jealousies, greed, and power that influence their lives. Fools I detest; nonetheless, I prefer them to the religious hypocrite, the bigoted politician, the insincere academic poser. My fascination and sympathy have always been with and for the rejects, the down-trodden, and the over-zealous who fail only because they believe and follow blindly. Even the truth must be proved. When I wrote my first play, *If Wishes Were Horses*, while a student at Rose Bruford College, I was mocked, ridiculed, and laughed at. When the play was accepted and broadcast by the BBC African Service it dawned on me that the mockery and laughter were the incentive, inspiration, and encouragement I needed which I never got from my tutors and those elites of my own kind. So I have continued to write.

It is true that my plays speak out on behalf of the masses. My protagonists are drawn mostly from among the underdogs, the underprivileged. I caution against despair, apathy, and inertia. I urge them to come to terms with the realities of the world they live in, to use their common sense, plan their own strategies, and take individual and collective decisions as men and women in control of their own principles, not those dictated to them. They should be people who respect themselves—who understand their indigenous traditions, love their country, are ready to make sacrifices, even to die for it; are willing to make mistakes and ready to correct those mistakes: all of which leads to individual freedom and self-determination. From this basis they are prepared to face the world as men and women in control of their own destinies.

If posterity judges my work adversely, as some critics have done, the youth will always be there to prove it wrong. I believe in the young and unafraid Africans. For them, I will continue to write as I feel and like and want.

* * *

Mixing absurdist comedy, ritualistic theater, and Brechtian alienation effects with dialect, African proverbs, satire, political and social allusions, a rich, highly poetic stage language, parodies (especially of Christian missionary songs), and his own songs, Yulisa Amadu Maddy has tried to move beyond elite art to a popular yet political theater for the African urban population. From the European fringe theater of the 1960s he returned to Africa, where he has increasingly worked in pidgin English and local languages. His published plays are similar to his partly autobiographical novel, *No Past, No Present, No Future*, in being critical of the characters and their actions and in not choosing sides between them. The plays present highly stylized versions of representative African social problems but offer no solutions. Maddy aims to demystify and raise consciousness.

The early one-act play *Yon-Kon* contains many of the ingredients developed at greater length in his other works, including the relationship of personal freedom to communal activity. Although the setting is an African prison (details suggest that Maddy has Sierra Leone in mind), it is symbolic of the prison of the world in which the convicts are forced to keep up an absurd, endless march—"Right, left, left, right." A store clerk who has received a two-week sentence objects to the march and is hurt by the others, who demand that he respect Yon-Kon, their leader, who makes them chant, "We must not steal, we must not fight, we must obey the laws." When the new convict continues to assert his rights, he is attacked and after a struggle is accused of killing another prisoner who probably died from a weak heart. When Yon-Kon asks for £200 to have the prison doctor testify that the dead man died of a stroke, the clerk foolishly says that he will trust justice. He is unjustly sentenced to a further seven years for manslaughter and loses his life savings as a consequence.

Yon-Kon illustrates both the insecurity of a life of routine and the ways in which the law responds to money, prestige, and the views of the community. The new convict believes in bourgeois ideals of truth, justice, and personal rights, but he cannot survive the cruelty and absurdity of the world as represented by the prison, where power and leadership are more important than truth. Bully, leader, cynic, hypocrite, middleman between the prisoners and prison officials, leader of a criminal gang, enforcer of prison discipline, Yon-Kon appears adjusted to the reality of his environment: "I don't feel free outside. I will never feel free or enjoy anything outside prison. Prison was built for people like me. I will always make new friends there. I will have people to command." At the play's end he is once more making the others march "Right, left, left, right," while the convicts chant, "We must behave—as good citizens should."

Alla Gbah, possibly influenced by Camus's *L'Étranger*, portrays the last hours of Joko Campbell, a 27-year-old student condemned to death for killing his mistress. Maddy is here particularly concerned with the relationship of love to freedom. Joko ran away from home because his mother made him feel helpless, "like a child." Claiming not to have time for the "ethics of decadent puritan society," he falls in love with a Mrs. Manly, a woman of his mother's age who is notorious for seducing students. He idealizes her and finds in his love a way of transforming his dull, purposeless existence into a new life. When he catches her making love to another man, Joko kills her in defense of his manhood. Although Joko is a Dostoevskian hero who defines himself by "creating and killing," his notions are tested by a moral realism. Rejecting "money, education, morals, society," Joko wants to find "Love, selfless love. Freedom" and "Above all, happiness" among the underprivileged. But despite his proud defiance, as the play ends he is alone in his cell with one hour to live, frightened, crying, "I need you mother." Independence means learning the hard facts of life through trial and error.

Obasai, another short play, is a farcical yet hard-boiled portrait of modern African society. It concerns the decision of a tough village schoolboy to leave his mother, brother, and "good society" to join some swindlers in creating a new life for himself as a fisherman. Women, as in all Maddy's plays, seem to be agents of conformity, seductively threatening and hypocritical, whom the protagonist must reject. Because society is corrupt, there is little to choose from between the good and the swindlers. The dialogue often takes on the power of Jacobean satire: "Easy, Dad. He's a real punk. Look how he's running to meet the bitch. She wears his trousers and he wears her frock." Maddy's dramas are Jonsonian comedies in which crooked characters play upon and bring out the hypocrisy of society, while the attractiveness of the swindlers puts the audience's own values into question.

A common Maddy target is the African ruling class, especially the Europeanized Creole elite of Sierra Leone, which is contrasted to the downtrodden laborers and peasants through whose eyes the dramatist attempts to see reality. The long play *Gbana-Bendu*, with its wry, arch, exaggerated, melodramatic style, is concerned with the robbery of Africa by the governing elite and the improbability of the people in a democracy willingly ridding themselves of their oppressors. The attempt by two drunken tramps to save a virgin from being sacrificed becomes symbolic of the condition of Africa. The traditional masqueraders are revealed to be thieves who rob the people's houses during ceremonies and keep the sacrificial maidens for their own sexual use. The rhetoric of tradition and convention sanctifies their misdeeds. When she refuses to be saved from the sacrifice and claims that she must fulfill her duty, the virgin at first appears a symbol for the self-repression of traditional Africa. In a surprising twist, however, we learn that she is in cahoots with the chief masquerader, whom she loves; she uses her supposed loyalty to convention as a means to trick others. Although Maddy demystifies both traditionalist and nationalist rhetoric, the ending of the play becomes confusing, for the tramps are unreliable and might be making up the explanations they offer. In a final irony, as the tramps discuss whether they are becoming corrupted by others, they are themselves trapped by the crowd.

Many of Maddy's later plays in Krio and pidgin have not been published. *Big Berrin*, for which he was imprisoned, concerns corruption in Sierra Leone and the hopeless condition of the urban poor. According to Michael Etherton in *The Development of African Drama* (1982), the central character is a schoolteacher who, not having been paid for months, creates his own church through which he can exploit others. The play shows that the local politicians, businessmen, religious leaders, and other members of the establishment have continued the ways of the colonial powers in robbing the people.

—Bruce King

MALPEDE, Karen

Nationality: American. **Born:** Texas, 29 June 1945. **Education:** University of Wisconsin, Madison, Wisconsin, 1963-67, B.S. (honors) 1967; Columbia University, New York, 1969-71, M.F.A. 1971. **Family:** Married 1) Bill Hash in 1974 (divorced 1986), one daughter; 2) George Bartenieff in 1995. **Career:** Cofounder and resident playwright, New Cycle Theater, Brooklyn, New York; field faculty, Norwich University, Vermont, 1979-87; adjunct faculty, Lang College, spring 1991, and Tisch School of the Arts, 1986-91. Professor, Tisch School of Arts, New York University, 1991—

Visiting lecturer, Smith College, Northhampton, Massachusetts, spring semesters, 1982-86. **Awards:** PEN writers grant, 1981; New York Foundation for the Arts Grant for playwrighting, 1982-83; Winner, Broadcloth series, Minneapolis, 1983; ART Matters, Inc. Artists fellowship, 1989; The Eastman Foundation, writer's grant, 1991; Goddard fellowship, New York University, 1994; McKnight National Playwright's fellowship, 1994-95; Semi-finalist, Essay, *New Letters* New Writing Contest, 1996; Vidda Foundation, Production Grants, 1995, 1996. **Member:** PEN; Dramatists Guild; The Center on Violence and Human Survival. **Agent:** Helen Merrill Ltd., 435 West 23rd Street, #1A, New York, New York 10011, U.S.A. **Address:** 289 Washington Avenue, Brooklyn, New York 11205, U.S.A.

Publications

Plays

A Lament for Three Women (produced New York, 1974). In *A Century of Plays by American Women,* edited by Rachel France, New York, Richards Rosen Press, 1979.

Rebeccah (produced New York, 1975).

Sappho & Aphrodite (produced New York, 1983).

A Monster Has Stolen the Sun (produced New York, 1984).

Us (produced New York, 1987). In *Women on the Verge: Seven Avant-garde American Plays,* edited by Rosette C. Lamont, New York, Applause Books, 1993.

A Monster Has Stolen the Sun and Other Plays (inlcudes *A Monster Has Stolen the Sun*; *The End of the War*; *Sappho & Aphrodite*). Marlboro, Vermont, The Marlboro Press, 1987.

Better People (produced New York, 1990). In *Angels of Power and Other Reproductive Creations,* edited by Susan Hawthorne and Renate Klein, West Melbourne, Australia, Spinifex, 1991.

Going to Iraq (produced New York, 1992).

Kassandra, adaptation of novel by Christa Wolf (produced New York, 1992).
The Beekeeper's Daughter (Veroli, Italy, and New York, 1994).

Screenplay: *The Beekeeper's Daughter,* 1997.

Television Plays: *The Open Theater and the Plays of Peter Handke* (wrote and narrated part 3), 1973; *Genetic Property,* 1990.

Video: *Underexposed: the Temple of the Fetus,* with Kathy High, 1993.

Other

People's Theater in America. New York, Drama Book Publishers, 1972.
Women in Theater: Compassion and Hope. New York, Drama Book Publishers, 1983; New York, Limelight Editions, 1985.

Editor, *Three Works by the Open Theater.* New York, Drama Book Publishers, 1974.

*

Critical Study: In *Artists Writing Ethnic Cleansing* by Steven M. Weine, Latham, Maryland, Rowan & Littlefield, 1986.

Karen Malpede comments:

My early work dealt most often with myth or history. For example, *Sappho & Aphrodite* is about the great Greek poet and the school she ran for women on Lesbos; *A Monster Has Stolen the Sun* is based upon the Celtic myth of the goddess Macha (in my play) made to wrestle the king when she is nine months pregnant. She wins and puts a curse on him so that he will never be able to fight again without being as overwhelmed as a woman in childbirth. *Making Peace: A Fantasy* is set in America during the visionary decade of the 1940s; it takes place on earth and in heaven, where the utopian thinkers Charles Fourier, Mother Ann Lee, and Mary Wollstonecraft vie for space on a heavenly mound.

Since 1986 I've dealt almost exclusively with contemporary characters and events: *Us* is about child abuse, incest, and war and their effects on the erotic lives of two sets of parents and their children; *Better People* is a surreal comedy about reproductive technologies and genetic engineering; *Going to Iraq* is about life in the United States during the Golf War; *The Beekeeper's Daughter* tells what happens when a human rights worker brings a woman who has been raped during the war in Bosnia home to her father. It was first produced in Italy and in New York during the war.

My work has been called, variously, poetic, feminist, political, spiritual, avant-garde. It's also often funny. Most recently my plays have been labeled "theater of witness." I've been influenced by all the usual suspects, but, especially, I would add by ancient Greeks and Isben as well as the Living Theater, Genet, Stein, Yeats, Augusta Gregory, and Duras and Christa Wold, whose *Cassandra* I adapted for the stage. I'm fascinated by character and language. I'm interested in the connections between personal and public violence. I think of the theater as a healing space in which characters make the turn from victims to survivors.

* * *

There is a persisting paradox at the heart of the work and witness of Karen Malpede. Critics regularly express surprise at the contrast between her acknowledged significance in the canon of contemporary American theater and her failure to impinge on the consciousness of the majority of theatergoers. In fact, this phenomenon is more prevalent than popularly supposed. With several professionally produced plays to her name, the award-winning Malpede is a relatively prolific writer, and, in applying her wide-ranging professional interests to making theater relevant, she has over the years developed an enthusiastic and informed audience for her work.

Malpede's work is founded on an approach to composition in which ideas are constantly being tested, reworked, and re-formed. *Going to Iraq,* for example, developed out of a collective theater piece, *Collateral Damage,* which itself grew out of a monologue, *Baghdad Bunker*. Of her plays the work *The Beekeeper's Daughter* brings together many thematic interests developed in earlier pieces, of which the better known are *Us, A Monster Has Stolen the Sun, The End of War, Sappho and Aphrodite, A Lament for Three Women,* and *Blue Heaven.*

Malpede's background consists of extensive exposure to and experience in the avant-garde theater, with close connections going back to LaMama, Judith Malina, Julian Beck's Living Theatre, the work of Joseph Chaikin, and Charles Marowitz's Open Theatre. She combines her pedagogic interest in her role as associate professor at the Tisch School of Arts with an interest in playwriting and direction for Theater Three Collective, a Brooklyn-based organization formed "to explore the human psyche as it intersects with history." She has written, contributed to, and edited several seminal books underpinning her interest in the role and significance of women in the theater, the most important being *People's Theatre in Amerika* (1972) and *Women in Theatre: Compassion and Hope* (1983). Her extensive contribution has been widely recognized as influential in the advancement of the interests of minority groups, from black theater to lesbian theater. True to her theatrical influences, however, the thrust of her work continues to be broadly humanitarian. This may be further qualified by accentuating Malpede's belief in the indissoluble link between personal and political ethics. Such a belief is explicit in most of her plays, for example, *Blue Heaven,* a work that collages the sensational story of the private violence and death of the artist Ana Mendieta, who fell from the window of her husband Carl Andre's SoHo apartment, with the public violence of the Desert Storm victory in the Persian Gulf War.

If Malpede's interdisciplinary and eclectic interests make her hard to categorize, she argues, characteristically supporting her theorizing with her theater practice, that her own life parallels the larger advances in the past 25 years of special-interest identity politics. This has created a situation in which gender, sexual orientation, ethnic origin, and disease or disability have "shown us how to recognise both self and other." Her response to this, in a phrase adapted from Carolyn Forché, is a "theatre of witness," which she describes as a way of "changing the self by communion with the other's situation and story . . . (as a means of) revitalising the individual and re-affirming the social contract."

In a defining article in *New Theatre Quarterly* in August 1996, Malpede further qualifies the theater of witness as "a new ritual and poetic theatre whose substance is the inner life as lived in the presence of history . . . which . . . by coming cognisant of the extremity of twentieth century violence poses the question: what does it take to be human in such an age as this?" In both the processes of its construction and in its dramatic content, *The Beekeeper's Daughter* in particular offers an exemplary paradigm of the theater of witness. Addressed to public questions hanging over a lack of empathy in the face of racial cleansing in the former Yugoslavia, the play came to fruition through the writer's accumulation of awareness of the reality of the situation in Bosnia as it impinged on the American people. Followings its premiere in Italy in 1994, Malpede conducted an undergraduate seminar in 1995 at the Tisch School of Arts supported by her collaborator, psychiatrist Stevan Weine. The theoretical strands of the teaching program modulated into a series of supporting testimonies from participants, thus providing the kind of synthesis that encourages Malpede to the view that two types of theater exist—the spectacular and the "necessary."

As a piece of entertainment, *The Beekeeper's Daughter,* with themes based on Greek tragedy linked to evocations of contemporary politics, led one critic to say that "it should be read not watched . . . (as it) was impossible to comprehend the play's subtle meanings." Nonetheless, Malpede's ongoing capacity to examine contemporary issues through her highly developed skill in characterization and dramatic economy continues to redefine theater as a necessary, sustainable, and innovative source of social and political action.

—Paul Hadfield

MAMET, David (Alan)

Nationality: American. **Born:** Flossmoor, Illinois, 30 November 1947. **Education:** Rich Central High School; Francis W. Parker School; Goddard College, Plainfield, Vermont, B.A. in English 1969; Neighborhood Playhouse School, New York, 1968-69. **Family:** Married 1) Lindsay Crouse in 1977 (divorced), one daughter; 2) Rebecca Pidgeon in 1991. **Career:** Actor in summer stock, 1969; stage manager, *The Fantasticks*, New York, 1969-70; lecturer in drama, Marlboro College, Vermont, 1970; artist-in-residence, Goddard College, 1971-73; founder and artistic director, St. Nicholas Company, Plainfield, Vermont, 1972, and St. Nicholas Players, Chicago, 1974-76; faculty member, Illinois Arts Council, 1974; visiting lecturer, University of Chicago, 1975-76 and 1979, and New York University, 1981; teaching fellow, Yale University School of Drama, New Haven, Connecticut, 1976-77; associate artistic director, Goodman Theatre, Chicago, 1978-84; associate director, New Theater Company, Chicago, 1985. Associate professor of film, Columbia University, New York, 1988—. Contributing editor, *Oui* magazine, 1975-76. **Awards:** Joseph Jefferson award, 1974; Obie award, 1976, 1983; New York State Council on the Arts grant, 1976; Rockefeller grant, 1976; CBS-Yale University fellowship, 1977; New York Drama Critics Circle award, 1977, 1984; Outer Circle award, 1978; Society of West End Theatre award, 1983; Pulitzer prize, 1984; Dramatists Guild Hull-Warriner award, 1984; American Academy award, 1986; Tony award, for *Glengarry Glen Ross,* and for *American Buffalo,* both 1984, and for *Speed-the-Plow,* 1988; American Academy and Institute of Arts and Letters award, 1986; Golden Globe award nomination for best screenplay, for *House of Games,* 1988; Writers Guild award nomination, for *The Untouchables,* 1988. **Agent:** Howard Rosenstone, Rosenstone/Wender, 3 East 48th Street, 4th Floor, New York, New York 10017, U.S.A.

Publications

Plays

Lakeboat (produced Marlboro, Vermont, 1970; revised version produced Milwaukee, 1980). New York, Grove Press, 1981.

Duck Variations (produced Plainfield, Vermont, 1972; New York, 1975; London, 1977). With *Sexual Perversity in Chicago,* New York, Grove Press, 1978; in *American Buffalo, Sexual Perversity in Chicago, Duck Variations*, 1978.

Mackinac (for children; produced Chicago, 1972?).

Marranos (produced Chicago, 1972-73?).

The Poet and the Rent: A Play for Kids from Seven to 8:15 (produced Chicago, 1974). Included in *Three Children's Plays*, 1986.

Squirrels (produced Chicago, 1974). New York, French, 1982.

Sexual Perversity in Chicago (produced Chicago, 1974; New York, 1975; London, 1977). With *Duck Variations*, New York, Grove Press, 1978; in *American Buffalo, Sexual Perversity in Chicago, Duck Variations, 1978.*

American Buffalo (produced Chicago, 1975; New York, 1976; London, 1978). New York, Grove Press, 1977; in *American Buffalo, Sexual Perversity in Chicago, Duck Variations*, 1978.

Reunion (produced Louisville, 1976; New York, 1979; London, 1981). With *Dark Pony*, New York, Grove Press, 1979.

The Woods (also director: produced Chicago, 1977; New York, 1979; London, 1984). New York, Grove Press, 1979.

All Men Are Whores (produced New Haven, Connecticut, 1977; London, 1990). Included in *Short Plays and Monologues*, 1981.

A Life in the Theatre (produced Chicago and New York, 1977; London, 1979). New York, Grove Press, 1978; London, Methuen, 1989.

The Revenge of the Space Pandas; or, Binky Rudich and the Two-Speed Clock (produced Chicago, 1977). Included in *Three Children's Plays*, 1986.

Dark Pony (produced New Haven, Connecticut, 1977; New York, 1979; London, 1981). With *Reunion*, New York, Grove Press, 1979.

The Water Engine: An American Fable (produced Chicago and New York, 1977; London, 1989). With *Mr. Happiness*, New York, Grove Press, 1978.

Prairie du Chien (broadcast 1978; produced New York, 1985; London, 1986). Included in *Short Plays and Monologues*, 1981; with *The Shawl*, London, Methuen, 1989.

American Buffalo, Sexual Perversity in Chicago, Duck Variations: Three Plays. London, Eyre Methuen, 1978.

Mr. Happiness (produced New York, 1978; London, 1984). With *The Water Engine*, New York, Grove Press, 1978.

Lone Canoe; or, The Explorer, music and lyrics by Alaric Jans (produced Chicago, 1979).

The Sanctity of Marriage (produced New York, 1979). With *Reunion* and *Dark Pony*, New York, French, 1982.

Shoeshine (produced New York, 1979). Included in *Short Plays and Monologues*, 1981.

A Sermon (also director: produced New York, 1981; London, 1987). Included in *Short Plays and Monologues*, 1981.

Short Plays and Monologues (includes *All Men Are Whores, The Blue Hour: City Sketches, In Old Vermont, Litko, Prairie du Chien, A Sermon, Shoeshine*). New York, Dramatists Play Service, 1981.

Edmond (produced Chicago and New York, 1982; London, 1985). New York, Grove Press, 1983; London, Methuen, 1986.

The Disappearance of the Jews (produced Chicago, 1983).
Glengarry Glen Ross (produced London, 1983; Chicago and New York, 1984). New York, Grove Press, and London, Methuen, 1984.
Red River, adaptation of a play by Pierre Laville (produced Chicago, 1983).
Five Unrelated Pieces (includes *Two Conversations*; *Two Scenes*; *Yes, But So What*) (produced New York, 1983). Included in *Dramatic Sketches and Monologues*, 1985.
The Dog (produced 1983). Included in *Dramatic Sketches and Monologues*, 1985.
Film Crew (produced 1983). Included in *Dramatic Sketches and Monologues*, 1985.
4 A.M. (produced 1983). Included in *Dramatic Sketches and Monologues*, 1985.
Vermont Sketches (includes *Pint's a Pound the World Around, Deer Dogs, Conversations with the Spirit World, Dowsing*) (produced New York, 1984). Included in *Dramatic Sketches and Monologues*, 1985).
The Frog Prince (produced Louisville, 1984; New York, 1985). Included in *Three Children's Plays*, 1986.
The Spanish Prisoner (produced Chicago, 1985).
The Shawl (produced Chicago and New York, 1985; London, 1986). With *Prairie du Chien*, New York, Grove Press, 1985; London, Methuen, 1989.
The Cherry Orchard, adaptation of a play by Chekhov (produced Chicago, 1985). New York, Grove Press, 1987.
Cross Patch (broadcast 1985; produced New York, 1990). Included in *Dramatic Sketches and Monologues*, 1985.
Goldberg Street (broadcast 1985; produced New York, 1990). Included in *Dramatic Sketches and Monologues*, 1985.
Vint, adaptation of a story by Chekhov, in *Orchards* (produced Urbana, Illinois, 1985; New York, 1986). New York, Knopf, 1986.
Dramatic Sketches and Monologues (includes *Five Unrelated Pieces, The Power Outrage, The Dog, Film Crew, 4 A.M., Food, Pint's a Pound the World Around, Deer Dogs, Columbus Avenue, Conversations with the Spirit World, Maple Sugaring, Morris and Joe, Steve McQueen, Yes, Dowsing, In the Mall, Cross Patch, Goldberg Street*). New York, French, 1985.
Goldberg Street: Short Plays and Monologues. New York, Grove Press, 1985.
Three Children's Plays. New York, Grove Press, 1986.
Speed-the-Plow (produced New York, 1987; London, 1988). New York, Grove Press, 1988; London, Methuen, 1989.
House of Games (screenplay). New York, Grove Press, 1987; London, Methuen, 1988.
Things Change, with Shel Silverstein (screenplay). New York, Grove Press, 1988; London, Methuen, 1989.
Where Were You When It Went Down? in *Urban Blight* (musical revue), based on an idea by John Tillinger, music by David Shire, lyrics by Richard Maltby, Jr. (produced New York, 1988).
Bobby Gould in Hell (produced New York, 1989; London, 1991).
Uncle Vanya, adaptation of the play by Chekhov (produced Harrogate, 1990). New York, Grove Press, 1989.
Five Television Plays (includes *A Waitress in Yellowstone, The Museum of Science and Industry Story, A Wasted Weekend, We Will Take You There, Bradford*). New York, Grove Weidenfeld, 1990.
We're No Angels (screenplay). New York, Grove Weidenfeld, 1990.
Three Sisters, adaptation of the play by Chekhov. New York, Grove Weidenfeld, 1991.
Homicide (screenplay). New York, Grove Weidenfeld, 1992.
Oleanna (produced New York, 1992; London, 1993).
Plays: One (includes *Chronology*; *Duck Variations*; *Sexual Perversity in Chicago*; *Squirrels*; *American Buffalo*; *The Water Engine*; *Mr. Happiness*). London, Methuen, 1994.
No One Will Be Immune and Other Plays and Pieces. New York, Dramatists Play Service, 1994.
The Cryptogram. New York, Dramatists Play Service, 1995.
American Buffalo: A Screenplay. 1995.
Plays: Two (includes *Reunion*; *Dark Pony*; *A Life in Theater*; *Lakeboat*; *Edmond*). London, Metheun, 1996.
Plays: Three (includes *Glengarry Glen Ross*; *Prairie du Chien*; *The Shawl*; *Speed the Plow*). London, Methuen, 1996.
The Old Religion. New York, Free Press, 1997.
The Spanish Prisoner (screenplay). In *Scenario* (New York), Spring 1998.
The Old Neighborhood: Three Plays. New York, Vintage Books, 1998.

Screenplays: *The Postman Always Rings Twice*, 1981; *The Verdict*, 1982; *The Untouchables*, 1987; *House of Games*, 1987; *Things Change*, with Shel Silverstein, 1988; *We're No Angels*, 1990; *Homicide*, 1991; *Glengarry Glen Ross*, 1992; *Hoffa*, 1992; *Oleanna*, 1994; *Uncle Vanya on 42nd Street*, 1994; *American Buffalo*, 1996; *Wag the Dog*, 1998.

Radio Plays: *Prairie du Chien*, 1978; *Cross Patch*, 1985; *Goldberg Street*, 1985; *Dintenfass*, 1989.

Poetry

The Hero Pony. New York, Grove Weidenfeld, 1990.

Other

Writing in Restaurants (essays). New York, Viking, 1986; London, Faber, 1988.
The Owl (for children), with Lindsay Crouse. New York, Kipling Press, 1987.
Warm and Cold (for children), with Donald Sultan. New York, Grove Weidenfeld, 1988.
Some Freaks (essays). New York, Viking, 1989; London, Faber, 1990.
On Directing (essays). New York, Viking, 1991.
The Village (novel). London, Faber and Faber, 1994.
A Whore's Profession: Notes and Essays. London and Boston, Faber and Faber, 1994.
The Duck and the Goat. New York, St. Martin's Press, 1996.
Passover. London, HarperCollins, 1996.
Make-believe Town: Essays and Remembrances. London, Faber and Faber, 1996.
True and False: Heresy and Common Sense for the Actor. New York, Pantheon Books, 1997.
Three Uses of the Knife: On the Nature and Purpose of Drama. New York, Columbia University Press, 1998.

*

Bibliography: *Ten Modern American Playwrights* by Kimball King, New York, Garland, 1982.

Critical Studies: *David Mamet* by C.W.E. Bigsby, London, Methuen, 1985; *David Mamet* by Dennis Carroll, London, Macmillan, and New York, St. Martin's Press, 1987; *David Mamet: A Casebook,* edited by Leslie Kane, New York, Garland, 1991; "How to Do Things with Salesmen: David Mamet's Speech-Act Play" by David Worster, in *Modern Drama Review* (Downsview, Ontario), Fall 1994; "Man among Men: David Mamet's Homosocial Order" by David Radavich, in *Fictions of Masculinity: Crossing Cultures, Crossing Sexualities,* edited by Peter F. Murphy, New York, New York University Press, 1994; "P.C. Power Play: Language and Representation in David Mamet's *Oleanna*" by Roger Bechtel, in *Theatre Studies* (Columbus, Ohio), 1996, pp. 29-48; Weasels *and Wisemen: Education, Ethics, and Ethnicity in David Mamet* by Leslie Kane, New York, St. Martin's Press, 1999.

Theatrical Activities:
Director: **Plays**—*Beyond the Horizon* by O'Neill, Chicago, 1974; *The Woods,* Chicago, 1977; *Twelfth Night,* New York, 1980; *A Sermon,* New York, 1981; *Oleanna,* New York, 1992. **Films**—*House of Games,* 1987; *Things Change,* 1988; *Homicide,* 1991; *Hoffa,* 1992; *Oleanna,* 1994. **Television**–*Ricky Jay and His 52 Assistants,* 1996.

Actor: **Television**–*The Water Engine,* 1992; *Dr. Katz: Professional Therapist,* 1995.

* * *

David Mamet's rise to the forefront of American drama has been seen as the triumph of the minimalist. Mamet has also been cast in the role of the theater poet who indulges in language for its own sake and as the apologist for the bigmouthed, home-baked philosopher. His plays have been attacked for their lack of clarity, for their plotlessness, for their obscenity, and for their articulation of a poetics of loss without any compensatory dimensions. Some critics said his work was without subtext; others implied it consisted of nothing but subtext. All this is true in one sense or other, but the stridency of response is itself an indicator that the Mamet phenomenon has implicated the audience as a vital constituent of what happens in the plays.

Most of Mamet's plays seem in some way fragmentary. Almost from the start his plays looked like something made on a film-editing table; he frequently made use of cinematic devices such as crosscutting. The 30 brief scenes that make up *Sexual Perversity in Chicago* do have a chronological linearity, but it is left to the audience—placed by the title as voyeurs of perversity—to read through the displacement activity that passes as dialogue and interpret its own construction of the homosocial sexuality behind the talk. Mamet's use of the fragment cogently illustrates the theorists' view that the audience's function is to "creatively fill in the gaps."

Like the presentation of behavior, the philosophies that spill out of Mamet's early characters are fractured slogans chipped out of a broader cultural context. These contexts are always so well known as to have their own mythology: the gangster, the real-estate salesman, the Jewish patriarch, the sexual hijacker—each has an ethic that has been articulated and elaborated by decades of film and popular culture. That the characters are "losers" does nothing to invalidate the myth, but it does open up the dimension of loss. In *American Buffalo* the failure of the three would-be crooks to achieve any part of their scheme does not undermine the notion of the big burglary as a faith to live by, any more than the males in *Sexual Perversity* will cease to live in hope of the big sexual coup. The reading of this as loss, meaninglessness, or sterility, however, is ambivalent, because the texture of language brings a lyricism that is both bonding and possibly healing, if not regenerative. *American Buffalo* ends with compassion. *The Disappearance of the Jews* may announce the disappearance of something but that does not mean that nothing is left. Whether they reach for fiction or for rhetoric, the characters seldom stop reaching.

Bonding may be loveless or even adversarial in Mamet. *Glengarry Glen Ross* has its four salesmen wedged within the real-estate system, a system that says that two of them must be laid off to become waste products, the condition of so many Mamet characters. The predatory cycle, however, takes in not only the salesmen themselves but also clients who are trapped by the wonderful spirals of sales blather into buying junk land. Again, language is the bond: the first act ends with Roma's virtuoso cadenza on the general theme of the human condition and the sudden—brilliantly comic—revelation that he is talking to a complete stranger. The laughter is also reflexive; the audience has been as absorbed in the barroom philosophy almost as much as the clients.

Mamet has not been averse to describing some of his plays as "classical tragedies," apparently because of their tone and themes of rejection and betrayal. It is also noticeable, however, that in these plays he moves beyond episodic structure to give a precisely defined diachronic placing that observes unities of both place and time. The whole claustrophobic action of *American Buffalo* takes place in a junk shop within a single day, while *The Woods* dramatizes the recurrent Mamet question—why men and women do not get along—by placing two characters in a cabin in the woods for a single night. Although in both plays the characters are firmly positioned within a fantasy social system, their more sustained action has gratified critics who want to give Mamet's characters an individual psychology. Deriving from the same period but not staged until 1994, *The Cryptogram* pivots on a related set of questions concerning interpersonal betrayals but scrutinizes them from the perspective of a boy nervously approaching adulthood.

That Mamet's plays look at gender delineations as well as sexuality is clear from the content of the male fantasies that pervade his work. The classification of characters through fantasy as well as through social constructions means, however, that female characters in particular can be ambivalent. This is especially clear in *The Shawl* and *Speed-the-Plow* when two male characters confront a woman who intrudes on their relationship. In the latter play, a conflict erupts when two Hollywood tycoons give a temporary secretary a script to read and her verdict divides them. The secretary can be played dumb or shrewd, as a product of the male gaze or as a generator of it, like the nonappearing woman in *A Life in the Theatre*. A similar complexity of female characterization can be found in Mamet's screenplay for the motion picture *House of Games* and in his sequel to *Speed-the-Plow, Bobby Gould in Hell.* Structurally, both may be seen as modern morality plays, a genre Mamet experimented with in *Edmond,* a descent into the hell of New York.

The same ambivalence is much more starkly visible in *Oleanna,* Mamet's gloss on the political correctness debates of the 1990s. Whatever Mamet's protestations about how the two characters should be played, the fact that their sexual-harassment duel has cogently been interpreted in radically different ways in New York and in London shows that once again the minimalist exterior is braced by a formidable subtext of power relations.

—Howard McNaughton

MANAKA, Matsemela

Nationality: South African. **Born:** Alexandra, South Africa in 1956. **Family:** Married in 1984; two children. **Career:** Artist, musician, poet, and playwright. Founder-member, Soyikwa Theatre Group, Soweto, 1976—. Lives in Diepkloof, Soweto. **Awards:** Freedom-to-write award, PEN, 1987; Edinburgh Fringe First award, for *Pula* and *Imbumba*. **Agent:** c/o PEN, 568 Broadway, 4th Floor, New York, New York 10012, U.S.A. **Address:** c/o The Market Theatre, P.O. Box 8656, Johannesburg 2000, South Africa.

Publications

Plays

The Horn (produced Soweto, 1978).
Egoli, City of Gold (produced Soweto, 1979; Erlangen, West Germany, 1980). Johannesburg, Soyinkwa-Ravan, 1979.
Pula (*Rain!*) (produced Soweto, 1982; Edinburgh, 1983; London, 1984). Published in *Market Plays*, edited by Stephen Gray, Johannesburg, Ad. Donker, 1986; Braamfontein, Skotaville, 1990.
Imbumba (*Unity*) (produced Soweto, n.d.; Edinburgh, 1983; London, 1984).
Children of Asazi (produced Soweto, 1985; New York, 1986).
Goree, music by Motsumi Makhene (produced Soweto, 1985; New York, 1989).
Blues Afrika Café (produced Johannesburg, 1990).
Ekhaya: Museum over Soweto (produced Johannesburg, 1991).
Yamina (produced Johannesburg, 1993).

Other

Echoes of African Art. Braamfontein, Skotaville, 1987.

*

Critical Studies: *"In Township Tonight!": South Africa's Black City Music and Theatre* by David Coplan, Johannesburg, Soyinkwa-Ravan, 1985; *Black Theater, Dance, and Ritual in South Africa* by Peter Larlham, Ann Arbor, Michigan, UMI Research Press, 1985; *Theatre and Cultural Struggle in South Africa* by Robert Mshengu Kavanagh, London, Verso, 1985; "*Repainting the Damaged Canvas: The Theatre of Matsemela Manaka*," in *Commonwealth: Essays and Studies* (Dijon), no. 14, vol. 1, 1991; "From Soweto to Goree: A South African Writer in Search of the African Heritage" by Geoffrey Davis, in *Matatu* (Amsterdam), 1994, pp. 25-38.

Theatrical Activities:
Director: **Plays**—All his own plays.

* * *

Matsemela Manaka's most anthologized play, *Children of Asazi,* was first produced in Soweto in 1985. It deals with homelessness, toys with incest, and exposes the systematic destruction of the black family unit under the then racist South African government. What is remarkable about the work, apart from a plot that makes ingenious use of the structure of indigenous African folktales, is that its very advocacy of resistance is rooted in love and attachment to place. Diliza, the hero, is a young, politically conscious firebrand who has sworn to defy the government bulldozers coming to mow down Alexandra, the city where he lives with his father in a shack. Against his father's instructions, he attends a meeting aimed at mobilizing the people against enforced evacuation. On his return he discovers that one of the most vocal men at the meeting, Ntate Majika, is actually a rich, sneaky, two-faced character who has evicted a poorer black neighbor, Ntate Mabu, from his house and sent him into the streets by offering bribes of whiskey to the administration officer responsible for allocating houses. Diliza unmasks Majika and forces him to confess several other acts of sabotage against the inhabitants of Alexandra, including the confiscation of the money collected by the residents to get a lawyer to defend them against forceful removal. Majika had actually invested the money for the benefit of his own stomach, wife, and children. His argument is that, when the period of investment elapses, the money will be used to defend all of the residents who have been arrested while protesting against removal. He claims that it is the devil that made him do it. Diliza summons the spirits of the land to assist him in exorcising the thieving devil in Majika. The spirits actually appear on stage in a mock ritual, thereby enhancing the work's visual effect.

Central to the play, however, is Diliza's love affair with Charmaine, who at the beginning of the play is pregnant with Diliza's child. In a complicated plot that unfolds through conflicting stories told by Nduna, Diliza's father, and his grandmother, Gogo, we learn first that Charmaine is Diliza's sister, only to be told later that Charmaine's mother was another woman who is dead. Before this revelation Charmaine had suggested to Diliza that they run away and resettle somewhere else or abort the child. The story comes to a happy ending when Diliza insists on finding out who his real mother is. This stubborn quest is a subtle metaphor for the average South African's yearning to be earthed where his umbilical cord is buried, namely, his native land. Thus, even though the play ends happily for the couple, a greater threat to their future and unborn child looms, for there is a palpable and audible menace in the play, the sound of bulldozers in the distance. This existential anguish is articulated by Gogo:

> As we were going up the hill from the bridge, I saw my best Sunday hat, rollerskating down the donga. . . . One of my little friends, a girl, noticed the hat and screamed: "There goes your hat!" . . . When she came back with the hat, she found us in tears. My home was no more. I looked at the little children and saw citizens whose citizenship was like an ice cream under the heat of the sun.

This thematic preoccupation is further pointed up when, out of compassion, Diliza takes in the homeless and disguised Gogo, not knowing that she is his grandmother. She is accepted into an already crowded shack:

> Nduna: There you are! It fits like a garage and two rooms in the backyards of Soweto. Look at that! It's a three room

house already. Innovation! . . . we grew up sleeping in the kitchen, maGogo. Thirteen of us . . . in a room divided into two rooms by means of a curtain. . . . We may not be able to stretch our feet, but one day we will.

Thus, naive and simple as the play may appear on the surface, a careful reading of *Children of Asazi* reveals that beneath the love story and the trite plot of mistaken identities lies a terrifyingly mapped geography of dispossession and its devastating impact on three generations of black South Africans who had never had a decent roof over their heads. Manaka's forte in the play is the traditional folktale technique into which he weaves songs, proverbs, ironies, idiomatic expressions, reversals, flashbacks, mime, and a measure of contemporaneity through jazz music. These elements reduce the tedium of words, and the racy, crisp, one-line dialogue suggests that the play moves swiftly in performance.

Manaka's other well-known play, *Egoli, City of Gold,* was devised in a workshop and performed to overwhelmingly high audience turnouts at the Space Theatre in 1979. It has also traveled abroad and was so provocative at the time that the South African government banned it. The play chronicles the experiences of two miners, both migrant laborers who are living in men's compounds and separated from their families. Surrounded by walls day and night, they see their lives as prison sentences. To them working in the mines for paltry pay is one long process of asphyxiation by inhaling gold dust. To make things worse, they realize that the huge profits from exported gold are used by the South African government to consolidate white rule and support an infrastructure and health and welfare systems for whites, while the black population is left to starve in ghettos, slums, and black townships. Manaka uses mime, songs, poetry, and symbolism to paint this canvas of exploitation in which human and economic energies are mined from the land without thought for its rightful owners. It is characteristic that the playwright empowers the characters with an insurrectionary consciousness, and in one of the scenes they dream and reenact through mime the process of freeing themselves from their bondage. Their desperation is embedded in the words "Egoli. City of misery. City of hate."

Both plays demonstrate successful experimentation with form and message. Manaka, however, leans quite often toward the sentimental and melodramatic instead of the deeper characterization that could give his plays a greater tragic force.

—Esiaba Irobi

MANIAM, K. S.

Nationality: Malaysian. **Born:** Subramaniam Krishnan, Bedong, Kedah, 4 March 1942. **Education:** Ibrahim Secondary school, Sungai Petani, Kedah, graduated 1960; The University of Birmingham, certificate in education, 1964; University of Cambridge, 1969; The University of Maylaya, Kuala Lumpar, B.A. in English, 1973, M.A. in English, 1979. **Family:** Married Saroja Muniandy in 1978, one daughter and one son. **Career:** Teacher, secondary schools in Kedah, 1965-69; English tutor, University of Malaya, 1973-75; lecturer, Taylor's college, Kuala Lumpar, 1975-79; lecturer, 1979-86, then associate professor, department of English, University of Malaya, Kuala Lumpar, 1986-97. Full-time writer, 1998—. **Awards:** First prize, the New Straits Times-Shell Short Story Competition, 1987, for *The Loved Flaw* and 1990, for *Haunting the Tiger*; Consolation prize, The New Straits Times-ESSO Play Writing competition, 1993, for *Skins Not Our Own.*

Publications

Plays

The Cord (produced Kuala Lumpar, 1984). Kuala Lumpar, Aspatra Quest Publishers, 1983.
The Sandpit: A Monologue (produced Kuala Lumpar, 1988). In *Southeast Asia Review of English* (Kuala Lumpar), 1987.
The Sandpit: Womensis (produced Kuala Lumpar, 1991). In *Southeast Asia Review of English* (Kuala Lumpar), 1992.
The Birch and the Rod (produced Perth, 1993).
Skins Not Our Own (produced Kuala Lumpar, 1995).
Skinned (produced Kuala Lumpar, 1995).
Our Own Skins (produced Kuala Lumpar, 1995).
Skin Trilogy (produced Kuala Lumpar, 1995).

Novel

In a Far Country. London, Skoob Books Publishing, 1993.

Short Stories

Plot, The Aborting, Parablames & Other Stories. Kuala Lumpar, AMK Interaksi, 1989.
Arriving and Other Stories. Singapore, Times Books International, 1995.
Haunting the Tiger. London, Skoob Books Publishing, 1996.

Other

The Return. London, Skoob Publishing, 1993.
Sensuous Horizons: The Stories and Plays. London, Skoob Books Publishing, 1994.

*

Critical Studies: "Linguistic Boundaries: K. S. Maniam's *The Return*" by Anne Brewster, in *A Sense of Exile: Essays in the Literature of the Asia-Pacific Region,* edited by Bruce Bennett and Susan Miller, Nedlands, University of Western Australia, 1988; "Ralph Ellison and K. S. Maniam: Ethnicity in America and Malaysia, Two Kinds of Invisibility" by Tang Soo Ping, in *MELLUS* (Amherst, Massachusetts), Winter 1993-94, pp. 81-97.

* * *

Better known as a fiction writer and academic, K. S. Maniam shot to theatrical fame in 1984 with the staging of his powerful play *The Cord.* Plays in English in Malaysia do not generally attract too much attention because their audiences are small, usually limited to university types. But word quickly spread that Maniam had written a play that demanded to be seen, a play that, according to some critics, transcended its own Malaysian setting and pervaded the sensibility of all who saw it. Whether or not such words become too fulsome, it can hardly be argued by anyone who knows *The Cord* that here is a play that probes deep into the human psyche. The play revolves around the character Muniandy who avoids confronting truths of his life, particularly his past life. It is the slow but sure impact that Muniandy's illegitimate son, Ratnam, and his wife, Leela, make on Muniandy's consciousness that finally gives him the much-needed courage to realize his own truth. Maniam has said (in a personal letter) that for him as playwright *The Cord* has "always landscaped the culture of self-delusion, the culture of despotism and the culture of release." Maniam is a firm believer that we each have to live out our own karma but that we can improve our karma through greater awareness of what it is we really are. When we try forever to avoid knowledge, such an awareness escapes us and we remain slaves of maya or appearances.

Maniam's other well-known play, *The Sandpit* (1991), develops at least one major aspect of *The Cord:* the spiritual. *The Sandpit* transports the ordinary and converts it into the extraordinary; common gestures, actions, words, and rituals suddenly become more than what they ordinarily are, taking on large dimensions of meanings both symbolic and literal. The play has a simple yet engaging plot: a man leaves home and does not return for three days. His two wives react differently: the first wife, the orthodox one, waits patiently at home staring at her husband's special chair. The second wife goes off to the brothel where she first met him. The complexities loom large as the audience awaits, with the two women, the return of this strange, mysterious husband. A unique bond develops between audience and wives, and through the sad, lyrical, poetic lamentations a new awareness begins to grow. Maniam is very skillful at handling the spiritual dimensions that crave attention and, sooner or later, demand a confrontation.

Maniam's plays deal with inner loneliness, spiritual emptiness, and crisis-driven angst, all of which lead individuals to a better understanding of themselves once they recognize their own deeper malaise. Outer symbols fuse and jell with inner meanings, and where these fusions are traumatic lies Maniam's strength as a playwright willing to give rein to an intense searching for the larger significance of human existence.

—Kirpal Singh

MANKOWITZ, (Cyril) Wolf

Nationality: British. **Born:** London, 7 November 1924. **Education:** East Ham Grammar School, London; Downing College, Cambridge, M.A. in English 1946. **Military Service:** Served as a volunteer coal miner and in the British Army during World War II. **Family:** Married Ann Margaret Seligmann in 1944; four sons. **Career:** Play and film producer: with Oscar Lewenstein, 1955-60; independently, 1960-70; with Laurence Harvey, 1970-72. Owner, Pickwick Club restaurant, London, 1963-70; also antique and art dealer. Moved to Ireland in 1971. Adjunct professor of English, 1982—, and adjunct professor of theatre arts, 1987-88, University of New Mexico, Albuquerque. Honorary consul to the Republic of Panama in Dublin, 1971. Exhibition of Collages, Davis Gallery, Dublin, 1990. **Awards:** Society of Authors award, for poetry, 1946; Venice Film Festival prize, 1955; BAFTA award, 1955, 1961; Oscar, for screenplay, 1957; Film Council of America golden reel, 1957; *Evening Standard* award, 1959; Cork Film Festival International Critics prize, 1972; Cannes Film Festival grand prize, 1973. **Address:** The Bridge House, Ahakista, Durrus, near Bantry, County Cork, Ireland; or, 2322 Calle Halcon, Santa Fe, New Mexico 87505, U.S.A.

Publications

Plays

Make Me an Offer, adaptation of his own novel (televised 1952; revised version, music and lyrics by Monty Norman and David Heneker, produced London, 1959).

The Bespoke Overcoat (produced London, 1953). London, Evans, 1954; New York, French, n.d.

The Baby, adaptation of a work by Chekhov (televised 1954; produced London, 1981). Included in *Five One-Act Plays*, 1955.

The Boychik (produced London, 1954).

It Should Happen to a Dog (televised 1955; produced Princeton, New Jersey, 1967; London, 1977). Included in *Five One-Act Plays*, 1955.

Five One-Act Plays. London, Evans, 1955; New York, French, n.d.

The Mighty Hunter (produced London, 1956). Included in *Five One-Act Plays*, 1955.

The Last of the Cheesecake (produced London, 1956). Included in *Five One-Act Plays*, 1955.

Expresso Bongo, with Julian More, music and lyrics by David Heneker and Monty Norman (produced London, 1958). London, Evans, 1960.

Belle; or, The Ballad of Dr. Crippen, with Beverley Cross, music by Monty Norman (produced London, 1961).

Pickwick, music and lyrics by Cyril Ornadel and Leslie Bricusse, adaptation of the novel by Dickens (produced London, 1963).

Passion Flower Hotel, music and lyrics by Trevor Peacock and John Barry, adaptation of the novel by Rosalind Erskine (produced London, 1965).

The Samson Riddle (produced Dublin, 1972; as *Samson and Delilah*, produced London, 1978). London, Vallentine Mitchell, 1972.

Jack Shepherd, music by Monty Norman (produced Edinburgh, 1972; as *Stand and Deliver*, produced London, 1972).

Dickens of London (televised 1976). London, Weidenfeld and Nicolson, 1976; New York, Macmillan, 1977.

The Hebrew Lesson (screenplay). London, Evans, 1976.

The Irish Hebrew Lesson (produced London, 1978; New York, 1980).

Iron Butterflies (produced Albuquerque, 1985). Two acts published in *Adam International Review* (London), 1984.

Screenplays: *Make Me an Offer*, with W. P. Lipscomb, 1954; *A Kid for Two Farthings*, 1955; *The Bespoke Overcoat*, 1955; *Trapeze*, 1955; *Expresso Bongo*, 1959; *The Two Faces of Dr. Jekyll* (*House of Fright*), 1960; *The Millionairess*, with Ricardo Aragno, 1960; *The Long and the Short and the Tall* (*Jungle Fighters*), with Willis Hall, 1961; *The Day the Earth Caught Fire*, with Val Guest, 1961; *Waltz of the Toreadors*, 1962; *Where the Spies Are*, with James Leasor and Val Guest, 1965; *Casino Royale*, with others, 1967; *La Vingt-cinquième Heure* (*The Twenty-fifty Hour*), 1967; *The Assassination Bureau*, with Michael Relph, 1969; *Bloomfield* (*The Hero*), with Richard Harris, 1970; *Black Beauty*, with James Hill, 1971; *The Hebrew Lesson*, 1972; *Treasure Island*, with Orson Welles, 1973; *The Hireling*, 1973; *Almonds and Raisins* (documentary), 1983.

Television Plays: *Make Me an Offer*, 1952; *The Baby*, 1954; *The Girl*, 1955; *It Should Happen to a Dog*, 1955; *The Killing Stones*, 1958; *Love Is Hell*, 1966; *Dickens of London* series, 1976; *Have a Nice Death*, from the story by Antonia Fraser (*Tales of the Unexpected* series), 1984.

Novels

Make Me an Offer. London, Deutsch, 1952; New York, Dutton, 1953.
A Kid for Two Farthings. London, Deutsch, 1953; New York, Dutton, 1954.
Laugh Till You Cry: An Advertisement. New York, Dutton, 1955; included in *The Penguin Wolf Mankowitz*, 1967.
My Old Man's a Dustman. London, Deutsch, 1956; as *Old Soldiers Never Die*, Boston, Little Brown, 1956.
Cockatrice. London, Longman, and New York, Putnam, 1963.
The Biggest Pig in Barbados: A Fable. London, Longman, 1965.
Raspberry Reich. London, Macmillan, 1979.
Abracadabra! London, Macmillan, 1980.
The Devil in Texas. London, Royce, 1984.
Gioconda. London, W.H. Allen, and New York, Freundlich, 1987.
The Magic Cabinet of Professor Smucker. London, W.H. Allen, 1988.
Exquisite Cadaver. London, Deutsch, 1990.
A Night with Casanova. London, Sinclair Stevenson, 1991.

Short Stories

The Mendelman Fire and Other Stories. London, Deutsch, and Boston, Little Brown, 1957.
Expresso Bongo: A Wolf Mankowitz Reader. New York, Yoseloff, 1961.
The Blue Arabian Nights: Tales of a London Decade. London, Vallentine Mitchell, 1973.
The Days of the Women and the Nights of the Men: Fables. London, Robson, 1977.

Poetry

XII Poems. London, Workshop Press, 1971.

Other

The Portland Vase and the Wedgwood Copies. London, Deutsch, 1952.
Wedgwood. London, Batsford, and New York, Dutton, 1953; revised edition, London, Barrie and Jenkins, 1980.
Majollika and Company (for children). London, Deutsch, 1955.
ABC of Show Business. London, Oldbourne Press, 1956.
A Concise Encyclopedia of English Pottery and Porcelain, with R.G. Haggar. London, Deutsch, and New York, Hawthorn, 1957.
The Penguin Wolf Mankowitz. London, Penguin, 1967.
The Extraordinary Mr. Poe: A Biography of Edgar Allan Poe. London, Weidenfeld and Nicolson, and New York, Summit, 1978.
Mazeppa: The Lives, Loves, and Legends of Adah Isaacs Menken: A Biographical Quest. London, Blond and Briggs, and New York, Stein and Day, 1982.

*

Manuscript Collection: Mugar Memorial Library, Boston University.

Theatrical Activities:
Director: **Film**—*The Hebrew Lesson*, 1972.

Wolf Mankowitz comments:

There have been some quite good notes and notices on odd works of mine from time to time, but I really could not give details. Let's just say that they all agreed that I was somewhat over-diversified and altogether too varied, and generally speaking, pragmatic, which means, I suppose, opportunistic in the way one tends to be if one is a professional writer. Lately my writing has been described as erudite, sophisticated, always funny, sometimes bizarre—so whether I'm getting better or worse, I am certainly continuing. I have never considered myself to be a playwright. I think of myself as a storyteller, and I tend to use whatever form the story seems to me to require.

* * *

In his early novels and short stories Wolf Mankowitz displayed a sure grasp of the dramatic, that sense of character and situation that makes for good theater. *Make Me an Offer* and *A Kid for Two Farthings* are both simple, direct narratives that are sensitive and funny, and it was natural enough to see them transcribed for the stage and the screen. Since then Mankowitz has joyfully embraced show business at all levels. He has become an impresario, he is a screenwriter who adapts his own scripts and those of others, and he has put every form of popular entertainment on celluloid. The films to which he has contributed range in their appeal from the glamorous (*The Millionairess*) to the horrific (*The Two Faces of Dr. Jekyll*) and from adventure (*The Day the Earth Caught Fire*) to schmaltz (*Black Beauty*).

Mankowitz has certainly found his spiritual home in Shaftesbury Avenue, but that has not shaken his allegiance to the basic principles of storytelling he first learned in the East End. He still employs a powerful mixture of cynicism and sentiment, still reveres the past, and still delights in patterns of speech and idiosyncrasies of behavior. At a guess, his central character in *Make Me an Offer* is something of a self-portrait: "Who knew better than he that nothing is given, that everything passes, the woods decay. He was the ultimate human being. He resigned himself to make a profit." *Expresso Bongo,* a musical set in Soho in which the promoters of pop live in the continued hope of overnight success and sudden fortune, is a further comment on commercialization.

Of Mankowitz's one-act plays *The Bespoke Overcoat* has always attracted praise for its technical skill and depth of feeling. It was published together with four smaller pieces, one entitled *It Should Happen to a Dog* and another *The Last of the Cheesecake*. As one might expect, these are anecdotes of Jewish life, poignant, comic, and shrewd. *The Bespoke Overcoat* is something more, a celebration of that stubborn reverence for life that the good adhere to however desperate their circumstances. Morry the tailor ("a needle like Paganini") can never give his friend the longed-for overcoat since Fender has died in poverty. But human values are not negated by death, a truth that is triumphantly stated in Morry's speeches and, at the close of the play, in his chanting of the Kaddish. Pathos is the dominant mood in another early play, *The Boychik.* This work is a study of hopeless ambition, that of an elderly actor who with his son dreams of reopening the decaying theater in which he was once a star.

Mankowitz has made an important contribution to postwar drama that is not always acknowledged by those who distrust box office success. As in *A Kid for Two Farthings*, his picture of Jewish life is convincing for its realism and memorable for its use of symbolism. He has eschewed the avant-garde but is nevertheless a highly sophisticated playwright who understands the traditions of the European theater and has worked against the parochialism of the English stage.

—Judy Cooke

MANN, Emily

Nationality: American. **Born:** Boston, Massachusetts, 12 April 1952. **Education:** Radcliffe College, Cambridge, Massachusetts, B.A. in English 1974 (Phi Beta Kappa); University of Minnesota, Minneapolis (Bush Fellow), 1974-76, M.F.A. in theater arts 1976. **Family:** Married Gerry Bamman in 1981 (divorced), one son. **Career:** Associate director, Guthrie Theatre, Minneapolis, 1978-79; resident director, BAM Theater Company, Brooklyn, New York, 1981-82; member of the board, 1983-87, and vice-president of the board, 1984-86, Theatre Communications Group, and director, New Dramatists workshop for play development, 1984-91, both New York; artistic director, McCarter Theatre Center for the Performing Arts, Princeton, New Jersey, 1989—; artistic associate, Crossroads Theatre, New Brunswick, New Jersey, 1990. Lecturer, Council of the Humanities and Theatre and Dance program, Princeton University, New Jersey, 1990—. Lives in Princeton, New Jersey. **Awards:** Obie award, 1981 (for writing and directing); Guggenheim fellowship, 1983; Rosamond Gilder award, 1983; National Endowment for the Arts grant, 1984, 1986; Creative Artists Public Service grant, 1985; Edinburgh Festival Fringe first award, 1985; McKnight fellowship, 1985; Dramatists Guild award, 1986; Playwrights USA award, 1986; Helen Hayes award, 1986; Home Box Office U.S.A. award, 1986; Greater Los Angeles NAACP Best Director award, for *Twilight*, 1992; The Beverly Hills/Hollywood Area NAACP Theatre award for best director, for *Twilight*, 1992; Tony, Outer Critics Circle, and Drama Desk award nominations for best play and director of a play, for *Having Our Say*, 1994; Jefferson award for best play and best direction, for *Having Our Say*, 1994; Dramatist Guilds' Hull Warriner award for best play, for *Having Our Say*, 1994; YWCA of Trenton Celebration of Women award, 1995; Brandeis University Women Achievement award, 1995; Douglas College of New Jersey Women of Achievement award, 1996. **Agent:** George Lane, William Morris Agency, 1325 Avenue of the Americas, New York, New York 10019, U.S.A.

PUBLICATIONS

Plays

Annulla, An Autobiography (as *Annulla Allen: The Autobiography of a Survivor*, also director: produced Minneapolis, 1977; revised version, as *Annulla, An Autobiography*, produced St. Louis, 1985; New York, 1988). New York, Theatre Communications Group, 1985.

Still Life (also director: produced Chicago, 1980; New York, 1981; Edinburgh and London, 1984). New York, Dramatists Play Service, 1982; published in *Coming to Terms: American Plays and the Vietnam War*, edited by James Reston, Jr., New York, Theatre Communications Group, 1985.

Execution of Justice (produced Louisville, 1984; also director: produced New York, 1986). Published in *New Playwrights 3*, edited by James Leverett and Elizabeth Osborn, New York, Theatre Communications Group, 1986.

Nights and Days, adaptation of a play by Pierre Laville, published in *Avant-Scène* (Paris), July 1984.

Betsey Brown, adaptation of the novel by Ntozake Shange, book by Shange and Mann, music by Baikida Carroll, lyrics by Shange, Mann, and Carroll (also director: produced Philadelphia, 1989).

Miss Julie, translation (produced 1992).

Having Our Say: The Delaney Sisters First 100 Years (produced 1994).

Greensboro, A Requiem (produced 1996).

The House of Bemerda Alba, translation (produced 1997).

Testimonies: Four Plays. New York, Theatre Communications Group, 1997.

Screenplay: *The Greensboro Massacre*, 1992.

*

Theatrical Activities:
Director: **Plays**—*Cold* by Michael Casale, Minneapolis, 1976; *Ashes* by David Rudkin, Minneapolis, 1977, and Cincinnati, 1980; *Annulla Allen*, Minneapolis, 1977; *Surprise, Surprise* by Michel Tremblay, Minneapolis, 1978; *On Mount Chimborazo* by Tankred Dorst, Minneapolis, 1978; *Reunion* and *Dark Pony*, by David Mamet, Minneapolis, 1978; *The Glass Menagerie* by Tennessee Williams, Minneapolis, 1979, Princeton, New Jersey, 1990; *He and She* by Rachel Crothers, New York, 1980; *Still Life*, Chicago, 1980, New York, 1986; *Oedipus the King* by Sophocles, New York, 1981; *A Tantalizing* by William Mastrosimone, Louisville, 1982; *The Value of Names* by Jeffrey Sweet, Louisville, 1982, and Hartford, Connecticut, 1984; *A Weekend near Madison* by Kathleen Tolan, Louisville and New York, 1983; *Execution of Justice*, Minneapolis, 1985, New York, 1986; *A Doll's House* by Ibsen, Hartford, Connecticut, 1986; *Hedda Gabler* by Ibsen, La Jolla, California, 1987; *Betsey Brown*, Philadelphia, 1989, Princeton, New Jersey, 1990; *The Three Sisters* by Chekhov, Princeton, New Jersey, 1991; *Cat on a Hot Tin Roof*, 1992; *Miss Julie*, 1992; *Three Sisters*, 1992; *Twilight*, Los Angeles, 1992, 1993; *The Perfectionist*, 1993; *The Matchmaker*, 1994; *Having Our Say*, Boston, 1995; *Betrayal*, 1997; *House of Bernarda Alba*, 1997; *Safe as Houses*, 1998.

* * *

Emily Mann has referred to her work as "theatre of testimony." Documentary drama is her métier, and contemporary history has provided her with subjects that range from the horrors of war, to peacetime violence, to the revolution in gender roles and sexual politics. Her first three stage plays are based wholly or in part on interviews with the people whose stories she tells.

Annulla, An Autobiography is the prototype. Mann visited the protagonist, a survivor of Nazism, in 1974, and the work hews so closely to what the playwright heard in Annulla Allen's London kitchen that she credits her as coauthor. The short play turns Annulla's own words into an uninterrupted monologue. Annulla's privileged girlhood in Galicia is only a distant memory that has been eclipsed by the Nazi terror. Her self-assurance and un-Semitic good looks helped her escape concentration camps and rescue her Jewish husband from Dachau. Now widowed, she cares for a demanding invalid sister. However compelling her harrowing story, Annulla insists, "It is not me who is interesting, it is my play." An enormous manuscript covers her kitchen table, stage center. Annulla's play argues for global matriarchy as the solution to evil and barbarism. "If women would only start thinking, we could change the world," she observes, declaring women incapable of the monstrous acts of Hitler or Stalin.

Still, Annulla is unable to read out representative passages from her work in progress. The manuscript is so disorganized and the need to get dinner for her ailing sister so pressing that she loses patience sifting through the jumbled pages. Therein lies Mann's point. However reasoned Annulla's thesis or promising her creativity, she is chronically distracted by more traditional female roles and by the anxieties and guilt that stem from her terrible past. Annulla can no more impose order on her play than she can on her life. Mann does not try to do that for her. In setting down the unmediated monologue of this scarred but plucky woman, Mann makes a statement about her own role. *Annulla* testifies to the freedom for creativity exercised by the playwright, who recognizes that it was by sheer accident of time and place that the life of her coauthor and subject was spared.

In *Still Life* Mann again draws on interviews with real people who become the dramatis personae. She calls the work a documentary, specifying that it be produced with that genre's characteristic objectivity. That tone is the first of the ironies that mark this work about the virulent psychic and emotional conditioning suffered by a Vietnam veteran and about the troubled society to which he returns. As a marine Mark learned that he could kill civilians as easily as enemy soldiers. After the war he cannot get rid of the memory of having wielded power over life and death. His obsession is alternately the source of rage, guilt, and physical pleasure. Incapable of talking either to those who were not in Vietnam or to those who were, Mark turns to drugs, crime, and domestic violence. He is not too self-centered to appreciate that his wife, Cheryl, whom he abuses, is as much a casualty of the war years as he is. Cheryl wants to return to the securities of a traditionalism more alive in her memories than in post-1960s America. She longs to play the roles her mother did, noting that, except in wartime, it is women who protect men, a point of view strikingly antithetical to that of Annulla Allen. Nadine, Mark's mistress, has done battle with all manner of "naughtiness." "A woman with many jobs and many lives," in Mann's words, Nadine describes herself as being so busy that she sleeps with her shoes on. The observation is metaphoric. Nadine steps over troubled waters, never feeling the cold or agitation and never plunging beneath the surface. Mark can tell Nadine his ugly truths, for absolutely nothing offends, disturbs, or even touches her.

Still Life is staged so as to make palpable the lack of genuine communication between Mark, who lives in the past, Cheryl, who yearns for an unrealizable future, and Nadine, who hovers above an unexamined present. The three characters sit side by side behind a table, like members of a panel discussion or witnesses at a trial. They talk about, but rarely to, one another, their intersecting speeches often juxtaposed ironically. Nadine's innocence about her near fatal pregnancies, for example, overlaps the ingenuous Cheryl's shock in coming upon Mark's pictures of war casualties. Projections on a screen behind the actors underscore the hopelessness of anyone's enjoying the full understanding of others. Gruesome pictures of those horribly mutilated in the war, for instance, illustrate Mark's inability to talk to his parents, who supported the war. Indeed, this seething play, whose self-possessed characters never touch one another on stage, ironically reflects a society where people, however uncommunicative, are continually in violent and destructive collision.

The notion of the audience as jury, implicit in *Still Life,* is central to *Execution of Justice*. It is significant that the work was commissioned by the Eureka Theatre of San Francisco. Its subject is the 1978 murder of George Moscone, the mayor of San Francisco, and Harvey Milk, a city supervisor and the first avowed homosexual voted into high public office. The play brings to the stage the case of the people against Dan White, the assassin. It demonstrates the instability of White, who had been elected a city supervisor, resigned, changed his mind, and when Moscone refused to reappoint him to his former post, vented his rage by shooting him and Milk. Mann bases her script on the transcript of the trial, reportage, and extensive interviews with some of the principals as well as what she calls in a prefatory note "the street." The play neatly synthesizes the background pertinent to the case, such as the evolution in the social and political spheres caused by the migration to San Francisco of a large homosexual population. It re-creates the climate of fear provoked by the mass deaths in Jonestown, Guyana, and the reputed connections between James Jones and liberal elements in San Francisco. The play effectively captures the unprecedented violence that stalked American political life in the 1970s.

As the testimony piles up, one appreciates the implausible defense arguments—for example, the "Twinkies defense" that attributed criminal behavior to the accused's junk food diet—and the unlikely claim that the murders were purely politically and not homophobically motivated. *Execution of Justice* shows that what was really on trial were conservative values, outraged and threatened by the growing power of the gay community. The use of video projections and film clips from documentaries intensify the passions of the trial, and the inclusion of reporters and photographers heightens its immediacy. Although Mann treats the explosive material with an even hand, there is no question that she wants the audience as jury to find that Dan White's conviction and light jail sentence for the lesser charges of voluntary manslaughter amount to the miscarriage of justice referred to in the play's title.

Mann's penchant for transforming life to the stage took a new turn with *Betsey Brown*, a rhythm and blues musical. She came to the project at the invitation of Ntozake Shange, who began it as a short story, turned it into a performance piece produced in 1979 at the Kennedy Center as *Boogie Woogie Landscapes,* and finally rewrote it as a novel. Shange and the jazz trumpeter-composer Baikida Carroll approached Mann for help in reworking the piece for the stage. The result was a full-fledged collaboration, a musical whose 28 songs color and interweave the various strands of a distinctly contemporary story.

The eponymous Betsey Brown is a young African American woman who comes of age in the Saint Louis of 1959. The first stirrings of the civil rights movement form the background for a number of issues the play explores. The most obvious is, of course, racism, both within the black community and from a white society threatened by integration. At least as consequential is the question of a role model for teenage Betsey. On one side is her mother, a "modern" woman who briefly abandons her family to pursue her own intellectual needs. Notwithstanding, she is genuinely concerned about educating her daughters to become cultivated members of a society that hardly encourages the self-actualization of black women. On the other side is the comforting figure of the Browns' housekeeper, a traditional woman who sings gospel songs with exquisite conviction. Her other accomplishments include commonsensical strategies for pleasing a man and consoling a crying child. Reviews of *Betsey Brown*'s premiere proved the success of the work in moving beyond its delineation of the tensions and beauties of black life to dramatize universal problems of parental responsibilities to children in a radically changing world.

In addition to her work for the stage, Mann has written three screenplays. *Naked* (1985), based on the book by Jo Giese Brown, is subtitled *One Couple's Intimate Journey through Infertility*. *Fanny Kelly* (1985) dramatizes the true story of an intrepid pioneer woman captured by the Sioux. *You Strike a Woman, You Strike a Rock* (1990) is a script on the Greensboro massacre that was commissioned by NBC Theatre. The scripts are distinguished by tight, suspenseful plots as well as the credible characterizations that Mann has made her signature.

—Ellen Schiff

MAPONYA, Maishe

Nationality: South African. **Born:** Johannesburg, 4 September 1951. **Education:** Diepkloof Secondary School, Soweto, 1969-71; Orlando High School, 1972-73; University of Leeds, 1986-87. **Career:** Supervisor, Liberty Life Assurance, Johannesburg, 1974-83; coordinator, Bahumuts (drama group), Diepkloof, 1976-88; vice chair, P.A.W.E., Johannesburg, 1991-93. **Awards:** Standard Bank Young Artists award, 1985; Wesley Guild's Best Diepkloof Poet prize, 1986. **Address:** Dramatic Art Department, University of Witwatersrand, PO Wits 2050, Johannesburg, South Africa.

Publications

Plays

The Hungry Earth (produced London, 1981). Johannesburg, Polyptoton, 1981.
Umongikazi (The Nurse) (produced Edinburgh and London, 1983). Johannesburg, Polyptoton, 1983.
Dirty Work (produced London, 1985). Johannesburg, Polyptoton, 1985.
Gangsters (produced London, 1985; New York, 1986). Johannesburg, Polyptoton, 1985; New York, Braziller, 1986.
The Valley of the Blind, with V. Amani Waphtali (also co-director; produced London, 1987).
Jika (produced New York, 1988).
Busang Meropa (*Bring Back the Drums*) (produced Birmingham, 1989).
Doing Plays for a Change: Five Works. Johannesburg, Witwatersrand University Press, 1995.

Radio Play: *Gangsters*, 1987.

Recordings: *Busang Meropa* (*Bring Back the Drums*), Johannesburg, S.F.B., 1988; *Azikho*, Johannesburg, Tusk Records, 1991.

*

Critical Study: "Staging Whiteness: Beckett, Havel, Maponya" by Anthony O'Brien, in *Theatre Journal* (Baltimore, Maryland), March 1994, pp. 45-61.

Theatrical Activities:
Director: **Plays**—Most of his own plays; *Changing the Silence* by Don Kinch, London, 1985; *The Coat* by Athol Fugard, Johannesburg, 1990; *Two Can Play* by Trevor Rhone, Johannesburg, 1992; *A Raisin in the Sun* by Lorraine Hansberry, 1992.

Actor: **Plays**—Roles in most of his own plays, and in *The Hungry Earth*, London, 1981.

* * *

Maishe Maponya's plays can be described as theatrical hand grenades to be detonated for maximum impact on the sensibilities of the audience. The themes are unabashedly political, and each work offers an excruciating insight into the impact the system of apartheid had on different segments of the black South African population. The playwright tries to assault the reader with knife blade images of the experiences of several classes of workers and other artistic professions straining against the strictures and structures of white-controlled establishments that were draconically manipulated to deny black South Africans maximum participation, career advancement, and self-fulfillment. Persecution and prejudice can be said to be Maponya's creative obsessions.

In *The Hungry Earth*, his earliest published play (1981), we are dragged on a tour of five symbolic settings that epitomized the degradation of black South African migrant laborers. In the first setting four men—Mathloko (Suffering), Usiviko (Shield), Beshwana (Loincloth), and Sethotho (Imbecile)—are asleep in a laborers' hostel when Usiviko wakes up from a nightmare in which he claims that he has seen Umlungu (Whiteman) leaving the land with goods plundered from the sweat and toil of the original owners of the land. The scene recaptures the history of their dispossession and the consequent hardship wrought upon them by European settlers. The imbecile Sethotho plays the devil's advocate, pointing out the material and economic benefits of the white man's control of South Africa. In a symbolic dance the four men mime their determination to reclaim their land and its bounties just as their ancestors resisted colonialism. Their act of defiance is traced to Isandlwana (Little Hill), where the Zulus fought a battle against the British in 1879 and inflicted heavy casualties on them. Also evoked through the dance is the memory of Umgungudlovu (Surrounding of the Elephant), another battlefield where the Zulus routed the Boers in 1838. Subsequent scenes expose the exploitation of children in sugar plantations, where they labored for 10 hours every day, after trekking six miles each morning, only to be paid 50 cents by the white owners. The beauty of this scene lies in the manner in which the four men transform themselves into children, with one of them doubling as a father, a visitor searching for his child in several plantation barracoons. The final scene displays the four men in a mine as the roof of the pit caves in on them and kills 41 black miners, hence the title of the play.

Maponya's other plays employ the same episodic structure, which makes for fluidity of scene changes and easy transformation of characters, typical of many South African protest plays. His major contribution to the corpus of plays created by other black and white liberal playwrights was the presentation of the experience and effects of segregation in an uncompromising and urgent manner, and he called for a pragmatic black blacklash instead of the survivalist tendency found, for example, in *Sizwe Bansi Is Dead.*

Umongikazi (The Nurse) portrayed the dilemma of black nurses working in a white-administered hospital. Through the maltreatment of three characters—Felize, Nyamezo, and Maria—the play highlights the bureaucratic double standards employed by the South African Nursing Association in the promotion of the workers, a strategy that left black nurses perennially at the foot of the career ladder. Generous with statistics, Maponya informs us that there were 4,000 black doctors for 23 million black people, whereas there were 12,000 for a mere 5 million whites. In one striking scene a white pediatrician refuses to treat a black newborn because "tomorrow it'll be the one that will snatch my bag."

Gangsters, however, is Maponya's masterpiece. Its edge over the other works is the dexterous use of flashbacks with which the playwright chronicles the hounding, arrest, torture, and death of Rasecheba, a poet accused of writing inflammatory verses. It starts at the end, and a carefully arranged sequence of past meetings and incidents leads to the theatrical finale in which the policemen who tortured the hero to death are at a loss as to the explanation they will give to the inquisition and the court. The suggestions that are rejected include "hanged himself from the cell window . . . fell to his death from a seventh storey floor trying to escape interrogation [the interrogation room is actually on the first floor] . . . slipped on a tablet of wet soap [this is rejected because it has been used too often to explain away the death of black people held in detention]." By shifting the emphasis from the poet's death to the process of his death, the playwright succeeds in presenting Rasecheba's tormentors as professional homicides who for once are embattled with guilt, thus giving the work a near tragic impetus. Another revealing insight in *Gangsters* is the nature of the circumstances, mainly economic, that forced black policemen to become informers or to persecute their own people. Jonathan, a black policeman in the play, becomes Whitebeard's hatchet man simply because Whitebeard, his boss, is paying for the education of Jonathan's children in Swaziland.

Dirty Work portrays a paranoid security officer, Peter Hannekon, giving a lecture on the state-of-the-art security equipment devised and imported by the then white South African government to forestall any invasion by black people. It is hilarious that any little sound offstage sends Hannekon trembling. Trying to exorcise the terror conjured up in him by "invade," a word he cannot pronounce, he dies of a heart attack toward the end of the lecture.

Maponya's weaknesses as a playwright include poor character development, speechifying, and an irritating tendentiousness that sometimes becomes overtly propagandist. His strengths include the "poverty" of his theater, its Brechtian dynamic, and the infusion of local color into his work through indigenous songs, dances, languages, and mime. The racy dialogue in the interrogation scenes of *Gangsters* and the macabre humor toward the end of the play are commendable. Maponya has a monochromatic imagination, however, rather than a deep insight into human nature.

—Esiaba Irobi

MARBER, Patrick

Nationality: British. **Born:** London, 19 September 1964. **Education:** Wadham College, Oxford. **Career:** Writer and director. **Awards:** Evening Standard award for best comedy and Writer's Guild award for best west end play, both, 1995, both for *Dealer's Choice*; Evening Standard award for best comedy, Critics Circle award for best play, and the Laurence Olivier award for best play, all 1997, all for *Closer.* **Agent:** Judy Daish Associates, 2 St. Charles Place, London W10 63G, England.

Publications

Plays

Dealer's Choice (also director: produced London, 1995). New York, Dramatists Play Service, 1998.

Closer (also director, produced London, 1997). London, Methuen, 1997.

After Miss Julie, adaptation for television of August Strindberg. London, Methuen, 1998.

Television Plays: *After Miss Julie.*

*

Theatrical Activities:
Director: **Plays**–*1953*; *Blue Remembered Hills*; *The Old Neighborhood* by David Mamet, 1998. **Television**–*After Miss Julie.*

* * *

Patrick Marber's writing career has been a diverse and a distinguished one, particularly in the context of British radio and television, where he was a member of the creative team behind such influential and popular successes as *On the Hour, The Day Today,* and *Knowing Me, Knowing You.* His career in the theater came later but has been equally successful. His plays *Dealer's Choice* (1995) and *Closer* (1997) both premiered at the Royal National Theatre. Both won critical and popular success and awards and audiences in generous measure.

Marber's first play, *Dealer's Choice,* is about men—the relationships between them and, most especially, the relationship between fathers and sons. Stephen runs a poker school every Sunday night in the basement of his restaurant. The poker game has become a familiar fixed point in the lives of the players: Mugsy, the good-natured habitual loser; Sweeney, a divorced father struggling to maintain a relationship with his young daughter; and Carl, Stephen's son, deeply in debt to the professional gambler Ash, who is, in turn, in debt to another player. While Carl may be addicted to gambling, and is hugely in debt as a result, Stephen is equally addicted to the ritual of the card game, its language and its familiarity. The irony is that the stability and order in the men's lives derive from a game of chance.

The gambling motif is deployed deliberately and expertly: it distills feelings of compulsion and obsession with a built-in narrative suspense. Marber uses the specific metaphor of the poker game as a quintessentially masculine ritual. The play's title reflects the rules of the poker school, i.e., that the dealer can choose the variations of the game—Hold 'em, Omaha, Irish, Lowball, Queen Follows, Chicago, Hedgehog, and Mugsy's Nightmare. The truth is that this is the only degree of "choice" available to the players.

Marber deals with an utterly male environment—there are scant few references to women in this community of men. The men inhabit a protected and private world, proscribed through the deployment of a hugely technical vocabulary. The dialogue is fast paced, vigorous, and edgy, filled with references to the rules and complexities of poker. Marber uses this language to construct the easy intimacy of familiarity, belonging, and community. For audiences the dense vocabulary of the poker game can seem to spiral into impenetrability, but it also demonstrates the nature of this ambiguous group. The technical vocabulary is less a means of communication than an evasive tactic, constructing a barrier against the outside world. The language marks the community of men as an exclusive space, in which they have some kind of authority, some kind of certainty. On the one hand poker terminology merely describes the game, but on the other it marks a complex strategy of displacement, setting up different social structures and counter communities. Marber is concerned to reveal the mendacity of this use of language: the men hide behind the poker game for they cannot talk about their real feelings without the ritual of the game. The play, however, has a sincere emotional core. The game is a backdrop to the story of Carl's relationship with Stephen, his actual father, and with Ash, his chosen father figure:

> Stephen: You've been coming in here every Sunday night "Hi Dad" "Bye Dad" and then you go straight off to a casino to gamble thousands of pounds with another man.
>
> Carl: And you're jealous.
>
> *Pause*
>
> Carl: I've played with real men for real money. Ash lost every penny he ever had in one night—
>
> Stephen: The object of the game is to win.
>
> *Pause*
>
> Carl: You don't understand.
>
> Stephen: Yes I do.
>
> *Pause*
>
> Carl: Same time next week?

Dealer's Choice is a bold first play in which Marber's interest in contemporary relationships, social structures and rituals is fully demonstrated. This theme is developed further in another of Marber's works. *After Miss Julie* is an exceptional, brutal, and sexually explicit re-imagining of August Strindberg's *Miss Julie,* relocated to an English country house. It was written as a BBC television production that aired in 1995. It is set on the evening of 26 July 1945, the night of the British Labour Party's landslide General Election victory. The recontextualization allows Marber to describe the decline of the English landed class. Together John and Christine (a figure Marber reinvents as a multifaceted character in her own right) represent a class on the rise. The metaphor sees Miss Julie as louche and decadent, succumbing to John (the master's chauffeur), an ambitious man whose unambiguous and predatory sexuality modernizes a physical, animalistic aggression.

Marber's second stage play, *Closer,* is also about sexual politics. It is a black and witty sex comedy, wholly urban in its execution and utterly contemporary in the fluid sexual morality it describes. As with *Dealer's Choice,* Marber quickly shows his ability to demonstrate characters and their histories through bantering conversation and repartee. The play lays bare the ironies of contemporary sexuality and modern relationships. Over a period of months and years, four characters meet, have relationships, fall out, and move on. Dan, a writer of newspaper obituaries and an aspiring novelist, begins a passionate affair with the mysterious and hedonistic Alice. He then meets the photographer Anna and begins an affair with her. There is a strong but far from explicit suggestion that Anna and Alice may have a sexual liaison. In a sex chat room on the Internet (using the assumed identity of Anna), Dan meets Larry, a rather boorish dermatologist. Larry marries Anna and later has an affair with Alice. Other than the cybersex encounter, however, none of these meetings or relationships is slight or without consequence. They are intense and authentic, occasionally obsessive and destructive, but always tempered by Marber's linguistic dexterity, sexual explicitness, and caustic and epigrammatic humor. The observation in *Dealer's Choice,* "Poker without gambling is like sex without orgasm," is matched in *Closer* by Anna's barb to Dan, "You're a man, you'd come if the tooth fairy winked at you." Humor is used expertly by Marber to weave together narrative and illuminate character.

These two stage plays reveal Marber's hugely entertaining and highly idiomatic dramaturgy as coolly contemporary and wickedly incisive in its analyses of the darker sides of modern society and the relationships it fosters. He is an assured commentator of current social and sexual mores.

—Adrienne Scullion

MARCHANT, Tony

Nationality: British. **Born:** London, 11 July 1959. **Education:** St. Joseph Academy School. **Awards:** Edinburgh Festival award, 1982; *Drama* award, 1982. **Agent:** Lemon, Unna, and Durbridge, 24 Pottery Lane, Holland Park, London W11 4LZ, England.

Publications

Plays

Remember Me? (produced London, 1980).

Thick as Thieves (includes *London Calling* and *Dealt With*) (produced London, 1981). London, Methuen, 1982.

Stiff (produced London, 1982).

Raspberry (produced Edinburgh and London, 1982). Included in *Welcome Home, Raspberry, The Lucky Ones*, 1983.

The Lucky Ones (produced London, 1982). Included in *Welcome Home, Raspberry, The Lucky Ones*, 1983.

Welcome Home (produced Hemel Hempstead, Hertfordshire, and London, 1983). Included in *Welcome Home, Raspberry, The Lucky Ones*, 1983.
Welcome Home, Raspberry, The Lucky Ones. London, Methuen, 1983.
Lazydays Ltd. (produced London, 1984).
The Attractions (produced London, 1987). Oxford, Amber Lane, 1988.
Speculators (produced London, 1987). Oxford, Amber Lane, 1988.

Television Plays: *Raspberry*, 1984; *Reservations*, 1985; *This Year's Model*, 1988; *The Money Men*, 1988; *Death of a Son*, 1989; *The Attractions*, 1989; *Take Me Home*, 1989; *Goodbye Cruel World*, 1992.

*

Tony Marchant comments:
I started writing at 20, and for the past seven or eight years I have written about my generation in various situations—unemployed, trapped in office conformity, at war, in a state of sexual confusion. The experiences of my characters differ vastly: from having fought in the Falklands (*Welcome Home*) to confronting the "stigma" of infertility (*Raspberry*). Generally the plays are about people attempting to confound the expectations of their environment. They are mostly excluded from the mainstream of society, but suffer from its judgement. They all question these judgements and ultimately defy them. Theirs is a plea for dignity.

* * *

Tony Marchant's work marks him as the spokesman for people not normally given a voice. His earliest plays toured schools and youth clubs, and he has tended to work in theaters that have a strong sense of community, such as the Theatre Royal at Stratford East, or a regular clientele, such as the now closed Soho Poly, or he has worked for touring companies like Paines Plough. In short, Marchant has worked in intimate locations that allow his greatest strengths free play. He has a sharp eye for the minutiae of characterization allied to the ability to endow his characters with a high level of articulacy that still seems to keep within the bounds of naturalism.

The two-part *Thick as Thieves,* for example, shows a group of unemployed London teenagers. The first play, *London Calling,* depicts them as merely wandering about and flirting with the notion of casual violence, but there is also a clear sense that at least some of them are thinking through their situation in a remarkably organized way. They take on the unthinking prejudices of Pimple, a mate who is toying with the ideas of the National Front, but while they are clear about who not to blame for their situation, they cannot conceive of a way out, so that their very real linguistic energy is dissipated in destructive self-parody. They are only too aware that they are prime subjects for well-meaning, ineffectual documentary, and when Pimple remembers bonfires on the tatty dump that is now their social space, Paul responds sardonically, "Our heritage—building things with rubbish and setting light to 'em." The idea of waste is made overt in the second play, *Dealt With,* in which Paul and the others confront a personnel officer who has rejected him. They harass him without much effect, and the play ends with the boys, except for Paul, who is now on the verge of suicide, on the run from the security guard. Here the focus is split. On the one hand there is a simple clash between the deprived and the prosperous and on the other a contrast between the dreams with which Paul invests this confrontation and the inadequacy of the personnel officer as a target for his rage. Marchant sometimes seems lost between the two, and the somewhat melodramatic ending looks like a way of dodging the issue.

In his play about the aftermath of the Falkland Islands War, *Welcome Home,* we are shown a group of young men who have found at least a temporary alternative—the army. Marchant gives a scrupulous account of both the benefits and the cost of this alternative on a personal level. In the discipline of the "cherry berets" the boys have found both self-image and self-respect. They have developed a comradeship that can show itself both in uproarious horseplay and also in their care that a comrade's funeral turn out well. In return the army demands not just their lives but also the right to control their self-expression. As the corporal points out, the funeral is part of their public duty to be heroes "as advertised on TV." When one of them messes up the discipline of the procession, he is not simply punished by the army for violating its image, but he assists the process, breaking down from pure shame. The corporal treats him with savage violence, but his motivation is not the reflex action of a man addicted to "bull." Rather, it is a clumsy attempt at shock therapy, an attempt to help while staying within the permitted boundaries of the Para image. This, Marchant implies, is the real cost of the army as an outlet for youthful energy and courage—the damage it does to the best human instincts.

Raspberry is perhaps the clearest celebration of the human ability to transcend immediate oppression. Two women share a gynecological ward—one for an abortion, the other for yet another operation for infertility. Despite the insensitivity of the system that has flung them together, symbolized by the hostility of the nurse toward the young abortion patient, they achieve a close and mutually comforting relationship. Lacking any common ground, they unite against their surroundings in an almost surreal spirit. What starts as a near quarrel turns, in the face of an angry nurse, into a mischievous assertion that they have been playing games. This then becomes something like fact as they improvise a party to transform the grimness of the preoperation evening, which leads, in turn, to a genuine relationship. The moment when they hold each other in the face of their shared pain is a touching moment of theater.

This ability to show the play instinct at work in the unlikeliest settings, along with the comradeship arising out of it, is perhaps Marchant's major strength. The naturalism of his sets and plots precludes a close analysis of the underlying politics. One simply accepts that, unjust as it is, this is the present situation. He clearly shows, however, the resources that are there to fight it, and the linguistic energy of his characters is a lively symbol of human energy in the face of oppression. For change to occur, Marchant implies, this energy needs only to be harnessed.

—Frances Gray

MARGULIES, Donald

Nationality: American. **Born:** Brooklyn, New York, 1954. **Education:** Pratt Art Institute; SUNY Purchase, B.F.A in visual art. **Family:** Married Lynn Street, one son. **Career:** Graphic artist,

1979-81; adaptor and playwright, Jewish Repertory Theatre; teacher of playwriting, Yale University School of Drama, New Haven, Connecticut. **Awards:** Pulitzer nomination, Dramatists Guild/Hull Warriner award, Burns Mantle best play, and Obie award, best new play, 1992, all for *Sight Unseen*; Drama-Logue award, 1995, and Obie award, both for *The Model Apartment*; Pulitzer prize nomination and Los Angeles Drama Critics Circle award, both 1997, both for *Collected Stories.* **Agent:** c/o Howard Rosenstone, Rosenstone/Wender, 3E 48 Street, New York, New York 10017, U.S.A.

PUBLICATIONS

Plays

Luna Park (produced New York, 1982).
Resting Place (produced New York, 1982).
Gifted Children (produced New York, 1983).
Found a Peanut (produced New York, 1984). New York, Dramatists Play Service, 1984.
What's Wrong With This Picture (produced New York, 1990). New York, Broadway Play Publishing, 1988.
Zimmer (produced New York, 1988).
The Model Apartment (produced Los Angeles, 1988; New York, 1995). New York, Dramatists Play Service, 1990.
The Loman Family Picnic (produced New York, 1989). Garden City, New York, 1990.
Pitching to the Star (produced New York, 1990). In *Best American Short Plays, 1992-93,* New York, Applause Books, 1994.
Pitching to the Star and Other Short Plays (includes *Pitching to the Star*; *L.A.*; *Space*; *Women in Motion*; *Zimmer*). New York, Dramatists Play Service, 1993.
Sight Unseen (produced Costa Mesa, California, 1991; New York, 1992). New York, Dramatists Play Service, 1992.
Sight Unseen and Other Plays (includes *Found a Peanut*; *What's Wrong with This Picture*; *The Model Apartment*; *The Loman Family Picnic*; *Sight Unseen*). New York, Theatre Communications Group, 1995.
July 7, 1994 (produced Louisville, 1995). In *Humana Festival '95,* Lyme, New Hampshire, Smith and Kraus, 1995.
July 7, 1994: Short Plays and Monologues. New York, Dramatists Play Service, 1997.
Broken Sleep, with Michael-John La Chiusa (short musical; produced Williamstown, Massachusetts, 1997).
Collected Stories: A Play (produced Costa Mesa, California, 1996). New York, Dramatists Play Service, 1998.
Dinner with Friends (produced Louisville, Kentucky, 1998). In *Human Festival '98,* Lyme, New Hampshire, Smith and Kraus, 1998.

*

Critical Study: "Ways of Seeing in Donald Margulies' *Sight Unseen*" by June Schlueter, in *Studies in American Drama, 1945-Present* (Columbus, Ohio), 1993, pp. 3-11.

* * *

Donald Margulies, the son of a Brooklyn wallpaper salesman, has written a wide range of powerful, well-crafted plays, from satiric comedies to sensitive, literate character studies. All draw deeply on his own experiences as an artist, a Jew, a father, and a husband to explore the web of influences that create the characters we play in our own lives. Provocative yet personal, Margulies deftly merges hilarity and heartbreak with sizable theatrical flair.

His early plays create antic comedy from near catastrophic situations: in *A Model Apartment*, a crazy daughter of two Holocaust survivors barges into their Florida condo for a surprise visit; in *What's Wrong with This Picture?* a young mother who choked to death on Chinese food returns as a ghost to straighten up her family's apartment; and in *The Loman Family Picnic* a boy deals with family tensions by writing a musical-comedy version of Arthur Miller's *Death of a Salesman.* Audiences who like their humor unleavened by dark hints of mortality or ironic commentary on Jewish-American middle-class life will have to stick to Neil Simon.

These earlier works, beginning with *Found a Peanut* and culminating in the bravura *Loman Family Picnic,* focus on childhood's impact on identity as parents and their offspring act out the rituals—bar mitzvahs, funerals, backyard games—that attempt to bind them into a cohesive community. The second act of Margulies's career begins with his breakthrough play *Sight Unseen.* In that and subsequent plays the conflicts center on mature protagonists who search for self-definition amid a confusing world: an artist's pursuit of fame has erased his connection to his own past in *Sight Unseen*; a doctor at an inner-city clinic must balance the needs of her patients and of her family in the 60-minute one-act *July 7, 1994;* a young writer plunders her mentor's life for material in *Collected Stories*; and a couple question their lives when two friends they thought they knew get divorced in *Dinner with Friends.*

Margulies often uses structural devices to heighten the theatricality of his storytelling. *Found a Peanut,* a play about a group of kids whose power struggles and backyard bickering are intensified when a Carvel ice cream bag full of money is discovered, has no grownup characters—just children to be played by adult actors. Many plays feature ghost characters, such as the young mother in *What's Wrong with This Picture?,* the daughter who died in the Holocaust in *The Model Apartment,* and Doris's Aunt Marsha in *The Loman Family Picnic.*

The Loman Family Picnic is the culmination of Margulies's investigation of the crucible of childhood. It is a wacky, full-tilt, genre-bending, heartbreaking farce. The play looks at one Brooklyn family's life through the eyes of its youngest member, Mitchell, whose parents, Herbie and Doris, lead unsatisfying lives. (He works 12-hour days selling lighting fixtures; she fixes him "dietetic" meals and plans brother Stewie's bar mitzvah, which they can't afford). Throughout, there are bravura playwriting touches. For example, at the dinner table Herbie and Doris suddenly launch into an animated conversation in which they laughingly and lovingly describe how each other has died. The lights shift abruptly and reality returns as their mutual boredom redescends like darkness. The act two opening is another gem: The family of four directly confides in the audience in a series of asides as they take turns freezing for the bar mitzvah photographer. Then, just after the big blowup at the climax when Herbie walks out, the family breaks into a song-and-dance routine from Mitchell's eponymous musical. Finally, the play ends with not one but three permutations of Herbie and Doris's reconciliation, including Doris jumping out the high-rise window. The final version is the most tragic, of course: nothing changes.

Of the later plays, *Sight Unseen* is the most ambitious. The eight scenes are neatly divided into two acts, but the action moves forward and backward in time, centering on the painter Jonathan Waxman's relationship with his college lover and former muse, Patricia, now married to an English archaeologist who is in the process of excavating a medieval garbage dump. Waxman, a hot, trendy artist, is doing his own bit of emotional archaeology, trying to dig out his past, to which he's feeling disconnected because of the very recent death of his father and because of his mounting fame. The play concerns itself with how these characters suppress emotions and are unable to deal truthfully with their feelings. Once Patricia sells Waxman a portrait of her that he painted when they first met, we sense that she will be able to live honestly with herself and her husband, untainted by this past romance. Unfortunately, no such revelation seems forthcoming from Jonathan, whose last name connotes an imitation of himself. Margulies, a one-time art student, seems to blame Waxman's condition on Jonathan's inability to assimilate his own Jewishness, a flaw brilliantly revealed in two interview scenes with a young German art critic.

Margulies further explores the way artists form their identities in *Collected Stories*, a two-hander set over the course of six years. Lisa, a graduate student fiction writer, and her teacher, the successful and established literary figure Ruth, form a relationship that progresses from pupil and teacher to equals as writers and colleagues. Eventually, Lisa eclipses her role model and mentor, largely because of a book that the young woman writes that baldly steals her one-time professor's life story. In a way, it is exactly what Margulies has done in his impressive body of work; only the playwright has mined his material from a writer closer to home—himself.

—John Istel

MARTIN, Jane

A pseudonym for an unidentified playwright. **Nationality:** American. **Born:** Kentucky. **Awards:** American Theatre Critics Association award for best new play, 1994, for *Keely and Du*, and 1997, for *Jack and Jill*; Best Foreign play of the year award, *Theater Haute* magazine, for *Talking With*. **Address:** c/o Sandy Speer, Actors Theatre of Louisville, 316 West Main Street, Louisville, Kentucky 40202, U.S.A.

Publications

Plays

Talking With (produced Louisville, 1981).
Summer (produced 1984).
Vital Signs (produced Louisville, 1990). New York, Samuel French, 1990.
Cementville (produced Louisville, 991). New York, Samuel French, 1991.
Criminal Hearts (produced Detroit, 1992). London, Samuel French, 1992.
Keely and Du (produced Louisville, 1993). New York, Samuel French, 1993.
Middle-Aged White Guys (produced Louisville, 1995). New York, Samuel French, 1995.
Jack and Jill (produced Louisville, 1996). New York, Samuel French, 1995.
Jane Martin: Collected Works, 1980-1995. Lyme, New Hampshire, Smith and Kraus, 1995.
Mr. Bundy (produced Louisville, 1998).

*

Critical Study: "The Lone Body on Stage" by Linda Ford Winans, in *Text and Presentation* (Athens, Georgia), 1993, pp. 97-101.

* * *

Jane Martin is a dramatist of mordant topical plays, but what is unusual about her is that she has been able to preserve her anonymity for so many years on the pretext that to reveal her identity would blight the muse. For some two decades Martin's career has mirrored the exponential growth of the Actors Theatre of Louisville, Kentucky, as a world center for new playwriting. This has given rise to a persistent belief, equally as often rebutted by John Jory, the artistic director of the theater, that Jory and Martin are one and the same. "Regardless of identity or gender," demurs Jory, "the point in the end is the plays themselves."

In this Jory is undoubtedly vindicated by the critical response bestowed on Martin's plays. *Keely and Du* in particular has received a succession of accolades. These include a nomination for a Pulitzer Prize and the American Theater Critics Award in 1994. A large proportion of her dramatic output has been published in *Jane Martin: Collected Works 1980-1985*. A collection of major writing to that date, the work includes *Talking With, Vital Signs, Cementville,* and *Criminal Hearts*. Since then she has written *Jack and Jill* and *Mr Bundy*. The former play, premiered at the 1996 Humana Festival of New American Plays, was, like *Keely and Du,* the winner of the American Theater Critics Award. The latter, produced for the 1998 Humana Festival, shows all of the signs of extending Martin's repute, if in no way clarifying her real identity.

It is certainly fair to say that, while not all of Martin's plays have been premiered at Louisville, the particular rhythms of the Actors Theatre are conducive to, and over the years have been supportive of, her distinctive creative style. Apart from the Humana Festival of New American Plays, the Actors Theatre has staged a Shorts Festival and, annually since 1979, a Ten Minute Play Competition. Jory views this as a valuable teaching tool for actors and directors, "providing a perfect study of theme, character and structure without the trappings of a full-length play." The discipline of the 10-minute play neatly meshes with the monologue form that Martin has adapted and developed with startling success. *Talking With* (1982), the first of Martin's blockbusters, is arranged as a series of 11 female monologues developed from a single short piece, *Twirler.* With *Vital Signs* (1990) Martin "proved again the infinite resonance of monologue [introducing] a gallery of characters who shatter expectation, reinvent the ordinary and dignify the bizarre."

Cementville (1991) and *Criminal Hearts* (1992), premiered at the Theatre Company in Detroit, laid to rest any remaining doubts that Martin was able to work within a traditional dramatic structure without losing her inimitable and distinctive approach to characterization. More important, after *Cementville* there was an expansion of Martin's thematic concerns. *Keely and Du* (1993), for example, is a significant advance not only in theme but also in structure. Further, it offers prophetic insight into what subsequently became the national controversy surrounding abortion. In the play Martin displays her usual penchant for the marginalized character and surreal situation to devastating effect. Kelly, a young women on her way to get an abortion, is kidnapped by a group of fundamentalist pro-lifers and shackled to an iron bed in a basement in the company of Du, an old nurse, with the intention of holding her beyond the time when an abortion can be carried out. The play was a brilliant critical and popular success. According to one critic, it has the ability to accommodate "with a quiet sense of vindication, both sides of the issue." It has been a clear box office hit, with well over 300 professional productions.

The tendency to deal with universal themes continued with Martin's next three plays. *Middle Aged White Guys* (1995) is a play about "the warped icons of Americana": a corrupt mayor, a Vietnam veteran turned mercenary, and a business tycoon. *Jack and Jill* (1996) is a comedy that captivates audiences through its ability to "hear what men and women actually say—and understands what they don't say—in the world at this moment." *Mr. Bundy* (1998), whose title refers to the notorious serial killer, deals with the vexing and extremely live issue of how a community comes to terms with a child molester once he completes his jail sentence.

—Paul Hadfield

MASTROSIMONE, William

Nationality: American. **Born:** Trenton, New Jersey, 19 August 1947. **Education:** Pennington Preparatory School, New Jersey, 1963-66; Tulane University, New Orleans, 1966-70; Rider College, Trenton, New Jersey, 1973-74, B.A. in English 1974; Rutgers University, New Brunswick, New Jersey, 1974-76, M.F.A. 1976. **Awards:** Los Angeles Drama Critics Circle award, 1982; Outer Circle award, 1983; John Gassner award, 1983; Los Angeles NAACP award Best Play, 1987; Roxanne Mueller award, Cleveland International Film Festival, 1988; New Jersey Governor's Walt Whitman award, 1989; Golden Globe award, 1992; Humanities award, 1995; Environmental Media award, 1995. Honorary degree: Rider College. **Agent:** George Lane, William Morris Agency, 1350 Avenue of the Americas, New York, New York 10019. **Address:** 46808 286th Avenue South East, Enumclaw, Washington 98022, U.S.A.

Publications

Plays

The Woolgatherer (produced New Brunswick, New Jersey, 1979; New York, 1980; London, 1985). New York, French, 1981.
Extremities (produced New Brunswick, New Jersey, 1980; New York, 1982; London, 1984). New York, French, 1984.
A Tantalizing (produced Louisville, 1982). New York, French, 1985.
Shivaree (produced Seattle, 1983). New York, French, 1984.
The Undoing (produced Louisville, 1984).
Nanawatai (produced in Norwegian, Bergen, Norway, 1984; produced in English, Los Angeles, 1985). New York, French, 1986.
Tamer of Horses (produced New Brunswick, New Jersey, 1985; revised version produced Los Angeles, 1986; revised version produced Seattle, 1987).
Cat's-Paw (produced Seattle, 1986). New York, French, 1987.
The Understanding (produced Seattle, 1987; New York, 1989).
Sunshine (produced New York, 1989).
Burning Desire. N.p., n.d.
Benedict Arnold. N.p., n.d.
William Mastrosimone: Collected Plays (includes *Sunshine*; *Tamer of Horses*; *A Stone Carver*; *Extremities*; *The Wool Gatherer*; *Nanawatai*; *Shivaree*). Newbury, Vermont, Smith and Kraus, 1993.
Like Totally Weird (produced Louisville, 1998). In *Humana Festival Anthology,* Newbury, Vermont, Smith & Kraus, 1998.

Screenplays: *Extremities*, 1986; *The Beast*, 1988; *The Burning Season,* 1995; *With Honors*; *Escobar.*

Television Play: *Sinatra* series, 1992.

*

Manuscript Collection: Boston University.

Critical Study: "Extremities and Masterpieces: A Feminist Paradigm of Art and Politics" by Tracy C. Davis, in *Feminist Theatre and Theory,* edited by Helene Keyssar, New York, St. Martin's, 1996.

* * *

When *Extremities* opened off-Broadway in 1982, it proved to be one of the most controversial plays of the season. Some critics suggested that William Mastrosimone's tense drama about a would-be rapist and his implacable female captor attracted audiences because there was not more powerful fare available. Some also dismissed the play as an exercise in old-fashioned melodrama, with onstage violence to whet the appetites of jaded television viewers. Actually, as he explained in "The Making of *Extremities,*" Mastrosimone had been inspired by a 55-year-old rape victim, but he touched a raw nerve among theatergoers in general and women in particular. The fear of, and revulsion against, violent, vicious, and unprovoked sexual attacks was very real. That some angry or unbalanced male members of some minority groups were often perceived as the usual rapists found resonance in the play, whose disturbed potential ravisher is named Raul. This choice by the playwright, some suggested, was invoking racial stereotypes. Confronting a seemingly helpless young woman, Marjorie, with this cunning, shifty criminal was also seen as a deliberate attempt to exploit people's fears.

These charges are unfair to Mastrosimone, who clearly cares more for victims' rights and safety than he does for those of wrongdoers. In *Extremities* the naked threat of violence and violation is presented almost immediately, but fortunately Marjorie is able to turn the tables and take Raul captive. As the play progresses, his deviousness and threats drive her to rage and lead her to decide to kill him and bury the body in her garden. When her roommates return, their reactions vary, suggesting standard social reactions to such a situation when it is merely hypothetical. At the close there is a somewhat schematic catharsis for both Raul and Marjorie, but it offers no magic solutions to the problem.

In addition to the exercise of physical violence onstage, Mastrosimone offers audiences a tightly constructed cat-and-mouse plot whose outcome is not easily guessed. What is especially appealing, however, as in other Mastrosimone plays, is his ability not only to capture the rhythms and idioms of the conversation of various social groups but also to make them the proper expression of his characters. David Mamet is often praised for his ear for common or raffish speech, and Mastrosimone is adept at the same thing but in a different way. Whereas Mamet's characters may seem involved in an aimless stream of consciousness, Mastrosimone's are generally trying to achieve some end, at the very least to move the plot forward.

In *The Woolgatherer* there is almost no major plot action. Rose, a fragile, disturbed girl who displaces her terrors and misadventures on a mythical friend, Brenda, brings home Cliff, a trucker looking for a sexual encounter. Their banter—his jocular, angry, or uncomprehending and hers tense, poetic, and pained—is the substance of the play as they come to know and trust each other. The title refers to her collection of men's sweaters, begged from previous visitors.

In *A Tantalizing*, a one-act play with two characters, it is the man, Ambrose, who is unbalanced. Dafne, a young woman who has watched this once well-dressed, confident lawyer spend his days in a parking lot doing imaginary business on a disconnected telephone he carries with him, has brought him to her apartment, although it is not clear why. No matter what comforts or refreshments she offers him, he is peremptory, corrective, and fussy, traits that reveal reasons for his failure in life. At the close she succeeds in getting him to lay aside his ragged clothes for some of her late father's fine clothing.

Mastrosimone can manipulate three or more characters with effective exchanges of dialogue onstage at the same time, but he seems to prefer confrontations between two people, with others brought on, if at all, only when required by the plot. *Shivaree* has echoes of *Butterflies Are Free,* with the difference being that Chandler, its protagonist, is hemophiliac, not blind. His overprotective mother drives a cab to pay the bills, while he saves ice cream money to pay for a session with a prostitute. He finds both himself and romance, however, with a neighboring exotic dancer named Shivaree.

Nanawatai deals with the fates of a Soviet tank team trapped in a mountain cul-de-sac by Afghan rebels. The title is supposedly the tribal word for "sanctuary," and, once it is uttered, enemies must protect the one who begs it. A Russian soldier claims sanctuary and is spared. Later, his former comrades do so as well, but implacable Afghan women, impatient with the seeming softness of their men, slaughter the helpless Soviets. It is interesting that the work was premiered in Norway rather than in the United States. The play was the basis for the film *The Beast.*

Cat's-Paw goes beyond *Extremities* in dealing with topical terrors and in subtly satirizing American manners and mores. Jessica Lyons, a weekend television anchorwoman who wants a major news scoop to improve her ratings, is taken blindfolded to interview Victor, who has just blown up a car loaded with explosives outside the Environmental Protection Agency in Washington, D.C. He and his small group are using terrorist tactics to protest the government's failure to protect the public from toxic wastes. To that end, he has kidnapped a culpable minor EPA official, David Darling, whom he threatens to kill. Lyons's past television coups have shown her to be unblinking in the face of horrors, and Victor hopes to use her talents to get his message to the world. Perhaps he will even blow up the White House as she reports the event on television. The willingness of the media to exploit or to trivialize horrors in order to win audiences, the real threat of toxic wastes and official cover-ups, and the various aspects of terrorism are all used effectively. It is especially provocative that the maniacal killer seems to espouse all the pieties of the Sierra Club and to be willing to destroy unknown innocents for the greater good of mankind. The verbal sparring between Victor and Lyons is notable, and the situation is cinematic.

There are overtones of Tennessee Williams in *The Undoing.* Lorraine Tempesta, who runs a chicken-slaughtering and dressing shop, drinks too much, longs for a man, and harasses her dating daughter. A year before, her husband Leo had been killed in a terrible traffic accident. At the site she laughed, but now she is overcome with guilt. A one-eyed man who wants to help out comes into the shop. He proves to be the driver of the other car, come to make amends. There is also a kind of Greek-Italian chorus of two old women, Mrs. Corvo and Mrs. Mosca.

Tamer of Horses combines elements familiar from other Mastrosimone plays. The childless Ty and Georgiane have taken a youthful black offender, Hector, as a foster child. Ty, orphaned and separated from his brother Sam, who died young as a criminal, wants to give another youth in trouble a chance for a new life. A classics teacher, Ty reaches Hector through a retelling of the *Iliad,* but he cannot break him of old thieving, lying ways. Especially chilling is Hector's re-creation of a subway mugging. Although he has been touched by the two and their care, Hector nonetheless departs. With Mastrosimone's talent for authentic ethnic dialogue and his apparent belief that one cannot teach even a young dog new tricks, he has found a voice and themes for the audiences of his time.

The Understanding, later retitled *A Carver of Stone,* is autobiographical in tone. It deals with a sternly independent immigrant Italian father, a stone carver in Tenafly, New Jersey, and his alienated son. The father threatens to shoot officials who, in order to build a freeway ramp, want to evict him from the stone house he built himself. His son Raff arrives, ostensibly to introduce his fiancée Janice but actually to persuade the old man to leave his home peacefully. Old wounds are probed and new threats explored. Father and son arrive at an understanding on two levels.

Sunshine, which the writer adapted for the screen, also probes emotional wounds. Sunshine is a stripper who performs for ogling males in a glass booth under seductive pink lights. At home she keeps a pet lobster in a glass tank, an obvious symbol. Repulsed by her life, she flees a murderous husband to take shelter with Nelson, a burned-out paramedic. He protects himself from the world with indifference, but she manages to get under his skin. Both are in glass booths, but they finally reach an understanding. The idea for the play came from a nine-hour talk with a stripper who took shelter with Mastrosimone from her porn king husband. The play, he says, is "about the effect pornography has on the people who perform it."

Although *Like Totally Weird* was written during a two-hour plane trip, it obviously had been gestating during Mastrosimone's experiences in writing for the screen and for television. The play crystallizes his fears for the future of a society whose culture is pervasively influenced by these media. Teenagers Kenny and his passive chum Jimmy break into the Beverly Hills mansion of Russ Rigel, a rich Hollywood producer who is best known for his high-grossing films of sex and violence. The boys know by heart some of the most sensual and horrific scenes of his films and love acting them out. Rigel's lavish postmodern split-level showplace is filled with priceless antiques and artworks, and it proves an ideal setting for replays of his films.

As Rigel and his mistress and star, Jennifer Barton, are on their way to receive yet another award, Kenny forces them at gunpoint to enter into his re-creations of Rigel's cinematic epics of violence. The gun is loaded, and Kenny is clearly capable of using it to get what he wants, just as he has seen guns used in Rigel's films. Kenny's idol is the psychotic killer Charles Manson, and media saturation has made him a boy-man with no sense of responsibility or morality. His and Jimmy's reality is what they see in films or on television. Kenny is a clever mimic not only of the actors and films he has seen but also of his parents and other adults he despises, and he offers some ironically comic impersonations that momentarily relieve the tension in what is a taut, threatening drama. Rigel is revealed as a totally unprincipled and manipulative person, one who will sacrifice anything or anyone to protect himself and his profits. Out of the final tragedy of the encounter, Rigel snatches the real-life materials of yet another major sex-and-violence motion picture triumph.

In *Like Totally Weird* Mastrosimone has ingeniously presented most of the violent menace in psychologically charged incidents and has avoided showing actual violence. Rigel may well be a composite of producers with whom the playwright has worked in Hollywood, allowing him to settle personal scores. He has said, however, "We don't need another Hollywood play. It's about America—not only about what is happening, but what it will become." He sees greed as the principal reason for Hollywood's production of films of ever increasing violence: "There are all these people who are making fortunes and have no idea about the lives they're destroying." He views producers as mad scientists who have created monsters that will turn on them: "The template for the entire process in the back of my mind was Frankenstein." As a writer for screen and television as well as a parent, Mastrosimone began to "connect all of my experiences" with the horrifying incidents of youthful violence: "I began to see myself as part of the problem." Neither Mastrosimone nor *Like Totally Weird* insists that movies make kids kill people, "but I think the accumulation of images—the breakdown of morality, and other things, over a lifetime just makes it more likely . . . That steady diet of murder and mayhem, without consequences, has now become real."

During the premiere of *Like Totally Weird* at the Humana Festival, Mastrosimone noted that he works on about two scripts a year. He does not lust after New York productions, for he believes that critics tend to have set expectations of writers whose work they think they know. "Some write the same play over and over. I don't want to do that. I prefer new plays on new themes," he has said. "But 'Mother Theatre' regards those who don't choose to write for it as traitors." He has noted that his plays are often done in Europe, where critics tend to be more perceptive about his work. Instead of coming cold to a production of a new play—followed by a hit or flop review—as is the custom in New York, he thinks that "critics should be part of the process." For Mastrosimone, who has had several productions by the Actors Theatre of Louisville, "This has been my best experience in working on a play."

As with so many other talented playwrights, Mastrosimone has found cinema and television more lucrative markets than the theater. Nonetheless, he once told an interviewer that he prefers the "instant gratification" a writer can get in the theater from both audience and critics. He also likes the fact that he can discover quickly what audiences and critics think, reactions that are delayed or muted with film and television. Further, his experiences with filmmaking have not always been positive ones. He was so disgusted with what was done to *Extremities,* for example, that he walked out in midproduction.

From the summaries of his plays, it is clear that the theme of people being held captive, sometimes through their own passivity or obsessions, is a continuing concern for Mastrosimone.

—Glenn Loney

MATURA, Mustapha

Nationality: Citizen of Trinidad and Tobago. **Born:** Trinidad, 17 December 1939. **Education:** Belmont Boys Roman Catholic Intermediate School, 1944-53. **Family:** Married Mary Margaret Walsh in 1964; three children. **Career:** Worked as an office boy and in a solicitor's firm, 1954-57, stocktaker in hotel, 1958-59, insurance salesman, 1959-60, and tally clerk on the docks, 1960-61, all in Trinidad; moved to England, 1961; hospital porter, 1961-62, display assistant in a cosmetic factory, 1962-65; stockroom assistant in a garment factory, 1966-70. Founding chair, Black Theatre Co-operative, London, 1978. **Awards:** Arts Council bursary, 1971; John Whiting award, for *As Time Goes By,* 1972; George Devine award, for *As Time Goes By,* 1973; *Evening Standard* award, 1975; *Caribbean Times* award, for directing, 1982; Trinidad and Tobago Government Scarlet Ibis award for achievement, 1991. **Agent:** Judy Daish Associates, 2 St. Charles Place, London W10 6EG, England.

Publications

Plays

Black Pieces (includes *Party, Indian, Dialogue, My Enemy*) (produced London, 1970). With *As Time Goes By*, London, Calder and Boyars, 1972.

As Time Goes By (produced Edinburgh and London, 1971). With *Black Pieces*, London, Calder and Boyars, 1972.

Bakerloo Line (produced London, 1972).

Nice (produced London, 1973). Included in *Nice, Rum an' Coca Cola, and Welcome Home Jacko*, 1980.

Play Mas (produced London, 1974; New York, 1976). London, Marion Boyars, 1976.

Black Slaves, White Chains (produced London, 1975).

Bread (produced London, 1976).

Rum an' Coca Cola (produced London, 1976; New York, 1977). Included in *Nice, Rum an' Coca Cola, and Welcome Home Jacko*, 1980.

More, More (produced London, 1978).

Another Tuesday (produced London, 1978).

Independence (produced London, 1979). Included in *Play Mas, Independence, and Meetings*, 1982.

Welcome Home Jacko (produced London, 1979; New York, 1983). Included in *Nice, Rum an' Coca Cola, and Welcome Home Jacko*, 1980.

A Dying Business (produced London, 1980).
Nice, Rum an' Coca Cola, and Welcome Home Jacko. London, Eyre Methuen, 1980.
One Rule, music by Victor Romero and John Laddis (produced London, 1981).
Meetings (produced New York, 1981; also director: produced London, 1982). New York, French, 1982; included in *Play Mas, Independence, and Meetings*, 1982.
Play Mas, Independence, and Meetings. London, Methuen, 1982.
The Playboy of the West Indies (produced Oxford and London, 1984; Chicago, 1988).
The Trinidad Sisters, adaptation of *The Three Sisters* by Chekhov (produced London, 1988; Washington, 1992).
The Coup (produced London, 1991).
A Small World (produced Washington D.C. and London, 1994).

Screenplay: *Murders of Boysie Singh*, 1972.

Television Plays: *No Problem* series, with Farrukh Dhondy, 1983; *There's Something Wrong in Paradise*, 1984; *Party at the Palace*, 1984; *Black Silk* series, with others, 1985; *Playboy of the West Indies*, 1985.

Other

Moon Jump (for children). London, Heinemann, and New York, Knopf, 1988.

*

Critical Study: "Mustapha Matura's *Playboy of the West Indies:* A Carnival Discourse on Imitation and Originality" by Sandra Pouchet Paquet, in *Journal of West Indian Literature* (Kingston, Jamaica), August 1992, pp. 85-96.

Theatrical Activities:
Director: **Plays**—*Meetings*, London, 1982; *Fingers Only by* Yemi Ajibade, London, 1982.

Mustapha Matura comments:
In my writing I have tried to examine the effects of colonialism, political and psychological, on the colonisers and the colonised, hoping that in the magic process of theatre these experiences will lead to eventual liberation.

* * *

The prolific Mustapha Matura was hailed as "the most perceptive and humane black dramatist presently writing in Britain" by Benedict Nightingale as early as 1979. Matura's earlier plays were taken up by the Royal Court and Theatre Upstairs and by the different sections of the London fringe represented by the ICA, the Almost Free, and the Bush. His *Play Mas* was the only work by a Caribbean writer to transfer to the West End. With *The Coup* in 1991 he became the first Caribbean writer to be staged by the National Theatre. In 1978 Matura cofounded the Black Theatre Co-operative with Charlie Hanson; the Co-op has produced his *Welcome Home Jacko* and *One Rule*. Matura gained wider exposure in the 1980s through television scripts: a musical examining black politics through Kid Creole's shipwreck in the Caribbean, *There's Something Wrong in Paradise*; a series devised with Rudy Narayan about a black barrister in London, *Black Silk*; and a Channel 4 comedy series about five young blacks, *No Problem*, written with Farrukh Dhondy. The 40-minute *Black Slaves, White Chains* is a curiosity in his work, an allegory in which three manacled slaves are discouraged from escape by tempters who offer sex, religion, and books. Two finally accept an offer of work, leaving the third still defiant.

Matura's other plays are best divided into those set among West Indians living in England and plays set in the Caribbean. *As Time Goes By* is the most entertaining of the former group. It concerns a plausible Trinidadian East Indian mystic and con man, a Jonsonian rogue living in Notting Hill who solves everyone's problems for a fee. Other characters include the West Indian father worried that his son has turned into a cockney skinhead and the white hippie couple who steal the con man's best marijuana. His wife longs to return to Trinidad: "Trinidad en much but is we own is a heaven compared to dis. . . . Look, child, is five years I here and every night a go ter bed a pray dat when a open my eyes in de morning a go see de sun shining, home." Matura wants his comedy taken seriously: "*As Time Goes By* is about a black man living in this country and how he's escaping from the realities of being a black man and not looking at the world, this country, in any political context. A lot of it is about his escapism and how he's pretending and not being himself, not being black, not being his own true identity." The jokes and high spirits cover a desperation and near despair about the struggle to make a bare living in a hostile environment. *Welcome Home Jacko* looks at unemployed boys in a run-down London youth club who profess faith in Rastafarianism but are eventually forced by the return of Jacko from prison into a more accurate perception of their blackness.

Play Mas is one of Matura's more ambitious dramas of change in Trinidad. The first half presents Samuel working as a drudge in a tailor's shop and being pushed around by his East Indian bosses, a mother and son. The time is the early 1950s, with the Peoples' National Movement emerging. When Samuel goes to a political meeting instead of sweeping the floor, he is sacked. Play Mas, the carnival, arrives, and people revel in the streets in striking costumes. The second half is set after independence, several years later. Samuel, who has become the local police chief, is seeking the source of arms coming to guerrillas on the island. Although the declaration of a state of emergency could prevent the carnival, Samuel is persuaded to lift the ban, and the carnival provides an apparent happy ending.

Rum an' Coca Cola has only two characters, composers of calypsos on a Trinidad beach. The very form of calypso is shown to be degraded by the need to perform "Rum an' Coca Cola," with its refrain "working for the Yankee dollar." As usual with Matura, the surface lightness is deceptive, for he feels passionately about the state of his own part of the Third World.

"In *Independence*," writes Matura in the author's note, "I wanted to show that colonialism is a state of mind as well as a political reality and to examine the conflicts created by the leftovers of such attitudes." In this drama two barmen in an old, little-used hotel offer contrasting views. The older clings to memories of the good old days when the hotel was full of tourists, while the younger wants to be a farmer and completely discard the colonialism that lingers with the hotel, which the older finally burns down.

Meetings focuses on another facet of independent Trinidad: the successful, though they have riches as well as self-government, are, in Matura's words, "people living outside their landscape, with problems that neither inheritance can solve." *Meetings* is about an affluent Americanized couple, seen in their sterile laborsaving kitchen and enjoying a Mercedes, air-conditioning, and a swimming pool. Both lead a hectic life of business meetings. The man, however, influenced by a new young cook in the household, discovers a preference for traditional foods, breadfruit and coconut leaves. This leads to a growing commitment to his roots, talking to old people with tales of slave revolts and taking part in a shango, an ecstatic African-based ritual, to the horror of his wife, who says that she did not marry a monkey man. She, meanwhile, sinks into the corruption that follows selling illegally imported cigarettes, and satire turns to tragedy.

The Coup, subtitled "a play of revolutionary dreams," is based on the attempted coup against Eric Williams in 1970. Here Matura uses farce to allude lightly to serious issues of power and the Third World.

The Playboy of the West Indies is an audacious rewriting of J. M. Synge's classic. Matura moves the location from County Mayo to the remote Trinidadian fishing village of Mayaro, so that one outpost of the English-speaking world becomes another. Widow Quin becomes Mama Benin, the shebeen becomes a rum shop, and the local girls bring gifts of molasses and freshwater oysters. The time is 1950, when many men are emigrating and the girls fear they will not find husbands. Synge's eloquent Irish poetry becomes a racy, idiomatic, earthily comic Caribbean speech.

The Trinidad Sisters transfers *The Three Sisters* to Port-of-Spain at the start of World War II, with the women dreaming of going to Cambridge. Vershinin is the only white. The colonial world will soon crumble, as Chekhov's Russia did. Matura justified his work by saying, "It's a wonderful vehicle for familiarising the European who knows the play with West Indian parallels, but also for black Europeans who are soon not going to know anything about the West Indies."

Matura has remarked, "I respond differently to each new play I write. . . . So it would be less than accurate, and misleading, to find one common perception throughout my work." Matura's subjects are the state of former black colonies and of blacks in Britain, usually treated with apparent lightness and with a mastery of all the possibilities of Trinidadian speech.

—Malcolm Page

McCABE, Eugene

Nationality: Irish. **Born:** Glasgow, Scotland, 7 July 1930. **Education:** Castleknock College, Dublin; University College, Cork, B.A. 1953. **Family:** Married Margôt Bowen in 1955; one daughter and three sons. **Career:** Farmer in County Monaghan, 1955—. Chair Patrick Kavanagh Society, 1970-73. **Awards:** *Irish Life* award, 1964; Prague Festival award, for television play, 1974; Irish Critics award, for television play, 1976; Royal Society of Literature Winifred Holtby prize, for fiction, 1977; Reading Association of Ireland award, for children's book, 1987. **Agent:** A. P. Watt Ltd., 20 John Street, London WC IN2DR, England. **Address:** Drumard, Clones, County Monaghan, Ireland.

Publications

Plays

The King of the Castle (produced Dublin, 1964; New York, 1978). Dublin, Gallery Press, and Newark, Delaware, Proscenium Press, 1978.

Breakdown (produced Dublin, 1966).

Pull Down a Horseman (produced Dublin, 1966). With *Gale Day*, Dublin, Gallery Press, 1979.

Swift (produced Dublin, 1969).

Victims (trilogy; includes *Cancer*, *Heritage*, *Victims*), adaptation of his own fiction (televised 1976; produced Belfast, 1981). Cork, Mercier Press, 1976; *Cancer* published Newark, Delaware, Proscenium Press, 1980.

Roma, adaptation of his own story (televised 1979). Dublin, Turoe Press, 1979.

Gale Day (televised 1979; produced Dublin, 1979). With *Pull Down a Horseman*, Dublin, Gallery Press, 1979.

Television Plays: *A Matter of Conscience*, 1962; *Some Women on the Island*, 1966; *The Funeral*, 1969; *Victims* (trilogy), 1976; *Roma*, 1979; *Gale Day*, 1979; *Music at Annahullion*, from his own short story, 1982; *The Year of the French*, with Pierre Lary, from the novel by Thomas Flanagan, 1983.

Novels

Victims: A Tale from Fermanagh. London, Gollancz, 1976.

Death and Nightingales. London, Secker and Warburg, 1992.

Short Stories

Heritage and Other Stories. London, Gollancz, 1978.

Other

Cyril: The Quest of an Orphaned Squirrel (for children). Dublin, O'Brien Press, 1986.

* * *

Eugene McCabe's output is small, and one could wish for more plays from such a talent. In the 1980s he turned more to fiction and television as his media, winning much acclaim for his adaptation of Thomas Flanagan's best-selling historical novel *The Year of the French*. As a playwright McCabe belongs to the 1960s, when he was instrumental, together with such dramatists as Brian Friel, Thomas Murphy, and John B. Keane, in revitalizing the moribund Irish theater, symptomatic of which was the Abbey Theatre's ultraconservatism of the period.

McCabe's plays have a forthrightness that must be seen in the context of theatrical and cultural conditions in an Ireland emergent from isolationism and about to come to terms with the changes and challenges brought by television, the EEC, air travel, and an affluence deriving from unprecedented industrial development. *The King of the Castle* challenged certain taboos in Irish society by presenting for contemplation the spectacle of a childless couple goaded by social attitudes toward sex and fertility into hiring a surrogate father. The setting is a farm in County Monaghan, where Scober Mac Adam is harvesting and has many hired hands and small farmers in assistance. A proud and powerful figure, Scober is all too sensitive to the mocks and jeers of those who look on his pretty wife Tressa and fault him for her childlessness. The imagery and atmosphere of the harvest reinforce Scober's bitter sense of sterility, and unknown to Tressa he encourages a young laborer, Matt Lynch, to think of her as in need of him. When she discovers the monstrous notion that Scober has planned, Tressa, a sympathetic character, is shattered. Ironically, Scober has succeeded only in driving her further away from him than ever, while the mockery of the "chorus" of Hardyesque locals is not silenced but increased. Written with sensitivity as well as appropriate frankness, the play is McCabe's greatest claim to attention as a dramatist. It is, one might say, an Irish *Desire under the Elms*. It won for McCabe the prestigious *Irish Life* Award.

Two unpublished plays, *Breakdown* and *Swift,* followed. Neither was a success. *Breakdown,* a play about the new Ireland of big business deals and shady ethical standards, could nevertheless be regarded as rather old-fashioned in its moral approach, "pure Ibsen through the idiom," as the *Irish Times* reviewer put it. *Swift* was a major production at the Abbey with Tyrone Guthrie directing, Tanya Moisiewitch designing, and Micheál MacLiammóir from the Gate Theatre starring as Swift. The *Irish Times* reviewer described the play as "an episodic, impressionistic chronicle" and found it somewhat tedious in spite of, or perhaps because of, the stars descending amid the homely Abbey company. The subsequent television adaptation of *Swift* indicated that the proper medium for McCabe's main theme, Swift's madness, was film rather than theater. But in tackling the theme for the stage he was joining a long and distinguished line of Irish dramatists—Yeats, Lord Longford, and Denis Johnston, for example—fascinated by the mysteries of Swift's biography,

The greater success of *Swift* on television may have inclined McCabe toward that medium and away from the stage. Yet he did, in fact, write once more for the stage with *Gale Day,* a short play about Patrick Pearse. This was written at a time when revisionist historians were depicting Pearse as less than heroic and, indeed, as seriously flawed. *Gale Day* puts Pearse on trial and presents him as sympathetic and courageous in spite of the charges laid against him. The play makes a pendant to an earlier short piece, *Pull Down a Horseman,* in which Pearse and James Connolly hold a debate over the true nature of Irish republicanism. McCabe does not take sides between the romantic idealist and the socialist.

With his three-part television drama on the Northern Ireland situation—*Cancer, Heritage,* and *Victims*—McCabe reached a wider audience with enormous success. Using fiction that McCabe had either already published or was about to publish, these plays carried a documentary quality that was both new and powerful on Irish television. From his native vantage point in the border county of Monaghan adjoining the rural population of Fermanagh that is sharply divided on sectarian lines, McCabe can communicate through codes of language and skillful subtext startling and even shocking insights into the ways violence blasts through coexistence and undermines human feeling. As one character puts it in *Heritage,* "Men who don't want to hate are pushed to it," and they must take sides. McCabe probably said all he wanted to say about the Northern Ireland tragedy in these three plays. He subsequently wrote a simple study of a tramp figure, an Irish Mad Tom, in *Roma,* based on a story with the same title already published in *Heritage and Other Stories*. The confused mind of the old man could be seen as an image of Irish consciousness strained by the twin forces of loyalty to traditional pieties and the necessity to see and accept changes in moral standards when doors are opened to foreign influences. The concern with breakdown under one kind of strain or another has been McCabe's enduring theme as a playwright, and it is found again even in so minor a piece as *Roma.*

—Christopher Murray

McCARTEN, Anthony (Peter Chanel Thomas Aquinas)

Nationality: New Zealander. **Born:** New Plymouth, 28 April 1961. **Education:** Francis Douglas Memorial College, New Plymouth, graduated 1979; Victoria University, Wellington, B.A. 1987. **Family:** Married Fiona Mathieson in 1988 (divorced 1992); two sons. **Career:** Journalist, Taranaki *Herald*, New Plymouth, 1979-82; musician, Anthony Takes A Bath, Wellington, 1989. **Awards:** Queen Elizabeth II Arts Council grant, 1989, 1990, 1991, 1996; New Zealand *Listener* award, 1991: Wellington Theatre Critics award, 1991. **Agent:** Playmarket, P.O. Box 9767, Wellington, New Zealand; and, Casarotto Ramsay, National House, 60-66 Wardour Street, London W1V 3HP, England.

Publications

Plays

Cyril Ellis, Where Are You? (produced Wellington, 1984).
Yellow Canary Mazurka (produced Wellington, 1987).
Ladies Night, with Stephen Sinclair (produced Auckland, 1988; Oldham, Greater Manchester, 1989; London, 1990).
Pigeon English (produced Wellington, 1989).
Weed (produced Wellington, 1990).
Via Satellite (produced Wellington, 1991).
Hang On a Minute Mate! (produced Wellington, 1992).
F.I.L.T.H.: Failed in London Try Hong Kong (produced Wellington, 1996).
Four Cities (produced Los Angeles, 1997).

Screenplay: *Via Satellite,* 1998.

Novels

Spinners. Aukland, Vintage, 1998.

Short Stories

A Modest Apocalypse. Auckland, Godwit Press, 1991.

*

Theatrical Activities:
Director: **Plays**—*Via Satellite,* 1998.

Anthony McCarten comments:

I come from out of a rural farming tradition, small towns and ordinary people are my characters. My plays, by and large, try to place these ordinary people in extraordinary situations, thereby forcing them to reveal their true character. Often as not, they are funny, but if I don't occasionally pull at a heart-string or two, then I know I've failed.

*   *   *

To write nine plays in nine years and have most of them staged at least once was not a bad start for a New Zealand playwright who had only passed his 30th birthday. When one of these plays also became a runaway success, toured extensively in Australasia, went on to three tours of Britain produced by Michael Codron and then to Europe in translation, and even made money, the playwright can be said to have arrived.

And yet there has always been the feeling that Anthony McCarten is searching for a winning formula rather than trying to express his own, deeply felt ideas.

In his first play, *Cyril Ellis, Where Are You?*, McCarten experimented with form and came up with a mixture of the bizarre and the comic. A group of widely disparate people travel by train on Christmas Eve in 1951, which all New Zealanders remember as the date of the Tangiwai disaster, in which a train plowed into a swollen river, causing many deaths. He was partly successful in showing the alienated condition of New Zealanders, and he was welcomed as a promising new talent.

Yellow Canary Mazurka addressed the plight of those lonely and rejected people who live in high-rise apartments and only just manage to communicate. Comedy was his mode, because that is what audiences in Wellington resolutely seemed to want, and the play was again well received and the tragicomedy of the situation recognized. A second production in Auckland was considered "as tight a piece of writing as one could wish for . . . a crazy love story, part black comedy, part Pinteresque farce, which functions as a perfect paradigm of urban angst."

In 1987 he collaborated with Stephen Sinclair to produce the phenomenally successful *Ladies Night*, which encouraged him to claim to be "the first New Zealander of his generation to emerge as an international force in the writing of plays". While this was too grandiose a claim at the time, it may well prove to be true.

Ladies Night tells of five despairing young men on the dole who decide to try anything to earn money, including stripping at a nightclub. Arrogantly confident at first that they have nothing to learn, they are forced to change their ideas about what women want and to sharpen their performance skills while improving their physiques. They learn some of life's lessons and emerge sharper, nastier, but certainly more confident—and much, much richer. Their highly charged strip acts end the play, each performer having developed his own specialty act to fit his personality. Audiences for *Ladies Night* came from the wider non-theater-going crowd, and many young women made multiple visits to watch what became a dramatized version of a sex show with laughs.

Although *Ladies Night* has resisted critical approval, it has had numerous productions, and it quickly became the most widely seen New Zealand play ever. Translated, it has gone to Germany, Austria, Spain, and Italy, proving that some pleasures are common to women the world over.

By the time his fourth play, *Pigeon English*, made it to the stage in 1989, it had been in preparation for three or four years. A whimsical satire on local government bureaucrats faced with the dilemma of removing pigeons from the town hall clock, it failed to live up to expectations.

Weed took up the plight of New Zealand farmers faced with financial ruin after oil shocks, stock market crashes, and European Community exclusions, with the happy suggestion that a really lucrative cash crop—marijuana—would help them trade their way out of difficulties in a truly monetarist manner. Originally titled *A Secret Economy*, this genuinely Kiwi play has proved popular and has had revivals throughout the country.

Consistent only in that he writes comedy in various shades of black, McCarten next explored the rich vein of domestic comedy in *Via Satellite*. A family consisting of a mother, four remaining daughters, and the husband of one of them wait for the appearance on television of a fifth daughter about to go for gold at the Olympic Games. They also await the even more disruptive arrival of a television crew to film the family watching the event for satellite relay to the waiting world. Civil war has been raging in the family for a long time, and each knows and dreads the moves the others will make. Each responds in her own way to the success of the famous sister, and the play gives fine opportunities for dynamic and comic performances from five women. When the crew arrives, the complications intensify, and all is only just resolved by curtain time. Farce hovers but is kept at bay. McCarten has laid claim in program notes and interviews to a more serious intent, saying that he is examining the way a family brings up its members and that there may be some connection between the success of one and the failure of another. The play does not justify these claims, but it has brilliant dialogue, funny situations, and skillful construction. In it McCarten is a master of comedy.

Barry Crump is a New Zealand writer of yarns about blokes in the bush, and McCarten's next enterprise, *Hang On a Minute Mate!*, was to adapt some of these stories into a full-length play. Overburdened by a complicated revolving set and a Model A Ford trundling on and off, the play was too long and cumbersome in performance, although the theater proved that careful marketing could find a new audience for this genre.

A solo piece for a modern young man who expresses his dislocation from and dysfunction in today's society, called *Let's Spend the Night Together*, emerged from workshop and rehearsal readings. Together with Sinclair, McCarten created *Legless*, or *The Curse of the Wedgecombes*. This comedy, a spoof murder mystery, has allegorical overtones of the split between Britain and her erstwhile dominions.

—Patricia Cooke

McCLURE, Michael (Thomas)

Nationality: American. **Born:** Marysville, Kansas, 20 October 1932. **Education:** University of Wichita, Kansas, 1951-53; University of Arizona, Tucson, 1953-54; San Francisco State University, B.A. 1955. **Family:** Married 1) Joanna Kinnison in 1954 (divorced in 1994), one daughter; 2) Amy Evans in 1997. **Career:** Assistant professor, 1962-77, associate professor, 1977, and professor, 1978—, California College of Arts and Crafts, Oakland. Playwright-in-residence, American Conservatory Theatre, San Francisco, 1975; associate fellow, Pierson College, Yale University, New Haven, Connecticut, 1982. Editor, with James Harmon, *Ark II/ Moby I*, San Francisco, 1957. **Awards:** National Endowment for the Arts grant, 1967, 1974; Guggenheim fellowship, 1971; Magic Theatre Alfred Jarry award, 1974; Rockefeller fellowship, 1975;

Obie award, 1978; Josephine Miles award, 1994; Lifetime Achievement award, National Poetry Association, 1995. **Agent:** Helen Merrill Ltd., 361 West 17th Street, New York, New York 10011. **Address:** 3200 Brunell Drive, Oakland, California 94602, U.S.A.

Publications

Plays

!The Feast! (produced San Francisco, 1960). Included in *The Mammals*, 1972.
Pillow (produced New York, 1961). Included in *The Mammals*, 1972.
The Growl, in *Four in Hand* (produced Berkeley, California, 1970; produced separately New York, 1976). Published in *Evergreen Review* (New York), April-May 1964.
The Blossom; or, Billy the Kid (produced New York, 1964). Milwaukee, Great Lakes Books, 1967.
The Beard (produced San Francisco, 1965; New York, 1967; London, 1968). Privately printed, 1965; revised version, New York, Grove Press, 1967.
The Shell (produced San Francisco, 1970; London, 1975). London, Cape Goliard Press, 1968; in *Gargoyle Cartoons*, 1971.
The Cherub (produced Berkeley, California, 1969). Los Angeles, Black Sparrow Press, 1970.
The Charbroiled Chinchilla: The Pansy, The Meatball, Spider Rabbit (produced Berkeley, California, 1969). Included in *Gargoyle Cartoons*, 1971.
Little Odes, Poems, and a Play, The Raptors. Los Angeles, Black Sparrow Press, 1969.
The Brutal Brontosaurus: Spider Rabbit, The Meatball, The Shell, Apple Glove, The Authentic Radio Life of Bruce Conner and Snoutburbler (produced San Francisco, 1970; *The Meatball* and *Spider Rabbit* produced London, 1971; New York, 1976; *The Authentic Radio Life of Bruce Conner and Snoutburbler* produced London, 1975). Included in *Gargoyle Cartoons*, 1971.
Gargoyle Cartoons (includes *The Shell, The Pansy, The Meatball, The Bow, Spider Rabbit, Apple Glove, The Sail, The Dear, The Authentic Radio Life of Bruce Conner and Snoutburbler, The Feather, The Cherub*). New York, Delacorte Press, 1971.
The Pansy (produced London, 1972). Included in *Gargoyle Cartoons*, 1971.
Polymorphous Pirates: The Pussy, The Button, The Feather (produced Berkeley, California, 1972). *The Feather* included in *Gargoyle Cartoons*, 1971.
The Mammals (includes *The Blossom, !The Feast!, Pillow*). San Francisco, Cranium Press, 1972.
The Grabbing of the Fairy (produced Los Angeles, 1973). St. Paul, Truck Press, 1978.
The Pussy, The Button, and Chekhov's Grandmother; or, The Sugar Wolves (produced New York, 1973).
McClure on Toast (produced Los Angeles, 1973).
Gorf (produced San Francisco, 1974). New York, New Directions, 1976.
Music Peace (produced San Francisco, 1974).
The Derby (produced Los Angeles, 1974; revised version produced New York, 1981).
General Gorgeous (produced San Francisco, 1975; Edinburgh, 1976). New York, Dramatists Play Service, 1982.
Two Plays. Privately printed, 1975.
Sunny-Side Up (includes *The Pink Helmet* and *The Masked Choir*) (produced Los Angeles, 1976). *The Pink Helmet* included in *Two Plays*, 1975; *The Masked Choir* published in *Performing Arts Journal* (New York), August 1976.
Minnie Mouse and the Tap-Dancing Buddha (produced San Francisco, 1978). Included in *Two Plays*, 1975.
Two for the Tricentennial (includes *The Pink Helmet* and *The Grabbing of the Fairy*) (produced San Francisco, 1976).
Range War (produced Tucson, 1976).
Goethe: Ein Fragment (produced San Francisco, 1977). Published in *West Coast Plays 2* (Berkeley, California), Spring 1978.
Josephine the Mouse Singer, adaptation of a story by Kafka (produced New York, 1978). New York, New Directions, 1980.
The Red Snake (produced San Francisco, 1979).
The Mirror (produced Los Angeles, 1979).
Coyote in Chains (produced San Francisco, 1980).
The Velvet Edge. Privately printed, 1982(?).
The Beard, and VKTMS: Two Plays, (*VKTMS* produced New York, 1988). New York, Grove Press, 1985.

Television Play: *The Maze* (documentary), 1967.

Video: *Love Lion*, 1991.

Novels

The Mad Cub. New York, Bantam, 1970.
The Adept. New York, Delacorte Press, 1971.

Poetry

Passage. Big Sur, California, Jonathan Williams, 1956.
Peyote Poem. San Francisco, Wallace Berman, 1958.
For Artaud. New York, Totem Press, 1959.
Hymns to St. Geryon and Other Poems. San Francisco, Auerhahn Press, 1959.
The New Book: A Book of Torture. New York, Grove Press, 1961.
Dark Brown. San Francisco, Auerhahn Press, 1961.
Two for Bruce Conner. San Francisco, Oyez, 1964.
Ghost Tantras. Privately printed, 1964.
Double Murder! Vahrooooooohr! Los Angeles, Wallace Berman, 1964.
Love Lion, Lioness. Privately printed, 1964.
13 Mad Sonnets. Milan, East 128, 1964.
Poisoned Wheat. Privately printed, 1965.
Unto Caesar. San Francisco, Dave Haselwood, 1965.
Mandalas. San Francisco, Dave Haselwood, 1966.
Dream Table. San Francisco, Dave Haselwood, 1966.
Love Lion Book. San Francisco, Four Seasons, 1966.
Hail Thee Who Play. Los Angeles, Black Sparrow Press, 1968; revised edition, Berkeley, California, Sand Dollar, 1974.
Muscled Apple Swift. Topanga, California, Love Press, 1968.
Plane Pomes. New York, Phoenix Book Shop, 1969.
Oh Christ God Love Cry of Love Stifled Furred Wall Smoking Burning. San Francisco, Auerhahn Press, 1969(?).
The Sermons of Jean Harlow and the Curses of Billy the Kid. San Francisco, Four Seasons, 1969.
The Surge. Columbus, Ohio, Frontier Press, 1969.
Hymns to St. Geryon, and Dark Brown. London, Cape Goliard Press, 1969; San Francisco, Grey Fox Press, 1980.
Lion Fight. New York, Pierrepont Press, 1969.

Star. New York, Grove Press, 1971.
99 Theses. Lawrence, Kansas, Tansy Press, 1972.
The Book of Joanna. Berkeley, California, Sand Dollar, 1973.
Transfiguration. Cambridge, Massachusetts, Pomegranate Press, 1973.
Rare Angel (writ with raven's blood). Los Angeles, Black Sparrow Press, 1974.
September Blackberries. New York, New Directions, 1974.
Solstice Blossom. Berkeley, California, Arif Press, 1974.
Fleas 189-195. New York, Aloes, 1974.
A Fist Full (1956-1957). Los Angeles, Black Sparrow Press, 1974.
On Organism. Canton, New York, Institute of Further Studies, 1974.
Jaguar Skies. New York, New Directions, 1975.
Man of Moderation. New York, Hallman, 1975.
Flea 100. New York, Hallman, 1975.
Ah Yes. Berkeley, California, Poythress Press, 1976.
Antechamber. Berkeley, California, Poythress Press, 1977.
Antechamber and Other Poems. New York, New Directions, 1978.
Fragments of Perseus. New York, Jordan Davies, 1978.
Letters. New York, Jordan Davies, 1978.
Seasons, with Joanna McClure, Berkeley, California, Arif, 1981.
The Book of Benjamin, with Wesley B. Tanner. Berkeley, California, Arif, 1982.
Fragments of Perseus (collection). New York, New Directions, 1983.
Fleas 180-186. Berkeley, California, Les Ferriss, 1985.
Selected Poems. New York, New Directions, 1986.
Rebel Lions. New York, New Directions, 1991.
Simple Eyes. New York, New Directions, 1994.
Three Poems. New York, Penguin Books, 1995.

Other

Meat Science Essays. San Francisco, City Lights, 1963; revised edition, San Francisco, Dave Haselwood, 1967.
Freewheelin' Frank, Secretary of the Angels, as Told to Michael McClure by Frank Reynolds. New York, Grove Press, 1967; London, New English Library, 1974.
Scratching the Beat Surface. Berkeley, California, North Point Press, 1982.
Specks (essays). Vancouver, Talonbooks, 1985.
Testa Coda. New York, Rizzoli, 1991.
Lighting the Corners: On Art, Nature, and the Visionary. New Mexico, University of New Mexico Press, 1997.

Editor, with David Meltzer and Lawrence Ferlinghetti, *Journal for the Protection of All Beings 1 and 3*. San Francisco, City Lights, 2 vols., 1961-69.

*

Bibliography: A *Catalogue of Works by Michael McClure 1956-1965* by Marshall Clements, New York, Phoenix Book Shop, 1965.

Manuscript Collections: Simon Fraser University, Burnaby, British Columbia; University of California, Berkeley.

Critical Studies: "This Is Geryon," in *Times Literary Supplement* (London), 25 March 1965; interview in *San Francisco Poets* edited by David Meltzer, New York, Ballantine, 1971, revised edition, as *Golden Gate*, San Francisco, Wingbow Press, 1976; "Michael McClure Symposium" in *Margins 18* (Milwaukee), March 1975; "An Interview with Michael McClure" by S. E. Gontarski, in *The Review of Contemporary Fiction* (Normal, Illinois) Fall 1990, pp. 116-23; "Reaching into the Stream: An Interview with Michael McClure" by Mitchell Smith, in *Kerouac Connection,* Spring 1994, pp. 31-38.

Theatrical Activities:
Actor: **Films**—*Beyond the Law*, 1968; *Maidstone*, 1971.

Michael McClure comments:

Theatre is an organism of poetry—weeping, and laughing, and crying, and smiling, and performing superhuman acts—on a shelf in space and lit with lights.

* * *

Michael McClure's curious and highly personal amalgams of Artaud, pop art playfulness, surrealism, and Eastern mysticism seek to bridge the romantic gap and to join the mind and body in what he calls "spiritmeat." His first attempt in this ambitious project was a succès de scandale, *The Beard,* in which two archetypes of American dreams, Jean Harlow and Billy the Kid, confront each other outside time and place. Harlow's challenge, "Before you can pry any secrets from me, you must first find the real me! Which one will you choose?" counterpoints Billy's "You're divine" and "You're a bag of meat," two McClurean identities. *The Beard* avoids the implied metaphysics of meaty divinity since rational argument could only intensify the split between the senses and the spirit. Instead, Billy and Harlow's verbal duel becomes increasingly sexual and violent, pulsating to an ecstatic climax rather than a resolution.

McClure has tried to extend our concept of what humanity is, first by emphasizing man's animality. *!The Feast!* was written in "grahr" language, sound poetry based on animal grunts, growls, howls, and groans, which gradually evolved into mystical imagery:

> There's no light in the closed rose but a tiny black cherub sleeps there and sings to the creatures that walk in the cliffs of the Lily's pollen, moving from shadow to light in the drips of rain. The seen is as black as the eye seeing it.

At its best such language is difficult to sustain in the theater, and for *Gargoyle Cartoons* and subsequent plays up to *Minnie Mouse and the Tap-Dancing Buddha* McClure returned to the more direct statement of *The Beard*. These plays present his metaphysics in what is almost a parody of Beat slang: "From the moment of birth till the hour we're zapped and boogie to the grave, we're thoroughly enwrapped in the realms of being. How can we know nothing, and know especially that even nothing isn't something, if there's always *Being* there?" Although these bald statements have little dramatic value, the best of the plays are oddly unsettling glimpses of human nature and of humans and nature. The combination spider and rabbit of *Spider Rabbit* wanders absentmindedly onstage and decides to show and tell. Producing a head from his bag, he saws it open: "BOY AM I HUNGRY! This is the brain of a soldier. BOY, do I hate war. (The head quivers as Spider Rabbit proceeds to eat it with the spoon.) I'M OUT OF CARROTS. BOY, DO I HATE WAR." Few of the plays blend social satire and sight gag so sharply, but they all have a reckless playfulness and a freedom to explore the theater's sensuous possibilities and the audience's expectations about the theater.

Despite their frequent childishness, McClure felt that these plays illustrated the universe's basic nature, which embraces the silly and shallow as well as the profound. More recently, however, he decided that he "had carried that stream of comedies where the universe created the plays to an extreme that completed my expectations and satisfactions in that mode. So at this time, I've nothing further to say in that vein." Since that time, in about 1978, his work has focused largely on the relation of art to society. In *Goethe: Ein Fragment,* Mephistopheles offers a callow, arrogant young Goethe a deal: if Goethe will write a play that immortalizes the devil, the playwright will receive a second life. This alternate life is the play called *Faust,* and with this arrangement McClure plays with the relative importance of the artist and his creation. Not only is the devil a more sympathetic character than Goethe, but both of them frequently become subordinate to the play *Faust.* As Mephistopheles says, "Everything real or imagined exists everywhere at once," and McClure suggests that what is imagined is less mortal than ordinary reality, a state that is performed behind a scrim in *Goethe: Ein Fragment.*

Like *Goethe* and the clumsy *The Red Snake,* which was based on James Shirley's 1641 *The Cardinal,* McClure's *Josephine the Mouse Singer* is drawn from existing literature, Kafka's delicate and eloquent short story. The play won an Obie Award for its script before it was produced in New York, and its best dialogue is the narration taken directly from Kafka. McClure, however, effectively dramatizes the central problem. Is Josephine's art, brilliant as it is, more important than the dull gray mouse society? Josephine, proud and demanding, is willing to break all of the rules of society in order to give it better art, but at the same time she threatens to destroy it. Neither Kafka nor McClure is foolhardy enough to try to resolve this dilemma, but in dramatizing it McClure produced some of the best writing of his career.

—Walter Bode

McDONAGH, Martin

Nationality: British. **Born:** 1970. **Education:** Dropped out of school at age 16. **Awards:** George Devine award, 1996, Writer's Guild award for best fringe play, Evening Standard award for most promising newcomer, nominations for six Tony awards, and Lawrence Olivier award, all for *The Beauty Queen of Leenane*; 1996 Pearson Television Theatre Writers' Scheme best play prize, for *The Cripple of Inishmaan.* **Agent:** The Rod Hall Agency Limited, 7 Goodge Place, London W1P 1FL, England.

Publications

Plays

The Beauty Queen of Leenane (produced Galway, 1996; London, 1996; New York, 1998). London, Methuen, 1996.
A Skull in Connemara. London, Methuen, 1997.
The Lonesome West. London, Methuen, 1997.
The Beauty Queen of Leenane and Other Plays (includes *The Beauty Queen of Leenane*; *A Skull in Connemara*; *The Lonesome West*). New York, Vintage Books, 1996.
The Cripple of Inishmaan (produced London, 1997; New York, 1998). New York, Vintage Books, 1998.
The Lieutenant of Inishmor. N.p., n.d.
The Banshees of Inisheer. N.p., n.d.

* * *

Critics have labeled Martin McDonagh's work "postmodern melodrama" and "Gothic soap opera." Such apt sobriquets have been accompanied by a level of critical and popular acclaim rarely seen this century. By his mid-20s the playwright had four plays running at prestigious London theaters backed by largely enthusiastic reviews. *The Beauty Queen of Leenane,* his first produced, attracted the most notice and went on to enjoy a Tony award-winning run on Broadway. Ultimately it may be one of his weaker scripts.

Whatever one's personal tastes, McDonagh's four major produced works—"The Leenane Trilogy" and *The Cripple of Inishmann*—are domestic tragicomedies set in the west of Ireland. They all display quirky, hapless Irish characters, dialogue that opens wounds and provokes laughs, and a love of language and storytelling (Johnnypateenmike in *Cripple of Inishmann* literally lives off his gift for gossip, trading tidbits of news for groceries). But the early jaunty tone quickly turns dark. Characters torment one another—most often, family members—before bashing or shooting each other. As the sad-sack, liquor-loving local priest in *The Lonesome West* says of the isolated village that lends the trilogy its name, "I thought Leenane was a nice place when I first turned up here, but no. Turns out it's the murder capital of fecking Europe."

In an interview the London-born writer suggests that Harold Pinter and David Mamet, as well as the stories of the Brothers Grimm, influenced his plays. Indeed McDonagh mixes Pinter's menace-filled narrative style with Mamet's virtuosic use of curses and speech rhythms for comic effect, while spinning yarns with a mythic, almost tragic Greek focus on primal family lusts and betrayals. A typical play has about seven or eight scenes. Older characters are embittered, grudge-harboring hectors, and the young people are dense-headed wastrels. Hovering over their lives is a vague sense of promise, not of the redemption offered by the ineffectual Catholic Church but of escape, either through drink, television, or dreams of America. (McDonagh's other major inspiration, Quentin Tarantino-type Hollywood gangster flicks, is evident in plays not set in Ireland; his *Dead Day in Coney,* for instance, takes place among a circle of low-life mobsters in and around Brooklyn's famous amusement park and boardwalk.)

The Cripple of Inishmann is also part of a trilogy (including *The Banshees of Inisheer* and *The Lieutenant of Inishmor*), with each work set on a different Aran Island in the 1930s. The young eponymous protagonist of the first, Cripple Billy, fibs his way onto a boat so that he can get to the next island, where an American film director is hiring actors for a documentary about Irish life, by claiming that he has tuberculosis and will die within months. Miraculously Billy makes it to Hollywood. In a typical turn of misfortune, a healthy American actor is cast as the Irish cripple, and Billy finds himself near death in a seedy hotel room. Like most McDonagh plays, the drama ends with a rapid succession of reversals as surprising for their dramaturgical clumsiness as for their shock value. First Billy suddenly reappears on Inishmann. Then, filled with hopelessness and despair, the orphan, who lives with two eccentric old women whom he calls "aunties," gets set to kill himself. But he aborts that plan when Slippy Helen, the love of his life, begrudgingly agrees to go "walking" with him and gives him a kiss, sending Billy into a paroxysm of joy. Just as audiences believe McDonagh may have indulged them a happy ending, Billy coughs up blood as the lights fade to their final black. Here, the only escape is death.

That fact of life does not stop Maureen, the title character of *Beauty Queen*, from trying to flee. A mature woman who lives with her cantankerous, conniving, and demanding mother, she gets her one chance to escape when her new lover Ray Dooley invites her to go to Boston. Of course he sends his younger, shiftless brother to deliver the invitation in a letter. So, before Maureen arrives home, the mother burns it. Sounding a bit like *Hedda Gabler*? Instead of dueling pistols, however, the younger Dooley early in the play picks up an iron fireplace poker and admiringly offers to buy it. Sure enough, that poker "goes off" at the end. But McDonagh mixes pedestrian twists with more clever tricks. For instance, hints are dropped about Maureen's mental health, and, just as audiences take Maureen's side against her mother, her vicious actions make them question their sympathies.

A Skull in Connemara and *The Lonesome West*, the second and third plays in the trilogy, rehash many of the same themes with similar imagery and dramaturgical strategies. The characters change, although earlier incidents and characters are alluded to. *Skull in Connemara* is the darkest, focusing on the late-middle-aged Mick. He is an un-gravedigger: every year, he must clear a section of the cemetery to make room for fresh corpses. He gathers the old bones and smashes them to dust before scattering them in the lake. This year, he must dig up the bones of his wife, whose death still causes suspicious villagers to whisper behind Mick's back. *The Lonesome West* is perhaps the funniest and best of the lot. The last third is particularly brilliant. Two brothers' Cain-and-Abel-like struggle is ameliorated momentarily when Father Welsh, the local priest, writes them a letter suggesting that if the brothers cannot find peace, the Father's soul will burn in hell. The two proceed to sit down and attempt to make peace by topping each other with harrowing confessions about past transgressions against each other. They try mightily to absolve each sin. Finally they cannot take it anymore, and the play ends with a tremendous burst of violence. Because neither sibling is physically harmed, however, the lights fade as one follows the other to the pub, a particularly Irish means of escape. It is a rare moment in which McDonagh allows a sliver of hope to infiltrate an otherwise bleak landscape.

—John Istel

McGEE, Greg(ory William)

Nationality: New Zealander. **Born:** Oamaru, 22 October 1950. **Education:** Waitaki Boys High School; University of Otago, Dunedin, LL.B. 1973. **Family:** Married Mary Davy; one daughter. **Career:** Literary fellow, University of Auckland, 1982. **Agent:** Playmarket, P.O. Box 9767, Wellington. **Address:** 8 John Street, Ponsonby, Auckland 2, New Zealand.

Publications

Plays

Foreskin's Lament (produced Auckland, 1980). Wellington, Victoria University Press, 1981.
Tooth and Claw (produced Wellington, 1983). Wellington, Victoria University Press, 1984.
Out in the Cold (produced Auckland, 1983). Wellington, Victoria University Press, 1984.
Whitemen (produced Auckland, 1986).

Television Plays: *Free Enterprise*, 1982; *Mortimer's Patch* series, 1984; *Roche* series, 1985.

*

Critical Studies: "A National Ethos in Three Dimensions: Rugby in Contemporary New Zealand Fiction" by Scott A. Crawford, in *Arete: The Journal of Sport Literature,* Fall 1986, pp. 57-72; "Playboys of the South Pacific: The Plays of Greg McGee" by Sebastian Black, in *Australasian Drama Studies* (Queensland), October 1990, pp. 183-201.

Greg McGee comments:

The colour, vitality, humour, and general excess I have tried to bring to my work, particularly *Foreskin's Lament*, *Out in the Cold*, and *Whitemen*, are reactions against the traditional literary perception of New Zealand as a dull, grey, colourless place which forced most of our writers and artists into cultural exile. Even those who stayed, like Frank Sargeson, seem in their work to share this "colonial" view of New Zealand as culturally bankrupt. It has been a view that has been too easily accepted by our novelists and short story writers, many of whom felt unable to work here.

I have no such difficulties and I glory in the idiosyncrasies of a very inventive New Zealand colloquial English. The burgeoning Maori writing presence does not seem to be having any difficulties, either, in throwing off the yoke of what, after all, was a very pakeha (white) perception of this land.

* * *

From its first production in 1980, Greg McGee's *Foreskin's Lament* was immediately recognized as the most strident piece of confrontational realism in New Zealand drama. For some theatergoers the play was simply about rugby: the first act set in a changing room on practice night, the second at a party after the Saturday match. Most people, however, also followed the argument of the character nicknamed Foreskin that the rugby player is "the heart and bowels" of New Zealand society, the greatest influence on New Zealand law and ethics. Rugby, with its associations of brutality and insensitivity, thus becomes a metaphor for New Zealand life, the "larger game." The team is a herd, which represents a society, and the action essentially consists of an individual's detaching himself from the herd, articulating his independence, and then being absorbed back into the herd. Foreskin's mission is not to undermine rugby or destroy the team, of which he is the valued fullback; he simply wants to encourage the members to play better rugby, to teach them a primitive altruism on the field. The coach, whose ethic is to "kick shit out of everything above grass height," protests that he "does not understand the meaning of the word," and in the second half of the play Foreskin's defeat is reflected in his retreat into the coach's language. As Foreskin realizes that his stance is hopeless, he moves into his "lament," which begins as a parody of a formal speech at the party; he echoes the speech the acting captain made at the beginning of the act, although the subject now is the death of a teammate. The speech gradually turns into a more general threnody for the lost heroes of New Zealand rugby, and the style becomes increasingly poetical, with invented verbs of loss and fragmentation.

The stance of the individual against the collective has obvious parallels in Ibsen and Bond, and the central action, a villainous scheme against the captain that results in his death, is the stuff of sporting melodrama. Nonetheless, McGee's depiction of the bonds that give cohesion to the team and the nuances of language in which the slogans are asserted, questioned, and reasserted constitute the finest piece of social realism in New Zealand drama to that point. The published script of *Foreskin's Lament* is based on the version used in the premiere productions. McGee has subsequently modified the play considerably, however, and the performance script held by his agents does not even contain the final poetical lament.

McGee's second play, *Free Enterprise*, was a situation comedy for television about the thwarting of a café owner, but it was a disappointment. His next two stage plays, however, were much more substantial. *Tooth and Claw* is set in a law office (McGee's own profession), with a large central screen serving sometimes as a window, suggesting that events in the city are being monitored from the executive tower, and sometimes as a depiction of the lawyer's mental state, thus illustrating his anxieties. Before the first lines of dialogue the lawyer views with dismay a black-and-white screen image of civic anarchy, suggesting that this play, too, will offer a metaphorical expansion of the action. It also becomes clear, however, that there really is disorder in the streets and that the lawyer's nightmare is derived from a recent incident in which he was assaulted and robbed by a Maori activist (who expressionistically appears on stage as a mime). The immediate action consists of politely veiled blackmail from a former student flatmate who is now a speculator and entrepreneur, manipulations that are reflected in two senior law partners as well. The guilty past is analyzed and confessed in clinical detail, a method that contrasts strongly with the remarkable vagueness with which the wider present and imminent future are depicted.

In the same year as *Tooth and Claw*, *Out in the Cold* was premiered as a stage play, although its outline was already familiar from McGee's short story of the same title. Summarized, it sounds like a situation comedy. Judy, a former student and now a single mother, tries to pass herself off as a man in order to get a well-paying job doing heavy labor in a meat-processing and freezing plant. The peripeteia that will occur when her real identity is discovered—as it is transparently obvious that it will be—means that there is a good deal of comic suspense pivoting on the inevitable rethinking of attitudes. Like rugby in the earlier play, however, the meat industry is here a metaphor for Kiwi masculinity—or the packaging of masculinity—and the facility with which it can be penetrated and possibly punctured means that the overt comedy is supported by rich implicit ironies. A 1985 television version began with a brief introduction without dialogue in which Judy, sunbathing naked, got up, cut her hair, and dressed as a man before going to the employment room at the slaughterhouse. This clarified some of the possible ambiguities in the stage version and generated strong sympathy with Judy from the start. The screen also allowed meticulous coverage of the butchering process, and the camera dwelt on the labyrinthine expanses of the works, which became even more clearly a physical correlative to a bizarre social system.

McGee's fourth stage play, *Whitemen*, was a resounding critical and commercial failure, and it has not been published. Such has been the continuing impact of his earlier works, however, that several companies have successfully mounted second productions that explored different approaches.

—Howard McNaughton

McGRATH, John (Peter)

Nationality: British. **Born:** Birkenhead, Cheshire, 1 June 1935. **Education:** Alun Grammar School, Mold, Wales; St. John's College, Oxford (Open Exhibitioner), 1955-59, B.A., Dip.Ed. **Military Service:** Served in the British Army (national service), 1953-55. **Family:** Married Elizabeth MacLennan in 1962; two sons and one daughter. **Career:** Farm worker, Neston, Cheshire, 1951; play reader, Royal Court Theatre, London, and television writer and director, 1959-65. Founder and artistic director, 7:84 Theatre Company, 1971-88 (divided into Scottish and English companies, 1973); founding director, Freeway Films, 1983—; director, Channel Four Television, London, 1989-95. Judith E. Wilson fellow, Cambridge University, 1979, 1989. Visiting writer, Bernard College, New York, 1994; visiting writer, Columbia University, New York, 1996; visiting professor of Media Arts, Royal Holloway, London University, 1996. **Agent:** Casarotto Ramsay Ltd., National House, 60-66 Wardour Street, London W1V 3HP, England. **Address:** c/o Freeway Films, 67 George Street, Edinburgh EH2 2JG, Scotland.

Publications

Plays

A Man Has Two Fathers (produced Oxford, 1958).

The Invasion, with Barbara Cannings, adaptation of a play by Arthur Adamov (produced Oxford and Edinburgh, 1958).

The Tent (produced Edinburgh and London, 1958).

Why the Chicken (produced Edinburgh, 1959; revised version produced on tour, 1960).

Tell Me Tell Me (produced London, 1960). Published in *New Departures* (London), 1960.

Take It (produced London, 1960).

The Seagull, adaptation of a play by Chekhov (produced Dundee, 1961).

Basement in Bangkok, music and songs by Dudley Moore (produced Bristol, 1963).

Events While Guarding the Bofors Gun (produced London, 1966). London, Methuen, 1966.

Bakke's Night of Fame, adaptation of the novel *A Danish Gambit* by William Butler (produced London, 1968). London, Davis Poynter, 1973.

Comrade Jacob, adaptation of the novel by David Caute (produced Falmer, Sussex, 1969).

Random Happenings in the Hebrides; or, The Social Democrat and the Stormy Sea (produced Edinburgh, 1970). London, Davis Poynter, 1972.

Sharpeville Crackers (produced London, 1970).

Unruly Elements (includes *Angel of the Morning, Plugged-in to History, They're Knocking Down the Pie-Shop, Hover Through the Fog, Out of Sight*) (produced Liverpool, 1971; *Plugged-in to History*, produced London, 1971; *Out of Sight, Angel of the Morning, They're Knocking Down the Pie-Shop*, and *Hover Through the Fog*, produced London, 1972). *Angel of the Morning, Plugged-in to History* and *They're Knocking Down the Pie-Shop*, published as *Plugged-in*, in *Plays and Players* (London), November 1972.

Trees in the Wind (also director: produced Edinburgh and London, 1971, New York, 1974).

Soft or a Girl (produced Liverpool, 1971; revised version, as *My Pal and Me*, also director: produced Edinburgh, 1975).

The Caucasian Chalk Circle, adaptation of a play by Brecht (produced Liverpool, 1972).

Prisoners of the War, adaptation of the play by Peter Terson (produced Liverpool, 1972).

Underneath (also director: produced Liverpool, 1972; London, 1978).

Serjeant Musgrave Dances On, adaptation of the play *Serjeant Musgrave's Dance* by John Arden (produced Stirling, 1972).

Fish in the Sea, music by Mark Brown (produced Liverpool, 1972; revised version produced London, 1975). London, Pluto Press 1977.

The Cheviot, the Stag, and the Black, Black Oil (also director: produced Edinburgh, 1973). Kyleakin, Isle of Skye, West Highland Publishing, 1973; revised version, 1975; revised version, London, Eyre Methuen, 1981.

The Game's a Bogey (also director: produced Aberdeen, 1974). Edinburgh, Edinburgh University Student Publications, 1975.

Boom (also director: produced Golspie, Sutherland, 1974; revised version produced Aberdeen, 1974). Published in *New Edinburgh Review*, August 1975.

Lay Off (also director: produced Lancaster and London, 1975).

Little Red Hen (also director: produced Edinburgh, 1975; London, 1976). London, Pluto Press, 1977.

Oranges and Lemons (also director: produced Amsterdam, 1975; Birmingham, 1977).

Yobbo Nowt, music by Mark Brown (also director: produced York and London, 1975; as *Mum's the Word*, produced Liverpool, 1977; as *Left Out Lady*, produced New York, 1981). London, Pluto Press, 1978.

The Rat Trap, music by Mark Brown (also director: produced Amsterdam and London, 1976).

Out of Our Heads, music by Mark Brown (also director: produced Aberdeen, 1976; London, 1977).

Trembling Giant (English version) (produced Lancaster, 1977).

Trembling Giant (Scottish version) (also director: produced Dundee and London, 1977).

The Life and Times of Joe of England (also director: produced Basildon, Essex, and London, 1977).

Big Square Fields, music by Mark Brown (produced Bradford and London, 1979).

Joe's Drum (also director: produced Aberdeen, 1979). Aberdeen, People's Press, 1979.

Bitter Apples, music by Mark Brown (produced Liverpool, 1979).

If You Want to Know the Time (produced London, 1979).

Swings and Roundabouts (also director: produced Aberdeen, 1980). Included in *Two Plays for the Eighties*, 1981.

Blood Red Roses (also director: produced Edinburgh, 1980; London, 1981; revised version produced Liverpool, 1982). Included in *Two Plays for the Eighties*, 1981.

Two Plays for the Eighties. Aberdeen, People's Press, 1981.

Nightclass, music by Rick Lloyd (also director: produced Corby, Northamptonshire, and London, 1981).

The Catch, music by Mark Brown (also director: produced Edinburgh, 1981).

Rejoice!, music by Mark Brown (also director: produced Edinburgh and London, 1982).

On the Pig's Back, with David MacLennan (produced Kilmarnock, Ayrshire, 1983).

The Women of the Dunes (produced in Dutch, Ijmuiden, Netherlands, 1983).

Women in Power; or, Up the Acropolis, music by Thanos Mikroutsikos, adaptation of plays by Aristophanes (also director: produced Edinburgh, 1983).

Six Men of Dorset, music by John Tams, adaptation of a play by Miles Malleson and Harry Brooks (produced Sheffield and London, 1984).

The Baby and the Bathwater: The Imperial Policeman (also director: produced Cumbernauld, Dunbartonshire, 1984; revised version produced Edinburgh, 1985; London, 1987).

The Albannach, music by Eddie McGuire, adaptation of the novel by Fionn MacColla (produced Edinburgh, 1985).

Behold the Sun (opera libretto), with Alexander Goehr, music by Goehr (produced Duisburg, West Germany, 1985).

All the Fun of the Fair, with others (produced London, 1986).

Border Warfare (also director: produced Glasgow, 1989).

John Brown's Body (also director: produced Glasgow, 1990).

Watching for Dolphins (also director: produced London, 1991).

The Silver Darlings (produced Glasgow, 1992).

Reading Rigoberta (also director: produced 1994).

Half the Picture, with Richard Norton Taylor (produced London, 1995).

Ane Satye of the Fourth Estate (produced 1996).

The Last of the MacEachans (also director: produced 1996).

Screenplays: *Billion Dollar Brain*, 1967; *The Bofors Gun*, 1968; *The Virgin Soldiers*, with John Hopkins and Ian La Fresnais, 1969; *The Reckoning*, 1970; *The Dressmaker*, 1989; *The Long Roads*, 1991; *Mairi Mhor*, 1994.

Television Plays: scripts for *Bookstand* series, 1961; *People's Property (Z Cars* series), 1962; scripts for *Tempo* series, 1963; *Diary of a Young Man* series, with Troy Kennedy Martin, 1964; *The Entertainers* (documentary), 1964; *The Day of Ragnarok*, 1965; *Mo* (documentary), 1965; *Shotgun*, with Christopher Williams, 1966; *Diary of a Nobody*, with Ken Russell, from the novel by George and Weedon Grossmith, 1966; *Orkney*, from stories by George Mackay Brown, 1971; *Bouncing Boy*, 1972; *Once upon a Union*, 1977; *The Adventures of Frank*, from his play *The Life and Times of Joe of England*, 1979; *Sweetwater Memories* (documentary), 1984; *Blood Red Roses*, 1986; *There Is a Happy Land*, 1987; *Border Warfare*, 1989; *John Brown's Body*, 1990; *Half the Picture*, with Richard Norton Taylor (from their play), 1995.

Other

A Good Night Out: Popular Theatre: Audience, Class and Form. London, Eyre Methuen, 1981; reprinted London, Nick Hern Books, 1996.
The Bone Won't Break: On Theatre and Hope in Hard Times. London, Methuen, 1990.
Six Pack, Six Plays for Scotland. Edinburgh, Polyson, 1996.

Translator, with Maureen Teitelbaum, *The Rules of the Game* (screenplay), by Jean Renoir. London, Lorrimer, 1970.

*

Bibliography: By Malcolm Page, in *New Theatre Quarterly* (Cambridge), November 1985.

Manuscript Collection: University of Cambridge; National Library of Scotland, Edinburgh.

Critical Studies: *Disrupting the Spectacle* by Peter Ansorge, London, Pitman, 1975; *British Theatre since 1955* by Ronald Hayman, London and New York, Oxford University Press, 1979; *Stages in the Revolution* by Catherine Itzin, London, Eyre Methuen, 1980; *Dreams and Deconstructions* edited by Sandy Craig, Ambergate, Derbyshire, Amber Lane Press, 1980; "Three Socialist Playwrights" by Christian W. Thomsen, in *Contemporary English Drama* edited by C. W. E. Bigsby, London, Arnold, and New York, Holmes and Meier, 1981, and "The Politics of Anxiety" by Bigsby, in *Modern Drama* (Toronto), December 1981; *Modern Scottish Literature* by Alan Bold, London, Longman, 1983; interview with Oscar Moore, in *Plays and Players* (London), April 1983; *The Moon Belongs to Everyone (Making Theatre with 7:84)* Metheun, 1990; *The Politics of Alternative Theatre in Britain, 1968-1990, the Case of 7:84* by Maria di Cenzo, Cambridge, 1996; *Scottish Theatre since the Seventies* edited by Stevenson and Wallace, Edinburgh University Press, 1996.

Theatrical Activities:
Director: **Plays**—Many of his own plays, and *Bloomsday* by Allan McClelland, Oxford, 1958; *The Birds* by Aristophanes, Oxford, 1959; Live New Departures series of plays, 1961-64; *The Eccentric* by Dannie Abse, London, 1961. **Television**—*Bookstand* series, 1961; *The Compartment* by Johnny Speight, 1961; *Z Cars* series (8 episodes), 1962; *The Fly Sham* by Thomas Murphy, 1963; *The Wedding Dress* by Edna O'Brien, 1963; *The Entertainers* (documentary), 1964; *The Day of Ragnarok*, 1965; *Mo* (documentary), 1965; *Shotgun* by McGrath and Christopher Williams, 1966; *Double Bill* by Johnny Speight, 1972; *Z Cars: The Final Episode*, 1978; *The Adventures of Frank*, 1979; *Come to Mecca* by Farrukh Dhondy, 1983; *Blood Red Roses*, 1986; *Border Warfare*, 1989; *John Brown's Body*, 1990.

John McGrath comments:

(1973) My plays, I now realize, have been from the beginning about the relationship of the individual to other individuals and thence to history. They have pursued this theme in many ways, poetic, comic, tragic, realistic, and latterly more and more freely. Music is now coming to play a more important part in my plays, to help break through the barriers of naturalism which I can no longer tolerate. My work has never suited London (West End) audiences or ways of thinking: it has been seen and enjoyed by working-class audiences from Orkney to Plymouth, and by young audiences all over the country in university theatres and art labs and studio theatres, via the 7:84 Theatre Company. I have also benefited from a thriving relation with the Everyman Theatre, Liverpool, under the direction of Alan Dosser, as previously from working with directors as perceptive and helpful as Ronald Eyre, Anthony Page, and Richard Eyre in Edinburgh.

My plays are not difficult to approach, although they tend to have many levels of meaning embedded fairly deeply under them as well as on the surface. The key, if key is needed, is a growing political consciousness allied to a growing feeling for individual human beings, with all the contradictions that alliance involves.

* * *

The enormity of John McGrath's contribution to the field of contemporary drama will probably never be fully realized, largely because of the way in which he has latterly chosen to direct his energies. Active in the theater as an undergraduate writer, he immediately went on to earn a place in history as one of the key developers of the dominant mode of modern television naturalism, and during his time with the BBC he was jointly responsible for the hugely influential *Z Cars* series. Rejecting a full-time career in television, he turned first to the conventional professional theater. The play *Events While Guarding the Bofors Gun* derived from his own experience in the army in the 1950s and was linkable thematically and in stature with Arnold Wesker's *Chips with Everything.* He then produced *Bakke's Night of Fame,* an adaptation of a novel, as well as working on a number of screenplays, including that for his own *The Bofors Gun.*

Interest in the political consciousness of his characters was apparent from the outset, but the demands of television and of the conventional professional theater for a well-crafted play with a resolved narrative proved inhibiting. The sense of class confrontation and ideological molding in *The Bofors Gun,* for instance, is never matched by any strand in the play that suggests a way out of the fatalistically conceived framework of plot and society. What McGrath sought was a way of presenting individuals in conflict with their social context but in ways that suggested the possibility of change through self-education and experience. This was to involve him in a conscious turning away from the conventional theater with what he saw as, at best, its minimally questioning analysis of capitalist society. The problem for him was as much that of audience as theatrical style: "The audience has changed very little in the theatre, the social requirements remain constant, the values remain firmly those of acceptability to a metropolitan middle-class audience, with an eye to similar acceptability on the international cultural market."

The real break with his past, and a consistent turning away from the politically restricting naturalistic mode, came in 1968. McGrath had started work on the first of a long series of plays about Scotland's history and its struggles, *Random Happenings in the Hebrides.* The play was to deal with the attempts of a young Scottish Labour M.P. to work for change for his island community within the confines of the parliamentary system. In the middle of writing the play, the barricades went up in Paris. McGrath went over and rethought the play, placing a greater emphasis on a nonparliamentary oppositional strategy but seeing all the time the conflict between the need for political organization and the immediacy of action that he had witnessed in France. It was a theme that was to dominate much of his later work, taking him progressively further away from naturalism and into various models of agitprop theater in pursuit of an audience that could be defined in terms of its political potential rather than its interest in the theater as such.

By 1970, when *Random Happenings* was first produced, McGrath had started a formative period of work with the Liverpool Everyman, including a series of playlets about contemporary Britain, *Unruly Elements,* which was later retitled *Plugged-in to History*. In 1971 McGrath founded 7:84, a socialist theater group intent on taking plays into the kind of nontheatrical venues shunned by the conventional theatrical establishment. Since then he has worked largely in Scotland, producing a string of plays dealing with Scottish socialist strategy in a variety of historical and contemporary contexts, with the occasional production for the English offshoot of 7:84. Productions have varied from the didactic intensity of the first 7:84 piece, *Trees in the Wind,* to offerings such as the political pantomime *Trembling Giant* that make use of the loosest of narrative structures to put across a deliberately crude analysis. McGrath's clear awareness of the dangers of arguing for an impossibly simple solution to a highly complex problem, the dilemma of all revolutionaries living in a nonrevolutionary age, is brilliantly articulated in the humor and wit of the plays, frequently inviting the audience into the never self-contained discourse. The general method is summed up well by Joe's tongue-in-cheek invitation to the audience to take its seats again after the interval in *Joe's Drum,* a play written in response to the election of a Conservative administration and the failure of the Scottish Assembly vote. They are assured that they should not be frightened off by the fear of weighty material: "It's yer ain true story told in biased argument, highly selective history and emotional folksong. Are ye all back that's comin' back? Right—lock the doors."

McGrath's and 7:84's insistence on a theater that should not only offer enlightenment but also entertainment is a key part of the play's acceptance. McGrath has moved progressively away from the kind of parody of a consumer society that has proved a staple of so much agitprop theater—as in the *Beat the System* TV show in *The Game's a Bogey*—in search of popular cultural roots that oppose those offered by the consumerist system. The use of the Highland *ceilidh* form for the first Scottish 7:84 tour, in 1973, of *The Cheviot, the Stag, and the Black, Black Oil* gave McGrath the structure of a traditional evening entertainment through which to tell the story of Scottish exploitation through history to the then oil boom. In subsequent plays he was to make the link between the music as part of an oppositional cultural history and the need to question contemporary representations a major part of the shows' dynamics.

McGrath's is a questioning development of agitprop, and his conclusions are usually open-ended, witnessing a small personal achievement perhaps but not proclaiming the imminence of revolutionary change. And in this context his depiction of the particular dilemma of women caught in the dual webs of capitalism and a male-oriented ideology has emerged as a major theme in his work. In *Joe's Drum* the wife is a continual presence, chipping away at masculine vanities, and in a play such as *Yobbo Nowt* all of the emphasis is placed on the struggles of a wife after she has ejected an unfeeling husband. Her discovery of the way in which the system operates against the have-nots parallels her own discovery of individual potential, and the play ends with a small personal leap forward.

McGrath has produced work at a prolific rate, always with a central interest in the way in which the individual can operate against the increasingly sophisticated and endlessly elastic models of late capitalist society. The overall effect is to suggest the way in which the various manifestations of authority and oppression are a part of a single system and thus linkable, as they are from one play to another, each then becoming just one in a series of views through the different windows of a part of the same enormous construction. In *Blood Red Roses* he traced the political struggles of Bessie from the 1950s to the present day, and she is just one of what is by now a very large political family assured of an audience away from the subsidized and commercial theaters of London where reputations are made. His insistence, however, on the continual tracing of that struggle has itself been a great struggle, and as he recounts in *The Bone Won't Break,* the establishment, in particular that part of the establishment holding the purse strings of the Arts Council, continually opposed the efforts of McGrath and 7:84 to the extent that the company at last ceased to operate. As a result stage productions from McGrath have become less frequent, although the 1990 *John Brown's Body* at Glasgow's Tramway, in which the dominant stage feature was a huge platform along three walls from which the ruling-class characters controlled and directed the workers and audience at stage level, saw him continue unabashed. More of his energy has inevitably gone into work for film and television. A popular writer in a genuine sense, McGrath will continue to be performed long after the reputations of many participants in what he sees as an integral part of the capitalist system have been forgotten.

—John Bull

McGRATH, Tom

Nationality: British. **Born:** Rutherglen, Lanarkshire, 23 October 1940. **Education:** Glasgow University, degree in drama and English. **Family:** Married; four daughters. **Career:** Director, Third Eye Centre, Glasgow; founding editor, *International Times* underground newspaper, London, 1960s; writer-in-residence, Traverse Theatre, Edinburgh, and University of Iowa, Iowa City. Since 1990 associate literary director, Scottish Arts Council, Edinburgh. Also a jazz pianist. **Agent:** Michael Imison Playwrights, 28 Almeida Street, London N1 1TD, England.

Publications

Plays

Laurel and Hardy (produced Edinburgh, 1976; as *Mr. Laurel and Mr. Hardy*, produced London, 1976).

The Hard Man, with Jimmy Boyle (produced Edinburgh and London, 1977). Edinburgh, Canongate, 1977.

The Android Circuit (produced Edinburgh, 1978).

Sisters (produced London, 1978; revised version produced Southampton, 1985).

Animal (produced Edinburgh, 1979).

The Innocent (produced London, 1979).

1-2-3: Who Are You Anyway?, *Very Important Business*, *Moondog* (produced Edinburgh and London, 1981).

The Phone Box (for children; produced on tour, 1983).
Pals (produced Cumbernauld, Dunbartonshire, 1984).
Kora (produced Edinburgh, 1986).
Thanksgiving (produced Glasgow, 1986).
Private View, with Mhairi Grealis (produced Edinburgh, 1987).
Trivial Pursuits (produced Edinburgh, 1988).

Radio Play: *The Silver Darling*, from the novel by Neil Gunn, 1982.

Televisions Plays: *The Nuclear Family*, 1982; *Blowout*, 1984; *The Gambler*, 1984; *End of the Line*, 1984.

Composer: music for *The Great Northern Welly Boot Show*, book by Tom Buchan, lyrics by Billy Connolly, Edinburgh and London, 1972.

Poetry

Birdcalls. Edinburgh, Shore Poets, 1996.

*

Critical Study: "Utopian Visions: Merlin in Edinburgh" by Ken Cockburn, in *Cahpman,* Summer 1992, pp. 47-49.

* * *

For a long time the original success of Tom McGrath's most completely achieved play, *Animal,* kept it out of circulation in England. Although the hit of the 1979 Edinburgh Festival, when it was presented as an official offering by the Traverse Theatre, it was snapped up by American entrepreneurs and the English rights were blocked. The absurdity of such absolute control was reflected by its middling success when it was finally produced south of the Scottish border long after its ecstatic notices. Nonetheless, it remains his most dazzling theatrical conceit.

Originally mounted in an ascending structure of scaffolds and platforms, the play observed the drama of life in a colony of apes and the intrusive presence of zoologists observing them. The real spectacle and abiding image of the play was the movement and relationships of the apes themselves. With the animals portrayed by loose-limbed actors and actresses, the effect was of life observed through a series of mirrors. The animals were watched by the humans, while the apes aped the humans they were watching. Insights and comedy came through the parallel dramas, and, ironically, dramatic communication was hindered most by the necessity of speech among the humans.

Before becoming a dramatist, McGrath was himself an outside observer of sorts. He edited Britain's most influential countercultural periodical, *International Times,* part of the exploding drug culture of the 1960s. That experience was brought to his play for the Royal Shakespeare Company, *The Innocent,* which followed a progression from the use of drugs for pleasure to addiction and withdrawal in an attempt to consider the implications of a selfish pursuit of pleasure on the dreams of the lost alternative society. It was the first of his plays even to suggest personal experience and observation, and most of his work through the 1970s was notable for his wide-ranging interests. Science fiction and dramatized biography were perhaps the strongest elements.

His first play, which appeared at the Edinburgh Festival in 1976 and later transferred to London, was *Mr. Laurel and Mr. Hardy,* a private view of the offscreen life of the best comic team of the first Hollywood era. McGrath takes the ambitious route of showing both lives independently as well as matching his two actors for some of the on-screen routines. For McGrath the attraction of Stan Laurel is obviously his Glasgow beginnings, but Oliver Hardy is given equal biographical substance. The play is notable for its contemplation of the team's pathetic final years, with Laurel alone still writing routines for himself and his old partner but speaking both parts.

McGrath's second play, a violent dramatization of the life of a reformed Glasgow gangster, appeared the following year. *The Hard Man* was written with Jimmy Boyle, who told the story under his own name in the book *A Sense of Freedom,* which McGrath had a hand in. The story is essentially an odyssey through childhood and gang warfare in the Glasgow slums, culminating in a criminal career that included brutal murder. There is a further dimension to the story, namely, Boyle's rehabilitation in prison and his emergence as a sculptor. The play does not go that far, however, but rather provides a form of ritual reenactment of the street violence that accentuates key moments in the life of Johnny Byrne, the fictional Boyle. Jailed for murder, Byrne remains the fiercely proud street fighter, resisting the regimentation and sadism of the prison and finally reaching a peculiar transcendence in a cramped cage where he squats and smears excrement over himself.

That power was missing from McGrath's fantasy *The Android Circuit* and from *Sisters,* his portrait of three girls growing up in London's East End. Moments of the force were again visible in a trilogy he wrote for the Traverse and BBC radio, *1-2-3,* which McGrath described as "plays about male identity written from a feminist viewpoint by a man." The plays are chiefly connected by a cast of three, two men and a woman, and the first play, *Who Are You Anyway?,* blazes a trail of gender confusion as male love and bonding are transferred to love of a woman. The final play appears to pick up the thread of *The Innocent* and shows the two men and woman reinventing a myth about woman as witch, specifically as priestess of the moon. *Moondog* begins with a drop-out Scot pictured in his chosen solitude in the Highlands and greeting the morning with a chant before being interrupted by an old friend who comes bearing unwanted business propositions. A further interruption is in the form of the woman who arrives with a different purpose, in the nature of human sacrifice.

The trilogy failed in London but found an audience for the same production at the Toronto Theatre Festival of 1981, and McGrath himself spent a year at the University of Iowa directing the Playwrights' Workshop there. Returning to Scotland, he returned to Scottish themes, notably with *Kora,* a documentary drama about the struggle of tenants in a Dundee housing estate to improve conditions but filled with flashes of McGrath's theatrical invention and optimism. His American experience was satirically reflected through the short play *Thanksgiving,* written for Glasgow's Tron Theatre. As part of a trilogy including plays by other Glasgow-based writers, it was designed to accommodate original music by Edward McGuire but rather more theatrically made use of the spectral presence of the musicians. In it McGrath dissected the consumerism of Thanksgiving Day in the United States, with a bossy television set and a woman reasonably declaring her love for two men during "the year of the Ayatollah." It passes more as amused observation than enlightening comment, and if McGrath's work in the 1980s was less visible than his work of the 1970s, it was similarly diverse and sympathetic.

While he continues to supply original plays and adaptations to the Scottish theater, from the Edinburgh Lyceum to Cumbernauld Theatre Company, by the 1990s McGrath has moved into a new role with perhaps even more influence on the future of Scottish drama. As associate literary director of the Scottish Arts Council, he masterminded training and astute subsidy to become regarded as a guru of Scottish playwrights. His own work still represents a major part of his time, but perhaps reverting to his early days, when as a founder member of the *International Times* he was concerned with enfranchising the disaffected into an alternative society, his inspiration to others has proved to be a major achievement.

—Ned Chaillet

McGUINNESS, Frank

Nationality: Irish. **Born:** Buncrana, Donegal, 29 July 1953. **Education:** Carndonagh College, Donegal, 1966-71; University College of Dublin, 1971-76, B.A., and M.Phil in medieval studies. **Career:** Lecturer, University of Ulster, Coleraine, Londonderry, 1977-79, University College of Dublin, 1979-80, and St. Patrick's College, Maynooth, County Kildare, 1984—. Director, The Abbey Theatre, Dublin, 1992—. Member of Aosdanna, 1991—. **Awards:** Rooney prize, 1985; Harvey's award, 1985; *Evening Standard* award, 1986; *Plays and Players* award, 1986; Cheltenham prize, 1986; Charrington award, 1987; Ewart-Biggs Peace prize, 1987; Edinburgh Fringe first, 1988; Prague prix des journalists, 1989. **Agent:** Sheila Lemon, Lemon, Unna, and Durbridge, 24 Pottery Lane, Holland Park, London W11 4LZ, England.

Publications

Plays

The Factory Girls (produced Dublin, 1982; London, 1988). Dublin, Monarch Line, 1983; revised edition, Dublin, Wolfhound, 1988.

Borderlands (produced Dublin, 1984). Published in *Three Team Plays*, edited by Martin Drury, Dublin, Wolfhound, 1988.

Observe the Sons of Ulster Marching Towards the Somme (produced Dublin, 1985; London, 1986; Boston, 1988). London, Faber, 1986.

Baglady (produced Dublin, 1985; London and Springfield, Connecticut, 1988). With *Carthaginians*, London, Faber, 1988.

Gatherers (produced Dublin, 1985).

Innocence: The Life and Death of Michelangelo Merisi Caravaggio (produced Dublin, 1986). London, Faber, 1987.

Yerma, adaptation of the play by Federico García Lorca (produced Dublin, 1987).

Rosmersholm, adaptation of the play by Henrik Ibsen (produced London, 1987).

Carthaginians (produced Dublin, 1988; London, 1989; Williamstown, New York, 1991). With *Baglady*, London, Faber, 1988.

Times in It (produced Dublin, 1988).

Peer Gynt, adaptation of the play by Henrik Ibsen (produced Dublin, 1988). London, Faber, 1990.

Mary and Lizzie (produced London, 1989). London, Faber, 1989.

Beautiful British Justice (sketch) in *Fears and Miseries of the Third Term* (produced Liverpool and London, 1989).

The Bread Man (produced Dublin, 1990).

Three Sisters, adaptation of the play by Anton Chekhov (produced Dublin and London, 1990). London, Faber, 1990.

Threepenny Opera, adaptation of the play by Bertolt Brecht (produced Dublin, 1991).

Someone Who'll Watch Over Me (produced London and New York, 1992).

Plays (includes *The Factory Girls*; *Observe the Sons of Ulster Marching Towards the Somme*; *Innocence*; *Carthaginians*; *Baglady*). London, Faber, 1996.

Mutabilitie. London, Faber, 1997.

Television Plays: *Scout*, 1987; *The Hen House*, 1990.

Poetry

Booterstown. Old Castle, Co. Meath, Gallery Press, 1994.

*

Manuscript Collection: National Library of Ireland.

Critical Study: *The Feast of Famine: The Plays of Frank McGuinness* by Eamonn Jordan, New York, Peter Lang, 1997.

Frank McGuinness comments:

After 20 years or more of civil war, Ireland still stumbles forward, keeping its head just above water. I want my plays to trace the steps of that stumbling, to be steeped in that unholy water. Having lost the certainness of faith and fatherland, this country is in the business of finding new languages, new laws. Theatre is likewise radically shaken. *Someone Who'll Watch over Me*, *Mutabilitie*, and another project will, I hope, form a contingently linked trilogy, giving what are new lives to those lies, the conflict of Ireland and England, the edging of Ireland to Europe.

* * *

"It is possible that there is no other memory than the memory of wounds." The epigraph to *Carthaginians*, taken from Czeslaw Milosz, could stand as epigraph to the whole of Frank McGuinness's work. The characteristic Irish preoccupation with (in his own words) "the effect that the past has on our present" finds distinctive form in his plays. These plays explore the relationship between culture (whether local or national) and personal identity, in which the past is experienced as both a burden and a source of energy. McGuinness has described his plays as "attempts to give what was lost a voice," and the constant formal and stylistic experimentation of his work evidences his continuing effort to articulate the relationship between the personal and the cultural spheres as part of a project of recuperation and regeneration. The necessity to give voice also guarantees the essentially theatrical nature of the work. McGuinness's plays find their resolutions in acts of utterance of a ritual or quasi-ritual nature: song, recitation, oratory, incantation, or naming. Above all, these plays are shaped by the imperative of confession, which, though sacramental in feeling, is valued as an act of human reciprocity. By giving voice we keep our words to the voiceless.

McGuinness's first play, *The Factory Girls*, prefigures the dramatic movement of his later ones. The confrontational response of a group of five women to the threat of redundancy leaves them in an apparently hopeless situation, but it also catalyses a realization in each of an independence gained through bonding. In this terminal situation, individuality and collectivity are found to be mutually sustaining. This realization, in a much more richly contextualized form, assumes a pivotal position in McGuinness's best-known (and best) play, the award-winning *Observe the Sons of Ulster Marching Towards the Somme.* As a piece in which a writer from a Catholic background addresses empathetically the experience of Protestant Ulstermen at one of the vital symbolic moments of Loyalist historical memory, the play was, quite properly, regarded as a significant act of fellowship. Yet it is the perception of "something rotten" at the heart of a "dying" Unionist culture that prompts the characters to question, in their different ways, both the idea of inevitable death as "sacrifice" and the familiar rhetoric of blood that embodies that idea. The play is in four named parts, each evoking a ritual of a secular character. Part 1, "Remembrance," is a monologue set in the present, in which the elderly Kenneth Pyper affirms his fidelity to the sacrifice of "the irreplaceable ones," his immediate comrades on the Somme in 1916, then calls up their ghosts to help him answer the question of "why we let ourselves be led to extermination." The "ghosts," including Pyper's own very different younger self, play out the events leading up to 1 July 1916. In "Initiation," the eight young Ulstermen gather in a makeshift barracks where the homosexual Pyper, failed sculptor and "black sheep" of an ascendancy family, mocks Unionist culture—by fierce parody—as only an insider could. With a disastrous French marriage behind him and a death wish driving him on, Pyper vows, "I'll take away your peace." In "Pairing" the stage is divided to evoke four numinous locations: Boa Island, a church, a rope bridge, and the Twelfth Field. The men are home on leave, but "the guns are home" too. The realization that "we *are* the sacrifice" brings about within each of the four pairings a dissolution of identity, personal and cultural. Yet the same moment also yields a visionary clarity of understanding. The fellowship and even (homosexual) love that enables each man to refashion himself as an independent being is finally tested and proven in Part 4, "Bonding." As they wait in the trenches to go over the top in this "last battle," their ritual preparations affirm the potency of Protestant rhetoric not as triumphalist threat and self-justification but as common inheritance and shared medium of identity. It is Pyper, remade in the bond, who delivers the final prayer; the battle cry of "Ulster" reaches paroxysm and his younger and elder selves join hands to "dance in this deserted temple of the Lord."

The symbolic mode developed through *Sons of Ulster*, *Innocence* (a play about Caravaggio, another homosexual artist figure), and the densely powerful monologue *Baglady*, finds its most daring embodiment—both visual and verbal—in McGuinness's play about Northern Catholic culture, *Carthaginians.* Once again the focus is on an isolated group of individuals in crisis, but here the isolation is self-imposed and the situation even more openly symbolic. This is a play of waiting. Although the setting is a real place in real time and the dialogue-style is predominantly naturalistic, the action is largely internalized, articulated not through conventional narrative but through image, symbol, and quasi-ritual utterance. Six people—three women and three men—are camped out in the Derry city graveyard awaiting the fulfillment of a vision of the dead rising in the burial ground. The world they create for themselves, in this place of ancient resonances, is one that effects strange inversions and suspensions of normal experience by the attempt to mediate between the living and the dead. The group is anchored to everyday fact and reality only through the kind offices of Dido Martin, "patriot and poof," the queen of this particular Carthage and the representative of quite another kind of camp. As with Pyper and Caravaggio, homosexuality here constitutes not a social "issue" but a perspective offering clarification and insight. By virtue of his gender position and through his theatricality (he even writes a parodic play for them), Dido delivers a criticism of the culture of the living even as he is mediating it to the group. Each of the graveyard dwellers nurses the "wound" of a deep personal loss or torment of political conscience, but these wounds are subsumed in the overshadowing memory of a great communal wound: Bloody Sunday, the day in 1971 when British troops shot dead thirteen civilians during a protest march in Derry. The confessional rites of personal release are finally sealed by the communal invocation, as Sunday dawns, of the names of the victims of the atrocity. The dead are present as silent "Listeners," and the living are enjoined to include themselves in a general forgiveness. As "they sleep in the graveyard," the vigilant Dido affirms the survival of the city ("Carthage has not been destroyed"), discards the accumulated detritus of Northern Catholic culture, and leaves Derry to "walk the earth."

Where the symbolic intensities of *Carthaginians* seem indebted to Lorca, the fantastic narrative of *Mary and Lizzie*, with its constant reference to "popular forms of English art" (pantomime and television comedy) and Irish folk tradition (ballad and myth), announces its affiliation to *Peer Gynt* (which McGuinness has translated). This is the playwright's most direct treatment of voicelessness. "Frederick Engels lived with two Irishwomen, Mary and Lizzie Burns"; they showed him the "Condition of the Victorian Working Class" in Manchester. For this reason they are, for McGuinness, "probably the most important Irish people of the nineteenth century, in terms of world history." Yet they are remembered only by the single line in Engels's Life: they are their name(s). Neither fully "historical" nor fully "mythical," Mary and Lizzie, like Pyper, Caravaggio, and Dido, move between two distinct realms. In the world of Myth, a nameless shadowy territory projected by Irish song, folklore, and ritual and defined by darkness and the earth, they are first sent out from the arboreal City of Women to "kiss and tell." They are then shown the future, in the forms of a Magical Priest (son of Mother Ireland), representing both Protestantism and Catholicism in a "killing combination," and a ritual Feast of Famine—complete with balladeering Pig. They escape to England and the realm of History, where, after "passing the time" with the young Queen Victoria (a pantomime dame), they descend to the "open sewer" of Manchester. There they agree to guide a fearful Engels through the nameless "dark" of the "dangerous poor," and so become silent collaborators in his project to "change the world." The sisters' insistence on sexuality and the body disrupts the philosophical double-act of Engels and Karl Marx. At "Dinner with Karl and Jenny" (Marx's wife, herself tormented by the suppression of her contribution) the reason and abstraction of "scientific" socialism is posed against the instinctive physicality and lyrical utterance of Mary and Lizzie. As Jenny reads Engels's terrible account of the Manchester Irish, the illiterate sisters counter his betrayal by singing the folk song "She Moved Through the Fair." Finally, the regenerative power of song and the earth is decisively affirmed in the face of a vision of the "night to come," brought about in the name of political ideologies and attested to by nameless "Women of the Camps" in choric song. Even after Mary's "death," song can unite the sisters with their mother to wander the earth (like McGuinness's other mediator figures) and "sing the songs of those who were never sung about." The linkage of myth, song, and the earth bears witness to the endurance of the voiceless.

McGuinness's most ambitious play about the relation of Ireland and England is the disappointing *Mutabilitie*, a historical fantasy set in Ireland in 1598, in the aftermath of the Munster wars. The action moves between the castle of the poet Spenser—mythologist of the virgin queen Elizabeth—and the forest exile of the dispossessed Irish king Sweney and his family. Between these locations move the bardic wise woman File and the king's son Hugh, plotting revenge even as they serve the English. The fugitive poet-playwright sheltered by Spenser and believed for a time by File to be the Bard from the River who will "sing the song of all songs," endowing the Irish with a voice and effecting reconciliation with the English, is Shakespeare himself, "on tour" in Ireland with his company. The demented Spenser, a mad father like King Sweney, finally fires his own castle and flees Ireland, leaving his own child to be discovered and fostered by the Irish aristocracy, now freed from the obligation of revenge and resolved to walk as beggarly penitents "through the earth." By way of song, stylized language, and pervasive allusion, both structural and verbal, the play itself attempts a specifically Irish engagement with Shakespeare, his medium, and the culture he represents. Unfortunately McGuinness's poetic dialogue is flat and his Shakespearean echoes often misjudged. More modest and more successful (commercially too, with a West End run) is *Someone Who'll Watch Over Me*. But this piece about an Irish journalist, an English lecturer, and an American doctor contriving to ensure their own mental survival while being held hostage in the Lebanon, is much less concerned with the relation of different nationalities (though there are the inevitable tensions) than with common humanity and the growth, through song, story, and imaginative utterance, of a profound fellowship between very different men. The play is quite unBeckettian in mood yet indebted to Beckett in more than just technique.

—Paul Lawley

McINTYRE, Clare

Nationality: British. **Career:** Member, Nottingham Playhouse TIE Company, 1977-78, The Women's Theatre Group, London, 1979-81, and Common Stock, London, 1981. **Awards:** Beckett award, 1989; *Evening Standard* award, 1990; London Drama Critics award, 1990.

Publications

Plays

Better a Live Pompey than a Dead Cyril, with Stephanie Nunn, adaptation of the poems and writings of Stevie Smith (produced London, 1980).

I've Been Running (produced London, 1986).

Low Level Panic (produced London, 1988). Published in *First Run*, edited by Kate Harwood, London, Hern, 1989.

My Heart's a Suitcase (produced London, 1990). London, Hern, 1990.

My Heart's a Suitcase and *Low Level Panic*. London, Nick Hern, 1994.

The Thickness of Skin. London, Nick Hern, 1996.

Radio Play: *I've Been Running*, 1990.

*

Theatrical Activities:

Actor: **Plays**—Role in *Better a Live Pompey than a Dead Cyril*, by McIntyre with Stephanie Nunn, London, 1980; Mrs. Kendal in *The Elephant Man* by Bernard Pomerance, Plymouth, 1982; Dawn in *Steaming* by Nell Dunn, Chester, 1985; Gwendolen in *The Importance of Being Earnest* by Oscar Wilde, Chester, 1985; Jane in *Crystal Clear*, Nottingham, 1986; Jan in *Bedroom Farce* by Alan Ayckbourn, Bolton, 1987; Linda in *Kafka's Dick* by Alan Bennett, Leeds, 1988. **Films**—*The Pirates of Penzance*, 1981; *Krull*, 1982; *Plenty*, 1984; *Empire State*, 1986; *Security*, 1987; *A Fish Called Wanda*, 1988. **Television**—*Hotel du Lac*, 1985; *Splitting Up*, 1990.

* * *

For several years before she turned to writing full-time, Clare McIntyre was an actress working in theater and film. As a member of the Women's Theatre Group she produced a delightful compilation of the work of Stevie Smith. Her first original play was *I've Been Running*, directed by Terry Johnson and performed at the Old Red Lion in London. It focuses on a female health freak whose fears are kept at bay by feverish activity. McIntyre is one of a long line of female playwrights whose work has been encouraged and nurtured by a combination of the Women's Playhouse Trust and Max Stafford-Clark at the Royal Court. Both *Low Level Panic* and *My Heart's a Suitcase* reveal an uncanny ability to reflect the obsessions and anxieties of contemporary women. Like Caryl Churchill, her plays attract a huge female following, but there is no reason men should not also enjoy her wit and shrewd observation.

The panic in *Low Level Panic* is engendered in a couple of females who share a flat when they are confronted with the images of women peddled by advertising and pornography. The territory is similar to Sarah Daniels's but without her aggression. Mary, Jo, and Celia are preparing for a party. McIntyre cleverly sets all but two of the play's scenes in the bathroom, the very place where women minutely examine their bodies and almost invariably find them wanting. Lying in the bath, Jo imagines herself as the heroine of a sexual fantasy, a leggy model gliding through the cocktail bars of London's hotels, clinking glasses of martini, and meeting the admiring eyes of a rich, handsome stranger across a crowded room. Such glacial perfection and anonymity is in complete contrast with Jo's vision of herself as overweight and overtalkative, especially when confronted with a roomful of people at a party. Far from being an expression of her own sensuality, her fantasy makes her feel both humiliated and undesirable. It is also in sharp contrast with the reality experienced by Mary when, in one of just two scenes set outside the bathroom, she is stopped on her way home and raped. As a result she can no longer dress up for a party without feeling that she is asking to be attacked again. The pornographic magazine she discovers in their dustbin appears to her to be a legal incitement to men to attack women. In contrast, Celia, the third member of the flat and the least developed as a character, dishes out advice on the right color of eye shadow as though life simply consists of trapping the right man. The intimate dialogue about spots, herpes, and even unattractive clitorises is sharply observed and very amusing. But above all it is the confusion and naïveté of her characters that McIntyre captures so accurately.

Anxiety is also a theme in *My Heart's a Suitcase*. Chris is 30 years old, a waitress, and distinctly unhappy about it: "What's wrong with being a waitress is that it's a shit job with shit money, no shitting pension and zero fucking prospects." She has a capacity to complain that rivals Jimmy Porter's in Osborne's *Look Back in Anger*. *My Heart's a Suitcase* is a play of the 1980s, a time when everybody was supposed to be getting richer, but Chris, who is middle-class, articulate, has a degree, and could presumably earn money if she set her mind to it, is paralyzed. Her life is drifting by while she is obsessed with the horrors of the world, an obsession intensified after being attacked on the tube by a man with a gun. Her more placid friend Hannah faces the possibility of real paralysis in the form of multiple sclerosis. The two of them travel together to the seaside, invited to spend the weekend in an empty flat belonging to a rich ex-boyfriend of Chris. Thus Chris is given plenty of opportunity to rail against the injustice that some people have money while she has a pittance. She is confronted with real riches when Colin's wife, Tunis, arrives at the flat trailing her consumer goods behind her and throws a tantrum when she discovers that her specially made curtains do not fit. Tunis does not even have to work for her money but fritters her time away in endless shopping sprees. McIntyre, however, avoids drawing too neat a moral, for Tunis is indolent but not a villain and is discontented without being wildly unhappy. It is not that Chris is particularly greedy; it is more that she imagines that wealth would make her happy, although a strange religious phantom called Luggage suggests that it is a woman's role in life to make do with her lot. The phantom and the man who attacks her are the least engaging aspects of the play. Most enjoyable is Chris's ability to articulate her discontent with such ferocious gusto. She may be maddening, but it is hard to dislike her, and McIntyre makes a rare attempt to present the rich complexities of female friendship onstage. She is a humorous, observant playwright with a deep understanding of the female psyche.

—Jane Edwardes

McLURE, James

Nationality: American. **Born:** Louisiana. **Address:** c/o Dramatists Play Service, 440 Park Avenue South, New York, New York, 10016, U.S.A.; and, Chappell Plays Ltd., 129 Park Street, London W1Y 3FA, England.

Publications

Plays

Lone Star (produced Louisville and New York, 1979; London 1980). New York, Dramatists Play Service, 1980.

Pvt. Wars (produced New York, 1979; London, 1980). New York, Dramatists Play Service, 1980.

1959 Pink Thunderbird (includes *Lone Star* and *Laundry and Bourbon*) (produced Princeton, New Jersey, 1980; London, 1989).

Laundry and Bourbon (produced Ashland, Oregon, 1980; London, 1986). New York, Dramatists Play Service, 1981.

The Day They Shot John Lennon (produced Princeton, New Jersey, 1983; London, 1990). New York, Dramatists Play Service, 1984.

Thanksgiving (produced Louisville, 1983).

Wild Oats: A Romance of the Old West, adaptation of the play by John O'Keeffe (produced Los Angeles, 1983). New York, Dramatists Play Service, 1985.

Lahr and Mercedes (produced Denver, 1984).

The Very Last Lover of the River Cane (produced Louisville, 1985).

Max and Maxie (produced New York, 1989). New York, Dramatists Play Service, 1989.

Ghost World. New York, Dramatists Play Service, 1995.

*

Theatrical Activities:

Actor: **Plays**—In *The Death and Life of Jesse James* by Len Jenkin, New York, 1978; *Music Hall Sidelights* by Jack Heifner, New York, 1978.

* * *

James McLure is a playwright and actor who became recognized for two one-acts, *Lone Star* and *Pvt. Wars*, that were produced on Broadway in 1979. It is *Lone Star* that best characterizes the nature and dilemma of McLure's favorite protagonist: a southwestern country bumpkin, a good ole boy who is a veteran returning as an adult to a tamer and duller world that both baffles and bores him. This character or his counterpart, who appears in several McLure plays, is a displaced romantic unable to function well in an adult world that no longer operates by his values.

Set in the littered backyard of a bar in a small town in Texas, *Lone Star* focuses on the swaggering figure of Roy, a former high school hero now back after a hitch in Vietnam but not adjusting well. He drinks Lone Star beer and gasses with his hero-worshiping but slower younger brother about his military and amorous exploits and his three loves: his wife, his country, and his 1959 pink Thunderbird convertible. At the evening's end only one love is left intact, for Roy learns that his brother has slept with his young wife and that his cherished Thunderbird has been borrowed and demolished by a fatuous hardware store clerk ever jealous of Roy. Though the symbols of Roy's youth are destroyed or tarnished, he bounces back at the conclusion, dimly realizing that he can no longer merely muse on the past. Validly praised by critics for its earthy humor and the salty regional idiom of its roistering language, the short play represents McLure at his most effective.

Less successful than its companion piece, *Pvt. Wars* is a black comedy set in an army hospital in which three recuperating Vietnam veterans tease, torment, and even solace one another to disguise their anxiety about returning to the uncertainties of civilian life. Like *Lone Star*'s Roy, they will have to confront a different world. The trio includes a Georgia hillbilly (Gately) given to fiddling with a dead radio, a streetwise hipster (Silvio) addicted to flashing nurses, even though he may now be impotent, and a prissy rich kid (Natwick) who misses his mother. The men's encounters, depicted in 12 sketchlike scenes, project an offbeat humor, but the play's episodic structure forces too fragmentary a quality on the action and characters.

Conceived as a companion piece to *Lone Star* and set in the latter's same mythical Texas town at the home of Roy and his wife Elizabeth, *Laundry and Bourbon* is a short comedy introducing three women on a hot summer afternoon. Elizabeth, the intelligent young lady of the house, folds laundry and sips bourbon while chatting with a gabby neighbor, Hattie. Their talk is interrupted by the self-righteous and unwelcome Amy Lee, the gossipy wife of the hardware clerk of *Lone Star*. Amid self-generated bits of gossip, Amy Lee purposefully blurts out that Roy has been seen with another woman. Displaying an inner strength and an understanding of her husband's turmoil since returning from Vietnam, Elizabeth realizes Roy's need for her and her love for him, and she resolves to be waiting for him when he returns home, whatever the opinion of others. In this comedy McLure's humor, characters, and dialogue are richly successful, and it stands alongside *Lone Star* as the playwright's strongest work.

Wild Oats is a loose adaptation of John O'Keeffe's eighteenth-century comedy of the same name, but while it keeps the plot structure of the original, it transfers the action's locale and characters to the legendary Old West. The plot and characters are a send-up of old-fashioned melodrama's clichés and stereotypes and involve long-lost sons found and forgiven, long-estranged parents reunited, and mistaken identities ultimately revealed. While *Wild Oats* suffers from a surfeit of complications and characters, it emerges as an amusing theatrical romp disclosing its author's hand for theatricality and parody.

The Day They Shot John Lennon is comprised of a series of encounters among strangers gathered at the New York site of John Lennon's assassination. The disparate group, whose motives vary from curiosity and shock to theft, includes the veterans Silvio and Gately (of *Pvt. Wars*), now out of the army hospital and practicing pickpockets. Caught in a theft, Gately reveals his serious mental disturbance and Silvio his protective overseeing of his friend. The total group's interaction throughout points up the assassination's larger significance: that violence and ugliness continue to exist in the communal soul and are too soon forgotten even when witnessed. McLure credibly portrays contemporary urbanites with point and poignancy, demonstrating that his territory goes beyond the Southwest.

That he is an actor as well as a writer contributes to McLure's strengths. These include a sharp eye for character, a gifted ear for regional idiomatic speech, and an uncommon comic flair that extends to the examination of American myths and mores.

—Christian H. Moe

McNALLY, Terrence

Nationality: American. **Born:** St. Petersburg, Florida, 3 November 1939. **Education:** Schools in Corpus Christi, Texas; Columbia University, New York (Evans Traveling Fellow, 1960), 1956-60, B.A. in English 1960 (Phi Beta Kappa). **Career:** Stage manager, Actors Studio, New York, 1961; tutor to John Steinbeck's children, 1961-62; film critic, *Seventh Art*, New York, 1963-65; assistant editor, *Columbia College Today*, New York, 1965-66. Vice-president, Dramatists Guild, 1981—. **Awards:** Stanley award, 1962; Guggenheim fellowship, 1966, 1969; Hull Warriner award, 1973, 1987, 1989; Obie award, for *Bad Habits*, 1974, for *The Ritz*, 1975; American Academy award, for *The Ritz*, 1975; Emmy award, for *Andre's Mother*, 1990; Tony, for best book of a musical, for *Kiss of the Spider Woman*, 1993; Pulitzer prize nomination, for *A Perfect Ganesh*, 1994; Tony award, best play, and Outer Critics' Circle award, for *Love! Valor! Compassion!*, 1995, and for *Master Class*, 1996. **Agent:** Gilbert Parker, William Morris Agency, 1325 Avenue of the Americas, New York, New York 10019. **Address:** 218 West 10th Street, New York, New York 10014, U.S.A.

Publications

Plays

The Roller Coaster published in *Columbia Review* (New York), Spring 1960.

And Things That Go Bump in the Night (as *There Is Something Out There*, produced New York, 1962; revised version, as *And Things That Go Bump in the Night*, produced Minneapolis, 1964; New York, 1965; London, 1977). Included in *The Ritz and Other Plays*, 1976.

The Lady of the Camellias, adaptation of a play by Giles Cooper based on the play by Dumas fils (produced New York, 1963).

Next (produced Westport, Connecticut, 1967; New York, 1969; London, 1971). Included in *Sweet Eros, Next, and Other Plays*, 1969.

Tour (produced Los Angeles, 1967; New York, 1968; London, 1971). Included in *Apple Pie*, 1969.

Botticelli (televised 1968; produced Los Angeles, 1971; London, 1972). Included in *Sweet Eros, Next, and Other Plays*, 1969; in *Off-Broadway Plays 2*, London, Penguin, 1972.

Sweet Eros (produced Stockbridge, Massachusetts, and New York, 1968; London, 1971). Included in *Sweet Eros, Next, and Other Plays*, 1969; in *Off-Broadway Plays 2*, London, Penguin, 1972.

¡Cuba Si! (produced Provincetown, Massachusetts, and New York, 1968). Included in *Sweet Eros, Next, and Other Plays*, 1969.

Witness (produced New York, 1968; London, 1972). Included in *Sweet Eros, Next, and Other Plays*, 1969.

Noon (in *Chiaroscuro* produced Spoleto, Italy, 1968; in *Morning, Noon, and Night*, produced New York, 1968). Published in *Morning, Noon, and Night*, New York, Random House, 1968.

Apple Pie (includes *Next*, *Tour*, *Botticelli*). New York, Dramatists Play Service, 1969.

Last Gasps (televised 1969). Included in *Three Plays*, 1970.

Bringing It All Back Home (produced New Haven, Connecticut, 1969; New York, 1972). Included in *Three Plays*, 1970.

Sweet Eros, Next, and Other Plays. New York, Random House, 1969.

Three Plays: ¡Cuba Si!, Bringing It All Back Home, Last Gasps. New York, Dramatists Play Service, 1970.

Where Has Tommy Flowers Gone? (produced New Haven, Connecticut, and New York, 1971). New York, Dramatists Play Service, 1972.

Bad Habits: Ravenswood and Dunelawn (produced East Hampton, New York, 1971; New York City, 1974). New York, Dramatists Play Service, 1974.

Let It Bleed, in *City Stops* (produced New York, 1972).

Whiskey (produced New York, 1973). New York, Dramatists Play Service, 1973.

The Ritz (as *The Tubs*, produced New Haven, Connecticut, 1973; revised version, as *The Ritz*, produced New York, 1975). Included in *The Ritz and Other Plays*, 1976.
The Ritz and Other Plays (includes *Bad Habits, Where Has Tommy Flowers Gone?, And Things That Go Bump in the Night, Whiskey, Bringing It All Back Home*). New York, Dodd Mead, 1976.
Broadway, Broadway (produced New York, 1978).
It's Only a Play (produced New York, 1982). New York, Nelson Doubleday, 1986.
The Rink, music by John Kander, lyrics by Fred Ebb (produced New York, 1984; Manchester, 1987; London, 1988). New York, French, 1985.
The Lisbon Traviata (produced New York, 1985). Included in *Three Plays*, 1990.
Frankie and Johnny in the Claire de Lune (produced New York, 1987; London, 1989). Included in *Three Plays*, 1990; in *Best American Plays*, New York, Crown, 1993.
Don't Fall for the Lights (dialogue only), with A.R.Gurney and Richard Maltby, Jr., *Street Talk*, and *Andre's Mother* in *Urban Blight*, (musical revue), based on an idea by John Tillinger, music by David Shire, lyrics by Richard Maltby, Jr. (produced New York, 1988).
Faith, Hope, and Charity, with Israel Horovitz and Leonard Melfi (produced New York, 1988). New York, Dramatists Play Service, 1989.
Prelude and Liebstod (produced New York, 1989).
Up in Saratoga (produced San Diego, 1989).
Three Plays (includes *The Lisbon Traviata, Frankie and Johnny in the Claire de Lune, It's Only a Play*). New York, New American Library, 1990.
Kiss of the Spider Woman, adaptation of the novel by Manuel Puig, music by John Kander, lyrics by Fred Ebb (produced Purchase, New York, 1990; London, 1992).New York, Samuel French, 1997.
Lips Together, Teeth Apart (produced New York, 1991).
Terrence McNally: 15 Short Plays. Lyme, New Hampshire, Smith and Kraus, 1994.
A Perfect Ganesh. New York, Dramatists Play Service, 1994.
Love! Valour! Compassion!. Garden City, New York, Fireside Theatre, 1995.
Andre's Mother and Other Short Plays. New York, Dramatists Play Service, 1995.
Terrence McNally: Collected Plays:
Volume II (includes *And Things That Go Bump in the Night; Where Has Tommy Flowers Gone?*). New York, Smith and Kraus, 1996.

Screenplays: *The Ritz*, 1976; *Frankie and Johnny*, 1991.

Television Plays: *Botticelli*, 1968; *Last Gasps*, 1969; *The Five Forty-Eight*, from the story by John Cheever, 1979, *Mama Malone series*, 1983.

Other

Master Class. London, Methuen, 1995.

*

Critical Studies: "*Lips Together, Teeth Apart:* Another Version of Pastoral" by Benilde Montgomery, in *Modern Drama* (Downsview, Ontario), December 1993, pp. 547-55; "Negative Identifications: HIV-Negative Gay Men in Representation and Performance: A Center for Lesbian and Gay Studies Book" by David Roman, in Queer *Representations: Reading Lives, Reading Cultures*, edited by Martin Duberman, 1997, New York, New York University Press, 1997; *Terrence McNally: A Casebook*, edited by Toby Silverman Zinman, New York, Garland, 1997.

* * *

It is a long way from Terrence McNally's one-act plays to the rather woozy *And Things That Go Bump in the Night*, to the manic antics of *The Ritz*, to the hilarious bitchiness of *The Lisbon Traviata*, to the wistful sadness of *Lips Together, Teeth Apart*, to the upbeat quirkiness of the characters in *Frankie and Johnny in the Claire de Lune*, and back to the sharp and incredibly funny goings-on in *It's Only a Play*.

There are a number of unifying elements that are evident in all of McNally's plays: a love of music and theater; a clever, often biting, wit; a sense of where Middle America thinks it is; and an aura of the confessional, with the characters as penitents and the audience as priest. In lazy writers this last characteristic simply takes the form of narrative monologue, but in McNally's work it can be genuinely revealing and often hilarious.

One-act plays seem slightly out of fashion these days, although they are wonderful entrances to production for new writers, but beginning in the 1960s McNally was pumping out biting and successful playlets. One favorite is *Whiskey*, which at times is as funny as any one-act play since *Box and Cox*. It begins with the disastrous appearance of a drunken television cast at the Houston Astrodome and eventually exposes an endearing bunch of fakers. What is clear in this play, as in so many of McNally's pieces, is his infatuation with and amusement by theater and show people.

Other one-act plays that should continue to find productions include *Tour*, which is a funny and very accurate portrait of an American couple abroad. They are an easy target, however, and McNally later finds more amusing Americans to tease. For those of us who saw James Coco as the reluctant and shy draftee in *Next*, this short play will always be a highlight of off-Broadway theater. In *Botticelli*, which is different in almost every way, we see two soldiers in Vietnam playing the word game Botticelli as they "kill a gook." What is truly frightening, and what provokes anger, in this one-act play is the fact that these Americans are intelligent, clever, and educated, and yet they have become murderers.

McNally wrote *Hope*, the middle play in *Faith, Hope, and Charity*. It is set in Central Park, and, as with a good many of McNally's plays, a number of brand products are named, a device that serves to locate the time and the characters but can be overdone. In *Hope* several characters wait on Easter Sunday for the sun to rise, which it almost fails to do. The sadness in the play is reflected in an exchange in which a nun says, "Sometimes I think that Christ died in vain. Isn't that terrible?" and another character replies, "Sometimes I think everyone dies in vain. Isn't that worse?" Heavy stuff indeed and a portent of heavier stuff to come with the age of AIDS.

With *Sweet Eros*, in which a young lady is tied to a chair and tormented, McNally achieved a good deal of notoriety, but the play flounders in a monologue that seems to be the purpose of the work itself. Likewise, *Witness* is basically one very long, funny speech by a window cleaner, again given a memorable performance by James Coco.

Given the nature of one-act plays, however, McNally's considerable reputation as one of America's leading playwrights rests on his full-length works. *And Things That Go Bump in the Night* received a lot of attention, in part because of its homosexual hero and its experimental format but also because at heart the play is honest and fascinating. It takes itself very seriously indeed. A later work, *Where Has Tommy Flowers Gone?,* brings to the foreground some of McNally's favorite leitmotivs: the theater, the outsider, and the long monologue with the hero addressing the audience as a character in the play. Theater and cinema references abound in Tommy's monologues, and the dramatic conventions that are routed in Tommy's various drag outfits are explored skillfully and with good humor. Again, products and product names are almost the "scenery" of the play, but beneath it all is a boy so alienated from the world that he is making a bomb to blow the whole thing up. Beneath the humor of *Where Has Tommy Flowers Gone?* there is a deep and disturbing anger that lifts the play from mere frippery to something more profound.

McNally has written at least four major theater pieces, all of which have had major success with audiences, just as did the earlier *The Ritz,* a commercial play that takes place in a gay bathhouse. *Lips Together, Teeth Apart* brings together two men and two women at a house on Fire Island. The brother of one of the women has died of AIDS, and she is deciding what to do with the place. McNally juggles his onstage and offstage characters with enormous skill, combining the running gags and an abiding sense of tragedy, death, fear, and loneliness. Chloe says, quite wisely, as she babbles incessantly, "I talk too much probably because it's too horrible to think about what's really going on." There is a sharp contrast between this sense of horror and death and the gays next door who are noisily celebrating the Fourth of July, suggesting that if we cannot laugh and at least pretend we all wallow in sadness and self-pity. There is much in McNally's *Lips Together, Teeth Apart* that echoes the best of Chekhov. This is a play that is much more than merely topical and clever, giving us four distinct and touching characters. It is a play that confronts a deep ache in most of us.

Frankie and Johnny in the Claire de Lune, on the other hand, is a realistic bringing together of two unheroic figures—a brassy, frightened waitress and her suitor, Johnny, who is hardly the hunk of the week. Together in Frankie's one-room walk-up apartment, they find and lose each other and finally find themselves. Another of McNally's devices is used here very successfully: the integration of appropriate music that which comes from "real" sources and is not merely background or mood-inducing pabulum. Frankie and Johnny talk and love and talk some more, but not for a moment are we, the audience, bored or alienated, for we find our own real or hoped-for love in these characters. The film version seemed less intimate but was equally moving, and it is likely that the play will continue to have a life of its own in theaters throughout the world. It deserves a returning audience.

The Lisbon Traviata is both an achingly funny play and a sad commentary on a love affair that is not just breaking up but is already broken to pieces. The "opera queens" who dote on, and live for, divas are hoist by their own petards. Mendy, the queen who has to have, absolutely must have, a copy of Maria Callas singing the "Lost One" in Lisbon, is one of the funniest and most pathetic characters of modern drama. A lonely man, he wants so much to be loved, but his caustic wit and his obsessions would frighten off a saint. Stephen knows that his relationship with Mike is over, that Paul has come between them, but he cannot quite accept his loss. McNally has created a poignant and very funny play. It may even now shock some audiences, but it will survive and thrive in theaters wherever humor, self-exploration, and honesty are permitted.

The funniest of the later plays is *It's Only a Play.* Not since Michael Frayn's *Noises Off* has there been a farce about theater and theater people to equal the sheer joy and madness of this work. *It's Only a Play* is an almost perfect reflection of what it is to produce a play on Broadway. (Is it McNally's own *The Ritz* that he is remembering?) The maniacal characters "celebrating" the opening night at the producer's smart apartment are so brilliantly drawn that one need never have seen a theater person to know that that these are the real thing, properly exaggerated for farce. In the fabled tradition of *The Torchbearers* (those inept amateurs) and *Light up the Sky* (those greedy professionals), McNally has skewered his beloved show business, and I honestly cannot remember a play at which the audience screamed with laughter in just this way. It is all outrageous, improbable, and absolutely on the mark.

It is safe to assume that Terrence McNally is not only a leading American playwright but also a caring, skillful, and successful man who has explored his theatrical territory with these diverse and wonderful plays. He is well beyond being promising, for he has delivered.

—Arthur H. Ballet

McPHERSON, Conor

Nationality: Irish. **Born:** Dublin, 1971. **Education:** University College Dublin. **Career:** Co-founder, Fly by night Theatre Company. Writer-in-residence, Bush Theatre, London, 1996—. **Awards:** Stewart Parker Trust award, 1995, for *The Good Thief*; Thames TV award and Guinness/National Theatre Ingenuity award, both 1996, both for *This Lime Tree Bower.* **Agent:** Curtis Brown, Ltd., 162-168 Regent Street, London W1R 5TB, England.

Publications

Plays

The Good Thief (produced Dublin).
Rum and Vodka (produced Dublin).
This Lime Tree Bower: Three Plays (includes *Rum and Vodka*; *The Good Thief*; *This Lime Tree Bower*). Dublin, New Island Books, 1996.
St. Nicholas & The Weir. Dublin and London, New Island Books, 1997.
I Went Down (screenplay). London, Nick Hern, 1997.
The Weir. London, Nick Hern, 1998.

Screenplay: *I Went Down.*

* * *

English drama, Kenneth Tynan once famously suggested, has been largely a procession of glittering Irishmen, and it is true that it has always depended heavily on the Irish for injections of verbal energy, black humor, and strong storytelling. Although Conor McPherson is the heir to an honorable tradition, what makes his work exciting is its capacity for growth. In the course of no more than five plays he has progressed from creating spellbinding monologues to drama of genuine interaction. With *The Weir,* a Royal Court Theatre hit destined for international success, he has written one of the most mature and moving plays to have emerged from any source in the 1990s.

McPherson's precocious talent was first revealed in two male monodramas, *The Good Thief* and *Rum and Vodka,* written for Dublin's Fly By Night Theatre Company. But it was *This Lime Tree Bower,* in its move from Dublin to London's Rush Theatre, that brought him a wider audience. Heavily influenced by Brian Friel's *Faith Healer,* the play consists of three interwoven, overlapping monologues, all dealing with events in a grotty seaside town within hailing distance of Dublin. The story hinges on the fraternal robbery of an extortionate bookmaker. But what grips audiences are McPherson's narrative gift, strong sense of place, and understanding of betrayal. One character, an impressionable schoolboy, is cruelly deceived by his best friend. His elder brother, in initiating the robbery, betrays his belief in the work ethic. And the third character, a preening philosophy lecturer with comic echoes of Kingsley Amis's Jim Dixon and David Lodge's Morris Zapp, betrays his own academic talent.

McPherson's next work, *St Nicholas,* reverted to the male monologue. It tells the strange story of a middle-aged Dublin drama critic who becomes erotically obsessed by a local actress, pursues her to London, and there falls in with a Mephistophelian vampire. The first half is a rivetingly funny account of Dublin theatrical politics and of the self-loathing of a seedy hack who decides to turn him himself into a "character" through his abrasive reviews and drunken behavior. But the play loses its grip in the second half when the hero acts as a pimp for the vampire, nightly luring the glittering young back to his master's pad. This is clearly intended as a metaphor for the critic's kinship with parasitic bloodsuckers and as a symbol of his attempt to revivify himself through the elixir of youth, but the move from stark reality to inner fantasy feels awkwardly contrived.

Challenged by the Royal Court's Ian Rickson to come up with a play using dialogue, McPherson responded magnificently with *The Weir,* even though the work is still built around a series of male monologues. A group of men meet in a small rural bar on a windy, wintry night and seek both to impress and scare a female newcomer to the area, Valerie, by telling her local ghost stores. Valerie, however, responds with a true and tragic tale of personal bereavement that not only leaves the men poleaxed but also changes the balance of power within the bar.

Technically, the play represents a considerable advance, for McPherson interweaves monologue, dialogue, and ruminative silence with prodigious skill. But his real achievement lies in his ability to build up a rich picture of Irish rural life: its superstitions, solitude, clannishness, resentment of outsiders—in particular the German tourists who arrive like swallows each summer—and equivocal attitudes of men toward women. Valerie acts as the catalyst who exposes the sadness of a series of disappointed lives, none more so than that of Jack, the local garage owner who once threw away the chance of married happiness and opted to become a "contrary bollocks." In the final monologue he describes his daily life: "Down in the garage. Spinning small jobs out all day. Taking hours to fix a puncture. Stops you thinking about what might have been and what you should have done." In his evocation of lost happiness and wasted potential, McPherson reveals a mature compassion and ability to universalize from the particular that links him across the century with Chekhov.

—Michael Billington

MDA, Zakes

Nationality: South African. **Born:** Zanemvula Kizito Gatyeni, near Sterkspruit in the Herschel District of the Eastern Cape Province, 1948. **Education:** St. Theresa Mission High school; Peka High school, Lesotho; educated in Switzerland and the United States; University of Capetown, Ph.D. in 1990. **Career:** Poet, playwright, and painter. Founding member, Martholi traveling theater, 1982; director, Theater for Development project, National University of Lethos, 1985. Fellow, South African Research Program, Yale University, New Haven, Connecticut, 1992—. Consultant, UNICEF, 1988—. **Awards:** South African Amstel Playwright's Merit award, 1978, for *We Shall Sing for Fatherland*; Christine Crawfor award of the American theatre Association, 1984, for *The Road.*

Publications

Plays

We Shall Sing for the Fatherland (produced 1978).
Dead End (produced Johhanesburg, 1979).
Dark Voices Ring. N.p., n.d.
We Shall Sing for the Fatherland and Other Plays. Johhanesburg, Ravan Press, 1980.
The Road (produced 1984).
The Hill. N.p., n.d.
The Plays of Zakes Mda (includes *Dead End*; *We Shall Sing for the Fatherland*; *Dark Voices Ring*; *The Hill*; *The Road*). Johhanesburg, Ravan Press, 1990.
And the Girls in Their Sunday Dresses: Four Works. Johhanesburg, Witwatersrand University Press, 1993.

Novel

She Plays with the Darkness. Florida Hills, South Africa, Vivlia Publishers, 1995.
Ways of Dying. Cape Town, Oxford University Press, 1995.

Poetry

Bits of Debris: The Poetry of Zakes Mda. Lesotho, Thapama Books, 1986.

Other

When People Play People: Development Communication through Theatre. London, Zed Books, 1993.

*

Critical Studies: "Dramatic Discourse in the Foreground of *The Hill*" by Michael Cosser, in *South African Theatre Journal* (Uniedal), September 1991, pp. 66-79; "When People Play People in (Post) Apartheid South Africa: The Theories and Practices of Zakes Mda" by Denis Salter, in *Brecht Yearbook* (Canada), 1997, pp. 283-303; "Catastrophe and Beauty: *Ways of Dying*, Zakes Mdas's Novel of the Transition" by Johan van Wyk, in *Literator, 2520, South Africa,* November 1997, pp. 79-90.

* * *

Zakes Mda is one of southern Africa's most gifted playwrights. His birth in South Africa and upbringing in Lesotho gave him first-hand experience of racial segregation. Like Athol Fugard, he is concerned with the destructive effects of apartheid on both individuals and society. His plays explore and articulate victims' feelings, and as political theater they empower the victim and echo Mda's own anguish at events in his society.

Mda's plays investigate racial segregation in southern Africa along with broad issues like social disintegration, labor migration, forced relocation, poverty, land, race relations, violence, and class tensions. These reverberate alongside specific themes like self-delusion and moral turpitude in *The Hill* and betrayal in *The Road, Dead End, We Shall Sing for the Fatherland,* and *Dark Voices Ring. Fatherland* also investigates neocolonialism in independent African countries, while *Smouldering* furthers the debate on police harassment, class tensions, and the choice between passive resistance and armed struggle in black communities. *At Dawn We Sang* revisits the absurdist elements of *The Road* and *Fatherland* and questions the sacrifice of the artist's integrity to materialistic capitalism. Each Mda play explores a different theme, but they embrace others, such as the writer's disillusionment with religion, as correlatives of a wider problem.

Mda uses few characters, ranging from two in *The Road* to seven in *The Hill.* The characters are marginalized people, those rejected by society and alienated by social inequities. Some, like Nontobeko in *Dark Voices Ring,* Lucy in *The Road,* and Voice in *Dead End,* are physically absent, yet they influence events onstage. Through the combination of stereotypes and individual attributes, Mda creates both memorable types and individualized characters. In Man, Woman, Farmer, and Labourer, for example, he explores character types and yet fashions them with convincing humanity and integrity. On the other hand, social outcasts like Charley in *Dead End* and Young Man in *The Hill* reveal a surprising touch of altruism and humanity and debunk notions of stereotypes.

Mda's characters are marginalized by the very economic and political structures their labors sustain and with which they must negotiate their survival, and this oppositional relationship creates a dramatic tension that is evident in the settings of his plays. The settings are small, enclosed spaces, such as the prison in *Dead End* or even worse places, where decay and privation among blacks are graphically presented against the opulence of white South Africa. The staging areas are thus extremely limited, even in such open settings as the veld in *The Hill* and *The Road* and the national park in *We Shall Sing for the Fatherland.* The starkness of the settings and the use of only a few properties symbolize the characters' material poverty. Mda's dialogue is also generally economical, with characters speaking only out of exigency, and it is with difficulty that audiences are drawn into their private and painful worlds. In *The Road,* for example, Koekemoer and Labourer engage in parallel dialectics with no real understanding of each other, yet their one moment of convergence and understanding over Lucy ends in tragedy.

Mda's theatrical style has resonances of Bertolt Brecht's epic theater and of absurdism, with his techniques being developed through the integration of traditional African theatrical and modern European dramatic forms. Characters and actions are presented and interpreted with typical Brechtian detachment and criticism. Mda's integration of flashbacks and his use of the play within the play link the past, present, and future and provide a wider socio-cultural context to the characters and their environment. The plays are structured and presented against the background of a resounding indictment of apartheid, and it is this desire to indict that is the problem with Mda's theater.

Mda's solution to apartheid is black armed struggle, but his new society offers little hope, for the heroes of the struggle are soon betrayed by erstwhile comrades. His viewpoint disregards dialogue for violence and is overtaken by the complexity of the issues he seeks to deconstruct. Mda creates neither credible nor redeemable white characters, for the decadent Frikkie of *Dead End* and the perverted Koekemoer of *The Road* are just as unlikely representatives of any race as are the black Charley and Labourer. His cause-and-effect plots and their resolutions in inevitable violence are predictable. He insufficiently explores characters such as Voice, Old Man, and Lucy and thus fails to effectively question their actions and motives.

Despite these flaws, the symbolic use of character and setting and the dynamism of his plays demonstrate Mda's unique theatrical style. His control of style and context and his subtle treatment of themes are unique and rare in a theater that is profoundly political and thus susceptible to moralizing and polemics. In the introduction to *The Plays of Zakes Mda* (1990) Andrew Horn insists that "what merits attention in Mda's plays is not only the nature of his critique, but the theatrical skill with which that critique is presented." Mda's work stands out for its use of a variety of theatrical devices, for its imagination, and for its urgency of thought.

—Victor I. Ukaegbu

MEDNICK, Murray

Nationality: American. **Born:** Brooklyn, New York, 24 August 1939. **Education:** Fallsburg Central School, New York; Brooklyn College, 1957-60. **Career:** Artistic co-director, Theatre Genesis, New York, 1970-74. Co-founder and artistic director, 1978—, Padua Hills Playwrights Workshop and Festival, Los Angeles, California. Playwright-in-residence, Florida State University, Tallahassee, 1972, State University of New York, Buffalo, 1973, California State University, Long Beach, 1973, La Verne College, California, 1978-82, and Pomona College, Claremont, California, 1983, 1984. **Awards:** National Endowment for the Arts grant, for poetry, 1967; Rockefeller grant, 1968, 1972; Obie award, 1970; Guggenheim grant, 1973; Creative Artists Public Service grant, 1973; Los Angeles Theatre League Ovation Lifetime Achievement award, 1992. **Address:** 10923 Ayres Avenue, Los Angeles, California 90064, U.S.A.

Publications

Plays

Sand (produced New York, 1967; London, 1970). Published in *The New Underground Theatre*, New York, Bantam, 1968.

The Hawk: An Improvisational Play, with Tony Barsha (produced New York, 1967). Indianapolis, Bobbs Merrill, 1968.

Willie the Germ (produced New York, 1968). Published in *More Plays from Off-Off-Broadway*, edited by Michael T. Smith, Indianapolis, Bobbs Merrill, 1972.

The Hunter (produced New York, 1968). Indianapolis, Bobbs Merrill, 1969.

The Shadow Ripens (also director: produced San Diego and New York, 1969).

The Deer Kill (produced New York, 1970). Indianapolis, Bobbs Merrill, 1971.

Cartoon (produced New York, 1971).

Are You Lookin'? (also director: produced New York, 1973).

Black Hole in Space (produced New York, 1975).

Taxes (also director: produced New York, 1976). Published in *Wordplays 3*, New York, Performing Arts Journal Publications, 1984.

The Coyote Cycle (7 plays) (also director: produced Los Angeles, 1978-80; produced Santa Fe, 1984). Published in *West Coast Plays* (Berkeley, California), 1981, Padua Hills Press, 1991; *Coyote V: Listening to Old Nana*, in *Plays from Padua Hills*, edited by Mednick, Claremont, California, Pomona College, 1983.

The Actors' Delicatessen, with Priscilla Cohen (produced New York, 1984).

Scar (also director: produced San Francisco, 1985).

The Pitch (produced San Francisco, 1985). Published in *Articles*, 1986.

Heads (produced Los Angeles, 1987).

Shatter 'n Wade (produced Los Angeles, 1990). Published in *Best of the West*, edited by Mednick, Los Angeles, Padua Hills Press, 1991.

Fedunn (produced Omaha, 1991; revised version produced Padua, 1991; Atlanta, 1997).

Switchback (produced Los Angeles, 1994). Los Angeles, Sun and Moon Press, 1997.

Skinwalkers (produced New York, 1995).

Baby Jesus! (produced Los Angeles, 1995).

Freeze (produced Los Angeles, 1995).

Joe and Betty (produced Atlanta, 1996)

Dictator (produced Los Angeles, 1997).

Sixteen Routines (produced New York, 1997).

Kesler's Defiance (produced Los Angeles, 1998).

Television Plays: *Iowa*, 1977; *Blessings*, 1978.

Other

Plays from Padua Hills. Claremont, California, Pomona College, 1983.

Editor, *Best of the West*. Los Angeles, California, Padua Hills Press, 1991.

*

Theatrical Activities:

Director: **Plays**—Several of his own plays, and *Blue Bitch* by Sam Shepard, New York, 1973.

Actor: **Plays**–*The Coyote Cycle*, 1983-89; *The Actors' Delicatessen*, San Francisco, 1984; *Theory of Miracles* by John Steppling, 1990.

* * *

Murray Mednick is one of the important American dramatists who came of age in the 1960s. Beginning in 1965 he produced some dozen plays, developing increasing technical strength, clarity, and complexity and extending his vision with passionate conviction. His plays and the worlds they evoke are often dominated by ugly, crushing economic and personal pressures that lie behind the American pretense of equality and social justice. The humor is often bitter. Another recurring feature has been the attempt to place contemporary experience in the context of Native American myth.

Mednick did most of his early work at Theatre Genesis, a church-sponsored theater on the Lower East Side in New York City. A poet before he turned to drama, he wrote several one-act plays in the mid-1960s, then moved on to larger forms. *Sand* presents an aging, used-up American couple who are visited by a formal ambassador; their horrible regressive stupor is unbroken by the news that their son has been killed in the Vietnam War. The dead soldier's body is brought in at the end on a meat hook. *Willie the Germ* is about a down-and-out man working as a dishwasher for a grotesque family of Coney Island freaks who endlessly seduce him into incomprehensible machinations that always get him into trouble. He yearns to escape but is kept in his place by put-downs and an invisible electric force field operated by an anonymous Button-Pusher in the audience. At the end he is destroyed and castrated by the monstrous representatives of "society."

Mednick has also created plays with groups of actors, using improvisation to draw material from their lives and imaginations into a form devised by the dramatist. *The Hawk* is a play about a drug pusher and his victims. The victims' self-revealing monologues were developed by the actors and framed in a formal, ritualistic structure. The play employed a novel and experimental set of technical acting devices and was remarkably successful in shaping very loose, idiosyncratic material into an elegantly disciplined and cohesive form. *The Shadow Ripens* was based on an Eskimo legend and embodied the idea of descending to dangerous nonrational depths of being in quest of wisdom and authenticity.

Mednick continued to produce plays that emphasized language and carefully crafted writing. *Are You Lookin'?* is a fragmented, highly subjective study of the effect of heroin use on personal emotional life. *The Hunter* depicts a hip, tight friendship between two men. They are united by a common enemy, a middle-aged hunter obsessed with the Civil War (they later nail him to a tree); and they are driven to mutual mistrust by a woman. The play's pared-down, ambiguous style shows Mednick moving toward the visionary.

The young hero of *The Deer Kill* has moved to an old farm seeking a simple, virtuous life. His good nature and well-being are sorely tried—by crazed friends from the city (one of whom kills himself), by his unfaithful wife, and by the local authorities, because his dog has killed a deer. The play is more realistic than

Mednick's earlier work, a clear, rich, and affecting study of the struggle to live morally in contemporary America.

In the mid-1970s Mednick, who was born in Brooklyn, moved from New York to Los Angeles, where he continued to broaden and deepen his achievement. The cartoonlike *Taxes*, his take on the vaunted California lifestyle, ironically recapitulates the devices of the freshly historic New York avant-garde. The playwright's biting clarity of vision communicates a new compassion for his characters.

In 1978 Maria Irene Fornés, John Steppling, Sam Shepard, and Mednick founded the Padua Hills Playwrights Workshop and Festival in Los Angeles, where he served as artistic director. Padua Hills took the form of theater without a theater—natural settings were the only stage available. This led to Mednick's extraordinary *The Coyote Cycle*, seven plays developed between 1978 and 1984. Drawing on Native American imagery, including the Coyote/Trickster tradition and the Hopi creation myths, as well as contemporary culture and experimental theater, *The Coyote Cycle* is an environmental warning and prayer for planetary salvation. All-night performances of the cycle took audiences into rugged landscapes for a unique theatrical and conceptual experience.

By the early 1990s Mednick had also written *Scar*, *Shatter 'n Wade*, and *Heads*. In *Scar*, set in the mountains of New Mexico, a successful rock musician encounters a "loser" from his past who forces him to confront deep responsibilities to earth and being. The teeming, finely honed talk in *Shatter 'n Wade* implies sharp contemporary anxieties and aggressions, its mounting menace and fear mirroring society at the raw interface with individual consciousness. The direct, apocalyptic *Heads* is clean, mean, and powerful, unflinchingly mythic, and beautifully spare in its language.

Mednick uses theater as a free poetic medium, and the dark intensity of his vision, as well as the intelligence of his forms, fuses many levels of meaning. His later works won fervent admiration, and he continued to enlarge the meaning, artistry, and emotional effect of his plays.

—Michael T. Smith

MEDOFF, Mark (Howard)

Nationality: American. **Born:** Mount Carmel, Illinois, 18 March 1940. **Education:** University of Miami, 1958-62, B.A. 1962; Stanford University, California, 1964-66, M.A. 1966. **Family:** Married Stephanie Thorne in 1972 (second marriage); three daughters. **Career:** Supervisor of publications, Capitol Radio Engineering Institute, Washington, D.C., 1962-64. Instructor, 1966-71, assistant professor, 1971-74, associate professor, 1974-79, professor of drama (currently head of the department of theatre arts), 1979—, dramatist-in-residence, 1975—, and artistic director, 1982-87, American Southwest Theatre Company, all at New Mexico State University, Las Cruces. Chair of the Awards Committee, American College Theatre Festival, 1985-86. **Awards:** Drama Desk award, 1974, 1980; New Mexico State University Westhafer award, 1974; John Gassner award, 1974; Joseph Jefferson award, for acting, 1974; Guggenheim fellowship, 1974-75; Tony award, 1980; Outer Circle award, 1980; Los Angeles Drama-Logue Critics' award for Playwrighting, 1980; New Mexico Governor's award, 1980; Society of West End Theatre award, 1982; Obie award, 1984; ACE Award Nomination, for *Apology*, 1986; Academy Award nomination, for Best Adapted Screenplay, for *Children of a Lesser God*, 1987; Distinguished Alumnus, University of Miami, 1987. D.H.L.: Gallaudet College, Washington, D.C., 1981. **Agent:** Gilbert Parker, William Morris Agency, 1325 Avenue of the Americas, New York, New York 10019, U.S.A. **Address:** Department of Theatre Arts, New Mexico State University, Las Cruces, New Mexico 88003, U.S.A.

PUBLICATIONS

Plays

The Wager (produced Las Cruces, New Mexico, 1967; New York, 1974). New York, Dramatists Play Service, 1975.

Doing a Good One for the Red Man (produced Las Cruces, New Mexico, 1969). Included in *Four Short Plays*, 1974.

The Froegle Dictum (produced Albuquerque, New Mexico, 1971). Included in *Four Short Plays*, 1974.

The War on Tatem (produced Las Cruces, New Mexico, 1972). Included in *Four Short Plays*, 1974.

The Kramer (produced San Francisco, 1972). New York, Dramatists Play Service, 1976.

When You Comin Back, Red Ryder? (produced New York, 1973). New York, Dramatists Play Service, 1974; included in *The Hero Trilogy*, 1989.

The Odyssey of Jeremy Jack (for children), with Carleene Johnson (produced Las Cruces, New Mexico, 1975). New York, Dramatists Play Service, 1974.

Four Short Plays (includes *The Froegle Dictum, Doing a Good One for the Red Man, The War on Tatem, The Ultimate Grammar of Life*). New York, Dramatists Play Service, 1974.

The Wager: A Play, and Doing a Good One for the Red Man, and The War on Tatem: Two Short Plays. Clifton, New Jersey, James T. White, 1975.

The Halloween Bandit (produced Huntington, New York, 1976; New York City, 1978).

The Conversion of Aaron Weiss (produced Minneapolis, 1977).

Firekeeper (produced Dallas, 1978).

The Last Chance Saloon (also director: produced Las Cruces, New Mexico, 1979).

Children of a Lesser God (produced Los Angeles, 1979; New York, 1980; London, 1981). New York, Dramatists Play Service, 1980; Ambergate, Derbyshire, Amber Lane Press, 1982.

The Hands of Its Enemy (produced Los Angeles, 1984; New York, 1986). New York, Dramatists Play Service, 1987.

The Majestic Kid, music by Jan Scarborough, lyrics by Medoff and Scarborough (produced San Francisco, 1985; New York, 1988). Included in *The Hero Trilogy*, 1989.

Kringle's Window (produced Las Cruces, New Mexico, 1985).

The Heart Outright (produced Santa Fe, 1986; New York, 1989). In *The Hero Trilogy*, 1989; New York, Dramatists Play Service, 1990.

The Hero Trilogy (includes *When You Comin' Back, Red Ryder?, The Majestic Kid, The Heart Outright*). Salt Lake City, Peregrine Smith, 1989.

Big Mary. New York, Dramatists Play Service, 1989.

Stefanie Hero. New York, Dramatists Play Service, 1994.

Kringle's Window. New York, Dramatists Play Service, 1994.

Stumps. New York, Dramatists Play Service, 1995.

The Homage That Follows. New York, Dramatists Play Service, 1995.
Showdown on Rio Road, with Ross Marks. New York, Dramatists Play Service, 1998.
Crunch Time, with Phil Treon. New York, Dramatists Play Service, 1998.

Screenplays: *Good Guys Wear Black,* with Bruce Cohn and Joseph Fraley, 1978; *When You Comin' Back, Red Ryder?*, 1979; *Off Beat,* 1986; *Apology,* 1986; *Children of a Lesser God,* with Hesper Anderson, 1987; *Clara's Heart,* 1988; *City of Joy,* 1992; *Homage,* 1995; *Santa Fe,* 1997.

Radio Plays: *The Last Chance Saloon,* 1980; *The Disintegration of Aaron Weiss,* 1979.

*

Critical Studies: "Mark Medoff" by Gail Willmott, in *Kaleidoscope: International Magazine of Literature, Fine Arts, and Disability,* Summer 1985, pp. 28-33; "The Western Holdup Play: The Pilgrimage Continues" by Rudolf Erben, in *Western American Literature* (Logan, Utah) February 1989, pp. 311-22; "Reading the Myth of the West" by Helen Lojek, in *South Dakota Review* (Vermillion, South Dakota) Spring 1990, pp. 46-61; "An Interview with Mark Medoff" by Mimi Gladstein, in *Studies in American Drama, 1945-Present* (Columbus, Ohio) 1993, pp. 61-83; "Mark Medoff" by Gladstein, in *Speaking on Stage: Interviews with Contemporary Playwrights,* edited by Philip C. Kolin and Colby H. Kullman, Tuscaloosa, University of Alabama Press, 1996.

Theatrical Activities:
Director: **Plays**—Some of his own plays; *Waiting for Godot* by Samuel Beckett; *The Effect of Gamma Rays on Man-in-the-Moon Marigolds* by Paul Zindel; *Jacques Brel Is Alive and Well and Living in Paris*; *The Birthday Party* by Harold Pinter; *One Flew over the Cuckoo's Nest* by Dale Wasserman; *Equus* by Peter Shaffer; *The Hotel Baltimore* by Lanford Wilson; *Head Act* by Mark Frost; *The Hold Out* by Tony Stafford; *Xmor* by Jan Scarborough and Barbara Kerr; *Vanities* by Jack Heifner; *A Flea in Her Ear* by John Mortimer; *Deadline for Murder.*

Actor: **Plays**—Andrei Bolkonski in *War and Peace*; Marat in *Marat/Sade* by Peter Weiss; Pozzo in *Waiting for Godot* by Samuel Beckett; Teddy in *When You Comin Back, Red Ryder?*; Harold Gorringe in *Black Comedy* by Peter Shaffer; Bro Paradock in *A Resounding Tinkle* by N.F. Simpson; Lenny Bruce in *The Soul of Lenny Bruce*; Dysart in *Equus* by Peter Shaffer; Deeley in *Old Times* by Harold Pinter; Scrooge in *A Christmas Carol*; Bellman in *The Hands of Its Enemy,* Los Angeles, 1984.

Mark Medoff comments:
My work is simply a reflection of my own spirit, my fears, sorrows, and fires.

* * *

Mark Medoff's characters are nostalgic, hoping for redemption in the face of a disappearing way of life. This life exists in various forms. In some of Medoff's plays we mourn the lost idealism of the 1960s and in some the disappearing myth of the West. In all of them characters are defending themselves against a changing world, whether through violence, verbal wit, or the hope of love.

The Kramer is a dream play depicting a power-hungry young man's seemingly gratuitous attempt to take over a secretarial school and simultaneously transform the lives of everyone in it. In a touch of rather heavy-handed symbolism, Kramer's profile is marred by a cancerous mole. Neither the men nor the women in his way—the obligatory conservative supervisor, the unambitious secretary Artie Malin—are a match for Kramer's cynicism, his verbal game playing, or his eventual transition from verbal to physical violence. Kramer's persuasiveness is based on his apparent ability to know verbatim the past lives of his antagonists. He easily persuades Judy Uichi to leave her Japanese amputee husband on the grounds that "the idealism of your youth having dissipated, he's a lodestone around your neck." Equally as easily, he persuades Artie Malin to leave his unattractive wife, Carol May. Ironically, it is Carol May, who seems to be Kramer's weakest opponent, who is actually his only true adversary. She is the only character who seems capable of genuine feeling, and it is her voice that we remember: "You understand you're trying to drown me. . . . Why are you doing this? . . . Is it me—or is it that you just want to destroy things? . . . Haven't you ever loved another person very, very much?"

Teddy in *When You Comin Back, Red Ryder?* is, like Kramer, a figure of violence who far exceeds everyone around him in both intelligence and physical strength. But Teddy is a more complex character. Though initially his disruption of the New Mexico diner appears as gratuitous as Kramer's takeover, it becomes evident that Teddy's real threat is not just his violence but also his ability to destroy the illusions around which lives are constructed. Teddy shares Kramer's uncanny insight into others' pasts, and his readings of people are both cruel and accurate. If Teddy is evil, he is also a catalyst for change, forcing decisions and realizations that have long been avoided. In addition, Medoff allows an insight that we do not get into Kramer, for we see what Teddy is mourning. Calling himself one of the "disaffected" youth, he asks of the old western heroes, "What in the hell happened to those people?" and announces at the end of the play, "This is the last dance then, gang. Time's gone and I'm gonna ride off into the sunrise." Teddy's tragedy is both his misused brilliance and his ability to accept life's divergence from myth.

The Wager is in many ways a transition between Medoff's earlier works and *Children of a Lesser God.* Leeds shares with Kramer and Teddy the qualities of violence, verbal wit, and cruel if brilliant insight. But the violence here is transformed to suggest emotional vulnerability. As in *The Kramer,* the protagonist's only real match is a woman. The verbal pyrotechnics between Leeds and Honor are clearly a defense against their attraction to one another. Leeds's ability to overcome this defensiveness, even if with great resistance, and Honor's recognition that words are often destructive to understanding suggest greater depth of character than that possessed by any of Medoff's earlier protagonists. In addition, for Medoff it is a change of key.

The singular quality of *Children of a Lesser God* is its lyricism, relying on the same fluid and dreamlike staging employed in *The Kramer.* The play begins and ends in James's memory. Like his predecessors, James is bright and somewhat disaffected, a former Peace Corps volunteer who tells us, "I saved Ecuador." Unlike his predecessors, however, he retains in the face of the cynicism of his somewhat stereotypical supervisor and the students at a school for the nonhearing both some measure of idealism and an openness to feeling, although his tendency to what Robert Brustein has called "pop psychoanalysis" can become annoying. Also unlike his predecessors, James shares the stage. He has a coprotagonist.

Sarah Norman, one of James's nonhearing students, who signs because she will not speak, provides the play with much of its lyrical eloquence. The relationship between James and Sarah, initially a power struggle between teacher and student, becomes a love affair and then reverts to a power struggle. The issues Medoff explored in earlier works are now complicated by the conflict between power and feeling. James acknowledges the inherent ambiguity of his motives—do they stem from a desire to help or a desire to control? For her part Sarah is "determined to preserve her wholeness inside a deaf world . . . deafness . . . is a condition of being 'other,' and this otherness has its sufficient rewards." She signs to James, "I live in a place you can't enter. It's out of reach. . . . Deafness isn't the opposite of hearing, as you think. It's a silence full of sound. . . ." Their final confrontation is a recognition of simultaneous love and difference, a difference that is, despite love, irresolvable. James acknowledges, "Yes, I'm a terrific teacher: Grow, Sarah, but not too much. Understand yourself, but not more than I understand you. Be brave, but not so brave you don't need me anymore." Sarah says, "I'm afraid I would just go on trying to change you. We would have to meet in another place; not in silence or in sound but somewhere else. I don't know where that is now."

It is paradoxical that the play's eloquence is inherent in its characters' inability to make themselves understood. The fact is that the two protagonists speak separate languages. Although this linguistic difference is muted by James's simultaneous translation of Sarah's signing, the play does at least give an indication of the imperative to understand those who are "inarticulate" in our language. Those who are nonvocal, Medoff suggests, do not necessarily have nothing to say. The struggle to be heard is a common theme, and in his review Brustein expresses his irritation, calling the play "a chic compendium of every extant cliché about women and minority groups. . . ." But the frequency with which a theme is explored is not necessarily related to its importance; if anything, the repetition of an idea may indicate the necessity of coming to terms with it. Gerald Weales has written of this play that "Since no marriage—however close, however loving—can make two people one . . . the special cases of James, as teacher, and Sarah, as unwilling pupil, can become metaphors for any marriage." James's final nostalgia for a love that is real and yet not realizable is at the heart of the play's poignance, something the later screenplay fails to retain by resorting to a happy ending.

Two later plays by Medoff are less successful in their reiteration of earlier themes. In the musical *The Majestic Kid* Aaron is like Leeds, concerned with issues of love and distance but with lost idealism. The characters, however, are unrealized. Aaron's love affair with Lisa is abrupt and therefore unimportant. It is difficult to know how to take the Laredo Kid, a movie character brought to life who knows all the old western plots by heart (movie as karma?) but cannot decipher the present script. And the ideological and political concerns of Aaron's longtime lover and coworker, A. J., jar with her flip one-liners. *The Hands of Its Enemy* also concerns a woman who cannot hear. But *Enemy* is more conceptional than *Children*, a play within a play that juxtaposes a psychological exploration of the characters of a playwright and her director with the rehearsal process for their play. The central theme again centers around issues of distance and the need to trust, but here the struggle is at times cloying and overdone.

At his weakest Medoff may occasionally go too far in one direction or the other, becoming either gratuitous or overly sentimental. But in his best plays he is able to combine a frighteningly realistic depiction of the cruelties we wittingly or unwittingly commit with a simultaneous acknowledgment of our tremendous vulnerability.

—Elizabeth Adams

MEE, Charles L., Jr.

Nationality: American. **Born:** Evanston, Illinois, 15 September 1938. **Education:** Harvard University, B.A. (cum laude) in 1960. **Family:** Married 1) Claire Lu Thomas in 1959 (divorced 1962); 2) Suzi Baker in 1962 (divorced), one son and one daughter; 3) Kathleen Tolan in 1983, two daughters. **Career:** Playwright and historian. Editor-in-chief, *Horizon Magazine,* 1971-75. Board of Directors, Theatre Communications Group. **Award:** National Book Critics Circle nomination for best literary work, for general nonfiction, 1987, for *The Genius of the People.* **Agent:** Lois Wallace, 177 East 70th Street, New York, New York 10021, U.S.A.

Publications

Plays

Players' Repertoire (produced Cambridge, Massachusetts, 1960).
Constantinople Smith (produced New York, 1961).
The Gate (produced New York, 1961).
Thee by Mee (produced New York, 1962).
Anyone, Anyone (produced New York, 1964).
Vienna: Lusthaus (produced New York, 1986).
The Imperialists at the Club Cave Canem (produced New York, 1988).
The Investigation of the Murder in El Salvador (produced New York, 1989). In *Wordplays 4,* New York, Performing Arts Journal Publications, 1984.
Another Person Is a Foreign Country (produced New York, 1991).
Orestes (produced Cambridge, Massachusetts, 1992).
The Bacchae (produced Los Angeles, 1993).
The War to End War (produced 1993).
Charles Mee: History Plays. Baltimore, Maryland, Johns Hopkins University Press, 1998.

Books for children

Lorenzo de Medici and the Renaissance, with others. American Heritage Press, 1968.
The Horizon Book of Daily Life in Renaissance Italy. American Heritage Press, 1975.
Happy Birthday, Baby Jesus, with Ken Munowitz. New York, Harper, 1976.
Moses, Moses, with Ken Munowitz. New York, Harper, 1977.
Noah, with Ken Munowitz. New York, Harper, 1978.

Other

White Robe, Black Robe. New York, Putnam, 1972.
Erasmus: The Eye of the Hurricane. Coward, 1973.
Meeting at Postdam. M.Evans, 1976.
A Visit to Haldeman and Other States of Mind. M. Evans, 1977.
Seizure. M. Evans, 1978.
The End of Order: Versailles, 1919. New York, Dutton, 1980.
The Ohio Gang: The World of Warren G. Harding. M. Evans, 1981.
The Marshall Plan: The Launching of the Pax Americana. New York, Simon and Schuster, 1984.
The Genius of the People. New York, Harper, 1987.
Rembrandt's Portrait: A Biography. New York, Simon and Schuster, 1988.
Playing God: Seven Fateful Moments When Great Men Met to Change the World. New York, Simon and Schuster, 1993.

*

Critical Study: "Charles L. Mee, Jr: The Theatre of History" by Alisa Solomon, in *Performing Arts Journal* (Baltimore, Maryland), 1988, pp. 67-76.

* * *

The text of Charles L. Mee's *Orestes* opens with the following stage direction: "Thrilling sounds of bombs, rockets, whistle flares, and other explosions and sonic marvels make the theater rock and shudder." In a way every Mee play, at one moment or another, fulfills this promise. His plays and his adaptations of classical literature require tremendous energy both from the production team and the audience.

A furious collage of sources that Mee credits Max Ernst's Fatagaga pieces with inspiring, his texts are acts of resistance that probe social class, politics, and ultimately American capitalism. They resist consumption in a society that craves consumption; they resist easy comprehension even as audiences' patience with nonlinear narrative and abstract verbal soundscapes seems at low ebb; and they insist on a political critique in a country where only a minority votes in most elections. They are postmodern, surreal, and subversive. Mee himself best describes the sensation caused by his work: "My plays are broken, jagged, filled with sharp edges, filled with things that take sudden turns, careen into each other, smash up, veer off in sickening turns."

The works of Mee are difficult to discuss as literature, especially since his plays have been staged by a succession of bravura directors who use the texts as a trampoline on which to bounce off vivacious, highly theatrical experiences. His most widely seen play may be *Vienna Lusthaus,* a short collage of texts staged by the director and choreographer Martha Clarke. In fact, so inseparable are the productions from the written texts that in *Vienna Lusthaus* the characters' names are often those of the actors who originated the roles. The dialogue—mainly a series of monologues—consists of a mélange of Freud, aristocratic musings taken from letters of the Austro-Hungarian imperial family, and other sources.

Mee's plays have been staged by some of America's foremost experimental artists—Anne Bogart (*Orestes, Another Person Is a Foreign Country*); Robert Woodruff (*Orestes, The Trojan Women a Love Story*); the adventurous Sledgehammer Theatre in San Diego (*The War to End War*); and Tina Landau (*Orestes, The Trojan Women a Love Story, Time to Burn, The Berlin Circle*).

Mee's adaptations of the Greek classics use their sources only as a touchstone. The major characters are present, but so are others of Mee's invention: the Tapemouth Man and the Forensics Expert in *Orestes,* for instance, or Bill and Ray Bob in *Trojan Women.* Each text includes snippets of dialogue lifted from a wide variety of writers and publications. *Orestes* mixes the French poet Apollinaire and the American writers Bret Easton Ellis and William Burroughs with bits from *Vogue* and *Soap Opera Digest.* This makes the madness of the central murder in *Orestes* literalized, most vividly brought to life when a chain-smoking Electra visits her brother in a hospital bed. Avowedly non-Aristotelian, the tragedy is not based on a heroic figure's downfall but on the barbarity of civilization and its detritus that incites such violence. *The Trojan Women* mixes an intoxicating update of Euripides in act 1, where the prisoners could be from any war-torn country, with a musical act 2 featuring a long encounter between Aeneas and Dido that begins when Dido enters the stage singing Linda Ronstadt's version of "When You Wish upon a Star." These adaptations thereby become cultural collisions between civilizations millennia apart. And in a typical Mee-like touch, the ending is left up to the director and performers. After Dido seemingly drowns Aeneas, the stage directions are "Aeneas drags himself from the hot tub. He is nearly dead—or else, he doesn't drag himself from the tub, and he is dead."

Time to Burn, inspired by Gorky's *Lower Depths,* is perhaps Mee's most focused and coherent text. Like Gorky's characters, a motley ensemble of people share a dank basement. In Mee's version, however, it is the basement of an abandoned factory, and the denizens are a hodgepodge of immigrants and outsiders, including a couple from Poland, an eastern European woman, a Brazilian transsexual, a disabled Mexican dwarf, an elderly African American matriarch, and Nikos, a former actor who recites whole sections of *Eumenides* in his native Greek. Symbols of capitalism's ironic triumph, these people argue and barbecue, sing and curse, while scratching out a living under the unforgiving thumb of Vinnie Pazzi, the landlord who lives upstairs. The Steppenwolf Theatre's production of the play was a stunning piece of work. The later play *The Berlin Circle,* a Chinese folktale set in 1989 in East Germany, again has the kind of high-impact cultural collisions that are embedded in all of Mee's bold theater.

—John Istel

MILLAR, (Sir) Ronald (Graeme)

Nationality: British. **Born:** Reading, Berkshire, 12 November 1919. **Education:** Charterhouse School, Surrey; King's College, Cambridge. **Military Service:** Served in the Royal Naval Volunteer Reserve, 1940-43: sub-lieutenant. **Career:** Deputy chair, Theatre Royal, Haymarket, London, 1977—. Knighted, 1980. **Agent:** Ian Bevan, 37 Hill Street, London W1X 8JY. **Address:** 7 Sheffield Terrace, London W.8, England.

Publications

Plays

Murder from Memory (produced London, 1942).
Zero Hour (produced London, 1944).

The Other Side, adaptation of the novel by Storm Jameson (produced London, 1946).
Frieda (produced London, 1946). London, English Theatre Guild, 1947.
Champagne for Delilah (produced London, 1949).
Waiting for Gillian, adaptation of the novel *A Way Through the Wood* by Nigel Balchin (produced London, 1954). London, French, 1955.
The Bride and the Bachelor (produced London, 1956). London, French, 1958.
A Ticklish Business (produced Brighton, 1958; as *The Big Tickle*, produced London, 1958). London, French, 1959.
The More the Merrier (produced London, 1960). London, French, 1960.
The Bride Comes Back (produced London, 1960). London, French, 1961.
The Affair, adaptation of the novel by C.P. Snow (produced London, 1961; Washington, D.C., 1964). New York, Scribner, 1962; London, French, 1963.
The New Men, adaptation of the novel by C.P. Snow (produced London, 1962). Included in *The Affair, The New Men, The Masters*, 1964.
The Masters, adaptation of the novel by C.P. Snow (produced London, 1963). Included in *The Affair, The New Men, The Masters*, 1964.
The Affair, The New Men, The Masters: Three Plays Based on the Novels and with a Preface by C.P. Snow. London, Macmillan, 1964.
Robert and Elizabeth, music by Ron Grainer, lyrics by Millar, adaptation of the play *The Barretts of Wimpole Street* by Rudolf Besier (produced London, 1964). London, French, 1967.
On the Level, music by Ron Grainer (produced London, 1966).
Number 10, adaptation of the novel by William Clark (produced Glasgow and London, 1967). London, Heinemann, 1967.
They Don't Grow on Trees (produced London, 1968). London, French, 1969.
Abelard and Heloise, based on *Peter Abelard* by Helen Waddell (produced Exeter and London, 1970; New York, 1971). London and New York, French, 1970.
Parents' Day, adaptation of the novel by Edward Candy (produced London, 1972).
Odd Girl Out, adaptation of the novel by Elizabeth Jane Howard (produced Harlow, Essex, 1973).
The Case in Question, adaptation of the novel *In Their Wisdom* by C.P. Snow (produced London, 1975). London, French, 1975.
Once More with Music (produced Guildford, Surrey, 1976).
A Coat of Varnish, adaptation of the novel by C.P. Snow (produced London, 1982). London, French, 1983.
A View from the Wings. Hodder & Stoughton, 1991.
A View from the Wings and West End, West Coast, Westminster. London, Weidenfeld & Nicholson, 1993.

Screenplays: *Frieda*, with Angus Macphail, 1947; *So Evil My Love*, with Leonard Spiegelgass, 1948; *The Miniver Story*, with George Froeschel, 1950; *Train of Events*, with others, 1950; *The Unknown Man*, with George Froeschel, 1951; *Scaramouche*, with George Froeschel, 1951; *Never Let Me Go*, with George Froeschel, 1953; *Rose Marie*, 1954; *Betrayed*, with George Froeschel, 1954.

*

Theatrical Activities:
Actor: **Plays**—In *Swinging the Gate* (revue), London, 1940; Prince Anatole Kuragin in *War and Peace* by David Lucas, London, 1943; Cully in *Mr. Bolfry* by James Bridie, London, 1943; David Marsden in *Murder for a Valentine* by Vernon Sylvaine, London, 1944; Flight Lieutenant Chris Keppel in *Zero Hour*, London, 1944; Penry Bowen in *Jenny Jones* by Ronald Gow, London, 1944; Roy Fernie in *We Are Seven* by Ian Hay, London, 1945; Colin Tabret in *The Sacred Flame* by W. Somerset Maugham, London, 1945; Smith in *Murder on the Nile* by Agatha Christie, London, 1946. **Films**—*The Life and Death of Colonel Blimp*, 1943; *Beware of Pity*, 1945.

* * *

Ronald Millar was born in Reading in 1919. When he was a small boy, his mother, an actress who wanted him to be protected from the glamorous uncertainties of stage life, sent him to a good preparatory school to receive a classical education. At the end of his time there he sat for scholarships at several of the great public schools. He was offered a scholarship at Harrow, but he refused it on the advice of his headmaster, who had his eye on Winchester. At the Winchester examination, however, he happened to be out of sorts and narrowly missed an award, but he did gain one at Charterhouse.

From his mother's point of view this was an unhappy accident, for at that time Charterhouse, of all the great public schools, had the closest connection with the theater and the largest number of old boys who were actors. And from there young Ronald went on to King's, which of all the colleges in Cambridge had the strongest theatrical tradition.

The outcome was fairly predictable. Millar joined various university acting clubs, showed talent, gained experience—he was, incidentally, given the leading part in the triennial Greek play that is traditionally a great dramatic event at Cambridge—and was inevitably attracted to the professional stage. Service in the Royal Navy delayed his final decision, but by the time he was invalided out he had made up his mind. He did not return to Cambridge to take his degree but turned actor at once.

The years spent with the classics, however, were not wasted. There are many worse forms of training for a writer, and Millar's ambition to be a dramatist was at least as strong as his desire to act and was to prove much more lasting. His second play, *Zero Hour,* was produced at the Lyric in June 1944, with himself in the cast, and his third, *Frieda,* about a girl escaped from Nazi Germany, at the Westminster in 1946. This had a fair success on the stage and a bigger one as a film.

In 1949 Millar suffered a deep disappointment. Returning to England after an interlude spent writing film scripts in Hollywood, he brought with him a light comedy, *Champagne for Delilah,* that was instantly accepted for West End production. To all of the experts who handled it, it seemed certain to have a huge success, and it was received with acclaim on its prior-to-London tour. But on arrival at the New Theatre it proved a dead failure, and nobody has ever been able to suggest why. Seven years later, however, Millar must have felt compensated by an ironic twist of fate when another play, *The Bride and the Bachelor,* ran for more than 500 performances after having been given a hostile reception by nearly all of the critics. Later still, in 1960, a sequel to this piece, *The Bride Comes Back,* also ran very well.

By this time Millar had enough successful work to his credit to prove that one of his outstanding qualities was his versatility. From the seriousness of *Frieda* to the frivolity of the two *Bride* plays was a big step and a vivid contrast in styles, and he now proceeded to demonstrate further uses to which his versatility might be put.

The year 1961 saw the beginning of a whole series of plays adapted by Millar from novels or other literary sources, the first of them being a stage version of C. P. Snow's story of college life at Cambridge, *The Affair*. As a Cambridge man himself, Millar was familiar with the atmosphere so truthfully rendered by the book and, given a free hand, matched the atmosphere quite perfectly. Then came a setback. Manager after manager refused to believe that a play so local in its application could interest the general public. At last Henry Sherek, who had been Millar's backer for *Frieda* and *Champagne for Delilah,* accepted the risk, and he was rewarded with critical favor and a year's run.

A second play from a Snow novel, *The New Men,* followed in 1962 and had no success, but a second Cambridge piece, *The Masters,* was staged in 1963 and ran even longer than *The Affair* had. In 1975 yet another play, *The Case in Question,* based on Snow ran very well.

The particular talent that carried Millar to his notable successes in this field is an ability to turn a novelist's narrative prose into dialogue without losing his personal flavor. Added to this is the ability where necessary to write scenes of his own invention in a style to fit with the rest.

This was perhaps not an especially difficult task in the case of the two Cambridge plays, where novelist and adapter had in common a detailed knowledge of and feeling for the atmosphere they wished to convey, but it became a problem of much delicacy in the case of Millar's next, and much more serious play, *Abelard and Heloise*. The main materials for this play were Helen Waddell's book about Peter Abelard and the famous letters, and the task was to find an idiom that would convey both of these elements. This was done with such skill that the play drew not only the more serious playgoers but also the general public. Produced in May 1970, it ran into 1972.

One other proof of Millar's versatility should be noted. In 1964 he wrote both the book and lyrics for *Robert and Elizabeth,* the musical version of *The Barretts of Wimpole Street.* It ran for two and a half years.

—W. A. Darlington

MILLER, Arthur

Nationality: American. **Born:** New York City, 17 October 1915. **Education:** Abraham Lincoln High School, New York, graduated 1932; University of Michigan, Ann Arbor (Hopwood Award, 1936, 1937), 1934-38, A.B. 1938. **Family:** Married 1) Mary Slattery in 1940 (divorced 1956), one son and one daughter; 2) the actress Marilyn Monroe in 1956 (divorced 1961); 3) the photographer Ingeborg Morath in 1962, one daughter. **Career:** Worked in automobile supply warehouse, 1932-34; member of the Federal Theatre Project, 1938; writer for CBS and NBC Radio Workshops. Associate professor of drama, University of Michigan, 1973-74. International president, PEN, London and New York, 1965-69. Lives in Connecticut. **Awards:** Theatre Guild award, 1938; New York Drama Critics Circle award, 1947, 1949; Tony award, 1947, 1949, 1953; Pulitzer prize, 1949; National Association of Independent Schools award, 1954; American Academy Gold medal, 1959; Brandeis University Creative Arts award, 1969; Peabody award, for television play, 1981; Bobst award, 1983; National Arts Club medal of honor, 1992; City University of New York Edwin Booth award, 1992; Commonwealth award, 1992. D.H.L.: University of Michigan, 1956. Honorary degree: Hebrew University, Jerusalem, 1959. Litt.D.: University of East Anglia, Norwich, 1984. **Member:** American Academy, 1981. **Agent:** Kay Brown, International Creative Management, 40 West 57th Street, New York, New York 10019, U.S.A.

Publications

Plays

Honors at Dawn (produced Ann Arbor, Michigan, 1936). *No Villain* (*They Too Arise*) (produced Ann Arbor, Michigan, 1937).

The Pussycat and the Expert Plumber Who Was a Man, and *William Ireland's Confession*, in *100 Non-Royalty Radio Plays*, edited by William Kozlenko. New York, Greenberg, 1941.

The Man Who Had All the Luck (produced New York, 1944; London, 1960). Published in *Cross-Section 1944*, edited by Edwin Seaver, New York, Fischer, 1944.

That They May Win (produced New York, 1944). Published in *Best One-Act Plays of 1944*, edited by Margaret Mayorga, New York, Dodd Mead, 1945.

Grandpa and the Statue, in *Radio Drama in Action*, edited by Erik Barnouw. New York, Farrar and Rinehart, 1945.

The Story of Gus, in *Radio's Best Plays*, edited by Joseph Liss. New York, Greenberg, 1947.

The Guardsman, radio adaptation of a play by Ferenc Molnár, and *Three Men on a Horse*, radio adaptation of the play by George Abbott and John Cecil Holm, in *Theatre Guild on the Air*, edited by William Fitelson. New York, Rinehart, 1947.

All My Sons (produced New York, 1947; London, 1948). New York, Reynal, 1947; in *Collected Plays*, 1957.

Death of a Salesman: Certain Private Conversations in Two Acts and a Requiem (produced New York and London, 1949). New York, Viking Press, and London, Cresset Press, 1949.

An Enemy of the People, adaptation of a play by Ibsen (produced New York, 1950; Lincoln, 1958; London, 1988). New York, Viking Press, 1951; London, Walker, 1989.

The Crucible (produced New York, 1953; Bristol, 1954; London, 1956). New York, Viking Press, 1953; London, Cresset Press, 1956; augmented version (with additional scene, subsequently omitted), New York, Dramatists Play Service, 1954.

A View from the Bridge (produced New York, 1955). With *A Memory of Two Mondays*, New York, Viking Press, 1955; revised version (produced London, 1956), New York, Dramatists Play Service, 1956; London, Cresset Press, 1957.

A Memory of Two Mondays (produced New York, 1955; Nottingham, 1958). With *A View from the Bridge*, New York, Viking Press, 1955; in *Collected Plays, 1957.*

Collected Plays (includes *All My Sons*, *Death of a Salesman*, *The Crucible*, *A Memory of Two Mondays*, *A View from the Bridge*). New York, Viking Press, 1957; London, Cresset Press, 1958.

After the Fall (produced New York, 1964; Coventry, 1967; London, 1990). New York, Viking Press, 1964; London, Secker and Warburg, 1965.

Incident at Vichy (produced New York, 1964; Brighton and London, 1966). New York, Viking Press, 1965; London, Secker and Warburg, 1966.
The Price (produced New York, 1968; also director: produced London, 1969). New York, Viking Press, and London, Secker and Warburg, 1968.
Fame, and The Reason Why (produced New York, 1970). *Fame* published in *Yale Literary Magazine* (New Haven, Connecticut), March 1971.
The Creation of the World and Other Business (produced New York, 1972; Edinburgh, 1974). New York, Viking Press, 1973; in *Collected Plays 2*, 1981; revised version, as *Up from Paradise*, music by Stanley Silverman (also director: produced Ann Arbor, Michigan, 1974; New York, 1983), New York, French, 1984.
The Archbishop's Ceiling (produced Washington, D.C., 1977; revised version produced Cleveland, 1984; Bristol, 1985; London, 1986). London, Methuen, 1984; with *The American Clock*, New York, Grove Press, 1989.
The American Clock, adaptation of the work *Hard Times* by Studs Terkel (produced Seattle, 1979; New York, 1980; Birmingham, 1983; London, 1986). London, Methuen, 1983; with *The Archbishop's Ceiling*, New York, Grove Press, 1989.
Playing for Time, adaptation of a work by Fania Fenelon (televised 1980; produced Edinburgh, 1986). New York, Bantam, 1981; in *Collected Plays 2*, 1981.
Collected Plays 2 (includes *The Misfits, After the Fall, Incident at Vichy, The Price, The Creation of the World and Other Business, Playing for Time*). New York, Viking Press, and London, Secker and Warburg, 1981.
Eight Plays (includes *All My Sons, Death of a Salesman, The Crucible, A Memory of Two Mondays, A View from the Bridge, After the Fall, Incident at Vichy, The Price*). New York, Doubleday, 1981.
Two-Way Mirror (includes *Elegy for a Lady* and *Some Kind of Love Story*) (also director: produced New Haven, Connecticut, 1982; Edinburgh, 1984; London, 1989). *Elegy for a Lady* published New York, Dramatists Play Service, 1982; *Some Kind of Love Story* published Dramatists Play Service, 1983; both plays published London, Methuen, 1984.
Danger! Memory! (includes *I Can't Remember Anything* and *Clara*) (produced New York, 1987; London, 1988). London, Methuen, 1986; New York, Grove Press, 1987.
Speech to the Neighborhood Watch Committee in *Urban Blight* (musical revue), based on an idea by John Tillinger, music by David Shire, lyrics by Richard Maltby, Jr. (produced New York, 1988).
Plays 3 (includes *The American Clock, The Archbishop's Ceiling, Two-Way Mirror*). London, Methuen, 1990.
Everybody Wins (screenplay). London, Methuen, 1990; New York, Grove Weidenfeld, 1990.
The Last Yankee (produced New York, 1991; London, 1993). New York, Dramatists Play Service, 1991.
The Ride Down Mount Morgan (produced London, 1991). London, Methuen Drama, 1991.
Broken Glass: A Play in Two Acts. New York, Penguin Books, 1994.
Plays: Two (includes *The Misfits*; *After the Fall*; *Incident at Vichy*; *The Price*; *The Creation of the World and Other Business*; *Playing for Time*). London, Methuen Drama, 1994.
Plays: Five (includes *The Last Yankee*; *The Ride Down Mount Morgan*; *Almost Everybody Wins*) . London, Methuen Drama, 1995.

Screenplays: *The Story of G.I. Joe* (uncredited), 1945; *The Witches of Salem*, 1958; *The Misfits*, 1961; *Everybody Wins*, 1990; *The Crucible*, 1992.

Radio Plays: *The Pussycat and the Expert Plumber Who Was a Man, William Ireland's Confession, Grandpa and the Statue, The Story of Gus, The Guardsman, Three Men on a Horse*, early 1940s; *The Golden Years*, 1987 (UK).

Television Play: *Playing for Time*, 1980.

Novels

Focus. New York, Reynal, 1945; London, Gollancz, 1949.
The Misfits (novelization of screenplay). New York, Viking Press, and London, Secker and Warburg, 1961.

Short Stories

I Don't Need You Any More. New York, Viking Press, and London, Secker and Warburg, 1967.
Homely Girl, A Life, and Other Stories. New York, Penguin Books, 1992.

Other

Situation Normal. New York, Reynal, 1944.
Jane's Blanket (for children). New York, Crowell Collier, and London, Collier Macmillan, 1963.
In Russia, photographs by Inge Morath. New York, Studio, and London, Secker and Warburg, 1969.
The Portable Arthur Miller, edited by Harold Clurman. New York, Viking Press, 1971; London, Penguin, 1977.
In the Country, photographs by Inge Morath. New York, Studio, and London, Secker and Warburg, 1977.
The Theater Essays of Arthur Miller, edited by Robert A. Martin. New York, Viking Press, and London, Penguin, 1978.
Chinese Encounters, photographs by Inge Morath. New York, Farrar Straus, and London, Secker and Warburg, 1979.
"Salesman" in Beijing. New York, Viking, and London, Methuen, 1984.
Timebends (autobiography). New York, Grove Press, and London, Methuen, 1987.

*

Bibliography: "Arthur Miller: The Dimension of His Art: A Checklist of His Published Works," in *Serif* (Kent, Ohio), June 1967, and *Arthur Miller Criticism (1930-1967)*, Metuchen, New Jersey, Scarecrow Press, 1969, revised edition as *An Index to Arthur Miller Criticism*, 1976, both by Tetsumaro Hayashi; *Arthur Miller: A Reference Guide* by John H. Ferres, Boston, Hall, 1979.

Manuscript Collections: University of Texas, Austin; University of Michigan, Ann Arbor; New York Public Library; Library of Congress, Washington, D.C.

Critical Studies (selection): *Arthur Miller*, Edinburgh, Oliver and Boyd, and New York, Grove Press, 1961, and *Miller: A Study of His Plays*, London, Eyre Methuen, 1979, revised edition as *Miller the Playwright*, Methuen, 1983, both by Dennis Welland;

Arthur Miller by Robert Hogan, Minneapolis, University of Minnesota Press, 1964; *Arthur Miller: The Burning Glass* by Sheila Huftel, New York, Citadel Press, and London, W.H. Allen, 1965; *Arthur Miller: Death of a Salesman: Text and Criticism* edited by Gerald Weales, New York, Viking Press, 1967; *Arthur Miller* by Leonard Moss, New York, Twayne, 1967, revised edition, 1980; *Arthur Miller, Dramatist* by Edward Murray, New York, Ungar, 1967; *Arthur Miller: A Collection of Critical Essays* edited by Robert W. Corrigan, Englewood Cliffs, New Jersey, Prentice Hall, 1969; *Psychology and Arthur Miller* by Richard I. Evans, New York, Dutton, 1969; *The Merrill Guide to Arthur Miller* by Sidney H. White, Columbus, Ohio, Merrill, 1970; *Arthur Miller: Portrait of a Playwright* by Benjamin Nelson, New York, McKay, and London, Owen, 1970; *Arthur Miller* by Ronald Hayman, London, Heinemann, 1970, New York, Ungar, 1972; *Twentieth-Century Interpretations of The Crucible* edited by John H. Ferres, Englewood Cliffs, New Jersey, Prentice Hall, 1972; *Studies in Death of a Salesman* edited by Walter J. Meserve, Columbus, Ohio, Merrill, 1972; *Critical Essays on Arthur Miller* edited by James J. Martine, Boston, Hall, 1979; *Arthur Miller: New Perspectives* edited by Robert A. Martin, Englewood Cliffs, New Jersey, Prentice Hall, 1982; *Arthur Miller* by Neil Carson, London, Macmillan, and New York, Grove Press, 1982; *Twentieth-Century Interpretations of Death of a Salesman* edited by Helene Wickham Koon, Englewood Cliffs, New Jersey, Prentice Hall, 1983; *Conversations with Arthur Miller* edited by Matthew C. Roudané, Jackson, University Press of Mississippi, 1987; *File on Miller* edited by C.W.E. Bigsby, London, Methuen, 1988; *Because It Is My Name: Problems of Identity Experienced by Women, Artists, and Breadwinners in the Plays of Henrik Ibsen, Tennessee Williams, and Arthur Miller* by Nada Zeineddine, Braunton, Devon, Merlin Books, 1991; *Communists, Cowboys, and Queers: The Politics of Masculinity in the Works of Arthur Miller* by David Savran, Minneapolis, University of Minnesota Press, 1992; *The Crucible: Politics, Property, and Pretense* by James J. Martine, New York and Toronto, Twayne Publishers, 1993; *Arthur Miller's Death of a Salesman* by Lloyd Cameron, Glebe, New South Wales, Pascal Press, 1995; *The Achievement of Arthur Miller: New Essays,* edited by Steve Centola, Dallas, Texas, Contemporary Research Press, 1995; *The Cambridge Companion to Arthur Miller,* edited by C.W.E. Bigsby, Cambridge, Cambridge University Press, 1997; *Arthur Miller's The Crucible,* edited by Harold Bloom, Broomall, Pennsylvania, Chelsea House, 1998; *Readings on The Crucible,* edited by Thomas Siebold, San Diego, California, Greenhaven Press, 1999.

Theatrical Activities:

Director: **Plays**—*The Price*, London, 1969; *Up from Paradise*, 1974; *Two-Way Mirror*, New Haven, Ann Arbor, Michigan, Connecticut, 1982; *Death of a Salesman*, Beijing, 1983, Stockholm, 1992.

Actor: **Play**—Narrator in *Up from Paradise*, Ann Arbor, Michigan, 1974. **Television**—*The Civil War.*

Arthur Miller comments:

I have, I think, provided actors with some good things to do and say. Beyond that I cannot speak with any certainty. My plays seem to exist and that's enough for me. What people may find in them or fail to find is not in my control anymore; I can only hope that life has not been made less for what I've done, and possibly a bit more.

* * *

> How may a man make of the outside world a home?
> I am constantly awed by what an individual is, by the endless possibilities in him for good and evil, by his unpredictability, by the possibilities he has for any betrayal, any cruelty, as well as any altruism, any sacrifice.
>
> —Arthur Miller

Arthur Miller writes primarily about man's relationship to society and the issues of personal identity and human dignity. Throughout, he has used the realistic form. His statement of purpose—to write "a drama of the whole-man"—conveys his interest in psychology as well as morality. Miller frequently uses what T. S. Eliot called the "objective correlative" ("a set of objects, a situation, a chain of events which shall be the formula of that *particular* emotion") in order to combine an extraordinarily forceful theater with uncanny psychological insights and lyrical and poetic vision. His aim is a theater that "teaches, not by proposing solutions but by defining problems."

The *Collected Plays* of 1957 portray the individual struggling against the laws of society, family, and even selfhood—torn either between the dreams the dog-eat-dog world has imposed upon him and his essential goodness or between his deepest wishes for the simple life and the needs he feels obliged to meet. Set against a ruthless capitalist system that ignores or uses the common man, Miller's plays explore an identity that frequently consists of merely accommodating oneself to an essentially alien universe (society) and the act of painstakingly supporting one's family. Sometimes, however, a person learns that, in fact, he never was connected with the family or job, let alone society, or that the values of each are equally spurious.

Miller's first successful play, *All My Sons,* portrays the conflict between the idealistic son (Chris) and his materialistically corrupted father (Joe Keller). To retain his business, Keller has shipped defective plane parts that have ultimately caused the deaths of many fliers. The seeds of the great *Death of a Salesman* are here—from the stage setting (with the Keller's house and the impinging presence of the more successful neighbors) to the use of poetic images (wind, the car), and even to specific rhetorical cadences ("Nobody in this house dast take her faith away"). Here are the eternally forgiving, self-deluding wife-mother, her idealistic sons (one has committed suicide for his principles), the poignant and misguided bond between father and son, and the father's suicide to expiate a lifetime of wrong commitment. Here is Miller's vision of the terrible rat race of ordinary business reality and of one's better knowledge of the need to love others. One bears a responsibility to the other and "can be better! Once and for all you can know there's a universe of people outside and you're responsible to it." This becomes increasingly difficult to enact, however, for a man's love for his family may also tear him apart: "There's nothin' he could do that I wouldn't forgive. Because he's my son. Because I'm his father and he's my son."

Miller's masterpiece, *Death of a Salesman,* measures the enormous gap between America's promise of inevitable success and the devastating reality of one man's concrete failure. Commitment to false social values blinds one to the true values of human experience—the comforts of personal relationships, of family and friendship, of love. Identity and commitment are again the subject. Willie Loman, who may well exemplify Miller's definition of the tragic hero as discussed in his essay "Tragedy and the Common Man," has completely sold himself to what is at best an anachronistic dream—that anyone can get ahead. This is what he has been brought up to believe, the promise of his mythic salesmen heroes. While Willie has pursued this promise for 40 years and has sold it to his two sons, he is blind to its contemporary meaninglessness and to his own, and their, failure. But Willie is a great salesman—as in the old American dream—and even his wife, the loyal Linda, lives in a world of self-generating lies and illusions. What Willie comes to realize on the single day of the play—his "recognition scene"—is that he has totally overlooked his true wealth, that he is a deeply loved father. Ironically, armed with this knowledge, he defies the system that has until now defeated him. He commits suicide to give his sons the only thing his society respects—cash. In defiance, irony, and profound bitterness, Miller sends Willie to his death with the same illusion he has lived by, although Willie is now fully aware of and in control of it. This is Miller's most bitter picture of the system that uses the little man, that eats the orange and throws away the peel. As tattered and self-pitying as Willie sometimes appears, he is one of the theater's most poignant and moving figures.

Miller has connected the origins of *The Crucible* with McCarthyism, with the "political, objective knowledgeable campaign from the far Right [which] was capable of creating not only a terror, but a new subjective reality, a veritable mystique which was gradually assuming even a holy resonance." Specifically about the Salem witch trials of 1692, the play also treats the national paranoia, hysteria, and general immorality that characterized the McCarthy witch-hunts. Miller bitterly attacks the society that rewards the suppression of freedom in the name of right and conformity. Two lines summarize his focus: the rhetorical question "Is the accusor always holy?" and the statement "You must understand . . . that a person is either with this court or he must be counted against it, there be no road between." Although it has been called a modern morality play, Miller goes beyond black-and-white characterizations to portray his figures' petty rivalries and moral ambiguities. He probes the political, social, and psychological needs of both those who capitulate and those who resist. Mr. Proctor, after defying the court's demands, finally regains his name, something that also is important to Willie and Keller, and dies in another act of defiance. Once again, Miller illustrates his conviction that a person can assert his "personal dignity" and "act against the scheme of things that degrades." As he puts it in *All My Sons,* one can be "better."

A Memory of Two Mondays, which Miller has expressed an especial fondness for, brings back the years of the Great Depression. It was initially produced with *A View from the Bridge,* which treats the hardworking and likable Eddie Carbone who, out of blind love toward his niece-ward, informs on the illegal immigrants he is presumably safeguarding (one of whom is his niece's boyfriend). Blind to what really drives him ("You can never have her") and defiant of community, family, and natural law, he endures public humiliation for his act of treason. His grief is overwhelming as he cries the familiar "I want my name." He draws a knife, and once again Miller's protagonist precipitates his own death. Although the play is, as Miller intended, simpler than *Salesman,* it recalls it in many ways: two men in conflict with a third, who is an authority figure; the (surrogate) father's blind worship of his charge ("She's the best"); and the ever supportive and loving wife. It also retains certain expressionistic elements; the narrator, for example, functions like a Greek chorus and frames each section in mythic terms.

For the next nine years Miller wrote short stories, prose essays (including "The Shadow of Gods"), and the screenplay *The Misfits*. With *After the Fall* he turned from the family and the obligation to connect with the social world to a more existential statement: the recuperative and regenerative powers of love, the question of personal or universal guilt, and the necessity of man to justify himself to himself rather than to the system. Emphasis thus shifted to the need for human community and love and to the fact that a person is his brother's keeper. Despite the many critical attempts to pigeonhole *After the Fall* autobiographically, Miller has said that the play is no more autobiographical than his other work. It treats, he has said, the self-destructiveness of a character who views herself as "pure victim." In this stream-of-consciousness drama, Quentin, the protagonist, subjects all of his values to scrutiny. His statement "The bench was empty. No judge in sight. And all that remained was the endless argument with oneself, this pointless litigation of existence before an empty bench," and the tone of the entire piece redefines Miller's conviction that a person must come to terms with his own acts and values. As Quentin confronts his parents, his wives, and the various situations of his recent and past life, Miller suggests that we all bear the mark of Cain; we are all born after the Fall and are responsible for our acts. After such knowledge comes forgiveness, and the play ends with the affirmative "Hello."

Themes of commitment, responsibility, and integrity continue in *Incident at Vichy,* in which the aristocrat Von Berg, the mirror image of Quentin, transfers his own freedom to the Jewish Leduc and accepts his own death. Miller raises questions about sacrifice and guilt ("the soul's remorse for his own hostility"). The play investigates the need we all have for scapegoats and for the suffering "other." "You must face your own complicity," he writes, "with . . . your own humanity." A person must accept not only his own evil, and goodness, but also the sacrifices and kindness of others.

The Price returns to two brothers, the poles of love and money, the sacrifices and selfishness of each, and the terrible lack of relationship that always existed between them—the terrible "price" that rivalry and lovelessness exact. Unlike Von Berg in *Incident,* the brothers have given nothing, and they therefore have nothing. Gregory Solomon, an antiques dealer, teaches that one must give without expecting repayment; he understands the gratuitousness of love. One must embrace community while realizing the utter isolation that is finally the human condition.

Although in 1972 Miller said that his plays were becoming more mythical, *The Creation of the World and Other Business,* which is about God's conflict with Lucifer over the behavior of Adam and Eve and of Cain and Abel, is an existential query into the nature of individual responsibility. Miller's later works have been less than successful. *The American Clock* is a series of vignettes in which the fate of a Depression family—the not particularly heroic Baums—is intertwined with that of a remarkably heroic nation during the 1930s. It is an overly ambitious effort, and Miller describes it "as though the whole country were really the setting"; it was intended, he explains, to be "a mural for the theater inspired by Studs Terkel's *Hard Times*." The two minidramas of *Two-Way Mirror,* on the other hand, are extremely modest, although they are intended as "passionate voyages through the masks of [agonizing] illusion." *Elegy for a Lady* focuses on a middle-aged man who, while selecting a gift for his dying mistress, indulges in a conversation with the boutique proprietress on the pain of love. In *Some Kind of Love Story* a detective visits an old girlfriend, now a call girl who may be the key figure in clearing a murder suspect. The 20-minute *The Last Yankee* treats two men—one an affluent businessman with seven children and the other a carpenter without children—who meet in a mental hospital. They are waiting to visit their wives, both of whom suffer from severe depression. The men discuss the possible reasons for their wives' illness, in the course of which they realize that the women's symptoms and their causes—specifically, their marriages—are totally different. At the end of the play, as the social and economic rivalries between the men become dominant, Miller evokes a subtle perspective on the ubiquitousness of human need and self-absorption, both of which inevitably destroy personal relationships.

The Ride Down Mount Morgan is presumably a "comedy" about bigamy, although Miller himself describes his somber subject as "what it takes out of a man to get everything he wants in marriage and life." While there are some comic moments, the play actually focuses on marital deception and responsibility. Miller portrays a husband in his 50s named Lyman Felt. He is a Willy Loman gone astray—a onetime poet and now an insurance magnate—who has gone to the limits of marital infidelity. Lyman is a nine-year bigamist who has negotiated "two sublimely happy marriages . . . without being humbled." Throughout the play Lyman (and Miller) rationalizes his clearly immoral life. That is to say, as he "loves each wife equally," he prides himself on his efforts to understand true selfhood. "You can either be true to yourself or to other people," he says, and "A loser lives someone else's life. I've lived my own life." The play is constructed as a series of flashbacks in Lyman's hospital room following a car accident on icy Mount Morgan. It is here that the two wives, Leah and Theodora (one a young Jewish businesswoman; the other an older Waspish woman) first meet and learn the truth. Ultimately, each rejects him as a liar. Miller has said of the play, "We have no solution to this problem. We have an instinctual life, and we have a social life," which is a variation of Lyman's remark to his lawyer—"Look, we're all the same." Perhaps more pertinent to Miller's audience, however, is Lyman's revelation: "I know what's wrong with me—I could never stand still for death! Which you've got to do, by a certain age, or be ridiculous—you've got to stand there nobly and serene and let death run his tape out your arms and around your belly and up your crotch until he's got you fitted for that last black suit. And I can't. I won't! So I'm left wrestling with this anachronistic energy which God has charged me with and I will use it till the dirt is shoveled into my mouth."

The English, who have revered Miller's work of the past two decades more than Americans have, awarded him the esteemed Olivier Prize for *The Broken Mirror,* a play that received many poor notices in the United States. Set in November 1938, the play, as the title suggests, is connected to Kristallnacht, the night the Nazis broke the windows of Jewish businesses and burned synagogues. The title also refers to the wine glass broken at traditional Jewish wedding ceremonies. The plot is relatively simple. Sylvia, an attractive, middle-aged Jewish woman, reads about the Nazi brutality toward the Jews, specifically a scene of elderly Jews scrubbing streets with toothbrushes, and this results in the hysterical paralysis of her legs. Such news does not move her husband, a self-hating Jew whose name, Philip Gellberg, he insists, is not to be confused with Goldberg. As he visits Sylvia's general practitioner, Harry Hyman, Philip is offended by any remark that touches on his ethnicity, takes pride in the fact that he is the only Jew to work in the Brooklyn Guaranty and Trust, and enjoys the fact that his son is the only Jew at West Point a potential general.

The sympathetic physician, married to a non-Jew, was a well-known flirt in his youth and has taken a special interest in Sylvia, presumably for purposes of research, although one soon observes the sexual overtones of their relationship. All the same, it seems unquestionable that the doctor's primary interest is in helping Sylvia recover. He urges the husband to be more patient and affectionate and elicits from him a confession that, shortly after their son was born and the couple attended a party at which pornographic photos were shared, he lost all sexual interest in his wife. She, in turn, has been quietly resentful that he never allowed her to return to her job as a bookkeeper after their son was born.

What is troubling about the play is its predictability, but what is extremely moving is the love each partner feels for the other and the mixture of fantasy and reality they create about their lives, including whether or not, at the doctor's advice, they have just shared a sexual liaison after 20 years of abstinence. Their many years of pain and frustration are clear. She, for example, says, "What I did with my life! Gave it away like a couple of pennies. I took better care of my shoes." The overall meaning of the play is also obvious. The wife associates her husband with the Nazis and has become the Jewish victim, one who might flee the situation but instead remains at home, paralyzed. In the event the audience has missed it, the doctor supplies the global connection: "She knows something . . . like she's connected to . . . some wire that goes half around the world." In the conclusion the husband suffers a heart attack, and Sylvia stands but does not walk. The doctor's last comments are "Everybody's persecuted."

—Lois Gordon

MILLER, Susan

Nationality: American. **Born:** Philadelphia, Pennsylvania, 6 April 1944. **Education:** Pennsylvania State University, University Park, B.A. 1965; Bucknell University, Lewisburg, Pennsylvania, M.A. 1970. **Career:** Instructor in English, Pennsylvania State University, 1969-73; lecturer in playwriting, University of California, Los Angeles, 1975-76; playwright-in-residence, Mark Taper Forum Theatre, Los Angeles, 1975; instructor, NYU Tisch School of the Arts, 1987-93; lecturer, Rutgers University, 1991; instructor, Westside YMCA, New York, 1992-94; director, The Legacy Project, 1994-97. **Awards:** Rockefeller grant, 1975; National Endowment for the Arts grant, 1976; Obie award, 1979, 1994; Susan Smith Blackburn prize, for *My Left Breast,* 1994; Robert Chesley Playwrighting award for lifetime achievement, 1996. **Member:** The Dramatists Guild; PEN; The Writers Guild of America. **Agent:** Joyce Ketay Agency, 1501 Broadway, suite 1908, New York, New York 10036, U.S.A.

Publications

Plays

No One Is Exactly 23 (produced University Park, Pennsylvania). Published in *Pyramid 1* (Belmont, Massachusetts), 1968.

Daddy, and A Commotion of Zebras (produced New York, 1970).

Silverstein & Co. (produced New York, 1972).

Confessions of a Female Disorder (produced Hartford, Connecticut, 1973). Published in *Gay Plays*, edited by William M. Hoffman, New York, Avon, 1979.
Denim Lecture (produced Los Angeles, 1974).
Flux (produced New York 1975; London, 1976).
Cross Country (produced Los Angeles, 1976; New York, 1977). Published in *West Coast Plays* (Berkeley, California), 1978.
Nasty Rumors and Final Remarks (produced New York, 1979). Published in *Amazon All Stars,* Applause Books, 1997.
Arts and Leisure (produced Los Angeles, 1985).
For Dear Life (produced New York, 1989).
It's Our Town, Too (produced Los Angeles, 1992). Published in *Actors' Book of Gay and Lesbian Plays,* Applause Books, 1992; *The Best American Short Plays, 1992-1993,* Applause Bocks, 1992.
My Left Breast (produced Louisville, 1994; New York, 1995). Published in *The Best American Short Plays, 1994-1995,* Applause Books, 1995; *Plays from the Human Festival,* Smith and Kraus; *The Breast: An Anthology,* Global City Press; *O Solo Homo,* Grove Atlantic Press, 1998.

* * *

In Susan Miller's *Arts and Leisure* the character J. D. Salinger inquires of the professor about a student's films, "Does her work astonish you?" Miller's startling explorations of women's minds and hearts do just that, especially creating the shock of recognition in spectators who, like her characters, write, teach, or experience turbulent relationships. Miller's plays most frequently explore issues of intimacy and of evolving sexual identity. In contrast to her self-protective Dina in *Flux*, who pleads, "I'm not eager to expose private agonies," Miller persists in such probing in plays characterized by their whimsy yet potential violence, their passion yet playfulness.

Most of Miller's full-length plays include a tap dance, and nearly all of her funny dramas or poignant comedies end on an upbeat note—with Jake's optimism, with Ronnie's self-discovery, with Jess regaining her confidence, with Salinger gladly relinquishing his manuscripts, with Perry beginning a new life. In fact, the last line of *Cross Country* finds Perry greeting new companions. Although the title of *Nasty Rumors and Final Remarks* suggests that Raleigh's demise concerns Miller, the dramatist actually focuses on the life of this quicksilver woman who can't be confined by her hospital bed or defined by her friends, lovers, or offspring. Hence, even after her stroke Raleigh seems affirmative. So does Miller's reply to the Republican Party's 1992 convention. Because it follows the structure of the model by Thornton Wilder, *It's Our Town, Too* ends at the graveyard, but it affirms respect for those who are different, for values other than those of fundamentalist Christians, and for families other than the old-fashioned model of the homemaker mother, wage-earning father, two children, and a dog.

Miller's language provides part of her plays' fascination. She builds her rhythms into her lines so that their catchy cadences prove actor-proof. In natural dialogue that is fragmented but also filled with expressive turns of phrase, her characters fumble to express their panic or pleasure, occasionally achieving eloquent accuracy. *Cross Country*, for instance, says of Perry's wrenching herself out of her marriage to take off in search of professional and personal fulfillment, "There is a moment, like the black holes in space, of complete and irrevocable loss. To allow that moment is to let go of the sides of time, to fall into another place where it is not likely any of your old friends will recognize you again." Miller's lines often provide witty insights into women's lives, as when a character remarks that, because women are so often interrupted while looking after others, "Women live longer just to finish their conversations."

Miller chooses as her characters writers and others in the arts, usually women in crisis or in transition, women experiencing problems living with others or in their own skin. One of several protagonists bearing names unusual for women, Ronnie in *Confessions of a Female Disorder* makes the transition from puberty to a marriage and career while struggling to avoid confronting her attraction to women. The title expresses both Ronnie's love of women and a female penchant for abnegation. Perry, in *Cross Country,* leaves her marriage to find herself. *Flux*'s iconoclast Jess, on the edge and unable to contain her emotions or control those she inspires in others, turns her students on to her considerable charms instead of to English, making a mess in the classroom and in her personal life as well. *Nasty Rumors and Final Remarks* takes dying Raleigh on an adventure of self-discovery; nobody else could tame her enough to know her. Catherine and Jake in *For Dear Life* differ too profoundly to sustain their relationship; she always expects the worst, while her husband flees her pessimism when it begins to infect him. Yet, ironically, she proves correct in her fears that their marriage will crumble.

Such early Miller works as the Jewish-American black comedy *Silverstein & Co.* and her one-act *No One Is Exactly 23* employ absurdist styles. As her craft developed, however, Miller suited her form to her objective, often combining presentational and representational conventions in the same play and varying her structure to fit her purpose. Although frequently employing surface verisimilitude, Miller sticks to that style throughout only in *Arts and Leisure*, in which the professor and Ginny break into the New Hampshire farmhouse of J. D. Salinger—"the Greta Garbo of American letters"—and threaten to blow up his home unless the reclusive but compulsive writer turns over all of his unpublished manuscripts. Establishing immediate suspense and then sustaining it throughout, Miller confines the action to less than 24 hours on a single set.

At the other extreme *Cross Country*, which is Miller's most surprising play structurally, employs huge chunks of narration distributed among the cast, rather than assigned to a single narrator, as well as stage directions the actors speak aloud, as in chamber theater. This highly episodic play dramatizes some scenes in a single sentence or gives one line to two characters who interact on stage simultaneously, but in fact separately, with the protagonist Perry. Miller begins by describing what happens after the play's middle, and the narrative occurs mostly in the past tense. After repeatedly jumping around in its chronology, *Cross Country* eventually moves forward to Perry's new life on the West Coast.

Miller experiments with chronology in another fashion in *For Dear Life*, which disrupts linear progression through time by moving from the present in act 1 to 18 years later in act 2 and to 16 years before that in act 3. In other words, act 3 occurs about two years after act 1, but the intervening act flashes far forward. The style, meanwhile, moves from mostly representational to presentational. Miller unifies the unusual construction with a speech we watch Jake prepare during the first act and that his son quotes at the end of the play, when he is supposed to be one year old (although we have see him as a teenager in the previous act). The disrupted chronology of the play's construction permits Miller to show us in act 3 the problems causing the divorce that act 2 has already shown occurring. The couple in the third act wait for their happiness to end, as we know it must. Not only act 2 but also the title tell us that they are hanging on for dear life, clinging to a relationship as though to a lifeline even though logic dictates letting go.

Confessions of a Female Disorder, perhaps the most fluid of all of Miller's unconventionally constructed plays, takes Ronnie from her first menstrual period and the start of her search for a man through her gathering with other women in her kitchen as they begin to explore various facets of themselves. So presentational and episodic is the work that Miller has Ronnie hop out of a shower straight into her psychiatrist's office in midlather and has husband David pop in "out of sequence," a line acknowledging to spectators that we all know this to be a play, not a slice of life. "Cheerleaders" and "lettermen" jump in and out of the action both to comment and to take minor roles, as, for example, the men who offer her a sexual encounter superior to her first experience. When coercing her into marriage, Ronnie's psychiatrist turns into a minister.

Although Miller has revised *Flux* several times, each version employs presentational, episodic scenes conveying the quality of dreams and nightmares that do for the collapse of female self-esteem what Arthur Miller (who is no relation) did for male disintegration in *Death of a Salesman*. Moving freely from the classroom, Saul's bedroom, Jess's house, Jess's office, and her mentor's office or classroom, Miller dramatizes Jess's disorienting mismatch of expectations with those of her students and partner. Such construction and style convey what Jess and her students experience emotionally rather than factually. Thus, the mentor performs a con artist's shell game, the students don pajamas and brush their teeth in the classroom, and a voice-over about student evaluations accompanies an orgy. Jess and her students clearly populate each other's dreams.

Miller's most unusual temporal distortions occur in *Nasty Rumors and Final Remarks*. While Raleigh experiences a cerebral hemorrhage on one side of the stage, others elsewhere deal with its aftermath. Only one preliminary scene has established Raleigh's personality before the stroke. As time passes, Raleigh begins narrating and describing herself in the third person and in the past tense. (The play is somewhat like *Cross Country* in this respect.) While she is supposed to be in a coma and dying, we see her talking to us and eavesdropping on her male lover, her female lover, and her friend. Raleigh's ramblings around the hospital are intersected by flashbacks that dramatize her relationships to the people who have gathered to wait for her death. Such presentational episodes connect so seamlessly in a montage of past events and present passions that we scarcely notice the technique until everyone gathers to bid good-bye to the dead woman.

Raleigh has proven unreliable, unpredictable, unfaithful, and unnerving to all who care about her. Yet when the play ends, we miss her, as we do all of Miller's protagonists—usually brilliant, beautiful, bisexual women who fascinate and bewilder their admirers and who cannot tame their whirlwind natures. In dramatizing them Miller explores such themes as how to couple successfully, how to balance professional and personal fulfillment, how to know and be oneself, and how to behave responsibly toward others without betraying oneself. Miller balances her evocation of anxiety and loneliness with a sense of elation at rising to the challenges of intimacy and career. She repeatedly achieves the trademark Miller effect of locating our hidden lacerations and then tickling the wounds until we are convulsed.

—Tish Dace

MILNER, Ron(ald)

Nationality: American. **Born:** Detroit, Michigan, 29 May 1938. **Education:** Northeastern High School, Detroit; Highland Park Junior College, Detroit; Detroit Institute of Technology; Columbia University, New York. **Career:** Writer-in-residence, Lincoln University, Pennsylvania, 1966-67; taught at Michigan State University, East Lansing, 1971-72. Founding director, Spirit of Shango theatre company, and Langston Hughes Theatre, Detroit. **Awards:** John Hay Whitney fellowship, 1962; Rockefeller grant, 1965. **Address:** c/o Crossroads Theatre Company, 7 Livingston Avenue, New Brunswick, New Jersey 08901, U.S.A.

Publications

Plays

Who's Got His Own (produced New York, 1966). Published in *Black Drama Anthology*, edited by Milner and Woodie King, New York, New American Library, 1971.

The Monster (produced Chicago, 1969). Published in *Drama Review* (New York), Summer 1968.

The Warning: A Theme for Linda (produced New York, 1969). Published in *A Black Quartet: Four New Black Plays*, New York, New American Library, 1970.

(M)Ego and the Green Ball of Freedom (produced Detroit, 1971). Published in *Black World* (Chicago), April 1971.

What the Wine-Sellers Buy (produced Los Angeles, 1973; New York, 1974). New York, French, 1974.

These Three (produced Detroit, 1974).

Season's Reasons (produced Detroit, 1976; New York, 1977).

Jazz Set, music by Max Roach (produced Los Angeles, 1979; New York, 1982).

Crack Steppin' (produced Detroit, 1981).

Roads of the Mountaintop (produced New Brunswick, New Jersey, 1986).

Don't Get God Started, music and lyrics by Marvin Winans (also director: produced New York, 1987).

Checkmates (produced Los Angeles, 1987; New York, 1988).

Other

Black Drama Anthology. New York, New American Library, 1971.

* * *

Playwright Ron Milner is considered one of the more exciting writers who came to national prominence during the explosive black theater movement of the 1960s. Much like his contemporaries Ed Bullins and Amiri Baraka, he was influenced by both the social and political conditions of the times. A native of Detroit, Milner has often been called "the people's playwright," and his works have been described as being rich in the authentic texture of life in the urban black setting. He has repeatedly been praised for his powerful use of language and observation of character. His characters often examine their self-perceptions and identity while questioning their place in a complex and oppressive world. This introspection enables them to come to a new understanding of themselves, thereby changing how they relate to the world.

Reminiscent of Lorraine Hansberry's *A Raisin in the Sun*, Milner's first full-length play, *Who's Got His Own*, portrays the damaged relationships of a recently widowed mother with her alienated son and embittered daughter. The drama explores the impact that living in a racist society has on black manhood. When the play opens with the funeral of the domineering patriarch, the son—Tim Junior—is forced to address the conflicting feelings of disgust and love he has had for his father. After Mrs. Bronson reveals several unspoken truths about her husband, Tim and his sister Clara are better able to understand their father in a new way, thereby coming to terms with their feelings.

Milner's next play, a one-act drama called *The Warning: A Theme for Linda*, again examines the theme of black manhood. Unlike *Who's Got His Own*, however, the issue is dealt with entirely through the unpleasant and whimsical experiences of women. Linda, a 17-year-old girl living in an impoverished section of Detroit, daydreams about men and what it means to be a woman. In contrast to her fantasies, Linda's alcoholic mother and resentful grandmother tell her of their disastrous encounters with men, warning her to stay clear of them. Finally, after deciding to discard both the imaginary men of her dreams and those of the stories told by her mother and grandmother, Linda instead decides to begin a serious sexual relationship with her boyfriend Donald. She confronts him with the challenge of sharing their futures together as equals in mind, body, and soul.

In 1973 Milner combined his concern for the temptations besetting urban black youth with an examination of the destructive role models of pimps and drug dealers created by Hollywood. Set in Detroit, *What the Wine-Sellers Buy* deals with a young high school boy choosing between good and evil. The boy, Steve Carlton, is forced to decide whether or not to follow the advice of a pimp named Rico, who suggests that he turn his girlfriend into a prostitute to raise money for Steve's sick mother. By following Rico's advice, Steve would simultaneously satisfy his mother's medical needs while condemning his girlfriend, Mae, to a life of depravity. Steve's struggle with his conscience allow Milner again to address the theme of black male responsibility. Steve finally comes to the correct moral decision by understanding that the cost would be too high for himself and his girlfriend.

Set in Detroit in the late 1980s, *Checkmates* depicts the vast differences in the value systems of two generations of African American couples: a young, upwardly mobile professional pair, and their older, middle-class, traditionally minded landlords. Milner shows the world in which we live as one devoid of the strong moral and social values it once had. The younger couple—Sylvester and Laura—initially appear to have it all: successful careers, good looks, love, and financial security. As the play progresses, however, their commitment to one another is tested as they confront growing individual needs. For Laura it is her desire for a career that justifies having an abortion without Sylvester's knowledge. Sylvester displays self-centeredness as he becomes physically abusive after increased feelings of paranoia regarding his job and the discovery of Laura's abortion. The distrust created between Laura and Sylvester eventually pushes them both into the arms of other lovers. Their code of behavior that anything goes actually helps to create a division in their relationship during times of strife. Rather than bringing them closer, Sylvester and Laura's troubles enlarge the division between them and eventually make their love for one another seem futile, finally leading to divorce.

In contrast, through reminiscent flashbacks we see that the older couple of Frank and Mattie have also dealt with infidelity, physical abuse, and the frustrations of racism on the job. In each of these experiences, however, Frank and Mattie chose personal sacrifice over self-centered behavior; children were not seen as being in conflict with individual desires, and adultery and physical abuse were simply not tolerated. It is through their lives that we see how these sacrifices for their marriage have strengthened the relationship. Because of their more traditional value system, Frank and Mattie's world is more stable. Theirs is a code of behavior that helps them live through troubled times.

—Gary Anderson

MINGHELLA, Anthony

Nationality: British. **Born:** Ryde, Isle of Wight, 6 January 1954. **Education:** University of Hull, Yorkshire (Reckitt Travel Award), B.A. (honours) 1975. **Career:** Lecturer in drama, University of Hull, 1976-81. Lives in London. **Awards:** London Theatre Critics award, 1984, 1986. **Agent:** Judy Daish Associates, 83 Eastbourne Mews, London W2 6LQ, England.

Publications

Plays

Mobius the Stripper, adaptation of the story by Gabriel Josipovici (also director: produced Hull, 1975).

Child's Play (also director: produced Hull, 1978).

Whale Music (also director: produced Hull, 1980; London, 1981). Included in *Whale Music and Other Plays*, 1987.

A Little Like Drowning (produced Hemel Hempstead, Hertfordshire, 1982; London, 1984). Included in *Whale Music and Other Plays*, 1987.

Two Planks and a Passion (produced Exeter, 1983; London, 1984). Included in *Whale Music and Other Plays*, 1987.

Love Bites (produced Derby, 1984).

What If It's Raining? (televized 1986). Included in *Interior: Room, Exterior: City*, 1989.

Made in Bangkok (produced London, 1986). London, Methuen, 1986.

Whale Music and Other Plays. London, Methuen, 1987.

Hang Up (broadcast 1987). Included in *Interior: Room, Exterior: City*, 1989.

Cigarettes and Chocolate (broadcast 1988). Included in *Interior: Room, Exterior: City*, 1989.

Interior: Room, Exterior: City (includes *Cigarettes and Chocolate, Hang Up, What If It's Raining?*). London, Methuen, 1989.

Living with Dinosaurs and One-Act Plays and Sketches. London, Methuen, 1991.

Plays 1 (includes *Made in Bangkok*; *Whale Music*; *A Little Like Drowning*; *Two Planks and a Passion*). London, Methuen, 1992.

Truly, Madly, Deeply (screenplay). London, Methuen, 1992.

Driven to Distraction. Cambridge, Cambridge University Press, 1994.

Plays 2 (includes *Cigarettes and Chocolate*; *Hang Up*; *What If It's Raining?*; *Truly, Madly, Deeply*; *Mosaic*; *Days Like These*). London, Methuen, 1997.

Screenplay: *Truly, Madly, Deeply*, 1991; *The English Patient*, based on the novel by Michael Odaatje.

Radio Plays: *Hang Up*, 1987; *Cigarettes and Chocolate*, 1988.

Television Plays: *Studio* series, 1983; *What If It's Raining?* 1986; *Inspector Morse*, from a novel by Colin Dexter, 1987; *Storyteller* series, 1987 (USA); *Signals* (opera), music by John Lunn and Orlando Gough, 1989; *Driven to Distraction*, episode in *Inspector Morse* series, 1990.

Novels

On the Line (novelization of television series). London, Severn House, 1982.

The Storyteller (novelization of television series). London, Boxtree, 1988.

*

Theatrical Activities:

Director: **Plays**—Some of his own plays. **Film**—*Truly, Madly, Deeply*, 1991.

* * *

Anthony Minghella emerged as one of the most consistently adventurous younger British dramatists of the 1980s. He is a writer refreshingly prepared to tackle a wide variety of subjects, and his plays have been marked by an unsentimental humanism and steadily growing technical confidence as he moved from relatively small-scale work in studio and fringe theaters to wider exposure in the commercial sector.

Whale Music was an early indication of Minghella's original voice. With an all-female cast (Minghella has continued to write superb roles for actresses), it is structured around a diverse group of women waiting in a seaside town for a student friend to have her baby. While the play at times seems overly schematic and, in its succession of short scenes, at points jerkily constructed (the dissolving scenes worked much more surely in a later television version), it still creates a recognizable milieu with understated precision. Tender, ironic, and funny, it contains some memorable writing, particularly a long speech from the drifting Stella, giving room to the pregnant Caroline, that is savagely corrosive in its picture of the men she encounters in her one-night stands.

A Little Like Drowning is also written in a succession of short scenes, but it spans many years, with its fulcrum on the breakup of an Anglo-Italian couple's marriage. Moving between the present on an English beach, where the old Leonora recalls her life to her granddaughter, to her 1920s marriage to Alfredo in Italy and his affair and later life in Dublin with Julia, the play seamlessly links time and space. A scene set in 1939, with Alfredo packing to leave Leonora, has both Leonora and Julia on stage but unaware of each other, the scene playing as if their dialogue were totally independent.

Minghella continued to explore and celebrate his own Anglo-Italian inheritance in *Love Bites,* this time on a more epic scale. The first act is set in wartime England and concentrates on two Italian immigrant brothers, Angelo and Bruno, who are establishing themselves in the ice cream business. Particularly impressive in this act is Minghella's handling of Angelo's affair with Elizabeth, a schoolteacher who becomes pregnant by him and to whose love he cannot finally respond. His suggestion of the curiously suspended quality of time during war is especially evocative. The second act, which leaps into the present, is set in a convention hotel, with Angelo about to be inaugurated as president of the Ice Cream Group of Great Britain. Minghella handles his large cast and canvas with a sharp sense of focus, painting a vivid picture of the family's tribal relationships among the different generations. Bruno, in disappointed middle age, realizes that he has let himself be trapped by the past, but he comes to realize in a powerfully written late scene that he and Angelo are essentially alike after all. In such scenes Minghella's control of the play's changes of mood is continuously sure.

Minghella moved completely away from such material in *Two Planks and a Passion,* set in late 14th-century York, in which a troubled Richard II, his wife, and his friend the Earl of Oxford have escaped the court's pressures while the workmen's guilds prepare the mystery plays for the Feast of Corpus Christi. The play weaves together several strands—the royals' mischievous exploitation of local bourgeois snobbery, rivalry among the artisans for patronage, and the workers' rehearsal of the Crucifixion—and includes scenes of high comedy, especially that involving the king mercilessly teasing the fawning mayor during an innovative golf game. As the rehearsal becomes a moving performance witnessed by the royal party, the play gradually draws these elements together. The play may occasionally suffer from the lack of one truly dynamic central character, but it remains an engaging, grave, and totally individual work.

Two Planks and a Passion gradually brought Minghella into the critical spotlight, and a Most Promising Playwright Award rightly came his way in 1984. That promise was amply confirmed by his first major West End play, *Made in Bangkok.* The play covers a group of English tourists and businessmen in Bangkok. It is often sharply and satirically funny, and its moods keep boldly changing, but it emerges as a very dark comedy indeed about personal as well as cultural exploitation. Minghella again created a challengingly complex leading female role in Frances, the wife of a devious and finally frightening businessman and the only character not tainted by some form of exploitation, and he again demonstrated his ability to handle a multiscene and intricately interlocking play with accomplished control. Minghella also reaffirmed the theater's ability to shock, to jolt an audience's moral attitude, as in the scene in which Edward, a repressed homosexual dentist, finally makes a sickeningly pathetic bid for the favors of the hotel worker guide who has helped him. Minghella's dispassionate and compassionate handling of all of his characters gives the play a depth of texture that made one intrigued to see in what direction he might travel next.

As with several other potentially major British dramatists, however, movies seem to have come to occupy Minghella exclusively. The modest worldwide success of his wry and tender *Truly, Madly, Deeply* was trumped by the fanfare and fuss surrounding his screenplay for and direction of the Oscar-winning *The English Pa-*

tient. Nonetheless, he is on record as saying that he does not rule out an eventual return to the theater.

—Alan Strachan

MITCHELL, Adrian

Nationality: British. **Born:** London, 24 October 1932. **Education:** Greenways School, Wiltshire; Dauntsey's School, West Lavington, Wiltshire; Christ Church, Oxford (editor, *Isis* magazine, 1954-55), 1952-55. **Military Service:** Served in the Royal Air Force, 1951-52. **Career:** Reporter, Oxford *Mail*, 1955-57, and *Evening Standard*, London, 1957-59; columnist and reviewer, *Daily Mail*, *Woman's Mirror*, the *Sun*, the *Sunday Times*, *Peace News*, *Black Dwarf*, *New Statesman*, and the *Guardian*, all London. Instructor, University of Iowa, Iowa City, 1963-64; Granada fellow in the arts, University of Lancaster, 1967-69; fellow, Wesleyan University Center for the Humanities, Middletown, Connecticut, 1971-72; resident writer, Sherman Theatre, Cardiff, 1974-75; visiting writer, Billericay Comprehensive School, Essex, 1978-80; Judith E. Wilson fellow, Cambridge University, 1980-81; resident writer, Unicorn Theatre for Young People, London, 1982-83. **Awards:** Eric Gregory award, 1961; P.E.N. prize for translation, 1966; Tokyo Festival award, for television, 1971. **Member:** Fellow, Royal Society of Literature, 1988. **Agent:** Peters, Fraser, and Dunlop Group, 503-504 The Chambers, Chelsea Harbour, Lots Road, London SW10 0XF, England.

Publications

Plays

The Ledge (libretto), music by Richard Rodney Bennett (produced London, 1961).

The Persecution and Assassination of Jean-Paul Marat as Performed by the Inmates of the Asylum of Charenton under the Direction of the Marquis de Sade [*Marat/Sade*], adaptation of a play by Peter Weiss (produced London, 1964; New York, 1965). London, Calder, 1965; New York, Atheneum, 1966.

The Magic Flute, adaptation of the libretto by Schikaneder and Giesecke, music by Mozart (produced London, 1966).

US, with others (produced London, 1966). Published as *US: The Book of the Royal Shakespeare Production US/Vietnam/US/Experiment/Politics . . .* , London, Calder and Boyars, 1968; as *Tell Me Lies*, Indianapolis, Bobbs Merrill, 1968.

The Criminals, adaptation of a play by José Triana (produced London, 1967; New York, 1970).

Tyger: A Celebration of the Life and Work of William Blake, music by Mike Westbrook (produced London, 1971). London, Cape, 1971.

Tamburlane the Mad Hen (for children; produced Devon, 1971).

Man Friday, music by Mike Westbrook (televised 1972; produced London, 1973). With *Mind Your Head*, London, Eyre Methuen, 1974.

Mind Your Head, music by Andy Roberts (produced Liverpool, 1973; London, 1974). With *Man Friday*, London, Eyre Methuen, 1974.

The Government Inspector (as *The Inspector General*, produced Nottingham, 1974; revised version, as *The Government Inspector*, produced London, 1985). London, Methuen, 1985.

A Seventh Man, music by Dave Brown, adaptation of the book by John Berger and Jean Mohr (produced London, 1976).

White Suit Blues, music by Mike Westbrook, adaptation of works by Mark Twain (produced Nottingham and London, 1977).

Houdini: A Circus-Opera, music by Peter Schat (produced Amsterdam, 1977; Aspen, Colorado, 1980). Amsterdam, Clowns, 1977(?).

Uppendown Mooney (produced Welwyn Garden City, Hertfordshire, 1978).

The White Deer (for children), adaptation of the story by James Thurber (produced London, 1978).

Hoagy, Bix, and Wolfgang Beethoven Bunkhaus (produced London, 1979; Indianapolis, 1980).

In the Unlikely Event of an Emergency, music by Stephen McNeff (produced Bath, 1979; London, 1988).

Peer Gynt, adaptation of the play by Ibsen (produced Oxford, 1980).

The Mayor of Zalamea; or, The Best Garrotting Ever Done, adaptation of a play by Calderón (produced London, 1981). Edinburgh, Salamander Press, 1981.

Mowgli's Jungle, adaptation of *The Jungle Book* by Kipling (pantomime; produced Manchester, 1981).

You Must Believe All This (for children), adaptation of "Holiday Romance" by Dickens, music by Nick Bicât and Andrew Dickson (televised 1981). London, Thames Television-Methuen, 1981.

The Wild Animal Song Contest (for children; produced London, 1982). Oxford, Heinemann, 1993.

Life's a Dream, with John Barton, adaptation of a play by Calderón (produced Stratford-on-Avon, 1983; London, 1984).

A Child's Christmas in Wales, with Jeremy Brooks, adaptation of the work by Dylan Thomas (produced Cleveland, 1983).

The Great Theatre of the World, adaptation of a play by Calderón (produced Oxford, 1984).

C'mon Everybody (produced London, 1984).

Animal Farm (lyrics only), book by Peter Hall, music by Richard Peaslee, adaptation of the novel by George Orwell (for children; produced London, 1984; Baltimore, 1986). London, Methuen, 1985; Chicago, Dramatic Publishing Company, 1986.

The Tragedy of King Real (screenplay), in *Peace Plays 1*, edited by Stephen Lowe. London, Methuen, 1985.

Satie Day/Night (produced London, 1986).

The Pied Piper (for children), music by Dominic Muldowney (produced London, 1986). Birmingham, Oberon, 1988.

Mirandolina, adaptation of a play by Goldoni (produced Bristol, 1987).

The Last Wild Wood in Sector 88 (produced Rugby, 1987).

Love Songs of World War Three (produced London, 1988).

Fuente Ovejuna, adaptation of the play by Lope de Vega (produced London, 1988).

Woman Overboard, adaptation of a play by Lope de Vega, music by Monty Norman (produced Watford, 1988).

The Patchwork Girl of Oz, adaptation of the story by L. Frank Baum (for children; produced Watford, 1988).

Anna on Anna (produced Edinburgh and London, 1988; Baltimore, 1990).

The Tragedy of King Real (produced Ongar, Essex, 1989).

Triple Threat (produced London, 1989).

Greatest Hits (produced London, 1992).
The Snow Queen, adaptation of Hans Christian Anderson. London, Oberon, 1996.
The Seige: A Play with Songs. London, Oberon Books, 1996.

Screenplays: *Marat/Sade*, 1966; *Tell Me Lies* (lyrics only), 1968; *The Body* (commentary), 1969; *Man Friday*, 1976; *The Tragedy of King Real*, 1983.

Radio Play: *The Island* (libretto), music by William Russo, 1963.

Television Plays: *Animals Can't Laugh*, 1961; *Alive and Kicking*, 1971; *William Blake* (documentary), 1971; *Man Friday*, 1972; *Somebody Down There Is Crying*, 1974; *Daft As a Brush*, 1975; *The Fine Art of Bubble Blowing*, 1975; *Silver Giant, Wooden Dwarf*, 1975; *Glad Day*, music by Mike Westbrook, 1979; *You Must Believe All This*, 1981; *Juno and Avos*, from a libretto by Andrei Voznesensky, music by Alexei Rybnikov, 1983.

Initiated and helped write student shows: *Bradford Walk*, Bradford College of Art; *The Hotpot Saga, The Neurovision Song Contest*, and *Lash Me to the Mast*, University of Lancaster; *Move Over Jehovah*, National Association of Mental Health; *Poetry Circus*, Wesleyan University; *Mass Media Mash* and *Mud Fair*, Dartington College of the Arts, 1976 and 1977.

Novels

If You See Me Comin'. London, Cape, and New York, Macmillan, 1962.
The Bodyguard. London, Cape, 1970; New York, Doubleday, 1971.
Wartime. London, Cape, 1973.
Man Friday. London, Futura, 1975.

Poetry

(Poems). Oxford, Fantasy Press, 1955.
Poems. London, Cape, 1964.
Peace Is Milk. London, Peace News, 1966.
Out Loud. London, Cape Goliard Press, and New York, Grossman, 1968; revised edition, as *The Annotated Out Loud*, London, Writers and Readers, 1976.
Ride the Nightmare: Verse and Prose. London, Cape, 1971.
Cease-Fire. London, Medical Aid Committee for Vietnam, 1973.
Penguin Modern Poets 22, with John Fuller and Peter Levi. London, Penguin, 1973.
The Apeman Cometh. London, Cape, 1975.
For Beauty Douglas: Collected Poems 1953-1979. London, Allison and Busby, 1982.
Nothingmas Day (for children). London, Allison and Busby, 1984.
On the Beach at Cambridge: New Poems. London, Allison and Busby, 1984.
Love Songs of World War Three (collected song lyrics). London, Allison and Busby, 1989.
Greatest Hits (collected song and lyrics). Newcastle upon Tyne, Bloodaxe, 1992.
Blue Coffee: Poems, 1985-1996. Newcastle upon Tyne, Bloodaxe, 1996.
Heart on the Left: Poems, 1953-1984. Newcastle upon Tyne, Bloodaxe, 1997.

Recording: *Poems*, with Stevie Smith, Argo, 1974.

Other (for children)

The Adventures of Baron Munchausen. London, Walker, 1985.
The Baron Rides Out [*on the Island of Cheese, All at Sea*]. London, Walker, and New York, Philomel, 3 vols., 1985-87.
Leonardo, The Lion from Nowhere. London, Deutsch, 1986.
Our Mammoth [Goes to School, in the Snow]. London, Walker, 3 vols., 1987-88; San Diego, Harcourt Brace, first 2 vols., 1987-88.
Rhinestone Rhino. London, Methuen, 1989.
All My Own Stuff. Hemel Hempstead, Simon & Schuster, 1991.
The Ugly Duckling, adaptation of Hans Christian Anderson, illustrated by Jonathan Hale. Houghton Mifflin, 1994.
Steadfast Tin Soldier, adaptation of Hans Christain Anderson, illustrated by Hale. New York, DK Publishers, 1996.
Maudie and the Green Children. Vancouver, Tradewind Books, 1996.
Gynormous: The Ultimate Book of Giants. London, Orion, 1996.
Balloon Lagoon and the Magic Islands of Poetry. London, Orchard Books, 1997.
Twice My Size. Brookfield, Connecticut, Millbrook Press, 1999.

Editor, *Strawberry Drums*. London, Macdonald, 1989.

Other

Naked In Cheltenham (miscellany). Cheltenham, Gastoday, 1978.
Tourist Snapshots of Chile. London, Chile Solidarity Campaign, 1985.
The Thirteen Secrets of Poetry. Hemel Hempstead, Simon & Schuster, 1993.

Editor, with Richard Selig, *Oxford Poetry 1955*. Oxford, Fantasy Press, 1955.
Editor, *Jump, My Brothers, Jump: Poems from Prison*, by Tim Daly. London, Freedom Press, 1970.

*

Critical Study: "Adrian Mitchell" by John L. DiGaetani, in *A Search for a Postmodern Theater: Interviews with Contemporary Playwrights,* New York, Greenwood, 1991.

Theatrical Activities:
Actor: **Plays**—*C'mon Everybody*, London, 1984; *Love Songs of World War Three*, London, 1988; *Triple Threat*, London, 1989; *Greatest Hits*, London, 1992.

* * *

"A truthful colour supplement. As you turn the pages, conflicting images hit you." Adrian Mitchell's description of his stage show *Mind Your Head* may to some extent be applied to all of his dramatic creations. Impossible to pigeonhole into any one form, they mingle genres indiscriminately, juxtaposing pathos with horror and ribald humor. Instead of adhering to the norms of dramatic artifice, Mitchell appears to seize the chaos and disturbance of modern life and transfer it whole to the stage. Constants of his work are its anarchic individualism and the opposition of its author to establishment mores.

Irony lies at the root of Mitchell's dilemma. A notable performance poet adept in a structured, concentrated medium, he nevertheless strives continually to dispense with the formal restraints of language. As a playwright he equally attempts to eschew established theatrical conventions. Overall, Mitchell's work recalls the 1960s and its legacy of protest, which had a profound influence on his thinking. Together with his contemporary Christopher Logue, he featured prominently in anti-Vietnam War demonstrations, taking part in public poetry readings and contributing to the radical stage show *US.*

All the same, this aspect of Mitchell's writing may be overstressed. His plays are perhaps more traditional and less unorthodox than they appear at first glance. Centuries ago Aristophanes combined fantasy, social comment, satire, and personal invective against establishment figures, the action interspersed with song and dance routines. In much the same way Mitchell's dramas blend the 1960s happening with elements of pantomime and old-time music hall, their seemingly random progress broken by songs and comic patter from various members of the cast. *Mind Your Head* typifies this approach, a surreal revamping of the Hamlet legend that is built around the passengers and crew of a London bus. Mitchell allows his humor a free rein, using parodies of comic and pop song styles for some of the key passages—Hamlet's soliloquy, for example, is performed as a Frankie Howerd monologue—and bestowing the names of jazz musicians on his characters. The pantomimic atmosphere of the show, with its songs and jokes, provides for audience participation, which accords with Mitchell's performance style. A similar work is *Tyger,* in which scenes from the daily life of the poet William Blake are expanded to include a fantasy moon voyage and several establishment names are mercilessly caricatured in song and dance form. Mitchell's affinity with Blake is spiritual rather than stylistic, and he is able to evoke the nature of the man by judicious quotation while retaining his own mixed-genre method of presentation.

Mitchell's television plays tend to show more formal organization than his stage dramas. An exception is *Glad Day,* another Blake tribute in which Mitchell manages to transfer some of the spontaneous energy of *Tyger* to the small screen. Like several of Mitchell's dramas, *Glad Day* involved the close cooperation of Mike Westbrook, whose musical accompaniments gave an added power to Blake's poetry, not least in the memorable "Song of the Slave" whose lyrics are intensified by the jazz arrangement. More typical of the television plays is *Man Friday,* a significant work that Mitchell later adapted for the stage and as a novel. It embodies many of Mitchell's most profound beliefs on the theory of white supremacy, which he contrasts with the foundations of so-called primitive societies. In a series of dialogues between Crusoe and the "savage" Friday, Mitchell adroitly ridicules not only the white man's "civilizing" mission but also popular concepts of nationalism, crime and punishment, and property ownership. The stage version, which allows for more audience interaction, is a strong work, but the original television play is the more enduring. Ironically, as with other Mitchell creations, its organized structure ensures its success.

The throwaway, instant quality of some of Mitchell's writing, his ability to create for specific occasions, may perhaps explain his skill in adapting the work of other writers. His earliest success in this field came in the 1960s with his verse translation of Weiss's *Marat/Sade,* whose blend of social comment and gallows humor evidently appealed to him. Since then he has produced versions of works by Dickens, Gogol, Calderón, Goldoni, Baum, and Lope de Vega. *You Must Believe All This,* taken from a Dickens original, shows Mitchell to be an adept writer for children, to whom audience participation is a natural response. It is a skill that is further confirmed by his rearrangement of L. Frank Baum's fables in *The Patchwork Girl of Oz* and, outside the field of drama, by a number of illustrated books for younger readers. Mitchell fractures the original texts to obtain the desired result, altering language and adding or deleting scenes, usually to good effect. His adaptation of Gogol's *The Government Inspector* inserts the famous troika scene and speech from *Dead Souls* and provides Khlestakov with a startling airborne departure, both of which work dramatically and are in keeping with the lurking unease that underlies this particular "comedy." Similarly, his versions of Calderón's *Life's a Dream* and *The Mayor of Zalamea* break with the fluency of their Spanish originals in favor of a popular, slangy English verse form that conveys greater impact than a strict translation. Calderón's exploration of major human themes, his matching of sentiment with grim humor, is clearly to Mitchell's taste, and the results have been interesting. The same may be said of *Woman Overboard,* his highly individual reworking of Lope de Vega's play *The Dog in the Manger.* This gift for adaptation is far from being the least of Mitchell's talents, and his efforts in this field deserve comparison with the best of his original plays.

Other examples of the latter include his one-act musical satire on the world's worst airline, *In the Unlikely Event of an Emergency,* and three longer productions that Mitchell describes as "compilation shows of songs and poems," namely, *Triple Threat, Love Songs of World War Three,* and *Greatest Hits.* These last had Mitchell appearing as a leading performer onstage as well as in his customary role of author and are proof that he has lost none of his power and drive. If anything, his creative energy seems to have increased, with fresh concepts and approaches being constantly sought in his latest dramas. *Anna on Anna,* his one-woman show portraying the life of poetess Anna Wickham and specially written for the actress Illona Linthwaite, is a perfect example in this respect.

—Geoff Sadler

MITCHELL, Julian

Nationality: British. **Born:** Epping, Essex, 1 May 1935. **Education:** Winchester College, Hampshire, 1948-53; Wadham College, Oxford, B.A. 1958; St. Antony's College, Oxford, M.A. 1962. **Military Service:** Served in the Royal Naval Volunteer Reserve, 1953-55: midshipman. **Career:** Member, Arts Council Literature Panel, 1966-69; formerly, Governor, Chelsea School of Art, London. Chair, Welsh Arts Council Drama Committee, 1988-92. Lives in Newport, Gwent, Wales. **Awards:** Harkness fellowship, 1959; Rhys Memorial prize, 1965; Maugham award, 1966; International Critics prize, for television play, 1977; Christopher award, for television play, 1977 (U.S.A.); Florio prize, for translation, 1980; Society of West End Theatre award, 1982. **Agent:** Peters, Fraser, and Dunlop Group, 503-504 The Chambers, Chelsea Harbour, Lots Road, London SW10 0XF, England.

Publications

Plays

A Heritage and Its History, adaptation of the novel by Ivy Compton-Burnett (produced London, 1965). London, Evans, 1966.
A Family and a Fortune, adaptation of the novel by Ivy Compton-Burnett (produced Guildford, Surrey, 1966; Seattle, 1974; London, 1975). London, French, 1976.
Shadow in the Sun (televised 1971). Published in *Elizabeth R*, edited by J.C. Trewin, London, Elek, 1972.
Half-Life (produced London, 1977; New York, 1981). London, Heinemann, 1977.
Henry IV, adaptation of the play by Pirandello. London, Eyre Methuen, 1979.
The Enemy Within (produced Leatherhead, Surrey, 1980).
Another Country (produced London, 1981; New Haven, Connecticut, 1983). Ambergate, Derbyshire, Amber Lane Press, 1982; New York, Limelight, 1984.
Francis (produced London, 1983). Oxford, Amber Lane Press, 1984.
After Aida; or, Verdi's Messiah (produced London, 1986). Oxford, Amber Lane Press, 1986.
The Evils of Tobacco, adaptation of a work by Chekhov, translated by Ronald Hingley (produced London, 1987).
Adelina Patti, The Queen of Song. (produced Wales, 1987-88).
Falling Over England (produced London, 1994). Oxford, Amber Lane Press, 1994.
August, adaptation of *Uncle Vanya* by Chekhov (produced Wales 1994). Oxford, Amber Lane Press, 1994.
Wilde. London, Orion Books Ltd, 1997.

Screenplays: *Arabesque*, with Stanley Price and Pierre Marton, 1966; *Another Country*, 1984; *Vincent and Theo*, 1990; *August*, 1995; *Wilde*, 1997.

Radio Documentary: *Life and Deaths of Dr. John Donne*, 1972.

Television Plays: *Persuasion*, from the novel by Jane Austen, 1971; *Shadow in the Sun*, 1971; *The Man Who Never Was*, 1972; *A Perfect Day*, 1972; *Fly in the Ointment*, 1972; *A Question of Degree*, 1972; *The Alien Corn*, from a story by W. Somerset Maugham, 1972; *Rust*, 1973; *Jennie*, 1974; *Abide with Me*, from the book *A Child in the Forest*, by Winifred Foley, 1976; *Staying On*, from the novel by Paul Scott, 1980; *The Good Soldier*, from the novel by Ford Madox Ford, 1981; *The Weather in the Streets*, from the novel by Rosamond Lehmann, 1984; episodes for *Inspector Morse* series, 1987-92; *All the Waters of Wye* (documentary), 1990; *Survival of the Fittest*, 1990.

Novels

Imaginary Toys. London, Hutchinson, 1961.
A Disturbing Influence. London, Hutchinson, 1962.
As Far as You Can Go. London, Constable, 1963.
The White Father. London, Constable, 1964; New York, Farrar Straus, 1965.
A Circle of Friends. London, Constable, 1966; New York, McGraw Hill, 1967.
The Undiscovered Country. London, Constable, 1968; New York, Grove Press, 1970.

Short Stories

Introduction, with others. London, Faber, 1960.

Other

Truth and Fiction (lecture). London, Covent Garden Press, 1972.
Jennie, Lady Randolph Churchill: A Portrait with Letters, with Peregrine Churchill. London, Collins, 1974; New York, St. Martin's Press, 1975.

Editor, with others, *Light Blue, Dark Blue: An Anthology of Recent Writing from Oxford and Cambridge Universities*. London, Macdonald, 1960.

* * *

Julian Mitchell's success as a playwright makes nonsense of claims that the well-made play is dead. He is a skillful craftsman whose work fits well into a British theatrical tradition as defined by, say, Terence Rattigan. Dialogue is all in his work, and the plays offer audiences an invitation into a world of polite discourse in which, if voices are occasionally raised, there is always someone present to push the argument forward into its next phase. He is not an innovative writer, but he is always a polished one, as might be expected from someone who came late to the stage after an extensive literary apprenticeship. The 1990s have seen him embarked in yet another direction with his screenplay for *Vincent and Theo,* but his reputation as a writer in the 1960s rested solely on his activities as a novelist. The 1970s saw him established as a regular writer and adapter for television—his work including dramatizations of Jane Austen's *Persuasion,* Paul Scott's *Staying On,* and Ford Madox Ford's *The Good Soldier,* as well as a contribution to the *Elizabeth R* series—and it was only in the 1980s that he really began to receive serious attention as a stage dramatist. Indeed, two of his earliest stage plays, *A Heritage and Its History* and *A Family and a Fortune,* were both adapted from novels by Ivy Compton-Burnett, and it is always apparent that he writes as a novelist converted to the stage.

Mitchell's first novel was compared by one critic with the work of Aldous Huxley, and his plays have a dedicated commitment to a series of theatrical debates that make the comparison only too inviting. At worst the characters serve as convenient mouthpieces for opposing views. For example, in *Half-Life* a country house weekend, that most predictable of all West End formats, is the venue for a political discussion with an assorted bunch of overly articulate people, and there is scarcely any sense of theater about the events depicted. All is wit and verbal swordplay. But at best the debate is more open, and this is nowhere more so than in his most successful play, *Another Country.*

In *Another Country* Mitchell offers one of many analyses of the "betrayal" of their class by the Cambridge communist school of the 1930s. What makes his account interesting is that he transfers the action back to the penultimate year of their public school days, placing the thoughts of the pro-Stalinist Judd and the flamboyantly gay Bennett (Guy Burgess in thin disguise, as is made explicit in the film version) in the context of the institution that is intended to mold them for their future roles as statesmen and administrators. The familiar use of the school as a metaphor of the state, not of the country at large but of its ruling class, allows Mitchell to show how an essentially apolitical Bennett might be led into the world of espionage both as a reaction to the brutal punishing of his sexual appetites by an institution that serves only to heighten their appeal and as an extension of the need to be continually in disguise, leading a double life, which he sees as his fate.

The economic need to restrict the size of the cast (although the play eventually transferred to the West End, it started its life at the Greenwich Theatre) does much to increase the sense of enclosure, of claustrophobia, that confronts any boy who cannot, or will not, fit into the system already created for him. Bennett actually spends a great deal of time in the play acknowledging the attention of his offstage and never seen young lover and in peering through binoculars at what is happening outside the particular room he is in, including the early sighting of the removal of the body of a boy who has hanged himself in the bell tower, a victim of the sexual double standards of the school.

After Aida presents a similarly enclosed stage, in this instance to consider the events leading up to Verdi's agreement to compose *Otello*. It is difficult not to compare the play with Shaffer's *Amadeus*, but it stands up very well to the exercise, being a much less pretentious reanimation of musical history. A preoccupation with the past is also evident in Mitchell's earlier play *Francis*, which takes a long sweep through the life of Saint Francis and his attempts to hang on to his ideal of poverty in the face of pressure from both the established church and his increasingly wealthy new order. As a character Francis is Mitchell's most successful creation, with a stronger sense of internal conflict apparent than his protagonists who are allowed to dominate the action simply by the superiority of their wit and rhetoric. Francis's attempt to relive the spartan life of his Christ unites the rebellious instincts of Bennett with the puritan discipline of Judd in *Another Country*, and here the corrupt oppression of church and papacy take the place of the school. As in all his plays, the voice of the rebel is allowed a place—as it is with the young Prue Hoggart in *Half-Life*—but the resolution of the plays, having suggested a plausible reason for the rebellion, is always to suggest the impossibility of real change.

For Mitchell history teaches a lesson of conflict in which the terms of reference remain essentially unchanged. In all of his plays there is little sense of new ground being broken, either theatrically or intellectually, but if the mainstream is to continue to demand a steady diet of well-made plays, then at least there is always evidence of an articulate intelligence behind Mitchell's work. This is certainly to be welcomed in the increasingly dull world of contemporary West End theater.

—John Bull

MITCHELL, Ken

Nationality: Canadian. **Born:** Moose Jaw, Saskatchewan, 13 December 1940. **Education:** University of Saskatchewan, 1962-65, B.A. 1965, M.A. 1967. **Family:** Married, five children. **Career:** Reporter, The Leader Post, Regina, Saskatchewan, 1959-60; editor, The Weekly Mirror, Regina, Saskatchewan, 1960; proofreader, Robert Simpson, Toronto, Ontario, 1960-61; miscellaneous trades including work at Wall's, P.B. Cow, and South London Decorating, London, 1961-62; sign painter, Saskatchewan Power Corporation, Regina, Saskatchewan, 1962; copy editor, The Leader Post, Regina, Saskatchewan, 1962-65; publicity writer, Saskatchewan Wheat Pool, Regina, Saskatchewan, 1965. Professor, University of Regina, Saskatchewan, 1967—. Director of Creative Writing, Saskatchewan Summer School of Arts, 1970-75. Visiting professor, University of Victoria, 1975-76; visiting professor, Banff School of Fine Arts, 1977, 1978, 1980; Scottish-Canadian Exchange fellow, University of Edinburgh, 1979-80; Foreign Expert, University of Nanjing, China, 1980-81; Foreign Expert, Foreign Affairs College, Beijing, China, 1986-87. **Awards:** W.P. Thompson Scholarship for academic excellence and student leadership, University of Saskatchewan, 1964; Robinson Memorial Scholarship, University of Saskatchewan, 1965; George William Brown Scholarship, University of Saskatchewan, 1965; First prize, Saskatchewan Arts Board short story competition, 1965; Best Supporting Actor, Dominion Drama Festival, 1970; First prize, National One Act Play competition, University of Regina, 1971; First prize, National Play competition, University of Regina, 1977; finalist, Chalmers award for Best Canadian play, 1978; Yaddo fellow, Yaddo arts Colony, New York, 1978; Arts A Grant, Canada Council, 1982; Founder's award, Saskatchewan Writers Guild, 1984; Best Canadian Play, Canadian Authors Association, 1985; Senior Arts Grant, Saskatchewan Arts Board, 1989; Alumni award for Excellence in Research, University of Regina, 1996. Honorary degree: Centre for Canadian Studies, Chongging, China, 1985. **Agent:** Bella Pomer Agency, 22 Shallmar Boulevard PH2, Toronto, Canada M5N 2Z8. **Address:** 209 Angus Crescent, Regina, Saskatchewan S4T 6N3, Canada.

Publications

Plays

Heroes (produced University of Surrey, England, 1972.) Toronto, Playwrits Co-op, 1973.

Pleasant Street (produced Saskatoon, 1972).

This Train (produced Toronto, 1973). Toronto, Playwrights Co-op, 1973.

Cruel Tears (produced Saskatoon, 1975). Vancouver, Talon Books, 1977.

The Meadowlark Connection. Regina, Piles of Bones, 1975.

Showdown at Sand Valley (produced Regina, 1975).

The Medicine Line (produced 1976).

The Shipbuilder (produced Regina, 1978). Saskatoon, Fifth House, 1990.

Davin: The Politician (produced Regina, 1978). Edmonton, NeWest Press, 1979.

The Great Cultural Revolution, with Michael Taylor (produced Vancouver, 1979). Toronto, Playwrights Canada, 1980.

Chautauqua Girl (produced Vancouver, 1982). Toronto, Playwrights Canada, 1982.

Spirit of Saskatoon, with Michael Taylor (produced Saskatoon, 1982).

Year of the Moose (produced1982).

Genesis, with Douglas Hicton (produced Toronto, 1982).

Laffin' Jack Rivers Show, with Michael Taylor (produced Saskatoon, 1983).

Gone the Burning Sun, with David Liang (produced Guelph, 1984). Toronto, Playwrights Canada, 1985.
The Plainsman (produced Saskatoon, 1985). Regina, Coteau Books, 1992.
Melody Farm (produced Saskatoon, 1987).
Save the Pigs! (produced 1990).
Future Harvest (produced Regina, 1990).
Grey Owl (produced Saskatoon, 1990).
That'll Be the Day (produced Weyburn, 1996).
The Great Electric Revolution (produced Regina, 1996).

Screenplays: *This Train,* 1977; *Striker,* 1977; *The Hounds of Notre Dame,* 1980; *The Shipbuilder,* 1985; *St. Laurent,* 1985; *The Medicine Line,* 1988; *The Giant,* 1988; *The Great Electrical Revolution,* 1989.

Radio Plays: *Sand Valley Centennial,* 1967; *A Very Loving Person,* 1967; *Showdown at Sand Valley,* 1969; *The Medicine Line,* 1970; *The Meadowlark Caper,* 1971; *The Bald Eagle,* 1976; *Cruel Tears,* 1976; *The Shipbuilder,* 1980; *The Promised Land,* 1991; *The Heavenly Kingdom,* 1984; *Going to Kithira,* 1989; *Five Stories of Sinclair Ross,* 1991.

Television Plays: *The Front Line,* 1985, *Ken Mitchell's Moose Jaw,* 1985; *The New Immigrants,* 1989; *Dream Seekers,* 1990-91.

Novels

Wandering Rafferty. Toronto, Macmillan, 1972.
Everybody Gets Something Here. Toronto, Macmillan, 1977.
Horizon. Toronto, Oxford University Press, 1977.
The Con Man. Vancouver, Talon Books, 1979.
Through the Nan Da Gate. Saskatoon, Thistledown Press, 1986.
Witches and Idiots. Maderia Park, Harbour Publishing, 1990.
Rebels in Time. Edmonton, NeWest Press, 1991.
The Stones of Dalai Lama. Toronto, Soho Press and Douglas & McIntyre, 1993.

Other

Sinclair Ross: A Reader's Guide. Moose Jaw, Coteau Books, 1981.
Ken Mitchell Country. Regina, Coteau Books, 1984.

*

Manuscript Collection: University of Regina Archives.

Theatrical Activities:
Actor: **Plays**–Nick in *Who's Afraid of Virginia Woolf,* 1970; Healey in *Roots,* Regina, 1972; Jamie in *Long Days Journey into Night,* Regina, 1975; "The Boos" in *Of Mice and Men,* Ontario, 1984; Bethune in *Gone the Burning Sun,* national tour of Canada, with international performances, 1991-93. **Films**–Narrator in *St. Laurent,* 1985; Larry in *Great Electric Revolution,* 1989; **Radio**–Four Horns in *The Bloodless Battle of White Forehead,* 1970; narrator in *The Great Electric Revolution,* 1980; Caplette in *The Promised Land,* 1980; Bender in *the Shipbuilder,* 1980; narrator in *Ernest Lidner,* 1981; **Television**–Host in *The Moose Jaw,* 1985; host in *The New Immigrants,* 1989; host in *The Dream Seekers,* 1990-91; narrator in *Harvest of Change,* 1992.

Ken Mitchell comments:
(1998) I don't like to analyze my work. It seems to thrive on multi-disciplinary, though I've recently re-focused on narrative fiction–that is, novels. Brecht was an influence (people say) and taking up acting was essential.

* * *

One of Ken Mitchell's most memorable characters is the Chinese playwright Wu Han, the tragic hero in *The Great Cultural Revolution,* a play based on events in China in the 1960s. In Wu Han, Mitchell creates a playwright willing to go to the wall to defend his belief in the power of the word. Mitchell and his character have much in common. Like Wu Han, Mitchell creates plays with a strong political position, and both speak passionately for the political and social values of art. In an introduction to the play, from the collection *Rebels in Time,* Mitchell bemoans a Canada where "Drama has become politically irrelevant, ideas virtually banned. Too many of our playwrights have become political eunuchs, purveying psychobabble and pandering to sentimentality. . . ."

With one notable exception, Mitchell's most important works have been historical tragedies. Whether centered in his home region in southern Saskatchewan, Canada, or looking out into revolutionary China or civil war-torn Spain, each work examines the life of a public figure who, as Mitchell says in his essay "Between the Lines," "chooses to carve his or her life out of the Precambrian rock, rather than proceed along the well-followed path." In a more colorful phrase, he prefers a protagonist who is a "disturber of the excrement." That is, Mitchell focuses on the fate of outsiders or eccentrics in conflict with the institutions, laws, or mindless common sense of the world around them. This individuality, reflected positively in characteristics that could help advance the community or the world, also contains negative traits of arrogance or stubborn pride that make the protagonists tragic targets for the less imaginative and less successful.

Mitchell does not create documentary plays. His sense of the relationship between historical authenticity and dramatic necessity has transformed radically over his career. For example, the earliest published version of *Davin: The Politician* (1979) calls for slides of newspaper headlines, photographs of historical figures, and so on, declaring "Anything which will cement the play to 'historical reality' will enhance dramatic values." Such instructions and intentions are missing from the most recently published version (1991).

Mitchell now seeks the truth of historical character in a more imaginative way, inventing scenes and conversations and experimenting with form. In one of his most popular works, *The Shipbuilder,* he calls his protagonist Jaanus Karhulainen to signify that the character is Mitchell's own exploration of what might lie behind events in the life of the historical original, Tom Sukanen. In *The Plainsman,* a rather sketchy play about Gabriel Dumont and the North West Rebellion of 1885, he invents freely.

The Shipbuilder combines with *Davin: The Politician* and *The Plainsman* as Mitchell's "Great Plains Trilogy." This study of the period of prairie settlement, with its New World-Old World conflicts and clashing utopian visions, clearly contains characteristics of the "settler society" category of postcolonial aesthetics.

Mitchell knows that theater must also entertain. Experiments with form enhance the meaning of an action and the quality of the character, as well as the entertainment value of the works. One early popular success, *Cruel Tears,* is a country music opera cowritten with the Saskatchewan group Humphrey and the Dumptrucks. Although characterization remains rather two-dimensional in this retake on *Othello*, choruses of mimes and of singers support the scenes or comment ironically on the action. Among the history plays form varies widely, from the Chinese opera style of the play-within-the-play of *The Great Cultural Revolution*, to the epic sweep of *Davin: The Politician*, to the 14-scene structure of *Gone the Burning Sun*, his frequently performed piece on the life of Norman Bethune. Mitchell likens this last structure to the Stations of the Cross, but he could equally well subtitle the piece "The Rake's Apotheosis" after Hogarth.

From his collaboration on *Cruel Tears*, Mitchell also learned of the "absolutely fundamental" dimension music brings to theater. Music has continued to play an important part in Mitchell's drama ever since, from the strong percussive background of *The Shipbuilder*, to the Chinese *pipa* accompanying *Gone the Burning Sun*, to the fiddle tunes that figure so prominently in *The Plainsman*.

The one prominent exception to the historical tragedies is *The Great Electrical Revolution*, a Depression-era domestic comedy. The familiar qualities of stubborn resistance to authority are still present, but the tone and resolution in this adaptation of a popular Mitchell short story mark an interesting departure. However, as of this writing it remains to be seen if this represents a momentary shift or the beginning of new phase in Mitchell's playwriting career. Certainly Mitchell's nondramatic works demonstrate a strong comic and satirical bent, and there are fine moments of humor in the historical tragedies, so it would be no surprise to find him writing more comic drama in the future.

—Don Perkins

MITCHELL, Loften

Nationality: American. **Born:** Columbus, North Carolina, 15 April 1919. **Education:** De Witt Clinton High School, Bronx, New York, graduated 1937; City College, New York, 1937-38; Talladega College, Alabama, B.A. in sociology 1943; Columbia University, New York, M.A. 1947-51. **Military Service:** Served in the United States Naval Reserve, 1944-45: seaman second class. **Family:** Married Helen Marsh in 1948; two sons. **Career:** Actor, stage manager, and press agent, 115th Street People's Theatre and Harlem Showcase, New York, 1946-52; social worker, with Gypsy families, 1947-58, and in Day Center Program for Older Persons, 1959-66, Department of Welfare, New York; professor of African-American Studies and Theatre, State University of New York, Binghamton, 1971-85, now professor emeritus. Editor, NAACP *Freedom Journal*, 1964. **Awards:** Guggenheim fellowship, 1958; Rockefeller grant, 1961; Harlem Cultural Council award, 1969; State University of New York Research Foundation award, 1974; Audelco award, 1979. **Address:** 88-45 163rd Street, Jamaica, New York 11432, U.S.A.

PUBLICATIONS

Plays

Shattered Dreams (produced New York, 1938).
Blood in the Night (produced New York, 1946).
The Bancroft Dynasty (produced New York, 1948).
The Cellar (produced New York, 1952).
A Land Beyond the River (produced New York, 1957). Cody, Wyoming, Pioneer Drama Service, 1963.
The Phonograph (produced New York, 1961).
Tell Pharaoh televised 1963; (produced New York, 1967). Published in *The Black Teacher and the Dramatic Arts*, edited by William R. Reardon and Thomas D. Pawley, Westport, Connecticut, Negro Universities Press, 1970.
Ballad for Bimshire, with Irving Burgie (produced New York, 1963; revised version produced Cleveland, 1964).
Ballad of the Winter Soldiers, with John Oliver Killens (produced New York, 1964).
Star of the Morning: Scenes in the Life of Bert Williams (produced Cleveland, 1965; revised version produced New York, 1985). Published in *Black Drama Anthology*, edited by Woodie King and Ron Milner, New York, New American Library, 1971.
The Final Solution to the Black Problem in the United States; or, The Fall of the American Empire (produced New York, 1970).
Sojourn to the South of the Wall (produced 1973; revised version produced 1983).
The Walls Came Tumbling Down, music by Willard Roosevelt (produced New York, 1976).
Bubbling Brown Sugar, concept by Rosetta LeNoire, music by Danny Holgate, Emme Kemp, and Lilian Lopez (produced New York, 1976; London, 1977). New York, Broadway Play Publishing, 1985.
Cartoons for a Lunch Hour, music by Rudy Stevenson (produced New York, 1978).
A Gypsy Girl (produced Pine Bluff, Arkansas, 1982).
Miss Waters, To You, concept by Rosetta LeNoire (produced New York, 1983).

Screenplays: *Young Man of Williamsburg*, 1954; *Integration: Report One*, 1960; *I'm Sorry*, 1965.

Radio Writing: *Tribute to C.C. Spaulding*, 1952; *Friendly Advisor* program, 1955; *The Later Years* program, 1959-62.

Television Plays: *Welfare Services*, 1960s; *Tell Pharaoh*, 1970.

Novel

The Stubborn Old Lady Who Resisted Change. New York, Emerson Hall, 1973.

Other

Black Drama: The Story of the American Negro in the Theatre. New York, Hawthorn, 1967.

Editor, *Voices of the Black Theatre*. Clifton, New Jersey, James T. White, 1975.

*

Manuscript Collections: State University of New York, Binghamton; Boston University; Talladega College, Alabama; Schomburg Collection, New York.

Critical Studies: *Negro Playwrights in the American Theatre 1925-1959* by Doris E. Abramson, New York, Columbia University Press, 1969; article by Ja A. Jahannes, in *Afro-American Writers after 1955* edited by Thadious M. Davis and Trudier Harris, Detroit, Gale, 1985.

Theatrical Activities:
Actor: **Plays**—With the Progressive Dramatizers and the Rose McClendon Players, both New York; Victor in *Cocktails*, and Aaron in *Having Wonderful Time* by Arthur Kober, 1938; Angel in *The Black Messiah* by Dennis Donoghue and James H. Dunmore, 1939.

* * *

For his work as a black theater historian, the American theater owes a great debt to Loften Mitchell. His books—*Black Drama* and *Voices of the Black Theatre*—and numerous essays contain invaluable information and insights on African American contributions. Mitchell's plays reflect his passionate interest in the black theater and in black American history in general. With few exceptions his plays and librettos inform the audience of the tribulations and achievements of well-known black entertainers and historical figures.

Black pride, unity, and perseverance during times of adversity form recurrent themes in Mitchell's plays. These concepts are often voiced in rhetorical discourses by characters drawn along simplistic, ideological lines. His protagonists are based on historical individuals, and they speak and act as though they are already aware of the significance of their achievements to future generations. After the black characters have suffered in conflicts with external forces motivated by racial prejudice and self-interest, the plays end on a triumphant note as the blacks learn how to endure the hardships and, in some cases, prevail over their adversaries.

Tell Pharaoh surveys the history of black Americans; the characters speak of their illustrious African heritage, bitter experiences as slaves, and ongoing struggles for the same civil rights and opportunities enjoyed by white Americans. The drama identifies black American heroes and martyrs and celebrates the contributions of blacks to various aspects of American life. As in most of his works, Mitchell includes a tribute to his beloved Harlem and uses music to set the mood and underscore the sentiments of the play. The concluding harangue against Pharaoh—a symbolic persecutor of blacks, Latins, Asians, Indians, and other groups—dates the work and typifies the rhetoric of the revolutionary activists of the 1960s.

Based on real events, *A Land Beyond the River* depicts the story of a rural black South Carolina community that, through the judicial system, sought the right to send its children to any school receiving public funds. In Mitchell's dramatization a sickly but courageous black woman—Martha Layne—proposes the lawsuit, and her husband—Joseph—rallies the support of other black citizens and a sympathetic white physician. Uncle Toms and white bigots attempt to undermine their efforts. Intimidating threats and the burning of the Layne home aggravate Martha's precarious condition and result in her death. The events create dissension among the blacks and encourage most to accept a local court decision to provide a "separate, but equal" school for blacks. In a stirring speech punctuated with biblical references, however, Joseph contends that black children would not receive parity with whites through the ruling. Instead, he convinces his peers to appeal the case to a higher court in order to achieve their original objective of obtaining equal access to services and facilities enjoyed by white students. Despite the clichés and simplistic characterizations, the drama provides a moving historical portrait of valiant individuals bound by a common cause in the civil rights movement.

A later work—*Miss Waters, To You*—is based on the life of Ethel Waters. A series of scenes with musical numbers depict Waters's transition from a struggling 17-year-old divorcée to an accomplished actress and singer. The play includes appearances by such noted entertainers as Bessie Smith, Lena Horne, Duke Ellington, and Cab Calloway. These blacks provide each other with moral support and teach Waters how to endure the racial prejudice and indignities of their profession. Such scenes, however, weaken the credibility of the play as a true portrait of Waters's life. In fact, her animosity toward black entertainers such as Horne was quite well known. The drama also glosses over certain of Waters's ignoble traits, which would place her in a less exalted light. As in his other tributes to black entertainers—*Bubbling Brown Sugar* and *Star of the Morning: Scenes in the Life of Bert Williams*—Mitchell chose to portray black role models of high esteem with few if any unadmirable attributes.

—Addell Austin Anderson

MOORE, (James) Mavor

Nationality: Canadian. **Born:** Toronto, Ontario, 8 March 1919. **Education:** University of Toronto secondary schools, graduated 1936; University of Toronto, 1936-41 (Leonard Foundation Scholar), B.A. (honours) in philosophy and English 1941. **Military Service:** Served in the Canadian Army Intelligence Corps, 1941-45: captain (psychological warfare). **Family:** Married 1) Darwina Faessler in 1943 (divorced), four daughters; 2) the writer Phyllis Grosskurth in 1969; 3) Alexandra Browning in 1982, one daughter. **Career:** Feature producer, Toronto, 1941-42, chief producer for the International Service, Montreal, 1944-45, and Pacific Region producer, Vancouver, 1945-46, CBC Radio; teacher, Academy of Radio Arts, Toronto, 1946-49; managing producer, New Play Society, Toronto, 1946-50, 1954-57; radio director, 1946-50, and executive television producer, 1954-60, United Nations Information Division, New York; chief producer, 1950-53, and assistant television program director, 1954, CBC Television, Toronto; drama critic, Toronto *Telegram*, 1958-60; stage director, Canadian Opera Company, Toronto, 1959-61, 1963; general director, Confederation Centre, Charlottetown, Prince Edward Island, 1963-65; founder and artistic director, Charlottetown Festival, 1964-67; general director, St. Lawrence Centre for the Arts, Toronto, 1965-70. President, Mavor Moore Productions Ltd., Toronto, 1961—; professor of theatre, York University, Downsview, Ontario, 1970—. **Awards:** Peabody award, 1947, 1949, 1957; Canadian Association of Authors and Artists award, for television writing, 1955; Centennial Medal, 1967. D.Litt.: York University, 1969; LL.D.: Mount Allison University, Sackville, New Brunswick, 1982. Officer, Order of Canada, 1973. **Member:** Executive Committee, 1975, and chair, Canada Council, 1979—. Board of Directors, 1953—, later senator, Stratford Festival, Ontario; chair, Canadian Theatre Centre, 1957-58; governor, National Theatre School, Montreal, 1958—; founding chair, Guild of Canadian Playwrights, 1977. **Agent:** (Canada) Canadian Speakers and Writers Service, 44 Douglas Crescent, Toronto, Ontario; (U.K. and U.S.A.): ACTAC Ltd., 16 Cadogan Lane, London S.W.1, England. **Address:** 176 Moore Avenue, Toronto, Ontario M4T 1V8, Canada.

Publications

Plays

Court Martial, with Earle Birney (broadcast 1946). Published in *Words on Waves: Selected Radio Plays* by Birney, edited by Howard Fink, Kingston, Ontario, Quarry Press, 1985.

Spring Thaw (revue; produced Toronto, 1947 and later versions, 1948-57, 1961-65). Sketch *Togetherness* published in *A Treasury of Canadian Humor*, edited by Robert Thomas Allen, Toronto, McClelland and Stewart, 1967.

Who's Who (also director: produced Toronto, 1949).

The Best of All Possible Worlds, adaptation of the novel *Candide* by Voltaire (broadcast 1952; revised version, as *The Optimist*, broadcast 1954; revised version, as *The Best of All Possible Worlds*, music and lyrics by Moore, produced Toronto, 1956).

The Hero of Mariposa, music and lyrics by Moore, adaptation of *Sunshine Sketches of a Little Town* by Stephen Leacock (broadcast 1953; as *Sunshine Town*, also director: produced Toronto, 1956).

The Ottawa Man, adaptation of a play by Gogol (televised 1958; revised version, also director: produced Toronto, 1961; revised version produced Lennoxville, Quebec, 1972).

Louis Riel (opera libretto), with Jacques Languirand, music by Harry Somers (produced Toronto, 1967; Washington, D.C., 1975).

Yesterday the Children Were Dancing, adaptation of a play by Gratien Gélinas (also co-director: produced Charlottetown, Prince Edward Island, 1967). Toronto, Clarke Irwin, 1969.

Johnny Belinda, lyrics by Moore, musical version of the play by Elmer Harris (produced Charlottetown, Prince Edward Island, 1968).

Getting In (broadcast 1968; as *The Interview*, televised 1973). New York, French, 1972.

The Pile (broadcast 1969). Included in *The Pile, The Store, Inside Out*, 1973.

Man Inc., adaptation of a play by Jacques Languirand (produced Toronto, 1970).

The Argument (broadcast 1970). Published in *Performing Arts in Canada* (Toronto), Winter 1973.

The Store (broadcast 1971). Included in *The Pile, The Store, Inside Out*, 1973.

Inside Out (televised 1971). Included in *The Pile, The Store, Inside Out*, 1973.

Anne of Green Gables (additional lyrics, with Elaine Campbell), book by Donald Harron, music by Norman Campbell, lyrics by Harron and Campbell, adaptation of the novel by L.M. Montgomery (produced Charlottetown, Prince Edward Island, 1971).

Come Away, Come Away (broadcast 1972). Published in *Encounter: Canadian Drama in Four Media*, edited by Eugene Benson, Toronto, Methuen, 1973.

Customs (broadcast 1973). Published in *Cues and Entrances*, edited by Henry Beissel, Toronto, Gage, 1977.

The Pile, The Store, Inside Out. Toronto, Simon and Pierre, 1973.

The Roncarelli Affair, with F.R. Scott (televised 1974). Published in *The Play's the Thing*, edited by Tony Gifford, Toronto, Macmillan, 1976.

Abracadabra, music by Harry Freedman (produced Courtenay, British Columbia, 1979).

Love and Politics, music and lyrics by Moore, adaptation of the play *The Fair Grit* by Nicholas Flood Davin (produced St. Catherines, Ontario, 1979).

Fauntleroy, music and lyrics by Johnny Burke, adaptation of the novel *Little Lord Fauntleroy* by Frances Hodgson Burnett (produced Charlottetown, Prince Edward Island, 1980).

A Christmas Carol, musical (produced Vancouver, 1988). Woodstock, Illinois, Dramatic Publishing, 1996.

Six Plays by Mavor Moore. Vancouver, Talon Books, 1989.

Radio Plays: more than 100 plays, including *Court Martial*, with Earle Birney, 1946; *The Best of All Possible Worlds*, 1952 (revised as *The Optimist*, 1954); *The Hero of Mariposa*, 1953; *Fast Forward*, 1968; *Getting In*, 1968; *The Pile*, 1969; *The Argument*, 1970; *The Store*, 1971; *A Matter of Timing*, 1971; *Come Away, Come Away*, 1972; *Customs*, 1973 (USA); *Time Frame*, 1974; *Freak*, 1975.

Television Plays: more than 50 plays, including *Catch a Falling Star*, 1957; *The Ottawa Man*, 1958; *The Well*, 1961; *The Man Born to Be King*, 1961; *The Man Who Caught Bullets*, 1962; *Mary of Scotland*, 1966; *Inside Out*, 1971; *The Interview*, 1973; *The Roncarelli Affair*, with F.R. Scott, 1974.

Poetry

And What Do You Do? A Short Guide to the Trades and Professions. Toronto and London, Dent, 1960.

Other

4 Canadian Playwrights: Robertson Davies, Gratien Gélinas, James Reaney, George Ryga. Toronto, Holt Rinehart, 1973.

Slipping on the Verge: The Performing Arts in Canada with Theatre as a Case Study. Washington, D.C., Canadian Embassy, 1983.

Reinventing Myself (memoirs). Toronto, Stoddart Publishing, 1994.

Editor, *The Awkward Stage: The Ontario Theatre Study*. Toronto, Methuen, 1969.

Editor, *An Anthology of Canadian Plays*. Toronto, New Press, 1973.

*

Theatrical Activities:
Director: **Plays**—*King Lear*, Toronto, 1948; *Heartbreak House* by Shaw, Toronto, 1948; *The Circle* by W. Somerset Maugham, Toronto, 1948; *The Government Inspector* by Gogol, Toronto, 1948; *Who's Who*, Toronto, 1949; *Macbeth*, Toronto, 1949; *The Tempest*, Toronto, 1949; *Sunshine Town*, Toronto, 1956; *The Ottawa Man*, Toronto, 1961, Charlottetown, Prince Edward Island, 1966; *The Fourposter* by Jan de Hartog, Halifax, Nova Scotia, 1963; *Dial M for Murder* by Frederick Knott, Halifax, 1963; *Floradora*, Vancouver, 1964; *Julius Caesar*, Vancouver, 1964; *An Evening with Wayne and Shuster*, Charlottetown, 1965; *Laugh with Leacock*, Charlottetown, 1965; *Yesterday the Children Were Dancing* (co-director), Charlottetown, 1967. **Television and Radio**—Productions for CBC, United Nations (New York), CBS and NBC (USA).

Actor: **Plays**—Roles with the New Play Society, Toronto, the Crest Theatre, the Charlottetown and Vancouver Festivals, and other theatre companies, including title role in *King Lear*, Toronto, 1948, 1963; title role in *Riel*, Toronto, 1948; Escalus in *Measure for Measure*, Stratford, Ontario, 1954; Caesar in *Caesar and Cleopatra* by Shaw, Toronto and Vancouver, 1962; Undershaft in *Major Barbara* by Shaw, Halifax, 1963. **Television**—Starring roles in numerous Canadian drama series. **Radio**—Roles in numerous CBC productions, CBS and NBC (USA), etc.

* * *

Mavor Moore is Canada's most ubiquitous man-about-theater. He has had great success as actor, producer, director, festival impresario, and theater administrator. His position as a professor of theater at York University in Toronto has given him a period of relative calm to concentrate on writing. For most of his career as a playwright for the stage, he has mainly adapted the work of other writers, very often for his own direction. He has also worked as a librettist in cooperation with composers and cowriters.

In the area of musical drama Moore created a lively version of Mariposa, that sleepy little town that Stephen Leacock wrote about in *Sunshine Sketches*. In *Sunshine Town* Moore wrote a book, music, and lyrics that had the right period feeling, and it has had several revivals.

On another occasion, for his Charlottetown Festival, he wrote a musical version of *Johnny Belinda* based on the Broadway play by Elmer Harris. Again, the quality of the writing and the success of his director, Alan Lund, made even the story of a deaf-mute who is raped a good and satisfying musical.

Louis Riel is an opera rather than a musical. With a score composed by Harry Somers, it was a notable addition to the Canadian Opera Company's repertoire for the centennial year of 1967. Moore went to history—Riel is a key figure in the French-English debate that still is a central part of Canada's polity—and managed to create a full-blooded set of characters, even though from time to time the dialogue is more operatic than dramatic. Generally, however, Moore's greatest gift as a dramatist is his skill in dialogue, perhaps because he has written so much for radio, a purely verbal medium.

Moore's best-known play is *The Ottawa Man*, an adaptation of Gogol's *The Government Inspector*. Only Moore's talent for dialogue could have made it the success it is, for the central situation, which is firmly rooted in the official corruption of czarist Russia, cannot be easily transplanted to the relative honesty of nineteenth-century pioneer Manitoba. But the fact is that one does not question this while the play is being acted, nor is one too aware of the fact that the characters are all stereotypes rather than people. What one is aware of is the farcical encounter between two Irishmen, a French-Canadian Catholic, a German immigrant, and an English remittance man, all of whom speak in an uncannily accurate style and accent.

Moore has written several one-act plays, mainly for radio and television. Character is not important in them, but ideas and verbal play on those ideas are. In fact, so little character is necessary for embodying the ideas that in some of the plays none of the characters has a name. In *Come Away, Come Away*, which is about an old man facing death and a little girl fascinated by the encounter, the characters are Old Man and Little Girl; in *The Pile*, a fable about modern business and ecology, the characters are X and Y; and in *Getting In*, a play with a truly strange resonance, P is the official and T is an applicant.

Perhaps the most significant of these plays is *The Argument*, which, through its dialogue alone, establishes characters who are identified only as M—a man—and W—a woman. But their dialogue, their argument, creates an interaction that convinces one that Moore is capable of writing longer and more solid work.

—Arnold Edinborough

MORNIN, Daniel

Nationality: British. **Born:** Belfast, 10 January 1956. **Education:** Orangefield Primary School, 1961-67, and Orangefield Secondary, 1967-71, both Belfast. **Military Service:** Served in the Royal Navy as ordinary seaman, 1974-77. **Family:** Married Aine Beegan in 1991; one son. **Agent:** Judy Daish, Judy Daish Associates, 2 St. Charles Place, Ladbroke Grove, London W10 6EC, England.

Publications

Plays

Mum and Son (produced London, 1981).
Kate (produced London, 1983).
Getting Out (as *Short of Mutiny*; produced London, 1983).
Comrade Ogilvy (produced London, 1984).
By the Border (produced London, 1985).
The Murderers (produced London, 1985).
Built on Sand (produced London, 1987).
Weights and Measures (produced London, 1987).
At Our Table (produced London, 1991).

Screenplay: *Nothing Personal*, 1996.

Television Play: *Border Country*, 1991.

Novel

All Our Fault. London, Hutchinson, 1991.

Other

Translator, *Muller's Dancers*, by Akos Nemeth. In *Hungarian Plays*, London, Nick Hern Books, 1996.

*

Daniel Mornin comments:

(1998) I seem to be attracted to themes that are (I hope) longer lasting than they are fashionable. This means that I am poor, but happy with my work. I like to work "between the lines" and feel that this approach provokes thought and excites curiosity so that the piece remains with the audience a bit longer than the time they have sat and watched it. Unfortunately I am attracted to a "Greek" view of human nature (that is, non-sentimental), and this has often meant that my characters are a little too honestly drawn for commercial theater. Recently I have become very interested in "Godless" morality, a fictive morality of the head, as opposed to handed down thou-shall-nots.

* * *

Daniel Mornin's plays are often seen as a direct response to the effects and influences of being raised in Belfast during "the Troubles." But the centrality of violence in much of his work suggests in its treatment that the author regards violence as part of a generic rather than local condition. His professional debut, *Mum and Son*, documents an oppressive relationship between a dutiful son and a predatory mother against a background of mystery surrounding the boy's father. This mystery is further intensified firstly in the presentation and subsequently in the rebuttal of apparently incontrovertible facts about the father.

Mornin's method—consistently to rework themes and situations until the possibilities inherent in them have been exhausted—suggests that he is challenged by the technical requirement to deliver a formal structure that matches the brilliance of his dialogue. This is illustrated—structurally and thematically—in his one-act play *By the Border*: regarding structure, he uses a "delaying" device that takes the form of a character who remains choric-like and silent on stage for the larger part of the play; Mornin's thematic concern is manifest in his use of the brother-sister motif that over the span of his plays is progressively understood consciously to exploit the relevance of Greek tragedy for the contemporary stage. The brother/sister theme is dramatized initially in *Kate* as a focused, painfully exact study of an incestuous relationship between the offspring of a "mixed" marriage. At the other end of the spectrum his play *At Our Table* attempts to reconcile the distinctions between modern and classical Greek theater. As in *By the Border* the characters in *At Our Table* grow in scale and significance throughout the play, a structural device delaying the revelation that will confirm the full horror of the apparently ordinary domestic situation.

Notwithstanding his obsession with particular themes, virtually all of Mornin's plays underpin his ongoing interest in experimentation. *Weights and Measures* is a striking example of the extent to which he will go to balance thematic interest against technical development. Based on the life of the serial killer Denis Nilssen, *Weights and Measures* is set in a house stratified to reveal activities played out on various levels. In the upper part of the house there are scenes between a "yuppie" and the two women who in the course of the play spiritually destroy him. In the lower level the Nilssen figure enacts a number of brilliant scenes with an actor appearing in various guises as different people. The play, however, is caught between the theoretical compactness of its formal symmetry and the practical problems of reconciling an audience to a rigid division of stage space across scenes of widely different dramatic interest.

Weights and Measures, however, is a pivotal play for Mornin, who with it was consciously working to consolidate his practical skill as a writer of gripping dialogue while seeking to develop a paradigm for expanding his imaginative repertoire. To this purpose *Built on Sand* is set on the island of Crete. As a reworking of *The Murderers*, though, it is lacking in the authority of the earlier play. *The Murderers,* in fact, is generally regarded as one of his best plays, a dramatic counterpoint to Martin Dillon's account of "The Shankill Butchers," a group of Protestant paramilitaries who achieved notoriety in the 1970s through a series of indiscriminate and bestial murders. The play's formal achievement is to extend the play's climax to an unbearable pitch. It anatomizes the psyche of working-class men, not undifferentiated but as a complex of interdependent relationships initiated in blood and secured by tribal fealty. *The Murderers* characteristically exemplifies Mornin's ability to sustain tension between character and action in a way that is profoundly shocking.

If in doing this *The Murderers* illustrates Mornin's skill in dramatizing homophile relationships, his work cannot be described as narrowly homoerotic and homosexual. Rather it gives an extraordinary insight into men's secretive and interdependent rituals. *Short of Mutiny*, set mainly below decks of a Royal Navy destroyer, is a custom-made context for this theme. Mornin dramatizes a situation in which predominantly young seamen work to discharge themselves dishonorably from the service so as to avoid paying themselves "out." Set against them, the ship's officers, aware of and circumscribed by the stratagem, cannily avoid confrontation. *Short of Mutiny*'s large cast is an indication of Mornin's primary interest in "pure drama." In later plays he subsequently writes more practically for smaller casts.

Mornin is hardly a prolific writer, though the quality of his work is highly regarded. He also writes for radio and television, and his first novel, *All Our Fault*, was screened as *Nothing Personal,* directed by Thaddeus O'Sullivan. Thematically it reworks material from *The Murderers*, which from Mornin's perspective gives rise to an absorbing question: if the political process underway in Ireland brings a "peace dividend," in what way will Mornin reconstruct himself?

—Paul Hadfield

MORRISON, Bill

Nationality: Irish. **Born:** Ballymoney, County Antrim, Northern Ireland, 22 January 1940. **Education:** Dalriada Grammar School, Ballymoney, 1951-58; Queen's University, Belfast, 1958-62, LL.B. (honours) 1962. **Family:** Married Valerie Lilley in 1968 (divorced 1986). **Career:** Actor in Belfast, Dublin, and London, from 1963; resident writer, Victoria Theatre, Stoke-on-Trent, Staffordshire, 1969-71; radio drama producer, BBC, Belfast, 1975-76; resident writer, Everyman Theatre, 1977-78, lecturer in creative writing, C.F. Mott College, 1977-78, drama producer, Radio City, 1979-81, and associate director, 1981-83, and artistic director, 1983-85, Playhouse Theatre, all Liverpool. Board member, Merseyside Young People's Theatre, Liverpool, 1978—; board member, Playhouse Theatre, 1981—; chair, Merseyside Arts Drama Panel, 1985—. **Awards:** Ford Foundation grant, 1972; Arts Council bursary, 1975; Pye award, for radio feature, 1981. **Member:** Writers' Guild of Great Britain. **Agent:** Michael Imison Playwrights, 28 Almeida Street, London N1 1TD, England.

Publications

Plays

Love and a Bottle, adaptation of the play by George Farquhar (produced Dublin, 1966; Nottingham, 1969).

Laugh But Listen Well (produced Dublin, 1967).

Conn and the Conquerors of Space (for children; also director: produced Falmer, Sussex, 1969; London, 1971).

Please Don't Shoot Me When I'm Down (produced Manchester, 1969; London, 1972).

Jupiter-5 (for children; produced Stoke-on-Trent, 1970; London, 1971).

Aladdin and His Magic Lamp (for children; also director: produced Stoke-on-Trent, 1971).
Tess of the d'Urbervilles, adaptation of the novel by Hardy (produced Stoke-on-Trent, 1971). London, Macmillan, 1980.
Sam Slade Is Missing (broadcast 1971; produced Derby, 1972; London, 1974). Published in *The Best Short Plays 1973*, edited by Stanley Richards, Radnor, Pennsylvania, Chilton, 1973.
The Time Travellers (for children; produced Stoke-on-Trent, 1971).
Patrick's Day (produced New Haven, Connecticut, 1972).
The Love of Lady Margaret (broadcast 1972; produced London, 1973).
Ellen Cassidy (broadcast 1974; produced Liverpool, 1978).
The Emperor of Ice-Cream, adaptation of the novel by Brian Moore (broadcast 1975; produced Dublin, 1977).
The Irish Immigrants Tale (produced Liverpool, 1976).
Flying Blind (produced Liverpool, 1977; London, 1978; New York, 1979). London, Faber, 1978.
Time on Our Hands (produced Belfast, 1979).
Dr. Jekyll of Rodney Street (produced Liverpool, 1979).
Scrap! (produced Liverpool, 1982; London, 1985).
Cavern of Dreams, with Carol Ann Duffy (produced Liverpool, 1984).
Run, Run, Runaway (for children; produced Liverpool and London, 1986).
Be Bop a Lula (musical; produced Liverpool, 1988).
The Little Sister, adaptation of the novel by Raymond Chandler (produced Plymouth and Liverpool, 1990).
A Love Song for Ulster (a trilogy of plays; produced London, 1993). London, Nick Hern Books, 1994.
Drive On (produced Belfast, 1996).

Radio Plays: *Sam Slade Is Missing*, 1971; *The Love of Lady Margaret*, 1972; *The Great Gun-Running Episode*, 1974; *Ellen Cassidy*, 1974; *Crime and Punishment*, from a novel by Dostoevsky, 1975; *Crow's Flight*, from a play by Dimitri Kehaidis, 1975; *The Emperor of Ice-Cream*, 1975; *Simpson and Son*, 1977; *The Big Sleep*, *The High Window*, *The Lady in the Lake*, *The Little Sister*, and *The Long Goodbye*, all from the novels by Raymond Chandler, 1977; *Maguire*, 1979; *The Spring of Memory* (feature), 1981; *Blues in A-Flat*, 1989; *Farewell My Lovely,* from the novel by Raymond Chandler, 1990; *Waiting for Lefty,* from the play by Clifford Odets, 1994; *Affair,* 1991; *Murder at the Cameo,* 1996.

Television Plays: *McKinley and Sarah*, 1973; *Joggers*, 1978; *Potatohead Blues*, 1982; *Shergar*, 1986; *A Safe House*, 1990; *Force of Duty,* 1992.

*

Theatrical Activities:
Director: **Plays**—*On Approval* by Frederick Lonsdale, Dublin, 1967; *The Lion in Winter* by James Goldman, London, 1969; *Two Gentlemen of Verona*, London, 1969; *Conn and the Conquerors of Space*, Falmer, Sussex, 1969; *Aladdin and His Magic Lamp*, Stoke-on-Trent, 1971; Playhouse Theatre, Liverpool: *A Doll's House* by Ibsen, *Ladies in Waiting* by Ellen Fox, *These Men* by Mayo Simon, *Skirmishes* by Catherine Hayes, *Walking on Walter* by Claire Luckham, *A Lesson from Aloes* by Athol Fugard, *I Want* by Nell Dunn and Adrian Henri, *Breezeblock Park* by Willy Russell, *Alfie* by Bill Naughton, *Cavern of Dreams*, and *The Divvies Are Coming* by Eddie Braben, 1981-85; *The Beastly Beatitudes of Balthazar B* by J.P. Donleavy, London, 1983.

Actor: **Plays**—Roles at Arts Theatre, Belfast, and with Ulster Theatre Company, 1963-65; Nick in *Who's Afraid of Virginia Woolf?* by Edward Albee, Dublin, 1966; Barney Muldoon in *Illuminatus!* by Robert Anton Wilson, Liverpool, 1978. **Film**—*Sinful Davey*, 1969.

Bill Morrison comments:

(1982) I was born in Ireland but I was born in the British part of it. I was born during a war and have lived in the shadow of war since. I am more an Ulster writer than an Irish one. My language has the particular rhythms of that place, my characters and subjects are violently shaped by it, my use of comedy is dictated by it. I write in order to try to make sense of what happens to me and what I see around me and I hope by that to make a record of how people felt and lived in a particular time and place, which I take to be the job of the writer in any society.

I also write for an audience. I am proud of the fact that my work has been performed in twelve countries. The excitement and persistence of theatre is that it is the form which depends on the creative participation of the audience to complete it. The audience always affects and often profoundly alters the quality of the artistic event. To me the theatre is a laboratory of human communication, a place of constant experiment. The glory of the nature of it is that it has to be on the human scale. Technology does change and improve but it barely affects the essential experience. Writing for radio, TV, or film is rewarding because of the audience it reaches but it is not the same. Theatre is the only human activity I have found which embraces and needs all levels of skill and talent in its making and where, despite all its internal conflicts, the need and advantage of cooperating always wins. The event is always greater than the individual. It is always communal.

That is how it should be. It is why I now run a theatre with other writers. However, I regret the fact that, apart from a community tour of a show *Time on Our Hands* which I devised with a company, my work remains unperformed in Northern Ireland.

(1988) The purpose of the writer in society is to record how people feel about the time they live in and the events in it. I try to make sense of what I feel and see around me, and mostly fail—which is why I write comedy and farce. The story of my time is the story of murder exposed as farce.

(1998) I have finally been performed in Ulster, *Drive On* at the Lyric, Belfast in 1996, a memory play.

My cautious optimism about my country's future is reflected in the trilogy of plays, *A Love Song for Ulster,* which portrays the complete history. It is as definitive as I can get. Perhaps we can all move on now from violence.

* * *

Following up his own proposition that since 1969 "the trouble with being an Ulster playwright has been trouble," Bill Morrison wrote in 1977, "the best of my work, or at least the most important to me, has been about my country and the people who try to survive in it. The plays have been about my struggle to understand the disease in my society which caused its intense, unbearably prolonged and homicidal breakdown. But they have also been about my struggle to find a form which would encompass it." This comment conveniently suggests the characteristics that give Morrison's drama its force: his exploration of the problematic relation between cultural and personal spheres in the Ulster context and the formal experimentation from play to play that such an exploration necessarily entails. Moreover, in a writer who believes, as Morrison does, that "the theatre is ultimately the only way of fully discovering oneself," the "struggle to find a form" makes itself felt as a moral as well as an artistic imperative.

The struggle was complicated for Morrison in the early 1970s by the lack of sympathy he encountered in theater (and television) for his exploratory treatment of the Ulster situation. Finding an outlet instead in radio, he experimented with the use of stereo in adaptations (notably *Crime and Punishment*). In his first original radio play, *The Love of Lady Margaret*, he also satisfyingly exploited the potential of the medium for narrative ambiguity in the rendering of an isolated consciousness and its labyrinth of ultimately self-thwarting fictions.

The aptness of the radio medium to the playwright's concerns is powerfully (though perhaps not consistently) apparent in *Ellen Cassidy*—a later stage version of which the author considers to have been unsatisfactory. Here the troubled consciousness belongs to the 34-year-old Armagh-born Protestant Ellen. Now in London, estranged from yet still haunted by her Irish husband, and awaiting the arrival of her young lover, she engages with the constraints and outcomes of an Ulster upbringing in a fluid series of recollections, reflective monologues, and flashbacks. The writing is often richly imaged; at the heart of the play is the symbolic opposition of blood—the issue of menstruation, sexual and sectarian violence, the pulsing badge of cultural belonging, something inside the self and controlling it—and water, an element outside the self that for Ellen promises cool, free-floating identity. As a woman, Ellen has experienced in both her upbringing and her relationships the stifling cultural consequences of the evolutionary determinism expatiated upon by her older lover, the biologist Gorman. When it becomes clear that the men in her life are, in their different ways, all pathetically enslaved by their cultural conditioning and its "stories," she finally proclaims her independence of all three and of "the old old days of pain": "My name is Ellen Cassidy and I live all alone."

Because of—or perhaps despite—the lyrical power of its monologues, *Ellen Cassidy* cannot help but bring to mind Morrison's admission that at this time he was "using plays as a form of psychoanalysis." *Flying Blind* signals a breakthrough for Morrison in its achievement of a decisively impersonal form for the articulation of his characteristic preoccupations. The brooding and often painful energies of *Ellen Cassidy* are here gathered, shaped, and endowed with a bitter comic trajectory by the crisp dialogue and coolly contrived sudden mayhem of farce. The result is, as one critic has put it, "a world where the laws of farce and tragedy are interchangeable."

The increasingly fevered comings and goings of *Flying Blind* take place in and around the "imaginatively furnished" living room of an Ulster medical representative, Dan Poots, a supplier of "happy pills" who has dedicated himself to survival in an environment he considers to be in the grip of a "perversion of the spirit." He retreats between stereo headphones, listening to the music of his hero, Charlie "Bird" Parker, who "found the terms of membership unacceptable"—as Dan now does. Even before the darkly funny (and, for him, bladder-stretching) incursions of two groups of terrorists—a Protestant murder-squad and vengeful Catholics—Dan's strategy for survival is seriously disturbed by the demands of his concerned wife Liz and by her old flame Michael. A sociologist, Michael has returned to his native Ulster, laden with simplistic sociopolitical solutions and a desperation born of childlessness, determined to "save" Liz (or, failing that, her babysitter). Meanwhile, the lawyer Boyd, recently forced out of politics by terrorist death threats, is alarmed to find his sexual impulses arising only in the revolver he brandishes—and even that fails to go off at the climactic moment. In fact sex, that generic stipulation of farce, is here ingeniously invested with a pivotal diagnostic function. The pathetic impotence of the men in the play is symptomatic of a diseased society in which, as Dan realizes, potency exists not in sexual relationships but in the self-destructive violence of history's "blind men," the terrorists. Hence the moral force behind the farce when Dan and his generous (though unfulfilled) neighbor Bertha confront imminent death by undressing to make love right in front of the panic-stricken terrorists who are threatening them. In the end a fatal mêlée (graced by a bucket of piss and a purblind terrorist called Magoo) disrupts the reconciliation of friends and neighbors, and happy ending gives way to familiar stalemate.

Following the success of *Flying Blind* and after a group of Raymond Chandler adaptations for radio, Morrison worked on radio scripts in the United States and on a number of British television projects, most of them either abortive or disappointing. His last important stage play before his spell as director at the Liverpool Playhouse (1981-1985) was *Scrap!* Here again farce is the formal basis, but the action is rather less riotous than in *Flying Blind*, and there are interwoven elements of the thriller mode—or even of the whodunnit.

Scrap! is centrally concerned with betrayal—personal, cultural, and political. The high-ranking English policeman Cleaver (a.k.a. Butcher) aims "to solve the problems of a whole country" by an appeal to what he considers to be the "eternal verities": "bribery, blackmail, and betrayal." His plan is to lure the key Protestant terrorist organizer Sidney Mulligan out of Belfast to Liverpool and to deliver him over to the Catholic terrorist leader Madigan as part of a deal involving the military-strategic cooperation with Britain of a prospective nonneutral "new" united Ireland. To this end Cleaver brings over to Liverpool Mulligan's schoolgirl daughter Kate, who has gone to the police with her father's operational notebooks in her possession. Kate, ironically, is glad to escape Belfast and with it the childhood innocence that makes her a potential blood sacrifice on the altar of Ulster's history, yet at the same time she is torn at the prospect of betraying her father and all that he stands for. She manages to deposit the vital documents with his cousin, the English scrap-dealer Tommy Atkins (who is unaware of the fact). When Mulligan himself arrives in Liverpool, impelled less by his concern for the notebooks than by the desperation and "black pain" he feels at the disappearance of the child in whose innocence he invests all his surviving values, he is drawn into a deadly, yet also farcical, pattern of intrigue and betrayal. The plainly allegorical design of the play is reinforced by the coordination of symbolic structure and setting: the mirror-lined basement bar of the second half realizes visually the darkly oppressive phantom world of Ulster history, which shuts out the "sweet daylight" of freedom and reduces the Protestants to the contorted scrap of Britain. At the climax Cleaver's underhanded plans go grotesquely wrong. The powerful Protestant Mulligan, having wrapped himself in a waistcoat of dynamite and lit the fuse, grasps the disarmed Catholic Madigan under one arm and the crooked Englishman Cleaver under the other as he asks: "which among us deserves to be saved?" This final stage image crystallizes the deadlock Morrison has always sought to confront and to understand through his drama, in the belief that such understanding would also constitute a kind of self-discovery.

A further strand of Morrison's work is constituted by his imaginative realizations of "true stories" that are in some way enigmatic or remarkable. Into this category fall the television films *Shergar* (about the kidnap of the racehorse) and *A Safe House* (about the Maguire case) and the stage play *Be Bop a Lula.* Based on research by Spencer Leigh, *Be Bop a Lula* tells the story of rock and rollers Gene Vincent and Eddie Cochran on their 1960 British tour, during which the latter died in a car crash. The narrative, woven around no less than 30 songs (performed live), concentrates on the relationship between the broodingly violent and self-destructive Vincent, with his crippled leg and black leathers, and the fresh but fated Cochran. Cochran is the rising star, but the final image of the play is of the already fading Vincent sitting on his friend's coffin. The play is a kind of requiem, a contribution to (pre-Beatles) rock mythology rather than an exploration of it. "Great drama it isn't," wrote one reviewer, "but it is good rock and roll."

Morrison's major work of the 1990s was the "Irish Trilogy," *A Love Song for Ulster* (comprising *The Marriage, The Son,* and *The Daughter*). Northern Ireland, from partition through the various phases of the Troubles, is allegorized as "a house set in a landscape, the ownership of which is constantly in dispute." The allegory is sustained to a remarkable degree: events and relationships presented as familial and domestic invite identification with specific historical equivalents throughout. The effect is resourceful and intermittently witty but ultimately unrelenting, and although the savagery of the playwright's stylization fits with the inevitable savagery of much of the action, necessary psychological development is often uncomfortably elliptical. Partition is imaged as an arranged marriage across the sectarian divide. From 1922 to 1992 three generations of the heroic, ordinary people of the house of Ulster are beset, corrupted, and crazed by the "orchestrators of discord"—priests and preachers, bigots and gangsters, in-laws and chancers, soldiers and murderers—until the dominant idea of filicide as necessary sacrifice is made horribly actual by the killing of a baby in its cradle. Forgetting and mutual trust are recognized (largely by the women) as the ways out of this "constant prison" of the past, but if one kind of love is the solution, another kind—"love of land"—is revealed to be the original and continuing problem.

—Paul Lawley

MORTIMER, John (Clifford)

Nationality: British. **Born:** Hampstead, London, 21 April 1923. **Education:** Harrow School, Middlesex, 1937-40; Brasenose College, Oxford, 1940-42, B.A. 1947; called to the bar, 1948; Queen's Counsel, 1966; Master of the Bench, Inner Temple, 1975. **Military Service:** Served with the Crown Film Units as scriptwriter during World War II. **Family:** Married 1) Penelope Dimont in 1949 (divorced 1971), one son and one daughter; 2) Penny Gollop in 1972, two daughters. **Career:** Drama critic, *New Statesman, Evening Standard,* and *Observer,* 1972, all London; member of the National Theatre Board, 1968-88; president, Berkshire, Buckinghamshire, and Oxford Naturalists' Trust, 1984—; chair, League of Dramatists; chair of the council, Royal Society of Literature, 1989—; chair, Royal Court Theatre, 1990—; president, Howard League for Penal Reform, 1992—. Lives in Henley-on-Thames, Oxfordshire. **Awards:** Italia prize, for radio play, 1958; Screenwriters Guild award, for television play, 1970; BAFTA award, for television series, 1980; *Yorkshire Post* award, 1983. D. Litt.: Susquehanna University, Selinsgrove, Pennsylvania, 1985; University of St. Andrews, Fife, 1987; University of Nottingham, 1989; Lifetime Achievement award, BANF festival, 1998. LL.D.: Exeter University, 1986. C.B.E. (Commander, Order of the British Empire), 1986. **Agent:** Peters, Fraser, and Dunlop Group, 503-504 The Chambers, Chelsea Harbour, Lots Road, London SW10 0XF, England.

Publications

Plays

The Dock Brief (broadcast 1957; produced London, 1958; New York, 1961). In *Three Plays,* 1958.

I Spy (broadcast 1957; produced Salisbury, Wiltshire, and Palm Beach, Florida, 1959). In *Three Plays,* 1958.

What Shall We Tell Caroline? (produced London, 1958; New York, 1961). In *Three Plays,* 1958.

Three Plays: The Dock Brief, What Shall We Tell Caroline?, I Spy. London, Elek, 1958; New York, Grove Press, 1962.

Call Me a Liar (televised 1958; produced London, 1968). In *Lunch Hour and Other Plays,* 1960; in *The Television Playwright: Ten Plays for B.B.C. Television,* edited by Michael Barry, New York, Hill and Wang, 1960.

Sketches in *One to Another* (produced London, 1959). London, French, 1960.

The Wrong Side of the Park (produced London, 1960). London, Heinemann, 1960.

Lunch Hour (broadcast 1960; produced Salisbury, Wiltshire, 1960; London, 1961; New York, 1977). In *Lunch Hour and Other Plays,* 1960; published separately, New York, French, 1961.

David and Broccoli (televised 1960). In *Lunch Hour and Other Plays,* 1960.

Lunch Hour and Other Plays (includes *Collect Your Hand Baggage, David and Broccoli, Call Me a Liar*). London, Methuen, 1960.

Collect Your Hand Baggage (produced Wuppertal, Germany, 1963). In *Lunch Hour and Other Plays,* 1960.

Sketches in *One over the Eight* (produced London, 1961).

Two Stars for Comfort (produced London, 1962). London, Methuen, 1962.

A Voyage round My Father (broadcast 1963; produced London, 1970). London, Methuen, 1971.

Sketches in *Changing Gear* (produced Nottingham, 1965).

A Flea in Her Ear, adaptation of a play by Feydeau (produced London, 1966; Tucson, Arizona, 1979). London and New York, French, 1967.

A Choice of Kings (televised 1966). In *Playbill Three,* edited by Alan Durband, London, Hutchinson, 1969.

The Judge (produced London, 1967). London, Methuen, 1967.

Desmond (televised 1968). In *The Best Short Plays 1971,* edited by Stanley Richards, Philadelphia, Chilton, 1971.

Cat among the Pigeons, adaptation of a play by Feydeau (produced London, 1969; Milwaukee, 1971). New York, French, 1970.
Come As You Are: Four Short Plays (includes *Mill Hill, Bermondsey, Gloucester Road, Marble Arch*) (produced London, 1970). London, Methuen, 1971.
Five Plays (includes *The Dock Brief, What Shall We Tell Caroline?, I Spy, Lunch Hour, Collect Your Hand Baggage*). London, Methuen, 1970.
The Captain of Köpenick, adaptation of a play by Carl Zuckmayer (produced London, 1971). London, Methuen, 1971.
Conflicts, with others (produced London, 1971).
I, Claudius, adaptation of the novels *I, Claudius* and *Claudius the God* by Robert Graves (produced London, 1972).
Knightsbridge (televised 1972). London, French, 1973.
Collaborators (produced London, 1973). London, Eyre Methuen, 1973.
The Fear of Heaven (as *Mr. Lucy's Fear of Heaven*, broadcast 1976; as *The Fear of Heaven*, produced with *The Prince of Darkness* as *Heaven and Hell*, London, 1976). London, French, 1978.
Heaven and Hell (includes *The Fear of Heaven* and *The Prince of Darkness*) (produced London, 1976; revised version of *The Prince of Darkness*, as *The Bells of Hell* produced Richmond, Surrey, and London, 1977). *The Bells of Hell* published London, French, 1978.
The Lady from Maxim's, adaptation of a play by Feydeau (produced London, 1977). London, Heinemann, 1977.
John Mortimer's Casebook (includes *The Dock Brief, The Prince of Darkness, Interlude*) (produced London, 1982).
When That I Was (produced Ottawa, 1982).
Edwin (broadcast 1982). In *Edwin and Other Plays*, 1984.
A Little Hotel on the Side, adaptation of a play by Feydeau and Maurice Desvalliers (produced London, 1984). In *Three Boulevard Farces*, 1985.
Edwin and Other Plays (includes *Bermondsey, Marble Arch, The Fear of Heaven, The Prince of Darkness*). London, Penguin, 1984.
Three Boulevard Farces (includes *A Little Hotel on the Side, A Flea in Her Ear, The Lady from Maxim's*). London, Penguin, 1985.
Die Fledermaus, adaptation of the libretto by Henri Meilhac and Ludovic Halévy, music by Johann Strauss (produced London, 1989). London, Viking, 1989.
A Christmas Carol, adaptation (produced 1994).

Screenplays: *Ferry to Hong Kong*, with Lewis Gilbert and Vernon Harris, 1959; *The Innocents*, with Truman Capote and William Archibald, 1961; *Guns of Darkness*, 1962; *I Thank a Fool*, with others, 1962; *Lunch Hour*, 1962; *The Running Man*, 1963; *Bunny Lake Is Missing*, with Penelope Mortimer, 1964; *A Flea in Her Ear*, 1967; *John and Mary*, 1969.

Radio Plays: *Like Men Betrayed*, 1955; *No Hero*, 1955; *The Dock Brief*, 1957; *I Spy*, 1957; *Three Winters*, 1958; *Lunch Hour*, 1960; *The Encyclopedist*, 1961; *A Voyage round My Father*, 1963; *Personality Split*, 1964; *Education of an Englishman*, 1964; *A Rare Device*, 1965; *Mr Luby's Fear of Heaven*, 1976; *Edwin*, 1982; *Rumpole*, from his own stories, 1988; *Glasnost*, 1988.

Television Plays: *Call Me a Liar*, 1958; *David and Broccoli*, 1960; *A Choice of Kings*, 1966; *The Exploding Azalea*, 1966; *The Head Waiter*, 1966; *Hughie*, 1967; *The Other Side*, 1967; *Desmond*, 1968; *Infidelity Took Place*, 1968; *Married Alive*, 1970; *Swiss Cottage*, 1972; *Knightsbridge*, 1972; *Rumpole of the Bailey*, 1975, and series, 1978, 1979, 1987, 1988; *A Little Place off the Edgware Road, The Blue Film, The Destructors, The Case for the Defence, Chagrin in Three Parts, The Invisible Japanese Gentlemen, Special Duties*, and *Mortmain* all from stories by Graham Greene, 1975-76; *Will Shakespeare*, 1978; *Rumpole's Return*, 1980; *Unity*, from the book by David Pryce-Jones, 1981; *Brideshead Revisited*, from the novel by Evelyn Waugh 1981; *Edwin*, 1984; *The Ebony Tower*, from the story by John Fowles, 1984; *Paradise Postponed*, from his own novel, 1986; *Summer's Lease*, from his own novel, 1989; *The Waiting Room*, 1989; *Titmuss Regained*, from his own novel, 1991.

Ballet Scenario: *Home*, 1968.

Son et Lumière scripts: *Hampton Court*, 1964; *Brighton Pavilion*, 1965.

Novels

Charade. London, Lane, 1948.
Rumming Park. London, Lane, 1948.
Answer Yes or No. London, Lane, 1950; as *The Silver Hook*, New York, Morrow, 1950.
Like Men Betrayed. London, Collins, 1953; Philadelphia, Lippincott, 1954.
The Narrowing Stream. London, Collins, 1954; New York, Viking, 1989.
Three Winters. London, Collins, 1956.
Will Shakespeare: The Untold Story. London, Hodder and Stoughton, 1977; New York, Delacorte Press, 1978.
Paradise Postponed. London and New York, Viking, 1985.
Summer's Lease. London and New York, Viking, 1988.
Titmuss Regained. London and New York, Viking, 1990.
The Rapstone Chronicles (includes *Paradise Postponed, Titmuss Regained*) London and New York, Viking, 1991.
Dunster. London and New York, Viking, 1992.

Short Stories

Rumpole. London, Allen Lane, 1980.
  Rumpole of the Bailey. London, Penguin, 1978; New York, Penguin, 1980.
  The Trials of Rumpole. London, Penguin, 1979; New York, Penguin, 1981.
Regina v. Rumpole. London, Allen Lane, 1981.
  Rumpole's Return. London, Penguin, 1980; New York, Penguin, 1982.
  Rumpole for the Defence. London, Penguin, 1982.
Rumpole and the Golden Thread. New York, Penguin, 1983.
The First Rumpole Omnibus (includes *Rumpole of the Bailey, The Trials of Rumpole, Rumpole's Return*). London, Penguin, 1983.
Rumpole's Last Case. London, Penguin, 1987; New York, Penguin, 1988.
The Second Rumpole Omnibus (includes *Rumpole for the Defence, Rumpole and the Golden Thread, Rumpole's Last Case*). London, Viking, 1987; New York, Penguin, 1988.
Rumpole and the Age of Miracles. London, Penguin, 1988; New York, Penguin, 1989.
Rumpole à la Carte. London and New York, Viking, 1990.

Other

No Moaning of the Bar (as Geoffrey Lincoln). London, Bles, 1957.
With Love and Lizards (travel), with Penelope Mortimer. London, Joseph, 1957.
Clinging to the Wreckage: A Part of Life. London, Weidenfeld and Nicolson, and New Haven, Connecticut, Ticknor and Fields, 1982.
In Character (interviews). London, Allen Lane, 1983.
The Liberty of the Citizen (lecture), with Franklin Thomas and Lord Hunt of Tanworth. London, Granada, 1983.
Character Parts (interviews). London, Viking, 1986.

Editor, *Famous Trials*, edited by Harry Hodge and James H. Hodge. London, Viking, and New York, Penguin, 1984.
Editor, *Great Law and Order Stories*. London, Bellew, 1990.

*

Manuscript Collections: Boston University; University of California, Los Angeles.

Critical Studies: *Anger and After* by John Russell Taylor, London, Methuen, 1962, revised edition, 1969, as *The Angry Theatre*, New York, Hill and Wang, 1962, revised edition, 1969; "Murder by Decree: An Interview with John Mortimer" by Rosemary Herbert, in *Armchair Detective: A Quarterly Journal Devoted to the Appreciation of Mystery, Detective, and Suspense Fiction* (New York), Fall 1987, pp. 340-49.

John Mortimer comments:
(1982) Comedy, I remember saying when my plays were first performed, is the only thing worth writing in this despairing age. Twenty years later the world has offered no call for a change of attitude. It may be that only in the most secure and optimistic ages can good tragedies be written. Our present situation, stumbling into a misty future filled with uncertainty and mistrust, is far too serious to be described in terms that give us no opportunity to laugh.

* * *

As a barrister John Mortimer has been a doughty advocate of the freedom of the stage from censorship, and as a public figure he is respected as a staunch left-wing intellectual, albeit with an uninhibited taste for the good life and a hearty dislike of what he is wont to call the "nanny state." His own most successful plays, however, have been agreeable and witty middle-class entertainments. They are deftly crafted and beautifully scripted, with well-observed characters who are sometimes presented in plots of such simplicity as to be little more than a single extended situation, and his theatrical style departs from traditional realistic canons only in a certain fluidity of staging. His remarkable expertise in the difficult form of the one-act play has tempted some critics to suggest that Mortimer is less at home with longer plays, but this is not entirely fair, for he does know how to develop ideas and characters. Mortimer's skilled theatrical craftsmanship is exemplified particularly well in his translations of *A Flea in Her Ear, Cat among the Pigeons,* and *The Lady from Maxim's,* three French farces by Georges Feydeau. Above all, however, Mortimer is associated in the public mind with the *Rumpole* television series. Rumpole is, in Mortimer's phrase, an Old Bailey hack, and each of the many half-hour episodes presents an entertaining if undemanding intertwining of three elements: the battles of a bumbling but liberal-minded barrister to defend the flawed individuals who are his clients against the English legal system; the everyday squabbles between the oddly assorted partners in chambers in London; and Rumpole's domestic difficulties with his harridan of a wife, Hilda, or, as the British public has come to call her, "She Who Must be Obeyed."

The Dock Brief, which was Mortimer's first play to be produced, contains much that is to be found again and again in his work. Set in the cells beneath the courtroom, it is economical to produce, but imagination and the provision of acting opportunities compensate for any lack of extravagance in staging. Hilariously funny yet sad in its implications, the play juxtaposes a very human prisoner charged with killing his wife and an aging, totally incompetent barrister who dreams that presenting the case for the defense will win him the reputation for which he has always yearned. In the cell he attempts to play out the courtroom drama he foresees, but in court, we are told, he fails dismally. A happy paradox, however, results in an unexpected happy ending.

Another of Mortimer's early plays, the very popular one-act *Lunch Hour,* illustrates two more characteristic aspects of his work. As a barrister specializing in divorce cases, Mortimer was well acquainted with the world of sleazy hotels and the clientele that used them for their assignations. With an attractive blend of wit and sympathy, *Lunch Hour* shows what this may well mean in personal terms. Sex, it turns out, is really only a secondary consideration here, and once again, as in *The Dock Brief,* there are beguiling episodes that raise the question of the relationship between individuals' true selves and the roles they are called upon to assume in life. Mortimer is also interested, in what some might regard as a very English way, with life in English private schools, and this is represented for the first time in the sensitive and closely observed early play *What Shall We Tell Caroline?* In the play, of course, it transpires that putting the question in quite these terms represents a fundamental misunderstanding of the headmaster's 18-year-old daughter.

Many theatergoers regard *A Voyage round My Father* as Mortimer's greatest achievement, and both on stage, with Alec Guinness in the lead, and on television, with Laurence Olivier, it made a great impression. Mortimer's father was a noted figure in the courts, both for the style of his advocacy and for the fact that he was blind, and *Voyage* is a marvelously rich portrayal of this impossibly difficult character in counterpoint to the son's life from childhood through adolescence to maturity. The situations can become hilarious, as the blind barrister deliberately flouts every bourgeois convention, and the dialogue has all the brilliance one might expect from men whose stock-in-trade is the ability to speak well. The social observation is sharp, and with all this there is also great sympathy for a wounded human being who fights to retain his dignity. Symbolic of the blind barrister's determination not to be daunted by his affliction is his passionate concern for the beauty of his garden. By the end the audience feels almost guilty for enjoying looking at the summer flowers he cannot see.

The Judge also explores the legal world, this time from the angle of a judge who, at the end of his career, returns not only to his hometown in the provinces but also to unresolved aspects of his past. The tone is more serious than in many of Mortimer's plays. The public has generally preferred rather lighter fare, such as *Collect Your Hand Baggage,* with its whimsically deflating ending,

Two Stars for Comfort, set in a modest hotel, and clever short plays like those collected in *Come As You Are,* which reveal, in a form and with an attitude that demands little of the audience, an acute awareness of just what makes people tick.

John Mortimer has since turned more toward television, fiction, and the writing of his memoirs, which give examples of the way he has turned his experiences as a barrister to good account in creating the character Rumpole. Insights into Mortimer's attitudes to his work as a playwright are to be found in the introduction to a Mark Pattenden selection of his plays—*Dock Brief, Marble Arch, The Prince of Darkness,* and *Rumpole and the Judge's Elbow*—that was intended for use in schools and colleges. Explaining that he came to writing for the stage only after experience in radio drama, Mortimer suggests that this is why the actual words of the text are always so important to him and why he has to find the right "voice" for his characters, which is not simply a matter of imitating realistic speech but also of capturing their rhythms as well as their vocabularies. He argues, too, that plays must have a theme, by which, as Mortimer puts it, he means "something to say which the audience may recognise and which may, with luck, help in our understanding of life on earth, and in our sympathy with others." Devising plots is, he admits, difficult for him, yet he knows that he must find them if he is to hold an audience's attention.

Making a comment about *Dock Brief* that is applicable to his work in general, Mortimer remarks that he believes that "our life is essentially comic and even our saddest moments have an element of comedy, just as our funniest experiences have some sadness in them." Declaring that his aim is to write "serious comedy," he goes on to say that "I want to make my audiences laugh, but I also wish to leave them with something to think about." Acknowledging how much he learned when translating into English the French farces of Feydeau, Mortimer notes that "farce is really tragedy played at about two hundred revolutions a minute," and he adds that "farce is played extremely seriously. The audience won't laugh if the actors give the slightest hint that they think it is funny." In a few very direct and unpretentious paragraphs Mortimer shows that he is well aware of the nature of his work in drama and that he sets about the task of amusing the public in a highly professional manner, without abandoning his moral principles and his political ideals.

—Christopher Smith

MOSEL, Tad

Nationality: American. **Born:** Steubenville, Ohio, 1 May 1922. **Education:** Amherst College, Massachusetts, B.A. 1947; Yale University, New Haven, Connecticut, 1947-49; Columbia University, New York, M.A. 1953. **Military Service:** Served in the United States Army Air Force, 1943-46: sergeant. **Career:** Clerk, Northwest Airlines, 1951-53. Visiting critic in television writing, Yale University School of Drama, 1957-58. Member of the Executive Board, *Television Quarterly*, Syracuse, New York; member of the Executive Council, Writers Guild of America. **Awards:** Pulitzer prize, 1961; New York Drama Critics Circle award, 1961. D. Litt.: College of Wooster, Ohio, 1963. D.F.A.: College of Steubenville, 1969. **Agent:** William Morris Agency, 1350 Avenue of the Americas, New York, New York 10019. **Address:** 400 East 57th Street, New York, New York 10022, U.S.A.

Publications

Plays

The Happiest Years (produced Amherst, Massachusetts, 1942).
The Lion Hunter (produced New York, 1952).
Madame Aphrodite (televised 1953; revised version, music by Jerry Herman, produced New York, 1962).
My Lost Saints (televised 1955). Published in *Best Television Plays*, edited by Gore Vidal, New York, Ballantine, 1956.
Other People's Houses: Six Television Plays (includes *Ernie Barger Is Fifty, The Haven, The Lawn Party, Star in the Summer Night, The Waiting Place*). New York, Simon and Schuster, 1956.
The Out-of-Towners (televised 1956). Published in *Television Plays for Writers: Eight Television Plays*, edited by A.S. Burack, Boston, The Writer, 1957.
The Five-Dollar Bill (televised 1957). Chicago, Dramatic Publishing Company, 1958.
Presence of the Enemy (televised 1958). Published in *Best Short Plays 1957-1958*, edited by Margaret Mayorga, Boston, Beacon Press, 1958.
All the Way Home, adaptation of the novel *A Death in the Family* by James Agee (produced New York, 1960). New York, Obolensky, 1961.
Impromptu (produced New York, 1961). New York, Dramatists Play Service, 1961.
That's Where the Town's Going (televised 1962). New York, Dramatists Play Service, 1962.

Screenplays: *Dear Heart*, 1964; *Up the Down Staircase*, 1967.

Television Plays: *Jinxed*, 1949; *The Figgerin' of Aunt Wilma*, 1953; *This Little Kitty Stayed Cool*, 1953; *The Remarkable Case of Mr. Bruhl*, 1953; *Ernie Barger Is Fifty*, 1953; *Other People's Houses*, 1953; *The Haven*, 1953; *Madame Aphrodite*, 1953; *The Lawn Party*, 1955; *Star in the Summer Night*, 1955; *Guilty Is the Stranger*, 1955; *My Lost Saints*, 1955; *The Waiting Place*, 1955; *The Out-of-Towners*, 1956; *The Five-Dollar Bill*, 1957; *The Morning Place*, 1957; *Presence of the Enemy*, 1958; *The Innocent Sleep*, 1958; *A Corner of the Garden*, 1959; *Sarah's Laughter*, 1959; *The Invincible Teddy*, 1960; *Three Roads to Rome: Venus Ascendant, Roman Fever, The Rest Cure*, from stories by Martha Gellhorn, Edith Wharton, and Aldous Huxley, 1960; *That's Where the Town's Going*, 1962.

Other

Leading Lady: The World and Theatre of Katharine Cornell, with Gertrude Macy. Boston, Little Brown, 1978.

*

Critical Study: "Tad Mosel, Ohio Playwright" by Janet Overmyer, in *Ohioana Quarterly,* Winter 1986, pp. 137-39.

* * *

Tad Mosel gained attention in the 1950s as one of the leading American writers for live television. His scripts were ideally suited to the medium in their restricted scope, focus on intimate details, and Chekhovian naturalism within a thoroughly contemporary

American suburban milieu. An earlier one-act play written for the stage, *Impromptu,* has become a minor classic in its treatment of illusion and reality by means of a theatrical metaphor. A group of actors find themselves on a stage to which they have been summoned in order to improvise a play. Their groping efforts point up the recognition that life itself is essentially an improvisation in which roles are assumed and identity elusive. Mosel handles this potentially trite and sentimental concept with wit and restraint.

Mosel's most successful work, however, was *All the Way Home,* a stage adaptation of James Agee's novel *A Death in the Family.* Mosel's play captures the essence of the subjective, introspective novel while providing it with an external, theatrical form. In its depiction of several generations of a family and its compassionate rendering of death, birth, and the process of emotional maturing, the work has echoes of Thornton Wilder, an impression that is reinforced by Mosel's fluid handling of time and space. Especially noteworthy is the economy of dialogue, which is related to Mosel's sure sense of the power of the stage to communicate in unverbalized, visual terms.

—Jarka M. Burian

MOTTON, Gregory

Nationality: British. **Born:** London, 17 September 1961. **Family:** Lives with Lotta Kjellberg; two daughters, one son. **Awards:** Arts Council bursary, 1989, 1993; Royal Literary Fund grant, 1991, 1995; Polonski Foundation, 1994.

PUBLICATIONS

Plays

Chicken (produced London, 1987). With *Ambulance*, London, Penguin, 1987.

Ambulance (produced London, 1987). With *Chicken*, London, Penguin, 1987.

Downfall (produced London, 1988). With *Looking at You (Revived) Again*, London, Methuen, 1989.

Looking at You (Revived) Again (produced Leicester and London, 1989). With *Downfall*, London, Methuen, 1989.

The Ghost Sonata, adaptation of the play by August Strindberg (produced London, 1989).

The Pelican, adaptation of the play by August Strindberg (produced London, 1989).

Picture of Dorian Gray, adaptation of the novel by Oscar Wilde (produced Leicester, 1990).

Woyzeck, adaptation of the play by Georg Büchner (produced London, 1992). London, Hern, 1992.

The Father, translation (produced Glasgow, 1993).

A Message for the Broken Hearted (produced Liverpool, 1993). London, Oberon.

The Terrible Voice of Satan (London, 1993). London, Oberon.

Cat and Mouse (Sheep) (Paris, 1994). London, Oberon.

Swanwhite (produced The Gate Theater, 1996).

A Little Satire (The Gate Theater, 1997). London, Oberon.

Radio Plays: *The Jug*, 1991; *Lazy Brién*, 1992; *Sleeping Beauty*, 1995; *In Praise of Progress*, 1997.

*   *   *

In a 1988 *Guardian* review of *Downfall,* Gregory Motton's third drama in two years, Michael Billington detected "the birth of a new genre: Urban Impressionism." Occasioned by the congruent staging of Nick Ward's *The Strangeness of Others,* to which many reviewers unfavorably compared Motton's work, the label is no less useful than many another. "Surrealism," Billington went on to suggest; "tragi-farcical nightmare," opined Paul Taylor of *The Independent.* Motton "[is] fast making a name for himself," Sheridan Morley ventured in *Punch*, as "the dramatic poet of urban disintegration." A drama willfully, if not always clearly, focused on social damage and dissidence and at the same time fashioning an expressionist, sometimes symbolist mode of address does not lend itself easily to a shorthand account. Abrupt shifts of mood and register, dialogue gracelessly demotic and then poetically or portentously inflected, and violence and comedy charged by incipient wandering and waste make clear that dramatic naturalism is as residual a feature of Motton's stagecraft as his characters are the residues and casualties of psychosocial development.

A break with naturalism is hardly apparent from the settings of the earlier plays, *Chicken*—"an abandoned working men's cafe" and "a street outside [a] doorway"—and *Ambulance*—"Ellis's room" and "the street, outside a launderette." The interplay between road and room, as it were, shapes a series of narratives in both plays, however, that elliptically explore what have become Motton's ruling concerns: commitment and communication, power and loss. Indeed, the title *Ambulance* has much to do with the impairment of the characters' motor functions. The crippled Clivey, locked into a relation with Louise, is then mothered by Mary, who is herself unable to carry her legs beyond a certain radius of Holloway Prison. Meanwhile, the uncertainly gendered Ellis injures herself in jumping from a stifling room onto the pavement outside, thus prompting the arrival of the ambulance. The men of the ambulance figure as anonymous powers of capture and disablement, much as in *Chicken* the "party" that the patriarch Pat menacingly invokes and the role he assumes as secretary of state for sanitation and education—to include "secrecy"—suggest individual disempowerment by bureaucracy and factional interests. Commitment, along with individual desire for personal and professional growth, is readily transmuted into involuntary committal.

Indeed, individuals, who periodically but always problematically form couples, wander through an increasingly fractured narrative line across the plays, forcing out an ever more compacted set of dramatic coordinates. Lost, abandoned, and imagined children, for example, along with the sense of continuity, history, and relation they suggest, are repeatedly invoked. The killing of the chicken in the play of that title is a matricidal act (no eggs), the breaking of a food chain by a usurping father. The "pain of separation," as Johnny terms it in *Ambulance*—even though on occasions it is separation from that which one never possessed—includes loss of memory, relation, and aspiration and of visible and attainable goals, even as seekers with binoculars search the skies and invoke the "cosmos." The same play's Pedro, increasingly wracked with bodily spasms, can still claim, however, that "life goes on," even when, at the play's close, the "battering ram" (an ambulance crew) comes into view.

Downfall, a drama divided into 56 brief scenes, is forbiddingly dense and oblique with a networks of verbal and circumstantial patterning. Its snatches of biblical and occult narrative and its characters (Tower Man, Spanish Lover, Violent Man) are emblematic rather than socially situated. More so than in the earlier dramas, dialogue swings from the barely articulate outburst or stumbling exchange to outpourings of garrulous but vacuous energy or fitfully focused portentousness. Pointed concentration slides off into offhand non sequitur. At the same time despite, or perhaps because, each scene is titled as an episode, Motton's dramatic, but more especially visual, imagination has developed to incorporate wildly different modes and circumstances. The Violent Man is hounded by a swooping helicopter, the itinerant Hetty and Rolo are grounded beneath the choric Tower Man, and the Secret Service man Geronimo is progressively losing power and position in respect of the "sides" that the play as carnival insists on dislocating. Such circumstances recur and are refashioned to punctuate material that might otherwise overreach itself.

A moment of tender, if not quite literally touching, intimacy between "two strays" just before the play's close ("There are lots of people in the world," remarks Clancy, not for the first time) serves to highlight Motton's emphasis on permissive rather than repressive commitment in a world open to surveillance, institutional power, and false prophets, all emanating from on high upon a falling world. In a shadowing of the Christian story—with "skulduggery" as Gethsemane and Dover "the nation's Calvary" at the play's end—*Downfall* enacts the struggle to remain upright, in every sense of the word, along a modern *via dolorosa* of betrayal, suffering, guilt, and despair. Along the way there are any number of false epiphanies, as well as a conspicuously unachieved annunciation, ending with "a long road stretching out" before three figures themselves stretched across the skyline and Motton's concluding dance (perhaps a dance of death).

The debt to Strindberg, several of whose plays Motton has translated for production, is most evident in his more tightly worked, economically constructed "ghost" play *Looking at You (Revived) Again.* It presents a triangle of figures—the man Abe; the "dark woman" Mrs. James, the wife, it seems, from reconstructed dramas of the past whom Abe has abandoned and whose children he affects to be seeking; and "Peragrin's daughter," whom Abe consorts with as "the dark side . . . the invisible side of (his) soul." The daughter, who is known as "p.d.," finally not only overshadows the crippled Mrs. James, who is now upstanding, and transforms herself into a figure of mannikin beauty, but she also overshadows Abe, who claims to have been "eclipsed" entirely, with the promise of a child that will stir him to a sense of responsibility. Inset narrated stagings of a wedding, threats from landlords and bailiffs, desolate settings, and sickness notwithstanding, the lack of social specificity and the more tightly worked psychodramas of repression, transference and working through make this a studied rejection of naturalism. One might indeed be forgiven for seeking the play's public concerns less with urban disintegration and contemporary British culture than with European Jewry and for locating its dramatic kinship within European expressionism.

—James Hansford

MOWAT, David

Nationality: British. **Born:** Cairo, Egypt, 16 March 1943. **Education:** Bryanston School, 1956-60; New College, Oxford, 1961-64, B.A. (honors) in English language and literature 1964; University of Sussex, Falmer, 1964-66. **Career:** Cilcennin fellow, University of Bristol, 1973-75; director of the Playwrights Workshop, University of Iowa, Iowa City, 1978; fellow, Virginia Center for Creative Arts, 1979. **Awards:** Arts Council awards, 1970, 1971, 1976, 1977, 1983. **Address:** 7 Mount Street, Oxford OX2 6DH, England.

Publications

Plays

Jens (produced Falmer, Sussex, 1965; London, 1969). Included in *Anna-Luse and Other Plays*, London, Calder and Boyars, 1970.
Pearl (produced Brighton, 1966).
1850 (produced London, 1967).
Anna-Luse (produced Edinburgh, 1968; London, 1971; New York, 1972). Included in *Anna-Luse and Other Plays*, 1970.
Dracula, with others (produced Edinburgh, 1969; London, 1973).
Purity (produced Manchester, 1969; London, 1970; New York, 1972). Included in *Anna-Luse and Other Plays*, 1970.
The Normal Woman, and Tyyppi (produced London, 1970).
Adrift, with others (produced Manchester, 1970).
The Others (produced London, 1970). London, Calder and Boyars, 1973.
Most Recent Least Recent (produced Manchester, 1970).
Inuit (produced London, 1970).
Liquid (produced London, 1971).
The Diabolist (produced London, 1971).
John (produced London, 1971).
Amalfi, based on *The Duchess of Malfi* by Webster (produced Edinburgh, 1972).
Phoenix-and-Turtle (produced London, 1972; New York, 1976). Published in *The London Fringe Theatre*, edited by Victor Mitchell, London, Burnham House, 1975.
Morituri (produced London, 1972).
My Relationship with Jayne (produced London, 1973).
Come (produced London, 1973).
Main Sequence (produced Bristol, 1974).
The Collected Works (produced London, 1974; New York, 1977).
The Memory Man (produced Bristol, 1974).
The Love Maker (produced Bristol, 1974).
X to C (produced Bristol, 1975).
Kim (produced Sheffield, 1977; London, 1980).
Winter (produced Iowa City, 1978; London, 1983).
The Guise (produced Birmingham and London, 1979; New York, 1991).
Hiroshima Nights (produced Milton Keynes, Buckinghamshire, and London, 1981).
The Midnight Sun (produced London, 1983).
Carmen (produced Chichester, 1984).
The Almas (produced London, 1989).
Jane, or the End of the World (produced London, 1992).

Radio Plays: *To Die in Africa*, 1989; *Singing and Dancing in Kanpur*, 1991.

Short Stories

New Writers 11, with others. London, Calder and Boyars, 1974.

* * *

The name of David Mowat is familiar to those who frequent experimental fringe theaters. He began his career as one of the band of writers who provide much of the repertoire of short plays produced on the lunchtime circuit.

Many of these playwrights seem almost indistinguishable from one another. Indeed, some half dozen of them indulge occasionally in corporate efforts. Their methods are freewheeling, their subject matter often sensational, and their intention to subvert the existing social structure by means of shock effects. They command respect on account of their talent and seriousness of purpose, although their playing out of sadistic and erotic fantasies induces doubt as often as cheers.

Mowat stands conspicuously apart from these writers, however. There is present in his work an obsessive search for truth. "What information, useful information for the living of our lives, are we getting from this person?" asks the narrator in a direct address to the audience in *Phoenix-and-Turtle*. In the same play he also observes, "There's no obscenity so obscene as the horrid spectra of untruth lurking in the centre of one's home." The speaker is a lecturer in English who has been sacked as a result of a liaison with a student, who has just burned the manuscript of his book on the subject of the eponymous Shakespeare poem, who feels compelled to tell his wife that she has not long to live, and who—after an incestuous attack on his daughter—discovers that the girl is already pregnant. All of these lies are brought into the open but, characteristically, the very act of telling the truth by means of the basic lie of theater is also questioned. The author likens art to putting a frame around lies and, by making them scan or rhyme, pretending to give them a moral purpose.

Fat-Man, from the same period but not produced, deals allegorically with rifts in the political left. Using as a motto a dictum of Mao Tse-tung's—"When the body is healthy, the feelings are correct"—the scene is set in a gymnasium threatened with demolition. The names of three of its four characters—Fatman, Cripple, and Little-Boy—indicate the satirical nature of the problem. Each one has passionate convictions regarding the desired use of the gymnasium. The play is subtitled "the exercise of power," but, needless to say, Mowat offers no easy solutions. His adaptation of *The Duchess of Malfi* and his approving quotation of Webster's remark that all life is a torture chamber may point to a vein of pessimism, but this, too, could be misleading. There is a quality of nagging obsession in Mowat's plays. His zeal for uncovering the truth has an echo of Ibsen, and his haunted, nightmarish fantasies remind one of Strindberg. Of living authors only Pinter comes to mind. Mowat, too, is a master of mystery and economy, and his plays, though often difficult to comprehend at first sight, share with Pinter's the power to keep an audience spellbound.

Mowat has traveled a long way since he wrote *Jens,* a comparatively straightforward piece of symbolism in which animals and humans mingle surrealistically. His most impressive early play was *Anna-Luse*. Here, a blind young girl gets up in the morning, goes through a ritual of stocktaking of her body and her possessions, and is visited by a girlfriend, who is also blind, a confused young man, and a dubious physical therapy instructor. The last was the victim of a gang of thugs on the way over. Drenched but undaunted, he proceeds to give the girls some strange therapy, which induces in Anna-Luse a phantom pregnancy and childbirth. It is, however, the instructor who is revealed most surprisingly, for he ends, curled up like a baby, at Anna-Luse's breast.

Mowat's plays are by no means solemn. In *The Diabolist,* for example, a worried mother is introduced to her daughter's new boyfriend. He is the epitome of the ordinary bloke, but he turns out unexpectedly to be a devil worshiper. Apart from a macabre and not altogether unsuccessful ending, this sketch is as funny as anything produced by the absurdists.

The surface of these plays is in most cases shabbily suburban and lower-middle-class. They gain from being staged with absolute naturalism, with the tension between manner and matter then becoming increasingly menacing. The rug is slowly and unnervingly pulled from under our feet, and we leave the theater with our heads buzzing with questions that have no easy or formal solutions but that demand to be asked, if not answered.

Mowat's full-length play *John* belongs in this category. Its hero spends the entire play in a catatonic trance. The unease engendered by his silence, along with its effect on the other, superficially "ordinary" characters, provides an exciting evening. Sudden irruptions of extreme violence occur regularly in Mowat's work, but they never appear gratuitously.

The short play *Come* seems to me to be willfully enigmatic. Here a distraught father attempts to persuade his estranged daughter to return to him. He lies in wait for her in a room adjoining an intellectual party that becomes an orgy. Nothing is achieved, and neither the motives nor the narrative makes any comprehensible sense.

The full-length play *The Collected Works* is Mowat's most lucid and fully realized work. The setting is a library, and the books, like the eyes of accumulated wisdom and disillusion, stare down at an emotional and a turbulent tangle that involves a researcher, who is a lovesick girl, the sterile chief librarian, and his beautiful wife. Taking as his theme the tensions between life and art, Mowat contrasts the messiness and unexpectedness of the former with the unalterable composure of the latter. There is much sly comedy as the characters explain themselves in lengthy monologues. Once again, he writes in a deliberate undertone, but the surface simmers with unease and bubbles with incipient volcanic explosions.

Mowat has shown sensitivity, depth, and an increasing technical assurance. To create a play of real significance, however, one with "useful information for the living of our lives," it would be necessary for him to emerge from his somewhat esoteric milieu.

—Frank Marcus

MTWA, Percy

Nationality: South African. **Born:** Wattville, Benoni. **Career:** Dancer and musician, Daveyton; stores clerk, Dunlop Industries, Johannesburg; founder-singer, Percy and the Maestros. **Award:** Edinburgh Fringe first, 1987. **Address:** c/o The Market Theatre, P.O. Box 8656, Johannesburg 2000, South Africa.

Publications

Plays

Woza Albert!, with Mbongeni Ngema and Barney Simon (produced Johannesburg, 1981; Edinburgh, London, and Los Angeles, 1982; New York, 1984). London, Methuen, 1983; published in *Woza Afrika! An Anthology of South African Plays*, edited by Duma Ndlovu, New York, Braziller, 1986.

Bopha! (Arrest!) (also director: produced Johannesburg, n.d.; New York, 1986; London, 1987). Published in *Woza Afrika! An Anthology of South African Plays*, edited by Duma Ndlovu, New York, Braziller, 1986.

*

Critical Studies: "*Woza Albert*" in *West Africa* (London), October 1982; "I've Been an Entertainer Throughout My Life. . . : Interview with Percy Mtwa" by Eckhard Breitinger, in *Matatu: Journal for African Culture and Society* (Amsterdam), 1988.

Theatrical Activities:
Director: **Play**—*Bopha!*, New York, 1986; London, 1987.

Actor: **Plays**—Role in *Mama and the Load* by Gibson Kente, Johannesburg, 1979, and roles in *Woza Albert!*

* * *

Although his international reputation rests on two plays, Percy Mtwa has had a substantial performing career in South Africa, Britain, and North America, which shows that his dramatic creativity goes far beyond verbal scripting to explore many areas of theater semiotics. While observing affinities with Grotowski's "poor theatre"—intense physicality with minimal props and costuming—critics have also complained that Mtwa's plays are unsophisticated and their thought not profound and that the actors' accents make what dialogue there is hard to follow. This failure to acknowledge that Mtwa's commitment is not to a Shavian theater of ideas but to a confrontational theater of resistance also evades a pivotal fact of his plays' theatrical interactiveness, that their politics of language casts the audience as complicit in the situation onstage.

Woza Albert!, cowritten with the actor Mbongeni Ngema and the white director Barney Simon, announces its activist function in the title. *Woza* means "rise up," whether from death, sleep, or passivity. Its running motif is what would happen if Morena, a Christ-like Messiah, should visit South Africa, and most of its 26 scenes present workplace situations showing black oppression, white exploitation, and police brutality. Long before he arrives, Morena serves as a catalyst for the aspirations of the ordinary people, but with his appearance and with his arrest, death, and resurrection the play takes on more overtly parabolic tones. In the final graveyard scene Morena searches for a name on a tombstone beginning with the letter *L* so that he can raise Lazarus, but he finds instead the name of the title figure, Albert Luthuli, the Zulu chief who was president of the ANC. The play ends with a dancing, celebratory invocation to other dead heroes of South African freedom, black and white, to rise up.

If the recurrent themes are of oppression, the tone of the play is of vitality, with the actors' bodies making an insistent statement of indefatigability and playfulness. The absurdities that surround the figure of Morena, arriving by jumbo jet and eventually gunned down by a military helicopter, merge with the playfulness of performance but only partly disguise the fact that basically this is a theological play, contesting the religious ideology of apartheid and advancing a Christianity of liberation. There is no subtlety in the indictment of white religious posturing when it turns out that Morena cannot understand Afrikaans, nor is it difficult to see white supremacist tactics when a black worker is paid to play Judas and another is imprisoned on Robben Island with only the Bible to read. Other religious allusions are less overt, for example, the longest scene in the play, in which the Coronation Brickyard recalls the Israelites in bondage in Egypt making bricks for Pharaoh.

Bopha! (Arrest!) does to the law what *Woza Albert!* does to religion, but it builds up to starker images of township violence. Here the Judas motif occupies the whole play in the form of a black police sergeant who forces the recruitment of his reluctant brother and also confronts his politically active son's resistance. If the brutality of the final episodes is grim, there is also a filament of rich comedy in the subversive behavior of the brother recruited into the force, and there is an optimistic ending to the violent absurdity of the police state with the resignation of the sergeant.

Although they were written as resistance plays, Mtwa's works looked forward to a unified, multicultural South African society. This vision was reinforced in production by the use of only two or three actors to play many characters. In the theater the actor's sometimes half-naked body became a screen onto which were projected many different identities, black and white, an effect of condensation not unlike the sequence of photographs of the dead heroes at the end of the BBC television abridgment of *Woza Albert!* The figure of the Messiah was inscribed on the martyrs. In addition, by parodying the idea of miracles, the plays did not run the risk of obsolescence with the collapse of apartheid. By the time Peter Brook directed his French version of *Woza Albert!* at the Théâtre des Bouffes du Nord, some sections required rewriting in the light of reform, but it was clear that the supporting social, economic, and religious system would remain highly problematic long after the legal demolition of apartheid.

Within the dialogue of resistance Mtwa casts the audience as a complicit mediator. When the actors play blacks in Johannesburg pleading with white motorists for jobs, the front of the stage becomes the car window, the auditorium the car interior, and the theatergoer the privileged minority with the power to act or ignore. In both plays the actors constantly work frontally, engaging the audience rather than each other even during dialogue, and their hand gestures speak a language of appeal, inquiry, and indictment.

Like much modern South African drama, both plays combine several languages, the meaning of which cannot always be easily inferred in performance. This sometimes works for comic irony, as when Zulu is used to abuse a white boss behind his back or when an Afrikaans policeman is confronted with "big English." But language is also used as a blocking device to prevent the access of other characters or a white audience, staking out a precise cultural territory through language and claiming it as one's own. For this reason the production history of Mtwa's plays is particularly interesting. Their political dynamics have fluctuated radically with every audience group, from their black township origins to their showcase status at international festivals like Edinburgh and Paris. Like the black actor's skin, black language—

including Black English—is a text that must be understood in a multicultural society.

—Howard McNaughton

MUNRO, Rona

Nationality: Scottish. **Born:** Aberdeen, 7 September 1959. **Education:** Mackie Academy, Stonehaven; Edinburgh University, 1976-80, M.A. in history (honours). **Family:** Married Edward Draper in 1981; one son. **Career:** Writer-in-residence, Paines Plough Theatre Company, London, 1985-86. One half the Scottish comedy/theatre duo the Misfits (with Fiona Knowles), 1985—. **Awards:** McClaren award for radio, 1986; Susan Smith Blackburn prize, 1991; *Evening Standard* award, 1991; London Theatre Critics Circle prize, 1992; *Plays and Players* award, 1992. **Agent:** Casarotto Ramsay Ltd., National House, 60-66 Wardour Street, London W1V 3HP, England.

PUBLICATIONS

Plays

The Salesman (produced Edinburgh, 1982).
The Bang and the Whimper (produced Edinburgh, 1982).
Fugue (produced Edinburgh, 1983). Edinburgh, Salamander, 1983.
Touchwood (for children; produced Aberdeen, 1984).
The Bus (for children; produced Edinburgh, 1984).
Ghost Story (for children; produced Glasgow, 1985).
Piper's Cave. Published in *Plays by Women: Five*, edited by Michelene Wandor and Mary Remnant, London, Methuen, 1985.
The Biggest Party in the World (produced Edinburgh, 1986).
Dust and Dreams (produced Fareham, Hampshire, 1986).
The Way to Go Home (produced London, 1987).
Winners (produced Leeds, 1987).
Off the Road (produced Leeds, 1988).
Saturday at the Commodore (produced Isle of Skye, 1989). Published in *Scot Free*, edited by Alasdair Cameron, London, Hern, 1990.
Bold Girls (produced Cumbernauld, Strathclyde, 1990; London, 1991). Published in *First Run 3*, edited by Matthew Lloyd, London, Hern, 1991.
Your Turn to Clean the Stair (produced Edinburgh, 1992).
The Maiden Stone. London, Nick Hern, 1995.

Radio Plays: *Kilbreck* series, 1983-84; *Watching Waiters*, 1986; *Dirt under the Carpet*, 1987; *Citizens* series, 1988; *Elsie*, 1990; *Elvis*, 1990; *Eleven*, 1990; *Three Way Split*, 1992.

Television Plays: *Hardware*, 1984; *Biting the Hands*, 1989; 3 episodes in *Dr. Who* series, 1989; *Say It with Flowers* in *Casualty* series, 1990.

*

Critical Study: In *Feminist Stages: Interviews with Women in Contemporary British Theatre,* edited by Lizbeth Goodman, Harwood Academic Press, 1996.

Rona Munro comments:

I am a Scottish playwright, a woman playwright, and an Aberdonian playwright, not necessarily in that order. All of these facts inform my writing but don't define it. Up till now a lot of my writing has concerned itself with issues around gender and sexual politics and as yet there's no sign of that preoccupation wearing off. I'm concerned to address these issues from a broad, human perspective, and as far as possible to write entertainingly and honestly, reflecting women's and men's lives as I perceive them rather than as I would choose them to be. I'm concerned to assert my place as part of a living tradition, a distinctive Scottish culture, and to explore the possibilities of writing in Scots as well as in English. I am also apparently incapable of writing anything without slipping a few gags in and will probably always choose to write drama that is liberally laced with comedy.

* * *

Rona Munro is one of Scotland's most innovative playwrights and performers. Her creative use of language (the Aberdonian dialect, in particular) and the integration of Celtic myth into her contemporary scenarios serve to enrich her theater writing immensely. Her own experiences as a student, cleaner, and traveler have also influenced her work, lending it a voice that is at once true to her working-class origins and informed by world affairs and global issues.

An early play, *Fugue,* was commissioned in 1982 and staged at the Traverse Theatre, Edinburgh, in 1983. Another early work, *Ghost Story,* was staged at the Tron Theatre, Glasgow, 1985. She has also written for television and radio, but her theater work is her true forte. She has been influenced by her work with both the Paines Plough Theatre Company and her own women's comedy duo: the Msfits, founded with colleague Fiona Knowles. Her best-known plays, however, are *Piper's Cave* and *Saturday at the Commodore.*

Piper's Cave is a curiously surreal play. The cast consists of a young woman (Jo) and a mysterious man who appears to be older than his 30 or so years (Alisdair). A third "character" is the unseen spirit of the landscape, personified quite literally by Munro who gives this spirit a "local habitation and a name," as well as a good number of lines in the script. The landscape is called Helen. Helen is present from the opening of the play, but she comes into her own about halfway through, speaking as frequently as do the two real characters. Whether or not she is speaking, however, Helen's presence is crucial throughout; this is a play about the power of the environment and one that challenges ingrained essentialist notions about Mother Nature. At the same time it addresses issues of gender and power and sex and violence.

Piper's Cave, as Munro reveals in the published afterword to the play, actually exists, though she exercised some creative license in terms of its location. Similarly, the issues that she deals with in the play are quite real. Yet the play experiments with reality and myth by combining them, drawing on one to enrich the other. The play introduces young Jo as a modern woman and Alisdair as a version of the legendary piper who walked into the hills and never returned. Helen is the natural world, and she has a mighty wit. Jo and Alisdair, however, also have their "otherworldly" sides. Alisdair is, or thinks he is, the legendary piper. Jo becomes, or thinks she becomes, the *selky,* or seal woman, of Celtic myth. At plays end, we hear splashing—the sound of waves that would be made by Jo, or by Helen, or that might be the sound of curtains closing on a thought-provoking play.

While only Alisdair in *Piper's Cave* spoke regularly in dialect, all of *Saturday at the Commodore* is written to be performed in a strong Aberdonian. The play is quite short (only five pages in the published version) and is a one-woman monologue of sorts, commissioned by the influential socialist theater companym, 7:84 Scotland as part of a series of short pieces by Voices of Today's Scotland. The use of dialect is crucial both to the setting of the play and to where it is performed. (It was first performed at the Isle of Skye in 1989.)

Lena is the 30-year-old central character, or narrator, who relates the story of *Saturday at the Commodore:* a story of one woman's memories of childhood and adolescence in Scotland. The play is a story, a narrative that conjures vivid images of other places and people, most notably Nora, Lena's "best mate" and the girl she fancied as well. She tells of her development into womanhood, as she recalls being a student and later becoming a teacher, and as she moves from one heterosexual relationship to a life of independence. All this is told in a narrative that is relaxed, wry, witty, and engaging. The dialect makes it Lena's story and a uniquely Scottish story. Yet Munro's ability to create likable characters and familiar, evocative situations makes it a larger story as well.

Munro has expressed her own views on the importance of women's theater and comedy writing. In an interview in 1995 (in *Feminist Stages: Interviews with Women in Contemporary British Theatre,* edited Lizbeth Goodman, 1996), she was asked whether she felt strongly either for or against working collaboratively with other women in theater:

> I feel strongly for, though when it happens it's not always a positive experience. We all know the Maggie Thatcher syndrome: beat the boys at their own game, etc. I think it's most energizing to work with women, but some women are exceptions. We can't generalize too much. But I like to think of the gender situation in theatre (or any art form) as a game of musical chairs. The game's been going on for ever, and only once in a great while does anyone add a new chair. But no matter how many people are playing and how many chairs there are, there's only ever one chair for women. Now we've added more chairs but not really enough. I'm an incurable optimist, and things have always gone reasonably well for me. But still, I think the establishment is slow to change, in the theatre and in academia and critical circles. Yet audiences out there are very hungry for reflections of women's stories which haven't been told.

Munro has continued to tell those stories in comedy and theater and increasingly in other media as well.

—Lizbeth Goodman

MURPHY, Tom

Nationality: Irish. **Born:** Thomas Murphy in Tuam, County Galway, 23 February 1935. **Education:** Vocational School, Tuam; Vocational Teachers' Training College, Dublin. **Family:** Married Mary Hippisley; three children. **Career:** Apprentice fitter and welder, Tuam, 1953-55; engineering teacher, Vocational School, Mountbellow, County Galway, 1957-62. Actor and director, 1951-62. Member of the Board of Directors, 1972-83, and writer-in-association, 1986—, Irish National Theatre (Abbey Theatre), Dublin; Regents lecturer, University of California, Santa Barbara, 1981; writer-in-association, Druid Theatre, Galway, 1983-85. Founding member, Moli Productions, Dublin, 1974. **Awards:** Irish Academy of Letters award, 1972; Independent Newspapers award, 1983; Harvey's award, 1983, 1986; *Sunday Tribune* award, 1985. **Member:** Irish Academy of Letters, 1982, and Aosdána, 1984. **Agent:** Alexandra Cann Representation, 68E Redcliffe Gardens, London SW10 9HE, England; and, Bridget Aschenberg, International Creative Management, 40 West 57th Street, New York, New York 10019, U.S.A. **Address:** 46 Terenure Road West, Dublin 6, Ireland.

Publications

Plays

On the Outside, with Noel O'Donoghue (produced Cork, 1961; New Haven, Connecticut, 1976). With *On the Inside*, Dublin, Gallery Press, 1976; included in *A Whistle in the Dark and Other Plays*, 1989.

A Whistle in the Dark (produced London, 1961; New Haven, Connecticut, and New York, 1969). New York, French, 1971; included in *A Whistle in the Dark and Other Plays*, 1989.

Famine (produced Dublin, 1966; London, 1969; New York, 1981). Dublin, Gallery Press, 1977; included in *Plays: One*, 1992.

The Fooleen (as *A Crucial Week in the Life of a Grocer's Assistant*, televised 1967; as *The Fooleen*, produced Dublin, 1969). Dixon, California, Proscenium Press, 1970; Dublin, Gallery Press, 1978; as *A Crucial Week in the Life of a Grocer's Assistant*, included in *A Whistle in the Dark and Other Plays*, 1989.

The Orphans (produced Dublin, 1968; Newark, Delaware, 1971). Newark, Delaware, Proscenium Press, 1974.

The Morning after Optimism (produced Dublin, 1971; New York, 1974). Cork, Mercier Press, 1973.

The White House (produced Dublin, 1972).

On the Inside (also director: produced Dublin, 1974; New Haven, Connecticut, 1976). With *On the Outside*, Dublin, Gallery Press, 1976; included in *A Whistle in the Dark and Other Plays*, 1989.

The Vicar of Wakefield, adaptation of the novel by Goldsmith (produced Dublin, 1974).

The Sanctuary Lamp (produced Dublin, 1975; New York, 1980). Dublin, Poolbeg Press, 1976; revised version, Dublin, Gallery Press, 1984.

The J. Arthur Maginnis Story (produced Dublin, 1976).

Conversations on a Homecoming (televised 1976; produced Galway, 1985; New York, 1986; London, 1987). Dublin, Gallery Press, 1986; included in *After Tragedy*, 1988.

Epitaph under Ether (also director: produced Dublin, 1979).

The Blue Macushla (produced Dublin, 1980). Included in *Plays: One*, 1992.

The Informer, adaptation of the novel by Liam O'Flaherty (also director: produced Dublin, 1981; Louisville, 1982).

She Stoops to Conquer, adaptation of the play by Goldsmith (produced Dublin, 1982).

The Gigli Concert (produced Dublin, 1983; Costa Mesa, California, 1984; London, 1992). Dublin, Gallery Press, 1984; included in *After Tragedy*, 1988.
Bailegangáire (produced Galway, 1985; London, 1986; New Haven, Connecticut, 1987). Dublin, Gallery Press, 1986; included in *After Tragedy*, 1988.
A Thief of a Christmas (produced Dublin, 1985).
After Tragedy: Three Irish Plays (includes *The Gigli Concert, Conversations on a Homecoming, Bailegangáire*). London, Methuen, 1988.
A Whistle in the Dark and Other Plays (includes *A Crucial Week in the Life of a Grocer's Assistant, On the Outside, On the Inside*). London, Methuen, 1989.
Too Late for Logic (produced Dublin, 1989). London, Methuen, 1990
The Patriot Game (produced Dublin, 1991). Included in *Plays: One*, 1992.
Plays: One (includes *Famine*; *The Patriot Game*; *The Blue Macushla*). London, Methuen, 1992.

Television Plays: *The Fly Sham*, 1963; *Veronica*, 1963; *A Crucial Week in the Life of a Grocer's Assistant*, 1967; *Snakes and Reptiles*, 1968; *Young Man in Trouble*, 1970; *The Moral Force, The Policy, Relief* (trilogy), 1973; *Conversations on a Homecoming*, 1976; *Speeches of Farewell*, 1976; *Bridgit*, 1981; *Fatalism*, 1981.

*

Bibliography: *Ten Modern Irish Playwrights* by Kimball King, New York, Garland, 1979.

Critical Studies: "Thomas Murphy Issue" of *Irish University Review* (Dublin), Spring 1987; *The Politics of Magic: The Work and Times of Tom Murphy* by Fintan O'Toole, Dublin, Raven Arts Press, 1987; *The Vital Role of Tom Murphy's Women* (dissertation) by Kathleen Hill-Phipps, Ann Arbor, Michigan, 1993; "Tom Murphy: Acts of Faith in a Godless World" by Richard Allen Cave, in *British and Irish Drama Since 1960*, Houndmills, England, Macmillan, 1993; "A Classic Portrayal of Violence: A Case Study of *A Whistle in the Dark* by Tom Murphy" by Martin J. Croghan, in *The Classical World and the Mediterranean*, edited by Giuseppe Serpillo and Donatella Badin, Cagliari, Italy, Tema, 1996.

Theatrical Activities:
Director: **Plays**—*On the Outside/On the Inside*, Dublin, 1974; *Famine*, Dublin, 1978; *The Well of the Saints* by J.M. Synge, Dublin, 1979; *Epitaph under Ether*, Dublin, 1979; *The Informer*, Dublin, 1981.

Tom Murphy comments:

My plays attempt to recreate the feeling or the mood of life rather than to represent it: they attempt to create something that can be identified with, felt or recognised. The emotional and/or spiritual truth is, if anything, more important than the intellectual truth. The mood can be the theme of the play.

* * *

Apart from *A Whistle in the Dark*, which made Kenneth Tynan and other notables sit up in the early 1960s, Tom Murphy's plays have not won the international recognition they deserve. It is significant that when *Conversations on a Homecoming* was staged by the Galway Druid Theatre Company at the Pepsico International Arts Festival in New York in 1986, he was spoken of in reviews as if he were new on the scene.

The main reason for this unwarranted neglect internationally seems to lie in Murphy's exploration of themes that are particularly, though not exclusively, Irish in a form that uncompromisingly makes strenuous demands on audiences. A typical Murphy play, while not necessarily set in Dublin and possibly as vague in setting as the dreamlike forest in *The Morning after Optimism*, is occupied with a spiritual deprivation and a social humiliation that are endemically Irish. The grounding, the objective correlative, is invariably a potentially explosive situation deriving from feelings that are powerfully responsive to defects in a particular community, society, or national institution. Unless one is familiar with the grounding, the plays may appear obscure or the level of feeling inexplicably intense, and the language, which is Murphy's strongest weapon, may seem to be in excess of the apparent facts. This is to say that atmosphere and mood are of primary importance. For example, to the puzzlement of some British reviewers covering the Dublin Theatre Festival in 1975, *The Sanctuary Lamp* caused disturbances among its first audiences at the Abbey Theatre, and comparison was made with the initial impact of O'Casey's *The Plough and the Stars* (1926), when riots occurred. Murphy's play was regarded by some as highly blasphemous. The satiric and iconoclastic feelings released in it arise out of a church setting. The church has been taken over by three outcast characters, Harry and Francisco, who used to have a circus act of a sleazy nature, and Maudie, a runaway orphan frightened into believing that Jesus has taken away her baby because she is bad. Francisco has pursued Harry for defecting and to spring upon him the shattering news that Harry's wife, who formed part of their dubious circus act in rich people's houses, is dead from an overdose of drugs. Harry, for his part, is heartsick at the death of his little daughter Teresa and is burning with feelings of revenge against life and God. He takes the job of sacristan and custodian of the lamp that signifies the divine presence. When Francisco arrives pursuing the fugitive from himself, they argue in the locked church at night over the effects on their lives of the "metaphysical monster" the Catholic Church. With a bottle of altar wine in one hand, Francisco delivers from the pulpit his bitter jeremiad against contemporary Catholicism. But when all passion is spent, the three characters settle down for the night in a confession box, forming a fellowship against the dark and tending the lamp as a gesture of human rather than of divine presence.

Murphy's plays, besides being uncompromising as passionate indictments of hypocrisy of every kind, are also theatrically demanding. Some, such as the historical drama *Famine*, are almost unrelieved theater of cruelty. One of his best and most ambitious plays, *The Gigli Concert*, ran for three and a half hours at the Abbey Theatre, and Murphy refused at the time to cut it. The director and cast of such plays face huge problems, but overcoming them provided the Irish theater with some of its greatest achievements in the 1970s and early 1980s. *The Gigli Concert* may be described as a fantastic reworking of the Faust story so as to explore and express in contemporary terms the nature of damnation and of magical release. The plot centers on the visit of a self-made Irish millionaire during a mental breakdown to one J. P. W. King, a professed "dynamatologist," actually an abandoned practitioner of an American quasi science. The "patient" wants to sing like Beniamino Gigli, an obsession arising from recurring depression caused by guilt. In this regard he could be compared with Ibsen's Solness (*The Master Builder*) and Osborne's Maitland (*Inadmissible Evidence*). King gets caught up in the pursuit of this impossible ambition, and Gigli's voice on record also begins to fascinate him. "He's the devil!" the Irish man warns him. But when the latter backs away, preferring to return to society with all of his neuroses intact, and King's Gretchen figure has told him that she is dying of cancer while Helen accuses him of making obscene telephone calls, King feels compelled to go on with the mad scheme of trying himself to sing like Gigli. He turns to conjuring, and in a theatrically challenging scene he manages to bring off the impossible. The magic of the theater and its illusions allows the audience to believe that this hopeless case has transcended the barriers of the normal. King then plugs in the cassette player once more and, pressing the repeat button, lets Gigli sing on forever while he takes off elsewhere.

Bailegangáire, another extraordinary play, breaks new ground. Written when Murphy was playwright in association at the Druid Theatre in Galway, it has a good deal of Irish (Gaelic) words and phrases, and it deals with Irish tragic material in a style that seems to marry Synge and Beckett. The play combines two levels and two situations in two time periods. On one level an old woman, Mommo, raves in a senile manner in bed, endlessly telling a story of a tragic event in her history but never finishing the tale. On another level her granddaughters, Mary and Dolly, try to come to terms with their own lives while caring for her. Their conversations often take place while at the same time Mommo is raving on. Each of the women is, in fact, trying to seize hold of her life, but it happens that Mommo holds the key to the happiness of all three. Mary, the nurse, realizing that Mommo's obsession with the story is related to her own need to shape her life, forces her to finish the tale for the first time. The story concerns a laughing contest in which Mommo's husband won over a local champion but caused his death and subsequently the death of another grandchild. The full facts have the effect of drawing Mary and Dolly closer to Mommo, and, rather like the three characters who settle down for the night at the end of *The Sanctuary Lamp,* these three women settle down in Mommo's bed and find peace in knowledge and understanding. The beautiful and moving ending was powerfully rendered by Siobhan McKenna as Mommo in the first production, which traveled to the Donmar Warehouse in London in 1986. The play, while being well received, was found to be somewhat mystifying by a number of English reviewers, who could make sense of it only as allegory, with Mommo as Ireland obsessed with her history.

Too Late for Logic tried to consolidate the new direction Murphy began to take with *The Gigli Concert* toward what he has called "after tragedy." These later plays tend to move beyond tragedy into a mood of acceptance. A new attitude toward women, now dramatized as holding the key to sanity and survival, has continued to develop. *Too Late for Logic* is in one sense merely a play about the suicide of an academic too bound up in Schopenhauer, but in a wider sense the play explores how the academic, Christopher, might have learned from the women in his life. Instructive as this learning process may be, it lacks the dramatic fire of Murphy's earlier plays, since the form chosen is to begin with the suicide of Christopher and make him the observer of his own self-defeat. This is a self-obsessive work in which the playwright fails to integrate his new quasi-feminist sympathies with dramatic inventiveness.

Murphy's only serious rival among his Irish contemporaries is Brian Friel, who in a program note for *The Blue Macushla* paid tribute to Murphy's unique talent, his restless and uncompromising imagination. By his refusal to write the popular play and by his digging afresh every time into the daunting recesses of passion and folly, Murphy has shown himself to be one of the best, if the most unpredictable, of modern Irish dramatists.

—Christopher Murray

MURRAY-SMITH, Joanna

Nationality: Australian. **Born:** Mornington, Victoria, 17 April 1964. **Education:** University of Melbourne, Victoria, 1982-86, B.A. (honors) 1986. **Family:** Married Raymond Gill in 1992, one son. **Awards:** Premier's literary award, Victoria. **Agent:** Sarah jane Leigh, ICM, 40 West 57th Street, New York, New York 10019, U.S.A. **Address:** 62 Bell Street, Fitzroy, Victoria, Australia.

Publications

Plays

Atlanta (produced Melbourne, 1990). Sydney, Currency Press, 1990.
Love-Child (produced Melbourne, 1993). Sydney, Currency Press, 1993.
Flame (produced Sydney, 1994). Sydney, Currency Press, 1994.
Honour (produced Melbourne, 1995). Sydney, Currency Press, 1997.
Redemption (produced Melbourne, 1997). Sydney, Currency Press, 1997.

Radio Plays: *Love-Child,* 1994; *The Anchor,* 1996; *Wings,* 1998.

Television Plays: *Cassidy,* 1989; *Mimi Goes to the Analyst,* 1992; *Greed,* 1993; *Flame,* 1995.

Other

Truce. Ringwood, Victoria, Penguin, 1994.
This Is Joseph Speaking (for children). Reed Books, 1994.

*

Joanna Murray-Smith comments:

It has only been with my more recent plays that the earliest signs of a distinctive style have been claimed by me as a writer and resolved as my "voice," for better or worse. This style, for want of a better word, is characterized by broken statements, ellipses, and repetitions, which is the way I "hear" characters while I am writing. My characters find eloquence through the struggle to be articulate. In their broken language, they are searching for understanding, both of others and themselves.

* * *

Joanna Murray-Smith is a young playwright whose increasingly prominent reputation is based mainly on the four plays she has had produced by the Playbox Theatre Centre in Melbourne since 1990, especially *Love Child* (1993), *Honour* (which premiered in 1995 and won the Victorian Premier's Literary Award for Drama in 1996) and *Redemption* (1997). After dabbling with a historical Australian literary scandal in her first play (*Angry Young Penguins* in 1987), Murray-Smith has since turned her attention almost exclusively to problematic relationships between educated, articulate, professional women and men of the 1990s. Ideas of family also figure prominently in her work. Her plays are carefully crafted, highly polished, and neatly structured "plays of ideas," generally in heightened naturalistic form. They sometimes resemble chamber-music pieces in the detailed way in which action among small groups of people (her casts vary in number, mostly from two to four) is developed in increasingly embroidered dialogues and occasional group scenes.

Murray-Smith's first play for Playbox (*Atlanta* in 1990) deals with the sense of loss felt by a tight-knit group of five young upwardly mobile people following the sudden death of their leading light—the Atlanta of the title. Atlanta is a constant spiritual influence and, by means of flashback, an actual presence throughout the play. By turns, different pairs and trios mourn the loss of Atlanta and reconstruct their past; occasionally the whole group meets at a holiday beach house or at a "yuppie" inner-city restaurant. Another early play, the hilarious if lightweight comedy *Ridge's Lovers* (first produced at La Mama in 1992), is also a mixture of duets (featuring the dilettante Ridge and his various lovers) and trios—especially one at the end between all three lovers, which cleverly sidelines Ridge and effectively ostracizes him from his own play. Despite their surface polish and structural intelligence, both plays were condemned by critics as much for their antifeminist stance as for their lack of depth of characterization.

Murray-Smith's fourth play for Playbox (*Redemption* in 1997) fared better with Australian critics, but it is still probably more remarkable for its extremely articulate dialogue and its musically structured form than for its characterization. The play is a set of sharp but brittle dialogues between thirtyish Edie and her brother-in-law Sam, who meet up after many years for the funeral of the noted cellist Jacob (the long-estranged husband and brother, respectively, of Edie and Sam), who was killed as a result of random violence. The musical "theme and variations" structure, in which dialogue is frequently cut into half-sentence fragments shared between the two antagonists, is appropriate enough given the career of the central but never-seen character.

Brilliance of form and depth of content, however, combine splendidly in Murray-Smith's best plays: the middle two of the four Playbox commissions. In *Love Child* Billie, a young iconoclastic television actress who was adopted out in her infancy by her would-be professional mother, arrives (in a carefully prearranged meeting) on the doorstep of Anna, a busy and socially committed film editor who had her infant daughter adopted out years earlier. Initially, the careful plotting leads us to believe that the two are, indeed, mother and daughter; however, a beautifully contrived set of cyclic dialogues (mirrored in the Playbox premiere by a small revolving stage separating the two women) lead us to wonder if the relationship is really all that it is set up to be. So intriguing is the resultant relationship that *Love Child* has been performed all over Australia (and on stages and radio stations abroad) in several productions since its premiere.

Even more effective are the four-way relationships established in *Honour*, Murray-Smith's most widely successful play. *Honour* is a spare and tightly focused study of a long-term marriage that is threatened when a physically and intellectually attractive young writer interviews the acclaimed but aging journalist Gus (husband of the title character, Honor, a published poet who has suppressed her career in order to nurture Gus and their daughter) for a book about celebrities. The alternating dialogues between all possible combinations of husband, interviewer, wife, and daughter—in a well-crafted cyclic structure—are witty and compressed, all four characters are strongly developed, and the action moves briskly and with admirable economy through a series of well-chosen, crucial events in the characters' lives. *Honour* has been re-produced by many Australian theater companies and gave the playwright her Broadway debut early in 1998. In this play and in several others, Joanna Murray-Smith gives articulate and witty voice to a rising generation of Australian women (and men) whose realistic concerns are largely seen on the Australian stage as material for social satire or stand-up comedy.

—Geoffrey Milne

MURRELL, John

Nationality: Canadian. **Born:** the United States, 15 October 1945. **Education:** Schools in Alberta; University of Calgary, Alberta, B.A. in drama. **Family:** Married; one daughter. Schoolteacher for five years; playwright-in-residence, Alberta Theatre Projects, Calgary, 1975; associate director, Stratford Festival, Ontario, 1978; head of the theatre section, Canada Council, 1988—. **Awards:** Clifford E. Lee award, 1975. **Address:** c/o Talonbooks, 104-3100 Production Way, Burnaby, British Columbia V5A 4R4, Canada.

Publications

Plays

Metamorphosis. Edmonton, Alberta Department of Culture, 1970.

Haydn's Head (produced Edmonton, 1973).

Power in the Blood (produced Edmonton, 1975).

Arena (produced Calgary, 1975).

Teaser, with Kenneth Dyba (produced Calgary, 1975).

A Great Noise, A Great Light (produced Calgary, 1976).

Waiting for the Parade: Faces of Women in War (produced Calgary, 1977; London, 1979; St. Paul, 1982). Vancouver, Talonbooks, 1980.

Memoir (produced Guelph, Ontario, 1977; London, 1978; revised version produced Calgary, 1981). New York, Avon, 1978.

Uncle Vanya: Scenes from Rural Life, adaptation of a play by Chekhov (produced Stratford, Ontario, 1978; Portsmouth, New Hampshire, 1979; London, 1982). Toronto, Theatrebooks, 1978.

Mandragola, adaptation of the play by Machiavelli (produced Calgary, 1978).

Bajazet, adaptation of the play by Racine (produced Toronto, 1979).

The Seagull, adaptation of a play by Chekhov (produced Stratford, Ontario, 1980).

Farther West (produced Calgary, 1982). With *New World*, Toronto, Coach House Press, 1985.

New World (produced Ottawa, 1984). With *Farther West*, Toronto, Coach House Press, 1985.

October (also director: produced Toronto, 1988).
Democracy (produced Douglas, Alaska, 1991).

*

Critical Study: "Ancestral Voices: The (European) Plays of John Murrell" by Denis Salter, in *On-Stage and Off-Stage,* edited by Albert Reiner Glaap and Rolf Althof, St. Johns, Breakwater, 1996.

Theatrical Activities:
Director: **Play**—*Mrs. Warren's Profession* by Shaw, Calgary, 1981.

* * *

Though John Murrell has several unpublished scripts and translations to his credit, he is known primarily for the internationally successful works *Memoir* and *Waiting for the Parade*. These were preceded by several other pieces. *Power in the Blood,* loosely about the American evangelist Aimee Semple McPherson, was followed by two comedies commissioned by Pleiades Theatre in Calgary and then by *A Great Noise, A Great Light,* about the late 1930s in Alberta.

Waiting for the Parade interweaves the stories of five women through several years of World War II in Calgary. The eldest, Margaret, is pessimistic, a widow with one son in the navy and one imprisoned for antiwar activities. Catherine, a factory hand, is a total contrast, a promiscuous extrovert whose husband is a prisoner of war. Eve is an idealistic teacher with a husband too old to join the army. They are bossed by the energetic, bigoted Janet, who is compensating for her spouse, a radio announcer who is not contributing to the war effort. (She is more thinly characterized than the others.) Detached from the foursome is a seamstress, German-born Marta, whose father is interned for supposed Nazi sympathies. These women variously talk, plan, and argue while rolling bandages and taking fruit to troop trains at the station, and the detail of wartime life, with appropriate songs, is good. *Waiting for the Parade* is gentle and poignant, sometimes comic.

Memoir is about 77-year-old Sarah Bernhardt in 1922, during the last year of her life, composing her memoirs on an island off the Brittany coast and occasionally acting a fragment from her greatest roles. The only other character is her pedantic, spinsterish middle-aged male secretary, dubious about the theater, a bad actor, who has to play the other parts—a manager, a doctor, and Oscar Wilde. Bernhardt's biography is obliquely revealed. "Old actors do not die; they simply rehearse their dying," Keith Garebian has commented. The play touches on such themes as the relationship between art and life and that between a great artist and lesser mortals. Murrell always writes eloquently, although he risks overwriting. An early work, this is marked by lines like "a tall gray woman with a voice like a clay jug thrown against a stone wall." The 1981 version of the play was substantially altered and improved. *Memoir* has been very successful, translated into more than 20 languages, and performed in 35 countries.

Two of Murrell's subsequent plays are more ambitious, with larger casts. Although directed by Robin Phillips, neither drew much national or international attention. *Farther West,* which the author labels "a romance," is loosely based on the life and death of an actual Calgary brothel mistress, May Buchanan. Starting in Rat Portage, Ontario, in 1886, she travels west to Calgary and then has to take refuge in Nose Creek. She is pursued by Seward, an obsessive, puritanical policeman who continues the hunt for her even after leaving the force, and Shepherd, a rancher who loves her and wants to marry her. They pursue her to Vancouver, where in 1892 Shepherd kills her. In a powerful final scene Seward pushes her corpse in a rowing boat out into English Bay. The play is strongly charged with sex—the first half ends in what Mark Czarnecki called "the most erotic simulated lovemaking ever to see the Canadian stage"—yet May can perform the sex act while keeping her true self inviolate. She never stops seeking the West: "Thomas Shepherd of Sheep River! That's not the sort of kindling to start fires under me. I've got to travel farther, much farther, before I find anybody." In her West there are "no rules, no laws, no judges." Instead, she seeks her independence: "I prefer my own kind of pleasure, my own kind of peace and my own pennies to anybody else's dimes!" The West as myth, in fact, is partly caught in this drama, though perhaps impossible to embody on the stage.

New World takes place on a summer day on China Beach on Vancouver Island, looking out to the Pacific. The seven characters include an unhappy English woman painter (Old World) and her brother, an American maker of rock videos (New World). Between the two worlds are a third sibling, an aging photographer (an Anglophone Canadian) and his assistant, and a cook and a bisexual (a Francophone Canadian). The sadness of both the failed painter and the successful photographer is exposed. There is a complicated plot; the French-Canadian goes off with the wife of the rock video man but includes him too, while her daughter starts to fall in love with the photographer's young apprentice. Yet *New World* is not centrally a play of character or plot. On the contrary, what matters for Murrell are the references to *The Tempest,* the sea, and the sun; the use of Puccini's music; the photographer taking endless self-portraits; and a beautiful blue Japanese fishing float found on the beach, which is admired, broken, and mended and which, at the last moment in the third scene, "spontaneously explodes into a thousand bright fragments." Murrell aspires here to write what Jamie Portman called a "tone poem" beyond the banalities of character and plot (it resembles some of Michel Tremblay's later work and David Storey's *Early Days*), but he has not achieved this difficult ambition.

Murrell's next three plays return to real people and to artists, whom he calls the most tormented and least successful of people. *October* is about an actress, a dancer, and a writer. Both acts take place outside an inn at Fiesole, near Florence. In the first half, in 1913, Eleanora Duse tries, in a personal and pessimistic way, to console Isadora Duncan, whose two children have just drowned. The encounter prompts Duse's return to the stage. The second half takes place 11 years earlier, with Duse having a ferocious quarrel with her lover, D'Annunzio. Murrell sees that genius and monstrosity may go together and that the passion and commitment of the Europeans "has something to teach us in this culture."

His subject is Americans in *Democracy,* Ralph Waldo Emerson visiting Walt Whitman in 1863, during the Civil War. The rationalist and the romantic discuss the war, their country, and its future. The play is static and subdued, of words and ideas. The other two characters are soldiers, one blinded, the other a deserter. Christopher Newton commented that "it is a dense set of variations on themes suggested by the writings of Emerson and Whitman. *Democracy* is a complex metaphor which addresses the problems that many of us face today when dealing with the deaths of young men, whether in war or, closer to home, from AIDS."

In *The Faraway Nearby* Murrell's subject is the painter Georgia O'Keeffe, living alone in remote New Mexico at age 83, and her evolving friendship with Juan Hamilton, who is 26. The play begins with a 50-minute monologue by O'Keeffe, through an evening, breakfast, walking dogs, sketching, and crawling under her house to pursue a rattlesnake. She relishes solitude, strives daily to catch the colors of the desert landscape around her, and free-associates about her art, her past, and her way of life. Juan arrives, first a handyman, later a close friend. He works at pottery, then takes her to his favorite place, the faraway, where a long-dried-out waterfall trickles again. Murrell has written that his especial concern is with the way "some creative people refine and restrict their personal lives, in order to channel maximum energy and focus into their work." He achieves three objectives: he makes us eager to look at O'Keeffe's paintings; he scrutinizes the temperament of the aged, dedicated genius; and he portrays delicately an unusual and moving intimacy, indeed eroticism, between a woman and a man young enough to be her grandson.

Murrell's theatrical career began with effective small-scale work, then in *New World* he groped toward the poetic, and in the audacious *Farther West* he encompassed epic and myth. In the last three dramas he studied artists and refined his literate language.

—Malcolm Page

MUSAPHIA, Joseph

Nationality: New Zealander. **Born:** London, England, 8 April 1935. **Education:** A primary school in Australia, and at Christchurch Boys' High School, New Zealand. **Family:** Married Marie Beder in 1966; one son and one daughter. **Career:** Shop assistant, Ballintyne's, Christchurch, 1950-51; motor mechanic, David Crozier's, Christchurch, 1951-54; commercial artist, Stuart Wearn, Christchurch, 1954-55, Wood and Braddock, Wellington, 1955, John Haddon, London, England, 1956-57, and for agencies, Wellington, 1958-60; cartoonist, New Zealand *Listener*, Wellington, 1958-60; fish and chip shop owner, Wellington, 1971-73. Columnist, the *Dominion* and *Sunday Times*, both Wellington, 1974—. Writing fellow, Victoria University, Wellington, 1979. **Awards:** New Zealand State Literary Fund grant, 1963; New Zealand Arts Council grant, 1974, 1976. **Agent:** Playmarket, P.O. Box 9767, Wellington. **Address:** 75 Monro Street, Wellington 3, New Zealand.

Publications

Plays

Free (produced Wellington, 1961). Published in *Landfall 68* (Christchurch), December 1963.
Virginia Was a Dog (broadcast 1963; produced Wellington, 1968).
The Guerilla (produced Sydney, 1971). Sydney, Currency Press, 1976.
Victims (produced Wellington, 1973). Published in *Act 20* (Wellington), August 1973.
Obstacles (produced Wellington, 1974). Published in *Act 25* (Wellington), December 1974.
Mothers and Fathers (produced Wellington, 1975). Sydney, Currency Press, 1977.
Hunting (produced Wellington, 1979).
Shotgun Wedding (produced Wellington, 1980). Wellington, Playmarket, 1981.
The Hangman (produced Wellington, 1983).
Mates (produced Wellington, 1986).

Screenplay: *Don't Let It Get You*, 1966.

Radio Plays: more than 120 plays, including *Out of the Passing Crowd*, 1962; *A Seat in the Sun*, 1963; *Bread Crumbs for the Pigeons*, 1963; *Suddenly It's Tomorrow*, 1963; *Virginia Was a Dog*, 1963; *This Business of Being Alive*, 1963; *The Cause of Something*, 1965; *This Side of Life*, 1965; *The Marriage*, 1965; *See Mr. Roberts*, 1966; *Too Many Cooks*, 1966; *The Listener with the Pop-up Toaster*, 1966; *Be Good If You Could but You Can't*, 1967; *Has Anybody Here Seen Christmas?*, 1967; *Once upon a Blind Date*, 1968; *Think!*, 1968; *A Fair Go for Charlie Wellman*, 1968; *The Spook*, 1968; *A Jolly Roger for Christmas*, 1969; *The Old Man and the Sea and Christmas Dinner*, 1973; *Going On*, 1974; *I Was a Teenage Matchmaker*, 1975; *Sound Furious*, 1976; *Never Let It Be Said*, 1977; *Flotsam and Jetsam*, 1977; *Hello Goodbye*, 1979; *Mind Jogging*, 1980; *Just Desserts*, 1982; *That'll Be the Day*, 1983.

Television Plays: episode in *Buck House* series, 1974; scripts for *Joe's World* and *In View of the Circumstances* series.

*

Joseph Musaphia comments:

While I have tried both serious and comedy writing and acting, I prefer comedy. Receiving an immediate, vocal response from the members of an audience is the one vital peculiarity comedy has that allows its creator conclusive proof that his effort was worthwhile. By the same token, I hope that what the audience initially laughed at supplies them with food for thought for some time after their amusement has died down. If I had to describe my attitude towards my writing, it would probably be best summed up by a description used by a local critic in reviewing *Mothers and Fathers*. Michael Dean referred to me in the New Zealand *Listener* as a "moral democrat." Having checked out his description in as many tomes as are available to me, I have decided that it just might be inoffensive enough to be acceptable to this playwright, who is not at all happy to be categorized or to write about his own work. I don't enjoy being asked what a play of mine "was getting at," because if the play worked on stage the question should not have to be asked. I can say that after a preposterously varied existence, I count myself very lucky indeed to be making such an enjoyable living out of a typewriter. If audiences continue to get half the pleasure out of watching my plays as I get writing them, I have no complaints.

* * *

In a sense all of Joseph Musaphia's plays for the theater develop out of the early one-act piece *Free*, which is about personal freedom. He has delighted in exploring the ways people hold down and exploit others, especially in sexual relationships, in order to satisfy purely selfish needs. His plays are comedies—in fact, more than any other New Zealand playwright he uses elements of nineteenth-century farce—but the moral implications seldom leave any doubt that it is his intention, as he would say, to hit his audience hard.

Musaphia found an apt vehicle for this in *The Guerilla.* Adam King, an ordinary man—although the name might suggest Original Egotism—frustrated by the minor indignities imposed by petty officialdom on suburban life, barricades himself in his house with hand grenades and his de facto wife and demands to see the prime minister. (It is characteristic that King's success in persuading the police to pass in to him an Armalite rifle, a farcical detail that seems to remove the play from the world of possibility, actually occurred in the incident on which the play is based.) Musaphia likes to use such a character, apparently harmless, whom life drives into aberration if not madness. In *Obstacles* a bedridden woman sexually teases her father's friend into a position from which she can blackmail them both into performing her slightest wish, yet she still needs their assistance to reach the loo. Much of the comedy rises out of situations thus extrapolated, so to speak, from ordinary life into the world of farce.

Farce is not often connected with strong moral concern, and it is a sign of Musaphia's not-so-farcical nature that he has more difficulty with his last than with his first acts. He can catch an audience's attention effortlessly. The bickering couple of a dead marriage in *Shotgun Wedding* are interrupted by the entry of the husband's partner from a recent naughty weekend in full bridal dress. It is a superb coup de théâtre. Equally fine is the opening of *Mothers and Fathers,* in which a suburban couple place by telephone the following advertisement: "Mature, liberated, rational, childless couple are willing to pay five thousand dollars to suitable woman prepared to volunteer her body for impregnation by male half of the aforementioned married couple."

Musaphia is unwilling to resolve the complications that arise from such openings with either a wedding or a pistol shot. Life is good for a laugh, but it is also a serious matter, and when all passions are spent, it returns to its habitual gray.

The more complicated plots tend to diverge rather than converge in the last act. *Victims,* which capitalizes splendidly on its 1900 setting and parallels the ignorance of straitlaced Victorian puritanism with modern societies for the preservation of community standards, opens with almost the entire cast standing around a grave, but it ends with couples separated into three different bedrooms. Even when violence is used, nothing is really resolved. In the underrated *Hunting,* for example, two middle-aged divorced people are feeling their way gingerly toward a relationship they both desperately want when they are interrupted by the return of their grown-up children, also the victims of sexual mistakes, clamoring for their parents' undivided protection and attention. This crisis of middle age also dominates Musaphia's play *Mates,* in which the same difficulty in finding a satisfying action or shape allows the initial power of the piece to drain away.

Mothers and Fathers, by far Musaphia's most successful play, avoids any madness or extreme nastiness and presents four characters not one of whom is really unsympathetic. Their sexual needs and antagonisms result in a realignment of forces. The two husbands, who are rendered irrelevant, are left confronting their two ex-wives, who have joined against the common enemy and occupied the house, an example of aggressive feminism paralleled in most of the other plays. If Musaphia's men are not quite so rampantly chauvinist as some of his women, Musaphia would no doubt agree that their world is so arranged that they do not need to be so self-centered to get their way.

Musaphia has often contributed to the successful production of his plays as either director or actor. His audiences, however, have been suspicious of the taste shown in exploiting such pitiful and sometimes unpleasant characters for such uproarious farcical laughter. There is not a doubt that Musaphia can make his audiences laugh, but they have not always liked being hit so hard at the same time.

—John Thomson

N

NAGY, Phyllis

Nationality: American (emigrated to England in 1992; became permanent resident of the United Kingdom in 1996). **Born:** New York, New York, 7 November 1962. **Education:** New York University, 1980-83, B.F.A. in 1986. **Career:** Playwright. Writer-in-residence, Royal Court Theatre, London. **Awards:** New York Foundation for the Arts fellowship, 1991; National Endowment for the Arts fellowships, 1991, 1993; McKnight fellowship, 1991; Mobil Playwriting prize, 1992, Susan Smith Blackburn runner-up, 1995, Eileen Anderson Playwrighting prize, 1995; Writers Guild of Great Britain Best Play award, 1995. **Agent:** Ms. Mel Kenyon, Casarotto Ramsay Ltd., National House, 60-66 Wardour Street, London W1V 4ND, England.

Publications

Plays

Weldon Rising (produced London, 1992). London, Methuen, 1994.
Girl Bar (produced Tampa, Florida, 1992; Los Angeles, 1994).
Entering Queens (produced London, 1993).
Butterfly Kiss (produced London, 1994). London, Nick Hern, 1994.
The Scarlet Letter, adaptation of the novel by Nathaniel Hawthorne (produced Denver and New York, 1994). New York, Samuel French, 1995.
Trip's Cinch (produced Louisville, 1994). Woodstock, Illinois, Dramatic Publishing, 1995.
Disappeared (also director: produced London, 1995). New York, Samuel French, 1995; London, Methuen, 1995.
The Strip (produced London, 1995). London, Nick Hern, 1995.
Never Land (produced London, 1998). London, Methuen, 1998.
Plays 1 (includes *Weldon Rising*; *Butterfly Kiss*; *Disappeared*; *The Strip*). London, Methuen Drama, 1998.

Screenplays: *Found in the Street,* 1998; *Carol,* 1998.

Radio Play: *The Strip,* 1995.

*

Critical Study: "The Violence of Civility" by Douglas Langworthy, in *American Theatre,* February 1995, pp. 22.

* * *

Phyllis Nagy is a distinctive figure in the British theater scene: a New Yorker by birth, she has been based in London since 1992, when her work was first premiered. Although closely connected with the Royal Court, Nagy's work was very different from the popular successes of Mark Ravenhill, Jez Butterworth, Sarah Kane, Anthony Neilson and others associated with that theater.

Her first play to be produced—a Royal Court production, in association with the Liverpool Playhouse—was *Weldon Rising* (1992). This was quickly followed with the production of *Entering Queens* (1993) by Gay Sweatshop and *Butterfly Kiss* (1994) at the Almeida. Interspersed were several American productions—*Trip's Cinch, Girls Bar,* and her version of *The Scarlet Letter* (all 1994). *Disappeared* (1995) opened at the Leicester Haymarket Studio, while her lays, *The Strip* (1995) and *Never Land* (1998), were premiered by the Royal Court.

All these plays are subtly wrought yet bold and determined in their characterization and narrative: big things happen in Nagy's plays. Her plays are full of murders; beatings; seductions and sex; brutal gay bashings on mean urban streets; erotic encounters in lofts, flats, and hotel rooms; kidnapping; and filicide, matricide, and suicide. These things, however, are rendered strangely familiar, comprehensible, significant, and meaningful, because they involve her extraordinarily memorable characters.

Already discernible in *Weldon Rising* is something of the skewed postmodern tone of Nagy's subsequent work. In *Weldon Rising* Nagy describes a bleak urban landscape, peopled by an eclectic range of finely drawn, wholly human characters: Marcel, a transvestite male prostitute, who refers to himself only in the third person ("Marcel IS the third person"); Jimmy, a beautiful young gay man, whose death is as a result of prejudiced, ignorant homophobia; the lovers, Tilly and Jaye, whose headily erotic encounters contrast with the murder of Jimmy and parallel the emotional rhythm of the drama's narrative; and Natty, Jimmy's insecure, self-conscious partner ("adrift, guilty, obsessive"), a contemporary hero who claims, "I'm not good-looking enough to have gay friends."

Set in a mythologized New York City, the play presents and then replays the violent attack on Jimmy by a nameless "Boy." The impact of the murder on its witnesses is described in heavily metaphorical terms, surreally matching the play's structural fluidity. The play ends with the fantastical, unexplained exit of Natty, out of the dramatic milieu and out of the narrative, the one melting and merging, the other deliberately collapsing in on itself.

Disappeared is a black, urban fairy tale and a tense and mysterious thriller beginning and also ending with another unexplained and unexpected exit—this time of Sarah Casey, the 25-year-old travel agent "who's never been anywhere," from a Hell's Kitchen bar. Sarah disappears and the play shifts from before to after the event. Nagy introduces witnesses, detectives, and suspects, but her audience never comes closer to the truth than the account given at the very start of the play to Sarah herself by the mysterious Elston Rupp: "I kill people. . . . I take them home. And then I do them. In my apartment. I tend to keep them alive for a few days. Before . . . I talk to them. For a while. Before."

This strange outsider figure reappears throughout Nagy's work, most clearly as Rupp in *Disappeared* and Otto Mink in *The Strip,* and is subsequently reworked as the malcontent, Henri Joubert, in *Never Land.* They are figures of unease, utterly knowing and more or less malevolent, and if not the perpetrators of violence, they can be the motive force behind others' violence. Nagy's return to this character and the idea of mysterious and unexplained disappearances are just two of the motifs and themes that run through her work. Across her oeuvre Nagy plays games of familiarity and repetition with her audience. For example, both Rupp in *Disappeared* and Martin in *The Strip* manage thrift stores; in *Disappeared* and *Butterfly Kiss* the name Eleanor is repeated with understated significance; while in all her plays very specific musical references—"Trampled Underfoot" by Led Zeppelin, "Mesopotamia" by the B-52's, "Go West" by the Pet Shop Boys, and "You Don't Have to Say You Love Me" by Dusty Springfield—comment on and support the narratives, while also contributing to the atmosphere and pace of the pieces.

The familiarity of Nagy's soundscape also extends to the plays' settings. The dramatic milieu of Nagy's plays is geographically highly specific—New York's meat-packing district, the Upper East Side, Hell's Kitchen, Queens, Fort Lauderdale, London's Earls Court, the Luxor Hotel in Las Vegas, a precipitous hillside village in the south of France—and yet simultaneously Nagy describes and references a fantastical world in which the extreme possibilities of an urban mythology affect the lives of her characters with dizzying frequency. For example, *Weldon Rising* is set in a rather conventional version of New York's mean streets; however, in Nagy's version, it is the hottest night of the year and rivers dry up, bridges collapse, and tunnels melt in the portentous heat. It is not just that New York so easily mutates into metaphoric ur-city but that Nagy re-creates the hyperreality of the urban landscape into a distinctive space, a queer space. The same transformation occurs in *The Strip* when all the characters find themselves at the Sphinx-like facade of the Luxor Hotel in Las Vegas.

This self-conscious awareness and celebration of the artificiality of the work also marked Nagy's dramaturgical projects as experiments in the nature of theater itself, which again set her apart from her Cool Britannia contemporaries. It is tempting to describe the technique and structure employed throughout her work as cinematic but, in fact, it is quintessentially theatrical. She uses the technique of cutting across space and time and employs elaborate rhythms of language. As Michael Coveney wrote in his introduction to an anthology of her plays, "Nagy writes sinuously and elegantly, working consistently towards a theatrical coalescence of plot, dialogue and swiftly changing scenic representation that is as exciting as it is unusual."

Despite her chosen context of theatrical London and her generous deployment of sex and violence, expletives and slang, Nagy's modern cityscape has all the exoticism and all the eroticism but none of the gratuitousness of some of her contemporaries. In this way Nagy's perspective on the modern condition is distinctive, more end of the world than fin de siècle.

—Adrienne Scullion

NASH, N. Richard

Pseudonym: N. Richard Nusbaum. **Nationality:** American. **Born:** Philadelphia, Pennsylvania, 7 June 1913. **Education:** University of Pennsylvania, B.S. in 1934. **Military Service:** Office of War Information, WWII. **Family:** Married 1) Helena Taylor, 1935 (divorced 1954), one son; 2) Janice Rule in 1956 (divorced 1956); 3) Katherine Copeland in 1956, two daughters. **Career:** Brief stint as a professional boxer; playwright, screenwriter, television writer, and novelist. Instructor in drama and philosophy at various institutions, including Bryn Mawr College, Haverford, Brandeis, and the University of Pennsylvania. **Awards:** Maxwell Anderson Verse Drama award, for *Parting at Imsdorf,* 1940; International Drama award and Prague award, both for *See the Jaguar,* 1954; Karl Gosse award, for *The Rainmaker,* 1957; Archer award, for *Handful of Fire,* 1960; Orbeal award; Cannes Theatre Laurel; Europa prize for literature. **Agent:** Joan Scott, Writers & Artists Agency, 162 West 56th Street, New York, New York 10019, U.S.A.

Publications

Plays

So Wonderful! (In White) (as N. Richard Nusbaum). New York, Samuel French, 1937.
Incognito (as N. Richard Nusbaum). New York, Samuel French, 1941.
Parting at Imsdorf (as N. Richard Nusbaum). New York, Samuel French, 1941.
Sky Road: A Comedy of the Airways (as N. Richard Nusbaum). Peterson & Company, 1941.
Second Best Bed (produced New York, 1946).
The Young and Fair (produced New York, 1948).
See the Jaguar (produced New York, 1952). New York, Dramatists Play Service, 1953.
The Rainmaker (produced New York, 1954). Random House, 1955; produced as *110 in the Shade* (produced New York, 1963).
Girls of Summer (produced New York, 1956). Samuel French, 1957.
Handful of Fire (produced New York, 1958). Samuel French, 1959.
Wildcat, musical adaptation (produced New York, 1960).
The Happy Time (produced New York, 1968). New York, Dramatic Publishing Company, 1969.
Echoes (produced New York, 1973). Samuel French, 1973.
Sarava, musical based on *Dona Flor and Her Two Husbands* by Jorge Amado (produced New York, 1979).

Screenplays: *Nora Prentiss,* 1946; *Welcome Stranger,* 1946; *The Sainted Sisters,* adaptation of the story "The Sainted Sisters of Sandy Creek" by Elisa Bialk, 1948; *Dear Wife,* 1950; *The Vicious Years,* 1950; *The Flying Missile,* with Harvey S. Haislip, 1951; *Molly,* with Gertrude Berg, 1951; *Maru Maru,* 1952; *Top of the World,* 1955; *The Rainmaker,* 1956; *Porgy and Bess,* adaptation of the folk opera by George Gershwin, 1959.

Television Plays: *House in Athens*; *The Rainmaker*; *The Brownstone*; *The Happy Rest*; *The Young and Fair*; *The Arena*; *Welcome Home*; *The Joker.*

Novels

Cry Macho. Delacorte, 1975.
East Wind Rain. Atheneum, 1977.
The Last Magic. Atheneum, 1978.
Aphrodite's Cave. Atheneum, 1980.
Radiance. Doubleday, 1983.

Other

The Athenian Spirit. N.p., n.d.
The Wounds of Sparta. N.p., n.d.

* * *

In a production note to *A Handful of Fire,* N. Richard Nash described himself as "a playwright romanticist." Throughout a long career that has included spectacular successes, Nash has remained true to this honest assessment of himself as a writer of poetic drama, folk fantasy, and musical comedy. During the mid-1950s Nash was one of six writers selected by Fred Coe to create serious drama for television. It was a distinguished group—including Tad Mosel, Horton Foote, and Paddy Chayefsky—and under Coe's tutelage they produced some remarkable plays. Although he seemed unable to contend with the changes that occurred during and after the Age of Aquarius, Nash's best works catch the folksy, innocent spirit of the earlier postwar period in a remarkable fashion.

From Colonial times to the present there has been a recognizable cyclical movement in the writing of poetic drama. Both poetry and poetic drama suffered in conflict with the rise of realism in late 19th-century literature and theater, and not until the period between the World Wars did the discernible weaknesses of language in American plays promote a renewed interest in poetic drama. Since World War II few poets have written for the theater. Furthermore, the postwar liberal definitions of poetic drama encouraged a creativity that promoted the uncontrollable thetrical experimentation of the time and eventually fell victim to political correctness. Following the success of Edna St. Vincent Millay, Maxwell Anderson, and Archibald MacLeish writing as N. R. Nusbaum, Nash dramatized a romantic war situation in *Parting at Imsdorf. See the Jaguar* combined his interest in folklife and verse drama and in a western setting introduced James Dean as, according to one critic, "a sort of human varmint."

Nash believes in the common touch. In the romantic lives of his folk people there is an abiding innocence that may be corrupted if nature's dictates are not followed and if people fail to reach out to one another. In Nash's singular world, however, romance exists in all of its beauty, supported by the author's wit and pervasive good humor. After writing an average comedy about Will Shakespeare entitled *Second Best Bed,* Nash wrote *The Young and the Fair,* which suggested a new pattern for his playwriting—a romantic melodrama in which integrity is corrupted by compromise and regained in the final act through native courage. He then produced his masterpiece, *The Rainmaker.*

In *The Rainmaker* a plain and plainspoken girl looks at herself at the insistence of a self-confessed con man, Starbuck, who tells her not to use the mirror on the wall to see her beauty: "It's in the wrong place. It's gotta be inside you." Originating as a television script, *The Rainmaker* was a success on Broadway as a thoughtful play ending with a great comic flourish and later had success both as a movie and as a musical entitled *110 in the Shade.* It is a superbly structured work, well tempered with humor and with a happy resolution for all romantics. Another work, *A Handful of Fire,* is a typical romantic comedy, carefully sprinkled with good humor. It features a folk setting in a Mexican border town and a naive young hero who, despite the overwhelming presence of evil in his town, is eventually instructed by love to reach for goodness.

In addition to *110 in the Shade,* Nash wrote two successful musicals. *Wildcat* described both the adventures of drilling for oil in 1912 and the character of the heroine, played by Lucille Ball. *The Happy Time,* starring Robert Goulet and David Wayne, was an adaptation of Robert Fontaine's book about family life in a Canadian town. More appropriate than *Wildcat* for Nash's approach to life and his theory of dramaturgy, *The Happy Time* was also more successful in the theater.

—Walter J. Meserve

NELSON, Richard

Nationality: American. **Born:** Chicago, Illinois, 17 October 1950. **Education:** Hamilton College, Clinton, New York, 1968-72, B.A. 1972. **Family:** Married Cynthia B. Bacon in 1972; one daughter. **Career:** Literary manager, BAM Theater Company, Brooklyn, New York, 1979-81; associate director, Goodman Theatre, Chicago, 1980-83; dramaturg, Guthrie Theatre, Minneapolis, 1981-82. **Awards:** Watson fellowship, 1972; Rockefeller grant, 1979; Obie award, 1979, 1980; National Endowment for the Arts fellowship, 1980, 1985; Guggenheim fellowship, 1983; ABC award, 1985; Playwrights USA award, 1986; HBO award, 1986; *Time Out* award (London), 1986; Giles Cooper award for best radio play, for *Languages Spoken Here,* 1988; Lila Wallace Writers Award, Reader's Digest Fund, 1991-93; Tony award nomination, best play, 1992, for *Two Shakespearean Actors.* **Agent:** Peter Franklin, William Morris Agency, 1325 Avenue of the Americas, New York, New York 10019. **Address:** 32 South Street, Rhinebeck, New York 12572, U.S.A.

Publications

Plays

The Killing of Yablonski (produced Los Angeles, 1975).

Conjuring an Event (produced Los Angeles, 1976; New York 1978). Included in *An American Comedy and Other Plays*, 1984.

Scooping (produced Washington, D.C., 1977).

Jungle Coup (produced New York, 1978). Published in *Plays from Playwrights Horizons*, New York, Broadway Play Publishing, 1987.

The Vienna Notes (produced Minneapolis, 1978; New York and Sheffield, 1979). Published in *Wordplays 1*, New York, Performing Arts Journal Publications, 1980.

Don Juan, adaptation of a play by Molière (produced Washington, D.C., 1979).

The Wedding, with Helga Ciulei, adaptation of a play by Brecht (produced New York, 1980).

The Suicide, adaptation of a play by Nikolai Erdman (produced Chicago, 1980).

Bal (produced Chicago, 1980). Included in *American Comedy and Other Plays*, 1984.

Rip Van Winkle; or, "The Works" (produced New Haven, Connecticut, 1981). New York, Broadway Play Publishing, 1986.

Il Campiello, adaptation of the play by Goldoni (produced New York, 1981). New York, Theatre Communications Group, 1981.

Jungle of Cities, adaptation of a play by Brecht (produced New York, 1981).

The Marriage of Figaro, adaptation of a play by Beaumarchais (produced Minneapolis, 1982; New York, 1985).

The Return of Pinocchio (produced Seattle, 1983; New York, 1986). Included in *An American Comedy and Other Plays*, 1984.

An American Comedy (produced Los Angeles, 1983). Included in *An American Comedy and Other Plays*, 1984.

Accidental Death of an Anarchist, adaptation of a play by Dario Fo (produced Washington, D.C., and New York, 1984). New York, French, 1987.

Three Sisters, adaptation of a play by Chekhov (produced Minneapolis, 1984).

Between East and West (also co-director: produced Seattle, 1984; London, 1987). Published in *New Plays USA 3*, edited by James Leverett and M. Elizabeth Osborn, New York, Theatre Communications Group, 1986.
An American Comedy and Other Plays. New York Performing Arts Journal Publications, 1984.
Principia Scriptoriae (produced New York and London, 1986). New York, Broadway Play Publishing, and London, English Theatre Guild, 1986.
Chess (revised version), with Tim Rice, music by Benny Andersson, lyrics by Björn Ulvaeus (produced New York, 1988).
Some Americans Abroad (produced Stratford-on-Avon, 1989; New York, 1990). London, Faber, 1989.
Eating Words (broadcast 1989). Published in *Best Radio Plays of 1989*, London, Methuen, 1990.
Sensibility and Sense (televized 1990). London, Faber, 1989.
Two Shakespearean Actors (produced Stratford-on-Avon, 1990; London, 1991). London, Faber, 1990.
Columbus and the Discovery of Japan (produced London, 1992). London, Faber, 1992.
Misha's Party, with Alexander Gelman (produced London, 1993).
Life Sentences (produced New York, 1993).
New England (produced London, 1995).
The School for Husbands, adaptation of Moliere (produced New York, 1995).
The Imaginary Cuckold, adaptation of Moliere (produced New York, 1995).
The Father (produced 1996).

Screenplay: *Ethan Frome*, 1993.

Radio Plays: *Languages Spoken Here*, 1987; *Roots in Water*, 1989; *Eating Words*, 1989; *Advice to Eastern Europe*, 1990; *The Unrequited Lovers' Manual*; *Hank Aaron's 715th*; *The Fall of Agnew*; *Watergate: An Audio Memory*.

Television Play: *Sensibility and Sense*, 1990; *The End of a Sentence*, 1991.

Other

Making Plays: The Writer-Director Relationship in Theatre Today, with David Jones. New York, Faber, 1995.

Editor, *Strictly Dishonorable and Other Lost American Plays*. New York, Theatre Communications Group, 1986.

*

Critical Studies: "Richard Nelson" by Craig Gholson, in *BOMB*, Summer 1990, pp. 46-49; "Creating a Self, Personal and National, in Richard Nelson's *Trilogy*" by Robert J. Andreach, in *University of Mississippi Studies in English*, 1993-95, pp. 329-43.

Theatrical Activities:
Director: **Play**—*Between East and West* (co-director, with Ted D'Arms), Seattle, 1984.

* * *

Richard Nelson is seriously funny. His writing is often comic, but it is never frivolous, and he uses laughter to deepen an audience's understanding of character and situation. Farcical misunderstanding is one of the ways he achieves this, and it is no surprise to find a Broadway adaptation of Dario Fo's *Accidental Death of an Anarchist*, along with versions of Goldoni and Molière, among his scripts. His plays, however, are perhaps even more notable for a rare thoughtfulness. For a few seasons this thoughtfulness caught audiences in his native United States by surprise, and he was considered suspiciously foreign and probably political.

In a nicely ironic turn of fortune, Nelson's reputation in the American theater grew when he achieved considerable success in a foreign country. His 1986 play *Principia Scriptoriae* was tepidly received on its first production in New York but won prizes and a flurry of admiring reviews when David Jones directed it for the Royal Shakespeare Company. It proved to be only the first of several highly successful plays for the RSC, plays that were subsequently produced to great effect in the United States.

His next play for the RSC, *Some Americans Abroad*, was a comedy about a group of American tourists on a cultural tour of the literary landmarks of England. A knowing and witty piece about American pretension, subterfuge, and enthusiasm, it ingeniously forced spectators into recognition of aspects of themselves. The majority of the audience naturally was British, but they laughed at the Americans onstage while sharing the theater with a healthy number of culture-hungry Americans who were finding large parts of their own itinerary re-created in the play.

The later long-running New York production at Lincoln Center demonstrated just how subtly Nelson had pitched his comedy. Whereas London audiences had been greatly amused by the eagerness of the tourists to experience British culture, New Yorkers accepted such enthusiasm as natural, an understandable Anglo-Saxon search for European roots. They found their laughter in the acutely observed academic rivalries in the play.

Some Americans Abroad shares with much of Nelson's work a concern with roots and rootlessness, with that endemic twentieth-century condition of exile. His play *The Return of Pinocchio* imagines that the wooden puppet who became a boy had left Italy to star in a Walt Disney movie and later became a wealthy entertainer. After World War II he returns to his Italian village, where he finds the misery of starvation, prostitution, and theft. But the play is about an American cloak of protective naïveté that permits the dream of "making it big" to thrive by ignoring the reality of the world.

Between East and West is another story of the uprooted. Gregor and Erna Hasek are Czech émigrés in their 50s who confront the American experience as Gregor attempts to rebuild his career as a stage and film director in the United States. By lying, the Communist party has made it possible for Gregor to return, but it succeeds only in luring back the homesick Erna. Gregor remains alone in a country he still sees as the land of opportunity, directing a play that is finally dismissed as "too European." It contains some of his finest writing, including a scene in which Gregor rehearses Erna in Chekhov's *Three Sisters*, trying to correct her English pronunciation while she defiantly reverts to Czech. The play is entirely acted in English and uses his own adaptation of Chekhov.

Between East and West also represents another of Nelson's concerns, the function of the intellectual in society. The play that most thoroughly examines the matter in an American context, however, is *Sensibility and Sense*. It is a fine and delicate drama about the aging of ideals and idealists that focuses particularly on two women as they were in 1937 and as they are in 1986. Their history parallels the history of the intellectual left during those years and articulates the painful divisions as one woman writes scathingly about the other, who is dying but certainly not going gently.

The RSC offered the premieres of the next two major plays by Nelson. *Two Shakespearean Actors* was his retelling of the rivalry of two actors, the American Edwin Forrest and the Englishman William Charles Macready. In 1849, while they were presenting competing Macbeths in neighboring theaters in New York's Astor Place, the jingoistic followers of Forrest started a riot that resulted in 34 deaths. Using simultaneous rehearsals of *Macbeth,* Nelson's play had fun re-creating the contrasting styles of the two actors, and there is loving comic detail in the backstage and barroom banter of the theatrical companies. The key to the play, however, is an artistic coming together of Forrest and Macready on the stage of a shuttered theater as the riot rages in the streets. Despite the posturing that has gone before, they find that their artistic intentions share a belief that could be called sacred. Like *Some Americans Abroad,* the play demonstrated Nelson's understanding of audiences on each side of the Atlantic. His British audiences chose the side of Macready and laughed at the American's perceived crudity. On Broadway, where the play proved itself as a large-scale work, it was injected with an American pace yet somehow tilted decisively in Forrest's favor.

Columbus and the Discovery of Japan, Nelson's contribution to the 500th anniversary of the discovery of America, suffered a severe critical divide on the RSC's main London stage. Many reviewers felt that the three-hour piece, mistakenly performed in rather small boxes on the vast Barbican stage, was a small-scale play. But the work effectively dramatizes the contradictions of Columbus himself. His greatness of vision and pettiness of character combine to get him his ships and get him to America, and the issues of the play are exceptionally large in scale. To achieve this, Nelson called on the opposing techniques of Brecht and Chekhov to create a "Chekhovian epic," vast and intimate. Passionate admirers of the play recognized this and also recognized the way in which his recurring theme of rootlessness applied to the drifting life of Columbus.

Perhaps his play *Roots in Water,* which has not received a full production on stage, contains Nelson's most specific statement on rootlessness. The work is a sequence of 12 short plays that span the years 1977 to 1988. A husband comforting his ex-wife as her new marriage fails recites something he has been writing: "'Roots in water. We live but there's nowhere to settle.' A poem. That I've been working on for a long time." Coming at the end of the sequence, when year by year Nelson has demonstrated the post-Vietnam, post-Watergate malaise that affected his generation in particular, it nonetheless seemed to indicate that he himself was continuing to work on the poem, on the clear statement about how Americans had come to that particular disaffected point.

Nelson's skill at mastering dramatic forms has also extended to prizewinning radio plays for the BBC in which Americans abroad are directly confronted with cultural conflicts in part prompted by their disaffection with their own country. In *Languages Spoken Here* a second-generation Polish-American in London finds himself out of his depth when he tries to help an exiled Polish novelist with a translation. In *Eating Words* a self-exiled American novelist finds a brotherhood through his friendship with an English novelist dying of AIDS. And in *Advice to Eastern Europe* a young American would-be filmmaker finds romance and utter political confusion when he gets romantically entangled with a young Czech woman, a filmmaker who idealizes the United States.

—Ned Chaillet

NEWMAN, G(ordon) F.

Nationality: British. **Born:** Kent. **Family:** Married to Rebecca Hall; two children. **Awards:** BAFTA award, 1992, 1994. **Agent:** Duncan Heath/Catherine King, ICM, 76 Oxford Street, London W1N OAX, England. **Address:** Kempley House, Kempley, Gloucestershire GL18 2BS, England.

Publications

Plays

Operation Bad Apple (produced London, 1982). London, Methuen, 1982.
An Honourable Trade (produced London, 1984). London, Methuen, 1984.
The Testing Ground, from his own novel (produced London, 1989).

Screenplay: *Number One*, 1985.

Television Plays: *Law and Order* series, 1978; *Billy,* 1979; *The Nation's Health,* 1984; *1996,* 1989; *Here Is the News,* 1990; *For the Greater Good,* 1991; *Black and Blue,* 1992; *The Heater,* 1994.

Novels

Sir, You Bastard. London, W.H. Allen, 1970; New York, Simon and Schuster, 1971; as *Rogue Cop*, New York, Lancer, 1973.
Billy: A Family Tragedy. London, New English Library, 1972.
The Player and the Guest. London, New English Library, 1972.
The Abduction. London, New English Library, 1972.
You Nice Bastard. London, New English Library, 1972.
Three Professional Ladies. London, New English Library, 1973.
The Split. London, New English Library, 1974.
The Price. London, New English Library, 1974.
You Flash Bastard. London, New English Library, 1974.
The Streetfighter. London, Star, 1975.
A Detective's Tale. London, Sphere, 1977.
The Guvnor. London, Hart Davis MacGibbon, 1977; as *Trade-Off,* New York, Dell, 1979.
A Prisoner's Tale. London, Sphere, 1977.
A Villain's Tale. London, Sphere, 1977.
The List. London, Secker and Warburg, 1979.
The Obsession. London, Granada, 1980.
Charlie and Joanna. London, Granada, 1981.
The Men with the Guns. London, Secker and Warburg, 1982.
The Nation's Health. London, Granada, 1983.
Law and Order. London, Granada, 1983.
Set a Thief. London, Joseph, 1986.
The Testing Ground. London, Joseph, 1987.
Trading the Future. London, Macdonald, 1992.
Circle of Poison. London, Simon and Schuster, 1995.

*

G. F. Newman comments:

I declare myself to be a radical vegan (pure vegetarian), one who has hitherto sought to change corrupt and oppressive institutions through political ideas. But lately I've realised that change comes only from the heart of man (and woman), rather than as a consequence of the political clothes he wears. It comes when we recognize a true ideal and are brave enough to run with it; when we see truth and are strong enough to stand and defend it. Recognizing that the exploitation of one species paves the way to the exploitation of all others is such a truth; acknowledging the interconnectedness of all living creatures on this planet is such an ideal. If we want to change society, if we want a fairer, more just, more compassionate society, first we must extend justice and compassion beyond our immediate family and our own kind to every living creature. Until we do so we will never be without racial or national or sexual strife; we will never sustain lasting beneficial change. To every action there is reaction; our troubled human condition is largely the result of what we do to the "other nations" who share this earth with us. If there were political solutions to be had we would almost certainly have them by now, and all of our problems would have been legislated away. Due process is part of the problem, not the solution; only when we gain self-recognition will we start to approach solutions. In my work I strive to create mirrors that reflect some of the problems that confront us to help me gain self-recognition.

*   *   *

G. F. Newman is known above all as the author of fiction, and though he has turned to the dramatic form from time to time, it is not in the theater that he has made his name. His *The Nation's Health* and *Law and Order,* for instance, created quite a stir on television, but that was more on account of their highly controversial content than because of specifically dramatic qualities, and the published versions take the form of novels.

Operation Bad Apple, which was given its first performance at the Royal Court Theatre in London on 4 February 1982, reveals both the strengths and weaknesses of Newman as a dramatist. There is a sense of commitment that has to be respected, and the action moves speedily to make its points. The play shares with several of Newman's novels the central character of Detective Chief Inspector Terry Sneed, and indeed the whole work might be well thought of as a deft dramatization of an episode from his chronicles of the world of dishonest London coppers, which had special relevance at the time. The first scene introduces the theme of the investigation, by police drafted in from Wiltshire, of complaints about possible misconduct in the Metropolitan Police. It is not long before we come to appreciate that there is indeed genuine cause for concern. As the investigators fret about the impact on their family lives of a lengthy absence from home in the debilitating moral atmosphere of the capital, they come into contact with corruption at every level, with brutal policemen abusing their power both in their relationships with brother officers and with the criminal classes. What becomes increasingly plain, however, is the fact that the powerful and cynical Sneed is the most guilty of all the policemen, though his subordinates, too, are portrayed as disreputable, grasping, and cowardly. To conclude this disheartening drama Newman offers a scene in which two pillars of the establishment are seen on a golf course organizing a totally immoral cover-up in an effort to avert any criticism of the status quo.

The effect is certainly striking, but there is no escaping the feeling that Newman is rather too keen to shock by exposing what he plainly feels are the disgraceful inadequacies of the police force. No doubt he has a point, but a little more balance and perspective might be fairer, and it would certainly make for better drama if the audience did not have quite the feeling of being pushed in one direction.

The dramatic style of the play is fluid, cutting swiftly from one brief scene to the next, almost in cinematic style, and with the audience largely left to make sense of the juxtapositions without formal explanations. Characters are used functionally, rather than developed for their own sake, and there is a certain reliance on social types, which is in harmony with the general thrust of a play that shows, in many ways, more interest in groups and classes than in people as such. Some quite lengthy speeches are the expression of the way certain individuals impose their will on those around them. The incessant use of foul language, which some might regard simply as realistic, also serves as an effective and constant reminder of moral degradation.

Moral degradation in political life is likewise the theme of *An Honourable Trade,* first performed at the Royal Court Theatre in October 1984. The title is blatantly ironic, for the play shows how an ineffectual attorney general is caught in a web of sexual intrigue only to end up by being promoted to the high office of lord chancellor (in effect, head of the British judicial system) when the prime minister decides on this as the best way of avoiding damaging scandal. The tone of the play is bitter and cynical throughout, but a tendency toward exaggeration turns what might have been damaging satire into something more like political farce that will amuse those who are already disabused without really wounding those whom it professes to attack. Once again, the dramatic method is based upon a series of brief quasi-cinematic scenes, framed by an opening scene in the House of Commons and a more striking final glimpse of what the audience will appreciate as empty and antiquated pomp and circumstance in the House of Lords. Newman shows particular skill in repeatedly capturing in a few words the typical linguistic usage and tone of voice of a wide variety of characters.

—Christopher Smith

NGEMA, Mbongeni

Nationality: South African. **Born:** Umkumbane, Durban, 1955. **Career:** Worked as a laborer, musician, and actor, 1976-78; performed with Gibson Kente's theater company, 1979-81; founder, playwright, and director, Committed Artists theater company, South Africa, 1982—. **Awards:** Tony award nomination; Edinburgh Fringe first, 1987. **Address:** c/o The Market Theatre, P.O. Box 8656, Johannesburg 2000, South Africa.

Publications

Plays

Woza Albert!, with Percy Mtwa and Barney Simon (produced Johannesburg, 1981; Edinburgh, London, and Los Angeles, 1982; New York, 1984). London, Methuen, 1983; published in *Woza Afrika! An Anthology of South African Plays*, edited by Duma Ndlovu, New York, Braziller, 1986.

Asinamali! (*We Have No Money!*) (also director: produced New York, 1986). Published in *Woza Afrika! An Anthology of South African Plays*, edited by Duma Ndlovu, New York, Braziller, 1986.
Sarafina!, music by Ngema and Hugh Masekela (produced New York, 1987).
Too Harsh (produced Johannesburg, n.d.).
The Last Generation (also director: produced Johannesburg, n.d.).

Screenplay: *Sarafina!*, with William Nicholson, 1992.

Other

The Best of Mbongeni Ngema: An Anthology. Braamfontein, Skotaville Publishers, 1995.

*

Critical Study: *Nothing Except Ourselves: The Harsh Times and Bold Theater of South Africa's Mbongeni Ngema* by Laura Jones, New York, Viking, 1994.

Theatrical Activities:
Director: **Plays**—Some of his own plays; *Sheila's Day* by Duma Dnlovu, New Brunswick, New Jersey, 1989.

Actor: **Plays**—Role in *Isigcino* by Lucky Mavundla; *Working Class Hero* by Kessie Govender; *Mama and the Load* by Gibson Kente, Johannesburg, 1979; *Woza Albert!*. **Films**—Role in *Sarafina!*, 1992.

* * *

Mbongeni Ngema gained world attention as a playwright with the production and publication of the critically acclaimed *Woza Albert!*, which he devised and cowrote with Percy Mtwa and Barney Simon. The play uses a minimum of stage props, lighting, and actors and instead employs dramatic devices such as songs, dance, and mime in a panoramic yet poignant examination of the quality of life in modern South Africa. The resilience of black people as they endured, challenged, and rebelled against the machinery of apartheid is its thematic province. But what sets it apart from many other South African plays that often use a tendentious manner to assault the readers or audience with these disturbing issues is Ngema's sense of humor. This helps the work's aesthetic distancing. But the comic potential of the work is disturbing, for it harbors a subterfuge. As we read the play, we can easily infer that the laughter in it is the only psychic valve for a people who can no longer cry.

Woza Albert! employs the ingenious concept of the Messiah (Morena) coming to visit South Africa. An invisible interviewer tries to get the reactions and opinions of a cross section of the black population, which is played by only two actors, Mtwa and Ngema. Their witty and sarcastic responses and their constant mutation into different characters fill the stage with a dynamic visual theatricality as well as historical insight into the origins of the dispossession of the black citizens. In one of the most stunning scenes two passengers traveling in a train are asked for their view of the visit. They answer, "He will be taken to all the nice places in the country. Like the game reserve where he can lie down with a leopard and a lamb. . . . And then on a Thursday—the gold mines to watch." At this point the actors mime deafening drills and perform a short, ironic dance routine that is supposed to signify the happiness of the black gold miners. They then suggest that Christ should also be taken to see Sun City, the Las Vegas of South Africa, where he will inspect a guard of honor mounted by prostitutes and gambling machines. Finally they ask, "When the television cameras turn on him, will he be smiling? Will he be joyous?" They conclude that he will be crying, and they go on to improvise a speech that articulates the reason for Christ's tears: "What place is this . . . where old people weep over the graves of children? . . . How was it permitted? I've passed people with burning mouths . . . and the other side I sèe people . . . living in glass and gold."

It is this interface between black and white, wealth and poverty, comfort and misery, and life and death that informs both the poetic framework and the political agenda of *Woza Albert!* Its dramatic strength lies in the improvisational latitude the imagined situation gives the actors for wry comment on a vast number of issues pertinent to the apartheid state, while also allowing them space to criticize the shortcomings of their own black people. The dialogue is crisp, the scenes brief, and the reenactments precise. The play ends on an affirmative note in a graveyard where Christ is asked to raise the spirits, not bodies, of the dead black African leaders who have championed the insurrection against racism. Notable among these names is Albert Luthuli, after whom the play is named.

Ngema's other technically competent work is *Asinamali!* (*We Have No Money!*), which as a slogan is the black South African equivalent of "Won't pay; can't pay!" It deals with the problems of unemployment, economic hardship, and homelessness, and it is in theatrical terms a bitter indictment of the white-controlled South African labor bureaucracy that existed under apartheid. Because black people could spend as long as six months looking for jobs in white-reserved townships, they logically could not pay their rents. *Asinamali!* uses vivid vignettes to re-create this vicious circle of orchestrated dehumanization and its aftermath, a protest that ends in a massacre as armed white police enforcements move in with tanks and decimate the agitating citizens.

Set in prison with five characters—Solomzi, Thami, Bongani, Bheki, and Bhoyi—the play makes a distinction between the image of the prisoners as they are stigmatized by members of society and the reality of the political and social conditions that led to their crimes and consequent incarceration. The play uses a series of brilliantly reenacted flashbacks to expose the humanity of the characters first appearing on stage as common felons. Employing a cinematographic technique characteristic of the dramaturgy of Ngema, these five characters people the stage with as many as 20 other human presences. Bongani alone plays 11 characters. The other characters almost equal his feat as they mimic and impersonate various absent people to give dramatic conviction to the stories of their lives.

One memorable flashback in the play deals with sexual politics and unfolds in the scene in which Thami recalls his seduction by the wife of a white pig farmer. The scene emphasizes again Ngema's gift for subversive humor:

> Mrs Van Niekerk always called me to come help buy her groceries on Saturdays. I would sit at the back seat of the car . . . . One day she started to ask me; "how do you feel when you see a white woman?" . . . I WANT THEM! . . . One night she called me in; "Thami, kom hier, come into

the house." A child asked from another room; "mommy, who is speaking Zulu in the house?" she said: "Ag . . . it's Radio Zulu, I am trying to learn Zulu, go to sleep honey. . . ." It became daily bread.

Thami continues to enjoy his daily bread until the day its ecstasy makes him forget to lock the pigsty gate and the pigs escape. The husband returns, and Thami is sent to prison.

These two plays are the most representative of Ngema's vision and craftsmanship as a playwright. His inspiration has been strongly rooted in the experience of apartheid.

—Esiaba Irobi

NGUGI, James T. ***See*** **NGUGI wa Thiong'o.**

NGUGI wa Thiong'o

Pseudonym: James T. Ngugi. **Nationality:** Kenyan. **Born:** Kamiriithu, near Limuru, Kiambu District, 5 January 1938. **Education:** Kamaand ra School, Limuru; Karing'a School, Maangu ; Alliance High School, Kikuyu; University College, Kampala, Uganda (editor, *Penpoint*), 1959-63, B.A. 1963; Leeds University, Yorkshire, 1964-67, B.A. 1964. **Family:** Married Nyambura in 1961; five sons and three daughters. **Career:** Columnist ("As I See It"), early 1960s, and reporter, 1964, Nairobi *Daily Nation*; editor, *Zuka*, Nairobi, 1965-70; lecturer in English, University College, Nairobi, 1967-69; fellow in creative writing, Makerere University, Kampala, 1969-70; visiting lecturer, Northwestern University, Evanston, Illinois, 1970-71; senior lecturer, associate professor, and chair of the Department of Literature, University of Nairobi, 1972-77; imprisoned under Public Security Act, 1977-78; left Kenya, 1982; now lives in London. **Awards:** East African Literature Bureau award, 1964. **Address:** c/o Heinemann Educational Books, Halley Court, Jordan Hill, Oxford OX2 8EJ, England.

Publications

Plays

The Black Hermit (produced Kampala, Uganda, 1962; London, 1988). London, Heinemann, 1968.

This Time Tomorrow (broadcast 1967). Included in *This Time Tomorrow*, 1970.

This Time Tomorrow (includes *The Rebels* and *The Wound in the Heart*). Nairobi, East African Literature Bureau, 1970.

The Trial of Dedan Kimathi, with Micere Mugo (produced London, 1984). Nairobi, Heinemann, 1976; London, Heinemann, 1977.

Ngaahika Ndeenda (in Kikuyu), with Ngugi wa Mirii (produced Limuru, 1977). Nairobi, Heinemann, 1980; as *I Will Marry When I Want*, London, Heinemann, 1982.

Radio Play: *This Time Tomorrow*, 1967.

Novels

Weep Not, Child. London, Heinemann, 1964; New York, Collier, 1969.

The River Between. London, Heinemann, 1965.

A Grain of Wheat. London, Heinemann, 1967.

Petals of Blood. London, Heinemann, 1977; New York, Dutton, 1978.

Caitaani Mutharaba-ini (in Kikuyu). Nairobi, Heinemann, 1980; as *Devil on the Cross*, London, Heinemann, 1982.

Matigari (in Kikuyu). Nairobi, Heinemann, 1986; translated by Wangui wa Goro, London, Heinemann, 1989.

Short Stories

Secret Lives and Other Stories. London, Heinemann, and New York, Hill, 1975.

Other

Homecoming: Essays on African and Caribbean Literature, Culture, and Politics. London, Heinemann, 1972; New York, Hill, 1973.

The Independence of Africa and Cultural Decolonisation, with *The Poverty of African Historiography*, by A.E. Afigbo. Lagos, Afrografika, 1977.

Writers in Politics: Essays. London, Heinemann, 1981; revised edition Oxford, James Currey, 1997.

Detained: A Writer's Prison Diary. London, Heinemann, 1981.

Education for a National Culture. Harare, Zimbabwe Publishing House, 1981.

Barrel of a Pen: Resistance to Repression in Neo-Colonial Kenya. London, New Beacon, and Trenton, New Jersey, Africa World Press, 1983.

Decolonising the Mind: The Politics of Language in African Literature. London, Currey, 1986.

Njamba Nene and the Cruel Chief (for children). Nairobi, Heinemann, 1986.

Njamba Nene's Pistol (for children). Nairobi, Heinemann, 1986.

Njamba and the Flying Bus. Nairobi, Heinemann, 1986.

Writing Against Neocolonialism. London, Vita, 1986.

Conversation with Ngugi wa Thiong'o. Evanston, Illinois, Northwestern University Press, 1986.

Walter Rodney's Influence on the African Continent. London, Friends of Bogle, 1987.

Moving the Centre: The Struggle for Cultural Freedoms. London, James Currey, 1993.

Penpoints, Gunpoints, and Dreams: Towards a Critical Theory of the Arts and the State of Africa. Oxford, Clarendon Press, 1998.

*

Bibliography: *Ngugi wa Thiong'o: A Bibliography of Primary and Secondary Sources 1957-1987* by Carol Sicherman, London, Zell, 1989.

Critical Studies: *Ngugi wa Thiong'o* by Clifford Robson, London, Macmillan, 1979, New York, St. Martin's Press, 1980; *Ngugi wa Thiong'o: An Exploration of His Writings* by David Cook and Michael Okenimkpe, London, Heinemann, 1983; *East African Writing in English* by Angela Smith, London, Macmillan, 1989; *Mother, Sing for Me: People's Theatre in Kenya* by Ingrid Björkman, London, Zed Books, 1989. *Ngugi wa Thiong'o: The Making of a Rebel: A Source Book in Kenyan Literature and Resistance* by Carol Sicherman, 1990; *Politics as Fiction: The Novels of Ngugi wa Thiong'o* by Harish Narang, New Dehli, Creative Books, 1995; *Beyond Ideology: Literary Technique in Ngugi's Petals of Blood and Devil on the Cross* by Koku Amuzu, Montreux and Washington, D.C., Minerva, 1997; *Ngugi wa Thiong'o: An Exploration of His Writings* by David Cook, Oxford and Portsmouth, New Hampshire, James Currey, 1997; *Ngugi and African Postcolonial Narrative: The Novel as Oral Narrative in Multigenre Performance* by F. Odun Balogun, St. Hyacinthe, Quebec, World Heritage Press, 1997.

* * *

Ngugi wa Thiong'o's plays are the minor works of a major novelist. Indeed, one book on his work tacitly ignores the plays. Nevertheless, his first play remains important for its historical priority, and in his later work he offers an aesthetic—indeed, moral—example of how dramatists may serve a popular audience. For several years after its production in 1962, Ngugi's *The Black Hermit* was the only full-length play in English from East Africa. Written just before Kenya achieved independence, the play is a pessimistic look at the rival claims of traditional and modern ways of life, traditional and modern religions, and public service and private fulfillment. Unfortunately, the claims of nation, ideology, family, and love are not explored, only touched upon. The shuffling of the different issues—now one, now another held before us—produces melodrama. The author himself has called the play "very confused."

Remi, the first of his tribe to go to college, loved Thoni, who married his brother while he was away. On the death of his brother Remi's father urged him to follow tradition and marry his brother's wife. This he did, though he felt that he could never love one who had been another's. He fled from her—and from the expectations of the tribe that he would be their political leader—to the city and the love of a white girl. The play opens with the efforts of his mother and wife to get him to return. The pastor will visit Remi on their behalf; meanwhile, the elders also send emissaries bearing "medicine." Weighing the Bible in one hand and the medicine in the other, Remi is moved by these "pieces of superstition" and returns home. He holds a successful political rally against tribalism, but while he discusses future plans, a woman enters with a letter from

> She who was kind.
> She who was true.
> A tender sapling growing straight.
> Though surrounded by weed.

Although his wife had loved him and deep down he had loved her, she had heard him say that he had been wrong to follow custom in marrying her. Thus, she commits suicide, leaving the letter to state that she has always loved him. The play ends with Remi kneeling beside her body and declaring, "I came to break Tribe and Custom, Instead, I've broken you and me."

More interesting is a short radio play, *This Time Tomorrow*. A slum, ironically named Uhuru (Freedom) Market, is to be bulldozed because "tourists from America, Britain and West Germany are disgusted with the dirt that is slowly creeping into a city that used to be the pearl of Africa." In the slum live Njango, wife of a freedom fighter, and her dreaming daughter Wanjiro. During the play Wanjiro's lover persuades her to move into his house, and Njango attends a protest meeting led by a former freedom fighter who is arrested. A bulldozer razes the hut as Njango ends the play: "If only we had stood up against them! If only we could stand together!" The actualities of the situation are caught in a soliloquy of Wanjiro's—"How often have I leaned against this very post, and watched the city awake. Just now, noise is dead in the city. It is so dark outside—the crawling maggots in the drains are hidden." Against this are set the bland phrases of the journalist, with which the play opens—"The filthy mushrooms—inhabited by human beings—besieging our capital city, came tumbling down yesterday."

As an epigraph to his collection of essays *Writers in Politics*, Ngugi quotes Karl Marx: "The profound hypocrisy and inherent barbarism of bourgeois civilization lies unveiled before our eyes, turning from its home, where it assumes respectable forms, to the colonies, where it goes naked. . . ." The struggle against colonialism is dramatized in *The Trial of Dedan Kimathi*, while *I Will Marry When I Want* attacks the new black bourgeois exploiters. Both dramatize Ngugi's views insistently and even stridently.

Kimathi was a leader of the Mau-Mau rebellion who was captured and shot by the British. In Ngugi's play Kimathi's brief arraignment and trial frame four "trials" of his resolution in his cell, reminiscent of the visits of the tempters to Eliot's Becket. The last of these is followed by a flashback to a trial, over which had Kimathi presided, to judge traitors in the guerrilla ranks. Woven between are scenes that focus on a boy and girl whom a female colleague of Kimathi's recruits for a rescue attempt. They allow Ngugi to describe the life of the most destitute, stress women's contribution to the liberation struggle, and show the spirit of revolt passed to the next generation. The complexity of the play's structure saves it from being too pietistic or too obviously didactic.

There are flashbacks to the independence struggle in *I Will Marry When I Want*, but they seem to serve more as excuses for the songs and dances that befit a popular piece than to have a dramatic purpose. The play has a narrower focus than *The Trial of Dedan Kimathi*, showing the destruction of a simple bourgeois family who is both hypocritically Christian and a black tool of foreign capitalism. The didactic message is spelled out by a neighbor *raisonneur*.

All of Ngugi's plays contrast tradition with the exploitation of (neo-)colonialists and their agents. Disgust at official and religious cant is sharpened by a sense that Uhuru has brought nothing to the common people. A believer in the collectivization of economic resources and the "release of a people's creative spirit [through] the active work of destroying an inhibitive social structure and building a new one" (*Homecoming*), Ngugi developed *I Will Marry When I Want* in his home village as "a community product." Its performance led to his being jailed for a year amid charges that he was subverting national unity by promoting the Kikuyu language in which it was written. A later attempt to develop a drama of the people, *Maitu Njuriga* ("Mother, Sing for Me"), used songs in five of Kenya's languages. Its performance was not allowed, but many people saw a series of "rehearsals."

—Anthony Graham-White

NICHOLS, Peter (Richard)

Nationality: British. **Born:** Bristol, 31 July 1927. **Education:** Bristol Grammar School, 1936-44; Bristol Old Vic Theatre School, 1948-50; Trent Park Teachers' Training College, Hertfordshire, 1955-57. **Military Service:** Served in the Royal Air Force, 1945-48. **Family:** Married Thelma Reed in 1959; three daughters (one deceased) and one son. **Career:** Actor, in repertory, television, and films, 1950-55; teacher in primary and secondary schools, 1957-59; has also worked as a park keeper, English language teacher in Italy, cinema commissionaire, and clerk. Visiting playwright, Guthrie Theatre, Minneapolis, 1977. Governor, Greenwich Theatre, London, 1970-76; member, Arts Council Drama Panel, 1972-75. **Awards:** Arts Council bursary, 1961; *Evening Standard* award, 1967, 1969, 1978, 1982; John Whiting award, for best musical, 1968; Ivor Novello award, 1977; Society of West End Theatre award, 1978, 1982; Tony award, 1985; New York Drama Critics Circle award, 1989. Fellow, Royal Society of Literature, 1983. **Agent:** Rochelle Stevens, 2 Terrett's Place, London N1 1QZ, England.

Publications

Plays

Promenade (televised 1959). Published in *Six Granada Plays*, London, Faber, 1960.
Ben Spray (televised 1961). Published in *New Granada Plays*, London, Faber, 1961.
A Day in the Death of Joe Egg (produced Glasgow and London, 1967; New York, 1968). London, Faber, 1967; as *Joe Egg*, New York, Grove Press, 1967.
The Gorge (televised 1968). Published in *The Television Dramatist*, edited by Robert Muller, London, Elek, 1973.
The National Health; or, Nurse Norton's Affair (produced London, 1969; Chicago, 1971; New York, 1974). London, Faber, 1970; New York, Grove Press, 1975.
Hearts and Flowers (televised 1970). Included in *Plays 1*, 1987.
Forget-Me-Not Lane (produced London, 1971; New Haven, Connecticut, 1973). London, Faber, 1971.
Neither Up nor Down (produced London, 1972). Included in *Plays 1*, 1987.
The Common (televised 1973). First version in *Plays 1*, 1987.
Chez Nous (produced London, 1974; New York, 1977). London, Faber, 1974.
The Freeway (produced London, 1974; Milwaukee, 1978). London, Faber, 1975.
Harding's Luck, adaptation of the novel by E. Nesbit (produced London, 1974).
Privates on Parade (produced London, 1977; New Haven, Connecticut, 1979; New York, 1989). London, Faber, 1977.
Born in the Gardens (also director: produced Bristol, 1979; London, 1980). London, Faber, 1980.
Passion Play (produced London, 1981). London, Eyre Methuen, 1981; as *Passion* (produced New York, 1983), New York, French, 1983.
Poppy, music by Monty Norman (produced London, 1982). London, Methuen, 1982; in *Plays 2*, 1987.
A Piece of My Mind (produced Southampton and London, 1987). London, Methuen, 1987.
Plays 1 (includes *Forget-Me-Not Lane, Hearts and Flowers, Neither Up nor Down, Chez Nous, The Common* revised version, *Privates on Parade*). London, Methuen, 1987; revised edition, as *Plays: One* (includes *A Day in the Death of Joe Egg, The National Health, Forget-Me-Not Lane, Hearts and Flowers, The Freeway*), London, Methuen, 1987.
Plays: Two (includes *Chez Nous, Privates on Parade, Born in the Gardens, Passion Play, Poppy*). London, Methuen, 1990.
Blue Murder (also director: produced Bristol, 1996). London, Methuen, 1996.

Screenplays: *Catch Us If You Can* (*Having a Wild Weekend*), 1965; *Georgy Girl*, with Margaret Forster, 1966; *A Day in the Death of Joe Egg*, 1972; *The National Health*, 1973; *Privates on Parade*, 1983.

Television Plays: *Walk on the Grass*, 1959; *After All*, with Bernie Cooper, 1959; *Promenade*, 1959; *Ben Spray*, 1961; *The Big Boys*, 1961; *The Reception*, 1961; *The Heart of the Country*, 1962; *Ben Again*, 1963; *The Hooded Terror*, 1963; *The Continuity Man*, 1963; *The Brick Umbrella*, 1964; *When the Wind Blows*, 1965; *The Gorge*, 1968; *Majesty*, from a story by F. Scott Fitzgerald, 1968; *Winner Takes All*, from a story by Evelyn Waugh, 1968; *Daddy Kiss It Better*, 1968; *Hearts and Flowers*, 1970; *The Common*, 1973; *Greeks Bearing Gifts*, 1991.

Other

Feeling You're Behind: An Autobiography. London, Weidenfeld and Nicolson, 1984.

*

Critical Studies: *The Second Wave* by John Russell Taylor, London, Methuen, and New York, Hill and Wang, 1971; interview in *Playback 2* by Ronald Hayman, London, Davis Poynter, 1973; *The New British Drama* by Oleg Kerensky, London, Hamish Hamilton, 1977, New York, Taplinger, 1979; *British Television Drama* edited by George W. Brandt, London, Cambridge University Press, 1981; *Landmarks of Modern British Drama: The Seventies* edited by Roger Cornish and Violet Ketels, London, Methuen, 1986; "Casting the Audience: Theatricality in the State Plays of Peter Nichols" by Andrew Parkin, in *British and Irish Drama since 1960* edited by James Acheson, Houndmills, England, Macmillan, 1993; "Adulteration as Clarity: Dramaturgical Strategy in Peter Nichol's Passion Play" by William Storm, in *Modern Drama* (Downsview, Ontario), Fall 1994, pp. 437-50; "Peter Nichols" by Kim L. Jones-Owen, in *British Playwrights, 1956-1995: A Research and Production Sourcebook* edited by William W. Demastes, Westport, Connecticut, Greenwood, 1996.

Theatrical Activities:
Director: **Plays**—*A Day in the Death of Joe Egg*, London, 1971; *The National Health*, Minneapolis, 1977; *Born in the Gardens*,

Bristol, 1979; *Forget-Me-Not Lane*, London, 1990; *Blue Murder*, Bristol, 1996.

* * *

Few dramatists have had more success than Peter Nichols in making characters reveal their attitudes toward a problem, toward one another, and toward society. In this media age, when everyone's opinion is solicited, known, and categorized, the writer who is an artist at encapsulating attitude is likely to achieve wide popularity.

In *A Day in the Death of Joe Egg,* for example, Nichols demonstrates admirably his ability to deal with a forbidden subject in 1967, that of the paraplegic, the spastic, the "vegetable," who is referred to in many ways during the course of the play. There was a surge of approval as a new barrier of inhibition was swept away, something very flattering to an audience. Nichols manages to present an uncomfortable subject in a kind of hectic, hectoring way that is contrived not to offend. He incorporates every possible range of emotional response, and we come away feeling that there is something in the problem for all of us.

Nichols's jokes always cut near the bone, and in the revival of *Joe Egg,* directed by the author himself, one sometimes had the feeling that there was no bone left to cut near. There may possibly be something too quiescent at the back of the parents' games, for they constantly exercise their instantly dismissable feelings at the expense of their "problem." One sometimes feels that a sustained and heartfelt cry of pain might be more cathartic, but pain is not an attitude. The main reservation, however, concerns the theme. One looks in vain for a guiding idea to capture the imagination. Here and there Nichols throws in a possibility, as when, for instance, he points out that we are all crippled, all limited, in some way. While the peripheries of the problem never relax their hold, a central issue obstinately fails to materialize. Nichols's method is to touch upon everything, moving forward with brittle and lightning force in case he loses his audience.

The National Health, produced at the National Theatre in 1969, combines many Anouilhesque qualities and shortcomings. Half of the play is a comic comment on the human race, the conclusion being that each of us is entitled to his own death. It is half a gallop through every known attitude to health. The result has a lively spontaneous progress and is well organized, but it ultimately is on the thin side.

In *Forget-Me-Not Lane* the debt to Anouilh appears even greater as a middle-aged man asks himself what went wrong in his marriages and reexamines his childhood and his life with his parents during World War II. The device of shuttling the action back and forth between past and present results in much high comedy and some sharp theatrical moments. *Chez Nous* presents the much trodden situation of two friendly married couples, Dick and Liz and Diana and Phil. On holiday in the Dordogne, they are driven to the brink of splitting up. The marital tug of war that we have already seen in *Joe Egg* and *Forget-Me-Not Lane* is organized in greater depth and comic intensity than Nichols had used previously, and in his presentation of the boulevard twist of fate—that Dick's daughter has given birth to Phil's son—Nichols pulls off a memorable coup de théâtre. Some critics found it highly improbable, but the combination of artificiality and the earthy, even squalid, way the couples express themselves toward each other produces an enjoyable, if not exactly profound, sense of truth.

In *Passion Play* Nichols drives even more relentlessly down the path of adultery by a device of splitting the main characters, Eleanor and James, into double identities, a device similar to that of Brian Friel in *Philadelphia, Here I Come!* Again, it is the many-sidedness of life he attempts to pay tribute to, but what promises much by way of exploring the inner states of the pair never lives up to expectations. No larger vision appears than that of lost apes in pursuit of ultimate sexiness. This may, of course, be sound comment, or it may equally point to the shortcoming that virtuosity has become an end in itself.

With minor plays such as *The Freeway* Nichols returned to the episodic comic style of *The National Health,* though with less success. A great motorway has been built running north to south, and in a weekend jam a number of marooned motorists commingle in the form of a glorified variety entertainment. Although there is some sharply observed satire, we seem, like the cars themselves, not to arrive anywhere in particular. But by the same token, *Privates on Parade* succeeds admirably. It is a mixture of the cynical comments and concert routines of an army entertainment troupe around 1950, and in it Nichols again demonstrates his skill as pure entertainer. *Harding's Luck* is a straightforward adaptation of E. Nesbit's children's novel that uses the author as narrator. The central character is Dickie, a crippled urchin from Deptford. He is elevated by the hospitality of a genteel family, finds out that he is well connected, and finally is submitted to a magical transformation backward in time, from an Edwardian childhood into a Jacobean youth.

Poppy is an ambitious attempt to do with pantomimic convention what *Privates on Parade* did with the concert party, but it is much less successful. Taking as his subject the Opium Wars in mid-nineteenth-century China, Nichols satirizes British imperial commercialism in a mixture of styles, but he ultimately reveals that he has little that is vitally comic or original to add to what became a hackneyed target for entertainers in the 1980s.

—Garry O'Connor

NKOSI, Lewis

Nationality: British. **Born:** Durban, South Africa, 5 December 1936. **Education:** Public schools in Durban; Zulu Lutheran High School; M.L. Sultan Technical College, Durban, 1961-62; Harvard University, Cambridge, Massachusetts (Nieman Fellow), 1962-63. **Family:** Married Bronwyn Ollerenshaw in 1965; twin daughters. **Career:** Staff member, *Ilanga Lase Natal* (Zulu newspaper), Durban, 1955-56, *Drum* magazine and *Golden City Post*, Johannesburg, 1956-60, and *South African Information Bulletin*, Paris, 1962-68; radio producer, BBC Transcription Centre, London, 1962-64; National Education Television interviewer, New York, 1963; literary editor, *New African* magazine, London, 1965-68; Regents lecturer on African Literature, University of California, Irvine, Spring 1971. Currently professor of English, University of Zambia, Lusaka. **Awards:** Dakar Festival prize, for essays, 1965; C. Day Lewis fellowship, 1977; Macmillan Silver Pen award, 1987. **Agent:** Deborah Rogers, Rogers, Coleridge, and White Ltd., 20 Powis Mews, London W11 1JN, England. **Address:** Department of English, University of Zambia, P.O. Box 31338, Lusaka, Zambia.

PUBLICATIONS

Plays

The Rhythm of Violence (produced London, 1963). London, Oxford University Press, 1964; in *Plays from Black Africa*, edited by Fredric M. Litto, New York, Hill and Wang, 1968.
Malcolm (televised 1967; produced London, 1972).
The Chameleon and the Lizard (libretto; produced London, 1971).

Screenplay: *Come Back Africa*, 1959.

Radio Plays: *The Trial*, 1969; *We Can't All Be Martin Luther King*, 1971.

Television Play: *Malcolm*, 1967 (Sweden).

Novels

Mating Birds. Nairobi, East African Publishing House, 1983; London, Constable, and New York, St. Martin's Press, 1986.
The Hold-up. Lusaka, Wordsmiths Zambia Ltd., 1989.

Other

Home and Exile (essays). London, Longman, 1965; revised edition, 1983.
The Transplanted Heart: Essays on South Africa. Benin City, Nigeria, Ethiope, 1975.
Tasks and Masks: Themes and Styles of African Literature. London, Longman, 1981.

*

Critical Studies: "An Ornithology of Sexual Politics: Lewis Nkosi's *Mating Birds*" by Andre Brink, in *English in Africa* (Grahamstown, South Africa), May 1992, pp. 1-20; "On Tradition, Madness, and South Africa: An Interview with Lewis Nkosi" by Janice Harris, in *Weber Studies: An Interdisciplinary Humanities Journal* (Ogden, Utah), Spring-Summer 1994, pp. 25-37; "Jackson 'Pollock' Moloi in Lewis Nkosi's *Under the Shadow of the Guns*" by Kenneth A. Robb and Harender Vasudeva, in *Notes on Contemporary Literature* (Carrollton, Georgia), May 1995, pp. 3-4.

Theatrical Activities:
Actor: **Play**—Father Higgins in *No-Good Friday* by Athol Fugard, Johannesburg, 1958.

* * *

When Lewis Nkosi's *The Rhythm of Violence* was published in 1964, it was hailed as the first play by a black South African to appear in print since Herbert Dhlomo's *The Girl Who Killed to Save* (1935). Because of its sensitive handling of the explosive issues of South African racism, the play was widely acclaimed, and Nkosi was seen by some as being in the vanguard of a new black South African theater. Since then Nkosi has published short stories and essays, a form in which he seems to excel, but his visible dramatic output has been limited to three radio and television plays.

After the mid-1960s the immediacy of the South African situation, the terrific tensions it created—which Nkosi himself has noted in his speculations on the dearth of contemporary plays and novels from South Africa—made it difficult for the black South African writer to do anything other than the personal forms of essay, short story, and autobiography. Drama is written for an audience, and the stricter, though more subtle, laws that developed after the Sharpeville massacre made it difficult for a mixed audience to come together in South Africa.

Thus, we are left with only one major work in the theater on which to judge Nkosi, *The Rhythm of Violence,* an outstanding first play and an important one. There are weaknesses in the play. Certain of the scenes tend to drag, and some of the characters seem static, almost unreal. This is especially the case with Tula and Sarie, the Zulu boy and Boer girl who are caught in the web of destruction. Nkosi's moral, however, that violence is mindless, that it destroys both the guilty and the innocent, and that violence begets more violence, is effectively acted out. Nkosi also does an excellent job of presenting the two Boer policemen, Jan and Piet, in such a way that we see beyond the harshness of their exterior into their confused souls. They are the most fully realized characters in the play, and in one masterful scene, in which Jan pretends to be a black politician and is carried away in his part ("You spoke just like a native communist," says Piet in a shocked voice), Nkosi makes it clear that the possibility for understanding between men does exist unless the rhythm of violence prevents such understanding from developing.

—Joseph Bruchac

NOONAN, John Ford

Nationality: American. **Born:** New York City, 7 October 1943. **Education:** Fairfield Preparatory School, Connecticut, graduated 1959; Brown University, Providence, Rhode Island, A.B. in philosophy 1964; Carnegie Institute of Technology, Pittsburgh, M.A. in dramatic literature 1966. **Family:** Married Marcia Lunt in 1962 (divorced 1965); three children. **Career:** Taught Latin, English, and history at Buckley Country Day School, North Hills, Long Island, New York, 1966-69; stage-hand, Fillmore East Rock Theatre, New York, 1969-71; stock-broker, E.F. Hutton Company, New York, 1971-72; professor of drama, Villanova University, Pennsylvania, 1972-73. **Awards:** Drama Desk award, 1972; Obie award, 1972; Rockefeller grant, 1973; Emmy award, 1984; Drama-Logue award, 1987. **Member:** French Society of Composers and Authors, 1989. **Agent:** Joan Scott Inc., 162 West 56th Street, New York, New York 10019. **Address:** 484 West 43rd Street, New York, New York 10036, U.S.A.

PUBLICATIONS

Plays

The Year Boston Won the Pennant (produced New York, 1969). New York, Grove Press, 1970.
Lazarus Was a Lady (produced New York, 1970).

Rainbows for Sale (produced New York, 1971). Published in *The Off-Off-Broadway Book*, edited by Albert Poland and Bruce Mailman, Indianapolis, Bobbs Merrill, 1972.
Concerning the Effects of Trimethylchloride (produced New York, 1971).
Monday Night Varieties (produced New York, 1972).
Older People (also director: produced New York, 1972).
Good-By and Keep Cold (produced New York, 1973).
A Noonan Night (produced New York, 1973).
A Sneaky Bit to Raise the Blind, and Pick Pack Pock Puck (produced New York, 1974).
Where Do We Go from Here? (produced New York, 1974).
Getting Through the Night (produced New York, 1976).
The Club Champion's Widow (produced New York, 1978).
A Coupla White Chicks Sitting Around Talking (produced New York, 1979; London, 1983). New York, French, 1981.
Listen to the Lions (produced New York, 1979).
Some Men Need Help (produced New York, 1982). New York, French, 1983.
Talking Things Over with Chekhov (produced Burbank, California, 1987; New York, 1990). New York, Samuel French, 1991.
Nothing But Bukowski (includes *The Raunchy Dame in the Chinese Raincoat, The Heterosexual Temperature in West Hollywood*) (produced New York, 1987).
Green Mountain (produced Los Angeles, 1987).
Mom Sells Twins for Two Beers (produced Los Angeles, 1987).
Spanish Confusion (produced Los Angeles, 1987).
Why Can't You Be Him? (produced Sarasota, Florida, 1987).
All She Cares About Is the Yankees. New York, French, 1988.
My Daddy's Serious American Gift (produced Los Angeles, 1989).
Stay Away a Little Closer (produced New York, 1990).
Recent Developments in Southern Connecticut (produced Cincinnati, 1990).
Music from Down the Hill: A Comic Drama in Two Acts. New York, Samuel French, 1995.
A Critic and His Wife. New York, Applause, 1997.

Screenplays: *Septuagenarian Substitute Ball*, 1970; *The Summer the Snows Came*, 1972.

Television Plays: "The Women" in *St. Elsewhere* series, 1984; *Some Men Need Help,* 1985.

*

Manuscript Collection: Lincoln Center Library of the Performing Arts, New York.

Critical Studies:"Theatre as Mystery," in *Evergreen Magazine* (New York), December 1969, and reviews in *Village Voice* (New York), May 1971 and May 1972, all by John Lahr; "John Ford Noonan Dons Glad Rags at Stockton" by Noreen Turner, in *The Press* (Atlantic City, New Jersey), June 1989; "John Ford Noonan" by Stuart Spencer, in *BOMB,* Summer 1989, pp. 16-17.

Theatrical Activities:
Director: **Play**—*Older People*, New York, 1972.

Actor: Since 1967 in summer stock, regional and off-Broadway theatres, and in television and films.

John Ford Noonan comments:
In *The Year Boston Won the Pennant*, Marcus Sykowski, a once legendary baseball pitcher who has mysteriously lost his glove arm and is now in search of a chrome limb to take its place, discusses pitching as follows:

> I am a pitcher. Pitching is my job. I have lost an arm, but I will earn it back. I have science on my side. I'm no college man. I never got a degree. I am no thinker, no man whose job it is to lead or be understood. I am a pitcher. I stand on the mound. I hold the ball, smile, get the feel I'm ready. I rear, I fire, and that ball goes exactly where I tell it 'cause I tell it to, 'cause it was me who threw it, the great Sykowski. What else must they know. . . . One strike, two strikes, three strikes, four, five, six, seven, eight, nine . . . the whole side, 'cause when you're pouring rhythm sweet, when you got it, really got it, they can't see it, they can't smell it, they can't touch it, they can't believe it. . . . It's yours, all yours . . . it's magic.

I believe Marcus is speaking of more than throwing a baseball.

* * *

John Ford Noonan's plays veer in style from conventional realism to fantasy and contain a range of American character types from baseball players and firemen to transvestites, gangsters, old people, and deserted wives. They have earned Noonan critical and popular attention since his first full-length play was produced in 1969. Themes interweaved throughout his plays encompass a Saroyanesque concern for the vulnerability of the world's little people and the need to help one another. While believing in the communion of saints, Noonan largely avoids sentimentality in his work and sees the dark forces lurking in the sunlight. Characters in his early plays tend toward caricatures and are often enmeshed in conflicts with mythic implications.

Noonan's later work discloses characters of realistic dimension while thematically supporting W. H. Auden's thought that "we must love one another or die." *A Coupla White Chicks Sitting Around Talking*, deservedly Noonan's most popular work, is a two-character comedy effectively emphasizing that good can come from unlikely relationships. In Westchester County suburbia a prim WASP housewife, Maude Mix, angry and lost at the latest desertion by her philandering husband, finds herself called upon by Hannah Mae, a prying Texan wife and new next-door neighbor, who makes uninvited daily visits and offers practical but unwelcome advice after deducing Maude's situation. Maude cannot rid herself of the loudmouthed do-gooder even when she truthfully reports that Hannah's oafish husband has forced her into bed on a surprise visit. Hannah leaves her husband and moves in with Maude, and a symbiotic friendship develops. Maude learns to accept the futility of her marriage, and she regains self-esteem and the strength to go it alone, while Hannah returns to her now penitent husband but promises to maintain daily visits to Maude. The comedy offers a perceptive look at two delightfully defined contemporary women undergoing loss and gain.

Although differing in details, a reverse-gender repetition of the above play appears in the later but less successful *Some Men Need Help*. Singleton, a young WASP advertising executive disillusioned with his career and deserted by his wife, is drowning himself in liquor and self-loathing in his Connecticut home when he is visited by an overbearing, lower-class ex-Mafioso neighbor who inexplicably insists on saving him. Singleton cannot eject the unwelcome Good Samaritan, even with racist slurs, and eventually he is persuaded to undergo detoxification and to change his self-destructive attitude. While overly reminiscent of its predecessor, this well-intentioned comedy about two men who grow to like each other relays Noonan's message that help is possible when you love your neighbor.

More characteristic of his individual voice, Noonan's earlier plays are often less realistic in style and context than the later ones. *The Year Boston Won the Pennant* employs fantasy and Brechtian techniques to chronicle the odyssey through a callous society of the maimed baseball pitcher Marcus Sykowski, who wishes to regain his former fame and the ability he enjoyed before mysteriously losing his arm. Throughout 14 scenes with mocking titles, the impractical but courageously aspiring Sykowski visits family and friends seeking solace and money to buy a prosthetic limb. But he is bewildered when he encounters attempted exploitation and unprovoked betrayal or violence, while at the same time, unnoticed by everyone, an antiwar revolution occurs in the streets. Constantly pursued by a mysteriously menacing gangster, Sykowski is assassinated while pitching a dreamlike comeback game. The victimized hero seems to be a metaphor for a baffled, maimed Vietnam-era America self-destructively pursuing an impossible quest for lost prestige and driven by forces of greed and unconscionable irrationality. This dark comedy, sometimes ambiguously uneven in style and characterization, does more than confirm Leo Durocher's observation that "good guys finish last."

The hysteria and the inclination toward fantasy of ordinary people are often subjects in Noonan's work of the 1970s. In *Rainbows for Sale* a youthful firehouse custodian meets his older self only to find him a deceased racist fireman who has gone on a maniacal shooting spree in an ethnic neighborhood. The play effectively mixes fantasy with forcibly graphic narrative. The difficulties of aging are represented with empathy and irony in *Older People,* a cycle of 15 sketchlike short plays with interludes of song—a Noonan characteristic—dealing with the new fears and waning sexual powers of the elderly. While the sketches range in quality, the work's contrast between its sad and wistful subject matter and its farcical form is engaging.

Concern with fantasy and the bizarre as well as with domestic alienation is sustained in several Noonan plays of the 1980s, which tend to be less successful than earlier works. In *Talking Things Over with Chekhov,* a budding playwright has hallucinatory conversations with Chekhov about literary philosophy. The playwright renews a friendship with a former actress-lover, desperate for a comeback after suffering a nervous breakdown, by offering her a starring role in his explicit autobiographical play about their past relationship. Her casting has been confirmed by a willing producer. When the playwright secures a more advantageous producer who will cast another actress, however, she is desolate despite the writer's claim that the play is the truly major star. The two-character piece begins awkwardly and totters between comedy and an uneven examination of obsession. *Listen to the Lions* deals with a Boston Irish family, peopled by insufficiently drawn yet colorful characters unable to relate to one another. *My Daddy's Serious American Gift* focuses on a girl who tells of having found her father dead in her home with a killer who wants her to call it suicide. The implausible story is not sufficiently rescued by its bizarre quality.

Three plays of the 1990s, ranging from fantasy to realism, focus on couples. *Stay Away a Little Closer,* set in a snowstorm-beset Vermont cabin, targets a dysfunctional married couple who are visited by the ghost of the cabin's former owner, sent to save their souls. Despite a vague theme, this contemporary ghost story offers interestingly complex characters. *A Critic and His Wife* centers on a self-obsessed couple who become rivals when the critic-husband turns novelist and his wife a noted newspaper columnist. That the characters need greater humanization does not negate Noonan's telling point that writing cannot substitute for living. *Music from Down the Hill* brings together two women of different generations who share a room in a mental health clinic and a belief in the power of rock music. The spoiled younger woman claims to have murdered college roommates, and the older, a former teacher, claims to have been a boogie champion and a participant in the music festival at Woodstock, also held in awe by her roommate. Revelations effectively, if too clearly, disclose that one woman is a self-deceiving liar and emotional cripple while the other is a healer.

In a 1989 interview Noonan claimed that a playwright has to listen to the child in himself and to write about things that pop into his head. This philosophy continues to be borne out, not always with success, in his work. Yet Noonan remains a talented dramatist with a zany, acerbic, and perceptive vision of the world. He has an individual voice worthy of attention.

—Christian H. Moe

NORMAN, Marsha

Nationality: American. **Born:** Marsha Williams in Louisville, Kentucky, 21 September 1947. **Education:** Durrett High School, Louisville; Agnes Scott College, Decatur, Georgia, B.A. in philosophy 1969; University of Louisville, 1969-71, M.A. 1971. **Family:** Married 1) Michael Norman in 1969 (divorced 1974); 2) Dann C. Byck, Jr., in 1978 (divorced 1986); 3) Tim Dykma in 1987, two children. **Career:** Worked with disturbed children at Kentucky Central State Hospital, 1969-71; teacher, Brown School, Louisville, 1973—; book reviewer and editor of children's supplement (*Jelly Bean Journal*), Louisville *Times*, mid-1970s; playwright-in-residence, Actors Theatre, Louisville, 1977-78, and Mark Taper Forum, Los Angeles, 1979; treasurer, the Dramatists Guild, 1988—. Lives in Long Island, New York. **Awards:** American Theater Critics Association prize, 1978; National Endowment for the Arts grant, 1978; Rockefeller grant, 1979; John Gassner award, 1979; Oppenheimer award, 1979; Susan Smith Blackburn prize, 1983; Pulitzer prize, 1983; American Academy award, 1986; Tony award, 1991, and Drama Desk award, 1991, both for *The Secret Garden.* **Agent:** Jack Tantleff, The Tantleff Agency, 375 Greenwich Street, New York, New York 10013, U.S.A.

Publications

Plays

Getting Out (produced Louisville, 1977; New York, 1978; London, 1988). New York, Avon, 1980.

Third and Oak: The Laundromat (produced Louisville, 1978; New York, 1979). New York, Dramatists Play Service, 1980.

Third and Oak: The Pool Hall (produced Louisville, 1978). New York, Dramatists Play Service, 1985.
Circus Valentine (produced Louisville, 1979).
Merry Christmas, in *Holidays* (produced Louisville, 1979).
'Night, Mother (produced Cambridge, Massachusetts, 1982; New York, 1983; London, 1985). New York, Hill and Wang, 1983; London, Faber, 1984.
The Holdup (produced San Francisco, 1983). New York, Dramatists Play Service, 1987.
Traveler in the Dark (produced Cambridge, Massachusetts, 1984; revised version produced Los Angeles, 1985; New York, 1990).
Four Plays (includes *Getting Out, Third and Oak, The Holdup, Traveler in the Dark*). New York, Theatre Communications Group, 1988.
Sarah and Abraham (produced Louisville, 1988).
The Secret Garden, music by Lucy Simon, adaptation of the novel by Frances Hodgson Burnett (produced Norfolk, Virginia, 1990; New York, 1991). London, French, 1993.
The Red Shoes (produced New York, 1993).
D. Boone (produced Louisville, 1992).
Trudy Blues. Lyme, New Hampshire, Smith and Kraus, 1995.
Marsha Norman: Collected Plays (includes *Getting Out*; *Third and Oak*; *Circus Valentine*; *The Holdup*; *Traveler in the Dark*; *Sarah and Abraham*; *Loving Daniel Boone*; *Three Speeches*). Lyme, New Hampshire, Smith and Kraus, 1998.

Screenplay: *'Night Mother,* 1986.

Television Plays: *It's the Willingness* (*Visions* series), 1978; *In Trouble at Fifteen* (*Skag* series), 1980; *Face of a Stranger,* 1991.

Novel

The Fortune Teller. New York, Random House, 1987; London, Collins, 1988.

*

Bibliography: "A Marsha Norman Bibliography" by Robert Conklin, in *Marsha Norman: A Casebook,* edited by Linda Ginter Brown, New York, Garland Publishers, 1996.

Critical Studies: "A Sisterhood of Women: Marsha Norman's *Getting Out* and *The Laundromat*" by Margarete Rubik, in *Gramma: Journal of Theory and Criticism,* 1994, pp. 141-47; "Marsha Norman" by Daryll Grantley, in *American Drama,* edited by Clive Bloom, New York, St. Martin's, 1995; "Locked behind the Proscenium: Feminist Strategies in *Getting Out* and *My Sister in This House*" by Patricia R. Schroeder, in *Feminist Theatre and Theory,* edited by Helene Keyssar, New York, St. Martin's, 1996; *Marsha Norman: A Casebook,* edited by Linda Ginter Brown, New York, Garland Publishers, 1996; "Suicide in Beth Henley's *Crimes of the Heart* and Marsha Norman's *"Night Mother*" by Lana A. Whited, in *Southern Quarterly* (Hattiesburg, Missouri), Fall 1997, pp. 65-74.

Theatrical Activities:
Director: **Play**—*Semi-Precious Things* by Terri Wagener, Louisville, 1980.

* * *

"I know now, all these years and plays later, that I always write about solitary confinement." If this realization only came to Marsha Norman with the anthologizing of *Getting Out* in 1988, it also eluded critics who generalized on her early successes and tended to find a playwright grasping at various fragments of social significance and dissecting them within a broad spectrum of dramaturgic experimentation. Yet the focalizing drive toward the character locked within herself certainly is a recurrent motif and is related suggestively to another of Norman's statements quoted in *The Feminist Companion to Literature in English:* "What you cannot escape seeing is that we are all disturbed kids."

Norman's perception derives from her early experience working with disturbed children, partly at the Kentucky Central State Hospital, and is most obviously illustrated in *Getting Out*. But most of her plays take place at the intersection of the confined and the disturbed. *Third and Oak: The Laundromat* parodies the idea of "standing by your man" in its portrait of two women accidentally meeting in the middle of the night carrying shirts that are the relics of relationships they want to think still survive. But the play ends with an assertion of the strength of solitude. If *The Holdup* presents itself as a parody of the frontier myth, it is also a study of a naive young man's detachment from a suffocating mother to a point of self-sufficient isolation. *Traveler in the Dark* is more complex in its structuring of relationships, but the same dynamics recur in the central character of Sam, a famous surgeon trying to place himself as father, husband, and son and fleeing back to his now absent mother when his professional skills leave him stranded and helpless beside a dying friend.

But it is Norman's two full-length plays with female protagonists that most amply illustrate her skills at feminizing and contemporizing the problem play. If the material of *Getting Out* sounds in synopsis rather like a case study with obvious elements of social didacticism, its technique is reminiscent of O'Neill's *Strange Interlude* in its schizoid presentation of the main character. The whole action follows the first day of notional freedom for Arlene, just released on parole after serving a murder sentence but unable to detach from her "criminal" self, Arlie, played by another actor. Detachment, however, is just the obverse of the integration she seeks into society, into a straight career, and into her fragmented family, but the quest for some kind of bonding is thwarted by the people she meets. These include her former pimp and her prison guard, both with an agenda of brutal exploitation, her mother, who in effect rejects her, and her new neighbor, another ex-con who still carries the ambience of the prison with her. Instead, integration comes with the self she has tried to exorcise, and the play's ending has Arlie and Arlene laughing playfully together, an interesting anticipation of Caryl Churchill's finale to *Cloud Nine*.

Jessie Cates, whose suicide is the entire action of *'Night, Mother,* is a restatement and development of this integration. As the often quoted introductory statement emphasizes, she has only just got herself together. Only in the last year has she "gained control of her own mind and body," and the choice of suicide is the triumphant result of this control. But in the period before control there was a quest for identity as daughter, wife, and mother, a search through pockets of silence most graphically illustrated by her epileptic fits. This abnormality, read as a biological deviance parallel to Arlie's antisocial propensities, means that Jessie, too, has constantly been generating her own state of solitary confinement.

Because they have in different senses been "inside," both Jessie and Arlene are highly receptive to reports of their personal history they have been out of touch with. The murder for which Arlie was locked up is relayed back to her by people who saw it covered on television. Jessie wants to know what she, her other self, looks like during fits, and this is directly related to the search for control that is central to all of Norman's protagonists. Arlene's hunt for normal work will bring her to meet strangers who nevertheless know the television image of Arlie, a gaze as brutal, as impersonal, and as invasive as the thought of the two-way mirrors in the prison washrooms. The reductiveness of this is severe, a total denial of adult dignity, as when Jessie regresses to a condition of infantile dependence when she wets herself during fits, only knowing that it has happened because others have told her that they cleaned her up.

Such a crisis of identity reflects the blur of social positioning that both women face. An absent father confronts them with an Oedipus/Electra ambiguity. Society tells both of them that they have failed as mothers of the sons who are having their own problems of integration. And both are threatened by the blackmail of dependence from one of Jane Gallop's "phallic mothers," through whom, in Luce Irigaray's terms, there is the prospect of "femininity" being "effaced to leave room for maternity," especially when these mothers do not hesitate to hit them with evidence of their own incompetence as mothers. But in their ultimate refusal to disavow themselves in the face of such pressures or to annihilate the "disturbed kid" in themselves and now in society at large, there is the defiant insistence that the dismantling of structures may not just be anarchic but may also bring a more integrated sense of self, even, if necessary, in confinement. Jessie's final wish for her son may serve as Norman's gloss on the anxieties of the craft of modern mothering: if he spends his inheritance on dope, she hopes that it is at least good dope.

—Howard McNaughton

NOWRA, Louis

Nationality: Australian. **Born:** Melbourne, Victoria, in 1950. **Education:** La Trobe University, Bundoora, Victoria. **Family:** Married Sarah de Jong in 1974. **Career:** Writer-in-residence, University of Queensland, Brisbane, 1979, Lighthouse Company, Adelaide, 1982, Playbox Theatre, Melbourne, 1985, and Capricornia Institute, 1987; associate artistic director, Sydney Theatre Company, 1980, and Lighthouse Company, 1983; guest lecturer, Yale University, New Haven, Connecticut, 1988; writer-in-residence, University of Queensland, 1994. **Awards:** Australian Literature Board fellowship, 1975, 1977-79, 1981, 1983; Prix Italia award, for *Summer of the Aliens,* 1990; NSW Premier's Prize, for *The Temple,* 1994; Australian Literary Society Gold Medal, 1994; Australia/Canada award, 1994; The Green Room award for Best New Play, 1995; A.F.I. award, Best Adapted Screenplay, for *Cosi,* 1996. Honorary doctorate: Griffiths University, 1996. **Agent:** Hilary Linstead and Associates, level 18, plaza 11, 500 Oxford Street, Bondi Junction, New South Wales 2022, Australia.

Publications

Plays

Kiss the One-Eyed Priest (produced Melbourne, 1973).

Albert Names Edward (broadcast 1975; produced Melbourne, 1976). Radio version published in *Five Plays for Radio*, edited by Alrene Sykes, Sydney, Currency Press, 1976; stage version published with *Inner Voices*, Currency Press, 1983.

Inner Voices (libretti) (produced Sydney, 1977; London, 1982). Sydney, Currency Press, 1978.

Visions (produced Sydney, 1978). Sydney, Currency Press, 1979.

The Lady of the Camellias, adaptation of a play by Dumas fils (produced Sydney, 1979).

Inside the Island (produced Sydney, 1980). With *The Precious Woman*, Sydney, Currency Press, 1981.

The Precious Woman (produced Sydney, 1980). With *Inside the Island*, Sydney, Currency Press, 1981.

Cyrano de Bergerac, adaptation of the play by Rostand (produced Sydney, 1980).

The Song Room (broadcast 1980). Stage version published in *Seven One-Act Plays*, edited by Rodney Fisher, Sydney, Currency Press, 1983.

Death of Joe Orton (produced Adelaide, 1980).

Beauty and the Beast (produced Sydney, 1980).

Lulu, adaptation of a play by Frank Wedekind (produced Adelaide, 1981).

Spellbound (produced Adelaide, 1982; London, 1986).

Royal Show (produced Adelaide, 1982).

The Prince of Homburg, adaptation of a play by Heinrich von Kleist (also director: produced Adelaide, 1982).

Sunrise (produced Adelaide, 1983). Sydney, Currency Press, 1983.

The Golden Age (produced Melbourne, 1985; Bristol, 1992). Sydney, Currency Press, 1985.

Whitsunday (opera), music by Brian Howard (produced Sydney, 1988).

Capricornia, adaptation of the novel by Xavier Herbert (produced Sydney, 1988). Sydney, Currency Press, 1988.

Ghosts, co-translated with May-Brit Ackerholt (produced 1988).

Byzantine Flowers (produced Sydney, 1989).

Summer of the Aliens (as *The Summer of the Aliens*, broadcast 1989; as *Summer of the Aliens* produced Melbourne, 1992). Sydney, Currency Press, 1992.

The Watchtower (produced Sydney, 1990). Yackandandah Press, 1992.

Love Burns (libretti), composed by Graeme Koehne (produced Adelaide, 1992).

Cosi (produced Sydney, 1992). Sydney, Currency Press, 1992; screenplay published as *Così*, Sydney, Currency Press, 1996.

The Temple (produced Melbourne, 1993). Sydney, Currency Press, 1993.

Radiance (produced Sydney, 1993). Sydney, Currency Press, 1993.

Crow (produced South Australian Theater Company, 1994). Sydney, Currency Press, 1994.

The Price of Prayer (produced Sydney, 1995).

The Incorruptible (produced Melbourne, 1995). Sydney, Currency Press, 1995.

Miss Bosnia (produced Brisbane, 1995).

The Jungle (produced Sydney, 1995). University of Woollongong Press, 1988.

Deceit (produced Zootango Theatre Company, 1996).

Screenplays: *Map of the Human Heart,* 1994; *Cosi,* 1996; *Heaven's Burning,* 1997; *The Matchmaker,* 1997; *Radiance,* 1998.

Radio Plays: *Albert Names Edward,* 1975; *The Song Room,* 1980; *The Widows,* 1986; *The Summer of the Aliens,* 1989; *Sydney,* 1993; *Moon of the Exploding Trees,* 1995.

Television Plays: *Displaced Persons,* 1985; *Hunger,* 1986; *The Lizard King,* 1987; *The Last Resort,* 1987; *Directly from My Heart to You,* 1996.

Novels

The Misery of Beauty: The Loves of Frogman. Sydney and London, Angus and Robertson, 1976.
Palu. Woollahara, New South Wales, Pan, 1987.
Red Nights. Sydney, Picador, 1997.

Other

The Cheated. Sydney, Angus and Robertson, 1979.

*

Critical Study: *Louis Nowra,* edited by Veronica Kelly, Amsterdam, Rodopi, 1987; *The Plays of Louis Nowra* by Veronica Kelly, Sydney, Currency Press, 1998.

Theatrical Activities:
Director: **Plays**—*For a Dancer,* Adelaide, 1982; *The Prince of Homburg,* Adelaide, 1982; *The Marriage of Figaro* by Beaumarchais, Adelaide, 1983; *Not about Heroes* by Stephen MacDonald, Melbourne, 1985; *The Lighthouse* by Peter Maxwell Davies, Sydney, 1985.

Actor: **Play**—*Summer of the Aliens,* 1992.

* * *

Louis Nowra was born in a working-class family in a new postwar outer-Melbourne suburb. His comic and savage theatrical parables obliquely image the cultural patterns of contemporary Australian experience. Yet his early performed plays puzzled some observers by their exotic locales, such as eighteenth-century Russia *(Inner Voices),* warlord China *(The Precious Woman),* or Paraguay during the genocidal 1870s War of the Triple Alliance *(Visions).* With its violence, farce, and formal stylization, his theater presents a wry view of the savageries of "history," its transformative powers, and the price of survival. Nowra was originally suspicious of naturalism and his early plays were imagistic and scene based: "I was bemused by American and English naturalism, which left me with the impression of whingeing men in grubby cardigans and women shouting at their husbands." Although his recent plays have been more character based and emotionally textured, the suspicion remains. He finds the post-1970s mainstage traditions of Australian naturalism, with its masculine focus, both theatrically and ideologically constricting, preferring the more extensive emotional opportunities afforded by female characters. Both his 1993 political farce *The Temple,* dealing with the resistible rise of 1980s junk millionaires, and the 1995 dystopian fantasy *The Incorruptible,* based on the careers of populist politicians, however, manipulate the Australian demotic masculine idiom as expertly as such writers of the 1970s New Wave as Jack Hibberd or David Williamson have done. Despite stylistic similarities with New Wave in his early writing, he resists what he sees as its programmatic closure of the Brechtian project, satirizing 1970s didactic theater in his 1992 rehearsal farce *Cosi.* His theater owes more to expressionistic, mythical, and musical modes, which produce an expansive, highly visual, and tonally mixed dramaturgy. Through this dramaturgy the contradictions and decentered consciousness of a multicultural and multiracial society are explored with complexity unequalled in contemporary Australian writing.

Ivan, true heir to the Russian throne *(Inner Voices),* has been imprisoned all his life in a fortress knowing no language but his name. Released to become a puppet-tsar, he is forced to mouth, with hilarious lack of polish or decorum, his mentors' political proclamations and trite Enlightenment philosophy. As the pathetically stunted consciousness of Ivan struggles towards expression, he becomes a tyrant, mutilating and imprisoning his tutors to drown out the sound of what have now become his own truly inner voices. Finally Ivan is imprisoned anew, a solitary figure screaming for silence like an image in a Francis Bacon painting. Nowra's motifs of crippled, mute, or aphasic characters, of language acquisition and the process of cultural transmission, suggest a postcolonial dimension. "Teaching" is a power maneuver, neither disinterested nor innocuous. Later plays continue to explore the marginalized state of colonized subjects and their gradual emergence into a new hybridized and empowering consciousness, signified, as in *The Golden Age,* by the invention of powerfully poetic creolized languages.

Visions enlarges upon the anti-imperial theme of *Inner Voices.* It introduces the first of Nowra's many powerful female roles in Eliza Lynch, a dubiously Parisian courtesan now married to Lopez, the military dictator of Paraguay. In this fantasia on historical themes, Lynch acts as the snobbish transmitter of haute bourgeoise European "culture" to a "backward" nation, leading to their own overthrow at the cost of Paraguay's catastrophic military defeat. Juana the blind girl, a brutalized victim of the invasion, speaks her mystical visions in a private language. As the first of Nowra's Aboriginal characters—figures whose dislocation and endurance embody the discursive position of black experience within white Australia—her fate is to eventually parrot Lynch's visions of "culture." But in *The Golden Age* and *Byzantine Flowers* the colonized character, frequently of mixed racial origin, is able to transcend the brutalities of colonization and use her acquired language to speak her own visions and procure her own autonomy. Since the adaptation of *Capricornia* for Belvoir Street Theater's national tour in 1988, Nowra has written major roles for Aboriginal actors; particularly *Crow* and the three-actor *Radiance.*

In 1980 Nowra shocked some and delighted others by setting *Inside the Island* in Australia. Its period is 1912, three years before Gallipoli, its location a remote wheat property whose semifeudal social relations, based on a suppressed history of black dispossession, are apocalyptically disrupted when a squad of young trainee soldiers are poisoned by ergotized flour at a bush picnic and run wild in a destructive orgy. Poisoned flour was a common method of massacre of Aboriginals. Expressionistic images of white cricket flannels streaked in blood, of raging bushfires, and violent self-mutilation show the eruption both of the suppressed past and of the immediate future, since the ergotism scenes draw on accounts of the hell of the Somme offensive: the true poisoned legacy is and remains imperialism. A more elliptical version of Australia's client-state status is central to the Chekhovian comedy *Sunrise*, the first of Nowra's plays to use his appreciation of comedy of manners. Bourgeois rituals are wittily explored at the Easter gathering of a privileged Adelaide family, whose various guilts and nightmares include collaboration in the 1950s British nuclear tests at Maralinga. A purgative bushfire threatens the resurgence of a violent past in a society that attempts to forget history.

The Golden Age, perhaps Nowra's most resonant play, examines Tasmanian history through the discovery in 1939 of a "lost" tribe of whites, descended from convict outcasts and speaking a richly earthy patois. Because of their inbred genetic degeneration, they bravely decide to seek reintegration with the world of "rack 'n' cat," which had so savagely exiled their ancestors. Once in Hobart, however, they are confined in a lunatic asylum, in the politically expedient belief that they provide evidence for Nazi eugenicism. This incarceration obviously alludes to the last Tasmanian Aboriginals, imprisoned in the nineteenth century in these same grim convict remnants. Betsheb, the last survivor, is returned to her forest home, but her lover Francis, the soldier traumatized by the European conflict, may not be able to survive there with her. In a powerful but ambiguous ending, Betsheb promises him "Nowt more outcastin."

In his adaptation of Xavier Herbert's novel *Capricornia*, in *Byzantine Flowers*, and in his Australian bicentennial opera *Whitsunday*, Nowra further empowers his part-Aboriginal or Kanak heroine. In the two latter pieces, by using the powers of love, sexual charisma, or survivor cunning, she comes into her own inheritance and begins to restore to her world something of what has been destroyed. *Crow*, a comic and fantastic play set in Darwin during the 1941 bombings, was written in the wake of the historically momentous High Court decision in June 1992 recognizing native title. The titular character Crow is an Aboriginal Mother Courage who doggedly and resourcefully fights the white power-holders and their court system for legal recognition of her family's claim to their land. The 1993 *Radiance*, however, explores the pains and guilts of a family of black women who reunite in a north Queensland beachside house for their mother's funeral. In a night of exorcism and anger, they confront the painful legacy of their mother, whom they all remember differently. Behind their story lies past governmental policies of separating children from black mothers. *Radiance* (subsequently filmed) is a tight play for three actors that uses the family reunion genre to explore the complexities of Australian black-white relations.

Most recently, Nowra has mined a rich vein of overtly semiautobiographical writing. The engaging *Summer of the Aliens*, the first of a projected trilogy, shows an adolescent Lewis attempting to understand his own sexual emotions plus a bizarre-seeming array of his family's and neighbor's activities. Perhaps they have been taken over by aliens from UFOs, he surmises, though he comes to realize that such perturbing behavior is merely an attribute of humanity, his own included. Its sequel, *Cosi*, one of recent theater's most awarded successes and adapted as a popular film, has the now 21-year-old drop-out directing Mozart's opera for the inhabitants of a mental institution. An extended homage to the high-comic style of its model, despite the black humor, *Cosi* is a witty example of the rehearsal play genre. It presents humanity as pitifully fragile, sometimes appalling, but always spiritually resilient, an endless source of delight and dismay that dogmas cannot easily contain.

Nowra's abiding interest in public Australian history produced his farce *The Temple* (loosely based on the career of Alan Bond) and *The Incorruptible*, which picks up the charismatic appeal and divisive populist policies of Australia's Johannes Bjelke-Peterson and America's Huey Long. In 1995 Nowra set his comic rehearsal play *Miss Bosnia* during the siege of Sarajevo, using as a factual base the historical beauty contest held in the besieged city. Like *Cosi*, but more problematically, *Miss Bosnia* celebrates the power of art to transcend historical brutalities and the survivor's faculty for self-invention. His scene-sequence *The Jungle*, like the radio play *Sydney*, is a Menippean satire set in the harbor city and depicting a haunted and vividly fragmented metropolis with its parade of lowlifes, debauchery, magic, and slapstick. Scenes of *The Jungle* have been performed separately, specifically the tightly confronting "The Price of Prayer," with its dissection of gay relationships and the discrepancies of social power affecting migrant Australians.

—Veronica Kelly

NUSBAUM, N. Richard. ***See* NASH, N. Richard.**

OAKES, Meredith

Nationality: Australian (resident of England since 1973). **Born:** Sydney, Australia, 18 September 1946. **Education:** University of Sydney, New South Wales, 1965-69, B.A. (with double honours, 1969). **Family:** Married Tom Sutcliffe in 1973; one son and one daughter. **Career:** Various jobs while in school including print room assistant, french teacher, plastic bottle trimmer, and filing clerk, all in Sydney; music critic, *Sydney Daily Telegraph,* 1968-70; music critic and editorial assistant, various publishers including *Music and Musicians, The Listener,* and *The Independent,* all London, 1971-93. Writer-in-residence, Gate Theatre, 1994, and Royal Court Theatre, 1995, London. **Agent:** Mel Kenyon, Casarotto Ramsay, National House, 60-66 Wardour Street, London W1V 4ND, England.

Publications

Plays

The Neighbor (produced London, 1993). London, Oberon Books, 1993.
The Editing Process (produced London, 1994). London, Oberon Books, 1994.
Mind the Gap (produced Hampstead Theatre, 1995). London, Oberon Books, 1995.
Faith (produced London, 1997). London, Oberon Books, 1997.

Radio Plays: *Glide,* 1998.

Television Plays: *Prime Suspect 4.*

* * *

The Editing Process shows Meredith Oakes at her very best as an alert observer of contemporary British life, on which she comments satirically with wit that is both amusing and cutting. The action of *The Editing Process*—a title that suggests the manipulation of creative talent as well as indicating the specific topic of the play—is set in the editorial offices of *Footnotes in History*, a small-scale periodical that has in the course of its 125-year history built up something of a reputation in its distinctly restricted field but whose very existence is challenged as a result of one of the many changes of ownership that have convulsed the world of publishing in recent decades. Everything takes place in the journal's offices, a setting familiar to many who witnessed the first production in London's Royal Court Theatre, and a good deal of quite easy humor springs from the interplay between character types who are easily recognizable.

William is a 60-year-old editor with a tendency to express himself from time to time in a paragraph of prose that might well be more suitable for the pages of *Footnotes in History* than for everyday conversation. Ted, his assistant, is 30 years younger and is impatient for greater scope for his skills and energies. Peggy has grown old in the service of the journal, unlike Eleanor, who, at the age of 22, has used nebulous family connections to secure an unpaid job in the office, hoping that this will be the first step in a career in what is commonly supposed to be the glamorous sphere of publishing. Lionel, the general manager of the firm that has taken over *Footnotes in History,* is the catalyst of change. He is suave and cruel, a clever operator with no true sense of values. This aspect is brought out even more strongly in the character of Tamara Del Fuego, whose very name is sufficient indication that Oakes is building up this remarkably expensive design consultant into something of a caricature. In a plot that moves forward quickly and clearly, the inevitable does not take long to occur. William is soon out of his depth, Peggy is left with nothing more than nostalgia for 15 years in a job that she had really liked, and Ted takes over. But for how long?

The Editing Process functions first as the depiction of a business situation typical of the present day, but it is also a comment on human values that has more general significance. Similar points can be made about *Faith,* in which the setting is a "remote island farmhouse in time of war, 1982." Although the play is not specifically "about" the Falklands Islands War, there could not be many in any British audience who would fail to make some connections. Once again, however, Oakes takes the opportunity to widen the implications of the play, going on, as she did in *The Editing Process,* from one particular pressing decision that understandably seems important to those involved to invite the audience to consider the event in a broader perspective.

The dramatic method is typically simple. Four British solders are holed up in the remote farmhouse. They are safe from the enemy, at least for the present, but communications with their superiors are difficult, which means that the men are left largely to sort things out on their own. Army ranks set up group hierarchies that are evident from the outset. Toby Spiers is the sergeant, which means that he should be in command, but his sore feet reflect the laming of his will. Advancing years and hopes of a comfortable retirement have sapped his appetite for combat, and a military career of obeying orders has undermined his mental independence. Just as the aging William is contrasted in *The Editing Process* with the thrusting determination of the younger Ted, so, too, energy is concentrated here in Adam Ziller, no more than a lance corporal but a character of vigor and determination who has more influence on the two privates than the sergeant does. Feminine interest is provided by Sandra, aged 30 and the only female in this dangerous and increasingly fraught situation.

Personality clashes have already produced tension when a new and unexpected element makes everything more difficult. Larry, an American mercenary who has fought for the "wrong" side, is brought in as a prisoner, and the question arises of what to do with him. Orders from higher authority are grim, for no benefit is perceived in upsetting the delicate balance of political interests maintained around the general situation. The sergeant, as is to be expected, plays for time, endeavoring to shift to others the responsibility for action, and it is Adam who has to show determination.

Military matters certainly create the tone of the play and give an edge to the debates that are presented by Oakes in dialogue that shows her usual command of laconic and occasionally earthy speech. The interest transcends the immediate situation, however, absorbing though that is. As it asks what is the "faith" that motivates people in their lives and their conduct toward others, the play reveals an understanding of the pull of group dynamics and a genuine sympathy with flawed humanity.

In *The Neighbour* Oakes transports us to a location that many would regard as an urban battlefield, a modern London council estate whose rootless and impoverished inhabitants live in a state of permanent friction. The young man John sums up the situation and his response to it early in the first scene:

> It's a beautiful summer night. You can hear the weeds growing. They're making fertile use of restricted space, like the rest of us. This estate won a design award for witty compact, provision, We've got a red toilet seat. The place is a blank to me. Unreal, No shelter. I believe it was completed five years ago. Before that, the weeds had all the space they wanted. Now they're fighting it out in two hundred garden plots, each the size of the grave but less nourishing. I don't feel lonely out here. In there with her [his mother] I feel lonely. But I mean to make this my home. The superior man creates, by his very existence, a place of safety.

The precision in detail, like the irony at the expense of well-meaning planners, even the touch of lyricism, give this speech its strength. The predicament presented in *The Neighbour* shows Oakes's response to humanity's plight. And with all of her accustomed dramatic flair for deftly creating powerful situations and involving us in problems, she shows her unreadiness to accept simplistic solutions.

—Christopher Smith

OBAFEMI, Olu

Nationality: Nigerian. **Born:** Akutupa-Bunu, Kogi State, 4 April 1950. **Education:** Methodist School, Kabba, 1956-64; Government Secondary school, Dekina, 1965-69; Titcombe College, Egbe, 1970-71; Ahmadu Bello University, Zaria, 1972-75, B.A. (honors) in English; University of Sheffield, England, 1977-78, M.A. in African Literature in English, 1978; University of Leed, 1981. **Family:** Married; three children. **Career:** Information officer, Kwara State, Ilorin, 1976; founder and director, Ajon players theater troupe, Ilorin and Dupelola, 1981—. Professor of English and dramatic literature, University of Ilorin, 1990—. Distinguished Scholar's lecturer, University of Toronto, 1984; visiting scholar, University of Leeds, 1989-90; visiting professor, University of York, Cambridge, London, Edinburgh, and England, 1990; visiting professor, Bayreuth University, Germany, 1992, 1993, 1996; British Council fellow, 1993. Member, Kwara State Council for Arts and Culture, 1986. Associate editor, *African Theater Review,* 1986-89. Editor, *Ilorin Journal of Language and Literature,* and *Ilorin Monograph Series,* 1990-93. Chairman, Association of Nigerian Authors, Kwara, 1993-98. Vice chairman, Kogi State Council for Arts and Culture, 1994-96. Member, Kogi State Graphic State Newspaper, 1994-96 and editorial board, Post Express newspapers, 1998. **Awards:** Guest writer award, Oyo State, Association of African authors, 1998.

Publications

Plays

Pestle on the Mortar (produced Zaria, 1974).
Nights of a Mystical Beast (produced Leeds, 1980). In *Collected Plays of Olu Obafemi,* Ilorin, 1983.
Collected Plays of Olu Obafemi. Ilorin, 1983.
The New Dawn (produced Ilorin, 1982). Benin City, Adena Press, 1986.
Nights of a Mystical Beast and The New Dawn. Benin City, Adena, 1986.
Suicide Syndrome (produced Ilorin, 1986).
Naira Has No Gender (produced Leeds, 1990). Ibadan, Kraft Books, 1993.
What Else, Gani? n.d.

Novel

Wheels. Ibadan, Kraft Books, 1997.

Poetry

Rising Voices. Lagos, Kraftbooks, 1990.
Songs of Hope. Joe-Noye Associate Press, 1997.

Other

Nigerian Writers and the Nigerian Civil War: Anguish, Commitment, Catharis. Ilorin, Christie-Davies, 1992.
Contemporary Nigerian Theatre. Bayreuth, Germany, Bayreuth University Press, 1997.

*

Theatrical Activities:
Director: **Plays**–*Suicide Syndrome,* 1997.

Actor: **Plays**–Bambulu in *This is Our Chance* by James Ene Henshaw, Dekina, 1966; Bluntscili, in *Arms and the Man* by Bernard Shaw, Dekina, 1969; Banquo in *Macbeth* by William Shakespeare, Egbe, 1970; blind man in *Nights of a Mystical Beast,* Leeds, 1980; Yonkon in *Yankon* by Amadu Maddy, Ilorin, 1984.

Olu Obafemi comments:

Creativity comes to me as a constant struggle with the complex problem of transforming social criticism, social ideals and ethos into a compelling, and compulsive theater, hence between scripting and staging, musing and acting, it is an on-going battle to separate the truth of life from the mode of confronting reality through the art of performance. And the struggle continues between the terrorism of social injustice, unjust rulers in an antagonistic society of our emergent nations of Africa on the one hand, the stge itself as a ritual of terror. So creativity is for me only one way of hoping, of stretching the dream of a new done beyond the unacceptable realities of today. And so the story and telling continue, and stage, in the media, and the solitude of the mind.

* * *

Olu Obafemi belongs to the generation of Nigerian dramatists who advocate a socialist theater aesthetic. For them the theater, when properly used, can become a weapon for raising the consciousness of the masses. Four of his five known plays are a testimony to the functional deployment of the theater for revolutionary ends. For Obafemi, the theater provides a context for demystifying the nature of social and power relations and the levels of exploitation of the masses. Thus, a constant theme that runs through his theater is economic and political exploitation, from *Pestle on the Mortar* to *Naira Has No Gender*.

Not much is known about the unpublished play *Pestle*, except that it was performed in 1981 at the launching of Obafemi's Ajon Players. His published plays—*Nights of a Mystical Beast, The New Dawn, Suicide Syndrome,* and *Naira Has No Gender*—show Obafemi's concern with unequal power relations that give rise to exploitation in neocolonial African states. The plays explore ways by which the oppressed can rise above this exploitation by taking their destinies in their own hands and overthrowing their oppressors. The plays also demonstrate his belief in the relevance of theater to the process of change.

Nights of a Mystical Beast borrows the myth of *agurumo*, the mystical beast, and uses it as a metaphor for the mystification of the exploitative process, in both colonial and contemporary neocolonial African societies. Although structurally the play seems composed of disparate elements, Obafemi's point is that the mystification of power and its attendant relations of exploitative oppression under colonialism and the slave era are surely being repeated in the power relations and patterns of exploitation in neocolonial Giro, where a very few control and enjoy the benefits of political and economic power at the expense of the majority. This theme is explored further in *The New Dawn*.

Structurally, the two plays are similar. Both open with historical incidents: *Mystical Beast* begins with the power relations and machinations in a chief's court in colonial times, and *Dawn* opens with the famed massacre of innocent children ordered by Emperor Bokassa of the Central African Republic. Both incidents are designed to show a continuity between the past, the present, and the future. The youth are the hope and the future, a future that both political and economic tyrants fear and would do anything to stop from asserting itself. *Dawn*, like *Mystical Beast,* conducts a critique of the role of the intellectual elite in the process of social change. Both plays also feature four key characters, a device Obafemi uses in all his plays. The setting in *Dawn*, as in *Mystical Beast,* is a drinking shed where most of the action unfolds through a series of flashbacks, dramatizations, and role play by the onstage characters. The drinking shed is very economical dramatic device that Obafemi employs in all his drama and often uses in conjunction with other folk forms, such as dance, music, riddling, storytelling, and children's games. These dramatic strengths notwithstanding, Obafemi reveals a naive idealism in the unity of the intellectuals, the peasants, and the workers in the pursuance of a socialist transformation. This weakness though is redeemed by the self-criticism conducted by the group of intellectuals in each play that exposes their inadequacy in leading the mass revolt against oppression. Evidence of Obafemi's optimism is the intellectuals' acceptance by the masses into their fold as the pool of mass protest swells to include anyone but the capitalist and political oppressors.

In *Suicide Syndrome* Obafemi alternates between scenes of poverty and scenes of affluence to expose the gulf between the lifestyles of the rich and the poor. In the poor worker's home hungry children question their mother about full bellies and hunger, about having wealth and not having it, questions that the poor woman is unable to answer convincingly because she simply does not seem to know herself. Set in counterpoint is the scene of the two mistresses of the very rich Alhaji and the Professor. The two women quibble over the small matter of two hundred thousand *naira* for Alahji's madam's minor shopping trip to London. *Suicide* is structurally a more ambitious play, starting innocuously with members of an audience who take over a theater to protest their dissatisfaction with the play they have just been shown. They subsequently put on their own play, relevant to their reality in a way the classical piece was not. Obafemi achieves two things here. First, he takes a swipe at both Wole Soyinka and John Pepper Clark-Bekederemo, first generation dramatists who have been accused of being exotic and irrelevant. Second, the play demonstrates Obafemi's belief in the function of theater as a platform for articulating and enacting revolutionary ideology.

In *Naira Has No Gender* Obafemi succeeds in distancing and controlling his anger against the wielders and abusers of power, such as Chief Awandu, a corrupt politician and businessman. Using the traditional marriage institution as a point of reference, Obafemi questions what he sees as an unnecessary and debilitating demand of traditional marriage rites, which, as the character Otunla points out to his bride-to-be, "needs an IMF loan to finance." Otunla's principled resistance to this imposition and his stubborn refusal to accept help win him support from his former classmate and Chief Awandu's heir.

One hallmark of Obafemi's theater is his optimistic and happy endings. All his plays end on a joyous note, with singing and dancing to celebrate the triumph of the masses and with no recriminations against the erstwhile oppressors. This tendency to achieve a joyous consensus is perceived by such critics as Chris Dunton as utopian naïveté. But for Obafemi the reordered society envisaged by his drama holds a place for everyone, and what is needed is the equitable redistribution of wealth by altering the social structures within which socio-economic relationships are conducted. He may not be a Soyinka in the mastery of language and sophisticated dramatic technique or an Osofisan in creative audacity and control of folk form and matter, but Obafemi makes up for these weaknesses with his passion for and belief in theater as a functional art form for the improvement of the lot of the masses. He is a dramatist whose love of humanity in general and the deprived in particular informs and somehow rescues his theater from a pedestrian lightness and a language that occasionally flounders into banality. On paper, his plays may seem light, but in performance they do provide a vibrant theatrical experience both for the actors and the audience through the use of the composite mediums of dance, music, songs, games, and riddles.

—Osita Okagbue

OGUNYEMI, Wale

Nationality: Nigerian. **Born:** Igbajo, Osun State, 1939. **Education:** Occasional student of School of Drama, University of Ibadan, 1966; Extra Mural Certificate in Drama, University of Ibadan, 1967. **Family:** Married; five children. **Career:** Member, Orisun Theatre, Ibadan, and University of Ibadan Theatre Arts Company; senior artist and writer, Institute of African Studies, University of Ibadan; writer-in-residence, the Workshop Theatre, University of Leeds, 1974-75; deputy project director, Unibadan Masques, Ibadan, 1976. **Awards:** Nigerian Writers Guild award, 1982; University of California African Arts award, 1971; First Prize at the 4th National Festival of Arts, University of Ibadan, 1974; Organization of African Unity Playwriting award, 1971; Writer of the Year, Nigerian Writers League, 1981; Association of Nigerian Authors Drama award, 1988; World Service Drama award, 1990; Commander of Nigerian Theatre, Dramatic Society of Obafemi Awolowo University, Ile Ife, 1995. **Address:** c/o Institute of African Studies, University of Ibadan, Ibadan, Nigeria, West Africa.

PUBLICATIONS

Plays

Business Headache (produced Ibadan, n.d.). Oshobogo, Adeyeye Print, 1966.
The Scheme (produced Ibadan, 1967). Published in *Three Nigerian Plays*, edited by Ulli Beier, London, Longman, 1967.
Be Mighty Be Mine (produced Ibadan, 1968). Published in *Nigeria Magazine* (Lagos), no.97, 1968.
Eshu Elegbara (produced Ibadan, 1968). Ibadan, Orisun, 1970.
Aare Akogun, adaptation of *Macbeth* by Shakespeare (produced Ibadan, 1968).
Obaluaye (musical; produced Ibadan, 1968). Ibadan, Institute of African Studies, University of Ibadan, 1972.
Ijaye War (produced Ibadan, n.d.). Ibadan, Orisun, 1970.
Kiriji (produced Ibadan, 1971). Lagos, African Universities Press, 1976.
Poor Little Bird. Published in *The Study of Literature in West African Countries,* edited by H.L.B. Moody, London, Allen & Unwin, 1972.
The Vow (produced Ibadan, 1972). London, Macmillan, 1985.
The Divorce (produced Ibadan, 1975). Ibadan, Onibonoje Press, 1977.
Langbodo, adaptation of a work by D.O. Fagunwa (produced Lagos, 1977; London, 1984). Lagos, Nelson, 1979.
Eniyan, adaptation of *Everyman* (produced Ibadan, 1982). Ibadan, Ibadan University Press, 1987.
The Sign of the Rainbow (produced Ibadan, n.d.). London, Heinemann Educational Books, 1973.
Partners in Business. 1991.
The First Time I Saw Him. Published in *Before Our Very Eyes: Tribute to Wole Soyinka,* edited by Dapo Adelugba, Spectrum Books, 1987.

Screenplays: *The Vow,* 1970; *The Divorce,* 1977; *Ipade,* 1977; *Ida Ahun,* 1982; *Eni A Wi Fun,* 1984; *Langbodo,* 1986; *Cult of the Buffalo,* 1992; *Teni N Teni,* 1994; *The Ultimate,* 1995; *Ire Olokun,* 1996; *Simia,* 1996; *Darker Night,* 1996; *Ayo Ni Mo Fe,* 1996; *Imputation,* 1996; *Ebenezer,* 1997; *Sango,* 1997.

Television Plays: *Be Mighty Be Mine*, 1968; *For Better for Worse* series; *Bello's Way* series, *Cock Crow at Dawn* series, 1978-82.

Radio Play: *We Can Always Create.*

*

Critical Studies: "Langbodo: The Concept of Theatre as Exploration" by Dapo Adelugba, in *Nigeria Magazine* (Lagos, Nigeria), April/June 1986, pp. 3-9; "Nigerian Dramatists in Search of a Theatrical Idiom: A Folkloristic Perspective on Wale Ogunyemi, Kola Ogunmola and Atiboroko Uyovbukerhi" by Austin Ovigue Asagba, in *Lore and Language* (Enfield Lock, England), July 1991, pp. 49-58.

* * *

As a playwright who has written for live theater as well as television and radio, Wale Ogunyemi is one of the most versatile theater practitioners in contemporary Nigeria. Although his work was popular with audiences, it received critical attention rather belatedly. Ogunyemi's later work revealed a greater depth of vision and subtlety of direction that gave aesthetic perspective to his theater oeuvre.

Ogunyemi may be categorized as a transitional dramatist. He occupies a position somewhere between the populist vernacular folk drama, pioneered by Ogunde and developed by Duro Ladipo, Oyin Adejobi, Moses Olaiya, Kola Ogunmola, and the 200 or more Yoruba traveling theaters, and the consciously exotic literary dramatic enterprises of English expression, pioneered by James Ene Henshaw and taken further by Wole Soyinka, J. P. Clark, Ola Rotimi, and the second generation of dramatists led by Femi Osofisan. It is for this reason that Ogunyemi's drama belongs more with total theater, which combines dance, music, spectacle, and dialogue, rather than with "profound" dramatic texts. Among Ogunyemi's most popular subjects are traditions/myths and conflicts, both of values and of cultures. He also explores history and employs social satire. Of his published texts, his major plays include *The Vow, The Scheme,* and *Obaluaye,* which deal with conflicts of values; *Ijaye War* and *Kiriji,* both historical dramas; *The Divorced,* and his television serials *For Better for Worse* and *Bello's Way,* all of which offer commentary on social and domestic problems in contemporary Nigerian society. He also adapted Shakespeare's *Macbeth* for the Nigerian stage (*Aare Akogun*).

The Vow contrasts indigenous African values with so-called modern European values. This, of course, is a well-worn dramatic path in Nigerian theater. The play tells the story of an ultraconservative king who sets out to thwart his Western-educated son's plan to marry a foreign girl who is pregnant with his child. The king hopes to force his son to accept a prearranged marriage in accordance with "our grandfathers' ways." Both father and son are firmly committed to their convictions, and tension mounts. Fearing disgrace, the father employs charm, which backfires and leads to his suicide. An atmosphere of tragedy surrounds the king, but he lacks the depth of character and complexity that would secure audience sympathy. The verse of the play is thin and the dialogue lacks the subtlety and richness of diction required of tragedy.

In *Obaluwaye,* Ogunyemi uses the techniques of Yoruba folk drama to examine individuals in a society that is in a state of cultural flux. The play relies heavily upon music and dance. Ogunyemi's protagonist, Baale, attempts to show how tragedy may be averted through the syncretic accommodation of indigenous African and nonindigenous Christian traditions, yet he treats his native traditions and customs with neglect and contempt. He refuses, and urges his people to refuse, to worship the gods of the land. The gods' anger is manifested in the visitation of the Smallpox King, Soponna, and the disease plagues the whole community with widespread mortal consequences. Baale's recommendation to increase vaccination fails, and Baale himself falls victim to Obaluaye's curse. He dies and is resurrected by an Ifa priest. Baale performs the required rites, and he pledges to observe them regularly. The king and the community are expiated and the moral is drawn: "Christianity does not say we shouldn't observe tradition."

A significant proportion of Ogunyemi's drama treats historical themes. *Ijaye War* represents the ceaseless battles among the Yorubas during the 1860s, known as the Ijaye-Ibadan Wars, which eventually fragmented the old Oyo Empire. In *Ijaye War,* Alafin Atiba defies age-old tradition by forcing the Kingmakers to appoint his first son, Adelu, as his successor. Even though Alafin Atiba's stated aim is to prevent the usual interminable crisis over succession, tradition holds that the crown prince is to die with the king, not succeed him. The would-be successor protests this breach with tradition, but it is the fierce opposition of Kurunmi, the Aare Ona Kakanfo (generalissimo) of Oyo and the Lord of Ijaye, that leads to the next round of wars. Kurunmi says tradition is inviolable and must be protected, and thus challenges Adelu's claim to the throne. Adelu gains the support of Ibadan, and Kurunmi forges an alliance with the Egba people. In the battle that ensues, Kurunmi loses his five sons and, deeply grieved, commits suicide. The play maintains extreme historical fidelity but to such and extent that it is ultimately more a reconstruction of events than a creative work. The same criticism can be applied to *Kiriji,* which dramatizes the late nineteenth-century revolt of the Ekiti and Ijesha peoples against the tyrannical imperialism of Ibadan, represented in the play by Aare Lasote and his inexhaustible appetite for new territory. The war ends in a stalemate, and the epilogue indicates that a mutually convenient truce is reached. Dramatic quality, however, is lacking in the play; its most laudable achievement being, perhaps, the effective depiction of battles on stage.

In terms of craft and dramaturgy, Ogunyemi's most accomplished play is *Langbodo,* Nigeria's main dramatic entry for the 1977 Second World Black and African Festival of Arts and Culture (FESTAC). A dramatization of Soyinka's novel *Forest of a Thousand Demons,* it is imaginatively translated from the Yoruba classical novelist D. O. Fagunwa's work, *Ogboju Ode Ninu Igbo Irunmole.* The play is in the heroic quest tradition but is adapted as a nationalist journey toward social redemption. Of epic proportions, it encompasses all the major political cultures in Nigeria and all the ethnolinguistic sectors of Nigerian society. In terms of dramaturgy, the play combines the forms of song, dance, narration, audience participation, and mime. The journey motif is embodied in the seven leading hunters who are asked by the king to undertake a journey to Mount Langbodo in the depths of the forest of demons and bring back peace and prosperity. The journey symbolizes a quest for the social regeneration and redemption sorely needed in a society in the throes of decadence and spiritual lassitude, as Nigeria was at the time play was produced.

Ogunyemi's mythohistorical body of work includes two other significant texts: *Sango: A Legendary African King,* a screenplay filmed by Afrika 'N Vogue: Even-Ezra Studios Lagos (1997) and *Queen Amina of Zazzau* (1993), an epic historical drama, originally titled *Praying Mantis. Sango* draws a highly engaging and sharp contrast between the Yoruba cosmogonic perception of thunder and lightning as attributes of the anthropomorphic deity, Sango (god of lightning and retribution), and the Western scientific perception of lightning as merely an electrical phenomenon. These two divergent views present the intense conflictual thrust through which Ogunyemi dramatizes Sango's ascendancy to the Oyo throne, his iconoclastic reign, and his self-exile following his destruction of his palace and his people. The play ends by hinting at Sango's eventual deification and thus validates the Yoruba cultural worldview. *Queen Amina of Zazzau* is a dramatic re-creation of the historical legend of Queen Amina, grandmother of the founder of the Zazzau Kingdom, which she later ruled with great authority and success. Although her reign is characterized by equity and justice, she is committed to enhancing the greatness of her kingdom and to fulfilling her own passions—but without the hindrances of wedlock. Her fierce commitment to her own glory and pleasure also supplies her tragic flaw. The play is spectacular and richly enacted with full complements of dance, dialogue, and proverbial and metaphorical songs. The play is also suspenseful, plausible, and esthetically satisfying.

—Olu Obafemi

O'MALLEY, Mary (Josephine)

Nationality: British. **Born:** Bushey, Hertfordshire, 19 March 1941. **Career:** Resident writer, Royal Court Theatre, London, 1977. **Awards:** *Evening Standard* award, 1978; Susan Smith Blackburn prize, 1978; Plays and Players award; Pye award, for television play.

Publications

Plays

Superscum (produced London, 1972).

A 'nevolent Society (produced London, 1974).

Oh If Ever a Man Suffered (produced London, 1975).

Once a Catholic (produced London, 1977; New York, 1979). Ashover, Derbyshire, Amber Lane Press, and New York, French, 1978.

Look Out . . . Here Comes Trouble (produced London, 1978). Ashover, Derbyshire, Amber Lane Press, 1979.

Talk of the Devil (produced Watford, Hertfordshire, 1986; revised version produced Bristol, 1986).

Television Plays: *Percy and Kenneth,* 1976; *Oy Vay Maria,* 1977; *Shall I See You Now?,* 1978; *On the Shelf,* 1984.

Poetry

Where the Rocks Float. Dublin, Salmon Publishing, 1993.

The Knife in the Wave. Cliffs of Moher, Salmon Publishers, 1997.

Other

A Consideration of Silk. Galway, Salmon Publishing, 1990.

Never Shake Hands with the Devil. Dublin, Elo Publications, 1990.

* * *

Mary O'Malley came into the public eye with her mischievous play *Once a Catholic,* which premiered at the Royal Court

Theatre in 1977 and then transferred to the West End. The play won awards from the *London Evening Standard* and from *Plays and Players*. It is a warm but sharply retrospective look at a Catholic convent of the 1950s, with the youth rebellion of that decade given added edge by the repressiveness of the nuns. All of the girls are called Mary, and the play is a witty and perceptive extended sitcom that is such good fun that it would undoubtedly offend no one. In its way it even was able to test the taboos of the commercial theater in a scene in which one of the shocked nuns discovers a packet of Tampax hidden in the lavatory. There is a final act of sacrilege when one of the girls affixes a plasticine penis to a statue of Christ in the school chapel, for which Mary the scapegoat, the only one who genuinely wants to become a nun, is blamed.

There is a satirical edge to O'Malley's writing that derives from her sensitivity to the ordinary pains and ironies of daily life and also to the iconography of domestic experience, which is so important to people. This latter was the main feature of her play *Look Out . . . Here Comes Trouble,* which was staged by the Royal Shakespeare Company at the Warehouse in London in 1978. The play, which was set in a psychiatric ward, floundered in its material detail, and although the comic pain was a feature in the lives of the characters, it never became part of the structural fabric of the play. O'Malley somehow appears to be caught between the potentialities of a more ruthless satirical approach and a familiar, lightly comic sitcom approach.

—Michelene Wandor

O'NEILL, Michael and Jeremy Seabrook

O'NEILL, Michael. Nationality: British. **Education:** Northampton Grammar School; Cambridge University. **Career:** Teacher. **Agent:** Curtis Brown, 162-168 Regent Street, London W1R 5TB, England.

SEABROOK, Jeremy. Nationality: British. **Born:** Northampton in 1939. **Education:** Northampton Grammar School; Gonville and Caius College, Cambridge; London School of Economics, diploma in social administration 1967. **Career:** Teacher in a secondary modern school for two years; social worker, Inner London Education Authority, 1967-69, and with Elfrida Rathbone Association, 1973-76.

PUBLICATIONS

Plays

Life Price (produced London, 1969).
Morality (produced London, 1971).
Millennium (produced London, 1973).
Our Sort of People (produced London, 1974).
Sex and Kinship in a Savage Society (produced London, 1975).
Sharing (produced London, 1980).
Black Man's Burden (produced London, 1980).

Radio Plays: *The Bosom of the Family*, 1975; *Living Private*, 1978; *Our Children's Children*, 1980; *Life Skills*, 1985.

Television Plays: *Skin Deep*, 1971; *Soap Opera in Stockwell*, 1973; *Highway Robbery*, 1973; *A Clear Cut Case*, 1973; *A Stab in the Front*, 1973; *Children of the Sun*, 1975; *Beyond the Call of Duty* (*Crown Court series*), 1976; *A State of Welfare*.

Plays by Jeremy Seabrook

Yesterday's News, with Joint Stock (produced Aldershot, Hampshire, and London, 1976).
Heart-Throb, with Caroline Hutchison and Anna Mottram (produced London, 1988).

Radio Plays: *Birds in a Gilded Cage*, 1974; *A Change of Life*, 1979; *A Mature Relationship*, 1979; *Golden Opportunities*, 1982.

Other by Jeremy Seabrook

The Unprivileged: A Hundred Years of Family Life and Tradition in a Working-Class Street. London, Longman, 1967.
City Close-Up. London, Allen Lane, and Indianapolis, Bobbs Merrill, 1971.
Loneliness. London, Temple Smith, 1971; New York, Universe, 1975.
The Everlasting Feast. London, Allen Lane, 1974.
A Lasting Relationship: Hormosexuals and Society. London, Allen Lane, 1976.
What Went Wrong? Working People and the Ideals of the Labour Movement. London, Gollancz, 1978; New York, Pantheon, 1979.
Mother and Son: An Autobiography. London, Gollancz, 1979; New York, Pantheon, 1980.
Working-Class Childhood. London, Gollancz, 1982.
Unemployment. London, Quartet, 1982.
The Idea of Neighbourhood: What Local Politics Should Be About. London, Pluto Press, 1984.
A World Still to Win: The Reconstruction of the Post-War Working Class, with Trevor Blackwell. London, Faber, 1985.
Landscapes of Poverty. Oxford, Blackwell, 1985.
Life and Labour in a Bombay Slum. London, Quartet, 1987.
The Politics of Hope: Britain at the End of the Twentieth Century, with Trevor Blackwell, London, Faber, 1988.
The Leisure Society. Oxford, Blackwell, 1988.
The Race for Riches: The Human Cost of Wealth. Basingstoke, Marshall Pickering, 1988.
The Myth of the Market. Hartland, Devon, Green Books, 1990.
Victims of Development: Resistence and Alternatives. New York, Verso, 1993.
The Revolt Against Change: Towards a Conserving Radicalism, with Trevor Blackwell. London, Vintage, 1993.
Global Parasites: 500 Years of Western Culture, with Winin Pereira. Bombay, Earthcare Books, 1994.
Pioneers of Change: Living Experiments for a Humane Future. New Society, 1994.
Notes from Another India. London, Pluto Press, 1996.
Travels in the Skin Trade: Tourism and the Sex Industry. Chicago, Pluto Press, 1996.
In the Cities of the South: Scenes from a Developing World. London, Verso, 1996.

* * *

It was Jean Genet whose beliefs about society radically changed when he discovered that, according to the most advanced and accurate statistics available, the percentage of criminals remained the same whichever class or system held power at a particular moment. Michael O'Neill and Jeremy Seabrook's early work suffers from the widespread delusion that it is only as a result of capitalism, the "ceaseless gutting of their body and spirit in the name of enterprise, profits, efficiency," that there is a social sediment at the bottom of society, providing both aggressors and victims for horrible crime. For in their first performed play, *Life Price,* the predestined victim, Debbie, and the typical child murderer, George Reginald Dunkley, are both observed against a landscape of "neglected mounds of detritus, crumbling terraces, derelict buildings, and the housing estate itself, all cabbage-stalks and dilapidated creosote fences, maculated concrete, rusting bed-springs and motorbikes, dead chrysanthemums and dingy paintwork."

A State of Welfare, a television play, is a much better organized work about the moving of an American scent spray firm into England and its impact on the household of an average worker. Here the theme of a working-class boy bettering himself, by taking French lessons with an executive's wife, and so coming into conflict with his father—the two sides of industry get together over dinner in a powerful scene reminiscent of Ibsen's *The League of Youth*—forms a substantial and colorful central thread.

Morality is an even more domestic story than *A State of Welfare*. A family called the Pargeters are trying to make their son Nick "get on" by passing his A-level exams and winning a place at a university. When it is discovered that Nick is having a homosexual affair with his progressive and sensitive teacher, Larry, the family is up in arms at the scandal this will cause in the neighborhood. Nick's parents manage to summon up the courage to go to see Larry, but he calms them down with a hypocritical assertion about morality. The psychology—and morality—may be crude compared with other plays about divided loyalty, but *Morality* is a lively portrayal of family conflict. As in *Life Price,* the authors seem to be saying that it is society that is to blame for the cynicism and destructiveness of young people toward their elders. This is an attitude supported by concrete, almost documentary writing, not by the continual assertion of a doctrinaire point of view.

In *Millennium,* which is set in a semidetached house on a Northampton estate, there is a gap of 53 years between the first part and the second. The authors present for comparison the lifestyle of Florrie's family and that of Doll her granddaughter in a broader and more sentimental way than in the earlier plays. In Florrie's family one of the girls is dying of scarlet fever, while about her rages the violence of poverty, the stringencies of life caused by the father's status as a hired man. The rebel son, common to both generations, in the first part merely burns his sister's boots, while in the second he has, as part of a gang, tied up a boy, cut his hair, and tried to extort money from his parents. The boot burning satisfies the instinct for anger at the circumstances, and it is punished and purged within the family unit. The second misdemeanor is a matter for the courts, showing the impersonality of justice and how the family has broken down. The time gap achieves a neat and forceful comparison.

Dramatically striking, too, is the Pirandellian twist by which Florrie's family members advance on their petty-minded, materialistic descendants and engage in a battle of wits. The authors' sympathies clearly lie with the earlier brood, on whom a huddled, statuesque dignity is conferred. Grim and monochrome as they appear, they have the virtue of discipline and look to the afterlife for their reward.

Sex and Kinship in a Savage Society is a less successful treatment of the same theme of family disintegration. In *Black Man's Burden* the family is Jamaican. We hear imposing astral voices with Jamaican accents telling the heroine Melvita that her child-to-be is the new Messiah. The family settles in England, and the problems of assimilating such a striking notion into a society with a National Health Service intent on imposing its own solution on visionaries give the authors the opportunity, once more, for striking contrasts. This time the contrasts are comic, beguiling speech rhythms and exact evocations of place.

—Garry O'Connor

OSOFISAN, Femi

Pseudonym: Okinba Launko. **Nationality:** Nigerian. **Born:** Babafemi Adeyemi Osofisan, 16 June 1946. **Education:** Schools in Ilesha, Ife-Ife, and Erunwon; Government College, Ibadan; University of Dakar, Senegal, D.E.S. 1968; University of Ibadan, B.A. 1969, Ph.D. 1974; University of Paris III, 1971-73. **Career:** Member of the faculty, 1973—, currently professor in theatre arts, University of Ibadan. Visiting professor, University of Benin, Lomé, Togo Republic, 1980, University of Pennsylvania, Philadelphia, 1983, University of Benin, Benin City, Nigeria, 1983-85, University of Ife, Ife-Ife, 1985-86, and University of Iowa, Iowa City, 1991; visiting fellow, University of Cambridge, 1986, Cornell University, Ithaca, New York, 1992, and St. Alfred College, England, 1992. Founding member of the Editorial Board, the *Guardian,* Lagos, 1984-85. Currently editor, *Opon Ifa: Ibadan Poetry Chapbooks*. Drama consultant, FESTAC 77, Lagos; artist-in-residence, Henri Clewes Foundation, La Napoule, France, 1990; guest writer, Japan Foundation, Japan, 1991; drama consultant, MAMSER, Abuja, 1991-92. Visiting writer, Emory University, Atlanta, 1994; visiting professor, University of Leeds, 1996. President, Association of Nigerian Authors, 1989, 1990; vice-president for West Africa, Pan-African Writers Association, from 1992. **Awards:** Association of Nigerian Authors prize, 1983, 1986, 1993; Fulbright fellowship, 1986. **Address:** Department of Theatre Arts, University of Ibadan, Ibadan, Nigeria.

Publications

Plays

Odudwa, Don't Go! (produced Ibadan, 1968).
You Have Lost Your Fine Face (produced Ibadan, 1969).
A Restless Run of Locusts (produced Akure, 1970). Ibadan, Onibonoje Press, 1975.
Red Is the Freedom Road (produced Ibadan, 1974). Included in *Morountodun and Other Plays*, 1982.
The Chattering and the Song (produced Ibadan, 1974). Ibadan, Ibadan University Press, 1977.
Who's Afraid of Solarin? (produced Ibadan, 1977). Calabar, Scholars Press, 1978.
Once upon Four Robbers (produced Ibadan, 1978). Ibadan, BIO, 1982.

Farewell to a Cannibal Rage (produced Ibadan, 1978; revised version produced Benin City, 1984). Ibadan, Evans, 1986.
Morountodun (produced Ibadan, 1979; revised version produced Ife-Ife, 1980). Included in *Morountodun and Other Plays*, 1982.
Fires Burn But They Die Hard (televized 1981). Included in *Birthdays Are Not for Dying and Other Plays*, 1991.
The Inspector and the Hero (televized 1981). Included in *Birthdays Are Not for Dying and Other Plays*, 1991.
Birthdays Are Not for Dying (produced Ibadan, 1981). Ibadan, Evans, 1987.
The Oriki of a Grasshopper (produced Ibadan, 1981; revised version produced Benin City, 1985). Included in *Two Short Plays*, 1986.
No More the Wasted Breed (produced Ibadan, 1982). Included in *Morountodun and Other Plays*, 1982.
Morountodun and Other Plays. Ikeja, Longman, 1982.
Midnight Hotel (produced Ibadan, 1982). Ibadan, Evans, 1986.
The Engagement (for children) (produced Benin City, 1984). Ibadan, Agbo Areo Publishers.
Altine's Wrath (televised 1983; produced Ibadan, 1983). Included in *Two Short Plays*, 1986.
Esu and the Vagabond Minstrels (produced Benin City, 1984; revised version produced Ife-Ife, 1986). Ibadan, New Horn Press, 1987.
Two Short Plays. Ibadan, New Horn Press, 1986.
Twingle-Twangle A-Twynning Tayle (produced Ibadan, 1988). Lagos, Longman, 1992.
Aringindin and the Nightwatchmen (produced Ibadan, 1989). Ibadan, Heinemann Educational, 1992.
Another Raft (produced Ibadan, 1989). Lagos, Malthouse Press, 1990.
Yungba-Yungba and the Dance Contest (produced Ibadan, 1990). Ibadan, Heinemann Educational, 1992.
Birthdays Are Not for Dying and Other Plays. Lagos, Malthouse Press, 1991.
Nkrumah-ni...Africa-ni! (Produced Accra, 1994; Colombo, 1995).
Tegonni, An African Antigone (produced Atlanta, 1994).
Reel, Rwanda! (Produced London, 1996).
Fiddlers on a Midnight Lark (produced Lagos, Maison de France, 1996).
One Legend, Many Seasons (produced Ibadan, 1996).
A Nightingale for Dr. DuBois (produced Accra, 1997).
Andorra Goes Kinshasa (produced Lagos Goethes Institut, 1997).
The Album of the Midnight Blackout (produced Ilorin, 1997). Ibadan, University Press, 1994.
Many Colors Make the Thunder-King (produced Minneapolis, 1997). Minneapolis, Guthrie Theatre Publications.
Making Children Is Fun. Ibadan, Mosuro Publishers.
Ònà Òmìnira, Ònà Èjè, adaptation of *Red Is the Freedom Road* by Ademola Aremu. London, Hakuna Matata Press.

Television Plays: *The Inspector and the Hero*, 1981; *Fires Burn But They Die Hard*, 1981; *Altine's Wrath, A Debt to the Dead, A Date with Danger, The New Cathedral, At the Petrol Station, Mission Abandoned, A Hero Comes Home, Operation Rat-Trap, To Kill a Dream* (all in *Visitors* series), 1983.

Novels

Kolera Kolej. Ibadan, New Horn Press, 1975.
Cordelia (as Okinba Launko). Lagos, Malthouse Press, 1990.
Ma'ami (for children). London, Heinemann.

Poetry

Minted Coins (as Okinba Launko). Ibadan, Heinemann Educational, 1986.
Dreamseeker On Divining Chain. Ibadan, Kraft Books.

Other

Beyond Translation: Tragic Paradigms and the Dramaturgy of Ola Rotimi and Wole Soyinka. Ife-Ife, Ife Monographs on African Literature, 1986.
The Orality of Prose: A Comparatist Look at the Works of Rabelais, Joyce, and Tutuola. Ife-Ife, Ife Monographs on African Literature, 1986.

Translator, *Theatre and Nationalism: Wole Soyinka and LeRoi Jones*, by Alain Ricard. Ife-Ife, University of Ife Press, 1978.

*

Critical Studies: *The Drama of Femi Osofisan: A Critical Perspective* by Muyiwa Awodiya, 1995; *Ancient Songs Set Ablaze: The Theatre of Femi Osofisan* by Sandra Richards, 1996.

Theatrical Activities:
Director: All of his own plays.

Actor: Since 1963 lead roles with many companies including The Orisun Theatre Company, the Unibadan Masques, the University of Ibadan Theatre Ensemble, and the Kakaun Sela Company.

Femi Osofisan comments:

My works belong to what is now customarily described as the second generation of modern Nigerian writing, following that of Wole Soyinka and Chinua Achebe. The distinctive features of our dramaturgy are (a) the concern to produce works that are directly relevant to the political and social struggles of our times, and particularly from a combattant, leftist perspective, without however being dogmatic or pedantic. In most cases, this had meant a violent rejection of the sometimes exotic, and sometimes anthropological works of our predecessors, and of the tragic-metaphysical emphasis of their explorations; and (b) the equal concern to produce works that are easily accessible, readable, and simple, without being simplistic. In my case, it has meant a predilection for plays which are more or less open-ended, in which the audience is called upon to involve itself, take positions, and, even, decide the resolutions for the actors. Thus we have created a novel aesthetics, based on a vigorous and lively experimentation with form and mechanics, and the resuscitation of the traditional resources of folklore and festival, masques and myth, ritual and extemporisation. The driving aim is to entertain our audience, but also, and crucially, to change our world.

* * *

University professor, theater director, newspaper columnist, and poet, Femi Osofisan is part of a generation that has experienced Nigerian independence only as an empty slogan. Thus, he fashions a committed literature designed to reawaken a collective, imaginatively self-critical sensibility and to break the enduring shackles of religion, custom, and colonialism in favor of a more humane egalitarian society. Within Nigeria he is often viewed as a radical who would completely destroy the past, but his radicalism actually builds positively upon the best of tradition while seeking to encourage pervasive change.

For analytical convenience Osofisan's works may be separated into the broad categories of realistic protest plays, satiric adaptations of European models, and a particularly African form of "total theater." *A Restless Run of Locusts, Red Is the Freedom Road,* and *The Oriki of a Grasshopper* fit into the first category. Here the playwright registers the widespread political corruption, brutality, intellectual failure, and rhythm of repression, coup, and countercoup of postindependence Nigeria. His *No More the Wasted Breed* rejects an acceptance of martyrdom, articulated in Wole Soyinka's *The Strong Breed,* and illuminates in persuasive dramatic form aspects of the quarrel, albeit friendly, that many younger intellectuals have with their distinguished mentor.

European dramatic literature provides a ready source for adaptation in such plays as *Who's Afraid of Solarin?* and *Midnight Hotel.* The former play is a loose adaptation of Gogol's *The Inspector General,* and the latter, through its use of farcical complications and acerbic songs rendered from an oversized songbook, borrows from both Feydeau and Brecht. More importantly for Nigerian audiences, which may be unaware of the European originals, these plays satirize the rampant materialism of the upper classes. As such they may be considered an ingenious contemporary development of traditional satires in which the unempowered expressed their dissatisfaction with the privileged.

Osofisan's most conceptually and stylistically complex plays are *The Chattering and the Song, Farewell to a Cannibal Rage, Once upon Four Robbers, Morountodun,* and *Esu and the Vagabond Minstrels.* Illustrative of an African concept of drama, these plays incorporate nonverbal elements like dance and music into a spoken text, insist upon theater as artifice through frequent role changes and storytelling techniques, conjoin spatial and temporal frames into a seamless experiential present, and place high value on episodic and open-ended structures that challenge audiences to impose meaning upon the event.

The Chattering and the Song, the first Osofisan play written in this genre, contains many of the themes upon which the playwright has subsequently elaborated. The play traces a path whereby university-trained supporters of a farmers' movement progress from an unfocused anger about social injustice to an active understanding of the process of social change. Games, or the construction of illusory systems in which the characters invest belief, are the vehicles through which this evolution is accomplished. Thus the characters play a number of riddling and card games, with each new round being a repetition with significant variation. Riddling, which is designed to develop intellectual prowess through experimentation with trope and which epitomizes the temporary resolution of apparent paradox, becomes a metaphor for an appropriate revolutionary stance that acknowledges dialectical development yet maintains commitment to an egalitarian ideal.

The initial irony of would-be revolutionaries unwittingly betraying espoused principles within the context of a game is repeated in their later reenactment of a play within the play, for the most flamboyant radical begins awkwardly in his role of ruler but grows more overbearing the longer he is called upon to defend his privileged position. The historical drama these characters enact is itself a radical reinterpretation of recorded fact, and the alteration enables Osofisan to posit identity as multiple, contextual, and susceptible to change, qualities that in turn necessitate the continuous reevaluation of material circumstances. The confrontational climax of the historical drama is rendered in song, dance, and drumming, sensorially rich devices that satisfy his audiences' inherited expectations concerning aesthetic structures most suited for conveying deep emotion. Yet this appeal to the senses is followed by an intellectual argument couched in terms of myth, another popular mode of expression that Osofisan has elsewhere characterized as a "pedagogical explanation of knowledge by means of metaphor." The abrupt disruption of the play within the play offers the audience a graphic image of its potential to reject and redirect a hegemonic social reality. The moment anticipates the final deconstruction of form, in which the actors jettison their roles entirely and encourage the audience to join in acknowledging the positive thrust of the farmers' movement.

Thus, Osofisan offers in plays like *The Chattering and the Song* what Brecht defined as a "fighting" popular theater. With sophisticated irreverence, he reinterprets core values, thereby challenging audiences to reclaim for themselves the power to alter their world.

—Sandra L. Richards

O'SULLIVAN, Vincent (Gerald)

Nationality: New Zealander. **Born:** Auckland, 28 September 1937. **Education:** University of Auckland, M.A. 1959; Lincoln College, Oxford, B.Litt. 1962. **Family:** Married. **Career:** Editor, *Comment,* 1963-66, and literary editor, New Zealand *Listener,* 1978-79, both Wellington; lecturer, Victoria University, Wellington, 1963-66; senior lecturer, 1965-75, and reader, 1977-78, Waikato University, Hamilton; visiting fellow, Yale University, New Haven, Connecticut, 1976; writer-in-residence, Victoria University, 1981, University of Tasmania, Hobart, 1982, and Deakin University, Geelong, Victoria, 1982; playwright-in-residence, Downstage Theatre, Wellington, 1983; ARGS research fellow, Flinders University of South Australia, Bedford Park, 1984-86; writer-in-residence, University of Queensland, St. Lucia, 1987. Professor of English, Victoria University, Wellington, 1988—. **Awards:** Commonwealth scholarship, 1960; Macmillan Brown prize, 1961; Jessie MacKay award, 1965; Farmers poetry prize, 1967, 1971; Fulbright award, 1976; Wattie Book award, 1979; New Zealand Book award, 1981. **Address:** c/o John McIndoe Ltd., 51 Crawford Street, P.O. Box 694, Dunedin, New Zealand.

Publications

Plays

Shuriken (produced Wellington, 1983). Wellington, Victoria University Press, 1985.
Ordinary Nights in Ward Ten (produced Wellington, 1984).
Jones and Jones (produced Wellington, 1988). Wellington, Victoria University Press, 1989.
Billy (produced Wellington, 1989). Wellington, Victoria University Press, 1990.
Cobbers (as *The Lives and Loves of Harry and George,* produced Wellington, 1990).

Novel

Miracle: A Romance. Dunedin, McIndoe, 1976.

Short Stories

The Boy, the Bridge, the River. Dunedin, McIndoe, 1978.
Dandy Edison for Lunch and Other Stories. Dunedin, McIndoe, 1981.
Survivals. Wellington, Port Nicholson Press, 1985.
The Snow in Spain. Wellington, Allen and Unwin, 1990.
Palms and Minarets: Selected Stories. Wellington, New Zealand, 1992.

Poetry

Our Burning Time. Wellington, Prometheus, 1965.
Revenants. Wellington, Prometheus, 1969.
Bearings. Wellington and London, Oxford University Press, 1973.
From the Indian Funeral. Dunedin, McIndoe, 1976.
Butcher & Co. Wellington, Oxford University Press, 1977; London, Oxford University Press, 1978.
Brother Jonathan, Brother Kafka. Wellington and Oxford, Oxford University Press, 1980.
The Rose Ballroom and Other Poems. Dunedin, McIndoe, 1982.
The Butcher Papers. Auckland, Oxford University Press, 1986.
The Pilate Tapes. Auckland, Oxford University Press, 1986.
Matters of Fallen Years. Edinburgh, Taraga Press, 1990.
Selected Poems. New York, Oxford University Press, 1992.
House of Sin. New York, Woodstock Books, 1995.

Other

New Zealand Poetry in the Sixties. Wellington, Department of Education, 1973.
Katherine Mansfield's New Zealand. Melbourne, Lloyd O'Neal, 1974; London, Muller, 1975.
James K. Baxter. Wellington, Oxford University Press, 1976; London, Oxford University Press, 1977.
Finding the Pattern, Solving the Problem: Katherine Mansfield the New Zealand European (lecture). Wellington, Victoria University Press, 1989.
Let the River Stand. New York, Penguin, 1993.
Selected Letters. Edinburgh, Taraga Press, 1995.

Editor, *An Anthology of Twentieth-Century New Zealand Poetry*. London, Oxford University Press, 1970; revised edition, Wellington and London, Oxford University Press, 1976; revised edition, 1987.
Editor, *New Zealand Short Stories 3*. Wellington, Oxford University Press, 1975; London, Oxford University Press, 1976.
Editor, *The Aloe, with Prelude*, by Katherine Mansfield. Wellington, Port Nicholson Press, 1982; Manchester, Carcanet, and Atlantic Highlands, New Jersey, Humanities Press, 1983.
Editor, with M.P. Jackson, *New Zealand Writing Since 1945*. Auckland, Oxford University Press, 1983.
Editor, with Margaret Scott, *The Collected Letters of Katherine Mansfield 1: 1903-1917*. Oxford and New York, Oxford University Press, 1984; *2: 1918-1919*, 1987.
Editor, *Collected Poems*, by Ursula Bethell. Auckland, Oxford University Press, 1985.
Editor, *The Poems of Katherine Mansfield*. Auckland, Oxford University Press, 1988.
Editor, *Selected Letters by Katherine Mansfield*. Oxford, Clarendon Press, 1989.

*

Critical Studies: "Tragic Power in Vincent O'Sullivan's *Shuriken*" by Phillip Mann, in *Australasian Drama Studies* (Queensland, Australia), April 1991, pp. 147-58; "Re-Orienting Australia Drama: Staging Theatrical Irony" by Joanne Tompkins, in *A Review of International English Literature* (Calgary), October 1994, pp. 117-33; "Setting Allegory Adrift in John Ashbery's *Mountains and Rivers,* James Joyce's *Portrait of an Artist as a Young Man,* and Vincent O'Sullivan's *Let the River Stand*" by Katrina Bachinger, in *Trends in English and American Studies: Literature and the Imagination,* Lewiston, New York, Mellen, 1996.

* * *

Vincent O'Sullivan's early poems, especially the *Butcher & Co.* sequences, demonstrated his gift for characterization, and it is not surprising that he should eventually turn his attention to the stage. In at least two respects his first play, *Shuriken,* established a pattern for most of his subsequent work. Like *Billy* and the unproduced *Yellow Brides,* which treats love in much the same way as *Shuriken* treats war, it dramatizes a clash between white antipodean society and the indigenous cultures of the Pacific Rim. And like all of his plays, it exhibits inventive mixing of theatrical modes.

Shuriken focuses on a fatal clash in a New Zealand prisoner-of-war camp holding Japanese in 1943. The prisoners and their minders inhabit different worlds, with only Tiny, the camp interpreter, and "Charlie," the most tractable of the Japanese, capable of any movement between the two. The camp commandant characterizes the difference as one between "thinking white and thinking yellow." Tiny sums it up less colorfully:

> The point is we can see history in two ways. . . . There's the bird's eye view that gives you the grand scale. The sweep of time where none of us individually matters a damn. . . . The Japs stand for [this view]. We stand for the opposite. . . . We don't think about history. We think about us.

Not surprisingly, then, the Japanese see their captors as

> a group of men . . . with no memory of the past, no sense of destiny for the future, a present defined by what? A certain number of sheep, a full stomach, a King on the other side of the world who regards your dead as his right. A king who is a man like yourselves.

The Japanese emperor is, of course, a god, and the Japanese prisoners' loyalty to him, coupled with their proud military tradition and their lack of concern for the individual, precludes any acceptance of defeat, surrender, or imprisonment. This intransigence leads eventually to the fatal showdown with their reluctant and uncomprehending captors. To accentuate the prisoners' proud sense of their culture, O'Sullivan builds certain Japanese theatrical conventions into the play, notably a snatch of No drama in act 1 that features the spirit of a dead prisoner.

The New Zealanders, "lost in the featureless landscape of a world without history," as one reviewer put it, lack such distinctive cultural forms and tend to lapse into the imported idiom of music hall for their more stylized moments. But one character among them, the Maori soldier Tai, does have an authentic culture, to which he gives memorable expression at the end of Act 1 when he delivers a moving elegy—"both a soliloquy and a traditional Maori lament"—for his brother-in-law killed in battle by the Japanese.

Tai remains on the fringe of the action in *Shuriken,* but in *Billy* O'Sullivan puts an Aboriginal character, loosely modeled on the famous Bennelong, firmly at the center of things. The play opens with a beautifully contrived image of the colonization of Australia. The principals enter one by one and remove dustcovers "suggesting mounds, hillocks etc." from the furniture, thus transforming an Australian landscape into a Victorian drawing room. The ensuing colonial ensemble eventually breaks down into a series of fragmentary scenes in which the Europeans one by one encounter Billy, who, unlike Bennelong, being a deaf-mute, serves as the other by which they define themselves. As one character puts it, "I am looking at something so empty, so foreign to me, that I only see back myself."

Through Billy's mime some startling sound effects—for example, the "clamour of magpies"—and a few vignettes of minor, mainly Irish, characters, a picture of a more authentic Australia slowly emerges. Apart from one highly stylized scene, however, in which Elizabeth acts as Billy's mouthpiece, this Australia remains below the symbolic threshold of language, as the final stage direction indicates:

> With the spot narrowing to his face, [Billy] opens his mouth, straining to utter some sound. It is painful, guttural, perhaps slowly developing into a painful scream. He sinks to his knees, still making this protracted sound. It is accompanied by or taken over by the sound of a didgeridoo. The lights snap back on, into mid-party. BILLY is still kneeling on the floor, the others dance gaily about him, a jig or reel.

Like *Shuriken, Billy* grafts stylized sequences of one kind or another onto a realistic base. O'Sullivan's other plays employ this same formula, generally drawing on music hall for the stylized episodes. *Jones and Jones,* the best and, since O'Sullivan is a noted Mansfield scholar, the most authoritative of the plays spawned by the centenary of Katherine Mansfield's birth, makes a particularly apt use of music hall. In his author's note O'Sullivan explains that his intention was "to present something that was faithful to my idea of the kind of woman she was, and yet to avoid any suggestions of 'naturalism' or stage biography. I took my lead from her own passion for music hall."

The play charts the relationship between Mansfield and Ida Baker, with cameo roles for a number of other notables, including D. H. Lawrence, who at one point "enters through a trap in the floor . . . wearing a miner's helmet." The stolid character of Baker often provides a linking device for the stylized antics of the others, but by the end Mansfield, too, is wanting to leave the superficial world of music hall behind. She "wouldn't mind being real . . . for a change," and as she sets out on her fateful final voyage to Fontainebleau, her husband, John Middleton Murry, comments, "She thinks the only way to truth is through shedding our false selves." Her own last speech expresses a wish "to become so simple that the light shines through me."

The development from role playing to sincerity is in effect reversed in *Cobbers*. This play works backward through the lives of two men who have lived together since their 20s. They initially appear to be harmless old codgers whose fondness for music hall merely underlines their appealing eccentricity. But the play eventually reveals that they are, and always have been, ruthlessly exploitative and manipulative. As with Mansfield, a love of music hall becomes in effect a metaphor for heartlessness.

O'Sullivan's best plays seldom range beyond this blend of realism and music hall, but he is certainly capable of a wider range of styles. *Ordinary Nights in Ward Ten,* an obscure allegory of love and time, is bewilderingly eclectic, while *Kurtspiel,* which has not been produced, uses Brechtian techniques effectively, especially in the first act, to depict the career of Kurt Weill.

—Richard Corballis

OVERMYER, Eric

Nationality: American. **Born:** Boulder, Colorado, 25 September 1951. **Education:** Reed College, Portland, Oregon, B.A. 1976; Florida State University, Tallahassee, 1977; Brooklyn College, City University of New York, 1979-81. **Family:** Married 1) Melissa Cooper in 1978; 2) Ellen McElduff in 1991. **Career:** Literary manager, Playwrights Horizons, New York, 1981-84; associate artist, Center Stage, Baltimore, Maryland, 1984-91; story editor, *St. Elsewhere* television series, 1986-87; visiting associate professor of playwriting, Yale University, and associate artist, Yale Repertory Theater, New Haven, Connecticut, 1991-92. **Awards:** Le Comte du Nouy, 1984; McKnight fellowship, 1986; National Endowment for the Arts fellowship, 1987; New York Foundation for the Arts fellowship, 1987; Rockefeller fellowship, 1987. **Agent:** George Lane, William Morris Agency, 1325 Avenue of the Americas, New York, New York 10019. **Address:** c/o Yale School of Drama, P.O. Box 208325, New Haven, Connecticut 06520-8325, U.S.A.

Publications

Plays

Native Speech (produced Los Angeles, 1983; New York, 1991). New York, Broadway Play Publishing, 1984.

On the Verge, or The Geography of Yearning (produced Baltimore, Maryland, 1985; New York, 1987; London, 1989). New York, Broadway Play Publishing, 1986.

The Double Bass, with Harry Newman, adaptation of the play by Patrick Süskind (produced New York, 1986).

In a Pig's Valise, music by August Darnell (produced Baltimore, Maryland, 1986; New York, 1989). New York, Broadway Play Publishing, 1989.

In Perpetuity Throughout the Universe (produced Baltimore, Maryland, and New York, 1988). New York, Broadway Play Publishing, 1988.

Hawker. Published in *Plays from New Dramatists,* edited by Christopher Gould, New York, Broadway Play Publishing, 1989.

Mi Vida Loca (produced New York, 1990). New York, Broadway Play Publishing, 1991.
Don Quixote de La Jolla (produced La Jolla, California, 1990). New York, Broadway Play Publishing, 1993.
Kafka's Radio (produced New York, 1990).
The Heliotrope Bouquet by Scott Joplin and Louis Chauvin (produced Baltimore, Maryland, 1991). New York, Broadway Play Publishing, 1993.
Dark Rapture (produced Seattle, 1992). New York, Broadway Play Publishing, 1993.
Eric Overmyer: Collected Plays (includes *Native Speech*; *On the Verge*; *In a Pig's Valise*; *In a Perpetuity throughout the Universe*; *The Heliotrope Bouquet by Scott Joplin and Louis Chauvin*; *Dark Rapture*). Newbery, Vermont, Smith and Kraus, 1993.
Amphitryon. New York, Broadway Play Publishing, 1996.
Marriage of Figaro/Figaro Gets a Divorce. New York, Broadway Play Publishing, 1996.
Alki, adaptation of *Peer Gynt* by Ibsen. New York, Broadway Play Publishing, 1997.

Television Plays: *St. Elsewhere* series, 1985-88; *The Days and Nights of Molly Dodd* series, 1988-90; *Sisters* series, 1990-91.

*

Critical Studies: "Eric Overmyer" in *A Search for a Postmodern Theater: Interviews with Contemporary Playwrights,* edited by John L. DiGaetani, New York, Greenwood, 1991; "Desultory Structures: Language as Presence in the Works of Overmyer, Wellman, and Jenkin" by Paul C. Castagno, in *The Journal of the Comparative Drama Conference* (Gainseville, Florida), 1991, pp. 1-7.

Eric Overmyer comments:

I am interested in the authentically theatrical. Hermann Broch stated that he wrote novels in order to discover that which can only be discovered by writing a novel. I write plays in order to discover what can only be discovered by writing plays. I am interested in discovering the limits of the theatre, its possibilities and its impossibilities. I am interested in language, first and always: a charged, mythic, poetic, theatrical language. And imagination: mythic, poetic, epic. I am interested in bravura performance style which is necessary to an authentically theatrical experience. I am not interested in naturalism, in small plays with small ideas which need small performances, in plays which are really faux cinema; in short, in the kind of plays the dramaturg James Magruder refers to as "talking about my problems in your living room." I am interested in plays which are contradictory, complex, many-layered, and many-faceted, which are unencumbered by reductive, mechanistic psychology, motive, and biography. In other words, I am interested in reversal instead of transition, in wrought language rather than humdrum speech, in leaps of the imagination not tedious exposition, in classic plays, and in contemporary plays which embody classical virtues and present classical challenges. I prefer to work with directors who direct classical plays as if they were contemporary, and contemporary plays as if they were classical. I am not an avant-gardist, I am a nouveau-classicist.

* * *

As one of only two playwrights toiling in the American theater for whom language is both object and muse (the other being Mac Wellman), Eric Overmyer suffers many fools. Directors, actors, and the critical establishment charge him with willful obscurity and arrant pedantry and chide him for a perceived resistance to closure. He runs afoul of editors and proofreaders, who insisted, for example, on changing his line "Give it me" in *In Perpetuity Throughout the Universe* to "Give it to me" through every stage of publication. The choice of "give it me" over "give it to me" is no trifling matter in an Overmyer play, and those deaf to the difference deny the characters their territory. Smoothing over this particular imperative or paraphrasing Overmyer into standard usage denies the author his right to remain a nonnaturalistic word jockey spinning lines outside the adamantly realist boundaries of the American theater. The standard new American play—standard play in standard prose—can be boiled down to the formula "Talking about *my* problems in *your* apartment." Apartments count for nothing in Overmyer's euphonic universe; his people more often than not turn up in dreams or on the airwaves or in terra incognita. Their language, their logorrheic pulse, is their main chance to talk their way into a known state of being and to recognize themselves. How well the audience knows them when they get there is another matter.

Overmyer's second play, *On the Verge, or The Geography of Yearning*, is one of the most important new works to emerge in American drama since 1960. Mary, Alex, and Fanny, three intrepid Victorian women explorers, set out for adventure in 1888 with machetes and pith helmets. As they progress, the terrain becomes increasingly unfamiliar. Unknown objects—eggbeaters, side-view mirrors—turn up; words and phrases they have never heard or used before—I like Ike, Cool Whip, "tractor opera"—spring to their lips. They discover that they are, in fact, bivouacking their way along the continuum of American pop. They pause in 1955, and Alex and Fanny, enthralled by the postwar consumer culture, remain in this most ideal of climates. They leave Mary to venture ever forward, yearning into the future. *On the Verge* traverses the twin peaks of American literature, the urge to know and the urge to go, and charts with unflagging theatricality the giddy debasement of American speech on the open market: "I have seen the future and it is slang."

The theme of what control an artist, particularly a writer, can exert over his work—in a sense, the question of reception theory—recurs throughout Overmyer's plays. *In Perpetuity Throughout the Universe* is a dark, vertiginous ride through the conspiratorial mentality of racist America in which a double cast of good guys and bad guys ghostwrite hate primers, creating enemies to keep the populace permanently paranoid and off-kilter. The title is a phrase from an author's contract regarding future rights to sequels and spin-offs. *Don Quixote de La Jolla*, built during five weeks of site-specific collaboration at the La Jolla Playhouse, is an insidiously faithful tweak on the tale of the mad knight and his doughty sidekick. Overmyer offers a baleful rumination on what weight, if any, the mighty and mightily unread sixteenth-century classic would have on a southern Californian populace raised on "Lady of Spain" and the terminally trashy *Man of La Mancha.* Not surprisingly, the *lambada* leaves Cervantes in the dust in another one of Overmyer's hilarious acts of cultural anthropology.

His 1991 play, *The Heliotrope Bouquet by Scott Joplin and Louis Chauvin*, was the fifth to be presented at Baltimore's Center Stage. In it Overmyer creates a fluid, overlapping dreamscape that encompasses both historical and hallucinatory locations. Joplin, the foremost composer of piano ragtime, and Chauvin, an illiterate contemporary whose musical gifts were said even to have surpassed Joplin's, wrote "The Heliotrope Bouquet," a slow-drag two-step, in 1906. This rhapsodic moment is the occasion of the play. Inasmuch as the historical material is scarce and largely conjectural, *Heliotrope* is less a historical restitution of Chauvin's place in American culture and African American history than it is a dialectical meditation on artistic collaboration. Although grounded in the sporting house context of ragtime America, the conflict between "slow and cautious Joplin," who lives with an eye on the future, and Chauvin, who burns brightly in the moment and believes that it only lasts "as long as a man stays awake," raises larger, unanswered questions "still to be heard in the ether and the House of God." What is posterity to a dead man? What is success? Does it come from a rag well performed before friends or in copies of sheet music tucked inside a stranger's piano bench? What is worth recalling—bundles of heliotrope set down on a table or notes bunched on the musical stave? Is art the moment of creativity or the fact of duration?

As with all of Overmyer's work, a main source of *Heliotrope*'s drama is its poetic idiom. As richly syncopated as ragtime, the play can be said to mimic the structure of a piano rag; certain lines are repeated throughout and passed from character to character like a musical phrase set in different keys. *Heliotrope*'s language is sensational; better than merely original, it is particular. Overmyer states his own case best when he wrote in his production notes for *On the Verge,* "The language of the play . . . cannot, must not, should not be naturalized or paraphrased. Rhythm and sound are sense."

—James Magruder

OWENS, Rochelle

Pseudonym for Rochelle Bass. **Nationality:** American. **Born:** Brooklyn, New York, 2 April 1936. **Education:** Lafayette High School, Brooklyn, graduated 1953; Alliance Francais, 1981; Université at Montreal, 1982; Université at Laual, Quebec, 1983; Sorbonne, 1985. **Family:** Married George Economou in 1962. **Career:** Worked as a clerk, typist, and telephone operator. Founding member, New York Theatre Strategy. Visiting lecturer, University of California, San Diego, 1982; adjunct professor and host of radio program *The Writer's Mind,* University of Oklahoma, Norman, 1984; distinguished writer-in-residence, Brown University, Providence, Rhode Island. **Awards:** Rockefeller grant, 1965, 1975; Ford grant, 1965; Creative Artists Public Service grant, 1966, 1973; Yale University School of Drama fellowship, 1968; Obie award, 1968, 1971, 1982; Guggenheim fellowship, 1971; National Endowment for the Arts grant, 1974; Villager award, 1982; New York Drama Critics Circle award, 1983; Bellagio fellowship, Rockefeller Foundation, Italy, 1993; distinguished writer-in-residence, University of Southwestern Louisiana, 1997. **Agent:** Dramatists Guild, 1501 Broadway, New York, New York 10036. **Address:** 1401 Magnolia, Norman, Oklahoma 73072, U.S.A.

Publications

Plays

Futz (produced Minneapolis, 1965; New York, Edinburgh, and London, 1967; produced Berlin, Paris, Zurich, Amsterdam, Stockholm, and New Zealand, 1970-85). New York, Hawk's Well Press, 1961; revised version in *Futz and What Came After,* 1968, in *New Short Plays 2,* London, Methuen, 1969.

The String Game (produced New York, 1965). Included in *Futz and What Came After,* 1968.

Istanboul (produced New York, 1965; London, 1982). Included in *Futz and What Came After,* 1968.

Homo (produced Stockholm and New York, 1966; London, 1969). Included in *Futz and What Came After,* 1968.

Beclch (produced Philadelphia and New York, 1968). Included in *Futz and What Came After,* 1968.

Futz and What Came After. New York, Random House, 1968.

The Karl Marx Play, music by Galt MacDermot, lyrics by Owens (produced New York, 1973). Included in *The Karl Marx Play and Others,* 1974.

The Karl Marx Play and Others (includes *Kontraption, He Wants Shih!, Farmer's Almanac, Coconut Folksinger, O.K. Certaldo*). New York, Dutton, 1974.

He Wants Shih! (produced New York, 1975). Included in *The Karl Marx Play and Others,* 1974.

Coconut Folksinger (broadcast 1976). Included in *The Karl Marx Play and Others,* 1974.

Kontraption (produced New York, 1978). Included in *The Karl Marx Play and Others,* 1974.

Emma Instigated Me, published in *Performing Arts Journal 1* (New York), Spring 1976.

The Widow, and The Colonel, in *The Best Short Plays 1977,* edited by Stanley Richards. Radnor, Pennsylvania, Chilton, 1977.

Mountain Rites, in *The Best Short Plays 1978,* edited by Stanley Richards. Radnor, Pennsylvania, Chilton, 1978.

Chucky's Hunch (produced New York, 1981). Published in *Wordplays 2,* New York, Performing Arts Journal Publications, 1982.

Who Do You Want, Peire Vidal? (produced New York, 1982). With *Futz,* New York, Broadway Play Publishing, 1986.

Three Front (produced Omaha, 1988; produced as *Guerra á Trois,* Teatro Nouveau, 1993). Published in French translation in *Europe Pluri Lingue,* 1997.

Screenplay: *Futz* (additional dialogue), 1969.

Radio Plays: *Coconut Folksinger,* 1976 (Germany); *Sweet Potatoes,* 1977.

Television Play (video): *Oklahoma Too: Rabbits and Nuggets,* 1987; *How Much Paint Does the Painting Need?* 1992; *Black Chalk,* 1994.

Short Stories

The Girl on the Garage Wall. Mexico City, El Corno Emplumado, 1962.

The Obscenities of Reva Cigarnik. Mexico City. El Corno Emplumado, 1963.

Poetry

Not Be Essence That Cannot Be. New York, Trobar Press, 1961.
Four Young Lady Poets, with others, edited by LeRoi Jones. New York, Totem-Corinth, 1962.
Salt and Core. Los Angeles, Black Sparrow Press, 1968.
I Am the Babe of Joseph Stalin's Daughter. New York, Kulchur, 1972.
Poems from Joe's Garage. Providence, Rhode Island, Burning Deck, 1973.
The Joe 82 Creation Poems. Los Angeles, Black Sparrow Press, 1974.
The Joe Chronicles 2. Santa Barbara, California, Black Sparrow Press, 1979.
Shemuel. St. Paul, New Rivers Press, 1979.
French Light. Norman, Oklahoma Press with the Flexible Voice, 1984.
Constructs. Norman, Oklahoma, Poetry Around, 1985.
Anthropologists at a Dinner Party. Tucson, Arizona, Chax Press, 1985.
W. C. Fields in French Light. New York, Contact II, 1986.
How Much Paint Does the Painting Need? New York, Kulchur, 1988.
Black Chalk. Norman, Oklahoma, Texture Press, 1992.
Paysanne and Selected Earlier Poems, 1961-1990. New York, Contact II Publications, 1993.
Rubbed Stones. Norman, Oklahoma, Texture Press, 1994.
Luca: Discourse on Life and Death. Blackwood Broadside Chaplet, 1995.
New and Selected Poems 1961-1996. New York, Junction Press, 1997.
The Wild River. World Wide Net, Light and Dust Books, 1997.

Recordings: *A Reading of Primitive and Archaic Poetry*, with others, Broadside; *From a Shaman's Notebook*, with others, Broadside; *The Karl Marx Play*, Kilmarnock, 1975; *Totally Corrupt*, Giorno, 1976; *Black Box 17*, Watershed Foundation, 1979.

Other

Spontaneous Combustion: Eight New American Plays. New York, Winter House, 1972.

Translator, *The Passerby*, by Lilian Atlan. Henry Holt & Company, 1993.

*

Manuscript Collections: Columbia University; Mugar Memorial Library, Boston University; University of California, Davis; University of Oklahoma, Norman; Lincoln Center Library of the Performing Arts, New York; Smith College, Northampton, Massachusetts.

Critical Studies: By Harold Clurman and Jerome Rothenberg in *Futz and What Came After*, 1968; review by Jane Augustine in *World 29* (New York), 1974; "Rochelle Owens Symposium" in *Margins 24-26* (Milwaukee), 1975; *American Playwrights: A Critical Survey* by Bonnie Marranca and Gautam Dasgupta, New York, Drama Book Specialists, 1981; *Women in American Theatre* edited by Helen Krich Chinoy and Linda Walsh Jenkins, New York, Crown, 1981; *American Women Writers* by Linda Mainiero, New York, Ungar, 1981; essay by Owens in *Contemporary Authors Autobiography Series 2* edited by Adele Sarkissian, Detroit, Gale, 1985; Len Berkman, in *Parnassus* (New York), 1985; in *Modern American Drama 1945-1990* by C. W. E. Bigsby, Cambridge University Press, 1992; essay on Rochelle Owens by Susan Smith Nash in *Talisman #12, A Journal of Contemporary Poetry and Poetics,* 1994; *Symposium on Rochelle Owens,* Light and Dust Books, World Wide Net, 1997.

Theatrical Activities:
Director and actor: **Television**—*Oklahoma Too: Rabbits and Nuggets*, 1987; *How Much Paint Does the Painting Need,* 1992; *Black Chalk,* 1994.

Rochelle Owens comments:

I am interested in the flow of imagination between the actors and the director, the boundless possibilities of interpretation of a script. Different theatrical realities are created and/or destroyed depending upon the multitudinous perceptions and points of view of the actors and director who share in the creation of the design of the unique journey of playing the play. There are as many ways to approach my plays as there are combinations of people who might involve themselves.

The inter-media videos *Oklahoma Too, Black Chalk,* and *How Much Paint Does the Painting Need* use poetry and images juxtaposed. The structures both linguistic and visual offer exciting projections of my continuous investigation of making art.

(1998) Oceanic Poetics

The process of writing must be marked with sensory surprises that paint dimensions of motion and energy crystallized in language that acts as a generative force: a spontaneity of the aesthetic, the organic, and the symbolic that reflect the mind's inner plateau and rhythm. My writing has been described as "protofeminist" by certain critics because I belong to the generation of experimental artists who gave rise to the present feminist movement. I also want to suggest the importance of the struggle to articulate the meaning of reality that goes beyond static notions of consciousness. Each generation of artists needs to seek a redefinition of aesthetic possibilities. For me, the writing process is a continual effort to expand my resources, to participate in the act of finding new reverberations in visual/verbal language. My writing is feminist because it has much to do with my personal and social identity as a woman in a patriarchal culture, and because it resists in both form and idea the absolute power of organized doctrine, principles, and procedures. One ought to question the assumptions of the culture which created the social role of women. As a poet I must be open to the expanded horizons of my own time. My concerns are to examine the real and invented borders of gender, identity, and human experience, and to keep my mind oceanic so that I can reconceptualize my poetry as transformation and as part of the reservoir of human history.

* * *

Rochelle Owens came to the attention of the theater public with her first play, *Futz,* whose shocking subject and inventive language launched her career. Owens's plays are distinguished by intense poetic imagery that springs from primordial human impulses of the subconscious and by the passionate and often violent struggle of her characters to survive within their repressive societies. Although a moralist who satirizes human frailty with parody, dialect, and the comic grotesque, Owens is also a compassionate observer who imbues her characters with tragic dimensions.

Futz is preceded by a quotation from Corinthians: "Now concerning the things whereof ye wrote to me: It is good for a man not to touch a woman." Cyrus Futz loves his pig, Amanda, and is persecuted by the community. Majorie Satz lusts for all men and wheedles an invitation to share Futz's sexual pleasure with his pig. Oscar Loop is driven to madness and murders Ann Fox when they inadvertently witness the Futz-Amanda-Majorie orgy. Majorie kills Amanda for revenge, Oscar is condemned to hang, and Futz is sent to prison, where he is stabbed by Majorie's brother. Puritanical society punishes innocent sensuality.

The String Game also explores the conflict between puritanism and natural impulse. Greenland Eskimos play the string game to ward off winter boredom. They are admonished for creating erotic images by their Italian priest, Father Bontempo, yet he longs for his own string game, warm spaghetti. The half-breed Cecil tempts Bontempo with a promise of pasta in exchange for the support of Cecil's commercial schemes. While gluttonously feasting, the priest chokes to death. The saddened Eskimos refuse to comply with Cecil's business venture and stoically return to their string games.

Istanboul dramatizes a cultural clash and *Homo* a class struggle. In *Istanboul* Norman men are fascinated by hirsute Byzantine women and their wives by the smooth-skinned Byzantine men. In a religious frenzy Saint Mary of Egypt murders the barbaric Norman Godfrigh, and sensual Leo makes love to Godfrigh's wife as they wait for the Saracens to attack. *Homo* presents the mutual greed and contempt of Nordic and Asiatic in a surrealistic exploration of racial and class conflict. In the dramatic energy of the play revolution comes and goes, and workers continue their brutality.

Human perversion and bloody primitive rites prevail in Owens's most savage play, *Beclch*. In a fantasy Africa four white adventurers intrude upon the natural innocence of a village. Queen Beclch, a monster of excess, professes her love for young Jose and then introduces him to the cruelty of cockfighting. She promises Yago kingship if he will contract elephantiasis. When Yago cannot transcend the pain of his deformity, he is forced mercilessly by the villagers to strangle himself. Beclch moves further into excess, and Jose flees in disgust. Since a queen cannot rule without a male consort, Beclch prepares herself for death as voluptuously as she has lived.

A promise of social progress resides in Owens's first play with music, *The Karl Marx Play*. As in *Homo*, linear time is ignored, and through a montage of scenes past and present a human portrait of Marx emerges in what is Owens's most joyful play. Her Marx is drained by illness, poverty, and lust for his aristocratic wife. All those who surround him, particularly his friend Engels and a twentieth-century American black, Leadbelly, demand that he complete *Das Kapital*. Although Marx denies his Jewish heritage, he invokes Yahweh for consolation, but it is finally Leadbelly who actively ignites the man of destiny to fulfill his mission.

He Wants Shih! is an elegant poetic tragedy. Lan, son of the last empress of the Manchu dynasty, abdicates the warlike legacy of his mother, ignores the adoring Princess Ling, loves his stepbrother Bok, and is enthralled with his stern mentor Feng. Steeped in Eastern philosophy and the supernatural, this surrealistic, archetypal myth of individuation is dramatized with ritual, masks, and pseudo-Chinese dialect. The dismembered head of the empress continues to speak on stage while Western imperialists decimate the Chinese. Acknowledging his homosexuality in the final scene, Lan-he is transformed into Lanshe. Total renunciation of sex and empire ends this fantastic play.

As *He Wants Shih!* explores the quest for selfhood, *Kontraption* examines dehumanization in a technological world. On an empty terrain Abdul and Hortten share their lives and sexual fantasies. Abdul's intolerance of their repulsive laundry man, Strauss, drives him to murder, and he is in turn transformed by a magician into a mechanical contraption. When Abdul attempts to transcend his own grotesque condition, he falls to his death, leaving behind a disconsolate Hortten.

Owens returns to historical biography in *Emma Instigated Me*. The life of Emma Goldman, the nineteenth-century anarchist, is juxtaposed against a contemporary author and director and against female revolutionaries. Once again linear time is dissolved. The characters change from one to another and from character into actor into bystander. The theatricality of the play becomes its most important objective.

Owens has continued to experiment. *Chucky's Hunch* was acclaimed by New York critics as hilarious and impelling. In this work, in contrast to her multicharacter dramas, the solitary Chucky, a middle-aged failure, narrates a series of recriminating letters to one of his three ex-wives. Similarly, in *Who Do You Want, Peire Vidal?*, two characters assume multiple roles. In this play within a play a Japanese-American professor is among the transformational characters in a series of episodic confrontations. Owens's fantastic imagery, charged language, and daring confrontation with subconscious impulse remain unique in American theater.

—Elaine Shragge

OWUSU, Martin

Nationality: Ghanaian. **Born:** Agona, Kwaman, 11 July 1943. **Education:** University of Ghana, Legon, 1963-66, diploma in drama and theatre studies 1966; University of Bristol, 1971-73, M. Litt. in drama 1975; Brandeis University, Waltham, Massachusetts, 1976-79, Ph.D. in English and American literature 1979. **Family:** Married Margaret Owusu in 1966; one daughter and two sons. **Career:** Tutor, St. Augustine's College, 1966-69, and Mfantsipim School, 1969-71, both Cape Coast; lecturer, University of Cape Coast, 1973-76; assistant professor, Mass Bay Community College, 1979-82, Brandeis University, 1981-82, University of Rhode Island, Kingston, 1982-83, and Emerson College, Boston, 1984, and 1986-87. Senior lecturer, 1987—, and drama coordinator, 1988-91, University of Ghana, Legon. **Awards:** British Council fellowship, 1971; ECRAG award, for acting, 1988, and for television, 1989. **Address:** c/o School of Performing Arts, University of Ghana, P.O. Box 25, Legon, Near Accra, Ghana.

Publications

Plays

The Story Ananse Told (produced Legon, 1967). London, Heinemann, 1971.

The Mightier Sword (produced Cape Coast, 1967). Included in *The Sudden Return and Other Plays*, 1973.

The Adventures of Sasa and Esi, Sasa and the King of the Forest. Accra, Ghana Publishing House, 1968.
The Adventures of Sasa and Esi, Sasa and the Witch of the Forest. Accra, Ghana Publishing House, 1968.
Anane (televised 1968; produced Legon, 1989). Included in *The Sudden Return and Other Plays*, 1973.
The Sudden Return (produced Legon, 1991). Included in *The Sudden Return and Other Plays*, 1973.
The Sudden Return and Other Plays (includes *The Mightier Sword, The Pot of Okro Soup, Anane, A Bird Called "Go-Back-for-the-Answer"*). London, Heinemann, 1973.
Python: The Legend of Aku Sika (produced Legon, 1989). Accra, Asempa Publishers, 1992.

Television Play: *Anane*, 1968.

Other

Drama of the Gods: A Study of Seven African Plays. Roxbury, Massachusetts, Omenana, 1983.
African Drama: Analysis and Interpretation: J.C. De Graft's Through a Film Darkly and Sons and Daughters. Legon, Soundstage Production, 1992.

*

Martin Owusu comments:

My plays are set in historic, mythological, and modern Ghana. I draw my material and forms largely from traditional sources. I am ceaselessly seeking to move in new directions. While I have a profound awareness of playwriting fashions in Europe and America, I am attempting to create forms that are more directly related to African experience. I am particularly interested in the mysterious and the supernatural. At the same time, I explore the effect of man's social background on his manners and morality.

* * *

Martin Owusu's first published play, *The Story Ananse Told*, taps the rich theatrical fount of the *anansesem* storytelling tradition of the Akans of Ghana. Owusu does not just flirt with the traditional storytelling form. Rather, he explores its essence and mode, which he then uses as his guiding aesthetic for creating a theater that is contemporary while being firmly rooted in tradition. It is the dialectical tension between the traditional and the modern that makes his plays so engaging. He seems chiefly concerned with experimenting with African traditional forms of song, dance, mime, and folklore in order to make these elements intrinsically part of contemporary African theater. It is in *The Sudden Return and Other Plays* that he successfully realizes this intention.

The five plays that make up the collection are *The Sudden Return, The Mightier Sword, The Pot of Okro Soup, Anane*, and *A Bird Called "Go-Back-for-the-Answer." The Sudden Return* possesses a "sparse and lyrical economy" and is a moving and truly "pathetic story of a middle aged revenu seeking spiritual solace for a tortured conscience." Kojo's sudden return after a 15-year absence startles as well as pleases members of his extended family, but only for a while, for he is a deeply troubled man virtually on the brink of a mental collapse. Through a series of flashbacks Owusu reveals to the audience that Kojo, in order to get rich, had killed his wife and two daughters through ritual magic and in doing so had set his soul on fire. The climax of the play is his psychic disintegration in full view of his people, for his guilt can no longer be hidden from the world. *The Sudden Return* is a play that aspires to the tense and emotional heights of tragedy but somehow falls short because the central character cannot rise above the flaccid image of a sad soul caught in a web of anguish and the trauma of a personal past. It is, however, richly textured by a neat mix of the indigenous myths, legends, and superstitions of Ghana.

The second play, *The Mightier Sword*, is a historical work with a tripartite structure that helps to control the terrain as well as the action of the drama. Although not as emotionally and theatrically powerful as *The Sudden Return*, it is successful as a re-creation of a past contained within a written history. It is concerned with dramatizing certain incidents in the history of the once powerful and extensive empire of Ghana, especially the internecine wars that raged endlessly between the Ashanti and Denkyira. The central conflict revolves around the rivalry between Osei Tutu of the Ashanti and Ntim Gyakari of the Denkyira, while the main action is the unprovoked insults and diplomatic blunders of the latter and his subsequent defeat in the war he brought about. As documentary drama it succeeds and is at times captivating, but as effective stage drama it is weak because its poetry limps, while the action and the lines remain static and narrative most of the time.

A Pot of Okro Soup and *A Bird Called "Go-Back-for-the-Answer"* return to the *anansesem* tradition of *The Story Ananse Told*. Here Ananse is up to his usual tricks, with his victims being a gullible couple, Apraku and Akosua, whom he deceives into giving him food in exchange for a useless piece of stone he claims is capable of making the most delicious soup. This is vintage Ananse, his scams being merely survivalist, never malicious. In *Bird* the indomitable hero tricks his way into the ranks of the elders of Nana Kuntu's court. Owusu exploits a rich tradition of storytelling theater in his Ananse plays, and with this character his audience can be assured of boundless comedies of delightful characters and lively situations. The Ananse plays are full of verve, for the *anansegoro* tradition provides a versatile and dynamic structure of music, mime, and dialogue that makes them interesting to read and stage.

The last play in the collection, *Anane*, is a tragicomedy. It also is influenced by the storytelling form, and it observes the formulaic opening and has a narrator who stands outside the action to tell and comment on the story. The play is about Anane, who as a baby is picked up in the bush by Bofo. He is brought up to believe that Bofo and his wife are his parents and that their only daughter is his sister. But when it appears that the hatred and taunts of the girl are going to lead to disaster and a sad end for Anane, his real father turns up as a stranger, actually a king. In this play Owusu explores another style of storytelling, one in which the narrator always remains outside the action. This style is unlike that used in the Ananse tales, in which Ananse is usually the narrator as well as the main character.

On the whole Owusu is to be commended for his sophisticated experiments with Ghanaian traditional forms, which he has successfully adapted for the modern theater. His plays blend music, song, dance, proverb, myth, and legend in a rich theatrical mix that can be best appreciated in performance. He has contributed immensely to the drive toward the creation of an African theater that can exist comfortably on the African stage as well as on the stages of the world. In general, although his universe is his African cultural environment, his characters and themes belong to all humanity.

—Osita Okagbue

OyamO

Nationality: American. **Born:** Charles F. Gordon in Elyria, Ohio, 7 September 1943. **Education:** Admiral King High School, Lorain, Ohio, graduated 1962; Miami University, Oxford, Ohio, 1963-65; studied journalism; New York University, 1967-68; theater lighting program, Brooklyn College, New York, 1968; Harlem Youth Speaks/First Light Video Institute, New York, 1974; College of New Rochelle, New York, B.A. 1979; Yale University School of Drama, New Haven, Connecticut, M.F.A. 1981. **Military Service:** U.S. Naval Reserve, 1966 (honorable discharge). **Career:** Assistant technical director, New Lafayette Theatre, 1967-69, assistant stage manager, American Place Theatre, 1970, founder, The Black Magicians, theatre company, 1970, and master electrician, Negro Ensemble Company, 1971, all New York; teacher in creative writing, Afro-American Cultural Center, Buffalo, New York, 1972, Street Theatre, Eastern Correctional Institute, Napanoch, New York, 1975-76, Afro-American Cultural Center, New Haven, Connecticut, 1978, and College of New Rochelle, New York, 1979-82; writer-in-residence, Emory University, Atlanta, Georgia, 1982-83, and Playwrights Center, Minneapolis, 1984; visiting lecturer, Playwrights Workshop, Princeton University, New Jersey, 1986-87. Adjunct associate professor in playwriting, 1989-90, and associate professor, University of Michigan, Ann Arbor, 1990—. **Awards:** Rockefeller grant, 1972, 1983; New York State Council on the Arts fellowship, 1972, 1975, 1982, 1985; Guggenheim fellowship, 1973; Ohio Arts Council award, 1979; Yale University School of Drama Molly Kazan award, 1980; McKnight fellowship, 1984; National Endowment for the Arts fellowship, 1985, 1992. **Address:** 814 Stimson, Ann Arbor, Michigan 48103; or, 157 West 120th Street, No. 3, New York, New York 10027, U.S.A.

Publications

Plays

Chumpanzees (produced New York, 1970).
The Negroes (produced New York, 1970). Published in *Black Troupe Magazine* (New York), vol.1, no.2, 1970.
Outta Site (produced New York, 1970). Published in *Black Theatre Magazine* (New York), vol.1, no.4, 1970.
The Thieves (produced Seattle, 1970).
Willie Bignigga (produced New York, 1970). Published in *Dramatika*, (New York), vol.3, no.1, 1970.
The Last Party (produced New York, 1970).
The Lovers (also director: produced New York, 1971).
The Advantage of Dope (produced Buffalo, New York, 1971).
His First Step in *The Corner* (produced New York, 1972). Published in *The New LaFayette Theatre Presents*, edited by Ed Bullins, New York, Grove Press, 1974.
The Breakout (produced Waterford, Connecticut, 1972; New York, 1975). Published in *Black Drama: An Anthology*, edited by Woodie King and Ron Milner, New York, n.p., 1972.
The Juice Problem (produced Waterford, Connecticut, 1974).
Crazy Niggas (produced Napanoch, New York, 1975).
A Star Is Born Again (for children) (produced New York, 1978).
Mary Goldstein and the Author (produced New York, 1979). Chicago, Third World Press, 1989.
The Place of the Spirit Dance (produced New Haven, Connecticut, 1980).
The Resurrection of Lady Lester (produced New Haven, Connecticut and New York, 1981). Published in *Plays U.S.A.: 1*, edited by James Leverett, New York, Theatre Communications Group, 1981.
Distraughter and the Great Panda Scanda (musical; produced Atlanta, Georgia, 1983).
Old Black Joe (produced San Francisco, 1984).
Every Moment (produced San Francisco, 1986).
The Temple of Youth (for children) (produced New York, 1987).
Fried Chicken and Invisibility (produced New York, 1988).
Singing Joy (produced New York, 1988).
An Evening of Living Colors, music by Olu Dara (produced Trenton, New Jersey, 1988; New York, 1989).
The Stalwarts (produced New York, 1988).
Return of the Been-To (produced New York, 1988).
Let Me Live (produced New York, 1991).
One Third of a Nation, adaptation of a play by Arthur Arent (produced Fairfax, Virginia, 1991).
Famous Orpheus (produced New Brunswick, New Jersey, 1991).
Angels in the Men's Room (produced New York, 1992).
Sanctuary (sketches) (produced New York, 1992).
I Am a Man. Washington, D.C., Arena Stage, 1995.

Other

The Star That Could Not Play (for children). New York, OyamO Ujamaa, 1974.
Hillbilly Liberation (collection of plays and prose). New York, OyamO Ujamaa, 1976.

* * *

The dramas of OyamO are rarely confined by a realistic style. His works often juxtapose myth and reality and require actors to play multiple roles. His gift for the use of language evokes an intense emotional impact, while creating vivid visual images.

Although inspired by the life of Lester Young, the author does not profess his play *The Resurrection of Lady Lester* to be a docudrama of the famed saxophonist. It is termed a "poetic mood song," and the lyrical quality of the dialogue provides impressions of the man and his music instead of the cold facts that usually encumber biographical dramas. Although not given in chronological order, scenes from the musician's life seem to flow seamlessly into one another as though streaming from Young's memory. Perhaps the most poignant of these scenes are those that illustrate his intimate professional and personal relationship with legendary singer Billie Holiday. In the end the play manages not to be a lament for Young's tragic death but rather celebrates a musician who plays his instrument from the depths of his soul.

Set in the early 1970s, *Fried Chicken and Invisibility* examines a former militant who believes that he has found a scheme to obtain success in a racist American society. Traveling to a writer's conference by train, William Price and Winston McRutherford share rum and fried chicken while discussing their experiences as African Americans. Price, a strong-willed young man in his late 20s, recalls his turbulent youth in an impoverished neighborhood and his revolutionary activities during the 1960s. Reminiscent of the hero in Ralph Ellison's novel *Invisible Man,* Price argues for invisibility as a strategy for survival. As long as he fits the ineffectual, stereotypical image whites have created for blacks, he believes that whites will not see him as a threat and therefore target him for death. Price assumes the posture of a black revolutionary, but by the end of the play his true disposition is revealed. The young man tries to proposition McRutherford's wife, whom he mistakenly assumes to be white, and the opinion of the whites at the writer's conference seems unduly important to him, even though McRutherford informs him of its ineffectuality in furthering one's career. Thus, the drama indicts Price as a hypocritical man of few convictions, except in regard to his own self-interest.

Set in Atlanta in 1932, *Let Me Live* gives a moving portrayal of men caught in an unjust and cruel penitentiary system. The drama provides glimpses into the lives of eight African American prisoners, with scenes alternating between their current predicament and episodes revealed by memory. Mirroring the prevailing sociopolitical conditions of the outside world, the penal system encourages the men to turn on one another for their basic needs or perversions. One recently imprisoned man, Angelo Herndon, struggles not to fall prey to the base intentions of his captors. An ardent communist jailed for organizing the disenfranchised, Herndon provides the other prisoners with the hope that his socialist allies will provide the legal assistance needed to free them from their hellish existence. Drawing on his strong convictions as a source of inspiration, he refuses to despair when one of his cell mates dies from lack of medical attention or when the attorney sent to advise them proves unsympathetic and ineffectual. Attempting to break his spirit, Shonuff, a masochistic prison informant and enforcer, brutally rapes Herndon after getting him intoxicated. At the end of the play, however, when given the opportunity to deal his abuser a fatal blow, Herndon decides against the animalistic action. Although another prisoner does decide to kill Shonuff, Herndon's personal stance against barbarism represents a tribute to those who refuse to relinquish their humanity under inhumane conditions.

Famous Orpheus is based on the mythological legend of the lovers Orpheus and Eurydice and was inspired by *Black Orpheus,* the film adaptation of the story. This poetic drama uses touches of humor to explore the connection between myth and reality. Guided by a calypsonian griot, a Trinidadian troupe of singers and dancers portrays the story. Orpheus, a famed guitarist, appears eager to marry his fiancée, Mariella, even though she does not share his passion for music. When he goes to collect a newly made guitar, however, Orpheus falls desperately in love with Eurydice, the niece of the instrument maker. During the revelry of carnival, a mysterious figure representing death stalks Eurydice, as he has done since she left her home in Tobago. When the figure reveals his presence to Eurydice, she runs for her life, with the figure in pursuit. Orpheus gives chase as far as the wharf and tries in vain to fight the figure. Eurydice becomes entangled in an electric cable and falls to her death in the ocean. Obsessed with his love for Eurydice, Orpheus attempts to retrieve her from the underworld. There he meets such mythological beings as Charon, Pluto, and Persephone. Ironically, these legendary figures speak in the rhythms and style of the Trinidadian people, sprinkling their dialogue with specific references to modern-day popular culture. Receiving his request to retrieve the dead Eurydice, they allow Orpheus to return with her to the land of the living provided that he does not look at her until they have left the underworld. Unfortunately, Eurydice's feelings of neglect compel Orpheus to look at her, thus breaking his agreement. A heartbroken Orpheus returns to his own world, only to be killed by his jealously insane ex-fiancée.

OyamO's most critically acclaimed play is *I Am a Man,* which tells the story of T. O. Jones, one of the leaders of the 1968 strike of sanitation workers in Memphis, Tennessee. Although historically Jones's work would be overshadowed by the assassination of Martin Luther King, Jr., in OyamO's dramatization the characters and events of the play are products of Jones's mind. Numerous brief scenes depict Jones at critical points as he incites the workers to unionize and strike for better working conditions. He faces halfhearted negotiations with city officials who are not beneath using black operatives to undermine the movement. He confronts national union leaders who believe him not savvy enough to see the strike through. He finds his marriage dissolving as his wife feels that the family should no longer play a secondary role to his union activities. Consequently, the once confident Jones succumbs to the compounding, debilitating pressures of his work. After King's assassination and the settlement of the strike, the men Jones had organized turn out to be his saving grace. He is the only person from whom they will take the order to return to work. In this way the brotherhood serves as a healing and rejuvenating power for a man who felt that he had lost his way.

—Addell Austin Anderson

P

PAGE, Louise

Nationality: British. **Born:** London, 7 March 1955. **Education:** High Storrs Comprehensive School, Sheffield; University of Birmingham, 1973-76, B.A. in drama and theatre arts 1976; University of Wales, Cardiff, 1976-77, post-graduate diploma in theatre studies 1977. **Career:** Yorkshire Television fellow in creative writing, University of Sheffield, 1979-81; resident playwright, Royal Court Theatre, London, 1982-83; associate director, Theatre Calgary, Alberta, 1987. **Awards:** George Devine award, 1982; J.T. Grein award, 1985. **Agent:** Phil Kelvin, Goodwin Associates, 12 Rabbit Row, London W8 4DX. **Address:** 6-J Oxford and Cambridge Mansions, Old Marylebone Road, London NW1 5EC, England.

Publications

Plays

Want-Ad (produced Birmingham, 1977; revised version produced London, 1979).
Glasshouse (produced Edinburgh, 1977).
Tissue (produced Birmingham and London, 1978; Connecticut, 1985; New York, 1992). Published in *Plays by Women 1*, edited by Michelene Wandor, London, Methuen, 1982.
Lucy (produced Bristol, 1979).
Hearing (produced Birmingham, 1979).
Flaws (produced Sheffield, 1980).
House Wives (produced Derby, 1981).
Salonika (produced London, 1982; New York, 1985). London, Methuen, 1983.
Falkland Sound/Voces de Malvinas (produced London, 1983).
Real Estate (produced London, 1984; Washington, D.C., 1985; New York, 1987). London, Methuen, 1985.
Golden Girls (produced Stratford-on-Avon, 1984; London, 1985). London, Methuen, 1985.
Beauty and the Beast (produced Liverpool and London, 1985). London, Methuen, 1986.
Goat (produced Croydon, Surrey, 1986).
Diplomatic Wives (produced Watford, 1989). London, Methuen, 1989.
Plays: One (includes *Tissue*, *Salonika*, *Real Estate*, *Golden Girls*). London, Methuen, 1990.
Adam Was a Gardener (produced Chichester, 1991).
Like to Live (produced New York, 1992).
Hawks and Doves (produced Nuffield, 1992).

Radio Plays: *Saturday, Late September*, 1978; *Agnus Dei*, 1980; *Armistice*, 1983.

Television Play: *Peanuts* (*Crown Court* series), 1982.

* * *

Although Louise Page's work may lack the strident militancy expected of modern women writers, her contribution lies in her singling out the experiences of women as keystones to an examination of social conditioning. These women are unexceptional, lacking in unique personality traits. Their right to be the center of the drama stems from the situations they are in, unremarkable situations in themselves but personal crises to the characters through whom we see the contradictions between our socially conditioned expectations and our private experience of life. By isolating these ordinary women and their mundane crises, Page explores and exposes the social preconceptions by which people define and judge, analyzing the ways in which these assumptions limit our lives, complicate our decisions, and contradict our experiences.

Page adopts different theatrical styles to highlight this tension between socially conditioned expectations and private experience. In plays as different in form as *Tissue, Salonika,* and *Real Estate,* the most frequent single word is "expect," and the action is played out against a background of expectations, making the audience aware of the contradictions and distortions these ingrained preconceptions place upon individual behavior. *Tissue,* for example, is not so much a play about breast cancer as a play in which the crisis of breast cancer serves as a focus for the examination of assumptions about female sexuality and value.

A straight narrative about a woman fighting breast cancer would, by definition, imply themes of personal heroism. The structure of *Tissue* changes the emphasis from personality and the fact of cancer to the associated ideas that make facing breast cancer more difficult for both victim and associates. Scenes from Sally's life, unconnected by time or space and irrelevant in themselves, are magnetized by Sally's cancer, and their juxtaposition highlights the complex socially conditioned assumptions that create the feminine mystique. Their sequence has the logic of memory, setting one another off through association of word, image, or emotional logic and building an analysis of the obsessive connections between breasts and sexuality, sex and love, and the evaluation of women by physical appearance absorbed from childhood. Sally herself is barely a character at all. She displays no individual personality traits, and her thoughts and reactions are not so much personal as situational, the responses of a woman who has breast cancer.

Breasts define womanhood. They are assumed to be the measure of attractiveness, synonymous with sexuality and prerequisites for love, happy partnership, and the future. The mystique created around the female body is shown through the play to prevent realistic and healthy attitudes toward oneself and others. Sally's mother, who treated Sally's growing breasts as objects of magical impurity, is afraid to touch her own to test for cancer. Sally's boss tells of his wife who "wrecked her life trying to keep her body whole. I did not ask her to be beautiful but to be there." Although we would consciously reject the evaluation of a woman solely on the size of her breasts, the progress of the play illuminates the way these assumptions infiltrate our lives and inform our behavior.

Through stylistic choices Page depersonalizes the characters in order to accentuate their situations and responses. All of the men and women, except Sally, are meant to be played by the same actor and actress. Direct speeches to the audience and other theatrical devices, like the content-related sequence of scenes and the quick-fire lists (for example, of possible causes of cancer in scene

28), serve to demystify by removing the personal elements and emphasizing the situational behavior and its constriction through preconceptions. The construction of the play encourages audiences to go beyond their fear of cancer and to recognize the social conditioning that exacerbates their fears but that, through unraveling and understanding, can be overcome. Cancer, terrifying as it is, becomes not the end of the road but a pathway through distorted preconceptions of femininity and the examination of the taboos of both cancer and sexuality.

Sally's greatest fear when she finds that she has cancer is not that she will die but that she will cease to be attractive to men and thus be unable to love and be loved. Only at the end, when she has a new lover and after she has confronted, with us, the moments of her life that make up the fearful, complex confusion between her appearance and her value as a woman, does she take joy in the very fact of living.

Salonika, too, celebrates the indefatigable life force that defies physical limitation while making us aware of our assumptions and their limiting effects on our lives. The play's dreamlike quality not only stems from the World War I soldier's ghost rising from the sands, but the situation itself flies in the face of expectation. The mother and daughter on holiday to visit the father's grave are 84 and 64 years old. The mother has a 74-year-old lover who has hitchhiked to Greece to be with her. In a world in which love is assumed to be the reserve of the young and beautiful, these very facts cause a sense of unreality and demand that we take note of our preconceptions.

Within the play, too, the characters are constantly evaluating the expectations they held in the light of experience:

> Ben: (the ghost)—I didn't think you'd be a daughter.
> Enid: Didn't you?
> Ben: No. That's why I said to call a girl Enid. Because I thought you'd be a boy.
> Leonard: You expect everything in you to shrivel. All the hate and the longing. The lust. You don't expect to have them any more. But there isn't much else so you have them all the more. I could kill now. If I had the strength. . . . That's not what you expect.

Life as we live it defies expectation. The young man on the beach suddenly dies, leaving the old to bury him.

This dichotomy between social preconceptions and personal experience is elaborated in a more realistic form in *Real Estate.* Here Gwen, a middle-aged woman, lives with Dick, her second husband, outside Didcot, where she runs a small real estate agency. Her daughter Jenny, a successful London buyer, returns for the first time since she ran away 20 years before. Jenny is pregnant and has come to claim the care and attention mothers are automatically expected to provide. Gwen, conventional as she appears, does not revert to type. Although she dreads losing contact with Jenny again, she resists her intrusion into her life.

Without thinking we assume that the younger modern woman would introduce a lifestyle free from preconceptions and conventions. But Jenny, the very image of the modern independent woman, demands conventional responses from others. The modernness she brings with her is calloused, self-centered, and totally material. She carelessly lets the dog out, and she refuses to marry Eric, the child's father, while demanding his attention. When she insinuates herself into the business Gwen has founded on honesty, loyalty, and personal concern, Jenny's first act is to encourage a client to gazump.

Almost by definition, we expect a middle-aged, middle-class woman's life to be circumscribed by convention and socially approved roles, but, without proselytizing, Gwen and Dick have evolved a lifestyle that suits them both: "I can't ask you to stay for supper because I don't know if there's enough. Are you expecting to be asked to stay? Dick's province, not mine. He's the one who knows how long the mince has been in the freezer. How many sheets there are which haven't been turned edge to edge." Dick even embroiders tapestries. Indeed, the men in the play could not be more amenable. Eric, though divorced, appears sympathetic to his wife and is actively committed to the care of his daughter. Jenny considers this a liability, and when her needs conflict with the child's, she demands priority, although she refuses Eric her commitment. While Gwen has no desire to be a mother again or a grandmother, Dick longs for a baby on whom to lavish loving care.

Gwen cannot share her life with Jenny. Their expectations and values are mutually exclusive. Without fuss, leaving to Dick the traditional role she once imagined for herself, Gwen takes the little acorn she planted at the play's start and plants it in the forest. Like Jenny, it is well able to continue its growth on its own, although probably more willing. The placing of Gwen at the center of the play challenges our assumptions. We are led to consider the limitations these preconceptions force upon individual lives and their lack of validity as bases for judgment and the evaluation of human behavior. While retaining our sympathy, Gwen foils our expectations, setting them in relief so that we can evaluate them.

Page structures her plays to call into question our assumptions about character, behavior, and role and to stress that the roots of these automatic expectations and responses are in social conditioning rather than personality and psychology. Her choice of unexceptional women in unexceptional circumstances places emphasis on the way these preconceptions infiltrate the very fabric of our lives, laying bases for misunderstanding and regret and corrupting moments of crisis and decision.

—Elaine Turner

PARKS, Suzan-Lori

Nationality: American. **Education:** Mount Holyoke College, South Hadley, Massachusetts, B.A. in English and German literature (Phi Beta Kappa) 1985. **Career:** Drama studio, London, 1986. Guest lecturer, Pratt Institute, New York, 1988, University of Michigan, Ann Arbor, 1990, and Yale University, New Haven, Connecticut, and New York University, both 1990 and 1991; playwriting professor, Eugene Lang College, New York, 1990; writer-in-residence, New School for Social Research, New York, 1991-92. **Awards:** Mary E. Woolley fellowship, 1989; Naomi Kitay fellowship, 1989; National Endowment for the Arts grant, 1990, and playwriting fellowship, 1990, 1991; New York Foundation for the Arts grant, 1990; Rockefeller Foundation grant, 1990; Obie award, 1990. **Agent:** Wiley Hausam, International Creative Management, 40 West 57th Street, New York, New York 10019, U.S.A.

Publications

Plays

The Sinner's Place (produced Amherst, Massachusetts, 1984).
Betting on the Dust Commander (produced New York, 1987). New York, Dramatists Play Service, 1990.
Imperceptible Mutabilities in the Third Kingdom (produced New York, 1989).
Greeks (produced New York, 1990).
The Death of the Last Black Man in the Whole World (produced New York, 1990). Published in *Theatre* (New Haven), Summer/Fall 1990.
The America Play (produced New York, 1991).
Devotees in the Garden of Love (produced Louisville, 1991).

Screenplay: *Anemone Me*, 1990.

Radio Plays: *Pickling*, 1990; *The Third Kingdom*, 1990; *Locomotive*, 1991.

Video: *Poetry Spots*, 1989; *Alive from Off Center*, 1991.

Recording: *Imperceptible Mutabilities, The Last Black Man,* 1991.

*

Critical Studies: "Signifying on the Signifyin': The Plays of Suzan Lori Parks" by Alisa Solomon, in *Theater* (New Haven, Connecticut), Summer-Fall 1990, pp. 73-80; "Suzan Lori Parks and Liz Diamond: Doo-a-Diddly-Dit-Dit" by Steven Drukman, in *The Drama Review: A Journal of Performance Studies* (Cambridge, Massachusetts), Fall 1995, pp. 56-75; "Interview with Suzan Lori Parks" by Shelby Jiggetts, in *Callaloo* (Baltimore, Maryland), Spring 1996, pp. 309-17.

* * *

Suzan-Lori Parks is a playwright with the linguistic sensibilities of a Gertrude Stein or James Joyce, who recognizes that "the world is in the word" and who attempts to stage that world following the example of Samuel Beckett. Citing the model of Shakespeare, she eschews stage directions: "If you're writing the play—why not put the directions in the writing." She draws on her own experiences as an African American woman living in a white male culture but denies that her works are only about being black: "I don't want to be categorized in any way."

Parks sees her main task as a writer being to "make words from world but set them on the page—setting them loose on the world." Others may employ neologisms, lexical transformations, phonetic shifts, spelling variations, and repetitions to further the plot and point to the theme. In Parks's plays language is the theme, and the omission of even a letter can change the direction of a play or the life of a people. "Before Columbus thuh worl usta be *roun* they put uh /d/ on thuh end of roun makin round. Thusly they set in motion thuh end. Without that /d/ we coulda gone on spinnin for ever. Thuh /d/ think ended things ended" says Queen-then-Pharaoh Hatshepsut in *The Death of the Last Black Man in the Whole Entire World.* Fixed in place by an imposed language that defines them but is not their own, Parks's people, like Joyce's and Beckett's, seek to get out from under the weight of words. "Talk right or you're outa here," Molly is told by her boss in *Imperceptible Mutabilities in the Third Kingdom.* A phoneme, the /sk/ in "ask," for example, defeats her as she struggles against a language and a world in which "everything in its place."

Parks's play *Imperceptible Mutabilities in the Third Kingdom* was a tetraptych whose title she carefully defined: *Imperceptible*—"That which by its nature cannot be perceived or discerned by the mind or the senses"; *Mutabilities*—"things disposed to change"; *in the Third Kingdom*—". . . that of fungi. Small, overlooked, out of sight, of lesser consequence. All of that. And also: the space between." The four playlets—"Snails," "Third Kingdom," "Open House," "Third Kingdom (reprise)," and "Greeks"—offer a composite picture of African American experience starting with contemporary time, moving backward to a mythic retelling of the forced journey from Africa, and concluding with two "family plays" that depict the terrible results of such displacement and estrangement from both language and self.

The absence of traditional narrative is counteracted by formal structures. All of the playlets have five characters whose names either rhyme or are the same. "Snails" is divided into six sections and "Open House" and "Greeks" into seven. Each makes use of slides and photographs offering an intertextual archival history. In each the angle of vision is, to invoke Beckett, "trine: centripetal, centrifugal and . . . not." The characters seen by white society see themselves thus reflected but still struggle to see beyond the stereotype, the "not."

"Snails" describes three roommates, each wounded by words and each carrying two names, the one she chooses and the one by which she is known in the white community, names that "whuduhnt ours." They are visited by a robber who "didn't have no answer cause he didn't have no speech" and his opposite, a loquacious naturalist named Lutsky who spouts the latest anthropological terminology and who comes to study the habits of the women. Disguised as a cockroach, the contemporary version of the fly on the wall, he also doubles as the exterminator called to rid the women of the pest. Of the two it is Lutsky, Parks suggests, who is the true thief, for he steals their voice by fixing them with his words, the better to classify and study them.

"Third Kingdom" offers a melodic, mythic retelling of the black voyage from Africa to America. It is chanted by characters whose names range from Kin-Seer, Us-Seer, Shark-Seer, and Soul-seer to Over-seer. A refrain opens the section and punctuates the piece and the reprise: "Last night I dreamed of where I comed from. But where I comed from diduhnt look like nowhere like I been." The speakers evoke images of a lost home, of a voyage, and of the boat that carried them. While Shark-Seer denies their collective experience—"But we are not in uh boat!"—Us-Seer insists, "But we iz."

"Open House" is a composite black/white family portrait in which Aretha Saxon, a black servant/surrogate mother to a white girl and boy is being "let go because she's gone slack." But before she leaves/expires, she is subjected to "an extraction" in which her teeth are tortuously yanked from her mouth by the efficient Miss Faith, who records in the process the parallel extraction/eradication of African American history from white memory.

The last playlet, "Greeks," is the most powerful. The modern retelling of the Odysseus legend, it focuses on the Smith family—Sergeant, Mrs. Sergeant, Buffy, Muffy, and Duffy—the mother and children awaiting the return of the father who will bring with him "his Distinction" won by faithfully serving his country in the white man's army. While they make periodic visits to "see their maker," each furlough followed by the birth of a child, and

Mrs. Smith takes pride in her own mark of distinction—looking as if "you ain't traveled a mile nor sweated a drop"—Sergeant Smith waits in vain, finally returning in old age, like Odysseus, to a family that barely recognizes him. Legless and broken, he helplessly explains his dream: "Always wanted to do me somethin noble. . . . Like what they did in thuh olden days." The only glory open to him, however, is to break the fall of "that boy fallin out thuh sky. . . . I saved his life. I aint seen him since." This section ends where the first play began, with the character recognizing the position of blacks in America: "We'se slugs."

The Death of the Last Black Man in the Whole Entire World is even more experimental and language centered. It includes a series of poetic phrases or melodious riffs depicting the life and times of Parks's composite African American couple (Black Man with Watermelon and Black Woman with Fried Drumstick), who are surrounded by characters with names evoking black soul food (Lots of Grease and Lots of Pork), literary figures (And Bigger and Bigger and Bigger—after Richard Wright), and ancient times (Queen-then-Pharaoh Hatshepsut).

Beginning with the line "The Black man moves his hands," Parks takes her people on a linguistic voyage back through African American experience, historic and literary. She animates her characters as she plays with a set of phrases and transformations, concluding with "Thuh black man he move. He move. He hans." They are words carved on a rock to be remembered "because if you dont write it down we will come along and tell the future that we did not exist." Unlike those in the earlier play, these characters laugh at the end, having thrown off and stomped on the controlling "/d/."

Again, strict form undergirds the work. The title is repeated nine times throughout the seven sections of the play, the first six times ending in "world" and the last three in "worl," allowing Black Man to go from a fixed figure in a borrowed language to a self-animated speaker. The commensurate female experience moves from being a provider of chicken to a supporter and an encourager. Her words end the play.

Parks's work is audacious, upending traditional dramaturgy and replacing action with language shifts. Building on the earlier experiments of Ntozake Shange and Adrienne Kennedy, she moves even further to create a theater of poetry in which the very power of language is reaffirmed by showing its potential to stand as subject and theme.

—Linda Ben-Zvi

PATEL, Gieve

Nationality: Indian. **Born:** Bombay, 18 August 1940. **Education:** St. Xavier's College, B.Sc.; Grant Medical College, M.B.B.S. **Family:** Married Toni Diniz in 1969; one daughter. **Career:** Medical doctor, painter, dramatist, and actor.

Publications

Plays

Princes (produced Bombay, 1971).
Savaksa (produced Bombay, 1982). In *Bombay Literary Review,* 1989.
Mister Behram (produced Bombay, 1987). Bombay, Praxis, 1988.

Poetry

Poems. Bombay, Ezekiel, 1966.
How Do You Withstand, Body. Bombay, Clearing House, 1976.
Mirrored, Mirroring. New Delhi, Oxford University Press, 1991.

*

Critical Studies: "Gieve Patel's *Savaksa*" by Karen Smith, in *New Literature Review* (Wollongong), 1984, pp. 48-63; "Gieve Patel: Poet as Clinician of Feelings" by Vrinda Nabar, in *The Indian Literary Review: A Tri-Quarterly of Indian Literature* (New Delhi), October 1985, pp. 49-55; "The Poetry of Gieve Patel: A Critical Scrutiny" by Vineypal Kaur Kirpal, in *Living Indian English Poets,* edited by Madhusudan Prasad, New Delhi, Sterling, 1989.

* * *

One of India's most celebrated dramatists, Gieve Patel is a medical doctor by training and profession. Some have said his obsession (others might prefer the term "preoccupation") with the body and all its encumbrances (e.g., disease, pain, desires, and instincts) is the direct result of his medical training. A Parsi by birth, he is also a painter and an accomplished poet.

As dramatist, Patel is both a playwright and an actor, and he has managed to convey fundamental human themes—and to express the frailties and suffering of his characters—through a concise and economical use of language. *Princes,* staged for the first time in 1970, launched Patel's career as a playwright of note. The play is a powerful depiction of the disintegration and fragmentation of a middle-class Parsi family in India. This morose attitude concerning Patel's Parsi background is also evident in his subsequent plays *Savaksa* (1982) and *Mister Behram* (1988). The Parsis are a small but highly cultured, educated, and influential community, but the pressures they face in India are immense, and Patel's plays document with acute sensitivity the complexities facing them. One of the fascinating aspects of Patel's plays is the way he skillfully uses English to represent a distinct Parsi "flavor" and to put across the sense of isolation felt by many Parsis in India.

As a student of the human body and all its passions, and as a writer who seeks to understand rather than explain human behavior, Patel has few peers in Indian theater. He has stated that Jean Racine is the great influence in his life and that psychoanalysis, with its power to reveal patterns of human behavior, has also played a significant role. For Patel plays are a form of therapy, much needed though differently prescribed in different cultures.

—Kirpal Singh

PATRICK, Robert

Nationality: American. **Born:** Robert Patrick O'Connor in Kilgore, Texas, 27 September 1937. **Education:** Eastern New Mexico University, Portales, three years. **Career:** Host, La Mama, 1965, secretary to Ruth Yorck, 1965, and doorman, Caffe Cino, 1966-68, all New York; features editor and contributor, *Astrology Magazine*, New York, 1971-72; columnist, *Other Stages*, New York, 1979-81. Artist-in-residence, Jean Cocteau Repertory Theater,

New York, 1984. **Awards:** *Show Business* award, 1969; Rockefeller grant, 1973; Glasgow Citizen's Theatre International play contest, first prize, for *Kennedy's Children,* 1973; Creative Artists Public Service grant, 1976; International Thespians Society award, 1980; Janus award, 1983; Robert Chesley Foundation Lifetime Achievement in Gay Playwrighting award, 1996. **Address:** 1837 North Alexandria Avenue, #211, Los Angeles, California 90027, U.S.A.

PUBLICATIONS

Plays

The Haunted Host (produced New York, 1964; London, 1975). Included in *Robert Patrick's Cheep Theatricks!*, 1972; in *Homosexual Acts,* London, Inter-Action, 1976.
Mirage (produced New York, 1965). Included in *One Man, One Woman,* 1978.
Sketches (produced New York, 1966).
The Sleeping Bag (produced New York, 1966).
Halloween Hermit (produced New York, 1966).
Indecent Exposure (produced New York, 1966).
Cheesecake (produced New York, 1966). Included in *One Man, One Woman,* 1978.
Lights, Camera, Action (includes *Lights, Camera Obscura, Action*) (produced New York, 1966; in *My Dear It Doesn't Mean a Thing*, produced London, 1976). Included in *Robert Patrick's Cheep Theatricks!*, 1972.
Warhol Machine (produced New York, 1967).
Still-Love (produced New York, 1968). Included in *Robert Patrick's Cheep Theatricks!*, 1972.
Cornered (produced New York, 1968). Included in *Robert Patrick's Cheep Theatricks!*, 1972.
Un Bel Di (produced New York, 1968). Published in *Performance* (New York), 1972.
Help, I Am (produced New York, 1968). Included in *Robert Patrick's Cheep Theatricks!*, 1972.
See Other Side (produced New York, 1968). Published in *Yale/Theatre* (New Haven, Connecticut), 1969.
Absolute Power over Movie Stars (produced New York, 1968).
Preggin and Liss (produced New York, 1968). Included in *Robert Patrick's Cheep Theatricks!*, 1972.
The Overseers (produced New York, 1968).
Angels in Agony (produced New York, 1968).
Salvation Army (produced New York, 1968).
Joyce Dynel: An American Zarzuela (as *Dynel*, produced New York, 1968; revised version, as *Joyce Dynel*, produced New York, 1969). Included in *Robert Patrick's Cheep Theatricks!*, 1972.
Fog (produced New York, 1969). Published in *G.P.U. News* (Milwaukee), 1980.
The Young of Aquarius (produced New York, 1969).
I Came to New York to Write (produced New York, 1969; Edinburgh, 1975). Included in *Robert Patrick's Cheep Theatricks!*, 1972.
Oooooooops! (produced New York, 1969).
Lily of the Valley of the Dolls (produced New York, 1969; Edinburgh, 1972).
One Person: A Monologue (produced New York, 1969; London, 1975). Included in *Robert Patrick's Cheep Theatricks!*, 1972.
Silver Skies (produced New York, 1969).
Tarquin Truthbeauty (produced New York, 1969).
Presenting Arnold Bliss (produced New York, 1969; in *The Arnold Bliss Show*, produced Edinburgh, 1972).
The Actor and the Invader (in *Kinetic Karma*, produced New York, 1969; in *The Arnold Bliss Show*, Edinburgh, 1972).
Hymen and Carbuncle (produced New York, 1970). Included in *Mercy Drop and Other Plays*, 1979.
A Bad Place to Get Your Head (produced New York, 1970).
Bead-Tangle (includes *La Répétition*) (produced New York, 1970).
Sketches and Songs (produced New York, 1970).
I Am Trying to Tell You Something (produced New York, 1970).
Angel, Honey, Baby, Darling, Dear (produced New York, 1970).
The Golden Animal (produced New York, 1970).
Picture Wire (produced New York, 1970).
The Richest Girl in the World Finds Happiness (produced New York, 1970). Included in *Robert Patrick's Cheep Theatricks!*, 1972.
A Christmas Carol (produced New York, 1971).
Shelter (produced New York, 1971).
The Golden Circle (produced New York, 1972). New York, French, 1977(?).
Ludwig and Wagner (produced New York, 1972). Included in *Mercy Drop and Other Plays*, 1979.
Youth Rebellion (produced New York, 1972).
Songs (produced New York, 1972).
Robert Patrick's Cheep Theatricks!, edited by Michael Feingold. New York, Winter House, 1972.
The Arnold Bliss Show (includes *Presenting Arnold Bliss, The Actor and the Invader, La Répétition, Arnold's Big Break*) (produced Edinburgh, 1972). Included in *Robert Patrick's Cheep Theatricks!*, 1972.
Play-by-Play (also director: produced New York, 1972; revised version produced Chicago and London, 1975). New York, French, 1975.
Something Else (produced New York, 1973; in *My Dear It Doesn't Mean a Thing*, produced London, 1976). Included in *One Man, One Woman*, 1978.
Cleaning House (produced New York, 1973). Included in *One Man, One Woman*, 1978.
The Track of the Narwhal (produced Boston, 1973).
Judas (produced New York, 1973). Published in *West Coast Plays 5* (Berkeley, California), Fall 1979.
Mercy Drop; or, Marvin Loves Johnny (produced New York, 1973). Included in *Mercy Drop and Other Plays*, 1980.
The Twisted Root (produced New York, 1973).
Simultaneous Transmissions (produced New York, 1973). Published in *The Scene/2 (Plays from Off-Off-Broadway)*, edited by Stanley Nelson, New York, The Smith/New Egypt, 1974.
Hippy as a Lark (produced New York, 1973).
Imp-Prisonment (produced New York, 1973).
Kennedy's Children (produced New York, 1973; London, 1974). London, French, 1975; New York, Random House, 1976.
Love Lace (produced New York, 1974). Included in *One Man, One Woman*, 1978.
How I Came to Be Here Tonight (produced Los Angeles, 1974).
Orpheus and Amerika, music by Rob Felstein (produced Los Angeles, 1974; New York, 1980).
Fred and Harold, and One Person (produced London, 1975). Published in *Homosexual Acts*, London, Inter-Action, 1976.
My Dear It Doesn't Mean a Thing (includes *Lights, Camera Obscura, Action*; *Something Else*) (produced London, 1976).

Report to the Mayor (produced New York, 1977).
Dr. Paroo (produced New York, 1981). Published in *Dramatics* (Cincinnati), 1977.
My Cup Ranneth Over (produced New York and London, 1978). New York, Dramatists Play Service, 1979.
Mutual Benefit Life (produced New York, 1978). New York, Dramatists Play Service, 1979.
T-Shirts (produced Minneapolis, 1978; New York, 1980). Published in *Gay Plays*, edited by William M. Hoffman, New York, Avon, 1979.
One Man, One Woman (produced New York, 1979). New York, French, 1978.
Bank Street Breakfast (produced New York, 1979). Included in *One Man, One Woman*, 1978.
Communication Gap (produced Greensboro, North Carolina, 1979; as *All in Your Mind*, produced New York, 1981).
The Family Bar (produced Hollywood, 1979). Included in *Mercy Drop and Other Plays*, 1979.
Mercy Drop and Other Plays (includes *The Family Bar* and *The Loves of the Artists: Ludwig and Wagner, Diaghilev and Nijinsky*, and *Hymen and Carbuncle*). New York, Calamus, 1979.
Diaghilev and Nijinsky (produced San Francisco, 1981). Included in *Mercy Drop and Other Plays*, 1979.
Sane Scientist (produced New York, 1981).
Michelangelo's Models (produced New York, 1981). New York, Calamus Press, 1983.
24 Inches, music by David Tice, lyrics by Patrick (produced New York, 1982).
The Spinning Tree (produced Ada, Ohio, 1982; New York, 1983).
They Really Love Roba (produced New York, 1982).
Sit-Com (produced Minneapolis, 1982). Published in *Blueboy* (New York), June 1982.
Willpower, published in *Curtain* (Cincinnati), May 1982.
Blue Is for Boys (produced New York, 1983).
Nice Girl (produced New York, 1983).
Beaux-Arts Ball (produced New York, 1983).
The Comeback (produced New York, 1983).
The Holy Hooker (produced Madison, Wisconsin, 1983).
50s 60s 70s 80s (produced New York, 1984).
Big Sweet, music by LeRoy Dysart (produced Richmond, Virginia, 1984). Published in *Dramatics* (Cincinnati), 1984.
That Lovable Laughable Auntie Matter in "Disgustin' Space Lizards" (produced New York, 1985).
Bread Alone (produced New York, 1985).
No Trojan Women, music by Catherine Stornetta (produced Wallingford, Connecticut, 1985).
Left Out (produced Arroyo Grande, California, 1985). Published in *Dramatics* (Cincinnati), 1985.
The Hostages (produced New York, 1985).
The Trial of Socrates (produced New York, 1986). Dallas, Texas, Dialogus Play Service, 1993.
Bill Batchelor Road (produced Minneapolis, 1986).
On Stage (produced Ralston, Nebraska, 1986).
Why Are They Like That? (produced Spokane, Washington, 1986).
Desert Waste (produced New York, 1986).
La Balance (produced New York, 1986).
Pouf Positive (produced New York, 1986). Published in *Out/Write* (San Francisco), 1988.
Lust (produced New York, 1986).
Drowned Out (produced New York, 1986). Published in *One-Acts for High Schools*, Montana, Merriwether Press, 1986.
The Last Stroke (produced New York, 1987).
Explanation of a Xmas Wedding (produced New York, 1987).
Let Me Not Mar That Perfect Dream (produced New York, 1988). Published in *The James White Review* (Minneapolis), 1987.
Untold Decades (produced New York, 1988). New York, St. Martin's Press, 1988.
The Trojan Women (produced New York, 1988).
Hello, Bob (produced New York, 1990). Published in *Stages* (New York), 1991.
Evan on Earth (produced Sacramento, California, 1991).
Un-tied States (produced Denver, Colorado, 1991).
Interruptions (produced Bakersfield, California, 1992).
Bread Alone. Dallas, Texas, Dialogus Play Service, 1993.

Screenplays: *The Haunted Host*, 1969; *The Credit Game*, 1972.

Novel

Temple Slave. Dayton, Texas, Starwolf Press, 1993.

*

Manuscript Collection: Lincoln Center Library of the Performing Arts, New York.

Theatrical Activities:
Director: **Plays**—*Wonderful, Wonderful* by Douglas Kahn, and excerpt from *The Approach* by Jean Reavey, La Mama, New York, 1965; artistic director of *Bb Aa Nn Gg!!!*, New York, 1965; created Comic Book Shows at the Caffe Cino, New York, 1966; assistant director to Tom O'Horgan and Jerome Savary, Brandeis University, Waltham, Massachusetts, 1968; originated *Dracula*, Edinburgh, 1968; reopened *Bowery Follies*, New York, 1972; *Silver Queen* by Paul Foster, New York, 1973; directed many of his own plays.

Actor: **Plays**—At Caffe Cino, La Mama, and Old Reliable in his own plays and plays by Powell Shepherd, Soren Agenoux, John Hartnett, Stuart Koch, H.M. Koutoukas, and William M. Hoffman.

Robert Patrick comments:

(1973) My plays are dances with words. The words are music for the actors to dance to. They also serve many other purposes, but primarily they give the actors images and rhythms to create visual expressions of the play's essential relationships. The ideal production of one of my plays would be completely understandable even without sound, like a silent movie. Most of my plays are written to be done with a minimum of scenery, although I have done some fairly lavish productions of them. My plays fall into three general classes: 1) simple histories, like *I Came to New York to Write*; 2) surrealistic metaphors, like *The Arnold Bliss Show, Lights, Camera, Action*, and *Joyce Dynel*, and 3) romances, like *Fog, Female Flower* (unproduced), and both *The Golden Animal* and *The Golden Circle*. Basically, I believe the importance of a play to be this: a play is an experience the audience has together; it is stylized to aid in perception and understanding; and, above all, it is done by live players, and it is traced in its minutest particulars, so that it can serve as a warning (if it is a tragedy or comedy) or as a good example. Nothing must be left out or it becomes merely ritual. The time of the ritual is over. The essential experience must replace it.

* * *

Robert Patrick's conception of theatrical form and purpose was molded at the Caffe Cino. He had been working there at odd jobs in the early 1960s and, influenced by Joe Cino's creative energy along with playwrights like Lanford Wilson, Paul Foster, David Starkweather, and the entire Cino gang, he wrote his first play, *The Haunted Host*. In fact, he got his name with that production in a typically haphazard Cino manner. Marshall Mason, later artistic director of Circle Repertory Company and chief interpreter of Lanford Wilson's dramas, was rushing out to get *The Haunted Host* programs printed. Patrick, who was acting in his own show, asked that Mason break up his name and list Robert Patrick and Bob O'Connor, one for playwright and the other for actor, because he did not want people concentrating on the fact that the playwright and actor were the same person. When Mason came back with the programs, Robert Patrick O'Connor was known as Robert Patrick, playwright.

The Caffe Cino was a place in which theatrical rules did not exist. Experimentation with form and content was common, and wits-only, wing-it living was the norm. Although when the Cino closed it was shrouded in tragedy, for most of its years the key word there was "fun." Entertainment was the only guideline anyone followed, and this freewheeling, fun-obsessed lifestyle turned a naive young Texan named Bob O'Connor into the most prolific playwright of his generation. As he says of the off-off-Broadway movement that began, in part, at the Cino, "For the first time a theatre movement began, of any scope or duration, in which theatre was considered the equal of the other arts in creativity and responsibility; never before had theatre existed free of academic, commercial, critical, religious, military, and political restraints. For the first time, a playwright wrote from himself, not attempting to tease money, reputation, or licences from an outside authority."

To analyze the numerous plays Patrick has written and produced since 1964 on a script-by-script basis would be to miss the profound contribution of the overall body of his work. His genius stems not from some artfully crafted style or from deep, intellectual questioning but rather from an uncanny ability to record and reflect the world around him. *Kennedy's Children,* his best-known play, captures the mood of an entire era and serves as a mirror of morals for a lost decade.

In *Kennedy's Children* the characters, all of whom we now recognize as 1960s stereotypes, sit separately in a bar. We are presented with their interior monologues. The alienation, the loneliness, and the confusion that were apparent in America's youth throughout the tumultuous years of Vietnam are so accurately portrayed in *Kennedy's Children* that it is difficult to imagine a more perfect example of the crumbling American dream post-Vietnam.

To read Patrick for clues to a specific style is to get trapped. For most of his career his style has been unique only in its absence, a fact that often drives his critics to despair. It could only be described, perhaps, as Cinoese or as off-off-Broadway eclectic. As he has continued to write, however, he has appeared to coalesce his vast mental resources into a genuine effort to produce works that deal with an unchanging human condition. The classical themes of love, greed, pride, and tormented self-doubt abound in all of his plays, but they are never as obviously mirrored as in his later works. In fact, he has said that he is striving to write "classical Greek drama." If his style is elusive, his subject certainly is not. Patrick is pure romantic, and in play after play he has written primarily about relationships and heterosexual marriage. He has also become known as a gay playwright, and although in his later works he has begun using gay themes again, most of his gay plays are, in fact, early works that have been rediscovered in the contemporary rage for gay theater. Although *Michelangelo's Models* is about a man and a boy who get together, theirs is a basically traditional relationship, and this play, too, is about how people do or do not form unions. It is this general appeal to the traditional that not only gives his plays an international popularity but that also accounts for his enormous effect on high school audiences. Young people are drawn to him as to a pied piper, and it is to them that he is most expressive about the great excitement the art of theater can generate. He has traveled extensively to high schools across the country to encourage students to write for and to become involved with theater.

Aside from stating the obvious, that his story is the subject of his plays, as apples are the subjects of a Cézanne painting, and that his stories are about couples getting together or not getting together and about society's effect on a relationship, there is no generalizing about a Patrick play. From the starkly classic tragedy of *Judas* to the innovative oratorio of an age, *Kennedy's Children,* to the retrograde Renaissance fantasia of *Michelangelo's Models,* he has been a man in love with playwriting. He has improvised full-scale musicals in four days (*Joyce Dynel* and *A Christmas Carol*), provided occasional entertainments (*The Richest Girl in the World Finds Happiness, Play-by-Play, Halloween Hermit*), whipped out formal experiments (*Lights, Camera, Action*; *Love Lace*; *Something Else*), manufactured commercial successes (*My Cup Ranneth Over, Mutual Benefit Life*), helped the developing gay theater (*Mercy Drop, T-Shirts, The Haunted Host*), and piled up eccentricities (*The Golden Animal, Lily of the Valley of the Dolls*, and the unproduced *Female Flower*). His first collection, *Robert Patrick's Cheep Theatricks!,* was only an arbitrary gleaning of the 150 works he had accumulated by 1972. His second, *One Man, One Woman,* ranged from 1964 to 1979, and his third, *Mercy Drop and Other Plays,* from 1965 through 1980. Many works are still unpublished and unproduced.

Patrick believes that words are music for actors to dance to and that rhythms have to help the actors build up emotions. He is highly conscious of vocabulary and of the ways in which words give the actors images to act out and tell an audience story facts and plot facts or jokes or bits of poetry. In *Michelangelo's Models* the peasant boy Ignudo, who wants to marry Michelangelo, talks in Okie dialect. And Michelangelo's speech varies between the formal patterns of the other characters and the slang that unites him to Ignudo. Patrick's fascination with words sometimes gets him tangled in verbiage, but it creates a type of security blanket for this off-off-Broadway baby. Playwrights who regularly work off-off-Broadway never know if they are going to have sets, lights, music, or anything, and writing for a bare floor and some actors is thus a form of artistic self-preservation. When it is possible to get lights and background music to set the mood, it is then all the better. If Patrick is sometimes overly expository, it can be traced directly to the Caffe Cino, where the lights sometimes went out and action had to be described to an audience in the dark.

—Leah D. Frank

PATTERSON, Peter. *See* **TERSON, Peter.**

PHILLIPS, Caryl

Nationality: British. **Born:** St. Kitts, West Indies, 13 March 1958; brought to England in 1958. **Education:** Schools in Leeds to 1974, and in Birmingham, 1974-76; Queen's College, Oxford, 1976-79, B.A. (honours) 1979. **Career:** Founding chair, 1978, and artistic director, 1979, *Observer* Festival of Theatre, Oxford; resident dramatist, The Factory, London 1981-82; writer-in-residence, Literary Criterion Centre, Mysore, India, 1987, and Stockholm University, Sweden, 1989. Visiting writer, Amherst College, Massachusetts, 1990—. Member of the Board of Directors, Bush Theatre, London, 1985-88; member, British Film Institute Production Board, London, 1985-88. Lives in London. **Awards:** Arts Council bursary, 1983; Malcolm X prize, 1985; Martin Luther King Memorial prize, 1987; *Sunday Times* Young Writer award, 1992. **Agent:** Judy Daish Associates, 83 Eastbourne Mews, London W2 6LQ; or, Curtis Brown, 162-168 Regent Street, London W1R 5TB, England.

PUBLICATIONS

Plays

Strange Fruit (produced Sheffield, 1980; London, 1982). Ambergate, Derbyshire, Amber Lane Press, 1981.
Where There Is Darkness (produced London, 1982). Ambergate, Derbyshire, Amber Lane Press, 1982.
The Shelter (produced London, 1983). Oxford, Amber Lane Press, 1984; New York, Applause, 1986.
The Wasted Years (broadcast 1984). In *Best Radio Plays of 1984*, London, Methuen, 1985.
Playing Away (screenplay). London, Faber, 1987.
The Nature of Blood. Toronto, Vintage, 1997.

Screenplay: *Playing Away*, 1986.

Radio Plays: *The Wasted Years*, 1984; *Crossing the River*, 1986; *The Prince of Africa*, 1987; *Writing Fiction*, 1991.

Television Plays: *The Hope and the Glory*, 1984; *The Record*, 1984; *Lost in Music*, 1985.

Novels

The Final Passage. London, Faber, 1985; New York, Penguin, 1990.
A State of Independence. London, Faber, and New York, Farrar Straus, 1986.
Cambridge. London, Bloomsbury, 1991; New York, Knopf, 1992.
Crossing the River. Toronto, Vintage, 1993.
Higher Ground. London, Picador, 1993.

Short Stories

Higher Ground. London, Viking, 1986; New York, Viking, 1989.

Other

The European Tribe (travel). London, Faber, and New York, Farrar Straus, 1987.

*

Caryl Phillips comments:

My dominant theme has been cultural and social dislocation, most commonly associated with a migratory experience.

* * *

Few British dramatists have been equally at home in fiction and in the theater, but Caryl Phillips is a playwright with a reputation that overlaps a variety of categories. Most of his work has been concerned with the immigrant experience of blacks in Britain, but his perspective is both historical and international, and he has applied his talent with success to drama for the stage, television, radio, and cinema. In addition, with his first two books he made a mark in the demanding form of the novel. Journalism, too, has proved a fruitful form, provoking thoughtful essays on such significant predecessors as James Baldwin. Indeed, Baldwin is an unmistakable model and inspiration, and the clear, passionate view of the United States that was seen in Baldwin's early essays, when he was able to combine a knowledge of the American South with a European perspective, is reflected in Phillips's view of Britain, although Phillips goes further and applies Baldwin's measures to Europe as well. For Phillips it is Europe that has made him a "black" writer. In the preface to his play in two parts, *The Shelter,* he says, "In Africa I was not black. In Africa I was a writer. In Europe I am black. In Europe I am a black writer. If the missionaries [for which read critics] wish to play the game along these lines then I do not wish to be an honorary white."

Although born in Saint Kitts in the West Indies and very conscious of his Caribbean heritage, Phillips is a child of Leeds in England, where he was reared, and his accent is Yorkshire. His plays have persistently explored the conflicts of immigration, looking at the yearning for a homeland that has achieved mythological significance and at the reality of life in a society that views the immigrant as an outsider because of color. While immigration has remained his major theme, he has maintained an ironic distance that sees slavery as the first immigration, an immigration imposed on the African by Europeans and North Americans.

Phillips's perspective is finally more mid-Atlantic than Caribbean, and the title of his first play, *Strange Fruit,* is drawn directly and knowingly from the Billie Holiday song about lynching. As in much of his later work, the subject is a West Indian family held together by a single parent but pulled between two hemispheres. Although Vivien has educated her sons in England, they feel drawn to the black culture of the Caribbean.

In Phillips's next and more ambitious play, *Where There Is Darkness,* the pull of the islands is felt by a West Indian man, Albert, who 25 years earlier fled his home for the promises of England after first making a girl pregnant so that her father would pay their passage to the "motherland." Phillips sets the play on the eve of Albert's return to the Caribbean, during and after a farewell party for the white friends and colleagues he has gathered in his years as a social worker. In his London garden Albert confronts the guilt of his betrayals, including the sacrifice of his first wife to his ambition, and his inability to bring the son he loves into his vision of success.

While remembering that his own father had advised him that the only way out of the gutters and up to the mountains was through exile and foreign wealth, the sacrifice he was prepared to make was the gift of his son to England. When he took his father-in-law's money for the passage, it was with the admonition that "the child belongs to England." His disappointment when his son announces that he is leaving the university to marry his pregnant black girlfriend proves the final blow in his struggle for self-justification. At the beginning of the play Albert's confrontation with his accommodations to white society has driven him into the garden with a raging headache. At the end of the play he has stripped down to his trousers to plunge into an imaginary sea. His Faustian bargain has torn his spirit apart.

Everywhere in his work Phillips is concerned with the price paid for admission into the white man's world, "the price of the ticket" in Baldwin's phrase. In his novel *The Final Passage,* as in his plays of immigration, it is confrontation with the bitter reality of England that is the revelation. But the final passage is not really a voyage made by choice. It is rather the completion of a journey that began with the so-called Middle Passage, the crossing of the Atlantic from Africa to the New World in English slave ships. For the black men and women of his dramas, every choice is the result of a desperate search for a homeland to replace the Africa they lost in generations past when their ancestors were ripped from their tribes. The final passage for the black people of the Commonwealth is the attempt to complete the voyage to English society.

In *The Shelter,* a play that takes on the potent image, taboo for so long, of black men with white women, Phillips first imagines a shipwreck that throws together a freed slave and a white widow on a desert island at the end of the eighteenth century. His use of period language is too fussy to wholly express his ideas, and the ex-slave is so demonstrably superior to the English woman in thought and poetic speech that his slow transformation in her mind from ape to man is devalued. But the first part does nicely prepare the way for the second act, an examination of a sexual relationship between a black immigrant and a white woman in the London of the 1950s. At that key moment in the history of immigration, the man and woman can only meet in a pub by pretending to be strangers. When their relationship is revealed by a kiss, they sacrifice their right to sit together, but a more fundamental decision is being made. The woman has chosen to bear the man's child despite his announcement that he wants to return "home" alone.

Radio is a medium that has allowed Phillips the means to explore his ideas with greater ambition, beginning with his prizewinning play *The Wasted Years*. In that piece he was able to re-create the pressures of school and family life on two brothers, products of the wave of immigration so ironically reflected by "news reports" describing the original arrival of the previous generation, "these dashing chaps in their colourful hats and big smiles." *Crossing the River,* a starkly refined short radio play, looked at the triangle of the slave heritage, from Africa to the United States and Britain, and *The Prince of Africa*, his most powerful radio piece, was the richly imagined story of the crossing of a slave ship. Although the destination of the ship was Boston, Massachusetts, it was a play that was firm in its condemnation of England as a nation of slavers, and it gave little sympathy to the guilty captain who refused to take personal responsibility for his cargo.

Phillips has a finely disciplined command of language and wide experience of a world well beyond the triangle of the slave heritage. He is a dramatist who broadens the understanding of his audiences, particularly when he is allowed to drop the burden of his label as a black writer.

—Ned Chaillet

PIELMEIER, John

Nationality: American. **Born:** Altoona, Pennsylvania, 23 February 1949. **Education:** Catholic University, Washington, D.C., 1966-70, B.A. (summa cum laude) in speech and drama 1970 (Phi Beta Kappa); Pennsylvania State University, University Park (Shubert Fellow), 1970-73, M.F.A. in playwriting 1978. **Family:** Married Irene O'Brien in 1982. **Career:** Actor, 1973-82: numerous roles in regional theatres, including Actors Theatre of Louisville, Guthrie Theatre, Minneapolis, Alaska Repertory Theatre, Anchorage, Center Stage, Baltimore, and Eugene O'Neill Playwrights Conference, Waterford, Connecticut. **Awards:** National Endowment for the Arts grant, 1982; Christopher award, for television play, 1984; Humanitas award, for television play, 1984. D.H.L.: St. Edward's University, Austin, Texas, 1984. **Agent:** William Craver, Writers and Artists Agency, 19 West 44th Street, Suite 1000, New York, New York 10036, U.S.A. **Address:** c/o Jeannine Edmunds, Curtis Brown Ltd., 10 Astor Place, New York, New York 10003, U.S.A.

Publications

Plays

Soledad Brother (produced University Park, Pennsylvania, 1971).

A Chosen Room (produced Minneapolis, Minnesota, 1976).

Agnes of God (produced Louisville, 1980; New York, 1982; London, 1983). New York, New American Library, 1985.

Jass (produced New York, 1980).

Chapter Twelve: The Frog (produced Louisville, 1981).

Courage (produced Louisville, 1983; New York, 1984).

Cheek to Cheek (produced Louisville, 1983).

A Gothic Tale (also director: produced Louisville, 1983). Included in *Haunted Lives*, 1984.

Haunted Lives (includes *A Witch's Brew*, *A Ghost Story*, *A Gothic Tale*) (produced Edinburgh, 1986). New York, Dramatists Play Service, 1984.

The Boys of Winter (produced New York, 1985).

Evening (produced Cincinnati, 1986).

In Mortality (produced Louisville, 1986).

Sleight of Hand (produced New York, 1987).

The Classics Professor (produced New York, 1988).

Steeple Chase (produced New York, 1989).

Impassioned Embraces. New York, Dramatists Play Service, 1989.

Willi, music by Matthew Selman (produced Big Fork, Montana, 1991).

Young Rube, music and lyrics by Matthew Selman (produced St. Louis, Missouri, 1992).

Voices in the Dark (produced New York, 1998).

Screenplay: *Agnes of God*, 1985.

Television Plays: *Choices of the Heart*, 1983; *The Last P.O.W.*; *The Billy Garwood Story*; *Stranger Within*; *An Inconvenient Woman*; *The Flock*; *Acts of Contrition*.

*

Theatrical Activities:
Director: **Play**—*A Gothic Tale*, Louisville, 1983.

Actor: **Plays**—Jasmine in *Memphis Is Gone* by Dick Hobson, New York, 1975; Tommy in *Female Transport* by Steve Gooch, Lymon in *Ballad of the Sad Café* by Edward Albee, and Boy in *Welcome to Andromeda* by Ron Whyte, all Louisville, 1975; Junior in *Waterman* by Frank B. Ford, Billy in *The Collected Works of Billy the Kid* by Michael Ondaatje, Burnaby in *The Matchmaker* by Thornton Wilder, and Kid in *Cold* by Michael Casale, all Minneapolis, 1976; Dorcas in *Gazelle Boy* by Ronald Tavel, and Dennis in *Scooter Thomas Makes It to the Top of the World* by Peter Parnell, both Waterford, Connecticut, 1977; roles in *Holidays*, and Mark in *The Shadow Box* by Michael Cristofer, both Louisville, 1979, Mark Levine in *Today a Little Extra* by Michael Kassin, Louisville, 1980; role in *The Front Page* by Ben Hecht and Charles MacArthur, Baltimore, 1980; Lysander in *A Midsummer Night's Dream*, Anchorage, Alaska, 1981; and numerous other roles.

John Pielmeier comments:

I consider myself primarily a writer for actors, and then a theatrical storyteller. I am fascinated with music and the myths of history, though *Agnes of God* is an exception to the latter. Some of my best work (*Jass* and *The Boys of Winter*) illustrates this fascination clearly. I consider writing a collaborative effort with actors and audience, and a play is never finished until it is on its feet for several weeks or for several productions. J.M. Barrie and Thornton Wilder are the playwrights closest to my heart—so in the end I suppose I am something of a theatrical romantic.

* * *

The playwright and actor John Pielmeier is indebted to regional theater, where much of his work has been developed and presented. He achieved national attention with *Agnes of God,* whose successful Broadway engagement was preceded by nine regional productions. (Pielmeier also wrote the screen version of the play.) The drama's concern with the conflict between the real and the imagined, the rational and the irrational, is one that constantly catches Pielmeier's interest.

In the introduction to the published play, Pielmeier confesses that *Agnes of God* sprang from his questioning concern as a lapsed Catholic with the possibility of saints and miracles today, augmented by a headline about an infanticide in a nunnery. The circumstances of the drama are that a stigmatic and emotionally disturbed young nun, who as a child was abused by a sadistic mother, gives birth in her convent to a child later found strangled in a wastebasket. The saintly nun, Agnes (from the Latin word for "lamb"), hears divine voices but claims to remember nothing about the child's conception, birth, or death. A court psychiatrist, a lapsed Catholic woman who harbors a grudge against nuns, is sent to discover if Agnes is sufficiently sane to stand trial for manslaughter. Proceeding as a narrator and detective-like investigator, the anticlerical doctor becomes absorbed with Agnes and begins to question her own pragmatic values in the face of the supernatural overtones of the situation. A conflict develops between the doctor and the convent's mother superior, later revealed to be Agnes's aunt, who is protective of Agnes and believes in the possibility of a parthenogenetic miracle. At the climax of the investigation, Sister Agnes reenacts under hypnosis the child's conception, leaving unanswered the question of divine or human fatherhood. It is the psychiatrist's anguished self-questioning that emerges as the central issue.

A comparison to Peter Shaffer's *Equus,* whose plot is similar, is unavoidable, although Shaffer's play is more successful in the depth of its physician-protagonist and in its examination of the questions raised. Nonetheless, Pielmeier has written a theatrically powerful play whose well-orchestrated female characters and strong dramatic climaxes provide an exciting theater experience. The question of faith and miracles it initially poses, while not answered, tends to become obscured by the psychological issues that trigger the revelations of the second act. The play stimulates the emotions but leaves the audience confused.

The enigmatic dichotomy of the natural and unnatural provides the connection among three three-character one-acts collectively titled *Haunted Lives*. In the least effective but still eerie *A Witch's Brew,* a brother engages his doubting sister and her boyfriend in a grisly childhood game in which he pretends that objects passed around in darkness are human body parts. The game takes place in a semidark farmhouse basement, where he claims that his mother murdered and buried his long absent father. *A Ghost Story,* a more successfully developed piece, presents two hiking strangers who seek shelter from a blizzard in an isolated Maine cabin. They are joined by a mysterious girl who participates in telling frightening stories, one involving an unknown murderer who cuts the throats of hikers. One hiker, once his companions fall asleep, tells the audience of a recurring dream, which is realized at the play's conclusion, in which his dead sister appears and cuts the throat of a hiker after she has seduced him. In *A Gothic Tale,* the final and most chilling tale, a young woman obsessed with the need to be loved and her manservant imprison a young rake in the tower of an island mansion, warning him that he will die unless he admits love for the woman. At the end of six weeks, depicted in six scenes, the gradually starving prisoner's aversion turns to terror and capitulation as he dies, discovering the skeletons of the men preceding him. The drama has a strong cumulative effect of impending doom. *Haunted Lives* is a well-crafted minor work that again demonstrates Pielmeier's theatrical skill.

In addition to *Courage,* a monodrama about J. M. Barrie, and *Choices of the Heart,* a teleplay about a religious worker murdered in El Salvador, two other works show an extension of Pielmeier's range. The musical *Jass* (dialect for "jazz"), with story and mood songs by the playwright, tells an unfocused story of a house facing legal closure in the red-light district of Storyville in New Orleans in 1917. An antiwar drama that was short-lived on Broadway, *The Boys of Winter* tells of seven Marines who are wiped out on a Vietnam hilltop in 1968 and whose lieutenant, on his return, kills seven innocent Vietnamese civilians in cold blood. The atrocity is rationalized in the men's monologues, offering the controversial premise that we all are guilty of My Lais. Despite flaws, the play's dialogue projects a salty reality, and its bloody incidents gather theatrical force.

Displaying Pielmeier's background as an actor, *Impassioned Embraces* consists of 14 short pieces dealing with the perils and pleasures of the acting profession and with aspects of love from the sublime to the ridiculous. For example, the pieces include an actor suffering a devastating rehearsal, a bridegroom realizing that he prefers the bridesmaid to the bride, a man about to undergo a vasectomy, a couple watching a 3-D horror movie, a cross-dresser mistaking the gender of another cross-dresser, and several monologues about acting. Designed for six actors, the inventive and amusing playlets can be presented separately without a formal setting. Revealing Pielmeier's interest in the form of the musical, *Young Rube* is a colorful chronicle, with music and lyrics by Mat-thew Selman, about the early career of the cartoonist Rube Goldberg, noted for drawing zany inventions connected to political satire. Pielmeier is a dramatist of proven theatrical expertise.

—Christian H. Moe

PINNER, David

Nationality: British. **Born:** Peterborough, Northamptonshire, 6 October 1940. **Education:** Deacon's Grammar School, Peterborough; Royal Academy of Dramatic Art, London, 2 years. **Family:** Married the actress Catherine Henry Griller in 1965; one daughter and one son. **Career:** Has acted with repertory companies in Sheffield, Coventry, Windsor, and Farnham, and in London. Playwright-in-residence, Peterborough Repertory Theatre, 1974 and the Unicorn Theatre, London, 1976. **Awards:** 4 Arts Council bursaries. **Agent:** Micheline Steinberg, Playwrights, 409 Triumph House, 187-191 Regent Street, London W1R 7WF, England. **Address:** 18 Leconfield Avenue, London SW13 0LD, England.

PUBLICATIONS

Plays

Dickon (produced Hornchurch, Essex, 1966). Published in *New English Dramatists 10*, London, Penguin, 1967.
Fanghorn (produced Edinburgh and London, 1967). London, Penguin, 1966.
The Drums of Snow. Published in *New English Dramatists 13*, London, Penguin, 1968; revised version (produced Stanford, California, 1970; Oxford, 1974), in *Plays of the Year 42*, London, Elek, 1972.
Marriages (also director: produced London, 1969).
Lightning at the Funeral (produced Stanford, California, 1971).
The Potsdam Quartet (produced Guildford, Surrey, 1973; revised version produced London, 1980; New York, 1982). Leominster, Herefordshire, Terra Nova, 1980; New York, French, 1982.
Cartoon (produced London, 1973).
An Evening with the GLC (produced London, 1974).
Hereward the Wake (produced Peterborough, 1974).
Shakebag (produced London, 1976). Published in *Green River Review* (University Center, Michigan), 1976.
Lucifer's Fair (produced London, 1976).
The Last Englishman (broadcast 1979; also director: produced Richmond, Surrey, 1990).
Screwball (produced Plymouth, 1982).
Revelations (produced Grinnell, Iowa, 1986).
The Teddy Bears' Picnic (produced Chester, 1988).
Skin Deep (produced Chester, 1989).
Sins of the Mother (produced London, 1996).

Radio Plays: *Dickon*, 1966; *Lightfall*, 1967; *Cardinal Richelieu*, 1976; *The Ex-Patriot*, 1977; *Keir Hardie*, 1978; *The Square of the Hypotenuse*, 1978, *Talleyrand*, 1978; *Drink to Me Only*, 1978; *The Last Englishman*, 1979; *Fings Ain't What They Used to Be*, 1979.

Television Plays: *Strange Past*, 1974; *Juliet and Romeo* (Germany), 1976; *The Potsdam Quartet*, 1979; *Leonora*, 1981, *The Sea Horse*, 1982.

Novels

Ritual. London, Hutchinson, 1967; later adapted for film as *The Wickerman,* 1993.
With My Body. London, Weidenfeld and Nicolson, 1968.
There'll Always Be an England. London, Blond and Briggs, 1985.

*

Manuscript Collection: Grinnell College, Iowa.

Theatrical Activities:
Director: **Plays**—*Marriages*, London, 1969; *All My Sons* by Arthur Miller, London, 1976; *The Three Sisters* by Chekhov, London, 1976, *The American Dream* by Edward Albee, London, 1977; *Suddenly Last Summer* by Tennessee Williams, London, 1977; *The Last Englishman*, Richmond, 1990; *Macbeth*, London, 1992; *Andromache* by Euripides, London, 1992.

Actor: **Plays**—Hornbeck in *Inherit the Wind* by Jerome Lawrence and Robert E. Lee, Perth, Scotland, 1960; Ross in *Macbeth* and Magpie in *Naked Island* by Russell Byaddon, Coventry, 1961, Gratiano in *The Merchant of Venice*, Newcastle upon Tyne, 1963; title role in *Billy Liar* by Keith Waterhouse and Willis Hall, Windsor, 1964; Cassius in *The Man Who Let It Rain* by Marc Brandel, London, 1964; Laertes in *Hamlet*, Bassanio in *The Merchant of Venice*, and Edmund in *King Lear*, Sunderland, 1964-65; Lopahin in *The Cherry Orchard* by Chekhov, Hornchurch, Essex, 1965; Sergeant Trotter in *The Mousetrap* by Agatha Christie, London, 1966; Joseph in *Revelations*, Grinnell, Iowa, 1986. **Film**—*Robbery*, 1967. **Television**—*The Growing Pains of P. C. Penrose* by Roy Clarke, 1975; *The Prince Regent* by Robert Muller, 1979, *Henry V*, 1979; *Fame Is the Spur*, by Howard Spring, 1982; *A Murder Is Announced* by Agatha Christie, 1985.

* * *

David Pinner's *Fanghorn* may have misfired in the 1967 production, and it may fail to sustain the comic impact and inventiveness of the first two acts in the third, but the talent is unmistakable. What is remarkable about the writing is its energy. It begins with a middle-aged man beheading roses with a sword, then fencing flirtatiously with his 16-year-old daughter before switching to making her jump by slashing at her legs. And it sustains a brisk pace in visual surprises and twists in the plot. An uncertain note is occasionally struck with deliberately overwritten lines like

"Look at that gull battering his whiteness against the hooks of the wind!" But there are also some very funny lines and plenty of intriguing changes of direction in the dialogue, which builds up to the entrance of Tamara Fanghorn, a tough-talking, leather-clad sophisticate who arrives from upstairs before she is expected. Subsequent developments make it look as though she is in league with the wife to humiliate the husband, who is first secretary to the minister of defense. Act 2 ends with him naked except for his pants, his hands tied with his belt and his feet with the telephone wire. As the curtain falls, Tamara is brandishing a cutthroat razor and threatening, "Now I am going to cut off what offends me most!" When the curtain rises on act 3, we find him denuded only of his mustache. The crucial twist comes when his disillusioned wife has walked out on him and we find that this is what he and Tamara had wanted all along.

Dickon is centered on more ordinary family relationships. It is vitiated by perfunctoriness and superficiality in most of its characterizations, but there is a glowingly affectionate portrait of a lower-middle-class father trying to fight off the awareness of cancer and then later fighting with pain. But the end piles on the drama too heavily, with one son powdering morphine tablets to put the dying man out of his agony, the other son giving them to him, and then the two of them fighting and laughing hysterically.

There is a curious reprise of these themes in *The Potsdam Quartet*. Act 1 ends with the leader revealing to the cellist that for 10 years he has been suffering from Parkinson's disease, and the cellist, who had thought he was going mad, reacting with a joyful demonstration of relief. How the cellist could have remained ignorant of his own condition is never adequately explained, and there are only cursory references to the illness in act 2. There the major climax is provided by a quarrel between the second violin and the viola player, who are lovers. John (second violin) threatens Ronald (viola) that he is going to have the boyfriend of the leader's daughter, and Ronald responds by swallowing a succession of sleeping pills.

The play is set in an anteroom at the Potsdam Conference in 1945. The string quartet, which is based on the Griller Quartet, play two quartets for Churchill, Stalin, and Truman. Act 1 takes place immediately after the first quartet, and act 2 immediately after the second. Apart from the four musicians, the only character is a Russian guard who hardly ever speaks. The characters are well contrasted, and there is some amusing dialogue, but it is a realistic play in which the action is limited to what can go on in one room between four men who know each other extremely well. Act 1 cannot always avoid the pitfall of making them tell one other things they all know in order to give information to the audience, and act 2 resorts to having them get drunk in order to increase the ratio of action to talk. The play lacks the energy and the courage of *Fanghorn,* but, after writing many unproduced plays in the six intervening years, Pinner cannot be blamed for playing safe. The theater, however, can be blamed for failing to nourish the talent he originally showed.

Perhaps Pinner's best plays are the two one-acters produced at the Soho Poly. *Cartoon* is about an alcoholic cartoonist drying out in a clinic just up the road from the pub where he customarily spends his lunch hour drinking grapefruit juice and weeping as he regularly wins money out of the fruit machine. *An Evening with the GLC* is set in a television studio, where a Labour councillor and his wife are exposed to a live interview conducted by their son. Both walk a little too willingly into the traps that are set for them, but the exposure of political dishonesties is nonetheless effective. Written when Pinner was resident playwright at Peterborough, *Hereward the Wake* is another historical play with dialogue in the modern idiom.

—Ronald Hayman

PINNOCK, Winsome

Nationality: British. **Born:** London in 1961. **Education:** Goldsmiths' College, London, B.A. (honours) in English and drama 1982. **Career:** Playwright-in-residence, Tricycle Theatre, London, 1989-90, and Royal Court Theatre, London, 1991—. Recipient of Junior Judith E. Wilson Fellowship, Cambridge University, 1997-98. **Awards:** Unity Theatre Trust award, 1989; George Devine award, 1991; Thames Television award, 1991. **Agent:** Lemon, Unna, and Durbridge, 24 Pottery Lane, Holland Park, London W11 4LZ, England.

PUBLICATIONS

Plays

The Wind of Change (produced London, 1987).
Leave Taking (produced Liverpool, 1988; London, 1990). Published in *First Run*, edited by Kate Harwood, London, Hern, 1989.
Picture Palace (produced London, 1988).
A Rock in Water (produced London, 1989). Published in *Black Plays: Two*, edited by Yvonne Brewster, London, Methuen, 1989.
A Hero's Welcome (produced London, 1989).
Talking in Tongues (produced London, 1991).
Mules. London, Faber, 1996.

Television Plays: episode in *South of the Border* series, 1988; episode in *Chalkface* series, 1991.

* * *

Winsome Pinnock's radical portrayals of black identities on the otherwise white-dominated stage of the Royal Court Theatre won her immediate recognition. Widely acknowledged as one of the leading young talents writing for the British theater, she is one of a very small circle of black women playwrights whose work was regularly produced at mainstream British theaters.

Though Pinnock was born and educated in London, her work is influenced by an awareness of the role of a Carribean heritage in the lives of England's black communities. Some of her work also deals with the theme of civil rights. These two interests combine and enrich the language as well as the themes of her plays.

One of Pinnock's best-known plays is *A Hero's Welcome,* first presented as a rehearsed reading at the Royal Court in 1986. It was given a full production—in a revised version—at the Theatre Upstairs in 1989 (produced by the Women's Playhouse Trust). The play is set in Jamaica and tells a story of family tension and young love, framed in the traditions and expectations of West Indian culture but informed by the British context of its writing and production. It centers on three young women: Minda, Sis, and

Ishbel. The action takes place in a small Caribbean community in 1947. The three young women are looking for better lives and an escape from poverty. Len, the returning "hero" (whose strong sexual drive is exciting and enticing to the young women) seems to symbolize that kind of possibility and hope. Only the two older women characters, Nana and Mrs. Walker, are able to offer the wisdom of age and experience that keeps the girls in line in their community. That such a play found a wide and diverse audience is itself a success but more important was the national recognition that this production brought Pinnock.

Also in 1989—in fact, one month before *A Hero's Welcome* was given its full production—the Theatre Upstairs premiered Pinnock's *A Rock in Water* (published in Methuen's *Black Plays: Two* [1989], edited by Yvonne Brewster). This play broke new ground for Pinnock and for London audiences with its powerful evocation of a historical figure: Claudia Jones, the founder of the Notting Hill Carnivals in the mid-1950s and a dedicated worker at the *West Indian Gazette,* one of the first black presses. In bringing Jones to public attention, Pinnock engaged in a process of "writing (black) women into history." The play also engaged audiences in a recognition of the importance of location and cultural identity in the lives of black women and men. The play chronicles the life of Claudia Jones in Trinidad and Harlem as well as in London (where she made her home following accusations of "un-American activities").

A Rock in Water was commissioned by the Royal Court's Young People's Theatre and was developed during workshops. Pinnock did her own research by interviewing people who had known Claudia Jones, bringing the characters of her play to life through the memories of Jones's contemporaries and co-workers including the actress Corinne Skinner-Carter who was later featured in *A Hero's Welcome.* The play was performed by 14 members of the Young People's Theatre, all of whom had been closely involved in the development of the ideas that Pinnock wove into the play.

Pinnock's *Picture Palace,* produced by the Women's Theatre Group, went on national tour in 1988. The play focused on the roles that women play and on the images used in advertising and the media in Britain. That same year *Leave Taking* was first produced at the Liverpool Playhouse Studio. Like *A Hero's Welcome,* it had a cross-cultural focus. *Leave Taking* was given a revival in 1990, directed by Jules Wright and produced by the Women's Playhouse Trust at the Royal Court. The play's popularity is related to its scope and its intelligent yet humorous view of relationships between individuals and their cultural identities. *Leave Taking* also introduced the theme of cultural difference in the coming of awareness of individuals and groups of black women and men—a topic that was rarely dealt with in British theater. *Leave Taking* was again revived for a run at the Belgrade Theatre, Coventry, in May 1992.

Pinnock's *Talking in Tongues* was performed at the Royal Court Theatre (directed by Hetty MacDonald) when Pinnock was writer in residence there during 1991. In this play Pinnock's concern with the intermingling of cultures and with identities and voices is further developed within the story of a number of black and white friends and colleagues who come together at a New Year's Eve party. Sexuality and interracial relationships are represented, as are the themes of competition and identification between blacks and whites, women and men. As in her other work, the use of dialect frames the play with the sound and rhythm of another language.

In most of Pinnock's work, the realist drama focuses on the central dilemma of the black woman coming to terms with (predominantly) white British society. Pinnock's talent as a playwright is enriched in all of her work by her keen awareness of the nuances of language and by her ability to reach out and communicate with the many different communities and individuals who make up the audiences of her plays.

—Lizbeth Goodman

PINTER, Harold

Nationality: British. **Born:** Hackney, London, 10 October 1930. **Education:** Hackney Downs Grammar School, 1943-47; Royal Academy of Dramatic Art, London, 1948. **Military Service:** Conscientious objector: no military service. **Family:** Married 1) the actress Vivien Merchant in 1956 (divorced 1980), one son; 2) the writer Lady Antonia Fraser in 1980. **Career:** Professional actor, 1949-60, and occasionally since then; also a director; associate director, National Theatre, London, 1973-83; director, United British Artists, 1983; editor and publisher Greville Press, Warwick, 1988—, and member of the editorial board, *Cricket World,* 1989—. Lives in London. **Awards:** *Evening Standard* award, 1960; Newspaper Guild of New York award, 1962; Italia prize, for television play, 1962; Berlin Film Festival Silver Bear, 1963; Screenwriters Guild award, for television play, 1963, for screenplay, 1963; New York Film Critics award, 1964; BAFTA award, 1965, 1971; Tony award, 1967; Whitbread award, 1967; New York Drama Critics Circle award, 1967, 1980; Shakespeare prize (Hamburg), 1970; Writers Guild award, 1971; Cannes Film Festival Golden Palm, 1971; Austrian State prize, 1973; Pirandello prize, 1980; Commonwealth award, 1981; Donatello prize, 1982; British Theatre Association award, 1983, 1985; Bobst award, 1984; David Cohen British Literature prize, 1995. D.Litt.: universities of Reading, 1970, Birmingham, 1971, Glasgow, 1974, East Anglia, Norwich, 1974, Stirling, 1979, Hull, 1986, Sussex, 1990, East London, 1994, Sofia, Bulgaria, 1995; Brown University, Providence, Rhode Island, 1982. Honorary fellow, Queen Mary College, London, 1987. C.B.E. (Commander, Order of the British Empire), 1966. **Member:** Fellow, Royal Society of Literature; honorary member, American Academy and Institute of Arts and Letters, 1984, and American Academy of Arts and Sciences, 1985. **Agent:** Judy Daish Associates, 83 Eastbourne Mews, London W2 6LQ, England.

Publications

Plays

The Room (produced Bristol, 1957; also director: produced London, 1960; New York, 1964). Included in *The Birthday Party and Other Plays*, 1960.

The Birthday Party (produced Cambridge and London, 1958; San Francisco, 1960; New York, 1967). London, Encore, 1959; included in *The Birthday Party and Other Plays*, 1960; revised version, London, Methuen, 1965.

Sketches in *One to Another* (produced London, 1959). London, French, 1960.

Sketches in *Pieces of Eight* (produced London, 1959). Included in *A Slight Ache and Other Plays*, 1961; in *The Dwarfs and Eight Revue Sketches*, 1965.

A Slight Ache (broadcast 1959; produced London, 1961; New York, 1962). Included in *A Slight Ache and Other Plays*, 1961; in *Three Plays*, 1962.

The Dumb Waiter (produced, in German, Frankfurt, 1959; London, 1960; Madison, Wisconsin, and New York, 1962). Included in *The Birthday Party and Other Plays*, 1960.

The Dwarfs (broadcast 1960; also director: produced London, 1963; revised version produced Edinburgh, 1966; Boston, 1967; New York, 1974). Included in *A Slight Ache and Other Plays*, 1961, in *Three Plays*, 1962.

The Birthday Party and Other Plays (includes *The Dumb Waiter* and *The Room*). London, Methuen, 1960; as *The Birthday Party and The Room* (includes *The Dumb Waiter*), New York, Grove Press, 1961.

The Caretaker (produced London, 1960; New York, 1961). London, Methuen, 1960; with *The Dumb Waiter*, New York, Grove Press, 1961.

Night School (televised 1960). Included in *Tea Party and Other Plays*, 1967; in *Early Plays*, 1968.

A Night Out (broadcast 1960; produced Dublin and London, 1961; New York, 1971). Included in *A Slight Ache and Other Plays*, 1961; in *Early Plays*, 1968.

A Slight Ache and Other Plays (includes *The Dwarfs*, *A Night Out*, and sketches). London, Methuen, 1961.

The Collection (televised 1961; also co-director; produced London, 1962; New York, 1963; revised version, televised 1978). London, French, 1962; in *Three Plays*, 1962.

Three Plays. New York, Grove Press, 1962.

The Lover (televised 1963; also director: produced London, 1963; New York, 1964). Included in *The Collection, and The Lover*, 1963; published separately, New York, Dramatists Play Service, 1965.

The Collection, and The Lover (includes the prose piece *The Examination*). London, Methuen, 1963.

The Compartment (unreleased screenplay), in *Project 1*, with Samuel Beckett and Eugène Ionesco. New York, Grove Press, 1963.

Dialogue for Three, published in *Stand* (Newcastle upon Tyne), vol. 6, no. 3, 1963.

Tea Party (televised 1965; produced New York, 1968; London, 1970). London, Methuen, 1965; New York, Grove Press, 1966; revised version, London, Karnac, 1968.

The Homecoming (produced London, 1965; New York, 1967). London, Methuen, 1965; New York, Grove Press, 1966; revised version, London, Karnac, 1968.

The Dwarfs and Eight Revue Sketches (includes *Trouble in the Works*, *The Black and White*, *Request Stop*, *Last to Go*, *Applicant*, *Interview*, *That's All*, *That's Your Trouble*). New York, Dramatists Play Service, 1965.

The Basement (televised 1967; produced New York, 1968; London, 1970). Included in *Tea Party and Other Plays*, 1967; in *The Lover, The Tea Party, The Basement*, 1967.

Tea Party and Other Plays. London, Methuen, 1967.

The Lover, The Tea Party, The Basement. New York, Grove Press, 1967.

Early Plays: A Night Out, Night School, Revue Sketches. New York, Grove Press, 1968.

Sketches by Pinter (produced New York, 1969). Included in *Early Plays*, 1968.

Landscape (broadcast 1968; produced London, 1969; New York, 1970). London, Pendragon Press, 1968; included in *Landscape, and Silence*, 1969.

Silence (produced London, 1969; New York, 1970). Included in *Landscape, and Silence*, 1969.

Landscape, and Silence (includes *Night*). London, Methuen, 1969; New York, Grove Press, 1970.

Night, in *Mixed Doubles* (produced London, 1969). Included in *Landscape, and Silence*, 1969.

Five Screenplays (includes *The Caretaker*, *The Servant*, *The Pumpkin Eater*, *Accident*, *The Quiller Memorandum*). London, Methuen, 1971; modified version, omitting *The Caretaker* and including *The Go-Between*, London, Karnac, 1971; New York, Grove Press, 1973.

Old Times (produced London and New York, 1971). London, Methuen, and New York, Grove Press, 1971.

Monologue (televised 1973; produced London, 1973). London, Covent Garden Press, 1973.

No Man's Land (produced London, 1975; New York, 1976). London, Eyre Methuen, and New York, Grove Press, 1975.

Plays 1-4. London, Eyre Methuen, 1975-81; as *Complete Works 1-4*, New York, Grove Press, 1977-81.

The Proust Screenplay: A la Recherche du Temps Perdu. New York, New Directions, 1977; London, Eyre Methuen-Chatto and Windus, 1978.

Betrayal (produced London, 1978; New York, 1980). London, Eyre Methuen, 1978; New York, Grove Press, 1979.

The Hothouse (also director: produced London, 1980). London, Eyre Methuen, and New York, Grove Press, 1980; revised version (produced Providence, Rhode Island, and New York, 1982), Methuen, 1982.

Family Voices (broadcast 1981; produced London and Cambridge, Massachusetts, 1981). London, Next Editions, and New York, Grove Press, 1981.

The Screenplay of The French Lieutenant's Woman. London, Cape, and Boston, Little Brown, 1981.

The French Lieutenant's Woman and Other Screenplays (includes *Langrishe, Go Down* and *The Last Tycoon*). London, Methuen, 1982.

Other Places (includes *Family Voices*, *Victoria Station*, *A Kind of Alaska*) (produced London, 1982). London, Methuen, 1982; New York, Grove Press, 1983; revised version, including *One for the Road* and omitting *Family Voices* (produced New York, 1984; London, 1985).

Precisely (sketch), in *The Big One* (produced London, 1983).

One for the Road (also director: produced London, 1984; in *Other Places*, produced New York, 1984). London, Methuen, 1984; revised version, Methuen, 1985; New York, Grove Press, 1986.

Mountain Language (also director: produced London, 1988). London, Faber, 1988; New York, Grove Press, 1989.

The Heat of the Day, adaptation of the novel by Elizabeth Bowen (televized 1989). London, Faber, 1989.

The Comfort of Strangers and Other Screenplays (includes *Reunion*, *Turtle Diary*, *Victory*). London, Faber, 1990.

Party Time (also director: produced London, 1991). With *Mountain Language*, London, Faber, 1991; separately London, Faber, 1991.

The Trial, adaptation of the novel by Franz Kafka. London, Faber, 1993.

The New World Order (also director: produced London, 1991). New York, Dramatists Play Service, 1991.

Moonlight: A Play. New York, Grove, 1993.

Ashes to Ashes. London, Faber, 1996.

Screenplays: *The Servant*, 1963; *The Guest* (*The Caretaker*), 1964; *The Pumpkin Eater*, 1964; *The Quiller Memorandum*, 1966; *Accident*, 1967; *The Birthday Party*, 1968; *The Go-Between*, 1971; *The Homecoming*, 1973; *The Last Tycoon*, 1976; *The French Lieutenant's Woman*, 1981; *Betrayal*, 1982; *Turtle Diary*, 1985; *The Trial*, 1989; *Reunion*, 1989; *The Handmaid's Tale*, 1990; *The Comfort of Strangers*, 1990; *The Remains of the Day*, 1991.

Radio Plays: *A Slight Ache*, 1959; *The Dwarfs*, 1960; *A Night Out*, 1960; *Landscape*, 1968; *Family Voices*, 1981; *Players*, 1985.

Television Plays: *Night School*, 1960; *The Collection*, 1961, revised version, 1978; *The Lover*, 1963; *Tea Party*, 1965; *The Basement*, 1967; *Monologue*, 1973; *Langrishe, Go Down*, from the novel by Aidan Higgins, 1978; *Mountain Language*, 1988; *The Heat of the Day*, 1989; *Party Time*, 1992.

Novel

The Dwarfs. London, Faber, and New York, Grove Weidenfeld, 1990.

Poetry

Poems, edited by Alan Clodd. London, Enitharmon Press, 1968; revised edition, 1971.
I Know the Place. Warwick, Greville Press, 1979.
Ten Early Poems. Warwick, Greville Press, 1992.

Other

Mac (on Anew McMaster). London, Pendragon Press, 1968.
Poems and Prose 1949-1977. London, Eyre Methuen, and New York, Grove Press, 1978; revised edition, as *Collected Poems and Prose*, Methuen, 1986.

Editor, with John Fuller and Peter Redgrove, *New Poems 1967: A PEN Anthology*. London, Hutchinson, 1968.
Editor, with Geoffrey Godbert and Anthony Astbury, *100 Poems by 100 Poets*. London, Methuen, 1986; New York, Grove Press, 1987.

*

Bibliography: *Pinter: A Bibliography: His Works and Occasional Writings with a Comprehensive Checklist of Criticism and Reviews of the London Productions* by Rudiger Imhof, London, TQ Publications, 1975; *Harold Pinter: An Annotated Bibliography* by Steven H. Gale, Boston, Hall, and London, Prior, 1978; *Harold Pinter Bibliography, 1993-1994* by Susan Holliscompiler Merritt, in *Pinter Review* (Tampa, Florida), 1995-1996, pp. 208-28.

Critical Studies (selection): *Harold Pinter*, New York, Twayne, 1967, revised edition, 1981, and *Harold Pinter*, New York, St. Martin's Press, 1975, London, Macmillan, 1976, both by Arnold P. Hinchliffe; *Harold Pinter* by Ronald Hayman, London, Heinemann, 1968, New York, Ungar, 1973, revised edition, Heinemann, 1980; *Harold Pinter* by John Russell Taylor, London, Longman, 1969; *Stratagems to Uncover Nakedness: The Dramas of Harold Pinter* by Lois Gordon, Columbia, University of Missouri Press, 1969; *Harold Pinter: The Poetics of Silence* by James H. Hollis, Carbondale, Southern Illinois University Press, 1970; *Harold Pinter* by Alrene Sykes, St. Lucia, University of Queensland Press, and New York, Humanities Press, 1970; *The Peopled Wound: The Plays of Harold Pinter* by Martin Esslin, London, Methuen, and New York, Doubleday, 1970, revised edition, as *Pinter: A Study of His Plays*, Methuen, 1973, New York, Norton, 1976, revised edition, Eyre Methuen, 1977, revised edition, as *Pinter: The Playwright*, Methuen, 1982; *The Dramatic World of Harold Pinter: Its Basis in Ritual* by Katherine H. Burkman, Columbus, Ohio State University Press, 1971; *Pinter: A Collection of Critical Essays* edited by Arthur Ganz, Englewood Cliffs, New Jersey, Prentice Hall, 1972; *The Plays of Harold Pinter: An Assessment* by Simon Trussler, London, Gollancz, 1973; *The Pinter Problem* by Austin E. Quigley, Princeton, New Jersey, Princeton University Press, 1975; *The Dream Structure of Pinter's Plays: A Psychoanalytic Approach* by Lucina Paquet Gabbard, Rutherford, New Jersey, Fairleigh Dickinson University Press, 1976; *Where the Laughter Stops: Pinter's Tragi-Comedy*, Columbia, University of Missouri Press, 1976, and *Harold Pinter*, London, Macmillan, and New York, Grove Press, 1982, both by Bernard F. Dukore; *Butter's Going Up: A Critical Analysis of Harold Pinter's Work* by Steven H. Gale, Durham, North Carolina, Duke University Press, 1977, and *Harold Pinter: Critical Approaches* edited by Gale, Madison, New Jersey, Fairleigh Dickinson University Press, 1986; *Harold Pinter: A Critical Evaluation* by Surendra Sahai, Salzburg, Austria, Salzburg Studies in English Literature, 1981; *Canters and Chronicles: The Use of Narrative in the Plays of Samuel Beckett and Harold Pinter* by Kristin Morrison, Chicago, University of Chicago Press, 1983; *Harold Pinter* by Guido Almansi and Simon Henderson, London, Methuen, 1983; *Pinter: The Player's Playwright* by David T. Thompson, London, Macmillan, and New York, Schocken, 1985; *Pinter's Comic Play* by Elin Diamond, Lewisburg, Pennsylvania, Bucknell University Press, 1985; *Harold Pinter: You Never Heard Such Silence* edited by Alan Bold, London, Vision Press, and New York, Barnes and Noble, 1985; *Making Pictures: The Pinter Screenplays* by Joanne Klein, Columbus, Ohio State University Press, 1985; *Harold Pinter: The Birthday Party, The Caretaker, and The Homecoming: A Casebook* edited by Michael Scott, London, Macmillan, 1986; *Pinter's Female Portraits: A Study of Female Characters in the Plays of Pinter* by Elizabeth Sakellaridou, London, Macmillan, 1988; *Harold Pinter: Towards a Poetics of His Plays* by Volker Strunk, Bern, Switzerland, Peter Lang, 1989; *Pinter in Play* by Susan Merritt, Durham, North Carolina, Duke University Press, 1990; *Harold Pinter: A Casebook* by Lois Gordon, New York, Garland, 1990; *Harold Pinter and the Language of Cultural Power* by Marc Silverstein, Lewisburg, Pennsylvania, Bucknell University Press, 1993; *Conversations with Pinter* by Mel Gussow, London, Nick Hern, 1994; *Gender and Power in the Plays of Harold Pinter* by Victor L. Cahn, Basingstoke, Macmillan, 1994; *The Pinter Ethic: The Erotic Aesthetic* by Penelope Prentice, New York, Garland, 1994; *Harold Pinter: A Question of Timing* by Martin S. Regal, Basingstoke, Hampshire, Macmillan Press, 1995; *Understanding Harold Pinter* by Ronald Knowles, Columbia, South Carolina, University of South Carolina Press, 1995; *The Plays of Harold Pinter: A Study of Neurotic Anxiety* by S. R. Jalote, New Dehli, Harman Publishing House, 1996; *The Life and Work of Harold Pinter* by Michael Billington, London, Faber, 1996; *Harold Pinter and the New British Theatre* by D. Keith Peacock, Westport, Connecticut, Greenwood Press, 1997.

Theatrical Activities:

Director: **Plays**—*The Birthday Party*, Oxford and Cambridge, 1958; *The Room*, London, 1960; *The Collection* (co-director, with Peter Hall), London, 1962; *The Lover*, London, 1963; *The Dwarfs*, London, 1963; *The Birthday Party*, London, 1964; *The Man in the Glass Booth* by Robert Shaw, London, 1967, New York, 1968; *Exiles* by James Joyce, London, 1970; *Butley* by Simon Gray, Oxford and London, 1971; *Next of Kin* by John Hopkins, London, 1974; *Otherwise Engaged* by Simon Gray, Oxford and London, 1975, New York, 1977; *Blithe Spirit* by Noël Coward, London, 1976; *The Innocents* by William Archibald, New York, 1976; *The Rear Column* by Simon Gray, London, 1978; *Close of Play* by Simon Gray, London, 1979; *The Hothouse*, London, 1980; *Quartermaine's Terms* by Simon Gray, London, 1981; *Incident at Tulse Hill* by Robert East, London, 1981; *The Trojan War Will Not Take Place* by Jean Giraudoux, London, 1983; *The Common Pursuit* by Simon Gray, London, 1984; *One for the Road, and Victoria Station*, London, 1984; *Sweet Bird of Youth* by Tennessee Williams, London, 1985; *Circe and Bravo* by Donald Freed, London, 1986; *Mountain Language*, London, 1988; *Vanilla* by Jane Stanton Hitchcock, Bath and London, 1990; *Party Time*, London, 1991; *The New World Order*, London, 1991. **Film**—*Butley*, 1976. **Television**—*The Rear Column* by Simon Gray, 1980; *The Hothouse*, 1981.

Actor (as David Baron and Harold Pinter): **Plays**—With Anew McMaster's theatre company in Ireland, 1950-52; with Donald Wolfit's theatre company, Kings Theatre, Hammersmith, London, 1953, numerous provincial repertory companies, 1953-60; Mick in *The Caretaker*, London, 1964; Goldberg in *The Birthday Party*, Cheltenham, 1964; Lenny in *The Homecoming*, Watford, Hertfordshire, 1969; Deeley in *Old Times*, Los Angeles, 1985; Hirst in *No Man's Land*, London, 1992. **Radio**—*Monologue*, 1975; *Rough for Radio* by Samuel Beckett, 1976; *Two Plays* by Václav Havel, 1977. **Films**—*The Servant*, 1963; *Accident*, 1967; *The Rise and Rise of Michael Rimmer*, 1970. **Television**—*Rogue Male*, 1976; *Langrishe, Go Down*, 1978; *The Birthday Party*, 1986.

* * *

In a remarkably prolific period between 1957 and 1965 Harold Pinter established himself as the most gifted playwright in England and the author of a unique dramatic idiom. Popularly labeled the "Pinteresque," his theater is not "of the absurd," nor is it a "drama of menace," both of which portray the gratuitous visitation upon innocent victims of external forces of terror or of the "absurd." Pinter's actually consists of a much more frightening visitation. At least through *Silence* and *Landscape,* his comfortable people, unlike the innocents of Kafka's or even Beckett's worlds, are besieged by their own internal fears and longings and their own irrepressible guilts and menacing sexual drives. It is these that invariably wage successful war against the tidy lifestyles the people have constructed in order to survive from day to day.

Pinter's characters, usually enclosed in a room, organize their lives with the games people play. But in their games, or role-playing—in which each has agreed to a specific scenario with implicit limits and taboos—they often say one thing but feel and communicate another. During their exchanges, in fact, the verbal is only the most superficial level of communication. The connotations of their words and their accompanying gestures, pauses, and double entendres—as well as their hesitations and silences—communicate a second level of meaning that is often opposed to the first. Pinter himself has said of language, "The speech we hear is an indication of that which we don't hear. It is a necessary avoidance, a violent, sly, and anguished or mocking smoke screen which keeps the other in its true place. When true silence falls we are left with echo but are nearer nakedness. One way of looking at speech is to say that it is a constant stratagem to cover nakedness." Indeed, one way of looking at Pinter's plays is to say that they are dramatic stratagems that uncover nakedness.

Into his characters' rooms, and into their ritualized and verbal relationships, a stranger invariably enters, whereupon language begins to disintegrate, and the protection promised by the room is threatened. The commonplace room, in fact, becomes the violent scene of mental and physical breakdown. What occurs, in effect, is that the characters project on to the stranger—an intruder into their precarious psychic stability—their deepest fears. The so-called victimizers—Goldberg and McCann in *The Birthday Party;* Riley in *The Room;* the blind, mute match seller in *A Slight Ache;* the visiting, unfamiliar sister-in-law in *The Homecoming;* the old, garrulous, and admittedly opportunistic Davies in *The Caretaker;* and even the mechanical dumbwaiter in *The Dumb Waiter*—all function as screens upon which the characters externalize their own irrationality, that side of themselves the games have ultimately been inadequate to hide. In a sense, Pinter's intruders are his technique for leading the characters to expose their true identities. What is, of course, simultaneously funny and horrific is that the games constructed—and even the intruders, or screens, which are mirror images of the characters—contain within themselves the boring lives already lived and the violence struggling for expression.

In Pinter's first play, *The Room,* Rose coddles, feeds, clothes, and emasculates her silent husband, Bert, fittingly portrayed as a child wearing a silly hat and reading comic books. (He has agreed to play the passive child in their relationship.) Protective of her precarious stability, she admits, "This is a good room. You've got a chance in a place like this. . . . It's cold out. . . . It's murder." When a young couple enter a mirror of Rose and Bert many years before, thinking that her flat is empty, she actually experiences them as potential "murderers." This is exacerbated by her landlord's (Kidd's) retaliatory remarks, prompted by her earlier put-down, and his mention that a blind black man in the basement, an obvious image of her subterranean mind, is waiting to "see" her. For the rest of the play Rose acts out her rage, sexual appetite, and then guilt toward the black Riley, as though she were reenacting an earlier Oedipal crime. From her "You're all deaf and dumb and blind, the lot of you," she succumbs to his "Sal [a childhood name]. . . . I want you to come home" and caresses his eyes and head. With Bert's return, following this enactment of the most basic instinctual and taboo behavior, she becomes blind.

In *The Birthday Party* a young man has similarly secluded himself in order to hide from some lingering childhood guilt. When the two strangers Goldberg and McCann enter his seaside retreat, Stanley becomes violent and projects upon them his own fantasies and guilt: "You stink of sin"; "You contaminate womankind. . . . Mother defiler. . . . You verminate the sheet of your birth." At a later "celebration" his landlady, Meg, with whom Stanley has structured a safe though flirtatious child-lover relationship, and the neighbor Lulu, along with Goldberg and McCann, act out both Stanley's taboo Oedipal impulses and his repulsion and guilt toward these drives. As Rose became blind, Stanley becomes mute. In *The Dumb Waiter* two hit men lose control when some very funny messages descend on the building's dumbwaiter and the w.c. (water closet) malfunctions, whereupon their carefully measured roles are upset. In *The Caretaker* the intrusion of a harmless, though manipulative and highly verbal, old man threatens the carefully designed relationship of two brothers. In *The Homecoming* a presumably stable, all-male household is exposed in all its rage, confused sexuality, and utter precariousness when an unknown woman (the visiting wife of a third son) appears. Her mere presence threatens everyone's identity. In *The Basement* and *Tea Party* Pinter returns to his earlier triangular patterns and focuses on the breakdown of orderly and controlled behavior for displays of cuckoldry and homosexuality.

Silence and *Landscape* indicate a new direction. The same childless couples inhabit these plays, but they have long ago learned that playing games will not assure their relationship. Nothing is certain in their isolated rooms, least of all identity or connection. Each person not only fails to understand himself, unable to distinguish fantasy from experience, but he can never know the stranger who calls himself his spouse. There is a type of finality in these plays but also a poignancy about the people so inextricably locked within themselves.

These plays demand a more poetic reading for the lyrical sense of the characters' rationalizations, hopes, fears, and fantasies, which are true at one and the same time. Still in the tradition of Joyce, Woolf, and Beckett, Pinter has moved in these works from earlier explorations of the underside of the self (what Freud called "the seething cauldron" beneath logical thought and act) to a dramatic rendering of the simultaneous levels of fantasy and real experience that equally occupy the individual. He has said of the complexities and ultimate mystery of human behavior, "The desire for verification on the part of us all, with regard to our own experience and the experience of others, is understandable, but cannot always be satisfied. I suggest there can be no hard distinctions between what is real and what is unreal, nor between what is true and what is false. A thing is not necessarily either true or false; it can be both true and false."

The details, characters, and images of *Silence* and *Landscape* are similar, as though each were two halves of a whole. Poetic images of growing old, they tell of brief and unfulfilled love affairs. Their details are of walks in the country, moments in pubs, and flights of birds; recollections are illuminated by memories of fading sunlight or gray clouds or gusts of rain. Speakers interrupt their wistful thoughts with lusty outbursts about the most mundane of matters. Every word, gesture, color, and mood reverberates, and each character's reveries define the others. Although their conversations are not directed to the other, each explains the way in which life has passed the other by, although to him the insight remains unfathomable. Just as these people fail to connect, their poetically connected insights, their common pain and joy, and their repetition of words and gestures suggest a universality about human nature. Pinter has clearly moved toward new, poetic dimensions. It is interesting to note that he also published his first volume of poems at this time, although they were written as early as his first plays.

Old Times returns to issues of possible and real homosexual and heterosexual commitment, fidelity, and friendship. Pinter's triangle, two women and a man, suggests any number of possibilities and combinations: "There are some things one remembers even though they may never have happened. There are things I remember which may never have happened but as I recall them so they take place." *No Man's Land* re-creates a male world of potential comforters and predators, with each man locked in a precarious linguistic world of identity. The no-man's-land here is that mysterious realm of truth and self-knowledge, of one's comprehension of oneself and of the world that "never moves, which never changes, which never grows older, but which remains forever, icy and silent."

Almost as though Pinter had begun with a line from *Old Times*, in which one man tells another that he proposed that his wife betray him, *Betrayal* treats multiple betrayals among friends, spouses, and lovers, and even within the self, in a fascinating structural manipulation of time. Pinter was perhaps inspired by his screenplay of Proust's *À la recherche du temps perdu*, for the play begins two years after an affair ended and in nine scenes moves back in time. Humor, banality, poetry, violence, diluted passion, and pain merge in a poignant evocation of time and of one's eternal separation from both innocence and responsibility.

The Hothouse, written in 1958 but not published until 1980, focuses on the sanatorium in which the mute Stanley in *The Birthday Party* might have been committed. Staff members chatter in banal, funny, and threatening conversations about sex and the variations of power and control. Playing with traditional symbolism—there has been both a birth and death; the play occurs on Christmas; the characters in this hothouse are named Roote, Cutts, Lush, and Lamb—Pinter raises serious and ambiguous issues about sanity and insanity and about so-called leaders and followers. At the end there is a gratuitous mass murder of the staff, but the identity of the perpetrator remains ambiguous. Is it one of the patients? Is it one of the staff?

The London production of *Other Places* included *Victoria Station*, *A Kind of Alaska*, and *Family Voices;* in New York *One for the Road* replaced *Family Voices*, which was originally a radio play. There is a curious unity in these works as they anatomize primitive responses to menace and loyalty. Tours de force in concreteness, they are finely chiseled portraits of the contingency of human experience, and they simultaneously evoke the most abiding of human encounters with evil or kindness.

The short *Victoria Station* portrays the conversation between a taxi dispatcher and a driver who, after picking up a female passenger, loses all sense of place and identity. The dispatcher becomes his brother's keeper. *One for the Road* conveys a series of frightening confrontations between a banal, Goldberg-like torturer, vaguely representative of God and country, and his victims—a tortured man, his brutally assaulted wife, and their son who is eventually murdered. In the most affecting of the group, *A Kind of Alaska*, a woman in her mid-40s "erupts to life" after nearly 30 years of sleeping sickness. Pinter depicts her rebellious, bewildered, foolish, angry, and gallant responses in a combination of hallucination, childlike language, and erotic wish fulfillment. The reality of her lost youth and lost love, along with her sister's and doctor's unshakable loyalty, create a powerful work.

Pinter's work since the late 1980s has been political in the extreme. He has announced, repeatedly, that he feels a responsibility to pursue his role as "a citizen of the world in which I live, [and] insist upon taking responsibility." This responsibility consists of both speaking out publicly and writing about the political oppression of the individual through the subversive function of language. As such, *Mountain Language* treats the oppression of an unnamed people in an unspecified totalitarian state for the crime of retaining their own (mountain) language. In the first of four brief scenes Pinter portrays a mother and a wife who wait an entire day before being permitted to visit their imprisoned son and husband—each man apparently arrested for retaining his now outlawed language. As one officer reminds the women: "Your language is forbidden. It is dead. No one is allowed to speak your language." Already terrorized by two guards and their dogs, the women, even when permitted to see the prisoners, are subjected to additional ridicule and sexual menace. As the elderly mother visits her son—with both forbidden to speak in their native language—a voice-over (tape) plays out their thoughts, but the guards' double-talk destroys any possibility of communication. In the next of these stark, rapid scenes, a young woman sees the hooded figure of her badly tortured husband and is told that she can save him only if she sleeps with an administrator. In the final scene, when the state arbitrarily changes the law and the mother is told that she "can speak in her own language. Until further notice," she has become too terrorized to do so, and her son collapses before her eyes. The play is a frightening image, as Pinter explained, of what happens when people are deprived of "expressing their own identity through their own language."

The New World Order, billed as "a short satiric response to the Gulf War," is a 10-minute play whose title is taken from one of U.S. President George Bush's political phrases. It portrays the gratuitous torture two men inflict upon an innocent. In a small room two captors stand and discuss what to do with their victim, who sits silent and blindfolded before them. As they play word games punctuated by Pinter's meticulous pauses, they increase the prisoner's apprehension of his impending torture. In essence the two men play ironic variations on the theme "He has no idea what we are going to do with him," and the victim, like the audience, has "some idea," "a faint idea," "a little idea" and constructs any series of possible tortures. The guards also remind each other about their power in language; for example, they tease their victim with contradictory and vulgar sexual epithets (he is called "a cunt" and then "a prick"), and they proceed to question whether he is a peasant or a theologian. At one point the more vocal terrorist becomes silent. "I feel pure," he says, as if through sheer power and authority he had reached a transcendent state. In Pinter's somewhat mysterious climax we are told that not only his partner but the prisoner as well will shake his hand "in about thirty-five minutes." It would appear that what was the peasant, theologian, or just plain Pinter innocent has either been driven entirely mad or has totally capitulated to authority. The new world order has reduced all dissent or individuality to blind conformity.

In his plays *Moonlight* and *Ashes to Ashes* Pinter works in yet another mode. While he retains the juxtaposition of brutality and the banal, he is now writing about the extremities of human experience and how at even those moments such interchanges continue. During the ordeal of dying, for example, an ambivalent love and hatred continue between spouses or their children. He has never been so subtle in his portrait of violence and suffering and of the various degrees of responsibility we all share as seeming victim or victimizer.

Moonlight portrays the dying Andy and his wife Bel, with flashes throughout of their caring but angry sons (Jake and Fred) and of their younger, somewhat mystical daughter (Bridget). They speak of their lives together. *Ashes to Ashes,* although visually about the relationship between a couple staying at their country home, is filled, in its details and in the wife's thoughts, with echoes of the Holocaust and of the bondage, helplessness, and perplexity wrought upon its victims. Despite Pinter's typical dialogue, which captures the quintessential banality of everyday verbal interchange (and there are hilarious moments in both these plays), the playwright has added a lyrical poetry in the spirit, if not the content, of *Silence* and *Landscape*. As life and death proceed with their attendant love, hatred, and brutality, a tenderness envelopes the characters, as does a totally new intimation of the possibilities of an afterlife.

At the end of both one remains, as ever, jolted by Pinter's imaginative evocation of the cruelty and kindness that we only half-knowingly impose on those closest to us. His more lyrical tone, however, transforms the plays into an emotional experience of the deepest sort. Audiences are undoubtedly as mystified in articulating this feeling as they were in response to his earliest great works.

—Lois Gordon

PISMIRE, Osbert. *See* **HIVNOR, Robert (Hanks).**

PLATER, Alan (Frederick)

Nationality: British. **Born:** Jarrow-on-Tyne, County Durham, 15 April 1935. **Education:** Pickering Road Junior and Infant School, Hull, 1940-46; Kingston High School, Hull, 1946-53; King's College, Newcastle upon Tyne (University of Durham), 1953-57; qualified as architect (Associate, Royal Institute of British Architects), 1961. **Family:** Married 1) Shirley Johnson in 1958 (divorced 1985), two sons and one daughter; 2) Shirley Rubinstein, three stepsons. **Career:** Worked in an architect's office, Hull, 1957-60. Full-time writer, 1960—. Co-founder, Humberside Theatre (formerly Hull Arts Centre), 1970; co-chair, Writers Guild of Great Britain, 1986-87; president, Writers Guild of Great Britain, 1991-95. Lives in London. **Awards:** Writers Guild award, for radio play, 1972; Sony award, for radio play, 1983; Royal Television Society award, 1984, 1985; New York and San Francisco film festival awards, 1986; Broadcasting Guild award, 1987; BAFTA writers and drama series award, 1988; Variety Club of Great Britain award, 1989; Grand Prix, Banff Festival, Canada, 1989; BAFTA CYMRU Writer's award, 1994. D. Litt.: Hull University, 1985. Honorary Fellow, Hull College of Higher Education, 1983; Fellow, Royal Society of Literature, 1985. Honorary Doctor of Civil Law, University of Northumbria, 1997. **Agent:** Alexandra Cann Representation, 12 Abingdon Road, London W8 6AF, England.

Publications

Plays

The Referees (televised 1961; produced Stoke-on-Trent, 1963).

The Mating Season (broadcast 1962; produced Stoke-on-Trent, 1963). Published in *Worth a Hearing: A Collection of Radio Plays*, edited by Alfred Bradley, London, Blackie, 1967.

A Smashing Day (televised 1962; revised version, music by Ben Kingsley and Robert Powell, produced Stoke-on-Trent, 1965; London, 1966).

The Rainbow Machine (broadcast 1962; produced Stoke-on-Trent, 1963).
Ted's Cathedral (produced Stoke-on-Trent and London, 1963).
A Quiet Night (televised 1963). Published in *Z Cars: Four Scripts from the Television Series*, edited by Michael Marland, London, Longman, 1968.
See the Pretty Lights (televised 1963; produced London, 1970). Published in *Theatre Choice: A Collection of Modern Short Plays*, edited by Michael Marland, London, Blackie, 1972.
The Nutter (televised 1965; revised version, as *Charlie Came to Our Town*, music by Alex Glasgow, produced Harrogate, Yorkshire, 1966).
Excursion (broadcast 1966). Included in *You and Me*, 1973.
The What on the Landing? (broadcast 1967; produced Coventry, 1968; London, 1971).
On Christmas Day in the Morning (*Softly, Softly* series; televised 1968). Included in *You and Me*, 1973.
Hop Step and Jump (produced Scarborough, Yorkshire, 1968).
Close the Coalhouse Door, music by Alex Glasgow, adaptation of stories by Sid Chaplin (produced Newcastle upon Tyne and London, 1968). London, Methuen, 1969.
Don't Build a Bridge, Drain the River!, music by Michael Chapman and Mike Waterson (produced Hull, 1970; revised version, music by Mike O'Neil, produced Hull, 1980).
Simon Says!, music by Alex Glasgow (produced Leeds, 1970).
And a Little Love Besides (produced Hull, 1970; London, 1977). Included in *You and Me*, 1973.
King Billy Vaudeville Show, with others (produced Hull, 1971).
Seventeen Per Cent Said Push Off (televised 1972). Included in *You and Me*, 1973.
The Tigers are Coming—O.K.? (produced Hull, 1972).
You and Me: Four Plays, edited by Alfred Bradley. London, Blackie, 1973.
Swallows on the Water (produced Hull, 1973).
When the Reds Go Marching In (produced Liverpool, 1973).
Annie Kenney (televised 1974). Published in *Act 3*, edited by David Self and Ray Speakman, London, Hutchinson, 1979.
Tales of Humberside, music by Jim Bywater (produced Hull, 1975).
Trinity Tales, music by Alex Glasgow (televised 1975; produced Birmingham, 1975).
Our Albert (produced Hull, 1976).
The Fosdyke Saga, with Bill Tidy (produced London, 1977). London, French, 1978.
Drums along the Ginnel (produced London, 1977).
Fosdyke 2, with Bill Tidy (produced London, 1977).
Short Back and Sides (televised 1977). Published in *City Life*, edited by David Self, London, Hutchinson, 1980.
Well Good Night Then . . . (produced Hull, 1978).
Skyhooks (produced Oldham, Lancashire, 1982).
On Your Way, Riley!, music by Alex Glasgow (produced London, 1982).
A Foot on the Earth (produced Newcastle upon Tyne, 1984).
Prez, music by Bernie Cash (produced Hull and London, 1985).
Rent Party, from an idea by Nat Shapiro (produced London, 1989).
Sweet Sorrow (produced Edinburgh and London, 1990). London, Square One, 1990.
Going Home (produced Newcastle upon Tyne, 1990). London, Square One, 1990.
I Thought I Heard a Rustling (produced London, 1991). Oxford, Amber Lane, 1991.
Shooting the Legend (produced Newcastle upon Tyne, 1995).
All Credit to the Lads (produced Sheffield, 1998).

Screenplays: *The Virgin and the Gypsy*, 1970; *Juggernaut*, 1974; *It Shouldn't Happen to a Vet* (*All Things Bright and Beautiful*), 1976; *Priest of Love*, 1982; *The Inside Man*, 1984; *Keep the Aspidistra Flying*, 1997.

Radio Plays: *The Smokeless Zone*, 1961; *Counting the Legs*, 1961; *The Mating Season*, 1962; *The Rainbow Machine*, 1962; *The Seventh Day of Arthur*, 1963; *Excursion*, 1966; *The What on the Landing?*, 1967; *Fred*, 1970; *The Slow Stain*, 1973; *5 Days in '55* (*The Gilberdyke Diaries*), 1976; *Tunes*, 1979; *Swallows on the Water*, 1981; *The Journal of Vasilije Bogdanovic* (*In a Strange Land* series), 1982; *Tolpuddle*, with Vince Hill, 1982; *Who's Jimmy Dickenson?*, from his play *Well Good Night Then . . .*, 1986; *All Things Betray Thee*, adaptation of Gwyn Thomas, 1996; *The Lower Depths*, adaptation of Maxim Gorky, 1997.

Television Plays: *The Referees*, 1961; *A Smashing Day*, 1962; *So Long Charlie*, 1963; *See the Pretty Lights*, 1963; *Z Cars* series (18 episodes), 1963-65; *Ted's Cathedral*, 1964; *Fred*, 1964; *The Incident*, 1965; *The Nutter*, 1965; *Softly, Softly* series (30 episodes), 1966-76; *To See How Far It Is* (trilogy), 1968; *The First Lady* series (4 episodes), 1968-69; *Rest in Peace, Uncle Fred*, 1970; *Seventeen Per Cent Said Push Off*, 1972; *The Reluctant Juggler* (*The Edwardians* series), 1972; *Tonight We Meet Arthur Pendlebury*, 1972; *It Must Be Something in the Water* (documentary), 1973; *Brotherly Love*, 1973; *The Land of Green Ginger*, 1974; *The Needle Match*, 1974; *Goldilocks and the Three Bears*, 1974; *Wish You Were Here* (documentary), 1974; *Annie Kenney* (*Shoulder to Shoulder* series), 1974; *The Loner* series, 1975; *The Stars Look Down*, from the novel by A.J. Cronin, 1975; *Trinity Tales* series, 1975; *Willow Cabins*, 1975; *Practical Experience*, 1976; *Oh No—It's Selwyn Froggit* series, 1976; *A Tyneside Entertainment* (documentary), 1976; *Seven Days That Shook Young Jim* (*Going to Work* series), 1976; *We Are the Masters Now*, 1976; *There Are Several Businesses Like Show Business*, 1976; *The Bike*, 1977; *Short Back and Sides*, 1977; *Middlemen* series, 1977; *By Christian Judges Condemned*, 1977; *For the Love of Albert* series, 1977; *Give Us a Kiss, Christabel*, 1977; *The Eddystone Lights* (documentary), 1978; *The Party of the First Part*, 1978; *Curriculee Curricula*, music by Dave Greenslade, 1978; *Night People*, 1978; *Flambards*, from works by K.M. Peyton, 1979; *The Blacktoft Diaries*, 1979; *Reunion*, 1979; *The Good Companions*, from the novel by J.B. Priestley, 1980; *Get Lost!* series, 1981; *Barchester Chronicles*, from novels by Trollope, 1981; *The Clarion Van*, from a work by Doris Neild Chew, 1983; *Feet Foremost*, from a story by L.P. Hartley, 1983; *Bewitched*, from the story by Edith Wharton, 1983; *The Consultant*, from the novel *Invitation to Tender* by John McNeil, 1983; *Pride of Our Alley*, 1983; *The Crystal Spirit: Orwell on Jura*, 1983; *Thank You, Mrs. Clinkscales*, 1984; *The Solitary Cyclist*, from a story by Arthur Conan Doyle, 1984; *Edward Lear: On the Edge of the Sand*, 1985; *The Beiderbecke Affair* series, 1985; *A Murder Is Announced*, from the novel by Agatha Christie, 1985; *Coming Through*, 1985; *The Man with the Twisted Lip*, from a story by Arthur Conan Doyle, 1986; *Death Is Part of the Process*, from a novel by Hilda Bernstein, 1986; *Fortunes of War*, from novels by Olivia Manning, 1987; *The*

Beiderbecke Tapes, 1987; *A Very British Coup*, from the novel by Chris Mullin, 1988; *The Beiderbecke Connection*, 1988; *Campion*, from the works of Margery Allingham, 1989; *A Day in Summer*, from the novel by J.L. Carr, 1989; *Misterioso*, from his own novel, 1991; *The Patience of Maigret*, from the novel by Georges Simenon, 1992; *Maigret and the Burglar's Wife*, from the novel by Georges Simenon, 1992; *Selected Exist,* adaptation of Gwyn Thomas, 1993; *Doggin' Around,* 1994; *Oliver's Travels,* 1995; *Simisola,* adaptation of Ruth Rendell, 1996; *A Clubbable Woman,* 1996; *An Advancement of Learning,* 1996; *Deadheads,* 1997; *Bones and Silence,* 1998.

Novels

The Beiderbecke Affair. London, Methuen, 1985.
The Beiderbecke Tapes. London, Methuen, 1986.
Misterioso. London, Methuen, 1987.
The Beiderbecke Connection. London, Methuen, 1992.
Oliver's Travels. London, Little Brown, 1994.

Other

The Trouble with Abracadabra (for children). London, Macmillan, 1975.

*

Critical Studies: Introduction to *Close the Coalhouse Door*, 1969, "What's Going On Behind the Coalhouse Door," *in Sunday Times* (London), 9 February 1969, "The Playwright and His People," in *Theatre Quarterly 2* (London), April-June 1971, "One Step Forward, Two Steps Back," in *New Statesman* (London), 3 November 1972, "Views," in *Listener* (London), 29 November 1973, and "Twenty-Five Years Hard," in *Theatre Quarterly 25* (London), 1977, all by Plater; "The London Show" by Yorick Blumenfeld, in *Atlantic* (Boston), August 1969; *The Second Wave* by John Russell Taylor, London, Methuen, and New York, Hill and Wang, 1971; "Trinity Collage" by Peter Fiddick, in *Guardian* (London), 12 December 1975; article by Albert Hunt, in *British Television Drama* edited by George W. Brandt, London, Cambridge University Press, 1981.

Alan Plater comments:

(1973) Authors introducing their work fill me with gloom, like people explaining jokes: if I didn't laugh or cry before the explanation, nothing is likely to change afterwards. Therefore all I can do is look down the laundry list of my work to date and try to work out why I bothered, apart from what Mr. Perelman calls "the lash of economic necessity."

The clue lies in the place of birth and the present address: I was born and have always lived in industrial communities. I live in a place that works for a living. I never ran barefoot other than from choice. I have always eaten well and have never been deprived of anything that mattered: but I have always been close enough to the inequalities and grotesque injustices of our society to get angry about them.

(1977) Essentially I am writing a segment of the history of a society that was forged by the Industrial Revolution. This is less earnest and painful than it sounds; if an idea is important enough it is worth laughing at and one professional associate defined my method as taking fundamentally serious concepts like Politics and Religion and Life and Death and kicking the Hell out of them with old jokes. At any rate, the evidence of the more-or-less knockabout shows we've done around the regions is that people laugh the louder if the fun is spiced with a couple of centuries of inherited prejudice.

The other thought prompted by the laundry list is that not many writers have tangled with as rich and diverse a company of people and subjects: D.H. Lawrence, Mrs. Pankhurst, Sandy Powell, and Les Dawson would look good on any music-hall poster, though there might be some dispute over billing. At any rate, it underlines my feeling that it's the job of the writer at all times to head for the nearest tightrope and, in the words of Max Miller, Archie Rice, or both: "You've got to admit, lady, I do have a go."

(1982) Very little changes. The inequalities and injustices of 1973 are still there and I'm still heading for the tightrope as in 1977. We've got a new dog called The Duke (after Ellington) and I've had a programme banned by the BBC, which is a distinction of a sort. I copied some words by Jean Rhys and pinned them on the wall behind my desk. She says: "All of writing is a huge lake. There are great rivers that feed the lake, like Tolstoy and Dostoevsky. And there are trickles, like Jean Rhys. All that matters is feeding the lake. I don't matter. The lake matters. Nothing else is important. . . ."

(1988) After all that worthy stuff about living in an industrial community, here I am writing this paragraph in downtown N.W.3. In the famous words of Mr. Vonnegut: so it goes. We grow older, we change, we pursue happiness and sometimes find it. Professionally, I still head for the tightrope and Jean Rhys is still with me. So, for that matter, is The Duke.

(1998)Ten years on and *The Duke,* may he rest in peace, no longer lies at my feet. After fourteen years in London my regional loyalties and Celtic inheritance burn more furiously than ever. The world is missing its chance. As global communication spreads, the stories should be more specific and localised, yes, even parochial. We should be trading tales from our own backyards, as a constructive alternative to warfare. In reality, screen and television writers have total freedom to write anything they choose providing it's about a detective or a doctor. We are singing fewer songs to more people that ever before. When I need an oasis, I work in the theatre: a strange place to look for sanity. To be sure, we live in interesting times.

* * *

Alan Plater is one of several dramatists whose work has done much to further the cause of British regional theater. Although some of his plays have been seen in London and he has written widely for national television and the cinema, for many years his energies were directed toward ensuring the success of the ambitious Hull Arts Centre, a small 150-seat theater. This physical home was also apparently a spiritual one, for his plays are set in the northeast of England and are largely concerned with the particular problems and history of the area. "Central to the greater part of my writing," he once stated, "is man's relationship to his work," and work in this context means particularly coal mining and deep-sea fishing, two regional industries. Plater admires the "genuine solidarity and craft-consciousness" of those whose jobs involve "hideous physical working conditions," and he has captured the sheer pride in overcoming fear and danger that distinguishes the miners in his highly successful musical documentary

Close the Coalhouse Door. Plater identifies wholeheartedly with the community he describes. He shares the passion for football, and once, when he was asked about his literary influences, he replied by mentioning the popular music hall names of his youth—Norman Evans, Mooney and King. He also expresses with great fire many of the social and political attitudes, which some might call prejudices, characterizing the region: a hatred of bosses, who are usually portrayed as effete southerners, a respect for the trade union tradition, a somewhat overgeneralized call for revolution coupled with a suspicion of change, a brashly extrovert dismissal of all forms of theater that lack working-class appeal, and a socialism that refuses to accept the possibility that Labour politicians are better than stooges for capitalistic con men.

Plater's work falls into two main categories. He has written several carefully observed naturalistic plays such as *See the Pretty Lights* and *A Smashing Day,* both of which were rewritten for the stage from television scripts. In 1966 Plater met the composer and songwriter Alex Glasgow, and together they have collaborated on several musical documentaries, among them *Charlie Came to Our Town* and *Close the Coalhouse Door*. Unlike the naturalistic plays, the documentaries combine many styles of writing—cross-talk sketches, songs, impassioned oratory, summaries of historical incidents, and much satire—all of which are loosely brought together by a general theme, the history of Hull or the struggle of miners to gain decent living standards.

These two styles reveal different qualities. *See the Pretty Lights* is a gentle, warm, and moving account of a meeting between a middle-aged man and a teenage girl at the end of a pier. Both lead dull lives, and the bright lights of the seaside and their momentary friendship help to relieve—but also to underline—their social frustrations. The hero of *A Smashing Day* is a young man, Lennie, who suffers from bored aimlessness. He meekly accepts his job, the odd nights with mates who never become friends, and the routine drink. But he senses that a more exciting life awaits him somewhere if only he could find out where. He goes steady with a girl, Anne, and drifts toward marriage, which he does not want, but the social pressures are such that he persists in marrying her even after meeting Liz, an independent and sensitive girl with whom he falls in love. Many critics felt that the increased length of the stage play failed to achieve the concentrated power of the television script, and *A Smashing Day* was not successful in London. But it did provide an excellent part for the then unknown actor Hywel Bennett, and it revealed Plater's ability to describe an apparently uninteresting person in some depth. Lennie is never allowed to be either a pathetic person or an angry young man, and despite a shy insecurity that leaves an impression of spinelessness, his situation is moving, credible, and strong enough to hold the play together.

If Plater's naturalistic plays are distinguished by restraint and accuracy, the documentaries have entirely the opposite qualities: panache, a cheerful display of class bias, and loose, anything-goes technique. The best known is *Close the Coalhouse Door,* which was remarkably successful in Newcastle but received only a limited run in London, a fact that could be interpreted in several ways. The episodes of mining history are told within the context of a golden wedding reception in the Millburn family, who step out of a photograph to tell stories of strikes and hardships. Some scenes are particularly powerful: the death of a miner, the rivalry between families and men, the bitterness against the blackleg miners who went back to work too soon after a strike. Plater stressed the complicated mixture of affection and fear for the pits, together with a scorn of modernization programs whose effect was to send miners back on the dole. The songs by Glasgow caught the friendly liveliness of music halls and pubs, and in Newcastle it became a cult show. "Workers turned up in their thousands once the word got round," recalled Plater. The large Playhouse Theatre was filled to capacity night after night, with the audiences sitting in the aisles and even on the steps to the stage.

Why did the show receive such a tepid reception in London? The answer is a complex one that reveals much about Plater's work. Plater has offered two reasons—that London audiences are prejudiced against working-class plays and that in any case they could not be expected to share the associations of the North. Both may be true, but is it not the job of a dramatist to convey the importance of his theme to those who do not belong to the background? London critics generally commented on the superficial characterizations of the play, on the rather simplistic dialogue and form, and on the one-sided interpretations of history. These objections to Plater's documentaries were confirmed by two subsequent shows that did not go to London: *Simon Says!,* a wholesale attack on the British ruling classes as represented by Lord Thing, the chairman of the MCC (the governing board of English cricket); and *And a Little Love Besides,* a scathing account of the uncharitable church. The critical charge against both these plays was that the satire was too sweeping and naive to hit any real targets. Plater's documentaries are seen at their best perhaps either when the subject contains real and deeply felt observations or when the general sense of fun takes over. *Charlie Came to Our Town,* Plater's first documentary with Glasgow, is a delightfully light-hearted musical about an eccentric anarchist.

Plater's two styles complement each other, and it is sad perhaps that they have not been combined in one play. The naturalistic plays are small-scale and lack the passionate energy of the documentaries, while the documentaries are too vaguely polemical and lack the construction of the naturalistic plays. Plater is a prolific writer whose talents seem hard to control. But his adaptability is shown by the skill with which he has adjusted to the various media. His contributions to the *Z Cars* detective series on television and his screenplay for D. H. Lawrence's *The Virgin and the Gypsy* have been rightly praised. This energetic eagerness to tackle any task that interests him helped revitalize the theater in the northeast.

—John Elsom

POLIAKOFF, Stephen

Nationality: British. **Born:** London, 1 December 1952. **Education:** Westminster School, London; King's College, Cambridge, 1972-73. **Family:** Married Sandy Welch in 1983; one daughter. **Career:** Writer-in-residence, National Theatre, London, 1976-77. **Awards:** *Evening Standard* award, 1976; BAFTA award, 1980; Venice Film Festival prize, 1989; Bergamo Film Festival prize, 1991; *Evening Standard* British Film Award, best film, 1992, for *Close My Eyes.* **Agent:** Casarotto Ramsay Ltd., National House, 60-66 Wardour Street, London W1V 3HP, England.

Publications

Plays

Granny (produced London, 1969).
Bambi Ramm (produced London, 1970).
A Day with My Sister (produced Edinburgh, 1971).
Lay-By, with others (produced Edinburgh and London, 1971). London, Calder and Boyars, 1972.
Pretty Boy (produced London, 1972).
Theatre Outside (produced London, 1973).
Berlin Days (produced London, 1973).
The Carnation Gang (produced London, 1974).
Clever Soldiers (produced London, 1974). Included in *Plays: One*, 1989.
Heroes (produced London, 1975).
Hitting Town (produced London, 1975; New York, 1979). Included in *Hitting Town, and City Sugar*, 1976.
City Sugar (produced London, 1975; New York, 1978). Included in *Hitting Town, and City Sugar*, 1976.
Hitting Town, and City Sugar. London, Eyre Methuen, 1976; revised edition 1978.
Strawberry Fields (produced London, 1977; New York, 1978) London, Eyre Methuen, 1977.
Shout Across the River (produced London, 1978; New York, 1979). London, Eyre Methuen, 1979.
American Days (produced London, 1979; New York, 1980). London, Eyre Methuen, 1979.
The Summer Party (produced Sheffield, 1980). London, Eyre Methuen, 1980.
Caught on a Train (televised 1980). With *Favourite Nights*, London, Methuen, 1982.
Favourite Nights (produced London, 1981). With *Caught on a Train*, London, Methuen, 1982.
Soft Targets (televised 1982). With *Runners*, London, Methuen, 1984.
Breaking the Silence (produced London, 1984). London, Methuen, 1984.
Runners (screenplay). With *Soft Targets*, London, Methuen, 1984.
Coming in to Land (produced London, 1987). London, Methuen, 1987.
Playing with Trains (produced London, 1989). London, Methuen, 1989.
She's Been Away, and Hidden City (screenplays). London, Methuen, 1989.
Plays: One (includes *Clever Soldiers, Hitting Town, City Sugar, Shout Across the River, American Days, Strawberry Fields*). London, Methuen, 1989.
Close My Eyes (screenplay). London, Methuen, 1991.
Sienna Red (produced London, 1992). London, Methuen, 1992.
Plays: Two (includes *Breaking the Silence*; *Playing with Trains*; *She's Been Away*; *Century*). London, Methuen, 1994.
Sweet Panic. London, Methuen, 1996.
Blinded by the Sun and Sweet Panic. London, Methuen, 1996.
Plays: Three (includes *Caught on a Train*; *Coming in to Land*; *Close My Eyes*). London, Methuen, 1998.
Talk of the City. London, Methuen, 1998.

Screenplays: *Runners*, 1983; *Hidden City*, 1988; *She's Been Away*, 1989; *Close My Eyes*, 1991; *Century*, 1993.

Television Plays: *Stronger Than the Sun*, 1977; *Bloody Kids*, 1980; *Caught on a Train*, 1980; *Soft Targets*, 1982.

*

Critical Studies: "Stephen Poliakoff's Drama for the Post-Scientific Age" by Matthew Martin, in *Theatre Journal* (Baltimore, Maryland), May 1993, pp. 197-211; "Stephen Poliakoff" by William W. Demastes, in *British Playwrights, 1956-1995: A Research and Production Sourcebook*, Westport, Connecticut, Greenwood, 1996.

Theatrical Activities:
Director: **Films**—*Hidden City*, 1988; *Close My Eyes*, 1991; *Century*, 1993.

* * *

Stephen Poliakoff first achieved recognition in 1975 with the two related plays *Hitting Town* and *City Sugar*. The plays attack a series of readily identifiable targets—the tackiness and squalor of new inner-city developments, the alienating effects of fast-food shops and discos, the banality of pop radio DJs. But here, as so often subsequently, the rather crude political context is less the real subject of the drama than a convenient backdrop against which a series of strangely vulnerable oddball characters rehearse their particular desperation. Poliakoff's is a theater of individual gesture rather than generalized political analysis. Although his plays appear to offer a series of thematically related attacks on contemporary society in loosely political terms, it is the emotional subtext that is most important.

In *Hitting Town* it is the awkward movement of a lonely woman and her waywardly embittered younger brother through a desolate provincial night on the town and toward an incestuous bed that creates most of the dramatic tension. Likewise, in the screenplay for *Runners* it is the tentative efforts of the father to achieve some kind of relationship with his young runaway daughter that holds the audience's attention, not the more general theme of hopelessness in the face of mass youth unemployment that the film presents as its primary concern. Indeed, the daughter is not presented as a passive victim of circumstances. Like so many of Poliakoff's central protagonists, she is a survivor, shell-shocked but still in possession of a tentative resilience and surviving in a half-glimpsed London world of the dispossessed by distributing advertising literature.

Poliakoff returns continually to city nightlife. This is the time when his characters can be displayed at their loneliest, a situation that brings about the very existence of the all-night radio phone-in that provides the structural continuity of *City Sugar*. And it is this pervading sense of isolation in supposedly crowded locations that gives his plays their peculiar clarity, for Poliakoff's stage city is a curiously unpopulated one. In *Hitting Town* the sister and brother first visit a Wimpy Bar in which the only other person present is a waitress, who will again be the sole witness to their dialogue in a shopping area. Whether other people are assumed to be present, and thus a further cause of the sister's worry at her brother's deliberately provocative behavior, is deliberately left unclear, but no such ambiguity exists by the time the three of them arrive at a disco in which the only direct evidence of the presence of others comes from the voice of the unseen DJ.

In *Favourite Nights* Catherine, a language teacher by day and an escort by night, takes her German businessman-student and her sister to a casino in which we otherwise see only a croupier, an American punter, and Alan, an official of the club. The absence of characters who must be understood to be present in places such as discos and casinos intensifies the way in which Poliakoff's characters see themselves as a part of, and yet separate from, the contemporary world. Catherine's manic attempts to beat the bank yet again in order to avoid the sexual compromise potentially involved in letting her client pay for their evening out is seen as if in a filmic close-up from which all the extras are excluded, and her attempts to communicate with her lover, Alan, in a locale in which contact between the staff and punters is banned is given a curious intensity by the presence of spy cameras unsupported by any other realized members of the casino management.

Given all of this, it is not surprising that the medium of film has come to seem increasingly attractive to Poliakoff. In *Hidden City,* the first film he directed, the fascination with the city as a secret world is still evident. A bored mathematical psychologist meets up with a strange young woman who reveals a literal underworld of tunnels and hidden chambers in pursuit of officially dead newsreel film footage but who stumbles by accident on evidence of a long since buried nuclear scandal. But afterward it is the image of the hidden city rather than the concern with the hidden scandal that remains in the mind.

Even when Poliakoff moves out of a city environment, as in *Strawberry Fields,* he takes his characters from London and up the motorway vertebrae of England and in and out of service stations and lay-bys that are as unpopulated as his all-night bars and casinos. Kevin and Charlotte set off to meet at prearranged points other members of the Fascist group to which they belong. In this instance the lack of contact with any other characters—with the exception of a police constable and a hitchhiker who are shot dead at the ends of the first and second acts, respectively—stresses their lack of contact with any reality, other than Kevin's half-remembered images of the 1960s, to support their ideology. They see themselves increasingly as latter-day Bonnies and Clydes, but the paranoia of persecution and pursuit on which their stance is built is undercut by the nonappearance of the police who are supposedly chasing them.

This thematic use of the journey is another manifestation of the characters as socially and politically rootless and as unconnected to the details of everyday life. In his 1980 television play *Caught on a Train,* Poliakoff uses a railway journey across Europe in which a series of characters—from a collection of anarchically politicized football hooligans to a young American thoroughly disenchanted with Europe—meet in transit without ever properly communicating as an informing metaphor for an account of contemporary malaise. The film marked a major development in his work, and it is interesting that he was to return to the central motif of the train journey in his most impressive stage play, *Breaking the Silence*.

For the first time since his earliest work, in *Breaking the Silence* Poliakoff moved the action into the past, Russia in the immediate aftermath of the Revolution. Nikolai, a wealthy Jewish aristocrat based loosely on the playwright's own Russian grandfather, is turned out of his spacious accommodations and is made a telephone surveyor of the Northern Railway. To this end he is given a train to patrol a region where telephone poles have yet to be erected, all the time working single-mindedly toward his life ambition of producing the first synchronized talking pictures. He is to be thwarted, however, and the play finishes as he prepares for exile in England, his pictures as silent as the northern region's telephone system. It is again a journey of isolation in which all attempts at communication are literally and metaphorically denied, but it is also another story of a survivor. Poliakoff has for the first time properly united the individual concerns of the narrative with a larger thematic structure. His concern with the links between the political worlds of the East and West, and thus with his own sense of cultural duality, was continued in *Coming in to Land,* which opened at the National Theatre in 1987, and in *Playing with Trains.*

—John Bull

POLLOCK, Sharon

Nationality: Canadian. **Born:** Sharon Chalmers, Fredericton, New Brunswick, 19 April 1936. **Education:** University of New Brunswick, Fredericton, 2 years. **Family:** Married Ross Pollock in 1954; six children. **Career:** Actress in New Brunswick, and with touring group, Prairie Players, Calgary; head of the playwriting division, Department of Drama, University of Alberta, Edmonton, 1976-77; director of the Playwrights' Colony, Banff School of Fine Arts, Alberta, 1977-81; playwright-in-residence, Alberta Theatre Projects, Calgary, 1977-79, National Arts Centre, Ottawa, 1981, 1982, and Regina Public Library, Saskatchewan, 1986-87; dramaturge, 1982-83, associate artistic director, 1983-84, and artistic director, 1984, Theatre Calgary. Member, 1979-80, and chair 1980-81, Canada Council Advisory Arts Panel; vice-chair Playwrights Canada National Executive, 1981-83. **Awards:** Dominion Drama Festival award, for acting, 1966; Nellie award, for radio play, 1981; Governor-General's award, 1981, 1986; Alberta award of excellence, 1983; Chalmers award, 1984; Canada Council Senior Arts grant, 1984; Alberta Writers Guild award, 1986; Alberta Literary Foundation award, 1987. Honorary Doctorate: University of New Brunswick, 1986. **Address:** 319 Manora Drive N.E., Calgary, Alberta T2A 4R2, Canada.

Publications

Plays

A Compulsory Option. Edmonton, Department of Culture, Youth, and Recreation, 1970; revised version (produced Vancouver, 1972; as *No! No! No!* produced Toronto, 1977), Vancouver, New Play Centre, 1972.

Walsh (produced Calgary, 1973). Vancouver, New Play Centre, 1972; revised version (produced Stratford, Ontario, 1974), Vancouver, Talonbooks, 1974.

New Canadians (for children; produced Vancouver, 1973).

Superstition Throu' the Ages (for children; produced Vancouver, 1973).

Wudjesay? (for children; produced Vancouver, 1974).

A Lesson in Swizzlery (for children; produced New Westminster, British Columbia, 1974).

The Rose and the Nightingale (for children), adaptation of the story by Oscar Wilde (produced Vancouver, 1974).

The Star-child (for children), adaptation of the story by Oscar Wilde (produced Vancouver, 1974).
The Happy Prince (for children), adaptation of the story by Oscar Wilde (produced Vancouver, 1974).
And Out Goes You? (produced Vancouver, 1975).
The Komagata Maru Incident (produced Vancouver, 1976; London, 1985). Toronto, Playwrights, 1978.
Blood Relations (as *My Name Is Lisbeth*, produced New Westminster, British Columbia, 1976; revised version, as *Blood Relations*, produced Edmonton, 1980; New York, 1983; Derby and London, 1985). Included in *Blood Relations and Other Plays*, 1981; in *Plays by Women 3*, edited by Michelene Wandor, London, Methuen, 1984.
Tracings: The Fraser Story (collective work), with others (produced Edmonton, 1977).
The Wreck of the National Line Car (for children; produced Calgary, 1978).
Mail vs. Female (produced Calgary, 1979).
Chautauqua Spelt E-N-E-R-G-Y (for children; produced Calgary, 1979).
One Tiger to a Hill (produced Edmonton, 1980; revised version produced Lennoxville, Quebec, and New York, 1981). Included in *Blood Relations and Other Plays*, 1981.
Generations (produced Calgary, 1980). Included in *Blood Relations and Other Plays*, 1981.
Blood Relations and Other Plays. Edmonton, NeWest Press, 1981.
Whiskey Six (produced Calgary, 1983).
Doc. Toronto, Playwrights, 1986.
Heroines: Three Plays. Red Deer, Red Deer College Press, 1992.
Saucy Jack. Winnipeg, Blizzard Publishing, 1994.
Fair Liberty's Call. Toronto, Coach House Press, 1995.

Other Play: *The Great Drag Race; or, Smoked, Choked, and Croaked* (for children).

Radio Plays: *Split Seconds in the Death Of*, 1971; *31 for 2; We to the Gods; Waiting; The B Triple P Plan; In Memory Of; Generation*, 1980; *Sweet Land of Liberty*, 1980; *Intensive Care; Mary Beth Goes to Calgary; Mrs. Yale and Jennifer* (8 episodes); *In the Beginning Was*.

Television Plays: *Portrait of a Pig*; *The Larsens*; *Ransom*; *Free Our Sisters, Free Ourselves*; *The Person's Case*; *Country Joy* (6 episodes).

*

Manuscript Collection: University of Calgary, Alberta.

Critical Studies: "Sharon Pollock" by Gilbert Reid, in *Profiles in Canadian Literature*, edited by Jeffrey Heath, Toronto, Dundurn, 1986; "Women Dramatists: Sharon Pollock and Judy Thompson" by Diane Bessai, in *Post-Colonial English Drama: Commonwealth Drama Since 1960*, edited by Bruce King, New York and London, St. Martin's, 1992; "Crossing Borders: Sharon Pollock's Revisitation of Canadian Frontiers" by Anne Nothof, in *Modern Drama* (Downsview, Ontario), Winter 1995, pp. 475-87; "Broken Toys: The Destruction of the National Hero in the Early History Plays of Sharon Pollock" by Heidi J. Holder, in *Essays in Theatre Etudes* (Canada), May 1996, pp. 131-45; "Painting the Background: Metadrama and the Fabric of History in Sharon Pollock's *Blood Relations*" by Herb Wylie, in *Essays in Theatre Etudes* (Canada), May 1997, pp. 1914-205.

Theatrical Activities:
Director: **Plays**—Some of her own plays; *Betrayal* and *A Slight Ache* by Harold Pinter; *The Mousetrap* by Agatha Christie; *Scapin* by Molière; *The Gingerbread Lady* by Neil Simon; *The Bear* and *A Marriage Proposal* by Chekhov; *Period of Adjustment* by Tennessee Williams; *The Indian Wants the Bronx* by Israel Horovitz; *The Effect of Gamma Rays on Man-in-the-Moon Marigolds* by Paul Zindel; *Buried Child* by Sam Shepard; and others.

Actress: **Plays**—Roles in some of her own plays; title role in *Lysistrata* by Aristophanes; Nancy in *The Knack* by Ann Jellicoe; Amanda in *Private Lives* by Noël Coward; Miss Cooper in *Separate Tables* by Terence Rattigan; Bunny in *The House of Blue Leaves* by John Guare; Nell in *Endgame* by Samuel Beckett; Maddy in *All That Fall* by Arthur Miller; Polina in *The Seagull* by Chekhov; title role in *Miss Julie* by Strindberg; Alison in *Look Back in Anger* by John Osborne; The Psychiatrist in *Agnes of God* by John Pielmeier; and others.

* * *

Like many Canadian plays of their period, Sharon Pollock's early plays explore the country's history, employing documents but moving from them in a subjective response to events, leading to an investigation of character and political process. In a note to the text of *The Komagata Maru Incident*, Pollock posits that drama "is a theatrical impression of an historical event seen through the optique of the stage and the mind of the playwright." Indeed, as Anne Nothof has pointed out, Pollock's history plays "are essentially iconoclastic, deconstructing comfortable assumptions about the growth of. . .nation and the peaceful integration of 'others'."

Pollock's second play, *Walsh*, first explores her "cynic[ism] about ideas, theories and ideologies," as Carl Berger puts it. It is also her first attempt to use documents to support her narrative. In the first draft, speeches reproduced from historical sources preceded each scene to provide exposition; this rather awkward device was replaced in the published version by a prologue that occurs out of time and that shows us the eventual moral decline of the protagonist. It also provides fewer but more easily assimilated historical details than the original speeches. The play recreates the dilemma of Major John Walsh of the Northwest Mounted Police, who in 1876 is caught between the Canadian government of Sir John A. MacDonald (hidden behind the symbol of Queen Victoria, as Great White Mother) and the American Indian Nations, symbolized by Chief Sitting Bull. Sitting Bull is cast as a shaman figure, and critics who have found the character so pious as to be unreal have ignored the fact that he is intended not as a rounded character in a drama but as a metonym of his dying race, a race caught in a modern European world it cannot resist but still true to the primitive but doomed values of the "Sacred Hoop" of life. Major Walsh, a strict militarist, attempts to extend white logic to the Indian view of the world and discovers that he does not himself wish to accept the detached political logic of his white superiors. He also discovers that legalities and self-interest motivate the Canadian government. In one short and highly dramatic speech, he capitulates in the face of these discoveries, reverting to his background and his sense of duty, and by doing so seals his own moral doom. The young recruit Clarence reverses Walsh's spiritual decline, learning to see native people as human beings even as Walsh forces himself to regard them merely as political pawns. Their dialectic expresses a central theme of the play: the man without responsibility can remain idealistic and humane; the bureaucrat trapped between forces he cannot control, but must administer, falls victim to the events of history. The staging echoes this stark reality—a few representative figures on an almost bare stage play out a moment in a larger event and do so in an unadorned and internalized landscape.

The trapped figure reappears in *The Komagata Maru Incident* in the person of the spy William Hopkinson. In this play Pollock returns to a form similar to that of *Walsh* after an experiment in burlesque history in *And Out Goes You? Komagata Maru* concerns the historic refusal of the turn-of-the century provincial government to allow a boatload of East Indian refugees to enter British Columbia. The ship remains in Vancouver harbor for two months, and the play explores the racial and legal aspects of the event. Sent as a spy, Hopkinson is forced to come to terms with his own racial self-image (he is half-East Indian) and with his attempts to survive in a white world. Hopkinson is a rounder character than Walsh; the issues are not as simple, and the protagonist confronts not only the social attitudes that surround him but also the weaker side of his own personality. The stagecraft is also more sophisticated than in early plays: the action moves back and forth from the ship to other locales; the secondary characters are interesting in themselves; the theme, though it centers on a serious local problem of a particular time, discusses universal issues of fear, envy, and ambition.

Although these first plays concern the reactions of men to historical events, the later plays show a growing interest by Pollock in the reactions of women in general and herself in particular. Her most successful play, *Blood Relations*, a reworking of an idea first written as *My Name Is Lisbeth*, is a study of the American murderer Lizzie Borden. In a powerfully metadramatic design, Lizzie switches roles with her actress friend (possibly lover) and watches "herself" repeat the action that led to the murder even as she struggles to resist a nineteenth-century construction of the female. The question of culpability ("Did you do it, Lizzie, did you?") is extended through an elaborate pattern of blood imagery to include the audience. As agents of the folklore that condemns her—the ending suggests—Americans and even Canadians are as guilty of the murder as is Lizzie. This contention is supported not only by the double action but by Pollock's most successful writing, a well-designed and intricate web of language that demonstrates a significant leap from the earlier dialogue.

The semiautobiographical *Doc* continues Pollock's search into the feminine memories of family and the formative effect of family on women. The play has attracted almost as much attention as *Blood Relations*, though it is arguably a less well designed and less original play. The speeches are often beautiful and compelling in themselves; the general tone, intimate and honest.

Pollock's play *Fair Liberty's Call* returns to Canadian history, this time the story of a United Empire Loyalist family. As in *Doc*, the play presents a domineering father. Ironically named (King) George, the UEL father is intent upon the acquisition of land and switches allegiances as necessary to further his own self-interest. His sons take ideological positions, one joining the American Revolution and the other joining a Loyalist regiment. When the Loyalist son is driven to suicide, his position is taken over by his sister, Emily, disguised under the name Eddie. Reconstructing her gender allows Emily/Eddie to escape restrictions on women and the fate of her mother, driven mad by events, but it exposes her to the horrors of war and eventually to a moral crisis. Although the action concerns men's wars, the play opens with a montage of women's voices (the mother and daughters), turns around cycles of bloodletting, and ultimately argues—once again—that history depends upon who is telling it and upon the teller's gender, race, and social position. Subthemes of the treatment of black refugees and First Nations People extend the feminist theme. The ending allows a hint of transformation as the daughter Annie convinces the vengeful Anderson that endless reprisals only bar the future for the children of both sides, and the mother is finally able to see her footprint in the soil of a new land. This ending, reminiscent of other feminist writings of transformation, is, however, acutely unhistorical, demonstrating Pollock's willingness to use documents loosely to achieve political effect.

In her own career, as in the women she creates, Sharon Pollock refuses compromise, resists male and established authority, and shatters historical myth. Consistent in her political vision, she is a compelling voice in Canadian theater.

—Reid Gilbert

POMERANCE, Bernard

Nationality: American. **Born:** Brooklyn, New York, in 1940. **Education:** University of Chicago. **Career:** Cofounder, Foco Novo theatre group, London, 1972. Lives in London. **Awards:** New York Drama Critics Circle award, Tony award, Obie award, and Outer Circle award, all 1979. **Address:** c/o Faber and Faber Ltd., 3 Queen Square, London WC1N 3AU, England.

Publications

Plays

High in Vietnam, Hot Damn; Hospital; Thanksgiving Before Detroit (produced London, 1971). Published in *Gambit 6* (London), 1972.

Foco Novo (produced London, 1972).

Someone Else Is Still Someone (produced London, 1974).

A Man's a Man, adaptation of a play by Brecht (produced London, 1975).

The Elephant Man (produced Exeter and London, 1977; New York, 1979). New York, Grove Press, 1979; London, Faber, 1980; in *Best American Plays*, New York, Crown, 1983.

Quantrill in Lawrence (produced London, 1980). London, Faber, 1981.

Melons (produced London, 1985; New Haven, Connecticut, 1987).

Novel

We Need to Dream All This Again. New York, Viking, 1987.

*

Critical Studies: "The Elephant Man as Romantic Critic of Shakespeare" by Frederick W. Shilstone, in *Studies in the*

Humanties (Indian, Pennsylvania), June 1985, pp. 29-38; "Multiple and Virtual: Theatrical Space in *The Elephant Man*" by Vera Jiji, in *The Theatrical Space,* edited by James Redmond, Cambridge, Cambridge University Press, 1987.

* * *

An American living in England, Bernard Pomerance found productions for his early plays in London's fringe theater of the 1970s. Yet it was his play *The Elephant Man*, produced on Broadway in 1979 subsequent to an English premiere and an off-off-Broadway presentation, that established Pomerance as a playwright. An immense critical and popular success, the play won several awards, including an Obie and one from the New York Drama Critics Circle.

The title of the biographical drama was a sideshow term applied to John Merrick (1863-90), a noted freak of Victorian England so hideously malformed by an incurable and then unknown disease, now diagnosed as neurofibromatosis, that he was cruelly exploited as a traveling show oddity. Rescued from exhibition by the anatomist Frederick Treves, he was given safe shelter in London Hospital in Whitechapel, which raised public donations for his maintenance and became his home for the six years before his death. Merrick became a curio studied by science and visited by fashionable society, which found him a man of surprising intelligence and sensitivity. Treves's published account of Merrick's life sparked Pomerance's interest in the subject.

In 22 often trenchant, short scenes identified by title placard, *The Elephant Man* effectively employs a presentational and Brechtian style to tell its story. In act 1 Treves encounters Merrick in a sideshow, later offers him shelter after a mob almost kills him, and determines with condescending compassion to create for his patient the illusion of normality. To this purpose he enlists the actress Mrs. Kendal to befriend Merrick. The second act shifts the focus from physician to patient as we watch the progress of Treves's social engineering. The man fits himself into the role of the correct Victorian gentleman, but not without questioning the rules he is told to obey.

As the metamorphosis continues, fashionable society lionizes Merrick, for he lets them see him not as an individual but as a mirror of qualities they like to claim. Noting to Mrs. Kendal that sexual loneliness continues to isolate him from other men and that he has never seen a naked woman, the actress kindly obliges by baring her breasts, only to be interrupted by a scandalized Treves who orders her out for her impropriety. She does not return. Interpreting the experience as defining his own limitations, Merrick realizes that his normality has been an illusion, and he suicidally lets his huge head drop unsupported, causing strangulation. Simultaneously with his patient's development, Treves comes to question his own principles and those of his class and painfully perceives Merrick's subtle exploitation by science and society. Pomerance is concerned with the themes that compassion, society and its conventional morality, and the idea of normality are at bottom destructive illusions.

Pomerance's play is at once theatrically effective, emotionally compelling, and intellectually provoking. Yet the drama has problems. More ideas are unleashed than are developed, and some of the ideas are overstated in the later scenes. Moreover, the shift in focus from Treves to Merrick and then back to the former near the conclusion unbalances the center of the play, and the physician's loss of self-assurance demands more preparation. But such problems are minor when considering the play's overriding strengths.

As John Merrick is an exemplary victim of nineteenth-century greed, intolerance, and samaritanism, the aging Apache leader Caracol, alias John Lame Eagle, in *Melons* is a noble turned vengeful savage who is exploited and oppressed by white civilization. Regarded as a messiah by his Pueblo settlement, Caracol confronts his old adversary, the U.S. cavalry, now representing an oil company with drilling rights on Indian land, recalls past humiliations at white hands, and ultimately reveals his ritual decapitation of two geologists sent by the company to find oil on the reservation. The revelation causes both his death and that of his white antagonist. Caracol's doomed attempts to hold onto ancient ways and his white enemy's callous materialism reflect the Indian's inability to accommodate the conquering culture. Pomerance employs as a narrator an Indian activist who was raised by whites and who encompasses the tension between both cultures but is powerless to prevent the conflict's bloody conclusion. The narrator strides back in time to tell the Caracol story in a fractured account burdened with commentary, flashbacks, and a lengthy debate with Caracol that hinders the forward momentum and immediate action of the play. While praising its ambitions, many critics who viewed the 1985 London production by the Royal Shakespeare Company faulted the play's structural and storytelling flaws and the consequent shortcomings in overall theatrical effectiveness.

Quantrill in Lawrence, an earlier play, displays similar deficiencies in craft and the playwright's characteristic attraction to historical settings and situations. The play combines a plot derived from Euripides' *Bacchae* with the burning of Lawrence, Kansas, in 1863 by the Confederate outlaw Quantrill. The liberation of women and of suppressed desires are the play's thematic concerns.

Pomerance is a talented playwright committed to tackling large themes. His work is notable for its interest in biographical and historical sources as a means by which to examine contemporary problems.

—Christian H. Moe

POWNALL, David

Nationality: British. **Born:** Liverpool, 19 May 1938. **Education:** Lord Wandsworth College, Long Sutton, Hampshire, 1949-56; University of Keele, Staffordshire, 1956-60, B.A. (honors) 1960. **Family:** Married 1) Glenys Elsie Jones in 1961 (divorced 1971), one son; 2) Mary Ellen Ray in 1972 (divorced 1990), one son; 3) Alex in 1993, one son. **Career:** Personnel officer, Ford Motor Co., Dagenham, Essex, 1960-63; personnel manager, Anglo-American, Zambia, 1963-69; resident writer, Century Theatre touring group, 1970-72, and Duke's Playhouse, Lancaster, 1972-75; founder and resident writer, Paines Plough Theatre, Coventry, 1975-80. **Awards:** Giles Cooper award, 1981, 1985; John Whiting award, for drama, 1982, 1986; Sony Gold award, 1995. **Member:** Royal Society of Literature, 1976. **Agent:** Andrew Hewson, John Johnson Ltd., 45-47 Clerkenwell Green, London EC1R 0HT, England.

PUBLICATIONS

Plays

As We Lie (produced Cheltenham, 1973). Zambia, Nkana-Kitwe, 1969.
How Does the Cuckoo Learn to Fly? (produced on tour, 1970).
How to Grow a Guerrilla (produced Preston, Lancashire, 1971).
All the World Should Be Taxed (produced, Lancaster, 1971).
The Last of the Wizards (for children; produced Windermere, Cumbria, and London, 1972).
Gaunt (produced Lancaster, 1973).
Lions and Lambs (produced on Lancashire tour, 1973).
The Dream of Chief Crazy Horse (for children; produced Fleetwood, Lancashire, 1973). London, Faber, 1975.
Beauty and the Beast, music by Stephen Boxer (produced Lancaster, 1973).
The Human Cartoon Show (produced Lancaster, 1974).
Crates on Barrels (produced on Lancashire tour, 1974; London, 1984).
The Pro (produced London, 1975).
Lile Jimmy Williamson (produced Lancaster, 1975).
Buck Ruxton (produced Lancaster, 1975).
Ladybird, Ladybird (produced Edinburgh and London, 1976).
Music to Murder By (produced Canterbury, 1976; Miami, 1984). London, Faber, 1978.
A Tale of Two Town Halls (produced Lancaster, 1976).
Motocar, and Richard III, Part Two, music by Stephen Boxer (produced Edinburgh and London, 1977). London, Faber, 1979.
An Audience Called Édouard (produced London, 1978). London, Faber, 1979.
Seconds at the Fight for Madrid (produced Bristol, 1978).
Livingstone and Sechele (produced Edinburgh, 1978; London, 1980; New York, 1982).
Barricade (produced on tour, 1979).
Later (produced London, 1979).
The Hot Hello (produced Edinburgh, 1981).
Beef (produced London, 1981; New York, 1986). Published in *Best Radio Plays of 1981*, London, Methuen, 1982.
Master Class (produced Leicester, 1983; London, and Washington, D.C., 1984; New York, 1986). London, Faber, 1983.
Pride and Prejudice, adaptation of the novel by Jane Austen (produced Leicester, 1983; New Haven, Connecticut, 1985; London, 1986).
Ploughboy Monday (broadcast 1985). Published in *Best Radio Plays of 1985*, London, Methuen, 1986.
The Viewing (produced London, 1987).
Black Star (produced Bolton, Lancashire, 1987).
The Edge (produced London, 1987).
King John's Jewel (produced Birmingham, 1987).
Rousseau's Tale (produced London, 1991).
My Father's House (produced Birmingham, 1991).
Nijinsky: Death of a Faun (produced Edinburgh, 1991).
Dinner Dance (produced Leicester, 1991; London, 1992).
Elgar's Rondo (produced Stratford and London, 1993).

Radio Plays: *Free Ferry*, 1972; *Free House*, 1973; *A Place in the Country*, 1974; *An Old New Year*, 1974; *Fences*, 1976; *Under the Wool*, 1976; *Back Stop*, 1977; *Butterfingers*, 1981; *The Mist People*, 1981; *Flos*, 1982; *Ploughboy Monday*, 1985; *Beloved Latitudes*, from his own novel, 1986; *The Bridge at Orbigo*, 1987; *A Matter of Style*, 1988; *Plato Not Nato*, 1990; *The Glossomaniacs*, 1990; *Bringing Up Nero*, 1991; *Kitty Wilkinson*, 1991; *Dreams and Censorship*, 1993; *Fishing for Ghosts*, 1994; *Selling the Archbishop*, 1994; *Curves of Clio*, 1995; *Under the Table*, 1995; *Something to Remember You By*, 1995; *Elgar's Third*, 1995; *Brahms on a Slow Train*, 1996; *Gift from the North*, 1997; *Pound on Mr. Greenhill*, 1997; *Satchel Mouth*, 1997; *Stolen Time*, 1998; *Making Love, War, and Peace*, 1998; *An Epiphanous Use of the Microphone*, 1998.

Television Plays: *High Tides*, 1976; *Mackerel Sky*, 1976; *Return Fare*, 1978; *Follow the River Down*, 1979; *Room for an Inward Light*, 1980; *The Sack Judies*, 1981; *Love's Labour* (*Maybury* series), 1983; *The Great White Mountain* (*Mountain Men* series), 1987; *Something to Remember You By*, 1991.

Novels

The Raining Tree War. London, Faber, 1974.
African Horse. London, Faber, 1975.
God Perkins. London, Faber, 1977.
Light on a Honeycomb. London, Faber, 1978.
Beloved Latitudes. London, Gollancz, 1981.
The White Cutter. London, Gollancz, 1988; New York, Viking, 1989.
The Gardener. London, Gollancz, 1990.
Stagg and His Mother. London, Gollancz, 1991.
The Sphinx and the Sybarites. London, Sinclair Stephenson, 1993.

Short Stories

My Organic Uncle and Other Stories. London, Faber, 1976.

Poetry

An Eagle Each: Poems of the Lakes and Elsewhere, with Jack Hill. Carlisle, Cumbria, Arena, 1972.
Another Country. Liskeard, Cornwall, Harry Chambers/Peterloo Poets, 1978.

Other

Between Ribble and Lune: Scenes from the North-West, photographs by Arthur Thompson. London, Gollancz, 1980.
The Bunch from Bananas (for children). London, Gollancz, 1980; New York, Macmillan, 1981.

Editor, with Gareth Pownall, *The Fisherman's Bedside Book*. London, Windward, 1980.

*

Critical Studies: "Individual Talent and the Will of the People in David Pownall's Master Class" by Bryon Nelson, in *Midwest Quarterly: A Journal of Contemporary Thought* (Pittsburg, Kansas) Winter 1988, pp. 157-70; "David Pownall's Master Class–Set Unseen?" by Trevor Cobain, in *Theatre History in Canada, Historie du Theatre au Canada* (Toronto, Ontario) Spring 1989, pp. 65-79.

* * *

Beginning in the 1970s David Pownall wrote prolifically, producing several novels and numerous plays for the stage, radio, and television. Partly because few of the plays are published, he had little attention until the success of *Master Class* at the Old Vic in 1984. A second well-known stage work is an adaptation of Jane Austen's novel *Pride and Prejudice*.

A few of Pownall's plays are conventional pieces of storytelling, for instance, *Ladybird, Ladybird*, which shows Miriam's return to Liverpool after 50 years in the United States. A young war widow, she had escaped her environment and left a baby son behind. Now she comes back for a first meeting with her grandchildren, two men and a girl in a wheelchair, and the play shows the twists, turns, shifts, and complexities in the new relationships. Other stories set in the present are *Fences*, for radio, in which an upper-class girl falls in love with a stable boy, and two for television, *Return Fare*, in which a discharged mental patient goes to live with his brother, and *Follow the River Down*, in which an old man relives his life as he follows a river to its mouth.

In Pownall's most distinctive plays something quite unexpected breaks through, identifiable reality changing to fantasy or taking on ritualistic aspects. In the early, strange *How to Grow a Guerrilla* an English garden has run wild and turned to jungle. A moronic youth plays soldiers, and a takeover by gangsters is followed by one by black police. *Motocar* is set in Rhodesia 10 days before independence (indefinitely in the future when Pownall wrote it in 1976), with the action taking place in a mental hospital run by whites for blacks. A suspected black terrorist named Motocar is brought in for psychiatric examination. A poetic ritual eventually develops in which the blacks force the four whites to relive aspects of the black experience of oppression.

Many of this group of plays uses historical events and changes and adapts them. *Richard* III, *Part Two* ingeniously weaves together George Orwell in 1984 and Richard III in 1484 by way of a board game about Richard called Betrayal. Games and men must both be properly marketed for success, and while Richard failed in this, Orwell knew it. The 30-character *Seconds at the Fight for Madrid* is set in November 1936. The audience meets English, Americans, Germans, a Russian, peasants, and beggars who discuss the fate of three showgirls and a musician who have blundered into the military zone. The picture of the Spanish Civil War is completed with appearances by the king, Franco, Hitler, and, since Pownall is ever imaginative, Don Juan and Don Quixote. *Barricade*, set in the Spanish countryside in May 1937, has anarchists joined by two gypsies and a young English army officer on a cycling holiday. In curiously stylized scenes the gypsies attempt to awaken the Englishman politically. *An Audience Called Édouard* starts with the pose of two men and two women as in *Le Déjeuner sur l'herbe,* with an unseen Manet imagined painting the work somewhere among the audience. The chatter of the foursome is disturbed by two intruders from the river, one of whom is Karl Marx, indeed a disrupter of the harmony of La Belle Époque. In *The Bridge at Orbigo*, for radio, a referee and a footballer retracing the pilgrim route to Santiago de Compostela are guided into the past by a priest. Most difficult of all, in *Music to Murder By* a Californian woman musicologist conjures up the ghosts of Gesualdo, an Italian Renaissance composer, and Philip Heseltine, alias Peter Warlock, a scholar and composer who killed himself in 1930. The play is an illustration of links between creativity and violence.

A third group of plays treats historical subjects more objectively. *All the World Should Be Taxed* emphasizes political elements in the Nativity story. *The Dream of Chief Crazy Horse*, with 70 parts and written for schools, surveys 10,000 years of Indian history. In *Livingstone and Sechele* the young missionary David Livingstone makes his first convert, Sechele, chief of the Crocodile people in South Africa and is obliged to scrutinize his own faith. The other characters are their wives, submissive Mary and Mokoton, a fifth wife who schemes to keep her man from the outsiders. *Black Star* takes as its obscure subject Ira Aldridge, a black American actor touring in Shakespeare in Poland in 1865. *Bringing Up Nero*, for radio, is a discussion between the young Nero and his tutor, the playwright Seneca, the theme being whether a writer can influence a tyrant.

Two plays of 20th-century local history were written for Lancaster. *Buck Ruxton* deals with two brutal murders by a Parsee doctor in 1935. *Lile Jimmy Williamson* looks at the man who was the "uncrowned king" of Lancaster from the 1880s to the 1920s. He was a millionaire linoleum manufacturer and Liberal M.P. from 1892 on. Pownall explained that Williamson "monopolised the city's industry so that he could pay subsistence wages and control the movement of employment. . . . I wasn't grinding any particular political axe. I was fascinated to find out what happened and why. Especially why it was allowed."

Birmingham Repertory Theatre commissioned *My Father's House*, a play about Joseph Chamberlain and his sons Neville and Austen, the most famous family in British politics. Pownall remarks that writing about real people "is a relief from creating fictional characters. It gives you a new flavour and uses a different part of your mind."

Pownall has also written three unique "danceplays." *Nijinsky: Death of a Faun*, set on the day Nijinsky hears of the death of Diaghilev, was written for Nicholas Johnson, a dancer who had never acted before. The others were written for the Kosh company. *The Edge*, for one voice, is about a mother estranged from her daughter, and *Dinner Dance* brings seven people into a kitchen. Pownall's work here is pioneering and original.

The wide-ranging historical interests and the musical aspect of *Music to Murder By* come together in *Master Class*, set in the Kremlin in 1948. Stalin, shown as a subtle manipulator, and the bully Zhdanov summon two famous composers to condemn their kind of music and to require them to meet Communist party expectations in the future. Shostakovich wants to be loyal, to work within the Soviet system, while Prokofiev feels himself outside it. Because Stalin has all the power, the conflict is uneven, and from outside the drama audiences may know that the composers survived the confrontation. The second half has additional interest when the men try to compose a Georgian folk cantata to show their conformity. Though some critics have argued that Pownall trivializes the issues, *Master Class* poses important questions about art and politics, elitism and social purpose, and the distance between modern music and the general public.

Pownall has been a man overflowing with ideas, eagerly moving on to the next work rather than perfecting the previous one. His difficulty in gaining wider recognition, however, arises from the demands he makes on his audiences, whether to care about controversy in Russia in 1948 or to go more than halfway toward him in the strange world of *Richard* III, *Part Two, An Audience Called Édouard,* or *Music to Murder By*.

—Malcolm Page

PROCACCINO, Michael. ***See* CRISTOFER, Michael.**

R

RABE, David (William)

Nationality: American. **Born:** Dubuque, Iowa, 10 March 1940. **Education:** Loras College, Dubuque, B.A. in English 1962; Villanova University, Pennsylvania, 1963-64, 1967-68, M.A. 1968. **Military Service:** Served in the United States Army, 1965-67. **Family:** Married 1) Elizabeth Pan in 1969, one son; 2) the actress Jill Clayburgh in 1979. **Career:** Feature writer, New Haven *Register*, Connecticut, 1969-70. Assistant professor, 1970-72, and consultant, 1972—, Villanova University. **Awards:** Rockefeller grant, 1967; Associated Press award, for journalism, 1970; Obie award, 1971; Tony award, 1972; Outer Circle award, 1972; New York Drama Critics Circle citation, 1972, and award, 1976; *Variety* award, 1972; Dramatists Guild Hull-Warriner award, 1972; American Academy award, 1974; Guggenheim fellowship, 1976. **Agent:** Ellen Neuwald Inc., 905 West End Avenue, New York, New York 10025. **Address:** c/o Grove/Atlantic Monthly Press, 841 Broadway, New York, New York 10003, U.S.A.

Publications

Plays

Sticks and Bones (produced Villanova, Pennsylvania, 1969; New York, 1971; London, 1978). With *The Basic Training of Pavlo Hummel*, New York, Viking Press, 1973.

The Basic Training of Pavlo Hummel (produced New York, 1971). With *Sticks and Bones*, New York, Viking Press, 1973.

The Orphan (produced New York, 1973). New York, French, 1975.

In the Boom Boom Room (as *Boom Boom Room*, produced New York, 1973; revised version, as *In the Boom Boom Room*, produced New York, 1974; London, 1976). New York, Knopf, 1975; revised version (produced New York, 1986), New York, Grove Press, 1986.

Burning (produced New York, 1974).

Streamers (produced New Haven, Connecticut, and New York, 1976; London, 1978). New York, Knopf, 1977.

Goose and Tomtom (produced New York, 1982). New York, Grove Press, 1986.

Hurlyburly (produced Chicago and New York, 1984; also director: revised version produced Los Angeles, 1988). New York, Grove Press, 1985; revised edition, New York, Grove Weidenfeld, 1990; in *Best American Plays*, New York, Crown, 1993.

Those the River Keeps (produced Princeton, New Jersey, 1991). New York, Grove Weidenfeld, 1991.

Recital of the Dog. New York, Grove Press, 1993.

The Vietnam Plays (includes *The Basic Training of Pavlo Hummel* and *Sticks and Bones*). New York, Grove Press, 1993.

Hurlyburly and Those the River Keeps: Two Plays. New York, Grove Press, 1995.

A Question of Mercy. In *American Theater*, July/August 1997; New York, Grove Press, 1998.

Screenplays: *I'm Dancing as Fast as I Can*, 1982; *Streamers*, 1983; *Casualties of War*, 1989; *The Firm*, 1993.

*

Bibliography: *David Rabe: A Stage History and a Primary and Secondary Bibliography* by Philip C. Kolin, New York, Garland, 1988.

Manuscript Collection: Mugar Memorial Library, Boston University.

Critical Studies: *David Rabe: A Casebook*, edited by Toby Silverman Zinman, New York, Garland, 1991; "David Rabe and the Female Figure: The Body in the Boom Boom Room" by Les Wade, in *Text and Performance Quarterly* (Annandale, Virginia), January 1992, pp. 40-53; "Collapsing Male Myths: Rabe's Tragicomic *Hurlyburly*" by David Radavich, in *American Drama* (Cincinnati, Ohio), Fall 1993, pp. 1-16; "David Rabe: *Streamers*–Vietnam and Postmodernism" by Hans Ulrich Mohr, in *Modern War on Stage and Screen*, Lewiston, New York, Mellen, 1997; "The Emotion of Multitude and David Rabe's *Streamers*" by Jack Barbera, in *American Drama* (Cincinnati, Ohio), Fall 1997; "When Reason Fails" by Stephanie Coen, in *American Theater*, July-August 1997, pp. 22.

* * *

David Rabe's corrosive portrait of American life evolves within a series of metaphoric arenas—living rooms, military barracks, disco bars—in which his characters collide violently against one another but where they primarily struggle with their own society-fostered delusions. The revised edition of *In the Boom Boom Room*, published in 1986, is mischievously dedicated to "the wolf at the door," but the creature is already well within Rabe's theatrical house and the psyches of those who dwell inside it.

Two Rabe plays, forming with *Streamers* what has come to be known as his Vietnam trilogy, burst onto the New York stage in 1971 when both were produced by Joseph Papp at the Shakespeare Festival Public Theatre. Rabe denies that they are specifically antiwar plays, maintaining that he neither expected nor intended them to wield any political effect, that they merely define a condition as endemic to the "eternal human pageant" as family, marriage, or crime. ("A play in which a family looks bad is not called an 'antifamily' play. A play in which a marriage looks bad is not called an 'antimarriage' play. A play about crime is not called an 'anticrime' play.")

But *The Basic Training of Pavlo Hummel* and *Sticks and Bones* portray the dehumanization and senseless horror of the Vietnam era with the sustained raw power now ordinarily associated only with certain films produced well after American troops withdrew (*Apocalypse Now, The Killing Fields, Platoon, Full Metal Jacket*). Poor Pavlo Hummel's basic training functions as ritual throughout the play, contributing significantly to Rabe's theatrical stylization of an essentially realistic dramatic structure. Rabe's realism is invariably a realism heightened, stretched beyond traditional limits through (as in *Sticks and Bones* and *Hurlyburly*) dazzling language play or (as in *Pavlo Hummel*) surreal fracturing of time and space and the ominous on- and offstage drifting of Ardell, a character seen only by Pavlo. Such blending of the real and surreal characterizes Rabe's style and serves both to rattle a viewer's preconceptions and to reinforce (as in *Sticks and Bones*) a given figure's alienation from those closest to him. It also prevents a play with a simpleminded hero from itself becoming simpleminded by complicating the theatrical conventions that develop Pavlo into an army-trained killer who is killed himself, ironically not on the battlefield but in a brothel squabble. A sense of verisimilitude nevertheless underpins Rabe's stylistic virtuosity, the details of the Vietnam plays clearly emanating not only from the playwright's imagination but from his own army experience in a hospital support unit at Long Binh as well.

While *Pavlo Hummel* focuses on precombat preparation for war, *Sticks and Bones* concerns its grotesque stateside aftermath. The naive Pavlo may be blind to the reality of war, but David, the embittered veteran of *Sticks and Bones,* has been literally—physically—blinded by it. Torn by the atrocities he has witnessed and tormented by his psychological and physical infirmity, David must be expelled from the bosom of the family whose artificial tranquillity he is determined to destroy. Pavlo knows too little, David too much, and both must therefore die.

Despite its intensely serious subject, the method of *Sticks and Bones* is often wildly comic, dependent upon the clichéd conventions of situation comedy that Rabe transforms into a vehicle for a macabre parody of American delusion. The play resonates, however, with overtones of American domestic tragedy, notably Miller's *Death of a Salesman* and O'Neill's *Long Day's Journey into Night.* Generically complex, articulated in language that alternates between poetic and vernacular extremes, *Sticks and Bones* remains the most important American play to come out of the Vietnam experience.

Streamers, adapted to the screen by Rabe and the director Robert Altman in 1983, expands the thematic scope of the earlier plays but most resembles *Pavlo Hummel* in its barracks setting. The violence inherent in the military system is here expanded, linked by Rabe to institutionalized racism and homophobia camouflaged in the rhetoric of patriotism.

Hurlyburly, a title that reflects the chaos of its characters' lives, veers in a different direction. The word appears in the opening lines of *Macbeth,* which Rabe considered using in their entirety to name each of his three acts, respectively, "When Shall We Three Meet Again?," "In Thunder Lightning or in Rain?," and "When the Hurlyburly's Done, When the Battle's Lost and Won." Although he rejected the idea, he writes in the afterword that he "felt for a long time that the play was in many ways a trilogy, each act an entity, a self-contained action however enhanced it might be by the contents of the other acts and the reflections that might be sent back and forth between all three." (Rabe is an astute commentator on the art of playwriting, his own and others'. See also his introduction to *Pavlo Hummel* and the author's note to *Sticks and Bones.*)

Like that of *Streamers* and *Pavlo Hummel,* the world of *Hurlyburly* is male centered, but the barracks of those plays shift to the living room of a small house in the Hollywood Hills inhabited by Rabe's least sympathetic outcasts. Cut off from their wives and children by divorce or separation, the men of *Hurlyburly* waver violently between macho boasting and episodes of confessional self-loathing as they seek solace in drugs, alcohol, and uncommitted affairs. Their hostility toward women, whom they regard as "broads" or "bitches," masks their inability to reconcile codes of male behavior learned as children with expectations demanded by their liberated partners. These boy-men lack a moral center and represent for Rabe a characteristically American rootlessness.

The men's anger is articulated in the stylized excesses and violence of the play's language and in the four-letter words that punctuate the dialogue but, more subtly, in the winding convolutions of speech: parenthetical expressions, self-interruptions, thoughts within thoughts, the repetitions and circularity that contribute to the work's considerable length and O'Neillian power. Eddie, Mickey, and Phil fear silence even more than they fear tuning into their own feelings, and they thus keep talking, even if doing so runs the risk of accidental self-revelation. In this regard an early stage direction notes that "in the characters' speeches phrases such as 'whatchamacallit,' 'thingamajig,' 'blah-blah-blah' and 'rapateta' abound. These are phrases used by the characters to keep themselves talking and should be said unhesitatingly with the authority and conviction with which one would have in fact said the missing word." The play's dialogue is extraordinary in its rich mix of funny, vulgar, savagely articulate language.

Rabe maintains that *Hurlyburly* contains no spokesman, that "no one in it knows what it is about." But the age of anxiety, documented by the disasters ticked off nightly on the 11 o'clock news determines how his characters, and his audience, live. Rabe may claim that no single person in his play knows what it means, but *Hurlyburly*'s thematic core is expressed clearly in the drunken Eddie's furious lament for an absent God:

> The Ancients might have had some consolation from a view of the heavens as inhabited by this thoughtful, you know, meditative, maybe a trifle unpredictable and wrathful, but nevertheless UP THERE—this divine onlooker—we have bureaucrats devoted to the accumulation of incomprehensible data—we have connoisseurs of graft and the filibuster—virtuosos of the three-martini lunch for whom we vote on the basis of their personal appearance. The air's bad, the water's got poison in it, and into whose eyes do we find ourselves staring when we look for providence? We have emptied out the heavens and put oblivion in the hands of a bunch of aging insurance salesmen whose jobs are insecure.

Hurlyburly is Rabe's most intricate, verbally dazzling theatrical statement, a view even more strikingly apparent since the publication of the dramatist's definitive edition of the play in 1990. In this version Rabe restored and revised text cut or altered for the 1984 production directed by Mike Nichols in Chicago and on Broadway. This new, even more corrosive version of *Hurlyburly* emerged from a process of revision that culminated in a 1988 production of the play directed by Rabe himself at the Westwood Playhouse in Los Angeles.

Also prominent in Rabe's later work are his screenplay for *Casualties of War,* a film with which Rabe has expressed dissatisfaction but one that searingly reflects his continuing obsession with the Vietnam conflict, and *Those the River Keeps,* a play that returns to the terrain of *Hurlyburly* from a fresh perspective.

—Mark W. Estrin

RAVENHILL, Mark

Nationality: British. **Born:** Gretna Green, Scotland, 7 June 1966. **Education:** Warden Park Comprehensive, Cuckfield. **Military Service:** Member of the Territorial Army. **Family:** Married Tracey Leeson in 1989 (divorced 1990). **Career:** Senior caller, Mecca Bingo Hall, Brighton, 1987-90; Front of House Executive, English National Opera, 1992-94; literary manager, Paines Plough Theatre Company. **Award:** Evening Argus Young Journalist award, 1975. **Agent:** Mel Kenyon, c/o Cassarotto Company, National House, 60-66 Wardour Street, London W1V 4ND England.

Publications

Plays

Fist (produced London).
His Mouth (produced London, 1995).
Shopping and Fucking (produced London, 1996; New York, 1998). London, Methuen, 1996.
Faust (produced 1997). London, Methuen, 1997.
Sleeping Around (produced Salisbury, 1998).

Radio Plays: *Mad Money,* adaptation of Ostrovsky, 1993; *Lulu,* adaptation of Wedekind, 1995.

* * *

Mark Ravenhill burst on the British theater scene with his remarkable play *Shopping and Fucking* (1996), in which he presents a remarkably destructive, but hugely marketable, version of *fin-de-siècle* London. He describes a city and a populace in headlong self-destruct mode. It is a play that not only captured but indeed epitomized the dark underbelly of the Cool-Britannia zeitgeist and became the totemic reference point for such "new-lad" icons as the magazine *Loaded,* Nick Hornby's novel *Fever Pitch,* and the band Oasis. *Shopping and Fucking* was the inevitable and epigrammatical culmination of and inspiration for plays like Sarah Kane's *Blasted* (1995) and *Closer* (1998), Jez Butterworth's *Mojo* (1995), Anthony Neilson's *The Censor* (1997), and Irvine Welsh's *You'll Have Had Your Hole* (1998). It was theater of and for the chemical generation, but it was also safely located at the Royal Court Theatre and enjoyed a series of enormously successful main stage national tours. Despite the reaction of the mainstream press to the title, the vomiting scene at the beginning, the drug dealing throughout, and the anal rape at the end, one might, therefore, consider the play more sensationalist than shocking.

Ravenhill's work is a bleak, cruel, but painfully funny play that offers a black spin on the aftermath of the 1980s and its Thatcherite values of monetarism, individualism, and consumerism. In Ravenhill's 1990s these ideologies have spun out of control and produced a world where everything and everyone has a price. Its amoral characters are set adrift in the lower depths of contemporary London, a society of clubbing, drinking, causal sex, drug use, and drug dealing. It is a world of buying and selling, where even personal relationships are reduced to retail transactions: "It wasn't an attachment. . . . More of a . . . transaction. I paid him. I gave him money. And when you're paying, you can't call it a personal relationship, can you? . . . We did a deal. I paid him. We confined it to the lavatory. It didn't mean anything."

The play is divided into some 14 short scenes, which interweave fragments of the lives of five characters and several stories through "snapshots" of meetings, conversations, and relationships. Mark is a 30-something former drug addict, who shares his life and flat with Lulu and Robbie, 20-something losers who survive by selling drugs, sex, and each other. In the boom of the 1980s, Mark was a trader on the stock exchange but, as he puts it, "a history of substance abuse" has taken its toll. He picks up Gary, a young prostitute with a history of sexual abuse, a cavalier attitude toward other people's credit cards, and a wildly self-destructive personality and sexuality. Their relationship is based on sadomasochistic sex and shopping for expensive designer clothes. In a surreal twist on the tart-with-a-heart motif, Ravenhill rewrites *Pygmalion* with Gary re-creating Mark as a pimp in designer clothes.

Robbie and Lulu make a disastrous attempt to deal ecstasy in a London club. Robbie fails as a dealer because he disobeys Lulu's one rule of dealing: "He who sells shall not use." Having lost 300 ecstasy tablets, Robbie and Lulu owe Brian, the threatening gangster and major vice dealer, £3,000. This they raise through a frenzied week operating telephone sex lines.

The two stories come together in a scene of violent abuse in which both Mark and Robbie have brutal sex with a blindfolded Gary while Lulu watches and ridicules him. The scene is in some measure archetypal of a whole genre of new writing in Britain. It claims shocking explicitness, utter topicality, and authentic social relevance.

A play that has already enacted stripping, rimming, fellatio, and snuff video has to find and present the next most excessive thing: Gary's self-hatred manifests itself in an extreme masochistic death wish and the scene ends with Mark set to penetrate him with a fork. In the theater this is potent stuff but emotionally and morally it may be construed as rather empty.

Citing the black comedy, sexual license, verbal sparring, and rich urban context, some critics have seen in Ravenhill a Joe Orton for the '90s. *Shopping and Fucking* does achieve the energy and topicality of Orton, and Ravenhill uses language and dialogue with assurance, demonstrating a sharp ear for contemporary idiomatic speech. He even creates scenes and moments of great amorality and huge absurdity, but Ravenhill's dramaturgy is far less concerned with formal experimentation than are Orton's plays. For all its graphic shock value and its bravura and explicit action, Ravenhill's play is formally conventional without the theatrical audacity or the political edge of Orton.

A further useful parallel must be to the plays of Bernard Marie Koltès and his exploration of "the deal." This is, perhaps, most explicit in his 1987 play *In the Solitude of the Cotton Fields,* in which the characters are known only as the Dealer and the Client. Koltès offers a very different kind of investigation of the same central metaphor—that everything and everyone has a price and that relationships are merely extended and elaborate negotiations about agreeing upon a price. Taken together both plays—*In the Solitude of the Cotton Fields* and *Shopping and Fucking*—reveal a very modern obsession with trading and with money, with relationships as commerce, and with individuals as commodities. By capturing such contemporary themes and then placing them at the center of London's hugely influential club culture, Ravenhill won huge success. *Shopping and Fucking,* quite simply, set the popular standard and violent-chic tone for new writing in London.

—Adrienne Scullion

RAYSON, Hannie

Nationality: Australian. **Born:** Brighton, Melbourne, 31 March 1957. **Education:** Brighton High School, Melbourne, 1969-72; Melbourne Church of England Girls Grammar, 1973-74; University of Melbourne, Parkville, Victoria, B.A. 1977; Victorian College of the Arts, Melbourne, Victoria, diploma of art in dramatic art 1980. **Family:** Married Michael Cathcart; one son. **Career:** Co-founder, writer and actor, Theatre Works, Melbourne, 1981-83; writer-in-residence, The Mill Theatre, Geelong, 1984, Playbox Theatre, Melbourne, 1985, LaTrobe University, Bundoora, Victoria, 1987, Monash University, Clayton, Victoria, and Victorian College of the Arts, Melbourne, 1990. **Awards:** Queen Elizabeth II Silver Jubilee award, 1981; Australian Writers Guild award, 1986, 1990; Victorian Green Room award, 1990; New South Wales Premier's Literary award, 1990, 1995; "The Age" Performing Arts award, 1995; The Sidney Myer Performing Arts award, 1996. Honorary degree: La Trobe University, Bundoora, Victoria. **Member:** Victorian Ministry for the Arts, 1986-87; Literature Board of the Australia Council, 1992-95. **Agent:** Hilary Linstead and Associates, Level 18, Plaza II, Bondi Junction, New South Wales 2022, Australia.

Publications

Plays

Please Return to Sender (produced Melbourne, 1980).
Mary (produced Melbourne, 1981). Montmorency, Victoria, Yackandandah, 1985.
Leave It Till Monday (produced Geelong, 1984).
Room to Move (produced Melbourne, 1985). Montmorency, Victoria, Yackandandah, 1985.
Hotel Sorrento (produced Melbourne, 1990). Sydney, Currency Press, 1990.
Wall Street Creche (produced 1992).
Falling from Grace (produced Melbourne, 1994). Sydney, Currency Press, 1994.
Scenes from a Separation (produced Melbourne, 1995). Sydney, Currency Press, 1996.
Competitive Tenderness (produced Melbourne, 1996). Sydney, Currency Press, 1997.

Screenplay: *Falling from Grace,* adapted from her own play, 1996.

Television Plays: *Sloth*, 1992; episode in *Sins* series, 1993.

*

Hannie Rayson comments:

My plays to date have been a response to particular contemporary social phenomena that at the outset I want to understand more fully. I seek subject matter that is full of contradiction and spend large tracts of time doing research. I begin with a big question, for example, in *Room to Move*: how has feminism affected Australian men, or, in *Hotel Sorrento*, how does the experience of expatriation alter one's perception of home?

Articulating the intellectual context occurs in tandem with the process of immersing myself in the world of the play: the characters, their lives, relationships, and so on. I am neither polemical nor didactic, but I do want my work to be dense with ideas that have a critical relationship with the narrative. My ambition is to write plays that send audiences into the night with much to talk about.

* * *

Hannie Rayson's early work was in collaborative and community theater, and the influence of that experience is evident in the problem-based plots and episodic structures that are characteristic of her writing. *Mary,* the first of her plays to achieve publication and some prominence, was directly a product of such involvement and was developed in close consultation with relevant interest groups. Rayson acknowledges in her foreword to the published text their contribution to the project. She also acknowledges the challenge she faced as a fifth-generation Australian in dramatizing authentically but humorously the experience of a teenage Greek girl caught between her parents' culture and the very different expectations and rituals of Australian adolescents.

Room to Move marked Rayson's transition into the mainstream subsidized theater, and it has proved a very popular piece. It was hailed at the time as representing a belated recognition of feminist concerns in the Australian theater. But Rayson's subject is less the reappraisal of the role of women in relationships and in the wider society than of the impact such changes have had in these areas, particularly on the men who have been challenged with adjusting to them. In a sense the practical consequence of this approach is the reinforcement of the privileged status that men have enjoyed, or suffered from, in contemporary Australian plays as the principal agents of wit and momentum in the dialogue. Reviewers have frequently likened Rayson's presentation of the comedy of marital strife to that of David Williamson.

Hotel Sorrento is Rayson's most ambitious play, and it established her as a playwright of real substance. At its center is the interaction, past and present, among three sisters. It has suitable Chekhovian elements of wryness and compassion and establishes credibly a number of lines of conflict, most of them unresolvable. There are other aspects reminiscent of Chekhov: a strong sense of nostalgia for a lovelier and more innocent past, which in Rayson's depiction of the little seaside town of Sorrento is allowed to pass largely without analysis; a lively and articulate range of surrounding characters with a tendency to pontificate on the state of the nation; and, most tellingly, a subtle and powerful sense of the dignity and beauty that can coexist with the silliness of people. The central images of the beach and the pier are handled evocatively and catch for the first time in Australian theater something of the mythological importance that looking out from the fringes of the continent to the water has in constructions of Australian identity. It is a way of seeing that is just as fundamental as the more characteristic literary stance that looks inward to the arid center. The great strengths of *Hotel Sorrento* are its authentic feeling and its intelligent talk, even if occasionally the debates about Australian identity become a little stodgy.

In Rayson's later work good conversation remains a powerful resource, although it is tempered by a number of experimental structural moves. *Falling from Grace,* which revisits the revolution in gender relationships to explore its effect on female friendships, is self-consciously cinematic in style. *Scenes from a Separation,* a collaboration with Andrew Bovell, is similarly episodic and counterbalances the emotional directness of the representative female perspective on the marriage breakdown with the acerbic self-justifications of Bovell's presentation of the male view. *Competitive Tenderness* enters new territory, its satirical treatment of economic rationalism becoming also an exercise in formal farce. But there seems little room for argument about Rayson's theatrical home ground. She has very impressively animated a range of contemporary attitudes to relationships, many nearly as reflective and ironic as the playwright who encompasses them all.

—Peter Fitzpatrick

REANEY, James (Crerar)

Nationality: Canadian. **Born:** South Easthope, Ontario, 1 September 1926. **Education:** Elmhurst Public School, Perth County; Central Collegiate Vocational Institute, Stratford, Ontario, 1939-44; University College, Toronto (Epstein award, 1948), B.A. 1948, M.A. 1949, graduate study, 1956-58, Ph.D. in English 1958. **Family:** Married Colleen Thibaudeau in 1951; two sons (one deceased) and one daughter. **Career:** Member of the English Department, University of Manitoba, Winnipeg, 1949-56; professor of English, Middlesex College, University of Western Ontario, London, 1960-92. Founding editor, *Alphabet* magazine, London, 1960-71. Active in little theatre groups in Winnipeg and London: founder, Listeners Workshop, London, 1966. Lives in London, Ontario. **Awards:** Governor-General's award, for poetry, 1950, 1959, for drama, 1963; President's medal, University of Western Ontario, 1955, 1958; Massey award, 1960; Chalmers award, 1975. D.Litt.: Carleton University, Ottawa, 1975. Officer, Order of Canada, 1975; Fellow, Royal Society of Canada, 1978. **Agent:** John Miller, Cultural Support Services, 14 Earl Street, Toronto, Ontario M4Y 1M3, Canada. **Address:** Department of English, University of Western Ontario, London, Ontario N6A 3K7, Canada.

Publications

Plays

Night-Blooming Cereus, music by John Beckwith (broadcast 1959; produced Toronto, 1960). Included in *The Killdeer and Other Plays*, 1962.

The Killdeer (produced Toronto, 1960; Glasgow, 1965). Included in *The Killdeer and Other Plays*, 1962; revised version (produced Vancouver, 1970), in *Masks of Childhood*, 1972.

One-Man Masque (also director: produced Toronto, 1960). Included in *The Killdeer and Other Plays*, 1962.

The Easter Egg (produced Hamilton, Ontario, 1962). Included in *Masks of Childhood*, 1972.

The Killdeer and Other Plays. Toronto, Macmillan, 1962.

The Sun and the Moon (produced London, Ontario, 1965). Included in *The Killdeer and Other Plays*, 1962.

Names and Nicknames (for children; produced Winnipeg, 1963). Rowayton, Connecticut, New Plays for Children, 1969.

Aladdin and the Magic Lamp, Apple Butter, Little Red Riding Hood (puppet plays; also director: produced London, Ontario, 1965). *Apple Butter* included in *Apple Butter and Other Plays*, 1973.

Let's Make a Carol (for children), music by Alfred Kunz. Waterloo, Ontario, Waterloo Music, 1965.

Ignoramus (for children; produced London, Ontario, 1966). Included in *Apple Butter and Other Plays*, 1973.

Listen to the Wind (also director: produced London, Ontario, 1966). Vancouver, Talonbooks, 1972.

The Canada Tree (produced by Girl Guides of Canada on Morrison Island, Ontario, 1967).

Colours in the Dark (produced Stratford, Ontario, 1967). Vancouver and Toronto, Talonbooks-Macmillan, 1970.

Geography Match (for children; produced London, Ontario, 1967). Included in *Apple Butter and Other Plays*, 1973.

Three Desks (produced London, Ontario, 1967). Included in *Masks of Childhood*, 1972.

Don't Sell Mr. Aesop (produced London, Ontario, 1968).

Genesis (also director: produced London, Ontario, 1968).

Masque, with Ron Cameron (produced Toronto, 1972). Toronto, Simon and Pierre, 1974.

Masks of Childhood, edited by Brian Parker. Toronto, New Press, 1972.

All the Bees and All the Keys, music by John Beckwith (for children; produced Toronto, 1972). Erin, Ontario, Press Porcépic, 1976.

Apple Butter and Other Plays for Children. Vancouver, Talonbooks, 1973.

The Donnellys: A Trilogy. Erin, Ontario, Press Porcépic, 1983.

1. *Sticks and Stones* (produced Toronto, 1973). Erin, Ontario, Press Porcépic, 1975.
2. *The St. Nicholas Hotel* (produced Toronto, 1974). Erin, Ontario, Press Porcépic, 1976.
3. *Handcuffs* (produced Toronto, 1975). Erin, Ontario, Press Porcépic, 1977.

Baldoon, with C.H. Gervais (produced Toronto, 1976). Erin, Ontario, Porcupine's Quill, 1976.

The Dismissal; or, Twisted Beards and Tangled Whiskers (produced Toronto, 1977). Erin, Ontario, Press Porcépic, 1979.

The Death and Execution of Frank Halloway; or, The First Act of John Richardson's Wacousta (produced Timmins, Ontario, 1977). Published in *Jubilee 4* (Wingham, Ontario), 1978; complete version, as *Wacousta!* (produced Toronto, 1978), Erin, Ontario, Press Porcépic, 1979.

At the Big Carwash (puppet play; produced Armstrong, British Columbia, 1979).

King Whistle! (produced Stratford, Ontario, 1979). Published in *Brick 8* (Ilderton, Ontario), Winter 1980.

Antler River (produced London, Ontario, 1980).

Gyroscope (produced Toronto, 1981). Toronto, Playwrights, 1983.

The Shivaree (opera), music by John Beckwith (produced Toronto, 1982).

I the Parade (produced Waterloo, Ontario, 1982).

The Canadian Brothers, from a novel by John Richardson (produced Calgary, 1983). Published in *Major Plays of the Canadian Theatre 1934-1984*, edited by Richard Perkyns, Toronto, Irwin, 1984.

Serinette (opera; produced Sharon Temple, Ontario, 1986).

Crazy to Kill (opera; produced Guelph, Ontario, 1988).

Sleigh without Bells (puppet play). Published in *Inter-Play: Works and Words of Writers and Critics*, Breakwater Books, 1994.

Alice Through the Looking Glass, adaptation of Lewis Carroll's novel (produced Erin, Ontario, 1994).

Radio Plays: *Blooming Cereus*, 1959; *Wednesday's Child*, 1962; *Canada Dash, Canada Dot* (3 parts), music by John Beckwith, 1965-67; *The Story of the Gentle Rain Food Co-op*, 1998.

Poetry

The Red Heart. Toronto, McClelland and Stewart, 1949.
A Suit of Nettles. Toronto, Macmillan, 1958.
Twelve Letters to a Small Town. Toronto, Ryerson Press, 1962.
The Dance of Death at London, Ontario. London, Ontario, Alphabet, 1963.
Poems, edited by Germaine Warkentin. Toronto, New Press, 1972.
Selected Shorter [and Longer] Poems, edited by Germaine Warkentin. Erin, Ontario, Press Porcépic, 2 vols., 1975-76.
Imprecations: The Art of Swearing. Windsor, Ontario, Black Moss Press, 1984.
Performance Poems. Goderich, Ontario, Moonstone Press, 1990.

Other

The Boy with an "R" in His Hand. Toronto, Macmillan, 1965.
14 Barrels from Sea to Sea. Erin, Ontario, Press Porcépic, 1977.
Take the Big Picture. Erin, Ontario, Porcupine's Quill, 1986.
The Box Social & Other Stories. Erin, Ontario, Porcupine's Quill, 1996.
Father Bought a Tollgate Company (for children). Erin, Ontario, Porcupine's Quill, 1998.

*

Manuscript Collections: University of Toronto; Toronto Public Library.

Critical Studies: *James Reaney* by Alvin A. Lee, New York, Twayne, 1968; *James Reaney* by Ross G. Woodman, Toronto, McClelland and Stewart, 1971; *James Reaney* by J. Stewart Reaney, Agincourt, Ontario, Gage, 1977; *Approaches to the Work of James Reaney* edited by Stan Dragland, Downsview, Ontario, ECW Press, 1982; "Three Desks: A Turning Point in James Reaney's Drama" by Tim McNamara in *Queen's Quarterly*, Kingston, Spring 1987, pp. 15-32; *How to Play: The Theatre of James Reaney* by Gerald D. Parker, Downsview, Ontario, ECW Press, 1991; "Playing with Time: James Reaney's *The Donnellys* as Spatial Form Drama" by Karen Grandy in *Modern Drama*, Downsview, Ontario, Winter 1995, pp. 462-74; "Alchemy in Ontario: Reaney's Twelve Letters to a Small Town" by Wanda Campbell in *Canadian Literature*, Vancouver, Winter 1996, pp. 102-17; "James Reaney's *The Donnellys* and the Recovery of 'The Ceremony of Innocence'" by Craig Stewart Walker in *Australian Drama Studies*, Queensland, October 1996, pp. 188-96.

Theatrical Activities:
Director: **Plays**—*One-Man Masque*, Toronto, 1960; *Aladdin and the Magic Lamp*, *Apple Butter*, and *Little Red Riding Hood*, London, Ontario, 1965; *Listen to the Wind*, London, Ontario, 1966; *Genesis*, London, Ontario, 1968.

Actor: **Plays**—In *One-Man Masque*, Toronto, 1960.

James Reaney comments:
These plays are interested in telling stories. I like using choral and collage techniques. The plays, particularly the children's plays, are based on watching children play on streets and in backyards. So–plays as play.

(1998) Now that I'm 70 and retired from academy, I have a lot more time to spend on theatrical writing, particularly my notion of Kanuki Theatre, which I gather, in the States, is called Oriental Fusion Theatre. As I begin to get productions abroad, and continual production in the school and college system here, with such playwrights as Allan Stratton and Tompson Highway, as disciples from my school, I sense how much a playwright can do in fathering "community" and a sense of identity that is an alternative to that fostered so strongly by the commercial media. I think the greatest influence on me has been the story of the Donellys, playing with my own children, and trying to imitate the Brontë children's storytelling techniques. I am at present working on a dramatic version of their childhood Angria and Gondal worlds–in desperation called "The Full Brontë." Branwell is the Brontë that I most care for right now–and, if I can resurrect him from the unheeding neglect of the Brontë fans, then I can die in peace.

* * *

When James Reaney turned to drama in the late 1950s, he had already won well-deserved recognition as a poet with the volumes *The Red Heart* (1949) and *A Suit of Nettles* (1958), both of which won the Governor General's Award. The early plays show Reaney struggling to master the elements of the dramatist's craft, a struggle that is not always successful. *The Killdeer*, first produced in 1960, reveals weaknesses typical of Reaney's work at the time. There is a sensational and melodramatic plot in which a female prisoner accused of murder is made pregnant by the protagonist to save her from the gallows, with Madame Fay unmasked in a final courtroom scene, all of which is accompanied by crude characterization and uncertain motivation. But if the other plays of this period—*The Easter Egg, The Sun and the Moon, Listen to the Wind,* and *Three Desks*—reveal similar weaknesses, they are also plays rich in poetry, and they feature a nonrealistic approach to theater that relies on nonlinear plots and the representation of mythic patterns through theatrical effects. If the reader or viewer is disconcerted by these early plays, it is because there are so many unexpected and unprepared-for shifts in Reaney's dramatic voice.

Some of Reaney's best work is represented by his 1960s plays for children—*Names and Nicknames, Geography Match,* and *Ignoramus*. *Colours in the Dark,* commissioned by the Stratford Festival and produced by John Hirsch at the Avon Theatre in Stratford in 1967, is the best of these, and it also appeals to adult audiences. The play dispenses almost entirely with plot, motivation, and conventional structure, replacing them with elements related to the play's thematic concerns—the letters of the alphabet, the books of the Bible, the seasons. The play's key structural element, which gives coherence to the multiple incidents and to the rapid switches in mood, is provided by poems that Reaney had already published and that are themselves given coherence by the dominant "Existence" poem. Central to these elements or motifs is the archetypal theme of a fall and possible redemption.

Many critics regard Reaney's Donnelly trilogy, produced between 1973 and 1975 by Toronto's Tarragon Theatre, as his best work. His re-creation of the events surrounding the 1880 murder of the Donnelly family of southwestern Ontario by Orangemen combines in a striking way history, folktales, myth, music, dancing, mime, and an inventive use of props. The first part, *Sticks and Stones,* is a vivid celebration of the Donnelly family and a powerful foreshadowing of their death. While rooted in naturalistic detail, the play suggests that the Donnellys are outsiders, as mythic in stature as Oedipus or the ancient mariner. The other two plays of the trilogy—*The St. Nicholas Hotel* and *Handcuffs*—are less effective, for they repeat the essential story of the murder of the Donnellys. In them the mythic gives way to the naturalistic, and drama is too often subsumed in literal documentary. But if the trilogy is marred by Reaney's excesses and if the published text seems confusing (9 actors must carry more than 70 roles), the true values of the work can best be seen in production, where the complex nexus of symbols and the larger-than-life characters carry dramatic conviction. Reaney's plays are best understood as process rather than in terms of the printed text.

Following the Donnelly trilogy Reaney turned to dramatizing Canadian historical themes, as in *Baldoon* (with C. H. Gervais), *The Dismissal, Wacousta!,* and *The Canadian Brothers,* the last two based on melodramatic novels by Major John Richardson, a deservedly neglected early 19th-century writer. The late plays have not been well received. In such 1980s plays as *King Whistle!* and *Antler River,* Reaney further reduced the scope of his themes by dramatizing incidents in the history of his own immediate neighborhood of Stratford and London, Ontario. These plays have not gained provincial or national attention. Reaney has also written a number of libretti: *The Shivaree: Opera in Two Acts* (1978) and *Crazy to Kill* (1988), both with music by John Beckwith, and *Serinette* (1990), with music by Harry Somers. His adaptation of Lewis Carroll's *Alice through the Looking-Glass* (1994) premiered at the Stratford Festival, Canada, in 1994. A retrospective volume of 11 short stories, *The Box Social,* was published in 1996.

Although Reaney is generally held in high regard as a dramatist, his work is uneven, revealing a conflict between his innate academicism and the populist theatricality to which he aspires.

—Eugene Benson

REARDON, Dennis J.

Nationality: American. **Born:** Worcester, Massachusetts, 17 September 1944. **Education:** Tulane University, New Orleans, 1962-63; University of Kansas, Lawrence (Hopkins Award, 1965, 1966), 1963-66, B.A. in English (cum laude) 1966; Indiana University, Bloomington, 1966-67; State University of New York, Albany, 1985-1990, Ph.D. in 1990. **Military Service:** Served in the United States Army, 1968-69. **Family:** Married in 1971 (divorced 1990); one daughter; 2) married in 1991 (divorced 1996). **Career:** Playwright-in-residence, University of Michigan, Ann Arbor (Shubert Fellow, 1970; Hopwood Award, 1971), 1970-71, and Hartwick College, Oneonta, New York; member of the English Department, State University of New York, Albany, 1985-87. Head of playwriting program, Indiana University, Bloomington, 1987—. Lives in Bloomington, Indiana. **Awards:** Creative Artists Public Service grant, 1984; Weissberger Foundation award, 1985; National Play award, 1986; National Endowment for the Arts fellowship, 1986; Indiana Arts Commission Master fellowship, 1992; winner of the Theatre Memphis new play competition, 1997, for *The Peer Panel.*

PUBLICATIONS

Plays

The Happiness Cage (produced New York, 1970). New York, French, 1971.
Siamese Connections (produced Ann Arbor, Michigan, 1971; New York, 1972).
The Leaf People (produced New York, 1975). Published in *Plays from the New York Shakespeare Festival,* New York, Broadway Play Publishing, 1986.
The Incredible Standing Man and His Friends (also co-director: produced Oneonta, New York, 1980).
Steeple Jack (produced Portland, Maine, 1983; New York, 1985).
Subterranean Homesick Blues Again (produced Louisville, 1983; New York, 1984). In *25 Ten-Minute Plays from the Actor's Theatre of Louisville,* New York, Samuel French, 1989.
Comment, music by Merrill Clark (produced New York, 1985).
New Cures for Sunburn (produced Albany, 1986).
Boone Descended (produced Chicago, 1992).
The Peer Panel. 1996.

*

Manuscript Collection: Lincoln Center Library of the Performing Arts, New York.

Critical Study: *Uneasy Stages* by John Simon, New York, Random House, 1975.

Theatrical Activities:
Director: **Play**—*The Incredible Standing Man and His Friends* (co-director), Oneonta, New York, 1980.

Dennis J. Reardon comments:

The central dynamic in my plays exists in the tension between what is "real" and what is "made up." I often mix carefully researched and recognizably topical material with the stuff of dreams, and I am seldom precise about where one mode leaves off and the other begins. My intent is to push beyond the suffocating ephemera of journalistic facts into a more iconic realm where the only reality is a metaphor.

(1998) The crux of my plays is the conflict between the irresistible force of Society and the inevitably futile opposition posed by a recalcitrant Individual. The leitmotif is failure: the failure of the Outsider to integrate productively within the encompassing entities of family, profession, community, or country; and, conversely, the failure of the encompassing entity to creatively engage the mutant soul of the willful Individual. Both forces lose.

I confess (somewhat sheepishly) that I am given to dramatic meditations upon the gulf between our aspirations and achievements, the enduring pain of the reach that forever exceeds our grasp, the entropic decay of Ideals, the maddening persistence of unfulfillable desire, and the dull ache in the gut by which we recognize these things.

Step right up, eh? What I hope redeems these dolorous themes somewhat is that I can't write about them without hearing a kind of laughter. A spectral laughter. Some ghost, or some god, is distantly amused. Or, as my kinsmen would put it, "Being Irish, I have an abiding sense of tragedy which sustains me through temporary periods of joy (Stop by if you're in the neighborhood. I'll stand you to a pint).

* * *

Among the plays of America's contemporary dramatists, Dennis J. Reardon's work is distinguished by an energy that assaults the intellect as well as the emotions. With an audacity arising first from his youthful enthusiasm and then from a greater understanding of his craft, Reardon has experimented with theatrical effect in order to enhance his stories and to communicate his vision of man. From audiences he clearly demands intellectual involvement, while he besieges their senses with a variety of staged actions. Yet he remains basically a storyteller, albeit one with a bit of the Irish dark side showing. His subject is the plight of man immemorial, a condition he explores with all of the anxieties, frustrations, and reactions to the violent freedoms of the 1960s that marked his own maturing years. His career divides into two distinct periods. *The Happiness Cage, Siamese Connections,* and *The Leaf People* brought him immediate recognition on Broadway as well as a sense of being both victor and victim in a world he did not fully understand. After a period of "self-willed" oblivion, he began writing again in 1980, and since then he has produced a half-dozen plays that reveal the vibrancy of his earlier work accentuated through experience and by the more balanced probing of the demons and saints, facts and fates, that persistently follow the modern everyman.

The plays of Reardon's early period remain as daringly theatrical as anything he has written. Because he is always idea oriented, however, his heavy emphasis upon a depressing view of humanity in these plays changes in subsequent work without bringing a complete denial of his philosophical stance. Feeling that he has "the power to bring an untold amount of happiness into this miserable world," Dr. Freytag of *The Happiness Cage* experiments upon his patients to find a cure for schizophrenia. One patient questions Freytag's assessment of his condition as "lonely, confused, frightened, and thoroughly unhappy" and asserts that he is simply a man, that he is a unique human being. Moreover, he wants to know what happiness means. Apparently sharing Nathaniel Hawthorne's definition of the "unpardonable sin," Reardon mocks the stupid cruelty of the veterans' hospital where Freytag works and the flagrant hypocrisy of its management toward the lonely, confused, frightened, and thoroughly unhappy doctor. The "brooding, barren immensity" of the Kansas farm in *Siamese Connections* provides a metaphor for the story of two brothers—the favored one who was killed in Vietnam and the one who survived but did not know how to kill the ghosts that made him into a homicidal monster, resentful of his brother, unable to escape, condemned. In *The Leaf People,* a demanding play for actors and technicians, Reardon underscores one of the ironies of life while dramatizing mankind's murderous pathway to power. The action takes place in the Amazon rain forest, where a rock star searches for his father, an Irish apostle named Shaughnessey who has discovered and wants to save the Leaf People. Internal conflict prevents the Leaf People from protecting themselves from the invisible greed of the outside world, the apostle dies, the son fails as a messenger of their danger, and disaster results. Eventually, new residents in the area say that they have "never heard of any tribe called the Leaf People."

In all of Reardon's plays since 1980 there has been a persistent probing of man's sensitivities and sensibilities, but his overall perspective is obviously comic. As he writes about the human comedy, however, laughter is not his objective; understanding is. If people laugh, it is as likely the laughter of pain or startled hilarity, a dark and improbable humor. The stereotypical characters in the absurd world of *The Incredible Standing Man and His Friends,* "a parody of dysfunction on both the societal and individual levels," may produce such confused laughter. Who helps and what happens to the inarticulate man in a situation people do not understand? *Steeple Jack,* Reardon's most balanced view of life, dramatizes the trials of a young girl, tortured by fears and despairs, who is guided to hope by an illiterate busboy and a self-anointed apostle who preaches at perpetual man as he trudges on toward Armageddon. In *Subterranean Homesick Blues Again* the cavern tour guide, Charon, appropriately delivers his querulous tourists with ironic politeness to that place where "the turbulence and confusion of your days beneath the Sun are ended." *Security* and *Club Renaissance* (unpublished) in *Unauthorized Entries* written 1984; both show the insubstantiality of modern times, in which a whimsical fate controls. A darker humor prevails in *New Cures for Sunburn,* in which the disastrous impulses of family cruelty and morbidity reach a climax in a loss of human dignity for all. In opposition to such bleak pictures of grotesque man, *Sanctuary for Two Violins* (*Under Assault*), written in 1984 but unpublished, repeats the hope of *Steeple Jack* as two old violinists heroically resist the assaults of life and survive to create the music described in the final line of the play, "How lovely!"

Reardon's major plays in the 1990s were *Boone Descended* (written in 1992, unpublished) and *The Pen Panel* (written in 1996, unpublished). Both plays reveal Reardon's view of a modern world that leaves much to be desired. Irony abounds. David Boone is a man of glorious disappointments, not the least of which is his umpteenth descendent, David Boone, who lives in present-day degradation and is tantalized by the "strong seed" that he presumably enjoys while proclaiming himself "king" of a universe alien to his own. *The Pen Panel,* almost an in-joke for playwrights, attacks the politically correct panel—a young idealist, a cynical journeyman playwright, a black woman, a lesbian, and a gay man—assembled by the New York Playwrights Endowment Council to pick three winners for a sponsored competition. A seriocomic but patently truthful absurdity, the abusive and agenda-ridden discussion is finally terminated by the contest administrator, whose comment—"Wasn't it fun?"—underscores the acerbic irony.

Having chosen the stage on which to project the conflicts and crises of modern man, Reardon finds that he has a great deal to say about moral obligations, a mechanical society, the illusions of security, destructive cynicism, fraudulence and perversity, and the destructive forces of vulgarity. In order to underline his concerns, he is an explorer in contemporary theater. Music—rock, popular ballads, a sonata for two violins—plays an important role in his art. Like many writers—such as Thornton Wilder, whom he appears to admire—Reardon experiments with the concept of time and the complexity of its adequate expression on stage. In *Siamese Connections* the dead and the living exist together; in *The Incredible Standing Man* life hangs waiting for a traffic light to change; in *Sanctuary for Two Violins* dance movements project timeless assaults on life. In *Boone Descended* past and present time merge to predicate the future. In these experiments with time, some of Reardon's plays suggest the vertical approach of No drama, unfettered by realistic representation or linear progression of thought. Space—on stage or imagined—also stabs Reardon's consciousness and moves him toward shifting scenes divided by numerous blackouts. His work is further marked by that relentless energy, carefully orchestrated in such plays as *Steeple Jack, Standing Man,* and *Boone Descended,* to produce compelling and thoughtful drama.

—Walter J. Meserve

RECKORD, Barry

Nationality: Jamaican. **Born:** Kingston, Jamaica, 1926. **Education:** Kingston College; Oxford University, 1952. **Career:** Teacher, Kingston College, 1956; teacher, Luse Secondary School, England and University of Alberta, Canada. Lived in London until 1970; now lives in Jamaica. **Awards:** Guggenheim fellowship, 1974. **Address:** c/o Tricycle Theatre, 269 Kilburn High Road, London NW6 7JR, England.

Publications

Plays

Adella (produced London, 1954; revised version, as *Flesh to a Tiger*, produced London, 1958).
You in Your Small Corner (produced Cheltenham, 1960; London, 1961).
Skyvers (produced London, 1963). Published in *New English Dramatists 9*, London, Penguin, 1966.
Don't Gas the Blacks (produced London, 1969).
A Liberated Woman (also director: produced New York, 1970; London, 1971).
Give the Gaffers Time to Love You (produced London, 1973).
X (produced London, 1974).
Streetwise, music and lyrics by Reckord (produced London, 1982).
White Witch (produced London, 1985).

Radio Play: *Malcolm X*, 1973.

Television Plays: *In the Beautiful Caribbean*, 1972; *Club Havana*, 1975.

Other

Does Fidel Eat More Than Your Father: Cuban Opinion. London, Deutsch, and New York, Praeger, 1971.

*

Theatrical Activities:
Director: **Play**—*A Liberated Woman*, New York, 1970.

Actor: **Play**—Guy in *A Liberated Woman*, London, 1971.

* * *

Barry Reckord's studies of the effects of exploitation are thorough and broad based. In his early play *Flesh to a Tiger* we are let in on the struggle of people in a Jamaican slum trying to emancipate themselves from superstition without falling under white domination. Della is a beautiful but poor woman, and her child is dying. She has to choose between the local "shepherd's" magic and the English doctor's medicine. Half-fearful of magic and half in love with the doctor, she encourages him to be insulted in the end for what he regards as his "weakness." She finally smothers the baby and stabs the shepherd.

But exploitation is basically a class evil rather than a racial one, and Reckord illustrates this impressively in his most famous play, *Skyvers,* which is an authentic picture of students in a London comprehensive school just before they drop out. The beautifully preserved Cockney patter is another triumph of the play. As with *Flesh to a Tiger,* it deals with the incipient violence that results from frustration and limited choice. The students are surrounded by parents and teachers who are social failures, and they dream about football stars, pop singers, and big-time criminals. Even if we deny that such schools are invented to suppress talent, the effect is the same. And the sight of "criminally ill-educated," uncertain boys suddenly acting with confidence and more than a hint of violence when they get together as a group should be a warning.

Having looked at exploitation of the group, Reckord then examined the other side of the coin, the liberation of the individual. In *Don't Gas the Blacks* he introduces a black lover to test the professed liberalism of a middle-class Hampstead couple and succeeds in exposing the racism of the one and in destroying the sexual fantasies of the white woman about the black man. In *A Liberated Woman* the experiment is taken a stage further, for here it is the husband who is black and the wife's lover white. Does the wife's liberation extend to her having a white lover?

Reckord is also interested in establishing the link between social and economic exploitation and the obsession of blacks to ape white bourgeois values. The aping can be seen in a lighter vein in *You in Your Small Corner,* where it is the black bourgeois family in Brixton who are the custodians of "culture." It is they who are educated and who "talk posh," and it is the English who are downtrodden and "common." The black mother, the successful owner of a club, does not want her son to get serious about the local girls but to wait until he goes up to Cambridge, where he will meet "people of his own class."

In the television play *In the Beautiful Caribbean,* however, the mood is darker. Nothing much seems to have changed in Jamaica since *Flesh to a Tiger* 14 years earlier except that now the class and race battles are fought to the death. The society does really seem to be in disintegration because of the many special interests that are hostile to each other. There is the American exploitation of bauxite, the drug industry, the subordination of the black working classes by the black middle classes, unemployment, the generation gap, and more.

This is not new in itself, but what is new is the people's refusal to be abused indefinitely, which brings about the black power uprising. We trace this from One Son, who is fired from his job as captain of a fishing boat, becomes interested in politics, and starts selling a black power newspaper. He is thrown in jail and beaten and killed because the police think that he knows where the black power guns are hidden. His friend Jonathan, a barrister and therefore middle-class, finally manages to forego the temptations of white power and becomes a persuasive black power orator instead. And as so often happens, the end is bloodshed and defeat.

—E. A. Markham

REDDIN, Keith

Nationality: American. **Born:** New Jersey, 7 July 1956. **Education:** Northwestern University, Evanston, Illinois, B.S. 1978; Yale University School of Drama, New Haven, Connecticut, M.A. 1981. **Family:** Married Leslie Lyles in 1986. **Awards:** McArthur award, 1984; San Diego Critics Circle award, 1989, 1990. **Agent:** Peter Franklin, William Morris Agency, 1325 Avenue of the Americas, New York, New York 10019, U.S.A.

Publications

Plays

Throwing Smoke (produced Atlanta, Georgia, 1980). With *Desperadoes* and *Keyhole Lover*, New York, Dramatists Play Service, 1986.

Life and Limb (produced Costa Mesa, California, 1984; New York, 1985). New York, Dramatists Play Service, 1985.

Desperadoes (produced New York, 1985). With *Throwing Smoke* and *Keyhole Lover*, New York, Dramatists Play Service, 1986.

Rum and Coke (produced New Haven, Connecticut, 1985; New York, 1986). New York, Broadway Play Publishing, 1986.

Keyhole Lover (produced New York, 1987). With *Desperadoes* and *Throwing Smoke*, New York, Dramatists Play Service, 1986.

Desperadoes, Throwing Smoke, Keyhole Lover. New York, Dramatists Play Service, 1986.

Highest Standard of Living (produced Costa Mesa, California and New York, 1986). New York, Broadway Play Publishing, 1987.

After School Special (produced New York, 1987; as *The Big Squirrel*, produced New York, 1987).

Plain Brown Wrapper (5 sketches) (produced New York, 1987).

Big Time (produced Chicago, Illinois, 1987; New York and London, 1988). New York, Broadway Play Publishing, 1988.

Nebraska (produced La Jolla, California, 1989; New York, 1991). New York, Broadway Play Publishing, 1990.

Life During Wartime (produced La Jolla, California, 1990; New York, 1991). New York, Dramatists Play Service, 1991.

Innocents' Crusade (produced New Haven, Connecticut, 1991; New York, 1992). New York, Dramatists Play Service, 1993.

Black Snow. New York, Dramatists Play Service, 1993.

Brutality of Fact. New York, Dramatists Play Service, 1995.

Television Plays: *Big Time*, 1988; *The Heart of Justice*, 1990; *Praha*, 1991.

*

Theatrical Activities:
Actor: **Plays**—Third red soldier, art student, fifth comrade, fourth airman, and Dockerill in *No End of Blame* by Howard Barker, New York, 1981; Geoffrey in *A Taste of Honey* by Shelagh Delaney, New York, 1981; Melvin McMullen in *Cliffhanger* by James Yaffe, 1985; Leo Davis in *Room Service* by John Murray and Allen Boretz, New York, 1986; Dr. William Polidori in *Bloody Poetry* by Howard Brenton, New York, 1987; role in *Precious Memories* by Romulus Linney, New York, 1988; role in *Just Say No* by Larry Kramer, New York, 1988; Dennis Post in *The Bug* by Richard Strand, Louisville, Kentucky, 1989; role in *Buzzsaw Berkeley* by Doug Wright, New York, 1989.

* * *

That Keith Reddin is considered one of America's most political playwrights is less an accurate assessment of his dramaturgical preoccupations than it is an indictment of a nation of historical amnesiacs. Indeed, Reddin is part of a disenchanted generation of American writers, baby boomers who were raised on television and the homespun, fictitious ideals of American supremacy. These writers, who came to maturity after Watergate, wish to combat the critical forces of amnesia and nostalgia in the national psyche. With varying degrees of naïveté, they display a political consciousness rather than particular agendas. Many of Reddin's plays are set around textbook topics and incidents like the Korean War (*Life and Limb*), the Cold War (*Highest Standard of Living*), the Bay of Pigs invasion (*Rum and Coke*), or the use of nuclear power (*Nebraska*). Like most American filmmakers and playwrights, what Reddin does is to use political events and cultural patterns as a backdrop for an individual's struggle with fractious personal relationships. The political is traduced by the personal, and the result is a sharply satirical, uneasy sketch about another episode in the ongoing saga of America's moral complacency.

A Reddin play typically centers around a well-meaning, bright, unsuspecting gull who joins a powerful organization only to gradually awaken to its incorporated evil. The hero is given opportunities to stand against the juggernaut or at least to get out, but he is shown to be either too powerless or too passive to make a difference. When he does speak out, events have passed him by, or he sustains a sudden and tragic personal loss. The play then becomes an opportunity for the sadder but wiser narrator to detail his loss of innocence for the audience. At the outset of *Rum and Coke*, for example, Jake, the raw CIA recruit who finds himself unable to stem the tide in Cuba, states, "This is how I got messed up in something called the Bay of Pigs."

Jake's admission, offhand yet personal and an invitation that deflects pain through mockery, is an example of Reddin's characteristic tone. Reddin is an actor, and although he does not perform in his own work, for better and for worse he writes for the actor. The scenes are taut, brisk, and highly verbal, and yet the characters often seem underwritten until actors flesh out the conflicts with their presence. Even the minor characters are provided with monologues or nonnaturalistic outbursts to the audience that showcase the actors' talents. A Reddin play is not concerned with subtextual moorings and structural transitions, and it is performed at high velocity and high pitch, the comedy arising from abrupt shifts in tone and emphasis and a predilection for the grotesque detail in everyday circumstances.

Reddin makes use of a postmodern sensibility. Having the theologian Calvin make a visit from the sixteenth century to deliver an ad hoc diatribe against the utter debasement of contemporary language and finish with a reference to Yul Brynner in *The King and I* is a typical Reddin moment. One of his themes is the anaesthetizing effect of popular culture and the media on the individual, and his plays bristle with references to advertising slogans, household products, songs, old movies, political buzzwords, and so forth. In production his comedies feature virtual sound tracks of popular recordings as commentary on the action. Reddin is also something of a fantasist. In two very different plays the love interests of the heroes die unexpectedly. In *Life and Limb*, just as things are finally looking better for Franklin and Effie in 1950s suburbia, Effie is killed in a freak movie theater accident, presumably because she has committed adultery and must pay for it. In *Life During Wartime* Gail is the victim of a senseless murder in which her young lover Tommy is an unwitting yet circumstantial accessory. These deaths of highly sympathetic characters are completely shocking. The playwright himself cannot seem to part with them or to face up to his dramaturgical choice, and so in each instance he has the dead woman return from the other world to console her grieving man.

Is this comic resurrection or infantile, patent wish fulfillment? Reddin would seem to want it both ways, seeking theatrical resolution while showing such a gesture to be false. His heroes and heroines connect best when they are in different spaces. While they walk the earth, they are pulled irresistibly to become like everyone else—amoral, compromised, money mad, power driven. Time and again Reddin shows that blows come when they are least expected, that people are much more evil than expected, and that the web of complicity is always more extensive than is assumed. In a society administered by the corrupt and controlled by the media, how can a person hope to keep his hands clean? All that one can do is bear witness. If Reddin's earliest plays can be seen as fashionably cynical political cartoons, his later work demonstrates a more profound treatment of individual loss. Small wonder then that his play opening in 1991 was titled the *Innocents' Crusade*.

—James Magruder

REID, Christina

Nationality: Irish. **Born:** Belfast, 12 March 1942. **Education:** Everton Primary School, 1947-49, Girls Model School, 1949-57, and Queens University, 1982-83, all Belfast. **Family:** Married in 1964 (divorced 1987); three children. **Career:** Worked in various office jobs in Belfast, 1957-70; writer-in-residence, Lyric Theatre, Belfast, 1983-84, and Young Vic Theatre, London, 1988-89. **Awards:** Ulster Television Drama award, 1980; Thames Television Playwriting award, 1983; George Devine award, 1986.

PUBLICATIONS

Plays

Did You Hear the One About the Irishman . . . ? (produced New York, 1982; London, 1987). With *The Belle of Belfast City*, London, Methuen, 1989.

Tea in a China Cup (produced Belfast, 1983; London, 1984). With *Joyriders*, London, Methuen, 1987.

Joyriders (produced London, 1986; New York, 1992). With *Tea in a China Cup*, London, Methuen, 1987.

The Last of a Dyin' Race (broadcast 1986). Published in *Best Radio Plays of 1986*, London, Methuen, 1986.

My Name, Shall I Tell You My Name (broadcast 1987; produced London, 1990).

The Belle of Belfast City (produced Belfast, 1989). With *Did You Hear the One About the Irishman . . .?*, London, Methuen, 1989.

Les Miserables, adaptation of the novel by Victor Hugo (produced Nottingham, 1992).

Joyriders and Did You Hear the One About the Irishman...? Oxford, Heinemann Educational, 1993.

Plays (includes *Tea in a China Cup*; *Did You Hear the One About the Irishman . . . ?*; *Joyriders*; *The Belle of Belfast City*; *My Name, Shall I Tell You My Name*; *Clowns*). London, Methuen Drama, 1997.

Radio Plays: *The Last of a Dyin' Race*, 1986; *My Name, Shall I Tell You My Name*, 1987; *The Unfortunate Fursey*, adaptation of the novel by Mervyn Wall, 1989; *Today and Yesterday in Northern Ireland*, for children, 1989.

Television Play: *The Last of a Dyin' Race*, 1987.

*

Critical Studies: "Dramatic Strategy in Christina Reid's *Tea in a China Cup*" by Diderik Roll-Hansen, in *Modern Drama* (Downsview, Ontario), September 1987, pp. 389-95; "Christina Reid" by Carla J. McDonaugh, in *Irish Playwrights, 1880-1995: A Research and Production Sourcebook*, edited by Bernice Schrank and William W. Demastes, Westport, Connecticut, Greenwood, 1997.

Christina Reid comments:

I come from a long line of Irish storytellers. The women of my mother's family didn't just sit still and tell tales, they dressed up and enacted a mixture of fact and fiction through song, dance, and dialogue, as much for their own enjoyment as to entertain us children. It is my earliest memory of theatre. In my plays, characters often tell their story as naturally in song and dance as they do in words, and much of my writing to date has been about the women and children of Northern Ireland. There are strong parts for men in the plays, but there are usually more women in the cast, and the main storyline tends to be mostly theirs. I don't set out to do this in any causal way; it is simply how I write, but I do think that too often Northern Ireland is portrayed on stage and screen as if "the troubles" and male violence is the whole rather than a part of life there, and that this leaves too many songs unsung.

* * *

Much as the weaver of homespun interlaces strands of yarn, Christina Reid alternates the tragedies of Belfast life with her ironic humor. Her plays are at once soft and abrasive, delicate and resilient, and they blanket us in warmth. Her portraits of working-class people are well crafted, their characters revealed quickly and neatly by series of humble incidents. Woven into the comfort of the ordinary is the horror of the extraordinary, and entwined in the pain is the ache of laughter. The effect is outrageous as prejudice, deprivation, and death are reduced to commonplace events that we can understand no matter where we live.

Outrage is a natural reaction to Reid's first play, the one-act *Did You Hear the One about the Irishman . . . ?* It is a 1980s romance à la Victor Hugo in that the sublime and the grotesque coexist. Allison, a Protestant, and Brian, a Catholic, are idealists in an imperfect world. Neither can understand why it could be dangerous for them to marry, even though Brian's father was murdered and both have relatives in Long Kesh, where political prisoners are held. Their dialogue is witty and gentle, in contrast to the pleading of their families and the warnings of the prisoners. Periodic appearances are made by an Irishman who reads from a list of "Permitted Christmas Parcels" for the prison, thereby injecting reality, and by a comedian whose anti-Irish jokes are increasingly ominous. In counterpoint to Allison's and Brian's joke about forming their own peaceful Apathy Party, the comedian talks of the inevitable violent deaths the Irish must suffer. The tragic conclusion is expected, yet the theatrical impact is not diminished. Reid makes effective use of black humor.

Tea in a China Cup is a lovely, quiet play. Although it takes place during the Troubles, it is concerned more with pride, making the proper impression, and not airing dirty linen in public. It is the maintenance of dignity that obsesses Beth's working-class Protestant family, and it is fear of becoming caught in the same domestic trap that motivates Beth. In the first scene Beth must buy a grave plot for her mother, Sarah, who is dying of cancer. Reid's ironic faculty is evident immediately as Beth must decide between the Catholic and Protestant sections of the new cemetery lest her mother stand out "like a sore thumb." Always aware of tradition, Sarah hopes only to live until the 12th of July, when the Orangemen will again march past her window. She cautions Beth to remember all of the family stories after she is gone, and Beth tells us about the men who went to war, the women who laid out the dead, her own friendship with a Catholic girl, and the importance of having what her grandmother called "a wee bit of fine bone china." But the china that to Sarah symbolizes the last vestige of civilization in a city of soldiers and Catholics is a bane to Beth. As Reid leads us through 30 years in the life of the family, Beth matures. In the end, still loving them all, she is able to break free of the restrictions that bound the women to home and custom. Superstition, prejudice, and tradition are cast aside in one last ironic act. Hope is possible.

Less optimistic is *Joyriders,* a spirited evocation of what it means to be a poor Catholic teenager in Belfast. Sandra, Maureen, Arthur, and Tommy are four residents of the deplorable Divis Flats housing development who are given a chance to prove themselves in a youth training program. Two are young offenders, one was scarred when the army accidentally shot him, and one lives alone with her glue-sniffing brother. Reid first places these characters in a theater, watching the end of Sean O'Casey's *Shadow of a Gunman* with their social worker Kate. By their reactions to the dialogue, their characters are instantly defined. Tommy, possibly a half-caste, is defensive; the disfigured Arthur is a joker; Sandra is practical; Maureen is a romantic. Together, they form a kind of family that Kate leads through various vicissitudes to a conclusion even she cannot control. The startling reversal is reminiscent of the well-made play. *Joyriders* is a particularly ironic title, since the activity brings the group only momentary joy and lasting misery. More ironic still is Kate's realization that the entire training course is the ultimate joyride since, when it ends, the participants have little chance of finding jobs. The course itself is constantly threatened with extinction. Sandra, Maureen, Arthur, and Tommy all rejoin the cycle of hopelessness. In several ways the play ends by coming full circle. Reid creates a sensitive portrait of teenagers trying to find their identities in a society that has no place for them. The issue is the fate of children from what Reid quotes as "the worst housing development in Western Europe."

The Belle of Belfast City takes its title from a music hall song sung by Dolly, the aging child star and matriarch of the play's family. As three generations gather, their reunion is marred by Jack, a loyalist who protests against the Anglo-Irish agreement with the Reverend Ian Paisley. All of Dolly's women—Belle, the half-caste granddaughter; the niece Janet, the victim of her brother Jack's incestuous attentions; the brave Vi and the idealistic Rose, Dolly's daughters—are subject to the males in power. Jack, the conservative Protestant zealot, and Tom, a strong-arm English "businessman," both harass the women. Each copes in her own valiant way, but each is swept along on the political undercurrent that ripples through the play. Vi is eventually persuaded to sell her shop. Rose fears the right-wing Catholic stand, so like Jack's, that limits women's rights. Reid is more straightforward about her politics than usual.

Reid's themes are women and their submissive role in Northern Ireland, their families, and the damage caused to both by the Troubles. She speaks sympathetically yet unsentimentally and with the authority of one who knows the people and the customs about which she writes. It is a tribute to her skill that we can receive her message while being entertained. In no sense do we feel that we have been subjected to a lecture, and yet we are filled with rage. In the midst of a lovely story is the inescapable presence of oppression, of a cycle of hopelessness despite courage. It is Reid's humor that gives resilience to her characters and provides a fascinating contrast to degradation and horror. Her frequent use of music also adds texture to her plays.

—Carol Banks

RENÉE

Nationality: New Zealander. **Born:** Renée Gertrude Jones in Napier, 19 July 1929. **Education:** Primary schools to age 12; extra-mural study at Massey University, Palmerston North, from 1967: B.A. (University of Auckland) 1979. **Family:** Married in 1949 (divorced); three sons. **Career:** English and drama teacher in secondary schools, Wairoa, and at Long Bay College, Auckland, 1975-81; member, Womenspirit Collective, 1979-85, and Broadsheet Collective, Auckland, 1982-84; organized and led several writing workshops, 1983-85; playwright-in-residence, Theatre Corporate, Auckland, 1986; Robert Burns fellow, Otago University, Dunedin, 1989. Actress and director with Napier Repertory Players, Wairoa Community Theatre, and in Auckland. National vice-president, P.E.N., 1992. Lives in Dunedin. **Awards:** Queen Elizabeth II Arts Council grant, 1982, and award, 1986; New Zealand Literary Fund Merit award, 1986; Robert Burns fellowship, University of Otago, 1989; Project Grant from Literature Boar, Queen Elizabeth II Arts Council, 1991; Scholarship in Letters from Queen Elizabeth II Arts Council, 1993; Writer's fellowship, University of Waikato, 1995. **Agent:** Playmarket, P.O. Box 9767, Wellington, New Zealand.

PUBLICATIONS

Plays

Secrets: Two One-Woman Plays (produced Auckland, 1982; revised version produced Auckland, 1987). With *Setting the Table*, Wellington, Playmarket, 1984.

Breaking Out (produced Wellington, 1982).

Setting the Table (produced Auckland, 1982). With *Secrets*, Wellington, Playmarket, 1984.
What Did You Do in the War, Mummy? (also director: produced Auckland, 1982).
Asking for It (also director: produced Kaikohe, 1983).
Dancing (produced Auckland, 1984).
Wednesday to Come (produced Wellington, 1984). Wellington, Victoria University Press, 1985.
Groundwork (produced Auckland, 1985).
Pass It On (produced Auckland, 1986). Wellington, Victoria University Press, 1986; reprint 1994.
Born to Clean, songs by Jess Hawk Oakenstar and Hilary King (produced Auckland, 1987).
Form (for children). Dunedin, McIndoe, 1990. Published in *Song of the Shirt*, Dunedin, McIndoe.
Jeannie Once (produced Dunedin, 1990). Wellington, Victoria University Press, 1991.
Touch of the Sun (produced Dunedin, 1991).
Missionary Position (produced Dunedin, 1991).
Te Pouaka Karaehe: The Glass Box (also director: produced Wellington, 1992).
Tiggy Tiggy Touch Wood (produced Dunedin, 1992). Published in *Playlunch*, edited by Christine Prentice and Lisa Warrington, University of Otago Press, 1996; published in *Intimate Acts: Eight Contemporary Lesbian Plays*, New York, Brito and Lair.
Pink Spots & Mountain Tops (for children; also director: produced, 1992).
Heroines, Hussies & High High Flyers (produced Dunedin, 1993).

Radio Plays: *The Snowball Waltz*, 1994; *Diversions for an Idle Hour*, 1994; *My Name is Marama Kingi*, 1994; *Rugosa Roses Are Very Hardy*, 1994; *Dreaming in Ponsonby*, 1994; *Sister to Dragons*, 1994; *Hard and Unfamiliar Words*, 1996; *Does This Make Sense To You?*, 1996.

Television Plays: *Husbands and Wives* (*Country G.P.* series), 1985; *Beginnings and Endings*, *Strings*, *Sheppard Street*, and *Journeys* (*Open House* series), 1986.

Novels

Willy Nilly. Auckland, Penguin, 1990.
Daisy and Lily. Auckland, Penguin, 1993.
Does This Make Sense To You?. Auckland, Penguin, 1995.
I Have To Go Home (for children). Auckland, Penguin, 1997.
The Snowball Waltz. Auckland, Penguin, 1997.

Short Stories

Finding Ruth. Auckland, Heinemann, 1987.

Uncollected Short Stories

"Old Movies" (in *Hero Paper*, 1994).
"Rarely Pure and Never Simple" (in *Metro Magazine*, January 1995).

*

Manuscript Collection: University of Canterbury, Christ-church; Playmarket, Wellington.

Theatrical Activities:
Director: **Plays**—*What Did You Do in the War, Mummy?*, New Zealand tour, 1982; *Asking for It*, New Zealand tour, 1983; *Te Pouaka Karaehe* (*The Glass Box*), Wellington, 1992.

* * *

Since she began writing plays, Renée has remained true to the principles that first inspired her. They are to celebrate the lives of ordinary working women and to give prominence to their undervalued struggles in times of social change. At the same time she writes with humor and a light touch. Widely respected as New Zealand's most prolific and versatile woman dramatist, she explores themes of gender, class, and race. Perhaps because her work coincided with the upsurge in feminist thinking and because it filled a need for more and better parts for women in plays, all of the major professional theaters performed her plays during the 1980s.

Setting the Table, written in January 1981, is a naturalistic play that shows women as intelligent, humorous, and strong and that also handles radical feminist questions. Set in a kitchen and revolving around four women who run a refuge for those who have been battered, the action arises from the actions of an angry husband who follows one of the workers home while he is looking for his wife. Sheila, who works at a public hospital, has become so angered by living in a culture that accepts rape that she takes the opportunity to intimidate a violent man. She injures him with a knife, ties a yellow ribbon around his penis, and hangs a sign on him saying, "This man is a rapist." The central issue that follows from this action is whether or not it is ever necessary or acceptable to retaliate with violence in a violent situation.

Renée's best-known work is a historical trilogy that began in 1984 with *Wednesday to Come* (set in the 1930s), followed by *Pass It On* (1951), and completed in 1990 with *Jeannie Once* (1879). The plays tell the stories of four generations of working-class women during times of upheaval. *Wednesday to Come* is also set in a kitchen, but this time during the Great Depression while a march of the unemployed to Parliament passes the house. Inside, a young woman is waiting for the body of her husband, who has committed suicide in a work camp, to be returned to her. Four generations of women live together, represented by five well-drawn characters who retain their individuality while signifying class oppression and working women's invincibility.

While keeping the teenagers Jeannie and her brother from the previous play, *Pass It On* takes the action forward to the 1951 waterfront confrontation in which men fought each other in the streets. Because it is against the law to help strikers or to publish any news about them, a handwritten broadsheet is being printed and distributed (hence the title). This time the technique is Brechtian rather than naturalistic, and several actors are used to fill many smaller roles. The effect is more didactic than in the earlier play.

Jeannie Once goes back to the first Jeannie, the grandmother of *Wednesday to Come*, and explores her first years in New Zealand in 1879. Renée again tries new ways of telling her story, using music hall songs and many characters in short scenes. Women are the strong center of a group of people from Britain trying to make a new life in a distant colony. Issues of racial prejudice appear in the victimization of 19-year-old Martha, a Maori accused of stealing.

A racial theme is also obvious in *Groundwork*, set during the 1981 South African Springbok rugby tour of New Zealand, which takes the play inside prison and in flashback to a suburban home. Lesbian relationships are also thematic in this play, as they were covertly in *Setting the Table* and *Breaking Out* and more overtly in *Belle's Place*.

Missionary Position is a full-length play in which three bag ladies seek refuge from life's realities at the bottom of the social heap by living in a film star fantasy in which they cast themselves as Garbo, Monroe, and Dietrich. As she has often done, Renée uses music to counterpoint the action. *Touch of the Sun* is a comedy with strong roles for two women who play sisters sorting through the extensive wardrobe of their dead mother and discovering that things were not quite as they imagined in her life. The dominant presence of the dead mother looms over their lives and, it appears, always will.

Maori values set alongside success in the European world is the theme of *Te Pouaka Karaehe* (*The Glass Box*). "I think people get caught up in the glass box [of the city] and that becomes a barrier. Just living in the city and learning city ways and playing city games, you forget some of the things about home," Renee has said of the play. Handicapped by three offstage characters who do not appear but who are constantly talked about, *The Glass Box* gives good opportunities for Maori women actors, but the focus is diffused over several cultural and political issues, which weakens the impact. *Tiggy Tiggy Touch Wood* is a tragicomedy about a woman who was brain damaged years before as the result of a vicious attack. She is cared for by a friend who loves her, but the time has come when a decision must be made about putting her in a home.

Renée has added television scripts, a collection of short stories (*Finding Ruth*), a film treatment, and a novel (*Willy Nilly*) to her output. Plays, however, continue to be her first line of creative communication with a society not by any means fully adjusted to the feminist point of view.

—Patricia Cooke

REZNIKOV, Hanon

Nationality: American. **Born:** New York, New York, 1950. **Education:** Yale University, B.A. in drama. **Family:** Married Judith Malina in 1988. **Career:** Joined the Living Theatre, 1973; executive director of the Living Theatre, 1985—. Also teacher of theater at various schools including New York University, the Eugene O'Neill Theater Center, American Conservatory Theater, and The New School for Social Research. **Awards:** Ninth Centennial Medal, University of Bologna, Bologna, Italy, 1988; Obie, for sustained achievement, 1989; Medaglia D'Onore, City of Palermo, Palermo, Italy.

PUBLICATIONS

Plays

Strike Support Oratorium (produced New York, 1973).
The Money Tower (produced Pittsburgh, 1975).
The Yellow Methuselah (produced Rome, 1982; New York, 1984).
Poland/1931 (produced New York, 1988).
The Tablets (produced New York, 1989).
Clearing the Streets (produced New York, 1989).
The Body of God (produced New York, 1989).
Rules of Civility and Decent Behavior in Company and in Conversation (produced New York, 1991).
The Zero Method (produced New York, 1991).
Waste (produced New York, 1991).
Anarchia (produced New York, 1993).
And Then the Heavens Closed (dproduced New York, 1995).
Utopia (produced Germany, 1995).
Capital Changes (produced New York, 1998).

*

Theatrical Activities:
Actor: **Plays**–*Seven Meditations on Political Sado-Masochism*, 1973-78; *Strike Support Oratorium*, 1973-78; *Six Public Acts*, 1975-78; *The Money Tower*, 1975-77; *Prometheus at the Winter Palace*, 1978-79; *Antigone*, 1979-84; *Masse-Mensch*, 1980-84; *The Archeology of Sleep*, 1983-84; *VKTMS: Orestes in Scenes*, 1988; *The Tablets*, 1990; *The Zero Method*, 1991; *Mysteries and Smaller Pieces*, 1992-96; *The Rape of Persephone*, 1997; *The Libation Beaters*, 1997.

* * *

Hanon Reznikov was an undergraduate at Yale University when the Living Theatre, then based in Europe, opened *Paradise Now* in New Haven on its 1968-69 American tour. At the end of the performance Judith Malina and Julian Beck, who had founded the theater in New York in 1947, led the audience into the streets to proclaim the Beautiful Nonviolent Anarchist Revolution, and they spent the night in jail. After receiving his B.A. in drama, Reznikov joined the company, and since 1973 he has devoted his considerable energies to working under the banner of the Living Theatre. Following Beck's death in 1985, he became executive director, with Malina as artistic director.

By the time of Reznikov's arrival, the work that had made Beck and Malina's reputation was behind them and the roving communal troupe dispersed, with commerce co-opting the cultural loosening of the 1960s. Collective creation had largely run its course, but the Living Theatre's working method remained intensely collaborative. Headquartered in Brooklyn after a harrowing sojourn in Brazil, the group continued to develop theater pieces in a unique style, at once confrontationally political, humane, and poetic.

From the start Reznikov worked both as an actor and as a playwright and director. During the Brooklyn period much of the work was site- or occasion-specific, including the *Strike Support Oratorium* of 1973 and *The Money Tower*, which was designed to be performed outside factory gates at the time of shift changes.

Systematically marginalized in its homeland by the evolving media culture, in 1975 the Living Theatre returned to Europe, took up residence in Rome, and toured widely over the next nine years. It presented the street plays made in New York, attracted a fresh troupe of young actors, and developed new expressionist works. The company returned to the United States in 1984 with a repertoire that included Reznikov's *The Yellow Methuselah*, an ambitious visual and mythopoetic spectacle inspired by Shaw's *Back to Methuselah* and the writings of the modernist painter Wassily Kandinsky. During the press performance at New York's Joyce Theatre, Beck as Shaw sat on the lap of the critic for the *New York Times*. The Living Theatre was scapegoated as representing a 1960s counterculture of liberation, and press hostility aborted the planned American tour. Practical difficulties as well as Beck's illness and death subsequently caused a hiatus in the Living Theatre's work.

In 1988 Malina and Reznikov married and resumed a vigorous schedule of productions. *Poland/1931* reintroduced the Living Theatre to the New York public. Reznikov, adapting poems by Jerome Rothenberg, used space and theatrical styles freely in dramatizing the text. The work illuminated the immigrant experience, which touched Reznikov too, with a sophisticated, sharply contemporary literary sensibility. A tender feeling for individual character complemented a harsh economic analysis and a witty, spontaneous sense of style.

The next year Malina and Reznikov opened a new Living Theatre in a makeshift space on East Third Street, a slum neighborhood respectable audiences shunned, and set about rebuilding the acting company. Poems by Armand Schwerner were the basis of Reznikov's *The Tablets,* an ensemble movement piece with a flavor of timeless ritual. The text was largely given to the narrator (Reznikov), who played in the local language on tour in Italy and Germany.

Rules of Civility and Decent Behavior in Company and in Conversation, adapted by Reznikov from a text by George Washington, was another semiabstract work on a Greek model. It played two costumed Washingtons against a unified chorus and invited the audience to challenge the ironies of the Founding Father's politesse. At the end of the play, both in New York and on tour in Europe, the cast led the audience into the streets for a candlelight vigil protesting the war against Iraq.

Two street plays, *Tumult, or Clearing the Streets* and *Waste,* were given frequent performances in open spaces in New York City, keeping the Living Theatre's revolutionary humanist philosophy in front of the public. Despite consistently greater respect and support in Europe, especially in Italy, with its responsive students and lively tradition of political theater, Malina and Reznikov were both New Yorkers and felt that their pacifist-anarchist message was most urgently needed at home. They struggled to keep their theater on Third Street open to the community, and Reznikov developed *The Body of God* in collaboration with a dozen homeless people for performances there.

Reznikov's final work in the Third Street theater was a highly personal two-character play. Exploring the philosophy of Ludwig Wittgenstein in the mocking style of classic film noir, *The Zero Method* was essentially a docudrama of Reznikov's love affair with Malina as they pursued the political and artistic work of the Living Theatre. The author performed the work with Malina in New York and abroad. His intellectual bent, dry wit, warm heart, and playful spirit gave this chamber play a rare charm.

After years of group discussions of a play elucidating the Living Theatre's theory of anarchism, Reznikov's *Anarchia* opened at Theater for the New City in New York in 1993. Malina and Reznikov continued to live in New York but did most of their work in Italy, both individually and touring with the Living Theatre company. *Utopia* (1995) opened in Germany and played in Poland, Portugal, and Italy. In New York, Reznikov collaborated with Joanie Fritz on *And Then the Heavens Closed . . .,* based on *The Memoirs of Glückl of Hameln.*

Capital Changes, which premiered at Theater for the New City in 1998, was inspired by Fernand Braudel's *Material Civilization and Capitalism: 1400-1800.* In keeping with the Living Theatre's aesthetic principle of directly engaging the audience, the 13 characters in the play each sold shares in their futures over the centuries. The shares were bought and redeemed in real money as a practical demonstration of how capitalism values the individual.

—Michael T. Smith

RHONE, Trevor D.

Nationality: Jamaican. **Born:** Kingston, 24 March 1940. **Education:** A school in St. Catherine; Beckford and Smith's School (now Jago High School), Spanish Town, 1952-57; Rose Bruford College, Sidcup, Kent, 1960-63. **Family:** Married Camella King in 1974; one daughter and two sons. **Career:** Writer, Jamaican Broadcasting Corporation, Kingston, 1958-60; teacher in Jamaica, 1963-64 and 1965-69; actor in England, 1964-65; founder, Theatre '77 (Barn Theatre), Kingston, 1965. Freelance writer, 1969— **Awards:** Gold medal from Virgin Islands film festival, 1974, for *Smile Orange*; Musgrave gold medal, 1988; Commander of the Order of Distinction. **Agent:** Wiley Hausam, International Creative Management, 40 West 57th Street, New York, New York 10019, U.S.A. **Address:** c/o Drumbeat Series, Longman Group Ltd., 5 Bentinck Street, London W1M 5RN, England.

Publications

Plays

Smile Orange (produced Kingston, 1971; Waterford, Connecticut, and London, 1972). Included in *Old Story Time and Other Plays,* 1981.

The Web (produced Waterford, Connecticut, 1972).

School's Out (produced Kingston, 1975; London, 1986). Included in *Old Story Time and Other Plays*, 1981.

Old Story Time (also director: produced Nassau, 1979; London, 1984). Included in *Old Story Time and Other Plays,* 1981.

Old Story Time and Other Plays. London, Longman, 1981.

Two Can Play (produced London, 1983; New York, 1985). With *School's Out,* London, Longman, 1986; published separately, Lexington, Kentucky, KET, 1986.

One Stop Driver, music by Louis Marriott (produced London, 1989).

Screenplay: *Smile Orange*, 1974.

*

Theatrical Activities:

Director: **Plays**—*Old Story Time*, Nassau, 1979, and London, 1984; *Smile Orange*, London, 1992. **Film**—*Smile Orange*, 1974.

Actor: **Play**—Russ Dacres in *School's Out*, Kingston, 1975.

* * *

Filmmaker, actor, and teacher of acting, Trevor Rhone is Jamaica's best-known playwright and one of the few Caribbean dramatists to be often performed outside the region. Having started the Barn Theatre in Kingston, he has a highly professional understanding of theater economics and the technical abilities and limitations of most drama groups. Written for small casts, using readily available stage props, requiring few set changes, his plays can be easily and inexpensively performed. They are entertaining while treating serious social problems. Rhone writes good acting parts and has a talent for suggesting dialect without clouding meaning for speakers of Standard English. He has a sense of what makes people tick, how they behave toward one other. While he shows people influenced by their environment, their problems are personal and require will to resolve. The plays are Jamaican in subject matter and nationalist in perspective, but their themes are universal. Rhone is especially concerned with domination on a personal and national level and with the ways in which self-interest destroys communal values.

Rhone's first success, *Smile Orange*, is built upon a contrast between the real and the tourist Jamaica as found at a third-rate Montego Bay hotel. Language is representative of cultural and racial identification, as is shown by the hotel telephone operator's shift from the Standard English she uses on her job to the dialect forms she uses in conversation with friends: "Me see one or two dry-up looking white people but [*hiss*] is today dem say di season start proper." In an impoverished society both personal and national relationships are established by financial considerations: "Is money I looking. Him have nutten to offer." Because the workers feel dependent on the American tourists, they suffer from racial self-hatred: "Di boss man have a black man out front as Assistant Manager. Di tourist don't like dat, you know, and I don't blame dem." A satire about the corrupting effect of the tourist economy on Jamaica, *Smile Orange* shows a society in which self-respect and sense of community have been lost, with the result that the characters feel trapped by circumstances, exploit one other, and look toward America for their redemption: "When it get down to di nitty-gritty is each man for himself." Driven rather by self-interest than vocation, dignity, ethics, or sense of community, the hotel employees are unreliable, even malicious. In the background a band plays cheerful music, but tableware is polished with spit and banana skins left lying on the floor.

School's Out, a satirical exposé of the failure of local schools since independence, offers a disillusioned view of Jamaica and of human motives. The missionary school, representative of the nation, is perhaps best symbolized by the nonfunctioning toilet to which the characters often refer. It has been overflowing for weeks, and its stink pervades the school, but no one will have it fixed since it is the responsibility of the apparently absent headmaster, whose unopened door is always present on stage. The teaching staff and chaplain are late to their classes, find excuses to dismiss them early, and by not doing their duty have left the school's canteen and other activities in the control of unsupervised students, whose hooliganism the teachers then use to justify themselves. When a new white teacher begins to restore order, he is accused of asserting himself and of racial pride. As the play's symbolism suggests, he is a Christlike leader whose involvement cuts through the stereotypes and who looks after the students' personal and moral welfare. Seeing their sinecures threatened, the other teachers start rumors of his sexual involvement with the students, which leads to his resignation and the return of disorder and incompetence.

In *School's Out* the staff is divided by politics. The conservatives do nothing to prevent a drop in standards, while praising the past when the school had high standards and excluded the masses. Meanwhile, the semiliterate products of recent mass education drive out the good and hire others like themselves. The obvious analogy is to Jamaican society since independence. The evil of self-interest triumphs over national reform.

The relationships between the political, racial, moral, and religious aspects of Rhone's writing are clear in *Old Story Time*, in which a black mother's initial hatred for and eventual acceptance of her black daughter-in-law is symbolic of Jamaica's coming to terms with itself and its overcoming both black and colonial self-hatred. As in the other plays, relations among characters are illustrative of the national mentality. The play covers 40 years of Jamaican social history, from a time when anything black was condemned as inferior to a present when many of the same prejudices linger on under the surface of national independence. The villain is "a high brown man" who ruthlessly pursues his own self-interest and cheats others, especially trusting blacks.

The use of a *conteur* in *Old Story Time* is a technically effective way of moving back and forth in time. While the use of a traditional oral literary frame reinforces the play's concern with the revaluation of blackness, it allows dramatization of revelations about the past. Similarly, the use of obeah by the mother, the highly educated son's belief in its effectiveness, and the exorcism, half obeah and half Christian, of the mother's hatred are both psychologically probable and a statement about African survival in the New World. The ending is sentimental, but the ceremonial exorcism is good spectacle.

Set in Kingston in the late 1970s, when politics had resulted in a near civil war, with people locking themselves in their houses while the sounds of machine guns are heard in the near distance, *Two Can Play* translates women's liberation to a Jamaican context. The national situation has contributed to the crisis of a marriage in which the husband has dominated, exploited, and humiliated his wife, leaving her sexually and emotionally unsatisfied. Unable to jump the legal and financial hurdles to emigrate to the United States, the husband collapses into futile incompetence, whereas the wife proves to be daring, disciplined, and quick thinking. Having reached the United States on her own, she returns to Jamaica, now conscious of her abilities, to demand that her husband treat her better. To a nation where violence appears to have destroyed society, the United States may seem a promised land, but by the play's conclusion, when the husband and wife can emigrate there, they have learned that American cities are also dangerously violent and marked by racial prejudice and conflict.

—Bruce King

RIBMAN, Ronald (Burt)

Nationality: American. **Born:** New York City, 28 May 1932. **Education:** Brooklyn College, New York, 1950-51; University of Pittsburgh, B.B.A. 1954, M.Litt. 1958, Ph.D. 1962. **Military Service:** Served in the United States Army, 1954-56. **Family:** Married Alice Rosen in 1967; one son and one daughter. **Career:** Assistant professor of English, Otterbein College, Westerville, Ohio, 1962-63. Lives in South Salem, New York. **Awards:** Obie award, 1966; Rockefeller grant, 1966, 1968, 1975; Guggenheim fellowship, 1970; Straw Hat award, 1973; National Endowment for the Arts grant, 1974, fellowship, 1986-87; Creative Artists Public Service grant, 1976; Dramatists Guild Hull-Warriner award, 1977; Playwrights U.S.A. award, 1984; Kennedy Center New American Play grant, 1991. **Agent:** Flora Roberts, Inc., 157 West 57th Street, New York, New York 10019.

Publications

Plays

Harry, Noon and Night (produced New York, 1965). With *The Journey of the Fifth Horse*, Boston, Little Brown, 1967.

The Journey of the Fifth Horse, based in part on "The Diary of a Superfluous Man" by Turgenev (produced New York, 1966; London, 1967). With *Harry, Noon and Night*, Boston, Little Brown, 1967; published separately, London, Davis Poynter, 1974.

The Final War of Olly Winter (televised 1967). Published in *Great Television Plays*, New York, Dell, 1969.

The Ceremony of Innocence (produced New York, 1967). New York, Dramatists Play Service, 1968.

Passing Through from Exotic Places (includes *The Son Who Hunted Tigers in Jakarta, Sunstroke, The Burial of Esposito*) (produced New York, 1969). New York, Dramatists Play Service, 1970.

The Most Beautiful Fish (televised 1969). Published in *New York Times*, 23 November 1969.

The Son Who Hunted Tigers in Jakarta (produced New York, 1989). Included in *Passing Through from Exotic Places*, 1970.

Fingernails Blue as Flowers (produced New York, 1971). Published in *The American Place Theatre*, edited by Richard Schotter, New York, Dell, 1973.

A Break in the Skin (produced New Haven, Connecticut, 1972; New York, 1973).

The Poison Tree (produced Philadelphia, 1973; revised version produced Philadelphia, 1975; New York, 1976). New York, French, 1977.

Cold Storage (produced New York, 1977; London, 1986). Garden City, New York, Nelson Doubleday, 1976.

Five Plays (includes *Cold Storage*; *The Poison Tree*; *The Ceremony of Innocence*; *The Journey of the Fifth Horse*; *Harry, Noon and Night*). New York, Avon, 1978.

Buck (produced New York, 1983). New York, Theatre Communications Group, 1983.

Sweet Table at the Richelieu (produced Cambridge, Massachusetts, 1987). Published in *American Theatre* (New York), July/August 1987.

The Cannibal Masque (produced Cambridge, Massachusetts, 1987).

A Serpent's Egg (produced Cambridge, Massachusetts, 1987).

The Rug Merchants of Chaos (produced Pasadena, California, 1991).

The Rug Merchants of Chaos and Other Plays (includes *The Rug Merchants of Chaos*; *Buck*; *Sweet Table at the Richelieu*). New York, Theatre Communications Group, 1992.

Screenplay: *The Angel Levine*, with Bill Gunn, 1970.

Television Plays: *The Final War of Olly Winter*, 1967; *The Most Beautiful Fish*, 1969; *Seize the Day*, from the novella by Saul Bellow, 1985; *The Sunset Gang* series (includes *Yiddish*, *The Detective*, *Home*), from the short stories by Warren Adler, 1991.

*

Bibliography: In *The Work of Ronald Ribman: The Poet as Playwright* by Susan H. Dietz, University of Pennsylvania, unpublished dissertation, 1974.

Manuscript Collection: New York Public Library.

Critical Studies: "Journey and Arrival of a Playwright" by Robert Brustein, in *New Republic* (Washington, D.C.), 7 May 1966; *The Jumping-Off Place*, New York, Harcourt Brace, 1969, and "Ronald Ribman: The Artist of the Failure Clowns," in *Essays on Contemporary American Drama* edited by Hedwig Bock and Albert Wertheim, Munich, Hueber, 1981, both by Gerald Weales; articles by Anne Roiphe, 25 December 1977, and by Leslie Bennetts, 6 March 1983, both in *New York Times* theatre section; *Harvard Guide to Contemporary American Writing* edited by Daniel Hoffman, Cambridge, Massachusetts, Harvard University Press, 1979; "Life Near Death: Art of Dying in Recent American Drama" by Margot A. Kelly, in *Text and Presentation,* edited by Karelisa Hartigan, Lanham, Maryland, Ups of America, 1988; "Ronald Ribman's Buck, Unsolved Mysteries, and the Television Simulators" by Elizabeth Klaver, in *American Drama* (Cincinnati, Ohio), Fall 1997, pp. 82-98.

* * *

Ronald Ribman is a difficult playwright to characterize. The surface dissimilarity among his works gives each of his plays a voice of its own, but all are variations on the dramatist's own voice—on his preoccupation with recurrent themes and on his commitment to language that is at once complex and dramatic. Perhaps because he is also a poet (although not so good a poet as playwright), he is essentially a verbal dramatist, fascinated by the nuances of language—the way a well-chosen adverb can alter the first meaning of a sentence or the way an extended metaphor can come to characterize its speaker through both content and style. Yet he is aware of, and often in key scenes dependent on, visual images that give particular force to the words. Consider, for example, the scene in *Harry, Noon and Night* in which Immanuel cleans a fish while sparring verbally with Archer, the aggressive chop, chop, chop altering seemingly innocent statements.

The chief thematic concern of Ribman is with man caught between aspiration and possibility. "Well, all my characters are crying out against the universe they can't alter," he once told an interviewer, but the inalterable force varies from play to play. Sometimes it seems to lie primarily within the character (Harry of *Harry, Noon and Night*), sometimes to be dictated by the assumptions of society (the prisoners in *The Poison Tree*). More often it is a combination of these two. Finally, in *Cold Storage* it lies in the fact of human mortality.

Ribman's first two plays—*Harry, Noon and Night* and *The Journey of the Fifth Horse*—deal with "failure clowns" and "fifth horses," to borrow the loser images of the plays. Underlying *Harry* is a conventional psychological drama about a young man perpetually in the shadow of his successful older brother. Yet Harry can be victimizer as well as victim, and so can Immanuel, who routs the brother in scene 2 but is himself the captive clown of scene 3. Add the German setting with its references to the Nazis, "the Dachau circus," and the metaphor of the failure clown spreads to suggest the human condition, all in a very funny comedy. The fifth horses of *Journey*, which grows out of Turgenev's "The Diary of a Superfluous Man," are Turgenev's hero and the publisher's reader who finally rejects the manuscript. The second character is only an ironic note in the original story, but Ribman creates him fully, including his real and his fantasy lives, and lets him recognize and cry out against the identification he feels with the man whose diary he is reading.

With his television play *The Final War of Olly Winter* and with *The Ceremony of Innocence*, Ribman seemed to be moving into overt social drama, into a direct pacifist statement brought on by the general distress with the American presence in Vietnam. Similarly, *The Poison Tree* seemed to some an explicit commentary on prison conditions and racial bigotry, a reading that perhaps contributed to its commercial failure as the theater moved away from the social and political concerns of the 1960s. Although the social implications of these dramas are real enough, they are plays that deal with familiar Ribman themes and display the complexities of structure and language already familiar from the early plays. *The Ceremony of Innocence* is a historical drama that uses flashback scenes to explain why Ethelred will not come out of seclusion to defend England against the Danish invasion. He prefers to stand aside from a society that, mouthing the rhetoric of honor, chooses war over peace and special privilege over public welfare. Still, the failures of his society—so forcefully expressed in a speech of the disillusioned idealist Kent—are reflections of Ethelred's inability to rule even himself as he gives way at crucial moments to an anger that belies his faith in the rational mind. In *The Poison Tree*, in which the prison is largely peopled by black convicts and white guards, Ribman develops his titular metaphor to show that all the characters are creatures of the situation. The manipulative guard who is his own victim, too easily a caricature in production, is actually the Kent of this play, finally as helpless as the leading prisoner, the one who prefers feeling to dehumanizing theory, but he is incapable of nonviolent, regenerative action.

With *Cold Storage* Ribman returned to the exuberance and inventiveness that characterized *Harry, Noon and Night*. Primarily a two-character play, *Cold Storage* is set in the terminal ward of a New York hospital. Given that setting, it is perhaps surprising to find such vitality, so much luxury of language, such wild humor, but these qualities are as important to the play's content as they are to its texture. Parmigian, a dying fruit merchant with an incredible frame of reference and a compulsive need to talk (silence is death), assaults Landau and gets him to release his secret guilt at having survived the Holocaust. As Landau learns to live, Parmigian comes to accept the fact of death. The play ends with a community of two, a conspiracy of sorts against the human condition, and leaves the audience with a marvelously replenishing sense of life.

The crying out is more muted in *Buck* and *Sweet Table at the Richelieu*, but these works provide opposition to the inevitable—the one an image, the other a character. The titular protagonist of *Buck*, a director for a sex-and-violence television company, fails to humanize his product, to modify the cruel behavior of his colleagues, or to solve his offstage personal problems, but the play ends with new snow falling, bringing the promise of cleansing even though the snow will quickly turn to dirt and slush. As the patrons of the Richelieu, a metaphorical luxury spa, exit for the last sleigh ride, the less self-obsessed of the guests is defined as the Lady of Enduring Hope, although she knows that no one can stay long enough to taste all of the glories on the sweet table.

There is a quartet of failing clowns in *The Rug Merchants of Chaos*, two couples who have wandered the world trying to succeed with one impossible business after another. When we meet them, escaping on a rattletrap ship from Cape Town after a fire they set for the insurance got out of hand, it is only the latest installment in lives that one character describes as "hanging so delicately between farce and destruction." At the end there is exhilaration when they go over the side of the ship, ready to risk themselves and their hopes in an open boat miles from any shore.

—Gerald Weales

RIDLER, Anne

Nationality: British. **Born:** Anne Barbara Bradby, Rugby, Warwickshire, 30 July 1912. **Education:** Downe House School; King's College, London, diploma in journalism 1932. **Family:** Married Vivian Ridler in 1938; two sons and two daughters. **Career:** Member of editorial department, Faber and Faber publishers, London, 1935-40. **Awards:** Oscar Blumenthal prize, 1954, and Union League Civic and Arts Foundation prize, 1955 (*Poetry*, Chicago). **Address:** 14 Stanley Road, Oxford OX4 1QZ, England.

Publications

Plays

Cain (produced Letchworth, Hertfordshire, 1943; London, 1944). London, Editions Poetry London, 1943.

The Shadow Factory: A Nativity Play (produced London, 1945). London, Faber, 1946.

Henry Bly (produced London, 1947). Included in *Henry Bly and Other Plays*, 1950.

Henry Bly and Other Plays. London, Faber, 1950.

The Mask, and The Missing Bridegroom (produced London, 1951). Included in *Henry Bly and Other Plays*, 1950.

The Trial of Thomas Cranmer, music by Bryan Kelly (produced Oxford, 1956). London, Faber, 1956.

The Departure, music by Elizabeth Maconchy (produced London, 1961). Included in *Some Time After and Other Poems*, 1972.

Who Is My Neighbour? (produced Leeds, 1961). With *How Bitter the Bread*, London, Faber, 1963.

The Jesse Tree: A Masque in Verse, music by Elizabeth Maconchy (produced Dorchester, Oxfordshire, 1970). London, Lyrebird Press, 1972.

Rosinda, translation of the libretto by Faustini, music by Cavalli (produced Oxford, 1973; London, 1975).

Orfeo, translation of the libretto by Striggio, music by Monteverdi (produced Oxford, 1975; London, 1981). London, Faber Music, 1975; revised edition, 1981.

Eritrea, translation of the libretto by Faustini, music by Cavalli (produced Wexford, Ireland, 1975). London, Oxford University Press, 1975.

The King of the Golden River, music by Elizabeth Maconchy (produced Oxford, 1975).

The Return of Ulysses, translation of the libretto by Badoaro, music by Monteverdi (produced London, 1978). Published in *The Operas of Monteverdi*, edited by Nicholas John, London, Calder, 1992.

The Lambton Worm, music by Robert Sherlaw Johnson (produced Oxford, 1978). London, Oxford University Press, 1979.

Orontea, translation of the libretto by Cicognini, music by Cesti (produced London, 1979).
Agrippina, translation of the libretto by Grimani, music by Handel (produced London, 1982).
La Calisto, translation of the libretto by Faustini, music by Cavalli (produced London, 1984).
Così fan Tutte, translation of the libretto by da Ponte, music by Mozart (produced London, 1986; broadcast, 1988). Oxford, Perpetua Press, 1987.
Don Giovanni, translation of the libretto by da Ponte, music by Mozart (produced London, 1990).
The Marriage of Figaro, translation of the libretto by da Ponte, music by Mozart (produced London, 1991).
The Coronation of Poppea, translation of the libretto by Busenello, music by Monteverdi (produced London, 1992). Published in *The Operas of Monteverdi*, edited by Nicholas John, London, Calder, 1992.

Television Play: *Così fan Tutte*, 1988; *The Marriage of Figaro*, 1991; *The Coronation of Poppea*, 1992.

Poetry

Poems. London, Oxford University Press, 1939.
A Dream Observed and Other Poems. London, Editions Poetry London, 1941.
The Nine Bright Shiners. London, Faber, 1943.
The Golden Bird and Other Poems. London, Faber, 1951.
A Matter of Life and Death. London, Faber, 1959.
Selected Poems. New York, Macmillan, 1961.
Some Time After and Other Poems. London, Faber, 1972.
Italian Prospect: Six Poems. Oxford, Perpetua Press, 1976.
Dies Natalist: Poems of Birth and Infancy. Oxford, Perpetua Press, 1980.
Ten Poems, with E.J. Scovell. Leamington, Other Branch Readings, 1984.
New and Selected Poems. London, Faber, 1988.
Collected Poems. Manchester, Carcanet Press, 1994.

Other

Olive Willis and Downe House: An Adventure in Education. London, Murray, 1967.
A Victorian Family Postbag. Oxford, Perpetua Press, 1988.
Profitable Wonders: Aspects of Thomas Traherne, with A.M. Allchin and Julia Smith. Oxford, Amate Press, 1989.
A Measure of English Poetry: Critical Essays. Oxford, Perpetua Press, 1991.

Editor, *Shakespeare Criticism 1919-1935*. London and New York, Oxford University Press, 1936.
Editor, *A Little Book of Modern Verse*. London, Faber, 1941.
Editor, *Time Passes and Other Poems*, by Walter de la Mare. London, Faber, 1942.
Editor, *Best Ghost Stories*. London, Faber, 1945.
Editor, *The Faber Book of Modern Verse*, revised edition. London, Faber, 1951.
Editor, *The Image of the City and Other Essays*, by Charles Williams. London, Oxford University Press, 1958.
Editor, *Selected Writings*, by Charles Williams. London, Oxford University Press, 1961.
Editor, *Shakespeare Criticism 1935-1960*. London and New York, Oxford University Press, 1963.
Editor, *Poems and Some Letters*, by James Thomson. London, Centaur Press, and Urbana, University of Illinois Press, 1963.
Editor, *Thomas Traherne: Poems, Centuries, and Three Thanksgivings*. London, Oxford University Press, 1966.
Editor, with Christopher Bradby, *Best Stories of Church and Clergy*. London, Faber, 1966.
Editor, *Selected Poems of George Darley*. London, Merrion Press, 1979.
Editor, *The Poems of William Austin*. Oxford, Perpetua Press, 1983.
Editor, *A Victorian Family Postbag*. Oxford, Perpetua Press, 1988.

*

Manuscript Collection: Eton College Library, Buckinghamshire.

Critical Studies: *The Christian Tradition in Modern British Verse Drama* by William V. Spanos, New Brunswick, New Jersey, Rutgers University Press, 1967; "Anne Ridler at Seventy" by Tracey Warr, in *Poetry Review* (London), March 1983, pp. 45-46.

Anne Ridler comments:

(1977) It is a great advantage for a dramatist to know the cast and place he is writing for, the audience he is addressing. Only rarely have I had this opportunity, and this is perhaps why *Thomas Cranmer*, commissioned for performance in the church where Cranmer was tried, has been judged my best play.

Writing words for music, however, gives a rare opportunity for a contemporary poet to use his particular talents in the theatre, and it is in this field (whether by original words, or fitting a translation to a musical line) that I prefer to work at present. Libretto-writing, as W.H. Auden said, gives the poet his one chance nowadays of using the high style.

* * *

Although Anne Ridler has to her credit a number of plays that have their place in the postwar revival of blank verse drama, it is more likely that she will be remembered for her volumes of poetry than for her work in the theater. She began by tackling the forbidding theme of Cain, presenting the characters from Genesis with the archangels Michael and Gabriel serving as chorus to the tragedy. *The Shadow Factory*, a most unusual Nativity play, is altogether more interesting, for it juxtaposes reflections on the birth of Jesus and some sharp criticisms of contemporary issues. In the factory the workers are reduced almost to robots, endlessly repeating the same pointless actions in the production line. The jingle "The Piece-Work Way/Means Better Pay" sums up the futility of it all, and the director is no doubt intentionally something of an Orwellian Big Brother. He has, however, had the idea of commissioning a large mural painting as an example of corporate sponsorship that will enhance the company's image. The artist who undertakes the work soon sizes up the situation and, having taken the precaution of obtaining a promise that nobody shall see what he is doing until it is finished, paints a picture that portrays the director as a masked figure playing chess heartlessly with the lives of his workers. Meantime, a parson, who is also admitted to the factory as part of a policy of good treatment for the staff, rehearses a Nativity play with the workers. The two strands come together as the director swallows his pride and accepts the mural and its message—or rather the message of the Nativity. With its concern for social injustice, the play strikes a chord, and if the director is a little too wooden in his attitudes and expression, there is certainly life in the portrayal of the workers, especially William, whose reactions to the birth of his first child are observed with affectionate accuracy. All the same, the mixture of realism and allegory is not altogether persuasive, and the optimism, as with many Nativity plays, is a little difficult to swallow except on Christmas Eve.

Henry Bly is more successful because its engaging plot, based on the Grimm Brothers' fairy tale "Brother Lustig," is realistic only in its depiction of characters, not of milieu. Henry is a picaresque rogue, always keen to enjoy a drink or to cadge a coin. On his feckless way through life he falls in with a tramp who never explains himself very fully but whom, when he works miracles without hope of any material reward, we soon come to recognize as some sort of Christ figure. For Henry he is at first merely a simpleton to be exploited, but by the end the ne'er-do-well comes to realize that what he is being offered is his chance for salvation. Folklore is also used as the basis for *The Mask,* which takes the form of a reworking of the moving Somerset folk song "The Shooting of His Dear" and manages to modernize the tale without destroying its charm.

Ridler turned to history with *The Trial of Thomas Cranmer,* written to mark the 400th anniversary of his death. When played in the University Church at Oxford, near so many of the sites mentioned by the characters, the tragedy must have been particularly moving, but even without local knowledge this simple and yet very sympathetic chronicle of inhumanity strikes home. Ridler's method is first to show Cranmer as a complete human being, naturally anxious to avoid the challenge of martyrdom, so that she can enlist all of our sympathies as he goes to his death. His persecutors seem all the more ignoble since he is not cast in the heroic mold, and his courage and faith impress us all the more since we know that he would sooner not be tested. There is, of course, also Cranmer's magnificent control of language, and this, perhaps as much as the obvious Oxford connection and reverence for one of the martyrs of the English church, must have attracted Ridler.

For Ridler verse drama is not a matter of grand phrases and extravagant imagery. Instead, she prefers a sober style, rarely enlivened by metaphor and spiced with just occasional dry wit. She knows the power of monosyllables and has enough confidence in the power of her verse to avoid gross effects. It is the rhythm, close to that of prose yet subtly more strict, that repeatedly lifts the speeches she puts into the mouths of her characters above the mundane matters they may be discussing and gives her dialogue the extra strengths of poetry. In her plays her constant concern is to present images of redemption within contexts that portray the pains, problems, and little joys of mankind. Her verse serves as one more element in the bridge she seeks to build between two worlds.

After her verse plays Ridler not only continued to write poetry and edit a variety of other works, but she also turned toward the world of opera. For the composer Elizabeth Maconchy, for instance, she provided the librettos for *The Departure* and *The King of the Golden River* (after Ruskin), and for Robert Sherlaw Johnson she refashioned a popular County Durham folktale for his opera *The Lambton Worm.* She has also produced translations—or, as she prefers to call them, with her typical precision of language, "singing versions"—of the texts of Monteverdi's *The Return of Ulysses,* Cavalli's *La Calisto,* Handel's *Agrippina,* and Mozart's *Così fan tutte.* These meticulously worked versions, which reveal a rare combination of verbal and musical sensitivity, have set high standards in this testing art form. They have made an important contribution to the growing trend, exemplified at its best by Kent Opera, of performing, both in the theater and on television, the masterpieces of the operatic repertory in English.

In 1994 Carcanet Press published Ridler's *Collected Poems,* with a second edition appearing three years later. The fact that it included the choruses from *The Trial of Thomas Cranmer* is an indication that she rated them an important part of her work.

—Christopher Smith

RITTER, Erika

Nationality: Canadian. **Born:** Regina, Saskatchewan in 1948. **Education:** McGill University, Montreal, B.A. 1968; University of Toronto, M.A. in drama 1970. **Career:** Teacher, Loyola College, Montreal, 1971-74; playwright-in-residence, Stratford Festival, 1985; host of *Dayshift*, CBC radio program, 1985-87. **Awards:** Chalmers award, 1980; ACTRA award, 1982. **Agent:** Shain Jaffe, Great North Artists, 350 DuPont Street, Toronto, Ontario M5R 1V9, Canada.

Publications

Plays

A Visitor from Charleston (produced Winnipeg, 1975). Toronto, Playwrights Co-op, 1975.
The Splits (produced Toronto, 1978). Toronto, Playwrights Co-op, 1978.
Winter 1671 (produced Toronto, 1979). Toronto, Playwrights Co-op, 1979.
Automatic Pilot (produced Toronto, Ontario, 1980). Toronto, Playwrights Co-op, 1980.
The Passing Scene (produced Toronto, 1982).
Murder at McQueen (produced Toronto, 1986).

Radio Plays: *Good Intentions, The Road to Hell*; *Miranda*; *Smith and Wesson*; *The Girl I Left Behind Me.*

Other

Urban Scrawl (essays and sketches). Toronto, Macmillan, 1984.
Ritter in Residence (essays and sketches). Toronto, McClelland and Stewart, 1987.
The Hidden Life of Humans (novel). Toronto, Key Porter Books, 1997.

*

Critical Study: *The Work: Conversations with English-Canadian Playwrights*, edited by Robert Wallace and Cynthia Zimmerman, Toronto, Coach House Press, 1982.

* * *

Erika Ritter's first published play, *A Visitor from Charleston,* produced in 1975, concerns Eva, a youngish divorcée and frustrated would-be actress who drowns the tedium of a routine library job and a dull ex-husband in a world of romantic fantasy created by repeated viewings of *Gone with the Wind.* The viewings have continued after her separation from her husband and number 47 as the play opens. Eva is deterred from seeing the film for the 48th time by a door-to-door cosmetic salesman pushing a line called Instant Fantasie that promises rejuvenation and glamour, the things Eva experiences vicariously in Rhett and Scarlett, who are eternally young, frozen in time on film. For the period of the play Eva heckles and badgers the salesman, distracting him from his patter to reveal her life's disappointments and expose his frauds and weaknesses, all in the hope that Instant Fantasie products will somehow prove to be her own personal *Gone with the Wind.* Peering into the mirror as she tries out the new blushers and mascaras, recalling the face of her youth, triggers a series of three memory scenes, each increasing her disillusionment and confirming her sense that love and artistic fulfillment are impossible except in the movies.

The two major themes of male/female relationships and the creating of art, along with a number of motifs and technical devices introduced in *A Visitor from Charleston,* continue with variations throughout the five following plays. With the exception of the anachronistic historical play *Winter 1671,* all are contemporary, urban, and full of corrosively witty one-liners and self-deprecating anecdotes.

The Splits, Ritter's next play, produced in 1978, is about Megan, a television scriptwriter who is trying to organize her career as well as come to terms with the three men in her life—Hal, the Tuesday-Thursday lover she met in group therapy; David, her story editor and well-meaning though weak friend; and Joe, her boorish, abusive, cadging ex-husband. In the end they all split—Hal willingly; Joe by force, trashing Megan's apartment while declaring that she is the only woman he ever loved; and David by default. Most important is Megan's departure. The play closes with her picking up her purse and typewriter from the wreckage and walking out, an upbeat ending by a courageous woman who has rejected palliatives and mediocre solutions for a creative life on her own terms.

The Automatic Pilot is Ritter's most accomplished work. It concerns Charlie, a writer of soap operas by day and a stand-up comedienne by night who uses the disasters of her personal life as material for her comic routines. Again, Ritter deals with male/female relationships, but this time she does so from both perspectives—Charlie's (the female lead) in the first act and Gene's (her lover) in the second. Because Ritter refuses to oversimplify the difficulties of the current situation for unattached, self-supporting, successful professional women who also want a fulfilling and secure love relationship with a decent man who can accept equality of the sexes, her plays never take a straight feminist direction. She refuses just to blame patriarchal society and insists that many women, like Charlie, are their own worst enemies. This leads to a shrewd analysis of elements of character that are self-defeating in women. Yet while Ritter sees their unhappiness as "largely a product of their own mentality and their attitude about themselves," she does recognize that there is a link between this and society as a whole: "My characters tend to do a lot of wistful wandering; they tend to be indecisive people because they live in an indecisive age." Both men and women are affected by this modern indecisiveness, as even macho Nick, one of Charlie's pickups in *The Automatic Pilot,* slumps wearily and says that he feels old. And the root of Charlie's difficulty, as both her lover Gene and her ex-husband Alan point out, is that, despite her independence and apparent cynical toughness, she ultimately depends on other people for respect and a sense of self. In reaction against this dependency, Charlie tries constantly to see herself as the victim of the people whose respect she feels she has lost. As Ritter explains, "[Charlie] wants to contrive circumstance so that she, in her own mind, is free from guilt or blame. . . . She manipulates situations so that the other person is responsible, because she's more comfortable with the role of the person who is acted upon."

The form this self-contempt takes is her routine as a comedienne at the Canada Goose, a nightclub that employs amateurs. On one level joking is Charlie's method of coming to terms with the harshness of experience by laughing at herself, but on another level it is an appeal for the audience's approval and sympathy. The technique of comic self-deprecation that started as a defense mechanism becomes an emotional necessity for her. She gradually starts to see her actual experience in terms of the show instead of vice versa. As the audience watches Charlie's routine in the "show within the play," it sees creation in process at the same time as it sees the destruction of Charlie's life. The saddest result is that when she does win the love of a totally decent man, Gene, she cannot accept it. She has to spoil it because she feels comfortable and safe only in her habitual mixture of self-contemptuous misery, which is projected as comedy to win the admiration of an audience.

In the meantime Gene, the only male character in all of the plays who represents Ritter's point of view, also turns his personal experience into a novel, comically entitled *Deathless Prose.* He is not hooked on the process as Charlie is, however, but uses his art to try to understand. Beneath the often farcical situations and constant wisecracks are extremely perceptive comments on human behavior and art, typical of the bittersweet, comic-sad mixture of most of Ritter's work.

Six years later *Murder at McQueen* was produced, a play again focusing on women and their relations with men and with their own particular forms of self-expression. Three of the four women, each a decade apart in age, has an affair with a macho, amoral talk show host, appropriately named Rex. The eldest, Mitzi, founds a successful women's club, McQueen, as therapy following the breakup, but after five years she still yearns for him. Her best friend, Norah, a beautiful young lawyer in her 20s, is annoyed by the chauvinist tack Rex takes in his talk show and telephones her protest. They are both intrigued, and they meet secretly and end up in bed. Despite numerous affairs Rex is enthralled for the first time, and Norah is attracted but feels that she has betrayed Mitzi. To Rex's astonishment and dismay she ultimately rejects him, but she also leaves the club and Mitzi.

The plot is framed by a chorus figure, Blythe, a writer and teacher of detective fiction and a nonmember of the club who observes and receives confidences from members. She suffers from the same unsatisfactory love experiences as the others—separation, rejection, fulfillment through fantasy. When her fictional detective, Butler, appears in the flesh to investigate a fire at the club and crank calls to Rex, she at first finds illusion merging wonderfully with reality until fantasy is overwhelmed by sordid facts. The murder of the play's title refers to the betrayal of friendships, the death of hope and trust, and, concomitantly, the growth of cynicism, despair, and loneliness.

Ritter's plays are all written in the style and tradition of the comedy of manners, in which a shrewd eye for yuppie attitudes and an ear for their ways of talking are captured in often brilliant verbal wit. In fact, the wit is so ubiquitous and sharp that the audience sometimes forgets Ritter's technical skill. The juxtaposing of two modes of fantasy, the movie and the cosmetics, in *A Visitor from Charleston,* which creates a kind of literary trompe d'oeil, and the mode of sliding into memory through the mirror are effects she varies imaginatively in later plays. She creates clever transitions from one level to another so that we see the relationship between real life and performance and between fantasy and human need that is central to Ritter's vision.

—Dorothy Parker

ROCHE, Billy

Nationality: Irish. **Born:** Wexford, 11 January 1949. **Education:** Mercy Convent School, Wexford, 1954-57; Christian Brothers, Primary and Secondary, 1957-66. **Family:** Married Patti Egan in 1973; three daughters. **Career:** Barman, Shamrock Bar, Wexford, 1967-69; upholsterer, Smiths Car Factory, Wexford, 1969-73 and 1978-80; builders' labourer, London, 1973-75; barman, Stonebridge Lounge, Wexford, 1976; factory worker, Wexford, 1976-78. Singer with The Roach Band, 1975-80; playwright-in-residence, The Bush Theatre, London, 1988. Lives in Wexford. **Awards:** *Plays and Players* award, 1988, 1989; John Whiting award, 1989; George Devine award, 1990; Edinburgh Fringe first, 1990; Thames Television award, 1990; London Theatre Fringe award, 1992; *Time Out* award, 1992. **Agent:** Leah Schmidt, Curtis Brown Group, 162-168 Regent Street, London W1R 5TB, England.

Publications

Plays

Johnny Nobody (produced Wexford, 1986).

A Handful of Stars (as *The Boker Poker Club*, produced Wexford, 1987; as *A Handful of Stars*, produced London, 1988). Published in *First Run*, edited by Kate Harwood, London, Hern, 1989.

Amphibians (produced Wexford, 1987; revised version produced London, 1992). London, Warner Chappell Plays, 1992.

Poor Beast in the Rain (produced London, 1989). London, Hern, 1990.

Belfry (produced London, 1991). Included in *The Wexford Trilogy*, 1992.

The Wexford Trilogy (includes *A Handful of Stars*, *Poor Beast in the Rain*, *Belfry*) (produced London, 1992). London, Hern, 1992.

The Cavalcaders. London, Nick Hern, 1994.

Trojan Eddie (screenplay). London, Methuen, 1997.

Screenplay: *Trojan Eddie.*

Novel

Tumbling Down. Dublin, Wolfhound Press, 1986.

*

Theatrical Activities:
Actor: **Plays**—Spud Murphy in *Johnny Nobody*, Wexford, 1986; Stapler in *The Boker Poker Club*, Wexford, 1987; Eagle in *Amphibians*, Wexford, 1987; Willy Diver in *Aristocrats* by Brian Friel, London, 1988. **Films**—Role in *Strapless* by David Hare, 1990. **Television**—*The Bill*, 1992.

Billy Roche comments:

It is my fascination with my hometown of Wexford in Ireland that forms the basis of all my work so far. I had hoped that I'd be over it all by now but instead I find my fascination deepens with every play I write. It is mainly the language of the people of Wexford that I'm after—poetic, strange, sly language that can be so devastatingly economic, particularly in the affairs of the heart, and yet has the knack of going right to the core of the matter. Like many other writers before me I keep returning to the place of my birth like a salmon swimming home perhaps because I just long to see my own face in the water or at the very least I really wouldn't mind finding the little fellow I used to be once upon a time.

* * *

"The play is set in Wexford, a small town in Ireland." The thematic territory of Billy Roche's *The Wexford Trilogy* is as economically defined and focused as its geographical setting. What is presented in each of the plays is less a plot than a situation of stagnation in which the thwarted energies and desires of the individual continually seek expression—or even resolution in action. The paralysis of a provincial milieu in which, although "it's nobody's fault," "everyone's to blame," is familiar from James Joyce's *Dubliners* and the stream of Irish writing that emerges from it, but Roche's treatment is distinctive in its particularity and resonance. Indeed, his writing is notable (especially in view of its themes) for its deep and unembarrassed relation to its artistic roots: not only Joyce and the Irish short story, but Anton Chekhov—mediated perhaps through the 1970s plays of Brian Friel. The affection manifest in the presentation of many of the characters and the fullness with which the Wexford context is suggested tend to pull against the astringencies of a Joycean or Chekhovian irony, but the sense of small-town stagnation is nevertheless potent. Not the least Joycean feature of Roche's writing is the pervasive reference to popular culture—film and pop song—which functions as ironic counterpoint to the action. Also noticeable is the way that stereotypes familiar from O'Casey are displaced and rotated. In all three plays, those who ultimately constrain, command, influence, or stand as symbols are versions of the stoical, forbearing mother and the feckless, extravagant father. But these figures are always unseen, offstage: their determining presence is made all the more apparent by their physical absence.

A Handful of Stars, the first play of the *Trilogy*, is set in a "scruffy pool hall," the favorite haunt of local teenage rebel and self-styled "King of the Renegades," Jimmy Brady. For Jimmy, to "grow up" would be for him to join the "livin' dead," wrapped up in a "nice neat little parcel." Progressively isolated by the loss of his girlfriend (who leaves him because he is "not going to change") and the impending marriage of his best friend, Jimmy realizes that he has not "a ghost of a chance" of avoiding the fate of his drunken ne'er-do-well father. He "wages war on everybody," and seals his alienation from local society by attempting to hold up a shop. Taking refuge in the pool hall, he wrecks the privileged preserve of its "élite" members. Before the Garda arrives, the over-the-hill local boxer, Stapler, a surrogate father for Jimmy, steadies him but can offer only weary words: "Most of us wage war on the wrong people." Jimmy would "rather be an ejit than a creep," and there seems no other option. His parents' momentary happiness now appears like a "mirage," and his arrest will, he knows, consign his mother to further silent torment. Among other things, the play is a tribute to the "young rebels" of 1950s and 1960s Hollywood—"Brando and Dean, Newman, Clift and McQueen." Yet the rebel here represents not a "misunderstood" generation posed against a smug "adult" orthodoxy but a culture split against itself and "screamin'."

For his second play Roche originally projected a piece that was to focus on a Jimmy-like rebel who would refuse his cultural identity, "run for the hills," and join the carnival. But the Bush Theatre prevailed on the playwright to reconsider, and he turned this scenario inside out, effecting in the process a decisive shift of thematic emphasis. *Poor Beast in the Rain* centers not on departure but on that most pervasive trope of Irish literature: return. According to Roche himself, this is "a rainy day sort of a play which is held together by an ancient Irish Myth as Danger Doyle returns like Oisín to the place of his birth, 'just because he wanted to see his auld mates again.' Danger Doyle, who is a sort of grown-up Jimmy Brady, ran away with another man's wife ten years ago and the play is really about all the people the pair of them left behind." The setting is an "old fashioned betting shop"—owned by the abandoned husband, Steven, and run by him and his daughter Eileen—on the weekend of the All-Ireland Hurling Final, in which the local team is successful. For the frequenters of the betting shop, "the ranks of the left behind," the most common strategy of consolation is the mythologization of the past and the veneration of its "characters," be they local wild boys or hurling heroes. Danger Doyle has escaped only to a depressed and workaday existence in England. Yet when he returns, feeling "like a fugitive," it is not to "kiss the past's arse" but to persuade Eileen to go back with him to visit her dejected mother. He also tries to set his "auld mates" free from their devotion to glamorized memories of himself. This task entails not a demythologization (which is revealed as the other, disillusioned, side of the rhetorical coin) but an assurance that, as he says to an embittered old flame, "I don't have what you seem to think I took from yeh." Only when his name is "washed away" will she cease to conceive of herself as a "poor beast" left out "in the rain": to those "reachin' for the moon," the here-and-now can only ever be an "auld snare."

The third play of the *Trilogy*, *Belfry*, signals an interesting formal shift. A split stage and retrospective structure permit a fluidity of action and promote an intimacy with the consciousness of a single individual. Events are framed, punctuated, and indeed ordered by an expansive and occasionally lyrical narrative addressed "to the audience." In it, the "little sacristan" Artie O'Leary discloses why, in his "queer auld whisperin' world," the "only life he's ever known," he now has "a story to tell." His story is of a furtive, though passionate, adulterous affair with the church helper Angela and of how she "tapped a hidden reservoir" by releasing him from a life dominated by a tyrannical mother and bounded by his necessary involvement with the rites of birth, marriage, and death. On his mother's death, the illegitimate Artie can become his "father's son again"—a wild "Jack-the-lad" in his free time. A small enough victory in a "small enough life," it is not an insignificant one when those around him are so thwarted. The young priest Pat laments a life "surrounded by dead and dying" and turns to drink again; Angela attempts to mend her continuing sense of exclusion from her husband's life by moving on to another affair; and the husband himself, Donal, having confronted Artie and then resumed their friendship, broods over his fading status as a local handball star. Only Dominic, the backward and endearingly sparky altar boy for whom Artie is a surrogate father, stands apart. He is beaten by Artie, who believes (wrongly) that he has revealed the affair to Donal, and he is killed in an accident whilst escaping from the special school to which he has been sent. But it is his surprise birthday party that Artie's narrative poignantly revisits; it is Dominic who, ringing out "I Can't Get No Satisfaction" on the church bells and announcing his ambition to make people happy, embodies the "capacity" for happiness in the play. In *Belfry*, as elsewhere in *The Wexford Trilogy*, Roche manages to avoid not just the sentimentality of a facile hope but the equally insidious sentimentality of a self-pitying despair.

The Cavalcaders supplements the *Trilogy*, though its charm is more deceptive and its ironies harsher. Its action flashes back and forth across a seven-year gap to chart the psychological consequences of the personal betrayals inflicted on and by a small-town shoemaker who runs a barbershop quartet in his spare time. The group's songs provide a sharp counterpoint to the destructive womanizing of the emotionally damaged "lovely liar" Terry, even as his quartet is itself "fallin' apart." Cultural change in Wexford forms a background to this play but is more fully and ambitiously addressed in Roche's little-noticed R.S.C. commission, *Amphibians*. As fishermen leave their boats to work in the local seafood factory, the stubborn individualist Eagle determines, before he too capitulates, to give his teenage son the traditional St. Martin's Eve rite-of-passage of camping out alone on nearby Useless Island. But a new, more violent, rite has been devised, and, after the discovery of an illicit family connection between the factory owner and a thwarted worker, the boy's vigil is savagely interrupted by the beating of the owner by the worker, who then mutilates himself. Wexford is still celebrated—but guardedly: once able to move in both elements, the amphibians now, it seems, grope between them.

—Paul Lawley

ROMERIL, John

Nationality: Australian. **Born:** Melbourne, Victoria, 26 October 1945. **Education:** Brighton Technical School and High School, Melbourne, Australia; Monash University, Clayton, Victoria, 1966-71, B.A. (honors) in English 1970. **Career:** Writer-in-residence, Australian Performing Group, Melbourne, 1974, Western Australian Institute of Technology, Bentley, 1977, University of Newcastle, New South Wales, 1978, Jigsaw Theatre Company, Canberra, 1980, Troupe, Adelaide, 1981, Flinders University, Bedford Park, South Australia, 1984, Magpie, Adelaide, 1985, and National University of Singapore, 1986-87; Mathew J. Cody artist-in-residence, Victorian Arts Centre, Melbourne, 1985. Also a director and actor. Chair, Australian National Playwrights Centre, 1998. **Awards:** Australian Council for the Arts travel grant, 1972; Canada-Australia prize, 1976; Victorian Government Drama fellowship, 1988; Australian Artists Creative fellowship, 1993-96. **Agent:** Almost Managing, P.O. Box 1034, Carlton, Victoria 3053, Australia.

Publications

Plays

A Nameless Concern (produced Melbourne, 1968).
The Kitchen Table (produced Melbourne, 1968). Included in *Two Plays*, 1971.
Scene One, with John Minter (produced Melbourne, 1969).
The Man from Chicago (produced Melbourne, 1969).
The American Independence Hour (produced Melbourne, 1969).
Mr. Big, The Big, Big Pig (produced Melbourne, 1969).
In a Place Somewhere Else (produced Melbourne, 1969).
I Don't Know Who to Feel Sorry For (produced Melbourne, 1969). Sydney, Currency Press, 1973; London, Eyre Methuen, 1975.
Chicago Chicago (produced Melbourne, 1970). In *Plays*, Melbourne, Penguin, 1970; in *Plays of the 60s*, Sydney, Currency Press, 1998.
200 Years (produced Melbourne, 1970).
Marvellous Melbourne, with Jack Hibberd (produced Melbourne, 1970). Published in *Theatre Australia* (Potts Point, New South Wales), July-September 1977.
Dr. Karl's Kure (produced Melbourne, 1970).
The Magnetic Martian Potato (produced Melbourne, 1971).
Whatever Happened to Realism (produced Melbourne, 1971).
Mrs. Thally F (produced Melbourne, 1971). In *Seven One-Act Plays*, edited by Rodney Fisher, Sydney, Currency Press, 1983; in *Plays of the 70s*, Sydney, Currency Press, 1998.
Two Plays (includes *The Kitchen Table* and *Brudder Humphrey*). Clayton, Victoria, Kosmos, 1971.
Rearguard Action (produced Melbourne, 1971).
Hackett Gets Ahead, with Bill and Lorna Hannan (produced Melbourne, 1972).
He Can Swagger Sitting Down (produced Melbourne, 1972).
Bastardy (produced Melbourne, 1972). Montmorency, Victoria, Yackandandah Playscripts, 1982.
A Night in Rio and Other Bummerz, with Tim Robertson (produced Melbourne, 1973).
The Earth, Air, Fire, and Water Show (produced Melbourne, 1973).
Waltzing Matilda: A National Pantomime with Tomato Sauce, with Tim Robertson (produced Melbourne, 1974). Montmorency, Victoria, Yackandandah Playscripts, 1984.
The Floating World (produced Melbourne, 1974). Sydney, Currency Press, 1975; London, Eyre Methuen, 1976; revised version, Currency Press, 1982.
The Golden Holden Show (produced Melbourne, 1975).
Dudders, with John Timlin (produced Melbourne, 1976).
The Radio-Active Horror Show (produced Melbourne, 1977).
The Accidental Poke (produced Melbourne, 1977). Published in *Popular Short Plays for the Australian Stage*, edited by Ron Blair, Sydney, Currency Press, 1985.
Mickey's Moomba (produced Melbourne, 1979).
Carboni (produced Melbourne, 1980).
700,000 (produced Canberra, 1980).
Samizdat (produced Adelaide, 1981).
Centenary Dance (produced Adelaide, 1984).
The Kelly Dance (produced Adelaide, 1984). Montmorency, Victoria, Yackandandah Playscripts, 1986.
Definitely Not the Last (produced Adelaide, 1985). Montmorency, Victoria, Yackandandah Playscripts, 1989.
Jonah, music by Alan John, adaptation of the novel by Louis Stone (produced Sydney, 1985; revised version, produced Adelaide, 1991).
Legends, with Jennifer Hill and Chris Anastassiades (produced Melbourne, 1985). Montmorency, Victoria, Yackandandah Playscripts, 1986.
Koori Radio (produced Hobart, 1987).
The Impostor, adaptation of a play by Sha Yexin (produced Melbourne, 1987).
Top End (produced Melbourne, 1988).
History of Australia, with Tim Robertson and Don Watson (produced Melbourne, 1989).
Lost Weekend (produced Adelaide, 1989).
Black Cargo, adaptation of a story by John Morrison (produced Melbourne, 1991).
The Reading Boy (produced Adelaide, 1991).
Working Out (produced Melbourne, 1991).
Bring Down the House (produced Melbourne, 1992).
Doing the Block (produced Melbourne, 1993).
Hanoi-Melbourne (produced Hanoi, 1995).
Red Sun Red Earth (produced Adelaide and Nago City, 1996).
Love Suicides, music by Peter Neville (produced Canberra and Melbourne, 1997).
Kate n Shiner (produced Perth, 1998).
XPO: The Human Factor (produced Brisbane, 1998).

Screenplays: *Nothing Like Experience*, 1969; *Bonjour Balwyn*, 1969; *The Great McCarthy*, from a novel by Barry Oakley, 1975; *Mr. Steam and Dry*, 1986.

Television Plays: *The Best of Mates*, 1972; *Charley the Chequer Cab Kid*, 1973; *6 of the Best* series, 1981-86; *Everything's A Hustle*, 1989.

Dramaturgy and Treatments: *The Ballad of Lois Ryan*, 1988; *State of Defense*, 1987; *Concepts Inc*, 1987; *The Firm*, 1989; *Making Trax*, 1998.

*

Critical Studies: Interview in *Meanjin* (Melbourne), no. 3, 1978; article by Romeril, in *Theatre Australia* (Potts Point, New South Wales), April 1979; interview in *Australian Drama Studies* (St. Lucia), no. 17, 1990; *State of Play* by Len Radic, Ringwood, Victoria, Penguin, 1991; "Unhappy the Land that Has a Need of Heroes: John Romeril's 'Asian Plays'" by Gareth Griffiths, in *Myths, Heroes and Anti-Heroes: Essays on the Literature and Culture of the Asia-Pacific Region* edited by Bruce Bennett and Dennis Haskell, Nedlands, University of Western Australia, 1992; *John Romeril* edited by Gareth Griffiths, Amsterdam, Rodopi, 1993; "The Japanese Version of *The Floating World:* A Cross-Cultural Event between Japan and Australia" by Keiji Sawada, in *Australasian Drama Studies* (Queensland, Australia), April 1996, pp. 4-19.

John Romeril comments:

I take my prime duty as a playwright to be the recording and representation of contemporary Australian reality on the stage. Politically I'm of a left-wing persuasion, hence interested in plays of ideas. However, I operate on the premise that if you want people to entertain ideas you must first entertain people. Thus the kind of theatre I try to make is above all lively, full of colour, movement, wit, and style, fused with content of pressing concern.

* * *

For more than a quarter of a century John Romeril has been Australia's most prolific yet neglected playwright. Few of his works are in print, and those mostly in small-run desktop editions, while critical comment has been almost nonexistent. Much of his output has been performed by community or school companies for particular occasions or audiences. An example is *Koori Radio,* which was devised for Hobart's Salamanca Theatre Company and dealt with the supposed genocide of Aboriginal people in that state. Other scripts as various as *The Kelly Dance*, about the nineteenth-century bushranger, and *Legends*, about young people groping toward self-esteem, have been worked up from improvisations with trainee actors in Adelaide and Melbourne, respectively. The latter even credits two students as coauthors.

One of only two writers to have made successful long-term professional careers in the Australian theater since the dramatic renaissance of the late 1960s (David Williamson is the other), Romeril nevertheless consciously welcomes collaborative and specialized projects as being consistent with his democratic political views, and they make up more than three-quarters of his dramatic opus. In nearly all such work the resulting scripts, though not necessarily the performances, lack the clarity of a final singular penning; many are unpublished, and most have had only the single originating production. The popular historical subject matter of *The Kelly Dance* has made it an exception, with minor publication and many subsequent productions throughout Australia, although all have been in small venues by amateur or semiprofessional companies. The play is a good introduction to Romeril's community-style pieces, with a bush dance setting maximizing audience participation and the consequent informal atmosphere unifying the short, episodic scenes and rambling structure. Such projects might best be characterized as "entertainments with ideas."

As well as being a "public servant of the pen," however, Romeril has occasionally had moderate success as a single author of mainstream, professionally performed plays, and he has insisted on being seen as a "hybrid" talent who works across the full spectrum of staging possibilities. Again, he has had specialized commissions such as *The Reading Boy*, a children's piece on an ecological theme that is performed by puppets, but after some 14 years during which his work was ignored by the mainstream professional companies, the 1980s brought him attention from larger theaters. Major restagings of his early success *The Floating World* in Melbourne in 1982 and in Sydney in 1986 can largely be attributed to its appearance on secondary school English syllabi at the time. But there also were state company productions of a musical adaptation of the Louis Stone novel *Jonah;* a community-style piece, *Top End*, set in Darwin and perhaps mistakenly given formalized staging by the Melbourne Theatre Company in 1988; and a Chekhovian, or perhaps more accurately Shavian, comedy, *Lost Weekend*, that had two major productions in 1989.

Lost Weekend pits a narrow-minded trade unionist recovering from a stroke against an aristocratic grazier and ex-army officer. The setting is a farm homestead that, like the stately homes of England, has been reduced to offering tourist accommodations. Romeril's allegory of an Australia caught between patronizing colonial and idealistic national constructions of society is finely balanced against the pragmatic response to new economic realities by the grazier's wife. A scatterbrained but sane serving girl acts as a disbelieving chorus to the eccentric gathering, but a weak ending mars the play. Romeril has had his biggest critical and commercial success with a revised 1991 production of *Jonah* in Adelaide. It is a sharp but colorful Brechtian satire that charts the uncheckable rise of a seedy street thug who turns from booting fallen rivals to making boots.

It is unfortunate that neither *Lost Weekend* nor *Jonah* has been published. As a consequence Romeril continues to be known in schools and universities, nationally and internationally, principally through *The Floating World*, a work of the 1970s. A formally experimental comedy-drama, it combines cartoon characters and an increasingly dreamlike narration to tell the story of Les Harding, a former prisoner of war on the notorious railway from Thailand to Burma who many years later reluctantly joins his wife on a holiday cruise to Japan. As the journey progresses, his oafish and bigoted behavior becomes increasingly disturbed when memories of horror, loss, and suffering begin to consume him. Originally staged in the characteristically informal surroundings that provide the warmth and vibrancy Romeril's hard-edged, antiromantic stories need to succeed as entertainment, *The Floating World* has adapted uneasily to proscenium production. It is no coincidence that the acclaimed production of *Jonah,* although done by a state company using star actors, avoided formal theater blocking and had the actors moving among the audience to clear a space for each successive location.

New productions of *The Floating World* have made significant script deletions and staging reinterpretations. These have had Romeril's consent, which is consistent with his belief in relating performances to contemporary social contexts. When it was first produced, the play was criticized as being racist, and while this was certainly not the author's intention, its increasingly subjective engagement with Harding's internal agony can be misinterpreted as an endorsement of his chauvinist outbursts, thus distorting the play in performance. The 1986 production by the Sydney Theatre Company removed a number of scenes satirizing cheap goods imported from Japan, replacing them with images of Japanese traditional culture. Such revisions have not been incorporated into the published script.

In an Australian theater industry that has increasingly marginalized political, experimental, and noncommercial work, Romeril has shown an exceptional ability to shift styles and subjects in order to survive. New editions and works of critical analysis might serve to revive interest in a writer poorly served by scholarship and the written record.

—Richard Fotheringham

ROTIMI, Ola

Nationality: Nigerian. **Born:** Sapele, 13 April 1938. **Education:** Methodist Boys' High School, Lagos, 1952-56; Boston University (president, African Students Union, 1962-63), 1959-63, B.F.A. 1963; Yale University School of Drama, New Haven, Connecticut (Rockefeller scholar, 1963-66; Student Drama prize, 1966), 1963-66, M.F.A. 1966. **Family:** Married Hazel Mae Gaudreau in 1965; three sons and one daughter. **Career:** Executive director and artistic director, University of Ife Theatre, Ife-Ife, 1973-77. Director of the university theatre, 1977—, dean of student affairs, 1979-80, dean of the faculty of humanities, 1982-84, and since 1982 head of the department of creative arts, all University of Port Harcourt. **Awards:** *African Arts* prize, 1969; Oxford University Press prize, 1970; Nigerian National Festival of the Arts prize, 1974. **Address:** Department of Creative Arts, University of Port Harcourt, P.M.B. 5323, Port Harcourt, Rivers State, Nigeria.

Publications

Plays

Our Husband Has Gone Mad Again (produced Ibadan and New Haven, Connecticut, 1966). Ibadan, Oxford University Press, 1977.
The Gods Are Not to Blame (produced Ife-Ife, 1968; London, 1978). Ibadan, Oxford University Press, 1971.
Kurunmi: An Historical Tragedy (produced Ife-Ife, 1969). Ibadan, Oxford University Press, 1971.
Holding Talks (produced Ife-Ife, 1970). Ibadan, Ibadan University Press-Oxford University Press, 1979.
Ovonramwen Nogbaisi (produced Ife-Ife, 1971). Benin City, Ethiope, and London, Oxford University Press, 1974.
Initiation into Madness, adaptation of a play by Adegoke Durojaiye (produced Ife-Ife, 1973).
Grip Am (produced Ife-Ife, 1973).
Akassa Youmi (produced Port Harcourt, 1977).
If: A Tragedy of the Ruled (produced Port Harcourt, 1979). Ibadan, Heinemann, 1983.
Hopes of the Living-Dead (produced Port Harcourt, 1985). Ibadan, Spectrum Books, 1988.

Recording: *When Criminals Turn Judges*, 1991.

*

Bibliography: By O. Lalude, in *Bibliographic Series 1*, Port Harcourt, University of Port Harcourt Library, 1984.

Critical Studies: Interview in *Dem Say* (Austin, Texas), 1974; *African Theatre Today* by Martin Banham and Clive Wake, London, Pitman, 1976; "Three Dramatists in Search of a Language" by Dapo Adelugba, in *Theatre in Africa* edited by Oyin Ogunba and Abiola Irele, Ibadan, Ibadan University Press, 1978; "Ola Rotimi's Search for Technique" by Akanju Nasiru, in *New West African Literature* edited by Kolawole Ogungbesan, London, Heinemann, 1979; "The Search for a Popular Theatre" by Biodun Jeyifo, in *Drama and Theatre in Nigeria* edited by Yemi Ogunbiyi, Lagos, Nigeria Magazine, 1981; article by Alex C. Johnson, in *African Literature Today 12* edited by Eldred Jones and Eustace Palmer, London, Heinemann, 1981; *Beyond Translation: Tragic Paradigms and the Dramaturgy of Ola Rotimi and Wole Soyinka* by Femi Osofisan, Ife-Ife, Ife Monographs on African Literature, 1986; "Ola Rotimi: The Man, the Playwright, and the Producer on the Nigerian Theatre Scene" by Chinyere G. Okafor, in *World Literature Today: A Literary Quarterly of the University of Oklahoma* (Norman, Oklahoma), Winter 1990, pp. 24-29; *Ola Rotimi: The Untold Stories* by Dayo Alao, Agidingbi, Ikeja, Daily Times of Nigeria, 1992; "Ola Rotimi and Wole Soyinka at UNIFE: A Newspaper Controversy" by Bernth Lindfors, in *Matatu: A Journal for African Culture and Society* (Amsterdam, Netherlands), 1994, pp. 171-89.

Theatrical Activities:
Director: **Plays**—All his own plays; *King Christophe* by Aimé Césaire, Ife-Ife, 1970; *Rere Run* by Dejo Okediji, Ife-Ife, 1973; *Wahala* by Babalola Fatunwase, Ife-Ife, 1973; *The Curse* by Kole Omotosho, Ife-Ife, 1975; *The Family* by Comish Ekiye, Ife-Ife, 1976; *Sizwe Bansi Is Dead* by Athol Fugard, John Kani, and Winston Ntshona, Port Harcourt, 1984; *The Emperor Jones* by Eugene O'Neill, Port Harcourt, 1985; *Behold My Redeemer* by Rasheed Gbadamosi, Port Harcourt, 1986.

Ola Rotimi comments:

My creative passion is for a people's theatre informed by that which also impels it, namely: the spasms of the socio-political tendons of Africa yesterday, today, and tomorrow.

* * *

Of the generation of Nigerian playwrights who began writing in the late 1960s, Ola Rotimi exhibits the surest sense of drama as a plastic, three-dimensional form incorporating spoken word, dance, music, mime, and the massing of bodies in space for the creation of spectacle. This sense of theatrical possibility is found equally in his high, or stylistically elevated, dramas and in his more realistic sociopolitical plays.

Characteristic of his high style are the tragedy *The Gods Are Not to Blame* and the historical dramas *Kurunmi* and *Ovonramwen Nogbaisi*. Each play distances its concerns by locating events in the previous century; treats the gods as an awesome, unseen presence rather than as a physical manifestation; molds music, mime, and ritual elements to create a varied social panorama; employs dance in an efficacious manner designed to enhance collective well-being; and makes extensive use of traditional poetic forms for the expression of values central to the community portrayed. The best-known play of the group, *The Gods Are Not to Blame,* is also a good example of the blend of theater traditions to which Rotimi is heir, for he obtained degrees in directing and playwriting from Boston and Yale universities in the United States and, following his return to Nigeria in 1966, began researching traditional Yoruba performance modes as part of his direction of the Ori Olokun Acting Company.

Adapted from the Oedipus story, *The Gods Are Not to Blame* strives to reject the fatalistic relationship of man to god contained in the Greek original by using as a central visual image the shrine of Ogun, the Yoruba god associated with iron and, by implication, with the creation of technologies designed to extend man's manipulation of the environment. In Rotimi's hands the source of the protagonist's downfall becomes the learned social conditioning of ethnic paranoia.

But this adaptation is not fully successful, for Yoruba attitudes concerning fate only superficially approximate an interpretation of Greek tragedy as attributable to a single character flaw. Furthermore, Rotimi's subsequent explanation that the drama, first produced in 1968 during the Nigerian civil war, was intended as a direct commentary on current events is not fully satisfactory. Such a position invalidates the centrality of the prophecy imposed by the original and runs the risk of reducing the war's complex causes to a single issue. Rather, it seems that in this instance the choice of material identifies Rotimi with the period in modern African literatures when writers were eager to validate their cultures in terms the former colonial masters could appreciate.

A similar borrowing from Western perspectives seems evident in *Kurunmi* and *Ovonramwen Nogbaisi,* for these historical dramas concerning internecine Yoruba wars and the British conquest of the Benin empire hinge upon the great-man theory of history, which is antithetical to an African emphasis on personality as collective. While the latter play is not entirely persuasive because the king's failure of will seems insufficiently motivated, *Kurunmi* is an impressive evocation of a world under fatal pressure. Through the manipulation in English of Yoruba expressive modes governing the use of proverbs and lyrical structures or the easy movement between the spiritual/tragic realm and the secular/comic world, Rotimi creates an effective defense of tradition and culture as the sole element that distinguishes humans from other life forms. Yet, true to historical accounts and his own contemporary reality, the playwright brings his protagonist to the ironic realization that this defense visits wide-scale destruction and eventual decline upon the entire nation.

In contrast, later realistic plays like *If: A Tragedy of the Ruled* and *Hopes of the Living-Dead* tackle current social concerns directly and explore the dynamic interplay between leaders and followers. The first play, loosely adapted from Errol John's Caribbean drama *Moon on a Rainbow Shawl,* is an impassioned plea for the rejection of self-interest in favor of a collective vision of national health. The latter play, while conforming to sketchy historical accounts, projects the sobering image of Nigeria as a nation of lepers threatened with sure extinction unless they learn to work collectively for the benefit of all.

In these sociopolitical works the playwright achieves a theatrical plasticity similar to that of the stylistically elevated plays. The simultaneous playing of several scenes and massing of actors in such a way as to convey separate foci that momentarily converge and allow for the settling on a common purpose, the successful integration of various Nigerian languages with pidgin and English to capture the dream of a truly pluralistic society, and the use of music to evoke a poignant sense of the possibility of a shared human grandeur—all of these distinguish Rotimi as one of the best playwrights of contemporary Nigerian drama.

—Sandra L. Richards

RUDKIN, (James) David

Nationality: British. **Born:** London, 29 June 1936. **Education:** King Edward's School, Birmingham, 1947-55; St. Catherine's College, Oxford, 1957-61, M.A. 1961. **Military Service:** Served in the Royal Corps of Signals, 1955-57. **Family:** Married Alexandra Margaret Thompson in 1967; two sons (one deceased) and two daughters. **Career:** Assistant master of Latin, Greek, and music, County High School, Bromsgrove, Worcestershire, 1961-64. **Awards:** *Evening Standard* award, 1962; John Whiting award, 1974; Obie award, 1977; New York Film Festival gold medal, 1987; Society of Authors scholarship, 1988; European Film Festival Special Jury award, 1990; Sony Silver Medal, 1993. **Agent:** Casarotto Ramsay Ltd., National House, 60-66 Wardour Street, London W1V 4ND, England.

Publications

Plays

Afore Night Come (produced Oxford, 1960; London, 1962). Included in *New English Dramatists 7*, London, Penguin, 1963; published separately, New York, Grove Press, 1966.

Moses and Aaron, translation of the libretto, music by Schoenberg (produced London, 1965). London, Friends of Covent Garden, 1965.

The Grace of Todd (opera libretto), music by Gordon Crosse (produced Aldeburgh, Suffolk, and London, 1969). London, Oxford University Press, 1970.

Burglars (for children; produced London, 1970). Published in *Prompt Two*, edited by Alan Durband, London, Hutchinson, 1976.

The Filth Hunt (produced London, 1972).

Cries from Casement as His Bones Are Brought to Dublin (broadcast 1973; produced London, 1973). London, BBC Publications, 1974.

Ashes (produced Hamburg, 1973; London, 1974; Los Angeles and New York, 1976). London, Pluto Press, 1978.

Penda's Fen (televised 1974). London, Davis Poynter, 1975.

No Title (produced Birmingham, 1974).

The Sons of Light (produced Newcastle upon Tyne, 1976; London, 1978). London, Eyre Methuen, 1981.

Sovereignty under Elizabeth (produced London, 1977).

Hippolytus, adaptation of the play by Euripides (produced Stratford-on-Avon, 1978; London, 1979). London, Heinemann, 1980.

Hansel and Gretel (produced Stratford-on-Avon, 1980; London, 1981).

The Triumph of Death (produced Birmingham, 1981). London, Eyre Methuen, 1981.

Peer Gynt, adaptation of the play by Ibsen (produced Stratford-on-Avon, 1982; London. 1983). London, Methuen, 1983.

Space Invaders (produced Stratford-on-Avon and London, 1984).

Will's Way (produced Stratford-on-Avon and London, 1985).

The Saxon Shore (produced London, 1986). London, Methuen, 1986.

Deathwatch, and The Maids, adaptations of plays by Jean Genet (produced London, 1987).

Rosmersholm, adaptation of a play by Isben (produced London, 1997). Bath, Absolute Press, 1990.

When We Dead Awaken, adaptation of a play by Ibsen (produced London, 1990). Bath, Absolute Press, 1990.

Broken Strings (opera libretto), music by Param Vir (produced Amsterdam and Munich, 1992).

Screenplays (additional dialogue, uncredited): *Fahrenheit 451*, 1966; *Mademoiselle*, 1966; *Testimony*, 1987; *December Bride*, 1989; *The Woodlanders,* 1998.

Radio Plays: *No Accounting for Taste*, 1960; *The Persians*, from the play by Aeschylus, 1965; *Gear Change*, 1967; *Cries from Casement as His Bones Are Brought to Dublin*, 1973; *Hecuba*, from the play by Euripides, 1975; *The Lovesong of Alfred J. Hitchcock,* 1993; *The Haunting of Mahler,* 1994.

Television Plays: *The Stone Dance*, 1963; *Children Playing*, 1967; *House of Character*, 1968; *Blodwen, Home from Rachel's Mar-*

riage, 1969; *Bypass*, 1972; *Atrocity*, 1973; *Penda's Fen*, 1974; *Pritan* and *The Coming of the Cross* (*Churchill's People* series), 1975; *The Ash Tree*, from the story by M.R. James, 1975; *The Living Grave* (*Leap in the Dark* series), 1981; *Artemis 81*, 1981; *Across the Water*, 1983; *White Lady*, 1987; *Gawain and the Green Knight*, from the Middle English poem, 1991.

Ballet Scenario: *Sun into Darkness*, 1966.

*

Critical Studies: *David Rudkin: Sacred Disobedience: An Expository Study of His Drama, 1959-96* by David Ian Rabey, Amsterdam, Harwood Academic Publishers, 1997.

Theatrical Activities:
Director: **Television**—*White Lady*, 1987.

* * *

David Rudkin's *Afore Night Come* is one of the most mature and assured first plays of the postwar period, although in retrospect it can be seen to contain its author's chief dramatic preoccupations only, as it were, in solution, uncrystalized. Primitive chthonic forces long repressed by culture and individual psychology reassert themselves with great violence when a group of fruit pickers on a Midlands farm single out a casual worker—a strange, "educated" Irish tramp—as scapegoat for their personal, moral, and economic failings and carry out his ritual murder in the sinister, though apparently numinous, presence of a crop-spraying helicopter. Thematic elements that are to become central in Rudkin's later work—homosexuality, sexual infertility, the threat of nuclear devastation, England's Irish problem—are present but not developed. Indeed, thematic coherence seems less important to Rudkin at this stage of his career than the recognizably Pinteresque menace that can be generated by the rhythms of a judiciously charged dialogue. It is perhaps for this reason that, although the crucial sacrificial event of *Afore Night Come* is obviously two-edged, the energy of the play makes itself felt as essentially negative.

By contrast, Rudkin's work after his 12-year self-imposed apprenticeship is energized by his passionate commitment to a powerful central idea. The primitive impulses of *Afore Night Come* reveal their creative aspect in the concentration on the reintegration and realization of the self that occurs in the gradual, painful liberation from a complex web of repression. On the evidence of his work, Rudkin believes that the power wielders of modern civilization, and especially the various Christian churches with their capacity for psychological conditioning, function only by burying or perverting for their own dark ends original natural forces and beliefs. His dramatic response is to affirm the continuity of these forces on several different levels simultaneously—psychological, sexual, cultural, historical—using the forms that many modern artists have regarded as the enduring repositories of nonrational or even antirational values—image, fable, and myth. The quasi-physical impact of Rudkin's dramatic language, with its intense compression and often eccentric syntax, itself reflects these values. Hence also the importance to Rudkin of dialect, the concrete, poetic language of the authentic, geographically rooted self that he repeatedly sets against abstract discourse, the rootless, "Flat Urban Academic" that "will bury our theatre." (The Norwegian acts of his *Peer Gynt* are translated into the "stylized rural Ulster speech" of his own childhood.)

Ashes is a harrowing autobiographical play that rotates the theme of sexual infertility through a series of wider perspectives—political, anthropological, and existential—in handling the problem of free will and determinism. The roughly contemporaneous television play *Penda's Fen,* however, offers a more satisfying dramatic realization of his preoccupations. The growth of an adolescent boy in Worcestershire away from social, religious, educational, and sexual constraints into mature selfhood is articulated through images of a local landscape in which the natural forces of Penda's Fen, the modern Pinvin, are being perverted to menacing scientific ends. This is done through suggestive sequences of music, which, together with sound effects, has always been more important to Rudkin than scenery or props, and through a series of dream images that reveal to the boy his homosexuality. Here as elsewhere in Rudkin's work, homosexuality is important less as a social reality than as an idea. It is the humane "mixed" state that stands as a critique of the conventional phallic "manliness" of society's power wielders. Having realized that Christianity has "buried" the authentic Jesus—just as Pinvin, a real place, has buried Penda's Fen—the boy Stephen rejects power and inherits, in a vision of Penda himself, the last of the English pagan kings, "the sacred demon of ungovernableness."

The key play in Rudkin's oeuvre, at which he worked from 1965 to 1976, is *The Sons of Light,* a massive, multilayered fable with science fiction elements and a tripartite mythic structure: "The Division of the Kingdom," "The Pit," and "Surrection." The ancient paradigm drawn on by Rudkin is perhaps most familiar from the Christian *Harrowing of Hell,* but the play's fundamental design, as well as its title, is indebted above all to the heresy of Manichaeanism, with its characteristic cosmological dualism. A new pastor and his three sons arrive on a remote Scottish Atlantic island to find it divided and in the grip of a patriarchal religion of wrath. The island's subterranean industrial complex, an obscene dystopia masterminded by an expressionist-style German scientist, dehumanizes and mechanizes its workers, allaying any residual stirrings with the purely functional promise of religious transcendence. Two of the pastor's sons are killed, but amid terrible violence and purgative suffering the third son, the "cold," burning "angel" John, descends into this "pit," initiates a fresh consciousness of self in the workers, and destroys the complex, thus uniting the body of the island and reclaiming it for its inhabitants. Simultaneously the identity of a schizophrenic girl, hitherto an outcast, is reintegrated, and she is made whole. The structural parallel is underscored by the destruction on several levels of the baneful father, the figure who, as always in Rudkin, holds in place the structures of repression—sexual, familial, and political. This extraordinary conjunction of Reichian psychotherapy and Artaudian theater within the arena of myth is a distinctive and powerful achievement.

Rudkin's fiercely idiosyncratic brand of psychohistory is most clearly embodied in *The Triumph of Death,* an extravagant gothic panorama that dramatizes the annihilation or demonization of natural modes of being and worship by medieval Christianity in its perverted ("Crosstian") project of ideological self-definition and cultural domination in the name of "Salvation." With its insistently excremental symbolism, its appropriation of Christian imagery for the evocation of polymorphous ("natural") sexuality, and its reconception of Christian mythological figures (most notably "Jehan"/Joan of Arc), this is undoubtedly Rudkin's riskiest and most challenging work. Indeed, its oddity is a strength, with the epigraph insisting that the past both is and is not "another country." Its gravest limitation is a degree of schematization that *The Sons of Light,* despite shared concerns and imagery and the fundamental dualism of its structure, largely avoids. *The Triumph of Death,* for all its antirationalist primitivism and its fluid Artaudian dramaturgy, is a thesis play: "Our fracture is our fall," and civilization is founded on repression.

The Saxon Shore attempts to combine an individual's quest for selfhood with a historical vision. The context is also implicitly political, and in Rudkin this means (as in *Ashes, Cries from Casement As His Bones Are Brought to Dublin,* and *Across the Water*) the Irish problem. The play is set in Britain in AD 410. The Roman empire is crumbling fast; on the North Sea coast the displaced native British Celts and a "plantationer" Saxon community face each other across Hadrian's Wall in the presence of a disgruntled and demoralized colonial army. The allegory of the Ulster situation—a Saxon defense regiment aids the scornful Roman soldiers and Saxons who have turned nocturnal werewolves compulsively perpetrate acts of terror—serves as framework for the story of Athdark, a "child growed stale" from mother domination but who shows "the beginnings of a man" by the end of the play. The structure of the story recalls that of a fable or folktale, while resemblances of narrative pattern and tone, as well as verbal echoes, indicate Rudkin's continuing creative and critical engagement with *Peer Gynt.* (*The Dream of Gerontius* and *King Lear* are also, as ever in Rudkin, important intertexts.) But despite the play's variety of English and a speculative version of Celtic, its dramatic language is disappointingly thin and lacking in resonance. Moreover, the relation between the historical conditions and the development of the individual is never as fully or coherently articulated as it is in Rudkin's best work.

—Paul Lawley

RUGANDA, John

Nationality: Ugandan. **Born:** Uganda, 1941. **Education:** Makerere University, Kampala, B.A. (honours) in English literature. **Career:** Member, the Makerere Free Travelling Theatre, and founder-member, the Makonde Group, editorial and sales representative, Oxford University Press's East Africa Branch, 1972, and senior fellow in creative writing, Makerere University, 1973, all Kampala. Founder-member, the Nairobi Travelling Theatre, Kenya. **Address:** c/o Heinemann Kenya, PO Box 45314, Nairobi, Kenya.

Publications

Plays

The Burdens (produced Kampala, 1972). Nairobi, Oxford University Press, 1972.

Black Mamba (produced Kampala, 1972). With *Covenant of Death,* Nairobi, East African Publishing House, 1973.

Covenant of Death. With *Black Mamba,* Nairobi, East African Publishing House, 1973.

The Floods (produced Nairobi, 1979). Nairobi, East African Publishing House, 1980.

Music Without Tears (also director: produced Nairobi, 1981). Nairobi, Bookwise, 1982.

Echoes of Silence (also director: produced Nairobi, 1985). Nairobi, Heinemann, 1986.

Television Plays: *The Secret of the Season,* 1973; *The Floods,* 1973; *The Illegitimate,* 1982.

Radio Plays: *My Father the Glutton,* 1971; *Covenant with Death,* 1974; *Black Mamba,* 1977.

Other

Telling the Truth Laughingly: The Politics of Francis Imbuga's Drama. Nairobi, East African Educational Publishers, 1992.

*

Critical Studies: *Notes on John Ruganda's "The Burdens,"* Nairobi, Heinemann, 1977; *Thematic Trends and Circumstances in John Ruganda's Drama* (dissertation) by Francis Davis Imbuga, University of Iowa, 1992.

* * *

It was *The Burdens* that brought John Ruganda to prominence as a playwright in Uganda. Wamala, the major character in the play, had once been a teacher but through two masterstrokes of chicanery wriggled himself into the post of a minister. His first political ploy was to seduce and marry Tinka, the daughter of an influential chief, thereby securing for himself a formidable political constituency. The second move was to give a demagogic speech on the eve of Uganda's independence, which won him the position he desired. With the extraordinary fringe benefits accompanying his post as a minister, Wamala and his family cut themselves off from ordinary people and preferred to drink only with kings. But Power and Time plan their revenge.

As the play opens, Wamala is at the bottom of the social heap. He can no longer feed his family. His wife, a more resourceful person, confronts their new, humiliating reality by brewing and selling a local brand of alcohol, *enguli.* Their two children starve. Unable to face the penury, Wamala escapes into alcohol. His favorite haunt is, ironically, The Republic, a bar where he recalls the more pleasant days of old with his former political cronies. Very late one night he returns and, inspired by alcohol, decides to meet an old architect, Vincent Kanagonago, a prospective politician, and to sell him on the idea of running Kanagonago's electioneering campaign as a master sloganeer and of becoming a partner in the establishment of a company that would manufacture matchsticks with two heads that can be lit when struck even on wet surfaces. In a brilliant play within a play he reenacts this meeting, with his wife acting as the rich, condescending Kanagonago. Somewhere along the line illusion blurs into reality, and Wamala attempts to strangle his wife, believing that she really is Kanagonago. Wamala's leap to murder comes after he realizes that Kañagonago, to whom he has sold his idea, is actually the owner of Associated Matches, the company with a match-manufacturing monopoly in the country. Another hilarious moment is the scene in which Wamala, in a reverie, relives his days of glory at a political rally by using the audience as the electorate. It ends tragically when Tinka murders her half-crazed husband, fearing that, with his progressing state of diminished responsibility, he might kill her first. *The Burdens* is a well-knit play that employs only four characters. The dialogue is precise and contrapuntal. It is a competent satirical study of postindependence disillusionment in African politics.

In *Music without Tears* Ruganda explores the collective hysteria that engulfed Uganda in the post-Idi Amin period of the country's turbulent history. Odie is bitter that his brother, Wak, had fled the country 10 years earlier to escape the tortures and disappearances. With the country liberated by a new military government, he returns but is insensitive to the brutalities still going on. Odie argues that the punishment for this nonchalance should be death. His sister, Stella, insists that Odie should see a psychiatrist in order to curb his blood lust. He turns on her and accuses her of betraying the honor of the family by sleeping with Ali, the army commander who signed the paper for the death of their father, a former minister for tourism. Ali was also in charge of a drunken platoon that raped Stella and her classmates, including some nuns, a few years ago. A study in tyranny, even within the family, *Music without Tears* reveals the aftereffects of military rule on the psyche of an abused and savaged populace.

In *The Floods* Ruganda again probes the psychosomatic disorder that befalls a society in which the craze for power and position makes meaningful human relationship impossible. Bwogo, a former chief of the State Research Bureau, the Ugandan version of the FBI and KGB, has been made redundant since the boss, Amin, was ousted from power. He lives with Nankya, a pseudointellectual who is bent on getting to the top of the academic ladder by fair or foul means. Bwogo, still suffering from the cannibalistic streak that characterized his days in power, announces on the radio that a flood is going to sweep off all of the inhabitants of a symbolic island on Lake Victoria. His scheme is to get Nankya and her mother on the government-approved Noah's Ark, a "rescue" boat whose passengers are consequently exterminated. Bwogo's actions stem from jealousy and guilt. In one of the phantasmagoric moments of this dark play, Bwogo sees apparitions of those he killed coming to take his life.

The Floods is a disturbing study in physical and verbal cannibalism. It is divided into waves instead of scenes and acts, with each wave symbolizing the wash of violence rising and ebbing in Bwogo's mind. Its greatest strength, however, is Ruganda's evocative language. Here is a memorable passage by a fisherman who functions as narrator and communal memory in the play:

> KYEYUNE: It was early evening when I set sail. . . . I paddled on and on to the centre of the lake. Then all of a sudden the net on my right became heavy. . . . I knew it was a big catch. Do you know what it was, son? A man. A military man. Dead. Three long nails in his head, his genitals sticking out in his mouth. A big stone round his neck. His belly ripped open and the intestines oozing out. . . . I looked at the body and froze with fright. Here was a man . . . who probably had a wife and children. . . . What had he done to come to such an unmourned-for end? Had he, perhaps, in a moment of enthusiasm, uttered an unwelcome word to his masters?

Ruganda's weaknesses as a playwright include sloganeering, poor character delineation through dialogue, excessive intellectualizing, and unrelieved cynicism. His strengths are the ferocious honesty with which he dissects his society and his experimentation with theatrical forms that, when they work, give his psychodramas both on the page and in performance a psychotherapeutic power.

—Esiaba Irobi

RUSSELL, Willy

Nationality: British. **Born:** Whiston, Lancashire, 23 August 1947. **Education:** Schools in Knowsley and Rainford, Lancashire; Childwall College of Further Education, Lancashire, 1969-70; St. Katharine's College of Higher Education, Liverpool, 1970-73, Cert.Ed. **Family:** Married Ann Margaret Seagroatt in 1969; one son and two daughters. **Career:** Ladies' hairdresser, Liverpool and Kirkby, 1963-68; labourer, Bear Brand warehouse, 1968-69, and teacher, Shorefields Comprehensive, 1973-74, Liverpool. Freelance writer, 1974—. Associate director, 1981-83, and honorary director, 1983—, Liverpool Playhouse; founding director, Quintet Films, London, 1982—. Writer-in-residence, C.F. Mott College of Education, Liverpool, 1976; fellow in creative writing, Manchester Polytechnic, 1977-79. Also folk song composer and singer: performances (with group Kirbytown Three) in clubs and on radio and television since 1965. **Awards:** Arts Council bursary, 1974; *Evening Standard* award, 1974; London Theatre Critics award, 1974; Society of West End Theatre award, 1980, 1983, 1988; Golden Globe award, 1984; Ivor Novello award, 1985. M.A.: Open University, Milton Keynes, Buckinghamshire, 1983. **Agent:** Casarotto Ramsay Ltd., National House, 60-66 Wardour Street, London W1V 3HP. **Address:** W.R. Ltd., 43 Canning Street, Liverpool L8 7NN, England.

Publications

Plays

Keep Your Eyes Down (produced Liverpool, 1971).

Blind Scouse (includes *Keep Your Eyes Down*, *Playground*, *Sam O'Shanker*) (produced Liverpool, 1972; revised version of *Sam O'Shanker*, music by Russell, produced Liverpool, 1973).

Tam Lin (for children), music by Russell (produced Liverpool, 1972).

When the Reds, adaptation of the play *The Tigers Are Coming—O.K.?* by Alan Plater (produced Liverpool, 1973).

Terraces, in *Second Playbill 1*, edited by Alan Durband. London, Hutchinson, 1973; collection published as *Terraces*, 1979.

John, Paul, George, Ringo and Bert (produced Liverpool and London, 1974).

The Cantril Tales, with others (produced Liverpool, 1975).

Breezeblock Park (produced Liverpool, 1975; London, 1977). London, French, 1978.

Break In (televised 1975). Published in *Scene Scripts 2*, edited by Michael Marland, London, Longman, 1978.

I Read the News Today (broadcast 1976). Published in *Home Truths*, London, Longman, 1982.

One for the Road (as *Painted Veg and Parkinson*, produced Manchester, 1976; as *Dennis the Menace*, produced Norwich, 1978; as *Happy Returns*, produced Brighton, 1978; as *One for the Road*, produced Nottingham, 1979). London, French, 1980; revised version (produced Liverpool, 1986; London, 1987), 1985.

Our Day Out (televised 1977). Published in *Act 1*, edited by David Self and Ray Speakman, London, Hutchinson, 1979; revised version, songs and music by Bob Eaton, Chris Mellors, and Russell (produced Liverpool and London, 1983), London, Methuen, 1984.
Stags and Hens (produced Liverpool, 1978; London, 1984). London, French, 1985.
Lies (televised 1978). Published in *City Life*, edited by David Self, London, Hutchinson, 1980.
Politics and Terror (televised 1978). Published in *Wordplays 1*, edited by Alan Durband, London, Hutchinson, 1982.
The Boy with the Transistor Radio (televised 1980). Published in *Working*, edited by David Self, London, Hutchinson, 1980.
Educating Rita (produced London, 1980; Chicago and New York, 1987). London, French, 1981.
Blood Brothers (produced Liverpool, 1981; revised version, music and lyrics by Russell, produced Liverpool and London, 1983). London, Hutchinson, 1986.
Educating Rita, Stags and Hens, and Blood Brothers. London, Methuen, 1986.
Shirley Valentine (produced Liverpool, 1986; London, 1988; New York, 1989). With *One for the Road*, London, Methuen, 1988.
Plays: One (includes *Breezeblock Park*; *Our Day Out*; *Stags and Hens*; *Educating Rita*). London, Methuen, 1996.

Screenplays: *Educating Rita*, 1983; *Shirley Valentine*, 1989; *Dancin' thru the Dark*, from *Stags and Hens*, 1990.

Radio Play: *I Read the News Today*, 1976.

Television Plays: *King of the Castle*, 1973; *Break In*, 1975; *The Death of a Young, Young Man*, 1975; *Our Day Out*, 1977; *Lies*, 1978; *Politics and Terror*, 1978; *The Daughters of Albion*, 1979; *The Boy with the Transistor Radio*, 1980; *One Summer* series, 1983.

Poetry

Sam O'Shanker: A Liverpool Tale. Liverpool, Mersey Yarns, 1978.

Other

Published Music: *I Will Be Your Love and OOee boppa OOee boppa*, RSO, 1974; *Dance the Night*, Paternoster, 1980; *Blood Brothers*, Paternoster-Russell Music, 1983; *The Show*, Timeact-Russell Music-Paternoster, 1985; *Mr. Love*, Russell Music-Warner Brothers, 1986.

Film Music: *Shirley Valentine*, with George Hatzinassios, 1989.

*

Critical Studies: "Willy Russell: The First Ten Years" by Timothy Charles, in *Drama* (London), Summer 1983; *Willy Russell and His Plays* by John Gill, Birkenhead, Merseyside, Countyvise, 1996.

Theatrical Activities:
Director: **Play**—*Educating Rita*, Liverpool, 1981.

Actor: **Plays**—Narrator in *Blood Brothers*, Liverpool, 1985, and *Shirley Valentine*, Liverpool, 1986. **Film**—*Educating Rita*, 1983.

Willy Russell comments:

I am loath to make any specific statement on the nature of my work as I reserve the right to dismiss on Thursday the statement I made on Wednesday. However, in a letter of 1984, written to a BBC producer to explain why I would not be writing a play I wrote the following (I think for me it will remain as true on a Thursday as it is on a Wednesday):

> To write a play one must passionately believe in something which one wants to communicate. The writer might want to tell of the ills of the world, or of his love for another, of society's folly, of mankind's goodness and baseness. He may want to argue a political cause or just show off his wit. Whatever, it is something which requires a passionate belief in telling what one has to tell. I heard David Edgar say recently that (to paraphrase) writing becomes more difficult as one gets older because as one gets older one gets less certain. Perhaps what he meant was that with age one sees the corollary to every argument, that the radical turns merely liberal. I don't want to be liberal. But *what* do I, personally, want to communicate? What is it that I am deeply concerned with at present? Am I being too heavy on myself? When going through this pre-play torture have I *ever* felt concerned with anything? Is total emptiness a necessary condition in the prelude to writing a play?
>
> I don't want to write what I've already written. I want to learn. I want to write a play which forces me to develop the talent I have. Talent must not go back on itself and stagnate. It is a nerve-wracking process but truly it is better to write nothing than to write something which one has already written. It's only with pushing against the barriers, stretching the boundaries, staring at the abyss that the imagination soars and poetry can be achieved. I believe that no great play was ever written at any significant distance from the abyss—they are all written on the edge. Think of Moss Hart saying that one never learns to be a playwright, only how to write one particular play. The next play, no matter how "successful" the playwright, is something about which he knows nothing. He cannot know how to write it, has no guidelines because, before he has written it, it has never existed. Every play is a trip back to the beginning and a walk through hell all over again.
>
> What do I want to say? What moves me? What story do I want to tell? I believe that every play I have ever written has, ultimately, been one which celebrates the goodness of man; certainly, the plays have included emptiness, despair, possibly even baseness. But it is the goodness that I hope the audience is left with. I really don't want to write plays which are resigned, menopausal, despairing, and whingeing. I don't want to use any medium as a platform for displaying the smallness and hopelessness of man. Man is man because madly, possibly stupidly but certainly wonderfully, he kicks against the inevitability of life. He spends his life looking for answers. There probably are no answers but the fact that man asks the questions is the reason I write plays.

* * *

What happens when you grow beyond the class and the culture you were born into? When is freedom real and when is it a fake? What is true knowledge? These are the central questions posed by Willy Russell's major plays since the mid-1970s.

Breezeblock Park is set in the houses of two sisters, Betty and Reeny. It is Christmas and therefore a time for competitive consumption. Betty and Reeny try to outdo each other over costly furniture, bathroom fittings, and central heating systems. Betty's husband Ted is obsessed with his new car and, with his knowledge of *Mastermind* and his ambitions as an author, sees himself as an intellectual. Betty's brother Tommy represents a vulgar alternative to this working-class gentility when he gives Betty a vibrator as a Christmas present and prefers to celebrate in the pub rather than in his sister's tasteful front room. Gender roles are strictly defined. The women's territory is the home, particularly the kitchen. Their talk is of clothes, food, children, and relationships. The men work away from home, and their talk is of sports, politics, and general knowledge. Everyone, however, closes ranks over the play's central issue—the pregnancy of Betty's daughter Sandra. Their code demands that she marry the father. There is no shame in "being in the club." As Tommy explains, "It's a bloody secret society they've got goin'. They have a great time." But Sandra is different. She reads, she is interested in ideas, and she hangs around with students. In fact, her lover, Tim, is a student. After a strong talking-to by the men, Tim is ready to do the decent thing, but Sandra stands firm. She will have the child, but she will live with Tim unmarried in a student house. "I want a *good* life, Mother," she shouts at Betty. "I want to sit around and talk about films and—and music." Betty replies, "You begrudge me every bit of pleasure I have ever had." The two cultures, gentility and bohemianism, are irreconcilable. In a skillful last scene Sandra breaks through the menacing circle of her relations, but only because her mother steps aside. Tim meekly follows her.

Another wedding fails and another escape takes place in *Stags and Hens*. It is stag night for Dave and hen night for Linda, who are to be married on the following day. But both parties have been booked into the same dance hall in Liverpool. On a single set, which consists of the ladies' and gents' loos side by side, the differing codes of sex, drink, and clothes are enacted in dialogue that is witty, vulgar, sentimental, and bitter. Linda, we discover, is uneducated but discontented with her girlfriends' cheerful acceptance of the conventions of their class. It is not so much the consumer world of *Breezeblock Park* that is satirized here as the competitive world of grabbing a girl or keeping a man. In a shrewd theatrical move Dave stays dead drunk throughout the play, which puts the spotlight even more fiercely on Linda. She finally rejects her world by leaving with Peter, the lead singer of the band and an old flame who has made good in London. But the last word is given to Eddy, the leader of Dave's friends. It is he, like Tommy in the earlier play, who organizes local solidarity against the outsider. "Don't you come makin' people unhappy," he warns Dave. "She's our mate's tart. We look after our mates. We stick with them." Eddy, however, is younger than Tommy. He has to construct a myth of freedom for his class and culture in the dead wastes of Merseyside. Peter may be a successful artist, but Eddy assures everyone that "You could do that, what he does if you wanted to. You can do anythin' he can do. We all can." All they can do is get drunk, draw their names on the toilet walls, and try to chat up women. Eddy is furious when Linda gets away, but he is still optimistic for the future. The play ends with his staggering out of the gents' loo carrying the still oblivious Dave over his shoulder and muttering, "She's gone. Well y've got no baggage weighin' y' down. There's nothin' holdin' us back now Dave. We can go anywhere."

With *Educating Rita* all of these themes are sharply expressed and focused by Rita herself. She has already outpaced Sandra and Linda by enrolling in an Open University course, but the early encounters between her directness and the cultured evasiveness of her tutor Frank reveal real cultural gulfs. As she shows in a series of brilliant observations in scene 4 of the first act, however, she knows very well what she is leaving behind and why she wants to change. Her class may have a certain level of affluence, but it does not have meaning. It does not have culture as meaningful life: "I just see everyone pissed, or on the Valium, tryin' to get from one day to the next." Since Rita does not believe in a distinct working-class culture—"I've read about that. I've never seen it though"—she wants the knowledge and skills that Frank can give her. "What do you want to know?" he asks her at their first tutorial. "Everything," she replies. By the end of the play she has certainly acquired poise and sophistication—"I know what clothes to wear, what plays to see"—along with a contempt for Frank, which she did not have at the beginning. She has escaped her origins, and she knows how much everyone resents this kind of mobility: "They hate it when one of them tries to break away."

In the musical *Blood Brothers* Russell shifts to men and their chances in life. Twin brothers who were separated at birth are brought up by two different mothers, one in a working-class and the other in a middle-class environment. Another Linda shuttles between the two. Each sees advantages in the other's situation, but it is the working-class Mickey who suffers unemployment, depression, and jealousy over Linda. Edward goes to a university and becomes a local politician. He helps his brother with housing and a job, but, in a melodramatic ending, Mickey shoots his brother because he thinks that Linda has slept with him and then gets shot down himself by the police. Once again, women progress as men go under.

This pattern is repeated in *Shirley Valentine,* which is the least complex of Russell's plays. It is a monologue in two acts by a 42-year-old Liverpool housewife who moves from her downbeat kitchen to a down-market taverna in Greece. She tells her tale of taking off for a holiday in Greece with a feminist friend, leaving her boorish husband and her two layabout children. She has an affair with a Greek waiter, and although she knows that he seduces all of his clients, she gains new confidence in herself from his flattery. She gives sharp verbal sketches of oafish English families abroad and a self-portrait in which stoicism and romanticism are equally mixed. Shirley is pre-Rita in her self-awareness, but she has made a decisive break in her life pattern by going to Greece and staying there, even though her linguistic and cultural resources are so slender that we have to doubt whether she really has achieved a breakthrough. The play ends with her waitressing at the taverna and waiting for her husband, who is desperate to get her back. It is a fantasy to think that she could stay on—she would be ostracized by all of the local women as a whore—but the hope is that her husband will treat her with new respect at home. *Shirley Valentine* is an entertaining piece that had a long London run, but it represents a step backward from Russell's earlier successes.

—Tony Dunn

S

SAINER, Arthur

Nationality: American. **Born:** New York City, 12 September 1924. **Education:** Washington Square College, New York University (John Golden award, 1946), 1942-46, B.A. 1946; Columbia University, New York, 1947-48, M.A. in literature 1948. **Family:** Married 1) Stefanie Janis in 1956 (divorced 1962); 2) Maryjane Treloar in 1981, two sons and two daughters. **Career:** New York editor, *TV Guide*, New York, 1956-61; founding editor, *Ikon*, New York, 1967. Book critic, 1961—, book editor, 1962, and drama critic, 1961-65 and 1969—, *Village Voice*, New York; film and theatre editor, *American Book Review*, New York, 1986-90. Member of the English or Theatre department, C.W. Post College, Brookville, New York, 1963-67, 1974-75, Bennington College, Vermont, 1967-69, Chautauqua Writers' Workshop, New York, 1969, Staten Island Community College, New York, 1974-75, Hunter College, New York, 1974, 1980-81, Adelphi University, Garden City, New York, 1975, Wesleyan University, Middletown, Connecticut, 1977-80, Middlebury College, Vermont, 1981-83, New School for Social Research, New York, 1985—, and Sarah Lawrence College, Bronxville, New York, 1990—. Member of the Academic Council and program adviser, Campus-Free College, Boston, 1971-74. Co-producer, Bridge Theatre, New York, 1965-66. **Awards:** Office for Advanced Drama Research grant, 1967; Ford grant, 1979, 1980; Berman award, 1984; New Play Commission in Jewish Theater, 1998. **Agent:** Anne Edelstein, 404 Riverside Drive, New York, New York 10025, U.S.A. **Address:** 462 First Street, Brooklyn, New York 11215, U.S.A.

Publications

Plays

The Bitch of Waverly Place (produced New York, 1964).
The Game of the Eye (produced Bronxville, New York, 1964).
The Day Speaks But Cannot Weep (produced Bronxville, New York, and New York City, 1965).
The Blind Angel (produced New York, 1965).
Untitled Chase (produced New York, 1965).
God Wants What Men Want (also director: produced New York, 1966).
The Bombflower (also director: produced New York, 1966).
The Children's Army Is Late (produced Brookville, New York, 1967; New York City, 1974).
The Thing Itself (produced Minneapolis, 1967; New York, 1972; Published in *Playwrights for Tomorrow 6*, edited by Arthur H. Ballet, Minneapolis, University of Minnesota Press, 1969.
Noses (produced New York, 1967).
OM: A Sharing Service (produced Boston, 1968).
Boat Sun Cavern, music by George Prideaux and Mark Hardwick (produced Bennington, Vermont, 1969; New York, 1978).
Van Gogh (produced New York, 1970).
I Piece Smash (produced New York, 1970). Published in *The Scene/ 2 (Plays from Off-Off-Broadway)*, edited by Stanley Nelson, New York, The Smith/New Egypt, 1974.
I Hear It Kissing Me, Ladies (produced New York, 1970).
Images of the Coming Dead (produced New York, 1971, 1980).
The Celebration: Jooz/Guns/Movies/The Abyss (produced New York, 1972).
Go Children Slowly (produced New York, 1973).
The Spring Offensive, music by Shimoda (produced New York, 1974).
Charley Chestnut Rides the I.R.T., music by David Tice (produced New York, 1975).
Day Old Bread: The Worst Good Time I Ever Had, music by David Tice and Robert Savage (produced New York, 1976).
The Rich Man, Poor Man Play, music by David Tice and Paul Dyer (produced New York, 1976; also director: 1982).
Witnesses, music by Ilan Mamber (also director: produced New York, 1977).
Carol in Winter Sunlight, music by George Prideaux (produced New York, 1977).
After the Baal-Shem Tov (produced New York, 1979).
Sunday Childhood Journeys to Nobody at Home (produced New York, 1980).
The Celebration Reclaimed (produced New York, 1993).
The Burning Out of 82, music by Sarah Snyder (produced New York, 1997).
Jews and Christians in the End Zone, music by Sarah Snyder (produced New York, 1998).

Television Plays: *A New Year for Margaret*, 1951; *The Dark Side of the Moon*, 1957; *A Man Loses His Dog More or Less*, 1972.

Other

The Sleepwalker and the Assassin: A Study of the Contemporary Theatre. New York, Bridgehead, 1964.
The Radical Theatre Notebook. New York, Avon, 1975.
The New Radical Theater Notebook. New York, Applause, 1997.
Zero Dances. New York, 1998.

*

Critical Studies: "The Greening of American-Jewish Drama" by Ellen Schiff, in *Handbook of American-Jewish Literature*, New York, Greenwood, 1988.

Theatrical Activities:
Director: **Plays**—Several of his own plays; *Lord Tom Goldsmith* by Victor Lipton, New York, 1979; *The Desire for a City* by Norah Holmgren, New York, 1985.

Actor: **Plays**—*OM: A Sharing Service*, Boston, 1968; *The Children's Army Is Late*, Parma, Italy, 1974.

Arthur Sainer comments:

(1973) I like to believe I write plays to find out something—about self, about self in cosmos, about the cosmos, I try to make something in order to understand something. Sometimes the plays use ideological material but they aren't ideological plays. Ultimately if they work they work as felt experience.

For some time I was fascinated by the juxtaposition of live performers and visual projections, concerned with an enlarged arrested image operating on a level other than that of the "real" performer. That period ran from *The Game of the Eye* (1964) through *Boat Sun Cavern* (written in 1967, produced in 1969). But I've lost interest in projections, I want the magic to be live, immediate, home-made. And I want the mistakes to be live ones.

Language—I've gone from many words, *God Wants What Men Want* (written in 1963), to few words, *The Blind Angel* (1965), *The Bombflower* (1966), to some words, *Images of the Coming Dead* (1971). None of these approaches is superior to the others. It depends on what the play needs and what the playwright needs at that time. Bodies are no more or less useful than the utterances that emerge from them. Only truth is useful.

Words are useful, but so is everything else. I don't hold with Grotowski's belief that every conceivable element other than the performer ought to be stripped away. Everything created by God, everything designed or decimated by the hands of man, is potentially viable and important, all of it is a testament to this life. But I've come lately (in *The Spring Offensive*) to believe in an economy of means—forget the lights, forget the setting—to believe in the magic of what is obviously being put together by hand before our eyes.

Much theatre leaves me cold, and most audiences disturb me. I don't want to make audiences particularly happy or excite them anymore. I don't want them to be sitting there judging the play, to be weighing its excellences and faults. I want the audiences to be seized and ultimately to become the play. We like to say that a really fine play changed its audience, but a really fine play also creates the condition where its audience can change it. The play ultimately is the product of this mutual vulnerability.

* * *

Theater's ability to reproduce the external, everyday details of human life is balanced by its need to incorporate the internal, imaginative reality of its characters. Arthur Sainer's plays combine the two kinds of reality by allowing the characters to retain their unique contributions to life while linking them into a living whole. Whether describing the radical politics of the 1960s, the shifting forces at work in love and marriage, the alienation of the poor and dispossessed, a subway conductor's imminent death, or other contemporary struggles with life, Sainer is sensitive to both the effect of daily routines and rituals and the pressure of people upon one another. His real subjects are not the events that happen to people in the course of a play but rather the way people change and are changed by life around them.

This concentration on people produces plays that are plotless in the usual sense but that obey a rigorous internal logic. Louis, the protagonist of *The Thing Itself,* says,

> In the theatre to which we are offering our blood, there are no characters to be created. There are no consistencies, no patterns. Instead there are irrelevancies, inconsistencies, mistakes, broken thoughts. There is an impulse toward chaos, another toward assimilation. In our theatre there is no stage and no story, there is only human life pushed into a corner, threatened with extinction. And human life threatened with human life. And always mistakes.

The statement is unusually blunt for Sainer, whose dialogue is most often more oblique and questioning, and *The Thing Itself* is unusually pessimistic and bitter, but Louis does describe Sainer's primary attitude toward drama's means and goals. Louis and his friends—Harold, who eats obsessively; Althea, a sympathetic prostitute who is brutal toward her brutal customers—are coping with the thing itself, the degradation of life in an impersonal, almost savage city environment.

As in most of Sainer's plays, *The Thing Itself* is frequently interrupted by mimed scenes, fantasies, monologues, songs, slides, and films. Sainer has used most of the techniques available to contemporary playwrights—from Brechtian alienation to improvisation and audience participation—quite skillfully, but in every case they are expressions of the contradictory, tumultuously human life of the plays. A trilogy—*Images of the Coming Dead, The Children's Army Is Late,* and *Carol in Winter Sunlight*—follows the growth and evolution of a family, with the shifting stresses on David and Carol resulting from David's immersion in filmmaking. Carol's increasing desire to escape the trap of the family, the love both bear for their children, and their concern for their aging parents combine to create a broad and penetrating portrait of the family. In addition, the logic of the portrait calls up a series of mythological and allegorical scenes: a group of figures who begin in naked innocence gradually become a mindlessly hardworking society and are beset by aggressive renegades; Hector and Achilles fight their epic combat; and two characters named Allan and Albert reenact the tragedy of Cain and Abel with a modern twist. The evolution of the human race vibrates against the evolution of the family, and the depiction of the family, sharp and sensitive as it is, is extended and expanded.

Sainer's ability to mesh the intimacy of everyday life and the development of civilization combines with his inquiries into the meaning of Jewish history to focus his plays on death. In *The Children's Army Is Late* David searches to find and film a dying man. *Charley Chestnut Rides the I.R.T.* is filled with the bewilderment and agony of an ordinary subway conductor who suddenly faces death from a terminal illness. The interest in death, however, stems from its use as a reflection of life. *After the Baal-Shem Tov* tells the story of a Jew who survives a German concentration camp to start life anew in the United States. Israel is an innocent, gentle man with an irritating habit of questioning everything. As he makes his way in America, visits a kibbutz in Israel, and becomes the editor of a respected Jewish newspaper, he loses his naïveté but not his questions. Recalling his liberation from the concentration camp, he sings,

> Here in the new world, the absent
> From the dead take on new life,
> The skeletons take on new flesh.
> What's it like now for the absent from the dead?
> What's it like now? Shoving, running,
> Piling up things, looking into faces.
> It's stupid life, it's joyous days.

Israel gives up everything and everyone he has gained in order to "redeem the promises," and there is throughout Sainer's plays an intensely human attempt to redeem the gift of life and to understand the death of people, of ideas, and of relationships in order to appreciate them more fully.

—Walter Bode

SÁNCHEZ-SCOTT, Milcha

Nationality: American. **Born:** Bali in 1955. Lived in Colombia and Mexico until 1969. **Education:** Educated in London and in California. **Career:** Has lived in California since 1969. **Member:** New Dramatists, New York. **Awards:** Drama-logue award (seven times); Vesta award, 1984; Rockefeller award, 1987. **Agent:** George Lane, William Morris Agency, 1325 Avenue of the Americas, New York, New York 10019. **Address:** 2080 Mount Street, Los Angeles, California 90068, U.S.A.

Publications

Plays

Latina (produced Los Angeles, 1980). Published in *Necessary Theater: Six Plays About the Chicano Experience*, edited by Jorge A. Huerta, Houston, Texas, Arte Publico Press, 1989.

Dog Lady and The Cuban Swimmer (produced New York, 1984; London, 1987). Published in *Plays in Process* (New York), vol.5, no.12, 1984.

Roosters (produced New York, 1987). Published in *On New Ground: Contemporary Hispanic-American Plays*, edited by M. Elizabeth Osborn, New York, Theatre Communications Group, 1987.

Evening Star (produced New York, 1988). New York, Dramatists Play Service, 1989.

Stone Wedding (produced Los Angeles, 1989).

El Dorado (produced Costa Mesa, California, 1990).

*

Critical Studies: "Language as a Cure: An Interview with Milcha Sánchez-Scott" by Jon Bouknight, in *Latin American Theatre Review* (Lawrence, Kansas), Spring 1990, pp. 63-74; *Chicana Voices in American Drama: Silviana Wood, Estela Portillo Trambley, Cherri Moraga, Milcha Sánchez-Scott,Josefina Lopez* (dissertation) by Virginia Derus McFerran, University of Minnesota, 1991; "Of Angels and Transcendence: An Analysis of *Fences* by August Wilson and *Roosters* by Milcha Sánchez-Scott" by Harry J. Elam, Jr., in *Staging Difference: Cultural Pluralism in American Theatre and Drama,* edited by Marc Maufort, New York, Peter Lang, 1995.

* * *

Despite or perhaps because of her international education and Pan-American, Pan-Pacific ancestry, Milcha Sánchez-Scott has felt the shock of sexist, racist prejudice against Latinas. She dramatizes the humor, resolution, and hope required of the unempowered. These qualities, along with the bonding and devotion of displaced communities, hold back for a moment the oppressions of economics and of negative assumptions. Harsh realities contain holes through which stream magical visions, supernatural spells, miraculous cures, transformations, and a religious faith in the past and future. Dual language allows her characters an alternative to the dominant culture, whether Spanish or English. Words let them escape the mundane to the uniquely eloquent. Such language supplies a scriptural correlative for the physical images. Her first play made Sánchez-Scott's bilingual and bilevel dramatic visions clear and effective, even for materialistic, English-speaking audiences.

In the prologue to *Latina,* which Sánchez-Scott wrote with Jeremy Blahnik, New Girl journeys from a Peruvian mountain village to cross the barbed wire U.S. border. Originally plaintive, a Peruvian flute resounds "triumphantly" with American pop music, as light shows a bus stop outside the sleazy Felix Sanchez Domestic Agency on Wilshire Boulevard. Two tan mannequins stand in the window: a maternal dummy in white holds a pink doll, and a naughty maid in black holds a feather duster. Dressed carefully to look like an American, Sarita enters briskly to say how embarrassing it is to be thought carless, a maid for hire, Latina, or available at age 23 in Los Angeles. Overhearing this but speaking no English, old Eugenia the *yu-yu* vendor and cleaning lady offers *"niña Sarita"* a cure for her sickness. Still in denial, Sarita answers in effortless Spanish, rebukes in English, and translates for the audience. As Eugenia ritually sprinkles water to sweep, Sarita hears a rooster and admits that she sees her grandmother sweeping a dirt road in 1915 in Juárez. Joking bawdily about using Lava soap, they reveal Sarita's frustrated career as a television actress and the old woman's affectionate pride in it. New Girl, dressed as a Peruvian and furtively seeking domestic work, panics at the word "immigration" in Sarita's reassurance and bites the hand that places Latinas in Anglo households. As Don Felix approaches to open his shop, Eugenia prays before placing her daily bet with Sarita: Is he wearing his Mickey Mouse or sailboat pajama tops today? What is the point of praying? Sarita asks in Spanish and, before going in, pauses to assure the audience, "I let her win."

These first few moments typify the play and Sánchez-Scott's approach. Seven comically disparate Latin women—eight with Sarita—wait at the agency for jobs and party and gossip about their desperate realities. The mannequins mock Sarita's abject servility to Anglos in not defending Alma, and they don rebozos and go to the park as sisters. What does one let oneself be called? New Girl lets them reduce her five names to Elsa Moreno, accepts Sarita's offer to exchange her carefully chosen disguise for her Peruvian dress, and, with the help of Eugenia's charm and prayer and everyone's generosity, gets a placement. Sarita—in learning to accept Eugenia's prayer and bet that her own audition overcame television's prejudice against "exotics" and in divesting herself to help others—gets beyond her *"mal educada"* to find her own dignity. Sarita Gomez will play her television role, and she attacks the intolerable Mrs. Camden. *Latina* ends with an immigration raid in which all of the "illegal" women are arrested and with another New Girl creeping toward the barbed wire.

As *The Cuban Swimmer* begins, the Suarez family from Long Beach is in the Pacific Ocean halfway to Catalina Island. The daughter Margarita is swimming in an invitational race, and the father (a coach), mother (a former Miss Cuba), grandmother (the praying Abuela), and younger brother, with binoculars and punk sunglasses, follow in their boat. Margarita loses her concentration and apparently is drowned by exhaustion, oil slicks ("rainbows"), and the family's hopes and demands but mostly by the condescension of being called a simple Cuban amateur and brave little loser by the sexist American television reporter in a helicopter. Sinking to the bottom, she strokes into blackout to the rhythm of a Hail Mary. Abuela, who shouts "Assholes!" at the vanishing helicopter, invokes ancestors and saints as the grieving family reports the swimmer lost: "My little fish is not lost!" In a nicely ambiguous phrase the same television reporter describes to the family and the world "a miracle." The lost Cuban swimmer "is now walking on the waters, through the breakers," and is first "onto the beach." Abuela recognizes "*sangre di mi sangre.*"

In *Dog Lady* pretty 18-year-old Rosalinda Luna is said to successfully, literally "run like a dog" to win her big race, and she runs on beyond the barrio's Castro Street. She does so with the prayerful support of her decorous mother and the *yu-yu* spell and incantation from old Luisa Ruiz, the mentally and physically unkempt dog keeper and healer next door. But it is Jesse, the 15-year-old tomboy, who receives the audience's attention, her mother's scolding, her sister's trust, and half of the bouquet an infatuated 18-year-old intended for the star. Suddenly a beautiful *señorita,* she asks, "You really turn into a dog?" Rosalinda puts the *yu-yu* around Jesse's neck: "You have to work very hard." The two actions—winning and reluctantly coming-of-age—frame soaring fantasies, functional but funny misunderstandings, and bright dialogue.

Evening Star features another two houses on Castro Street and another reluctant coming-of-age. Olivia Peña, in parochial school uniform at age 14, and Junior Rodriguez, age 16, search for stars from his roof. A local vendor—like Eugenia, Abuela, the dog lady, and the stage manager of Thornton Wilder's *Our Town*—is the keeper of lore and cures. The grandmother, Tina Peña, is puzzled and agrees with the vendor—before old man Peña, throwing rocks, drives him off—that the white rose miraculously appearing in her garden on this morning should signify birth. Both are hardworking, impoverished households that have troubled daughters. Peña drove off their lost Sarita, who left her baby Olivia, and the abandoned Mrs. Rodriguez next door does the same when her 15-year-old admits her pregnancy. As Lilly Rodriguez gives birth upstairs in the Peñas' house, epiphanies, tendernesses, and strengths bloom like roses. Mama Rodriguez rushes in to help her baby, and old Peña, who cannot go in and who cannot pray, throws a humanistic rock at heaven. The vendor is heard saying, "The sun is rising. Another day of life. Try not to abuse it." Despite gritty details, poetic monologues, and Peña's comic grouchiness and daily ritual—penuriously updating his mailing list by crossing off Hispanic names from the day's obituaries—too much of the affirmation seems gratuitous and the theatrical without magic.

Roosters, set where farmworkers labor to achieve dignity and respite, divides allegorically named males and females into contrasting types and lets the drama bring them to fertile reconciliation. In a prologue the handsome Gallo, who is in his 40s, explains that he has served a prison term for manslaughter. He was caught breeding another's high-flying ("like dark avenging angels") Filipino Bolina with his scruffy red Cuban hen ("a queen" who killed every "stag") to create the prize fighting cock Zapata. As he stalks and pricks his crossbred Hispanic-Pacific rooster, a male dancer, with a stiletto, Gallo croons, "Show Daddy whatcha got." He exults when the "son" Zapata attacks and draws blood. Everyone anxiously awaits the homecoming of the husband-lover, brother, and father. The women preparing food anticipate more hardship and loneliness. The grandfather has willed Zapata to 20-year-old Hector during the father's absence. The boy plans first to fight Zapata tonight and then to sell him to finance a better life for his mother Juana, his tortilla-rolling aunt Chata, and his mystical younger sister Angelita. With her cardboard wings and tombstones, prayers to saints, disappearances, and imaginary tea parties, Angelita sees the shadows stalking her father and brother. She must choose sides. The predicted cockfight between Hector and Gallo allows rightful shares of nobility to each generation, character, and way of living, something that Sánchez-Scott shows persuasively.

—John G. Kuhn

SAUNDERS, James A.

Nationality: British. **Born:** Islington, London, 8 January 1925. **Education:** Wembley County School; University of Southampton. **Family:** Married Audrey Cross in 1951; one son and two daughters. **Career:** Formerly taught English in London. Full-time writer, 1962—. Lives in Twickenham, Middlesex. **Awards:** Arts Council bursary, 1960, 1984; *Evening Standard* award, 1963; Writers Guild award, 1966; Art Vouncil of Great Britain major bursary, 1984; BBC radio play award, 1986, for *Menocchio*; Moliere award, 1990, for *Fall.* **Agent:** Casarotto Ramsay Ltd., National House, 60-66 Wardour Street, London W1V 3HP, England.

PUBLICATIONS

Plays

Cinderella Comes of Age (produced London, 1949).

Moonshine (produced London, 1955).

Dog Accident (broadcast 1958; revised version produced London, 1969). Published in *Ten of the Best,* edited by Ed Berman, London, Inter-Action Imprint, 1979.

Barnstable (broadcast 1959; produced Dublin and London, 1960). London, French, 1965.

Alas, Poor Fred: A Duologue in the Style of Ionesco (produced Scarborough, 1959; London, 1966). Scarborough, Studio Theatre, 1960.

The Ark, music by Geoffrey Wright (produced London, 1959).

Ends and Echoes: Barnstable, Committal, Return to a City (produced London, 1960). *Return to a City* included in *Neighbours and Other Plays,* 1968.

A Slight Accident (produced Nottingham, 1961; London, 1971; Chicago, 1977). Included in *Neighbours and Other Plays,* 1968.

Double, Double (produced London, 1962). London, French, 1964.

Next Time I'll Sing to You, suggested by a theme from *A Hermit Disclosed* by Raleigh Trevelyan (produced London, 1962; revised version produced London and New York, 1963). London, Deutsch, and New York, Random House, 1963.

Who Was Hilary Maconochie? (produced London, 1963). Included in *Savoury Meringue and Other Plays,* 1980.

The Pedagogue (produced London, 1963). Included in *Neighbours and Other Plays,* 1968.

Neighbours (produced London, 1964; New York, 1969). Included in *Neighbours and Other Plays,* 1968.

A Scent of Flowers (produced London, 1964; New York, 1969). London, Deutsch, and New York, Random House, 1965.

Triangle, with others (produced Glasgow, 1965; London, 1983).

Trio (produced Edinburgh, 1967). Included in *Neighbours and Other Plays,* 1968.

The Italian Girl, with Iris Murdoch, adaptation of the novel by Murdoch (produced Bristol, 1967; London, 1968). London, French, 1969.

Neighbours and Other Plays (includes *Trio*; *Alas, Poor Fred*; *Return to a City*; *A Slight Accident*; *The Pedagogue*). London, Deutsch, 1968.

Haven, later called *A Man's Best Friend*, in *We Who Are about to . . .*, later called *Mixed Doubles* (produced London, 1969). London, Methuen, 1970.

The Travails of Sancho Panza, based on the novel *Don Quixote* by Cervantes (produced London, 1969). London, Heinemann, 1970.

The Borage Pigeon Affair (produced London, 1969). London, Deutsch, 1970.

Savoury Meringue (produced London, 1971; New York, 1981). Included in *Savoury Meringue and Other Plays* 1980.

After Liverpool (broadcast 1971; produced Edinburgh and London, 1971; New York, 1973). London, French, 1973.

Games (produced Edinburgh and London, 1971; New York, 1973). London, French, 1973.

Opus (produced Loughton, Essex, 1971).

Hans Kohlhaas, adaptation of the story by Heinrich von Kleist (produced London, 1972; as *Michael Kohlhaas*, produced London, 1987).

Bye Bye Blues (produced Richmond, Surrey, 1973; London, 1977). Included in *Bye Bye Blues and Other Plays*, 1980.

Poor Old Simon (in *Mixed Blessings*, produced Horsham, Sussex, 1973; produced separately, New York, 1981). Included in *Savoury Meringue and Other Plays*, 1980.

Random Moments in a May Garden (broadcast 1974; produced London, 1977). Included in *Bye Bye Blues and Other Plays*, 1980.

A Journey to London, completion of the play by Vanbrugh (produced London, 1975).

Play for Yesterday (produced Richmond, Surrey, 1975; London, 1983). Included in *Savoury Meringue and Other Plays*, 1980.

The Island (produced London, 1975). Included in *Bye Bye Blues and Other Plays*, 1980.

Squat (produced Richmond, Surrey, 1976).

Mrs. Scour and the Future of Western Civilisation (produced Richmond, Surrey, 1976; London, 1983).

Bodies (produced Richmond, Surrey, 1977; London, 1978; New Haven, Connecticut, 1981). Ashover, Derbyshire, Amber Lane Press, and New York, Dramatists Play Service, 1979.

Over the Wall (produced London, 1977). Published in *Play Ten*, edited by Robin Rook, London, Arnold, 1977.

What Theatre Really Is, in *Play Ten*, edited by Robin Rook. London; Arnold, 1977.

Player Piano, adaptation of the novel by Kurt Vonnegut (produced London, 1978).

The Mountain (produced Bristol, 1979).

The Caucasian Chalk Circle, adaptation of a play by Brecht (produced Richmond, Surrey, 1979).

Birdsong (produced Richmond, Surrey, 1979; New York, 1984). Included in *Savoury Meringue and Other Plays*, 1980.

The Girl in Melanie Klein, adaptation of the novel by Ronald Harwood (produced Watford, Hertfordshire, 1980).

Savoury Meringue and Other Plays, Ambergate, Derbyshire, Amber Lane Press, 1980.

Bye Bye Blues and Other Plays (includes *The Island* and *Random Moments in a May Garden*). Ambergate, Derbyshire, Amber Lane Press, 1980.

Fall (produced Richmond, Surrey, 1981; London, 1984). London, French, 1985.

Nothing to Declare (broadcast 1982; produced Richmond, Surrey, 1983).

Menocchio (broadcast 1985). Published in *Best Radio Plays of 1985*, London, Methuen, 1986.

Redevelopment, adaptation of a play by Václav Havel (produced Richmond, Surrey, 1990). London, Faber, 1990.

Making It Better (broadcast 1991; produced London, 1992). London, French, 1992.

Retreat. London, First Writes, 1995.

Playforms. Cambridge, England, Cambridge University Press, 1997.

Screenplay: *The Sailor's Return*, 1970.

Radio Plays: *Love and a Limousine*, 1952; *The Drop Too Much*, 1952; *Nimrod's Oak*, 1953; *Women Are So Unreasonable*, 1957; *Dog Accident*, 1958; *Barnstable*, 1959; *Gimlet* (version of *Double, Double*), 1963; *It's Not the Game It Was*, 1964; *Pay As You Go*, 1965; *After Liverpool*, 1971; *Random Moments in a May Garden*, 1974; *The Last Black and White Midnight Movie*, 1979; *Nothing to Declare*, 1982; *The Flower Case*, 1982; *A Suspension of Mercy* (*Murder for Pleasure* series), from the novel by Patricia Highsmith, 1983; *Menocchio*, 1985; *The Confidential Agent*, from the novel by Graham Greene, 1987; *Headlong Hall*, from the novel by Thomas Love Peacock, 1988; *Making It Better*, 1991; *The Three Musketeers*, from the novel by Alexandre Dumas, 1993.

Television Plays: *Just You Wait* (version of *Double, Double*), 1963; *Watch Me I'm a Bird*, 1964; *The White Stocking*, *New Eve and Old Adam*, *Tickets Please*, *Monkey Nuts*, *Two Blue Birds*, *In Love*, and *The Blue Moccasins*, all from works by D.H. Lawrence, 1966-67; *The Beast in the Jungle*, from the story by Henry James, 1969; *Plastic People*, 1970; *The Unconquered*, 1970; *Craven Arms*, from a story by A.E. Coppard, 1972; *The Mill*, 1972; *The Black Dog*, 1972; *Blind Love*, from the story by V.S. Pritchett, 1977; *The Healing Nightmare*, 1977; *People Like Us*, with Susan Pieat and Ian Curteis, from the novel by R.F. Delderfield, 1978; *Bloomers* series, 1979; *The Sailor's Return*, from the novel by David Garnett, 1980; *The Captain's Doll*, from the story by D.H. Lawrence, 1983; *The Magic Bathroom*, 1987.

*

Critical Studies: "A Hermit Dramatized" by Kathy J. Gentile, in *Modern Drama* (Downsview, Ontario), September 1985, pp. 490-99; "Giggling at the Arts: Tom Stoppard and James Saunders" by Neil Sammells, in *Critical Quarterly* (Oxford), Winter 1986, pp. 71-78.

* * *

James Saunders's work is characterized by a diversity of styles, which is unusual even among the more eclectic of his contemporaries. He can be compared to a startling variety of other writers, and should his scripts survive without attribution, future generations of scholars might assign them in something like this fashion: to Harold Pinter the revue sketch investment of the commonplace with interest found in *Double, Double* and the schematic exploration of open marriage found in *Bye Bye Blues*; to John Mortimer the charming coincidence of complementary handicaps that permits two self-pitying people to unite in *Blind Love*; to Samuel Beckett the seemingly plotless philosophizing of *Next Time I'll Sing to You*; to John Arden and Margaretta D'Arcy the episodic structure and satire of inept and hypocritical public officials in *The Borage Pigeon Affair*; to Eugène Ionesco or N. F. Simpson the absurdist farce of such one-acts as *Who Was Hilary Maconochie?*, *Alas, Poor Fred*, and *A Slight Accident*; to Simon Gray the mutual torment inflicted by sophisticates in extremis found in *Bodies*; to Peter Handke the invitation to spectators to reject the play found in the fragmented *Games*; to Henry Livings the music hall flavor of *Savoury Meringue*; and to any one of dozens of realistic dramatists the belligerence and bewilderment of the interracial psychological study *Neighbours*.

Although Saunders's stylistic range is breathtaking, future literary detectives might discover his authorship by recognizing distinctive situations and themes. His dramatis personae are frequently couples, and he is constantly investigating how people relate to others, care about others, commit themselves to others, and sustain the relationships long-term. The alienated Saunders character often lives close to the edge. He or she finds difficulty wrenching meaning from a life rendered pointless by death and unbearable by loneliness or, paradoxically, by the proximity of people. He probes the false values exemplified in various interpersonal relations, and he illuminates the responsibility people assume or evade for the choices they make. He is a humanist sympathetic to the underdog or the rebel and is deeply suspicious of the games people play to keep their emotions at bay or to score points off others. Yet he is expert at dramatizing those often urbane games, and such is the ambiguity of his situations—particularly in his later work—that spectators may be forgiven for wondering whether his commiseration for the losers is not balanced by a certain admiration for the victor's skill.

Saunders has created a constellation of wonderfully ineffectual characters. There is the driver in *Gimlet* whose bus passes through—but is really bypassed by—life. There is the befuddled actor in *Triangle* who is "not quite sure whether I'm trying to play myself or trying not to play myself." There are the musicians in *Trio* who cannot perform because they are under attack by flies. There is the teacher in *The Pedagogue* who loses control of his pupils as well as his faith in mankind. There are the men and women in *After Liverpool* who often botch their desultory attempts to talk to one other. There is the wife in *A Slight Accident* who is flustered by her husband's failure to get up off the floor after she has murdered him and poor Pringle's confusion when he is reminded that he killed the title character in *Alas, Poor Fred*. There is the deceased protagonist of *A Scent of Flowers*, whose inability to inspire in her family any accessible love has led her to suicide. In *Next Time I'll Sing to You* there is little Lizzie who is lost because she is replacing her twin sister in the role without benefit of either rehearsal or script. There are the ridiculous attempts of the macho men in *The Island* to bully their superiors (the women) into liking them. ("If I had been expecting anything," quips one of the gals, "they'd be a disappointment.") And there are those archetypal sufferers of indignity in *The Travails of Sancho Panza*.

Saunders has repeatedly dramatized the tension between such poles as independence and dependence or our responsibility for choices versus our lack of control over events. In an early radio play that later became the street theater piece *Dog Accident*, for instance, Saunders confronts passersby with a dispute that is seemingly between two of their number over a dog who has just been run over. They disagree over whether the dog's demise was its own fault and, later, over whether the dog is really dead or still suffering. Why, argues the indifferent one, should they care about a dying dog when large-scale catastrophes strike people every day? The other momentarily opts for bothering, then either cannot sustain or cannot stomach the pain and prefers to go to lunch. Our mutual interdependence and the complex determinants of an event also inform *Bye Bye Blues*, in which three separate couples discuss one or more automobile accidents in which they are all somehow involved or implicated.

Saunders's best-known play, *Next Time I'll Sing to You*, picks as its subject a hermit, Jimmy Mason, who died in Essex in 1942. Another writer might have considered Mason's solitary life and death more conventionally and sentimentally. But Saunders suggests the aimlessness of life with a form that itself rambles. This presentational style and nonlinear "plot" may communicate subliminally that life is disordered suffering. Ostensibly, however, the play is a comedy in which the characters are actors making disconnected attempts to put on a play about Mason. They crack jokes, discuss whether they are asleep, and confuse the actress who is supposedly a substitute for her sister. Perhaps five minutes is devoted to conveying the facts of Mason's life. Gradually, such philosophical issues as the nature of man and the purpose of life are raised. *Next Time I'll Sing to You*, like *Waiting for Godot*, employs offbeat characters and an unusual structure to raise fundamental human questions. After we wonder why Mason lived alone—or, indeed, why he lived—we come to wonder whether his solitude differs only superficially from our own. If we are better off than Mason, the reason may only be "One thing about us—at least we're not dead."

Although well known, *Next Time I'll Sing to You* has been regarded by some critics as pretentious or incomprehensible. Neither charge could be leveled at Saunders's best play, *Bodies*. Though seemingly more realistic because it is set in recognizable contemporary homes, *Bodies* is one of Saunders's many plays that combine presentational and representational styles. It also epitomizes his highly verbal work; hearing it is much more important than seeing it.

In *Bodies* Saunders portrays two couples who many years before had affairs with one another's mates. Act 1 intercuts monologues, in which each of the four recalls the affairs, with duologues on their approaching reunion with their ex-lovers. Act 2 brings them, at that reunion, into present confrontation with their pasts. The couples have handled their midlife crises—or passages—quite differently. Anne and Merwyn, who have considered themselves unromantic pragmatists, muddle along, experiencing their anxiety at reaching middle age, their panic at disillusionment in the things they once held dear, and their terror at lack of self-esteem. On the other hand, by means of a new therapy David and Helen have reached a state untroubled by emotions of any kind. They insist that people are only bodies and that happiness and unhappiness do not exist.

We are meant to wonder whether feelings are valuable. Especially if such passions are painful, is it preferable, like tranquil and twitchless David and Helen, to be therapeutically freed from suffering, from the insistence on finding meaning in experience? Or is that solution insensitive, unresponsive to life, and is one therefore better off—as Peter Shaffer's *Equus* and innumerable other contemporary British plays suggest—with one's neuroses intact? But if Saunders initially sets up a dichotomy between detached David and Helen and the troubled teacher Merwyn, he subtly suggests that the latter also escapes his emotional traumas, though his means is not therapy but mental agility liberally laced with alcohol. An offstage student, meanwhile, has left Merwyn's English seminar and fled his feelings still more effectively by killing himself. Ultimately, what Saunders has dramatized, then, are alternative routes to wasting one's personal emotional riches.

Saunders has been blessed with sufficient royalties from his German productions to earn a living, and he has benefited the long-term willingness of two London groups, the Questors and the Richmond Fringe at the Orange Tree, to try whatever he happens to write. Free from worry over whether each new work will prove a commercial success, Saunders has been able to write to please himself. Perhaps this has encouraged self-indulgence in scenes sometimes simultaneously cerebral and long-winded. Yet when he avoids verbosity, Saunders succeeds with versatility, ingenuity, whimsy, suspense, wit, and an emotional sensitivity that permits him to touch us without growing maudlin. Both in depth and in range, his plays continue to intrigue longer than might the work of a more uniform playwright.

—Tish Dace

SCHENKAR, Joan M.

Nationality: American. **Born:** Seattle, Washington, 15 August 1950. **Education:** St. Nicholas School, Bennington College, Bennington, Vermont, and a collection of graduate schools. **Career:** Advertising copywriter, social worker, and researcher, all New York, 1960s; coffee and doughnut vendor, 1973, and church organist, Congregational Church, 1974, both Vermont; playwright-in-residence, Joseph Chaikin's Winter Project, New York, 1977 and 1978, Polish Laboratory, New York, 1977, Florida Studio Theatre, Sarasota, Florida, 1980, Changing Scene, Denver, Colorado, 1982, Centre d'essai des auteurs dramatiques, Montreal, and Composer-Librettist's Workshop, New York, both 1985, Minnesota Opera New Music Theatre Ensemble, Minneapolis, 1986-88, and Kentucky Foundation for Women, Louisville, Kentucky, 1988. Visiting fellow, Cummington Community Arts, Cummington, Massachusetts, 1978, Ragdale Foundation, Lake Forest, Illinois, 1979, and MacDowell Art Colony, Peterborough, New Hampshire, 1980; teacher, School of Visual Arts, New York, 1978-91; founder and artistic director, Force Majeure Productions, New York, from 1987; director, The Performance Series, North Bennington, Vermont, 1992. **Awards:** National Endowment for the Arts grant, 1977, 1978, 1980, 1982, fellowship, 1981; Creative Artists Public Service fellowship, 1979-80; Lowe Foundation grant, 1983; Playwrights Forum award, 1984; Arthur Foundation grant, 1984, 1989; New York State Council on the Arts grant, 1986, 1989, 1992; Schubert Travel grant, 1988; Vermont Community grant, 1991; and 30 other grants and awards. **Agent:** Samuel French Ltd., 45 West 25th Street, New York, New York, 10010, U.S.A. **Address:** P.O. Box 814, North Bennington, Vermont 05257, U.S.A.; 29 Cornelia Street, Apartment 6, New York, New York 10014, U.S.A.; 5, rue de Jarente, 75004 Paris, France. **Online address:** JMSchenkar@aol.com.

Publications

Plays

The Next Thing (produced Los Angeles, 1976).
Cabin Fever (produced Los Angeles, 1976; New York, 1977; London, 1986). New York, French, 1984.
Last Words (produced New York, 1977).
Signs of Life (produced New York, 1979; London, 1983). Published in *The Women's Project Anthology*, edited by Julia Miles, New York, Performing Arts Journal Publishers, 1980.
The Lodger (produced New York, 1979).
Mr. Monster (produced New York, 1980).
The Last of Hitler (also director: produced New York, 1981).
Between the Acts (also director: produced New York, 1984, 1989).
Fulfilling Koch's Postulate (also director: produced New York, 1985; London, 1986; Berlin, 1996).
Joan of Arc (produced Minneapolis, 1986).
Family Pride in the 50s (produced New York, 1986). Published in *The Kenyon Review* (Kenyon, Ohio), Spring 1993.
Fire in the Future (produced Minneapolis, 1987; also director: produced New York, 1988).
Hunting Down the Sexes (includes *Bucks and Does*, *The Lodger*) (produced New York, 1987).
Nothing Is Funnier than Death (produced New York, 1988).
The Universal Wolf (produced New York, 1991; Universal Wolf Providence, 1994; Los Angeles, 1995). New York, Applause Books, 1992.

Other

Truly Wilde. New York, Basic Books, 1999; London, Virago Press, 1999.

*

Critical Studies: "Foodtalk in the Plays of Caryl Churchill and Joan Schenkar" by Vivian M. Patraka, in *The Theatre Annual* (Akron, Ohio), 1985; "Mass Culture and Metaphors of Menace in Joan Schenkar's Plays" by Vivian M. Patraka, in *Making a Spectacle, Feminist Essays on Contemporary Women's Theatre* edited by Lynda Hart, Ann Arbor, Michigan, University of Michigan Press, 1989; "History and Hysteria, Writing the Body in *Portrait of Dora* and *Signs of Life*" by Ann Wilson, in *Modern Drama* (Toronto, Ontario), March 1989; "Crossing the Corpus Callosum" by Elin Diamond, in *The Drama Review* (New York), Summer 1991; introduction to *Signs of Life: Six Comedies of Menace* by Vivian Patraka, Middletown, Connecticut, Weslyan University Press, 1997.

Theatrical Activities:
Director: **Plays**—*The Last of Hitler*, New York, 1981; *Between the Acts*, New York, 1984, 1989; *Fulfilling Koch's Postulate*, New York, 1985; *Fire in the Future*, New York, 1988; *Murder in the Kitchen*, Vermont, 1992, New York, 1993.

Joan Schenkar comments:

My most serious intention as a writer for the stage is to enter a clear condition of nightmare through the comedy of precise vernacular. . . . Some truths are so terrible they can only be approached by laughter—which is why I write comedies of menace. In the best of all possible productions, I will have made you laugh at something horrible.

(1998) Writing is a life sentence to solitude. Writing for theatre is a life sentence to standing on a stage with your skirt up over your head. Between utter seclusion and total exposure, I have tried to locate an even more extreme position: the theatricalization of feelings so complex that the only way to access them is laughter. I cannot forget that The Last Laugh is always (literally) on us. After the flesh is gone, every skeleton sports a persistent smile.

Each of my plays was composed as much as possible as a piece of music. Each one has movements, developed themes, arias, duets, etc. I have always meant to mark the plays for performance much as music is marked—for prose language does not offer us the nice distinctions of pitch, stress, tempo, and juncture that music does. I have always paid more attention to the sound of language than to the sense of it, figuring that if I get the sound right, the sense will take care of itself. It usually does.

Plays happen, for an audience, in the dark. Reading them requires a very good light. I love this apparent contradiction and am encouraged by it, for it turns the act of reading plays—which for me is often more interesting than seeing them—into a waking dream.

* * *

Dreams, history, and fantasy serve as raw material for the elliptical, determinedly nonnaturalistic plays of Joan Schenkar. Her style is heavily influenced by cartoons, comic strips, feminist theory and literature, radio, television, the circus, and the sideshow. Schenkar's stated purpose "is to make comedies of tragic subjects," and she wields her macabre, demonic sense of humor like a scalpel in dissecting varied topics—the Victorians' destructive attitude toward women, the insidious spread of anti-Semitism, the power and precariousness of a scientific outlook, and the surreal normality of American suburbia.

Schenkar gives a number of her plays the subtitle "a comedy of menace." Her three primary works in this vein—*Cabin Fever*, *Fulfilling Koch's Postulate*, and *Family Pride in the 50s*—all share this subversive manic humor. *Cabin Fever*, the funniest and most menacing, reads like a Stephen King story as dramatized by Samuel Beckett. Three characters, called One, Two, and Three, never move from their dilapidated New England front porch as they try to stave off the dreaded disease of the title. Underneath their reserved, almost formal manner, however, terror lurks. They know that "It comes in threes." "What does?" one character asks. "Death," assures another. Their anxiety spirals with each repetition of this litany. When talk turns to the cannibalism that has been running rampant in this backwoods community, One twitches in her seat as Two and Three recall the last time they sampled human flesh. Although they jocularly threaten to eat One, she gets the last laugh, and the play ends with her brandishing knife and fork.

Influenced by the "Katzenjammer Kids" comic strip, Schenkar purposefully confines herself to a 300-word vocabulary for *Fulfilling Koch's Postulate*. As in *Cabin Fever*, Schenkar provides her characters with a one-line litany: "Nothing is funnier than death." Her sets are always exaggerated metaphors that serve as an extra character, and this play features a lip-shaped proscenium and a playing space made into an esophagus. Within this frame the stage is split between the kitchen, from which a household chef based on the infamous historical figure known as Typhoid Mary, spreads her deadly contagion, and the laboratory in which Dr. Koch tries to track down the root of the disease. As the cook cooks and the scientist probes, the culinary activities take on shades of sinister experimentation while Koch's dissections become utterly domestic. *Family Pride in the 50s* is a heavy-handed satire on an easy target: the idyllic postwar decade dominated by frosted flakes, family holiday dinners, and fights over the television set. Everyone resembles everyone else—two brothers married two sisters, each with two children. As the eldest child Joan retches violently, everyone blithely continues their family squabbles. When the children "play doctor," they use real knives and instruments, much as the dramatist did: "When I was a kid I used to collect knives. . . . I had a surgeon's puncture tool. . . . And I'd take people's blood samples." The play ends with the children sitting around the table:

> Maureen: You gonna deal those cards? Or do I have to cut 'em with my knife.
>
> Joan: Tch tch. Such language sis. Tch tch tch. Such *language* at the *dinner* table.

Schenkar's preoccupation with science—what she calls "false science"—underlies two other historically based plays, *The Last of Hitler* and *Signs of Life*. The former is a dream play picturing the führer in what Schenkar envisions as his version of hell—a "Kozy Kabin" in Florida, a state with a large population of Jews. Once again Schenkar works with a split stage, but this time it is divided by an enormous 1940s radio that spews anti-Semitism, which is less visible than Typhoid Mary's infection but just as deadly. As Dr. Reich and his office skeleton perform ventriloquist routines reminiscent of Charlie McCarthy's, Hitler and Eva Braun fight off cancer and their own Jewishness. *Signs of Life*, the most successful of Schenkar's imaginative treatments of history, features Henry James and Dr. Sloper, the inventor of the "uterine guillotine," taking tea and toasting "the ladies" who, Schenkar believes, helped make the men famous—Henry's invalid sister Alice, and Jane Merritt, P. T. Barnum's sideshow star dubbed the Elephant Woman, on whom Sloper performed experimental surgery. The play clearly demonstrates how both women were transformed into freaks, victims of Victorian patriarchy's malevolence toward women.

Between the Acts, an absurdist, surreal fairy tale set in the garden of the wealthiest man in the world, gives allegorical voice to Schenkar's feminist and political concerns. At a climactic moment the rich capitalist Martin Barney and his daughter's lesbian lover, the artist Romaine Brooks, circle each other like boxers. Instead of trading physical blows, they shout out famous names. When Barney yells, "J. P. Morgan," Romaine is momentarily staggered, but she strikes back with "Emily Brontë, Emily Dickinson, Virginia Woolf!" and crumples the industrialist, who wails, "Genius! Good God! I have nothing to fight genius with." Featuring a gigantic Venus's-flytrap that serves as a trysting spot, a riding crop that spews magic dust, and a dog in a tutu that performs bourrées in silhouette, this is one of Schenkar's wildest efforts.

Hunting Down the Sexes, composed of two compact and vicious one-acts, makes these gender wars literal. The first part, *Bucks and Does*, focuses on three men—Rap, Ape, and Ab—at their hunting cabin. The play opens with Rap masturbating in synchronized motion with Ab's ritualistic cleaning of the guns. Schenkar then takes Freud's theories to their harrowing extreme. Rap, who insists on calling does "pretty brown girls," tells his mates, "There's nothing like pulling a trigger and watching 'em drop. I always come when they drop." Of course, the does, portrayed by actresses, get their final revenge when Rap staggers into the cabin with his crotch bloodied by a stray bullet. In the second part, *The Lodger*, a pair of spinsterish women debate the tortures they will inflict on their male prisoner, captured in the guerrilla war between genders raging around their Victorian New England home.

Schenkar's works all limn the body/brain duality. Images of blood, ritualistic "bloodings," and blood samples appear in virtually every play, while the fragile intellectual systems holding reality together go haywire. In the best of her work Schenkar's stagecraft, using varied performance traditions—from cartoons to shadow puppets—and structural devices—from entr'actes to epilogues—matches her imagination to provide insightful entrées to the dualities dueling for body and soul in Western society.

—John Istel

SCHEVILL, James (Erwin)

Nationality: American. **Born:** Berkeley, California, 10 June 1920. **Education:** Harvard University, Cambridge, Massachusetts, B.S. 1942. **Military Service:** Served in the United States Army, 1942-46. **Family:** Married Margot Helmuth Blum in 1966; two daughters by an earlier marriage. **Career:** Member of the faculty, California College of Arts and Crafts, Oakland, 1950-59; member of the Faculty, 1959-68, and director of the Poetry Center, 1961-68, San Francisco State College. Professor of English 1969-85, professor emeritus, 1985—, and director of the creative writing program, 1972-75, Brown University, Providence, Rhode Island. Founding member, Wastepaper Theatre, Providence. **Awards:** National Theatre Competition prize, 1945; Dramatists Alliance Contest prize, 1948; Fund for the Advancement of Education fellowship, 1953; Phelan prize, for biography, 1954, for play, 1958; Ford grant, 1960; Rockefeller grant, 1964; William Carlos Williams award (*Contact* magazine), 1965; Roadstead Foundation award, 1966; Rhode Island Governor's award, 1975; Guggenheim fellowship, 1981; McKnight fellowship, 1984; American Academy award, 1991, literary award, 1992. M.A. (ad eundem): Brown University, 1969. D.H.L.: Rhode Island College, Providence, 1986. **Agent:** Helen Merrill Ltd., 435 West 23rd Street, No. 1A, New York, New York 10011. **Address:** 1309 Oxford Street, Berkeley, California, U.S.A.

Publications

Plays

High Sinners, Low Angels, music by Schevill, arranged by Robert Commanday (produced San Francisco, 1953). San Francisco, Bern Porter, 1953.

The Bloody Tenet (produced Providence, Rhode Island, 1956; Shrewsbury, Shropshire, 1962). Included in *The Black President and Other Plays*, 1965.

The Cid, adaptation of the play by Corneille (broadcast 1963). Published in *The Classic Theatre 4*, edited by Eric Bentley, New York, Doubleday, 1961.

Voices of Mass and Capital A, music by Andrew Imbrie (produced San Francisco, 1962). New York, Friendship Press, 1962.

The Master (produced San Francisco, 1963). Included in *The Black President and Other Plays*, 1965.

American Power: The Space Fan, and The Master (produced Minneapolis, 1964). Included in *The Black President and Other Plays*, 1965.

The Black President and Other Plays. Denver, Swallow, 1965.

The Death of Anton Webern (produced Fish Creek, Wisconsin, 1966). Included in *Violence and Glory: Poems 1962-1968*, 1969.

This Is Not True, music by Paul McIntyre (produced Minneapolis, 1967).

The Pilots (produced Providence, Rhode Island, 1970).

Oppenheimer's Chair (produced Providence, Rhode Island, 1970).

Lovecraft's Follies (produced Providence, Rhode Island, 1970). Chicago, Swallow Press, 1971.

The Ushers (produced Providence, Rhode Island, 1971). Included in *Five Plays*, 1993.

The American Fantasies (produced New York, 1972).

Emperor Norton Lives! (produced Salt Lake City, 1972; revised version, as *Emperor Norton*, music by Jerome Rosen, produced San Francisco, 1979).

Fay Wray Meets King Kong (produced Providence, Rhode Island, 1974). Published in *Wastepaper Theatre Anthology*, edited by Schevill, 1978.

Sunset and Evening Stance; or, Mr. Krapp's New Tapes (produced Providence, Rhode Island, 1974). Published in *Wastepaper Theatre Anthology*, edited by Schevill, 1978.

The Telephone Murderer (produced Providence, Rhode Island, 1975). Published in *Wastepaper Theatre Anthology*, edited by Schevill, 1978.

Cathedral of Ice (produced Providence, Rhode Island, 1975). Wood Hole, Massachusetts, Pourboire Press, 1975; reprinted in anthology *Plays of the Holocaust*, edited by Elinor Fuchs, New York, Theatre Communications Group, 1987.

Naked in the Garden (produced Providence, Rhode Island, 1975).

Year after Year (produced Providence, Rhode Island, 1976).

Questioning Woman (produced Providence, Rhode Island, 1980).

Mean Man I (also director: produced Providence, Rhode Island, 1981).

Mean Man II (also director: produced Providence, Rhode Island, 1982).

Edison's Dream (produced Providence, Rhode Island, 1982).

Galileo, with Adrian Hall, adaptation of the play by Brecht (produced Providence, Rhode Island, 1983).

Cult of Youth (produced Minneapolis, 1984).

Mean Man III (also director: produced Providence, Rhode Island, 1985).

Time of the Hand and Eye (produced Providence, Rhode Island, 1986).

The Planner (also director: produced Providence, Rhode Island, 1986).

Collected Short Plays. Athens, Swallow Press-Ohio University Press, 1986.

The Storyville Doll Lady (also director: produced Providence, Rhode Island, 1987).

Perelman Monologue (produced Providence, Rhode Island, 1987).

Mother O; or, The Last American Mother (produced Providence, Rhode Island, 1990). Included in *Five Plays*, 1993.

Sisters in the Limelight (produced Providence, Rhode Island, 1990).

American Fantasies (produced Rostock, East Germany, 1990).

The Garden on F Street, with Mary Gail (produced Providence, Rhode Island, 1992).
The Phantom of Life: A Melville Play (produced Kingston, 1993).
Five Plays (includes *Lovecraft's Follies*, *The Ushers*, *The Last Romantics*, *Mother O; or, The Last American Mother*, *Shadows of Memory: A Double Bill About Dian Fossey and Djuna Barnes*). Athens, Ohio, Swallow Press, 1993.
The Last Romantics (produced Berkeley, California, 1997).

Radio Plays: *The Sound of a Soldier*, 1945; *The Death of a President*, 1945; *The Cid*, 1963 (Canada); *The Death of Anton Webern*, 1972.

Novel

The Arena of Ants. Providence, Rhode Island, Copper Beech Press, 1977.

Poetry

Tensions. San Francisco, Bern Porter, 1947.
The American Fantasies. San Francisco, Bern Porter, 1951.
The Right to Greet. San Francisco, Bern Porter, 1955.
Selected Poems 1945-1959. San Francisco, Bern Porter, 1960.
Private Dooms and Public Destinations: Poems 1945-1962. Denver, Swallow, 1962.
The Stalingrad Elegies. Denver, Swallow, 1964.
Release. Providence, Rhode Island, Hellcoal Press, 1968.
Violence and Glory: Poems 1962-1968. Chicago, Swallow Press, 1969.
The Buddhist Car and Other Characters. Chicago, Swallow Press, 1973.
Pursuing Elegy: A Poem about Haiti. Providence, Rhode Island, Copper Beech Press, 1974.
The Mayan Poems. Providence, Rhode Island, Copper Beech Press, 1978.
Fire of Eyes: A Guatemalan Sequence. Providence, Rhode Island, Copper Beech Press, 1979.
The American Fantasies: Collected Poems 1: 1945-1981. Athens, Swallow Press-Ohio University Press, 1983.
The Invisible Volcano. Providence, Rhode Island, Copper Beech Press, 1985.
Ghost Names/Ghost Numbers. Providence, Rhode Island, Walter Feldman, 1986.
Ambiguous Dancers of Fame: Collected Poems 2: 1945-1985. Athens, Swallow Press-Ohio University Press, 1987.
Quixote Visions. Providence, Rhode Island, Ziggurat Press, 1991.
The Complete American Fantasies. Athens, Ohio, Ohio University Press, 1996.

Recording: *Performance Poems*, Cambridge, 1984.

Other

Sherwood Anderson: His Life and Work. Denver, University of Denver Press, 1951.
The Roaring Market and the Silent Tomb (biographical study of the scientist and artist Bern Porter). Oakland, California, Abbey Press, 1956.
Bern Porter: A Personal Biography. Gardiner, Maine, Tilbury House, 1992.
Editor, *Six Historians*, by Ferdinand Schevill. Chicago, University of Chicago Press, and London, Cambridge University Press, 1956.
Editor, *Break Out! In Search of New Theatrical Environments*. Chicago, Swallow Press, 1973.
Editor, *Wastepaper Theatre Anthology*. Providence, Rhode Island, Pourboire Press, 1978.

*

Manuscript Collection: John Hay Library, Brown University, Providence, Rhode Island.

Critical Study: Unpublished thesis by Wanda Howard, University of Rhode Island, Kingston, 1981.

Theatrical Activities:
Director: **Plays**—Wastepaper Theatre, Providence: *Mean Man I-III*, 1981-85; *The Planner*, 1986; *The Storyville Doll Lady*, 1987.

James Schevill comments:

(1973) My early plays were verse plays. Recently, my plays have been written in prose. However, as a poet, I still believe in poetry as the roots of the theatre, and do my best to upend a theatre that is too literal and prosaic. I want an action that is both theatrical and poetic, that can use the disturbing images of our time to create a new vitality on stage. To achieve this vitality, I like to use dramatic, historical contrasts to give a play depth and perspective. Today the great possibilities of playwriting lie in the recognition that a play can range in time and space as widely as a film, that it can be as exciting in movement as a film, and that the great advantage it continues to have over film is the live actor who is capable of instantaneous, extraordinary transformations in character and situation.

* * *

A lyric poet, James Schevill has been consistently drawn to the theater, but his plays are written largely in prose. Composed of history, current events, and fantasy, they theatricalize injustice in contemporary America.

The Bloody Tenet takes its title from the self-defense of Roger Williams when he was persecuted for religious unorthodoxy. Schevill's play sets Williams's story as a play within a play, and the outer frame is a dialogue between a middle-aged journalist and a voluptuous evangelist. As the inner play dramatizes Williams's condemnation by orthodox authority, the frame play dramatizes a facile orthodoxy paying lip service to liberty. Schevill's play finally confronts his modern audience with Williams himself, who refuses to choose between the journalist's critique of his inadequacies and the evangelist's idolization of him. In verse Williams reemphasizes his belief in individual paths to God.

Moving from religion to politics, Schevill paired his next two plays under the title *American Power*. The first, *The Space Fan*, is subtitled a play of escape, and the second, *The Master*, a play of commitment. The titular space fan is a zany lady who communicates with beings in outer space, and a suspicious government assigns an investigator to spy on her activities. During the course of the play the space fan converts the investigator to her free way of life, and as they join in a dance, the investigator declares, "For the first time in my life, I feel that I've become a real investigator."

In the companion play, *The Master*, the investigation is more insidious. An attractive young woman, the candidate, is guided by a master in examinations that will culminate in a degree of general mastery. During the examination the master imposes various roles on the candidate, including that of an army officer, an Indian squaw, a minuteman, a Southern rebel, and, finally, a corpse. The master and candidate then oppose each other with their respective autobiographies, which erupt into scenes that glorify American power. The subtitles of both plays emerge as ironic: *The Space Fan* is a play of escape from American power, and *The Master* is a play of commitment that satirizes, and implicitly condemns, the commitment to American power.

Schevill's next play, *The Black President*, is rooted in American oppression of blacks, but it reaches out to indict the whole white racist world. Moses Jackburn, a black American, is captain of a facsimile slave ship that is manned by the blacks of many countries. He sails the ship up the Thames to London, demanding to speak with the British prime minister. He is met with pious platitudes, then mercantile bargaining, and finally threats of force. Rather than surrender the ship, Jackson orders his crew to blow it up. While awaiting extradition to America, he is visited by the Spanish Carla, with whom he shares a fantasy life in which she helps him campaign for the presidency. Back in the reality of his prison, Jackburn denounces his dream, but he still hopes for "a little light."

In *Lovecraft's Follies* Schevill indicates his concern about man's enslavement by technology. H. P. Lovecraft, a Rhode Island recluse, was one of the first science fiction writers to stress its gothic horrors. The protagonist of Schevill's play, Stanley Millsage, is a physicist at a space center who has developed a Lovecraft fixation on the horrors that science can perpetrate. These terrors are theatricalized scenically to serve as a cathartic journey for the protagonist. Thus freed from his Lovecraft fixation, Millsage declares, "Well, that's the end of Lovecraft's follies. . . ." But the figure of Lovecraft, alone on stage, says mockingly to the audience, "Maybe!"

This note of indecision leads to Schevill's next major play, *Cathedral of Ice*, in which technology again brings horror. On stage is a dream machine: "With our machine's modern computer device/We conjure up a vast Cathedral of Ice./ . . . I become Dream-Fuehrer, power to arrange." The drama fancifully traces the results of Hitler's mania for power as, in seven scenes, he confronts historical and imaginary figures. Inspired by Napoleon and Charlemagne, Hitler summons an architect to "create for eternity our famous German ruins." Converting people's weaknesses into cruel and theatrical strengths, Hitler builds on the legends of Karl May and Richard Wagner. He refuses to tarnish his own legend by marrying Eva Braun. Above all he harnesses science to his monstrous, destructive dream. But night and fog, who are characters in the play, erode his structures. Even as the gas chambers destroy their multitudes, the Nazis are destroyed by their own manias, so that Hitler finally seeks glory in a *Liebestod* in the Cathedral of Ice.

With fantastic theatrical shapes Schevill's drama explores the realities of power and politics. Using music, dance, ritual, and projections, Schevill the poet has reached out to embrace many possibilities of theater.

—Ruby Cohn

SCHISGAL, Murray (Joseph)

Nationality: American. **Born:** Brooklyn, New York, 25 November 1926. **Education:** Brooklyn Conservatory of Music; Long Island University, New York; Brooklyn Law School, LL.B. 1953; New School for Social Research, New York, B.A. 1959. **Military Service:** Served as a radioman in the United States Navy, 1944-46. **Family:** Married Reene Schapiro in 1958; one daughter and one son. **Career:** Jazz musician in 1940s; lawyer, 1953-55; English teacher, Cooper Junior High School, East Harlem, and other private and public schools in New York, 1955-59. Full-time writer, 1960—. Lives in New York City. **Awards:** Vernon Rice award, 1963; Outer Circle award, 1963; Los Angeles and New York Film Critics award, National Society of Film Critics award, and Writers Guild award, all for screenplay *Tootsie*, 1983. **Agent:** Arthur B. Greene, 101 Park Avenue, 26th Floor, New York, New York 10178, U.S.A.

Publications

Plays

The Typists, and The Tiger (as *Schrecks: The Typists, The Postman, A Simple Kind of Love*, produced London, 1960; revised versions of *The Typists* and *The Postman* produced as *The Typists, and The Tiger*, New York, 1963; London, 1964). New York, Coward McCann, 1963; London, Cape, 1964.

Ducks and Lovers (produced London, 1961). New York, Dramatists Play Service, 1972.

Luv (produced London, 1963; New York, 1964). New York, Coward McCann, 1965.

Knit One, Purl Two (produced Boston, 1963).

Windows (produced Los Angeles, 1965). Included in *Fragments, Windows and Other Plays*, 1965.

Reverberations (produced Stockbridge, Massachusetts, 1965; as *The Basement*, produced New York, 1967). Included in *Fragments, Windows and Other Plays*, 1965.

Fragments, Windows and Other Plays (includes *Reverberations, Memorial Day, The Old Jew*). New York, Coward McCann, 1965.

The Old Jew, Fragments, and Reverberations (produced Stockbridge, Massachusetts, 1966). Included in *Fragments, Windows and Other Plays*, 1965.

Fragments (includes *The Basement* and *Fragments*) (produced New York, 1967). Included in *Fragments, Windows and Other Plays*, 1965.

Memorial Day (produced Baltimore, 1968). Included in *Fragments, Windows and Other Plays*, 1965.

Jimmy Shine, music by John Sebastian (produced New York, 1968; revised version, as *An Original Jimmy Shine*, produced Los Angeles, 1981). New York, Atheneum, 1969.

A Way of Life (produced New York, 1969; as *Roseland*, produced Berlin, 1975; as *The Downstairs Boys*, produced East Hampton, New York, 1980).

The Chinese, and Dr. Fish (produced New York, 1970). New York, Dramatists Play Service, 1970.

An American Millionaire (produced New York, 1974). New York, Dramatists Play Service, 1974.

All Over Town (produced New York, 1974). New York, Dramatists Play Service, 1975.

Popkins (produced Dallas, 1978). New York, Dramatists Play Service, 1984.
The Pushcart Peddlers (produced New York, 1979). Included in *The Pushcart Peddlers, The Flatulist, and Other Plays*, 1980.
Walter, and The Flatulist (produced New York, 1980). Included in *The Pushcart Peddlers, The Flatulist, and Other Plays*, 1980.
The Pushcart Peddlers, The Flatulist, and Other Plays (includes *A Simple Kind of Love Story, Little Johnny, Walter*). New York, Dramatists Play Service, 1980.
Twice Around the Park (includes *A Need for Brussels Sprouts* and *A Need for Less Expertise*) (produced New York, 1982; Edinburgh, 1984). Included in *Luv and Other Plays*, 1983.
Luv and Other Plays (includes *The Typists, The Tiger, Fragments, The Basement, The Chinese, The Pushcart Peddlers, The Flatulist, Twice Around the Park*). New York, Dodd Mead, 1983.
The New Yorkers (produced New York, 1984).
Jealousy (produced New York, 1984). With *There Are No Sacher Tortes in Our Society!*, New York, Dramatists Play Service, 1985.
Closet Madness and Other Plays (includes *The Rabbi and the Toyota Dealer* and *Summer Romance*) (produced Sicily and Tokyo, 1991). New York, French, 1984.
The Rabbi and the Toyota Dealer (produced Los Angeles, 1985). Included in *Closet Madness and Other Plays*, 1984.
Old Wine in a New Bottle (produced in Flemish, Antwerp, 1985). New York, Dramatists Play Service, 1987.
Schneider (produced Stockbridge, Massachusetts, 1986).
Road Show (produced New York, 1987). New York, Dramatists Play Service, 1987.
Man Dangling. New York, Dramatists Play Service, 1988.
The Songs of War (produced Garden Grove, California, 1989).
Popkins (produced Paris, 1990; Rome, 1991). New York, Dramatists Play Service, 1984, 1990.
Oatmeal and Kisses. New York, Dramatists Play Service, 1990; revised as *The Death of Bacon and Eggs*, 1993.
Play Time (produced Denver, 1991).
74 Georgia Avenue (produced West Bloomfield, Michigan, 1992). Published in *Man Dangling*, Dramatists Play Service, 1988.
The Japanese Foreign Trade Minister (produced Cleveland, 1992).
The Cowboy, the Indian, and the Fervent Feminist (produced New York, 1993). Published in *Best American Short Plays, 1992-1993*, Applause Theater and Cinema Books, 1993.
Extensions (produced New York, 1994). Published in *Best American Short Plays 1991-1992*, Applause Theater and Cinema Books, 1992.
Angel Wings (produced New York, 1994).
Sexaholics and Other Plays (includes *1995, Sexaholics, The Artist and the Model, The Artist and the Model 2, The Cowboy, the Indian, and the Fervent Feminist: Extensions*). Dramatists Play Service, 1995.
Circus Life (produced New York, 1995).
Slouching Towards the Millennium (three one-act plays; produced New York, 1997).
An Occasion for Celebration (one act play). New York, Watermill, 1997.
Fifty Years Ago. Published in *Best American Short Plays*, New York, Applause Theatre and Cinema Books, 1998.

Screenplays: *The Tiger Makes Out*, 1967; *Tootsie*, with others, 1983; *Snowball*, with David Ives, 1994; *A Hero of Our Times*, 1994; *Pen Pals*, 1995; *Medusa*, 1995-96; *Night Cries*, 1996; *Call Me Lucky*, 1997.

Television Plays: *The Love Song of Barney Kempinski*, 1966; *Natasha Kovolina Pipishinsky*, 1976.

Novel

Days and Nights of a French Horn Player. Boston, Little Brown, 1980.

* * *

In the mid-1960s Murray Schisgal's plays were hailed as a step ahead of the avant-garde and as more absurd than the work of the absurdists. He was frequently grouped with the new star authors of American theater—Edward Albee, John Guare, Arthur Kopit, Jack Gelber—whose work, like Schisgal's, was first seen in the United States off-Broadway. As Schisgal notes with irony in the preface to his plays *The Typists, and The Tiger,* this recognition by American critics came only after he had achieved significant success as a playwright in England. *The Typists* and *The Tiger,* two one-acts, and the full-length play *Ducks and Lovers* were, in fact, all first produced in London, and Schisgal's eventual Broadway hit, *Luv,* was optioned in London as early as 1961. After the popular success of *Luv,* which opened in London in 1963 and New York in 1964, Schisgal's career as a playwright seemed assured. He continued to write new plays at a remarkably steady pace through the 1960s and 1970s, and most of his new works were produced and published. Critics, however, quickly lost interest in his work, and he has thus become one of the few American playwrights who has genuinely sustained a career in the theater but who has no defined place in American culture or drama history.

Much of the oddity of Schisgal's reception can be discovered in the comic constancy and contemporaneity of his work. He is a satirist of daily life in America and of the clichés of that life. His plays evoke a zany world that teeters between lunacy and good sense. In each of his plays there is at least one character whose social role is ostensibly ordinary but whose manner of inhabiting that role is eccentric and perverse. Nowhere is this disclosure of the volatile, chaotic energy of ordinary people better accomplished than in *The Tiger*. The plot is simply and potentially melodramatic. Ben, a postman, kidnaps Gloria, a suburban housewife, and he intends to rape her. We encounter the two as Ben enters his dingy, cluttered basement apartment with Gloria slung over his shoulder. Any expections we might have of soap opera melodrama are quickly thwarted by the peculiar behavior of both characters. Ben's notion of rape begins with a peck on Gloria's cheek and includes playing her a recording of Tchaikovsky's first piano concerto. Gloria is so impressed by Ben's quasi-philosophic utterances that she repeatedly forgets that she, not he, is the victim in this situation. Ben's hyperbolic frustration turns out to be the perfect match for Gloria's fertile boredom, and as we laugh at the two equally naive lovers groping for each other like adolescents, we are finally able to laugh, too, at the self-indulgence of our own overly promoted ennui.

The Tiger delights both because it enables us to laugh at our inflation of contemporary causes and because almost every line is a surprise. While remaining within a recognizable world, Schisgal captures the inanity of our assertions and our memories. Like *The Tiger*, Schisgal's full-length work *Luv* is a comedy of contemporary manners and obsessions. The classic triangle—a man, his wife, and his best friend—erupts and renegotiates its connections in *Luv* with much the same irreverence for marriage and other institutions that emerged in *The Tiger*. Milt, Harry, and Ellen of *Luv* clearly deserve each other, for no one else would take any one of them as seriously as they do each other or themselves. In this play, as in *The Tiger,* Schisgal's magic is that of the true clown, and he makes us laugh at every near catastrophe, including the suicide attempts of each character. In the end, however, *Luv* does not sustain its wit, and one is left with the uneasy sense that, having displayed love itself as a false totem, the play's most lasting image is of a dog peeing on someone's leg.

Relentless in his deflation of each new passion in American society, Schisgal's plays since the late 1960s have become less funny and more acute in the social issues they address. Of the plays written since *Luv, Jimmy Shine* and *All Over Town,* are particularly rich in the experience they provide for an audience. *All Over Town* assaults every facile "solution" that was embraced in the late 1960s and early 1970s. Welfare, psychiatry, ecology, liberalism, and racial and sexual "liberation" are all reduced to confetti in an upper-class New York apartment that becomes a carnival of errors. Although Schisgal has since written other plays in his distinctive satiric mode, *All Over Town* so expands the madness and so multiplies the cast of characters that it conveys an aura of finality, at least in this mode. In contrast, *Jimmy Shine,* while orthodox in dramaturgy, exemplifies a powerful new mode in Schisgal's writing. In *Jimmy Shine* Schisgal quietly controls the tentative, unsatisfied struggles of his artist-hero to find meaning without ornamentation. Schisgal's persistent presentation of the humorous aspects of sexuality and the painful burdens of human love are presented in *Jimmy Shine* without the usual parodic refractions. Perhaps it is the integrity so transparent in *Jimmy Shine* that continues to draw community and academic theater companies to Schisgal's plays.

—Helene Keyssar

SCHWARTZ, Jerome. ***See*** **LAWRENCE, Jerome.**

SELBOURNE, David

Nationality: British. **Born:** London, 4 June 1937. **Education:** Manchester Grammar School; Balliol College, Oxford, B.A. (honours) 1958; Inner Temple, London, called to the Bar, 1959. **Career:** Lecturer, University of Aston, Birmingham, 1963-65; Tutor in Politics, Ruskin College, Oxford, 1965-86. **Awards:** Aneurin Bevan Memorial fellowship, 1975; Southern Arts Association award, 1979; Indian Council of Social Science research award, 1979; Social Science Research Council award, 1980; Periodical Publishers Association award, 1986. **Address:** c/o Xandra Hardie, 9 Elsworthy Terrace, London NW3 3DR, England.

Publications

Plays

The Play of William Cooper and Edmund Dew-Nevett (produced Exeter, 1968). London, Methuen, 1968.
The Two-Backed Beast (produced Liverpool, 1968). London, Methuen, 1969.
Dorabella (produced Edinburgh, 1969). London, Methuen, 1970.
Samson (produced London, 1970). With *Alison Mary Fagan*, London, Calder and Boyars, 1971.
Alison Mary Fagan (produced Auckland, New Zealand, 1972). With *Samson*, London, Calder and Boyars, 1971.
The Damned. London, Methuen, 1971.
Class Play (produced London, 1972). Published in *Second Playbill 3*, edited by Alan Durband, London, Hutchinson, 1973.
Three Class Plays (for children; produced London, 1973).
What's Acting? and Think of a Story, Quickly! (for children; produced London, 1977). London, Arnold, 1977.
A Woman's Trial (produced in Bengali, as *Shrimatir Bichar*, Calcutta, 1982).

Other

Brook's Dream: The Politics of Theatre. London, Action Books, 1974.
An Eye to China. London, Black Liberator Press, 1975.
An Eye to India: The Unmasking of a Tyranny. London, Penguin, 1977.
Through the Indian Looking-Glass: Selected Articles on India 1976-1980. Bombay, Popular Prakashan, and London, Zed Press, 1982.
The Making of A Midsummer Night's Dream: An Eye-Witness Account of Peter Brook's Production. London, Methuen, 1982.
Against Socialist Illusion: A Radical Argument. London, Macmillan, and New York, Schocken, 1985.
Left Behind: Journeys into British Politics. London, Cape, 1987.
Death of the Dark Hero: Eastern Europe 1987-1990. London, Cape, 1990.
The Spirit of the Age. London, Sinclair-Stevenson, 1993.
Not an Englishman: Conversations with Lord Goodman. London, Sinclair-Stevenson, 1993.
The Principle of Duty: An Essay on the Foundations of Civic Order. London, Sinclair-Stevenson, 1994.

Editor, *In Theory and in Practice: Essays on the Politics of Jayaprakash Narayan*. New Delhi, Oxford University Press, 1985; Oxford and New York, Oxford University Press, 1986.
Editor, *A Doctor's Life: The Diaries of Hugh Selbourne M.D., 1960-1963*. London, Cape, 1989.

*

Critical Studies: Introductions by John Russell Brown to *The Play of William Cooper and Edmund Dew-Nevett*, 1968, by Stuart Hall to *An Eye to China*, 1975, and by Selbourne to *What's Acting? and Think of a Story, Quickly!*, 1977.

* * *

David Selbourne writes with consistent strategy. He chooses simple actions that involve basic motives, providing only a minimum of complication with his story and the representation of the process of everyday living. He is thus free to move his characters into ever-changing relationships with each other and with their own reactions. In the one-act *Samson* (consisting of 12 short scenes), a boy tries to break away from his father. In *Dorabella* a spinster is attracted to the boyfriend of her hairdresser. In *The Play of William Cooper and Edmund Dew-Nevett*, a simple-minded would-be artist seeks happiness and finds corruption.

These are intellectual plays in that they are based on a clear view of how time, power, imagination, thought, and passions work together. But they are realized with a sensual awareness that seeks to create brilliant juxtapositions. Activity and language take actors and audiences directly to total, undisguised confrontations.

Almost all the dialogue is in a verse form that serves to accentuate thrust and concision. It also contains echoes from mystical poets and the Old Testament that play a large part in creating the overall impression of the plays. The echoes are purposefully easy to catch and are well integrated with a lively reproduction of ordinary talk. With its radiant images, this style offsets the restricted nature of the play's action, where man is repeatedly shown caught by his own condition of living. *The Damned* presents self-deception and domination with calculated ruthlessness, but even in this painful drama the words spoken show how the hope of a free life is still the characters' true source of energy. At the end of *William Cooper* the simpleton can "fly no more," but he has only just recognized again "light blazing into my head."

Two plays of Selbourne's belong in a separate category. In both *Alison Mary Fagan* and *Class Play* , Selbourne has placed real people in a dramatic context. In *Alison Mary Fagan* an actress faces herself, her life, and her career; in *Class Play* three pupils and a teacher confront school and life. These are difficult plays to perform, for the dialogue is shockingly direct and the situations continually changing. At the center of one drama is a person who performs and at the center of the other are children who are manipulated, and these are to be seen without artifice, recognized as if outside theater.

Selbourne stopped writing for the stage in the early 1980s, but his body of work demonstrates that he is a writer of teeming imagination and clear determination. He never fell in with a fashionable mode of writing for the stage; he worked on his own, confident in the validity of his purpose. His work is exhilarating and demanding and has left a permanent mark.

—John Russell Brown

SEWELL, Stephen

Nationality: Australian. **Born:** Sydney in 1953. **Education:** University of Sydney, B.S. 1975. **Career:** Writer-in-residence, Nimrod Theatre, Sydney, 1981-82. **Awards:** Australian Writers Guild award, 1982; New South Wales Premier's award, 1985. **Agent:** c/o Currency Press, 87 Jersey Road, Woollahra, NSW 2025, Australia.

Publications

Plays

The Father We Loved on a Beach by the Sea (produced Brisbane, 1978). Sydney, Currency Press, 1976.

Traitors (produced Melbourne, 1979; London, 1980). Sydney, Alternative Publishing Co-operative, 1983.

Welcome the Bright World. Sydney, Alternative Publishing Co-operative, 1983.

The Blind Giant Is Dancing (produced Adelaide, 1983). Sydney, Currency Press, 1983; revised version, 1985.

Burn Victim, with others (produced Sydney, 1983).

Dreams in an Empty City (produced Adelaide, 1986; London, 1988). Sydney, Currency Press, 1986.

Hate (produced Sydney, 1988).

Miranda (produced Brisbane, 1989).

Sisters (also director: produced Melbourne, 1991; London, 1992).

King Golgrutha (produced Adelaide, 1991).

In the City of Grand-Daughters (produced Melbourne, 1993). Sydney, Currency Press, 1993.

Dust (produced Adelaide, 1993). Sydney, Currency Press, 1996.

The Boys (screenplay). Sydney, Currency Press, 1998.

Screenplay: *Isabelle Eberhardt*, 1993; *The Boys*.

*

Critical Studies: "The World Outside: Cosmopolitanism in the Plays of Nowra and Sewell" by John McCallum, in *Meanjin*, June 1984, pp. 286-96; "Interview: Stephen Sewell Talks to Mary Ann Hunter" by Mary Ann Hunter, in *Australasian Drama Studies* (Queensland, Australai), April 1989, pp. 33-45; *Setting the Stage: A Semiotic Re-reading of Selected Australian Plays by Dorothy Hewett, Jack Hibberd, Louis Nowra, and Stephen Sewell* (dissertation) by Joanne Tompkins, York University, 1993.

* * *

The first production of *Traitors* in 1979 established Stephen Sewell as one of the most exciting and challenging of the new generation of Australian playwrights. His work is distinctive for the power and complexity of its political vision, and in this sense it is perhaps more appropriately compared with contemporary left-wing British theater than with the mostly comic, mostly celebratory style of satire that has dominated Australian theater.

The Blind Giant Is Dancing and *Dreams in an Empty City* share some of the central concerns of the local tradition, however. This is the case in the ways they present patterns of social, and particularly marital, interaction, offering distinctive images of contemporary Australia. But always in Sewell's work the analysis of interpersonal politics is conducted in the context of structures of power that exist beyond the individual and beyond the immediate culture. Even in his early period as an avowed Marxist, Sewell was cautious about ideologies, and some of the critics who find his work ponderous and propagandistic seem to be responding to his overtly ideological approach to theater rather than to the complex political vision the plays actually present. Sewell's description of Marxism as a "tenable hypothesis" indicates his own awareness of the complexity of the issues he deals with. It does not, however, give a sense of the desperate importance in the disintegrating world his plays depict of finding some system of value that is tenable or of the passion with which such a commitment can be held.

The Father We Loved on a Beach by the Sea, Sewell's first play, was to some extent a dress rehearsal for later presentations of aspects of family culture in terms that attempt to define the forces that create them. It also anticipated something of the structural complexity of these more elaborate explorations of political cause and effect. In *The Father* the juxtaposition of two time frames—with remembrances of the past as experienced by Joe, a quintessential Aussie "battler," and a hypothetical revolutionary future focused on Dan, his activist son—entails an ambitious mixture of playing styles that is developed in a still more challenging way in subsequent plays. Whereas the treatment of little people in Sewell's later work reflects his premise that the political and the personal are inextricable or identical, the image of the family in *The Father* appeals directly to the feelings of unresolved guilt, love, and resentment that most people have for their parents.

Traitors and *Welcome the Bright World* were greeted as distinguished examples of the new internationalism in Australian drama that followed the self-consciously new wave movement of the late 1960s and early 1970s. The settings of the two plays—respectively, Stalinist Russia between the World Wars and Germany through the 1970s—certainly looked like a conspicuous refusal to be parochial. But the relevance of a concept like internationalism to Sewell's work can be sought more profitably in the nature of his political analysis and the theatrical company he (metaphorically) keeps than in matters of literal placement.

Traitors is the most concentrated of Sewell's plays. The historicity and episodic structure look Brechtian, but there is not much ground for rational reflection. The play's intensity comes from the unrelenting pressure of its depiction of the efforts of individuals to find a place for love and a sense of personal purpose in a society in which betrayal and oppression appear to preempt such things.

Soviet factionalism provided a somewhat esoteric basis for *Traitors.* The combination of revolutionary politics in Germany, different forms of the consciousness of being Jewish, and the state of contemporary physics made a more demanding basis for *Welcome the Bright World.* This play confirmed a general critical conception of Sewell as a playwright whose reach, excitingly but rather willfully, would always exceed his grasp. As in *Traitors,* there is a great deal going on, most of it powerful and disturbing and all of it suggesting that this is a writer who will not make theatrical compromises in his mission to address an audience intelligently. In a sense the unwieldiness of the structure, in its seeming to guarantee that there are forces here beyond containment, becomes an aspect of the play's power.

The two plays that followed found forms of containment but not at the expense of the intensity of the ideas. In returning to aspects of Australian society as his subject, Sewell drew in both cases on a central myth to encompass action beyond the immediate political references. In *Blind Giant* this was the Faust story, and in *Dreams in an Empty City* it was the Christ story.

Blind Giant deals with political corruption at all levels of Australian society, although its focus is on the corrosiveness of compromise in the development of its central character, a crusader on the Labor left. There is nothing simplistic about this concern, however. The exploration of power structures, from the domestic to the international, is complicated in the action by the elusiveness of answers to all questions about the sources of power and by individual psychological patterns of assertion and submission. It is perhaps in the latter area that the play's major strength lies. Its treatment of sexual and family politics seems to offer more durable insights than the remarkably accurate short-term prophecies that emerge from its presentation of Australian political life.

The force that in *Blind Giant* threatens to undermine all positions of integrity is cynicism, and no one in the play, apart from a rather unlikely Chilean freedom fighter, seems to find an answer to it. In *Dreams in an Empty City* this force is given its full spiritual dimension in the form of corrupting despair. Even the most venal of the financial predators in the play appeal at some point to a perception of the world as irredeemably fallen in order to mask their opportunism with moral repugnance. The enemy of political change is not the dominant system in itself but rather the sickness that breeds it. Like *The Father* and *Blind Giant, Dreams in an Empty City* ends on a note of apocalyptic fantasy, here nothing less than the collapse of international capitalism. But for all of the risks involved in its giant subject and in its allegorical methods that transpose Christian virtue into a context of secular revolution, it works as a powerful and moving play.

Sewell moved away from the panoramic mythic play in his subsequent work. The cinematic chamber plays *Miranda* and *Sisters* focus on the convolutedly personal, with little developed sense of the political at all. *The Garden of Grand-Daughters* resolves or abandons its analysis of family love and resentment in a mood of bittersweet comic acceptance. *King Golgrutha,* while it presents its monstrous capitalist on the grand scale, does so with a wild grotesquerie that preempts analysis. In *Hate*, however, Sewell triumphantly reconciles the impulse to political and metaphorical breadth with a concentrated focus on the messiness of the family. As with the house of Atreus, the gothic corruption of the Truscott house becomes representative of a wider cultural rottenness, its old guilts suggestive of unresolved sins, in particular against the country's original inhabitants.

Sewell may stand on the margin of Australian theater, but his voice remains distinctive and essential to its health.

—Peter Fitzpatrick

SHAFFER, Anthony (Joshua)

Nationality: British. **Born:** Liverpool, Lancashire, 15 May 1926; twin brother of Peter Shaffer, *q.v.* **Education:** St. Paul's School, London; Trinity College, Cambridge (co-editor, *Granta*), graduated 1950. Conscript coalminer, Kent and Yorkshire, 1944-47. **Family:** Married 1) Carolyn Soley, two daughters; 2) the actress Diane Cilento in 1985. **Career:** Barrister, 1951-55; journalist, 1956-58; partner in advertising film production agency, 1959-69. Lives in Wiltshire. **Awards:** Tony award, 1971; Mystery Writers of America Edgar Allan Poe award, for screenplay, 1973. **Agent:** Peters, Fraser, and Dunlop Group, 503-504 The Chambers, Chelsea Harbour, Lots Road, London SW10 0XF, England.

Publications

Plays

The Savage Parade (produced London, 1963; as *This Savage Parade*, produced London, 1987).

Sleuth (produced London and New York, 1970). New York, Dodd Mead, 1970; London, Calder and Boyars, 1971.

Murderer (produced Brighton and London, 1975). London, Boyars, 1979.

Widow's Weeds (produced Brisbane, Queensland, 1977; Plymouth, 1987).

Whodunnit (as *The Case of the Oily Levantine*, produced Guildford, Surrey, 1977; London, 1979; revised version, as *Whodunnit*, produced New York, 1982; Brighton, 1987). New York, French, 1983.

Screenplays: *Mr. Forbush and the Penguins*, 1971; *Frenzy*, 1972; *Sleuth*, 1973; *The Wicker Man*, 1974; *Masada*, 1974; *The Moonstone*, 1975; *Death on the Nile*, 1978; *Absolution*, 1981; *Evil Under the Sun*, 1982; *Appointment with Death*, 1988.

Television Play: *Pig in the Middle*.

Novels

How Doth the Little Crocodile? (as Peter Antony, with Peter Shaffer). London, Evans, 1952; as Peter and Anthony Shaffer, New York, Macmillan, 1957.

Withered Murder, with Peter Shaffer. London, Gollancz, 1955; New York, Macmillan, 1956.

The Wicker Man (novelization of screenplay), with Robin Hardy. New York, Crown, 1978; London, Hamlyn, 1979.

Absolution (novelization of screenplay). London, Corgi, 1979.

*

Critical Studies: *Peter and Anthony Shaffer: A Reference Guide* by Dennis A. Klein, Boston, Hall, 1982; "Twins in the Theater: A Study of Plays by Peter and Anthony Shaffer" by Jules Glenn, in *Blood Brothers: Siblings as Writers,* edited by Norman Kiell, New York, International UP, 1983.

* * *

It is not often that a writer has the opportunity to create a literary fashion and even a new genre, but theatrical thrillers and mysteries can legitimately be divided into pre-*Sleuth* and post-*Sleuth*, indicating more than their date of composition. The traditional stage or film mystery is a variant on the classic English country house mystery novel, a whodunit in which a crime is committed and the audience tries to guess which of several suspects is the criminal, while the author carefully directs our suspicions in the wrong directions. In *Sleuth* Anthony Shaffer created the "whodunwhat," in which both the identity of the criminal and the nature of the crime—indeed, the reality and reliability of everything we have seen with our own eyes—are part of the mystery.

Sleuth begins in an orthodox way, as a man enlists the aid of his wife's lover in a complex plot to rob himself; this way lover and wife can afford to run off, husband will be free to marry his own mistress, and the insurance company will pay for everything. No sooner has the audience settled in to see whether they will pull it off and whether one will double-cross the other than we discover that this is not what has been going on at all; the whole project is a convoluted cover for a murder. And no sooner is that fact absorbed than we are told that the murder we thought we watched happening did not really happen. (Oh yes it did, we are told a moment later. Oh no it did not, we are shown a bit after that.) A policeman has come to arrest the murderer. (Oh no he has not. Oh yes he has.) In fact, a second murder entirely has happened offstage (Oh no . . .), and the murderer has planted clues implicating the innocent party, whom he dares the policeman to find since the police are really coming this time (Oh no . . .). Even the program and cast list cannot be trusted.

Of course *Sleuth* has its antecedents, among them Patrick Hamilton's *Gas Light* and the Hitchcock film *Suspicion*—Is the man really trying to kill his wife, or is she imagining it?—and the Clouzot film *Diabolique*—Who of the three main characters are the murderers and who the victims? But Shaffer concentrates and multiplies the questions and red herrings and dresses them in an entertaining mix of psychology (the husband is a compulsive games player), social comment (husband is a snob, lover working class), in-jokes (husband writes mysteries of the classic whodunit kind), and black humor (one plot twist somehow requires a character to dress as a clown). And everything moves so quickly and effortlessly that there is added delight in the author's skill and audacity in so repeatedly confusing us. *Sleuth* was an immense worldwide success that quickly bred dozens of other thrillers of the new genre, notable among them Ira Levin's *Deathtrap* and Richard Harris's *The Business of Murder*. The Agatha Christie-type whodunit, with corpses that did not get up again and a murderer who was "someone in this room," seemed hopelessly old-fashioned when compared to plays in which the audience had to figure out what was really happening before moving on to the question of who was guilty.

Oddly, Shaffer's own follow-ups in the genre he created were rather limp. *Murderer* opens with a 30-minute silent sequence during which we watch a particularly gruesome murder and dismemberment, followed by the arrival of a policeman, the discovery of the grisly evidence, and the confession of the criminal—only to be told then that it was all a fake, the pastime of a crime buff reenacting a famous murder. So far, so good, but when the buff then turns his hand to an actual murder, the plot twists are less inevitable and less delightful than in *Sleuth*. Two actual murders take place, one with the wrong victim and one with the wrong murderer, but everything seems forced and unlikely and requires extensive advance setups or after-the-fact explanations. It is ultimately an unpleasant play, working too hard to shock and surprise and thus removing the pleasure of shock and surprise.

The Case of the Oily Levantine, revised for the United States as *Whodunnit,* is openly labeled "A Comedy Thriller" and is lighter and more entertaining than *Murderer,* though sometimes just as strained and self-conscious. Its first act is a high-spirited parody of the whodunit genre, with the title character blackmailing everyone in sight—titled dowager, retired officer, debutante, even the butler—until an unidentified one of them murders him. The best touch, which has some of *Sleuth*'s flair, is that we periodically hear the disguised voice of the murderer giving teasing clues; the voice refers, for example, to lighting a cigarette, only to have each character onstage light up as our hope of catching the criminal fades. As one might predict by now, act 2 begins with the discovery that nothing seen in act 1, except the murder, was real. This twist owes a debt to the 1973 film *The Last of Sheila*, and the working out of the new version of the murder is unconvincing and unengrossing, despite forced in-jokes both literary and theatrical. There is a satisfying final joke, however, as the solution is shown to be a twist on one of the traditional whodunit's oldest clichés.

Shaffer's skill as a craftsman of mystery and thrills is seen in his film work, notably for the film version of *Sleuth* and in Hitchcock's *Frenzy*. In the theater, however, his reputation must rest on *Sleuth* and on the genre it created.

—Gerald M. Berkowitz

SHAFFER, Peter (Levin)

Nationality: British. **Born:** Liverpool, Lancashire, 15 May 1926; twin brother of Anthony Shaffer, *q.v.* **Education:** A preparatory school in Liverpool; Hall School, London; St. Paul's School, London; Trinity College, Cambridge (co-editor, *Granta*), 1947-50, B.A. in history 1950. Conscript coalminer, Chislet colliery, Kent, 1944-47. **Career:** Worked in Doubleday bookstore, an airline terminal, at Grand Central Station, Lord and Taylor department store, and in the acquisition department, New York Public Library, all New York, 1951-54; staff member, Boosey and Hawkes, music publishers, London, 1954-55; literary critic, *Truth*, London, 1956-57; music critic, *Time and Tide*, London, 1961-62. Lives in New York City. **Awards:** *Evening Standard* award, 1958, 1980, 1988; New York Drama Critics Circle award, 1960, 1975; Tony award, 1975, 1981; Outer Critics Circle award, 1981; Vernon Rice award, 1981; New York Film Critics Circle award, 1984; Los Angeles Film Critics Association award, 1984; Oscar, for screenplay, 1985; Hamburg Shakespeare prize, 1989; William Inge award for Distinguished Achievement in the American Theatre, 1992. C.B.E. (Commander, Order of the British Empire), 1987. **Member:** Royal Society of Literature. **Agent:** Macnaughton Lowe Representation, 200 Fulham Road, London SW10 9PN, England; or, Robert Lantz, The Lantz Office, 888 Seventh Avenue, New York, New York 10106, U.S.A.

Publications

Plays

Five Finger Exercise (produced London, 1958; New York, 1959). London, Hamish Hamilton, 1958; New York, Harcourt Brace, 1959.

The Private Ear, and The Public Eye (produced London, 1962; New York, 1963). London, Hamish Hamilton, 1962; New York, Stein and Day, 1964.

The Merry Roosters' Panto, music and lyrics by Stanley Myers and Steven Vinaver (produced London, 1963; as *It's about Cinderella*, produced London, 1969).

Sketch in *The Establishment* (produced New York, 1963).

The Royal Hunt of the Sun: A Play Concerning the Conquest of Peru (produced Chichester and London, 1964; New York, 1965). London, Hamish Hamilton, and New York, Stein and Day, 1965.

Black Comedy (produced Chichester, 1965; London, 1966; New York, 1967). Included in *Black Comedy, Including White Lies*, 1967.

White Lies (produced New York, 1967). Included in *Black Comedy, Including White Lies*, 1967; as *White Liars* (produced London, 1968), London, French, 1967; revised version (produced London and New York, 1976), French, 1976.

Black Comedy, Including White Lies: Two Plays. New York, Stein and Day, 1967; as *White Liars, Black Comedy: Two Plays*, London, Hamish Hamilton, 1968.

Shrivings (as *The Battle of Shrivings*, produced London, 1970; revised version, as *Shrivings*, produced York, 1975). London, Deutsch, 1974; with *Equus*, New York, Atheneum, 1974.

Equus (produced London, 1973; New York, 1974). London, Deutsch, 1973; with *Shrivings*, New York, Atheneum, 1974.

Amadeus (produced London, 1979). London, Deutsch, 1980; revised version (produced New York, 1980; London, 1981), New York, Harper, and London, Penguin, 1981.

The Collected Plays of Peter Shaffer (revised texts; includes *Five Finger Exercise*, *The Private Ear*, *The Public Eye*, *The Royal Hunt of the Sun*, *White Liars*, *Black Comedy*, *Equus*, *Shrivings*, *Amadeus*). New York, Harmony, 1982.

Black Mischief (produced Bristol, 1983).

Yonadab (produced London, 1985).

Lettice and Lovage (produced Bath and London, 1987; revised version, produced London, 1988; New York, 1990). London, Deutsch, 1988; New York, Harper and Row, 1990.

Whom Do I Have the Honour of Addressing? (broadcast 1989). London, Deutsch, 1990.

The Gift of the Gorgon (produced London, 1992). London and New York, Viking, 1993.

The White Liars and Black Comedy: Two One-Act Plays. New York, Samuel French, 1995.

Screenplays: *Lord of the Flies*, with Peter Brook, 1963; *The Public Eye* (*Follow Me!*), 1972; *Equus*, 1977; *Amadeus*, 1984.

Radio Plays: *Alexander the Corrector*, 1946; *The Prodigal Father*, 1957; *Whom Do I Have the Honour of Addressing?*, 1989.

Television Plays: *The Salt Land*, 1955; *Balance of Terror*, 1957.

Novels

The Woman in the Wardrobe (as Peter Antony). London, Evans, 1951.

How Doth the Little Crocodile? (as Peter Antony, with Anthony Shaffer). London, Evans, 1952; as Peter and Anthony Shaffer, New York, Macmillan, 1957.

Withered Murder, with Anthony Shaffer. London, Gollancz, 1955; New York, Macmillan, 1956.

Other

Editor, *Elisabeth Frink Sculpture: Catalogue Raisonne*. Trafalger Square, 1988.

*

Critical Studies: *Peter Shaffer* by John Russell Taylor, London, Longman, 1974; *Peter Shaffer* by Dennis A. Klein, Boston, Twayne, 1979; *File on Shaffer* edited by Virginia Cooke and Malcolm Page, London, Methuen, 1987; *Peter Shaffer: Roles, Rites and Rituals in the Theater* by Gene A. Plunka, Teaneck, New Jersey, Fairleigh Dickinson University Press, 1988; *Peter Shaffer* by C. J. Gianakaris, Basingstoke, Macmillan, 1992; *Peter Shaffer: Theatre and Drama* by M.K. MacMurraugh-Kavanagh, Basingstoke, Hampshire, Macmillan Press, 1998.

* * *

In 1958, when Peter Shaffer's *Five Finger Exercise* achieved critical acclaim in London, it was difficult to reconcile its middle-class tone and formal elements with the breed of theater of Britain's angry young men, which was then flourishing. A well-made drawing room drama set in a weekend cottage in Suffolk, *Five Finger*

Exercise probed the Harringtons' marital strife and its devastating effects upon their nervous literary son and the young, secretive German tutor brought into the household to educate their volatile 14-year-old daughter. The intricately wrought monologues of the five characters are played and replayed against a background of music. The family relationships are dangerously out of balance, and the intrusion of the outsider threatens to destroy them. Only after numerous variations of the same theme does the play find resolution.

Five Finger Exercise placed Shaffer in the tradition of the well-made play, while he was also compared briefly with John Osborne and Harold Pinter. Other plays by Shaffer show his flair for the highly theatrical spectacle and epic theater. His use of framing and narration derive from dramatists such as Thornton Wilder, Tennessee Williams, Robert Bolt, and Bertolt Brecht. His narrators control the prism through which the work is viewed and provide a structure that offers his play of intellect a wider range.

Shaffer's use of the conventions of presentational aesthetics emerges clearly in *The Royal Hunt of the Sun*, *Equus*, *Amadeus*, and *Yonadab*. His narrators interrupt the action and dart backward and forward, violating the conventions of the fourth wall, addressing the audience directly, and inviting them to participate in the experience of epic theater as it was articulated by Brecht. The epic mode provides solutions to some of the technical problems apparent in *Five Finger Exercise* and very much evident in *Shrivings*, a work marred by too much ideological talkiness and an inadequate objective correlative for the play's ideas. His brilliantly conceived narrators—Old Martin in *The Royal Hunt of the Sun*, the analyst Dysart in *Equus*, Salieri in *Amadeus*, and Yonadab in the eponymous play—rivet the audience's attention, offering a self-conscious examination of the play's narration and story line without diminishing its nakedly dramatic elements.

Two later works—the stage play *Lettice and Lovage* and the broadcast play *Whom Do I Have the Honour Of Addressing?*—more nearly resemble his comedies of the 1960s. Abandoning the conventions of the frame and epic theater, they nonetheless display his interest in narrative technique.

Lettice, a whimsical tour guide, has been hired by the Preservation Trust (a thinly disguised National Trust) to show parties around Britain's historical houses. She is a devotee of history and invention, and her creative spirit is too restless to allow her merely to recite her official text. The play opens with Lettice regaling a group of tourists with stories about a great staircase constructed from Tudor oak that dominates the grand hall of the all-too-dreary Fustian House. After several more recitations she constructs ever more melodramatic accounts of the stairs and the house's inhabitants, introducing the Virgin Queen herself, Gloriana, into her tale. She thrives on her own theatrical romanticizing and role playing, deviating wildly from historical fact in her desperate attempts to make one of the dullest Elizabethan houses in England more interesting. The first act concludes with her being fired by the severe, duty-bound Lotte. Act 2 finds Lotte befriending Lettice, and the two women quaff Lovage, an herbal brew, enlarging, enlivening, and enlightening their souls, spirits, and eyes as they share their pasts and rebel against the drabness of their lives. In the third act Lettice coaxes her apparent accuser, Lotte, into allowing her to replay their enactment of Charles I's beheading in front of Bardolph, an attorney who has come to defend Lettice from Lotte's charges of attempted murder. In both the first and third acts Shaffer breaks the fourth wall with entrances from the auditorium and with addresses to both an onstage and offstage audience. Throughout the play there are readings of letters as well as constant variations on an official transcribed text. Both devices thicken the play's texture. In all these small ways Shaffer manipulates techniques of narrative to interrupt the dramatic mode.

Angela Parsons, the deeply self-deluded monologuist of the radio play *Whom Do I Have the Honour of Addressing?*, similarly interweaves readings of her correspondence into her stage narration as she speaks her supposed last and only words about her life and death into a tape recorder. Shaffer sets both of these later works in the present and abandons the use of flashbacks and the presence of a narrator. In the radio play he offers another level of mediation of the dramatic action through the device of the tape recorder, which is used in a manner reminiscent of Beckett in *Krapp's Last Tape*.

Two other elements have been staples of almost all of Shaffer's plays. Music is an integral aspect of their soundscape, and elements from detective fiction figure prominently in the treatment of plot and character. He served for a number of years as music critic for *Time and Tide* in London, and before he became a successful playwright, he coauthored two detective novels with his brother, Anthony Shaffer, author of *Sleuth*. Shaffer's light and playful one-act work *The Public Eye* presents Julian Christoforou, a raisin-and-yogurt-eating private eye who meddles in the domestic life of Charles and Belinda Sidley, prying in a detective-like way into their souls and psyches. Ultimately, this British eccentric teaches the couple how to experience love again and how to play. Shaffer uses the character of the detective and the devices of detective fiction—disguised identities, the dreary business of sleuthing, the perfunctory discovery scene, the interrogation scene, the establishing of fees—to structure his frivolous one-act play. Many of the same devices can be found in Shaffer's superbly crafted farce *Black Comedy,* as well as in *Equus*, *Amadeus*, *Lettice and Lovage*, and *Whom Do I Have the Honour of Addressing?*

Black Comedy depends for its comic effect on a clever theatrical trick of the eye and mind. While the stage is lit, its fictive world is dark; when the stage is black, the characters are inhabiting a fully lit fictive world. Because of this simple reversal the audience relishes the delight of watching a stage full of characters groping around in the darkness, although actually flooded with light, as a result of a blown fuse in the London flat of Brindsley Miller. Miller, a young sculptor, is trying to impress his debutante fiancée's father, Colonel Melkett, by selling one of his sculptures to an elderly, deaf millionaire art collector. To ensure the evening's success, Brindsley and his fiancée have swiped numerous pieces of elegant Regency furniture from the flat of his modish neighbor, a closet homosexual and owner of an antique china shop. As the evening advances toward its complete dissolution, Brindsley is forced to drag the furniture from his apartment back to its owner's, right in front of the darkened eyes of the owner, his father-in-law-to-be, a mistress who has paid a surprise visit, a spinster, his alcoholic upstairs neighbor, and his silly, spoilt fiancée. The scene is hilarious, and comic timing is essential to its success. Brindsley's misstep, which causes him to fall neatly down the entire flight of stairs as he attempts to return calmly from his bedroom, requires that the actor display no trace of the knowledge that he is facing an uncomfortable fall. The moment at which Brindsley, with a Regency chair in one hand and a Wedgwood bowl in the other, passes under the outstretched arms of his father-in-law and fiancée as they exchange a glass of lemonade is another brilliant comic moment. The deft timings of exits and entrances, sudden falls, and rapid movements of major pieces of stage furniture, combined with the sharp white light that glaringly exposes the goings-on to the audience, testify to the importance of the genre of detective fiction and film in Shaffer's imagination. The exposed lightbulb and the interrogation scenes of detective fiction probably contributed to the game of hide-and-seek executed in this delightful farce.

In *Amadeus* the debt is even more apparent. The play opens with the word "assassin" hissed and savagely whispered by the chorus of rumor on the stage; it rises in a crescendo and is punctuated with the names of Mozart and Salieri. By the end of the second scene Salieri, the narrator, promises the audience one final performance, to be entitled "The Death of Mozart; or, Did I Do It?" The audience is plunged into a world of a whodunit in which they are the detective and Salieri is the villain. Shaffer's revised version clarified the London version's dramatic structure, implicating Salieri more directly in Mozart's death and replacing Greybig with Salieri as the Masked Figure and Messenger of Death who appears to Mozart in the penultimate.

Yonadab continues in this tradition. Yonadab, the cousin of Amnon and Absalom, David's sons, is the treacherous confidant of both brothers. He plays the one against the other, abetting the scene of Tamar's incestuous rape by her half brother Amnon and later assisting Absalom in the slaying of Amnon. He is also the reporter of the lurid scene to the audience. Again, the play's focus on reporters and news, on a lurid tale of intrigue, ambition, incest, and murder, on the cunning ways such plots transpire, and on the way villains are punished reflects the sure hand of a writer familiar with detective fiction.

In both *Lettice and Lovage* and *Whom Do I Have the Honour of Addressing?* the protagonists are guilty of assault, in one case accidental and in the other a justifiable, albeit violent, reaction to the sordid happenings resulting from Angela's infatuation with a Hollywood stage idol half her age. Both plays can be seen as the confessions of confused, romantic souls, their crimes being an overactive imagination in a colorless world.

Music is also an essential aspect of Shaffer's theatrical talent. In *White Lies*, later revised as *White Liars*, Shaffer used a tape recording to surround the audience with the inner monologues and dialogues of Sophie, his fortune-telling protagonist. In *The Private Ear* Bob's great passion is music and the gramophone, and his failed romance is with a girl he met at a concert. *Five Finger Exercise* depends on the music of Bach and Brahms and on the stuck recording of a gramophone repeating over and over a portion of Mahler's Symphony no. 4 to dramatize the suicide attempt of the young German tutor whose father's participation in the Nazi party has driven him to England. Shaffer described *The Royal Hunt of the Sun*'s brilliant score, written by Marc Wilkinson, in this way: "To me its most memorable items are the exquisitely doleful lament which opens Act II, and, most amazing of all, the final Chant of Resurrection, to be whined and whispered, howled and hooted, over Atahuallpa's body in the darkness, before the last sunrise of the Inca Empire." *Amadeus* soars with the music of Mozart and Salieri and reflects how Salieri probably imagined Mozart's music. *Lettice and Lovage* opens with lugubrious Elizabethan music. In its final, farcical act Bardolph is marching about the stage banging on an invisible drum and calling out his "PAMTITITI-PAMS," and he is joined by Lettice's soprano doubling of his cries in imitation of the martial music that accompanied King Charles I's execution in 1649.

Finally, Shaffer is a playwright of ideas. Perhaps his eloquent exposition of them failed in *Shrivings*, but the battles between Dysart and Alan Strang in *Equus*, Pizarro and Atahuallpa in *The Royal Hunt of the Sun*, Salieri and Mozart in *Amadeus*, and Yonadab and David's brothers all intelligently explore man's struggle for meaning in a world in which death dominates and religion holds no salvation. Alan Strang, the boy who blinded six horses, knows a savage god; Atahuallpa is the Son of the Sun God; and Pizarro has neither faith nor, until the very end, love or passion. East and West collide, and faithfulness is played against faithlessness, passion and violence against impotence, passivity and Eastern love against skepticism and violence, and passionate creativity against classical balance and duty.

Some have criticized Shaffer's later plays for owing too much of their success to the brilliance of the leading actors and too little to the themes and plots. *Lettice and Lovage* was written for Maggie Smith, who brilliantly captured Lettice's extravagance of nature, but the third act is slightly forced, even in its revised version. The play originally concluded with Lettice and Lotte setting out to bomb a select number of London's most abominable post-World War II municipal monstrosities. In the revised version they set out to create their own "E.N.D. Tours" to London's aesthetically disgusting buildings. The radio play also exploits Dame Judi Dench's voice and relies upon the eccentricities of its protagonist and the lurid details of its close to carry it. But both are plays for women, a departure for Shaffer, whose earlier plays lacked major women's roles, and both have a whimsicality and winning poignancy.

It is to Shaffer's credit that he has excelled in creating plays with stunning spectacles, lavish soundscapes, dramatic action, and a powerful artillery of rhetoric as well as more theatrically modest ones in which it is the delicious play of words and invention that charms us.

—Carol Simpson Stern

SHANGE, Ntozake

Nationality: American. **Born:** Paulette Williams in Trenton, New Jersey, 18 October 1948; took name Ntozake Shange in 1971. **Education:** Schools in St. Louis and New Jersey; Barnard College, New York, 1966-70, B.A. (cum laude) in American studies 1970; University of Southern California, Los Angeles, 1971-73, M.A. in American studies 1973. **Family:** Married David Murray in 1977 (2nd marriage; divorced); one daughter. **Career:** Faculty member, Sonoma State College, Rohnert Park, California, 1973-75, Mills College, Oakland, California, 1975, City College, New York, 1975, and Douglass College, New Brunswick, New Jersey, 1978. Associate professor of drama, University of Houston, 1983—. Artist-in-residence, Equinox Theatre, Houston, 1981—, and New Jersey State Council on the Arts. **Awards:** New York Drama Critics Circle award, 1977; Obie award, 1977, 1980; Columbia University medal of excellence, 1981; Los Angeles *Times* award, 1981; Guggenheim fellowship, 1981; Nori Eboraci award, Bernard College, 1988; Lila Wallace-Reader's Digest Fund annual writer's award, 1992; Paul Robeson Achievement award, National Coalition of 100 Black Women, 1992; Living Legend award, National Black Theatre festival, 1993; Claim Your Life award, 1993; Monarch Merit award; Pushcart prize. **Address:** Department of Drama, University of Houston-University Park, 4800 Calhoun Road, Houston, Texas 77004, U.S.A.

PUBLICATIONS

Plays

For Colored Girls Who Have Considered Suicide When the Rainbow Is Enuf (produced New York, 1975; London, 1980). San Lorenzo, California, Shameless Hussy Press, 1976; revised version, New York, Macmillan, 1977; London, Eyre Methuen, 1978.

A Photograph: Lovers-in-Motion (as *A Photograph: A Still Life with Shadows*, *A Photograph: A Study of Cruelty*, produced New York, 1977; revised version, as *A Photograph: Lovers-in-Motion*, also director: produced Houston, 1979). New York, French, 1981.

Where the Mississippi Meets the Amazon, with Thulani Nkabinda and Jessica Hagedorn (produced New York, 1977).

Spell #7 (produced New York, 1979; London, 1985). Included in *Three Pieces*, 1981; published separately, London, Methuen, 1985.

Black and White Two-Dimensional Planes (produced New York, 1979).

Boogie Woogie Landscapes (produced on tour, 1980). Included in *Three Pieces*, 1981.

Mother Courage and Her Children, adaptation of a play by Brecht (produced New York, 1980).

From Okra to Greens: A Different Kinda Love Story (as *Mouths* produced New York, 1981; as *From Okra to Greens*, in *Three for a Full Moon*, produced Los Angeles, 1982). New York, French, 1983.

Three Pieces: Spell #7, A Photograph: Lovers-in-Motion, Boogie Woogie Landscapes. New York, St. Martin's Press, 1981.

Three for a Full Moon, and Bocas (produced Los Angeles, 1982).

Educating Rita, adaptation of the play by Willy Russell (produced Atlanta, 1983).

Three Views of Mt. Fuji (produced New York, 1987).

Betsey Brown, adaptation of her own novel, with Emily Mann, music by Baikida Carroll, lyrics by Shange, Mann, and Carroll (also director: produced Philadelphia, 1989).

The Love Space Demands: A Continuing Saga (produced London, 1992). New York, St. Martin's Press, 1991; included in *Plays: One*, 1992.

Plays: One (includes *For Colored Girls Who Have Considered Suicide When the Rainbow Is Enuf, Spell #7, I Heard Eric Dolphy in His Eyes, The Love Space Demands: A Continuing Saga*). London, Methuen, 1992.

Novels

Sassafrass: A Novella. San Lorenzo, California, Shameless Hussy Press, 1977.

Sassafrass, Cypress and Indigo. New York, St. Martin's Press, 1982; London, Methuen, 1983.

Betsey Brown. New York, St. Martin's Press, and London, Methuen, 1985.

Liliane. New York, Picador USA, 1994.

Poetry

Melissa and Smith. St. Paul, Bookslinger, 1976.

Natural Disasters and Other Festive Occasions. San Francisco, Heirs, 1977.

Nappy Edges. New York, St. Martin's Press, 1978; London, Methuen, 1987.

A Daughter's Geography. New York, St. Martin's Press, 1983; London, Methuen, 1985.

From Okra to Greens: Poems. St. Paul, Coffee House Press, 1984.

Ridin' the Moon West in Texas: Word Paintings. New York, St. Martin's Press, 1988.

I Live in Music. New York, Welcome Enterprises, 1994.

Other

See No Evil: Prefaces, Essays, and Accounts 1976-1983. San Francisco, Momo's Press, 1984.

Whitewash. New York, Walker & Company, 1997.

If I Can Cook, You Know God Can. Boston, Beacon Press, 1998.

*

Critical Studies: "Writing the Body: Reading Joan Riley, Grace Nichols, and Ntozake Shange" by Gabriele Griffin, in *Black Women's Writing*, edited by Gina Wisker, New York, St. Martin's, 1993; "Dancing out of Form, Dancing into Self: Genre and Metaphor in Marshall, Shange, and Walker" by Barbara Frey Waxman, in *The Journal of the Society for the Study of the Multi-Ethnic Literature of the United States* (Amherst, Massachusetts), Fall 1994, pp. 533-55; *Ntozake Shange: A Critical Study of the Plays* by Neal A. Lester, New York, Garland Publishing, 1995; "Unmasking the Minstrel Mask's Black Magic in Ntozake Shange's *Spell # 7*" by Karen Cronacher, in *Feminist Theatre and Theory*, edited by Helene Keyssar, New York, St. Martin's, 1996.

Theatrical Activities:
Director: **Plays**—*The Mighty Gents* by Richard Wesley, New York, 1979; *The Spirit of Sojourner Truth* by Bernice Reagon and June Jordan, 1979; *A Photograph: Lovers-in-Motion*, Houston, 1979; *Betsey Brown*, Philadelphia, 1989.

Actor: **Plays**—The Lady in Orange in *For Colored Girls Who Have Considered Suicide When the Rainbow Is Enuf*, New York, 1976; in *Where the Mississippi Meets the Amazon*, New York, 1977; in *Mouths*, New York, 1981.

* * *

The production of *For Colored Girls Who Have Considered Suicide When the Rainbow Is Enuf* established Ntozake Shange as a major force in American theater. True to the Xhosa name she had received in 1971, she was indeed "one who brings her own things" and "walks with lions." Shange has since moved from the spotlight, but she remains one of the finest English-language verse dramatists, forging a poetry compelling in both its social immediacy and its broad vision.

For Colored Girls is a collage of poems mixed with song and dance that celebrates the lives of black girls who previously had not been considered a fit subject for dramatic presentation. Structured around rhythmic pulses, the play charts the passage from the self-conscious bravado of "we waz grown," proclaimed at the moment of high school graduation and loss of virginity, through a variety of alternatively funny and painful experiences with men, to the hard-gained knowledge of one's self-worth found in the closing affirmation—"i found god in myself & i loved her fiercely."

Belying the women's anguish and seeming predilection toward the negative is their willingness to dance, with dance and music being metaphors for the courage to venture into the world with grace, to seek intimate connections with others, and to celebrate the nearly limitless potentiality of life.

The play unlocked emotional doors rarely touched in American theater. For many women experiencing a performance of the play became a quasi-religious moment in which some of their deepest feelings were acknowledged and a healing of wounds achieved. For countless other audiences it energized a highly charged debate about male-female relationships and the image of black men in American literature.

Shange's subsequent plays *A Photograph: Lovers-in-Motion* and *Boogie Woogie Landscapes* continue to use a rite-of-passage theme, but the exploration is carried forth within a more clearly delineated social context and a more conventional dramatic form. Thus, in *A Photograph* the male protagonist's identification with both Alexandre Dumas *père* and the illegitimate Dumas *fils* serves as a metaphor for his confusion, and the shedding of this fantasy is an indication of the extent to which he moves toward a healthier creative vision. Similarly, Layla in *Boogie Woogie Landscapes* relives her own emotional geography in order to reconcile the possibility of personal love with social struggle. But given the ways in which society distorts personality, love is tenuous, more often a momentary grasping for, rather than solid achievement of, unity.

With *Spell #7* the playwright moves further into the public arena by tackling the iconography of the "nigger." Manipulating the power of music, minstrel performers banish a huge, all-seeing blackface mask along with their stage personae in order to create a safe space in which secret hopes, fears, and dreams may be articulated. But two confessions centering around the shattering of faith puncture the whimsical or contained quality of most of the fantasies and reveal an almost overwhelming anguish. Although the master of ceremonies intervenes to reassure the audience that it will enjoy his black magic and although the actors conjure forth the joyous spirit of a black church with the chant "bein colored and love it," the mask returns. In reading the play we are left to wonder whether the actors and audience have indeed enjoyed the freedom of their own definitions or whether Shange has performed a sleight of hand that simply allows the drama to end on a positive note. The answer lies finally in the extent to which the communion between actors and audience creates a countervailing force to the hideous minstrel mask and in the audience members' ability to find within their own lives resolutions to the play's purposeful contradictions.

The play *From Okra to Greens: A Different Kinda Love Story* explores further the intersection of the personal and the political. Present are the now familiar Shange themes of nearly overwhelming brutalization balanced by the transcendence of dance, music, and poetry. But significantly new is the shared articulation of many of these experiences by both a male and female protagonist and the effective merger of the personal and the political into a whole that allows them to move forward. Thus, the play closes with the couple bidding their "children" to emerge from the ghettoes, Bantustans, barrios, and favelas of the world to fight against the old men who would impose death, to dance in affirmation of their unbreakable bond with nature itself.

Within a black theater tradition Shange seems to have been influenced most by Amiri Baraka and Adrienne Kennedy. Characteristic of her dramaturgy are an attack upon the English language that she as a black woman finds doubly oppressive, a self-consciousness as a writer linked to a determination to reclaim for oppressed peoples the right of self-definition, and a use of poetry, music, and dance to approximate the power of nonlinear, suprarational modes of experience. A poet, Shange brings to the theater a commitment as a locus of eruptive, often contradictory, and potentially healing forces whose ultimate resolution lie beyond the performance space.

—Sandra L. Richards

SHANLEY, John Patrick

Nationality: American. **Born:** New York City, 13 October 1950. **Education:** New York University, B.S. 1977. **Awards:** Oscar, 1987; Writers Guild of America award, 1987; Los Angeles Drama Critics Circle award, 1987. **Agent:** Esther Sherman, William Morris Agency, 1350 Avenue of the Americas, New York, New York 10019. **Address:** 630 Ninth Avenue, Suite 800, New York, New York 10036, U.S.A.

Publications

Plays

Saturday Night at the War (produced New York, 1978).

George and the Dragon (produced New York, 1979).

Welcome to the Moon and Other Plays (includes *The Red Coat, Down and Out, Let Us Go out into the Starry Night, Out West, A Lonely Impulse of Delight*) (produced New York, 1982). New York, Dramatists Play Service, 1985.

Danny and the Deep Blue Sea (produced Waterford, Connecticut, 1983; New York, 1984; London, 1985). New York, Dramatists Play Service, 1984.

Savage in Limbo (produced New York, 1985; London, 1987). New York, Dramatists Play Service, 1986.

the dreamer examines his pillow (produced Waterford, Connecticut, 1985; New York, 1986). New York, Dramatists Play Service, 1987.

Women of Manhattan (produced New York, 1986). New York, Dramatists Play Service, 1986.

All for Charity (produced New York, 1987).

Italian American Reconciliation (also director: produced New York, 1988). New York, Dramatists Play Service, 1989.

The Big Funk (produced New York, 1990). New York, Dramatists Play Service, 1991.

Beggars in the House of Plenty (produced New York, 1991). New York, Dramatists Play Service, 1992.

Collected Plays. New York, Applause, 1992.

Thirteen by Shanley (includes *Danny and the Deep Blue Sea, The Red Coat, Down and Out, Let Us Go out into the Starry Night, Out West, A Lonely Impulse of Delight, Welcome to the Moon, Savage in Limbo, Women of Manhattan, the dreamer examines his pillow, Italian American Reconciliation, The Big Funk, Beggars in the House of Plenty*). New York, Applause, 1992.

What Is This Everything? (produced New York, 1992).

Four Dogs and a Bone and The Wild Goose. New York, Dramatists Play Service, 1995.

Moonstruck, Joe Versus the Volcano, and Five Corners (screenplays). New York, Grove Press, 1996.
Missing/Kissing: Missing Marisa, Kissing Christine. New York, Dramatists Play Service, 1997.
Psychopathia Sexualis. New York, Dramatists Play Service, 1998.

Screenplays: *Moonstruck,* 1987; *Five Corners,* 1988; *The January Man,* 1989; *Joe Versus the Volcano,* 1990; *Alive,* 1993.

*

Critical Study: "John Patrick Shanley" by Craig Gholson, in *BOMB,* Summer 1988, pp. 21-25.

* * *

The theater of John Patrick Shanley is primarily about the loss and pain caused by love. In Shanley's plays love leaves none of its converts with sufficient air. It robs people of options, stultifies, sends reason packing, and embraces suffering. People truly suffer in Shanley's plays. They are primed for pain, they cannot wait to taste its joys, and such longed-for suffering is fully orchestrated through the arrival of love, the protagonist. Love creates a state in which everything diminishes except the pain it generates. People seem to understand that they have lost something, but love holds them in a delicious stupor. They do not seem to know what has been lost, and they spend their days heaving, sighing, and breathing heavily.

Shanley has important strengths, in particular a wonderful ear for the sound of working-class Italian-Americans. He portrays the language as having too many syllables by adopting a flatfooted formality, a kind of hard hat existentialism. Probably nobody speaks like this character in *Italian American Reconciliation:*

> Aldo: A lot of people have an expression of this problem. They had something horrible for a long time, and then they get away from it, and then they miss it.

Or like this one:

> Huey: I feel this pain that makes me weak. The pain is that place in me where I'm hurt from the divorce. . . . I tried to go into the future and be new, but it don't work for me.

But for all their verbal constructions and cadences with an authentic ring, for all their rhetorical poetry of loss and exhortation of grief and baying to the heavens, Shanley's characters inhabit a self-perpetuating prison. These protagonists have not found a way of moving past self-absorption into that place where the world transacts its mundane but necessary business.

Shanley's early collection *Welcome to the Moon and Other Plays* contains some seemingly uncertain, sometimes uncontrolled pieces, but they do display an engaging energy and a foreshadowing of both the strengths and weaknesses of his later works.

Down and Out is raw Shanley, a work consciously without subtext that comes at us from that cloudy lyricism fashioned by William Saroyan in his early plays. The allegorical figures are named Love and Poet. Love is fixing a dinner of water and beans when Poet arrives home sick and discouraged. He wanted a library book, but the library was not open. A shrouded figure comes to the house and demands his library card. Poet wants to write new poems, but "I cannot write them. Because I have no pencil." Another shrouded figure holds out "Money! Money! Money!"

> Love: Look how green it is! How green!
> Poet: It's beautiful! Can I have it?
> Figure: Give me your soul. Give me your soul.
> Love: Never! Get out get out get out!

Later Poet laments:

> Poet: No one wants my poetry. The man in the newspaper said I am an untalented fool. The man in the newspaper was right. We are alone. Unknown. We live on beans.

But Love inspires Poet:

> Love: The darkest thing has come and led to a moment of despair. But look! See here! I am your Love who has never left you! I can turn a tiny lock and open up your soul again! (She opens the box, which is his soul. It plays music. The poet is bathed in a powerful light. He rises up.)

In *Let Us Go Out into the Starry Night* ghosts and monsters are chewing at the head of a tormented young man and clawing at his stomach. The man explains to the young woman who seeks him out that one of these monsters is the ghost of his mother:

> Man: She doesn't look too bad today really. Some nights she visits me looking like a rotting side of beef and carrying a big knife.

They kiss and decide to merge their dreams:

> Man: How did we get here?
> Woman: We got here by being serious.

In *Welcome to the Moon* Stephen abandons his wife and returns to the Bronx, to a "lowdown Bronx bar." He confides in his old buddy Vinnie that he has never got over his girlfriend Shirley, whom he has not seen for 14 years but whose memory has poisoned his marriage. Stephen breaks down and weeps and is shortly joined in his weeping by Ronny, another member of the old Bronx gang who has been trying to kill himself because of his own unrequited love. It is hard to establish where Shanley is positioning himself. His overlay of irony seems to be a defense against the expected charge of sentimentality. One is left suspecting that Shanley's characters are unable to deal with the world, that they need to surrender to that controlling creature love, who will mend all pencils, retrieve library cards, cook beans, and keep one from loneliness and suicide.

By 1988 Shanley had developed an almost seamless aesthetic. In *Italian American Reconciliation* Huey desperately wants to return to his former wife, Janice, who not only detested him but also shot his dog and threatened him with the same gun. Janice is a nightmare, and Huey has everything a man could want in sweet, gentle Teresa, but he is convinced that Janice took "his power to stand up and be a man and take. I want it back. I think Janice has it. I think she took that power from me, or it's sitting with her." Shanley seems to identify with Huey's belief system, his people seeing only themselves. Huey is blinded by his belief in the castrating powers of Janice, and in an important sense Huey has created his Janice, a woman he cannot possibly see. One has to question what kind of consuming love is taking place, how the world of the Bronx and of broken people is ever going to mend. Perhaps Shanley has to borrow Janice's gun and shoot love right out the door. But then what are we left with?

—Arthur Sainer

SHAWN, Wallace

Nationality: American. **Born:** New York City, 12 November 1943; son of the editor William Shawn. **Education:** Dalton School, New York, 1948-57; Putney School, Vermont, 1958-61; Harvard University, Cambridge, Massachusetts, 1961-65, B.A. in history 1965; Magdalen College, Oxford, 1966-68, B.A. in philosophy, politics, and economics 1968, M.A.; studied acting with Katharine Sergava, New York, 1971. **Family:** Lives with Deborah Eisenberg. **Career:** English teacher, Indore Christian College, Madhya Pradesh, India, 1965-66; teacher of English, Latin, and drama, Church of Heavenly Rest Day School, New York, 1968-70; shipping clerk, Laurie Love Ltd., New York, 1974-75; Xerox machine operator, Hamilton Copy Center, New York, 1975-76. **Awards:** Obie award, 1975, 1986, 1991; Guggenheim fellowship, 1978. **Agent:** Casarotto Ramsay Ltd., National House, 60-66 Wardour Street, London W1V 3HP, England.

Publications

Plays

Our Late Night (produced New York, 1975). New York, Targ, 1984.

In the Dark, music by Allen Shawn (also director: produced Lenox, Massachusetts, 1976).

A Thought in Three Parts (as *Three Short Plays: Summer Evening, The Youth Hostel, Mr. Frivolous*, produced New York, 1976; as *A Thought in Three Parts*, produced London, 1977). Published in *Wordplays 2*, New York, Performing Arts Journal Publications, 1982.

The Mandrake, adaptation of a play by Machiavelli (produced New York, 1977; as *Mandragola*, music and lyrics by Howard Goodall, produced London, 1984).

The Family Play (produced New York, 1978).

Marie and Bruce (produced London, 1979; New York, 1980). New York, Grove Press, 1980; with *My Dinner with André* (screenplay), London, Methuen, 1983.

My Dinner with André, with André Gregory (produced London, 1980).

My Dinner with André (screenplay), with André Gregory. New York, Grove Press, 1981; with *Marie and Bruce*, London, Methuen, 1983.

The Hotel Play (produced New York, 1981). New York, Dramatists Play Service, 1982.

Aunt Dan and Lemon (produced London and New York, 1985). London, Methuen, and New York, Grove Press, 1985.

The Fever (produced New York and London, 1991). New York, Farrar Straus, and London, Faber, 1991.

The Designated Mourner. London, Faber, 1996.

Four Plays. New York, Noonday, 1997.

Plays One. London, Faber and Faber, 1997.

Screenplay: *My Dinner with André*, with André Gregory, 1981.

*

Critical Studies: "He's Still Falling: Wallace Shawn's Problem of Morality" by Gay Brewer, in *American Drama* (Cincinnati, Ohio), Fall 1992, pp. 26-58; *Writing Wrongs: The Work of Wallace Shawn* by W. D. King, Philadelphia, Temple University Press, 1997; "Wallace Shawn" by Patrick McGrath, in *BOMB*, Spring 1997, pp. 24-27.

Theatrical Activities (selected):
Director: **Play**—*In the Dark*, Lenox, Massachusetts, 1976.

Actor: **Plays**—In *Alice in Wonderland*, New York, 1974; Prologue and Siro in *The Mandrake*, New York, 1977; Ilya in *Chinchilla* by Robert David MacDonald, New York, 1979; in *My Dinner with André*, London, 1980; Father, Jasper, and Freddie in *Aunt Dan and Lemon*, London and New York, 1985; *The Fever*, New York and London, 1991. **Films**—*Manhattan*, 1979; *Starting Over*, 1979; *All That Jazz*, 1980; *Atlantic City*, 1980; *Simon*, 1980; *My Dinner with André*, 1981; *Lovesick*, 1983; *Strange Invaders*, 1983; *Deal of the Century*, 1983; *Micki and Maude*, 1984; *Crackers*, 1984; *The Bostonians*, 1984; *The Hotel New Hampshire*, 1984; *Heaven Help Us*, 1985; *Prick Up Your Ears*, 1987; *Radio Days*, 1987; *The Moderns*, 1989; *We're No Angels*, 1990; *Mom and Dad Save the World*, 1992; *Nickel and Dime*, 1992; *Shadows and Fog*, 1992; *The Cemetery Club*, 1993; *The Double O Kid*, 1993; *Meteor Man*, 1993; *Mrs. Parker and the Vicious Circle*, 1994; *Vanya on 42nd Street* (title role), 1994; *Kalamazoo*, 1994; *A Goofy Movie*, 1995. **Television**—*Saigon: Year of the Cat*, 1983; *Matrix*, 1993; also appeared on episodes of *Taxi*, *The Cosby Show*, and *Murphy Brown*.

* * *

Shock has always been one side effect of Wallace Shawn's dramatic writing, a rather curious side effect when one thinks of the man himself in his amiable and benign intelligence. Joint Stock's 1977 production of *A Thought in Three Parts* at London's ICA Theatre started the forces of oppression on a particularly merry chase. Within 24 hours of the play's opening there were calls for prosecution on the grounds of obscenity, and there were detectives sitting in the audience. Within a week the charity commissioners had initiated an inquiry into the ICA's charitable status. Within two months the government had announced that it was setting up a committee to consider the law of obscenity generally, at the same time specifically declining to prosecute *A Thought in Three Parts*.

After the dust had settled, the reputation of the three one-act plays that made up the evening was invisible for the outrage that had been engendered. Rarely had London's critics been so disturbed by a theatrical event, and the event showed the danger of taking sex seriously in the theater. The clownish romping of such shows as *Oh! Calcutta!* had given way to something considerably more threatening.

A dangerous aura of violence hung over the evening despite the jokey comedy and naked sexual frolicking of the actors in the second of the plays, the one that caused the greatest outrage. Something more akin to horror than joy came through, and rather than real copulation there was real fear. The first part, *Summer Evening,* takes place in a hotel room in a foreign city, where a man and a woman exchange trivial words about eating, reading, and card playing. Underneath the conversation is the specter of brutal sexuality, and phrases break through the trivia to reveal the real state of play: "I just had a picture. I thought of you strangling me."

Rather than viewing sex as communication, the second play analyzes the essentially solitary experience of orgasm. The selfishness of much sexual gratification percolates through the distractions presented of oral foreplay, intercourse, and group masturbation in *The Youth Hostel.* Shawn compresses time and emotional responses so that the blinding number of orgasms signal changing relationships between five young people spending the night together. The comedy of the dialogue, in language suitable for *True Teenage Romances,* is a deceiving technique that sharpens the human isolation of the characters when their sexual energies are exhausted.

Mr. Frivolous, the final play, begins and remains with the isolation of an individual, an elegant man breakfasting alone in an elegant room. His monologue skates through idle sexual fantasy, from basic heterosexuality to images of gropes with a priest and the possibilities of bondage. Shawn's very public musings on sexuality are finally too dour to be erotic. He stimulates the mind, not the body.

Shawn first made an impact on the off-off-Broadway scene when André Gregory directed the play *Our Late Night* for the experimental company called the Manhattan Project. An obvious precursor to *A Thought in Three Parts,* the play dramatized the drifting unconscious thoughts of two young people quietly going to bed. Around the two there was a swirl of couples discussing sexuality, food, and other encounters.

Shawn's collaboration with Gregory on that production led to the remarkable play by Shawn and Gregory called *My Dinner with André,* which was made into a film by Louis Malle. Gregory had spent the best part of two decades exploring the expanding boundaries of the theatrical avant-garde, finally chasing the aesthetic experience into a forest in Poland, to the Findhorn community in Scotland, and to India, Tibet, and the Sahara. Shawn had spent those years consolidating a reputation as an actor in films with Woody Allen and with such plays as *Marie and Bruce* that drew attention to him without intensifying the scandal.

The form of *My Dinner with André* is seductive and misleading. It pretends to be an account of an actual dinner that Shawn had with Gregory, "a man I'd been avoiding literally for years," and Shawn himself became the character who introduces and frames the play, indeed playing the part of Wally Shawn opposite Gregory's André in both the stage version and the film. The play's conflict is Shawn's New York rationality confronted with Gregory's telling of the "para-theatrical" activities he had had since quitting the theater after directing *Our Late Night* in 1975.

No such dinner occurred, but the conversation actually took place, extended well beyond the 100 or so pages of the final script. Shawn and Gregory taped lengthy meetings in which Gregory detailed his adventures and conclusions against the curious and sane encouragement of Shawn's skepticism. Gregory talked of the project he undertook in a Polish forest with 40 musicians, creating "experiences" with the encouragement of his friend the Polish director Jerzy Grotowski. He elaborated on his search by telling of a Japanese monk he befriended and with whom he ate sand in the desert. Shawn responded that he liked electric blankets and that happiness could be a cup of cold coffee in which no cockroach had drowned during the night.

The piece is an aesthetic debate of great interest and value, and while the bulk of the ideological contribution is Gregory's, Gregory credits Shawn with the dramatic sensibility that shaped the debate and made the unfolding of the story so mesmerizing. It is Shawn's own characterization of himself as a cynic that gives a forum to Gregory's ideas, and it makes for a significant contribution to the search for artistic forms and meaning that followed the explosion of experiment in the 1960s. Shawn's own openness to thoughtful and radical inquiry into the nature of art and human experience is hearteningly matched by his disciplined skills of expression.

The amused cynicism evident in his own plays was reflected in Shawn's translation and adaptation of Machiavelli's *Mandragola,* with its jaundiced view of human relationships, but it was his original play *Aunt Dan and Lemon* that again stirred the audience into shock. In some ways a meditation on Nazi atrocities, it was most disturbing for the cold way in which it portrayed the spiritually damaged woman called Lemon, the narrator of the piece. She began by welcoming the audience, including the "little children. How sweet you are, how innocent," and she went on to tell the story of a friend of her parents, an American academic teaching at Oxford called Aunt Dan, who had regaled her with strange tales when she was 11. Aunt Dan's stories were sometimes about the heroism of Henry Kissinger when he ordered bombing attacks on Vietnam or about a woman who had been Aunt Dan's lesbian lover and who had killed a man by strangling him with her stockings. The lesson Lemon learns is that comfort is bought by assigning the killing to others and that it is really hypocritical to condemn the Nazis, who, after all, had been very successful against the Jews. Profoundly disturbing, the play is a mesmerizing blend of narration and enactment that tries, with mixed success, to comprehend the nature of human cruelty and the negotiated truce with justice that affects all nonpolitical people.

Shawn's 1991 play for one character, *The Fever,* was an even more specific meditation on justice and injustice, virtually a call for revolution. "This piece was written," he has said, "so that it could be performed in anyone's flat or home, for an audience of 10 or 12, as well as in public places, and it was designed to fit a very wide spectrum of performers." Shawn himself has performed it in dining rooms and at London's Royal National Theatre, and it would be very hard to measure its impact, for it is basically a call for people to change, for those theater-going civilized people who have money to switch sides and join the poor.

The performer describes waking up in a hotel room in a poor country and reviewing his or her own reconsideration of the privilege that has come with money. In a post-Marxist world, it rehearses with passion Marx's analysis of the value of things, of commodities, so that the value of labor is recognized. By graphic reference to the torture and oppression that protects privilege, he indicts his audience and the comfortable notion of gradual change, but finally the character speaking cannot relinquish his or her own wealth. The dramatic and political journey is never completed.

—Ned Chaillet

SHEARER, Jill

Nationality: Australian. **Born:** Melbourne, 14 April 1936. **Career:** Secretary, Japanese Consulate-General, Brisbane, 1966-79. **Awards:** Big River Festival prize, for poetry, 1973; Monash Alexander Special award, 1976; New South Wales Society of Women Writers award, 1976; Utah Cairns Centenary award, 1976; McGregor Literary award, 1987; Australia Council grant, 1989. **Address:** c/o Playlab Press, P.O. Box 185, Ashgrove, Brisbane 4060, Queensland, Australia.

Publications

Plays

The Trouble with Gillian (produced Brisbane, 1974).
The Foreman (produced Brisbane, 1976). Sydney, Currency Press, 1979.
The Boat (produced Brisbane, 1977). Published in *Can't You Hear Me Talking to You*, St. Lucia, University of Queensland Press, 1978.
The Kite (produced Brisbane, 1977). Included in *Echoes and Other Plays*, 1980.
Nocturne (produced Brisbane, 1977). Included in *Echoes and Other Plays*, 1980.
Catherine (produced Goulburn, New South Wales, 1978). Melbourne, Edward Arnold, 1977.
Stephen (produced Brisbane, 1980). Included in *Echoes and Other Plays*, 1980.
Echoes and Other Plays (includes *The Kite, Nocturne, Stephen*). Ashgrove, Playlab Press, 1980.
Release Lavinia Stannard (produced Brisbane, 1980).
A Woman Like That (produced Brisbane, 1986).
Shimada (produced Melbourne, 1987; New York, 1992). Sydney, Currency Press, 1989.
Comrade (produced Brisbane, 1987). Ashgrove, Playlab Press, 1987.
The Family. Sydney, Currency Press, 1995.

Radio Play: *A Woman Like That*, 1989.

*

Manuscript Collection: Fryer Library, University of Queensland, St. Lucia, Brisbane.

Critical Studies: "Telling It in Multiple Layers: An Interview with Jill Shearer" by Helen Gilbert, in *Australasian Drama Studies* (St. Lucia, Brisbane), 21, October 1992; "Distinguishing Desire: Gender and Imperialism in Jill Shearer's *Shimada*" by Leigh Dale and Helen Gilbert, in *Myths, Heroes and Anti-Heroes: Essays on the Literature and Culture of the Asia-Pacific Region*, Nedlands, University of Western Australia Press, 1992; "Looking the Same? A Preliminary (Post-Colonial) Discussion of Orientalism and Occidentalism in Australia and Japan" by Leigh Dale and Helen Gilbert, in *Yearbook of Comparative and General Literature* (Bloomington, Indiana), 1993, pp. 35-50.

Jill Shearer comments:

Whilst I'm interested in all aspects of contemporary society, I'm drawn to writing about individuals and families often caught up in larger events. Living and working in Australia I'm increasingly interested in exploring Asian cultures (as I did in my play *Shimada*) increasingly linked as they are with my own.

* * *

Beginning with numerous one-act plays written in the 1970s and produced mostly by amateur companies, Jill Shearer's work exhibits a passionate concern with social issues and tackles such wide-ranging and often controversial topics as abortion, industrial work practices, conservation, race relations, and foreign economic influence in Australia. These broader issues are most often played out in localized settings through the representation of ordinary people and family situations. *The Foreman*, for example, condemns racism not through a primary focus on interactions between Aboriginal and non-Aboriginal Australians but by revealing the effects of prejudice on an Aboriginal family whose relationships become strained when the breadwinner is rejected by his white "mates" after he receives a well-deserved promotion.

Other plays such as *Echoes, The Trouble with Gillian, Stephen*, and *The Boat* also foreground family tensions, although these are often more powerfully suggested by the characters' desperate attempts to sustain some semblance of harmony or normality than by any overt confrontations. *The Boat* depicts a man's regression into a childlike fantasy world after he loses his job and sense of purpose. His wife and son choose not to disabuse him of his belief that the daily fishing trips played out in the living room of their conventional suburban home are mere fictions. In *Echoes* the representation of a family on holiday at the beach is similarly energized by a forced but unsustainable congeniality that sidesteps problems and masks hostilities. In both texts subterranean conflict is kindled by an outsider who threatens to fracture the fragile integrity of the family unit, but despite its fissures the structure proves resistant to the "truths" the outsider might offer. Short, sharp, and narrowly focused, both plays construct vivid impressions of the roles people play in order to cope with difficult situations. Characterized by deft touches of the bizarre combined with a vague sense of threat, they are strongly evocative of Pinter's work. This is also the case with *Nocturne*, a very short scenario that positions a cellist at the top of a mountain road playing with wild abandon, oblivious to all else but the music, while a walker becomes increasingly frustrated and aggressive as she tries to make conversation. Here Shearer's use of silence and the unfinished line or trail-away phrase also owes much to Pinter's influence.

To the extent that she evokes clearly recognizable images of tropical Australia, Shearer could be called a regionalist writer. *Nocturne* owes something of its uncomfortable ambience to the disjunction between a highly minimalist set, an abstract tree beside a white strip of road, and the dialogue's insistent references to the panoramic view from the tangled rain forest where the antagonists sit to the nearby coastline and beyond. *Echoes* features the Great Barrier Reef as a deceptively calm retreat in which nature's bounty is balanced only by its potential destructiveness. This dual aspect of nature that represents both threat and promise acts here as a metaphorical parallel for the characters themselves, while in *The Kite* the healing powers of the beach and the sand are harnessed to dissuade a young woman from committing suicide.

Though not pursuing an obvious feminist agenda, Shearer consistently creates strong women characters, and her one historical play, *Catherine*, clearly argues for a reconsideration of women's roles in Australia's past and present. Constructed as a play within a play, *Catherine* explores the relationship between a female convict on the second fleet and a rakish upper-class gentleman who has taken her by intimidation, if not force, for his mistress. While the viewer's interest is directed toward this tale, the framing narrative questions the passivity attributed to Catherine when the actor who plays her insists on presenting a character with more verve than the director sees fit. The play sets out to rescue Catherine and other convict women from the margins of imperial history, but it also voices a powerful indictment of the convict system even while celebrating the tenacity of the oppressed and dispossessed who were transported to Australia to found a nation.

In terms of style, Shearer's later work strives toward heightened expression through spare dialogue and dramatic uses of the mise-en-scène. *Shimada,* her most acclaimed play, shows the theatrical influences of Japanese forms such as No and Kabuki. Also set on Queensland's tropical coast, *Shimada* tackles the difficult issue of Asian-Australian relations. Eliding past and present, the play interweaves two narratives of cultural conflict. The contemporary scenes focus on a group of Australians struggling to avoid Japanese control of a small bicycle factory, but their efforts are clearly motivated less by a commitment to national economic growth than by xenophobic fears inflamed by wartime memories, for the ending looks to American capital investment to keep the factory viable. One of the older workers, Eric, believes that the Japanese businessman Toshio, who comes to discuss the merger, is the dreaded guard of the camp in Burma where he was interned during World War II. Through flashbacks and effective uses of role doubling the text does indeed suggest that Toshio might be Shimada, but it is equally probable that the two are related only in Eric's mind. While the Australian's suspicion of the cultural other is matched by Toshio's inscrutability, suggesting that relationships between the two nations are destined to remain problematic, *Shimada*'s primary appeal lies in precisely those differences that make interactions between characters and the cross-fertilization of forms so theatrically charged.

Shearer's work is not easily categorized in terms of themes and styles, for it ranges freely through diverse topics and experiments with a number of dramatic modes of expression. One recurrent element in her work, however, is a cautious celebration of Australians' abilities to cope with the vicissitudes of modern life.

—Helen Gilbert

SHEPARD, Sam

Nationality: American. **Born:** Samuel Shepard Rogers in Fort Sheridan, Illinois, 5 November 1943. **Education:** Duarte High School, California, graduated 1960; Mount San Antonio Junior College, Walnut, California, 1960-61. **Family:** Married O-Lan Johnson in 1969 (divorced), one son; one daughter by the actress Jessica Lange. **Career:** Worked as hot walker at the Santa Anita Race Track, stable hand, Connolly Arabian Horse Ranch, Duarte, herdsman, Huff Sheep Ranch, Chino, orange picker in Duarte, and sheep shearer in Pomona, all in California; actor with Bishop's Company Repertory Players, Burbank, California, and U.S. tour, 1962; car wrecker, Charlemont, Massachusetts; bus boy, Village Gate, 1963-64, waiter, Marie's Crisis Café, 1965, and musician with the Holy Modal Rounders, 1968, all in New York; lived in England, 1971-74, and in California, 1974—. Founder, with Murray Mednick, John Steppling, and others, Padua Hills Playwrights Workshop and Festival, Los Angeles, 1978. **Awards:** Obie award, 1967, 1970, 1973, 1975, 1977, 1978 (twice), 1980, 1984; Yale University fellowship, 1967; Rockefeller grant, 1967; Guggenheim grant, 1968; American Academy grant, 1974; Brandeis University Creative Arts award, 1976, 1985; Pulitzer prize, 1979; New York Drama Critics Circle award, 1986; Outer Circle award, 1986; Drama Desk award, 1986; Theater Hall of Fame, 1994. **Agent:** Toby Cole, 234 West 44th Street, New York, New York 10036, U.S.A.

Publications

Plays

Cowboys (produced New York, 1964).

The Rock Garden (produced New York, 1964; excerpt produced in *Oh! Calcutta!*, New York, 1969; London, 1970). Included in *The Unseen Hand and Other Plays*, 1971; in *Angel City and Other Plays*, 1976.

Up to Thursday (produced New York, 1965).

Dog (produced New York, 1965).

Rocking Chair (produced New York, 1965).

Chicago (produced New York, 1965; London, 1976). Included in *Five Plays*, 1967.

Icarus's Mother (produced New York, 1965; London, 1970). Included in *Five Plays*, 1967.

4-H Club (produced New York, 1965). Included in *The Unseen Hand and Other Plays*, 1971.

Fourteen Hundred Thousand (produced Minneapolis, 1966). Included in *Five Plays*, 1967.

Red Cross (produced New York, 1966; Glasgow, 1969; London, 1970). Included in *Five Plays*, 1967.

La Turista (produced New York, 1967; London, 1969). Indianapolis, Bobbs Merrill, 1968; London, Faber, 1969.

Melodrama Play (produced New York and London, 1967). Included in *Five Plays*, 1967.

Forensic and the Navigators (produced New York, 1967). Included in *The Unseen Hand and Other Plays*, 1971.

Five Plays: Chicago, Icarus's Mother, Red Cross, Fourteen Hundred Thousand, Melodrama Play. Indianapolis, Bobbs Merrill, 1967; London, Faber, 1968: as *Chicago and Other Plays*, New York, Urizen, 1981; Faber, 1982.

Cowboys #2 (produced New York, 1967; London, 1980). Included in *Mad Dog Blues and Other Plays*, 1971; in *Angel City and Other Plays*, 1976.

The Holy Ghostly (produced on tour, 1969; New York, 1970; London, 1973). Included in *The Unseen Hand and Other Plays*, 1971.

The Unseen Hand (produced New York, 1969; London, 1973). Included in *The Unseen Hand and Other Plays*, 1971; with *Action*, London, Faber, 1975.

Operation Sidewinder (produced New York, 1970). Indianapolis, Bobbs Merrill, 1970; in *Four Two-Act Plays*, 1980.

Shaved Splits (produced New York, 1970). Included in *The Unseen Hand and Other Plays*, 1971.

Cowboy Mouth, with Patti Smith (produced Edinburgh and New York, 1971; London, 1972). Included in *Mad Dog Blues and Other Plays*, 1971; in *Angel City and Other Plays*, 1976.

Mad Dog Blues (produced New York, 1971; Edinburgh, 1978). Included in *Mad Dog Blues and Other Plays*, 1971; in *Angel City and Other Plays*, 1976.
Back Bog Beast Bait (produced New York, 1971). Included in *The Unseen Hand and Other Plays*, 1971.
The Unseen Hand and Other Plays. Indianapolis, Bobbs Merrill, 1971.
Mad Dog Blues and Other Plays. New York, Winter House, 1971.
The Tooth of Crime (produced London and Princeton, New Jersey, 1972; New York, 1973). With *Geography of a Horse Dreamer*, New York, Grove Press, and London, Faber, 1974.
Blue Bitch (televised 1972; produced New York, 1973; London, 1975).
Nightwalk, with Megan Terry and Jean-Claude van Itallie (produced New York and London, 1973). Published in *Open Theater*, New York, Drama Book Specialists, 1975.
Little Ocean (produced London, 1974).
Geography of a Horse Dreamer (also director: produced London, 1974; produced New Haven, Connecticut, 1974; New York, 1975). With *The Tooth of Crime*, New York, Grove Press, and London, Faber, 1974.
Action (produced London, 1974; New York, 1975). With *The Unseen Hand*, London, Faber, 1975; in *Angel City and Other Plays*, 1976.
Killer's Head (produced New York, 1975; London, 1979). Included in *Angel City and Other Plays*. 1976.
Angel City (also director: produced San Francisco, 1976; New York, 1977; London, 1983). Included in *Angel City and Other Plays*, 1976.
Angel City and Other Plays (includes *Curse of the Starving Class, Killer's Head, Action, Mad Dog Blues, Cowboy Mouth, The Rock Garden, Cowboys #2*). New York, Urizen, 1976; London, Faber, 1978.
Suicide in B Flat (produced New Haven, Connecticut, 1976; New York and London, 1977). Included in *Buried Child and Other Plays*, 1979.
The Sad Lament of Pecos Bill on the Eve of Killing His Wife (produced San Francisco, 1976; New York, 1983). With *Fool for Love*, San Francisco, City Lights, 1983; London, Faber, 1984.
Curse of the Starving Class (produced New York, 1976; London, 1977). Included in *Angel City and Other Plays*, 1976.
Inacoma (produced San Francisco, 1977).
Buried Child (produced San Francisco and New York, 1978; London, 1980). Included in *Buried Child and Other Plays*, 1979; New York, Dramatists Play Service, 1997.
Seduced (produced Providence, Rhode Island, and New York, 1978; London, 1980). Included in *Buried Child and Other Plays*, 1979.
Tongues, with Joseph Chaikin, music by Shepard, Skip LaPlante, and Harry Mann (produced San Francisco, 1978; Edinburgh, 1987; London, 1991). Included in *Seven Plays*, 1981.
Savage/Love, with Joseph Chaikin, music by Shepard, Skip LaPlante, and Harry Mann (produced New York, 1979; London, 1984). Included in *Seven Plays*, 1981.
Buried Child and Other Plays. New York, Urizen, 1979; as *Buried Child, and Seduced, and Suicide in B Flat*, London, Faber, 1980.
True West (produced San Francisco and New York, 1980; London, 1981). London, Faber, 1981; in *Seven Plays*, 1981.
Jackson's Dance, with Jacques Levy (produced New Haven, Connecticut, 1980).
Four Two-Act Plays (includes *La Turista, The Tooth of Crime, Geography of a Horse Dreamer, Operation Sidewinder*). New York, Urizen, 1980; London, Faber, 1981.
Seven Plays (includes *Buried Child, Curse of the Starving Class, The Tooth of Crime, La Turista, True West, Tongues, Savage/Love*). New York, Bantam, 1981; London, Faber, 1985.
Superstitions, music by Shepard and Catherine Stone (produced New York, 1983).
Fool for Love (also director: produced San Francisco and New York, 1983; London, 1984). With *The Sad Lament of Pecos Bill on the Eve of Killing His Wife*, San Francisco, City Lights, 1983; London, Faber, 1984.
Fool for Love and Other Plays (includes *Angel City, Cowboy Mouth, Suicide in B Flat, Seduced, Geography of a Horse Dreamer, Melodrama Play*). New York, Bantam, 1984.
Paris, Texas (screenplay), with Wim Wenders, edited by Chris Sievernich. Berlin, Road Movies, 1984.
A Lie of the Mind (also director: produced New York, 1985; London, 1987). New York, New American Library, 1986; London, Methuen, 1987.
The War in Heaven (broadcast 1985; produced London, 1987). New York, New American Library, 1986.
Hawk Moon (produced London, 1989).
States of Shock (produced New York, 1991). New York, Dramatists Play Service, 1992.
Simpatico: A Play in Three Acts. New York, Vintage Books, 1995.
Plays: 3 (includes *A Lie of the Mind*; *States of Shock*; *Simpatico*). London, Methuen Drama, 1996.
Plays: 2 (includes *True West*; *Buried Child*; *Curse of the Starving Class*; *The Tooth of Crime*; *La Turista*; *Tongues*; *Savage/Love*). London, Faber and Faber, 1997.

Screenplays: *Me and My Brother*, with Robert Frank, 1969; *Zabriskie Point*, with others, 1970; *Ringaleevio*, 1971; *Paris, Texas*, 1984; *Fool for Love*, 1985; *Far North*, 1988; *Silent Tongue*, 1992.

Radio Play: *The War in Heaven*, 1985.

Television Play: *Blue Bitch*, 1972 (UK).

Other

Hawk Moon: A Book of Short Stories, Poems, and Monologues. Los Angeles, Black Sparrow Press, 1973.
Rolling Thunder Logbook. New York, Viking Press, 1977; London, Penguin, 1978.
Motel Chronicles (includes *Hawk Moon*). San Francisco, City Lights, 1982; as *Motel Chronicles and Hawk Moon*, London, Faber, 1985.
Joseph Chaikin and Sam Shepard: Letters and Texts 1972-1984, edited by Barry V. Daniels. New York, New American Library, 1989.
Joseph Chaikin and Sam Shepard: Letters and Texts, 1972-1984. New York, Theatre Communications Group, 1994.
Cruising Paradise: Tales. New York, Vintage Books, 1996.

*

Bibliography: *Ten Modern American Playwrights* by Kimball King, New York, Garland, 1982.

Critical Studies: *American Dreams: The Imagination of Sam Shepard* edited by Bonnie Marranca, New York, Performing Arts Journal Publications, 1981; *Sam Shepard, Arthur Kopit, and the Off Broadway Theater* by Doris Auerbach, Boston, Twayne, 1982; *Inner Landscapes: The Theater of Sam Shepard* by Ron Mottram, Columbia, University of Missouri Press, 1984; *Sam Shepard* by Don Shewey, New York, Dell, 1985; *Sam Shepard* by Vivian M. Patraka and Mark Siegel, Boise, Idaho, Boise State University, 1985; *Sam Shepard: The Life and Work of an American Dreamer* by Ellen Oumano, New York, St. Martin's Press, 1986, London, Virgin, 1987; *Sam Shepard's Metaphorical Stages* by Lynda Hart, Westport, Connecticut, Greenwood Press, 1987; *Sam Shepard: A Casebook* by Kimball King, New York, Garland, 1988; *File on Shepard* edited by Simon Trussler, London, Methuen, 1989; *Sam Shepard* by David J. DeRose, New York, Twayne, 1992; *Sam Shepard on the German Stage: Critics, Politics, Myths* by Carol Benet, New York, Peter Lang, 1993; *Rereading Shepard: Contemporary Critical Essays on the Plays of Sam Shepard,* edited by Leonard Wilcox, Basingstoke, Macmillan, 1993; *Sam Shepard and the American Theatre* by Leslie A. Wade, Westport, Connecticut, Greenwood Press, 1997; *The Theatre of Sam Shepard: States of Crisis* by Stephen J. Bottoms, Cambridge, Cambridge University Press, 1998.

Theatrical Activities:
Director: **Plays**—Many of his own plays. **Film**—*Far North,* 1988; *Silent Tongue,* 1992.

Actor: **Plays**—With Bishop's Company, Burbank, California; role in *Cowboy Mouth,* New York, 1971. **Films**—*Brand X,* 1970; *Days of Heaven,* 1978; *Resurrection,* 1981; *Raggedy Man,* 1981; *Frances,* 1982; *The Right Stuff,* 1983; *Country,* 1984; *Fool for Love,* 1985; *Crimes of the Heart,* 1987; *Baby Boom,* 1987; *Steel Magnolias,* 1989; *The Hot Spot,* 1990; *Defenseless,* 1991; *Voyager,* 1991; *Thunderheart,* 1992; *The Pelican Brief,* 1993; *Safe Passage,* 1994.

Sam Shepard comments:

(1973) I'm interested in exploring the writing of plays through attitudes derived from other forms such as music, painting, sculpture, film, all the time keeping in mind that I'm writing for the theatre. I consider theatre and writing to be a home where I bring the adventures of my life and sort them out, making sense or nonsense out of mysterious impressions. I like to start with as little information about where I'm going as possible. A nearly empty space which is the stage where a picture, a sound, a color sneaks in and tells me a certain kind of story. I feel that language is a veil hiding demons and angels which the characters are always out of touch with. Their quest in the play is the same as ours in life—to find those forces, to meet them face to face and end the mystery. I'm pulled toward images that shine in the middle of junk. Like cracked headlights shining on a deer's eyes. I've been influenced by Jackson Pollock, Little Richard, Cajun fiddles, and the Southwest.

* * *

In spite of his prolific output—some 40 plays since the mid-1960s—Sam Shepard's invention never flags, and his achievements sometimes tower high. More than any contemporary American playwright, he has woven into his own dramatic idiom the strands of a youth culture thriving on drugs, rock music, astrology, science fiction, old movies, detective stories, cowboy films, and races involving cars, horses, and dogs. He has also come to strive for mythic dimensions in family plays.

Growing up in southern California, Shepard fell into playwriting almost by accident when he went to New York City: "The world I was living in was the most interesting thing to me, and I thought the best thing I could do maybe would be to write about it, so I started writing plays." Since the time was the 1960s and the place was the Lower East Side, Shepard's short plays were produced off-off-Broadway. Today he finds it difficult to remember these early efforts, which tend to focus on a single event, the characters often talking past one another or breaking into long monologues. However puzzling the action, these plays already ring out with Shepard's deft rhythms.

Within three years of these first efforts, in 1966, the 23-year old Shepard produced his first full-length play, *La Turista,* punning on the Spanish word for tourist and the diarrhea that often attacks Americans traveling to Mexico. Perhaps influenced by Beckett's *Waiting for Godot, La Turista* is composed of two acts in which the second virtually repeats the first. Questionable identities and mythic roles are at once more blatant and more realistic than in Beckett, however. In both acts Kent is sick, and his wife Salem—both named for cigarette brands—sends for a doctor who, more or less aided by his son, essays a cure. But the first act is set in a Mexican hotel room and the illness is *la turista,* whereas the second act is set in an American hotel room and the illness is sleeping sickness. Playing through film stereotypes, Kent breaks out of the theater and perhaps out of illness as well.

Other plays followed swiftly, with a number published in 1971 in two volumes aptly named for the first and longest play in each book. In the six plays of *The Unseen Hand* almost all of the main characters are threatened by unseen hands. Two plays of *Mad Dog Blues* camp the popular arts they affectionately embrace. In the title play two friends, Kosmo, a rock star, and Yahoudi, a drug dealer, separate to seek their respective fortunes. Kosmo takes up with Mae West and Yohoudi with Marlene Dietrich. Each pair becomes a triangle when Kosmo annexes Waco, Texas, and Yahoudi Captain Kidd, for whose treasure they all hunt. Tumbling from adventure to adventure, Yahoudi shoots Captain Kidd, Marlene goes off with Paul Bunyan, and Kosmo and Mae find the treasure, but Jesse James makes off with the treasure and Mae West. Finally Mae suggests that they all go to the Missouri home of Jesse James, and the play ends in festive song and dance.

A longer play from 1970 also ends in comic celebration. The punning title *Operation Sidewinder* refers to an American army computer in the shape of a sidewinder rattlesnake. By the play's end, however, it becomes an actual snake and Hopi Indian religious symbol through whose symbiotic power a disoriented young couple is integrated into an organic society, even as in New Comedy. To attain this, the pair has to avoid a revolutionary conspiracy, a military backlash, several corpses, and their own highly verbal confusion.

It is generally agreed that *The Tooth of Crime* is Shepard's most impressive play. He has commented, "It started with language—it started with hearing a certain sound which is coming from the voice of this character, Hoss." The play's strength remains its language, a synthesis of the slangs of rock, crime, astrology, and sports. Hoss has played by the code and moved by the charts, but he senses that he is doomed. The doom gradually takes the shape and name of Crow, a gypsy killer. Alerted by Eyes, warned by the charts of Galactic Jack, doped by his doctor, comforted by his moll, Hoss prepares for his fate: "Stuck in my image." In the second act Hoss and Crow, the has-been and would-be, duel with words and music—"Choose an argot"—as Referee keeps score. In the third round the Referee calls a TKO, and Hoss kills him. Unable to bend to Crow's wild ways, Hoss prefers to die in the manner of classical heroes but in contemporary idiom: "A true gesture that won't never cheat on itself 'cause it's the last of its kind."

Ironically, this American tragedy was written when Shepard was living in London, where his *Geography of a Horse Dreamer* sprang from English dog racing. On home ground in California, Shepard wrote *Action,* about two passive American couples, *Killer's Head,* about a cowboy in the electric chair, *Angel City,* about horror and horror movies in Hollywood, and *Suicide in B Flat,* about pressures leading to artistic suicide. These plays are at once newly inventive and stylistically consistent in their non-realistic images, unpredictable characters, and rich language grounded in colloquialism and soaring to manic monologue. Shepard's most mercurial achievement in pure monologue is the two pieces created for the actor Joseph Chaikin—*Tongues and Savage/Love*.

While becoming more involved in his career as a film actor, Shepard has written what he himself calls a "family trilogy," although there is no carryover of characters in *Curse of the Starving Class, Buried Child,* and *True West.* In these plays Shepard follows Eugene O'Neill in dramatizing a tragic America mired in sin. In *Curse* the sin is betrayal of the land to soulless speculators. In *Buried Child* it is incest, cruelty, and murder that stifle freedom and creativity in the young. In its opposition of two brothers with divergent lives and attitudes toward the West, *True West* is at once funnier on its surface and more focused.

The love/hate relationship within a pair carries over from *True West* to *Fool for Love,* but the pair are now half siblings and whole lovers. May and Eddie are alternately ecstatic and sadistic in one another's presence in a tawdry motel room, while their father observes them from an offstage vantage. When, at the play's end, the motel room goes up in flames, it is not only the end of their inconclusive incest but also of Shepard's own subjection to conventional playmaking, with exposition, plot, and resolution. Shepard punctuated this stage of his career by acting the part of Eddie in the movie version, where, unfortunately, flashbacks were shown.

A Lie of the Mind divides the stage among a rootless and a rooted family, a violent representative of the old West, and a family where the victimized women exude tenderness. Shepard implies that America must look forward with a gentleness that belies its violent past. More boldly, Shepard denounces the violence of war in *States of Shock.* A nameless American colonel wheels a wounded young veteran, Stubbs, who may prove to be his son, into a family restaurant. As conflict escalates between the bellicose colonel and the injured Stubbs, a white man and woman think only of their own appetites, but the black waitress finally heals Stubbs. Percussion and projections cause the action to resonate far beyond the confines of a family restaurant.

Shepard has absorbed American pop art, media myths, and the southwestern scene to recycle them in many—perhaps too many—image-focused plays in which the characters speak inventive idioms in vivid rhythms. But at his best—*La Turista, Mad Dog Blues, The Tooth of Crime, A Lie of the Mind*—Shepard achieves his own distinctive coherence through beautifully bridled fantasy.

—Ruby Cohn

SHERMAN, Martin

Nationality: American. **Born:** Philadelphia, Pennsylvania, 22 December 1938. **Education:** Boston University, 1956-60, B.F.A. 1960. **Career:** Playwright-in-residence, Playwrights Horizons, New York, 1976-77. **Awards:** Wurlitzer Foundation grant, 1973; National Endowment for the Arts fellowship, 1980; Dramatists Guild Hull-Warriner award, 1980; Rockefeller fellowship, 1985. **Agent:** Casarotto Ramsay Ltd., National House, 60-66 Wardour Street, London W1V 3HP, England. **Address:** 35 Leinster Square, London W.2, England.

Publications

Plays

A Solitary Thing, music by Stanley Silverman (produced Oakland, California, 1963).

Fat Tuesday (produced New York, 1966).

Next Year in Jerusalem (produced New York, 1968).

The Night Before Paris (produced New York, 1969; Edinburgh, 1970).

Things Went Badly in Westphalia (produced Storrs, Connecticut, 1971). Published in *The Best Short Plays 1970*, edited by Stanley Richards, Philadelphia, Chilton, 1970.

Passing By (produced New York, 1974; London, 1975). Published in *Gay Plays 1*, edited by Michael Wilcox, London, Methuen, 1984.

Soaps (produced New York, 1975).

Cracks (produced Waterford, Connecticut, 1975; New York, 1976; Oldham, Lancashire, 1981; London, 1982). Published in *Gay Plays 2*, edited by Michael Wilcox, London, Methuen, 1986.

Rio Grande (produced New York, 1976).

Blackout (produced New York, 1978).

Bent (produced Waterford, Connecticut, 1978; London and New York, 1979). Ashover, Derbyshire, Amber Lane, 1979; New York, Avon, 1980.

Messiah (produced London, 1982; New York, 1984). Oxford, Amber Lane, 1982.

When She Danced (produced Guildford, Surrey, 1985; London, 1988; New York, 1990). Oxford, Amber Lane, 1988.

A Madhouse in Goa (includes *A Table for a King* and *Keeps Rainin' All the Time*) (produced London, 1989; New York, 1997). Oxford, Amber Lane, 1989.

Some Sunny Day (produced London, 1996). Oxford, Amber Lane, 1996.

Screenplays: *The Clothes in the Wardrobe*, adaptation of Alice Thomas Ellis's *The Summerhouse Trilogy*, 1993; *Alive and Kicking,* 1997; *Bent,* 1997.

*

Critical Studies: "Images of the Gay Male in Contemporary Drama" by James W. Carlsen, in *Gayspeak: Gay Male and Lesbian Communication,* edited by James W. Chesebro, New York, Pilgrim, 1981; "Inventing History: Toward a Gay Holocaust Literature" by Kai Hammermeister, in *The German Quarterly* (Cherry Hill, New Jersey), Winter 1997, pp. 18-26.

Theatrical Activities:
Director: **Play**—*Point Blank* by Alan Pope and Alex Harding, London, 1980.

* * *

Although Martin Sherman is an American playwright born and bred, his parentage is Russian, and he displays a European consciousness as well as an unusual sensitivity to the music of language. Small wonder he prefers historical periods, including the early twentieth century, to the present day and European settings to American. Although *Bent* and *Passing By* focus on male-identified men, in the leading roles of *Rio Grande, Messiah, When She Danced,* and *A Madhouse in Goa* Sherman has created remarkably complex and individualized portraits of women. He brings a keen intellect to bear on his materials, yet crafts plays that, far from being aridly cerebral, are palpably permeated with the deepest feeling. Generalizations about his work, however, are dangerous, for he does not repeat himself. Equally at home with comedy and drama, Sherman works in styles as diverse as his subjects, and his eccentric characters populate works of often audacious originality.

Sherman's volatile and varied subjects include a satire of soap operas (*Soaps*); a dying woman who, when visited by an alien from another planet, is tempted to go off with him in his spaceship (*Rio Grande*); a charming light comedy about two gay men who develop hepatitis shortly after meeting and care for each other (*Passing By*); and a hippie whodunit so crazed that the killer's identity is never revealed (*Cracks*). This madcap comedy of death, described by a British critic as "Agatha Christie on acid," is a counterculture *Ten Little Indians*, but it is also a satire of narcissism that Joe Orton might have written had he spent the 1960s in California.

The characters in these and other Sherman plays are outsiders because they are gay or Jewish or foreign or female or strangers in a strange land. In *Messiah* seeing the Cossacks torture her husband to death has rendered Rebecca mute, while in *A Madhouse in Goa* aphasiac Daniel's language is as dislocated as this gay genius—an "other"—is from his world. Seven languages are spoken in *When She Danced* since nearly everyone in the play is an expatriate from another country. The men in *Bent* represent exiles within their own country, because of their differences thrown into a concentration camp to die.

Although this literal and metaphorical alienation devastates spectators, Sherman's survival kit, above all, contains humor. In *Messiah* his Rachel, a skeptical yet compassionate figure who seems to embody the author's spirit more than any of Sherman's other creations, endures because she is blessed with an ironic sensibility that perceives God's exquisite humor and turns even her denial of God's existence into a scream directed at the deity.

This dark, personal, and painful play set in seventeenth-century Poland and Turkey concerns not the title character, who never appears, but a clever yet homely woman whose life the news of the "false Messiah" Sabbatai Sevi profoundly alters. From a claustrophobic village to a barren foreign shore, Rachel and what family remains after her husband dies in a literal leap of faith journey in search of salvation. In liberation from dogma and sexual repression and in self-reliance, however, fear and doubt accompany the removal of boundaries. Such exiles must do without both restrictions and security equally. Rich in eroticism, brooding mysticism, and earthy humor, *Messiah* dramatizes a courageous, autonomous woman, a resilient and female Job who experiences metaphysical conflicts often reserved for male heroes. In her soul, as well as in the play as a whole, doubt, superstition, and disillusionment war against buoyant spirits, wit, kindness, and faith in God, in the future, and in the self.

Whereas religion opposes sexuality in *Messiah,* in *Bent* the source of oppression is government. A play that has changed the popular perception of Holocaust victims as solely Jewish, *Bent* has been staged in countries worldwide. Its initial urbane comedy quickly moves into a nightmare about men whom the Nazis required to wear not yellow stars but pink triangles. Forced into complicity in his lover's murder, Max also denies his homosexuality and, in order to survive, proves that he is not "bent" by having sex with the corpse of a 13-year-old girl. Yet Max moves beyond betrayal and self-contempt. In the dehumanizing circumstances of Dachau his humanity emerges as he affirms the possibility of love and self-sacrifice, embraces his gay identity, and defies those who imprison his soul. In the play's most amazing scene Max even makes love to another prisoner without their ever making physical contact.

When She Danced finds affirmation not through intense suffering but in comedy of wit. This day in the life of Isadora Duncan takes its tone from the 1940s films of Preston Sturges, the writer and director who grew up around the Duncan household. A touching and amusing valentine to genius, the comedy finds the 46-year-old improvident, charismatic dancer living in Paris with her young husband Sergei, with whom she shares no common tongue. Much of the humor derives from the troubles the characters have in trying to communicate in the seven languages they speak and from the arrival of a translator. Isadora's instincts that language is highly overrated—"We never had it in America"—prove prophetic as the attempts to communicate promote discord and chaos as well as hilarious misunderstandings.

Like *Bent, A Madhouse in Goa* moves from wit to poignance. Of course, neither of its two parts takes place in Goa. The brittle, mannered comedy of *A Table for a King* unfolds at a Corfu resort in the 1960s, while the stormy weather of *Keeps Rainin' All the Time* occurs on Santorini "one year from now," after nuclear accidents have altered world weather patterns so drastically that rain continually drenches the Greek isles. The former's narrator is a gay, Jewish, socially awkward young American whose insecurities are assailed by a garrulous southern matron who mocks and mothers him and whose loneliness is momentarily assuaged by the clever Greek waiter who seduces him.

This fellow's wallowing in melancholy seems only minor self-indulgence when contrasted to a second assortment of self-pitying people wrapped up in their own needs but none too adept at satisfying them. Only gradually does a spectator appreciate that among this self-absorbed crew is the same American, this time in his 40s. Not exactly the same man, however, for it appears that Daniel is the author of the first part, which dramatizes not the real events of 20 years before but rather a fictionalization that conveniently omits the painful truths that would have reduced his novel's commercial appeal. This sellout, however, is minor compared to plans for a musical film version of *A Table for a King* presented by a born-again Hollywood producer, who may be the most mercilessly satirized Sherman creation. The self-preoccupied Daniel's stroke-induced aphasia prevents his communicating with the others surrounding him—his male nurse, his dying friend Heather, her hacker son, the producer's girlfriend. Thus, when Heather's fears of religious extremists, carcinogenic food, AIDS, and getting nuked require reassurance, Daniel intones "Apple sauce."

The despair underlying Sherman's humor and the imaginative situation and plotting recall David Mercer, particularly his *Duck Song*. Underneath the jokes lurks anguish for a doomed world, a perception that prompted the comical woman of part 1 to commit herself to the titular Indian asylum. Sherman smashes his other characters' lives, leaving Daniel no audience for his incomprehensible and bitter wit. Unlike the Sherman plays that have dramatized survival, *A Madhouse in Goa*—like Beckett's *Endgame*—distills dread for the very future of humanity.

—Tish Dace

SHERMAN, Stuart

Nationality: American. **Born:** 9 November 1945. **Career:** Has worked at the Kitchen and the Performing Garage, New York. **Awards:** National Endowment for the Arts fellowship; Creative Artists Public Service grant; New York State Council on the Arts grant; Northwest Area Foundation grant; Massachusetts Council for the Arts and Humanities grant; Art Matters grant; MacDowell Colony residency; Asian Cultural Council travel grant; prix de Rome, 1991. **Address:** 166 West 22nd Street, 6A, New York 10011, U.S.A.

Publications

Plays

Spectacles (produced New York, Amsterdam, Paris, Frankfurt, Hamburg, Sydney, and Tokyo, 1975-90).
The Classical Trilogy: Hamlet, Oedipus, Faust.
Hamlet (produced Amsterdam, 1981; New York, 1982).
Faust (produced Frankfurt, 1982).
Oedipus (produced Minneapolis, 1984).
The Second Trilogy: Chekhov, Strindberg, Brecht (produced New York, 1986).
Chekhov (produced Cambridge, Massachusetts and New York, 1985).
Brecht (produced Frankfurt, 1985; New York, 1986).
Strindberg (produced Melbourne, Australia, 1986; New York, 1986).
The Man in Room 2538 (produced New York, 1986).
It is Against the Law to Shout "Fire!" in a Crowded Theater: or, "Fire! Fire!" (produced New York, 1986).
This House Is Mine Because I Live in It (produced New York, 1986).
Endless Meadows, and So Forth (produced New York, 1986).
Chattanooga Choo-Choo (Für Elise) (produced New York, 1987).
An Evening of One-Act Plays (produced New York, 1987).
Slant (produced Amherst, Massachusetts, 1987).
Crime and Punishment; or, The Book and the Window (produced New York, 1987).
"A" is for "Actor" (produced New York, 1987).
The Yellow Chair (produced New York, 1987).
One Acts and Two Trilogies. Imperial Beach, California, Video Research Institute Theater Library, Contemporary Scripts, Series 1, No.10, 1987.
But What Is the Word for "Bicycle"? (produced New York, 1988). As *Aber wie heisst das Wort für "Fahrrad"?*, Cologne, Kölner Ensemble Publication, 1990.
In a Handbag; or, Oscar's Wilde: or, The Importance of Being More or Less Earnest (produced New York, 1988).
Objects of Desire (produced New York, 1989).
The Play of Tea; or, Pinkies Up! (produced New York, 1989).
Knock, Knock, Knock, Knock (produced New York, 1989).
Taal Eulenspiegel (produced Ghent, Belgium, 1990).
Solaris, adaptation of the novel by Stanislaw Lem (produced Aachen, Germany, 1992). Cologne, Kölner Ensemble Publication, 1992.

*

Theatrical Activities:
Plays—Acted in and directed all his own plays.

* * *

It is difficult to write about Stuart Sherman's theater, for his work is often complex. Yet at moments the complexity speaks to something quite simple.

Sherman's work is generally described as performance art, under which rubric might be grouped works as diverse as Charlotte Moorman's naked cello recitals, the Spalding Gray meditative monologues about wonders and miseries recalled in tranquillity, and George Jessel's telephone calls to his mother. One of the elements in Sherman's work that assures the categorizers that he is doing performance art is its nonlinear, nonsequential narrative, but sometimes his plots are sequential and his plays nonnarrative. Another element is Sherman's use of the presentational, the mode indicating that the players, even when they do not speak directly to the audiences, are always aware of them. Heightening the presentational mode is an absence of psychological depth, whereby the player often takes on an allegorical persona, for example, good dental hygiene, or becomes a metaphor for urban anxiety. We thus understand that the player is presenting rather than being, and even as it distances us from emotional catharsis, it permits us to collaborate in the understanding that presumably we, performer and spectator, are all thinking together. What we are all thinking about is not always clear.

In the early 1970s Sherman would set up a small card table on West Broadway in the heart of Soho in New York City. It was always at some daytime hour. A handful of pedestrians might wander by and a few stop out of curiosity, allowing themselves to be amused or not, and then move on. No one was threatened by the man who stood behind the card table. If the work was not always accessible, it was modest enough not to challenge whatever agenda people might be developing for themselves. In fact, there was something almost incorrigibly domestic, and therefore incorrigibly reassuring, about these ostensibly sober and brief cartoonlike romps. The very card table looked as if it had been lifted out of his mother's kitchen, and the objects used by Sherman might have come out of that same kitchen—for example, a homely set of salt and pepper shakers or some plastic cups and saucers. The whole arsenal of props suggested banal domesticity, since before the street audience there floated unthreatening plastic, dime store paper, cellophane, kitchen variety glass, bits of linoleum, and the inevitable Formica. The Sherman work might speak of magical or homely events that could befall any reasonable middle-class urban type, or there might be an abstract portrait of some local celebrity from the downtown art scene. There was something particularly engaging and refreshing about the modesty of means, about the self-effacement of the performer who plied his art with the homeliest of weapons in full daylight, open to the scrutiny of whoever might be passing. Granted that the street chosen was fast becoming a major thoroughfare for downtown gallery hoppers, there was still a beguiling innocence about the herky-jerky, open-faced Sherman performance and its rickety card table technology.

Sherman had already been performing indoors, but within a year or two he shifted to more sophisticated sites like the Kitchen and the Performing Garage. His work began to embrace the more complex technology of lights, projections, and other staples from the arena of mixed media. And now it was customary to see other performers working in tandem with Sherman. What these performers very often had in common was a seeming ability to convey that not only were they not acting but that they had not the first clue as to how one might create a character onstage. In a very real sense one was still in the kitchen of Stuart's mother, and the performers had decided to dress up in "acting clothes" and do something that somebody said was "acting." It is not that one or more of them might not have had considerable training in performance, but rather that what seemed to be required for Sherman's material, which still dealt with abstract portraits and nonlinear narratives, was a kind of somnambulant persona that acted as cipher rather than character. So the acting, it seemed, needed to conform to the comforting artifice of gracelessness, to material that was graceless but at the same time particularly heartfelt.

In 1986 Sherman premiered *The Man in Room 2538,* a two-character play set in a bar-restaurant atop a hotel in Tokyo. The customer, played by Sherman, is waiting at the bar; he wants to eat his dinner at a window seat, but all such seats are occupied. While he waits, he and the bartender carry on a low-key philosophical discourse. The customer, who dines here every night on "the usual," steak teriyaki and Kirin beer, recounts how he took the elevator to the 25th floor and stood outside room 2538:

> I don't see, inside the room, a man sitting by the window, looking out, holding a book on his lap. I don't see this. I don't see the color of the walls, which are slightly blue. I don't feel the fit of the man's shoes. . . . I don't see, feel, or hear any of these things.

Later the customer sees himself "more and more clearly, sitting by a window . . . and I order something to eat and something to drink. . . ." The customer is either recounting last night's usual or tonight's usual, which will materialize when a window seat becomes vacant. What seems to connect what he does not see inside room 2538 with what he does see in the bar-restaurant are 2,538 dots of light, precisely 2,538 dots joined to make the seen and the unseen. The bartender, a rationalist, is slowly drawn into the customer's mathematical fixation.

The narrative here is linear, but what gives the play its substance is not simply the apparent content, the intellectual, discursive byplay, but also the exterior of the byplay, the hallucinatory manner within which the byplay carries on its life. The content and its exterior manner are both shaped in the spirit of the mathematical logic of Kurt Godel and the hallucinatory loop drawings of M. C. Escher, in which phenomena come together in an endless mirrorlike reality. It seems that Sherman has come into his own in this work. He has tried to see into things, and many of his works, which he sometimes calls "spectacles" or "portraits," have to do with this attempt at seeing. Perhaps that is why representational acting is not appropriate. If one were to accept the premise that representation is the grossest of lies, then there is a particular value in devising the obvious artifice of structures wherein performers perform separate events side by side and over and over, sometimes with variations and sometimes with ritual-like actions, none especially convincing except that we are convinced that someone is performing them.

Sherman's *Classical Trilogy,* comprising *Hamlet, Faust,* and *Oedipus,* and his *Second Trilogy,* comprising *Chekhov, Brecht,* and *Strindberg,* combine ritual abstractions with readings of fragments from various plays, and they seem to be an attempt to "play" these plays in the manner children might play them at home. The trilogies could be regarded as analogs, abstractions of the plays, but the obviousness of the playing suggests that this is Sherman's way of making the plays his own, of finding a new reality, of seeing that he is seeing, as if once again he were making a play in the Sherman kitchen of days gone by.

—Arthur Sainer

SIMON, Barney

Nationality: South African. **Born:** Johannesburg, 13 April 1933. **Education:** Fairview Junior School, Jeppe Preparatory School, and Jeppe Boys High, all Johannesburg. **Career:** Copywriter, E. Lindsay Smithers, 1958-62, copy chief, J. Walter Thompson, 1962-66, editor, *The Classic Magazine*, 1964-71, founder-director, Phoenix Players, 1965-68, and creative director, Central Advertising, 1966-68, all Johannesburg; associate editor, *New American Review*, New York, 1969-70; founder-director, Mirror 1, 1970-72; founder, with Mannie Manim, and director, The Company, 1973-76. Beginning 1976 founder, with Mannie Manim, and artistic director, The Market Theatre and, beginning 1990, The Market Theatre Laboratory, both Johannesburg. Chair of Celebration, Derry, 1992. **Awards:** Ford Foundation grant, 1970; Edinburgh Festival Fringe award, 1982, 1987; Los Angeles Critics award, 1982; Bay Area award, 1983; *City Limits* award, 1984; Obie award, 1984, 1986; Vita award, 1985, 1991, 1992; Rockefeller grant, 1989, 1992. **Agent:** Patricia MacNaughton, MacNaughton Lowe Representation, 200 Fulham Road, London SW10 9PN, England. **Address:** c/o The Market Theatre, P.O. Box 8656, Johannesburg 2000, South Africa.

Publications

Plays

Phiri, with others (produced Johannesburg, 1972).
Hey Listen (produced Johannesburg, 1973).

Six Characters in Search of an Author, adaptation of a play by Pirandello (produced Johannesburg, 1973).
People, with others (produced Johannesburg, 1973).
People Too, with others (produced Johannesburg, 1974).
Joburg, Sis! (includes *Men Should Cry More Often, Miss South Africa, I Live in a Building, Cape Town Is Fantastic, Our War*) (also director: produced Johannesburg, 1974). Johannesburg, Bataleur Press, 1974.
Storytime, with others (includes *The Yellow Star*) (also director: produced Johannesburg, 1975). *The Yellow Star* published Johannesburg, Quarry, 1976.
Medea, adaptation of a play by Franz Grillparzer (also director: produced Cape Town, 1978; Edinburgh, 1983; London, 1983).
Cincinatti, with others (produced Johannesburg, 1979). Johannesburg, Haum Educational, 1984.
Call Me Woman, with others (produced Johannesburg, 1980).
Cold Stone Jug, adaptation of the play by Stephen Gray (also director: produced Cape Town, 1980). Cape Town, Human and Rousseau, 1982.
Marico Moonshine and Manpower, with others (produced Johannesburg, 1981).
Woza Albert!, with Mbongeni Ngema and Percy Mtwa (also director: produced Johannesburg, 1981; Edinburgh, London, and Los Angeles, 1982; New York, 1984). London, Methuen, 1983; in *Woza Afrika! An Anthology of South African Plays*, edited by Duma Ndlovu, New York, Braziller, 1986.
Black Dog-Inj Mayama, with others (also director: produced Johannesburg, Edinburgh, and London, 1984).
Born in the R.S.A., with others (also director: produced Johannesburg, 1985; New York, Edinburgh, and London, 1986). In *Woza Afrika! An Anthology of South African Plays*, edited by Duma Ndlovu, New York, Braziller, 1986; as *Born in the R.S.A.: Four Workshopped Plays*, Johannesburg, Witwatersrand University Press, 1997.
Outers, with others (produced Johannesburg, 1985).
The Dybbuk, adaptation of the play by S. Ansky (produced Johannesburg, 1986).
Klaaglied vir Kous (produced Johannesburg, 1986).
Written by Hand, with others (produced Boston, Massachusetts, 1987).
Score Me with Ages, with others (produced Johannesburg, 1989).
Eden and Other Places, with others (produced Johannesburg, 1989).
Inyanga—About Women in Africa, with others (produced Johannesburg, 1989).
Singing the Times, with others (produced Johannesburg, 1992).

Television Plays: *Six Feet of the Country*, 1982; *Good Climate, Friendly Inhabitants*, 1982; *City Lovers*, 1982; *Born in the R.S.A.*, 1986; *Woza Albert!*, 1987.

Other

Familiarity Is the Kingdom of the Lost, by Dugmore Boetie. London, Cresset Press, 1969; New York, Dutton, 1970.

*

Critical Study: *The Best of Company: The Story of Johannesburg's Market Theatre* by Pat Schwartz, Johannesburg, Ad Donker, 1988; *Athol Fugard and Barney Simon: Bare Stage, a Few Props, Great Theatre* by Mary Benson, Randburg, Ravan Press, 1997.

Theatrical Activities:
Directed, adapted, and workshopped many plays.

Barney Simon comments:

Because of my opposition to the segregation of audiences and players in apartheid South Africa, I never considered a professional career in South African theatre. From 1954 to 1958 I lived in London. For a short period, around 1957, I worked backstage for Joan Littlewood's Theatre Workshop. This was a definitive influence on my understanding of the horizons and freedoms of theatre and its role in the life of a community.

When I returned to South Africa I met Athol Fugard, then struggling to make theatre in the black townships. Our communication was immediate and electric. In 1961 Fugard was employed to run a workshop theatre at the African Music and Drama Association at Dorkay House, Johannesburg. His first production was *The Blood Knot* which he had just written. He was directing and performing in the play. He invited me to participate as "third eye." This was the beginning of a long and committed association. When he moved to Port Elizabeth I continued to work at Dorkay House with a multi-racial group. I earned my living as an advertising copywriter.

In the mid-sixties, because of political pressures we were forced to leave Dorkay House and I founded Phoenix Players (in a condemned mansion) which performed to invited, free audiences which rendered multi-racial theatre legal. You could have blacks as guests as long as you didn't serve liquor.

Between 1968 and 1970, I lived and worked in America as a director, writer, and editor. Upon my return to South Africa I founded a company called Mirror 1—"a reflecting surface in which we might find an image of ourselves." We performed plays relevant to our situation on campuses, in backyards and lounges. Concurrently I began to work in mission hospitals in the Transkei and Zululand, working with black nurses in the creation of songs to traditional melodies and plays through which they communicated with traditional, largely illiterate communities. The work extended to urban communities and squatter camps. We once played in a backyard next door to a man under house arrest so that he could watch over his fence. The procedure with the nurses was to begin with awareness exercises and gossip, followed by incognito field-trips into their villages where they "spied" on their potential subjects and audiences and considered their lives. Subsequently I used the same procedure with professional actors in Johannesburg, and in this way many Market Theatre pieces were created. There is an Ehassidic saying "God created man because He loves to listen to stories." I believe that actors and audiences are made in His image. My procedure is (without knowledge of him) similar to Mike Leigh's, except that the majority of my "made" plays were made within a normal four-week period. I slept with my lights on and a pen clutched in my hand. At present I am negotiating to have a decade of this work published.

* * *

Barney Simon is known for his work as a theater director, but essentially he has been "happiest creating plays, including musicals, through workshops with actors." The genesis of Simon's interest in improvised theater may be traced to his having worked with Joan Littlewood in the 1950s and with Athol Fugard, the South African playwright and director who has done similar work, notably with Winston Ntshona and John Kani, to produce the highly successful and internationally acclaimed *Sizwe Bansi Is Dead* and *The Islands*. Simon worked with Fugard in the first production of the latter's *The Blood Knot* in 1961.

Simon is credited with a number of plays, most of which have emerged from workshops and improvisations with the members of the multiracial Market Theatre in Johannesburg. Among his written plays are *Phiri* (described as a black musical version of *Volpone*) *Cold Stone Jug, Joburg, Sis!,* and *Miss South Africa*. His works collectively devised with actors include *People, Storytime, Call Me Woman, Cincinatti* [sic], *Woza Albert!,* and *Born in the R.S.A.* The last two are the best known of his workshop creations.

Woza Albert! and *Born in the R.S.A.* represent a tradition of theater and performance much influenced by the philosophy and experiments of the Polish director Jerzy Grotowski. This style of playmaking and performance, known as "poor theater," has become a hallmark of much contemporary political theater of South Africa from Fugard onward. Usually such plays are collectively devised and are process rather than product oriented, and they often employ nonnaturalistic styles of performance to inform while entertaining their readers and audiences. The characters in the plays are very often drawn from the suppressed communities of South African apartheid society. *Woza Albert!* and *Born in the R.S.A.* also represent the dream of crossing the racial barriers to bring much needed peace to South Africa's segregated and intensely troubled sociocultural milieu.

Woza Albert!, which first brought Simon and Mbongeni Ngema and Percy Mtwa, his two black actors/collaborators, into the international limelight, has been described as "an act of affirmation," for it testifies to the ability of the human spirit and imagination to rise creatively above the soul-deadening repression of an inhuman social system. The characters/actors in this play of racial agony manage to wrest hope from the pits of despair, and it is this they offer to the audience. It is a play that offers laughter through a torrent of tears.

In theatrical terms the play is simple. Two black actors come upon an empty stage/space and with minimal props begin to present to the audience poignant and hilarious images of South African urban life. The stage becomes filled with villains, heroes, and clowns, clearly understating the sheer will and defiance that makes survival possible in an inhuman environment. What amazes most in this theater of "poor means" is the enormous amount of histrionic ability required of the actors in order to actualize for the audience the gripping reality of this drama of racial and communal anguish. Over an exhilarating period of two hours, the two actors range freely and effortlessly through a wide spectrum of characters and situations that reflect the gory details of life for blacks under apartheid. The play's strength lies in its simple details, which challenge and force the audience to become cocreators with the performers of the mise-en-scène.

Born in the R.S.A., while in the mold of the earlier play, is more of a docudrama. The seven actors/characters actually play themselves and only occasionally assume other personae. The play employs the traditional storytelling style of collective narration, with all of the actors/characters talking about themselves in relay mode, but while they are doing this, they are actually talking about one another and about South Africa. The work is structurally complex, with each personal story maintaining a linear continuity that is often broken by other stories. Yet all create a uniquely clear and unbroken narrative. A viewer can pick a character/actor and follow his or her narration, but each acquires a broader perspective and a deeper significance when seen in the context of the whole that is the human anguish and tension of the South African situation.

This new direction in Simon's work and the fact that the Market Theatre, which he founded with Mannie Manim, was for a long time South Africa's only integrated theater, clearly show him to be an artist who is politically committed and who believes in utilizing the resources of the theater medium to examine the human condition and dilemma in a racially repressive and inhuman environment. In an interview Simon aptly stated the philosophy behind his work in the theater, which is to "present plays that are relevant to our lives, that open hearts and minds," and he does this through helping his actors to "create personal texts" from their South African landscape. In doing so, he seems to have moved away from the mere directing and adapting of *Phiri* to genuinely creating plays of the moment that fuse the traditional elements of his South African culture while using and extending the techniques of poor theater, as illustrated by the work he and his collaborators have done in *Woza Albert!* and *Born in the R.S.A.*

—Osita Okagbue

SIMON, (Marvin) Neil

Nationality: American. **Born:** The Bronx, New York, 4 July 1927. **Education:** De Witt Clinton High School, New York, graduated 1943; New York University, 1944-45; University of Denver, 1945-46. **Military Service:** Served in the United States Army Air Force, 1945-46: corporal. **Family:** Married 1) Joan Baim in 1953 (died 1973), two daughters; 2) the actress Marsha Mason in 1973 (divorced 1983); 3) Diane Lander in 1987. **Career:** Radio and television writer, 1948-60. **Awards:** Emmy award, for television writing, 1957, 1959; Tony award, 1965, 1970, 1985, 1991; London *Evening Standard* award, 1967; Shubert award, 1968; Writers Guild of America West award, for screenplay, 1969, 1971, 1976; PEN Los Angeles Center award, 1982; New York Drama Critics Circle award, 1983; Outer Circle award, 1983, 1985; New York State Governor's award, 1986; Pulitzer prize, 1991; Peggy V. Helmerich Distinguished Author award, 1996. L.H.D.: Hofstra University, Hempstead, New York, 1981; Williams College, Williamstown, Massachusetts, 1984. **Address:** c/o G. DaSilva, 10100 Santa Monica Boulevard, No. 400, Los Angeles, California 90067, U.S.A.

Publications

Plays

Sketches (produced Tamiment, Pennsylvania, 1952, 1953).

Sketches, with Danny Simon, in *Catch a Star!* (produced New York, 1955).

Sketches, with Danny Simon, in *New Faces of 1956* (produced New York, 1956).

Adventures of Marco Polo: A Musical Fantasy, with William Friedberg, music by Clay Warnick and Mel Pahl. New York, French, 1959.

Heidi, with William Friedberg, music by Clay Warnick, adaptation of the novel by Johanna Spyri. New York, French, 1959.

Come Blow Your Horn (produced New Hope, Pennsylvania, 1960; New York, 1961; London, 1962). New York and London, French, 1961.

Little Me, music by Cy Coleman, lyrics by Carolyn Leigh, adaptation of the novel by Patrick Dennis (produced New York, 1962; London, 1964; revised version produced New York, 1982; London, 1983). Included in *Collected Plays 2*, 1979.

Barefoot in the Park (as *Nobody Loves Me*, produced New Hope, Pennsylvania, 1962; *as Barefoot in the Park*, produced New York, 1963; London, 1965). New York, Random House, 1964; London, French, 1966.

The Odd Couple (produced New York, 1965; London, 1966; revised [female] version produced New York, 1985). New York, Random House, 1966.

Sweet Charity, music by Cy Coleman, lyrics by Dorothy Fields, based on the screenplay *Nights of Cabiria* by Federico Fellini and others (produced New York, 1966; London, 1967). New York, Random House, 1966.

The Star-Spangled Girl (produced New York, 1966). New York, Random House, 1967.

Plaza Suite (includes *Visitor from Mamaroneck, Visitor from Hollywood, Visitor from Forest Hills*) (produced New York, 1968; London, 1969). New York, Random House, 1969.

Promises, Promises, music and lyrics by Burt Bacharach and Hal David, based on the screenplay *The Apartment* by Billy Wilder and I.A.L. Diamond (produced New York, 1968; London, 1969). New York, Random House, 1969.

Last of the Red Hot Lovers (produced New York, 1969; Manchester and London, 1979). New York, Random House, 1970.

The Gingerbread Lady (produced New York, 1970; Windsor and London, 1974). New York, Random House, 1971.

The Prisoner of Second Avenue (produced New York, 1971). New York, Random House, and London, French, 1972.

The Sunshine Boys (produced New York, 1972; London, 1975). New York, Random House, 1973.

The Comedy of Neil Simon (includes *Come Blow Your Horn*; *Barefoot in the Park*; *The Odd Couple*; *The Star-Spangled Girl*; *Plaza Suite*; *Promises, Promises*; *Last of the Red Hot Lovers*). New York, Random House, 1972.

The Good Doctor, music by Peter Link, lyrics by Simon, adaptation of stories by Chekhov (produced New York, 1973; Coventry, 1981; London, 1988). New York. Random House, 1974; London, French, 1975.

God's Favorite (produced New York, 1974). New York, Random House, 1975.

California Suite (includes *Visitor from New York, Visitor from Philadelphia, Visitor from London, Visitor from Chicago*) (produced Los Angeles. New York, and London, 1976). New York, Random House, 1977.

The Goodbye Girl (screenplay 1977) stage version, music by Marvin Hamlisch, lyrics by David Zippel (produced Chicago, 1992; New York, 1993).

Chapter Two (produced Los Angeles and New York, 1977; London, 1981). New York. Random House, and London, French, 1979.

They're Playing Our Song, music by Marvin Hamlisch, lyrics by Carol Bayer Sager (produced Los Angeles, 1978; New York, 1979; London, 1980). New York, Random House, 1980.

Collected Plays 2 (includes *The Sunshine Boys*, *Little Me*, *The Gingerbread Lady*, *The Prisoner of Second Avenue*, *The Good Doctor*, *God's Favorite*, *California Suite*, *Chapter Two*). New York, Random House, 1979.

I Ought to Be in Pictures (produced Los Angeles and New York, 1980; Perth, Scotland, 1983; London, 1986). New York, Random House, 1981.

Fools (produced New York, 1981). New York, Random House, 1982.

Brighton Beach Memoirs (produced Los Angeles, 1982; New York, 1983; London, 1986). New York, Random House, and London, French, 1984.

Actors and Actresses (produced Stamford, Connecticut, 1983).

Biloxi Blues (produced Los Angeles, 1984; New York, 1985). New York, Random House, 1986.

Broadway Bound (produced New York, 1986; London, 1991). New York, Random House, 1987.

Rumors (produced New York, 1988; revised version produced Chichester, West Sussex, 1990). New York, Random House, 1990.

Jake's Women (produced San Diego, 1990; revised version produced New York, 1992). New York, Random House, 1993.

Lost in Yonkers (produced New York, 1991; London, 1992). New York, Random House, 1991.

Collected Plays 3 (includes *Sweet Charity*; *They're Playing Our Song*; *I Ought to Be in Pictures*; *Fools*; *The Odd Couple* [female version]; *Brighton Beach Memoirs*; *Biloxi Blues*; *Broadway Bound*). New York, Random House, 1992.

Laughter on the 23rd Floor (produced New York, 1993).

London Suite: A Comedy (produced New York, 1993). New York, Samuel French, 1996.

Neil Simon Monologues. Rancho Mirage, California, Dramaline Publications, 1996.

Proposals (produced New York, 1997).

Collected Plays 4 (includes *Rumors*; *Lost in Yonkers*; *Jake's Women*; *Laughter on the 23rd Floor*; *London Suite*). New York, Touchstone, 1998.

Screenplays: *After the Fox*, with Cesare Zavattini, 1966; *Barefoot in the Park*, 1967; *The Odd Couple*, 1968; *The Out-of-Towners*, 1970; *Plaza Suite*, 1971; *The Heartbreak Kid*, 1972; *The Last of the Red Hot Lovers*, 1972; *The Prisoner of Second Avenue*, 1975; *The Sunshine Boys*, 1975; *Murder by Death*, 1976; *The Goodbye Girl*, 1977; *The Cheap Detective*, 1978; *California Suite*, 1978; *Chapter Two*, 1979; *Seems Like Old Times*, 1980; *Only When I Laugh*, 1982; *I Ought to Be in Pictures*, 1982; *Max Dugan Returns*, 1983; *The Lonely Guy*, with Ed Weinberger and Stan Daniels, 1984; *The Slugger's Wife*, 1985; *Brighton Beach Memoirs*, 1987; *Biloxi Blues*, 1988; *The Marrying Man*, 1991; *Lost in Yonkers*, 1993; *Jake's Women*, 1996.

Radio: scripts for *Robert Q. Lewis Show*.

Television: *Phil Silvers Show*, 1948; *Tallulah Bankhead Show*, 1951; *Your Show of Shows*, 1956; *Sid Caesar Show*, 1956-57; *Jerry Lewis Show*; *Jacky Gleason Show*; *Red Buttons Show*; *Sergeant Bilko* series, 1958-59; *Garry Moore Show*, 1959-60; *The Trouble with People*, 1972; *Happy Endings*, with others, 1975; *Broadway Bound*, 1992.

Other

Rewrites: A Memoir. New York, Touchstone, 1996.

*

Bibliography: *Ten Modern American Playwrights* by Kimball King, New York, Garland, 1982.

Manuscript Collection: Harvard University, Cambridge, Massachusetts.

Critical Studies: *Neil Simon* by Edythe M. McGovern, New York, Ungar, 1979; *Neil Simon* by Robert K. Johnson, Boston, Twayne, 1983; "Neil Simon" by Michael Woolf, in *American Drama,* edited by Clive Bloom, New York, St. Martin's, 1995; *Neil Simon's Laughter on the 23rd Floor* by John C. Carr, Washington D.C., Performance Plus Program, 1995; *Neil Simon: A Casebook,* edited by Gary Konas, New York, Garland, 1997.

* * *

In continuing times of turmoil and despair in the commercial theater, both in Britain and in the United States, it is encouraging to note that neither Neil Simon nor Alan Ayckbourn has been seriously deterred by dismissive or hostile criticism. Some 50 years ago, on both sides of the Atlantic, there were a number of playwrights who regularly produced new works for each new season, confidently expecting professional productions. Today writers' grants and play workshops proliferate as producers, directors, actors, critics, and even audiences wonder where the interesting new plays are to be found. At least in the commercial sector some already renowned playwrights find it difficult to get a Broadway or even an off-Broadway production. In the United States, Simon is almost alone as a successful dramatist who is expected to continue concocting comedies and musicals that audiences will enjoy.

Unlike Ayckbourn, who is able to develop and test his new works at Scarborough's Stephen Joseph Theatre before they are shown in the West End, Simon's scripts are customarily commercially mounted and tried out in Los Angeles and elsewhere in regional theaters before going to Broadway. In terms of royalties and other income from his varied ventures on stage, in films, and on television, it has been suggested that Simon may well be the most successful playwright who has ever lived. At various times he has had three and four productions running simultaneously on Broadway, not to mention touring ensembles, stock and amateur productions, and foreign stagings.

Simon's fortunes with many critics, however, have been rather different. Initially, with early domestic comedies such as *Come Blow Your Horn* and *Barefoot in the Park,* he was welcomed as a fresh new voice with a particular comic talent for pointing up the pangs and problems of urban family life. He was also fortunate in receiving slickly professional productions with impressive performers that brought his vision of contemporary middle-class angst to life. The fact that most new Simon scripts rapidly became long-running hits—significant commercial money spinners—helped attract even wider audiences. It is axiomatic that people would rather see hits than flops. Once in the theater, however, spectators were obviously amused by Simon's comic techniques, but they also clearly responded to characters and situations they could recognize. Laughter was aroused, as it still is in Simon's plays, not only by obvious comic devices and one-liners but also by the vagaries of characters and awkward situations with which many metropolitan spectators could identify.

It has been repeatedly pointed out by regional and foreign critics and by producers that the farther removed from New York a Simon production is the less easily audiences respond and empathize. Some explain this by suggesting that Simon's concerns are largely with urban and suburban New Yorkers, which, not striking any personal sparks of instant recognition, may well be of more limited interest to audiences elsewhere. A few of Simon's detractors, however, insist that his comedy is not only one of New York insularity but more specifically of materialistic, middle-class New York Jews, thus making it less immediately accessible to non-Jews beyond the Hudson or across the Atlantic. Whatever the merits of this argument, in the mid-1980s such Simon successes as his autobiographical *Brighton Beach Memoirs* and *Biloxi Blues* were produced by Britain's subsidized Royal National Theatre rather than by a West End commercial management.

While some object to what they perceive as a regional, cultural, economic, or even ethnic bias in Simon's choice of subject matter, others—notably critics rather than audiences—complain about what is often seen as the playwright's major fault—his obvious addiction to the one-liner that seems to elicit boisterous laughter regardless of the dramatic context in which it occurs. A cursory look at Simon's comedies and musical comedy books readily reveals this penchant for the quick, often sarcastic quip that, in fact, is more often to be heard in New York conversations than elsewhere in the United States. This is a distinctive element in Simon's comic writing, and its genesis can be traced to his early collaboration with his brother Danny when they were gag writers for such television series as the Phil Silvers and Sid Caesar shows, where the smart retort and the devastating comic put-down were major means of provoking laughter. The gift of making people laugh in the theater is to be prized, but this talent in Simon has been viewed by critics who concede his comedic talents as rather a curse than a dramatic strength.

Despite his commercial success and even such official recognition as the Pulitzer, Kennedy Center, Tony, Shubert, and *Evening Standard* awards, Simon has been sensitive to critical objections and reservations about his work. In conversation he is an informed, concerned, compassionate, serious human being, and a Simon interview is not a barrage of hilarious one-liners. To answer charges that his comedies are all artificial constructs, with characters that are manipulations of stereotypes in stock situations, he has repeatedly pointed out that from the first the most successful of his works have been firmly rooted in his personal experience or in that of close friends and family. That is certainly true of *Come Blow Your Horn* and *The Odd Couple.* As television collaborators, Simon has noted, his brother Danny was rumpled and disorganized, while Neil was always neat and tidy, out of which came the comic conflicts of sloppy Oscar and fussy Felix. *Barefoot in the Park* reprised the New York apartment experiences of the newlywed Simons.

Last of the Red Hot Lovers, which shows a series of amorous miscarriages on the part of a frustrated fish merchant with variously fixated women, was inspired by the so-called sexual revolution of the 1960s, when many middle-aged men and women feared that the new freedoms were passing them by. (Women in the Broadway audience would shout advice to James Coco, who played the forlorn would-be seducer: "Jimmy! She's not right for you!") Whatever demanding critics may say, popular audiences readily respond to Simon's view of people and life.

The Star-Spangled Girl is a construct, as Simon has admitted, acknowledging that it did not work as he had hoped it would. *Plaza Suite,* in which the identical suite in the famed New York hotel is the scene of three quite different but amusing encounters, may be viewed as a comic tour de force, but the situations are all based on reality. (In fact, Simon's film *The Out-of-Towners* is a dramatized expansion of an opening *Plaza Suite* monologue that was omitted on Broadway. It depicts various hilarious but believable misadventures that can befall unwary visitors to Manhattan.)

When Simon tried to show critics and the public that he was capable of dealing thoughtfully and dramatically with a serious subject, his effort, *The Gingerbread Lady,* was dismissed or disparaged as having been damaged by his recourse to the familiar device of the comic quip. The play was clearly inspired by the self-destructiveness of the much loved actress and singer Judy Garland. While Simon explored the possible reasons for her loss of confidence and development of bad habits and addictions, he also was intrigued by the idea of an often hurt, but still loving, daughter effectively becoming a mother to her own mother in order to protect her from herself. Another show business situation was probed in *The Sunshine Boys,* which explored the behind-the-scenes hostilities of vaudeville teams such as Smith and Dale that continued into old age.

The Prisoner of Second Avenue continues to excite interest, however, with its mordant humor all the more relevant as seemingly successful and highly paid executives are suddenly fired with no prospects of reemployment. As if to answer those who complain that Simon writes only about New Yorkers, *California Suite* did for Los Angeles what *Plaza Suite* did for Manhattan. Unfortunately, the formula did not work. The 1995 *London Suite,* although cast in the same pattern and given a handsome production, was staged off-Broadway. It also had a rather short run of only 169 performances despite, or perhaps because of, its usual Simon slickness.

Chapter Two, in which Simon came to terms with his sorrow and rage at the loss of his first wife from cancer and told of beginning a new relationship, at last was a serious subject that critics and the public could accept as an honest, deeply felt vision of suffering and redemption, leavened as it was with sharp personal satire and comic quips. Curiously, Simon's subsequent semiautobiographical trio of comedies—the saga of a young playwright's growing up—have been critically praised as a breakthrough in comic technique. Actually, however, *Brighton Beach Memoirs* (about his childhood in Brooklyn), *Biloxi Blues* (about his 1940s army experiences), and *Broadway Bound* (about an ambitious young man with a typewriter) exemplify one of the oldest known dramatic structures. Simon's alter ego, Eugene Morris Jerome (pace Eugene O'Neill), functions as a genial narrator who interrupts his first-person story to step into dramatized episodes. It is efficient as a technique, but it is hardly an innovation.

After the trilogy *Rumors* was a disappointment, for the basic situation and characters were stereotypical constructs of no particular interest, animated merely by the confusions and misunderstandings rumors make possible. Simon himself described it as a farce, but, except for a setting with a number of doors, it lacked the essential elements of farce. Unlike Feydeau, however, Simon did not know how to use the doors for suspense or comic effect. A colorful, manic Broadway production with some exemplary comic performers glossed over the weakness of the script.

After this slump *Lost in Yonkers* was doubly welcomed by critics and the public. It was hailed as even more honest and autobiographical than the trilogy. The play focused again on two boys—Simon brother surrogates—growing up with a tyrannical, embittered, and crippled grandmother in a shabby Yonkers flat, while their loving but feckless father tries to survive the Depression on the road. A gangster uncle and a childlike aunt provide love and occasional adventure for the boys. For the play Simon was awarded a Pulitzer Prize, as well as the 1991 Tony for best play, his work at last being deemed sufficiently serious. It is true that the characters were much more distinctive and less generic, but, as in previous Simon plays, every one of them had a string of smart one-liners that were vintage Simon and yet not out of character.

Jake's Women, which was tried out in San Diego in 1990 only to be halted on its way to Broadway by Simon himself, was rethought and rewritten to achieve a popular, if not critical, success in New York. The dramaturgy is intricate and engaging as Jake, a Simon-like playwright, summons up his own imaginings of the women in his fantasy and real lives. His long dead first wife turns up at will, but she can express only the thoughts, emotions, and words the playwright assigns her in his fantasies. This is also the comedic limitation for his more recent and now estranged wife, a possible future wife, and his daughter by the first wife, who is seen at two different ages. This play is, in effect, "Chapter Two 1/2." Like *Chapter Two,* it is autobiographical in that the specter of a beloved but deceased first wife is ruining the playwright's emotional relationships with subsequent lovers. Even the writer's female therapist is made to see things his way. The work is a clever conceit in performance, but it plumbs no new depths in the Simon or the general human psyche that were not already explored in *Chapter Two.*

Laughter on the 23rd Floor was based on Simon's most formative experience as a playwright of comedies, his apprenticeship as a gag writer for television comedians. At a brainstorming session in a Manhattan high-rise, highly competitive writers are trying to devise comedy routines for an extremely demanding, neurotic, and insecure star. Critics detected elements of Sid Caesar in this provocative portrait. To insiders the writers themselves seemed to be inspired by well-known talents. Part of the comic tension was generated by their almost desperate desire to please their employer. But trying to top each other, especially in the distinctively New York comedy of insult, also held the audience's attention and produced a steady stream of amusing one-liners. There was no better excuse for an evening of Simon gags than a session in a gag-factory. Of course, the gags had to be good, or the comedian's show would be canceled and the writers out of work.

Despite a handsome Broadway production staged by Joe Mantello and designed by John Lee Beatty, *Proposals* had a very short run. Opening in November 1997, it closed only two months later after 76 performances and 11 previews. Despite favorable reviews, sustaining audiences did not develop. One reason for this may be that Simon's longtime fans have been growing older, and a play narrated by an African American maid who has been dead for some years about a white man who is living his last days and hours may not have appealed to those who are only too conscious of their mortality. The heart of the comedy, however, is a kind of mating carousel that is centered on the man's disaffected daughter, who is still suffering from the effects of her father's neglect and unwise divorce from her mother. He has focused his life too much on his business and not enough on his family, a mistake he comes to understand and regret as he prepares to take leave of life. The play is not, however, gloomy and depressing but rather is tender, amusing, loving, and healing.

Over the years Simon has also shown himself a skilled adapter of other materials, as in the musicals *Little Me* (Patrick Dennis's novel), *Sweet Charity* (Federico Fellini's film), and *Promises Promises* (Billy Wilder's film) and in the plays *The Good Doctor* (Chekhov's short stories), *God's Favorite* (the Book of Job set on Long Island's North Shore, Simon's answer to Archibald MacLeish's *J.B.*), and *Fools* (suggested by Sholem Aleichem's stories of Chelm). For the cinema he has drafted effective screenplays of some of his own works as well as originals such as *The Goodbye Girl* and *Murder by Death.* The first was a popular romantic screen comedy and later a stage musical; the second, a puzzling disaster.

Despite periodic renunciations of Broadway, carping critics, the frantic pace of New York life, or East Coast values, Simon seems to draw his primary inspiration and stimulation from this scene. Some denigrators would insist that with Simon nothing succeeds like excess. But his large, impressive, continuing body of comedies—endorsed to a greater or lesser degree by audiences at home and abroad—is an undeniable achievement by a distinctive talent with a penetrating intelligence. It is a record all the more impressive in a time when so few playwrights are regularly creating effective comedies for the stage.

—Glenn Loney

SIMONS, Beverley

Nationality: Canadian. **Born:** Beverly Rosen, Flin Flon, Manitoba, 31 March 1938. **Education:** Banff School of Fine Arts, Alberta, 1956; McGill University, Montreal, 1956-57; University of British Columbia, Vancouver, 1958-59, B.A. (honours) in English and theatre 1959. **Family:** Married to Sidney B. Simons; three sons. **Career:** Lived in Europe, 1959-61. Lives in Vancouver. **Awards:** Canada Council grant, 1967, and award, 1972.

Publications

Plays

Twisted Roots (as Beverley Rosen), in *First Flowering*, edited by Anthony Frisch. Toronto, Kingswood House, 1956.

The Birth (produced Montreal, 1957).

A Play (produced Montreal, 1957).

The Elephant and the Jewish Question (produced Vancouver, 1968). Vancouver, New Play Centre, n.d.

Green Lawn Rest Home (produced Burnaby, British Columbia, 1969). Toronto, Playwrights, 1973.

Crabdance (produced Seattle, 1969). Vancouver, In Press, 1969; revised version (produced Vancouver, 1972), Vancouver, Talonbooks, 1972.

Preparing (produced Burnaby, British Columbia, 1973). Vancouver, Talon Books, 1974; in *Preparing* (collection), 1975; in *Canadian Literature in the 70s,* Toronto, Holt Rinehart & Winston, 1980.

Preparing (includes *Prologue*, *Triangle*, *The Crusader*, *Green Lawn Rest Home*). Vancouver, Talonbooks, 1975.

Prologue, *Triangle*, *The Crusader* (produced Toronto, 1976). Included in *Preparing*, 1975.

If I Turn Around Quick, published in *Capilano Review* (North Vancouver), Summer 1976.

Leela Means to Play (produced Waterford, Connecticut, 1978). Published in *Canadian Theatre Review 9* (Downsview, Ontario), Winter 1976.

Television Play: *The Canary*, 1968.

*

Critical Studies: "Beverley Simons Issue" of *Canadian Theatre Review 9* (Downsview, Ontario), Winter 1976.

* * *

Crabdance is Beverley Simons's best-known work and remains her outstanding achievement. In it the commonplace world is transformed by Sadie Golden's hypersensitive perceptions, salesmen becoming sons, lovers, and husband as she projects onto them her feelings about sex, motherhood, and her femaleness. At the critical hour of 3 p.m. she dies out of the lacerating existence in which "Mama's gone a-hunting/She's taken off her own white skin. . . ." The salesmen are recognizably objective figures as well as emanations from Sadie, and the play's relation to experience is powerfully present through distorted images. The great success of *Crabdance* lies in the perilous balance between observation and feeling, between the known world and Sadie's vision of it.

In the earlier one-act play *Green Lawn Rest Home,* less ambitious than *Crabdance* but the most finished and unified of her plays, Simons also makes the internal perceptions of the characters modify the presentation of outward reality and brilliantly fuses lyrical and satirical perspectives. Society's prettification of senility and dying is critically observed while, at the same time, the mortifications before death, the leaking away of life in anguish, and the tiny passions of the geriatrics are seen and felt from within. For the old couple a date, which consists of a walk to the gate of the rest home, is subjectively presented, the equivalent of the most violent adolescent sexuality. Simons conveys feelingly the real hardness of the green pebbles that, from a little distance away, give the illusion of lawns.

Leela Means to Play sporadically presents clear moral views of the operation of justice through a judge's trial by encounters. The play is a full-length aggregation of very short scenes, related in theme but not through plot or sequence. They are gobbets of allegory in which the representation of modern life is distorted by an intensely feeling consciousness. There is no equivalent of Sadie Golden, however, to give focus and coherence to the play. In this work Simons relies too naively on her audience's recognition of the personality behind it. The play seems to have been untimely snatched from the authorial womb, still trailing unsynthesized bits of Beckett, Genet, Albee, and No theater by way of Yeats, unfinished though very much alive.

Like *Crabdance,* the title piece of *Preparing* gives us a dramatization of the passionately sensitive perceptions of Simons. This monologue requires an actress skilled in mime and with a set of voices adequate to portray the several ages of woman. From adolescence to womanhood the speaker undertakes preparations for imposed sexual roles that end with ultimate resistance ("fuck 'em all") to the impositions. Two other short pieces in this collection are too clamantly experimental. One, *The Crusader,* employs masks in a novel but clumsy way, and in the other, *Triangle,* light and movement give us the geometry of bonding and victimization in the relationships of three characters. In both the moral view is rather heavily imposed and not offset by studious theatricality.

In the earlier play *The Elephant and the Jewish Question,* which was published in mimeographed form, Simons showed herself capable of handling a conventional structure and natural speech, though the piece is rather stickily embedded in Jewish atmosphere. The great development from this to *Crabdance* is an indication of Simons's strengths. Her work is marked by her exploration of various ways of presenting lyrical, internalized characters within an objective framework. But her genuine distinctiveness seems to be overlaid and obscured by studious imitation and anxiety about form.

—Michael Sidnell

SINCLAIR, Stephen (Kennedy)

Nationality: New Zealander. **Born:** Auckland, 30 December 1956. **Education:** Victoria University of Wellington, B.A. in Maori studies 1980. **Career:** Warehouse employee, Lands Bags, 1977; dishwasher, Plimmer House Restaurant, 1978-79; research assistant, Maori Studies Department, Victoria University of Wellington, 1979; writer, actor, director, Wellington Arts Centre, 1980-81; translator of Maori manuscripts, National Archives, 1982; writer, actor, director, Taotahi Maori and Polynesian Theatre Group, 1982-84; postman, New Zealand Post Office, 1983-85; and administration officer, New Zealand Actors Equity, Wellington Branch and New Zealand Writers Guild, Southern Branch, 1986-87, all Wellington. **Agent:** Playmarket, P.O. Box 9767, Wellington, New Zealand; and, Casarotto Ramsay, National House, 60-66 Wardour Street, London W1V 3HP, England. **Address:** 6 Hauraki Road, Takapuna, Auckland 9, New Zealand.

PUBLICATIONS

Plays

Le Matau (The Hook), with Samson Samasoni (produced Wellington, 1984).
Ladies Night, with Anthony McCarten (produced Auckland, 1987; London, 1990).
Big Bickies, with Frances Walsh (produced Dunedin, 1988).
The Sex Fiend, with Danny Mulheron (produced Wellington, 1989).
Caramel Cream (produced Wellington, 1991).
Ladies Night 2: Raging On, with Anthony McCarten (produced Auckland, 1992).
Legless, with Anthony McCarten (produced Christchurch, 1993).
The Alhambra's Master (produced Wellington, 1993).
Braindead the Musical (produced Auckland, 1995).

Screenplays: *Meet the Feebles*, with Peter Jackson & Francis Walsh, 1991; *Braindead*, with Frances Walsh and Peter Jackson, 1992.

Novel for Children

Thief of Colours. Penguin Books, 1995.

* * *

Stephen Sinclair can turn his hand to any form or genre. Film scripts with Peter Jackson, such as *Meet the Feebles,* the first splatter-puppet movie, and the zombie comedy *Braindead* come as easily to him as a musical or drama. His historical epic *The Alhambra's Master* is a drama with chorus about betrayal among Wellington seafarers at beginning of the twentieth century, and, with evocations of Wellington's harbor and the city of that time, it has great potential for staging on a bare platform. He also can write parody or parable with ease and has made collaborative writing almost his trademark.

A poet with published work in *Landfall*, Sinclair's first production, *The Howzie Show*, was a 1981 group effort about inner-city living that set the pattern for cowriting. *Scars of Welfare* pilloried the social welfare dole queues long before they became a scandal. In 1984 he wrote *Le Matau* ("The Hook") with Samson Samasoni for the Maori and Polynesian theater group Taotahi. It is a work about the changes made by a Samoan immigrant as he adapts to New Zealand life and values. The play was the first exploration of the Pygmalion theme in Sinclair's work, and it also shows his interest in race relations and in lives lived in the modern city.

The film *Braindead* was conceived as a musical in collaboration with Frances Walsh in 1987. The screenplay has a number of difficult technical requirements, some of which are gory.

Again in collaboration with Walsh, Sinclair wrote the musical *Big Bickies*, a grotesque parable about an archetypal New Zealand couple who win the big prize in a lottery. Deliberately using clichés for satirical purposes, *Big Bickies* exposes the cynical way society exploits the naive.

Sinclair's next and most widely performed collaborative work, the commercial blockbuster *Ladies Night,* was written with Anthony McCarten, and it brought him fame and financial rewards. It has had numerous productions and tours in New Zealand, Australia, Canada, and Britain, and it has resisted critical disapproval to become the New Zealand play seen by the biggest audiences ever. Translated, it has gone to Germany, Austria, Spain, and Italy, proving that some pleasures are common to women the world over.

Ladies Night tells of five despairing young men on the dole who decide to try anything to earn some money, including stripping at a nightclub. Arrogantly confident at first that they have nothing to learn, they are forced to change their ideas about what women want and to sharpen their performance skills while improving their physiques. Each develops his own specialty act. They learn some lessons and emerge sharper, nastier but more confident, and much, much richer. Their highly charged strip acts end the play. Audiences for *Ladies Night* came from the wider non-theater-going crowd, and many young women have made multiple visits to watch what became a dramatized version of a sex show with laughs.

Collaboration with Danny Mulheron resulted in the farce *The Sex Fiend.* Their close work on the structure of this notoriously difficult form paid off, for the play is well paced and has proved extremely popular as well as critically acceptable. Matthew, a sensitive New Age man, has just been elected the sexual harassment officer at a university. One evening his live-in girlfriend Anna invites a lesbian feminist poetry group to use their flat for a reading. At the same time the staunch lad Brent arrives armed with porno videos and hunting for booze and birds. In true farcical style these and other disparate elements have to be kept apart by the increasingly frenetic Matthew, who makes full use of doors, stairs, mistaken identity, and discarded clothes, both his own and other people's. There is much harassment of the feminist poets, and unexpected encounters enliven everyone's evening. All kinds of extreme attitudes of the modern postfeminist age get a sound thrashing in this very funny farce.

Sinclair next tried his hand alone at a straight comedy-drama about race and sexual relations called *Caramel Cream.* Performed in 1991, the play is completely different in feeling from his preceding work, although it touches again on the Pygmalion theme of *Le Matau* and continues to demonstrate the surprising versatility of this writer. The plot concerns two inept burglars who avoid the police by hiding in a social welfare office, where they are disturbed by the lonely Claire, who is working late. She befriends them, and an attraction begins to form between her and Mitch, a Maori. Peter, a European, becomes suspicious of their friendship. The comic mood at the start does not last, and we can see that the affair is doomed. Sinclair apparently does not want us to think that anything can halt the slide back into the violence and mindless crime from which Claire has tried to rescue Mitch. The title, with its contrast of brown on the outside and white inside, is of course satirical. Structural weakness, in that there is no satisfactory dramatic climax, and the numerous short scenes in four separate settings make *Caramel Cream* disjointed on stage. Perhaps it would be better suited to film, but it shows that Sinclair has continued to experiment.

Sinclair has also collaborated with McCarten on *Legless*, a satire of the English country house murder mystery with a New Zealand twist. Its alternative title, *The Curse of the Wedgecombes*, better conveys its flavor. On one level a simple comedy, it also can be seen as an allegory of relations between xenophobic Britain and her old dominions now that the European Community looms as the new club to belong to. Sinclair thus remains a clever and always interesting writer.

—Patricia Cooke

SLADE, Bernard

Nationality: Canadian. **Born:** New-bound in St. Catherines, Ontario, 2 May 1930. **Education:** 13 schools in England and Wales, including John Ruskin School, Croydon, Surrey, and Caernarvon Grammar School. **Family:** Married Jill Hancock in 1953; one daughter and one son. **Career:** Moved to Canada in 1948; worked in a customs office, 1948; actor, 1949-57; cofounder, Garden Centre Theatre, Vineland, Ontario, 1954; television writer, 1957-74; wrote scripts for Canadian Broadcasting Corporation, CBS, ABC, and NBC; guest lecturer, Columbia University, New York, New York University, and University of California, Los Angeles. **Awards:** Drama Desk award, 1975. **Agent:** Jack Hutto, 405 West 23rd Street, New York, New York 10011. **Address:** 11500 San Vincente Blvd., Apt 204, Los Angeles, California 90049, U.S.A.; and, Flat 3, 4 Egerton Place, London S.W.3., England.

PUBLICATIONS

Plays

Simon Says Get Married (produced Toronto, 1960).
A Very Close Family (produced Winnipeg, 1963).
Same Time, Next Year (produced Boston and New York, 1975; London, 1976). New York, Delacorte Press, 1975.
Tribute (produced Boston and New York, 1978; Northampton, 1984). New York, French, 1978.
Romantic Comedy (produced New York, 1979; Watford, Hertfordshire, and London, 1983). Garden City, New York, Doubleday, 1980.
Fling! New York, French, 1979.
Special Occasions (produced New York, 1982; revised version, also director: produced London, 1983). New York, French, 1982.
Fatal Attraction (produced Toronto, 1984; London, 1985). New York, French, 1986.
An Act of the Imagination (produced as *Sweet William*, Guildford, Surrey, 1987). New York, French, 1988.
Return Engagements (produced Westport, Connecticut and New York, 1988). New York, French, 1989.
I Remember You (produced Madach Theatre, Budapest). New York, Samuel French, 1994.
Every Time I See You, musical (produced Budapest, 1995).
Same Time Another Year (produced Pasadena and Berlin). New York, Samuel French, 1996.
You Say Tomatoes (produced 1996). New York, Samuel French, 1996.

Screenplays: *Stand Up and Be Counted*, 1972; *Same Time, Next Year*, 1978; *Tribute*, 1980; *Romantic Comedy*, 1983.

Television Plays: *The Prize Winner*, 1957 (revised version, as *The Long, Long Laugh*); *Men Don't Make Passes*, *Innocent Deception*, *The Gimmick*, *Do Jerry Parker*, *The Most Beautiful Girl in the World*, *The Big Coin Sound*, *The Oddball*, *The Reluctant Angels*, *A Very Close Family* and *Blue Is for Boys*, 1958-64; *Bewitched* series (16 episodes), 1963-64; pilot films for series: *Love on a Rooftop*, *The Flying Nun*, *The Partridge Family*, *Bridget Loves Bernie*, *The Girl with Something Extra*, *Mr. Deeds Goes to Town*, *The Bobby Sherman Show*, and *Mr. Angel*, 1964-74; 80 scripts for other series.

*

Manuscript Collection: Special Collections, Boston University, Massachusetts.

Critical Studies: Article by Robert Berkvist, in *New York Times*, 13 April 1975; article by William A. Davis, in *Critical Survey of Drama* edited by Frank N. Magill, Englewood Cliffs, New Jersey, Salem Press, 1985.

Theatrical Activities:
Director: **Play**—*Special Occasions*, London, 1983; *Same Time Another Year,* Pasadena, 1996.

Actor: **Plays**—Roles in 200 plays throughout Canada, and on Canadian television, 1949-57; George in *Same Time, Next Year*, Edmonton, 1977.

* * *

Bernard Slade, while not as prolific as Neil Simon, has been Simon's only serious rival as a consistently commercially successful Broadway dramatist in recent years. His work is ultraprofessional and, while occasionally unusually adventurous technically, artfully tailored to the prevailing Broadway taste.

He had a phenomenally long-running early hit with *Same Time, Next Year*, a rare example of a successful two-character play that recalled Jan de Hartog's *The Fourposter*, with adultery instead of marriage at its center and a similar span of years. It follows the love affair of Doris and George, both happily married to their respective partners and with children, in a California hotel room (hardly changing in the play's six scenes), an affair that occupies one weekend every year between 1951 and 1975. The play is an accomplished laughter rouser, especially in the scene in which an all too pregnant Doris appears for the 1961 weekend. Although somewhat overreliant on strings of smart one-liners and with noticeably grinding gear changes at more serious moments, as when George cracks up over the death of his son in Vietnam, it never descends into a sniggering comedy of adultery. In fact, a genuine relationship emerges as Slade traces the changes in the couple over a quarter of a century of shifting middle-class American values.

In *Special Occasions* Slade again used only two characters in a shifting timescale. In 14 scenes moving from 1970 to 1979 and set in various locales in California, New York, and Colorado, the play uses the "special occasions"—weddings, christenings, anniversaries, funerals—in the lives of a divorced couple, Amy and Michael. Slade often writes with economy and with insight into the different levels of the couple's dependence, although, as in *Same Time, Next Year* the play is at its happiest in the groove of broad mainstream comedy. In the handling of the time shifts in an unnaturalistic manner through the use of almost filmic dissolves and links between the major scenes, the play is technically adventurous, but the technique cannot compensate for a distinct air of predictability in its substance.

Romantic Comedy, a valentine to the kind of charmingly elegant comedy that once dominated Broadway and an unabashed star vehicle, cunningly updated an apparently moribund genre, complete with a glimpse of 1970s nudity. Set in the luxurious New York penthouse of Jason Carmichael, a successful Broadway dramatist looking for a new collaborator on the eve of his marriage, the play has a setting, style, and tone that recall the world of Philip Barry in the developing relationship (again over a period of years—here the mid-1960s to 1979) between Carmichael and Phoebe Craddock, a classic ugly duckling who develops into a beautiful swan. The play has one memorably funny scene involving the collaborators and Carmichael's sharp female agent after a disastrous opening night, but it becomes a great deal too lachrymose for a bittersweet light comedy and is stiltedly overwritten in its final scenes. Even more manipulative as a star vehicle was *Tribute*, initially set in a Broadway theater at a tribute to Scottie Templeton, a middle-aged screenwriter described as "a mixture of Noël Coward, the Marx Brothers, and Peter Pan." The participants include his agent, his doctor (it transpires that Scottie has terminal cancer), and his son. In the flashback scenes into which the play dissolves behind the scrim of the theater setting and that take place in Scottie's townhouse, the complex relationship between father and son comes to be the emotional fulcrum of the evening as the two men, both wary of each other, finally make their peace. The play certainly delivered a juicy central role (performed by Jack Lemmon) and adroitly mixed pathos with slapstick comedy. It never risked alienating its public, however, always recovering with a cleverly timed gag from any hint of overseriousness, especially evident in the sentimental ending.

Slade's later play *Fatal Attraction* was a would-be glossy thriller involving a famous actress under a death threat. It was a disappointingly muddled farrago that fell well beneath the standards of models such as *Deathtrap*. His follow-up to *Same Time, Next Year* lacked both the zest and the heart of its original. *I Remember You*, essentially a nostalgic comedy, was an interesting experiment technically. Its best scenes are set in the nonnaturalistic setting of a contemporary New York piano bar, where the play's Peter Pan of a hero, Austin "Buddy" Bedford, plays and sings classic '30s and '40s numbers (Kern, Coward, Mercer, Porter, Berlin, etc.), which often counterpoint the action. But its love story involving Buddy, a smart Manhattan career girl, and her English-born mother, with whom it transpires Buddy had a past affair, is soft centered and sabotaged by too many poor wisecracks. Another comedy, *You Say Tomatoes*, involving a pukka English writer and his brash younger American fan, had a promising central situation for a comedy of American vs. Anglo-Saxon manners. This play, too, however, never gets genuinely airborne and becomes progressively strained as the action shifts from the English shires to New York with, for Slade, surprisingly overwritten dialogue.

—Alan Strachan

SMITH, Anna Deavere

Nationality: American. **Born:** Baltimore, Maryland, 18 September 1950. **Education:** American Conservatory Theatre, M.F.A. in 1976. **Career:** Assistant professor of theater, Carnegie-Mellon University, Pittsburgh, Pennsylvania, 1978-79; acting teacher, New York University, 1983-84; master teacher of acting, American Conservatory Theatre, 1986; assistant professor of acting, University of Southern California, Los Angeles; teaching artist, Lincoln Center Institute. Professor of theater, Stanford University, Stanford, California, 1990—. Visiting artist, Yale University, New Haven, Connecticut, 1982; visiting teacher, National Theatre Institute, 1986. **Awards:** Drama-Logue award; Obie award; Drama Desk award; Lucille Lortel award; George and Elizabeth Marton award; Kesselring prize and Pulitzer prize nomination, all 1992, all for *Fires in the Mirror: Crown Heights, Brooklyn, and Other Identities*; Antoinette Perry award, best play, Antoinette Perry award nomination, best actress, Obie award, and Drama Desk award, all 1993, all for *Twilight*; fellow of Bunting Institute, Radcliffe College. Honorary degree: Beaver College. **Agent:** c/o David Williams, International Creative Management, 40 West 57th Street, New York, New York 10019, U.S.A.

Publications

Plays

On the Road (produced New York, 1982).
A Birthday Party (produced New York, 1983).
Aunt Julia's Shoes (produced Ward Nasse Gallery, 1984).
Charlayne Hunter Gault (produced Ward Nasse Gallery, 1984).
Aye, Aye, Aye, I'm Integrated (produced New York, 1984).
Building Bridges, Not Walls (produced New York, 1985).
Voices of Bay Area Women (produced Phoenix, 1988).

Clorophyll Post-Modernism and the Mother Goddess: A Conver/Ation (produced Hahn Cosmopolitan Theatre, 1988).
Gender Bending: On the Road Princeton University (produced Princeton, New Jersey, 1989).
Piano (produced Los Angeles, 1989). New York, Theatre Communications Group, 1989.
On Black Identity and Black Theatre (produced New Brunswick, New Jersey, 1990).
From the Outside Looking In (produced San Francisco, 1990).
Fragments (produced Bellagio, Italy, 1991).
Identities, Mirrors, and Distortions I (produced Calistoga, California, 1991).
Identities, Mirrors, and Distortions II (produced San Francisco, 1991).
Identities, Mirrors, and Distortions III (produced Stanford, California, 1991).
Identities, Mirrors, and Distortions IV (produced New York, 1991).
Fires in the Mirror: Crown Heights, Brooklyn, and Other Identities (produced Joseph Papp Public Theatre, 1992; London, 1993). New York, Anchor Books, 1993.
Hymn (ballet, with Judith Jamison; produced New York, 1993).
Twilight: Los Angeles, 1992 (produced Los Angeles, 1993). As *Twilight–Los Angeles, 1992 on the Road: A Search for American Character.* New York, Anchor Books, 1994.

Television Play: *Fires in the Mirror,* 1993.

*

Critical Studies: "Anna Deavere Smith" by Thulani Davis, in *BOMB,* Fall 1992, pp. 40-43; "Anna Deavere Smith: The World Becomes You: An Interview" by Carol Martin, in *The Drama Review: A Journal of Performance Studies* (Cambridge, Massachusetts), Winter 1993, pp. 45-62; "Anna Deavere Smith: Acting as Incorporation" by Richard Schechner, in *The Drama Review: A Journal of Performance Studies* (Cambridge, Massachusetts), Winter 1993, pp. 63-64; "Anna Deavere Smith: Perspectives on Her Performance within the Context of Critical Theory" by Charles R. Lyons and James C. Lyons, in *Journal of Dramatic Theory and Criticism* (Lawrence, Kansas), Fall 1994, pp. 43-66; "Performing Race: Anna Deavere Smith's *Fires in the Mirror*" by Janelle Reinelt, in *Modern Drama* (Downsview, Ontario), Winter 1996, pp. 609-17; "Doing Justice to the Subjects: Mimetic Art in a Multicultural Society: The Work of Anna Deavere Smith" by Tania Modleski, in *Female Subjects in Black and White: Race, Psychoanalysis, Feminism,* edited by Elizabeth Abel and Barbara Christian, Berkeley, California, University of California Press, 1997.

Theatrical Activities:
Actor: **Plays**–Performs in all her own plays. Role in *Horatio,* San Francisco, California, 1974; role in *Alma, the Ghost of Spring Street,* New York, 1976. **Film**–*Soup for One,* 1982; *Dave,* 1993; *Philadelphia,* 1993. **Television**–*All My Children,* 1983; *The Issue Is Race,* 1992.

* * *

Although Anna Deavere Smith has written conventional plays with fictional characters, her widespread acclaim rests on two works, *Fires in the Mirror* and *Twilight: Los Angeles, 1992,* from her grandiosely titled series "On the Road: A Search for American Character." Smith uses a unique playwriting process for all the works in this project, which began in the early 1980s: She interviews dozens, even hundreds, of people from a specific community or a widespread area about a single set of social issues. She then selects excerpts from the interview transcripts and performs her "characters" using their own words and speech patterns.

The result is a different kind of documentary history play. Unlike conventional pageants that focus narrowly on great leaders, epic battles, treaty signings, or fictitious walks in the woods, Smith performs a large, democratic cast of characters on a minimally dressed set to offer a conversation of colorful voices, whether the piece is constructed from interviews with women at an academic conference or with participants in the 1992 Los Angeles riots. Much of the power of these pieces comes from the author's virtuosic ability to portray dozens of people. One critic likened her performance to an act of shamanism.

Whether they are "plays" has been subject to debate. Although the Tony Award voters nominated *Twilight* for Best Play after it moved to Broadway in 1994, the Pulitzer committee refused to consider it a play. The New York Drama Critics' Circle neatly circumvented the debate by giving Smith an award for "unique contribution to theatrical form." Another critic resorted to a series of hyphens to describe *Twilight* as "a two-hour (no intermission) collage-drama-documentary-epic-poem-living movie."

Smith searches for the "American character" in speech; the voices she gathers on her tape recorder become her entree to her subjects' souls. She doesn't do imitations; "I'm a repeater," she insists, performing her "characters" with vocal tics, pauses, and repetitions included. In a sense, by revealing character through speech patterns, the one-time Stanford acting professor has discovered a new performance tool for creating characters onstage.

Fires in the Mirror, Smith's most cohesive and powerful work, includes about two dozen characters who talk about African-American and Jewish race relations in response to a three-day riot in the Crown Heights section of Brooklyn. Hours after a car in a motorcade escorting the Grand Rebbe of the Lubavitcher sect careened out of control and killed Gavin Cato, a young Caribbean-American boy, an angry mob of blacks stabbed a young Hasidic scholar walking down the street.

Fires in the Mirror contains not only a cross section of residents that comment on the specific events but also a number of famous pundits—author and activist Angela Davis, *Ms.* magazine cofounder Letty Cottin Pogrebin, the Reverend Al Sharpton—who speak to the issues in a larger context. The play is broken into sections with titles like "Race," "Mirrors," and "Seven Verses," which contain anywhere from one to five characters. The last section, "Crown Heights, Brooklyn, August 1991" is the longest and deals with the particular events leading to the rioting. Each character's one- to three-minute piece also has a title, which in production is projected on a screen. The strength of the play lies in Smith's ability to find common ground amid the cacophony of voices. In the section called "Hair," for instance, Sharpton talks about how his coif is an homage to James Brown; next, a Lubavitch housewife explains her thoughts about wearing the wigs traditional to her faith.

Because of the success of *Fires in the Mirror* (it was filmed for the PBS series "American Playhouse"), Smith was commissioned to create a similar piece around the riots that occurred in Los Angeles after the police officers who beat Rodney King were acquitted. *Twilight: Los Angeles, 1992* is similarly structured, except certain characters return and interweave themselves into the narrative and multimedia was used more extensively (the famous video footage of King's beating, for example, was shown). As in *Fires in the Mirror,* Smith focused on the clash of cultures. Beginning with a Mexican-American man talking about being beaten by police in the 1940s, the piece features a Korean shopkeeper whose store was looted, gang members (the name of one gave the play its title), and city figures from Mayor Tom Bradley to police chief Daryl Gates. Although a critical success, it could not sustain a long commercial Broadway run.

Smith was then commissioned by a consortium of nonprofit regional theaters to create a piece based on the presidential election in 1996. The initial production at Arena Stage was a fascinating disaster: instead of focusing solely on politics, power, and the media, as was the original intent, the piece ballooned to include a fictitious theater company putting on a play about presidential power; women prisoners; and even a spinning exercise class. Clearly, Smith wanted to write a "play" this time; the interview material became a kind of sidelight to the melodramatic conflicts that arise within the theater company. Nevertheless, the interviews as performed by a multicultural and multigenerational cast (a young boy played FDR, for instance) were spellbinding, and Smith's ability to capture and hone poetic snatches from diverse people was undiminished. Ironically, instead of investigating power, Smith's excessive, indulgent script, at least in its initial incarnation, suggested that she had been seduced by it.

Anyone skeptical that history does not repeat itself, however, should hear Smith repeat it for you. By embodying disparate Americans and giving them voice, she questions conventional notions of history and playmaking. By revealing the multiplicity of perspectives that can be brought to bear on an event, an issue, or a community, Smith offers audiences a chance to listen to "others"—and thereby to hear themselves.

—John Istel

SMITH, Michael T(ownsend)

Nationality: American. **Born:** Kansas City, Missouri, 5 October 1935. **Education:** Hotchkiss School, Lakeville, Connecticut, 1951-53; Yale University, New Haven, Connecticut, 1953-55. **Family:** Married Michele Marie Hawley in 1974 (divorced 1989); two sons. **Career:** Theatre critic, 1959-74, and associate editor, 1962-65, *Village Voice*, New York (Obie award judge, 1962-68 and 1972-74); teacher, New School for Social Research, New York, 1964-65, Project Radius, Dalton, Georgia, 1972, and Hunter College, New York, 1972; instrument maker, Zuckermann Harpsichords, Stonington, Connecticut, 1974-77 and 1979-85; arts editor, Taos *News*, New Mexico, 1977-78; music, art, and theatre critic, New London *Day*, Connecticut, 1982-86; assistant press secretary to Edward I. Koch, Mayor of New York City, 1986-89; music critic, Santa Barbara *News-Press,* 1992—. Also director, lighting designer, and musician: manager, Sundance Festival Theatre, Upper Black Eddy, Pennsylvania, 1966-68; producer, Caffe Cino, New York, 1968; director, Theatre Genesis, New York, 1971-75, and Boston Early Music Festival and Exhibition, 1983-85; manager, 14th Street Lighting, New York, 1989-90; since 1990 lighting director, The Living Theater, New York. **Awards:** Brandeis University Creative Arts award, 1965; Obie award, for directing, 1972; Rockefeller grant; 1975; MacDowell Colony fellowship, 1991. **Address:** 1801 Olive Avenue, Santa Barbara, California 93101, U.S.A.

Publications

Plays

I Like It (also director: produced New York, 1963). Published in *Kulchur* (New York), 1963.
The Next Thing (produced New York, 1966). Published in *The Best of Off-Off-Broadway*, edited by Smith, New York, Dutton, 1969.
More! More! I Want More!, with John P. Dodd and Remy Charlip (produced New York, 1966).
Vorspiel nach Marienstein, with John P. Dodd and Ondine (also director: produced New York, 1967).
Captain Jack's Revenge (also director: produced New York, 1970; London, 1971). Published in *New American Plays 4*, edited by William M. Hoffman, New York, Hill and Wang, 1971.
A Dog's Love, music by John Herbert McDowell (produced New York, 1971).
Tony (produced New York, 1971).
Peas (also director: produced Denver, 1971).
Country Music (also director: produced New York, 1971). Published in *The Off-Off-Broadway Book*, edited by Albert Poland and Bruce Mailman, Indianapolis, Bobbs Merrill, 1972.
Double Solitaire (also director: produced Denver, 1973).
Prussian Suite (also director: produced New York, 1974).
A Wedding Party (also director: produced Denver, 1974; New York, 1980).
Cowgirl Ecstasy (also director: produced Denver, 1976; New York, 1977).
Life Is Dream, adaptation of a play by Calderón (also director: produced Taos, New Mexico, 1979).
Heavy Pockets (also director: produced Westerly, Rhode Island, 1981).
Sameness, with Alfred Brooks (produced Denver, 1990).

Poetry

American Baby. Westerly, Rhode Island, Fast Books, 1983.
A Sojourn in Paris. Westerly, Rhode Island, Fast Books, 1985.

Other

Theatre Journal, Winter 1967. Columbia, University of Missouri Press, 1968.
Theatre Trip (critical journal). Indianapolis, Bobbs Merrill, 1969.

Editor, with Nick Orzel, *Eight Plays from Off-Off-Broadway*. Indianapolis, Bobbs Merrill, 1966.
Editor, *The Best of Off-Off-Broadway*. New York, Dutton, 1969.
Editor, *More Plays from Off-Off-Broadway*. Indianapolis, Bobbs Merrill, 1972.

*

Theatrical Activities:
Director: **Plays**—Many of his own plays, and *Three Sisters Who Are Not Sisters* by Gertrude Stein, New York, 1964; *Icarus's Mother* by Sam Shepard, New York, 1965; *Chas. Dickens' Christmas Carol*

by Soren Agenoux, New York, 1966; *Donovan's Johnson* by Soren Agenoux, New York, 1967; *With Creatures Make My Way* by H.M. Koutoukas, New York, 1967; *The Life of Juanita Castro* by Ronald Tavel, Denver, 1968; *Dr. Kheal* by Mariá Irene Fornés, Denver, 1968; *Hurricane of the Eye* by Emmanuel Peluso, New York, 1969; *Eat Cake* by Jean-Claude van Itallie, Denver, 1971; *XXX* by William M. Hoffman, Denver, 1971; *Bigfoot* by Ronald Tavel, New York, 1972; *Tango Palace* by Mariá Irene Fornés, New York, 1973; *Krapp's Last Tape* by Beckett, *The Zoo Story* by Albee, and *West Side Story* by Arthur Laurents, Taos, New Mexico, 1977-78; *A Shot in the Dark* by Harry Kurnitz, Kingston, Rhode Island, 1985; *Curse of the Starving Class* by Sam Shepard, New London, Connecticut, 1985.

Michael T. Smith comments:

Circumstances too narrowly personal to be called historical have more to do with the extent and character of my plays than any political or career agenda I may have chosen and willed. It has seemed to me that the real (as opposed to manifest) content of anything I write produces itself from affinities and perceptions that I haven't much control over. In fact they control me, define me. The challenge is to find a form that transmits them, that enables me to share these infinitely intimate flashes of truth and beauty.

* * *

> It all seems to refer to something else, but it is difficult to figure out what that something else is.
>
> —*Country Music*

I offer the following tale as a model for the unconscious process that seems to underlie the plays of Michael T. Smith.

He has gone to a lot of trouble to arrange his materials. The plantain was picked while Venus was ascendant, the hair was surreptitiously cut from the sleeping girl, the circle was drawn in clean sand by the flowing stream, and now the words so carefully memorized are pronounced correctly. All of these elements must be in order to produce the event.

He dutifully summons demons to aid him. From the inner recesses of his consciousness and the stream, from his spinal column and the beech tree, from his shoulder and his dog, demons fly to him. He is protected from danger by the limits of his circle.

He perceives the demons as scraps of old arguments, flashes of relieved emotions, a slight feeling of unease. Is he coming down with a cold? Why did he think of his mother? Will he stay with his lover?

His experience tells him to say to the demon thoughts, "Get ye hence." He must go further. He is tired of emotion and bored with dialectic. "There must be something else," he thinks.

What does he want tonight? To be loved? To hate? Make fertile? Kill? None of these. Tonight he wants to be wise. He does not want information; he has plenty of facts. He knows that hens lay eggs, soldiers kill, and lovers love. No, he wishes to know how and where to stand in relation to his knowledge.

He throws a little something on the fire. It flares briefly, and suddenly a similar flare lights his mind. He thinks of nothing at all for some moments of eternity. The muscles of his neck relax, after which he addresses the world as the wind makes his hair fly: "Who are you, Moon? Who are you, Stream? Who are you, Dog? Who are you, Man?"

I certainly do not wish to say that Smith is a practitioner of black or white arts. What I do mean to suggest is that Smith, like many other artists of his age, wants to explore lines of inquiry that in earlier times might have been called religious.

As the magician or priest juxtaposes disparate and often illogical elements toward a magical goal, Smith arranges his material without the superficially logical glue that audiences since Ibsen have come to expect.

Smith's stories often seem discontinuous in characterization and time. The actress playing the daughter in *Peas* is also asked to play her own mother, grandmother, and lover's other girlfriend. In *Country Music* costumes and makeup are changed drastically and abruptly. In *The Next Thing* the sequence of events is arranged aesthetically; reaction does not necessarily follow action, although within any small section time is normal. In *Point Blank,* which has not been produced, the opening stage direction reads, "This is a loop play. Begin anywhere, repeat several times, stop anywhere."

Thus, in spite of fairly naturalistic dialogue the audience is somewhat disoriented by a Smith play. In fact, because the dialogue is so normal, Smith creates enormous tension by letting his characters play freely with their roles and time.

Smith's homely subject matter, which is most often the family, also is at variance with his treatment. Unlike most playwrights who write about the family, Smith is not interested in commenting either unfavorably or favorably on the subject.

As the priest or witch places such ordinary elements as bread, wine, and plants in the context of the cosmos, so Smith exposes his characters to time, nature, and politics.

In *Country Music* two couples are exposed to the vagaries of time and weather. Their loves seem more affected by these elements than by psychology. Change seems to occur the way buds grow. In *Captain Jack's Revenge* the characters are subject to art and politics. In the first act the people consciously try to order their awareness by means of television, radio, stereo, slide and movie projectors, telephone, and doorbell. In the second act we see how the minds of these same people have been shaped by the actions of remote figures in American history.

Yet Smith does not tell us that we are doomed by weather, time, politics, psychology, or the media. He is pointing two ways at once, both at the solidity of certain facts, the bread and the wine, and at the cosmic context of these facts.

Yes, the couple in *Country Music* are subject to powerful forces outside their control, but look at the stars, look at the different kinds of light we can see—candlelight, sunshine, moonlight, twilight, dawn. The actors prepare food on stage and then eat it. All of these experiences are called for by the author as his characters love, grow apart, and leave.

Yes, the white people in *Captain Jack's Revenge* are doomed to the Indians' revenge for the crimes of their ancestors, but notice the beauty of the revenge, the glorious but mind-numbing media, the alluring but confusing drugs.

From Smith's magical (I might say "objective") point of view comes the curiously unemotional language. Rarely do his people lose their cool. They love passionately, they hate, and they murder, but their language does not often reflect this. Does the playwright feel that emotion is such a heavy element onstage that the total picture would be unduly dominated by it? As the son says in *Peas,* "I want other people to be there without making a point of it."

Smith's plays are not designed to weigh 10 tons of emotions. The audience must not be distracted from being aware that they are seeing a model, not a slice, of life. The altar or voodoo dolls are not naturalistic representations either. Perhaps the logic of a Smith play is this: If you can portray a situation objectively, with the freedom to be playful, if you can see the total picture, if you can arrange the elements of existence, you can induce a state of mind that allows us to see the magic of everyday life.

—William M. Hoffman

SOFOLA, Zulu

Nationality: Nigerian. **Born:** Issele-Uku, 22 June 1935. **Education:** Virginia Union University, Richmond, B.A. in English (cum laude) 1959; Catholic University of America, Washington, D.C., M.A. in drama 1966; University of Ibadan, Ph.D. in tragic theory 1977. **Family:** Married J.A. Sofola in 1960; four sons and one daughter. **Career:** Coordinator of extra-mural program, University of Ibadan, 1968-70; acting head of the performing arts department, 1985-87, and head of department, 1989—, University of Ilorin, Kwara State; senior visiting professor, State University of New York, Buffalo, New York, 1988-89. **Awards:** African-American scholarship, 1961-62; Ford Foundation fellowship, 1969-72; University of Missouri award, 1971; African Writers Project award, 1980; Ife International Book Fair award, 1987; Fulbright fellowship, 1988. **Address:** c/o Department of the Performing Arts, Faculty of Arts, University of Ilorin, Ilorin, Kwara State, Nigeria.

Publications

Plays

The Disturbed Peace of Christmas (produced Ibadan, 1969). Ibadan, Daystar Press, 1971.
Wedlock of the Gods (also director: produced Columbia, Missouri, 1971). London, Evans Brothers, 1973.
The Operators (produced Ibadan, 1973). Included in *Lost Dreams and Other Plays*, 1992.
King Emene (produced Ibadan, 1975). Ibadan, Heinemann, 1974.
Old Wines Are Tasty (produced Ibadan, 1975). Ibadan, University Press, 1981.
The Sweet Trap (produced Ibadan, 1975; also director: produced Buffalo, New York, 1988). Ibadan, University Press, 1977.
The Wizard of Law. London, Evans Brothers, 1976.
The Deer and the Hunters Pearl (produced Ibadan, 1976).
Memories in the Moonlight (produced Ibadan, 1977). London, Evans Brothers, 1986.
Song of a Maiden (produced Ilorin, 1977). Ibadan, University Press, 1991.
Queen Omu-Ako of Oligbo (also director: produced Buffalo, New York, 1989).
Eclipso and the Fantasia (produced Ilorin, 1990).
Lost Dreams (produced Ilorin, 1991). Included in *Lost Dreams and Other Plays*, 1992.
The Showers (produced Ilorin, 1991). Included in *Lost Dreams and Other Plays*, 1992.
The Love of the Life. Included in *Lost Dreams and Other Plays*, 1992.
Lost Dreams and Other Plays (includes *Lost Dreams*, *The Operators*, *The Love of the Life*, *The Showers*). Ibadan, Heinemann, 1992.

Other plays: *The Ivory Tower*; *A Celebration of Life*.

*

Critical Studies: "Sofola's Place in the West African Women Writers Canon" by Olusegun Adesina Adekoya, in *Glendora Review*, 1996; "African Feminism and the Theatres of Zulu Sofola and Tess Onwueme: A Celebration" by I. I. Uko, in *Africana Marburgensia* (Marburg, Germany), 1996, pp. 4-10.

Theatrical Activities:
Director: **Plays**—*Wedlock of the Gods*, Columbia, Missouri, 1971; *King Emene*, Ibadan, 1978; *The Sweet Trap*, Buffalo, New York, 1988; *Queen Omu-Ako Oligbo*, Buffalo, New York, 1989.

Zulu Sofola comments:

My main areas of research are into the African concept of tragedy, the creative process, the artist in traditional societies and African aesthetics. In my plays I explore the tragic factor in African cosmology in a search for an Afro-centric theory that may help the African scholar to better define African humanity. Consequently in my plays I have treated the aspects in traditional society where customs and moral precepts set themselves at war against individual citizens, as is the case in: *Wedlock of the Gods*; *Song of a Maiden*, where a university intelligentsia reject the philosophy of "town and gown" and become irrelevant; *Queen Omu-Ako of Oligbo*, where the traditional female arm of government confronts the warring camps of the Federal Government of Biafra in defence of the citizens in the Ani'ocha area of Delta State; and in *The Sweet Trap* where a misguidéd elite engage in a meaningless gender debate, a battle of the sexes.

* * *

Zulu Sofola is the first published and established female Nigerian dramatist and theater practitioner of English expression. The main thematic concerns and preoccupations of her textual and dramatic output are the utilization of tradition to address various contemporary issues and concepts, including the state and status of women in modern society, the individual in contending Western and indigenous African cultures, and individual and group moralities as influenced and determined by religious persuasions, social and communal ethics, and history.

Sofola's plays employ elements of magic, legend, myth, ritual, and folklore to explore the enduring conflicts between indigenous African traditionalism and Western-induced modernism, with an often undisguised preference for the former. In her exploration and examination of this conflict, the patriarchal male supremacy survives or is at best gently admonished to accommodate and recognize the importance of women in a male-dominated society. Some of her major plays also manifest her vision of individual and group tragedy, mainly derived from her indigenous African perception and cosmology. Again, this conception of tragedy arises from individual protagonists and female representatives of the women's liberation movement who attempt to break the existing harmonious culture of patriarchy. Her most produced play, *Wedlock of the Gods,* explores the repercussions of an attempt to violate traditional lore and order. Her other important plays that examine traditional issues include *King Emene, Old Wines Are Tasty,* and *Memories in the Moonlight.* Her more contemporary plays that deal with women's struggle for liberation and the conflict between academia (gown) and the macrosociety (town) are, respectively, *The Sweet Trap* and *Song of a Maiden.*

Myth, legend, and magic enrich and structure Sofola's dramaturgy in traditional themes in which characters who defy age-old conventions are revealed as treading tragic paths. Uloko and Ugwoma in *Wedlock of the Gods* are passionate and genuine lovers who cannot consummate their love in marriage because an older and, to the parents, more acceptable suitor exists. As it turns out, the older suitor dies shortly after marrying Ugwoma, and the two lovers return to their original purpose of getting married without waiting for the prescribed mourning period and rites for the late husband to pass. As expected, the enraged mother-in-law makes it her responsibility to set tradition back on course by evoking her magical powers to destroy the new couple. Here is an oversimplified mythopoeia in which tragedy is equated with defiance of traditional codes and mores.

This tradition of imposing an elderly man on an unwilling young girl who has already chosen her partner recurs in the play *Memories in the Moonlight.* In the end Abiona marries her dream man, and the plot is resolved via metaphysics and traditional contrivance in which an arranged reconciliation between the parent and suitor takes place.

The Sweet Trap employs a traditional cleansing ceremony (the Okebadan festival, an exclusive male cult that is associated with license and abuse of the female sex) to celebrate a traditionally Nigerian supremacy of the man over his wife or wives. In this play, using the three-act dramatic structure, Sofola counsels against the growing wave of feminism in the country, particularly in university circles where she teaches, advocating instead that harmonious matrimony requires a wife to recognize and accept her husband's supremacy, with, of course, a gentle appeal to husbands to accord their wives due emotional regard. The plot begins in Femi Sotubo's university residence. Femi applies brute force and chauvinism to deny his wife the right to celebrate her birthday. Encouraged by her friends and with the promise of a venue to celebrate the birthday, Clara Sotubo changes from an initial position of docility and submission to one of violent defiance and self-assertion. The party goes on. As it turns out, the birthday party ends in a fiasco and humiliation as the Okebadan celebrants intrude on the arena and generously dole out abuse to the women, who in confusion blame each other for being responsible for initiating the party. After the disruption the resolution of the play comes from Dr. Jinadu, who advises Clara to apologize to her husband, advice she gleefully takes and complies with. She cringes on her knees for stubbornly going against tradition. The thesis of the play is that female submission is necessary to avert matrimonial disharmony.

Sofola's conceptual vision of tragedy grows out of her traditionalist vision of a particular African worldview that emphasizes that iconoclasm and unorthodoxy disrupt cosmic harmony and wreak historical discontinuity in the communal psyche. In this view an individual is independent within a communal equilibrium. Tragedy occurs when the independence is extended beyond the communal ethos and cosmos. Tragedy can be averted through conformity or atonement and expiation. In the play *King Emene* a usurpation of the throne has taken place through intrigue and a murder contrived by Emene's mother to deprive the deceased of his due right of ascendancy. Disharmony inevitably occurs, and the kingdom is troubled. King Emene aggravates the situation when he rejects the admonition of elders that he not perform the rites that usher in the Peace Week because a heinous crime needing cleansing and propitiation has been committed. Oblivious of the facts of the situation, Emene interprets this as a plot against him and proceeds with the rites, during which he is suddenly and mysteriously attacked by a boa. He is shamed and inevitably commits suicide. Thus, unexpiated crime and defiance of traditional wisdom occasion the tragedy of King Emene.

Sofola's thematic concerns with tragedy, metaphysics, gender problems, and individual and social conflict with a growing Western modernism are all anchored structurally and perceptually in certain traditionalist aesthetics. Technically, her plays are simple and accessible, at times bordering on oversimplification. Her dialogue and characterization oscillate between the sketchy and the profound. Her language is clear and unobtrusive, ranging between standard English usage and direct translation from her vernacular African linguistic sources and background, which is partly responsible for the audience interest in her theater.

—Olu Obafemi

SOLIS, Octavio

Nationality: American. **Education:** Trinity University, San Antonio, Texas, B.A. in 1980; Dallas Theater Center, M.F.A. in 1983. **Career:** Playwright and director. **Awards:** Wallace Alexender Gerbodie Foundation playwrighting award, 1992; Barrie and BC Stavis playwrighting award, 1992-93; Lila Wallace Reader's Digest fund, 1992-93; Will Glickman award for best new play in the Bay Area, 1993; Goldie award, outstanding artist in the Bay Area, The Bay Guardian, 1994; The Roger L. Stevens award from the Kennedy Center's fund for new American plays, 1994; playwright fellowship, National Endowment for the Arts, 1995-97. **Agent:** Peter Hagan, 130 West 42nd Street, New York, New York 10036, U.S.A.

Publications

Plays

Prospect (produced 1988). In *Theatreforum* (San Diego, California), 1994.

Man of Flesh (produced 1988). In *Plays from South Coast Repertory,* New York, Broadway Play Publishing.

Scrappers (produced 1992).

Santos & Santos (produced 1993). In *American Theatre* (New York), November 1995.

El Paso Blue (produced 1994).

La Posada Magica (produced 1994).

Dreamlandia (produced Dallas, 1996).

*

Critical Studies: "Customizing Culture" by Douglas Langworthy, in *American Theatre,* November 1995, pp. 34.

Theatrical Activities:
Director: **Plays—**Most of his own plays; *Slaughterhouse* by Greg Sarris, San Francisco, 1994; *Cleveland Raining* by Sung Rno, San Francisco, 1995.

* * *

Born and raised in El Paso, Texas, a southwestern city with a majority population that is bilingual (Spanish-English) and Chicano (Mexican-American), Octavio Solis has written plays that reflect his border experiences. His works deal in one way or another with the juxtaposed realities of living in a part of the United States that was once Mexico. He came to be based in San Francisco and has had his plays produced by a number of regional theaters throughout the country. He has also directed several productions of his plays.

Man of the Flesh, the first of Solis's play to be produced, is a Chicano adaptation of the classic Don Juan legend. In Solis's vision Juan is the reprobate son of a Mexican gardener for the Downey's, a wealthy Anglo family. As in the other versions of this classic, Juan is visited by the dead. It is the ghost of Juan's mother, formerly the Downey's maid, who returns at the climactic ending of this play, however, and who takes him to his just reward in hell. Much of the play, which incorporates music, is written in verse, with "code switching" between English, Spanish, and a street patois that is often found in Chicano plays. Solis also translated the play into Spanish for a production in both languages by the San Diego Repertory Theatre in 1991. In both the English and Spanish versions code switching is prominent, reflecting the patterns of border language.

Prospect revolves around a young Chicano named Scout, a self-avowed "computer nerd" who has denied his Mexican heritage but who rediscovers his cultural and linguistic roots when he finds himself in an all-night drinking, smoking, and snorting binge with strangers. A Chicana who is dying of cancer reminds Scout of his grandmother, and he is momentarily taken back in time to fond memories of this old Mexican woman who tried to teach him to speak Spanish. Requiring only two settings, the work is Solis's most naturalistic play. The action begins with a brief scene in a bar, where Scout meets the people with whom he will spend the rest of the night, and then moves to the run-down house of the cancer victim and her husband. The house and the people in it become metaphors for society at large. The play offers a harsh view of working-class people from various cultures, while gently revealing the Chicanos' search for identity.

La posada magica centers on Gracie, a young Chicana whose brother's death has caused her to lose faith in God. She rediscovers her faith on Christmas Eve when a traditional Mexican Christmas processional, La Posada, comes to her home. A work for young audiences, this is written as a play within a folk play. It exposes multiple realities as the action shifts from narration to a metatheatrical re-creation of Joseph and Mary's search for *posada* (lodging). The play uses music and incorporates elements of the traditional Spanish and Mexican Christmas celebrations with contemporary dramatizations of the Chicano experience.

El Paso Blue is a more complicated play than any of Solis's other works. Here he attempts to re-create archetypal struggles when a young Chicano's Anglo-American wife leaves him for his own father. Set in the southwestern desert, the action shifts from site to site as the playwright exposes the characters and their conflicts. The play is accented with songs. Much of the dialogue is written in free verse, with code switching that may confuse the audience member who is not bilingual. Rich poetry permeates this abstract look at cultural, ethnic, and generational conflicts.

Santos & Santos is a powerful examination of a fictitious family of young, successful Chicano brothers who have used the family furniture business to launder drug sales. The central figure is the youngest brother, who has returned to El Paso to join in the family business but who is appalled by the realization of how they are making their fortune. The entire family is destroyed by the greed, leaving no one unharmed by the events that transpire. Multiple settings, flashbacks, poetic language, and visions from the past give the play a classic, epic scope as the playwright develops the characters and their devastating downfall.

All of Solis's plays are written in formal and informal verse, a bilingual poetry that manages to capture the spirit and the conflict of border existence. His imagery ranges from appearances of the dead to poetic descriptions of the human condition. The plays range from the playful comedy of *Man of the Flesh* to the deadly seriousness of *Santos & Santos*. Some of his plays employ live music and songs to enhance the celebratory nature of the writing, and in each the rhythms of the language provide a vivid score. Solis often contrasts the Chicano characters with non-Chicano adversaries and allies. Each of his plays investigates the cultural and spiritual nature of the Mexican-American, from a traditional Christmas play to a play about a family of brothers whose last name is Santos (saints).

—Jorge Huerta

SOREL, Julia. ***See*** **DREXLER, Rosalyn.**

SOWANDE, Bode

Nationality: Nigerian. **Born:** Kaduna, Nigeria, 2 May 1948. **Education:** University of Ife (now Obafemi Awolowo University), Ife-Ife, 1967-71, B.A. in French (honours) 1971; University of Dakar, Senegal, 1969, diplôme d'études françaises 1970; University of Sheffield, England, 1973-77, M.A. in dramatic literature 1974, Ph.D. 1977. **Family:** Married with children. **Career:** Resident playwright, Orisun Theatre, Ibadan, 1968-71; founder, 1972, and resident playwright Odu Themes, 1972—, and Odu Themes Meridian (drama studio), 1986, both Ibadan; senior lecturer, department of theatre arts, University of Ibadan, 1977-90; visiting lecturer, universities of Sheffield, Leeds, and Kent, England, 1988, and universities of Rome, L'Aquila, and Lecce, Italy, 1990-91; international theatre residence, France, 1990; visiting writer, University of Turin, 1995; visiting writer, University of Rome, 1997; visiting writer, Brooklyn, New York, 1997; visiting writer, Lincoln Center Theater, New York, 1998. **Awards:** T.M. Aluko prize, for creative writing, 1966; University of Ife creative writing prize, 1968; University of Sheffield Edgar Allen award, for academic proficiency, 1975; Association of Nigerian Authors Drama award, 1987, 1989; British Council fellowship, 1988; French National award, 1991; Pan African Association Patron of the Arts award, 1992. **Address:** c/o Odu Themes Meridian, 33 Oyo Road, Orita, U.I., P.O. Box 14369, U.I. Post Office, Ibadan, Nigeria.

Publications

Plays

The Night Before (produced Ibadan, 1972). Included in *Farewell to Babylon and Other Plays*, 1979.
Lamps in the Night (produced Ibadan, 1973).
Bar Beach Prelude (televised 1974; produced London, 1976).
A Sanctus for Women (as *The Angry Bridegroom*, produced Sheffield, England, 1976). Included in *Farewell to Babylon and Other Plays*, 1979.
Afamako—the Workhorse (produced Ibadan, 1978). Included in *Flamingo and Other Plays*, 1986.
Farewell to Babylon (produced Ibadan, 1978). Included in *Farewell to Babylon and Other Plays*, 1979.
Kalakutu Cross Currents (produced Ibadan, 1979).
The Master and the Frauds (produced Geneva, Switzerland, 1979). Included in *Flamingo and Other Plays*, 1986.
Farewell to Babylon and Other Plays. London, Longman, 1979.
Barabas and the Master Jesus (produced Ibadan, 1980).
Flamingo (produced Ibadan, 1982; London, 1992). Included in *Flamingo and Other Plays*, 1986.
Circus of Freedom Square (produced L'Aquila, Italy, 1985). Included in *Flamingo and Other Plays*, 1986.
Flamingo and Other Plays. London, Longman, 1986.
Tornadoes Full of Dreams (produced Lagos, 1989). Lagos, Malthouse Press, 1990.
Arede Owo, adaptation of *The Miser* by Molière (produced Lagos, 1990).
Ajantala-Pinocchio (produced Chieri, Italy, 1992).

Radio and Television Plays: *Bar Beach Prelude*, 1974; *Get a Pigeon from Trafalgar Square*, 1975; *Beggar's Choice*, 1976; *Acada Campus* series, 1980-82; *Flamingo* series, 1982; *Penance* series, 1983; *My Brother's Keeper* (13 episodes), 1983; *Without a Home* series, 1984; *Dream for the Sun*, 1988.

Novels

Our Man the President. Ibadan, Spectrum, 1981.
Without a Home. London, Longman, 1982.
The Missing Bridesmaid. Ibadan, A.B.M, 1988.

*

Theatrical Activities:
Director: **Plays**–*The Divorce* by Wale Ogunyemi, 1997.

Actor: **Plays**—Baba Fakunle in *The Gods Are Not to Blame* by Ola Rotimi, Ibadan, 1968; chorus leader in *Chaka* by Léopold Sedar Senghor, Ibadan, 1970; Old man in *A Sanctus for Women*, Sheffield, 1976; Bello in *Afamako—the Workhorse*, Ibadan, 1978; Monrian in *Farewell to Babylon*, Ibadan, 1978; Monrian in *Flamingo*, Ibadan, 1982.

Bode Sowande comments:

Writing came to me and from within me as a pleasure but the creative sensibility teaches me its attendant responsibility. Whatever the roots of my African self, I realize that in the global continent the human spirit flows into the countless branches of the same expression. At every turn values should be naturally renewed, and in a crisis-torn world, a militant hope is the needed virtue for today's heroism.

I dread pigeon-holing, but I celebrate the variety of nature's expression in man, and salute the original genius of creating names for the world's objects and people.

I consider today's man as an exile from his natural heritage. If only to go back "home," I believe that fine creative writing is a necessary compass for today's map in education and in leisure.

In the creative arts, in the living theatre, in "good" television, story telling and documentation, I am in my element.

* * *

Bode Sowande belongs to the second generation of dramatists in Nigeria who are noted for their conscious, materialist approach to society. Sowande's major plays draw dramatic conflicts around class antagonism and attempt a dialectical interpretation of this problem, proposing successful ethical solutions that favor the underprivileged working class and the peasant masses. Sowande can be distinguished, however, from his colleagues of the avant-garde generation of Nigerian dramatists (Femi Osofisan, Kole Omotoso and Tunde Fatunde) by his philosophy of spiritual nationalism, a vision that circumscribes ideology within metaphysical consciousness. The play that established this philosophy of nationalism is *Farewell to Babylon,* the sequel to *The Night Before* Sowande's other major plays, apart from his many television scripts and radio dramas include, *Circus of Freedom Square, Afamako, the Workhorse,* and *Tornadoes Full of Dreams,* this last a drama commissioned by the French Cultural Centre in Lagos to commemorate the bicentenary of the French Revolution. *Arede Owo* , a free adaptation into Yoruba of Molière's *The Miser* was also commissioned by the French Cultural Centre.

Sowande employs the method and format of the traditional Yoruba performance theater of song, poetry, dance, storytelling, and improvisation to enrich the topical contemporary message of his work. This can be seen in plays such as *Mummy Water's Wedding, Ajantala-Psnochio* , and his re-creation of Amos Tutuola's *My Life in the Bush of Ghosts*, as the drama entry for the Africa '95 Arts Festival, staged in London's Royal Court Theatre for Young People. The latter production sustains the spectacle and the folkloric universe of its origins with a conscious slant toward social relevance and moral instruction. All of these plays, too, speak eloquently of the dramatist's identification with the issues that plague contemporary society. The issues range from oppression and exploitation of the underprivileged by a political elite, to the alienation and disillusionment of young people, to the growing aggressive materialism with its lethal potential for a virile social culture, and general social incoherence.

Most of these features of social decadence are already amply evident in Sowande's early play, *The Night Before*. The play features a nonlinear, episodic narrative of the experiences of six undergraduate students on the eve of their graduation ceremony. The anticipated euphoria of the moment is submerged for these young intellectuals, however, by somber reflections upon a past that casts shadows on the promise of a bright future. The night turns into an opportunity for confession. Their individual and collective activism has been marred by certain personal failings that leave them ill at ease with the challenges of the outside world. Nita, a perceptive artist, is unable to reconcile herself to the banality of the environment. Moniran's optimism is blighted by memories of his students' union election campaigns. Dabira burns his academic gown as a symbol of his renunciation of the group. Nibidi and Moye make up their minds to join the aggressive, acquisitive world outside. The central theme of the play, which is conveyed through a combination of the play-within-a-play device, role playing, flashbacks, and the direct-address formula (all of which are experiments with the Brechtian epic dramatic mode), is the inevitable sense of defeat and frustration that a thoroughly corrupt social order engenders in otherwise idealistic young people. There is a kind of critical realism in this play that is rather cynical, given the revolutionary promise of the beginning. Rather than gathering the strands of the struggle that the students' idealism could manifest, the play degenerates into a cataloguing of the tales and narratives of failed progressives. A revolutionary outlook gives way to cynicism and outright despair.

Farewell to Babylon is a more purposeful and more emphatic statement than *The Night Before.* The individual characters in the play are committed and have definite programs of action. Onita and Moniran, erstwhile colleagues in the earlier play, join opposing sides of the social system. Moniran joins the military dictatorship while Onita joins the farmers' movement. The play's events bear a strong resemblance to the Agbekoya uprising of the late 1960s in the Western Region of Nigeria, in which the military government smashed a massive people's revolt. Moniran's fiancée, Jolomitutu, becomes a police detective and infiltrates the farmers' movement. She successfully undermines the farmers' leader, Dansaki, and extracts vital information in the process. Onita, a university don who resigns his lecturing job to join the farmers' movement, is arrested and during the process of interrogation meets his old friend and colleague Moniran. The encounter leads to a revelation of their positions as revolutionaries during which Onita contemptuously spits in the face of his former friend. The death of Onita at the hands of Cookey, his psychopathic fellow inmate in prison, denies him the knowledge of the true and continuing identity of Moniran, who later participates in a coup that dethrones the dictatorial president. As a result, a compromise with the farmers is reached, and the promise of a civilian democracy is made. Using the dramaturgical devices of pantomime, visual and kinetic effects, songs, and dialogue, Sowande proposes a revolution that is political as well as spiritual and abstract.

A recognition of metaphysics and spiritualist abstractions as viable instruments for attaining an alternative social order is presented in *A Sanctus for Women,* in which the Yoruba legend of Olurombi is evoked as a caution against aggressive and uncritical materialism in society. Both in his plays and in his radio and television series such as *Acada Campus* and the serialized novel *Without a Home,* sociopolitical transformation is shown to be at the center of Sowande's creative ideology and vision.

—Olu Obafemi

SOYINKA, Wole

Nationality: Nigerian. **Born:** Akinwande Oluwole Soyinka, Abeokuta, 13 July 1934. **Education:** St. Peter's School, Ake, Abeokuta, 1938-43; Abeokuta Grammar School, 1944-45; Government College, Ibadan, 1946-50; University College, Ibadan (now University of Ibadan), 1952-54; University of Leeds, Yorkshire, 1954-57, B.A. (honours) in English. **Family:** Married; has children. **Career:** Play reader, Royal Court Theatre, London, 1957-59; Rockefeller research fellow in drama, University of Ibadan, 1961-62; lecturer in English, University of Ife, IfeIfe, 1963-64; senior lecturer in English, University of Lagos, 1965-67; head of the department of theatre arts, University of Ibadan, 1969-72 (appointment made in 1967); professor of comparative literature, and head of the department of dramatic arts, University of Ife, 1975-85; Goldwin Smith professor of Africana studies and theatre, Cornell University, Ithaca, New York, from 1988. Visiting fellow, Churchill College, Cambridge, 1973-74; visiting professor, University of Ghana, Legon, 1973-74, University of Sheffield, 1974, Yale University, New Haven, Connecticut, 1979-80, and Cornell University, 1986. Founding director, 1960 Masks Theatre, 1960, and Orisun Theatre, 1964, Lagos and Ibadan, and Unife Guerilla Theatre, IfeIfe, 1978; co-editor, *Black Orpheus*, 1961-64; editor, *Transition* (later *Ch'indaba*) magazine, Accra, Ghana, 1975-77. Secretary-general, Union of Writers of the African Peoples, 1975. Tried and acquitted of armed robbery, 1965; political prisoner, detained by the Federal Military Government, Lagos and Kaduna, 1967-69. **Awards:** Dakar Festival award, 1966; John Whiting award, 1967; Jock Campbell award (*New Statesman*), for fiction, 1968; Nobel prize for literature, 1986; AGIP-Mattei award, 1986; Benson medal, 1990; Premio Letterario Internazionale Mondello, 1990; Prisoner of Conscience prize, Amnesty International. D.Litt: University of Leeds, 1973; Yale University, 1981; Paul Valéry University, Montpellier, France, 1984; University of Lagos; Morehouse College, Atlanta, 1988; University of Bayreuth, Germany, 1989. **Member:** Fellow, Royal Society of Literature; American Academy, and Academy of Arts and Letters of the German Democratic Republic. Commander, Federal Republic of Nigeria, 1986, Legion of Honour (France), 1989, and Order of the Republic of Italy, 1990; Akogun of Isara, 1989; Akinlatun of Egbaland, 1990. **Agent:** Morton Leavy, Leavy Rosensweig and Hyman, 11 East 44th Street, New York, New York 10017; or Carl Brandt, Brandt and Brandt, 1501 Broadway, New York, New York 10036, U.S.A. **Address:** P.O. Box 935, Abeokuta, Nigeria.

PUBLICATIONS

Plays

The Swamp Dwellers (produced London, 1958; New York, 1968). Included in *Three Plays*, 1963; in *Five Plays*, 1964.

The Lion and the Jewel (produced Ibadan, 1959; London, 1966). Ibadan, London, and New York, Oxford University Press, 1963.

The Invention (produced London, 1959).

A Dance of the Forests (produced Lagos, 1960). Ibadan, London, and New York, Oxford University Press, 1963.

The Trials of Brother Jero (produced Ibadan, 1960; Cambridge, 1965; London, 1966; New York, 1967). Included in *Three Plays*, 1963; in *Five Plays*, 1964.

Camwood on the Leaves (broadcast 1960). London, Eyre Methuen, 1973; in *Camwood on the Leaves, and Before the Blackout*, 1974.

The Republican and *The New Republican* (satirical revues; produced Lagos, 1963).

Three Plays. Ibadan, Mbari, 1963; as *Three Short Plays*, London, Oxford University Press, 1969.
The Strong Breed (produced Ibadan, 1964; London, 1966; New York, 1967). Included in *Three Plays*, 1963; in *Five Plays*, 1964.
Childe Internationale (produced Ibadan, 1964). Ibadan, Fountain, 1987.
Kongi's Harvest (produced Ibadan, 1964; New York, 1968). Ibadan, London, and New York, Oxford University Press, 1967.
Five Plays: A Dance of the Forests, The Lion and the Jewel, The Swamp Dwellers, The Trials of Brother Jero, The Strong Breed. Ibadan, London, and New York, Oxford University Press, 1964.
Before the Blackout (produced Ibadan, 1965; Leeds, 1981).Ibadan, Orisun, 1971; in *Camwood on the Leaves, and Before the Blackout*, 1974.
The Road (produced London, 1965; also director: produced Chicago, 1984). Ibadan, London, and New York, Oxford University Press, 1965.
Rites of the Harmattan Solstice (produced Lagos, 1966).
Madmen and Specialists (produced Waterford, Connecticut, and New York, 1970; revised version, also director: produced Ibadan, 1971). London, Methuen, 1971; New York, Hill and Wang, 1972.
The Jero Plays: The Trials of Brother Jero, and Jero's Metamorphosis. London, Eyre Methuen, 1973.
Jero's Metamorphosis (produced Lagos, 1975). Included in *The Jero Plays*, 1973.
The Bacchae: A Communion Rite, adaptation of the play by Euripides (produced London, 1973). London, Eyre Methuen, 1973; New York, Norton, 1974.
Collected Plays:
1. *A Dance of the Forests, The Swamp Dwellers, The Strong Breed, The Road, The Bacchae*. London and New York, Oxford University Press, 1973.
2. *The Lion and the Jewel, Kongi's Harvest, The Trials of Brother Jero, Jero's Metamorphosis, Madmen and Specialists*. London and New York, Oxford University Press, 1974.

Camwood on the Leaves, and Before the Blackout: Two Short Plays. New York, Third Press, 1974.
Death and the King's Horseman (also director: produced Ifelfe, 1976; Chicago, 1979; also director: produced New York, 1987; Manchester, 1990). London, Eyre Methuen, 1975; New York, Norton, 1976.
Opera Wonyosi, adaptation of *The Threepenny Opera* by Brecht (also director: produced Ifelfe, 1977). Bloomington, Indiana University Press, and London, Collings, 1981.
Golden Accord (produced Louisville, 1980).
Priority Projects (revue; produced on Nigeria tour, 1982).
Requiem for a Futurologist (also director: produced Ifelfe, 1983). London, Collings, 1985.
A Play of Giants (also director: produced New Haven, Connecticut, 1984). London, Methuen, 1984.
Six Plays (includes *The Trials of Brother Jero, Jero's Metamorphosis, Camwood on the Leaves, Death and the King's Horseman, Madmen and Specialists, Opera Wonyosi*). London, Methuen, 1984.
A Scourge of Hyacinths (broadcast 1990). Published with *From Zia with Love*, London, Methuen, 1992.
The Beautification of Area Boy; A Lagosian Kaleidoscope. London, Methuen Drama, 1995.

Screenplay: *Kongi's Harvest*, 1970.

Radio Plays: *Camwood on the Leaves*, 1960; *The Detainee*, 1965; *Die Still, Dr. Godspeak*, 1981; *A Scourge of Hyacinths*, 1990.

Television Plays: *Joshua: A Nigerian Portrait*, 1962 (Canada); *Culture in Transition*, 1963 (USA).

Novels

The Interpreters. London, Deutsch, 1965; New York, Macmillan, 1970.
Season of Anomy. London, Collings, 1973; New York, Third Press, 1974.

Poetry

Idanre and Other Poems. London, Methuen, 1967; New York, Hill and Wang, 1968.
Poems from Prison. London, Collings, 1969.
A Shuttle in the Crypt. London, Eyre Methuen-Collings, and New York, Hill and Wang, 1972.
Ogun Abibimañ. London, Collings, 1976.
Mandela's Earth and Other Poems. New York, Random House, 1988; London, Deutsch, 1989.
Early Poems. Oxford, Oxford University Press, 1997.

Other

The Man Died: Prison Notes. London, Eyre Methuen-Collings, and New York, Harper, 1972.
In Person: Achebe, Awoonor, and Soyinka at the University of Washington. Seattle, University of Washington African Studies Program, 1975.
Myth, Literature, and the African World. London, Cambridge University Press, 1976.
Aké: The Years of Childhood (autobiography). London, Collings, 1981; New York, Vintage, 1983.
The Critic and Society (essay). Ifelfe, University of Ife Press, 1981.
The Past Must Address Its Present (lecture). N.p., Nobel Foundation, 1986; as *This Past Must Address Its Present*, New York, Anson Phelps Institute, 1988.
Art, Dialogue and Outrage: Essays on Literature and Culture. Ibadan, New Horn, 1988.
Isara: A Voyage Around "Essay." New York, Random House, 1989; London, Methuen, 1990.
Ibadan: The Penkelemes Years: A Memoir. Ibadan, Spectrum Books, 1994.
Soyinka: A Collection of Critical Essays. Ibadan, Syndicated Communications, 1994.
The Open Sore of a Continent: A Personal Narrative of the Nigerian Crisis. Oxford, Oxford University Press, 1997.

Editor, *Poems of Black Africa*. London, Secker and Warburg, and New York, Hill and Wang, 1975.

Translator, *The Forest of a Thousand Daemons: A Hunter's Saga*, by D.O. Fagunwa. London, Nelson, 1968; New York, Humanities Press, 1969.

*

Bibliography: *Wole Soyinka: A Bibliography* by B. Okpu, Lagos, Libriservice, 1984.

Critical Studies: *Wole Soyinka* by Gerald Moore, London, Evans, and New York, Africana, 1971, revised edition, Evans, 1978; *The Writing of Wole Soyinka* by Eldred D. Jones, London, Heinemann, 1973, revised edition, 1983, 2nd revised edition, London, Curry, 1988; *The Movement of Transition: A Study of the Plays of Wole Soyinka* by Oyin Ogunba, Ibadan, Ibadan University Press, 1975; *Komik, Ironie, und Satire im Dramatischen Werk von Wole Soyinka* by Rita Bottcher-Wobcke, Hamburg, Buske, 1976; *A Dance of Masks: Sengher, Achebe, Soyinka* by Jonathan Peters, Washington, D.C., Three Continents, 1978; *Notes on Wole Soyinka's The Jero Plays* edited by E.M. Parsons, London, Methuen, 1979; *Critical Perspectives on Wole Soyinka* edited by James Gibbs, Washington, D.C., Three Continents, 1980, London, Heinemann, 1981, and *Wole Soyinka* by Gibbs, London, Macmillan, and New York, Grove Press, 1986; *The Lion and the Jewel: A Critical View* by Martin Banham, London, Collings, 1981; *Theatre and Nationalism: Wole Soyinka and LeRoi Jones* by Alain Ricard, Ife-Ife, University of Ife Press, 1983; *A Writer and His Gods: A Study of the Importance of Yoruba Myths and Religious Ideas in the Writing of Wole Soyinka* by Stephan Larsen, Stockholm, University of Stockholm, 1983; *Wole Soyinka and Modern Tragedy: A Study of Dramatic Theory and Practice* edited by Ketu E. Katrak, Westport, Connecticut, Greenwood Press, 1986; *Wole Soyinka: An Introduction to His Writing* by Obi Maduakar, London, Garland, 1986; *Before Our Very Eyes: Tribute to Wole Soyinka* edited by Dapo Adelugba, Ibadan, Spectrum, 1987; *Index of Subjects, Proverbs and Themes in the Writings of Wole Soyinka* by Greta M.K. Coger, New York, Greenwood, 1988; *The Essential Soyinka: A Reader*, edited by Henry Louis Gates, Jr., New York, Pantheon, 1991; *Wole Soyinka: An Appraisal,* edited by Adewale Maja-Pearce, Oxford, Heinemann, 1994; *The Politics of Wole Soyinka* by Tunde Adeniran, Ibadan, Fountain Publications, 1994; *Talking with Paper: Wole Soyinka at the University of Leeds, 1954-1958, the Making of a Playwright* by James Gibbs, Powis, Wales, Nolisment Publications, 1995; *Wole Soyinka: A Life, Work and Criticism* by Derek Wright, Fredericton, N.B., York Press, 1996.

Theatrical Activities:
Director: **Plays**—By Brecht, Chekhov, Clark, Easmon, Eseoghene, Ogunyemi, Shakespeare, Synge, and his own works; *L'Espace et la Magie*, Paris, 1972; *The Biko Inquest* by Jon Blair and Norman Fenton, IfeIfe, 1978, and New York, 1980.

Actor: **Plays**—Igwezu in *The Swamp Dwellers*, London, 1958; Obaneji and Forest Father in *A Dance of the Forests*, Lagos and Ibadan, 1960; Dauda Touray in *Dear Parent and Ogre* by R. Sarif Easmon, Ibadan, 1961; in *The Republican*, Lagos, 1963; **Film**—*Kongi's Harvest*, 1970; **Radio**—Konu in *The Detainee*, 1965.

* * *

Wole Soyinka's dramatic concerns are as varied as the universal setting that forms the canvas for his plays. Key themes that run through Soyinka's plays are his preoccupation with death, his fascination with the creative-destructive principle (as embodied in the contradictory essence of Ogun [his creative muse]), a belief in the recurring cycle of human stupidity and violence, and a preoccupation with the brutality of dictatorships, especially the military in Nigeria. Added to these concerns is his abiding faith in special individuals whose singular acts of courage may save a humanity that is always on the verge of self-destruction.

Death holds a unique place in Soyinka's dramatic consciousness as can be seen from *The Road, Death and the King's Horseman, The Strong Breed, Requiem for a Futurologist, Camwood on Leaves, A Dance of the Forests,* and *The Bacchae of Euripides.* The first two explore death as both a ritual process and a phenomenon of transition in Yoruba metaphysics. *The Road* deals with the Yoruba ritual of *agemo,* the neither-nor phase between the moment of death and physical dissolution of flesh. The character Professor interrupts the death process of Murano in order to study the transition from one plane of existence to another. The tragedy in the play arises from this sacrilege and act of hubris, and Professor pays for this with his own life. In *Death and the King's Horseman*, a similar interruption of ritual by the character Pilkings leads to tragedy for Elesin and the Yoruba world. Soyinka's explorations are linked to the notion that death, like birth, is merely a stage in the process of life and that life exists on three planes—crossing from one to another requires a rite of passage and a journey through the gulf of transition. An understanding of this notion helps in the explication of Soyinka's dramas, especially the complex ones like *A Dance of the Forests* in which the intercrossings between the planes of the dead, the living, the unborn, and the gods provide the dynamics and tension and *Death and the King's Horseman* in which Elesin is expected to commit suicide so as to accompany his dead Alafin to the world of the ancestors.

In *The Strong Breed*, Eman belongs to the strong breed of the title whose duty it is to carry the sins of the community every year. His tragedy is that in trying to avoid this lighter fate of "carrier" for his own community, he has to accept the heavier fate of "scapegoat" for another community. In all these plays Soyinka asks his audience to understand death not as an occasion of finality and sorrow, as it is in some cultures, but rather as a journey into knowledge and life. *Requiem for a Futurologist* is a satiric reaction to a 1983 prediction that a prominent Nigerian dramatist would die in an accident. Despite treating Godspeak's "death" as a farce, Soyinka probes the deeper significance of death. The play asks very disturbing questions and leaves them unanswered.

What Soyinka does very brilliantly in his "death" plays is examine the notion of tragedy. Tragedy for Soyinka does not always mean death for the main character. The tragic moments are often those moments when the central character courageously enters the gulf of transition, confronts the forces that guard it, and finally emerges with new knowledge to energize his community. Soyinka's tragedy is therefore an individual experience on behalf of the community. Pentheus dies that Thebes might be saved from the vengeance of Dionysus, and it is thus not surprising that at the end of *The Bacchae of Euripides* the entire community celebrates with the wine that spurts from his impaled head. Olunde's death in *Death and the King's Horseman*, Professor's in *The Road*, Eman's in *The Strong Breed,* and Erinjobi's in *Camwood on Leaves* all have this quality of communal beneficence. This view of tragedy is peculiarly African.

The recurring cycle of human stupidity is the theme of *A Dance of the Forests* in which the human community, while celebrating its history, refuses to acknowledge its crimes of the past. The cycle of crime and violence will persist unless a courageous individual breaks it. Demoke could have been this individual, but he returns the Half-Child to its dead mother and the cycle continues.

Mad Men and Specialists is Soyinka's exploration of this cycle in a Nigeria just recovering from a civil war. In the nihilist philosophy of AS, he states the eternal futility of human action: "AS was the Beginning, AS is Now, AS ever shall be. . . ." This philosophy of despair asserts that there is never change in human existence; life will return to its ordained path. Even when the power-crazy Bero kills Old Man, his action promises no escape, instead it is back to another cycle of human misery and cannibalism that is the reality of war.

Soyinka creates strong characters by endowing them with the creative-destructive impulse of Ogun, god of war and of creativity. Most of his heroes—Elesin in *Death and the King's Horseman*, Professor in *The Road*, Demoke in *A Dance of the Forests*, Eman in *The Strong Breed*, Dionysus in *The Bacchae of Euripides*, Daoudu and Segi in *Kongi's Harvest*—all share in the singular ability to be both creative and destructive. They all also in some way breach the gulf of transition as Ogun did as the first victim-hero of Yoruba tragic rites. Thus Soyinka's heros' vitality stems from the tension between their contradictory essences.

Although Soyinka writes about the myths, rituals, and metaphysics of the Yoruba, his plays escape parochialism. He uses his Yoruba origins merely as a creative fount and anchor in his exploration of contemporary Nigerian and universal concerns. His plays are statements about prevailing political, ethical, and social issues. Even his most ritualistic plays are politically and socially meaningful and indicate that his is a mind sensitive to the environment. In the delightful *The Lion and the Jewel,* he looks at the modern world versus the traditional, as represented by Lakunle and Baroka. In the hugely successful Jero plays, in which he satirizes religious charlatanism and susceptibility, in *The Swamp Dwellers,* in which he pits the near-violent but deep-seated anguish of Igwezu against the corrupt priesthood of Kadiye, and even in the domestic comedy, *Childe Internationale*, Soyinka shows himself to be the barometer of his society.

His most political plays are *Kongi's Harvest, Opera Wonyosi,* and *A Play of Giants. Kongi's Harvest* is an attack on the burgeoning of dictatorships all over the African continent. In *Opera Wonyosi* he deals with madness and corruption in Jean-Bédel Bokassa's Central African Republic. In *A Play of Giants* he attacks Africa's well-known quartet of dictators—Bokassa, Idi Amin, Francisco Macias Nguema, and Mobutu Sese Seko. He portrays the four dictators as unfortunate aberrations that are only fit for Madame Tussaud's chamber of horrors. Soyinka is at his satiric best as he paints these human monstrosities as oversized and grotesque buffoons who have no place in human society and history.

In later plays such as *From Zia with Love, A Scourge of Hyacinths* , and *The Beatification of Area Boy,* Soyinka turns his eye on his Nigerian landscape. In the first two he uses an real situation—a retroactive decree of the Buhari/Idiagbon military regime that made drug trafficking an offence punishable by death. Soyinka uses the invading water hyacinths as a metaphor for the military intrusion that is choking the civil liberties of the Nigerian peoples. *The Beatification of Area Boy* deals with the direct and indirect activities of the military as these affect the lives of street traders on Broad Street in Lagos. He subtitled the play "a Lagosian kaleidoscope," and it looks at one incident-filled day in the lives of these marginalized members of Nigerian society and their methods of survival under a regime that is so terribly corrupt and unconcerned with its people's welfare. Most of the action in the play is perceived through the eyes of Sanda, a university dropout who leads the street vendors in their toothless fight against the system. In the three plays there is no mistaking Soyinka's anger and disapproval of the scourge of military dictators who are as corrupt as the civilian politicians they replaced. There is also evidence of his love and hope for his homeland, especially in *The Beatification of Area Boy* with its cast of lovable rogues. In these plays, Soyinka serves in both the traditional role of the artist and as the conscience and mouthpiece of his society.

Soyinka's major contribution may be the creation of a theater that is genuinely African. He draws upon his Yoruba heritage and enriches his writing with its rituals, dances, songs, and beliefs. Above all, however, he borrows and adapts for contemporary African and non-African audiences the very rich Yoruba theater sensibility and integrates it with a solid knowledge of world theater styles and traditions.

—Osita Okagbue

SPEIGHT, Johnny

Nationality: British. **Born:** Canning Town, London, 2 June 1920. **Education:** St. Helen's School. **Family:** Married Constance Barrett in 1956; two sons and one daughter. **Career:** Worked in a factory, as a jazz drummer and insurance salesman; then writer for BBC radio and television. **Awards:** Screenwriters Guild award, 1962, 1966, 1967, 1968; *Evening Standard* award, 1977; Pye award, for television writing, 1983. **Address:** Fouracres, Heronsgate, Chorleywood, Hertfordshire, England. **Died:** 5 July 1998.

Publications

Plays

Mr. Venus, with Ray Galton, music and lyrics by Trevor H. Stanford and Norman Newell (produced London, 1958).
Sketches in *The Art of Living* (produced London, 1960).
The Compartment (televised 1961; produced Pitlochry, Perthshire, 1965).
The Knacker's Yard (produced London, 1962).
The Playmates (televised 1962; as *Games*, produced London, 1971).
If There Weren't Any Blacks You'd Have to Invent Them (televised 1965; produced Loenersloot, Holland, and London, 1965). Loenersloot, Holland, Mickery, 1965; London, Methuen, 1968.
Sketches in *In the Picture* (produced London, 1967).
The Salesman (televised 1970; produced London, 1970).
Till Death Us Do Part. London, Woburn Press, 1973.
The Thoughts of Chairman Alf (produced London, 1976).
Elevenses (sketch), in *The Big One* (produced London, 1983).
For Richer, for Poorer...(television play). BBC Books, 1991.

Screenplays: *French Dressing*, with others, 1964; *Privilege*, with Norman Bogner and Peter Watkins, 1967; *Till Death Us Do Part*, 1968; *The Alf Garnett Saga*, 1972.

Radio Writing: for the *Edmondo Ros*, *Morecambe and Wise*, and *Frankie Howerd* shows, 1956-58; *Early to Braden* show, 1957-58; *The Deadly Game of Chess*, 1958; *The April 8th Show* (*7 Days Early*), 1958; *Eric Sykes* show, 1960-61.

Television Writing: for the *Arthur Haynes* show; *The Compartment*, 1961; *The Playmates*, 1962; *Shamrot*, 1963; *If There Weren't Any Blacks You'd Have to Invent Them*, 1965; *Till Death Us Do Part* series, 1966-75, 1981; *To Lucifer a Sun*, 1967; *Curry and Chips* series, 1969; *The Salesman*, 1970; *Them* series, 1972; *Speight of Marty* series, 1973; *For Richer . . . For Poorer*, 1975; *The Tea Ladies* series, with Ray Galton, 1979; *Spooner's Patch* series, with Ray Galton, 1980; *The Lady Is a Tramp* series, 1982; *In Sickness and in Health*, 1985.

Other

It Stands to Reason: A Kind of Autobiography. London, Joseph-Hobbs, 1973.

The Thoughts of Chairman Alf: Alf Garnett's Little Blue Book; or, Where England Went Wrong: An Open Letter to the People of Britain. London, Robson, 1973.

Pieces of Speight. London, Robson, 1974.

The Garnett Chronicles: The Life and Times of Alf Garnett, Esq. London, Robson, 1986.

*

Theatrical Activities:

Actor: **Films**—*The Plank*, 1967; *The Undertakers*, 1969; *Rhubarb*, 1970.

* * *

Johnny Speight is one of those writers whose success in television became a trap. Unlike almost every other writer of comic series for prime-time viewers, he has been a source of controversy, scandal, and outrage, as well as having been rewarded with a popularity that proved to be less than totally advantageous. He was a factory worker before World War II, and it was not until 1955 that his determination to succeed as a writer bore any fruit. His first work was writing scripts for such comedians as Frankie Howerd, Arthur Askey, Cyril Fletcher, and Eric Sykes. When he began to write for Arthur Haynes, he showed an ability to create unusual material rather than the power to exploit the familiar gifts of an established comedian. For Haynes, Speight created the character of a tramp whose aggressive, rebarbative personality had a striking originality.

It was through a series of programs for BBC television, *Till Death Us Do Part*, that Speight became a household name. His work became a battleground over which so-called permissive liberals fought old-fashioned viewers who believed in verbal restraint, the importance of good taste, and the banishment of certain topics, notably religion, from light entertainment. What Speight wrote was in essence originally a cartoon, a Cockney version of the North Country Andy Capp, in which attitudes almost everybody would condemn as antisocial were derided. Four people—husband and wife and their daughter and son-in-law—inhabit the sitting room of a slum house; they have nothing in common except their bitter dislike for each other. The father, Alf Garnett, is barely literate and full of misconceived, misunderstood, and ignorant prejudices about race, politics, and religion; his language is atrocious. His wife is reduced almost to the state of a vegetable, coming to life only when her detestation of her husband finds some opportunity of expressing itself. The son-in-law, as ignorantly and stupidly of the left as Garnett is of the right, is a Liverpudlian-Irish Roman Catholic who dresses flamboyantly, wears his hair long, and does no work whatever; his only spell of activity was an inefficient attempt to swindle social security officials. The daughter agrees in all things with her husband, but it is plain that her agreement is the result of his effectiveness as a lover rather than of any intellectual processes of argument.

Through these appalling people Speight was able to lambaste senseless racial and political prejudices while making cheeky fun of the royal family, the church, and anything else that drifted into what passed in the Garnett household for conversation. For a time Garnett was a very effective weapon against bigotry and stupidity. Unfortunately, his effectiveness as a vehicle for satire tended to diminish as the monstrous energy with which he was created slipped out of control and allowed him to take possession of each episode. The series continued long after the original impetus had exhausted itself, and it began to show something dangerously ambivalent in Speight's attack on racism. The creation of two Garnett films demonstrated that Speight's monsters were at their most popular when there was nothing left to say about them, so that *Till Death Us Do Part* seemed to turn into an incubus from which the author was unable to escape.

Curry and Chips, another effort to stifle racial prejudice by allowing it to be voiced in its most extreme forms by the stupid, lacked the vitality of *Till Death Us Do Part.* A later series, *Them*, in which two tramps dreamed of grandeur, their dreams contrasting sharply with the reality of their way of life, was notable only for the gentleness of its comedy, proving that Speight was capable of more than the stridency of life with the Garnett family.

Such work, for all the energy of Garnettry and the strength with which the leading monster had been created, made it seem that Speight had moved a long way in the wrong direction. His first television play proper, *The Compartment* (1961), had nothing to do with the sort of writing that later made him notorious. In a compartment of an old-fashioned train that has no corridor, a businessman is alone with a practical joker who persecutes him for the length of the journey. It becomes the joker's amusement to convince his pompous, easily frightened companion that he is helpless in the company of an armed, murderous psychopath. There are no motives, no explanations, no rationalizations; the events simply happen with a sort of uneasy humor. A year later the same joker, selling "jokes" and tricks from door to door, finds himself sheltered for a night by a strange psychopathic girl who is the only inhabitant of a large house. *The Playmates*—for the girl wants to join in the fun with the traveler's samples—shares the disregard for motives and explanations already shown by *The Compartment.* A third play, which it seems offers another aspect of the experience of the joker, was equally effective. The ideas were fashionable at the time when it was avant-garde and exciting to offer allegiance to the theater of the absurd, but Speight produced his genuine shocks and frissons.

Both *The Compartment* and the later television play *If There Weren't Any Blacks You'd Have to Invent Them* were adapted for stage performances, but despite some success they proved to belong to the screen rather than the stage. *If There Weren't Any Blacks* exploited Speight's reputation, won from the Garnett series, as a passionate opponent of racism, and it makes its point amusingly and convincingly. There is none of the ambivalence that crept into *Till Death Us Do Part* when Garnett took control of the series and began to speak as a character in his own right rather than as an instrument designed by his creator to ridicule the politically idiotic. Speight's only genuine play for the theater not adapted from television material, *The Knacker's Yard*, won praise for the vigor and imaginativeness of its dialogue.

It is impossible not to think of Speight as a creator of grotesque, disturbing characters who became trapped by television into a situation demanding that he repeat, with diminishing returns, a success that rapidly lost its inventiveness. It is thus that he paid the penalty of his originality.

—Henry Raynor

SPURLING, John

Pseudonym: Henry Tube. **Nationality:** British. **Born:** Kisumu, Kenya, 17 July 1936. **Education:** Dragon School, Oxford, 1946-49; Marlborough College, Wiltshire, 1950-54; St. John's College, Oxford, 1957-60, B.A. 1960. **Military Service:** Served in the Royal Artillery (national service), 1955-57. **Family:** Married Hilary Forrest (the writer Hilary Spurling) in 1961; one daughter and two sons. **Career:** Plebiscite officer for the United Kingdom in Southern Cameroons, 1960-61; announcer, BBC Radio, London, 1963-66; radio and book reviewer (under the pseudonym Henry Tube), the *Spectator*, London, 1966-70, and other publications. Henfield fellow, University of East Anglia, Norwich, 1973, art critic, *New Statesman*, London, 1976-88. Lives in London. **Agent:** Patricia MacNaughton, MacNaughton Lowe Representation, 200 Fulham Road, London SW10 9PN, England.

Publications

Plays

Char (produced Oxford, 1959).
MacRune's Guevara As Realised by Edward Hotel (produced London, 1969; Walla Walla, Washington, 1971; New York, 1975). London, Calder and Boyars, 1969.
Romance, music and lyrics by Charles Ross (produced Leeds and London, 1971).
In the Heart of the British Museum (produced Edinburgh and London, 1971). London, Calder and Boyars, 1972.
Shades of Heathcliff (produced Sheffield, 1971; London, 1972). With *Death of Captain Doughty*, London, Boyars, 1975.
Peace in Our Time (produced Sheffield, 1972).
Death of Captain Doughty (televised 1973). With *Shades of Heathcliff*, London, Boyars, 1975.
McGonagall and the Murderer (produced Edinburgh, 1974).
On a Clear Day You Can See Marlowe (produced London, 1974).
While Rome Burns (produced Canterbury, 1976).
Antigone Through the Looking Glass (produced London, 1979).
The British Empire, Part One (produced Birmingham, 1980). London, Boyars, 1982.
Coming Ashore in Guadeloupe (produced Harrogate and London, 1982).
Racine at the Girls' School (produced Chettenham, 1992; London, 1993).
Achilles on the Beach at Troy (produced Yorkshire, 1994).

Radio Plays: *Where Tigers Roam*, 1976; *The Stage Has Nothing to Give Us* (documentary), 1980; *The British Empire: Part One: Dominion over Palm and Pine*, 1982, *Part Two: The Christian Hero*, 1982, *Part Three: The Day of Reckoning*, 1985; *Daughters and Sons*, from the novel by Ivy Compton-Burnett, 1985; *Fancy Pictures: A Portrait After Gainsborough*, 1988; *Discobolus*, 1989; *The Butcher of Baghdad*, 1993; *MacRune's Guevara*, 1993.

Television Plays: *Hope*, 1970; *Faith*, 1971; *Death of Captain Doughty*, 1973; *Silver*, 1973.

Novels

The Ragged End. London, Weidenfeld and Nicolson, 1989.
After Zenda. London, Andre Deutsch, 1995.

Other

Beckett: A Study of His Plays, with John Fletcher. London, Eyre Methuen, and New York, Hill and Wang, 1972; revised edition, Eyre Methuen, 1978; revised edition, as *Beckett the Playwright*, Methuen, and New York, Farrar Straus, 1985.
Graham Greene. London, Methuen, 1983.

Editor, *The Hill Station: An Unfinished Novel, and An Indian Diary*, by J. G. Farrell. London, Weidenfeld and Nicolson, 1981.

*

John Spurling comments:

(1977) *MacRune's Guevara* was written from a desire to create an event in space rather than to turn out something recognisable as a play (I imagined it being performed in an art gallery rather than a theatre): at the same time I wanted to represent to myself my own conflicting reactions to Che Guevara and to attack certain forms of artistic and political cant which were dominant in the theatre at the time—perhaps still persist.

I found the idea for the more complex structure of *In the Heart of the British Museum* in Frances Yates's book on Renaissance theories of *The Art of Memory*, but after completing five scenes I put the play away. I took it up again as a commission for the Traverse Workshop Theatre, under Max Stafford-Clark's direction. The piece, with its emphasis on song and dance, was finished with this particular company in mind, but since I had felt the need for just such a company to perform it even before I knew of the company's existence, the original structure did not have to be altered. The subject matter comprises Aztec and Chinese legend, the recent Chinese Cultural Revolution, the exile of the Roman poet Ovid, and some of the subject matter of Ovid's own poems. The central theme is also Ovid's, the idea of Metamorphosis, and this is an important element in the structure.

Shades of Heathcliff grew directly out of being commissioned for Ed Thomason's Crucible Vanguard Theatre in Sheffield. A play for Sheffield seemed to call for a version of *Wuthering Heights*; the company consisted only of three actors and one actress, and, performing in a small space, dictated that it be a chamber piece and that the characters of the four Brontë children and of the novel itself be melted together.

Peace in Our Time was commissioned by the Crucible Theatre, Sheffield. It is the first part of a larger work called *Ghosts and Monsters of the Second World War*, which I have yet to finish. This first part is set in Hell, where the characters (Hitler, Stalin,

Mussolini, Chamberlain, et al.) replay some of the political games of 1935-39.

McGonagall and the Murderer is a short play commissioned by the Pool Theatre, Edinburgh. A man who has failed to assassinate Queen Victoria and is now confined in Broadmoor tries to win a second chance by entering the mind of the poet McGonagall, himself on the road to Balmoral. *On a Clear Day You Can See Marlowe* was first written in 1970 and revised in 1974 for the Major Road Company. The play is something of a companion piece to *MacRune's Guevara*—a collage of the few known facts about the playwright Marlowe, much speculation (both reasonable and ludicrous), and versions of his own work in modern rehearsal.

(1988) *While Rome Burns*, commissioned by the Marlowe Theatre, Canterbury under its then director, David Carson, is a futuristic version of Edgar Allan Poe's story "The Masque of the Red Death." A company of travelling players visits an island off the coast of Britain, the last refuge of a group of well-heeled, middle-class people who have fled from a major catastrophe on the mainland. *Antigone Through the Looking Glass*, also commissioned by David Carson for a production at the King's Head, Islington, London, is roughly the same length as Sophocles' *Antigone* which is being acted off-stage, while we watch the performers coming and going in the green-room.

The British Empire trilogy, covering the period 1820-1911, with a cast of over 200 characters, was intended for the stage. Part One was performed in the studio at Birmingham Rep as a promenade production (directed by Peter Farago with a cast of only 9) and then adapted for BBC Radio 3, which also commissioned Parts Two and Three. I am still hoping to see the whole seven-hour work on the stage, preferably performed in one day or at least on successive evenings.

Coming Ashore in Guadeloupe was started in 1973 for a Dutch company which folded, but substantially revised in 1982 for the Cherub Theatre Company and its director Andrew Visnevski. It is a panorama (in fairly concise form) of the European discovery and conquest of America, featuring Columbus, Cortes, Pizarro, Raleigh, Verrazzano, and others, but viewed much of the time through the eyes of the Indian inhabitants.

(1998) The subject of *Racine at the Girls' School* is Racine's last-but-one play *Esther,* originally performed in 1689 by the girls of Madame de Maintenon's school at St. Cyr, near Versailles. My play deals with various crises, personal and religious, during the rehearsals, directed by Racine himself, for a significant change of cast in the fourth performance of *Esther.* This performance was attended not only by Madame de Mainteon and her lover (probably secret husband) King Louis XIV, but also by the recently exiled King James II of England and his queen, Maria of Modena. My own play is Racinean in style and observes Aristotle's classical unities. It was commissioned by the Cheltenham Literary Festival and was performed entirely by schoolgirls from Cheltenham Ladies' College and, a year later, by pupils at St. Paul's Girls' School in London.

The Butcher of Baghdad was written for the Cherub Company of London and combines the old story of Shahrazad and the Caliph of Baghdad (from *The Arabian Nights*) with the Gulf War of 1991. *Achilles on the Beach at Troy,* in which the Security Council are trying to cope with various contemporary wars and suddenly find themselves overseeing, like the Greek gods, the Trojan War, was commissioned by the Yorkshire Sculpture Park, near Wakefield, to coincide with the exhibition there of Sir Anthony Caro's Trojan War sculptures.

* * *

John Spurling's work has veered from the technically innovative and exciting to the commonplace, and some of it—for example, the sentimental musical drawing room comedy *Romance*—is probably best forgotten. He has, however, produced three plays that will almost certainly survive: *MacRune's Guevara, In the Heart of the British Museum*, and *While Rome Burns.*

There is in most of Spurling's work a profound concern with history and experience, and indeed with what happens to history. In *MacRune's Guevara* it is suggested that the real Guevara was an enigmatic figure of whom we are unlikely to know anything that finally matters. History, present in the play in the form of press reports and problematic enough by itself, is only one of the ways in which the audience sees Guevara. Other viewpoints come from the actors in the play, as well as from the narrator, Edward Hotel, who is the supposed dramatist. Hotel has recently occupied a room in which the failed Scots-Irish artist MacRune lived just before his death. MacRune had covered the walls of the room with pencil sketches of 17 scenes of Guevara's Bolivian campaign. The sketches, now faint and sometimes indistinguishable from other marks on the wall, are a parallel to the press reports about Guevara. Everything is thrown into a discussion of the nature of history, including Hotel's own views on the subject and MacRune's supposed views, which, we are told with questionable reliability, are heretical from a Marxist point of view. From all of this Guevara emerges as partly ineffectual and partly valiant guerrilla hero but also as a dupe of higher powers. On the one hand he is an inspirer of love who does not allow himself to be swayed by it from his cause, and on the other, in an interlude located in the Congo, he is a merely simpleminded killer of bourgeois Belgians. At the end of his life he appears disillusioned, although he is as brave as ever. He appears to be a man who did not amount to much in life but who has acquired mythic dimensions in death. One critic called the play "an honest magnification of the author's own confusion." In fact, it is the exact opposite, a sophisticated attempt to show the king without his clothes. Through Guevara, Spurling is also making a point about all contemporary heroes.

The technique of multiple viewpoints used in *MacRune's Guevara,* of which Spurling was one of the pioneers, was further elaborated in his next notable play, *In the Heart of the British Museum.* Here three narratives are interwoven: the disgrace and rehabilitation of a Chinese professor during the Cultural Revolution, the exile and death of Ovid, and the temptation and fall of the Aztec god Quetzalcóatl and his succession by the grimmer Texcatlipoca. These themes elaborate and comment on one another. In contrasting power and war with culture and intelligence and in setting history against myth and reputation against reality, Spurling does not take sides. He makes it clear that he is not quarreling with others; it is of his quarrel with his own multitudinous and contradictory responses to Guevara, myth, history, power, and intelligence that Spurling makes his artistic work. By his omnivorous, witty plays he hopes to make us experience all of reality and thus progress to that profound understanding that is at the heart of all things.

Yet the understanding toward which Spurling stretches his hands is nothing if not radically critical, especially of contemporary fads and blind spots. Witness the concern in the title of *While Rome Burns,* which is loosely structured on Poe's "The Masque of the

Red Death." In this play a privileged few escape from Britain to an island fortress where they are burdened neither with incomes nor with taxes and are protected from news of the world without. War games and cricket, costume balls and leisured adultery, all suggestive of a luxury cruise without a destination, are what constitute their concerns. The island sanctuary is approached by an assassin, and disconnected set pieces provide mannered comic moments that reveal the butterfly character of the protagonists and their growing sense of dread. We identify with their fear, and yet we cannot help seeing that this beauty is terrible and deserves to be destroyed.

Spurling has written conventional plays with competence. At his best, however, he avoids the comforts of security. Melodrama and the music hall, comedy and tragedy, the neat plot and the predictable one—all are alike eschewed. Sometimes Spurling pares away, peels off layer after layer. At other times he takes strange or unexpected angles, comparing like with what appears at first glance to be wholly unlike. Finally, his work functions as parable, icon, and mystic text, and at his finest he persuades drama to aspire to the condition of poetry.

—Prabhu S. Guptara

STARKWEATHER, David

Nationality: American. **Born:** Madison, Wisconsin, 11 September 1935. **Education:** University of Wisconsin, Madison, 1953-57, B.A. in speech 1957. **Career:** Freelance legal proofreader, New York. **Awards:** Creative Artists Public Service grant, 1975; Rockefeller grant, 1978. **Address:** 340 West 11th Street, New York, New York 10014, U.S.A.

PUBLICATIONS

Plays

Maggie of the Bargain Basement, music by Starkweather (ballad opera; produced Madison, Wisconsin, 1956).
Excuse Me, Pardon Me (produced Madison, Wisconsin, 1957).
You May Go Home Again (produced New York, 1963). Published in *The Off-Off-Broadway Book*, edited by Albert Poland and Bruce Mailman, Indianapolis, Bobbs Merrill, 1972.
So Who's Afraid of Edward Albee? (produced New York, 1963).
The Love Pickle (produced New York, 1963; Edinburgh, 1971).
The Family Joke (produced New York, 1965).
The Assent (produced New York, 1967).
Chamber Comedy (produced Washington, D.C., 1969).
A Practical Ritual to Exorcise Frustration after Five Days of Rain, music by Allan Landon (also co-director: produced New York, 1970).
The Poet's Papers: Notes for an Event (produced Boston, 1971). Published in *New American Plays 3*, edited by William M. Hoffman, New York, Hill and Wang, 1970.
The Straights of Messina (produced New York, 1973).
Language (also director: produced New York, 1974).
The Bones of Bacon (produced New York, 1977).

*

Manuscript Collection: Lincoln Center Library of the Performing Arts, New York.

Theatrical Activities:
Director: Several of his own plays.

David Starkweather comments:

(1973) Two mirrors facing what do they reflect?

Slice the mind in fives, Consciousness stage center. One way wings of Memory, staging areas of attention seeking self-ordering re-experience, detouring terror into ritual belief: Subconscious. Opposite wings of Appetite, senses drawn to sources of actuation, pulled always into foreign homes: Superconscious. Deeper still surrounding wings as well as centers, forms in the mind's structure beneath conception, containing all potential concepts like the possibilities of a medium; Unconscious. Facing Other Consciousness awareness of other centers of awareness, the possibilities of union/conflict with/within all potential spectators. The boundaries between these modes of mindworks the symbol, always blocking one way, all ways disappearing another.

My current vision of theatre is a head, the bodies of the audience resonating chambers like the jugs beneath the stage in the classic N , feeling their behavioral imaginations. Sound surrounds but the eyes are in front perceiving SENSES in terms of each other. Vision is figure to sound's ground and vice versa because each word has an aural and visual component. A noun is a picture (visual/spatial) and a verb is a melody (aural/temporal) relation. The split between being and doing dissolves when nouns are just states verbs are in at a given moment. The central human art form is the spoken word.

We laugh at people who are out of control. We laugh with people who are shoulder to shoulder. And we call it tragedy when a hero who is behind us loses.

If you write a play and do it badly that play is about incompetence. My plays in their forms hope to suggest what competence is. Moving toward an ideal. And I deal this round. Place your bets. It's a show of competence. All plays are about knowing. Being is where they're at. What I seek in a word is Order. In a feeling a release of energy.

For themes I have recognized a clear line of development in my last three plays: 1) there is nothing you can know without limiting your ability to know something equally true; 2) the only thing we need to believe is that there is nothing we need to believe; and 3) the only taboo is on taboos.

I write consistently about changing minds.

A number of works, my most ambitious, are as yet unproduced: *Owey Wishey Are You There?*, 1965, *The Wish-House*, 1967, a bianry set "Taste and Sense: A Love Story," 1985, and (either to be seen first) "On Western Siv," 1991.

(1998) I have been working since on my most ambitious work, a trilogy, I hope to finish before the millennium and have produced before the following one.

* * *

Ham: And where are you?
Noah: I am here and it is now. And all around is mystery.

—*A Practical Ritual to Exorcise Frustration after Five Days of Rain*

It is not that he hates his family, his religion, or the rest of society. It is just that he cannot stand their noise. Most people he knows participate in the trivia of family life and the charades of state. They believe that somewhere there is one person who will solve the riddle of their emotional needs, that the state must be protected, especially from within, that there is a god who sits on a throne.

So the young man leaves his home, not to be mean or ornery but because he will go crazy if he stays. He goes downtown, where there are so many people that no one will notice him, or downtown to the wilderness, where there are no people. And now he is in the downtown part of his mind, where memories of his former life rise and beckon him to return and resume the old ties. He replies to their telephone calls and to his dreams that their lives are meaningless and that their ways are mindless and hold no allure.

But the old ways are alluring to him in his solitude, and part of him wants to go home. Gradually, painfully, he withdraws into the land of light, however, and now he is totally alone with his mind. Soon he is his mind, and alone he is together. At this still point fears arise in their pure form and threaten his sanity. They are fears of pain, of people, of death, of bodily functions.

He discovers that these fears cannot be conquered in their essence but must be met in their actuality, and so he goes back to the world to conquer his fears. But this time he is armed. Around his waist he carries self-containment, his vest is armored with enlightenment, and his helmet is pure reason.

There are no trumpets on his return. People have scarcely noticed that he has been gone, so busy have they been with their own wars and marriages. When he approaches the natives, he finds that things are as they have always been between him and them. They do not see what he sees. So he withdraws and returns again armed with new weapons. The cycle is endless, and the man is lonely but filled with love. His attitude is increasingly ironic.

This portrait of the saintly exile is a composite of the heroes and mock heroes that form the core of David Starkweather's work, the recalcitrant lover Colin of *So Who's Afraid of Edward Albee?,* the errant son David of *You May Go Home Again,* the would-be suicidal Alan of *The Assent,* the wandering Poet of *The Poet's Papers,* and both Sonny and Pittsburgh, who together form the hero of *Language*. They are all versions of the Odysseus/Christ/dropout antiheroes of our time.

Colin, one of Starkweather's earliest creations, is merely disgusted by the system and puzzled by his disgust. David, created later, is overwhelmed by his ambiguous feelings toward his family and goes into exile. Alan, guilty in exile, longs for death. The Poet, more comfortable in his separation from society, wanders the earth and watches it destroy itself. And Sonny and Pittsburgh, who have in different ways plumbed the mysteries of isolation, now seek a way back into a society they have left.

In all of his plays, but especially in *The Family Joke* and *The Wish-House,* which has not been produced, Starkweather provides ample reason for self-exile and incidentally offers savage but concerned criticism of Western society. In *The Family Joke* the nuclear family is seen as the system's breeding factory. Children must be raised, no matter what the cost to the parents. *The Wish-House* presents an almost paranoid view of the methods of mind control that the system is willing to employ. For the enemy, here represented by a Dr. Brill, is in possession of the same knowledge that Starkweather's exiled heroes have struggled so hard to obtain: "All that you consider yourself to be is merely the stopper to contain what you really are. All that you do most easily, by habit and without thought, is only to avoid your most beautiful and dangerous nature."

In counterpoint to some of the most glorious abstractions in contemporary theater, architectural visions that spring from contemplation of the basic dualities of thought, Starkweather weaves the anxieties that often accompany advanced thought—fears of death, impotence, blood, piss, and shit.

In *The Poet's Papers* the war between the two divisions of mankind, the Orals and the Anals, is conducted in lyrical language. In *The Assent* the system prefers control of urination to control of theft: "Petty theft raises the living standard of the worker . . . and stimulates cash flow. Whereas urine . . . involves the production of a nonsalable commodity and is therefore a general drain on the corporate effort." In *Language* the virgin Sonny admits, "I think that potency has something to do with murder."

The plays of Starkweather give a complete view of what in olden times would have been called a saint: the man who leaves his society, goes into physical and psychical exile, searches for his god, and brings back the golden fleece to an indifferent world. In play after play and in growing clarity, Starkweather shows us the dangerous yet exciting journey, the abandoned society, and the funny, heartbreaking return. He even allows us glimpses of the fleece:

> He goes away within
> miles from the common road
> to bring back for this world
> something lovely something pure
> Thank you, man.

—William M. Hoffman

STAVIS, Barrie

Nationality: American. **Born:** New York City, 16 June 1906. **Education:** New Utrecht High School, Brooklyn, New York, graduated 1924; Columbia University, New York, 1924-27. **Military Service:** Served in the Army Signal Corps, Plans and Training section, 1942-45: technical-sergeant. **Family:** Married 1) Leona Heyert in 1925 (divorced 1939); 2) Bernice Coe in 1950, one son and one daughter. **Career:** Foreign correspondent in Europe, 1937-38; freelance journalist after World War II. Co-founder, and member of the board of directors, New Stages theatre group, 1947, and United States Institute for Theatre Technology, 1961-64 and 1969-72; visiting fellow, Institute for the Arts and Humanistic Studies, Pennsylvania State University, University Park, 1971. Lives in New York City. **Awards:** Yaddo fellowship, 1939; National Theatre Conference award, 1948, 1949. Fellow, American Theatre Association, 1982.

Publications

Plays

In These Times (produced New York, 1932).

The Sun and I (produced New York, 1933; revised version produced New York, 1937).

Refuge: A One-Act Play of the Spanish War (produced London, 1938). New York, French, 1939.

Lamp at Midnight: A Play about Galileo (produced New York, 1947; Bristol, 1956). New York, Dramatists Play Service, 1948; revised version, South Brunswick, New Jersey, A.S Barnes, and London, Yoseloff, 1966; revised version, Chicago, Dramatic Publishing Company, 1974; one-hour school and church version (produced Chicago, 1972; New York, 1973), Dramatic Publishing Company, 1974.

The Man Who Never Died: A Play about Joe Hill (produced St. Paul, 1955; New York, 1958). New York, Haven Press, 1954; revised version, South Brunswick, New Jersey, A.S. Barnes, and London, Yoseloff, 1972.

Banners of Steel: A Play about John Brown (produced Carbondale, Illinois, 1962). South Brunswick, New Jersey, A.S. Barnes, and London, Yoseloff, 1967; revised version, as *Harpers Ferry: A Play about John Brown* (produced Minneapolis, 1967).

Coat of Many Colors: A Play about Joseph in Egypt (produced Provo, Utah, 1966). South Brunswick, New Jersey, A.S. Barnes, and London, Yoseloff, 1968.

Joe Hill (opera libretto), music by Alan Bush, adaptation of the play *The Man Who Never Died* by Stavis (produced Berlin, 1970).

Galileo Galilei (oratorio) music by Lee Hoiby, adaptation of the play *Lamp at Midnight* by Stavis (produced Huntsville, Alabama, 1975).

The Raw Edge of Victory (as *Washington*, produced Midland, Texas, 1976). Published in *Dramatics* (Cincinnati), April and May 1986.

Video: *The Man Who Never Died,* 1990.

Novels

The Chain of Command (novella). New York, Ackerman, 1945.

Home, Sweet Home! New York, Sheridan House, 1949.

Other

John Brown: The Sword and the Word. South Brunswick, New Jersey, A. S. Barnes, and London, Yoseloff, 1970.

Editor, with W. Frank Harmon, *The Songs of Joe Hill.* New York, People's Artists, 1955.

*

Manuscript Collections: Lincoln Center Library of the Performing Arts, New York; Pennsylvania State University, University Park.

Critical Studies: "Barrie Stavis: The Humanist Alternative" by Herbert Shore, in *Educational Theatre Journal* (Washington, D.C.), December 1973; interview in *Astonish Us in the Morning: Tyrone Guthrie Remembered* by Alfred Rossi, London, Hutchinson, 1977, Detroit, Wayne State University Press, 1981; "Humanism Is the Vital Subject" (interview), in *Dramatics* (Cincinnati), March-April 1978; "A History, A Portrait, A Memory" by Stavis, in *Time Remembered: Alan Bush: An Eightieth Birthday Symposium* edited by Ronald Stevenson, Kidderminster, Worcestershire, Bravura, 1981; "How Broad Should the Theatre's Concerns Be?" by Daniel Larner, in *Dramatics* (Cincinnati), May 1981; "Barrie Stavis Issue" of *Religion and Theatre* (St. Paul), August 1981; *American Theater of the 1960s* by Zoltán Szilassy, Carbondale, Southern Illinois University Press, 1986; "Barrie Stavis: Sixty Years of Craft and Commitment" by Ezra Goldstein, in *Dramatics* (Cincinnati), April 1986; *The Galileo Plays of Bertolt Brecht and Barrie Stavis* (dissertation) by David Ward Larson, University of Illinois, 1989; "The Passionate, Personal Plays of Barrie Stavis" by Ezra Goldstein, in *Cardozo Studies in Law and Literature* (New York), Fall-Winter 1990, pp. 279-88; "Anywhere But Home: The Life and Work of Barrie Stavis" by Daniel Larner, in *American Drama* (Cincinnati, Ohio), Fall 1994, pp. 39-61.

Barrie Stavis comments:

(1973) I wrote my first full-length play when I was 19 years old. I had my first production when I was 26. Fortunately there are no scripts in existence. About a dozen plays followed—all since destroyed.

The material and form of these early plays were derivative, echoing closely the dominant writing and production modes of the American stage. I refer to the Theatre of Illusion where the play is naturalistic in concept and style, generally romantic in approach. The physical envelope of such plays consists of a box set, usually a four-walled room with the fourth wall removed so that the audience can "peek in" and see what happens to those "real" people on the stage.

I was gradually becoming dissatisfied with this kind of stage and its "imitation of life." It could not contain the statements I was trying to make in the theatre. But at that time I did not know how to break away from the narrow restrictions of the romantic-naturalism and the pseudo-realism of the Theatre of Illusion. I knew (though certainly not as clearly as I know it now) that I was concerned with writing plays where the driving force of the characters was the clash of their *ideas*, not their subjective emotions.

Form is dictated by content and should grow out of function. Thus, I was also searching for a form which would be consonant with my material. I was seeking a freedom and a plastic use of the stage which the box set could not give me. I began studying Shakespeare intensively. Shakespeare was, and remains even to this day, my major theatre influence, followed by the Bible for its style, and its ruthlessly candid and objective way of telling a story. My study of the Elizabethan theatre, along with Greek theatre and the Roman amphitheatre, gradually led me to devise what I designated (1933-34) as "Time-Space Stage"—a stage where both time and space could be used with fluidity.

In 1939 I began to work on *Lamp at Midnight*. It took three years to complete. It was in this play that I first achieved a successful synthesis of content and form. The characters in the play are embattled over basic philosophic concepts; and the plastic use of time and space on the stage proved to be the perfect medium for expressing the conflict of ideas.

It was then that I realized I wanted to write further plays exploring this use of the stage. Although all the plays in the series would have the same major theme, each play would be independent unto itself with the common theme developed from a different axis of observation.

The series proved to be a tetralogy exploring the problems of men who have ushered in new and frequent drastic changes in the existing social order—men who are of their time and yet in advance of their time. And I have been concerned with examining the thrust they exercise on their society, and the counter-thrust society exerts on them.

It is the essence of nature and of man to undergo continual change. New forms evolve from old, mature, and, as the inevitable concomitant of their maturation, induce still newer forms which replace them. This is the historical process.

This process of change is gradual. It is not always perceived nor clearly apparent. Yet it is constant and inexorable. At a given moment when historical conditions are ripe, a catalyst enters and fragments the existing culture, setting into motion a new alignment of forces, a new series of relationships, which gradually become stabilized, codified.

It is this process of change that I endeavor to capture in my plays: the precise moment in history when society, ripe for change, gives birth to the catalyst who sets the dynamics of change into accelerated motion.

The four plays in their order are: *Lamp at Midnight* (Galileo Galilei), *The Man Who Never Died* (Joe Hill), *Harpers Ferry* (John Brown), *Coat of Many Colors* (Joseph in Egypt). In the first of these plays, *Lamp at Midnight,* I dramatize the story of Galileo Galilei, the first human being to turn his new, powerful telescope to the night skies, there to discover the true motion of our solar system, a discovery unleashing a host of scientific and social consequence which heralded the coming Industrial Age. In *The Man Who Never Died* I dramatize the story of Joe Hill, troubador, folk poet, and trade union organizer, who was framed on a murder charge and who, during the 22 months of his prison stay, grew to heroic proportions. In *Harpers Ferry* I dramatize the story of John Brown's raid on Harpers Ferry, a raid which was the precursor to the Civil War. In *Coat of Many Colors* I dramatize the story of Joseph in Egypt, the world's first great agronomist and social planner, and I explore the theme of power and its uses. These four plays have been so designed that they can be performed by a single basic acting company. Further, all four plays can be produced on the same basic unit set.

Galileo Galilei, Joe Hill, John Brown, Joseph—these men have certain things in common. They were put on trial for their thoughts and deeds, found guilty, and punished. Yet their very ideas and acts achieved their vindication by later generations. Thus does the heresy of one age become the accepted truth of the next.

I have chosen to write plays about men who have an awareness of social and moral responsibility, plays that have faith in man's capacity to resolve his problems despite the monumental difficulties facing him. Why? Because I believe in ethical commitment. I believe that man is capable of ultimately solving the problems of the Nuclear Age.

Today, much theatre writing is obsessed with frustration and defeat. One trend of such playwriting deals with personality maladjustments and sexual aberration. This theatre is preoccupied with such matters as who goes to bed with whom, the gap in communication between parent and adolescent, the need to show that sex is either rape or submission. There is intense concern with subjective, neurotic problems, very little concern with the objective and social conditions of the world in which the characters live and the impact of the world upon them. It is as though the characters were living in a vacuum tube. Outside is the pulsating, throbbing world, but within the tube they function only insofar as their psyches collide with one another. Of the outside world, there is barely a reflection. A second contemporary trend is the writing of plays which explore the thesis that the human condition is hopeless because man is utterly dislocated in his society, that rational thought is a snare, that human life is purposeless, that action is without point for it will accomplish no result. There is in such plays no release for the affirmative emotion of an audience.

However, I believe with Chekhov that "Every playwright is responsible not only for what man is, but for what man can be." With Aristophanes, I seek to banish the "little man and woman affair" from the stage and to replace it with plays which explore ideas with such force and clarity as to raise them to the level of passion. Today especially, it should be the responsibility of the playwright to search out those situations which, by the inherent nature of the material, will capture the emotions and the intellect of an audience and focus it on men and women striving creatively for a positive goal.

(1988) I am now engaged in another tetralogy. The overall thematic examination of these four plays is *War, Revolution, and Peace*. In them, I explore George Washington, Abraham Lincoln, Miguel Hidalgo, and Simon Bolivar. Thus, I deal with the four liberators of the Western Hemisphere. In these plays I am concerned with the movement of colony to nation, of subject to citizen.

The material I handle is historical, but like the four plays of my first tetralogy, they are highly contemporary. We have been living in a century of war. There was the Japanese-Russian war in the first years of the century. Then came the famous/infamous assassination in Sarajevo which ushered in World War I. From then on until today, the world has been embroiled in wars, large and small. At this moment, there are over *50* different wars raging throughout the world. Thus, focusing on the theme of *War, Revolution, and Peace* is very much of our time.

I have completed the first play of the tetralogy: *The Raw Edge of Victory*, which deals with George Washington and the Revolutionary War. I'm half way through the second play, which focuses on Abraham Lincoln and the Civil War. Since I spend approximately five years on each play, it is obvious that I have accounted for the next ten years of my writing life!

* * *

A mere glance at the men Barrie Stavis has chosen to write about is indicative of his own passions, goals, and intentions: John Brown, Joe Hill, Galileo, and the biblical Joseph, and, in various stages of completion, works about George Washington, Hidalgo, Bolívar, and Lincoln.

There is about Stavis an almost Talmudic fury when he discusses his work and when he writes. This is in strange contrast to the man himself, for he is warm, friendly, hopeful, and eager. Stavis is intellectually always aware ("conscious" might be an even better word) of what he is doing dramaturgically and theatrically. His experience in theater goes back further than most, and he has worked with almost every kind of theater, getting his plays on stages everywhere.

Beyond grassroots experiences there is the playwright Stavis who is very like the protagonists in his own plays—a man with a vision. It is a driving, almost monomaniacal vision that he, the artist, holds in careful check.

Just as his first tetralogy dealt with, in his words, "four aspects of mankind," all of his plays are precisely predicated. *Lamp at Midnight,* which was seen by 20 million in one night on a Hallmark Hall of Fame telecast, is "about Truth," no small feat to undertake in a single play. *The Man Who Never Died* is "about

Human Dignity"; *Harpers Ferry* is "about Freedom"; and *Coat of Many Colors* is "about Power." Stavis writes this kind of play deliberately, and there are abundant audiences and theaters in the United States and elsewhere eagerly seeking such plays. They have something to say, say it clearly, and are about something. As with good textbooks—good textbooks, mind—his work is pedantic, fascinating, and satisfying.

Stavis celebrated his 80th birthday shortly after the first play in his projected second tetralogy was published in *Dramatics*. This drama is about George Washington's heroic efforts to hold together the colonial army in the face of foreign intrigues, English military superiority, congressional neglect, domestic opportunism, and defeatism, despair, and dissatisfaction in the ranks. Stavis called this epic drama *The Raw Edge of Victory,* and it is a potent brew of all of the conflicts that raged as the Revolutionary War dragged on and on. The real role of black slaves and women in the war is forcefully demonstrated, as are the grim realities of keeping the troops in line, which Washington does with unflinching severity even as he understands the reasons for rebellion in the ranks. Unlike the earlier plays there are touches of humor here, even gallows humor, as well as contrasts between the roughness of camp life and the sophisticated court of King Louis XVI. Stavis's extensive research fortunately does not parade itself, and it is abundantly evident in the dramatic revelation of how Washington and his army won the war and at what cost.

As with any conscientious teacher, Stavis is a superb researcher who reads and studies about and around the men he will put onstage. Out of that research eventually comes the spine of the play, the direction dictated by the material. His own humanistic background, of course, controls the aesthetics and even the politics of the play, and his experience controls the shape of the work, but the man and the artist avoid the merely pedantic, the narrowly polemic, the purely didactic. The five years he works on any single play make it fairly inevitable as a work: big, intellectual, and more than a little preachy but almost always theatrical.

Stavis is a grassroots playwright. Middle America listens to the voice of history, and it is history that Stavis purveys most astutely and clearly. Grandeur and pageantry are second nature to the themes and the shapes of his work. His best work, I think, is *The Man Who Never Died.* It is no small accident that the play deals with an early "liberal," an American labor leader martyred and misplaced in time and place. That the play comes most successfully to the stage finally in the form of a German opera is really no surprise to those most familiar with Stavis's work.

He denies a tendency to romanticism and insists on the classicistic nature of his work. As did Brecht, Stavis claims to be more concerned with the how of an action than with the why. In fact, his plays, with possibly the Joseph play excepted, tend to Seriousness with a capital *S.* There is generally little to amuse one in a Stavis play, for the solemnity of the central figure is reflected in the almost complete lack of humor in the play itself. Even love is dealt with clinically and analytically. He leaves it to the total action to move his audiences: the themes that last, the appeal to noble if belated stances, the hero out of time.

Stavis, quite seriously and realistically, sees his own work as primarily influenced by both Shakespeare and the Holy Bible. If there are more rabbinic research and prophetic polemics than there are lyricism and joy, Stavis cannot be faulted. He is, after all, very much a writer of his time and place, but with a keen eye on the lessons of the past.

Stavis is a pro. Methodical, organized, enthusiastic, and almost pristinely professional as he is, there is a double irony in the fact that he has never had a hit on Broadway. Yet he represents professional theater to literally dozens of colleges and repertory companies not only in the United States but also around the world. To non-Americans particularly, as Tyrone Guthrie once indicated, Stavis represents the clearest and "most American" voice of the time. As perhaps is still true with O'Neill, Stavis seems most American to those who are least American, and he seems most universal to his American audiences.

In any event there is no mistaking Stavis's intent and purpose. If heroic drama has gone out of fashion in an era of the antihero, Stavis persistently views history and man's passage through that history as essentially heroic.

Finally, Stavis is quite the opposite in one crucial aspect from the heroes of his plays. While each of them is a man out of joint with his own time, Stavis is of his time and writes for that broadest, most fundamental of audiences—people—and not for critics.

—Arthur H. Ballet

STEPPLING, John

Nationality: American. **Born:** California, 18 June 1951. **Career:** Founder, with Sam Shepard and others, Padua Hills Playwrights Workshop and Festival, Los Angeles, 1978; founder and co-artistic director, Heliogabalus Company, 1986-89. **Awards:** Rockefeller fellowship, 1984; National Endowment for the Arts grant; PEN West award, 1989. **Agent:** Michael Peretzian, William Morris Agency, 151 El Camino Drive, Beverly Hills, California 90212.

Publications

Plays

Shaper (produced Louisville, Kentucky, 1985).
The Dream Coast (produced Los Angeles, 1986). New York, Dramatists Play Service, 1987.
Pledging My Love (produced San Francisco, 1986).
Standard of the Breed (produced Los Angeles, 1988).
Teenage Wedding (produced Los Angeles, 1990; New York, 1991).
Deep Tropical Tan (produced Los Angeles, 1990; New York, 1992).
The Thrill (produced Los Angeles, 1991).
Storyland and Theory of Miracles. Published in *Best of the West*, edited by Murray Mednick, Los Angeles, Padua Hills Press, 1991.
Sea of Cortez (produced Los Angeles, 1992).
Sea of Cortez and Other Plays. Los Angeles, California, Sun & Moon Press, 1996.

Screenplay: *52 Pick-up*, with Elmore Leonard, 1986.

*

Critical Studies: "John Steppling" by Harvey Perr, in *BOMB,* Spring 1990, pp. 20-22; "John Steppling's Drama of the Dream Coast" by Neena Beber, in *Theater* (New Haven, Connecticut), Summer-Fall, 1990, pp. 16-20.

* * *

In John Steppling's enigmatic evocations of life on the edge of the emotional abyss, the American dream has been neither deferred nor exploded. Instead, his characters' aspirations have leaked from their souls like corrosive toxic sludge. His four major full-length plays—*The Shaper, The Dream Coast, Standard of the Breed,* and *The Thrill*—are all set on a West Coast whose spiritual, if not physical, focus is the scuzzy underside of Los Angeles and Hollywood.

All of the plays are written in short, enigmatic blackout scenes that resolutely avoid a traditional dramatic trajectory composed of rising and falling action. Structurally they therefore mimic the emptiness of the characters' emotional lives, which seem measured out in small epiphanies that come across as continuous denouements. Steppling's spare use of language and heavy emphasis on silence and pauses are reminiscent of the German playwright Franz Xaver Kroetz. The sometimes glacial pace of his action coupled with his low-life subjects help inject all of his plays with a dark, unseen but pervasive sense of danger and potential menace.

Wilson, the aging owner of a rundown Los Angeles motel in *The Dream Coast,* perhaps best describes the worldview of Steppling's characters when he remembers being with his son: "I took him out—and everything seemed fine. He'd be having fun—he was only a little boy, three, four years old, so it was a kind of fun that little kids have, like it's an easy thing—but it was drab; underneath it not very deep, right under the surface was this drabness—sordid, sad—yeah, very sad, an awful sickness, an illness of sadness. . . ." The play, a *Grapes of Wrath* for the 1980s, finds two transplanted Okies—Marliss, a pliable 23-year-old, and Weldon, approaching 40—in residence at Wilson's motel. Marliss does not "have any dreams about California"; instead, she is content to hang out by the pool and pop whites, smoke joints, and score some coke. She ends up naked and semiconscious on a transvestite's motel room floor as Bill, a grease-stained auto mechanic, drops his pants and lowers himself onto her. Wilson, haunted throughout the play by his ex-wife's harping injected onstage via audiotape, finally allows his financially strapped motel to be torched for the insurance money.

The Shaper also explores failed dreams through the increasing insolvency of a small business. The play is set in Bud and Del's rundown surfboard shop, and the title literally refers to Bud's occupation as a surfboard sculptor. Metaphorically, however, it suggests the influence of Del, who is in jail at the play's outset for possession of cocaine possession and who lures Bud not only into acts of infidelity and petty larceny but also into the whole soulless environment in which their dissipation has occurred. Reesa, Del's half sister, has recently arrived in California from Ohio, and she ogles the other characters' tans and tells them how she always imagined Bud as a "shiny golden beach boy." The great distance between her ideal and the sordid reality forms the vacuous grand canyon at the heart of Steppling's plays.

The Thrill, like *The Dream Coast,* is an ironic title. Linda, another of Steppling's young, impressionable women unable to generate any self-motivation, hangs out at a southern California shopping mall. There she encounters two small-time con artists working their way west from Providence, Rhode Island. Walter found Nat when he was 19 and reminds his partner that he was "the most beautiful thing I'd ever seen." But their partnership, like Bud and Del's, is doomed since Nat has managed to seduce the docile Linda by force. (One scene consists solely of Nat forcing himself sexually on Linda in a telephone booth in the mall while her friend Beverly watches.) The thrill of her relationship is all that Linda has to fill her life, and her passivity is such that, when her father sends her a large check for her 21st birthday, she willingly hands it over to Nat, who then disappears with the money. The play ends with Linda sharing lunch with her aunt, who runs a small fabric store in the mall—a perfect image of bland domesticity—in which she has recently started working now that the source of her thrills has vanished.

Standard of the Breed departs slightly from the other plays in that it takes place not in the Los Angeles area but in Jack's Nevada desert home outside Las Vegas where he raises mastiffs, "the largest dogs in the world." The dreams, however, crash just as resoundingly there as in Los Angeles. A more significant difference is that the characters have not yet completely surrendered their hopes and dreams to despair. The play unfolds at a dreamlike pace over the course of one night, beginning when 20-something Cassie, a mixed-up young L.A. girl, arrives at Jack's doorstep after having left her unwitting boyfriend asleep in their room at a Vegas hotel. She has come to buy a mastiff puppy and to escape her relationship. Jack explains that the standard for breeding dogs is "perfection," a metaphor for these humans as well, although such a project is ultimately destined for failure. The play is also about leaving, and, as in all of Steppling's work, the characters are in transit to or from some half-idealized existence. Reese, Jack's boss at the casino, deserts his girlfriend Teela, who had hoped to go to Los Angeles to try to make it as a singer. Jack decides to head to Sacramento and to get drunk for a while, and he encourages Cassie to dump her life and head out into the desert with her puppy by her side: "Leave it—That's a fine thing to do. All you need to take is the yearning." The play ends with Jack letting his prized mastiffs loose into the desert morning, where they will surely die slow, painful deaths.

Some critics take exception to Steppling's plays not only for the manner in which they continually portray young females as hapless victims of older, predatory males but also for their perceived soullessness. In an interview Steppling has maintained his prerogative: "We live in patriarchy, it's very sexist. I'm writing what I see. . . . And everyone's a victim, really. Men and women are just subjugated in different kinds of ways." To Steppling's admirers such arguments are beside the point, for they feel that few American dramatists so effectively describe the underbelly of human aspiration and futility.

—John Istel

STONE, Peter

Nationality: American. **Born:** Los Angeles, California, 27 February 1930. **Education:** Bard College, Annandale-on-Hudson, New York, 1947-51, B.A. 1951; Yale University, New Haven, Connecticut, 1951-53, M.F.A. 1953. **Family:** Married Mary O'Hanley in 1961. **Career:** Playwright and film scenarist. **Awards:** National Academy of Television Arts and Sciences Emmy award, for *The Defenders,* 1962; Writers Guild of America award nomination for television play, for *The Benefactors,* 1962, for *Charade,* 1964; Mystery Writers Guild of America award for best mystery play, 1963; Academy award for best original story and screenplay, for *Father Goose,* 1964; Tony award, for best musical, 1969, 1981; Drama Desk award for best book of a musical, 1969; New York Drama Critics Circle award, 1970; Plays and Players award for best new musical, 1970. **Member:** Dramatists Guild (president), 1981—. **Agent:** Sam Cohn, c/o ICM, 40 West 57th Street, New York, New York 10019, U.S.A. **Address:** Stony Hill Road, Amagansett, New York 11930, U.S.A.

Publications

Plays

Friend of the Family (produced St. Louis, Missouri, 1958).

Kean, music and lyrics by Robert Wright and George Forrest (produced New York, 1961).

Skyscraper, music by James Van Heusen, lyrics by Sammy Cahn (produced New York, 1965).

1776, music and lyrics by Sherman Edwards (produced New York, 1969).

Two by Two, adaptation of the play *The Flowering Peach* by Clifford Odets, music by Richard Rodgers, lyrics by Martin Charmin (produced New York, 1970).

Sugar, adaptation of the film *Some Like It Hot,* music by Jule Styne (produced New York, 1972).

Full Circle, with Erich Maria Remarque (produced New York, 1973).

Woman of the Year, adaptation of the film (produced Boston and New York, 1981).

Grand Hotel. N.p., n.d.

My One and Only. N.p., n.d.

The Will Rogers Follies. N.p., n.d.

Titanic, musical (produced New York).

Screenplays: *Charade,* 1963; *Father Goose,* 1964; *Mirage,* adaptation of the novel *Fallen Angel* by Howard Fast, 1965; *Arabasque,* 1966; *The Secret War of Harry Frigg,* with Frank Tarloff, 1968; *Sweet Charity,* adaptation of the play by Neil Simon, 1969; *Skin Game,* 1971; *1776,* 1972; *The Talking of Pelham 1-2-3,* 1974; *The Silver Bears,* 1978; *Who's Killing the Great Chefs of Europe,* 1978; *Why Would I Lie?* 1980; *Just Cause,* n.d.

Television: scripts for *Studio One,* 1956; *Brenner,* 1959; *Witness,* 1961; *Asphalt Jungle,* 1961; *The Defenders,* 1961-62; *Espionage,* 1963; *Androcles and the Lion,* music and lyrics by Richard Rodgers, 1968; creator of *Adam's Rib,* and *Ivan the Terrible,* 1976.

* * *

Peter Stone's contribution to American drama and theater is remarkable in two areas. Since 1982 he has served as president of the Dramatists Guild, begun in 1912 as a division of the Authors League of America and now the main support organization for playwrights in the United States. During his tenure Stone has successfully led the guild through a number of challenging issues with various groups of theaters and artists.

Referred to in playbills and scripts as the librettist or the creator of the book, Stone will be remembered as a traditional dramatist who does what all fine dramatists have always done: find an idea or concept that interests people and provide the appropriate dramatic construction for that concept. It is a simply stated but extremely difficult task. Finding himself interested in the musical theater during a troubling time for the genre, Stone brought wit and intelligence, along with the substantive beliefs of the well-read man, to his chosen field. His skills helped the American musical during those uncertain years of reassessment and into the challenging decade of the 1990s. Basic to his success is his theory of dramaturgy, firmly based on classical tenets and solidly dependent on the conventions of theater that have instructed Western dramatists for more than 2,000 years. Construction, Stone believes, is everything in a musical, as is an adherence to Aristotle's elements—plot, character, thought, poetry, spectacle, and music—and the classical theories of aesthetic distance and of the willing suspension of disbelief.

Following a popular current trend in musical theater, most of Stone's works have been skillful adaptations of successful books, movies, or plays. His first effort, *Kean,* was based on Jean-Paul Sartre's play of that title, which he saw in Paris and was asked to adapt for the musical stage. Although not a box office hit in New York, it was considered a succès d'estime and essentially started Stone on his career. Nor was *Skyscraper* remarkably successful. It was an adaptation of Elmer Rice's last commercial hit, *Dream Girl* (1945), an expressionistic comedy that follows a woman's fantasies from youth to old age. Tied to a story by Cy Feuer and Earnest Martin about a woman whose little house was surrounded by skyscrapers, Stone's work lacked the unity that Aristotle would have demanded.

Two by Two was an adaptation of Clifford Odets's last play of any consequence, *The Flowering Peach,* in which Odets used Noah and his ark to suggest that the corrupt world would find redemption in the strong family unit. Stone's work showed good potential on stage until his leading actor, Danny Kaye, injured a leg and played his role on crutches or in a wheelchair, with the predictable result that Stone's concept was upstaged. Stone was brought in to save *Sugar* when previous librettists had failed to capture the popularity of the movie *Some Like It Hot* for a live audience. *My One and Only* and *Will Rogers Follies* were shows of spectacle and dance in which concept overwhelmed structure.

Both *1776* and *Titanic* illustrate Stone's remarkable ability to take a historical event of which everyone knows the climax and to discover the right and appropriate dramatic device that melds concept and structure into successful theater. More than most librettists, Stone carefully structures his musical theater piece by blending the inherent features of poetry, music, and spectacle with the dramatic elements of plot, character, and thought. The independent natures so obvious among the characters in *1776* clearly reveal the contentiousness that underscores every meeting of the members of the Continental Congress. The first line of the play, spoken by John Adams, establishes both the concept and the atmosphere: "I have come to the conclusion that one useless man is called a disgrace, that two are called a law firm, and that three or more become a congress." When the stubborn issue of slavery is raised, it proves to be as disruptive in 1776 as later generations would find it. Quite distinct from what other librettists frequently do, Stone displays the sensible thought that people should know more about their country.

Stone is also the author of numerous television scripts, and, unique among his contemporaries, he has received two Tony Awards, an Oscar, and an Emmy.

—Walter J. Meserve

STOPPARD, Tom

Nationality: British. **Born:** Tom Straussler in Zlin, Czechoslovakia, 3 July 1937; moved to Singapore, 1939, Darjeeling, India, 1942, and England, 1946. **Education:** Dolphin School, Nottinghamshire, 1946-48; Pocklington School, Yorkshire, 1948-54. **Family:** Married 1) Jose Ingle in 1965 (marriage dissolved 1971), two sons; 2) Miriam Moore-Robinson (i.e., the writer Miriam Stoppard) in 1972 (marriage dissolved 1992), two sons. **Career:** Journalist, *Western Daily Press*, Bristol, 1954-58, and Bristol *Evening World*, 1958-60; freelance journalist and writer; drama critic, *Scene*, London, 1962-63. Member of the board, Royal National Theatre, London, 1989—. Lives in Iver, Buckinghamshire. **Awards:** Ford grant, 1964; John Whiting award, 1967; *Evening Standard* award, 1967, 1973, 1975, 1979, 1983, 1997; Italia prize, for radio play, 1968; Tony award, 1968, 1976, 1984; New York Drama Critics Circle award, 1968, 1976, 1984; Shakespeare prize (Hamburg), 1979; Outer Circle award, 1984; Drama Desk award, 1984. M.Lit.: University of Bristol, 1976; Brunel University, Uxbridge, Middlesex, 1979; University of Sussex, Brighton, 1980. Honorary degrees: Leeds University, 1980; University of London, 1982; Kenyon College, Gambier, Ohio, 1984; York University, 1984. Fellow, Royal Society of Literature. C.B.E. (Commander, Order of the British Empire), 1978; Knighthood, 1997. **Agent:** Peters, Fraser, and Dunlop Group, 503-504 The Chambers, Chelsea Harbour, Lots Road, London SW10 0XF, England.

Publications

Plays

A Walk on the Water (televised 1963; produced Hamburg, 1964); revised version, as *The Preservation of George Riley* (televised 1964); as *Enter a Free Man* (produced London, 1968; New York, 1974). London, Faber, 1968; New York, Grove Press, 1972.

The Dissolution of Dominic Boot (broadcast 1964). Included in *The Dog It Was That Died and Other Plays*, 1983.

"M" Is for Moon among Other Things (broadcast 1964; produced Richmond, Surrey, 1977). Included in *The Dog It Was That Died and Other Plays*, 1983.

The Gamblers (produced Bristol, 1965).

If You're Glad I'll Be Frank (broadcast 1966; produced Edinburgh, 1969; London, 1976; New York, 1987). With *Albert's Bridge*, London, Faber, 1969; revised version, published separately, New York and London, French, 1978.

Tango, adaptation of a play by Slawomir Mrozek, translated by Nicholas Bethell (produced London, 1966). London, Cape, 1968.

A Separate Peace (televised 1966). London, French, 1977; in *Albert's Bridge and Other Plays*, 1977.

Rosencrantz and Guildenstern Are Dead (produced Edinburgh, 1966; revised version produced London and New York, 1967). London, Faber, and New York, Grove Press, 1967; screenplay published as *Rosencrantz and Guildenstern Are Dead: The Film*, London, Faber, 1991.

Albert's Bridge (broadcast 1967; produced Edinburgh, 1969; New York, 1975; London, 1976). With *If You're Glad I'll Be Frank*, London, Faber, 1969; in *Albert's Bridge and Other Plays*, 1977.

Teeth (televised 1967). Included in *The Dog It Was That Died and Other Plays*, 1983.

Another Moon Called Earth (televised 1967). Included in *The Dog It Was That Died and Other Plays*, 1983.

Neutral Ground (televised 1968). Included in *The Dog It Was That Died and Other Plays*, 1983.

The Real Inspector Hound (produced London, 1968; New York, 1972). London, Faber, 1968; New York, Grove Press, 1969.

After Magritte (produced London, 1970; New York, 1972). London, Faber, 1971; New York, Grove Press, 1972.

Where Are They Now? (broadcast 1970). With *Artist Descending a Staircase*, London, Faber, 1973; in *Albert's Bridge and Other Plays*, 1977.

Dogg's Our Pet (produced London, 1971). Published in *Ten of the Best*, edited by Ed Berman, London, Inter-Action Imprint, 1979.

Jumpers (produced London, 1972; Washington, D.C., and New York, 1974). London, Faber, and New York, Grove Press, 1972; revised version, Faber, 1986.

Artist Descending a Staircase (broadcast 1972; produced London, 1988; New York, 1989). With *Where Are They Now?*, London, Faber, 1973; in *Albert's Bridge and Other Plays*, 1977.

The House of Bernarda Alba, adaptation of the play by García Lorca (produced London, 1973).

Travesties (produced London, 1974; New York; 1975). London, Faber, and New York, Grove Press, 1975.

Dirty Linen, and New-found-land (produced London, 1976; Washington, D.C., and New York, 1977). London, Faber, and New York, Grove Press, 1976.

The Fifteen Minute Hamlet (as *The [Fifteen Minute] Dogg's Troupe Hamlet*, produced London, 1976). London, French, 1978.

Albert's Bridge and Other Plays (includes *Artist Descending a Staircase, If You're Glad I'll Be Frank, A Separate Peace, Where Are They Now?)*. New York, Grove Press, 1977.

Every Good Boy Deserves Favour: A Play for Actors and Orchestra, music by André Previn (produced London, 1977; Washington, D.C., 1978; New York, 1979). With *Professional Foul*, London, Faber, and New York, Grove Press, 1978.

Professional Foul (televised 1977). With *Every Good Boy Deserves Favour*, London, Faber, and New York, Grove Press, 1978.

Night and Day (produced London, 1978; Washington, D.C., and New York, 1979). London, Faber. 1978; New York, Grove Press, 1979; revised version, Faber, 1979.

Albert's Bridge Extended (produced Edinburgh, 1978).

Undiscovered Country, adaptation of a play by Schnitzler (produced London, 1979; Hartford, Connecticut, 1981). London, Faber, 1980.

Dogg's Hamlet, Cahoot's Macbeth (produced Warwick, London, Washington, D.C., and New York, 1979). London, Faber, and New York, French, 1980.

On the Razzle, adaptation of a play by Johann Nestroy (produced Edinburgh and London, 1981; Washington, D.C., 1982). London, Faber, 1981.

The Real Thing (produced London, 1982). London, Faber, 1982; revised version (produced New York, 1984), 1984.

The Dog It Was That Died (broadcast 1982). Included in *The Dog It Was That Died and Other Plays*, 1983.

The Love for Three Oranges, adaptation of the opera by Prokofiev (produced on tour, 1983).

The Dog It Was That Died and Other Plays (includes *The Dissolution of Dominic Boot, "M" Is for Moon among Other Things, Teeth, Another Moon Called Earth, Neutral Ground, A Separate Peace*). London, Faber, 1983.

Rough Crossing, adaptation of a play by Ferenc Molnár (produced London, 1984; revised version produced New York, 1989; London, 1990). London, Faber, 1985.

Squaring the Circle: Poland 1980-81 (televised 1984). With *Every Good Boy Deserves Favour* and *Professional Foul*, London, Faber, 1984.

Four Plays for Radio (includes *Artist Descending a Staircase, Where Are They Now?, If You're Glad I'll Be Frank, Albert's Bridge*). London, Faber, 1984.

Dalliance, adaptation of a play by Schnitzler (produced London, 1986). With *Undiscovered Country*, London, Faber, 1986.

Largo Desolato, adaptation of the play by Václav Havel (produced Bristol, 1986; London, 1987). London, Faber and New York, Grove Press, 1987.

Brazil (screenplay), in *The Battle of Brazil* by Jack Mathews. New York, Crown, 1987.

Hapgood (produced London, 1988). London, Faber, 1988.

The Radio Plays 1964-1983. London, Faber, 1990.

The Television Plays, 1965-1984. London, Faber & Faber, 1993.

Arcadia (produced London, 1993). London, Faber, 1993.

Indian Ink. London and Boston, Faber and Faber, 1995.

Plays. London, Faber, 1996.

Plays One: The Real Inspector Hound and Other Entertainments. London and Boston, Faber & Faber, 1996.

Plays Two. London and Boston, Faber & Faber, 1996.

The Invention of Love. New York, Grove Press, 1998.

Screenplays: *The Romantic Englishwoman*, with Thomas Wiseman, 1975; *Despair*, 1978; *The Human Factor*, 1980; *Brazil*, with Terry Gilliam and Charles McKeown, 1985; *Empire of the Sun*, 1988; *Rosencrantz and Guildenstern Are Dead*, 1990.

Radio Plays: *Dissolution of Dominic Boot*, 1964; *"M" Is for Moon among Other Things*, 1964; *If You're Glad I'll Be Frank*, 1966; *Albert's Bridge*, 1967; *Where Are They Now?*, 1970; *Artist Descending a Staircase*, 1972; *The Dog It Was That Died*, 1982; *In the Native State*, 1991.

Television Plays: *A Walk on the Water*, 1963 (revised version, as *The Preservation of George Riley*, 1964); *A Separate Peace*, 1966; *Teeth*, 1967; *Another Moon Called Earth*, 1967; *Neutral Ground*, 1968; *The Engagement*, from his radio play *The Dissolution of Dominic Boot*, 1970 (USA); *One Pair of Eyes* (documentary), 1972; *The Boundary* (*Eleventh Hour* series), with Clive Exton, 1975; *Three Men in a Boat*, from the novel by Jerome K. Jerome, 1975; *Professional Foul*, 1977; *Squaring the Circle*, 1984.

Novel

Lord Malquist and Mr. Moon. London, Blond, 1966; New York, Knopf, 1968.

Short Stories

Introduction 2, with others. London, Faber, 1964.

*

Bibliography: *Tom Stoppard: A Reference Guide* by David Bratt, Boston, Hall, 1982.

Critical Studies: *Tom Stoppard* by C. W. E. Bigsby, London, Longman, 1976, revised edition, 1979; *Tom Stoppard* by Ronald Hayman, London, Heinemann, and Totowa, New Jersey, Rowman and Littlefield, 1977, 4th edition, Heinemann, 1982; *Beyond Absurdity: The Plays of Tom Stoppard* by Victor L. Cahn, Madison, New Jersey, Fairleigh Dickinson University Press, 1979; *Tom Stoppard* by Felicia Hardison Londré, New York, Ungar, 1981; *Tom Stoppard: Comedy as a Moral Matrix* by Joan Fitzpatrick Dean, Columbia, University of Missouri Press, 1981; *The Stoppard Plays* by Lucina Paquet Gabbard, Troy, New York, Whitston, 1982; *Shakespearean Parallels and Affinities with the Theatre of the Absurd in Stoppard's Rosencrantz and Guildenstern Are Dead* by Anja Easterling, n.p., 1982; *Tom Stoppard's Plays* by Jim Hunter, London, Faber, and New York, Grove Press, 1982; *Tom Stoppard* by Thomas R. Whitaker, London, Macmillan, and New York, Grove Press; 1983; *Stoppard: The Mystery and the Clockwork* by Richard Corballis, New York, Methuen, 1984, Oxford, Amber Lane Press, 1985; *Tom Stoppard: An Assessment* by Tim Brassell, London, Macmillan, and New York, St. Martin's Press, 1985; *File on Stoppard* edited by Malcolm Page, London, Methuen, 1986, *Tom Stoppard* by Susan Rusinko, Boston, Twayne, 1986; *Stoppard the Playwright* by Michael Billington, London, Methuen, 1987; *The Theatre of Tom Stoppard* by Anthony Jenkins, London and New York, Cambridge University Press, 1987, revised edition, 1989; *Tom Stoppard: A Casebook* edited by John Harty, III, New York, Garland, 1987; *Tom Stoppard: The Artist as Critic* by Neil Sammells, London, Macmillan, 1988; *Tom Stoppard: Rosencrantz and Guildenstern Are Dead, Jumpers, Travesties: A Casebook* edited by T. Bareham, London, Macmillan, 1990; *Tom Stoppard: The Moral Vision of the Major Plays* by Paul Delaney, London, Macmillan, 1990; *Tom Stoppard's The Real Thing* by Lloyd Cameron, Glebe, NSW, Pascal Press, 1994; *Conversations with Stoppard* by Mel Gussow, London, Nick Hern, 1995; "Tom Stoppard" by Richard Corballis, in *British Playwrights, 1956-1995: A Research and Production Sourcebook*, edited by William W. Demastes, Westport, Connecticut, Greenwood, 1996; "Tom Stoppard: His Life and Career before *Rosencrantz and Guildenstern*" by John Fleming, in *Library Chronicle of the University of Texas* (Austin, Texas), 1996, pp. 111-61.

Theatrical Activities:

Director: **Play**—*Born Yesterday* by Garson Kanin, London, 1973; *The Real Inspector Hound*, London, 1985. **Film**—*Rosencrantz and Guildenstern Are Dead*, 1990.

* * *

Tom Stoppard came to prominence in 1967 with *Rosencrantz and Guildenstern Are Dead*, the play that remains perhaps most identified with his name in the public consciousness. Yet his steadily maturing dramaturgy has yielded a succession of works hailed by critics as the "masterpiece," notably *Arcadia* and *The Invention of Love* in the 1990s. A characteristic verbal agility anchors Stoppard's *oeuvre*, while he demonstrates increasing finesse at orchestrating his complex narratives and even begins to probe the emotional lives of his characters, including—in some later plays—the women. Many of the full-length plays reflect extensive research into topics as various as modern philosophical schools, particle physics, mathematics, horticulture, art and history of India, and classical Latin poetry. He has developed his craft by working in a variety of dramatic modes: radio, television, and motion pictures as well as the stage, including translation-adaptations of modern classic plays from other languages.

After several years as a journalist and sometime theater reviewer Stoppard in 1960 wrote his first play, *A Walk on the Water*, which did not reach the legitimate stage until 1968 (in a revised version titled *Enter a Free Man*). Meanwhile it was a series of radio and television plays that launched him as a professional dramatist. Several of those early radio plays—including *If You're Glad I'll Be Frank*, *Albert's Bridge*, and *Artist Descending a Staircase*—were brought to the stage two decades later. Their creative use of the radio medium, however, tends to gimmickry at the expense of character, as in *Artist Descending a Staircase*, an ingenious search backward and forward in time for the truth about the circumstances of the artist's death, which had been captured on a tape recording that lends itself to clever ambiguity of interpretation. The 1991 radio play *In the Native State* more subtly and gracefully explores the medium's unique properties, fueling the story's implicit eroticism and placing the focus on an intriguing web of human interactions: between English and Indian people, between people in 1930 and in the present. Such treatment of parallel or overlapping pasts and presents may be seen also in plays like *Travesties*, *Arcadia*, *Indian Ink*, and *The Invention of Love*.

Stoppard's early full-length plays tended to rely on literary sources or influences. Critic Mel Gussow referred to *Rosencrantz and Guildenstern Are Dead*, for example, as "riding the coat-tails of *Hamlet*," but the play also betrays its debts to Samuel Beckett and Luigi Pirandello. The play's title characters are the school chums of Shakespeare's Hamlet and have been summoned to Elsinore without knowing what is expected of them. Stoppard's play shows two characters adrift in somebody else's plot, just as the absurdists focused upon modern man's rudderlessness in a world he cannot control. While the action of *Hamlet* proceeds in the background, the two innocents play games to pass the time in a manner clearly inspired by Beckett's *Waiting for Godot*. Their desire to overcome the fixity of the work of art in which they must function echoes the premise of Pirandello's *Six Characters in Search of an Author*. The complex interrelationships of life and art are demonstrated with particular theatrical flair in the pair's scenes with the Players who come to perform for Claudius at Elsinore.

Two recurring themes in Stoppard's short plays of the 1960s and early 1970s, as well as in his novel *Lord Malquist and Mr. Moon*, are the relativity of truth and the urge to discern some pattern in the world's chaos. In *Albert's Bridge* a well-educated young man opts to spend his life painting a suspension bridge, because it sets him above the fray of daily existence that can now be perceived as "dots and bricks, giving out a gentle hum." *The Real Inspector Hound* amusingly toys with the boundary between art and life by having two theater critics get caught up in the murder mystery drama they are watching. The stage picture at the beginning of *After Magritte* is like a surrealist painting, but the action of the play reveals a kind of manic logic behind the visual nonsense.

The same concerns reappear in *Jumpers* and *Travesties*. Although the philosophical discourse may become a bit heavy-handed in *Jumpers*, this must still be counted among Stoppard's major plays for the brilliance of its theatrical conceits. The intellectual argument of the play, a dialectic between moral philosophy and logical positivism, is reified in stage metaphors like the human pyramid of middle-aged philosophers in jump suits, whose shaky performance inadvertently demonstrates the false logic of a relativistic philosophical system. But the search for absolutes by philosopher George Moore is constantly subverted by events in his own household that cannot be understood at face value. *Travesties* is a dazzling foray into a crucial moment in political and cultural history—filtered through the self-serving memory of a senile minor figure, Henry Carr, who worked at the British Consulate in Zurich during World War I. He comes into contact with Lenin, who is preparing the way for a revolution in Russia; Tristan Tzara, who seeks through dadaism to overthrow 25 centuries of artistic convention; and James Joyce, who is already working on the novel that will revolutionize modern literature. Fitting these characters into the borrowed structure of *The Importance of Being Earnest* (which was produced by the English Players under Joyce's direction in Zurich in 1917), Stoppard examines the responsibility of the artist to society.

Stoppard made fun of the arbitrariness of language in several pieces beginning with the one-act farce *Dogg's Our Pet*, in which some of the characters speak Dogg's language, which is composed of English words used to mean different things. He pursued this conceit in paired one-act spin-offs of Shakespeare, *Dogg's Hamlet* and *Cahoot's Macbeth*. The stage action is the construction of a speaker's platform, a stage, or a wall using slabs, planks, bricks, and cubes—just as language uses parts of speech to construct a meaning. *Dogg's Hamlet* incorporates an earlier playlet, *The [Fifteen-Minute] Dogg's Troupe Hamlet*, which is a very funny condensation of Shakespeare's *Hamlet*, followed by a two-minute version as an encore. Another set of related one-acts places the shorter piece *New-found-land* as the filling in a farcical sandwich called *Dirty Linen*. Set in a House of Commons meeting room, *Dirty Linen* shows the foibles of members of the Select Committee on Promiscuity in High Places. They come to accept the common-sense opinions of the attractive Maddie Gotobed who has been sexually involved with most of them. When the Committee adjourns for 15 minutes two new characters use the room to discuss another matter, and this business is the pretext for *New-found-land*, which culminates in a panegyric monologue about America as seen through foreign eyes.

Violations of human rights in totalitarian regimes fueled several plays in the late 1970s. Invited by André Previn to write a play that would involve a collaboration of actors and a live orchestra on the stage, Stoppard realized that by making the orchestra a figment of one character's imagination, he could set the play in an insane asylum and write about the Soviet practice of confining political prisoners there along with genuine lunatics. For all its serious subject matter, *Every Good Boy Deserves Favour* contains some supremely witty dialogue. It also features a child, Sacha, whose observation of the system's injustice and of his dissident father's integrity has matured him beyond his years. A boy named Sacha also plays a crucial role in the television play *Professional Foul*, which draws its metaphors from a soccer match that is played in Czechoslovakia while British philosophers attend a conference there. In the course of the tense drama Sacha courageously helps one of them to smuggle his father's doctoral thesis to England for publication. Another television play, *Squaring the Circle*, traces the 1980-81 workers' Solidarity movement in Poland and makes of that complex history a clear and absorbing narrative for the layman. Stoppard's premise is that the concept of a free trade union like Solidarity is as irreconcilable with the Communist bloc's definition of socialism as is the mathematical impossibility of turning a circle into a square of the same area. *Cahoot's Macbeth* must also be classed as one of Stoppard's "plays of commitment."

Night and Day continued Stoppard's expressions of concern for human rights under totalitarian regimes, but it also marks a turning point in that Stoppard began here to deal with romantic love as an aspect of his characters' emotional lives. The main subject of *Night and Day* is journalism, especially the pros and cons of a free press. The action—set in a fictitious African country where a British-educated black dictator's rule is challenged by a Soviet-backed rebel—brings together three journalists and the wife of a British mine owner. In *The Real Thing* Stoppard finally allowed the human story to take precedence over ideological concerns or stylistic conceits. With a playwright as protagonist this romantic comedy touches on a number of Stoppard's familiar themes from politics to language. A central speech, using a cricket-bat metaphor to uphold standards in language and thought, is dramatic writing at its best, a stylistic high point in the work of a writer for whom style has always been the strong suit.

During the increasingly long periods between his plays, Stoppard has devoted himself to writing screenplays, directing stage plays, and adapting plays in translation. His adaptations differ from literary translation in that he allows himself considerable liberty, especially in the handling of dialogue and metaphor. *Rough Crossing* uses the situation and characters from Ferenc Molnár's *The Play at the Castle* (also known as *The Play's the Thing*) but moves them from a castle on the Italian Riviera to a transatlantic ocean liner. *On the Razzle* is a free-wheeling version of Johann Nestroy's *Einen Jux will er sich machen* (the same play that spawned Thornton Wilder's *The Matchmaker*). *Dalliance* and *Undiscovered Country* both have their origins in plays by Arthur Schnitzler. Critic Michael Bywater commented of Stoppard's version of *The Seagull*: "It's Chekhov's play, but there's Stoppard's voice, clear as a bell, dry, ironic and, on the page, almost uninflected" (*New Statesman & Society*, 9 May 1997).

Hapgood combines espionage melodrama and a touch of romantic comedy in a complicated plot illustrating the premise that the truth depends upon where you are standing. Using subatomic particles (impossible to pin down by both position and momentum) as a metaphor, Stoppard employs two real sets of twins and one fake pair to give dramatic shape to the notion that there is no fixity in human affairs. *Arcadia*, similarly challenging in its complexity, found greater favor with audiences. Set in a stately country home in 1809 and in 1989, *Arcadia* juxtaposes the ordered universe of the Enlightenment (including Newtonian science and geometric landscaping) with subsequent disarray exemplified by romantic notions of untrammeled nature as well as sloppy historical scholarship that gives rise to misapprehensions about the past. Past and present intersect in the same space—often employing the same props—to dazzling theatrical effect. The character of Thomasina Coverly, a 13-year-old mathematical genius, is one of Stoppard's most remarkable creations.

Like *Arcadia*, *Indian Ink* privileges the audience with insight into what really happened in the past, while contemporary characters overlook or misinterpret crucial evidence. Flora Crewe, a free-spirited English poet visiting India in 1930, is herself oblivious to the political upheaval going on around her, while artistic communion brings her to a moment of intense intimacy with an Indian painter. There is a charming dialogue passage touching upon A. E. Housman's translation of classical Roman love poetry, and this prefigures the subject of Stoppard's next play, *The Invention of Love*. Housman is the central character in *The Invention of Love*, both as the recently deceased poet-scholar being ferried across the Styx by Charon and as the younger self he observes rowing with his college chums Pollard and Jackson. Housman struggles against his homosexuality in the days before it even had a name ("beastliness" is used) but finds fulfillment in perfecting translations from the Latin. With dialogue to savor, *The Invention of Love* is both hilarious and poignant, a play of ideas and of human emotion. Stoppard's craft has never been so sure.

—Felicia Hardison Londré

STOREY, David (Malcolm)

Nationality: English. **Born:** Wakefield, Yorkshire, 13 July 1933; brother of the writer Anthony Storey. **Education:** Queen Elizabeth Grammar School, Wakefield, 1943-51; Wakefield College of Art, 1951-53; Slade School of Fine Art, London, 1953-56, diploma in fine arts 1956. **Family:** Married Barbara Rudd Hamilton in 1956; two sons and two daughters. **Career:** Worked as an art teacher, farm worker, postman, tent erector, and bus conductor; played professionally for the Leeds Rugby League Club, 1952-56; associate artistic director, Royal Court Theatre, London, 1972-74. Fellow, University College, London, 1974. **Awards:** Macmillan award (U.S.) for fiction, 1960; Rhys Memorial award, for fiction, 1961; Maugham award, for fiction, 1963; *Evening Standard* award, 1967, 1970; New York Drama Critics Circle award, 1971, 1973, 1974; Faber Memorial prize, 1973; Los Angeles Drama Critics Circle award, 1973; Obie award, 1974; Booker prize, for fiction, 1976. **Address:** c/o Jonathan Cape Ltd., 20 Vauxhall Bridge Road, London SW1V 2SA, England.

Publications

Plays

The Restoration of Arnold Middleton (produced Edinburgh, 1966; London, 1967). London, Cape, 1967; New York, French, 1968.

In Celebration (produced London, 1969; Los Angeles, 1973; New York, 1984). London, Cape, 1969; New York, Grove Press, 1975.

The Contractor (produced London, 1969; New Haven, Connecticut, 1970; New York, 1973). London, Cape, 1970; New York, Random House, 1971.

Home (produced London and New York, 1970). London, Cape, 1970; New York, Random House, 1971.

The Changing Room (produced London, 1971; New Haven, Connecticut, 1972; New York, 1973). London, Cape, and New York, Random House, 1972.

The Farm (produced London, 1973; Washington, D.C., 1974; New York, 1976). London, Cape, 1973; New York, French, 1974.

Cromwell (produced London, 1973; Sarasota, Florida, 1977; New York, 1978). London, Cape, 1973.

Life Class (produced London, 1974; New York, 1975). London, Cape, 1975.

Mother's Day (produced London, 1976). London, Cape, 1977.

Sisters (produced Manchester, 1978; London, 1989). Included in *Early Days, Sisters, Life Class*, 1980.

Early Days (produced Brighton and London, 1980). Included in *Early Days, Sisters, Life Class*, 1980.
Early Days, Sisters, Life Class. London, Penguin, 1980.
Phoenix (produced London, 1984). New York, Dramatic Publishing, 1993.
The March on Russia (produced London, 1989; Cleveland, Ohio, 1990). London, French, 1989.
Stages (produced London, 1992). Included in *Plays 1*, 1992.
Plays 1 (includes *The Contractor*; *Home*; *Stages*; *Caring*). London, Methuen, 1992.
Plays 2 (includes *Restoration of Arnold Middleton*; *In Celebration*; *March on Russia*). London, Methuen, 1994.
The Changing Room. London, Methuen, 1996.
Plays 3 (includes *The Changing Room*; *Cromwell*; *Life Class*). London, Methuen, 1998.

Screenplays: *This Sporting Life*, 1963; *In Celebration*, 1976.

Television Play: *Grace*, from the story by James Joyce, 1974.

Novels

This Sporting Life. London, Longman, and New York, Macmillan, 1960.
Flight into Camden. London, Longman, 1960; New York, Macmillan, 1961.
Radcliffe. London, Longman, 1963; New York, Coward McCann, 1964.
Pasmore. London, Longman, 1972; New York, Dutton, 1974.
A Temporary Life. London, Allen Lane, 1973; New York, Dutton, 1974.
Saville. London, Cape, 1976; New York, Harper, 1977.
A Prodigal Child. London, Cape, 1982; New York, Dutton, 1983.
Present Times. London, Cape, 1984.

Poetry

Storey's Lives: Poems 1951-1991. London, Cape, 1992.

Other

Writers on Themselves, with others. London, BBC Publications, 1964.
Edward, drawings by Donald Parker. London, Allen Lane, 1973.

*

Manuscript Collection: Boston University, Massachusetts.

Critical Studies: "No Goodness or No Kings" by Susan Shrapnel in *Cambridge Quarterly*, Autumn 1970; *The Second Wave*, London, Methuen, and New York, Hill and Wang, 1971, and *David Storey*, London, Longman, 1974, both by John Russell Taylor; "David Storey: Novelist or Playwright?" by Mike Bygrave, in *Theatre Quarterly 1* (London), April-June 1971; by Marie Peel, in *Books and Bookmen* (London), March 1972; interview in *Plays and Players* (London), September 1973; "The Ironic Anger of David Storey" by William J. Free, in *Modern Drama* (Toronto), December 1973; "Poetic Naturalism in David Storey" in *New British Drama on the London Stage 1970-1985* by Richard Allen Cave, Gerrards Cross, Smythe, 1987; *The Plays of David Storey: A Thematic Study* by William Hutchings, Edwardsville, Illinois, Southern Illinois Press, 1988; *David Storey*, edited by William Hutchings, 1992; "Man as Working Animal: Work, Class, and Identity in the Plays of David Storey" by Rakesh H. Solomon, in *Forum for Modern Language Studies* (Oxford), July 1994, pp. 193-203; *The Dramatic Art of David Storey: The Journey of a Playwright* by Herbert Liebman, Westport, Connecticut, Greenwood Press, 1996.

Theatrical Activities:
Director: **Television**—*Portrait of Margaret Evans*, 1963; *Death of My Mother* (D.H. Lawrence documentary), 1963.

* * *

David Storey's achievement as a dramatist has to be measured alongside the contribution made by Lindsay Anderson, who directed several of Storey's productions at London's Royal Court Theatre. Anderson may well have inspired Storey to branch out into the theater following his auspicious beginning as a realistic novelist in the early 1960s. Anderson was certainly largely responsible for transforming Storey's most minutely detailed scripts into viable theatrical experiences.

Storey began as a playwright with *The Restoration of Arnold Middleton*, a play about a free spirit who rebels against conventional suburban mores. Both in style and in outlook, the piece resembled a number of other plays of the time by Tom Stoppard, David Mercer, and John Antrobus, and, though competent, it was not truly indicative of Storey's main direction in the theater.

In Celebration and *The Contractor* were far more distinctive. Each drew from the original novel a quality that was completely Storey's own in the matter-of-fact rendering of northern working-class life. Not quite as grim as Lawrence's earlier evocations of Nottinghamshire mining communities, these were more subdued in tone, seeking simply to render a portrait of the way industrial life had fragmented family relationships, though the undercurrents of almost tribal unity and custom remained. *In Celebration* provides pointed comparisons with Mercer's *Ride a Cock Horse* in its refusal to let migration southward develop into Mercer's celebrated northern chip on the shoulder. Storey's family of working-class lads return home for their parents' wedding anniversary, but the scars of upbringing are manifest as are the recriminations. The protest is muted, however, less by inertia than by the sheer inability to come to terms with transition, even to the point of articulating that something is wrong.

It was an impressive feat, not least because Storey had dared to present something "internal" and "reflective" on a London stage and at a time when the waves of agitprop were beginning to break. Anderson's production concentrated on ensemble playing to underscore the theme of kinship, and Alan Bates and Constance Chapman gave memorable performances in an unglamorous evening that was, nonetheless, compelling.

The Contractor developed these strands as far as they can go. Each of the untoward elements of the earlier play were now fully exploited. Storey refined narrative to the point where there were no further dramatic cruces to be explored. Several itinerant laborers appear on stage in desultory fashion to assemble a marquee for a wedding. The audience watches as actors simulate the very business their characters are required to do. They remain in role, but most of the theatricality is provided by their common initiative in successfully performing a set task by the time the act concludes. After the break the actors repeat the process in reverse, and when the marquee is finally dismantled the play ends, as unceremoniously as it had begun.

For ensemble playing, this could only be matched by an audience being invited to attend a workshop of actors working with a given group in some highly organized game playing. As a piece of scripted theater, it bypassed areas of sleight-of-hand to emerge as a genuine piece of naturalism, closer to real experience than Arnold Wesker's *The Kitchen* had been, because the suspension of disbelief was "unnecessary." Life and art mirrored each other as they had never done before.

To say that Storey had set himself an impossible task by trying to move on from that point is to give a far more rounded picture of Storey's career than he does himself. He continued to write plays interspersed with as many novels. Most of them, too, reveal a ready ability to experiment. All of the subsequent plays are at least watchable, and even when he relies too heavily on existing models, including his own, he does so with the clear aim of creating something new.

The Changing Room and *Home*, for example, closely followed *The Contractor* in Anderson productions at the Royal Court. But if the one suggested that writer and director were using a formula (with a still-life depiction of a northern amateur rugby team), the other compelled audiences to look at Storey anew. *Home*'s lingering achievement is likely to be as the vehicle for the Gielgud-Richardson double act late in their careers when the public was eager to see two lions of the London stage performing the epitome of their talents. The production duly transferred to the West End and enabled the English Stage Company, at the Royal Court, to enter a turbulent decade of fringe production at least financially solvent. As a play *Home may* bear too many traces of Samuel Beckett's influence to be seen as a development of Storey's canon. *Mother's Day* is Ortonesque, while *Sisters* (an early play staged at Manchester) betrays so many uncomfortable similarities to *A Streetcar Named Desire* that it is tempting to wonder why the author did not simply write a transatlantic version of that Tennessee Williams play.

On more native ground, however, Storey has enjoyed both critical and popular success with further examples of working-class life. The apparent absence of a center to Storey's work may be owing to the fact that he trained as an artist at London's Slade School of Fine Art and that the point of a play like *Early Days*, which depicts a politician living out his retirement in bemused and gentle autocracy, may be less to raise searching questions about the condition of England than to offer an impressionistic pastoral better suited to comparison with John Constable's landscapes than with the crazy-quilt landscape of left-wing drama. (The play, incidentally, enabled Ralph Richardson to end his career on a note of triumph.)

Painting (and art generally) was the theme of the earlier *Life Class*, which presents a group of faintly motivated art students trying to create something out of ubiquitous drabness. They fail, as the play fails, to catch hold of anything substantial.

The Farm, *Cromwell*, *The March on Russia*, and *Stages* were produced in the late 1980s and early 1990s. Storey said that he used the Brontës as inspiration in writing the first of these, and although the information is of tangential significance, this return to the theme of northern family life, with women at the center, is a solid achievement. *Cromwell* with its epic structure is more circumspect, though Brian Cox held the production together and revealed the author's mordant wit. *The March on Russia* was very much a reprise. At work again with Anderson (who has since died), Storey seemed content to revive their earliest collaboration under a new title—it is difficult, at any rate, to view the play as very much more than that. With that play Storey may have been searching for a center to his dramatic work. More likely this is to be found, however, in the one milestone of his career, *The Contractor*.

—James MacDonald

STOTT, Mike

Nationality: British. **Born:** Rochdale, Lancashire, 2 January 1944. **Education:** Attended Manchester University. **Career:** Stage manager, Scarborough Library Theatre, Yorkshire, and playreader, Royal Shakespeare Theatre, 3 years; script editor, BBC Radio, London, 1970-72; Thames Television resident writer, Hampstead Theatre Club, London, 1975. **Agent:** Michael Imison Playwrights, 28 Almeida Street, London N1 1TD, England.

Publications

Plays

Mata Hari (produced Scarborough, 1965).

Erogenous Zones (produced London, 1969).

Funny Peculiar (produced Bochum, Germany, 1973; Liverpool, 1975; London, 1976). Ashover, Derbyshire, Amber Lane Press, 1978.

Lenz, adaptation of the story by Georg Büchner (produced London, 1974; New York, 1979). Todmorden, Lancashire, Woodhouse, 1979.

Plays for People Who Don't Move Much (produced London, 1974; section produced as *Men's Talk*, Edinburgh, 1974).

Midnight (produced London, 1974).

Other People (produced London, 1974).

Ghosts, adaptation of a play by Wolfgang Bauer (produced London, 1975).

Lorenzaccio, adaptation of the play by Alfred de Musset (produced Exeter, 1976).

Followed by Oysters (produced London, 1976; as *Comings and Goings*, produced Liverpool and London, 1978).

The Scenario, adaptation of a play by Anouilh (produced Bellingham, Northumberland, 1976).

Soldiers Talking, Cleanly (televised 1978). London, Eyre Methuen, 1978.

The Boston Strangler (produced London, 1978).

Grandad (produced Croydon, Surrey, 1978).

Strangers (produced Liverpool, 1979).

Ducking Out, adaptation of a play by Eduardo De Filippo (produced London, 1982).

Dead Men (produced Southampton, 1982).

Pennine Pleasures (produced Oldham, Lancashire, 1984).

The Fling, adaptation of a work by Asher (produced London, 1987).

The Fancy Man (broadcast 1987; produced London, 1988). Published in *Plays International* (Shrewsbury, Shropshire), November 1988.

Radio Plays: *Lucky*, 1970; *When Dreams Collide*, 1970; *Early Morning Glory*, 1972; *Lincoln*, 1973; *Richard Serge*, 1973; *The Bringer of Bad News*, 1973; *The Doubting Thomases*, 1973; *The Fancy Man*, 1987.

Television Plays: *The Flaxton Boys*, 1969; *Susan*, 1973; *Thwum*, 1975; *Our Flesh and Blood*, 1977; *Pickersgill People* series, 1978; *Soldiers Talking, Cleanly*, 1978; *One in a Thousand*, 1981; *The Last Company Car*, 1983; *The Practice* series, 1985-86.

* * *

Mike Stott's 1976 West End success with his comedy *Funny Peculiar* may well represent the culmination of his search for an ideal, or at least a clinching, formula for the permissive sex comedy.

Stott's search began with *Erogenous Zones,* a collection of sketches for performance by a company of six and centered around the twin themes of love and homicide. The mixture here is one of cartoon strip wit and women's magazine cliché, the main charm residing in the way passion is reduced to absurdity through being couched in dumb and deadpan phrases. The types are instantly recognizable—the doughy sweetheart, the sadistic cop, the clean-limbed officer doing press-ups, the big, beefy success, the mad gunman, the obsessive lawyer—with the point always clear before the payoffs. Stott shows cleverness in catching the comedy of the obvious while managing to avoid repetition.

In *Other People* the form is sometimes labored although the dialogue is often sharp. It begins with an arresting image of a flasher naked under his plastic see-through mac and a pretty Czech girl who frightens him away by her eagerness to participate in anything he might suggest. But an arresting image does not make a play, and the web of relationships Stott establishes—between a successful businessman, Dave, who ends his life by taking an overdose; an out-of-work Italian, a father of five who is given a check by the dying man to solve all of his problems; a lonely widow of 51 who lacks love; and her daughter, married to Dave's friend Geoff—fails to form a coherent pattern of comic interest. The writing is often vivid, as in the Italian's fantasy of selling underwear to Arabs in hair-covered boxes—"We buy the hair, we comb it, shampoo, and we stick it on the boxes. And those Arabs, those Greeks, they go CRAZY in the shops, just to stroke our sexy hairy boxes. Believe me, Mr. Brock, I know those men, the foreigners, the Aristotles, the Ahmeds. They KILL each other to be stroking a hairy English box." The theme of sexual permissiveness is provocatively explored, with the sound of couples making love upstairs and one couple trying to initiate group sex. But it is hard to make out what Stott's intention is, whether he is attempting genuine social observation or merely exploiting current fashion.

Funny Peculiar has a mock moral ending. When the hero Trevor, a North Country grocer proclaiming the virtues of sexual freedom, is pursued by a sex-hungry puritan lady of advanced years and falls into his cellar, he is consequently rendered helpless in plaster and straps on a hospital bed. There he becomes the passive object of his wife's and mistress's oral lust. The play is a new and up-to-date version of the "tu l'a voulu, Georges Dandin" idea, and Trevor's obsession with sex is kept simmering in naked cavorting among the council estate's flower beds and in his attempts to preach to the unconverted customers of his shop, losing business as a result.

The best writing is found in the scenes in which he tries to convince his wife to leap on the freedom bandwagon and when he upbraids her for sexual ordinariness. Her defense is so heartfelt and real that her subsequent conversion to his way of thinking seems to be engineered for the sake of the plot. There is one piece of slapstick, a fight with confectionary between a visiting salesman and Trevor, which must rate as one of the best scenes of comic anarchy ever seen on the West End stage.

In his versions of Büchner's *Lenz* and of Wolfgang Bauer's *Ghosts,* Stott demonstrates more fragmented skills as an adaptor and translator from the German. *Lenz,* originally a short story about a Strasbourg intellectual who believes that he can raise a girl from the dead, is written in numerous short scenes, in Büchner's own expressionistic manner, that fail to come to grips with any central issue. The original of *Ghosts* is a roughed-up rewrite of Brecht's satire on a lower-middle-class wedding party that uses socially more sophisticated though dramatically more crude characters.

In later plays Stott has not shown that he can move beyond formula writing. *The Boston Strangler,* for all its rape and murder in intended subtle variations—ensuring constant changes of wigs and underwear by the actress playing all of the victims—cumulatively diminishes interest in the crimes of a psychopath. *Comings and Goings* promises to be better. Jan, a teacher who is married to a cream cracker executive, deserts him and arrives in the household of a pair of homosexuals. But development is lost in favor of generalized encounters confirming the rule of license and ending with vapid literary parallels. The characters have little genuineness, and the comings and goings lack dramatic direction. Stott seems to have come to the position of despising the people he writes about. *Grandad,* too, displays a tawdry lack of charity and becomes unrelievedly tedious. Stott returned to formula writing in the television series *The Practice,* an examination of life in a medical center.

—Garry O'Connor

SUNDE, Karen

Nationality: American. **Career:** Actor, Colorado Shakespeare Festival, Boulder, Colorado, 1967, The New Shakespeare Company, San Francisco, 1967-68, Arrow Rock Lyceum, Arrow Rock, Missouri, 1969-70, and CSC Repertory, New York, 1971-85; associate director, CSC Repertory, New York, 1975-85. **Awards:** Bob Hope award, 1963; American Scandinavian Foundation travel grant, 1981; Finnish Literature Center Production grant, 1982; Villager award (three times), 1983; McKnight fellowship, 1986; Aide de la Création grant, 1987. **Address:** 23 Leroy Street, Number 8, New York, New York 10014, U.S.A.

Publications

Plays

The Running of the Deer (produced New York, 1978).

Balloon (produced New York, 1983). New York, Broadway Play Publishing, 1983.

Philoctetes, adaptation of the play by Sophocles (also director: produced New York, 1983).
Dark Lady (produced Santa Maria, California, 1986). Woodstock, Illinois, Dramatic Publishing, 1988.
Kabuki Othello (produced Philadelphia, 1986).
To Moscow (produced Ankara, Turkey, 1994-95; New York, 1996). Woodstock, Illinois, Dramatic Publishing; in *Scenes and Monologues from the Best New Plays,* edited by Roger Ellis, Colorado Springs, Meriwether Publishing Ltd.,1992.
Quasimodo (musical), adaptation of Victor Hugo's *The Hunchback of Notre Dame*, with Christopher Martin (produced Woodstock, New York, 1987).
Anton, Himself (produced Louisville, Kentucky, 1989). In *Moscow Art Theatre*, edited by Michael Bigelow Dixon, Louisville, Kentucky, Actors' Theatre of Louisville, 1989; in *Scenes and Monologues from the Best New Plays,* edited by Roger Ellis, Colorado Springs, Meriwether Publishing Ltd., 1992.
Kabuki Macbeth (produced New York, 1989).
Haiti: A Dream (produced Atlanta, Georgia, 1990). In *Facing Forward,* New York, Broadway Play Publishing, 1994.
Masha, Too (produced Philadelphia, 1991). In *Scenes and Monologues from the Best New Plays,* edited by Roger Ellis, Colorado Springs, Meriwether Publishing Ltd., 1992.
Achilles (produced Kourian, Cyprus, Budapest, Hungary, and Philadelphia, 1991).
Scenes and Monologs from the Best New Plays, edited by Roger Ellis. Colorado Springs, 1992.
In a Kingdom by the Sea (produced Madison, New Jersey and New York, 1992).
La Pucelle (Me and Joan) (produced Philadelphia, 1993).
Daddy's Gone A-Hunting (produced Philadelphia, 1995).
Oh Wild West Wind (produced Madison, New Jersey, 1997). Woodstock, Illinois, Dramatic Publishing, 1998.

Radio Plays: *The Sound of Sand*, 1963; *Balloon*, 1987; *Haiti: A Dream*, 1991.

*

Manuscript Collection: Lincoln Center Library for the Performing Arts, New York.

Critical Studies: "Kabuki Macbeth" by Charles West, in *Shakespeare Bulletin: A Journal of Performance Criticism and Scholarship* (Easton, Pennsylvania) May-June 1988, pp. 18-19.

Theatrical Activities:
Director: **Plays**—*Exit the King* by Ionesco, New York, 1978; *Philoctetes* by Sophocles, New York, 1983.

Actor: **Plays**—Some 60 roles performed off Broadway including: Ruth in *The Homecoming* by Pinter, 1972-76; Celimene in *The Misanthrope* by Molière, and Viola in *Twelfth Night*, 1973-74; Hedda in *Hedda Gabler* by Ibsen, 1974-77; Antigone in *Antigone* by Anouilh, 1975-77; Isabella in *Measure for Measure*, 1975; Hesione in *Heartbreak House* by Shaw, 1976-77; Rebekka West in *Rosmersholm* by Ibsen, 1977-78; Countess Aurelie in *The Madwoman of Chaillot* by Giraudoux, 1978; Portia in *The Merchant of Venice*, 1980; Jocasta and Antigone in *Oedipus Rex*, *Antigone*, and *Oedipus at Colonus* by Sophocles, 1980-81; Aase in *Peer Gynt* by Ibsen, 1981-82; Lotte in *Big and Little* by Botho Strauss, 1983-84; Alice in *Dance of Death* by Strindberg, 1984; Clytemnestra in *The Orestia* by Aeschylus, 1984-85. **Television**—Mary Brewster in *The Mayflower*, 1980.

Karen Sunde comments:

I follow my nose—and here's all I know: that rhythm is important to me. And economy. And passion. That the live current between audience and stage is everything.

(1998) When I wanted a life in art, but didn't know whether to act or write, I learned that art . . . only lives in the air between. As actor, I must ignite, by my life onstage, a current, for the audience's imagination to be lit by the writer's. As writer my words are only a step toward this moment when the air vibrates with life surging between actors and audience.

Audience is an organism of all who gather at one time. Initially, they share humanity, but what they become, as the current flows among them and from them, is community. That's why I want my plays to speak to any person—whatever race, age, sex, religion, or culture—who happens to come. Theatre's power and purpose is to create, from any group that gathers, a community celebrating itself. It tells us who we are, and that we are *together.* When it works, it's magic. And holy.

* * *

With a voice both poetic and theatrical, Karen Sunde writes plays that dramatize historical epochs in epic scope. Hers is a distinctive, even unique, contemporary American drama, more akin to European than to other American plays. She tackles topics of war and politics to produce usually presentational, often explosive theater that many would swear could not have been created by a woman. Yet she imbues her mythic vision of the bellicose and patriarchal nature and direction of the United States and the world with a sense of what women can or do contribute to modifying these.

Sunde's works for the stage and screen fall into three related groups: the historical plays, the treatments of classics, and the glimpses of a painful present that shapes a deplorable but possibly salvageable future.

The first of her three consecutive plays set during or immediately after the American Revolution, *The Running of the Deer* has a huge canvas and varied vistas. It dramatizes the ravages of cold, starvation, and battle on George Washington's troops in order to probe the character of American male heroes. The second play, *Balloon*, achieves the same goal by setting, in a theatrical framework worthy of Jean Genet, another American founding father, Benjamin Franklin, so that he can spar with his Tory son and woo his French mistress, Helvetius, who fears losing her autonomy in marriage to a man as passionately committed to his vocations as to his lovers. An appropriate protagonist for a play about hope and progress, Franklin strives and achieves, yet his painful interpersonal relations have diluted his triumphs.

Deborah: The Adventures of a Soldier, an unproduced television play, is like several of Sunde's subsequent plays that investigate female heroism. In this case the subject is the male model of heroism achieved by the astonishing woman warrior Deborah Sampson, who enlists in the Continental army as Robert Shurtliffe and rises to leadership among men while battling the British. As Sunde remarks of her version of this historical woman's triumph, "When war is real, issues confused, deaths bitter, a woman has to finally decide who she is." This woman can outshoot, outthink, and outrun men, but should she continue to do so? Sunde humorously recounts Deborah's adventures both as a soldier and as a woman trying to pass for a man (with women coming on to "him") and falling in love with a sergeant who thinks that she is male. Sunde's background as an actor in Shakespeare's plays has certainly sensitized her to the comedic possibilities of employing a woman playing a man. But the dramatist also conveys the war's pathos, its pain, and its cost in lives lost.

Sunde continued to explore female heroism in *The Flower's Lost Child,* an unproduced play that portrays what the playwright describes as "America's romance with violence." Instead of showing colonists who resist taxation without representation and throw off an oppressor's rule, Sunde chooses hippie revolutionaries in 1970s New York. The shift in period changes the perspective, forcing us to distance ourselves from terrorists and to question the appropriateness of bombs in the pursuit of peace. Yet she dramatizes these idealists sympathetically. A resourceful and brave leader, the character Anne has worked with Martin Luther King and embraced nonviolence. Now, disillusioned by his assassination, she has abandoned marches and rallies in favor of dynamite. The tragedy creates a powerful sense of fate, as Sunde frames the entire play as a flashback by beginning with firemen sifting through rubble and dismembered bodies and then enhances the suspense by surrounding her characters with explosives.

In an unproduced and untitled gothic thriller about the British serial killer John George Haigh, set in 1948, Sunde builds tension by hinting at a murder and the threat to the lives of two courageous women, a spirited teenager and another more mature woman who struggle to foil an amoral terrorist.

Sunde again depicts a female hero in *Dark Lady*, which, set against the slaughter of the plague, dramatizes the relationship between Shakespeare and Renaissance England's best-known woman poet, Emilia Bassano. Sunde creates in her a passionate woman whose humanity, courage, spirit, and generosity equal, and ultimately exceed, Shakespeare's.

In three further plays Sunde dramatizes actual characters in events that might plausibly have occurred. *To Moscow* concerns Chekhov, his actress wife Olga Knipper, Konstantin Stanislavsky, and the beginnings of the Moscow Art Theatre. The title evokes Chekhov's three sisters' unrealized intention to return from their provincial backwater to Moscow. Sunde chooses as four of the six central characters women whom Chekhov exploits. But in one, Olga, he finds, like Shakespeare in Emilia, his equal. Sunde completes the Russian trilogy with two matching one-act portraits—one of the narcissist Chekhov titled *Anton, Himself* and the other, *Masha, Too*, of his sister as she struggles to summon the courage to tell him that she plans to marry. We conclude from *Anton* that her brother will not let her leave him. While viewers need know nothing about Chekhov to enjoy these three, Sunde interlards the action with jokes about his plays and stories, making her plays especially intriguing to knowledgeable viewers.

While penning her history plays, Sunde undertook a related approach to indicting human folly by means of literary myths—one from Victor Hugo, three from Shakespeare's plays, and one from Homer's *Iliad.* Sunde's musical version of *The Hunchback of Notre Dame*, which she wrote with director Christopher Martin, fashions the novel into a fluid work that contrasts with the long, carefully demarcated scenes in that other musical version of Hugo, *Les Misérables*. More opera than musical and boasting a score ranging from ecclesiastic to gypsy, the galvanic *Quasimodo* dramatizes the theme that people should experience, not repress, their passions: "Man is man, not stone."

Providing further evidence of her versatility, Sunde created four Kabuki plays for the Japanese director Shozo Sato, who has staged them in Kabuki style but with American performers. Although *Kabuki Othello* preserves the Shakespearean outlines, Sunde makes Iago's motivation clearer and eliminates Shakespeare's racism and sexism. Asian ritual reinforces the tragedy's inevitability. Far from inviting unfavorable comparisons to the original, Sunde creates her own distinctive imagery—delicate, tender, and eventually heroic for Desdemona and demonic for the Ainu Othello—and in Emilia's lines she creates a healthy sarcasm about machismo and female subservience. In *Kabuki Macbeth* and the unproduced *Kabuki Richard* the dramatist also evokes a theatrical mixture of the original plots and their archetypes with Eastern culture, with samurai, shoguns, karma, and Siva intertwined with ghosts, witches, and severed heads.

In *Achilles* Sunde converts material from the *Iliad* into a mythic antiwar tragedy. She emphasizes the macho lust for glory that leads to the razing of Troy and the massive, senseless slaughter, reminding us of the continuing cost of personal and international bravado. Sunde's searing script dramatizes pride, arrogance, and savagery and shows the aftermath of grief, in which Achilles joins Priam in mourning Hector's death after the bereaved father kisses the "victor's" hand. Focusing her work through the eyes of the enslaved Briseis, "only a woman," a prize of battle who has learned that "the purpose of life is war," Sunde employs an archetypal example to promote peace and the recognition of our common humanity.

Sunde likewise dramatizes conflicts from a humanist perspective in a series of prescient plays looking toward the global future. The unproduced *House of Eeyore,* which takes its title from A. A. Milne's *Winnie the Pooh* stories, employs dream research, a gubernatorial campaign, and an ageless Native American psychic named for the female spirit Gaia to awaken a prominent American family to its spiritual and social responsibilities.

Whereas the visionary middle-class women in *House of Eeyore* works as a research physician, Gaye in the unproduced screenplay *Countdown: Earth* saves the western half of the planet though her skill as a geophysicist, not to mention her bravery in carrying out a daredevil rescue while dangling above a volcano starting to erupt. Still a third woman scientist, this one discovering a cure for cancer, plays a prominent role in the unproduced screenplay *Over the Rainbow,* but here Sunde chooses as her protagonist another healer, the scientist's little girl. Both *Countdown: Earth* and *Over the Rainbow* employ science fiction to arouse concern about the planet's survival.

In three further plays Sunde hopes for a better tomorrow even as she explores the roots of today's misery. The prophetic *Haiti: A Dream* dramatizes the flight to Florida of Haitian boat people by focusing on a man and his wife and on the old woman empowered by voodoo who tries unsuccessfully to inspire them both to recognize their own strength to lead their people. In a similar spirit of fantasizing about a better way, the unproduced *How His Bride Came to Abraham* creates an extraordinary modern pacifist myth in which a wounded male Israeli soldier and a female Palestinian terrorist experience each other's passionate hunger for their homes and rights. Sunde describes this tragedy as "today's violent news stories in fairy-tale form," but it indelibly etches itself upon viewers' souls because of the human encounter as wary people drop their guard with an enemy.

The multimedia *In a Kingdom by the Sea*, based upon the abduction of Marine Lt. Col. William Higgins, presents simultaneously the efforts of the UN peacekeepers to free one of their own, here named Hogan, and Hogan himself. Hogan appears in both past and present and in both monologue and dialogue to share with the audience the "key to America" and to his character—football and women, in Hogan's case the woman whom, since high school, he has tried to impress with a uniform. In contrast to the wartime dream of peace and love in *How His Bride Came to Abraham, In a Kingdom by the Sea* dramatizes the subversion of the UN peacekeeping forces' efforts in Lebanon by those on both sides for whom macho bravado means more than an end to hostility.

A balloon will rise, but what, Sunde inquires in *Balloon*, of humanity? Her plays consider whether we have reason to hope.

—Tish Dace

T

TABORI, George

Nationality: British. **Born:** Budapest, Hungary, 24 May 1914. **Education:** Zrinyl Gymnasium. **Military Service:** Served in the British Army Middle East Command, 1941-43; lieutenant. **Family:** Married 1) Hanna Freund (divorced 1954); 2) the actress Viveca Lindfors (divorced), one son, one daughter, and one stepson. **Career:** Former artistic director, Berkshire Theatre Festival, Stockbridge, Massachusetts. **Awards:** British Film Academy award, 1953. **Address:** c/o Suhrkamp Verlag, Lindenstrasse 29-35, Postfach 4229, 6000 Frankfurt am Main, Germany.

PUBLICATIONS

Plays

Flight into Egypt (produced New York, 1952). New York, Dramatists Play Service, 1953.
The Emperor's Clothes (produced New York, 1953). New York, French, 1953.
Miss Julie, adaptation of a play by Strindberg (also director: produced New York, 1956).
Brouhaha (produced Brighton and London, 1958; New York, 1960).
Brecht on Brecht (produced New York and London, 1962). New York, French, n.d.
The Resistible Rise of Arturo Ui: A Gangster Spectacle, adaptation of the play by Brecht (produced New York, 1963; Edinburgh, 1968; London, 1969). New York, French, 1972.
Andorra, adaptation of the play by Max Frisch (produced New York, 1963).
The Guns of Carrar, adaptation of a play by Brecht (produced Syracuse, New York, 1963; New York City, 1968). New York, French, 1970.
The Niggerlovers: The Demonstration, and Man and Dog, music by Richard Peaslee (produced New York, 1967).
The Cannibals (produced New York, 1968). Published in *The American Place Theatre*, edited by Richard Schotter, New York, Dell, 1973; published separately, London, Davis Poynter, 1974.
Mother Courage, adaptation of a play by Brecht (produced Washington, D.C., 1970).
Pinkville, music by Stanley Walden (produced Stockbridge, Massachusetts, 1970; New York, 1971).
Clowns (also director: produced Tübingen, 1972).
Talk Show (produced Bremen, 1976).
Changes (produced Munich, 1976).
Mein Kampf: A Farce (produced Edinburgh and London, 1989).
Weisman and Copperface (produced London, 1991).

Screenplays: *I Confess*, with William Archibald, 1953; *The Young Lovers*, with Robin Estridge, 1954; *The Journey*, 1959; No Exit, 1962; *Secret Ceremony*, 1968; *Parades*, 1972; *Insomnia*, 1975.

Novels

Beneath the Stone the Scorpion. London, Boardman, 1945; as *Beneath the Stone*, Boston, Houghton Mifflin, 1945.
Companions of the Left Hand. London, Boardman, and Boston, Houghton Mifflin, 1946.
Original Sin. London, Boardman, and Boston, Houghton Mifflin, 1947.
The Caravan Passes. London, Boardman, and New York, Appleton Century Crofts, 1951.
The Journey: A Confession. New York, Bantam, 1958; London, Corgi, 1959.
The Good One. New York, Pocket Books, 1960.

Other

Ich wollte, meine Tochter läge tot zu meinen Füssen und hätte die Juwelen in den Ohren: Improvisationen über Shakespeares Shylock: Dokumentationen einer Theaterarbeit. Munich, Hanser, 1979.

*

Critical Studies: "*Othello* in Vienna" by Marvin Carlson, in *Shakespeare Quarterly* (Washington, D.C.), Summer 1993, pp. 228-30; "George Tabori's Bair Essentials: A Perspective on Beckett Staging in Germany" by Julian A. Garforth, in *Forum Modernes Theater* (Turbingen, Germany), 1994, pp. 59-75.

Theatrical Activities:
Director: **Plays**—*Miss Julie* by Strindberg, New York, 1956; *Brecht on Brecht*, toured, 1962; *Hell Is Other People*, New York, 1964; *The Cannibals* (co-director, with Marty Fried), Berlin, 1970; *Pinkville*, Berlin, 1971; *Clowns*, Tübingen, 1972; *Kohlhaas*, Bonn, 1974; *Emigrants*, Bonn, 1975; *Afore Night Come* by David Rudkin, Bremen, 1975; *The Trojan Women* by Euripides, Bremen, 1976.

* * *

George Tabori's world recalls the Sherwood Anderson title *Dark Laughter*. What a world—betrayal, repression, violence, cannibalism, and, unlike the Greeks, no redemption. And this world is envisioned more and more as a black comedy, but not quite. The flavor is sardonic and tongue-in-cheek, but beneath there is absolutely no acceptance of the world as it is. Beneath the sardonic tone we can apprehend the eyes of an anguished, lacerated soul who has seen mankind in one perversion and one degradation after another, seen Hungary in its fascistic period earlier in the century, Germany in the Nazi era, and America in its growing role as policeman-butcher of the world, has seen it all, and yet whose outcry marks him as one who still believes in the impossible dream of brotherhood. I have the sense that Tabori is too angry, too disgusted to want to believe, but that past his disgust, past his disillusionment, there is a tremendous, cavernous yearning to believe in the possibility of a decent society.

Early Tabori is represented by *The Emperor's Clothes*, the tale of what might be called a "fuzzy-headed idealist" intellectual in Budapest who appears to renounce all of his beliefs when he falls into the hands of the secret police but who emerges as a man with backbone. Under torture he rediscovers his manhood. In short, this is Tabori at his most idealistic.

But then the world grew darker, and Tabori began to shift from naturalism toward a more abstract, less lyrical, and far harsher theater. He began adapting Brecht, for example, *Brecht on Brecht* and *Arturo Ui,* and his own work became more detached, more sardonic, and more abstract. By the time of *The Cannibals* in 1968, the work was dry, dark, bitter, and removed. The prisoners in a Nazi concentration camp decide to cook and eat their friend Puffi, the fat man who has just died. To Uncle, who is protesting the cannibalism, Hirschler says:

> Listen, Uncle, let's have some perspective. The cake is too small. Whenever you eat, you take a crumb out of someone else's mouth. At this very moment, while you're making such a fuss, millions are starving to death in India; but today we may have stumbled on the most elegant solution. The graveyards are full of goodies; the chimneys are going full blast, and nice fat suicides come floating down every river and stream. All that perfectly good stuff going to waste.

This is shades of Swift's *A Modest Proposal.* And the cannibalism, which Tabori treats both literally and as a metaphor, is painted as inexorable. At the end of the play loudspeakers place the action in historic context:

> some savages eagerly desire the body of a murdered man
> So that his ghost may not trouble them,
> For which reason I recommend, dear brethren in Christ,
> The Jew's heart, in aspic or with sauce vinaigrette,
> So soft it will melt in your mouth.

In *The Niggerlovers* Tabori views the racial tensions that afflict the United States, but any sympathy is sublimated. No one comes off with any saving grace, for the white liberals are stupid, saccharine, or slightly perverted, and the blacks are corroded with cynicism. No action seems to be of any help, and there is no way out.

Pinkville studies the development of an American killer, specifically how the U.S. army takes a nonviolent, righteous young man and, using his very righteousness, subverts him into the killer it needs to massacre Vietnamese. Again, the action is inexorable. Everything becomes grist for the army's purpose, and the world is so self-enclosed that there is no way out.

And yet the way out is through the action of Tabori's art. The very work is a cry. The sardonic element has within it a taint of satisfaction, as if the worst is always somehow satisfying, but the worst is also an indictment of us and ultimately a call. For the early heroes are gone, and no heroes are left in the later plays, where there is nothing for us to emulate. You and I become the only possible heroes left to Tabori and to the world.

—Arthur Sainer

TALLY, Ted

Nationality: American. **Born:** Winston-Salem, North Carolina, 9 April 1952. **Education:** Yale University, New Haven, Connecticut (John Golden fellowship 1976-77; Kazan award, 1977; Field prize, 1977), B.A. 1974, M.F.A. 1977. **Family:** Married; one son and one daughter. **Career:** Taught at Yale University; artist-in-residence, Atlantic Center for the Arts, 1983. Lives in Pennsylvania. **Awards:** CBS-Yale fellowship, 1977; Creative Artists Public Service grant, 1979; John Gassner award, 1981; National Endowment for the Arts fellowship, 1983; Obie award, 1984; Guggenheim fellowship, 1985; Christopher award, 1988; Oscar, 1992; Writers Guild award, 1992; Chicago Film Critics award, 1992; Saturn award, 1992; Edgar award, 1992. **Member:** Dramatists Guild, Writers Guild, Academy of Motion Picture Arts and Sciences, and the Artistic Board, Playwrights Horizons, New York. **Agent:** (theatre) Helen Merrill Ltd., 425 West 23rd Street, New York, New York 10011, U.S.A.; (film) Arlene Donovan, International Creative Management, 40 West 57th Street, New York, New York 10019, U.S.A.

Publications

Plays

Terra Nova (produced New Haven, Connecticut, 1977; Chichester, Sussex, 1980; London, 1983; New York, 1984). London, French, 1981; New York, Dramatists Play Service, 1982.

Word of Mouth (revue), with others (produced New York, 1978).

Hooters (produced New York, 1978). New York, Dramatists Play Service, 1978.

Coming Attractions, music by Jack Feldman, lyrics by Feldman and Bruce Sussman (produced New York, 1980). New York, French, 1982.

Silver Linings: Revue Sketches. New York, Dramatists Play Service, 1983.

Little Footsteps (produced New York, 1986; London, 1987). New York, Dramatists Play Service, 1986.

Taxi from Hell in *Urban Blight* (musical revue), based on an idea by John Tillinger, music by David Shire, lyrics by Richard Maltby, Jr. (produced New York, 1988).

The Gettysburg Sound Bite (produced New York, 1989).

Screenplays: *White Palace*, with Alvin Sargent, 1990; *The Silence of the Lambs*, 1991; *The Juror,* 1995; *Before and After,* 1995.

Television: *The Comedy Zone* series, 1984; *The Father Clements Story*, with Arthur Heineman, 1987.

*

Critical Studies: "Coming Attractions: Theater and the Performance of Television" by Elizabeth Klaver, in *Mosaic: A Journal for the Interdisciplinary Study of Literature* (Winnipeg, MB), December 1995, pp. 111-27; "Tally's *Terra Nova*: From Historical Journals to Existential Journey" by Robert J. Andreach, in *Twentieth Century Literature: A Scholarly and Critical Journal* (Albany, New York) Spring 1989, pp. 65-73.

Ted Tally comments:

I have sometimes been asked whether my plays share any particular theme. Though they have been diverse both stylistically and in terms of subject matter, I think there are at least two common threads: a fascination with rites of passage, and a concern for the prices one must pay in pursuit of a dream.

* * *

Ted Tally writes in versatile voices. Since 1977 productions of his plays at showcase American theaters—including the Yale Repertory Theater; the O'Neill Theater Center in Waterford, Connecticut; the Mark Taper Forum in Los Angeles; and the audaciously innovative Playwrights Horizons in New York—in Stockholm, and at the Chichester Festival Theatre have earned him recognition as an important dramatic talent.

Tally's prodigious promise is revealed stunningly in *Terra Nova,* his most widely produced and justifiably praised work. His subject is specific and based in reality—the Englishman Robert Scott's doomed 1911-12 race to the Antarctic against the Norwegian Roald Amundsen. But the play's method and implications are mythic and poetic. They free Tally from the confines of a history play and enable him to universalize his literal subject through stylized language, setting, and dramatic structure. Set in the mind of the dying Scott as he records final entries in his diary, *Terra Nova* portrays its hero's hallucinatory evaluation of the sources that have driven him and his unlucky band of men to the Antarctic. The procession of stage images shifts seamlessly and cinematically within the frozen present, the past, and the future, and all are reflected through the anguished mind of Scott, whose story coexists as an exciting theatrical adventure and as the wellspring for a series of complex moral debates.

Tally dissects the core of heroism even as he concedes the need of nations to create heroes and the symbiotic needs of special men, sometimes tragic men like Scott, to enact the roles their societies write for them. Related to the play's central, ambivalent issue are the vanishing points between national pride and jingoism, patriotic sacrifice and familial irresponsibility, and a shrinking British Empire and a future, toward which the play points, bereft of old-style heroes. "The world is changing," Amundsen says in Scott's imagined future: "England, Norway, Europe—The Great War changed everything, you wouldn't know it today [1932]. It's a smaller place, but not a more neighbourly one. A frightened place, a world of shopkeepers and thieves. Where is the heroic gesture in such a world? The man who can keep his bread on the table is a hero. Where on such an earth are men who walk like gods? Dead and gone, with Columbus and Magellan." In his haunted fear of failure and conflicting drive to defy man's ordinary boundaries, Scott resembles Ibsen's master builder Solness. He is possibly, as Amundsen calls him, "the most dangerous kind of decent man," possibly a true representative of the last breed of genuine hero, or possibly a complete sham. Scott is one of the few realized tragic heroes in contemporary American drama.

In *Coming Attractions* the subject is still celebrity, but the mode is wild satire. Amundsen's prediction in *Terra Nova* has come true: no heroes are left. But television and the tabloids and memoir publishers and movie writers, hungry for heroes to feed an insatiable American public, fabricate them out of killers, madmen, and real people. *Coming Attractions* takes deadly aim at many targets: Miss America contests, television news, talk and variety shows, inept law enforcement, an even more inept judicial system, old-time religion, advertising, and, especially, an American society that encourages fleeting fame or infamy to masquerade as authentic accomplishment. To appear on television even for a moment is the promised end. Tally's shift from the poetic voices of *Terra Nova* to the parodies in *Coming Attractions* of showbiz vernacular, press agentry, and media hype is dazzling. Outrageous puns (Criminal to Judge: "I demand that you give me the chair!" Judge: "Then where would I sit?"), burlesque routines, movie clichés, and mordantly hilarious situations (with the play concluding with the televised musical electrocution of its killer-hero: "Live from Death Row—it's—The Execution of Lonnie Wayne Burke!") combine in a lunatic blend of the Marx Brothers, Artaudian theater of cruelty, Paddy Chayefsky's *Network,* and Sinclair Lewis's *Elmer Gantry.*

Tally's other work reflects his discomfort with stylistic uniformity. *Hooters* is a rites-of-passage sex comedy. Three early unproduced film scripts belong to three separate genres: situation comedy (*Couples Only*); epic (*Empire,* on which Tally worked for a year with director Lindsay Anderson); and New York police thriller (*Hush-a-Bye*). In the underrated play *Little Footsteps*—"an exceptionally literate sitcom," *New York Times* critic Frank Rich called it—the teenage courtship dance of *Hooters* evolves into marriage and legal rituals as a young couple await the arrival of their firstborn. "We've got nothing against your religion, Ben; it's you we hate," his mother-in-law casually informs the beleaguered hero in the play's pungent dialogue.

Like most serious contemporary American playwrights, Tally deplores the exorbitant costs of Broadway theater, which result in productions appealing to "the widest possible audience" and having "more and more to do with sensation and effect, less to do with any food for thought." His plays are primarily associated with strong regional theater companies and with Playwrights Horizons in New York City, the highly regarded company with which he has been identified periodically since the beginning of his career.

Tally's disenchantment with the theater appears to have driven him entirely to screenwriting, a shift that, with his adaptation of *The Silence of the Lambs,* has brought him financial reward and critical acclaim, including an Oscar, rarely earned for his stage work. He embraces film writing for its opportunities to reach "a wider audience and to be less subject to the whims of critics." He rejects the notion that Hollywood "sucks up writers and destroys them," maintaining that his work with director Jonathan Demme on *The Silence of the Lambs* was a thoroughly enjoyable collaborative effort.

In recognition of what he calls the inevitable "streamlining" that must occur in screen adaptation, Tally's screenplay for the film eliminates the multiple points of view that occur in Thomas Harris's novel. "The book goes inside the minds not just of Clarice Starling, but of Lecter, of Gumb, the killer she is pursuing, and of Jack Crawford, her mentor at the F.B.I.," Tally told a *New York Times* interviewer. "I thought really that the entire story had to concentrate on Clarice, that every scene had to concentrate as much as possible on what she is seeing and what she is feeling and what she is thinking. The heart of the story was between Clarice and Lecter, that strange sexual power struggle, that chess game between this young woman and this man—this monster." That "this monster," performed memorably by Anthony Hopkins, becomes the film's unforgettable character, a Norman Bates for the 1990s, is a particular consequence of Tally's dialogue, which manages to externalize Lecter's dangerous complexity and dark humor without turning him into a caricature.

"Success is a bitch. Grab her, and have her—but don't stand under her window with a mandolin," says Amundsen, the cynical, pragmatic leveler of Scott's romantic imagination in *Terra Nova.*

"Ain't life a bitch?" muses theatrical agent Manny Alter to the man condemned to electrocution in *Coming Attractions*. In *Terra Nova* heroism comes to an end, but genuine myths are born. In *Coming Attractions* travesty is the only legitimate vehicle for a society in which violence and bad taste alone capture the public imagination. Hannibal "The Cannibal" Lecter sprang to mythical status as an icon of popular cinema culture following the release of *The Silence of the Lambs*. It is no small irony that Ted Tally's most explicit flirtation with violence and bad taste captured the public imagination as none of his plays has been able to do.

—Mark W. Estrin

TAVEL, Ronald

Nationality: American. **Born:** Brooklyn, New York, 17 May 1941. **Education:** Brooklyn College; University of Wyoming, Laramie, B.A., M.A. 1961. **Career:** Screenwriter, Andy Warhol Films Inc., 1964-66; playwright-in-residence, Play-House of the Ridiculous, New York, 1965-67, Theatre of the Lost Continent, New York, 1971-73, Actors Studio, New York, 1972, Yale University Divinity School, New Haven, Connecticut, 1975, 1977, Williamstown Theatre Festival, Massachusetts, Summer 1977, New Playwrights Theatre, Washington, D.C., 1978-79, Cornell University, Ithaca, New York, 1980-81, Centrum Foundation, Fort Worden State Park, Washington, 1981, and Millay Colony for the Arts, New York, 1986; lecturer in foreign languages, Mahidol University, Thailand, 1981-82; visiting professor of creative writing, University of Colorado, Boulder, 1986; lecturer, University of New Orleans, 1991. Member of the Education Division, Theater for the New City, New York, 1984—. Literary adviser, *Scripts* magazine, New York, 1971-72; drama critic, *Stages* magazine, Norwood, New Jersey, 1984; theatre editor, *Brooklyn Literary Review*, 1984-85. **Awards:** Obie award, 1969, 1973; American Place Theatre grant, 1970; Creative Artists Public Service grant, 1971, 1973; Rockefeller grant, 1972, 1978; Guggenheim fellowship, 1973; National Endowment for the Arts grant, 1974; New York State Council on the Arts grant, 1975; ZBS Foundation grant, 1976; New York Foundation for the Arts fellowship, 1985; Yaddo fellowship, 1986; Senior Fulbright scholar, Taiwan. **Agent:** Helen Merrill Ltd., 361 West 17th Street, New York, New York 10011. **Address:** 5980 Shore Boulevard South, Diplomat 212, Gulfport, Florida 33707.

Publications

Plays

Christina's World, published in *Chicago Review*, Winter-Spring 1963.

The Life of Juanita Castro (produced New York, 1965). Included in *Bigfoot and Other Plays*, 1973.

Shower (produced New York, 1965). Included in *Bigfoot and Other Plays*, 1973.

Tarzan of the Flicks (produced Plainfield, Vermont, 1965). Published in *Blacklist 6* (Maplewood, New Jersey), 1965.

Harlot (scenario), published in *Film Culture* (New York), Spring 1966.

The Life of Lady Godiva (produced New York, 1966). Published in *The New Underground Theatre*, edited by Robert Schroeder, New York, Bantam, 1968.

Indira Gandhi's Daring Device (produced New York, 1966). Included in *Bigfoot and Other Plays*, 1973.

Screen Test (produced New York, 1966).

Vinyl (produced New York, 1967). Published in *Clyde* (New York), vol. 2, no. 2, 1966.

Kitchenette (also director: produced New York, 1967). Included in *Bigfoot and Other Plays*, 1973.

Gorilla Queen (produced New York, 1967). Published in *The Best of Off-Off-Broadway*, edited by Michael T. Smith, New York, Dutton, 1969.

Canticle of the Nightingale (produced Stockholm, 1968).

Cleobis and Bito (oratorio; produced New York, 1968).

Arenas of Lutetia (also director: produced New York, 1968). Published in *Experiments in Prose*, edited by Eugene Wildman, Chicago, Swallow Press, 1969.

Boy on the Straight-Back Chair, music by Orville Stoeber (produced New York, 1969). Included in *Bigfoot and Other Plays*, 1973.

Vinyl Visits an FM Station (produced New York, 1970). Published in *Drama Review* (New York), September 1970.

Bigfoot, music by Jeff Labes (produced New York, 1970). Included in *Bigfoot and Other Plays*, 1973.

Words for Bryan to Sing and Dance (produced New York, 1971).

Arse Long—Life Short (produced New York, 1972).

Secrets of the Citizens Correction Committee (produced New York, 1973). Published in *Scripts 3* (New York), January 1972.

Bigfoot and Other Plays. New York, Winter House, 1973.

Queen of Greece (produced New York, 1973).

The Last Days of British Honduras (produced New York, 1974).

Playbirth (produced New York, 1976).

The Clown's Tail (produced New York, 1977).

Gazelle Boy (produced Waterford, Connecticut, 1977).

The Ovens of Anita Orangejuice: A History of Modern Florida (produced Williamstown, Massachusetts, 1977; New York, 1978).

The Ark of God (produced Washington, D.C., 1978).

The Nutcracker in the Land of Nuts, music by Simeon Westbrooke (produced New York, 1979).

My Foetus Lived on Amboy Street (broadcast 1979; also director: produced New York, 1985).

The Understudy (produced Ithaca, New York, 1981).

Success and Succession (produced New York, 1983).

Notorious Harik Will Kill the Pope (also director: produced New York, 1986).

Thick Dick (also director: produced New York, 1988).

Screenplays: *Harlot*, 1964; *Phillip's Screen Test*, 1965; *Screen Test*, 1965: *Suicide*, 1965; *The Life of Juanita Castro*, 1965; *Horse*, 1965; *Vinyl*, 1965; *Kitchen*, 1965; *Space*, 1965; *Hedy; or, The 14-Year-Old Girl*, 1966; *Withering Sights*, 1966; *The Chelsea Girls*, 1966; *More Milk Evette*, 1966.

Radio Play: *My Foetus Lived on Amboy Street*, 1979.

Novel

Street of Stairs. New York, Olympia Press, 1968.

*

Manuscript Collections: Mugar Memorial Library, Boston University: Lincoln Center Library of the Performing Arts, New York; University of Wisconsin Center for Theatre Research, Madison.

Critical Studies: "The Pop Scene," in *Tri-Quarterly 6* (Evanston, Illinois), 1966, and "Pop Goes America," in *New Republic* (Washington, D.C.), 9 September 1967, both by Peter Michelson; "Ronald Tavel: Ridiculous Playwright" by Dan Isaac, in *Drama Review* (New York), Spring 1968; "Toward Eroticizing All Thought," in *New York Times*, 5 January 1969, and "Ronald Tavel: Celebration of a Panic Vision," in *Village Voice* (New York), 6 March 1969, both by Gino Rizzo; "A Kid Named Toby" by Jack Kroll, in *Newsweek* (New York), 24 March 1969; *American Playwrights: A Critical Survey* by Bonnie Marranca and Gautam Dasgupta, New York, Drama Book Specialists, 1981.

Theatrical Activities:
Director: **Plays**—*The Life of Juanita Castro*, Chicago, 1967; *Kitchenette*, New York, 1967; *Arenas of Lutetia*, New York, 1968; *Infinity*, New York, 1972; *A Streetcar Named Desire* (in Thai, as *Ourrat*) by Tennessee Williams, Bangkok, 1981; *The Zoo Story* (in Thai) by Edward Albee, Bangkok, 1982; *Clash of the Bra Maidens*, New York, 1984; *My Foetus Lived on Amboy Street*, New York, 1985; *The Tell-Tale Heart*, East Meadow, New York, 1985; *Talent*, East Meadow, New York, 1985; *Notorious Harik Will Kill the Pope*, New York, 1986; *Thick Dick*, New York, 1988. **Films**—*Harlot*, 1964; *Phillip's Screen Test*, 1965; *Screen Test*, 1965; *The Life of Juanita Castro*, 1965; *Horse*, 1965; *Vinyl*, 1965; *Space*, 1965; *It Happened in Connecticut*, 1965; *Hedy; or, The 14-Year-Old Girl*, 1966; *Withering Sights*, 1966; *The Chelsea Girls* (*Toby Short* and *Hanoi Hanna episodes*), 1966.

Actor: **Plays**—Roles in *In Search of the Cobra Jewels* by Harvey Fierstein, New York, 1972, and in all his directed plays. **Films**—In all his directed films, and in *Fifty Fantasticks*, 1964; *Bitch*, 1965; *Jail*, 1967; *Suicide Notations: Fire Escape*, 1972; *Infinity*, 1974.

Ronald Tavel comments:

(1973) My earliest tales were delivered Homerically. At the age of six or seven I took the first step toward giving them permanent form: comic books. While these comics were shameless imitations of the pictorial styles featured in the funnies we read at that time, there was, I fancy, something more urgent in my stories and characterizations. I wrote my first (verse) play (or fragment of one) in my sophomore year in high school and ten verse plays (or fragments of ones) followed that effort. The last of these have reached print but only one (*Cleobis and Bito*) was ever produced. In 1965, after two years of writing, directing, and acting in films, I turned again to playwriting. These were the one-acters that inaugurated The Theatre of the Ridiculous movement—a term I invented to catch the attention of critics and lower them into a category in order to facilitate their work. The term "Ridiculous" should not be taken too seriously (!) unless you want to re-define that word as Professor Peter Michelson did in his essay on the new American absurdity (*New Republic*, 9 September 1967). I sought in these abstract satires to find a distinctly American language for the stage and that is a continuing preoccupation in my later and mercilessly longer "tragedies." In the early plays I also attempted to destroy plot and character, motivation, cause, event, and logic along with their supposed consequences. The word was All: what was spoken did not express the moment's preoccupation; rather, the preoccupation followed the word. In *The Life of Lady Godiva* I reached, cynically, for the Aristotelian principles of playmaking. While cynicism is the major thrust of *Godiva*, a near decade of concern with *The Poetics* was worming its way, re-evaluated, to the core of my chores. *Gorilla Queen* progresses by building and abolishing, rebuilding and reabolishing, etc., the Aristotelian constructs. The full-length plays after *Gorilla Queen* obey, I believe, without too much objection, the Greek's difficult insights. While I have no single favorite, I am particularly fond of *Shower* because it continues to mystify me, am protective of *Arenas of Lutetia* because no one else will be, and consider *Bigfoot* (if you will allow me to play critic) my most ambitious and best play to date.

(1988) Although my recent fellowships and judging and teaching appointments are apparently for my abstract work in theatre, I have continued to create as many formal pieces: partly because I feel that formal values, following the disappearance of American education, are threatened in serious contemporary theatre; and partly because I believe that our present situation is not more keenly scrutinized by the abstract than the formal. (My previous solution, in larger works, was always to combine the two.)

Because of the growing idiosyncratic nature of serious plays, it has become common in the last decade for American dramatists to direct their own work. Reluctantly, I have joined their ranks. Since directing forces a stronger confrontation with space, time, flesh, clothes, and light than words alone do, and requires no rewards or rejuvenations outside itself, it helps the playwright to that closer understanding of the unity of theatre which he irresponsibly surrendered in the past century and a half.

* * *

Ronald Tavel is one of the originators of the mode Susan Sontag identified as "camp." From the start he writes with an unmistakable voice, relentlessly punning and answering back to his own wordplays; he is philosophizing, art-conscious, joking, and as ridiculous as the Marx Brothers. He turns his formidable energy to the service of justice, with a Cassandra's terror of self-righteousness, and a not-to-be-thwarted demand for meaning and self-knowledge.

This thrust is evident even in a pop joke like *The Life of Juanita Castro* , which takes its authenticity from *Life* magazine. *Indira Gandhi's Daring Device* drew a swift protest from the government of India, and *How Jacqueline Kennedy Became Queen of Greece* was muted (in title only) to *Queen of Greece*. These plays are travesty, but Tavel is out for serious game, and loads his plays with real facts and arguments.

Gorilla Queen, his first play on a large scale, is a spoof on jungle movies, unique in its crazy playfulness, smart-alecky language, outlandishly scrambled sexuality, and self-consciousness about art. From the epilogue (delivered by a gibbon holding a purple rose): ". . . art ain't never 'bout life, but life *is* only 'bout art. Dis rose?—oh, it ain't no symbol like ya mighta thought, an dat's cause it ain't got nothin' to do wit life either. Dis here rose is all 'bout art. Here, take it—(He throws the rose into the audience.)"

In *Bigfoot* the work began to reveal, not just refer to, its depth and power. Here Tavel's subject is brothers in the image of Jacob and Esau. One brother, an intellectual monastic and schoolteacher, suspects the other, a forest ranger, of not being human, confusing him with the Bigfoot, the legendary man-ape of the Pacific Northwest. Set in the majestic forest and the monastery schoolroom,

Bigfoot is a play of immense complexity. The surface is no longer pop or campy, but the postrealist strategies are in flood: a fictional lighting girl gets caught up in the "more real" fiction of the play's far-fetched story; the Playwright's Brother is a character *ex machina*, played in the production Tavel supervised by his own brother—what a thing to do in a play about mythic fratricide!

The Ovens of Anita Orangejuice is a boisterous, savage satire about Anita Bryant's 1977 campaign against gay rights. Subtitled "A History of Modern Florida," it is a wisecrack that turns into a nightmare. For all its frenzied hilarity, it makes a thought-provoking, emotionally compelling case. In *Gazelle Boy* a middle-aged missionary in the North Woods loses her head over a wild boy, which leads to tragedy of profoundly unsettling dimensions. It is a beautiful play, dense with religion. Here sex represents a reaching for the divine. *The Understudy* is about sex murders. The play's playwright may have done the killings he has written about, which the audience is ultimately shown in literal gore; a demented understudy tries to save him, and steal the writer's being, by recommitting the murders himself.

My Foetus Lived on Amboy Street takes a far more tender tone. The play appears to be a prenatal autobiography. The writer experiments with an expressionistically abstracted, outwardly geometrical stagecraft. The persona of the play's ego imagines himself as a spider, while the company of players patch in the various roles as freely as the author counterposes multiple vernaculars of lyricism and melodrama. *Notorious Harik Will Kill the Pope*, which Tavel himself staged at the Theatre for the New City in New York in 1986, crammed the stage with movie types (Turhan Bey and Lana Turner are among the characters) in a flashy complexity of scenes. The frivolity of its trashy satirical style—Tavel never resists a pun—masks a sustained demolition of the religious establishment that, like all his themes, the writer gives every sign of meaning.

—Michael T. Smith

TERRY, Megan

Nationality: American. **Born:** Marguerite Duffy in Seattle, Washington, 22 July 1932. **Education:** Banff School of Fine Arts, Alberta, summers 1950-53, 1956; University of Washington, Seattle, 1950, 1953-56, B.Ed. 1956; University of Alberta, Edmonton, 1951-53. **Career:** Drama teacher and director of the Cornish Players, Cornish School of Allied Arts, Seattle, 1954-56; founding member, 1963, and director of the playwrights workshop, 1963-68, Open Theatre, New York; writer-in-residence and ABC Fellow, Yale University School of Drama, New Haven, Connecticut, 1966-67; founding member, Women's Theatre Council, 1971; founding member and treasurer, New York Theatre Strategy, 1971; Bingham professor of humanities, University of Louisville, 1981; Hill professor of fine arts, University of Minnesota, Duluth, 1983; visiting artist University of Iowa, Iowa City, 1992, Emory University, 1996, Bucknell University, 1996, Texas Tech, 1997. Resident playwright and literary manager, Omaha Magic Theatre, 1971—. **Awards:** Stanley award, 1965; Office of Advanced Drama Research award, 1965; ABC-Yale University fellowship, 1966; Rockefeller grant, 1968, 1987; Obie award, 1970; National Endowment for the Arts grant, 1972, fellowship, 1989; Earplay award, 1972; Creative Artists Public Service grant, 1973; Guggenheim fellowship, 1978; Dramatists Guild award, 1983; Nebraska Artist of the Year Governors award, 1992; Lifetime award, American Theatre Fellow, 1994. **Agent:** Tonda Marton, E. Marton Agency, Room 612, One Union Square West, New York, New York 10003-3303, U.S.A. **Address:** 2309 Hanscom Boulevard, Omaha, Nebraska 68105; or, c/o Omaha Magic Theatre, Nebraska 68102, U.S.A.

Publications

Plays

Beach Grass (also director: produced Seattle, 1955).
Seascape (also director: produced Seattle, 1955).
Go Out and Move the Car (also director: produced Seattle, 1955).
New York Comedy: Two (produced Saratoga, New York, 1961).
Ex-Miss Copper Queen on a Set of Pills (produced New York, 1963; Edinburgh, 1987). With *The People vs. Ranchman*, New York, French, 1968.
When My Girlhood Was Still All Flowers (produced New York, 1963).
Eat at Joe's (produced New York, 1964).
Calm Down Mother (produced New York, 1965; London, 1969). Indianapolis, Bobbs Merrill, 1966.
Keep Tightly Closed in a Cool Dry Place (produced New York, 1965; London, 1968). Included in *Four Plays*, 1967.
The Magic Realists (produced New York, 1966). Included in *Three One-Act Plays*, 1972.
Comings and Goings (produced New York, 1966; Edinburgh, 1968). Included in *Four Plays*, 1967.
The Gloaming, Oh My Darling (produced Minneapolis, 1966). Included in *Four Plays*, 1967.
Viet Rock: A Folk War Movie (also director: produced New York, 1966; London, 1977). Included in *Four Plays*, 1967.
Four Plays. New York, Simon and Schuster, 1967.
The Key Is on the Bottom (produced Los Angeles, 1967).
The People vs. Ranchman (produced Minneapolis, 1967; New York, 1968). With *Ex-Miss Copper Queen on a Set of Pills*, New York, French, 1968.
Home; or, Future Soap (televised 1968; revised version, as *Future Soap*, produced Omaha, 1987). New York, French, 1972.
Jack-Jack (produced Minneapolis, 1968).
Massachusetts Trust (produced Waltham, Massachusetts, 1968). Published in *The Off-Off-Broadway Book*, edited by Albert Poland and Bruce Mailman, Indianapolis, Bobbs Merrill, 1972.
Changes, with Tom O'Horgan (produced New York, 1968).
Sanibel and Captiva (broadcast 1968). Included in *Three One-Act Plays*, 1972.
One More Little Drinkie (televised 1969). Included in *Three One-Act Plays*, 1972.
Approaching Simone (produced Boston and New York, 1970). Old Westbury, New York, Feminist Press, 1973.
The Tommy Allen Show (also director: produced Los Angeles and New York, 1970). Published in *Scripts 2* (New York), December 1971.
Grooving (produced New York, 1972).
Choose a Spot on the Floor, with Jo Ann Schmidman (produced Omaha, 1972).
Three One-Act Plays. New York, French, 1972.

Couplings and Groupings (monologues and sketches). New York, Pantheon, 1973.
Susan Peretz at the Manhattan Theatre Club (produced New York, 1973).
Thoughts (lyrics only), book by Lamar Alford (produced New York, 1973).
Nightwalk, with Sam Shepard and Jean-Claude van Itallie (produced New York and London, 1973). Published in *Open Theater*, New York, Drama Book Specialists, 1975.
St. Hydro Clemency; or, A Funhouse of the Lord: An Energizing Event (produced New York, 1973).
The Pioneer, and Pro-Game (produced Omaha, 1973; New York, 1974). Holly Springs, Mississippi, Ragnarok Press, 1975.
Hothouse (produced New York, 1974). New York, French, 1975.
Babes in the Bighouse (produced Omaha, 1974; New York, 1976). Omaha, Magic Theatre, 1979.
All Them Women, with others (produced New York, 1974).
We Can Feed Everybody Here (produced New York, 1974).
Hospital Play. Omaha, Magic Theatre, 1974.
Henna for Endurance. Omaha, Magic Theatre, 1974.
The Narco Linguini Bust (produced Omaha, 1974).
100,001 Horror Stories of the Plains, with others (produced Omaha, 1976). Omaha, Magic Theatre, 1979.
Sleazing Towards Athens. Omaha, Magic Theatre, 1977; revised version (produced Omaha, 1986), 1986.
Willie-Willa-Bill's Dope Garden. Birmingham, Alabama, Ragnarok Press, 1977.
Brazil Fado (produced Omaha, 1977). Omaha, Magic Theatre, 1977; revised version (produced Santa Fe, 1978), 1979.
Lady Rose's Brazil Hide Out (produced Omaha, 1977).
American King's English for Queens (produced Omaha, 1978). Omaha, Magic Theatre, 1978.
Goona Goona (produced Omaha, 1979). Omaha, Magic Theatre, 1985; New York, Broadway Play Publishing, 1992.
Attempted Rescue on Avenue B: A Beat Fifties Comic Opera (produced Chicago, 1979). Omaha, Magic Theatre, 1979.
Fireworks, in Holidays (produced Louisville, 1979). Colorado Springs, Meriwether Publishing, 1992.
Running Gag (lyrics only), book by Jo Ann Schmidman (produced Omaha, 1979). Omaha, Magic Theatre, 1981.
Objective Love I (produced Omaha, 1980). Omaha, Magic Theatre, 1985.
Scenes from Maps (produced Omaha, 1980). Omaha, University of Nebraska, 1980.
Advances (produced Omaha, 1980). Omaha, Magic Theatre, 1980.
Flat in Afghanistan (produced Omaha, 1981). Omaha, Magic Theatre, 1981.
Objective Love II (produced Omaha, 1981). Omaha, Magic Theatre, 1985.
The Trees Blew Down (produced Los Angeles, 1981). Omaha, Magic Theatre, 1981.
Winners (produced Santa Barbara, California, 1981).
Kegger (produced Omaha, 1982).
Fifteen Million Fifteen-Year-Olds (produced Omaha, 1983). Omaha, Magic Theatre, 1983.
Mollie Bailey's Traveling Family Circus, Featuring Scenes from the Life of Mother Jones, music by Jo Anne Metcalf. New York, Broadway Play Publishing, 1983.
X-rayed-iate (produced Omaha, 1984).
Katmandu, published in *Open Spaces* (Columbia, Missouri), 1985.
Family Talk (produced Omaha, 1986).
Sea of Forms (collaborative work), text and lyrics with Jo Ann Schmidman (produced Omaha, 1986). Omaha, Magic Theatre, 1987.
Walking Through Walls (collaborative work), text and lyrics with Jo Ann Schmidman (produced Omaha, 1987). Omaha, Magic Theatre, 1987.
Dinner's in the Blender (produced Omaha, 1987). Omaha, Magic Theatre, 1987.
Retro (produced Omaha, 1988).
Amtrak (produced Omaha, 1988). Hattiesburg, University of Southern Mississippi Press, 1990.
Headlights (produced Little Rock, Arkansas, 1988).
The Snow Queen (produced Omaha Theater for Young People, 1990). Omaha, Magic Theater, 1990.
Do You See What I'm Saying? (produced Chicago, 1990). New York, French, 1991.
Body Leaks, with Sora Kimberlain and Jo Ann Schmidman (produced Omaha, 1990). Published in anthology *Theatre Alive*, Meriwether, 1994.
Breakfast Serial (produced Omaha, 1991). Published in *Facing Forward*, B.P.P. Inc, 1995; published in *Take Ten: New Ten Minute Plays*, 1997.
Sound Fields (produced Omaha, 1992). Omaha, Magic Theater, 1993.
Belches on Couches, with Jo Ann Schmidman and Sora Kimberlain (produced Omaha, 1994).
STARPATHMOON STOP, with Jo Ann Schmidman (produced Dallas, 1996).

Radio Plays: *Sanibel and Captiva*, 1968; *American Wedding Ritual Monitored/Transmitted by the Planet Jupiter*, 1972.

Television Plays: *The Dirt Boat*, 1955; *Home; or, Future Soap*, 1968; *One More Little Drinkie*, 1969.

Other

Editor and photographer, *Right Brain Vacation Photos: New Plays and Production Photographs 1972-1992*, Omaha, Magic Theatre, 1992.

*

Manuscript Collections: Kent State University, Kent, Ohio; Hope College, Holland, Michigan; Lincoln Center Library of the Performing Arts, New York; Omaha Public Library; Harvard University (video collection); University of California at Berkley.

Critical Studies: "Who Says Only Words Make Great Drama?" by Megan Terry, in *New York Times*, 10 November 1968; "Megan Terry" in *Dictionary of Literary Biography* by P. J. Rose, 1981; "Megan Terry" in *Women in American Theater*, edited by Chiuoy and Jenkins, New York, Crown, 1981; New York, Theater Communications Group, 1981; "Megan Terry: Mother of American Feminist Theatre," in *Feminist Theatre* by Helene Keyssar, London, Macmillan, 1984, New York, Grove Press, 1985; "Megan Terry" in *Interviews with Contemporary Women Playwrights* by K. Betskot and R. Koenis, New York, William Morrow, 1986; "Megan Terry's Transformational Drama: The Possibilities of Self" by June Schlueten, University of Mississippi Press, 1987; "(Theoretically) Approaching Megan Terry" by Elin Diamond, in *Art and Cinema 3* (New York), 1987; "Megan Terry" in *In Their Own*

Words by David Savran, New York, Theater Communications Group, 1988; "Megan Terry" in *American Playwrights Since 1945,* edited by P. C. Kolin, New York, Greenwood Press, 1989; "Making Magic Public: Megan Terry's Traveling Family Circus" in *Making a Spectacle*, edited by Lynda Hart, Ann Arbor, University of Michigan Press, 1989; "Megan Terry–Speaking on Stage: Interviews with Contemporary Playwrights," Tuscaloosa and London, University of Alabama Press, 1996; "Megan Terry and Asian Women in Theater" by Joan Soon Shim, Seoul, Soungsil University, 1997.

Theatrical Activities:
Director: **Plays**—With the Cornish Players, Seattle: *Beach Grass*, *Seascape*, and *Go Out and Move the Car*, 1955; with the Open Theatre's Playwrights Workshop, New York, 1962-68; *Viet Rock*, New York, 1966; *The Tommy Allen Show*, Los Angeles, 1970; and other plays. **Television**—*The Dirt Book*, 1955.

Actor (as Maggie Duffy): **Plays**—Hermia in *A Midsummer's Night Dream*, title role in *Peter Pan* by J. M. Barrie, Kate in *Taming of the Shrew*, and other roles, Banff School of Fine Arts, Alberta, 1950-53; (as Megan Terry): roles in *Body Leaks*, 1991, *Sound Fields*, 1992, both Omaha; *STARPATH MOONSTOP,* Omaha, 1996.

Megan Terry comments:
I design my plays to provoke laughter—thought may follow.

* * *

"Roughly political, generally unintelligible, devoutly gymnastic." Walter Kerr's assessment seems strikingly at odds with the playwright who later came to be acknowledged as the "Mother of American Feminist Drama." Yet the energy, vitality, and diversity of Megan Terry's work in the 1960s was often mistaken for lack of control or purpose, especially since many of the plays seemed to merge with the cultures of pop, protest, and the hippies. She became best known for *Viet Rock: A Folk War Movie*, a pivotal theatrical rallying point against the Vietnam War. It could too easily be dismissed as politically superficial without acknowledging the dramaturgically innovative features it shared with most of her early work.

Calm Down Mother was Terry's first major contribution to a feminist theater. It is subtitled "A Transformation for Three Women," referring to an improvisatory technique developed by Terry and Joseph Chaikin in the early period of the Open Theatre. To the audience the transformation appeared simply as a dissolving of character, location, or any other apparently concrete reality so that the given circumstances that might be thought to define roles were constantly protean. Many different fragments of identity crystallize briefly in *Calm Down Mother,* and they provide a tapestry of female experience similar to Ntozake Shange's notion of the choreopoem. Although some found the play shocking for its up-front physicality, it was also generally received as celebratory of women reclaiming their bodies in the theater.

The transformation was conceptualized more intellectually within psychoanalysis to reveal fragments of personality or roles that are not easily integrated into one's preferred identity. Thus, the "tapestry" of *Calm Down Mother* is also a condensation. This becomes clearer in two plays dealing with male criminals, *The People vs. Ranchman* and *Keep Tightly Closed in a Cool Dry Place*. The latter has three actors in a prison cell working through a murder and a trial in which they were complicit. The clustering of responses to the event, the exposure of repressed self-images, and the merging of figures from history and the screen constitute the central action, with the notion of transformation being facilitated by the actors occasionally connecting to form a machine.

Other plays of the 1960s experimented with other styles. *Ex-Miss Copper Queen on a Set of Pills* can be read as gothic realism in its picturing of two female scavengers encountering the title character in a New York street at night, but it also has an hallucinatory fabric as the queen "fights through drugs and drink" to make contact with them. *The Magic Realists* is transformational in its whimsical presentation of a businessman paranoically in retreat from his family and other responsibilities, but it also has elements of dream, jazz, male fantasy, and consoling retreat into an ersatz pioneering ethos that is derived from stage and screen more than from history books. *Home; or, Future Soap*, written for television and rescripted for stage, is a science fiction vision of population explosion carried to an extreme in which its nine characters are born and die in the same room. It too, however, has a social concern as it scrutinizes principles such as home, family, and children.

Terry's most lasting play as a reading script has been *Approaching Simone*, ostensibly a stage biography of Simone Weil. The play's seriousness and appeal to authenticity acted as a corrective to those who had found her earlier work trite, and it was widely praised both for its audacity in presenting an affirmative portrait of a genius and for finding theatricality in an apparently untheatrical life. Yet Terry also saw the play as the culmination of 15 years of developing her dramatic technique. In its combination of stark statements to the world, couched in a context of sometimes severe or shocking stylization, there is a boldness of dramatic strategy that matches the choice of subject.

At the height of her New York success, and having won an extensive international reputation, Terry joined the Omaha Magic Theatre in the early 1970s. She has been highly productive with the group, but much of her work there has been local or regional in its application. Her "social action theater" and "community problem plays" are extensively researched and workshopped within the community they document, and on tour their performance is accompanied by a "scholar," such as a psychiatrist or historian, who facilitates discussion afterward with the audience. Subjects like juvenile alcohol abuse (*Kegger*), domestic violence (*Goona Goona*), and incarceration of women (*Babes in the Bighouse*) are of obvious community concern, but her plays also deal with issues such as illiteracy (*Headlights*), how behavior is shaped by imbalance in language (*American King's English for Queens*), and communication within families (*Family Talk* and *Dinner's in the Blender*). Seriousness of social commitment could be found in Terry from the start, however. There is, for example, a case study in *Copper Queen* that might almost offer a gloss to *Kegger*. And nor has sheer playfulness deserted her in the face of earnestness. She can still write plays like *Amtrak*, about a pickup on a train, which combines satire, iconoclasm, and a self-reflexive structure with a hint of the artistic anarchy of the 1960s.

—Howard McNaughton

TERSON, Peter

A pseudonym for Peter Patterson. **Nationality:** British. **Born:** Newcastle upon Tyne, Northumberland, 24 February 1932. **Edu-**

cation: Heaton Grammar School; Newcastle upon Tyne Technical College; Redland Training College, Bristol, 1952-54. **Military Service:** Served in the Royal Air Force, 1950-52. **Family:** Married Sheila Bailey in 1955; two sons and one daughter. **Career:** Draughtsman, 1948-50; games teacher, 1953-65. Resident writer, Victoria Theatre, Stoke-on-Trent, Staffordshire, 1966-67; associated with the National Youth Theatre. **Awards:** Arts Council bursary, 1966; John Whiting award, 1968; Writers Guild award, 1971. **Agent:** Alan Williams Associates, S8 M. House, 1, Shaw Lane, Lichfield, Stafts WS 13 7AN, England.

PUBLICATIONS

Plays

A Night to Make the Angels Weep (produced Stoke-on-Trent, 1964; London, 1971). Published in *New English Dramatists 11*, London, Penguin, 1967.
The Mighty Reservoy (produced Stoke-on-Trent, 1964; London, 1967). Published in *New English Dramatists 14*, London, Penguin, 1970.
The Rat Run (produced Stoke-on-Trent, 1965).
All Honour Mr. Todd (produced Stoke-on-Trent, 1966).
I'm in Charge of These Ruins (produced Stoke-on-Trent, 1966).
Sing an Arful Story, with others (produced Stoke-on-Trent, 1966).
Jock-on-the-Go, adaptation of the story "Jock-at-a-Venture" by Arnold Bennett (produced Stoke-on-Trent, 1966).
Holder Dying (extracts produced Stoke-on-Trent, 1966).
Mooney and His Caravans (televised 1966; produced London, 1968). With *Zigger Zagger*, London, Penguin 1970.
Zigger Zagger (produced London, 1967). With *Mooney and His Caravans*, London, Penguin, 1970.
Clayhanger, with Joyce Cheeseman, adaptation of the novel by Arnold Bennett (produced Stoke-on-Trent, 1967).
The Ballad of the Artificial Mash (produced Stoke-on-Trent, 1967).
The Apprentices (produced London, 1968). London, Penguin, 1970.
The Adventures of Gervase Beckett; or, The Man Who Changed Places (produced Stoke-on-Trent, 1969). Edited by Peter Cheeseman, London, Eyre Methuen, 1973.
Fuzz (produced London, 1969).
Inside-Outside (produced Nottingham, 1970).
The Affair at Bennett's Hill, (Worcs.) (produced Stoke-on-Trent, 1970).
Spring-Heeled Jack (produced London, 1970). Published in *Plays and Players* (London), November 1970.
The 1861 Whitby Lifeboat Disaster (produced Stoke-on-Trent, 1970; London, 1971). Todmorden, Yorkshire, Woodhouse, 1979.
The Samaritan, with Mike Butler (produced Stoke-on-Trent and London, 1971). Published in *Plays and Players* (London), July 1971.
Cadium Firty (produced London, 1971).
Good Lads at Heart (produced London, 1971; New York, 1979).
Slip Road Wedding (produced Newcastle upon Tyne and London, 1971).
Prisoners of the War (produced Newcastle upon Tyne, 1971; London, 1983).
But Fred, Freud Is Dead (produced Stoke-on-Trent, 1972). Published in *Plays and Players* (London), March 1972.
Moby Dick, adaptation of the novel by Melville (produced Stoke-on-Trent, 1972).
The Most Cheerful Man (produced Stoke-on-Trent, 1973).
Geordie's March (produced London, 1973).
The Trip to Florence (produced London, 1974).
Lost Yer Tongue? (produced Newcastle upon Tyne, 1974).
Vince Lays the Carpet, and Fred Erects the Tent (produced Stoke-on-Trent, 1975).
The Ballad of Ben Bagot (televised 1977). Published in *Prompt 2*, edited by Alan Durband, London, Hutchinson, 1976.
Love Us and Leave Us, with Paul Joyce (produced London, 1976).
The Bread and Butter Trade (produced London, 1976; revised version produced London, 1982).
Twilight Joker (produced Brighton, 1977; London, 1978).
Pinvin Careless and His Lines of Force (produced Stoke-on-Trent, 1977).
Family Ties: Wrong First Time; *Never Right, Yet Again* (produced London, 1977). Published in *Act 2*, edited by David Self and Ray Speakman, London, Hutchinson, 1979.
Forest Lodge (produced Salisbury, 1977).
Tolly of the Black Boy (produced Edinburgh, 1977).
Rattling the Railings (produced London, 1978). London, French, 1979.
The Banger (produced Nottingham, 1978).
Cul de Sac (produced Chichester, 1978; London, 1979).
England, My Own (produced London, 1978).
Soldier Boy (produced London, 1978).
VE Night (produced Chichester, 1979).
The Limes, and I Kid You Not (produced London, 1979).
The Pied Piper, adaptation of the poem by Robert Browning, music by Jeff Parton (produced Stoke-on-Trent, 1980). London, French, 1982.
The Ticket (produced London, 1980).
The Night John (produced London, 1980).
We Were All Heroes (produced Andover, Hampshire, 1981).
Aesop's Fables, music by Jeff Parton (produced Stoke-on-Trent, 1983). London, French, 1986.
Strippers (produced Newcastle upon Tyne, 1984; London, 1985). Oxford, Amber Lane Press, 1985.
Hotel Dorado (produced Newcastle upon Tyne, 1985).
The Weeping Madonna. Published in *New Plays 1: Contemporary One-Act Plays*, edited by Terson, Oxford, Oxford University Press, 1988.
Under the Fish 8 Over the Water (produced Bradford on Avon).
Have You Seen This Girl? (produced Kent).
Twin Oaks (produced Lille).
The Sailor's Horse (produced Minehead).

Radio Plays: *The Fishing Party*, 1971; *Play Soft, Then Attack*, 1978; *The First Flame*, 1980; *The Rundle Gibbet*, 1981; *The Overnight Man*, 1982; *The Romany Trip* (documentary), 1983; *The Top Sail at Imberley*, 1983; *Madam Main Course*, 1983; *Poole Harbour*, 1984; *Letters to the Otter*, 1985; *When Youth and Pleasure Meet*, 1986; *The Mumper*, 1988; *Blind Down the Thames*, 1988; *Stones, Tops, and Tarns*, 1989; *Tales My Father Taught Me*, 1990; *Getting to Know Mr. Scmeigelow.*

Television Plays: *Mooney and His Caravans*, 1966; *The Heroism of Thomas Chadwick*, 1967; *The Last Train Through the Harecastle Tunnel*, 1969; *The Gregorian Chant*, 1972; *The Dividing Fence*, 1972; *Shakespeare—or Bust*, 1973; *Three for the Fancy*, 1973; *Dancing in the Dark*, 1974; *The Rough and the

Smooth, 1975; *The Jolly Swagman*, with Paul Joyce (*Crown Court* series), 1976; *The Ballad of Ben Bagot*, 1977; *The Reluctant Chosen*, 1979; *Put Out to Grass*, 1979; *Atlantis*, 1983; *Salvation Army* series.

Other

The Offcuts Voyage. Oxford, Oxford University Press, 1988.

Editor, *New Plays 1: Contemporary One-Act Plays*. Oxford, Oxford University Press, 1988.
Editor, *New Plays 2: Contemporary One-Act Plays*. Oxford, Oxford University Press, 1988.
Editor, *New Plays 3: Contemporary One-Act Plays*. Oxford, Oxford University Press, 1989.

* * *

Peter Terson has been called a "primitive," a term that in its complimentary sense is intended to mean that his technique is artless, his observation fresh and original, and his naturally prolific talent untainted by too much sophistication. This somewhat backhanded tribute, however, belittles his ability. Few dramatists have the sheer skill to write successfully for both the small in-the-round theater company at the Victoria in Stoke-on-Trent and the large casts of the British National Youth Theatre, whose London productions take place in conventional proscenium arch theaters. Nor is Terson unknowledgeable about contemporary trends in the theater. He insisted, for example, that Harry Philton in *Zigger Zagger,* the boy who escapes from the mindless enthusiasm of a football crowd to learn a trade, should not "mature or have a *Roots*-like vision of himself," thus pushing aside one cliché of contemporary naturalistic drama. One underrated aspect of Terson's style is the way in which he either avoids an idea that has become too fashionable or twists it to his own ends. In *The Mighty Reservoy* he plays with the Lawrentian theme of the dark, elemental forces of nature and makes it seem both credible as a psychological obsession and, through this haunting power over the mind, a force indeed to be feared. Terson is, however, ruthless with the pretentiousness of middle-class theater. On receiving a Promising Playwright's Award from Lord Goodman, for example, he inquired whether Green Shield stamps went with it. This latent cheekiness is also part of his plays. Although he rarely ventures into the class polemic of some of Alan Plater's documentaries, he usually caricatures people in authority: magistrates and social workers (in *Zigger Zagger*), scientists and business tycoons (in *The Ballad of the Artificial Mash*) and the paternalistic firm (in *The Apprentices*). He chooses working-class rather than middle-class themes and environments, and he writes with particular passion about his own childhood in Newcastle upon Tyne and the poverty and unemployment of the 1930s. This refusal to accept the normal attitudes of the West End, coupled with his strong regional loyalties, may help to account for his reputation as a primitive, but for this very reason the term is misleading. He does not write popular West End comedies because he does not choose to do so, and he does not write about middle-class families in the grip of emotional dilemmas because the problems he tackles seem to him more important. He is a highly skilled writer with a particular insight into northern working-class societies and whose plays have, at best, a richness of imagination and an infectious humor.

Terson's first plays were produced at the Victoria Theatre in Stoke-on-Trent, a pioneering Midlands company directed by Peter Cheeseman, whose work concentrated on productions in the round and on plays with local associations and on documentary plays. Terson immediately caught the company style and became their resident playwright in 1966. His first plays, *A Night to Make the Angels Weep* and *The Mighty Reservoy,* were naturalistic comedies but with strong underlying themes. *The Mighty Reservoy* is set in the Cotswolds, on a large reservoir built on a hill that is guarded by Dron. The reservoir is presented as a passionate force of water that might at any time swamp the surrounding villages. Dron has an affectionate pride toward it, and he introduces his friend Church to its mysteries, among them that the water demands a human sacrifice before it will be satisfied. Church eventually becomes the sacrifice. But the dialogue between the two men ranges from intimate, slightly drunken chat over their dissatisfactions about life to a passionate yearning for union with nature. *Mooney and His Caravans,* another two-person play written for the Victoria Theatre, represents a different type of "drowning." A couple on a caravan site are gradually driven away from their home by the aggressive commercialism of Mooney, whom they admire and who owns the site. With these small-cast and tightly knit naturalistic plays, Terson also wrote several looser and more flexible and easygoing works. They included *Jock-on-the-Go,* a picaresque tale about a lad on the make in nineteenth-century Yorkshire, and *The Ballad of the Artificial Mash,* a horror story about the effect of hormone poultry foods on a salesman, one of the first and most effective plays about environmental pollution. Both of these plays were in the style of the Stoke documentaries, with short scenes, mainly satirical, brought together by songs and dances written and performed by the company. Although Terson left the Victoria Theatre in 1967, the influence of its informal atmosphere, the economy of means, and the easiness of storytelling—using a narrator and props to indicate change of locale—remained with him as a formative inspiration. He has since written other plays for the company, including *But Fred, Freud Is Dead,* an amusing northern comedy.

In 1966 Michael Croft, the director of the National Youth Theatre, invited Terson to write a play for his largely amateur group of schoolchildren and young adults. Terson's first play for the company, *Zigger Zagger,* was enormously successful, although its story seems flimsy and episodic. Harry Philton, sustained at first by his love of football, leaves school without distinction and drifts from one job to another and from his unhappy home to his well-intentioned brother-in-law. Eventually, however, the craze for football leaves him, and he settles down to a proper trade apprenticeship. Terson sets the story against a background of a prehooligan football terrace, with fans whose songs and attitudes comment on the main events of the story. The exuberance of the production and the nostalgia and fervor of the football crowds provide an unforgettable image of surging humanity charged with a youthful energy that only heightens the sad frustrations of Harry's career. *The Apprentices* tackled a somewhat similar theme but did so more naturalistically. Bagley, a young tearaway, works reluctantly in a local factory and plays football whenever he has the opportunity. He deliberately scorns all opportunities for promotion and is determined to leave the town and his job as soon as he can. But he is trapped in an unwise marriage, and at the end of the play he is resigned to a dull, frustrating future. *Spring-Heeled Jack* and *Good Lads at Heart,* two other plays written for the National Youth Theatre, explore the frustrations of misfits in an impoverished society.

Although Terson's plays have a much greater variety and range than is often supposed, he usually limits himself to social surroundings with which he is familiar. Perhaps the least satisfactory part of this limitation is that he shares some stock reactions, say, about the awfulness of progress and the craftsmanship of the past, that are expressed rather too often in his plays. He also fails to pare down his documentary plays to the dramatic essentials. But his influence on British regional theater has been considerable, and more than any other contemporary dramatist he carries forward the ideas of social drama pioneered by Joan Littlewood.

—John Elsom

THOMPSON, Judith

Nationality: Canadian. **Born:** Montreal, 20 September 1954. **Education:** Queen's University, Kingston, Ontario, 1973-76, B.A. in English drama 1976; National Theatre School, Montreal, 1976-79. **Family:** Married Gregor Campbell in 1983; four children. **Career:** Nurse aide, Ongwanada Hospital, 1974, and social worker, Ministry of Social Services, 1977, both Kingston, Ontario; private tutor, Toronto, 1979; professor of drama, University of Guelph. Lives in Toronto. **Awards:** Governor-General's award, 1984, 1990; Chalmers award, 1988, 1991; Nellie award, for radio, 1989; Toronto Arts award, 1990; B'nai B'rith Media Human Rights award, for *White Sand,* 1991. **Agent:** Great North Artists, 350 Dupont Street, Toronto, Ontario M5R 1V9, Canada.

PUBLICATIONS

Plays

The Crackwalker (produced Toronto, 1980; also director: New York, 1987; London, 1992). Toronto, Playwrights, 1988.
White Biting Dog (produced Toronto, 1984). Toronto, Playwrights, 1984.
Pink (produced Toronto, 1986). Included in *The Other Side of the Dark,* 1989.
Tornado (broadcast 1987). Included in *The Other Side of the Dark,* 1989.
I Am Yours (produced Toronto, 1987). Included in *The Other Side of the Dark,* 1989.
The Other Side of the Dark. Toronto, Coach House, 1989; Toronto, Canada Playwrights Press, 1997.
Lion in the Streets (also director: produced Toronto, 1990). Toronto, Coach House, 1991; Toronto, Playwrights Canada Press, 1997.
White Sand (radio play). In *Airborne,* Blizzard Publishing, 1991.
Hedda Gabler, adaptation of the play by Ibsen (also director: produced Niagara-on-the-Lake, Ontario, 1991).
Sled (produced Toronto, 1997). Toronto, Playwrights Canada Press, 1997.

Radio Plays: *Quickening,* 1984; *A Kissing Way,* 1986; *Tornado,* 1987; *White Sand,* 1991.

Television Plays: *Turning to Stone,* 1986; *Don't Talk,* 1992.

*

Critical Studies: "'Cause You're the Only One I Want: The Anatomy of Love in the Plays of Judith Thompson" by George Totes in *Canadian Literature* (Vancouver), 118, 1988; "Spatial Metaphor in the Plays of Judith Thompson" by Robert Nunn, in *Theatre History in Canada* (Toronto, Ontario), Spring 1989, pp. 3-29; "Women Dramatists: Sharon Pollock and Judy Thompson" by Diane Bessai, in *Post-Colonial English Drama: Commonwealth Drama Since 1960,* edited by Bruce King, London, St. Martin's, 1992.

Theatrical Activities:
Director: **Plays**—*The Crackwalker,* New York, 1987; *The Crucible* by Arthur Miller, Fredericton, New Brunswick, 1989; *Lion in the Streets,* Toronto, 1990; *Hedda Gabler,* Niagara-on-the-Lake, Ontario, 1991.

Judith Thompson comments:

I believe that the voice is the door to not only the soul of an individual, but the soul of a nation, and within that, the soul of a culture, a class, a community, a gender. When I write a play it is as if I am walking into dark woods—do not know what I will find, but the most interesting stories happen when I stumble on raw mythology. I have worked in radio, television, and film, but I believe that the stage has by far the most power. There is a rock, an actor and words—when the technology all collapses—the play will survive.

* * *

Judith Thompson's haunting and challenging plays evaluate love relationships and betrayals, the destructive force of cities and contemporary lifestyles, and physical and spiritual pain. Dreams and the effects of dreams expressionistically shape theplays, which have had a considerable impact in Canada beginning in the 1980s. The evil beast that exists in every subconscious, and that sometimes results in murder, confronts good, though not in a didactic manner. Thompson's plays refer to worms, snakes, and lions, and they are sometimes punctuated by screams of agony that are frequently difficult to decipher. The characters try to deal with their evil, peeling back the layers of the selves they have constructed to hide the nightmares. Because of the self-protection that many characters engage in, they do not listen to the seers and psychics.

Class and generational tensions exist in every play, with birth being a recurrent image of the search for love, acceptance, and belonging in this world. The characters of Thompson's plays are people for whom life means psychic hardship and pain, but they are not extraordinary people. They are merely undisguised versions of everyman and thus deserving of empathy. Reflecting both this tension and the ordinariness of the characters, bodily functions and fluids, epilepsy, and cancer are not modestly overlooked.

The plays are not naturalistic in style. Much of the dialogue, however, is naturalistic, and the accents and pronunciations clearly indicate the ages, education, and frames of mind peculiar to each character. Thompson talks of standing in her characters' blood to really feel who they are.

The Crackwalker centers on two couples who are friends. Sandy and Joe are working-class, while Theresa and Alan are unable to hold jobs and to react independently. They unsuccessfully imitate Joe and Sandy. A desperate Alan helplessly kills his baby in fear and in an ironic gesture of protection. As Alan slips between the cracks to the world "below" the sidewalk, he finds the company of the Crackwalker, a "drunken Indian" who symbolizes, among other things, social and economic failure. Joe and Sandy, sickened by Alan and by the naive Theresa's acceptance of the horrifying world around her, escape to Alberta, but they will never escape from their fear of the Crackwalker.

Pink is a brief monologue about Lucy, a white South African girl whose black nurse, Nellie, is killed in an uprising. It explores the insidiousness of apartheid through Lucy's insistence that the pink color of her favorite cake is real and through her demands that nothing, insidious or not, is her fault. Pink is not real; black is.

The radio drama *Tornado* pursues the struggle of having babies and stealing babies that is developed in *I Am Yours*. Dee in *I Am Yours* must accept her mother's death, represented by the evil blob she paints that lives behind the wall. Encephalitis is the metaphor Dee uses to describe the nightmarish control her subconscious has over her, and Toilane also talks of his head filling with water. Dee's one-night stand with Toilane produces a baby that Toilane abducts, with the help of his mother, because he needs to care for someone. The title, from a locket Dee's father had given to her, refers to all of the characters, each of whom seeks love, understanding, and belonging.

White Biting Dog is also about possession and the fear of losing one's self and others. Pony, a psychic, arrives at the Race household, feeling that she is on a mission. Her dog, recently dead, appeared to Cape Race, who was about to jump to his death. The dog convinced him that if he saved his father from death Cape too would experience a salvation. Dogs reappear throughout the play, and Pony especially misses her white biting dog. Desperately searching for his release, Cape tries to bring his estranged parents back together. The only two surviving characters are Cape and his mother, Lomia, who hope that the deaths—one metaphoric, two literal—will at least provide the hope that they need to keep living. Pony's suicide is the blood sacrifice that will, she hopes, effect the change in Cape. The play uses music, particularly drumbeats and song, to provide a rhythm. Once again the nightmares terrorize many of the characters, who frequently try to create other selves to survive, covering up the "bad" implicit in everyone.

Lion in the Streets presents a devilish creature who is haunting a murdered, intellectually disadvantaged Portuguese girl. She must both warn others of the lion and decipher what happened to her before she can be released from its clutches and the hold that life still has on her. The girl becomes a Cassandra figure to the other characters, who attempt to cope with cancer, poverty, child care, and weight problems. The play ends with the girl's crucifixion-cum-wedding, which expiates her lion only. The other characters must fight their own lions.

Thompson's plays are also visually exciting. Favoring a staging that allows for different levels, the plays graphically demonstrate the evils that everyday life uncovers in the world and in the characters considering ways to exorcise their beasts.

—Joanne Tompkins

THOMSON, Katherine

Nationality: Australian. **Born:** Sydney, New South Wales, 25 July 1955. **Education:** Macquarie University, Sydney, 1973-76, B.A. **Career:** Freelance writer, 1977—. Writer-in-residence, Magpie Theatre, Adelaide, 1988, Deckchair Theatre, Fremantle, 1990-91, and Fringe Theatre, Hong Kong, 1994. **Awards:** Victorian Premier's Literary award, 1992; Australian Writers' guild award, for best community play, 1992; Australian Writers' Guild award, for best script for television, 1993; Australian Council fellowship to Yaddo, 1993; Distinctly Australian fellowship, 1997. **Agent:** James Laurie Management, Suite 4A1, 410 Elizabeth Street, Surry Hills, Sydney 2010, Australia. **Address:** e-mail: kt@triode.net.au.

Publications

Plays

A Change in the Weather (produced Wollongong, 1982).
Tonight We Anchor in Twofold Bay (produced Eden, New South Wales, 1984).
A Sporting Chance (produced State Theatre Company, 1987).
Darlinghurst Nights (produced Sydney, 1988).
Diving for Pearls (produced Melbourne, 1991). Sydney, Currency Press, 1992.
Barmaids (produced Fremantle, 1991). Sydney, Currency Press, 1992.
Navigating (produced Queensland and Melbourne, 1997).

Radio Plays: *Diving for Pearls,* 1997.

Television Plays: *Mirror, Mirror I,* 1995; *Mirror, Mirror II, 1996*; *Halifax f.p. II,* 1995; *Fallen Angels,* 1996; *"G.P.",* 1994-96; *Wildside, 1997*; *Halifax f.p. III,* 1997.

Audio: *Diving for Pearls,* 1997.

*

Manuscript Collection: National Library of Australia.

Theatrical Activities:
Actor: **Play**–In *An Ideal Husband* by Oscar Wilde.

Katherine Thomson comments:

From an early age, even before I went to high school, I became aware that whenever I read reports of industrial action in the newspapers the bias seemed to be on the company's side. My uncle and cousins in Wollongong had all worked down in the mines, and when I visited them, and if there was something "going on," I would be privy to their side of the industrial story, the (usually) Byzantine build-up to a strike or walk-out that, no surprise, one didn't read in the press.

So if the subject area of my plays usually has something to do with contemporary working class issues, I have my relatives to thank. When I began to write for the theater people were telling me I was "giving a voice to people we don't usually hear onstage." Like much feedback one receives, this was somewhat of a surprise. I was just writing about people I knew. Or people who tell me their stories. My plays have always been the product of extensive research not only in my "community plays" (partly verbatim works like *Twofold Bay*, *A Change in the Weather*) but also for my other, so-called mainstage work (*Darlinghurst Nights*, *Barmaids*, *Diving for Pearls*, *Navigating*).

Up until now a common thread in my work has been the characters coping with rapid change, people trying to re-invent themselves, or maintain their moral stand in a shifting landscape. The themes might be serious, but the characters are survivors, and, thankfully they (so far!) have emerged from the page brandishing humor as their weapon.

None of this work has been done in isolation–actors and directors have been great supporters of my work (indeed to date there have been nine wonderful women biting off the role of Barbara in *Diving for Pearls*), and I've also enjoyed rigorous dramaturgical from: Des Davis, Ros Horin, May-Brit Akerholt and, particularly, dramaturg Paul Thompson (now at NYU).

* * *

Having worked for a time as an actor with Theatre South, a regional theater company in New South Wales, Katherine Thomson was commissioned by the company in 1985 to research and write a play based on the community of the south coast fishing town of Eden. *Tonight We Anchor in Twofold Bay,* which premiered in 1986, took the form of a quasi-documentary history of the town, with episodes from the gold rushes and whaling days, a bushfire, and other significant incidents portrayed in brief vignettes punctuated with songs and poetry. The play revealed a lively sense of character, rhythm, and theatricality.

Thomson's next major work was *Darlinghurst Nights,* written for the Sydney Theatre Company in 1988. It was a musical play based on Kenneth Slessor's poems celebrating the seamy heyday of King's Cross in the 1920s and 1930s, with characters like Green Rolls Royce Woman, Gunman, Gunman's Girl, and Girl from the Country. The work was a nostalgic and mellow entertainment well suited to Sydney's bicentennial celebration.

Thomson's two subsequent plays, which first appeared on different sides of Australia in 1991, differed markedly from the historical montage style of the first two. *Diving for Pearls,* which was premiered by the Melbourne Theatre Company, is a largely naturalistic study of contemporary working-class people in a large industrial port city at a time when economic rationalism and industrial reconstruction are having a dire impact on the lives and aspirations of its inhabitants. The local engineering works is preparing for a takeover that will put one of the central characters out of work, while a smart new hotel development promises (falsely) to give work to another. It is a mark of Thomson's skill as a writer and of her respect for her characters that the tragic events that unfold avoid bathos and mawkishness. In fact, *Diving for Pearls* is a very moving play that gets to the heart of the way ordinary people endure intolerable hardship and loss. A number of other productions of the play followed its premiere.

Barmaids, which was first produced by Deck Chair Theatre in Fremantle in Western Australia, is different again. This is a two-handed play faintly reminiscent of the Englishman John Godber's *Shakers.* It is set in a bar in which two live characters (the eponymous barmaids) serve drinks, topical references, and witty repartee to life-sized effigy characters in a largely plotless presentational, rather than naturalistic, style. The audience is also directly implicated in this brash and bawdy, but at the same time deeply poignant, portrayal of five days and nights in the working lives of two middle-aged workers. Their livelihoods are also threatened by the onset of new initiatives, mainly the introduction of topless barmaids to enliven the flagging trade at a time of economic recession. *Barmaids* has come to be one of the most frequently produced plays in Australia, with separate productions in all major cities, and it owes its enduring popularity as much to the truth and actability of its characters as to the relative inexpensiveness of its production.

In her play *Navigating,* written for the Queensland Theatre Company in 1997, Thomson returned some way toward the style of *Diving for Pearls*. This work is a mostly naturalistic narrative, although it has moments of symbolism and historical parable, about past and present events in the once thriving but now moribund fictional seaside town of Dunbar. The central character, a 49-year-old local council employee named Bea Samson, is still mourning the death of most of her school friends in a boating accident 35 years earlier. She then happens to discover evidence of massively corrupt business dealings on the part of the leading councillor, Ian, who is also having an affair with her sister, in his bid to win the town renewed financial viability through a contract to build a private prison for an American company. Bea innocently decides to expose the corrupt practice, whereupon the community turns against her despite the fact that most of them also have grievances against Ian. She is seen as an enemy of progress and thus as an enemy of the people. In scenes of savage and ignorant persecution, Bea is forced to navigate a difficult path to truth and survival, just as the captain of the historical ship *Dunbar* did to avoid being wrecked on the rocks of the treacherous entrance to the town.

Thomson has a deeper understanding of the economic wrongs and social injustices in contemporary Australian society than do most of her peers. Notwithstanding criticism of plotlessness and other structural flaws in some of her plays and overindulgence in symbolism and allegory in others, she also has a powerful capacity to embody these problems in dramatic terms.

—Geoffrey Milne

TOWNSEND, Sue

Nationality: British. **Born:** Leicester, 2 April 1946. **Education:** South Wigston Girls High School, Leicestershire. **Family:** Married 1) in 1964 (divorced 1971), two sons and one daughter; 2) Colin Broadway in 1985, one daughter. **Career:** Member of the Writer's Group, Phoenix Arts Centre, Leicester, 1978. Lives in Leicester. **Awards:** Thames Television bursary, 1979. **Agent:** Sheil Land Associates, 43 Doughty Street, London WC1N 2LF, England; Curtis Brown Literary Agents, 28-29 Haymarket, London, England; Tessa Sayle Agency, 11 Jubilee Place, London, SW3 3TE, England.

Publications

Plays

In the Club and Up the Spout (produced on tour, 1979).

Womberang (produced London, 1980; as *The Waiting Room*, produced Leicester, 1982). Included in *Bazaar and Rummage, Groping for Words, and Womberang*, 1984.

The Ghost of Daniel Lambert, music by Rick Lloyd (produced Leicester, 1981).

Dayroom (produced Croydon, Surrey, 1981).

Bazaar and Rummage (produced London, 1982). Included in *Bazaar and Rummage, Groping for Words, and Womberang*, 1984.
Captain Christmas and the Evil Adults (produced Leicester, 1982).
Groping for Words (produced Croydon, Surrey, 1983; revised version, as *Are You Sitting Comfortably?*, produced Watford, Hertfordshire, 1986; as *Groping for Words*, produced London, 1988). Included in *Bazaar and Rummage, Groping for Words, and Womberang*, 1984.
Clients (produced Croydon, Surrey, 1983).
Bazaar and Rummage, Groping for Words, and Womberang. London, Methuen, 1984.
The Great Celestial Cow (produced Leicester and London, 1984). London, Methuen, 1984.
The Secret Diary of Adrian Mole Aged 13 3/4, songs by Ken Howard and Alan Blaikley (produced Leicester and London, 1984). London, Methuen, 1985.
Ear, Nose and Throat (produced Chichester, West Sussex, 1988). London, Methuen, 1989.
Ten Tiny Fingers, Nine Tiny Toes (produced Manchester, 1989). London, Methuen, 1990.
Disneyland It Ain't (produced London, 1990).

Radio Plays: *The Diary of Nigel Mole Aged 13 3/4*, 1982; *The Growing Pains of Adrian Mole*, 1984; *The Great Celestial Cow*, 1985; *The Ashes*, 1991; *A Ladder in the Stocking*, 1991.

Television Plays: *Revolting Women* series, 1981; *Bazaar and Rummage*, 1984; *The Secret Diary of Adrian Mole* series, 1985; *The Growing Pains of Adrian Mole*, 1987; *The Refuge* series, with Carole Hayman, 1987; *Think of England* series, 1991.

Novels

The Adrian Mole Diaries. London, Methuen, 1985; New York, Grove Press, 1986.
The Secret Diary of Adrian Mole Aged 13 3/4. London, Methuen, 1982; New York, Avon, 1984.
The Growing Pains of Adrian Mole. London, Methuen, 1984.
Rebuilding Coventry: A Tale of Two Cities. London, Methuen, 1988; New York, Grove Weidenfeld, 1990.
Adrian Mole from Minor to Major. London, Methuen, 1991.

Other

The True Confessions of Adrian Albert Mole, Margaret Hilda Roberts, and Susan Lilian Townsend. London, Methuen, 1989.
Mr. Bevan's Dream. London, Chatto and Windus, 1989.
The Queen and I. New York, Soho Press, 1992.
The Wilderness Years. London, Methuen, 1993.
Ghost Children. New York, Soho Press, 1997.

*

Sue Townsend comments:

I suppose I write about people who do not live in the mainstream of society. My characters are not educated; they do not earn high salaries (if they work at all). I look beneath the surface of their lives. My plays are about loneliness, struggle, survival, and the possibility of change.

Strangely, they are also comedies. Comedy is the most tragic form of drama.

* * *

Sue Townsend writes compassionate comedy whose power comes from its intermittently hard edge. A comedy with serious intentions is nothing new, but what is distinctive about the sometimes gentle, sometimes tough comedy Townsend writes is her ability to balance buoyant laughter with biting social commentary. In what she has called "problem plays," Townsend presents groups whose troubles are conventionally ignored: agoraphobics, adult illiterates, Asian women immigrants. In her later work she has written increasingly on politically volatile issues like national health and institutional attitudes toward childbearing and children. She is optimistic that by comically encouraging awareness of such groups and issues in a diverse audience (she hopes to attract working-class people back to the theater) her plays can contribute to social change.

In *Bazaar and Rummage* genial comedy cushions the revealing and disturbing study of three agoraphobics and their two social workers. Here Townsend refines the tendencies already apparent in her early theater script *Womberang*, tendencies that characterize most of her plays: a group and not an individual is at the center of the action, the play refuses conventional descriptions of its plot, and the comedy is generated by community and concern. Townsend describes plays like *Bazaar*, which offers a "group against the world," as "closet plays" or "enclosed plays" so as to emphasize her focus on neglected social problems. In *Bazaar* she engages her predilection for dealing with "the change in [such] a group" by presenting a trio of agoraphobics venturing from home for the first time in years while flanked by the two amateur social workers attempting to aid them. Instead of focusing on one of the characters and her progress toward health, Townsend balances the advances and setbacks in the lives of all five women; progress toward self-understanding is not a function of individual awareness but of group members supporting one another through crises. The plot that such communal character development creates is more circular than linear. There is a passing of awareness from one character to another until the group achieves a collective courage. Townsend's approach to comedy in this play occasioned a notable critical debate. The marriage of very funny lines to a feminist message moved some reviewers to dismiss the effort as "glib," "quirky," or "not too seriously meant" and motivated Michael Billington to warn the playwright that laughter "can't be used simply to decorate." But Townsend herself describes the combination of comedy and women as natural. Laughter, she explains, is "how women cope and have coped for centuries." She sees comedy as the most powerful tool available to her for reaching people, and in *Bazaar*, by allowing her audience to laugh with the agoraphobics, she encourages compassion and enables reflection. While theater critics have found comedy variously revolutionary or reactionary, Townsend uses it to approach tough social issues and sees it—perhaps for that reason—as "a basic need of the human body."

Townsend's concern turns from women's special problems to the class issue of illiteracy in *Are You Sitting Comfortably?* (An earlier version was called *Groping for Words.*) The play shares its class-conscious focus with *The Secret Diary of Adrian Mole Aged 13 3/4*, the stage version of Townsend's successful novel. Both plays portray working-class characters seeking personal and social validation, but to the very light touch of *Adrian Mole* Townsend adds a pointed political message in *Are You Sitting Comfortably?*—a condemnation of a British class structure that seems to require illiterates. The play's class conflict is manifest in the encounter of the well-positioned, middle-class Joyce—the novice literacy instructor—and her three working-class students—George, Thelma, and Kevin. As in *Bazaar*, Townsend again keys the play's action to the symbiotic developments within the group. By the end of the play Joyce must acknowledge that her liberalism effects little social change, but Kevin vocalizes what all the others are afraid to say. In the play's chilling ending he realizes that the world does not "want us to read! There ain't room for all of us is there?" This painful truth gels not just in Kevin, however, but also in the group. The audience, too, must join in this difficult collective realization, for as it laughs, it is being asked, "Are *you* sitting comfortably?" The play may be the clearest example of Townsend's comic gifts, but it is also evidence of her commitment to using comedy to urge rethinking and reconsidering.

In two later works Townsend moved further in her engagement with political issues. *Ten Tiny Fingers, Nine Tiny Toes* is set in a future in which two couples are curiously joined in their attempt to maintain a measure of control over their offspring. In a right-wing society strictly compartmentalized by class, Lucinda and Ralph, the equivalent of an upper-working-class couple, conceive a baby in a government-sanctioned laboratory procedure. In distinct contrast Dot and Pete, unskilled laborers relegated to perish on the fringes of organized society, conceive naturally—and illegally. When the two mothers meet, awaiting childbirth in a shared hospital room, they bond through recognition of how much the institutions around them devalue both women and the life they produce. Their connection empowers them to challenge the government hegemony. When Lucinda's daughter is destroyed by the authorities because of a deformity (a missing toe), the two conspire to share the breast-feeding and rearing of Dot's baby boy. With both husbands rejected for their failure to behave admirably to the stress of births gone wrong, the two women face an uncertain future together; yet, as in previous plays, Townsend provides an upbeat ending in which the women brave the future on their own terms. In the one-act *Disneyland It Ain't* children again provide the focus as Maureen pleads with Mr. Mouse to visit her dying 10-year-old daughter. As the British mother and the American carnival worker puzzle through his reluctance to help, her rage and his fear frame a discussion that ranges from national health insurance to consumerism and religious apostasy. All the while, the grim specter of the dying child shadows the caustic and clever dialogue. In theatrical shorthand Townsend displays her ability to combine the trials of day-to-day survival with a hope that she and her most burdened characters manage to eke out.

In fiction as well as in drama, Townsend has fused comedy and serious matter. In her novel *Rebuilding Coventry* Townsend creates a slightly bizarre, often comic, but deadly serious narrative centered on a woman who discovers that she has options in her life only as a result of unintentionally murdering a man who was strangling his wife. Townsend's feminism and class consciousness—active in both genres—have led her on a constant quest for new forms and formats. But it is in her plays especially that she has used comedy to bring people together both inside and outside of the dramatic frame.

—Susan Carlson

TREVOR, William

A pseudonym for William Trevor Cox. **Nationality:** Irish. **Born:** Mitchelstown, County Cork, 24 May 1928. **Education:** St. Columba's College, Dublin, 1942-46; Trinity College, Dublin, B.A. 1950. **Family:** Married Jane Ryan in 1952; two sons. **Career:** History teacher, Armagh, Northern Ireland, 1951-53; art teacher, Rugby, England, 1953-55; sculptor in Somerset, 1955-60; advertising copywriter, Notley's, London, 1960-64. Lives in Devon, England. **Awards:** *Transatlantic Review* prize, for fiction, 1964; Hawthornden prize, for fiction, 1965; Society of Authors travelling fellowship, 1972; Allied Irish Banks prize, for fiction, 1976; Heinemann award, for fiction, 1976; Whitbread award, 1976, 1983; Irish Community prize, 1979; BAFTA award, for television play, 1983; Hudson Review Bennett prize; The Sunday Express Book of the Year, 1995; The Whitbread Book of the Year, 1995. D. Litt.: University of Exeter, 1984; Trinity College, Dublin, 1986; D. Litt.: University of Exeter, 1984; Trinity College, Dublin, 1986; Queen's University, Belfast, 1989; National University, Cork, 1990. **Member:** Irish Academy of Letters. C.B.E. (Commander, Order of the British Empire), 1977. **Agent:** Peters, Fraser, and Dunlop Group, 503-504 The Chambers, Chelsea Harbour, Lots Road, London SW10 0FX, England; and Sterling Lord Literistic Inc., 1 Madison Avenue, New York, New York 10010, U.S.A.

Publications

Plays

The Elephant's Foot (produced Nottingham, 1965).

The Girl (televised 1967; produced London, 1968). London, French, 1968.

A Night with Mrs. da Tanka (televised 1968; produced London, 1972). London, French, 1972.

Going Home (broadcast 1970; produced London, 1972). London, French, 1972.

The Old Boys, adaptation of his own novel (produced London, 1971). London, Davis Poynter, 1971.

A Perfect Relationship (broadcast 1973; produced London, 1973). London, Burnham House, 1976.

The 57th Saturday (produced London, 1973).

Marriages (produced London, 1973). London, French, 1973.

Scenes from an Album (broadcast 1975; produced Dublin, 1981). Dublin, Co-op, 1981.

Beyond the Pale (broadcast 1980). Published in *Best Radio Plays of 1980*, London, Eyre Methuen, 1981.

Autumn Sunshine, adaptation of his own story (televised 1981; broadcast 1982). Published in *Best Radio Plays of 1982*, London, Methuen, 1983.

Radio Plays: *The Penthouse Apartment*, 1968; *Going Home*, 1970; *The Boarding House*, from his own novel, 1971; *A Perfect Relationship*, 1973; *Scenes from an Album*, 1975; *Attracta*, 1977; *Beyond the Pale*, 1980; *The Blue Dress*, 1981; *Travellers*, 1982; *Autumn Sunshine*, 1982; *The News from Ireland*, from his own story, 1986; *Events at Drimaghleen*, 1988; *Running Away*, 1988; *Mr. McNamara*, 1995; *The Piano Tuner's Wives*, 1997.

Television Plays: *The Baby-Sitter*, 1965; *Walk's End*, 1966; *The Girl*, 1967; *A Night with Mrs. da Tanka*, 1968; *The Mark-2 Wife*,

1969; *The Italian Table*, 1970; *The Grass Widows*, 1971; *O Fat White Woman*, 1972; *The Schoolroom*, 1972; *Access to the Children*, 1973; *The General's Day*, 1973; *Miss Fanshawe's Story*, 1973; *An Imaginative Woman*, from a story by Thomas Hardy, 1973; *Love Affair*, 1974; *Eleanor*, 1974; *Mrs. Acland's Ghosts*, 1975; *The Statue and the Rose*, 1975; *Two Gentle People*, from a story by Graham Greene, 1975; *The Nicest Man in the World*, 1976; *Afternoon Dancing*, 1976; *The Love of a Good woman*, from his own story, 1976; *The Girl Who Saw a Tiger*, 1976; *Last Wishes*, 1978; *Another Weekend*, 1978; *Memories*, 1978; *Matilda's England*, 1979; *The Old Curiosity Shop*, from the novel by Dickens, 1979; *Secret Orchards*, from works by J.R. Ackerley and Diana Petre, 1980; *The Happy Autumn Fields*, from a story by Elizabeth Bowen, 1980; *Elizabeth Alone*, from his own novel, 1981; *Autumn Sunshine*, from his own story, 1981; *The Ballroom of Romance*, from his own story, 1982; *Mrs. Silly (All for Love* series), 1983; *One of Ourselves*, 1983; *Broken Homes*, from his own story, 1985; *The Children of Dynmouth*, from his own novel, 1987; *August Saturday*, from his own novel, 1990; *Events at Drimaghleen,* from his own story, 1991.

Novels

A Standard of Behaviour. London, Hutchinson, 1958.
The Old Boys. London, Bodley Head, and New York, Viking Press, 1964.
The Boarding-House. London, Bodley Head, and New York, Viking Press, 1965.
The Love Department. London, Bodley Head, 1966; New York, Viking Press, 1967.
Mrs. Eckdorf in O'Neill's Hotel. London, Bodley Head, 1969; New York, Viking Press, 1970.
Miss Gomez and the Brethren. London, Bodley Head, 1971.
Elizabeth Alone. London, Bodley Head, 1973; New York, Viking Press, 1974.
The Children of Dynmouth. London, Bodley Head, 1976; New York, Viking Press, 1977.
Other People's Worlds. London, Bodley Head, 1980; New York, Viking Press, 1981.
Fools of Fortune. London, Bodley Head, and New York, Viking Press, 1983.
The Silence in the Garden. London, Bodley Head, and New York, Viking, 1988.
Two Lives (includes *Reading Turgenev* and *My House in Umbria*). London and New York, Viking, 1991.
Felicia's Journey. New York, Penguin, 1994.
Death in Summer. Toronto, Alfred Knopf, 1998.

Short Stories

The Day We Got Drunk on Cake and Other Stories. London, Bodley Head, 1967; New York, Viking Press, 1968.
Penguin Modern Stories 8, with others. London, Penguin, 1971.
The Ballroom of Romance and Other Stories. London, Bodley Head, and New York, Viking Press, 1972.
The Last Lunch of the Season. London, Covent Garden Press, 1973.
Angels at the Ritz and Other Stories. London, Bodley Head, 1975; New York, Viking Press, 1976.
Lovers of Their Time and Other Stories. London, Bodley Head, 1978; New York, Viking Press, 1979.
The Distant Past and Other Stories. Dublin, Poolbeg Press, 1979.
Beyond the Pale and Other Stories. London, Bodley Head, 1981; New York, Viking Press, 1982.
The Stories of William Trevor. London and New York, Penguin, 1983.
The News from Ireland and Other Stories. London, Bodley Head, and New York, Viking, 1986.
Nights at the Alexandra (novella). London, Century Hutchinson, and New York, Harper, 1987.
Family Sins and Other Stories. London, Bodley Head, and New York, Viking, 1990.
The Collected Stories. London, Penguin, 1992.
Outside Ireland: Selected Stories. London, Penguin Books, 1995.
Making Conversation. London, Penguin, 1995.
Matilda's England. London, Penguin, 1995.
Cocktails at Doney's and Other Stories. London, Bloomsbury Classics, 1996.
After Rain. London, Penguin, 1997.

Other

Old School Ties (miscellany). London, Lemon Tree Press, 1976.
A Writer's Ireland: Landscape in Literature. London, Thames and Hudson, and New York, Viking, 1984.
Juliet's Story (for children). Louisville, Kentucky, 1991.
Excursions in the Real World. New York, Penguin, 1993.

Editor, *The Oxford Book of Irish Short Stories*. Oxford and New York, Oxford University Press, 1989.

*

Manuscript Collection: University of Tulsa, Oklahoma.

Critical Studies: "Trevor's System of Correspondences" by Kristin Morrison, in *Massachusetts Review,* Autumn 1987; *Trevor: A Study of His Fiction* by Gregory A. Schirmer, London, Routledge, 1990; *William Trevor, A Study of the Short Fiction* by Suzanne Morron Paulson, New York, Twayne, 1993; *William Trevor* by Kristin Morrison, New York, Twayne, 1993; *William Trevor: The Writer and the Man* by Dolores MacKenna, 1997.

* * *

A successful novelist and prolific television and radio dramatist before turning in any real measure toward the theater, William Trevor has been somewhat unlucky in his career as far as full-length plays are concerned. *The Elephant's Foot* closed during its tour before reaching London. *The Old Boys* had a particularly unfortunate opening in London, with its star's first-night nerves hindering the flow of a play whose full effect depended on the subtleties of its verbal nuances, and although the central performance improved immeasurably during its original limited Mermaid Theatre run and throughout a subsequent provincial tour, the play did not find a West End theater.

The Elephant's Foot, along with his early one-acter *The Girl,* represents something of a false start for Trevor. Both reveal his unusual gift for dialogue, particularly for characters enmeshed in their own sense of failure and for those verging on the sinister or seedy. Both plays, however, remain somewhat inert, heavily relying as they do on a central situation of strange intruders entering domestic scenes, itself something of a cliché in the theater of the early 1960s. *The Girl* is set in suburban London, one of Trevor's favorite locales both in his novels and plays. In the play a mysterious teenage girl descends on the Green household, convincingly claiming to be Mr. Green's daughter, the result of a single drunken escapade with a prostitute. Not unsurprisingly, her arrival divides the family until it is revealed, with the arrival of the girl's violent young friends, that Green is only the latest in a long list of the prostitute's clients to be descended on and terrorized by the loutish teenage gang. It is adroit and suspenseful enough to sustain its length, although the ghost of Pinter looms heavily over the play, even to some extent over the dialogue. This is particularly so in the opening sections between the Green family, which are laden with pauses and the reiteration of the clichés of suburban small talk.

The Elephant's Foot is similarly burdened with a top-heavy plot and reliance on a closing surprise. An elderly couple, Colonel and Mrs. Pocock, live apart except for their Christmas reunion with their twin children. They are in the midst of preparing their Christmas meal when they are invaded by the bizarre stranger Freer (first cousin to the splendid con man Swingler in *The Old Boys*) and his mute associate Tiger. Freer gradually unsettles the Pococks, frightening them by anticipating the nonarrival of their children, but he fails to insinuate Tiger into the household in the twins' place. The play closes with the Pococks alone again, preparing to resume their old domestic battle. After a promising opening, with a very funny verbal tussle between the Pococks over the unfortunate selection of the Christmas brussels sprouts, the play collapses in the second act, and it sustains itself to the final curtain only by resorting to coincidence and unconvincing metaphysical overtones. Nevertheless, *The Elephant's Foot* revealed that Trevor was capable of an individual dramatic verbal style, which his early novels, largely in dialogue, had pointed toward. It is a stylized counterpointing of the colloquial with the rhetorical that owes a little to Ivy Compton-Burnett but essentially remains very much his own.

This was further developed in *The Old Boys*, his own adaptation of his Hawthornden Prize-winning novel of the same name. This work, too, revealed Trevor's special understanding of elderly characters, particularly in the scenes set in a London residential hotel populated entirely by old boys of the same minor public school and tyrannized over by a dragoness of a matron surrogate. In its study of a schoolboy rivalry extending from out of the past to influence a struggle over the presidency of the Old Boys' Association, the play is by turns hilarious and deeply touching, although the first act never satisfactorily solves problems of construction in the adaptation process. But the climatic scene, in which Mr. Jaraby at last realizes the futility of his grudges and ambitions and, now a widower preparing to join the other old men at the Rimini Hotel, launches into a speech of life-affirming anarchy at the expense of the bullying proprietrix, stands as one of Trevor's finest achievements.

After *The Old Boys* Trevor enjoyed considerable success with one-act plays often adapted from previous television and radio plays or from short stories. Most of these are acutely observed and tightly written duologues between different kinds of victims—the lonely, deserted, or repressed characters Trevor reveals so compassionately. Some of these, such as *A Night with Mrs. da Tanka*, an encounter in a hotel between a sad, drunken divorcée and a shy bachelor, suffer in the transition to the stage and seem curiously artificial. But the best of them—especially *Going Home*, in which a precocious schoolboy and a spinster assistant matron, traveling in a train compartment together for the holidays, painfully realize their mutual loneliness—capture moments of crisis in their characters' lives and give them a genuine life on stage beyond the confines of the original medium from which they were adapted. Likewise, some of the best scenes in *The Old Boys* are those not in or most freely adapted from the original novel.

—Alan Strachan

TUBE, Henry. ***See* SPURLING, John.**

U-V

UHRY, Alfred

Nationality: American. **Born:** Atlanta, Georgia, 3 December 1936. **Education:** Brown University, Providence, Rhode Island, 1958. **Family:** Married Joanna Kellogg in 1959; four daughters. **Career:** Instructor in English and drama, Calhoun High School, New York, 1963-1980. Member, 1987, and president, 1990—, Young Playwrights Foundation, New York; council member, Dramatists Guild, New York, 1988—; member of the faculty, New York University School of the Arts, 1991—. Lives in New York. **Awards:** Pulitzer prize, for *Driving Miss Daisy,* 1988; Marton award, 1988; Outer Critics Circle award, 1988; Los Angeles Drama Critics Circle award, 1989; Oscar, for *Driving Miss Daisy,* 1990. **Agent:** Flora Roberts, 157 West 57th Street, New York, New York 10019, U.S.A.

Publications

Plays

Here's Where I Belong, adaptation of *East of Eden* by John Steinbeck, book by Alex Gordon, music by Robert Waldman (produced New York, 1968).

The Robber Bridegroom, adaptation of the novella by Eudora Welty, music by Robert Waldman (produced New York, 1974). New York, Drama Book Specialists, 1978.

Swing, book by Conn Fleming, music by Robert Waldman (produced Washington, D.C., 1980).

Little Johnny Jones, adaptation of a musical by George M. Cohan (produced New York, 1982).

America's Sweetheart, adaptation of a novel by John Kobler, with John Weidman, music by Robert Waldman (produced Hartford, Connecticut, 1985).

Driving Miss Daisy (produced New York, 1987; Ipswich, Suffolk, 1990). New York, Dramatists Play Service, 1987.

The Last Night of Ballyhoo. New York, Dramatists Play Service, 1997.

Screenplays: *Mystic Pizza*, 1988; *Driving Miss Daisy*, 1989; *Rich in Love*, 1992.

*

Critical Studies: "Southern Society in *Driving Miss Daisy*" by Beverly Branch, in *Motion Pictures and Society,* edited by Douglas Umstead Radcliff, Kent, Ohio, Romance Languages Department, Kent State University, 1990; "*Driving Miss Daisy:* A Sociosemiotic Analysis" by Angela J. Mason and Timothy J. Viator, in *The Southern Quarterly: A Journal of the Arts in the South* (Hattiesburg, Missouri), Fall 1994, pp. 55-63; "Alfred Uhry" by Paul Rudd, in *BOMB,* Summer 1997, pp. 36-40; "Ballyhoo and Daisy, Too" by Don Shewey, in *American Theatre,* April 1997, pp. 54-55.

* * *

Alfred Uhry was awarded the Pulitzer Prize in 1988 for his first and only full-length play, *Driving Miss Daisy,* and an Oscar for best screenplay for his adaptation of the play. Uhry's earlier work was primarily as a lyricist and librettist. His longtime collaboration with composer Robert Waldman resulted in Tony and Drama Desk Award nominations in 1976 as lyricist and librettist for *The Robber Bridegroom.* Waldman composed the incidental music for the Playwrights Horizons premiere of *Driving Miss Daisy.* Uhry's work prior to the success of *Driving Miss Daisy* was primarily on lesser-known musicals, including *Here's Where I Belong,* based on Steinbeck's *East of Eden*; *Swing*; *Little Johnny Jones,* which starred Donny Osmond; and *America's Sweetheart,* about Al Capone. None of these musicals received critical acclaim. Even *The Robber Bridegroom,* a musical based on the novella by Eudora Welty, met with mixed reviews, with one reviewer noting that the score was "self-consciously rural" with "few bright moments." Uhry's work on such musicals, however, along with his stint as a teacher of play- and lyric writing, proved to be beneficial once he decided to write about his childhood in Atlanta and of his grandmother, an elderly southern woman with a black chauffeur who drove her for nearly 25 years.

Driving Miss Daisy is actually a long one-act that takes place in various locations in Atlanta from 1948 to 1973. There are 24 shifts in scene, although the play is not formally divided into scenes. The action centers around Daisy Werthan, a widow who progresses in age from 72 to 97 during the course of the play. Her son Boolie Werthan, who ages from 40 to 65, hires a black chauffeur, Hoke Coleburn. Hoke is 60 when the play begins.

The play is deceptively simple in presentation. There is no traditional plot or conflict. The structure is episodic, moving chronologically forward, but the large span of time does not resonate with meaning, nor does it punctuate any vast issues or polemics. The dramatic action is sustained through the growing relationship between Daisy and Hoke. Boolie serves more as a transitional device than as a pivotal character, although the playwright does use Boolie to demonstrate the up-and-coming southern Jewish businessman.

What distinguishes *Driving Miss Daisy* from other plays written during the 1980s is the subtlety with which the playwright empowers his dramaturgy, enabling him to address issues of race and ethnicity and to explore conflicts of old versus young, rich versus poor, and Jew versus gentile while maintaining the emphasis on the human relationship that develops between Daisy and Hoke. Uhry's dramaturgy is economical in every way. Exposition is provided by way of dialogue concerning cars and insurance and the church that people attend, so that necessary information regarding geography, economy, and time is provided by scant verbal signposts.

When the subject of hiring a driver for the aging Miss Daisy is broached by Boolie, Daisy responds innocently with "I still have rights. And one of my rights is the right to invite who I want—not who you want—into my house. . . . What I do not want—and absolutely will not have is some—some chauffeur sitting in my kitchen. . . ." This technique of introducing ideas and issues, in this case, that of human rights, is a technique Urhy employs subtly but also deftly. The notion of prejudice is handled in the same way. Both issues are strong undercurrents in the play, and they are issues that Daisy comes to understand better through her friendship with Hoke, although she never articulates anything beyond saying to him, "You're my best friend."

Uhry is a master of understatement. What is not said in *Driving Miss Daisy* is significant. Equally compelling is Uhry's use of metaphor that serves both to punctuate the humor and to reveal the differences in characters' lifestyles and points of view. Hoke's response to Boolie's inquiry regarding Hoke's ability to handle Miss Daisy is a good example. Hoke replies, "I use to wrastle hogs to the ground at killin' time, and ain' no hog get away from me yet."

Driving Miss Daisy is a play about dignity in which all of the characters strive to hold onto their personal integrity against an environment of prejudice, change, and economic instability. The southern dialect in counterpoint with the colloquial expressions create a lyrical rhythm that greatly contributes to the overall effect of the play. The simple images called for by Uhry throughout the play are meant to capture glimpses of these characters' lives, so that in effect the people become representative of types as well as individuals. The play, then, becomes representative of a time in history and tells about that time by means of this one story.

Perhaps the only drawback of Uhry's play is that with the simplicity of the dramaturgy the play requires a strong cast to sustain its subtextual notions as well as to sustain the constant leaps in time and place. In addition, the juxtaposition of one "scene" to the next has no symbolic meaning, so that the shifts become predictable and the tension difficult to sustain. Still, *Driving Miss Daisy* reflects Uhry's expertise in cinematic dramaturgy, and it is a play that continues to be produced successfully in regional theaters.

—Judy Lee Oliva

USTINOV, Peter (Alexander)

Nationality: British. **Born:** London, 16 April 1921. **Education:** Gibbs Preparatory School, London; Westminster School, London, 1934-37; London Theatre Studio, 1937-39. **Military Service:** Served in the Royal Sussex Regiment, Royal Army Ordnance Corps, 1942-46; with Army Kinetograph Service, 1943, and Directorate of Army Psychiatry. **Family:** Married 1) Isolde Denham in 1940 (divorced 1950), one daughter; 2) Suzanne Cloutier in 1954 (divorced 1971), two daughters and one son; 3) Hélène du Lau d'Allemans in 1972. **Career:** Actor, writer, and director. Codirector, Nottingham Playhouse, 1963. Rector, University of Dundee, 1968-73. Goodwill Ambassador, Unicef, 1969—. **Awards:** Golden Globe award, 1952; New York Drama Critics Circle award, 1953; Donaldson award, 1953; *Evening Standard* award, 1956; Royal Society of Arts, Benjamin Franklin medal, 1957; Emmy award, for acting, 1957, 1966, 1970; Oscar, for acting, 1961, 1965; Peabody award, for acting, 1972; Unicef award, 1978; Jordanian Independence medal, 1978; Prix de la Butte, 1978; Variety Club award, for acting, 1979; City of Athens gold medal, 1990; Greek Red Cross medal, 1990; medal of honour, Charles University, Prague, 1991; Critics' Circle award, 1993; Ordem Nacional do Cruzerio do Sul, Brazil, 1994; German Cultural award, 1994; German Bambi, 1994; International Child Survival award, 1995; German Video prize, 1997. D.M.: Cleveland Institute of Music, 1967. D.L.: University of Dundee, 1969, University of Ottawa, 1991. D.F.A.: La Salle University, Philadelphia, 1971. D. Litt.: University of Lancaster, 1972; University of Toronto, 1984; St. Michael's College, 1995; University of Brussels, 1995. D.H.L.: Georgetown University, Washington, D.C., 1988. Fellow, Royal Society of Arts; fellow, Royal Society of Literature, 1978. C.B.E. (Commander, Order of the British Empire), 1975; Commander, Order of Arts and Letters (France), 1985; Order of Istiglal, Hashemite Kingdom of Jordan; Order of the Yugoslav Flag; elected to the Académie des Beaux-Arts, Paris, 1988; knighted, 1990; chancellor, University of Durham, 1992. **Agent:** William Morris Agency, 31-32 Soho Square, London W1V 5DG, England. **Address:** 11 rue de Silly, 92110 Boulogne, France.

Publications

Plays

The Bishop of Limpopoland (sketch: produced London, 1939).

Sketches in *Swinging the Gate* (produced London, 1940).

Sketches in *Diversion* and *Diversion 2* (produced London, 1940, 1941).

Fishing for Shadows, adaptation of a play by Jean Sarment (also director: produced London, 1940).

House of Regrets (produced London, 1942). London, Cape, 1943.

Beyond (produced London, 1943). London, English Theatre Guild, 1944; in *Five Plays*, 1965.

Blow Your Own Trumpet (produced Liverpool and London, 1943). Included in *Plays about People*, 1950.

The Banbury Nose (produced London, 1944). London, Cape, 1945.

The Tragedy of Good Intentions (produced Liverpool, 1945). Included in *Plays about People*, 1950.

The Indifferent Shepherd (produced London, 1948). Included in *Plays about People*, 1950.

Frenzy, adaptation of a play by Ingmar Bergman (produced London, 1948).

The Man in the Raincoat (also director: produced Edinburgh, 1949).

Plays about People. London, Cape, 1950.

The Love of Four Colonels (also director: produced Birmingham and London, 1951; New York, 1953). London, English Theatre Guild, 1951; New York, Dramatists Play Service, 1953.

The Moment of Truth (produced Nottingham and London, 1951). London, English Theatre Guild, 1953; in *Five Plays*, 1965.

High Balcony (produced London, 1952).

No Sign of the Dove (also director: produced Leeds and London, 1953). Included in *Five Plays*, 1965.

Romanoff and Juliet (produced Manchester and London, 1956; New York, 1957). London, English Theatre Guild, 1957; New York, Random House, 1958; revised version, as *R Loves J*, music by Alexander Faris, lyrics by Julian More (produced Chichester, 1973).

The Empty Chair (produced Bristol, 1956).

Paris Not So Gay (produced Oxford, 1958).

Photo Finish: An Adventure in Biography (also director: produced Dublin and London, 1962; New York. 1963). London, Heinemann, 1962; Boston, Little Brown, 1963.

The Life in My Hands (produced Nottingham, 1964).

Five Plays: Romanoff and Juliet, The Moment of Truth, The Love of Four Colonels, Beyond, No Sign of the Dove. London, Heinemann, and Boston, Little Brown, 1965.
Halfway Up the Tree (produced on tour, Germany, 1967; also director: produced New York and London, 1967). New York, Random House, 1968; London, English Theatre Guild, 1970.
The Unknown Soldier and His Wife: Two Acts of War Separated by a Truce for Refreshment (produced New York, 1967; also director: produced Chichester, 1968; London, 1973). New York, Random House, 1967; London, Heinemann, 1968.
Who's Who in Hell (produced New York, 1974).
Overheard (produced Billingham, County Durham, and London, 1981).
The Marriage, adaptation of an opera libretto by Gogol, music by Mussorgsky (also director: produced Milan, 1981; Edinburgh, 1982).
Beethoven's Tenth (produced Paris, 1982; Birmingham, London, and Los Angeles, 1983; New York, 1984).
An Evening with Peter Ustinov (produced London, 1990).

Screenplays: *The New Lot* (documentary), 1943; *The Way Ahead*, with Eric Ambler, 1944; *The True Glory* (documentary), with others, 1944; *Carnival*, with others, 1946; *School for Secrets* (*The Secret Flight*), 1946; *Vice Versa*, 1948; *Private Angelo*, with Michael Anderson, 1949; *School for Scoundrels*, with others, 1960; *Romanoff and Juliet*, 1961; *Billy Budd*, with Robert Rossen and De Win Bodeen, 1962; *Lady L.*, 1965; *Hot Millions*, with Ira Wallach, 1968; *Memed, My Hawk*, 1984.

Television Plays: *Ustinov ad lib*, 1969; *Imaginary Friends*, 1982; *Inside the Vatican*, 1993.

Novels

The Loser. London, Heinemann, and Boston, Little Brown, 1961.
Krumnagel. London, Heinemann, and Boston, Little Brown, 1971.
The Old Man and Mr. Smith. London, O'Mara, 1990; New York, Arcade, 1991.
Monsieur René. Cologne, Germany, Verlag Kiepenheuer, 1998.

Short Stories

Add a Dash of Pity. London, Heinemann, and Boston, Little Brown, 1959.
The Frontiers of the Sea. London, Heinemann, and Boston, Little Brown, 1966; as *God and the State Railways*, 1993.
The Disinformer. London, O'Mara, and New York, Arcade, 1989.

Other

Ustinov's Diplomats: A Book of Photographs. New York, Geis, 1961.
We Were Only Human (caricatures). London, Heinemann, and Boston, Little Brown, 1961.
The Wit of Peter Ustinov, edited by Dick Richards. London, Frewin, 1969.
Rectorial Address Delivered in the University, 3rd November 1972. Dundee, University of Dundee Press, 1972.
Dear Me (autobiography). London, Heinemann, and Boston, Little Brown, 1977.
Happiness (lecture). Birmingham, University of Birmingham, 1980.
My Russia. London, Macmillan, and Boston, Little Brown, 1983.
Ustinov in Russia. London, O'Mara, 1987; New York, Summit, 1988.
Ustinov at Large (articles). London, O'Mara, 1991.
Still At Large (articles). London, O'Mara, 1993.

Recordings: Writer and performer—*Mock Mozart, and Phoney Folk Lore*, Parlophone; *The Grand Prix of Gibraltar*, Orpheum; narrator—*Peter and the Wolf*; *The Nutcracker Suite The Soldier's Tale*; *Háry János*; *The Little Prince*; *The Old Man of Lochnagar*; *Grandpa*; *Babar and Father Christmas*.

*

Critical Studies (includes filmographies and bibliographies): *Peter Ustinov* by Geoffrey Willans, London, Owen, 1957; *Ustinov in Focus* by Tony Thomas, London, Zwemmer, and Cranbury, New Jersey, A. S. Barnes, 1971; *The Universal Ustinov* by Christopher Warwick, London, Sidgwick & Jackson, 1990.

Theatrical Activities:
Director: **Plays**—*Fishing for Shadows*, London, 1940; *Squaring the Circle* by Valentine Katayev, London, 1941; *The Man in the Raincoat*, Edinburgh, 1949; *Love in Albania* by Eric Linklater, London, 1949; *The Love of Four Colonels*, Birmingham and London, 1951; *A Fiddle at the Wedding*, by Patricia Pakenham-Walsh, Brighton, 1952; *No Sign of the Dove*, Leeds and London, 1953; *Photo Finish*, Dublin and London, 1962; *Halfway up the Tree*, New York, 1967; *The Unkown Soldier and His Wife*, Chichester, 1968, London, 1973; *Jolanthe*, 1993; *Francesca da Rimini*, 1993. **Films**—*School for Secrets* (*The Secret Flight*), 1946; *Vice Versa*, 1948; *Private Angelo*, with Michael Anderson, 1949; *Romanoff and Juliet*, 1961; *Billy Budd*, 1962; *Lady L.*, 1965; *Hammersmith Is Out*, 1972, *Memed, My Hawk*, 1984. **Operas**—*L'Heure Espagnole* by Ravel, *Gianni Schicchi* by Puccini, and *Erwartung* by Schoenberg (triple bill), London, 1962; *The Magic Flute* by Mozart, Hamburg, 1968; *Don Quichotte* by Massenet, Paris, 1973; *Don Giovanni* by Mozart, Edinburgh, 1973; *Les Brigands* by Offenbach, Berlin, 1978; *The Marriage* by Mussorgsky, Milan, 1981, Edinburgh, 1982; *Mavra* and *The Flood* by Stravinsky, Milan, 1982; *Katja Kabanowa* by Janá ek, Hamburg, 1985; *The Marriage of Figaro* by Mozart, Salzburg and Hamburg, 1987; *The Love of the Three Oranges*, Moscow, 1997.

Actor: **Plays**—Waffles in *The Wood Demon* by Chekhov, Shere, Surrey, 1938; in *The Bishop of Limpopoland*, London, 1939; Aylesbury Repertory Company: in *French Without Tears* by Terence Rattigan, *Pygmalion* by G. B. Shaw, *White Cargo* by Leon Gordon, *Rookery Nook* by Ben Travers, and *Laburnum Grove* by J. B. Priestley, 1939; Reverend Alroy Whittingstall in *First Night* by Reginald Denham, Richmond, Surrey, 1940; *Swinging the Gate* (revue), London, 1940; M. Lescure in *Fishing for Shadows*, London, 1940; *Hermione Gingold Revue*, London, 1940; *Diversion and Diversion 2* (revues), London, 1940, 1941; Petrovitch in *Crime and Punishment* by Rodney Ackland, London, 1946; Caligula in *Frenzy*, London, 1948; Sergeant Dohda in *Love in Albania* by Eric Linklater, London, 1949; Carabosse in *The Love of Four Colonels*, London, 1951; The General in *Romanoff and Juliet* London, 1956, New York, 1957; Sam Old in *Photo Finish*, London, 1962, New York, 1963; Archbishop in *The Unknown Soldier and His Wife*, Chichester, 1968, London, 1973; Boris

Vassilevitch Krivelov in *Who's Who in Hell*, New York, 1974; title role in *King Lear*, Stratford, Ontario, 1979, 1980; Stage Manager in *The Marriage*, Milan, 1981, Edinburgh, 1982; Ludwig in *Beethoven's Tenth*, Paris, 1982, Birmingham, London, and Los Angeles, 1983, New York, 1984; *An Evening with Peter Ustinov*, London, 1990, San Francisco, 1991; *Beethoven's Tenth*, 1995. **Films**—*Hullo Fame!*, 1941; *Mein Kampf, My Crimes*, 1941; *One of Our Aircraft Is Missing*, 1941; *The Goose Steps Out*, 1942; *Let the People Sing*, 1942; *The New Lot*, 1943; *The Way Ahead*, 1944; *The True Glory* 1945; *School for Secrets* (*The Secret Flight*), 1946; *Vice Versa*, 1947; *Private Angelo*, 1949; *Odette*, 1950; *Quo Vadis*, 1951; *Hotel Sahara*, 1951; *The Magic Box*, 1951; *Beau Brummell*, 1954; *The Egyptian*, 1954; *Le Plaisir* (*House of Pleasure*) (narrator), 1954; *We're No Angels*, 1955; *Lola Montès* (*Lola Montez, The Sins of Lola Montes*), 1955; *I girovaghi* (*The Wanderers*), 1956; *Un angel paso sobre Brooklyn* (*An Angel over Brooklyn, The Man Who Wagged His Tail*), 1957; *Les Espions* (*The Spies*), 1957; *The Adventures of Mr. Wonderful*, 1959; *Spartacus*, 1960; *The Sundowners*, 1960; *Romanoff and Juliet*, 1961; *Billy Budd*, 1962; *La donna del mondo* (*Women of the World*) (narrator), 1963; *The Peaches* (narrator), 1964; *Topkapi*, 1964; *John Goldfarb, Please Come Home*, 1964; *Lady L.*, 1965; *The Comedians*, 1967; *Blackbeard's Ghost*, 1967; *Hot Millions*, 1968; *Viva Max!*, 1969; *Hammersmith Is Out*, 1972; *Big Truck and Sister Clare*, 1973; *Treasure of Matecumbe*, 1976; *One of Our Dinosaurs Is Missing*, 1976; *Logan's Run*, 1976; *Robin Hood* (voice in animated film), 1976; *Un Taxi mauve* (*The Purple Taxi*), 1977; *The Last Remake of Beau Geste*, 1978; *The Mouse and His Child* (narrator), 1978; *Doppio delitto* (*Double Murders*), 1978; *Death on the Nile*, 1978; *Tarka the Otter* (narrator), 1978; *Winds of Change* (narrator), 1978; *Ashanti*, 1979; *Charlie Chan and the Curse of the Dragon Queen*, 1981; *The Great Muppet Caper*, 1981; *Grendel, Grendel, Grendel* (voice in animated film), 1981; *Evil under the Sun*, 1982; *Memed, My Hawk*, 1984; *Appointment with Death*, 1988; *The French Revolution*, 1989; *Lorenzo's Oil*, 1991; *The Phoenix and the Magic Carpet*, 1995; *Stiff Upper Lips*, 1996. **Television**—*The Life of Dr. Johnson*, 1957; *Barefoot in Athens*, 1966; *In All Directions* series; *A Storm in Summer*, 1970 (USA); *Lord North*, 1972; *The Mighty Continent* (narrator), 1974; *A Quiet War*, 1976 (USA); *The Thief of Bagdad*, 1978; *Jesus of Nazareth*, 1979; *Einstein's Universe* (narrator), 1979; *Imaginary Friends* (5 roles), 1982; *The Well-Tempered Bach*, 1984; *13 at Dinner*, 1985; *Dead Man's Folly*, 1986; *Peter Ustinov's Russia*, 1986 (Canada); *World Challenge*, 1986 (Canada); *Murder in Three Acts*, 1986; narrator for *History of Europe*, *The Hermitage* and *The Ballerinas*; *Peter Ustinov in China*, 1987; *Around the World in Eighty Days*, 1988-89; *The Secret Identity of Jack the Ripper*, 1989-90; *The Mozart Mystique*, 1990; *Ustinov on the Orient Express*, 1991-92; *Old Curiosity Shop*, from the novel by Dickens, 1995; *Haydn Gala*, 1995; documentaries of Thailand and Hong Kong, 1995; *Peter Ustinov's Mendelssohn*, 1997; *Following the Equator*, 1998.

Peter Ustinov comments:

I believe that theories should emerge as a logical consequence of practice, and not be formulated in a coldly intellectual climate for eventual use. I therefore regard myself as a practical writer who began to write in the period of the proscenium arch, but who survived into the epoch of the arena and platform stages. The theatre, to survive, must do what film and television cannot do, and that is to exploit the physical presence of the audience. Naturalism was the logical reaction against romanticism, but the poetry inherent in all valid works of any school emerges more easily on film and even more easily on television than on the stage, and the time of the "fourth wall" has passed. Also, with the extraordinarily graphic quality of current events diffused by the news media, and the growing public sense of irony and scepticism about the nature and possibilities of government, tragedy and comedy have been chased forever from their ivory towers. This is the time of the tragic farce, of the comic drama, of the paradox, of the dramatized doubt. In my plays as in my non-dramatic works I have always been interested in the comic side of things tragic and in the melancholy side of things ribald. Life could not exist without its imperfections, just as the human body could not survive without germs. And to the writer, the imperfections of existence are life-blood.

* * *

Like Noël Coward, with whose versatility his own was often compared when he was establishing himself, Peter Ustinov had a dazzling early break in his career. While he was appearing in a Herbert Farjeon revue, Farjeon gave one of Ustinov's manuscripts to James Agate, then at the height of his influence on the *Sunday Times*. Following Agate's lavish praise of *House of Regrets*, it was produced in 1942. It is very much a young man's play. Its story of Russian émigrés living in genteel poverty in wartime London is an often self-consciously atmospheric piece, but it shows Ustinov's sympathetic identification with eccentrics and the aged in his picture of the old admiral and general plotting their coup to reenter Russia. In the immediately following period Ustinov's plays appeared with impressive frequency, perhaps too frequently for their own good. Too many could be described in the terms he uses to label *Blow Your Own Trumpet*, a fantasy set in an Italian restaurant—"An idea rather than a play in the ordinary sense of the word." *The Tragedy of Good Intentions*, a chronicle play about the Crusades, is unfocused and verbose. *The Indifferent Shepherd*, centered around a clergyman's crisis of conscience and his closest approach to a conventional well-made West End play, is lackluster despite its sincerity. *No Sign of the Dove*, a resounding critical failure, is a reworking of the Noah legend, but, despite a fine neo-Firbankian opening of high style, it dwindles into a tepid mixture of late Shaw and bedroom door farce. The initial impetus in these earlier plays is rarely sustained consistently.

At the same time Ustinov's unique gift for the fantastic was developing more surely. *The Banbury Nose*, tracing a great military family through three generations in reverse order (a kind of *Milestones* backwards), is a technical tour de force, but in the scenes between the wife and the men who have loved her Ustinov also reveals a sure understanding of the threads of response between people. Although his 1950s work produced some oddly muffled efforts—such as *The Moment of Truth*, an overinflated political drama—he also produced *The Love of Four Colonels* and *Romanoff and Juliet*, and he was at his inventive best in both. *The Love of Four Colonels*, set in a European state disputed by the Allies, enjoys satirizing national characteristics as the four colonels try to awaken the Sleeping Beauty's love in pastiche scenes in which they play out their own hopes and ideals. *Romanoff and Juliet* adapts the Romeo and Juliet story to the Cold War context of rival Russian and American embassies in "the smallest country in Europe." Underneath the fairy tales and Ruritanian trappings there is a shrewd core of humanist understanding of contemporary problems, although with Ustinov's polyglot ancestry this inevitably emerges in an international rather than a local context.

His later output continued to develop earlier themes. *Photo Finish* recalls *The Banbury Nose* in its flashback time sequence, presenting a famous writer in confrontation with his younger selves as he contemplates the mirror of the past. *The Unknown Soldier and His Wife* is a further exploration of material in *The Tragedy of Good Intentions,* but it is a much surer play. It sweeps from ancient Rome to medieval England to modern times, with links provided by recurring characters who emerge whenever war comes and who control its course. The play occasionally threatens to become a series of admittedly amusing antiwar sketches, but it contains some of Ustinov's most pungent writing.

Few of Ustinov's plays have a tight plot progression; as in his novels, he is happier in a more picaresque style. His ancestry perhaps partly explains his drawing on the Russian literary tradition that blends tragedy and comedy, and his best plays have a strong tension between the two. He once stressed the influence of music on his work, and there is indeed a Mozartian strain that informs the best plays. Despite an apparent surface plotlessness, they have an internal rhythm that gives them strong theatrical movement. This could hardly be said of a string of disappointing later work, however. *Halfway up the Tree*, a tired comedy of the dropout generation, was sadly jaded, but it was still not so distressingly feeble as *Who's Who in Hell.* This latter play has a splendid initial idea; it is set in an anteroom of hell where the ultimate destination of new arrivals, including the U.S. president and the Russian premier, is decided. But the promise of a sharp political comedy is torpedoed by stale jokes and a woefully jejune level of intellectual argument. *Overheard*, a lachrymose comedy of diplomatic life, was similarly thin, while *Beethoven's Tenth* was not entirely a return to form. Again, there is a hugely promising initial premise; Beethoven, speaking perfect English, materializes as the result of a trance by a psychic au pair in the house of a London music critic and is shortly cured of his deafness. The play seems poised to take off into an exhilarating comedy of ideas, but, apart from a closing scene to the first act in which the critic's wife, an ex-singer, performs "An die ferne Geliebte" to the composer's accompaniment—as good a scene as anything Ustinov has written—the work never recovers the buoyancy of the opening. Ustinov had the chance to revise *Beethoven's Tenth* for a Chichester Festival revival, when he again played the title role. But he did not take it, and in a lackluster production the play seemed even more of a missed opportunity. Ustinov's theatrical excursions have come to consist of lucrative but somewhat automatic-pilot runs of his solo anecdotal show.

—Alan Strachan

VALDEZ, Luis (Miguel)

Nationality: American. **Born:** 26 June 1940. **Education:** San Jose State University, California. **Family:** Married Guadalupe Valdez in 1969; three children. **Career:** Union organizer, United Farmworkers, Delano, California, to 1967. Founding director, El Teatro Campesino, Delano, 1965-69, Fresno, 1969-71, and since 1971 San Juan Bautista, California. **Awards:** Obie award, 1968; Emmy award, for directing, 1973; Rockefeller grant, 1978. **Address:** Teatro Campesino, P.O. Box 1240, San Juan Bautista, California 95045, U.S.A.

Publications

Plays

Las dos caras del patroncito (produced Delano, 1965). Included in *Actos*, 1971.
La quinta temporada (produced Delano, 1966). Included in *Actos*, 1971.
Los vendidos (produced Delano, 1967). Included in *Actos*, 1971.
The Shrunken Head of Pancho Villa (produced Delano, 1968). In *Necessary Theater,* Houston, Arte Publico Press, 1989.
La conquista de Mexico (puppet play; produced Delano, 1968). Included in *Actos*, 1971.
No saco nada de la escuela (produced Fresno, 1969). Included in *Actos*, 1971.
The Militants (produced Fresno, 1969). Included in *Actos*, 1971.
Vietnam campesino (produced Fresno, 1970). Included in *Actos*, 1971.
Soldado razo (produced Fresno, 1970; New York, 1985). Included in *Actos*, 1971.
Huelguistas (produced Fresno, 1970). Included in *Actos*, 1971.
Bernabé (produced Fresno, 1970). Published in *Contemporary Chicano Theatre*, edited by Roberto Garza, Notre Dame, Indiana, University of Notre Dame Press, 1976.
Actos. San Juan Bautista, Cucaracha, 1971.
El Virgen del Tepeyac (produced San Juan Bautista, 1971).
Dark Root of a Scream (produced Los Angeles, 1971; New York, 1985). Published in *From the Barrio: A Chicano Anthology*, edited by Lillian Faderman and Luis Omar Salinas, San Francisco, Canfield Press, 1973.
Los olivos pits (produced San Juan Bautista, 1972).
Mundo (produced San Juan Bautista, 1973).
La gran carpa de los rasquachis (produced San Juan Bautista, 1973).
El baille de los gigantes (produced San Juan Bautista, 1973).
El fin del mundo (produced San Juan Bautista, 1975).
Zoot Suit (produced Los Angeles, 1978; New York, 1979).
I Don't Have to Show You No Stinking Badgers (produced Los Angeles, 1986).
Zoot Suit and Other Plays. Houston, Texas, Arte Publico Press, 1992.
Frida: A Screenplay. Los Angeles, California, Writers and Artists Agency, 1993.
Bandido! (produced 1994).

Screenplays: *Zoot Suit*, 1982; *La Bamba*, 1987; *Frida Kahlo,* 1992; *The Crisco Kid,* 1993.

Other

Pensamiento Serpentino: A Chicano Approach to the Theatre of Reality. San Juan Bautista, California, Cucaracha, 1973.
Luis Valdez–Early Works. Houston, Arte Publico Press, 1990.

Editor, with Stan Steiner, *Aztlan: An Anthology of Mexican American Literature*. New York, Knopf, 1972.

*

Critical Studies: "Chicano Cinema: A Dialectic between Voices and Images of the Autonomous Discourse Versus Those of the

Dominant" by Victor Fuentes, in *Chicanos and Film: Representation and Resistence,* edited by Chon A. Noriega, Minneapolis, University of Minnesota Press, 1992; "Zoot Suit: The Return to the Beginning" by Rose Linda Fregoso, in *Mediating Two Worlds: Cinematic Encounters in the Americas,* edited by John King and Ana M. Lopez, London, British Film Institute, 1993; *Man's Inhumanity to Man: Justice and Injustice in Three Mexican-American Playwrights* (dissertation) by Joshua Al Mora, Texas Tech University, 1994; *Taking It to the Street: The Social Protest Theater of Luis Valdez and Amiri Baraka* by Harry Justin Elam, Ann Arbor, University of Michigan Press, 1997; "Luis Miguel Valdez" by Jaime Herrera, in *Updating the Literary West,* edited by Max Westbrook and Dan Flores, Fort Worth, Texas, Texas Christian University Press, 1997.

Theatrical Activities:
Director: **Plays**—Most of his own plays. **Films**—*Zoot Suit,* 1982; *La Bamba,* 1987.

Actor: **Film**—*Which Way Is Up*?, 1977. **Television**—*Visions* series, 1976.

* * *

Best known as the founder of the Teatro Campesino (Farmworkers Theatre) in 1965, Luis Valdez is a man of many talents: actor, playwright, screenwriter, essayist, stage and film director, and the leading practitioner of Chicano theater in the United States. From the earliest agitprop pieces (*actos*) he directed and wrote to his professionally produced *Zoot Suit,* first a play and then a film, Valdez has attempted to portray the Chicano's reality.

The very term "Chicano" connotes a political attitude that is cognizant of a distinctive place in the so-called American melting-pot, and Valdez became a major proponent of this self-imposed designation when his theater toured the country asserting a cultural and political distinction. Valdez has termed *Zoot Suit* an "American play," this in deference to his belief that Chicanos are a part of American society and should not be excluded from what the society has to offer its citizens. Valdez's dramatic themes always reflect Chicanos in crisis, never pretending that they have been fully accepted into the American mainstream. His characters are always in conflict with some aspect of the system, and more often than not the manifestation of the power structure is presented by non-Chicanos, or Anglos. Although the characters in power find it easy to manipulate the subordinate Chicanos, Valdez's audiences discover that, whether the heroes win or lose, it is they who can win through collective action.

Las dos caras del patroncito ("The Two Faces of the Boss") and *La quinta temporada* ("The Fifth Season") are *actos* that reveal the problems of striking farmworkers solved through unionization. When Valdez decided to leave the union in 1967, he sought an independent theater company not focused solely on labor movement and farmworker themes. The next *acto, Los vendidos* ("The Sellouts"), explored various stereotypes of Chicanos and satirized the person who attempted to assimilate into a white racist society. *No saco nada de la escuela* ("I Don't Get Anything Out of School") exposed inequities in the educational process, and *La conquista de Mexico* ("The Conquest of Mexico") drew a parallel between the fall of the Aztecs and the disunity of Chicano activists. The use of masks, farcical exaggeration, stereotyped characters, improvisation, and social commentary in the *actos* reflects Valdez's work with the San Francisco Mime Troupe prior to the founding of his own theater. While the *actos* are brief agitprop statements, Valdez's plays explore other theatrical forms.

Beginning with his first play, *The Shrunken Head of Pancho Villa,* originally written and produced while he was a student, Valdez has written nonrealistic statements that mingle fantasy and farce, comedy and pathos. All of Valdez's plays issue forth from a family structure. *The Shrunken Head of Pancho Villa* pits the assimilationist against the *pachuco* social bandit, two brothers whose lifestyles reflect the extremes within the barrio. *Bernabé* revolves around a village idiot who gains a spiritual release when he symbolically marries *La Tierra* (Earth), which appears to him as a symbol of the Mexican Revolution of 1910.

There is much of the Spanish religious folk theater in Valdez's plays, which are combined with a new message of social justice. The playwright uses allegorical and mythological figures to present his messages, for example, to combat the evils of the war in Vietnam in the *actos Vietnam campesino* and *Soldado razo* ("Private Soldier") or in the expressionist play *Dark Root of a Scream.* He exposes the need for a balance with nature in the ritualistic *El fin del mundo* ("The End of the World"), in *La gran carpa de los rasquachis* ("The Great Tent of the Underdogs"), and in *Mundo,* a title based on the name of the protagonist, Reimundo, or "king of the world." Beginning with *Bernabé,* each of the plays combines indigenous mythology with contemporary problems. *La gran carpa de los rasquachis* unites the Virgin of Guadalupe with Quetzalcóatl, the Mesoamerican Christ figure, calling for unity among all people.

In *Zoot Suit* Valdez unites all of the elements of his theater to create a statement that cannot be classified without listing its parts: the *acto,* living newspaper, *corrido* (dramatized Mexican ballad), selective realism, and fantasy. The play is narrated by an archetypal *pachuco,* a barrio character type that has always fascinated the playwright. This enigmatic figure glides in and out of the action, a fantastical symbol of the Chicano's defiance and ability to survive between the Mexican and the Anglo cultures. *Zoot Suit* was the first Chicano play to reach Broadway, and though the New York critics generally disliked it, the play broke box office records in Los Angeles. The play reminded its audiences that modern Chicano struggles have their precedents in such events as the Sleepy Lagoon murder trial, which exposed a biased system of justice in the 1940s. Valdez's hit film *La Bamba,* the story of Chicano pop singer Ritchie Valens, was a big hit with the Anglo audience in 1987.

From *actos* to *Zoot Suit* Valdez remains a singular example of a playwright who has consistently re-created the struggles and successes of Chicanos. His clarity of vision and style, however controversial the themes, makes him a true man of the theater.

—Jorge A. Huerta

van ITALLIE, Jean-Claude

Nationality: American. **Born:** Brussels, Belgium, 25 May 1936; moved to the United States, 1940; became citizen, 1952. **Education:** Great Neck High School, New York; Deerfield Academy, Massachusetts; Harvard University, Cambridge, Massachusetts,

A.B. 1958; New York University, 1959; studied acting at the Neighborhood Playhouse, New York. **Career:** Editor, *Transatlantic Review*, New York, 1960-63; playwright-in-residence, Open Theatre, New York, 1963-68; freelance writer on public affairs for NBC and CBS television, New York, 1963-67; taught playwriting at the New School for Social Research, New York, 1967-68, 1972, Yale University School of Drama, New Haven, Connecticut, 1969, 1978, 1984-85, and Naropa Institute, Boulder, Colorado, 1976-83; lecturer, Princeton University, New Jersey, 1973-86, New York University, 1982-86, 1992, University of Colorado, Boulder, Fall 1985, 1987-91, and Columbia University, New York, Spring 1986; visiting Mellon professor, Amherst College, Massachusetts, Fall 1976, and Middlebury College, Vermont, 1990. Teacher of Healing Power of Theater Workshops, Rowe Conference Center, Rowe, Massachusetts, Omega Institute, New York, and at other institutes, 1991-98. **Awards:** Rockefeller grant, 1962; Vernon Rice award, 1967; Outer Circle award, 1967; Obie award, 1968; Guggenheim fellowship, 1973, 1980; Creative Artists Public Service grant, 1973; National Endowment for the Arts fellowship, 1986; Achievement award from the Strobe Foundation, 1987. Ph.D.: Kent State University, Kent, Ohio, 1977. **Address:** 63 Davenport Road, Rowe, Massachusetts 01367, U.S.A.

Publications

Plays

War (produced New York, 1963; Edinburgh, 1968; London, 1969). Included in *War and Four Other Plays*, 1967; in *America Hurrah: Five Short Plays*, 1967.

Almost Like Being (produced New York, 1964). Included in *War and Four Other Plays*, 1967; in *America Hurrah: Five Short Plays*, 1967.

I'm Really Here (produced New York, 1964; London, 1979). Included in *War and Four Other Plays*, 1967.

The Hunter and the Bird (produced New York, 1964). Included in *War and Four Other Plays*, 1967.

Interview (as *Pavane*, produced Atlanta, 1965; revised version, as *Interview*, produced New York, 1966; London, 1967). Included in *America Hurrah: Five Short Plays*, 1967.

Where Is de Queen? (as *Dream*, produced New York, 1965; revised version, as *Where Is de Queen?*, produced Minneapolis, 1965). Included in *War and Four Other Plays*, 1967.

Motel (as *America Hurrah*, produced New York, 1965; revised version, as *Motel*, produced New York, 1966; London, 1967). Included in *America Hurrah: Five Short Plays*, 1967.

America Hurrah (includes *Interview*, *TV*, *Motel*) (produced New York, 1966; London, 1967). New York, Coward McCann, 1967; with *War* and *Almost Like Being*, as *America Hurrah: Five Short Plays*, London, Penguin, 1967.

The Girl and the Soldier (produced Los Angeles, 1967). Included in *Seven Short and Very Short Plays*, 1975.

War and Four Other Plays. New York, Dramatists Play Service, 1967.

Thoughts on the Instant of Greeting a Friend on the Street, with Sharon Thie (produced Los Angeles, 1967; in *Collision Course*, produced New York, 1968). Included in *Seven Short and Very Short Plays*, 1975.

The Serpent: A Ceremony, with the Open Theatre (produced Rome, 1968; New York, 1970). New York, Atheneum, 1969.

Take a Deep Breath (televised 1969). Included in *Seven Short and Very Short Plays*, 1975.

Photographs: Mary and Howard (produced Los Angeles, 1969). Included in *Seven Short and Very Short Plays*, 1975.

Eat Cake (produced Denver, 1971). Included in *Seven Short and Very Short Plays*, 1975.

Mystery Play (produced New York, 1973). New York, Dramatists Play Service, 1973; revised version, as *The King of the United States*, music by Richard Peaslee (also director: produced New York, 1973), New York, 1975.

Nightwalk, with Megan Terry and Sam Shepard (produced New York and London, 1973). Published in *Open Theater*, New York, Drama Book Specialists, 1975.

The Sea Gull, adaptation of a play by Chekhov (produced Princeton, New Jersey, 1973; New York, 1975). New York, Harper, 1977.

A Fable, music by Richard Peaslee (produced New York, 1975). New York, Dramatists Play Service, 1976.

Seven Short and Very Short Plays (includes *Photographs*, *Eat Cake*, *The Girl and the Soldier*, *Take a Deep Breath*, *Rosary*, *Harold*, *Thoughts on the Instant of Greeting a Friend on the Street*). New York, Dramatists Play Service, 1975.

The Cherry Orchard, adaptation of a play by Chekhov (produced New York, 1977). New York, Grove Press, 1977.

America Hurrah and Other Plays (includes *The Serpent*, *A Fable*, *The Hunter and the Bird*, *Almost Like Being*). New York, Grove Press, 1978.

Medea, adaptation of the play by Euripides (produced Kent, Ohio, 1979).

Three Sisters (produced New York, 1979). New York, Dramatists Play Service, 1979.

Bag Lady (produced New York, 1979). New York, Dramatists Play Service, 1980.

Uncle Vanya, adaptation of a play by Chekhov (produced New York, 1983). New York, Dramatists Play Service, 1980.

Naropa, music by Steve Gorn (produced New York, 1982). Published in *Wordplays 1*, New York, Performing Arts Journal Publications, 1980.

Early Warnings (includes *Bag Lady*, *Sunset Freeway*, *Final Orders*) (produced New York, 1983). New York, Dramatists Play Service, 1983.

The Tibetan Book of the Dead; or, How Not to Do It Again, music by Steve Gorn (produced New York, 1983). New York, Dramatists Play Service, 1983.

Pride, in *Faustus in Hell* (produced Princeton, New Jersey, 1985).

The Balcony, adaptation of a play by Jean Genet (produced Cambridge, Massachusetts, 1986).

The Traveler (produced Los Angeles, Leicester, and London, 1987).

Struck Dumb (produced Los Angeles, 1989; New York, 1991). Published in *Best One-Act Plays: 1990-1991*, New York, Applause, 1991.

Ancient Boys (produced Boulder, Colorado, 1990; New York, 1991).

Chekhov, The Major Plays. New York, Applause, 1995.

The Tibetan Book of the Dead for Reading Aloud. Berkeley, North Atlantic, 1998.

Guys Dreamin' (produced Shelburne Falls, Massachusetts and New York, 1997).

War, Sex, Singing, and Dancing (produced Shelburne Falls, Massachusetts 1998).

Screenplays: *The Box Is Empty*, 1965; *Three Lives for Mississippi*, 1971.

Television Writing: *Look Up and Live* series, 1963-65; *Hobbies; or, Things Are All Right with the Forbushers*, 1967; *Take a Deep Breath*, 1969; *Picasso: A Painter's Diary*, 1980.

Other

Calcutta (journal). Kent, Ohio, Kent State University Libraries, 1987.
The Playwright's Workbook. New York, Applause, 1997.

*

Manuscript Collections: Kent State University, Ohio; Harvard University Library, Cambridge, Massachusetts.

Critical Studies: By Walter Kerr, in *New York Times*, 11 December 1966; "Three Views of America," in *The Third Theatre* by Robert Brustein, New York, Knopf, 1969, London, Cape, 1970; *Up Against the Fourth Wall* by John Lahr, New York, Grove Press, 1970; "Jean-Claude van Itallie Issue" of *Serif* (Kent, Ohio), Winter 1972; "Jean-Claude van Itallie" by Gene A. Plunka in *The Playwright's Art: Conversations with Contemporary American Dramatists,* edited by Jackson R. Bryer, New Brunswick, New Jersey, Rutgers University Press, 1995; "Jean-Claude van Itallie" by Alexis Greene in *Speaking on Stage: Interviews with Contemporary American Playwrights,* edited by Philip C. Kolin and Colby H. Kullman, Tuscaloosa, University of Alabama Press, 1996.

Theatrical Activities:
Director: **Plays**—*The King of the United States*, New York, 1973; *The Tempest* by Shakespeare, New York, 1984; *The Balcony*, New York, 1989.

Actor: **Plays**—*Guys Dreamin'*, Shelburne Falls, Massachusetts Boston, and New York, 1997; *War, Sex, Singing, & Dancing,* Shelburne Falls, Massachusetts, 1998.

Jean-Claude van Itallie comments:

I seem to have been most intent on playing with new forms that might express a clear theatre optic. I have worked as a playwright in solitude. I have adapted and translated into English from a foreign language. I have worked as a poet in collaboration with a theatre director and actors, and with actors alone. I have written for puppets. I have written screenplays and specifically for television. I question theatre but I remain married to it, more or less. I agree that language itself helps to keep us isolated but I continue to write. I want to write with greater clarity, but from the heart. I like to work with other artists in the theatre, and to imagine the audience as a community of friends.

The 1960s were an exciting time of revolt and reformation. In the vanguard, theater destroyed preconceptions and invented new disciplines to express re-found truths underlying the mendacity of the commercial and political world. The 1970s were a time of retrenchment; I worked on new versions of classics making contact with my heritage as a playwright, my lineage. What now? In form, I'm working to synthesize the discoveries of the 1960s, and the rediscoveries of the 1970s. Political lies and corruption of power have become mundane; we are concerned now with our self-caused possible destruction of the world. What is the relationship between runaway technology and short-sighted pollution of air, food, and water, on the one hand, and spiritual poverty on the other? This is a time to clarify and acknowledge the split between body and mind in the individual and the world, and in that acknowledgement to effect a healing.

(1998) Intent on bringing my own spiritual and artistic practices together, I have transformed the farmhouse where I live into Shantigar Foundation "for where artistic and spiritual practices meet." Workshops are held here, and the barn is being renovated to provide a venue for making plays and dance pieces to send out into the world as well as for workshops and retreats.

I teach "Healing Power of Theater" workshops around the United States, combining writing exercises, performance exercises, meditation, movement, storytelling, and voice work—using tools of theater as a way for anyone to heal, and as a way for actors to build solo performance pieces. Theater started as a healing, disciplined, joyous ceremony in which anyone was free to participate. Performing, like singing and dancing, is everyone's right, not the exclusive domain of the professional. What's more, performing your own stories is good for you; it's healing.

Putting my body where my mouth is, I have started performing my own (autobiographical) words. I wrote my own part and performed in *Guys Dreamin'* with two other actors and a drummer. We performed in Shelburne Falls, Massachusetts, in Boston and at LaMama ETC in New York City. I'm now performing *War, Sex, Singing and Dancing,* a solo piece I've written with piano accompaniment.

Scratch a dramatist, find a performer. On stage I feel I've come home, my body has finally caught up with my mind.

* * *

In terms of their brevity, wit, and social commentary, the early plays of Jean-Claude van Itallie may be taken to resemble the early one-acts of Ionesco or, better, Chekhov. Later in his career van Itallie composed luminous American versions of the major Chekhov plays. The decisive difference between van Itallie's drama and that of the classic moderns lies in the realm of form. He is preoccupied with multiple levels of experience, with the mask behind the mask and with states of awareness outside the province of the everyday. His crystalline perceptions give rise to complex modes of characterization, a concern with indeterminate time, and a montage approach to dramatic activity and language.

Van Itallie's essential stage vocabulary is present at the start, in his off-off-Broadway debut with *War*. He describes the play as a "formal war game, a duel" between two male actors of different generations who metamorphose into father and son. They are visited by the shimmering vision of a nameless great actress of the Edwardian era who addresses them as her children and transforms their gritty New York loft, which is crammed with theatrical paraphernalia, into a sunny, cheerful park. At the end the men form an emblem of a two-headed eagle of war, each male identity locked into that of the other.

The rich theatrical implications of this meditation on appearances, on essential conflict, and on the role and nature of personality quickly matured when in the same year van Itallie began writing for the newly organized Open Theatre under the direction of Joseph Chaikin. In its shattering of received theatrical forms, its canonization of the workshop process, and its philosophical daring, the Open Theatre provided van Itallie with a subtle instrument for testing the limits of theatrical representation. For the Open Theatre he contributed numerous sketches, improvisations, and short plays, including *The Hunter and the Bird.* Among his most successful were the pop-art Hollywood comedies informally known as "the Doris Day plays": *Almost Like Being* and *I'm Really Here,* with a wacky Doris D. in love with Just Rock and then the deadly Rossano.

Van Itallie's chief works for the Open Theatre came in his last years with the company. A triptych of one-acts under the title *America Hurrah* begins with *Interview,* a rhythmic weaving of ritualized daily behavior and speech that starts and concludes in the anonymous offices of an employment agency in which all of the applicants are named Smith. *TV* dramatizes the menace and trivializing power of the mass media, with a trio watching television in the viewing room of a ratings company as the images break free of the set and engulf them. *Motel: A Masque for Three Dolls* unfolds within a tacky Midwestern motel room in which the huge Doll Motel-Keeper spews forth an unctuous monologue about the room and its furnishings, which represent the mail-order-catalogue surface of a violent America. Man Doll and Woman Doll enter the room and proceed to tear the place apart, have sex, and destroy the Motel-Keeper.

The theme of violence done to persons through the exigencies of the social contract is taken up again in *The Serpent.* Here in an even more sophisticated interplay of layered actions, contemporary violence is linked to its ancient sources and seen as a central aspect of the human condition. As it simultaneously presents and confronts the values in its story, this "ceremony" for actors explores the themes and the events of Genesis, and the tree of life is a tangle of men who embody the serpent. God's fixing of limits upon Adam and Eve is viewed as humanity's projection of its own need for limits, and the self-consciousness that results from the Fall leads to Cain and Abel and the unending human battle in which each is "caught between the beginning and the end" and unable to remake the past.

After leaving the Open Theatre, van Itallie wrote and staged *The King of the United States,* a stark political fable about the need for an office of rule supported by agents of the status quo to give order to life. *Mystery Play* recycles the characters and themes of *The King* and inverts its tone and style in an elegantly paced farce-parody of the whodunit presided over by a Mystery Writer who likes to play detective.

In 1975 van Itallie collaborated again with Chaikin on *A Fable,* a folktale for adults. In picaresque episodes the Journeyor leaves her impoverished village in search of help, and in her wanderings over a wide and storied landscape she comes to celebrate the need to transcend the beast within.

With *Early Warnings* van Itallie returned to smaller forms and a second triptych, this time on the theme of accommodation. The warnings are directed at the audience, for the characters already have made their choices. *Bag Lady* presents a day in the street life of the witty Clara, who is organizing her bags and keeping only the essential shards of her identity. The perky actress Judy Jensen in *Sunset Freeway* breezes along in her car at dusk on the L.A. freeway, immersed in her identity as a commercial actress. She speaks to her toy giraffe, imagines a nuclear holocaust, spots Warren Beatty, and, looking out upon the glories of consumer culture, is in heaven. In *Final Orders* space program agents Angus and Mike listen to instructions from a computer and hold on to one another, poised for the holocaust that now is at hand.

Among van Itallie's most ambitious projects is a theatrical version of *The Tibetan Book of the Dead; or, How Not to Do It Again,* a ritual for the dead in which the characters are emanations of the Dead One, speaking, chanting, and dancing within a huge skull and upon a floor mandala. In its style and complexity and in its debt to an ancient text, the work resembles *The Serpent,* but its landscape lies beyond history and legend in an essentialized world of the spirit.

The whole of van Itallie's dramatic universe is dedicated to a process of vital experimentation through the counterpoint of language, mask, and gesture. His is a philosophy of theatrical play underscored with social critique. Central to his vision are the inadequacies of being and a knowledge of exile. And above all there is a knowledge of the brutalities that are visited upon the self as it seeks to make its way in a world almost willfully estranged from organic life.

—Bill Coco

VIDAL, Gore

Pseudonym: Edgar Box. **Nationality:** American. **Born:** West Point, New York, 3 October 1925. **Education:** Los Alamos School, New Mexico, 1939-40; Phillips Exeter Academy, New Hampshire, 1940-43. **Military Service:** Served in the United States Army, 1943-46: warrant officer. **Career:** Editor, E.P. Dutton, publishers, New York, 1946. Lived in Antigua, Guatemala, 1947-49, and Italy, 1967-76. Member of the advisory board, *Partisan Review,* New Brunswick, New Jersey, 1960-71; Democratic-Liberal candidate for Congress, New York, 1960; member of the President's Advisory Committee on the Arts, 1961-63; co-chair, New Party, 1968-71. **Awards:** Mystery Writers of America award, for television play, 1954; Cannes Film Critics award, for screenplay, 1964; National Book Critics Circle award, for criticism, 1983; named honorary citizen, Ravello, Italy, 1983; Prix Deauville, for *Creation,* 1983; National Book award for nonfiction, for *United States: Essays, 1952-1992,* 1993. **Address:** La Rondinaia, Ravello, Salerno, Italy; or c/o Random House Inc., 201 East 50th Street, New York, New York 10022, U.S.A

Publications

Plays

Visit to a Small Planet (televised 1955). Included in *Visit to a Small Planet and Other Television Plays*, 1956; revised version (produced New York, 1957; London, 1960), Boston, Little Brown, 1957; in *Three Plays*, 1962.

Honor (televised 1956). Published in *Television Plays for Writers: Eight Television Plays*, edited by A.S. Burack, Boston, The Writer, 1957; revised version as *On the March to the Sea: A Southron Comedy* (produced Bonn, Germany, 1961), in *Three Plays*, 1962.

Visit to a Small Planet and Other Television Plays (includes *Barn Burning, Dark Possession, The Death of Billy the Kid, A Sense of Justice, Smoke, Summer Pavilion, The Turn of the Screw*). Boston, Little Brown, 1956.

The Best Man: A Play about Politics (produced New York, 1960). Boston, Little Brown, 1960; in *Three Plays*, 1962.
Three Plays (includes *Visit to a Small Planet, The Best Man, On the March to the Sea*). London, Heinemann, 1962.
Romulus: A New Comedy, adaptation of a play by Friedrich Dürrenmatt (produced New York, 1962). New York, Dramatists Play Service, 1962.
Weekend (produced New York, 1968). New York. Dramatists Play Service, 1968.
An Evening with Richard Nixon and . . . (produced New York, 1972). New York, Random House, 1972.

Screenplays: *The Catered Affair*, 1956; *I Accuse*, 1958; *The Scapegoat*, with Robert Hamer, 1959; *Suddenly, Last Summer*, with Tennessee Williams, 1959; *The Best Man*, 1964; *Is Paris Burning?*, with Francis Ford Coppola, 1966; *Last of the Mobile Hot-Shots*, 1970; *The Sicilian*, 1970; *Gore Vidal's Billy the Kid*, 1989.

Television Plays: *Barn Burning*, from the story by Faulkner, 1954; *Dark Possession*, 1954; *Smoke*, from the story by Faulkner, 1954; *Visit to a Small Planet*, 1955; *The Death of Billy the Kid*, 1955; *A Sense of Justice*, 1955; *Summer Pavilion*, 1955; *The Turn of the Screw*, from the story by Henry James, 1955; *Honor*, 1956; *The Indestructible Mr. Gore*, 1960; *Vidal in Venice* (documentary), 1985; *Dress Gray*, from the novel by Lucian K. Truscott IV, 1986.

Novels

Williwaw. New York, Dutton, 1946; London, Panther, 1965.
In a Yellow Wood. New York, Dutton, 1947; London, New English Library, 1967.
The City and the Pillar. New York, Dutton, 1948; London, Lehmann, 1949; revised edition, Dutton, and London, Heinemann, 1965.
The Season of Comfort. New York, Dutton, 1949.
Dark Green, Bright Red. New York, Dutton, and London, Lehmann, 1950.
A Search for the King: A Twelfth Century Legend. New York, Dutton, 1950; London, New English Library, 1967.
The Judgment of Paris. New York, Dutton, 1952; London, Heinemann, 1953; revised edition, Boston, Little Brown, 1965; Heinemann, 1966.
Messiah. New York, Dutton, 1954; London, Heinemann, 1955; revised edition, Boston, Little Brown, 1965; Heinemann, 1968.
Three: Williwaw, A Thirsty Evil, Julian the Apostate. New York, New American Library, 1962.
Julian. Boston, Little Brown, and London, Heinemann, 1964.
Washington, D.C. Boston, Little Brown, and London, Heinemann, 1967.
Myra Breckinridge. Boston, Little Brown, and London, Blond, 1968.
Two Sisters: A Memoir in the Form of a Novel. Boston, Little Brown, and London, Heinemann, 1970.
Burr. New York, Random House, 1973; London, Heinemann, 1974.
Myron. New York, Random House, 1974; London, Heinemann, 1975.
1876. New York, Random House, and London, Heinemann, 1976.
Kalki. New York, Random House, and London, Heinemann, 1978.
Creation. New York, Random House, and London, Heinemann, 1981.
Duluth. New York, Random House, and London, Heinemann, 1983.
Lincoln. New York, Random House, and London, Heinemann, 1984.
Empire. New York, Random House, and London, Deutsch, 1987.
Hollywood. New York, Random House, and London, Deutsch, 1990.
Live from Golgotha: The Gospel According to Gore Vidal. New York, Random House, 1992.
The Smithsonian Institute. Rockland, Massachusetts, 1998.

Novels as Edgar Box

Death in the Fifth Position. New York, Dutton, 1952; London, Heinemann, 1954.
Death Before Bedtime. New York, Dutton, 1953; London, Heinemann, 1954.
Death Likes It Hot. New York, Dutton, 1954; London, Heinemann, 1955.

Short Stories

A Thirsty Evil: Seven Short Stories. New York, Zero Press, 1956; London, Heinemann, 1958.

Other

Rocking the Boat (essays). Boston, Little Brown, 1962; London, Heinemann, 1963.
Sex, Death, and Money (essays). New York, Bantam, 1968.
Reflections upon a Sinking Ship (essays). Boston, Little Brown, and London, Heinemann, 1969.
Homage to Daniel Shays: Collected Essays 1952-1972. New York, Random House, 1972; as *Collected Essays 1952-1972*, London, Heinemann, 1974.
Matters of Fact and of Fiction: Essays 1973-1976. New York, Random House, and London, Heinemann, 1977.
Sex Is Politics and Vice Versa (essay). Los Angeles, Sylvester and Orphanos, 1979.
Views from a Window: Conversations with Gore Vidal, with Robert J. Stanton. Secaucus, New Jersey, Lyle Stuart, 1980.
The Second American Revolution and Other Essays 1976-1982. New York, Random House, 1982; as *Pink Triangle and Yellow Star and Other Essays*, London, Heinemann, 1982.
Vidal in Venice, edited by George Armstrong, photographs by Tore Gill. New York, Summit, and London, Weidenfeld and Nicolson, 1985.
Armegeddon? Essays 1983-1987. London, Deutsch, 1987; as *At Home*, New York, Random House, 1988.
A View from the Diner's Club: Essays 1987-1991. London, Deutsch, 1991.
Screening History. Cambridge, Massachusetts, Harvard University Press, 1992.
The Decline and Fall of the American Empire. Berkeley, California, Odonian Press, 1992.
United States: Essays, 1952-1992. New York, Random House, 1992.
Palimpsest: A Memoir. New York, Random House, 1995.
Virgin Islands: A Dependency of United States: Essays 1992-1997. London, Deutsch, 1997.
The Essential Vidal. New York, Random House, 1998.

Editor, *Best Television Plays*. New York, Ballantine, 1956.

*

Bibliography: *Gore Vidal: A Primary and Secondary Bibliography* by Robert J. Stanton, Boston, Hall, and London, Prior, 1978.

Manuscript Collection: University of Wisconsin, Madison.

Critical Studies: *Gore Vidal* by Ray Lewis White, New York, Twayne, 1968; *The Apostate Angel: A Critical Study of Gore Vidal* by Bernard F. Dick, New York, Random House, 1974; *Gore Vidal* by Robert F. Kiernan, New York, Ungar, 1982; "The Romantics of Gore Vidal" by James Tatum, in *Raritan: A Quarterly Review* (New Brunswick, New Jersey), Spring 1992, pp. 99-122; *Gore Vidal: Writer Against the Grain,* edited by Jay Parini, New York, Columbia University Press, 1992; "First Person Singular I: The Importance of Being Gore" by Andrew Kopkind, in *Nation,* July 1993, pp. 16-20; "Gore Vidal and the Erotics of Masculinity" by Robert J. Corber, in *Western Humanities Review* (Salt Lake City, Utah), Spring 1994, pp. 30-52; "Gore Vidal's Satire" by M. D. Fletcher and Kate Feros, in *Studies in Contemporary Satire* (Kearney), 1996, pp. 160-64; *Gore Vidal: A Critical Companion* by Susan Baker, Westport, Connecticut, 1997.

Theatrical Activities:
Actor: **Film**—*Roma* (*Fellini Roma*), 1972.

* * *

Eschewing all consideration of Gore Vidal as a novelist and short story writer, the critic must associate his theatrical production with its kinship to cinema and television. That is, Vidal's plays are quite stageable yet are intrinsically cinematographic or televisionistic. They have a modernity about them that facilitates their being restructured for each medium, for they are thematically and linguistically loose but integrally hinged. The characters are drawn in such a manner that, in displacing a character, changing a tempo, or shifting the psychology for a particular medium, Vidal does not violate the play's integrity. Critics have envied Vidal's facile success on television and on the stage, but his success would not be forthcoming were he not an extremely proficient stylist. True, Vidal has a grudge against a complacent bourgeois society and likes to jab at sensitive and vulnerable spots, and he succeeded cinematographically in *Suddenly Last Summer*. The film *Lefthanded Gun,* based on his television play on the Billy the Kid legend, also succeeded, but *Myra Breckinridge* failed because the producers were not faithful to Vidal.

Vidal's themes, which are extreme and tabooistic in his novels, are more traditional in his plays, involving mainly war and politics. But the persistent leitmotiv in all of his works is man bereft in the modern world. Should man relinquish certain values? Find new ones? Vidal assigns satire for the first alternative, irony for the second. Vidal the person seems to opt for relative values, and he creates types, as do all playwrights, to epitomize these values. Yet, in creating antagonistic types to exemplify certain absolutes, Vidal finds himself with characters possessing more dramatic qualities and effectiveness, which indicates that Vidal the writer is instinctively more sage than Vidal the person. Since the antagonist stands well in his own defense, he wins dramatic or tragic sympathy. Hence the thesis comes to no social conclusion, and the spectator is left with the unresolved futility of modern life. This is good dramaturgy.

Weekend is the least effective of Vidal's plays. It is an attempt to profit from the topical concern about miscegenation, which the author encrusts on a political campaign, not unlike *The Best Man.* But the situation and the characters are not real enough for good satire, nor are they exaggerated enough to make good farce. Vidal's merit as a playwright is best demonstrated in his trilogy *Visit to a Small Planet, On the March to the Sea,* and *The Best Man.*

Visit to a Small Planet is the story of a one-man invasion from outer space by an extraterrestrial being who is intent on creating a state of war between his world and ours. This "man" is called Kreton, an epithet all warmongers should bear, and he almost succeeds in creating a war hysteria on earth through certain well-conceived comic situations. It was because of these situations that the play became a very successful television series. Its antiwar theme is ineffective, however, because we cannot associate the Kreton's world with our own cretin world. After all, it is they, not we humans, who want war. The audience cannot help but feel self-righteous at the end when Kreton is led off to his celestial kindergarten. In attempting a satire on war, Vidal created an excellent science fiction farce with characterizations that are memorable—the pixie Kreton, the prototype of the war-loving general, Tom Powers, and Roger Felding, an equally ambitious television commentator.

Although the theme of *On the March to the Sea* is shopworn—the disasters wrought on Southern families, particularly that of John Hinks, by the ravages of the Civil War—the play is poignant and highly dramatic. With the possible exception of Captain Taylor of the Union army, who is flamboyant and too philosophical, the characters are all believable. (Participants in war are never introspective or contemplative, at least about ethical or social problems, during bellicose engagements.) Vidal thought a lot of the character and gave him the final words, but the character really caught in the maelstrom of life and war, Hinks, is the authentic tragic figure of the play. The war pervades all, yet as the title aptly indicates, the main theme is not Sherman's march to the sea but rather a series of incidents that take place during the march. The question of what is human dignity (the answer to one's own conscience) and honor (the answer to social conscience) is literally put through a trial by fire. Except for Colonel Thayer, who is the heavy, the characters, even though intentionally depicted as types, are all quite well drawn. But Thayer is too much of a celluloid character to be really cruel. The prize for cruelty goes to Clayton, son of Hinks, too young and self-centered to understand his father's anguish. Though *Visit to a Small Planet* was intended as a satire on war, *On the March to the Sea* is infinitely more effective as an antiwar drama.

The Best Man shows the struggle between two presidential aspirants who are jockeying, scratching, and grubbing for the nomination of their party. The play is a well-wrought urn, perfectly structured, and contains political characters that emulate Hollywood stereotypes—with Vidal having every intention of doing this—and effective dialogue, with each character keeping to his program. The suspenseful outcome of the nomination is solved by an honorable, classical, and justified theatrical technique, the president *ex machina.* The solution is not only theatrically but also thematically perfect, in that the person eventually to be nominated is of little importance. The play asks if one has to be a demagogue to be successful in political life. Vidal gives such a selection of presidential aspirants that they seem *inverosimil* and incredible. But as the old Italian quip says, "If it's not a wolf, it's a dog." This is ingeniously planted in the mind of the spectator, and this is why *The Best Man* is extremely good satire.

—John V. Falconieri

VOGEL, Paula (Anne)

Nationality: American. **Born:** Washington, D.C., 16 November 1951. **Education:** Bryn Mawr College, Pennsylvania, 1969-70, 1971-72; Catholic University, Washington, D.C., 1972-74, B.A.; Cornell University, Ithaca, New York, 1974-77, A.B.D. **Career:** Lecturer in women's studies and theatre, Cornell University, Ithaca, New York, 1977-82; artistic director, Theater with Teeth, New York, 1982-85; production supervisor, theatre on film and tape, Lincoln Center, New York, 1983-85; professor and director of graduate playwriting program, Brown University, Providence, Rhode Island, 1985—. **Awards:** Heerbes-McCalmon award, 1975, 1976; American College Theatre Festival award, 1976; Samuel French award, 1976; American National Theatre and Academy-West award, 1977; National Endowment for the Arts fellowship, 1980, 1991; MacDowell Colony, 1981, 1989; Bunting fellowship, 1990; Yaddo fellowship, 1992; McKnight fellowship, 1992; Bellagio fellowship, 1992; AT&T award, 1992; Governor's Award for the Arts, 1992; Obie award, 1992, 1997; Guggenheim fellow, 1995; Lucille Lortel award, 1997; Drama Desk Outer Critics Circle award, 1997; New York Drama Critics award, 1997; George and Elizabeth Morton award, 1997; The Fund for New American Plays, 1997; Robert Chesley Award in Playwrighting, 1997; Pew Charitable Trust Senior Residency award, 1997; Rhode Island Pell Award in the Arts, 1998; Pulitzer prize, for drama, 1998, for *How I Learned to Drive*. **Member:** New Dramatists. **Agent:** Peter Franklin, William Morris Agency, 1325 Avenue of the Americas, New York, New York 10019. **Address:** c/o Box 1852, Brown University, Department of Creative Writing, Providence, Rhode Island 02912, U.S.A.

Publications

Plays

Meg (produced Ithaca, New York, 1977; New York, 1979). New York, French, 1977.

The Last Pat Epstein Show Before the Reruns (produced Ithaca, New York, 1979).

Desdemona (produced Ithaca, New York, 1979; New York, 1985).

Bertha in Blue (produced New York, 1981).

The Oldest Profession (produced New York, 1981).

And Baby Makes Seven (produced San Francisco, 1986).

The Baltimore Waltz (produced New York, 1992). New York, Dramatists Play Service, 1992.

Hot 'n' Throbbing (produced New York, 1992).

The Baltimore Waltz and Other Plays. New York, Theatre Communications Group, 1995.

The Mineola Twins (produced Juneau, 1996; New York, 1998).

How I Learned to Drive (produced New York, 1997).

The Mammary Plays (includes *The Mineola Twins*; *How I Learned to Drive*) . New York, Theatre Communications Group, 1998.

*

Critical Study: "Time to Laugh" by Kathy Sova, in *American Theatre,* February 1997.

* * *

Paula Vogel's plays, while imaginatively dramatizing the conflict between the life force and death, prompt us to reexamine such topics as the feminization of poverty, the nontraditional family, the AIDS epidemic, and domestic violence—both in late twentieth-century America and in the context of a revisit to Shakespeare's *Othello.* Despite the topicality of her comedies, which sport a sting, the plays tend to praise the salutary nature of fantasy. Although clearly written from a feminist perspective, Vogel does not portray her women uncritically or her men unsympathetically.

Nonetheless, Vogel laments the unnecessarily Darwinian nature of people's odds of survival, a sort of law of the jungle by which the more muscular, wealthy, or powerful white, Protestant men enjoy an advantage. Prodigy Cecil, one of three fantasy children in *And Baby Makes Seven,* quotes Darwin to this effect: "Never forget that every single organic being around us strives to increase in numbers; that each lives by a struggle at some period in its life; that heavy destruction inevitably falls either on the young or the old. . . . Thus, from war or nature, from famine and death, all organic beings advance by one general law—namely, Multiply, Vary, Let the Strongest Live, and the Weakest Die. . . ."

The Oldest Profession depicts the effects wrought by the feminization of poverty among the elderly during the Reagan years. In a tiny New York City park at Seventy-second and Broadway, four prostitutes still working in their 70s and their madam, age 83, quietly chat about their fees, their clients, and their simple meals, which, given their low incomes, provide a precarious pleasure as well as sustenance. The hookers preserve their self-respect and their dignity, except when it occasionally becomes necessary to beat off a rival's attempt to encroach on their territory. Although Vogel's premise that ladies of the night keep plying their trade until they drop might seem far-fetched, *The Oldest Profession* reflects the reality that senior citizens do service their own generation in this manner. What else are they trained to do, and how else, deprived of health insurance and Social Security payments, can they eke out an existence? Vogel's shrewd social criticism even locates the characters in the building occupied by Zabar's Delicatessen, which actually did evict elderly tenants living upstairs when it expanded into selling housewares.

Vogel evinces a keen ear for her characters' colloquial speech, an intuitive understanding of their honor, pride, and enjoyment in their work, and subtlety in dramatizing their deprivations, ambitions, conflicts, and mutual nurturing. She gives the audience 10 minutes or so to warm to these women before we learn that they are anything more than just widows enjoying the sun. By this time we are perfectly prepared to recognize their importance to clients and their value as people, for Vogel's work represents the most respectful play ever written on the topic. As we laugh at such quips as "Vera's not just a woman with a Past; she's a woman with an Epic," we respond to Vogel's views of their struggle to survive on income that is insufficient to meet expenses, their efforts to exercise some control over their destinies, their compassion, their sisterhood, their respect for others and themselves, and their loneliness as, one by one, they die.

Although it is a comedy, *The Oldest Profession* is like Vogel's other plays in stressing the women's mortality. *And Baby Makes Seven* initially seems a more carefree comedy about a contented though nontraditional family composed of Ruth, her pregnant partner Anna, the gay man Peter, and three imaginary children made quite real to the adults and to the audience by Ruth and Anna. The situation quickly grows sinister, however, after Peter, who has fathered Anna's child, insists that the kids must go before the baby arrives. Once more Vogel hooks the audience with her characters' charm before telling us the truth about them. When we hear the boys talking in the dark about how babies are made, we cannot resist lovable Henri from Albert Lamorisse's 1955 film *The Red Balloon*, prodigy Cecil, and Orphan, a wild boy brought up by a pack of dogs who wants to name the baby Lassie. Soon infanticide occupies the grown-ups. Combining whimsy and menace, the fantasy threatens to careen off into violence while still encompassing the playful interaction of the lesbian lovers and their friend. After eight-year-old Henri tries to blackmail Anna into buying him a pony by claiming to be the father of her child, all three kids are killed off. (Orphan dies of rabies while quoting dog references from Shakespeare, including "Out, damned spot.") Yet the parents come to appreciate their need for both illusions and playfulness and, in Vogel's happiest ending, quickly recapture both.

Vogel repeats this mingling of fantasy and death in *The Baltimore Waltz*, this time replacing the earlier plays' realism with a fluid presentational approach that combines narrative, lectures, language lessons, a slide show, and quick two- and three-person scenes set in the United States and Europe. Vogel simultaneously creates a compassionate comedy about death, a bedroom farce, and a satire on American AIDS policy, which fails urgently to pursue a cure because so many of the victims have been those who are powerless and "different" from our rulers. "If just one grandchild of George Bush caught this thing during toilet training, that would be the last we'd hear about the space program," laments a character.

But Vogel conjures a disease that targets single teachers in elementary schools, who do not have a mother's immunity to their pupils' viruses. Although set in a ward at Baltimore's Johns Hopkins Hospital, the fantasy waltzes protagonist Anna around Europe in a twofold quest: to find a cure for Acquired Toilet Disease, and to enjoy sex so that she can, before her untimely demise, make up for all of those years of celibacy while she forced herself to remain a good little girl. Vogel forces spectators not in a high-risk group to consider for the first time the possibility of their own impending deaths, struck down by a mysterious illness the government does not care to fight fiercely. An AIDS play for those unaware souls who ignore the epidemic's ravages, *The Baltimore Waltz* proves to be another Vogel comedy that wins our sympathies before showing its hand. Only after we cannot help caring about Anna does the play, by substituting slides of Baltimore for views of Europe, let us know that she is merely a surrogate for her dying sibling Carl, an AIDS victim (Vogel's brother, to whose memory she dedicates the play "because I cannot sew"). This ferocious comedy, playful and poignant and written in lieu of a panel for the AIDS memorial quilt, veers quickly then from nightmarish satire of medical quackery, to bereavement, to a magical waltz.

The plays that tackle violence, however, cannot offer such an upbeat conclusion. *Hot 'n' Throbbing* tells the truth: domestic violence escalates to murder. And *Desdemona* creates no happy ending to avoid its protagonist's death. We are stuck with how Shakespeare ends his play, though Vogel stops her comedy's action before that tragedy's crisis. Yet the intersection of their plots at *Desdemona*'s conclusion in the hair-brushing scene renders chilling the loss of life awaiting the high-spirited woman we have delighted in earlier.

Vogel's imaginative re-creation of Desdemona provides the audience with everything Shakespeare denies us: full portraits of the three women (the only characters here), high spirits that do not willingly suffer their men's foolishness, no easy acquiescence to being victimized, and even a lusty, frank sexuality. This provocative, startling comedy takes from Shakespeare its setting in Cyprus, Amelia's theft of the handkerchief, and the women's names. But whereas Shakespeare's Desdemona must today appear foolish to endure Othello's violent and unwarranted jealousy, Vogel's character gives him cause to be jealous by exulting in an earthy, exuberant sexuality as she beds every man on the island save Cassio. Weaving such irony through her short, pithy episodes, Vogel depicts women as often coarse, mainly honest, and so sensual that they seem on the verge of seducing one another. The women's relations are marred, however, by petty jealousies, betrayals, and rivalries.

Vogel shows us that we must blame the social system, which is implicitly responsible for denying the women sisterhood in a common cause, forcing them instead to depend on destructive men who exercise over them the power of life and death. Denied meaningful, remunerative employment, a woman can slave in a kitchen while promoting the advancement of a husband she despises (Amelia), run a bawdy house (Bianca), or prostitute herself (Desdemona). Separated by class, financial status, and education—like the women in Wendy Kesselman's *My Sister in This House*—the women trust one another too little, too late. Because of this Desdemona will die, ironically having just made plans to leave her husband the next morning.

Ostensibly more in control, Charlene, an empowered professional woman and feminist in *Hot 'n' Throbbing,* has obtained a restraining order against the husband who has beaten her for years. Working at her computer, she supports herself and her kids by writing women's erotica for a feminist film company; like Desdemona's hooking, this has earned her independence. Yet gender power imbalances leave her vulnerable to violence. The husband breaks down the door, manipulates both her compassion for him and their teenagers' responses, and finally kills her.

Charlene has created powerful images of a dominant woman and submissive partner, but, later, just before she is murdered, a male crew reverses the roles and turns the script into a snuff film. Even the daughter has fantasized about bondage and pain. If Vogel permits any hope for women at the conclusion of this funny but dark and frightening play, it emerges when the daughter dons kneesocks, flannel shirt, overalls, and heavy boots, thereby ensuring that she is no sex object before she takes her own place at the computer. There she begins to write the play we have just seen, the sort of play Vogel writes, with the power to transform people and thus alter the world.

—Tish Dace

WALCOTT, Derek (Alton)

Nationality: British. **Born:** Castries, St. Lucia, West Indies, 23 January 1930. **Education:** St. Mary's College, Castries, 1941-47; University College of the West Indies, Mona, Jamaica, 1950-54, B.A. 1953. **Family:** Married 1) Fay Moyston in 1954 (divorced 1959), one son; 2) Margaret Ruth Maillard in 1962 (divorced), two daughters; 3) Norline Metivier in 1982. **Career:** Teacher, St. Mary's College, Castries, 1947-50 and 1954, Grenada Boy's Secondary School, St. George's, Grenada, 1953-54, and Jamaica College, Kingston, 1955; feature writer, *Public Opinion*, Kingston, 1956-57; feature writer, 1960-62, and drama critic, 1963-68, *Trinidad Guardian*, Port-of-Spain. Co-founder, St. Lucia Arts Guild, 1950, and Basement Theatre, Port-of-Spain; founding director, Little Carib Theatre Workshop (later Trinidad Theatre Workshop), 1959-76. Assistant professor of creative writing, 1981, and visiting professor, 1985—, Boston University. Visiting professor, Columbia University, New York, 1981, and Harvard University, Cambridge, Massachusetts, 1982, 1987. **Awards:** Rockefeller grant, 1957, 1966, and fellowship, 1958; Arts Advisory Council of Jamaica prize, 1960; Guinness award, 1961; Ingram Merrill Foundation grant, 1962; Borestone Mountain award, 1964, 1977; Royal Society of Literature Heinemann award, 1966, 1983; Cholmondeley award, 1969; Audrey Wood fellowship, 1969; Eugene O'Neill Foundation fellowship, 1969; Gold Hummingbird medal (Trinidad), 1969; Obie award, for drama, 1971; Jock Campbell award (*New Statesman*), 1974; Guggenheim award, 1977; *American Poetry Review* award, 1979; Welsh Arts Council International Writers prize, 1980; MacArthur fellowship, 1981; Los Angeles *Times* prize, 1986; Queen's gold medal for poetry, 1988; W.H. Smith award, for poetry, 1991; Nobel prize, for literature, 1992; St. Lucia Cross, 1993. D. Litt.: University of the West Indies, Mona, 1973. O.B.E. (Officer, Order of the British Empire), 1972. **Member:** Fellow, Royal Society of Literature, 1966; Honorary Member, American Academy, 1979. **Agent:** Bridget Aschenberg, International Famous Agency, 1301 Avenue of the Americas, New York, New York 10019, U.S.A. **Address:** 165 Duke of Edinburgh Avenue, Diego Martin, Trinidad.

Publications

Plays

Cry for a Leader (produced St. Lucia, 1950).

Senza Alcun Sospetto (broadcast 1950; as *Paolo and Francesca*, produced St. Lucia, 1951?).

Henri Christophe: A Chronicle (also director: produced Castries, 1950; London, 1952). Bridgetown, Barbados Advocate, 1950.

Robin and Andrea, published in *Bim* (Christ Church, Barbados), December 1950.

Three Assassins (produced St. Lucia, 1951?).

The Price of Mercy (produced St. Lucia, 1951?).

Harry Dernier (as *Dernier*, broadcast 1952; as *Harry Dernier*, also director: produced Mona, 1952). Bridgetown, Barbados Advocate, 1952.

The Sea at Dauphin (produced Trinidad, 1954; London, 1960; New York, 1978). Mona, University College of the West Indies Extra-Mural Department, 1954; in *Dream on Monkey Mountain and Other Plays*, 1970.

Crossroads (produced Jamaica, 1954).

The Charlatan (also director: produced Mona, 1954?; revised version, music by Fred Hope and Rupert Dennison, produced Port-of-Spain, 1973; revised version, music by Galt MacDermot, produced Los Angeles, 1974; revised version produced Port-of-Spain, 1977).

The Wine of the Country (also director: produced Mona, 1956).

The Golden Lions (also director: produced Mona, 1956).

Ione: A Play with Music (produced Kingston, 1957). Mona, University College of the West Indies Extra-Mural Department, 1957.

Ti-Jean and His Brothers (produced Castries, 1957; revised version, also director: produced Port-of-Spain, 1958; Hanover, New Hampshire, 1971; also director: produced New York, 1972; London, 1986). Included in *Dream on Monkey Mountain and Other Plays*, 1970.

Drums and Colours (produced Port-of-Spain, 1958). Published in *Caribbean Quarterly* (Mona), vol. 7, nos. 1 and 2, 1961.

Malcochon; or, The Six in the Rain (produced Castries, 1959; as *The Six in the Rain*, produced London, 1960; as *Malcochon*, produced New York, 1969). Included in *Dream on Monkey Mountain and Other Plays*, 1970.

Jourmard; or, A Comedy till the Last Minute (produced St. Lucia, 1959; New York, 1962).

Batai (carnival show; also director: produced Port-of-Spain, 1965).

Dream on Monkey Mountain (also director: produced Toronto, 1967; Waterford, Connecticut, 1969; New York, 1970). Included in *Dream on Monkey Mountain and Other Plays*, 1970.

Franklin: A Tale of the Islands (produced Georgetown, Guyana, 1969; revised version, also director: produced Port-of-Spain, 1973).

In a Fine Castle (also director: produced Mona, 1970; Los Angeles, 1972). Excerpt, as *Conscience of a Revolutionary*, published in *Express* (Port-of-Spain), 24 October 1971.

Dream on Monkey Mountain and Other Plays (includes *Ti-Jean and His Brothers*, *Malcochon*, *The Sea at Dauphin*, and the essay "What the Twilight Says"). New York, Farrar Straus. 1970; London, Cape, 1972.

The Joker of Seville, music by Galt MacDermot, adaptation of the play by Tirso de Molina (produced Port-of-Spain, 1974). With *O Babylon!*, New York, Farrar Straus, 1978; London, Cape, 1979.

O Babylon!, music by Galt MacDermot (also director: produced Port-of-Spain, 1976; London, 1988). With *The Joker of Seville*, New York, Farrar Straus, 1978; London, Cape, 1979.

Remembrance (also director: produced St. Croix, U.S. Virgin Islands, 1977; New York, 1979, London, 1980). With *Pantomime*, New York, Farrar Straus, 1980.

The Snow Queen (television play), excerpt published in *People* (Port-of-Spain), April 1977.

Pantomime (produced Port-of-Spain, 1978; London, 1979; Washington, D.C., 1981; New York, 1986). With *Remembrance*, New York, Farrar Straus, 1980.

Marie Laveau, music by Galt MacDermot (also director: produced St. Thomas, U.S. Virgin Islands, 1979). Excerpts published in *Trinidad and Tobago Review* (Tunapuna), Christmas 1979.
The Isle Is Full of Noises (produced Hartford, Connecticut, 1982).
Beef, No Chicken (produced New Haven, Connecticut, 1982; London, 1989). Included in *Three Plays*, 1986.
Three Plays (includes *The Last Carnival*; *Beef, No Chicken*; *A Branch of the Blue Nile*). New York, Farrar Straus, 1986.
The Last Carnival (produced Stockholm, Sweden, 1992). Included in *Three Plays*, 1986.
To Die for Granada (produced Cleveland, Ohio, 1986).
The Odyssey, adaptation of the epic by Homer (produced Stratford-on-Avon, 1992). New York, Farrar, Straus, 1993.

Radio Plays: *Senza Alcun Sospetto*, 1950; *Dernier*, 1952.

Poetry

25 Poems. Port-of-Spain, Guardian Commercial Printery, 1948.
Epitaph for the Young: XII Cantos. Bridgetown, Barbados Advocate, 1949.
Poems. Kingston, Jamaica, City Printery, 1951.
In a Green Night: Poems 1948-1960. London, Cape, 1962.
Selected Poems. New York, Farrar Straus, 1964.
The Castaway and Other Poems. London, Cape, 1965.
The Gulf and Other Poems. London, Cape, 1969; as *The Gulf*, New York, Farrar Straus, 1970.
Another Life. New York, Farrar Straus, and London, Cape, 1973.
Sea Grapes. London, Cape, and New York, Farrar Straus, 1976.
The Star-Apple Kingdom. New York, Farrar Straus, 1979; London, Cape, 1980.
Selected Poetry, edited by Wayne Brown. London, Heinemann, 1981.
The Fortunate Traveller. New York, Farrar Straus, 1981; London, Faber, 1982.
The Caribbean Poetry of Derek Walcott and the Art of Romare Bearden. New York, Limited Editions Club, 1983.
Midsummer. New York, Farrar Straus, and London, Faber, 1984.
Collected Poems 1948-1984. New York, Farrar Straus, and London, Faber, 1986.
The Arkansas Testament. New York, Farrar Straus, 1987; London, Faber, 1988.
Omeros. New York, Farrar Straus, 1989; London, Faber, 1990.
Poems, 1965-1980. London, Cape, 1992.
Derek Walcott: Selected Poems. Harlow, Longman, 1993.
The Bounty. New York, Farrar, Straus, 1997.

Recording: *Derek Walcott Reads*, New York, Cademon, 1994.

Other

The Poet in the Theatre. London, Poetry Book Society, 1990.
Antilles: Fragments of Epic Memory. New York, Farrar, Straus, 1993.
Conversations with Derek Walcott, edited by William Baer. Jackson, University of Mississippi, 1996.
Homage to Frost, with Seamus Heaney and Joseph Brodsky. New York, Farrar, Straus, 1996.
What the Twilight Says: Essays. New York, Frrarar, Straus, 1998.

*

Bibliography: *Derek Walcott: An Annotated Bibliography of His Works* by Irma E. Goldstraw, New York, Garland, 1984.

Critical Studies: *Derek Walcott: Memory as Vision* by Edward Baugh, London, Longman, 1978; *Derek Walcott: Poet of the Islands* by Ned Thomas, Cardiff, Welsh Arts Council, 1980; *Derek Walcott* by Robert D. Hamner, Boston, Twayne, 1981; *The Art of Derek Walcott* edited by Stewart Brown, Bridgend, Glamorgan, Seren, 1989; *Derek Walcott's Poetry: American Mimicry* by Rei Terada, Boston, Northeastern University Press, 1992; *Derek Walcott and West Indian Drama: Not Only a Playwright but a Company, The Trinidad Theatre Workshop, 1959-1993* by Bruce Alvin King, Oxford and New York, Clarendon Press, 1995; *Poetics of Derek Walcott: Intertextual Perspectives,* edited by Gregson Davis, Durham, North Carolina, Duke University Press, 1997; *Critical Perspectives on Derek Walcott,* edited by Robert D. Hammer, Boulder, Colorado, Lynne Reinner, 1997.

Theatrical Activities:
Director: Many of his own plays.

* * *

Although primarily a poet—and, as such, one of the best writing in English today—Derek Walcott is also an accomplished playwright whose interest in drama was kindled at an early age. A youthful stage designer, he has for some time supervised acting workshops in Trinidad, where he has also campaigned for the establishment of a national Caribbean theater. His plays afford dramatic treatment to themes expressed in his poetry, exploring concepts of personal and racial identity, the brooding presence of evil, and the inevitability of exile and separation. Walcott's efforts to comprehend and utilize the nature of his own mixed ancestry in his writing explain much of the tension and conflict that underlie his work. The descendant of European masters and African slaves officially denied a history of their own, he strives in poems and dramas alike to maintain a balance between the two. Walcott's affection for European literature, demonstrated clearly in his mastery of poetic and dramatic styles, is genuine but wary, and in his play *The Last Carnival* he indicates the dangers of wholesale acceptance of European models by Caribbean artists. At the same time he strongly asserts the heritage of his black forebears, drawing on patterns of Caribbean speech and African-derived chanting, drumming, and dance in many of his plays. His vision focuses powerfully on the quest for self-knowledge and self-realization in a world in which, as the child of two conflicting cultures, he might fairly claim with his fictional character Shabine, "I had no nation now but the imagination."

Walcott's early dramas present native Caribbean figures in heroic and tragic roles, countering the accepted European pantheon of greats. For a writer trying to re-create a history with meaning for his black compatriots, the Haitian revolution offers evident attractions. *Henri Christophe: A Chronicle* portrays the life, ambition, and eventual downfall of the rebel who became the self-proclaimed king of Haiti, and Walcott returned later to the events of this period with *Haitian Earth,* which has not been produced. More typical of his work as a dramatist are those plays that have lowly, downtrodden peasants as their leading characters. In *Malcochon, The Sea at Dauphin,* and *Dream on Monkey Mountain* woodcutters, charcoal burners, and fishermen take center stage, their subsistence lifestyles presented in the bleakest possible light.

Walcott strips away all heroic pretensions from them, revealing his creations as squalid, vulnerable individuals. Makak, for instance, whose nightmare vision provides the core of the play in *Dream on Monkey Mountain,* bears a name that invites comparison with the macaque. This allusion to mankind's prehuman ancestry is clear in the text itself: "In the beginning was the ape, and the ape had no name, so God called him man." A further, sinister dimension is also suggested in the dehumanizing racist stereotype of all blacks as monkeys. In his dream Makak struggles to free himself from the power of the White Goddess, whiteness here—as in *Moby Dick*—symbolizing death and negation. With its bleak, compelling insights and its presentation of "the wretched of the earth," *Dream on Monkey Mountain* ranks among Walcott's strongest dramatic statements.

Another significant work, *Ti-Jean and His Brothers,* makes effective use of drumming and chanting as background to a play whose dialogue is imbued with Creole speech patterns. Ti-Jean, the untutored peasant, holds the central role in a Caribbean morality play, encountering and overcoming the devil in his many guises by a combination of luck and mother wit. His victory, achieved at tragic cost, is given a native context by its "chorus" of chants and drum rhythms. *The Joker of Seville* reveals talent of another kind, being a remarkable reworking of the Don Juan legend from Molina's Spanish original in which Walcott reshapes the classic material to a valid creation of his own. Following Juan, the amoral, heartless lecher-hero, to his final destruction, he sets the action not in Spain but in Trinidad, where Latin and African cultures fuse uneasily together. The stage is devised as a symbolic bullring in which stick fighters and masked dancers echo the dialogue with comments and chanted choruses. *O Babylon!* has a more modern setting, its action centering on a confrontation between developers and Rastafarian squatters on the eve of Haile Selassie's visit to Jamaica. Walcott presents scenario and players in a manner at once comic and profound, the complex natures and motives of his characters displayed in speeches that make inspired use of Rastafarian, Jamaican, and English languages. Music and dance again complement the inevitable irony of the play's conclusion.

Three Plays, an impressive triptych from the 1980s, shows Walcott once more exploring major themes in a contemporary Trinidadian setting. *The Last Carnival* traces the shared relationships of a landowning Creole family and their "adopted" English sibling as colonialism gives way to independence and the trauma of revolution. The image of the carnival, at once a vain attempt by the thwarted artist Victor to impose the canons of European culture on his unresponsive audience and a symbolic final gesture of the old order, is effectively contrasted with the surface radicalism of the young revolutionaries, for whom war is another kind of carnival and one equally doomed to failure. The gradual change in Agatha, the working-class English woman who renounces her own radical politics on Victor's death to become the mainstay of the establishment, is convincingly shown, as is her tense relationship with the isolated, unbalanced Victor and his earthy, Creolized brother Oswald. In the end the one hope for salvation is the exile chosen by Clodia, the Agatha of a new generation.

Beef, No Chicken, like *O Babylon!,* presents the conflict of developers and the little man in terms of comic farce. Its central theme is the struggle of small-time restaurateur Otto Hogan to fight off the efforts of a corrupt council to bypass his premises with a major highway. Modern reality is represented by the shopping mall magnate Mongroo, who regards bribery and coercion as an integral part of civilization, and a mayor who sees pollution as evidence of progress. Otto's futile attempts to hold up the road by haunting workmen in the guise of a female ghost are complicated by a hilariously varied cast that includes a television crew, Cuban revolutionaries, and the members of the council. In the end he is forced to abandon his principles and join the rat race, running for mayor as the council and Mongroo are exposed on television. *A Branch of the Blue Nile,* which is set in a small theater workshop in Port of Spain, follows the lives of actors and the director as they examine their relationships through rehearsals, improvisations, and performance in a modern version of *Antony and Cleopatra.* Walcott depicts the players and setting superbly in a powerful, moving drama in which acting is presented as a holy or profane transformation, a state of grace or possession that defines and limits the continuing flux of life. The poetic strength of his dialogue—in blank verse speeches, taped conversations, and island dialect—lends an individual voice to all three plays and in particular to the last, which is surely one of his most impressive achievements.

—Geoff Sadler

WALKER, George F(rederick)

Nationality: Canadian. **Born:** Toronto, Ontario, 23 August 1947. **Education:** Riverdale Collegiate, Toronto, graduated 1965. **Family:** Married Susan Purdy in 1980; two daughters. **Career:** Playwright-in-residence, 1971-76, and artistic director, 1978-79, Factory Theatre Lab, Toronto; resident playwright, New York Shakespeare Festival, 1981. **Awards:** Canada Council grant, 1971 (and 4 subsequent grants); Chalmers award, 5 times; Governor-General's award, 1986, 1988. **Agent:** Great North Artists, 350 Dupont Street, Toronto, Ontario M5V 1V9, Canada.

PUBLICATIONS

Plays

The Prince of Naples (produced Toronto, 1971). Toronto, Playwrights, 1972.

Ambush at Tether's End (produced Toronto, 1971). Toronto, Playwrights, 1972.

Sacktown Rag (produced Toronto, 1972). Toronto, Playwrights, 1972.

Bagdad Saloon (produced Toronto and London, 1973). Toronto, Playwrights, 1973.

Demerit (produced Toronto, 1974).

Beyond Mozambique (produced Toronto, 1974). Toronto, Playwrights, 1975.

Ramona and the White Slaves (also director: produced Toronto, 1976). Included in *Three Plays*, 1978.

Gossip (produced Toronto and Chicago, 1977). Toronto, Playwrights, 1980.

Zastrozzi, The Master of Discipline (produced Toronto, 1977; London, 1978; Seattle, 1979; New York, 1982). Toronto, Playwrights, 1977.

Three Plays (includes *Bagdad Saloon*, *Beyond Mozambique*, *Ramona and the White Slaves*). Toronto, Coach House Press, 1978.

Filthy Rich (produced Toronto, 1979; Evanston, Illinois, 1982; London, 1984; New York, 1985). Toronto, Playwrights, 1981.
Rumours of Our Death, music by John Roby, lyrics by Walker and Roby (also director: produced Toronto, 1980). Published in *Canadian Theatre Review* (Downsview, Ontario), Winter 1980.
Theatre of the Film Noir (also director: produced Toronto, 1981; London, 1983). Toronto, Playwrights, 1981.
Science and Madness (produced Toronto, 1982). Toronto, Playwrights, 1982.
The Art of War: An Adventure (also director: produced Toronto, 1983; New York 1987). Toronto, Playwrights, 1983.
Criminals in Love (produced Toronto, 1984). Toronto, Playwrights, 1985.
The Power Plays (includes *Gossip, Filthy Rich, The Art of War*). Toronto, Coach House Press, 1984.
Better Living (produced Toronto, 1986; Poughkeepsie, New York, 1987). Included in *East End Plays*, 1987.
Beautiful City (produced Toronto, 1987). Included in *East End Plays*. 1987.
East End Plays (includes *Criminals in Love, Better Living, Beautiful City*). Toronto. Playwrights, 1987.
Nothing Sacred, adaptation of Turgenev's *Fathers and Sons* (produced Los Angeles, 1988; New York, 1992). Toronto, Coach House Press, 1988.
Love and Anger. Toronto, Coach House Press, 1990.
Escape from Happiness (produced Vassar College, 1991). In *Shared Annxiety: Selected Plays,* Vancouver, Talonbooks, 1994.
Tough! In *Shared Anxiety: Selected Plays,* Vancouver, Talonbooks, 1994.
Shared Anxiety: Selected Plays (includes *Beyond Mozambique*; *Zastroxxi*; *The Master of Discipline*; *Theatre of the Film Noir*; *The Art of War*; *Criminals in Love*; *Better Living*; *Escape from Happiness*; *Tough*). Vancouver, Talonbooks, 1994.
Suburban Motel. Burnaby, Talonbooks, 1997.

Radio Plays: *The Private Man*, 1973.

Television plays: *Sam, Grace, Doug, and the Dog*, 1976; *Microdrama*, 1976; *Strike*, 1976; *Overlap*, 1977; *Capital Punishment*, 1977.

*

Critical Studies: *Factory Lab Anthology* edited by Connie Brissenden, Vancouver, Talonbooks, 1974; "Playnotes" by Richard Horenblas, in *Scene Changes* (Toronto) October 1975; in *University of Toronto Quarterly*, Spring 1980; "Slashing the Pleasantly Vague: George F. Walker and the Word" by Stephen Haff, in *Essays in Theatre Etudes* (Guelph), November 1991, pp. 59-69; "George F. Walker" by Chris Johnson, in *Post-Colonial English Drama: Commonwealth Drama Since 1960,* edited by Bruce King, New York and London, St. Martin's, 1992; "Out with the Queers: Moral Triage and George F. Walker's *Theatre of the Film Noir*" by Ed Nyman, in *Australasain Drama Studies* (Queensland), October 1996, pp. 57-65; "George Walker" by Stephen Haff, in *BOMB,* Spring 1997, pp. 36-39; "Three Tutorial Plays: *The Lesson, The Prince of Naples,* and *Oleanna*" by Craig Walker, in *Modern Drama* (Downsview, Ontario), Spring 1997, pp. 149-62.

Theatrical Activities:
Director: **Plays**—Some of his own plays; *The Extremist* by Ilya Denykin, Toronto, 1976.

* * *

George F. Walker's origins are in theater of the absurd. In *Ambush at Tether's End* , a corpse hangs upstage while Galt and Bush engage in dialogue much like that of Vladimir and Estragon or Rosencrantz and Guildenstern as they wait for someone to take responsibility. Notes found on the corpse humorously introduce themes of free will and determinism, liberty, and responsibility. Trapped in a situation they did not create, unable to act, the two repeatedly attempt suicide but lack the courage. The play is characterized by verbal wit, idiomatic absurdities ("you're here to put your foot down if it gets out of hand"), and economical development of character.

Written during a time when American legends were becoming the subject matter of literature, *Bagdad Saloon* shows the inappropriateness of applying American myths to other nations. Such "mythical" American figures as Henry Miller, Gertrude Stein, and Doc Holliday assume they are famous and as a result act capriciously, whereas the non-Americans seek a formula to imitate. This chaotic, highly fragmented, cartoonlike drama, with its exaggerated actions and simplified characters, continues in *Beyond Mozambique*. While the natives beat drums and collect arms to rebel, the mad Europeans, like many of Walker's characters, can no longer distinguish between reality and fantasy. The bleak vision of *Ramona and the White Slaves* probes the depths of the psyche, its perversions, the nature of power, and the wild instability of emotions. Although the setting is once again "exotic,"—Hong Kong in 1919—the play may be an opium dream; the slavery, mutilation, rape, and guilt serving as a metaphor for "the story of a family."

The investigation of power and evil is central to *Zastrozzi*, *The Master of Discipline*. A study in obsessive revenge and the will to dominate, Zastrozzi appears as a creature from the feudal past with his whips, demand for slavelike obedience, and hatred (in 1896) of impressionist art. He is driven by a code of honor and refuses to question his motives or examine rights and wrongs. Underlying his brutality is his perception of life as arbitrary. Zastrozzi is opposed by Victor, the modern, liberal, rational man who is unable to kill Zastrozzi when he has the opportunity, and, like many of Walker's voices of conscience, is bound to fail. *Zastrozzi* is more unified than the plays that preceded it. The characters are representative archetypes of Western civilization. As Walker's work developed, narrative became increasingly important, as is the opposition between the power of evil and the weakness of good.

Walker's aesthetics—based on parody, pastiche, and caricature—is a product of postmodernism. In the three "power plays"—*Gossip, Filthy Rich,* and *The Art of War*—Walker imitates the conventions of popular art forms in order to meditate on the nature, use, and misuse of power. Tyrone M. Power (the name ironically alludes to the movie star, although this Tyrone Power is short and balding) is first an investigative reporter (a parody of the hardboiled films of the '30s and '40s) and later a hard-drinking, cynical, but soft-hearted, private detective. Power is at first a loner, but in *Filthy Rich* he is joined by Jamie, a young working-class Sancho Panza. Power quixotically takes on the local political establishment, uncovers their crimes, but gains nothing and becomes more cynical. In *Gossip* he finds that he is being used by those whose motive for seeing corruption exposed is revenge. The romantic individualism of the investigative reporter and private eye pays off neither financially nor emotionally. By *The Art of War*, Power has become a sort of ineffectual Sherlock Holmes, fighting a losing battle against his Moriarty. While the criminal laughs at him and escapes, Power can only ponder upon his inaction.

The struggle between good and evil continues in *Science and Madness* with its horror-film conventions. The difference between good and evil becomes less clear in *Theatre of the Film Noir*, which begins with a French police inspector—in a pastiche of cheap French detective fiction and B movie voiceovers—warning that, as Paris has just been liberated from German occupation, all order has broken down, and there is no clear standard of morality. Power investigates the recent killing of a young Resistance fighter. The suspects include the Communists, the young man's homosexual lover (a dangerous psychopath), and the young man's sister, a Nazi collaborator with whom he had an incestuous relationship. Walker is concerned with the breakdown of significance and the instability and unpredictability of character. Morality has become a question of circumstance.

Many of Walker's later plays use the family as a source of and metaphor for society and ideology. *Better Living* is the first of a series about the Toronto East End working class of Walker's youth. Nora Quinn is a charmingly tuned-out mother to three bickering daughters. Her husband, Tom, who left years ago returns now as Tim and initiates a patriarchal, neofascist "consumer socialism." Jack, Nora's brother, is an indecisive liberal unwilling to accept that violence may be necessary in order to end Tim's rule. The play raises questions about identity, memory, and the price of order.

Beautiful City looks at three families in relation to the ideal of community. Toronto is being ruined by unscrupulous architects, corrupt real-estate developers, criminals, and an uncaring local government. What can be done? Such themes are examined again in *Love and Anger* in which a lawyer fights the system by manufacturing evidence for a black woman who hopes to get her husband released from prison.

The Toronto plays treat the lives of characters who live in a chaotic and corrupt world in which the sins of the past are visited upon the children. In *Criminals in Love* Gail and her boyfriend Junior are two innocents who, trapped by their environment, lack the will to break free. By allowing themselves to be manipulated by the strong and unprincipled, Junior and Gail are transformed from unwilling accomplices to defiantly armed terrorists.

Escape from Happiness like *Beautiful City* is nearly allegorical. Junior, now Gail's husband, is beaten up by thugs; this produces no reaction from his blinkered mother-in-law, Nora. Unable to accept the past and forgive, the family agrees on nothing. Nora still refuses to accept that the man in bed upstairs, a former policeman, is her husband. When drugs are found in the basement, Nora is framed as two policemen quarrel about law, justice, and evidence. Each of the plays ends with a small ironic flicker of hope. Here there is a rapid happy ending of hugs and reconciliation.

In his short recent plays Walker comes even closer to a theater that seeks to solve social problems. *Tough Talk* mixes talk show and public trial. A girl is pregnant; her friend guards her while grilling the philandering boyfriend. *Problem Child* is about a blue-collar couple's battle with a welfare agency over their baby. It is part of a series of six, all set in the same motel room. Although his plays have progressed from nihilism toward commitment, Walker has warned against imposing a consistent interpretation. The sympathies and analysis are socialist, but his vision remains a mixture of parody, skeptical lunacy, and concern.

—Bruce King

WALKER, Joseph A.

Nationality: American. **Born:** Washington, D.C., 23 February 1935. **Education:** Howard University, Washington, D.C., B.A. in philosophy 1956; Catholic University, Washington, D.C., M.F.A. 1970. **Military Service:** Served in the United States Air Force: 2nd lieutenant. **Family:** Married 1) Barbara Brown (divorced 1965); 2) Dorothy A. Dinroe in 1970. **Career:** Worked as taxi driver, salesman, and postal clerk; English teacher in Washington, D.C., and New York; actor with the Negro Ensemble Company, New York, 1969—; playwright-in-residence, Yale University, New Haven, Connecticut, 1970; taught at City College, New York, 1970s; currently member of the drama department, Howard University. **Address:** Department of Drama, Howard University, 2400 6th Street, N.W., Washington, D.C. 20059, U.S.A.

PUBLICATIONS

Plays

The Believers, with Josephine Jackson, music and lyrics by Benjamin Carter and others (produced New York, 1968).
The Harangues (produced New York, 1969). Shortened version, as *Tribal Harangue Two*, in *The Best Short Plays 1971*, edited by Stanley Richards, Philadelphia, Chilton, 1971.
Ododo (also director: produced New York, 1970). Published in *Black Drama Anthology*, edited by Ron Milner and Woodie King, New York, New American Library, 1971.
The River Niger (produced New York, 1972). New York, Hill and Wang, 1973.
Yin Yang, music by Dorothy A. Dinroe-Walker (also director: produced New York, 1973).
Antigone Africanus (produced New York, 1975).
The Lion Is a Soul Brother (also director: produced New York, 1976).
District Line (produced New York, 1984).

Screenplay: *The River Niger*, 1976.

*

Critical Studies: "Mother, Sister, Wife: A Dramatic Perspective" by Anthony Barthelemy, in *The Southern Review* (Baton Rouge, Louisiana), Summer 1985, pp. 770-789; "The Thousand and First Face of the Hero" by Rebecca Phillips, in *The Bulletin of the West Virginia Association of College English Teachers* (Montgomery, West Virginia), Fall 1991, pp. 91-102.

Theatrical Activities:
Director: Several of his own plays.

Actor: **Plays**—*The Believers*, New York, 1968; *Cities in Bezique* by Adrienne Kennedy, New York, 1969. **Films**—*April Fools*,

1969; *Bananas*, 1971. **Television**—*NYPD* series; *In Black America* (narrator).

* * *

The dramas of Joseph A. Walker explore various aspects of black life, including male-female relationships, interracial strife, and family and community bonds. The focus of most of his work, however, is on the psyche of black American males. Cut off from their ancestral home and exploited by whites, these disoriented men are portrayed as lacking a sense of identity, purpose, and self-worth. Efforts by some of the men to obtain power and wealth are most often thwarted by white America's black sycophants. Whether or not one agrees with this simplistic ideology, frequently espoused in the 1960s and 1970s, Walker's plays are still relevant because of their compelling depiction of those black males stagnated by feelings of impotence, frustration, and hopelessness.

While the black male characters are deftly drawn and complex, Walker's portraits of black women and whites rarely escape the limitations of stereotypes. Black women seldom have any personal goals but instead function as either supporters or castrators of their men. White women serve as sexual playmates and status symbols for their black lovers. White men exploit blacks and destroy those who pose a threat to their way of life. Lacking depth and plausible motivations for their actions, these characters weaken the credibility of Walker's plays.

As its title suggests, *The Harangues* is used as a vehicle for the playwright to vent his opinions. Composed of two episodes and two one-act plays, the work has a despairing view of black life. In the first episode a fifteenth-century West African man chooses to kill his son rather than subject him to life as a slave in the New World. The second episode mirrors the first by showing a contemporary black American revolutionary who kills his child rather than allow him to grow up in a despondent society. Black women plead for their children's lives in both episodes, but they are conspicuously absent in the one-acts. The first one-act, set in Washington, D.C., concerns a black male and his pregnant white fiancée. Incredibly, with little hesitation, the white woman agrees to assist her lover in the murder of her father, who will disinherit her if she marries. The plan backfires, however, and because of the actions of a traitorous black "friend" results in the death of the scheming black man. In the second one-act, unless they can convince him of their worthiness to live, a deranged black man threatens to kill his three captives: a white liberal and an assimilationist black man and his white lover. After their perverted lives are exposed, only the white woman, who endures several sexual indignities, is deemed to be virtuous. As the death penalty is being carried out, however, the woman takes a bullet meant for her contemptible black lover. In an ensuing struggle the assimilationist gains control of his captor's gun and kills him. As in the first one-act, a desperate black man dies at the hands of a black minion of the white race.

In sharp contrast to the pessimistic outlook that envelopes *The Harangues, The River Niger* celebrates the enduring qualities of the black man and offers a hopeful vision of the future. Johnny Williams, a middle-aged house painter and poet living in Harlem, uses liquor to escape the bleak reality of a life that has become stagnated by unrealized dreams. Johnny places his hopes for the future in his son Jeff's career in the air force. But his son's homecoming brings another disappointment to Johnny's life. Jeff admits that he has been dismissed from the military, which he abhorred. He contends that his ouster was due to his refusal to be a "supernigger"—a black man who tries to prove that he has capabilities comparable to whites. He further announces that he will no longer be bound by familial and social expectations but will instead seek only to fulfill his own needs and desires. Despite his intentions Jeff soon finds himself involved in the self-destructive affairs of his former gang. When Jeff and the gang are betrayed by one of the members and prison terms appear imminent, Johnny has a shoot-out with the traitor, which results in both of their deaths. But before Johnny dies, he demands to take the rap for the shooting and the gang's alleged offense. Johnny's wife, Mattie, admonishes her family and the gang not to fail to cooperate and to carry out her husband's wishes. Johnny's heroic gesture provides Jeff and the other gang members with a new lease on life and a powerful example of the unconditional selfless love that a father can have for his son.

The portraits of the men are well crafted and realistic. The characters function as representatives of differing moral values, abilities, aspirations, and perspectives within the black community. Johnny emerges as the most eloquent and convincing spokesman who, through his poem "The River Niger," speaks of the need to be cognizant of one's unbreakable link to all people of African descent.

Although the play's black women represent various age groups and cultures, they share similar attitudes toward their men. The women serve their men's needs with little concern for their own desires or ambitions. Mattie even accepts the fact that her husband chooses to confide in his West Indian friend instead of her. Incredibly, during a conversation between Mattie and Jeff's South African lover, Johnny's wife agrees with the younger woman that women are incapable of having a similar type of relationship because "women don't trust one another." Despite this and several other questionable remarks made by the women, their behavior as selfless and loyal supporters of their men foreshadows the concluding message of the play. As Johnny's final actions and his demand for cooperation demonstrate, the survival of the race requires a communal effort with little thought of self-interest.

A Washington, D.C., taxi stand serves as the setting for *District Line*. The play depicts a day in the lives of six cab drivers—two white and three black males and one black female. The drivers reveal their past experiences and present their concerns and aspirations as they interact with one another and their passengers. Black males continue to be Walker's most poignant characterizations. Of greatest interest are the scenes concerning two drivers: Doc, a moonlighting Howard University professor, and Zilikazi, an exiled South African revolutionary. Female characters, whether black or white, appear to be gratuitous in the drama and remain stereotypes. The playwright does, however, portray white men in roles other than the liberal or the oppressor of blacks. Still, the work suffers in comparison to Walker's other plays because of its fundamental flaws. The dramatic action is not adequately developed or sustained throughout the play, and the work lacks a central theme to tie the scenes together. Consequently, the drama fails to create the intense emotional impact characteristic of Walker's other plays.

—Addell Austin Anderson

WALLACE, Naomi

Nationality: American. **Born:** Prospect, Kentucky, 17 August 1960. **Education:** Hampshire College, Amherst, Massachusetts, B.A. in 1982; University of Iowa, M.F.A. in poetry, 1986; M.F.A. in playwriting, 1993. **Family:** Three children. **Career:** Graduate instructor, University of Iowa, 1991-1993; playwright-in-residence, Illinois State University, Norman, Illinois, fall, 1994; guest speaker, Yale University, 1994; invited speaker, Grinnell College, 1995. **Awards:** Eugene O'Neill National Playwright's festival, 1989; *The Nation's* Discovery award for poetry, 1990; Jane Chamber's student playwriting award, 1992; winner, National Poetry competition, 1993; British national Poetry competition, 1994; Mobil playwriting award, 1994; Susan Smith Blackburn award, 1995, 1996; AT&T award for new plays, 1996; fellowship of southern writers Bryan family award for playwriting, 1996; Kesselring prize for drama, 1996; Obie award, for best play, 1997. **Agent:** U.S. agent: Joyce Ketay, 1501 Broadway, Suite 1910, New York, New York 10036, U.S.A; U.K. agent: Rod Hall, AP Watt Ltd., 20 John Street, London WCIN 2DR, England.

PUBLICATIONS

Plays

In the Fields of Aceldama (produced Des Moines, Iowa, 1991).
The War Boys (produced 1993).
The Fish Story. In *Monologues by Women for Women,* edited by T. Haring-Smith, Heinemann Press, 1994.
The Girl Who Fell Through a Hole in Her Sweater, with Bruce McLeod (for children; produced London, 1994).
In the Heart of America (produced London, 1994; New Haven, Connecticut, 1994). In *Staging Gay Lives: An Anthology of Gay Male Theater,* edited by John Clum, Boulder, Colorado, Westview Press, 1995; in *American Theater,* March 1995.
Slaughter City (produced Norman, Illinois, 1994; London, 1996). London, Faber and Faber, 1996.
One Flea Spare (produced London, 1995; New York, 1997). New York, Broadway Play Publishing, 1997.
Birdy (produced London, 1996; Philadelphia, 1998). London, Faber and Faber, 1997.
Collected Plays. New York, Broadway Play Publishers, 1997.
The Trestle at Pope Lick Creek (produced Louisville, 1998).

Screenplay: *Lawn Dogs,* 1998.

Poetry

To Dance a Stony Field. Calstock, Cornwall, Peterloo Poets Press, 1995.

*

Critical Studies: "Forging Links" by John Istel, in *American Theatre,* March 1995, pp. 26.

* * *

Naomi Wallace's plays use a brutal poetic lyricism and heightened, sometimes surreal, theatricality to expose the complex nexus of sex, race, social class, and politics in postindustrial capitalist society. In her best work, like *One Flea Spare,* set during a seventeenth-century plague, the characters' transcend their roles as depictions of class struggle and power negotiations; their yearnings and passions startle audiences and induce an uneasy empathy. The characters in efforts like *The War Boys,* in which three men prowl the Mexican border for illegal immigrants and play macho games, seem heavy-handed, groaning noisily under the symbolic freight with which they are laden.

American audiences' discomfort with overtly political drama may partly explain why, like her friend and mentor, Tony Kushner, Wallace has had most of her plays first produced in Britain—and has received greater critical acclaim there. Few other contemporary American dramatists, besides Kushner, match Wallace's marriage of poeticism and politics (other influences would have to include Brecht and Edward Bond). Her plays are structurally adventurous, with characters jumping around in time. The panoramic *In the Heart of America* centers on an Arab-American woman's search for the fate of her gay brother in the military during the Gulf War, but the cast includes Lue Ming, the ghost of a Vietnamese victim of the My Lai massacre destined to haunt all American "conflicts" in her search for Lt. Calley. *Slaughter City,* a play set in a Louisville, Kentucky, slaughterhouse, has characters from the industrial past mingle with the contemporary American workers—Cod claims his mother died in the Triangle Shirtwaist Factory fire and a sausage grinder symbolizes industrialists through the ages. Wallace uses this fluidity of time to suggest that the exploitation of labor—for war or capitalist gain—is grounded in historical circumstances that transcend any present-day conflagration. Likewise, her dialogue often will jump styles within a play and move from gritty naturalism to heightened poetic outbursts, stylized song, or the occasional archaic usage. The playwright requests a design scheme to match in almost all of her playscripts; she recommends a minimal setting that should in no way be "realistic."

Within these fluid structures, Wallace, a published poet, often creates startling, haunting stage images to embody her themes: in *The Trestle at Pope Lick Creek,* a mother's hands are permanently died blue from working in a china plate factory; in *One Flea Spare,* the quarantined child Morse trades an orange for a favor and tosses it into the air as the lights black out to end the play. More often, the images find vibrancy in the very viscera of the human body. Although most obvious in *Slaughter City,* in all of Wallace's plays the characters' bodies bleed, piss, and pus—victimized by the twin evils of war and oppressive industrialization.

Yet Wallace's plays are all love stories at heart, revealing her fascination with how the human body can experience both exquisite desire and acute pain. Her characters literally eviscerate or penetrate one another in paroxysms of lust, love, or disgust. A Gulf War soldier from *In the Heart of America* recalls stepping into the ribcage of an enemy infantryman and proclaiming, "Hey, boys, now I'm really standing in Iraq." In *One Flea Spare,* the aristocratic Mrs. Snelgrave rediscovers her sensuality thanks to a scurvy sailor with whom she's been quarantined; their foreplay includes a moment when she squiggles her fingers in his festering wound. Likewise, in *The Trestle at Pope Lick Creek,* a tragic tale of teenage love set during the end of the Great Depression in rural America, the eccentric teen Pace recalls her father sticking her hand in a bucket of frogs. Later, a character claims, "The only way to love someone is to kill them." In *One Flea Spare,* that is just what the young girl Morse does: following the orders of Mrs. Snelgrave, who has become a kind of foster mother to the orphan, the girl plunges a knife into the woman's heart. In Wallace's stage adaptation of William Wharton's novel *Birdy,* Al feeds his psychotic would-be feather friend by chewing food and regurgitating it into his mouth.

Wallace mines humanity's inability to escape their own physicality, no matter how heightened the poetry or brutal the battle. The playwright, while puncturing the myth that America is a classless society and delineating the toll industrialization takes on our bodies, reminds us that our common genetic code can be found in the armpit and the groin as well as in the heart.

—John Istel

WANDOR, Michelene (Dinah)

Nationality: British. **Born:** London, 20 April 1940. **Education:** Chingford Secondary Modern School, 1954-56, and Chingford County High School, 1956-59, both Essex; Newnham College, Cambridge, 1959-62, B.A. (honors) in English 1962; University of Essex, Colchester, 1974-75, M.A. in sociology 1975; Trinity College of Music, degree in Renaissance and Baroque music. **Family:** Married the literary agent Ed Victor in 1963 (divorced 1975); two sons. **Career:** Poetry editor, *Time Out* magazine, London, 1971-82; regular contributor, *Spare Rib* magazine, London, 1972-77; reviewer, *Plays and Players*, *Listener*, and *New Statesman*, all London; presenter *Kaleidoscope* programme, BBC Radio, and *Spirit of the Age,* early music programme. Playwright-in-residence, University of Kent, Canterbury, 1982-83. **Awards:** Arts Council bursary, 1974, 1983; Emmy award, 1987. **Address:** 71 Belsize Lane, London NW3 5AU, England.

Publications

Plays

You Too Can Be Ticklish (produced London, 1971).
Brag-a-Fruit (produced London, 1971).
The Day after Yesterday (produced London, 1972).
Spilt Milk, and Mal de Mère in *Point 101* (produced London, 1972). Published in *Play Nine*, edited Robin Rook, London, Arnold, 1981.
To Die among Friends (includes *Mal de Mère*, *Joey*, *Christmas*, *Pearls*, *Swallows*) (produced London, 1974). Included in *Sink Songs*, 1975.
Friends and Strangers (produced on tour, 1974).
Sink Songs, with Dinah Brooke. London, Playbooks, 1975.
Penthesilia, adaptation of the play by Heinrich von Kleist (produced London, 1977).
The Old Wives' Tale (produced London, 1977). Included in *Five Plays*, 1984.
Care and Control (produced London, 1977). Published in *Strike While the Iron Is Hot*, edited by Wandor, London, Journeyman Press, 1980.
Floorshow, with others (produced London, 1978).
Whores d'Oeuvres (produced London, 1978). Included in *Five Plays*, 1984.
Scissors (produced London, 1978). Included in *Five Plays,* 1984.
Aid Thy Neighbour (produced London, 1978). Included in *Five Plays*, 1984.
Correspondence (broadcast 1978; produced London, 1979).
Aurora Leigh, adaptation of the poem by Elizabeth Barrett Browning (produced London, 1979). Published in *Plays by Women 1,* edited by Wandor, London, Methuen, 1982.
Future Perfect, with Steve Gooch and Paul Thompson (produced on tour, 1980).
The Blind Goddess, adaptation of a play by Ernst Toller (produced on tour, 1981).
Five Plays (includes *To Die among Friends*, *The Old Wives' Tale*, *Whores d'Oeuvres*, *Scissors*, *Aid Thy Neighbour*). London, Journeyman Press, 1984; New York, Riverrun Press, 1985.
The Wandering Jew, with Mike Alfreds, adaptation of a novel by Eugène Sue (produced London, 1987). London, Methuen, 1987.
Wanted (produced London, 1988). London, Playbooks, 1988.

Radio Plays and Serials: *Correspondence*, 1978; *The Unlit Lamp*, from the novel by Radclyffe Hall, 1980; *Precious Bane*, from the novel by Mary Webb, 1981; *Lolly Willowes*, from the novel by Sylvia Townsend Warner, 1983; *An Uncommon Love*, 1984; *Kipps*, from the novel by H.G. Wells, 1984; *Venus Smiles*, from the story by J.G. Ballard, 1985; *The Brothers Karamazov*, from a novel by Dostoevsky, 1986; *The Nine Tailors*, from the novel by Dorothy L. Sayers, 1986; *Persuasion*, from the novel by Jane Austen, 1986-87; *Helbeck of Bannisdale*, from the novel by Mrs. Humphry Ward, 1987; *Gardens of Eden*, 1987; *Whose Body?*, from the novel by Dorothy L. Sayers, 1987; *The Dwelling Place*, from the novel by Catherine Cookson, 1988; *Frenchman's Creek*, from the novel by Daphne du Maurier, 1989; *Ben Venga Maggio*, 1990; *The Courtier, the Prince and the Lady*, 1990; *The Mill on the Floss*, from the novel by George Eliot, 1991; *A Summer Wedding*, 1991; *Killing Orders*, from the novel by Sara Paretsky, 1991; *A Question of Courage*, from the novel by Marjorie Darke, 1992; *The King's General*, from the novel by Daphne du Maurier, 1992; *Deadlock*, from the novel by Sara Paretsky, 1993; *Jane Eyre,* from the novel by Charlotte Bronte, 1994; *The Jungle Book,* from the stories of Rudyard Kipling, 1995; *The Piano,* from the book of the film, 1995; *Pride and Prejudice,* from the novel by Jane Austen, 1996; *Body of Glass,* from the novel by Marge Piercy, 1996; *The Castle of Otranto,* from the novel by Horace Walpole, 1996; *Ethan Frome,* from the novel by Edith Wharton, 1997; *The Queen of Spades,* from the novel by Pushkin, 1997; *The Moonstone,* from the novel by Wilkie Collins, 1998.

Television Plays: *The Belle of Amherst*, from the play by William Luce, 1987; *The Story of an Hour*, adaptation of a story by Kate Chopin, 1988.

Novel

Arky Types, with Sara Maitland. London, Methuen, 1987.

Short Stories

Tales I Tell My Mother, with others. London, Journeyman Press, 1978; Boston, South End Press, 1980.
Guests in the Body. London, Virago Press, 1986.
More Tales I Tell My Mother, with others. London, Journeyman Press, 1987.

Poetry

Upbeat: Poems and Stories. London, Journeyman Press, 1982; New York, Riverrun Press, 1985.
Touch Papers, with Judith Kazantzis and Michèle Roberts. London, Allison and Busby, 1982.
Gardens of Eden: Poems for Eve and Lilith. London, Journeyman Press, 1984; New York, Riverrun Press, 1985.
Gardens of Eden: Selected Poems. London, Random Century, 1990.

Other

The Great Divide: The Sexual Division of Labour; or, Is It Art?, with others. Milton Keynes, Buckinghamshire, Open University Press, 1976.
Understudies: Theatre and Sexual Politics. London, Eyre Methuen, 1981; revised edition, as *Carry On, Understudies*, London, Routledge, 1986.
Look Back in Gender: Sexuality and the Family in Post-1956 British Drama. London, Methuen, 1987.
Wandor on Women Writers: Antonia White, Elizabeth Barrett Browning, Hannah Culwick, Dorothy Richardson, Jean Rhys. London, Journeyman Press, 1988.
Once a Feminist: Stories of a Generation. London, Virago, 1990.

Editor, *The Body Politic: Writings from the Women's Liberation Movement in Britain 1969-1972*. London, Stage 1, 1972.
Editor, with Michèle Roberts, *Cutlasses and Earrings* (poetry anthology). London, Playbooks, 1977.
Editor, *Strike While the Iron Is Hot: Three Plays on Sexual Politics*. London, Journeyman Press, 1980.
Editor, *Plays by Women 1-4*. London, Methuen, 4 vols., 1982-85.
Editor, *On Gender and Writing*. London, Pandora Press, 1983.

*

Critical Studies: "The Personal Is Political: Feminism and the Theatre" by Wandor, in *Dreams and Deconstructions* edited by Sandy Craig, Ambergate, Derbyshire, Amber Lane Press, 1980; *Feminist Theatre* by Helene Keyssar, London, Macmillan, 1984, New York, Grove Press, 1985.

Michelene Wandor comments:

I began writing plays in 1969, when the "fringe" began. I also was writing poetry and theatre reviews. For me the activities of fiction/non-fiction have always been complementary. At that time I became aware of, and developed, socialist and feminist convictions. For about ten years I wrote plays just for the stage, in a variety of forms—social realism, collage, surreal, comedy, abstract: whatever. Since 1979 I have written extensively for radio, a stimulating medium. I have dramatised/transposed a number of texts for radio—a way of working with the voices and styles of other writers that is both exciting and rewarding. I have absolutely no pre-conceived ideas about the appropriateness or otherwise of dramatic form. For me the appropriate form arrives as a combination of content and my approach to it. Having said that, I can also be lured by any subject. I have written a lot of female-centred work and male-centred work, and am always as aware as I can be of the way an inevitable (though variable) gender-bias operates in every drama.

* * *

Michelene Wandor is well known and respected in the United Kingdom and abroad both as a playwright and as a writer of poetry, fiction, and adaptations for radio and television. She is equally well known for her influential writing about theater and culture. In her theater writing, Wandor established her reputation with two key texts: *Understudies* (1986) and *Look Back in Gender* (1987).

As a playwright, Wandor worked in a wide variety of contexts, from her early work with feminist collectives and fringe theater companies to her work for the National Theatre and the BBC. Some of her plays were published in anthologies with playwrights such as Howard Brenton and Frank Marcus, which marked her as one of the most notable "political playwrights" of her generation. She is also one of the few women—along with more mainstream playwrights such as Caryl Churchill, Pam Gems, and Louise Page—who was a part of the watershed of women's alternative theater in the 1970s. She worked with Monstrous Regiment, Mrs. Worthington's Daughters, and Gay Sweatshop as an independent playwright and as a commissioned writer of radio and television drama.

Of all her plays, Wandor is best known for a few early stage plays and for a number of highly successful radio dramas. She attributes the high profile of her radio plays to the fashion in contemporary theater for "conservative" forms, styles, and themes including the current popularity of dramatic adaptations:

> If theatre had not become so conservative so quickly, and if the theatre had retained its early 1970s openness, more of my work would be done in the theatre. Basically, to be successful in the theatre as a woman playwright, you need to have patrons who will bandwagon you. To work well in radio some similar things apply, but I genuinely believe that there are more radio producers whose commitment is to the work rather than to the fashion.

Wandor's comments reflect on the nature of her writing, which is always informed by politics; whether social, cultural, sexual, or personal. Thus it has been Wandor's adaptations that on the whole have best suited the "conservative" trend of theater production. Her best radio work includes *Ben Venga Maggio,* a dramatic poem in the voice of the popular character Columbina that blends spoken language and Italian carnival music (produced in 1990 for Radio 3 and nominated for both a Sony Award and the Prix Italia). Another notable radio play of the same period is *The Courtier, the Prince and the Lady.* The play is set in Renaissance Italy and draws on Machiavelli and Castiglione as source material and incorporates the music of Josquin and his contemporaries (produced in 1990 for Radio 3 and nominated for a Sony Award in 1991). In 1991 Wandor also adapted George Eliot's *The Mill on the Floss* in a five-part dramatization (broadcast on Radio 4). She has since adapted feminist detective stories by Sara Paretsky and some of the writings of Olive Shreiner and Marjorie Darke.

Wandor had considerable success in television drama. She won an international Emmy Award for her adaptation of William Luce's play about the life of Emily Dickinson, *The Belle of Amherst,* which starred Claire Bloom (Channel Four, 1987). In 1988 she wrote a short film adaptation of Kate Chopin's *The Story of an Hour* (broadcast by Thames TV).

Wandor's most characteristic work, however, is found in her own original stage plays. One important contribution to British theater was her scripting, from improvised and group-researched material, of Gay Sweatshop's *Care and Control* in 1977. That play was among the first political theater pieces to address the issue of the state and motherhood. It had a considerable social impact as well as theatrical and critical success, as did *Aid Thy Neighbor*, produced at London's New End Theatre in 1978. The latter play offered a frank treatment of the process of artificial insemination by donor—another crucial issue for contemporary women. In these and many of her other stage plays, Wandor combined her feminist politics and social activism in her writing for the stage. While some of her work could be described with labels such as agitprop or social realism, Wandor would herself be the first to qualify and explain these terms. In fact, analysis of the influence of politics on the theater of the 1970s and '80s is one of the threads running through Wandor's critical writing about the theater. For Wandor, playwriting and political involvement (real and representational) tended to go hand in hand.

Partly for reasons related to the politics (and fashionability) of radio and theater production, Wandor wrote an increasing number of adaptations during the 1980s including *Aurora Leigh*—an adaptation of Elizabeth Barrett Browning's long blank-verse poem—produced by Mrs. Worthington's Daughters in 1979 and revived at the National Theatre in 1981. Her major main stage theater success was also an adaptation, *The Wandering Jew*, cowritten with Mike Alfreds (adapted from Eugène Sue's novel of the same name) and produced at the National Theatre in 1987.

During the late 1980s and early '90s, Wandor's stage plays began to convey more of her own voice. In *Wanted*, for instance, she took an experimental tack in her depiction of a mixed bag of characters (an angel, an unborn being, and the biblical Sarah) all engaged in a witty and topical theatrical representation of the issue of surrogacy. Here, as in her earlier plays *Care and Control* and *Aid Thy Neighbor*, the concern for gender relations and family structure are central. Yet the style of *Wanted* revealed a developmental shift in Wandor's work: a move away from social realism and the structure of adaptations to the refinement of a distinctive personal voice.

—Lizbeth Goodman

WARD, Douglas Turner

Nationality: American. **Born:** Burnside, Louisiana, 5 May 1930. **Education:** Xavier University Preparatory School, New Orleans, 1941-46; Wilberforce University, Ohio, 1946-47; University of Michigan, Ann Arbor, 1947-48; Paul Mann's Actors Workshop, New York, 1955-58. **Family:** Married Diana Hoyt Powell in 1966; one son and one daughter. **Career:** Co-founder, 1967, and artistic director, Negro Ensemble Company, New York. **Awards:** Vernon Rice award, 1966; Obie award 1966, 1970, for acting, 1973; Drama Desk award, for acting, 1970; Boston Theatre Critics Circle award, for directing, 1986. **Agent:** William Morris Agency, 1325 Avenue of the Americas, New York, New York 10019.

PUBLICATIONS

Plays

Happy Ending, and Day of Absence (produced New York, 1965; *Day of Absence* produced Edinburgh, 1987). New York, Dramatists Play Service, 1966; as *Two Plays*, New York, Third Press-Viking Press, 1971.

The Reckoning (produced New York, 1969). New York, Dramatists Play Service, 1970.

Brotherhood (also director: produced New York, 1970). New York, Dramatists Play Service, 1970.

Redeemer, in *Holidays* (produced Louisville, 1979; in *About Heaven and Earth*, also director: produced New York, 1983).

*

Critical Studies: Introduction by Sheila Rush to *Two Plays* by Ward, New York, Third Press-Viking Press, 1971; "A Conversation with Douglas Turner Ward" by AnEta Sewell, in *Literature in Performance: A Journal of Literary and Performing Art* (Chico, California), April 1986, pp. 83-93; *A Critical Overview of Selected Work and Accomplishments of Douglas Turner Ward and Their Impact on American Theatrical Arts* (dissertation) by Clifford Arnold Reed, Detroit, Michigan, Wayne State University, 1987; "A Vanishing Race" by Howard J. Faulkner, in *College Language Association Journal* (Atlanta, Georgia), March 1994, pp. 274-92.

Theatrical Activities:
Director: **Plays**—*Daddy Goodness* by Richard Wright and Louis Sapin, New York, 1968; *Man Better Man* by Errol Hill, New York, 1969; *Contribution* by Ted Shine, New York, 1969; *Brotherhood and Day of Absence*, New York, 1970; *Ride a Black Horse* by John Scott, New York, 1971; *Perry's Mission* by Clarence Young III, New York, 1971; *The River Niger* by Joseph A. Walker, New York, 1972; *A Ballet Behind the Bridge* by Lennox Brown, New York, 1972; *The Great MacDaddy* by Paul Carter Harrison, New York, 1974, 1977; *The First Breeze of Summer* by Leslie Lee, New York, 1975; *Waiting for Mongo* by Silas Jones, New York, 1975; *Livin' Fat* by Judi Ann Mason, New York, 1976; *The Offering* by Gus Edwards, New York, 1977; *The Twilight Dinner* by Lennox Brown, New York, 1978; *The Raft* by John Pepper Clark, New York, 1978; *Black Body Blues* by Gus Edwards, New York, 1978; *Zooman and the Sign* by Charles Fuller, New York, 1980, 1981; *Home* by Samm-Art Williams, New York, 1980; *Weep Not for Me* by Gus Edwards, New York, 1981; *A Soldier's Play* by Charles Fuller, New York, 1981; *The Isle Is Full of Noises* by Derek Walcott, Hartford, Connecticut, 1982; *About Heaven and Earth* by Ward, Julie Jensen, and Ali Wadad, New York, 1983; *Manhattan Made Me* by Gus Edwards, New York, 1983; *District Line* by Joseph A. Walker, 1984; *Ceremonies in Dark Old Men* by Lonne Elder III, New York, 1985; *The War Party* by Leslie Lee, New York, 1986; *Jonah and the Wonder Dog* by Judi Ann Mason, New York, 1986; *Louie and Ophelia* by Gus Edwards, New York, 1986; *We* (includes *Sally* and *Prince*) by Charles Fuller, New York, 1988; *Jonquil* by Charles Fuller, New York, 1990; *Lifetimes on the Streets* by Gus Edwards, New York, 1990.

Actor as Douglas Turner and Douglas Turner Ward: **Plays**—Joe Mott in *The Iceman Cometh* by O'Neill, New York, 1957; Matthew Kumalo in *Lost in the Stars* by Maxwell Anderson, New York; Moving Man, then Walter Younger, in *A Raisin in the Sun* by Lorraine Hansberry, New York, 1959, then tour, 1960-61; Archibald in *The Blacks* by Jean Genet, New York, 1961; Porter in *Pullman Car Hiawatha* by Thornton Wilder, New York, 1962; understudied Fredericks in *One Flew over the Cuckoo's Nest* by Dale Wasserman, New York, 1963; Zachariah Pieterson in *The Blood Knot* by Athol Fugard, New York, 1964 and tour; Fitzroy in *Rich Little Rich Girl* by Hugh Wheeler, Philadelphia, 1964; Roman Citizen in *Coriolanus*, New York, 1965; Arthur in *Happy Ending*, New York, 1965; Mayor and Clan in *Day of Absence*, New York, 1965; with the Negro Ensemble Company, New York—Oba Danlola in *Kongi's Harvest* by Wole Soyinka, 1968, in *Summer of the Seventeenth Doll* by Ray Lawler, 1968, Thomas in *Daddy Goodness* by Richard Wright and Louis Sapin, 1968, Russell B. Parker in *Ceremonies in Dark Old Men* by Lonne Elder III, 1969, 1985, Scar in *The Reckoning*, 1969, Black Man and Asura in *The Harangues* by Joseph A. Walker, 1969, in *Frederick Douglass Through His Own Words*, 1972, Johnny Williams in *The River Niger* by Joseph A. Walker, 1972, Harper Edwards in *The First Breeze of Summer* by Leslie Lee, 1975, Mingo Saunders in *The Brownsville Raid* by Charles Fuller, 1976, Bob Tyrone in *The Offering* by Gus Edwards, 1977, Fletcher in *Black Body Blues* by Gus Edwards, 1978, Flick in *The Michigan* by Dan Owens, 1979, Technical Sergeant Vernon C. Waters in *A Soldier's Play* by Charles Fuller, Edinburgh, 1984, Jonah Howard in *Jonah and the Wonder Dog* by Judi Ann Mason, 1986, and Louie in *Louie and Ophelia* by Gus Edwards, 1986; Papa in *This Isle Is Full of Noises* by Derek Walcott, New Haven, Connecticut, 1982; New Ice Age and New Ice Age II in *Lifetimes on the Streets* by Gus Edwards, New York, 1990.

Douglas Turner Ward comments:

I am a black playwright, of black sensibilities, primarily utilizing the devices of satire, exaggeration, and mordant humor to explore and express themes of contemporary life, particularly as they relate to black survival.

* * *

The black American Douglas Turner Ward is one of those rare individuals who have successfully combined careers as actor, writer, and director. He has twice won Obie Awards for plays he wrote and in which he performed: in 1966 for *Happy Ending* and *Day of Absence*, and in 1970 for *The Reckoning*. In 1967 he became artistic director of the Negro Ensemble Company, an important repertory company that he and actor-director Robert Hooks founded.

Despite his success as an actor, Ward is better known as a dramatist, particularly for his first two plays, *Happy Ending* and *Day of Absence,* which treat satirically the relationships between blacks and whites. The history of these award-winning one-acts is almost as ironic as their subject matter. Although both plays were completed by 1960, Ward could not find a producer until, five years later, Hooks, operating on limited financing, arranged to have them produced at Saint Mark's Theatre.

As *Happy Ending* opens, two black female domestics are lamenting their employer's decision to divorce his promiscuous wife. Their sorrow is interrupted by their dapper nephew, who rebukes them for pitying people who have overworked and underpaid them. This, he informs them, is their chance to escape from domestic labor. They then educate him to the ironies of life. As middle-aged black women with limited formal education—four strikes against them—they can expect only low-paying jobs that will barely provide subsistence. In contrast, as domestic laborers, although they have received little money, they have provided their nephew with fashionable clothes not missed from the employer's wardrobe and with food smuggled from the employer's larder. As the nephew joins in their sorrows, they receive the happy news that the employers have become reconciled.

Day of Absence is a one-act satirical fantasy about the turmoil in a southern city on a day when all blacks disappear. White couples begin to argue as they discover that they have no experience tending the house or caring for their children. The Ku Klux Klan is bitter because, with the black people gone, it no longer has a pretext for existence or victims for its sadistic practices. Elected repeatedly on a campaign of keeping blacks in their places, the mayor proves incompetent to manage the affairs of the town. In the midst of the despair the reappearance of one black reassures the whites that others will return. The play ends, however, with the question of whether the whites have fully learned how much they depend on blacks.

Ward's first full-length play, *The Reckoning,* produced by the Negro Ensemble Company in 1969, focuses on a confrontation between a black pimp and a southern governor. Ward continued his satire in the one-act *Brotherhood,* in which a white husband and wife try to mask their antiblack sentiments from a middle-class black couple whom they have invited to their house. The blacks are not deceived.

In 1966, in an article published in the *New York Times,* Ward adumbrated the need for a predominantly black audience "to readily understand, debate, confirm, or reject the truth or falsity" of the creations of the black playwright. Ward insisted that whenever a black playwright writes for a predominantly white audience—"least equipped to understand his intentions, woefully apathetic or anesthetized to his experience, often prone to distort his purpose"—the writer must restrict himself to the rudimentary reeducation of the audience. Consequently, the playwright has no opportunity to develop artistically. Although he admitted that a black playwright could gain the necessary "theatre of Negro identity" in a black community, Ward saw no possibility for such a theater until there was massive reconstruction of urban ghettos.

Walker's hope of such a black-oriented theater inspired the founding of the Negro Ensemble Company. Its notable successes have included Lonne Elder III's *Ceremonies in Dark Old Men* and Charles Fuller's *A Soldier's Play.*

—Darwin T. Turner

WASSERSTEIN, Wendy

Nationality: American. **Born:** Brooklyn, New York, 18 October 1950. **Education:** Calhoun School, Manhattan; Mount Holyoke College, South Hadley, Massachusetts, B.A. 1971; City College, City University of New York, M.A. 1973; Yale University School of Drama, New Haven, Connecticut, M.F.A. 1976. **Career:** Playwright and actress. Teacher at Columbia University and New York University; member of artistic board of Playwrights Horizons. Lives in New York. **Awards:** Pulitzer prize, 1989; New York Drama Critics Circle award, 1989; Susan Smith Blackburn award, 1989; Tony award, 1989; National Endowment for the Arts grant; Guggenheim grant; Outer Critics Circle award, for *The Sisters Rosensweig,* 1993. **Agent:** Royce Carlton Inc., 866 United Nations Plaza, Suite 4030, New York, New York 10017, U.S.A.

Publications

Plays

Any Woman Can't (produced New Haven, Connecticut, 1973).
Happy Birthday Montpelier Pizz-zazz (produced New Haven, Connecticut, 1974).
When Dinah Shore Ruled the Earth, with Christopher Durang (produced New Haven, Connecticut, 1975).
Uncommon Women and Others (produced New Haven, Connecticut, 1975; New York, 1977; Edinburgh, 1985). New York, Avon, 1979.
Isn't It Romantic (produced New York, 1981; revised version produced New York, 1983). New York, Dramatists Play Service, 1985.
Tender Offer (produced New York, 1983).
The Man in a Case, adaptation of a story by Chekhov, in *Orchards* (produced Urbana, Illinois, 1985; New York, 1986). New York, Knopf, 1986.
Miami, music and lyrics by Bruce Sussman and Jack Feldman (produced New York, 1986).
Smart Women/Brilliant Choices in *Urban Blight* (musical revue), based on an idea by John Tillinger, music by David Shire, lyrics by Richard Maltby, Jr. (produced New York, 1988).
The Heidi Chronicles (produced Seattle, Washington and New York, 1988). New York, Dramatists Play Service, 1990.
The Heidi Chronicles and Other Plays (includes *Uncommon Women and Others, Isn't It Romantic*). San Diego, California, Harcourt Brace, 1990.
The Sisters Rosensweig (produced New York, 1992). New York, Harcourt, 1993.
An American Daughter. New York, Harcourt Brace & Company, 1998.

Television Play: *Uncommon Women and Others*, 1978; *The Sorrows of Gin*, from the story by John Cheever, 1979.

Other

Bachelor Girls (essays). New York, Knopf, 1990.
Pamela's First Musical (for children), illustrated by Andrew Jackness. New York, Hyperion, 1996.

*

Critical Studies: "*The Heidi Chronicles*: The Big Chill of Feminism" by Jan Balakian, in *South Atlantic Review* (Atlanta, Georgia), May 1995, pp. 93-101; "Drama and the Dialogic Imagination: *The Heidi Chronicles* and *Fefu and Her Friends*" by Helene Keyssar, in *Feminist Theatre and Theory*, edited by Helene Keyssar, New York, St. Martin's, 1996; "Wendy Wasserstein and the Crisis of (Jewish) Identity" by Stephen J. Whitfield, in *Daughters of Valor: Contemporary Jewish American Women Writers*, edited by Jay L. Halio and Ben Siegel, Newark, Delaware, University of Delaware Press, 1997; "Women Who Choose: The Theme of Mothering in Selected Dramas" by Becky K. Becker, in *American Drama* (Cincinnati, Ohio), Spring 1997, pp. 43-57; *Wendy Wasserstein: Dramatizing Women, Their Choices and Their Boundaries* by Gail Ciociola, Jefferson, North Carolina, McFarland, 1998.

Theatrical Activities:
Actress: **Play**—In *The Hotel Play* by Wallace Shawn, New York, 1981.

* * *

Identity is the theme in all of Wendy Wasserstein's plays, but it is most fully integrated in her major works—*Uncommon Women and Others, Isn't It Romantic,* and *The Heidi Chronicles*. Wasserstein's commercial success with *The Heidi Chronicles,* which received both the Pulitzer Prize and the Tony Award for best play in 1989, has placed her in the slippery position of championing women's causes and feminist concerns. The playwright, however, is more concerned with genetics than gender and more likely to employ humor than humanism in creating her female characters. Her early works, which are not published, are precursory exercises that explore themes of sexuality, marriage, and relationships through episodic structure, music, and comic caricatures. Male characters are primarily used as foils and are rarely fully developed. Most of Wasserstein's female characters are not traditionally developed either and are often representative of types. What unifies and sustains her dramaturgy is Wasserstein's coy sense of humor, supported by keen observations of everyday life.

Wasserstein uses American rituals as a means to exploit traditional roles. In two early plays, *When Dinah Shore Ruled the Earth* and *Any Woman Can't,* she uses a beauty pageant and a dance audition, respectively, to both exhort and extol the eclectic roles of ambitious females in a male-dominated society. In *Happy Birthday, Montpelier Pizz-zazz* a college party scene is the backdrop for the exploitation of both the stereotypical roles and expectations of college students. The primary issues center around women's options, but the play depends too much on caricature to be taken seriously. *Uncommon Women and Others,* Wasserstein's first major work, makes better use of college rituals as a means to explore both characters and issues.

Uncommon Women and Others is not unique, but it is risky in terms of subject matter. The reunion format of five women who meet in 1978 and then travel back six years to their final year at Mount Holyoke College provides the structure of the all-female play. What makes the play compelling are the concerns that each of the five women has regarding her role in society, both in relation to the others and to herself. There is no real plot that unifies the play and no real ending. A disembodied male voice is heard between each scene reciting extracts from a traditional graduation address. The technique serves to unify the play not only structurally but also thematically, since each excerpt raises issues the women are trying to work through and choices they are facing in the future.

Isn't It Romantic is similar to *Uncommon Women and Others* in terms of episodic structure, the use of music to create mood and exploit ritual, and the use of a disembodied voice, which takes the form of telephone messages from various characters in the play and characters who are not physically present. *Isn't It Romantic* offers a better-developed plot and characters with more dimension, and its theme has the strongest philosophical bent of any Wasserstein work. The play, which benefited from major rewrites after its New York premiere, contains the playwright's best linguistic foreplay of wit and wisdom, stemming from her keen sense of irony and honest portrayal of the two major characters.

The central character, Janie Blumberg, is "a little kooky, a little sweet, a little unconfident." By contrast, her best friend, Harriet

Cornwall, could be "the cover girl on the best working women's magazine." With Janie, her friends, and her parents, along with Harriet and her mother, Wasserstein creates a Chekhovian *Cherry Orchard,* in which the plot is simple and the characters, each of whom is a bit eccentric and lives in his or her own world, discover that each must fulfill his or her own desires and that each must have his or her own dream. Janie grows by recognizing the discrepancies in everyone else's desires. The final tableau shows Janie as she begins to dance to "Isn't It Romantic" while the audience hears the voice of a friend leaving a desperate message on the answering machine. Janie's dancing becomes more confident until she is "dancing beautifully," symbolizing her growth and celebrating an optimistic future.

The final tableau in Wasserstein's most celebrated work, that of Heidi sitting in a rocker singing softly to her adopted child, is in stark contrast to that of Janie's ebullient face and dancing silhouette. Unfortunately, *The Heidi Chronicles* overshadows the merits of *Isn't It Romantic*. The plays are similar, both dealing with a single woman looking for her place in society and in life. Heidi, however, more closely resembles Harriet or Kate from *Uncommon Women and Others*. All are successful in their careers, but all have paid a price for success.

The Heidi Chronicles has won more prizes than any other Wasserstein play. It is not without merit, but it does not live up to its potential as a well-documented play that promises a comparison of "lost women painters" from the sixteenth century to the "lost feminists" of the twentieth century. Heidi, an art historian, opens the play in midlecture in front of a slide screen of a Sofonisba Anguissola painting. The painting and the lecture serve as both a literal and a symbolic framing device. Scenes move in time from 1965 to 1977 and from 1980 to 1989. The play explores Heidi's disillusionment with the women's movement, dramatizing its history at the same time. It raises serious and important issues only to undercut them with a loosely constructed plot and a contrived ending. Homosexuality, single parenting, politics, and art are all subjects that remain unexplored. As the heroine of the play, Heidi has an unusual role in that much of the time she is a spectator. And most of the action is that of encountering and reencountering the various people in her life who have influenced her. The humor is closer to that of television sitcom and lacks the risqué verbiage of *Uncommon Women and Others* or the strong philosophical wit of *Isn't It Romantic*.

Wasserstein's strengths lie in her ability to create characters who laugh at themselves while questioning others. She serves as a role model for women who wish to be successful in the New York theater venue. All of her plays are quirky and interesting and offer strong roles for women.

—Judy Lee Oliva

WEINSTEIN, Arnold

Nationality: American. **Born:** New York City, 10 June 1927. **Education:** Hunter College, New York, B.A. in classics 1951 (Phi Beta Kappa); University of London, 1949-50; Harvard University, Cambridge, Massachusetts, A.M. in comparative literature 1952; University of Florence (Fulbright Fellow), 1958-60. **Military Service:** Served in the United States Navy, 1944-46. **Family:** Married Suzanne Burgess in 1969. **Career:** Visiting lecturer, New York University, 1955-56, and University of Southern California, Los Angeles; United States Information Service Lecturer, Italy, 1958-60; director of Drama Workshop, Wagner College, Staten Island, New York, summers 1964, 1965; visiting professor, Hollins College, Virginia, 1964-65; professor of dramatic literature, New School for Social Research, New York, 1965-66; chair of the department of playwriting, Yale University, New Haven, Connecticut, 1966-69; visiting professor, University of Colorado, Boulder, Summer 1969; chair of the department of drama, Columbia College, Chicago, 1969-70; visiting professor, Southampton College, Southampton, New York, 1978-79, and Columbia University, New York, from 1979. Co-director, with Paul Sills, Second City, and other improvisational groups; director, Free Theatre, Chicago, Actors Studio, New York and Los Angeles, and Rock Theatre and Guerilla Theatre, Los Angeles. **Awards:** Guggenheim fellowship, 1965. **Agent:** Sam Cohn, International Creative Management, 40 West 57th Street, New York, New York 10019. **Address:** Department of English and Comparative Literature, Columbia University, New York, New York 10027, U.S.A.

Publications

Plays

Red Eye of Love (produced New York, 1958). New York, Grove Press, 1962.

White Cap (produced New York, 1960).

Fortuna, music by Francis Thorne, adaptation of a play by Eduardo De Filippo and Armando Curcio (produced New York, 1962).

The Twenty Five Cent White Hat (in *3 x 3*, produced New York, 1962).

Food for Thought: A Play about Food, with Jay and Fran Landesman (produced St. Louis, 1962).

Dynamite Tonite, music by William Bolcom (produced New York, 1963; revised version produced New York, 1964; revised version produced New Haven, Connecticut, 1966). New York, Trio Music, 1964.

Party (produced New York, 1964; revised version, music by Laurence Rosenthal, produced New York, 1976).

They (produced Philadelphia, 1965).

Reg. U.S. Pat. Off., in *Pardon Me, Sir, But Is My Eye Hurting Your Elbow*, edited by Bob Booker and George Foster. New York, Geis, 1968.

Story Theatre (produced New Haven, Connecticut, 1968).

Greatshot, music by William Bolcom (produced New Haven, Connecticut, 1969).

Ovid, music by The True Brethren, adaptation of *Metamorphoses* by Ovid (produced Chicago, 1969; New York, 1971).

Mahagonny, adaptation of the libretto by Brecht, music by Kurt Weill (produced New York, 1970). Excerpts published in *Yale/Theatre* (New Haven, Connecticut), 1969.

The American Revolution, with Paul Sills, music by Tony Greco, lyrics by Weinstein (produced Washington, D.C., 1973).

More Metamorphoses, adaptation of the work by Ovid (produced Spoleto, Italy, 1973).

Gypsy New York (produced New York, 1974).

Lady Liberty's Ice Cream Cone (produced New York, 1974).

Captain Jinks, adaptation of the play by Clyde Fitch, music arranged by William Bolcom (produced New York, 1976).

America More or Less, music by Tony Greco (produced San Francisco, 1976).
Monkey, with Paul Sills (produced New York, 1978).
Stories for Theatre (produced Southampton, New York, 1979).
Casino Paradise, with Thomas Babe, music by William Bolcom (produced Philadelphia, 1990).

Improvisational Material: *Second City*, New York, 1963-64.

Television Plays: *Improvisation*; *The Last Ingredient*, music by David Amram.

Poetry

Different Poems by the Same Author. Rome, United States Information Service, 1960.

Recording: lyrics for *Black Max: Cabaret Songs*, music by William Bolcom, RCA, 1985.

*

Manuscript Collection: Yale University, New Haven, Connecticut.

Critical Studies: *American Drama since World War II*, New York, Harcourt Brace, 1962, and *The Jumping-Off Place*, Harcourt Brace, 1969, both by Gerald Weales; *A Theatre Divided*, Boston, Little Brown, 1967, and *Opening Nights*, New York, Putnam, 1969, both by Martin Gottfried; *Common and Uncommon Masks* by Richard Gilman, New York, Random House, 1971.

Theatrical Activities:
Director: **Plays**—*Second City* (co-director, with Paul Sills), and other improvisational groups; his own and other plays at the Free Theatre, Chicago, Actors Studio, New York and Los Angeles, and the Rock Theatre and the Guerilla Theatre, Los Angeles; *A Memory of Two Mondays* by Arthur Miller, Southampton, New York, 1979; *The White House Murder Case* by Jules Feiffer, New York, 1980.

Arnold Weinstein comments:
I try to write the history and mythology of today. The schoolroom, the churchroom, the theatre are one, or all are lost. Drama and karma are one. Look them up. Look them up and down. The audience is half the action, the actors the other half; the author starts the fight. Power. The passing of power. It really is life there in the dark, here. The lightning of television terrifies most. Right in the word the intrusion of fear—fear of loss of control, loss of sale, loss of sorcery. Loss of power. Our fear sends us through the channels, puts us on our tracks. If the trinity does not control the power, what's left? Only everything. Everything running around in formless rampant ranks waiting for daring brutes to pick up the wire reins.

* * *

The generation of American playwrights that followed Arthur Miller and Tennessee Williams was a troubled one, reflecting a country that was emerging from a history of brute domination into a future of questions and complexities. These playwrights were similarly trapped between the theater styles and values of an outgoing past and the uncertainty of a fast-approaching future. Such writers as Jack Gelber and Jack Richardson never fulfilled their early promise, but Arnold Weinstein's inability to find himself as a playwright is perhaps the most painful, for he is the most artistic, talented, and original of the lot. But he has been hurt by a combination of critical rejection and changing taste, and although he is the author of charming plays and librettos, his career seems frustrated.

Weinstein's New York professional debut was a production by the Living Theatre of *Red Eye of Love,* which remains his best-known full-length play. At the time the Living Theatre was in its Brecht stage and so was Weinstein, who was to prove too affected by changing fashion and too insecure in his own style. The play is a romantic fable about American capitalism. Its hero is a toy inventor in love with a girl who feels it her "duty to marry money." She turns to the owner of a 13-story meat market, which grows beyond 40 stories as the play progresses. The girl vacillates between the inventor (artist) and the butcher (capitalist), while the play does vaudeville turns to Joycean word games with a whimsicality that would prove a Weinstein signature. The author's stage energy, his antic humor, his feel for America, and his deep love of cheap sentiment are established as they would persist throughout his subsequent work, but the play is too often precious and almost blatantly Brechtian.

In 1962 Weinstein wrote the libretto for *Fortuna,* an off-Broadway musical of inspired zaniness. (One of America's rare playwrights to appreciate their artistic value, he was to become involved with many musical projects, but although several were planned, none reached Broadway.) *Fortuna,* adapted from an Italian comedy, tells of the impoverished and luckless title character who inherits a fortune on the condition that he have no sons. After a series of farcical complications, Fortuna gets his fortune. Once again, Weinstein deals with a Schweikian hero-victim, another indication that expressionist and absurdist influences would for too long influence his work and keep him from self-discovery.

Weinstein's one-act absurdist play, *The Twenty Five Cent White Hat,* opened and closed off-Broadway, unappreciated by New York's critics. Although the play was a trite plea for the importance of individuality, it was filled with Weinstein's lively and poetic comic writing.

The turning point in the playwright's career came with *Dynamite Tonite,* a "comic opera for actors" written with composer William Bolcom. Although not without relation to Brecht, the work had a brisk originality of its own. For though it was a legitimate opera, it was indeed written for actors, that is, for nonsingers. Weinstein's libretto was intensely pacifist, yet it was romantic and comic and tender and suffused with affection for a vulnerable mankind. Its operetta-style hero and heroine sang hilarious Wagnerian parodies in counterpoint to flat-footed soldiers doing soft-shoe dances. Set as the work was on the battleground of a never-never land, it had an odd mixture of expressionism and Americana that somehow worked.

Dynamite Tonite is a superb theater work, but it was so brutally criticized that it closed on its first night. Several attempts were made to revive it, first by the Repertory Theatre at Yale Drama School and once more off-Broadway, but it seemed doomed to rejection despite, or perhaps because of, its artistic superiority.

Greatshot, another musical work with Bolcom and also produced at Yale, was in the style of the then popular self-creative companies, such as Weinstein's friends at the Living Theatre had developed, but there was no soul or clarity of intention to the work. The structured, verbal theater to which the playwright naturally inclined did not mesh with the physical, improvisational, antiverbal theater he was emulating.

Meanwhile, Weinstein long had been preparing a new translation of the great Brecht-Weill opera *Mahagonny.* When after many years of effort it was finally produced, the work proved mediocre, although it was hardly showcased by the disastrous production.

Weinstein's history, then, is one of victimization by the American theater's commercialism, which leaves little room for so creative, artistic, and poetic a playwright. It is a victimization by British-American theater generally, with its overwhelming sense of trends. (Absurdism, for example, once hailed as the style for moderns, was obsolete after no more than five years of fashion.) And it is a victimization by rejection.

—Martin Gottfried

WELLER, Michael

Nationality: American. **Born:** New York City, 26 September 1942. **Education:** Stockbridge School; Windham College; Brandeis University, Waltham, Massachusetts, B.A. in music 1965; Manchester University, Lancashire. **Awards:** Creative Artists Public Service grant, 1976. **Agent:** Joyce Ketay, 1501 Broadway, Suite 1908, New York, New York 10036, U.S.A. **Address:** 215 East 5th Street, New York, New York 10003, U.S.A.

Publications

Plays

Cello Days at Dixon's Palace (produced Cambridge, Massachusetts, 1965).

Fred, music by Weller, adaptation of the novel *Malcolm* by James Purdy (produced Waltham, Massachusetts, 1965).

How Ho-Ho Rose and Fell in Seven Short Scenes, music by Weller (produced Manchester, 1966; London, 1972).

The Making of Theodore Thomas, Citizen, adaptation of the play *Johnny Johnson* by Paul Green (produced London, 1968).

Happy Valley (produced Edinburgh, 1969).

The Bodybuilders, and Now There's Just the Three of Us (produced London, 1969). With *Tira Tells Everything There Is to Know about Herself*, 1972; in *Off-Broadway Plays 2*, London, Penguin, 1972.

Poison Come Poison (produced London, 1970).

Cancer (produced London, 1970). London, Faber, 1971; as *Moonchildren* (produced Washington, D.C., 1971; New York, 1972), New York, French, 1971.

Grant's Movie (produced London, 1971). With *Tira*, London, Faber, 1972.

Tira Tells Everything There Is to Know about Herself (produced London, 1971). With *The Bodybuilders*, 1972; as *Tira* (produced New York, 1975), with *Grant's Movie*, London, Faber, 1972.

The Bodybuilders, and Tira Tells Everything There Is to Know about Herself. New York, Dramatists Play Service, 1972.

More Than You Deserve, music by Jim Steinman, lyrics by Weller and Steinman (produced New York, 1973).

Twenty-Three Years Later (produced Los Angeles, 1973).

Fishing (produced New York, 1975; London, 1976). New York, French, 1975.

Alice, in *After Calcutta* (produced London, 1976).

Split (one-act version; produced London, 1977; New York, 1978). New York, French, 1979; *as Abroad* in *Split* (full-length version), 1981.

Loose Ends (produced Washington, D.C., and New York, 1979; London, 1981). New York, French, 1980.

Barbarians, with Kitty Hunter Blair and Jeremy Brooks, adaptation of a play by Gorky (produced New York, 1980). New York, French, 1982.

Dwarfman, Master of a Million Shapes (produced Chicago, 1981).

At Home (produced London, 1981). Included in *Split* (full-length version), 1981.

Split (full-length version; includes *At Home* [*Split*, part 1] and *Abroad* [*Split*, part 2]. New York, French, 1981.

The Ballad of Soapy Smith (produced Seattle, 1983; New York, 1984). New York, French, 1985.

Ghost on Fire (produced La Jolla, California, 1985; New York, 1998). New York, Grove Press, 1987; New York, French, 1998.

A Dopey Fairy Tale, adaptation of a story by Chekhov, in *Orchards* (produced Urbana, Illinois, 1985; New York, 1986). New York, Knopf, 1986.

Spoils of War (produced New York, 1988). New York, French, 1989.

Lake No Bottom (produced New York, 1989). New York, French, 1990.

Buying Time (produced Los Angeles, 1993).

Help! (produced Cincinnati, 1994).

Dogbrain (for young audiences; produced Louisville, 1996).

The Heart of Art (produced Boston, 1997).

Momentum (unproduced); 1997.

Five Plays (includes *Moonchildren*, *Fishing*, *At Home*, *Abroad*, *Loose Ends*). New York, Theatre Communications Group, 1998.

What the Night Is For (unproduced); 1998.

Screenplays: *Hair*, 1979; Ragtime, 1982; *Lost Angels*, 1989; *God Bless You Mr. Rosewater*, 1991; *Spoils of War,* 1992; *Getting Rid of Alex,* 1993; *The 16 Pleasures,* 1996; *In the Blue Light of African Dreams,* 1998.

*

Theatrical Activities:
Actor: **Play**—Star-Man in *The Tooth of Crime* by Sam Shepard, London, 1972.

* * *

Chronicling his own generation, Michael Weller has sent interim reports from the frontlines of bourgeois American youth as students moved from universities into communes, from the city to the country, and from idealism to Madison Avenue competitiveness. Whatever the surrounding environment, his basic concern has been with personal relationships and their vulnerability.

Many of Weller's early plays were introduced to London by the American expatriate Charles Marowitz of the Open Space Theatre, and Weller had an English reputation before he had an

American one, despite earning his first production while ne was still a student at Brandeis University. His plays generally appeared in a kind of hyperventilating realism that matched the extremes of emotion afflicting his characters without detailing too completely their day-to-day existence.

Weller's first play to have a genuine transatlantic impact was the very specifically American drama that was called *Cancer* when it had its premiere at London's Royal Court Theatre. Cancer is, of course, an astrological sign as well as a disease, and the play was retitled *Moonchildren* for its first American performance at Arena Stage in Washington D.C. Although written and first produced in 1970, there was something nostalgic and historical in its portrait of a group of college students sharing an apartment during the heady days of resistance to President Nixon and the war in Vietnam.

Perhaps Weller drew the battle lines too clearly, placing his young people in a sort of drug-armed camp that opposed the adult society represented by police, landlords, and relatives. The sharp details of the young people's conversational exchanges spoke well for his dramatist's ear, however, and there was an optimism in his writing suggesting that goodwill, high spirits, and visionary certitude would break down the barriers between police and students. It was an idea that grew sour in the later plays, where the broken barriers more often represented a capitulation of idealism. What balanced the comical anarchy in *Cancer* was finally the familial call across generations, the news given to one boy that his mother was dying of cancer—actually, painfully, and beyond the relief of metaphor.

Grant's Movie followed *Cancer* almost immediately and drew harsher lines between the generations. Police and antiwar demonstrators have come to serious violence, and a policeman is kidnapped by three peace-seeking hippies who believe that the man might have murdered the brother of a friend during a demonstration. The friend is Grant, and the torment planned for the policeman is according to his script. Everybody is in Grant's movie.

Weller's next leap was *Fishing,* a review of the hippie alternative as it appeared in 1975. It was a play that came to be seen as the second part of an extended trilogy that began with *Cancer.* Three dropouts are discovered in a backwater of the Pacific Northwest, short on cannabis and cash and exploring a new fantasy of beginning a commercial fishery, if they can raise $1,500 to buy a boat. In the course of the play real death again enters the fable when the man who was selling the boat dies and when the chicken that was becoming a pet is killed, plucked for eating, and pulled apart in rage. Another death is flirted with when one of the three plans suicide on his motorcycle before changing his mind in favor of the fishing: "Oh you're right, it's a dumb idea, no doubt about it. You and me. Two of the finest minds of our generation. But it's something to do. And, you know, if we approach it just the right way, after a while, if we manage to stick to it, and we don't get seasick and we do catch fish we might find there's a good reason for doing it."

Weller's ear for dialogue had become more acute by then, and the acid wit was refined, but the play that best represented his developing perspective was *Loose Ends,* his 1979 report on the progress of the alternative society of the 1960s. It was panoramic in intention, first evoking an accidental meeting on the hippie road to paradise when a young couple come together on a beach in Bali, he returning to the United States from a depressing tour in the Peace Corps and she on her way to enlightenment in India. Weller's comedy and optimism survive his story of the relationship, which stretches forward from 1970 across the decade of Vietnam, Watergate, and disillusion.

With the panoramic structure of *Loose Ends,* Weller constructed a play consisting entirely of dramatic touch points. The form remained realistic, but every meeting was a contrast to what had gone before. What would have been a gradual evolution of a dropout into a hip property speculator becomes a comical commentary as the woodsman becomes a long-haired man in a business suit. Gurus and passing fashions are recorded for their worth and then brushed aside while the original couple fall into competition with each other, rejecting and then courting financial success. Their path is to divorce rather than seek enlightenment, and although their careers remain on the edge of art, in photography and filmmaking, the world is busy overcoming their ideals.

With *Cancer* and *Fishing, Loose Ends* forms a rounded trilogy of reportage, and the plays make a dramatic document of value. Weller remains a writer for the theater, contributing new, short pieces such as *Split* and important longer works such as *Ghost on Fire* and *Spoils of War.* With adaptations for the cinema, such as his screenplay for E. L. Doctorow's *Ragtime,* his reputation has also grown elsewhere.

—Ned Chaillet

WELLMAN, Mac (John McDowell)

Nationality: American. **Born:** Cleveland, Ohio, 7 March 1945. **Education:** University School, Shaker Heights, Ohio, graduated 1963; School of International Service, American University, Washington D.C., B.A. in international relations and organization 1967; University of Wisconsin, Madison, M.A. in English literature 1968. **Career:** Associate professor of English, Montgomery College, Rockville, Maryland, 1969-72; playwright-in-residence, New York University, 1981-82, Yale University School of Drama, New Haven, Connecticut, 1992, and Princeton University, New Jersey, 1992-93; teacher of playwriting, Mentor Playwrights' Project at the Mark Taper Forum, Los Angeles, University of New Mexico, Albuquerque, New York University, Iowa Playwright's Lab, Iowa City, Brown University, Providence, Rhode Island, and New Dramatists, New Voices, Boston, Massachusetts, 1984-92; resident, Bellagio Study and Conference Centre, the Rockefeller Foundation, Bellagio, Italy, 1991; PNM distinguished chair in playwriting, University of New Mexico, Albuquerque, 1991; master artist, Atlantic Center for the Arts, New Smyrna, Florida, 1991. Lives in New York. **Awards:** New York Foundation for the Arts fellowship, 1986, 1990; McKnight fellowship, 1989; Rockefeller fellowship, 1989; Guggenheim fellowship, 1990; National Endowment for the Arts fellowship, 1990, 1995; Obie award, 1990 (three times), 1991; Outer Circle Critics award, 1990; Bessie award, for *7 Blowjobs,* 1992; American Theater Critics Association award, 1992; Commission for the McCarter Theatre, Princeton, 1994; resident at Yaddo, 1995, 1998; Lila Wallace-Reader's Digest Writers' award, 1996; honored in A Horizontal Avalanche: the Mac Wellman Festival, October 1997-March 1998. **Agent:** Wiley Hausam, International Creative Management, 40 West 57th Street, New York, New York 10019, U.S.A.

Publications

Plays

Fama Combinatoria (broadcast 1973; produced Amsterdam, The Netherlands, 1975).
The Memory Theatre of Giordano Bruno (broadcast 1976).
Opera Brevis. San Francisco, Heron Press, 1977.
Starluster (produced New York, 1979). Published in *Wordplays 1*, edited by Bonnie Marranca, New York, Performing Arts Journal Publications, 1980.
Dog in the Manger, adaptation of a play by Lope de Vega (produced New York, 1982).
The Self-Begotten (produced New York, 1982).
Phantomnation, with Constance Congdon and Bennett Cohen, music by James Ragland (produced Mill Valley, California, 1983).
The Professional Frenchman (produced Minneapolis, 1984). Published in *Theatre of Wonders*, edited by Wellman, Los Angeles, Sun and Moon Press, 1985.
Bodacious Flapdoodle (produced Woodstock, 1984; New York, 1985). Auburn, California, Video Research Institute Library, 1987.
Harm's Way, music by Bob Jewett and Jack Maeby (broadcast 1984; produced New York, 1985). New York, Broadway Play Publishing, 1984.
Energumen (produced New York, 1985). Published in *Women with Guns*, edited by Christopher Gould, New York, Broadway Play Publishing, 1986.
The Bad Infinity (produced Minneapolis, 1985). Published in *7 Different Plays*, edited by Wellman, New York, Broadway Play Publishing, 1988; Baltimore, Johns Hopkins University Press, 1994.
1951, with Anne Bogart and Michael Roth (produced San Diego, California and New York, 1986).
The Nain Rouge, music by Michael Roth (produced New York, 1986).
The Distance to the Moon, music by Melissa Shiftlett (produced New York, 1986).
Cleveland (produced New York, 1986). Published in *Short Plays for Young Actors,* edited by Craig Slaight and Jack Sharrar, Lyme, New Hampshire, Smith and Kraus, 1996.
Dracula, adaptation of the novel by Bram Stoker (produced Woodstock, New York, 1987; New York, 1992).
Albanian Softshoe (produced New York, 1988).
Peach Bottom Nuclear Reactor Full of Sleepers (produced New York, 1988).
Cellophane (produced New York, 1988). Hadley, Massachusetts, Playwrights Press, 1988; in *Plays for the End of the Century,* edited by Bonnie Marranca, Johns Hopkins University Press, 1996.
Without Colors, adaptation of *Cosmicomics* by Italo Calvino, music by Melissa Shiftlett (produced Minneapolis, 1989).
Whirligig (produced New York, 1989). Published in *Plays in Process* (New York), vol.10, no.7, 1989.
Bad Penny (produced New York, 1989; London, 1993). Los Angeles, Sun and Moon Press, 1990.
The Ninth World (produced San Diego, California, 1989; New York, 1991).
Terminal Hip (also director: produced New York, 1989;London, 1993). Published in *Performing Arts Journal* (New York), no. 40, 1992.
Crowbar (produced New York, 1990).
Sincerity Forever (produced New York, 1990).
7 Blowjobs (produced San Diego, California, 1991; New York, 1992).Published in *Theater Forum* (New York), no. 1, 1992.
A Murder of Crows (produced Dallas, Texas, 1991; New York, 1992). Published in *Plays in Process* (New York), 1992.
Tallahassee, adaptation of Ovid's *Metamorphoses*, with Len Jenkin, (produced New Smyrna Beach, Florida, 1991; New York, 1995).
Coathanger (produced New Haven, Connecticut, 1992).
Strange Feet (produced Washington, D.C. and New York, 1993).
The Land of Fog and Whistles (produced New York, 1993). Published in *Theater* (New Haven), vol. 24, no. 1, pp. 52-8, March/April 1993.
Three Americanisms (produced New York, 1993; Seattle, 1994). Published in *50: A Celebration of Sun and Moon Classics,* Los Angeles, Sun and Moon Press, 1995.
The Hyacinth Macaw (produced New York and Dallas, 1994).
Why the Y? (In Ybor) (produced Tampa, 1994).
Swoop (produced New York, 1994).
Absence of Mallets, with David Van Tieghem (New York, 1994).
The Sandalwood Box (produced San Francisco, 1994; New York, 1996; with *The Damned Thing,* New York, 1998). Published in *The Best American Short Plays,* edited by Howard Stein and Glenn Young, New York, Applause Books, 1996.
The Land Beyond the Forest: Dracula and Swoop. Los Angeles, Sun and Moon Press, 1995.
London (In 10 Cities) (produced New York, 1996).
Second-Hand Smoke (produced New York, 1996).
The Lesser Magoo (produced Los Angeles, 1997).
*tiger**tiger**tiger* (produced Washington DC, 1995).
Infrared (produced San Francisco and New York, 1996).
Fnu Lnu (produced New York, 1996).
My Old Habit of Returning to Places (produced Los Angeles, 1997).
The Porcupine Man and *Three Other Plays (No Smoking Piece, the Distance to the Moon,* and *Eyes of the Panther;* produced New York, 1998).
I Don't Know Who He Was and I Don't Know What He Said (produced New York, 1998).
The Difficulty of Crossing a Field (produced Waco, Texas, 1998).
Cat's Paw (produced New York, 1998). Published with *The Difficulty of Crossing a Field* in *Theater* (New Haven), vol. 27, nos. 2 &3, pp. 65-137, May 1997.

Radio Plays (all broadcast in The Netherlands): *Nobody*, 1972; *Fama Combinatoria*, 1973; *Mantices*, 1973; *Two Natural Drummers*, 1973; *The Memory Theatre of Giordano Bruno*, 1976; *Harm's Way*, 1984.

Novels

The Fortuneteller. Los Angeles, Sun and Moon Press, 1991.
Annie Salem. Los Angeles, Sun and Moon Press, 1996.

Poetry

In Praise of Secrecy. Washington, D.C., Word Works, 1977.
Satires. Minneapolis, New Rivers Press, 1985.
A Shelf in Woop's Clothing. Los Angeles, Sun and Moon Press, 1990.

Other

Breathing Space: An Anthology of Sound-Text Art. Washington, D.C., Blackbox, 1977.

Editor, *Theatre of Wonders*. Los Angeles, Sun and Moon Press, 1985.
Editor, *7 Different Plays*. New York, Broadway Play Publishing, 1988.
Editor, *Slant Six*. Minneapolis, New Rivers Press, 1990.

*

Critical Studies: "Mac Wellman's Horizontal Avalanches" by Eric Overmyer, in *Theater* (New Haven), Summer/Fall 1990, pp. 54-56; "Seven Avenues Towards the Heart of a Mystery" by Carey Perloff in *Theater* (New Haven), vol. 27, nos. 2 & 3, pp. 61-3, Spring 1997; "Werewolves, Fractals and Forbidden Knowledge: An Interview with Mac Wellman" by Shawn Garrett in *Theater* (New Haven), vol. 27, nos. 2 & 3, pp. 87-95, Spring 1997.

Theatrical Activities:
Director: **Play**—*Terminal Hip*, New York, 1990.

* * *

Mac Wellman is one of the most original, daring, and important playwrights in America. His work is spiky, challenging, fiercely funny, radical in its formal strategies and in its politics, and in every line a rebuke to the timid, dull, stultifying, and sentimental naturalism that still dominates the American theater. Consequently, except for small fringe theaters, his work has rarely been produced outside New York City. It is seldom, if ever, performed on the stages of the straitlaced, mainstream regional theaters. Artistic directors may admire Wellman's work, but few have the courage or recklessness to produce his plays and risk awakening and alienating their slumbering subscription audiences.

Wellman is also a poet and novelist, and he is one of a handful of American playwrights who care about writing, who investigate the possibilities of the American language, whose language is carefully wrought and poetically charged, and whose plays are always in some part, whatever their other concerns, about the American language and hence about American culture and politics. In his disdain for naturalism, his rejection of linear narrative, psychological subtext, and traditional notions of character, his deliberate subversion and mockery of mainstream theatrical convention, and his love of, in his words, "Gritty, dirty, slimy American language when spoken in the theatre," Wellman is colleague and kindred spirit to a group of playwrights who include Len Jenkin, Eric Overmyer, and Jeffrey Jones, writers who are, in Jones's words, "the Huck Finns" of the American theater.

Wellman is also a critic, editor, and teacher, and with these playwrights he has tried to generate a new movement in American playwriting, a movement based in American language and in rebellion against mainstream American playwriting, against the kind of play characterized by the dramaturge James Magruder as "the talking about my problems in your living room kind of play." To this end he has edited two influential anthologies, *Theatre of Wonders* and *7 Different Plays*, and published numerous articles.

Wellman was born and raised in Cleveland, Ohio, and his writing evinces the dry humor and flat twang of his Midwestern roots. This can be seen, for example, in *A Murder of Crows:*

> *Lights up on a pair of boots protruding from a washtub.*
> Nella: That's not Andy. That's dad, and he's dead.
>
> Nella: When the kids were young the sea was normal. Of the logic of the sea my younger one, Susannah, said: It's lucky the shallow end is near the beach.

Wellman's Cleveland background shows in recurring images of toxicity and pollution; the plays are full of poisoned landscapes and poisoned families. It is not surprising that a playwright from Cleveland should be concerned with blight, death, and decay. After all the river that flows through the middle of the city was once so polluted that it caught on fire, a landmark event in the history of the American ecology movement. That image, a burning river of sludge, seems to inform Wellman's work in a pervasive, subterranean way, its smudgy fumes percolating up from the depths of his writing.

> Nella: Not to mention the county dump, where that hellacious grease pit is. The rivers in this part of the state all look like bubble baths, and the air's all mustardy. Even the local ocean's a little oily and waxy. Like a big bowl of custard, wiggly custard.
> Howard: Nella's alright. Only she's never been the same since the avalanche by the . . . grease pit. Landfill or whatever it was. Godawful sludge heap. That ghastly, wolfish slime.

Wellman's concern with blight extends, of course, to the American language "as she is spoke" in the theater. He has attempted to dig himself out from under the avalanche of advertising hype, sentimental clichés, received ideas, politically correct jargon, and sheer mendacity that poison public discourse, tyrannize and terrorize the artist in America, and reduce most American theater to ersatz television. Two of his plays, *7 Blowjobs* and *Sincerity Forever*, are direct responses to the right-wing attack on art and artists in America and to the assault on the National Endowment for the Arts led by the conservative senator from North Carolina, Jesse Helms. Among other things *Sincerity Forever* is about the Ku Klux Klan, and with typically puckish humor Wellman dedicated the play to Senator Helms and sent him a copy. *7 Blowjobs* was inspired by the furor over Robert Mapplethorpe's homoerotic photographs. Both pieces generated considerable public controversy. Ironically, the terrified bureaucrats at the NEA tried to disassociate themselves from *Sincerity Forever*, not wanting the unreliable Wellman as an ally.

Wellman has said that he is interested in "bad language," a term that means nonstandard language and that originated with H. L. Mencken. In a 1992 interview with Allan Havis, Wellman said, "I think there are deep truths about the American psyche that you can understand better by a little of the downside, the dark side of American language. There is a powerful yearning that is present there, a powerful urge for transcendence. A very deep and spiritual side to all Americans that's most evident when we're not being correct grammatically or stylistically, in our use of language."

A typical example of Wellman's bad language, in which he mines American folk talk and twists and forges it into his own idiom, occurs in *A Murder of Crows:*

> Raymond: Crows jerk and juke about and the winds wind up a medley of talkative hacksaws. We edge near the pit, back off and think by baking apple pie we've got the key to the whole shitwagon and maybe we do. Maybe we don't. I'd love to know what the inside of a storm feels like to be one. I really do. But if it were up to me I'd skin the cat with a touch more care, seeing as how the consequences of what passes for luck at gin rummy, poker and horses has a strange way of barking up the wrong tree.

Another of Wellman's principal linguistic strategies is the use of free verse. His lines are broken in such a way and with such care that they acquire a terrific sprung rhythm, a tin-can-tied-to-a-tailpipe sort of clatter, great energy, and unexpected humor. The use of verse also acts as a series of linguistic speed bumps, slowing the headlong hurtle of the actor and the audience as one speaks and the other listens, revitalizing the language, and subverting expectations and assumptions. Much of Wellman's work, for example, *Cellophane*, a long dramatic poem for an ensemble of actors, and *Terminal Hip*, a demented tour de force monologue, is pure language without conventional narrative or action or character. They are tirades from the edge of darkness that harangue an American culture twisted and scarred and maimed by advertising and television and politics.

Wellman's other major works include *Harm's Way*, *The Bad Infinity*, *Crowbar*, and *Bad Penny*. *Harm's Way*, a western (or rather a midwestern), is a meditation on violence, on the language of violence, and on the American culture of violence. Violence is America's original sin, the dark stain on the country's psyche and a subject too little explored in serious nonexploitative endeavors in any medium and almost never in the theater. *Harm's Way* is a dark, brooding meditation on the conquest of the frontier and, by extension, on subsequent American foreign policy. It is an X ray of American myth and history, both official and countercultural. Its hero is a gunfighter named Santouche, a glorified psychopath and serial killer, and the play probes the American penchant for making heroes of such monsters. (This is illustrated by the popularity of Hannibal Lecter in the film *The Silence of the Lambs*.) The play ends with Santouche murdering his woman, a whore named Isle of Mercy, while a crowd of children taunt the gunslinger: "You gonna kill everyone, Mister? You gonna kill everyone, Mister? You gonna kill everyone, Mister?" It is a haunting refrain that evokes the scorched-earth tragedy of Vietnam as well as countless Hollywood movies, both western and contemporary. *Harm's Way* is an American *Woyzcek*.

Wellman's *The Bad Infinity* takes another approach:

> You know the story of Rip
> Van Winkle? Well the true
> story of Rip Van Winkle
> runs as follows: there's
> this old fart who went
> to sleep for twenty years
> and woke up to find
> everything. THE SAME.
> (pause)
> Except him. He was twenty
> years older.
> Was he ever surprised.
> And horrified.
> EXACTLY THE SAME.

> A bad infinity, like most human systems, is a flawed system that replicates itself forever. Historically, the term was used by Hegel to mean a series of logical operations that never reaches a final result or accelerates to another level, a dialectic that never achieves synthesis or transcends itself. In *The Bad Infinity* Wellman explores a number of such systems: geopolitics, fashion, economics, professional sports, crime, international banking, art, criticism, media, and the shopworn conventions of the conventional theater. The American theater is a bad infinity if ever there was one.

Crowbar and *Bad Penny* are site-specific pieces written for En Garde Arts, a New York-based producing organization run by Anne Hamburger that produces such theatrical events. *Crowbar* was written for and produced in the Victory Theatre, an old grande dame of a Broadway house that was reclaimed and refurbished for the event. (The theater, which had fallen on hard times, had long ago been abandoned as a legitimate theater and had become a porno house showing terrifying triple bills at bargain-basement prices.) *Crowbar* used the history of the Victory Theatre as the inspiration for an evocative, ghostly, and ultimately tender and sad piece about the decay of Broadway, the theater, and the city itself—its crime-ridden, derelict, end-of-days condition as a great, hulking, once magnificent but now dangerous ruin.

Bad Penny is one of Wellman's best plays, playful, funny, and exhilarating. Written for and produced at Bow Bridge in Central Park, it is a comic sonata of urban life, alienation, and insanity. A hapless motorist from Big Ugly, Montana, breaks down in the big city and finds himself stranded in the middle of Central Park, surrounded by inspired New York lunacy. *Bad Penny* is spare and taut, and it contains some of Wellman's most inspired writing. The following passage is the monologue that ends the play:

> First Woman: For all things beneath the sky are lovely, except those which are ugly; and these are odious and reprehensible and must be destroyed, must be torn limb from limb howling, to prepare the ritual banquet, the ritual of the Slaughter of Innocents. For the Way is ever difficult to discover in the wilderness of thorns and mirrors and the ways of the righteous are full strange and possess strange hats and feet. For the Way leads over from the Fountains of Bethesda, where the Lord performed certain acts, acts unknown to us, across the Bow Bridge of our human unknowability, pigheadedness, and the wisenheimer attitude problem of our undeserving, slimeball cheesiness; and scuttles into the Ramble, there, of utterly craven, totally lost, desperate and driven incomprehensibility—friend neither to fin, to feather, nor tusk of bat, bird, weasel, porcupine, nor gnat. And we who are not who we are must forever bury the toxic waste of our hidden hates in the dark, plutonic abysm of our human hearts, and be always blessed in the empty promise of the sky that looks down upon us with a smile, a divine smile, even as she crushes us all beneath her silver foot.

Wellman's plays are political in every line. They are not direct. They are oblique and ironic and have multiple, even contradictory, meanings. They are many-faceted. They are dense and extraordinary. In a word they are poetic, theatrical. They are, to use an image from *The Bad Infinity*, like horizontal avalanches. An avalanche of images, language, and ideas moving the viewer from his or her received ideas and assumptions as relentlessly and irresistibly as a wall of mud or a glacier grinding down a canyon. I understand Wellman's plays as I understand poetry, on a deep, cellular level that almost resists reason and explanation. There is much in life that is mysterious, that resists reduction and categorization and simpleminded explanation. Such are Wellman's plays. They are beautiful, subversive, and important works, and they deserve to be more frequently produced and better known.

—Eric Overmyer

WERTENBAKER, (Lael Louisiana) Timberlake

Nationality: British. **Education:** Schools near St. Jean-de-Luz, France; attended university in the United States. **Career:** Journalist in London and New York; teacher of French in Greece, one year. Resident writer, Shared Experience, 1983, and Royal Court Theatre, 1985, both London. Lives in London. **Awards:** Arts Council of Great Britain bursary, 1981, grant, 1983; Thames Television bursary, 1984, 1985; *Plays and Players* award, 1985; *Evening Standard* award, 1988; Olivier award, 1988; Whiting award, 1989; London Theatre Critics Circle award, 1991, 1992; Writers Guild Macallan award, 1992. **Agent:** Michael Imison Playwrights, 28 Almeida Street, London N1 1TD, England.

Publications

Plays

This Is No Place for Tallulah Bankhead (produced London, 1978).
The Third (produced London, 1980).
Second Sentence (produced Brighton, 1980).
Case to Answer (produced London, 1980; Ithaca, New York, 1981).
Breaking Through (produced London, 1980).
New Anatomies (produced London, 1981; New York, 1990). Published in *Plays Introduction*, London, Faber, 1984.
Inside Out (produced Stoke-on-Trent, 1982).
Home Leave (produced Ipswich, Suffolk, 1982).
False Admissions, adaptation of a play by Marivaux (produced London, 1983).
Successful Strategies, adaptation of a play by Marivaux (produced London, 1983).
Abel's Sister, based on material by Yolande Bourcier (produced London, 1984; New York, 1985).
The Grace of Mary Traverse (produced London, 1985). London, Faber, 1985.
Léocadia, adaptation of the play by Jean Anouilh (broadcast 1985). Published in *Five Plays*, by Anouilh, London, Methuen, 1987.
Mephisto, adaptation of the play by Ariane Mnouchkine, based on a novel by Klaus Mann (produced London, 1986).
Our Country's Good, adaptation of *The Playmaker* by Thomas Keneally (produced London, 1988; Los Angeles, 1989; New York, 1991). London, Methuen, 1988; revised edition, 1990.
The Love of the Nightingale (produced Stratford-on-Avon and London, 1988). With *The Grace of Mary Traverse*, London, Faber, 1989.
Pelléas and Mélisande, adaptation of the play by Maeterlinck (broadcast 1988; produced London, 1989).
Three Birds Alighting on a Field (produced London, 1991). London, Faber, 1991.
The Thebans, adaptation of three plays by Sophocles (includes *Oedipus Tyrannos*, *Oedipus at Colonus*, *Antigone*) (produced Stratford-on-Avon and London, 1992).
The Break of Day. London, Faber, 1995.
Plays (includes *New Anatomies*; *The Grace of Mary Traverse*; *Our Country's Good*; *The Love of the Nightingale*; *Three Birds Alighting on a Field*). London, Faber, 1996.

Radio Plays: *Léocadia*, 1985; *La Dispute*, from the play by Marivaux, 1987; *Pelléas and Mélisande*, from the play by Maeterlinck, 1988; *Our Country's Good.*

Television Plays: *Do Not Disturb*, 1991; *The Children*, adaptation of a novel by Edith Wharton, 1992.

*

Critical Studies: "Recasting the Phaedra Syndrome: Myth and Morality in Timberlake Wertenbaker's *The Love of the Nightingale*" by Joe Winston, in *Modern Drama* (Downsview, Ontario), Winter 1995, pp. 510-19; "Timberlake Wertenbaker" by Carla J. McDonough, in *British Playwrights, 1956-1995: A Research and Production Sourcebook*, edited by William W. Demastes, Westport, Connecticut, Greenwood, 1996; "The Play's the Thing: The Metatheatre of Timberlake Wertenbaker" by Christine Dymkowski, in *Drama on Drama: Dimensions of Theatricality on the Contemporary British Stage*, edited by Nicole Boireau, New York, St. Martin's, 1997.

Timberlake Wertenbaker comments:

I like monologues. I think they are an unused and rather beautiful form of communication. I do not like naturalism. I find it boring. My plays are an attempt to get away from the smallness of naturalism, from enclosed rooms to open spaces, and also to get ideas away from the restraints of closed spaces to something wider. My plays often start with a very ordinary question: If women had power, would they behave the same way as men? Why do we seem to want to destroy ourselves? Is the personal more important than the political? If someone has behaved badly all of their lives, can they redeem themselves? Parallel to this will be some story I may have heard, some gossip about somebody, a sentence heard or read. A friend of mine once told me his mother had been taught how to be a good hostess by being made to talk to empty chairs. I used that as the opening scene of *The Grace of Mary Traverse*. I once heard about a young couple where the woman, for no apparant reason, had come out of the bath and shot herself. That became *Case to Answer*. Somebody showed me a print of the Japanese courtesan Ono No Komachi. I wrote a play about her. Everything gets collected and used at some point. I'm sure it's the same for all writers, but I haven't asked. Once I have the idea and the people, I do a lot of research. I think plays should be accurate, whatever their subject. Then the imagination can be let free, but only after a solid knowledge of the world, the people, the age, whatever is the world of the play.

I don't think you can leave the theatre and go out and make a revolution. That's the naivety of the 1970s. But I do think you can make people change, just a little, by forcing them to question something, or by intriguing them, or giving them an image that remains with them. And that little change can lead to bigger changes. That's all you can hope for. Nor do I think playwrights should have the answers. A play is like a trial: it goes before the jury, the audience, and they decide—to like or not like the people, to agree or not to agree. If you really have the answers, you shouldn't be a writer but a politician. And if you're only interested in slice of life, then you should make documentaries. The theatre is a difficult place; it requires an audience to use its imagination. You must accept that and not try to make it easy for them. You must give them language, because it is best heard in the theatre, and language is a potent manifestation of hope. In some theatres in ancient Greece the number of seats corresponded to the number of adult males with voting rights. I think that is right: theatre is for people who take responsibility. There is no point in trying to attract idiots. Theatre should never be used to flatter, but to reveal, which is to disturb.

* * *

There is a wonderful continuity in the work of Timberlake Wertenbaker, which is nonetheless full of surprise, invention, and delight in inversion. It is never possible to predict how she may wish to say something, although familiarity with her work shows themes and preoccupations that are part of her powerful personal identity as a writer. In form and setting, however, her dramas roam freely over historical periods and cultures: from antique Greece to a Japanese story that spans centuries, and from an Australian penal colony to Islamic cross-dressing and the art world of London in the 1990s.

With the worldwide success of her major play *Our Country's Good,* originally performed at London's Royal Court Theatre, Wertenbaker moved from the ranks of the much courted and professionally admired—she is that rarity, a writers' writer who repeatedly demonstrates the potential of dramatic composition—to the genuinely popular. The play came about when the theater's director, Max Stafford-Clark, gave her Thomas Keneally's novel *The Playmaker,* a historical retelling of a production of Farquhar's *The Recruiting Officer* by prisoners at a penal settlement in Australia.

Although it springs from Keneally's novel, *Our Country's Good* is richly original theater in its own right. A densely populated play, it maintains a constant focus on the individuals in the story and finds in the convict population a creative and positive energy that is lacking in the British officers who oppress them. As much as any of her plays, it demonstrates her sure instinct for the theatrical situation, as, for instance, in her development of the character of a woman rehearsing her role despite a sentence of death that will mean her execution before the first performance.

Such skills did not come about overnight, although they seemed to flower spectacularly in the collaborative creative atmosphere of the Royal Court. Before her first four major plays—*The Grace of Mary Traverse, Our Country's Good, The Love of the Nightingale,* and *Three Birds Alighting on a Field*—she had established an intriguing and peculiar body of work. There was individuality and dramatic inversion in even the most straightforward of her plays, such as *Home Leave,* which she wrote about women working in a factory at the end of World War II. Her opening stage directions present her leading character with calculated ambiguity: "She's in overalls, her hair hidden in a cloth cap and it should be impossible to tell she's a woman." Often the tilt of her writing explores a fluidity between the sexes that is far more revolutionary than any declaration of equality, and she does not hesitate to subvert legend or history in her examinations of human nature.

Perhaps the most elaborate statements about the intentions of Wertenbaker's early work appear in her play *Inside Out,* borrowed from the Japanese legend of Komachi, a famous beauty and poet who was doomed to suffer because of the task undertaken by one of her admirers that led to his death. Unable to match the poetic speech of Komachi in his declaration of love, he vowed to return from an arduous journey every night for 100 nights but returned only 99 times. In Wertenbaker's version Komachi first appears as an old woman who has survived into the present and who has become interchangeable with Shosho, the lover. When the story of the love affair is retold, the old woman becomes Shosho, and another actress plays the young Komachi, who first rebuffs him and then, through desire, regrets the delay. Shosho remains steadfast in his promise.

As if that were not enough sexual ambiguity, it is by draping Shosho in her clothes and exchanging roles with him that Komachi extracts the promise of the 100 visits. Because it is by imagining himself as Komachi that Shosho has invented the idea of the poetic action, it is forever unclear who really suggested the task, but what remains equally unclear is the function of gender in Wertenbaker's version of the story. The chorus reports, "They say a woman is a man turned inside out. Most evident in the genitals, his turned out, hers turned in, hers waiting for his, waiting for completion, that's what they say." But while that may be what "they say," it is obvious that Wertenbaker is not convinced. The chorus also asks, "Question: what is the anatomy of a woman?" and is answered by Komachi's companion Li: "Not what you imagine through your genitals."

Another of Wertenbaker's plays, *New Anatomies,* tackles that physical question more directly. It tells the story of Isabelle Eberhardt, a young woman who dresses as a male Arab to find acceptance among the Muslims and, ironically, is persecuted by the French. In her Arab persona as Si Mahmoud she seeks spiritual enlightenment, and although the Arabs have more than a fair idea that she is actually a woman, they befriend her and accept her own determination of her sex. In the stage version, written for a women's theatrical troupe, all of the roles, male and female, are taken by women. The ambiguity is not helpful, for the issue of Isabelle's self-determined sexuality is profound, and the dressing-up of other women undermines both the spiritual search and the intended clash of Western and Oriental cultures. As a text, however, it carefully and provocatively defines its arguments.

As a woman of American heritage, educated in France and resident in Britain, Wertenbaker herself juggles cultures and influences, and in addition to her original work she has made significant contributions to translation from the French, particularly with her translations of Marivaux. His stylish comic knowingness about sexuality and faithlessness has been well reflected in her English versions of *False Admissions, Successful Strategies,* and *La Dispute,* in which she has maintained a cool ironical posture that admirably suggests the French originals. Although she has also provided convincing versions of Jean Anouilh's *Léocadia* and Ariane Mnouchkine's *Mephisto,* it is in Marivaux's writing that her own preoccupations are best reflected.

Ancient Greek is another of Wertenbaker's languages, and her notable plainspoken version of the Oedipus plays of Sophocles—*Oedipus Tyrannos, Oedipus at Colonus,* and *Antigone*—were presented successfully by the Royal Shakespeare Company as *The Thebans*. She has also explored the radicalization of Electra in her short, and relatively minor, *Agamemnon's Daughter,* a reshaping of the *Oresteia* that has not been produced.

Possibly the most straightforward of Wertenbaker's original plays is *Abel's Sister*, written with material provided by Yolande Bourcier. It is, nonetheless, emotionally complex. Although set in the English countryside, the play has some of the mythical aspirations of Sam Shepard's versions of the American family. Sandra, the "spastic" twin sister of Howard, has removed herself from the center where she lives to move in on her brother and his girlfriend. When she announces that her favorite story is Cain and Abel, because it was right that Cain should at least kill the brother who suffocated him, she prepares the way for an attack on her brother by an American neighbor who has been led to believe that Howard is dangerously violent. It is typical of Wertenbaker that she should turn to a biblical source, again inverting the sexes, to explain the motivation of her characters.

Wertenbaker's own most radical historical revision is her dramatic fantasia *The Grace of Mary Traverse,* in which she portrays Lord Gordon, the disaffected peer accused of treason after the destructive Gordon riots of 1780, as a man who discovers power through the impulsive rape of a woman in the streets. In her version of events he is a peripheral character, and the dramatic catalyst is Mary Traverse, a young woman trained only in polite conversation by her father. After witnessing the rape by Gordon, she determines not to be a victim and decides to enter Georgian London as an equal of the rapacious men. She gambles with them, hires a male whore to deflower her, prostitutes herself to her father, and buys the sexual services of a woman for her own pleasure. She, too, finds power a seduction and helps reignite the hatred for Catholics, though the horrors of mass violence finally chill her.

The classicism and cosmopolitan dramaturgy of Wertenbaker's writing seem to mark her out from most of her contemporaries as a writer who deals with the present only through metaphor. Her play for the Royal Shakespeare Company, *The Love of the Nightingale,* reinforced this perception, but when she returned to the Royal Court for *Three Birds Alighting on a Field,* she was to provide one of the most articulate deconstructions of the 1980s to appear on a stage.

Wertenbaker's central characters are Biddy, an English society woman who is ordered by her wealthy Greek husband to become interesting, and Stephen, a painter of English landscapes who has been exiled for a decade in the countryside for being unfashionable. In the original production the play included scenes that retold the parallel story of Philoctetes, the Greek hero abandoned on an island by Odysseus because of the smell of a wound. In order to win the Trojan War, Odysseus needed to trick Philoctetes back into his service, and in order for the gallery owner in Wertenbaker's play to survive the recession of the 1990s, he needs to lure Stephen back into his fold.

When the play was revived by the Royal Court a year after its first production, Wertenbaker dispensed with the enacted scenes of the Philoctetes story and allowed the modern story to stand on its own, secure in its parallels and confident of its own message. Events conspire to remove Biddy from her wealth and the limitations of her class, while she becomes the agent who restores Stephen to the society of art. In the years covered by his exile the world has changed. The ideological certainties of the left and the right have been vanquished by the collapse of Eastern Europe and the Western economies, and Wertenbaker's play is witty, knowing, and eloquent in its depiction of the results.

Even in her most explicitly classical plays, Wertenbaker manages to wear her erudition lightly. What she demonstrates in *Three Birds Alighting on a Field* is the enduring strength of these classical values in the most topical of dramas. With her grasp of classical storytelling, her great gift of language, and her individuality of perception, she has provided some of the most enduring drama of the late twentieth century.

—Ned Chaillet

WESKER, Arnold

Nationality: English. **Born:** Stepney, London, 24 May 1932. **Education:** Upton House Technical School, Hackney, London, 1943-48; London School of Film Technique, 1955-56. **Military Service:** Served in the Royal Air Force, 1950-52. **Family:** Married Doreen Bicker in 1958; two sons and two daughters. **Career:** Furniture-maker's apprentice and carpenter's mate, 1948; bookseller's assistant, 1949 and 1952; plumber's mate, 1952; seed sorter on farm, 1953; kitchen porter, 1953-54; pastry cook, London and Paris, 1954-58; founder and director, Centre 42, 1961-70. Chair of the British Centre, 1978-83, and president of the Playwrights Permanent Committee, 1981-83, International Theatre Institute. Lives in London. **Awards:** Arts Council grant, 1958; *Evening Standard* award, 1959; Encyclopaedia Britannica award, 1959; Marzotto prize, 1964; Best Foreign Play award (Spain), 1979; Goldie award, 1987. Fellow, Royal Society of Literature, 1985. Litt.D.: University of East Anglia, Norwich, 1989; Denison University, Ohio, 1997. Honorary fellowship: Queen Mary College, London, 1995. **Agent:** Jan Morris, Hay-on-Wye, Hereford HR3 5RJ, England.

Publications

Plays

The Wesker Trilogy. London, Cape, 1960; New York, Random House, 1961.

Chicken Soup with Barley (produced Coventry and London, 1958; Cleveland, 1962). Published in *New English Dramatists 1*, London, Penguin, 1959.

Roots (produced Coventry and London, 1959; New York, 1961). London, Penguin, 1959.

I'm Talking about Jerusalem (produced Coventry 1960; revised version produced London, 1960). London, Penguin, 1960.

The Kitchen (produced London, 1959; New York, 1966). Published in *New English Dramatists 2*, London, Penguin, 1960; expanded version (produced Coventry and London, 1961; New York, 1966), London, Cape, 1961; New York, Random House, 1962.

Chips with Everything (produced London, 1962; New York, 1963). London, Cape, 1962; New York, Random House, 1963.

The Nottingham Captain: A Moral for Narrator, Voices and Orchestra, music by Wilfred Josephs and Dave Lee (produced Wellingborough, Northamptonshire, 1962). Included in *Six Sundays in January*, 1971.

Menace (televised 1963). Included in *Six Sundays in January*, 1971; in *The Plays of Arnold Wesker 2*, 1977.

Their Very Own and Golden City (produced Brussels, 1965; revised version produced London, 1966). London, Cape, 1966; revised version (also director: produced Aarhus, Denmark, 1974), in *The Plays of Arnold Wesker 2*, 1977.

The Four Seasons (produced Coventry and London, 1965; New York, 1968). London, Cape, 1966; in *The Plays of Arnold Wesker 2*, 1977; revised version in *The Plays of Arnold Wesker 2*, 1990.

The Friends (also director: produced Stockholm and London, 1970). London, Cape, 1970; in *The Plays of Arnold Wesker 2*, 1977.

The Old Ones (produced London, 1972; New York, 1974). London, Cape, 1973; revised version, edited by Michael Marland, London, Blackie, 1974; in *The Plays of Arnold Wesker 2*, 1977.

The Wedding Feast, adaptation of a story by Dostoevsky (produced Stockholm, 1974; Leeds, 1977; revised version produced Birmingham, 1980). Included in *The Plays of Arnold Wesker 4*, 1980.

The Journalists (produced Coventry, 1977; Los Angeles. 1979). London, Writers and Readers, 1975.

Love Letters on Blue Paper, adaptation of his own story (televised 1976; produced Syracuse, New York, 1977; also director: produced London, 1978; New York, 1984). London, TQ Publications-Writers and Readers, 1978.

The Plays of Arnold Wesker:

1. *The Kitchen, Chips with Everything, The Wesker Trilogy*. New York, Harper, 1976; revised edition as *The Wesker Trilogy* (includes *Chicken Soup with Barley, Roots, I'm Talking About Jerusalem*), London, Penguin, 1979.
2. *The Four Seasons, Their Very Own and Golden City, Menace, The Friends, The Old Ones*. New York, Harper, 1977; revised edition as *The Kitchen and Other Plays* (includes revised version of *The Four Seasons*; *The Kitchen*; *Their Very Own and Golden City*), London, Penguin, 1990.
3. *Chips with Everything, The Friends, The Old Ones, Love Letters on Blue Paper*. London, Penguin, 1980; revised edition as *Chips with Everything and Other Plays*, 1990.
4. *The Journalists, The Wedding Feast, The Merchant*. London, Penguin, 1980; revised edition as *Shylock and Other Plays* (includes *The Journalists, The Wedding Feast, The Merchant* as *Shylock*), 1990.
5. *One Woman Plays*: *Yardsale, Whatever Happened to Betty Lemon?, Four Portraits of Mothers, The Mistress, Annie Wobbler*. London, Penguin, 1989.
6. *Lady Othello and Other Plays*: *One More Ride on the Merry-Go-Round, Caritas, When God Wanted a Son, Lady Othello, Bluey*. London, Penguin, 1990.
7. *Wild Spring and Other Plays* (includes *Badenheim 1939*; *Beorhtel's Hill*; *Three Women Talking*; *Letter to a Daughter*; *Blood Libel*; *Wild Spring*). London, Penguin, n.d.

The Merchant (produced Stockholm, 1976; revised version produced Philadelphia and New York, 1977; revised version produced Birmingham, 1978). Included in *The Plays of Arnold Wesker 4*, 1980; revised version published separately, London, Methuen, 1983; revised version as *Shylock* included in *The Plays of Arnold Wesker 4*, 1990.

Caritas (produced London, 1981). London, Cape, 1981.

Mothers: Four Portraits (produced Tokyo, 1982; as *Four Portraits of Mothers*, produced Edinburgh, 1984; Colorado, 1985; London, 1987). As *Four Portraits of Mothers*, included in *The Plays of Arnold Wesker 5*, 1989.

Annie, Anna, Annabella (broadcast 1983; as *Annie Wobbler*, also director: produced Birmingham and London, 1983; New York, 1986). As *Annie Wobbler*, included in *The Plays of Arnold Wesker 5*, 1989.

Sullied Hand (produced Edinburgh, 1984).

Yardsale (broadcast 1984; produced Edinburgh, 1985; also director: produced London, 1987; New York, 1988. Included in *The Plays of Arnold Wesker 5*, 1989.

Bluey (broadcast 1985). Included in *The Plays of Arnold Wesker 6*, 1990.

One More Ride on the Merry-Go-Round (produced Leicester, 1985). Included in *The Plays of Arnold Wesker 6*, 1990.

Whatever Happened to Betty Lemon? (produced Paris, 1986; also director: produced London, 1987; New York, 1988). Included in *The Plays of Arnold Wesker 5*, 1989.

Little Old Lady (for children; produced Sigtuna, Sweden, 1988). Published in *New Plays 1*, edited by Peter Terson, Oxford, Oxford University Press, 1988.

Beorhtel's Hill (produced Basildon, Essex, 1989).

Shoeshine (for children). Published in *New Plays 3*, edited by Peter Terson, Oxford, Oxford University Press, 1989.

The Mistress (also director: produced Arezzo, Italy, 1991). Included in *The Plays of Arnold Wesker 5*, 1989.

Three Woman Talking (produced Evanston, Illinois, 1992).

Letter to a Daughter (televised in Norway, 1992; produced Seoul, South Korea, 1992).

Circles of Perceptiopn (produced 1996).

Denial (produced 1997).

Screenplay: *The Kitchen*, 1961; *Maudie*, adaption of Doris Lessing novel *The Diary of Jane Somers*.

Radio Plays: *Annie, Anna, Annabella*, 1983 (Germany); *Yardsale*, 1984; *Bluey*, 1985 (Germany).

Television Plays: *Menace*, 1963; *Love Letters on Blue Paper*, from his own story, 1976; *Diary of a Good Neighbour*, adaptation of Doris Lessing's *The Diary of Jane Somers*, 1989; *Letter to a Daughter*, 1992 (Norway).

Short Stories

Love Letters on Blue Paper. London, Cape, 1974; New York, Harper, 1975.

Said the Old Man to the Young Man: Three Stories. London, Cape, 1978.

Love Letters on Blue Paper and Other Stories. London, Penguin, 1980; revised edition, 1990.

Other

Labour and the Arts: II, or, What, Then, Is to be Done? Oxford, Gemini, 1960.

The Modern Playwright; or, "O Mother, Is It Worth It?" Oxford, Gemini, 1961.

Fears of Fragmentation (essays). London, Cape, 1970.

Six Sundays in January (miscellany). London, Cape, 1971.
Say Goodbye—You May Never See Them Again: Scenes from Two East-End Backgrounds, paintings by John Allin. London, Cape, 1974.
Words as Definitions of Experience. London, Writers and Readers, 1976.
Journey into Journalism. London, Writers and Readers, 1977.
Fatlips (for children). London, Writers and Readers, and New York, Harper, 1978.
The Journalists: A Triptych (includes the play *The Journalists, A Journal of the Writing of "The Journalists,"* and *Journey into Journalism*). London, Cape, 1979.
Distinctions (essays, lectures, journalism). London, Cape, 1985.
As Much As I Dare. New York, Random House, 1994.
The BIRTH of Shylock and the DEATH of Zero Mostel (diaries of rehearsals). Quartet Books, 1997.
The King's Daughters (erotic stories). Quartet Books, 1998.

*

Critical Studies: *Mid-Century Drama* by Laurence Kitchin, London, Faber, 1960, revised edition, 1962; *The Writer and Commitment* by John Mander, London, Secker and Warburg, 1961; *Anger and After* by John Russell Taylor, London, Methuen, 1962, revised edition, 1969, as *The Angry Theatre*, New York, Hill and Wang, 1962, revised edition, 1969; "Two Romantics: Arnold Wesker and Harold Pinter" by Clifford Leech, in *Contemporary Theatre*, edited by John Russell Brown and Bernard Harris, London, Arnold, 1962, New York, St. Martin's Press, 1963; *Arnold Wesker* by Harold U. Ribalow, New York, Twayne, 1966; "Arnold Wesker, The Last Humanist?" by Michael Anderson, in *New Theatre Magazine* (Bristol), vol.8, no.3, 1968; *Arnold Wesker* edited by Michael Marland, London, Times Newspapers, 1970; *Arnold Wesker* by Ronald Hayman, London, Heinemann, 1970, revised edition, New York, Ungar, 1973, Heinemann, 1979; *The Plays of Arnold Wesker: An Assessment* by Glenda Leeming and Simon Trussler, London, Gollancz, 1971, and *Arnold Wesker*, London, Longman, 1972, and *Wesker the Playwright*, London, Methuen, 1983, both by Leeming, and *Wesker on File* edited by Leeming, Methuen, 1985; "Production Casebook 2: Arnold Wesker's *The Friends*" by Garry O'Connor, in *Theatre Quarterly* (London), April 1971; *Theatre Language: A Study of Arden, Osborne, Pinter, and Wesker* by John Russell Brown, London, Allen Lane, and New York, Taplinger, 1972; article by Margaret Drabble, in *New Review* (London), February 1975; *Stages in the Revolution* by Catherine Itzin, London, Eyre Methuen, 1980; *Understanding Arnold Wesker* by Robert Wilcher, Columbia, University of South Carolina Press, 1991.

Theatrical Activities:
Director: **Plays**—*The Four Seasons*, Havana, 1968; *The Friends*, Stockholm and London, 1970; *The Old Ones*, Munich, 1973; *Their Very Own and Golden City*, Aarhus, Denmark, 1974; *Love Letters on Blue Paper*, London, 1978, and Oslo, 1980; *Annie Wobbler*, Birmingham and London, 1983, London, 1984; *Yardsale*, Stratford-on-Avon, 1985, London, 1987; *Whatever Happened to Betty Lemon*, London, 1987; *The Merry Wives of Windsor* by Shakespeare, Oslo, Norway, 1990; *The Kitchen*, Madison, Wisconsin, 1990; *The Mistress*, Rome, 1991.

Arnold Wesker comments:

(1982) It is really for others to write about me. I try every so often to explain myself in lectures, articles, interviews. Never satisfactorily. Certain themes and relationships seem to pre-occupy me: the relationship between lovers, husband and wife, parent and child, friends, state and the individual; the themes of injustice, defiance, the power of knowledge.

I have no theories about the theatre writing through which I pursue these themes and relationships. Each play comes to me with its own metaphor, dictates its own form, creates its own atmosphere. All literature contains a mixture of poetry and journalism. Poetry in the theatre is that indefinable *sense* of truth which is communicated when two dissimilar or unrelated moments are placed side by side. "Sense" of truth, not *the* one and only truth. I would like to think my plays and stories have a larger proportion of poetry than journalism, and that if I have any talent it is for identifying the metaphors which life contains for the purpose of illuminating itself.

One day I hope someone may write as generously of me as Ruskin did of Turner:

> This you will find is ultimately the case with every true and right master; at first, while we are tyros in art, or before we have earnestly studied the man in question, we shall see little in him; or perhaps see, as we think, deficiencies; we shall fancy he is inferior to this man in that, and to the other man in the other; but as we go on studying him we shall find that he has got both that and the other; and both in a far higher sense than the man who seemed to possess those qualities in excess. Thus in Turner's lifetime, when people first looked at him, those who liked rainy weather said he was not equal to Copley Fielding; but those who looked at Turner long enough found that he could be much more wet than Copley Fielding when he chose. The people who liked force said that "Turner was not strong enough for them; he was effeminate; they liked De Wint,—nice strong tone;—or Cox—great, greeny, dark masses of colour—solemn feeling of the freshness and depth of nature; they liked Cox—Turner was too hot for them." Had they looked long enough they would have found that he had far more force than De Wint, far more freshness than Cox when he chose,—only united with other elements; and that he didn't choose to be cool, if nature had appointed the weather to be hot . . . . And so throughout with all thoroughly great men, their strength is not seen at first, precisely because they united, in due place and measure, every great quality. . . .

* * *

In a 1978 interview Arnold Wesker characterized himself as "world-weary" . . . "over-whelmed with a sense of frustration and impotence. . . . For reasons which I don't understand, I do seem to arouse hostilities and irritations." Nevertheless, Wesker has continued to write, and if he can find no place, or small room, in the British theater, his plays enjoy a considerable success in other countries. The paradox of a major British writer premiering his work abroad and in translation is heightened when one considers the obsessive concern in his earlier plays with the necessity of acting in community to transform and transcend the immediate environment in order to live authentically and fully.

Wesker's plays are plays of ideas, dramatized in debate and expressed in passionate terms, about the complexity and necessity of moral choices when there is no clear precept to follow. In the earlier plays these moral dilemmas are often laid out in set pieces. In *Roots,* for example, Beatie tells the story of the girl in love with one man who deserts her and loved by another who rejects her because she has given herself to the first. Idealism is seen very early on to contain its own negative dialectic. "Tell me your dreams," says Peter in *The Kitchen,* and he unleashes the dream of a man who wants to drop a bomb on the CND marchers because they hold up the buses.

Ironically, Wesker enjoyed much more success with his earlier plays, in which the dialectics between idealism and frustration were presented more simply, than with his later plays, in which the issues are much more complex. Values that had been seen positively in the earlier plays are often revealed to be illusory. The search for words through which to apprehend the world, express one's thoughts and feelings, and build bridges fails to achieve these aims and becomes a way of obscuring or evading the issues. The realization of self through education and culture, which is to be the means of Beatie's liberation, becomes in *The Friends* a source of frustration, isolation, and contempt for others.

Wesker's stature in the theater declined during the 1960s and 1970s. Until 1964 his battle against apathy and purely materialist values and for the individual's right to life, liberty, and the pursuit of happiness through the orderly and gradual reform of society could be seen as a feasible course of socialist action. The political and economic crises of the mid-1960s through the 1970s called for either a cynical withdrawal from these aims, a dropping out into anarchistic individualism, or a commitment to a program, however vague, for mass revolution. Wesker's concern with values that surmount the material has embarrassed his opponents. His concern with the individual has led those who share his own passionate concern for the realization of working-class potential to brand his work as elitist, subjective, and ultimately conformist.

From Wesker's plays it is easy to select quotations that support a critique of counterrevolutionary idealism. After all, in *The Friends* Manfred has a speech in which he says, "The working class! Hate them! It's coming, Macey. Despise them! I can hear myself, it's coming. Hate them! The working class, my class, offend me. Their cowardly acquiescence, their rotten ordinariness—everything about them—Hate them! There!" Wesker leaves himself open to such criticisms not because he necessarily agrees with such views but because, recognizing that such thoughts and feelings are part of the dialectics of his own makeup, he allows his characters to express them with extreme feeling and does not explicitly deny them by suppressing or taking a committed authorial stance against them. Examined closely, Wesker's later plays present a complex dialectical discourse of contrasting and often contradictory views as to what the central issue involves. Friend and foe alike might condemn this as nit-picking over the dead ground of a perverse adherence to idealism in the stern face of reality. Politicos may call for a sword to cut through the Gordian knots with which Wesker becomes enmeshed. He himself relentlessly pursues metaphysical values in an increasingly materialistic world, charting as he goes the deepening frustrations of compromise and the high price exacted for sticking to one's beliefs.

What is clear from the line of development through Wesker's plays is the continual decrease of the spatial area in which the individual can act. The major shift in his work occurred in the mid-1960s and coincided with his withdrawal from public action, as expressed through his involvement with CND, the Committee of 100, and Centre 42. There are fewer scenes of concerted action in the later plays to mark the potential power of the working class as shown in the first act of *The Kitchen* or the coal-stealing scene in *Chips with Everything*. The size of the community participating in the ritual celebrations becomes smaller and more enclosed. In the first act of *Chicken Soup with Barley* the setting is a room, but there is constant reference to the world outside. The streets of the East End and the battlefields of Spain are arenas of political action. Education will make the world Beatie Bryant's oyster. In *The Old Ones* both the streets and the classroom are potential areas of mindless violence. In *The Merchant* Shylock's actions are confined within the space and rules of the ghetto. The line culminates in the walling up of the nun Christine in *Caritas* while she repeats, "This is a wall, this is a wall. . . ." The area of the action shrinks, and the concerns become more metaphysical.

Wesker's world-weariness and his sense of isolation and impotence are nihilistic only if he sees them subjectively. A move out into the world would reveal them as a common feature of the contemporary human condition. If it is harder to keep faith with Sarah Kahn's injunction to "care," her corollary still stands: "If you don't care you'll die." The struggle might be harder and the issues less clear-cut than they appeared before, but the battle must still be waged. But to do this the ghetto has to be broken out of, and being walled up for one's beliefs is too high a price to pay for integrity.

Since 1981 Wesker's work has marked time, with no major play coming from him. There have been signs, however, of the resurgence of lightheartedness and fun, if not optimism. *One More Ride on the Merry-Go-Round* is Wesker's attempt at writing pure comedy, but, not unexpectedly, serious themes intrude. The main action of the comedy is the revival of energy and purpose in a 50-year-old academic and his wife. Two further plays, *When God Wanted a Son* and *Lady Othello,* continue the theme of a middle-aged academic in affairs with younger women. Through these plays Wesker explores further the process first encountered in *Roots,* the education and culturalization of women by an autodidactic male. In these plays the issues become more complex. *When God Wanted a Son* centers on a wife separated from her husband, who returns obsessively to exasperate and infuriate her. In *Lady Othello,* Wesker's finest play for some time, the couple in the relationship are incompatible in terms of age, color, race, and his feelings of guilt. In both of these plays the destructive and divisive effects of education and learning are explored along with the positive. Wesker also has written a series of one-woman plays, the best known and most often performed being *Annie Wobbler.* These serve to remind us that Wesker is, above all, a great writer of character parts. His reputation internationally remains unabated, but at home he remains bitter and alienated by the lack of respect for and production of his plays.

—Clive Barker

WESLEY, Richard (Errol)

Nationality: American. **Born:** Newark, New Jersey, 11 July 1945. **Education:** Howard University, Washington, D.C., 1963-67, B.F.A. 1967. **Family:** Married Valerie Deane Wilson in 1972; four children. **Career:** Passenger service agent, United Airlines, Newark, 1967-69; member of the New Lafayette Theatre Company and managing editor of *Black Theatre* magazine, New York, 1969-73; founding member, 1973, and member of the Board of Directors,

1976-80, Frank Silvera Writers Workshop, New York; teacher of black theatre history, Manhattanville College, Purchase, New York, Wesleyan University, Middletown, Connecticut, 1973-74, and Manhattan Community College, New York, 1980-83; member of the board of directors, Theatre of Universal Images, Newark, 1979-82; teacher, Rutgers University, New Brunswick, New Jersey, 1984. Assistant professor, Tisch School of the Arts, New York, 1995—. **Awards:** Drama Desk award, 1972; Rockefeller grant, 1973; Audelco award, 1974, 1977; NAACP Image award, 1974, 1975. **Agent:** Innovative Artists, 141 5th Avenue, New York, New York 10010, U.S.A. **Member:** Writers Guild of America, 1994—; National Film Preservation Board, Library of Congress, Washington, D.C., 1997—. **Address:** c/o Jay C. Kramer, 135 East 55th Street, New York, New York 10022, U.S.A.

Publications

Plays

Put My Dignity on 307 (produced Washington, D.C., 1967).
The Street Corner (produced Seattle, 1970; New York, 1972).
Headline News (produced New York, 1970).
Knock Knock, Who Dat (produced New York, 1970).
The Black Terror (produced Washington, D.C., 1970; New York, 1971). Published in *The New Lafayette Theatre Presents*, edited by Ed Bullins, New York, Doubleday, 1974.
Gettin' It Together (produced Roxbury, Massachusetts, 1971; New York, 1972). With *The Past Is the Past*, New York, Dramatists Play Service, 1979.
Strike Heaven on the Face! (produced New York, 1973).
Alicia (produced Waterford, Connecticut, 1973; as *Goin' Thru Changes*, produced New York, 1974).
Eight Ball (produced Waterford, Connecticut, 1973; as *The Past Is the Past,* New York, 1974).
The Sirens (produced New York, 1974). New York, Dramatists Play Service, 1975.
The Mighty Gents (produced Waterford, Connecticut, 1974; as *The Last Street Play*, produced New York, 1977; as *The Mighty Gents*, produced New York, 1978). New York, Dramatists Play Service, 1979.
The Past Is the Past (produced Waterford, Connecticut, 1974; New York, 1975). With *Gettin' It Together*, New York, Dramatists Play Service, 1979.
On the Road to Babylon, music and lyrics by Peter Link, based on a concept by Brent Nicholson (produced Milwaukee, 1980).
Butterfly (produced Waterford, Connecticut, 1985).
The Dream Team, with music and lyrics by Tom Tigrney and John Forster (produced Chester, Connecticut, 1985).
The Talented Tenth (produced New York, 1989).
Heaven and the Homeboy, with music and lyrics by Shelton Becton and George Faison (produced Montclair, New Jersey, 1997).

Screenplays: *Uptown Saturday Night*, 1974; *Let's Do It Again*, 1975; *Fast Forward*, 1985; *Native Son*, 1986.

Television Play: *The House of Dies Drear*, from the novel by Virginia Hamilton, 1984; *Murder without Motive,* 1992; *Fearless,* adapted from Walter Mosley, 1996; *Mandela and Deklerk,* 1997.

*

Manuscript Collection: Dramatists Play Service, New York.

* * *

Richard Wesley writes about the black community of America's urban ghettos. He charts the stoops, poolrooms, and tenements of the inner city and the ways of the people who live there: pimps, prostitutes, derelicts, street gangs. While his sensibility is lyrical, his intentions are political. Wesley questions the values that entrap his characters in aimless days and barren futures. He examines the rules by which they try to survive and the human and social costs when these rules prove inadequate.

While black playwrights such as Ed Bullins and Ron Milner really came from the ghettos they dramatize, Wesley grew up in a middle-class family in Newark, New Jersey. He was, he says, nearly a teenager before he discovered that college was not compulsory. At Howard University he not only came under the influence of the fabled Owen Dobson, mentor of many black theater artists, but also embraced the black nationalist movement that took root on campuses in the 1960s. Upon graduation in 1967 he joined Bullins at the Black Playwrights Workshop of Harlem's New Lafayette Theatre, known for its activist posture and the cross-pollination it encouraged between the stage and the surrounding street culture.

His early play *The Black Terror* is a satire on the contradictions Wesley detected in cultural nationalism. The playwright introduces us to members of a radical cadre pledged to revolutionary suicide in the service of urban guerrilla warfare. Through the character of Keusi, a pragmatic Vietnam veteran, Wesley debates the movement's tactics and its leaders' image of themselves as a kamikaze vanguard. "To die for the revolution is the greatest thing in life," says one of the militants. "But revolution is about life, I thought," Keusi answers. "Our first duty as revolutionaries is to live. . . . Why we gotta fight a revolution with a value system directed toward death?"

Although its ideological emphasis is unique among his plays, *The Black Terror* incorporates many stylistic traits, blended impressionistically, that Wesley would refine in his increasingly humanistic later works. Raised more on television than live entertainment, he favors the stage equivalents of filmic cross-fades, superimpositions, and jump cuts to shift locations rapidly, juxtapose moods, and suggest simultaneous action, an approach that subsequently brought him several Hollywood contracts. From the classics he borrows choral and ritualistic elements that he mingles with characters and scenes more typical of contemporary naturalistic drama. His dialogue, a pungent street argot, is expanded by poetic rhythms and refrains, while his monologues approach soliloquies of direct address.

For the series of short plays he produced between 1972 and 1974, Wesley muted the stylistic exuberance of *The Black Terror* in favor of compassionate yet unsentimental character studies. In *Gettin' It Together* and *Goin' Thru Changes* polarized young couples struggle both against each other and against cheapening odds to piece together a future. *Strike Heaven on the Face!* brings a war hero home to peacetime defeat. *The Past Is the Past* is set in a poolhall where a son in search of his heritage confronts the father who long ago abandoned him. Inspired in part by Fellini's *Nights of Cabiria,* a second reunion play, *The Sirens,* probes the life of a prostitute who is eventually faced with a choice between her hard-won but precarious independence and reconciliation with the husband who vanished a decade before to chase a dream now belatedly come true.

Individually, the plots of these five miniatures are casual, mere hooks on which Wesley's hangs family portraits. Taken as montage, however, they together gain a thematic solidarity that presents the scenography of a condition. A number of issues that played supporting roles in *The Black Terror* here become Wesley's preoccupations: the breakdown of family structures that leads to alienation between men and women and between parents and children; connections between past and present, through which a legacy of defeat passes from generation to generation; and thwarted efforts to wrench self-worth from deluded hopes and to stake out a little turf from which pride can be harvested. How, Wesley asks, can the quest for manhood succeed opposite frustrations that lead to inertia on the one hand and savagery on the other?

His cinematic style refined and his ability to draw tenderly detailed characters having matured, Wesley assembled his thematic concerns in a full-length drama about the important present and harsh destiny in store for the remnants of an expired Newark street gang. *The Last Street Play* opened to enthusiastic reviews, some of which compared Wesley's inner-city tragedy to Kurosawa's *The Seven Samurai* and Fellini's *I vitelloni*, film classics concerning disoriented young toughs, now past their prime, who confront tomorrow with a gallows bravado as deluded as it is fatal. Under the title *The Mighty Gents,* the play transferred to Broadway, a commercial tribute that remains rare for legitimate dramas by black authors and that italicizes the universality of Wesley's subject—the American dream examined from a black perspective. Frankie Sojourner, onetime Gents leader, owes a debt to Studs Lonigan, the Irish Catholic title character of James T. Farrell's Depression novel of another squandered youth and another wasted generation. Among fellow playwrights who came of age in the 1970s, Wesley has most in common with David Mamet, whose *American Buffalo* in many ways resembles *The Mighty Gents*. In both plays might-have-been men cling to a past in which, briefly, they were somebody. In both, desperation ignites violent schemes to regain self-esteem in the eyes of a world where, as Frankie puts it, "The census don't count us and welfare don't even know we alive." More largely, each evaluates American society in our times and the standards we use to govern it.

—C. Lee Jenner

WHELAN, Peter

Nationality: British. **Born:** Newcastle-under-Lyme, 3 October 1931. **Education:** Hanley High School, Stoke-on-Trent, 1941-49; Keele University, Staffordshire, 1951-55. **Military Service:** National Service, 1950-51. **Family:** Married Ffrangcon Price in 1958; two sons and one daughter. **Career:** Assistant surveyor, Town Planning Office, Stoke-on-Trent, 1949-50; farm worker, Endon Farm, Staffordshire, 1950; manservant, Uffington Hall, Lincolnshire, and demolition worker, Staffordshire, both 1955; hall porter, English Speaking Union Hotel, London, 1956; advertising copywriter, A.S. Dixon Ltd., London, 1956-57; English teacher, Berlitz School, Bergen, Norway, 1957-58; teacher, West London College, London, 1958; advertising copywriter and director, various agencies in London, 1959-90. Lives in London. **Awards:** Ford Foundation grant, 1964; Sony Radio award, 1990; Writers' Guild Nominations, 1995, 1997; T.M.A. awards, 1997; Lloyd's Private Banking Bewst Play, 1997. **Agent:** The Agency, 24 Pottery Lane, Holland Park, London W11 4LZ, England.

Publications

Plays

Lakota, with Don Kincaid (produced London, 1970).
Double Edge, with Les Darbon (produced London, 1975). London, French, 1976.
Captain Swing (produced Stratford-on-Avon, 1978; London, 1979). London, Collings, 1979.
The Accrington Pals (produced London, 1981; New York, 1984). London, Methuen, 1982.
Clay (produced London, 1982). London, Methuen, 1983.
A Cold Wind Blowing Up, with Les Darbon (produced Cologne, Germany, 1983).
World's Apart, adaptation of a work by Jose Triana (produced Stratford-on-Avon, 1986; London, 1987).
The Bright and Bold Design (produced London, 1991; Washington, D.C., 1992). London, Warner Chappell, 1991.
The School of Night (produced Stratford-on-Avon, 1992). London, Warner Chappell, 1992.
Shakespeare Country (produced for Little Theater Guild, 1993). London, Warner Chappell, 1993.
The Tinder Box, adapted from Hans Anderson (produced Newcastle-under-Lyme, 1994). London, Samuel French, 1995.
Divine Right (produced Birmingham, 1996). London, Warner Chappell, 1996.
The Herbal Bed (produced Stratford-on-Avon, 1996; London, 1997; New York, 1998). London, Warner Chappell, 1996; New York, Dramatists Play Service, 1998.
Overture (produced Newcastle-under-Lyme, 1997).

*

Peter Whelan comments:

The wastage of human conflict—often seen against a background of larger conflict—is, I suppose, my preoccupation.

I was a late starter, 40 before my first play, *Captain Swing*. I was drawn to it by wishing to counteract despairing visions of humanity as innately violent or socially brutalised. *The Accrington Pals*, *The Bright and Bold Design*, and *Clay* form almost a trilogy, drawing on my extended family background in the potteries and Salford. At the centre of it is the force of attraction and repulsion between people swept along by the times they live in and yearning for some peace in one another. And though my subsequent work has moved well beyond this family connection, the persistent theme of division and conciliation—of survival—is something I'm always conscious of.

* * *

Autumn 1830. Within sight of the harvest they have gathered, the farm labourers of Britain are starving while the gentry rejoice in their new threshing machines. Fires flare in Kent. In a small Sussex village, Mathew Hardness, wheelwright and committed democrat ("It's the people who keep the law . . . let those who govern break it. . . . No making revolution but restoring our natural right") encourages peaceful confrontation between labourers and landowners. Meanwhile, the gentry receive threatening letters from "Captain Swing, avenger of the people."

The gentry are engulfed by terror, their guilt sowing fear of anarchy in dynamic contrast to the reason and restraint of the local Swing rebels. However, the infiltration of an Irishman, O'Neil, professional revolutionary hot from the fires of France, greedy for power and violent rebellion, creates factions and confusion amongst the workers, and the arrival of a badly burned soldier, Farquare, on the run from the Dragoons and near death, inflames revolutionary zeal. Gemma, barmaid and town whore, in a passion for Farquare, embraces the revolution with fanatical fervour, vows celibacy, and proclaims Farquare to be Captain Swing.

Flails strike against the bare stage; tri-colour and black flags fly; the menacing presence of giant corn men provides a dark sense of historical and metaphysical necessity setting the immediate moment of history ringing with the energy of unresolved patterns of historical and imminent crisis.

Peter Whelan's *Captain Swing* was an impressive stage debut. The scope of the action, the impressive use of stage space, and the powerful construction of dramatic image heralded an exciting new writer. Whelan gives even the most minor characters distinction by activating their personal demands in relation to the historical situation. From Mathew to Agnes, who seeks justice from the committee for her husband's murder of their child, each character is unmistakably both a private individual with personal needs and concerns and an active, unavoidable member of the social context.

On the one hand, this economic approach to character development creates the sensation that every possible attitude toward the immediate crisis and its implications has been argued for our assessment. On the other, it forms the very core of Whelan's structure and themes. The tension between the characters' individual and social identities and responsibilities provides the central dynamic of his work and arguably its most dramatically powerful element.

In *The Accrington Pals* the interdependence between the individual and the community is created by presenting World War I from the perspective of the home front. May, a fiercely independent woman who runs a fruit and vegetable stall, is unable to confess her love for Tom, an artist, partly because she knew him as a child, partly because she is older than he is, but mainly because, against her deepest fears, he has enlisted. Whelan describes the play as "a story of a class-cum-love relationship between a strong-minded, rugged individualist woman and a dreamy, Utopian idealist young man." This relationship provides the framework for an intense discussion about personal will and success, community responsibility, and, as in *Captain Swing,* the personal and social consequences of social and historical power struggles. Occasional letters from the front and a remarkable scene in which May meets Tom's corpse bring the war onto the stage, and when the town learns of the deaths of the Accrington pals, they turn on their own leaders. The relationship between the individual and the social context is, however, typically ambiguous and complex. Despite its futile waste of human resources, the war affords May the chance to achieve her dream of owning a shop.

Whelan's plays are most successful when his overt question—"How shall we live?"—is set in the conundrum of incorporating private needs and expression with the recognition and responsibility of social demands. His attempt to explore these themes in the drawing room through the discussion of personal experience is both less engaging and less revealing. *Clay* lacks the social context and social commitment of the first two plays and, hence, both their dramatic dynamism and their complexity. Micky and her husband Ben, Staffordshire potters, are visited by old friends, Win and Pat, recently returned from West Germany. A close foursome as teenagers, the middle-class, middle-aged couples struggle to recapture their relationships, both group and personal. (Win and Pat's marriage has nearly failed.) Although "How shall we live?" is still on the tip of Whelan's tongue, it is literally and simplistically stated here. The translation of the question to personal angst reduces the discussion to specific personal experience, and the issues, like the characters, are limited and hypothetical. The four characters never take on the weight that would allow them to stand as analogous examples. Win does not come to "stand for all of us who have ever looked for a refuge from that future." Rather, her obsessive idealizing suggests a pathetic, private pathology. Whelan's occasional insistence on extended relevance—clay is "tough. You can't get rid of it. It looks fragile but in five thousand years they'll still be digging lots of it up. . . . When everyone's gone and the churchyard's empty. And that's the ultimate satisfaction of being a potter. Finally, you get buried in your work"—is self-conscious and literary. Separate from the necessities of social interaction and responsibility, the characters are credible but rather unengaging stage people whose personal problems may be viewed with detached sympathy and discarded when the curtain descends.

In *The Bright and Bold Design,* however, a return to historical context seems to reinspire Whelan's courageous dramatization of unresolved complexities. In his introduction Whelan implies that he intends to celebrate individualism, and in a manner unusual to his work he isolates Jessie, a talented freehand painter and designer working in a Staffordshire pottery in the 1930s, focusing on her personal experience and emotions. But the effect of the play is more complex. Jessie seeks recognition and self-expression through painting and eventually leaves the factory to stay with an aunt, help in her shop, and paint. She braves the pressures of Jack, the new design manager who recognizes her talent and promotes her designs but demands that she amend them to his ideas, and of the community, represented by the other painters and by Jack's ideal of bringing beautiful tableware to the workers. Whelan's unwillingness, however, to simplify the issues at stake makes the intended celebration of individualism ambivalent and more dramatic, demanding further contemplation of the relationship between the community and the individual. Jack's ideals are tinged and distorted by his personal desires. Simultaneously, Jessie's isolation and the drabness of her self-fulfillment make her apparent victory less glitteringly absolute, especially since she is still, willy-nilly, dependent on others for her independence. It is notable that we last see Jessie back in the community for Jack's funeral. The play asks whether individuality and talent cannot be better used by the community, or even, more pertinently, how we might organize our world so that both society and the individual can benefit and grow.

Whelan is constantly exploring how the values in conflicting ideals might be synthesized to mutual advantage. Given that we are both uniquely ourselves and inescapably members of our world and responsible to it, "How shall we live?"

—Elaine Turner

WHITE, Edgar Nkosi

Nationality: American. **Born:** Montserrat, West Indies, 4 April 1947. Brought to the United States in 1952. **Education:** City College, City University of New York, 1964-65; New York University, 1966-69, B.A.; Yale University School of Drama, New Haven, Connecticut, 1971-73; New York Theological Seminary, 1992—. **Career:** Playwright-in-residence, Yale University School of Drama, New Haven, Connecticut, New York Shakespeare Festival Joseph Papp Public Theater, 1971-72, and Cafe La Mama, New York, 1992; artistic director, Yardbird Players Company, New York, 1974-77. **Awards:** New York State Council on the Arts grant, 1975; O'Neill award, 1977; Rockefeller grant, 1989. **Agent:** Helen Merrill, 361 West 17th Street, New York, New York 10011, U.S.A; and, Marion Boyars, 24 Lacy Road, London SW15 1NL, England.

Publications

Plays

The Mummer's Play (produced New York, 1965). Included in *Underground*, 1970.
The Wonderful Yeare (produced New York, 1969). Included in *Underground*, 1970.
The Figures at Chartres (produced New York, 1969).
The Life and Times of J. Walter Smintheus (produced New York, 1971). With *The Crucificado*, New York, Morrow, 1973.
The Burghers of Calais (produced Boston, 1971; New York, 1972). Included in *Underground*, 1970.
Fun in Lethe; or, The Feast of Misrule (produced Providence, Rhode Island, 1974). Included in *Underground*, 1970.
Underground: Four Plays. New York, Morrow, 1970.
Seigismundo's Tricycle: A Dialogue of Self and Soul (produced New York, 1971).
Lament for Rastafari (produced New York, 1971; London, 1978). Included in *Lament for Rastafari and Other Plays*, 1983.
Transformations: A Church Ritual (produced New York, 1972).
The Crucificado (produced New Haven, Connecticut, 1972; New York, 1972). With *The Life and Times of J. Walter Smintheus*, New York, Morrow, 1973.
La Gente (produced New York, 1973).
Ode to Charlie Parker (produced New York, 1973).
Offering for Nightworld (produced New York, 1973).
Les Femmes Noires (produced New York, 1974; London, 1981). Included in *Redemption Song and Other Plays*, 1985.
The Pygmies and the Pyramid (produced New York, 1976).
The Defense (produced Waterford, Connecticut and New York, 1976).
Trinity: The Long and Cheerful Road to Slavery (includes *Man and Soul, The Case of Dr. Kola, That Generation*) (produced London, 1982; New York, 1987). Included in *Lament for Rastafari and Other Plays*, 1983.
Lament for Rastafari and Other Plays. London, Boyars, 1983.
Like Them That Dream (produced New York, 1988). Included in *Lament for Rastafari and Other Plays*, 1983.
The Nine Night (produced London, 1983). With *Ritual by Water*, London, Methuen, 1984.
Ritual by Water (produced London, 1983). With *The Nine Night*, London, Methuen, 1984.
Redemption Song (produced London, 1984). Included in *Redemption Song and Other Plays*, 1985.
The Boot Dance (produced London, 1984). Included in *Redemption Song and Other Plays*, 1985.
Ritual (produced London, 1985).
Redemption Song and Other Plays. London, Boyars, 1985.
Moon Dance Night (produced London, 1987).
I Marcus Garvey (also director: produced Jamaica and New York, 1992).
Live from Galilee (produced New York, 1992).

Other

Sati, the Rastafarian (for children). New York, Lothrop, 1973.
Omar at Christmas (for children). New York, Lothrop, 1973.
The Yardbird Reader. Privately printed, 1973.
Children of Night (for children). New York, Lothrop, 1974.
The Rising. London, Boyars, 1988.

*

Critical Studies: *The Drama of Nommo* by Paul Carter Harrison, New York, Grove, 1972; *Drumbeats, Masks, and Metaphors: Contemporary Afro-American Theatre* by Genevieve Fabre, Cambridge, Massachusetts, Harvard University Press, 1983; "Flight from Non-Existence" by John Kraniauskas, in *Index on Censorship* (London, England), February 1989, pp. 23-25; "Identity, Exile and Migration: The Dialectics of Content and Form in West Indian Literature" by Osy Okagbue, in *New Literature Review* (Wollongong, New South Wales), Summer 1990, pp. 14-23.

Edgar Nkosi White comments:

My work mainly has to do with ritual. The central theme of my work is the business between man and God. My interest in theatre began with the church (African, Caribbean, American). I am at present studying for my Masters in Divinity at the New York Theological Seminary.

I am a very slow writer. I have no control over what direction my work, my interest, my craft will lead me. I also find myself falling in love with film. I am still a black writer. After 20 years of writing I am beginning to learn the craft. My perspective is global.

* * *

Edgar Nkosi White's drama is concerned with the black predicament within a predominantly white universe. And for him a black is a black whether he comes from Africa or the Caribbean, and he is even more so to the white man. His plays highlight the deprivation and hardship of the developing nations and the usual dreams of a better life in the developed nations. It is hardly surprising that migration, exile, and alienation are the central focus as he follows black exiles through their humiliations and disappointments in the cities of Europe and North America.

White's first collection of plays, *Underground*, contains *The Burghers of Calais*, *Fun in Lethe*, *The Mummer's Play*, and *The Wonderful Yeare*. *The Burghers of Calais* deals with the wrongful conviction of the Scottsboro boys for rape. The play centers around Bagatelle and his mates in prison as their fate is thrown from one court to another without much hope for a reprieve. White here shows his concern with the manifest injustice that black people face. Of the four plays in the collection this is the one with the largest focal range and the one in which White is closest to his fellow victims of racism. The play's structure is complex, displaying the playwright's bold experiments with dramatic form. Of especial interest is his application of a highly developed cinematic sensibility to create plays that very often challenge the audience's ability to integrate diverse material. His scenes are as varied as the huge canvas on which his characters conduct their complex relationships.

Fun in Lethe explores the theme of migration, exile, and alienation by dramatizing the journey of a West Indian poet through Great Britain. Harmatia represents the numerous citizens of the former empire who return to claim their own piece of the motherland, and his experience typifies the problems and disillusionment of the black son who stakes his claim on mother England. It is even worse for the pretentious ones like Harmatia and like Legion in *Redemption Song* who are writers trying to eke out a living through their craft in a hostile environment. The play is typically a mishmash of characters, events, and ideas, and though amusing, it is not always effective structurally.

The Mummer's Play returns to an America described as "one large unflushed toilet." A note of impatient anger creeps into White's writing, a note that he retains up to *Redemption Song*. Because they merely lie around and do nothing to help themselves, the black victims get sympathy neither from White nor from the audience. Here as in other plays White explores the various myths about West Indians, and in the end he tries to explode some of them. When he looks at alienation in *Redemption Song*, *The Mummer's Play*, *The Wonderful Yeare*, and *The Boot Dance*, he does not simply blame America or Europe but also holds responsible the victims, who through an enervating anguish allow themselves to become alienated. And when he deals with migration and exile, as he does in most of his plays, he seeks to expose the deeper structures of social inequality in Caribbean society that are responsible for the famed migratory consciousness of West Indians. He does this well in *Redemption Song* as he follows Legion, the failed and alienated migrant who returns to his island only to face further alienation and subsequent death from the oppressors of Redemption City.

The Wonderful Yeare is set in a New York slum and deals with social deprivation and petty racial jealousies among America's oppressed ethnic minorities. This deeply ironic play, in which White shows his understanding of the *lazzi*s and of the improvisation of the commedia dell'arte, is about the "gift of life in the midst of death." Even as the plague rages, life goes on, and on a positive note, unlike White's other artists, Misserimus does something in the end—he marries Maria and goes to work.

White's second collection contains *Lament for Rastafari, Like Them That Dream*, and *Trinity*. *Lament for Rastafari* is structurally episodic, with narrative continuity maintained safely through characters. It is about the spiritual as well as physical journey of a West Indian family first to England and then to America. Lindsay, Barret, and Laputa, like White's other migrants and exiles, are driven by want and racial oppression to leave home and scour the cities of Europe and North America. In this play White begins his experiments with the West Indian dialect that we see in full flow in *Redemption Song*. *Like Them That Dream* is about Sparrow, a South African painter who flees apartheid only to encounter it in other forms in America. In the end he has to make a choice, either to keep running or to stand and confront apartheid head-on. And it is only when he does the latter that he is able to appreciate the love and stability that Sharon offers him. The play is in many respects like *The Boot Dance*, which concerns Lazarus, another exile who, in fleeing oppressive apartheid, finds himself oppressed and powerless in an English mental asylum where only blacks are the inmates and the doctor is white. All in all, what emerges from this and other plays is White's extremely despairing vision of the black condition.

Trinity is a group of three plays. *Man and Soul* deals with misunderstanding and antagonism between blacks from Africa and those from the West Indies, as well as racist law that lumps them together as criminals. *The Case of Dr. Kola* shows the idiocies of African governments and corrupt politicians, as well as the equally hopeless military men who replace them through coups. Finally, *That Generation* follows Wallace and Phyllis on their journey from a comfortable life in the West Indies to one of penury and denigration in England. Again, a sense of despair pervades these plays, which are colored by White's essential pessimism.

Les Femmes Noires displays all of the characteristics of White's dramaturgy, and as he himself points out, it is "polyscenic" and conceived as representing the "viewpoint of a blind man perceiving sound." The action progresses as if seen through the roving lens of a movie camera or the playing-out of sounds and motion in a dream. The play follows the dreary lives, individual anguish, and fading hopes of a group of black women in New York City, but it is rescued from White's usual pessimism by the sisterly striving and support these women offer to one another. It is their basic humanity that survives.

White's plays suggest that each is a personal journey, and the central characters, often black artists struggling to survive in the unfriendly cities of Europe and North America, are projections of his own psyche that he probes in order to come to terms with exile and alienation. His central characters are thus the same person seen in different situations, sometimes speaking the same lines, as in *Fun in Lethe* and *Lament for Rastafari,* but always the exile. Through their cinematic structure the plays capture White's lonely and restless search for meaning. It is this dialectic between content and form that makes White an interesting dramatist.

—Osita Okagbue

WHITE, John (Sylvester)

Nationality: American. **Born:** Philadelphia, Pennsylvania, 31 October 1919. **Education:** Gonzaga High School, Washington, D.C., 1933-37; University of Notre Dame, Indiana, 1937-41, A.B. in English 1941. **Family:** Married Vasiliki Sarant in 1966. **Career:** Actor for 25 years: charter member, Actors Studio, New York. Lives in Hawaii.

Publications

Plays

Twist (produced New York, 1963).

Bugs (produced New York, 1964). With *Veronica*, New York, Dramatists Play Service, 1966.

Sand (produced New York, 1964).

Veronica (produced New York, 1965). With *Bugs*, New York, Dramatists Play Service, 1966.
Bananas (produced New York, 1968).
The Dog School (produced New York, 1969).
Lady Laura Pritchett, American (produced Southampton, New York, 1969).
Mirage (produced Hanover, New Hampshire, 1969).
The Passing of Milldown Muldern (produced Los Angeles, 1974).
Ombres (produced Paris, 1975).
Les Punaises (produced Paris, 1975).

Screenplay: *Skyscraper*, 1959.

Other

Report from Palermo, by Danilo Dolci. New York, Orion, 1958.

*

Manuscript Collection: Lincoln Center Library of the Performing Arts, New York.

Theatrical Activities:
Actor: **Plays**—As John Sylvester: roles in *Richard III*, New York, 1943; *Sundown Beach* by Bessie Brewer, New York, 1948; *Danny Larkin* by James V. McGee, New York, 1948; *All You Need Is One Good Break* by Arnold Manoff, New York, 1950. **Television**—Mr. Woodman in *Welcome Back, Kotter* series, 1975-79; roles in other television and radio plays.

John White comments:
(1973) Unless writing for hire, I write privately, from within, using for material the backwash of fifty years of existence, sometimes even living. I cannot work from the daily paper or the latest vogue. Indeed, I am turned off by the world. When I think about it, I can't write. I have been accused of being formless and have been applauded, on the other hand, for good form. I detest critics (in the main; there are a few splendid exceptions) and professional "knowers-how." Lonely is the word.

* * *

Although represented by professional productions of just one full-length and a few one-act plays, John White in the 1960s established himself as one of the freshest and most talented playwrights in America. Writing in a strikingly idiosyncratic style, the hallmark of any artist, he applied modern surrealism—less than absurdist, more than naturalistic—to find a mythology in American roots. His small body of work is uneven. *Bugs* is a good one-act play, *Veronica* is a superlative one, and *Bananas* is a prematurely produced full-length play that, with polishing, would have been a major work. But like too many playwrights producing in New York during the period, White was hurt by a powerful and ignorant fraternity of critics. (It was an era when *Waiting for Godot, Entertaining Mr. Sloane,* and *The Homecoming* by, respectively, Beckett, Orton, and Pinter were rejected.) The playwright fled to Hollywood to seek a living wage at least. Ironically, the style he plumbed has since become familiar, and therefore palatable, through the work of playwrights from Pinter to Sam Shepard.

Bugs, American vernacular for "mad," is about a disturbed young man who has escaped from a hospital and returned to a home where things are not much saner. His mother and girlfriend are respectively and insanely cheerful and stupid. His father, when not hidden behind a newspaper, is a ranting menace. Though the play might have been more, it gave clear promise of the author's specialness.

Veronica fulfilled the promise. Its central characters are a popular American songwriting team of the 1930s. They are holed up in a hotel room, trying desperately to repeat the huge success they had with a song called "Veronica." They are interrupted by a most peculiar burglar whose very philosophy of life, as it turns out, was inspired by the lyrics of the song. The lyrics, in an accurate satire of the period's popular music, spell out the passé, nostalgic American dream as once advertised, a dream of beautiful blonds and money and trips to tropical islands. But has this sweet, silly dream now grown obsolete, only to be superseded by mundane social responsibility? One of the songwriters is too absorbed by war and disease to write again about June and moon. His partner is furious—"People haven't changed—a kiss is still a kiss, a sigh is still a sigh."

This yearning for a country once foolish and lovable, the choice of innocence over sophistication, is more deeply explored in the ambitious *Bananas*. The play is set in a period burlesque house during a rehearsal by three comics and an actress. A critic arrives. A series of sketches begins in which the author relates the techniques for burlesque to those of absurdism, suggesting that, in a nostalgic and truthful and sardonic way, everything is bananas, another American slang word for "madness," obviously White's view of existence. As the play continues, the metaphor of a show as life changes from the burlesque theater to a modern television studio, but everyday conversation remains like a replica of dialogue we have heard on a stage somewhere. The idea is excellent and much of the technique virtuosic, but the play was produced prematurely and is ultimately confusing. Its argument, however, seems clear enough—a preference for the innocence of actors, for entertainment, over the hopeless attempts by intellectuals to make sense of life.

Without being repetitious, White, like most fine playwrights, has had from the start a consistency to his style and content.

But sadly, a start seems to be all there is to White's playwriting career. Like too many in the brutal, competitive, business-controlled, and mindlessly commercial and antiartistic American theater, he has a sensitivity as a playwright that seems to have been beaten down by senseless rejection and unappreciation.

—Martin Gottfried

WHITEHEAD, Ted (Edward Anthony Whitehead)

Nationality: British. **Born:** Liverpool, Lancashire, 3 April 1933. **Education:** St. Francis Xavier's Jesuit College; Christ's College, Cambridge, B.A. (honours) in English 1955, M.A. **Military Service:** Served in the King's Regiment, 1955-57. **Family:** Married 1) Kathleen Horton in 1958 (marriage dissolved 1976), two daughters; 2) Gwenda Bagshaw in 1976. **Career:** Milkman, postman, bus conductor, sales promotion writer, salesman, and teacher, 1959-65; advertising copywriter and account executive, 1965-71; resident dramatist, Royal Court Theatre, London, 1971-72; fellow in creative writing, Bulmershe College, Reading, Berkshire, 1975-76. **Awards:** George Devine award, 1971; *Evening Standard* award, 1971. **Agent:** Casarotto Ramsay Ltd., National House, 60-66 Wardour Street, London W1V 3HP, England.

Publications

Plays

The Foursome (produced London, 1971; Washington, D.C., 1972; New York, 1973). London, Faber, 1972.

Alpha Beta (produced London, 1972; New York, 1973). London, Faber, 1972.

The Punishment (televised 1972). Published in *Prompt Three*, edited by Alan Durband, London, Hutchinson, 1976.

The Sea Anchor (produced London, 1974; New York, 1982). London, Faber, 1975.

Old Flames (produced Bristol, 1975; London, 1976; New York, 1980). London, Faber, 1976.

Mecca (produced London, 1977; New York, 1980). London, Faber, 1977.

The Man Who Fell in Love with His Wife, adaptation of his television series *Sweet Nothings* (produced London, 1984). London, Faber, 1984.

Dance of Death, adaptation of a play by Strindberg (produced Oxford, 1984; London, 1985).

Radio Play: *The Old Goat Gone*, 1987.

Television Plays: *Under the Age*, 1972; *The Punishment*, 1972; *The Peddler*, 1976; *The Proofing Session*, 1977; *The Irish Connection* (*Crown Court* series), 1979; *Sweet Nothings* series, 1980; *World's End* series, 1981; *The Detective* serial, from the novel by Paul Ferris, 1985; *The Life and Loves of a She-Devil* serial, from the novel by Fay Weldon, 1986; *First Born*, from a novel by Maureen Duffy, 1988; *Jumping the Queue*, from the novel by Mary Wesley, 1989; *The Free Frenchman*, from the novel by Piers Paul Read, 1989; *Murder East Murder West*, 1990.

Novel

World's End (novelization of television series). London, BBC Publications, 1981.

*

Critical Study: "The Life and Loves of a She-Devil (Fay Weldon & Ted Whitehead)" by Liz Bird and Jo Eliot, in *British Television Drama in the 1980s*, edited by George W. Brandt, Cambridge, Cambridge University Press, 1993.

* * *

Ted Whitehead's chosen dramatic territory is marriage and the impossible demands the institution makes on love and fidelity. His principal characters are most often drawn from the white-collar working class. They are witty and articulate but not intellectuals. His dialogue is a rapid verbal sparring, which frequently breaks down into hysteria or physical violence. His writing drives toward as plain a style as possible in the exposition of his emotional and sexual themes, although he is capable of occasional passages of lyrical beauty. "Escape" and "freedom" are key positive terms in his vocabulary, but they turn out to be chimeras for both men and women. His plays chart accurately the major debates around the family, sex, and marriage since the early 1960s, and while he has little interest in plot or character development, his ear is sharp for the changing discourse of males and females in this area.

A comparison between Whitehead's first stage success, *Alpha Beta*, and the later play *The Man Who Fell in Love with His Wife* is immediately instructive. *Alpha Beta* has only two characters, Mr. and Mrs. Elliot, and covers the years from 1962 to 1971. Elliot is a manager on the Liverpool docks, and she is a housewife. When the play opens, he is 29 and she is 26. They have two children who remain as an offstage audience to the bickering, fighting, violence, and hysteria that make up the play. Mr. Elliot already has a mistress, Eileen, and wants a divorce. His wife will not give him one. Although marriage has turned into a bitter trap for both of them, Mrs. Elliot stands by the moral law of until death us do part. For Mr. Elliot they are dead already. He wants the freedom to "fuck a thousand women." He is no different, he claims, from all his male friends, except that they sublimate their desires in blue movies and dirty jokes. "I'm sick of fantasy," he says, "I want reality." Elliot's view is that he married too young and too early for the permissive 1960s. Marriage is changing, he warns his wife, and in the future even a woman like her will "want a bit of what's going, for herself." A mutual enslavement like theirs should not last: "Man and women are going to share free and equal unions that last because they want them to last. Not because they're forced!" Mrs. Elliot has only contempt for his "honesty" and his sociology. In her view he is retarded. He has never grown out of the role of working-class bucko, tomcatting around after eternal youth. She will not let him escape his duties as head of the household. Over the years of the play they evolve a type of compromise. Mr. Elliot pays the bills and resides in the house, but he pursues his extramarital affairs. His wife runs the house and just about hangs onto her sanity. The play ends with a suicide threat by Mrs. Elliot that her husband takes half seriously but that fires no buried love or affection in him. It is an unsatisfactory ending, for there can be no ending to a war on these terms. As the title suggests, this couple must go through the alphabet of their hatred and then start all over again.

The Man Who Fell in Love with His Wife begins with just that change in women's status that Mr. Elliot foresaw. Mary Fearon, who is in her late 30s, has got her first job working in civil service. Her husband Tom, age 41, is also employed as a dock manager in Liverpool. Mary's office life causes him extreme jealousy but also refuels his sexual passion for her. Suspender belts and instant photos play their part in maintaining an ardor that Mary, who still loves her husband deeply, cannot match. Thus, love in marriage can be as stifling as hatred. Tom wants to replay their adolescence and courtship, and the Platters and Ike and Tina Turner are his favorite music. In freezing weather he drags his wife out to a favorite beach near Liverpool. Mary wants to move on, however, and eventually she moves out. By then Tom has given up his job to monitor his wife throughout the day. The roles and emotions of *Alpha Beta* have been reversed, and there is now a chance for the kind of freedom for both sexes that Mr. Elliot prophesied. For this is the 1980s, and there is a new role model, Julia, a divorcée in her 30s. She is an office friend who supports Mary's bid for independence and counters Tom's arguments with reason and confidence. "Is it selfish for me to want my wife to love me?" he asks. "It's selfish to demand it regardless of what she wants," Julia replies. In the end the two have to settle for separate lives, although old connections cannot be broken. "I love you—even if I can't live with you," says Mary, and Tom, now a cab driver, has to become an adult out of his own resources.

Glimpses of this comparative optimism can be seen in other Whitehead plays of the 1970s. In *The Sea Anchor* men and women friends wait on Dublin Bay for the arrival of the daredevil Nick after his solo voyage across the Irish Sea in a 10-foot dinghy. Since all of the characters are engaged in adulterous relationships, the play is also about the other side of marriage. Nick is their hero, for he "does exactly what he wants to do" while the others cover up in various ways. Whitehead's theme of the trapped, randy male is complemented by that of the calculating, randy female, and in the character of Jean we see a coarser precursor to Julia. The backchat is vulgar and witty, but Andy is given two lyrical passages. They occur when he recalls a shoal of mackerel at night, "a giant ripple, V-shaped . . . it came hissing along beside the boat," and the time he and Nick heard black bodies barking in the silver sea and discovered that they were porpoises, which sharply contrast with the brutality of the sexual relationships. Nick's boat comes in empty. His sea anchor, "a kind of parachute, keeps you steady," has not saved him. A lost hero is useless, and the sea is a false escape from domestic complexity.

Nor is there any solution abroad. The group of English tourists in *Mecca* brings its marital conflicts and emotions intact to Morocco. Middle-aged Andrew sublimates his desire for the 20-year-old Sandy into a false fatherly protectiveness. His wife Eunice is not fooled, but her verbal barbs have an articulateness that Mrs. Elliot lacked. Ian is young and fancy-free, and Martin is the gay protector for the defensive bravado of Jill, 38, divorced, and feeling herself caught between the insouciance of Sandy and the certainties of Eunice. "She's not afraid of sex," says Jill to Eunice, "and neither is her generation. That's why they don't get used-up like us." But Sandy's innocence leads her, dressed only in a towel, outside the compound in which the tourists live into the poor and violent world of Arab North Africa. She is raped, and a boy who hangs round the compound is suspected. When the boy is cornered, Andrew beats him to death. His desire is displaced into murderous aggression. The police and courts are finally bought off, and the tourists leave for "civilization" with relief. But back home, as Whitehead's other plays show, the war goes on.

—Tony Dunn

WHITEMORE, Hugh (John)

Nationality: British. **Born:** Tunbridge Wells, Kent, 16 June 1936. **Education:** Judd School, Tunbridge Wells, 1945-51; King Edward VI School, Southampton, 1951-55; Royal Academy of Dramatic Art, London, 1956-57. **Family:** Married 1) Jill Brooke in 1961 (marriage dissolved); 2) Sheila Lemon in 1976; one son. **Career:** Freelance writer: drama critic, *Harpers and Queen*, London, 1970. Lives in London. **Awards:** Emmy award, 1971, 1984; Writers Guild award, 1971, 1972; RAI prize, 1979; Italia prize, 1979; Neil Simon Jury award, 1984; Rpyal Film Performance, Christopher award, BAFTA nomination for best adapted screenplay, and Scriptor award, all 1987, all for *84 Charing Cross Road*; New York Joint Policy Board for Mathematics Communications award, 1987, for *Breaking the Code*; Emmy nominations for outstanding writing in a TV special, 1987 and 1989. **Agent:** Judy Daish Associates, 83 Eastbourne Mews, London W2 6LQ, England; or, Phyllis Wender, Rosenstone and Wender, 3 East 48th Street, 4th Floor, New York, New York 10017, U.S.A.

Publications

Plays

Horrible Conspiracies (televised 1971). Published in *Elizabeth R*, edited by J.C. Trewin, London, Elek, 1972.
Stevie: A Play from the Life and Work of Stevie Smith (produced Richmond, Surrey, and London, 1977; New York, 1979). London, French, 1977; New York, Limelight, 1984.
Pack of Lies (produced Brighton and London, 1983; New York, 1985). Oxford, Amber Lane Press, 1983; New York, Applause, 1986.
Breaking the Code, adaptation of the book *Alan Turing: The Enigma of Intelligence* by Andrew Hodges (produced London, 1986; New York, 1987). Oxford, Amber Lane Press, 1987.
The Best of Friends (produced London, 1987). Oxford, Amber Lane Press, 1988.
The Towers of Trebizond (produced Edinburgh, 1991).
It's Ralph (produced London, 1991).
A Letter of Resignation. Oxford, Amber Lane, 1997.

Screenplays: *Decline and Fall . . . of a Birdwatcher!*, with Ivan Foxwell and Alan Hackney, 1968; *All Neat in Black Stockings*, with Jane Gaskell, 1968; *Man at the Top*, with John Junkin, 1973; *All Creatures Great and Small*, 1975; *The Blue Bird*, 1976; *Stevie*, 1978; *The Return of the Soldier*, 1983; *84 Charing Cross Road*, 1987.

Television Plays: *The Full Chatter*, 1963; *Dan, Dan the Charity Man*, 1965; *Angus Slowly Sinking*, 1965; *The Regulator*, 1965; *Application Form*, 1965; *Mrs. Bixby and the Colonel's Coat*, from a story by Roald Dahl, 1965; *Macready's Gala*, 1966; *Final Demand*, 1966; *Girl of My Dreams*, 1966; *Frankenstein Mark II*, 1966; *Amerika*, from the novel by Kafka, 1966; *What's Wrong with Humpty Dumpty?*, 1967; *Party Games*, 1968; *The Last of the Big Spenders*, 1968; *Hello, Good Evening, and Welcome*, 1968; *Mr. Guppy's Tale*, from a story by Dickens, 1969; *Unexpectedly Vacant*, 1970; *The King and His Keeper*, 1970; *Killing Time*, 1970; *Cider with Rosie*, from the book by Laurie Lee, 1971; *Horrible Conspiracies* (*Elizabeth R* series), 1971; *An Object of Affection*, 1971; *Act of Betrayal*, 1971; *Breeze Anstey* (*Country Matters* series), from the story by H.E. Bates, 1972; *The Strange Shapes of Reality*, 1972; *The Serpent and the Comforter*, 1972; *At the Villa Pandora*, 1972; *Eric*, 1972; *Disappearing Trick*, 1972; *Good at Games*, 1972; *Bedtime*, 1972; *Intruders*, 1972; *The Adventures of Don Quixote*, from a novel by Cervantes, 1973; *Deliver us from Evil*, 1973; *The Pearcross Girls*, 1973; *A Thinking Man as Hero*, 1973; *Death Waltz*, 1974; *Outrage*, 1974; *David Copperfield*, from the novel by Dickens, 1974; *Trilby*, from the novel by George du Maurier, 1975; *Goodbye*, 1975; *84 Charing Cross Road*, from the book by Helene Hanff, 1975; *Moll Flanders*, from the novel by Defoe, 1975; *The Eleventh Hour*, with Brian Clark and Clive Exton,

1975; *Censors*, with David Edgar and Robert Muller, 1975; *Brensham People*, from novels by John Moore, 1976; *William Wilson*, from the story by Poe, 1976; *Moths*, from the novel by Ouida, 1977; *Exiles*, from the book by Michael J. Arlen, 1977; *Dummy*, 1977; *Mrs. Ainsworth*, from a novel by E.F. Benson, 1978; *Losing Her*, 1978; *Rebecca*, from the novel by Daphne du Maurier, 1979; *Contract*, 1981; *A Dedicated Man*, from the story by Elizabeth Taylor, 1982; *I Remember Nelson*, 1982; *A Bit of Singing and Dancing*, from the story by Susan Hill, 1982; *Lovers of Their Time*, from the story by William Trevor, 1982; *My Cousin Rachel*, from the novel by Daphne du Maurier, 1983; *Office Romances*, from stories by William Trevor, 1983; *Down at the Hydro*, from a story by William Samsom, 1983; *Concealed Enemies*, 1984; *The Boy in the Bush*, from a story by D.H. Lawrence, 1984; *The Final Days*, from a novel by Bob Woodward and Carl Bernstein, 1989.

*

Critical Study: "Hugh Whitemore" by Walter H. Placzek, in *British Playwrights, 1956-1995: A Research and Production Sourcebook*, edited by William Demastes, Westport, Connecticut, Greenwood, 1996.

* * *

Hugh Whitemore is best known as a writer for television, and since 1963 he has had a long list of plays to his credit both as parts of series and as individual efforts. His adaptation of Laurie Lee's *Cider with Rosie* won a Writers Guild Award, as did his contribution to *Country Matters* in 1972. *Elizabeth R,* a series of six plays, one of which, *Horrible Conspiracies,* was provided by Whitemore, received an Emmy Award. *Horrible Conspiracies* deals with events surrounding the execution of Mary, Queen of Scots, and its fascination with the world of spying and conspiracy was to become a recurrent theme in his work. Gloriana is presented as an aging queen, ruled by superstition and fear and fixated on thoughts of death, with a court that is far from magnificent.

The predominant style of *Horrible Conspiracies* is that of conventional television naturalism, although the play is prefaced by a grim masque portending death, and the piece jumps quickly through a series of locations that suggest the complexities of espionage and counterespionage lurking immediately beneath the outward display of power. Little interest is shown in the intricacies of psychological behavior or in any larger political context, and the play seems very much a part of a larger series in which each individual writer is considerably restrained by the overall structure. Over the years Whitemore has shown himself as adept at meeting the strictures of such demands and as able to turn out a consistently well-crafted piece.

The influence of Whitemore's work on television is evident in his belated stage entrance. *Stevie: A Play from the Life and Works of Stevie Smith* makes few bows in the direction of the stage. Information is given in the conventional format of recalled anecdotes raised in the course of a series of conversations between Stevie and the aunt she lived with for most of her life. The atmosphere of suburban London comes across well, as does Stevie's delight in the absurdity of her life there, but we gain little insight into her obsession with death and her failed attempt at suicide. It is a well-made play, offering the kind of "coffee table" approach to biography so frequently to be found on television. Its chief virtue lies in Whitemore's success in creating in the central character a plausible human being, even if we learn little more than superficial things about her. That this was done in a beautifully realized suburban set does little to take the edge off the feeling that *Stevie* is essentially a television play put on stage.

Whitemore's next stage play, *Pack of Lies,* was exactly this, having started life as the successful BBC *Play for Today* under the title *Act of Betrayal.* The play concerns the intrusion into a suburban family of the British secret service, intent on trapping as Russian spies their close friends and neighbors, the Krogers. The play, which is based on real events of 1960-61, again captures well the restrictions and niceties of suburban life and builds to a traditional theatrical climax as the host family becomes increasingly and ambivalently involved in the inquiry. But again it is difficult to see what exactly is added to the piece by its adaptation to the stage. The direct narrative asides to the audience apart, its predominant tone is still that of a safe naturalism. It asks no questions that cannot be contained within the confines of plot and set, and it is hard not to think that the chief reason for its appearance in London's West End was the latest bout of interest in Burgess, Philby, et al. One obvious attraction to theatrical managements was that it was a cheap production in a theatrical world dominated by excessively expensive musicals.

Whitemore's fourth stage-play, *Breaking the Code,* did, however, succeed in making the break from the small screen to the stage. Far more ambitious than his two earlier efforts, it presents the story of Alan Turing, the man who broke the German Enigma code in World War II and pioneered the development of computers. Taking on the difficult task of elucidating the theory behind Turing's work, and succeeding surprisingly well, the play blends the theme of scientific exploration with its depiction of an establishment England that could have the scientist's name obliterated from the record book because he was a practicing homosexual—the two sets of broken codes in conflict. Whitemore has been fortunate in having Derek Jacobi play his protagonist, but it says much for the play's superiority to its predecessors that the actor is able to fill the part so well. *Breaking the Code* is, no less than all of Whitemore's work, a classically well-made play produced to a given West End formula, but the difference is that here, for the first time, the formula has been stretched to fit what the writer wants to say rather than acting as a straitjacket.

Although Whitemore has continued to work for television, the commercial success of his first stage plays has led to further productions. *The Towers of Trebizond* was produced in Edinburgh, and *The Best of Friends* and *It's Ralph* were both produced in London's West End. The latter fitted the familiar pattern of small-cast, single-set domestic dramas. The rural home of a successful journalist and his music publisher wife is invaded by the unwelcome Ralph, an old friend of the husband and a guest whose presence, in the traditional manner, allows an even greater articulation of midlife crisis and marital depression. With this play Whitemore was compared inevitably to Ayckbourn, although the sudden removal of the by now emotionally involved Ralph toward the end promises, without properly delivering, a new permutation of the theme.

—John Bull

WILKINSON, Christopher

Nationality: British. **Born:** 4 May 1941. **Address:** 33 Yates Lane, Milnsbridge, Huddersfield HD3 4NW, England.

Publications

Plays

Their First Evening Alone Together (produced Sheffield, 1969; London, 1971).
Wally, Molly and Polly (produced Sheffield, 1969).
Teasdale's Follies, with Frank Hatherly, music by Jeremy Barlow (produced Sheffield, 1970).
Strip Jack Naked (produced Sheffield, 1970; London, 1971).
Dynamo (produced London, 1971).
Plays for Rubber Go-Go Girls (produced London, 1971).
I Was Hitler's Maid (also director: produced Sheffield and London, 1971).
Sawn Off at the Knees, with Veronica Thirlaway (produced Sheffield, 1978).

*

Theatrical Activities:
Director: **Play**—*I Was Hitler's Maid*, Sheffield and London, 1971.

Actor: **Plays**–Jonathan Brester in *Arsenic and Old Lace,* 1989; Frank Crawley in *Rebecca,* 1990; Peter Desmond in *The Seagull,* 1992; Uncle Ben in *Death of a Salesman,* 1993; Jaggers and Orlick in *Great Expectations,* 1993; Egeus, Starveling, and Cobweb in *Midsummer Night's Dream,* 1994; Duncan in *Macbeth,* 1995; Graham in *Talking Heads,* 1995; Narrator, Jenkins, and Edwards in *Under Milkwood,* 1996; Michael Watters in *Someone Who'll Watch Over Me,* 1997; Candy in *Of Mice and Men,* 1997; Scrooge in *A Christmas Carol,* 1997-98; Travis Flood in *Ghost From a Perfect Place,* 1998. **Film**–In *Cardiac Arrest,* 1995; in *Brass Eye,* 1996; in *KISZKO,* 1998. **Television**–In *The Beiderbecke Tapes, Coronation Street, Criminal,* and *Crimewatch File,* all 1995; in *In Suspicious Circumstances,* 1995; in *Brookside,* 1996; in *Emmerdale,* 1996; in *Beck,* 1996; in *Heartbeat,* 1997; in *Hetty Wainthrop,* 1998.

* * *

Christopher Wilkinson is best known for his work with two fringe companies. One is the touring Portable Theatre and the other is the Vanguard Theatre Club, now the Crucible Theatre-in-Education group that is attached to Sheffield's main repertory theater, the Crucible. His close associations with these companies have influenced his work. Wilkinson has written ordinary scripts, such as *Strip Jack Naked,* that reveal his wit, his ear for a good line of dialogue, and his delight in a Grand Guignol situation. But he later chose not to write formal scripts but rather to suggest themes and games for the acting companies to explore in improvisation and other ways.

I Was Hitler's Maid is an example of such a nonscripted play. Wilkinson offered the actors stories taken from semipornographic men's magazines and full of blood, sex, and action. The magazines were of a type distributed to American troops in Vietnam and were therefore considered to be related in some way to a real political situation. The stories were all exceptionally violent. Some were set in World War II among SS officers and patriots of the French Resistance and others in South America among guerrilla bands and the forces of law and order. But the settings were almost irrelevant, for the situations were pointedly similar. A girl is tortured and repeatedly raped by the enemy before being rescued by the hero. In the opening scene she is whipped by Hitler, and in a later scene she becomes Calamity Jane, the whipping Wild West heroine. The dialogue is based on the clichés of the genre, with the actors encouraged to break up the story patterns, the snatches of rehearsed scenes, and even the moments of violence in order to emphasize the arbitrary lack of logic of the fantasies. The production progresses toward two main climaxes—an orgy scene in which three men rape one girl and a disemboweling scene in which three soldiers attack a lifelike female doll hanging in a cupboard.

Some critics thought that *I Was Hitler's Maid* was not so much a comment on pornography as pornography itself, while others deplored the deliberate lack of construction. But few productions could have achieved such a telling diatribe against sex-and-violence comics without seeming lofty and puritanical. Wilkinson, by presenting the stories on stage, where actors leapt up in astonishing health after being beaten senseless, and by denying the elementary logic that kept the stories credible, brought out the full sadomasochistic absurdity of the genre.

A somewhat similar production, *Dynamo,* was less successful, perhaps because Wilkinson's moral intentions had to be more overtly expressed. *Dynamo* is set in a strip club, and the first section consists of ordinary, dull strip routines performed by gum-chewing, bored girls. We watch them preparing to go onstage, collecting their props and records, and adjusting their hair, and then we see the routines. But after a time the strip club becomes an interrogation cell in which a girl is tortured by a police chief, kicked around the floor, and finally hung up naked. Wilkinson wants to draw the parallel between ordinary pornographic fantasies and the political torture of an Algerian suspect by the French police, but the play fails because the association between the two events seems at best clichéd and at worst tenuous and unconvincing. If Wilkinson means to imply that in both cases women were treated like mere objects of male desire, the theme is convincing enough but rather obvious and could have been developed in many other ways. If he is suggesting that pornography leads to political violence, then the fact that there is no logical connecting link between the scenes damages his argument.

Wilkinson's most successful work, however, is *Plays for Rubber Go-Go Girls.* These are sketch sequences loosely linked by an attack on American imperialism and on the sexual fantasies supporting repression. The first half of the production consists of various sex-and-violence stories in the style of *I Was Hitler's Maid,* but the deliberate disorganization of the earlier plays is replaced by a solemn burlesque treatment in high camp. The stories could come from an outrageous adventure story in the style of James Bond, with beautiful girls from Vietnam and Latin America submitting with delight to Commie-hating GIs. The second half is an amusing skit on childhood training in America. A cop warns his daughter, Fuzz Child, against everything, from drugs to long hair, that might threaten the purity of American middle-class life. The juxtaposition of the repressed fantasies with the formal teaching are related to the Vietnam War until the war itself is shown to be an effect of various cultural forces.

Among these forces is perhaps Wilkinson's most typical preoccupation, the maltreatment of women by men. Women are presented as rubber girls who can be endlessly stabbed either with a phallus or a bayonet. This serious theme is treated with an immense satirical verve and accuracy. The fantasies are funny and familiar, and, shocking out of their usual contexts, they are presented to the public as grotesque art objects, as being representative of our civilization just as the pyramids were of ancient Egypt. Wilkinson's great achievement as a writer is to make us look afresh at the clichés surrounding our lives.

—John Elsom

WILLIAMS, Heathcote

Nationality: British. **Born:** Helsby, Cheshire, 15 November 1941. **Career:** Associate editor, *Transatlantic Review*, London and New York; founding editor, *Suck*, Amsterdam. **Awards:** *Evening Standard* award, 1970; George Devine award, 1970; John Whiting award, 1971; Obie award, 1971. **Agent:** Judy Daish Associates, 83 Eastbourne Mews, London W2 6LQ, England.

Publications

Plays

The Local Stigmatic (produced Edinburgh, and London, 1966; Boston, 1967; New York, 1969). Published in *Traverse Plays*, London, Penguin, 1965; with *AC/DC*, New York, Viking Press, 1973.
AC/DC (produced London, 1970; New York, 1971). London, Calder and Boyars, 1972; with *The Local Stigmatic*, New York, Viking Press, 1973.
Remember the Truth Dentist, music by Bob Flagg (produced London, 1974). With *The Speakers*, London, Calder, 1980.
The Speakers (produced Birmingham, 1974). With *Remember the Truth Dentist*, London, Calder, 1980.
Very Tasty—A Pantomine (produced London, 1975).
An Invitation to the Official Lynching of Michael Abdul Malik (produced Newcastle upon Tyne, 1975).
Anatomy of a Space Rat (produced London, 1976).
Hancock's Last Half-Hour (produced London, 1977; Huntington Station, New York, 1978). London, Polytantric Press, 1977.
Playpen (produced London, 1977).
The Immortalist (produced London, 1977). London, Calder, 1978.
At It, in *Breach of the Peace* (produced London, 1982; produced separately Edinburgh and London, 1983).
Whales (produced Liverpool and London, 1986).

Screenplay: *Malatesta*, 1969.

Television Play: *What the Dickens!*, 1983.

Poetry

Whale Nation. London, Cape and New York, Crown, 1988.
Falling for a Dolphin. London, Cape, 1988; New York, Crown, 1989.
Sacred Elephant. London, Cape and New York, Crown, 1989.
Autogeddon. London, Cape and New York, Arcade, 1991.

Other

The Speakers. London, Hutchinson, 1964; New York, Grove Press, 1967.
Manifestoes, Manifesten. Rotterdam, Cold Turkey Press, 1975.
Severe Joy. London, Calder, 1979.
Elephants. London, Knockabout Comics, 1983.

*

Critical Study: "Heathcote Williams Issue" of *Gambit 18-19* (London), 1971; "A Note on *The Lost Stigmatic*" by Bert Cardullo, in *Notes on Contemporary Literature* (Boulder, Colorado), January 1988, pp. 11-12.

Theatrical Activities:
Actor: **Films**—*The Tempest*, 1980; *Little Dorrit*, 1987; *Orlando*, 1993.

* * *

Often regarded as a one-play dramatist, Heathcote Williams merits praise not only for his acknowledged counterculture classic of the 1960s, *AC/DC,* but also for plays that have received only cursory critical treatment. All of his plays center on social misfits who either hope for the reformation of a corrupt society or erect barriers against the void that threatens to engulf them.

The spectacular setting and visceral, and often unintelligible, dialogue of *AC/DC* dazzled audiences in the 1960s. In an amusement arcade three hippies meet two schizophrenics, Maurice and Perowne; all are trying to shed media-induced personalities. Maurice helps Perowne achieve the goal by speaking long, fantastic monologues. Maurice's monologues so intimidate two of the hippies, a couple, that they are silenced and drop out of the play altogether.

Bludgeoning dialogue threads through *AC/DC,* although it is not of thematic importance. Sadie, the remaining hippie, competes with Maurice for control of Perowne. Like Maurice, she relies on long, unrelated fantasies to free Perowne from his enslavement to the video screens, television, and radio that are the environment for the second half of the play. Besides fantasizing to Perowne, she also trepans him, thus freeing him from media personalities. Sadie thereby overwhelms Maurice, and she dismisses him for being "into the same territory-sex-adrenalin-bullshit" as everyone else. Sadie looks for a revolution that will destroy such alienation.

Like *AC/DC,* the earlier play *The Local Stigmatic* dramatizes a Pinteresque struggle for dominance. Ray often contradicts and challenges Graham, but ultimately he accedes to the latter's game of assaulting strangers. The games lend form to their otherwise pointless existence.

Like *The Local Stigmatic, Hancock's Last Half-Hour* pits an individual against meaninglessness, but in this play the individual loses. Hancock, a former clown, desperately performs comedy to keep the silence from deafening him. He has locked himself in a hotel room and there engages in the performance that is the play. The performer's fear of audience indifference drives Hancock and accounts for the desperation of his monologue, which includes jokes, readings from encyclopedias, Freud's *Jokes,* press clippings, and parodies of such set pieces as Hamlet's soliloquy. Fear also accounts for his self-mockery and for his final suicide.

The Immortalist is not as compressed or exciting a play as *AC/DC,* nor does it question existence as do *The Local Stigmatic* and *Hancock's Last Half-Hour*. The play is essentially and atypically didactic. The immortalist will not die of natural causes, but he can be killed. Consequently, he would preserve the earth and its inhabitants from human desecration. He argues against passivity: "Listen, people foul up because they stay in the same place. They've traded Utopia for reality. . . . Consuming as a substitute for being. . . . You have radio as a substitute for telepathy, television as a substitute for astral projection. Aeroplanes are a substitute for inner fire."

Williams's freaks indict a society that fosters passivity and consumerism through its mass media. As individuals, they can find no structures or values by which to order and give meaning to their lives.

—Frances Rademacher Anderson

WILLIAMS, Nigel

Nationality: British. **Born:** Cheadle, Cheshire, 20 January 1948. **Education:** Highgate School, London; Oriel College, Oxford. **Family:** Married; three sons. **Career:** Writer and television executive. **Awards:** Somerset Maugham award, for fiction, 1978. **Agent:** Judy Daish Associates, 2 St. Charles Place, London W10 6EG, England. **Address:** c/o Faber and Faber, 3 Queen Square, London WC1N 3AU, England.

Publications

Plays

Double Talk (produced London, 1976).
Snowwhite Washes Whiter, and Deadwood (produced Bristol, 1977).
Class Enemy (produced London, 1978; New York, 1979). London, Eyre Methuen, 1978.
Easy Street (produced Bristol, 1979).
Sugar and Spice (produced London, 1980). With *Trial Run*, London, Eyre Methuen, 1980.
Line 'em (produced London, 1980). London, Eyre Methuen, 1980.
Trial Run (produced Oxford and London, 1980). With *Sugar and Spice*, London, Eyre Methuen, 1980.
W.C.P.C. (produced London, 1982). London, Methuen, 1983.
The Adventures of Jasper Ridley (produced Hull, 1982; London, 1983).
My Brother's Keeper (produced London, 1985). London, Faber, 1985.
Deathwatch, adaptation of a play by Jean Genet (produced Birmingham and London, 1985).
Country Dancing (produced Stratford-on-Avon, 1986; London, 1987). London, Faber, 1987.
As It Was, adaptation of a book by Helen Thomas (produced Edinburgh, 1987).
Nativity (produced London, 1989).
Two and a Half Men in a Boat. London, Spectre, 1993.
Lord of the Flies, adaptation of the novel by William Golding (produced 1995).
Harry and Me (produced London, 1996). London, Faber, 1996.
The Last Romantics (produced Greenwich, 1996).

Screenplay: *The Canterville Ghost.*

Television Plays: *Talkin' Blues*, 1977; *Real Live Audience*, 1978; *Baby Talk*, 1981; *Let 'em Know We're Here*, 1981; *Johnny Jarvis* series, 1983; *George Orwell* (documentary), 1983; *Charlie*, 1984; *Breaking Up*, 1986; *Centrepoint*, 1990; *The Last Romantics*, 1991; *Witchcraft*; *Skallagrigg,* adaptation of the William Horwood novel; *The Wimbledon Poisoner,* from his novel, 1994; *It Could Be You,* 1995.

Novels

My Life Closed Twice. London, Secker and Warburg, 1977.
Jack Be Nimble. London, Secker and Warburg, 1980.
Charlie (novelization of television play). London, Methuen, 1984.
Star Turn. London, Faber, 1985.
Witchcraft. London, Faber, 1987.
Breaking Up (novelization of television play). London, Faber, 1988.
Black Magic. London, Hutchinson Books, 1988.
The Wimbledon Poisoner. London, Faber, 1990.
They Came from SW19. London, Faber, 1992.
East of Wimbledon. London, Faber, 1993.
Scenes from a Prisoner's Life. London, Faber, 1994.
From Wimbledon to Waco. London, Faber, 1995.
The Wimbledon Trilogy. London, Faber, 1995.
Stalking Fiona. London, Granta Books, 1997.

Other

Johnny Jarvis (for children). London, Penguin, 1983.
Buttons in the Marsh. London, Faber, 1989.

*

Critical Study: *Angry Young People: The Working-Class Adolescent in Contemporary English Drama as Portrayed in Selected Plays by Peter Terson, Barrie Keefe, Nigel Williams, and Stephen Poliakoff* (dissertation) by Spencer Gates, New York University, 1991.

Theatrical Activities:
Director: **Television**—*George Orwell*, 1983; *Cambodian Witness* (documentary) by James Fenton, 1987.

* * *

Each of Nigel Williams's early plays (1977-80) explores the interaction of and relations among a handful of sharply distinguished individuals who have been isolated by some circumstance, or who isolate themselves, to form a closed group. A convincing, and relishful, rendering of Cockney speech rhythms enables Williams to generate considerable claustrophobic intensity within this dramatic framework. The intensity, however, is largely negative. The plays are dominated by variations on one particular figure—an overbearingly voluble and physically aggressive embodiment of destructive energy. The figure stands outside every recognizable position, whether social, sexual, or political, and aims to discredit and destroy the positions represented by the other characters through violence both verbal and physical. Although the theme of each play, be it class, race, or sex, is at least implicitly political, the presence of the central figure ensures that the dramatic treatment is less political than psychological. The figure catalyzes and externalizes hidden tensions, sometimes with self-destructive consequences, tearing away civilized constraints in such a way as to lay bare not political or economic causes but atavistic, tribal impulses.

The tribal emerges clearly in *Class Enemy.* The growing tension and final conflict take place not between groups but within a single group. Six fifth formers in a London school fill up an unsupervised afternoon by each "teaching a lesson" on his pet subject. The friction between Iron, the voluble, violent representative of inner-city despair, who cherishes his pessimism and seems to relish debasement, and Sky-Light (the nicknames, of course, being significant), who despite the social circumstances retains trust in the essential goodness of human nature and a radiant perception of the world, erupts into a fight for leadership of the group. Iron wins the fight, but as Sky-Light realizes, the self-directed violence of Iron's moral nature and the frustration of his fevered demand for an indefinable knowledge reveal him as the real victim, the loser.

Sky-Light stands against and illuminates the moral collapse of Iron, but in *Sugar and Spice,* which focuses on sex hatred as *Class Enemy* focuses on class hatred, neither the prostitute Suze nor the lovers Carol and Steve are strong enough to counter the disruptive force of the lesbian Sharon and her male counterpart, the Iron-like John. Each contrives a ritual sexual humiliation, by stripping, of a member of the other sex, and each addresses a savage, climactic speech to the naked victim's genitals. The hatred embodied in Sharon and John represents not just a critique of society's distortion of sexuality but also a mutual revulsion of the sexes that seems to extend to a revulsion from sexuality itself.

Although they are no less bleak in tone than the previous plays, *Trial Run* and *Line 'em* both conclude more decisively. In *Trial Run* Gange, a young Sikh, and Billy, who is of mixed parentage, stage a mock trial with hostages they have taken while holed up waiting for the police to surrender a man from a special patrol group upon whom Gange wants revenge. But the disruptive Billy, with his hatred of society in general, wants more than personal revenge. After Gange has been killed by police marksmen, Billy mysteriously and unexpectedly assumes the posture of inner stillness and blank patience of his Eastern ancestors. His abandonment of the social will makes itself felt as an affirmation, yet in *Line 'em* it is precisely this social will, represented by a solidarity that seems less political than tribal, that is finally affirmed. The anarchistic Foreman mocks and undermines the picket line organized by the old-style union man Sam, yet when soldiers arrive to break the picket, he reunites his own ranks by causing insubordination in those of the enemy and by questioning the validity of the commanding officer's values. In the final tableau the two "armies" confront one another.

It is apparent from these accounts that the power of Williams's drama is cumulative, for each play concentrates on a single situation and builds up to an explosive climax. His two comic-satiric plays of the early 1980s, *W.C.P.C.* and *The Adventures of Jasper Ridley,* which is his most explicitly political play, depart from this pattern by adopting a more obviously scenic form for the presentation of the experiences of the naive, innocent central figures within their respective milieus. *My Brother's Keeper,* however, again focuses intensely on a single, although this time familial and significantly middle-class, situation. As an old actor lies dying in a hospital after a severe stroke, he is visited by his immediate family. His will to live is insistently provoked by his playwright son Tony, whose own thwarted energy arises out of a sense of life wasted through the withholding of feelings, especially love, within this "ordinary" middle-class family. Although vehemently opposed by his brother Sam, a successful businessman with an enduring sense of exclusion from the aesthetic side of the family, Tony attempts to break the maternal domination that he sees as having crippled the family emotionally by encouraging a confrontation, between his parents especially, and a purgation through speaking out. A point of resolution is reached only when the dying actor-father stumblingly articulates the necessity for mutual acceptance within a family of relationships as "states of conflict." Unusually for Williams, and this can be seen as a significant shift of emphasis in his drama, the energies of the play and of its central figure Tony make themselves felt as positive. Yet one does suspect that, more strongly than in Williams's previous work, a great deal of dramatic heat is being expended in the generation of a rather ordinary light.

In *Country Dancing* Williams's work takes on a historical focus. Within a narrative framework provided by an encounter in 1914 between the folk song collector Cecil Sharp and an ancient village fiddler born in the year of Waterloo, the story of the fiddler's life and relationships is played out. It is a story of deprivation, love, betrayal, oppression, and abandonment, but it is one in which the fate of the individual is shown to be inextricably linked to, and even determined by, the enormous social shifts occurring in the century between the two moments of "pointless slaughter." The experience and consequences of rural protest and depopulation and of urbanization and mass industrialization are suggested with point and ingenuity by the songs and dances that punctuate the action. Dance functions as invocation, provocation, and counterpoint and, above all, as a complex metaphor of social, personal, and labor relations, larger patterns shaping the lives of individuals. As life becomes a business and political economy triumphs, the cosmopolitan individualism of the waltz displaces the rooted community of country dance, and the uprooted fiddler loses both his wife and his musical gift. But music is "the only certain thing," and the gift revives just at this moment of impending European holocaust. In its formal fluidity and lucid stylization, quite different from the dense naturalism with which Williams originally made his mark, *Country Dancing* seems to represent a significant shift in his writing for the stage.

—Paul Lawley

WILLIAMSON, David (Keith)

Nationality: Australian. **Born:** Melbourne, Victoria, 24 February 1942. **Education:** Monash University, Clayton, Victoria, B.E. in mechanical engineering 1964; Melbourne University. **Family:** Married 1) Carol Anne Cranby in 1965 (divorced 1972), two children; 2) Kristin Ingrid Lofvén in 1974, two foster children. **Career:** Design engineer, General Motors-Holden's, Melbourne, 1965; lecturer, Swinburne College of Technology, Melbourne, 1966-72. Visiting professor, University of Aarhus, Denmark, 1978.

Commissioner, Australian Broadcasting Corporation, 1978-79; chair, Australian National Playwrights Conference, 1979-80; president, Australian Writers Guild, 1979-86. **Awards:** George Devine award, 1971; Australian Writers Guild award, 1972, 1973, 1977, 1979, 1980; London *Evening Standard* award, 1974; Australian Film Institute award, 1974, 1975, 1976, 1977, 1981, 1987; Best Screenplay award, Oxford Film Festival, 1976; Sydney Critics award, 1983; Penguin award for best mini-series, 1985; Christopher award, 1981. Officer, Order of Australia, 1983. **Agent:** Anthony Williams Management, The Basement, 55 Victoria Street, Potts Point, New South Wales 2011, Australia.

Publications

Plays

The Coming of Stork (produced Melbourne, 1970). Included in *The Coming of Stork, Jugglers Three, What If You Died Tomorrow*, 1974.

The Removalists (produced Melbourne, 1971; London and Cleveland, 1973; New York, 1974). Sydney, Currency Press, 1972; London, Eyre Methuen, 1973.

Don's Party (produced Melbourne, 1971; London, 1975). Sydney, Currency Press, and London, Eyre Methuen, 1973.

Jugglers Three (produced Melbourne, 1972). Included in *The Coming of Stork, Jugglers Three, What If You Died Tomorrow*, 1974.

What If You Died Tomorrow (produced Melbourne, 1973; London, 1974). Included in *The Coming of Stork, Jugglers Three, What If You Died Tomorrow*, 1974.

The Coming of Stork, Jugglers Three, What If You Died Tomorrow. Sydney, Currency Press, and London, Eyre Methuen, 1974.

The Department (produced Adelaide, 1974). Sydney, Currency Press, 1975; London, Eyre Methuen, 1976.

A Handful of Friends (produced Adelaide, 1976). Sydney, Currency Press, 1976.

The Club (produced Melbourne, 1977; London, 1980; as *Players*, produced New York, 1978; as *The Team*, produced Toronto, 1981). Sydney, Currency Press, 1978.

Travelling North (produced Sydney, 1979; London, 1980). Sydney, Currency Press, 1980.

Celluloid Heroes (produced Sydney, 1980).

Gallipoli (screenplay), in *The Story of Gallipoli*, by Bill Gammage. Melbourne, Penguin, 1981.

The Perfectionist (produced Melbourne, 1982; London, 1983). Sydney, Currency Press, 1983.

Sons of Cain (also director: produced Melbourne, 1985; London, 1986). Sydney, Currency Press, 1985.

Collected Plays 1 (includes *The Coming of Stork, The Removalists, Don's Party, Jugglers Three, What If You Died Tomorrow*). Sydney, Currency Press, 1986.

Emerald City (produced Sydney, 1987; London and New York, 1988). Sydney, Currency Press, 1987.

Top Silk. Sydney, Currency Press, 1989.

Siren (produced Sydney, 1990).

Money and Friends (produced Los Angeles, 1992).Sydney, Currency Press, 1992.

Collected Plays 2 (includes *Handful of Friends*; *The Club*; *The Perfectionist*; *Travelling North*). Sydney, Currency Press, 1993.

Brilliant Lies (produced Brisbane, 1993).

Sanctuary (produced Melbourne, 1994). Sydney, Currency Press, 1994.

Dead White Males (produced Sydney, 1995). Sydney, Currency Press, 1995.

Heretic (produced Sydney, 1996). Melbourne, Penguin Books, 1996.

After the Ball. Sydney, Currency Press, 1997.

Third World Blues. Sydney, Currency Press, 1997.

Screenplays: *Stork*, 1971; *The Family Man* (episode in *Libido*) 1972; *Petersen*, 1974; *The Removalists*, 1975; *Don's Party*, 1976; *Mrs. Eliza Fraser*, 1976; *The Club*, 1980; *Gallipoli*, 1981; *Partners*; *The Year of Living Dangerously*, with Peter Weir and C.J. Koch, 1983; *Phar Lap*, 1983; *Travelling North*, 1986; *Emerald City*, 1989; *Brilliant Lies*, 1994; *Sanctuary*, 1995.

Television Plays: *The Last Bastion*, 1985; *The Perfectionist*, 1985; *The Four-Day Revolution*, 1988; *The Four-Minute Mile*, 1988 (U.K.).

Other

Counterpointforum: The Australian Image, with Geoffrey Bolton. Murdoch, Western Australia, Murdoch University, 1981.

*

Critical Studies: "Mask and Cage: Stereotype in Recent Drama" by Margaret Williams, in *Meanjin* (Melbourne), September 1972; in *Southerly* (Sydney), June 1973; "*The Removalists*: A Conjunction of Limitations" by Williamson, in *Meanjin* (Melbourne), no. 4, 1974; "Australian Bards and British Reviewers" by Arlene Sykes, in *Australian Literary Studies* (Hobart, Tasmania), May 1975; "The Games People Play: The Development of David Williamson," in *Contemporary Australian Drama* edited by Peter Holloway, Sydney, Currency Press, 1981, and "David Williamson's Plays since *The Department*," in *Southerly* (Sydney), March 1986, both by Brian Kiernan; *Modern Australian Styles* by Mark O'Connor, Townsville, Queensland, Foundation for Australian Literary Studies, 1982; "A New Map for Australia: The Plays of David Williamson" by John McCallum, in *Australian Literary Studies* (St. Lucia, Queensland), May 1984; interview with Paul Kavanagh and Peter Kuch, in *Southerly* (Sydney), June 1986; *David Williamson* edited by Ortrun Zuber-Skerritt, Amsterdam, Rodopi, 1988; *David Williamson: A Writer's Career* by Brian Kiernan, Sydney, Currency Press, 1996.

Theatrical Activities:
Director: **Play**—*Sons of Cain*, Melbourne, 1985.

David Williamson comments:

I would regard my early plays as mounting a satiric-ironic attack, albeit with a modicum of ambivalent affection, on the conformist philistine, materialist, sexist, and aggressive aspects of the Australian social ethos. In my later plays the personal as distinct from the sociological observations are accorded more weight but the ironic-satiric stance of the earlier plays is, I think, maintained.

* * *

David Williamson is Australia's most widely produced playwright at home and abroad as well as its busiest screenwriter. He communicates an accurate, often unflattering, view of Australia's urban middle class. His dramas tend to be heightened naturalistic portraits with which audiences can identify, while they also make satiric comments on what Williamson describes as "the conformist, philistine, materialistic, sexist, and aggressive aspects of the Australian social ethos." Embodied in his work are serious thematic concerns arising from the tensions of group interaction, power struggles, violence, sexual insecurity, the failure to recognize one's potential, the search for self-discovery, and the struggle of pragmatism versus idealism.

Using aggressively honest language, Williamson's early plays focus with sharp-edged criticism on sociological observations, and they adopt an implicit moral stance, without judgmental proscription, that underlies all of his work. Outstanding among his early plays is *The Removalists,* which later became a successful screenplay. The action centers on an idealistic rookie policeman so humiliated by his cynical superior that he angrily beats to death a feisty working-class wife basher who has resisted the policeman's imperious involvement in the repossession of his estranged wife's furniture by an indifferent removalist (mover). The victim represents the very image of macho fighter and lover, but his fate nevertheless engages the audience's sympathy. *The Removalists* attacks not the police so much as authoritarianism, in a powerful portrayal of the lurking violence in humanity and in male-dominated Australian society in particular. Williamson questions whether violence's arousal and acceptance can be ended in any society that vicariously relishes it.

Other plays of the 1970s also established Williamson's craftsmanship and satiric-ironic bent. With critical affection he explores patterns of social interaction within the darkly humorous rituals of a gathering, party, or meeting. The title character of *The Coming of Stork*—and of the film *Stork*—is a gauche, antiestablishment "ocker" (proletarian) student who disrupts a Melbourne gathering, drunkenly protests a couple's contemplated marriage, and reveals his own hypocrisy. More notable than this somewhat uneven play's attack on middle-class propriety is its new prototype of the urban male. The disrupted ritual of a party also forms the center of the more successful *Don's Party.* Here the interaction of a group of university-educated men in their 30s reflects failed ambitions and hopes as they are caught up in a world of materialistic concerns. This effective social comedy presents well-realized characters and carries an undertone of indictment. *A Handful of Friends* compellingly, if bleakly, treats the betrayal of friendship, as a failed academic, a filmmaker, and their wives conclude a reunion after having torn one another apart, revealing subtle threads that bind them all. In the somewhat autobiographical *What If You Died Tomorrow,* a novelist and his journalist wife find themselves playing hosts to an odd assortment of unexpected guests whose acidulous revelations underscore the play's thematic concern with the loss of never-to-be-regained systems of definite values.

By 1977 Williamson admitted that his plays were becoming less committed to social change, while maintaining their strong moral concern. This is apparent in three plays about institutional or professional environments. *The Club,* which was a popular success, depicts a football club's infighting that results in two self-aggrandizing administrators holding onto power and winning out over coaches representing the true spirit of the game. Amid comically veined confrontations there is a trenchant look at the failure of democracy within a sports club. Academic idealism foiled by institutional bureaucracy and personal interest is the outcome of an engineering faculty-staff meeting in *The Department,* a work drawing on the author's experience as a lecturer in a technical college. The well-integrated play focuses on power struggles and relationships when a self-protective department head subverts a pragmatic solution to a pressing boiler problem and misdirects resources away from the department's ostensible goals. The comic absurdity of the situation is artfully emphasized and enhanced by strong characterizations. In *Sons of Cain* Williamson sardonically views the press through an aggressive newspaper editor's crusade that uncovers high-level corruption involving a government that nevertheless has achieved commendable social reform. The editor worriedly foresees his efforts as leading to the government being superseded by another equally corrupt but less progressive.

Returning to the exploration of moral duty as it clashes with claims of self, Williamson inaugurated his work in the 1980s with *Travelling North.* This excellent bittersweet comedy traces the autumnal relationship between a retired, widowed construction engineer of socialistic opinions and prickly temperament and a conventional middle-aged divorcée ridden with guilt about her neglectful mothering of grown daughters with troubled marriages. Displaying Williamson's maturing theatrical craftsmanship, *Travelling North* presents multidimensional characters in an unsentimental voyage toward self-fulfillment, and it exceeds national bounds to examine questions more universal than peculiarly Australian. Less successful in its plumbing of relationships, *The Perfectionist* examines the need for give-and-take in a marriage between a self-absorbed perfectionist academic and a wife who wants attention and independence. Her attachment to a Danish student hired as house help results in a failed attempt toward freedom but initiates more respectful awareness from the husband.

Williamson's work of the late 1980s and the early 1990s continued to offer perceptive explorations of contemporary problems. *Emerald City* is an effective comedy with autobiographical underpinnings that treats the issue of pragmatism versus idealism. A highly principled screenwriter and his book editor wife move to Sydney, where both are seduced by the Emerald City's magnetic pull toward commercialism. At the conclusion the couple have undergone disillusionment, although they remain in Sydney, sadder but wiser. *Money and Friends* is an acid-laced comedy whose central character is a kindly, tactful man emotionally relied upon by a dysfunctional, money-motivated, self-centered circle of urbane friends. When he abandons tact for truth and also admits facing financial ruin, his friends save one refuse to help. An amusing resolution concludes this sardonic portrait of middle-class values.

Two of Williamson's plays of the 1990s are particularly representative of his diversity in style, subject matter, and thematic focus. *Dead White Males* intermixes realistic with surrealistic scenes in depicting the attack upon liberal humanism—represented by Shakespeare's recurring figure—by poststructuralists—represented by young feminists and a professor not above brainwashing and propositioning female students. A feminist undergoes self-discovery when she learns that her parsimonious grandfather actually has been a generous contributor to the family of a needy coworker. The discovery forces her to reject her antihumanistic professor's agenda and her family's prejudices. *Heretic* covers the efforts of the Australian anthropologist Derek Freeman in the 1980s to discredit the research of the American anthropologist Margaret Mead for her 1928 book on Samoa, which claimed that it was a utopian society free of Western social strictures toward sex and other matters. Although Freeman proves Mead's findings false, an ironic counterpoint to the anthropological story is the play's subplot involving the egocentric Freeman and his subservient wife, who wins emancipation as her husband gains insight. Both plays earned mixed critical reviews, although they merited praise for their substance.

For more than three decades Williamson has drawn a social map of urban Australia, on which he has plotted with developing craftsmanship the personal issues that he and his characters confront. Whether or not he has been successful in transmitting his experience of Australian society to theatergoers outside his native land is less important than the fact that his plays collectively encompass many vital issues faced by middle-class audiences.

—Christian H. Moe

WILSON, August

Nationality: American. **Born:** Pittsburgh, Pennsylvania, 27 April 1945. **Education:** Gladstone High School, Pittsburgh, 1960-61. **Family:** Married Constanza Romero; two daughters. **Career:** Founder, Black Horizons Theatre Company, Pittsburgh, 1968. **Awards:** Jerome fellowship, 1980; Bush fellowship, 1982; Rockefeller fellowship, 1984; McKnight fellowship, 1985; New York Drama Critics Circle award, 1985, 1986, 1990, 1992, 1996; Guggenheim fellowship, 1986; Whiting Foundation award, 1986; American Theatre Critics award, 1986, 1989, 1990, 1991, 1992, 1998; Outer Circle award, 1987; Drama Desk award, 1987; John Gassner award, 1987; Tony award, 1987; Pulitzer prize, 1987, 1990; Helen Hayes award, 1988; Los Angeles Drama Critics Circle award, 1988. **Member:** American Academy of Arts and Sciences; New Dramatists, New York. **Address:** 600 First Avenue, Suite 301, Seattle, Washington 98104-2239, U.S.A.

Publications

Plays

Black Bart and the Sacred Hills (produced St. Paul, 1981).
Jitney (produced Pittsburgh, 1982; revised productions in Pittsburgh and New Brunswick, New Jersey, 1997).
The Mill Hand's Lunch Bucket (produced New York, 1983).
Ma Rainey's Black Bottom (produced New Haven, Connecticut, and New York, 1984; London, 1989). New York, New American Library, 1985; with *Fences*, London, Penguin, 1988.
Fences (produced New Haven, Connecticut, 1985; New York, 1987; Liverpool, 1990). New York, New American Library, 1986; with *Ma Rainey's Black Bottom*, London, Penguin, 1988.
Joe Turner's Come and Gone (produced New Haven, Connecticut, 1986; New York, 1988; London, 1990). New York, New American Library, 1988.
The Piano Lesson (produced New Haven, Connecticut, 1987; revised version produced New York, 1990). New York, New American Library, 1990.
Two Trains Running (produced New Haven, Connecticut, 1990; New York, 1992).
Three Plays (includes *Ma Rainey's Black Bottom, Fences, Joe Turner's Come and Gone*). Pittsburgh, University of Pittsburgh Press, 1991.
Seven Guitars (produced Chicago, Boston, and New York, 1996).

*

Critical Studies: *May All Your Fences Have Gates: Essays on the Drama of August Wilson,* edited by Alan Nadel, Iowa City, University of Iowa Press, 1994; *August Wilson and the African-American Odyssey* by Kim Pereira, Urbana, Illinois, University of Illinois Press, 1995; *The Dramatic Vision of August Wilson* by Sandra Garrett Shannon, Washington, D.C., Howard University Press, 1995; *I Ain't Sorry for Nothin' I Done: August Wilson's Process of Playwrighting* by Joan Herrington, New York, Limelight Editions, 1998; *August Wilson: A Research and Production Sourcebook* by Yvonne Shafer, Westport, Connecticut, Greenwood Press, 1998.

August Wilson comments:

I write about the black experience in America and try to explore in terms of the life I know best those things which are common to all cultures. I see myself as answering James Baldwin's call for a profound articulation of the black experience, which he defined as "that field of manners and ritual of intercourse that can sustain a man once he has left his father's house." I try to concretize the values of the black American and place them on stage in loud action to demonstrate the existence of the above "field of manners" and point to some avenues of sustenance.

* * *

August Wilson is one of America's most significant playwrights. His major works include his proposed cycle of dramas depicting African American life in each decade of the twentieth century. Cut off from their African roots by the legacy of slavery, Wilson's black characters are often victims of racism and economic oppression. Feeling powerless to change their bleak condition, some vent their frustrations on one another. Those able to reclaim their history and spirituality not only find a way to survive but also are inspired to challenge the injustices that plague their lives.

Set in a Pittsburgh boardinghouse in 1911, *Joe Turner's Come and Gone* portrays a man, Herald Loomis, in search of "his song"—that elusive element that would make his life meaningful. Before his journey to Pittsburgh, Loomis lived in Tennessee with his wife and young daughter. Falsely jailed on a trumped-up charge, he was forced to work in one of the chain gangs run by the governor's brother. The years of hard labor broke Loomis's spirit. When he was released from jail, he found that his wife had left his daughter in the care of her mother. Loomis and his daughter travel to Pittsburgh, ostensibly in search of his wife. A "conjure" man named Bynum shows him, however, that it is not the loss of his wife but rather a lack of direction in his life that has been plaguing him. Despite the painful hardships he has endured, Loomis learns to look within himself to find the unique and life-affirming quality that will serve as the source of inspiration and guidance throughout the remainder of his years.

One of Wilson's few plays set outside Pittsburgh, *Ma Rainey's Black Bottom* examines the consequence of black rage when it can find no outlet for expression other than through violence. Set in Chicago in 1927, the play has less to do with the famed blues singer Gertrude "Ma" Rainey than with her studio band. Most of the musicians trade retorts and stories about life, while accepting the exploitation of their talents by whites as an inherent part of the entertainment business. A cocky but gifted young trumpeter, Levee, mistakenly believes that he can break through the racial barriers that have prohibited his peers from reaping their rightful rewards. When rebuffed by the establishment he sought to join, however, he does not lash out at his oppressors. Instead, his wrath results in the death of one of his black musician colleagues. Thus, the playwright suggests that black-on-black crime is a direct result of the prevailing inequitable socioeconomic system.

Set in 1936 in Pittsburgh, *The Piano Lesson* concerns the trials and tribulations a family endures over the legacy of a piano. As slaves in the mid-19th century, two members of the Charles family were exchanged by their owners, the Sutter family, for a piano. When the Sutters order one of the remaining members of the Charles family to carve decorations into the piano, the sculptor instead creates a memorial not only to those recently sold but also to his ancestors who survived from the Middle Passage to the present time. Stolen from the Sutter family by the grandsons of the sculptor, 80 years later the piano is in the possession of Berniece, whose father was killed in retaliation for the theft. Two of the Charles descendants, Berniece and her brother Boy Willie, fight over the piano, not fully understanding its symbolic and emotional worth. Obsessed with the anguish suffered by her mother over the piano, Berniece fails to recognize the more important connection it has with her family's legacy. Boy Willie sees more value in the piano as a commodity to sell in order to purchase land. At the end of the play the family is reconciled, as each member comes to realize that the piano must remain as a living symbol of the family's painful yet proud heritage.

Fences tells the story of a bitter garbageman named Troy Maxson and his family. A former player in the Negro baseball leagues, Troy had developed into a fine batter. When the major leagues finally opened their doors to black athletes, however, he was past his prime and could not compete with younger players. In Pittsburgh he married a woman named Rose, who bore him a son, Cory. Troy found himself in a seemingly endless routine revolving around his work and family responsibilities. He also recognized bitterly that he could not have purchased his house or adequately supported his family if it had not been not for the supplemental income from his brother's disability checks. Thus, Troy understands that poverty and racism have kept him from achieving the American dream. His dissatisfaction with his life consequently leads Troy to betray his family through infidelity and a misguided sense of what is best for them. His ill-fated actions threaten to tear the family apart, while leaving deep emotional scars on those he loves the most. Through the play Wilson teaches that blacks cannot survive on bitterness or thoughts of what should have been. Instead, blacks must learn that adaptation is the key to their survival. Indeed, it is this ability to adjust to new situations that has allowed African Americans to endure horrific experiences.

Although *Two Trains Running* is set in the volatile 1960s, the great political and social upheavals of the times seem to have little effect on the characters of the play. This play is also set in Pittsburgh, and the characters who pass through a diner owned by Memphis Lee appear to have a passive view of life as they spin their tales. Memphis, a frustrated and embittered man, struggles with his own feelings of self-worth as exemplified by the conflict he has with white city officials over the price offered for his home for an urban development project. Ironically, it is a mentally impaired handyman who illustrates that one does not have to accept the role of being a victim in a racist society. Each day for nine years he demands the agreed-upon payment of a ham for the painting of a butcher's fence. His refusal to acquiesce to the butcher's offer of a chicken as compensation inspires others finally to take a stand for their own rights. With the added encouragement and wisdom of an ancient sage, Memphis is motivated to demand and acquire his just rewards from those formerly thought to be immovable, omnipotent opponents.

Set in 1977 at a gypsy cab station in Pittsburgh, *Jitney* is a realistic drama noted for the fidelity with which it portrays black urban speech and life. Becker, the manager of the cab company, and his drivers face the bleak prospect of having their business destroyed by a highway project. Such a plan threatens the economic and social fabric of their African American community, but they initially feel powerless to assert their right to direct their own fate. A responsible and pragmatic man, Becker has been a father figure and friend to his employees. His station serves as a home where they can play checkers or trade stories and dreams. Becker shows little compassion toward his son Booster, recently released from prison. Believing that his imprisonment had caused Booster's mother to suffer undeservedly, Becker sees little of himself in his streetwise son. Soon after Becker decides to fight against the urban renewal scheme, he dies in a freak accident while moonlighting at a steel mill. Realizing the true nature of his father's legacy, Booster now seems ready to lead the men in their struggle for empowerment.

—Addell Austin Anderson

WILSON, Doric

Nationality: American. **Born:** Los Angeles, California, 24 February 1939. **Education;** Studied with Lorraine Larson, Tri-Cities, Washington, 1955-58; apprenticed to Richland Players, Washington, 1952-58; attended University of Washington, Seattle, 1958-59. **Career:** Founding member and playwright-in-residence, Barr/Wilder/Albee Playwrights Unit, New York, 1963-65; artistic director, Ensemble Project, New York, 1965-68; founding member and playwright-in-residence, Circle Repertory Company, New York, 1969-71; founding, artistic director, TOSOS Theatre Company, New York, 1973-77; playwright-in-residence, The Glines, New York, 1978-82, and Jerry West's Funtastic Shows, Portland, Oregon, 1983-84; director, New City Theatre Playwright's Workshop, Seattle, 1985. Director and playwright-in-residence, Pioneer Square Theater, Seattle, 1986—. **Awards:** San Francisco Cable Car award, 1981; Chambers-Blackwell award, 1982; Villager award, 1983; Newsmaker award, 1984. **Address:** 506 9th Avenue, Apartment 3FN, New York, New York 10018, U.S.A.

Publications

Plays

And He Made a Her (produced New York, 1961).
Babel, Babel, Little Tower (produced New York, 1961).

Now She Dances! (produced New York, 1961; revised version produced New York, 1975).
Pretty People (produced New York, 1961).
In Absence (produced New York, 1968).
It Was a Very Good Year (produced New York, 1970).
Body Count (produced New York, 1971).
The West Street Gang (also director: produced New York, 1977). Included in *Two Plays*, New York, Sea Horse Press, 1979.
Ad Hoc Committee (produced New York, 1978).
Surprise (produced New York, 1978).
Turnabout (as Howard Aldon) (produced Richland, Washington, 1979).
A Perfect Relationship (produced New York, 1979). Included in *Two Plays*, New York, Sea Horse Press, 1979; New York, Sea Horse press, 1983.
Forever After: A Vivisection of Gaymale Love, Without Intermission (also director: produced New York, 1980). New York, JH Press, 1980.
Street Theater: The Twenty-Seventh of June, 1969 (produced New York, 1981). New York, JH Press, 1983.

*

Manuscript Collection: Lincoln Center Library of the Performing Arts, New York.

Critical Studies: Introduction by William M. Hoffman to *Gay Plays*, New York, Avon, 1979; *Lavender Culture* by Karla Jay and Allen Young, New York, Jove, 1979: "Caffe Cino" by Wilson, in *Other Stages* (New York), 8 March 1979; interview with Robert Chesley, in *Advocate* (San Francisco), 5 April 1979; "Gay Plays, Gay Theatre, Gay Performance" by Terry Helbing, in *Drama Review* (New York), March 1981; "Images of the Gay male in Contemporary Drama" by James W. Carlsen, in *Gayspeak: Gay male and Lesbian Communication,* edited by James W. Chesebro, New York, Pilgrim, 1981.

Theatrical Activities:
Director: **Plays**—Many productions in New York, most recently *The Madness of Lady Bright* by Lanford Wilson, 1974; *The Hostage* by Brendan Behan, 1975; *What the Butler Saw* by Joe Orton, 1975; *Now She Dances!,* 1976; *The West Street Gang*, 1977; *Forever After*, 1980.

* * *

Doric Wilson is a quintessentially urban dramatist who grew up in rural Washington State but who lived in New York City for more than two decades. He specializes in stylish farce, ironic comedy of wit, and urbane satire. His combination of fantasy and whimsy and his intellectual dialectic may suggest the touch of a Giraudoux or a Shaw, a Wilder or a Wycherley. Yet underlying his often caustic comedy is a surprisingly romantic sensibility that finds him subtly rooting for happy ever-afters.

And He Made a Her (1961) may have been the first play written specifically for Caffe Cino, and therefore for off-off-Broadway. Like many of the Cino writers, Wilson is gay, and, after stints as an original member of both the Barr/Wilder/Albee Playwrights Unit and the Circle Repertory Company, in 1973 he formed the first professional gay company, TOSOS (The Other Side of Silence), which he founded with his income as a bartender.

Wilson excels at accurate observation of life, particularly gay life, which he satirizes but with which he also sympathizes. He was the first to write openly about gay characters who are neither sick nor miserable. Although he dislikes the word "gay," it is a linguistic rather than a political stance. A pioneer in his efforts to write about gay subjects and produce for gay audiences, Wilson has been a leader among up-front homosexuals combating gay self-hatred, and his sharpest satire is reserved for homophobes, whether straight or gay. Wilson's plays speak particularly to gay spectators, but they promote tolerance, affection, honesty, and understanding among people of any sexuality.

Wilson's work is characterized by its playfulness, its fantasy, and its feminism. *And He Made a Her*, for example, dramatizes the displeasure among Adam and the angels caused by Eve's creation. The angelic host—including one being described as "of liberal size and liberal party but not left winged enough to fly—or fall—with Lucifer"—worry about Eve, who is disturbing the natural animosity of the animals, domesticating the plants, and intent upon reproduction. Clearly superior to Adam, she provokes amazement "that woman is able to look up at someone shorter than she is." Perhaps even more surprising is Wilson's substitution, as early as 1961, of the response "A Women" for "Amen." Other early Wilson one-acts that exemplify these characteristics are his satire of narcissism *Pretty People*, set in a museum that displays live people, and the political satire *Babel, Babel, Little Tower*, in which the narcissists are warmongers and religious freaks from several historical periods.

Although these early Wilson plays are not specifically gay in subject, another piece from the period is concerned with homosexuality and has been expanded into a full-length play. *Now She Dances!* comments upon both Oscar Wilde's imprisonment and contemporary America by dramatizing the Salome story according to the dramatic conventions of *The Importance of Being Earnest.* As Lane the butler—"with excellent references from another play"—puts it, *Now She Dances!* gives us "farce fencing force over tea." In both versions Lady Herodias's daughter, Miss Salome, demands and finally receives a man's head on a tray covered with a tea cozy; in the full-length version the word "head" is a double entendre that may go over the heads of some. In the original Wilde is the prisoner who will not come out of the closet; in the rewrite the prisoner is an unashamed and clever contemporary American homosexual whom Salome tries to seduce. The words she speaks as she unbuttons her bodice typify Wilson's simultaneous accomplishment of more than one objective: "In years to come, when you talk of this, and you will, be kind."

Those famous lines, directed in Robert Anderson's *Tea and Sympathy* toward a boy who is sympathetic because he is not gay, serve as an implicit critique of years of theatrical treatment of the homosexual, who until recently was usually ignored or despised or pitied. Wilson hardly misses an opportunity to mix comments on the theater with his wider political satire. Among jabs at animal symbols of women (seagull, wild duck), Actors Studio nonsense about an actress who plays a maid "identifying" with the soup she is serving, and tedious first scenes ("a lovely bouquet of blue expositions"), Wilson spoofs gay dramatists such as Genet and Wilde who do not give a reasonable facsimile of the life thousands of homosexuals actually live.

Street Theater is a play about the hours preceding the Stonewall riots, which gave birth to the gay rights movement. Wilson mocks the self-contemptuous pair from *The Boys in the Band* and a closet queen, as well as the heterosexual mobster bar owner who exploits his "queer" customers and a couple of vice squad cops, one of whom arrests the other. Set on the street near the Stonewall bar, the comedy offers politically provocative wit plus an array of deftly characterized New York homosexuals, and it suggests what sort of homophobic treatment prompted them to turn on their tormentors in revolt.

Another treatment of the street and bar scene by one of its aficionados is found in *The West Street Gang*, which likewise dramatizes the victimization of gays by homophobes, opportunists, and one another. Set in a downtown West Side leather bar, it was also performed in one (Spike). It shows the bar's patrons threatened by a gang of teenage fag bashers of the type who regularly try to murder gays with baseball bats and tire chains. Their efforts at self-protection are led by a transvestite but hampered by a so-called gay rights leader, Arthur Klang (a thinly disguised Arthur Bell of the *Village Voice*), and by Bonita Aryant (a still more thinly disguised Anita Bryant, then waging a nationwide crusade against homosexuality). *The West Street Gang* offers more than simply appropriate politics. It is a hilarious treatment of some familiar New Yorkers who turn out to be more than mere stereotypes. There is a hustler who gets rolled, a pacifist who urges violence, and, best of all, a drag queen who leads the fight against the marauding street gang. On entering "she" follows the butch dress code, but she goes to the john and then simpers back onstage in a dress. Whether hero or heroine, she stands up well not only to the homophobic cops and bar owner and to Bonita, who mistakes the bar's patrons for longshoremen, but also to her less than broad-minded fellow patrons in the bar. Indeed, the varied characters lead us to conclude that tolerance, cooperation, and mutual respect are the qualities Wilson most admires.

Among his domestic love stories *Turnabout* is one of several Wilson satires of straight relationships. *A Perfect Relationship* depicts the friendship of two men who do not recognize that they ought to be lovers, and *Forever After* is both a romantic comedy and a parody of same.

Written under the pseudonym Howard Aldon, *Turnabout* is a suburban sitcom in which a wife teaches her adulterous husband a lesson without actually sleeping with other men. A play in which nonstop one-liners compete with very funny situations as sources of humor, *Turnabout* devastates the complacent husband's double standard. It demonstrates Wilson's capacity for the kind of heterosexual commercial comedy he could regale Broadway with if he were not more interested in a different type of dramaturgy. He has, however, written several other satires of heterosexual relationships, including *In Absence*, *It Was a Very Good Year*, *Body Count*, and *Surprise*.

In *A Perfect Relationship* the protagonists, Ward and Greg, are roommates whose lifestyle is built upon a commitment to noncommitment. Both thrive on cruising, which Greg practices at discos and Ward at backroom bars. Although they are not lovers, they bicker as though they were—over who does the laundry, cooks dinner, or takes the first shower. They even keep score, as though it were an organized sport, while denigrating each other's masculinity. They have a "perfect" relationship until both sleep with the same trick, a young opportunist who uses this one-night stand to acquire Ward and Greg's desirable Christopher Street apartment. Along the way to discovering that they ought to be lovers, Ward and Greg deal with the kooky heterosexual woman from whom they are subletting. She and her boyfriends behave as though they are at a zoo, with the young men the animals, yet her preconceptions about gays are not much sillier than their own. Although she outdoes them in promiscuous noninvolvement, she helps the roommates to recognize that they share a lot more than the rent.

The kind of love story Wilson writes in *A Perfect Relationship* he sets out to parody in *Forever After*, but at the same time he maintains an effective tension in the latter between amusement at romanticism and acceptance of long-term commitment between men. Tom and David's amorous remarks are jeered at by two mocking muses in drag seated in proscenium boxes. It actually is Melpomene, the tragic muse, who sets out to destroy the affair. It is her descent into the fray to coach the lovers in suspicion and disharmony that prompts the comic muse Thalia to follow and defend the playwright's prerogative to give the young men a happy-ever-after conclusion. Something of a descendant of Sheridan's *The Critic* or of the Duke of Buckingham's *The Rehearsal*, *Forever After* mixes presentational and representational styles while lampooning such theatrical targets as Sam Shepard's *Buried Child*, Martin Sherman's *Bent*, Edward Albee's *The Lady from Dubuque*, Robert Patrick's *T-Shirts*, general negativity in drama, and the claims made by performers in gay plays that they are straight. The particular object of Wilson's wrath and wisecracks, however, is melodrama in which the homosexual is a tormented degenerate.

Wilson's ear for the varieties of gay attitudes, jargon, and quips is as good as ever in *Forever After*, and his penchant for punning is true to his best form. The dialogue is among his most raunchy and real. As to his appraisal of the dispute between the muses, Wilson shares Thalia's views; he sees the funny and playful side of everything, including love, but on the subjects of human relations and aesthetics he is not a cynic. Although *Forever After* demonstrates that it is easier to fight than to sustain a relationship, Wilson sets us to cheering those who succeed at commitment.

—Tish Dace

WILSON, Lanford (Eugene)

Nationality: American. **Born:** Lebanon, Missouri, 13 April 1937. **Education:** Ozark High School, Missouri; Southwest Missouri State College, Springfield, 1955-56; San Diego State College, California, 1956-57; University of Chicago, 1957-58. **Career:** Worked at various jobs, including advertising, Chicago, 1957-62; director, actor, and designer for Caffe Cino and Cafe La Mama theatres, New York, and other theatres. Co-founder and resident playwright, Circle Repertory Company, New York, 1969—. **Awards:** Rockefeller grant, 1967, 1974; Vernon Rice award, 1968; ABC-Yale University fellowship, 1969; New York Drama Critics Circle award, 1973, 1980; Obie award, 1973, 1975, 1983, 1997; Outer Circle award, 1973; American Academy award, 1974; Drama-Logue award, 1978, 1979; Pulitzer Prize, 1980; Brandeis University Creative Arts award, 1981; John Steinbeck award, 1989. **Agent:** Bridget Aschenberg, International Creative Management, 40 West 57th Street, New York, New York 10019, U.S.A. **Address:** P.O. Box 891, Sag Harbor, New York 11963, U.S.A.

Publications

Plays

So Long at the Fair (produced New York, 1963).
No Trespassing (produced New York, 1964).
Home Free! (also director: produced New York, 1964; London, 1968). Included in *Balm in Gilead and Other Plays*, 1965; with *The Madness of Lady Bright*, London, Methuen, 1968.
Balm in Gilead (produced New York, 1964; Edinburgh, 1986). Included in *Balm in Gilead and Other Plays*, 1965.
The Madness of Lady Bright (also director: produced New York, 1964; London, 1968). Included in *The Rimers of Eldritch and Other Plays*, 1967; with *Home Free!*, London, Methuen, 1968.
Ludlow Fair (produced New York, 1965; Edinburgh, 1967; London, 1977). Included in *Balm in Gilead and Other Plays*, 1965.
Balm in Gilead and Other Plays. New York, Hill and Wang, 1965.
Sex Is Between Two People (produced New York, 1965).
The Rimers of Eldritch (also director: produced New York 1965). Included in *The Rimers of Eldritch and Other Plays*, 1967.
This is the Rill Speaking (also director: produced New York, 1965). Included in *The Rimers of Eldritch and Other Plays*, 1967.
Days Ahead (produced New York, 1965). Included in *The Rimers of Eldritch and Other Plays*, 1967.
The Sand Castle (produced New York, 1965). Included in *The Sand Castle and Three Other Plays*, 1970.
Wandering: A Turn (produced New York, 1966). Included in *The Rimers of Eldritch and Other Plays*, 1967.
The Rimers of Eldritch and Other Plays. New York, Hill and Wang, 1967.
Miss Williams: A Turn (produced New York, 1967).
Untitled Play, music by Al Carmines (produced New York, 1967).
The Gingham Dog (produced Washington, D.C., 1968; New York, 1969; Manchester, 1970). New York, Hill and Wang, 1969.
The Great Nebula in Orion (produced Manchester, 1970; New York, 1972; London, 1981). Included in *The Great Nebula in Orion and Three Other Plays*, 1973.
Lemon Sky (produced Buffalo and New York, 1970). New York, Hill and Wang, 1970.
Serenading Louie (produced Washington, D.C., 1970; New York, 1976). New York, Dramatists Play Service, 1976; revised version (produced New York, 1984), New York, Hill and Wang, 1984.
The Sand Castle and Three Other Plays (includes *Wandering*, *Stoop: A Turn*, *Sextet (Yes): A Play for Voices*). New York, Dramatists Play Service, 1970.
Sextet (Yes): A Play for Voices (produced New York, 1971). Included in *The Sand Castle and Three Other Plays*, 1970.
Summer and Smoke, music by Lee Hoiby, adaptation of the play by Tennessee Williams (produced St. Paul, 1971; New York, 1972). New York, Belwin Mills, 1972.
Ikke, Ikke, Nye, Nye, Nye (produced New Haven, Connecticut, 1971; New York, 1972; London, 1981). Included in *The Great Nebula in Orion and Three Other Plays*, 1973.
The Family Continues (produced New York, 1972). Included in *The Great Nebula in Orion and Three Other Plays*, 1973.
The Great Nebula in Orion and Three Other Plays (includes *Ikke, Ikke, Nye, Nye, Nye*; *The Family Continues*; *Victory on Mrs. Dandywine's Island*). New York, Dramatists Play Service, 1973.
The Hot l Baltimore (produced New York, 1973; London, 1976). New York, Hill and Wang, 1973.
The Mound Builders (produced New York, 1975). New York, Hill and Wang, 1976.
Brontosaurus (produced New York, 1977; London, 1982). New York, Dramatists Play Service, 1978.
5th of July (produced New York, 1978; Bristol, 1987). New York, Hill and Wang, 1979.
Talley's Folly (produced New York, 1979; London, 1982). New York, Hill and Wang, 1980.
Bar Play, in *Holidays* (produced Louisville, 1979).
Talley and Son (as *A Tale Told*, produced New York, 1981; revised version, as *Talley and Son*, produced New York, 1985). New York, Hill and Wang, 1986.
Angels Fall (produced New York, 1982). New York, Hill and Wang, 1983.
Thymus Vulgaris (produced New York, 1982). New York, Dramatists Play Service, 1982.
Three Sisters, adaptation of a play by Chekhov (produced Hartford, Connecticut, 1985; New York, 1986; revised version produced Hartford, Connecticut, 1992).
Say deKooning (produced Southampton, New York, 1985). Included in *Hall of North American Forests*, 1988.
Sa-Hurt? (produced New York, 1986).
A Betrothal (produced London, 1986; New York, 1987). Included in *Hall of North American Forests*, 1988.
Burn This (produced Los Angeles and New York, 1987; London, 1990). New York, Hill and Wang, 1988.
Dying Breed (produced New York, 1987).
A Poster of the Cosmos (produced New York, 1987; London, 1992).
Hall of North American Forests (includes *The Bottle Harp*, *Say deKooning*, *A Betrothal*) (produced New York, 1987). New York, Dramatists Play Service, 1988.
The Moonshot Tape (produced New York, 1990).
Redwood Curtain (produced Seattle, Washington, 1992; New York, 1993).
A Sence of Place (produced Sag Harbor, 1997). New York, Dramatists Play Service.
Sympathetic Magic (produced New York, 1997). New York, Dramatists Play Service.
Book of Days (produced Chelsea, Michigan, 1998).

Screenplays: *One Arm*, 1970; *Burn This*, 1992; *Talley's Folly*, 1992.

Television Plays: *The Migrants*, from a story by Tennessee Williams, 1974; *Taxi!*, 1979.

*

Bibliography: *Ten Modern American Playwrights* by Kimball King, New York, Garland, 1982.

Critical Studies: "The Comic Vision of Lanford Wilson" by Martin J. Jacobi, in *Studies in the Literary Imagination* (Atlanta), Fall 1988; "Wilson Lanford" by John L. DiGaetani, in *A Search for a Postmodern Theater: Interviews with Contemporary Playwrights*, New York, Greenwood, 1991; "An Interview with Lanford Wilson" by John C. Tibbetts, in *Journal of Dramatic Theory and Criticism* (Lawrence, Kansas), Spring 1991; *A Comfortable House: Lanford Wilson, Marshall W. Mason, and the Circle Repertory* by Philip Middleton Williams, Jefferson, North Carolina, McFarland & Company, 1993; *Discovery and Invention: The Urban Plays of*

Lanford Wilson by Anne Dean, Rutherford and London, Fairleigh Dickinson University Press, 1995.

Theatrical Activities:
Director: **Plays**—Many of his own plays, including *The Rimers of Eldritch*, New York, 1965; *This Is the Rill Speaking*, New York, 1965; *Indecent Exposure* by Robert Patrick, New York, 1968; *Not to Worry* by A. E. Santaniello, New York, 1975; *In Vienna* by Roy London, New York, 1980.

Actor: **Plays**—In *The Clown*, New York, 1968; *Wandering*, New York, 1968; *Him* by E. E. Cummings, New York, 1974.

* * *

Lanford Wilson's plays are deeply concerned with the conflict between the traditional values of the past and the insidious pressures of modern life. While he has been only intermittently successful at resolving this conflict, it has provided him with dramatic material of great variety and interest. The eccentric characters of *Balm in Gilead* and *The Madness of Lady Bright* fight or flee convention, and their desperation is sharply and sympathetically drawn. *The Rimers of Eldritch* or *This Is the Rill Speaking* ridicule the hypocrisy, bigotry, and convention of a small town while they rejoice in the confused innocence and energy of its adolescents. These collage plays, in which different strands of dialogue interweave, scenes overlap, and actors double their roles, allowed Wilson deftly to juxtapose the rooted strengths and values of the old with the energy and explorations of the young.

Wilson's experiments with the collage style resolved themselves in *The Hot l Baltimore*, which is set in a deteriorating flophouse whose sign has lost its *e* and which is peopled by whores, retirees, outcasts, and deadbeats. At the Hotel Baltimore, however, it is the old who have rejected convention and the young girl who fights to recover the past. This call girl is as dismayed that no one will fight to save the hotel—"That's why nothing gets done anymore. Nobody's got the conviction of their passions"—as she is furious that a young stranger gives up the search for his grandfather too easily. More naturalistic than earlier plays, *The Hot l Baltimore* uses a clear and simple prose and the physical symbol of the hotel to focus on Wilson's basic concerns.

Wilson's trilogy about the Talley family again uses buildings as the symbol of an emotional and social conflict between past and present. *5th of July,* set in the present, reunites the scattered Talleys: Aunt Sally Talley, her nephew Ken and his homosexual lover, and Sally's niece June and her illegitimate daughter. Since Ken, whose legs were paralyzed in Vietnam, and June are offering the house to two old friends who were fellow radicals in the 1960s, the play was frequently described as an evaluation of the decade's politics. The politics are not deeply felt, however, and quickly become secondary to the sale of the house, which comes to represent the rejection of the family's roots in favor of a future they do not want or like. *Talley and Son,* set in World War II but the last play to be written, hinges on the struggle between Sally Talley's father and grandfather over control of the family business. While this play is excessively and clumsily complex, *Talley's Folly,* whose action is concurrent with that of *Talley and Son,* concerns the elegantly compact and dramatically clear courtship of Sally Talley by a New York lawyer, Matt Friedmann. Described as "a valentine" by Matt, who frequently and nonnaturalistically addresses the audience, the play unites tradition and progress through his warm, obstinately honest, and ultimately successful wooing of Sally.

While *Talley's Folly* avoids topical issues to its benefit, *Angels Fall* uses an accident at a nearby nuclear plant to trap characters in a small Catholic church (compare *Bus Stop*). Paralleling a young, intelligent Navaho's rejection of his responsibility to his community with an art historian's sudden and violent rejection of his life's work, the play's pretext seems gratuitous and its resolution of the characters' spiritual crises mechanical.

A talented craftsman of dialogue, Wilson often fails to weld his situations seamlessly to his deepest concerns. When, however, his primary values—honesty and the love of friends, family, and home—are tied closely to the dramatic situations, his plays enact crucial questions about how the fabric of society is woven and cared for over generations.

—Walter Bode

WILSON, Robert M.

Nationality: American. **Born:** Waco, Texas, 4 October 1941. **Education:** University of Texas, Austin, 1959-62; Pratt Institute, Brooklyn, New York, 1962-65, B.F.A. 1965; studied painting with George McNeil, Paris, 1962; apprentice in architecture to Paolo Soleri, Acrosanti community, Phoenix, Arizona, 1966. **Career:** Artistic director, Byrd Hoffman Foundation, New York, 1970—; frequent lecturer at seminars and workshops, 1970—. Artist: individual shows, 1971—. **Awards:** Best Foreign Play award (France), 1970; Guggenheim fellowship, 1971, 1980; Drama Desk award, for directing, 1971; Obie award, for directing, 1974, 1986; Rockefeller fellowship, 1975, and award, 1981; Maharam award, for design, 1975; BITEF, Belgrade Grand prize, 1977; Lumen award, for design, 1977; French Critics award, for musical theatre, 1977, for best foreign play, 1987; German Critics award, 1979; Der Rosenstrauss, Munich, 1982; Harvard University citation, 1982; San Sebastian Film Festival award, 1984; Berlin Theatre Festival award, 1984, 1987; Malaga Theatre Festival Picasso award, 1986; Boston Theatre Critics Circle award, 1986; Skowhegan medal, for drawing, 1986; Bessie award, 1987; American Theatre Wing Design award, for noteworthy unusual effects, 1987; Mondello award, Palermo, 1988; The American Institute of Architects honor, 1988; New York Public Library Lion of the Performing Arts, 1989; São Paulo great prize, for best event, 1989; Italian Theatre Critics award, 1989; Barcelona Festival of Cinema Art grand prize, for video, 1989; Paris Film Festival special mention, for video, 1989; German Theatre Critics award, 1990. **Address:** Byrd Hoffman Foundation, 131 Varick Street, Number 908, New York, New York 10013, U.S.A.

PUBLICATIONS

Plays

Dance Event (produced New York, 1965).
Solo Performance (produced New York, 1966).
Theater Activity (produced New York, 1967).
ByrdwoMAN (produced New York, 1968).
Alley Cats (produced New York, 1968).

Watermill (produced New York, 1969).
The King of Spain (produced New York, 1969). Published in *New American Plays 3*, edited by William M. Hoffman, New York, Hill and Wang, 1970.
The Life and Times of Sigmund Freud (produced New York, 1969).
Deafman Glance (produced Iowa City, 1970; New York, 1971).
Program Prologue Now, Overture for a Deafman (produced Paris, 1971; New York, 1972).
Overture (produced New York, 1972).
Ka Mountain and GUARDenia Terrace: A Story about a Family and some People Changing (produced Shiraz, Iran, 1972).
King Lyre and Lady in the Wasteland (produced New York, 1973).
The Life and Times of Joseph Stalin (produced Copenhagen and New York, 1973).
Dia Log/A Mad Man a Mad Giant a Mad Dog a Mad Urge a Mad Face (produced Rome and Washington, D.C., 1974).
The Life and Times of Dave Clark (produced São Paulo, 1974).
"Prologue" to A Letter for Queen Victoria (produced Spoleto, Italy, 1974).
A Letter for Queen Victoria (produced Spoleto, Italy, on tour, and New York, 1974). New York, Byrd Hoffman Foundation, 1974.
To Street (Bonn, 1975).
The $ Value of Man (produced New York, 1975).
Dia Log, with Christopher Knowles (produced New York, 1975).
Spaceman, with Ralph Hilton (produced New York, 1976).
Einstein on the Beach, music and lyrics by Philip Glass (produced Avignon, France and New York, 1976). New York, EOS Enterprises, 1976.
I Was Sitting on My Patio This Guy Appeared I Thought I Was Hallucinating (produced Ypsilanti, Michigan, and New York, 1977; London 1978). New York, Byrd Hoffman Foundation, 1978.
Dia Log/Network, with Christopher Knowles (produced Boston, 1978).
Overture to the Fourth Act of Deafman Glance (produced Purchase, New York, 1978; New York, 1987).
Death, Destruction, and Detroit (produced Berlin, 1979). New York, Gnome Baker, 1978.
Dia Log/Curious George, with Christopher Knowles (produced Brussels, 1979; New York, 1980).
Edison (produced Lyon, France, and New York, 1979).
The Man in the Raincoat (produced Cologne, 1981).
Medea, with Gavin Bryars (produced Washington, D.C., 1981; New York, 1982).
Great Day in the Morning, with Jessye Norman (produced Paris, 1982).
The Golden Windows (produced Munich, 1982; New York, 1985). Munich, Hanser, 1982.
the CIVIL warS: a tree is best measured when it is down (sections produced Rotterdam, 1983; with Heiner Müller, Cologne, 1984; with Maita di Niscemi, Rome, 1984; with *The Knee Plays*, music and lyrics by David Byrne, Minneapolis, 1984; Tokyo, 1984: Marseille, 1984; Cambridge, Massachusetts, 1985). Sections published Amsterdam, Meulenhoff Landshoff, 1983; Frankfurt, Suhrkamp, 1984; Rome, Edizioni del Teatro dell' Opera, 1984; Los Angeles, Otis Art Institute, 1984; with *The Knee Plays*, with David Byrne, Minneapolis, Walker Art Center, 1984; with Heiner Müller, Cambridge, Massachusetts, American Repertory Theater, 1985.
King Lear (produced Hollywood, 1985).
Readings (produced Dublin, 1985).
Alcestis, adaptation of the play by Euripides, with Heiner Müller (produced Cambridge, Massachusetts, 1986). Stuttgart, Staatstheater Stuttgart, 1987.
Death, Destruction, and Detroit II (produced Berlin, 1987).
Parzival, with Tankred Dorst (produced Hamburg, 1988). Hamburg, Thalia Theatre, 1987.
Cosmopolitan Greetings (book only), music by Rolf Liebermann and George Gruntz, text by Allen Ginsberg (produced Hamburg, 1988).
The Forest (book only), music by David Byrne, text by Heiner Müller and Darryl Pinckney (produced Berlin and New York, 1988). Berlin, Theater der Freien Volksbuhne, 1988.
De Materie, music by Louis Andriessen (produced Amsterdam, 1989).
Orlando, adaptation of the novel by Virginia Woolf, text by Darryl Pinckney (produced Berlin, 1989).
The Black Rider: The Casting of Magic Bullets, music and lyrics by Tom Waits, text by William S. Burroughs (produced Hamburg, 1990).
Steel Velvet. Munich, Prestel, 1997.
Robert Wilson: RWWM. Zurich and New York, Memory/Cage Editions, 1997.

Screenplay: *Overture for a Deafman*, 1971.

Video: *Spaceman*, with Ralf Hilton, New York, 1976, Amsterdam, 1984; *Video 50*, Ecublens, Switzerland, 1978; *Deafman Glance*, 1981; *Stations*, 1982; *La Femme à la Cafetière*, Paris, 1989; *The Death of King Lear*, 1989.

Recordings: *The Life and Times of Joseph Stalin*, Byrd Hoffman Foundation, 1973; *Einstein on the Beach*, music and lyrics by Philip Glass, CBS, 1979; *the CIVIL warS: Knee Plays*, music and lyrics by David Byrne, Warner Brothers, 1985.

*

Manuscript Collection: Rare Book and Manuscript Library, Columbia University, New York.

Critical Studies (selection): *The Theatre of Visions: Robert Wilson* by Stefan Brecht, Frankfurt, Suhrkamp, 1979, London, Methuen, 1982; *Robert Wilson: The Theater of Images* edited by Craig Nelson, Cincinnati, Contemporary Arts Center, 1980, revised edition, New York, Harper, 1984; "The Forest as Archive: Wilson and Interculturalism" by Bonnie Marranca, in *Performing Arts Journal* (Baltimore, Maryland), 1989, pp. 36-44; *Robert Wilson and His Collaborators* by Laurence Shyer, New York, Theatre Communications Group, 1990; *Robert Wilson's Vision: An Exhibition of Works*, edited by Trevor J. Fairbrother, Boston, Massachusetts, Museum of Fine Arts, 1991; "Robert Wilson: Is Postmodern Performance Possible?" by Katherine Arenas, in *Theater Journal* (Baltimore, Maryland), March 1991, pp. 14-40; "Time, Wilson, and What a Play Should Do" by Gordon Rogoff, in *Theater* (New Haven, Connecticut), Summer-Fall 1991, pp. 52-53; *Alone in a Crowd: A Reception-History of Avant-Garde Productions in the United States: Samuel Beckett, The Living Theater, Robert Wilson* (dissertation) by Edmond Loren Gaible, University of California (Berkeley), 1993; *The Language of Visual Theater: Sign and Context in Josef Svoboda, Meredith Monk, and Robert Wilson* (dissertation) by Robert Dean Wilcox, University of

Washington, 1994; "Robert Wilson's Theater of Images and the Japanese Theater" by Sang-kyong Lee, in *The Force of Vision, I: Dramas of Desire; Visions of Beauty,* edited by Earl Miner, Tokyo, International Comparative Literature Association, 1995; "Poet from Another World: Robert Wilson in France" by Laurence Romero, in *The French Review: Journal of the American Association of Teachers of French* (Champaigne, Illinois), February 1995, pp. 487-500.

Theatrical Activities:
Director and Designer: **Plays**—All his own plays; *American Hurrah* by Jean-Claude van Itallie, New York, 1966 (design only); *A Letter to Queen Victoria,* Spoleto, Italy, on tour, and New York, 1974; *Hamletmachine* by Heiner Müller, New York, and Hamburg, 1986, London, Paris, on tour, Madrid, and Palermo, 1987; *Quartet* by Heiner Müller, Stuttgart, 1987, Cambridge, Massachusetts, 1988; *Swan Song* by Chekhov, Munich, 1989, Tokyo, 1990; *King Lear* by Shakespeare, Frankfurt, 1990; *When We Dead Awaken,* adaptation of the play by Ibsen, Cambridge, Massachusetts, 1991. **Opera**—*Medée* by Marc-Antoine Charpentier, Lyon, France, 1984; *Alceste* by C.W. Gluck, Stuttgart, 1986, Chicago, 1990; *Salome* by Richard Strauss, Milan, 1987; *Le Martyre de Saint Sebastian* by Claude Debussy (choreographed with Suzushi Hanayagi), Paris and New York, 1988; *Doktor Faustus,* adaptation of the novel by Thomas Mann, music by Giacomo Manzoni, Milan, 1989; *La Nuit d'avant le jour* (inauguration of the Opera Bastille), Paris, 1989; *Parsifal* by Richard Wagner, Hamburg, 1991. **Films**—*The House,* 1963; *Slant,* 1963; *Overture for a Deafman,* 1971.

* * *

Robert M. Wilson is an atypical dramatist in that he composes with pictures rather than words, and he creates through directing his works, few of which have been published, on the stage. Early productions with his Byrd Hoffman School of Byrds, named after Wilson's dance therapist, had affinities with the 1930s surrealists. Drama therapy work with a deaf mute and with a man with severe brain damage showed that one picked up sounds in the form of vibrations, or "interior impressions," while the other created a "graphic" logic from the aural shape of words independent of conventional sense.

Wilson's performance pieces express this "autistic" perception of the world, from his first, relatively simple piece—*Deafman Glance,* which formed part of the epic *Ka Mountain and GUARDenia Terrace*—to later collaborations with Heiner Müller. Their structure is an architectural arrangement of sounds, words, and movements in which images are restated or varied to form thematic motifs. The presentation is designed to sensitize the spectator to the same subliminal range of nuances as a brain-damaged deaf mute. Wilson sees autism as an increasingly common psychological response to the pressures of contemporary life, and his aim is therapeutic, to open the audience to interior impressions. The result is an audiovisual collage of dreamlike and seemingly disconnected images that are deliberately presented with obsessive repetitiveness and painful slowness. This kind of temporal fourth dimension reached its fullest extension with *Ka Mountain* at the Shiraz festival, spreading over seven days and moving from a picture frame stage to cover a whole mountainside.

At one point the only movement was that of a live turtle crossing the empty stage, which took almost an hour, while the mountain behind was dotted with unrelated two-dimensional cardboard cutouts—Noah's ark, a dinosaur, flamingos, the Acropolis surrounded by a ring of ICBM rockets, Jonah's whale, and a graveyard, with the Manhattan skyline on the summit. This last cutout was burnt to the ground on the final day of the performance and replaced by a Chinese pagoda with the Lamb of God inside. (The original plan, vetoed by the Iranian festival authorities, had been to blow up the mountaintop or paint it entirely white.) There was no intellectual sense to be made out of this apocalyptic collage. The dialogue resembled automatic writing or dadaist free association. Yet there were obvious mythical connotations: the creation of the world corresponding to the seven-day performance of the play, "ka" representing the soul, and a seasonal birth/death/resurrection pattern.

Wilson's "chamber" pieces tend to draw their dream imagery from social rather than religious archetypes, as in *A Letter for Queen Victoria.* Queen Victoria listens while a long and totally meaningless letter is read aloud. Couples in white sit at café tables gesticulating frenetically and speaking the same lines—"chitter-chatter, chitter-chatter"—simultaneously. The effect is disorienting rather than satiric, however, with two ballet dancers slowly spinning on either side of the stage throughout the performance and somnambulistic characters talking in endless non sequiturs. Again, there are apocalyptic overtones: a sniper shoots the couples, who collapse one by one across their tables, and the performance ends with a long drawn-out scream. But the focus is on perception itself instead of on what is perceived. Four aviators/Lindberghs stand with their backs to the audience, looking at a changing land-/cloudscape through a huge window; a Chinese man stands behind another enormous window frame, staring out at the audience through a continually opening and closing venetian blind.

Coexisting independently in their collaborative work, Müller's verbal poetry and Wilson's visual imagery—like the separated halves of metaphor—form overlapping layers of sign versus signifier. The possible multiple meanings are more than the sum of the statements, making rational comprehension almost impossible. This surrealistic unrelatedness and conflict of opposites, the hallmark of Wilson's later drama, is represented by *the CIVIL warS: a tree is best measured when it is down.*

Originally intended for performance at the 1984 Olympic Games, this multilingual, multimedia epic has reached the stage only in fragmented segments. Texts by both Wilson and Müller—plus excerpts from letters by Frederick the Great and Kafka and fragmented passages from Empedocles, Goethe, Hölderlin, Shakespeare, and Racine—accompanied a sequence of pictures drawn by Wilson, in any of his productions the initial step from which movements and tableaux are developed. The flow of images turned history into a multinational stream of consciousness, and a major theme was the way events get recorded in art. The starting point of scene E of the third act—produced with scene A of the fourth act and the epilogue in Cologne and at the ART—was Mathew Brady's American Civil War photographs, with the anachronistic presence of Frederick the Great leading to other types of conflict: Frederick's invasion of neighboring territories to unify Germany, which spread to North America and became a prototype for modern world wars; Frederick's battles with his father, representing familial conflict; and Frederick's schizoid combination of Enlightenment liberalism and militaristic brutality as the emblem of a single person at war with himself. The apocalyptic final section presented documentary film of New York high-rise buildings being demolished.

Although the material can be described in such linear terms, the effect was hallucinatory. Fantastical figures—elongated black scribes bearing huge black quills like swords; a white scribe dressed in ornate folds of paper and transfixed by a massive pencil; a half human dog; waltzing polar bears—share the stage with historical characters. Frederick the Great was played by several different actors, both male and female. In the epilogue Abraham Lincoln—a sticklike, 20-foot, top-hatted puppet that topples like a felled tree—is juxtaposed with mythical Hopi Indian beings—Snow Owl, and Earth Mother—and with King Lear mourning the dead Cordelia (actually a pile of crumpled newspaper).

History as hallucination, time scales that distort conventional modes of perception, and deconstructed reality as myth—these are the defining features of Wilson's drama.

—Christopher Innes

WILSON, Snoo (Andrew Wilson)

Nationality: British. **Born:** Reading, Berkshire, 2 August 1948. **Education:** Bradfield College, Berkshire, 1962-66; University of East Anglia, Norwich, 1966-69, B.A. (upper second) in English and American studies 1969. **Family:** Married Ann McFerran in 1976; two sons and one daughter. **Career:** Founding director, Portable Theatre, Brighton and London, 1968-75; script editor, *Play for Today* series, BBC Television, 1972; dramaturge, Royal Shakespeare Company, 1975-76; director, Scarab Theatre, 1975-80. Henfield fellow, University of East Anglia, 1978. **Awards:** John Whiting award, 1978; US Bicentennial fellowship, 1980; San Diego Theater Critics Circle award, 1988. **Agent:** Casarotto Ramsay Ltd., National House, 60-66 Wardour Street, London W1V 3HP. **Address:** 41 The Chase, London SW4 0NP, England.

Publications

Plays

Girl Mad as Pigs (produced Norwich, 1967).
Ella Daybellfesse's Machine (produced Norwich, 1967).
Between the Acts, adaptation of the novel by Virginia Woolf (produced Canterbury, 1969).
Charles the Martyr (produced Southampton, 1970).
Device of Angels (produced Edinburgh and London, 1970).
Pericles, The Mean Knight (also director: produced London, 1970).
Pignight (also director: produced Leeds and London, 1971). With *Blowjob*, London, Calder, 1975.
Blowjob (produced Edinburgh and London, 1971). With *Pignight*, London, Calder, 1975.
Lay By, with others (also director: produced Edinburgh and London, 1971). London, Calder and Boyars, 1972.
Reason (as *Reason the Sun King*, produced Edinburgh, 1972; as *Reason: Boswell and Johnson on the Shores of the Eternal Sea*, in *Point 101* produced London, 1972; as *Reason*, produced Chicago, 1975). Published in *Gambit* (London), vol. 8, no. 29, 1976.
England's Ireland, with others (also director: produced Amsterdam and London, 1972).
Vampire (produced London, 1973). Published in *Plays and Players* (London), July 1973; revised version (produced London, 1977; New York, 1979), Ashover, Derbyshire, Amber Lane Press, 1979.
The Pleasure Principle: The Politics of Love, The Capital of Emotion (produced London, 1973). London, Eyre Methuen, 1974.
The Beast (produced London, 1974; New York, 1977). Published in *Plays and Players* (London), December 1974 and January 1975; revised version, as *The Number of the Beast* (produced London, 1982), with *Flaming Bodies*, London, Calder, and New York, Riverrun Press, 1983.
The Everest Hotel (also director: produced London 1975). Published in *Plays and Players* (London), March 1976.
A Greenish Man (televised 1975; produced London, 1978). London, Pluto Press, 1979.
The Soul of the White Ant (produced London, 1976). London, TQ Publications, 1978; New York, French, 1983.
Elijah Disappearing (produced London, 1977).
England-England, music by Kevin Coyne (produced London, 1977).
The Glad Hand (produced London, 1978). London, Pluto Press, 1979.
In at the Death, with others (produced London, 1978).
The Language of the Dead Is Tongued with Fire (produced London, 1978).
Flaming Bodies (produced London, 1979). With *The Number of the Beast*, London, Calder, and New York, Riverrun Press, 1983.
Magic Rose (produced London, 1979).
Spaceache, music by Nick Bicât (produced Cheltenham and London, 1980).
Salvation Now (produced Seattle, 1981).
The Grass Widow (produced Seattle, 1982; London, 1983). London, Methuen, 1983.
Our Lord of Lynchville (produced New York, 1983; as *Lynchville* produced London, 1990).
Loving Reno (produced New York, 1983; also co-director: produced London, 1983).
La Colombe, music by Gounod, adaptation of the libretto by Barbier and Carré (produced Buxton, Derbyshire, 1983).
Hamlyn (produced Loughborough, Leicestershire, 1984).
Orpheus in the Underworld, with David Pountney, music by Offenbach, adaptation of the libretto by Crémieux and Halévy (produced London, 1985).
More Light (also co-director: produced London, 1987). Oxford, Mandrake, 1990.
80 Days, music and lyrics by Ray Davies (produced La Jolla, California, 1988).
Walpurgis Night (produced London, 1992).

Screenplay: *Shadey*, 1986.

Television Plays: *The Good Life*, 1971; *Swamp Music*, 1972; *More about the Universe*, 1972; *The Barium Meal*, 1974; *The Trip to Jerusalem*, 1975; *A Greenish Man*, 1975; *Don't Make Waves* (*Eleventh Hour* series), with Trevor Griffiths, 1975.

Novels

Spaceache. London, Chatto and Windus, 1984.
Inside Babel. London, Chatto and Windus, 1985.

*

Critical Studies: Interview in *Theatre Quarterly* (London), Spring 1980; "Theatre on the Wrong Side of the Law: An Interview with Snoo Wilson" by Joel Schecther, *Theater* (New Haven, Connecticut), Spring 1981, pp. 56-60; "Snoo Wilson: Enfant Terrible on the English Stage" by James Bierman, in *Modern Drama* (Downsview, Ontario), December 1981, pp. 424-35; "Snoo Wilson" by Simon Trussler, Malcom Page and Elaine Turner, in *New Theatre Quarterly* (Cambridge, England), February 1989, pp. 86-96; "Snoo Wilson" by Dawn Dietrich, in *British Playwrights, 1956-1995: A Research and Production Sourcebook*, edited by William Demastes, Westport, Connecticut, Greenwood, 1996.

Theatrical Activities:
Director: **Plays**—*Pericles, The Mean Knight*, London, 1970; *Pignight*, Leeds and London, 1971; *Lay By*, Edinburgh and London, 1971; *England's Ireland*, Amsterdam and London, 1972; *Bodywork* by Jennifer Phillips, London, 1974; *The Everest Hotel*, London, 1975; *Loving Reno* (co-director, with Simon Callow), London, 1983; *More Light* (co-director, with Simon Stokes), London, 1987.

Actor: **Plays**—*Lay By*, London, 1971; The Porpoise in *Fresh-water* by Virginia Woolf, London, 1983; Andy Warhol in *Warhola!*, London, 1990.

Snoo Wilson comments:

(1973) More than anything else the proscenium arch theatre suggests the success of drawing room conversation as a mirror for a mature civilization. In these mirrors, the even keel of the state slices through the waters of unconsciousness, and very few playwrights have managed to knock any holes in the boat, though a number have suggested that the ship was sinking without their assistance, and others, like the stewards on the *Titanic*, bicycle gaily round the first-class gym, declaring that there is no list to the ship. These last are the ones most likely to be rewarded by the first-class passengers for their élan vital, even while the bilge water is rising round the ankles of the steerage families. The bicycling stewards are most likely to be able to command support that is quite independent of anything except people's gratitude at being amused, and many of them die peacefully in their beds declaring that there was always a slight list to port anyhow, and their reward was plainly a just one since people came and gave willingly, and were briefly happy.

A different brand of steward feels considerable unease at the condition of the ship, and his actions are likely to be much less popular at first than the bicyclists, though as time passes and his costume becomes charmingly archaic his pieces will be revived as Art, safe now from the Life he tried to redirect, which will have moved on in a lateral, unexpected direction. Television in Britain created a brand of "responsible" playwrights whose reputations at first were large and abrasive but now have stabilised in characteristic and therefore unsurprising because recognisable positions of social dynamism, and there the matter rests, a compromise acceptable both to producers who would like to produce more radical plays but have taken "Grandmother's footsteps" as far as they think the head of drama will let them, and to an audience stunned by tedium and kept alive by a feeling they ought to watch plays, sustained by tiny whiffs of excellence that occur in the smog of apathy. Both television and the theatre with one or two exceptions had failed either to make any formal advances in technique or to investigate areas of emotion which would force advances on them: I say "failed" because I believe that there must always be a technical evolution in theatre if only to remind audiences that they are watching a particular genre: playwrights who are adept at naturalism can take the edge off the most workmanlike oeuvre by making its naturalism subliminal.

The small groups who started with very little assistance at first—sometimes none—from the Arts Council in the late 1960s had a different sort of audience, a different sort of motive, and were a growth outside the conventional structure of theatre in Britain largely because it was dull and extremely conservative and did not provide outlets for the sort of things they wanted to do, or, in the case of Portable Theatre, a writer's theatre first, to write. Since there was very little money anyway the opportunity to write what the writer wanted to write and put it on in the way he wanted was possible, and a series of one night stands provided continuous platforms for plays which in the beginning we were prepared to take anywhere.

Now, there are a large number of studio theatres, almost a circuit, round the country. The success of *Lay By*, a group play written round a newspaper story, at the Edinburgh Festival, suggested that it was desirable and possible to launch a play about contemporary events to tour large theatres round England and Scotland. After six months of extreme difficulty we managed to set up a tour of a play about Northern Ireland, called *England's Ireland*, which had its first three weeks in Holland because we were unable to find theatres in England in sufficiently large numbers prepared to take the risk of an unknown play by a previously, quote, experimental group.

When we did bring the play to England, sadly it was in Chalk Farm at the Roundhouse rather than in Glasgow where it drew a significant response, and Lancaster and Nottingham were the only large repertory companies which would have it.

This demonstrates, among other things, the self-stultifying conservatism of the control of British theatre boards who believe that their audiences should be fed what they are accustomed to consume, either the costume drama of Ibsen's Choice, or on plays which by ignoring all but the most trivial of human difficulties and miseries close minds rather than open them in a stuffy two hours at the theatre.

The title I would choose for this essay, *The Freudian Landscape and the Proscenium Mind*, suggests that the middle-class mind is firmly ensconced on stage; this is true only by its being a self-perpetuating situation: it is not true that if we want to widen the range of theatrical experience we have to abandon the theatre. The theatre has always been a whore to safe fashion, but at the moment there is a pressure for a particular sort of awareness and articulacy which hopefully may lead to the good lady opening her legs to a different position, and renewed and enlarged clientele being the result. The plangent cries of either the affronted audience or management should not be an invitation to a secondary dialogue, whose end is respectability. Nor should this secondary dialogue be mistaken for a play, for the theatre is not that self-sufficient, being old, and bloated with the worst vices of time serving and sycophancy: and these will show through shallow devices. It is ourselves, finally, rather than the civilisation, who we have to prove mature; so, paradoxically, the struggle for exposure which shapes the ideas must not dent them, any more than an achieved articulacy within theatrical convention supplants the need for further thought.

* * *

Snoo Wilson began his writing career in the late 1960s with Portable Theatre, of which he was a founding director along with two friends from Cambridge, David Hare and Tony Bicât. Wilson himself studied at the then new University of East Anglia. His earlier plays, particularly *Pignight* and *Blowjob,* are extremely clever and dark works that reflect a good many of Wilson's general preoccupations. Though never an overtly political dramatist, Wilson has always been concerned with problems of individual psychology, in particular schizophrenia, with moral anarchy, and, most specifically, with the threat of pollution on a planet that, like the absurdists with whom he has so much in common, he shows to be in direct if often comic opposition to man's dreams and aspirations. In *Pignight* a Lincolnshire farm is taken over by a sinister gangster and turned into a machine for the organized butchering and processing of the animals in question. Underneath this surface violence runs a thread of eeriness. Smitty, a psychopathic farm laborer inherited by the new owners, is a running reminder of the war. He suffers from mysterious brain damage and takes delight in committing acts of savagery, including the blowing up of the farm dog, Robby. *Blowjob* is an equally violent exercise in alienation, with two skinheads planning to blow up a safe in a factory, an act they bungle. During their travels they meet up with a homosexual security guard who tries unsuccessfully to pick them up and with a girl student who, typically for the time of the play, is alienated from her academic environment. The whole play acts as a caustic comment on role playing and its stultifying effect on personality.

Both *Vampire* and *The Pleasure Principle* are plays that further develop Wilson's preoccupation with external ethical codes and their effect on individual freedom. *Vampire,* which has been both revived and revised by Wilson, has a conventional three-act structure that moves from a late nineteenth-century Presbyterian parsonage and a scene of astral sex in an Edwardian cricket pavilion to a contemporary scene of youthful disquiet and finishes with Enoch Powell, risen vampirelike from his coffin and delivering his famous "Rivers of Blood" speech. (The setting has been altered in a subsequent version from a secular funeral parlor to the pagoda in Kew Gardens.) The second act of *Vampire* is a neat example of Wilson's developing style.

In tune with a belief that the stage is the freest medium, Wilson concentrates on sharp juxtapositions that transcend conventional unities of time and place and, despite Wilson's often underestimated gift for composition, that continually upstage the dialogue spoken by his characters. Sarah, an upper-class girl, is wooed by a handsome young cricketer called Henry, who was killed in World War I. He returns in his astral form to try to make love to Sarah, who is frightened of being seen. Freud and Jung suddenly appear on stilts to discuss her hang-up in their own jargonistic fashion, while a talking ox grunts, "Let's go to my place and fuck." *The Pleasure Principle* concentrates on the almost undefined relationship between two characters whose opposing ideas of pleasure prevent them from consummating their mutual attraction until the last act. In fact, Robert and Gale make it after a seduction sequence played out in a cardboard swan, while the nervous breakdown of Robert, an aggressive businessman with a great belief in capitalism, is prefigured by the entrance of a pair of dancing gorillas bearing messages.

Although Wilson is something of a grand old man of the British fringe, he refuses, or is unable, to be assimilated into the mainstream despite a belief on his own part that his plays are designed to be both popular and fun. Indeed, he has developed an eclectic and mercurial interest in occult subjects and in trendy pseudoscience. In *The Beast* and *The Soul of the White Ant,* the latter a quite breathtaking short play, he has explored the worlds of two dead cult figures, the satanist Aleister Crowley and the South African naturalist Eugène Marais, whose reputation, part visionary and part charlatan, is tested by the methods of free association that characterize Wilson's work at its best. The title of the play derives from one of Marais's works about the corporate soul that Wilson employs as a metaphor for the collective insanity of his characters, a group of white South Africans who congregate in and around a bar run by a boozy eccentric, Mabel. In typical Wilsonian fashion the bar is caked with mud and threatened by etymological disaster, while Marais himself enters as a backstreet abortionist, white suited, visionary, and also corrupt, a combination of killer and life giver as symbolized by an act he performs when Mabel goes mad and shoots her houseboy, whose carefully collected sperm is now filling her freezer. When the stuff is thrown into the local river, two of Mabel's friends, Edith and June, are impregnated, and it is Marais who saves them, but only after Mabel's bizarre act of racial and sexual mutilation.

Wilson's most ambitious and perfectly realized play is probably *The Glad Hand,* which works on many levels both as a political thriller and as a bizarre and often wacky study in synchronization. On the surface the piece concerns the attempt of one Ritsaat, a fascistic South African, to locate and confront the anti-Christ who he claims was present on earth during a cowboy strike in Wyoming in 1886. Ritsaat's plan is simple. He will charter an oil tanker and by time travel via the Bermuda Triangle confront the anti-Christ in person. In fact, Ritsaat, through ingenuously offering "cowboy fun" in his recruiting advertisement, acquires two camp actors as part of the crew, along with a family of stock Paddies, a portly American scriptwriter, a Cuban cook, a CIA agent, and a dubious psychic surgeon who performs an operation on board. Indeed, the ship acts as the setting for the re-created cowboy strike, which includes passages of riveting documentary description of conditions prevailing at the time of an incident that did, in fact, happen. There is also the arrival on board of a raunchy American lesbian who sparks off several more of the play's coincidences until a final mutiny against Ritsaat's rule develops into an alliance of Cuban cook and chauvinist Irishman. Before dying Ritsaat manages to utter, "Between you and your perceptions is the mirror which you think reflects reality." It is a comment that sums up a good deal of Wilson's own intentions. Indeed, in showing that reality is something that can be changed or at least rearranged, he is making both a theatrical point about naturalism and a political point about the world as it exists, although how much real substance there is behind the technique is open to serious questioning.

In *A Greenish Man* Wilson employs his associative powers on the subject of Northern Ireland. Troy Phillips, a half-Irish Liverpudlian, is sent to Kilburn on an errand of revenge. There he encounters an IRA dinner being organized by the local Irish publican, as well as a bedraggled factory owner who has perfected a formula for green paint made entirely from grass clippings and a battered divorcée with a liberal conscience and a tax lawyer. It is a play that fell down in production because the knots Wilson used to tie up the different strands of his ideas did not survive the tug of live performance.

Flaming Bodies is set in the smart and characterless office of a Los Angeles film producer whose overweight, compulsively hungry script editor, Mercedes, has just been sacked but refuses to leave the office. Again, Wilson uses this Hockneyesque setting as a launching pad for a trip in which Mercedes rediscovers herself, but only after experiencing such events as a Chevy from another film crashing through the window of the office block, King Herod discovering his love of small boys (the film she is working on at the time of her sacking is a life of Christ), Mary and Joseph (both pregnant) turning up on an inflatable donkey, and her mother's ashes turning up in a film producer's lunch. Indeed, Mercedes spends a good deal of the time on the phone talking to her mother, to whom she protests her lesbianism, and to her psychiatrist, to whom she protests her sanity. In the flip, weight-conscious world of California film production, Mercedes is attacked on all sides, even by her dead father, who hovers in the air outside the office's huge picture window.

In the cartoon play *Spaceache* Wilson created an Orwellian world in which the unwanted and unemployed are cryogenically freeze-dried and reduced to milk bottle size before being sent into orbit until their time comes for resurrection. The play certainly does not exhibit Wilson's talents at their most representative, unlike those in which surface organization is being continually broken up and re-created, and, in an often mundane theatrical terrain, supernatural forces or natural powers are often the real arbiters of the proceedings.

Wilson's refusal to compromise on his chosen artistic progression has continued to cause him problems. Although he has moved with some success into novels, films, and opera, his work refuses to find a home on the main stages of any of Britain's premier subsidized companies despite initial plans and interest from both the National and the Royal Shakespeare Company. *The Grass Widow,* done for the Royal Court, was a rather unsuccessful jumble of ideas and effects inspired by a year's sabbatical in California. *The Number of the Beast* was an effectively reworked version of *The Beast.* Wilson's obsession with Aleister Crowley has continued to produce dividends, and the piece was an immensely entertaining essay on Crowley's bizarrely revolutionary life. Wilson's film *Shadey,* with Antony Sher as the eponymous sexually confused character, was well reviewed. And he had stunning success with the libretto for David Pountney's production of Offenbach's *Orpheus in the Underworld,* a much seen version for the English National Opera. Here it seemed that Wilson's ability to challenge accepted notions of taste and presentation and his impressive grasp of theatrical metaphor were welded to a firm base. It is sad that, although his work is increasingly produced abroad, notably in the United States, he has not realized his enormous potential at home.

—Steve Grant

WOLFE, George C.

Nationality: American. **Born:** Frankfort, Kentucky in 1954. **Education:** Pomona College, Claremont, California, B.A.; New York University, M.F.A. in dramatic writing and musical theatre. **Career:** Playwright, actor and director, 1978—. Producer of New York Shakespeare festival, 1993—. **Awards:** Hull-Warriner award, 1986; Playwrights U.S.A. award, 1988; Obie award, for direction, 1990 Tony award, 1992, for best director of a play, for *Angels in America,* 1994; HBO/USA Playwrights award; New York Distinguished Alumni award; Drama Desk award, 1992; Dorothy Chandler award, 1992; AUDELCO award; Oppenheimer award; Hull-Warner "Spirit of the City" award; LAMDA Liberty award; recognized as a "Living Landmark," New York Landmarks Conservancy, 1995. **Address:** c/o Grove/Atlantic Monthly Press, 841 Broadway, New York, New York 10003, U.S.A.

Publications

Plays

Paradise!, music by Robert Forest (produced Cincinnati, 1985; New York, 1985).

The Colored Museum (produced New Brunswick, New Jersey and New York, 1986; London, 1987). London, Methuen, 1987; New York, Grove, 1988.

Queenie Pie, music by Duke Ellington (produced New York, 1987).

Over There in *Urban Blight* (musical revue), based on an idea by John Tillinger, music by David Shire, lyrics by Richard Maltby, Jr. (produced New York, 1988).

Spunk, adaptation of stories by Zora Neale Hurston, music by Chic Street Man (includes *Sweat, Story in Harlem Slang, The Gilded Six-Bits*) (also director: produced New Brunswick, New Jersey, 1989; New York, 1990).

Blackout (produced New York, 1991).

Jelly's Last Jam (also director: produced New York, 1992).

Television Plays: *Hunger Chic,* 1989; *The Colored Museum,* 1991; *Jammin': Jelly Roll Morton on Broadway,* 1992.

*

Critical Studies: "Angels in America, Devils in the Wings" by Gordon Rogoff, in *Theater* (New Haven, Connecticut), 1993, pp. 21-29; "George C. Wolfe: Playwright, Director, and Producer" in *Callaloo: A Journal of African American and African Arts and Letters* (Baltimore, Maryland), Summer 1993, pp. 591-629; "Theatre and the Wolfe" by Ed Morales, in *American Theatre,* December 1994, pp. 14-20; "George C. Wolfe" by Bell Hooks, in *BOMB,* Winter 1994-1995, pp. 46-51; "Modern Morality Plays on Broadway: *Jelly's Last Jam* and *Angels in America*" by Ulrich Muller, in *Trends in English and American Studies: Literature and the Imagination,* Lewiston, New York, Mellen, 1996.

Theatrical Activities:
Director: **Plays**–Many of his own plays; *Angels in America* by Tony Kushner, 1994.
Television–*The Colored Museum,* 1991; *Jammin': Jelly Roll Morton on Broadway,* 1992; *In the Wings: Angels in America on Broadway,* 1993; *Fires in the Mirror,* 1993.

Actor: **Television**–*Finding Christa,* 1991; *Fresh Kill,* 1993.

* * *

Besides August Wilson, George C. Wolfe is probably the most prominent African American dramatist of contemporary times. Wolfe's most popular play, *The Colored Museum*, presents 11 satirical skits, called "exhibits," that deftly portray modern-day African American life. The first exhibit, "Git on Board," depicts a gleeful stewardess on a "celebrity slaveship" who takes her passengers on a trip at a warped speed through African American history. In "Cookin' with Aunt Ethel" an earthy black woman recalling an Aunt Jemima stereotype sings a biting blues song about the ingredients needed to make up a "batch of Negroes." "The Photo Session" lampoons blacks who are stylish in dress but lack substantive thoughts or feelings. "Soldier with a Secret" portrays a facet of black life characterized by a sense of hopelessness, which drives people to seek desperate measures to eliminate the pain of their existence. In this skit the ghost of a Vietnam soldier kills members of his platoon to spare them from enduring the lives of anguish they are sure to experience once they return home. "The Gospel according to Miss Roj" depicts a "snap queen" who initially compels us to laugh at his outrageous attire, speech, and behavior. Just as we become comfortable being amused by this self-styled "extraterrestrial" being, however, he forces us to examine our own smugness and disinterest in the well-being of others. "The Hairpiece" is a hilarious look at the preoccupation blacks have in reconciling their dual identities as Africans and Americans. "The Last Mama-on-the-Couch Play" parodies such dramas as Lorraine Hansberry's *A Raisin in the Sun* and Ntozake Shange's *For Colored Girls Who Have Considered Suicide*, while also satirizing classical training for blacks and the unrealistic portrayal of blacks in musicals. In "Symbiosis" a middle-class black man finds that he cannot discard his ethnic past in order to assimilate more easily into the dominant white society he wants so desperately to be a part of. "Lala's Opening" reveals an entertainer of international prominence who, like the man in the previous skit, tries unsuccessfully to ignore all traces of her African American heritage. In "Permutations" a once neglected and denigrated young woman creates a new image of self-worth through the experience of giving birth and nurturing her newborn. In the final exhibit, "The Party," a number of famous African Americans gather to celebrate their cultural heritage. Through the character of Topsy Washington the play's theme is revealed: the survival of blacks as a people comes from an appreciation of one's past and from a "madness" that allows one to adapt to and endure the absurdities and needless pain of African American life.

Wolfe's next major work, *Spunk*, was based on three short stories concerning male-female relationships by the writer, folklorist, and anthropologist Zora Neale Hurston. Throughout the show the songs of the Guitar Man and the Blues Speak Woman complement the scenes. The first tale, *Sweat*, depicts a destructive relationship in rural Florida. Delia, the sole support of the household, leads an unpleasant life with Sykes, her abusive and adulterous husband. Although Delia has purchased and cared for their home, Sykes decides to drive her out of it so that he can share the house with his lover Bertha. Knowing that his wife is greatly afraid of reptiles, Sykes attempts to terrorize her by bringing a rattlesnake into the house. Though frightened, Delia refuses to succumb to his act of intimidation. Growing impatient, Sykes decides to attack Delia in bed, but he ironically meets his own doom when the snake gives him a fatal bite. In stark contrast to the preceding, *Story in Harlem Slang* is a comical look at male-female relations as told in the vernacular of the people of Harlem. Two gigolos, Jelly and Sweet Back, boast of their seductive talents and decide to test their appeal on a young woman. After sizing them up, however, the woman quickly deflates their egos as she belittles them for believing her to be so naive as to yield to their dubious charms. Perhaps the most poignant of the three tales is *The Gilded Six-Bits*. The wife in a once happy marriage is seduced by the allure of gold possessed by a businessman. Catching his wife in an adulterous act, the husband proves her lover to be nothing more than a con artist deceiving people with his gilded coins. Although the couple remain married, their relationship changes drastically as the husband takes an aloof attitude toward his wife. After she gives birth to a son, however, the husband finds that he can forgive her, and he begins to nurture their relationship once again. Thus, the power of love overcomes the deceptions of the past.

Wolfe wrote the book for a later work, the musical *Jelly's Last Jam*, based on the life of the first great jazz composer, Jelly Roll Morton. The play is unlike those musicals that are little more than an excuse for blacks to sing and dance or those historical dramas that provide only praise for their subjects. Instead, the musical takes a critical look at Morton's accomplishments, as well as his ignoble traits. Set on the eve of his death, the play dramatizes events of his life and dares to question whether the Creole musician neglected to credit his African American heritage for the uniqueness and appeal of the musical style he helped to make popular.

—Addell Austin Anderson

WONG, Eleanor

Nationality: Malaysian. **Born:** Singapore, 6 February 1962. **Education:** National University of Singapore, LLB; New York University, law degree. **Career:** Lawyer with international firm. **Awards:** First prize, Singapore's First National Short Play Competition, 1985, for *Peter's Passionate Pursuit*; National Book Development Council Book award, 1996.

Publications

Plays

Peter's Passionate Pursuit (produced Singapore, 1985). NUS Shell Series, 1986.
To Touch the Soul of a God (produced Singapore, 1987).
Jackson on a Jaunt (produced Singapore, 1987).
Real Life? (produced Singapore, 1989).
The Joust (produced Singapore, 1991).
Mergers and Accusations (produced 1995).
Block Sale (produced Singapore, 1996).
Wills and Secession. In *Playful Phoenix,* Singapore, 1996.

* * *

The appearance of Eleanor Wong on the Singapore theater scene marks an important point in that nation's stage history. Here was a woman—a young, bright, witty lawyer—prepared to say things straight from a woman's point-of-view. Though Singapore has some very fine female actors, fine women playwrights are rare, the scene being dominated, as it were, by the "male giants": Kuo Pau Kun, Haresh Sharma, Desmond Sim, Robin Loon, and Robert Yeo. Though Stella Kon's *Emily of Emerald Hill* explored a woman's world in a historically set Singapore, Kon's play does not deal with the inner tensions of women—the tensions that women feel when their lives are ruined by their own choices, choices that society cannot accommodate without some form of punishment.

Wong's first major play, *Peter's Passionate Pursuit* (1985), is a strangely beautiful play that has as its basis a strong critique of Singapore's broad political culture. One of Wong's major preoccupations seems to be "compromise," and the play reveals how compromise becomes a kind of ethic by which people—especially those for whom power is the underlying foundation for good living—trade and exchange their values. This witty, in part funny, in part tragic, play explores the tensions that develop in the course of a lifestyle where honesty and truth are only very gradually surfacing to haunt the major players. The play was performed with high-tech props, and audiences were delighted by a treat of fantasy interwoven neatly with familiar echoes from their own lives and surroundings.

The broad political critique apparent in *Peter's Passionate Pursuit* is carried on, from one point of view at least, into the main themes of *The Joust* (1991), which looks at the question of dramatic political change. How is transition from a totalitarian state to a democratic state achieved, especially in a society that finds it hard to recognize the true (or real) meaning of democracy? This play was actually staged in the middle of Singapore's 1991 general elections and provided an interesting backdrop as it were for the choices before the electorate. Though the main characters carry vague Slavic names, the play could be said to be about Singapore itself—a nation asking itself how best to change without losing the good that had been achieved through some harsh measures taken in times of political crises.

Mergers and Accusations (1992) was a groundbreaking production; it featured for the first time in mainstream Singapore theater a lesbian principal. The play hauntingly explores deceit, cunning, love, pain, and suffering that result when society cannot accept an open homosexual relationship. The homosexual theme is also evident in the earlier play *Jackson on a Jaunt* (1987, but withdrawn from the stage on account of its "explicit" homosexual theme and then reworked and finally staged in 1989); in this play the whole question of "truth" in human relationships is raised when Jackson, its protagonist, discovers he has HIV, which puts at risk his fiancee, his mistress, and himself. The sequel to *Mergers and Accusations, Wills and Secession,* explores the received definition of "family" and challenges the notion that a homosexual partnership cannot constitute a family unit. This play, more mature and in some ways more substantial than *Mergers and Accusations,* also discusses crucial issues of religion (linking it with another of Wong's plays, *To Touch the Soul of a God*), love, and loyalty (bringing audiences back to *Peter's Passionate Pursuit,* which is also about loyalty) and gives to Wong's work a breadth that is quite rare in Singapore theater.

It is early yet to place Eleanor Wong within the context of Singapore theater, but her confidence and courage in willing to deal with themes and problems that many in Singapore find disturbing cannot be left unnoticed. Wong has written (in a personal letter): "I could wish for nothing better than, through my writing, to highlight some issues, concerns, injustices, opportunities, and wonders of the Singaporean experience and to stimulate fresh and creative thinking about them." This she certainly does, probably more than most have so far cared to acknowledge.

—Kirpal Singh

WOOD, Charles (Gerald)

Nationality: British. **Born:** St. Peter Port, Guernsey, Channel Islands, 6 August 1932. **Education:** Chesterfield Grammar School, 1942-45; King Charles I School, Kidderminster, Worcestershire, 1945-48; Birmingham College of Art, 1948-50. **Military Service:** Served in the 17/21st Lancers, 1950-55: corporal. **Family:** Married Valerie Elizabeth Newman in 1954; one son and one daughter. **Career:** Factory worker, 1955-57; designer, scenic artist, and stage manager, Theatre Workshop, London, 1957-59; staff member, Bristol *Evening Post*, 1959-62. **Awards:** *Evening Standard* award, 1963, 1973; Screenwriters Guild award, 1965; prix Italia Rai, 1988; BAFTA award, 1988; Royal Television Society award, 1988. Fellow, Royal Society of Literature, 1985. **Agent:** Jane Annakin, London Management, 2-4 Noel Street, London W1V 3RB, London. **Address:** Long Barn, Sibford Gower, Near Banbury, Oxfordshire OX15 5RT, England.

Publications

Plays

Prisoner and Escort (televised 1961; produced in *Cockade*, London, 1963).

Cockade (includes *Prisoner and Escort, John Thomas, Spare*) (produced London, 1963). Published in *New English Dramatists 8*, London, Penguin, 1965; published separately, New York, Grove Press, 1967.

Tie Up the Ballcock (produced Bristol, 1964; New York, 1986). Published in *Second Playbill 3*, edited by Alan Durband, London, Hutchinson, 1973.

Don't Make Me Laugh (produced London, 1965).

Meals on Wheels (produced London, 1965; shortened version produced Liverpool, 1971).

Fill the Stage with Happy Hours (produced Nottingham, 1966; London, 1967). Published in *New English Dramatists 11*, London, Penguin, 1967.

Dingo (produced Bristol and London, 1967). London, Penguin, and New York, Grove Press, 1969; London, Oberon Books, 1998.

Labour (produced Bristol, 1968).

H, Being Monologues at Front of Burning Cities (produced London, 1969). London, Methuen, 1970; London, Oberon Books, 1998.

Colliers Wood (produced Liverpool, 1970; London, 1971).

Welfare (includes *Tie Up the Ballcock, Meals on Wheels, Labour*) (produced Liverpool, 1971).

Veterans; or, Hair in the Gates of the Hellespont (produced Edinburgh and London, 1972). London, Eyre Methuen, 1972; London, Oberon Books, 1997.

The Can Opener, adaptation of a play by Victor Lanoux (produced London, 1974).

Jingo (produced London, 1975). London, Oberon Books, 1998.

The Script (produced London, 1976).

Has "Washington" Legs? (produced London, 1978; Cambridge, Massachusetts, 1981). With *Dingo*, London, Eyre Methuen, 1978.

The Garden (produced Sherborne, Dorset, 1982).

Red Star (produced London, 1984).

Across from the Garden of Allah (produced Guildford, Surrey, and London, 1986). London, Oberon Books, 1997.

Tumbledown: A Screenplay (televised 1988). London, Penguin, 1987.

The Plantagenets, adaptation of Shakespeare's *Henry VI* plays (produced Stratford-on-Avon, 1988). London, Penguin, 1989.

Man, Beast and Virtue, adaptation of a play by Pirandello (produced London, 1989). London, Oberon Books, 1989.

The Mountain Giants, adaptation of a play by Pirandello (produced London, 1993). London, Oberon Books, 1993.

The Tower, adaptation of a play by Dumas (produced London, 1995). London, Oberon Books, 1995.

Screenplays: *The Knack*, 1965; *Help!*, from Mark Behm, 1965; *Tie Up the Ballcock*, 1967; *How I Won the War*, 1967; *The Charge of the Light Brigade*, from John Osborne, 1968; *The Long Day's Dying*, 1968; *The Bed-Sitting Room*, an adaptation of a screenplay by Spike Milligan and John Antrobus, 1969; *Fellini Satyricon* (English dialogue), 1969; *Cuba*, 1980; *Vile Bodies*, 1981; *Red Monarch*, from stories by Yuri Krotkov, 1983; *An Awfully Big Adventure,* 1994; *Mary Stewart,* 1998.

Radio Plays: *Cowheel Jelly*, 1962; *Next to Being a Knight*, 1972.

Television Plays: *Prisoner and Escort*, 1961; *Traitor in a Steel Helmet*, 1961; *Not at All*, 1962; *Drill Pig*, 1964; *Drums along the Avon*, 1967; *A Bit of a Holiday*, 1969; *The Emergence of Anthony Purdy, Esq.*, 1970; *A Bit of Family Feeling*, 1971; *A Bit of Vision*, 1972; *Death or Glory Boy*, 1974; *Mützen ab*, 1974; *A Bit of an Adventure*, 1974; *Love Lies Bleeding*, 1976; *Do as I Say*, 1977; *Don't Forget to Write!* series, 1977, 1979; *Wagner*, 1984; *Puccini*, 1984; *Dust to Dust* (*Time for Murder* series), 1985; *My Family and Other Animals*, from the book by Gerald Durrell, 1987; *Tumbledown*, 1988; *The Setting of the Sun* (*Inspector Morse* series), 1989; *Sharpe's Company,* 1995; *Breed of Heros,* 1995; *England, My England,* with John Osborne, 1995; *Sharpe's Regiment,* 1996; *Sharpe's Waterloo,* 1997; *Mute of Malice* (KQC series), 1997; *Briefs Trooping Gaily* (KQC series), 1998.

*

Critical Studies: *The Second Wave* by John Russell Taylor, London, Methuen, and New York, Hill and Wang, 1971; *Revolutions in Modern English Drama* by Katharine J. Worth, London, Bell, 1973.

Theatrical Activities:
Director: **Film**—*Tie Up the Ballcock*, 1967.

Actor: **Film**—*The Knack*, 1965.

* * *

Charles Wood grew up in a theatrical family, and he served five years as a soldier. In both theater and war he sees a sordid reality sold to the public as glamorous. A line from one of his earliest plays, *Spare*, epitomizes his vision: "He . . . wet hisself grotesque at Waterloo." His most interesting works and perhaps his most and least successful, respectively, are *Dingo* and *H, Being Monologues at Front of Burning Cities,* in both of which the interest in theater and war come together.

The two acts of *Dingo* give equally desolate views of World War II. The first is in a desert emplacement during the North African campaign. Various soldiers drop in on its two occupants, Dingo and Mogg, the most notable being a comic who attempts to entertain the troops. Some of the same characters, including the comic, are in the internment camp of the second act. There he functions as the master of ceremonies for a camp entertainment that provides cover for an escape by the officers. The play ends with the liberation of the camp, and even Churchill arrives to "urinate on the West Wall of Hitler's Germany."

In *Dingo* Wood protests against the glamorization of World War II and even suggests that its conduct was affected by how it could be sold to the public. The grim reality is made all the more horrific by being constantly counterpointed against culturally approved and sanitized images of war. Consider, for example, the character Tanky, whose screams as he burns to death in his tank come right after the opening dialogue of the play and whose seated, charred form is carried around by his mate like a ventriloquist's dummy. At the end of the play, through the camp's liberation and the beginning of the glorification of the now finished war, he repeats, "He killed me." While the stubborn fact of the phrase and the charred corpse do not change, "he" seems to shift references, from NCO to officer to Churchill, so that the simple statement becomes an indictment of a system. The phrase is repeated three times and is the last line of the play. It is appropriate that the dead should have the last word.

H, written in rough and often awkward verse, dramatizes the Indian Mutiny in spectacular Victorian style, with set-piece battles, *tableaux vivants* that show actors in the positions of imperial paintings, painted backdrops, and front cloths that fall as charging officers stagger or slide beneath them. Extraordinary staging demands are made: sepoys advance from beneath an elephant, "five men are mutilated in a horrible manner," and a rebel soldier is tied over the mouth of a cannon and blown to bits, raining pieces of flesh in the form of rose petals into the audience. But as this last stage direction suggests, all is subverted by Wood's mid-twentieth-century theatrical consciousness. The dramatic interest lies in the different characters of the commanders and officers and in a captain's wife who is raped by an Indo-Irish rebel and who bears his child at the end of the play. One can admire the play's ambitiousness and ingenuities, but there are too many assaults and too long a deathbed scene at the end.

The sense that we are watching theatrical "turns" is strong in all of Wood's plays. His characters often try out attitudes on one another, as in *Veterans*, or parody beliefs they do not share, as in *Dingo.* Thus, the audience is more than usually aware of the transitions from one unit, or "beat," to the next. In addition, Wood brings theatrical performance into the script itself. To take *Dingo* as an example, besides the corpse treated as a ventriloquist's dummy, there is also the comedian who attempts to entertain the soldiers stuck in their desert emplacement, sits on a toilet with Churchill and Eisenhower glove puppets arguing about Arnhem, and emcees a climactic POW camp concert with the men in drag. There is nothing so scabrous in *How I Won the War*, directed by Richard Lester with John Lennon in the lead role and for which Wood was the scriptwriter, but he brought to it a similar presentational style. As men are killed, each is dyed a different color and continues marching with his platoon.

Wood has twice written plays about making films about war. *Veterans* was inspired by Wood's experience as scriptwriter for *The Charge of the Light Brigade*. We see the aging stars engaging in sometimes bitchy banter and in reminiscence while waiting for their call. The overall tone is nostalgic, even elegiac. In contrast, *Has "Washington" Legs?* deals with the business of making movies and shows the emptiness not of the performers' assumed or faked emotions but of American corporate happy talk, of manipulative psychobabble, as various financial or artistic claimants to a piece of the action jockey over a lamentably unclear project to film the American Revolution. Wood's fierceness is undiminished, and his mockery of the mythification of war continues, but his target has changed to the mediators and middle managers of a service industry society.

Wood's one play directly about the theater, *Fill the Stage with Happy Hours*, may be one of the sourest comedies ever written. The characters, especially Albert, who is the manager of a tatty rep company, and his wife Maggie, whose acting career has given way to managing the bar, try on various attitudes as though to see if they fit the situation. For example, at one point Albert affects moral indignation at the juvenile lead's supposed seduction of his son, and at another he offers his son a man-to-man chat about seizing career opportunities when the sexual interest of a visiting grande dame of the stage is evident. Genuine emotion is either no longer possible for them or, ironically, can only be shown through the adoption of an appropriate borrowed attitude. At the end of the play Maggie tells Albert what he has refused to recognize, that she is dying of cancer. The curtain falls slowly as she sings "Smiling Through" and he turns heroic: "By God, I'll do *Ghosts*, I'll show this bloody town. . . . Isn't she marvellous, your mother—that's what it's about, son—that's how to use it. . . . It's given us a good life, hasn't it Maggie? . . ." Her reply ends the play: "Shut up, dear—you're not very good at it are you?" In the original production the actors, game troupers all, stopped the fall of the curtain to bow and blow kisses to the audience.

—Anthony Graham-White

WRIGHT, Nicholas

Nationality: British. **Born:** Cape Town, South Africa, 5 July 1940. **Education:** Rondebosch Boys' School, Cape Town; London Academy of Music and Dramatic Art. **Career:** Director, Theatre Upstairs, Royal Court Theatre, London, 1970-75; joint artistic director, Royal Court Theatre, 1976-77; associate director of new writing 1984, literary manager, 1987, and associate director, 1992—, Royal National Theatre, London. **Awards:** Arts Council bursary, 1981. **Agent:** Judy Daish Associates, 83 Eastbourne Mews, London W2 6LQ. **Address:** 33 Navarino Road, London E.8, England.

Publications

Plays

Changing Lines (also director: produced London, 1968).
Treetops (produced London, 1978).
The Gorky Brigade (produced London, 1979).
One Fine Day (produced London, 1980; New York, 1986).
The Crimes of Vautrin, adaptation of a novel by Balzac (produced Stockton-on-Tees, County Durham, and London, 1983). London, Joint Stock, 1983.
The Custom of the Country (produced London, 1983). London, Methuen, 1983.
The Desert Air (produced Stratford-on-Avon, 1984; London, 1985). London, Methuen, 1985.
Six Characters in Search of an Author, adaptation of a play by Pirandello (produced London, 1987).
Mrs. Klein (produced London, 1988; Washington D.C., 1992). London, Hern, 1988.
Thérèse Raquin, adaptation of the novel by Zola (produced Chichester, West Sussex, 1990).

Other

99 Plays (essays). London, Methuen, 1992.

*

Critical Study: "The Persistence of Cervantine Romance in Nicholas Wright's *The Custom of the Country*" by Clark A. Colahan and Celia E. Weller, in *Cervantes: Bulletin of the Cervantes Society of America* (Granville, Ohio), Spring 1990, pp. 69-77.

* * *

Nicholas Wright's first play appeared as early as 1968, but although he has spent most of his professional life in the theater, he has not produced a large body of work. It is not possible to speak of a development in his writing, yet certain definite shifts of emphasis can be discerned within a drama that is notable for combining a careful eclecticism of form and mode with steady concentration on a large but well-defined thematic territory.

Wright's work focuses on periods of social and political change or transition and seeks to explore, in a wide range of ways, the relation of the individual, whether as agent or as victim, to the large historical movement. *Treetops,* his earliest success, is typical in its South African setting, Cape Town in 1952, the year of the death of George VI and of the accession of Elizabeth II. The action is basically naturalistic, but the sunstroke-induced hallucination that prompts the disillusioned English liberal "Rusty" Walker to leave home and family, secede from the reactionary Torch Commando organization for ex-servicemen, and make an illegal gesture is presented surrealistically. Rusty realizes that he is standing within the footprint of a giant, and a chimpanzee on a bicycle brings an enigmatic message from the dead king that nonetheless makes it clear that the giant is the British Empire, within whose soon-to-be-dismembered body Rusty has been living. Rusty's political activism is a matter of quasi-physical impulse rather than of "correct analysis," but his liberal gestures serve to awaken the hitherto dormant energies of the friend to whom he appeals for help and advice, Leo Skiba, an émigré Lithuanian socialist ideologue and organizer. The personal and political symbiosis that finally moves Leo to action and that affords Rusty "moments of the most intense joy" is throughout paralleled, indeed partly articulated, by the movingly realized relationship of affection and provocation, of need and violence, between Rusty's son Rupert and Leo's son Mark.

The debt to Brecht evident in Wright's formal strategies throughout his work is most clearly felt in *The Gorky Brigade,* which again scrutinizes the relation between political organization, energy for action, and individual dissent at a time of historical change. In the third year of the Soviet revolution (1920-21), the revolutionary teacher Ekaterina undertakes the supervision and instruction of a colony of teenage "bourgeois anarchists." In act 1 her initial despair, her new "scientific" (dialectical) teaching methods, and her eventual success in enabling the colonists to form themselves into the Gorky Brigade, under which banner they rob rich peasants in order to further their own revolutionary purposes, are presented in a series of scenes after the Brechtian epic model, some of them attached to rubrics taken from Gorky. The Gorky sentences, however, are rotated ironically in act 2 when Ekaterina's star student, Minnie, who has been away at a university for six years, returns to the colony. Gorky himself is at last to visit his admirers, and she has come to request his help and influence in the case of a professor of hers who is being condemned and persecuted for his work in genetics. The colony, once in the vanguard of the revolution but now isolated and out of touch by virtue of its very idealism, humiliates and rejects Minnie. And Gorky, feeling himself Europeanized into doubt and noncommitment after his sojourn in Italy, can respond to her appeals, despite his climactic public reaffirmation of Soviet aims and thinking, only with gestures of impotence and bad faith. Yet Minnie will not retreat into individual dissent. She refuses to leave the colony again, and as the play ends, she is trying to call a meeting of the colonists in order to regalvanize revolutionary principles and action.

In both *Treetops* and *The Gorky Brigade,* different though they are formally and stylistically, the exploration of the role of individual dissent in the process of political change is clearly shaped and underwritten by a commitment to socialism. In his plays of the 1980s, however, Wright's dramatic attitude toward the individual as a motive force in history is firmly ironic, and his treatment is less direct than in the plays of the late 1970s. The tendency, already apparent in the earlier plays, to make a character represent or embody an attitude or class or group emerges with increasing strength through a more obvious stylization of action. In reference to *The Desert Air,* "embody" is emphatically the word. The enormous central figure, memorably incarnated in the Royal Shakespeare Company production by Geoffrey Hutchings, is a caricature on a heroic scale. Colonel—later Brigadier—"Hippo" Gore is a "vulgar toad" in whose "swollen and distended" gut is embodied a whole social movement and moral attitude. Put in charge of a secret service unit in wartime Cairo (1942-43), Hippo dedicates himself to "wangling" his way up through the class-determined hierarchy of the British army, a "stumpy" intent on toppling "those long, tall, *pointy* bastards." Thus, the class war cuts across and usurps in importance World War II, and the transference of British support in occupied Yugoslavia from the royalist Chetniks to the communist-led Partisans is effected not by principle or decisive strategic thinking but by the Hippo's self-interested wangling. The physical state figures forth the moral one, often hilariously, sometimes painfully, in Hippo and his agents, and although he is eventually disgraced, Gore is allowed a final apotheosis through a self-interested self-sacrifice, his distended body blown apart at last for the sake of glory in posterity as the man who literally had "the *guts* to change" British policy.

Wright's handling of the ironic interaction of representative figures is even more impressive in *The Custom of the Country,* all the more so as it is negotiated within the strict generic framework of romantic comedy. Title and plot both derive from Fletcher and Massinger, and there is an authentically Jacobean relish of pace and event in the conduct of a narrative charged with the pathos of yearning and unfulfillment. Wright's decision to set the play in the cultural melting pot of the southern Africa of the 1890s, mostly Johannesburg, serves to introduce a political dimension into the comedic action. It is the plot's several plotters rather than the young married lovers they manipulate who are the central representative figures: the self-deluding "entrepreneuse" Daisy Bone, a brothel keeper who is persuaded to cast the missionary hero Paul as her "perfect love"; her business manager, the eastern European Jewish intellectual Lazarus, who looks forward to a moral apocalypse and finds union in death with Daisy; the Afrikaner gold mine owner Henrietta van Es, whose hitherto frustrated femininity finds its sexual object in Paul's "gentleman of leisure" brother Roger and its maternal project in the reclamation of her errant "zombie" son Willem; and Dr. Jamieson, the agent of British imperialist designs on the African interior whose ultimate success ensures the preparation and impending dispatch of a Pioneer Column to the territory that will eventually become Rhodesia. Happy ending and historical implication are thus posed in an ironic counterpoint that is emphasized by the innocently portentous curtain speech of Paul's African bride Tendai. Such precision of dramatic nuance is characteristic of this play and indeed of Wright's work at its best.

The historical and political dimensions hitherto characteristic of Wright's work are effectively absent from *Mrs. Klein.* But although the play is not a satire, its dominating, egotistical central figure can be seen as a distant cousin of Hippo. In *Mrs. Klein* an irony that is at once astringent and sympathetic operates within a tightly patterned and witty meditation upon the complexity of maternal-filial relationships. Set in London in 1934, it is an intimate trio that dramatizes an episode in the life of the émigré psychoanalyst Melanie Klein. The journey through the "primitive jungle" of mourning for the death of her son triggers a crisis in the relationship of Mrs. Klein with her daughter Melitta, who is also an analyst. Their encounters play out in real terms the familiar categories of analysis. The confrontation turns on rival interpretations of the son's apparent suicide. But Mrs. Klein's assistant, Paula, extricates herself from this conflict, gathers the available facts, and constructs an alternative narrative. The truth of the son's death is a truth not of the suicidal energy of transference of feeling—as Mrs. Klein and Melitta, despite their conflict, both believe—but of freedom and contingency. The death was the result of an accident that befell a happy man. This truth forces a self-confrontation on Mrs. Klein, which in turn lifts the veil of mourning and enables a reaffirmation of her professional calling. The end is open, understated, and intriguingly poised.

—Paul Lawley

WYMARK, Olwen

Nationality: American. **Born:** Olwen Buck, Oakland, California, 14 February 1932. **Education:** Pomona College, Claremont, California, 1949-51; University College, London, 1951-52. **Family:** Married the actor Patrick Wymark in 1950 (died 1970); two daughters and two sons. **Career:** Writer-in-residence, Unicorn Theatre for Young People, London, 1974-75, and Kingston Polytechnic, Surrey, 1977; script consultant, Tricycle Theatre, London; lecturer in playwriting, New York University; part-time tutor in playwriting, University of Birmingham, 1989-91. Member, Arts Council of Great Britain Drama Panel, 1980-84. Lives in London. **Awards:** Zagreb Drama Festival prize, 1967; Actors Theatre of Louisville Best New Play award, 1978. **Agent:** Lemons Unna, and Durbridge, 24 Pottery Lane, Holland Park, London W11 4LZ, England.

PUBLICATIONS

Plays

Lunchtime Concert (produced Glasgow, 1966). Included in *Three Plays*, 1967; in *The Best Short Plays 1975*, edited by Stanley Richards, Radnor, Pennsylvania, Chilton, 1975.
Three Plays (as *Triple Image: Coda, Lunchtime Concert, The Inhabitants*, produced Glasgow, 1967; *The Inhabitants*, produced London, 1974). London, Calder and Boyars, 1967.
The Gymnasium (produced Edinburgh, 1967; London, 1971). Included in *The Gymnasium and Other Plays*, 1971.
The Technicians (produced Leicester, 1969; London, 1971). Included in *The Gymnasium and Other Plays*, 1971.
Stay Where You Are (produced Edinburgh, 1969; London, 1973). Included in *The Gymnasium and Other Plays*, 1971; in *The Best Short Plays 1972*, edited by Stanley Richards, Philadelphia, Chilton, 1972.
No Talking (for children; produced London, 1970).
Neither Here nor There (produced London, 1971). Included in *The Gymnasium and Other Plays*, 1971.
Speak Now (produced Edinburgh, 1971; revised version produced Leicester, 1975).
The Committee (produced London, 1971). Included in *Best Friends, The Committee, The Twenty-Second Day*, 1984.
The Gymnasium and Other Plays. London, Calder and Boyars, 1971.
Jack the Giant Killer (produced Sheffield, 1972). Included in *The Gymnasium and Other Plays*, 1971.
Tales from Whitechapel (produced London, 1972).
Daniel's Epic (for children), with Daniel Henry (produced London, 1972).
Chinigchinich (for children; produced London, 1973).
Watch the Woman, with Brian Phelan (produced London, 1973).
The Bolting Sisters (for children; produced London, 1974).
Southwark Originals (collaborative work for children; produced London, 1975).
The Twenty-Second Day (broadcast 1975; produced London, 1975). Included in *Best Friends, The Committee, The Twenty-Second Day*, 1984.
Starters (collaborative work for children; includes *The Giant and the Dancing Fairies, The Time Loop, The Spellbound Jellybaby, The Robbing of Elvis Parsley, I Spy*) (produced London, 1975; Wausau, Wisconsin, 1976).
Three For All (collaborative work for children; includes *Box Play, Family Business, Extended Play*) (produced London, 1976).
We Three, and After Nature, Art (produced London, 1977). Published in *Play Ten*, edited by Robin Rook, London, Arnold, 1977.
Find Me (produced Richmond, Surrey, 1977; Louisville, 1979). London, French, 1980.
The Winners, and Missing Persons (for children; produced London, 1978).
Loved (produced London, 1978; Syracuse, New York, 1979). London, French, 1980.
The Child (broadcast 1979). London, BBC Publications, 1979.
Please Shine Down on Me (produced London, 1980).
Female Parts: One Woman Plays (includes *Waking Up, A Woman Alone, The Same Old Story, Medea*), adaptations of plays by Dario Fo and Franca Rame, translated by Margaret Kunzle and Stuart Hood (produced London, 1981). London, Pluto Press, 1981.
Best Friends (produced Richmond, Surrey, 1981). Included in *Best Friends, The Committee, The Twenty-Second Day*, 1984.
Buried Treasure (produced London, 1983).
Best Friends, The Committee, The Twenty-Second Day. London, Calder, and New York, Riverrun Press, 1984.
Lessons and Lovers (produced York, 1985). London, Faber, 1986.
Nana, adaptation of the novel by Zola (produced Winchester and London, 1987). London, Absolute Press, 1990.
Strike Up the Banns (produced Mold, Clwyd, 1988). London, French, 1988.
Brezhnev's Children (produced London, 1991). London, French, 1992.
Mirror Mirror (opera; produced London, 1992).

Radio Plays: *The Ransom*, 1957; *The Unexpected Country*, 1957; *California Here We Come*, 1958; *The Twenty-Second Day*, 1975; *You Come Too*, 1977; *The Child*, 1979; *Vivien the Blockbuster*, 1980; *Mothering Sunday*, 1980; *Sea Changes*, 1984; *A Wreath of Roses*, from the novel by Elizabeth Taylor, 1985; *Mothers and Shadows*, from a novel by Marta Traba, 1987; *Christopher Columbus*, from the novel by Elizabeth von Arnim, with Barbara Clegg, 1989; *Oroonoko*, from the novel by Aphra Behn, 1990.

Television Plays: *Mrs. Moresby's Scrapbook*, 1973, *Vermin*, 1974, *Marathon*, 1975, *Mother Love*, 1975, *Dead Drunk*, 1975, and *Her Father's Daughter*, 1984 (all in *Crown Court* series); *Oceans Apart*, 1984; *Not That Kind of People*, 1984.

*

Olwen Wymark comments:

I didn't start writing plays until my mid-thirties and for the first few years wrote only one-act, rather experimental plays; Harold Hobson called them "atonal." I also wrote about eight plays for children. Since 1977 I've written full-length plays in a more naturalistic form as well as some adaptations. I've recently written an opera which was performed in 1992 and hope I will write more. I'm currently concentrating on writing for television.

* * *

Olwen Wymark has written some three dozen plays for radio, television, and stage. These range from one-act plays through full-length ones, and her children's plays typify the playful side of her personality. Indeed, smallness figures again and again in her work, though, like so much else, one has to unmask it from her work even as she herself relies on a series of unmaskings for dramatic effect. *Find Me*, for example, is a documentary play about a mentally disturbed girl who had, in real life, died in a special hospital. Those expecting the play to concentrate sympathy on Verity, the little girl, must have been disappointed, for it is far easier to sympathize with the restaurant owners, friends, and family who have their peace and property destroyed by the girl's predilection for starting fires. Indeed, though she died in the hospital, viewers find themselves sympathizing with the desperate hospital authorities rather than with Verity. She is so small as to disappear in the maelstroms she creates, and it is difficult to find her, let alone love her. The play was sparked by letters that the girl had written and that her family had allowed Wymark to read; one began "Dear Whoeveryouare. Please find me and have me as your beloved." Here, in Wymark's view, is everyman's dilemma: one feels unsure of oneself, and yet it is precisely this self-doubt that fuels creativity. At least it was so in this girl's case.

Wymark's early plays are exteriorizations of internal anguish, games devised by the characters to reflect and exercise their grief and dissatisfactions. In *The Gymnasium* two friends begin a friendly boxing match, with the elderly and gentlemanly friend requesting his pretty Cockney partner not to talk. They have hardly commenced sparring when the boy turns on a stream of vitriolic abuse. There is plenty of time to attempt to puzzle this through before one realizes that this is a marriage therapy session; the Cockney plays the gentleman's wife and incites his partner to beat him instead of the wife, who is protected by the fine walls of custom and civility.

Most of Wymark's plays are about boringly familiar situations, rooted as they are in the emotional hothouse of upper-middle-class life. What makes the plays dramatic is a lively sense of timing, for she offers to her audience the pleasure of solving marvelously constructed puzzles. It is not always possible to sort out the stories, however, and, as Irving Wardle said in his *Times* review of *Neither Here nor There*, "A series of false certainties recede in infinite perspective. Her characters fall through one trapdoor to the solid ground beneath, only to find that collapsing beneath them as well." Is the play a comment on the nightmarish quality of experience? Hardly, for the schoolgirls are inventing the whole game themselves.

Situation and theme; anxieties, tensions, and emotional states; guilt, futility, and desperation—these come across in Wymark's bizarre and intense plays much more strongly than do characters and situations, though these are presented starkly enough. Whenever it is possible to piece her stories together, one begins to care for her characters. Otherwise her plays remain merely ingenious. Witty and at their best arresting, they have a lack of shape that reflects a deeper problem. *Stay Where You Are* shows us a girl at the mercy of two people who appear to be lunatics. Their lunacy turns out, however, to be designed to wake her from her complacency. Quasi existentialism no longer brings the excitement it did in the 1960s, and this is Wymark's biggest problem; she needs to find something new or fresh or more substantial that she can say through the pressure and sparkle of her work.

What saves Wymark's work is that she is aware of this and that she laughs at herself. *The Technicians,* for example, is a marvelous attack on technical cunning that operates in a moral vacuum. Modern experimental theater is here hoist with its own petard, and what makes the attack poignant is that Wymark loves modern theater. In it she lives and moves and has her being.

—Prabhu S. Guptara

Y-Z

YANKOWITZ, Susan

Nationality: American. **Born:** Newark, New Jersey, 20 February 1941. **Education:** Sarah Lawrence College, Bronxville, New York, B.A. 1963; Yale University School of Drama, New Haven, Connecticut, M.F.A. 1968. **Family:** Married Herbert Leibowitz in 1978; one son. **Awards:** Vernon Rice award, 1970; MacDowell Colony fellowship, 1971, 1973; National Endowment for the Arts fellowship, 1972, 1979; Rockefeller grant, 1973; Guggenheim fellowship, 1974; Creative Artists Public Service grant, 1974; New York State Council on the Arts grant, 1984; Japan/US Friendship Commission grant, 1985; WGA finalist for *Sylvia Plath* teleplay, Best Documentary of 1988; Berrilla Kerr award, 1997. **Agent:** Mary Harden, Harden-Curtis Associates, 850 Seventh Avenue, New York, New York, 10019, U.S.A. **Address:** 205 West 89th Street, Apartment 8F, New York, New York 10024, U.S.A.

PUBLICATIONS

Plays

The Cage (produced New York, 1965).
Nightmare (produced New Haven, Connecticut, 1967; New York, 1968).
Terminal (produced New York, 1969). Published in *Three Works by the Open Theatre*, edited by Karen Malpede, New York, Drama Book Specialists, 1974.
The Ha-Ha Play (produced New York, 1970). Published in *Scripts 10* (New York), October 1972.
The Lamb (produced New York, 1970).
Slaughterhouse Play (produced New York, 1971). Published in *New American Plays 4*, edited by William M. Hoffman, New York, Hill and Wang, 1971.
Transplant (produced Omaha, 1971).
Basics, in *Tabula Rasa* (produced New York, 1972).
Positions, in *Up* (produced New York, 1972).
Boxes (produced New York, 1972). Published in *Playwrights for Tomorrow 11*, edited by Arthur H. Ballet, Minneapolis, University of Minnesota Press, 1973.
Acts of Love (produced Atlanta, 1973).
Monologues for *Wicked Women Revue* (produced New York, 1973).
Wooden Nickels (produced New York, 1973).
America Piece, with the Provisional Theatre (produced Los Angeles, 1974).
Still Life (produced New York, 1977).
True Romances, music by Elmer Bernstein (produced Los Angeles, 1977).
Qui Est Anna Marks? (Who Done It?) (produced Paris, 1978).
A Knife in the Heart (produced Williamstown, Massachusetts, 1983).
Baby (original story), book by Sybille Pearson, music by David Shire, lyrics by Richard Maltby, Jr. (produced New York, 1983).
Alarms (produced London, 1987).
Night Sky (produced New York, 1991). London and New York, French, 1992.
1969 Terminal 1996, with Joseph Chaikin (produced Belgrade, 1996; Atlanta and New York). PAJ, 1997.

Screenplays: *Portrait of a Scientist as a Dumb Broad; Danny AWOL*, 1968; *The Land of Milk and Funny*, 1968; *Silent Witness*, 1979.

Radio Plays: *Rats' Alley*, 1969; *Kali*, 1969.

Television Writing: *The Prison Game (Visions* series), 1976; *The Forerunner: Charlotte Perkins Gilman*, 1979; *Arrow to the Sun: The Poetry of Sylvia Plath*, 1987.

Novel

Silent Witness. New York, Knopf, 1976.

*

Manuscript Collection: Kent State University, Kent, Ohio.

Critical Studies: Interviews with Erika Munk in *Performance* (New York), December 1971, and Arthur Sainer in *The Radical Theatre Notebook* edited by Sainer, New York, Avon, 1975; *Interviews with Contemporary Women Playwrights* edited by Kathleen Betsko and Rachel Koenig, New York, Beech Tree, 1987.

Susan Yankowitz comments:

(1973) Most of my work for the theatre has been an attempt to explore what is intrinsically unique in the theatrical situation. That is, I've been interested in sound, gesture, and movement as a corollary to language; in the interaction between the visual and verbal elements of stage life; in the fact of live performers engaged with live audience members in an exchange; and in the development of a theatrical vocabulary. My work has been generally informed by the social and political realities which impinge on all our lives; these, to a large extent, influence and shape my plays. In addition, I have been interested in a collective or collaborative approach to evolving works for the theatre and in working improvisationally with actors and directors to "find" a play which is a creative expression of our shared concerns.

At present, I am growing more concerned with the question of language—its limits and possibilities—and am moving into the realm of fiction which I feel is a more appropriate medium for that adventure.

* * *

Susan Yankowitz enlivens nonrealistic, highly theatrical images of sociological problems with music, dance, pantomime, patterned speech, and bold sets and costumes. These devices reinforce her verbal attacks on such contemporary social sins as conformity, alienation, racism, and sexism. The devices also enable her to avoid didacticism. Yankowitz's emphasis on the theatrical was undoubtedly encouraged by the Open Theatre, whose ensemble work contributed to the several versions of the published text of *Terminal*. The work cannot be understood apart from the Open Theatre production, for the text merely suggests the performance and may be altered by other groups.

Terminal achieves unity through ritual rather than through coherent plot. It argues that people must face their deaths, and it satirizes people who do not. The dying in *Terminal* turn to so-called Team Members who offer them a mass-produced panacea for death. The living conduct this impersonal ritual, and they also embalm and touch up the dead to hide the fact of death. The dead pierce the subterfuge practiced by and upon the dying; they "come through" the dying to judge the living and themselves. The enactment of necrophilia or the graphic description of embalming involves the audience in this common human fate.

As ritual is the binding thread in *Terminal,* so the structure of a parable unifies *The Ha-Ha Play*. Like *Terminal,* this play exposes a general human failing, but it emphasizes rectification rather than exposure. Children who are abducted to a woods, in which the audience sits, by hyenas wearing masks learn to communicate through laughter. Communication is thus not only possible between groups, but it also dissolves enmity between them.

In contrast to *Terminal* and *The Ha-Ha Play, Slaughterhouse Play* traces the growth of consciousness of a unifying character, the black slaughterhouse worker Junius. *Slaughterhouse Play* attacks racism. Its central symbol is the slaughterhouse, which whites run and in which blacks work, slaughtering black troublemakers and selling their "meat" to whites. As in *Terminal,* action and dialogue involve the audience. The most prized black meat is that of the male genitals, which a white butcher displays in his shop and which Junius and other rebellious blacks steal to wear around their necks as symbols of their rebellion. *Slaughterhouse Play* ends with a sequence in which blacks stab whites and whites shoot blacks repeatedly.

Not only is *Boxes* in a much lighter vein than *Slaughterhouse Play,* but literal boxes function theatrically as a fictional slaughterhouse cannot. Characters carve windows in boxes, and from within those boxes they define themselves according to type and speak in clichés. Yankowitz underlines the conformity by having the characters wear hats with boxes that match their box dwellings. People in their separate boxes perform their daily chores at the same time that others experience great pain or joy. Such caricature unifies *Boxes*. The boxes ultimately become coffins.

Yankowitz dramatizes individual or social problems and involves her audience either by shock or mimicry. Once engaged, the audience is forced to admit its responsibility for such failures as avoiding death, alienation, conformity, and racism. This is Yankowitz's aim.

—Frances Rademacher Anderson

ZEDER, Suzan L.

Nationality: American. **Born:** Los Angeles, California, 18 February 1948. **Education:** Trinity University, San Antonio, Texas, B.F.A. 1969; Southern Methodist University, Dallas, Texas, M.F.A. 1972; Institute of Education, University of London, (Fulbright-Hayes Scholar) 1972-73; Florida State University, Tallahassee, Florida, 1975-98, Ph.D. 1979. **Family:** Married Jim R. Hancock. **Career:** Assistant professor, Director of Developmental Drama Program, Florida State University, Tallahassee, Florida, 1975-77; assistant professor, Director of Child Drama Program, University of Washington, Seattle, 1977-82; adjunct professor, Southern Methodist University, Dallas, Texas, 1982-89; adjunct professor, University of Dallas, 1982-85. Professor, chair University of Texas, Austin, Texas, 1985—. Visiting writer, Northwestern University, 1989-97; University of Illinois, 1989; Arizona State University, Indiana University, Florida State University, Interlochen Arts Academy, and Ball State University. **Awards:** John Rosenfield award in playwriting, Southern Methodist University, 1971; Fulbright-Hayes scholarship to England, 1972-73; Charlotte Chorpenning award for Outstanding Playwright for Plays for Young People, 1978; Distinguished play award, American Alliance for Theatre and Education, 1987; inducted into Southwest Theatre Association Hall of Fame, 1988; National Endowment for the Arts grant, 1991-93; Distinguished Achievement in Playwrighting, New England Theatre Conference, 1994; inducted into College of Fellows of the American Theatre, 1996. **Agent:** Bruce Ostler, Bret Adams Agency, 448 West 44th Street, New York, New York 10036, U.S.A. **Address:** Department of Theater and Dance, University of Texas at Austin, Winship Building, Austin, Texas 78712-1168, U.S.A.

Publications

Plays

Wiley and the Hairy Man (produced Dallas, 1972). New Orleans, Anchorage Press, 1978.

The Play Called Noah's Flood (produced Flint, Michigan, 1984). New Orleans, Anchorage Press, 1985.

Step on a Crack (produced Dallas, 1974). New Orleans, Anchorage Press, 1976.

Ozma of Oz: A Tale of Time (produced Seattle, 1978). New Orleans, Anchorage Press, 1981.

Doors (produced Seattle, 1980). New Orleans, Anchorage Press, 1985.

Spa! (produced Dallas, 1982).

Mother Hicks (produced Seattle, 1983). New Orleans, Anchorage press, 1986.

In A Room Somewhere (produced 1985). New Orleans, Anchorage Press, 1988.

An Evening at Versailles featuring The Miser, adaptation of Moliere (produced Dallas, 1986).

The Death and Life of Sherlock Holmes (produced Louisville, 1986; New York, 1991). New Orleans, Anchorage Press, 1996.

Wish in One Hand and Spit in the Other: A Collection of Plays by Suzan Zeder, edited by Susan Pearson-Davis, New Orleans, Anchorage Press, 1988.

Do Not Go Gentle (produced New York, 1991). Dramatic Publishing, 1996.

The Macbeth Project, co-adapted with Jim Hancock (produced Austin, 1993).

The Taste of Sunrise (produced Seattle, 1996).

Screenplays: *Mother Hicks,* 1994.

*

Manuscript Collection: Arizona State University, Child Drama Collections at Hayden Library, under direction of Kathy Krzys.

* * *

Around the world from East to West children have enjoyed and responded to the magic of theater. From the earliest times they have eagerly suspended their disbelief; they have learned accepted behavior, rituals, and history; they have sat in concentrated awe of the spectacles of mankind presented to them. But the concept of a theater for children, limited by the liberal imagination of the modern world, is a phenomenon of the twentieth century. The first Children's Educational Theatre was formed in 1903 with the goals of learning and of community-approved and personal creativity that inform many of its institutions today. In the 1920s Winifred Ward brought greater acceptance to children's theater, and in the 1940s Charlotte Chorpenning set out rules for writing for the child audience. By the 1960s formats more imaginative than the usual dramatized fairy tale, fantasy, or high adventure were created by the Paper Bag Players. New and more realistic subject matter, such as divorce, death, and prejudice, appeared during the 1970s and 1980s as children's theater became enmeshed in the political, financial, and labor problems that engaged all theaters. By this time, however, the idea of theater for young audiences was firmly established within the broader field of entertainment, and during the final quarter of the twentieth century Suzan Zeder, with her spectacular energy as a teacher, lecturer, and theater artist, has emerged as the pivotal playwright in the progress and process of young people's theater in the United States.

Zeder has established herself as an original and distinctive voice in her field. In terms of dramatic style she is a constant experimenter, building upon traditional forms but quickly emphasizing the imaginative aspect of scenic investiture and lighting techniques that today's creative technology makes possible. Always responsive to and respectful of the searching and frequently troubled minds of her audience, she addresses the serious and emotionally charged issues of contemporary young people without feeling obligated to provide a popularly acceptable solution or obviously promote the agenda of any recognizable interest group.

Zeder is at her best when creating a child protagonist, although she has also written plays for adult players and audiences. Within her plays featuring children and their challenges she provides entertainment that easily reaches a multigenerational audience. *Step on a Crack* illuminates the problems of Ellie, a spoiled 13-year-old who bitterly resents the fact that her widowed father, with whom she has enjoyed a wonderfully happy relationship, has remarried. With malicious care Ellie tries to undermine her stepmother, until the consequences of winning her campaign stimulate more thoughtful responses. Girl, in *Mother Hicks,* is perhaps Zeder's most honest and successful child character. Intelligent, imaginative, independent, and totally appealing, Girl forces the action of the play along the lines of discovery that reveal the thematic needs of Tuc, the deaf mute, and Mother Hicks, the witch who tells Girl, "I'm just a left over person, just like you!" In a play of swift and purposeful movement, Zeder employs the character of Girl to dramatize the universal needs for love, for taking care of weaker things, for understanding, and for belonging. *Doors* is another play in which a child protagonist, Jeff, becomes the means through which an impending crisis—divorce—is traced to a meaningful conclusion if not a resolution. Zeder is carefully aware that dramatic conclusions do not necessarily provide acceptable resolutions.

One of the most recognizable characteristics of Zeder's work is her attitude toward the performance space itself. In most of her plays she envisions the stage as a place of action—a space delineated by light, by actors in costume, by properties carried on stage by actors and then transformed by the addition of other properties, or by locales and atmospheres established by the rearrangement of simple set pieces. In all instances space is intended for and dependent upon the eyes of an accepting audience.

In like fashion, fantasy characters inhabit Zeder's fantasy space. Ellie has two make-believe friends who are essentially her "bad angels" and who must be left behind if she is to grow. *Wiley and the Hairy Man,* based on folk legends of good and evil, effectively uses conjuring and employs a chorus that constantly changes its role—mud, a fireplace, a cauldron. *Ozma of Oz,* employing characters from L. Frank Baum's story, is a distinctly different play of fantasy and magic that depends upon Ozma's ability to "see behind the mind and into the heart." A variety of impersonations in *The Death and Life of Sherlock Holmes* is essential as Sir Arthur Conan Doyle plays his own fictitious villains in an attempt to free himself from the "sterile stereotype" of Holmes.

Above all, Zeder is a collaborative artist. Her plays are generally developed as she watches various performances of each work over a period of years; seeks input from actors, directors, and designers; and scrupulously revises. To Zeder theater is always "risky," as she shows in her "fascination with the possibilities of centering a play around the feelings and instincts and possibly heroic responses of a young person." This is Zeder's stated objective as a playwright working with the diversity of style, form, and content that characterize her plays.

—Walter J. Meserve

ZINDEL, Paul

Nationality: American. **Born:** Staten Island, New York, 15 May 1936. **Education:** Port Richmond High School, Staten Island; Wagner College, New York, B.S. in chemistry 1958, M.Sc. 1959. **Family:** Married Bonnie Hildebrand in 1973; one son and one daughter. **Career:** Technical writer for chemical company, New York, 1959; chemistry teacher, Tottenville High School, New York, 1960-69; playwright-in-residence, Alley Theatre, Houston, 1967. Lives in New York City. **Awards:** Ford grant, 1967; Obie award, 1970; Vernon Rice award, 1970; New York Drama Critics Circle award, 1970; Pulitzer prize, 1971; American Library Association's Best Young Adult citation, 1971, 1975, 1976, 1977, 1980, 1982; Media and Methods Maxi award, 1973, for *The Pigman*; New York Library "books for the teen age" citations, 1980, 1981, 1982. D.H.L.: Wagner College, 1971. **Agent:** Curtis Brown, 10 Astor Place, New York, New York 10003. **Address:** c/o Harper and Row, 10 East 53rd Street, New York, New York 10022, U.S.A.

Publications

Plays

Dimensions of Peacocks (produced New York, 1959).

Euthanasia and the Endless Hearts (produced New York, 1960).

A Dream of Swallows (produced New York, 1964).

The Effect of Gamma Rays on Man-in-the-Moon Marigolds (produced Houston, 1965; New York, 1970; Guildford, Surrey, and London, 1972). New York, Harper, 1971; in *Plays and Players* (London), December 1972.

And Miss Reardon Drinks a Little (produced Los Angeles, 1967; New York, 1971; London, 1976). New York, Random House, 1972.
Let Me Hear You Whisper (televised 1969). New York, Harper, 1974.
The Secret Affairs of Mildred Wild (produced New York, 1972). New York, Dramatists Play Service, 1973.
The Ladies Should Be in Bed (produced New York, 1978). With *Let Me Hear You Whisper*, New York, Dramatists Play Service, 1973.
Ladies at the Alamo (also director: produced New York, 1975).
A Destiny with Half Moon Street (produced Coconut Grove, Florida, 1983), revised version as *Amulets Against the Dragon Forces* (produced New York, 1989). New York, Dramatists Play Service, 1989.
Amulets against the Dragon Forces (produced New York, 1989). New York, Dramatists Play Service, 1990.
Every Seventeen Minutes the Crowd Goes Crazy! Lyme, New Hampshire, Smith and Kraus, 1996.

Screenplays: *Up the Sandbox*, 1973; *Mame*, 1974; *Maria's Lovers*, with others, 1984; *Runaway Train*, with Djordje Milicevic and Edward Bunker, 1985; *Babes in Toyland*, with Leslie Bricusse, 1986.

Television Play: *Let Me Hear You Whisper*, 1969.

Novel

When a Darkness Falls. New York, Bantam, 1984.

Fiction (for children and young adults)

The Pigman. New York, Harper, 1968; London, Bodley Head, 1969.
My Darling, My Hamburger. New York, Harper, 1969; London, Bodley Head, 1970.
I Never Loved Your Mind. New York, Harper, 1970; London, Bodley Head, 1971.
I Love My Mother, illustrated by John Melo. New York, Harper, 1975.
Pardon Me, You're Stepping on My Eyeball! New York, Harper, and London, Bodley Head, 1976.
Confessions of a Teenage Baboon. New York, Harper, 1977; London, Bodley Head, 1978.
The Undertaker's Gone Bananas. New York, Harper, 1978; London, Bodley Head, 1979.
The Pigman's Legacy. New York, Harper, and London, Bodley Head, 1980.
A Star for the Latecomer, with Bonnie Zindel. New York, Harper, and London, Bodley Head, 1980.
The Girl Who Wanted a Boy. New York, Harper, and London, Bodley Head, 1981.
To Take a Dare, with Crescent Dragonwagon. New York, Harper, 1982.
Harry and Hortense at Hormone High. New York, Harper, 1984; London, Bodley Head, 1985.
The Amazing and Death-Defying Diary of Eugene Dingman. New York, Harper, and London, Bodley Head, 1987.
A Begonia for Miss Applebaum. New York, Harper, and London, Bodley Head, 1989.
The Pilgrim's Legacy. New York, HarperCollins, 1989.
Attack of the Killer Fishsticks. New York, Bantam, 1993.
The Fifth-Grade Safari. New York, Bantam, 1993.
Fright Party. New York, Bantam, 1993.
The Freaky Facts Club. London, Random House, 1993.
David & Della. New York, HarperCollins, 1993.
One Hundred Percent Laugh Riot. New York, Bantam, 1994.
Loch. New York, HarperCollins, 1994.
The Doom Stone. New York, HarperCollins, 1995.
Raptor. New York, Hyperion Books, 1998.
Reef of Death. New York, HarperCollins, 1998.

Other

The Pilgrim and Me: A Memoir. Oxford, New Windmills, 1991.

*

Manuscript Collection: Boston University.

Critical Studies: *Presenting Paul Zindel* by Jack Jacob Forman, Boston, Twayne, 1988; "Paul Zindel" by John L. DiGaetani, in *A Search for a Postmodern Theater: Interviews with Contemporary Playwrights*, edited by John L. DiGaetani, New York, Greenwood, 1991; "A Fellowship of Madness: Williams' *Blanche Dubois* and Zindel's *Anna Reardon*" by James R. Keller, in *Notes on Contemporary Literature* (Carollton, Georgia), November 1993, pp. 2-3.

Theatrical Activities:
Director: **Play**—*Ladies at the Alamo*, New York, 1975.

* * *

Most parts in most plays are male. In the work of the realist and humorist Paul Zindel, however, almost all of the roles are for women. They are not nice women, for they tend, like so many of Tennessee Williams's women, to be neurotic freaks. The tormented women who people Zindel's plays are dumpy and defensive, lonely and lacerating, bitter and—psychologically, at least—brutal. Yet he stirs our compassion by imparting to them a vulnerability, guaranteeing that they must endure at least as much pain as they inflict.

Not all of Zindel's characters are adults. Perhaps because he was initially a high school chemistry teacher on his native Staten Island, he has taken an interest in the distress of young people. This is the case in his best-known play, *The Effect of Gamma Rays on Man-in-the-Moon Marigolds*, and also in such teen novels as *My Darling, My Hamburger*, *The Pigman*, and *The Pigman's Legacy*. He also introduces animals in his scripts with considerable frequency.

Regardless of who their victims may be, Zindel's characters damage those for whom they have reason to feel affection and to whom they are bound either by blood or in other ways. Where the relationship is familial or a surrogate for the sibling, parental, or conjugal bond, the suffocating intimacies create a dramatic tension familiar from the work of such other American writers of domestic drama as Inge, Williams, O'Neill, and Miller. Most of Zindel's characters are sexually unfulfilled. Despite their tenacity in surviving, his creations cling to unlived lives or, in the nuclear terminology of *Marigolds*, half-lives that in some of the plays are shadowed by the dead and the doomed. Yet the terrible plight in which

Zindel's characters find themselves is relieved by considerable humor.

The melodrama *Marigolds* has enjoyed far more success than any other of Zindel's plays. Its original New York production ran for over two years and won its author several prizes. The play takes its remarkable title from the project on the subject that withdrawn Tillie, a girl in her early teens, has prepared for her school science fair. Tillie finds solace in the perspective of her place in the whole history of evolution, beginning with the creation of the universe. Understanding the continuity of life, of energy and matter, encourages her to look beyond her own squalid surroundings. Her attitude contrasts sharply with the narcissism shared by her crude older sister Ruth and cynical mother Beatrice.

Beatrice is at once eccentric, selfish, and pathetic. She forces Tillie to miss school and then lies about it to the teacher. When she is angry at the other kids' derision of Tillie, her resentment stems not from sympathy with her daughter but from a suspicion that they are really ridiculing her. She flirts with the teacher on the phone but insults him behind his back, talks constantly of hair-brained get-rich-quick schemes, and taunts and torments her helpless senile boarder and her emotionally crippled daughters. She also kills the girls' pet rabbit.

Yet we grow fond of Beatrice and of Ruth, in spite of her resemblance to her mother, with whom she shares lipstick, cigarettes, hostilities, and neuroses. We observe Ruth's dread of thunder and death and her mother's fear of failure and life, we watch them wound and comfort each other, and we find Zindel's craft compelling us to care for women who might well have seemed monsters. When Ruth destroys her mother's confidence and makes her miss the science fair in which Tillie's project wins first prize, we even appreciate the agony out of which she chloroforms Ruth's rabbit.

Marigolds dramatizes a recurrent Zindel subject, disturbed women, and a recurrent Zindel theme, the suffering that friends and relatives inflict on their "loved ones." All three women are "crazies" whose behavior reflects that of more controlled but no less destructive "normal" people. Just as the marigolds have been exposed to gamma rays, these women have been subjected to high concentrations of anguish; Ruth and Beatrice correspond to the dwarfed plants and Tillie to the rare mutants made beautiful by more moderate radiation.

In *And Miss Reardon Drinks a Little*, another play that depicts women who both cause pain and suffer from it, Zindel sides with the vulnerable but abnormal against the ruthless and insensitive but normal. Each Miss Reardon—one alcoholic, the other depressive—is harmless compared to their executive sister and her unsupportive husband. In one respect the couple resemble Mildred and her spouse in *The Secret Affairs of Mildred Wild*. The sexual repression that is mostly implicit in the earlier play, however, becomes an explicit issue in the latter. Mildred absorbs herself in movie magazines and cinematic fantasies instead of her marriage, and in turn her husband fails to consummate an extramarital affair because he is distracted by his sweet tooth. While Mildred watches movies day and night, her diabetic candy store owner of a husband is swallowing all of his merchandise. Naturally, both the business and the relationship are bankrupt. Yet the pair somehow survive their eccentricities and, more importantly, their disillusionment with each other to subscribe to the further fantasy of reconciliation.

The farce of *Mildred Wild*—complete with a modernization of the screen scene from *The School for Scandal*—is less successful than the acerbic wit—replete with profanity and obscenity—of *Ladies at the Alamo*. More of a catfight than a literal shoot-out, the play takes place in Texas, where control of a regional theater constitutes the stakes of the battle. Even though the Alamo is only a theater, a massacre of sorts does occur, with devastating destruction wrought to each of the five women's egos. Funny, foul-mouthed insults fly amid women feuding over whether the artistic director, Dede, will continue to run the theater she has built from a little box into an empire. The loyalties are complex, the betrayals still more so. Dede is far from admirable and probably wins because she is the biggest bully, but when the dust settles, we are somehow glad that she has survived. *Alamo* is another Zindel triumph in the manipulation of audience sympathies.

The drunken neurotics of the play resemble the bridge players of the short work *The Ladies Should Be in Bed*. The principal action of this play forms a minor incident in *Alamo* as well, when one of the women maliciously phones parents of teenagers and reports sexual activity with a "pervert." But it is the ladies themselves who are obsessed with sex and, therefore, "should be in bed." Sexuality is likewise a subject of *Amulets Against the Dragon Forces*, in which a boy unsure of his sexual preference is thrust temporarily, by his mother's employment as a nurse, into a gay male household. But with the alcoholic longshoreman Floyd and the teenage Chris, Zindel especially depicts the products of dysfunctional families. The play rivals *Marigolds* in its dramatization of a youngster's effort at self-protection when threatened by tormented and tormenting adults. *Amulets* is unusual in Zindel's menagerie of female misfits, for its neurotics, or dragons, include both men and women.

—Tish Dace

NATIONALITY INDEX

Below is the list of entrants divided by nationality. The nationalities were chosen largely from information supplied by the entrants. It should be noted that "British" was used for all English entrants and for any other British entrant who chose that designation over a more specific one, such as "Scottish."

American

JoAnne Akalaitis
Edward Albee
Robert Anderson
George Axelrod
Thomas Babe
Jon Robin Baitz
Amiri Baraka
Eric Bentley
Kenneth Bernard
George Birimisa
Lee Blessing
Eric Bogosian
Lee Breuer
Kenneth H. Brown
Ed Bullins
Charles Busch
Lewis John Carlino
Lonnie Carter
Frank Chin
Darrah Cloud
Constance S. Congdon
Ron Cowen
Michael Cristofer
Ossie Davis
Phillip Hayes Dean
Steven Dietz
Charles Dizenzo
Rosalyn Drexler
Martin Duberman
Christopher Durang
Jules Feiffer
Harvey Fierstein
Horton Foote
Richard Foreman
María Irene Fornés
Paul Foster
Mario Fratti
Bruce Jay Friedman
Charles Fuller
George Furth
Frank Gagliano
Herb Gardner
Larry Gelbart
William Gibson
Frank D. Gilroy
James Goldman
Philip Kan Gotanda
Spalding Gray
Richard Greenberg
David Greenspan
John Guare
A. R. Gurney
William Hanley
William Hauptman
Allan Havis
Beth Henley
Dick Higgins
Errol Hill
Robert Hivnor
William M. Hoffman
Joan Holden
Israel Horovitz
Tina Howe
David Henry Hwang
Albert Innaurato
Len Jenkin
Lee Kalcheim
Adrienne Kennedy
Wendy Kesselman
Kenneth Koch
Arthur Kopit
H. M. Koutoukas
Tony Kushner
Arthur Laurents
Jerome Lawrence
Romulus Linney
Quincy Long
Craig Lucas
Ken Ludwig
Jackson Mac Low
Eduardo Machado
Karen Malpede
David Mamet
Emily Mann
Donald Margulies
Jane Martin
William Mastrosimone
Michael McClure
James McLure
Terrence McNally
Murray Mednick
Mark Medoff
Charles L. Mee, Jr.
Arthur Miller
Susan Miller
Ron Milner
Loften Mitchell
Tad Mosel
Phyllis Nagy
N. Richard Nash
Richard Nelson
John Ford Noonan
Marsha Norman
Eric Overmyer
Rochelle Owens
OyamO
Suzan-Lori Parks
Robert Patrick
John Pielmeier
Bernard Pomerance
David Rabe
Dennis J. Reardon
Keith Reddin
Hanon Reznikov
Ronald Ribman

Australian

British

Christopher Fry
Tom Gallacher
Jonathan Gems
Pam Gems
Peter Gill
John Godber
Steve Gooch
Simon Gray
Trevor Griffiths
Wilson John Haire
John Hale
Willis Hall and Keith Waterhouse
David Halliwell
Christopher Hampton
Chris Hannan
David Hare
Richard Harris
Tony Harrison
Ronald Harwood
Michael Hastings
Ronald Hayman
Iain Heggie
Robert Holman
John Hopkins
Debbie Horsfield
Donald Howarth
Dusty Hughes
Ron Hutchinson
Debbie Isitt
Stephen Jeffreys
Ann Jellicoe
Terry Johnson
Keith Johnstone
Sarah Kane
Charlotte Keatley
Barrie Keeffe
Tom Kempinski
Hanif Kureishi
Kevin Laffan
David Lan
Bryony Lavery
Mike Leigh
Doris Lessing
Deborah Levy
Stephen Lowe
Doug Lucie
Peter Luke
Sharman Macdonald
Wolf Mankowitz
Patrick Marber
Tony Marchant
Martin McDonagh
John McGrath
Tom McGrath
Clare McIntyre
Ronald Millar
Anthony Minghella
Adrian Mitchell
Julian Mitchell
Daniel Mornin
John Mortimer
Gregory Motton
David Mowat
G. F. Newman
Peter Nichols
Lewis Nkosi
Mary O'Malley
Michael O'Neill and Jeremy Seabrook
Louise Page
Caryl Phillips
David Pinner
Winsome Pinnock
Harold Pinter
Alan Plater
Stephen Poliakoff
David Pownall
Mark Ravenhill
Anne Ridler
David Rudkin
Willy Russell
James A. Saunders
David Selbourne
Anthony Shaffer
Peter Shaffer
Johnny Speight
John Spurling
Tom Stoppard
David Storey
Mike Stott
George Tabori
Peter Terson
Sue Townsend
Peter Ustinov
Derek Walcott
Michelene Wandor
Timberlake Wertenbaker
Arnold Wesker
Peter Whelan
Ted Whitehead
Hugh Whitemore
Christopher Wilkinson
Heathcote Williams
Nigel Williams
Snoo Wilson
Charles Wood
Nicholas Wright

Canadian

Ted Allan
Carol Bolt
Sally Clark
David Fennario
Brad Fraser
David Freeman
David French
Jack Gray
John Gray
Tom Hendry
John Herbert
Tomson Highway
Margaret Hollingsworth
Wendy Lill

TITLE INDEX

The following list includes the titles of all stage, screen, radio, and television plays cited in the entries with *Contemporary Dramatists*. The name in parenthesis directs the reader to the appropriate entry where fuller information is given. The date is that of first production or publication. These abbreviations are used: s, screenplay; r, radio play; and t, television play.

$ Value of Man (Wilson, R.), 1975
1-2-3: Who Are You Anyway? (McGrath, T.), 1981
2 (Linney), 1990
2 Children Free to Wander (r Hampton), 1969
2 Monologos, 2 Obras Cartas (Fratti), 1992
2 Samuel 11, Etc (Greenspan), 1989
4 A.M (Mamet), 1983
4-Channels (r Bermange), 1989
4-H Club (Shepard), 1965
5 Days in '55 (r Plater), 1976
5th of July (Wilson, L.), 1978
6 of the Best (t Romeril), 1981-86
7 Blowjobs (Wellman), 1991
8 x Gray (Gray, Spalding), 1982
8th Ditch (Baraka), 1964
16 Pleasures (Weller), 1996
17 Loves and 17 Kisses (Birimisa), 1966
18 Wheels (Gray, John), 1977
23 Pat O'Brien Movies (Friedman), 1966
24 Inches (Patrick), 1982
26 Mountains for Viewing the Sunset From (Higgins), 1981
27 Episodes for the Aquarian Theatre (Higgins), 1959
31 Ejaculations (Bogosian), 1996
31 for 2 (r Pollock)
34th Star (t Linney), 1976
47 Beds (Gray, Spalding), 1981
50s 60s 70s 80s (Patrick), 1984
52 Pick-up (s Steppling), 1986
57th Saturday (Trevor), 1973
74 Georgia Avenue (Schisgal), 1992
75th (Fratti), 1974
75th (Horovitz), 1977
80 Days (Wilson, S.), 1988
84 Charing Cross Road (t Whitemore), 1975
102 Boulevard Haussmann (t Bennett), 1990
200 Years (Romeril), 1970
1000 Airplanes on the Roof (Hwang), 1988
1001 Arabian Nights (s Allan), 1959
1776 (Stone), 1969
1841 (Gow), 1988
1850 (Mowat), 1967
1861 Whitby Lifeboat Disaster (Terson), 1970
1918 (s Foote), 1984
1949 (French), 1989
1951 (Wellman), 1986
1959 Pink Thunderbird (McLure), 1980
1959/60 (Higgins), 1985
1969 Terminal 1996 (Yankowitz), 1996
1984 Here and Now (Kee), 1985
1985 (Holden), 1985
1995 (Schisgal), 1995
1996 (t Newman), 1989
100,001 Horror Stories of the Plains (Terry), 1976
700,000 (Romeril), 1980
"A" is for "Actor" (Sherman, S.), 1987
A-A-America: Grandma Faust, and The Swing (Bond, E.), 1976
Aare Akogun (Ogunyemi), 1968
Abel's Sister (Wertenbaker), 1984
Abelard and Heloise (Millar), 1970
Abide with Me (t Mitchell, J.), 1976
Abigail's Party (Leigh), 1977
Abingdon Square (Fornés), 1984
Able's Will (t Hampton), 1977
Abortive (r Churchill), 1971
Abracadabra (Moore), 1979
Abroad (Weller), 1981
Absence of Mallets (Wellman), 1994
Absence of War (Hare), 1993
Absent Forever (Hopkins), 1987
Absent Friends (Ayckbourn), 1974
Absolute Beginners (t Griffiths), 1974
Absolute Decline (r Jeffreys), 1984
Absolute Power over Movie Stars (Patrick), 1968
Absolute Strangers (t Anderson), 1991
Absolution (s Shaffer, A.), 1981
Absurd Person Singular (Ayckbourn), 1972
Abugida Transform (Gabre-Medhin), 1976
Abundance (Henley), 1989
Acada Campus (t Sowande), 1980-82
Academic Murders (Koch), 1966
Academy (Fratti), 1963
Academy-Return (Fratti), 1967
Acapulco (Berkoff), 1986
Access to the Children (t Trevor), 1973
Accident (s Pinter), 1967
Accidental Death of an Anarchist (Nelson), 1984
Accidental Poke (Romeril), 1977
According to Plan (r Elyot), 1987
Accrington Pals (Whelan), 1981
AC/DC (Williams, H.), 1970
Aces High (s Barker), 1976
Aces Wild (Hendry), 1972
Achilles (Sunde), 1991
Achilles Heel (t Clark, B.), 1973
Achilles on the Beach at Troy (Spurling), 1994
Acid (Edgar), 1971
Acrobats (Horovitz), 1968
Across from the Garden of Allah (Wood), 1986
Across Oka (Holman), 1988
Across the River and into the Jungle (Kopit), 1958
Across the Water (t Rudkin), 1983
Act (Furth), 1977
Act (Higgins), 1974
Act of Betrayal (t Whitemore), 1971
Act of the Imagination (Slade), 1987
Acting Exercize (Barnes)
Action (Patrick), 1966
Action (Shepard), 1974

NOTES ON ADVISERS AND CONTRIBUTORS

ADAMS, Elizabeth. Freelance writer, Cleveland, Ohio. Author of fiction and essays in *The Massachusetts Review, Yale Theatre, The North American Review, The Chicago Review, The Alaska Quarterly Review,* and other journals. **Essay:** Mark Medoff.

ANDERSON, Addell Austin. Director, Black Theatre Program, Wayne State University, Detroit, Michigan; managing director, Plowshares Theatre Company, Detroit. Author of articles in *The Drama Review, College Language Association Journal, Theatre Survey,* and other journals and in books, including *Masterplots II, The Feminist Director, African-American Encyclopedia, Theatrical Directions,* and *American Playwrights, 1880-1945.* Editor of *The Black Theatre Directory.* **Essays:** Loften Mitchell; OyamO; Joseph A. Walker; August Wilson; George C. Wolfe.

ANDERSON, Frances Rademacher. Freelance writer, Sacramento, California. **Essays:** Heathcote Williams; Susan Yankowitz.

ANDERSON, Gary. Co-founder and artistic director, Plowshares Theatre, Detroit, Michigan; publicist, Black Theatre Network; executive administrator, Arts Centered Education, Wayne State University, Detroit. Author of articles in the *African-American Encyclopedia* and *BT News.* **Essay:** Ron Milner.

APPLE, Thomas. Lecturer in Renaissance and modern drama, University of Canterbury, Christchurch, New Zealand. Professional actor and former lecturer, Bryn Mawr College, Pennsylvania. **Essays:** Thomas Babe; Horton Foote.

BALLET, Arthur H. Professor emeritus of theater, University of Minnesota, Minneapolis. Consultant to various funding organizations in the United States. Advisory editor of *New Theatre Quarterly.* Former program director for theater, National Endowment for the Arts, Washington, D.C.; executive director, Office for Advanced Drama Research, Minneapolis; and dramaturge, Guthrie Theatre, Minneapolis, and American Conservatory Theatre, San Francisco. Editor of *Playwrights for Tomorrow,* vols. 1-13. **Essays:** Steven Dietz; Nick Enright; Lee Kalcheim; Terrence McNally; Barrie Stavis.

BANHAM, Martin. Professor of drama and theater studies, University of Leeds. Author of *Osborne,* 1969, and *African Theatre Today,* 1976. Editor of *Plays by Tom Taylor,* 1985, and *The Cambridge Guide to World Theatre,* 1988 and 1992. Co-editor (with John Hodgson) of three volumes of *Drama in Education,* 1972, 1973, and 1975.

BANKS, Carol. Independent scholar. Former dramaturge and high school English teacher. **Essay:** Christina Reid.

BARKER, Clive. Senior lecturer in theater studies, University of Warwick, Coventry. Joint editor of *New Theatre Quarterly,* Cambridge. Author of *Theatre Games,* 1977. **Essay:** Arnold Wesker.

BARLOW, Judith E. Professor of English and women's studies, State University of New York, Albany. Author of *Final Acts: The Creation of Three Late O'Neill Plays,* 1985, and many theater reviews and articles on O'Neill, Rachel Crothers, Tina Howe, and American drama. Editor of *Plays by American Women (1900-30),* 1981, and O'Neill centennial issue of *Theatre Survey,* 1988, and *Plays by American Women (1930-1960),* 1994. **Essay:** Tina Howe.

BARNETT, Gene A. Professor of English, Department of English, Languages, and Philosophy, Fairleigh Dickinson University, Teaneck, New Jersey. Author of *Denis Johnston,* 1978, *Lanford Wilson,* 1987, and articles on modern drama and American literature. **Essay:** Thomas Kilroy.

BENEDIKT, Michael. Author of several books of poetry, including *Night Cries,* 1976, and *The Badminton at Great Barrington,* 1980, and the plays *The Vaseline Photographer, The Orgy Bureau,* and *Clyde's Wife.* Editor (with G. E. Wellwarth) of anthologies of plays in translation, including *Modern French Plays: From Jarry to Ionesco,* 1964, *Postwar German Theatre,* 1965, and *Modern Spanish Theatre,* 1967. Editor of anthologies of poetry and teacher at several American universities.

BENNATHAN, Joss. Freelance writer and critic, drama teacher, actor, and community theater worker. **Essays:** Doug Lucie.

BENSON, Eugene. Professor of English, University of Guelph, Ontario. Editor of journal, *Canadian Drama.* Former chair of Writers' Union of Canada, 1983-84. Author of plays *Joan of Arc's Violin,* 1972, and *The Gunners' Rope,* 1973; also author of novels *The Bulls of Ronda,* 1976, and *Power Game,* 1980; and author of critical monograph *J. M. Synge,* 1980. Librettist of operas *Heloise and Abelard,* 1973, *Everyman,* 1974, and *Psycho Red,* 1980. Co-editor with L. W. Connolly of *English-Canadian Theatre,* 1980, *The Oxford Companion to Canadian Theatre,* 1989, and *Encyclopedia of Post-Colonial Literatures in English,* 2 vols., 1994. Co-editor with William Toye of *The Oxford Companion to Canadian Literature,* 1997. **Essay:** James Reaney.

BENTLEY, Eric. See his own entry.

BEN-ZVI, Linda. Professor of English and theater, Colorado State University, Fort Collins. Editor of *Samuel Beckett,* 1986, *Women in Beckett,* 1991, *Susan Glaspell: A Collection of Critical Essays,* 1993, and *Vital Voices: An Anthology of Contemporary American Women Playwrights,* 1993. **Essay:** Suzan-Lori Parks.

BERKOWITZ, Gerald M. Professor of English, Northern Illinois University, DeKalb. Author of *David Garrick: A Reference Guide,* 1980, *Sir John Vanbrugh and the End of Restoration Comedy,* 1981, *New Broadways: Theatre across America 1950-1980,* 1982, *American Drama of the Twentieth Century,* 1992, and *New Broadways: Approaching a New Millennium.* Editor of *The Plays of David Garrick,* 1981. **Essays:** Tom Kempinski; Anthony Shaffer.

BERTIN, Michael. Play reviewer; graduate of the Yale School of Drama; employee of Salvation Army at Alexandria Community Shelter for the Homeless in Virginia. Editor of *The Play and Its Critic: Essays for Eric Bentley,* 1986. **Essay:** Eric Bentley.

BIGSBY, C. W. E. Professor of American studies, University of East Anglia, Norwich. Author of *Confrontation and Commitment: A Study of Contemporary American Drama,* 1967, *Edward Albee,* 1969, *Tom Stoppard,* 1976 (revised 1979), *The Second Black Renaissance,* 1980, *Contemporary English Drama,* 1981, *Joe Orton,* 1982, *A Critical Introduction to Twentieth-Century American Drama,* 3 vols., 1982-85, *David Mamet,* 1985; also author of television play, *The After Dinner Game* (with Malcolm Bradbury),

1975. Editor of *Three Negro Plays,* 1969, *The Black American Writer,* 1970, *Dada and Surrealism,* 1972, *Superculture,* 1974, *Edward Albee: A Collection of Critical Essays,* 1976, *Approaches to Popular Culture,* 1976, *The Radical Imagination and the Liberal Tradition* (with Heide Ziegler), 1982, *Cultural Change in the United States since World War II,* 1986, *The Plays of Susan Glaspell,* 1987, *Miller on File,* 1988, *Miller and Company,* 1990, and *American Drama 1945-1990,* 1992. **Essay:** Robert Anderson.

BILLINGTON, Michael. Theater critic for *The Guardian* since 1971 and London correspondent for *New York Times* since 1978; author and broadcaster. Former theater, film, and television critic for *The Times,* 1965-71. Author of *The Modern Actor,* 1973, *How Tickled I Am,* 1977, *Alan Ayckbourn,* 1983, *Tom Stoppard: Playwright,* 1987, and *Peggy Ashcroft,* 1988. Editor of *The Performing Arts,* 1980, *The Guinness Book of Theatre Facts and Feats,* 1982, and *Director's Shakespeare: "Twelfth Night,"* 1990. **Essays:** Preface to the fifth edition; Jim Cartwright; Conor McPherson.

BLAU, Herbert. Distinguished professor of English and comparative literature, University of Wisconsin, Milwaukee. Former artistic director of Kraken, cofounding director of Actors Workshop, San Francisco, and codirector of Repertory Theater of Lincoln Center, New York. Director of American premieres of *Mother Courage, Serjeant Musgrave's Dance,* and *The Condemned of Altona.* Author of *The Impossible Theater,* 1964, *Take Up the Bodies: Theater at the Vanishing Point,* 1982, *Blooded Thought,* 1982, *The Eye of Prey: Subversions of the Postmodern,* 1987, *The Audience,* 1990, *To All Appearances: Ideology and Performance,* 1992; also author of plays *Telegraph Hill* and *A Gift of Fury,* and texts for Kraken.

BODE, Walter. Editor in chief, Grove Press, New York. Editor of *Audition Pieces: Monologues for Student Actors.* **Essays:** Richard Foreman; Michael McClure; Arthur Sainer; Lanford Wilson.

BOWEN, John. See his own entry. **Essays:** Stephen Bill; John Hale; David Lan.

BRADISH, Gaynor F. Late adjunct associate professor, Union College, Schenectady, New York. Author of the introduction to Arthur Kopit's *Oh Dad, Poor Dad . . . ,* 1960. Director of Kopit's *Asylum,* New York, 1963, and of many plays for drama workshops and university groups. Died 1988 or 1989. **Essays:** Michael Cristofer; Albert Innaurato.

BRISBANE, Katharine. Founding publisher of Currency Press Pty. Ltd., Sydney. Author of introductions to works by Alexander Buzo, Peter Kenna, Jim McNeil, Katharine Susannah Prichard, John Romeril, Patrick White, and David Williamson; also author of drama section *The Literature of Australia,* 1976, *Companion to Theatre in Australia,* 1995, *World Encyclopaedia of Contemporary Theatre,* vol. 4, 1998. Contributor of articles to *Contemporary Australian Drama,* 1981. Editor of *Entertaining Australia,* 1991, a history of the performing arts in Australia. **Essays:** Janis Balodis; Alexander Buzo; Jack Davis; Dorothy Hewett.

BRISSENDEN, Constance. Freelance writer and editor based in Vancouver, British Columbia. Former dramaturge, Playwrights Canada; managing editor of EXPO 86, Vancouver; and editor of five anthologies of Canadian plays. **Essay:** Carol Bolt.

BROWN, John Russell. Consultant, Middlesex University. Former professor of theater, University of Michigan, Ann Arbor; head of drama, University of Birmingham; professor of English, University of Sussex; and literary manager and associate of National Theatre of Great Britain. Author of *Shakespeare and His Comedies,* 1957, *Shakespeare's "Macbeth,"* 1963, *Shakespeare's Plays in Performance,* 1966, *Effective Theatre,* 1969, *Shakespeare's "The Tempest,"* 1969, *Shakespeare's Dramatic Style,* 1970, *Theatre Language: A Study of Arden, Osborne, Pinter, Wesker,* 1972, *Free Shakespeare,* 1974, *Shakespeare in Performance,* 1976, *Discovering Shakespeare,* 1981, *Shakespeare and His Theatre,* 1982, *A Short Guide to Modern British Drama,* 1982, and *Studying Shakespeare: A Casebook,* 1990. General editor of Stratford-upon-Avon Studies, 1960-67, and Theatre Production Studies. Editor of Shakespeare's *The Merchant of Venice,* 1955, Webster's *The White Devil,* 1960, and *The Duchess of Malfi,* 1965, and Shakespeare's *Henry V,* 1965. **Essay:** David Selbourne.

BRUCHAC, Joseph. Editor of *Greenfield Review,* Greenfield Center, New York. Author of 14 collections of poetry, several novels, and five collections of retellings of Native American stories. Editor of numerous anthologies, including *Breaking Silence: Asian American Poetry,* 1984, and of *Survival This Way: Interviews with American Indian Poets,* 1987. **Essays:** R. Sarif Easmon; Obi B. Egbuna; Lewis Nkosi.

BULL, John. Lecturer in English literature and drama, University of Sheffield. Author of *New British Political Dramatists,* 1984, *Stage Right: The Recovery of the Mainstream,* 1988, and articles on modern British drama. Editor of *Howard Brenton: Three Plays,* 1988, and *The Penguin Book of Pastoral Verse,* 1988. **Essays:** Peter Barnes; John Godber; John McGrath; Julian Mitchell; Stephen Poliakoff; Hugh Whitemore.

BURIAN, Jarka M. Professor emeritus of theater, State University of New York, Albany. Author of *The Scenography of Josef Svoboda,* 1971, *Svoboda: Wagner,* 1983, and many articles on scenography, design, and Czechoslovakian theater for *Theatre Journal, Theater Crafts, Drama Review, Modern Drama, American Theater,* and other journals. Editor and translator of Svoboda's *Secret of Theatrical Space,* 1993. **Essay:** Tad Mosel.

CAMERON, Alasdair. Lecturer in theater studies, University of Glasgow. Theater reviewer in Scotland for *The Times* and *The Sunday Times.* Author of *A Critical History of Twentieth-Century Scottish Theatre and Drama,* 1989 (revised ed., 1993). Editor of *Scot-Free,* an anthology of new Scottish plays, 1989. **Essay:** Neil Bartlett.

CARLSON, Susan. Professor of English, Iowa State University, Ames. Author of *Women of Grace: Henry James's Plays and the Comedy of Manners,* 1985, *Women and Comedy: Rewriting the British Theatrical Tradition,* 1991, and articles in *Modern Drama, New Theatre Quarterly, Themes in Drama, Theatre Research International, Journal of Dramatic Theory and Criticism,* and other journals. **Essay:** Sue Townsend.

CARRAGHER, Bernard. Freelance writer. **Essays:** Lonnie Carter; Charles Dizenzo.

CHAILLET, Ned. Producer, BBC Radio Drama, London. Former writer for *Washington Star* and *Times Literary Supplement;* deputy drama critic, *The Times;* and London theater critic, *Wall Street Journal,* Europe. **Essays:** John Robin Baitz; Steven Berkoff; Richard Crane; Nick Dear; Marcella Evaristi; Athol Fugard; Barrie Keeffe; Hugh Leonard; Tom McGrath; Richard Nelson; Caryl Phillips; Wallace Shawn; Michael Weller; Timberlake Wertenbaker.

CHAMBERS, Colin. Literary manager, 1981-97; repertoire consultant, since 1997, Royal Shakespeare Company. Senior research fellow, De Montfort University. Formerly freelance journalist and theater critic. Author of *Other Spaces: New Theatre and the RSC, The Story of Unity Theatre,* and *Peggy: The Life of Margaret Ramsay, Play Agent,* winner of inaugural Theatre Book Prize, 1998. Co-author of *Playwrights' Progress: Patterns of Postwar British Drama,* with Mike Prior, and *Kenneth's First Play,* with Richard Nelson. Editor of *Making Plays: The Writer-Director Relationship in the Theatre Today* by Richard Nelson and David Jones. **Essay:** Preface to the sixth edition.

CHAMBERS, D. D. C. Associate professor of English, Trinity College, Toronto. Author of *Thomas Traherne,* 1987. **Essays:** Jack Gray; John Herbert.

CHRISTIANSEN, Richard. Entertainment editor, *Chicago Tribune.*

CLURMAN, Harold. Critic and lecturer. Author of *The Fervent Years: The Story of the Group Theatre,* 1945, *Lies like Truth: Theatre Essays and Reviews,* 1958, *All People Are Famous: Instead of an Autobiography,* 1974, *The Divine Pastime: Theatre Essays,* 1974, and *Ibsen,* 1977. Producer and director of many plays beginning in the 1920s. Died 1980.

COCO, Bill. Contributing editor of *Performing Arts Journal;* member of drama faculty, Columbia University, New York; dramaturge for Joseph Chaikin and Living Theatre. Author of articles in *Theatre Journal, Performing Arts Journal, Drama Review,* and *Performance.* Currently editing the papers of Joseph Chaikin. **Essays:** Lee Breuer; Jean-Claude van Itallie.

COHN, Ruby. Professor of comparative drama, University of California, Davis; member of editorial boards of *Modern Drama, Theatre Journal,* and *Cambridge Guide to World Drama.* Author of *Samuel Beckett: The Comic Gamut,* 1962, *Currents in Contemporary Drama,* 1969, *Edward Albee,* 1969, *Dialogue in American Drama,* 1971, *Back to Beckett,* 1971, *Modern Shakespeare Offshoots,* 1976, *Just Play: Beckett's Theatre,* 1980, *From Desire to Godot,* 1987, *Retreats from Realism in Recent English Drama,* 1990, and *New American Dramatists 1960-1990,* 1991. **Essays:** Preface to the third edition; Edward Bond; Christopher Hampton; Joan Holden; James Schevill; Sam Shepard.

COLOMBO, John Robert. Freelance writer, editor, and communications consultant. Author or editor of more than 80 books, including poetry, science fiction, lore, literature, cultural guides, and *The Dictionary of Canadian Quotations,* 1991. Translator of works by Robert Zend, Eva Lipska, Lyubomir Levchev, Ludwig Zelle, George Faludy, and others.

COLVIN, Clare. Freelance writer, reviewer, and critic for *The Times, The Sunday Times, Sunday Express,* and other newspapers and magazines. **Essays:** Nell Dunn; Hanif Kureishi.

COOK, Albert. Professor of classics, English, and comparative literature and Ford Foundation Professor, Brown University, Providence, Rhode Island. Author of several plays, four books of poetry, and many critical works, including *Enactment: Greek Tragedy,* 1971, *Shakespeare's Enactment,* 1972, *Myth and Language,* 1980, *French Tragedy,* 1981, *Changing the Signs: The Fifteenth-Century Break-through,* 1985, *Thresholds: The Romantic Experience,* 1985, and *Soundings: On Shakespeare, Modern Poetry, Plato, and Other Subjects,* 1991.

COOKE, Judy. Editor of *Fiction Magazine,* London, and of anthology *The Best of Fiction Magazine,* 1986. **Essay:** Wolf Mankowitz.

COOKE, Patricia. Theater critic for *Dominion Sunday Times,* Wellington. Former teacher of English and drama; tutor, Victoria University of Wellington; and secretary, Shakespeare Globe Centre, New Zealand. **Essays:** John Broughton; David Geary; Stuart Hoar; Anthony McCarten; Renée; Stephen Sinclair.

CORBALLIS, Richard. Professor of English, Massey University, Palmerston North, New Zealand. Author of *Stoppard: The Mystery and the Clockwork,* 1984, and *Introducing Witi Ihimaera* (with Simon Garrett), 1984. Editor of *George Chapman's Minor Translations: A Critical Edition of His Renderings of Musaeus, Hesiod and Juvenal,* 1984. **Essay:** Vincent O'Sullivan.

CORRIGAN, Robert W. Dean, School of Arts and Humanities, University of Texas at Dallas. Author of *Theatre in Search of a Fix,* 1973, *The World of the Theatre,* 1979 (2nd ed., 1992), and *The Making of Theatre,* 1980. Editor of *Arthur Miller: A Collection of Critical Essays,* 1969, several anthologies of plays, and volumes on comedy and tragedy. Founding editor of *Tulane Drama Review* (later *Drama Review*).

DACE, Tish. Professor of English, Southeastern Massachusetts University, North Dartmouth; contributor to *Plays International, Plays and Players, Theater Week, Theatre Crafts, Other Stages, Village Voice, New York Times, American Theatre, Playbill,* and other publications. Author of *LeRoi Jones (Imamu Amiri Baraka): A Checklist of Works by and about Him,* 1971, *The Theatre Student: Modern Theatre and Drama,* 1973, and *Langston Hughes: Early Critical Responses,* 1991. **Essays:** Harvey Fierstein; Spalding Gray; John Guare; Wendy Kesselman; Susan Miller; James A. Saunders; Martin Sherman; Karen Sunde; Paula Vogel; Doric Wilson; Paul Zindel.

DARLINGTON, W. A. Member of editorial staff and chief drama critic, 1920-68, *Daily Telegraph,* London. Author of *Alf's Button,* 1919 (novel), 1924 (play); *I Do What I Like,* 1947; *The Actor and His Audience,* 1949; and *Six Thousand and One Nights,* 1960. C.B.E., 1963. Died 1979. **Essay:** Ronald Millar.

DAWSON, Terence. Lecturer in English literature at National University of Singapore, since 1988. Contributor of articles on both English and French literature to numerous journals, including *Modern Language Review.* **Essay:** Peter Luke.

DIAMOND, Elin. Associate professor of English, Rutgers University, New Brunswick, New Jersey. Author of *Pinter's Comic Play,* 1985, and articles on Pinter, Beckett, Churchill, Benmussa, and Duras in *Theatre Journal, Modern Drama, Comparative Drama,* and other journals. **Essay:** Adrienne Kennedy.

DUNN, Tony. Senior lecturer in literary and cultural studies, Portsmouth University, Hampshire; editor of *Gambit,* London. Author of articles on Howard Barker, British theater in the 1980s, and reviews, features, and interviews in *Gambit, Drama, Plays and Players,* and *Tribune.* **Essays:** Howard Barker; Alan Bleasdale; Deborah Levy; Willy Russell; Ted Whitehead.

EDINBOROUGH, Arnold. President, Council for Business and the Arts in Canada; member of board of governors, Stratford Festival, Ontario. Author of *Canada,* 1962, *Some Camel . . . Some Needle,* 1974, *The Enduring Wood,* 1978, *The Festivals of Canada,* 1981, *Winston's: The Life and Times of a Great Restaurant,* 1988, and articles in the *Financial Post, Canadian Churchman,* and other periodicals. **Essay:** Mavor Moore.

EDWARDES, Jane. Theater editor, *Time Out,* London. Contributor to *Kaleidoscope,* BBC Radio. **Essays:** Debbie Isitt; Clare McIntyre.

ELSOM, John. Senior lecturer, City University, London. Author of *Theatre Outside London,* 1972, *Post-War British Theatre,* 1976 (revised 1979), *The History of the National Theatre* (with Nicholas Tomalin), 1978, and *Post-War British Theatre Criticism,* 1981. Editor of *Is Shakespeare Still Our Contemporary?,* 1989. **Essays:** Barry Bermange; Chris Bond; J. P. Donleavy; Wilson John Haire; Willis Hall and Keith Waterhouse; Alan Plater; Peter Terson; Christopher Wilkinson.

ESTRIN, Mark W. Professor of English and director of film studies, Rhode Island College, Providence, since 1966. Editor of *Lillian Hellman: Plays, Films, Memoirs,* 1980, *Critical Essays on Lillian Hellman,* 1989, and *Conversations with Eugene O'Neill,* 1990. Contributor of essays and reviews to numerous publications, including *Resources for American Literary Study, Modern Drama, Literature/Film Quarterly, The Journal of Narrative Technique,* and *Choice.* **Essays:** David Rabe; Ted Tally.

FALCONIERI, John V. President emeritus, American University of Rome; editor of *Theatre Annual;* member of the editorial board, *International Drama.* Author of *A History of the Commedia dell'Arte in Spain.* **Essay:** Gore Vidal.

FEINGOLD, Michael. Drama critic, *Village Voice,* New York. Director of productions of plays by John Arden, Lanford Wilson, and others. Translator of plays by Brecht, Ibsen, Molière, Prévert, Diderot, Bernhard, and others. Literary director of Guthrie Theatre, Minneapolis, 1970-79. **Essay:** Kenneth Bernard.

FITZPATRICK, Peter. Associate professor and head, Centre for Drama and Theatre Studies, Monash University, Clayton, Victoria. Author of *After "The Doll": Australian Drama since 1955,* 1979; also author of books on the plays of David Williamson and Stephen Sewell, dual biography *Pioneer Players: The Lives of Louis and Hilda Esson,* 1995. Contributor of articles on Australian drama. **Essays:** Hannie Rayson; Stephen Sewell.

FOTHERINGHAM, Richard. Reader in drama, University of Queensland, Brisbane. Author of *Sport in Australian Drama,* 1992. Editor (with Veronica Kelly) of *Australasian Drama Studies,* since 1982, and editor of *Community Theatre in Australia,* 1987. **Essay:** John Romeril.

FRANK, Leah D. Theater critic, *New York Times,* Long Island Supplement; theater critic and feature writer for many newspapers and magazines, including *New York Times, New York Daily News, Elle, Other Stages* (founding editor), *Stamford (Connecticut) Advocate,* and *New York Theater Review.* **Essays:** Frank D. Gilroy; Robert Patrick.

FRIEDMAN, Melvin J. Professor of comparative literature, University of Wisconsin, Milwaukee; advisory editor of *Journal of Popular Culture, Studies in the Novel, Renascence, Journal of American Culture, Studies in American Fiction, Fer de Lance, Contemporary Literature, Journal of Beckett Studies, International Fiction Review, Arete, Journal of Modern Literature,* and *Yiddish.* Author of *Stream of Consciousness: A Study in Literary Method,* 1955. Author or editor of works about Beckett, Flannery O'Connor, Styron, Catholic novelists, Ezra Pound, and Ionesco. **Essay:** Bruce Jay Friedman.

GILBERT, Helen. Lecturer, Monash University, Clayton, Victoria. Co-author (with Joanne Tompkins) of *Re-acting (to) Empire: Performance and Post-Colonial Drama,* 1993, and *Post-Colonial Drama: Theory, Practice, Politics,* 1996. Author of *Sightlines: Race, Gender and Nation in Contemporary Australian Theatre,* 1998. **Essays:** Alma De Groen; Jill Shearer.

GILBERT, Reid. Professor of English, Capilano College, North Vancouver, British Columbia. Author of play *A Glass Darkly,* 1973, *A Short Guide to Writing about Literature: First Canadian Edition,* 1997, and numerous articles and reviews in *Theater Research in Canada, Theatre Journal TDR, Modern Drama, SCL, Canadian Theatre Review, Capilano Review,* and other periodicals. Author in Profiles in Canadian Literature Series. **Essays:** David Fennario; David Freeman; John Gray; Tom Hendry; Sharon Pollock.

GILMAN, Richard. Professor of drama, Yale University, New Haven, Connecticut. Author of *The Confusion of Realms,* 1970, *Common and Uncommon Masks,* 1971, *The Making of Modern Drama,* 1975, *Decadence,* 1979, and *Faith, Sex, Mystery: A Memoir,* 1987. Former literary editor of *New Republic* and drama critic for *Commonweal* and *Newsweek.*

GOODMAN, Lizbeth. Lecturer in literature, Open University, Milton Keynes; director of Shakespeare Multimedia Project for the BBC; member of editorial committee for *New Theatre Quarterly.* Author of *Contemporary Feminist Theatres: To Each Her Own,* 1993. Co-editor of *Imagining Women: Cultural Representations and Gender,* 1992, and *Shakespeare, Aphra Behn & the Lavan,* 1996, and editor of *Literature & Gender,* 1996, and *Feminist Stages,* 1996. **Essays:** Sarah Daniels; Debbie Horsfield; Charlotte Keatley; Bryony Lavery; Rona Munro; Winsome Pinnock; Michelene Wandor.

GORDON, Lois. Professor, Department of English and Comparative Literature, Fairleigh Dickinson University, Teaneck, New Jersey. Author of *Stratagems to Uncover Nakedness: The Dramas of Harold Pinter,* 1969, *Donald Barthelme,* 1981, *Robert Coover:*

The Universal Fiction-making Process, 1983, *American Chronicle: Six Decades in American Life 1920-1980,* 1987, *American Chronicle: Seven Decades in American Life 1920-1989,* 1990, *Harold Pinter: A Casebook,* 1990, *The Columbia Chronicles of American Life, 1910-1992,* 1995, and *The World of Samuel Beckett, 1906-1946,* 1996; also author of articles on Arthur Miller, Tennessee Williams, Samuel Beckett, T. S. Eliot, William Butler Yeats, William Faulkner, Randall Jarrell, Philip Roth, Elizabeth Bishop, William Gaddis, and other writers. **Essays:** Arthur Miller; Harold Pinter.

GOTTFRIED, Martin. Freelance writer, drama critic, and lecturer. Author of *A Theater Divided,* 1968, *Opening Nights,* 1970, *Broadway Musicals,* 1979, *Jed Harris: The Curse of Genius,* 1984, *In Person: The Great Entertainers,* 1986, *All His Jazz,* 1990, *More Broadway Musicals,* 1991, and *Sondheim,* 1993. **Essays:** Lewis John Carlino; Arnold Weinstein; John White.

GRAHAM-WHITE, Anthony. Professor, Department of Communication and Theater, University of Illinois, Chicago. Author of *The Drama of Black Africa,* 1974; contributor of articles to various journals. Former editor of *Educational Theatre Journal* (now *Theatre Journal*). **Essays:** Ama Ata Aidoo; J. P. Clark Bekederemo; David Campton; Frank Chin; David Cregan; Tsegaye Gabre-Medhin; Philip Kan Gotanda; Len Jenkin; Ngugi wa Thiong'o; Charles Wood.

GRANT, Steve. Assistant editor of *Time Out,* London. Author of five plays, essays on fringe theater in *Dreams and Deconstructions,* 1980, and articles in *The Guardian, The Observer, The Times, The Sunday Times, Morning Star, Cosmopolitan,* and other periodicals. **Essays:** John Byrne; Snoo Wilson.

GRAY, Frances. Lecturer in drama, University of Sheffield. Author of *John Arden,* 1982, and *Noël Coward,* 1987; also author of radio plays, including *Mary,* 1983, *Neverland,* 1985, and *Dawnhorse,* 1991. Contributor of articles on radio drama, modern theater, and women in comedy. Editor of *Second Wave at the Albany.* **Essay:** Tony Marchant.

GUERNSEY, Otis L., Jr. Author and editor of Applause-Best Plays Series of theater yearbooks, since 1964, *Dramatists Guild Quarterly,* since 1964, *The Directory of the American Theater 1894-1971,* 1971, *Curtain Times: The New York Theater 1965-1987,* 1987, and anthologies *Playwrights, Lyricists, Composers on Theater,* 1974, and *Broadway Song and Story,* 1986.

GUPTARA, Prabhu S. Professor, European Institute of Purchasing Management, France, and chair, Advance Management Training Ltd. Freelance writer, lecturer, and broadcaster. Author of two books of poetry, *Beginnings,* 1975, and *Continuations,* 1976; contributor of articles to *Encyclopaedia Iranica, The Oxford Companion to English Literature,* 1985, and *Times Literary Supplement,* and other periodicals. **Essays:** Michael Abbensetts; John Antrobus; Michael Hastings; John Spurling; Olwen Wymark.

HADFIELD, Paul J. A. Senior lecturer in theater studies, University of Ulster, Coleraine, Londonderry. Director of Theatre Ireland since 1982. Member of Association of International Theatre Critics since 1987 and of advisory board for Yeats International Festival since 1991. **Essays:** John B. Keane; Stephen Lowe; Karen Malpede; Jane Martin; Daniel Mornin.

HAMMOND, Jonathan. Late vice president, National Union of Journalists; former editor, Penguin Books, London. Author of articles in *Culture and Agitation* and *Plays and Players.* Died 1983. **Essays:** John Burrows and John Harding; Stewart Conn.

HANSFORD, James. Teacher of English, Royal Grammar School, Guildford; tutor in literature, Open University, Milton Keynes; and tutor in literature, Surrey University Extra-Mural Department. Author of essays on Beckett for *The Journal of Beckett Studies* and *Studies in Short Fiction,* on Conrad for *The Conradian* and *Conradiana,* on Gabriel Josipovici and Alan Burns in *Prospice,* and a pamphlet on postwar British drama for the English Association. **Essays:** Sarah Kane; Gregory Motton.

HAYMAN, Carole. Actress, writer, and director. Actress at Bristol Old Vic, Traverse Theatre Workshop, Edinburgh, and Joint Stock Theatre Group and in more than 20 productions at the Royal Court Theatre, London. Since 1980 has directed plays by Sue Townsend, Jane Thornton, Andrea Dunbar, and Sarah Daniels at the Royal Court and Soho Poly and for Joint Stock. Associate director at Royal Court, 1986-87. Author of radio play *Letters from Kim,* 1986, *All the Best Kim,* 1988, *Ladies of Letters,* 1991, and television series *Rides,* 1992-93. Editor (with Dale Spender) of *How the Vote Was Won and Other Suffragette Plays,* 1985.

HAYMAN, Ronald. See his own entry. **Essays:** Ted Allan; David Caute; Nick Darke; Donald Howarth; Doris Lessing; David Pinner.

HERN, Nick. Publisher of Nick Hern Books since 1988. Lecturer in drama, University of Hull, 1967-72, and University of Glasgow, 1972-74. Drama editor, Methuen, 1974-88.

HIGGINS, Dick. See his own entry. **Essay:** Jackson Mac Low.

HILL, Errol. See his own entry. **Essay:** Amiri Baraka.

HOBSON, Harold. Special writer for *The Sunday Times,* London. Author of *The First Three Years of the War,* 1942, *The Devil in Woodford Wells* (novel), 1946, *Theatre,* 1948, *Theatre II,* 1950, *Verdict at Midnight,* 1952, *The Theatre Now,* 1953, *The French Theatre of Today,* 1953, *Ralph Richardson,* 1958, *The French Theatre since 1830,* 1978, *Indirect Journey* (autobiography), 1978, and *Theatre in Britain: A Personal View,* 1984. Editor of five volumes of *International Theatre Annual.* Knighted 1977. **Essay:** Charles Dyer.

HOFFMAN, William M. See his own entry. **Essays:** Michael T. Smith; David Starkweather.

HOROWITZ, Arthur. Adjunct member, Theatre Arts faculty, Marymount Manhattan College, New York. Contributor of articles and reviews in *Western European Stages* and *Journal of Beckett Studies.* **Essay:** Jez Butterworth.

HUERTA, Jorge A. Professor of drama, University of California, San Diego. Author of *A Bibliography of Chicano and Mexican Dance, Drama, and Music,* 1971, *Chicano Theater: Themes and Forms,* 1982, and many articles. Editor of *El Teatro de la*

Esperanza: An Anthology of Chicano Drama, 1973, and *Necessary Theatre: Six Plays about the Chicano Experience,* 1989. Producer and director of several plays. **Essays:** Octavio Solis; Luis Valdez.

INNES, Christopher. Distinguished research professor, York University, Toronto, Ontario. Author of *Erwin Piscator's Political Theatre,* 1972, *Modern German Drama,* 1979, *Holy Theatre: Ritual and the Avant Garde,* 1981, *Edward Gordon Craig,* 1983, *Modern British Drama: 1890-1990,* 1992, *Avant Garde Theatre: 1892-1992,* 1992, and articles on drama and theater. General editor of Directors in Perspective Series for Cambridge University Press; co-editor of *Modern Drama.* Member of editorial board of *Cambridge Guide to World Theatre.* **Essays:** Michael Frayn; Pam Gems; Robert M. Wilson.

IROBI, Esiaba. Senior lecturer, School of Media, Critical and Creative Arts, Liverpool John Moores University. Author of articles and books, including *Politics and Aesthetics in West African Cinema,* 1993. **Essays:** Matsemela Manaka; Maishe Maponya; Mbongeni Ngema; John Ruganda.

ISTEL, John. Editor in chief, *Stagebill.* Former contributing editor of *American Theatre* magazine; associate editor for Back Stage Books. Author of articles and reviews in *Atlantic Monthly, Newsday, New York, Village Voice, American Theatre,* and *Mother Jones.* **Essays:** Darrah Cloud; Richard Greenberg; Donald Margulies; Martin McDonagh; Charles L. Mee, Jr.; Joan M. Schenkar; Anna Deavere Smith; John Steppling; Naomi Wallace.

JENNER, C. Lee. Freelance writer, New York. **Essays:** William H. Hoffman; Richard Wesley.

KAUFFMANN, Stanley. Visiting professor of drama, City University of New York Graduate Center; film critic, *New Republic.* Author of several books of film criticism, including *A World of Film,* 1966, *Figures of Light,* 1971, *Living Images,* 1975, *Before My Eyes,* 1980, and *Field of View,* 1986. Author of theater criticism, including *Persons of the Drama,* 1976, and *Theater Criticisms,* 1984, and of a volume of memoirs, *Albums of Early Life,* 1980.

KELLY, Veronica. Senior lecturer in English, University of Queensland, Brisbane; editor (with Richard Fotheringham) of *Australasian Drama Studies,* since 1982. Author of *Louis Nowra,* 1987, and articles on contemporary Australian drama for *Australasian Drama Studies, Kunapipi, Southerly, Modern Drama,* and other periodicals. Editor of Garnet Walch's *Australia Felix; or, Harlequin, Laughing Jackass and the Magic Bat,* 1988, and *Our Australian Theatre in the 1990s,* 1998. **Essays:** Hilary Bell; Michael Gow; Louis Nowra.

KEMP, David E. Head of Drama Department, Queen's University, Kingston, Ontario; actor, writer, and director. Author of book *A Different Drummer* and of performance piece *A Child Growing Up.* **Essay:** Ronald Harwood.

KENDLE, Burton S. Professor of English emeritus, Roosevelt University, Chicago. Author of articles on D. H. Lawrence, John Cheever, William March, Tennessee Williams, Paul Bowles, and other writers and on screenwriting. **Essay:** Alan Bennett.

KEYSSAR, Helene. Associate professor of communications and drama, University of California, San Diego. Author of *The Curtain and the Veil: Strategies in Black Drama,* 1981, *Feminist Theatre,* 1985, *Remembering War: A U.S.-Soviet Dialogue* (with Vladimir Pozner), 1990, *Robert Altman's America,* 1991, and articles in *Educational Theatre Journal, Prospects,* and other journals. Director and actor with Eureka Ensemble and other groups. **Essay:** Murray Schisgal.

KHAN, Naseem. Freelance writer; member of editorial board, *Drama,* London. Author of *The Arts Britain Ignores: The Arts of Ethnic Minorities in Britain,* 1976, and many articles and reviews.

KING, Bruce. General editor of series *Modern Dramatists* and *English Dramatists.* Former professor and visiting professor of English at universities in the United States, Canada, Scotland, France, Israel, Nigeria, and New Zealand. Author of *Dryden's Major Plays,* 1966, *Marvell's Allegorical Poetry,* 1977, *The New English Literatures: Cultural Nationalism in a Changing World,* 1980, *History of Seventeenth Century English Literature,* 1988, *Modern Indian Poets: Ezekiel, Ramanujan and Moraes,* 1991, *V. S. Naipaul,* 1993, and *Derek Walcott and West Indian Drama,* 1995. Editor of *Twentieth Century Interpretations of "All for Love,"* 1968, *Dryden's Mind and Art,* 1969, *Introduction to Nigerian Literature,* 1971, *Literatures of the World in English,* 1974, *A Celebration of Black and African Writing,* 1976, *West Indian Literature,* 1979, *Contemporary American Theatre,* 1991, *The Commonwealth Novel since 1960,* 1991, *Post-Colonial English Drama: Commonwealth Drama since 1960,* 1992, *The Later Fiction of Nadine Gordimer,* 1993, and *New National and Post-Colonial Literatures: An Introduction,* 1996. **Essays:** Yulisa Amadu Maddy; Trevor D. Rhone; George F. Walker.

KITCHIN, Laurence. Former professor of liberal arts, City University of New York; former teacher at Bristol, Tufts, Stanford, and Simon Fraser universities. Author of *Len Hutton,* 1953, *Three on Trial,* 1959, *Mid-Century Drama,* 1960 (revised 1962), *Drama in the Sixties,* 1966, and numerous radio scripts.

KLAUS, H. Gustav. Part-time professor of English, University of Osnabrück, Germany. Former visiting professor, University of Queensland and University of Edinburgh. Author of *Caldwell in Kontext,* 1978, and *The Literature of Labour,* 1985. Editor of *The Socialist Novel in Britain,* 1982, *The Rise of Socialist Fiction 1880-1914,* 1987, and *Tramps, Workmates and Revolutionaries,* 1991. **Essays:** Shelagh Delaney; Trevor Griffiths.

KOSTELANETZ, Richard. Writer and artist. Author of radio plays, several books of poetry, including *Arenas Fields Pitches Turfs,* 1982, collections of short stories, including *More Short Fictions,* 1980, and *Epiphanies,* 1983, volumes of experimental prose, including *Aftertexts/Prose Pieces,* 1986, and critical works, including *The Theatre of Mixed-Means,* 1968, *The End of Intelligent Writing,* 1974, *Twenties in the Sixties,* 1979, *The Old Poetries and the New,* 1981, *The Old Fictions and the New,* 1986, *On Innovative Music(ian)s,* 1989, *The New Poetries and Some Old,* 1991, *On Innovative Art(ist)s,* 1992, *On Innovative Performance(s),* 1993, *Radio Writings,* 1996, and *Vocal Shorts: Collected Performance Texts,* 1998. Editor of many collections and anthologies of experimental writing. Visual poetry and related language art exhibited at galleries and universities since 1975. **Essays:** Robert Hivnor; Kenneth Koch.

KUHN, John G. Professor of English and theater and director of theater, Rosemont College, Pennsylvania. **Essays:** María Irene Fornés; Milcha Sánchez-Scott.

LANGE, Bernd-Peter. Professor of English, University of Magdeburg, Germany. Former editor of *Gulliver* and *German-English Yearbook.* Author of *Charles Dickens,* 1969, *George Orwell,* 1975, *The Theory of Genres,* 1979, *Orwell, "1984,"* 1982, *Cultural Studies,* 1984, *The Spanish Civil War in British and American Literature,* 1988, *Classics in Cultural Criticism 1: Britain,* 1990, and *Contemporaries in Cultural Criticism,* 1991. **Essay:** Steve Gooch.

LAWLEY, Paul. Senior lecturer in English, University of Plymouth, Exmouth, Devon. Author of essays and reviews in *Journal of Beckett Studies, Modern Drama, Modern Fiction Studies, Theatre Journal,* and *Modern Language Review*; contributor of chapters to *The Cambridge Companion to Beckett Studies* and *"Make Sense Who May": Essays on Samuel Beckett's Later Works.* **Essays:** Brian Clark; David Edgar; Ron Hutchinson; Terry Johnson; Frank McGuinness; Bill Morrison; Billy Roche; David Rudkin; Nigel Williams; Nicholas Wright.

LEECH, Michael T. Freelance writer. Author of *Italy,* 1974 (revised 1987), *Amsterdam,* 1985, *Exploring Rural Italy,* 1988, and *Essential Kenya,* 1991. **Essay:** Jerome Lawrence.

LINDSAY, Maurice. Consultant at Scottish Civic Trust, Glasgow. Co-editor of *Scottish Review.* Author of more than 20 books of poetry, including *Collected Poems,* 1990, *On the Face of It: Collected Poems Volume 2,* 1993, and *News of the World,* 1995; of plays and travel and historical works; of critical studies, including *Robert Burns: The Man, His Work, The Legend,* 1954 (revised 1968, 1978), *The Burns Encyclopaedia,* 1959 (revised 1970, 1980), *History of Scottish Literature,* 1977 (revised 1992), and *Francis George Scott and the Scottish Renaissance,* 1980; and of an autobiography, *Thank You for Having Me,* 1983. Editor, with Joyce Lindsay, of various books, including *The Scottish Dog,* 1989, and *The Scottish Quotation Book,* 1992. **Essays:** Iain Heggie; A. L. Kennedy.

LONDRÉ, Felicia Hardison. Curators' professor of theater, University of Missouri, Kansas City; dramaturge for Missouri Repertory Theatre and for Nebraska Shakespeare Festival. Honorary co-founder of Heart of America Shakespeare Festival. Author of *Tennessee Williams,* 1979, *Tom Stoppard,* 1981, *Federico Garcia Lorca,* 1984, *The History of World Theatre, 2,* 1991, and articles on continental European and American theater history for essay collections, casebooks, and various journals, including *Theatre Research International, Theatre History Studies, Theatre Journal, Theater Week, Slavic and East European Arts, Studies in Popular Culture,* and *Comparative Drama.* Co-editor of *Shakespeare Companies and Festivals,* 1995, and *Love's Labour's Lost: Critical Essays,* 1997. **Essays:** William Hauptman; Tom Stoppard.

LONEY, Glenn. Professor emeritus of theater, City University of New York; secretary of New York Outer Critics Circle, American Theatre Critics Association, International Theatre Critics Association, and Music Critics Association; editor of *Art Deco News* and *The Modernist*; contributing editor of *Theatre Crafts International* and *Western European Stages*; associate editor of *Opera Monthly*; founder and editor of *Arts Archive.* U.S. critic and representative for *New Theatre Quarterly,* and principal correspondent for *NY Theatre-Wire, NY Museum-Wire,* and *Curator's Choice* on the Internet. Author or editor of many books, including *The Shakespeare Complex,* 1972, *Peter Brook's Royal Shakespeare Company Production of A Midsummer Night's Dream,* 1974, *The House of Mirth: The Play of the Novel,* 1980, *Your Future in the Performing Arts,* 1980, *Twentieth-Century Theatre* (chronology), 2 vols., 1983, *California Gold-Rush Plays,* 1983, *Musical Theatre in America,* 1984, *Unsung Genius: Jack Cole,* 1984, *Staging Shakespeare: Seminars on Production Problems,* 1990, and articles and reviews in *Opera News, Dance, Stages, Theatre Crafts, Performing Arts Journal,* and other journals. **Essays:** William Mastrosimone; Neil Simon.

MacDONALD, James. Fellow in drama, University of Exeter; play reader for Northcott Theatre, Exeter. Former associate editor of *The Freethinker.* Reviewer and author of articles on humanism and arts for *The Freethinker,* 1977-81. **Essay:** David Storey.

MAGRUDER, James. Resident dramaturge, Center Stage, Baltimore, Maryland. Former literary manager of La Jolla Playhouse, California. Author of plays and adaptations, including *Nesteggs for Armageddon, Turcaret, The Triumph of Love,* and *The Sinking of the Titanic*; contributor of articles and theater criticism to *Theater, American Theatre,* and *The Village Voice.* **Essays:** Charles Busch; Eric Overmyer; Keith Reddin.

MAKEHAM, Paul. Lecturer in drama, Academy of the Arts, Queensland University of Technology. Has background as professional actor and has published widely on contemporary Australian drama. Doctoral thesis, completed in 1996, examines representations of landscape in twentieth-century Australian drama. **Essay:** Andrew John Bovell.

MARCUS, Frank. See his own entry. **Essay:** David Mowat.

MARKHAM, E. A. Freelance writer. Author of several books of poetry, including *The Lamp,* 1978, *Pierrot,* 1979, *Love Poems,* 1979, *Games and Penalties,* 1980, *Human Rites,* 1984, *Living in Disguise,* 1986, *Lambchops in Papua/New Guinea,* 1986, and *Towards the End of the Century,* 1989, and of *Love, Politics, and Food,* 1982, and *Something Unusual* (stories), 1986. Editor of *Hinterland,* 1989. **Essay:** Barry Reckord.

MARKUS, Thomas B. Artistic director, Theatre by the Sea, Portsmouth, New Hampshire. Author of *The Professional Actor: From Audition to Performance,* 1980, and essays on Genet and Albee. Former director and actor in New York and Hollywood. **Essays:** Ron Cowen; Martin Duberman.

MARRANCA, Bonnie. Publisher and editor (with Gautam Dasgupta) of *Performing Arts Journal* and Performing Arts Journal Publications, New York. Author of *American Playwrights: A Critical Survey* (with Dasgupta), 2 vols., 1981, *Theatre-writings,* 1984, and numerous essays. Editor of *The Theatre of Images,* 1977, *American Dreams: The Imagination of Sam Shepard,* 1981, *American Garden Writing,* 1988, *Hudson Valley Lives,* 1991, and *Interculturalism and Performance,* 1991.

MARTIN, John. Artistic director, Pan Project, London. **Essay:** Girish Karnad.

McCALLUM, John. Senior lecturer in theater studies and director of Australian Theatre Studies Centre, University of New South Wales, Kensington. Author of many articles on recent Australian drama. **Essay:** Ray Lawler.

McGILLICK, Paul. Lecturer in applied linguistics, University of Sydney; theater critic for *Australian Financial Review.* Former editor of *New Theatre Australia.* Author of *Jack Hibberd,* 1988, and numerous monographs and articles on theater and visual arts. **Essay:** Jack Hibberd.

McNAUGHTON, Howard. Associate professor of English, University of Canterbury, Christchurch, New Zealand. Author of *Bruce Mason,* 1976, *New Zealand Drama,* 1981, and section on drama in *The Oxford History of New Zealand Literature,* 1991, 1998. Editor of *Contemporary New Zealand Plays,* 1976, and *James K. Baxter: Collected Plays,* 1982. **Essays:** John Bowen; Barry Collins; Rosalyn Drexler; Ron Elisha; Paul Foster; Peter Gill; Clem Gorman; Roger Hall; Tony Harrison; Hone Kouka; David Mamet; Greg McGee; Percy Mtwa; Marsha Norman; Megan Terry.

MESERVE, Walter J. Distinguished professor of theater and English, Graduate School, City University of New York; co-editor of *Journal of American Drama and Theatre.* Former professor of theater and drama and director of Institute for American Studies, Indiana University, Bloomington. Author of *An Outline History of American Drama,* 1965 (revised ed., 1994), *Robert Sherwood: Reluctant Moralist,* 1970, *An Emerging Entertainment: The Drama of the American People to 1828,* 1977, *American Drama* (with others), vol. 8 of the Revels History, 1977, *American Drama to 1900: A Guide to Reference Sources,* 1980, and *Heralds of Promise: The Drama of the American People during the Age of Jackson 1829-1849,* 1986. Editor of *The Complete Plays of William Dean Howells,* 1960, *Discussions of Modern American Drama,* 1966, *American Satiric Comedies,* 1969, *Modern Drama from Communist China,* 1970, *The Rise of Silas Lapham by Howells,* 1971, *Studies in Death of a Salesman,* 1972, and *Modern Literature from China,* 1974. Compiler of *Who's Where in the American Theatre,* 1990, *A Chronological Outline of World Theatre* (with M. A. Meserve), 1992, and *On Stage America!,* 1996. **Essays:** George Axelrod; Herb Gardner; William Hanley; Arthur Laurents; N. Richard Nash; Dennis J. Reardon; Peter Stone; Suzan L. Zeder.

MILNE, Geoffrey. Lecturer in theater and drama, La Trobe University, Bundoora, Victoria; drama critic for Australian Broadcasting Corporation (radio). Author of numerous articles on Australian dramatists and theater organizations. Contributor to *The Australian Encyclopaedia,* 1988, and *Companion to the Theatre and Dance in Australia.* **Essays:** Barry Dickins; Daniel Keene; Joanna Murray-Smith; Katherine Thomson.

MITCHELL, Louis D. Associate professor of English, University of Scranton, Pennsylvania. Author of songs and lyrics for *Star of the Morning,* 1971; contributor of many articles to *Theatre Notebook, Eighteenth Century Studies, Crisis,* and other journals. **Essays:** Ossie Davis; Errol Hill.

MITCHELL, Tony. Lecturer in performance studies, University of Technology, Sydney. Author of *Dario Fo: People's Court Jester,* 1986, *File on Brenton,* 1987, and *File on Dario Fo,* 1989. **Essay:** Tes Lyssiotis.

MOE, Christian H. Professor and chair of theater, Southern Illinois University, Carbondale; member of advisory board of Institute of Outdoor Drama; member of Dramatists Guild. Author or co-author of *Creating Historical Drama,* 1965, an essay on Nathaniel West, and several adult dramas and plays for youth. Co-editor of *Six New Plays for Children,* 1971, and *Eight Plays for Youth: Varied Theatrical Experiences for Stage and Study,* 1991. **Essays:** Christopher Durang; William Gibson; Dusty Hughes; Romulus Linney; James McLure; John Ford Noonan; John Pielmeier; Bernard Pomerance; David Williamson.

MURRAY, Christopher. Statutory lecturer in English, University College, Dublin; member of executive board of *Irish University Review.* Author of *Robert William Elliston, Manager,* 1975. Editor of *St. Stephen's Green* (an Irish Restoration comedy), 1980, *Selected Plays of Lennox Robinson,* 1982, and *Yeats and the Noh: A Comparative Study* (with Masara Sepine), 1990. **Essays:** Brian Friel; Eugene McCabe; Tom Murphy.

NIGHTINGALE, Benedict. Freelance writer. Former drama critic for *New Statesman,* London, 1969-86; former professor of English, University of Michigan, Ann Arbor, 1986-87. Author of *An Introduction to Fifty Modern British Plays,* 1982 (as *A Reader's Guide to Fifty Modern British Plays,* 1982), and *Fifth Row Center: A Critic's Year On and Off Broadway,* 1986. **Essays:** Beverley Cross; John Hopkins.

OBAFEMI, Olu. See his own entry. **Essays:** Wale Ogunyemi; Zulu Sofola; Bode Sowande.

O'CONNOR, Garry. Playwright and biographer. Author of *French Theatre Today,* 1975, *The Pursuit of Perfection* (biography of Maggie Teyte), 1979, *Darlings of the Gods: One Year in the Lives of Laurence Olivier and Vivien Leigh,* 1984, *Ralph Richardson: An Actor's Life,* revised ed., 1986, *Sean O'Casey: A Life,* 1988, *The Mahabharata,* 1989, *Party of the Gods* (novel), 1990, *William Shakespeare: A Life,* 1991, and seven stage and radio plays, including *The Musicians, Semmelweis,* and *The Kingdom of Allemonde.* Editor of *Laurence Olivier: In Celebration,* 1987. **Essays:** Peter Nichols; Michael O'Neill and Jeremy Seabrook; Mike Stott.

O'CONNOR, Marion. Lecturer in English, University of Kent, Canterbury. Author of *William Poel and the Elizabethan Stage Society,* 1987. Editor of *Shakespeare Reproduced: The Text in History and Ideology* (with Jean E. Howard), 1987. **Essay:** Tom Gallacher.

OKAGBUE, Osita. Senior lecturer in theater studies, School of Humanities and Performance, University of Plymouth, Exmouth, Devon. Author of articles on theater in *Maske Unikothurne, Okike, New Literatures Review, Theatre Research International,* and *Assaph,* and of chapters in *African Writers I & II, Culture and Identity: Selected Aspects and Approaches,* and *African Theatre Development.* **Essays:** Biyi Bandele-Thomas; James Ene Henshaw; Gibson Kente; Olu Obafemi; Martin Owusu; Barney Simon; Wole Soyinka; Edgar Nkosi White.

O'LEARY, John. Freelance writer, London. **Essay:** Mike Leigh.

OLIVA, Judy Lee. Assistant professor of theater, University of Tennessee, Knoxville; chair of Theatre History Focus Group of the Association for Theatre in Higher Education. Author of *David Hare: Theatricalizing Politics,* 1990; also author of essays in *Casebook on Howard Brenton,* 1992, *Dictionary of Stage Directors,* 1993. Contributor of articles to *Theatre Journal, Theater Three, Theatre Studies,* and *Journal of Dramatic Theory and Criticism.* **Essays:** Lee Blessing; Beth Henley; Alfred Uhry; Wendy Wasserstein.

OSBORN, M. Elizabeth. Freelance writer, editor, and dramaturge. Editor of *On New Ground: Contemporary Hispanic-American Plays,* 1987, and *The Way We Live Now: American Plays and the AIDS Crisis,* 1990. Former book editor, Theatre Communications Group, New York. **Essays:** Constance S. Congdon; David Greenspan; Allan Havis; Tony Kushner; Eduardo Machado.

OVERMYER, Eric. See his own entry. **Essay:** Mac Wellman.

PAGE, Malcolm. Professor of English, Simon Fraser University, Burnaby, British Columbia. Author of *John Arden,* 1984, *Richard II* (critical study), 1987, and *Howards End* (critical study), 1993. Editor of *File on Arden,* 1985, *File on Stoppard,* 1986, *File on Shaffer,* 1987, *File on Osborne,* 1988, *File on Ayckbourn,* 1989, *File on Hare,* 1990, *File on Pinter,* 1993, and *File on Fray,* 1994. Co-editor of *File on Edgar* (with Simon Trussler), 1991. **Essays:** Alan Ayckbourn; Peter Flannery; David Hare; Tomson Highway; Margaret Hollingsworth; Ann Jellicoe; Wendy Lill; Mustapha Matura; John Murrell; David Pownall.

PALMER, Richard H. Professor of theater, College of William and Mary, Williamsburg, Virginia. Associate editor of *Theatre Annual.* Author of *The Lighting Art,* 1985 (2nd ed., 1994), *The Critics Canon,* 1988, *Tragedy and Tragic Theory: An Analytic Guide,* 1992, and *The Contemporary British History Play,* 1998. **Essay:** Stephen Jeffreys.

PARKER, Dorothy. Associate professor of English, Victoria College, University of Toronto. Editor of *Modern American Drama: Williams, Miller, Albee, and Shepard,* 1986, and *Modern Drama.* **Essays:** David French; Erika Ritter.

PERKINS, Don. Research associate, Edmonton Professional Theatre Project. Author of "Necessary Adjustments? The Problem of Community Solidarity in *Paper Wheat, The Fighting Days,* and *The Shipbuilder,*" *Prairie Forum* 21:1, 1996, and "Shifting Loyalties: The Indigenous Indigenisation in Canadian Historical Drama of Cultural Contacts," *Essays in Theatre/Etudes Theatrales* 15:2. **Essay:** Ken Mitchell.

PETERSON, William. Professor of Theatre Arts, California State University, San Bernardino. Author of articles and reviews in *Asian Theatre Journal, Australasian Drama Studies, Theatre Journal, The Journal of Dramatic Theory and Criticism, SPACLAS Journal, SPAFA Journal, High Performance, Performance* (London), and *Theatre Insight.* **Essays:** Michael Gurr; Kuo Pao Kun.

PETZOLD, Roxana. Editor, Grove Weidenfeld, New York. **Essay:** JoAnne Akalaitis.

POUNTNEY, Rosemary. Lecturer in English, Jesus College, University of Oxford; honorary research fellow in drama, King Alfred's College, Winchester. Former professional actress. Author of *Notes on "Waiting for Godot,"* 1981, *Theatre of Shadows: Samuel Beckett's Drama, 1956-76,* 1988, and articles and reviews on Beckett and contemporary theater. **Essay:** Howard Brenton.

PRENTICE, Chris. Lecturer in New Zealand and postcolonial literatures and theory, University of Otago. Author of essays in various journals and co-editor (with Lisa Warrington) of *Playlunch: Five Short New Zealand Plays,* 1996. **Essay:** Michaelanne Forster.

RAYNOR, Henry. Schoolmaster and freelance writer. Author of *Joseph Haydn,* 1962, *Wagner,* 1970, *Radio and Television,* 1970, *A Social History of Music from the Middle Ages to Beethoven,* 1972, *Mahler,* 1975, *Music and Society since 1815,* 1976, *The Orchestra,* 1978, *Mozart,* 1978, and *Music in England,* 1980. **Essays:** Terence Frisby; Kevin Laffan; Johnny Speight.

READ, Leslie du S. Lecturer in drama, University of Exeter, Devon. Contributor to *The Cambridge Guide to World Theatre,* 1988, *The Cambridge Encyclopaedia,* 1990, *Encyclopaedia of Literature and Criticism,* 1990, and *The Oxford Illustrated History of Theatre,* 1992. **Essay:** Robert Holman.

REILLY, John M. Professor of English, State University of New York, Albany. Author of many articles on African American literature, popular crime writing, and social fiction and of bibliographical essays in *Black American Writers,* 1978, and *American Literary Scholarship.* Editor of *Twentieth-Century Interpretations of Invisible Man,* 1970, *Richard Wright: The Critical Reception,* 1978, and reference book *Twentieth Century Crime and Mystery Writers,* 1980 (2nd ed., 1985). **Essay:** Ed Bullins.

RICHARDS, Sandra L. Assistant professor of drama and director of Committee on Black Performing Arts, Stanford University, California. Author of the introduction to *Center Stage: An Anthology of Twenty-one Black American Plays,* 1981; contributor of articles on Amiri Baraka, actor Bert Williams, and Nigerian playwrights to *Theatre Journal, Mime,* and *San Francisco Theatre.* **Essays:** Charles Fuller; Femi Osofisan; Ola Rotimi; Ntozake Shange.

ROOSE-EVANS, James. Director and founder of Hampstead Theatre, London. Author of plays, including *84 Charing Cross Road, Re:Joyce!, Cider with Rosie,* and *Augustus;* radio documentaries, including *The Female Messiah* and *The Third Adam, The Adventures of Odd and Elsewhere.* Author of *Directing a Play,* 1968, *Experimental Theatre from Stanislavsky to Peter Brook,* 1970 (revised 1984 and 1989), *London Theatre: From the Globe to the National,* 1977, and novel *Inner Journey: Outer Journey,* 1987. Director of many plays, including works by Hugh Whitemore, Václav Havel, Anthony Stevens, Sean Mathias, Christopher Fry, and Pam Gems. **Essay:** James Forsyth.

SADLER, Geoff. Assistant librarian, Local Studies, Chesterfield, Derbyshire. Author of 18 Western novels (as Jeff Sadler and Wes Calhoun), including *Ghost Town Guns,* 1990, and *Headed North,* 1992 (as Sadler), and *Texas Nighthawks,* 1990 (as Calhoun), as well as the *Justus* trilogy of plantation novels (as Geoffrey Sadler), 1982, *Journey to Freedom* (a war memoir with Antoni Snarski), 1990, and *Shirebrook: Birth of a Colliery* (with Ernest I. Roberts), 1991. Co-author of *Tom's Times,* a cooperatively written play by the Shirebrook Writers' Group, 1991. Editor of *Twentieth Century Western Writers,* 1991. **Essays:** Ray Cooney; Adrian Mitchell; Derek Walcott.

SAINER, Arthur. See his own entry. **Essays:** Israel Horovitz; John Patrick Shanley; Stuart Sherman; George Tabori.

SCHECHNER, Richard. Founding director, Performance Group, New York; professor of performance studies, New York University. Author of *Public Domain,* 1968, *Environmental Theatre,* 1973, *Theatres, Spaces, and Environments* (with Jerry N. Rojo and Brooks McNamara), 1975, *Essays in Performance Theory,* 1977 (revised 1988), *The End of Humanism,* 1982, *Performative Circumstances,* 1983, and *Between Theater and Anthropology,* 1986. Joint editor of *Free Southern Theatre,* 1969, *Ritual, Play, and Performance,* 1976, and *By Means of Performance: Intercultural Studies of Theatre and Ritual,* 1990. Director for Wooster Group.

SCHECHTER, Joel. Chair of Theatre Arts Department, San Francisco State University, California. Former dramaturge and professor of dramatic criticism, Yale School of Drama, New Haven, Connecticut, and literary adviser, American Place Theatre, New York. Author of *Durov's Pig: Clowns, Politics and Theatre,* 1985; contributor to *American Theatre, The Drama Review, In These Times, The Nation, New York Times, The Partisan Review,* and other journals and periodicals. Editor of *Theater* magazine at Yale, 1977-92; guest editor of *Teatr,* Moscow, 1989.

SCHIFF, Ellen. Professor emeritus of French and comparative literature, North Adams State College, Massachusetts. Author of *From Stereotype to Metaphor: The Jew in Contemporary Drama,* 1982; contributor of articles to *New York Times, Massachusetts Review,* and *Modern Drama,* and chapters in *Holocaust Studies Annual, Anti-Semitism in American History,* and *Handbook of American Jewish Literature.* **Essay:** Emily Mann.

SCHNEIDER, Alan. Late professor of drama, University of California, San Diego. Director of Broadway and off-Broadway plays by Albee, Beckett, Edward Bond, Grass, Preston Jones, Pinter, Saroyan, Ted Whitehead, Tennessee Williams, Elie Wiesel, and Lanford Wilson. Died 1984.

SCULLION, Adrienne. Lecturer, Department of Theatre, Film, and Television Studies, University of Glasgow. Editor of *Female Playwrights of the Nineteenth Century,* 1996. Author of articles on Scottish theater for several essay collections and various journals. **Essays:** Sebastian Barry; Kevin Elyot; Chris Hannan; Liz Lochhead; Sharman Macdonald; Patrick Marber; Mark Ravenhill.

SHOSTAK, Elizabeth. Contributing editor of *Boston Book Review.* Author of essays and reviews in *Publishers Weekly, Boston Globe, The Women's Review of Books,* and elsewhere. **Essays:** Dick Higgins; Quincy Long.

SHRAGGE, Elaine. Freelance writer, San Francisco. **Essay:** Rochelle Owens.

SIDNELL, Michael. Professor, Graduate Centre for the Study of Drama, University of Toronto; actor and director. Co-author of *Druid Craft* (on Yeats), 1971, and *The Secret Rose,* 1981; author of *Dances of Death: A History of the London Group Theatre,* 1984, *Mode Narratif et Mode Dramatique,* 1992, and articles on Irish and theater subjects. **Essay:** Beverley Simons.

SINGH, Kirpal. Head of Literature and Drama, Nanyang Technological University, Singapore. Editor of *World Literature Written in English.* Author of more than 10 books, including *Critical Engagements,* 1986, and *The Writer's Sense of the Past,* 1989. **Essays:** Kee Thuan Chye; K. S. Maniam; Gieve Patel; Eleanor Wong.

SMITH, Christopher. Senior fellow (formerly reader) in French and comparative literature, University of East Anglia. Author of *Jean Anouilh: Life Work and Criticism; Alabaster, Bikinis and Calvados,* 1985; contributor of numerous articles on drama and translation. Editor of Jean de Taille's *Dramatic Works,* Jacques de la Taille's *Alexandre,* A. Montchrestien's *Two Tragedies,* and of the journal *Seventeenth-Century French Studies.* **Essays:** Edward Albee; Keith Dewhurst; Ronald Hayman; Earl Lovelace; John Mortimer; Phyllis Nagy; G. F. Newman; Meredith Oakes; Anne Ridler.

SMITH, Michael T. See his own entry. **Essays:** George Birimisa; William H. Hoffman; H. M. Koutoukas; Murray Mednick; Hanon Reznikov; Ronald Tavel.

SOGLIUZZO, A. Richard. Theater critic, historian, and professor of drama; assistant editor of *Theatre Annual.* Author of *Luigi Pirandello, Director,* 1982; also author of articles on Italian theater, Arthur Miller, and Eugene O'Neill in *A Handbook of Modern Drama, A History of the Theatre,* and periodicals. **Essays:** Mario Fratti; Frank Gagliano.

SPURLING, John. See his own entry. **Essays:** Stanley Eveling; David Halliwell.

STERN, Carol Simpson. Professor and chair, Department of Performance Studies, Northwestern University, Evanston, Illinois. Past president of American Association of University Professors. Author of articles and theater and book reviews in *Victorian Studies, Literature in Performance,* and *British Mystery and Thriller Writers since 1940.* Author of *Performance: Texts and Contexts* (with Bruce Henderson), 1993. **Essays:** Eric Bogosian; Kenneth H. Brown; Caryl Churchill; James Goldman; Simon Gray; Peter Shaffer.

STRACHAN, Alan. Theater director. Productions in London included *The Watched Pot* by Saki, 1970; *John Bull's Other Island,* 1971, and *Misalliance,* 1973, by Shaw; *The Old Boys* by William Trevor, 1971; *A Family and a Fortune* by Julian Mitchell, 1975; and *Just between Ourselves* by Alan Ayckbourn, 1977. Devised and codirected *Cowardy Custard,* 1972, *Cole,* 1974, *Shakespeare's People,* 1975, and *Yahoo,* 1976. At Greenwich Theatre, 1978-88, productions included many new plays, such as *An Audience Called Édouard* by David Pownall, *The Paranormalist* by Jonathan Gems, and *One of Us* by Robin Chapman, and revivals, such as *Private Lives and Present Laughter* by Noël Coward and *A Streetcar Named Desire* and *The Glass Menagerie* by Tennessee Williams. **Essays:** George Furth; Larry Gelbart; Jonathan Gems; A. R. Gurney; Richard Harris; Keith Johnstone; Craig Lucas; Ken Ludwig; Anthony Minghella; Bernard Slade; William Trevor; Peter Ustinov.

STYAN, J. L. Franklyn Bliss Snyder Professor of English Literature and professor of theater emeritus, Northwestern University, Evanston, Illinois. Author of *The Elements of Drama,* 1960, *The*

Dark Comedy, 1962 (revised 1968), *The Dramatic Experience,* 1965, *Shakespeare's Stagecraft,* 1967, *Chekhov in Performance,* 1971, *The Challenge of the Theatre,* 1972, *Drama, Stage and Audience,* 1975, *The Shakespeare Revolution,* 1977, *Modern Drama in Theory and Practice,* 3 vols., 1981, *Max Reinhardt,* 1982, *The State of Drama Study,* 1984, *All's Well That Ends Well* (Shakespeare in Performance Series), 1984, *Restoration Comedy in Performance,* 1986, and *The English Stage: A History of Drama and Performance,* 1996. **Essay:** Christopher Fry.

TAUBMAN, Howard. Drama critic, 1960-66, and critic at large, 1966-75, *New York Times.* Adviser to Exxon Corporation on its "Theatre in America" series and other arts programs. Author of *The Making of American Theatre,* 1965, and of several books on music.

TAYLOR, John Russell. Art critic, *The Times,* London. Author of many books, including *Anger and After,* 1962 (revised 1969), *The Second Wave,* 1971, *Directors and Directions,* 1975, *Hitch: The Life and Work of Alfred Hitchcock,* 1978, *Strangers in Paradise,* 1981, and *Impressionist Dreams: The Artists and the World They Painted,* 1990. Author of studies of Pinter, David Storey, Peter Shaffer, Ingrid Bergman, Alec Guinness, Vivien Leigh, Orson Welles, and Edward Wolfe. Editor of *Look Back in Anger: A Casebook,* 1968, and of film criticism of Graham Greene.

THOMSON, John. Research associate in English, Victoria University, Wellington. Author of *New Zealand Drama 1930-1980,* 1984. **Essay:** Joseph Musaphia.

THOMSON, Peter. Professor of drama, University of Exeter, Devon. Author of *Brecht* (with Jan Needle), 1981, *Shakespeare's Theatre,* 1983, and *The Everyman Companion to the Theatre* (with Gamini Salgado), 1985. Editor of *Julius Caesar* by Shakespeare, 1970, *Essays on Nineteenth-Century British Theatre* (with Kenneth Richards), 1971, *The Eighteenth-Century English Stage* (with Richards), 1973, *Lord Byron's Family* by Malcolm Elwin, 1975, and *Plays* by Dion Boucicault, 1984. **Essay:** Martin Crimp.

TOMPKINS, Joanne. Lecturer in English and drama, University of Queensland, Brisbane, Australia. Author of *Post-Colonial Drama: Theory, Practice, Politics* (with Helen Gilbert), 1996, and editor of *Performing Women/Performing Feminisms: Interviews with International Women Playwrights* (with Julie Holledge), 1996. **Essays:** Sally Clark; Brad Fraser; Judith Thompson.

TREWIN, J. C. Late drama critic, *Illustrated London News, The Lady,* and *Birmingham Post.* Author of more than 40 books, including *Mr. Macready,* 1955, *Benson and the Bensonians,* 1960, *Shakespeare on the English Stage 1900-1964,* 1964, *Peter Brook: A Biography,* 1971, *Theatre Bedside Book,* 1974, *The Edwardian Theatre,* 1976, *Going to Shakespeare,* 1978, *Companion to Shakespeare,* 1981, and *Five and Eighty Hamlets,* 1987. Codeviser of *Farjeon Reviewed,* 1975. Editor of *Plays of the Year* series, 1949-81, and of many other books. O.B.E., 1981. Died 1990.

TURNER, Darwin T. University of Iowa Foundation Professor of English and head of African American world studies, University of Iowa, Iowa City. Author of *Katharsis* (poetry), 1964, *Nathaniel Hawthorne's The Scarlet Letter,* 1967, *Afro-American Writers,* 1970, *In a Minor Chord: Three Afro-American Writers,* 1971, and *The Teaching of Literature by Afro-American Writers,* 1972. Editor of several books, including *Images of the Negro in America,* 1965, *Black American Literature,* 3 vols., 1969, *Black Drama in America,* 1971, *Voices from the Black Experience,* 1972, *The Wayward and the Seeking: A Collection of Writings by Jean Toomer,* 1980, *The Art of Slave Narrative,* 1982, and *Cane: An Authoritative Text, Backgrounds, and Criticism,* 1988. **Essay:** Douglas Turner Ward.

TURNER, Elaine. Lecturer in drama, University of Warwick; teacher at Central School of Speech and Drama and British American Drama Academy. Member of editorial board of *New Theatre Quarterly.* **Essays:** John Arden; Louise Page; Peter Whelan.

UKAEGBU, Victor. Lecturer in drama, Nene-University College, Northampton. Author of essay on Athol Fugard in African Writers Series, 1996. **Essay:** Zakes Mda.

WANDOR, Michelene. See her own entry. **Essay:** Mary O'Malley.

WARDLE, Irving. Drama critic, *The Times,* London. Author of *The Houseboy* (play), 1974, and *The Theatres of George Devine,* 1978.

WATERS, Erika. Professor of English, University of the Virgin Islands, St. Croix Campus. Author of articles and reviews on Caribbean literature, and editor of *The Caribbean Writer,* an annual anthology that premiered in 1987. Co-editor of *Critical Issues in West Indian Literature,* 1984, and editor of *New Writing from the Caribbean,* 1994. **Essay:** David Edgecombe.

WEALES, Gerald. Professor emeritus of English, University of Pennsylvania, Philadelphia; drama critic for *Reporter* and *Commonweal.* Author of *Religion in Modern English Drama,* 1961, *American Drama since World War II,* 1962, *A Play and Its Parts,* 1964, *Tennessee Williams,* 1965, *The Jumping-Off Place: American Drama in the 1960's,* 1969, *Clifford Odets,* 1971 (revised 1985), and *Canned Goods as Caviar: American Film Comedy in the 1930's,* 1985. Editor of several collections of plays and essays and of *The Complete Plays of William Wycherley,* 1966. **Essays:** Phillip Heyes Dean; Jules Feiffer; David Henry Hwang; Arthur Kopit; Ronald Ribman.

WETZSTEON, Ross. Theater editor, *Village Voice,* New York. Editor of *The Obie Winners,* 1980, and of *Fool for Love and Other Plays* by Sam Shepard, 1984.

ISBN 1-55862-371-X